The Role of the Father in Child Development *edited by Michael E. Lamb*

Handbook of Behavioral Assessment *edited by Anthony R. Ciminero, Karen S. Calhoun, and Henry E. Adams*

Counseling and Psychotherapy: A Behavioral Approach *by E. Lakin Phillips*

Dimensions of Personality *edited by Harvey London and John E. Exner, Jr.*

The Mental Health Industry: A Cultural Phenomenon *by Peter A. Magaro, Robert Gripp, David McDowell, and Ivan W. Miller III*

Nonverbal Communication: The State of the Art *by Robert G. Harper, Arthur N. Wiens, and Joseph D. Matarazzo*

Alcoholism and Treatment *by David J. Armor, J. Michael Polich, and Harriet B. Stambul*

A Biodevelopmental Approach to Clinical Child Psychology: Cognitive Controls and Cognitive Control Theory *by Sebastiano Santostefano*

Handbook of Infant Development *edited by Joy D. Osofsky*

Understanding the Rape Victim: A Synthesis of Research Findings *by Sedelle Katz and Mary Ann Mazur*

Childhood Pathology and Later Adjustment: The Question of Prediction *by Loretta K. Cass and Carolyn B. Thomas*

Intelligent Testing with the WISC-R *by Alan S. Kaufman*

Adaptation in Schizophrenia: The Theory of Segmental Set *by David Shakow*

Psychotherapy: An Eclectic Approach *by Sol L. Garfield*

Handbook of Minimal Brain Dysfunctions *edited by Herbert E. Rie and Ellen D. Rie*

Handbook of Behavioral Interventions: A Clinical Guide *edited by Alan Goldstein and Edna B. Foa*

Art Psychotherapy *by Harriet Wadeson*

Handbook of Adolescent Psychology *edited by Joseph Adelson*

Psychotherapy Supervision: Theory, Research and Practice *edited by Allen K. Hess*

Psychology and Psychiatry in Courts and Corrections: Controversy and Change *by Ellsworth A. Fersch, Jr.*

Restricted Environmental Stimulation: Research and Clinical Applications *by Peter Suedfeld*

Personal Construct Psychology: Psychotherapy and Personality *edited by Alvin W. Landfield and Larry M. Leitner*

Mothers, Grandmothers, and Daughters: Personality and Child Care in Three-Generation Families *by Bertram J. Cohler and Henry U. Grunebaum*

Further Explorations in Personality *edited by A.I. Rabin, Joel Aronoff, Andrew M. Barclay, and Robert A. Zucker*

Hypnosis and Relaxation: Modern Verification of an Old Equation *by William E. Edmonston, Jr.*

Handbook of Clinical Behavior Therapy *edited by Samuel M. Turner, Karen S. Calhoun, and Henry E. Adams*

Handbook of Clinical Neuropsychology *edited by Susan B. Filskov and Thomas J. Boll*

The Course of Alcoholism: Four Years After Treatment *by J. Michael Polich, David J. Armor, and Harriet B. Braiker*

Handbook of Innovative Psychotherapies *edited by Raymond J. Corsini*

The Role of the Father in Child Development (Second Edition) *edited by Michael E. Lamb*

Behavioral Medicine: Clinical Applications .... Hughes, and W.W. Wenrich

Handbook for the Practice of Pediatric Psyc

Change Through Interaction: Social Psychol............................therapy *by Stanley R. Strong and Charles D. Claib*

Drugs and Behavior (Second Edition) *by Fr*

Date Due

MAR 1 4 1990	FEB 7 2003	
FEB 2 6 1993		
JUL 2 3 1993		
MAY 0 8 1996		
FEB 0 2 1999		
Feb 23 98		
March 17 98		
APR 1 2 1999		
OCT 1 4 1999		
DEC 1 3 1999		
JUL 3 1 2001		

BRODART, INC.   Cat. No. 23 233   Printed in U.S.A.

DES PLAINES, ILLINOIS   60016

Handbook of
Infant Development

Handbook of Infant Development

SECOND EDITION

Edited by

JOY DONIGER OSOFSKY

Departments of Pediatrics and Psychiatry
Louisiana State University Medical Center
New Orleans, Louisiana

A WILEY-INTERSCIENCE PUBLICATION

JOHN WILEY & SONS, INC.

New York • Chichester • Brisbane • Toronto • Singapore

Library of Congress Cataloging-in-Publication Data

Handbook of infant development.

  (Wiley series on personality processes)
  "Wiley-Interscience publication."
  Includes bibliographies and indexes.
  1. Infant psychology. 2. Infants—Development.
I. Osofsky, Joy D. II. Series. [DNLM: 1. Child
Behavior. 2. Child Development. 3. Infant.
4. Parent-Child Relations. WS 105 H236]
BF719.H36 1987   155.4'22   86–28906
ISBN 0–471–88565–7

Printed in the United States of America

10 9 8 7 6 5 4 3 2 1

Contributors

RICHARD N. ASLIN, Department of Psychology, University of Rochester, Rochester, New York.

ROGER BAKEMAN, Department of Psychology, Georgia State University, Atlanta, Georgia.

KAREN CAPLOVITZ BARRETT, Department of Psychology, University of Wyoming, Laramie, Wyoming.

ELIZABETH BATES, Department of Psychology, University of California, San Diego, California.

JOHN E. BATES, Department of Psychology, University of Indiana, Bloomington, Indiana.

KATHLEEN M. BERG, Department of Psychology, University of Florida, Gainesville, Florida.

W. KEITH BERG, Department of Psychology, University of Florida, Gainesville, Florida.

T. BERRY BRAZELTON, Child Development Unit, Children's Hospital Medical Center, Boston, Massachusetts.

INGE BRETHERTON, Department of Human Development, Colorado State University, Fort Collins, Colorado.

JOSEPH J. CAMPOS, Department of Psychology, University of Illinois, Urbana-Champaign, Illinois.

BERTRAND B. CRAMER, Service de Guidance Infantile, Geneva, Switzerland.

PETER DE CHATEAU, St. Goran's Hospital, Karolinska Institute, Stockholm, Sweden.

ROBERT N. EMDE, Department of Psychiatry, University of Colorado Health Sciences Center, Denver, Colorado.

TIFFANY FIELD, Mailman Center for Child Development, University of Miami Medical School, Miami, Florida.

PATRICIA L. FRANCIS, Department of Psychology, University of Oklahoma, Norman, Oklahoma.

JOHN M. GOTTMAN, Department of Psychology, University of Seattle, Seattle, Washington.

GERALD GRATCH, Department of Psychology, University of Houston, Houston, Texas.

FRANCES DEGEN HOROWITZ, Department of Human Development, University of Kansas, Lawrence, Kansas.

CARROLL E. IZARD, Department of Psychology, University of Delaware, Newark, Delaware.

JEROME KAGAN, Department of Psychology and Social Relations, Harvard University, Cambridge, Massachusetts.

CLAIRE B. KOPP, Department of Psychology, University of California, Los Angeles, California.

ANNELIESE F. KORNER, Department of Psychiatry and Social Sciences, Stanford University School of Medicine, Stanford, California.

BARRY M. LESTER, Bradley Hospital, East Providence, Rhode Island.

MICHAEL LEWIS, Department of Pediatrics, Rutgers Medical School, Piscataway, New Jersey.

CAROL Z. MALATESTA, Department of Psychology, New School for Social Research, New York, New York.

ROBERT B. MCCALL, Office of Child Development, University of Pittsburgh, Pittsburgh, Pennsylvania.

ELIZABETH MOLLNOW, Clinical Psychologist, Psychology Program, University of Cincinnati, Cincinnati, Ohio.

J. KEVIN NUGENT, University of Massachusetts at Amherst, and Child Development Unit, The Children's Hospital, Harvard Medical School, Boston, Massachusetts.

BARBARA O'CONNELL, Consultant, Graduate School of Education, University of California, San Diego, California.

HANŬS PAPOUŠEK, Developmental Psychobiology, Max-Planck-Institute for Psychiatry, Munich, Federal Republic of Germany.

MECHTHILD PAPOUŠEK, Developmental Psychobiology, Max-Planck-Institute for Psychiatry, Munich, Federal Republic of Germany.

ROSS D. PARKE, Department of Psychology, University of Illinois, Urbana-Champaign, Illinois.

ROBERT PLOMIN, College of Human Development, Pennsylvania State University, University Park, Pennsylvania.

SUSAN A. ROSE, Department of Psychiatry, Albert Einstein College of Medicine, Yeshiva University, Bronx, New York.

CAROLYN ROVEE-COLLIER, Department of Psychology, Rutgers University, New Brunswick, New Jersey.

HOLLY RUFF, Department of Pediatrics, Albert Einstein College of Medicine, Yeshiva University, Bronx, New York.

MICHAEL RUTTER, Honorary Director, Medical Research Council Child Psychiatry Unit, Institute of Psychiatry, London, England.

GENE P. SACKETT, Primate Center, University of Washington, Seattle, Washington.

JOSEPH A. SCHATZ, Department of Psychology, University of Houston, Houston, Texas.

PATRICIA A. SELF, Department of Psychology, University of Oklahoma, Norman, Oklahoma.

CECILIA SHORE, Miami University of Ohio, Department of Psychology, Oxford, Ohio.

BARBARA J. TINSLEY, Department of Speech Communication, University of Illinois, Urbana-Champaign, Illinois.

CHARLES V. VORHEES, Department of Pediatrics and Developmental Biology Program, Children's Hospital Research Foundation, University of Cincinnati, Cincinnati, Ohio.

Series Preface

This series of books is addressed to behavioral scientists interested in the nature of human personality. Its scope should prove pertinent to personality theorists and researchers as well as to clinicians concerned with applying an understanding of personality processes to the amelioration of emotional difficulties in living. To this end, the series provides a scholarly integration of theoretical formulations, empirical data, and practical recommendations.

Six major aspects of studying and learning about human personality can be designated: personality theory, personality structure and dynamics, personality development, personality assessment, personality change, and personality adjustment. In exploring these aspects of personality, the books in the series discuss a number of distinct but related subject areas: the nature and implications of various theories of personality; personality characteristics that account for consistencies and variations in human behavior; the emergence of personality processes in children and adolescents; the use of interviewing and testing procedures to evaluate individual differences in personality; efforts to modify personality styles through psychotherapy, counseling, behavior therapy, and other methods of influence; and patterns of abnormal personality functioning that impair individual competence.

IRVING B. WEINER

Fairleigh Dickinson University
Rutherford, New Jersey

Preface

In planning the Second Edition of the *Handbook of Infant Development,* I thought a great deal about my graduate student years, when I would have appreciated a new and up-to-date version of the infancy books that we were using at that time. I decided to plan a second edition reflecting the growth, expansion, and "information explosion" in the field. Although some second editions present updated reviews of old chapters, this volume includes a new set of contributions. Reviews and perspectives are presented by major researchers and teachers. The field of infancy has changed an enormous amount because of accumulated findings, discoveries, and new methodologies that have emerged in the last decade. While it is not possible to be inclusive, a few examples will suffice to illustrate some of the changes. In the last decade, some new areas or those in which much work has been done include perceptual development, cross-modal representation, memory, developmental behavioral genetics, innovative methodological approaches, risk factors and preventive interventions, continuities and discontinuities, and infant mental health. All of these areas and more are presented in this book, which will be useful as a resource volume for researchers in the field of infancy and also will serve as a place to begin for serious students. The material ranges from a comprehensive presentation of normal development in infancy to development in risk groups, methodological, design, and analysis issues, clinical approaches and interventions, and current issues and perspectives. International chapters have been included to broaden the focus of the volume. Although it is not possible to be totally comprehensive, many important areas are covered. As the reader will see in reviewing the chapters, the richness of the contributions and the programmatic perspectives of individuals have made the book of outstanding quality and utility.

In addition to changes in the content of this volume, I have made stylistic and section changes that I believe will be helpful to the reader. A stylistic change has been to include an introduction and integrative summary at the beginning of each section to highlight the issues. These introductions will provide the reader with an overview of the material that is covered in that section and, where appropriate, will present a perspective on the content area. The reader will also note that, in addition to reviews of new areas of research, more material is presented in this volume in the areas of risk, intervention, and applied aspects. Much more research is now available in prevention, clinical, and applied areas. The growth of knowledge allows for more application. Furthermore, there is national recognition of the importance of infant health factors and preventive intervention, which can be carried out much more effectively and scientifically than had been thought previously.

The first section, Developmental Perspectives, offers an overview of major areas for understanding development. Richard Aslin reviews audition and visual perception, Carolyn Rovee-Collier covers learning and memory, Elizabeth Bates, Barbara O'Connell, and Cecilia Shore discuss language development, Gerald Gratch and Joseph Schatz present the development of thought and language, and Keith and Kathleen Berg cover psychophysiological development. Cross-modal representation, a relatively new area of emphasis, is reviewed by Susan Rose and Holly Ruff. Developmental behavioral genetics, an important and growing area of research, is covered by Robert Plomin.

In the second section, Social, Emotional, and Interactive Perspectives, family and parent–child interaction, socialization, and social and emotional development are reviewed. Theories of social development are presented by Michael Lewis, and two perspectives on emotional development are presented, one by Carroll Izard and Carol Malatesta, and the other by Karen Barrett and Joseph Campos. Parent–infant and family interaction are reviewed by Ross Parke and Barbara Tinsley and parent–infant socialization in Western Europe by Peter de Chateau. An intuitive parenting approach from cross-cultural perspectives is discussed by Hanŭs and Methilde Papoušek.

The importance of assessment and methodology has grown in the last few years, with increasing concern about ways to understand observational and interactional research. Therefore, several chapters in this area have been included in the section entitled Assessment, Methodology, and Analysis. Two chapters cover assessment of the newborn: a general one by Patricia Francis, Patricia Self, and Frances Degen Horowitz, and a specific one on the Brazelton Neonatal Behavioral Assessment Scale by T. Berry Brazelton, Kevin Nugent, and Barry Lester. Gene Sackett discusses analysis in interaction research and presents a new technique, and Roger Bakeman and John Gottman review applications of observational methods.

As infancy has been studied more intensively and thoroughly from multidisciplinary perspectives, there has been growing awareness of the importance of risk factors and interventions. In the section entitled Risk Factors, Clinical Approaches, and Interventions, some of the important work in this area is reviewed. Claire Kopp presents historical reflections on developmental risk, and the specific influence of behavioral teratogenesis is reviewed by Charles Vorhees. Tiffany Field provides an overview of parent–infant interaction and interactive disturbances in high-risk infants, and Anneliese Korner presents a preventive intervention perspective with high-risk newborns. Moving to more clinically oriented interventions, Bertrand Cramer reviews subjective and objective aspects of the parent–infant relationship.

In the final section of the volume, Current Issues and Perspectives, I have identified topics that have emerged as important in the area of infant development. An attempt has been made both in the editor's introduction and throughout the chapters to point out areas of controversy and different theoretical and empirical positions. Work on attachment is reviewed by Inge Bretherton, and work on temperament by Jack Bates. Jerome Kagan presents perspectives on infancy that are important for understanding individual differences and development. Robert McCall covers the media, society, and child development research. The topic of continuities and discontinuities from infancy, a concern that continues to be extremely important to the very notion of development as well as to problems in adjustment and psychopathology, is discussed by Michael Rutter. Finally, infant mental health, an area in which there has been much recent work relating developmental science to clinical activity, is reviewed by Robert Emde.

This second edition of the *Handbook of Infant Development* presents a comprehensive perspective on new and important ideas in the area of infant development. It covers the field, ranging from traditional developmental processes to issues of risk and intervention. Methodological concerns are also stressed. This book should prove valuable as a reference volume for researchers, educators, and students interested in learning about infancy.

JOY DONIGER OSOFSKY

New Orleans, Louisiana
January 1987

Acknowledgments

In planning this volume, I want to give special thanks to my colleagues in the field of infant development who encouraged me and advised me that to prepare a second edition of the *Handbook of Infant Development* would be a worthwhile endeavor and an important one for the field. Several individuals have been particularly helpful in offering advice, support, and editorial assistance. Dr. Robert N. Emde has provided advice about overall structure and chapters and excellent editorial assistance. Dr. Rex Culp graciously did much reviewing for the volume and frequently consulted with me about the chapters. Dr. Della Hann contributed many hours to carefully proofing of the final manuscript for which I am most appreciative. I also want to thank the many other individuals who reviewed the chapters, offering guidance and perspectives for both the authors and the editor.

My editor at Wiley-Interscience, Mr. Herbert Reich, has been extremely helpful not only in supporting the project and encouraging me but in offering useful advice at times regarding content and audience for the volume. Ms. Judith Overton, editorial assistant at Wiley, has been very efficient in keeping the many details in order for both the editor and the publisher. Michael Flaherty has been most conscientious and patient in the final processing of the manuscripts.

Again, as with the first edition, this handbook could not have been completed without the enormous effort and talent of all of the contributors. Their excellent contributions have made this fine volume a reality.

Finally, I would like to thank my husband, Howard, and my three children, Hari, Justin, and Michael, for bearing with me during those many long hours when I was less available to them or at least distracted during the preparation of this volume. Their support has been crucial for the completion of such an undertaking. Through raising the children and observing their individual differences and growth, I have learned much about the complexities of infant and child development that cannot come from books.

J.D.O.

Contents

Handbook of
Infant Development

Developmental Perspectives

Part One of this volume, "Developmental Perspectives," includes an overview and perspective on topics considered to be extremely important for understanding infant development. Because of the space constraints, at times the reader is referred to other relevant reviews and references are cited that will guide the interested reader.

In the first chapter, Richard Aslin provides an overview of basic research and theory on visual and auditory development during human infancy. As Aslin notes, this is a very large task because of the significant advances in this area since the first edition of the *Handbook* was published in 1979. He emphasizes that, while it is not possible to provide a totally comprehensive review, he is covering the basic research of the past decade, highlighting the most relevant findings. He also refers the readers to recent reviews of visual and auditory development.

In Chapter 2, Carolyn Rovee-Collier proposes that the emphasis on the form instead of the function of learning has been an obstacle in the quest for understanding how infants benefit from experience. She feels that the ways in which such development occurs are not encompassed by the traditional learning models because they present a reductionistic view assumed to describe all instances of learning. In her chapter, Rovee-Collier reviews the current status of research and theory on infant learning, points to historical links, and discusses factors that influence the acquisition and expression of learning in infants and its ontogeny. She also presents data and theory on memory, its relationship to learning, and the significance for future research.

Because of the importance of research in the area of language development, a chapter on language and communication in infancy has been included in this volume. In Chapter 3, Elizabeth Bates, Barbara O'Connell, and Cecilia Shore present the view that language and communication are an integral part of infancy at every level of development. Their position is an interactionist one, proposing that language development is a process that begins early in infancy and depends on skills from a variety of domains, including perception, cognition, motor development, and socialization. The interactionist view holds for the emergence of both single words and their meanings and the more strictly linguistic (according to the authors) areas of phonology and grammar. In their chapter, they focus on major milestones of language development, including prespeech (0–10 months), first words (10–14 months), first sentences (18–22 months), and grammaticization (24–30 months). Within this developmental framework, three kinds of additional information are presented: (1) continuity between and within levels of development; (2) individual differences; and (3) cognitive parallels. In this last section, the authors note nonlinguistic cognition that parallels each of the major milestones of language development, feeling that the cognitive bases approach will allow us to evaluate the claim that language is an independent domain. A perspective on language development is very important for understanding normal development and may have significant implications for the study of risk and developmentally delayed groups, which are discussed in other sections of this volume.

In Chapter 4, Gerald Gratch and Joseph Schatz present results of initial attempts to examine Piaget's *processes* as contrasted with *products* and the importance of the processes for his observations. Focusing on Piaget's first two infancy books, *The Origins of Intelligence* and *The Construction of Reality in the Child,* Gratch and Schatz provide a sense of what Piaget and his intellectual context were like before he began to observe his three infants and then deal with observations and the ways in which they changed over time. The objective of their chapter is to stimulate the reader to consider Piaget and infancy in a somewhat different way from that which has been used. The authors feel strongly that, though we have learned much about infants, we must be patient in understanding the minds of such complex and important individuals. Further, they attempt to convey to the reader their belief that we need to spend more time looking carefully at babies and less time worrying about coming up with precise explanations of limited observations in restricted contexts.

The next chapter in Part One is entitled "Psychophysiological Development in Infancy: State, Startle, and Attention." In this chapter, Keith and Kathleen Berg focus on three topics: sleeping and waking states, the startle reflex and its modulation by nonstartle stimuli, and the development of attentional processes such as orienting and habituation. They chose these topics because the recording of physiological activity in these areas has had a considerable impact on the field. In introducing the chapter, they raise the interesting distinction between psychological development called *overt,* in which newborns' choices of behaviors are limited because they are not mature enough to provide meaningful data, and physiological activity called covert, which even in the premature infant is both abundant and relatively well developed. They emphasize that there is a relative wealth of information available from birth on related to physiological development. They make an important distinction between the labeling of physiological responses as indirect and the labeling of psychological ones as direct, suggesting that, while this approach may be useful for descriptive heuristic reasons, it does not indicate that one type of response is more valid. Further, they feel that both are modulated by CNS mechanisms and can be either comparatively overt or covert. They are types of behaviors that differ only in the degree to which they are typically overt or require electrical aids to be observed; thus they discard the fundamental behavior–physiology dichotomy.

In Chapter 6, "Cross-Modal Abilities in Human Infants," Susan Rose and Holly Ruff focus on an important and growing area of research in the field of infant development. Work in this area has not only resulted in a new understanding of development but has also been used to sensitize both researchers and clinicians to the variety of interactive interchanges that can occur between infants and caregivers (see Stern, 1985). According to the authors, cross-modal matching and cross-modal transfer require that the experience in the two perceptual systems be equivalent in some respect. There are two general views about how the equivalence comes about. One is that the systems can only be related through experience. The other is that equivalences are thought to exist by virtue of the fact that the different systems detect invariants specifying the same properties of objects and events. Therefore, there is no need for "transfer" because the response is based on the direct perception of the same object in both modalities. These issues are discussed in detail in the chapter. Historically, in terms of the developmental perspective, two fundamentally different assumptions were made about how cross-modal or intermodal integration develops: through either an initial separation of the systems or an initial unity. In this chapter, Rose and Ruff review how cross-modal abilities develop with age, raising several important issues, such as the following: Can the development of cross-modal abilities be accounted for solely by the development of intramodal abilities, or is something else required? What is the nature of information underlying equivalent involvement in cross-modal matching and transfer? How does the nature of information gathered change with age? How much of development is dependent on changing strategies of acquiring information about objects? How much is dependent on increasing experience in which there is simultaneous stimulation of the different modalities by objects and events?

As Robert Plomin points out in his chapter, "Developmental Behavioral Genetics," the timing is right for adding a chapter on behavioral genetics to the second edition of this handbook, because exciting discoveries have been made recently in applying this approach to the study of development in infancy. In his chapter, Plomin provides a brief overview of the field of developmental behavioral genetics and its relationship to infant development. He feels that the theory and methodology are extremely useful for the description and explanation of individual differences in infancy. There is much potential for meaningful research in this area. Plomin suggests some very interesting hypotheses for future research in this area, including the possibility of the influence of genetic mechanisms on the relationship between individual differences in infancy and adult development, the issue of whether infant mental development is general and undifferentiated, possible genetic influences on temperamental traits of emotionality, activity, and sociability/shyness, the relative magnitude of genetic impact at different stages and ages of development, and the possible mediating factor of genetics on environmental measures. He also discusses a very important issue in relation to work in behavioral genetics. Plomin suggests that genetic effects are not immutable; the more that is known about a trait genetically as well as environmentally, the greater the likelihood that rational interventions can be devised. This is a very hopeful position in relation to prospects for prevention and intervention with groups that are at high risk for both environmental and genetic disadvantage.

CHAPTER 1

Visual and Auditory Development in Infancy

RICHARD N. ASLIN

The purpose of this chapter is to provide an overview of basic research and theory on visual and auditory development during human infancy. This is a prodigious task given the impressive advances in these areas since the first edition of this handbook. Visual development, the traditional focus of researchers studying infant perception, was covered in 37 pages in the first edition, whereas a more recent treatment of this topic spanned two chapters and 175 pages (Banks & Salapatek, 1983; Gibson & Spelke, 1983). Auditory development and speech perception were covered in no more than a few selected paragraphs in the first edition, whereas a recent review encompassed 98 pages (Aslin, Pisoni, & Jusczyk, 1983) and an entire edited volume has recently been published (Trehub & Schneider, 1985). From this perspective, it should be clear that the present chapter cannot attempt to duplicate the incredible level of detail that has been attained in the past 8 years since the appearance of the first edition of this handbook. However, within the constraints of a general overview, an attempt will be made to cover the basic findings of the past decade, highlighting the most recent discoveries that have the greatest relevance to a broad readership.

METHODOLOGICAL ISSUES

The field of infant perception would not exist if researchers had failed to develop sensitive methods of assessing visual and auditory functioning. Fantz's (1958, 1961) early work on visual preferences demonstrated that young infants could provide reliable perceptual data, and subsequent methods have capitalized on various aspects of infants' fixational behaviors. Siqueland and Delucia's (1969) development of the high-amplitude sucking technique provided perhaps the greatest impetus for studies of auditory development, most notably in the area of infant speech perception. Variants of these pioneering techniques, along with newer methods for studying infant perception, have been reviewed in a recent volume by Gottlieb and Krasnegor (1985).

Preparation of this chapter was made possible by research grants from NIH (EY-05976 and HD-20286) and by a sabbatical award from the James McKeen Cattell Fund. The helpful critical comments provided by Sandy Shea, Robin Panneton, Terri Lewis, and Ben Stephens are gratefully acknowledged.

Methods for studying infant perception can most generally be differentiated into those employing spontaneously emitted (i.e., unconditioned) responses versus those employing conditioned responses. Table 1.1 lists a wide range of spontaneous and conditioned responses that have been used to assess visual and auditory functioning in young infants. The choice of a response is jointly dependent on pragmatic concerns (e.g., ease of recording) and on the specific question of interest to the researcher. For example, startle responses are quite easy to elicit in young infants by presenting a very intense acoustic stimulus. Startle responses are also quite easy to record, either by simple on-line observation or by videorecording for later off-line scoring. However, startle responses have not proven to be sensitive indices of auditory function, but rather provide a global assessment of the capacity of the auditory and/or tactile systems to detect *some* sensory input. If this level of evaluation is sufficient for the researcher (e.g., in the case of suspected congenital deafness), then the startle response may provide an adequate measure. However, if the researcher is interested in the capacity to discriminate between sounds differing in frequency, then the startle technique will prove to be virtually useless.

Another general consideration in choosing a method of assessment concerns the interpretation of developmental change. The most ubiquitous finding in developmental research is that infants show more adultlike performance as they grow older.

TABLE 1.1.   Methods Used to Study Visual and Auditory Development in Human Infants

Spontaneous Responses	Conditioned Responses
Vision	
Elicited motor responses	High-amplitude suck-
Blinking	ing
Pupillometry	Operant conditioning
Accommodation	Head turning
Eye movements	Foot kicking
Reaching	
Locomotion	
Brain wave responses	
Visual fixation responses	
Preferential looking	
Habituation	
Audition	
Elicited motor responses	Sucking
Startle activity	High amplitude
Blinking	Two interval
Eye blink inhibition	Operant head turning
Head orientation	Contingent orienting
Psychophysiological responses	Visual fixation
Heart rate	Head turning
Respiration	
Skin potential	
Cortical and brain stem evoked	
responses	
Habituation of visual fixation	

If one is simply concerned with the ability of infants to show evidence of respon-siveness, then any change in that level of responsiveness is of interest. However, if one is interested in the *capacity* of infants at a given age, and how that capacity changes over time, then developmental changes in responsiveness may be difficult to interpret. For example, young infants are notoriously uncooperative, inattentive, and unmotivated on many behavioral tasks. Many researchers assume that by using the same stimuli, the same response, and the same testing situation with infants at different ages (and with adults) one can rule out nonsensory factors. Unfortunately, it is virtually impossible to rule out all nonsensory factors because *absolute* changes in the level of performance may result *in part* from nonsensory factors, such as attentiveness or differences in the willingness to respond under uncertainty (so-called criterion effects).

There are essentially two strategies for dealing with these potential interpretive problems associated with nonsensory factors. First, one can employ a psychophys-ical approach to assess performance at more than one level along a stimulus di-mension of interest (e.g., intensity, wavelength, or "facelikeness"). If the measured response to all stimulus levels improves by a constant amount with age, then one cannot eliminate nonsensory factors as a potential explanation of this develop-mental improvement. However, if the pattern of improvement is not uniform at all stimulus levels, then the developmental difference (a significant Age × Stimulus Level interaction) is more likely a result of sensory rather than nonsensory factors. Unfortunately, there are always alternative explanations for these interactions, such as the choice of stimulus levels that are not within the range of responsiveness at all ages (i.e., floor or ceiling effects) or the selection of some stimuli that are qual-itatively different along the selected stimulus dimension (e.g., shifting from eco-logically relevant to non–ecologically relevant stimuli).

A second strategy for determining the presence of nonsensory factors in percep-tual development is to employ multiple response measures to assess the same un-derlying capacity. This strategy, sometimes referred to as converging operations, is based on the assumption that assessment tasks do not share all of the potential types of nonsensory factors that could influence an infant's level of performance. If sev-eral tasks, with clearly different nonsensory factors, converge on the same level of performance, then it is more likely that the level of performance reflects the capacity of the infant. Unfortunately, most *behavioral* assessment tasks have many nonsen-sory factors in common. Thus the most convincing evidence of converging opera-tions involves distinctly different tasks, for example, behavioral and psychophys-iological. As summarized by Yonas and Pick (1975), and elaborated on by Banks and Dannemiller (1986), another strategy that can be employed to differentiate be-tween sensory and nonsensory factors in perceptual development requires a link-age from predicted sensory thresholds to actual performance. However, unless one has excellent data on which to base these sensory predictions, any discrepancy be-tween predicted and obtained performance will be ambiguous.

In summary, when interpreting developmental improvements in perceptual per-formance, one must be cautious in concluding that infants at a particular age have deficits in their perceptual capacity. Measured performance should be taken as a conservative estimate of an infant's actual capacity because under other circum-stances improved performance may be obtained. In fact, the past 25 years of re-search on infant perception are a testimonial to the ingenuity of researchers in devising techniques that reveal greater sensitivity in infants' sensory and perceptual functioning. Although many of these techniques are quite robust under diverse testing situations, it is important to be aware that each has both advantages and limitations.

THE VISUAL SYSTEM

Investigators of sensory and perceptual development in both humans and nonhumans have studied all sensory modalities, but the visual system has commanded the attention of the vast majority of these studies. This singling out of the visual system is apparently the result of its relatively accessible receptor surface, its well-understood anatomy, and its role as the most important modality for many behaviors, including locomotion and pattern recognition. During the past 30 years, detailed reports of the responses of individual neurons in the mammalian visual system have also helped to guide investigations of human visual development by uncovering neural mechanisms that could support nearly every aspect of visual function. In addition, studies of neural development have uncovered both genetic constraints and experiential influences on the course of visual development, including the important concept of a sensitive period. A description of the neural properties of the visual system is beyond the scope of this chapter, but it is important to note that many of the experiments conducted with human infants are motivated in part by findings from the nonhuman literature. The interested reader may wish to consult several excellent reviews of this literature (e.g., Mitchell & Timney, 1984; Movshon & Van Sluyters, 1981).

The challenge to investigators of infant vision is to ask the right questions, choose the best methods, and formulate the most plausible explanation of a particular perceptual ability. Of course, there are considerable disagreements about what is "right," "best," and "most plausible" among researchers in this area. Some investigators present stimuli that are extremely simple, varying along only a single dimension, so that precise control over resulting response differences can be more easily interpreted (cf. Banks, 1985). Other investigators present stimuli that are multidimensional (complex) because subtle unidimensional stimulus variations rarely occur in the natural environment (cf. Johnston, 1985). In addition, some investigators employ spontaneous response measures that are extremely easy to record from most infants, while others use highly contrived conditioned responses that are difficult to obtain from the majority of tested infants. Clearly, the choice of stimulus and methodology is partially dependent on the question of interest to the investigator as well as on assumptions about what types of stimuli are most relevant to provide a complete understanding of perceptual development. Thus the following description of visual development will contrast two general approaches: psychophysical and ecological. The former approach assumes that stimuli must be varied along simple dimensions if one is to characterize the *capacity* of the infant visual system. The latter approach assumes that stimulus variations are multidimensional (yet specifiable) for organisms in the natural environment, and one must focus on the development of functional responses to these complex stimuli rather than the capacity to detect simple stimulus dimensions under simplified testing conditions.

In short, the psychophysical approach emphasizes what an infant *can* do and the ecological approach emphasizes what an infant *does* do.

Oculomotor Development

The mammalian visual system has evolved a number of oculomotor mechanisms that modulate the quantity and quality of visual stimulation reaching the retina. Because most of these oculomotor mechanisms are likely to be functionally immature in early infancy, they have been a topic of considerable interest to investigators of visual development. Moreover, they have been used as dependent measures of visual function in young infants; thus it is important to understand the integrity of their underlying motor control so that interpretations of sensory and perceptual development are not confounded by oculomotor developments that occur in early infancy (see Aslin, 1985, in 1986, for extensive reviews of these oculomotor systems).

The Lens

The function of the lens within the eyeball is to optimize the focus of the image of external objects onto the retinal surface. Two factors determine whether the retinal image will be optimally focused: the fixed refractive power of the cornea and the variable refractive power of the lens. Refraction refers to the bending of light rays from an object, and it is typically expressed in diopters. A diopter is the reciprocal of viewing distance in meters; for example, 1 diopter corresponds to 1 m, 2 diopters to ½ m, 3 diopters to ⅓ m, and so on. Thus, for an eyeball whose length matches the combined refractive power of the cornea and lens, objects at a far viewing distance will be in optimal focus (a condition called emmetropia). As objects approach, however, more refractive power is needed to maintain optimal retinal image focus at the plane of the retina. Thus the lens increases its refractive power by a process called accommodation in which the ciliary muscle puts tension on the lens capsule, thereby increasing the curvature of the posterior lens surface.

Accommodation also occurs in individuals who are not emmetropic. If the eyeball is too long relative to the refractive power of the cornea, then the retinal image of a distant object will be optimally focused in front of the plane of the retina. This condition is called nearsightedness (myopia) because near objects, which require more refractive power, can be brought into clear focus with little or no need for accommodation, whereas distant objects can only be focused with the aid of concave (minus) lenses. Similarly, if the eyeball is too short, then the retinal image of a distant object will be optimally focused behind the plane of the retina. This condition is called farsightedness (hyperopia) because far objects can be focused with the aid of accommodation, but maximum accommodation is reached at a relatively far distance and near objects can only be focused with the aid of convex (plus) lenses. Thus the ability of the visual system to maintain optimal retinal image focus is a joint function of the refractive power of the cornea, the accommodative accuracy of the lens, and the distance of the object. The smaller size of the newborn eyeball compared to the adult (17 mm vs. 24 mm) is closely matched to its greater refractive power (85 diopters vs. 60 diopters: Bennett & Francis, 1962; Lotmar, 1976). Although most infants are slightly hyperopic (Banks, 1980a), it appears that sufficient accommodation can be activated to overcome image blur except at very near viewing distances (Brookman, 1983).

The classic data on the accuracy of infant accommodation were provided by Haynes, White, and Held (1965) using a tehnique called dynamic retinoscopy. This technique employs a device called a retinoscope that directs a beam of light into the eyeball and enables an observer to view the beam as it is reflected from the retina. If the subject is accommodating accurately to the distance of the retinoscope, then the reflected beam will appear constant regardless of the distance to the retinoscope. However, if the subject accommodates nearer (myopically) or farther (hyperopically) than the retinoscope, the observer can estimate this focusing error. Haynes et al. (1965) reported that infants under 3 months of age show gross accommodative errors within the range of distances they studied (8–100 cm) and that until 1 month of age infants appear to adopt a fixed state of accommodation at approximately 20 cm. The implication of these data was that young infants must be confronted with a defocused retinal image unless the object is located at the fixed distance of accommodation.

Banks (1980b) provided a more extensive study of infant accommodation that has clarified some of the data and interpretations offered by Haynes et al. (1965). First, Banks noted that Haynes and colleagues used a small bull's-eye target attached to the retinoscope to elicit accommodation in their infant subjects. Although this target was clearly visible to all the infants tested at the nearest viewing distances, it may not have been visible to the younger infants at the farther viewing distances because visual resolution is based on retinal size (which decreases with increasing viewing distance for any physically invariant object). At the farther viewing distances, therefore, the accommodative state of the youngest infants may have simply reverted to what has been called the tonic or resting state of accommodation. To test this hypothesis, Banks created targets for accommodation that provided identical retinal images at several viewing distances. The resultant accuracy of accommodation, again assessed with retinoscopy, was considerably better than reported by Haynes and colleagues, although at the youngest age tested (1 month) there was still significant accommodative inaccuracy. These general conclusions have been confirmed using both photorefraction (Braddick, Atkinson, French, & Howland, 1979) and the visual evoked potential (VEP: Sokol, Moskowitz, & Paul, 1983).

Banks (1980b) was also interested in determining whether this accommodative inaccuracy resulted from the inability of the infant visual system to analyze precisely the retinal image blur that acts as a stimulus for accommodation. In other words, if infants cannot detect changes in the amount of blur, they have no functional reason for adjusting their accommodation. Based on estimates of the depth of focus of the infant visual system (primarily determined by eyeball size, pupil size, and visual acuity), Banks discovered that the accommodative errors measured in young infants never exceeded the depth of focus estimates. In other words, deficits in the sensory signal that drives the accommodative motor response were sufficient to account for the focusing errors observed in young infants. The functional implication of this finding is that the infant visual system is not deprived of clear retinal images by focusing errors as long as these errors fall within the sensory tolerance of the blur detection system that controls accommodation.

The foregoing description of retinal image focus was based on the assumption that the refractive power of the eye was constant for all stimulus orientations, that is, that the cornea is a sphere. If the corneal surface is not spherical, but rather is more curved (has higher refractive power) at certain meridia, then not all object orientations can be focused on the retina at any given time. This nonspherical refractive power is called astigmatism. Interestingly, the incidence of astigmatism appears to be greater in early infancy than in later childhood and adulthood (Atkinson, Braddick, & French, 1980; Dobson, Fulton, & Sebris, 1984; Gwiazda, Scheiman, Mohindra, & Held, 1984; Howland & Sayles, 1984). Moreover, this astigmatism is primarily the result of the cornea rather than the lens (Howland & Sayles, 1985). Because spectacle corrections are rarely prescribed for children prior to preschool age, it is unlikely that image clarity contributes to this developmental reduction in astigmatism.

Stabilizing Eye Movements

The spatial stability of the retinal image is determined by two underlying systems: the vestibular–ocular reflex (VOR) and optokinetic nystagmus (OKN). The VOR relies on sensory input from the vestibular system to signal changes in head velocity that counterroll the position of the eyes. For example, when the head is rotated side to side in the dark, the eyes do not remain fixed with respect to the head but rotate in the direction opposite to the direction of head rotation. Under normal illumination conditions, this counterrolling of the eyes would function to maintain the direction of gaze at a given fixed position in space. The VOR is also activated in the other two planes of head movement (tilted forward–back: the doll's eye reflex; tilted right–left: cyclotorsional eye movements). Of particular interest is the fact that these VOR responses occur extremely rapidly (latencies in adults are approximately 10 msec), thereby bypassing any volitional control and working very effectively to stabilize the retinal image during self-produced movements. Unfortunately, despite observational reports that have documented the presence of the VOR in newborns (cf. Peiper, 1963), VOR gain (the ratio of head movement velocity to eye movement velocity) has not been measured in young infants.

In a manner analogous to the VOR, the oculomotor system has evolved another stabilizing system that relies on visual information to compensate for motion of the entire retinal image. Whole-field movement elicits a smooth tracking eye movement that matches the velocity of the retinal motion. As the eyeball deviates from its central orbital position, a rapid eye movement (saccade) returns the eye to its previous position. The resulting alternation of smooth and rapid eye movements is called OKN. As in the case of the VOR, several observational reports have documented the presence of OKN in newborns (e.g., McGinnis, 1930), although it is clearly not as consistently elicited as in alert adults. However, most recordings of OKN in young infants have been unable to provide a quantitative measure of gain (e.g., Atkinson & Braddick, 1981; Kremenitzer, Vaughan, Kurtzberg, & Dowling, 1979; Naegele & Held, 1982). Hainline, Lemerise, Abramov, and Turkel (1984) measured OKN gains of 0.7, but only in somewhat older infants and with small-field gratings that may have underestimated peak gain. Thus at present it remains unclear whether the gain of newborn OKN is near 1.0 as in normal adults. If OKN gain is not nearly 1.0 in newborns, then they may have difficulty differentiating movement of objects in the visual field from movements of the eyeball in the orbit.

Saccadic Eye Movements and Scanning

The evolution of the fovea, a small retinal region with enhanced powers of spatial resolution, presumably led to the development of eye movements that move the fovea rapidly to sample specific regions of the visual field. These rapid rotations of the eyeball, interspersed with steady fixations of at least 200 msec, are called saccadic eye movements. In normal adults, saccades can have velocities as high as 900 deg per second, and typical saccade durations are 10–40 msec. Moreover, through a process called saccadic suppression, the smearing of the retinal image that would occur at such high velocities is apparently reduced or eliminated in adults (Volkmann, Riggs, Moore, & White, 1978). Thus saccadic eye movements provide a means of rapidly and efficiently moving the region of the retina with the highest spatial resolution so that specific locations of the visual array can be examined.

The earliest measures of saccadic eye movements in infants ignored the saccades themselves and analyzed the fixations that occur between saccades. Two hypotheses motivated these studies of visual scanning. First, given the knowledge that adult pattern vision is far superior if a target is imaged onto the fovea, it seemed reasonable to assume that infant pattern vision would also be heavily dependent on the specific regions of a visual stimulus that were fixated directly (i.e., onto the fovea rather than onto the peripheral retina). Second, an important theory of visual development outlined by Hebb (1949) proposed a necessary role for sequential fixations of a visual stimulus as a mechanism for infant pattern perception. Thus it was important at the time (early 1960s) to examine in as much detail as possible the pattern of fixations, or visual scanning, in very young infants.

Fortunately, a methodology was developed that enabled such detailed scanning data to be collected from young infants. The technique is called corneal reflection photography, and it is based on the fact that a light source, fixed in space and directed toward the eyeball, creates a reflection on the front surface of the cornea. If the infant looks directly at the light source, the corneal reflection appears in the center of the pupil. Because this light source is fixed and the corneal surface is convex, any movement of the eyeball results in a translation of the corneal reflection with respect to the infant's pupil. By using one or more light sources, covered with infrared filters to render them invisible to the infant, and a camera utilizing infrared-sensitive film, it is possible to record unobtrusively (with an accuracy of $+/-$ 5 deg) the individual fixations made by an infant who is viewing a visual stimulus. Initially, the sampling rate of the camera was set at 4 frames per second so that all fixations were captured (maximum fixation rates in adults are 4–5 per second), and any blurred film frames were assumed to be samples that occurred during a saccade.

Unfortunately, two factors complicated the use of corneal reflection photography as a measure of pattern perception in young infants. First, it became apparent that the center of the pupil was not an accurate reference point for judging the actual location of the fovea. In adults, the fovea is displaced 3–5 deg from the optic axis (pupil center), and Slater and Findlay (1972, 1975b) provided evidence that in newborns this displacement may be as large as 8–10 deg and may differ considerably between subjects. Thus these measurement errors rendered the corneal reflection technique less precise, though admittedly superior to simple observation. Second, the motor theory of pattern perception proposed by Hebb (1949) was based on some assumptions that were proven incorrect. For example, the sequence of saccades that leads to scanning during stimulus inspection is not randomly initiated. Rather, even in the earliest postnatal periods, infants are capable of directing their saccades to fixate specific stimulus targets that were initially imaged on the peripheral retina (Harris & MacFarlane, 1974; Lewis, Maurer, & Kay, 1978; MacFarlane, Harris, & Barnes, 1976; Mohn & van Hof-van Duin, 1985; Schwartz, Dobson, Sandstrom, & van Hof-van Duin, 1985). Thus it does not appear likely that the infant visual system "learns" about a visual pattern by making saccades along that pattern's contours. Rather, the visual information required to program these saccades must already be present prior to the saccade itself. There are, however, some limitations to the infant's ability to make saccades to peripheral targets. For example, several studies have reported that the probability of eliciting a saccadic eye movement is an inverse function of retinal eccentricity (Aslin & Salapatek, 1975; Bronson, 1982; Harris & MacFarlane, 1974; Tronick, 1972). Lewis, Maurer, and Blackburn (1985) have also shown that 1-month-olds are much less sensitive to targets located in the nasal visual field than are 2-month-olds who show little nasal–temporal asymmetry. Schonen, McKenzie, Maury, and Bresson (1978) also showed that detection of peripheral targets is impaired if they are presented at a different viewing distance than the initial central fixation stimulus. These findings indicate not only that the peripheral retina is important for pattern perception, but also that significant developments in the control of saccadic eye movements occur during the first several postnatal months. However, at least some of the peripheral targets that do *not* elicit a saccade are detected by the infant visual system as indicated by changes in heart rate (Finlay & Ivinskis, 1984).

Given the finding that young infants are capable of initiating saccades in the direction of a peripheral target, could they also accurately program and execute a magnitude-appropriate saccade? This question was addressed in a study by Aslin and Salapatek (1975). A technique called electrooculography (EOG) was used to record the size of saccades in 1- and 2-month-olds. A small target was presented for fixation and then displaced suddenly to a peripheral location 10, 20, 30 or 40 deg away. The vast majority of *initial* saccades were in the direction of the target, but they did not take the form of adult saccades. Adults employ a single saccade that is very nearly the same size as the target displacement (typically less than a 10 percent undershoot error). Infants, however, executed a series of saccades that grossly undershot the target (rarely greater than 50 percent of the target displacement). Moreover, each of these so-called multiple saccades was approximately 5–7 deg. Thus, on many trials, particularly for displacements of 20–40 deg, three or more saccades were executed, with intersaccadic intervals of approximately 400 msec.

Although the mechanism underlying immature infant saccades is unknown at present (see Aslin, in press, 1986, for a discussion of several potential explanations), it is not clear that multiple saccades are a significant constraint on infant perception. Under free-scanning conditions, the majority of adult saccades are 15 deg or less in magnitude (Bahill, Adler, & Stark, 1975). Moreover, when presented with a complex visual stimulus, rather than a single small target that is suddenly displaced, infants employ saccades that are typically 5–7 deg in magnitude, and these saccades typically show the same amplitude–velocity profile as adult saccades (Hainline, Turkel, Abramov, Lemerise, & Harris, 1984). Thus it would appear that infants are not necessarily at a functional disadvantage simply because they cannot (or will not) execute larger magnitude-appropriate saccades.

Pursuit Eye Movements

Saccadic eye movements function to move the fovea to fixate specific regions of the visual array. Pursuit eye movements function to follow a moving target that has already been imaged on the fovea. If the velocity of the eye matches the velocity of the target (i.e., the gain is 1.0), then spatial resolution of the moving target is not degraded despite its translation in space because there is no slippage of the retinal image across the retinal surface. The traditional view of smooth pursuit movements in young infants is that they are absent until the second postnatal month (McGinnis, 1930; Dayton & Jones, 1964; Dayton, Jones, Steele, & Rose, 1964). In early infancy, tracking of a smoothly moving target is accomplished solely by saccadic eye movements, and retinal velocity never matches target velocity. The only evidence for smooth pursuit in newborns comes from an EOG study by Kremenitzer et al. (1979), but they used an extremely large target that may have triggered OKN. Moreover, the gain of these smooth movements was considerably below 1.0 and saccades were interspersed to alter fixation rapidly to "catch up" to the moving target.

A more recent study of pursuit eye movements in somewhat older infants employed a smaller target and a more accurate corneal reflection recording system (Aslin, 1981). In support of the earlier studies by McGinnis (1930) and Dayton et al. (1964), no evidence of smooth pursuit was found until at least 6 weeks after birth. Brief segments of smooth pursuit were interspersed with saccadic tracking and the gain of the smooth segments was at best 0.50. However, another EOG study by Roucoux, Culee, and Roucoux (1983) reported evidence of smooth pursuit segments in newborns if the target velocity was slower than that used by Aslin (1981). In addition, Hainline (1985) reported smooth pursuit at slow target velocities in 1-month-olds. Thus, although there is some disagreement about the onset age for smooth pursuit, it is clear that the smooth pursuit system does not accurately match target velocity until several weeks after birth. Moreover, the evidence of smooth components of OKN in young infants demonstrates that even the newborn oculomotor apparatus is capable of executing smooth eye movements. It is possible that sensory information for translation of the target's image across the retina is degraded or that very young infants do not have a sufficiently well developed fovea to warrant accurate fixation and smooth tracking. Another intriguing possibility is that infants require *differential* motion of pattern elements in the visual array for consistent tracking to occur. Harris, Cassel, and Bamborough (1974) reported that infants 10–27 weeks old showed more consistent visual following of a target if the target's motion was different from a patterned background (either by having the background stationary or by moving it in the direction opposite to the target). These and other potential explanations of inefficient smooth pursuit in young infants await further empirical study.

Vergence Eye Movements

All of the preceding types of eye movements involve ocular rotations that are equal in both eyes. In contrast, vergence eye movements rotate the two lines of sight in opposite directions: either toward each other (convergence) to fixate near objects or away from each other (divergence) to fixate more distant objects. A very important function of vergence eye movements is to maintain the image of an object on both foveas. Failure to do so results either in the perception of double images (diplopia) or in a sensory adaptation (suppression) that eliminates diplopia by blocking the transfer of one eye's image to higher regions of the visual system.

There have been numerous observational reports that newborns are either incapable of converging to fixate a near object binocularly or sometimes appear cross-eyed when no near target is present (e.g., Peiper, 1963). Film records of infant binocular fixation (Ling, 1942) verified that convergence to a near target was absent until approximately 8 weeks of age. Initial attempts to use corneal photography to assess the accuracy of vergence (Maurer, 1974; Wickelgren, 1967) led to the conclusion that newborns are consistently walleyed, but at least some of this vergence inaccuracy was undoubtedly the result of the measurement error associated with the fact that the center of the pupil does not correspond exactly with the line of sight. Two more recent studies that used corneal photography and adjusted for this measurement problem (Aslin, 1977; Slater & Findlay, 1975a) found that newborns and 1-month-olds change their vergence angle appropriately as a target changes in distance, but vergence accuracy is limited to certain viewing distances. Specifically, near target viewing leads to an actual walleyed condition that cannot be attributed to a measurement error of corneal photography. Thus, on average, young infants make appropriate changes in vergence, but they are limited to intermediate viewing distances and they may be quite inaccurate on any given trial. However, corneal photography does not have sufficient resolution to estimate vergence accuracy with great precision.

Vergence inaccuracies may be mediated by deficiencies in the processing of the two major types of sensory information that control vergence in adults: blur and disparity. Slater and Findlay (1975a) suggested that the inability of young infants to accommodate may interfere with convergence to near target distances. Aslin and Jackson (1979) demonstrated that there is a link between accommodation and vergence in early infancy, a finding that is consistent with Slater and Findlay's hypothesis.

The second type of sensory information that leads to vergence responses in adults is based on the fact that each of the two eyes receives a slightly different image of objects located at near viewing distances. This interocular difference in the retinal images results from the fact that the eyes are separated slightly in the skull. The adult visual system is able to combine these slightly different images into a single (or fused) percept of objects, provided that the two images are not too discrepant and they are imaged onto so-called corresponding retinal areas. That is, pairs of locations on each retina are linked at a higher level of the visual system in such a way that fusion results rather than diplopia. When noncorresponding retinal locations are stimulated by an object, vergence eye movements can be executed to bring the two retinal images onto corresponding locations, thereby restoring fusion. The quantitative measure of noncorrespondence is called retinal disparity.

There have been no direct tests of the accuracy of fusional vergence eye movements (based solely on retinal disparity) in young infants because movement of a real object in distance triggers both blur and disparity. However, one study (Aslin, 1977) has provided an indirect measure of fusional vergence by inducing retinal disparity (but no accommodative stimulus) using wedge prisms. Prisms that displaced the image 2.5 or 5 deg were not sufficient to induce a fusional vergence eye movement in infants until the fifth postnatal month. In contrast, normal adults respond to prisms as small as 1–2 deg (Jampolsky, 1964). Thus it would appear that the sensory signal required to trigger a fusional vergence eye movement is not as finely tuned in young infants as it is in adults.

Summary

This brief review of the various oculomotor mechanisms utilized by the infant visual system to modulate the quantity and quality of retinal stimulation illustrates the complexity of the sensory and motor aspects of visual development. On the one hand, motor systems are used extensively as indices of sensory and perceptual development in the infant visual system. On the other hand, the development of these motor responses may be a function of nonsensory factors, including the independent development of the motor systems themselves. Thus it is important to understand the underlying mechanisms of all oculomotor systems that are used to estimate sensory and perceptual development. The visual system is unique in that the oculomotor systems are guided by sensory information and in turn alter that sensory input as a result of the motor output. This synergistic relation is both powerful, in that responses are tightly linked to sensory inputs, and complex, in that sensory and motor influences on the output are difficult to differentiate. However, it is clear that these oculomotor systems may place constraints on the higher-level aspects of visual perception to be discussed in the following sections.

Spatial Vision: Acuity and Contrast Sensitivity

Spatial resolution refers to the ability of the visual system to detect very small elements of contour (light–dark borders). Traditionally, spatial resolution has been assessed by presenting letters of varying size to subjects who can use verbal identification as a dependent response. Because infants cannot provide a verbal response, spatial resolution has been estimated with gratings (repetitive light–dark stripes). Gratings have also proven to be an important class of visual stimuli because they provide a measure of lateral interactions between adjacent contour elements, whereas a single contour (or bar) does not involve lateral interactions and has been shown to be largely independent of pattern vision (Cornsweet, 1970). By systematically varying the width of the stripes in the grating, one can estimate the stripe width that is just detectable. This threshold estimate of minimum detectable stripe width is one measure of acuity.

Three different techniques have been used to estimate acuity in infants: preferential looking, OKN, and the VEP. With each technique, acuity is defined as the smallest stripe width that reliably elicits a criterion response. A number of studies, employing slight variations in stimulus variables and procedures, have yielded quite consistent estimates of visual acuity in young infants (see review by Dobson & Teller, 1978). As shown in Figure 1.1, acuity corresponds to a stripe width of approximately 30–40 min of arc at birth, and there is a three- to fourfold improvement in acuity during the first 6 postnatal months. However, there are discrepancies between acuity estimates obtained with the three techniques. As discussed by Dobson and Teller (1978), and elaborated on by Banks and Dannemiller (1986), a variety of factors could contribute to these discrepancies, including the use of different stimulus variables (stationary vs. flickering vs. drifting gratings), different criteria for defining threshold, and different underlying neural mechanisms. Three recent studies have provided additional evidence in support of different acuity estimates using different

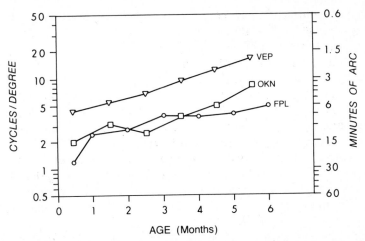

Figure 1.1. The development of visual acuity between birth and 6 months of age based on data collected with three techniques: preferential looking, optokinetic nystagmus (OKN), and the visual evoked potential (VEP). (From "Visual Acuity in Human Infants: A Review and Comparison of Behavioral and Electrophysiological Studies" by V. Dobson and D. Y. Teller, 1978, *Vision Research, 18,* p. 1480.) Reprinted with permission.

techniques (Maurer, Lewis, & Brent, in press; Norcia & Tyler, 1985; Sokol & Moskowitz, 1985). Despite these discrepancies, however, it appears that there is a very substantial improvement in acuity between birth and the second half of the first postnatal year.

An issue of considerable concern to both basic researchers and practitioners dealing with visual impairments is whether the acuity estimates obtained from infants are poorer than in adults simply because of poor attention or motivation. Harris, Hansen, and Fulton (1984) attempted to address this concern by constructing acuity stimuli that may enhance the infant's interest. They created a series of schematic face stimuli composed of black and white line segments varying in width. Groups of 1-, 3-, and 5-month-olds were tested with these schematic face stimuli and with standard gratings. No differences in acuity were obtained using the two types of stimuli, although there was some evidence that infants were more consistently attentive during the testing sessions with the facial stimuli.

Another important issue in the study of infant acuity is whether the fovea is actually used to fixate a stimulus. Although it is natural for normal adults to use the fovea for fixation, primarily because it is the retinal region with greatest resolving powers, there is anatomical evidence that the fovea is not fully mature until at least the fourth postnatal month (Abramov et al., 1982; Hendrickson & Yuodelis, 1984; Mann, 1964). A number of studies have attempted to document that infants under 4 months of age use the fovea for fixation and that spatial resolution is higher in the fovea than in the retinal periphery (Atkinson, Pimm-Smith, Evans, & Braddick, 1983; Lewis & Maurer, 1980; Spinelli, Pirchio, & Sandini, 1983). However, it has been impossible to rule out the alternative explanation that young infants use a nonfoveal retinal region for fixation and that this nonfoveal region has spatial resolution superior to the retinal periphery.

Another type of visual acuity involves the resolution of offsets (lateral displacements) for high-contrast targets. For example, adults are extremely sensitive to the lateral displacement of the middle dot in a vertically aligned array of three dots (2–10 sec of arc; Berry, 1948). This type of spatial resolution is called vernier acuity. Two studies (Manny & Klein, 1984; Shimojo, Birch, Gwiazda, & Held, 1984) have provided estimates of vernier acuity in infants 1–9 months old. Both studies used the preferential looking procedure to present two square wave gratings, one of which contained a subregion that was displaced laterally or vertically with respect to the background grating. As shown in Figure 1.2, both studies found a superiority of vernier over grating acuity, an effect also found in adults. Moreover, a follow-up study by Manny and Klein (1985) resolved the discrepancy between the absolute estimates of vernier acuity in the two previous studies by showing that the superior performance of the infants in the Shimojo and colleagues study could be replicated if several procedural variables more closely approximated those employed by Shimojo et al.

Although acuity is an important aspect of spatial resolution, there are many aspects of pattern vision that do not require excellent acuity. For example, subtle facial features often contain large contour elements. It has been suggested by researchers studying the adult visual system that a complete description of spatial resolution should include an estimate of contrast sensitivity (Cornsweet, 1970; Ginsburg, 1977). *Contrast* refers to the difference in luminance between adjacent light and dark stripes, and it is typically expressed as a percentage of this luminance difference compared to the combined luminance of the entire grating pattern (i.e., Lmax − Lmin/Lmax + Lmin × 100). *Contrast sensitivity* refers to the smallest amount of contrast required to detect the presence of a grating. One salient aspect of the adult visual system is that contrast sensitivity varies with the size of the stripes

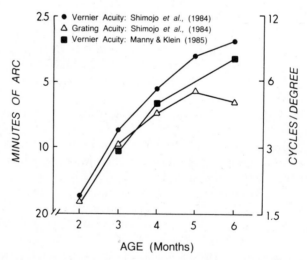

Figure 1.2. The development of vernier and grating acuity between birth and 12 months of age. (Reprinted with permission from "A Three Alternative Tracking Paradigm to Measure Vernier Acuity of Older Infants" by R. E. Manny and S. A. Klein, 1985, *Vision Research, 25*, p. 1250; Pergamon Journals Ltd. "Development of Vernier Acuity in Infants" by S. Shimojo, E. E. Birch, J. Gwiazda, and R. Held, 1984, *Vision Research, 24*, p. 725.)

in a grating pattern. For a variety of reasons, including the fact that any feature (i.e., spatial distribution of luminance) can be constructed from different-sized stripes with blurry edges, the standard stimulus used to assess contrast sensitivity is a sine wave grating. A sine wave grating is simply a set of stripes whose luminance profile changes gradually in a sinusoidal manner. Thus, to obtain an estimate of contrast sensitivity for stripes of different width, one can present sine wave gratings with different distances between the peaks of the sinusoidal luminance profile. Stripe width is best expressed in terms of retinal image size or visual angle rather than linear units like inches. Thus the width of the stripes in a grating can be expressed as cycles of the sine wave per visual degree (or cyc/deg). This unit of measurement is called spatial frequency. Thus narrow stripes have a high spatial frequency because many cycles (changes from light to dark to light) are contained within a single visual degree of retinal angle, and wide stripes have a low spatial frequency.

As shown in Figure 1.3, the contrast sensitivity function (CSF) of a normal adult is characterized by a peak at approximately 3 cyc/deg, corresponding to a stripe width of ⅙ deg (16 min of arc), a minimum detectable contrast of less than 1 percent, and a falloff in contrast sensitivity for both lower and higher spatial frequencies (wider and narrower stripes, respectively). The high spatial frequency falloff illustrates the decreasing sensitivity of the visual system to smaller contour elements, and an estimate of acuity is the highest spatial frequency that can be detected at 100 percent contrast (typically 30 cyc/deg or 1 min of arc in adults). The low spatial frequency falloff is associated with a mechanism called lateral inhibition. *Lateral inhibition* refers to the mutual inhibitory effect of adjacent pattern elements differing in luminance. If these pattern elements are of medium size, then lateral

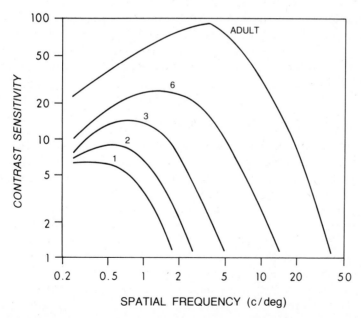

Figure 1.3. Schematized contrast sensitivity functions (CSFs) for adults and for infants 1–6 months of age.

inhibition can enhance the luminance difference. However, if the pattern elements are larger, then lateral inhibition cannot enhance the luminance difference. Thus the low spatial frequency falloff reflects the enhancement resulting from lateral inhibition at the medium spatial frequencies.

Figure 1.3 also illustrates CSFs for infants between 1 and 6 months of age. Notice three important features of this figure. First, the overall level of contrast sensitivity improves markedly between birth and adulthood. For example, an adult contrast threshold at 3 cyc/deg is approximately 1 percent, whereas even 100 percent contrast at 3 cyc/deg is not sufficient for detection by a 1-month-old and 20 percent contrast at 3 cyc/deg is required for detection by a 3-month-old. Recently, Adams and Maurer (1984) showed that contrast sensitivity in newborns for a low spatial frequency checkerboard is at least 11 percent. Second, the high-frequency cutoff of the CSF, which can be taken as an acuity estimate, improves markedly between birth and adulthood (from 0.5 cyc/deg to 30 cyc/deg). Third, there does not appear to be a low spatial frequency falloff in the CSF prior to 2 months of age, suggesting that the important mechanism of lateral inhibition is not functional until that age. As in the case of the development of acuity, both the preferential looking and VEP techniques have provided CSF estimates, and the general features illustrated in Figure 1.3 have been confirmed.

One important implication of the development of contrast sensitivity is that the detection of differences in stimulus blur, which depends on the detection of contrast differences, must be poorer in infants than in adults. First, infants are apparently unable to detect even medium spatial frequencies that are easily detected by adults. Second, great amounts of contrast are required for infants to detect even low spatial frequencies. As discussed earlier in the section on accommodation, Banks (1980b) has calculated the ability of the infant visual system to detect differences in stimulus blur given the very significant deficit in their CSF compared to adults. His estimates of blur detection thresholds suggest that the infant visual system is initially insensitive to what for adults would be easily detectable amounts of stimulus blur. Thus the accommodative inaccuracies measured in young infants appear to result from an inability to detect the sensory information required to trigger an accurate accommodative response.

Pattern Perception: The Linear Systems Approach

A potentially important approach to the understanding of infant pattern vision builds upon the notion that the CSF acts as a spatial filter for the visual system as a whole. In other words, there are many combinations of stimulus size (spatial frequency) and contrast that simply are not detectable by the visual system. The area under the CSF includes those combinations of spatial frequency and contrast to which the visual system is responsive. From Figure 1.3 it is quite apparent that the infant visual system filters out much more spatial information than the adult visual system. The linear systems approach is based on the assumption that a reasonable first approximation to an understanding of infant pattern vision consists of using the CSF to filter a potential visual stimulus to determine what spatial information is available to the infant visual system at a given age.

The actual computation involved in "filtering" the visual input with the CSF requires three steps. Consider a one-dimensional image of the visual stimulus. First, this stimulus is broken down into its so-called Fourier components. This analysis is based on the fact, described by Fourier's theorem, that any waveform can be decomposed into a finite set of sine waves that differ only in frequency (in this case, spatial extent or size), amplitude (in this case, contrast), and phase (in this case, relative spatial position within the image). Thus, as shown in Figure 1.4, a square wave can be created by summing together a series of sine waves whose frequencies are f, $3f$, $5f$, $7f$, . . . , whose amplitudes are 1, $\frac{1}{3}$, $\frac{1}{5}$, $\frac{1}{7}$, . . . , and whose phase is zero (i.e., all the sine waves begin at the same point). Similarly, although clearly in a more complicated way, any two-dimensional visual image can be decomposed into a series of so-called fundamental Fourier components with different orientations. This decomposition, performed by an image analysis system controlled by a computer, yields a representation of the visual stimulus that can be plotted in the Fourier domain (frequency $\times$ amplitude). This Fourier representation can then be "filtered" by the CSF by multiplying each spatial frequency component in the image by its relative weight based on the height of the CSF at that spatial frequency. Once "filtered" in the Fourier domain, the image can be transformed back into the image domain (space $\times$ luminance) by an inverse Fourier transform. The resultant image, then, is a representation of the spatial information that is actually available to the infant visual system after the visual stimulus has been "filtered" by the CSF.

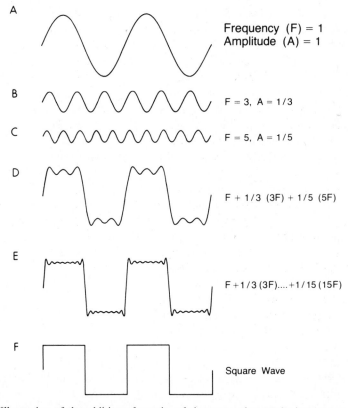

Figure 1.4. Illustration of the addition of a series of sine waves that results in a square wave and the application of this process to a grating pattern.

Although this "filtered" visual stimulus provides a nice demonstration of the transformed representation as "seen" by the infant's visual system, it does not provide a quantitative estimate of infant pattern vision (i.e., what the infant actually sees and how well different stimuli can be discriminated). However, if one makes a few simple assumptions, it is possible to predict a wide variety of phenomena in the infant pattern vision literature. For example, the vast majority of studies of infant pattern vision have used preferential looking as a measure of stimulus discrimination. A variety of constructs have been proposed as mediators of the infant's preference for one pattern over another, including complexity, discrepancy, and contour density. All of these constructs involve a developmental component, in that specific preferences change with age, and the factor underlying this development is a shift in "optimal" or preferred complexity, discrepancy, or contour density.

An alternative viewpoint, originally suggested and implemented by Banks and Salapatek (1981) and then elaborated on by Banks and Stephens (1982), Gayl, Roberts, and Werner (1983), and Banks and Ginsburg (1985), is a model of pattern preferences based on the CSF-filtered image of the visual stimulus and an assumption of maximum-contrast preference. In other words, once the visual stimulus has been "passed through" the CSF to obtain a representation of the visual information actually detectable by the infant visual system, the total amount of contrast contained in the two stimuli presented on a given preference test is compared. If the total stimulus contrast is detectably greater for one stimulus, then that stimulus will be preferred. Reanalyses of several previous preference studies revealed a remarkable correspondence between preferences predicted by this maximum-contrast model and actual preference results (see Fig. 1.5). This is quite impressive because the linear systems approach is presumably applicable only to threshold or near-threshold stimuli, and the stimuli used in the experiments represented in Figure 1.5 were clearly suprathreshold. It is important to note that, in its present form, the linear systems approach is applicable only to preference experiments and does not bear on infants' discriminative capacities per se.

It is clear that the linear systems approach will not be able to account fully for pattern preferences in older infants, as meaningfulness and familiarity become salient aspects of visual stimuli, nor will it be able to account fully for discriminative abilities that are assessed by habituation techniques, because the transformed stimulus representation according to the linear systems model is constant across repeated exposures. However, the approach has been applied successfully to preferential looking and habituation data collected from newborns (Slater, Earle, Morison, & Rose, 1985). Slater et al. (1985) demonstrated that stimuli equated on contour density but differing on overall contrast after filtering by the newborn CSF yielded preference data consistent with the linear systems model of Banks and Salapatek (1981). Moreover, they showed that strong initial preferences for certain stimuli are *not* shifted by habituation trials, whereas initially *non*preferred stimuli are subject to a novelty preference after habituation. Thus the linear systems approach has proven useful in pointing out the sensory information that is actually available to the infant visual system at different ages. When the model predicts empirical data, it provides a good account of that aspect of perception. When the model fails to account for empirical data, it must be modified appropriately. However, even if the model fails, it has the advantage of providing testable, quantitative predictions. This is a feature that is quite rare in the infant pattern perception literature.

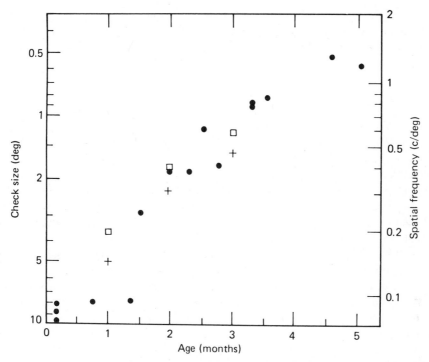

Figure 1.5. Predictions of pattern preference based on the linear systems approach implemented by Banks and colleagues. (From "Infant Visual Preferences: A Review and New Theoretical Treatment" by M. S. Banks and A. P. Ginsburg, 1985, in *Advances in Child Development and Behavior* by H. W. Reese (Ed.), New York: Academic Press. Reprinted with permission.)

Pattern Perception: Higher-Order Properties

Although much of the foregoing information on relatively low-level constraints on visual perception is important for setting an upper bound on the young infant's capacities, it does not account for many of the higher-order properties of visual perception associated with the adult visual system. These so-called higher-order properties include the segregation of figure from ground, the appreciation of pattern based on element arrangement, the organization of contours into a shape, and the identification of faces. Although there are more aspects of higher-order pattern perception to summarize than space allows, some of the more recent empirical demonstrations in young infants will be highlighted. This section will be limited to static two-dimensional patterns. Dynamic and three-dimensional patterns will be discussed in the later section on object perception.

The Externality Effect

One of the earliest empirical findings on the scanning of two-dimensional patterns was a developmental shift from fixation of external contours to fixation of internal contours (Salapatek, 1975). That is, when confronted with a pattern containing contours located within other contours, newborns and 1-month-olds tended to fixate exclusively the external contours, whereas older infants tended to fixate predominantly the internal contours (see also Maurer, 1983). It is important to note that young infants, who do not fixate an internal pattern element when it is surrounded by other pattern elements, do fixate that same smaller pattern element in the absence of the surrounding elements. An interpretive difficulty associated with scanning data is the inability to conclude from the absence of direct fixation that young infants fail to perceive internal pattern elements. The scanning technique only allows for an estimate of which aspects of a pattern are fixated directly (presumably with the fovea). It is quite possible, as in adults, that all aspects of a complex pattern are perceived via the combined input from the fovea and peripheral retina. For example, Maurer and Lewis (1979) have demonstrated that by 3 months of age infants can discriminate pattern differences when two stimuli are presented only to the peripheral retina. Thus scanning data are not sufficient to conclude that young infants do not perceive the internal elements of a complex two-dimensional pattern. Another technique is required to provide a measure of perception that is not dependent on inferences from scanning.

Milewski (1976) used the high-amplitude sucking technique to assess discrimination of the same visual patterns that Salapatek (1975) had used in his scanning studies. Separate groups of 1- and 4-month-olds were presented with patterns whose (1) internal element, (2) external element, (3) internal and external elements, or (4) neither internal nor external elements (control) were altered. Postshift sucking increased in all three experimental groups among the 4-month-olds, indicating that both internal and external pattern elements were perceived. However, the 1-month-olds who received a shift in only the internal element did not show evidence of an increase in sucking, whereas a shift in the external element did lead to an increase in sucking. A follow-up experiment demonstrated that this apparent failure to discriminate changes in the internal pattern element was not attributable to an inability to discriminate changes in the small pattern element when it was presented in isolation. These findings support the contention that there is a close correspondence between the elements of pattern that are fixated directly and the perception of those pattern elements. However, because the HAS technique requires encoding of these pattern elements and a subsequent comparison of pre- and postshift pattern elements, it is possible that the failure to exhibit recovery of sucking is the result of an encoding or retrieval deficit rather than a deficit in perception per se.

An obvious question that arose from these findings on the so-called externality effect is why young infants fail to deploy their fixation (and/or attention) to a smaller pattern element embedded in a larger pattern element. Milewski (1978) reported that a change in a small pattern element located adjacent to a larger pattern element was not discriminated by 1-month-olds. Thus, it appears that young infants, for as yet unexplained reasons, prefer to fixate primarily the larger of two or more pattern elements. Presumably, this fixation preference leads to an ineffective encoding/retrieval (and possibly perception) of the nonfixated pattern elements. However, Bushnell (1979) reported that 1-month-olds *are* capable of discriminating a change in an internal pattern element if the internal element is flashed or moved. Similarly, flashing or moving a smaller element located adjacent to a larger element enables 1-month-olds to discriminate a change in the smaller element. These results were extended by Ganon and Swartz (1980), who reported that 1-month-olds can discriminate a *static* internal pattern element if it has much higher salience than the external pattern element, for example, a bull's-eye surrounded by a circle. However, the same patterns used by Ganon and Swartz with 1-month-olds did not prove successful in overriding the externality effect in newborns (Bushnell, Gerry, & Burt, 1983). Thus at present it appears that the so-called externality effect is the result of a bias on the part of young infants to fixate and/or attend to the most salient pattern element in a multielement array. Salience is apparently defined as the largest continuous region of pattern or the region containing highest contour density. Alternatively, application of the linear systems approach may reveal that discrimination of larger or smaller pattern elements is a by-product of the spatial filtering properties of the infant visual system. To date, this approach has not been applied to the results on the externality effect.

Face Perception

These findings on the externality effect with geometric stimuli have been extended to more natural stimuli—faces—that contain both internal and external pattern elements. A number of scanning studies have confirmed that the externality effect is present in young infants presented with both real and schematic faces (Hainline, 1978; Haith, Bergman, & Moore, 1977; Maurer & Salapatek, 1976), although the effect is less evident in newborns presented with schematic faces (Maurer, 1983). Several aspects of this research on face perception now seem clear (see review by Maurer, 1985). First, prior to 2 months of age, infants do not appear capable of discriminating between an arrangement of contours that comprise a schematic face and a scrambled arrangement of these same contours. For example, although newborns will track a moving face farther than a moving gray region of the same size and mean luminance, they will also track a scrambled array of contours as far as the schematic face (Maurer & Young, 1983). In addition, 1-month-olds do not show differential fixation of a schematic face versus a scrambled face and fail to show recovery of fixation to the schematic face after habituation to the scrambled face, whereas 2-month-olds do fixate the schematic face longer and show evidence of discriminating between the schematic and the scrambled face (Maurer & Barrera, 1981). Although Haaf, Smith, and Smitley (1983) found little evidence for preference of schematic faces over scrambled faces even in 3-month-olds, there is some evidence that a more sensitive testing procedure can reveal such a face preference (see Maurer, 1985). Second, infants as young as 5 weeks of age are capable of discriminating between photographs of different faces (Bushnell, 1982). However, the basis for this discrimination is likely to be mediated by the external features of the faces because standardizing the hairline (using a bathing cap) led to a failure of face discrimination in 5-week-olds. In contrast, infants' discrimination of differences in facial expressions (mediated by internal facial features) has been demonstrated by 3 months of age (Barrera & Maurer, 1981; Young-Browne, Rosenfeld, & Horowitz, 1977), as well as by 5–7 months (Nelson, Morse, & Leavitt, 1979; Schwartz, Izard, & Ansul, 1985; see review by Nelson, 1985). However, even 9-month-olds show inconsistent evidence of extracting the emotional category (e.g., anger) from static faces independently of specific features correlated with that emotion (e.g., presence of teeth; see Caron, Caron, & Myers, 1985). Nevertheless, the foregoing findings suggest that the configuration of pattern elements in a facial stimulus (real or schematic) takes on special significance during the third postnatal month and that limitations on scanning and/or extraction of facial features constrain the discrimination of two-dimensional facial stimuli in early infancy.

Although these findings on face perception in young infants are consistent with the data on the externality effect with nonfacial stimuli, it is not clear why faces take on special significance once the externality effect has been overcome. For example, it is possible that infants learn through visual exploration that some faces are familiar and that faces in general are correlated with pleasant social interactions. In contrast, preferences for facial stimuli may emerge developmentally according to a maturational sequence that is little affected by visual experience. As pointed out in a recent study by Dannemiller and Stephens (submitted), the degree of face-likeness has not been manipulated independently of correlated physical attributes. For example, a preference for a face may arise because the face is facelike or because the face has configurations of contours that are attractive regardless of their presence in faces. This is a classic problem of differentiating between proximal and distal cues for a perceptual phenomenon. Dannemiller and Stephens (submitted) attacked this problem by creating facelike stimuli that were equated on all physical dimensions except spatial phase. In other words, the faces were contrast reversals, with the black elements in one pattern corresponding to the white elements in the other pattern, and vice versa. They reported that 12-week-olds preferred to fixate the face stimulus with dark facial features and a dark external contour, whereas 6-week-olds showed no preference for either of the two phase-reversed stimuli. In addition, the 12-week-olds showed no fixation preference for nonfacial stimuli that differed only in their spatial phase. Thus by 3 months of age infants have extracted some meaning (or significance) to the pattern of facial features to which they have been exposed during early postnatal life. Moreover, this face preference cannot be attributed to any of the proximal physical attributes of facial stimuli that covary with facelikeness.

Configurations and Gestalt Principles

It seems clear from the data on scanning of two-dimensional patterns that by 2 months of age infants engage in a comprehensive series of fixations of both the internal and external elements of a complex pattern. However, an extensive scanpath may not be sufficient for extracting some of the organizational properties of complex patterns. These organizational properties include the so-called Gestalt laws of good continuation, common fate, symmetry, and proximity. Salapatek (1975) developed a particularly interesting set of displays to examine some of these Gestalt laws in young infants. A matrix (rows and columns) of small identical elements was presented on both sides of a preferential looking display. One matrix contained 14-by-14 identical elements, whereas the other matrix contained 14-by-14 identical elements except for a small (2 by 2, 4 by 4, or 6 by 6) region of elements that differed from the background elements. This "discrepant" region of elements could only be detected if it differed on some basis from the background elements. Salapatek reported that 2- to 3-month old infants reliably fixated the matrix containing the discrepant elements, but only if the elements contained higher contour density than the background elements. Thus, if the discrepant elements were vertical lines and the background elements were horizontal lines, infants did not reliably fixate the matrix containing this discrepancy. Moreover, if the discrepant region contained the *absence* of elements, infants did not reliably fixate this discrepancy, even though adults and preschoolers reported that the "hole" in the matrix was perceptually compelling. Thus, Salapatek did not find evidence in 2- and 3-month-olds for the detection of grouping principles among identical elements in a texturelike display.

Recently, Van Giffen and Haith (1984) extended the use of this matrix technique to other variations in element arrangement. They presented 1- and 3-month-olds with circles and squares composed of many small elements (i.e., the contours comprising the elements were not joined). Each of the circles and squares contained a single element (located at the top or bottom of the figure) that was either displaced outward from the center of the figure or oriented 90 deg with respect to the adjacent elements. Thus to adults the discrepant element was easily detectable and was perceived as a discrepancy in the overall organization of the arrangement of pattern elements. A corneal reflection video system recorded each infant's fixations to several discrepant pattern arrangements as well as to a nondiscrepant control arrangement. The results indicated that 3-month-olds tend to fixate in the direction of the discrepant element, whereas the fixation data from the 1-month-olds were less consistently directed to the discrepant element. Thus, with a simple set of pattern elements, Van Giffen and Haith have provided the earliest indication that element arrangement operates as a Gestalt principle in 3-month-olds.

Another approach to the study of infants' perception of element arrangement is to habituate the infant to a particular arrangement of elements and then present test stimuli that contain either the same elements in a different arrangement or different elements in the same arrangement. If arrangement has been perceived in the habituation stimuli, then a novelty effect should be evident only to the test stimulus consisting of a change in arrangement. Vurpillot, Ruel, and Castrec (1977) conducted such a habituation experiment with 2- and 4-month-olds and reported that with small element sizes the novelty effect was present for the change in arrangement. Unfortunately, this change in element arrangement was accompanied by a local change in many regions of contour. Thus infants may have detected the change in these local features rather than appreciating the arrangement of the elements per se. Milewski (1979) conducted a similar experiment with 3-month-olds using three dots arranged in a vertical alignment. After habituation to this three-dot array, infants increased their fixation duration to a novel three-dot array whose middle dot was displaced laterally with respect to the other two dots. Although this could be interpreted as evidence of the perception of element arrangement, it could also have resulted from a local detection of contour displacement, similar to the displacement that is detected in a vernier acuity task (see Fig. 1.2).

In an attempt to overcome this problem of dissociating local changes in contour with changes in element arrangement, Bertenthal, Campos, and Haith (1980) employed a type of display whose element arrangement induces in adults the illusory perception of pattern contours. These so-called subjective contours are created by a particular configuration of pattern elements containing information for the corners of a larger shape. If these corner elements are altered even slightly, the perception of subjective contours disappears. Bertenthal and colleagues habituated 5- and 7-month-olds to an arrangement that did not induce a subjective contour in adults and then presented posthabituation test trials consisting of a subjective contour display and a novel but nonsubjective contour display. The 7-month-olds showed a novelty response only to the subjective contour display, whereas the results from the 5-month-olds were inconsistent. These results support the conclusion that

7-month-olds are capable of extracting a particular form of element arrangement from a complex two-dimensional display. Moreover, the results cannot be attributed to the detection of a local contour difference because of the absence of a novelty effect between the two nonsubjective contour displays.

One of the interesting features of the element arrangement in a subjective contour display is the symmetry among the elements. For example, in the display used by Bertenthal and colleagues (1980), all of the elements contained a notch that was oriented toward the center of the arrangement of elements. This possible role of symmetry in infant pattern perception was investigated by Bornstein and his colleagues. Bornstein, Ferdinandsen, and Gross (1981) reported that 4-month-olds habituated more rapidly to patterns with vertical symmetry (right–left mirror images) than to patterns with horizontal symmetry or no symmetry. Similarly, 4-month-olds tested in a habituation novelty task showed evidence of discriminating a pattern containing vertical symmetry from a pattern containing either horizontal or no symmetry, but did not show evidence of discriminating horizontal symmetry from no symmetry (Fisher, Ferdinandsen, & Bornstein, 1981). A similar primacy of vertical symmetry was reported by Humphrey, Humphrey, Muir, and Dodwell (1986) in a series of experiments with 4-month-olds, but they also reported that diagonally symmetrical patterns were encoded whereas nonsymmetrical patterns were not.

Bornstein and Krinsky (1985) extended these findings in a series of follow-up experiments. They reported that 4-month-olds (1) habituate more rapidly to vertically symmetrical patterns than to patterns that contain two vertically oriented elements that are not vertically symmetrical, (2) habituate more rapidly to vertically symmetrical patterns whose elements are spatially adjacent (0 or 2.5 deg separation) than to vertically symmetrical patterns that are spatially disparate (5 or 10 deg separation), and (3) discriminate between a vertically symmetrical pattern and a nonsymmetrical pattern composed of two identical vertically oriented elements. These last data were interpreted as evidence that 4-month-olds appreciate the configuration of the pattern elements rather than simply the local pattern differences. However, it would appear that this conclusion is not fully justified, because local pattern differences were present in the symmetrical and nonsymmetrical stimuli. Thus, as in the Vurpillot et al. (1977) and Milewski (1979) studies, infants may have shown pattern discrimination simply by detecting any local pattern difference without appreciating the arrangement of the pattern elements. This local versus global issue in pattern discrimination was also a problem in a recent study of element arrangement in *newborns* (Antell & Caron, 1985). The authors attempted to overcome the local contour confound by changing the absolute location of the pattern elements within the field of view across successive habituation trials. However, if the newborns had simply fixated only the top (or bottom) of the array of elements on each trial, discrimination of the rearrangement of elements could have been based on the detection of a change in local contour density rather than on the arrangement of the pattern elements.

One important aspect of pattern perception that may constrain the infant's perception of symmetry is the ability to discriminate stimulus orientation. Maurer and Martello (1980) demonstrated that infants 5–6 weeks old dishabituate to a grating of a novel orientation. This novelty effect was not attributable to scanning biases because no recovery of fixation was shown to the same grating orientation when the white and black bars were reversed in location (thereby inducing a local change in pattern unrelated to orientation). However, this study was limited to the two oblique (135 and 45 deg) orientations. Thus it was not informative about the limits of the infant's orientation discrimination. Nevertheless, this positive evidence for oblique orientation discrimination in young infants is important given several failures to find such a capacity (Colombo, Laurie, Martelli, & Hartig, 1984; Essock & Siqueland, 1981). Bomba, Eimas, Siqueland, and Miller (1984) also reported poor performance by 3- and 4-month olds on a horizontal or vertical versus oblique discrimination task, but they found significant orientation discrimination performance when the stimuli were embedded in a context containing different orientations. Finally, Bomba (1984) investigated 2-, 3-, and 4-month-olds' novelty preferences for oblique gratings at 45-, 25-, 22.5-, 14.5-, and 2.5-deg orientations after habituation to a vertically oriented grating. He reported that 2-month-olds did not discriminate among any of the oblique orientation differences. In contrast, 3-month-olds discriminated between 45 deg and 14.5 deg and between 25 deg and 2.5 deg, but not between 45 deg and 22.5 deg. Four-month-olds discriminated between 45 deg and 14.5 deg, 45 deg and 22.5 deg, and 25 deg and 2.5 deg. Thus, it appears that orientation sensitivity, particularly among the class of obliques, develops significantly during the first 4 months of age. It is interesting to note that the infant's ability to convert orientation information into a well-controlled behavioral response may require several months of visual-motor experience. Lockman, Ashmead, and Bushnell (1984) showed that 9-month-olds, but not 5-month-olds, are quite accurate in orienting their hand during the early phase of a reaching response to correspond to the orientation of a graspable object (a vertical or horizontal dowel).

A final, and perhaps most complex, aspect of the perception of two-dimensional patterns is the issue of shape perception. That is, are infants capable of recognizing that an arrangement of contours (either open or closed) has the same shape despite transformations in orientation or size? A comprehensive set of experiments by Schwartz and Day (1979) examined shape perception in 2- and 4-month-olds using the habituation-novelty paradigm. They presented evidence that variations in orientation and size had little effect on posthabituation fixation durations, thereby implying that pattern shape was extracted during the habituation sequence. However, as pointed out in a commentary to that monograph (Cohen, 1979), nearly all of the results could be accounted for by assuming that the infants were responding to the angles and/or the length of the line segments that comprised the shapes. That is, as in most other tests of higher-order pattern perception in infants, a local aspect of the entire configuration of contours may have provided the basis for the obtained results. This does not mean that young infants are incapable of shape perception. It simply means that the available data cannot differentiate between an explanation based on local features and an explanation based on an invariant property (shape) of the combination of features.

A particular aspect of the Schwartz and Day (1979) experiments was recently replicated and extended by Cohen and Younger (1984). Schwartz and Day had concluded, in part, that infants have an innate ability to perceive the relational information contained in the specific shapes they employed in their experiments. In particular, they concluded that "the angular relationship between edges and not the orientation of edges is the primary discriminative variable of shape in early infancy" (p. 21). Cohen and Younger noted that data from 2- and 4-month-olds do not answer the question of the innateness of this relational perceptual information. Moreover, the specific stimuli used by Schwartz and Day confounded the angular relations in the shape with the orientation of the individual line segments comprising the shape. Thus, Cohen and Younger tested 3-month-olds with stimuli that did not confound angular relations with line segment orientation, and they tested 6-week-olds to determine whether the perception of angular relations was present at an earlier age. Their results from 3-month-olds replicated the findings of Schwartz and Day, indicating that infants by this age respond to the angular relations of the line segments rather than to the orientation of the line segments. However, the 6-week-olds did not provide evidence of responding to the angular relations. Rather, they responded to the absolute orientations of the line segments comprising the shapes. Thus, Cohen and Younger proposed that relational information about shape is not innate but is acquired during the second postnatal month. In addition, they noted that younger infants may be *capable* of perceiving relational information if tested with a procedure that allows the infant to encode the shape of the habituation stimulus more effectively.

Another recent experiment indicates that 3- to 4-month-olds can use relational information to extract shape information, and the specific selection of stimulus materials made it unlikely that local features mediated the infants' performance. Bomba and Siqueland (1983) constructed shapes (square, triangle, circle) composed of dots and distortions of those shapes by shifting one or more of the dots. After familiarization with several different exemplars of a distorted shape, each infant was presented with a preference test that paired the *un*distorted (prototypical) shape with an undistorted *novel* shape. Infants reliably preferred to fixate the novel shape even though both shapes presented during this preference test differed from the distorted familiarization stimuli. A follow-up experiment verified that this preference for a novel shape was not simply the result of a failure to discriminate the nondistorted shapes from the distorted shapes. Thus, Bomba and Siqueland provided compelling evidence for the categorization of shapes based on prototypes, even though those prototypes had not been previously presented to the infants.

In summary, the area of two-dimensional pattern perception by infants continues to stimulate the interest and experimental efforts of a number of researchers. There appears to be a developmental progression of perceptual mechanisms that analyze patterns at relatively low levels (attributes), mid-levels (features), and high levels (configurations). However, it is not clear to what extent these findings are determined by the particular test procedures used with infants at different ages and the oculomotor developments that may initially constrain the type of information actually registered by the visual system. Moreover, as discussed in a later section on object perception, certain dynamic aspects of stimulus presentation appear to facilitate the extraction of pattern information. Thus at least part of the apparent developmental progression in the perception of static, two-dimensional patterns may result from an early dependence on attentional mechanisms that are only activated by high-contrast, flashing, or moving stimulus characteristics.

Color Vision

The ability to perceive chromatic differences between objects may at first appear to be an aesthetic "bonus" rather than a functionally useful capacity. However, there are many instances in the natural environment when color can permit object perception that would be nearly impossible without it. For example, in a heavily "cluttered" or camouflaged visual array, color perception allows an observer to detect easily an object whose hue is dramatically different from the hue of the background (e.g., a cardinal perched on a branch in a forest). A color-blind observer would be forced to rely on other visual information (e.g., luminance differences, relative motion, stereopsis) that typically require more subtle discriminations or longer detection times. For both aesthetic and functional reasons, researchers have long wondered whether young infants have color vision. Surprisingly, most aspects of infant color vision have only been conclusively documented in the past 10 years, in large part because of the technical difficulties of isolating chromatic information in a nonverbal organism.

There are essentially three questions that have been examined in infants with respect to color vision. First, what is the relative sensitivity of the infant visual system to different wavelengths? Second, can infants discriminate between different wavelengths of light independently of the luminance differences that typically covary with wavelength? Third, what are the perceptual categories used by infants when they group different wavelengths? Studies that have addressed these three questions have been summarized recently in an extensive review by Teller and Bornstein (1986).

Spectral Sensitivity

There are two basic types of photoreceptors in the primate retina: rods and cones. Rods are more sensitive to low-intensity (scotopic) stimuli, whereas cones are only sensitive to relatively high-intensity (photopic) stimuli. Although only a single photopigment (the chemical that absorbs light energy) is present in all rods, there are three different types of cone photopigments. These cone photopigments correspond to long (red), medium (green), and short (blue) wavelengths of light. Spectral sensitivity refers to the minimum amount of light energy at a given wavelength that is just detectable. Thus one can obtain a measure of scotopic spectral sensitivity by first dark-adapting the infant to eliminate the contribution of the cones and then presenting targets of varying intensity limited to a narrow band of wavelengths. The resultant scotopic spectral sensitivity function represents the efficiency with which the rod photopigment absorbs light at different wavelengths. Two studies of infants (Powers, Schneck, & Teller, 1981; Werner, 1982) used preferential looking and VEPs, respectively, to estimate infant scotopic spectral sensitivity. As shown in Figure 1.6, although infants are generally less sensitive than adults to light of a given absolute intensity, even 1-month-olds show a *relative* spectral sensitivity that is nearly identical to that of adults. Thus it would appear that the rod photopigment (rhodopsin) is the same from birth to adulthood.

Photopic spectral sensitivity is more complex in that three different photopigments contribute to the overall function. Although the output of these three photopigments for a stimulus containing many different wavelengths could simply be the summation of the three underlying photopigments, the overall function could also reflect complex inhibitory or multiplicative interactions. Moreover, in adults the overall shape of the photopic spectral sensitivity function is dependent on a variety of testing conditions (see Hurvich, 1981), for example, target size and duration, retinal eccentricity, and adaptation level (time at a given light intensity). Three studies have provided estimates of photopic spectral sensitivity in young in-

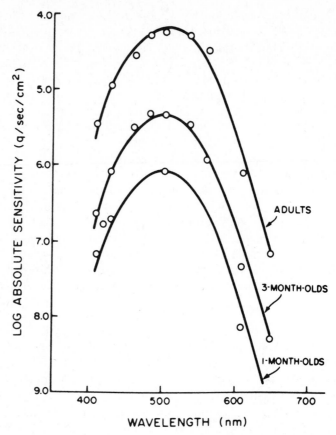

Figure 1.6. Scotopic spectral sensitivity in 1-month-olds, 3-month-olds, and adults. (From "Spectral Sensitivity of Human Infants at Absolute Visual Threshold" by M. K. Powers, M. Schneck, and D. Y. Teller, 1981, *Vision Research, 21,* p. 1013. Reprinted with permission.)

fants (Dobson, 1976; Moskowitz-Cook, 1979; Peeples & Teller, 1978). As shown in Figure 1.7, the *relative* shape of the curves obtained from infants matches closely the adult curve obtained under similar testing conditions. However, there is some evidence at the short wavelengths that infants are somewhat more sensitive than adults. It has been speculated that this enhanced relative sensitivity is the result of developmental changes in macular and/or lens pigmentation (the less yellowish macula/lens in infants may absorb/filter less blue light; Werner, 1982).

Although these data on photopic spectral sensitivity are important for studies of wavelength discrimination, they do not bear directly on the question of whether young infants have more than one cone photopigment, because a single photopigment, with a spectral sensitivity broader than any of the three adult cone photopigments, could yield an overall photopic spectral sensitivity function that was nearly identical to that of the adult. A technique called chromatic adaptation, however, can reveal the presence of more than one cone photopigment. If a target of a particular band of wavelengths (the adaptor) is presented for several minutes, then sensitivity to all wavelengths will be reduced temporarily if there is only a single

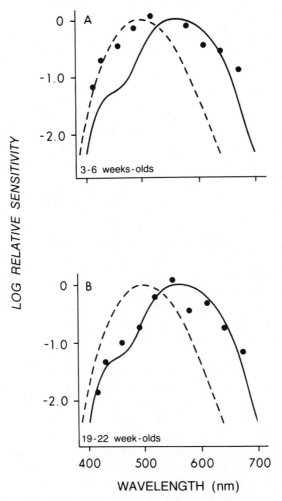

Figure 1.7. Photopic spectral sensitivity in 1-month-olds and 5-month-olds along with standard adult functions. (Reprinted with permission from "The Development of Photopic Spectral Sensitivity in Human Infants" by A. Moskowitz-Cook, 1979, *Vision Research*, *19*, p. 1139, Pergamon Journals Ltd.)

cone photopigment. However, if there are at least two cone photopigments maximally sensitive in different regions of the spectrum, then the sensitivity of only a limited region of the spectrum will be reduced. Pulos, Teller, and Buck (1980) measured the effects of chromatic adaptation in 2- and 3-month-olds and found evidence of at least two cone photopigments in 3-month-olds (and adults), but the data from 2-month-olds were inconsistent. However, the type of chromatic adaptation involved only a search for a short wavelength-sensitive (blue) cone photopigment. Schanel-Klitsch and Woodruff-Pak (1985) also measured the effects of chromatic adaptation in newborns and found evidence of at least two cone photopigments. Thus it appears that infants under 2 months of age have at least two cone photopigments, although the so-called blue cone system may be relatively immature until the third postnatal month.

Discrimination of Hue

The foregoing summary of spectral sensitivity has little direct relevance to the commonsense notion of color vision: the appreciation of differences in hue between two objects. However, the discrimination of hue is a specific aspect of the generic view of color vision. For example, two stoplights that appear to be slightly different shades of red may differ not at all in wavelength (hue), but only in brightness (intensity). This is because our perception of "color" is a combination of three variables: hue, saturation (the amount of white light added to the hue), and brightness. Many different combinations of these three variables can lead to the same color percept. Similarly, two colors may appear different because they differ on any one of the three variables. Thus to determine whether an infant can discriminate on the basis of wavelength information alone, it is necessary to equate the two wavelengths for brightness and saturation. Saturation can be equated simply by using narrow-band stimuli (essentially no added white light). However, brightness must be equated in a more complicated manner. Perhaps the simplest way to illustrate the complexity of this brightness match problem is to imagine a visual system with a single photopigment (as in the case of scotopic vision; see Fig. 1.6). This "color-blind" visual system is quite capable of detecting the difference between wavelengths unless those wavelengths are matched in intensity with respect to the spectral sensitivity function. For example, if the two wavelengths were selected by drawing a horizontal line through the middle of Figure 1.6, the relative sensitivity of the visual system would be identical at those two wavelengths and they could not be discriminated unless they differed in intensity. In contrast, a visual system with at least two photopigments would be able to discriminate most wavelength differences even if one equated their relative intensities. This is because wavelength information can be extracted from the unique combination of outputs of the two photopigments.

Early attempts at studying wavelength discrimination in infants assumed that one could equate the luminances of different wavelengths by using adult brightness match data. However, these adult data only reflect group averages and do not control for individual differences between adult observers. Moreover, photopic spectral sensitivity data from infants indicate that adult and infant brightness matches are unlikely to be identical at all wavelengths. Thus the Fagan (1974) study that used checkerboard stimuli composed of two wavelengths matched in brightness on the basis of adult averages may have allowed infants with a single photopigment to detect the presence of a pattern (the checkerboard) based on differences in shades of gray rather than on differences in hue.

More recent attempts to study wavelength discrimination have acknowledged this potential brightness artifact and controlled for it by systematically varying the relative intensities of the two wavelengths. For example, Peeples and Teller (1975) presented a red target on a white background and varied the intensity of the target around the adult brightness match. Thus, by using very small differences in intensity, they searched for a brightness match between target and background. Failure to find a brightness match implied the presence of at least two cone photopigments. Two-month-olds continued to detect the presence of the red target on the white background even at relative intensities that surely would have included a brightness match (in fact, a gray-vs.-gray control condition indicated that infants were quite sensitive to brightness mismatches in the range used to study wavelength discrimination).

Three other approaches have been used to control for potential brightness artifacts in infants' wavelength discrimination data. Schaller (1975) used an operant technique to reinforce fixation of a chromatic checkerboard whose luminance varied unsystematically from presentation to presentation. Despite luminance variations that certainly encompassed the potential brightness match, 3-month-olds provided evidence of wavelength discrimination. Similarly, Oster (1975) embedded a chromatic check into the middle of an achromatic checkerboard whose checks varied in intensity. The achromatic check luminances differed by an amount greater than the expected chromatic brightness mismatch. Using preferential looking, she paired this chromatic–achromatic checkerboard with a completely achromatic checkerboard and found that 2-month-olds preferred the chromatic–achromatic checkerboard. Adams, Maurer, and Davis (1986) used a similar procedure with newborns and reported evidence of discrimination of green, yellow, and red from gray, but not blue from gray. Teller, Peeples, and Sekel (1978) also reported some failures to discriminate wavelength in 2-month-olds. However, because of the many successful demonstrations of wavelength discrimination, it is clear that even newborns have at least two cone photopigments.

A recent study by Maurer, Lewis, Cavanagh, and Anstis (submitted) has provided data on spectral brightness matching using a clever method developed by Cavanagh, Anstis, and Mather (1984). A color television display presents either red and green stripes or blue and yellow stripes that rapidly change screen position to simulate stripe movement. The relative intensity of the red-green or blue-yellow stripes determines the perceived direction of stripe movement (left or right), and the stripes appear stationary when they are matched in relative luminance. Maurer and colleagues reported that the luminance matches in young infants were virtually identical to those in adults tested under the same conditions. The fact that these luminance matches in 1- and 3-month-olds occurred at the same relative intensities as in adults indicates the presence of at least two cone photopigments.

Overall, then, these studies provide evidence that infants as young as newborns have at least two functional cone photopigments. However, it was not clear until very recently whether infants had the same *three* cone photopigments as in adults. In other words, are infants trichromats? This question has generated a considerable amount of debate in the literature (see the most recent exchange in a long-standing controversy: Werner & Wooten, 1979; Bornstein, 1981a; Werner & Wooten, 1985b; Bornstein, 1985; Werner & Wooten, 1985a). At issue is the interpretation of infant wavelength discrimination data that would appear to rule out the presence of any of the three standard forms of dichromacy (only two photopigments). Bornstein (1976) and Hamer, Alexander, and Teller (1982) showed that by 3 months of age infants can make wavelength discriminations that would not be possible without the red and green photopigments. Packer, Hartmann, and Teller (1984) showed that larger test fields than those used by Hamer et al. (1982) improved the wavelength discrimination performance of 1- and 2-month-olds, implying that spatial summation is greater in younger infants and that red and green cone photopigments are present prior to 3 months of age. Finally, Varner, Cook, Schneck, McDonald, and Teller (1985) showed that by 3 months of age infants can make wavelength discriminations that would not be possible without a blue cone photopigment. These infant data, taken as a whole, provide compelling evidence that by 3 months of age infants are not classic protanopes (missing the red cones), deuteranopes (missing the green cones), or tritanopes (missing the blue cones). That is, they are able to discriminate wavelengths that are not discriminated by adults who are missing one of these cone photopigments. Of course, it is possible that these infants are making such "critical" wavelength discriminations even though they are lacking one of the three cone photopigments because the photopigment they are lacking does not correspond exactly in spectral sensitivity to one of the three adult photopigments. Thus, Werner and Wooten (1985a, 1985b) continue to argue that "conclusive proof" of trichromacy, even in infants older than 3 months, has not as yet been provided. Although strictly correct, their position is extremely implausible given the many other aspects of infant color vision that are consistent with the conclusion that 3-month-olds have all three cone photopigments.

Color Categories

An interesting aspect of color perception in adults is the fact that the verbal labels for hues are generally consistent between individuals and even across different language communities. Bornstein (see reviews, 1978, 1981b) has provided an extensive series of experiments aimed at determining whether these color categories are learned or innate. His strategy has been to assume that any consistency between the color categories used by adults and by preverbal infants must be the result of nonlinguistic factors. The paradigm he chose to investigate color categories in infants was to habituate infants to one hue and then present test hues, equally discrepant in wavelength from the habituation hue, but residing in different adult color categories. If infants show a novelty preference only for the between-category hue differences, and not for the within-category hue differences, then infants must share the same color categories as adults. Evidence for such an infant–adult correspondence in color categories was demonstrated in 4-month-olds by Bornstein, Kessen, and Weiskopf (1976). Moreover, the "failure" to show a novelty preference for within-category hue changes was not the result of an inability to discriminate these within-category differences. Bornstein (1981b) showed that 4-month-olds habituate more rapidly to a single wavelength than to a set of wavelengths drawn from within an adult color category. Thus, although there are some inconsistencies between adult and infant color categories, it appears that in general by 4 months of age infants group wavelengths into the same color categories as adults.

In summary, it is now clear that young infants have overall scotopic and photopic spectral sensitivity functions that are quite similar to those of adults. Moreover, infants as young as the first week after birth appear to be at least dichromats (i.e., they have two cone photopigments). There is also very strong, though perhaps not definitive, evidence that by the third postnatal month infants are trichromats. Finally, in many respects, 3-month-olds appear to categorize colors in much the same manner as adults, even though their wavelength discrimination powers are considerably greater than the wavelength differences within color categories. These findings, taken together, indicate that by 3 months of age infants are quite mature in their processing of wavelength information.

Temporal Vision and Motion Perception

Nearly all of the objects and events in the visual array undergo changes over time, either because of dynamic properties of the stimulus or because of the translation of the retinal image resulting from eye, head, and body movements. Thus it is important to determine the sensitivity of the infant visual system to rapidly changing stimuli and to relate this sensitivity to the perception of object motion. Recent reviews of both temporal vision (Banks & Dannemiller, 1986) and motion perception (Nelson & Horowitz, 1986) provide more extensive treatments of these topics.

Critical Flicker Fusion

Perhaps the most basic aspect of temporal vision is the fact that events with a very rapid time course are "fused" by the perceptual system. For example, the single film frames in a movie occur 24 times per second, yet the visual system "smooths out" these discrete samples by a process called temporal integration. *Critical flicker frequency* (CFF) refers to the lowest rate of oscillation of luminance changes (dark–light–dark–light) that is still perceived as nonflickering. In adults, the CFF is approximately 60 Hz within the photopic range of luminances and much slower at very low luminances. Only two behavioral studies of the CFF in infants have been reported. Nystrom, Hansson, and Marklund (1975) and Regal (1981) used the preferential looking technique to examine the CFF in infants 6–10 weeks old and 4–12 weeks old, respectively. The Nystrom and colleagues study presented all possible pairings of several different flicker rates, whereas the Regal study paired a variable flicker rate with a standard rate (100 Hz) considered to be well above the infant CFF. Regal found that the CFF is nearly adultlike by 2 months of age and 1-month-olds show only about a 20–25 percent deficit compared to 3-month-olds. Although no behavioral data are available in infants younger than 4 weeks of age, electrophysiological findings using the electroretinogram (ERG: a procedure for assessing the whole electrical potential from the retina) are equivocal at present. One study indicates a rapid and dramatic increase in the CFF between birth and 2 months (Heck & Zetterstrom, 1958) whereas the other study indicates nearly adultlike CFF at all ages (Horsten & Winkelman, 1964). Thus it would appear to be important to determine behaviorally whether the CFF undergoes any significant change between birth and 1 month of age.

Temporal and Spatiotemporal CSF

The CFF is only one aspect of temporal vision, namely, the ability of the visual system to detect the temporal variation in a high-contrast stimulus event (on–off luminance). Another aspect of temporal vision is the temporal CSF in which the observer must detect flicker for a patch of light that is sinusoidally modulated in luminance over time. In adults, the temporal CSF has a shape similar to the CSF for spatial stimuli (Kelly, 1961); that is, contrast sensitivity is best at mid-temporal frequencies (typically 5 Hz at low luminances and 20 Hz at high luminances). To date, however, this aspect of infant temporal vision has not been systematically investigated.

Preliminary data have been reported on a more complex form of temporal vision, namely, the contrast sensitivity of the visual system to sinusoidal gratings varying in temporal frequency. That is, a sinusoidal grating of a particular spatial frequency (stripe width) is presented and the light–dark bars are counterphase flickered (i.e., the position of the light and dark bars is alternated over time) at a fixed rate. The contrast of the bars is varied to determine the CSF at various flicker rates. Hartmann and Banks (1984) have reported that, as in the case of stationary gratings, the temporal CSF shows a band-pass characteristic (poorer contrast sensitivity at high and low temporal frequencies compared to medium temporal frequencies). They also found that more contrast was required for 6- and 12-week-olds to detect the grating at any flicker rate compared to adults, and that 12-week-olds were more sensitive than 6-week-olds. Moreover, there appeared to be little if any low temporal frequency insensitivity in the 6-week-olds.

Motion Sensitivity

Surprisingly little research has been directed to the question of infants' sensitivity to motion. One of the big problems in this area is that the actual retinal stimulus is difficult to define in infants because eye movements introduce uncontrolled variations in retinal image motion that may confound the detection of the actual motion of a stimulus within a given display. In adults, this problem can be minimized or eliminated either by asking the subject to fixate a stationary target as the moving stimuli are presented or by using a stabilized image device to prevent eye movements from introducing retinal image movements in addition to the actual movement of the stimulus.

Of course, it is not possible to instruct an infant to hold steady fixation, nor do current eye monitoring systems allow for the stabilization of the retinal image in infants. Thus all studies of infant motion sensitivity have employed unrestricted viewing that could generate retinal image motion from either actual object movement or eye movements. An initial attempt at specifying motion sensitivity in young infants was a study by Volkmann and Dobson (1976). They used the preferential looking technique to present a stationary checkerboard paired with a checkerboard that oscillated at velocities ranging from 0.9–31.2 deg/sec. They reported that 1-, 2-, and 3-month-olds preferred the moving over the stationary stimulus. Unfortunately, the range of stimulus velocities did not allow for an accurate estimation of a motion threshold.

A recent study by Kaufmann, Stucki, and Kaufmann-Hayoz (1985) provides the first systematic measure of motion sensitivity in young infants. They presented a circular array of 16 dots on each side of a preferential looking display. One of the dot arrays remained stationary and the other rotated at a set of fixed velocities. One-month-olds preferred the moving array of dots when its velocity was 84 min of arc/sec or greater whereas 3-month-olds preferred velocities of 56 min of arc/sec or greater. Slower velocities were not preferred over the stationary array of dots. These results indicate that there is a developmental improvement in motion sensitivity and that infants are considerably less sensitive than adults whose thresholds are 1–2 min of arc/sec. However, it is not possible to compare directly the absolute level of infant and adult motion sensitivity because of the different task demands of these age groups. What is clear from this study is a significant developmental improvement in motion sensitivity that corresponds to the one-octave (i.e., a doubling) improvement in spatial resolution for stationary grating patterns within this age range of 1 to 3 months.

Kaufmann et al. (1985) also assessed infants' sensitivity to rapid stimulus velocities to investigate an analog of the adult experience of stimulus fusion. That is, at
very rapid velocities adults perceive a set of discrete changes in object position as
a blurred or fused object trajectory. Using infants of the same age and the same apparatus, they paired a very rapidly rotating set of dots (above the adult fusion velocity) with a less rapidly rotating set of dots. Both 1- and 3-month-olds preferred
to fixate the less rapidly rotating set of dots at velocities of 118 deg/sec or less.
Thus there was no apparent age difference in infants' perception of stimulus fusion
within this age range. These results could be interpreted to mean that the visual
system is relatively mature in its processing of rapid spatiotemporal events, an interpretation consistent with Regal's (1981) findings on the CFF. In contrast, the visual
system is apparently quite immature in its processing of slow spatiotemporal events,
which presumably depend on the pattern-detecting system mediated by the visual
cortex. One potential problem with the presumed linkage between spatial resolution
and slow-motion perception is the possibility that slow-motion sensitivity is limited
by the differentiation of retinal image motion associated with object movement from
retinal image motion associated with eye movements. This may have less to do with
the sensory aspects of spatial resolution than with the accuracy of internal signals
(efferent or proprioceptive) for eye position within the orbit.

It is interesting to note that several studies (Hofsten, 1980, 1983; Hofsten & Lindhagen, 1979) have shown that infants are adept at "catching" a moving object. For
example, Hofsten (1983) reported that 9-month-olds synchronize their grasping response to an object moving at 30, 45, or 60 cm/sec within $\frac{1}{20}$ sec of the moment
of contact with the infant's hand. These studies demonstrate that as soon as infants
can reach for a stationary object (approximately 5 months of age) they can predict
the complex velocities in the path of object movement and program an arm and
hand movement that intercepts the moving object. Thus both the sensory capacities
and the sensorimotor skills required for "catching" a moving object are quite mature by the end of the first 6 postnatal months.

Depth Perception

The study of depth and distance perception has intrigued scholars and researchers
for centuries. The basic question is how the visual system is able to extract information about the three-dimensional aspects of the environment from visual images
that are inherently two-dimensional. There are three general classes of stimulus information that have proven sufficient for adults to appreciate the depth relations
in the environment: binocular, kinetic, and pictorial (see review by Yonas & Granrud, 1985). *Binocular information* refers to the fact that the two eyes, by virtue of
their lateral separation in the skull, receive slightly different retinal images for objects located at near distances (i.e., within 5 m). *Kinetic information* refers to the
fact that objects at different distances create differential retinal image velocities as
they change spatial location with respect to the retina. *Pictorial information* refers
to the static simulation of relative distance on a two-dimensional surface. Each of
these three types of depth information has been studied extensively in the past 5
years, and these studies have revealed that depth perception based on all three types
of information emerges in infants between 3 and 7 months of age.

Binocular Information

There are two aspects of binocular information that could enable infants to perceive relative depth: convergence angle and disparity. Convergence angle is the angle formed by the two lines of sight at the point of binocular fixation (larger angles correspond to nearer distances). Although convergence angle would seem to be a relatively ambiguous metric for object distance, primarily because of the developmental increase in interocular separation, it does appear to affect infants' reaching behavior. Hofsten (1977) showed that infants 5–8 months old, who wore wedge prisms that altered convergence angle, reached for objects at a distance appropriate for the new convergence angle.

Despite the potential role of convergence angle in depth perception, it is clear that disparity information is the primary binocular cue to depth in adults. *Disparity* refers to the change in convergence angle that would be required to fixate an object at a different distance. The appreciation of relative depth based on retinal disparity is called stereopsis. Stereopsis can be measured by presenting a slightly different retinal image to each eye. The slight differences between the lateral position of elements within each retinal image simulate the actual retinal image differences present in a real-world scene containing objects at different distances. The sensitivity of the visual system to retinal disparity (the smallest detectable depth difference) is called stereoacuity, and it is in the range of 10 sec of arc in normal adults (Berry, 1948). Notice that this value for adult stereoacuity is an order of magnitude better than grating acuity (60 sec of arc) and thus has been termed a form of hyperacuity. Also note that 10 sec of arc at a viewing distance of 1 m corresponds to a depth difference of less than 1 mm.

Stereopsis was first studied by Atkinson and Braddick (1976) and Appel and Campos (1977) using preferential looking and habituation. Appel and Campos used pictorial displays that, unfortunately, contained monocular cues as well as retinal disparity. Thus infants could detect a disparity from a no-disparity display without perceiving the depth relations in the display. An improved display that does not contain monocular cues was developed by Julesz (1960) and consists of an array of randomly arranged dots with a subregion of the dots containing retinal disparity. If the infant views the display with a single eye, only a field of randomly arranged dots is visible. However, if the infant views the display with both eyes, and the region of dots containing disparity is segregated and fused, it appears as a shape located at a different distance from the background of random dots. This so-called random-dot stereogram was used by Atkinson and Braddick with 2-month-olds. However, their results were inconsistent, with only two of four infants providing some evidence of detecting the display that contained disparity.

The first compelling demonstration of stereopsis in infants was reported by Fox, Aslin, Shea, and Dumais (1980). They also used a random-dot stereogram, but they moved the region of dots containing disparity to elicit changes in the infant's fixation. Moreover, they tested a broader age range than Atkinson and Braddick (1976). The results from the Fox and others study indicated that above-chance performance on this preferential looking task was not present until the fourth postnatal month. Thus the inconsistent findings from Atkinson and Braddick may have been the result of selecting an age range that did not (or could not) exhibit stereopsis.

Nearly simultaneously, Held, Birch, and Gwiazda (1980) reported similar findings on infant stereopsis using a so-called line stereogram display. This display is similar to the one used by Appel and Campos, but Held et al. conducted a number of control experiments to rule out the possibility of confounding monocular cues. An important feature of the Held et al. study was an assessment of stereoacuity. They varied the amount of disparity to determine the minimum amount required by infants at different ages to discriminate between a depth (disparity) and a no-depth (zero disparity) display. As in the Fox et al. (1980) study, Held et al. found that sensitivity to disparity emerges in the fourth postnatal month. In addition, stereoacuity improves very rapidly between 16 and 20 weeks of age, reaching near-adult levels by the sixth postnatal month.

A third study of infant stereopsis appeared shortly after these first two studies. Petrig, Julesz, Kropfl, Baumgartner, and Anliker (1981) used the visual evoked potential and a random-dot stereogram to assess the onset of stereopsis in infants 2–5 months old. They also found that stereopsis appears to emerge in the fourth postnatal month. Thus, as summarized in Figure 1.8, three different studies, from different labs, employing different displays and different methods, converged on the same finding that stereopsis appears to emerge in the fourth postnatal month. Of course, there are many potential reasons for this emergence, including the possibility that the neural mechanism underlying stereopsis does not become functional until that age. Several simple explanations have already been ruled out. First, the elements in the stereograms were well above infant acuity thresholds. Second, control conditions indicated that infants at young ages could provide reliable detection data for nonstereoscopic displays. Third, gross misalignments of the two eyes (which prevent stereopsis in adults) do not appear to account for the emergence of stereopsis at 4 months (Birch, Gwiazda, & Held, 1982, 1983). It is possible that differences in spatial resolution between the two eyes, which degrade stereoacuity in adults (Simons, 1984), also degrade stereoacuity in young infants. Birch (1985) showed that infants under 6 months of age have larger interocular acuity differences

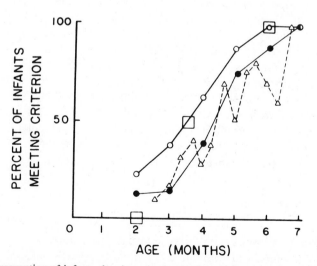

Figure 1.8. The proportion of infants showing criterion-level stereopsis performance during the first 6 months. (From "Scotopic Vision, Color Vision, and Stereopsis in Infants" by D. Y. Teller, 1982, *Current Eye Research,* p. 208. Reprinted with permission.)

than older infants. Moreover, infants 3–5 months old who have stereopsis show smaller interocular acuity differences than similar-aged infants with no measurable stereopsis. Thus at present it appears that the neural mechanism for stereopsis may not be functional in the first 3 postnatal months for most infants.

Other assessments of binocular function in young infants support the conclusion that a general neural property of binocularity emerges at approximately 4 months of age. For example, Birch, Shimojo, and Held (1985) presented two patterns to infants 1–6 months old using the preferential looking technique. One of the patterns was identical in each eye whereas the other pattern was different in each eye. This interocular difference consisted of reversing the black and white elements in the pattern as viewed by the two eyes. Such a pattern induces binocular rivalry in adults, whereas the pattern that is identical in the two eyes induces fusion. The onset age for stereopsis, assessed with the procedure used by Held et al. (1980), was found to coincide quite closely to the onset age for preferring the fusable pattern over the rivalrous pattern. These results suggest that both sensory fusion and stereopsis emerge at the same age and that they may share the same underlying neural mechanism. A follow-up study by Shimojo, Bauer, O'Connell, and Held (1986) confirmed that infants begin to prefer a fusable stimulus at the same age as they first demonstrate stereopsis. However, infants younger than the onset age for stereopsis actually prefer to fixate the *rivalrous* stimulus. Shimojo et al. (1986) attributed this finding to the fact that the orthogonally oriented gratings used to create binocular rivalry were apparently "superimposed" by the immature infant visual system, thereby creating a gridlike perception of the two images presented separately to the two eyes. Because this "grid" has more contour than the fusable stimulus (a horizontal or vertical grating), the prestereopsis infants preferred the rivalrous pattern. This is a very intriguing set of results because it suggests that binocular integration in young infants can occur with patterns that are not identical in the two eyes (a requirement in adults). An alternative interpretation of these findings suggests that the onset of stereopsis is correlated with the development of a greater neural specificity for concordant interocular orientations, and binocular rivalry is absent until this orientation specificity matures. In other words, perhaps a general neural mechanism does not simply emerge developmentally in the fourth postnatal month. Rather, different levels of binocular function can be specified, and some of these levels are present even in newborns. Support for this interpretation comes from a study by Slater, Morison, and Rose (1983), who showed that newborns who are habituated to a color or shape under monocular viewing conditions exhibit a posthabituation novelty preference when tested in the other eye. This interocular transfer of color or shape information implies some level of binocular function. Similarly, Shea, Doussard-Roosevelt, and Aslin (1985) showed that there is an interocular pupillary response to luminance signals presented to a single eye in prestereopsis infants.

Kinetic Information

The earliest tests for depth perception in young infants employed kinetic information. Walk and Gibson's (1961) classic visual cliff studies demonstrated that by the age of 6–7 months, when infants can locomote by crawling, they are sensitive to depth relations and avoid the more distant of two patterned surfaces. However, because infants at this age exhibited avoidance of the "deep" side of the visual cliff even while wearing an eye patch (Walk, 1968), it was clear that monocular information was *sufficient* to mediate this form of depth perception. The most plausible type of monocular depth information was motion parallax. *Motion parallax* refers to the relative velocity information that is contained in the retinal image of objects located at different distances as the head undergoes a lateral translation. Under conditions of stable fixation, the retinal image of a near object has a higher velocity than the retinal image of a more distant object. Thus motion parallax information provided by lateral head movements could provide the infant with information about the relative distance of two objects or surfaces. Unfortunately, to date there are no data specifying the sensitivity of the infant visual system to small amounts of motion parallax at different ages. Another complicating factor in the study of motion parallax is that fixation of an object at an intermediate distance can be maintained via the compensatory eye–head system. As a result, objects nearer *or* farther than this fixation distance give rise to more rapid retinal image velocities. Thus, although motion parallax provides accurate *differential* depth information, it does not provide unambiguous information about whether the nonfixated object is at a nearer or farther distance.

A recent study of a type of motion parallax called concurrent motion suggests that motion information alone, if not in conflict with other information, can induce the perception of relative depth. Kellman, Hofsten, and Soares (in press) habituated 4-month-olds to a set of three lights that moved toward and away from each other in an otherwise darkened room. To adults, this display induces the perception of a surface approaching and receding in distance. After habituation, infants were presented with two test trials under normal room illumination. One test display consisted of a triangular surface, with a light at each angle, that actually moved toward and away from the infant. The other test display consisted of a triangular surface that did not change in distance, but the lights at each angle moved toward and away from each other along the surface of the triangle. Thus in both test displays the pattern of retinal motion of the three lights was identical, but the actual movement of the triangular surface was quite different. Infants reliably dishabituated only to the triangle that did not change distance, suggesting that the triangle that did change distance was judged to be similar to the habituation stimulus.

Many of the stimulus parameters that influence another powerful depth effect—optical looming—have been studied in young infants. Research with nonhumans by Schiff (1965) documented that an avoidance response is elicited by an object traveling on a path that will lead to collision with the animal. Moreover, the optical information contained in the rapid expansion of the retinal image as the object approaches the animal is sufficient to trigger this avoidance response. Impending collisions created by real objects and simulated by optical expansion patterns have been presented to young infants to determine whether they exhibit avoidance responses to this dynamic distance information. This research has been reviewed by Yonas (1981), but several important findings will be summarized here.

Several investigators have reported that infants as young as 1 week after birth become upset, raise their arms in front of their faces, and/or turn their heads to avoid an approaching object simulated by a rapid optical expansion pattern (Ball & Tronick, 1971; Ball & Vurpillot, 1976; Bower, 1977; Bower, Broughton, & Moore, 1971). However, a series of experiments by Yonas et al. (1977) appears to have dispelled the interpretation that these infant responses are defensive in nature. It appears that the configuration of the optical expansion pattern included an upward movement of the stimulus contour. Very young infants, who were tested in an upright seated posture, fixated and followed the upward movement of the contour as the stimulus expanded. This visual following led to a backward movement of the head (initially interpreted as avoidance) and eventually a loss of balance that triggered an upward movement of the arms along the infant's midline (initially interpreted as the placement of the hands in a defensive position in front of the face). The larger backward head movement on looming trials than on minification (zooming) trials was verified with a pressure device by Yonas, Pettersen, and Lockman (1979). However, because the stimulus contour was rising on looming trials and falling on zooming trials, it is unlikely that this backward head rotation was a component of an avoidance response. Thus it does not appear that young infants exhibit avoidance responses to the kinetic information that signals a change in object distance as originally interpreted in these looming studies. However, 3-month-olds *are* apparently capable of differentiating a looming object from a looming aperture (Carroll & Gibson, 1981). That is, a looming object occludes the texture present in the background whereas a looming aperture reveals more background texture. Yet both displays contain a contour (the object or the aperture) that is expanding. Carroll and Gibson showed that the amount of backward head pressure was much greater in the looming target condition than in the looming aperture condition.

An additional response elicited on some trials by an optical expansion pattern is an eye blink. Yonas, Pettersen, Lockman, and Eisenberg (1980) reported that blinking is more frequently elicited by a looming stimulus than by a zooming stimulus in 3-month-olds, but they did not find this differential blinking response in 1-month-olds. Thus blinking may prove to be a sensitive index of distance perception to kinetic displays signaling impending collision in somewhat older infants.

A final type of kinetic information that is effective in eliciting relative depth perception in adults is the accretion and deletion of contour elements as one surface passes in front of another. As in the case of looming, this accretion–deletion can be presented on a two-dimensional surface to simulate the three-dimensional percept. Granrud, Yonas, Smith, et al. (1984) presented 5- and 7-month-olds with a television display containing two equal-sized regions of texture that were moving in opposite directions on the screen. One of these regions of texture elements was moved laterally across the other region of texture elements, thereby defining (at least for adults) the percept of a surface located nearer in distance than the texture elements defining the nonmoving background. Based on several studies that demonstrated that infants older than 4 months will reach for the nearer of two objects (Granrud, Yonas, & Pettersen, 1984), Granrud, Yonas, Smith, et al. (1984) measured whether infants' reaching responses were directed more frequently to the texture region that appeared nearer to adults. They found that both 5- and 7-month-olds reached more frequently to this "nearer" region of texture, thereby demonstrating that infants of this age can utilize the kinetic information of accretion–deletion to make distance-appropriate reaching responses.

Pictorial Information

One of the more intriguing questions concerning depth perception is how static pictorial (two-dimensional) information can lead to the perception of differences in object distance. A variety of pictorial "cues" to depth were documented systematically by artists such as Leonardo da Vinci in the seventeenth century, including linear perspective, shading, interposition, and familiar size. Until recently, however, it has proven quite difficult to study the pictorial cues to depth in young infants. A series of studies conducted by Yonas and his colleagues has employed a seemingly simple response, reaching, to assess a wide variety of these pictorial cues. The basis of the technique is the finding (discussed above) that infants older than 4 months of age will consistently reach for the nearer of two objects. Yonas, Cleaves, and Pettersen (1978) capitalized on this method to study a classic pictorial display called the Ames window. The Ames window is a two-dimensional trapezoidal display that contains a number of pictorial cues to depth, including relative size, linear and angular perspective, and shading. The longer lateral edge of the trapezoid appears to most adults, under *monocular* viewing conditions, to be nearer than the shorter edge because the display depicts a rectangular window that has been rotated at a 45-deg angle with respect to the viewer's frontoparallel plane. Yonas et al. (1978) found that 7-month-olds who viewed the display under monocular conditions consistently reached for the apparently nearer edge, and a nondepth control display ruled out the possibility that infants simply reach for the larger of two edges. In contrast, 5-month-olds did not consistently reach for the apparently nearer edge, although they did so under binocular conditions for a rectangle that was actually rotated at 45 deg. Thus pictorial information for relative depth contained in the Ames window was effective under monocular conditions in eliciting distance-appropriate reaching in 7-month-olds but not in 5-month-olds.

In an interesting follow-up to this study by Yonas et al. (1978), Kaufmann, Maland, and Yonas (1981) actually rotated the photograph of the Ames window so that the apparently more distant (smaller) edge was nearer than the apparently nearer (larger) edge. Under monocular viewing conditions, 5-month-olds reached for the physically nearer edge (ignoring the pictorial information), whereas 7-month-olds reached for the apparently nearer edge even though it was physically more distant. Thus it appears that 5-month-olds are not strongly influenced by the types of pictorial depth cues contained in the Ames window display whereas 7-month-olds are quite strongly influenced by these pictorial cues and ignore monocular kinetic information that can specify relative object distance.

Another important pictorial cue to depth is the relative size of objects. Although retinal size is not always correlated with actual size, it does provide a coarse metric for the actual size of objects located at similar viewing distances. Because infants do not readily attend to distant objects (McKenzie & Day, 1972), relative size may provide a useful form of pictorial depth information to young infants. Relative size was investigated in a study by Yonas, Granrud, and Pettersen (1985) using the same two-choice reaching technique described earlier. Two objects of unequal size were presented side by side at the same distance. The logic of the experiment is that under monocular conditions the smaller retinal image should be interpreted as a more distant object and reaching should be directed to the larger object. In contrast, under binocular conditions, there should be no preference for either object because they are presented at the same distance. If infants always reached for the larger object under binocular conditions, then any preferential reaching for the larger object under *monocular* conditions would be difficult to interpret. The results of this study indicated that 5½- and 7-month-olds reached for the larger object under monocular conditions but did not show preferential reaching under binocular conditions. Thus infants at these ages showed evidence that relative size was an effective pictorial cue to relative object distance. In contrast, 5-month-olds preferred to reach for the larger object under both monocular and binocular conditions. Thus the utilization of relative size at this age is equivocal (either it was not used under monocular conditions or it was overridden under binocular conditions by a preference for the larger real size).

The preceding studies of relative size employed objects that had no consistent actual size in the environment of the observers. There are many objects, however, whose actual size falls within a restricted range (e.g., faces). Our everyday exposure to such objects presumably leads us to expect that, as the retinal size of these familiar objects varies, their distance must also vary (i.e., we do not perceive faces as expanding and shrinking in actual size). Yonas, Pettersen, and Granrud (1982) investigated infants' sensitivity to the pictorial cue of familiar size by presenting photographs of familiar (face) and nonfamiliar (checkerboard) objects to 5- and 7-month-olds. On each preferential reaching trial, two identical photographs differing only in actual size were presented side by side at the same distance. Under monocular conditions, 7-month-olds reached for the larger of the two photographs when they were faces but not when they were checkerboards. Under binocular conditions, there was no preference for either face size. In contrast, 5-month-olds showed no preference for either the facial or checkerboard photographs. Their results indicate that 7-month-olds, like adults, treat a larger retinal image of a familiar object as if it were nearer in distance. This interpretation was supported by a follow-up experiment by Granrud, Haake, and Yonas (1985). They used a preexposure period to allow 5- and 7-month-olds to manipulate and visually explore two previously unfamiliar objects that differed in actual size. During a subsequent preferential reaching test, each infant was presented with two new objects located at the same distance. These new objects were identical to the preexposure objects except that they were now identical in actual size. Reaching under monocular conditions by the 7-month-olds was directed to the smaller of the two preexposure objects, a finding that is consistent with the interpretation that the actual size of the preexposure objects had been remembered and used to guide the subsequent reaching responses. The 5-month-olds did not show evidence of preferential reaching, indicating either that they did not rely on familiar size as a cue to direct their reaching responses or that they could not remember the actual size of the objects from the preexposure exploration.

Another effective pictorial cue to relative distance is the fact that in the real world nearer objects typically occlude portions of more distant objects. This interposition cue was studied by Granrud and Yonas (1984) in 5- and 7-month-olds by presenting a two-dimensional display containing three textured areas. Successive occlusion of the texture by adjacent areas of the display resulted, for adults tested under monocular conditions, in the percept of three surfaces at different distances. The nearest surface corresponded to the textured area that was not occluded. Under monocular conditions, 7-month-olds, but not 5-month-olds, consistently reached for this apparently nearer surface of the display. Control conditions (e.g., displays with similar shapes but no apparent texture occlusion) did not result in preferential reaching to the "nearer" surface, and no preferential reaching was present under binocular conditions. Thus interposition appears to be an effective pictorial cue for relative distance in 7-month-olds.

Finally, the pictorial cue of shading was investigated in a study by Granrud,

Yonas, and Opland (1985). They presented 5- and 7-month-olds with either a display containing an actual convexity (a bump) and an actual concavity (an indentation) or a photograph of this convex–concave display. For the actual three-dimensional display, both 5- and 7-month-olds reached preferentially for the bump under both monocular and binocular conditions. Thus either kinetic or binocular information was sufficient to elicit a preference for the bump over the indentation. However, the pictorial cue of shading presented in the photograph led the 7-month-olds, but not the 5-month-olds, to reach for the apparent bump under monocular conditions. Thus 7-month-olds appear to utilize shading as an effective pictorial cue to depth.

In summary, as discussed in detail by Yonas and Granrud (1985), there appears to be a developmental sequence in the unfolding of stimulus information utilized by the infant visual system to perceive depth relations. Kinetic information appears to emerge first, certainly by 3 months of age, as shown by the studies of blinking to looming stimuli. Disparity information becomes effective by 4–5 months of age as shown by the studies of stereopsis. Finally, pictorial cues to depth become effective between 5–7 months of age.

Constancies

An important distinction can be made in the study of perception between proximal and distal stimulation. Proximal stimuli are those physical attributes of energy (e.g., wavelength) that are available at the organism's receptors. Distal stimuli are the perceptual attributes (e.g., color) of the object or event in the organism's environment. One of the classic questions in the study of perception is how the developing organism correctly interprets the proximal stimulation so that knowledge (and perceptual experiences) of objects and events is veridical. Perhaps in no aspect of perception is this distinction between proximal and distal stimulation more sharply drawn than in the study of perceptual constancies. The mature visual system is able to perceive a relatively stable visual environment despite vast changes in many aspects of proximal stimulation. The brightness, contrast, color, size, and shape of objects remain invariant to the perceptual system even in the face of dramatic shifts in luminance, distance, and point of view.

Brightness

The mature visual system is sensitive to a tremendous range of light intensities (at least a factor of 10 to the tenth power). Despite this great overall range, however, the mature visual system is sensitive to very small *differences* in light intensity (approximately 1 percent). The basic mechanism that permits this seemingly impossible feat (large dynamic range with excellent sensitivity) is called light adaptation. Light adaptation is a neural process whereby a relatively small portion of the entire operating range, corresponding to the mean illumination of the environment, is functionally magnified to optimize sensitivity to *differences* in intensity. The process of light adaptation also permits significant shifts in the intensity of reflected light *within* the current operating range to yield an invariant percept of stimulus brightness. For example, a black sheet of paper still appears black when a light source increases its reflected intensity by a factor of 100. The disadvantage of light adaptation is that sudden shifts in the mean level of illumination render the organism "blind" until the region of high sensitivity can be shifted to the new level of illumination (e.g., when leaving a darkened movie theater or when driving into a tunnel).

One way to study this process of light adaptation is to obtain what is called an increment threshold function. An increment threshold is the amount of light intensity required just to detect that a stimulus is brighter. In adults, the amount of light required just to detect that a stimulus has been incremented in intensity is a constant proportion of the mean background illumination (Barlow, 1972). This invariant relation is called Weber's law, and it holds except at very low intensities where the *absolute* amount of stimulus evergy determines the increment threshold. A study of infants by Dannemiller and Banks (1983) used the preferential looking technique to study increment thresholds in 7- and 12-week-olds. A grating located on one of the two sides of an even-luminance background was incremented in intensity to estimate the increment threshold across a fourfold level of background intensities. The 12-week-olds showed increment threshold functions with a slope of unity, thus conforming to Weber's law in adults. The 7-week-olds, however, showed functions with slopes less than 1.0, indicating that Weber's law did not hold across the range of background intensities used in this study. Dannemiller and Banks concluded that this developmental difference was most likely the result of two factors: spatial summation or gain.

The explanation of shallower slopes for the 7-week-olds' increment threshold functions based on gain is that a greater amount of light intensity is needed at higher background levels to obtain the same level of perceived brightness. If this were true, then young infants would not have brightness constancy even within the operating range that functions in a normally illuminated environment. However, based on more recent data, it appears that this explanation is not entirely correct. The alternative explanation of shallower slopes for the 7-week-olds' increment threshold functions based on spatial summation comes from the finding in adults (Barlow, 1972) that stimulus size beyond a certain limit is no more effective on an increment threshold task (i.e., the total amount of light that can be captured has a spatial limit). The size of the test grating used in the Dannemiller and Banks (1983) study was 6 deg, clearly covering the size of the adult spatial summation area. However, based on recent estimates of the spatial summation area in infants (Hamer & Schneck, 1984; Schneck, Hamer, Packer, & Teller, 1984), it appears that spatial summation is effective over a much larger area of the retina in young infants than in adults. A direct test of this hypothesis (Dannemiller, 1985) revealed that the increment threshold function of 7-week-olds had a slope of 1.0 if the test stimulus was 8 deg in diameter. Thus it appears that the spatial summation explanation of the developmental difference in increment threshold function slopes between 6 and 12 weeks of age is most likely the correct one. The implication of this finding on spatial summation is that small surfaces will render Weber's law ineffective in maintaining brightness constancy. Of course, small objects are not typically attended to by very young infants, though they are certainly within the limits of the young infant's spatial resolution if they have sufficient contrast. Thus at present it is unclear whether the spatial summation constraint on brightness constancy is a serious perceptual impediment to young infants.

Contrast

Like brightness, the *difference* in brightness (contrast) between adjacent surfaces of an object remains perceptually invariant despite changes in viewing distance from those surfaces. An intriguing aspect of contrast constancy is its relation to the CSF.

Recall that the CSF represents the minimum amount of contrast that is required at different spatial frequencies just to detect the presence of a grating. For example, at medium spatial frequencies much less contrast is required for detection than at higher or lower spatial frequencies (see Fig. 1.3). Thus one might predict that at suprathreshold levels of contrast an object that receded in distance, thereby increasing its spatial frequencies, would appear to change in contrast. However, in adults the shape of the CSF does not provide a good representation of the perception of high-contrast objects. Gratings at high contrast, regardless of spatial frequency, are perceived as equal in contrast when they have the same *physical* contrast (Georgeson & Sullivan, 1975). Thus the shape of the CSF does not conform to contrast-matching judgments at suprathreshold contrast levels, and this apparent compensation enables contrast constancy to operate so that changing object distance does not alter perceived contrast.

A recent study by Stephens and Banks (1985) examined this issue of contrast constancy in 6- and 12-week-olds by presenting two gratings, one of fixed contrast and spatial frequency and the other of variable contrast and spatial frequency, in the preferential looking technique. They assumed that infants would prefer to look at neither grating if they were perceived as matching in contrast. Thus they obtained contrast matches from the infants for gratings differing in spatial frequency at both near-threshold and suprathreshold levels of contrast. The 12-week-olds, like adults, showed contrast matches that conformed to the *physical* contrast of the gratings when the gratings were suprathreshold. The 6-week-olds, however, showed contrast matches that conformed to their CSF at both near-threshold and suprathreshold contrast levels. Thus the 12-week-olds but not the 6-week-olds showed evidence of contrast constancy. As discussed by Stephens and Banks (1985) and supported by the data from Banks, Stephens, and Hartmann (1985), it appears that the 6-week-old infant does not have an adultlike multiple-channel visual system for analyzing spatial frequencies. However, there is evidence for more mature multiple-channel mechanisms in one 6-week-old based on VEP data (Fiorentini, Pirchio, & Spinelli, 1983). Thus the development of multiple channels tuned to narrow bands of spatial information requires further clarification. Nevertheless, certain perceptual phenomena, such as contrast constancy, do not appear to be operative until some time after the second postnatal month.

Color

Color constancy refers to the invariant perception of stimulus hue despite differences in the wavelength of light reflected from a surface. One convenient way to demonstrate color constancy is to note that a white surface appears white even if the color of the light source illuminating the surface changes (e.g., the more "reddish" sunlight at dawn and dusk). Dannemiller and Hanko (1985) recently tested 4-month-olds for color constancy by presenting two colored surfaces (Munsell chips) in a paired comparison test after familiarization to one of the colored surfaces. The critical test was to familiarize the infant with one Munsell chip illuminated by one of the light sources and then to present two Munsell chips illuminated by a different light source. One of the test chips was identical to the familiarization chip (distal match) but was different because of the different light source (proximal mismatch). The second test chip was different from the familiarization chip (distal mismatch) but was identical to the familiarization chip because of the different light source (proximal match). Color constancy would have been indicated if the infants had preferred the novel chip (distal mismatch) over the familarization chip (distal match), since such a novelty preference would imply recognition of the old chip as familiar and the new chip as novel. However, if the infants preferred the familiarization chip under new lighting conditions (proximal mismatch) to the novel chip under the new lighting conditions (proximal match), then infants presumably rely on proximal information and do not have color constancy. The results indicated that infants preferred the familiarization Munsell chip after the change in light source, presumably because this chip was novel on the basis of proximal stimulation. Therefore, at present color constancy has not been demonstrated in 4-month-olds.

Size

Our perception of object size remains invariant despite the fact that changes in object distance create changes in the size of the retinal image. Size constancy in adults is so compelling that most observers must be convinced that retinal image size actually undergoes a large change under typical viewing conditions. The issue of size constancy in infancy has been a topic of considerable interest for many decades (cf., Cruikshank, 1941), but positive evidence was not forthcoming until Bower's (1964) classic experiment. Bower used an operantly conditioned headturn response and purported to demonstrate rudimentary size constancy in 5-month-olds. However, several nonreplications of this finding have been published (Day & McKenzie, 1977; McKenzie & Day, 1972, 1976), along with at least one demonstration of size constancy in older infants (McKenzie, Tootell, & Day, 1980). Finally, Day and McKenzie (1981) reported evidence of size constancy in 4-month-olds, thus supporting Bower's (1964) study.

A recent study by Granrud (1986) appears to offer a potential explanation of the majority of these seemingly contradictory results. First, Granrud replicated the finding from Granrud, Yonas, and Pettersen (1984) that 5- and 7-month-olds reach to the nearer of two retinally equivalent objects more consistently under binocular than under monocular viewing conditions. Second, Granrud found that 4-month-olds also reach more consistently to the nearer of two retinally equivalent objects under binocular conditions than under monocular conditions, but that this binocular advantage was much less than in 5- and 7-month-olds. Third, Granrud pretested groups of 4-month-olds for their ability to detect the binocular disparity in a stereogram. Those 4-month-olds who were disparity sensitive reached more for the nearer of two retinally equivalent objects under binocular than under monocular conditions, whereas the disparity-insensitive 4-month-olds did not show more consistent reaching to the nearer object under binocular conditions. Thus it appears that binocular disparity is an important cue to distance perception as assessed in a preferential reaching task (though not an essential cue given the above-chance reaching to the nearer object under monocular conditions in the older infants). Finally, Granrud tested both disparity-sensitive and disparity-insensitive 4-month-olds on a size constancy task. The size constancy task consisted of habituating each infant to an object that moved through a range of distances, thereby presenting a variety of retinal image sizes. After habituation, the same object and an identical but different-sized object were presented singly on test trials. The range of retinal image sizes for both test objects overlapped the range presented during habituation, thereby ruling out retinal size as a proximal cue to distance perception. The disparity-sensitive 4-month-olds showed a significant increase in fixation to the novel-sized object and no significant increase in fixation to the familiar-sized object. Thus these infants evidenced size constancy. In contrast, the disparity-insensitive 4-month-olds did not show a significant increase in fixation to either the novel- or the familiar-sized objects. Thus it appears that sensitivity to object distance, which is clearly enhanced by the presence of sensitivity to disparity, is required to exhibit size constancy. Moreover, previous evidence of size constancy in older infants and inconsistent evidence of size constancy in 4-month-olds may be accounted for by the fact that disparity sensitivity does not appear to emerge until the fourth postnatal month (see Fig. 1.8). Apparently, the evidence of size constancy provided by the 4-month-olds in the Day and McKenzie (1981) study was the result of a sample containing many disparity-sensitive infants.

Shape

Shape constancy refers to the perception of invariant object shape despite transformations of the two-dimensional shape of the retinal image. As in the case of size constancy, shape perception presumably requires some information about object distance (e.g., the degree of surface slant). Information about object distance can be gained from several cues, including monocular information (motion parallax and changes in texture gradients) as well as binocular information (stereopsis and convergence). As in the case of size constancy, the earliest experiments were conducted by Bower (1966), who used the operant headturning procedure to assess generalization to objects that had the same retinal shape but a different actual shape (or vice versa). Although Bower (1966) provided evidence of shape constancy in 5-month-olds, there remained grave concern over the validity of these data because of several unpublished nonreplications. However, Day and McKenzie (1973) and Caron, Caron, and Carlson (1979) have provided evidence of shape constancy in 3-month-olds. Unfortunately, each of these studies suffers from a number of minor flaws that render any strong conclusions about shape constancy in young infants uncertain at present. For example, a recent study by Cook and Birch (1984) replicated the results of Caron and colleagues, who used rectangles tilted at various angles to test for shape constancy. However, when nonrectangular shapes were used, no evidence for shape constancy was obtained. Cook and Birch interpreted their results, and those of Caron and others, as evidence for the discrimination of the local feature of orthogonality (nonparallel contours) rather than as shape constancy per se.

Another question regarding shape constancy is whether infants recognize that a rotated object has an invariant shape despite a discriminable change in orientation and the resultant change in the position of local object features. Bornstein, Krinsky, and Benasich (1986) examined this question using the habituation technique in 4-month-olds. They reported that infants discriminated changes in orientation of 10 deg, but infants presented with several orientations of the same object during habituation did not dishabituate to that same object in a novel orientation. Thus shape constancy in 4-month-olds appears to be present for orientation variations in the frontoparallel plane but not necessarily for variations in depth (slant or tilt).

Object Perception

The vast majority of the present review of visual development has summarized proximal stimulus variables that could enable the infant to perceive, encode, and recognize specific objects in the natural environment. Thus an important final step in any explanation of visual development is to determine whether infants have the capacity to recognize that objects have an invariant size, shape, distance, and existence despite variations in proximal stimulation. This final section, then, is directed to studies of the shape of three-dimensional objects and the role of dynamic visual information in specifying object identity.

An elementary aspect of object perception is the ability to differentiate a rigid object from a nonrigid (deformable) object. Gibson, Owsley, and Johnston (1978) investigated this question in 5-month-olds by habituating infants to an object undergoing three different types of rigid motion. After habituation, each infant received test trials containing either a novel (fourth) rigid motion or a deformation of the object. Infants showed greater dishabituation to the deformation than to the novel rigid motion. Gibson, Owsley, Walker, and Megaw-Nyce (1979) replicated and extended this finding in 3-month-olds by presenting two different-shaped objects undergoing a single rigid motion during habituation. They reported greater dishabituation to the same shapes undergoing deformation than to the same shapes undergoing a new rigid motion. Thus it appears that infants 3–5 months old can perceive the important difference between object rigidity and deformation.

A number of studies have been directed to a related question: Can infants extract the three-dimensional shape of objects? Gibson et al. (1979) investigated this question by habituating 3-month-olds to an object of a particular shape undergoing two types of rigid motion and then testing for dishabituation to a new-shaped object that either underwent the same two rigid motions or was stationary. In both cases, infants dishabituated more to the new object shape regardless of whether the test object was moving or stationary. Owsley (1983) extended these findings by having 4-month-olds view the habituation object under monocular conditions, thereby eliminating binocular information for object shape. During habituation, the object was presented either dynamically as a rotating solid wedge or statically as a wedge in a single position. After habituation, the infants were presented with three test objects under *binocular* conditions: (1) the same wedge in a familiar position; (2) the same wedge in a novel position; and (3) a new object (a cube). Dishabituation was greater for the cube than for either wedge for infants who were habituated to the rotating wedge. Thus dynamic monocular information is sufficient to extract object shape as tested under static binocular conditions. For the infants who were limited to a static view of the wedge during habituation, there was no differential dishabituation to the three stimuli, indicating that static monocular information was not sufficient to extract object shape under these testing conditions. A follow-up experiment verified that the *dynamic* information during habituation was critical to subsequent shape discrimination rather than the fact that this dynamic presentation format allowed for multiple static perspectives of the wedge. When multiple static presentations of the wedge were presented during habituation, no differential dishabituation to the three test objects was obtained.

These findings on infants' ability to extract object shape from real three-dimensional stimuli has been extended to dynamic two-dimensional projections that induce three-dimensional percepts in adults. Kellman (1984) presented 4-month-olds with a videotape of either a continuously rotating object or a series of static views of the rotating object. After habituation, each infant viewed a new object undergoing a new type of rotation or the old object undergoing the same new rotation.

Infants who were habituated to the continuous object rotation dishabituated to the new object but not to the old object, despite the fact that the old object was now undergoing a novel type of rotation. Infants who were habituated to multiple static views of the object did not show dishabituation to either the old or new object. Thus it appears that 4-month-olds can extract object shape from dynamic two-dimensional information.

Both the Kellman (1984) and Owsley (1983) studies employed stimuli (either real or pictorial) that contained multiple dynamic cues, including changes in linear perspective, texture gradients, and shading. Shaw, Roder, and Bushnell (in press) attempted to eliminate all information about object shape except the perspective transformations that occur during object rotation. This type of display can be created by casting a shadow of an object onto a rear-projection screen as the object undergoes rotation behind the screen and has been termed the *kinetic depth effect* in studies of adults (Wallach & O'Connell, 1953). Shaw and colleagues habituated 4- and 6-month-olds to a dynamic shadow-cast display of a particular object and then presented a paired fixation test with two real objects, one of which was identical to the habituation stimulus but differed in texture and retinal size as well as now being static and three-dimensional. The 6-month-olds, but not the 4-month-olds, preferentially fixated the novel object during the test trials after habituation. Thus it appears that two-dimensional perspective transformations alone are sufficient for 6-month-olds to extract object shape. Kellman and Short (in preparation) have also studied the kinetic depth effect in 4-month-olds using videotapes of three-dimensional rotating wire frames that eliminate all cues to object shape except dynamic linear perspective. They reported dishabituation to a novel wire-framed object undergoing a novel rotation but no dishabituation to the familiar object also undergoing a novel rotation. Although this study did not assess object recognition using a transfer paradigm (as in Shaw et al., in press), these results suggest that 4-month-olds are sensitive to the dynamic proximal information contained in perspective transformations.

A recent study by Yonas, Arterberry, and Granrud (in press) examined why the 4-month-olds in the Shaw et al. (in press) study failed to show transfer of object recognition from a kinetic to a binocular display. After habituation to a rear-projected kinetic display created by rotation of an object in front of a light source, infants viewed a stereogram of the same object and a novel object. As in the Granrud (1986) study of size constancy, only those 4-month-olds who were disparity sensitive showed a preference for the novel object. These results suggest that 4-month-olds who have stereopsis can transfer their perception of object shape from one mode of depth information to another. In addition, these results suggest that the failure of the 4-month-olds in the Shaw et al. (in press) study to show transfer between kinetic and binocular modes of stimulus presentation may have been the result of a sample of disparity-*in*sensitive infants.

A more complex type of dynamic motion information that can be used by adults to recognize objects has been termed *biological motion* (Johansson, 1973). For example, if small lights are attached to the joints of a person who is walking on a treadmill, and this person is photographed in total darkness, the configuration of moving lights is sufficient for identification of the array as a walking human. This perceptual phenomenon in adults raises an interesting developmental question: Does the perception of biological motion arise from visual experience or is it based on a genetically specified visual mechanism? To address this question, Fox and McDaniel (1982) tested 2-, 4-, and 6-month-olds using the preferential looking technique. They presented the infants with pairs of videotaped point-light displays depicting a human running in place and a random configuration of moving lights. The 4- and 6-month-olds, but not the 2-month-olds, preferred to fixate the biological motion display. Follow-up experiments showed that 4- and 6-month-olds preferred to fixate a point-light display of an upright runner versus an inverted runner and that 6-month-olds preferred to fixate a point-light display of a hand grasping a glass versus a similar display that adults judged as nonbiological.

A more recent set of experiments by Bertenthal, Proffitt, and Cutting (1984) employed computer-generated point-light displays that simulated a walker presented in an upright and an inverted orientation. Both 3- and 5-month-olds dishabituated to this change in display orientation. A follow-up experiment showed that 5-month-olds did not discriminate a change in a point-light display that consisted of local motions identical to a walker but arranged in a configuration that adults judged as random motion. As discussed by Bertenthal et al. (1984), these results support the conclusion that infants *can* extract complex configural information from the motion contained in point-light displays. However, they do not force the conclusion that infants perceive biological motion of a human walker from these displays.

Further evidence for the importance of figural coherence in infants' perception of point-light displays was provided by Bertenthal, Proffitt, Kramer, and Spetner (in press).They reported that 3-month-olds show faster rates of habituation, implying more rapid encoding, to point-light displays that depict a walker compared to a scrambled version of the walker's moving lights. Once the infants met the criterion of habituation, however, they showed evidence of discriminating the walker display from the scrambled display. A control experiment documented the fact that the habituation and dishabituation findings were not the result of preferences for one of the two displays. Finally, Bertenthal, Proffitt, Spetner, and Thomas (1985) reported that 9-month-olds are sensitive to the occlusion of point-lights that occurs as the joints on the far side of the body translate behind the torso. The 9-month-olds, but not 5- or 7-month-olds, showed dishabituation to a shift from the walker display containing point-light occlusion to the walker display without point-light occlusion. No evidence of discriminating the occlusion information was evident in a scrambled version of the point-light display, and the positive evidence of occlusion discrimination in 9-month-olds was not the result of differential preference. In a final experiment, 9-month-olds showed evidence of discriminating appropriate occlusion (as in the walker display) from inappropriate occlusion (a random occlusion that was locally equivalent to the walker display). This discrimination of occlusion information was not shown by 9-month-olds who viewed either a scrambled point-light display or an inverted-walker point-light display.

Taken together, these several experiments on biological motion suggest that infants are capable of extracting complex forms of configural motion from point-light displays. Moreover, they suggest that certain proximal variables (e.g., display orientation) facilitate the encoding and discrimination of this so-called biological motion. However, until a transfer experiment is conducted (i.e., the point-light display is shown to be judged equivalent to a real object), it will remain uncertain whether infants perceive the distal object information that is correlated with the proximal information contained in point-light displays.

A final topic on object perception is the ability of infants to segregate the visual array into units that adults commonly call objects. This may seem to be a trivial ability until one considers the complexity involved in assigning edges, textures, and colors to separable entities when these physical attributes overlap in the visual array. A series of experiments by Kellman and Spelke (1983) provided important new insights into the process by which objects are segregated by 4-month-olds and whether infants perceive occluded objects as continuous forms rather than discrete segments of contour. Their first experiment provided the most basic finding. Infants were presented with a stationary block behind which a rod was oscillated laterally. After habituation to this display, each infant viewed two test trials, one containing the complete rod undergoing movement and the other containing two rod segments with the middle section, corresponding to what was occluded by the block during habituation, missing from this broken rod. Infants showed dishabituation only to the broken rod, indicating that the complete rod was judged as similar to the rod behind the block during habituation trials. Several follow-up experiments demonstrated that a stationary object located behind the stationary block was not sufficient to induce dishabituation to the broken version of the occluded object. Moreover, only movement of the occluded object, and not the relative motion created by movement of the occluding block, induced dishabituation to the broken object. Finally, if the two halves of an occluded object were quite different, suggesting to adults that parts of two objects were occluded by the block, infants still showed dishabituation to the broken object as long as the "dual" object underwent movement during habituation. These experiments provide rather strong evidence that 4-month-olds define object identity on the basis of common motion and infer the existence of a complete object even though only portions of the object are visible during occlusion.

An extension of this work by Kellman, Spelke, and Short (1986) attempted to define which types of occluded object motion were sufficient to induce the perception of object identity. Rather than lateral movement of the object behind the occluding block, they presented either movement in depth or vertical movement. In both cases, provided that the infants could detect the presence of object movement behind the occluder, 4-month-olds dishabituated to the broken object display. Kellman, Gleitman, and Spelke (submitted) examined another aspect of the type of object movement required to induce the perception of object identity. They moved the infant laterally rather than moving the object behind the occluder. In this condition, the retinal image of the occluded object translated with respect to both the occluder and the background texture. In a second condition of infant movement, the occluded object was attached to a rod under the infant's chair. Thus, as the infant was moved leftward, the occluded object moved rightward, and vice versa. In this condition, there was little or no relative motion of the occluded object, although there was absolute object motion with respect to the occluder and the background. The results showed that 4-month-olds did not dishabituate to the broken object after viewing a stationary display under conditions of self-movement. However, 4-month-olds did dishabituate to the broken object after identical self-movement that triggered an actual displacement of the occluded object. These results are important for two reasons. First, they suggest that infants who view a stationary display while they are undergoing self-movement perceive the objects as stationary. Second, they suggest that actual object movement can be detected even in the presence of self-movement. This latter result also implies that 4-month-olds can accurately determine the contribution of differential retinal image motion from objects at different distances.

The foregoing experiments address the issue of what types of information for object identity are detected by infants. A final question is whether this information can actually be utilized in a behaviorally relevant way. Hofsten and Spelke (1985) attempted to investigate this question by measuring the reaching responses of 5-month-olds presented with two objects. Recall from the work of Yonas and Granrud (1985; see section on depth perception) that 5-month-olds reach consistently for the nearer of two objects. Hofsten and Spelke were interested in what aspects define an object for infants' reaching responses. They arranged two objects so that the smaller object was located in front of the larger object. The smaller object was either thin or thick, so that its front surface was always the same distance from the front surface of the larger object. Thus for the small, thin object there was depth information supporting the perception of two different objects. However, for the small, thick object there was depth information supporting the perception of a single object consisting of a smaller segment attached directly to a larger segment. They reported that reaches were directed to the small, thin object rather than to the larger, more distant object. This result is consistent with the findings of Granrud and Yonas because the small, thin object was located nearer than the larger object. In contrast, for the small, thick object, infants reached for the larger, more distant object. Apparently, the infants perceived the two surfaces of the small and large object as attributes of a single object. Thus they reached for the edge of the larger object, which was the more distant surface.

Hofsten and Spelke (1985) extended these findings to cases of object motion. First, the display consisting of a small, thick object in front of a larger object was moved laterally so that the two objects oscillated together. Second, the two objects were moved laterally at different rates to create relative motion. When the objects moved together, 5-month-olds reached equally often to the larger and the smaller objects. However, when the objects moved differentially, infants reached consistently to the smaller object. The consistent reaching to the smaller object in the differential motion condition was not simply the result of the smaller object's moving more rapidly, because a similar reaching preference for the smaller object was present if only the larger object underwent movement as the smaller object remained stationary. Finally, if the small and large objects remained stationary against a moving background, infants reached for the larger object. Thus it appears that infants organize their perception of objects on the basis of the differential motion of multiple surfaces. If two surfaces undergo identical motions, they tend to be identified as a unified object. However, if two surfaces undergo different motions, they tend to be identified as two different objects.

In summary, the infant's perception of objects has been approached from an ecological perspective by considering the dynamic invariants that specify the rigidity of surfaces, the shape of objects, the connectivity of object elements, and the coherence of partly occluded and adjacent objects. The ecological perspective has resulted in several demonstrations that the functional significance of objects and events in the infant's environment is an important determinant of the infant's perception of those objects and events. However, this perspective has not provided a detailed account of the underlying mechanisms that enable the infant to extract dynamic invariants. A psychophysical approach to the search for these underlying mechanisms may be a potentially fruitful means of providing a more detailed specification of the rich stimulus information that determines object perception in infants.

Summary of Visual Development

During the past decade, research on infant visual perception has generated an overwhelming number of new findings on the capacity of infants to detect, discriminate, and categorize visual stimulation. The foregoing sections on the infant visual system have summarized only a limited subset of these new findings. It seems clear that the motivation for many of these studies was a search for the origins of perceptual function, and the development of more sensitive methods of measurement has uncovered perceptual capacities that just a few years earlier would not have been attributed to young infants. The oculomotor system, spatial and temporal vision, pattern perception, color vision, depth perception, perceptual constancies, and object perception are certainly underdeveloped in the newborn. However, the time course of perceptual development within each of these domains is more rapid than previously thought possible. These rapid developments raise questions about underlying mechanisms, and hypotheses about these mechanisms have been generated from analogous research on human adults and nonhuman animals. The challenge for the future is to move toward greater specificity in characterizing the stimuli that mediate visual perception and to determine the functional significance of underdeveloped perceptual abilities. Thus the psychophysical approach may prove invaluable in defining precisely the stimulus variables that enable veridical perception to occur. Similarly, an ecological approach may prove invaluable in guiding researchers toward classes of stimuli that carry functionally relevant information, such as the class of dynamic invariants for object perception. Armed with a combination of psychophysical and ecological perspectives, the future researcher of infant visual perception will undoubtedly have a clearer path to important new discoveries.

THE AUDITORY SYSTEM

The development of the human auditory system has been investigated from two quite different perspectives. A "bottom-up" approach has been followed in studies of basic psychoacoustic abilities, whereas a "top-down" approach has been followed in studies of speech and other complex acoustic signals. The advantage of the bottom-up approach is that it permits the specification of thresholds for detecting and discriminating differences between acoustic stimuli varying along simple dimensions, such as intensity and frequency. The disadvantage of this approach is its potential for suggesting that the perception of complex auditory stimuli can be explained solely on the basis of psychoacoustic principles. That is, the psychoacoustic approach can often lead to reductionistic accounts that may not be appropriate for all acoustic signals. The advantage of the top-down (or functional) approach is that it circumvents the reductionism of the psychoacoustic approach by focusing on higher-order or relational aspects of complex acoustic signals. The disadvantage of this approach is that it requires a precise specification of the higher-order information that allows for the discrimination or categorization of these complex acoustic signals. Unfortunately, the absence of an adequate description of these higher-order invariants renders any conclusions about underlying mechanisms somewhat ambiguous. Despite the problems associated with these two general approaches to the study of auditory development, there have been many important discoveries in the past 15 years.

Detection Thresholds

Perhaps the most basic aspect of auditory development is the onset of the ability to detect the presence of an acoustic stimulus. Several studies have demonstrated that the auditory system is functional several weeks prior to birth, based on changes in fetal heart rate (Grimwade, Walker, Bartlett, Gordon, & Wood, 1971) and the presence of brain wave activity in the fetus (Sakabe, Arayama, & Suzuki, 1969) and the premature newborn (Starr, Amlie, Martin, & Sanders, 1977). Moreover, several recent studies have documented auditory preferences immediately after birth that could only have been induced by prenatal auditory exposure (DeCasper & Fifer, 1980; Panneton, 1985; DeCasper & Spence, in 1986). Thus both direct and indirect evidence confirms the onset of auditory function prior to birth.

A second basic aspect of auditory development is the absolute sensitivity of the auditory system. Although sounds of high intensity may be detected by the fetus, particularly since sounds below 1000 Hz are attenuated very little as they pass through the mother's abdomen to the amniotic sac (Armitage, Baldwin, & Vince, 1980; Querleu & Renard, 1981), it is likely that significant changes in absolute sensitivity occur postnatally as neural structures mature and the peripheral auditory apparatus adapts to the analysis of sounds carried by airborne pressure variations. There were several classic studies of auditory thresholds prior to 1975 (see review by Eisenberg, 1976). However, it was not until the development of two methodological techniques—the auditory brain stem response (ABR) and the operant head-turning procedure—that researchers were able to collect reliable data from young infants. The first ABR studies of newborns were conducted by Hecox and Galambos (1974; see also Hecox, 1975; Hecox & Deegan, 1985). These findings indicated that absolute thresholds were 10–17 dB* poorer in newborns than in adults, and this result has been replicated by several investigators (e.g., Schulman-Galambos & Galambos, 1979).

Unfortunately, there are a number of interpretive problems associated with ABR data. First, because the latency of the ABR is very short (2–8 msec), it is necessary to employ either clicks or brief (e.g., 5 msec) tone pips as eliciting stimuli. As a result, it is difficult to examine absolute thresholds as a function of stimulus frequency because such brief stimuli contain a broad range of spectral information. Second, the ABR reflects the transmission of auditory information to relatively low levels of the auditory pathway (Buchwald & Huang, 1975; Starr & Hamilton, 1976). Thus an intact ABR is a necessary but not sufficient index of processing by higher levels of the auditory system, particularly those levels that presumably mediate a

---

*The term *decibel* (dB) refers to a logarithmic scale for representing sound intensities. A logarithmic scale is used because of the large dynamic range of the auditory system (approximately 15 factors of 10). A decibel is defined as $10 \log E1/E2$, where $E1$ is the intensity of the sound and $E2$ is a reference intensity such as absolute threshold in a normal adult. Thus, a 20 dB difference denotes a factor of 1000.

behavioral or perceptual response. Despite these limitations, the ABR has been a very useful screening technique for detecting conductive (i.e., peripheral) hearing losses in newborns.

The most productive behavioral technique for providing reliable assessments of auditory thresholds is the operant headturning procedure. This technique has the unfortunate disadvantage of being suitable only for infants older than 5 months of age (Moore, Wilson, & Thompson, 1977). A recent observational technique developed by Olsho (1984b) has promise for younger infants (e.g., 3-month-olds), but to date nearly all of the behavioral data on auditory thresholds have been gathered using one or more versions of the operant headturning procedure. The first reports of auditory thresholds using this technique were published by Schneider, Trehub, and Bull (1980) and Trehub, Schneider, and Endman (1980). These studies used a two-alternative version of the headturning technique that requires the infant to turn in the direction of one of two loudspeakers through which a narrow-band sound of varying intensity was presented. As shown in Figure 1.9, by varying stimulus intensity at several frequencies, they generated sensitivity functions for infants ranging in age from 6 to 24 months of age. Notice that infant thresholds were more similar to adult thresholds at the higher frequencies. Thus, the development of absolute thresholds appeared to consist of a gradual improvement in sensitivity to the lower frequencies. Similar findings were reported by Berg and Smith (1983) and by Sinnott, Pisoni, and Aslin (1983) using pure-tone stimuli and a unidirectional headturning procedure (see Fig. 1.9).

A subtle interpretive issue surrounding these data was raised by Aslin et al. (1983).

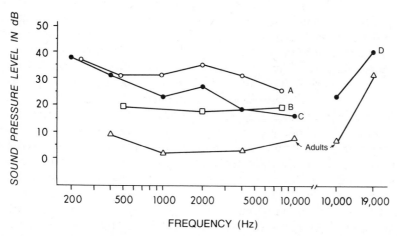

Figure 1.9. Absolute auditory thresholds as a function of stimulus frequency in infants and adults. (From "Behavioral Thresholds for Tones During Infancy" by K. M. Berg and M. C. Smith, 1983, *Journal of Experimental Child Psychology, 35,* p. 414; "High-Frequency Sensitivity in Infants" by B. A. Schneider, S. E. Trehub, and D. Bull, 1980, *Science, 207,* p. 1004; "A Comparison of Pure Tone Auditory Thresholds in Human Infants and Adults" by J. M. Sinnott, D. B. Pisoni, and R. N. Aslin, 1983, *Infant Behavior & Development, 6,* p. 13; "Developmental Changes in Infants' Sensitivity to Octave-Band Noises" by S. E. Trehub, B. A. Schneider, and M. Endman, 1980, *Journal of Experimental Child Psychology, 29,* p. 289.)

Although several of these studies of absolute thresholds also tested adults under identical conditions to provide the best possible developmental comparison, it is impossible to equate exactly the response criterion used at each age. For example, young infants may detect a sound but fail to respond because their criterion for judging detection is more stringent than that of adults. If there were an overall criterion effect between infants and adults, then the infant functions in Figure 1.9 would actually be shifted downward with respect to the adult function. Such a shift would imply that infants have *greater* high-frequency sensitivity than adults. A recent report by Schneider, Trehub, Morrongiello, and Thorpe (1986) is consistent with such a conclusion. They reported that 3-, 4-, and 5-year-olds were more sensitive than adults at 20 kHz. Thus, if there is a gradual developmental loss of high-frequency sensitivity, as suggested by Green (1985), then high-frequency sensitivity in infants may in fact be better than that in 6-year-olds and adults. Alternatively, high-frequency sensitivity may show a developmental improvement between 6 months and 6 years, followed by a decline between 6 years and adulthood. Nevertheless, the absolute magnitude of improvement in low-frequency sensitivity between 6 months of age and adulthood remains uncertain. Clearly, some improvement occurs regardless of the shift in sensitivity attributed to criterion effects.

Discrimination

Detection is an obvious requirement for functional hearing. However, most of the information carried by auditory signals is based on differences in intensity, frequency, duration, and patterning. These discriminative abilities require underlying mechanisms that can differentiate between *supra*threshold auditory signals. Although many early studies attempted to examine auditory discrimination (Eisenberg, 1976), they did not employ a psychophysical approach. That is, they presented only one or two stimulus differences rather than a series of stimulus differences lying along some simple physical dimension. As a result, failure to obtain evidence of discrimination for a limited number of stimulus differences was ambiguous because the method of measurement, rather than the infant's auditory system, may have been the critical limiting factor in obtaining positive evidence of discrimination. Moreover, because these early studies assessed only group performance rather than individual performance, they were not applicable in a clinical setting. Recently, several studies have employed the operant headturning technique and a psychophysical approach to guarantee that *some* stimulus differences were discriminated, thereby documenting the sensitivity of the method. In addition, by presenting many trials to each infant, it was possible to make statements about individual infants' discriminative abilities.

Intensity discrimination is a fundamental aspect of auditory function because the natural environment is rarely, if ever, completely quiet. Thus, in contrast to absolute thresholds, it is necessary to describe the ability to detect a signal in noise. Sinnott and Aslin (1985) used the unidirectional headturning procedure to assess intensity discrimination for pure tones of 1000 Hz. They found that the minimum intensity increment, or difference limen (DL), was approximately 3–12 dB in infants 6–9 months old in contrast to 1–2 dB in adults tested under identical conditions. DLs of similar intensity have been reported by Schneider and Trehub (1985) for narrow-band noises and by Bull, Eilers, and Oller (1984) for speech stimuli. Although the reported differences between infant and adult DLs were statistically significant, it is clear that by 6 months of age infants are quite good at discriminating the subtle intensity differences that signal stress in multisyllabic utterances. Unfortunately, the absence of any data on intensity DLs in infants younger than 6 months precludes any statements about the salience of syllable stress in the early postnatal period.

Another paradigm that has been used to assess infants' sensitivity to intensity variations consists of embedding a test signal within a broad-band masking stimulus. Bull, Schneider, and Trehub (1981), Nozza and Wilson (1984), and Trehub, Bull, and Schneider (1981) used the operant headturning procedure with this masking paradigm to investigate the magnitude of threshold deficit induced by different masker intensities. The *proportional* threshold elevation induced by different levels of masking was the same in infants and adults, although the infants' absolute thresholds were poorer than the adults'. Thus the basic mechanism that enables the auditory system to process differences in intensity appears to be remarkably mature by 6 months of age. The only qualitative developmental difference in intensity discrimination is that infants are apparently insensitive to rather large (15 dB) *decrements* in intensity, whereas adults show no asymmetry between DLs for intensity increments and intensity decrements (Sinnott & Aslin, 1985).

Frequency discrimination is another important aspect of auditory function that permits the differentiation of complex acoustic signals such as speech. Several recent reports (Olsho, 1984a; Olsho, Schoon, Sakai, Turpin, & Sperduto, 1982; Sinnott & Aslin, 1985) have employed the operant headturning procedure to investigate frequency DLs in infants 6–9 months old. In general, infants are able to discriminate a 2 percent change in the frequency of a pure tone (e.g., 20 Hz at 1000 Hz), although Olsho (1984a) has reported somewhat better frequency DLs at higher frequencies. In contrast, adult frequency DLs are approximately 0.5–1 percent. Despite these statistically significant developmental differences, it is clear that infants by 6 months of age are quite sensitive to variations in frequency. Moreover, in contrast to intensity discrimination, infants do not show an asymmetry between DLs for frequency increments and frequency decrements.

Another task that can assess frequency resolution is a masking paradigm in which a pure-tone background (masker) of variable frequency is presented simultaneously with a pure-tone target of fixed frequency. If the auditory system is able to process frequency information in narrow channels, then only masker frequencies very similar to the target frequency will interfere with the detection of the target. Olsho (1985) used this pure-tone masking paradigm and the operant headturning procedure with infants 5–8 months old. As shown in Figure 1.10, the masker intensity required to bring the target to threshold was smallest when the masker was the same frequency as the target. For masker frequencies more discrepant from the target frequency, the masker intensity required to bring the target to threshold was progressively greater. The resultant tuning function represents the susceptibility of the infant auditory system to the effects of masking at frequencies surrounding the target frequency. Although the unmasked thresholds differed between infants and adults, it is apparent from Figure 1.10 that the shape of the tuning curves was the same at the two ages. Thus it seems likely that the mechanism that mediates frequency analysis in the auditory system is quite mature by 6 months of age.

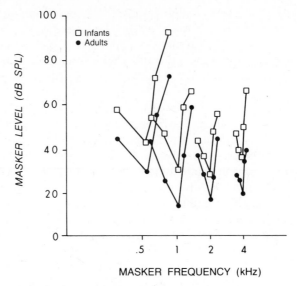

Figure 1.10. Psychophysical tuning curves for auditory frequency selectivity in 6-month-olds. (From "Infant Auditory Perception: Tonal Masking" by L. W. Olsho, 1985, *Infant Behavior & Development, 8,* p. 380. Reprinted with permission.)

A similar masking paradigm has been used with the ABR in an attempt to assess the underlying frequency selectivity of the infant auditory system. Folsom (1985) presented 3-month-olds with filtered clicks of limited bandwidth either with a continuous pure-tone masker of variable frequency or without a masker. As in the Olsho (1985) study, ABR latency and amplitude were attenuated maximally at the frequency of the pure-tone masker. The amount of masking at adjacent frequencies had the same general shape in infants and adults, but in infants there was greater masking by the low-frequency pure tones than in the adults. That is, the spread of masking from low frequencies to high frequencies was greater in infants, implying that frequency tuning at high frequencies was poorer in infants than in adults. An interesting hypothesis was raised by Folsom (1985) to acount for this poorer high-frequency tuning. Several studies in nonhumans have documented a postnatal shift in frequency coding along the basilar membrane (Harris & Dallos, 1984; Lippe & Rubel, 1983; Rubel & Ryals, 1983). Frequencies that are represented near the apex of the adult cochlea are represented more toward the base of the infant cochlea. Thus, if a similar developmental shift occurred in human infants, then lower frequencies would result in excitation of more basal (high frequency) regions of the basilar membrane, creating a mismatch between the frequency of stimulation and the neural tuning characteristic of the adult. This hypothesis is consistent with Hecox's (1975) report of high-pass masking in which low frequencies contribute more to the ABR in infants than in adults. Unfortunately, many of these issues are subject to a variety of competing explanations because of the complexity of recording, analyzing, and interpreting the ABR.

An extension of the foregoing findings on frequency discrimination to more speechlike stimuli was made by Aslin (1986) in a recent series of studies on frequency modulation. Much of the information contained in consonants is carried by changes in frequency that occur in the brief (20–80 msec) formant transitions (see later section on speech perception). The operant headturning procedure was used to assess DLs for frequency sweeps varying around a steady 1000-Hz standard. When the duration of the frequency sweep was long (300 msec), DLs were approximately 2 percent, a value indistinguishable from that obtained in studies of frequency DLs. However, when the frequency sweep was rapid (50 msec or less), DLs were larger (approximately 4 percent). Thus it appears that infants, like adults, are able to discriminate small frequency sweeps, but their performance is limited by the duration (or rate) of frequency modulation. These results may establish limits for the discrimination of speech sounds that contain variations in the duration of formant transitions.

Surprisingly little research has been directed to the question of duration discrimination. Eilers, Bull, Oller, and Lewis (1984) reported that infants 5–11 months old discriminated a change in vowel duration from 300 msec to 400 msec when the vowel was embedded in single-, double-, and triple-syllable words. Morrongiello (1984), in a control experiment for a larger study on melody perception, reported that 6-month-olds discriminated a change in component-tone duration from 200 msec to 160 msec (with a complementary change in intertone interval from 200 msec to 260 msec). Thus by 6 months of age infants are capable of discriminating a change of 20–33 percent in pure-tone duration and a 33 percent change in vowel duration. Unfortunately, neither of these studies was designed to assess the DL for duration.

In adults, the combination of discrete frequencies and durations leads to the perception of simple melodies. Chang and Trehub (1977a), using a heart rate measure, reported that 5-month-olds discriminated between two different six-tone melodies, but not when the melody change consisted of a transposition to an adjacent key (i.e., proportional increases or decreases in each component tone). Trehub, Bull, and Thorpe (1984) extended these early findings to infants 8–11 months old using the operant headturning procedure. They introduced four changes in a six-tone melody: (1) a transposition in key; (2) a change in the absolute frequencies of the component tones that retained the pattern of increments and decrements in frequency (the same melodic contour); (3) a change in the range of component-tone frequencies that retained the same melodic contour; and (4) a change in the range of component-tone frequencies that altered the melodic contour. They reported that infants discriminated all four of these alterations in the six-tone melody, and they hypothesized that the use of short intermelody intervals (800 msec, compared to the 15-sec intervals used in Chang & Trehub, 1977a) enabled the infants in this more recent study to retain information about the absolute frequencies of the component tones. In a second experiment, the discrimination task was made more difficult by presenting a distractor between each repetition of the melody. In addition to the four change conditions used in the first experiment, they presented a change in melodic contour that did not contain a change in the range of component frequencies. The results of this second experiment indicated that infants did not discriminate the transposition in key or the change in component frequencies that preserved melodic contour, unless the range of component frequencies was altered. Changes in melodic contour, regardless of the range of component frequencies, were discriminated. These findings are consistent with adult experiments that showed that memory for detailed information about the absolute frequencies of component tones and the absolute intervals between component tones is less robust than memory for melodic contour (e.g., Bartlett & Dowling, 1980).

A subsequent experiment by Trehub, Thorpe, and Morrongiello (1985) reported that a change in the frequency of a single component tone in a six-tone melody was sufficient for 6- to 8-month-olds to discriminate between two melodies. When the single altered tone was outside the frequency range of the standard melody, discrimination performance was better than when the altered tone was within the frequency range of the standard melody. However, when a distractor was introduced between each repetition of the standard melody, the magnitude of the change in frequency of the altered tone did not result in differential performance. This result was interpreted as evidence that melodic contour, and not absolute change in component-tone frequency, was the most robust information for discrimination of melodies varying in a single component tone.

Another aspect of melodies is their temporal grouping. Chang and Trehub (1977b), using a heart rate measure, reported that 5-month-olds discriminated a six-tone melody that changed from a 2-4 grouping to a 4-2 grouping based on the relative duration of intertone intervals. Similar results were reported by Demany, McKenzie, and Vurpillot (1977) in infants 1–3 months old using a habituation of visual fixation procedure. More recently, Morrongiello (1984) examined 6- and 12-month-olds' perception of groups of noise bursts. Noise bursts rather than pure tones were used in an attempt to remove spectral information as a potential cue to perceptual grouping. A nine-component noise burst pattern consisting of three groups of three bursts (3-3-3) served as the standard against which four types of comparisons were made: (1) a grouping of 4-1-4; (2) a grouping of 2-5-2; (3) a grouping of 5-4; and (4) a single sequence of 9. Twelve-month-olds discriminated all four changes whereas 6-month-olds discriminated only the changes that altered the *number* of groupings (i.e., 5-4 and 9). A follow-up experiment demonstrated that even the 6-month-olds were quite sensitive to changes in the relative duration of the component noise bursts and the intergroup intervals. Thus it seems most likely that the failure of the 6-month-olds to discriminate the changes from 3-3-3 to 4-1-4 and to 2-5-2 was the result of a limitation in the ability to perceive the *relative* timing information that enables adults to group component noise bursts.

Localization

Detection and discrimination of sounds in the environment are essential for the effective use of auditory information. However, locating a sound source is also important for tasks requiring the apprehension or avoidance of objects that are not easily detected by information from other sensory modalities. For many years there was no objective evidence that newborns could localize a sound source, primarily because of methodological difficulties. However, an early report by Wertheimer (1961) on bilateral sound localization by a single newborn, followed by several non-replications, led to a definitive demonstration of newborn sound localization nearly 20 years later (Muir & Field, 1979). The key to this demonstration was fourfold. First, it was essential to make the observer of the newborn's behavioral responses unaware of the actual location of the sound source so that observer bias was not a significant factor (this control was not used in many earlier studies). This was accomplished by the use of videotapes that were scored by observers who had no information about the location of the sound source. Second, it was important to support the body and head of the newborn in such a way that headturns were possible. This was accomplished by having an adult hold the newborn in the supine position on her lap while the newborn's head was gently supported by the holder's hand. Third, it was important to allow the newborn sufficient time to organize and implement a headturning response, particularly since response latencies were often as long as 10 sec. Subsequent research (Clarkson, Clifton, & Morrongiello, 1985) failed to find that longer stimulus durations enhanced the proportion or accuracy of newborn head turns, suggesting that response latency is determined by motor rather than sensory factors. Finally, it was important to take into account the occurrence of no-response trials when computing the accuracy of directional headturns, as well as the fact that newborn headturning responses habituate rapidly (Zelazo, Brody, & Chaika, 1984). In many previous studies, the percentage of correct head turns toward a sound source was expressed as a function of the total number of stimulus presentations, rather than as a function of the number of actual headturn responses. Muir and Field (1979) reported that newborns reliably made directionally appropriate headturns toward a bilateral sound source (a rattle), even though the proportion of no-response trials was quite high (20 percent or more). Moreover, only a limited number of trials (e.g., 6–10) was presented to reduce the effects of response habituation. Thus, provided that newborns respond, they consistently make headturns toward a sound located on the right or left.

This first definitive demonstration of newborn sound localization was followed by several studies that replicated the phenomenon and extended it to older infants (Clifton, Morrongiello, Kulig, & Dowd, 1981; Field, Muir, Pilon, Sinclair, & Dodwell, 1980; Muir, Abraham, Forbes, & Harris, 1979). An interesting outcome of these follow-up experiments was the finding that the accuracy of sound localization declines between birth and 2 months of age, followed by a reemergence by 4 months of age. This developmental decline is not the result of a growing conflict with visual information, but seems to be consistent with a shift from reflexive orienting to intentional orienting. Moreover, an auditory illusion called the precedence effect, in which a single sound is perceived when two identical sounds are presented from two lateralized loudspeakers with a delay in the onset of one sound, does not appear to emerge developmentally until the fourth postnatal month (Clifton et al., 1981; Morrongiello, Clifton, & Kulig, 1982; Clifton, Morrongiello, & Dowd, 1984). This illusion, which presumably functions to eliminate the perception of short-duration echos, is not perceived by animals with cortical lesions. Thus both the reemergence of intentional sound localization and the onset of the precedence effect may be mediated by cortical development. Although the precedence effect is present in 4-month-olds, the onset asynchrony between the two sounds required to detect a single source rather than two sounds is smaller in adults and 5-year-olds than in 6-month-olds (Morrongiello, Kulig, & Clifton, 1984), suggesting that temporal processing improves considerably during infancy.

A final aspect of sound localization is the issue of spatial resolution. That is, what is the minimum angle between two sound sources that can be reliably discriminated? This minimum audible angle is based on three types of information: (1) the difference in intensity between the sound reaching the two ears; (2) the difference in time of arrival of the sound wave at the two ears; and (3) the difference in the phase of the sound wave at the two ears. Unfortunately, despite evidence that phase information can be detected by 4-month-olds (Bundy, 1980), it is not clear that such information can be utilized effectively to guide a motor response. Preliminary evidence on the minimum audible angle in 7-month-olds (Ashmead & Perris, 1986) suggests that one or more of these three types of information is ineffective in eliciting a headturn to a change in sound location of less than 19 deg. These issues of spatial resolution and the auditory information that guides localization remain important questions for future research.

Preferences

The preceding sections on auditory detection, discrimination, and localization have described assessment techniques that rely on either spontaneously emitted or conditioned responses. Each of these abilities was investigated with the aim of determining the capacities of the infant at various ages. Although such data are important for understanding what an infant *can* do, they may tell us little about what infants *prefer* to do when listening to auditory stimuli. Auditory preferences may reveal whether certain types of suprathreshold stimuli are more salient than others or whether they differentially engage the attention of infants at different ages and/ or after different types of auditory exposure.

The first preference technique was based on a discrimination procedure developed by Horowitz (1975) and her colleagues. In the discrimination procedure, the infant's fixation of a visual pattern triggered the presentation of an auditory stimulus. After fixation duration met a predetermined criterion of habituation, the auditory stimulus was altered but the visual stimulus remained unchanged. Posthabituation recovery of visual fixation indicated that auditory discrimination had occurred. This habituation procedure was subsequently modified by Colombo and Bundy (1981) for use as a measure of auditory preferences. The infant's fixation of one of two identical visual stimuli triggered the presentation of one of two different auditory stimuli. If infants reliably preferred to fixate one of the two visual stimuli, then they must have (1) discriminated between the two auditory stimuli, and (2) preferred one auditory stimulus over the other. As in the preferential looking procedure used in research on infant vision, failure to show a preference for one of two suprathreshold stimuli leads only to the conclusion that no preference was shown (i.e., infants may have discriminated the stimuli but not preferred to fixate one over the other). Using this technique, Colombo and Bundy (1981) reported that 4-month-olds prefer to listen to a human voice over either silence or white noise. Colombo and Bundy (1983) reported that 4-month-olds show novelty preferences after the brief presentation of an initially nonpreferred auditory stimulus. Sullivan and Horowitz (1983) reported that 2-month-olds prefer certain speech stimuli with a rising–falling pitch contour. In addition, Colombo and Horowitz (1986) reported that 4-month-olds show no preference for a large frequency sweep over a smaller frequency sweep or over a flat (no-sweep) pure tone.

A variant of this preference technique has proven useful in studies of auditory signals containing features referred to as "motherese" (Newport, 1977). Fernald and Simon (1984) and Stern, Spieker, and MacKain (1982) reported that high pitch and exaggerated pitch contours are typical of maternal speech to infants and young children. Fernald (1985) presented female voices containing either normal or motherese pitch contours depending on the direction in which infants turned their heads. Four-month-olds reliably turned in the direction that led to the presentation of the motherese voice. A second experiment, in which a pure tone was varied in frequency to match the pitch contour of normal and motherese voices, showed that pitch contour information alone was sufficient to support 4-month-olds' preference for motherese.

Another technique that has been used to assess auditory preferences is a variant of the high-amplitude sucking procedure. DeCasper and Fifer (1980) demonstrated that newborns will alter their sucking behavior to listen to their own mothers' voices rather than the voices of strange females. Because the newborns had limited postnatal exposure to their own mothers' voices, this result suggested that the maternal voice preference may have been induced by prenatal exposure. Follow-up experiments added strong support to this hypothesis. First, intrauterine heartbeat sounds are effective as a reinforcer of newborn sucking responses (DeCasper & Sigafoos, 1983). Second, the father's voice is not preferred by newborns over another male voice (DeCasper & Prescott, 1984), although intrauterine heartbeat sounds are preferred over a male voice (Panneton & DeCasper, 1984). Finally, newborns prefer to listen to a tape-recorded prose passage that was read aloud by the mother during the latter stages of her pregnancy compared to a prose passage not read during her pregnancy (DeCasper & Spence, 1986), and newborns prefer a melody that was sung by the mother during her pregnancy compared to a melody that was not sung during her pregnancy (Panneton, 1985). These results strongly suggest that prenatal auditory exposure is sufficient to induce an auditory preference during the immediate postnatal period.

The findings on both infants' preferences for motherese and their preferences for auditory signals presented prenatally raise many questions about the mechanism underlying such preferences. Clearly, 4-month-olds' preferences for motherese could have been induced by postnatal exposure to environmental events that sensitized the infant to attend to exaggerated pitch contours. Alternatively, large frequency excursions may be particularly salient because of basic properties of the auditory system that are independent of auditory experience. Finally, it is possible that preferences for exaggerated pitch contours are induced by prenatal auditory experience. The filtering characteristics of the uterus limit high-amplitude auditory signals to frequencies below 1000 Hz (Armitage et al., 1980; Querleu & Renard, 1981). Moreover, the mother's voice is the auditory signal of greatest amplitude because it is carried to the uterus via both external (airborne) and internal (body cavity) routes. If frequency sensitivity is poor during the prenatal period, then the ability of the fetus to detect changes in low-frequency signals carried by the mother's voice may be limited to large pitch excursions. Although speculative, this hypothesis is consistent with a study by Mehler, Bertoncini, Barriere, and Jassik-Gerschenfeld (1978), who reported that 1-month-olds preferred the voice of their mother over the voice of a strange female, but only if both voices had normally intonated pitch contours. Clearly, many additional empirical tests of this prenatal induction hypothesis are required to differentiate the effects of genetic and experiential influences on infants' postnatal preferences for voices.

Speech Perception

Historically, the rationale for studying speech perception in infants was twofold. First, young children progress from virtually no productive articulations at 12 months of age to a rich repertoire of grammatical rules and semantic relations by

36 months of age (Brown, 1973). Because this rapid period of language development occurs despite little formal language training, many speech perception skills must be well developed prior to the onset of functional articulations. Second, given Chomsky's (1965, 1968) dominating influence as a proponent of innate syntactic mechanisms, researchers were sensitized to search for and to accept empirical findings that supported innate perceptual mechanisms that could facilitate the acquisition of language. These two factors, coupled with findings from two decades of research on adult speech perception, led to the first important empirical study of infant speech perception.

The now classic study by Eimas, Siqueland, Jusczyk, and Vigorito (1971) demonstrated that infants 1–4 months of age can discriminate subtle acoustic properties that differentiate for English-speaking adults the stop-consonant–vowel (CV) syllables /ba/ from /pa/. Although this study was important in demonstrating that very young infants had the sophisticated perceptual mechanism required for speech discrimination, it was also important for documenting that infants did *not* discriminate other speech contrasts. Computer-generated (synthetic) speech sounds differing along a single acoustic dimension called voice onset time (VOT) were presented in pairs to infants for testing with the high-amplitude sucking procedure. Only one of these VOT pairs spanned the boundary between English-speaking adults' phonemic* categories for /ba/ and /pa/. This between-category VOT pair was discriminated by the infants, whereas several other within-category VOT pairs were not discriminated, even though the physical difference between each pair was identical (20 msec). These results led Eimas et al. (1971) to conclude that infants had an innate mechanism for perceiving speech sounds in a categorical manner.

Given the historical context, these findings on infant speech perception were both startling, because they implied a sophisticated perceptual system in young infants, and easily accepted, because they conformed to expected views of linguistic innateness. Additional evidence from adult speech perception (Liberman, Harris, Kinney, & Lane, 1961) supported the interpretation that infants' perception of speech was not simply based on the acoustic differences between the VOT pairs. When presented with single exemplars of CV syllables from the VOT continuum, adults consistently label them as /ba/ or /pa/, thereby generating an identification (ID) function. This ID function is quite discrete in adults, with virtually no confusions between categories except at the steep category boundary between VOT values labeled /ba/ and VOT values labeled /pa/. For stop consonants, adults show chance levels of discrimination for any two exemplars drawn from the same phonemic category, but they show nearly perfect discrimination for any two exemplars drawn from different phonemic categories. For example, in English-speaking adults the category boundary between /ba/ and /pa/ is at a VOT value of approximately 25–30 msec. Thus a contrast between VOT values of 20 msec and 40 msec is easily discriminated,

---

*The term *phonemic* refers to a particular level of abstraction linking the acoustic (physical) properties of speech sounds to their function as components of a language. A phoneme is the smallest unit of sound that contrasts a difference in meaning in a given natural language. However, not all languages share all phonemes. Thus, if a range of acoustic differences could be used in some natural language, they comprise a phonetic segment. Those phonetic segments that are functional in a particular language comprise that language's set of phonemes, with the proviso that more than one phonetic segment may be contained in a phoneme.

whereas contrasts between VOT values of 0 msec and 20 msec or between 40 msec and 60 msec are difficult or impossible to discriminate. These two findings, a sharp category boundary based on labeling data and good between-category but poor within-category discrimination, became known as categorical perception (Liberman, Harris, Hoffman, & Griffith, 1957).

The functional implication of Eimas et al.'s (1971) claim that categorical perception was innate is the resulting simplification of the process of acquiring phonemic categories. Moreover, because categorical perception in adults had never been documented for nonspeech sounds, it seemed plausible to assume that categorical perception itself was a mechanism unique to speech. The plausibility of these conclusions underwent a series of challenges during the succeeding decade. These challenges took the following forms: (1) demonstrations of within-category speech discrimination in adults; (2) demonstrations of categorical perception for nonspeech signals in adults and infants; (3) demonstrations of categorical speech perception in nonhumans; and (4) inconsistencies in the categorical perception of foreign speech contrasts by infants and adults.

The early studies of categorical perception in adults employed a discrimination procedure that required the subject to remember two different speech sounds and compare a third sound to these stored exemplars. This discrimination procedure, called ABX, obviously placed some demands on the subject's memory for speech. More recent studies of speech discrimination (e.g., Carney, Widin, & Viemeister, 1977) employed a discrimination procedure used in psychoacoustic research called the repeating standard or AX procedure. A single exemplar is repeated and occasionally interrupted by the presentation of a different speech sound. Under these reduced memory conditions, adults can make within-category discriminations of stop consonants, for example, between VOT values of 0 and 20 msec. Thus the original finding that stop-consonant discrimination is impossible for within-category contrasts appears to be correct only if the subject is required to encode the sounds in short-term memory. Of course, in the natural environment we must encode speech sounds for seconds and minutes as we process ongoing fluent speech. The point here is simply that the correspondence between labeling of speech and poor within-category discrimination is largely a result of task demands and not the result of limitations of basic discriminative mechanisms.

The second challenge to the hypothesis that speech sounds are processed by adults (and infants) in a specialized manner was provided by several studies in which nonspeech sounds were perceived categorically just like speech sounds. The original claim of a specialized speech mechanism relied on the finding that nonspeech signals were not perceived categorically. This claim was based on studies of the discrimination of speech sounds that were played backwards or speech segments that were isolated from speech syllables (Liberman et al., 1961; Mattingly, Liberman, Syrdal, & Halwes, 1971). In both cases, these sounds were not perceived as speech and were not perceived categorically. However, some of these nonspeech sounds were grossly different from speech; for example, their durations were very brief. Miller, Wier, Pastore, Kelly, and Dooling (1976) and Pisoni (1977) constructed complex nonspeech stimuli that were not perceived by adults as speech but were nonetheless perceived categorically. Moreover, Jusczyk, Pisoni, Walley, and Murray (1980) presented one of these types of nonspeech stimuli, which varied along a tone onset time (TOT) continuum similar to VOT, to young infants and found nearly exactly the same type of categorical discrimination as Eimas et al. (1971) had found for VOT. A follow-up experiment with /ba/-/pa/, /du/-/tu/, and TOT continua found that infants' categorical discrimination boundaries were the same for all three continua (Jusczyk, Rosner, & Reed, Kennedy, submitted).

These results were extended to another nonspeech continuum after Eimas and Miller (1980) reported that infants' category boundary for a /ba/-/wa/ continuum shifts with a change in vowel duration. This boundary shift was demonstrated in adults (Miller & Liberman, 1979) and interpreted as a compensatory mechanism for changes in speaking rate. However, precisely the same shifts in infants' categorical discrimination shown by Eimas and Miller for a /ba/-/wa/ continuum were shown for an analogous nonspeech continuum in adults (Pisoni, Carrell, & Gans, 1983) and in infants (Jusczyk, Pisoni, Reed, Fernald, & Myers, 1983). Thus, if nonspeech stimuli share some of the gross acoustic features of speech stimuli, even though they are *not* perceived as meaningful speech sounds, they can be perceived in a categorical manner by both adults and infants.

The third challenge to the hypothesis that speech sounds are processed by a specialized mechanism unique to the human species was provided by the pioneering work of Kuhl and Miller (1975, 1978), who showed that chinchillas perceive human speech sounds in a categorical manner. Subsequent studies have extended this demonstration of categorical perception to nonhuman primates (Kuhl & Padden, 1982, 1983). Thus it is now clear that the mechanism that supports categorical perception is neither unique to speech nor limited to the human species. Although these findings do not rule out the possibility that human infants process speech with a specialized mechanism, they do demonstrate that such a specialized mechanism is not required to account for nearly all of the findings on speech perception in infants.

The final issue that must be confronted in attempting to understand the mechanism by which infants perceive speech sounds is the effect of early language input on the formation of speech categories. Even before the Eimas et al. (1971) study, it was known that adults from different language communities categorize the same physical dimension (e.g., VOT) in different ways (Lisker & Abramson, 1970). For example, the /ba/-/pa/ boundary in English-speaking adults corresponds to a VOT value of approximately 25–30 msec, the /ba/-/pa/ boundary in Spanish-speaking adults is approximately 0 msec, and there are two boundaries in Thai-speaking adults, one near the English boundary and one at approximately *minus* 25 msec. Thus Thai adults employ *three* categories in their language whereas English and Spanish adults utilize only two categories. These findings illustrate that there must be plasticity in the formation of speech categories, including the possibility of shifts in boundary locations and the addition (or subtraction) of entire categories.

Several studies of VOT discrimination have been conducted on infants from non–English-speaking environments to determine whether VOT categories are learned from exposure to a specific language or whether they are specified innately and susceptible to postnatal rearrangement or loss based on exposure to a specific language. Nearly all evidence to date supports the innateness hypothesis for stop-consonant categories. That is, it appears that infants from all language environments are capable of perceiving a limited set of speech categories that could be used in one or more of the world's languages. However, after exposure to a specific native language, those categories that are not used in the native language become less effective and eventually drop out completely. Some of these categories can be reactivated by nonnative language exposure (Pisoni, Aslin, Perey, & Hennessy, 1982; Tees & Werker, 1984; Werker & Tees, 1984b), whereas others appear quite resistant to reactivation despite extensive training (MacKain, Best, & Strange, 1981; Miyawaki, Strange, Verbrugge, Liberman, Jenkins, & Fujimura, 1975; Strange & Dittmann, 1984).

Evidence for the presence of nonnative speech categories in infants is considerable. For example, along the VOT continuum it appears that infants from any language environment can discriminate between /ba/ and /pa/ even if that distinction is not used in their native language (Lasky, Syrdal-Lasky, & Klein, 1975; Streeter, 1976). Although early evidence showed that only infants from a non-English environment could discriminate the VOT contrast that is used in Spanish or Thai (Eilers, Gavin, & Wilson, 1979; Eimas, 1975; Lasky et al., 1975; Streeter, 1976), subsequent research showed that even infants from an English-speaking environment could discriminate these contrasts (Aslin, Pisoni, Hennessy, & Perey, 1981). Moreover, infants from an English-speaking environment can discriminate a variety of speech contrasts other than those cued by VOT, even though English-speaking adults are initially unable to make such discriminations (Trehub, 1976; Werker, Gilbert, Humphrey, & Tees, 1981).

Perhaps the clearest demonstration of the loss of perceptual categories between infancy and adulthood has been provided by Werker and Tees (1983, 1984a). They showed that infants from an English-speaking environment were able to discriminate two speech contrasts that were native to Hindi and Salish (a North American Indian language). English-speaking adults, as well as English-speaking 4-year-olds, were unable without training to discriminate these two nonnative contrasts. However, as shown in Figure 1.11, infants from an English-speaking environment gradually lost their ability to discriminate these contrasts during the second six months of life. Thus, at least for the specific acoustic information utilized in the discrimination of these two nonnative speech contrasts, there appears to be a clear *loss* of a perceptual ability during infancy. To date, it remains unclear whether other nonnative speech contrasts, follow a similar time course for the loss of perceptual discriminability. However, it appears likely that robust acoustic information that signals nonnative speech contrasts can be used to reactivate the loss of speech categories (Pisoni et al., 1982). Those nonnative speech categories that show permanent losses (e.g., Hindi /ṭa/–/ta/ for speakers of English; English /r/–/l/ for speakers of Japanese) are distinguished by rather subtle acoustic information.

In general, then, what can we conclude about the mechanism that underlies infant speech perception? First, if infants process speech in a specialized manner, then it is likely that other complex nonspeech stimuli are also processed by the same underlying mechanism. It seems unlikely that infants actually hear speech as meaningful units until sometime in later infancy when they begin to associate sounds with meanings. Thus it seems premature to characterize infant speech perception as phonemic. However, there does appear to be a period beginning in the second six months of life when speech perception becomes language specific. This may indicate that speech sounds are grouped into phonetic categories, even though these categories may not be closely tied to the meanings used in the native language. Prior to 6 months of age, it seems likely that infants are performing their analysis of speech sounds solely on the basis of acoustic differences. These acoustic differences are sufficient to permit categorical perception, just as similar acoustic mechanisms

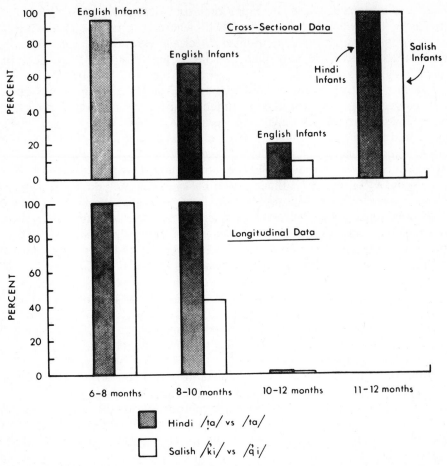

Figure 1.11. Discrimination performance for infants from an English-speaking environment on two non-English speech contrasts illustrating the decline in performance between 6–12 months of age. (From "Cross-Language Speech Perception: Evidence for Perceptual Reorganization During the First Year of Life" by J. F. Werker and R. C. Tees, 1983, *Canadian Journal of Psychology, 37,* p. 61. Reprinted with permission.)

presumably support the processing of nonspeech by infants and the processing of speech by nonhumans. Second, there is good evidence that every speech contrast used in one of the world's native languages can be discriminated by 6 months of age (see reviews by Aslin et al., 1983; Jusczyk, 1981). Although some contrasts were initially thought to be impossible for young infants to discriminate, subsequent methods proved these failures to be false negatives.

If we grant infants the ability to discriminate all language-relevant speech contrasts, what additional abilities are required to process speech at a phonemic level? First, infants must be able to recognize that different acoustic cues can signal the same phonemic category. In adult speech perception, this phonemic categorization ability is manifested in two quite different forms: (1) categorical perception that appears to be mediated by limitations at peripheral auditory levels; and (2) the assignment of discriminably different acoustic exemplars to speech categories. Both of these forms of categorization become automatized in adults so that the efficient processing of fluent speech is possible. In fact, given the ability of adults to discriminate within-category differences under certain testing conditions and not under other testing conditions, the two forms of categorization may actually represent a continuum of task difficulty rather than two discrete underlying processes. However, for a given task, it is clear that some speech sounds (e.g., stop consonants) are categorized by a mechanism based on sensory limitations, whereas other speech sounds (e.g., vowels) are categorized on the basis of experience with specific linguistic input.

One of the recurrent puzzles in the area of speech perception is the mechanism that maps variable acoustic cues onto invariant phonemic categories. For example, as shown in Figure 1.12, the distinction between /ba/ and /da/ is apparently carried by the direction (rising vs. falling) of the second format transition that leads into the steady-state vowel. However, the syllable /di/ has the same rising second-formant transition as the /b/ in /ba/, yet in the context of the vowel /i/ it is perceived as /d/. Thus the acoustic cue to the stop consonant interacts with the formant values of the following vowel. This example of the contextual nature of acoustic–phonemic relations would seem to suggest that perceiving speech as speech involves a complex interplay between various acoustic cues, a process that is unlikely to be mediated by a lower-level acoustic mechanism like the one that may account for categorical perception of speech and nonspeech by young infants (and nonhumans).

These issues of whether infants can form speech categories and what mechanism mediates such categorization have been the focus of several recent studies. Perhaps

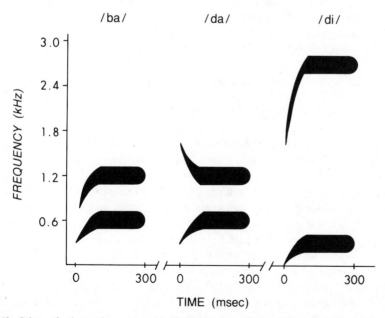

Figure 1.12. Schematized sound spectrograms illustrating how the same acoustic information for a syllable-initial stop consonant results in different perceptual categories as a function of vowel context.

the biggest limitation in these studies is methodological. Ideally, one would like to ask infants to indicate to which of several possible phonemic categories in the native language a particular speech sound belongs. Of course, this question is impossible to ask a preverbal organism. At best, one can ask the infant to sort exemplars into categories, by noting either the relative ease of habituation to multiple tokens or the relative ease of learning to respond to certain tokens and not to others.

A variety of studies have reported that infants, like adults, are influenced by contextual aspects of acoustic cues present in speech sounds. For example, Fodor, Garrett, and Brill (1975) used the operant headturning procedure to assess 4-month-olds' perception of a noise burst preceding a steady-state vowel. In adults, appending the noise burst from the syllable /pi/ to the steady-state vowel /a/ leads to the percept /ka/. Fodor et al. trained infants to make a head turn in one direction to /pi/ and in the other direction to /pu/, and then asked which direction infants would turn to /ka/. Their results, though marginally significant, indicated that infants generalized the /ka/ stimulus to the /pi/ response, a finding that is consistent with the hypothesis that infants perceived the combination of acoustic cues for stop consonants in an adultlike manner.

Other attempts have been made to use the two-alternative headturning procedure to assess speech categorization in infants. Aslin, Perey, Hennessy, and Pisoni (1977) trained 6-month-olds to make a unidirectional head turn to the change from /a/ to /i/ and to inhibit that same head turn to a change from /a/ to /u/. Although some infants performed at above-chance levels on this task, it appeared to be too difficult for infants when the discrimination between exemplars was made more difficult. Katz and Jusczyk (1980) attempted to replicate the two-alternative headturning procedure used by Fodor et al. (1975) but with the consonants /b/ and /d/. After initial training on /ba/ versus /da/, generalization was assessed for /b/ and /d/ in three new vowel contexts. As in the Fodor et al. study, performance during generalization was above chance but only marginally significant. A recent variant of the two-alternative headturning procedure has been developed by Burnham, Earnshaw, and Quinn (in press), but poor levels of performance on the endpoints of a VOT continuum rendered ambiguous any interpretation of subsequent categorization on intermediate VOT values. Thus it appears that variants of the headturning procedure do not provide a clear-cut analog to the two-alternative labeling procedure used with adults, perhaps because associating two responses with two speech sounds is a difficult task for the infant.

A number of other methods have been used to circumvent the task difficulty of a two-alternative headturning procedure. Unfortunately, none of these methods is a direct measure of categorization. However, they provide information on the ease with which infants ignore initially discriminable acoustic differences. Kuhl and her colleagues (Hillenbrand, 1983, 1984; Holmberg, Morgan, & Kuhl, 1977; Kuhl, 1979, 1983, 1985) employed a transfer of training paradigm using the operant headturning procedure. After 6-month-olds met a preset criterion of unidirectional headturning to a change from a single background exemplar to a single target exemplar, a number of discriminably different exemplars were added to a background set and to a target set. Thus, after training with the single exemplars, the infant heard a random variation in background exemplars and any headturns to these background exemplars were not reinforced. However, headturns to any of the several target exemplars were reinforced. The ease (number of trials to criterion or overall percent correct) with which infants generalized their headturning responses to the target exemplars and refrained from making headturns to the background exemplars provided an index of categorization. The types of categories studied included both vowels and consonants, and the types of phonemically irrelevant variations that the infant was "instructed" to ignore included pitch contour and fundamental frequency for vowels and vowel context and syllable position for consonants. In nearly all cases, 6-month-olds showed rapid generalization of correct responding to the new target exemplars. Thus for many important aspects of speech perception infants apparently "solved" the categorization problem with very little training. However, infants in these experiments received implicit feedback that their headturns to the background exemplars were "incorrect," but these false alarms were not recorded in these experiments (though if they had been persistent the transfer of training would not have occurred). Thus, if infants can *learn* to categorize rapidly, the findings using this procedure may not indicate precisely what speech categories infants use spontaneously (i.e., without any training or feedback).

Another important aspect of speech categorization is the manner in which different acoustic cues that could signal the same perceptual category are combined. This aspect of speech perception has been termed *trading relations* (Repp, 1982) because different acoustic cues, each of which alone signals the same phonetic distinction, can combine to determine the category boundary. The presence of trading relations has been documented in adults and in 5-year-olds (Morrongiello, Robson, Best, & Clifton, 1984), although in children the weights attached to different acoustic cues may not be the same as in adults. Unfortunately, the study of trading relations in infants is a nearly insurmountable task. For example, labeling data are needed for two synthetic continua to establish the category boundary for each acoustic cue, and then additional labeling data are needed for the combined acoustic cues to determine whether the category boundary has undergone a shift. However, there are some studies that suggest a process like trading relations may be operating in infancy. Morse, Eilers, and Gavin (1982) examined 6-month-olds' discrimination of a /slit/-/split/ continuum in which the /p/ in /split/ can be signaled either by formant transitions or by a brief gap. Using the operant headturning procedure, Morse and associates reported that infants discriminated both the natural /slit/-/split/ contrast and a contrast in which natural /slit/ was paired with this same /slit/ stimulus in which a silent gap was inserted after the /s/ (perceived by adults as /split/). Infants discriminated the natural /slit/ from this /slit/+ gap stimulus, but they did not show evidence of discriminating the natural /split/ from this /slit/ +gap stimulus. Although there are some methodological problems associated with this study, the results suggest that infants perceive the formant transitions for /p/ in /split/ to be equivalent to the combination of /slit/ plus a silent gap after the /s/.

Another indirect demonstration of trading relations has been reported by Levitt, Jusczyk, Murray, and Carden (submitted). A previous study of adults by Carden, Levitt, Jusczyk, and Walley (1981) had shown that the fricatives /fa/ and /θa/ are differentiated by the combination of a frication noise and formant transitions. However, if the frication noise is held constant, the formant transition differences are sufficient to differentiate two phonemic categories. Similarly, if the formant transition is held constant, the different frication noises are sufficient to differentiate two phonemic categories. However, without the frication noises, the different formant transitions lead to the uniform percept of the syllable /ba/. The results from infants paralleled the adult findings. Infants discriminated the /fa/–/θa/ contrast containing both frication noise and formant transition differences, the contrast containing the different frication noises with formant transitions held constant, and the contrast containing constant frication noises with different formant transitions. However, infants did not discriminate the contrast in which formant transition differences were presented without the frication noises. As in the Morse et al. (1982) study, these findings can be interpreted as evidence of trading relations if the failure to discriminate is actually indicative of perceptual equivalence.

In addition to the ability to categorize speech sounds on the basis of multiple acoustic cues, infants must be able to segment running speech into units such as phonemes, syllables, and words. We know a great deal about the perception of isolated speech syllables, but to date there have been no studies of infants' perception of running speech. Infants may be capable, under ideal laboratory conditions, of discriminating and categorizing isolated speech syllables, but they may be overwhelmed by the processing demands placed upon their perceptual and memory systems when confronted with real-time speech input.

An implicit assumption in past research on infant speech perception is that segmentation is focused on the phonemic level because for adults the phoneme is the smallest unit of language that signals a difference in meaning. Bertoncini and Mehler (1981) have provided evidence that the syllable is a more natural unit for infants' perception of speech. Similarly, Bertoncini, Bijeljac-Babic, Jusczyk, and Kennedy (submitted) have provided compelling evidence that in early infancy the syllable, particularly the vowel, is a very salient unit for speech categorization. Attempts to show that infants can use the phoneme or even a phonetic feature, such as voicing, to guide their perception of speech have met with equally plausible alternative explanations based on the level of the syllable (e.g., see Miller & Eimas, 1979, and an alternative account offered by Aslin et al., 1983, pp. 655–656).

The foregoing hypothesis that young infants attend to more global (syllable) levels of speech sounds should not be interpreted as the inability to perceive phonetic differences under some conditions. For example, in single syllables young infants are quite capable of discriminating a phonetic segment in CV, VC, and CVC contexts (Jusczyk, 1977). Moreover, in bisyllabic utterances, young infants are quite capable of discriminating a single phonetic difference regardless of its syllable position and whether it appeared in a stressed or an unstressed syllable (Jusczyk, Copan, & Thompson, 1978; Jusczyk & Thompson, 1978; Williams, 1977). Despite these capacities to discriminate phonetic segments in different syllable positions, in multisyllabic utterances, and without regard to syllable stress, there is recent evidence that discrimination performance is affected by other segmental information. For example, Goodsitt, Morse, Ver Hoeve, and Cowan (1984) used the operant head-turning procedure to examine 6-month-olds' discrimination of a /ba/–/du/ contrast embedded in trisyllabic utterances. There was no effect of syllable position; that is, discrimination performance was the same in initial, medial, and final position. However, there was an effect of syllable redundancy. That is, if the two nontarget syllables were identical rather than different (e.g., /ko-ba-ko/ rather than /ko-ba-ti/), discrimination performance was enhanced. This effect suggested that duplication of syllables is an effective means for highlighting acoustic differences in multisyllabic utterances.

A recent study by Karzon (1985) provides evidence that young infants' discrimination of syllables within multisyllabic utterances is facilitated by *supra*segmental information. The high-amplitude sucking procedure was used with infants 1–4 months old who were presented with the trisyllable contrast /ma-ra-na/ versus /ma-la-na/. In six experiments, a variety of additional acoustic cues were added to the segmental information for the medial /ra/–/la/ contrast: exaggerated pitch contour, greater amplitude, and longer duration. Only when these acoustic cues were present in combination did the infants show evidence of discriminating the medial /ra/–/la/ contrast. Although these results are subject to a variety of interpretations, it appears that the acoustic correlates of motherese are effective only when they occur in combination because pitch contour alone was insufficient to support discrimination. Alternatively, trisyllabic utterances may be more difficult for young infants to discriminate than for 6-month-olds, the high-amplitude sucking procedure may be less sensitive than the operant headturning procedure, or the acoustic salience of different phonetic segments may interact with suprasegmental cues (e.g., /r/–/l/ may be less salient than /ba/–/du/ even when enhanced by motherese).

Two additional studies have examined infants' sensitivity to suprasegmental information. Hirsh-Pasek, Kemler-Nelson, Jusczyk, Wright, and Kennedy (submitted) used the preferential headturning procedure developed by Fernald (1985) to determine whether infants 7 to 10 months old are sensitive to the acoustic correlates of English clausal structure. They took a naturally produced prose passage and added additional 1-sec segments of silence either at the English clause boundaries or in the middle of the clauses. Infants made headturns to listen more often to the "appropriately" modified passage that conformed to the clausal structure of English. However, they only exhibited this preference when the prose passage was spoken in motherese. It is unlikely that this preference was based on the infants' interpretation of the meaning of the words in the prose passage. Rather, it seems likely that the infants were sensitive to the prosodic features of the passages that were violated when silence was inserted at "inappropriate" locations. The absence of preference in the nonmotherese condition suggests that infants are more attentive to prosodic aspects of language when the linguistic input is delivered as motherese.

Another experiment by Halstead, Jusczyk, and Mehler (in preparation) used the habituation of visual fixation technique to examine 2-month-olds' sensitivity to the prosodic features of English, Italian, French, and Russian. Infants were presented with passages spoken in one of these languages whenever they fixated a visual stimulus. After meeting a preset criterion of habituation, the language was switched (or not switched for control subjects). Infants showed significant dishabituation of fixation for the contrast between English and Italian but not for the contrast between French and Russian. Although this pattern of results suggests that some familiarity with the native language is required for discrimination, a test of that hypothesis requires studies of infants from non–English-speaking environments. It is also unclear whether English–Italian discrimination was based on prosodic or segmental information, although prosodic information seems more likely. Finally, it is unclear whether the prosodic information was induced by postnatal or prenatal experience (or both). Studies of newborns will be needed to determine the origins of this discriminative ability and studies of low-pass filtered speech will be needed to determine whether prosodic or segmental information was the essential discriminative cue.

The final step in the process of achieving a phonemic level in the processing of speech is the assignment of meaning to phonetic segments. This process undoubtedly involves the assignment of differential weightings to the various acoustic cues that signal phonemic categories in a particular native language. Jusczyk (1985, 1986) has outlined a preliminary model for this process of assigning differential weightings during the course of phonological development. Although the model has not received a direct test, it is consistent with a large set of findings on infant speech perception, adult perception of speech and nonspeech, and speech perception by bilinguals. This link between speech perception and language development will certainly be a focus of research in the near future.

SUMMARY AND CONCLUSIONS

The area of infant perceptual development has undergone a remarkable period of growth in the past decade. The present coverage of the visual and auditory systems represents only a fraction of the voluminous literature in this area. Nevertheless, it is apparent that many important aspects of perceptual development have been discovered and clarified since the last edition of this handbook. Within the visual modality, we now know much more about oculomotor systems, visual acuity, pattern perception, color vision, depth perception, the perceptual constancies, and object perception than could have been predicted just a few years ago. Within the auditory modality, basic psychoacoustic studies have revealed important aspects of auditory capacity and studies of speech perception have changed our perspective on the process of language development.

Prospects for future research in the area of infant perception are unlimited. There is already a clear subinterest in aspects of visual and auditory development that may have clinical implications for the diagnosis and treatment of sensory anomalies. More sophisticated methods are continually evolving to provide a better indication of perceptual capacities. Finally, new approaches to the modeling of perceptual development are beginning to emerge as researchers strive for greater specificity in their hypotheses about the mechanisms underlying visual and auditory development. Although there is currently no all-encompassing theory of perceptual development, there are certainly many unanswered questions that will continue to provide future investigators with a rich source of exciting ideas and important discoveries.

REFERENCES

Abramov, I., Gordon, J., Hendrickson, A., Hainline, L., Dobson, V., & LaBossiere, E. (1982). The retina of the newborn human infant. *Science, 217,* 265–267.

Adams, R. J., & Maurer, D. (1984). Detection of contrast by the newborn and 2-month-old infant. *Infant Behavior & Development, 7,* 415–422.

Adams, R. J., Maurer, D., & Davis, M. (1986). Newborns' discrimination of chromatic from achromatic stimuli. *Journal of Experimental Child Psychology, 41,* 267–281.

Antell, S. E. G., & Caron, A. J. (1985). Neonatal perception of spatial relationships. *Infant Behavior & Development, 8,* 15–23.

Appel, M. A., & Campos, J. J. (1977). Binocular disparity as a discriminable stimulus parameter for young infants. *Journal of Experimental Child Psychology, 23,* 47–56.

Armitage, S. E., Baldwin, B. A., & Vince, M. A. (1980). The fetal sound environment of sheep. *Science, 208,* 1173–1174.

Ashmead, D. H., & Perris, E. (1986, April). *Accuracy of auditory localization in 7-month-old human infants.* Paper presented at the meeting of the International Conference on Infant Studies, Los Angeles.

Aslin, R. N. (1977). Development of binocular fixation in human infants. *Journal of Experimental Child Psychology, 23,* 133–150.

Aslin, R. N. (1981). Development of smooth pursuit in human infants. In D. F. Fisher, R. A. Monty, & J. W. Senders (Eds.), *Eye movements: Cognition and visual perception* (pp. 31–51). Hillsdale, NJ: Erlbaum.

Aslin, R. N. (1985). Oculomotor measures of visual development. In G. Gottlieb & N. A. Krasnegor (Eds.), *Measurement of audition and vision in the first year of postnatal life: A methodological overview* (pp. 391–417). Norwood, NJ: Ablex.

Aslin, R. N. (1986, February). *Discrimination of frequency modulation by human infants.* Paper presented at the Association for Research in Otolaryngology, Clearwater Beach, FL.

Aslin, R. N. (1986). Motor aspects of visual development in infancy. In P. Salapatek & L. B. Cohen (Eds.), *Handbook of infant perception* (pp. 43–113). New York: Academic.

Aslin, R. N. (in press). Anatomical constraints on oculomotor development: Implications for infant perception. In A. Yonas (Ed.), *The Minnesota symposium on child psychology* (Vol. 20). Hillsdale, NJ: Erlbaum.

Aslin, R. N., & Jackson, R. W. (1979). Accommodative-convergence in young infants: Development of a synergistic sensory-motor system. *Canadian Journal of Psychology, 33,* 222–231.

Aslin, R. N., Perey, A. J., Hennessy, B. L., & Pisoni, D. B. (1977, December). *Perceptual analysis of speech sounds by prelinguistic infants: A first report.* Paper presented at the ninety-fourth meeting of the Acoustical Society of America, Miami Beach.

Aslin, R. N., Pisoni, D. B., Hennessy, B. L., & Perey, A. J. (1981). Discrimination of voice onset time by human infants: New findings and implications for the effects of early experience. *Child Development, 52,* 1135–1145.

Aslin, R. N., Pisoni, D. B., & Jusczyk, P. W. (1983). Auditory development and speech perception in infancy. In M. M. Haith & J. J. Campos (Eds.), *Handbook of child psychology: Vol. II. Infancy and developmental psychobiology* (pp. 573–687). New York: Wiley.

Aslin, R. N., & Salapatek, P. (1975). Saccadic localization of peripheral targets by the very young human infant. *Perception & Psychophysics, 17,* 293–302.

Atkinson, J., & Braddick, O. (1976). Stereoscopic discrimination in infants. *Perception, 5,* 29–38.

Atkinson, J., & Braddick, O. (1981). Development of optokinetic nystagmus in infants: An indicator of cortical binocularity? In D. F. Fisher, R. A. Monty, & J. W. Senders (Eds.), *Eye movements: Cognition and visual perception* (pp. 53–64). Hillsdale, NJ: Erlbaum.

Atkinson, J., Braddick, O., & French, J. (1980). Infant astigmatism: Its disappearance with age. *Vision Research, 20,* 891–893.

Atkinson, J., Pimm-Smith, E., Evans, C., Braddick, O. J. (1983). The effects of screen size and eccentricity on acuity estimates in infants using preferential looking. *Vision Research, 23,* 1479–1483.

Bahill, A. T., Adler, D., & Stark, L. (1975). Most naturally occurring human saccades have magnitudes of 15 degrees or less. *Investigative Ophthalmology & Visual Science, 14,* 468–469.

Ball, W., & Tronick, E. (1971). Infant responses to impending collisions: Optical and real. *Science, 171,* 818–820.

Ball, W., & Vurpillot, E. (1976). La perception du mouvement en profundur chez le nourrisson. *L'Annee Psychologique, 76,* 383–400.

Banks, M. S. (1980a). Infant refraction and accommodation. *International Ophthalmology Clinics, 20,* 205–232.

Banks, M. S. (1980b). The development of visual accommodation during early infancy. *Child Development, 51,* 646–666.

Banks, M. S. (1985). How should we characterize visual stimuli? In G. Gottlieb & N. A. Krasnegor (Eds.), *Measurement of audition and vision in the first year of postnatal life: A methodological overview* (pp. 31–51). Norwood, NJ: Ablex.

Banks, M. S., & Dannemiller, J. L. (1986). Infant visual psychophysics. In P. Salapatek & L. B. Cohen (Eds.), *Handbook of infant perception* (pp. 115–184). New York: Academic.

Banks, M. S., & Ginsburg, A. P. (1985). Early visual preferences: A review and new theoretical treatment. In H. W. Reese (Ed.), *Advances in child development and behavior.* (Vol. 19) (pp. 207–246). New York: Academic.

Banks, M. S., & Salapatek, P. (1981). Infant pattern vision: A new approach based on the contrast sensitivity function. *Journal of Experimental Child Psychology, 31,* 1–45.

Banks, M. S., & Salapatek, P. (1983). Infant visual perception. In M. M. Haith & J. J. Campos (Eds.), *Handbook of child psychology: Vol. II. Infancy and developmental psychobiology* (pp. 435–571). New York: Wiley.

Banks, M. S., & Stephens, B. R. (1982). The contrast sensitivity of human infants to gratings differing in duty cycle. *Vision Research, 22,* 739–744.

Banks, M. S., Stephens, B. R., & Hartmann, E. E. (1985). The development of basic mechanisms of pattern vision: Spatial frequency channels. *Journal of Experimental Child Psychology, 40,* 501–527.

Barlow, H. B. (1972). Dark and light adaptation: Psychophysics. In D. Jameson & L. Hurvich (Eds.), *Handbook of sensory physiology: Vol VII/4. Visual psychophysics.* New York: Springer-Verlag.

Barrera, M. E., & Maurer, D. (1981). The perception of facial expressions by the three-month-old. *Child Development, 52,* 203–206.

Bartlett, J. C., & Dowling, W. J. (1980). Recognition of transposed melodies: A key distance effect in developmental perspective. *Journal of Experimental Psychology: Human Perception & Performance, 6,* 501–515.

Bennett, A. G., & Francis, J. L. (1962). The eye as an optical system. In H. Davson (Ed.), *The eye: Vol 4. Visual optics and the optical space sense.* New York: Academic.

Berg, K. M., & Smith, M.C. (1983). Behavioral thresholds for tones during infancy. *Journal of Experimental Child Psychology, 35,* 409–425.

Berry, R. N. (1948). Quantitative relations among vernier, real depth, and stereoscopic depth acuities. *Journal of Experimental Psychology, 38,* 708–721.

Bertenthal, B. I., Campos, J. J., & Haith, M. M. (1980). Development of visual organization: The perception of subjective contours. *Child Development, 51,* 1072–1080.

Bertenthal, B. I., Proffitt, D. R., & Cutting, J. E. (1984). Infant sensitivity to figural coherence in biomechanical motions. *Journal of Experimental Child Psychology, 37,* 213–230.

Bertenthal, B. I., Proffitt, D. R., Kramer, S. J., & Spetner, N. B. (in press). Infants' encoding of kinetic displays varying in relative coherence. *Developmental Psychology.*

Bertenthal, B. I., Proffitt, D. R., Spetner, N. B., & Thomas, M. A. (1985). The development of infant sensitivity to biomechanical motions. *Child Development, 56,* 531–543.

Bertoncini, J., Bijeljac-Babic, R., Jusczyk, P. W., & Kennedy, L. J. (submitted). An investigation of young infants' perceptual representation of speech sounds. *Journal of Experimental Psychology: General.*

Bertoncini, J., & Mehler, J. (1981). Syllables as units in infant speech perception. *Infant Behavior & Development, 4,* 247–260.

Birch, E. E. (1985). Infant interocular acuity differences and binocular vision. *Vision Research, 25,* 571–576.

Birch, E. E., Gwiazda, J., & Held, R. (1982). Stereoacuity development for crossed and uncrossed disparities in human infants. *Vision Research, 22,* 507–513.

Birch, E. E., Gwiazda, J., & Held, R. (1983). The development of vergence does not account for the onset of stereopsis. *Perception, 12,* 331–336.

Birch, E. E., Shimojo, S., & Held, R. (1985). Preferential-looking assessment of fusion and stereopsis in infants aged 1–6 months. *Investigative Ophthalmology & Visual Science, 26,* 366–370.

Bomba, P. C. (1984). The development of orientation categories between 2 and 4 months of age. *Journal of Experimental Child Psychology, 37,* 609–636.

Bomba, P. C., Eimas, P. D., Siqueland, E. R., & Miller, J. L. (1984). Contextual effects in infant visual perception. *Perception, 13,* 369–376.

Bomba, P. C., & Siqueland, E. R. (1983). The nature and structure of infant form categories. *Journal of Experimental Child Psychology, 35,* 294–328.

Bornstein, M. H. (1976). Infants are trichromats. *Journal of Experimental Child Psychology, 21,* 425–445.

Bornstein, M. H. (1978). Chromatic vision in infancy. In H. W. Reese & L. P. Lipsitt (Eds.), *Advances in child development and behavior* (Vol. 12) (pp. 117–182). New York: Academic.

Bornstein, M. H. (1981a). "Human infant color vision and color perception" reviewed and reassessed: A critique of Werner and Wooten (1979a). *Infant Behavior & Development, 4,* 119–150.

Bornstein, M. H. (1981b). Psychological studies of color perception in human infants: Habituation, discrimination and categorization, recognition, and conceptualization. In L. P. Lipsitt & C. K. Rovee-Collier (Eds.), *Advances in infancy research* (Vol. 1) (pp. 1–40). Norwood, NJ: Ablex.

Bornstein, M. H. (1985). Human infant color vision and color perception. *Infant Behavior & Development, 8,* 109–113.

Bornstein, M. H., Ferdinandsen, K., & Gross, C. G. (1981). Perception of symmetry in infancy. *Developmental Psychology, 17,* 82–86.

Bornstein, M. H., Kessen, W., & Weiskopf, S. (1976). Color vision and hue categorization in young human infants. *Journal of Experimental Psychology: Human Perception & Performance, 2,* 115–129.

Bornstein, M. H., & Krinsky, S. J. (1985). Perception of symmetry in infancy: The salience of vertical symmetry and the perception of pattern wholes. *Journal of Experimental Child Psychology, 39,* 1–19.

Bornstein, M. H., Krinsky, S. J., & Benasich, A. H. (1986). Fine orientation discrimination and shape constancy in young infants. *Journal of Experimental Child Psychology, 41,* 49–60.

Bower, T. G. R. (1964). Discrimination of depth in premotor infants. *Psychonomic Science, 1,* 368.

Bower, T. G. R. (1966). Slant perception and shape constancy in infants. *Science, 151,* 832–834.

Bower, T. G. R. (1977). Comment on Yonas et al.'s "Development of sensitivity to information for impending collision." *Perception & Psychophysics, 21,* 281–282.

Bower, T. G. R., Broughton, J. M., & Moore, M. K. (1971). Infants' responses to approaching objects: An indicator of response to distal variables. *Perception & Psychophysics, 9,* 193–196.

Braddick, O., Atkinson, J., French, J., & Howland, H. C. (1979). A photorefractive study of infant accommodation. *Vision Research, 19,* 1319–1330.

Bronson, G. W. (1982). *The scanning patterns of human infants: Implications for visual learning.* Norwood, NJ: Ablex.

Brookman, K. E. (1983). Ocular accommodation in human infants. *American Journal of Optometry & Physiological Optics, 60,* 91–99.

Brown, R. (1973). *A first language: The early stages.* Cambridge: Harvard University Press.

Buchwald, J. S., & Huang, C. M. (1975). Far-field acoustic response: Origins in the cat. *Science, 189,* 382–384.

Bull, D., Eilers, R. E., & Oller, D. K. (1984). Infants' discrimination of intensity variation in multisyllabic stimuli. *Journal of the Acoustical Society of America, 76,* 13–17.

Bull, D., Schneider, B. A., & Trehub, S. E. (1981). The masking of octave-band noise by broad-spectrum noise: A comparison of infant and adult thresholds. *Perception & Psychophysics, 30,* 101–106.

Bundy, R. S. (1980). Discrimination of sound localization cues in young infants. *Child Development, 51,* 292–294.

Burnham, D. K., Earnshaw, L. J., & Quinn, M. C. (in press). The development of categorical identification of speech. In B. E. McKenzie & R. H. Day (Eds.), *Perception in infancy: Problems and issues.* New York: Academic.

Bushnell, I. W. R. (1979). Modification of the externality effect in young infants. *Journal of Experimental Child Psychology, 28,* 211–229.

Bushnell, I. W. R. (1982). Discrimination of faces by young infants. *Journal of Experimental Child Psychology, 33,* 298–308.

Bushnell, I. W. R., Gerry, G., & Burt, K. (1983). The externality effect in neonates. *Infant Behavior & Development, 6,* 151–156.

Carden, G., Levitt, A., Jusczyk, P. W., & Walley, A. (1981). Evidence for phonetic processing of cues to place of articulation: Perceived manner affects perceived place. *Perception & Psychophysics, 29,* 26–36.

Carney, A. E., Widin, G. P., & Viemeister, N. F. (1977). Noncategorical perception of stop consonants differing in VOT. *Journal of the Acoustical Society of America, 62,* 961–970.

Caron, A. J., Caron, R. F., & Carlson, V. R. (1979). Infant perception of the invariant shape of objects varying in slant. *Child Development, 50,* 716–721.

Caron, R. F., Caron, A. J., & Myers, R. S. (1985). Do infants see emotional expressions in static faces? *Child Development, 56,* 1552–1560.

Carroll, J. J., & Gibson, E. J. (1981, April). *Infants' differentiation of an aperture and an obstacle.* Paper presented at the meeting of the Society for Research in Child Development, Boston.

Cavanagh, P., Anstis, S., & Mather, G. (1984). Screening for color blindness using optokinetic nystagmus. *Investigative Ophthalmology & Visual Science, 25,* 463–466.

Chang, H.-W., & Trehub, S. E. (1977a). Auditory processing of relational information by young infants. *Journal of Experimental Child Psychology, 24,* 324-331.

Chang, H.-W., & Trehub, S. E. (1977b). Infants' perception of temporal grouping in auditory patterns. *Child Development, 48,* 1666-1670.

Chomsky, N. (1965). *Aspects of the theory of syntax.* Cambridge, MA: M.I.T. Press.

Chomsky, N. (1968). *Language and mind.* New York: Harcourt, Brace & World.

Clarkson, M. G., Clifton, R. K., & Morrongiello, B. A. (1985). The effects of sound duration on newborns' head orientation. *Journal of Experimental Child Psychology, 39,* 20-36.

Clifton, R. K., Morrongiello, B. A., & Dowd, J. M. (1984). A developmental look at an auditory illusion: The precedence effect. *Developmental Psychobiology, 17,* 519-536.

Clifton, R. K., Morrongiello, B. A., Kulig, J. W., & Dowd, J. M. (1981). Newborns' orientation toward sound: Possible implications for cortical development. *Child Development, 53,* 833-838.

Cohen, L. B. (1979). Commentary on M. Schwartz & R. H. Day's "Visual shape perception in early infancy." *Monographs of the Society for Research in Child Development, 44*(7, Serial No. 182), 58-63.

Cohen, L. B., & Younger, B. A. (1984). Infant perception of angular relations. *Infant Behavior & Development, 7,* 37-47.

Colombo, J., & Bundy, R. S. (1981). A method for the measurement of infant auditory selectivity. *Infant Behavior & Development, 4,* 219-233.

Colombo, J., & Bundy, R. S. (1983). Infant response to auditory familiarity and novelty. *Infant Behavior & Development, 5,* 305-311.

Colombo, J., & Horowitz, F. D. (1986). Infants' attentional responses to frequency modulated sweeps. *Child Development, 57,* 287-291.

Colombo, J., Laurie, C., Martelli, T., & Hartig, B. (1984). Stimulus context and infant orientation discrimination. *Journal of Experimental Child Psychology, 37,* 576-586.

Cook, M., & Birch, R. (1984). Infant perception of the shapes of tilted plane forms. *Infant Behavior & Development, 7,* 389-402.

Cornsweet, T. N. (1970). *Visual perception.* New York: Academic.

Cranford, J., Ravizza, R., Diamond, I., & Whitfield, I. (1971). Unilateral ablation of the auditory cortex in the cat impairs complex sound localization. *Science, 172,* 286-288.

Cruikshank, R. M. (1941). The development of visual size constancy in early infancy. *Journal of Genetic Psychology, 58,* 327-351.

Dannemiller, J. L. (1985). The early phase of dark adaptation in human infants. *Vision Research, 25,* 207-212.

Dannemiller, J. L., & Banks, M. S. (1983). The development of light adaptation in human infants. *Vision Research, 23,* 599-609.

Dannemiller, J. L., & Hanko, S. A. (1985, April). *A test of color constancy in 4-month-olds.* Paper presented at the biennial meeting of the Society for Research in Child Development, Toronto.

Dannemiller, J. L., & Stephens, B. R. (submitted). A critical test of infant pattern preference models. *Child Development.*

Day, R. H., & McKenzie, B. E. (1973). Perceptual shape constancy in early infancy. *Perception, 2,* 315-320.

Day, R. H., & McKenzie, B. E. (1977). Constancies in the perceptual world of the infant. In W. Epstein (Ed.), *Stability and constancy in visual perception: Mechanisms and processes.* New York: Wiley.

Day, R. H., & McKenzie, B. E. (1981). Infant perception of the invariant size of approaching and receding objects. *Developmental Psychology, 17,* 670–677.

Dayton, G. O., Jr., & Jones, M. H. (1964). Analysis of characteristics of fixation reflexes in infants by use of direct current electrooculography. *Neurology, 14,* 1152–1156.

Dayton, G. O., Jr., Jones, M. H., Steele, B., & Rose, M. (1964). Developmental study of coordinated eye movements in the human infant. II: An electrooculographic study of the fixation reflex in the newborn. *Archives of Ophthalmology, 71,* 871–875.

DeCasper, A. J., & Fifer, W. P. (1980). Of human bonding: Newborns prefer their mothers' voices. *Science, 208,* 1174–1176.

DeCasper, A. J., & Prescott, P. (1984). Human newborns' perception of male voices: Preference, discrimination, and reinforcing value. *Developmental Psychobiology, 17,* 481–491.

DeCasper, A. J., & Sigafoos, A. D. (1983). The intrauterine heartbeat: A potent reinforcer for newborns. *Infant Behavior & Development, 6,* 19–25.

DeCasper, A. J. & Spence, M. J. (1986). Prenatal maternal speech influences newborns' perception of speech sounds. *Infant Behavior & Development, 9,* 133–150.

Demany, L., McKenzie, B., & Vurpillot, E. (1977). Rhythm perception in early infancy. *Nature, 266,* 718–719.

Dobson, V. (1976). Spectral sensitivity of the two-month infant as measured by the visually evoked cortical potential. *Vision Research, 16,* 367–374.

Dobson, V., Fulton, A., & Sebris, L. (1984). Cycloplegic refractions of infants and young children: The axis of astigmatism. *Investigative Ophthalmology & Visual Science, 25,* 83–87.

Dobson, V., & Teller, D. Y. (1978). Visual acuity in human infants: A review and comparison of behavioral and electrophysiological studies. *Vision Research, 18,* 1469–1483.

Eilers, R. E., Bull, D. H., Oller, D. K., & Lewis, D. C. (1984). The discrimination of vowel duration by infants. *Journal of the Acoustical Society of America, 75,* 1213–1218.

Eilers, R. E., Gavin, W., & Wilson, W. R. (1979). Linguistic experience and phonemic perception in infancy: A cross-linguistic study. *Child Development, 50,* 14–18.

Eimas, P. D. (1975). Speech perception in early infancy. In L. B. Cohen & P. Salapatek (Eds.), *Infant perception: Vol. 2. From sensation to cognition* (pp. 193–231). New York: Academic.

Eimas, P. D., & Miller, J. L. (1980). Contextual effects in infant speech perception. *Science, 209,* 1140–1141.

Eimas, P. D., Siqueland, E. R., Jusczyk, P., & Vigorito, J. (1971). Speech perception in infants. *Science, 171,* 303–306.

Eisenberg, R. B. (1976). *Auditory competence in early life.* Baltimore, MD: University Park Press.

Essock, E. A., & Siqueland, E. R. (1981). Discrimination of orientation by human infants. *Perception, 10,* 245–253.

Fagan, J. F. (1974). Infant recognition memory: The effects of length of familiarization and type of discrimination task. *Child Development, 45,* 351–356.

Fantz, R. L. (1958). Pattern vision in young infants. *Psychological Record, 8,* 43–47.

Fantz, R. L. (1961). The origin of form perception. *Science, 204,* 66–72.

Fernald, A. (1985). Four-month-old infants prefer to listen to motherese. *Infant Behavior & Development, 8,* 181–195.

Fernald, A., & Simon, T. (1984). Expanded intonation contours in mothers' speech to newborns. *Developmental Psychology, 20,* 104–113.

Field, J., Muir, D., Pilon, R., Sinclair, M., & Dodwell, P. (1980). Infants' orientation to lateral sounds from birth to three months. *Child Development, 50,* 295–298.

Finlay, D., & Ivinskis, A. (1984). Cardiac and visual responses to moving stimuli presented either successively or simultaneously to the central and peripheral visual fields in 4-month-old infants. *Developmental Psychology, 20,* 29–36.

Fiorentini, A., Pirchio, M., & Spinelli, D. (1983). Electrophysiological evidence for spatial frequency selective mechanisms in adults and infants. *Vision Research, 23,* 119–127.

Fisher, C. B., Ferdinandsen, K., & Bornstein, M. H. (1981). The role of symmetry in infant form discrimination. *Child Development, 52,* 457–462.

Fodor, J. A., Garrett, M. F., & Brill, S. L. (1975). Pi ka pu: The perception of speech sounds by prelinguistic infants. *Perception & Psychophysics, 18,* 74–78.

Folsom, R. C. (1985). Auditory brain stem responses from human infants: Pure-tone masking profiles for clicks and filtered clicks. *Journal of the Acoustical Society of America, 78,* 555–562.

Fox, R., Aslin, R. N., Shea, S. L., & Dumais, S. T. (1980). Stereopsis in human infants. *Science, 207,* 323–324.

Fox, R., & McDaniel, C. (1982). The perception of biological motion by human infants. *Science, 218,* 486–487.

Ganon, E. C., & Swartz, K. B. (1980). Perception of internal elements of compound figures by one-month-olds. *Journal of Experimental Child Psychology, 30,* 159–170.

Gayl, I. E., Roberts, J. O., & Werner, J. S. (1983). Linear systems analysis of infant visual pattern preferences. *Journal of Experimental Child Psychology, 35,* 30–45.

Georgeson, M. A., & Sullivan, G. D. (1975). Contrast constancy: Deblurring in human vision by spatial frequency channels. *Journal of Physiology, 252,* 627–656.

Gibson, E. J., Owsley, C. J., & Johnston, J. (1978). Perception of invariants by five-month-old infants: Differentiation of two types of motion. *Developmental Psychology, 14,* 407–415.

Gibson, E. J., Owsley, C. J., Walker, A., & Megaw-Nyce, J. (1979). Development of the perception of invariants: Substance and shape. *Perception, 8,* 609–619.

Gibson, E. J., & Spelke, E. S. (1983). The development of perception. In J. H. Flavell & E. M. Markman (Eds.), *Handbook of child psychology: Vol. III. Cognitive development* (pp. 1–76). New York: Wiley.

Ginsburg, A. P. (1977). *Visual information processing based on spatial filters constrained by biological data.* Unpublished doctoral dissertation, University of Cambridge, Cambridge, England.

Goodsitt, J. V., Morse, P. A., VerHoeve, J. N., & Cowan, N. (1984). Infant speech recognition in multisyllabic contexts. *Child Development, 55,* 903–910.

Gottlieb, G., & Krasnegor, N. A. (Eds.). (1985). *Measurement of audition and vision in the first year of postnatal life: A methodological overview.* Norwood, NJ: Ablex.

Granrud, C. E. (1986). Binocular vision and spatial perception in 4- and 5-month-old infants. *Journal of Experimental Psychology: Human Perception & Performance, 12,* 36–49.

Granrud, C. E., Haake, R. J., & Yonas, A. (1985). Infants' sensitivity to familiar size: The effect of memory on spatial perception. *Perception & Psychophysics, 37,* 459–466.

Granrud, C. E., & Yonas, A. (1984). Infants' perception of pictorially specified interposition. *Journal of Experimental Child Psychology, 37,* 500–511.

Granrud, C. E., Yonas, A., & Opland, E. A. (1985). Infants' sensitivity to the depth cue of shading. *Perception & Psychophysics, 37,* 415–419.

Granrud, C. E., Yonas, A., & Pettersen, L. (1984). A comparison of monocular and binocular depth perception in 5- and 7-month-old infants. *Journal of Experimental Child Psychology, 38,* 19–32.

Granrud, C. E., Yonas, A., Smith, I. M., Arterberry, M. E., Glicksman, M. L., & Sorknes, A. C. (1984). Infants' sensitivity to accretion and deletion of texture as information for depth at an edge. *Child Development, 55,* 1630–1636.

Green, D. M. (1985). Commentary on chapters 3, 4, 5, and 6. In S. E. Trehub & B. Schneider (Eds.), *Advances in the study of communication and affect: Vol. 10. Auditory development in infancy* (pp. 127–129). New York: Plenum.

Grimwade, J. C., Walker, D. W., Bartlett, M., Gordon, S., & Wood, C. (1971). Human fetal heart rate change and movement in response to sound and vibration. *American Journal of Obstetrics & Gynecology, 109,* 86–90.

Gwiazda, J., Scheiman, M., Mohindra, I., & Held, R. (1984). Astigmatism in children: Changes in axis and amount from birth to six years. *Investigative Ophthalmology & Visual Science, 25,* 88–92.

Haaf, R. A., Smith, P. H., & Smitley, S. (1983). Infant response to facelike patterns under fixed-trial and infant-control procedures. *Child Development, 54,* 172–177.

Hainline, L. (1978). Developmental changes in visual scanning of face and nonface patterns by infants. *Journal of Experimental Child Psychology, 25,* 90–115.

Hainline, L. (1985). Oculomotor control in human infants. In R. Groner, G. W. McConkie, & C. Menz (Eds.), *Eye movements and human information processing* (pp. 71–84). Amsterdam: Elsevier (North-Holland).

Hainline, L., Lemerise, E., Abramov, I., & Turkel, J. (1984). Orientational asymmetries in small-field optokinetic nystagmus in human infants. *Behavioural Brain Research, 13,* 217–230.

Hainline, L., Turkel, J., Abramov, I., Lemerise, E., & Harris, C. M. (1984). Characteristics of saccades in human infants. *Vision Research, 24,* 1771–1780.

Haith, M. M., Bergman, T., & Moore, M. J. (1977). Eye contact and face scanning in early infancy. *Science, 198,* 853–855.

Halsted, N., Jusczyk, P. W. & Mehler, J. (in preparation). Discrimination of native from non-native languages in 2-month-old infants.

Hamer, R. D., Alexander, K. R., & Teller, D. Y. (1982). Rayleigh discriminations in human infants. *Vision Research, 22,* 575–587.

Hamer, R. D., & Schneck, M. E. (1984). Spatial summation in dark-adapted human infants. *Vision Research, 24,* 77–85.

Harris, D. M., & Dallos, P. (1984). Ontogenetic changes in frequency mapping of a mammalian ear. *Science, 225,* 741–743.

Harris, P. L., Cassel, T. Z., & Bamborough, P. (1974). Tracking by young infants. *British Journal of Psychology, 65,* 345–349.

Harris, P., & MacFarlane, A. (1974). The growth of the effective visual field from birth to seven weeks. *Journal of Experimental Child Psychology, 18,* 340–348.

Harris, S. J., Hansen, R. M., & Fulton, A. B. (1984). Assessment of acuity in human infants using face and grating stimuli. *Investigative Ophthalmology & Visual Science, 25,* 782–786.

Hartmann, E. E., & Banks, M. S. (1984, April). *Development of temporal contrast sensitivity.* Paper presented at the International Conference on Infant Studies, New York.

Haynes, H., White, B. L., & Held, R. (1965). Visual accommodation in human infants. *Science, 148,* 528–530.

Hebb, D. O. (1949). *The organization of behavior.* New York: Wiley.

Heck, J., & Zetterstrom, B. (1958). Analyse des photopischen Flimmerelektroretinogramms bei Neugeborenen. *Ophthalmologica, 135,* 205–210.

Hecox, K. (1975). Electrophysiological correlates of human auditory development. In L. B. Cohen & P. Salapatek (Eds.), *Infant perception: From sensation to cognition: Vol. 2. Perception of space, speech and sound* (pp. 151–191). New York: Academic.

Hecox, K., & Deegan, D. M. (1985). Methodological issues in the study of auditory development. In G. Gottlieb & N. A. Krasnegor (Eds.), *Measurement of audition and vision in the first year of postnatal life: A methodological overview* (pp. 367–389). Norwood, NJ: Ablex.

Hecox, K., & Galambos, R. (1974). Brainstem auditory evoked responses in human infants and adults. *Archives of Otolaryngology, 99,* 30–33.

Held, R., Birch, E. E., & Gwiazda, J. (1980). Stereoacuity of human infants. *Proceedings of the National Academy of Sciences, U.S.A., 77,* 5572–5574.

Hendrickson, A. E., & Yuodelis, C. (1984). The morphological development of the human fovea. *Ophthalmology, 91,* 603–612.

Hillenbrand, J. (1983). Perceptual organization of speech sounds by infants. *Journal of Speech & Hearing Research, 26,* 268–282.

Hillenbrand, J. (1984). Speech preception by infants: Categorization based on nasal consonant place of articulation. *Journal of the Acoustical Society of America, 75,* 1613–1622.

Hirsh-Pasek, K., Kemler-Nelson, D. G., Jusczyk, P. W., Wright, K., & Kennedy, L. J. (submitted). Clauses are perceptual units for prelinguistic infants. *Cognition.*

Hofsten, C. von (1977). Binocular convergence as a determinant of reaching behavior in infancy. *Perception, 6,* 139–144.

Hofsten, C. von (1980). Predictive reaching for moving objects by human infants. *Journal of Experimental Child Psychology, 30,* 369–382.

Hofsten, C. von (1983). Catching skills in infancy. *Journal of Experimental Psychology: Human Perception & Performance, 9,* 75–85.

Hofsten, C. von, & Lindhagen, K. (1979). Observations on the development of reaching for moving objects. *Journal of Experimental Child Psychology, 28,* 158–173.

Hofsten, C. von, & Spelke, E. S. (1985). Object perception and object-directed reaching in infancy. *Journal of Experimental Psychology: General, 114,* 198–212.

Holmberg, T. L., Morgan, K. A., & Kuhl, P. K. (1977, December). *Speech perception in early infancy: Discrimination of fricative consonants.* Paper presented at the ninety-fourth meeting of the Acoustical Society of America, Miami Beach.

Horowitz, F. D. (Ed.). (1975). Visual attention, auditory stimulation, and language discrimination in young infants. *Monographs of the Society for Research in Child Development, 39*(5–6, Whole No. 158).

Horsten, G. P. M., & Winkelman, J. E. (1964). Electro-retinographic critical fusion frequency of the retina in relation to the histological development in man and animals. *Documenta Ophthalmologica, 18,* 515–521.

Howland, H. C., & Sayles, N. (1984). Photorefractive measurements of astigmatism in infants and young children. *Investigative Ophthalmology & Visual Science, 25,* 93–102.

Howland, H. C., & Sayles, N. (1985). Photokeratometric and photorefractive measurements of astigmatism in infants and young children. *Vision Research, 25,* 73–81.

Humphrey, G. K., Humphrey, B. E., Muir, D. W., & Dodwell, P. C. (1986). Pattern perception in infants: Effects of structure and transformation. *Journal of Experimental Child Psychology, 41,* 128–148.

Hurvich, L. M. (1981). *Color vision.* Sunderland, MA: Sinauer Associates.

Jampolsky, A. (1964). The prism test for strabismus screening. *Journal of Pediatric Ophthalmology, 1,* 60–64.

Johansson, G. (1973). Visual perception of biological motion and a model of its analysis. *Perception & Psychophysics, 14,* 201–211.

Johnston, T. D. (1985). Environmental constraints and the natural context of behavior: Grounds for an ecological approach to the study of infant perception. In G. Gottlieb & N. A. Krasnegor (Eds.), *Measurement of audition and vision in the first year of postnatal life: A methodological overview* (pp. 91–108). Norwood, NJ: Ablex.

Julesz, B. (1960). Binocular depth perception of computer-generated patterns. *Bell System Technical Journal, 39,* 1125–1162.

Jusczyk, P. W. (1977). Perception of syllable-final stop consonants by 2-month-old infants. *Perception & Psychophysics, 21,* 450–454.

Jusczyk, P. W. (1981). Infant speech perception: A critical appraisal. In P. D. Eimas & J. L. Miller (Eds.), *Perspectives on the study of speech.* Hillsdale, NJ: Erlbaum.

Jusczyk, P. W. (1985). On characterizing the development of speech perception. In J. Mehler & R. Fox (Eds.), *Neonate cognition: Beyond the blooming buzzing confusion* (pp. 199–229). Hillsdale, NJ: Erlbaum.

Jasczyk, P. W. (1986). Toward a model of the development of speech perception. In J. S. Perkell & D. H. Klatt (Eds.), *Invariance and variability in speech processes* (pp. 1–19). Hillsdale, NJ: Erlbaum.

Jusczyk, P. W., Copan, H. C., & Thompson, E. J. (1978). Perception by two-month-olds of glide contrasts in multisyllabic utterances. *Perception & Psychophysics, 24,* 515–520.

Jusczyk, P. W., Pisoni, D. B., Reed, M., Fernald, A., & Myers, M. (1983). Durational context effects in the processing of nonspeech sounds by infants. *Science, 222,* 175–177.

Jusczyk, P. W., Pisoni, D. B., Walley, A., & Murray, J. (1980). Discrimination of relative onset time of two-component tones by infants. *Journal of the Acoustical Society of America, 67,* 262–270.

Jusczyk, P. W., Rosner, B. S., Kennedy, L. J. & Reed, M. A. (submitted). Do temporal order differences underlie 2-month-olds' discrimination of English voicing contrasts? *Journal of the Acoustical Society of America.*

Jusczyk, P. W., & Thompson, E. (1978). Perception of a phonetic contrast in multisyllabic utterances by two-month-old infants. *Perception & Psychophysics, 23,* 105–109.

Karzon, R. G. (1985). Discrimination of polysyllabic sequences by one- to four-month-old infants. *Journal of Experimental Child Psychology, 39,* 326–342.

Katz, J., & Jusczyk, P. W. (1980, April). *Do six-month-olds have perceptual constancy for phonetic segments?* Paper presented at the International Conference on Infant Studies, New Haven, Connecticut.

Kaufmann, F., Stucki, M., & Kaufmann-Hayoz, R. (1985). Development of infants' sensitivity for slow and rapid motions. *Infant Behavior & Development, 8,* 89–98.

Kaufmann, R., Maland, J., & Yonas, A. (1981). Sensitivity of 5- and 7-month-old infants to pictorial depth information. *Journal of Experimental Child Psychology, 32,* 162–168.

Kellman, P. J. (1984). Perception of three-dimensional form by human infants. *Perception & Psychophysics, 36,* 353–358.

Kellman, P. J., Gleitman, H., & Spelke, E. S. (submitted). Object and observer motion in the perception of objects by infants. *Journal of Experimental Psychology: Human Perception & Performance.*

Kellman, P. J., Hofsten, C. von, & Soares, J. (in press). Concurrent motion in infant event perception. *Infant Behavior & Development.*

Kellman, P. J., & Short, K. R. (in preparation). Infant form perception from perspective transformation.

Kellman, P. J., & Spelke, E. S. (1983). Perception of partly occluded objects in infancy. *Cognitive Psychology, 15,* 483–524.

Kellman, P. J., Spelke, E. S., & Short, K. R. (1986). Infant perception of object unity from translatory motion in depth and vertical translation. *Child Development, 57,* 72–86.

Kelly, D. H. (1961). Visual responses to time-dependent stimuli. I. Amplitude sensitivity measurements. *Journal of the Optical Society of America, 51,* 422–429.

Kremenitzer, J. P., Vaughan, H. G., Jr., Kurtzberg, D., & Dowling, K. (1979). Smooth-pursuit eye movements in the newborn infant. *Child Development, 50,* 442–448.

Kuhl, P. K. (1979). Speech perception in early infancy: Perceptual constancy for spectrally dissimilar vowel categories. *Journal of the Acoustical Society of America, 66,* 1668–1679.

Kuhl, P. K. (1983). Perception of auditory equivalence classes for speech in early infancy. *Infant Behavior & Development, 6,* 263–285.

Kuhl, P. K. (1985). Methods in the study of infant speech perception. In G. Gottlieb & N. A. Krasnegor (Eds.), *Measurement of audition and vision in the first year of postnatal life: A methodological overview* (pp. 223–251). Norwood, NJ: Ablex.

Kuhl, P. K., & Miller, J. D. (1975). Speech perception by the chinchilla: Voiced–voiceless distinction in alveolar plosive consonants. *Science, 190,* 69–72.

Kuhl, P. K., & Miller, J. D. (1978). Speech perception by the chinchilla: Identification functions for synthetic VOT stimuli. *Journal of the Acoustical Society of America, 63,* 905–917.

Kuhl, P. K., & Padden, D. M. (1982). Enhanced discriminability at the phonetic boundaries for the voicing feature in macaques. *Perception & Psychophysics, 32,* 542–550.

Kuhl, P. K., & Padden, D. M. (1983). Enhanced discriminability at the phonetic boundaries for the place feature in macaques. *Journal of the Acoustical Society of America, 73,* 1003–1010.

Lasky, R. E., Syrdal-Lasky, A., & Klein, R. E. (1975). VOT discrimination by four to six and a half month old infants from Spanish environments. *Journal of Experimental Child Psychology, 20,* 215–225.

Levitt, A., Jusczyk, P. W., Murray, J., & Carden, G. (submitted). The perception of place of articulation contrasts in voiced and voiceless fricatives by 2-month-old infants. *Cognition.*

Lewis, T. L., & Maurer, D. (1980). Central vision in the newborn. *Journal of Experimental Child Psychology, 29,* 475–480.

Lewis, T. L., Maurer, D., & Blackburn, K. (1985). The development of young infants' ability to detect stimuli in the nasal visual field. *Vision Research, 25,* 943–950.

Lewis, T. L., Maurer, D., & Kay, D. (1978). Newborns' central vision: Whole or hole? *Journal of Experimental Child Psychology, 26,* 193–203.

Liberman, A. M., Harris, K. S., Hoffman, H. S., & Griffith, B. C. (1957). The discrimination of speech sounds within and across phoneme boundaries. *Journal of Experimental Psychology, 54,* 358–368.

Liberman, A. M., Harris, K. S., Kinney, J. A., & Lane, H. (1961). The discrimination of relative-onset time of the components of certain speech and nonspeech patterns. *Journal of Experimental Psychology, 61,* 379–388.

Ling, B. C. (1942). A genetic study of sustained visual fixation and associated behavior in the human infant from birth to six months. *Journal of Genetic Psychology, 61,* 227–277.

Lippe, W., & Rubel, E. W. (1983). Development of the place principle: Tonotopic organization. *Science, 219,* 514–516.

Lisker, L., & Abramson, A. S. (1970). The voicing dimension: Some experiments in comparative phonetics. *Proceedings of the Sixth International Congress of Phonetic Sciences, 1967.* Prague: Academia.

Lockman, J. J., Ashmead, D. H., & Bushnell, E. W. (1984). The development of anticipatory hand orientation during infancy. *Journal of Experimental Child Psychology, 37,* 176-186.

Lotmar, W. (1976). A theoretical model for the eye of new-born infants. *Albrecht v. Graefes Arch. klin. exp. Ophthal., 198,* 179-185.

MacFarlane, A., Harris, P., & Barnes, I. (1976). Central and peripheral vision in early infancy. *Journal of Experimental Child Psychology, 21,* 532-538.

MacKain, K. S., Best, C. T., & Strange, W. (1981). Categorical perceptions of English /r/ and /l/ by Japanese bilinguals. *Applied Psycholinguistics, 2,* 369-390.

Mann, I. C. (1964). *The development of the human eye.* London: British Medical Association.

Manny, R. E., & Klein, S. A. (1984). The development of vernier acuity in infants. *Current Eye Research, 3,* 453-462.

Manny, R. E., & Klein S. A. (1985). A three alternative tracking paradigm to measure vernier acuity of older infants. *Vision Research, 25,* 1245-1252.

Mattingly, I. G., Liberman, A. M., Syrdal, A. K., & Halwes, T. (1971). Discrimination in speech and non-speech modes. *Cognitive Psychology, 2,* 131-157.

Maurer, D. (1974). The development of binocular convergence in infants. (Doctoral dissertation, University of Minnesota, 1974). *Dissertation Abstracts International, 35,* 6136B.

Maurer, D. (1983). The scanning of compound figures by young infants. *Journal of Experimental Child Psychology, 35,* 437-448.

Maurer, D. (1985). Infants' perception of facedness. In T. M. Field & N. A. Fox (Eds.), *Social perception in infants* (pp. 73-100). Norwood, NJ: Ablex.

Maurer, D., & Barrera, M. (1981). Infants' perception of natural and distorted arrangements of a schematic face. *Child Development, 52,* 196-202.

Maurer, D., & Lewis, T. L. (1979). Peripheral discrimination by three-month-old infants. *Child Development, 50,* 276-279.

Maurer, D., Lewis, T. L., & Brent, H. P. (in press). The effects of deprivation on human visual development: Studies of children treated for cataracts. In F. J. Morrison, C. E. Lord, & D. P. Keating (Eds.), Applied Developmental Psychology (Vol. 3). Orlando: Academic.

Maurer, D., Lewis, T. L., Cavanagh, P., & Anstis, S. (submitted). *A new test of luminous efficiency for babies. Investigative Ophthalmology & Visual Science.*

Maurer, D., & Martello, M. (1980). The discrimination of orientation by young infants. *Vision Research, 20,* 201-204.

Maurer, D., & Salapatek, P. (1976). Developmental changes in the scanning of faces by young infants. *Child Development, 47,* 523-527.

Maurer, D., & Young, R. (1983). Newborns' following of natural and distorted arrangements of facial features. *Infant Behavior & Development, 6,* 127-131.

McGinnis, J. M. (1930). Eye movements and optic nystagmus in early infancy. *Genetic Psychology Monographs, 8,* 321-430.

McKenzie, B. E., & Day, R. H. (1972). Distance as a determinant of visual fixation in early infancy. *Science, 178,* 1108-1110.

McKenzie, B. E., & Day, R. H. (1976). Infants' attention to stationary and moving objects at different distances. *Australian Journal of Psychology, 28,* 45-51.

McKenzie, B. E., Tootell, H. E., & Day, R. H. (1980). Development of visual size constancy during the first year of human infancy. *Developmental Psychology, 16,* 163–174.

Mehler, J., Bertoncini, J., Barriere, M., & Jassik-Gerschenfeld, D. (1978). Infant recognition of mother's voice. *Perception, 7,* 491–497.

Milewski, A. E. (1976). Infants' discrimination of internal and external pattern elements. *Journal of Experimental Child Psychology, 22,* 229–246.

Milewski, A. E. (1978). Young infants' visual processing of internal and adjacent shapes. *Infant Behavior & Development, 1,* 359–371.

Milewski, A. E. (1979). Visual discrimination and detection of configurational invariance in 3-month infants. *Developmental Psychology, 15,* 357–363.

Miller, J. D., Wier, C. C., Pastore, R., Kelly, W. J., & Dooling, R. J. (1976). Discrimination and labeling of noise-buzz sequences with varying noise-lead times: An example of categorical perception. *Journal of the Acoustical Society of America, 60,* 410–417.

Miller, J. L., & Eimas, P. D. (1979). Organization in infant speech perception. *Canadian Journal of Psychology, 33,* 353–367.

Miller, J. L., & Liberman, A. (1979). Some effects of later-occurring information on the perception of stop consonant and semivowel. *Perception & Psychophysics, 25,* 457–465.

Mitchell, D. E., & Timney, B. (1984). Postnatal development of function in the mammalian visual system. In J. M. Brookhart & V. D. Mountcastle (Eds.), *Handbook of physiology: The nervous system III* (pp. 507–555). Bethesda, MD: American Physiological Society.

Miyawaki, K., Strange, W., Verbrugge, R., Liberman, A. M., Jenkins, J. J., & Fujimura, O. (1975). An effect of linguistic experience: The discrimination of [r] and [l] by native speakers of Japanese and English. *Perception & Psychophysics, 18,* 331–340.

Mohn, G., & van Hof-van Duin, J. (1985). The development of the binocular and monocular visual field in fullterm and preterm human infants. *Supplement to Investigative Ophthalmology & Visual Science, 26,* 137.

Moore, J. M., Wilson, W. R., & Thompson, G. (1977). Visual reinforcement of headturn responses in infants under 12 months of age. *Journal of Speech & Hearing Disorders, 42,* 328–334.

Morrongiello, B. A. (1984). Auditory temporal pattern perception in 6- and 12-month-old infants. *Developmental Psychology, 20,* 441–448.

Morrongiello, B. A., Clifton, R. K., & Kulig, J. W. (1982). Newborn cardiac and behavioral orienting responses to sound under varying precedence-effect conditions. *Infant Behavior & Development, 5,* 249–259.

Morrongiello, B. A., Kulig, J. W., & Clifton, R. K. (1984). Developmental changes in auditory temporal perception. *Child Development, 55,* 461–471.

Morrongiello, B. A., Robson, R. C., Best, C. T., & Clifton, R. K. (1984). Trading relations in the perception of speech by 5-year-old children. *Journal of Experimental Child Psychology, 37,* 231–250.

Morse, P. A., Eilers, R. E., & Gavin, W. J. (1982). The perception of the sound of silence in early infancy. *Child Development, 53,* 189–195.

Moskowitz-Cook, A. (1979). The development of photopic spectral sensitivity in human infants. *Vision Research, 19,* 1133–1142.

Movshon, J. A., & Van Sluyters, R. C. (1981). Visual neuronal development. *Annual Review of Psychology, 32,* 477–522.

Muir, D., Abraham, W., Forbes, B., & Harris, L. (1979). The ontogenesis of an auditory localization response from birth to four months of age. *Canadian Journal of Psychology, 33,* 320–333.

Muir, D., & Field, J. (1979). Newborn infants orient to sounds. *Child Development, 50,* 431–436.

Naegele, J. R., & Held, R. (1982). The postnatal development of monocular optokinetic nystagmus in infants. *Vision Research, 22,* 341–346.

Nelson, C. A. (1985). The perception and recognition of facial expressions in infancy. In T. M. Field & N. A. Fox (Eds.), *Social perception in infants* (pp. 101–125). Norwood, NJ: Ablex.

Nelson, C. A., & Horowitz, F. D. (1986). Visual motion perception in infancy: A review and synthesis. In P. Salapatek & L. B. Cohen (Eds.), *Handbook of infant perception* (pp. 123–153). New York: Academic.

Nelson, C. A., Morse, P. A., & Leavitt, L. A. (1979). Recognition of facial expressions by seven-month-old infants. *Child Development, 50,* 1239–1242.

Newport, E. L. (1977). Motherese: Speech of mothers to young children. In N. J. Castellan, D. B. Pisoni, & G. R. Potts (Eds.), *Cognitive theory* (Vol. 2). Hillsdale, NJ: Erlbaum.

Norcia, A. M., & Tyler, C. W. (1985). Spatial frequency sweep VEP: Visual acuity during the first year of life. *Vision Research, 25,* 1399–1408.

Nozza, R. J., & Wilson, W. R. (1984). Masked and unmasked pure-tone thresholds of infants and adults: Development of auditory frequency selectivity and sensitivity. *Journal of Speech & Hearing Research, 27,* 613–622.

Nystrom, M., Hansson, M. B., & Marklund, K. (1975). Infant preference for intermittent light. *Psychological Research Bulletin, Lund U., 15,* 1–11.

Olsho, L. W. (1984a). Infant frequency discrimination. *Infant Behavior & Development, 7,* 27–35.

Olsho, L. W. (1984b, April). *Preliminary results of an observer-based method for infant auditory testing.* Paper presented at the International Conference for Infant Studies, New York.

Olsho, L. W. (1985). Infant auditory perception: Tonal masking. *Infant Behavior & Development, 8,* 371–384.

Olsho, L., Schoon, C., Sakai, R., Turpin, R., & Sperduto, V. (1982). Auditory frequency discrimination in infancy. *Developmental Psychology, 18,* 721–726.

Oster, H. (1975, April). *Color perception in ten-week-old infants.* Paper presented at the meeting of the Society for Research in Child Development, Denver.

Owsley, C. (1983). The role of motion in infants' perception of solid shape. *Perception, 12,* 707–717.

Packer, O., Hartmann, E. E., & Teller, D. Y. (1984). Infant color vision: The effect of test field size on Rayleigh discriminations. *Vision Research, 24,* 1247–1260.

Panneton, R. K. (1985). *Prenatal auditory experience with melodies: Effects on postnatal auditory preferences in human newborns.* Unpublished doctoral dissertation, University of North Carolina at Greensboro.

Panneton, R. K., & DeCasper, A. J. (1984, April). *Newborns prefer intrauterine heartbeat sounds to male voices.* Paper presented at the International Conference for Infant Studies, New York.

Peeples, D. R., & Teller, D. Y. (1975). Color vision and brightness discrimination in two-month-old human infants. *Science, 189,* 1102–1103.

Peeples, D. R., & Teller, D. Y. (1978). White-adapted photopic spectral sensitivity in human infants. *Vision Research, 18,* 49–53.

Peiper, A. (1963). *Cerebral function in infancy and childhood.* New York: Consultants Bureau.

Petrig, B., Julesz, B., Kropfl, W., Baumgartner, G., & Anliker, M. (1981). Development of stereopsis and cortical binocularity in human infants: Electrophysiological evidence. *Science, 213,* 1402–1405.

Pisoni, D. B. (1977). Identification and discrimination of the relative onset of two component tones: Implications for voicing perception in stops. *Journal of the Acoustical Society of America, 61,* 1352–1361.

Pisoni, D. B., Aslin, R. N., Perey, A. J., & Hennessy, B. L. (1982). Some effects of laboratory training on identification and discrimination of voicing contrasts in stop consonants. *Journal of Experimental Psychology: Human Perception & Performance, 8,* 297–314.

Pisoni, D. B., Carrell, T. D., & Gans, S. J. (1983). Perception of the duration of rapid spectrum changes in speech and nonspeech signals. *Perception & Psychophysics, 34,* 314–322.

Powers, M. K., Schneck, M., & Teller, D. Y. (1981). Spectral sensitivity of human infants at absolute visual threshold. *Vision Research, 21,* 1005–1016.

Pulos, E., Teller, D. Y., & Buck, S. (1980). Infant color vision: A search for short wavelength-sensitive mechanisms by means of chromatic adaptation. *Vision Research, 20,* 485–493.

Querleu, D., & Renard, K. (1981). Les perceptions auditives du foetus humain. *Medicine et Hygiene, 39,* 2102–2110.

Regal, D. M. (1981). Development of critical flicker frequency in human infants. *Vision Research, 21,* 549–555.

Repp, B. H. (1982). Phonetic trading relations and context effects: New experimental evidence for a speech mode of perception. *Psychological Bulletin, 92,* 81–110.

Roucoux, A., Culee, C., & Roucoux, M. (1983). Gaze fixation and pursuit in head free human infants. In A. Roucoux & M. Crommelinck (Eds.), *Physiological and pathological aspects of eye movements* (pp. 23–31). The Hague: Dr. W. Junk.

Rubel, E. W., & Ryals, B. M. (1983). Development of the place principle: Acoustic trauma. *Science, 219,* 512–514.

Sakabe, N., Arayama, T., & Suzuki, T. (1969). Human fetal evoked response to acoustic stimulation. *Acta Oto-Laryngologica, Supplementum, 252,* 29–36.

Salapatek, P. (1975). Pattern perception in early infancy. In L. B. Cohen & P. Salapatek (Eds.), *Infant perception: From sensation to cognition: Vol 1. Basic visual processes* (pp. 133–248). New York: Academic.

Schaller, M. J. (1975). Chromatic vision in human infants: Conditioned operant fixation to "hues" of varying intensity. *Bulletin of the Psychonomic Society, 6,* 39–42.

Schanel-Klitsch, E., & Woodruff-Pak, D. S. (1985). Sensitivity of the human neonate to short- and long-wavelength stimuli. *Vision Research, 25,* 1641–1646.

Schiff, W. (1965). The perception of impending collision: A study of visually directed avoidant behavior. *Psychological Monographs, 79* (11, Whole No. 604).

Schneck, M. E., Hamer, R. D., Packer, O. S., & Teller, D. Y. (1984). Area-threshold relations at controlled retinal locations in 1-month-old infants. *Vision Research, 24,* 1753–1763.

Schneider, B. A., & Trehub, S. E. (1985). Behavioral assessment of basic auditory abilities. In S. E. Trehub & B. Schneider (Eds.), *Advances in the study of communication and affect: Vol. 10. Auditory development in infancy* (pp. 101–114). New York: Plenum.

Schneider, B. A., Trehub, S. E., & Bull, D. (1980). High-frequency sensitivity in infants. *Science, 207,* 1003–1004.

Schneider, B. A., Trehub, S. E., Morrongiello, B. A., & Thorpe, L. A. (1986). Auditory sensitivity in preschool children. *Journal of the Acoustical Society of America, 79,* 447–452.

Schonen, S. de, McKenzie, B., Maury, L., & Bresson, F. (1978). Central and peripheral object distances as determinants of the effective visual field in early infancy. *Perception, 7,* 499–506.

Schulman-Galambos, C., & Galambos, R. (1979). Brain stem evoked response audiometry in newborn hearing screening. *Archives of Otolaryngology, 105,* 86–90.

Schwartz, M., & Day, R. H. (1979). Visual shape perception in early infancy. *Monographs of the Society for Research in Child Development, 44,* (7, Serial No. 182).

Schwartz, G. M., Izard, C. E., & Ansul, S. E. (1985). The 5-month-old's ability to discriminate facial expressions of emotion. *Infant Behavior & Development, 8,* 65–77.

Schwartz, T. L., Dobson, V., Sandstrom, D. J., & van Hof-van Duin, J. (1985). Kinetic perimetry in newborn infants. *Supplement to Investigative Ophthalmology & Visual Science, 26,* 137.

Shaw, L., Roder, B., & Bushnell, E. W. (in press). Infants' identification of three-dimensional form from perspective transformations. *Perception & Psychophysics.*

Shea, S. L., Doussard-Roosevelt, J. A., & Aslin, R. N. (1985). Pupillary measures of binocular luminance summation in infants and stereoblind adults. *Investigative Ophthalmology & Visual Science, 26,* 1064–1070.

Shimojo, S., Bauer, J., Jr., O'Connell, K. M., & Held, R. (1986). Pre-stereoptic binocular vision in infants. *Vision Research, 26,* 501–510.

Shimojo, S., Birch, E. E., Gwiazda, J., & Held, R. (1984). Development of vernier acuity in infants. *Vision Research, 24,* 721–728.

Simons, K. (1984). Effects on stereopsis of monocular versus binocular degradation of image contrast. *Investigative Ophthalmology & Visual Science, 25,* 987–989.

Sinnott, J. M., & Aslin, R. N. (1985). Frequency and intensity discrimination in human infants and adults. *Journal of the Acoustical Society of America, 78,* 1986–1992.

Sinnott, J. M., Pisoni, D. B., & Aslin, R. N. (1983). A comparison of pure tone auditory thresholds in human infants and adults. *Infant Behavior & Development, 6,* 3–17.

Siqueland, E. R., & Delucia, C. A. (1969). Visual reinforcement of non-nutritive sucking in human infants. *Science, 165,* 1144–1146.

Slater, A., Earle, D. C., Morison, V., & Rose, D. (1985). Pattern preferences at birth and their interaction with habituation-induced novelty preferences. *Journal of Experimental Child Psychology, 39,* 37–54.

Slater, A. M., & Findlay, J. M. (1972). The measurement of fixation position in the newborn baby. *Journal of Experimental Child Psychology, 14,* 349–364.

Slater, A. M., & Findlay, J. M. (1975a). Binocular fixation in the newborn baby. *Journal of Experimental Child Psychology, 20,* 248–273.

Slater, A. M., & Findlay, J. M. (1975b). The corneal reflection technique and the visual preference method: Sources of error. *Journal of Experimental Child Psychology, 20,* 240–247.

Slater, A., Morison, V., & Rose, D. (1983). Locus of habituation in the human newborn. *Perception, 12,* 593–598.

Sokol, S., & Moskowitz, A. (1985). Comparison of pattern VEPs and preferential-looking behavior in 3-month-old infants. *Investigative Ophthalmology & Visual Science, 26,* 359–365.

Sokol, S., Moskowitz, A., & Paul, A. (1983). Evoked potential estimates of visual accommodation in infants. *Vision Research, 23,* 851–860.

Spinelli, D., Pirchio, M., & Sandini, G. (1983). Visual acuity in the young infant is highest in a small retinal area. *Vision Research, 23,* 1133–1136.

Starr, A., Amlie, R. N., Martin, W. H., & Sanders, S. (1977). Development of auditory function in newborn infants revealed by auditory brainstem potentials. *Pediatrics, 60,* 831–839.

Starr, A., & Hamilton, A. E. (1976). The correlation between confirmed sites of neurological lesions and abnormalities of far-field auditory brainstem lesions. *Electroencephalography & Clinical Neurophysiology, 41,* 595–608.

Stephens, B. R., & Banks, M. S. (1985). The development of contrast constancy. *Journal of Experimental Child Psychology, 40,* 528–547.

Stern, D. N., Spieker, S., & MacKain, K. (1982). Intonation contours as signals in maternal speech to prelinguistic infants. *Developmental Psychology, 18,* 727–735.

Strange, W., & Dittmann, S. (1984). Effects of discrimination training on the perception of /r–l/ by Japanese adults learning English. *Perception & Psychophysics, 36,* 131–145.

Streeter, L. A. (1976). Language perception of 2-month-old infants shows effects of both innate mechanisms and experience. *Nature, 259,* 39–41.

Sullivan, J., & Horowitz, F. D. (1983). The effects of intonation on infant attention: The role of the rising intonation contour. *Journal of Child Language, 10,* 521–534.

Tees, R. C., & Werker, J. F. (1984). Perceptual flexibility: Maintenance or recovery of the ability to discriminate non-native speech sounds. *Canadian Journal of Psychology, 38,* 579–590.

Teller, D. Y. (1982). Scotopic vision, color vision, and stereopsis in infants. *Current Eye Research, 2,* 199–210.

Teller, D. Y., & Bornstein, M. H. (1986). Infant color vision and color perception. In P. Salpatek & L. B. Cohen (Eds.), *Handbook of infant perception* (pp. 185–236). New York: Academic.

Teller, D. Y., Peeples, D. R., & Sekel, M. (1978). Discrimination of chromatic from white light by two-month-old human infants. *Vision Research, 18,* 41–48.

Trehub, S. E. (1976). The discrimination of foreign speech contrasts by infants and adults. *Child Development, 47,* 466–472.

Trehub, S. E., Bull, D., & Schneider, B. A. (1981). Infants' detection of speech in noise. *Journal of Speech & Hearing Research, 24,* 202–206.

Trehub, S. E., Bull, D., & Thorpe, L. A. (1984). Infants' perception of melodies: The role of melodic contour. *Child Development, 55,* 821–830.

Trehub, S. E., & Schneider, B. A. (Eds.). (1985). *Advances in the study of communication and affect: Vol. 10. Auditory development in infancy.* New York: Plenum.

Trehub, S. E., Schneider, B. A., & Endman, M. (1980). Developmental changes in infants' sensitivity to octave-band noises. *Journal of Experimental Child Psychology, 29,* 282–293.

Trehub, S. E., Thorpe, L. A., & Morrongiello, B. A. (1985). Infants' perception of melodies: Changes in a single tone. *Infant Behavior & Development, 8,* 213–223.

Tronick, E. (1972). Stimulus control and the growth of the infant's effective visual field. *Perception & Psychophysics, 11,* 373–376.

Van Giffen, K., & Haith, M. M. (1984). Infant visual response to Gestalt geometric forms. *Infant Behavior & Development, 7,* 335–346.

Varner, D., Cook, J. E., Schneck, M. E., McDonald, M., & Teller, D. Y. (1985). Tritan discriminations by 1- and 2-month-old human infants. *Vision Research, 25,* 821–831.

Volkmann, F. C., & Dobson, M. V. (1976). Infant responses of ocular fixation to moving visual stimuli. *Journal of Experimental Child Psychology, 22,* 86–99.

Volkmann, F. C., Riggs, L. A., Moore, R. K., & White, K. D. (1978). Central and peripheral determinants of saccadic suppression. In J. W. Senders, D. F. Fisher, & R. A. Monty

(Eds.), *Eye movements and the higher psychological functions* (pp. 35–54). Hillsdale, NJ: Erlbaum.

Vurpillot, E., Ruel, J., & Castrec, A. (1977). L'organisation perceptive chez le nourrisson: Response au tout ou a ses elements. *Bulletin de Psychologie, 327,* 396–405.

Walk, R. D. (1968). Monocular compared to binocular depth perception in human infants. *Science, 162,* 473–475.

Walk, R. D., & Gibson, E. J. (1961). A comparative and analytical study of visual depth perception. *Psychological Monographs, 75* (15, Whole No. 519).

Wallach, H., & O'Connell, D. N. (1953). The kinetic depth effect. *Journal of Experimental Psychology, 45,* 205–217.

Werker, J. F., Gilbert, J. H. V., Humphrey, K., & Tees, R. C. (1981). Developmental aspects of cross-language speech perception. *Child Development, 52,* 349–355.

Werker, J. F., & Tees, R. C. (1983). Developmental changes across childhood in the perception of non-native speech sounds. *Canadian Journal of Psychology, 37,* 278–286.

Werker, J. F., & Tees, R. C. (1984a). Cross-language speech perception: Evidence for perceptual reorganization during the first year of life. *Infant Behavior & Development, 7,* 49–63.

Werker, J. F., & Tees, R. C. (1984b). Phonemic and phonetic factors in adult cross-language speech perception. *Journal of the Acoustical Society of America, 75,* 1866–1878.

Werner, J. S. (1982). Development of scotopic sensitivity and the absorption spectrum of the human ocular media. *Journal of the Optical Society of America, 72,* 247–258.

Werner, J. S., & Wooten, B. R. (1979). Human infant color vision and color perception. *Infant Behavior & Development, 2,* 241–274.

Werner, J. S., & Wooten, B. R. (1985a). Two perspectives on infant color vision research. *Infant Behavior & Development, 8,* 115–116.

Werner, J. S., & Wooten, B. R. (1985b). Unsettled issues in infant color vision. *Infant Behavior & Development, 8,* 99–107.

Wertheimer, M. (1961). Psychomotor coordination of auditory and visual space at birth. *Science, 134,* 1692.

Wickelgren, L. W. (1967). Convergence in the human newborn. *Journal of Experimental Child Psychology, 5,* 74–85.

Williams, L. (1977, October). *The effects of phonetic environment and stress placement on infant discrimination of place of stop consonant articulation.* Paper presented at the Second Boston University Conference on Language Development, Boston.

Yonas, A. (1981). Infants' responses to optical information for collision. In R. N. Aslin, J. R. Alberts, & M. R. Petersen (Eds.), *Development of perception: Vol. 2. The visual system* (pp. 313–334). New York: Academic.

Yonas, A., Arterberry, M. E., & Granrud, C. E. (in press). Four-month-old infants' sensitivity to kinetic and binocular information for three-dimensional object shape. *Child Development.*

Yonas, A., Bechtold, A. G., Frankel, D., Gordon, F. R., McRoberts, G., Norcia, A., & Sternfels, S. (1977). Development of sensitivity to information for impending collision. *Perception & Psychophysics, 21,* 97–104.

Yonas, A., Cleaves, W., & Pettersen, L. (1978). Development of sensitivity to pictorial depth. *Science, 200,* 77–79.

Yonas, A., & Granrud, C. E. (1985). The development of sensitivity to kinetic, binocular and pictorial depth information in human infants. In D. Ingle, D. Lee, & M. Jeannerod (Eds.), *Brain mechanisms and spatial vision.* Dordrecht, Netherlands: Nijoff.

Yonas, A., Granrud, C. E., & Pettersen, L. (1985). Infants' sensitivity to relative size information for distance. *Developmental Psychology, 21,* 161–167.

Yonas, A., Pettersen, L., & Granrud, C. E. (1982). Infants' sensitivity to familiar size as information for distance. *Child Development, 53,* 1285–1290.

Yonas, A., Pettersen, L., & Lockman, J. (1979). Young infants' sensitivity to optical information for collision. *Canadian Journal of Psychology, 33,* 268–276.

Yonas, A., Pettersen, L., Lockman, J., & Eisenberg, P. (1980, April). *The perception of impending collision in 3-month-old infants.* Paper presented at the International Conference of Infant Studies, New Haven.

Yonas, A., & Pick, H. L. (1975). An approach to the study of infant space perception. In L. B. Cohen & P. Salapatek (Eds.), *Infant perception: From sensation to cognition: Vol. 2. Perception of space, speech and sound* (pp. 3–31). New York: Academic.

Young-Browne, G., Rosenfeld, H. M., & Horowitz, F. D. (1977). Infant discrimination of facial expressions. *Child Development, 48,* 555–562.

Zelazo, P. R., Brody, L. R., & Chaika, H. (1984). Neonatal habituation and dishabituation of head turning to rattle sounds. *Infant Behavior & Development, 7,* 311–321.

CHAPTER 2

Learning and Memory in Infancy

CAROLYN ROVEE-COLLIER

There is general agreement that learning is "a more or less permanent change in a behavior which occurs as a result of practice" (Kimble, 1961, p. 2). This definition excludes temporary changes due to arousal, fatigue, illness, medication, or biological rhythms as well as more permanent changes associated with aging, growth, or physiological intervention. There is a strong consensus that the resulting behavioral change should be adaptive (Thorpe, 1956), although the time frame over which the costs and benefits of a given instance of learning are calculated may be quite broad. Although this definition does not suffice in all instances—learning can occur in a single trial, for example—it holds for the greatest number of cases. On the other hand, there is little agreement about what the organism learns, the role of reinforcement in learning, or the process by which it occurs.

The categories of learning that are most often distinguished by authorities are *habituation, classical and instrumental conditioning,* various types of *complex learning, concept learning,* and *language acquisition.* Considerable evidence has been amassed linking these to a phylogenetic continuum, with the simplest organisms who occupy the lowest levels of the continuum being capable only of habituation and the most complex organisms, humans, being uniquely capable of language acquisition (Buss, 1973; Razran, 1971). Over the past 25 years, there has been increasing popular support for a hierarchical ontogeny of learning skills that parallels this continuum. The most widely accepted timetable for the initial appearance of these different categories holds that: (1) habituation cannot be demonstrated in premature newborns and can be achieved by full-term newborns only with difficulty; (2) classical conditioning cannot be established before 3 weeks of age; (3) categorization and other types of complex learning do not appear until the second half of the infant's first year; and (4) concept formation is not possible prior to the second half of the infant's second year. Although this progression is based exclusively on acceptance of the null hypothesis and, as such, can hardly be considered diagnostic, it is consistent with the theoretical zeitgeist and dominates current thinking about the infant's early learning abilities (e.g., Rosenblith & Sims-Knight, 1985; Sameroff

---

Preparation of this manuscript was supported by Grant No. MH32307 from the National Institute of Mental Health. The generous assistance of Judy Butler, Carolyn Greco, and Wendy Hill is gratefully acknowledged. Special thanks are due Benjamin Rovee, for help with the bibliography and word processing; Harlene Hayne, for critical suggestions and unselfish assistance during the preparation of this manuscript; and George Collier, for encouragement and moral support as well as insightful and critical analyses of many earlier drafts.

& Cavanagh, 1979). Recent research in behavioral ecology and animal cognition suggests that the abilities of animals to represent their environments has been greatly underestimated (e.g., Roitblat, Bever, & Terrace, 1984), raising new challenges to the evolutionary analysis described above. In addition, recent research on learning by human infants has cast further doubt on the evolutionary analogy and has revealed that the developmental timetable for various learning abilities is incorrect.

Over the last decade and particularly within the last 2 or 3 years, it has become increasingly fashionable to view the learning that takes place early in infancy (and particularly during the first few postnatal months) as bearing little or no relation to human cognitive development (Kagan, 1984; Moscovitch, 1984; Sameroff & Cavanaugh, 1979; Strauss & Carter, 1984). The theoretical commitment to this position has become so strong that an intellectual myopia has developed with respect to evidence to the contrary (e.g., Olson & Strauss, 1984). At the same time, an experimental void has steadily developed in the study of infant learning, with the result that the researchers who study infant learning today can be counted on one hand. Ironically, over the same period there has been a major theoretical and empirical renaissance in learning in other areas of psychology, including the newly emerging areas of behavioral ecology and behavioral neuroscience. Much of this work offers new and different perspectives on the significance of early experience and, in particular, of early learning (cf. Rovee-Collier, 1986).

Although the theoretical bias of the present chapter reflects the concept of the infant as a product of evolution, it rejects a simple ontogenetic–phylogenetic analogy. Instead, the evidence of infant learning is weighed in terms of its adaptive and functional significance. One aspect of an evolutionary approach is the recognition that human infants, like the young of all species, display behaviors that have been maximized by selection. Because human infants share a number of common, survival-related problems with infants of other mammalian species, they must also share with them a number of common behavioral and physiological solutions. At the same time, it is recognized that infants of different species face a number of *unique* problems that require unique biological and behavioral solutions. A second and equally important aspect of an evolutionary approach is the recognition that infants and adults of a given species occupy different niches. Because different selection pressures operate at different points in development, the problems that infants share with adults of the same species may be even more disparate than those they share with infants of other species. From this perspective, it is seen as inappropriate to ask them experimental questions in paradigms that were based on models developed for human adults. Their answers will surely be different and will tell us nothing about how they are "adultlike." By the same token, it is a mistake to believe that testing infants in paradigms developed for other nonverbal organisms—animals— will simply reveal how infants are "animallike" (cf. Strauss & Carter, 1984). Learning *procedures* transcend both phylogeny and ontogeny. They do not dictate the nature of either the particular problems or their solutions. Only through adapting the different procedures to reflect age- and species-appropriate problems can we hope to gain some insights into the structure of the infant's niche and the general principles that underlie the infant's behavioral solutions.

In the following chapter, I review the current status of what is known about infant learning and the research that has been conducted on this topic since the publication of the 1979 edition of this handbook. Coverage includes the major categories indicated above with the exception of language acquisition, which is a topic that merits extensive coverage in its own right. In addition, I consider briefly the relation between learning and memory and some of the recent data that address this relation.

HABITUATION

Habituation is defined as a "stimulus specific response decrement resulting from repeated or constant exposures to the response eliciting stimulus" (Wyers, Peeke, & Herz, 1973, p. 12). The defining characteristics of habituation have been delineated by Thompson and Spencer (1966).

Several aspects of this definition deserve comment. First, because habituation requires repeated stimulus presentations, it cannot be inferred from response to a test stimulus following a single stimulus presentation; at a minimum, two habituation trials must precede the test (Wyers et al., 1973). Second, habituation cannot be inferred from the presentation of a constant stimulus to which the infant cannot selectively orient its sensory receptors (e.g., a particular ambient temperature, illumination condition, swaddling, etc.). Response decrement resulting from continuous stimulation such as this (e.g., Brackbill, 1970) is *acclimatization,* not habituation. Third, the stipulation that responding to a particular stimulus must decrease with repeated presentations is operationally different from *familiarization.* In habituation, the emphasis is on changing response; the stimulus remains constant. Familiarization, which is *exposure learning* or *perceptual learning,* requires neither repeated stimulus presentations nor response decrements. When a response decrement is seen following a familiarization period, it is assumed that this reflects changes in the perception of the stimulus, not in response strength. The response remains stimulus appropriate, changing only because the properties of its eliciting stimulus become subjectively different. Finally, the phrase "stimulus specific response decrement" means that response to an altered stimulus on test trials will reflect the extent to which the infant discriminates the stimulus change. If the infant does not discriminate it, the response suppression will generalize to the test stimulus; if the infant does discriminate the stimulus change, the response suppression will not generalize; and so forth.

Recently, there has been widespread misapplication by infancy researchers of the term *dishabituation* (see Thompson & Spencer, 1966) to the phenomenon of *generalization* during a test with an altered stimulus (but see Bartoshuk, 1962; Clifton & Nelson, 1976; Field, Dempsey, Hatch, Ting, & Clifton, 1979; Jeffrey, 1976; Kisilevsky & Muir, 1984; Ruff, 1975). Unfortunately, the confusion of these two learning phenomena is unique to the infancy literature, doing little to enhance the general perception of the level of scholarship in developmental research with infants.

Theoretical Accounts

Pavlovian Model

In actuality, habituation is the progressive decrement in the strength of an *unconditional reflex* over repeated presentations of the unconditional stimulus. Pavlov (1927) accounted for habituation in the same manner as the extinction of a *con-*

ditional reflex, that is, in terms of the growth of an active inhibitory process that suppresses response. The only difference was in terms of how the eliciting stimulus became effective in the first place (unlearned or learned, respectively). Because stimuli elicit responses, it was presumed that the original habituation stimulus becomes an inhibitor of the response. That habituation results from an active inhibitory process is inferred from the response recovery seen to the original habituation stimulus following the intrusion of a strong external stimulus that temporarily disrupts the inhibitory process and allows the response to be expressed. This phenomenon is known as *dishabituation;* in extinction, the parallel phenomenon is known as *disinhibition.* As noted above, the label *dishabituation* has been incorrectly used to refer to responding that occurs directly to the interpolated stimulus instead of to the original habituation stimulus following the interpolated event. Common principles describe the generalization of inhibition and excitation during tests with altered stimuli.

Evolutionary Account

Considerable lip service has been paid to the adaptive benefits of habituation in terms of the savings, in time and energy, that accrue as a result of eliminating nonessential responding to biologically irrelevant stimuli (Lorenz, 1965; Thorpe, 1963). More recently, however, behavioral ecologists have argued that the real benefits of habituation derive from shifting the organism's behavioral priorities to other biologically significant events or activities (Wyers et al., 1973). Complex environments provide multiple stimuli and response opportunities. During habituation, when responding begins to decline to one stimulus, it increases compensatorily to another, and so forth, with the result that the total amount of time spent responding remains constant, irrespective of the specific activities to which the organism's time and energy are allocated (Hill, Rovee-Collier, Collier, & Wasserloos, 1986). Thus the adaptive value of habituation is realized not in terms of response suppression but in terms of the increased *response variability* and *response selection* that the suppression affords. This, in turn, reveals the hierarchy of stimuli and responses that are critical to the organism.

Most studies of habituation, irrespective of subject age or species, have not been designed to reveal this function (but see Pecheux & Lecuyer, 1983). Rather, designs have reflected the classic refinement paradigm in which all stimuli other than the target event, and all response opportunities other than the one being measured, are eliminated or minimized so that changes in only a single behavior can be attributed to the repetition of only a single stimulus. In addition, researchers typically use very simple stimuli and measure only a single component of a given response. These conditions offer no opportunity to observe an increase in alternative responses to other stimuli during habituation. The robust response to novel test stimuli following a series of habituation trials offers a glimpse of this adaptive function—the robustness of the phenomenon, in fact, can be taken as evidence of its adaptive significance. However, when the novel test stimulus, like the habituation stimulus, is presented singly, the subject can only either respond or not respond to it. The failure to provide alternative response opportunities has resulted in an underestimation of the functional significance of habituation and its fundamental properties (Wyers et al., 1973).

There have been two exceptions to the typical experimental approach in infant habituation research. The first is seen in tests of Jeffrey's (1968) serial habituation hypothesis, which assumes that the components of complex visual stimuli are serially processed in an order that reflects their initial salience. Presumably, processing of successively less salient elements results from the habituation of the element higher in rank. Miller (1972), for example, obtained initial visual preference scores for the individual elements of a complex stimulus and then repeatedly exposed infants to the compound for a fixed number of trials. During posttests with the individual elements, infants spent less time fixating the elements that were originally most preferred.

The second instance is seen in the use of repeated trials of paired stimuli when the two targets on a given trial differ (e.g., Cornell, 1974; Fantz, 1964; Greco & Daehler, 1985; Ruff, 1975). When two stimuli are presented simultaneously, infants can selectively shift fixations from one stimulus to the other. If both targets were identical, the response selection advantage of habituation to one of them would not be realized; functionally, there would not be an alternative stimulus to fixate. As a result, total looking time per trial (summed over both stimuli) would decrease. Experiments have often failed to consider, however, that infants fixate stimuli other than those provided as specific targets. Because the infant's eyes are not shut, this decrease in target fixation over trials must result in an increase in *unmeasured* fixation time to nonspecified stimuli in the test setting (e.g., the infant seat, the hands, other parts of the apparatus, the ceiling and walls, the mother) or an increase in other behaviors that may (e.g., crying) or may not (e.g., escape attempts) compete with visual fixation. Only when the pair offers a response *choice* is there an opportunity to observe the adaptive advantage of habituation.

In the Fantz (1964) study, for example, infants 2–6 months of age were presented with pairs of complex visual stimuli for 10 trials of 60 sec. One member of the pair remained the same from trial to trial, and one changed. As predicted, as infants spent less time looking at the stimulus that remained constant over trials, they spent more time looking at the variable member, with the result that *total looking time was conserved*. This is a very different result from that typically obtained in habituation studies.

Ironically, Jeffrey and Cohen (1971, p. 82) questioned a habituation interpretation of the Fantz data on the grounds that the novel member of the stimulus pair may have contributed to the attentional decline to the invariant member. However, this criticism is flawed on three counts. First, the total fixation time allocated to both stimuli did not account for the total fixation time available on a given trial, indicating that infants had ample time to sample both stimuli as well as to look elsewhere. Second, there is little conceptual distinction between providing a single compound stimulus with many parts that presumably compete for attention (e.g., Miller, 1972) and providing two different stimuli, as Fantz did, once the initial assumption is made that the infant fixates only a small segment of any stimulus. And third, an ecological analysis of the adaptive benefits of habituation is based on the real-world consideration that organisms live not in a stimulus vacuum but in a complex environment in which many stimuli continuously and simultaneously compete for attention. It is *only* in this situation that selection pressures historically have operated, and it is *only* in this situation that the response selection consequences of response suppression can be realized. In these conditions, habituation is seen as the underlying mechanism that allows attention to wax and wane, shifting from one aspect of the environment to the next as the relative weighting of competing stimuli also shifts.

In recent studies of categorization involving visual attention measures, the Fantz design has been used except that both stimuli change from one trial to the next while the *category membership* of one member of the pair remains constant and the other varies (e.g., Greco & Daehler, 1985).

Sokolov's Model

Most of the current research on habituation in infants is based on Sokolov's *neuronal model of the stimulus*. Sokolov (1963, pp. 282–294) postulated that a certain cell system stores information regarding the properties of a repeatedly presented stimulus and serves as a template against which information from subsequent stimulus presentations is compared. When an aspect of a future stimulus does not correspond exactly to this neuronal template, then an orienting reflex is produced. As the details of the template are progressively filled in over successive repetitions of a given stimulus, it elicits a progressively smaller orienting reflex. When the correspondence is perfect, the orienting reflex no longer occurs (i.e., habituation is complete). Sokolov proposed that the orienting reflex to individual components of habituated compound stimuli is elicited by the *omission* of the remaining parts, which produces a mismatch with the template. Thus discrepancies between the perceived stimulus and the representation of it produce orienting behavior. The reduction of the discrepancy over successive trials accounts for the habituation curve. This is similar to the CS-reduction account of classical conditioning (Pearce & Hall, 1980), described below. Graham (1973, p. 166) has noted that Sokolov's model does not address habituation of either defensive reflexes, which are elicited by intense stimulation and are relatively nonhabituable, or specific (adaptational) reflexes.

Dual-Process Theory

Less theoretical or empirical attention has been devoted to the dual-process theory of habituation (Groves & Thompson, 1970; Thompson & Spencer, 1966). This account attributes changes in response during repetitive stimulation to the interaction between two different underlying neural processes in different parts of the nervous system. Presumably, *habituation* (a decrease in responsivity to a specific stimulus) occurs in a specific S–R pathway that forms the appropriate reflex arc, while *sensitization* (an increase in general responsiveness) occurs in the parts of the nervous system that control arousal level or state. The habituation process is highly stimulus specific, whereas the sensitization process is initiated by a range of stimuli. Although sensitization persists for only seconds or minutes, depending upon stimulus intensity, habituation is relatively more permanent. Both processes can occur simultaneously, and the empirical function reflects their sum. However, its shape will essentially reflect the extent to which sensitization is maximized or minimized, particularly in the early trials. By this account, dishabituation results from a temporary increase in sensitization.

The hypothesized interplay between habituation and sensitization has strong implications for interpreting ontogenetic differences in habituation, particularly in light of age differences in sleep–wake cycles, state stability, and absolute thresholds. It is possible, for example, that age differences primarily reflect differences in sensitization, particularly during the early trials of a habituation series (e.g., Dannemiller

& Banks, 1983). Even within ages, patterns of individual differences are likely to reflect the interaction of these two processes (e.g., Bornstein & Benasich, 1986). The Sokolov (1963) and Thompson and Spencer (1966) models have been compared in an excellent review by Graham (1973) that includes infant habituation data. However, neither model can adequately account for recent evidence (Whitlow & Wagner, 1984) of two qualitatively different types of habituation (short-term and long-term) with different temporal characteristics. The latter finding has been interpreted in an information-processing context and has major implications for infant learning and memory.

Research Findings

Prior to 1960, studies of habituation in infants were rare (Lipsitt, 1963, 1967). Habituation had been demonstrated, however, in decorticate animals (Sharpless & Jasper, 1956) and at the level of the cochlear nucleus (Hernandez-Peon & Scherrer, 1955) and was widely considered to be the most primitive form of learning. As such, the habituation paradigm offered promise as a means for studying infant autonomic and sensory development.

A series of studies in the 1960s and early 1970s suggested that infants could habituate to auditory, visual, tactile, and olfactory stimuli during the newborn period. In these studies, investigators typically measured changes in general reactions to stimulation (e.g., heart rate, movement or general activity, respiration, sucking suppression, startle reflex, color changes); less often did they index habituation in terms of changes in the specific reflexes to the eliciting stimulus (e.g., fixation of a visual stimulus; head turning toward an auditory stimulus). However, many of the original findings appeared to be interpretable in terms of processes other than habituation. These considerations led Jeffrey and Cohen (1971) to conclude that:

> Habituation is not readily obtained in the neonate. A possible exception to that statement is the case of olfactory stimulation, but perhaps habituation is common to any situation involving observations of arousal from sleep rather than the more specific components of orienting behavior. By 2 or 3 months of age, however, habituation of orienting behavior is clearly observable in a variety of modalities. (p. 92)

In the 1970s, habituation research was strongly influenced by Sokolov's (1963) publication on the orienting reflex and its role in conditioning. For the most part, this work focused on the dimensions of visual or auditory stimulation that infants of different ages could discriminate and on their information-processing abilities (but see Jeffrey, 1976; McCall, 1971, 1979). The infant habituation literature has been reviewed extensively elsewhere (Berg & Berg, 1979; Bornstein, 1985; Clifton & Nelson, 1976; Cohen, 1976; Cohen, DeLoache, & Strauss, 1979; Cohen & Gelber, 1975; Graham, 1973; Jeffrey, 1976; Jeffrey & Cohen, 1971; Kessen, Haith, & Salapatek, 1970; Lipsitt, 1963; McCall, 1971; Olson, 1976; Olson & Sherman, 1983; Rovee-Collier, in press; Werner & Perlmutter, 1979).

Because habituation has been assumed to reflect central nervous system functioning, the rate of habituation has been viewed by many as an index of maturity. Thus for example the finding that girls habituate more rapidly than boys has been taken as evidence that girls are maturationally more advanced (e.g., Creighton,

1984). Although Richardson and McCluskey (1983) found that younger infants had a higher rate of attrition from habituation studies involving auditory–visual stimuli than older subjects, attrition was not differentially related to infant sex. Subjects who did not complete the procedures performed differently on the completed portions than those who remained in their study, raising significant questions about the generality of findings based on biased samples. The latter findings were confirmed by Wachs and Smitherman (1985), who also found that attrition was predicted by parental ratings of their infant's fussiness and nonadaptability on a standard infant temperament questionnaire; this relation was unrelated to infant age. Their finding that females showed greater attrition than males was at variance with the earlier report and was attributed to differences in session duration: Females failed earlier in the experimental session than males.

The questionable status of newborn habituation cast serious doubt on the prospect of habituation on the part of premature newborns or infants lacking cortex. In the last 5 years, however, researchers have presented compelling evidence of the habituability of newborn responses to auditory (Brody, Zelazo, & Chaika, 1984; Field et al., 1979; Krafchuk, Tronick, & Clifton, 1983; Zelazo, Weiss, Randolph, Swain, & Moore, 1986), visual (Slater, Morison, & Rose, 1982, 1984), and tactile (Field et al., 1979; Kisilevsky & Muir, 1984) stimulation. In addition, there is strong evidence of the habituability of premature newborns (Field et al., 1979; Krafchuk et al., 1983). However, the preterm studies have revealed a dissociation between behavioral and autonomic indicators of habituation, with a response decrement appearing *only* in the behavioral measures. Rose et al. (1976) had previously observed that, although both preterm and full-term newborns exhibited an increase in motor activity to strong tactile stimulation, only the full-terms had displayed a concomitant increase in heart rate. In the latter study, however, neither group had displayed a response decrement. Their observations indicated that the cardiac measure was more sensitive than the behavioral index to the parameters of stimulation for the full-term infants, whereas the opposite was true for the preterm group.

Graham (1979) has recently distinguished two acceleratory heart rate responses in the newborn. The *short-latency startle reflex* to stimuli with rapid rise times habituates, whereas the *long-latency defensive reflex* to high-intensity stimuli does not. The short-latency startle has been found to habituate rapidly in infant chimpanzees and apes (Berntson & Boysen, 1984). Krafchuk and colleagues (1983) proposed that the premature infants in their study who did not habituate were exhibiting cardiac responses of the defensive type—presumably a more primitive response. In their view, the high sensory thresholds of the premature infant are adaptive, protecting against unnecessary and energetically expensive arousal; however, once these thresholds are exceeded (i.e., a sufficiently intense stimulus is presented), the premature infant becomes highly aroused and reacts with defensive responses that are resistant to habituation.

Recent data have confirmed earlier evidence that responses of decerebrate infants as young as 20–30 days can habituate (Aylward, Lazzara, & Meyer, 1978; Berg, Clarkson, Eitzman, & Setzer, 1981; Graham, Leavitt, Strock, & Brown, 1978). In addition, infants with particular medical complications perform differently than normal infants in different components of a habituation/discrimination test procedure. Infants with Down's syndrome, for example, showed a deficit in discrimination following habituation to visual stimuli when tested at 19 and 23 but not at

28 weeks (Cohen, 1981). Similarly, cerebral palsied infants take longer to orient to the habituation stimulus than normal infants, but thereafter the two groups are equivalent in terms of fixation duration and posttest discrimination performance (McDonough & Cohen, 1982). Recently, Landry, Leslie, Fletcher, and Francis (1985) found that 7-month-old preterm infants with respiratory distress syndrome and intraventricular hemorrhage had longer latencies to orient to the habituation stimulus than either preterms with respiratory distress syndrome but without intraventricular hemorrhage or full-term infants. On measures of attention holding, habituation rate, and discrimination following habituation, however, the groups did not differ. Whether this reflected a motoric deficiency, a deficit in inhibiting response to the blinking light that precedes each trial, or a problem in detecting the contingency associated with orienting was not determined. Taken together, these findings suggest that Cohen's (1972, 1973) original distinction between attention-getting and attention-holding processes may have diagnostic value.

There have been only a few recent reports addressing procedural issues. These have focused almost exclusively on trial (Columbo & Horowitz, 1985) or habituation (Dannemiller, 1984; Sherman & Olson, 1982; see also Nelson & Horowitz, 1983) criteria. Dannemiller's analysis of the statistical bias associated with various habituation criteria is of critical importance in design decisions in habituation research. The greatest number of recent studies have used habituation as a tool for assessing cognitive functioning (but see Sophian, 1980), with emphasis on *individual differences* and the relation of various habituation measures to *later performance on intelligence tests* (Bornstein, 1985; Bornstein & Benasich, 1986; Bornstein & Sigman, 1986; Lewis & Brooks-Gunn, 1981), *perception* (Bornstein, 1981; Cohen et al., 1979; Keane & Swartz, 1981; Kellman, Spelke, & Short, 1986; Nelson & Horowitz, 1983; Quinn & Eimas, 1986; Streri & Pecheux, 1986), *categorization* (Caron, Caron, & Glass, 1983; Caron, Caron, & Myers, 1982; Caron, Caron, & Myers, 1984; Greco, 1985; Greco & Daehler, 1985; Olson & Sherman, 1983; Reznick & Kagan, 1983; Ross, 1980; Swartz, 1982; Sherman, 1985; Sherman & Olson, 1982; Strauss, 1979, 1981; Younger, 1985; Younger & Cohen, 1983), and *memory* (Greco & Daehler, 1985; Olson & Sherman, 1983; Olson & Strauss, 1984; Sherman, 1985; Strauss, 1981; Strauss & Curtis, 1981; Werner & Perlmutter, 1979; Zelazo et al., 1986). Much of the work previously cited has involved face perception in either live models, videotapes, photographs, or line drawings.

Conclusions

The past 5 years of habituation research have witnessed attempts to develop procedures appropriate for testing the limits of habituation to stimuli of different modalities in younger and compromised subjects. Over the same time, a relatively sophisticated methodology has grown up around the study of older infants and has been exploited for the study of perceptual–cognitive abilities. There has been little focus on the properties of habituation as a learning procedure, and experimental designs have precluded documentation of its adaptive function.

In the first instance, it has been documented that the full-term newborn infant can habituate to repetitive stimulation in every sensory modality. It has also been demonstrated that preterm newborns and decerebrate infants can habituate to some stimuli under some circumstances. Whether they do or not depends upon the measures that are used and the parameters of stimulation. It is significant that the conditions that produce habituation in preterm and decerebrate infants as well as their response characteristics differ from those of full-term infants. Whether their response decrements reflect the same process or different processes, mediated by the same or different brain mechanisms, remains to be seen.

The greatest number of studies of the second type have focused on the infant's early categorization abilities. The data have revealed that infants in their first year can selectively habituate to invariant, often subtle features of discriminably different, repeatedly encountered stimuli. These demonstrations have fostered considerable debate about the manner in which the infant detects and represents the structure of its environment—and *if* it does. However, thus far all conclusions have been inferred from a generalized lack of attention that can be observed for only a brief period following the initial train of closely spaced stimuli. They have yielded no evidence of either the adaptive benefits or the retention advantage that categorization presumably affords. While these data permit us to conclude that the infant is capable of the *precursor of categorization*—a short-term visual sampling or perceptual bias—they provide no direct evidence of categorization per se. Without this selective attentional bias, however, categorization would not be possible.

CLASSICAL CONDITIONING

Classical conditioning is the process by which organisms learn the structure of their niche and the economic relations that define it. Like habituation, it involves the repetitious presentation of a stimulus. As is not the case with habituation, however, the stimulus in classical conditioning bears a predictive relation to other stimuli in the environment; in effect, the organism learns which events in nature go with which others. Because many events in nature occur in an orderly fashion, classical conditioning permits organisms to exploit this orderliness and anticipate events instead of simply reacting to them.

Theoretical Accounts

The Pavlovian model dominated research and thinking about classical conditioning until the last decade, when western conceptualizations of classical conditioning came under the influence of two models (Pearce & Hall, 1980; Rescorla & Wagner, 1972) that expanded the traditional account to encompass a number of phenomena previously considered to be the exclusive domain of cognitive psychology.

Pavlovian Model

In both the basic Pavlovian model and subsequent elaborations of it, the two essential components are: (1) an unconditional stimulus (US) that reliably elicits a reflex without any prior training or prerequisites (i.e., unconditionally); and (2) a conditional stimulus (CS) that is within the organism's sensory range but that is initially "neutral" with respect to the reflex elicited by the US. According to Pavlov (1927), each presentation of these stimuli excites their corresponding cortical sites, and when they are presented repeatedly in close temporal contiguity, a temporary neural connection (*association*) is established between them. When excitation originating with the CS courses over this connection to the US site and stimulates it, this in turn triggers the unconditional response (UR) via excitation traveling over an inborn neural pathway. Thus once the cortical pathway between the CS and US is formed, the previously neutral CS can evoke the UR in the physical absence of the US. Because the appearance of the UR in the absence of the US is conditional upon the prior pairing of the CS and US, the UR elicited in this way is called a conditional response (CR). This response is an inevitable consequence of the CS–US pairing, and its appearance is taken as evidence of their association. For this reason, classical conditioning is considered a type of stimulus–stimulus (Pavlov, 1928) or stimulus–substitution (Buss, 1973) learning. A primary emphasis in Pavlovian conditioning is on the interplay of excitation and inhibition associated with stimulation, and the characteristic phenomena of conditioning (extinction, spontaneous recovery, generalization, discrimination, etc.) are interpreted in this context.

Rescorla-Wagner Model

This account of classical conditioning (Rescorla & Wagner, 1972; Wagner & Rescorla, 1972) is an elaboration of the original Pavlovian model but is devoid of its reflexology. The fundamental aspect of classical conditioning, according to this model, is what the occurrence of the CS signals regarding the occurrence of the US (an "expectancy"). The requirement that there be a *contingency* or correlation between the CS and the US has been substituted for the original requirement that the CS and the US be *contiguous*. What the organism learns, then, is this contingency. Because the CS and the US may each occur alone, the organism must detect that the conditional probability that the US will occur given that the CS has occurred *exceeds* the probability that the US will occur in its absence. Conditioning reflects the appreciation of this difference. Rescorla (1967) has demonstrated that the contingency can be either positive (the CS predicts that the US will occur) or negative (the CS predicts that the US will not occur).

In the Rescorla-Wagner model, the surprisingness of the US (cf. Kamin, 1969) determines the strength of its association with the CS on any trial, and the intensity and salience of the CS and US determine the rate of conditioning. As the US becomes increasingly well predicted by the CS over trials, the US loses its surprisingness (i.e., it becomes increasingly expected). This progressive decrease in the discrepancy between what the subject expects to occur and what actually occurs accounts for the negatively accelerated learning curve. As long as the expectation of the subject differs from the actual event (US), the CS can continue to acquire predictive value (associative strength). However, when the US is completely expected, conditioning is complete. The CR is an operational definition of the surprisingness of the US, and the progressive *reduction of the US* over trials in terms of its surprisingness accounts for learning.

Pearce-Hall Model

This account (Pearce & Hall, 1980) is very similar to the Rescorla-Wagner account except that its central emphasis is on the CS, the salience of which is the important determinant of conditioning. As the organism progressively learns the predictive relation between the CS and the US, there is progressively less new information that the CS can provide regarding this relation. This progressive *reduction of the CS* over trials in terms of its predictive value accounts for the negatively accelerated learning curve. An important consequence of the reduction in new information from the CS is a shift in attention to other, potentially more informative environmental stimuli. This theoretical account is reminiscent of the evolutionary account of habituation in that a benefit of learning is to free the organism to interact with other potentially significant aspects of its environment, to engage in other activities, or to learn other predictive relations.

Developmental Considerations

Because URs were thought to be exclusively subcortical and CRs exclusively cortical, Soviet psychologists originally saw the cortex as an "organ of ontogenetic behavior" (Elkonin, 1957, p. 48) and classical conditioning as a means by which to study its functioning. In 1913 Krasnogorskii, one of Pavlov's students, concluded that the cortex of infants less than 6 months old was insufficiently innervated to permit the formation of cortical connections, becoming "fully developed and functionally complete" only "during the second year" (cited in Elkonin, 1957, p. 50). Subsequently, however, Koltsova (1949) reported conditioned sucking reactions at the breast during the third postnatal week, and Kasatkin (1948) observed conditioned aural reflexes in infants more than 2 months premature between the actual and the expected date of birth. This was interpreted as evidence that cortical development is speeded by extrauterine stimulation.

Recent demonstrations of classical conditioning in decerebrate preparations of many species, including adult cats (Norman, Buchwald, & Villablanca, 1977), adult rabbits (McCormick & Thompson, 1984), and human infants—both full-term (Berntson, Tuber, Ronca, & Bachman, 1983) and preterm (Tuber, Berntson, Bachman, & Allen, 1980)—have discounted the necessity of cortical involvement in the formation of conditioned associations. These findings, together with the demonstration that classical conditioning in the simple invertebrate *Aplysia* results from functional and structural changes of specific nerve cells and their interconnections (Kandel, 1979), suggest that classical conditioning can be modulated at many different levels of neural organization (Rovee-Collier, 1986). Recent findings that the neural substrate for classical conditioning is functional in the rat fetus (Smotherman, 1982; Stickrod, Kimble, & Smotherman, 1982) and newborn rat pups (Johanson & Teicher, 1980; Rudy, Vogt, & Hyson, 1984; Smith & Spear, 1980) and in newborn human infants (Blass, Ganchrow, & Steiner, 1984; Cantor, Fischel, & Kaye, 1983) provide convergent evidence of classical conditioning as a fundamental mechanism by which even the youngest organisms learn the significant relations in their niche.

In light of current evidence, we must conclude that *previous theoretical attempts to define the appearance of the first classically conditioned responses in the human infant as the third postnatal week are completely without empirical foundation* (Sameroff, 1971, 1972; Sameroff & Cavanagh, 1979).

Classical Conditioning Research with Infants

Pavlov's early research focused exclusively on associations involving feeding reflexes and defensive reflexes. These were defined in terms of the USs that elicited them.

Subsequent researchers have expanded these classifications to include stimuli that elicit approach responses (classical appetitive conditioning) and withdrawal responses (classical aversive conditioning). Heart rate deceleration and pupillary dilation are usually classified with approach responses, while heart rate acceleration and pupillary constriction are usually classified with withdrawal responses.

The research and theory on infant classical conditioning have been reviewed extensively (Berg & Berg, 1979; Brackbill & Fitzgerald, 1969; Brackbill & Koltsova, 1967; Elkonin, 1957; Fitzgerald & Brackbill, 1976; Fitzgerald & Porges, 1971; Kasatkin, 1972; Lipsitt, 1963; Mateer, 1918; Olson & Sherman, 1983; Peiper, 1963; Razran, 1933; Rovee-Collier, 1986; Rovee-Collier, in press; Rovee-Collier & Lipsitt, 1982; Sameroff, 1972; Sameroff & Cavanagh, 1979; Siqueland, 1970). In the last decade there has been a significant hiatus in classical conditioning research with infants (cf. Rovee-Collier, 1986), and only a few reports have appeared since 1979. Not surprisingly, these have continued to focus on the feeding and defensive reflexes.

Classical Appetitive Conditioning

The predictive relations in the feeding context have proven to be a fertile source of information about the infant's early learning abilities. Researchers from many laboratories using a variety of CSs and task parameters have repeatedly found that classical conditioning increases the efficiency of food getting (rooting, head turning), consumption (sucking, mouthing, swallowing), and digestion (secretions of salivary and gastric juices, leucocytosis, blood sugar level) in the first few hours, days, weeks, and months following birth. The first study of infant classical conditioning (Krasnogorskii, 1907) demonstrated conditioned feeding responses in a 14-month-old to the presentation of a glass of milk (CS). The CRs included sucking, swallowing, and mouth opening. When the sight of the milk was subsequently paired with a second CS, a bell, swallowing came to be evoked by that CS as well. Krasnogorskii observed that conditioned sucking movements might provide the most objective means of studying classical conditioning in younger infants. This observation set the stage for much of the infant classical conditioning research that followed for the next 75 years.

With the advent of the contingency analysis of classical conditioning (Rescorla & Wagner, 1972) and the recognition of state as a significant variable in infant research (e.g., Ashton, 1973; Korner, 1972), many of the studies performed earlier came under sharp criticism for the failure to include appropriate contingency/state control groups. In retrospect, many of these criticisms were unjustified. In most of the studies, infants had been tested at a particular time in relation to a feeding (in animal research this is the typical operational definition of level of motivation) or at a common point in the sleep–wake cycle, and specific respiratory or activity conditions that subsequently became incorporated into formal state criteria had been specified as criteria for a stimulus presentation (see also Kantrow, 1937).

Although truly random control groups were not a part of earlier designs (Rescorla, 1967), a good number did include age and arousal control groups. The latter typically received the same total intensity of stimulation as the experimental group except that the CS was presented after the US—a backward conditioning procedure that does not lead to excitatory conditioning. Rescorla's original insight was that a backward conditioning paradigm could result in learning of a negative contingency and that this could be revealed if the CS had an opportunity to depress overt behavior below some baseline value greater than zero. Thus for example if a CS that signaled a no-shock period was presented during an instrumental avoidance procedure in which a stable response rate had been established (e.g., every 20 sec the animal received a shock unless it ran to the other side of a two-way avoidance chamber), a *decrease in the instrumental response rate* would be seen. In a traditional classical procedure where the CR is either made or not made, the negative contingency cannot be revealed (i.e., the extent to which the subject is responding below zero cannot be measured). Because a learning interpretation requires a difference in responding between the experimental and the control group, both random and backward conditioning control groups should remain at baseline, albeit for different reasons (as a result of either not learning or learning not to respond, respectively). Ironically, those who held that infants could not learn predictive relations between environmental events in the first few weeks of life also argued that learning was not conclusively demonstrated in these studies because of the opportunity afforded by the backward arrangement for *learning a negative contingency* between the CS and US!

Since chance acquisition has occasionally been reported in random control groups, many experimenters now prefer an *explicitly unpaired control* condition in which the CS precedes the US at nonoptimal intervals (Gormezano & Kehoe, 1978). Recent studies that have included either random control groups or explicitly unpaired control groups have confirmed the original conclusion that infants can be classically conditioned during the newborn period.

The notion that state should be held constant in studies of infant learning reflects our historical commitment to the refinement paradigm. However, this commitment may not be justified. Frequent state changes are a fact of early infancy. Most if not all of what infants normally learn, particularly in the newborn period, is embedded in a context of changing states. It is possible that these changing states may not be a source of extraneous variation but may serve in a manner analogous to conditional discriminative stimuli, sharpening the discrimination of the predictive relation between the CS and the US and increasing the probability that these events will be remembered on a future occasion (cf. Butler, 1986; Rovee-Collier, Griesler, & Earley, 1985). Removing an event from its normal context creates an artificial situation and presents the infant with a problem very different from the one that it was selected to solve as well as with different information for its solution.

Haroutunian and Campbell (1979) reported that infant rats could use an interoceptive cue as a CS prior to the time at which the same stimulus, applied externally, was effective. Their data are consistent with the notion that very young infants may be particularly sensitive to interoceptive stimuli associated with state changes. This possibility was tested by Cantor and colleagues (1983). In their study, feedback from the infant's own sucking activity served as a CS that predicted a tactile US (a palm press). The US elicited the Babkin reflex, which is incompatible with sucking. The strength of the association, measured in an extinction phase, was indexed by the extent of sucking suppression and by changes in the parameters of the infant's characteristic sucking burst following a CS presentation. All infants were tested in a quiet alert state. Three stimulation groups received palm press stimulation (the US) following either the first, third, or fifth suck (CS) of each sucking burst. Two nonstimulation control groups, whose hands remained loosely held throughout the acquisition phase, received "blank" stimulus presentations after the first or third suck of each burst. During the extinction test, the group that had received the US after the third suck showed a significant suppression of sucking, differing from both of the other stimulation groups and from the nonstimulation controls in both burst length and burst duration. The suppression that was shown by only this group was attributed to the optimal temporal interval between the initiation of sucking and the palm press stimulation (see also Lasky & Spiro, 1980; Little, 1970). The other groups functioned as explicitly paired controls at intervals that do not normally support conditioning in young infants. Also, because the group that received the US after the first suck did not differ from the two nonstimulation control groups, the effect of stimulation per se could not account for the results. The authors concluded that their conditioning procedure

> may have made not only the overt responses but also the underlying state changes incompatible. If so, the newborn may use this preceding state shift as a self-generated cue for the suppression of the sucking response in a period following the pairing of the two systems.
>
> *(Cantor et al., 1983, pp. 411–412)*

A second study, also concerned with the feeding reflexes, has provided unequivocal evidence that human newborns as young as 2 hr of age can learn predictive relations within a classical conditioning paradigm (Blass et al., 1984). Here, the CS was a tactile stimulus—stroking of the forehead. In many infant mammals, vigorous tactile stimulation regularly precedes nursing but does not directly induce sucking responses. In the present study also this stimulation was neutral with respect to the UR. The US was a sucrose solution, delivered into the infant's mouth via a pipette, and the primary URs, scored from videotapes, were *head-orient* and *pucker-suck*. Sessions took place 2 hr after a feeding and lasted 45–50 min. The experimental group and an explicitly paired control group received the same number of CS–US trials, but the experimental group received the US *immediately* after the CS, and the control group received it after a longer, variable delay. A sensitization control group received the US only, with no exposure to the CS prior to the extinction phase.

During acquisition, the experimental and the explicitly paired control groups exhibited the same incidence of head-orienting responses, but those of the experimental group were confined to the CS portion of the trial. Similarly, only the experimental group exhibited a high level of pucker-sucks during the CS. In the extinction phase, infants in the experimental group showed a classic extinction function, with the sharpest decline in conditioned responding occurring between the first and second trials. Infants in the sensitization control group displayed no evidence of a similar behavioral change.

Of particular interest were other changes shown by the experimental group during extinction:

> After 1 or 2 extinction trials, the infant's expression appeared to be that of surprise, which gave way to a frowning or angry face, to be followed by crying or whimpering. Crying was short-lived; and at its termination, the infants generally slept.
>
> *(Blass et al., 1984, p. 230)*

Their crying was not elicited by withdrawing sucrose per se; only 1 of the 16 infants in the two control groups cried during the extinction phase, yet all had received sucrose during training. This suggests that infants in the experimental group had learned the predictive relation between stroking and sucrose delivery and cried because their *expectancy was violated*. This same phenomenon was described in one of the earliest infant feeding studies (Marquis, 1941).

The Blass et al. data reflect a more general observation that extinction tests and their variant, interpolated US omission tests, may be particularly revealing of whether the contingency has been learned (Krachkovakaia, 1959; Marquis, 1941). In infant classical eyelid conditioning, for example, a greater percentage of CRs occurred on US omission trials than in the CS–US interval, although the latter measure also indicated that learning had occurred (Little, Lipsitt, & Rovee-Collier, 1984). In classical heart rate conditioning of newborns and decerebrate infants, responding within the CS–US interval is often precluded by the temporal parameters of stimulation in relation to the parameters of responding. Here as well the US omission procedure is particularly sensitive to the effects of conditioning, revealing a cardiac change when the predicted US does not occur (Berntson et al., 1983; Clifton, 1974; Stamps, 1977; Stamps & Porges, 1975; Tuber et al. 1980; Turco & Stamps, 1980). The direction of heart rate change may reflect the quality of the omitted US (i.e., acceleration during an aversive US omission, deceleration during an appetitive US omission) or the age and/or neurological status of the infant (e.g., acceleration in very young or decerebrate infants).

Sameroff and Cavanagh (1979) have argued that the Clifton (1974) and Stamps and Porges (1975) findings did not demonstrate initial acquisition of a CR, thereby precluding a description in terms of classical conditioning: " . . . why should the classical conditioning paradigm be twisted to incorporate these anomalous data? Would it not be better to utilize a paradigm in which the definitions need not be interpreted in such a convoluted form?" (Sameroff & Cavanagh, 1979, p. 355). This criticism is puzzling because the appearance of a CR when the US was omitted *is the evidence* that infants had learned the contingency. Not only is it common to assess conditioning in an extinction phase, but it is often preferred, both in classical and in instrumental procedures. In studies of the ontogeny of learning and memory in both animal (Amsel, 1979) and human (Rovee-Collier & Fagen, 1981) infants, for example, responding during an extinction phase following training provides a sensitive index of retention that veridically reflects the parameters of conditioning. In fact, data from the Clifton and Stamps-Porges studies as well as from the other studies previously cited are completely consistent with a contingency analysis of classical conditioning in which the CR is viewed as an index of an expectancy (Rescorla & Wagner, 1972; Wagner, 1978). Sameroff and Cavanagh's conclusions, therefore, are unjustified and appear to reflect an uncompromising theoretical commitment to the notion that newborns cannot be classically conditioned.

More serious, however, are the implications of their analysis for the field of infancy research more generally. The critical concern should not be whether a particular set of data fits a particular experimental procedure or not but what the data reveal about the structure of the infant's niche and its predictive relations. As scientists, we seek answers. By selectively dismissing answers, *however gained,* that do not fit into our prestructured conceptions, we misrepresent the course of infant development (cf. Olson & Strauss, 1984; Strauss & Carter, 1984). The increasing numbers of demonstrations of early learning and memory phenomena must not continue to be selectively ignored or dismissed because they fly in the face of the current zeitgeist. If we wish to *understand* early infant development, it will be necessary for us to modify and update our conceptions and models to incorporate these new answers as they are put forth.

Temporal Conditioning

Temporal information may be one of the earliest aspects of the environment to be incorporated into the infant's representation of the structure of its niche. For the young of many mammalian (Hudson & Distel, 1982) and avian (Gaioni & Evans, 1984) species, the ability to learn the particular timing of critical events and to anticipate them has immediate and direct survival implications. A number of earlier studies confirmed that very young human infants also are highly sensitive to the timing of spaced events (e.g., Lasky & Spiro, 1980; Little, 1973; Panneton & DeCasper, 1980). They can use time passage as the sole CS, that is, *temporal conditioning* (Brackbill & Fitzgerald, 1972; Bystroletova, 1954, cited in Brackbill & Koltsova, 1967; Cantor et al., 1983; Krachkovskaia, 1959; Lipsitt & Ambrose, 1967; Marquis, 1941; Stamps, 1977; for discussion, see Brackbill & Koltsova, 1967; Rovee-Collier & Lipsitt, 1982), and they can discriminate the interval by which the CS precedes the US, that is, *inhibition of delay* (Hoffman, Cohen, & DeVido, 1985; Krasnogorskii, 1908; Little, 1973).

The relative facility with which infants use temporal cues may reflect a number of factors. First, temporal information is provided in utero by the mother's cyclical metabolic and hormonal rhythms as well as by her grosser activity cycles. Second, because temporal cues are not unique to a particular modality, their efficacy does not depend on ontogenetic development within and across modalities. Moreover, because all modalities are sensitive to temporal information, this is a source of redundant information about the structure of the environment, further enhancing the reliability of temporal information as a predictive cue. And, third, because there are no orienting responses to be habituated following a temporal CS, conditioning may proceed more quickly.

The latter factor reflects the hypothesis that the habituation of reflexes to the CS in the CS–US interval is a major determinant of whether classical conditioning will or will not be achieved (Kimmel, 1973). A similar relation between habituation and exploratory behavior has been described by Pecheux and Lecuyer (1983). Papousek (1967a) observed that habituation of the infant's nonspecific orienting responses to the CS usually preceded the appearance of the first CR, and Berntson et al. (1983) found that the three decerebrate infants who displayed habituation of the cardiac response during conditioning trials with visual and/or auditory stimuli also displayed a heart rate change (acceleration) indicative of classical conditioning on US omission test trials (see also Ingram & Fitzgerald, 1974). Little (1973) provided convergent evidence of this relation in a study of infant eyelid conditioning. Her data suggested that the necessity for the orienting reflex to the *offset* of the CS in a trace interval to habituate contributed to the greater efficacy of delay relative to trace conditioning procedures.

With the exception of conditioned pupillary constriction (Brackbill & Fitzgerald, 1972), most of the successful instances of temporal conditioning have involved appetitive conditioning and, in particular, the feeding reflexes. This suggests that, unlike appetitive events, aversive events that the infant is likely to encounter do not recur at constant intervals in natural settings, or the infant does not have to learn about them; this protective function is assumed by the parents. Those aversive events that are predicted at particular times of the day or night (e.g., thermal extremes, predators) are usually met by morphological and physiological adaptations as well as by behavioral adaptations that need not involve learning (e.g., occupying a diurnal or nocturnal niche, death feigning or torpor, extended sleep periods, etc.). Aversive conditioning paradigms have revealed, however, infants' ability to time their conditioned responses until they just approximate the onset of the US (Hoffman et al., 1985; Little, 1973).

Classical Aversive Conditioning

The defensive reflexes are among the most primitive URs of phylogeny and ontogeny, yet there is little evidence of classical aversive conditioning in young infants. While young infants must feed and can increase the efficiency with which they locate, procure, ingest, and digest food through learning the predictive relations in their feeding context, they lack the motoric competence to escape or avoid noxious events. Because altricial young usually remain under the protective auspices of one or both parents, they do not need to protect themselves. In fact, there is evidence that the neural mechanisms that mediate associations between aversive exteroceptive cues and their consequences mature much later than those that, for example, mediate interoceptive cues and their consequences (Haroutunian & Campbell, 1979).

In primitive hunter–gatherer societies, human infants are thought to have remained in continuous physical contact with an adult during their first year (Konner, 1977). Under these circumstances, there would have been no selection pressures for the very young to anticipate noxious events, although they would have needed emergency defensive reactions for intense, momentary irritants. Even though slightly older infants exhibit anticipation of aversive events by crying, this principally serves to alert the parent, who reacts protectively. In effect, then, the classical aversive conditioning paradigm simply does not simulate a significant problem that very young infants in natural circumstances must solve. From this perspective, it is not surprising that successful attempts to document classical aversive conditioning (with the exception of odor or taste aversions) in infants of most altricial species either coincide with or just antedate the onset of independent locomotion. In human infants this relation is reflected in the timing of the appearance of fear of strangers and fear of the visual cliff.

Most of the early studies of aversively motivated behavior in human infants followed the example of adult research in which either electric shock, loud noise, or a corneal air puff was the noxious US. These initial attempts to demonstrate conditioning were largely unsuccessful with rat pups less than 8–10 days of age and with human infants less than 3–5 weeks.

Conditioned Fear

The best-known study of classical aversive conditioning in infants was reported by Watson and Rayner (1920). A careful reading of the original report, however, reveals that the US was initially administered only when 11-month-old Albert touched the rat. This and the descriptions of Albert's behavior at the sight of the rat indicate that Watson and Rayner used an instrumental punishment procedure that led to a suppression of touching the rat, a high-frequency behavior at the outset of the study (Church, 1966).

Recently, Gunnar (1980; Gunnar, Leighton, & Pellaux, 1984) has explored whether predictable aversive events are less fear provoking for 12-month-old infants than events that are unpredictable. Once the infant learns that a CS (a bell) predicts the onset of a noxious US (the noise produced by a cymbal-clapping toy monkey), the US should then predict a succeeding "safe" period, with the result that anxiety should be reduced during the intertrial interval. However, in both studies the data-collection procedure cut across CS and US presentations, precluding evaluating distress in relation to the US, and the contingency between turning on the toy and the noise it produced in study 1 was another instance of an instrumental punishment procedure.

Conditioned Eyelid Responses

The most widely studied response in the classical conditioning literature, irrespective of species or age, is the eyelid response. The eye blink is a protective reflex. When the US is a corneal air puff, a well-learned CR that just immediately anticipates the US is also a functional avoidance response. Many of the early failures to establish a conditioned eyelid reflex probably resulted from the use of a nonoptimal inter-stimulus interval (ISI). Little (1970) found that the optimal interval for eyelid conditioning in young infants is three times longer than the 500-msec ISI that is optimal for eyelid conditioning in adult humans and animals (Kimble, 1961). Similar evidence that longer ISIs are required for younger organisms has been reported in the animal infant literature (Caldwell & Werboff, 1962).

In a recent developmental analysis of eyelid conditioning, Little and colleagues (1984) used the nonoptimal 500-msec ISI as the explicitly paired control condition and a 1500-msec ISI as the experimental condition. Infants were trained for a single session at either 10, 20, or 30 days of age with a tone (CS) and air puff (US) and received a second session 10 days later. A random control group for each ISI condition was introduced at 30 days of age. A state criterion had to be met prior to trial initiation, and sessions began after a nap and when half of the normal ration had been consumed. Only the 1500-msec group learned the association, doing so at every age. The percentage of CRs increased with age, and the oldest group attained a higher level of conditioning than the youngest. All 1500-msec groups showed savings 10 days later, but only the groups that were first trained at 20 and 30 days of age also performed above age controls after that retention interval—a particularly impressive feat in view of their age, the small *number* of reinforced presentations (50), the relatively small *percentage* of reinforced trials (71 percent), and the brevity of training (20 min) in session 1. This finding is consistent with earlier observations of retention of classical conditioning after long intervals by older infants (Jones, 1930; Marinesco & Kriendler, 1933).

The recent development of devices by which the infant's eyelid reflex can be elicited and recorded unobtrusively has enhanced the prospect for infant eyelid conditioning as a model system for the study of learning (Balaban, Anthony, & Graham, 1985; Hoffman, Cohen, & English, 1985; Little, 1973; Little et al., 1984). Hoffman, Cohen, & DeVido (1985) presented a tone (CS) and, 500 msec later, a tap to the glabella (US) to infants from a wide age range and college students and found evidence of anticipatory responding in both groups. Although the conditioning of the infants was slower and less robust than that of the adults, it was more efficient: The infants' CRs more nearly overlapped the US.

There has been an increasing interest in the possibility that nonassociative, reflex *preconditioning* effects may provide a window on the functional maturity of the developing nervous system (Anthony & Graham, 1983). The preconditioning procedure involves presenting either a brief or a sustained stimulus immediately prior to a startle-eliciting US. Preconditioning phenomena may persist for many hours, and the prestimulus and the US need not be in the same modality. Because two stimuli are similarly paired in classical conditioning, habituation and sensitization (with short ISIs), and dishabituation, it is possible that preconditioning effects may be seen in such studies when stimulation parameters are appropriate (cf. Kisilevsky & Muir, 1984). Hoffman, Cohen, & DeVido (1985) found that newborns who received tones of different intensity (60, 70, 80, or 90 dB) prior to the glabellar tap exhibited a robust augmentation of blinks when the US was preceded by any of the three most intense tones; adults, however, showed the augmentation effect following the most intense tone only. In other manipulations, infants gave no indication of reflex inhibition over an ISI range of 75–600 msec or when tactile prestimulation was substituted for the tone; in contrast, reflex inhibition was observed in adults at all ISIs. These data were consistent with the earlier suggestion of Ziegler, Strock, and Graham (1979) that the neural system responsible for reflex inhibition is not fully developed at birth.

Balaban et al. (1985) found that the failure of transient stimuli to inhibit infant startle blinking to a US did not reflect an afferent processing deficit related to either the brevity or the low intensity of the prestimulus required to activate a mature neural mechanism for inhibition. They used either an acoustic or a visual stimulus as the US and stimuli from either the same or the other modality as the prestimulation agent. They hypothesized that if S_1 and S_2 were from the same modality and were processed, then short-term habituation should proceed more rapidly than if they were from different modalities, and more rapidly than if S_2 were presented repeatedly alone (see also Whitlow, 1975). In addition, the pairs of stimuli were presented against foregrounds that matched the modality of either S_1 or S_2. This presentation procedure increases attention, as measured by cardiac deceleration, but has different effects depending upon whether S_1 and S_2 are from the same modality. If they are, there is no observable effect of the foreground; if the two stimuli are from different modalities, then facilitation is expected if S_2 and the foreground match (different from S_1), and inhibition is expected if S_1 and the foreground match (different from S_2).

As predicted, stimuli from the same modality yielded smaller responses than stimuli from different modalities. Adults in a parallel experiment had longer UR latencies when the paired stimuli matched. Although UR latencies of infants and adults did not differ, the effect was not reliable for the infants. In addition, both infants and adults had longer blink latencies when S_1 and the foreground matched, but the foreground did not interact with S_2 for the infants; all showed heart rate deceleration over a trial, irrespective of same–different content. These data revealed that *infants were able to process an initial transient prestimulus in a relatively mature fashion.*

Conclusions

The current evidence unequivocally confirms earlier conclusions that, even within hours of birth, infants can learn and exploit the predictive relations in their environment *when those relations are presented in a biologically meaningful context*. The adaptive significance of this has been realized as an increase in behavioral and physiological efficiency. The facility with which infants learn contingencies associated with the feeding context and the difficulty with which they learn contingencies associated with noxious stimulation (with the exception of defensive reflexes such as the eyelid response, which require minimal coordinated movement) provide insights into the structure of their niche.

Newborns display considerable facility in exploiting temporal and interoceptive cues. In laboratory studies, state has been viewed as an extraneous stimulus that can interfere with learning. Yet it is likely that the infant's changing states, and perhaps even the direction of the change, act as setting events for certain kinds of predictive relations; for example, when aroused and crying, footsteps or the sight of an approaching adult predict distress relief (cf. Gekoski, Rovee-Collier, & Carulli-Rabinowitz, 1983). In addition, selective, state-related threshold changes may also influence which contingencies are most likely to be learned in association with which states (Pomerleau-Malcuit & Clifton, 1973). For this reason, the finding that some kinds of conditioning occur more readily in some states than in others should not be surprising (Brackbill, 1977; Clifton, Siqueland, & Lipsitt, 1972). Our insistence on maintaining a constant internal state in laboratory studies, along with a constant external milieu, may actually prevent infants from recognizing or learning the predictive relations that we structure for them.

Finally, it is safe to conclude that the manner in which we have framed our experimental questions, and not the infant's developmental or neurological status, has been the rate-limiting step in acquiring insights into the infant's early learning abilities.

INSTRUMENTAL LEARNING

Instrumental conditioning and its variant, operant conditioning, are distinguished from classical conditioning in that the production of a conditioned response is controlled not by an eliciting stimulus that precedes it but by a reinforcing stimulus that follows it (*operant control*). The critical distinction between the *eliciting* and the *reinforcing* properties of stimuli, and between elicited and emitted behavior, has been increasingly overlooked or confused in interpretations of learning and memory data gathered within instrumental procedures (e.g., Ruff, 1984; Schacter & Moscovitch, 1984); even in discrimination learning, a stimulus (S^+) that is correlated with reinforcement neither elicits nor otherwise forces the response to occur; rather, it merely sets the occasion for responding, providing information about the availability of reinforcement. Once the subject responds selectively in the presence of the S^+, behavior is under *discriminative control* but is still not elicited. Were the response initially elicited by S^+, it would not be possible to demonstrate the increase in the frequency or rate of responding that characterizes operant learning.

The greater concern in studies of instrumental learning is that the observed increase in response frequency or rate may reflect an increase in arousal induced by the reinforcing stimulation without regard to the contingency or by other sources that influence state changes (e.g., increasing irritability as a function of time in the session). As in Pavlovian conditioning, control groups for behavioral arousal or the eliciting effects of the reinforcer would receive the same number of reinforcements as the experimental group but their delivery would be either noncontingent upon responding or contingent but after a delay too long to support acquisition.

Theoretical Accounts

Most of the early research on instrumental learning derived from Thorndike (1911) and Skinner (1938), although the origins of subsequent work on concept formation and place learning are closely linked to Harlow (1949) and Tolman (1932, 1948), respectively. These accounts are presented in detail in Koch (1955). While Thorndike and Harlow both emphasized that the elimination of incorrect responses was central to learning, Thorndike and Skinner shared a commitment to the Law of Effect. Skinner's different approach to the analysis of behavior led to the elaboration of operant conditioning as a variety of Thorndike's prototypic instrumental paradigm.

Thorndike used a *discrete trials* procedure in which the experimenter initiates a trial (e.g., by presentation of a cue, placing the subject in a problem situation, etc.) and the subject terminates the trial when it performs the correct response (e.g., escaping from the box). Because the experimenter, not the subject, controls the intertrial interval, the number of responses and associated rewards as well as their distribution in time are limited. The traditional measures of instrumental learning, then, are the number of correct responses over trial blocks, the latency of responding, or the speed of responding.

Skinner assigned control of the intertrial interval to the subject. He termed his apparatus a *repeating problem box* and let the subject respond at whatever rate it chose, self-presenting, as it were, its own trials. In effect, Skinner substituted a single lever press or operant response for the extensive chain of behavior (finding and pulling a latch or loop and escaping from a box) that constituted the base of Thorndike's response measures—obviously the time it took to depress a lever was trivial; in addition, when the subject controlled the frequency of responding, there was no clear stimulus event from which to time a response latency. The time between successive responses, then, is the reponse measure in *free-operant procedures;* this is usually expressed as the number of responses over time (response rate).

Premack (1965) proposed a revision of the Law of Effect. He argued that any more probable response could potentially reinforce any less probable response. Moreover, the hierarchy of relative response probabilities could be rearranged. This approach inspired several studies on infant sucking behavior in the early 1970s (Brassell & Kaye, 1974; Brown, 1972) but has received no attention in recent studies of infant learning. Kimmel's (1973) model, which has special implications for infant learning, has received no research attention at all. Kimmel, like Premack, focused on the relation between responses during acquisition. He distinguished two classes of reflexes, positive and negative feedback reflexes, that differed both in habituability and in their reinforcing efficacy. Positive feedback reflexes (e.g., orienting and searching) increase afferent input to the CNS, habituate readily, and are non-reinforcing. Negative reflexes (e.g., nocioceptive, righting, withdrawal, or ingestion reflexes) reduce afferent input, habituate slowly if at all, and are reinforcing. Kimmel proposed that the relative habituability of the two reflexes determined the type of conditioning: If the first member of the pair were readily habituable, (e.g., a positive feedback reflex), then classical conditioning would occur; if the first member were nonhabituable, then it could gain in strength or frequency, that is, instrumental conditioning. We have previously cited examples that suggest that habituation of the orienting reflex to the CS is prerequisite for classical conditioning. By the same token, the resilience of recurrent responses (e.g., nonnutritive sucking) over time could be viewed as the basis for the facility with which they are instrumentally conditioned.

Finally, conspicuous for its absence has been infancy research motivated by Hullian theory (Hull, 1943, 1952). This is particularly curious because (1) his formal system specifically accommodated performance changes as a function of changes in arousal level, and (2) his theoretical approach was a major factor in research with children in the 1950s and early 1960s.

Instrumental Conditioning Research

Prior to 1960, there were no reports of simple instrumental conditioning in the infancy literature (Lipsitt, 1963), although studies of complex discrimination learning by older infants appeared in the 1940s. Beginning in the 1960s, there was interest in whether responses of younger infants could be instrumentally conditioned and, in particular, the earliest age at which this could be achieved. Because it was widely thought that the control of behavior progressed from reflexive to voluntary, instrumental learning was assumed to be a later ontogenetic achievement. This view was consistent with Piaget's contention that the means by which infants altered their environment for its interest value, that is, secondary circular reactions, did not develop until sensorimotor stage 3, between 4–8 months of age (see Flavell, 1963). However, it was subsequently documented that infants 2–3 months of age would work to produce visual and auditory stimulation (Rovee & Rovee, 1969; Sheppard, 1969), and several unpublished reports describing instrumental learning in newborns, including premature newborns, were widely circulated (Butterfield, 1968a, 1968b; Siqueland, 1968a, 1968b, 1969).

Research in the 1970s focused on *what responses* were influenced by *what reinforcers* delivered under *what conditions* (schedule, delay) to infants of *what age*. As a result, considerable evidence of operant learning, even in the earliest hours and days following birth, has been obtained. This work has been extensively reviewed (Brackbill & Koltsova, 1967; Fitzgerald & Porges, 1971; Fitzgerald, Strommen, & McKinney, 1977; Horowitz, 1968; Hulsebus, 1973; Kessen et al., 1970; Lipsitt, 1969, 1971; Millar, 1976; Olson & Sherman, 1983; Reese & Lipsitt, 1970; Rovee-Collier, in press; Rovee-Collier & Gekoski, 1979; Rovee-Collier & Lipsitt, 1982; Sameroff, 1972; Sameroff & Cavanagh, 1979).

In the 1980s, researchers began to exploit instrumental paradigms to investigate infant *perception* (Aslin, Pisoni, Hennessy, & Perey, 1981; DeCasper & Fifer, 1980; DeCasper & Prescott, 1984; Eimas & Miller, 1980; Essock & Siqueland, 1981; Fifer, 1980; Fifer & Moon, 1984; Olsho, 1985; for reviews, see Aslin, Pisoni, & Jusczyk, 1983; Jusczyk, 1985), *information processing* (Butler, 1986; DeCasper & Spence, 1986; Fagen, 1980; Gekoski & Fagen, 1984; Greco, Hayne, & Rovee-Collier, 1986;

Hayne, Rovee-Collier, & Perns, in press; Heth & Cornell, in press; Watson, 1984), *memory* (Brody, 1981; Butler, 1986; Earley, Griesler, & Rovee-Collier, 1985; Enright, 1981; Enright, Rovee-Collier, Fagen, & Caniglia, 1983; Fagen, 1984; Fagen, Morrongiello, Rovee-Collier, & Gekoski, 1984; Fagen & Ohr, 1985; Fagen, Ohr, & Fleckenstein, 1985; Fagen & Rovee-Collier, 1983; Fagen, Yengo, Rovee-Collier, & Enright, 1981; Gekoski, Fagen, & Pearlman, 1984; Griesler, Earley, & Rovee-Collier, 1985; Hayne et al., in press; Hayne & Rovee-Collier, 1985; Mast, Fagen, Rovee-Collier, & Sullivan, 1980; Ohr, Fagen, Rovee-Collier, & Vander Linde, 1986; Panneton & DeCasper, 1982; Rovee-Collier, Butler, & Hayne, 1985; Rovee-Collier, Enright, Lucas, Fagen, & Gekoski, 1981; Rovee-Collier, Griesler, & Earley, 1985; Rovee-Collier, Patterson, & Hayne, 1985; Rovee-Collier & Sullivan, 1980; Rovee-Collier, Sullivan, Enright, Lucas, & Fagen, 1980; Sullivan, 1982; Vander Linde, 1982; Watson, 1984), and *motoric development* (Brinker, Wilson, & Deni, 1985; Thelen & Fisher, 1983).

In addition, the *diagnostic and therapeutic value* of instrumental conditioning procedures has been explored in samples of developmentally disabled infants (Brinker, 1981; Brinker & Lewis, 1982a, 1982b), and the relations among *temperament* (Dunst & Lingerfelt, 1985; Fagen & Ohr, 1985), *affect* (DeCasper & Carstens, 1981; Fagen & Ohr, 1985; Fagen, Ohr, Fleckenstein, & Ribner, 1985; Levitt, 1980; Lewis, Sullivan, & Brooks-Gunn, 1985; Mast et al., 1980) and operant conditioning have begun to be investigated. For reviews of recent work, see Fagen and Rovee-Collier (1982), Olson and Sherman (1983), Rovee-Collier (1983, 1984, in press), Rovee-Collier and Fagen (1981, 1984), Rovee-Collier and Hayne (in press), and Watson (1984).

As was the case in classical conditioning, behaviors associated with foraging (rooting or head turning, mouthing) and feeding (sucking) have been most widely exploited in newborn studies of instrumental conditioning. The events that infants will work to produce by these means, however, need not bear any essential biological or "prewired" relation to the response. Thus in the work cited previously we see that the infant readily learns to suck with a given amplitude to turn on its mother's voice (DeCasper & Fifer, 1980), music (Panneton & DeCasper, 1982), a speech syllble (Jusczyk, 1985), or a visual stimulus (cf. Rovee-Collier & Lipsitt, 1982) and to withhold responding when the withdrawal of reinforcement is made contingent upon high-amplitude sucking (e.g., Siqueland, 1968a)—an operant punishment procedure. The same principles guide the behavior of premature infants, who learn to suck to produce a visual stimulus (Werner & Siqueland, 1978) and to keep their eyes open when music is synchronized with the duration of eye opening (Siqueland, 1969), as well as the more energetically costly behavior of older infants, whose operant kicks or arm pulls operate a visual stimulus (Brinker et al., 1985; Fagen, 1980; Fagen & Rovee-Collier, 1982; Hayes, Ewy, & Watson, 1982; Lewis et al., 1985; Watson, 1984). Taken together, these observations suggest that very young infants bring into the world a repertoire of responses that have been selected for their biologically significant consequences. These responses predict significant outcomes but not necessarily "what" outcome. The current consequences of responding, rather than a preprogrammed stimulus–response connection, determine the infant's current behavior.

Also as was the case in infant classical conditioning, in the current theoretical zeitgeist, the preceding evidence that even newborn infants can and do learn the relation between their own behavior and its environmental consequences is often dismissed or selectively ignored. Olson and Strauss (1984), for example, recently concluded that "there is no strong evidence of operant conditioning with neonates." In support of this conclusion, they cited no data but invoked Piaget's distinction between the stage 1 infant and the stage 2 infant: "Piaget *believed* [italics added] that newborns are not capable of "true learning" and that true learning and accommodative behavior did not emerge until the second sensorimotor stage at around 3 months of age" (Olson & Strauss, 1984, p. 33). An unfortunate consequence of the current dissatisfaction with conditioning analyses of infant development is that the data have been cast out with the perspective, resulting in a rather limited view of early infant behavior.

The types of reinforcers for which infants of different ages will work provide some critical insights into *what* infants perceive as important and *how* important it is. This is illustrated in recent work by DeCasper and Fifer and their associates (DeCasper & Sigafoos, 1983; DeCasper & Fifer, 1980; DeCasper & Prescott, 1984; DeCasper & Spence, 1986; Fifer, 1980; Fifer & Moon, 1984). Using the high-amplitude sucking paradigm, they found that the newborn discriminates and prefers its mother's voice to that of either a stranger or its own father. The reinforcing value of the mother's voice is apparently established in utero as a result of the selective screening of all sounds except the mother's voice and heartbeat, which also is a potent reinforcer for newborn sucking (DeCasper & Sigafoos, 1983). These operant preferences are not influenced by perceptual learning during the postnatal period prior to testing (DeCasper & Prescott, 1984). What are the adaptive benefits of such learning? There is evidence that learning the mother's voice may increase feeding efficiency (Noirot & Algeria, 1983) and contribute to the mother's ability to inhibit her infant's distress (Thoman, Korner, & Beason-Williams, 1977). More generally, the mother's voice, her heartbeat, and perhaps even her smell (Cernoch & Porter, 1985) provide a familiar context that is likely to facilitate new learning (cf. Henderson & Dias, 1985; Parry, 1972).

In contrast, experience with visual stimuli can only be acquired postnatally. Although newborns prefer to look at faces (Hainline, 1978) and discriminate facial expressions (Field, Woodson, Greenberg, & Cohen, 1982), the weight of current evidence indicates that faces do not acquire special significance until the fourth postnatal month (Dolgin & Azmitia, 1985). It appears that what defines a stimulus as significant to the infant prior to that time is whether or not it responds contingently to the infant (cf. Meltzoff, 1985; Watson, 1972). Because the critical features of "social" reinforcers also characterize many "nonsocial" reinforcers that are made contingent upon behavior in laboratory settings (e.g., contrast, movement), it is not surprising that social and nonsocial reinforcers appear to be functionally equivalent over the first few postnatal months. The generalized reinforcing efficacy of social reinforcers may buffer infants against the loss or inaccessibility of the mother as a sole caregiver in the perinatal period. Although concern over the *releasing* characteristics of adults who provide social reinforcement occasionally surfaces (Bloom, 1984), Poulson (1983, 1984) has provided convincing evidence of the reinforcing effects of social reinforcers in a single-subject design.

Infants are also sensitive to the *control* they exercise over the consequences of their own responding, and this becomes reinforcing in its own right (cf. Rovee-Collier & Gekoski, 1979; Skinner, 1953). Recently there has been considerable concern that extensive exposure to noncontingent stimulation early in infancy can result in future maladaptive behavior ranging from retarded learning and insecure attachment to failure to thrive and clinical depression (cf. Cicchetti & Aber, 1986). This concern was inspired by the finding of Overmier and Seligman (1967) that a large proportion of dogs who received repeated, highly traumatic shocks that were neither contingent upon behavior nor controllable subsequently could not learn to avoid them when a contingency was introduced—a phenomenon termed *learned helplessness* (Seligman, 1975).

There has been an increasing tendency for instances of retarded learning to be indiscriminately characterized in terms of learned helplessness. Although this implies an abnormal condition of pervasive behavioral apathy that generalizes to all instances of new learning, generalization tests for this profound response apathy often either have been missing or have been conducted with procedures that accommodate alternative interpretations. There are a number of conditions that typically yield retarded acquisition following prior exposure to noncontingent stimulation, none of which produces a pervasive, psychopathological state that, in turn, depresses all learning. Rather, the retardation is usually highly *context specific* and can be interpreted in terms of negative transfer, latent inhibition, conditioned inhibition, learned irrelevance, changes in perceptual salience, and so forth. Moreover, prior exposure to noncontingent stimulation can influence some measures of acquisition but not others. Gamzu and Williams (1971), for example, found that prior exposure to noncontingent reinforcement affected subsequent response rate but not speed of learning.

DeCasper and Carstens (1981) found that acquisition was impaired in newborns who had received prior noncontingent presentations of the auditory stimulus that was subsequently used as a reinforcer. However, Gekoski and Fagen (1984), using the mobile conjugate reinforcement paradigm with 3-month-olds, found that neither short- nor long-term preexposure either to noncontingent mobile movement (noncontingent reinforcement, as in the DeCasper-Carstens study) or to a nonmoving mobile (equivalent to CS preexposure) retarded subsequent acquisition in the same context with a second but similar mobile. Only if infants were later trained in the *same context* with the *same mobile* was their acquisition retarded, but this occurred *in the no-movement condition only.* This finding reveals the specificity of the infant's early exposure learning and suggests that learning deficits following exposure to uncontrollable stimulation should be assessed in terms of the traditional variables that are known to influence performance on retardation tests, including the subject's prior history of contingent and noncontingent reinforcement and the similarity of the contexts within which the experiences occur.

Summary

Although infants have been viewed as being primarily reflexive creatures at birth who only gradually become able to manipulate their environments actively, over the past 5 years there have been a number of reports documenting that very young infants, including newborns, can learn the contingencies between their own responses and the consequences they produce. These behavioral changes are not elicited, nor are they a reflection of general behavioral arousal. While some response-reinforcement contingencies are acquired more slowly by younger (Gekoski, 1977;

Papousek, 1970) or premature (Gekoski et al., 1984) infants, the rapidity of acquisition is specific to the nature of the response and reinforcer and the task parameters. Responses associated with feeding or responses that provide auditory access to the mother, for example, are learned very rapidly even by newborns.

In general, discrete trials procedures with younger infants have been less successful except in those instances when the critical natural parameters of tightly knit consummatory sequences, such as natural foraging–feeding sequences or those involving orienting responses to auditory or visual stimuli, have been experimentally mimicked (e.g., Caron & Caron, 1978; DeCasper & Fifer, 1980; Fifer, 1980; Papousek, 1959, 1961). These procedures reflect the types of problems that very young infants must solve. In retrospect, it is possible that some of the earlier difficulties encountered in classical conditioning studies stemmed from problems more generally associated with discrete trials. Free-operant procedures that allow the younger infant greater *environmental control* have produced evidence of robust and rapid learning during the first 6 months.

COMPLEX LEARNING AND CONCEPT FORMATION

Complex learning is not easily interpreted in terms of classic reinforcement theory, which holds that specific responses are strengthened or weakened by their immediate consequences (the Law of Effect) and that specific responses become associated with specific stimuli. In complex learning, subjects appear to learn something more conceptual, more general—perhaps a strategy or a rule. Earlier studies of complex learning had shown that infants can use *tools* (Richardson, 1932, 1934), develop *discrimination learning sets* (Fagen, 1977), and exploit landmarks or *place cues* to locate objects (Acredolo, 1978, 1979; Bremner & Bryant, 1977; Bremner, 1978a, 1978b; Cornell & Heth, 1979; Rieser, 1979). Recent research has continued to develop evidence on place learning (Bertenthal et al., 1984; Keating, McKenzie, & Day, 1986; McKenzie, Day, & Ihsen, 1984; Presson & Ihrig, 1982; Rieser & Heiman, 1982) and additionally has addressed the infant's ability to solve *barrier problems* (Henderson & Dias, 1985) and acquire *artificial categories* (Greco et al., 1986; Hayne et al., in press) and *same–different concepts* (Fagen et al., 1984).

Place Learning

Research on place versus response learning typically involves training the infant to anticipate a given event in a fixed location, changing either the infant's orientation or location, and then ascertaining whether the first response following the reorientation is based on the prior response or the prior location. Savings scores (trials to reattain the learning criterion) are also calculated. Thus far, it has been found that the ability to localize objects in space is influenced by a number of factors, including familiarity with the environment, stimulus salience, affective state, and age-related locomotor experience. Younger infants tend to localize objects in relation to the position of their own bodies; older infants more readily exploit salient landmarks or place cues that are unaffected by their own spatial location or orientation (Acredolo & Evans, 1980; Cornell & Heth, 1979; Presson & Ihrig, 1982) but have difficulty using place cues exclusively well into their second year (Cornell & Heth, 1979; Reiser & Heiman, 1982). The earlier reliance on response rather than on place cues parallels the earlier emergence of interoceptive over exeroceptive behavioral control during early infancy (e.g., Haroutunian & Campbell, 1979).

Most recently, investigators have sought to increase the amount of geographic information available in order to assess what factors contribute to place cue use (Keating et al., 1986), while others have attempted to isolate the types of response changes (spatial position, direction of facing) that may disrupt localization (Acredolo & Evans, 1980; McKenzie et al., 1984). These studies have shown that when only the direction of orientation changes, infants aged 8 months can localize on the basis of place cues (McKenzie et al., 1984). Their use of place cues is influenced both by the spatial relation between the landmark and the object or event to be located and by the frame of the room within which testing occurs (Keating et al., 1986).

Another approach has been to enrich the experience of the infant, thereby increasing the infant's exposure to changing spatial orientation in relation to its changing body position (Bertenthal et al., 1984). Using a task originally developed by Acredolo and Evans (1980), Bertenthal et al., (1984) placed infants in a movable high chair in a relatively small room with a plain window on one wall and a distinctive window on the other. Three groups of 8-month-olds—an independent locomotor group, a prelocomotor group, and a prelocomotor group with 4–10 weeks of walker experience—were trained to orient toward the distinctive window when a buzzer sounded. Three sec later an experimenter appeared in the window and talked briefly to the infant. After reaching criterion, infants were rotated 180 deg and were given five extinction test trials. During test trials, the independent locomotor group and the prelocomotor group with walker experience used place cues almost exclusively, whereas the prelocomotor group used place cues only half of the time.

Bertenthal et al., (1984) report a similar pattern of cue use by an orthopedically handicapped infant before and after self-produced locomotor experience. Initially, when the infant could neither creep nor crawl, he exploited place cues—usually in combination with response cues—on less than half of the trials. At 8.5 months, his orthopedic harness was removed for 4 hr per day, allowing an opportunity for self-produced locomotion. Subsequently, his use of place cues dramatically increased, reaching 80 percent and 100 percent by 9 and 10 months, respectively.

The work of Bertenthal and colleagues underscores the adaptive significance of place cues for infants who are increasingly likely to distance themselves from the caregiver. In fact, 9-month-olds readily use the mother as a stationary landmark (Presson & Ihrig, 1982). These acquire significance at approximately the same time that *social referencing* appears (Campos & Stenberg, 1981; Feinman, 1985), suggesting a functional link between these as two types of distal cues that guide behavior. Apparently the use of more distal cues is achieved not through the exclusion of response cues but as a result of *expanding* the variety of cues that can contribute to the solution of spatial localization problems (Cornell & Heth, 1979). The use of distal contextual cues, however, does not suddenly emerge in the second half of the first year of life; infants as young as 3 months reliably exploit distal contextual cues in ambiguous situations, such as when proximal cues are insufficiently remembered (Butler, 1986; Hayne & Rovee-Collier, 1985).

Categorization

In a variable environment, stimuli rarely occur in the same way twice. Although stimuli may be discriminably different from one another, many share common physical or functional properties. When responding is systematically organized on the basis of these common properties, infants are said to be responding categorically. There is considerable controversy about the nature of the representation, if any, that underlies categorical responding. We have argued (Rovee-Collier & Hayne, in press) that categorization can be understood in terms of a selective retrieval process and is described by the same principles that describe retrieval processes in general. By this account, the selective attentional bias that has been demonstrated in visual attention studies involving habituation or paired comparison procedures is the precursor for retrieval, which is automatically initiated when features of a contemporaneous cue that match stored features of a previous event are noticed. A similar memory model of categorization that emphasizes the contribution of contextual cues and retrieval has recently been proposed by Medin and Reynolds (1985).

Using the mobile conjugate reinforcement paradigm, Hayne et al., (in press) trained 3-month-olds to respond to a novel stimulus based on its membership in an artificial category (A or 2). Performance indicative of categorization was demonstrated 24 hr after the conclusion of training on a transfer test during an extinction phase. Performance during the transfer test was, in turn, predictive of the selective efficacy of a novel stimulus as a retrieval cue in a reactivation procedure administered 2 weeks after the conclusion of training when forgetting was complete. At that time, only a novel member of the original training category was effective in reinstating performance 24 hr later during the 14-day transfer test (also during an extinction phase) with yet another novel member of the training category; a novel stimulus from another category was no more effective than no reminder at all for subjects who were otherwise identically trained and tested. The predictive relation between performance on a 24-hr transfer test with a novel member of the same or a different category and the effectiveness of a novel member of the same or a different category in alleviating forgetting were confirmed in a subsequent experiment. This demonstration is particularly striking because novel stimuli are otherwise ineffective reminders for infants of this age (Enright, 1981); in fact, changes in a five-component mobile of more than a single object are discriminated 24 hr after training and also are ineffective reminders 2 weeks later (Rovee-Collier, Griesler, et al., 1985; Rovee-Collier, Patterson, et al., 1985), indicating the high degree of specificity required for a reactivation procedure to be effective. The general relation between the efficacy of a retrieval cue in a 24-hr transfer test and its efficacy as a reminder in a reactivation procedure administered after forgetting is complete ("Hayne's law") has not been disconfirmed in numerous subsequent studies (Butler, 1986; Greco et al., 1986; Rovee-Collier, Patterson, et al., 1985) over a 2-year period in our laboratory and provides strong support for a retrieval analysis of categorization.

In the categorization training procedure, infants had been trained with a succession of three mobiles, one per day for 9 training min each. The components of each mobile displayed a two-dimensional cue (form, color), one of which defined the category (form) and remained constant from session to session and one of which changed from session to session. Infants who received an invariant training series prior to the 24-hr transfer test with the same novel stimuli as those who received the variable training series (and also with a stimulus differing only in form) showed no transfer. This indicated that 3-month-olds *discriminated changes in a single dimension* and that transfer depended upon prior exposure to *multiple examples* of the category. Recent evidence indicates that varied training may not be a prerequisite for retrieval of category information at 24 months (Greco & Daehler, 1985).

More recently, Greco et al. (1986) have documented the conditions under which a physically dissimilar stimulus that is initially discriminated 24 hr after variable training can be included as a member of a functional category. Only then can it serve as a reminder for the original members of that category 2 weeks later.

The robustness of these findings for infants so young and with a category that has no obvious biological significance suggests that categorization is a basic means by which previously successful responses are transferred to novel situations that share critical common features with situations for which they have acquired responses. This is the first evidence in infants of the retention advantage that categorization presumably affords. It is likely that the extensive spacing between successively encountered examples of the category was a major factor underlying the infants' performance; from a memory perspective, this would have permitted each stimulus to be encoded as a different memory episode while simultaneously serving as a retrieval cue for the previous episode. Not only would this offer more addresses for the retrieval process to search, but also, over the course of successive retrievals, category-specific cues may have become hierarchically organized with respect to their accessibility to retrieval. (Rovee-Collier, in press).

Concept Learning

Whereas the term *category* referred to specific shared features of discriminably different stimuli, the term *concept* is used here to refer to rule-based responding to discriminably different events. The rule derives from the *relational* rather than the absolute properties of stimuli (e.g., an oddity concept, matching concept, same–different concept, etc.). Fagen (1977), for example, found that 10-month-olds used a "win–stay, lose–shift" strategy in the solution of object discrimination learning sets.

The decision that events are the same or are different is thought to be one of the most fundamental and primitive of cognitive processes. Of these, the decision that events are "different" is usually slower, even though it can be made at any point that a difference has been detected. Recently, Fagen and colleagues (1984) provided evidence that 3-month-olds acquire a same–different concept on the basis of the *serial order* in which they encounter discriminably different, novel events. Infants responded during transfer tests on the basis of the relation of the test stimulus to the prior stimulus series rather than on the basis of absolute information contained in the physical stimulus per se. As in the preceding studies (Greco et al., 1986; Hayne et al., in press), 3-month-olds were trained in the mobile conjugate reinforcement paradigm for 3 days with either the same or a different mobile (this time displaying storybook, zoo, or circus figures) in each session. During the 24-hr transfer test with yet another novel mobile, the variable training group exhibited complete transfer whereas the constant training group exhibited none. Of interest, however, was the performance of a third group that had received variable training but whose 24-hr transfer test was with the training stimulus of session 1. Infants in this group exhibited poor transfer to the familiar mobile, treating it as if it were "different," in spite of the fact that their variable training counterparts displayed complete transfer to a completely novel mobile. Had the infants forgotten the details of the session 1 mobile, previously encountered 72 hr earlier, they would simply have treated it as "just another novel mobile" and transferred responding to it. That they did not indicates that they still remembered the specific detail information of the mobile; that is, it selectively influenced their responding. What was "different" about the physically same stimulus was that it was "out of order"; that is, it violated the established scheme of "a different mobile each day," just as a completely novel mobile violated the scheme of "the same mobile each day," established for infants whose training mobile did not change.

To test this hypothesis, groups of infants were trained for only 2 days with either the same mobile each day (A-A) or a different one on successive days (A-B); on day 3, half of the infants in each group received a continuation of the training series (A-A-*A* or A-B-*C*), and half received a reversal (A-A-*B* or A-B-*A*, respectively). This problem is an analog of a *successive oddity problem* in that a minimum of three samples is necessary in order to determine "odd" or "different." Here, infants were asked to indicate whether the final stimulus did or did not belong on the basis of the previous stimulus series. Infants who received a violation of their training sequence in the 24-hr transfer test showed no generalization, irrespective of the specific stimulus with which they were tested; infants who received a continuation of the training sequence displayed complete transfer, irrespective of the specific test stimulus. In each instance, whether the physical characteristics of the test mobile were novel or familiar did not predict responding, nor did the frequency of encounter of previous events; only the *relation* of the characteristics to the succession of previously encountered mobiles was relevant.

These data demonstrate that infants respond to events as same and different on the basis of relations other than those specifically contained in the physical stimulus per se. The readiness with which they respond on the basis of minimal necessary information supports our conclusion that the formation of same–different concepts is a fundamental cognitive ability. These data further imply that the memories of 3-month-olds may be time bound, that is, encoded with reference to a particular time. Together with evidence that memories of 3-month-olds are also encoded with reference to a particular place (Butler, 1986; Hayne & Rovee-Collier, 1985), these findings challenge the popular contention that long-term memory requires a functional hippocampus, hence does not develop prior to 9 months of age (cf. Moscovitch, 1984). From an adaptive perspective, these findings indicate that infants, as a result of their accumulated prior experiences, not only learn how to behave to particular events but learn rules for behaving to novel events that bear absolute or relational similarities to those previously encountered. Moreover, they seem to learn *where* and *when* to expect *what* (either a particular event or variations of it) to occur.

Barrier Problems

Detour problems pose another challenge to classic learning theory in that subjects can reach a goal by performing responses for which they have not specifically been reinforced when access to the goal is blocked. Very young infants may solve barrier problems by crying or otherwise behaving in such a way that someone intervenes in their behalf; older infants can solve these problems directly.

A promising approach to the study of this problem was reported by Henderson and Dias (1985), who observed infants aged 2–12 months engaging in their normal daily activities in their own homes over a 5-month period. Narrative records were coded for ongoing activity, the type of blocking condition (physical, social, or cognitive) and the infant's response to it, the effectiveness of the response in removing the barrier, and how the response influenced the infant's subsequent behavior. In this natural setting, infants encountered approximately one block every 3 min. Most of the barriers were social and physical, and infants tended to respond in kind. Infants solved the majority of the problems themselves, by removing the block. It is interesting that they were most successful in the presence of a parent, even when the parent did not intervene.

These data confirm that problem solving is a major component of the infant's normal daily behavior (cf. Rovee-Collier, 1983). The frequency with which infants encounter problems and solve them in complex natural settings raises serious questions regarding the inability of researchers to document this competence in the laboratory. It is likely that this has resulted from our historical commitment to the refinement paradigm, which has stripped the typical experimental setting of the multiple sources of contextual information as well as of the response opportunities that infants normally exploit in the course of solving these types of problems. When more cues have been provided in experimental settings, one discovers that even young infants are quite able to exploit them (Butler, 1986).

Summary

Complex learning and concept formation are usually viewed as late-developing capacities that emerge during the last quarter of the first year of life. However, artificial categories with no obvious biological "hardwiring" as well as some concepts (e.g., same–different) can be acquired within the first 3 postnatal months. The ease with which this learning is achieved suggests that it is an important facet of early adaptive behavior. Infants increasingly exploit information in the physical setting to locate objects or events displaced in space, and this is strongly linked to their self-produced locomotor experience; infants much younger, who historically would have been carried by an adult, tend to base their behavior on proximal cues but resort to distal contextual cues to "disambiguate" the "instructions" in the test context. Finally, recent data on barrier problems suggest that we have grossly underestimated the incidence and diversity of problems that infants encounter *and solve* in natural settings. This, in turn, has led many to misjudge the structure of the younger infant's niche. Humans have evolved as efficient problem solvers, and infants have not escaped this contribution of their phylogeny. Future research in this area should explore how infants efficiently exploit the multiple sources of information available in a variable environment to solve these various problems, what information they use, the strategies they exercise given what information, and what factors determine when (or whether) they give up.

Conditioning Analyses of Infant Long-Term Memory

In most studies of memory involving learning procedures, steps are taken to ensure that the subject can perform the task it will subsequently be asked to remember. Therefore, greater attention is focused on the retrieval and expression of that memory than on its initial encoding, although it is clear not only that the conditions of original training influence what is learned and how well it is remembered but also that these conditions have different effects on memory processing by infants of different ages (Enright et al., 1983; Vander Linde et al., 1985). These findings notwithstanding, because retrieval is prerequisite in order for a memory to be expressed, a first line of attack on the problem of infant memory has been to analyze retention deficits in terms of retrieval deficits. This has led, in turn, to an emphasis on factors that *impair retrieval,* such as the contextual changes between training and retention testing (Butler, 1986; Rovee-Collier & Fagen, 1981; Rovee-Collier, Butler, et al., 1985; Rovee-Collier, Griesler, et al., 1985) and on procedures that *facilitate retrieval,* such as prior cuing or reactivation procedures (Fagen & Rovee, 1983; Rovee-Collier et al., 1980; for reviews, see Rovee-Collier & Fagen, 1981; Rovee-Collier & Hayne, in press).

Even very young infants have shown strong evidence of remembering what they have learned from one occasion to the next, whether the learning has involved *simple instrumental contingencies* (Davis & Rovee-Collier, 1983; Enright, 1981; Enright et al., 1983; Fagen & Ohr, 1984; Fagen & Rovee-Collier, 1983; Gekoski et al., 1984; Mast et al., 1980; Panneton & DeCasper, 1982; Rovee-Collier et al., 1981; Rovee-Collier & Sullivan, 1980; Rovee-Collier et al., 1980; Sullivan, 1982; Vander Linde, 1982; Vander Linde et al., 1985; Watson, 1984; Werner & Siqueland, 1978), *instrumental discrimination learning* (Fagen et al., 1981), *Pavlovian contingencies* (Gekoski et al., 1983; Jones, 1930; Little, 1973; Little et al., 1984), *complex learning* involving contextual cues (Butler, 1986; Hayne & Rovee-Collier, 1985; Rovee-Collier, Butler, et al., 1985; Rovee-Collier, Griesler, et al., 1985), or *concept learning* (Fagen, 1977; Fagen et al., 1984; Greco et al., 1986).

In their studies of fetal exposure learning, DeCasper and Fifer (DeCasper & Spence, 1986; Fifer, 1980) tested infants 34–96 hr after birth, indicating that they were capable not only of remembering for at least several days the events to which they had been exposed prenatally but also of discriminating them from other, similar events. Panneton and DeCasper (1982) found that newborns 55 hr old could remember for 6–10 hr the reinforcement schedule on which an auditory reinforcer had been delivered; Papousek (1977) found that newborns remembered the effects of prior training from 1 day to the next; Ungerer, Zelazo, and Brody (1978) found that infants 14–28 days of age could remember speech sounds for up to 2 days; and Little and colleagues (1984) found that 20- and 30-day-olds could remember the relation between a CS tone and a US air puff for at least 10 days. Infants 8–12 weeks of age, given the appropriate training conditions, remember for periods of up to 14 days without the benefit of a reminder; with a reminder, the retention intervals they can tolerate at least double. Eight-week-olds (Early et al., 1985; Vander Linde, 1982; Vander Linde et al., 1985) and premature infants (Gekoski et al., 1984) tend to forget more rapidly than older and age-matched infants, respectively, who are trained on the same task with the same parameters. By 3 months of age, not only do infants learn the proximal and distal details of their context, but for periods of days and even weeks thereafter, those contextual cues can selectively influence retrieval (Butler, 1986; Fagen, 1984; Fagen et al., 1981; Fagen et al., 1984; Fagen, Ohr, & Fleckenstein, 1985; Fagen, Ohr, Fleckenstein, et al., 1985; Gekoski & Fagen, 1984; Griesler et al., 1985; Hayne & Rovee-Collier, 1985; Mast et al., 1981; Rovee-Collier, Griesler, et al., 1985; Rovee-Collier, Patterson, et al., 1985; Rovee-

Collier & Sullivan, 1980). However, distal contextual details appear to be forgotten more slowly than proximal contextual details and control behavior after intervals when memories of proximal cues become "fuzzy" (Butler, 1986).

Short-Term and Long-Term Memory Processes

It has been proposed that a sensory or short-term memory (STM) process is necessary to account for the initial association of two events (e.g., the CS and US, the response and reinforcer, or the S^+ and reinforcer) that are separated by a relatively short period in a learning paradigm, whereas a long-term memory (LTM) process is necessary to describe how the subject remembers the now-associated events from trial to trial and/or from session to session. These distinctions correspond to Revusky's (1971) distinction between *associative memory* and *retentive memory* and to Watson's (1984) distinction between *memory in learning* and *memory of learning*.

In general, data from studies of STM in nonhuman primates (D'Amato, Salmon, & Colombo, 1985) and human infants (Brody, 1981) and children (Timmons, Lapinski, & Worobey, 1986) indicate that STM is on the order of seconds or minutes and is relatively invariant over ages, species, tasks, and measures. As in the primate research, the delays that human infants tolerate in STM tasks correspond closely to the delays they tolerate between the CS and US in classical conditioning procedures (Cantor et al., 1983; Little et al., 1984), between the response and the reinforcer in operant conditioning procedures (Millar & Watson, 1979; Watson, 1984), between the final habituation or paired comparison trial and a posttest (Cohen & Gelber, 1975; Olson, 1976; Werner & Perlmutter, 1979; Zelazo et al., 1986), between the prestimulus and a reflex elicitor (Anthony & Graham, 1983; Balaban et al., 1985), and between successive stimuli in a short-term habituation paradigm (Whitlow, 1975). This suggests that these various phenomena may be mediated by a single STM mechanism.

Reactivation of Infant Memory

The conditions that determine whether a memory that has become inactive (i.e., has been forgotten) will be restored to an active status, or *reactivated* (Fagen, Ohr, Fleckenstin, et al., 1985; Fagen & Rovee-Collier, 1983; Rovee-Collier et al., 1980; Rovee-Collier et al., 1981; Rovee-Collier, Patterson, et al., 1985; Sullivan, 1982), will not be elaborated. Reactivation procedures have indicated that many forgotten memories remain available even though they have temporarily become inaccessible to the retrieval process. Under these conditions, there is a continuing possibility that they could influence or guide subsequent behavior after lengthy developmental periods. Whether previously encoded memories are recoded during the retrieval process, thereby becoming inaccessible in their original form, is a problem for future research.

We have seen that contextual information (Butler, 1986; Hayne & Rovee-Collier, 1985; Rovee-Collier, Butler, et al., 1985; Rovee-Collier, Griesler, et al., 1985) as well as the specificity of the reminder (Enright, 1981; Fagen et al., 1981; Fagen, Ohr, & Fleckenstein, 1985; Greco et al., 1986; Hayne et al., in press; Rovee-Collier, Patterson, et al., 1985) influences whether a memory is reactivated or not (Hayne & Rovee-Collier, 1985; Rovee-Collier, Butler, et al., 1985), as do the extent and nature of an infant's prior experience with varied exemplars (Greco et al., 1986; Hayne, 1985) and the timing of the retention test in relation to when the reactivation cue was encountered (Fagen & Rovee-Collier, 1983; Rovee-Collier et al., 1980; Rovee-Collier et al., 1981). Once a memory has been reactivated, however, it slowly becomes accessible (at least in 3-month-olds) and remains so for a relatively lengthy period (Enright, 1981; Fagen & Rovee-Collier, 1983; Rovee-Collier et al., 1981). However, different memory attributes appear to be forgotten (Rovee-Collier & Sullivan, 1980) and retrieved (cf. Rovee-Collier & Hayne, in press) at different rates. Although the details of a particular memory are initially forgotten before the more general aspects of an event, they are the last to be remembered following a reactivation procedure. Because memories are the infant's behavioral predictions, the factors that influence the conditions under which they are selectively forgotten, reactivated, and altered will be critical for understanding how the infant's past experiences influence solutions to current problems.

Summary

Estimates of infant retention based on conditioning procedures contrast sharply with those based on measures of visual attention from habituation or paired comparison procedures. Whereas the latter measures have typically been calibrated in seconds or minutes, conditioning procedures have yielded evidence of robust retention after hours, days, and even weeks in extremely young infants. The magnitude of this discrepancy is the clue that the different kinds of procedures reflect very different memory processes (STM and LTM processes, respectively). The confusion that this discrepancy has generated has been perpetuated by a failure to consider the function of memory. It is not the mere existence of a memory that is important but the fact that it can be retrieved and used to facilitate adaptive, efficient behavior. It is, in essence, the prediction that guides future behavior.

With few exceptions (Olson & Sherman, 1983), most recent reviews of infant memory either have made no reference to findings of long-term memory obtained via learning procedures or have dismissed them as being of little value to the understanding of human memory (Olson & Strauss, 1984; Schacter & Moscovitch, 1984; Strauss & Carter, 1984; see also Moscovitch, 1984). The underlying premise has been that conditioning tasks developed with animals can provide little information about cognitive processes presumed to be unique to humans. Ironically, these discussions of infant memorial abilities have been almost exclusively based on indirect measures of visual short-term memory obtained from the infant's response to novelty—in reality, an analog of the classic matching-to-(non) sample paradigm developed for adult pigeons and nonhuman primates!

A complete understanding of the role of early experience and of developmental continuities and discontinuities will be possible only when we understand both STM and LTM processes and how they interact. Without knowledge of the changing types of cues that infants are likely to notice at different points in ontogeny, for example, it is difficult to appreciate whether the functional context of later retention testing is the same or different (Spear, 1984; Vander Linde et al., 1985). Thus the findings from visual recognition studies of STM memory provide the grist for analyses of LTM. From this perspective, our understanding of the infant's ability to exploit information in a variable environment will require extending selective attention research to more complex settings.

CONCLUSIONS

The success of any learning paradigm with infants reflects the extent to which that paradigm presents the essence of the problems that have been posed to mammalian young throughout phylogeny. In the last 25 years, we have learned a great deal about the stimuli to which infants respond, their short-term memory, their motor and perceptual development, their physiology, their social and emotional development, and their learning in relatively simple environments. Yet we have little understanding of the infant's behavior in a complex environment that contains a variety of sources of *predictive information*. Humans have evolved in a variable environment, yet our typical experimental environments have been relatively barren. The context may provide information that facilitates performance in natural settings, yet we have traditionally considered such information to be a source of extraneous variation that must be eliminated either experimentally or statistically. In this judgment, we may have been wrong. The few studies that are available on responding in a complex environment indicate that infants are active problem solvers. There is evidence that some of their behavior is rule based as early as 3 months, and additional evidence that rules guide their solutions to more complex problems at 6–10 months.

Our traditional descriptions of infant development, both Piagetian and those based on classic learning theory, are not adequate to account for recent findings. New theoretical formulations will be necessary. These will have to focus on different questions and consider different units of analysis. The determination of how the infant negotiates passage through a variable environment is a formidable task but not an impossible one. The task requires abandoning the refinement procedure— but not our technology or experimental control—and adopting an approach that recognizes the variability in the environment as well as the economic structure of the infant's niche. In addition to asking how the infant acquires the predictive relations in a variable environment, we must begin to consider how the infant uses the predictive information he or she has acquired to choose among items and activities when there are various costs and benefits associated with these choices. Moreover, we must begin to consider how the infant's current choices and experiences influence future behavior and the mechanism by which this occurs. These questions have only begun to be asked, much less answered. This should take at least another 25 years.

REFERENCES

Acredolo, L. P., & Evans, D. (1980). Developmental changes in the effect of landmarks on infant spatial behavior. *Developmental Psychology, 16,* 312–318.

Amsel, A. (1979). The ontogeny of appetitive learning and persistence in the rat. In N. E. Spear & B. A. Campbell (Eds.), *Ontogeny of learning and memory.* Hillsdale, NJ: Erlbaum.

Anthony, B. J., & Graham, F. K. (1983). Evidence for sensory-selective set in young infants. *Science, 230,* 742–743.

Ashton, R. (1973). The state variable in neonatal research. *Merrill-Palmer Quarterly, 19,* 3–20.

Aslin, R. N., Pisoni, D. B., & Jusczyk, P. W. (1983). Auditory development and speech perception in infancy. In M. M. Haith & J. J. Campos (Eds.), *Handbook of child psychology: Vol. 2. Infancy and developmental psychobiology* (4th ed.). New York: Wiley.

Aslin, R. N., Pisoni, D. B., Hennessy, B., & Perey, A. J. (1981). Discrimination of voice onset time by human infants: New findings and implications for the effects of early experience. *Child Development, 52,* 1135–1145.

Aylward, G. P. (1981). The developmental course of behavioral state in preterm infants: A descriptive study. *Child Development, 52,* 564–568.

Aylward, G. P., Lazzara, A., & Meyer, J. (1978). Behavioral and neurological characteristics of a hydraencephalic infant. *Developmental Medicine & Child Neurology, 24,* 211–217.

Balaban, M. T., Anthony, B. J., & Graham, F. K. (1985). Modality-repetition and attentional effects on reflex blinking in infants and adults. *Infant Behavior & Development, 8,* 443–457.

Bartoshuk, A. K. (1962). Human neonatal cardiac acceleration to sound: Habituation and dishabituation. *Perceptual & Motor Skills, 15,* 15–27.

Berg, W. K., & Berg, K. M. (1979). Psychophysiological development in infancy: State, sensory function and attention. In J. D. Osofsky (Ed.), *Handbook of infant development.* New York: Wiley.

Berg, W. K., Clarkson, M. G., Eitzman, D. V., & Setzer, E. S. (1981, April). *Habituation in infants lacking cortex.* Paper presented at the meeting of the Society for Research in Child Development, Boston.

Berntson, G. G., & Boysen, S. T. (1984). Cardiac startle and orienting responses in the great apes. *Behavioral Neuroscience, 98,* 914–918.

Berntson, C. G., Tuber, D. S., Ronca, A. E., & Bachman, D. S. (1983). The decerebrate human: Associative learning. *Experimental Neurology, 81,* 77–88.

Bertenthal, B. I., Campos, J. J., & Barrett, K. C. (1984). Self-produced locomotion. In R. N. Emde & R. J. Harmon (Eds.), *Continuities and discontinuities in development.* Hillsdale, NJ: Erlbaum.

Blass, E. M., Ganchrow, J. R., & Steiner, J. E. (1984). Classical conditioning in newborn humans 2–48 hours of age. *Infant Behavior & Development, 7,* 223–235.

Bloom, K. (1984). Distinguishing between social reinforcement and social elicitation. *Journal of Experimental Child Psychology, 38,* 93–102.

Bornstein, M. H. (1981). Psychological studies of color perception in human infants: Habituation, discrimination and categorization, recognition, and conceptualization. In L. P. Lipsitt (Ed.), *Advances in infancy research* (Vol. 1). Norwood, NJ: Ablex.

Bornstein, M. H. (1985). Habituation of attention as a measure of visual information processing in human infants: Summary, systematization, and synthesis. In G. Gottlieb & N. A. Krasnegor (Eds.), *Measurement of audition and vision during the first year of postnatal life: A methodological overview.* Norwood, NJ: Ablex.

Bornstein, M. H., & Benasich, A. A. (1986). Infant habituation: Assessments of individual differences and short-term reliability at five months. *Child Development, 57,* 87–99.

Bornstein, M. H., & Sigman, M. D. (1986). Continuity in mental development from infancy. *Child Development*, Vol. 57.

Bouton, M. E., & Bolles, R. C. (1985). Contexts, event-memories, and extinction. In P. D. Balsam & A. Tomie (Eds.), *Context and learning.* Hillsdale, NJ: Erlbaum.

Brackbill, Y. (1970). The cumulative effects of continuous stimulation on arousal level in infants. *Child Development, 42,* 17–26.

Brackbill, Y., & Fitzgerald, H. E. (1969). Development of sensory analyzers during infancy. In L. P. Lipsitt & H. W. Reese (Eds.), *Advances in child development and behavior* (Vol. 4). New York: Academic.

Brackbill, Y., & Fitzgerald, H. E. (1972). Stereotype temporal conditioning in infants. *Psychophysiology, 9,* 569–577.

Brackbill, Y., & Koltsova, M. M. (1967). Conditioning and learning. In Y. Brackbill (Ed.), *Infancy and early childhood*. New York: Free Press.

Brackbill, Y., & Thompson, G. G. (Eds.). (1967). *Behavior in infancy and early childhood*. New York: Free Press.

Brassell, W. R., & Kaye, H. (1974). Reinforcement from the sucking environment and subsequent modification of sucking behavior in the human neonate. *Journal of Experimental Child Psychology, 18,* 448–463.

Brinker, R. P. (1981, April). *Patterns of learning by handicapped infants*. Paper presented at the meeting of the Society for Research in Child Development, Boston.

Brinker, R. P., & Lewis, M. (1982a). Contingency intervention in infancy. In J. Anderson & J. Cox (Eds.), *Curriculum materials for high risk and handicapped infants*. Chapel Hill, NC: Technical Assistance Development Systems.

Brinker, R. P., & Lewis, M. (1982b). Discovering the competent handicapped infant: A process approach to assessment and intervention. *Topics in Early Childhood Special Education, 2,* 1–16.

Brinker, R. P., Wilson, S., & Deni, R. (1985, April). *Is a response that is predisposed by an infant's physical position more easily learned?* Paper presented at the meeting of the Society for Research in Child Development, Toronto.

Brody, L. R. (1981). Visual short-term cued recall memory in infancy. *Child Development, 52,* 242–250.

Brody, L. R., Zelazo, P. R., & Chaika, H. (1984). Habituation–dishabituation to speech in the neonate. *Developmental Psychology, 1,* 114–119.

Brown, J. (1972). Instrumental control of the sucking response in human newborns. *Journal of Experimental Child Psychology, 14,* 66–80.

Buss, A. (1973). *Psychology: Man in perspective*. New York: Wiley.

Butterfield, E. C. (1968a). *An extended version of modification of neonates' sucking with auditory feedback*. Unpublished manuscript, University of Kansas Medical Center, Children's Rehabilitation Unit.

Butterfield, E. C. (1968b). *Modification of neonates' sucking with auditory feedback*. Unpublished manuscript, University of Kansas Medical Center, Children's Rehabilitation Unit.

Butler, J. (1986). *A contextual hierarchy in infant memory*. Unpublished master's thesis, Rutgers University, New Brunswick, NJ.

Bystroletova, G. N. (1954). Obrazovanie u novorozhdennykh detei uslovnogo refleksa na vremia v sviazi a sutochnym ritnom kormleniia. *Zhurnal Vysshei Nervnoi Deiatel'nosti, 4,* 601–609. (Cited in Brackbill & Koltsova, 1967.)

Caldwell, D. F., & Werboff, J. (1962). Classical conditioning in newborn rats. *Science, 136,* 1118–1119.

Campos, J. J., & Stenberg, C. R. (1981). Perception, appraisal and emotion: The onset of social referencing. In M. E. Lamb & L. R. Sherrod (Eds.), *Infant social cognition*. Hillsdale, NJ: Erlbaum.

Cantor, D. S., Fischel, J. E., & Kaye, H. (1983). Neonatal conditionability: A new paradigm for exploring the use of interoceptive cues. *Infant Behavior & Development, 6,* 403–413.

Caron, A. J., Caron, R. F., & Glass, P. (1983). Responsiveness to relational information as a measure of cognitive functioning in nonsuspect infants. In T. Field & A. Sostek (Eds.), *Infants born at risk: Physiological, perceptual, and cognitive processes*. New York: Grune & Stratton.

Caron, A. J., Caron, R. F., & Myers, R. S. (1982). Abstraction of invariant face expressions in infancy. *Child Development, 50,* 1008–1015.

Caron, R. F., & Caron, A. J. (1978). Effects of ecologically relevant manipulations on infant discrimination learning. *Infant Behavior & Development, 1,* 291–397.

Caron, R. F., Caron, A. J., & Myers, R. S. (1985). Do infants see emotional expressions in static faces? *Child Development, 56,* 1552–1560.

Cernoch, J. M., & Porter, R. H. (1985). Recognition of maternal axillary odors by infants. *Child Development, 56,* 1593–1598.

Cicchetti, D., & Aber, J. L. (1986). Early precursors of later depression: An organizational perspective. In L. P. Lipsitt & C. Rovee-Collier (Eds.), *Advances in infancy research* (Vol. 4). Norwood, NJ: Ablex.

Church, R. M. (1966, September). *The role of fear in punishment.* Symposium paper presented at the meeting of the Eastern Psychological Association, New York.

Clifton, R. K. (1974). Heart rate conditioning in the newborn infant. *Journal of Experimental Child Psychology, 18,* 9–21.

Clifton, R. K., & Nelson, M. N. (1976). Developmental study of habituation in infants: The importance of paradigm, response system, and state. In T. J. Tighe & R. N. Leaton (Eds.), *Habituation: Perspectives from child development, animal behavior, and neurophysiology.* Hillsdale, NJ.: Erlbaum.

Clifton, R. K., Siqueland, E. R., & Lipsitt, L. P. (1972b). Conditioned headturning in human newborns as a function of conditioned response requirements and states of wakefulness. *Journal of Experimental Child Psychology, 13,* 43–57.

Cohen, L. B. (1972). Attention-getting and attention-holding processes of infant visual preferences. *Child Development, 43,* 869–879.

Cohen, L. B. (1973). A two-process model of infant visual attention. *Merrill-Palmer Quarterly, 19,* 157–180.

Cohen, L. B. (1976). Habituation of infant visual attention. In T. J. Tighe & R. N. Leaton (Eds.), *Habituation: Perspectives from child development, animal behavior, and neurophysiology.* Hillsdale, NJ: Erlbaum.

Cohen, L. B. (1981). Examination of habituation as a measure of aberrant development. In S. C. Friedman & M. Sigman (Eds.), *Preterm birth and psychological development.* New York: Academic.

Cohen, L. B., DeLoache, J. S., & Strauss, M. S. (1979). Infant visual perception. In J. D. Osofsky (Ed.), *Handbook of infant development.* New York: Wiley.

Cohen, L. B., & Gelber, E. R. (1975). Infant visual memory. In L. B. Cohen & P. Salapatek (Eds.), *Infant perception: From sensation to cognition* (Vol. 1). New York: Academic.

Columbo, J., & Horowitz, F. D. (1985). A parametric study of the infant control procedure. *Infant Behavior & Development, 8,* 117–121.

Cornell, E. H. (1974). Infants' discrimination of photographs of faces following redundant presentations. *Journal of Experimental Child Psychology, 18,* 98–106.

Cornell, E. H., & Heth, C. D. (1979). Response versus place learning by human infants. *Journal of Experimental Psychology: Human Learning & Memory, 5,* 188–196.

Creighton, D. E. (1984). Sex differences in the visual habituation of 4-, 6-, and 8-month-old infants. *Infant Behavior & Development, 7,* 237–249.

D'Amato, M. R., Salmon, D. P., & Colombo, M. (1985). Extent and limits of the matching concept in monkeys (*Cebus apella*). *Journal of Experimental Psychology: Animal Behavior Processes, 11,* 35–51.

Dannemiller, J. L. (1984). Infant habituation criteria: I. A Monte-Carlo study of the 50% decrement criterion. *Infant Behavior & Development, 7,* 147–166.

Dannemiller, J. L., & Banks, M. S. (1983). Can selective adaptation account for early infant habituation? *Merrill-Palmer Quarterly, 29,* 151–158.

Dashkovskaia, V. S. (1953). Pervye uslovnye reaktsii u novorozhdennykh detei v norme i pri nekotorykh patologicheskikh sostoiniiakh. *Zhurnal Vysshei Nervnoi Deiatelnosti, 3,* 247–259. (Cited in Brackbill & Koltsova, 1967.)

Davis, J. M., & Rovee-Collier, C. K. (1983). Alleviated forgetting of a learned contingency in 8-week-old infants. *Developmental Psychology, 19,* 353–365.

DeCasper, A. J., & Carstens, A. A. (1981). Contingencies of stimulation: Effects on learning and emotion in neonates. *Infant Behavior & Development, 4,* 19–35.

DeCasper, A. J., & Fifer, W. P. (1980). Of human bonding: Newborns prefer their mothers' voices. *Science, 208,* 1174–1176.

DeCasper, A. J., & Prescott, P. A. (1984). Human newborns' perception of male voices: Preference, discrimination, and reinforcing value. *Developmental Psychobiology, 17,* 481–491.

DeCasper, A. J., & Sigafoos, A. D. (1983). The intrauterine heartbeat: A potent reinforcer for newborns. *Infant Behavior & Development, 6,* 19–25.

DeCasper, A. J., & Spence, M. J. (1986). Prenatal maternal speech influences newborns' perception of speech sounds. *Infant Behavior & Development, 9,* 133–150.

Dolgin, K. G., & Azmitia, M. (1985). The development of the ability to interpret emotional signals—What is and is not known. In G. Zivin (Ed.), *The development of expressive behavior: Biology–environment interactions.* Orlando, FL: Academic.

Dunst, C. J., & Lingerfelt, B. (1985). Maternal ratings of temperament and operant learning in two- to three-month-old infants. *Child Development, 56,* 555–563.

Early, L. A., Griesler, P. C., & Rovee-Collier, C. (1985, April). *Ontogenetic changes in retention in early infancy.* Paper presented at the meeting of the Society for Research in Child Development, Toronto.

Eimas, P., & Miller, J. L. (1980). Contextual effects in infant speech perception. *Science, 209,* 1140–1141.

Elkonin, D. B. (1957). The physiology of higher nervous activity and child psychology. In B. Simon (Ed.), *Psychology in the Soviet Union.* London: Routledge & Kegan Paul.

Enright, M. K. (1981). *A comparison of newly acquired and reactivated memories of three-month-old infants.* Unpublished doctoral dissertation, Rutgers University, New Brunswick, NJ.

Enright, M. K., Rovee-Collier, C. K., Fagen, J. W., & Caniglia, K. (1983). The effects of distributed training on retention of operant conditioning in human infants. *Journal of Experimental Child Psychology, 36,* 209–225.

Essock, E. A., & Siqueland, E. R. (1981). Discrimination of orientation by human infants. *Perception, 10,* 245–253.

Fagen, J. W. (1977). Interproblem learning in ten-month-old infants. *Child Development, 48,* 786–796.

Fagen, J. W. (1980). Stimulus preference, reinforcer effectiveness, and relational responding in infants. *Child Development, 51,* 372–378.

Fagen, J. W. (1984). Infants' long-term memory for stimulus color. *Developmental Psychology, 20,* 435–440.

Fagen, J. W., Morrongiello, B. A., Rovee-Collier, C., & Gekoski, M. J. (1984). Expectancies and memory retrieval in three-month-old infants. *Child Development, 55,* 936–943.

Fagen, J. W., & Ohr, P. S. (1985). Temperament and crying in response to the violation of a learned expectancy in infancy. *Infant Behavior & Development, 8,* 157–166.

Fagen, J. W., Ohr, P. S., & Fleckenstein, L. K. (1985, April). *A recency effect in the reactivation of infant memory.* Paper presented at the meeting of the Society for Research in Child Development, Toronto.

Fagen, J. W., Ohr, P. S., Fleckenstein, L. K., & Ribner, D. R. (1985). The effect of crying on long-term memory in infancy. *Child Development, 56,* 1584–1592.

Fagen, J. W., & Rovee-Collier, C. K. (1982). A conditioning analysis of infant memory: How do we know they know what we know they knew? In N. E. Spear & R. L. Isaacson (Eds.), *The expression of knowledge.* New York: Plenum.

Fagen, J. W., & Rovee-Collier, C. K. (1983). Memory retrieval: A time-locked process in infancy. *Science, 222,* 1349–1351.

Fagen, J. W., Yengo, L. A., Rovee-Collier, C. K., & Enright, M. K. (1981). Reactivation of a visual discrimination in early infancy. *Developmental Psychology, 17,* 266–274.

Fantz, R. L. (1964). Visual experience in infants: Decreased attention to familiar patterns relative to novel ones. *Science, 46,* 668–670.

Feinman, S. (1985). Emotional expression, social referencing, and preparedness for learning in infancy—Mother knows best, but sometimes I know better. In G. Zivin (Ed.), *The development of expressive behavior: Biology–environment interactions.* Orlando, FL: Academic.

Field, T. M., Dempsey, J. R., Hatch, J., Ting, G., & Clifton, R. K. (1979). Cardiac and behavioral responses to repeated tactile and auditory stimulation by preterm and term neonates. *Developmental Psychology, 15,* 406–416.

Field, T. M., Woodson, R., Greenberg, R., & Cohen, D. (1982). Discrimination and imitation of facial expressions by neonates. *Science, 218,* 179–181.

Fifer, W. P. (1980). *Early attachment: Maternal voice preference in one- and three-day-old infants.* Unpublished doctoral dissertation, University of North Carolina at Greensboro.

Fifer, W. P., & Moon, C. (1984, October). *Discrimination and preference for voices in newborns.* Paper presented at the meeting of the International Society for Developmental Psychobiology, Baltimore.

Fitzgerald, H. E., & Brackbill, Y. (1976). Classical conditioning in infancy: Development and constraints. *Psychological Bulletin, 83,* 353–376.

Fitzgerald, H. E., & Porges, S. W. (1971). A decade of infant conditioning and learning research. *Merrill-Palmer Quarterly, 17,* 79–117.

Fitzgerald, H. E., Strommen, E. A., & McKinney, J. P. (1977). *Developmental psychology: The infant and young child.* Homewood, IL: Dorsey.

Flaherty, C. F. (1985). *Animal learning and cognition.* New York: Knopf.

Flavell, J. (1963). *The developmental psychology of Jean Piaget.* Princeton, NJ: Van Nostrand.

Gaioni, S. J., & Evans, C. S. (1984, October). *The role of frequency modulation and temporal patterning in mallard duckling recognition of distress calls.* Paper presented at the meeting of the International Society for Developmental Psychobiology, Baltimore.

Gamzu, E., & Williams, D. R. (1971). Classical conditioning of a complex skeletal response. *Science, 171,* 923–925.

Gekoski, M. J. (1977). *Visual attention and operant conditioning in infancy: A second look.* Unpublished doctoral dissertation, Rutgers University, New Brunswick, NJ.

Gekoski, M. J., & Fagen, J. W. (1984). Noncontingent stimulation, stimulus familiarization, and subsequent learning in young infants. *Child Development, 55,* 2226–2233.

Gekoski, M. J., Fagen, J. W., & Pearlman, M. A. (1984). Early learning and memory in the preterm infant. *Infant Behavior & Development, 7,* 267–276.

Gekoski, M. J., Rovee-Collier, C. K., & Carulli-Rabinowitz, V. (1983). A longitudinal analysis of inhibition of infant distress: The origins of social expectations? *Infant Behavior & Development, 6,* 339–351.

Gormezano, I., & Kehoe, J. E. (1978). Classical conditioning: Some methodological conceptual issues. In W. K. Estes (Ed.), *Handbook of learning and cognitive processes: Vol. 2. Conditioning and behavior therapy.* Hillsdale, NJ: Erlbaum.

Graham, F. K. (1973). Habituation and dishabituation of responses innervated by the autonomic nervous system. In H. V. S. Peeke & M. J. Herz (Eds.), *Habituation I.* New York: Academic.

Graham, F. K. (1979). Distinguishing among orienting, defense, and startle reflexes. In H. D. Kimmel, E. H. van Olst, & J. F. Orlebeke (Eds.), *The orienting reflex in humans.* Hillsdale, NJ: Erlbaum.

Graham, F. K., Leavitt, L., Strock, B., & Brown, H. (1978). Precocious cardiac orienting in a human anencephalic infant. *Science, 199,* 322–324.

Greco, C. (1985). *Infant categorization of basic-level objects: The roles of parts and overall contour.* Unpublished doctoral dissertation, University of Massachusetts, Amherst.

Greco, C., & Daehler, M. W. (1985). Immediate and long-term retention of basic-level categories in 24-month-olds. *Infant Behavior & Development, 8,* 459–474.

Greco, C., Hayne, H., & Rovee-Collier, C. (1986, April). *Concept acquisition in three-month-olds.* Paper presented at the meeting of the Eastern Psychological Association, New York.

Griesler, P. C., Earley, L. A., & Rovee-Collier, C. (1985, March). Detection *of retrieval cues by 2-month-old infants: The effect of altered contexts on retention.* Paper presented at the meeting of the Eastern Psychological Association, Boston.

Groves, P. M., & Thompson, R. F. (1970). Habituation: A dual-process theory. *Psychological Review, 77,* 419–450.

Gunnar, M. R. (1980). Control, warning signals, and distress in infancy. *Developmental Psychology, 16,* 281–289.

Gunnar, M. R., Leighton, K., & Peleaux, R. (1984). Effects of temporal predictability on the reactions of 1-year-olds to potentially frightening toys. *Developmental Psychology, 20,* 449–458.

Hainline, L. (1978). Developmental changes in visual scanning of faces and nonface patterns by infants. *Journal of Experimental Child Psychology, 25,* 90–115.

Harlow, H. F. (1949). The formation of learning sets. *Psychological Review, 56,* 51–65.

Haroutunian, V., & Campbell, B. A. (1979). Emergence of interoceptive and exteroceptive control of behavior in rats. *Science, 205,* 927–929.

Hayes, L. A., Ewy, R. D., & Watson, J. S. (1982). Attention as a predictor of learning in infants. *Journal of Experimental Child Psychology, 34,* 38–45.

Hayne, H., & Rovee-Collier, C. (1985, April). *Contextual determinants of reactivated memories in infants.* Paper presented at the meeting of the Society for Research in Child Development, Toronto.

Hayne, H., Rovee-Collier, C., & Perris, E. E. (in press). Categorization and memory retrieval by 3-month-old infants. *Child Development.*

Henderson, B. B., & Dias, L. (1985, April). *An exploratory study of infant problem solving in natural environments.* Paper presented at the meeting of the Society for Research in Child Development, Toronto.

Hernandez-Peon, R., & Scherrer, H. (1955). Habituation to acoustic stimuli in cochlear nucleus. *Federation Proceedings, 14,* 71.

Heth, C. D., & Cornell, E. H. (in press). A comparative description of representation and processing during search. In H. M. Wellman (Ed.), *The development of search ability.* Hillsdale, NJ: Erlbaum.

Hill, W. H., Rovee-Collier, C., Collier, G., & Wasserloos, L. (1986). Time budgets in growing chicks. *Physiology & Behavior, 37,* 353–360.

Hoffman, H. S., Cohen, M. E., & DeVido, C. J. (1985). A comparison of eyelid conditioning in adults and infants. *Infant Behavior & Development, 8,* 247–254.

Hoffman, H. S., Cohen, M. E., & English, L. M. (1985b). Reflex modification by acoustic signals in newborn infants and in adults. *Journal of Experimental Child Psychology, 39,* 562–579.

Horowitz, F. D. (1968). Infant learning and development: Retrospect and prospect. *Merrill-Palmer Quarterly, 14,* 101–120.

Horowitz, F. D., Paden, L., Bhana, K., & Self, P. (1972). An infant-control procedure for studying infant visual fixations. *Developmental Psychology, 7,* 90.

Hudson, R., & Distel, H. (1982). The pattern of behaviour of rabbit pups in the nest. *Behaviour, 79,* 255–271.

Hull, C. L. (1943). *Principles of behavior.* New York: Appleton-Century-Crofts.

Hull, C. L. (1952). *A behavior system.* New Haven: Yale University Press.

Hulsebus, R. C. (1973). Operant conditioning of infant behavior: A review. In H. W. Reese (Ed.), *Advances in child development and behavior* (Vol. 8). New York: Academic.

Ingram, E., & Fitzgerald, H. E. (1974). Individual differences in infant orienting and autonomic conditioning. *Developmental Psychobiology, 7,* 359–367.

Jeffrey, W. E. (1968). The orienting reflex and attention in cognitive development. *Psychological Review, 75,* 323–334.

Jeffrey, W. E. (1976). Habituation as a mechanism for perceptual development. In T. J. Tighe & R. N. Leaton (Eds.), *Habituation: Perspectives from child development, animal behavior, and neurophysiology.* Hillsdale, NJ: Erlbaum.

Jeffrey, W. E., & Cohen, L. B. (1971). Habituation in the human infant. In H. W. Reese (Ed.), *Advances in child development and behavior* (Vol. 6). New York: Academic.

Johanson, I. B., & Teicher, M. H. (1980). Classical conditioning of an odor preference in 3-day-old rats. *Behavioral & Neural Biology, 29,* 132–136.

Jones, H. E. (1930). The retention of conditioned emotional reactions in infancy. *Journal of Genetic Psychology, 37,* 485–498.

Jusczyk, P. W. (1985). The high-amplitude sucking technique as a methodological tool in speech perception research. In G. Gottlieb & N. A. Krasnegor (Eds.), *Measurement of audition and vision during the first year of postnatal life: A methodological overview.* Norwood, NJ: Ablex.

Kagan, J. (1984). *The nature of the child.* New York: Basic.

Kamin, L. J. (1969). Predictability, surprise, attention, and conditioning. In B. A. Campbell & R. M. Church (Eds.), *Punishment and aversive behavior.* New York: Appleton-Century-Crofts.

Kandel, E. R. (1979). Cellular insights into behavior and learning. *The Harvey Lectures, Series 73.* New York: Academic.

Kasatkin, N. I. (1972). First conditioned reflexes and the beginning of the learning process in the human infant. In G. Newton & A. H. Riesen (Eds.), *Advances in psychobiology* (Vol. 1). New York: Wiley.

Keane, T., & Swartz, K. B. (1981, April). *Visual habituation to sad and happy facial expressions in three- and six-month-old infants.* Paper presented at the meeting of the Society for Research in Child Development, Boston.

Keating, M. B., McKenzie, B. E., & Day, R. H. (1986). Spatial localization in infancy: Position constancy in a square and circular room with and without a landmark. *Child Development, 57,* 115–124.

Kellman, P. J., Spelke, E. S., & Short, K. R. (1986). Infant perception of object unity from translatory motion in depth and vertical translation. *Child Development, 57,* 72–86.

Kimble, G. (Ed.). (1961). *Hilgard and Marquis' conditioning and learning.* New York: Appleton-Century-Crofts.

Kimmel, H. D. (1973). Habituation, habituability, and conditioning. In H. V. S. Peeke & M. J. Herz (Eds.), *Habituation I.* New York: Academic.

Kisilevsky, B. S., & Muir, D. W. (1984). Neonatal habituation and dishabituation to tactile stimulation during sleep. *Developmental Psychology, 20,* 367–373.

Koch, S. (Ed.). (1955). *Psychology: A study of a science* (Vol. 2). New York: McGraw-Hill.

Koltsova, M. M. (1949). On the rise and development of the second signal system in the child. *Researches of the Laboratory of I. P. Pavlov, 4,* 49–102.

Konner, M. (1977). Evolution of human behavior development. In P. H. Leiderman, R. S. Tulkin, & A. Rosenfeld (Eds.), *Culture and infancy: Variations in human experience.* New York: Academic.

Korner, A. F. (1972). State as variable, as obstacle, and as mediator of stimulation in infant research. *Merrill-Palmer Quarterly, 18,* 77–94.

Krachkovskaia, M. V. (1959). Conditioned leukocytosis in newborn infants. *Pavlov Journal of Higher Nervous Activity, 9,* 193–199.

Krafchuk, E. E., Tronick, E. Z., & Clifton, R. K. (1983). Behavioral and cardiac responses to sound in preterm infants varying in risk status: A hypothesis of their paradoxical reactivity. In T. Field & A. Sostek (Eds.), *Infants born at risk: Physiological, perceptual, and cognitive processes.* New York: Grune & Stratton.

Krasnogorskii, N. I. (1967). The formation of conditioned reflexes in the young child. Translated in Y. Brackbill & G. G. Thompson (Eds.), *Behavior in infancy and early childhood.* New York: Free Press. (Original work published 1907)

Landry, S. H., Leslie, N. A., Fletcher, J. M., & Francis, D. J. (1985). Visual attention skills of premature infants with and without intraventricular hemorrhage. *Infant Behavior & Development, 8,* 309–321.

Lasky, R. E., & Spiro, D. (1980). The processing of tachistoscopically presented visual stimuli by five-month-old infants. *Child Development, 51,* 1292–1294.

Levitt, M. J. (1980). Contingent feedback, familiarization, and infant affect: How a stranger becomes a friend. *Developmental Psychology, 16,* 425–432.

Lewis, M., & Brooks-Gunn, J. (1981). Visual attention at three months as a predictor of cognitive functioning at two years of age. *Intelligence, 3,* 131–140.

Lewis, M., Sullivan, M. W., & Brooks-Gunn, J. (1985). Emotional behavior during the learning of a contingency in early infancy. *British Journal of Developmental Psychology: Special Infancy Issue, 3,* 307–316.

Lipsitt, L. P. (1963). Learning in the first year of life. In L. P. Lipsitt & C. C. Spiker (Eds.), *Advances in child development and behavior* (Vol. 1). New York: Academic.

Lipsitt, L. P. (1967). Learning in the human infant. In H. W. Stevenson, E. H. Hess, & H. L. Rheingold (Eds.), *Early behavior: Comparative and developmental approaches.* New York: Wiley.

Lipsitt, L. P. (1969). Learning capacities of the human infant. In R. J. Robinson (Ed.), *Brain and early behavior.* New York: Academic.

Lipsitt, L. P. (1971). Infant learning: The blooming, buzzing confusion revisited. In M. E. Meyer (Ed.), *Second western symposium on learning: Early learning.* Bellingham, WA: Western Washington State College.

Lipsitt, L. P., & Ambrose, J. A. (1967). *A preliminary report of temporal conditioning to three types of neonatal stimulation*. Paper presented at the meeting of the Society for Research in Child Development, New York.

Little, A. H. (1970). *Eyelid conditioning in the human infant as a function of the interstimulus interval*. Unpublished master's thesis, Brown University, Providence, RI.

Little, A. H. (1973). *A comparative study of trace and delay conditioning in the human infant*. Unpublished doctoral dissertation, Brown University, Providence, RI.

Little, A. H., Lipsitt, L. P., & Rovee-Collier, C. (1984). Classical conditioning and retention of the infant's eyelid response: Effects of age and interstimulus interval. *Journal of Experimental Child Psychology, 37,* 512–524.

Lorenz, K. (1965). *Evolution and modification of behavior*. Chicago: University of Chicago Press.

Marinesco, G., & Kreindler, A. (1933). Des reflexes conditionnels: L'organization des reflexes conditionnels chez l'enfant. *Journal de Psychologie, 30,* 855–886.

Marquis, D. P. (1941). Can conditioned responses be established in the newborn infant? *Journal of Genetic Psychology, 39,* 479–492.

Mast, V. K., Fagen, J. W., Rovee-Collier, C. K., & Sullivan, M. W. (1980). Immediate and long-term memory for reinforcement context: The development of learned expectancies in early infancy. *Child Development, 51,* 196–202.

Mateer, F. (1918). *Child behavior: A critical and experimental study of young children by the method of conditioned reflexes*. Boston: Gorham.

McCormick, D. A., & Thompson, R. F. (1984). Cerebellum: Essential involvement in the classically conditioned eyelid response. *Science, 223,* 296–299.

McDonough, S. C., & Cohen, L. B. (1982). Attention and memory in cerebral palsied infants. *Infant Behavior & Development, 5,* 347–353.

McKenzie, B., Day, R. H., & Ihsen, E. (1984). Localization of events in space. Young infants are not always egocentric. *British Journal of Developmental Psychology, 2,* 1–9.

Medin, D. C., & Reynolds, T. J. (1985). Cue–context interactions in discrimination, categorization, and memory. In P. D. Balsam & A. Tomie (Eds.), *Context and learning*. Hillsdale, NJ: Erlbaum.

Mehler, J., Bertoncini, J., Barriere, M., & Jassik-Gerschenfeld, D. (1978). Infant recognition of mother's voice. *Perception, 7,* 491–497.

Meltzoff, A. N. (1985). The roots of social and cognitive development: Models of man's original nature. In T. M. Field & N. Fox (Eds.), *Social perception in infants*. Norwood, NJ: Ablex.

Millar, W. S. (1976). Operant acquisition of social behaviors in infancy: Basic problems and constraints. In H. W. Reese (Ed.), *Advances in child development and behavior* (Vol. 11). New York: Academic.

Millar, W. S., & Watson, J. S. (1979). The effect of delayed feedback on infant learning reexamined. *Child Development, 50,* 747–751.

Miller, D. J. (1972). Visual habituation in the human infant. *Child Development, 43,* 481–493.

Moscovitch, M. (Ed.). (1984). *Advances in the study of communication and affect: Vol. 9. Infant memory*. New York: Plenum.

Nelson, C. A., & Horowitz, F. D. (1983). The perception of facial expression and stimulus motion by two- and five-month-old infants using holographic stimuli. *Child Development, 54,* 868–877.

Noirot, E., & Algeria, J. (1983). Neonate orientation towards human voice differs with type of feeding. *Behavioral Processes, 8,* 65–71.

Norman, R. J., Buchwald, J. S., & Villablanca, J. R. (1977). Classical conditioning with auditory discrimination of the eye blink in decerebrate cats. *Science, 195,* 551–553.

Ohr, P. S., & Fagen, J. W. (1984, April). *The effect of crying on long-term memory in young infants.* Paper presented at the meeting of the Eastern Psychological Association, Baltimore.

Ohr, P. S., Fagen, J. W., Rovee-Collier, C. K., & Vander Linde, E. (1986, April). *Memory retrieval in infancy as a function of amount of training.* Paper presented at the International Conference on Infant Studies, Los Angeles.

Olsho, L. W. (1985). Infant auditory perception: Tonal masking. *Infant Behavior & Development, 8,* 371–384.

Olson, G. M. (1976). An information processing analysis of visual memory and habituation in infants. In T. J. Tighe & R. N. Leaton (Eds.), *Habituation: Perspectives from child development, animal behavior, and neurophysiology.* Hillsdale, NJ: Erlbaum.

Olson, G. M., & Sherman, T. (1983). Attention, learning, and memory in infants. In P. H. Mussen (Ed.), M. M. Haith & J. J. Campos (Vol. Eds.), *Handbook of child psychology: Vol II. Infancy and developmental psychobiology* (4th ed.). New York: Wiley.

Olson, G. M., & Strauss, M. S. (1984). The development of infant memory. In M. Moscovitch (Ed.), *Advances in the study of communication and affect: Vol. 9. Infant memory.* New York: Plenum.

Overmier, J. B., & Seligman, M. E. P. (1967). Effects of inescapable shock upon subsequent escape and avoidance learning. *Journal of Comparative & Physiological Psychology, 63,* 28–33.

Panneton, R., & DeCasper, A. (1982, March). *Newborns are sensitive to temporal and behavioral contingencies.* Paper presented at the meeting of the International Conference on Infant Studies, Austin, TX.

Papousek, H. (1959). A method of studying conditioned food reflexes in young children up to the age of six months. *Pavlov Journal of Higher Nervous Activity, 9,* 136–140.

Papousek, H. (1961). Conditioned head rotation reflexes in infants in the first months of life. *Acta Paediatrica, 50,* 565–576.

Papousek, H. (1967). Conditioning during early postnatal development. In Y. Brackbill & G. G. Thompson (Eds.), *Behavior in infancy and early childhood: A book of readings.* New York: Free Press.

Papousek, H. (1970). The development of higher nervous activity in children in the first half-year of life. In *Cognitive development in children: European research in cognitive development.* Chicago: Society for Research in Child Development and University of Chicago Press.

Papousek, H. (1977). The development of learning ability in infancy. In G. Nissen (Ed.), *Intelligence, learning, and learning disturbances.* New York: Springer-Verlag.

Parry, M. H. (1972). Infants' responses to novelty in familiar and unfamiliar settings. *Child Development, 43,* 233–237.

Pavlov, I. P. (1927). *Conditioned reflexes* (G. V. Anrep, Trans.). London: Oxford University Press.

Pavlov, I. P. (1928). *Lectures on conditioned reflexes* (W. H. Gantt, Trans.). New York: Liveright.

Pearce, J. M., & Hall, G. (1980). A model for Pavlovian learning: Variations in the effectiveness of conditioned but not unconditioned stimuli. *Psychological Review, 87,* 532–552.

Pecheux, M.-G., & Lecuyer, R. (1983). Habituation rate and free exploration tempo in 4-month-old infants. *International Journal of Behavioral Development, 6,* 37–50.

Peiper, A. (1963). *Cerebral function in infancy and childhood.* New York: Consultants Bureau.

Pomerleau-Malcuit, A., & Clifton, R. K. (1973). Neonatal heart rate response to tactile, auditory, and vestibular stimulation in different states. *Child Development, 44,* 485–496.

Poulson, C. L. (1983). Differential reinforcement of other-than-vocalization as a control procedure in the conditioning of infant vocalization rate. *Journal of Experimental Child Psychology, 36,* 471–489.

Poulson, C. L. (1984). Operant theory and methodology in infant vocal conditioning. *Journal of Experimental Child Psychology, 38,* 103–113.

Premack, D. (1965). Reinforcement theory. In D. Levine (Ed.), *Nebraska symposium on motivation.* Lincoln, NB: University of Nebraska Press.

Presson, C. C., & Ihrig, L. H. (1982). Using mother as a spatial landmark: Evidence against egocentric coding in infancy. *Developmental Psychology, 18,* 699–703.

Quinn, P. C., & Eimas, P. D. (1986). Pattern-line effects and units of visual processing in infants. *Infant Behavior & Development, 9,* 57–70.

Razran, G. H. S. (1933). Conditioned responses in children: A behavioral and quantitative review of experimental studies. *Archives of Psychology, 23,* 120.

Razran, G. (1971). *Mind in evolution: An east-west synthesis of learned behaviour and cognition.* Boston: Houghton Mifflin.

Reese, H., & Lipsitt, L. P. (1970). *Experimental child psychology.* New York: Academic.

Rescorla, R. A. (1967). Pavlovian conditioning and its proper control procedures. *Psychological Review, 74,* 71–80.

Rescorla, R. A., & Wagner, A. R. (1972). A theory of Pavlovian conditioning: Variation in the effectiveness of a reinforcement and nonreinforcement. In A. H. Black & W. F. Prokasky (Eds.), *Classical conditioning II: Current research and theory.* New York: Appleton-Century-Crofts.

Revusky, S. (1971). The role of interference in association over a delay. In W. K. Honig & P. H. R. James (Eds.), *Animal memory.* New York: Academic.

Reznick, J. S., & Kagan, J. (1983). Category detection in infancy. In L. P. Lipsitt (Ed.), *Advances in infancy research* (Vol. 2), Norwood, NJ: Ablex.

Richardson, G. A., & McCluskey, K. A. (1983). Subject loss in infancy research: How biasing is it? *Infant Behavior & Development, 6,* 235–239.

Rieser, J. J. (1979). Spatial orientation of six-month-old infants. *Child Development, 50,* 1078–1087.

Rieser, J. J., & Heiman, M. L. (1982). Spatial self-reference systems and shortest-route behavior in toddlers. *Child Development, 53,* 524–533.

Riksen-Walraven, J. M. (1978). Effects of caregiver behavior on habituation rate and self-efficacy in infants. *International Journal of Behavioral Development, 1,* 105–130.

Roitblat, H. L., Bever, T. G., & Terrace, H. S. (Eds.). (1984). *Animal cognition.* Hillsdale, NJ: Erlbaum.

Rose, S. A., Schmidt, K., & Bridger, W. H. (1976). Cardiac and behavioral responsivity to tactile stimulation in premature and full-term infants. *Developmental Psychology, 12,* 311–320.

Rosenblith, J. F., & Sims-Knight, J. E. (1985). *In the beginning: Development in the first two years.* Monterey, CA: Brooks-Cole.

Ross, G. S. (1980). Categorization in 1- to 2-year-olds. *Developmental Psychology, 16,* 391–396.

Rovee-Collier, C. K. (1982, August). *Sensitivity to frequency-of-encounter information in infancy.* Symposium paper presented at the meeting of the American Psychological Association, Washington, D.C.

Rovee-Collier, C. K. (1983). Infants as problem-solvers: A psychobiological perspective. In M. D. Zeiler & P. Harzem (Eds.), *Advances in analysis of behaviour: Vol. 3. Biological factors in learning.* Chichester: Wiley.

Rovee-Collier, C. (1984). The ontogeny learning and memory in human infancy. In R. Kail & N. E. Spear (Eds.), *Comparative perspectives on the development of memory.* Hillsdale, NJ: Erlbaum.

Rovee-Collier, C. (1986). The rise and fall of infant classical conditioning research: Its promise for the study of early development. In L. P. Lipsitt & C. Rovee-Collier (Eds.), *Advances in infancy research* (Vol. 4). Norwood, NJ: Ablex.

Rovee-Collier, C. (in press). *Infant learning and memory.* Norwood, NJ: Ablex.

Rovee-Collier, C., Butler, J., & Hayne, H. (1985, October). *Contextual determinants of retention in 3-month-old infants.* Paper presented at the meeting of the International Society for Developmental Psychobiology, Dallas, TX.

Rovee-Collier, C. K., Enright, M. K., Lucas, D., Fagen, J. W., & Gekoski, M. J. (1981). The forgetting of newly acquired and reactivated memories of 3-month-old infants. *Infant Behavior & Development, 4,* 317–331.

Rovee-Collier, C. K., & Fagen, J. W. (1981). The retrieval of memory in early infancy. In L. P. Lipsitt (Ed.), *Advances in infancy research* (Vol. 1). Norwood, NJ: Ablex.

Rovee-Collier, C. K., & Fagen, J. W. (1984). La memoire des nourrissons. *La Recherche (Paris), 15,* 1096–1104.

Rovee-Collier, C. K., & Gekoski, M. J. (1979). The economics of infancy: A review of conjugate reinforcement. In H. W. Reese & L. P. Lipsitt (Eds.), *Advances in child development and behavior* (Vol. 13). New York: Academic.

Rovee-Collier, C. K., Griesler, P. C., & Earley, L. A. (1985). Contextual determinants of retrieval in three-month-old infants. *Learning & Motivation, 16,* 139–157.

Rovee-Collier, C., & Hayne, H. (in press). Reactivation and infant long-term memory. In H. W. Reese (Ed.), *Advances in child development and behavior* (Vol. 20). New York: Academic.

Rovee-Collier, C. K., & Lipsitt, L. P. (1982). Learning, adaptation, and memory. In P. M. Stratton (Ed.), *Psychobiology of the human newborn.* London: Wiley.

Rovee-Collier, C. K., Patterson, J., & Hayne, H. (1985). Specificity in the reactivation of infant memory. *Developmental Psychobiology, 18,* 559–574.

Rovee-Collier, C. K., & Sullivan, M. W. (1980). Organization of infant memory. *Journal of Experimental Psychology: Human Learning & Memory, 6,* 798–807.

Rovee-Collier, C. K., Sullivan, M. W., Enright, M., Lucas, D., & Fagen, J. W. (1980). Reactivation of infant memory. *Science, 208,* 1159–1161.

Ruff, H. A. (1975). The function of shifting fixations in the visual perception of infant. *Child Development, 46,* 857–865.

Ruff, H. A. (1984). An ecological approach to infant memory. In M. Moscovitch (Ed.), *Advances in the study of communication and affect: Vol. 9. Infant memory.* New York: Plenum.

Ruff, H. A. (1986). Components of attention during infants' manipulative exploration. *Child Development, 57,* 105–114.

Sameroff, A. J. (1971). Can conditioned responses be established in the newborn infant: 1971? *Developmental Psychology, 5,* 1–12.

Sameroff, A. J. (1972). Learning and adaptation in infancy: A comparison of models. In

H. W. Reese (Ed.), *Advances in child development and behavior* (Vol. 7). New York: Academic.

Sameroff, A. J., & Cavanagh, P. J. (1979). Learning in infancy: A developmental perspective. In J. D. Osofsky (Ed.), *Handbook of infant development*. New York: Wiley.

Schacter, D. L., & Moscovitch, M. (1984). Infants, amnesics, and dissociable memory systems. In M. Moscovitch (Ed.), *Advances in the study of communication and affect: Vol. 9. Infant memory*. New York: Plenum.

Seligman, M. E. P. (1975). *Helplessness: On depression, development, and death*. San Francisco: Freeman.

Sharpless, S. K., & Jasper, H. (1956). Habituation of the arousal reaction. *Brain, 79,* 655–680.

Sheppard, W. C. (1969). Operant control of infant vocal and motor behavior. *Journal of Experimental Child Psychology, 7,* 36–51.

Sherman, T. L. (1985). Categorization skills in infants. *Child Development, 56,* 1561–1573.

Sherman, T., & Olson, G. M. (1982, April). *A cross-sectional study of infant long-term memory*. Paper presented at the meeting of the International Conference on Infant Studies, Austin, TX.

Siqueland, E. R. (1968a). Reinforcement patterns and extinction in human newborns. *Journal of Experimental Child Psychology, 6,* 431–432.

Siqueland, E. R. (1968b, March). *Visual reinforcement and exploratory behavior in infants*. Paper presented at the meeting of the Society for Research in Child Development, Worcester, MA.

Siqueland, E. R. (1969). *Further developments in infant learning*. Paper presented at the meeting of the Nineteenth International Congress of Psychology, London.

Siqueland, E. R. (1970). Basic learning processes. I. Classical conditioning. In H. W. Reese & L. P. Lipsitt (Eds.), *Experimental child psychology*. New York: Academic.

Skinner, B. F. (1938). *The behavior of organisms*. New York: Appleton-Century-Crofts.

Skinner, B. F. (1953). *Science and human behavior*. New York: Macmillan.

Slater, A., Morison, V., & Rose, D. (1982). Visual memory at birth. *British Journal of Psychology, 73,* 519–525.

Slater, A., Morison, V., & Rose, D. (1984). Habituation in the newborn. *Infant Behavior & Development, 7,* 183–200.

Smith, G. J., & Spear, N. E. (1980). Facilitation of conditioning is two-day-old rats by training in the presence of conspecifics. *Behavioral & Neural Biology, 28,* 491–495.

Smotherman, W. P. (1982). Odor averison learning by the rat fetus. *Physiology & Behavior, 29,* 769–771.

Sokolov, E. N. (1963). *Perception and the conditioned reflex*. New York: Macmillan.

Sophian, C. (1980). Habituation is not enough: Novelty preferences, search, and memory in infancy. *Merrill-Palmer Quarterly, 26,* 239–257.

Spear, N. E. (1984). Ecologically determined dispositions control the ontogeny of learning and memory. In R. Kail & N. E. Spear (Eds.), *Comparative perspectives on the development of memory*. Hillsdale, NJ: Erlbaum.

Stamps, L. E. (1977). Temporal conditioning of heart rate responses in newborn infants. *Developmental Psychology, 13,* 624–629.

Stamps, L. E., & Porges, S. W. (1975). Heart rate conditioning in newborn infants: Relationships among conditionability, heart rate variability, and sex. *Developmental Psychology, 11,* 424–431.

Stickrod, G., Kimble, D. P., & Smotherman, W. P. (1982). In utero taste/odor aversion conditioning in the rat. *Physiology & Behavior, 28,* 5–7.

Strauss, M. S. (1979). Abstraction of prototypical information by adults and 10-month-old infants. *Journal of Experimental Psychology: Human Learning & Memory, 5,* 618–632.

Strauss, M. S. (1981, April). *Infant memory of prototypical information.* Paper presented at the meeting of the Society for Research in Child Development, Boston.

Strauss, M. S., & Carter, P. (1984). Infant memory: Limitations and future directions. In R. Kail & N. E. Spear (Eds.), *Comparative perspectives on the development of memory.* Hillsdale, NJ: Erlbaum.

Strauss, M. S., & Curtis, L. E. (1981). Infant perception of numerosity. *Child Development, 52,* 1146–1152.

Streri, A., & Pecheux, M.-G. (1986). Tactual habituation and discrimination of form in infancy: A comparison with vision. *Child Development, 57,* 100–104.

Sullivan, M. W. (1982). Reactivation: Priming forgotten memories in human infants. *Child Development, 53,* 516–523.

Swartz, K. B. (1982, March). *Comparative studies of social categorization in primate infants.* Paper presented at the meeting of the International Conference on Infant Studies, Austin, TX.

Thelen, E., & Fisher, D. M. (1983). From spontaneous to instrumental behavior: Kinematic analysis of movement changes during very early learning. *Child Development, 54,* 129–140.

Thoman, E. G., Korner, A. F., & Beason-Williams, L. (1977). Modification of responsiveness to maternal vocalization in the neonate. *Child Development, 48,* 563–569.

Thompson, R. F., & Spencer, W. A. (1966). A model phenomenon for the study of neuronal substrates of behavior. *Psychological Review, 73,* 16–43.

Thorndike, E. L. (1911). *Animal intelligence.* New York: MacMillan.

Thorpe, W. H. (1956). *Learning and instinct in animals.* London: Methuen.

Thorpe, W. H. (1963). *Learning and instinct in animals.* Cambridge. MA: Harvard University Press.

Timmons, C. R., Lapinski, K., & Worobey, J. (1986, April). *Delayed matching-to-sample performance by young Homo sapiens.* Paper presented at the meeting of the Eastern Psychological Association, New York.

Tolman, E. C. (1932). *Purposive behavior in animals and men.* New York: Century.

Tolman, E. C. (1948). Cognitive maps in rats and men. *Psychological Review, 55,* 189–208.

Tuber, D. S., Berntson, G. G., Bachman, D. S., & Allen, J. N. (1980). Associative learning in premature hydraencephalic and normal twins. *Science, 210,* 1035–1037.

Turco, T. L., & Stamps, L. E. (1980). Heart rate conditioning in young infants using a visual conditional stimulus. *Journal of Experimental Child Psychology, 29,* 117–125.

Ungerer, J., Brody, L., & Zelazo, P. (1978). Long-term memory for speech in 2- to 4-week-old infants. *Infant Behavior & Development, 1,* 177–186.

Vander Linde, E. (1982). *The effects of training factors on acquisition and retention in early infancy.* Unpublished doctoral dissertation, Rutgers University, New Brunswick, NJ.

Vander Linde, E., Morrongiello, B. A., & Rovee-Collier, C. K. (1985). Determinants of retention in 8-week-old infants. *Developmental Psychology, 21,* 601–613.

Wachs, T. D., & Smitherman, C. H. (1985). Infant temperament and subject loss in a habituation procedure. *Child Development, 56,* 861–867.

Wagner, A. R. (1978). Expectancies and the priming of STM. In S. H. Hulse, H. Fowler, & W. K. Honig (Eds.), *Cognitive processes in animal behavior.* Hillsdale, NJ: Erlbaum.

Wagner, A. R., & Rescorla, R. A. (1972). Inhibition in Pavlovian conditioning: Application of a theory. In R. A. Boakes & M. S. Halliday (Eds.), *Inhibition and learning.* London: Academic.

Watson, J. B., & Rayner, R. (1920). Conditioned emotional reactions. *Journal of Experimental Psychology, 3,* 1–14.

Watson, J. S. (1972). Smiling, cooing and "the game." *Merrill-Palmer Quarterly, 18,* 323–329.

Watson, J. S. (1984). Memory in learning: Analysis of three momentary reactions of infants. In R. Kail & N. E. Spear (Eds.), *Comparative perspectives on the development of memory.* Hillsdale, NJ: Erlbaum.

Weiss, M. U. (1986). *Newborns' response to auditory stimulus discrepancy.* Unpublished doctoral dissertation, Tufts University, Medford, MA.

Welch, M. J. (1974). Infants' visual attention to varying degrees of novelty. *Child Development, 45,* 344–350.

Werner, J. S., & Perlmutter, M. (1979). Development of visual memory in infants. In H. W. Reese & L. P. Lipsitt (Eds.), *Advances in child development and behavior* (Vol. 14). New York: Academic.

Werner, J. S., & Siqueland, E. R. (1978). Visual recognition memory in the preterm infant. *Infant Behavior & Development, 1,* 79–84.

Whitlow, J. W., Jr. (1975). Short-term memory in habituation and dishabituation. *Journal of Experimental Psychology, 104,* 189–206.

Whitlow, J. W., Jr., & Wagner, A. R. (1984). Memory and habituation. In H. V. S. Peeke & L. Petrinovich (Eds.), *Habituation, sensitization, and behavior.* New York: Academic.

Wyers, E. J., Peeke, H. V. S., & Herz, M. J. (1973). Behavioral habituation in invertebrates. In H. V. S. Peeke & M. J. Herz (Eds.), *Habituation I.* New York: Academic.

Younger, B. A. (1985). The segregation of items into categories by 10-month-old infants. *Child Development, 56,* 1574–1583.

Younger, B. A., & Cohen, L. B. (1983). Infant perception of correlations among attributes. *Child Development, 54,* 858–867.

Zeigler, B. L., Strock, B. D., & Graham, F. K. (1979, March). *Facilitatory and inhibitory reflex preconditioning in early infancy.* Paper presented at the meeting of the Society for Research in Child Development, San Francisco.

Zelazo, P. R., Brody, L. R., & Chaika, H. (1984). Neonatal habituation and dishabituation of head turning to rattle sounds. *Infant Behavior & Development, 7,* 311–321.

Zelazo, P. R., Weiss, M. J., Randolph, M., Swain, I. U., & Moore, D. S. (1986). *The effects of delay on dishabituation of localized head-turning in neonates.* Unpublished manuscript, Montreal Children's Hospital, Montreal.

CHAPTER 3

Language and Communication in Infancy

ELIZABETH BATES, BARBARA O'CONNELL, and CECILIA SHORE

For most parents, language acquisition signals the end of infancy. Other milestones come and go—walking, weaning, the great independence signaled by toilet training—but you know your child is no longer an infant when she tells you about her day, reconstructs Little Red Ridinghood almost intact, and talks about needs and feelings that you had to guess about just a few short months before. In fact, the word *infant* is taken from the Latin *in-* + *fants, fans,* participle of *fari,* literally "incapable of speech."

Perhaps for this reason, popular books on infancy typically say very little about the development of language, except for a few lines about the child's first words. But the absence of a significant section on language is more puzzling in scientific volumes on infancy. There is now a huge literature on language development during the first 2 years: evidence for speech perception in the first 6 months, the passage from cooing into successive stages of babbling, aspects of vocal and gestural communication prior to speech, the emergence of first words and reorganizations in single-word speech that continue across the second year, the passage into multiword speech, and (finally) the onset of "grammaticization" around the age of 2. In fact, language development is a window through which we can witness changes in infant ability that begin at birth.

Some infancy researchers may avoid psycholinguistics not because they find the subject matter unconvincing, but because it is such an insular field. The methods and jargon of psycholinguistics are very hard to penetrate—and certainly hard to summarize in a single chapter. Perhaps more important, however, the insularity of this science is often mirrored in a view of language itself as an insular system, a "mental organ" that is autonomous from other aspects of the developing mind (Chomsky, 1980, 1981). For those who embrace this theory, "true" language begins with a sudden burst of grammar around 2 years of age. The various aspects of speech and communication evidenced before that point are not only prelinguistic, they may actually have very little to do with the principles and mechanisms of language itself (e.g., Bickerton, 1984). This emphasis on *domain specificity* and *discontinuity* is usually accompanied by an emphasis on *innateness*. The orderly un-

We gratefully acknowledge the John D. and Catherine T. MacArthur Foundation Research Network on the Transition from Infancy to Early Childhood for funds supporting bibliographic work and manuscript preparation.

folding of language is explained in terms of a maturational timetable that (presumably) reflects the emergence of special neural mechanisms devoted almost exclusively to phonological, semantic, and grammatical processing (Fodor, 1983; Gardner, 1983). The phonological and grammatical aspects of language are considered to be particularly good candidates for this kind of innate, "modular" status. The same investigators are usually more willing to believe that semantics is connected up with the rest of the mind (including both lexical, or single-word, semantics, and relational, or sentence-level, semantics). Gardner puts it like this:

> Syntactic and phonological processes appear to be special, probably specific to human beings, and unfolding with relatively scant need for support from environmental factors. Other aspects of language, however, such as the semantic and pragmatic domains, may well exploit more general human information-processing mechanisms and are less strictly or exclusively tied to a "language organ."
>
> *(Gardner, 1983, p. 81)*

In this chapter, we will take a different view:

> Language development is a process that begins early in infancy, and depends crucially on skills from a variety of domains including perception, cognition, motor development, and socialization. This interactionist view includes not only the emergence of single words and their meanings, but also the more strictly linguistic areas of phonology and grammar.

In our brief overview of early language development, we will focus on major milestones of development in chronological order:

> Prespeech (0–10 months), including speech perception, babbling, and the expression of prelinguistic intentional communication through gesture and sound
> First words (10–14 months), that is, the passage from presymbolic vocal and gestural routines to an understanding of the idea that things have names
> First sentences (18–22 months), including a shift toward *sentential meanings* (from referential use of single words in naming and requests to predicational use of single words to express relationships between individual referents), and an accompanying shift toward *sentential forms* (i.e., from single-word utterances to word combinations)
> Grammaticization (24–30 months), that is, the passage from telegraphic or formulaic word combinations to productive control over aspects of word order and grammatical marking

Within this developmental framework, we will present three kinds of additional information:

> *Continuity between and within levels of development.* To what extent can we predict quantitative and qualitative aspects of language ability from performance at previous stages? Do the separate linguistic domains of phonology, semantics, and grammar develop on separate schedules, or are they tied together within and between stages? We will present evidence from 9 through 30 months suggesting that all the major content domains of language develop together, reflecting com-

mon styles as well as a common rate of development, in a fashion that suggests a complex pattern of mutual support and causation.

Individual differences. We will also consider some of the burgeoning evidence for individual differences in language development at each stage. This focus on variation raises further problems for those who would like to view language as an insular system that unfolds in a universal and orderly way.

Cognitive parallels. Finally, we will consider some aspects of nonlinguistic cognition that parallel each of the major milestones of language development. This cognitive bases approach will permit us to evaluate the claim that language is an independent domain (Bates & Snyder, in press; Johnston, 1986; Rice, 1982). In the early 1970s, there was a veritable explosion of theoretical papers proposing such a cognitive explanation for prelinguistic and linguistic transitions (Bates, 1976; Beilin, 1975; Bever, 1970; Bruner, 1975a; Corrigan, 1978; Cromer, 1974; Edwards, 1973; Hayes, 1970; Ingram, 1978; Karmiloff-Smith, 1979a, 1979b; Macnamara, 1972; Moore, 1973; Nelson, 1974, 1977). Most of these papers put forth some form of Piaget's approach to language–cognition relationships, pointing out parallels and explaining them in terms of stages—which are in turn defined in terms of an underlying and very general logic of action that reorganizes over time. Subsequent research has offered little support for the global stage approach to language–thought relations. However, there is now an ample body of evidence supporting the idea that *specific* linguistic skills are linked to *specific* changes in nonlinguistic cognition, although the nature of that relationship may differ from one point in development to another. We will offer a few highlights from this rather complex literature on the cognitive bases of language.

With this approach, we will be able to give only a brief impression of early language development, a summary of main points at best. But we do hope to convince our readers that language and communication are an integral part of infancy, at every level of development.

PRESPEECH: 0–10 MONTHS

The border between prespeech and speech is traditionally marked by the child's first words, somewhere between 10 and 14 months of age on the average (Bates, 1976; Greenfield & Smith, 1976; McCarthy, 1954; Nelson, 1973). The first evidence for systematic comprehension of language begins only slightly before that, around 9 months (Bates, Bretherton, & Snyder, 1985; Benedict, 1979; Greenfield & Smith, 1976; Oviatt, 1979; Snyder, Bates, & Bretherton, 1981). Nevertheless, there is a great deal of preparation for language in the months before that point, inside and outside of the speech channel. We will divide our consideration of prespeech into three parts: the development of sound (both perception and production), the development of gesture, and concomitant changes in nonlinguistic cognition.

Development of the Sound System

Speech Perception

After 15 years of research on infant speech perception, it now seems fair to conclude that infants in the first few weeks of life can hear most and perhaps all of the phonological contrasts that are used by human languages (for reviews see Aslin &

Pisoni, 1980; Aslin, Pisoni, & Jusczyk, 1983; Jusczyk, 1981, 1985; Kuhl, 1986). Why should this be a surprise? In an era of $5 calculators and $25 tape recorders, it seems at first glance that speech perception should be a relatively easy problem to solve. Speech-perceiving computers are such a common part of our science fiction landscape that most laypersons believe they exist already. They don't. After decades of expensive research by government and industry, it is still not possible for any native speaker to go up to an automatic bank teller, speak his or her number into a microphone, and see that number registered on the machine. The psychoacoustic problems of speech perception are legion, and though progress has been made, we still do not understand the process well enough to simulate it with anything resembling the efficiency of a human listener. Two of the most difficult problems include *linearity* and *invariance* (Chomsky & Miller, 1963; Aslin et al., 1983).

Linearity refers to the assumption that a physical stimulus unfolds in time in a way that corresponds to our phenomenal experience of that stimulus. So, for example, it sounds as though the noises that distinguish a *ka* from a *da* come at the front of the syllable. Unfortunately for engineers and the telephone company, this is not the case. Somewhere between the physical input and our phenomenal experience, there seems to be a process of transformation or reordering, so that bits and pieces of energy that come after the onset of the stimulus are made to sound as though they occurred at the beginning.

Invariance refers to the assumption that an invariant psychological entity (e.g., the *k* sound in both *ka* and *ku*) corresponds to an invariant physical entity, that is, a physical unit that is just as similar across contexts as it seems to be when we hear it. But this assumption is also violated by human speech. The burst of energy that distinguishes a *k* sound before an *a* does not look at all on spectographic analysis like the pattern that distinguishes a *k* before a *u*. But, alas, the *k* part of *ka does* look like the pattern that creates a *d* before a *u*. According to the *motor theory of speech perception,* these chaotic mappings between sound and experience make sense only if the listener knows something about the motor system that produced those sounds, and makes use of that knowledge in perception (Liberman, Cooper, Shankweiler, & Studdert-Kennedy, 1967; Stevens & House, 1972). The apparent psychological unity of various *d* and *k* sounds across contexts comes not from the physical shape of the sounds themselves, but from the fact that they are made through certain positionings of the tongue in the mouth, and the shunting of airwaves through different chambers with the voice turned on or off.

Because these nonlinear and context-dependent phenomena present such problems for a psychoacoustic model of speech, many researchers have come to accept the idea that the fundamentals of speech perception cannot be learned—although, of course, they can be "tuned" to fit a particular language (Abramson & Lisker, 1967, 1973; Lieberman, 1970, 1973). Eimas (1985), among others, has proposed that human beings are born with an innate, species-specific perceptual system that evolved to pick up the peculiar packages of sound that we make to one another. This belief follows not only from the fact that we can hear these sounds *at all,* but from the *way* that we hear them.

One distinctive aspect of speech perception is a phenomenon called *categorical perception.* To illustrate, consider the distinction between sounds like *pa* and *ba*. This consonant contrast is based on a dimension called voice onset time, or VOT, referring to the point at which the vocal cords begin to vibrate before or after we

open our lips. In sounds that we experience as a *b,* voicing begins before or simultaneous with the consonantal burst. In sounds that we experience as *p,* voicing
begins after the burst. It is possible to construct synthetic speech stimuli that vary
continuously along this VOT continuum, for example, from −150 to 0 to +150
msec from voice to burst. Despite this continuous variation, human listeners appear
to have strong perceptual biases about where the border between phonemes *ought
to be,* resulting in a discontinuous change in perception when a particular VOT
border is crossed. For the *pa/ba* contrast, the preferred boundary falls around +20
msec. When two stimuli straddle this border, they sound very different (e.g., a stimulus with a VOT of +10 sounds like a *b* while another with a VOT of +30 sounds
quite clearly like a *p*). But if two stimuli that are just as different *physically* from
one another do *not* straddle the border, people have a very hard time telling them
apart. A stimulus with a VOT of +30 and another with a VOT of +50 both sound
like *p.* Furthermore, human listeners cannot really decide whether these two *p*'s are
different from one another at all, or simply repetitions of the same stimulus. The
same is true for two *ba* stimuli that fall below the border (e.g., −10 and +10).
This kind of categorical perception seems to be quite different from the graded
judgments that we find in other perceptual domains, for example, color or light
intensity, providing still more evidence that speech is somehow "special." The finding that human infants show the same biases in the first few months of life added
fuel to our belief that these special speech processors are innate (Eimas, Siqueland,
Jusczyk, & Vigorito, 1971).

More recently, however, we have been forced to reexamine the case for special
speech detectors. If the apparently innate phenomenon of categorical perception
derives from a special mechanism evolved entirely for speech, then two predictions
should hold:

1. We should not find evidence for categorical perception in any other percep-
    tual domain—at least not in a form that resembles the boundary effects of
    speech.
2. We should not find evidence for categorical perception of speech stimuli in
    nonhuman species.

As reviewed recently by Kuhl (1986), Juscyk (1985), and Aslin and Pisoni (1980),
both of these predictions have been disconfirmed.

First, investigators have been able to elicit categorical perception for pairs of
simple pure-tone stimuli (Pisoni, 1977). Human listeners are able to discriminate
reliably between stimuli only when the differential onset of two tones straddles a
particular set of on–off boundaries. Most important, these are the same boundaries
that underlie categorical perception of VOT contrasts in most languages, and they
are the boundaries that infants innately prefer regardless of their native language.
In other words, the "special" acoustic boundaries that underlie categorical perception of speech are apparently not restricted to speech itself.

As Kuhl has pointed out, this evidence may be less disturbing than it seems at
first. It is possible that these boundaries show up in nonspeech stimuli only because
the pure-tone stimuli "mimic" the special properties of speech that we evolved to
meet. This would be similar to the kind of mimicry that ethologists use in trying to
determine the key stimuli that control many kinds of species-specific behavior. For

example, we know that robins will attack a clump of red feathers left out on the lawn overnight. The red clump is certainly not a robin, but it mimics that aspect of "robinness" that triggers aggressive behavior in another male. The fact that robins will attack the ethologists' decoy does not mean that the male robin has no "special" innate perceptual mechanism for dealing with other members of the species. It simply means that we have figured out enough about that perceptual mechanism to fool it with a specially designed laboratory stimulus.

Suppose, however, that the red feathers are attacked not only by the robin, but by a host of other species that do not bear the male robin any grudge at all. Now we would have to worry about the "special" nature of red feather detectors in our theory of robins. By the same token, suppose we find categorical perception of speech stimuli in animals that make no use at all of speech sounds? As first reported by Kuhl and Miller (1975, 1978), chinchillas apparently do evidence categorical perception for certain stop consonants. Similar findings have now been reported for nonhuman primates, using a variety of different phonemic contrasts (Kuhl & Padden, 1982, 1983; Morse & Snowden, 1975; Waters & Wilson, 1976).

The issue is certainly not settled; a great deal more animal research needs to be done before we can specify all the similarities and differences between the "innate" speech perception mechanisms of infancy and the "innate" auditory biases shown by other species. For example, Kuhl and Meltzoff (1982, 1984) have shown that infants 3–5 months old can "lip-read." Specifically, these infants will look preferentially at a close-up film of a human mouth corresponding to either an "ooo" or an "eee" sound emanating from a central speaker. It is difficult to imagine that nonhuman animals are capable of a similar cross-modal match. On the other hand, it was also difficult to imagine 10 years ago that chinchillas would be capable of categorical perception for stop consonants. (See McGurk (1984) for some arguments suggesting that the integration of acoustic and visual–labial cues actually takes many years to develop in human children.)

It is not only *possible* to build an animal model of speech perception, it is *essential* if we are going to make further sense of a large literature on speech perception in human infants. We rushed too quickly to the conclusion that the speech perception abilities of the human infant are based on innate mechanisms evolved especially for speech. The infant's abilities do indeed seem to involve a great deal of innately specified information processing. But we do not yet have firm evidence that *any* of this innate machinery is speech specific. We assumed that the human auditory system evolved to meet the demands of language; perhaps, instead, language evolved to meet the demands of the mammalian auditory system. This lesson has to be kept in mind when we evaluate other claims about the innate language acquisition device.

To summarize so far, human infants seem to be capable of discriminating most and perhaps all of the major phonemic contrasts used by natural languages. Some investigators have reported that a few phonemic contrasts are acquired relatively late, including fricative contrasts like *th* and *f* (Eilers & Minifie, 1975). But these contrasts are also relatively difficult for adults to hear under noisy conditions. This means that late developments in speech perception may not be late at all; they may simply be harder to demonstrate in a highly distractible infant. To explain the remarkable perceptual abilities of the human infant, we must assume that the ability to perceive speech is innate, at some level. However, because many of the same abilities have now been demonstrated in nonhuman species, it is no longer clear that we have to invoke "special" innate processors devoted entirely to the perception of speech.

There are, however, many aspects of speech perception that do have to change with experience. Paradoxically, some of the major developments involve a *loss* of discrimination. For example, Japanese infants can easily discriminate the *ra/la* contrast; Japanese adults have difficulty making the same discrimination even after hundreds of trials. When does the child lose the ability to hear discriminations that are outside her language? Research by Werker, Gilbert, Humphrey, and Tees (1981) suggests that a major change takes place around 10 months of age—corresponding to the period where we first find systematic evidence for comprehension of meaningful speech. We will return to this point later, in our effort to account for the transition from prespeech to language.

Finally, children will have to learn through experience to take advantage of what are called *coarticulation cues*. Fluent speakers do not pronounce the phonemes of their language like separate building blocks, one at a time. Each time we begin a new syllable, we are already getting our mouths ready for the kind of vowel that must occur within the syllable, and perhaps for the transition that the vowel itself must make to the consonant the follows still further on. Hence the *b* in *boat* is pronounced differently from the *b* in *bee*. Fluent listeners take advantage of such coarticulation phenomena, anticipating the identity of a word or syllable to come just on the basis of slight differences in pronunciation at or before the initial phoneme. However, because the use of coarticulation cues depends on experience with word and syllable structures that vary from one language to another, this aspect of speech perception has to be learned.

At the moment, we know very little about the perception of coarticulation cues in human infants (Aslin et al., 1983). It seems logical, however, that this aspect of perception will track stages in the development of language proper. That is, if children are using early phonetic cues to anticipate the structure of words to come, they must by definition know something about words. We will return to this point shortly, with reference to the emergence of coarticulation phenomena in the child's *production* of speech.

Speech Production

Discoveries in the field of infant speech perception are relatively recent, due to some technical innovations that took place in the 1960s. By contrast, investigators have written about speech production in infancy for literally centuries (Jakobson, 1968/1941; Leopold, 1939-1949; McCarthy, 1931; Pollack, 1878; Taine, 1877; Schultze, 1971/1880; Wundt, 1971/1900). Nevertheless, the real breakthroughs in infant babbling have happened in the last few years, due to painstaking longitudinal research in a handful of laboratories (Ferguson, 1978, 1984; Ingram, 1974, 1976, 1979; Menn, 1983; Stoel-Gammon & Cooper, 1982; Vihman, 1985; Vihman, Ferguson, & Elbert, in press).

In the first 2-3 weeks of life, infant sounds are restricted primarily to crying and a familiar set of "vegetative noises." Laughing and cooing begin at 2-3 months of age, and systematic play with speech sounds is usually not reported until 3 months (when infants also begin to play games of reciprocal imitation or "vocal tennis" with their caretakers (Uzgiris & Hunt, 1975).

At least for some children, we may hear vocal play along a wide pitch and volume range, an up-and-down coloratura performance that can appear as early as 5 months of age. But the systematic production of consonantal sounds is rarely reported before 5–6 months. When consonants do appear, there is reason to believe that the child is aiming at an environmental sound target. It is not the case, as folk wisdom once had it, that infants in the first year systematically try out all the speech sounds of human natural languages, before their language environment has any influence at all (Jakobson, 1968). This was a convenient theory for those who believed in language acquisition through operant reinforcement: If infants produced all possible sounds, then we could easily shape in a natural language by selective reinforcement of the environmentally relevant sounds (Mowrer, 1960). However, it now seems more likely that perception precedes production, and that the first consonant sounds produced by the infant reflect efforts to match environmental input.

This point has been made most clearly by Boysson-Bardies, Sagart, and Durand (1984), who collected samples of babble from infants growing up in French-, Chinese-, and Arabic-speaking households. The tapes were made at several points in development, from 4 through 10 months of age. Trained phoneticians as well as naive listeners were presented with the tapes and asked to classify infants according to their language environment. These results clearly suggest that there is a "drift" in the direction of language-specific sounds at 4–7 months—right before the point at which consonantal forms begin to appear with any regularity.

With the subjective rating method used by Boysson-Bardies et al., we have no idea which phonetic cues are responsible for the adult listener's subjective judgment. Thevenin, Eilers, Kimbrough, and Lavoir (1985) failed to replicate the findings on phonological drift, using shorter segments of infant babbling than the ones adopted by Boysson-Bardies. They suggest that the original findings were based not on consonantal forms in infant babbling, but on intonational differences among the three languages that are evident to the raters only when long segments of sound are being judged. On the other hand, it is also true that longer and more intonationally varied segments of babbling present more opportunities for the raters to hear fledgling consonant structures. So the matter is not settled. The important point seems to be that hearing children move in the direction of their target language by 5 months, producing intonational and/or segmental forms that match their language environment.

Although some signs of drift toward the phonological environment are demonstrable by 5 months, the onset of *canonical babbling* is typically very sudden, occurring at 6–10 months in the normal child. Canonical babbling is the systematic production of consonant–vowel or CV sequences (e.g., "ma" or "dah"). Often, when these CV patterns appear, they are repeated two or more times (e.g., "dadada"). This has led some researchers to refer to the transition between 6–10 months as *reduplicated babbling* (Stark, 1979).

Canonical or reduplicated babbling is easily noticed by most parents (Koopmans-van Deinum & van der Stelt, 1985), who sometimes eagerly mistake these CV sequences for meaningful speech (e.g., taking "dahdah" for "daddy"). Careful study of the contexts in which these sounds first occur suggests that canonical babbling does not really have any symbolic content when it is first produced. Babbling is not language—at least not initially. However, babbling does seem to indicate that children are "tuned in" to language, in a new and very explicit way. Systematic evidence for language comprehension occurs shortly thereafter, and children begin to lose sensitivity to phonemic contrasts that are not used by their native language. From this point on, changes in the organization of babbling will be linked to reorganizations in the comprehension and production of meaningful speech.

Although this takes us forward out of the prespeech era, we think it would be useful to review the next few stages in phonology very briefly—just to give the reader an idea how speech production tracks major developments in language. Most of the evidence on links between language and babbling that we will review here comes from a series of recent reports from the Stanford Child Phonology Project (hereafter CPP). For a more detailed view of phonological development, the reader is referred to these papers, and to a series of review papers by other investigators (Ferguson, 1978, 1984; Ferguson & Farwell, 1975; Ferguson & Macken, 1983; Leonard, Newhoff, & Mesalam, 1980; Macken, 1979; Macken & Ferguson, 1983; Menn, 1983; Vihman, 1985; Vihman & Carpenter, 1984; Vihman et al., in press; Vihman & Miller, in press; Yeni-Komshian, Kavanagh, & Ferguson, 1980a, 1980b).

First, at the point where mothers report a cumulative vocabulary of around 10 words, the children studied by CPP all showed a consistent preference for stop consonants in their babbling. By the time each child's reported vocabulary averaged 30 words, there was a marked increase in the percentage of vocalizations that include one "true" consonant (excluding glottals and glides). Between these two points, variegated or nonreduplicated babbling appears, where mixed consonants and vowel types occur in a single vocalization (e.g., C1V1C2V1 as in [bada] or C1V1C1V2 as in [dadu]). Another way of putting it is that babbling becomes more wordlike during early language development, as though the child's new experience with language is spilling over into sound play. This is clear counterevidence to claims by Jakobson and others that there is a sharp discontinuity between babbling and true speech.

Many investigators have claimed that sentencelike intonation contours also develop during this period, even before the child has a systematic set of contrasts that distinguish one word from another in the adult system (e.g., Dore, 1975; Ferguson & Macken, 1983; Halliday, 1975). This is sometimes called "learning the tune before the words." This issue remains controversial because of methodological difficulties in the collection and analysis of intonational data. Children typically acquire one or perhaps two intonation contours from the adult language during the babbling period, but they may or may not attach distinctive meanings to these contours. In other words, it is not clear that intonational contrasts form a *system* prior to the development of a sentence-level grammar. The most persuasive longitudinal evidence for a systematic contrast between intonation patterns comes from Halliday (1975), who suggests that a simple rise versus fall pattern on a single sound may indicate the contrast between a vocalization for which the child expects a response (rising tone) and a vocalization for which the child does not expect a response (falling tone). This is an area particularly in need of further research, and it may be an important domain of individual differences. For example, based on impressionistic evidence from two case studies, Dore (1975) has proposed two different styles that children may demonstrate during the prespeech period. "Word babies" concentrate on the referential aspects of language, showing early evidence for word comprehension and concentrating on wordlike sounds in their babbling. "Intonation babies" play more with sentencelike intonation contours and seem to be more interested in imitating sound "envelopes" than they are in breaking language down into meaningful components. This proposal bears an interesting relationship to patterns of individual variation that are well documented at later stages of development—as we shall see in more detail later.

Somewhere in the middle of the second year, most children go through a "vocabulary burst," with a move from 50 to over 100 words in a few weeks' time. This is usually slightly before the point where words are combined into novel multiword utterances (Bates et al., 1985). Phonological organization around this time can be characterized in terms of what CPP calls *whole word processes*. There are severe limits on what constitutes a possible word in the child's vocabulary. For example, a particular child may have a rule or bias that excludes any word containing both a velar stop (*k* or *g*) and an alveolar stop (*t* or *d*); hence the child may say [g ∧ k] for the adult word *duck* even though she is able to say *d* in other words (e.g., [da] for *doll)*. In their discussion of phonological "errors" during this period, Leonard and Brown (1984) suggest that children organize their sound system around a basic set of word prototypes. Any new words that enter their vocabularies during this time are deformed to fit one of these basic blueprints for how a word must sound.

At 24–30 months in most normal children, we find another shift in language development, referred to as the grammaticization process. We will describe this process in more detail later in the chapter. For present purposes, the point is that children acquire a more productive and systematic control over grammatical morphemes in just a few weeks' time, with a concomitant increase in the complexity of both syntactic and semantic relations. At this level, phonological organization evolves from whole word processes to the entire set of phonological contrasts that occur in the target language. Like the morphological elements that make up a grammar, phonology can now be described in terms of operations or rules for combining phonemic and allophonic segments. Segment substitution patterns generally apply to all words in the vocabulary, regardless of the overall consonant structure of the word. Syllable deletion rules may still play a role in reducing longer words to a shorter form (e.g., "giraffe" becomes "raffe"). But like the segment substitution rules, they apply regularly. For example, all voiced interdental fricatives (the sound corresponding to *th* in *that*) may be substituted with the single sound *d,* resulting in typical baby forms like [daet] for *that.* This contrasts with the previous stage, when substitution was based on particular word configurations. In other words, phonology has become a *system.*

There is an interesting irony in this developmental progression. For a brief period, word-based knowledge actually seems to *interfere* with the developing sound system. The child is freed from whole word phonology around the same time that he moves from word-based to sentence-based planning in the rest of his language development. This is one more illustration of the integral relationship between developments at the levels of sound, meaning, and form.

Recent evidence (Sereno & Lieberman, 1985) suggests that major changes in phonological development continue into middle childhood. In particular, the child learns to produce the kinds of anticipatory adjustments that we discussed in the section of speech perception, that is, *coarticulation phenomena.* It is not until this point that we can really call the child a fluent speaker of her native language. It is actually quite surprising that coarticulation effects appear so late, since younger children do sound like native speakers of their language—at least to the untrained ear. If Lieberman's new findings hold up to further scrutiny, then we have the first evidence for a major change in phonology to accompany all the known changes of linguistic and cognitive organization that happen at 3–7 years of age. Although it is completely speculative at this point, it is interesting that the latest shift in sound production occurs around the time that children begin to find it difficult to acquire a new language without an accent (see Krashen, Scarella, & Long, 1982). In any case, one conclusion should be clear: Phonological development is not restricted to the prespeech era, and it does not end in infancy. Instead, speech is linked stage by stage to changes in language ability.

Because the study of phonology involves a great deal of technical expertise, and a considerable amount of patience for detail, it is an area that is avoided by many developmental psycholinguists. Many of us assume that the most important developments in phonology take place long before the child tackles the problems of grammatical and lexical organization. And in any case, we assume that the problems of phonology form an isolated and constrained set that are not relevant to the "larger" issues of linguistic structure and content. This is a mistaken view. The sound system goes through reorganizations that are similar and perhaps causally related to developments in meaning and form. And because the "pieces" that make up a phonological system are finite and available to observation, phonology is an excellent domain for investigating abstract principles of structural reorganization in infancy (Macken, in press).

Development of Gesture

Before children begin to use words to refer to objects or classes of objects, three important components of word use first appear in prelinguistic communication, in both the vocal and the gestural modality. These are *intentionality, convention,* and *reference.* These transitions have now been exhaustively described in a series of longitudinal and cross-sectional studies, including several of our own (Atkinson, 1979; Bates, Benigni, Bretherton, Camaioni, & Volterra, 1979; Bates, Bretherton, Shore, & McNew, 1983; Bates, Camaioni, & Volterra, 1975; Bretherton, in press; Bretherton & Bates, 1979; Bretherton, McNew, & Beeghly-Smith, 1981; Bruner, 1975a, 1975b, 1983; Carter, 1978; Clark, 1978; Golinkoff, 1983; Greenfield, 1980; Greenfield & Smith, 1976; Harding & Golinkoff, 1979; Lock, 1978, 1980; Morford & Goldin-Meadow, 1983; Schaeffer, 1977; Sugarman, 1982c, 1983; Sugarman-Bell, 1978). In our brief review of prespeech, we will begin with a consideration of evidence for intentional communication prior to language. Then we will discuss the emergence of prelinguistic reference, through an examination of the pointing gesture. Finally, we will look at the emergence of presymbolic, but nevertheless social, conventions within these communicative frames.

Intentional Communication in Sound and Gesture

The human infant manages to communicate from the first few moments of life by emitting a series of positive and negative signals that have a predictable effect on adult members of our species. However, it is not until around 9 months of age that the same infant offers evidence of an intentional or planned control over her signals. How can we operationalize something as nebulous as intentionality? In their study of the emergence of *proto-imperatives* (i.e., preverbal requests), Bates and colleagues (1975) describe three kinds of changes that take place during episodes in which the child wants to have an object:

Gaze alternation.   If the adult listener and the object goal are not in the same line of vision (e.g., if mother is not holding the desired cookie), a 7-month-old usually looks directly at the cookie and reaches toward it without turning back to the adult—unless he becomes so frustrated that he begins to fuss, in which case he is likely to look to the mother for comfort. Around 9 months this behavior begins to change; the child often looks back and forth from the goal to the potential adult agent—as though he expects the adult to help out in some way.

Repair of failed messages.   If an initial gestural and/or vocal signal fails to move an adult into action, the child will repeat, augment, and/or substitute signals until the goal is reached. An initial reaching gesture may be repeated with an accompanying and rather insistent fuss, and the child may even reach out and nudge the parent. Furthermore, this repeat/repair sequence seems to be contingent not just on obtaining the goal, but on some kind of evidence that the adult is going to comply (e.g., the child may calm down or at least change the nature of his fussing when mother gets up to get him the cookie).

Ritualization of previously instrumental gestures.   Reaching usually begins as a "true" instrumental gesture; similarly, the fussing sound a child makes while reaching for a goal may begin as a genuine effort noise or a sound of distress. Around 9 months, when appeals are directed at adult agents rather than the goal itself, the same instrumental behaviors are transformed into ritualized sounds and movements that have no function at all except as signals. For example, a full reach may be turned into an abbreviated grasping motion or an open-and-shut gesture with the hands. And a full fuss may become a short and insistent "mmmm" sound.

Taken together, these three changes in signaling behavior suggest that the child now understands something about how communication works and intends to use those behaviors to communicate.

In these proto-imperative sequences, the child uses an adult as a means of obtaining a desired object. But children do not communicate solely in the service of external goals; sometimes the goal of an interaction is the interaction itself. Around 9 months, Bates and others (1975) also describe a reorganization in what they call *proto-declaratives,* that is, sequences in which the child uses an object as a means of obtaining adult attention and interest. The earliest form that they describe is the gesture of *showing:* The child is playing with an object and lifts it in the direction of the adult, the adult smiles or responds in some positive way, and the child goes back to playing, or puts the object down. Within 2 or 3 weeks, the showing gesture becomes more and more frequent and insistent, passing gradually into the new proto-declarative gesture of *giving.* When this behavior is at its peak, a visiting adult may find almost every movable object in the living room piled up at her feet—as long as she continues to respond to each gift with some kind of appreciative comment.

These proto-imperative and proto-declarative sequences all appear before the child begins to make systematic use of pointing in communication, around 11 months of age on the average. Interestingly enough, during the prepointing phase from 9 to 11 months, we often find a *noncommunicative* use of pointing, as the child extends an index finger to inspect or examine objects close at hand. So the *form* of pointing is there, even though the *function* seems to be delayed by weeks or even months. This brings us to the second major precursor to language: the development of reference.

Referential Communication in Sound and Gesture

Pointing is the quintessential act of reference, that is, an act by which one human being singles out an object of contemplation and offers it for another human being to consider (Werner & Kaplan, 1963). And because it seems to play such a peculiar and important role in human communication, the pointing gesture has received more attention than any other aspect of gestural communication in infancy (Bates et al., 1975; Bates et al., 1979; Leung & Rheingold, 1981; Murphy, 1978; Murphy & Messer, 1977; Petitto, 1983, 1985).

There is a sense in which the giving and showing gestures of the 9-month-old can be viewed as a primitive kind of reference: By seeking the adult's acknowledgment of an interesting toy or object, the child has become an active partner in establishing a shared object world. So why is communicative pointing delayed by 2 months or more? Bates and colleagues (1979) have argued that the exploratory pointing gestures of the 9-month-old *cannot* be used for communication until the child has worked out the principles of referential communication at a simpler level, with objects close at hand (or indeed quite literally in the hand). In other words, giving and showing are necessary precursors to pointing, external evidence that the child is coming to terms with the "idea" of referential communication (see also Sugarman-Bell, 1978). In defense of this position, Bates et al. cite studies with relatively large samples of children, demonstrating robust correlations between the emergence of communicative pointing and the previous onset of giving, showing, and ritualized request gestures (e.g., an open-and-shut movement of the hands). Because these gestures are so strongly correlated with one another, Bates et al. refer to them as the *gesture complex*. And the role of the gesture complex in the establishment of reference is further underscored by the fact that these communicative routines are highly correlated (in the +.70 range) with the subsequent appearance of naming.

Although all normal children do seem to show a version of the gesture complex, children vary considerably in the extent to which they use objects as a means of interaction with an adult (Goldfield, 1985). As we shall see later, these variations in prelinguistic communication about objects predict different styles in language use during both single- and multiword speech. There is also evidence from children outside the normal range (Snyder, 1975) indicating that the absence of protodeclarative behavior is associated with significant delays in language development.

In stressing the cognitive–referential nature of prelinguistic gesture, Bates et al. are siding with Werner and Kaplan (1963) in an old argument about the origins of pointing. Traditionally, pointing was viewed as a kind of reaching gesture, based on the primitive grasping scheme and aimed at literally obtaining an out-of-reach object. Werner and Kaplan (1963) suggest instead that pointing carries out a *cognitive* function for our species. It begins outside of communication, as the child explores the world and sets up *objects of contemplation*—as though the index finger helped in some way to clarify the distinction between subject and object. In other words, pointing serves not to *take an object in,* but to *push it away.*

Although this is a rather metaphysical notion, it does fit the behavioral evidence. Chimpanzees and other primates seem to produce something that looks superficially like a pointing gesture. However, formal and functional analysis of pointinglike movements in nonhuman primates suggests that their gestures are quite different, more similar to the imperative reaching gestures of the 9-month-old human. The body is inclined toward the goal, and the animal is not satisfied until the goal is reached. In nonimperative pointing, as Lock, Young, and Service (1985) have shown, the child's body tends to assume a more erect position. Most important, the terminating signal for such a pointing sequence is usually adult attention ("Yes, Eric, that's a doggie.") and not the attainment of some objective goal.

Along the same lines, Kinsbourne and Lempert (1978) and Bates and associates (1975) have suggested that pointing has its origins in attention rather than communication, as an extension of the orienting reflex. For example, the infant Carlotta studied by Bates et al. (1975) first pointed to objects out of reach when no one was in the room, while orienting to the sound of a dog barking outside the window (observed by her mother, who was peeking around the corner from another room). Although the evidence is slim, such a cognitive interpretation of pointing could explain the mysterious lack of such gestures in other species (at least in their declarative form), as well as the repeated finding that the appearance of pointing predicts subsequent progress in language development (Bates et al., 1979; Snyder, 1975).

Although parents do not report the appearance of pointing in their children before 9 months of age, Hannan (1982) and Fogel and Hannan (1985) have presented evidence to suggest that a pointinglike gesture occurs in infants as young as 9 weeks of age. Even though the gesture does not seem to have a communicative value, it has several features in common with communicative pointing later on: Points are longer and more frequent with the dominant hand, compared with other manual movements (see also Bates, O'Connell, Vaid, Sledge, & Oakes, 1985), and they occur more often when the child is excited about an object (as opposed to face-to-face interaction with the mother). Hannan argues that our species is biologically prepared to produce the pointing gesture, and to produce that gesture in contexts associated with orienting toward objects. This would certainly constitute a good innate head start toward referential communication. And yet the early pointing gestures do not seem to be under the child's intentional, communicative control. In this regard, early pointing may be similar to the walking reflex that infants show in the first days of life. The walking reflex is involuntary and seems to disappear across the first year of life; the same motor organization reappears, bit by bit, as the child learns (or "relearns") how to walk on his own, making adjustments for gravity and shifts in his own weight. Nature seems to provide a crude motor blueprint for some of our most important motor programs; but we have to conquer the system again later on, fine-tuning the initial program to fit with experience and with a series of new plans and goals.

Several other aspects of pointing have been explored in the developmental literature. For example, pointing is one aspect of communication where production seems to proceed ahead of comprehension. The average 1-year-old has been pointing for at least a month and seems to be able to indicate the general direction of a target with some accuracy. However, research on the comprehension of pointing suggests that 1-year-olds are rather bad at finding a visual target on the basis of an adult pointing gesture (Murphy & Messer, 1978). As Butterworth (1978, cited in Bruner,

1980) and Scaife and Bruner (1975) have shown, infants as young as 6 months of age will follow adult gaze at better than chance levels. And yet before 10 months of age they react to a pointing gesture by simply staring at the adult's finger. By 10 months, pointing can serve to direct the child's attention in some general direction (Butterworth, personal communication); however, the child is still unable to locate specific referents within a pointing angle of 60–90 deg. This is particularly clear and quite frustrating to deaf parents of deaf children, because the pointing gesture plays such an important role in both prelinguistic and linguistic communication (Newport & Supalla, personal communication; Petitto, 1983). Children have to *learn* how to follow a pointing gesture produced by another individual. Because comprehension does follow production to such a surprising extent, it seems unlikely that the child "learns" to point in the same way that she "learns" to name objects. In fact, we are tempted to conclude that pointing—an act that is carried out in the visual-gestural modality—may be one innate component of the human language acquisition device.

Another peculiarity in this literature is the almost complete absence of pointing to self in children under 18 months of age. In fact, pointing to self does not appear systematically until the phase in which hearing children refer to themselves quite explicitly in speech (with the pronouns *I* and *me,* with their own proper names, or both). This is also true for deaf children acquiring a signed language like ASL where points take on a systematic lexical–grammatical function (i.e., serving as pronouns in the language). Indeed, deaf children may avoid pointing to themselves or the listener around 18 months, as though the problem of working out first- and second-person reference is so hard that they don't want to deal with the issue at all. During this phase, they refer to themselves and the listener by name instead.

Petitto (1985) has used this *U*-shaped function in the development of pointing to argue for discontinuity between prelinguistic and linguistic forms. That is, she believes that the child ceases to use the prelinguistic form because the linguistic uses of the pointing gesture are becoming apparent and need to be sorted out before progress can be made. This is an interesting hypothesis, in line with the modular view of language that we referred to earlier. However, Petitto's argument for discontinuity is complicated by the fact that hearing children not exposed to sign also fail to point systematically to themselves before 18 months. Petitto does not offer evidence from hearing controls. However, our own observations of hearing children in the range of 12–20 months suggest that they also find the shifting reference from self to other quite confusing—in language and in gesture. The use of a pointing gesture to refer to speaker and listener may seem quite transparent to an adult, because that adult has been working with a systematic concept of self for a very long time. However, many independent lines of evidence have been offered to suggest that a concept of self as object does not emerge in normal children until the second half of the second year (Kagan et al., 1982). Hence the discontinuities that we see in pointing may depend not on the child's exposure to a grammaticized pointing gesture, but on a new and troublesome awareness of self as a social object, and a problem sorting out the shifting nature of first- and second-person reference within that framework. If, as Werner and Kaplan argue, third-person pointing at 9–11 months marks the emergence of the distinction between subject *and* object, then first-person pointing after 18 months may reflect the emergence of the concept of subject *as* object.

Conventional Communication in Sound and Gesture

The ritualization of previously instrumental behaviors in infant imperative communication is actually a crude beginning of what language philosophers call *convention* (Searle, 1969). A convention is a behavior or a display that conveys a meaning or carries out a social function, not because of a natural link between the behavior and some goal, but because some group of individuals has arbitrarily decided to behave that way. The use of a knife to cut meat is not in itself a convention. Knives are used to cut meat because they work well for that purpose; if our society died away, another society would probably reinvent the knife for exactly the same function. However, various rules of etiquette about which knife to use and where to place it on the table are based primarily on convention. If our society died away, it is unlikely that the same rules would be discovered all over again.

Conventions play a role in every aspect of human culture, but conventionality is particularly important for language. Except for a few onomatopoeic words like *cough* or *clang,* there are no natural links between words and their meanings. Words refer to or stand for their meanings only because a society has decided that it shall be so. For a child to break into her native language, she must figure out how to acquire completely arbitrary relationships between sounds or signs and socially imposed meaning. We suggest that two distinct learning processes are involved in the acquisition of cultural conventions—including the referential conventions of language. These are *imitation* (the ability to reproduce an arbitrary sound or movement, whether the child understands it or not), and *ritualization* (the ability to produce streamlined versions of a sound or movement, at predictable points in a specified social context).

First let us review the application of these two learning processes in the acoustic-articulatory modality. As we noted in the section on speech production, babbling "drifts" in the direction of the child's phonological environment at 4–7 months of age. This finding is consonant with what we know about the origins of vocal imitation. At 2 months of age the child can return a "vocal volley" that is initiated by an adult, as long as the adult produced a sound that is already in the child's vocabulary. This is not true imitation, but it seems to be part of the same kind of game (Piaget, 1962; Uzgiris & Hunt, 1975). By 3–4 months, the child is able to "serve" at vocal tennis, taking the initiative in an exchange of reciprocal imitation. But the elements of the game still come from sounds that are already in the child's repertoire. From 5 months onward, he begins to shape or modify his own sound system to resemble the sounds produced by others–even though he does not appear to have any insight into the meaning or function of speech sounds. At this point, we at last have true imitation, that is, imitation used as a vehicle to master new forms. But it is not until around 10 months (Piaget's stage 5—see Bates et al., 1979) that the child imitates new sounds frequently and systematically. This is the point, as we noted earlier, at which sounds become routinized and predictable in context.

A similar process takes place in the gestural modality, but it seems to take a little more time—at least in hearing children. The infant 3–4 months old is becoming adept at object manipulation and often spends a great deal of time watching his hands. However, there are few clear-cut gestural analogues of vocal tennis, or reciprocal imitation (cf. Meltzoff & Moore, 1977, 1982, on neonatal imitation of hand movements). According to Uzgiris and Hunt (1975), children may try to imitate simple gestures like banging one hand on the table during the transition from sensorimotor stage 3 to stage 4 (around 6 months). However, most children will not systematically imitate a new gestural model (i.e., a movement that is not already in their repertoire) until sensorimotor stage 5, at 9–12 months of age on the average. In other words, imitation becomes a vehicle for learning new behaviors around the same time in both the gestural and the vocal modalities.

Ten months is also the time in which we find robust naturalistic evidence of imitative and routinized gestural games like "pattycake" or "bye-bye" or "sooo-big." Notice that the *function* of showing off for the adult appears well before this point. For example, Bates and colleagues (1975) report that the 7-month-old Carlotta developed a vocal–gestural game of "giving the raspberries." However, the source of this particular game was not imitation of a conventional adult model. Instead, Carlotta had provoked an adult reaction of laughter when she hit upon the raspberries sound by accident; she repeated her performance, was reinforced again, and so the game continued. This kind of acquisition by operant conditioning does not seem to be the same thing as the imitatively derived games that proliferate from 10 months onward. And as reported by Bates et al. (1979), early "showing off" is not correlated significantly with the complex of conventional and/or referential gestures that precede and predict language development.

In hearing children, the imitatively derived gestural games are often paired with some kind of linguistic input: "clap your hands," "do pattycake," "wave to grandma," "bye-bye," or "how big is Jennifer?" Hence the onset of imitative-conventional games coincides with the first naturalistic evidence for comprehension of words, which in turn parallels the onset of intentional communication as it was discussed above. In other words, a lot of changes are taking place at the same time. Furthermore, these changes appear to be correlated across children in group studies (Bates et al., 1979). Later on we will consider some possible cognitive explanations for the array of changes that take place in communication at this point.

To summarize so far, the evidence from hearing children suggests that imitation of new, conventional hand movements does not occur before 9 months of age—2–3 months after the incorporation of conventional phoneme contrasts into babbling. However, observations of manual babbling in deaf children yield a different picture. Deaf parents who are native speakers of American Sign Language report that their children begin to produce signs as early as 5 months of age (Bonvillian, Orlansky, & Novack, 1983; Bonvillian, Orlansky, Novack, & Folven, 1983; Folven & Bonvillian, 1985; Hoffmeister, 1978a, 1978b; Newport & Supalla, personal communication; Prinz & Prinz, 1979). According to Bonvillian, Orlansky, and Novack (1983) and Bonvillian, Orlansky, Novack, and others (1983), the early onset of sign provides direct counterevidence to the hypothesis that naming is linked to cognitive changes that occur at 9–12 months (i.e., the hypothesis that Bates and her colleagues have maintained across several studies of hearing children). This apparent precocity of sign seems to be restricted to the first manual conventions; at later stages (e.g., the 10-sign point, or the emergence of sign combinations), there are few if any differences between milestones in the acquisition of sign and speech (Volterra & Caselli, 1983). So where do these early signs come from?

We suggest that the 5-month signs are really nothing more than manual babbling, directly parallel to the drift toward environmental input that we find in the vocal modality around the same time (Boysson-Bardies et al., 1984). These manual forms can become conventional, if the parents respond to them in a systematic way—like Carlotta's raspberries. But to call them names or symbols is probably an overestimate—similar to claims by enthusiastic hearing parents that a 6-month-old's reduplicated babbling (e.g., "dahdah") is also a word ("He said 'daddy'!"). In fact, it may be easier for the eager parent to make her overestimates in the manual modality, where the individual articulators are so much easier to observe. In support of this idea, Petitto (personal communication) showed films of a hearing infant who had never been exposed to American Sign Language to a hearing speaker of ASL. Without informing the judge that this was a hearing child, Petitto asked her to record any signs that she might see the infant produce. The adult "identified" several primitive baby signs in the infant's gestural activity. Imagine how much easier it would be to "read in" signs in the manual activity of a child who really is exposed to a constant barrage of gestural language. Parents are very good at reporting what their children do (Bates et al., 1985); they are not always good at figuring out what this behavior means from a developmental point of view. A serious test of the "early sign" hypothesis will require the application of a single set of criteria that distinguish symbols from other kinds of imitative and/or routinized behavior—criteria that can be fairly applied to both manual and vocal behaviors (Bates et al., 1983; Volterra & Caselli, 1983). We will return to this point in the next section.

To summarize, imitation and routinization are both required for the acquisition of cultural conventions. Certain forms of imitation appear as early as 3 months— and perhaps at birth, if Meltzoff and Moore (1977) are correct. Actions can also become routinized through nonimitative operant conditioning within the first half of the first year—although the child may not play a very active or anticipatory role in using the routine before 7–9 months. There are also robust individual differences in the *frequency* with which children engage in imitation and in social games or routines, at this stage and at every other level of language development (Bates et al., 1979). From a normative point of view, the important point about the 9-month transition is that imitation and routinization come together to form an efficient system for the acquisition of cultural conventions—in gesture and in sound.

There is still one more dimension we have not considered. For an imitative routine to become a convention, it must also be "agreed upon" by a community of users—even if there are only two members in the community. There is now a very large literature on caretaker–child interaction in the first year of life (Bell, 1970; Brazelton, Kozlowski, & Main, 1974; Bretherton, 1985; Bretherton & Beeghly, 1982; Bretherton et al., 1981; Bruner, 1977; Butterworth, 1979; Campos & Stenberg, 1981; Clarke-Stewart, 1973; Edwards, 1978; Lewis & Brooks-Gunn, 1979; Newson, 1977; Papousek, 1979; Ratner & Bruner, 1978; Sander, 1977; Stern, 1977, in press; Trevarthen & Hubley, 1979; Wolf, 1982). Without attempting a review of that literature here, it seems fair to conclude that a system of reciprocal expectations is established between child and parent within the first half of the first year. This system becomes quite explicit around 9 months—for the child as well as the parent—when the child develops intentional control over her communicative signals. Hence conventionality and intentionality merge together to set the stage for language acquisition, within a framework of social interaction that has been prepared for many months (Ratner & Bruner, 1978).

The importance of this "social scaffolding" for conventional communication is underscored by research on the early stages of communicative development in deaf and blind children (Andersen, Dunlea, & Kekelis, 1984; Urwin, Volterra & Caselli, 1983) and in perceptually intact children of blind mothers (Bohannon & Warren, 1984). These are, of course, populations in which at least one of the partners is missing information from the other in at least one modality.

Development in these early stages seems to be particularly limited for the blind child, who cannot see the world of referents shared by her parent and cannot easily determine when her partner is trying to establish joint reference. Perhaps for this reason, early communication between blind children and their parents seems to consist primarily of physical games and routines in which the referent is the interaction itself (e.g., a repetitive game of "bouncy-bouncy" in which the child learns to anticipate her parent's physical position at different points in the sequence). This means, in turn, that the merger between conventionality and external reference will be delayed. Not surprisingly, then, we find that blind children are often delayed by many months in the passage from prespeech to speech; once this infrastructure is laid down, however, language development proceeds at a much more rapid pace.

The problem is less severe for a sighted child of a blind parent. The child does have access to his parent's communication intentions, and can see the referent world that the parent is trying to share. This child's problem consists primarily in making is own referential intentions known, particularly in the prespeech phase when he cannot simply shout out the object's name. Preliminary research by Bohannon and Warren (1984) suggests that these children do experience a delay in the early stages of language. However, by 20 months they seem to be quite adept at compensating for the blind parent's problem, placing the parent's hand on a referent object and/ or dragging the parent over in the direction of a goal before a communication about that goal is made.

In deaf children and/or in deaf parents of hearing children, the first stages of conventional and referential communication are much more easily established. There is no evidence whatsoever of a delay in the prespeech stages for deaf families, where objects of contemplation are directly in view and each partner can signal her intentions visually to the other. Like the child of a blind parent who learns alternate ways to obtain adult attention, deaf children and deaf parents rapidly converge on a set of physical means to ensure that the listener is attending to a visual signal (e.g., thumping the floor next to a deaf parent to make him turn around). Also, in the absence of vocal signals to signal emotion and attitude, deaf children seem to make a much greater use of compensatory visual signals. This includes a particularly animated use of the face (Reilly, McIntire, & Bellugi, 1985). In ASL, the face is used in several ways. The more strictly linguistic uses of facial expression (e.g., a particular mouth configuration to modify the verb) are acquired around the same time that hearing children learn the corresponding lexical–grammatical functions in spoken language. Paralinguistic uses of the face (similar to intonational coloring in speech) occur within the second year, in parallel with the acquisition of systematic intonational contrasts in speech. Hence the more systematic or "codified" uses of facial expression, like the acquisition of various hand sign functions, seem to be locked into the same developmental chart that we find in hearing children. Nevertheless, ASL researchers note that deaf infants in the prespeech period display a much more animated albeit nonlinguistic use of the face in communicative interactions with the parent, when compared with hearing children of the same age. And the use of exaggerated facial expression is certainly a well-documented aspect of motherese among the deaf.

Our point is simply this: Caretakers of children in the prespeech period will exploit whatever resources are available to them to establish a communicative exchange and to keep it going. By the fourth quarter of the first year, children become active participants in this effort, converging on a set of agreed-upon and hence conventional procedures for sharing and obtaining objects. If the standard means of ensuring communication are not available, an alternative set of procedures are soon established. Hence by the end of the first year several strands of communication are in place: intentional communication, a primitive notion of reference, and a set of conventions consisting of imitatively derived, routinized signals that are agreed upon by the small community of caretaker and child. The stage is set for the next transition: the emergence of symbols, in particular the symbolic function of naming.

Nonlinguistic Correlates of Changes in Prespeech

Why do so many aspects of vocal and gestural communication change at around the same time? What is so special about the border of 9–10 months? Here we have our first evidence that language development is paced by other cognitive systems.

In a reanalysis of the Berkeley and Fels longitudinal studies, McCall, Eichorn, and Hogarty (1977) conclude that there are four major reorganization points in early cognitive development: 9–10 months; 12–13 months; 18–20 months; and 30 months. Their conclusions are based on changes in the factor structure and range of variation within traditional tests of infant intelligence. Nevertheless, it is difficult to avoid parallels between these global transition points and major milestones in language development: intentional communication and word comprehension at 9–10 months; first words at 12–13 months; first sentences at 18–20 months; and grammaticization by 30 months.

Of course this kind of "bottom-up" correlational study is more useful for its descriptive than for its explanatory value. Any study demonstrating correlations between linguistic and nonlinguistic development can provide only indirect evidence for a causal–mechanistic model of language change. However, many separate lines of evidence suggest that the child's entire cognitive system is undergoing radical change—particularly at the border that we have examined here.

For example, Bates and colleagues (1979) point out that proto-declarative and proto-imperative communication is significantly correlated not only with concurrent changes in imitation, but with noncommunicative changes in the ability to use tools (see also Harding & Golinkoff, 1979; Snyder, 1975; Sugarman-Bell, 1978). They suggest that object-to-object tool use draws on the same analytic capacities that are involved in the use of people as a means to obtain objects and the use of objects as a means to obtain adult attention.

Other nonlinguistic changes around the border of 9–10 months include the ability to learn a novel object category based on arbitrary correlations between perceptual features (Younger, 1985; Younger & Cohen, 1985). This kind of new correlational approach to learning could be involved in the child's emerging ability to comprehend words. We know that children can perceive most phonemic contrasts during the first weeks of life. But to perceive a bounded word, and to recognize that word in a variety of contexts, the child has to learn an arbitrary set of correlations among phonemic features. Similarly, in order to form a "whole" made up of a word and its contextual–perceptual meaning, the child must have the ability to pick up arbitrary amalgams of sound, gesture, and their situational associates.

There is a lot that we still do not know about cognitive reorganization at this stage or at any other stage in intellectual development (Case, 1985; Flavell, 1970, 1971; Mandler, 1981). Our point is, simply, that the first stages of language and communication seem to be inexorably linked to changes in other aspects of learning and behavior. These empirical facts must be kept in mind when we try to develop a theory of the mechanisms responsible for language acquisition.

FIRST WORDS: THE EMERGENCE OF NAMING (10–13 MONTHS)

We will divide this section into four parts: single-word comprehension; single-word production; individual differences in single-word use; and the development of a class of gestures that seem—at least for a short time—to have the functional status of words or *enactive names*.

Single-Word Comprehension

For most children, systematic evidence of word comprehension begins around 9–10 months. Usually, the child starts by responding more reliably to her name, or to the word *no*. But it soon becomes easier and easier to direct the child's attention to objects in the world by naming them (e.g., "Look at the doggie, Eric, the doggie."). Children vary markedly after this point in the rate at which their receptive vocabularies expand. According to Bates and others (1985), by 13 months the receptive vocabularies of middle-class children can range from 17 to 97. For present purposes, the interesting point is that these diverse learning curves all seem to begin at the same 9-month boundary.

Parents occasionally report an isolated instance of word comprehension well before this point. For example, Bates and associates (1975) report that their subject Carlotta looked up toward the ceiling in response to "Where's the light?" at 6 months of age. But the child looked toward the ceiling on command whether or not there was a light there and did not seem at all perplexed if no light was found. This routine seemed to be the product of several hundred trials and may reflect a completely different mode of acquisition than the one that underlies receptive language from 9 months onward. An experiment in novel word learning by Oviatt (1979) illustrates that the course of word comprehension is very different before and after the 9-month boundary. The youngest children in her study learned to respond appropriately to two new words (a noun for a novel animal, and a verb for a bar-pressing behavior), but only after many trials (i.e., with a very gradual learning curve). The older children (averaging 10 months) gave the same evidence for comprehension in relatively few trials, (i.e., with a very steep learning curve).

As we mentioned earlier, children also tend to pick up gestural games like "pattycake" and "bye-bye" around this same transition point. More often than not, these games are elicited by verbal cues like "clap your hands" or "say bye-bye to

Grandma.'' At the beginning, our parents tell us that the verbal cue has to be repeated, usually with a stereotyped intonation, and that success is much more likely if the parent is clapping or waving too. In other words, the performance needs a lot of support. Children become more and more efficient at anticipating the game to come, however, so that by 11 months many children will produce the requisite scheme to a minimal cue, for example, waving as soon as a guest gets up and moves toward the door. In the same vein, the child may begin to respond to key words embedded in a phrase that is not directed to him at all (e.g., a child who waves upon hearing her mother say, ''Jennifer learned how to say 'bye-bye' when my parents were visiting.''). These anecdotes suggest that word comprehension itself is becoming ''routinized,'' and that the child is becoming more and more skilled at picking target forms out of the sound stream. Indeed, some of our parents report that they have to start spelling words like *bottle* or *candy* in front of children as young as 14 months of age.

The integration of rapid language comprehension and imitation of novel schemes place the child at a qualitatively new level in the ability to acquire conventional signals. We would expect these developments to lead directly into word production, in each and every child. Instead, comprehension and production prove to be remarkably dissociable in this age range. In our first large longitudinal study (Bates et al., 1979), comprehension and production vocabularies were correlated at 12 months of age; but the correlation was barely significant, and accounted for only 16 percent of the variance. In subsequent group studies, comprehension and production totals were completely unrelated in this age range (Snyder et al., 1981; see also Benedict, 1979). This ''unhooking'' of receptive and expressive processing comes from a group of children who understand far more than they produce. Most of these children catch up in production, and are often among the most advanced talkers by 28 months of age (Bates et al., 1985). So the reason for a sharp comprehension–production lag is not entirely clear. We will return to this point later, in a summary view of individual differences in early language development.

Single-Word Production

When does a child produce his first word? The answer to this question depends on whether we distinguish between the *form* and the *function* of naming. As reviewed by Snyder et al. (1981), researchers have suggested three different developmental moments as ''the'' transition point into true naming:

1. 9–10 months, when children first produce conventional sounds and show comprehension of at least a few words and phrases
2. 12–13 months, when most children produce at least a few sound sequences that function like names from an adult point of view
3. 16–18 months, when there is a sudden surge in vocabulary growth and an increased use of single words to convey combinatorial or sentential meanings

Given this array of possibilities, when do we decide that the child has uttered her first ''real'' word? Children may begin, like the infant Carlotta (Bates et al., 1975), with grunts and effort noises that become intentional, conventional communications only in a very primitive sense—for example, the insistent sound ''mmm-mmm'' in requests. We infer that this sound is intentional by the three criteria described earlier (eye contact between listener and goal, changes in the signal contingent upon adult behavior, and abbreviation in the form of the signal toward a purely communicative function). Also, this sound is conventional in its stereotyped form, and in the fact that it is recognized and agreed upon by a community of at least two individuals (the child and her caretaker). Nevertheless most researchers would be uncomfortable in concluding that "mmm-mmm" is a word, much less a true name or vocal symbol for a class of referents.

From 9 to 13 months, we find more ambiguous cases in the gradual move toward naming. For example, Carlotta had a clear consonant–vowel combination, "nana," which was used for all types of requests. Unlike the "mmm" sound, which derived initially from effort noises, this combination seemed quite arbitrary in form. Indeed, it was quite unlike other calls, cries, and babbles in the same period. Another subject, Marta, invented her own peculiar vocal convention, "ayi." This was used not for requesting but for exclaiming or commenting on interesting objects—a vocal realization of the gestural proto-declarative, usually accompanied by pointing or giving. These wordlike sounds are conventions according to the above criteria. But can we call them words?

Sometimes, in the same developmental period, the child may choose an existing adult word to perform exactly the same functions as Carlotta's "nana" or Marta's "ayi." For example, Piaget's daughter Jacqueline (Piaget, 1962) used a word for grandfather ("panama") as an all-purpose request that bore no apparent relation to the presence or absence of grandfather himself—although her favorite slave must have played some role in the origins of this sound. In the grown-up world, *grandfather* is a name. In Jacqueline's world, however, it seems to be a pure performative routine for obtaining good things.

The problem of locating first words becomes even greater for very specific games like "bye-bye." Carlotta used the sound "bam" in a game of knocking over towers, at a regular point in that routine. Similarly, "brrr" was a sound made while moving vehicles. Svachkin (in Ferguson & Slobin, 1973) reports on his daughter's first word, "kitty," used only after throwing her toy cat out of the crib, at which point father was supposed to restore the toy (no doubt having said more than once, "Here's your kitty."). Marta used the Italian word "da" ("give") while giving or taking objects in a ritual exchange—a routine clearly related to the observation that adults say "da" over and over again in games of object exchange. These examples all involve uses of adult words. For the child, however, they all seem to be language games, procedures derived from imitating adult behaviors within a narrowly defined situation or script.

Let us consider, however, the subsequent history of Carlotta's "bam." Several weeks after the game had become a well-established routine, Carlotta was seated among her toys momentarily silent and empty-handed. She looked up, said the word "bam," and after a brief hesitation, turned to bang on her toy piano. Note that the sound has become in some sense decontextualized or "unstuck" from the original "bam" script, so that it is now used in advance as a kind of tag, reminder, or perhaps an announcement of the action to follow. The utterance "bam" is now functioning as a kind of primitive verb. At the beginning it was a procedure, an action, an equal among other related procedures, actions, and routines. Now it begins to signify or stand for the rest of the script, or some portion of the script.

It has been selected out and elevated to a different status from the other elements in the original routine—and as such, it has begun to function as a *symbol*.

Around the same time that "bam" evolved to a new status, other procedures also evolved into primitive nouns or names for objects. For example, Carlotta first used the vocal routine "woowoo" exclusively within a book-reading game, in response to the adult signal, "How does the doggie go?" By 13 months, she began to use "woowoo" to comment on the presence of a whole class of dogs, in books and in real life, including the sound of a dog barking somewhere in the distance. Perhaps because they are so well prepared by preexisting book routines, animal names are frequent in the early noun vocabularies of middle-class children (cf. Werner & Kaplan, 1963). However, names for food and water also appeared quickly in Carlotta's requests, and she soon began to collect names for toys, clothing, and other relevant objects in her world. Volterra, Bates, Benigni, Bretherton, and Camaioni (1979) traced the same kind of development from performative routines to acts of reference in the early speech records of 25 infants (the same infants studied by Bates et al., 1979). By their criteria, most of the children had made the transition into reference by 13 months (see also Bretherton, in press).

But is the flexible use of a small number of words really sufficient evidence to conclude that children understand the idea that things have names? To examine this issue in more detail, Snyder and colleagues (1981) developed a detailed coding scheme for classifying maternal reports of language use in 32 middle-class infants, at 13 months of age. In their study, mothers participated in a lengthy interview based on a checklist of 100 words and phrases likely to occur in the comprehension and production vocabularies of children 10–15 months of age (drawn from their own earlier work and that of other investigators). For every item that the mother recognized, in either production or comprehension, the interviewer probed for detailed anecdotes on how the word or phrase was used. For example, if the mother said that the child understood "bath," the interviewer would try to determine whether the child's understanding was restricted to a context of clothes being taken off, water running, and so forth—or whether he would react (positively or negatively) to the word in a systematic way when none of these usual bath-time clues were present. Similarly, if the mother reported that the child said "bow-wow" in reference to dogs, the interviewers would ask whether the word occurred only in the context of pointing at dog pictures in a book (perhaps in response to "How does the doggie go?") or whether he would label two or more live dogs, pictures of dogs in books, and so forth. On the basis of these anecdotal records, the authors placed all comprehension and production items into one of two categories: *context bound* and *context flexible*. (Actually, the dimension of context flexibility should be viewed as a continuum, with words at different points along the continuum throughout development.)

This coding yielded several findings about individual differences in the discovery of object naming: (1) Comprehension and production vocabularies were only slightly related, due to a group of children who understood far more than they produced, but (2) children with a high proportion of object names in production also tended to specialize in object names in comprehension; (3) furthermore, children with a high proportion of object names in either modality also tended to have larger vocabularies overall. For present purposes, the most important finding was that (4) 1-year-olds with a high proportion of context-flexible object names in their expressive vocabulary were generally more advanced in language development. That is, they had higher vocabularies overall in *both* production and comprehension. Furthermore, a longitudinal report of the same children at 28 months showed strong correlations between the early context flexibility measure and mean length of utterance, grammatical productivity, and several other measures of progress in language development (Bates et al., 1985).

Why should this single, rather odd measure predict so many aspects of later language? Snyder and others suggest that children who are high on the context flexibility measure are the "first in their class" to achieve an understanding of the idea that things have names, that is, the referential–symbolic function of words. Eventually, all normal children will make this discovery. But those who make it early will also have a head start in later stages of language development—including the acquisition of grammar. From a practical point of view, these findings underscore the difference between words as pure performatives (i.e., context-bound routines) and words as symbols. The fact that a child is using words is not sufficient evidence for real language understanding. Two children with equivalent vocabularies in terms of overall size may be at completely different levels.

Although children do seem to achieve insight into the symbolic function of naming by 13 months of age, vocabulary growth is rather slow and steady for several more months. Somewhere around 16-20 months, on the average, there is a sudden acceleration in the rate of single-word learning. This vocabulary burst seems to happen when cumulative vocabulary reaches 50 words; the same child's vocabulary may reach 400 words in just a few short weeks (Bates et al., 1985). Because this change is so dramatic, many investigators believe that the nominal insight has not occurred until this point. In other words, they deny our contention that word use is truly symbolic by 13 months (Dore, 1975; Nelson, 1985; Zukow, 1981). For Nelson, all of the examples that we have listed in this section would belong within a single prelexical stage, including Carlotta's very flexible and general word for "dogs." Partial support for this hypothesis comes from two sources. First, many children will begin systematically asking for the names of things around this time (e.g., "Whazzat?"). Second, bilingual children rarely pick up two equivalent words for the same referent during the first 50 words, as though they were working on the theory that objects can only have one name (Volterra & Taeschner, 1977). For example, a child might have only the German word for "cup," but acquire only the Italian word for "bow." After the 50-word border, they begin to acquire equivalent terms for new words in both languages—as though they have some insight now into the arbitrary and interchangeable status of object labels.

This position has the advantage of explaining why vocabulary growth takes off so suddenly in the middle of the second year (i.e., children start collecting names for things because they finally understand what names are for). But it leaves us at a loss to explain the systematic and very general use of a limited set of names (e.g., "doggie," "birdie") during the first 50-word phase. We will return to this problem shortly, when we examine the subsequent shift from single words to sentences.

Individual Differences in Single-Word Use

There is now a large body of evidence concerning individual differences in style as well as rate in language development in the single-word stage. We have talked so far as if all children begin to learn language by focusing on names for objects.

However, in one of the first systematic group studies of early lexical development, Nelson (1973) reports a surprisingly wide range of variation in the use of nominal expressions. For children at the referential end of the continuum, the first 50 words consist primarily of object names plus a few routines like "hi" or "up." These children tend to be early talkers and spend more of their time involved in social interactions that are mediated through objects. For children at the other end of the continuum, the first 50 words were drawn from many different categories (prepositions, adverbials, etc.). They even included some multiword formulas like "stop it" or "love you," expressions that challenge the meaning of the term *one-word stage*. Nelson coined the term *expressive style* to describe this approach to language, because the heterogeneous vocabularies of these children contain so many social routines and instrumental–regulatory expressions. Note also, however, that expressive-style children tend to be slower overall in early language development (cf. Horgan, 1981; Starr, 1975).

Snyder and colleagues (1981) showed that this referential–expressive dimension begins as early as 13 months of age and shows up in comprehension as well as production. More recently, Goldfield (1985) has uncovered evidence suggesting that referential–expressive style may actually begin prior to speech. In her longitudinal study, children who engaged in more proto-declarative, object-oriented communication in the preverbal stage were more likely to dislay a referential approach once language got under way. By contrast, children who engaged in less giving, showing, and pointing prior to speech tended later on to have more heterogeneous vocabularies and more social formulas. In other words, the referential–expressive dimension may have its roots in processing variables that are operating weeks or months before children begin to talk. Later on we will review some possible explanations for individual differences in early language—differences that seem to hold up at every stage of development that has been studied to date.

Gestural Naming

Around the time that children make the transition from vocal routines to naming, there is a parallel shift taking place in the gestural modality. As we noted above, two kinds of gestures can be found in the prespeech era:

1. Referential gestures (giving, showing, pointing) that are used intentionally to communicate about objects
2. Conventional games or routines ("pattycake," "bye-bye") that are acquired through imitation and carried out systematically in a social context that has been agreed upon by the child's small community

Like their vocal equivalents (e.g., "mmmm" or "bam"), these gestures do not seem to fit our implicit criteria for symbolic activity. Following Bates and associates (1979), we will define symbols as follows:

> The comprehension or use, inside or outside of communicative situations, of a relationship between a sign and its referent, such that the sign is treated as belonging to and/or substitutable for its referent in a variety of contexts; at the same time the user is aware that the sign is separable from its referent, that is, not the same thing. (p. 43)

In the same framework, following Bates et al. (1983), we will define naming as follows:

> The use of a symbol to recognize, categorize, identify or otherwise label a referent as a member of some known class of entities, or as an instantiation of a known unique individual. This naming act may be carried out for the purpose of identifying that referent for an intended listener, or in a private act of recognition for oneself. When used communicatively, a naming act may be the major point of an utterance or it may be a subsidiary act in the service of making further points about that referent. Similarly, in private cognition a naming act may be carried out in isolation, or as a subsidiary act within a higher relational or predicative construction. (p. 60)

Notice that these definitions are intentionally modality free. There is no reason why a gesture could not be used for symbolic naming—as indeed they are in a visual–manual language like ASL. But in children exposed to a spoken language, there is also a nonlinguistic equivalent to naming in the gestural modality.

Escalona (1973) and Werner and Kaplan (1963) were among the first to argue that hearing children engage in *enactive naming* toward the end of the first year, using a conventional gesture associated with an object (e.g., drinking from a cup, or combing with a comb) to recognize or classify members of that object class. These brief "I know what to do with this" gestures are extremely common in the age range of 10–16 months, and they seem to be related to the emergence of vocal naming along several different dimensions. Bates and Volterra (1985) have summarized several lines of evidence in support of the idea that object-associated, or *recognitory,* gestures serve as a kind of naming (Acredolo & Goodwyn, 1985a, 1985b; Bates et al., 1979; McCune-Nicolich, 1981; McCune-Nicolich & Bruskin, 1982; Volterra & Caselli, 1983).

1. *Onset time.* Children begin to produce object names and object-associated gestures around the same time in development, that is, at 11–13 months. Sometimes gestural versions of naming appear slightly ahead of language, but in normal children words are rarely very far behind the appearance of recognitory gestures with objects.

2. *Correlations.* In this initial phase of symbol use (i.e., 11–16 months), the number of recognitory gestures and the number of object names in a given child's repertoire are positively correlated. This is particularly true for recognitory gestures that are carried out empty-handed, or with some kind of substitute object.

3. *Content.* During this phase, gestures and words tend to refer to the same basic stock of referents or meanings: words and gestures for eating, drinking, greeting, bathing, dressing, certain household activities, vehicles, appearance and disappearance of objects, and so forth.

4. *Form.* Enactive gestures, like early names, are very brief and stylized in form. The child who touches cup to lip in object recognition seems to know the difference between this act and "real drinking" and shows no surprise or disappointment if there is nothing there to quench his thirst.

5. *Decontextualization.* Words and gestures that began as context-bound routines start to become "unstuck" from their initial context around the same time, generalized to an increasingly broad set of referents and situations. For example, the child may only put a phone to her ear at first in a stereotypic telephone game

with mother. Later she may produce the same gesture to anything vaguely resembling a phone (e.g., a pocket calculator with buttons, or a cylindrical block that bulges at both ends), by herself or with anyone interested enough to play the game. Words and gestures may also be used to refer to absent referents, and to past or future events (Acredolo & Goodwyn, 1985a, 1985b)—although there is considerable variation among children in the tendency to use gestures in this way (e.g., making a drinking gesture in a request for juice, even when the desired juice is out of sight).

It appears, then, that the two modalities are developing in parallel during the first few months of symbol use. By the middle of the one-word stage, things start to change. In particular, normal hearing children start to give much more priority to the vocal channel. For example, Bretherton, Bates, and others (1981) presented familiar objects one at a time to the same children at 13 and 20 months of age. Although at 13 months these children had roughly similar vocabularies in gesture and speech, they were significantly more likely to produce a recognitory gesture than a vocal label—as though the threshold for eliciting gestural schemes were somehow lower. By 20 months of age, results were in exactly the opposite direction: Vocal naming had increased markedly, and the probability of producing a recognitory gesture had dropped to much lower levels than were evident at 13 months of age.

We do not know at this point whether the drop in gestural reference is "caused by" the changes in language, but it is noteworthy that the shift takes place around the linguistic vocabulary burst. In arguing that words are essentially prelexical before the vocabulary burst, Nelson (1985) suggests that the equivalence between sound and gesture is evidence that *neither* type of scheme has a truly symbolic status. Both are, instead, context-bound routines for dealing with global object–event structures. From this point of view, then, the unhooking of sound and gesture by 20 months of age reflects the fact that words have become truly symbolic; hence the nonlinguistic gestures used by hearing children begin to drop out. As we shall see, however, links between language and gesture will occur again on a completely different plane, in the passage from single units to planned combinations of symbols at 20 months of age.

WORD COMBINATIONS

We will divide this section into three parts: (1) harbingers of word combinations during the one-word period; (2) the nature of first word combinations, including evidence for individual differences; and (3) parallel developments that take place outside of language.

From Single Words to Sentences

The child's first multiword combinations typically appear at 18–24 months. This is, on the average, 8–12 months after the same child produced his first words. In the world of child language, where so many things can happen in a brief period, this is really an incredibly long time. What is the child waiting for? When we look carefully at the last months of the so-called one-word stage, it is apparent that many of the components of sentences are already present.

One of the most important aspects of a sentence is its underlying *predication,* defined as *a state or quality attributed to one entity or a relationship attributed to two or more entities.* In the first part of the one-word stage (10–15 months), single-word use is referential rather than predicative. That is, single words are used primarily to label and/or to ask for objects and people—save for a few idiosyncratic nonnominal terms like "bye-bye" and "up," which seem to be what Greenfield and Smith (1976) call *pure performatives,* or speech acts that are essentially self-referring (see Gopnik, 1981, for a detailed consideration of early nonnominal expressions). Somewhere in the middle of the second year (16–20 months), the composition of vocabulary begins to change (Bates et al., 1985; Nelson, 1973). In particular, children begin to achieve productive control over verbs (e.g., "play," "kiss," "go") and adjectives (e.g., "pretty," "hot," "dirty"). Of course, this is also the point at which most children undergo a marked expansion of vocabulary overall, sometimes jumping from 50 to 400 words in a few short weeks. However, the appearance of verbs and adjectives cannot be attributed simply to the fact that vocabularies are getting larger, since the absolute *proportion* of the vocabulary that is made up of verbs and modifiers is increasing, too (Bates et al., 1985). Instead, the appearance of verbs and adjectives seems to reflect a change in the range of meanings that a child intends to convey—in particular, the emergence of predication.

This interpretation receives support from a change in the way that nouns are used around this time. For example, instead of pointing to daddy's shoe and saying "shoe," the child may point to daddy's shoe and say "daddy"—as though to indicate something like "This shoe belongs to daddy." This phenomenon has been noticed since the first published diary studies of early child language. DeLaguna (1927) coined the term *holophrase* to refer to such events, suggesting that the child has a sentence meaning in mind. However, she believed that such meanings are represented by the child as global and unanalyzed events and hence can only be referred to by a single word that stands for the whole. Greenfield and Smith (1976) argued instead that these holophrases represent well-articulated semantic or "case" relations like agent–object, object–location, possessor–possessed. In their view, these case relations are indeed analyzed by the child. However, only a portion of the meaning can be conveyed at the symbolic level; the rest of the meaning remains at the sensorimotor level, conveyed through gesture and context. In this sense, the child's single-word utterance is similar to the single-word exclamation of a football fan who says "Fantastic!" when commenting on a play that is perfectly obvious to his fellow fans attending the game. The comment is a predication, but the topic is so obvious to the listener that it doesn't have to be made explicit.

Howe (1976) has criticized the so-called method of rich interpretation, arguing that its exponents have overinterpreted single-word utterances that in reality convey little more than a simple association between the elements of highly familiar scenes and events. But even if the shift in the second year involves association rather than predication, it does involve a clear increase in complexity. The fact that multicomponent meanings seem to be available during the single-word stage has led investigators to look for processing explanations for the single-word limit.

Among the phenomena that argue for a processing limitation between single- and multiword speech is the occurrence of *successive single-word utterances* (e.g., Greenfield & Smith, 1976; Scollon, 1976; Werner & Kaplan, 1963). These usually begin with what Scollon calls *vertical constructions,* where the child adds a bit of meaning onto an adult utterance (e.g., in question-answering sequences like "What did the birdie do?"—"Away," or in bits of dialogue like "Let's have Cheerios"—"Milk"). But in the same time period, or shortly thereafter, we also find what Scollon calls *horizontal constructions*. In these cases, the child seems to build up relational, sentencelike meanings on her own, one word at a time (e.g. "daddy . . . car . . . garage."). Such successive single-word utterances are usually identified by the pauses that occur between individual words. However, Branigan (1979) carried out spectrographic analyses of such utterances and found that they had sentencelike intonational properties (e.g. an initial rise with a falling final tone) despite the perceived pauses. Hence at some level the individual words must have been planned as a unit.

Branigan's observations suggest that there might be something in the child's speech production system that prevents her from getting out more than one word at a time. However, whatever this something is, it cannot be a simple peripheral motor limitation. MacWhinney (personal communication) notes that children acquiring a richly inflected language like Hungarian sometimes produce single words that are several syllables long—even though they are incapable of combining the same number of syllables when each syllable represents an independent lexical item. Similarly, in children acquiring English we sometimes find formulaic phrases like "want it" (Nelson, 1973) during what we persist in calling the one-word stage. This interpretation is justified by the fact that the individual elements in early formulaic expressions never appear separately, nor in combination with other units. Hence the child seems to be treating a whole phrase like a single polysyllabic unit (i.e., a "giant word").

And yet many one-word children do seem to be aware that sentences are made up of "other stuff" in addition to the single word that conveys their intended meaning. Some children produce a kind of verbal scribbling, where they add an invented sound or "dummy word" to their one-word utterance (Bloom, 1970; Leonard, 1976). The most famous example is the sound "wida," which Bloom's daughter Allison added to many of her single-word utterances during the period before recognizable two-word utterances appeared. The sound "wida" had no detectable semantic-pragmatic function, but it was added at will to a wide variety of single-word utterances, as though Allison were simply trying to give her utterances a more grown-up sound.

In trying to explain the mystery of "wida," Bloom suggests that children in the one-word stage have all the semantic, auditory, and articulatory resources that they need to produce sentences. What they lack is a set of *syntactic principles* for putting individual elements together. This argument is compatible with the notion of grammar as a mental organ that develops on a separate timetable from semantics and phonology. The problem with this explanation is that the correlation between grammar and the onset of multiword speech isn't very good, either. As Horgan (1976) has shown, many children use the same ordering principles in their successive single-word descriptions that they use in multiword speech a few weeks later. So there does not seem to be a "new" ordering principle to explain the change in word packaging. Conversely, Braine (1976) has pointed out that many children begin their multiword careers with utterances that seem to be randomly ordered. This is particularly true outside of English, in richly inflected languages that vary word order extensively for pragmatic purposes. Since we can have single-word speech with ordering, and multiword speech without ordering, it is not clear that syntax plays any causal role in the passage from single words to sentences.

It can be argued, then, that all of the *linguistic* components necessary for multiword speech are present weeks or months before the child produces two-word combinations. This has led some investigators to consider the possibility that a *nonlinguistic* limitation is responsible for the transition from single words to sentences. Later on we will examine evidence suggesting that the shift from one word to two words, does indeed involve cognitive changes that transcend language proper.

First Word Combinations

On the average, most children are producing their first word combinations by 20 months of age. This is true not only for speaking children, but for children acquiring a visual–manual language (Newport & Supalla, 1980; Volterra & Caselli, 1983). The fact that sentences appear around the same time regardless of modality suggests (again) that the transition involves mechanisms that transcend simple modality-specific motor limitations.

However, some two-sign combinations have been reported for deaf children as early as 11–12 months of age. These are almost always combinations made up of one deictic or pointing sign plus a signed content word (e.g., the child points at a bird, then makes the sign for bird, perhaps returning to point once again—Newport, personal communication). This kind of phenomenon has been used by Bonvillian, Orlansky, and Novack (1983) and Bonvillian, Orlansky, Novack, and others (1983) to argue that sign is acquired weeks or months before the equivalent milestones are reached in spoken language. However, as Volterra and Caselli have pointed out, these particular sign combinations are really identical in form and function to utterances by a hearing child 11–12 months old who points to a bird while simultaneously saying "bird" (see also Petitto, 1985). In these early point + word and point + sign combinations, the pointing gesture and the name both have the same referent; that is, they are both about "one thing." It is not until late in the one-word stage that deaf children will produce point + sign constructions in which each element refers to a *different referent,* or a *different aspect* of a complex meaning (e.g., pointing to a small blackboard and signing "away," as if to indicate "Put that away."). This is similar to the kinds of utterances produced by hearing children in the same age range (e.g., a child who points to daddy's jogging shoes and says "daddy"). Finally, combinations involving two different content-bearing signs are rarely reported before 20 months—the age at which hearing children are also able to produce strings of two different content words. In short, there seems to be a universal starting point for grammar regardless of the modality in which a child is acquiring her language.

Across natural languages, there is also extraordinary commonality in the meanings that children express with their first sentences (Braine, 1976; Slobin, 1973). Twenty-month-old children like to talk about simple transitive events (actors, actions, objects that are acted upon), facts about possession and location, disappearance and reappearance, various kinds of negation (e.g., denial and protest), and a handful of states and qualities that people and objects can have (e.g., "hot," "cold," "pretty," "dirty," "nice"). These meanings also show up in both signed and spoken languages.

Given the universal starting point for word combinations, and the common semantic structures that underlie first sentences, we might also expect to find great
commonality in the *forms* used to express those meanings. Indeed, some of our
older textbooks still suggest that Stage I grammar looks the same across children
and across natural languages. Much to our surprise, research in the 1970s showed
that this is not the case.

Some of the first longitudinal studies of child language had discussed early grammar in terms of *pivot–open* combinations (Braine, 1963; Brown, Cazden, & Bellugi,
1969; Miller & Ervin, 1964). The term *pivot* refers to a small class of high-frequency
words (e.g., "more," "no," "allgone," "it"). Pivots, which usually occur in only
one position, can be combined with a wide variety of content words (e.g., "shoe
allgone," "more milk," "no bed," "kiss it"). Researchers initially believed that
the child's grammatical knowledge could be characterized in terms of rules for combining abstract classes of pivot words and content words (McNeill, 1966). However,
as Braine (1976) and others have argued, pivot–open combinations are probably
better characterized in terms of word-based formulas, that is, frame + slot rules
based on a single word and the kinds of arguments that it can take. The difference
may seem trivial to an outsider, but these different characterizations of pivot–open
sentences differ so much in level of abstraction that they presuppose very different
kinds of mechanisms for language learning.

Other studies emphasized the telegraphic nature of first word combinations, that
is, the fact that they tend to be made up of two or three content words with no
grammatical morphology (e.g., "mommy sock" or "doggie bed"—see Bloom, 1970;
Bowerman, 1969; Brown, 1973). In these structures, sentence position is tied not to
a particular word but to an abstract relationship of some kind (e.g., agents tend to
be ordered before the things that they act on; objects tend to be ordered before their
locations). Investigators argued about the best way to characterize this underlying
abstract knowledge: in syntactic terms (e.g., subject + verb + object) or in semantic terms (e.g., agent + action + patient). But they did not question the universal nature of the underlying system.

It was generally believed, despite differences in interpretation, that some universal amalgam of word-based principles and abstract rules would ultimately prove
sufficient for a characterization of the innate semantic–grammatical knowledge that
underlies the universal process of language acquisition. Some serious problems for
this view were raised in a monograph by Braine (1976), who reviewed the first word
combinations produced by children acquiring English, Finnish, Samoan, and Hebrew. Braine demonstrated that individual children vary markedly in the extent to
which they produce pivot–open versus telegraphic forms, and in the extent to which
they observe word order principles for each kind of construction. Hence if we want
to account for Stage I speech in abstract grammatical terms, then it may be necessary to write different grammars for different children, with considerable variation in the number and abstractness of the rules that make up each system.

Needless to say, this created problems for those who hoped to find "the" universal Stage I grammar. However, because Braine's review covered children who
were acquiring very different kinds of languages (e.g., English vs. Samoan), the
message about individual differences was still not driven home. Bloom, Lightbown,
and Hood (1975) presented still more troublesome evidence from four children who
were all acquiring English. Two of these children produced the kind of telegraphic

speech in Stage I that we had all come to expect, with minimal use of inflections of grammatical function words. These two children avoided first- and second-person pronouns, referring to themselves and the listener by name, leading Bloom and colleagues to characterize their approach to grammar as nominal style. The other two children used pronouns from the very beginning of multiword speech, together with a heterogeneous set of other inflections and function words, leading Bloom and colleagues to refer to their approach as *pronominal style.* Their output bore more relationship to the pivot–open grammar discussed by earlier investigators. This difference in form cannot be attributed to a difference in the underlying meanings that the children wanted to express, since all four children tended to express the same number and range of semantic relations. For example, one child might insist on her right to play with a toy truck by saying "Katherine play"; another child in similar circumstances would say something like "I do it."

There is an obvious similarity between nominal–pronominal style in early grammar and the referential–expressive dimension that appears in the single-word stage. Several longitudinal studies have now shown that referential children are indeed more likely to develop a nominal approach to first word combinations, while expressive children are more likely to make use of pronouns and other aspects of grammatical morphology during Stage I (Bates et al., 1985; Bretherton, McNew, Snyder, & Bates, 1983; Nelson, 1973, 1975, 1981). In the Bloom and colleagues study, these two "styles" of grammar disappeared by 24–28 months, as all children converged on a correct use of English names and pronouns. However, research by Horgan (1979) suggests that a similar difference between "noun lovers" and "noun leavers" shows up in later stages of language acquisition as well. We will say more later about alternative explanations for individual variation in early child language. For present purposes, the point is that children vary markedly in the way that they break into grammar—despite the fact that they all start at more or less the same time, trying to find a way to talk about the same basic stock of meanings and intentions. Stage I is not quite as universal as we hoped that it would be.

First Sentences Inside and Outside Language

Parallels to the passage from single- to multiword speech have been observed around 20 months in several other areas of development: gestural imitation (McCall, Parke, & Kavanaugh, 1977); classification of objects (Sugarman, 1982a, 1982b); a shift from single isolated gestures to multigesture strings in symbolic play (Fenson & Ramsay, 1980; McCune-Nicolich, 1981; McCune-Nicolich & Bruskin, 1982; Shore et al., 1984); and a variety of other behaviors (Case, 1985; Case & Khanna, 1981). According to Case, these limits may reflect global changes in mental working space or chunking—similar to the "seven plus or minus two" limit that seems to operate in adult short-term memory (Chi, 1976, 1977; Chi & Klahr, 1975; Miller, 1956). We can think of these limits in terms of memory, attention, and/or changes in the flexibility–automaticity of the individual units that are manipulated in a single cognitive act (Shore, 1986). For present purposes, the most important point is this: The transition from single words to sentences seems to reflect cognitive reorganizations that transcend language proper.

Shore and her colleagues have tried to understand the nature of this link between linguistic and gestural sequencing, in a series of large-sample longitudinal and cross-sectional studies. Shore, O'Connell, and Bates (1984) followed up suggestions by McCune-Nicolich (1981), in a longitudinal study of 30 children at 20 and 28 months of age. They extracted the usual measures of vocabulary and mean length of utterance from free speech records, together with estimates of style and rate of development taken from maternal interviews at 20 months. In addition, they used segments of elicited symbolic play to extract estimates of vocabulary and mean length of sequence in symbolic gesture, again at both age levels. At the 20-month session, there were striking parallels between the vocal and gestural modalities in the average length of an unbroken sequence and in the longest chain of different elements that a child could produce (averaging two with a range from one to four). They also found significant correlations between combinations of content words and gestural sequencing, correlations that held up even when size of vocabulary (in either modality) was partialed out. Hence the grammatical link between language and play is not simply a by-product of the semantic knowledge shared by the two modalities. By 28 months these links had disappeared—a finding that we will address in the next section on grammaticization.

Shore (1986) showed that the variance shared by gestural sequencing and word combinations is also accounted for by a measure that taps into the range and flexibility of individual words. In other words, the ability to combine words and/or gestures seems to be tied to the efficiency and/or automaticity of individual items (see also Bloom et al., 1975). This finding is compatible with arguments by Case (1985) that changes in chunking capacity or working memory are produced by changes in the amount of storage capacity required to produce a single unit. In other words, children do not "grow" more memory space from one stage to another. Rather, they become more efficient in the planning and execution of individual cognitive schemes, so that more and more of these schemes can be packed into the same mental space. However, because so many different aspects of cognition seem to be changing around the same time, there probably is a common underlying factor of some kind that permits increases in the efficiency of individual linguistic and non-linguistic chunks.

Yet another aspect of the word–gesture transition has been studied by Shore and Bauer (1983) and Bauer (1985), who compare individual differences in language with individual differences in symbolic play. They find, among other things, that the pattern of correlations between language and play differs for children of nominal-referential versus those of pronominal-expressive styles. For nominal-referential children, language abilities are most highly correlated with play involving object substitution; for pronominal-expressive children, language measures are instead correlated more highly with play involving realistic objects. This result is compatible with case studies by Wolf and Gardner (1979), who have described a distinction between "patterners" and "dramatists." Patterners tend to analyze a symbol system into its component parts (permitting referential style in language, and object substitution of play), while dramatists are more interested in the reproduction of reality through symbols (resulting in expressive style in language, with all the imitativeness that it involves, and realistic approaches to symbolic play). We will say more about this shortly, in an overview of possible explanations for individual differences in language development.

To summarize so far, there is good reason to believe that the transition from single words to sentences is just one manifestation of a change from "oneness" to "twoness" that is taking place in many other aspects of cognition. This point is made particularly clearly in studies of symbolic play, where we can find parallels to language in style as well as rate of acquisition. Now let us turn to the final phase of language development in infancy, the period of grammaticization.

GRAMMATICIZATION

Grammars are traditionally divided into two components: morphology and syntax. The morphological component provides a description of the rules governing bound morphology (i.e., the suffixes, prefixes, and infixes that can be used to build words and to modify lexical "roots"), as well as free-standing grammatical morphemes (i.e., the small set of high-frequency words that serve a primarily grammatical or "phrase-building" function, including determiners, pronouns, verb auxiliaries, prepositions, and a limited set of adverbials and other particles). The syntactic component concentrates, instead, on principles governing the hierarchical structure of sentences, and the way that constituents can be ordered within both simple and complex sentences. Even the most ardent believer in discontinuity (e.g., Bickerton, 1984) will admit that "true" language is under way when children finally begin to conquer these two aspects of grammar.

Most normal children acquire the fundamentals of syntax and morphology in their language between the ages of 20 and 30 months. The process begins at what Brown (1973) calls Stage II, when mean length of utterance begins to move beyond 1.5 morphemes. By 36 months, the average child has reached Brown's Stage IV— which means, in lay terms, that the child sounds very much like a competent speaker of her native language. She still commits morphological errors from time to time (e.g., "bringed" or "footses"), and she is not yet very handy with the complex syntactic forms like the passive ("The ball was kicked by John") or the cleft ("It was the ball that John kicked"). As Karmiloff-Smith (1979a, 1979b) has argued, many aspects of grammar may be under the control of a discourse-based system whose primary function is not the expression of basic event information, but the achievement of text cohesion, setting up transitions between sentences and clarifying shifts in reference from one sentence to another. Discourse-based grammar may not appear before 6–7 years of age, when the child has had ample experience with the structure of oral and perhaps written narratives. Before that point, grammars are organized primarily around sentence-level expressions. Nevertheless, within the limited communicative goals that preschool children set for themselves, a 36-month-old looks so radically different from a 20-month-old that it is easy to see why some psycholinguists favor discontinuous models of language development.

There are four lines of evidence that have been cited in support of the idea that grammaticization is discontinuous with the rest of cognition: the rulelike nature of morphosyntactic behavior, the speed with which basic morphemes are acquired, similarity across languages and children in the nature and sequence of grammatical development, and the uniqueness of language development in this age range.

Rules

A typical sequence in the acquisition of English verb morphology goes something like this. First, children use the same form of the verb to talk about past, present, and future events—usually the frequent and relatively simple third-person singular form (e.g., "daddy go"), though this may vary from one kind of verb to another (Bloom, Hafitz, & Lifter, 1980). Second, children begin to discriminate between the past and present forms of the most frequent verbs. Because the most frequent verbs are usually irregular, this means that the child will produce correct forms for such contrasting pairs as "go/went" and "come/came." Third, we begin to see the first evidence for *overgeneralization,* that is, the extension of a regular ending to an irregular form, as in "daddy goed" or "daddy comed." Children may vacillate between correct irregulars and overgeneralizations for many months (and sometimes for many years), but they eventually settle into an adultlike steady state in which overgeneralizations are very rare.

Overgeneralizations like these have been used for many years as evidence for the existence of rules (Berko, 1958; see McClelland & Rumelhart, in press; Mac-Whinney, 1978, for a discussion of this issue). This is particularly true when children demonstrate that they can add the appropriate ending to a word that they have never heard before (e.g., "This is a wug; this is another wug; now there are two wugs."). Furthermore, because children begin to produce overgeneralizations after a long period of producing the correct form, it is difficult to explain their behavior in terms of old learning principles like environmental frequency, practice, and reinforcement. The proliferation of rulelike behavior at 20–36 months of age thus provides grounds for the argument that the child is acquiring a new cognitive system that is discontinuous with his last 2 years of perceptual–motor learning.

However, there is now reason to believe that we overestimated the role of abstract rules in early morphological development. MacWhinney (1978) argued that many of the morphological errors produced by young children could result from a productive process of *analogy.* For example, the child may produce the new form "wugs" by noting an analogy between the nonsense word "wug" and a well-known pair of real words like "rug" and "rugs." More recently, McClelland and Rumelhart (in press) have simulated the course of verb tense learning in English children with a computer system that works entirely on the basis of multiple parallel analogies from known words to new forms. The system was never "taught" a rule, nor did it extract a single unitary rule in the traditional sense. And yet, as pairs of past and present forms were gradually fed into the system (beginning with higher-frequency pairs and moving gradually to lower- and lower-frequency exemplars), the computer produced a series of "guesses" about the past tense of new words that mimicked the *U*-shaped progression that we just described above: an initial use of correct irregular forms, followed by a period of vacillation between overregularized and correct irregular forms, eventually settling into the correct distribution of the various past–present pairings that are permissible in English. The period of overgeneralization was the emergent product of changes in the statistical composition of the "competition pool" of analogies at successive stages of learning (see also Bates & MacWhinney, in press).

This simulation certainly does not prove one way or another how human children acquire verb morphology. It does prove, however, that it is neither *logically* nor *empirically* necessary to postulate abstract rules in order to account for *U*-shaped functions and creative overgeneralizations in development. The kind of parallel, distributed learning system adopted by McClelland and Rumelhart can be used to account for many other aspects of memory and learning (e.g., visual pattern recognition). In that sense, then, it is at least possible that the acquisition of morphology is continuous with other kinds of learning that take place in the same age range.

Speed

Because so many aspects of syntax and morphology get underway in 4–8 months' time, the grammaticization period can be viewed as a kind of cognitive cataclysm. As far as we know, there are few other domains of cognition that develop so quickly. The closest analogue is the vocabulary burst in single-word development—again a development within the language domain.

In the earlier stages of language development, studies of retarded children overwhelmingly suggest that language is correlated with mental age (Miller, in press; Miller, Chapman, & Bedrosian, 1977; Miller & Yoder, 1973). This is certainly true for Down's syndrome children, who go through the earlier stages of language in slow motion, months or indeed many years after normal children. The "stretching out" of language acquisition also applies to the various nonlinguistic correlates of language discussed earlier. For example, Down's syndrome children develop single- and multischeme symbolic play around the time that they develop single- and multiword speech (Beeghly, Weiss, & Cicchetti, 1985). However, a recent study by Gleitman (1983) suggests that Down's children—once they reach Stage II (Brown, 1973)—go through the preliminary stages of morpheme acquisition in a few short weeks, in about the time that it takes a normal 2-year-old to acquire the same elements. They suggest that grammaticization requires a certain baseline level of cognition before it can begin; but once that baseline is established, an innate grammatical system is triggered and proceeds on its natural biological course independent of cognition (not unlike the phenomenon of imprinting in ducks—see Gleitman, 1981, for a more detailed discussion of the biological bases of language).

This seems to provide compelling evidence that grammaticization is independent of mental age. However, if McClelland and Rumelhart are correct (see above), the acquisition of basic morphology may actually involve relatively low-level processes—a kind of skill acquisition that is well within the reach of a 9-year-old Down's syndrome child with a mental age of 2. If this argument holds, then we must instead explain why the earlier developments took so long! Recall that McClelland and Rumelhart assumed that the system could map present-tense *meanings* onto past-tense *meanings*. This may in fact be the most demanding aspect of morphological development from a cognitive point of view, that is, figuring out the meaning and function of the contrasts involved in tense, aspect, case, number, person, and so on. The Down's syndrome child may take an abnormally long time in creating these mappings because of her cognitive limitations; but once those form–function mappings are achieved, the statistical analysis involved in acquiring different morphological variations could be carried out by lower-level mechanisms that operate at close to normal speed. Our point is, simply, that we don't know enough about the mechanisms involved in early morphosyntactic development; until we know more, we should not make too much out of the time required for the development to take place.

Universal Sequences

In the 1960s, most psycholinguists were convinced that the important aspects of language development would prove to be universal, that is, to occur in the same way and in the same sequence in every natural language (e.g., McNeill, 1970). How-ever, as we saw earlier, claims about universality cannot be maintained even for the stage of first word combinations. There are marked individual differences among children learning English in the extent to which they make use of morphology in Stage I. There are also marked differences across languages in, for example, the probability that two-word combinations will observe word order regularities (Bates & MacWhinney, 1979; and Braine, 1976) and the probability that children will omit verbs in their telegraphic speech (Bates, 1976). If Stage I shows so much variability, what hope is there for later stages in the acquisition of grammar?

In fact, the argument could be made that variability is maximal during Stage I—precisely because this represents an inherently prelinguistic or at least pregrammat-ical stage of development. However, individual styles do seem to hold up into the grammaticization period—for example, in the noun lovers and noun leavers studied by Horgan (1979). And successive stages in the acquisition of grammar also look very different from one language to another. For example, Turkish children—who are acquiring a morphological system that is exceptionally regular, clear, and se-mantically transparent—seem to have acquired all of the basic case morphology contrasts in their language by 24 months of age (Slobin, 1983). Russian and Serbo-Croatian children, who must acquire a very irregular and arbitrary system of case contrasts, do not reach an equivalent level before 6 or 7 years of age.

Slobin and his colleagues have recently documented variations in the acquisition of grammar across a large range of typologically distinct languages (Slobin, 1986). Based on this work, Slobin presents a lengthy list of operating principles that seem to govern the acquisition of every natural language. These include a tendency to avoid discontinuous morphemes (e.g., "call" and "up" in "Call the girl up."), a preference for locating morphemes at the end rather than the beginning or the mid-dle of a word, a belief that some meanings are inherently "grammaticizable" (e.g., person, gender, tense) while other meanings are not likely to be coded in the gram-mar (e.g., color, time of day), and a host of other probabilistic biases about what a language should be like. Notice that these operating principles represent *universal processes,* but they do not require children to come up with the same *universal content* at every stage of development. Because natural languages do vary a great deal, a fact that is compounded by variations in the individual child's language learning environment (e.g., whether she is learning primarily from parents or peers), children may look quite different from one another at any given stage. However, Slobin argues that the various hypotheses children entertain in the course of gram-matical development can all be explained with reference to this universal set of biases about language. The operating principles could be viewed as the prisms in a kalei-doscope: The basic underlying structure is constant, but an infinite set of variations are possible as a function of random, unsystematic, or partially systematic data.

Slobin has provided a richly detailed theoretical framework for considering all the variation we see in the acquisition of grammar (see also papers in MacWhinney, in press). Certainly he is correct in urging us to abandon the simpler "universalism" of our innocent past. But assuming that these principles prove to be correct, one very serious question remains: Where do the operating principles come from? Slobin is convinced that they represent an innate and domain-specific set of constraints on learning, quite independent from the rest of cognition. We are not so sure. Many of these principles could be viewed as language-specific applications of very general principles that constrain many aspects of perception and motor skill. For example, the tendency to avoid discontinuous morphemes could derive from the Gestalt principle of closure: Where possible, use a closed contour to form the boundary of an object. This kind of argument brings us to the fourth and final argument in favor of the independence of grammar in development.

Uniqueness

Within the period from 20 to 30 months there are no obvious analogues to the grammaticization process outside of language. Of course this may be partially due to our ignorance of cognitive development during the 1–3 age range (Emde & Harmon, 1984; Kagan, 1971). McCall, Eichhorn, and others (1977) find evidence for major reorganizations in the composition of intelligence (or whatever it is that infant intelligence scales measure) at 20 months and again at 30 months. So the grammaticization period is certainly bracketed by across-the-board changes in cognitive ability. But, perhaps because language development is such an effective "scene stealer" between these two points, very litte else is known about the intellectual achievements of toddlerhood (e.g., changes in spatial cognition, event representation, pattern recognition, motion detection, and/or classification—cf. Langer, 1980; Stiles-Davis, Sugarman, & Nass, in press; Sugarman, 1982a, 1982b).

Some recent studies of elicited symbolic play at 20–36 months suggest that children may learn to put cultural acts into a conventional sequence during this period (McCune-Nicolich, 1981; McCune-Nicolich & Bruskin, 1982; O'Connell & Gerard, 1985; Shore et al., 1984). Before this point, even though the 20-month-old can produce sequences of two or three gestures, the sequence in which those gestures are produced tends to be random from the point of view of conventional adult "scripts." For example, a child may carry out a bath sequence by first soaping the teddybear, then wrapping it in a towel, and only then placing it in the bathtub. By 28 months, in both spontaneous and imitative play, the child is much more likely to act the sequence out in its canonical order (e.g., put the teddy in the bathtub, soap it up, take it out, and dry it off). Furthermore, if props are missing for a correct execution of the script, the child will try to make the necessary plans in advance (e.g., finding a wooden block that can serve as the soap). As O'Connell and Gerard put it, the 20-month-old seems to know *that* certain acts belong together in a script; but she does not know *how* they go together. By 28 months, the child also understands the principles that hold an ordered sequence together (Gerard, 1984; O'Connell, 1984). Because the period from 20 to 28 months is so important in the acquisition of grammar, this raises the interesting possibility that grammaticization and conventional sequencing in play are based on some common change in the capacity to order a series of arbitrary cultural units.

Until we know more about cognitive development in the 1–3 age range, claims about these and other nonlinguistic analogues to grammar are pure speculation (cf. Curtis, Yamada, & Fromkin, 1979; Greenfield, Nelson, & Saltzman, 1972; for a more detailed discussion, see Bates & Snyder, in press; Johnston, 1986). At all the previous stages that we have reviewed, a specific set of nonlinguistic skills are reliably correlated with language—although this set of nonlinguistic correlates varies from one age to another. We have no reason to believe that the process stops cold at 2 years of age. But it is simply too soon to tell. A different kind of uniqueness argument applies not to the contrast between language and the rest of cognition, but to the relationship between grammar and the other domains of language—in particular, phonology and syntax. Here considerably more information is available.

In the section on speech production, we pointed out that changes in phonology are linked to both lexical and grammatical development throughout the first years of life. More recent evidence by the Stanford CPP suggests that these links involve style as well as rate of development. They find correlations between "phonological inconsistency" and "syntactic inconsistency" at 3 years of age. Furthermore, this style dimension in 3-year-old phonology is predicted by style (but not rate) of phonological development at one year (Vihman, 1985; Vihman et al., in press). In other words, individual children seem to take the same approach to grammar that they take to phonology, during the grammaticization period and at earlier stages of development.

Even stronger links can be found between the domains of grammar and lexical development. With regard to variation in rate, Bates and colleagues (1985) report that half the variance in mean length of utterance at 28 months (as well as a variety of associated grammatical measures) can be predicted by variation in a handful of lexical measures taken at 13 months of age. When scores on a single lexical measure at 20 months are added to the equation, *all* the predictable variance in 28-month MLU can be accounted for. This finding strongly suggests that children are using the same basic mechanisms in the acquisition of grammar that they used in the acquisition of single lexical items during the earlier stages.

With regard to variation in style, we have already pointed out evidence for continuity between referential–expressive style during the one-word stage and pronominal–nominal style during the stage of first word combinations. But what about the later stages in grammar? At 28 months of age, *all* normal children are hard at work analyzing the morphology and syntax of their native language. Bates and associates provide evidence suggesting that the holistic–Gestalt approach to grammar at 20 months is in fact of relatively little use at this later stage (cf. Nelson, 1985). For example, they report a significant *negative* correlation between the tendency to produce function words at 20 months and the same measure 8 months later—suggesting that the children who leave these morphemes out of their speech in Stage I are ultimately more successful in the acquisition of productive control over grammar. In a sense, the production of telegraphic speech presupposes some kind of analysis; grammatical inflections and function words have to be identified if the child is going to delete them systematically from his speech. This kind of analytic approach to language may provide at least a short-term advantage in the acquisition of grammar. However, whether or not an expressive–holistic style is associated with temporary setbacks, there is reason to believe that the two styles of language persist for years to come (Fillmore, 1979; Horgan, 1981).

This brings us to an overview of individual differences in language development, with at least some speculation about the mechanisms that may be responsible for the strands of variation that appear at 10–28 months of age (Bates et al., 1985; Kempler, 1980; Nelson, 1981, 1985; Peters, 1983). Table 3.1 (from Bates et al., 1985) summarizes some of the phonological, semantic, grammatical, and nonlinguistic variables that have been associated with a proposed "two-strand" theory of language development. Remember that these summary statements are drawn from many separate studies and might well fail to hold together as a block if all these factors

TABLE 3.1.   Individual Differences in Language Development: Summmary of Evidence

Strand 1	Strand 2
Semantics	
High proportions of nouns	Low proportions of nouns
Single-word utterances only in first 50 words	Some whole phrases and formulas in first 50 words
High adjective use	Low adjective use
Greater variety with lexical categories	Less variety with lexical categories
Imitation of object labels	Unselective imitation
Faster development of vocabulary	Slower development of vocabulary
Greater flexibility in use of single words	Contextual rigidity in use of single words
Grammar	
Telegraphic speech omitting functions	Early sentences contain inflections and function words
Refers to self and others with full noun phrase	Refers to self and others in pronominal form
Novel combinations	Frozen forms
Meaningful elements only	Some use of dummy words
Imitations are not more advanced grammatically than spontaneous speech	Imitations are more advanced grammatically than spontaneous speech
Greater consistency in word order rules	Less consistency in word order rules
Pragmatics	
Focus on object labeling	Focus on interpersonal regulation through language
Less variety of speech acts	Greater variety of speech acts
Phonology	
Better articulation and intelligibility	Less articulation and intelligibility
More use of consonants in babbling	Less use of consonants in babbling
Greater consistency in pronunciation across word tokens	More variability in pronunciation across word tokens
Demographic Variables	
Firstborn	Later born
Female	Male
Higher SES	Lower SES

Source: From "From First Words to Grammar: Individual Differences and Dissociable Mechanisms" by E. Bates, I. Bretherton, and L. Snyder. Unpublished manuscript, 1985.

were examined together in a single sample. Remember also that these variable are almost all continuous and normally distributed, with most children demonstrating a mixture of both styles.

The referential approach to language begins with an orientation toward individual words or wordlike sounds in the prespeech era, together with a particularly marked interest in interactions that are mediated through objects. This orientation toward objects shows up in the single-word stage in a high proportion of object names, which is in turn associated with more rapid expansion of the vocabulary and higher levels of language comprehension. Pronunciation at this and subsequent stages seems to be relatively more articulate and crisp—an impression based on the greater consistency with which such children apply their limited set of phonological principles or rules. By the stage of first word combinations, this style of language is associated with nominal constructions and a telegraphic avoidance of pronouns and other forms of grammatical morphology. By the time grammatical morphology comes under productive control, these children may also be more advanced in grammar—even though they seemed superficially to be less advanced in Stage I. The initial orientation toward nouns may persist into later stages of development, with greater expansion of noun phrases through adjectives and other descriptive terms. With regard to nonlinguistic variables, referential children are (in some studies, but not in others) more likely to be firstborn and female, to engage in longer bouts of play with objects, and to engage in play that involves object substitution (e.g., using a shoe or a wooden block for a baby in a game of putting baby to bed).

The expressive style begins in the prespeech era with an orientation toward the "intonational packaging" of language rather than individual word units. These children are less oriented toward interactions involving objects, and more likely to engage directly in social interaction. They may be more gregarious overall, and more prone to imitate sounds and gestures without understanding the nature or purpose of those activities. In the single-word stage, these children have fairly heterogeneous vocabularies, sometimes consisting of sentence-length formulas. It is in fact difficult to locate the border between single- and multiword speech, as more and more frozen formulas and partially productive frame + slot sentences appear in the child's repertoire. When sentences are produced, they are likely to contain pronouns and other grammatical morphemes from the very beginning, so it is also difficult to determine when a given morpheme is being used productively. This style is associated with a slower pace of development overall, although such children may seem very precocious at the early stages. Their pronunciation can be highly variable from one utterance to another; hence despite their efforts to sound like other people, these children may be harder to understand at the early stages. Also, because they are more prone to imitate whole forms without analysis, comprehension may actually appear to lag behind production at certain points. The noun avoidance so evident at the earlier stages may continue into later stages of language, so that an expressive child who is matched in mean length of utterance to a referential child may "buy" her MLU through the expansion of verb phrases rather than nouns and their modifiers. Nonlinguistic associates that are reported in some studies (but not others) include a more social orientation at every age, a more impulsive "leap before you look" approach to life. These children are somewhat more likely to be later born, and male. They seem to be somewhat more oriented toward reproduction of reality in their play, and less interested in breaking a symbolic array down into its component parts.

Assuming that these two strands do hang together (which they do to a limited and rather complicated degree—see Bates et al., 1985), how can we explain them? Almost every conceivable kind of explanation has been offered, including the following:

1.   Differences in maternal style, with the parents of referential children using strategies that foster communication about objects

2.   Differences in brain organization (including purported differences in rate of maturation between the analytic left hemisphere and the holistic right hemisphere, and/or differences in the development of Broca's area and Wernicke's area within the left hemisphere)

3. Temperamental factors (i.e., referential children are reflective, inhibited, shy; expressive children are impulsive, gregarious, sociable)

4. Differences in cognitive style (i.e., referential style is analytic, field independent; expressive style is holistic, Gestalt oriented, field dependent)

5. Differences in language modality (i.e., referential style results from greater emphasis on comprehension; expressive style results from greater emphasis on production)

It is sometimes difficult to distinguish between wisdom and cowardice, but we think it would be wiser at this point not to recommend *any* of the proposed explanations until more information is available. These proposals are not mutually exclusive, and they all may contribute to the variation that we see in early language development. One conclusion does seem warranted at this point, however: Whatever the cause of these variations in style, they do seem to cut across the traditional domains of language development, that is, phonology, semantics, and grammar. To that extent, they can be used to argue for an interactionist approach to the study of language.

CONCLUSION

Language is by definition a public behavior, wherein the child displays in exquisite detail the inner workings of the mind. As a result, we know much more about language than about any other aspect of cognition and behavior. It is certainly possible that language involves unique mental organs, structures that are used for no other purpose than the computations involved in comprehension, production, and/ or acquisition of language. But it is too early to say at this point. And because it is too early to know, we think it would be wiser to proceed with the assumption that language reflects other aspects of cognition.

The Italians have an expression: *Il calzolaio parla solo di scarpe*—"The shoemaker speaks only of shoes." Psycholinguists, like the Italian shoemaker, have made it difficult to carry out a conversation with investigators struggling to understand the rest of human development. We propose a different metaphor: If we assume instead that language acquisition participates in and displays the many other contents of mind, then psycholinguistics can become a window onto the rest of cognitive–affective development. If that is our working assumption (and if it proves to be true), we can use information on language to understand far less accessible aspects of development, as children make the transition from infancy to childhood.

REFERENCES

Abramson, A., & Lisker, L. (1967). Discriminability along the voice continuum: Cross-language tests. *Proceedings of the Sixth International Congress of Phonetic Sciences.* Prague: Academic, 1970.

Abramson, A., & Lisker, L. (1973). Voice-timing perception in Spanish word-initial stops. *Journal of Phonetics, 1,* 1–8.

Acredolo, L., & Goodwyn, S. (1985a, April). Spontaneous signing in normal infants. Paper presented at the biennial meeting of the Society for Research in Child Development, Toronto, Ontario.

Acredolo, L., & Goodwyn, S. (1985b). Symbolic gesturing in language development. *Human Development, 28,* 40–49.

Andersen, E., Dunlea, A., & Kekelis, L. (1984). Blind children's language: Resolving some differences. *Journal of Child Language, 11,* 645–664.

Aslin, R., & Pisoni, D. (1980). Some developmental processes in speech perception. In G. H. Yeni-Komshian, J. F. Kavanagh, & C. A. Ferguson (Eds.), *Child phonology: Vol. 2. Perception* (pp. 67–96). New York: Academic.

Aslin, R., Pisoni, D., & Jusczyk, P. (1983). Auditory development and speech perception in infancy. In M. Haith & J. Campos (Eds.), *Handbook of child psychology: Infant development.* New York: Wiley.

Atkinson, M. (1979). Prerequisites for reference. In E. Ochs & B. Schieffelin (Eds.), *Developmental pragmatics* (pp. 215–247). New York: Academic.

Bates, E. (1976). *Language and context: The acquisition of pragmatics.* New York: Academic.

Bates, E., Benigni, L., Bretherton, I., Camaioni, L., & Volterra, V. (1979). *The emergence of symbols: Cognition and communication in infancy.* New York: Academic.

Bates, E., Bretherton, I., Shore, C., & McNew, S. (1983). Names, gestures and objects: Symbolization in infancy and aphasia. In K. Nelson (Ed.), *Children's language* (Vol. 4) (pp. 59–123). Hillsdale, NJ: Erlbaum.

Bates, E., Bretherton, I., & Snyder, L. (1985). From first words to grammar: Individual differences and dissociable mechanisms. Manuscript.

Bates, E., Camaioni, L., & Volterra, V. (1975). The acquisition of performatives prior to speech. *Merrill-Palmer Quarterly, 21,* 205–226.

Bates, E., & MacWhinney, B. (1979). A functional approach to the acquisition of grammar. In E. Ochs & B. Schieffelin (Eds.), *Developmental pragmatics* (pp. 167–211). New York: Academic.

Bates, E., & MacWhinney, B. (in press). Competition, variation, and language learning. In B. MacWhinney (Ed.), *Mechanisms of language acquisition.* Hillsdale, NJ: Erlbaum.

Bates, E., & Snyder, L. (in press). The cognitive hypothesis in language development. In I. Uzgiris & J. McV. Hunt (Eds.), *Research with scales of phychological development in infancy.* Champaign-Urbana: University of Illinois Press.

Bates, E., & Volterra, V. (1985). On the invention of language: An alternative view. Commentary on S. Goldin-Meadow & C. Mylander. Gestural communication in deaf children: Some effects and non-effects of parental input on early language development. *Monographs of the Society for Research in Child Development,* Serial No. 207, Vol. *49,* Nos. 3 & 4.

Bates E., Whitesell, K., & Oakes, L. (in preparation). *Referential style in language and gesture.* Manuscript, University of California, San Diego.

Bauer, P. (1985). *Referential and expressive styles in linguistic and nonlinguistic domains: A longitudinal examination.* Unpublished doctoral dissertation, Miami University, Oxford, OH.

Beeghly, M., Weiss, B., & Cicchetti, D. (1985, October). *Structural parallels between symbolic play and language in children with Down's syndrome.* Paper presented at the Tenth Annual Boston University Conference on Language Development, Boston.

Beilin, H. (1975). *Studies in the cognitive basis of language acquisition.* New York: Academic.

Bell, S. (1970). The development of the concept of object as related to infant–mother attachment. *Child Development, 41,* 291–313.

Benedict, H. (1979). Early lexical development: Comprehension and production. *Journal of Child Language, 6,* 183–200.

Berko, J. (1958). The child's learning of English morphology. *Word, 14,* 150–177.

Bever, T. (1970). The cognitive basis for linguistic structures. In J. Hayes (Ed.), *Cognitive and the development of language.* New York: Wiley.

Bickerton, D. (1984). The language bioprogram hypothesis. *The Behavioral and Brain Sciences, 7:2,* 173–187.

Bloom, L. (1970). *Language development: Form and function in emerging grammars.* Cambridge, MA: M.I.T. Press.

Bloom, L., Hafitz, E., & Lifter, K. (1980). Schematic organization of verbs in child language and the acquisition of grammatical morphemes. *Language, 6,* 380–420.

Bloom, L., Lightbown, P., & Hood, L. (1975). Structure and variation in child language. *Monographs of the Society for Research in Child Development, 40* (Serial No. 160).

Bohannon, J. N., III, & Warren, A., (1984, April). *Verbal interaction patterns of blind mothers and sighted children.* Paper presented to the Southeast Conference on Human Development. Athens, GA.

Bonvillian, J., Orlansky, M., & Novack, L. (1983). Developmental milestones: Sign language acquisition and motor development. *Child Development, 54,* 1435–1445.

Bonvillian, J., Orlansky, M., Novack, L., & Folven, R. (1983). Early sign language and cognitive development. In D. Rogers & J. Sloboda (Eds.), *The acquisition of symbolic skills* (pp. 207–214). Chicago: Plenum.

Bowerman, M. (1973). Structural relationships in children's utterances: Syntactic or semantic? In T. Moore (Ed.), *Cognitive development and the acquisition of language* (pp. 197–214). New York: Academic.

Boysson-Bardies, B., Sagart, L., & Durand, C. (1984). Discernible differences in the babbling of infants according to target language. *Journal of Child Language, 11,* 1–15.

Braine, M. (1963). The ontogeny of English phrase structure: The first phase. *Language, 39,* 3–13.

Braine, M. (1976). Children's first word combinations. *Monographs of the Society for Research in Child Development, 41* (1, Serial No. 164).

Branigan, G. (1979). Some reasons why successive single word utterances are not. *Journal of Child Language, 6,* 411–421.

Brazelton, T., Kozlowski, B., & Main, M. (1974). The origins of reciprocity: The early mother–infant interacion. In M. Lewis & L. Rosenblum (Eds.), *The effect of the infant on its caregiver* (pp. 49–75). New York: Wiley.

Bretherton, I. (1985). Attachment theory: Retrospect and prospect. In I. Bretherton & E. Waters (Eds.), Growing points of attachment theory and research. *Monographs of the Society for Research in Child Development, 50,* #209, No. 1 and 2.

Bretherton, I. (in press). How to do things with one word: The ontogenesis of intentional message-making in infancy. In M. Smith & J. Locke (Eds.), *The emergent lexicon.* New York: Academic.

Bretherton, I., Bates, E. (1979). The emergence of intentional communication. In I. Uzgiris (Ed.), *New directions for child development* (Vol. 4) (pp. 81–100). San Francisco: Jossey-Bass.

Bretherton, I., Bates, E., McNew, S., Shore, C., Williamson, C., & Beeghly-Smith, M. (1981). Comprehension and production of symbols in infancy. *Developmental Psychology, 17,* 728–736.

Bretherton, I., & Beeghly, M. (1982). Talking about internal states: The acquisition of an explicit theory of mind. *Developmental Psychology, 18,* 906–921.

Bretherton, I., McNew, S., & Beeghly-Smith, M. (1981). Early person knowledge as expressed in gestural and verbal communication: When do infants acquire a "theory of mind"? In M. E. Lamb & L. R. Sherrod (Eds.), *Infant social cognition* (pp. 333–373). Hillsdale, NJ: Erlbaum.

Bretherton, I., McNew, S., Snyder, L., & Bates, E. (1983). Individual differences at 20 months: Analytic and holistic strategies in language acquisition. *Journal of Child Language, 10,* 293–320.

Brown, R. (1973). *A first language: The early stages.* Cambridge, MA: Harvard University Press.

Brown, R., Cazden, C., & Bellugi, U. (1969). The child's grammar from I to III. In J. Hill (Ed.), *Minnesota symposium on child psychology* (Vol. 2) (pp. 28–73). Minneapolis: University of Minnesota Press.

Bruner, J. (1975a). The ontogenesis of speech acts. *Journal of Child Language, 2,* 1–19.

Bruner, J. (1975b). From communication to language: A psychological perspective. *Cognition, 3*(3), 17–48.

Bruner, J. (1977). Early social interaction and language acquisition. In H. Schaffer (Ed.), *Studies in mother–infant interaction.* New York: Academic.

Bruner, J. (1980). Afterword. In D. Olson (Ed.), *The social foundations of language and thought* (pp. 376–386). New York: Norton.

Bruner, J. (1983). *Child's talk: Learning to use language.* New York: Norton.

Butterworth, G. (1979, September). *What minds have in common with space: A perceptual mechanism for joint reference in infancy.* Paper presented to the Developmental Section, British Psychological Society, Southampton.

Campos, J., & Stenberg, C. (1981). Perception, appraisal and emotion: The onset of social referencing. In M. Lamb & L. Sherrod (Eds.), *Infant social cognition* (pp. 273–314). Hillsdale, NJ: Erlbaum.

Carter, A. (1978). From sensorimotor vocalizations to words: A case study of the evolution of attention-directing communication in the second year. In A. Lock (Ed.), *Action, gesture, and symbol: The emergence of language* (pp. 309–350). London: Academic.

Case, R. (1985). *Intellectual development: From birth to adulthood.* New York: Academic.

Case, R., & Khanna, F. (1981). The missing links: Stages in children's progression from sensorimotor to logical thought. In W. Fischer (Ed.), *New directions for child development* (Vol. 12) (pp. 21–32). San Francisco: Jossey-Bass.

Chi, M. (1976). Short-term memory limitations in children: Capacity or processing deficits? *Memory & Cognition, 4,* 559–572.

Chi, M. (1977). Age differences in memory span. *Journal of Experimental Child Psychology, 23,* 266–281.

Chi, M., & Klahr, D. (1975). Span and rate of apprehension in children and adults. *Journal of Experimental Child Psychology, 19,* 434–439.

Chomsky, N. (1980). *Rules and representation.* New York: Columbia University Press.

Chomsky, N. (1981). *Lectures on government and binding: The Pisa lectures.* Dordrecht: Foris.

Chomsky, N., & Miller, G. (1983). Introduction to the formal analysis of natural languages. In R. D. Luce, R. Busch, & E. Galanter (Eds.), *Handbook of mathematical psychology.* New York: Wiley.

Clark, E. (1978). From gesture to word: On the natural history of deixis in language acquisition. In J. S. Bruner & A. Garton (Eds.), *Human growth and development: Wolfson College lectures,* 1976. Oxford: Clarendon.

Clarke-Stewart, A. (1973). Interactions between mothers and their young children: Characteristics and consequences. *Monographs of the Society for Research in Child Development, 37* (Serial No. 153).

Corrigan, R. (1978). Language development as related to stage 6 object permanence development. *Journal of Child Language, 5,* 173–189.

Cromer, R. (1974). The development of language and cognition: The cognition hypothesis. In B. Foss (Ed.), *New perspectives in child development.* Harmondsworth: Penguin.

Curtis, S., Yamada, J., & Fromkin, V. (1979). How independent is language? On the question of formal parallels between action and grammar. *UCLA Working Papers in Cognitive Linguistics, 1,* 131–157.

DeLaguna, G. (1927). *Speech: Its function and development.* Bloomington, IN: Indiana University Press.

Dore, J. (1975). Holophrase, speech acts, and language universals. *Journal of Child Language, 2,* 21–40.

Edwards, D. (1973). Sensory motor intelligence and semantic relations in early child grammar. *Cognition, 2,* 395–434.

Edwards, D. (1978). Social relations and early language. In A. Lock (Ed.), *Action, gesture and symbol* (pp. 449–470). London: Academic.

Eilers, R., & Minifie, F. (1975). Fricative discrimination in early infancy. *Journal of Speech & Hearing Research, 18,* 158–167.

Eimas, P. (1985). The perception of speech in early infancy. *Scientific American, 252*(1), 46–61.

Eimas, P., Siqueland, E., Jusczyk, P., & Vigorito, J. (1971). Speech perception in infants. *Science, 171,* 303–306.

Emde, R., & Harmon, R. (Eds.). (1984). *Continuities and discontinuities in development.* New York: Plenum.

Escalona, S. (1973, October). *On precursors of language.* Paper presented at Teachers College, Columbia University, New York.

Fenson, L., & Ramsay, D. (1980). Decentration and integration of the child's play in the second year. *Child Development, 51,* 171–178.

Ferguson, C. (1978). Learning to pronounce: The earliest stages of phonological development in the child. In F. D. Minifie & L. L. Lloyd (Eds.), *Communicative and cognitive abilities: Early behavioral assessment.* Baltimore: University Park Press.

Ferguson, C. (1984, April). *From babbling to speech.* Invited address to the International Conference on Infant Studies, New York.

Ferguson, C., & Farwell, C. (1975). Words and sounds in early language acquisition. *Language, 51,* 419–439.

Ferguson, C., & Macken, M. (1983). The role of play in phonological development. In K. Nelson (Ed.), *Children's language* (Vol. 4). Hillsdale, NJ: Erlbaum.

Ferguson, C., & Slobin, D. (Eds.). (1973). *Studies in child language development.* New York: Holt, Rinehart & Winston.

Fillmore, L. (1979). Individual differences in second language acquisition. In C. Fillmore, D. Kempler, & W. Wang (Eds.), *Individual differences in language ability and language behavior.* New York: Academic.

Flavell, J. (1970). Concept development. In P. Mussen (Ed.), *Carmichaels's manual of child psychology* (Vol. 1). New York: Wiley.

Flavell, J. (1971). Stage-related properties of cognitive development. *Cognitive Psychology, 2,* 421–453.

Fodor, J. (1983). *The modularity of mind.* Cambridge, MA: M.I.T. Press.

Fogel, A., & Hannan, T. (1985). Manual actions in nine- to fifteen-week old infants during face-to-face interaction with their mothers. *Child Development, 56,* 1271–1279.

Folven, R., & Bovillian, J. (1985, April). *Nonlinguistic gestures and early sign language acquisition.* Paper presented at the biennial meeting of the Society for Research in Child Development, Toronto.

Gardner, H. (1983). *Frames of mind.* New York: Basic.

Gerard, A. (1984). *Imitation and sequencing in early childhood.* Unpublished doctoral dissertation, University of California, San Diego.

Gleitman, L. (1981). Maturational determinants of language growth. *Cognition, 10,* 103–114.

Gleitman, L. (1983). Biological predispositions to learn language. In W. Demopolous & A. Marras (Eds.), *Language learning and concept acquisition.* Norwood, NJ: Ablex.

Goldfield, B. (1985). *The contribution of child and caregiver to referential and expressive language.* Manuscript under review.

Golinkoff, R. (1983). The preverbal negotiation of failed messages. In R. Golinkoff (Ed.) *The transition from prelinguistic to linguistic communication* (pp. 57–78). Hillsdale, NJ: Erlbaum.

Gopnik, A. (1981). The development of non-nominal expressions: Why the first words aren't about things. In D. Ingram & P. Dale (Eds.), *Child language: An international perspective.* Baltimore: University Park Press.

Greenfield, P. (1980). Toward an operational and logical analysis of intentionality: The use of discourse in early child language. In D. R. Olson (Ed.), *The social foundations of language and thought* (pp. 254–279). New York: Norton.

Greenfield, P., Nelson, K., & Saltzman, E. (1972). The development of rulebound strategies for manipulating seriated cups: A parallel between action and grammar. *Cognitive Psychology, 3,* 291–310.

Greenfield, P., & Smith, J. (1976). *The structure of communication in early development.* New York: Academic.

Halliday, M. (1975). *Learning how to mean: Explorations in the development of language.* London: Edward Arnold.

Hannan, T. E. (1982). Young infants' hand and finger expressions: An analysis of category reliability. In T. M. Field & A. Fogel (Eds.), *Emotion and early interaction.* Hillsdale, NJ: Erlbaum.

Harding, C., & Golinkoff, R. (1979). The origins of intentional vocalizations in prelinguistic infants. *Child Development, 50,* 33–40.

Hayes, J. (Ed.). (1970). *Cognition and the development of language.* New York: Wiley.

Hoffmeister, R. (1978a). *The development of demonstratives, pronouns, locatives, and personal pronouns in the acquisition of American Sign Language by deaf children of deaf parents.* Unpublished doctoral dissertation, University of Minnesota, Minneapolis.

Hoffmeister, R. (1978b). An analysis of possessive constructions in the ASL of a young deaf child of deaf parents. Unpublished manuscript, Temple University.

Horgan, D. (1976). Linguistic knowledge at early Stage I: Evidence from successive single word utterances. *Papers and reports in child language development.* Stanford: Stanford University Committee on Linguistics.

Horgan, D. (1979, May). *Nouns: Love 'em or leave 'em.* Address to the New York Academy of Sciences.

Horgan, D. (1981). Rate of language acquisition and noun emphasis. *Journal of Psycholinguistic Research, 10:6,* 629–640.

Howe, C. (1976). The meanings of two-word utterances in the speech of young children. *Journal of Child Language, 3,* 29–47.

Ingram, D. (1974). Phonological rules in young children. *Journal of Child Language, 1,* 49–64.

Ingram, D. (1976). Current issues in child phonology. In O. Morehead & A. Morehead (Eds.), *Normal and deficient child language* (pp. 3–27). Baltimore: University Park Press.

Ingram, D. (1978). Sensori-motor intelligence and languge development. In A. Lock (Ed.), *Action, gesture and symbol.* London: Academic.

Ingram, D. (1979). Phonological patterns in the speech of young children. In P. Fletcher & M. Garman (Eds.), *Language acquisition* (pp. 133–148). Cambridge, Eng.: Cambridge University Press.

Jakobson, R. (1968). *Child language, aphasia and phonological universals* (A. Keiler, Trans.). The Hague: Mouton. First published 1941 as *Kindersprache, aphasie und allegmeine lautgesetze.* Uppsala: Almqvist and Wiksell.

Johnston, J. (1986). Cognitive prerequisites: The evidence from children learning English. In D. I. Slobin (Ed.), *The cross-linguistic study of language acquisition.* Hillsdale, NJ: Erlbaum.

Jusczyk, P. (1981). Infant speech perception: A critical appraisal. In P. Eimas & J. Miller, (Eds.), *Perspective on the study of speech.* Hillsdale, NJ: Erlbaum.

Jusczyk, P. (1985). On characterizing the development of speech perception. In J. Mehler & R. Fox (Eds.), *Neonate cognition: Beyond the blooming, buzzing confusion* (pp. 199–230). Hillsdale, NJ: Erlbaum.

Kagan, J. (1971). *Change and continuity in infancy.* New York: Wiley.

Kagan, J. (1981). *The second year: the emergence of self-awareness.* Cambridge, MA: Harvard University Press.

Karmiloff-Smith, A. (1979a). *A functional approach to child language: A study of determiners and reference.* Cambridge, Eng.: Cambridge University Press.

Karmiloff-Smith, A. (1979b). Micro- and macrodevelopmental changes in language acquisition and other representational systems. *Cognitive Science, 3,* 91–118.

Kempler, D. (1980). Variation in language acquisition. *UCLA Working Papers in Cognitive Linguistics, 2,* 1–20.

Kinsbourne, M., & Lempert, H. (1978). Does left brain lateralization of speech arise from right-biased orienting to salient percepts? *Human Development, 22,* 270–275.

Koopmans-van Deinum, & van der Stelt, B. (1985). Early stages in the development of speech movements. In B. Lindblom & R. Zetterstrom (Eds.), *Precursors of early speech.* Basingstrake, Hampshire: MacMillan.

Krashen, S., Scarella, R., & Long, M. (Eds.). (1982). *Child-adult differences in second language acquisition.* Rowley, MA: Newbury House.

Kuhl, P. (1986). The special-mechanisms debate in speech: Contributions of tests on animals (and the relations of these tests to studies using non-speech stimuli). In S. Harnad (Ed.), *Categorical perception.* Cambridge, Eng.: Cambridge University Press.

Kuhl, P., & Meltzoff, A. (1982). The bimodal perception of speech in infancy. *Science, 218,* 1138–1141.

Kuhl, P., & Meltzoff, A. (1984). The intermodal representation of speech in infants. *Infant Behavior and Development, 7,* 361–381.

Kuhl, P., & Miller, J. (1975). Speech perception by the chinchilla: Voiced-voiceless distinction in alveolar plosive consonants. *Science, 190,* 69–72.

Kuhl, P., & Miller, J. (1978). Speech perception by the chinchilla: Identification functions for synthetic VOT stimuli. *Journal of the Acoustical Society of America, 63,* 905–917.

Kuhl, P., & Padden, D. (1982). Enhanced discriminability at the phonetic boundaries for the voicing feature in macaques. *Perception & Psychophysics, 32,* 542–550.

Kuhl, P., & Padden, D. (1983). Enhanced discriminability at the phonetic boundaries for the place feature in macaques. *Journal of the Acoustical Society of America, 73,* 1003–1010.

Langer, J. (1980). *The origins of logic.* New York: Academic.

Leonard, L. (1976). *Meaning in child language.* New York: Grune & Stratton.

Leonard, L., & Brown, B. (1984). Nature and boundaries of phonologic categories: A case study of an unusual phonologic pattern in a language impaired child. *Journal of Speech & Hearing Disorders, 49,* 419–428.

Leonard, L., Newhoff, M., & Mesalam, L. (1980). Individual differences in early childhood phonology. *Applied Psycholinguistics, 1,* 7–30.

Leopold, W. F. (1939–1949). *Speech development of a bilingual child* (Vols. 1–4). Evanston, IL: Northwestern University Press.

Leung, E., & Rheingold, H. (1981). The development of pointing as a social gesture. *Developmental Psychology, 17,* 215–220.

Lewis, M., & Brooks-Gunn, J. (1979). Toward a theory of social cognition: The development of self. In I. Uzgiris (Ed.), *New directions for child development* (pp. 1–20). New York: Academic.

Lewis, M., & Freedle, R. (1973). Mother-infant dyad: The cradle of meaning. In P. Pliner, L. Krames, & T. Alloway (Eds.), *Communication and affect* (pp. 127–155). New York: Academic.

Liberman, A., Cooper, F., Shankweiler, D., & Studdert-Kennedy, M. (1967). Perception of the speech code. *Psychological Review, 74,* 431–461.

Lieberman, P. (1970). Towards a unified phonetic theory. *Linguistic Inquiry, 1,* 307–322.

Lieberman, P. (1973). On the evolution of human language: A unified view. *Cognition, 2,* 59–94.

Lock, A. (Ed.). (1978). *Action, gesture, and symbol.* New York: Academic.

Lock, A. (1980). *The guided reinvention of language.* New York: Academic.

Lock, A., Young, A., & Service, V. (1985, April). *The development of the pointing gesture: Some normative and microanalytic data.* Paper presented at the biennial meeting of the Society for Research in Child Development, Toronto.

Macken, M. (1979). Developmental reorganization in phonology: A hierarchy of basic units. *Lingua, 49,* 11–49.

Macken, M. (in press). Algebraic and stochastic aspects of phonological learning. In B. MacWhinney (Ed.), *Mechanisms of language acquisition.* Hillsdale, NJ: Erlbaum.

Macken, M., & Ferguson, C. (1983). Cognitive aspects of phonological development: Model, evidence and issues. In K. Nelson (Ed.), *Children's language* (Vol. 4). Hillsdale, NJ: Erlbaum.

Macnamara, J. (1972). Cognitive basis of language learning in infants. *Psychological Review, 79,* 1–13.

MacWhinney, B. (1978). The acquisition of morphophonology. *Monographs of the Society for Research in Child Development, 43* (1–2, Serial No. 174).

MacWhinney, B. (Ed.). (in press). *Mechanisms of language acquisition.* Hillsdale, NJ: Erlbaum.

Mandler, J. (1981). Structural invariants in development. In L. Liben (Ed.), *Piaget and the foundations of knowledge.* Hillsdale, NJ: Erlbaum.

McCall, R., Eichorn, D., & Hogarty, P. (1977). Transitions in early mental development. *Monographs of the Society for Research in Child Development* (Serial No. 171).

McCall, R., Parke, R., & Kavanaugh, R. (1977). Imitation of live and televised models by children one to three years of age. *Monographs of the Society for Research in Child Development, 42* (5, Serial No. 173).

McCarthy, D. (1931). Language development. In C. Murchison (Ed.), *A handbook of child psychology* (pp. 278–313). Worcester, MA: Clark University Press.

McCarthy, D. (1954). Language development in children. In L. Carmichael (Ed.), *Manual of child psychology* (pp. 452–630). New York: Wiley.

McClelland, J., & Rumelhart, D. (in press). In B. MacWhinney (Ed.), *Mechanisms of language acquisition*. Hillsdale, NJ: Erlbaum.

McCune-Nicolich, L. (1981). Toward symbolic functioning: Structure of early pretend games and potential parallels with language. *Child Development, 52,* 785–797.

McCune-Nicolich, L., & Bruskin, C. (1982). Combinatorial competency in play and language. In K. Rubin (Ed.), *The play of children: Current theory and research*. Basel, Switzerland: Karger.

McGurk, H. (1984). *The developmental origins of bimodal speech perception*. Paper presented to the International Conference on Infant Studies, New York, New York.

McNeil, D. (1966). Developmental psycholinguistics. In F. Smith & G. Miller (Eds.), *The genesis of language: A psycholinguistic approach* (pp. 15–84). Cambridge, MA: M.I.T. Press.

McNeil, D. (1970). *The acquisition of language: The study of developmental psycholinguistics*. New York: Harper & Row.

Meltzoff, A., & Moore, K. (1977). Imitation of facial and manual gestures by human neonates. *Science, 198,* 75–78.

Meltzoff, A., & Moore, K. (1982). The origins of imitation in infancy: Paradigm, phenomena and theory. In L. Lipsitt & C. Rovee-Collier (Eds.), *Advances in infancy research* (Vol. 2). Norwood, NJ: Ablex.

Menn, L. (1983). Development of articulatory, phonetic and phonological capabilities. In B. Butterworth (Ed.), *Language production* (Vol. 2) (pp. 3–50). London: Academic.

Miller, G. (1956). The magical number seven plus or minus two: Some limits on our capacity for processing information. *Psychological Review, 63,* 81–97.

Miller, J. (in press). Language and communication characteristics of children with Down syndrome. In A. Crocker, S. Paschel, J. Rynders, & C. Tinghey (Eds.), *Down Syndrome: The state of the art*. Baltimore: Brooks.

Miller, J., Chapman, R., & Bedrosian, J. (1977, October). *Defining developmentally disabled subjects for research: The relationship between etiology, cognitive development and language and communicative performance*. Paper presented at the Second Annual Boston University Conference on Language Development.

Miller, J., & Yoder, D. (1973, September). *Assessing the comprehension of grammatical form in mentally retarded children*. Paper presented at the International Association for the Scientific Study of Mental Deficiency, The Hague.

Miller, W., & Ervin, S. (1964). The development of grammar in child language. In U. Bellugi & R. Brown (Eds.), *The acquisition of language*. Chicago: University of Chicago Press.

Moore, T. (1973). *Cognitive development and the acquisition of language*. New York: Academic.

Morford, M., & Goldin-Meadow, S. (1983, April). *Gestural harbingers of two-word speech*. Paper presented at the biennial meeting of the Society for Research in Child Development, Detroit.

Morse, P., & Snowdon, C. (1975). An investigation of categorical speech perception by rhesus monkeys. *Perception & Psychophysics, 17,* 9–16.

Mowrer, O. (1960). *Learning theory and the symbolic processes.* New York: Wiley.

Murphy, C. (1978). Pointing in the context of a shared activity. *Child Development, 49,* 371–380.

Murphy, C., & Messer, D. (1977). Mothers, infants, and pointing: A study of gesture. In H. R. Schaffer (Ed.), *Studies in mother–infant interaction.* London: Academic.

Nelson, K. (1973). Structure and strategy in learning to talk. *Monographs of the Society for Research in Child Development, 38* (Serial No. 149).

Nelson, K. (1974). Concept, word and sentence: Interrelations in acquisition and development. *Psychological Review, 81,* 267–285.

Nelson, K. (1975). The nominal shift in semantic development. *Cognitive Psychology, 7,* 461–479.

Nelson, K. (1977). The conceptual basis for naming. In J. Macnamara (Ed.), *Language learning and thought.* New York: Academic.

Nelson, K. (1981). Individual differences in language development: Implications for development and language. *Developmental Psychology, 17,* 170–187.

Nelson, K. (1985). *Making sense: The acquisition of shared meaning.* New York: Academic.

Newport, E., & Supalla, T. (1980). Clues from the acquisition of signed and spoken language. In U. Bellugi & M. Studdert-Kennedy (Eds.), *Signed and spoken languages: Biological constraints on linguistic form* (pp. 187–212). Weinheim: Verlar Chemiie GmbH.

Newson, T. (1977). An intersubjective approach to the systematic description of mother–infant interaction. In H. R. Schaffer (Ed.), *Studies in mother–infant interaction.* London: Academic.

O'Connell, B. (1984). *The development of sequential understanding revisited: The role of meaning and familiarity.* Unpublished doctoral dissertation, University of California, San Diego.

O'Connell, B., & Gerard, A. (1985). Scripts and scraps: The development of sequential understanding. *Child Development, 56,* 671–681.

Oviatt, S. (1979, April). *The developing awareness of linguistic generality in 9- to 17-month-old infants.* Paper presented at the biennial meeting of the Society for Research in Child Development, New Orleans.

Papousek, H. (1979). From adaptive responses to social cognition: The learning view of development. In M. Bornstein & W. Kessen (Eds.), *Psychological development from infancy: Image to intention.* Hillsdale, NJ: Erlbaum.

Peters, A. (1983). *The units of language acquisition.* Cambridge, Eng.: Cambridge University Press.

Petitto, L. (1983). *From gesture to symbol: The relationship between form and meaning in the acquisition of personal pronouns in American Sign Language.* Unpublished doctoral dissertation, Harvard University.

Petitto, L. (1985, October). *On the use of prelinguistic gestures in hearing and deaf children: Implications for theories of language acquisition.* Paper presented at the Tenth Annual Boston University Conference on Language Acquisition.

Piaget, J. (1962). *Play, dreams, and imitation in childhood.* New York: Norton.

Pisoni, D. (1977). Identification and discrimination of the relative onset time of two-component tones: Implications for voicing perception in stops. *Journal of the Acoustical Society of America, 61,* 1352–1361.

Pollack, F. (1878). An infant's progress in language. *Mind, 3,* 392–401.

Prinz, P., & Prinz, E. (1979). Simultaneous acquisition of American Sign Language and spoken English in a hearing child of a deaf mother and hearing father: Phase I—early lexical development. *Sign Language Studies, 25,* 283–296.

Ramer, A. (1976). Syntactic styles in emerging language. *Journal of Child Language, 3,* 49–62.

Ratner, N., & Bruner, J. (1978). Games, social exchange, and the acquisition of language. *Journal of Child Language, 5,* 391–401.

Reilly, J., McIntire, M., & Bellugi, U. (1985, October). *Faces: The relationship between language and affect.* Paper presented at the Tenth Annual Boston University Conference on Language Development.

Rice, M. (1982). Cognitive aspects of communicative development. In R. Scheifelbusch & J. Pickar (Eds.), *Communicative competence: Acquisition and intervention.* Baltimore: University Park Press.

Sander, L. (1977). The regulation of exchange in the infant–caregiver system and some aspects of the context–content relationship. In M. Lewis & L. Rosenblum (Eds.), *Interaction, conversation and the development of language.* New York: Academic.

Scaife, M., & Bruner, J. (1975). The capacity for joint visual attention in the infant. *Nature, 253,* 265–266.

Scollon, R. (1976). *Conversations with a one year old: A case study of the developmental foundation of syntax.* Honolulu: University Press of Hawaii.

Schaffer, H. (Ed.). (1977). *Studies in mother–infant interaction.* London: Academic.

Schultze, F. (1971). The speech of the child. In A. Bar-Adon & W. Leopold (Eds.), *Child language: A book of readings.* Englewood-Cliffs, NJ: Prentice-Hall (pp. 28–29). (Reprinted in translation by the editors from F. Schultze, *Die Sprache des Kindes.* Leipzig: Gunther, 1880, pp. 44–46.)

Searle, J. (1969). *Speech acts.* Cambridge, Eng.: Cambridge University Press.

Sereno, J., & Lieberman, P. (1985, October). *The development of anticipatory labial coarticulation in a child: Acoustic and perceptual data.* Paper presented at the Tenth Annual Boston University Conference on Language Acquisition.

Shore, C. (1986). Combinatorial play, conceptual development and early multiword speech. *Developmental Psychology, 22:*2.

Shore, C., & Bauer, P. (1983). *Individual styles in language and symbolic play.* Paper presented at the American Psychological Association Annual Convention, Anaheim, CA.

Shore, C., O'Connell, B., & Bates, E. (1984). First sentences in language and symbolic play. *Developmental Psychology, 20*(5), 872–880.

Slobin, D. (1973). Cognitive prerequisites for the acquisition of grammar. In C. Ferguson & D. Slobin (Eds.), *Studies of child language development.* New York: Holt, Rinehart & Winston.

Slobin, D. (1983). Universal and particular in the acquisition of language. In E. Wanner & L. Gleitman (Eds.), *Language Acquisition: The state of the art,* (pp. 128–170). Cambridge, Eng.: Cambridge University Press.

Slobin, D. (1986). *The cross-linguistic study of language acquisition,* (Vols. 1 & 2). Hillsdale, NJ: Erlbaum.

Snyder, L. (1975). *Pragmatics in language deficient children: Prelinguistic and early verbal performatives and presuppositions.* Unpublished doctoral dissertation, University of Colorado, Boulder.

Snyder, L., Bates, E., & Bretherton, I. (1981). Content and context in early lexical development. *Journal of Child Language, 8,* 565–582.

Stark, R. (1979). Prespeech segmental feature development. In P. Fletcher & M. Garman (Eds.), *Language acquisition* (pp. 15–32). Cambridge, Eng.: Cambridge University Press.

Starr, S. (1975). The relationship of single words to two-word sentences. *Child Development, 46,* 701–708.

Stern, D. (1977). *The first relationship*. Cambridge, MA: Harvard University Press.

Stern, D. (in press). Affect attunement: The sharing of feeling states between mother and infant by means of intermodal fluency. In T. Field & N. Fox (Eds.), *Social perception in infants*. Norwood, NJ: Ablex.

Stevens, K., & House, A. (1972). Speech perception. In J. Tobias (Ed.), *Foundations of modern auditory theory* (Vol. 2). New York: Academic.

Stiles-Davis, J., Bates, E., & Nass, R. (in press). The development of spatial and class relations in four young children with right cerebral hemisphere damage: Evidence for an early spatial-constructive deficit. *Brain & Cognition*.

Stoel-Gammon, C., & Cooper, J. (1982). Patterns of early phonological and lexical development. *Journal of Child Language, 11,* 247–271.

Sugarman, S. (1982a). Developmental change in early representational intelligence: Evidence from spatial classification strategies and related verbal expressions. *Cognitive Psychology, 14,* 410–449.

Sugarman, S. (1982b). Transitions in early representational intelligence: Changes over time in children's production of simple block structures. In G. Forman (Ed.), *Action and thought: From sensorimotor schemes to symbolic operations*. New York: Academic.

Sugarman, S. (1982c). The development of preverbal communication: Its contribution and limits in promoting the development of language. In R. Schiefelbusch & J. Pickar (Eds.), *Communicative competence: Acquisition and intervention*. Baltimore: University Park Press.

Sugarman, S. (1983). Empirical versus logical issues in the transition from prelinguistic to linguistic communication. In R. Golinkoff (Ed.), *The transition from prelinguistic to linguistic communication: Issues and implications*. Hillsdale, NJ: Erlbaum.

Sugarman-Bell, S. (1978). Some organizational aspects of preverbal communication. In I. Markova (Ed.), *The social context of language* (pp. 49–66). London: Wiley.

Taine, H. (1877). The acquisition of language by children. *Mind, 2,* 252–259.

Thevenin, D., Eilers, R., Kimbrough, D., & Lavoir, L. (1985). Where's the drift in babbling drift? A cross-linguistic study. *Applied Linguistics, 6,* 3–15.

Trevarthen, C., & Hubley, P. (1979). Secondary intersubjectivity: Confidence, confiding, and acts of meaning in the first year. In A. Lock (Ed.), *Action, gesture, and symbol* (pp. 183–229). London: Academic.

Urwin, C. (1978). *The development of communication between blind infants and their parents: Some ways into language*. Unpublished doctoral dissertation, Cambridge University.

Uzgiris, I., & Hunt, J. McV. (1975). *Assessment in infancy: Ordinal scales of psychological development*. Urbana, IL: University of Illinois Press.

Vihman, M., (1985). Individual differences in babbling and early speech: Predicting to age three. In B. Lindblom & R. Zetterstrom (Eds.), *Precursors of early speech*. Basingstroke, Hampshire: MacMillan.

Vihman, M., & Carpenter, K. (1984, February). *Linguistic advance and cognitive style in language acquisition*. Proceedings of the tenth annual meeting of the Berkeley Linguistic Society.

Vihman, M., Ferguson, C., & Elbert, M. (in press). Phonological development from babbling to speech: Common tendencies and individual differences. *Applied Psycholinguistics*.

Vihman, M., & Miller, R. (in press). Word and babble at the threshold of lexical acquisition. In M. Smith & J. Locke (Eds.), *The emergent lexicon*. New York: Academic.

Volterra, V., Bates, E., Benigni, L., Bretherton, I., & Camaioni, L. (1979). First words in language and action: A qualitative look. In E. Bates, L. Benigni, I. Bretherton, L. Camaioni, & V. Volterra (Eds.), *The emergence of symbols: Cognition and communication in infancy* (pp. 141–222). New York: Academic.

Volterra, V., & Caselli, C. (1983). From gestures and vocalizations to signs and words. In W. Stokoe & V. Volterra (Eds.), *SLR, 1983, Proceedings of the Third International Symposium on Sign Language Research,* Rome.

Volterra, V., & Taeschner, T. (1977). The origin and development of child language by a bilingual child. *Journal of Child Language, 5,* 311–326.

Waters, R., & Wilson, W. (1976). Speech perception by rhesus monkeys: The voicing distinction in synthesized labial and velar stop consonants. *Perception & Psychophysics, 19,* 285–289.

Werker, J., Gilbert, J., Humphrey, K., & Tees, R. (1981). Developmental aspects of cross-language speech perception. *Child Development, 52,* 349–355.

Werner, H., & Kaplan, B. (1963). *Symbol formation.* New York: Wiley.

Wolf, D. (1982). Understanding others: A longitudinal case study of the concept of independent agency. In G. Forman (Ed.), *Action and thought: From sensorimotor schemes to symbol use.* New York: Academic.

Wolf, D., & Gardner, H. (1979). Style and sequence in symbolic play. In M. Franklin & N. Smith (Eds.), *Early symbolization.* Hillsdale, NJ: Erlbaum.

Wundt, W. (1971). Exchanges and mutilations of sounds in child language. In A. Bar-Adon & W. Leopold (Eds.), *Child language: A book of readings.* Englewood Cliffs, NJ: Prentice-Hall (pp. 43–45). (Reprinted in translation by the editors from *Volkerpsychologie,* 1900; 3rd.)

Yeni-Komshian, G., Kavanagh, J., & Ferguson, C. (Eds.). (1980a). *Child Phonology, I: Production.* New York: Academic.

Yeni-Komshian, G., Kavanagh, J., & Ferguson, C. (Eds.). (1980b). *Child phonology, II: Perception.* New York: Academic.

Younger, B. (1985). The segregation of items into categories by 10-month-old infants. *Child Development, 56,* 1574–1583.

Younger, B., & Cohen, L. (1985). How infants form categories. In G. Bower (Ed.), *The psychology of learning and motivation: Advances in research and theory* (Vol. 19) (pp. 211–247). New York: Academic.

Zukow, P. (1981). *A microanalytic study of the role of caregiver in the relationship between symbolic play and language acquisition during the one-word period.* Unpublished doctoral dissertation, University of California, Los Angeles.

CHAPTER 4

Cognitive Development: The Relevance of Piaget's Infancy Books

GERALD GRATCH and JOSEPH A. SCHATZ

I believe with Schopenhauer, that one of the strongest motives that lead men to attempt science is to escape from everyday life with its painful crudity and hopeless dreariness from the fetters of one's own ever shifting desires. With this negative motive there goes a positive one. Man tries to make for himself, in the fashion that suits him best, a simplified and intelligible picture of the world. He then tries to substitute this cosmos of his for the world of experience and thus to overcome it. This is what the painter, the poet, the speculative philosopher, and the natural scientist do each in his own fashion. Each makes his cosmos and its construction the pivot of his emotional life, in order to find in this way the peace and security which he cannot find in a narrow whirlpool of personal experience.

(Einstein, quoted in Singer, 1981, pp. 40–41).

For many people, babies are boring. And the more such people are interested in abstract intelligence or scientific knowledge, the more boring babies appear to be. . . . Part of Piaget's achievement is that he showed how fundamentally mistaken such an attitude is.

(Boden, 1979, p. 22)

A foolish consistency is the hobgoblin of little minds.

(Emerson)

For the past 20-plus years, the phrase *infant cognitive development* and Piaget's account of it have almost been synonomous. Within an observational framework that derived in part from infant behavioral schedules, he went beyond describing whether and when to provide a relatively contextualized picture of how individual infants achieve various behavioral milestones. He redescribed those milestones in terms of stages of progress relevant to major preoccupations of his and our times. Thus in *The Origins of Intelligence* (1936/1952a; referred to hereafter as *O.I.*) he pictured six emergent stages in the development of intelligence. The infant progresses toward symbolically based planfulness by becoming more flexible and coherent in its actions. In *The Construction of Reality in the Child* (1937/1954; hereafter *C.R.*) he related his observations to the categories Kant used to analyze how scientific knowledge is possible. The infant, again, was imagined as progressing through six stages in which it organized its knowledge in terms of the categories of object, space, cause, and time. In *Play, Dreams, and Imitation* (1945/1962; hereafter *P.D.I.*) he provided an account of the development of symbols and dreams that was an alternative to viewing their origins in language or in sensory-based processes of an empiricist or psychoanalytic character.

Along with this stage picture, Piaget developed a language for describing the infant as an active construer and problem solver. The language described the infant in the same terms as the child and the adult and provided a mechanism for bridging their differences. Piaget's language is one of schemes, assimilation, and accommodation. The schemes are adaptive, or purposive, coherent organizations of elements. They selectively guide what is perceived and done about the world. The infant, child, and adult experience the world and themselves by assimilating inputs, with ease or difficulty, in terms of their network of schemes. They change their schemes and their networking by a slow process of accommodating them to refractory inputs. They differ in terms of the complexity and organization of their schemes, and these differences are bridged through their efforts to accommodate. Piaget did not view his description of the development of the logic and content of the mind in terms of problem-solving processes as an alternative to accounts in terms of mechanisms of biological maturation. Rather, his account was intended to reveal an aspect of what is entailed in the adaptive process of maturation, namely, the importance of experience from the infant's point of view.

The "packages" of observation and argument Piaget provided were not easy for contemporary English-speaking psychologists to assimilate. Many have commented on the difficulties, (e.g., Boden 1979; Flavell 1963). One is Piaget's writing style. At times, it appears that Piaget used the texts more as frames within which to work out his own thoughts than as occasions to make his thoughts plain to readers. That difficulty is compounded by the fact that his reference figures tended to be Continental Europeans whose ideas Piaget used but tended not to explicate. As such, Piaget has provided us with little help as we have tried to narrow the gap between his intellectual context and our own. Not only are his infancy books distant from us in time, but they are situated in an intellectual and methodological context rather different from our own largely behavioral and experimental traditions.

Another source of difficulty is his pretentiousness. His pretentiousness is a quality he was fully aware of and sometimes made fun of; for example, he refers to the unexpected importance readers from Anglo-Saxon countries attributed to the initial books of a mere youth (1952b). Examples of his pretentious simplifications are easy to find. He proposed his ideas as dialectical resolutions of classical themes that he cast as clear antitheses, for example, empiricism and rationalism, empiricism and nativism. He sought and claimed to find lawful correspondences between the stages he identifies in infancy and stages in later child and adult thought and in the history of science. He studied his three infants, but he presumed to write his books about *the* infant and *the* epistemic subject. He organized his studies of them in terms of stages that claim to capture the essential forms that underlie the many diverse things infants do in diverse contexts.

Piaget's approach to observations is a third source of difficulty. He presents an almost overwhelming number of them. Moreover, the observations were made in many different types of situations. At a given age level, this situational variation does not present too many problems. However, across ages, it does. It raises the question of whether the age differences described by Piaget are due to stage or to situation. Further, Piaget discussed and rediscussed his observations. Sometimes the vantage was the same, but the many rephrasings make it hard to find his exact meaning. Sometimes he discussed the same observations from several different points of view, and that leads to questions about the support for the various interpretations. To add to such difficulties, sometimes he discussed observations made on only one of the infants as if they applied to all three, and often he discussed observations that came from the three infants at quite disparate ages as if they came from the same kind of mind.

However, his pretentiousness and his approach to observations also had a positive feature in that they promised much and enabled us to focus our attention on those promises. We now could think that we were not studying a local phase of life in a number of disparate local ways. In trying to understand *the* infant, we could be working toward an understanding of such fundamental questions as the foundations of knowledge in general and of logic and science in particular. Even if we were not attracted to his placing infant study on such lofty planes, his detailed and contextualized descriptions of his infants offered us many surprises. Time and time again, he showed that our usual ways of describing the behavior of infants would lead us to expectations that were contradicted by their subsequent behavior. As such, the theories of mind or behavior that were more or less explicit in our descriptions would have failed to capture the bases on which the infant behaved. One oft-cited and studied example, which we will dwell on later, is the stage–4 object concept error (e.g., Harris, 1983). A well-oriented and seemingly competent infant readily finds an object hidden at place A. It then attentively watches the hiding of the object at place B and, as soon as it disappears completely, turns to A and searches there.

Small wonder then that Piaget dominated the study of infant cognition for so many years. He seemed to be saying something of great significance. He provided us with a relatively unique lode of detailed, interesting, and often counterintuitive observations that somehow seemed related to his claims. For many years, we have labored long and hard to make empirical and theoretical sense of those books. We have spent many years attempting to discover whether some of his observations are replicable. We have devoted a great deal of energy to trying to clarify his terms: for example, are schemes repeatable sequences of behavior or ways of sizing up and operating on the world, and how can we capture the difference? We have tried to make sense of his macro- and microdevelopmental claims: for example, are the stages real or nominal; does the coordination between vision and touch stem from a process of overlapping practice of disparate ways of acting or are there some kinds of prior coordinations?

Two plain consequences have emerged from the long labors of so many over Piaget's dense and difficult books about his infants and infancy. One is that we now have far more knowledge about cognitive development than before. Harris (1983) does an exceptional job of reviewing much of the experimental and theoretical literature that revolves around Piaget's ideas and observations, and his review is complemented by such excellent reviews, addressed to related themes, as those by Gibson and Spelke (1983), Mandler (1983), and Olson and Sherman (1983). The other is that Piaget's ideas are no longer ascendant. Thoughtful commentators on the state of developmental psychology such as Beilin (1983), Kessen (1983), and White (1980) point out that there is a general turning away from Piaget's notions of the saltatory progress of general intelligence, his structural views of concepts, and the tasks he used to embody his views. Infants and development are seen in more complex terms. There appears to be a general consensus that infants have more and earlier competences that Piaget claimed. Investigators examine more local themes than the grand simplifications Piaget focused our attention on and tend to emphasize the importance of such notions as the context dependence of reasoning and concepts, domain specifities, and specific innate preparedness. Alternative general notions are advanced such as the Gibsons' (1977, 1979) theme of ecological optics, neo-Vygotskian emphases on the social context of knowing (e.g., Kaye, 1982), Bruner's (1970) "modular" play on the metaphor of skill, and various other forms of an information-processing point of view. There tends to be a general belief that we should be looking into the "black box" to try to find a network of components and processes that can capture our intuitions about a developing mind that is more shifting and loosely coupled then the one Piaget sought.

We think that the present state of affairs is a salutary one. It is fitting that infant cognitive development no longer be so synonomous with Piaget. He opened our eyes to new ways of looking at infants, but we no longer need be dominated by him. However, we also believe that the present state of affairs may lead to an unfortunate consequence, namely that we no longer are likely to take his infancy books seriously enough to read them thoroughly. We think that would be a mistake. We have taken him too seriously in some ways and not seriously enough in others. We have looked too hard at his products and not hard enough at his processes. We have taken too seriously his conceptualizations of general cognitive development and of particular phenomena such as object permanence. But our many new metaphors of mind and our growing store of information about infants and how to study them put us in a position to look more seriously at Piaget's infancy books in a different way. We propose that we should be looking at the kinds of observations he made and the processes he went through to make them and to assemble them in book form. We believe that looking at him in such a light can lead us both to understand better what he did and claimed and to put our own efforts to understand infants into perspective.

In the remainder of this chapter, we present some results of our initial attempts to examine Piaget's processes and how they figured in the observations he made. Our presentation will focus on Piaget's first two infancy books, *O.I.* and *C.R.* It is organized in five sections. In the first, we put together some well-known facts in an attempt to provide a sense of what Piaget and his intellectual context were like before he began to observe his three infants. The remaining sections focus on his observations. The second presents statistical evidence that Piaget made important changes in his manner of observing with each successive infant. The next three sections present evidence of those changes in more concrete form by considering observations that are relevant to three of his major conceptual themes. The first is the shortest and has to do with his concept of reflexes as active rather than responsive systems. The second is the longest and takes up the theme of circular reactions. Under this head, Piaget examined the key theme of how intellectual structures are changed through function and its feedback. The third has to do with infants' concepts of reality, includes some of our own observations, and examines the relationship between concepts and intelligence.

In our presentation, we will make some unsurprising points the net effect of which we hope will incline you to look at Piaget and infants in a somewhat different way than heretofore. We will make such points as the following: Piaget's ideas, like ours, were in part a function of his historical context. He had to work long and hard to see infants' behavior in ways that were relevant to his presuppositional framework. In looking at his infants, he noticed many things that led to changes in how he observed and to some changes in his presuppositions. But he, in largest part, assimilated what he saw so that it fit with his presuppositions. We hope that the cumulative effect of our own presentation of such points will incline you to be sympathetic to two of our beliefs. One is that we be humble and patient in the face of the problem of understanding the minds of creatures so strange and important to us as infants. We have come a long way in the relatively short time we have studied them systematically—100 or 200 years, depending on how one counts—but that is a very short time in the face of so awesome a task. The other is that we are at a time where we need to do more looking at babies and less worrying about coming up with precise explanations of limited looks in restricted contexts. Here is where we can use Piaget, once again, as a guide. In many ways, our present search for an understanding of infants' minds through viewing them as dynamic, multi-componential systems is not so different from Piaget's. Moreover, some of his kinds of observations, and what he had to do to produce them, are the kinds of matters we presently do not engage in or, at the least, do not report. In particular, some of Piaget's detailings of how infants web together the many strands of themselves and their worlds in concrete situations to achieve limited adaptations are the kinds of stuff we need to be looking for if we are to arrive at a picture of a developing mind that is commensurate with our present sense of its dynamic multicomponential nature. As Einstein once said somewhere, our explanations should be as simple as they can be but no simpler.

A VIEW OF WHAT PIAGET BROUGHT TO THE STUDY OF HIS INFANTS

There are two strands in Piaget's autobiography (1952b) in terms of which we will attempt to picture Piaget before he began to observe his infants. One has to do with his naturalistic interests. He began them early and pursued them throughout his life. Piaget credits these activities with giving him an appreciation for the importance and difficulty of observation and classification. They also led him to have an abiding interest in the question of how adaptation to circumstances is related to the evolution of the species. For example, he published papers in 1929 in which he described how the shape of mollusks adapted to the varying action of shallow and deep shorelines and how the local adaptations became hereditary. He returned to those "soft" or neo-Lamarckian themes of inheritance, in the context of plants as well as mollusks, in some of his last books (e.g., 1980). In his autobiography, he comments on his 1929 papers by saying: "That experience taught me not to explain the whole of mental life by maturation alone!" (1952b, p. 250). Mental life was rooted in biological processes and biological processes are viewed in terms of adaptive changes.

The other strand was his passion for understanding how parts relate to the whole, how an order can be found among diverse individuals, societies, and species that could account for how such entities could change adaptively and yet cohere as systems of parts. Piaget was born (1896) and grew up at a time when change was in the air—evolution, relativity, World War I, nationalism and revolution, science versus religion, and so on—and when many intellectuals found it natural to feel obligated to answer the question of whether there was any unity in all the diversity at both the most personal and the most general of levels (e.g., Hughes, 1958). At the personal level, Piaget went through his own *Sturm und Drang* when he tried to unify his many selves, and he published an autobiographical novel that presented a solution to his own personal chaos as part of a general solution to how parts relate to a whole. He revisited those themes years later in his volume *Insights and Illusions in Philosophy* (1971). He continued to try to find a philosophy that would unite the many threads of intellectual life. He describes how he was reading William James and Pierre Janet around 1915. He was attracted to their pragmatic functionalism and their emphasis on the multiplicities of minds or personalities. However, he was dissatisfied with what he saw as James's, overly functionalist and antirationalistic emphases, his refusal to see mind as a logically coherent entity. He wrote what he characterized as a crude and pretentious "sketch of neo-pragmatism" in which, influenced by Janet's emphasis on acts, he tried to wed structure to function, saying: "Logic stems from a sort of spontaneous organization of acts" (1952b, p. 241). How to achieve a reconciliation between such dichotomies as part and whole, form and matter, logic and content was a preoccupation throughout his life. His later founding of the International Center for Genetic Epistemology is a clear sign of that abiding aim.

In the shorter term, he resolved some of those concerns by turning to the study of clinical and experimental psychology at age 25, the year after he received his doctorate in zoology. He spent a year in such study and then spent the following year (1920) working with Simon in the Paris laboratory of the deceased Binet. That is the time that American psychologists have marked well because he began his studies of children's thinking. It was a time when it seemed reasonable to make a working distinction between intelligence and knowledge and between intelligence and sensory and motor processes. Intelligence was identified with judgment and the capacity to vary the relation of means to ends and was believed to emerge sometime during infancy on a nonlinguistic basis, (e.g., Binet & Simon, 1905/1962). Piaget was put to work evaluating some analogy problems developed by Burt for the assessment of intelligence. In that context, Piaget's naturalistic interests came to the fore and led him to make his "great discovery": Children's mistakes are more interesting than their right answers. Piaget found it more interesting to understand how children's minds work by observing them directly in action. The child's point of view is critical and can be discovered: "Rousseau loved to say that the child is not a small grown-up, but has needs of his own, and a mentality adapted to those needs" (1924/1959, p. 199). Through the study of the development of children's intelligence and concepts, Piaget had found a way to merge his naturalistic and philosophical interests. Thus when he left Simon to go to the Institute J. J. Rousseau in Geneva, Piaget says:

"Being of a systematic turn of mind (with all the hazards that this implies) I made plans which I then considered final: I would devote two or three more years to the study of child thought, then return to the origins of mental life, that is, study the emergence of intelligence during the first two years. . . . I would be in a position to attack the problem of thought in general and construct a psychological and biological epistemology. (1952b, p. 246)

Piaget went on to conduct his child studies, and they took many more years than he had planned. During that period, there was a synergism between his child studies and his interests in the nature of knowledge in the sciences and in general. He wrote his books about the development of children's concepts of the natural and social world and how those relate to the development of logic and language. He taught philosophy and the history of the sciences. Those were times that were dominated by the search for a basis for thinking about progress in science and in mental life (e.g., Carr, 1961; Dyson, 1983). The nineteenth century idea that physics and mathematics rested on firm foundations was no longer accepted, nor was the idea that there was a simple progression from ''primitive'' to ''civilized'' minds. But it was a period when much effort was expended on finding an alternative foundation upon which to rest the sciences and culture. There were concerted efforts to establish a firm foundation for mathematics on which the language and observations of physics could rest, for example, by Whitehead and Russell, and by the logical positivists of the Vienna Circle. Piaget invested himself deeply in such issues.

He believed a developmental analysis could establish how knowing both in children and in science developed from a primitive or transductive confounding of the logic and content of inquiry to their relative independence. Both in the development of the child and in science, our concepts of reality become more objective because we come to think about our experiences more logically. The concepts would always have to be revised in the light of new experiences, but with the development of logic, we could at least be certain about how we reason about contingent facts. Piaget believed he could trace out the natural origins of such a basis for certainty by finding the changes in the hows of acting that underlie the particularities of our experiences. During this period, he was especially attracted to that movement in mathematics that attempted to base all of mathematics on the language of set theory. The mathematical object, the group, came to be Piaget's initial model of a logical knower in the infancy books. He was attracted to this object because it described how a set of elements could be kept track of, be closed, under a set of operations on them. What particularly attracted him to the group was the fact that its elements were actions themselves, sets of transformations on objects rather than sets of objects. To him it promised a way of describing when an actor could be so organized that there was a separation between intelligence and concepts, logic and subject matter, how and what.

Another feature of his thinking during this period was his commitment to an emergent embryological view of change in individuals, species, and societies. On this view there was *a* course of progress. Each stage was a complex organization of parts that had its own point of view and had to be understood in its own terms. Progress occurred because of a clash of perspectives, clashes between the multiple perspectives within the organization and between the perspectives of the organization and ''reality''. The aim of progress was the development of a coherent and consistent system of parts. In his child books, Piaget used various dialectical metaphors to try to account for the process of change and developed various concepts in terms of which to comprehend the child's developing intelligence and conceptions.

We now will describe the course of a few of the themes he developed in his early child books that he later elaborated in his infancy studies. One is the notion of *assimilation.* He seems to have gotten it in 1915 when he read Le Dantec, a French biologist, who used the notion in the context of his deductive account of biology.* However, Piaget used the term only in a general sense in his first two child books. But the term began to take on a technical quality in *The Child's Conception of the World* (1926/1951). In that work, he cited with approval William Stern's notions and language of an actively adapting mind. He now used Stern's notions of a *mental chemistry* of *schemes* that *assimilate* reality and *adapt* to it. In this volume, *adaptation* is used in the copy-sense, and it appears that he does not adopt, until the infancy books, J. M. Baldwin's (1906) term *accommodation* to capture that sense of the process of adaptation.*

In his child books, Piaget relies on J. M. Baldwin for his theme of reflexes as dynamic adaptive modes of apprehending the world. Further, he uses Baldwin's notion of the circular reaction as the means by which he imagines the role that function plays in the development of the mind. The attempt to recapture the interesting and unintended effect becomes the means by which the child goes beyond its existent networks of acting. "Skills in the making" provide a motive for a mind that will construct both itself and the world it adapts to.

A final example of Piaget's development of themes comes from the last section of the *Child's Conception of Physical Causality* (1927/1960). Piaget begins it with the sentence "Experience fashions reason, and reason fashions experience" (p. 301). How is that interaction to be understood? At every stage of development, the child has a unique point of view that involves both logic and concepts of the "real." But with maturity, those aspects become relatively independent, thought becomes deductive, and concepts are free of "realism." How does such progress occur? "Is it the real content of thought that fashions the logical form or is the converse the truth?" (p. 305). Piaget concludes the book by saying the main features of an answer to such a question " . . . will be found in a more searching study of the nature of assimilation" (p. 305). This book was published during the year Piaget's second child, Lucienne, was born. Piaget had already studied Jacqueline. Not only did he have many of his concepts in place, but he already seemed to have the organization of his first two books in mind, the study of the origins of intelligence (*O.I.*) and the concepts of the "real" (*C.R.*). Moreover, his study of infancy seemed to promise an understanding of "the problem of thought in general" (1952b, p. 246).

PIAGET'S OBSERVATIONS: A STATISTICAL ANALYSIS

The birthdates of Piaget's infants and the publication dates of his infancy books frame the time within which he conducted his infancy studies. Jacqueline was born in 1925, Lucienne in 1927, and Laurent in 1931. Thus Piaget and his wife had more than 7 years to make their observations. He published *O.I.* in 1936, *C.R.* in 1937, and *P.D.I.* was a caboose published in 1945. There were about 13 years between the publication of *C.R.* and Piaget's first observations of Jacqueline. We already have indicated that Piaget was conceptually prepared to find specific things about how their minds would function and develop. How did he go about grounding his

---

*We thank David Smillie for sharing with us these points from his historical investigations.

conceptions in terms of their behavior? Were there changes in that process and how often and why? Were there changes in his presuppositions? In what follows, we try to provide some partial answers to such questions.

We begin by presenting the results of our first attempt to look at *O.I.* and *C.R.* from the point of view of examining Piaget's processes. That inquiry consisted in making simple tallies of his reported observations. In making such an analysis, we have no idea of how many unreported observations were made nor what kind of editing process went into the observations that were reported. Tables 4.1, 4.2, 4.3 present our findings. Table 4.1, based on *O.I.,* presents a tally of the number of times Piaget cited an age at which one of his three infants did something of note. On a given day there might be one or more episodes. The tallies are grouped by stage, and each stage includes all of the episodes described in the chapter devoted to that stage. That way of tallying gives only an approximate number of stage-typed episodes because in most of the chapters Piaget also describes a small number of episodes that refer to earlier or later stages.

With those qualifications in mind, we think Table 4.1 is revelatory about Piaget's processes in several ways. First, it is striking to note that there are more episodes involving the third child, Laurent, than involving Jacqueline and Lucienne combined. Second, Piaget reported relatively few stage 1 or stage 6 episodes. Third, the modal stage decreases with each successive infant. The mode for Jacqueline is stage 5, Lucienne's modes are stages 2 and 3, and Laurent's mode is stage 2, and only in his case are there an appreciable number of stage 1 episodes. Plainly, Piaget changed in not only how often he looked but where he focused his attention.

Tables 4.2 and 4.3 are presented in order to indicate that these patterns do not entirely reflect how he proceeded and also to provide some sense of the observations reported in *C.R.* Table 4.2 presents tallies of the observations reported in the object chapter and Table 4.3 presents tallies of the observations reported in the space chapter. We do not present tallies for the cause and time chapters in part for reasons of

TABLE 4.1. Piaget's *The Origins of Intelligence:* **Number of Observational Episodes, Tallied by Infants and Stage**

	Stages						
	1	2	3	4	5	6	Total
Jacqueline	1	39	30	28	73	4	175
Lucienne	1	70	70	3	17	7	148
Laurent	18	162	86	44	17	9	336
Total	20	271	186	75	107	20	659

TABLE 4.2. Piaget's *The Construction of Reality in the Child:* **Number of Observational Episodes, in the Object Chapter, Tallied by Infants and Stage**

	Stages					
	1, 2	3	4	5	6	Total
Jacqueline	1	22	11	13	4	51
Lucienne	3	14	3	6	1	27
Laurent	2	33	17	3	0	55
Total	6	69	31	22	5	133

TABLE 4.3. Piaget's *The Construction of Reality in the Child:* Number of Observational Episodes, in the Space Chapter, Tallied by Infants and Stage

	Stages					
	1, 2	3	4	5	6	Total
Jacqueline	0	19	9	15	5	48
Lucienne	0	3	9	26	1	39
Laurent	3	60	36	31	5	135
Total	3	82	54	72	11	222

brevity and in part because the observations reported under those heads, especially time, primarily refer to episodes reported in *O.I.* and/or involve very similar situations or themes. That confounding also is present for object and space but to a much lesser extent. We used a slightly different method of tallying to create Tables 4.2 and 4.3. We did not count episodes that also were reported in *O.I.* Episodes that were discussed in the context of one stage but were classified by Piaget as belonging to another stage were tallied under the latter headings. Finally, Piaget cites a small number of "residual behaviors," things infants of a given stage did that were appropriate to earlier stages. We did not include these in our tallies.

Table 4.2 reveals that Jacqueline was observed as often as Laurent and that stage 3 was the mode for both. Within this series of observations, Piaget does not appear to change in the ways reflected in Table 4.1. However, the picture in Table 4.3 is very similar to that of Table 4.1 save for two reversals. Jacqueline's mode is stage 3 and Lucienne's mode is stage 5.

The tallies show that Piaget observed the three infants in different ways, but they don't indicate the character of the differences. We first will briefly describe some changes that depended upon Piaget's reliance on other observers of infants. Then we will take up our major focus, an attempt to trace some changes in how he investigated three of the themes he brought to the study of his infants.

Piaget's references to the literature make plain that his initial studies of Jacqueline were based in large part on his reading of the baby biographies of Preyer (1888–1889) and the Sterns (e.g., 1927) and of the reports of Karl and Charlotte Bühler and their associates (e.g., 1930). Their observational procedures and themes formed a frame that he continued to use with all three infants. Some examples are his pursuit of Stern's investigation of the development of depth perception and the Bühlers' investigation of the development of finding hidden objects and tool use. Within the framework of their procedures, he developed innovations and made some changes in who he observed. For example, Piaget not only used the Bühlers' idea of observing the infant's removal of a cover from its own face but contrasted that with the task of removing the cover from the face of the examiner. He also extended their hidden object series by creating the invisible displacement task in an attempt to identify representationally guided search. He made the latter kinds of observations with Jacqueline and Lucienne but not with Laurent.

However, he also opportunistically changed some of his observational procedures and themes when he read a research report that he found interesting. For example, he read a study by Szuman (1927) which he replicated with Laurent. He supported Szuman's observation. Laurent will or won't reach for a desirable object as a function of the size of the support upon which it rests. It appears that a similar thing happens in the case of his study of how Laurent comes to rotate his feeding bottle so that he can find its occluded nipple. This and other kinds of searches for the occluded "good parts" of objects and various other kinds of rotational activity are only studied with Laurent. Piaget makes reference to a similar bottle study by Rubinow and Frankl (*C.R.*, p. 90).

We think careful study of the relationship between the ideas and procedures of Piaget and those of his peers would teach us a great deal both about his thoughts about infants and about our infants or our thoughts about infants. We have not attempted to carry this out. Instead, we now turn to a consideration of how he changed in his attempts to ground observationally three of his presuppositions.

PIAGET'S OBSERVATIONS OF REFLEXES

Consider the theme of reflexes. It is a key issue for Piaget. His vision of the development of knowing as a constructive process rested on his assumption that reflexes are actively adaptive learning systems that are relatively independent of one another. If his vision were to prove reasonable, then he would have to find evidence of such kinds of processes in the first 2 months of life. Given the importance of the reflex theme, it is striking to note how he reported on Jacqueline neither very frequently nor very searchingly during this period of her life. At birth, along with Lucienne and Laurent, he reports on her sucking patterns (*O.I.*, obs. 1). He provides a brief but nicely detailed picture of their common pattern of sucking—lip and tongue movements—and their accompanying lateral head movements. They can suck their fingers, but their uncooperative arm movements keep them from retaining their fingers and they don't know where to seek for them. It's not clear whether this report about Jacqueline, and Lucienne, was based on direct observations or was a reconstruction based on some impressions and direct observations of Laurent. We raise this question because of the sparseness of his observations during Jacqueline's and Lucienne's first 2 months of life. Thus Piaget reports that Jacqueline at 1-24 (1 month, 24 days) turns her head in the correct direction when she is taken from one breast and is placed on the other (*O.I.*, obs. 26) and that she can bring her hand to her mouth at 1-28 (*O.I.*, obs. 24). For vision, he reports that she doesn't track a flame at 20 cm at 16 days (*O.I.*, obs. 28). He provides a general description of how her vocalizing shifts from wailing and violent crying to more differential and less need-tied vocalizing in the first 2 months (*O.I.*, obs. 40). Along with similar descriptions of Lucienne and Laurent, he describes how at 1 month she interrupts her crying when she hears an agreeable voice and then later comes to smile or frown in response to different voices; she does not attempt to localize the sounds (*O.I.*, obs. 43). But she does so at 2-12 (*O.I.*, obs. 44). He notes how, at 1-28, she moves her hands over her face while learning to suck her fingers (*O.I.*, obs. 55), and that she doesn't look at her hands before 2-30 (*O.I.*, obs. 61).

The observations of Lucienne are comparable in kind and number, and we will not detail them. However, two are noteworthy relative to the theme we will discuss after reflexes, circular reactions, and so we describe them here. Piaget reports that she plays with her tongue at 1-24 and over days extends the play to sucking her thumb and "beyond" (*O.I.*, obs. 13), and he reports on how she manages to get her thumb to her mouth and keep it there between 1-25 and 2-2 (*O.I.*, obs. 23).

This state of affairs changes dramatically with Laurent. He makes many observations on the reflexes described above in Laurent's first 2 months. Most of them bear on Laurent's second month of life, and we will return to some of them when we discuss circular reactions. However, Piaget made an extended number of daily observations of Laurent's sucking behavior in his first month of life (*O.I.*, obs. 2–10; 25). On Laurent's second day, Piaget makes further notes on the complexity and effectiveness of Laurent's sucking system. Laurent seizes the nipple without having to have it held in his mouth. Between meals on that day, Laurent repeatedly opens and closes his lips and moves his head laterally, seemingly searching for nurturance. On subsequent days, Piaget describes how he becomes increasingly discriminative about the surfaces he contacts, how his groping becomes increasingly directed, far ranging, and persistent, and how he may have formed associations between how and where he is placed and whether he will be fed. In this context, Piaget does not systematically study the last observation, and he doubts that Laurent had formed such connections in his first days of life. But he does experimentally evaluate the first two trends by studying how Laurent behaves when he is in different states and bodily positions, and when his lips are in touch with different surfaces. Piaget is convinced by those experiments that the improvements in Laurent's ability to adapt to his world in terms of his sucking reflex are real and that the observations documented his view of the importance of active practice in the development of reflexes. Whether one shares his view or not, what reading Piaget's observations of Laurent clearly brings out, in a way our synopses of them cannot, is how much there is to see if one will just look.

The principal point we want to make about Piaget's study of reflexes is how long it took him to begin to study their development in a concerted fashion. It is possible that he did not realize when he began to study Jacqueline how important that theme was for his argument. This possibility cannot be completely discounted, but we think it is an unlikely one given his preconceptions about the nature and origins of knowing and his acquaintance with Preyer's (1888–1889) observations. We rather think that this period of infancy was just too strange for him. Like an anthropologist visiting a strange culture, he had to "find his feet" (Geertz, 1973, 1983). We think it took living with and noticing first Jacqueline and then Lucienne before he could begin the process of looking at the myriad particulars of Laurent's behavior in a focal manner. Piaget's observations of Laurent's first month of life are preliminary and incomplete. For example, Piaget made nice descriptions of aspects of Laurent's early sucking and rooting, but he did not ask how the limitations in Laurent's early searching for breast and thumb might relate to the kind of nurturing context human neonates typically are born into. Given the ways humans typically feed their neonates, how ably must they search or control their limbs? These are the kinds of questions that ethologists have made us sensitive to, but they were not at the center of Piaget's attention. Both here and elsewhere Piaget asks questions about function but tends not to complement them with questions about niche.

However, Piaget's observations do provide a grounding for a view of infantile reflexes that remains controversial and has important implications for what we observe and think about the first weeks of life. Prechtl, the eminent neonatal neurologist, illustrates in his own field of study the present controversial nature of an organismic view of reflexes such as the one Piaget held. Consider Prechtl's passionate characterization of the neonate, and of reflexes, as:

not a bundle of reflexes, imperative in character. . . . . This approach became obsolete when the neural functions of healthy infants were studied in their own right and in more detail. The complexity, variability, and gracefulness of the infant's behavior are so fundamentally different from those of animal preparations or of brain-damaged adults that these pathological reflexes appear as artificial fragments of normal functions rather than homologies of the normal young nervous system. (1981, p. 198)

The poetry and passion of Prechtl's description can in part be attributed to the long wars this former student of Konrad Lorenz waged in behalf of such a view of the actively adapting infant, but they also are a testimony to how strongly such a view must be advocated to get a hearing. An illustration of how hard it is to look at and think about reflexes is the current controversy about the nature and fate of the stepping reflex relative to walking. Does that neonatal reflex disappear in the course of encephalization unless practiced (e.g., Zelazo et al., 1972) or does it never disappear because it is the kicking of an infant supported in an upright position (Thelen & Fischer, 1982)? We don't raise this issue because we know how to resolve it nor because a reading of Piaget will provide direct guidance; he did not systematically study the development of locomotion. Rather, we call attention to this controversy because Thelen and Fisher's analyses of the stepping reflex provide an example of how a generally accepted unit of behavior can come to be understood from a different perspective if we carefully look at the how of it in the light of questions about its functions and ecological circumstances.

Viewed in this general spirit, we believe Piaget's observations and his struggles to identify both what to observe and how to do so remain important sources of information about very early infant functioning and development. Near the close of the next section, on circular reactions, we will describe in detail an example of reflex functioning that illustrates this, namely, how Laurent came to capture his thumb with his mouth through practice.

PIAGET'S OBSERVATIONS OF CIRCULAR REACTIONS

We now consider another of Piaget's key themes and do so at some length. In this section, our intent is to go beyond simply documenting the claim that Piaget changed in what he observed and to try to capture some of the character of those changes and what they tell us about infants.

The idea of the circular reaction provided Piaget with a vehicle for observing and understanding how cognitive development is influenced by experience. Through the infant's attempts to make sense of new experiences, its reflex schemes and their networking would be reorganized. One facet of the idea provides an index of when such an emergent process would be occurring. When the infant engages in repeated cycles of an activity, then that activity is likely to be a skill in the making. The infant is likely to be motivated by a desire to recapture and control the novel experience. Examination of the course of the infant's practice can reveal the nature of the whats and hows of the experience that the infant is establishing a basis for controlling. Another facet of the idea has to do with identifying the emergent progress of the whats and hows and their relations. Within that frame, Piaget distinguishes between primary, secondary, and tertiary circular reactions. These changing patternings describe the progress of the infant toward forming objective concepts of objects and events and establishing coherent and flexible organizations of action schemes.

Piaget, with Jacqueline, had no difficulty in finding and exemplifying the circular reaction process when she was around 1 year of age. We will not describe those observations in detail. Rather, we present a brief and abstract picture of them to provide a context for a case we will consider in detail. During this period of her life, Piaget studied how she came to cope with such instrumentalities as sticks and strings. He provides the reader with a detailed view of the many aspects of her body and the objects that she unexpectedly encounters, the many repetitions she engages in before she webs those aspects together so that she can use the instruments, and how often she resets herself the problem after she has gained the desired object. Piaget was well prepared to observe such matters with Jacqueline, at least in part, because he was well acquainted with Köhler's (1917/1959) study of tool use in chimpanzees and the related work with infants of the Bühlers and their associates (e.g., 1930). Given this background, he also was prepared to look for precursors of such tertiary circular activity in Jacqueline, and we now will examine an instance of how, in the context of strings, he did this, first with Jacqueline and then with Lucienne and Laurent.

Secondary Circular Reaction or "Excitement"?

Piaget's initial observation involving strings was accidental and occurred when Jacqueline was 5–8 (*O.I.*, obs. 96). He reports that she looks at a doll attached to a string that is stretched from the hood to the handle of her bassinet. The doll hangs at foot level, and when she moves her feet, she strikes the doll and sets it in motion. A repetitive cycle ensues during which Jacqueline seems to become more skillful. Piaget establishes that she wants to kick the doll because she doesn't kick when the doll is removed. He also believes that she doesn't understand the causal relation between her kick and the doll's motion because she wiggles her feet, arms, and torso even when she can see the doll but it is too distant from her to reach with her feet. However, he does not ask whether her kicking and wiggling may be an artifact of her excitement over seeing the doll's movement rather than a secondary circular reaction, an instance of "procedures destined to make interesting sights last" (*O.I.*, p. 153).

This question, or its force, does not occur to him at the time, but it does afterwards. He raises it 2 months later with Jacqueline in a slightly altered context, and he raises it again with Lucienne and then with Laurent. When Jacqueline is 7–16 (*O.I.*, obs. 100), he now suspends a doll by a string from the hood of her bassinet. She grasps the doll in order to shake the hood 20 times and does so with increasing force and laughter. He concludes that she has been engaged in a secondary-circular reaction. On that day, he also evaluates whether she has causal understanding (*O.I.*, obs. 113). He concludes she does not because she pulls the string to "cause" Piaget to continue to swing his watch even when he is distant from the bassinet. In subsequent days, he observes how she remembers and generalizes the procedure. Thus at 7–23, Piaget, unseen, shakes the hood, and Jacqueline pulls the string even though the doll is not present. She repeats the string pulling on many days and extends the pattern to cause the shaking of the sides and the grate of the bassinet. She also comes to vary the angle at which she moves her arm (*O.I.,* obs. 101).

Given his observation of Jacqueline at 5-8, Piaget prepares to investigate the "excitement" question with Lucienne, and he makes his first observation when she is 3-5 (*O.I.,* obs. 94). Cloth dolls hang from the hood of her bassinet, and he notes how she bends and unbends her legs and thereby shakes her bassinet and the cloth dolls. The phenomenon is present, and on 3-6, he examines it again. He thinks her kicking seems purposive as she kicks as soon as the dolls are attached and does so unsmilingly and with "intense and sustained concentration" (*O.I.,* p. 158). At 3-8, Piaget is convinced that she is engaged in a circular reaction. He notes that when she is watching, with pleasure, her hands come and go, she also shakes herself. The shake reminds her of her dolls because she then looks to them and begins to shake herself regularly while watching the dolls with unsmiling concentration . At 3-9 (*O.I.,* 94R), he observes that she generalizes her shaking procedure. Piaget, unseen, shakes the bassinet, sans dolls. Lucienne shows interest and with a serious demeanor repeatedly shakes the bassinet and repeats the process in the evening. At 3-13 (*O.I.,* obs. 94), the dolls hang from the hood of her bassinet. She is watching her hands come and go with pleasure and happens to shake herself. She then looks to the dolls and the moving hood, then looks back and forth between her hands, the dolls, and the hood, and then shakes regularly and watches the dolls with concentration. On 3-16, she shakes the dolls with precise rhythmical movements and unsmilingly watches the dolls "as if studying the phenomenon." After awhile, she smiles at the dolls. A similar episode occurs at 3-24. It seems as if she has formed a skill, has control of the process.

At 4-27 (*O.I.,* obs. 94R), Piaget recreates the context in which he made his initial observation of Jacqueline at 5-8 (*O.I.,* obs. 96). The dolls hang over Lucienne's feet. She gives a big kick and is delighted with the effect. She briefly looks at her motionless foot and then begins again. Piaget wonders whether vision plays a role in guiding her kicking and concludes that it doesn't: She kicks the same whether she looks at the doll or has her head covered; when she misses, she varies her foot movements slowly but does not look at them.

Thus with Lucienne, Piaget attempts to document the early presence of purposive shaking and kicking. In this context, he continues to try to articulate criteria, for example, unsmiling concentration, and he begins to raise questions about how such skills or schemes are related to other skills or schemes, for example, her looking at hands, dolls, and hood; the visual guidance of her kicking. With Laurent, he looks even earlier. He continues to try to establish criteria that will differentiate excitement from intention and to describe the course of the formation of the scheme. But he also now begins to look even more searchingly for evidence of when and how different schemes come to be coordinated. We describe this process in the next two subsections.

The Early Use of Strings and Chains

At 2-17 (*O.I.,* obs. 97), there are toys hanging from the hood of Laurent's bassinet. Piaget notes that Laurent's wiggling causes the toys to move and that Laurent watches them. When they stop, he restarts his shaking, but Piaget does not believe that a secondary circular reaction is present. To examine the issue more thoroughly,

Piaget capitalizes on the fact that Laurent's arms are tied by strings to the handles of his bassinet to keep him from sucking his thumbs. At 2–24, Piaget attaches the strings to balls containing rattles that are hanging from the hood. Laurent chances to shake the balls by moving his hands. He then goes on to arch himself and wave his arms and legs. Piaget attributes this behavior to "joy" rather than to a circular reaction. On 2–25, he creates the conditions for a more careful evaluation of the issue. He lengthens the string so that slight arm movements will not shake the balls, and he attaches the string to Laurent's right arm. Laurent moves both arms equally and only episodically shakes the balls. But the arm movements do become more regular and more extensive. Something is happening, and on 2–27, Piaget now believes that "conscious coordination seems definite" (*O.I.,* p. 161). On that day, Laurent is surprised and frightened by his first shake. But by his second or third shake, he swings only his right arm and his movements become regular and more skilled. He reveals expectations. When he moves his arm, he blinks before the balls move. He intensifies his interest on subsequent days, and he swings his arm as soon as he hears the balls rattle as Piaget attaches them to the hood. Moreover, at 3–0, he reveals cross-manual transfer. The string is attached to his left arm. The first shake is by chance. and Laurent is frightened and then curious. With his right arm outstretched and immobile, he swings his left arm and watches the rattle.

Laurent has been grasping what he sees since 3–7, and on 3–12, the balls are attached to Piaget's watch chain and the chain hangs above Laurent's face (*O.I.,* obs. 98). Will Laurent adapt his scheme to this modest change in context? Will that adaptation also involve the use of visually guided reaching? On 3–10 (*O.I.,* obs. 97), Piaget had placed the string to which the balls were attached in Laurent's hand. After an accidental shake, Laurent had looked at the ball and then had struck with his right arm and continued to do so for a quarter of an hour with great laughter. Thus Laurent could swing the balls while grasping the string. When he sees the chain, will he reach for it and grasp and swing it? The result is negative. When Piaget puts the chain in his hand, he shakes the rattles by chance. He hears the noise, lets go of the chain, and waves his hand. But he does not go on to grasp the chain.

On 3–13 (*O.I.,* obs. 98), the same process occurs. Laurent now waves his hand repeatedly, occasionally striking the chain and shaking the rattles. Then without looking, Laurent grasps his sheet, as if to suck it. He has the chain in the folds of the sheet, thereby leading the rattles to sound. Laurent is interested, and he now slowly searches for the chain with his fingers but not with his eyes. As soon as he feels the chain free of the sheet, he grasps the chain, lets go of the sheet, and swings his arm and watches the rattle. After awhile, he looks at his hand and then looks up and down the chain. He seems to understand the connection. That evening, he hears the rattle and then looks at the chain. Now looking only at the chain, he reaches around for it, contacts it, grasps it, and then shakes. After awhile, he turns to sucking his fingers. The chain touches his fingers. He grasps it and pulls it slowly, expecting the noise. Then he pulls harder. Success leads to much laughing, babbling, and chain swinging. Also that evening (*O.I.,* obs. 106), he grasps the chain and, while looking at the rattle, he studies the relationship between the vigor of his swings of the chain and the movement of the rattles. On 3–14 (*O.I.,* obs. 98), he looks at the rattle and haptically searches for the chain with his left hand. He brushes the chain with his hand, grasps it, and systematically varies his swing. He loses the chain and now shakes his left hand, while looking at the rattle, for 5 minutes! It appears that he does and doesn't understand the connection! On the following days, he continues to grope for the chain with his hand and does not use vision to guide his hand. But on 3-18, he looks first at the rattle, then at the chain, and then he grasps it and swings it. Laurent appears to now understand the various connections.

But again, a modest change in context reveals the limits of Laurent's understanding. On 3-20 (*O.I.*, obs. 112), Laurent is offered a doll by Piaget. As soon as he sees it, he grasps it with his right hand and sucks it. The doll is attached by a long string to a rattle hanging from the hood of his bassinet. Laurent sucks the doll for 10 min, during which time the rattle neither moves nor sounds. Laurent then lets his arm drop to the side, and he continues to hold the doll. Piaget then shakes the rattle without causing the string on Laurent's hand to move. Laurent hears the rattle, looks at it, and neatly stretches out his right arm and causes the rattle to shake. A moment later, he is touching the doll with his right hand but is not holding it. Piaget shakes the rattle. Laurent moves his empty right hand without attempting to grasp the doll!

In presenting this series of observations, we hope several things are apparent. One is the long process Piaget had to go through to establish evidence about circular reactions in the early phases of infancy. He chances on a repetitive behavior of Jacqueline and decides he has not analyzed its purposefulness carefully enough. With Lucienne, he creates a context for study at an earlier age. He is able to refine his criteria for intentionality. But further issues arise: He had little opportunity to observe her behavior before she established the secondary circular reaction; he notices her kicking is not visually guided. With Laurent, he begins even earlier. He further refines his criteria, and he now looks systematically for evidence of how an effective procedure comes to be coordinated with other effective procedures and is extended into new contexts. He now is able to present a richly detailed picture of a slowly enlarging web of nested connections. With the formation of each, there is evidence of practice and study. Their coordinations and extensions sometimes occur rapidly, for example, the transfer of the use of the right hand as a means to the use of the left hand; the transfer from the chain-pulling context to the doll-pulling context. More often the process proceeds very slowly and results in a shifting understanding that indicates that his newly formed organizations coexist with his prior ones, for example, the oscillations between visual and haptic searches for the chain; Laurent's initial recognition that he must pull the doll to shake the rattle and his subsequent wave of his empty hand.

Thumb Sucking

Piaget's description of the complexity of the formation of Laurent's secondary circular reactions was foreshadowed in his observation of how Laurent, but not Jacqueline and Lucienne, came to be able to bring his thumbs to his mouth and keep them there. Thus while Piaget may or may not have noted in detail Jacqueline's thumb sucking at birth (*O.I.*, obs. 1), he reports only two subsequent brief observations (*O.I.*, obs. 24). At 1-28, he notes that she puts her left hand in her mouth when she is very hungry, and he notes that by 4 months she must put her thumb in her mouth in order to go to sleep. However, he got curious about the phenomenon of learning to suck with Lucienne. At 1-24 (*O.I.*, obs. 13), he observes that she plays with moving her tongue over her lower lip. At 1–25 and 1–26 (*O.I.*, obs. 23), he reports that her hands move to her mouth constantly but that she can't hold or find her fingers once she loses them. At 2–2, he notes that she sucks her fingers, the back of her hand, her wrist, and that when her hand escapes it approaches her mouth. That evening, he observes that her hand remains still for long moments, and her mouth opens to grasp it at the same time her hand approaches her mouth. At 2–3, her hand gropes in the right direction and then there is an abrupt movement of her fingers into her open and motionless mouth.

Given such observations of Lucienne, Piaget was prepared to study how Laurent achieved control of that important tool, his thumb. At 0–21 (*O.I.*, obs. 7), Piaget observes Laurent lying on his right side and sucking his thumb. His hands are clasped, his arms are tight against his body, and his body is immobile. Piaget removes his thumb and Laurent finds it three times. But the test does not assess whether Laurent can direct his hand and arm to his mouth as his arms are immobile. Piaget lays him on his back. His arms draw back as his head and lips seek without success. At 0–24, Piaget notes his body is immobile when he sucks his thumb. But when his hand is free and grazes his mouth, he does not direct it to his mouth. At 1–1 (*O.I.*, obs. 16), Piaget observes Laurent when he is held in a vertical position. Laurent roots and makes large, rapid arm movements and often knocks them against his face. Piaget assesses what Laurent will do when his hand is laid on his cheek. He twice turns his head to his right and tries to suck his fingers. On the second occasion, he manages to grasp his fingers. But his arms move, and he loses his fingers. Later, when his body is immobilized, his right hand happens to grasp his left arm and his left hand presses against his mouth. Laurent pauses and then grasps his thumb and sucks. At this point, Laurent does not appear to be able to direct his arm to his mouth, and it is unclear whether he can direct his hand there. It does appear that his mouth seeks his fingers. Piaget notes that Laurent immobilizes his arms and hands when he is sucking his thumb. He wonders if that is a reflex coordination or an achieved one.

At 1–2 (*O.I.*, obs. 17), Piaget begins to note definite coordinations. Laurent is being held in a vertical position. He is crying from hunger. He calms himself, but his arms move without direction. Then the arms seem to approach his mouth and at times brush his lips, and his mouth is open and grasping. Laurent then accidentally catches his left thumb, and his arms become rigid. However, they then move, he loses his thumb, and he gets very angry, cries, and tries to suck. Then again his arms seem to approach his mouth, and his mouth tries to catch the fingers that touch it. At 1–3, when he is again held vertically, his arm movements seem more directed. Further, when the hand contacts his mouth, it seems as if the mouth and hand seek each other. Laurent succeeds several times and immobilizes his arms and hands for a few seconds each time. That evening (*O.I.*, obs. 18), Piaget evaluates whether Laurent can hold his thumb in his mouth. He grasps Laurent's right arm and holds Laurent's right hand to his mouth. When his hand contacts his lips, he sucks it and immobilizes his arms. He loses his hand but now is able to direct it back to his lips 13 times. Piaget notes that in this process Laurent simultaneously opens his mouth and moves his hand toward his mouth. Even his failures reveal a coordination. When his fingers touch his cheek, his mouth is open to receive them.

On the next day, at 1–4 (*O.I.*, obs. 19), he shows even clearer signs of directed searching and of selective sucking. His right hand approaches his mouth and touches his lower lip. He grasps his index finger and then lets it fall out. Next he gets his thumb in his mouth and has his index finger between his gum and his lip. Laurent removes his hand to a distance of 5 cm and returns it so his thumb is in his mouth. He sucks and immobilizes his hands, arms, and body. He withdraws his thumb and again moves his hand to his mouth, only to catch three fingers. He removes his hand and returns it. He grasps his thumb and sucks it. Piaget removes his thumb. Laurent seems to give up but then brings his hand to his face. That involves a struggle, and after initially gaining his fingers, he grasps his thumb and sucks it. Piaget again removes his thumb and again Laurent succeeds. In the vertical position, Laurent has coordinated his hand and thumb with his mouth and can keep his thumb in his mouth.

When Laurent is at 1-5 and 1-6 (*O.I.,* obs. 20), Piaget observes whether the coordination is present when Laurent lies on his back. Laurent moves his hands to his face but doesn't find his mouth. However, when he is held in a vertical position, he quickly finds his thumb. At 1-7, he again is on his back. His arm movements are more directed, but he doesn't get his thumb far enough into his mouth and keeps losing it. But at 1-9, he is successful. Moreover, when Piaget removes his thumb, he brings it almost immediately to his mouth and holds it there. On occasion, he misses, but they are near misses, contacts of his mouth and nose. By the end of the month, Laurent can suck his left as well as his right thumb.

The Development of Circular Reactions, or How to Separate Means from Ends

Our presentation of Piaget's observations relative to the circular reaction theme has been selective and lengthy. Our hope is that we have helped highlight why his labors thereon are so golden, so worthy of replication and extension. With Laurent, we have in the literature at least one relatively contextualized and detailed description of how, from birth on, one infant worked at weaving together some of its many strands relative to one another and to those of the variegated world it encountered. However, such an instantiation of the circular reaction theme was only part of Piaget's aim. He also wanted to capture the progress of *the* infant's intelligence and concepts. On the one hand, he recognized that marking the phases of that progress was a relative matter, and on the other hand, he didn't quite act on that view. He indicated the former when he raised such questions as when we should attribute intentionality and intelligence and objective awareness to the infant's circular reaction (*O.I.,* p. 147). He argued that such examples as Laurent's persistent attempts to direct his thumb to his mouth and hold it there indicated how unreasonable it would be to reserve the attribution of intentionality until the infant acted on the basis of representations, particularly verbal ones. But to call acts intentional when they evidence meaning would be to include too much, even reflexes. The term should be used to mark the kind of progress that occurred between Laurent's searches for his thumb and searches for such matters as hidden objects. So too for "intelligence which presupposes intention" (*O.I.,* p. 147). One can describe Laurent's problem solving in gaining his thumb as employing variable means to an end, "but it is clear that such a description does not correspond to anything from the point of view of the subject himself, since the thumb is not known independently of the act which consists of sucking it" (*O.I.,* p. 180).

The last quotation gives some indication of the "other hand" of Piaget's solution to the demarcation problem. He posited stages that he tended to cast in definitive terms. Thus Laurent's searches for his thumb are stage 2 primary circular reactions. Laurent's searches for the chain are stage 3 secondary circular reactions; "the chain serving to shake the rattle has been perceived and manipulated before being conceived as 'means' and does not cease to be regarded as distinct from the rattle" (*O.I.*, p. 180). But the secondary circular reaction only involves the intention to recapture the interesting spectacle. The intention is aroused only after the event; there is no obstacle that intervenes between finding the means and the goal. Only in stage 4 do the infants' actions bear the clear hallmarks of intentionality. In situations involving hidden objects and demands for detours, such an infant intends to achieve the goal from the start, and, when confronted with an obstacle, perseveres toward the goal while deploying various familiar means to eliminate the obstacle. In stage 5, the infant now is able to engage in tertiary circular reactions; it now searches for new means and novel properties of objects and events.

This is the solution that so many have found so problematic. As working criteria for distinguishing phases of a problem-solving process, the stage definitions can serve a useful purpose. But how could Piaget describe so clearly Laurent's lack of control of his arms, hand, and torso and not see them as obstacles Laurent came to surmount through his various attempts to get his thumb into his mouth and keep it there? How could Piaget invoke the metaphor of mental chemistry and work so hard to show that the achieved coordinations of relatively independent schemes lead to readaptations that are both narrow in scope and variable in occurrence, and simultaneously argue so strongly for a description of that lengthy, iterative, and multidimensional process of webbing in terms of six neat emergent stages? We don't pretend to be able to answer such questions, but we can offer a few ideas from the perspective we have taken.

Part of an answer has to do with the task he faced in ordering his many diverse observations so that they could be presented in book form. The six stages are a device for classifying that almost overwhelming variety, and he did not always adhere to that six-stage ordering; for example, in *O.I.*, under stage 2, he describes the development of visually guided reaching in five stages. Part of an answer may lie in the kinds of mental chemistry models that were available to him. He rejected the prevailing ones, associationism and reflexology. They pictured the actor and world in terms that were too mechanical and that failed to capture the emergent reorganizations that he believed in and observed. As we indicated earlier, he found William James's (1890/1950) metaphor of a mind made up of many active parts congenial. But it also was unacceptable to him because it promised a mind that cohered only locally. For James, both the world the mind knows and the mind that knows it were untidy affairs. Concepts were never definitive but only tools for ordering the world. Their meaning changed with changes in their context of use, and even in given contexts they had to be found and refound. No sharp demarcations could be made between how you reasoned and what you reasoned about, nor could one easily distinguish between ability and performance. For us, James's characterization of adult thought intuitively captures Piaget's observations of the course of Laurent's early coping with the use of strings and chains. In part, Piaget plainly was comfortable with viewing the young infant's activities, and the young child's symbolic activities, in such transductive terms. But he was not comfortable with viewing the toddler's sensorimotor activities or the older child's representational activities in such terms.

When he wrote the infancy books, he was committed to a belief in which reasoning came to be logically consistent and concepts became more objective. In science, the concepts might have to be revised in the light of new experiences, but we, at least, could develop the ability to reason with certainty about such contingent matters as our concepts of the "real." Piaget sought a comparable kind of progress at the sensorimotor level. The infant's schemes and their organization would progress from ways of viewing the features of the world as affordances for action—objects as suckables and graspables; the infantile analogues of "holes are to dig" and "bikes are to ride"—to ways of distinguishing between the what and how of knowing.

We live in very different times than did the Piaget of the infancy books. We tend to think not of *the* species but rather of populations of individuals, and we assign class membership in terms of a family of criteria that do not form a consistent structure (Mayr, 1982). As such, we do not tend to expect to be able to find a set of essential features that partition all members of one species from all members of a related one. We no longer tend to think that the evolution of species can be comprehended without a careful specification of the niches they occupy. The pictures of the evolution of species are now messy bushes rather than tidy lines or trees. Certainly Piaget was not unaware of the importance of individuality and niche, but his views and his times led him to believe he could abstract essential features of mental development that went beyond such contingent matters.

Today, we are far less likely to think of the maturation and organization of the nervous system as progress toward a hierarchically organized control system. Some try to capture its staggered, multifaceted development by focusing not on *organogenesis*—when ears, eyes, limbs develop their hookups—but on *systemogenesis*—when subsets of these organs are organized to perform specific adaptive functions (Anokhin, 1964). Increasingly the metaphor of a cascade, a historical confluence of complex stochastic interactions between various elements, is used to picture a maturational process that is far more complex than the unfolding of a genetic program (e.g., Lewin, 1984). At a gross level, a maturational process can be pictured as a typical series of phases, but different individuals take many different routes to each phase. Rather than speaking of a hierarchically organized nervous system or mind, we frequently employ the notion of *heterarchy* (e.g., Minsky, 1982b), the idea being that what is a control mechanism at one moment may be a subsidiary mechanism at another.

Mathematicians and philosophers who are interested in the foundations of mathematics no longer seek to give it a firm foundation but rather seek to understand how such a variegated and unsettled domain can be so firm. They often find that the coherence and only local consistency of mathematical and other knowledge lie in the actors who rest their knowing on a web of metaphors (e.g., Davis & Hersh, 1980; Goodman, 1978; Lakoff & Johnson, 1980). In psychology, the dramatic split-brain investigations of Sperry and his associates have spurred a renewed interest in thinking about multiple minds and personalities in a Jamesian spirit. It is a view that leads one to expect conduct to be shifting rather than consistent and to view such themes as context, emotion, intention, and individuality as playing a central role in cognitive functioning (e.g., Hebb, 1980; Mandler, 1984; Sperry, 1982). In the domain of artificial intelligence, comparable metaphors are being developed, some examples being the various attempts by Minsky and Papert to motivate the search for a description of a society of mind (1980, 1982b), Doyle's theory of reasoned assumptions (1982), and Schank's ideas about the role of reminding in the organization of memory (1982). The stress is on picturing mind, as James did in his celebrated metaphor of the stream of consciousness, as a large set of parallel processors that carry on multiple functions and cohere only episodically as focal attention or consciousness. There is a search to formulate the units of such processors in terms that do not separate knowledge from action but rather combine both features of the world and purposes and procedures in units. The aim is to describe reasoning and knowing at any stage of development as being "common sense" in nature rather than as becoming progressively more logical. In other words, how can the mind be construed so that it can appear to grow in attention span and functional single-mindedness and yet be capable of noticing features that are not related to our intentions? Tolman (1932) directed our attention generatively to aspects of those issues on a molar level when he distinguished between instrumental and latent learning. There now is the promise that we can implement that kind of a notion in componential terms that can lead us to a better understanding of behavior and its relation to the brain.

We believe this changing context is a welcome one from which will emerge a more adequate model in terms of which to understand developing minds. It leads us to seek to see different facets of conduct and to try to formulate a different kind of model of their organization. Would Piaget have interpreted his observations differently if he were writing his books at this time? We think so, but we do not know. However, we do believe that the development of such a model demands that we seek the kinds of contextualized and detailed observations that Piaget provided, above all with Laurent. We don't pretend to be able to say how or where to make them, but we can note some things that enabled Piaget to report what he did.

Piaget focused on individuals. He looked at them often and so developed a particularized sense of them and the contexts he observed them in. As such, he often was in a position to study how they went about solving problems they came upon rather than simply studying how they coped with the problem he as experimenter imposed upon them. Moreover, when the latter was the case, his particularized sense of them put him in a position to attempt to look at their behavior from their point of view as well as his own. To put it in other terms, we quote Lorenz's account of what led Tinbergen to be such an able experimenter and modeler of behavior:

> It takes a very long period of watching to become truly familiar with an animal and to attain a deeper understanding of its behavior; and without the love for the animal itself, no observer, however patient, could ever look long at it enough to make valuable observations on its behavior.
>
> (*Tinbergen, 1967, p. xiii*)

INTELLIGENCE AND CONCEPTS OF REALITY

We end by presenting some more observations of the kind we believe beg extending and explaining. With these, we have several purposes. One is to describe some examples from older infants. We fear that our dwelling on how hard and rewarding it was for Piaget to see the complexity of ever younger infants may have conveyed the impression that we all must follow him in kind. That hardly is our intention.

Another is to take a somewhat different look at the difficulties Piaget had in trying to describe cognitive development in terms of the emergence of a distinction between intelligence and concepts. Another is to illustrate how different one line of current research on infants' concepts that Piaget spawned may look if we try to make observations in Piaget's spirit.

There are at least two ways to look at the organization of Piaget's first two infancy books, *O.I.* and *C.R.* One is to ask whether he succeeded in showing how infants come to separate intelligence from concepts of the "real," to shift from procedural or functional knowledge to possessing a coherent set of ways of operating on a store declarative knowledge. Viewed from such a perspective, Piaget was a self-declared failure. He didn't give up his intention to find a way of distinguishing operative from mere figurative knowledge in the books or in his later writings. But in the infancy books he concludes he simply has shown correlative changes in intelligence and concepts at each stage of development.

If we view Piaget from such a perspective, we think it is easy to lose sight of what a heroic and monumental labor he engaged in and to ask too much of him, and, implicitly, of ourselves. Another way to look at him, as we suggested earlier, is to ask how he managed to order the immense number of observations that varied so greatly in terms of infant, age, situation, and theme. If we put ourselves in his shoes in that way, we think a rather different view of his problematical assertions about development can emerge. His distinctions between intelligence and concepts and between stages thereof can be looked upon as a provisional classification system. Once the many observations were arrayed in those few terms, he could think about them and present his findings and thoughts to others. The classification system he used, of course, was not theoretically neutral and was tailored to his intellectual context. We hope our prior discussion has made plain many of the reasons that his presuppositional system was bound to lead his reasoning about his observations in some directions that presently do not make sense. But we believe that thinking about his grand distinctions as classificatory devices has the advantage that it better fits with what he did and frees us to capitalize on what he observed.

One source of support for such a view has to do with how Piaget used the Kantian categories of object, space, cause, and time. He plainly did not systematically attempt to study his infants' sense of time, and it is very hard to separate what is classified under the heading of cause in *C.R.* from what is considered under the *O.I.* headings at any stage. On the other hand, the observations are relevant to the Kantian categories, and Kant's ideas about the relation of reasoning to concepts of the "real" played a central role in the thinking of Piaget and his intended audience. As such, Piaget's use of this classification system can be viewed as a dramatic, useful, and provisional way of organizing and calling attention to what he had observed.

The loose fit between Piaget's observations and his classification system can be seen in other ways. One has to do with the observations that are described as residual reactions, things an infant did that were appropriate to an earlier stage, and with a number of observations that are not easily captured by the categories but were too interesting to omit. The former provide further indications that Piaget was able to note, and not accommodate to, evidence of the more loosely coupled organizations of his infants. We now describe one of the isolated examples in the hope that it will illustrate one of the principal messages that inhered in Piaget's observations, namely, the many facets of a situation that are conceptually problematic to infants that no longer appear problematic to us.

The example involves Jacqueline at 1-8-30 ((*O.I.,* obs. 182). There is an ivory plate in front of Jacqueline that is pierced by three holes that vary from 1 to 2 mm in diameter. She observes Piaget put the sharpened point of a short green pencil into one of the holes. She laughs, grasps the pencil, and imitates Piaget. Then Piaget offers her a longer brown pencil with the unsharpened end directed toward the plate. Jacqueline grasps the pencil, does not turn it over, and tries to put it into each of the three holes, including the hole occupied by the other pencil. She visits the three holes repeatedly. Piaget then removes the first pencil and offers it to her point down. She immediately places it in a hole. But now, Piaget offers her the pencil again but the unsharpened end faces toward the plate. Jacqueline rotates the pencil so that the point faces down and inserts the point. Piaget offers her the second pencil, now with the point facing down. She inserts the point. But when he offers her the second pencil with the point facing up, she does not turn it over and tries to insert its unsharpened end into the hole! Over the next 30 trials, Piaget sometimes offers her the first pencil, sometimes the second pencil, sometimes their points face down and sometimes up. Jacqueline always gets the first pencil point into a hole. She never rotates the upward-facing point of the second pencil, and she often tries to insert its unsharpened end into the hole occupied by the other pencil. At about the thirtieth attempt, Jacqueline correctly rotates the second pencil and then is able consistently to place both pencils into a hole.

We find this to be a striking example, and we imagine you will have no difficulty in finding analogous examples from your own adult experiences. We will shortly discuss what we think is an analogous example, Piaget's "typical" stage 4 object concept error. Piaget's discussion of this episode focuses on the suddenness of Jacqueline's "insight." We think that is right. Given all she appears to know about the situation and how to operate in it, how could it be otherwise? But a large part of the wonder of this example lies not there but in how to describe what she did before she achieved the solution. Note how descriptions of her knowledge of hows and whats in terms of abstract mental capabilities fail to prepare us for her course of behavior. She plainly discriminates between the two similar pencils and is aware that one of them has two ends that can be interchanged by rotating the pencil and inserting its point. In Piaget and/or the literature, there are beliefs that by Jacqueline's age or stage infants have concepts of *in, on, under,* and so forth, that they perceive objects categorically and relationally, and perhaps that they have the concept that two objects cannot occupy the same location at the same time (e.g., Harris, 1983; Mandler, 1983). Why doesn't Jacqueline use her considerable capabilities in this case? Perhaps, it is the difference between competence and performance? Perhaps, but such distinctions both reduce the wonder of such examples and beg the question of why such events are so frequent if we will but notice them (e.g., Minsky, 1982a; Perkins, 1981).

We now turn to our final set of observations. They bear, in general, on Piaget's typical stage 4 object concept error. We dwell on this context for three kinds of reasons. One is that performance on the delayed reaction task historically has been used as a marker of higher mental processes and infants in this age range seem to have hooked up many of their mental parts on a behavioral and neurological level (e.g., Gibson, 1982; Goldman-Rakic et al., 1983; Touwen, 1976). The others are that the intensive experimental study of the error makes many of its aspects clearer and that the error plays a key role in Piaget's account of when infants know objects conceptually. It forms a major component of his argument that search for hidden objects is not guided by representation or recall or imagining of the hidden object until stage 6. We will not take up this issue because it leads to murky issues involving the status of mental images in mental life (e.g., Jaynes, 1976; Mandler, 1983). It also plays an important role in his ideas about organization or structure, and this will be what we focus upon.

As described by Piaget, the typical stage 4 error occurs during a period when Piaget characterizes the infant as in relatively good control of its sensory and motor parts and able to think about events, at least on a sensorimotor level. An infant of about 8–10 months of age is easily able to find a desirable object that is hidden under one or two, and sometimes more, covers. Piaget interprets this feat as one that demands the coordination of a considerable number of elements. The infant somehow is able to attend to the goal of attaining the object even though, while the object is out of view, it must divert its attention to the cover and the nontrivial tasks of grasping, removing, and releasing the cover. The infant then attentively watches the object being hidden under the second cover. However, when the object is occluded, the infant immediately turns toward the first cover and searches there, a strange and surprising thing for a seemingly competent infant to do. The event is not unlike the surprises Piaget later gave us through the conservation problems. A seemingly trivial change in the situational circumstances leads someone who seemed to understand events in terms much like our own to do something nonsensical from our point of view. Piaget considers the possibility that the phenomenon is not a sign of a strange mind in action. The infants' processes and understanding can be viewed as not unlike our own, just different in some detail involving a memory or motor or perceptual process. Piaget rejects that possibility. Such processes are involved; for example, the infant perceives the new information but its memory of its past solutions overrides the new. However, the immediacy of the error points to the need for an explanation that focuses on how such processes are combined. He proposes that the infant does not hold onto the new information because that information is incorporated into its prior organization of notions of action, objects, and space. For infants at this stage, objects in space are still conceived of as being tied to effective ways of acting rather than to their objective properties.

The error and Piaget's explanation of it have been the subject of much dispute and experimental study. There are excellent recent reviews of this literature (e.g., Harris, 1983; Schuberth, 1982). We will describe some very general trends. One is that the error has proved to be far more episodic than seems to be implied by a stage notion. Secondly, systematic variation of a number of situational circumstances is associated with variation in the likelihood of the error. Third, many of these carefully designed studies have been motivated by thoughtful attempts to explain the error in terms of specific factors that would be relevant to an information-processing account of the error, for example, the role of delay length, distractors, and landmarks. In large part, these explanations have been successful in making the infants' errors appear less strange.

However, something about the error remains strange because there have been a growing number of reports that the error sometimes occurs even when the object is not occluded. Such investigators as Butterworth (1982), Harris (1983), and Wishart and Bower (1984) have attempted in different ways to cast both the in-view and out-of-view errors in a common explanatory framework that can be called neo-Piagetian because of their focus on organizational themes.

But there is something even more strange about the reports in the literature. The experimental studies have not examined Piaget's description of how the error is made. The studies primarily focus on documenting correlations between where and how objects are placed and where infants search. There is very little, if any, attention given to what the infants do in the interim between the two classes of events nor, within the classes, to the diverse ways in which they may behave. As such, the studies have not really addressed the event that led Piaget to view the error as so anomalous.

We now describe an episode from our studies of infants that we imagine was like the phenomenon that caught Piaget's eye. Nine-month-old Lisa watches and reaches with her left hand for a necklace that is hidden under a cover on her right. When the necklace is covered, Lisa strains to grasp the cover but the hiding tray is too distant. She sits up and looks toward the left cover. As the hiding tray is moved within her reach, she looks first at the experimenter, then to the right cover, and then uses her right hand to remove it and grasp the necklace. Thus despite distractions Lisa is able to keep her mind on the covered object. On the next trial, the toy is hidden under an identical cover on her left side. She reaches with her left hand for the toy as it is covered. She continues to reach for the left cover for a brief moment after the toy is covered. But almost in that same moment, she begins to turn toward and to look at the right cover. She then reaches directly for the right cover with her left hand and removes the cover. She frowns, stares, and then attempts to correct herself but is not permitted to do so. A very similar pattern occurs on the next trial.

We cannot explain Lisa's behavior, and we don't want to suggest that Piaget was correct on either an observational or an explanatory level. While Piaget described some episodes like that of Lisa's, many of his descriptions of the typical error simply note where he hid the toy and where his infants searched. Our own impression is that Lisa's pattern is not typical and that both she and other infants find many different routes to the error, vary them at different times, and sometimes do and sometimes don't err.

As such, one might well ask why one should dwell on such patterns. We will try to answer such a question in two ways. We will shortly describe three episodes that we hope you will find intriguing enough to make our second answer superfluous. In each case, an infant will take a different route to the error and in each case the object will be in view. Our second answer is the point we have made repeatedly in this chapter. Looking at such details is the only way to arrive at the phenomena that our models of the mind are to be explanations of. That answer, of course, begs the questions of what assurance there is that we won't get lost in details and why we should focus on stage 4 errors.

Part of an answer lies in the fact that we know a good deal more about these situations than Piaget did. Our large body of excellent parametric studies provides a ground within which we can work at ordering the confusing detail through repeated cycles of observing and attempting to represent what we have seen. The situations all have the feature that infants are likely to repeat a prior action when they observe a desirable object moved to a new location. Thus, like adults, infants in such situations can be seen to repeat past solutions to new problems that retain some features of the old. As such, infants are in a context in which they face a learning or insight problem that has the nice feature that we have relatively good control of their intentions: Do they want the toy? Therefore, we can focus our efforts on trying to identify and understand when and how they attempt to reorganize their many parts so that they not only can notice but can appreciate the new information. We further believe that the changing intellectual context we described earlier promises that we will be looking at such details with a fresher eye and that the new things we will see will lead us to new ways to represent how minds are so organized that they can adapt old knowledge to a changing world. In that framework, we think one feature of the stage 4 error is particularly relevant, namely, the transient and context-dependent nature of the phenomenon.

We now end with the promised episodes. The first we owe to our reading of a most interesting paper by Bremner and Knowles (in press). James, 8–10, is seated at a table. On his right is a transparent container from which he previously had removed toys. An opaque container is introduced on his left. He plays with it. Then he observes that a bell is hidden in it. James orients and reaches toward the container. When it is moved within his reach, he leans toward it, looks into it, and recovers the bell. The bell then is placed in the transparent container on his right. As James observes this, he tightens, stares intently, and frowns. He then puts his fingers in his mouth. He looks at the container as the experimenter audibly counts, "One, two. . . . "As three is reached, James looks at the experimenter and continues to do so as the containers are moved within his reach. After they are in front of him, James smiles and turns directly to his left and searches in the opaque container. He then picks it up, mouths it, and turns to his right and manages to drop the container into the transparent one. He then picks the opaque container up, throws it away, and takes the bell.

James shows a different pattern of erroneous search than Lisa and does so in a different context, one less likely to elicit stage 4 errors. Perhaps one need not think his behavior is unusual. Perhaps he erred because he was distracted by the experimenter's count and forgot the toy in view. Perhaps he was thinking about the "other toy" because, as Harris (1983) suggests, he has not yet learned that objects can be in one and only one place at a time. Perhaps it was James's "set" that led to his error. Perhaps James became concerned because the experimenter violated his expectation of where the object would be placed. Perhaps that led him to look at the experimenter and thus to forget where he saw the object placed and to search at the expected place. We are sure the reader can come up with other accounts as good or better. We have reported the episode only to bring out two things. One is that James, before the distraction, experienced the new placement of the toy as problematical, and, without Piaget's observations, we probably would not have noticed that or been prepared to try to understand the situation. The other is that Piaget described a similar phenomenon in which distraction did not appear to play a role (*C.R.*, obs. 39). At 10–3, Jacqueline finds an object hidden at one place and then makes the stage 4 error when the object is hidden at a second place. Piaget then places the object off to the side and leaves it in full view. Jacqueline searches for it in the first place.

We now turn to our last two episodes. They occur in a somewhat different spatial context, and we owe them to Diamond (1981), who has made a remarkable series of longitudinal observations, some involving occluded objects, some involving a revisiting of a transparent barrier problem. In particular, she, and we, have seen a striking type of stage 4 error in a transparent container context, one which appears to demand the reorganization of deeper-seated schemes than were involved in the prior episodes. We present it in part for its intrinsic interest and in part to set the stage for the last incident. The first trial to be described reveals that Mikaela, 10–5, has mastered a very difficult task. Mikaela carefully watches as a toy is moved from her right side into a transparent container that rests on its side and whose open side is on her right. The toy is placed inside the container next to its left wall. Mikaela has learned to inhibit her well-established tendency to reach for the toy on her line of sight. Instead, she has developed a pattern of leaning to her right, looking into the container, and then reaching in an awkward backhand fashion into the container with her left arm. She performs this sequence of actions and gains the toy. On the next trial, the container is rotated so that its opening faces to Mikaela's left. Mikaela watches as the toy is moved into the container and is left in front of the right wall. She looks at the toy and then appears to understand the problem for she leans to her left and looks at the left side of the container. She talks to herself for a moment as she looks at the left side of the container; then she brightens, and then she directly moves to her right and attempts to reach through the back of the container with her left hand.

The episode of Mikaela further illustrates the point that Piaget's stage 4 error is not specific to the issue of how infants process information about occluded objects but rather bears on more general organizational issues. Like Lisa, Mikaela notices and even appears to appreciated the new information. Yet, without seeming distraction, she leaps to the conclusion that a prior solution is appropriate to the changed but similar circumstances. Both Lisa and Mikaela don't hold onto the new information but seem to do so in a different fashion. Lisa's change seemed to occur without benefit of choice, whereas in Mikaela's case, her change of mind seemed to occur after a course of pondering. It's interesting to note that Mikaela's shift was not preceded by a look at the object on the right side. Her search seemed to be guided by some kind of control structure other than vision. Finally, her awkward backhand pattern of reaching also is of interest. This awkward use of the contralateral arm is a common occurrence in this context. The infants could much more easily reach into the container and grasp the toy if they used the same-side arm. How they develop this indirect procedure and how they come to use the more direct procedure raise interesting questions about the relationship between vision, motor procedures, and "concepts" (e.g., Moll & Kuypers, 1977).

The final episode we will describe shares some features with the episode of Mikaela and involves an opaque container. Eric, 8–9, has become quite good at retrieving a toy when it is moved into an opaque container whose opening is on his right side. On the first of the two trials we describe, Eric watches as the toy is moved into the container. He then leans to his right, looks into the container, and, like Mikaela, bring his left hand to the top edge of the opening. His awkward backhand method of reaching into the container leads him into difficulty. He then stops reaching with his left hand and reaches in with his right hand and takes the toy. On the next trial, the container is rotated so that its open side is on his left. Eric appears to understand the change. Eric watches the toy move into the container. He then leans to his left, looks in, and brings his right hand to the top edge of the opening. He has difficulty reaching in. But instead of persevering or using his alternate hand as he did on the previous trial, he moves his right hand to the right side of the container and attempts to reach in several times as he continues to look into the container. He then sits up, leans to his right, and looks at the right side of the container. Then he leans to the left and looks into the container. But instead of reaching in, he again leans to the right and looks at that side of the container. Finally, he again leans to his left and this time despite difficulty, uses his right hand to reach in and gain the toy.

With Eric's stage 4 error, we hope it is even more evident that it is interesting to look at the details of infants' conduct in terms of intuitions about the dynamic, multicomponential nature of their developing minds. Eric's sequence of actions indicate that he knows where the object disappears, what to do to get it, and how to evaluate the situation when that knowledge fails. His sequence of actions also provides some sense of how those aspects are organized. When his search procedure runs into difficulty on the second trial, he does not interrupt his search for the toy to investigate the nature of the obstacle (nor does he do so when frustrated on the first trial). Rather, he continues to look at the toy and uses the search procedure that was effective on the previous trial. Only when that procedure fails does he look away from the toy and conduct an examination of the obstacle. The course of that examination leads him to strengthen his belief in his initial procedure while he does not forget or lose interest in the toy. Is his pattern a general one? We doubt it. Does he err because he lacks a conception of a container? In one sense, yes; why else would he reach through its back side? But what led Eric to profit from his examination of the container? He certainly has some sense of the container, and like ours, his concept is not a complete one nor do all of its features come to the fore in a given moment. Like ours, his concepts appear to have both procedural and declarative aspects and their mix varies in the context of his shifting intentions. The mix seems to lead him sometimes to treat the new problem as a version of an old one and sometimes to appreciate its new features. Looking at him from such a Jamesian perspective enables one, in context, to explore both the similarities and the differences between the organization of his conduct and our own. It is in this sense that a number of recent theorists have recommended that we cast our observing and thinking about minds in terms of the metaphor of "insight" (e.g., Minsky, 1982a, 1982b; Newell, 1981).

IN SUM

In what ways do these last episodes and our attempts to examine Piaget's processes speak to the continued relevance of Piaget's infancy books? We hope our general answer is plain. To understand other minds and how they change, we need to have a sense of how they operate in their contexts, and we can only achieve that sense in part. That answer bears both on infants and on those who study them. We now often tend to operate in Jamesian terms. The cognitive revolution in large part is that we now tend to view actors as having minds of a general sort (e.g., Bruner, 1983). We tend to think of minds as webs of parallel processors whose relations are shifting and context dependent and result in a stream of consciousness. Piaget's thinking was a major source of inspiration for the emergence of such a view, and his books provide us with an almost unique set of observations relevant to coming to an understanding of infants in terms of such intuitions. Our present views tend to emphasize the context bound limits of the knowledge we obtain from our personal inquiries both in our everyday lives and in science. We seek and find certainties and consistencies among them, but we also know that we must remind ourselves that they are local matters that rest on larger webs of more loosely formed and coupled beliefs. In many ways, our present views of knowledge and knowing are more analogous to Piaget's views of infants than to his view of adults. A major limitation of Piaget's representation of the development of mental processes lies in his identification of the "aim" of development largely in terms of one form of adult activity, namely, how we try to form the products of our inquiries into precisely defined concepts about which we make logically consistent arguments. We need to avoid an analogous limitation as we use our present intuitions about minds to come to an understanding of the development of infants' minds.

The excitement and promise of our new intuitions lie in the fresh eyes they provide us. We believe we should not devote too much of our early efforts to attempts to construct formal representations of our intuitions or the first products we have gained through their use. Their meaning for the development of infants' minds will emerge through lengthy cycles of using them in particular contexts and reflecting on their use. Those are the morals that Geertz (1983) and Mayr (1982) have drawn from their reflections on thought in anthropology and biology, respectively. It has only been a little while since we shifted from thinking about infants' mental processes in terms of Piaget's perspective (e.g., Gratch, 1975) to thinking about them from our new perspectives. We devoted this chapter to Piaget because we believed that looking at him in terms of our new perspectives might not only lead to a different sense of his work but might offer guidance about how to use our new eyes. Our principal discovery about Piaget's work was how long and hard he had to work to ground his intuitions in the context of infancy and how his intuitions, in some measure, were changed in that process.

We also believe we discovered some reasons why Piaget's attempts to understand infants were so seminal, and those reasons provide general guidelines for how we should conduct our studies. Those guidelines bear more on how to look than on where. Piaget's focus was on the role of functioning in development and how to capture changes in the organization of reasoning and conception that resulted from such functioning. There was no general point of view that guided his choice of "where," of which contexts to use to study problem solving. He used contexts that were imminent in infant tests and prior research and/or emerged in the context of his infants' everyday activities. Sometimes the contexts bore on the issue of how to understand the relationships of maturational processes to mental development, for example, eye–hand and mouth–thumb coordination, and sometimes they bore on the issue of the social context of infancy, for example, imitation. Piaget did not offer, nor did he attempt to offer, a complete theory of mental development (although sometimes it appears he or we thought so). His thoughts and findings continue to be relevant to our search for such a theory. But at present, we are lucky to be operating in times when we are aware of how interesting and difficult it is to understand the interactions of such complex processes as maturation, socialization, and learning in local contexts (e.g., Bruner, 1983; Gottlieb, 1983).

However, we believe Piaget's practices do tell us important things about how to learn about infants' minds in particular contexts that we decide are relevant. We conclude by summarizing the hows we have considered and do so by describing some general guidelines for reducing the strangeness of other minds that have emerged from the artificial intelligence community. The most general guideline to be described stems from attempts to develop computer programs that model human problem solving (e.g., Boden, 1979; Minsky, 1982a, 1982b). Such modelers have found that it is easier to write programs that solve "hard" problems like algebraic ones formulated in ordinary language than programs that solve "easy" problems like placing and stacking blocks. In other words, they find it easier to model the minds of older and seemingly more complex actors than those of simpler, younger actors. The source of the difficulty for the modelers is located in the "strangeness" of the operating context of the younger actor. Two morals are drawn from this generalization. One is that the strangeness can be reduced by making detailed observations of how the actors operate in their contexts. The other is that such observations inform us about limitations in our understanding of our own minds by making explicit how many aspects of the world and ourselves we take for granted.

The second guideline suggests that making such contextualized observations of specific individuals is an effective way of understanding classes of "strange" minds. For example, Ericcson and Chase (1982) have made it intelligible to think of exceptional memory as a result of unexceptional individuals arriving at particularized and unexceptional ways of reformulating memory materials over the course of exceptional periods of efforts. These two guidelines capture, in large part, why we think Piaget's observations and his processes have current relevance. His detailed observations of individual infants operating in particular contexts are almost unique, and his exceptional amount of effort can afford insights into his, and our own, ways of operating.

There also is a more particularized guideline that indicates the relevance of one of Piaget's central themes, problem solving. Many now look at the problem of learning as the problem of achieving insights in a particular sense of that old term (e.g., Minsky, 1980, 1982b; Newell, 1981). The problem of learning is seen to be an issue of how the actor reformulates its old network of knowledge of facts and procedures so that a problem can be solved that is both similar to and yet different from prior problems that have been solved. This framing implies that one cannot go far beyond one's prior knowledge and that the gap can be hard to bridge. The difference between the scope of the insights of adults and that of the insights of infants is to be explained in terms of the level of abstraction of the mental elements that the actor is working with and their organization. The list of candidate processes is long and open: shifts in set and mood and attention, noticing, reminding, censors, trial and error, logical reasoning, modal reasoning, incubation, and so on. The goal of this return to the theme of insight is to create a frame within which we will focus on a search for how such processes are organized and come to change in particularized contexts. Such descriptions would then be used as the basis for the iterative process of observing and creating multicomponential models of minds that can cohere and yet adapt to the new.

That was Piaget's aim as well. He used a comparable perspective to describe how his infants groped to limited solutions of Köhler's (1917/1959) insight problems. His abstract model of the actor as problem solver—webs of schemes and processes of assimilation and accommodation—is a way of describing that theme, and so is his play on circular reactions. We dwelt at length on Laurent's early use of strings and chains both to illustrate the course of such a process of learning and to bring out how hard Piaget had to work to get into a position to observe that course. Our descriptions of the various episodes of the stage 4 error were an attempt to illustrate the value and difficulty of looking at particular infants in such a fashion in a limited framework, limited in both age and problem type. Which contexts are to be studied in this fashion must be determined by considerations that neither Piaget nor we can specify. We only hope we have made it plausible that if we exercise our fresh eyes we will discover much to wonder about.

REFERENCES

Anokhin, P. K. (1964). Systemogenesis as a general regulator of brain development. *Progress in Brain Research, 9,* 54–86.

Baldwin, J. M. (1906). *Mental development in the child and the race* (3rd ed.). New York: Macmillan.

Beilin, H. (1983). The new functionalism and Piaget's program. In E. Scholnick (Ed.), *New trends in conceptual representation.* Hillsdale, NJ: Erlbaum.

Binet, A., & Simon, T. (1962). The development of the Binet-Simon scale. In J. F. Rosenblith & W. Allensmith (Eds.), *The causes of behavior,* (pp. 286–290). Boston: Allyn & Bacon. (Original work published 1905)

Boden, M. A. (1979). *Jean Piaget.* New York: Viking.

Bremner, J. G., & Knowles, L. S. (in press). Piagetian stage iv search errors with an object that is directly accessible both visually and manually. *Perception.*

Bruner, J. S. (1970). The growth and structure of skill. In K. J. Connolly (Ed.), *Mechanisms of motor skill development.* New York: Academic.

Bruner, J. S. (1983). *In search of mind: Essays in autobiography.* New York: Harper Colophon.

Bühler, C. (1930). *The first year of life.* New York: Day.

Butterworth, G. (1982). Object permanence and identity in Piaget's theory of infant cognition. In G. Butterworth (Ed.), *Infancy and epistemology,* (pp. 137–169). New York: St. Martin's.

Carr, E. H. (1961). *What is history?* New York: Vintage.

Davis, P. J., & Hersh, R. (1980). *The mathematical experience.* Boston: Birkhauser.

Diamond, A. (1981 April). Retrieval of an object from an open box: The development of visual-tactile control of reaching in the first year of life. Paper presented at biennial meeting of the Society for Research in Child Development, Boston. *Society for Research in Child Development Abstracts,* 1981, p. 78.

Doyle, J. (1982). *Some theories of reasoned assumptions.* Unpublished manuscript, Computer Science Department, Carnegie-Mellon University, Cleveland.

Dyson, F. J. (1983). Review of mathematics and physics by Yu. I. Manin. *The Mathematical Intelligencer, 5,* 54–57.

Ericsson, K. A., & Chase, W. G. (1982). Exceptional memory. *American Scientist, 70,* 607–615.

Flavell, J. H. (1963). *The developmental psychology of Jean Piaget.* Princeton, NJ: Van Nostrand.

Geertz, C. (1973). *The interpretation of cultures.* New York: Harper Torch Books.

Geertz, C. (1983). *Local knowledge.* New York: Basic.

Gibson, E. J. (1977, August). *The ecological optics of infancy: The differentiation of invariants given by optical motion.* Unpublished presidential address, Division 3, American Psychological Association, San Francisco.

Gibson, E. J., & Spelke, E. S. (1983). The development of perception. In P. H. Mussen (Ed.), *Handbook of child psychology* (Vol. 3) (pp. 1-76). New York: Wiley.

Gibson, J. J. (1979). *The ecological approach to visual perception.* Boston: Houghton Mifflin.

Gibson, K. R. (1982). Comparative neuro-ontogeny; its implications for the development of human intelligence. In G. Butterworth (Ed.), *Infancy and epistemology* (pp. 52-82). New York: St. Martin's.

Goldman-Rakic, P. S., Isseroff, A., Schwartz, M. L., & Bugbee, N. M. (1983). The neurobiology of cognitive development. In P. H. Mussen (Ed.), *Handbook of child psychology* (Vol. 2) (pp. 281-344). New York: Wiley.

Goodman, N. (1978). *Ways of world making.* Indianapolis: Hackett.

Gottlieb, G. (1983). The psychobiological approach to developmental issues. In P. H. Mussen (Ed.), *Handbook of child psychology* (Vol. 2) (pp. 1-26). New York: Wiley.

Gratch, G. (1975). Recent studies based on Piaget's view of object concept development. In L. Cohen & P. Salapatek (Eds.), *Infant perception: From sensation to cognition* (Vol. 2). New York: Academic.

Harris, P. H. (1983). Infant cognition. In P. H. Mussen (Ed.), *Handbook of child psychology* (Vol. 2.) (pp. 689-782). New York: Wiley.

Hebb, D. O. (1980). *Essay on mind.* Hillsdale, NJ: Erlbaum.

Hughes, H. S. (1958). *Consciousness and society.* New York: Knopf.

James, W. (1950). *The principles of psychology.* New York: Dover. (Original work published 1890)

Jaynes, J. (1976). *The origins of consciousness in the breakdown of the bicameral mind.* Boston: Houghton Mifflin.

Kaye, K. (1982). *The mental and social life of babies.* Chicago: University of Chicago Press.

Kessen, W. (1983). The child and other cultural inventions. In F. S. Kessel & A. W. Siegel (Eds.), *Psychology and society: The child and other cultural inventions.* New York: Praeger.

Köhler, W. (1959). *The mentality of apes.* New York: Vintage. (Original work published 1917)

Lakoff, G., & Johnson, M. (1980). *Metaphors we live by.* Chicago: University of Chicago Press.

Lewin, R. (1984). Why is development so illogical? *Science, 224,* 1327-1329.

Mandler, G. (1984). *Mind and body.* New York: Norton.

Mandler, J. G. (1983). Representation. In P. H. Mussen (Ed.), *Handbook of child psychology* (Vol. 2) (pp. 420-494). New York: Wiley.

Mayr, E. (1982). *The growth of biological thought.* Cambridge, MA: Belknap.

Minsky, M. (1980). K-lines: A theory of memory. *Cognitive Science, 4,* 117-133.

Minsky, M. (1982a). Why people think computers can't. *The AI Magazine,* fall, pp. 3-15.

Minsky, M. (1982b). *Learning meaning.* Unpublished draft, M.I.T. Artificial Intelligence Laboratory.

Moll, L., & Kuypers, H. G. J. M. (1977). Premotor cortical ablations in monkeys: Contralateral changes in visually guided reaching behavior. *Science, 198,* 317-319.

Newell, A. (1981). *Duncker on thinking: An inquiry into progress in cognition.* Unpublished manuscript, Department of Computer Science, Carnegie-Mellon University, Cleveland.

Olson, G. M. & Sherman, T. (1983). Attention, learning and memory in infants. In P. H. Mussen (Ed.), *Handbook of child psychology,* (Vol. 2) (pp. 1001–1080). New York: Wiley.

Perkins, D. N. (1981). *The mind's best work.* Cambridge, MA: Harvard University Press.

Piaget, J. (1951). *The child's conception of the world.* London: Routledge & Kegan Paul. (Original work published 1926)

Piaget, J. (1952a). *The origins of intelligence.* New York: International Universities Press. (Original work published 1936)

Piaget, J. (1952b). Autobiography. In C. A. Murchison (Ed.), *History of psychology in autobiography.* Worcester, MA: Clark University Press (Vol. 4) (pp. 237–256).

Piaget, J. (1954). *The construction of reality in the child.* New York: Basic. (Original work published 1937)

Piaget, J. (1959). *Judgement and reasoning in the child.* Paterson, NJ: Littlefield, Adams. (Original work published 1924)

Piaget, J. (1960). *The child's conception of physical causality.* Paterson, NJ: Littlefield, Adams. (Original work published 1927)

Piaget, J. (1962). *Play, dreams and imitation in childhood.* New York: Norton. (Original work published 1945)

Piaget, J. (1971). *Insights and illusions of philosophy.* New York: World.

Piaget, J. (1980). *Adaptation and intelligence.* Chicago: University of Chicago Press.

Prechtl, H. F. R. (1981). The study of neural development as a perspective of clinical problems. In K. J. Connolly & H. F. R. Prechtl (Eds.), *Maturation and development* (pp. 198–215). Philadelphia: Lippincott.

Preyer, W. (1888–1889). *Mind of the child* (Vol. 1 & Vol. 2). New York: Appleton.

Schank, R. C. (1982). *Dynamic memory.* New York: Cambridge University Press.

Schuberth, R. E. (1982). The infant's search for objects: Alternatives to Piaget's theory of object concept development. In L. P. Lipsitt & C. K. Rovee-Collier (Eds.), *Advances in infancy research* (Vol. 1). Norwood, NJ: Ablex.

Singer, I. M. (1981). Mathematics. In W. Shropshire, Jr. (Ed.), *The joys of research* (pp. 38–46). Washington, D.C.: Smithsonian Institution Press.

Sperry, R. W. (1982). Some effects of disconnecting the cerebral hemispheres. *Science, 217,* 1223–1226.

Stern, W. (1927). *Psychologie die Fruhling Kindheit* (4th ed.). Leipzig: Quelle & Myer.

Szuman, S. (1927). Observations on syncretic perception in children. *Archives Psychologie,* 2, No. 1.

Thelen, E., & Fisher, D. M. (1982). Newborn stepping: An explanation for a "disappearing" reflex. *Developmental Psychology, 18,* 760–775.

Tinbergen, N. (1967). *The herring gulls' world.* New York: Doubleday Anchor Books.

Tolman, E. C. (1932). *Purposive behavior in animals and men.* New York: D. Appleton-Century.

Touwen, B. (1976). *Neurological development in infancy.* Philadelphia: Lippincott.

White, S. H. (1980). Cognitive competence and performance in everyday environments. *Bulletin of the Orton Society, 30,* 29–45.

Wishart, J. G., & Bower, T. G. R. (1984). Spatial relations and the object concept: A normative study. In C. K. Rovee-Collier (Ed.), *Advances in infancy research* (Vol. 3). Norwood, NJ: Ablex.

Zelazo, P. R., Zelazo, N., & Kolb, S. (1972). "Walking" in the newborn. *Science, 176,* 314–315.

CHAPTER 5

Psychophysiological Development in Infancy: State, Startle, and Attention

W. KEITH BERG and KATHLEEN M. BERG

INTRODUCTION

A major problem faced by the investigator interested in studying psychological development in infancy is the limited choice of behaviors sufficiently mature to provide meaningful data, especially for the very young and prematurely born infant. Though this limitation is true for the overt, easily observed behaviors, the more covert behavior of the infant, often denoted as *physiological* activity, is both abundant and relatively well developed, even in the premature. The heart has been beating since the fourth week after conception, and both sympathetic and parasympathetic systems exert at least some control at birth or before (Eichorn, 1970). The presence of clear sinus arrhythmia in the full-term infant indicates a definite cardiorespiratory coordination by well-known brain structures and may signal tonic parasympathetic control (Porges, 1983). Skin potential responses are readily recorded in the newborn, and electroencephalographic activity is observable early in gestation. Of course, these systems are not fully mature at birth, but they exemplify the relative wealth of information available from physiological activity.

For many investigators, the dichotomization of response measures into those that are *physiological* and those that are *behavioral* is not simply descriptive, but represents a fundamental and functional distinction. Responses labeled *physiological* are sometimes perceived as more indirect indicants of psychological constructs of interest since they do not conform to the common meaning of *behavior*. We would argue, however, that, while the dichotomy provides a useful descriptive heuristic, there are no grounds for a clear functional distinction nor for a hierarchical one in which one type of response is considered, a priori, to be more valid or direct. Both are controlled and modulated by central nervous system mechanisms, and it is possible for either to be comparatively overt or covert. We suggest that both are types of behavior differing only in the degree to which they are typically overt or require electrical aids to be observed.

Preparation of this manuscript was supported in part by grant #12–65 from the March of Dimes Foundation.

Discarding the fundamental behavior–physiology dichotomy avoids a logical problem, but it leaves us with the question of what to cover in a chapter on psychophysiological development, or for that matter why a separate chapter is required at all. A separate chapter serves to emphasize and outline the information that covert behaviors are able to add to that available from overt ones. However, we shall often be including research employing relatively overt behavior where it bears upon issues and problems that have been illuminated by the use of physiological responses, just as we know other chapters in this volume will include relevant research based on physiological behavior. In large part the physiological responses discussed will be heart rate, electroencephlography, and electromyography. Electrodermal activity (skin potential and resistance), respiration, and cardiovascular activity other than heart rate are only briefly mentioned since for infants there is little work available directed toward psychologically relevant questions.

The chapter is organized around three central topics: sleeping and waking states, the startle reflex and its modulation by nonstartle stimuli, and the development of attentional processes such as orienting and habituation. These are areas where the recording of physiological activity has had an important impact on our understanding of infant behavior and development. Development of sensory maturation as reflected in the sensory evoked potential was covered in the first edition of this chapter but is now dealt with in Aslin's chapter in this volume. Even with these restrictions we have had to limit discussion of a number of areas of importance and provide literature references as exemplars rather than being encyclopedic. For example, space was insufficient to cover fully the rapidly growing and important new research on the uses of physiological measures in the prematurely born infant, fetal heart rate monitoring, and the sinus arrhythmic and direct pharmacologic blocking measures of parasympathetic development in rodent pups and human infants. Recent reviews by Von Bargen (1983) on infant heart rate and by Shields (1983) on autonomic nervous system development cover several of these issues. Our choices have been guided by an emphasis on developmental changes in normal, full-term infants, with the hope that this information may serve to provide a useful comparison for work with infants at risk.

STATE, SLEEP, AND BIOLOGICAL RHYTHMS

A great deal has been written about state in the developmental literature; much of it, as Ashton (1973a) has pointed out, is difficult to interpret due to a general lack of agreement concerning the number and naming of states observed in young infants, as well as the criteria to be used in defining such states. This lack of agreement can be partly attributed to the instability of behavioral organization during early infancy. Spontaneous behaviors do tend to occur in clusters during this period, but these poorly organized clusters are quite different from the distinctive patterns of autonomic and central activity that occur in an orderly sequence as states in adults.

Although the complexities of waking states in adult subjects are still a matter of controversy, it is generally agreed that adult sleep may be classified into at least five stages: rapid eye movement (REM) sleep and four stages of non-REM or NREM sleep. During a typical night, the REM state and one or more stages of NREM sleep alternate with a period of approximately 90 min. After sleep onset there is a progression from stage 1 to stage 4 of NREM sleep, and an associated decrease in levels of central, autonomic, and motor activity. Electroencephalographic tracings recorded from the scalp show a gradual slowing of wave frequencies, heart rate and respiration become slow and regular, and there is general muscular relaxation (Williams, Holloway, & Griffiths, 1973). A notable exception is spontaneous electrodermal activity, which shows a dramatic increase during stages 3 and 4, frequently referred to as electrodermal *storms* (Johnson & Lubin, 1966). These patterns are reversed in REM sleep; the EEG changes to a low-amplitude, mixed-frequency pattern characteristic of increased activation, heart rate and respiration become irregular, and spontaneous electrodermal activity decreases to waking levels. Most characteristic of the REM state are discrete bursts of rapid eye movements and phasic movements of the face and extremities, which are superimposed on a background of profound inhibition of tonic muscle activity (Williams et al., 1973).

From a developmental perspective, REM sleep has generally been regarded as the most primitive of states. It was initially thought to be mediated exclusively by lower brain stem mechanisms and to be nearly mature at birth, while the development of NREM and wakefulness awaited the maturation of higher levels of the brain. More recently, it has become apparent that, although brain stem structures may be responsible for final expression of the REM state, many areas of the forebrain probably participate in its control. Considerable evidence also suggests that REM sleep may be more accurately described as two distinct states of phasic and tonic REM, marked by the presence or absence of eye movement activity. Behavioral response thresholds are significantly lower during tonic than phasic segments of a REM period (Price & Kremen, 1980). Both sympathetic activity, which is tonically reduced, and parasympathetic activity, which is tonically increased during the REM state, show phasic changes in the opposite direction during eye movement bursts (Parmeggiani, 1984), and spinal motoneurons, which are tonically suppressed throughout the REM state, exhibit an additional reduction in excitability when eye movements are present (Chase & Morales, 1985). This important distinction is only just beginning to be investigated in the infant.

The well-organized patterns of activity observed in the adult are not fully developed in the human infant until well into the first year of life. In the newborn, at least three distinct states can be identified: wakefulness and two stages of sleep that are the precursors of adult REM and NREM sleep. A variety of terminologies for these sleep states are currently in use, but the terms *active* and *quiet* sleep recommended by Anders, Emde, and Parmelee (1971) will be used here.

Organization of States

Observations reported by Dreyfus-Brisac (1967, 1968) in previable prematures 24–27 weeks of conceptional age indicate that at this stage of development infants exhibit only a single state that cannot be classified as sleep or wakefulness. Body movements, generally localized to the extremities, are almost continuous, with little periodic fluctuation. Eye movements are absent or very infrequent, heart rate is fixed and unvarying, and respiration is predominantly irregular and unrelated to body activity. Scalp recordings from these infants show short bursts of activity alternating with periods of quiescence that may last as long as 2–3 min.

With further maturation, eye movements gradually become more frequent, and by 28–30 weeks of conceptional age they may occur quite regularly at a rate of 1–4 per min (Dreyfus-Brisac, 1967). Spontaneous skin potential responses can first be recorded from the palms and soles of the feet during this period, but they occur infrequently and are unrelated to other phasic events (Curzi-Dascalova, Pajoc, & Dreyfus-Brisac, 1973).

The first signs of behavioral state organization appear at approximately 32 weeks of conceptional age with the emergence of two distinguishable EEG patterns. One of these, an intermittent pattern of slow wave clusters interspersed with periods of relative inactivity, later develops into the *trace alternant* pattern characteristic of quiet sleep in the full-term newborn. The second is a continuous pattern of mixed frequencies with predominant slow waves, the precursor of EEG patterns later associated with wakefulness and active sleep (Dreyfus-Brisac & Monod, 1975; Parmelee, Wenner, Akiyama, Stern, & Flescher, 1967). A tendency toward organization of other elements also appears at this time. Eye movements, body movements, and spontaneous skin potential responses continue to occur in association with both EEG patterns, but are most frequent during the mixed-frequency continuous pattern (Parmelee, Wenner, Akiyama, Stern, et al., 1967; Curzi-Dascalova et al., 1973; Curzi-Dascalova, Pajoc, & Dreyfus-Brisac, 1973, 1974).

Between 32 weeks and 40 weeks (term), interrelationships between different elements become more clearly defined and the various patterns of activity gradually become organized into the two groupings termed active and quiet sleep. Dreyfus-Brisac (1970) viewed this as a process in which states independently emerged from disorganized patterns of activity, culminating in the appearance of typical active sleep by 35 weeks and typical quiet sleep by 37 weeks of conceptional age. More recently, Prechtl and associates (Nijhuis, Prechtl, Martin, & Bot, 1982; Prechtl, Fargel, & Weinmann, 1979) have argued that the emergence of organized states represents the gradual synchronization of a number of independent state parameters, each with its own periodicity. They suggested that prior to 36 weeks of conceptional age the coincidence of parameters appropriate for a given state occurs only by chance. According to Nijhuis and colleagues (1982), coherent states are not present in the human fetus and newborn until approximately 36–38 weeks, when a linkage between components becomes evident and changes in the various state parameters begin to occur simultaneously.

Although the infant at term exhibits three distinguishable patterns that are recognizable as the precursors of wakefulness, REM, and NREM states in the adult, the interrelationships among elements of the patterns are not yet stable enough to place all periods of observation in these categories. The typical approach to this problem is to select several criteria for each state and require that some preset portion of these be met before a particular period of observation can be classified as one state or another. Periods not satisfying these criteria are then classified as transitional or undefined (e.g., Anders et al., 1971). In a variant of this approach, Prechtl (e.g., 1974) has proposed that each state be described as a vector in which the presence of a particular behavioral characteristic is assigned a positive value and its absence a negative value. Transitional states are not undefined in this system since vectors can be described for them.

As might be expected, the particular criteria selected and the number of criteria that must be met for classification may have a marked influence on the results, especially in young premature infants when state organization is just emerging. Parmelee, Wenner, Akiyama, Schultz, and others (1967) illustrated this influence in a comparison of two methods of defining sleep states in preterm infants. In the first method they classified each 20-sec period as either active sleep or quiet sleep if it included any four of six defining characteristics for each state. Analyzing the records in this way, they found that amounts of active sleep were greatest in the youngest prematures and gradually decreased in older infants. The opposite trend was obtained for quiet sleep, which was infrequent in young prematures and increased with further maturation. When they selected the three most useful state parameters and reanalyzed the records with the requirement that all three criteria be met for classification, the results for quiet sleep were unchanged but active sleep showed a very different developmental course; it was infrequent in very young prematures, increased to a peak at 34 weeks, and then steadily declined in older infants.

Definition of states is considerably less difficult in full-term infants than in prematures, but state components still show varying degrees of immaturity at term. Rapid eye movements, along with other physiological parameters characteristic of active sleep, can be observed in nonsleep states when the eyes are open or during crying (Emde & Metcalf, 1970). Penile erections, which are a concomitant of REM sleep in adults, may occur during any state in the newborn, although they tend to be more frequent during active sleep (Korner, 1968; Wolff, 1966). And other criteria, such as body movements and respiratory and EEG patterns, show varying degrees of overlap between the different states (Parmelee, Akiyama, Schultz, Wenner, Schulte, & Stern, 1968; Parmelee, Wenner, Akiyama, Stern, et al., 1967). These unstable patterns disappear during the first few months of life with the development of adult sleep stages.

Maturation of Specific Elements

EEG Patterns

Although the EEG of prematures is routinely described as less complex than that of older infants, there is still considerable diversity in the EEG patterns observed in young preterm infants. Parmelee, Schulte, Akiyama, Wenner, Schultz, and Stern (1968) were able to identify at least nine different EEG patterns in sleeping infants at 30–40 weeks of conceptional age, and Dreyfus-Brisac and her colleagues have typically distinguished at least four different patterns: those most characteristic of the two stages of sleep and two that appear to be transitional (e.g., Dreyfus-Brisac, 1970). Such transitional patterns are seen at all ages but change in character as the EEG matures (Parmelee, Wenner, Akiyama, Stern, et al., 1967).

After term, developmental changes in the EEG pattern of active sleep are for the most part limited to changes in wave amplitudes and frequencies (e.g., Parmelee, Wenner, Akiyama, Stern et al., 1967). More striking developmental changes are seen in quiet sleep patterns. The intermittent pattern that Dreyfus-Brisac has termed *trace alternant* is most typical of quiet sleep in the full-term newborn. This pattern develops as the low-level activity during "flat" periods of the discontinuous EEG characteristic of young prematures gradually increases in amplitude. The result consists of bursts or clusters of high-amplitude slow waves interspersed with periods of more attenuated activity (Parmelee, Akiyama, Stern, & Harris 1969). Parmelee and colleagues have noted that the burst-to-burst time appears to remain a constant 9–

10 sec in both newborn infants and prematures as young as 29 weeks of conceptional age. With increasing maturation the duration of the bursts gradually increases, reducing the duration of the flat periods until the pattern becomes one of continuous slow waves of approximately 3–4 weeks after term. Burst durations are significantly longer and the trace alternant pattern disappears earlier in prematures than in full-term infants of the same conceptional age, suggesting that extrauterine experience may accelerate EEG maturation (Ellingson & Peters, 1980b, Parmelee et al., 1969).

A second significant change in the EEG of quiet sleep occurs sometime during the second month of life with the appearance of sleep spindles, a waveform characteristic of NREM stage 2 in the adult. Spindles are brief bursts of rhythmic activity of 12–15Hz that are most prominent at the vertex and central regions of the scalp. They are typically fusiform in shape and may range from 400 msec to 3–5 sec in duration. According to Sterman and Bowersox (1981), they are generated by pacemakers in the lateral nuclei of the thalamus, and are believed to be associated with general sensorimotor inhibition in both sleeping and waking states. In the young infant, they are seen superimposed on the dominant slow wave activity of quiet sleep. Although similar rapid rhythms are frequently observed in preterm infants, they differ from sleep spindles in a number of respects and are generally regarded as a different phenomenon (Ellingson, 1982).

When spindle bursts first appear, they are brief and variable in frequency. After first appearance their development takes place within a period of approximately 2 weeks, during which they rapidly become more regular, longer in duration, and higher in amplitude (Metcalf, 1970a). Like burst duration in the trace alternant, their development appears to be accelerated in prematures compared to full-term infants of the same conceptional age (Ellingson & Peters, 1980b; Metcalf, 1969). By approximately 3–6 months of postnatal age, spindle activity in the infant is typically much stronger than in the adult and may occur with equal power throughout a quiet sleep phase (Schulte & Bell, 1973). This increase in spindle activity is also accompanied by less striking but significant increases in the spectral density of other EEG frequency bands (e.g., Samson-Dollfus, Nogues, Menard, Bertoldi-Lefever, & Geffroy, 1983; Sterman, 1979; Sterman et al., 1977; Sterman, McGinty, Harper, Hoppenbrouwers, & Hodgman, 1982), and by 3 months of age, quiet sleep can be differentiated into stages resembling the four stages of adult NREM (Coons & Guilleminault, 1982; Crowell, Kapuniai, Boychuk, Light, & Hodgman, 1982). Spindles remain a prominent feature of NREM sleep until approximately 2 years of age, when they rapidly decrease in duration and become restricted to a relatively short period of stage 2 at the beginning of a NREM episode (Lenard, 1970b).

The spontaneous K-complex, a second waveform characteristic of stage 2 sleep in the adult, first appears in infants at approximately 5–6 months of age (Metcalf, Mondale, & Butler, 1971). This vertex-dominant pattern generally consists of an initial sharp surface-negative wave followed by a large slow positive wave and is thought to be homologous to sensory-evoked responses to external or interoceptive stimulation. In the adult, their occurrence appears, in part, to be related to events of the cardiac cycle, suggesting that some percentage of these apparently spontaneous waveforms may be evoked by receptors of the cardiovascular system (Fruhstorfer, Partanen, & Lumio, 1971). Monod and Garma (1971) have reported that K-complexes may be observed in response to external stimuli in premature infants at approximately 32–34 weeks after conception but then become obscured with further development of EEG patterns.

At 5–6 months after birth K-complexes are poorly formed and may be seen over large areas of the scalp, although they are larger and better differentiated at the vertex. Vertex dominance gradually increases over the first 18–24 months of life. Metcalf and others (1971), rating development of K-complexes with respect to four different criteria, reported that after their first appearance these waveforms show rapid changes in maturation until about 2 years of age when development reaches a plateau. A second more gradual period of developmental change then begins after age 5.

Until approximately 5–8 months after birth there is no specific EEG pattern associated with drowsiness. Instead, this state is characterized by a gradual increase in amplitude and slowing of activity (Dreyfus-Brisac & Curzi-Dascalova, 1975). By 8 months, a specific pattern of high-amplitude regular theta activity of 4–5 Hz is present in most infants during drowsiness (Schulte & Bell, 1973). This pattern, which is occasionally referred to as *hypnagogic hypersynchrony,* is characteristic of the drowsy state until at least 2–3 years of age.

Throughout early development, EEG patterns for wakefulness and active sleep remain quite similar. The two states cannot be differentiated until approximately 36 weeks of conceptional age, when patterns associated with active sleep become slightly more rhythmic and regular (Parmelee, Wenner, Akiyama, Stern, et al., 1967). Evidence reviewed by Dreyfus-Brisac and Curzi-Dascalova (1975) indicates that by 3 months after birth the precursor of alpha can be distinguished in the occipital regions during the waking state. This pattern consists of an irregular frequency of 3–4 Hz rather than the alpha activity of 8–12 Hz seen in adults, but, like the adult alpha rhythm, it can be blocked by opening of the eyes. This rhythm increases in regularity and frequency to reach 6–8 Hz by 12 months of age.

Rapid Eye Movements

REMs, which are infrequent in very young preterm infants during sleep, rapidly increase to a high level by term (Petre-Quadens, De Lee, & Remy, 1971; Parmelee & Stern, 1972). A brief decrease in the incidence of eye movements between 37 and 39 weeks of conceptional age has been described by Petre-Quadens and colleagues (1971), who attributed this transient decrease in activity to the development of cortical inhibitory effects. In the newborn, REMs are superimposed on slow rolling movements of the eyes, which precede the appearance of the first rapid movements by 2–4 min and continue for several minutes after the REMs have disappeared (Prechtl & Lenard, 1967). This is not the case in adult subjects, although similar slow eye movements have been described in adults during sleep onset (Snyder & Scott, 1972).

It is generally agreed that REMs in the young infant do not reflect a simple random process, since nonsequential histograms of the intervals between eye movements show a higher incidence of short intervals than would be expected by chance (Dittrichova, Paul, & Pavlikova, 1972; Prechtl & Lenard, 1967). Although REMs in the neonate occur more frequently during some periods than others, they do not appear to show the "burst" pattern typical in adults. Interval histograms reported by Prechtl and Lenard (1967) for newborns and by Aserinsky (1971) for adults show similar maxima at inter-REM intervals of approximately 300 msec, but a second mode corresponding to the longer intervals between bursts is present only in the adult histogram. Evidence reviewed by Lenard (1970a) suggests that the burst pattern is present by 3–4 months of age.

Dittrichova and associates (1972) examined the incidence of REMs in 2- and 20-week-old infants and found that the frequency of eye movements occurring at intervals of less than 1 sec increased with age. However, a number of other investigators have reported a decrease in REM activity after term (De Lee & Petre-Quadens, 1976; Parmelee & Stern, 1972; Petre-Quadens et al., 1971). Becker and Thoman (1981, 1982) described bursts of intense, high-amplitude REM activity that were frequent during the neonatal period but decreased rapidly after 5 weeks of age. The incidence of such REM storms was found to be negatively correlated with state stability during the first weeks of life and negatively correlated with cognitive development in older infants.

Animal studies have indicated that REM bursts and isolated eye movements are controlled by different neural mechanisms. Lesions of the pontine vestibular nuclei selectively prevent REM bursts without affecting other eye movements (Pompeiano & Morrison, 1965), while removal of the cortex results in disappearance of single eye movements and facilitation of REM bursts (Jeannerod, Moret, & Jouvet, 1965). The number of eye movement bursts is increased after removal of frontal cortex but decreased after occipital decortication, suggesting that frontal and visual cortex normally have opposite effects on REM activity.

In infants, as in adults, periods of dense REM are associated with increases in the rate and irregularity of respiration and heart rate (Dittrichova, et al., 1972; Prechtl & Lenard, 1967; Spreng, Johnson, & Lubin, 1968). However, other phenomena, such as suppression of temperature regulation and CO_2 sensitivity, seen during phasic REM in adults, have not been observed in young infants (Darnall & Ariagno, 1982; Guthrie, Standaert, Hodson, & Woodrum, 1981). Vestibular stimulation in the form of continuous sinusoidal rocking reduces spontaneous REM activity in the newborn (Bernuth & Prechtl, 1969) but increases it in young children (Ornitz, Forsythe, & de la Pena, 1973). Similarly, presentation of brief auditory stimuli increases the frequency of REMs in 12-week-olds, but not in younger infants, and visual stimuli affect REM activity only after 20 weeks (Dittrichova, Paul, & Pavlikova, 1978). Ornitz, Ritvo, Carr, Panman, and Walter (1967) and Ornitz, Ritvo, Lee, Panman, and Walter (1969) have also reported that auditory evoked responses recorded from the scalp are suppressed during bursts of eye movements in adults and children older than 19 months of age, but not in infants 6–12 months old. All of these findings suggest that, despite the absence of significant changes in the EEG patterns of active sleep during early infancy, other characteristics of this state continue to change throughout the first year of life.

Electrodermal Activity

On their first appearance in young preterm infants, spontaneous skin potential responses are not consistently associated with a particular EEG pattern or with the occurrence of other measurable activity. However, by 31–36 weeks of conceptional age, they occur significantly more frequently in active than in quiet sleep and are usually associated with the presence of REMs (Curzi-Dascalova et al., 1973). This is the reverse of the pattern seen in adult subjects, who show greater spontaneous electrodermal activity during NREM than REM states (Johnson & Lubin, 1966; Koumans, Tursky, & Solomon, 1968).

Curzi-Dascalova and Dreyfus-Brisac (1976) have reported an abrupt increase in electrodermal responses in active sleep during the first month of life. Frequency of spontaneous skin potential responses during active sleep appears to stabilize at a higher level than that seen in adults during REM and remains at that level for at least 6 months, the oldest group tested. The authors suggested that this high frequency of spontaneous activity may be attributable to the immaturity of descending inhibitory influences in young infants during active sleep. The frequency of spontaneous electrodermal responses in quiet sleep also increases during this period but appears to be related to the appearance of EEG sleep spindles rather than to chronological age. With the development of spindle activity sometime during the second month of life, response frequency in quiet sleep increases rapidly to exceed frequencies seen during active sleep and approaches levels typical of NREM electrodermal storms in adults (Curzi-Dascalova & Dreyfus-Brisac, 1976).

In contrast to phasic skin potential responses, skin potential level does not differentiate between sleep states. However, it is lower during sleep than during wakefulness in both newborn infants (Bell, 1970) and adults (Koumans et al., 1968).

Respiration

Studies of respiratory activity in the fetal lamb during the last third of gestation have indicated that breathing movements change from a nearly continuous pattern to one in which periods of irregular respiration alternate with long intervals of apnea. These bursts of fetal breathing gradually become correlated with periods of rapid eye movement and, with the exception of infrequent, randomly occurring gasps or sighs, they are seen only during active sleep until after birth when respiration again becomes continuous (Boddy & Dawes, 1975; Maloney, Bowes, & Wilkinson, 1980).

With the advent of ultrasonic scanning techniques it has also become possible to examine respiratory activity in the human fetus in utero. Evidence reviewed by Boddy and Dawes (1975) indicates that fetal breathing movements can be detected as early as 11 weeks. Unlike the lamb, the human fetus near term does occasionally exhibit regular respiratory movements during periods of quiescence (Timor-Tritsch, Dierker, Hertz, Chik, & Rosen, 1980). However, breathing movements remain intermittent and tend to cluster during periods of probable active sleep (Junge & Walter, 1980).

According to Dreyfus-Brisac (1968), the respiration of young infants born very prematurely shows a continuous semiregular pattern that does not change with variations in amount of body activity. This is gradually replaced by less stable patterns in slightly older prematures, and by 30 weeks after conception the most common type of respiration is an irregular pattern characterized by unequal breath-to-breath intervals (Parmelee, Stern, & Harris 1972). Periodic respiration, a pattern in which respiratory episodes alternate with apneic episodes, is present approximately 25 percent of the time in premature infants 30–36 weeks of conceptional age, but gradually becomes less frequent with further maturation of respiratory control centers. Finley and Nugent (1983) have detected a low-frequency periodicity that approximates the frequency of periodic breathing in both normal respiration and heart rate in the newborn and suggest that periodic breathing represents an exaggeration of rhythmic activity normally present in both respiratory and cardiovascular functions.

Regular respiration, which is very rare in young preterm infants, increases rapidly after 36 weeks of conceptional age to become one of the most reliable state criteria by term. Data reported by Parmelee, Wenner, Akiyama, Stern, et al. (1967) indicate that, while regular respiration is present during only 25 percent of quiet sleep at 36 weeks, it is present during 78 percent of quiet sleep and only 10 percent of active sleep by 40 weeks of conceptional age.

Respiratory rates are reportedly higher during active sleep than quiet sleep in both prematures and full-term infants (Curzi-Dascalova, Lebrun, & Korn, 1983; Siassi, Hodgman, Cabal, & Hon, 1979), although state differences in rate may be temperature dependent. In a study of 1- and 4-week-old infants, Steinschneider and Weinstein (1983) found higher rates of respiration during active sleep when ambient temperature was 24 deg C, but not when room temperature was maintained at 32 deg C. Within an episode of active sleep, respiratory rates were highest during periods of frequent eye movements (Haddad, Lai, & Mellins, 1982).

As one might expect, respiratory variability is also consistently higher in active than in quiet sleep (e.g., (Finer, Abroms, & Taeusch, 1976; Haddad, Leistner, & Mellins, 1982; Hoppenbrouwers, Ugartechea, Combs, Hodgman, Harper, & Sterman, 1978). Haddad, Leistner, and Mellins (1982) have reported that this increase in variability during active sleep is primarily due to an increase in the variability of expiration time while variability of inspiration remains unchanged. Breathing irregularities associated with REM sleep persist after denervation of peripheral respiratory inputs and are therefore believed to be centrally mediated (Phillipson, 1978). Both respiratory rate and variability decrease in all states during the first few months of life but continue to be highest during wakefulness and lowest during quiet sleep (Curzi-Dascalova, Gaudebout, & Dreyfus-Brisac, 1981; Haddad, Epstein, Epstein, Leistner, & Marino, 1979; Hoppenbrouwers, Ugartechea, Combs, Hodgman, Harper, & Sterman, 1978).

The relationship between thoracic and abdominal respiratory movements may also discriminate between sleep states in the young infant (Curzi-Dascalova, 1978, 1982; Curzi-Dascalova & Plassart, 1978). During normal inspiration, the intercostal muscles and diaphragm contract together, resulting in expansion of the chest and outward movement of the abdominal wall. However, in active sleep, chest and abdominal respiratory movements are frequently out of phase so that the chest appears to collapse as the abdomen expands. Curzi-Dascalova (1978, 1982) has reported that this paradoxical breathing pattern is prevalent during active sleep in prematures as well as full-term newborns and persists without significant change in 3-month-old infants. EMG recordings have indicated that it is associated with inhibition of the intercostal muscles (Curzi-Dascalova, 1982). These inhibitory influences are also present during REM sleep in adults but do not result in noticeable chest distortion because of greater stability of the chest wall (Bryan & Muller, 1980).

It is generally agreed that breathing is regulated by two anatomically distinct systems. One of these is an "automatic" system in the brain stem based on chemoreceptor mechanisms, while the other is a forebrain "behavioral" system involved in voluntary control of respiration. On the basis of studies demonstrating that sensitivity to CO_2 is suppressed during REM sleep in adult humans and dogs, Phillipson (Phillipson, 1978; Sullivan, Murphy, Kozar, & Phillipson, 1979) argued that respiration is controlled by the automatic system in NREM sleep but that during REM the central chemoreceptors are bypassed and regulation is accomplished primarily by activation of behavioral system pathways.

Whether or not similar state differences in respiratory control are present early in development is not yet clear, although this type of organization is consistent with the finding that respiratory movements are seen only during active sleep in the fetal lamb. One preliminary report (Bryan, Hagan, Gulston, & Bryan, 1976) described an adultlike depression in response to CO_2 during REM in young human infants but attributed it to the peripheral effect of rib cage distortion. Numerous other studies have found no differences in CO_2 sensitivity between states (e.g., Anderson, Martin, Abboud, Dyme, & Bruce, 1983; Davi, Sankaran, MacCallum, Cates, & Rigatto, 1979; Haddad, Leistner, Epstein, Epstein, Grodin, & Mellins, 1980). In a study of respiration in infant monkeys, Guthrie et al. (1981) found that sensitivity to CO_2 during NREM sleep progressively increased with age to become significantly different from sensitivity during REM at 3 weeks after term. These results suggest that state differences in chemoreceptor function may gradually become evident with the maturation of NREM sleep. In a related study, Rigatto et al. (1982) examined ventilatory responses to brief hypoxia in healthy human prematures and found that the infants responded with an increase in ventilation during quiet sleep but exhibited a paradoxical decrease in ventilation during wakefulness and REM. The authors interpreted these state differences as further support for the notion of dual-system control of respiration in early infancy and speculated that the behavioral system regulating breathing during wakefulness and REM may be more susceptible to depression by hypoxia than the automatic system in preterm infants.

The occurrence of apneic periods during sleep has recently become a topic of considerable interest due to evidence linking sleep apneas with instances of sudden infant death (e.g., Guilleminault, Peraita, Souquet, & Dement, 1975; Steinschneider, 1972). Although numerous inconsistencies exist in this rapidly expanding literature, the general pattern of results suggests that short respiratory pauses on the order of 2–5 sec in duration are quite common in the young infant and are significantly more frequent in active than in quiet sleep (e.g., Curzi-Dascalova, Christova-Gueorguieva, Lebrun, & Firtion, 1984; Flores-Guevara et al., 1982; Waite & Thoman, 1981). Apneas of slightly longer duration may occur either more frequently in active sleep (Curzi-Dascalova & Plassart, 1978; Gabriel, Albani, & Schulte, 1976; Gould et al., 1977) or equally often in both sleep states (Curzi-Dascalova et al., 1984; Flores-Guevara et al., 1982; Krauss, Solomon, & Auld, 1977; Waite & Thoman, 1981).

The incidence of apnea is consistently higher in prematures than in full-term infants but decreases abruptly between approximately 37 and 40 weeks of conceptional age (Booth, Morin, Waite, & Thoman, 1983; Curzi-Dascalova & Christova-Gueorguieva, 1983; Ellingson, Peters, & Nelson, 1982; Gould et al., 1977; Krauss et al., 1977; Siassi et al., 1979). Schulte and associates (Gabriel et al., 1976; Schulte, Busse, & Eichhorn, 1977) have noted that apneic episodes are invariably associated with depression of monosynaptic reflexes and have attributed them to inhibitory influences known to act on spinal motoneurons, including respiratory motoneurons, during REM sleep. They suggest that the higher incidence of apnea in premature infants may be due to a relatively greater strength of inhibition early in development.

After term, apneic episodes decrease in both frequency and duration until 2–3 months of age and then remain fairly stable. Current evidence suggests that this trend is primarily due to a decrease in the frequency of longer-duration apneas in active sleep (Gould et al., 1977; Hoppenbrouwers et al., 1977).

Instances of prolonged apnea exceeding 15–20 sec in duration are rare in normal infants, but studies of clinical populations suggest that in certain at-risk infants, prolonged apneas of clinical significance occur predominantly in quiet or indeterminant sleep (Guilleminault et al., 1975; Watanabe, Inokuma, & Negoro, 1983). Apneas of this nature are believed to result from a failure of central chemoreceptors, or possibly defective integration of chemoreceptor information (Guilleminault et al., 1982; Shannon, 1980; Shannon et al., 1976). A number of investigators (e.g. Baker & McGinty, 1977; Watanabe et al., 1983) have suggested that the phasic stimulation provided by REM mechanisms during active sleep may actually serve to protect the at-risk infant from prolonged sleep apnea.

Heart Rate

Like respiration, heart rate is fixed and unvarying in previable prematures 24–27 weeks of conceptional age but becomes more irregular as central control mechanisms develop (Dreyfus-Brisac, 1968). Watanabe, Iwase, and Hara (1973) have reported that the mature pattern begins to emerge after 30 weeks of conceptional age, with a marked increase in heart rate range during active sleep, accompanied by only slight increases in variability during quiet sleep and wakefulness. A number of studies of heart rate during the neonatal period have distinguished between the more traditional measures of the variability of individual beats, referred to as *long-term* variability, and the variability of differences between sequential beats, which is usually described as *short-term* or *beat-to-beat* variability. These studies indicate that long-term variability is consistently higher in active sleep than in quiet sleep, but that the reverse is true for estimates of short-term variability (DeHaan, Patrick, Chess, & Jaco, 1977; Haddad, Epstein, Epstein, Leistner, & Mellins, 1980; Radvanyi & Morel-Kahn, 1976; van Geijn, Jongsma, DeHaan, Eskes, & Prechtl, 1980). It is generally agreed that both measures drop sharply from birth to approximately 1 month of age. After 1 month, increases in short-term varibility are seen in both sleep stages but are considerably larger in quiet sleep (Haddad, Epstein, et al., 1980; Leistner et al., 1980). There is less agreement about the developmental course of long-term variability, which has been reported to increase, decrease, or remain fairly stable during the postnatal period (Haddad, Epstein, et al., 1980; Harper, Hoppenbrouwers, Sterman, McGinty, & Hodgman, 1976; Harper, Leake, Hodgman, & Hoppenbrouwers, 1982; Leistner et al., 1980).

The greater long-term variability in active sleep has been attributed to the combined effect of phasic increases in sympathetic activity and phasic decreases in vagal activity that occur during periods of rapid eye movement (Baust & Bohnert, 1969). Short-term variability, on the other hand, appears to be associated with respiratory movements and is believed to be mediated solely by the vagus (Chess, Tam, & Calaresu, 1975; Radvanyi & Morel-Kahn, 1976; van Geijn et al., 1980). Studies of the development of respiratory–heart rate coupling have indicated that it is first observed during quiet sleep in prematures older than 37 weeks of gestation (Radvanyi & Morel-Kahn, 1976). The degree of coupling drops sharply during the immediate postnatal period but then rapidly increases between 1 and 6 months of age (Harper et al., 1978; Katona, Frasz, & Egbert, 1980). This pattern of increasing respiratory arrhythmia appears to be consistent with results of animal studies indicating that there is a gradual transition from sympathetic to parasympathetic dominance in quiet sleep during the postnatal period (Egbert & Katona, 1980).

Several authors have reported that average heart rate levels are higher during active than quiet sleep (e.g., DeHaan et al., 1977; Haddad, Epstein, et al., 1980; van Geijn et al., 1980; Watanabe, Iwase, & Hara, 1973), while others have found no difference in heart rate between the two states (Harper et al., 1976; Siassi et al., 1979). These inconsistencies may reflect the fact that autonomic function during active sleep does not exhibit a uniform pattern of effects, but is characterized by periodic fluctuations in sympathetic and parasympathetic influences (Baust & Bohnert, 1969).

Electromyogram

During the transition from wakefulness to sleep there is a gradual reduction in tonic activity of postural muscles. In certain of these muscles, activity remains at moderate levels throughout NREM sleep but is profoundly suppressed during REM. The specific muscle groups exhibiting this pattern vary across species, presumably reflecting differences in typical sleep postures. In the human adult, suppression of tonic EMG activity is most reliably found in muscles of the head and neck, particularly in the antigravity muscles of the chin; tonic activity in muscles of the trunk and limbs apparently does not discriminate between sleep stages but persists at a moderate level throughout both REM and NREM states (Jacobson, Kales, Lehmann, & Hoedemaker, 1964).

Developmental studies of EMG activity during sleep have suggested that it may be the most immature of state-specific measures in early infancy. Petre-Quadens (1967) reported that in premature infants 28–30 weeks of conceptional age the chin EMG is characterized by a constant low-amplitude activity that shows no state-dependent variations. By approximately 33 weeks, tonic EMG activity presents a more adultlike pattern but is not consistently suppressed during active sleep. Muscle activity in the infant at term has been extensively studied by Schloon, O'Brien, Scholten, and Prechtl (1976), who recorded EMG from a number of different sites and concluded that in the newborn, as in the adult, muscles in the vicinity of the chin are most sensitive to differences in state. Their results indicated that tonic activity was present in chin EMG during 85 percent of quiet sleep; it was also occasionally present during active sleep, but was never sustained for longer than 30 sec. Data reported by Petre-Quadens (1967) suggest that EMG activity recorded from the chin does not reliably discriminate between states until approximately 7 months of postnatal age.

States and Biological Rhythms

Within the past few years, considerable progress has been made toward an understanding of the neural mechanisms responsible for the timing of sleep and wakefulness. Current evidence suggests that in the adult the cyclic alternation of states, as well as other rhythmic processes, is controlled by two major pacemakers that function as a mutually interacting system (Aschoff & Wever, 1976; Moore-Ede, Sulzman, & Fuller, 1982). One of these, located in the suprachiasmatic nuclei of the hypothalamus, appears to be responsible for the circadian distribution of NREM sleep; animal studies have demonstrated that after lesions of this area total sleep time remains unchanged, but sleep periods become randomly distributed throughout the 24-hour day (Groos, 1984; Moore-Ede et al., 1982). The second pacemaker regulates the distribution of REM and circadian variations in core body temperature. These two rhythms are very closely coupled, and it has been suggested that REM-generating mechanisms may be directly sensitive to temperature (Syzmusiak & Satinoff, 1985).

Under natural conditions, the two pacemakers operate in synchrony with each other and with a 24-hour geophysical day. In human adults living on an entrained 24-hour schedule, body temperature reaches a maximum toward the end of the period of daytime wakefulness, then declines through the night to reach its minimum toward the end of the period of sleep (Wever, 1984). When sleep occurs during the nocturnal hours, sleep onset invariably begins with an episode of NREM. Periods of REM are quite short early in the night but gradually increase in duration toward morning. This trend continues during the morning hours after awakening, as evidenced by a high proportion of REM sleep in morning naps (Webb, Agnew, & Sternthal, 1966). When the sleep period is shifted to a different portion of the day, the distribution of REM continues to follow the circadian rhythm of body temperature, with greatest REM propensity occurring near the minimum of the temperature cycle (Czeisler, Weitzman, Moore-Ede, Zimmerman, & Knauer, 1980; Czeisler, Zimmerman, Ronda, Moore-Ede, & Weitzman, 1980; Wever, 1984). Subjects choosing to initiate sleep during this phase of the temperature cycle consistently show reduced latency to the first REM period and frequent instances of sleep onset REM (Czeisler, Zimmerman, Ronda, Moore-Ede, & Weitzman, 1980).

As every parent knows, young infants show no evidence of circadian variations in either sleep or waking states. The typical newborn sleeps approximately 16–17 hours per day, with periods of sleep and wakefulness evenly distributed between day and night (Parmelee, Wenner, & Schultz, 1964). Evidence of a circadian cycle begins to emerge by about 5–6 weeks of age as sleep becomes more concentrated during the night hours and wakefulness increases during the day. However, the consolidation of states and their synchronization with a 24-hour day appear to be independent processes, and although both sleep and waking periods continue to increase in duration, they may drift with respect to clock time during the first few weeks of life (Kleitman & Engleman, 1953; Meier-Koll, Hall, Hellwig, Kott, & Meier-Koll, 1978). A diurnal pattern of sleep and wakefulness is clearly established by 12–16 weeks of age, with daytime sleep consolidated into well-defined naps (Parmelee & Stern, 1972). Day–night differences apparently develop independently for various physiological functions. Some, such as skin resistance level, show evidence of diurnal cycles within the first weeks of life, while others, such as aspects of kidney function, do not show a mature diurnal pattern until approximately 2 years of age (Hellbrugge, Lange, Rutenfranz, & Stehr, 1964).

Changes in the circadian distribution of sleep and waking episodes are also accompanied by changes within the sleep cycle itself. During the neonatal period, infants, unlike adults, typically begin a sleep episode in active sleep and spend approximately equal amounts of time in each of the two sleep states, epochs of active and quiet sleep alternating with a period of 50–60 min (Roffwarg, Muzio, & Dement, 1966; Stern, Parmelee, Akiyama, Schultz, & Wenner, 1969). Within the first few weeks of life there is a rapid decrease in active sleep during the day, accompanied by a large increase in quiet sleep at night (Coons & Guilleminault, 1982; Fagioli & Salzarulo, 1982; Navelet, Benoit, & Bouard, 1982). Although there are numerous reports in the literature purporting to show a dramatic increase in quiet sleep in early infancy, more recent evidence suggests that quiet sleep actually increases not in amount, but only as a proportion of total sleep time. In a study of sleep–wake patterns in infants ranging from 3 weeks to 6 months of age, Coons and Guilleminault (1982) found that the amount of time spent in quiet or NREM sleep during a 24-hour day was remarkably constant over this age range. In contrast, time spent in active sleep declined in reciprocal proportion to increased wakefulness. When day and nocturnal sleep periods are examined separately, it is clear that the amount of active sleep decreases significantly during daytime naps (Ellingson & Peters, 1980a; Emde & Walker, 1976), but remains fairly constant during the night (Coons & Guilleminault, 1982; Fagioli & Salzarulo, 1982; Navelet et al., 1982). In terms of relative proportions of sleep stages, daytime naps are clearly different from nocturnal sleep periods by 3 months of age (Coons & Guilleminault, 1982).

At least two studies have also reported differences in the temporal distribution of active and quiet sleep during nocturnal sleep episodes. In an observational study of sleep in the home, Anders (1978) found a clear predominance of quiet sleep during the first third, and a predominance of active sleep in the last third of the night in a group of 9-month-old infants but not in 2-month-olds. Hoppenbrouwers, Hodgman, Harper, and Sterman (1982) found a similar difference in the nightly distribution of sleep stages by 4 months of age. Two additional studies by Fagioli and Salzarulo (1982) and Navelet and others (1982) examined age trends in active and quiet sleep during the night rather than directly comparing proportions of time spent in each sleep stage. Although neither study found significant developmental differences in the temporal distribution of active sleep, Fagioli and Salzarulo (1982) did report a tendency for quiet sleep to become concentrated in the early portion of the night in older infants.

The changeover from active sleep onset to the pattern of quiet sleep onset characteristic of the adult circadian sleep–wake organization occurs sometime during the first 6–12 months but is very susceptible to disruption by a number of factors, including feeding schedules (Harper et al., 1977), duration of prior wakefulness (Schulz, Salzarulo, Fagioli, & Massetani, 1983), and aspects of the laboratory situation (Bernstein, Emde, & Campos, 1973). As one might expect, studies of this transition have reported a great deal of variability, both between subjects and from one sleep period to the next within the same subject (Ellingson & Peters, 1980a; Kligman, Smyrl, & Emde, 1975). However, the data do appear to show a circadian trend. For a morning sleep period in the laboratory, Ellingson and Peters (1980a) found that the percentage of active sleep onsets decreased from 80 percent during the first 3 weeks of life to 5–10 percent by 3 months, becoming quite rare after 6 months. In a study of nocturnal sleep in the home, Anders (1978, 1979) reported that approximately two-thirds of the subjects entered sleep with an initial active sleep phase at both 2 and 9 months of age, although the duration of this episode was shorter in older infants. The results of Coons and Guilleminault (1984) appear to fall between these two extremes. These investigators examined sleep patterns over a 24-hour recording period and found that approximately 20 percent of sleep episodes still began with active sleep at 6 months of age.

To date, only Schulz and colleagues (1983) have directly examined circadian influences on the phase of sleep at onset. They found no significant effect of time of day on the proportion of active sleep onsets in infants younger than 4 months of age, but a group of infants 4–13 months old did show a circadian difference, with sleep onset and short-latency active sleep periods occurring most frequently between 4 and 8 A.M., and least frequently between noon and 4 P.M. These findings suggest a REM propensity rhythm similar to the adult, but appear to be inconsistent with the reports by Ellingson and Peters (1980a) and Emde and Walker (1976) that infants, unlike adults, show very little REM during morning naps. Both sets of investigators have suggested that stress associated with the laboratory situation may have reduced the proportion of active sleep observed in their subjects.

The relationship between body temperature and REM sleep propensity has not yet been investigated in young infants, but available evidence suggests that circadian variations in body temperature become apparent at about the same time as circadian variations in active sleep. Significant day–night differences in temperature have been reported by 3 months of age, although the rhythmic aspect of the variations is still obscure (Abe & Fukui, 1979; Abe, Sasaki, Takebayashi, Fukui, & Nambu, 1978; Hellbrugge et al., 1964; Kleitman, 1963). After 3 months, the rhythm gradually becomes more stable and regular, but the timing of crests and troughs does not approach that of the adult rhythm until 10–12 months of age (Abe & Fukui, 1979; Abe et al., 1978).

Within recent years there has been a trend toward viewing developmental changes in the organization of states not as the maturation of a single sleep–wakefulness cycle but in terms of the developing interactions between a number of independent biological rhythms. This view was originally proposed by Kleitman (1963), who argued that the cyclic alternations of active and quiet sleep seen in the newborn were manifestations of a biological rhythm more fundamental than sleep–wakefulness, which he termed the *basic rest–activity cycle,* or BRAC. Kleitman maintained that this periodicity did not disappear with the development of advanced states of sleep and wakefulness, but remained present in the adult as the regular recurrence of REM periods during sleep, and in cycles of increased alertness or efficiency during wakefulness.

There is now considerable evidence that cyclic variations approximating the 90-min period of the REM cycle do occur during the waking state in adults. Such variations have been reported in a variety of measures, including performance on both motor and perceptual tasks, ability to fall asleep, and numerous physiological indices thought to reflect alertness or arousal (Lavie, 1982; Lavie & Scherson, 1981; Manseau & Broughton, 1984). However, several recent reports suggest that there is a discontinuity in cycles of the BRAC at sleep onset, and a consensus has not yet been reached on the question of whether the periodic variations in alertness during wakefulness and the REM cycle during sleep are generated by the same mechanism (Johnson, 1980; Lavie, 1982; Schulz, Dirlich, Balteskonis, & Zulley, 1980).

It is clear that cyclic alternations in activity indicative of Kleitman's BRAC can be detected very early in development. In a study of fetal activity recorded in utero from electrodes placed on the mothers' abdomens, Sterman and Hoppenbrouwers (1971) found that activity showed an irregular alternation of peaks and troughs with one significant periodicity of 30–50 min, which they attributed to the fetus, and a second periodicity of 80–110 min, which appeared to correspond to maternal REM periods. These rhythms were detectable by 21 weeks of gestation, well before sleep and wakefulness can be distinguished in preterm infants. More recently, Dierker, Rosen, Pillay, and Sorokin (1982) examined cycles of fetal activity in normal gravidas between 27–42 weeks of gestation. Although the data were quite variable, they did find a significant increase in cycle length from approximately 12 min at 27 weeks to 60 min by term.

Conclusions drawn from studies of fetal activity appear to be consistent with estimates of state periodicities in infants born prematurely. In two studies examining both short and all-night sleep episodes, Parmelee and associates found that state cycle duration, as measured either from one period of active sleep to the next or from one period of quiet sleep to the next, was very short at 32 weeks of conceptional age but then remained consistently in the range of 40–60 min from 36 weeks after conception to 8 months past term (Stern et al., 1969; Stern, Parmelee, & Harris, 1973). Several additional studies (e.g., Anders, 1978; Coons & Guilleminault, 1984; Navelet et al., 1982) have also reported no significant differences in duration of the sleep cycle in infants 1–9 months of age. Although Harper, Leake, Miyahara, and others did find a significant decrease in cycle length from 64 to 52 min between 1 and 6 months of age, these results were obtained during a nocturnal recording session and may be secondary to the increasing consolidation of nocturnal sleep. Brezinova (1974) has reported that brief episodes of wakefulness increase cycle duration in adult subjects. The longer cycle length in younger infants may therefore have been the result of more frequent nocturnal awakenings in these subjects. Harper, Leake, Miyahara, and others also found considerable variability in temporal state sequencing in younger infants, which gradually decreased by 3–4 months of age as nocturnal waking episodes diminished.

Since Sterman and Hoppenbrouwers' (1971) initial report of both a cycle of 30–50 min and an adultlike cycle of 80–110 min in fetal activity, a number of studies have demonstrated similar periodicities in heart rate and respiration in the fetus and newborn (e.g., Baust & Gagel, 1977, Hoppenbrouwers, et al., 1981; Hoppenbrouwers, Ugartechea, et al., 1978). Attempts to relate these rhythms to the maternal REM cycle have proved unsuccessful, suggesting that both short- and long-duration cycles are endogenous to the fetus (Anders & Roffwarg, 1973b; Hoppenbrouwers et al., 1981; Hoppenbrouwers, Ugartechea, et al., 1978). The significance of the adultlike slower rhythm is not yet clear, particularly since the spectral analysis of states reported by Harper, Leake, & Miyahara (1981) suggests that it may disappear within the first 6 months of life. According to evidence compiled by Sterman (1972), the state cycle does not approach the average adult length of 90 min until late childhood or perhaps early adolescence.

The characteristics of infant state cycles have stimulated considerable speculation on the function of various sleep states during development. The role of active sleep has been of particular interest since it constitutes approximately 50 percent of total sleep time in the newborn, but only 20 percent of sleep in the adult (Roffwarg et al., 1966). The large amount of active sleep in the young infant and its gradual decrease with age led Roffwarg et al. (1966) to propose that these periods of intense central activation may serve to facilitate neural development in the immature organism. Others have suggested that the increased amounts of active sleep in infancy may be attributable to a higher metabolic rate, or perhaps to the incomplete development of neural mechanisms mediating wakefulness (McGinty, 1971). Within the past decade, evidence has been slowly accumulating in support of the view that protein synthesis plays a critical role in the generation of REM sleep. Protein concentrations in the brain have been found to increase during REM and to decrease during REM deprivation. Further, REM is reduced after administration of protein synthesis inhibitors. (e.g., Drucker-Colin, 1979; McGinty & Drucker-Colin, 1982). On the basis of these findings, Drucker-Colin (1979) suggested that the large amounts of active sleep observed in young infants may reflect increased levels of protein synthesis during this period of rapid growth and development. McGinty and Drucker-Colin (1982) have recently speculated that the cycles of the BRAC may be related to cycles of an intrinsic protein synthesis rhythm.

In addition to the 50- to 60-min cycles of the BRAC, Kleitman (1963) noted a 3- to 4-hour periodicity in episodes of wakefulness in the neonate but attributed these to the periodic recurrence of hunger. Kleitman believed wakefulness in the newborn infant to be a primitive arousal state that occurred as a result of discomfort or pain and terminated when the discomfort was removed. Results of subsequent studies have suggested that, contrary to Kleitman's belief, the newborn's 4-hour sleep–wakefulness cycle is probably an endogenous rhythm unrelated to the degree of hunger (Emde, Swedberg, & Suzuki, 1975; Gaensbauer & Emde, 1973; Morath, 1974). Additional support for this view has been provided by reports that a 3- to 4-hour periodicity is also evident in cycles of heart rate and heart rate variability in the fetus (Hoppenbrouwers et al., 1981), as well as in the ability to fall asleep in adults (Lavie & Zomer, 1984; Nakagawa, 1980).

The question of how the various biological rhythms interact during development has been addressed by Meier-Koll and associates (Meier-Koll, 1979; Meier-Koll et al., 1978). Their results indicate that these rhythms do not run independently, but form a hierarchically organized system of interacting oscillators. In a longitudinal study of one infant from birth to 4 months of age, they found that during the first 4 weeks periods of sleep and wakefulness were organized according to a 4-hour cycle exhibiting six crests within a 24-hour day, equally distributed between day and night. Within this 4-hour cycle, the timing and duration of sleep and waking episodes suggested that state transitions were triggered by Kleitman's BRAC, with most awakenings occurring when an epoch of active sleep would have been expected had the infant continued sleeping. After the fifth week, the sleep–wakefulness cycle continued to show a 4-hour periodicity during the day, but the mean period at night gradually increased from 4 to approximately 12 hours. Meier-Koll and colleagues (1978) speculated that the developing circadian rhythm modulated the frequency of the 4-hour cycle by decelerating it during the nocturnal hours and were able to simulate the sleep-waking behavior of their subject with a computer model based on this principle.

Factors Modulating States

One of the most effective means of altering the composition of sleep in adult subjects is to impose a period of sleep deprivation. In the adult, selective deprivation of REM periods produces a marked "rebound" or elevation of REM time on recovery nights, which has been interpreted as the reflection of a biological need for REM sleep (Dement, 1969). Anders and Roffwarg (1973a) reasoned that, if REM or active sleep serves a vital function during early development, the REM rebound effect should be particularly strong in the newborn. Initially, they attempted selectively to disturb either active or quiet sleep, but found it impossible to eliminate a single sleep stage. After awakening, infants, unlike adults, either returned to the same sleep stage or remained awake. In a second experiment, infants were kept awake during a 4-hour interfeeding period. Contrary to expectations, there was a significant reduction rather than a rebound of active sleep during the recovery period.

Other investigators have described a similar alteration of the state cycle after extended periods of wakefulness. Theorell, Prechtl, Blair, and Lind (1973) compared the distribution of various states in newborn infants on the first and fifth days after birth and found that infants spent considerably more time in waking states on the first day of life. The proportion of quiet sleep remained constant from the first to the fifth day, but the amount of active sleep nearly doubled, suggesting that the increased wakefulness on day 1 was maintained at the expense of active sleep. Similarly, Monod and Pajot (1965) reported that the proportion of active sleep was selectively reduced when more than 60 percent of a state cycle was spent in the waking state, and Ashton (1971) also noted a significant reduction in the first epoch of active sleep following a feeding and its associated period of wakefulness.

The results of at least one study suggest that REM rebound effects may occur in the young infant when the deprivation of active sleep is not accompanied by increased wakefulness. Gabriel and Albani (1977) found a reduction in active sleep and increased quiet sleep in a group of young prematures during a 3-day period of phenobarbital administration. After withdrawal of the drug, quiet sleep decreased and active sleep rebounded to exceed pretreatment levels. The REM rebound phenomenon is not well understood, but the reciprocal relationship between active sleep and wakefulness suggests that during early infancy these states are similar in some biologically significant respect.

In recent years there has been increasing evidence that several areas of the brain implicated in the control of sleep are also intimately involved in the regulation of basic biological processes. With the recognition of this correspondence, it is gradually becoming clear that not only do states alter physiological functions, but many physiological functions are able to alter states as well. One group of factors recently demonstrated to play a role in sleep regulation are those associated with feeding and metabolism. Studies recently reviewed by Danguir and Nicolaides (1985) indicate that both REM and NREM sleep are progressively reduced during starvation and immediately return to control levels after feeding or intravenous infusion of glucose. These effects appear to be associated with cellular utilization of the metabolites, since similar glucose infusions in nonstarved animals are ineffective unless insulin is also administered. Additional studies have demonstrated that REM and NREM states may be differentially affected by various metabolic substrates; for example, infusion of amino acid solution increases REM but has no observable effect on NREM sleep (Danguir & Nicolaides, 1985).

Metabolic influences on sleep have not been systematically investigated in young infants, but the few scattered reports available suggest that they also play an important role in state organization early in development. Steinschneider and Weinstein (1983) compared breast- and formula-fed infants on a number of sleep characteristics and found significantly less active sleep in breast-fed subjects. A disruption of sleep–wake patterns, including a marked decrease in the proportion of active or REM sleep, has been observed in infant rats during periods of maternal separation (Hofer, 1976). This disturbance of state organization was determined to be primarily due to factors associated with feeding, and could be prevented by appropriate formula composition and an intermittent schedule of delivery (Hofer & Shair, 1982).

More general effects of feeding have been reported by Harper and colleagues (1977), who found that young infants were significantly more likely to enter active sleep after periods of wakefulness accompanied by feeding than after similar periods of nonfeeding wakefulness. A study of Salzarulo, Fagioli, Salomon, and Ricour (1982) suggests that prolonged malnourishment also affects sleep patterns in infants older than approximately 4 months of age. They reported less quiet sleep and more active sleep in a group of infants suffering malnutrition as a result of gastrointestinal pathology than in control infants of the same age. This trend was reversed after nutritional rehabilitation.

Environmental temperature has been demonstrated significantly to affect both amount and composition of sleep in a variety of species, including the human. Current evidence suggests that REM sleep is severely depressed in ambient temperatures either above or below the neutral range, and brief skin temperature changes in the direction of thermoneutrality in either warm or cold environments may trigger REM episodes (Szymusiak, Satinoff, Schallert, & Wishaw, 1980). Non-REM sleep appears to be less sensitive to temperature variations, but also declines when deviations from neutral temperatures are extreme (e.g., Haskell, Palca, Walker, Berger, & Heller, 1981; Szymusiak & Satinoff, 1985).

Data presented by McGinty and Drucker-Colin (1982) show a similar relationship between temperature and sleep states in the young kitten, but there is little comparable information available in human infants. In a study of the effect of continuous stimulation on arousal levels, Brackbill (1971) noted that an increase in ambient temperature from 26 to 31 deg C produced an increase in quiet sleep but had no effect on active sleep in 1-month-old infants. Although temperatures in the range of 32–34 deg C are generally considered neutral when infants are unclothed (e.g., Parmelee, Bruck, & Bruck, 1962), for Brackbill's clothed subjects the temperature change presumably represented an increase above thermoneutral levels. Parmelee et al. (1962) have reported observations for two premature infants in both neutral temperatures and temperatures slightly below the neutral range. In contrast to results described by Brackbill, these infants showed decreased quiet sleep and an increase in active sleep when ambient temperature was reduced. Curiously, active temperature regulation, which is absent during REM in adults, appears to be present during active sleep in the young infant (Darnall & Ariagno, 1982). This REM-related suspension of temperature regulation in the adult is believed to be due to an inhibition of hypothalamic thermoregulatory mechanisms (Parmeggiani, 1985).

Alterations in atmospheric concentrations of oxygen and carbon dioxide are also effective in disrupting sleep patterns early in development. Baker and McGinty (1977, 1979) have reported that kittens exposed to hypoxia show a dramatic suppression of active sleep and increased quiet sleep compared to controls maintained in a normal environment. Since victims of the sudden death syndrome show indications of chronic hypoxemia, one might also expect similar alterations in the sleep organization of infants at risk for SIDS. Recent evidence suggests that sleep organization is disrupted in these infants, but the pattern appears to be one of increased rather than decreased active sleep (Haddad, Walsh, Leistner, Grodin, & Mellins, 1981; Navelet, Payan, Guilhaume, & Benoit, 1984), and a reduction in sleep–wake transitions (Harper, Frostig, Taube, Hoppenbrouwers, & Hodgman, 1983; Harper, Leake, Hoffman, et al., 1981).

As previously noted, conditions considered to be stressful are particularly effective in modulating the composition of sleep. Indeed, it has been suggested that all environmental manipulations that alter sleep may do so by means of their common effect on stress mechanisms (e.g., Szymusiak et al., 1980). In animals and human adults, the aspect of sleep most sensitive to environmental stress is the proportion of REM; REM is inhibited during stress and may be triggered by relief from stress in a number of forms (McGinty & Drucker-Colin, 1982; Szymusiak et al., 1980). Under mildly stressful conditions, compensation for decreased REM generally results in an increase in NREM stages 1 and 2, while stages 3 and 4 and total sleep time remain unaffected (e.g., Scott, 1972).

Comparable studies of infant sleep suggest that, although decreases in active sleep are frequently seen under conditions considered stressful, the most reliable effect of stress early in development is probably an increase in NREM or quiet sleep. In two experiments, Emde, Harmon, Metcalf, Koenig, and Wagonfeld (1971) found a significant increase in the proportion of quiet sleep during a 10-hour period following routine circumcision without anesthesia, while neither active sleep nor wakefulness was significantly affected. This increase in quiet sleep was reflected both in decreased latency to the first quiet sleep episode and in increased length of quiet sleep episodes. Theorell and associates (1973) have also reported an increase in the proportion of quiet sleep that they ascribed to stress factors. In a comparison of infants whose umbilicals were clamped early (within 10 sec) and late (longer than 3 min), Theorell and associates found only a higher percentage of quiet sleep and decreased wakefulness in late-clamped infants on both the first and the fifth day of life. They attributed these differences to the physiological stress of increased blood volume that may occur when cord clamping is delayed.

An additional study by Gabriel, Grote, and Jonas (1981) did find differences in active sleep under conditions that may be considered to represent different degrees of stress. These investigators compared state organization in two groups of young prematures during a 4-day observation period. One group received routine hospital care, while the other was left undisturbed as much as possible. Their results showed a number of differences between the two groups, including a considerably lower percentage of active sleep and increased wakefulness in infants who experienced frequent interventions.

A number of studies have examined the effects of various types of sensory stimulation on infant states. These are consistent in showing increased quiet sleep and decreased wakefulness, particularly crying wakefulness, during stimulation, but have reported inconsistent effects on active sleep. Reports by Schmidt, Rose, and Bridger (1980), Murray and Campbell (1971), and Brackbill (1970, 1975) described significant decreases in active sleep during various types of auditory stimulation, with more intense stimuli producing greater effects on sleep. Similarly, Wolff (1966) reported that, when infants were in active sleep, presentation of white noise or turning on overhead lights in the nursery consistently produced a transition to quiet sleep, while turning off these stimuli produced a change from quiet to active sleep in most instances. In three additional studies, Edelmann, Kraemer, and Korner (1982) and

Brackbill (1971, 1973) examined changes in infant states during stimulation in vestibular, visual, tactile, and auditory modalities. The results of all three studies showed increased quiet sleep accompanied by large decreases in crying wakefulness, but an increase rather than a decrease in active sleep. Theorell and others (1973), who also failed to find decreased active sleep in stressed infants, reported a similar decrease in wakefulness in their subjects. This pattern is consistent with the view that active sleep and waking states are in some sense interchangeable early in development, and it suggests that many of the inconsistencies observed in effects of stress and stimulation on infant sleep may be attributable to the apparent reciprocal relationship between these states.

Beyond the newborn period, stress-induced alterations in infant sleep become both more consistent and more adultlike. The majority of studies of sleep organization in older infants have examined changes in sleep patterns when sleep occurs in the laboratory rather than in the familiar home environment, and have found effects very similar to the "first night effect" widely reported in adult subjects (Agnew, Webb, & Williams, 1966). Bernstein and others (1973) compared sleep patterns under home and laboratory conditions in a group of 4-month-olds and found that the percentage of active sleep was reduced in a simulated laboratory environment compared to home naps. In a study of 2- and 8-week-old infants, Sostek and Anders (1975) monitored sleep–waking behavior over a 24-hour period that included 12 hours of polygraph recording. They found that both transportation to the laboratory and application of recording electrodes resulted in increased fussiness and crying in both age groups, but only the 8-week-olds showed a significantly reduced proportion of active sleep during the 12 hours of polygraph recording. These infants also failed to show evidence of diurnal variation in the periods immediately following transportation to the laboratory and application of electrodes, although diurnal variation was present, at least in older infants, during subsequent periods (Sostek, Anders, & Sostek, 1976).

STARTLE REFLEX EXCITATION AND MODULATION

Evaluation of various reflexes and their changes during infancy has long been an important source of information regarding basic neurological status and development taking place within the nervous system. Virtually all of the infant test protocols (e.g., Self's chapter, this volume) include some estimate of reflex responding. For the most part these tests are viewed, correctly or not, as an assessment of relatively low-level capabilities, both in the neurological levels tapped and in the psychological functioning required. However, research from a variety of disciplines, medicine, psychology, and neuroscience, is making it increasingly evident that at least some of these so-called low-level reflexes are remarkably sensitive to the modulating influence of neural structures up to and including the cortex, and that within the appropriate paradigm psychological processes mediated by such higher-level structures may be reflected in alterations of basic reflexes. The use of basic reflexes is of particular importance for the study of infants, since it can provide a valuable method for examining more complex processes within the limited behavioral repertoire.

The study of reflexes to assess higher or more general aspects of stimulus processing is only just beginning with infant populations. Virtually all of such work has been done with the blink reflex (or squint in the case of sleeping infants), usually as part of startle reflex elicitation. Much of the recent work has involved recording the electromyographic activity of the muscles surrounding the eye, collectively called the orbicularis oculi, since such activity can be readily recorded from awake or sleeping infants and it closely parallels the responses measured from the actual movement of the eyelid or other electrical activity associated with lid movement (Clarkson & Berg, 1984; Simons & Zelson, 1985). In this section we will briefly review developmental changes in the reflex itself and then consider the modulation of the reflex both by manipulation of the eliciting stimulus and by other accompanying stimuli. Modulatory effects are discussed in the context of the development of transient versus sustained auditory processing systems.

Development of the Startle and Other Blink-Eliciting Reflexes

The pioneering work of Landis and Hunt (1939) was among the first to suggest that the startle reflex, especially as distinguished from the moro reflex, is not fully developed at birth. In general, it appeared that components of the startle reflex emerged as the moro reflex declined over the first 2–4 months of life. In a few cases, some aspects of the startle, such as the blink, were observed simultaneously with the moro in infants older than 6 weeks. These workers noted that in infants as well as adults the blink is perhaps the most persistent and reliable of the various motor components making up the startle complex. Many years later, neurologists began to examine the development of another blink reflex, which is elicited by stimulation of the trigeminal nerve in the face, usually electrically. Detailed recordings of the orbicularis oculi electromyographic activity in adults had demonstrated that the reflex involved two components: a unilateral, monosynapic, short-latency response, sometimes called R1, and a polysyaptic, longer-latency activity, called R2, which appeared bilaterally even with unilateral stimulation. It was R2 that was most closely associated with the overt muscle activity and the blink itself. Two initial reports, Hopf, Hufschmidt, and Stroder (1965) and Clay and Ramseyer (1976), both reported inability to obtain any R2 in infants under 10 months or 20 months, respectively. Thereafter, they reported only long-latency or unilateral R2 responses up to about 36 months. Since Clay and Ramsayer readily obtained R1 responses at the earliest ages (1 month), and reported blinks with other stimuli, they concluded there was an immaturity of the polysynaptic connections in the brain stem or midbrain, rather than a sensory or motor pathway immaturity. A more determined effort by Kimura, Bodensteiner, and Yamada (1977) demonstrated that an R2 could be elicited in about two-thirds of healthy neonates, with sufficiently intense stimulation, but it was longer in latency and unilateral, being restricted to the side stimulated. All the reports agreed that the R2 reflex did not reach adult latency, form, and amplitude until about age 6. The difficulty in eliciting the R2 component in early infancy fits well with the Landis and Hunt report and the more recent data described below showing that blink responses to both acoustic and cutaneous (air puff) stimulation have a higher threshold in infants than in adults. The results remain consistent with the view that the deficit is related to the central pathway rather than to the peripheral afferents or efferents.

Graham and co-workers (e.g., Balaban, Anthony, & Graham, 1985; Graham,

Strock, & Zeigler, 1981) have proposed that this difficulty in eliciting blink responses and in other related blink modulation phenomena is indicative of a much more general developmental pattern. They note that in both the visual and auditory systems distinction has been made by some between those brain structures or neuron types that process the transient aspects of a stimulus (e.g., the onset and offset) and the sustained aspects of a stimulus (Gersuni, 1971; Norman, Pettigrew, & Daniels, 1977). Other work suggests such a distinction can also be made for the tactile system (Gescheider, 1976; Verillo, 1968). In the visual system the neurophysiology of the two systems has been fairly well worked out, and research in the kitten suggests that the transient processing cells, the so-called X cells, develop later than the cells specialized for processing of the sustained aspects of a stimulus (Norman et al., 1977). Graham argues that in general the young infant's ability to process transient aspects of stimuli is underdeveloped compared to the processing ability for sustained aspects of stimuli. Since startle blink is especially dependent on the transients for at least acoustic stimuli (K. M. Berg, 1973; Blumenthal, 1985; Blumenthal & W. K. Berg, 1982), immaturity in the transient system should result in the relatively poor startle blink responding.

Modification of Blinks by Manipulation of the Eliciting Stimulus:
A Test of the Transient–Sustained Hypothesis

In two studies carried out in our laboratory, Blumenthal (Blumenthal, 1982, 1985; Blumenthal & W. K. Berg, 1982) directly tested Graham's hypothesis by comparing infant and adult startle blinks in response to manipulations of transient and sustained aspects of auditory stimuli. In the first study (Blumenthal, 1982; Blumenthal & W. K. Berg, 1982) the rise and fall times of 95-dB white noise were varied from an abrupt 1 msec to a more gradual 10 msec. Each infant (4–6 weeks of age) and each adult received up to eight presentations of each rise–fall time stimulus. The results, shown in Figure 5.1, demonstrate that, while adults were able to maintain the amplitude of their blink as the transient was reduced over this range, the infants' responses declined. Examination of the response probability showed that even at the optimal 1-msec rise–fall condition, infants responded about 76 percent of the time whereas adults were at about 97 percent. The hypothesis was that faster rise times improved synchrony of neural firing in the startle pathway, a factor more critical to infants than to adults.

In the second study (Blumenthal, 1985), stimulus duration was varied. Noise stimuli with abrupt onsets were presented at 95 dB to adults and at 100 dB to neonates, the increased intensity employed partially to compensate for the lower sensitivity of the neonate. The results were clearest for response probability (Fig. 5.2).* With the brief 3-msec stimulus, a "transient-only" condition, the neonates' response was essentially at threshold—50 percent probability—whereas the adults were responding with measurable blinks on 80 percent of the trials. The impact of the

---

*Both of the Blumenthal studies make it clear that, when stimuli are employed that produce less than near 100 percent responding, stimulus variables may have different effects on the response probability than on the amplitude of responses that do occur. Something similar to this was noted by K. M. Berg (1973) whereby blink thresholds were affected differently than blink amplitude in supra threshold conditions.

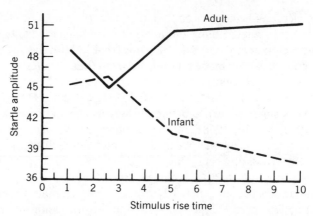

Figure 5.1. Startle response amplitude as a function of rise time in infants and adults. (From "Developmental Differences in the Temporal Summation of Transient and Sustained Auditory Stimuli" by T. D. Blumenthal, 1985, unpublished doctoral dissertation, University of Florida, Gainesville. Adapted with author's permission.)

sustained portion of the stimulus became evident as the stimulus duration was extended. The response probability gradually converged toward that for adults up until the 50-msec durations whereafter the neonates remained about 5–8 percentage points below the adults. Other results of the study confirm the relatively greater contribution of the sustained versus transient aspects of the stimuli for startle blinks. Responses were obtained for sustained stimuli and for pairs of transient pulses whose interpulse intervals were matched to the onset and offset of the sustained stimuli. For adults, pulse pairs (containing transient information only) were very nearly as

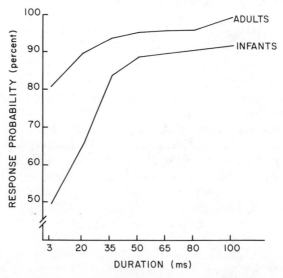

Figure 5.2. Probability of eliciting a startle response in newborns and adults as a function of duration of a continuous noise stimulus. (From "Developmental Differences in the Temporal Summation of Transient and Sustained Auditory Stimuli" by T. D. Blumenthal, 1985, unpublished doctoral dissertation, University of Florida, Gainesville. Used with author's permission.)

effective as sustained stimuli for durations or intervals out to 50 msec, but for infants equivalent effects were evident only out to 20 msec. Thus after 20 msec the
sustained aspect of the stimulus contributes more heavily to the neonate blink probability than to that of the adults. Anthony, Zeigler, and Graham (in press) report
data very consistent with both results. They find that increasing duration of either
visual or auditory startle stimuli has a greater impact on probability and latency of
startle responding in infants than it does in adults.

Modulation of Blink Reflexes with Additional Stimuli

A major source of information leading Graham to propose the lag in development
of transient stimulus processing was not effects of the blink-eliciting stimulus itself,
but the modulation of the blink reflex by other stimuli. Both inhibition and facilitation of the reflex can be produced under a variety of circumstances (Anthony,
1985; Graham et al., 1981), but the effect of primary interest to the hypothesis is
the potent inhibition that occurs when a nonstartling stimulus is presented about
60–300 msec prior to the onset of blink elicitation. For example, with adult humans,
a 75-dB, 20-msec tone pip presented about 100 msec prior to a startle-eliciting noise
will reduce the blink amplitude by about one-half compared to what the noise burst
alone would produce. Even greater amounts of inhibition are often reported. It can
be shown that this effect can occur cross-modally, in a variety of animal species,
without conditioning or learning, and regardless of the attentive state of the subject
(Graham et al., 1981; Hoffman & Ison, 1980). Neurophysiological studies indicate
that the effect requires only the integrity of the midbrain structures and below (Davis
& Gendelman, 1977; Leitner, Powers, Stitt, & Hoffman, 1981). Not only is the
effect large, it is very reliable; under optimal conditions virtually every adult subject
will show the effect. The surprise is that this powerful, ubiquitous effect organized
at a low level in the brain is in the human infant comparatively weak, capricious,
and unreliable.

The initial studies of blink inhibition in the infant were encouraging. Marsh,
Hoffman, and Stitt (1978) reported significant inhibition of an air-puff-elicited blink
by a 70-db tone in 6 of 9 infants under 15 months of age, though two of the negative
cases were 14 weeks or less. When present, the inhibition decreased the amplitude
by about half, compared with about a 75 percent reduction in adults tested under
similar conditions. Subsequently, W. K. Berg, Clarkson, and Silverstein (1979) reported mean inhibition of only 16 and 26 percent by 250- and 1000-Hz tones presented at 15–55 dB above adult thresholds, but inhibition of at least 10 percent was
present in 15 of 18 subjects tested. These two preliminary reports were followed by
several attempts to verify the original effects and to examine the impact of several
important parameters. However, subsequent reports from both these laboratories
as well as from Graham and coworkers made it clear that the effects were neither
so large nor so consistent as the initial work suggested. The subsequent work has
been directed at assessing the impact of several variables that may account for some
of the variability in the immature system.

Among the most important parameters in the adult reflex modulation work is
the time elapsed from onset of the modulatory lead stimulus to onset of the reflex-
eliciting stimulus, the stimulus onset asynchrony (SOA). In both mature animals
and adult humans, the inhibitory effect is maximized at SOAs of about 60–120 msec,

regardless of arousal state (Graham & Murray, 1977; Hoffman & Ison, 1980; Silverstein, Graham, & Callaway, 1980). However, some inhibition has been reported at SOAs as long as 2–3 sec (Clarkson, W. K. Berg, & Boettcher, 1980). Graham and co-workers (Graham et al., 1981) reported 84-dB lead tones produced acoustic startle inhibition of about 25–30 percent for infants 6–9 weeks old with SOAs of 225 and 275 msec, but not at shorter SOAs. For infants 16–24 weeks old, similar inhibition was produced at SOAs as short as 175 msec. Similarly, unpublished work in our laboratory* indicates that for prematurely born infants tested 3–18 weeks after delivery (gestationally corrected ages of 3 weeks before to 3–11 weeks following expected date of birth) 75-dB tones of a duration of 50 msec produce a 10–15 percent inhibition of an air-puff-elicited blink for an SOA of 250 msec, but not for SOAs of 150, 350, or 450 msec. This study and the Graham and associates work indicate that the SOA critical for producing inhibition may be very narrow in the young infant. Hoffman, Cohen, and English (1985) tested neonates with yet a third blink-eliciting reflex, the glabella reflex, elicited by a tap to the forehead. Lead tones of 90 dB were ineffective in significantly altering the blink at 75-, 150-, 200-, 300-, or 600-msec SOAs, but did produce significant facilitation of the blink when presented *simultaneously* with the glabella tap. Adults tested under similar conditions showed clear inhibition for all lead conditions *except* the simultaneous one. The finding of the blink facilitation in neonates for the simultaneous condition, together with the adult data, indicates that the lack of effect with the various SOAs cannot be attributed to an inability of the infants to detect the lead tone. However, if the narrow SOA window for blink inhibition falls very near 250 msec, as the Graham and colleagues and W. K. Berg laboratory studies suggest for the very young infant, it is just possible that the Hoffman and associates tests at SOAs of 200 and 300 msec fell just either side of that window. All three studies, while differing somewhat in their outcome, demonstrate that the blink reflex in infants is subject to modulation. In addition to the relevance of the SOA, several other aspects of testing have been shown to be important.

One of the most potentially powerful variables influencing virtually all psychophysiological responding is sleep–wake state. Only a few studies have examined this factor for reflex inhibition. With adult subjects, Silverstein and others (1980) found no differences between REM and NREM stages of sleep on the extent of inhibition, even though there was a substantial effect on the amplitude of the reflexive blink in the absence of any inhibiting lead stimuli. Furthermore, the inhibitory effects in sleeping subjects were comparable to those from the awake subject tested under similar stimulus conditions. In contrast, Strock's (1981) study of sleeping infants found differences in REM and NREM not only for the reflex itself, as had been seen with adults, but for the inhibitory effects as well. She reports significant inhibition of about 45–50 percent for 84-dB lead stimuli presented 225 or 275 msec prior to an acoustic startle stimulus with infants 6–9 weeks of age, but only when they were in quiet sleep. Furthermore, this inhibition appeared to be more substantial than seen with other infants tested similarly during waking periods. In preliminary work from our laboratory*, we have found that 75-dB lead stimuli pre-

---

*The research was carried out with the valuable collaborative efforts of Alonzo Avendano, Terry Blumenthal, Margarete Davies, Thomas Harbin, and Barry Hurwitz. It was funded in part by grant #12-65 from the March of Dimes Foundation.

sented 225 msec prior to an air-puff in infants 2–14 weeks old produced inhibition when they were judged to be in quiet sleep, but not when in active sleep or in drowsy or alert states. Also noteworthy is that the significant inhibition reported earlier for prematures was obtained during quiet sleep only. In the Hoffman and others (1985) study of neonates in which inhibition was not obtained, infants were generally asleep but sleep stage was not assessed. Since neonates spend at least 50 percent of the sleep time in the active/REM stages (Roffwarg et al., 1966), it is possible that the Hoffman and associates study may have missed some inhibition occurring during quiet sleep.

A recent study by Balaban and colleagues (1985) provided evidence for another important factor influencing the extent to which lead stimuli may modify the blink reflex. These authors assessed the inhibition in infants and adults for lead and blink-eliciting stimulus pairs (250-msec onset-to-onset intervals) when the pairs were presented either in the same modality (auditory–auditory or visual–visual) or in con-trasting modalities (auditory–visual or visual–auditory). They found that for the 16-week-old infants as well as the adult subjects blinks elicited by stimuli in the same modality as the lead stimulus were about 30 percent smaller than for mis-matched stimulus pairs. For reasons related to other aspects of the design, blink-eliciting stimuli were never presented alone, so the absolute extent of inhibition cannot be determined for the cross-modal pairs. However, based on previous work from this laboratory (e.g., Strock, 1981), acoustic–acoustic pairs tested under sim-ilar circumstances produced about 35 percent inhibition in infants, thus suggesting that, when lead stimuli were not of the same sensory modality as the blink-eliciting stimulus, little inhibition remains for infants, and inhibition would be reduced for adults (as was reported by Graham, 1980). The use of cross-modal paradigms in both the Berg, Hoffman and colleagues (1985) studies cited earlier could account for their reports of smaller magnitudes of inhibition (or no inhibition) as compared to much of the data from the Graham laboratory.

As Balaban and associates (1985) point out, differences between within- and between-modality effects may occur as a result of engagement of different neural mechanisms. The within-modality inhibition may reflect a more neurally peripheral event—a refractorylike effect—than the inhibition found with cross-modal stimulus pairs. The cross-modally supported inhibition would appear to be controlled by more central, polysensory pathways extrinsic to the primary sensorimotor circuits that mediate the reflex. Based on the Balaban and colleagues work, it appears that it is this latter mechanism that is especially immature in the infant, and whose lack of effect is responsible for the major differences between the adult and infant reflex inhibition. And it is this latter mechanism, still only poorly localized in the brain, that Graham argues is especially sensitive to the transient aspect of the lead stimulus.

Since adults readily exhibit a robust inhibitory reflex modulation whereas young infants do not, it is evident that a major developmental change occurs. Until re-cently, most investigators anticipated that these changes would occur sometime dur-ing the infancy or early childhood period. However, two recent studies suggest oth-erwise. W.K. Berg and others (1985) examined inhibition of air-puff-induced blink responses by 55- and 75-dB tones. The lead stimulus was a 2000-Hz tone of a du-ration of 25 msec whose onset preceded puffs by 225 msec. Averaged electromy-ographic activity of periorbital muscles provided information on blink amplitude. Subjects were tested at 2, 4, and 7 months of age, and at 2, 6, 9, 12, and 25 years of age, with numbers varying from 9 to 19 per age group. The very small and non-significant inhibition found in the two youngest infant groups grew gradually throughout the childhood years but did not approach adult levels until 12 years. This gradual increase in mean inhibition was accompanied by a gradual increase in the reliability of the effect across subjects, with 30 of the 31 subjects tested at 12 and 25 years showing the effect. These data show the development of cross-modal inhibition (auditory lead and tactile blink stimulus), but Ornitz, Guthrie, Kaplan, Lane, and Norman (in press) demonstrated a very similar function for within-modality stimulus pairs in children 3–8 years of age and adults. Using a 75-dB, 1000-Hz tone leading a blink-eliciting, 104-dB white noise burst by 120 msec, these investigators did not find adult levels of inhibition until the children reached 8 years of age. When the lead interval was extended to 250 msec, 8-year-olds produced less inhibition than adults. Lack of inhibition in the younger children was not attributable to a general inability to modulate the reflex since longer-duration, continuous lead tones produced facilitatory effects on blink amplitude, an effect also reported by Graham and colleagues (1981) for infants.

The most straightforward interpretation of the extended developmental trend in the reflex inhibition phenomenon is that the neurological mechanisms involved are very late maturing, at least in humans. Leitner and associates (1981) provide convincing evidence that the lateral tegmentum, an area within the midbrain reticular formation, is critical for producing both cross- and within-modality effects in rats. Myelination of some neurons within this region is very late in humans (Yakovlev & LeCours, 1967), and while myelination is not necessary for neural functioning, it may serve as a marker for an extended development sequence for this area generally.

Another more complex interpretation of the long developmental trend may also be warranted. It is possible that the resistance to blink inhibition present in the infant and young child is the result of suppression of the midbrain mechanisms by other immature areas within the brain, most notably the forebrain structures. Thus by this hypothesis it is not the critical mechanisms themselves that lack the ability to produce the effect, but rather their vulnerability to interference from immature higher-level neural structures that modulate the primary structures. The work of Graham, Leavitt, Strock, and Brown (1978) illustrated this possibility in the case of the cardiac orienting response by demonstrating the "precocious" deceleratory responses of a young anencephalic infant. In collaboration with Dr. Marsha Clarkson, we have tested a similarly damaged infant for blink reflex inhibition and found in this infant what could be termed "precocious" inhibitory responses. Infant RC was a black male infant delivered following an apparently uneventful pregnancy. The infant was normal in appearance and had no negative indications on the initial neonatal examination. Subsequent behavioral unresponsiveness and suggestions of convulsions led to the discovery of severe hydranencephaly. Transillumination and radiological imaging techniques indicated total lack of tissue in the brain cavity in the supratentorial compartment, approximately the level of the midbrain and above in the normal infant. Initial testing indicated lack of behavioral reactions to speech stimuli below 92 dB SPL, but a clear reaction at 94 dB and above. In no case was there evidence of heart rate changes to this or other stimuli. At 3½ weeks of age, electromyographic activity from the eyelid was recorded in response to air puffs near the eye. The infant was probably blind and remained quiet with eyes closed throughout the test. Inhibition was tested with 1- and 2-kHz tones at 94-, 99-, 104-, and 109-dB as lead stimuli as well as a puff-alone control condition. Scorable responses were obtained for 12 to 15 repetitions of each condition except the 94 dB. The results indicate increasing inhibition with intensity increases, asymptoting at a statistically significant 41 percent for the highest two intensities. Because of the substantial number of stimulus repetitions we are reasonably confident of these results. Occasionally we will see this level of inhibition in a normal child of this age, but not when responses are averaged over 10 or more presentations, such as was the case here. Of course, our normal subjects have not been tested at such high intensities, but since there was strong evidence of a considerable hearing loss in the infant, it is unlikely the lead tones were substantially above his acoustic threshold. Tests with two other hydranencephalic infants showed consistent though more modest inhibition for lead stimuli of 80–90 dB. The results for baby RC, though not unequivocal, argue that we should not yet reject the possibility that the weak inhibition in infants and young children may be a result of slowly maturing forebrain structures interfering with a more mature midbrain inhibitory mechanism.

Although the majority of studies of reflex modulation involve measurement of skeletal muscle activity, a few have examined autonomic reflexes as well. In an early study with adult rats, Chalmers and Hoffman (1973) reported that a monophasic accelerative response produced by a startle-eliciting noise burst was reduced by about a third when the startle stimulus was preceded by a brief 80-dB sound. However, motor components were almost completely inhibited by the prepulse. Further, there was no correlation between cardiac and motor components, indicating some dissociation of the two systems under these test conditions. Graham and associates (1981) report that 70-dB lead stimuli also reduced accelerative reactions in human adults when presented at 175 and 275 msec but not 75 msec before startle stimulation. Again, this was an indication of dissociation between systems, since the three intervals were equally effective in inhibiting blink responses. Graham and colleagues also report that lead stimululi of 1–4 sec elicit increases in heart rate accelerations as well as blink amplitude.

Although several studies have been carried out with infants, review of the results does not provide a consistent picture of the effects. For infants 6–9 weeks old, Graham and colleagues (1981) report that a 25-msec lead stimulus of 79–84 dB reduced the size of acceleration occurring to an acoustic startle stimulus. The effect was evident for an acceleration peaking 3–4 sec after the startle-eliciting stimulus onset, and again later in the response. A comparison of lead intervals of 75, 175, 225, and 275 indicated the effect was greatest at the longest interval. At 24 weeks of age, the startle response is deceleratory, and the lead stimulus reduced that response as well. Sustained lead stimuli of a duration of 1–4 sec had the effect of increasing the magnitude of the accelerative response in infants 6–9 weeks old, just as they had for adults. These data were for awake infants, but in related work, Strock (1981) found no significant effects of lead stimulus on heart rate responses of sleeping infants 6–9 weeks old, whether in active or quiet stages of sleep.

In contrast, Ver Hoeve and Leavitt (1985) found no effect of state for the direction or extent of cardiac response inhibition. However, these investigators did not employ stimuli explicitly designed to elicit the startle reflex, but rather elicited cardiac accelerative responses with a low-frequency square wave stimulus of 83 dB. The effect of a 75-dB tone turned on and sustained for the 100 msec prior to the square wave tone was to reduce the size of the acceleration in much the same manner as reported by Graham and associates (1981) for older infants. The surprise was that the same sustained stimulus presented at a 250-msec lead interval, as well as a 4000-msec lead stimulus, had the opposite effect; it produced a relative facilitation by extending an initial acceleration seen in the no-lead condition. Preliminary work in our laboratory with neonates in quiet sleep also suggests this relative facilitatory effect, present with a brief lead stimulus presented 250 msec prior to onset of a puff of air near the eye. The effect was reduced somewhat at lead intervals of 350–550 msec. A subsequent study by Ver Hoeve (1984) did not completely replicate his earlier results in that both discrete (duration of 40 msec) and sustained stimuli presented 240 msec prior to an acceleration-generating square wave had the effect of reducing the size of the initial acceleration.

In sum, there seem to be two effects reported. One is the inhibitory reduction of a brief acceleration peaking at about 3–4 sec after onset of the eliciting stimulus. This effect is very similar to that seen with adult humans and rats. Also, there has been reported a facilitatory effect using both discrete and sustained lead stimuli presented at shorter lead intervals. In this case the accelerative response is maintained and extended for a period of a few seconds rather than immediately returning toward baseline. The difficulty is that no consistent pattern of conditions has emerged that leads to one or the other of these autonomic modulations. Sustained lead stimuli of several seconds' duration have generally been reported to increase accelerative reactions, but it is not clear whether these effects are independent of the recovery following responses to the lead stimuli themselves. The only report of a reduced deceleratory response was with 24-week-old infants (Graham et al., 1981). Interpretation of the heart rate data is complicated by the fact that the response sometimes changes in overall shape (e.g., Ver Hoeve, 1984) as well as amplitude, thereby making it difficult to identify simple inhibition and facilitation effects.

ORIENTING AND ATTENTION

Development of Cardiac Orienting

In 1966 Lipton, Steinschneider, and Richmond reported, as part of a series of studies detailing infants' autonomic functioning, that there were pronounced changes in the form of the heart rate response to a brief airstream stimulus during the early months of life: Monophasic acceleration at birth shifted to a predominantly deceleratory response by 2½ months of age. In that same year Graham and Clifton (1966) reviewed a wide variety of evidence and hypothesized that heart rate deceleration was associated with generalized orienting* and attentive behavior, while acceleration above prestimulus levels was a component of the defensive response. Based on this, Graham and colleagues in this and later publications (e.g., Graham, Anthony, & Zeigler, 1984; Graham & Jackson, 1970) argued that the change from neonatal heart rate acceleration to the predominantly decelerative response of the older infant may reflect development of the orienting response.** Because Sokolov

---

**The term *orienting response* is used throughout this chapter in its more general sense, as Sokolov (1963) used it, to refer to a central mechanism that enhances the processing of information in all sensory systems. Other literature may use the term more restrictively to refer only to the physical orientation of the head, eyes, or ears toward a peripherally presented stimulus. Any of these would be considered components of the general mechanism evaluated here.

(1963) has hypothesized that orienting is part of a basic perceptual system geared toward taking in and processing information, in contrast to the protective and information-limiting systems engaged during defensive responding, the suggestion of development of orienting had important implications for the emergence of cognitive and learning capabilities (Sameroff, 1971). Further, the suggestion implied that the changes in heart rate response form during early infancy reflect development of brain systems responsible for relatively high-level behavior. In contrast to this position, Lipton and others (1966, p. 14) argued against such an interpretation of the developmental changes in cardiac response form and attributed them to autonomic nervous system (ANS) development, probably an increasing control by the vagus nerves and maturation of baroreceptor reflexes. Of course, it is also possible that during early infancy there is development of *both* central cognitive mechanisms and peripheral ANS control. An assessment of any of these possibilities requires separate evaluation of each position.

Ideally, we would evaluate the independent influences of each system on cardiac response development. Unfortunately, evaluation of ANS development and its influences on cardiac responding is very difficult in the human infant. In animals and in some cases adult humans, influence of peripheral or central mechanisms may be directly assessed by surgical or pharmacological intervention. Recent work with indirect measures such as heart rate variability (e.g., Katona et al., 1980; Porges, 1983) has provided some information on changes in tonic control of heart by the vagus in human infants, but these approaches do not evaluate ANS control of phasic responding (W. K. Berg & Hurwitz, 1983).

Since the orienting response is basically a hypothetical construct, its neurological control mechanisms remain unknown, and its influence, too, is difficult to test directly. However, indirect procedures may be employed with human infants to evaluate the likelihood that development of central orienting mechanisms is occurring. Such an approach would, first, supply evidence that neonates' autonomic and cardiovascular systems are capable of producing a deceleratory response like that of more mature infants and adults, at least under some conditions. The second and more convincing step would be to provide evidence that circumstances that alter the likelihood of decelerative responses in neonates and older infants are predictable from the constructs underlying the concept of orienting. This would help provide the convergence needed to demonstrate that developmental changes in orienting mechanisms are major contributors to changes in deceleratory responding early in infancy. In the remainder of this section we will evaluate this possibility, considering the evidence for deceleratory responses in neonates and the conditions under which they occur, and examining the developmental progression of the response and its controlling factors. A detailed evaluation of the evidence for development of ANS control over deceleratory responses is not possible within the space limitations of this chapter, but the topic will be briefly considered in conjunction with a summary evaluation of orienting development.

Importance of Response Topography

Following the Graham and Jackson (1970) conclusion that sustained deceleratory responses in neonates had not been unequivocally demonstrated, a concerted effort was made on the part of a number of investigators to elicit such a response. Review of this work indicates a number of false starts and dubious claims preceding the eventual success. A persistent problem was the failure to recognize the distinction

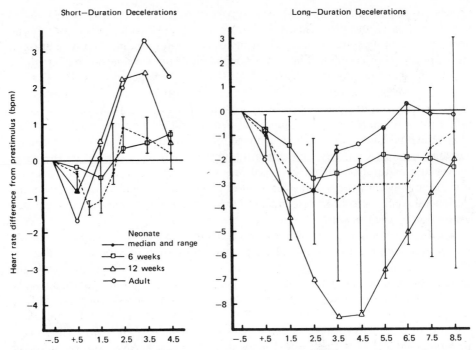

Figure 5.3. Illustrative short-latency (left panel) and long-latency (right panel) deceleratory responses in infants and adults. The median and range (vertical lines) of data from several studies are shown for newborns. (Short-duration newborn curve based on data from Porges et al., 1974, onset response of high-variability subjects; Schachter et al., 1971, means of individual subjects. Long-duration newborn curve based on data from Adkinson & Berg, 1976, onset response of older newborns on Trial Block 1 and offset response of older newborns on Trial Block 3; Clarkson & Berg, 1983, response to pulsed speech; Clifton & Nelson, 1976, subjects awake longer than 10 min; Pomerleau-Malcuit & Clifton, 1971, responses to auditory and vestibular stimuli; Porges et al., 1974, offset responses of both high- and low-variability subjects; Sameroff et al., 1973, response to checkerboards. Older infant and adult data are adapted from single response curves as described in the text.)

between what appear to be two types of cardiac deceleration: a brief initial deceleration, typically preceding an acceleration above baseline, and a longer sustained deceleration.

The general form of the brief deceleration is illustrated in the left panel of Figure 5.3. A curve showing the median heart rate response in three studies of neonates may be compared with responses in sleeping 6- and 12-week-olds (Rewey, 1973) and adults (W. K. Berg, Jackson, & Graham, 1975). In two of the studies with neonates, click stimuli were presented repeatedly regardless of state over a period of several hours (Schachter et al., 1971; Williams, Schachter, & Tobin, 1967).* In a third study, results are from the onset of 30-sec increase in room illumination in awake subjects with higher prestimulus heart rate variability (Porges, Stamps, & Walter, 1974). Two other reports using somewhat different measures of heart rate activity in neonates appear also to demonstrate the brief deceleration. Crowell, Kapuniai, and Jones

---

*The data from these studies as represented in Figure 5.3 were obtained by averaging data points from the published individual response curves.

(1985) used *t* statistics of heart rate deviations to assess responses to 63- and 80-dB 4.1-sec tones and Lippsitt and Jacklin (1971) used number of instances of heartbeats below and above prestimulus level to evaluate response to an odor. In all cases the brief initial deceleration was followed by an acceleration above baseline. There is little variation in response shape or latency across age or stimulus duration.

The right panel of Figure 5.3 illustrates the sustained, monophasic deceleratory response with its longer latency to peak. Again the median response for a number of studies of neonates (see legend to Fig. 5.3) is compared with illustrative responses to 75-dB auditory stimuli in awake 6- and 12-week-olds (Rewey, 1973) and to a 50-dB tone in awake adults (K. M. Berg, 1970). Though the latency to the peak of this longer deceleration is somewhat more variable across ages than for the brief response, none of these decelerations is followed by accelerations above baseline. Few examples of responses intermediate between these forms were locatable, suggesting these are representative of a true dichotomy. Further, these two distinct forms of heart rate response are associated with different stimulus conditions. The brief decelerations are typical in sleeping subjects, at least in older infants and adults, and they appear to habituate slowly if at all (Crowell et al., 1985; Schachter et al., 1971; Williams, Schachter, & Tobin, 1967), though the later acceleratory component may. In contrast, the sustained, monophasic decelerations are rarely found in sleeping infants or adults and they habituate rapidly, even in neonates (Adkinson & Berg, 1976). Stimulus duration may play some role since thus far the sustained decelerations have not been reported with very brief stimuli, though both types of responses have been seen with stimuli of longer duration. The sensory modality affected by the stimulus (auditory, visual, vestibular, and olfactory) appears not to determine the response type.

As noted by Graham (1984), the characteristics of the brief deceleration are reminiscent of what Lacey and Lacey (1980) referred to as the *primary* bradycardia. This was a lengthening of the single beat coincident with stimulus onset or the beat immediately following. Most of the work cited above has not examined this single beat separately, but the brief nature of the response suggests it must be occurring within just a beat or two following the stimulus, and the Schachter and colleagues (1971) work seems to confirm this. The results also suggest that this response may be reflecting primarily the transient aspect of the stimulus (Graham, Anthony, & Ziegler, 1983). This hypothesis could be readily explored by employing stimulus manipulations similar to those described in the section on blink responses.

Evidence of Long-Duration Decelerative Responses in Neonates

Though it is clear that sustained decelerations are difficult to elicit in very young infants, a sizable number of studies have reported unequivocal instances of sustained deceleratory responses in awake neonates to stimuli in a variety of modalities. Studies employing visual stimuli were among the first to provide clear evidence. Sameroff, Cashmore, and Dykes (1973) elicited a large (8 beats per minute) sustained deceleration to onset of a 12-by-12 checkerboard and Adkinson and Berg (1976) obtained sustained deceleration to both onset and offset of a field of color. In the latter study, onset responses rapidly habituated with stimulus repetition and dishabituated when a new color matched for brightness was introduced; both habituation and dishabituation are qualities expected of an orienting response. Long-duration decelerations to onsets of auditory stimuli have only been reported more recently for neonates. Clarkson and Berg (1983) and LeVita, Kush, Rothstein, and Brown (1980) obtained sustained, significant decelerations to onsets of pulsing stimuli, and both had some suggestive evidence of deceleratory responses to the offset of these stimuli as well. Decelerations occurred only at offset of the auditory stimulus employed by Porges, Arnold, and Forbes (1973) and the offset of room illumination examined by Porges and associates (1974). In studies of laterally presented "rattle" sounds in Clifton's laboratory (Morrongiello & Clifton, 1984; Morrongiello, Clifton, & Kulig, 1982), neonates turned their heads approximately half the time, and produced sustained deceleratory responses on the remaining trials when the motor activity was minimized. Though these studies provide clear evidence that the response can be elicited under a variety of circumstances, a number of other studies have found the effect only when rather stringent and sometimes contradictory conditions have been specified. Sustained decelerations have been reported to offset of room illumination on later trials for neonates whose resting heart rate variability is high (Porges et al., 1974), to onset and offset of later trials (but not trial 1) of low-frequency tones for higher-birth-weight babies (Stamps, 1980), and to the onset of square wave tone and to rocking (but not a tactile stimulus) only for infants tested after feeding (Pomerleau-Malcuit & Clifton, 1973). These studies provide ample evidence that, although the neonate seems able to produce the response, it does so with great reluctance. It is not yet possible to specify all the conditions necessary to elicit the long-duration deceleration in the neonate, but several important parameters have been identified. These parameters, as described in the next two sections, often influence the cardiac responding in older infants as well as neonates.

Variables Influencing Decelerative Responses

A number of variables that may be expected to influence orienting also appear to affect heart decelerations of neonates as well as older infants and adults. Sokolov (1969) outlines several basic criteria that may be used to identify orienting responses and distinguish them from defense responses: (1) Orienting should be elicited by stimuli of low to moderate intensity, whereas high intensities should produce defensive reactions; (2) orienting is initiated by any change detected in stimulation, including the offset as well as the onset of discrete stimuli of sufficient duration; (3) orienting responses should habituate rapidly, provided the stimulus does not serve as a signal for another important event and the stimulus can be easily "modeled" by the nervous system; and (4) once the stimulus is modeled, discriminable alterations from the model should reelicit the orienting response (dishabituation should occur). Sokolov also provided evidence that orienting should be accompanied by vasodilation of cerebral blood vessels, but attempts to replicate this have not been successful in adults (e.g., K. M. Berg, 1970). As Graham and coworkers have noted (e.g., Graham & Clifton, 1966; Graham & Jackson, 1970). Sokolov's theoretical description of orienting and stimulus modeling allows us to generate some additional criteria that have proven useful, most particularly the sleep–wake state of the infant. The control of deceleratory responding in neonates and infants will be evaluated later in terms of the original and several of the derived criteria.

Subject State

The theoretical relevance of state to orienting can be reasonably inferred since the awake subject is in a state more conducive to optimal information processing and therefore to orienting than is the sleeping subject. We will examine this variable first, since it so strongly influences the evaluation of other parameters. Data on heart rate responses indicate they are profoundly influenced by sleep–wake states at all ages. During all stages of sleep the cardiac response of the adult always has a prominent accelerative component regardless of stimulus intensity though the brief decelerative component may occur as well (W. K. Berg et al., 1975). In contrast, with appropriately moderate stimulus intensities and rise times, the awake adult has a monophasic decelerative response.

The arousal state of the subject is a much greater problem when testing the neonate and young infant, since sleep occurs with much greater frequency and unpredictability than in older subjects, and is under little or no control by the experimenter. Marked state-dependent differences in the form of the cardiac response have been shown to occur in infants 4 months of age (K. M. Berg, W. K. Berg, & Graham, 1971), 6 and 12 weeks of age (Rewey, 1973), and 2–8 weeks of age (Lewis, Bartels, & Goldberg, 1967), and in neonates (Jackson, Kantowitz, & Graham, 1971). Like adults, the sleeping infants in all age groups had responses that included a prominent acceleratory component. During the awake, quiet state sustained monophasic decelerations were seen in infants older than 12 weeks of age, while for younger subjects reactions were not always clearly decelerative, but they lacked the significant acceleration seen during sleep. In view of this it is not surprising that all successful attempts to elicit sustained deceleratory responses in neonates have, with one exception (Pomerleau-Malcuit, Malcuit, & Clifton, 1975), resulted from tests of only alert infants. A subsequent study by Pomerleau and Malcuit (1981) reported decelerations only for awake infants. Thus in the neonate as well as in the more mature subject a relaxed, alert state can be considered a necessary though not sufficient condition for eliciting monophasic, long-duration decelerations associated with orienting.

Although state seems to influence cardiac responses at all ages, evidence suggests that responses of neonates may be more sensitive to this variable than those of older infants. Clifton and colleagues (e.g., Clifton & Nelson, 1976) have found that responses of neonates who are judged to be alert at the time of testing differ depending upon the length of the alert period. Neonates tested at the beginning of an alert period of at least 10 min responded with a deceleration to the initial presentation of an intermittent auditory stimulus while those tested during periods of alertness of less than 5 min had no clear response to the stimulus. Clifton (1977) notes that the same phenomenon can be observed in a study of habituation of cardiac responses in infants 1–4 weeks old by Campos and Brackbill (1973), and Leavitt, Brown, Morse, and Graham (1976) have reported a similar effect for 6-week-olds. Clarkson and Berg (1983) found that, compared with more sustained periods of alertness, transitory alert periods in neonates attenuated but did not eliminate deceleratory responses, an effect also found in 4-month-olds (K. M. Berg et al., 1971). In any case, it is clear that deceleratory cardiac responses of neonates and very young infants are sensitive to even subtle state variations.

Stimulus Intensity

It is obvious that major changes in stimulus intensity are likely to influence cardiac responses as well as any other. However, Sokolov's predictions regarding stimulus intensity were unusual in that they include two nonmonotonic effects on orienting. First, increasing stimulus intensity would increase orienting only up to the point where the defense system became active and would thereafter decline as a result of the increased and competing defense response. Second, at intensities near absolute sensory threshold, orienting should be somewhat greater than that for intensities somewhat above threshold because the poorly perceived threshold-level stimuli would require greater processing activity than weak but clearly perceived stimuli (Graham & Clifton, 1966). There is some evidence for both effects in infants, though there are surprisingly few systematic studies of intensity effects on heart rate in the awake infant.

W. K. Berg and Graham (1970) summarized a number of adult studies and, consistent with Sokolov's theory, found decelerative responses to increase in magnitude up to about 60–70 dB or so and then decline thereafter. The entire function has not been evaluated in infants, but K. M. Berg and colleagues (1971) found that for 4-month-old, awake infants deceleration increased as intensity rose from 50 to 75 dB (such a differentiation was not evident for the accelerative responses occurring during sleep), and W. K. Berg (1975) reported that the increment from 75 to 90 dB caused a shift from deceleration to acceleration in both 4- and 10-month-olds tested while alert. However, the accelerative effect of the louder stimulus was much more consistent in the older group. Kearsley (1973) also reports shifts from deceleration to acceleration in neonates when stimulus intensities reach 90 dB, but the reliability of the effect is not clear in these data. Demonstrations of the second nonmonotonic effect of intensity, the enhancement of orienting to near-threshold stimuli, are even more infrequent. W. K. Berg, Silverstein, Verzijl-Tweed, and Clarkson (1977; see also W. K. Berg, 1985) tested sleeping infants 2–4 months old with 2-sec tones at 40, 45, 50, and 55 dB. The result was a significant quadratic effect of intensity on the initial deceleration very much like that reported by Jackson (1974) for adults. The infants' responses to the lower-intensity 40- and 55-dB tones were greater than at intermediate intensities. The effect was replicated for three different tone frequencies, and found again in a second study. Interpretation of the effect is complicated because stimulation produced the brief form of deceleration described earlier (Fig. 5.3), which does not conform to the orienting concept. To our knowledge, systematic assessment of low-intensity stimuli on heart rate has not been carried out in awake infants.

As previously noted, the range of intensities over which orienting can occur in adults is bounded by the absolute sensory threshold on the lower end and the threshold for defensive responding on the upper end. A variety of research with infants suggests a substantial variation in this range with age and health status, with both the lower and upper bound being affected. Two research groups (Field, 1981; Krafchuk, Tronick, & Clifton, 1983) have offered the hypothesis that prematurely born infants, especially ones at higher risk, have a very narrow window for orienting as a combined result of an elevated threshold for orienting and a lowered threshold for defensive responses. This hypothesis can nicely account for the contradictory reports of both hypo- and hyperreactivity in prematures. The hyporesponsivity may result from the elevation of orienting threshold, and hyperresponsivity may be due to the lowered defensive threshold (Krafchuk et al., 1983). It has the important implication that the premature will optimally process stimuli only when they are carefully presented within a narrow intensity range. The difficulty with the hypothesis is that it is based solely on studies that found accelerative responses in sleeping prematures. Given the difficulty in obtaining decelerative responding from full-term neonates, and the great percentage of time prematures sleep, it is not surprising that most investigations of premature cardiac activity report only accelerative responses.

Despite the lack of direct validation of this hypothesis regarding premature infant orienting, we believe that developmental changes in orienting and defense responses can be usefully conceived of in terms of changes in the orienting window. In particular, we suggest that the upper and lower intensity boundaries for orienting may vary independently as a function of normal development, and that the premature data could represent the lower developmental extreme of that function. With regard to the upper boundary, the zone where orienting shifts to defensive responding, the data reviewed earlier on orienting responses in neonates certainly suggest a lower boundary than that for older infants. W. K. Berg (1975) suggested that this boundary did increase over the first few months of life, providing an increased range over which orienting could occur, and thereafter began to decline again to an intermediate level. This decline in the range of stimuli to which orienting was exhibited was attributed to a decrease in the threshold for defenselike responding. In Figure 5.4 the attenuated response to the 90-dB stimulus by 4-month-olds resulted not from overall smaller responding, but from a mixture of acceleration under some conditions and large decelerations under others. In contrast, the 10-month-olds were unvarying in their accelerative response to this stimulus. Almost no data exist to evaluate possible changes in the lower bound of orienting, though stimulus thresholds are generally reported to be at least somewhat elevated during the neonatal period (Aslin, this volume). The work cited earlier by W. K. Berg and others (1977) hints of an elevated threshold for orienting when compared with the Jackson (1974) adult work, but parametric studies with awake infants will be required to provide such information. Thus the hypothesis must remain speculative, but it proposes that mechanisms controlling orienting are responsive to a narrow range of stimuli early in ontogeny, especially so in the premature. In the full-term infant the window for orienting is constrained at both the lower and upper bounds, but soon the upper boundary begins to rise (i.e., the threshold for the defense response increases), and the lower boundary may possibly decrease. This process continues throughout the first half-year of life or so, but thereafter, the defense threshold begins to decrease once again. Of course, this hypothesis has few data in support of it as yet, but it is testable and could integrate a good deal of evidence on information gathering and protective processes early in life.

Additional lines of support for the hypothesis are available if the hypothesis were broadened to include variables other than stimulus intensity. For example, one might suggest that the orienting window of the neonate is restricted not only to optimal intensity levels, but also to optimal levels of transient input or complexity. The results reported by Clarkson and Berg (1983) are consistent with this view. McGuire and Turkewitz (1983) took a similar tack when examining Schneirla's (1959) concepts of approach and withdrawal processes, notions quite similar to orienting and

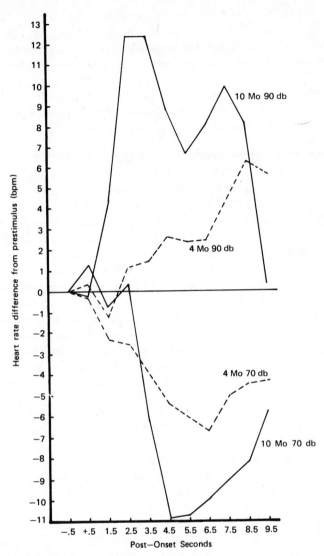

Figure 5.4. Cardiac rate response to 2-sec bursts of white noise at 70 and 90 dBA (re .0002 microbar) of infants 4 and 10 months of age.

defense responses. They argued that dimensions such as contour density, stimulus size, and number of stimulus elements could be usefully included in the notion of effective intensity. In doing so, they were able to account for a substantial set of data. The work demonstrating that accelerative heart rate responses accompany the development in the second half-year of life of negative reactions to visual cliff (Schwartz, Campos, & Baisel, 1973), presence of a stranger (Campos, Emde, & Gaensbauer, 1975; Waters, Matas, & Sroufe, 1975), and masks covering a mother's face (Sroufe, Waters, & Matas, 1974) may also fit with a multidimensional lowering of the defensive response threshold during this period of development.

Relating Orienting to the Transient–Sustained Dichotomy

A cornerstone of Sokolov's concept of the orienting response is that it occurs as a result of stimulus change. Since the change can occur either as an increase (onset) or decrease (offset) in stimulation, we should expect that cardiac deceleration could be initiated in both circumstances. Further, manipulations of these transitions, such as by altering the rise or fall time of an auditory stimulus or by producing multiple transitions with a pulse train of stimulation, should alter the orienting response. However, stimulus transitions are also important to the startle system, as was noted in the previous section, and this response is not completely compatible with orienting. Graham (1979) has directly addressed the distinctions among orienting, defense responding, and startle, and more recently has proposed a general organization to encompass these processes (Graham, 1984). The proposal is that the transient–sustained dichotomy described earlier in the context of the startle response may be usefully conceived of as orthogonal to systems adapted for processing intense or low to moderate stimulation levels. In her 1984 chapter, Graham proposed a two-by-two organization as shown in Table 5.1. In this view, orienting and defense responses are both aspects of the sustained processing system, differentiated by the intensity of the stimulus involved. Startle, as described earlier, is considered to be a transient processing system invoked when stimulus increases are sufficiently high. Most important for the present concern, however, is the fourth, and heretofore undefined, component of this organization, the nonstartle transient-detecting response (TDR). The TDR would be engaged by transient aspects of a stimulus but would be be superseded by the startle response when the threshold for this response was exceeded. It is the TDR that Graham proposes is responsible for the brief, slowly habituating heart rate decelerations shown in the left panel of Figure 5.3

TABLE 5.1.   A Two-by-Two Organization of Transient Versus Sustained Processing Systems and High-Versus Low-Intensity Stimulation[a]

	High Intensity	Low Intensity
Transient processing	*Startle*	*Transient detection response (TDR)*
	Short latency, brief response.	Short latency, brief response
	HR acceleration	HR deceleration
	Rapid habituation	Slow habituation
	May occur in sleep and awake states	May occur in sleep and perhaps awake states
Sustained processing	*Defense response*	*Orienting response*
	Longer latency, sustained response	Longer latency, sustained response
	HR acceleration	HR deceleration
	Slow habituation	Rapid habituation
	May occur in sleep and awake states	Occurs in awake states

Source: From "An Affair of the Heart" by F. K. Graham, in M. G. H. Coles, J. R. Jennings, and J. Stern (Eds.), *Psychophysiology: A Festschrift for John and Beatrice Lacey.* Copyright 1984 by Van Nostrand Reinhold. Adapted by permission.
[a]The predicted response in each of the four conditions is shown in italics, and the characteristics of that response are listed below it.

(Graham, 1984). Graham concurs with our view that only the more extended decelerations appear clearly to qualify as cardiac components of orienting, and places such responses into the low-intensity, sustained processing quadrant of the model.

Based on this theoretical construct and the data presented in Figure 5.3, we would be obliged to infer that the most significant developmental change occurs in the *sustained* processing system, at least as far as lower-intensity stimuli are concerned, since it is the sustained decelerations associated with orienting that show the dramatic development in the first few months of life. The brief deceleration, consistent with the TDR, appears rather similar for neonates, young infants, and adults. However, as described earlier, Graham has provided considerable evidence based on the startle response and its inhibition that it is the transient rather than the sustained processing system that undergoes the principal developmental change.

There are several ways in which this apparent contradiction can be resolved. One possibility is that rapid developmental changes are occurring in the two diagonally opposite quadrants of Table 5.1: (1) the transient system associated with higher intensities, the startle system; and (2) the sustained system associated with the lower-intensity system, the orienting response. Note from Table 5.1 that, though this grouping may seem awkward, only these two systems share the characteristic of rapid habituation. Nonetheless, at least the appearance of greater parsimony is achieved with Graham's focus on development occurring primarily within the transient system. This concept can be retained if one assumes that the entire orienting sequence requires *both* transient and sustained systems from the low-intensity side; the transient system to trigger the response and the sustained system to provide processing of the information available.* Immaturity in the transient processing system would limit the initiation of orienting, but once initiated, should not be a factor in evaluating information in any sustained component of a stimulus. The influence on infant heart rate of stimulus transitions and their manipulation and the sustained component information will be evaluated in the next two sections.

Influence of the Transient Component of a Stimulus

The transient component of a stimulus occurs at that point where there is a rapid shift in stimulus intensity, either increasing or decreasing. The effects of varying stimulus transients have been investigated in three ways: by comparing the responses at onset and offset of a sustained stimulus; by comparing stimuli with a single on and off with those having a series of such transitions (a pulse train); and by varying how abruptly the intensity transitions take place (the rise and fall times). Responses occurring to the offset of a sustained stimulus provide very important support for the argument that orienting in infants is reflected in cardiac deceleration. Unlike stimulus onset, offset of a stimulus is a change that could not result in a defense response, since the sustained stimulation that follows offset is at or near zero. Nor could it result in startle since this system is sensitive only to transients involving intensity increases. At all ages tested, awake infants consistently demonstrate decelerative responses to the offset of a sufficiently long continuous stimulus. Several studies have found monophasic bradycardia to offset of auditory and visual stimuli

---

*The segregation of orienting into an initiation component and an information-processing component seems to parallel the *attention-getting* and *attention-holding* processes proposed by Cohen (1972, 1973) for the visual system.

uninterrupted for 18–20 sec with neonates (Adkinson & Berg, 1976), 10-week-olds (Davies, 1982, 1985), and 12-week olds (Rewey, 1973). With stimuli much shorter than 15 sec or so it may be difficult to detect offset responses, since deceleratory offset responses may be masked by ongoing recovery from the earlier deceleratory response. Nonetheless, using 10-sec tones, both Clifton and Meyers (1969) and Berg (1972) report that 4-month-olds show evidence of decelerative responses to offset of continuous tones, and Bohlin, Lindhagen, and Hagekull (1981) find the effect in infants 7 months old, but not those 3–4 months. In some cases, offset responses have been evident even when onsets did not produce deceleration (e.g., Porges et al., 1974).

When the stimulus is a pulse train, offset is signaled not by a transient but by the lack of one. It is perhaps not surprising, therefore, that responses to offset of these stimuli are more difficult to produce. Most of the studies above (Berg, 1972; Bohlin et al., 1981; Clifton & Meyer, 1969; Davies, 1985; Rewey, 1973) reporting offset responses to continuous stimuli also employed pulsed stimuli matched for overall duration and failed to find any significant response to the termination of these stimuli. The exceptions to this pattern come from Leavitt and colleagues (1976) and LeVita and others (1980), who do find offset decelerations with a pulsed stimulus, but in both cases the offset occurred after 4 min or more of the pulsing pattern. Davies (1985) found no offset response to a stimulus pulsing for 1 min.

A pulse train stimulus provides a series of transients within a short period of time. If it is the case that infants are inefficient in processing transients, as Graham and others (1983) have argued, then the repeated presentation of transients should increase the likelihood or magnitude of the decelerative response provided the transient influences can summate. This is just what is reported in nearly all of the studies cited above as well as others that compared pulsed and continuous stimuli (Berg, 1972; Bohlin et al., 1981; Clarkson & Berg, 1983; Clifton & Meyers, 1969). There is, however, evidence of interactions with age. With neonates, only the multiple onsets appear to be able to produce deceleration in the case of auditory stimuli. At older ages, continuous auditory stimuli begin to produce deceleratory responding, but pulsed stimuli produce larger responses. Finally, there is some evidence that developmentally the effectiveness of the continuous stimulus catches up with that of pulsed ones, since Bohlin and colleagues (1981) show a decline in the differences in response magnitude for the two stimulus types in their older age groups. This may be due to ceiling effects at the older ages. The effectiveness of pulsing stimuli is apparently not limited to the decelerative response since Miller and Byrne (1983) report that accelerative responses elicited from sleeping neonates were significantly extended when pulsed speech was employed.

Graham and others (1983) have noted one exception to this pattern that could be important. The Clarkson and Berg (1983) study of heart rate responses in alert neonates varied the spectral complexity of the stimulus (pure tone, square wave tone, and synthesized vowel) as well as the temporal pattern (pulsed and continuous) in a counterbalanced, within-subject design. All three spectral complexities of pulsed stimuli produced deceleration, though only for the most complex one, the vowel sound, was the response significant. Onset of the continuous square wave and vowel stimuli produced significant acceleration, more so for the vowel, but the pure tone produced an extended deceleration. Clarkson and Berg argued that the deceleration to the latter stimulus was probably anomalous since the shape of the response was unusual: a slow decline that never began a return toward baseline in the 14-sec analysis interval. The other continuous stimuli produced accelerations typical in form and magnitude. The Graham and associates position is that the decelerative response to the simple, continuous tone was an example of an orienting response. It occurred, in their view, because neonates can respond adequately to a single transient if it has a controlled, slow onset, which was the case with these stimuli. Drawing a parallel to the work with visual stimuli, such as that reported by Karmel and Maisel (1975), they suggest that the neonates respond optimally to simple stimuli, but with age the preference shifts to greater complexity. They suggest that the accelerative responses Clarkson and Berg report for the continuous square wave and vowel stimuli were probably a result of uncontrolled transients inherent in the stimuli, and these transients were capable of eliciting startle responses and the associated accelerative reaction.

For several reasons we do not feel that this interpretation of the responding to continuous tones is adequate. First, previous attempts to elicit deceleration with controlled onset, pure tones in awake neonates have been unsuccessful (Graham & Jackson, 1970; Jackson et al., 1971). Also, the recent data evaluating neonate startle (Blumenthal, 1985) indicate that the 75-dB complex stimuli Clarkson and Berg employed were probably some 20–30 dB or more below the neonate's startle threshold. And finally, any uncontrolled transients in these spectrally complex stimuli should mitigate against orienting in pulsed as well as continuous stimuli, but Clarkson and Berg found the largest decelerations in response to pulsed stimuli. We would suggest either that the more spectrally complex sounds were closer to the optimal level of complexity than were pure tones or that the transients in the spectrally complex stimuli assisted in driving the sluggish neonate TDR needed to initiate an orienting response. In summary, we continue to argue that continuous stimuli are unlikely to be effective in eliciting orienting in neonates since single, widely separated transients are not usually going to be able to overcome the poor handling of transients by the immature nervous system.

One reason the transient processing of the infant may be deficient is the lack of synchrony in firing among neurons sensitive to onsets and offsets, perhaps as a result of poorly or unevenly myelinated neurons (Yakovlev & Lecours, 1967). Poor synchrony would result in reduced responding because it would decrease the likelihood of such neurons producing temporal and spatial summation in those neurons with which they synapse. If this is the case, one would expect that stimuli with rapid rise times would produce better synchrony than those with slower rise times, and therefore be more likely to elicit responding in transient sensitive systems. The rise time variable has been studied extensively in animal and adult human research, but few studies have examined its influence with infants. The Blumenthal (1982) data described previously demonstrated that shorter rise times were more likely to elicit startle in 6-week-olds, and that response magnitude dropped off quite rapidly as rise time was lengthened.

A different picture is suggested when lower-intensity stimuli are employed, those that are below the startle threshold and that could elicit the TDR or orienting. Graham and colleagues (e.g., Graham et al., 1983) argue that for the neonate it would be the slowly rising, controlled-onset stimuli that would be more effective because the young infants are insensitive to rapid transients. In support of this, they present evidence from two parallel studies of intensity and rise time effects with sleeping neonates and older infants. Only stimuli with slower rise times (300 msec) produce accelerative responses in neonates, whereas the short rise time stimuli were more effective in eliciting acceleration in the older sleeping infants. In neither age group was the effect significant with awake infants. Miller and Byrne (1983) report larger accelerative responses in sleeping neonates for slow vowel transitions (500 msec) than when the transitions were nearly instantaneous. In awake neonates, Kearsley (1973) reported no consistent effect of rise time on heart rate, but slow rise time stimuli were more likely to elicit widening of the eye opening, a response consistent with orienting. Unfortunately, these studies are difficult to interpret in terms of neonates' ability to orient since rise time effects have been reported only for accelerative responses in sleeping neonates. Clearly this is an area in need of further empirical work.

Influence of Amount of Information in the Sustained Portion of the Stimulus

The research described in the previous section is consistent with the view that the transient aspect of the stimulus is important, at least for initiating the orienting response. But for orienting, Graham's orthogonal organization of intensity and transient–sustained effects places emphasis on the importance of the sustained aspects of the stimulus. The quantity and quality of information inherent in a stimulus can only be manipulated to any great extent during the sustained portion of the stimulus. In this section we will consider a number of variables that may be considered as manipulations of stimulus information.

In the visual domain, a number of variables that have been shown to have a potent effect on visual orientation also appear to exert an effect on cardiac deceleration. Both visual fixation and amplitude of visual event-related potentials show an inverted-U-shaped relationship with the number and size of checks in a checkerboard stimulus. Based on this and further work, Karmel (e.g., Karmel & Maisel, 1975) interprets these data in terms of the variable, contour density, which could also be considered density of visual information. J. Keen (1974) reported more extended fixation and larger and longer decelerations for longer-contour stimuli (24-by-24 checkerboards) than for shorter ones (4-by-4 checkerboards). The effect was especially marked on the initial trial block. McCall and Kagan (1967) employed random polygons and found that both visual fixation and the number of infants decelerating were inverted-U-shaped functions of perimeter length, the analog to Karmel's contour length. McCall and Melson (1970) also reported the incidence of decelerations and visual fixation to covary with changes in contour length.

A variety of evidence also points to the preference for curved lines over straight lines for infants 2 months and older (Fantz, Fagan, & Miranda, 1975), and a perhaps related preference for faces. Though there have been no direct tests of heart rate responses to curved versus straight lines, McCall and Kagan (1967) found significantly less fixation and reduced heart rate deceleration in 4-month-olds to straight-lined polygons than to a variety of schematic and real faces. Field (1979) reports both longer looking and lower heart rate levels during a 3-min period of a still, schematic face (Raggedy Ann) than to the same face when moving or to the active mother's face. Both studies are consistent with a preference for distinct curved lines rather than the social value of a face per se. Finally, in a number of studies Lewis and coworkers have found both heart rate and visual fixation to covary directly with the "complexity" of a pattern of blinking lights (Kagan & Lewis, 1965; Lewis,

Kagan, Campbell, & Kalafat, 1966) and number of items (Lewis, Wilson & Baumel, 1971). Overall, the results seem to suggest that cardiac and visual fixation components of orienting are influenced similarly by a number of parameters of visual stimuli. However, there have been few attempts to examine visual orienting and cardiac responding in infants less than 3 months of age.

The manipulation of auditory complexity has principally involved variation in the number and organization of different spectral (frequency) components in a stimulus. In this domain, a sine wave (pure tone) stimulus would be the simplest since it has a single spectral component. At the opposite extreme would be white noise, which includes all spectral components. A substantial body of data indicates that with neonates, at least, pure tone stimuli are less effective in eliciting electrophysiological responding than are intensity-matched stimuli having a wider bandwidth. Pure tones have been demonstrated as less effective in producing accelerative cardiac responses than square wave and synthetic speech stimuli (Clarkson & Berg, 1983), two- or three-tone chords (Turkewitz, Birch, & Cooper, 1972a), and narrowband noise (Schulman, 1973). Similar effects have been reported for event-related potential and electromyographic reactions (Hutt, Bernuth, Lenard, Hutt, & Prechtl, 1968; Lenard, Bernuth, & Hutt, 1969). These results would be consistent with the typical psychoacoustic finding that wider-band stimuli are perceived as louder than narrower ones. All of the infant data cited are directed toward the neonate, and only Clarkson and Berg (1983) examine this dimension for decelerative cardiac responses. They report that increasing bandwidth increases the amplitude of the response, regardless of its direction, deceleration, or acceleration. There is need to explore this domain in older infants where deceleration is more prevalent.

One could also manipulate spectral variation over time, such as providing a sequence of different tones (e.g., a melody) rather than a repetition of the same tone. Complexity of the auditory stimulus could also be varied by altering the temporal aspects of the stimulus such as the rate or evenness with which tone pulses are given. Earlier, continuous, and pulsed stimuli were contrasted in terms of number of transients. It could be argued that this also varies the amount of information, thereby confounding transient and sustained manipulations. Rewey (1973) included several of these factors by comparing heart rate responses to a continuous pure tone with an irregularly pulsing, two-tone chord stimulus, referring to the latter as the complex stimulus. This more complex stimulus enhanced decelerative responses in awake 6-week-old but not 12-week-old infants. Independent manipulation of temporal and spectral variables will be required to clarify the contributions of transient and sustained effects of stimulation.

Perinatal Events and Risk Factors

The events associated with birth, including physical stress, adaptation to an independent existence, and recovery from maternal medication, and the various factors that can put an infant at risk for brain damage, would not be expected to provide optimal conditions for the perceiving and processing of sensory stimulation. This consideration has led a number of investigators to examine whether perinatal events and risk factors might have temporary or extended effects on orienting responses.

Evidence of temporary influence of perinatal events has led to what might be called the "birthday" effect. Adkinson and Berg (1976) reported sustained decelerations to visual stimuli only in infants older than the median sample age of 35 hours, and with pulsed auditory stimuli, LeVita and others (1980) found significantly larger decelerations for the older neonates using a similar age split. Similarly, Friedman (1972) reported that the visual fixation responses of 2-day-old neonates habituated, but those of babies tested on the day of birth did not. Indirect confirmation of these findings comes from Porges's laboratory. In several studies Porges and colleagues have reported decelerations in neonates who have higher than the median prestimulus heart rate variance. However, in two of the three reports (Arnold & Porges, 1972; Porges et al., 1973), prestimulus heart rate variability was greater on the second day of life. This led Adkinson and Berg (1976) to suggest that it was not the heart rate variance but the time since birth that was critical. In any case, both the Adkinson and Berg and the Porges reports attributed the birthday effect to recovery from undetermined events associated with the birth process rather than to any extraordinary neural maturation occurring in the brief period following birth, as was proposed by Friedman (1972). Since evidence indicates that birthday effects occur in both the autonomically ennervated cardiac system and the somatically ennervated oculomotor system, it is likely that the influence is centrally rather than peripherally mediated. These results also have practical importance. With many hospitals shortening the length of nursery care, sometimes to 24 hr or less, the influence of perinatal factors will make it increasingly difficult to test adequately for orienting in neonates.

A number of studies of the effects of risk factors on heart rate, especially those of medical condition, birth weight, and prematurity, have been reported (see Von Bargen, 1983, for a review). Because of the difficulty in obtaining data from awake and alert premature infants near or before the age at which they would have normally been born, only a few studies have been able to provide a clear and direct test of orienting ability in this group. Schulman (1968, 1969) tested 1- to 7-week-old low-birth-weight and prematurely born infants who were otherwise relatively free from negative indications (low risk), and a similar group who had additional medical problems (high risk). An 80-dB buzzer presented for 10 trials elicited deceleration only in the low-risk group. In the second study four low-risk preterm infants were tested longitudinally and found first to exhibit deceleration when they were 33–36 weeks of conceptual age, 7–10 weeks of postnatal age. This finding was surprising because of the difficulty in eliciting deceleration in even full-term infants at this postnatal age, especially with a stimulus of the intensity and quality employed, and because responses were averaged over 10 trials. Subsequently, Berkson, Wasserman, and Behrman (1974) attempted to replicate closely Schulman's procedures, including use of the same buzzer device, and failed to find even a brief deceleration in either high- or low-risk subjects up to 5 weeks of postnatal age. Three studies evaluated older prematures at 3 months (Fox & Lewis, 1983) and 5 months (O'Conner, 1980) of age relative to their expected date of birth. They found that either synthetic speech or pure tones were capable of eliciting decelerative responses in prematures born with or without medical difficulties, and that these responses did not differ from those elicited from full-term infants matched on conceptual age. In contrast, Field (1979) finds longer visual fixations and larger deceleratory reactions to a variety of face stimuli in 3 month old infants born 8 weeks premature. However, this latter study differed from the former ones in that it examined heart rate averaged over 3-min viewing periods rather than moment-by-moment phasic changes.

Two studies report that even for full-term infants birth weight may influence cardiac responding. Both LeVita et al. (1980) and Stamps (1980) suggest that within the normal weight range lower-weight infants may be less likely to orient than higher-birth-weight infants. However, LeVita and associates found this true only for responses to changes occurring amidst ongoing periods of stimulation, not to the initial stimulus onset, and Stamps based his conclusions on groups of four subjects and did not find consistent decelerations in either group.

Concomitant Somatic and Sucking Activity

As Obrist (1976) has reminded us, the primary function of the cardiovascular system is not to reflect attentional influences, but to meet the varying metabolic demands of the body. Therefore, it should be expected that changes in somatic activity would be one of the important factors influencing heart rate and other cardiovascular variables, and must be carefully considered when evaluating circumstances aimed toward eliciting the cardiac decelerative component of orienting. Obrist and colleagues (e.g., Obrist, 1976) have provided ample evidence of this cardiac–somatic relationship in adults and older children. If one proposes that it is the development of autonomic control of the heart that produces the age-related changes in heart rate response form, then it is reasonable to presume that this increase in ANS control should be reflected in development of the cardiac–somatic relationship.

The most detailed evidence on cardiac–somatic relationships in infants stems from studies of heart rate and sucking activity. In a series of studies in neonates, Lipsitt, Crook, and colleagues reported increased heart rate levels during both nutritive and nonnutritive sucking bursts compared to nonsucking periods. Field, Clifton, and colleagues (Field, Dempsey, Hatch, Ting, & Clifton, 1979; Nelson, Clifton, Dowd, & Field, 1978) confirmed this result, and showed that it also pertained to a prematurely born group tested at a conceptual age of 37 weeks (24 days after their birth). This pattern clearly suggested a cardiac–somatic coupling, but when the Lipsitt and Crook group compared different levels of fluid sweetness, they found that sweeter fluids produced higher levels of heart rate even though sucking rates within a sucking burst were slower (e.g., Ashmead, Reilly, & Lipsitt, 1980; Crook & Lipsitt, 1976; Lipsitt, Reilly, Butcher, & Greenwood, 1976). Apparently nonsomatic factors, possibly the hedonic effects of the fluid, can modulate the overall somatic influences of the sucking activity.

Other types of stimuli may be able to alter the somatic effects of sucking on neonatal heart rate, but they appear to be far less effective than sweetening a fluid. In the Nelson and colleagues (1978) study, when an auditory stimulus that had proved effective in eliciting deceleration in nonsucking infants was presented at predetermined points in the sucking bursts, no influence of the stimulus could be detected; that is, heart rate changes that occurred appeared to be the same as those that would have resulted during a sucking burst alone. Gregg, Clifton, and Haith (1976) more directly compared the effects of stimulation in the presence and absence of sucking in a study of visual tracking. Here, neonates who were sucking on a pacifier had accelerative heart rates while nonsucking infants did not. Clarkson and Berg (1983) report that presence of a pacifier (a nonnutritive sucking opportunity) attenuated but did not eliminate a decelerative response in neonates.

More recently, interactions of heart rate and more gross somatic behaviors have also been examined in neonates. Work with awake, alert neonates by Morrongiello and Clifton (Morrongiello & Clifton, 1984; Morrongiello et al., 1982) indicates that laterally presented complex sounds, which elicit head turns on some trials but not on others, will also elicit heart rate deceleration but only in the absence of a head turn. When present, the decelerations were of the long, monophasic type described in Figure 5.3, and were substantial in size (8–12 bpm). In the presence of a head turn, heart rate acceleration occurred coincident with the initiation of the overt behavior. In sleeping neonates, Pomerleau and Malcuit report similar effects on heart rate for presence or absence of a head turn elicited by stroking of the cheek (Pomerleau-Malcuit et al., 1975) and for presence or absence of gross body movements elicited by a rocking stimulus (Pomerleau & Malcuit, 1981). However, only accelerations were obtained in response to an ear pinch regardless of head turning (Pomerleau-Malcuit et al., 1975).

The studies just described that categorize trials on the basis of magnitude of motor activity share a common problem when attempting to interpret the heart rate changes. The selection process may capitalize on variations in motor activity unrelated to the presentation of the stimulus. For trials classified as *decreased movement* the bias would be toward decelerative responses. The same would be true for trials classified as *no motor activity*, if the trial onset interrupted ongoing, prestimulus motor activity. This potential source of bias could explain some surprising reports of decelerative responses in sleeping neonates for trials on which motor activity was judged absent following stimulus onset (e.g., Pomerleau & Malcuit, 1981; Pomerleau-Malcuit et al., 1975), and it indicates the need for caution in interpreting such responses, even in awake neonates where decelerative responses are more likely (e.g., Morrongiello & Clifton, 1984; Morrongiello et al., 1982). What is needed is a comparison of heart rate during both stimulus and pseudo-stimulus periods using the same motor activity selection criteria.

Whatever potency sucking and other somatic activity have for disrupting deceleratory heart rate responses in newborns, it appears largely to have dissipated by about 9 weeks of age. Brown, Leavitt, and Graham (1977) reported significant deceleration in 9-week-olds even for a subgroup of subjects who sucked throughout the test session, as did Morrongiello & Clifton (1984) when testing 5-month-olds who turned their heads toward a laterally presented sound. This increased likelihood of decelerative responding in the presence of ongoing motor activity does not appear to result from a decrease in the cardiac–somatic coupling per se. In the Brown and colleagues study, they found heart rate was still coupled to sucking rates, and correlations between the two measures were about the same for the 6-week-old and 9-week-old subjects tested in this study as for the neonates tested in Nelson and others (1978). Also, judging from published curves, the range over which heart rate fluctuates during sucking bursts and pauses remains at about $+/-5$ beats per minute during the first 9 weeks (Brown et al., 1977, Fig. 2; Nelson et al., 1978, Fig. 2 & Fig. 3). Apparently, the basic cardiac–somatic relationship remains fairly constant; what seems to change is the extent to which external stimuli can compete with it for the control of heart rate.

Habituation and Dishabituation

The occurrence of habituation and dishabituation can indicate fundamental cognitive processes and provide evidence of basic sensory capacity. In the mature subject, orienting responses to nonsignal stimuli (those stimuli not signaling significant events through prior experience or genetic programming) will, in most circumstances, rapidly habituate as the stimulus is presented repeatedly. However, the habituation phenomenon is not limited to orienting responses. Though not always rapid, habituation does occur for startle and other reflexes (e.g., Graham et al., 1983) and under limited circumstances can occur for defense responses as well (Graham & Clifton, 1966; Sokolov, 1960). Habituation has been demonstrated throughout the range of phylogeny (Ratner, 1970), at every level of the nervous system (Thompson & Spencer, 1966), and across all age levels in humans. In its many formats and guises, the habituation and dishabituation paradigm is probably the procedure most often employed in the experimental study of human infant behavior. However, due to limitations of space, discussion will be restricted to questions closely related to the evaluation of orienting and attentional development. These include the importance of cortical structures and arousal states, and the recent work on habituation of heart rate activity in the premature infant. The influence of stimulus type as well as other questions will not be considered in detail, but may be found in work devoted to the topic of habituation in infants (Clifton & Nelson, 1976; Jeffrey & Cohen, 1971).

For our purposes, the definition of habituation only as a decrement in responding with repeated stimulus presentation is not wholly adequate. Using this definition, other phenomena such as adaptation occurring at the level of the sensory receptor and fatigue of response effectors are confounded with the more selective and centrally mediated process we propose to examine. The required addition to the simple definition is that the observed response decrement be mediated by the central nervous system and be specific to the stimulus being tested. The requirement of central nervous system mediation eliminates processes such as receptor adaptation, which can also be stimulus specific. The stimulus specificity requirement means that a response decrement resulting from a generalized attenuation of responding to all stimuli, such as might occur when arousal state changes, would not qualify as habituation (Hutt, Lenard, & Prechtl, 1969). These two restrictions also conform to Sokolov's (1960, 1963) concepts of the neuronal model as the process that generates the rapid habituation of orienting. Thompson and Spencer (1966) have described habituation characteristics, some of which can be used as tests for receptor adaptation and effector fatigue, but it appears that the only adequate test of the stimulus specificity is presentation of a different stimulus than that used during habituation, a procedure often referred to as a dishabituation paradigm.

Dishabituation, the increase in response that may be produced following a habituation series, has been assessed with two different paradigms. Unfortunately, the dishabituation obtained in these two procedures may evolve from two different phenomena. In the procedure classically used in the animal literature, a dishabituation stimulus, usually rather intense, is presented following the presentation of a series of habituation stimuli. Thereafter, the stimulus used during habituation is presented once again. Dishabituation effects are evaluated by assessing the response difference to the same stimulus when presented just prior to and following the dishabituating stimulus. In this procedure, response to the dishabituating stimulus itself is not a measure of dishabituation. Thompson and Spencer (1966) have argued that dishabituation occurring in this paradigm results from an independent sensitization action that is evoked by the dishabituation stimulus. Once produced, the sensitization decays slowly, during which time it can enhance responses to any stimulus that may occur. As such, dishabituation produced in this manner would not adequately test stimulus specificity since the sensitizing process would not be selective to the habituation stimulus. The second procedure, one more commonly used in infant research, is to follow the series of habituation stimuli with one or more presentations of a different or "novel" stimulus, typically one equivalent in response effectiveness to that used for habituation if tested prior to any habituation. In this case, dishabituation is inferred from an increased response to the new stimulus compared to the response to the last in the series of habituating stimuli. Though interpretation of such results is complicated by possible generalization of habituation to the dishabituation stimulus (Graham, 1973), they provide the best test of stimulus specificity of a "model" generated during habituation. With proper choice of stimuli, the procedure provides a powerful method for testing stimulus discrimination abilities, as well (e.g., W. K. Berg, 1972).

Cortical and Other Forebrain Involvement

Much of the interest in habituation can be attributed to the suggestion by Sokolov (1963) and others that the cortex was involved in the process. If true, tests of habituation might provide a way to track and assess the myelination and dendritic arborization of cortex that continues for some time after birth in the normal infant (Conel, 1952; Dobbing & Sands, 1973), and possibly indicate cortical dysfunction in the infant at risk. However, a point often ignored is that Sokolov proposed the cortical modeling system only for the habituation of the orienting response. This is an important caveat, since there are numerous demonstrations of habituation in the absence of cortex for given response systems. There are demonstrations of habituation in many species that have no cortex (Ratner, 1970) and in animal preparations in whom normally present cortex has been surgically removed, and even in the single cells of the isolated spinal cords of cats. In the latter work, Groves and Thompson (1970) proposed that this habituation occurs right at the synapse, and that the same may be true for responses mediated at higher levels of the nervous system.

Sokolov's model of habituation of orienting proposes that on each stimulus presentation characteristics of the stimulus are extracted and stored in the cortex. With continued stimulus presentation this information accumulates into an increasingly accurate representation of the stimulus, this representation referred to as the neuronal model. In Sokolov's theory, when a stimulus is presented, it is compared with the existing model in the cortex. To the extent that there is a match between them, the orienting response is inhibited and over trials habituation occurs as a result. When a mismatch occurs, such as when a novel stimulus is presented, the orienting response is allowed to occur uninhibited. Though it is perhaps possible to reconcile the Thompson view with that of Sokolov, the complex level of information that the model system appears able to maintain and the active inhibitory nature of Sokolov's concept of habituation suggest it would be difficult to conceptualize the neuronal model only in terms of synaptic adaptation. Although Sokolov emphasized the cortex as the site of the model, others (e.g., Graham & Jackson, 1970) have proposed that limbic structures such as the hippocampus play an important role.

The evidence for orienting does appear to support the functional nature of Sokolov's model comparator system in humans (e.g., Graham, 1973), but there is increasing evidence from both animal and human work that neither cortex nor other forebrain structures are *necessary* for rapid habituation of orienting. Evidence supporting the role of cortex comes from: (1) some Russian studies cited by Sokolov (1963) indicating disruption of orienting response habituation with cortical damage; (2) dishabituation produced by the change in a semantic aspect of visually presented words (Siddle & Spinks, 1979), which presumably requires cortical input; and (3) the often-cited study by Brackbill (1971), which found little habituation in an anencephalic infant.

The subject of Brackbill's research was a 3-month-old infant with an intact cerebellum and brain stem but no telecephalon (status of midbrain and diencephalon are not noted). The arousal state of the infant could not be determined except to distinguish REM and non-REM periods. Habituation was tested in three sessions by examining motor reactions to an 80-dB stimulus presented at 20-, 30-, or 40-sec intervals. A habituation criterion of 5 consecutive no-response trials was not reached in any of the 180–200 trial sessions even though similarly tested 2- to 28-day normal infants reached such a criterion in an average of 22–23 trials. The conclusion drawn was that, while the cortex may not be important in elicitation of the orienting response, it is essential to its inhibition. Since there is no certain evidence that orienting rather than startle or defense responses was elicited and the infant may have lost forebrain structures other than cortex, this conclusion should be viewed cautiously.

Graham et al. (1978) provided the first human data clearly demonstrating the considerable ability of lower brain structures to mediate what appear to be cardiac components of orienting that both habituate with stimulus repetition and dishabituate with stimulus change. Like Brackbill (1971) they tested an anencephalic infant, but when only 3–6 weeks of age. An autopsy performed after the infant's death indicated that the brain was no more complete and perhaps even less so than that of the infant tested by Brackbill. Brain weight was 11 percent of the expected value and only the brain stem and cerebellum were grossly normal, though they too were underdeveloped. As with the Brackbill subject, state was difficult to assess, but was predominantly REM. Over a number of test sessions, a total of 330 auditory stimuli were presented, with various frequencies and qualities evaluated in different sessions. Virtually all stimuli elicited sustained heart rate decelerations comparable to those in older, normal infants. With stimulus repetition, the deceleratory responses habituated to zero in only 7 or 8 trials, and were reelicited with a change in stimulus. The magnitude of the cardiac response and the stable occurrence of habituation and dishabituation were judged not just equivalent to but more advanced than those of normal subjects of the same age, since such effects are not usually seen until infants are 3–4 months of age. The interpretation made by Graham and colleagues is that in the normal infant the activity of lower brain structures may be suppressed by immature higher structures. The anencephalic infant appears precocious because the interfering immature forebrain structures are not present.

The results of these two case studies appear to be contradictory, and they point to very different conclusions regarding the necessity of cortical structures in habituation of orienting. However, it is especially difficult to compare such studies since they involve single subjects and different response systems and quality and quantity of the remaining functional brain tissue can only be roughly estimated. Several subsequent studies of severely brain-damaged infants have provided some clarification of the situation.

In a study of five hydranencephalic and hydrocephalic infants varying from 1 to 52 months of age at testing, Berntson, Tuber, Ronca, and Bachman (1983) confirmed the Graham and colleagues finding of deceleratory responding in the absence of all or most cortical tissue, and also find evidence of a form of associative learning.* The latter was demonstrated by presenting pairs of tones or lights for 50–150 trials or so, and interspersing test trials in which the second of the two stimuli was omitted. Three of the five infants responded with a marked *accelerative* response on test trials in contrast with the small decelerative response to stimulus pairs or the same stimulus prior to pairing. This effect might also be viewed as dishabituation except for two difficulties. First, although the authors conclude there is evidence of habituation in the same three subjects, this is not readily evident from the figures provided except in one subject (Berntson et al., 1983, Fig. 3), and apparently there were too few data to analyze statistically. Second, in a parallel study done with surgically decerebrated rat pups, Ronca, Berntson, and Tuber (1985) did find clear habituation of deceleratory responding in the pups, and for test trials report recovery of the deceleration rather than the acceleration seen in the infants. Nonetheless, both studies provide clear evidence of deceleratory responding during the habituation phase and an apparent change in response form when the stimulus was altered. One further item of importance in the Ronca and others (1985) study was that surgical decerebration has greater effects in older pups than in younger ones, though the effect was most evident in the magnitude of the deceleratory response rather than the rate of habituation. This would suggest that the age difference at time of testing, 3 months for Brackbill and 4–6 weeks for Graham and others, could be important.

W. K. Berg, Clarkson, Eitzman, and Setzer (1981) evaluated three hydranencephalic infants and provided information allowing some comparison of response mode. The three infants were born without a forebrain and tested when less than 1 month of age. Heart rate responding was assessed in one infant, gross motor activity in two, and air-puff-elicited blink reflexes in two infants. As with Graham and others (1978) and Berntson and colleagues (1983), the infant from whom heart rate responses could be recorded showed sustained deceleratory responses to synthetic vowels presented at 74–80 dB. A response of 20 beats per minute occurred on the initial trial of the initial session, habituating within 6 trials. The simultaneously recorded gross body movements for this infant (behavioral ratings of limb and body activity) also habituated within a few trials, as they did in a second infant responding to tactile stimuli. In other sessions, two infants were presented air puffs near the eye to elicit blink reflexes. These responses declined slowly over 30–45 trials in one infant, as was not the case with a group of 10 normal infants tested similarly. In the second infant blink responding appeared to increase over trials.

Habituation was evaluated in these infants as a substantial or significant decline in responding, whether or not it reached a zero response level. For gross body activity, both infants appeared to show declines that were asymptotic at a level above zero. A similar phenomenon has been noted for a variety of responses in sleeping adults, as will be described in the next section. If a similar response pattern occurred in the Brackbill infant, the criterion of *no* response for 5 consecutive trials could

---

*Tuber, Berntson, Bachman, and Allen (1980) also report evidence of heart rate responding and associative learning in a hydranencephalic infant, but the later Berntson et al. (1983) report appears to include this same infant.

miss this initial decline, and might explain the apparent discrepancy between the Brackbill and Graham and others reports.

It would appear that brain stem or midbrain structures are capable of supporting orienting-like cardiac and motor responses, and their habituation as well as dishabituation. This may be more evident in the younger infants; in the case of gross bodily movements, responding may not habituate to a zero asymptotic level. It is also notable that in all cases the arousal state of the severely brain damaged infant is very difficult or impossible to assess with any certainty. To the extent that state effects alter habituation and dishabituation, this problem could considerably complicate interpretation of the several case studies of infants lacking cortex.

Habituation and the Influence of State

Waking State

In our review for the first edition of this book we found that for both visual and auditory stimuli there was disagreement as to whether the deceleratory heart rate and visual fixation responses of awake, young infants would reliably habituate. Since that publication there have been many published reports of habituation in infants 4 months and younger (for reviews see Graham et al. 1983; Von Bargen, 1983), suggesting that failure to find it should be viewed as the exception. We will not attempt to review this work further here, since the majority of recent studies resuppose the reliability of habituation, at least in infants older than 2–3 months, and use it together with dishabituating stimuli to evaluate sensory, perceptual, and cognitive abilities.

Sleep

In contrast to the work with awake infants, there were a large number of early studies reporting evidence of habituation in the sleeping neonate (e.g., Bartoshuk, 1962; Bridger, 1961; Engen, Lipsitt, & Kay, 1963; Keen, 1964; Leventhal & Lipsitt, 1964). Few, however, made the distinction between active and quiet sleep stages. The Hutts in particular (Hutt, Bernuth, et al., 1968; Hutt et al., 1969) have pointed out the dangers of ignoring state changes when studying habituation. Their reports indicated that, depending upon the state at the beginning of the session and the session length, either habituation or dishabituation could be mimicked by spontaneous state changes. Since they found no evidence of habituation within a state, the Hutts concluded that convincing evidence of habituation independent of state changes had not been demonstrated for the neonate. Rose, Schmidt, and Bridger (1978) provide further evidence of the difficulties in interpreting apparent response decrement during sleep. They found that tactile responsivity declines only after the completion of the first cycle of active and quiet sleep and does not differ between active and quiet sleep within the initial cycle of these states. However, as they note, it was not possible to determine whether the decline in responding during the later cycles of sleep was due to the length of time asleep or to a slow habituation process.

It is still the case that evidence for habituation within sleep states is sparse, but some early work is relevant to the question and there has been additional work since the Hutts' report. The bulk of the research has been with neonates. In the work by Engen (Engen et al., 1963; Engen & Lipsitt, 1965) sleep state was not explicitly noted, but the procedure of presenting stimuli only in the presence of even respiration and the absence of motor activity provided some assurance that testing took place in quiet sleep. In both studies they report significant decrement of respiratory, motor, and a combined autonomic measure within 10 repetitions of 10-sec odorant presentations to neonates. Change to a different odorant or removal of an element of a combined odorant resulted in response recovery. Ashton (1973) carefully controlled state in his evaluation of auditory habituation in neonates. Habituation of an accelerative HR response occurred for both 75-and 85-dB tones presented in the first period of active sleep, and with the 85-dB tone in the following quiet sleep. Dishabituation was not assessed, so the specificity of the decremental response could not be evaluated. Field, Dempsey, Hatch, Ting, and Clifton (1979) also tested habituation for neonates in active sleep. In a within-subject design, three types of stimuli were tested in separate habituation–dishabituation trial sequences: a rattle sound, a buzzer (both at 90-dB SPL), and tactile stimulation to the abdomen from a nylon filament (15–20 grams of pressure). The heart rate response to all three stimuli was an acceleration, and this response declined significantly from an average of about 7 beats per minute on the initial two trials to about 3 beats per minute by the last two habituation trials, 9 and 10. These results contrast with those of Rose, Schmidt, and Bridger (1976), who did not find habituation to a tactile stimulus like that used by Field et al. In the Field and colleagues study habituation trials were followed by the dishabituation stimulus, dropping of one end of the bassinet a few inches, which elicited a moro/startle reflex, and a large accelerative response. Subsequent presentation of the original habituating stimulus elicited a recovered accelerative response about like that produced when it was initially presented; that is, there was evidence of dishabituation as the term is used in this paradigm. Measures of gross motor activity indicated a similar pattern for the two auditory stimuli. Preterm infants were also tested in this study and results were similar to those for full-term infants for motor responses, but the preterm infants showed no evidence of habituation or dishabituation of the accelerative heart rate responses. The full-term data provide quite strong evidence for the presence of habituation during active sleep, with only two qualifications. With the use of 10 habituation trials we cannot discern whether the failure to reach a zero response level has an effect like that seen in adults, or whether the response would have continued to zero with additional trials, as some of the earlier infant studies had shown. In addition, the response recovery following the dishabituation trial could have been due to general but undetected shift in state produced by presentation of the strong moro/startle stimulus. Thus the stimulus specificity of the habituation again cannot be determined. Kisilevsky and Muir (1984) carried out a very carefully designed extension of the Field study covering the behavioral measures of tactile habituation in neonates. These researchers added vitally important control groups to assess the effects of time in the sleep state with and without the interposed dishabituation stimulus. Their stimulus was a brushing of the earlobe with an artist's brush, and the dishabituation stimulus was an 86-dB rattle sound. As in the Field study, subjects in active sleep received 10 presentations of tactile stimulation followed by the acoustic dishabituator, followed by a return to the tactile stimulus. The gross motor response declined about 40 percent within 6 trials and appeared to asymptote there. The dishabituation stimulus failed to produce recovery of response to the original stimulus. Results from the control groups convincingly demonstrated that their failure to find dishabituation resulted from a *suppressing* effect of the interposed acoustic dishabituation stimulus. This effect was not related to the prior habituation in any way since it occurred even when no habituating stimuli had preceded the acoustic stimulus. However, as the authors note, these data should not be viewed as contradicting the dishabituation of the type shown by Field and others (1979) since the use of different habituation and dishabituation stimuli could account for the differences in outcome. In the second study of their report, Kisilevski and Muir (1984) replicated the habituation results and utilized the dishabituation paradigm in which a qualitative change in stimulus is introduced following habituation. Both a cross-modal change to a moderate acoustic stimulus and a within-mode change of site of tactile stimulation produced full recovery of the motor reaction. Thus these data provide some of the strongest evidence to date of a response decrement during a single stage of sleep that is specific to at least some aspects of the repeated stimulus. The combination of the two papers provides unusually convincing evidence of true habituation in the neonate during active sleep. Schaefer (1975) provides some evidence of the same in quiet sleep with EEG reactions. This study examined both habituation and dishabituation of neonates' EEG desychronization responses at both anterior and posterior head regions to presentations of both tone and white noise. Though habituation over 15 trials was significant only for white noise and for the posterior recording site, dishabituation to change from noise to tone was also demonstrated.

There are almost no studies of habituation in the older sleeping infant, and the few that exist do not clearly distinguish between sleep states. Lewis, Dodd, and Harwitz (1969) reported significant habituation of cardiac responses to 30 repetitions of tactile stimuli in sleeping infants 2–6 weeks old. Subjects were believed to be in quiet sleep but this was not confirmed with specific observations. These stimuli did not produce habituation in awake infants, but their procedures, which allowed long interruptions and the restarting of sessions when awake infants became upset, would not be optimal to produce habituation. Campos and Brackbill (1973) presented 80-dB bursts of white noise at 40-sec intervals to infants 1–4 weeks old, some of whom remained asleep throughout testing. Habituation to a criterion occurred, but reportedly only about half of this group reached criterion before state changed, apparently from active to quiet sleep.

Habituation in sleeping infants, at least neonates, does appear to differ from that in sleeping adults. Although a number of the early adult studies suggested lack of habituation for any of a number of response measures (e.g., Johnson & Lubin, 1967), more recent reports have indicated that, when the results of adult studies are analyzed on a trial-by-trial basis, heart rate, vasomotor, and skin potential responses all seem to decline within about 10 trials. However, unlike habituation in the awake adult or apparently sleeping infant, responding asymptotes at a level well above zero (Firth, 1973; Johnson, Townsend, & Wilson, 1975; McDonald & Carpenter, 1975). It would appear that both the neonate and the adult have a period of rapid habituation during sleep, but only the adult maintains reduced responding over an extended number of trials. Stimulus-specific dishabituation has not been demonstrated in the adult, to our knowledge.

This review of habituation in sleep indicates some important advances in describing the process in neonates, but there is an obvious need to fill in the great gap between birth and adulthood. We might expect substantial changes to take place during the initial year of life when sleep mechanisms themselves are undergoing such marked changes. In particular, we would look forward to research on habituation in older infants that would: (1) distinguish between quiet and active sleep; (2) compare quiet and active sleep in separate groups to avoid carryover of habituation from one stage to the next; and (3) assess the stimulus specificity of response decrements with qualitative changes in stimuli to test dishabituation. With the Kisilevsky and Muir (1984) study this step has been taken for neonates in active sleep with tactile stimuli, and the Schaeffer (1975) results provide some evidence for quiet sleep as well. Nonetheless, it is clear that further research is needed for neonates as well as the older infants. As yet, data are too few to make any certain statements regarding developmental changes, but available results suggest that neonates habituate in sleep at least as rapidly as and probably more completely than adults. The habituation in sleeping infants can have stimulus specificity, an effect not yet demonstrated with sleeping adults.

Electrocortical Evidence of Orienting and Attention: Long-Latency Components of Event-Related Potentials

In psychophysiological research with adults, our understanding of orienting, attention, and stimulus processing capabilities have been greatly expanded by the study of brain potentials elicited by discrete stimulus events (now usually referred to as *event-related potentials* or ERPs), especially those components that have latencies longer than about 250 msec or so and that are enhanced by or occur only in the presence of significant attentional or orienting activity. The one initially identified was a surface-positive component occurring at about 300 msec after stimulus onset (e.g., Sutton, Braren, Zubin, & John, 1965; Sutton, Tueting, Zubin, & John, 1967), referred to as P3 or P300. Since then, the research literature has expanded greatly, and now it discusses a half-dozen or more late positive and negative components of the ERP, as well as modulation of various earlier components. Unfortunately there is considerable disagreement as to the cognitive specificity, reliability, and validity of many of the components. Nonetheless, there is no doubt that a subject's evaluation of the stimulus and its context can produce substantial alteration of ERP late components (e.g., Picton & Stuss, 1980; Sutton & Ruchkin, 1984). If such brain potentials exist and can be recorded in infants, they could provide important new sources of information regarding attentional processes in infants and brain development.

The first attempt to demonstrate late ERP components in infants was not published until some 13 years following the pioneering adult work by Sutton's group. Schulman-Galambos and Galambos (1978) provided the initial exploratory data on ERP late components in infants 7–52 weeks old, comparing responses to a variety of events designed to be interesting with those to out-of-focus slide presentations, events presumably of less interest. Late components, both negative (500–650 msec) and positive (about 1000 msec), were found, but did not differ between conditions as they had in adult subjects. The first well-controlled studies appeared in 1981. Courchesne, Ganz, and Norcia (1981) presented infants 4–7 months old (mean age = 6.2 months) with a series of brief (100 msec) exposures to two human faces. Utilizing what is called the "oddball" paradigm in adult work, they presented one face 88 percent of the trials on average, and the other the remaining 12 percent.

Both types of stimuli elicited a substantial, negative-going wave, which Courchesne and colleagues called Nc, peaking about 650 msec, and a very late positive wave, referred to as Pc, peaking somewhere about 1300 msec. These bear some similarity to those found by Schulman-Galambos and Galambos. Both components were present in the more frontal recording sites on the head for both stimuli, but only the negative wave was significantly larger in response to the infrequent stimulus and also shorter in latency. That same year Hofman and Salapatek published two reports of late ERP components in infants (Hofman & Salapatek, 1981; Hofman, Salapatek, & Kuskowski, 1981). In both, 3-month-old infants were presented with vertically striped stimuli differing in orientation or width. The paradigm was similar to that used by Courchesne and associates with one exception: These investigators preceded the test phase, in which two stimuli were intermixed in an 80/20 percent ratio, with a familiarization phase in which there were only presentations of that stimulus to be used as the frequent stimulus in the later test phase (i.e., 100 percent). They report increased positivity during the period from 300 to 600 msec after stimulus onset in the occipital (Oz) lead for the infrequent stimulus. Responses to the infrequent stimulus were compared with responses to the frequent stimulus (80 percent) in the same phase and the frequent stimulus (100 percent) presented in the preceding familiarization phase. The effect seemed to be more reliable across studies for the latter comparison. Hofman and Salapatek (1981) suggested that their positive component found in 3-month-olds and Courchesne's negative, frontally focused component found in 6-month-olds may together indicate a developmental progression from more sensory-dominated analyses occurring in the occipital region (for visual stimuli) to a more comprehensive, amodal stimulus analysis occurring in frontal regions.

This hypothesis and several others offered to explain the differences found in the two laboratories (Courchesne, 1983) were tested in a recent study by Nelson and Salapatek (in press). Like Courchesne and colleagues (1981), these investigators used face stimuli, 6-month-old infants, brief (100 msec) stimulus durations, extended response analysis periods, and longer interstimulus periods, and they examined frontal (Fz) as well as more posterior brain sites. Nelson and Salapatek retained, however, the 100 percent familiarization phase preceding the phase in which frequent and infrequent stimuli are interspersed with one another. Their initial study replicated the earlier Hofman and others (1981) work with vertical stripes, again finding greater positivity in the region of 300–450 msec. However, the effect was significant at the central (Cz) site rather than the occipital one, and only for the infrequent stimulus presented in the second phase when compared to the familiar stimulus presented in the earlier 100 percent phase. Ironically, the grand average waveforms actually appeared similar to that reported by Courchesne and colleagues in showing a substantial negative wave at the Cz and Fz sites, though peak latency appeared somewhat shorter than that reported by Courchesne et al. The increased positivity Nelson and Salapatek report mostly occurs during the recovery limb of this negative peak (Fig. 5.5), and therefore could just as well be described as a reduction in negativity. Nonetheless, the data certainly are not wholly consistent with Courchesne and associates since infrequent stimuli did not produce greater negativity, even at frontal regions. The second and third experiments in the Nelson and Salapatek paper support the indications from experiment 1 that the effects reported were only evident for comparisons *between* phase 1 and 2, not for compar-

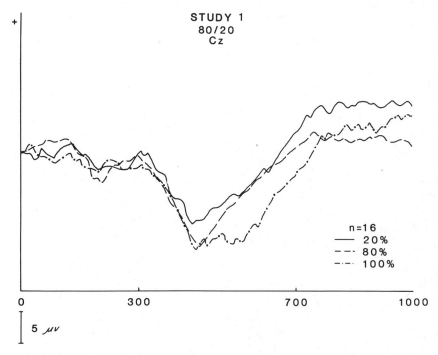

STUDY 1
80/20
Cz

n=16
——— 20%
— — 80%
—·— 100%

0   300   700   1000

5 μν

Figure 5.5. Event-related brain potential from 6-month-old infants for three conditions. Curves labeled "100%" is from the initial familiarization period. Curves labeled "20%" and "80%" are from the later test period (see text). (From "Electrophysiological Correlates of Infant Recognition Memory" by C. A. Nelson and P. Salapatek, in press, *Child Development*. Used with permission of the Society for Research in Child Development).

isons within phase 2 alone (20 percent versus 80 percent). As such, the necessary stimulus conditions for this effect appear to differ from those critical to the effect reported by Courchesne and others (1981).

Two other recent reports appear generally to support the Courchesne findings. Using face stimuli and a somewhat modified oddball paradigm, Karrer and Ackles (Ackles, Karrer, & McDonough, 1986; Karrer & Ackles, in press) report a substantial negative component for frontal, central, and parietal leads in 6-month-olds peaking at about 500–700 msec (Fig. 5.6). As with Courchesne's work, the Nc component was significantly more negative for infrequent presentations, though, contrary to Courchesne's evidence, the effect was more central than frontal. In the preliminary work with 6-week-olds, there was no Nc readily visible, and the investigators found no effects of stimulus probability. Using synthetic speech stimuli, Kurtzberg (1985) also finds that a late negative, more anterior component is enhanced in response to infrequent phonemes. This work is important since it indicates that late component effects are not specific to the use of faces or even to visual stimuli. Both these works also provide some evidence of the even later positive component labeled Pc by Courchesne and others.

To summarize the status of research on infant ERP late components, evidence increases for the development by at least 6 months of a so-called Nc component, a negative-going wave reaching a peak at about 400–700 msec after stimulus onset

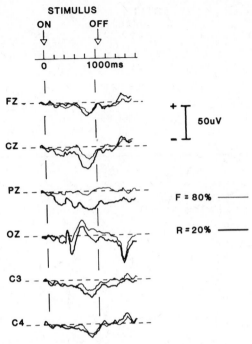

Figure 5.6. Event-related brain potentials from 6-month-old infants for frequent (F = 80%) and rare (R = 20%) conditions. In this study, a 100% condition did not preceed testing of the 80% and 20% conditions as it did in Figure 5.5. (From: "Brain organization & perceptual/cognitive development in normal and Down syndrome infants: A research program," by R. Karrer and P. Ackles, in (P. Vietze & H. Vaughan, Eds. *Early Identification of Infants at Risk for Mental Retardation,* Orlando, FL: Grune & Stratton, in press. Reprinted with permission.)

that is most prominent in frontal and central sites of the brain. When the typical oddball paradigm is employed, the infrequent stimulus appears to enhance the magnitude of the wave. When the block of intermixed frequent and infrequent stimuli is preceded by a substantial block of the to-be-frequent stimulus, such as the Salapatek group has used, an enhancement of Nc by rarely presented stimuli has not been demonstrated. A later positive component, Pc, has also been reported in several of the studies, but it does not appear to be influenced by stimulus probability in any of the work. The status of the earlier positive (or less negative) influence demonstrated by the Salapatek group is less clear. Important differences between the sets of studies have yet to be evaluated. As noted above, the paradigm used by the Salapatek group and the others differ somewhat, and they have yet to be directly compared. Further, scoring differences could play some role since Courchesne (1983) argues that one should not arbitrarily attribute all potentials occurring in electrodes placed near the eyes as due to blinks or eye movements, artifacts that are used to eliminate possibly contaminated trials. When brain potentials are occurring in the far frontal region, these can be expected to show up on eye electrodes. Use of monopolar eye electrodes allows one to evaluate selectively the source of the potential, and avoid discarding strong frontal brain signals. The monopolar eye lead arrangement and selective artifact rejection procedure were used in the Karrer and Ackles study, which replicated Courchesne's work, but were not employed in the work by the Salapatek group. And finally, the Karrer and Ackles, the Kurzberg, and the Courchesne and others studies used considerably longer time constant settings (less filtering of relatively slow-changing signals) than did the studies by the Salapatek group. Nelson and Salapatek (in press), who employed an unusually short time constant (0.3 sec) for late component work, argued that a time constant of this value should not significantly change the shape of the response, but based this on an assessment of adult ERPs (Duncan-Johnson & Donchin, 1979), which do not contain components nearly so slow changing as those found in infants. This difference would be unlikely artifactually to produce the early positive effect the Salapatek group describe, but it certainly could attenuate the Nc effect seen by the other investigators. Thus while there is evidence for two different cognitively related late ERP components in infants, only the Nc enhancement presently receives very strong support.

REFERENCES

Abe, K., & Fukui, S. (1979). The individual development of circadian temperature rhythm in infants. *Journal of Interdisciplinary Cycle Research, 10,* 227–232.

Abe, K., Sasaki, H., Takebayashi, K., Fukui, S., & Nambu, H. (1978). The development of circadian rhythm of human body temperature. *Journal of Interdisciplinary Cycle Research, 9,* 211–216.

Ackles, P. K., Karrer, R., & McDonough, S. (1986, April). Development of event-related potentials (ERP) as measures of information processing. In R. Karrer (Chair), *Event-related potentials and infant visual information processing.* Symposium conducted at the International Conference on Infant Studies. Los Angeles, CA.

Adkinson, C., & Berg, W. K. (1976). Cardiac deceleration in newborns: Habituation, dishabituation, and offset responses. *Journal of Experimental Child Psychology, 21,* 46–60.

Agnew, H. W., Webb, W. B., & Williams, R. L. (1966). The first night effect: An EEG study of sleep. *Psychophysiology, 2,* 263–266.

Anders, T. (1978). Home-recorded sleep in 2- and 9-month-old infants. *Journal of the American Academy of Child Psychiatry, 17,* 421–432.

Anders, T. (1979). Night waking in infants during the first year of life. *Pediatrics, 63,* 860–864.

Anders, T., Emde, R., & Parmelee, A. (1971). *A manual of standardized terminology, techniques and criteria for scoring of states of sleep and wakefulness in newborn infants.* Los Angeles: UCLA Brain Information Service.

Anders, T. F., & Roffwarg, H. P. (1973a). The effects of selective interruption and deprivation of sleep in the human newborn. *Developmental Psychobiology, 6,* 77–89.

Anders, T. F., & Roffwarg, H. P. (1973b). The relationship between maternal and neonatal sleep. *Neuropadiatrie, 4,* 151–161.

Anderson, J. V., Martin, R. J., Abboud, E. F., Dyme, I. Z., & Bruce, E. N. (1983). Transient ventilatory response to CO_2 as a function of sleep state in full-term infants. *Journal of Applied Physiology: Respiratory, Environmental & Exercise Physiology, 54,* 1482–1488.

Anthony, B. J. (1985). In the blink of an eye: Implications of reflex modification for information processing. In P. K. Ackles, R. Jennings, & J. M. Coles (Eds.), *Advances in psychophysiology* (Vol. 1). Greenwich, CT: AI Press.

Anthony, B. J., & Graham F. K. (1983). Evidence for sensory-selective set in young infants. *Science, 220,* 742–744.

Anthony, B. J., Zeigler, B. L., & Graham, F. K. (in press). Stimulus duration as an age-dependent factor in reflex blinking. *Developmental Psychobiology*.

Arnold, W. R., & Porges, S. W. (1972). *Heart rate components of orientation in newborns as a function of age and experience*. Paper presented at the meeting of the Eastern Psychological Association, Boston.

Aserinsky, E. (1971). Rapid eye movement density and pattern in the sleep of normal young adults. *Psychophysiology, 8*, 361–375.

Aschoff, J., & Wever, R. (1976). Human circadian rhythms: A multi-oscillatory system. *Federation Proceedings, 35*, 2326–2332.

Ashmead, D. H., Reilly, B. M., & Lipsitt, L. P. (1980). Neonates' heart rate, sucking rhythm, and sucking amplitude as a function of the sweet taste. *Journal of Experimental Child Psychology, 29*, 264–281.

Ashton, R. (1971a). Behavioral sleep cycles in the human newborn. *Child Development, 42*, 2098–2100.

Ashton, R. (1971b). The effects of the environment upon state cycles in the human newborn. *Journal of Experimental Child Psychology, 12*, 1–9.

Ashton, R. (1973a). The state variable in neonatal research. *Merrill-Palmer Quarterly, 19*, 3–20.

Ashton, R. (1973b). The influence of state and prandial condition upon the reactivity of the newborn to auditory stimulation. *Journal of Experimental Child Psychology, 15*, 315–327.

Baker, T., & McGinty, D. (1977). Reversal of cardiopulmonary failure during active sleep in hypoxic kittens: Implications for sudden infant death. *Science, 198*, 419–421.

Baker, T., & McGinty, D. (1979). Sleep–waking patterns in hypoxic kittens. *Developmental Psychobiology, 12*, 561–575.

Balaban, M. T., Anthony, B. J., & Graham, F. K. (1985). Modality-repetition and attentional effects on reflex blinking in infants and adults. *Infant Behavior & Development, 8*, 443–457.

Bartoshuk, A. K. (1962). Human neonatal cardiac acceleration to sound: Habituation and dishabituation. *Perceptual & Motor Skills, 15*, 15–27.

Bartoshuk, A. K. (1964). Human neonatal cardiac responses to sound: A power function. *Psychonomic Science, 1*, 151–152.

Baust, W., & Bohnert, B. (1969). The regulation of heart rate during sleep. *Experimental Brain Research, 7*, 169–180.

Baust, W., & Gagel, J. (1977). The development of periodicity of heart rate and respiration during sleep in newborn babies. *Neuropadiatrie, 8*, 387–396.

Becker, P., & Thoman, E. (1981). Rapid eye movement storms in infants: Rate of occurrence at 6 months predicts mental development at 1 year. *Science, 212*, 1415–1416.

Becker, P., & Thoman, E. (1982). Intense rapid eye movements during active sleep: An index of neurobehavioral instability. *Developmental Psychobiology, 15*, 203–210.

Bell, R. Q. (1970). Sleep cycles and skin potential in newborns studied with a simplified observation and recording system. *Psychophysiology, 6*, 778–786.

Berg, K. M. (1970). *Heart rate and vasomotor responses as a function of stimulus duration and intensity*. Unpublished master's thesis, University of Wisconsin, Madison.

Berg, K. M. (1973). *Elicitation of acoustic startle in the human*. Unpublished doctoral dissertation, University of Wisconsin, Madison.

Berg, K. M., Berg, W. K., & Graham, F. K. (1971). Infant heart rate response as a function of stimulus and state. *Psychophysiology, 8*, 30–44.

Berg, W. K. (1972). Habituation and dishabituation of cardiac responses in four-month-old, awake infants. *Journal of Experimental Child Psychology, 14,* 92–107.

Berg, W. K. (1974). Cardiac orienting responses of 6- and 16-week-old infants. *Journal of Experimental Child Psychology, 17,* 303–312.

Berg, W. K. (1975). Cardiac components of defense responses in infants. *Psychophysiology, 12,* 224.

Berg, W. K. (1985). Physiological measures of auditory sensitivity: Near-threshold intensity effects. In S. Trehub & B. Schneider (Eds.), *Advances in the Study of Communication and Effect: Vol 10. Auditory Development in Infancy,* New York: Plenum.

Berg, W. K., Berg, K. M., Harbin, T. J., Davies, M. G., Blumenthal, T., & Avendano, A. (1985). Comparisons of blink inhibition in infants, children, and young and old adults. *Psychophysiology, 22,* 572–573.

Berg, W. K., Clarkson, M. G., Eitzman, D. V., & Setzer, E. (1981, April). *Habituation in infants lacking cortex.* Paper presented at the meeting of the Society for Research in Child Development. Boston, MA.

Berg, W. K., Clarkson, M. G., & Silverstein, L. D. (1979). Inhibition of infants' reflex blinks by near-threshold auditory stimuli. *Psychophysiology, 16,* 191.

Berg, W. K., & Graham, F. K. (1970). Reproducible effects of stimulus intensity on heart rate response curves. *Psychophysiology, 6,* 653.

Berg, W. K., & Hurwitz, B. (1983). *Development of autonomic control of heart rate responding in infant rats: A possible animal model.* Workshop on phasic cardiovascular changes as tools in psychophysiological research, Monterey, CA.

Berg, W. K., Jackson, J. C., & Graham, F. K. (1975). Tone intensity and rise–decay time effects on cardiac responses during sleep. *Psychophysiology, 12,* 254–261.

Berg, W. K., Silverstein, L. D., Verzijl-Tweed, N., & Clarkson, M. G. (1977). Enhanced cardiac decelerations to near-threshold stimuli in infants. *Psychophysiology, 14,* 98.

Berkson, G., Wasserman, G., & Behrman, R. (1974). Heart rate response to an auditory stimulus in premature infants. *Psychophysiology, 11,* 224–246.

Bernstein, P., Emde, R., & Campos, J. (1973). REM sleep in four-month infants under home and laboratory conditions. *Psychosomatic Medicine, 35,* 322–329.

Berntson, G., Tuber, D., Ronca, A., & Bachman, D. (1983). The decerebrate human: Associative learning. *Experimental Neurology, 81,* 77–88.

Bernuth, H., & Prechtl, H. F. R. (1969). Vestibulo-ocular response and its state dependency in newborn infants. *Neuropadiatrie, 1,* 11–24.

Blumenthal, T. D. (1982). *Stimulus rise time and developmental differences in startle responding.* Unpublished master's thesis, University of Florida, Gainesville.

Blumenthal, T. D. (1985). *Developmental differences in the temporal summation of transient and sustained auditory stimuli.* Unpublished doctoral dissertation, University of Florida, Gainesville.

Blumenthal, T. D., & Berg, W. K. (1982). Developmental differences in startle response to stimulus onset transition. *Psychophysiology, 19,* 551–552.

Boddy, K., & Dawes, G. S. (1975). Fetal breathing. *British Medical Bulletin, 31,* 3–7.

Bohlin, G., Lindhagan, K., & Hagekull, B. (1981). Cardiac orienting to pulsed and continuous auditory stimulation: A developmental study. *Psychophysiology, 18,* 440–446.

Booth, C., Morin, V., Waite, S., & Thoman, E. (1983). Periodic and non-periodic sleep apnea in premature and fullterm infants. *Developmental Medicine & Child Neurology, 25,* 283–296.

Brackbill, Y. (1970). Acoustic variation and arousal level in infants. *Psychophysiology, 6,* 517–526.

Brackbill, Y. (1971a). Cumulative effects of continuous stimulation on arousal level in infants. *Child Development, 42,* 17–26.

Brackbill, Y. (1971b). The role of the cortex in orienting: Orienting reflex in an anencephalic human infant. *Developmental Psychology, 5,* 195–201.

Brackbill, Y. (1973). Continuous stimulation reduces arousal level: Stability of the effect over time. *Child Development, 44,* 43–46.

Brackbill, Y. (1975). Continuous stimulation and arousal level in infancy: Effects of stimulus intensity and stress. *Child Development, 46,* 364–369.

Brezinova, V. (1974). Sleep cycle content and sleep cycle duration. *Electroencephalography & Clinical Neurophysiology, 36,* 275–282.

Bridger, W. (1961). Sensory habituation and discrimination in the human neonate. *American Journal of Psychiatry, 117,* 991–996.

Brown, J., Leavitt, L., & Graham, F. K. (1977). Response to auditory stimuli in 6- and 9-week-old human infants. *Developmental Psychobiology, 10,* 255–266.

Bryan, A. C., & Muller, N. (1980). Lung mechanics and gas exchange during sleep. *Sleep, 3,* 401–406.

Bryan, H. M., Hagan, R., Gulston, G., & Bryan, A. C. (1976). CO_2 response and sleep state in infants. *Clinical Research, 24,* 689A.

Campos, J., & Brackbill, Y. (1973). Infant state: Relationship to heart rate, behavioral response and response decrement. *Developmental Psychobiology, 6,* 9–20.

Campos, J., Emde, R., Gaensbauer, T., & Henderson, C. (1975). Cardiac and behavioral interrelationships in the reactions of infants to strangers. *Developmental Psychology, 11,* 589–601.

Chalmers, D. V., & Hoffman, H. S. (1973). Cardiac and startle responses to acoustic stimuli in the rat. *Physiological Psychology, 1,* 74–76.

Chase, M. H., & Morales, F. R. (1985). Postsynaptic modulation of spinal cord motoneuron membrane potential during sleep. In D. McGinty, R. Drucker-Colin, A. Morrison, & P. Parmeggiani (Eds.), *Brain mechanisms of sleep.* New York: Raven.

Chess, G., Tam, R., & Calaresu, F. (1975). Influence of cardiac neural inputs on rhythmic variations of heart period in the cat. *American Journal of Physiology, 228,* 775–780.

Clarkson, M. G., & Berg, W. K. (1983). Cardiac deceleration and vowel discrimination in newborns: Crucial parameters of acoustic stimuli. *Child Development, 54,* 162–171.

Clarkson, M. G., & Berg, W. K. (1984). Bioelectric and potentiometric measures of eyeblink amplitude in reflex modification paradigms. *Psychophysiology, 21,* 237–241.

Clarkson, M. G., Berg, W. K., & Boettcher, M. C. (1980). Inhibition of startle at long lead stimulus intervals. *Psychophysiology, 17,* 325.

Clarkson, M. G., Clifton, R. K., & Morrongiello, B. A. (1985). The effects of sound duration on newborns' head orientation. *Journal of Experimental Child Psychology, 39,* 20–36.

Clay, S. A., & Ramseyer, J. C. (1976). The orbicularis oculi reflex in infancy and childhood. *Neurology, 26,* 521–524.

Clifton, R. K. (1977). The relation of infant cardiac responding to behavioral state and motor activity. In W. A. Collins (Ed.), *Minnesota symposia on child psychology* (Vol. 11). Chicago: Crowell.

Clifton, R. K., & Meyers, W. J. (1969). The heart-rate response of four-month-old infants to auditory stimuli. *Journal of Experimental Child Psychology, 7,* 122–135.

Clifton, R. K., & Nelson, M. N. (1976). Developmental study of habituation in infants: The importance of paradigm, response system and state. In T. J. Tighe & R. N. Leaton (Eds.), *Habituation: Perspectives from child development, animal behavior, and neurophysiology.* Hillsdale, NJ: Erlbaum.

Cohen, L.B. (1972). Attention-getting and attention-holding processes of infant visual preferences. *Child Development, 43,* 869–879.

Cohen, L. B. (1973). A two-process model of infant visual attention. *Merrill-Palmer Quarterly, 19,* 157–180.

Conel, J. L. (1952). Histologic development of the cerebral cortex. In *Biology of mental health and disease, the twenty-seventh annual conference of the Milbank Memorial Fund.* New York: Hoeber.

Coons, S., & Guilleminault, C. (1982). Development of sleep–wake patterns and non-rapid eye movement sleep stages during the first six months of life in normal infants. *Pediatrics, 69,* 793–798.

Coons, S., & Guilleminault, C. (1984). Development of consolidated sleep and wakeful periods in relation to the day/night cycle in infancy. *Developmental Medicine & Child Neurology, 26,* 169–176.

Courchesne, E. (1983). Cognitive components of the event-related brain potentials: Changes associated with development. In A. W. K. Gaillard & W. Ritter (Eds.), *Tutorials in ERP research: Endogenous components.* Amsterdam: North Holland.

Courchesne, E., Ganz, L., & Norcia, A. (1981). Event-related brain potentials to human faces in infants. *Child Development, 52,* 804–811.

Crook, C. (1976). Neonatal sucking: Effects of quantity of response-contingent fluid upon sucking rhythm and heart rate. *Journal of Experimental Child Psychology, 21,* 539–548.

Crook, C., & Lipsitt, L. P. (1976). Neonatal nutritive sucking: Effects of taste stimulation upon sucking rhythm and heart rate. *Child Development, 47,* 518–522.

Crowell, D., Kapuniai, L., Boychuk, R., Light, M., & Hodgman, J. (1982). Daytime sleep stage organization in three-month-old infants. *Electroencephalography & Clinical Neurophysiology, 53,* 36–47.

Crowell, D. H., Kapuniai, L., & Jones, R. (1982). Detection of averaged heart rate response to tones in human newborns. *Psychophysiology, 22,* 697–706.

Curzi-Dascalova, L. (1978). Thoracico-abdominal respiratory correlations in infants: Constancy and variability in different sleep states. *Early Human Development, 2,* 25–38.

Curzi-Dascalova, L. (1982). Phase relationships between thoracic and abdominal respiratory movement during sleep in 31–38 weeks CA normal infants. Comparison with full-term (39–41 weeks) newborns. *Neuropediatrics, 13* (Suppl.), 15–20.

Curzi-Dascalova, L., & Christova-Gueorguieva, E. (1983). Respiratory pauses in normal prematurely born infants. *Biology of the Neonate, 44,* 325–332.

Curzi-Dascalova, L., Christova-Gueroguieva, L., Lebrun, F., & Firtion, G. (1984). Respiratory pauses in very low risk prematurely born infants reaching normal term. A comparison to full-term newborns. *Neuropediatrics, 15,* 13–17.

Curzi-Dascalova, L., & Dreyfus-Brisac, C. (1976). Distribution of skin potential responses according to states of sleep during the first months of life in human babies. *Electroencephalography & Clinical Neurophysiology, 41,* 399–407.

Curzi-Dascalova, L., Gaudebout, C., & Dreyfus-Brisac, C. (1981). Respiratory frequencies of sleeping infants during the first months of life: Correlations between values in different sleep states. *Early Human Development, 5,* 39–54.

Curzi-Dascalova, L., Lebrun, E., & Korn, G., (1983). Respiratory frequency according to sleep states and age in normal premature infants: A comparison with full term infants. *Pediatric Research, 17,* 152–156.

Curzi-Dascalova, L., Pajot, N., & Dreyfus-Brisac, C. (1973). Spontaneous skin potential responses in sleeping infants between 24 and 41 weeks of conceptional age. *Psychophysiology, 10,* 478–487.

Curzi-Dascalova, L., Pajot, N., & Dreyfus-Brisac, C. (1974). Spontaneous skin potential responses during sleep: Comparative studies in newborns and babies between 2 and 5 months of age. *Neuropadiatrie, 5,* 250–257.

Curzi-Dascalova, L., & Plassart, E. (1978). Respiratory and motor events in sleeping infants: Their correlation with thoracico-abdominal respiratory relationships. *Early Human Development, 2,* 39–50.

Czeisler, C., Weitzman, E., Moore-Ede, M., Zimmerman, J., & Knauer, R. (1980). Human sleep: Its duration and organization depend on its circadian phase. *Science, 210,* 1264–1267.

Czeisler, C., Zimmerman, J., Ronda, J., Moore-Ede, M., & Weitzman, E. (1980). Timing of REM sleep is coupled to the circadian rhythm of body temperature in man. *Sleep, 2,* 329–346.

Danguir J., & Nicolaidis, S. (1985). Feeding, metabolism, and sleep: Peripheral and central mechanisms of their interaction. In D. McGinty, R. Drucker-Colin, A. Morrison, & P. Parmeggiani (Eds.), *Brain mechanisms of sleep.* New York: Raven.

Darnall, R., & Ariagno, R. (1982). The effect of sleep state on active thermoregulation in the premature infant. *Pediatric Research, 16,* 512–514.

Davi, M., Sankaran, K., MacCallum, M., Cates, D., & Rigatto, H. (1979). Effect of sleep state on chest distortion and on the ventilatory response to CO_2 in neonates. *Pediatric Research, 13,* 982–986.

Davies, M. C. (1982). *Time perception in infants.* Unpublished master's thesis, University of Florida, Gainesville.

Davies, M. C. (1985). *Infants' responses to temporally regular events and their omission.* Unpublished doctoral dissertation, University of Florida, Gainesville.

Davis, M., & Gendelman, P. M. (1977). Plasticity of the acoustic startle response in the acutely decerebrate rat. *Journal of Comparative & Physiological Psychology, 91,* 549–563.

DeHaan, R., Patrick, J., Chess, G. F., & Jaco, N. T. (1977). Definition of sleep state in the newborn infant by heart rate analysis. *American Journal of Obstetrics & Gynecology, 127,* 753–758.

De Lee, C., & Petre-Quadens, O. (1976). Eye-movement density during sleep in normal and pathological neonates and infants. *Waking & Sleeping, 1,* 45–48.

Dement, W. C. (1969). The biological role of REM sleep (circa 1968). In A. Kales (Ed.), *Sleep: Physiology and pathology.* Philadelphia: Lippincott.

Dierker, L., Rosen, M., Pillay, S., & Sorokin, Y. (1982). Correlation between gestational age and fetal activity periods. *Biology of the Neonate, 42,* 66–72.

Dittrichova, J. (1966). Development of sleep in infancy. *Journal of Applied Physiology, 21,* 1243–1246.

Dittrichova, J., Paul, K., & Pavlikova, E. (1972). Rapid eye movements in paradoxical sleep in infants. *Neuropadiatrie, 3,* 248–257.

Dittrichova, J., Paul, K., & Pavlikova, E. (1978). Responsiveness to stimulation during paradoxical sleep in infants. *Early Human Development, 2,* 39–51.

Dobbing, J., & Sands, J. (1973). Quantitative growth and development of the human brain. *Archives of Disease in Childhood, 48,* 757–767.

Dorros, K., Brody, N., & Rose, S. (1979). A comparison of auditory behavior in the premature and full-term infant: The effect of intervention. In H. D. Kimmel, E. H. Van Olst, & J. F. Orlebeke (Eds.), *The Orienting Reflex in Humans.* Hillsdale, NJ: Erlbaum.

Dreyfus-Brisac, C. (1967). Ontogenese du sommeil chez le premature humain: etude polygraphique. In A. Minkowski (Ed.), *Regional development of the brain in early life.* Oxford: Blackwell.

Dreyfus-Brisac, C. (1968). Sleep ontogenesis in early human prematures from 24 to 27 weeks of conceptional age. *Developmental Psychobiology, 1,* 162–169.

Dreyfus-Brisac, C. (1970). Ontogenesis of sleep in human prematures after 32 weeks of conceptional age. *Developmental Psychobiology, 3,* 91–121.

Dreyfus-Brisac, C., & Curzi-Dascalova, L. (1975). The EEG during the first year of life. *Handbook of electroencephalography and clinical neurophysiology* (Vol. 6B). Amsterdam: Elsevier.

Dreyfus-Brisac, C., & Monod, N. (1975). The electroencephalogram of full-term newborns and premature infants. *Handbook of electroencephalography and clinical neurophysiology* (Vol. 6B). Amsterdam: Elsevier.

Drucker-Colin, R. (1979). Protein molecules and the regulation of REM sleep: Possible implications for function. In R. Drucker-Colin, M. Shkurovich, & M. B. Sterman (Eds.), *The functions of sleep,* New York: Academic.

Duncan-Johnson, C., & Donchin, E. (1979). The time constant in P300 recording. *Psychophysiology, 16,* 53–55.

Edelman, A., Kraemer, H., & Korner, A. (1982). Effects of compensatory movement stimulation on the sleep–wake behaviors of preterm infants. *Journal of the American Academy of Child Psychiatry, 21,* 555–559.

Egbert, J., & Katona, P. (1980). Development of autonomic heart rate control in the kitten during sleep. *American Journal of Physiology, 238,* H829–H835.

Eichorn, D. (1970). Physiological development. In P. H. Mussen (Ed.), *Carmichael's Manual of Child Psychology.* New York: Wiley.

Ellingson, R. (1982). Development of sleep spindle bursts during the first year of life. *Sleep, 5,* 39–46.

Ellingson, R., & Peters, J. (1980a). Development of EEG and daytime sleep patterns in normal full-term infants during the first 3 months of life: Longitudinal observations. *Electroencephalography & Clinical Neurophysiology, 49,* 112–124.

Ellingson, R., & Peters, J. (1980b). Development of EEG and daytime sleep patterns in low risk premature infants during the first year of life: Longitudinal observations. *Electroencephalography & Clinical Neurophysiology, 50,* 165–171.

Ellingson, R., Peters, J. F., & Nelson, B. (1982). Respiratory pauses and apnea during daytime sleep in normal infants during the first year of life: Longitudinal observations. *Electroencephalography & Clinical Neurophysiology, 53,* 48–59.

Emde, R., Harmon, R., Metcalf, D., Koenig, K., & Wagonfeld, S. (1971). Stress and neonatal sleep. *Psychosomatic Medicine, 33,* 491–497.

Emde, R. & Metcalf, D. (1970). An electroencephalographic study of behavioral rapid eye movement states in the human newborn. *Journal of Nervous & Mental Disease, 150,* 376–386.

Emde, R., Swedberg, J., & Suzuki, B. (1975). Human wakefulness and biological rhythms after birth. *Archives of General Psychiatry, 32,* 780–789.

Emde, R., & Walker, S. (1976). Longitudinal study of infant sleep: Results of 14 subjects studied at monthly intervals. *Psychophysiology, 13,* 456–461.

Engen, T., & Lipsitt, L. P. (1965). Decrement and recovery of responses to olfactory stimuli. *Journal of Comparative & Physiological Psychology, 59,* 312–316.

Engen, T., Lipsitt, L. P., & Kaye, H. (1963). Olfactory responses and adaptation in the human neonate. *Journal of Comparative & Physiological Psychology, 56,* 73–77.

Fagioli, I., & Salzarulo, P. (1982). Sleep states development in the first year of life assessed through 24-h recordings. *Early Human Development, 6,* 215–228.

Fantz, R. L., Fagan, J., & Miranda, S. (1975). Early visual selectivity. In L. B. Cohen & P. Salapatek (Eds.), *Infant perception: From sensation to cognition: Vol 1. Basic visual processes.* New York: Academic.

Field, T. M. (1979). Visual and cardiac responses to animate and inanimate faces by young term and preterm infants. *Child Development, 50,* 188–194.

Field, T. M. (1981). Infant arousal, attention and affect during early interactions. In L. P. Lipsitt & C. Rovee-Collier (Eds.), *Advances in Infancy Research* (Vol 1). Norwood, NJ: Ablex.

Field, T. M., Dempsey, J. R., Hatch, J., Ting, G., & Clifton, R. (1979). Cardiac and behavioral responses to repeated tactile and auditory stimulation by preterm and term neonates. *Developmental Psychology, 15,* 406–416.

Finer, N., Abroms, I., & Taeusch, H. W. (1976) Ventilation and sleep states in newborn infants. *Journal of Pediatrics, 89,* 100–108.

Finlay, D., & Ivenskis, A. (1982). Cardiac and visual responses to stimuli presented both foveally and peripherally as a function of speed of moving stimuli. *Developmental Psychology, 18,* 692–698.

Finley, J. P., & Nugent, S. T. (1983). Periodicities in respiration and heart rate in newborns. *Canadian Journal of Physiology & Pharmacology, 61,* 329–335.

Firth, H. (1973). Habituation during sleep. *Psychophysiology, 10,* 43–51.

Flores-Guevara, R., Plouin, P., Curzi-Dascalova, L., Radvanyi, M.-F., Guidasci, S., Pajot, N., & Monod, N. (1982). Sleep apneas in normal neonates and infants during the first 3 months of life. *Neuropediatrics, 13* (Suppl.), 21–28.

Fox, N. (1983). Maturation of autonomic activity in preterm infants. *Developmental Psychobiology, 16,* 495–504.

Fox, N., & Lewis, M. (1983). Cardiac response to speech sounds in preterm infants: Effects of postnatal illness at three months. *Psychophysiology, 20,* 481–488.

Friedman, S. (1972). Habituation and recovery of visual response in the alert human newborn. *Journal of Experimental Child Psychology, 13,* 339–349.

Fruhstorfer, H., Partanen, J., & Lumio, J. (1971). Vertex sharp waves and heart action during onset of sleep. *Electroencephalography & Clinical Neurophysiology, 31,* 614–617.

Gabriel, M., & Albani, M. (1977). Rapid eye movement sleep, apnea, and cardiac slowing influenced by phenobarbital administration in the neonate. *Pediatrics, 60,* 426–430.

Gabriel, M., Albani, M., & Schulte, F. J. (1976). Apneic spells and sleep states in preterm infants. *Pediatrics, 57,* 142–147.

Gabriel, M., Grote, B., & Jonas, M. (1981). Sleep–wake pattern in preterm infants under two different care schedules during four-day polygraphic recording. *Neuropediatrics, 12,* 366–373.

Gaensbauer, T., & Emde, R. (1973). Wakefulness and feeding in human newborns. *Archives of General Psychiatry, 28,* 894–897.

Gescheider, G. A. (1976). Evidence in support of the duplex theory of mechanoreception. *Sensory Processes, 12,* 238–248.

Gould, J. B., Lee, A. F. S., James, O., Sander, L., Teager, H., & Fineberg, N., (1977). The sleep state characteristics of apnea during infancy. *Pediatrics, 59,* 182–194.

Graham, F. K. (1973). Habituation and dishabituation of responses innervated by the autonomic nervous system. In H. V. S. Peeke & M. J. Herz (Eds.), *Habituation: Behavioral studies and physiological substrates.* New York: Academic.

Graham, F. K. (1979). Distinguishing among orienting, defense, and startle reflexes. In H. D. Kimmel, E. H. von Olst, & J. F. Orlebeke (Eds.), *The orienting reflex in humans.* Hillsdale, NJ: Erlbaum.

Graham, F. K. (1980). Control of reflex blink excitability. In R. F. Thompson, L. H. Hicks, & V. B. Shvyrkov (Eds.), *Neuromechanisms of goal-directed behavior and learning.* New York: Academic.

Graham, F. K. (1984). An affair of the heart. In M. G. H. Coles, J. R. Jennings, & J. Stern (Eds.), *Psychophysiology: A Festschrift for John and Beatrice Lacey.* New York: Van Nostrand Reinhold.

Graham, F. K., Anthony, B. J., & Zeigler, B. L. (1983). The orienting response and developmental processes. In D. Siddle (Ed.), *Orienting and habituation: Perspectives in human research.* New York: Wiley.

Graham, F. K., & Clifton, R. K. (1966). Heart-rate change as a component of the orienting response. *Psychological Bulletin, 65,* 305–320.

Graham, F. K., & Jackson, J. C. (1970). Arousal systems and infant heart rate responses. In L. P. Lipsitt & H. W. Reese (Eds.), *Advances in child development and behavior* (Vol. V). New York: Academic.

Graham, F. K., Leavitt, L., Strock, B., & Brown, J. (1978). Precocious cardiac orienting in a human, anencephalic infant. *Science, 199,* 322–324.

Graham, F. K., & Murray, G. M. (1977). Discordant effects of weak prestimulation on magnitude and latency of the reflex blink. *Physiological Psychology, 5,* 108–114.

Graham, F. K., Strock, B. D., & Zeigler, B. L. (1981). Excitatory and inhibitory influences on reflex responsiveness. In W. A. Collins (Ed.), *Aspects of the development of competence. The Minnesota Symposia on Child Psychology* (Vol 14). Hillsdale, NJ: Erlbaum.

Gregg, C., Clifton, R. K., & Haith, M. (1976). A possible explanation for the frequent failure to find cardiac orienting in the newborn infant. *Developmental Psychology, 12,* 75–76.

Groos, G. (1984). The physiological organization of the circadian sleep–wake cycle. In A. Borbely & J. L. Valatx (Eds.), *Sleep Mechanisms. Experimental Brain Research Supplementum 8.* Berlin: Springer-Verlag.

Groves, P. M., & Thompson, R. F. (1970). Habituation: A dual-process theory. *Psychological Review, 77,* 419–450.

Guilleminault, C., McQuitty, J., Ariagno, R., Challamel, M., Korobkin, R., & McClead, R. (1982). Congenital central alveolar hypoventilation syndrome in six infants. *Pediatrics, 70,* 684–694.

Guilleminault, C., Peraita, R., Souquet, M., & Dement, W. (1975). Apneas during sleep in infants: Possible relationship with sudden infant death syndrome. *Science, 190,* 677–679.

Gersuni, G. V. (1971). Temporal organization of the auditory function. In G. V. Gersuni (Ed.), *Sensory Processes at the Neuronal and Behavioral Levels.* New York: Academic.

Guthrie, R., Standaert, T., Hodson, W. A., & Woodrum, D., (1981). Development of CO_2 sensitivity: Effects of gestational age, postnatal age, and sleep state. *Journal of Applied Physiology: Respiratory, Environmental & Exercise Physiology, 50,* 956–961.

Haddad, G., Epstein, R., Epstein, M., Leistner, H., Marino, P., & Mellins, R. (1979). Maturation of ventilation and ventilatory pattern in normal sleeping infants. *Journal of Applied Physiology: Respiratory, Environmental & Exercise Physiology, 46,* 998–1002.

Haddad, G., Epstein, R., Epstein, M., Leistner, H., & Mellins, R. (1980). The R-R interval and R-R variability in normal infants during sleep. *Pediatric Research, 14,* 809–811.

Haddad, G., Lai, T. L., Epstein, M., Epstein, R., Yu, K., Leistner, H., & Mellins, R. (1982).

Breath-to-breath variations in rate and depth of ventilation in sleeping infants. *American Journal of Physiology, 243,* R164–R169.

Haddad, G., Lai, T. L., & Mellins, R. B. (1982). Determination of ventilatory pattern in REM sleep in normal infants. *Journal of Applied Physiology: Respiratory, Environmental & Exercise Physiology, 53,* 52–56.

Haddad, G., Leistner, H., Epstein, R., Epstein, M., Grodin, W., & Mellins, R. (1980a). CO$_2$-induced changes in ventilation and ventilatory pattern in normal sleeping infants. *Journal of Applied Physiology: Respiratory, Environmental & Exercise Physiology, 48,* 684–688.

Haddad, G., Walsh, E., Leistner, H., Grodin, W., & Mellins, R. (1981). Abnormal maturation of sleep states in infants with aborted sudden infant death syndrome. *Pediatric Research, 15,* 1055–1057.

Hall, P. S., Thomas, S. A., Friedman, E., & Lynch, J. J. (1982). Measurement of neonatal blood pressure: A new method. *Psychophysiology, 19,* 231–236.

Harper, R. M., Frostig, Z., Taube, D., Hoppenbrouwers, T., & Hodgman, J. (1983). Development of sleep–waking temporal sequencing in infants at risk for the sudden infant death syndrome. *Experimental Neurology, 79,* 821–829.

Harper, R. M., Hoppenbrouwers, T., Bannett, D., Hodgman, J., Sterman, M., & McGinty, D. (1977). Effects of feeding on state and cardiac regulation in the infant. *Developmental Psychobiology, 10,* 507–517.

Harper, R. M., Hoppenbrouwers, T., Sterman, M., McGinty, D., & Hodgman, J. (1976). Polygraphic studies of normal infants during the first six months of life: I. Heart rate and variability as a function of state. *Pediatric Research, 10,* 945–951.

Harper, R. M., Leake, B., Hodgman, J., & Hoppenbrouwers, T. (1982). Developmental patterns of heart rate and heart rate variability during sleep and waking in normal infants and infants at risk for the sudden infant death syndrome. *Sleep, 5,* 28–38.

Harper, R. M., Leake, B., Hoffman, H., Walter, D., Hoppenbrouwers, T., Hodgman, J., & Sterman, M. (1981). Periodicity of sleep states is altered in infants at risk for the sudden infant death syndrome. *Science, 213,* 1030–1032.

Harper, R. M., Leake, B., Miyahara, L., Mason, J., Hoppenbrouwers, T., Sterman, M., & Hodgman, J. (1981). Temporal sequencing in sleep and waking states during the first 6 months of life. *Experimental Neurology, 72,* 294–307.

Harper, R. M., Walter, D., Leake, B., Hoffman, H., Sieck, G., Sterman, M., Hoppenbrouwers, T., & Hodgman, J. (1978). Development of sinus arrhythmia during sleeping and waking states in normal infants. *Sleep, 1,* 33–48.

Haskell, E., Palca, J., Walker, J., Berger, R., & Heller, H. (1981). The effects of high and low ambient temperatures on human sleep stages. *Electroencephalography & Clinical Neurophysiology, 51,* 494–501.

Hellbrugge, T., Lange, J., Rutenfranz, J., & Stehr, K. (1964). Circadian periodicty of physiological functions in different stages of infancy and childhood. *Annals of the New York Academy of Sciences, 117,* 361–373.

Hofer, M. (1976). The organization of sleep and wakefulness after maternal separation in young rats. *Developmental Psychobiology, 9,* 189–205.

Hofer, M., & Shair, H. (1982). Control of sleep–wake states in the infant rat by features of the mother–infant relationship. *Developmental Psychobiology, 15,* 229–243.

Hoffman, H. S., Cohen, M., & English, L. (1985). Reflex modification by acoustic signals in newborn infants and in adults: A new approach to the objective assessment of hearing in difficult to test subjects. *Journal of Experimental Child Psychology, 39,* 562–579.

Hoffman, H. S., & Ison, J. R. (1980). Reflex modification in the domain of startle: I. Some empirical findings and their implications for how the nervous system processes sensory input. *Psychological Review, 87,* 175–189.

Hofmann, M. J., & Salapatek, P. (1981). Young infants' event-related potentials (ERPs) to familiar and unfamiliar visual and auditory events in a recognition memory task. *Electroencephalography & Clinical Neurophysiology, 52,* 405–417.

Hofmann, M. J., Salapatek, P., & Kuskowski, M. (1981). Evidence for visual memory in the averaged and single evoked potentials of human infants. *Infant Behavior & Development, 4,* 185–205.

Hopf, H., Hufschmidt, H., & Stroder, J. (1965). Development of the "trigemino-facial" reflex in infants and children. *Annales Paediatrici, 204,* 52–64.

Hoppenbrouwers, T., Combs, D., Ugartechea, J., Hodgman, J., Sterman, M., & Harper, R. (1981). Fetal heart rates during maternal wakefulness and sleep. *Obstetrics & Gynecology, 57,* 301–309.

Hoppenbrouwers, T., Harper, R., Hodgman, J., Sterman, M., & McGinty, D. (1978). Polygraphic studies of normal infants during the first six months of life: II. Respiratory rate and variability as a function of state. *Pediatric Research, 12,* 120–125.

Hoppenbrouwers, T., Hodgman, J., Harper, R., Hofmann, E., Sterman, M., & McGinty, D. (1977). Polygraphic studies of normal infants during the first six months of life: III. Incidence of apnea and periodic breathing. *Pediatrics, 60,* 418–425.

Hoppenbrouwers, T., Hodgman, J., Harper, R., & Sterman, M. (1982). Temporal distribution of sleep states, somatic activity, and autonomic activity during the first half year of life. *Sleep, 5,* 131–144.

Hoppenbrouwers, T., Ugartechea, J., Combs, D., Hodgman, J., Harper, R., & Sterman, M. (1978). Studies of maternal–fetal interaction during the last trimester of pregnancy: Ontogenesis of the basic rest–activity cycle. *Experimental Neurology, 61,* 136–153.

Hutt, C., Bernuth, H., Lenard, H., Hutt, S., & Prechtl, H. F. R. (1968). Habituation in relation to state in the human neonate. *Nature, 220,* 618–620.

Hutt, S. J., Hutt, C., Lenard, H., Bernuth, H., & Muntjewerff, W. (1968). Auditory responsivity in the human neonate. *Nature, 218,* 888–890.

Hutt, S. J., Lenard, H., & Prechtl, H. F. R. (1969). Psychophysiological studies in newborn infants. In L. P. Lipsitt & H. W. Reese (Eds.), *Advances in child development and behavior.* New York: Academic.

Jackson, J. C. (1974). Amplitude and habituation of the orienting reflex as a function of stimulus intensity. *Psychophysiology, 11,* 647–659.

Jackson, J., Kantowitz, S., & Graham, F. K. (1971). Can newborns show cardiac orienting? *Child Development, 42,* 107–121.

Jacobson, A., Kales, A., Lehmann, D., & Hoedemaker, F. (1964). Muscle tonus in human subjects during sleep and dreaming. *Experimental Neurology, 10,* 418–424.

Jeannerod, M., Mouret, J., & Jouvet, M. (1965). Etude de la motricite oculaire au cours de la phase paradoxale du sommeil chez le chat. *Electroencephalography and Clinical Neurophysiology, 18,* 554–566.

Jeffrey, W. E., & Cohen, L. B. (1971). Habituation in the human infant. In H. Reese (Ed.), *Advances in child development and behavior* (Vol. 6). New York, Academic.

Johnson, L. (1980). The REM cycle is a sleep-dependent rhythm. *Sleep, 2,* 299–307.

Johnson, L., & Lubin, A. (1966). Spontaneous electrodermal activity during sleeping and waking. *Psychophysiology, 3,* 8–17.

Johnson, L., & Lubin, A. (1967). The orienting reflex during waking and sleeping. *Electroencephalography & Clinical Neurophysiology, 1967, 22,* 11–21.

Johnson, L., Townsend, R., & Wilson, M. (1975). Habituation during sleeping and waking. *Psychophysiology, 12,* 574–584.

Junge, H. D., & Walter, H. (1980). Behavioral states and breathing activity in the fetus near term. *Journal of Perinatal Medicine, 8,* 150–157.

Kagan, J., & Lewis, M. (1965). Studies of attention in the human infant. *Merrill-Palmer Quarterly, 11,* 95–127.

Karmel, B. Z., Lester, M. L., McCarvill, S. L., Brown, P., & Hofmann, M. L. (1977). Correlation of infants' brain and behavioral response to temporal changes in visual stimulation. *Psychophysiology, 14,* 134–142.

Karmel, B. Z., & Maisel, E. B. (1975). A neuronal activity model for infant visual attention. In L. B. Cohen & P. Salapatek (Eds.), *Infant perception: From sensation to cognition: Vol 1. Basic Visual Processes.* New York: Academic.

Karrer, R., & Ackles, P. (in press). Brain organization and perceptual-cognitive development in normal and Down syndrome infants: A research program. In P. Vietze, & H. Vaughan (Eds.), *Early identification of infants at risk for mental retardation.* Orlando, FL: Grune & Stratton.

Katona, P., Frasz, A., & Egbert, J. (1980). Maturation of cardiac control in full-term and preterm infants during sleep. *Early Human Development, 4,* 145–159.

Kearsley, R. B. (1973). The newborn's response to auditory stimulation: A demonstration of orienting and defensive behavior. *Child Development, 44,* 582–590.

Keen, R. (1964). Effects of auditory stimuli on sucking behavior in the human neonate. *Journal of Experimental Child Psychology, 1,* 348–354.

Keen, J. K. (1974). *Fixation and cardiac responses of four-month infants to repeated visual stimuli of varying complexities.* Unpublished master's thesis, University of Iowa, Iowa City.

Kimura, J., Bodensteiner, J., & Yamada, T. (1977). Electrically elicited blink reflex in normal neonates. *Archives of Neurology, 34,* 246–249.

Kisilevsky, B. S., & Muir, D. W. (1984). Neonatal habituation and dishabituation to tactile stimuli during sleep. *Developmental Psychology, 1984, 20,* 367–373.

Kleitman, N. (1963). *Sleep and Wakefulness.* Chicago: University of Chicago Press.

Kleitman, N., & Engelmann, T. (1953). Sleep characteristics of infants. *Journal of Applied Physiology, 6,* 269–282.

Kligman, D., Smyrl, R., & Emde, R. (1975). A "nonintrusive" longitudinal study of infant sleep. *Psychosomatic Medicine, 37,* 448–453.

Korner, A. (1968). REM organization in neonates. *Archives of General Psychiatry, 19,* 330–340.

Koumans, A., Tursky, B., & Solomon, P. (1968). Electrodermal levels and fluctuations during normal sleep. *Psychophysiology, 5,* 300–306.

Krafchuk, E. E., Tronick, E., & Clifton, R. K. (1983). Behavioral and cardiac responsiveness to sound in preterm neonates varying in risk status: A hypothesis of their paradoxical reactivity. In T. Field & A. Sostek, (Eds.), *Infants born at risk.* New York: Grune & Stratton.

Krauss, A., Solomon, G., & Auld, P. (1977). Sleep state, apnea and bradycardia in pre-term infants. *Developmental Medicine & Child Neurology, 19,* 160–168.

Kurtzberg, D. (1985, April). *Late auditory potentials and speech sound discrimination by infants.* Paper presented at the meeting of the Society for Research in Child Development, Toronto.

Kurtzberg, D., Vaughan, H. G., Jr., Courchesne, E., Friedman, D., Harter, M. R., & Putnam, L. (1984). Developmental aspects of event-related potentials. In R. Karrer, J. Cohen, & P. Teuting (Eds.), *Brain and information: Event-related potentials. Annals of the New York Academy of Sciences* (Vol 425). New York: New York Academy of Sciences.

Lacey, B. C., & Lacey, J. I. (1980). Cognitive modulation of time-dependent primary bradycardia. *Psychophysiology, 17,* 209–222.

Landis, C., & Hunt, W. A. (1939). *The Startle Pattern.* New York: Farrer & Rinehart.

Lavie, P. (1982). Ultradian rhythms in human sleep and wakefulness. In W. B. Webb (Ed.), *Biological rhythms, sleep, and performance.* New York: Wiley.

Lavie, P., & Scherson, A. (1981). Ultrashort sleep–waking schedule. I. Evidence of ultradian rhythmicity in "sleepability." *Electroencephalography & Clinical Neurophysiology, 52,* 163–174.

Lavie, P., & Zomer, J. (1984). Ultrashort sleep-waking schedule. II. Relationship between ultradian rhythms in sleepability and the REM-non-REM cycles and effects of the circadian phase. *Electroencephalography & Clinical Neurophysiology, 57,* 35–42.

Leavitt, L. A., Brown, J., Morse, P., & Graham, F. K. (1976). Cardiac orienting and auditory discrimination in 6-week-old infants. *Developmental Psychology, 12,* 514–523.

Leistner, H., Haddad, G., Epstein, R., Lai, T., Epstein, M., & Mellins, R. (1980). Heart rate and heart rate variability during sleep in aborted sudden infant death syndrome. *Journal of Pediatrics, 97,* 51–55.

Leitner, D. S., Powers, A. S., Stitt, C. L., & Hoffman H. S. (1981). Midbrain reticular formation involvement in the inhibition of acoustic startle. *Physiology & Behavior, 26,* 259–268.

Lenard, H. (1970a). Sleep studies in infancy: Facts, concepts, and significance. *Acta Paediatrica Scandinavica, 59,* 572–581.

Lenard, H. (1970b). The development of sleep spindles in the EEG during the first two years of life. *Neuropadiatrie, 1,* 264–276.

Lenard, H., Bernuth, H., & Hutt, S. (1969). Acoustic evoked responses in newborn infants: The influence of pitch and complexity of the stimulus. *Electroencephalography & Clinical Neurophysiology, 27,* 121–127.

Lester, B. (1975). Cardiac habituation of the orienting response to an auditory signal in infants of varying nutritional status. *Developmental Psychology, 11,* 432–442.

Leventhal, A., & Lipsitt, L. P. (1964). Adaptation, pitch discrimination and sound localization in the neonate. *Child Development, 35,* 759–767.

LeVita, E. M., Kush, L. K., Rothstein, G. D., & Brown, J. W. (1980). *Auditory discrimination in human infants.* Paper presented at the meeting of the Western Psychological Association, Honolulu.

Lewis, M. (1967). A developmental study of the cardiac response to stimulus onset and offset during the first year of life. *Psychophysiology, 8,* 689–698.

Lewis, M., Bartels, B., & Goldberg, S. (1967). State as a determinant of infant's heart rate response to stimulation. *Science, 155,* 486–488.

Lewis, M., Dodd, C., & Harwitz, M. (1969). Cardiac responsivity to tactile stimulation in waking and sleeping infants. *Perceptual & Motor Skills, 29,* 259–269.

Lewis, M., Goldberg, S., & Campbell, H. (1969). A developmental study of information processing within the first three years of life: Response decrement to a redundant signal. *Monographs of the Society for Research in Child Development, 34,* (9, Ser. 133).

Lewis, M., Kagan, J., Campbell, H., & Kalafat, J. (1966). The cardiac response as a correlate of attention in infants. *Child Development, 37,* 63–71.

Lewis, M., Wilson, C., & Baumel, M. (1971). Attention distribution in the 24-month-old child: Variations in complexity and incongruity of the human form. *Child Development, 42,* 429–438.

Lipsitt, L., & Jacklin, C. (1971). Cardiac deceleration and its stability in human newborns. *Developmental Psychology, 5,* 535.

Lipsitt, L., Reilly, B., Butcher, M., & Greenwood, M. (1976). The stability and interrelationships of newborn sucking and heart rate. *Developmental Psychobiology, 9,* 305–310.

Lipton, E., Steinschneider, A., & Richmond, J. (1966). Autonomic function in the neonate: VII. Maturational changes in cardiac control. *Child Development, 37,* 1–16.

Maloney, J., Bowes, G., & Wilkinson, M. (1980). "Fetal breathing" and the development of patterns of respiration before birth. *Sleep, 3,* 299–306.

Manseau, C., & Broughton, R. (1984). Bilaterally synchronous ultradian EEG rhythms in awake adult humans. *Psychophysiology, 21,* 265–273.

Marsh, R., Hoffman, H. S., & Stitt, C. L. (1978). Reflex inhibition audiometry. *Acta Otolaryngologica, 85,* 336–341.

McCall, R., & Kagan, J. (1967). Attention in the infant: Effects of complexity, contour, perimeter, and familiarity. *Child Development, 1967, 38,* 939–952.

McCall, R., & Melson, W. (1970). Complexity, contour and area as determinants of attention in infants. *Developmental Psychology, 1970, 3,* 343–349.

McDonald, D., & Carpenter, F. (1975). Habituation of the orienting response in sleep. *Psychophysiology, 12,* 618–623.

McGinty, D. J. (1971). Encephalization and the neural control of sleep. In M. B. Sterman, D. J. McGinty, & A. M. Adinolfi (Eds.), *Brain development and behavior.* New York: Academic.

McGinty, D. J. (1985). Physiological equilibrium and the control of sleep states. In D. J. McGinty, R. Drucker-Colin, A. Morrison, & P. Parmeggiani (Eds.), *Brain mechanisms of sleep.* New York: Raven.

McGinty, D. J., & Drucker-Colin, R. (1982). Sleep mechanisms: Biology and control of REM sleep. *International Review of Neurobiology, 23,* 391–436.

McGuire, I., & Turkewitz, G. (1979). Approach–withdrawal theory and the study of infant development. In M. Bortner (Ed.), *Cognitive growth and development: Essays in memory of Herbert G. Birch.* New York: Bruner/Mazel.

Meier-Koll, A. (1979). Interactions of endogenous rhythms during postnatal development. *International Journal of Chronobiology, 6,* 179–189.

Meier-Koll, A., Hall, U., Hellwig, U., Kott, G., & Meier-Koll, V. (1978). A biological oscillator system and the development of sleep–waking behavior during early infancy. *Chronobiologia, 5,* 425–440.

Metcalf, D. (1969). The effects of extrauterine experience on the ontogenesis of EEG sleep spindles. *Psychosomatic Medicine, 31,* 393–399.

Metcalf, D. (1970a). EEG sleep spindle ontogenesis. *Neuropadiatrie, 1,* 428–433.

Metcalf, D. (1970b). The ontogenesis of sleep–wake states from birth to 3 months. *Electroencephalography & Clinical Neurophysiology, 28,* 421.

Metcalf, D., Mondale, J., & Butler, F. (1971). Ontogenesis of spontaneous K-complexes. *Psychophysiology, 8,* 340–347.

Miller, C. L., & Byrne, J. M. (1983). Psychophysiologic and behavioral response to auditory stimuli in the newborn. *Infant Behavior & Development, 6,* 369–389.

Monod, N., & Garma, L. (1971). Auditory responsivity in the human premature: *Biologia Neonatorum, 17,* 292–316.

Monod, N., & Pajot, N. (1965). Le sommeil du nouveau-ne et du premature: I. Analyse des etudes polygraphiques (mouvements oculaires, respiration et E.E.G.) chez le nouveau-ne a terme. *Biologia Neonatorum, 8,* 281–307.

Moore-Ede, M., Sulzman, F., & Fuller, C. (1982). *The clocks that time us: Physiology of the circadian timing system.* Cambridge, MA: Harvard University Press.

Morath, M. (1974). The four-hour feeding rhythm of the baby as a free running endogenously regulated rhythm. *International Journal of Chronobiology, 2,* 39–45.

Moreau, T. (1976). Modality differences in habituation and dishabituation of cardiac responsiveness in the human newborn. *Developmental Psychobiology, 9,* 109–118.

Morrongiello, B. A., & Clifton, R. K. (1984). Effects of sound frequency on behavioral and cardiac orienting in newborn and five-month-old infants. *Journal of Experimental Child Psychology, 38,* 429–446.

Morrongiello, B. A., Clifton, R. K., & Kulig, J. W. (1982). Newborn cardiac and behavioral orienting responses to sound under varying precedence-effect conditions. *Infant Behavior & Development, 5,* 249–259.

Murray, B., & Campbell, D. (1971). Sleep states in the newborn: Influence of sound. *Neuropadiatrie, 2,* 335–342.

Nakagawa, Y. (1980). Continuous observation of EEG patterns at night and in daytime of normal subjects under restrained conditions. I. Quiescent state when lying down. *Electroencephalography & Clinical Neurophysiology, 49,* 524–537.

Navelet, Y., Benoit, O., & Bouard, G. (1982). Nocturnal sleep organization during the first months of life. *Electroencephalography & Clinical Neurophysiology, 54,* 71–78.

Navelet, Y., Payan, C., Guilhaume, A., & Benoit, O. (1984). Nocturnal sleep organization in infants "at risk" for sudden infant death syndrome. *Pediatric Research, 18,* 654–657.

Nelson, C. A. (1985, April). *Electrophysiological correlates of infant recognition memory: The late positive components.* Paper presented at the meeting of the Society for Research in Child Development. Toronto, Canada.

Nelson, C. A., & Salapatek, P. (in press). Electrophysiological correlates of infant recognition memory. *Child Development.*

Nelson, M., Clifton, R. K., Dowd, J., & Field, T. (1978). Cardiac responding to auditory stimuli in newborn infants: Why pacifiers should not be used when heart rate is the major dependent variable. *Infant Behavior & Development, 1,* 277–290.

Nijhuis, J., Prechtl, H., Martin, C., & Bots, R. (1982). Are there behavioural states in the human fetus? *Early Human Development, 6,* 177–195.

Norman, J. L., Pettigrew, J. D., & Daniels, J. D. (1977). Early development of X-cells in kitten lateral geniculate nucleus. *Science, 198,* 202–204.

O'Conner, M. J. (1980). A comparison of preterm and full-term infants on auditory discriminations at four months and on Bayley scales of infant development at eighteen months. *Child Development, 51,* 81–88.

Obrist, P. (1976). The cardiovascular–behavioral interaction—As it appears today. *Psychophysiology, 13,* 95–107.

Ornitz, E., Forsythe, A., & de la Pena, A. (1973). The effect of vestibular and auditory stimulation on the rapid eye movements of REM sleep in normal children. *Electroencephalography & Clinical Neurophysiology, 34,* 379–390.

Ornitz, E., Guthrie, D., Kaplan, A., Lane, S., & Norman, R. (in press). Maturation of startle modulation in children. *Psychophysiology.*

Ornitz, E., Ritvo, E., Carr, E., Panman, L., & Walter, R. (1967). The variability of the averaged evoked response during sleep and dreaming in children and adults. *Electroencephalography & Clinical Neurophysiology, 22,* 514–524.

Ornitz, E., Ritvo, E., Lee, Y., Panman, L., Walter, R., & Mason, A. (1969). The auditory evoked response in babies during REM sleep. *Electroencephalography & Clinical Neurophysiology, 27,* 195–198.

Parmeggiani, P. (1984). Autonomic nervous system in sleep. In A. Borbely & J. L. Valat (Eds.), *Sleep mechanisms. Experimental Brain Research Supplementum 8.* Berlin: Springer-Verlag.

Parmeggiani, P. (1985). Homeostatic regulation during sleep: Facts and hypotheses. In D. J. McGinty, R. Drucker-Colin, A. Morrison, & P. Parmeggiani (Eds.), *Brain mechanisms of sleep.* New York: Raven.

Parmelee, A., Akiyama, Y., Schultz, M., Wenner, W., Schulte, F., & Stern, E. (1968). The electroencephalogram in active and quiet sleep in infants. In P. Kellaway & I. Petersen (Eds.), *Clinical electroencephalography of children.* New York, Grune & Stratton.

Parmelee, A., Akiyama, Y., Stern, E., & Harris, M. (1969). A periodic cerebral rhythm in newborn infants. *Experimental Neurology, 25,* 575–584.

Parmelee, A., Bruck, K., & Bruck, M. (1962). Activity and inactivity cycles during the sleep of premature infants exposed to neutral temperatures. *Biologia Neonatorum, 4,* 317–339.

Parmelee, A., Schulte, F., Akiyama, Y., Wenner, W., Schultz, M., & Stern, E. (1968). Maturation of EEG activity during sleep in premature infants. *Electroencephalography & Clinical Neurophysiology, 24,* 319–329.

Parmelee, A., & Stern, E. (1972). Development of states in infants. In C. B. Clemente, D. P. Purpura, & F. E. Mayer (Eds.), *Sleep and the maturing nervous system.* New York: Academic.

Parmelee, A., Stern, E., & Harris, M. (1972). Maturation of respiration in prematures and young infants. *Neuropadiatrie, 3,* 294–304.

Parmelee, A., Wenner, W., Akiyama, Y., Schultz, M., & Stern, E. (1967). Sleep states in premature infants. *Developmental Medicine & Child Neurology, 9,* 70–77.

Parmelee, A., Wenner, W., Akiyama, Y., Stern, E., & Flescher, J. (1967). Electroencephalography and brain maturation. In A. Minkowski (Ed.), *Symposium on regional development of the brain in early life.* Philadephia: Davis.

Parmelee, A., Wenner, W., & Schulz, H. (1964). Infant sleep patterns from birth to 16 weeks of age. *Journal of Pediatrics, 65,* 576–582.

Petre-Quadens, O. (1966). On the different phases of the sleep of the newborn with special reference to the activated phase, or phase d. *Journal of Neurological Sciences, 3,* 151–161.

Petre-Quadens, O. (1967). Ontogenesis of paradoxical sleep in the human newborn. *Journal of Neurological Sciences, 4,* 154–157.

Petre-Quadens, O., De Lee, C., & Remy, M. (1971). Eye movement density during sleep and brain maturation. *Brain Research, 26,* 49–56.

Phillipson, E. A. (1978). Respiratory adaptations in sleep. *Annual Review of Physiology, 40,* 133–156.

Picton, T., & Stuss, P. T. (1980). The component structure of human event-related potentials. In H. H. Kornhuber & L. Deeke (Eds.), *Motivation, motor and sensory processes in the brain: Progress in brain research* (Vol 54). Amsterdam: Elsevier.

Pomerleau, A., & Malcuit, G. (1980). Development of cardiac and behavioral responses to a three-dimensional toy stimulation in one- to six-month-old infants. *Child Development, 51,* 1187–1196.

Pomerleau, A., & Malcuit, G. (1981). State effects on concomitant cardiac and behavioral responses to a rocking stimulus in human newborns. *Infant Behavior & Development, 4,* 163–174.

Pomerleau-Malcuit, A., & Clifton, R. K. (1973). Neonatal heart-rate response to tactile, auditory, and vestibular stimulation in different states. *Child Development, 44,* 485–496.

Pomerleau-Malcuit, A., Malcuit, G., & Clifton, R. K. (1975). An attempt to elicit cardiac orienting and defense responses in the newborn to two types of facial stimulation. *Psychophysiology, 12,* 527–535.

Pompeiano, O., & Morrison, A. (1965). Vestibular influences during sleep. I. Abolition of the rapid eye movements of desynchronized sleep following vestibular lesions. *Archives of Italian Biology, 103,* 569–595.

Porges, S. (1974). Heart rate indices of newborn attentional responsivity. *Merrill-Palmer Quarterly, 20,* 231–254.

Porges, S. (1983). Heart rate patterns in neonates: A potential diagnostic window to the brain. In T. Field & A. Sostek (Eds.), *Infants born at risk: Physiological, perceptual and cognitive processes.* New York: Grune & Stratton.

Porges, S., Arnold, W., & Forbes, E. (1973). Heart rate variability: An index of attentional responsivity in human newborns. *Developmental Psychology, 8,* 85–92.

Porges, S., Stamps, L., & Walter, G. (1974). Heart rate variability and newborn heart rate responses to illumination changes. *Developmental Psychology, 10,* 507–513.

Prechtl, H. F. R. (1974). The behavioral states of the newborn infant (a review). *Brain Research, 76,* 185–212.

Prechtl, H. F. R., Fargel, J., Weinmann, H., & Bakker, H. (1979). Postures, motility and respiration of low-risk preterm infants. *Developmental Medicine and Child Neurology, 21,* 3–27.

Prechtl, H. F. R., & Lenard, H.G. (1967). A study of eye movements in sleeping newborn infants. *Brain Research, 5,* 477–493.

Price, L., & Kremen, I. (1980). Variations in behavioral response threshold within the REM period of human sleep. *Psychophysiology, 17,* 133–140.

Radvanyi, M., & Morel-Kahn, F. (1976). Sleep and heart rate variations in premature and full term babies. *Neuropadiatrie, 7,* 302–312.

Ratner, S. C. (1970). Habituation: Research and theory. In J. Reynierse (Ed.), *Current issues in animal learning.* Lincoln: University of Nebraska Press.

Rewey, H. (1973). Developmental change in infant heart rate response during sleeping and waking states. *Developmental Psychology, 8,* 35–41.

Rigatto, H., Kalapesi, Z., Leahy, F., Durand, M., MacCallum, M., & Cates, D. (1980). Chemical control of respiratory frequency and tidal volume during sleep in preterm infants. *Respiration Physiology, 41,* 117–125.

Rigatto, H., Kalapesi, Z., Leahy, F., Durand, M., MacCallum, M., & Cates, D. (1982). Ventilatory response to 100 percent and 15 percent O_2 during wakefulness and sleep in preterm infants. *Early Human Development, 7,* 1–10.

Roffwarg, H., Muzio, J., & Dement, W. (1966). Ontogenetic development of the human sleep-dream cycle. *Science, 152,* 604–619.

Ronca, A. E., Berntson, G., & Tuber, D. S. (1985). Cardiac orienting habituation to auditory and vibrotactile stimuli in the infant decerebrate rat. *Developmental Psychobiology, 18,* 545–558.

Rose, S. A. (1983). Behavioral and psychophysiological sequelae of preterm birth: The neonatal period. In T. Field & A. Sostek (Eds.), *Infants born at risk.* New York: Grune & Stratton.

Rose, S. A., Schmidt, K., & Bridger, W. (1976). Cardiac and behavioral responsivity to tactile stimulation in premature and full-term infants. *Developmental Psychology, 12,* 311–320.

Rose, S. A., Schmidt, K., & Bridger, W. (1978). Changes in tactile responsivity during sleep in the human newborn. *Developmental Psychology, 14,* 163–172.

Rose, S. A., Schmidt, K., Reese, M. L., & Bridger, W. (1980). Effects of prematurity and early intervention on responsivity to tactile stimuli: A comparison of preterm and full-term infants. *Child Development, 51,* 416–425.

Salzarulo, P., Fagioli, I., Salomon, F., & Ricour, C. (1982). Developmental trend of quiet sleep is altered by early human malnutrition and recovered by nutritional rehabilitation. *Early Human Development, 7,* 257–264.

Sameroff, A. J. (1971). Can conditioned responses be established in the newborn infant? *Developmental Psychology, 5,* 1–12.

Sameroff, A., Cashmore, T., & Dykes, A. (1973). Heart rate deceleration during visual fixation in human newborns. *Developmental Psychology, 8,* 117–119.

Samson-Dollfus, D., Nogues, B., Menard, J., Bertoldi-Lefever, I., & Geffroy, D. (1983). Delta, theta, alpha and beta power spectrum of sleep electroencephalogram in infants aged two to eleven months. *Sleep, 6,* 376–383.

Schachter, J., Williams, T., Khachaturian, Z., Tobin, M., Kruger, R., & Kerr, J. (1971). Heart rate responses to auditory clicks in neonates. *Psychophysiology, 8,* 163–179.

Schaefer, A. B. (1975). Newborn responses to nonsignal auditory stimuli: I. Electroencephalographic desynchronization. *Psychophysiology, 12,* 359–366.

Schloon, H., O'Brien, M., Scholten, C., & Prechtl, H. F. R. (1976). Muscle activity and postural behavior in newborn infants. *Neuropadiatrie, 7,* 384–415.

Schmidt, K., Rose, S., & Bridger, W. (1980). Effect of heartbeat sound on the cardiac and behavioral responsiveness to tactual stimulation in sleeping preterm infants. *Developmental Psychology, 16,* 175–184.

Schneirla, T. C. (1959). An evolutionary and developmental theory of biphasic processes underlying approach and withdrawal. In M.R. Jones (Ed.), *Nebraska Symposium on Motivation* (Vol 7). Lincoln: University of Nebraska Press.

Schulman, C. (1968). *Differentiation in the neonatal period between infants at high risk and infants at low risk for subsequent severe mental retardation.* Paper presented at the meeting of the Eastern Psychological Association, Washington D.C.

Schulman, C. (1969). Effects of auditory stimulation on heart rate in premature infants as a function of level of arousal, probability of CNS damage, and conceptional age. *Developmental Psychobiology, 2,* 172–183.

Schulman, C. (1973). Heart rate audiometry: Part I. An evaluation of heart rate response to auditory stimuli in newborn hearing screening. *Neuropadiatrie, 4,* 362–374.

Schulman-Galambos, C., & Galambos, R. (1978). Cortical responses from adults and infants to complex visual stimuli. *Electroencephalography & Clinical Neurophysiology, 45,* 425–435.

Schulte, F. J., & Bell, E. F. (1973). Bioelectric brain development. An atlas of EEG power spectra in infants and young children. *Neuropadiatrie, 4,* 30–45.

Schulte, F. J., Busse, C., & Eichhorn, W. (1977). Rapid eye movement sleep, motoneurone inhibition, and apneic spells in preterm infants. *Pediatric Research, 11,* 709–713.

Schulz, H., Dirlich, G., Balteskonis, S., & Zulley, J. (1980). The REM-NREM sleep cycle: Renewal process or periodically driven process? *Sleep, 2,* 319–328.

Schulz, H., Salzarulo, P., Fagioli, I., & Massetani, R. (1983). REM latency: Development in the first year of life. *Electroencephalography & Clinical Neurophysiology, 56,* 316–322.

Schwartz, A., Campos, J., & Baisel, E. (1973). The visual cliff: Cardiac and behavioral responses on the deep and shallow sides at five and nine months of age. *Journal of Experimental Child Psychology, 15,* 86–99.

Scott, T.D. (1972). The effects of continuous, high intensity, white noise on the human sleep cycle. *Psychophysiology, 9,* 227–232.

Shannon, D. (1980). Pathophysiologic mechanisms causing sleep apnea and hypoventilation in infants. *Sleep, 3,* 343–349.

Shannon, D., Marsland, D., Gould, J., Callahan, B., Todres, D., & Dennis, J. (1976). Central hypoventilation during quiet sleep in two infants. *Pediatrics, 57,* 342–346.

Siassi, B., Hodgman, J., Cabal, L., & Hon, E. (1979). Cardiac and respiratory activity in relation to gestation and sleep states in newborn infants. *Pediatric Research, 13,* 1163–1166.

Siddle, D. A., & Spinks, J. A. (1979). Orienting response and information processing: Some theoretical and empirical problems. In H. D. Kimmel, E. H. van Olst, & J. F. Orlebeke (Eds.), *The orienting reflex in humans.* Hillsdale, NJ: Erlbaum.

Silverstein, L. D., Graham, F. K., & Calloway, J. M. (1980). Preconditioning and excitability of the human orbicularis oculi reflex as a function of state. *Electroencephalography & Clinical Neurophysiology, 48,* 406–417.

Simons, R. F., & Zelson, M. (1985). Engaging visual stimuli and reflex blink modification. *Psychophysiology, 22,* 44–49.

Snyder, F., & Scott, J. (1972). The psychophysiology of sleep. In N. S. Greenfield & R. A. Sternbach (Eds.), *Handbook of psychophysiology.* New York: Holt, Rinehart & Winston.

Sokolov, E. N. (1963). *Perception and the Conditioned Reflex.* New York: MacMillan.

Sokolov, E. N. (1969). The modeling properties of the nervous system. In M. Cole & I. Maltzman (Eds.), *A handbook of contemporary Soviet psychology.* New York: Basic.

Sostek, A. M., & Anders. T. F. (1975). Effects of varying laboratory conditions on behavioral state organization in two- and eight-week-old infants. *Child Development, 46,* 871–878.

Sostek, A. M., Anders, T., & Sostek, A. J. (1976). Diurnal rhythms in 2- and 8-week-old infants: Sleep–waking state organization as a function of age and stress. *Psychosomatic Medicine, 38,* 250–256.

Spreng, L. F., Johnson, L. C., & Lubin, A. (1968). Autonomic correlates of eye movement bursts during stage REM sleep. *Psychophysiology, 4,* 311–323.

Sroufe, L., Waters, E., & Matas, L. (1974). Contextual determinants of infant affective response. In M. Lewis & L. Rosenblum (Eds.), *The origins of fear.* New York: Wiley.

Stamps, L. E. (1980). Relationship between heart rate indices of the orienting response and birth weight in normal full-term newborns. *Developmental Psychobiology, 13,* 33–35.

Steinschneider, A. (1968). Sound intensity and respiratory responses in the neonate. *Psychosomatic Medicine, 30,* 534–541.

Steinschneider, A. (1972). Prolonged apnea and the sudden infant death syndrome: Clinical and laboratory observations. *Pediatrics, 50,* 646–654.

Steinschneider, A., Lipton, E., & Richmond, J. (1966). Auditory sensitivity in the infant: Effect of intensity on cardiac and motor responsivity. *Child Development, 37,* 233–252.

Steinschneider, A., & Weinstein, S. (1983). Sleep repiratory instability in term neonates under hyperthermic conditions: Age, sex, type of feeding, and rapid eye movements. *Pediatric Research, 17,* 35–41.

Sterman, M. B. (1972). The basic rest–activity cycle and sleep. In C. B. Clemente, D. P. Purpura, & F. E. Mayer (Eds.), *Sleep and the maturing nervous system.* New York: Academic.

Sterman, M. B. (1979). Ontogeny of sleep: Implications for function. In R. Drucker-Colin, M. Shkurovich, & M. B. Sterman (Eds.), *The functions of sleep.* New York, Academic.

Sterman, M. B., & Bowersox, S. (1981). Sensorimotor electroencephalogram rhythmic activity: A functional gate mechanism. *Sleep, 4,* 408–422.

Sterman, M. B., Harper, R., Havens, B., Hoppenbrouwers, T., McGinty, D. J., & Hodgman, J. (1977). Quantitative analysis of infant EEG development during quiet sleep. *Electroencephalography & Clinical Neurophysiology, 43,* 371–385.

Sterman, M. B., & Hoppenbrouwers, T. (1971). The development of sleep–waking and rest–activity patterns from fetus to adult in man. In M. B. Sterman, D. J. McGinty, & A. M. Adinolfi (Eds.), *Brain development and behavior.* New York: Academic.

Sterman, M. B., McGinty, D. J., Harper, R. M., Hoppenbrouwers, T., & Hodgman, J. (1982). Developmental comparison of sleep EEG power spectral patterns in infants at low and high risk for sudden death. *Electroencephalography & Clinical Neurophysiology, 53,* 166–181.

Stern, E., Parmelee, A., Akiyama, Y., Schultz, M., & Wenner, W. (1969). Sleep cycle characteristics in infants. *Pediatrics, 43,* 65–70.

Stern, E., Parmelee, A., & Harris, M. (1973). Sleep state periodicity in prematures and young infants. *Developmental Psychobiology, 6,* 357–365.

Strock, B. D. (1981). *Infant reflex excitability during quiet and active sleep.* Unpublished doctoral dissertation, University of Wisconsin, Madison.

Sullivan, C., Murphy, E., Kozar, L., & Phillipson, E. A. (1979). Ventilatory responses to CO_2 and lung inflation in tonic versus phasic REM sleep. *Journal of Applied Physiology: Respiratory, Environmental & Exercise Physiology, 47,* 1304–1310.

Sutton, S., & Ruchkin, D. (1984). The late positive complex: Advances and new problems. In R. Karrer, J. Cohen, & P. Tueting (Eds.), *Brain and information: Event-related potentials. Annals of the New York Academy of Sciences*, (Vol. 425). New York: New York Academy of Sciences.

Sutton, S., Braren, M., Zubin, J., & John, E. R. (1965). Evoked potential correlates of stimulus uncertainty. *Science, 150,* 1187–1188.

Sutton, S., Tueting, P., Zubin, J., & John E. R. (1967). Information delivery and the sensory evoked potential. *Science, 155,* 1436–1439.

Szymusiak, R., & Satinoff, E. (1985). Thermal influences on basal forebrain hypnogenic mechanisms. In D. J. McGinty, R. Drucker-Colin, A. Morrison, & P. Parmeggiani (Eds.), *Brain mechanisms of sleep.* New York: Raven.

Szymusiak, R., Satinoff, E., Schallert, T., & Wishaw, I. (1980). Brief skin temperature changes toward thermoneutrality trigger REM sleep in rats. *Physiology & Behavior, 25,* 305–311.

Theorell, K., Prechtl, H., Blair, A., & Lind, J. (1973). Behavioral state cycles of normal newborn infants: A comparison of the effects of early and late cord clamping. *Developmental Medicine & Child Neurology, 15,* 597–605.

Thompson, R. F., & Spencer, W. A. (1966). Habituation: A model phenomenon for the study of neuronal substrates of behavior. *Psychological Review, 73,* 16–43.

Timor-Tritsch, I., Dierker, L., Hertz, R., Chik, L., & Rosen, M. (1980). Regular and irregular human fetal respiratory movement. *Early Human Development, 4,* 315–324.

Tuber, D. S., Berntson, G. G., Bachman, D. S., & Allen, J. N. (1980). Associative learning in premature hydrancephalic and normal twins. *Science, 210,* 1035–1037.

Turkewitz, G., Birch, H., & Cooper, K. (1972a). Patterns of response to different auditory stimuli in the human newborn. *Developmental Medicine & Child Neurology, 14,* 487–491.

Turkewitz, G., Birch, H., & Cooper, K. (1972b). Responsiveness to simple and complex auditory stimuli in the human newborn. *Developmental Psychobiology, 5,* 7–19.

van Geijn, H., Jongsma, H., DeHaan, J., Eskes, T., & Prechtl, H. F. R. (1980). Heart rate as an indicator of the behavioral state. *American Journal of Obstetrics & Gynecology, 136,* 1061–1066.

Ver Hoeve, J. N. (1984). Newborn cardiac indices of processing transient versus steady-state acoustic stimuli. *Infant Behavior & Development, 7,* 372.

Ver Hoeve, J. N., & Leavitt, L. A. (1985). Neonatal acoustically elicited cardiac response: Modulation by state and antecedent stimulation. *Psychophysiology, 22,* 231–236.

Verillo, R. T. (1968). A duplex mechanism of mechanoreception. In D. R. Kenshalo (Ed.), *The skin senses.* Springfield, IL: Charles C. Thomas.

Von Bargen, D. M. (1983). Infant heart rate: A review of research and methodology. *Merrill-Palmer Quarterly, 29,* 115–149.

Waite, S., & Thoman, E. (1981). Brief apneas and reliable assessment of respiratory instability. *Sleep, 4,* 61–69.

Watanabe, K., Inokuma, K., & Negoro, T. (1983). REM sleep prevents sudden infant death syndrome. *European Journal of Pediatrics, 140,* 289–292.

Watanabe, K., Iwase, K., & Hara, K. (1973). Heart rate variability during sleep and wakefulness in low birthweight infants. *Biologia Neonatorum, 22,* 87–98.

Waters, E., Matas, L., & Sroufe, L. A. (1975). Infants' reactions to an approaching stranger: Description, validation, and functional significance of wariness. *Child Development, 46,* 348–356.

Webb, W. B., Agnew, H., & Sternthal, H. (1966). Sleep during the early morning. *Psychonomic Science, 6,* 277–278.

Wever, R. (1984). Circadian aspects of human sleep. In A. Borbely & J. L. Valatx (Eds.), *Sleep mechanisms. Experimental Brain Research Supplementum 8.* Berlin: Springer-Verlag.

Williams, H., Holloway, F., & Griffiths, W. (1973). Physiological psychology: Sleep. *Annual Review of Psychology, 24,* 279–316.

Williams, T. A., Schachter, J., & Tobin, M. (1967). Spontaneous variation in heart rate: Relationship to the average evoked heart rate response to auditory stimuli in the neonate. *Psychophysiology, 4,* 104–111.

Wolff, P. H. (1966). The causes, controls and organization of behavior in the neonate. *Psychological Issues, 5,* 1–105.

Yakovlev, P. I., & Lecours, A. (1967). The myelogenic cycles of regional maturation of the brain. In A. Minkowski (Ed.), *Regional development of the brain in early life.* Philadelphia: F. A. Davis.

CHAPTER 6

Cross-Modal Abilities in Human Infants

SUSAN A. ROSE and HOLLY A. RUFF

INTRODUCTION

The acquisition of knowledge about the world requires that information about the environment and about the self in the environment be picked up by the various perceptual systems (Gibson, 1966). How the different perceptual systems cooperate in the pickup of this information is a major epistemological issue as well as a perceptual one (Pick, in press). A special manifestation of this cooperation lies in the various cross-modal abilities seen in both humans and animals. Adult humans, for example, readily recognize many objects whether they are only touching them, listening to them, or looking at them; in some cases, they can identify objects by one perceptual system even though their previous experience of those objects has been limited to one of the others. This ability is referred to as *cross-modal transfer.* When an adult recognizes that two objects simultaneously experienced are the same even though each is perceived with a different system, the ability is referred to as *cross-modal matching.* How are these abilities to be understood, and how do they develop?

Cross-modal matching and cross-modal transfer require that the experience in the two perceptual systems be equivalent in some respect. How does this equivalence come about? By what means are the different systems related? Two general views prevail. One is that the systems can be related only through experience. This view is strongly associated with the legacy of the British empiricists. To quote from Bishop Berkeley:

> Sitting in my study I hear a coach drive along the street; I look through the casement and see it; I walk out and enter it. Thus, common speech would incline one to think I heard, saw and touched the same thing, to wit, the coach. It is nevertheless certain the ideas intromitted by each sense are widely different and distinct from each other, but having been observed constantly to go together, they are spoken of as one and the same thing.

> *(Boring, p. 185)*

The authors contributed equally to the writing of this chapter. Work on the chapter was supported by a Behavioral Sciences Research Grant from the National Foundation/March of Dimes and by grants HD 13810 and HD 19696 from the National Institutes of Health. We would like to express our appreciation to Gerald Turkewitz and David Lewkowicz for carefully reading earlier versions of this manuscript. Special thanks go to Emily Bushnell for her comprehensive review of the chapter and for comments that were very helpful in making the final revisions.

Equivalences must be achieved by the imposition of a mediating process that is attached to the sensations in both modalities and that serves to bridge a gap that exists between the modalities. Language has been postulated as one such mediator. Visual imaging is another. So, for example, one comes to know that certain visual features go with certain tactual features because some mediating link has been established between them.

What evidence is there for such a view? It is certainly the case that the receptors and the cortical pathways to some extent are unique for each system and that each is sensitive to a different form of energy. If we focus on these differences, how a unique pattern of stimulation in one modality becomes equivalent to another unique pattern in a second modality is a major issue. A number of investigators have also noted psychological ways in which the modalities differ in what is perceived and how information is stored. In a discussion of tactile perception, Revesz (1933/1950) suggested that the laws governing vision were not necessarily generalizable to touch and that modality differences in processing information were often profound. Studies of the blind do suggest that they perceive form and space differently from the sighted and that the errors made in tactual identification are quite different from those made in visual identification (Worchel, 1950). Even in the sighted, information picked up by hand and that picked up by eye are not always equivalent (Friedes, 1974). Touch, for example, has proved to be more sensitive to changes in curvature than orientation, whereas the reverse is true for vision (Goodnow, 1969). Some research suggests that visual information and tactual information are stored separately and that their decay rates are different (Heller, 1980; Posner, 1967). In line with these differences, there are asymmetries in cross-modal matching. For example, it is sometimes easier to select the correct tactual match for stimuli that were previously seen than to select the correct visual match for stimuli previously touched (e.g., Milner & Bryant, 1968; Rose, Blank, & Bridger, 1972). If touch and vision sample different properties, use different strategies, and follow different laws, then how an object may be recognized from information acquired by different systems becomes a matter of some concern (e.g., Birch & Lefford, 1963, 1967). Pick (1970, 1974), in fact, has suggested that haptic information about shape and spatial position is translated into a visual code, thereby raising the possibility that cross-modal transfer requires the translation of information from the code of one system into that of another.

In contrast, in a second view of how the systems are related, equivalences are thought to exist by virtue of the fact that the different systems detect invariants specifying the same properties of objects and events. In this view, therefore, there is no need for "transfer" because the response is now based on the direct perception of the same object in both modalities. For example, the fact that infants and chimpanzees show transfer from tactual experience with an object to line drawings of the object (Davenport, Rogers, & Russell, 1975; Rose, Gottfried, & Bridger, 1983) suggests that haptic exploration leads to information about contour that is not specific to a pattern of pressures on the hand and fingers or to a pattern of brightness differences on the retina. The information might better be conceived of as a pattern of spatiotemporal changes that can be picked up in a number of different ways. Research on sensory substitution underscores this possibility. For example, White, Saunders, Scadden, Bach-y-Rita, and Collins (1970) found that the image of an object could be conveyed through a camera to a matrix of 400 vibrators on the back; they report that blindfolded subjects required very little experience to be able to recognize common objects and to perceive the position in space of the objects. This work is not necessarily directly relevant to the process of gathering information from the movement of fingers over an object, but it does raise the possibility that recognition is tied more to a particular pattern of stimulation than to a particular system.

If some of the information obtained by various systems is abstract, then we can ask how the system extracts such abstract information from specific kinds of stimulation. One view is that the brain progressively reduces input as impulses travel from the peripheral nervous system through the primary cortical sites to the association areas; the terminal areas of the brain, therefore, are responding to a more abstract and less complex stimulus than the peripheral receptors responded to. It is possible that the final abstract description is represented in the same parts of the brain or by the same mechanism regardless of the system that responded to the input in the first place. If this were so, then the theoretically amodal nature of some stimulation would have a physical base.

A primary concern of the chapter is naturally with development. There are a number of accounts of how cross-modal or intermodal integration develops. Historically speaking, however, such views tend to revolve around one of two fundamentally different assumptions: There exists an initial separation of the systems or an initial unity. Many theorists consider that the modalities are independent at birth and that only coordinated experience leads to an integration of these originally independent systems. Piaget (1952; Piaget & Inhelder, 1956), for example, states that the child constructs separate action schemata for seeing, touching, and hearing, and only later coordinates them in a way that allows for intermodal correspondences. The lawful nature of these coordinations is thought to lead to *reciprocal assimilation* in which, for example, distinct visual sensations are associated with distinct tactual sensations.

Although there is little direct experimental evidence to indicate how cross-modal connections might actually be formed by associative experience, Bushnell (1981) provides a thoughtful account of how such coordination could develop between the tactual and visual systems. She suggests, for example, that the tonic neck reflex and the rooting reflex are two built-in means by which the infant comes to learn that what is seen in one place can also be touched. Initially, therefore, there is equivalence of location. Later, when the infant can reliably reach for and grasp objects, it can begin to learn that the tactual perception of an object and its properties is related to the visual perception of that object. In this way, combinations of modality-specific properties become part of the object's identity (Bushnell, in press).

An initial unity of the systems is frequently considered to be related to the pickup of amodal properties, such as shape, size, substance, duration, and intensity. Since by their very nature these properties can be picked up by different systems without prior coordinated experience, matching or transfer between the systems could theoretically be present from the beginning. As Walker-Andrews and Gibson (in press) note: "There is not enrichment through reference to a category organized from earlier experience. Instead, the invariants are revealed through movements of the object and/or observer which in and of themselves specify the enduring properties of the distal object." The modality detecting the invariants is irrelevant; development in all modalities basically consists of the extraction of invariants and the progressive differentiation of distinctive features.

In a more explicit statement of initial unity, Bower (1974) suggests that the newborn infant is born with the systems undifferentiated so that the infant does not "know" whether it is seeing or hearing or feeling something; it simply responds to the object. Development then involves differentiation. In this view, certain phenomenal aspects of stimulation are initially perceived regardless of modality, *not* because invariants are extracted, but rather because the modalities themselves are not differentiated. Turkewitz, Gardner, and Lewkowicz (1984) have proposed a variant of this view in which the initial unity is based on the effective intensity, or the quantitative aspects, of the stimuli. So, for example, size and brightness are not viewed as separate and distinct attributes of stimulation. Instead, size differences are responded to in terms of how much stimulation is produced by the corresponding larger and smaller objects; similarly, brightness is responded to in terms of "how much" rather than "how bright." The underlying metric is considered to be units of effective intensity.

There have been a number of recent studies of cross-modal transfer in infants, the primary focus of this chapter. What do these studies tell us about how the ability develops with age? Can the development of cross-modal abilities be accounted for solely by the development of intramodal abilities, or is something else required? What is the nature of the information that underlies the equivalences involved in cross-modal matching and transfer? And how does the nature of the information picked up change with age? How much of development is dependent upon changing strategies of acquiring information about objects? How much is dependent upon increasing experience in which there is simultaneous stimulation of the different modalities by objects or events?

In order to examine these issues, we will first review the existing studies on infants. The purpose of this review is to acquaint the reader with the phenomena that have been established. The discussion that follows will focus first on how the studies illuminate the different points of view on the relationship between perceptual systems and then on some specific developmental issues. We will try to place the current studies in perspective and to suggest other ways of approaching the general problem.

REVIEW OF THE CURRENT LITERATURE

Since it is essential to place some limits on the topic being covered in this chapter, we will exclude from consideration all studies that focus solely on how stimulation in one modality may serve as a cue that information is available in another modality (e.g., Mendelson & Haith, 1976; Turkewitz, Birch, Moreau, Levy, & Cornwell, 1966) or may modify the general responsiveness to stimulation in a second modality (Horowitz, 1974; Lawson & Ruff, 1984). We make these exclusions because in these cases the information in the two modalities does not have to be equivalent in any way. Recent reviews of intermodal perception by Harris (1983) and Spelke (1984) provide a thorough discussion of the literature available in these areas. We will focus, therefore, on studies in which the information in both modalities specifies the same object or event. Our review is further limited, with very few exceptions, to studies published in refereed journals. Because there are very few studies that are developmental in the sense that they assess performance over age, the review has generally been organized according to the age of the subjects in order to facilitate discussion of what happens with age. Tactual–visual and auditory–visual studies will be considered separately.

Methods

Several methods have been used to study cross-modal abilities. One of these is the matching experiment in which the subject is given the opportunity to explore simultaneously an object in one modality and another object in another modality. If, for example, two objects are visible while an object identical to one is being explored tactually, either a trained or spontaneous response to the visible object like the one being touched represents matching. A variant of this technique is used in auditory–visual studies where the source of a sound track is located between two films; in this case, looking more to the sound-specified film is evidence for matching. In both cases, two systems are simultaneously picking up equivalent information. When the experiences of the two systems are separated in time, the task is referred to as *cross-modal transfer*. Subjects are given a period of time to become familiar with the aspects of an object or event that are available to one system, or they are trained to make a response to a particular object in one system. Then the subjects are tested with a different system in isolation to determine whether they can recognize the object or event or respond correctly according to their previous training. That is, does the subject transfer information from one system to another?

Although both techniques are used successfully to demonstrate that there is coordination between different systems, the two techniques may be said to be assessing this coordination at different levels. In matching, the subject must respond to the equivalence or discrepancy between the information being picked up simultaneously by the two systems. Certain phenomena that operate in these circumstances may work against the subject's noticing discrepancies. For example, several studies with distorting prisms (Hay, Pick, & Ikeda, 1965; Rock & Victor, 1964) suggest that vision dominates when touch and vision are put into conflict and does so to such an extent that the location and even the shape of the felt object are perceived as equivalent to the visual object. Vision may dominate in localization in that sound may be perceived as coming from a visual source even though it is in actuality displaced from it. A clear auditory rhythm, on the other hand, may impose structure on the perception of a random visual event (Welch & Warren, 1980). Even if the perception through one system is not distorted in any way, simultaneous stimulation allows one system to guide and focus the attention of the observer. For example, different aspects of a visual event may be detected in the presence and absence of a particular sound (see Bahrick, Walker, & Neisser, 1981, for a good example).

These influences cannot operate directly in the transfer paradigm. Consequently, the transfer paradigm would seem to be better suited to the issue of whether information in the two modalities specifies the same object or event. If a subject can feel an object or hear a particular rhythm without any accompanying visual experience, and subsequently recognize that object or rhythm when it is presented only visually, then it would appear that what was specified by the stimulation of the first system is still relevant despite the switch in systems. Negative evidence, on the other hand, may stem from a failure to remember information from familiarization to test, a problem that does not exist in the matching paradigm.

Probably most people would agree that the highest level of coordination exists when the experience with one system leads directly to expectations about what will be experienced through another system; for example, when a subject feels an object and expects it to look a certain way. Some investigators may consider the existence of transfer to be evidence for such expectations, but because something is recognized on the basis of past experience does not logically imply that the previous experience led to any particular expectations. The least-used technique of violation of expectancy where some indication of surprise or puzzlement is measured would seem to provide the most straightforward evidence for the presence of specific expectations. The problem in this technique is to decide what behavior can be used to index the surprise or puzzlement. The studies to be reviewed involve all of these methods; it is important to consider what inferences can be drawn from different methods and what level of cross-modal functioning is being assessed.

Transfer Between the Haptic/Tactual and Visual Systems

The youngest age at which tactual–visual transfer has been demonstrated is 1 month. Meltzoff and Borton (1979) examined oral–visual transfer in infants in the age range of 26–37 days. These investigators used the familiarization–response to novelty paradigm that has been popular in cross-modal studies of vision and touch. One object, shielded from view, was presented tactually (orally) to the infant for a period of time. Then, as a test of recognition, the familiar and a novel object were simultaneously presented for visual inspection. The critical measure was whether the infant differentiated between novel and familiar by looking significantly more at one or the other. Specifically, a plain, smooth sphere or a nubby one was attached to a pacifier and inserted into the infant's mouth for 90 sec of oral familiarization. Afterwards, the infant was presented with both objects for a 20-sec visual test. The objects used for visual presentation were considerably larger than those used for oral familiarization. Even so, the infants showed a significant preference for looking at the object of the same shape as the one they had sucked on previously; that is, there was a familiarity preference. These findings were replicated in a second identical experiment. Meltzoff and Borton suggest that the transfer of information across modalities is a fundamental characteristic of the human being's perceptual-cognitive system and does not depend upon learning.

In another experiment with 1-month-olds, Gibson and Walker (1984) investigated oral–visual transfer of information about substance. In this study, infants were presented orally with a rigid or an elastic cylinder for 60 sec; they then watched a visual display in which a rigid and an elastic cylinder were simultaneously manipulated by two black-gloved hands for 60 sec. The lengths of the objects presented orally and visually were the same, but the diameters were larger for the visual display. The infants differentiated between novel and familiar, but in this study the significant preference was for the novel object. Gibson and Walker conclude that information about substance is picked up by infants as young as 1 month.

The results of the two studies with 1-month-olds are consistent in that oral experience with one object is followed by visual differentiation. It is somewhat troublesome that there was a familiarity preference in one study and a novelty preference in the other, but the discrepancy may be related to the length of familiarization and the nature of the information to be picked up. Although both demonstrations are provocative, a systematic search for the basis of the discriminations is required. The use of only a single pair of objects necessarily leaves the interpretation open, since the infants could be responding to a number of dimensions, such as texture, amount of contour, or overall intensity differences. This is a critical issue that will be dealt with more completely in the discussion.

A recent unpublished study of cross-modal transfer of form in 5-month-olds (Streri, Pecheux, & Vurpillot, 1984) is reported here because of the completeness of the design. This study included both intramodal conditions (visual–visual and tactual–tactual) and both cross-modal conditions (visual–tactual and tactual–visual). As was not the case with most of the other studies to be reviewed, the authors used a habituation paradigm with the infant control procedure in which trial duration is determined by each infant's behavior. In this case, trial length was defined as equivalent to the duration of the infant's first look or first grasp. Habituation trials continued to a criterion in which two consecutive looks (or grasps) lasted for less than half the duration of the first two looks (or grasps) or for a maximum of 10 trials. A single posthabituation trial followed. In the intramodal conditions, either the novel or the familiar member of the pair was presented in the same modality; in the cross-modal conditions, either the familiar or the novel object was presented to the other modality. Since grasps and looks are not equivalent response measures (looks are shorter than grasps) and since enhanced attention might be anticipated on cross-modal posthabituation trials simply because of the change in modality, the response on posthabituation trials could not be compared directly with the response on prior criterion trials. Therefore, cross-modal performance was evaluated by including posthabituation trials with both objects in the new modality and then comparing the responses to the novel and familiar objects on these trials.

In the visual–tactual condition, the new shape attracted significantly more attention; in the tactual–visual condition, no differentiation between novel and familiar occurred. This latter failure cannot be attributed to differences in the abilities of the two systems to pick up information both because intramodal transfer was found in both modalities and because cross-modal transfer occurred in one direction. Nevertheless, the fact that there was visual–tactual transfer and not tactual–visual transfer suggests that the information available for transfer was different after the tactual and visual habituation periods. It is possible that some difference would have arisen from differential constraints on tactual and visual exploration; any active attempts to manipulate the object, for example, may have caused the infant to drop it and terminate the trial. It is clear, however, that some information was obtained from the successive grasps, and it is possible that the infants obtained as much information as would be possible at that age. The study has the cardinal virtue of including all possible conditions, a factor that will be increasingly important to our understanding of developmental trends in cross-modal transfer and to our understanding of the processes underlying recognition by the different systems.

The familiarization–response to novelty technique has been used in several studies with 6-month-olds. In a study by Ruff and Kohler (1978), infants were given either a sphere or a cube to hold in one hand for 30 sec; they were then visually presented with both the sphere and the cube for two 10-sec trials. Although there was no overall preference for either the novel or the familiar objects, once a strong spontaneous preference for the sphere was taken into account, a preference for the familiar object emerged. That is, although the infants looked more at the sphere than at the cube on the test trials, those who had previously felt the sphere looked significantly more at it than did the infants who had felt the cube.

Rose, Gottfried, and Bridger (1981b) also investigated tactual–visual transfer of information about shape in 6-month-olds. In the first experiment, one object, shielded from view, was presented orally or manually to the infant for 30 sec and then the familiar and a novel object were simultaneously presented visually for two 10-sec trials. Three pairs of objects were used, one in the oral–visual task (a sphere and a cube) and two in the manual–visual tasks. In the latter, one pair consisted of a cross and a tapered ellipsoid, the other of a cylinder and a cylinder incised with curved indentations. In this experiment, infants failed to demonstrate tactual–visual transfer on any task, even though the conditions were identical to those that had been used successfully with 12-month-olds (Gottfried, Rose, & Bridger, 1977). A second experiment suggested that the younger infants were hampered by a slower rate of acquiring information. When the familiarization times were increased to 60 sec on each problem, 6-month-olds then showed successful transfer on both manual–visual problems; there was still no evidence for oral–visual transfer. In the third experiment, a matching design was used. Here the familiarization time was reduced to 30 sec again, but after the familiarization period ended, the infants were allowed to keep the object in their hands or mouths during the visual test. Even with this briefer familiarization period, 6-month-olds were successful in one of the manual–visual problems. As in the first two experiments, however, infants again showed no evidence of oral–visual transfer. Unlike Meltzoff and Borton (1979) and Gibson and Walker (1984), who used enlarged versions of their familiarization objects for the visual test, Rose and colleagues (1981b) used identical objects in both phases of all three experiments. Failure in these oral–visual conditions cannot, however, be attributed to the object's small size, since the results of a fourth experiment showed that infants could readily discriminate the cube and the sphere visually. Since the objects in this series of experiments were the same as those used with older infants, the authors concluded that cross-modal transfer is less robust at 6 months than at older ages.

Bryant, Jones, Claxton, and Perkins (1972) reported results on subjects who averaged 8 1/2 months. Their procedure, which had three stages, was based on the observation that infants are attracted to and reach for sound-producing objects. First a pair of objects were presented visually, silently and out of reach. Then both objects were removed from sight and one member was put into one of the infant's hands and made to produce a sound; the infant could not see the object. Finally, both members of the pair were again presented visually and the infant was permitted to reach for one. Two pairs of objects were used: Pair A consisted of an ellipsoid and an incomplete ellipsoid with an indentation; pair B consisted of a cube and similarly imcomplete cube. Significantly more infants reached for the member of pair A that they had previously handled; infants did not reach differentially for the objects in pair B. In a visual intramodal condition, the first and third stages were the same, but in the second stage, one of the objects was presented visually, instead of tactually, and made to produce its sound. Here, with both pairs, significantly more infants reached for the object previously presented with sound. The cross-modal results were replicated in a double-blind experiment where, as before, only pair A led to significant results. The failure of infants to show cross-modal recognition with pair B, where both stimuli had straight contours, led Bryant and colleagues to suggest that a "straight–straight discrimination is a very difficult one whether tactually or cross-modally" (p. 304).

Bushnell (1982) conducted a study of the cross-modal abilities of infants 8–11 1/2 months old using a violation of expectancy paradigm in which an arrangement of mirrors allowed one object to be seen at a particular location while a second, sometimes different, object was actually located there. When the infant reached into the apparatus and grasped the object, the expectancy formed from looking at it could be confirmed or violated. Comparisons were made between the infants' reactions on trick trials, when the seen object and the felt object were different, and their reactions on control trials where the seen and felt objects were identical. Trials lasted for 20 sec, beginning from the child's first voluntary touch of the object. Bushnell scored both the infant's looking and touching; more important, however, naive observers made forced choices from the videotapes on each pair of trick and control trials; they had to judge whether the trick or control trial occurred first. The observers, who were reliable in their judgments, reported basing their decisions on a variety of behavioral clues such as facial expressions of surprise or puzzlement, accuracy and confidence of grasp, and the presence or absence of reaching movements around the area of the object after contact. In this study, where the objects differed on both shape and texture (a fur-covered cylinder vs. a smooth plastic object that had protruding knobs), 9 1/2- and 11-month-olds responded differentially to trick and control trials while 8-month-olds did not.

In a recent unpublished study (Bushnell, Weinberger, & Polan, 1984) 11-month-olds differentiated a smooth egg-shaped block from a furry cube and a smooth cross from a furry cube, but failed to differentiate similar objects that differed along only one dimension (cross–cube and smooth–furry), suggesting that in some conditions cross-modal matching is easier when more than one dimension of difference exists. Although the 11-month-olds showed evidence of noticing the discrepancy when the cross was presented visually and the cube tactually, they did not seem to notice the difference when the cube was presented visually and the cross tactually. The authors suggest that infants may note distinctive features of what is seen and then search for these features with their hands. It is possible that a cross's intersection, once seen, is a more distinctive feature for which to search than are features such as corners, which are common to both the cube and cross. Interpretation would be helped by results from conditions in which the tactual experience precedes the visual one.

In an extension of their previous work on visual differentiation of elastic and rigid objects (Gibson, Owsley, & Johnston, 1978; Gibson, Owsley, Walker, & Megaw-Nyce, 1979; Walker, Gibson, Owsley, Megaw-Nyce, & Bahrick, 1980), Gibson and Walker (1984) investigated tactual–visual transfer of information about substance in 12-month-olds. The infants explored rigid (wooden) or elastic (sponge) objects tactually in the dark for 60 sec; the wooden objects were covered with a thin layer of foam so that surface properties were equivalent in the two conditions. The infants were then shown two movies in which an elastic object underwent deformation and a rigid object rotated around the horizontal and vertical axes. In the 30-sec visual test, the duration of first look was longer to the movie of the familiar substance; the overall proportion of time spent looking at the movies was not significantly different. In a second experiment, the conditions and objects were the same, but during familiarization, the infants handled the objects in the light thereby obtaining both visual and tactual information about substance, a task similar to one used by Gottfried and Rose (1980). In this study, a significant preference for the "familiar" movie was obtained with total looking as well as for the length of the first look. In both of the studies, the exploratory activities of the infants were different for the two kinds of objects. The infants tended to strike the rigid objects against the table more than the elastic ones while they pressed the elastic objects more than the rigid ones.

Rose and her colleagues have studied cross-modal transfer extensively in 12-month-olds. In the first study (Gottfried et al., 1977), infants were given three tactual–visual tasks (one oral–visual, two manual–visual) and three visual–visual tasks. A different pair of objects was used on each task, with members of a pair differing principally in shape. In this and subsequent studies by this group, the shapes were generally paired so as to pit angular against curvilinear forms, and topologically open against closed forms. Stimulus differences, however, were not systematically studied. Each task consisted of a 30-sec familiarization period, during which the infant mouthed, handled, or viewed one member of a pair, then a visual test during which both members of the pair were presented together visually for 20 sec, and finally a reaching test during which the infant was permitted to pick up one member of the pair. On all six tasks, the infants looked significantly more at the novel object and reached significantly more often for it as well.

Another study (Rose et al., 1983) begins to approach the issue of the nature of the information that is picked up. Infants were either visually or tactually familiarized with objects and then tested with the objects themselves, silhouette pictures of the objects, or line drawings of the objects. These test objects were selected to reflect degrees of pictorial abstractness with the outline drawing being more abstract than the pictures. In the first experiment, one group of 12-month-olds was tested for visual transfer after 30 sec of visual familiarization whereas a second group was tested for visual transfer after 30 sec of tactual familiarization. Infants showed visual–visual transfer to all three types of displays but showed tactual–visual transfer only to the objects. A second experiment suggested that infants need to feel the object longer before they can recognize its contour in a pictorial display. Here, where the infants were given 45 sec of tactual familiarization time, tactual–visual transfer was successful in all three conditions. The results of a third experiment lend support to the idea that recognition on the basis of pictorial contour alone is relatively difficult even visually. When visual familiarization was reduced to 15 sec, visual–visual transfer was successful only with the objects. These results are important in that they suggest that the tactual system requires more time to pick up the same information as the visual system. Even more important, they reveal the abstract nature of the information that is apparently used in recognizing objects in either modality (see also Rose, in press).

The relative difficulty of the cross-modal tactual–visual tasks found in several of these studies could occur because infants have difficulty with transfer across modalities or because infants experience difficulty in acquiring or retaining tactual information. The assessment of tactual recognition, however, required a new technique; Gottfried and Rose (1980) examined infants' manipulation of novel and familiar objects in darkness, videotaping their behavior under infrared light. In this study, 12-month-olds were administered two tasks. In both tasks, there was a 60-sec familiarization period in the light during which the infant was presented with five identical objects to look at and manipulate. In the 2-min test period that followed the infant was presented with the five original objects and five replicas of a novel object. In one task the test took place in the light and in the other the test took place in the dark. The comparison, therefore, was between a visual–tactual test and a solely tactual test. Two sets of objects were used; one consisted of star- and disc-shaped objects, the other of hexagonal and hourglass-shaped objects. The sets were counterbalanced across tasks. The results showed that, whether the test took place in light or darkness, the infants engaged in significantly more manipulation, more mouthing, and more hand-to-hand transfers of the novel shapes. In other words, infants recognized the objects by touch alone. These results were consistent with those of Soroka, Corter, and Abramovitch (1979).

In a follow-up study (Rose, Gottfried, & Bridger, 1981a) this measure of tactual recognition was used to assess tactual–tactual performance and to compare it with visual–tactual cross-modal performance. All tactual exploration, either during familiarization or during test, was carried out in total darkness. In the first of two experiments, which used the same two sets of objects used in Gottfried and Rose (1980), infants successfully differentiated novel from familiar objects by tactual exploration after 60 sec of either visual or tactual familiarization. In both tests, infants spent significantly more time manipulating the novel shapes. In the tactual–tactual condition, but not in the visual–tactual condition, they also engaged in more manipulatory episodes with novel shapes and exhibited more hand-to-hand transfer of the novel objects. Neither type of transfer was shown with shorter (30 sec) familiarization periods. The finding of successful tactual–tactual transfer with 60 sec of familiarization was confirmed in a second experiment using different stimuli, a sphere and a sphere with an indentation, and a modified procedure that more closely approximated the paired-comparison procedure used in studies of visual–visual and tactual–visual transfer. In both experiments there was evidence that performance in the tactual–tactual problems surpassed performance in the visual–tactual transfer.

Finally, two studies suggest that cross-modal transfer reflects a cognitive process or at least the integrity of the nervous system by showing that performance on such tasks varies with SES and risk (Rose, Gottfried, & Bridger, 1978) and that it is predictive of later cognitive status (Rose & Wallace, 1985).

Summary of Studies of Vision and Touch

Many of the studies are demonstrations that some equivalence between the two systems exists. Only one of the studies included more than one age group (Bushnell, 1982). In that study, there seemed to be a difference between 8 months and 9 1/2 months in whether a discrepancy in information from the two systems was noted; the negative results at 8 months, of course, could be due to an inappropriateness of the procedures for that age. The only other developmental data come from a comparison of different age groups in different studies; this is difficult, of course, because of differences in procedures and objects used. The easiest comparison can, perhaps, be made between the 6-month-olds in the study by Rose and colleagues (1981b) and the 12-month-olds in the study by Gottfried and colleagues (1977) because the same stimuli, procedures, and apparatus were used to test both age groups. The combined results of the two studies strongly suggest that cross-modal transfer, at least in the particular context, is a weaker phenomenon in 6-month-olds; that is, it is more vulnerable to delay and requires longer familiarization time. Since the same is true, however, for intramodal functioning (Rose, 1983), it is not possible to attribute the age difference to development of cross-modal abilities in particular.

One puzzle in the combined literature is why Meltzoff and Borton (1979) and Gibson and Walker (1984) find evidence of oral–visual transfer in 1-month-olds, while Rose and colleagues (1981b) do not find such transfer at 6 months. The differences might lie in the nature of the information or the mechanism required for the differentiations in each of the studies; we know relatively little, however, about what information was actually being obtained in the different studies. The results also need to be considered in light of developmental changes in other areas; there may be some reason why information from the mouth is not as salient at 6 months as it is at 1 month. It should be noted that Brown, Baker, and Gottfried (in press) failed to find oral–visual transfer at 1, 3, or 5 months. This failure occurred whether the objects were presented successively or simultaneously to the two modalities. Since each infant received four problems with different procedures, however, there could easily have been too much information for these young infants to handle.

All of the studies use small objects as stimuli. Pairs of objects representing dimensions of difference have varied in terms of texture, substance, and form. The texture differences have involved nubby versus smooth (Meltzoff & Borton, 1979) and furry versus smooth (Bushnell, 1982). Substance has been varied by comparing elastic and rigid objects (Gibson & Walker, 1984). The majority of studies have looked at form, and the two dimensions studied most often are curved versus straight and open versus closed. In no case, however, have object properties been systematically varied, leaving us with little definitive information about the actual basis for responding.

Neither has there been much exploration of the conditions under which cross-modal transfer takes place. Rose and colleagues (1981a, 1981b, 1983; see also Wagner & Sakovitz, in press) varied familiarization time and found that increasing the length of the infants' tactual experience with an object increases the degree to which they differentiate that object from another on a visual test and enhances the extent to which they prefer a novel object over the familiar one. The length of time required for recognition seems to be longer for the tactual system than for the visual system, but without further work it is hard to know whether familiarization time interacts with the nature of the information as well as modality. For example, it could conceivably take the infant longer to show visual recognition of a subtle texture than it would to show the same discrimination and recognition tactually. In addition to familiarization time, there seems to be some effect of having the object still in the hand or mouth during the visual test. The effect of simultaneity of input, however, is not as consistent an effect as length of familiarization time.

Transfer Between Auditory and Visual Systems

The studies of auditory–visual cross-modal functioning have been even less developmental in nature than the tactual–visual studies, and more concerned with the matching of information simultaneously available to two modalities than with transfer of information across modalities. It is also a little less satisfactory to organize these studies according to age of the subjects, but to be consistent, we will continue to use age as the primary organizer.

The only study carried out with very young infants (3-week-olds) involved auditory–visual cross-modal transfer of intensity. Using a cardiac habituation–recovery method, Lewkowicz and Turkewitz (1980) repeatedly presented infants with a white light of constant intensity; during the latter half of the session, white noise of different intensities was interspersed with the presentation of light. There were six intensities of sound in the range of 70–80 dB in 2-dB steps. The response measure was mean heart rate change; it was scored by comparing the mean cardiac rate immediately before and after stimulus presentation. Although the dependent measure was magnitude of cardiac change, regardless of direction, the authors report that the predominant response was acceleration. The magnitude of cardiac change was minimal at 74 dB with the magnitude increasing both above and below this value. Since the particular sound levels had been selected on the basis of intensity judgments made by adults, it is of interest that the infants' minimal response was at the sound intensity that adults had selected as equivalent to the light. That is, infants showed least recovery to the presumed intensity match and increasingly greater recovery to both more and less intense sounds. A separate group tested with a more intense light showed a generalization gradient around a higher-intensity sound. The authors suggest that very young infants respond to the quantity of stimulation, regardless of its source and, indeed, that infants of this age do not discriminate between the different sources.

While these data are important in suggesting that infants respond equivalently to intensities of sound and light that are also matched by adults, two observations can be made about the conclusion that qualitative differences between the stimuli are essentially ignored. First, the infants' response to qualitative differences was not studied. It would be important to know whether infants discriminate the sources of stimulation while responding equivalently, and, if so, what factors affect selective attention to quantitative over qualitative aspects of events. Second, several recent studies on adult rats' perception of duration suggest that sensory-specific storage exists even though light and sound durations appear to be timed by the same internal clock (Meck & Church, 1982; Roberts, 1982). Similarly, there could in infants be a common pathway for the intensity information and still be some preservation of information about the source of the stimulation.

The age that has been been studied most often is 4 months. Spelke (1976, 1979, 1981; see review, 1984) has carried out an extensive investigation of auditory–visual perception in this age group. Her paradigm, now widely adopted, addresses the problem of infants' perception of auditory–visual relationships through an observation of the effects of sound on infants' visual exploration. In most of these studies, infants view films of two events, shown side by side about 8 cm apart; as the films are projected, a sound track approriate to one of the events is played through a centrally placed speaker. If infants are sensitive to the temporal patterning of sights and sounds, it is anticipated that they will look longer or more often at the event specified by the sound track. The results, therefore, give us some information about cross-modal matching.

In her initial study (Spelke, 1976), the two events were a person playing a game of "peek-a-boo" and a hand repeatedly and rhythmically striking a wooden block and a tambourine. While the infants viewed the films, the sound tracks were played alternately for 2 1/2 min in temporal synchrony with the visible events. The infants looked longer at the film appropriate to the sound track. These findings have been confirmed and extended by others (e.g., Bahrick et al., 1981). Although it is not entirely clear why infants should look longer at the sound-specified film, one possibility is that the matching sound is heard to come from the same location as the film and thereby creates a preference for sounding objects over silent ones (e. g., Lawson & Ruff, 1984). Such an explanation assumes that infants detect the relationship between sights and sounds. It is not clear, however, whether this detection is based on the infants' having learned the relationships involved or whether it reflects an ability to pick up temporal invariants common to both aspects of the event.

In order to investigate infants' perception of temporal invariants per se, Spelke (1979) designed three experiments using less familiar events so that previously learned associations would be a less likely explanation. In the first experiment, infants were presented with two films, each with a different puppet moving at a different speed. One puppet moved up and down slowly at the rate of once every 2 sec (30 cycles per minute); the other moved at the faster rate of four times every 2 sec (120 cycles per minute). A different percussive sound accompanied each puppet with a discrete sound occurring with every impact of the puppet on the ground. Infants showed a slight visual preference for the visually synchronized event, but the preference was not as strong as in the previous study (Spelke, 1976). In this and subsequent experiments, the preference test was followed by a "search test" in which the paired films remained continuously visible while 5-sec segments of the sound tracks were played intermittently. The infant's attention was always brought back to center before a new sound was initiated. This measure proved to be more sensitive; when the sound occurred, infants directed more of their first looks to the synchronized event and did so more quickly.

A second experiment suggested that infants of this age could detect the tempo common to the visual and auditory aspects of the event, even in the absence of synchrony. Here the associated sound track was played at the same tempo but out of phase with the visual event. Infants showed no tendency to look longer at the acoustically specified event in the preference phase, but they again looked first and more often to the acoustically specified event on the search task. The differentiation between the specified and nonspecified films was evident only in the presence of the slow tempo.

A third experiment indicated that infants can also detect the presence of temporal synchrony in these events. When the pair of films involved two puppets moving at the same slow tempo but out of synchrony with each other, infants looked longer at the film moving in synchrony with the sound on the preference test and looked first and more often at it in the search test.

Spelke concludes from this series of studies that infants, like adults, can respond to the temporal equivalences between auditory and visual events. Two cautions seem to be in order, however. First, the infants' sensitivity to common tempo is not a robust phenomenon; most differences were significant at the .05 level and only when one-tailed tests were used. Second, any equivalence that was perceived cannot be related unambiguously to tempo. As noted by Lewkowicz (1985), since one object moved twice as fast, and therefore, more frequently, the matches could have been based on the total amount of stimulation rather than on the detection of tempo, as such.

Lewkowicz (1985) has tried to separate the contributions of tempo or rate, stimulus duration, and stimulus intensity in auditory–visual matches. In several studies, 4-month-olds viewed pairs of checkerboards flashing at different rates. All possible pairs were presented for a series of twelve 15-sec trials. Preferences for the paired visual stimuli were studied in the absence of sound and in the presence of concurrent tones presented in synchrony with one member of the pair of visual stimuli.

In the first experiment, rate varied (2, 4, 8 Hz) while the density of stimulation was kept constant at 50 percent. This is, for each cycle of stimulation, where a cycle consists of a single "on" and "off" phase, the stimulus was "on" 50 percent of the time. As a result, the intensity of stimulation was constant across the rates. In this situation, infants failed to show any evidence of cross-modal matching of rates; that is, they did not look preferentially at the visual frequency corresponding to the auditory frequency. In a second experiment, the duration of each sound and flash was kept constant across the three frequencies; therefore, intensity increased with frequency. Although, in this case, rate and intensity covaried, as they had in Spelke's study (1979, experiments 1 and 2), there was still no evidence of matching across modalities. In fact, the 4-Hz and 8-Hz sounds led to a shift in looking toward the 2-Hz light. This effect was interpreted as evidence of an intensity-modulating mechanism. To determine more directly whether this was the case, in experiment 3, rate was kept constant at 2 Hz while intensity was manipulated by varying the proportion of the cycle that the stimulus was "on." Again, no matching was found, but the same shift in preference occurred. Lewkowicz concluded that the infants' looking was influenced by the intensity of the sound, but not the temporal frequency, and that there was no matching in either case.

Lewkowicz's point about the confounding of tempo and intensity is well taken, but his failure to find matching on the basis of tempo or intensity is not directly relevant to Spelke's work. First of all, Lewkowicz used faster tempos; it is possible that the faster tempos could affect arousal level and selectivity, as his results suggest, but be too fast for cross-modal matching. Second, his trials were only 15 sec long compared to trials of at least 90 sec in Spelke's technique. At this age, matching may very well require more than 15 sec. The fact that Spelke obtains more clear-cut results with her search task *after* a second trial of 90–120 sec in which the sounds and films are presented simultaneously supports this notion. Finally, Lewkowicz's visual stimuli consisted of a series of flashes whereas Spelke's involved spatial displacement as a result of an object's movements. Fraisse (1981) suggests that the difficulty in perceiving static visual displays is due to inertia of the visual system in that aftereffects of the lights may disrupt the perception of the temporal separation of the lights. He writes: "As soon as visual rhythm has spatial dynamics, there is no problem—as can be observed by watching dancers" (p. 225). In sum, Lewkowicz's subjects may have encountered more difficulty than Spelke's in matching on the basis of tempo.

Rhythm, of course, involves more than frequency and duration. Mendelson and Ferland (1982) present evidence of cross-modal transfer of information about rhythm when auditory and visual events were presented successively to 4-month-olds. The infants were presented with a 60-sec recording of an auditory rhythm consisting of a syllable repeated in either a regular or irregular pattern. Each sequence was composed of identical 0.2-sec tones. In the regular rhythm, the tones were separated alternately by 0.2-sec and 0.5-sec intervals; in the irregular rhythm, the average frequencies and durations were maintained by rearranging the intervals in the sequence. After hearing one sequence for 90 sec infants viewed a 90-sec silent film of a puppet opening and closing its mouth in either the familiar or novel rhythm. Infants looked significantly longer at the novel rhythm, an effect interpreted as recognition of the previous rhythm despite the change in modality. Since average frequency and duration were controlled, the results had to be based on the structure of the sequence. It should be noted that the effect was most striking in the groups who viewed the irregular rhythm on the test trials. It may be important to note as well that Mendelson and Ferland's visual event was not stationary and may, therefore, have more in common with Spelke's bouncing puppets.

The above studies by Spelke, Lewkowicz, and Mendelson and Ferland all used discrete sounds of given tempos and rhythms. A second series of studies by Spelke (Spelke, Born, & Chu, 1983) delved into the nature of the changes in the visual display that seem to match the auditory discontinuities. The overall design was similar to that of Spelke (1979), with preference trials followed by a series of search trials; the stimulus displays involved two real puppets rather than films and their rates of movement were slower, about 20 cycles per minute. In the first experiment, the two different puppets moved at slightly different speeds and a different percussive sound was synchronized with each impact of one of the puppets on the floor of the stage. Infants looked longer at the visually synchronized event in the preference phase and directed more attention to it during the search phase, looking to the sound-specified event more often, more quickly, and for a longer duration. These results replicated earlier findings. The results of a second experiment indicate that infants relate the same sounds to abrupt changes in the puppet's direction of movement even when there is no impact. In this experiment, the sounds were synchronized with the brief halt in midair that occurred as the puppets changed direction from ascent to descent, not with the puppets' impacts on the floor. Yet the infants' behavior in both the preference and search episode was essentially the same as their behavior in the first experiment. The results of a third experiment lend confirmation to the conclusion that visual impacts are not essential for detecting an auditory–visual relationship between puppet and sound. Here, two puppets moved up and down at the same rate, but while one halted in midair, the other halted in contact with the ground. Both sounds were synchronized to one puppet's impacts and to the other puppet's pauses in midair. Infants showed no differential looking in the preferences or search phases. The findings from two further experiments show that these results are not restricted to vertical movement. The sounds proved to be similarly related to abrupt reversals of direction along circular paths, and these relationships were independent of the spatial location along the paths where the reversals occurred. As the authors suggest, the observed results appear to be based on the infants' detection of the relationship of discrete sounds and a wide variety of discontinuities in an object's movement. A final study with adults suggests that development may involve increasing specificity since the adults showed strong results only for the displays involving impacts with the ground.

Bahrick (1983) extended the study of auditory–visual matching to the ability of 4-month-olds to detect the auditory–visual information specifying substance, in this case, elasticity and rigidity. Using the same paradigm as Spelke, Bahrick presented infants with a film of blocks hitting against each other and producing banging sounds and a film of water-filled sponges squeezing against each other to produce "squishing" sounds. The films were presented for two 90-sec trials, with the sound tracks counterbalanced; these trials were followed by the search test. Infants looked significantly longer at the sound-synchronized, appropriate film in the preference test and directed more first looks to it in the search test. In a second experiment, synchrony and substance information were placed in conflict by putting each sound track in synchrony with the wrong film. Infants now showed no preference for either film, suggesting that neither synchrony nor substance was sufficient by itself to allow the relationship between these complex sounds and events to be detected. In a third experiment, Bahrick presented the sound and films successively, as in the Mendelson and Ferland study. The sound track was played first and then the films of the blocks and sponges were projected silently and simultaneously. Infants spent more time watching the film whose sound track they had heard previously; these results suggest that the infants detected the temporal structure specifying the substances, even in the absence of a synchronized presentation of the sound track and the film. Bahrick concluded that infants perceive sound–object correspondences by detecting information about the properties of objects from both auditory and visual modalities. As in Spelke's studies, however, it could be that the infants were relating the stimuli on some simpler basis. As Spelke (1984) suggests, the discrete sounds may be matched or transferred to abrupt changes in direction of motion and the relatively continuous sounds may be matched to the slower transitions in the motion of the elastic objects.

Walker-Andrews and Lennon (1985) studied 5-month-olds' ability to detect auditory–visual information specifying distance and direction of movement. Using the Spelke paradigm, they presented infants with two films; in one, an automobile approached the point of view, and in the other, it retreated. The films were presented side by side for two 25-sec trials accompanied by the sound track of a motor, either continuously increasing or decreasing in volume. Infants looked longer at the visual display that matched the sound. Preferential looking was observed, however, only when the films were paired (study 2) and not when they were presented successively (study 1). The authors suggest that infants perceive the auditory–visual correspondences specifying direction of motion by relating the increase in the projected size of an object to the increase in volume of the sound. The authors acknowledge, however, that their results could have been based on cross-modal matching of intensity levels rather than on the perception of an event in which an object changed distance from the observer. In fact, either interpretation is qualified by the finding that the preferences for the sound-matched film *within* trials was significant only when the sound track of increasing volume was played.

The issues of synchrony and structure have been dealt with in several studies of the relationship between speaking and movements of the mouth. Infants as young as 10–16 weeks are sensitive to some aspects of the synchrony between auditorially and visually presented speech. This was demonstrated when infants looked longer at the experimenter's face when the speech sounds and lip movements of the nursery rhyme she was reading were in synchrony than when they were out of synchrony (Dodd, 1979). Two recent reports suggest that infants 4–6 months old are sensitive to specific natural structural correspondences between the acoustic and visual properties of articulation, not just to a general temporal synchrony of the two.

Kuhl and Meltzoff (1982) carried out two experiments examining the ability of infants 18–20 weeks old to detect the correspondences involved in two different vowel sounds. In the first study, the infants were familiarized with two films, one of a woman repeating /a/ sounds (once every 3 sec), and another film of the woman repeating /i/ sounds at the same rate. After being presented with each film successively for 10 sec, the infants were then presented with the two films simultaneously and the sound track corresponding to one of the films was played from a central location for 2 min. Infants looked significantly longer at the face that matched the sound. In the second experiment, the original auditory stimuli were altered in order to remove the formant frequencies, which is the spectral information necessary to identify the sounds as vowels, while preserving the temporal characteristics of the stimuli, that is, their amplitude and duration. When this was done, performance dropped to chance; these results suggest, therefore, that spectral information was necessary for the match.

The results of a study by MacKain, Studdert-Kennedy, Spieker, and Stern (1983) are compatible with those of Kuhl and Meltzoff (1982). Infants were presented simultaneously with video displays of two women articulating different speech patterns; the sounds were three pairs of consonant–vowel–consonant–vowel disyllables: /mama, lulu/; /bebe, zuzi/; and /vava, zuzu/. The articulatory movements of both women were temporally synchronized with the acoustic passage, but only one contained a structural correspondence (e.g., mouth opening synchronized with rise in amplitude, mouth closing synchronized with fall in amplitude). Each infant was presented with each of the three stimulus pairs on four trials. Each trial lasted 20 sec and consisted of 11 auditory–visual repetitions of the disyllable. Infants looked longer at the display that corresponded to the sound track being played. This effect, however, was observed only while infants were looking rightward. Such rightward orienting is thought to accompany verbal processing in adults (Kinsbourne & Hiscock, 1983), presumably because attention to the right side of space reflects relatively greater activation of the language-processing left hemisphere. The authors suggest that facilitation of intermodal speech perception by a rightward gaze indicates that the left hemisphere is already predisposed in infancy to process such cross-modal speech–speaker correspondences. However, asymmetries of lateral gaze have not been validated as an index of cerebral lateralization. Moreover, while the direction of eye turning may be influenced by the nature of the material being processed, it is not clear why the direction of eye turning would affect cross-modal transfer or how it would selectively prime the left hemisphere for such activity.

The results of these studies on infants' detection of auditory–visual structural correspondences have important implications for language development. If infants are sensitive to the temporal and structural congruence of auditory and visual speech information, then intermodal perception may play a critical role in speech perception (see McGurk & MacDonald, 1976, for supporting evidence).

In a very different kind of investigation of the relationship between face and voice, Walker (1982) tested the ability of 5- and 7-month-olds to detect equivalent expressions of emotion by face and voice. Infants were presented with two filmed facial expressions accompanied by a vocal expression corresponding to one of them for 2 min. The expressions paired, in different experiments, were happy–neutral, happy–sad, and happy–angry. As was not the case for many of the other studies reported, Walker compared looking to the same facial expression *across* trials, that is, under conditions of match and mismatch. The infants spent a greater proportion of total looking time looking at the happy and nonhappy faces when each was paired with its appropriate sound track. Without any consideration of absolute looking times, however, it is impossible to know whether there was any preference for the sound-specified film within trials. Even when comparing responses across trials, there could have been more looking directed at the nonhappy faces under the happy voice condition than under the appropriate voice condition; that is, the proportions could be mainly a function of looking time to the happy face. On the other hand, the fact that there was no change with sound condition when the films were presented upside down, as they were in a fourth experiment, suggests that the happy voice was having some specific effect. With these results, Walker found support for her hypothesis that infants are sensitive to some commonalities between affective facial expression and vocal expression. She concluded that infants detect a number of auditory–visual relationships, thereby perceiving the bimodally presented expressions as unitary, meaningful events.

As can be seen in the studies reviewed so far, most have used matching paradigms; there has been relatively little work on the actual transfer of information gained auditorially to visual events and vice versa. Mendelson and Ferland (1979), Lewkowicz and Turkewitz (1980), and Bahrick (1983) did single studies that fit this category, and these suggest that there is transfer of intensity, temporal, and perhaps structural information by 4–5 months. In the first auditory–visual study of transfer to be done, Allen, Walker, Symonds, and Marcell (1977) habituated 7-month-olds to either an auditory or a visual rhythm over 15 consecutive trials and then assessed recovery to a different rhythm presented in either the same or different modality. Two temporal sequences were used, each consisting of identical light flashes or sounds, each of which was 0.25 sec in duration. In one sequence, each element was separated by 0.9 sec; in the other, elements were alternately separated by 0.3 and 0.9 sec. The infants who were presented with a different temporal sequence on recovery trials showed greater response recovery than did infants presented again with the same sequence. Recovery, as indexed by an increase in cardiac deceleration and an increase in negative skin potential, occurred to the new sequence regardless of whether the modality changed. The study by Allen and colleagues is the only visual–auditory one to include both intramodal and cross-modal conditions. The results suggest that recovery was greatest in the cross-modal conditions. As in some of the other studies, the basis of the response is not clear, since the two sequences differed in duration and the length of the first interstimulus interval, as well as in overall configuration. However, since the overall duration and initial intervals were the same in the two sequences used by Mendelson and Ferland (1982) and infants seemed to perceive the structure in that study, it is likely that they could do so in this study as well.

Starkey, Spelke, and Gelman (1983) examined the ability of infants 6–8 months old to detect numerical correspondences between sets of visible objects and sounds. Infants were presented with two photographic displays consisting of heterogeneous collections of two or three household items in different spatial arrangements. While the infants viewed these displays, they heard two or three drumbeats played from a central speaker; their looking time at the displays was then recorded for 10 sec after the offset of sound. In each of the three experiments, the infants received two blocks of 16 trials. In the first experiment and its replication, where drumbeats were played at the rate of 1.33 beats per second, infants attended longer to the numerical display corresponding to the number of drumbeats in each auditory sequence, although this preference was largely limited to the second block of trials. Since the duration of the two- and three-beat sequences differed, the infants' preference could have been based on temporal rather than numerical information, with the greater scanning time necessitated by the three-object sequence corresponding to the greater duration of the three-beat sequence. This issue was addressed in the third experiment by equating the overall durations of the two- and three-beat sequences. Infants still displayed a tendency to look at the visually corresponding display, although the preference was significant only when the infants' responses were averaged across both blocks of trials. The authors conclude that infants possess a mechanism that enables them to obtain information about number, irrespective of modality. The experimental design, however, did not permit the authors to separate the overall size of the visual display from its numerosity. The infants could have been responding to the relationship between the amount of visual stimulation and the amount of auditory stimulation via some intensity-based mechanism. If the same results were obtained when overall size of the visual display was held constant while its numerosity was varied, such a lower-level explanation would be ruled out.

Finally, a study by Wagner, Winner, Cicchetti, and Gardner (1981) investigated "metaphorical" matching in infants with a mean age of 11 months. They presented the infants with pairs of sounds and visual stimuli that they considered to have no physical similarity, for example, an ascending tone and an arrow pointing up versus a descending tone and an arrow pointing down; there were eight such pairs. Each pair was presented twice in 10-sec trials; one of the sounds was presented in the first 3 sec of the trial and then the visual pair was displayed while the sound continued. With three of the pairs, there was some evidence for the expected matches; that is, on both trials for a given pair, more infants preferred the visual stimuli that matched the sound being played than preferred the nonmatching stimuli. These results are confirmed by the looking times to each stimulus of a pair for those same three pairs. All comparisons were made between matching and nonmatching patterns of looking (that is, looking at the matching display on both trials versus looking at the non-matching displays on both trials), even though these patterns were not the most common. The justification for one-tailed tests is not clear; although the predictions were made on the basis of the discrepancy hypothesis, it seems possible that the nonmatching, rather than the matching, stimulus could have provided the optimal degree of discrepancy. If the use of one-tailed tests is accepted, then the probability of obtaining significant results in three out of eight cases by chance is .04. Although the results cannot be considered strong, it is of interest that two of the three pairs on which matching appeared to occur involved a discontinuous–continuous comparison for both visual and auditory stimuli.

One might take issue with the authors' contention that the auditory and visual stimuli of these pairs had no physical similarity. Such a contention assumes that our physical descriptions of these stimuli are adequate. Until we have a better understanding of the spatiotemporal relationships involved in vision, however, we are not in a good postion to know whether auditory and visual stimuli are physically or only "metaphorically" alike. Indeed, Marks's (1978) review of adult psychophysical studies suggests that many cross-modal matches between ostensibly unrelated stimuli may very well be rooted in psychophysical equivalences.

The conditions under which auditory–visual relationships are detected have been examined in several studies. Infants as young as 3 months have clearly learned some fairly arbitrary sound–object relationships (Spelke & Owsley, 1979). Two factors that are likely to be important for such learning are spatial coincidence (where the sights and sounds come from the same location) and temporal synchrony (where the sights and sounds are in phase with one another). Lyons-Ruth (1977) conducted one of the first studies of 4-month-old infants' ability to learn an arbitrary association between the sounds and visual characteristics of objects. She familiarized infants with a toy whose movements were synchronized with a sound coming from the same location. She then assessed how the infants' subsequent looking was affected when the same sound presented in a new location accompanied the same or a different object. Infants received eight 8-sec familiarization trials in which the sound-producing toy was presented at midline and then six 10-sec test trials in which the familiar sound came from 90 deg to the right of midline. On the test trials, the infants looked away more often when the novel toy was encountered. These results were interpreted as distress at the violation of the expectancy that the familiar object would be present at the site of the familiar sound. If so, this expectation would be due to the previous experience with an object whose movements were synchronized with a sound in the same location as the object.

In a recent study (Spelke, 1981), 4-month-olds showed evidence of learning about the temporally synchronized relationship between auditory and visually specified tempos even when the two were not precisely colocated; the sound, which emanated from the centrally placed speaker, was actually located 4 cm to either side of the visual events. In the initial phase of each of four experiments in the study, the infants were presented with two different puppets that bounced at the same rate, one bounce every 2 sec, but out of phase with one another. For the first 100 sec a sound synchronized to one puppet was played and for the second 100 sec a different sound synchronized with the other puppet was played. The synchrony was the only information tying each sound to its respective object. In two of the experiments (1 and 3), the initial phase was followed by a search task, in which the sound was out of synchrony with either puppet. Even though the infants did not look differentially in the initial preference phase, on the search task they more often looked first at the object that had been in synchrony with the sound. In two other experiments (2 and 4), the initial phase was followed by a transfer test where the sound track and visual stimuli were presented successively; the sound track for 50 sec and then the visual displays alone in silence for a 30-sec preference test. Here, infants selectively looked at the "novel" object, that is, the object that had not been associated with the immediately preceding sound. These results suggest that witnessing an object moving in synchrony with a sound for a few minutes is sufficient to establish a link between them. Precise spatial colocation is obviously not a necessary condition. Nonetheless, it should be noted that the evidence for the relationship was stronger during the search task when the two sources of information were present simultaneously than in the transfer tasks, and stronger when the infant could use a previously learned directional response.

Neither Lyons-Ruth nor Spelke manipulated spatial and temporal congruence. Spelke's results, however, suggest that, once an auditory–visual relationship has been established between temporally synchronized sounds and objects, then the infant continues to recognize that relationship even in the absence of synchrony.

Humphrey, Tees, and Werker (1979) assessed 4-month-olds' ability to learn auditory–visual temporal correspondences when lights and sounds were in and out of synchrony during familiarization. One group of infants was presented with temporally synchronized lights and sounds for ten 15-sec habituation trials, and then was presented with asynchronous signals for five 15-sec recovery trials. A second group of infants received the opposite sequence. Auditory and visual events were spatially congruent for both groups in this first experiment. The group receiving synchronized sound and light showed significant habituation and recovery of looking time while the group receiving nonsynchronized presentations showed neither. Similar results were obtained in a second experiment, where the sound source was placed 90 deg right or left of the infant's line of sight. These results suggest that infants can perceive the temporal synchrony between visual and auditory signals even when the light and sound are not colocated. The results of this study, though not bearing directly on the relationship between particular sounds and particular objects, suggest that temporally synchronous auditory and visual signals are more predictable and therefore may be more conducive to learning.

Lawson (1980) explicitly varied both spatial and temporal factors in order to study the learning of auditory–visual relationships in 6-month-olds. In each of four experiments, infants were familiarized for 90 sec with a moving object accompanied by a sound; they then received two 20-sec tests with two stationary objects, one familiar and one novel. On one test, the objects were accompanied by the familiar sound, and on the other, by a novel sound. The experiments differed in terms of the spatial and temporal relations that obtained during familiarization. In the first experiment, the object moved periodically, once every 2 sec, in synchrony with a sound emanating directly from it. When the familiar sound was played in the test phase, infants looked longer at the object with which the sound had been paired. Thus when the sound and the object were colocated and temporally synchronized infants learned that they were related. In the second experiment, the object again moved in synchrony with the sound during familiarization, but the sound emanated from a speaker placed above and 90 deg to the infant's left. Here, the infants did not look preferentially at either object on the test. In the third and fourth experiments, the sounds and objects were colocated in space but were not synchronized temporally; the object moved in a continuous fashion and the sound was periodic, or the object moved in a periodic fashion while a continuous sound emanated from it. In the first case, the pattern of preferential looking suggested that the infants had established some connection between the two; there was no such evidence in the second case. These results suggest that learning the relationship between auditory and visual aspects of an event occurs most easily when both those aspects are spatially congruent and temporally synchronous. Results reported by Spelke (1981) and Humphrey and colleagues (1979) further suggest that temporal congruence may be the more important of the two.

Summary of Studies of Audition and Vision

There are a number of studies of auditory–visual matching and transfer that suggest that the infant is able to detect complex temporal correspondences. While this work began by showing that infants detected auditory–visual correspondences between familiar objects and events, like mother's face and voice, it soon became apparent that infants were able to detect such correspondences between sights and sounds that had not been related in prior experience. The studies suggest that infants are capable of cross-modal matching and transfer of auditory and visual information specifying intensity (Lewkowicz & Turkewitz, 1980), rhythm (Allen et al., 1977; Mendelson & Ferland, 1979), tempo (Spelke, 1979, but see Lewkowicz, 1985, for qualifications), substance (Bahrick, 1983), number (Starkey et al., 1983), the structure common to speech production and facial patterns of movement (Kuhl & Meltzoff, 1982; MacKain et al., 1983), and the structure common to vocal affect and facial expression (Walker, 1982).

These studies encompass a greater range of phenomena than does the work in tactual–visual transfer. Also, as was not the case for the tactual–visual studies, more attention has been devoted to the conditions under which cross-modal relationships are detected and learned. Temporal synchrony has attracted the most attention. In the matching paradigm, Spelke (1979) found that infants attend visually more to an object moving in synchrony with a sound than to an object moving out of synchrony with the sound. Whether some degree of synchrony is critical to the match is less clear. Bahrick's (1983) findings suggest that synchrony may play a role in detecting auditory–visual information for substance. Spelke (1979), on the other hand, found that common tempos can be detected even when the sound is not synchronized with either visual display. When the relationships are of a more arbitrary nature, synchrony appears to facilitate the detection of and learning about those relationships (Humphrey et al., 1979; Lawson, 1980). In these cases, spatial colocation of sights and sounds (Lawson, 1980) may also be very important. In many of the matching studies, relationships seem to be readily detected even though some degree of spatial separation of sounds and visual events characterizes the experimental design (e.g., Bahrick, 1983; Kuhl & Meltzoff, 1982; MacKain et al., 1983; Spelke, 1979, 1981; Spelke et al., 1983), but the separation is very small. It is not clear how separated sounds and objects can be and still be perceived as related, nor is it clear what the boundaries are for the detection of synchrony. Further work with both of these factors could elucidate the role they play at different ages. More work on the effect of context is needed; for example, the role of movement has not been given any systematic consideration, although it appears likely that sounds may more readily be associated with visual movements, such as puppets jumping up and down, than with stationary visual displays, such as lights flashing on and off (Fraisse, 1981).

The work on infants' perception of the temporal structure common to auditory and visual events has tended to center around different issues, paradigms, and age groups than the work in tactual–visual transfer. The work in auditory–visual matching tends to stand as a monolithic investigation of abilities of the 4-month-old! The fact that so few studies use other age groups precludes serious consideration of developmental trends. In addition, studies tend to use only two exemplars of tempo, rhythm, or substance. Little rationale is given for the selection of particular exemplars and relatively little consideration is given to the constraints on the detection of correspondences. For our eventual understanding of the development of these abilities, we need more information about the time span over which successive stimuli are perceived as related, the differences in tempo that can be perceived, and the threshhold for temporal acuity in each modality, and we need to know how all of these change with age.

Like the tactual–visual studies, these studies leave unanswered many questions about the stimulus bases for these correspondences. Although certain findings seem to reflect a response to complex events, many may be explained in terms of detection of a few basic attributes of stimulation. Lewkowicz (1985) has suggested that matching of auditory–visual tempos may sometimes be based on the intensity differences that are confounded with tempo differences. The same can be said for matching number. As was pointed out before, Bahrick's (1983) findings that infants match auditory and visual information specifying rigidity and elasticity may instead be a matching of continuities and discontinuities in stimulation. It is possible, therefore, that infants' matching is sometimes based on more primitive or abstract properties than is considered in most interpretations of results.

Finally, it should be noted that comparisons between tactual–visual and auditory–visual studies are complicated by the fact that the former have generally used a transfer paradigm, where the stimuli to the different modalities are presented successively, while most of the auditory–visual studies use a matching paradigm where the stimuli are presented simultaneously. As noted before, successful performance with these two paradigms may depend upon somewhat different processes. Our understanding of development will require that we explore more systematically these different processes at different ages.

DISCUSSION

We began this chapter with a brief discussion of some theoretical points of view concerning the way the different systems are related. How do the results of the infant studies done to date bear on these points of view?

First, as has been observed before, the data from infant studies, as well as data from recent animal work, provide unambiguous evidence that language is not a necessary mediator for cross-modal transfer. Since every study reviewed was carried out with preverbal infants, the weight of evidence is overwhelming and should effectively put to rest this untenable assumption. Language mediation may, of course, be involved in some types of transfer at older ages, but it is clearly not a sine qua non for all types. The role of visual imagery cannot be addressed by the data at hand, so the possible existence of some mediation is not ruled out.

Second, the demonstration of transfer in infants only a few weeks old suggests that at least some form of cross-modal ability is possible without any, or with only minimal, bimodal experience. In particular, it seems unlikely that the oral–visual cross-modal transfer (Gibson & Walker, 1984; Meltzoff & Borton, 1979) seen in 1-month-olds would have resulted from coordinated oral and visual experience. As Harris (1983) points out, since the infant cannot visually inspect what it has in its mouth, simultaneous oral and visual exploration is not possible, at least with these small objects. The same general point can be drawn from the auditory–visual literature, where the stimuli share amodal properties, such as tempo or rhythm, but where the particular properties are unlikely ever to have occurred together, if at all, before the experimental session. While the basis of these responses may be more primitive than sometimes supposed, and although the basis is no doubt altered by experience, the ability to respond equivalently to information from different modalities is certainly present early on.

Theoretical positions tend toward dichotomies, and the results cited above could be used to argue for direct pickup of amodal properties and against the view that experience is necessary. It seems important to recognize, however, that the time at which a behavior appears in development does not, in itself, say very much about the mechanism for that behavior. On the one hand, relationships may be learned very rapidly, in only a few minutes, as several studies suggest, and, on the other hand, direct perception may require time.

The interaction of experience and maturation surely underlies both learned relationships between modality-specific properties and the detection of amodal properties. To take the latter as an example: An identical, amodal description of an object perceived through two different modalities may be possible because the object eventually stimulates a group of cells that receive input from more than one modality. These cells, however, might not be active or developed at birth; response to amodal properties across systems would not be possible, then, until the appropriate neural substrate had developed. The development of this substrate might result from maturation, or it might depend on specific kinds of multimodal experience where inputs to two or more systems occur simultaneously and are generated by the same objects (see, e.g., Knudsen, 1983). Once developed, the response of these cells could lead to direct perception of the object within and across modalities. What is needed, therefore, is a more precise definition of the experience that is required for certain abilities to become manifest.

Third, despite this caveat, the work with infants certainly suggests that abstract amodal properties are readily detected by the different systems under some circumstances. Even within the category of amodal properties, however, some properties may be detected more easily than others. For example, certain temporal properties, such as tempo and rhythm, can be considered to correspond in a one-to-one fashion. Other amodal properties, such as those common to objects experienced tactually and visually, may require more complex descriptions gathered from the pattern of temporal–spatial changes in both systems. Overall, however, even though individual systems may be using different strategies and may be governed by somewhat different principles, the infant is able to pick up a good deal of amodal information.

Fourth, several studies (Humphrey et al., 1979; Lawson, 1980; Spelke, 1981; Spelke et al., 1983) address the issue of what makes the detection of cross-modal relationships between properties and events that are specific to single modalities possible. These relationships are frequently referred to as arbitrary; because the properties are not amodal, stimulation in one modality does not provide identical information as stimulation in another modality. The identity of an object, however, may be learned initially on the basis of conjoint information, or as Bushnell (in press) suggests, *multimodal compounds*. The identity of an individual by face and voice can serve as an example. The conditions under which this learning takes place make it possible to perceive that a relationship between face and voice exists. That is, in normal circumstances, a particular face and a particular voice generally occur at the same time (when one disappears, the other tends to as well), they are located in the same place, and movements of the mouth and face are frequently synchronous with discontinuities in the vocal sounds. Spelke (1984) suggests that there may be further constraints having to do with the quality of the sound; that is, the infant is more likely to perceive a relationship between a face and a voice than between a face and a buzzer even if the above conditions hold. Within these conditions, learning leads to the ability to identify a person through only hearing the voice or only seeing the face. The experiences necessary for detecting and learning such relationships may be quite different from those required for detecting amodal properties, but they are amply provided for in the early social play of infants and their mothers (Stern, Hofer, Haft, & Dore, 1984). Once such relationships have been established, they serve as a basis for the same kind of expectations—that a particular sound will lead to a particular visual experience.

The relevance of infant studies to any consideration of how the relationships between the systems develop is more difficult, since developmental data are surprisingly sparse. Most investigators have included only a single age group in any one study. Taken as a whole, the infant studies show that cross-modal abilities are present at most ages tested. Otherwise, the studies have little bearing on the issue of whether the systems are initially undifferentiated or not. No study has adequately addressed the issue of whether the systems are initially separated or unified, and none have sought to link developments in coordination, such as eye–hand coordination, with developments in cross-modal abilities.

What Develops with Age?

Developmental Changes in the Separate Modalities

While little attention has been focused on developmental aspects of cross-modal abilities, developmental data from other sources are relevant to the topic. Since cross-modal abilities depend upon intramodal abilities, information about developmental changes within the separate modalities is useful. One question of importance is how the separate systems go about extracting information, or to what extent there are modality-specific differences in the style of gathering information. Strategies may also change with age, difficulty of the task, and familiarity with the stimuli.

THE TACTUAL/HAPTIC SYSTEM. There have been studies on both oral and manual behavior. Although there is a large literature on sucking, little attention has been given to the function that sucking or other oral responses may play in discrimination and recognition of objects. A recent study by Rochat (1983) represents a move in this direction. Rochat polygraphically recorded pressure variations applied by newborns and infants of 1 and 4 months to nipples varying in shape and the presence or absence of rigid features. In the analysis of the infants' oral activity, Rochat separated sucking responses, which have a distinctive burst–pause pattern, from nonrhythmical mouthing, which he termed *oral exploratory behavior.* Although the exploratory activity increased with age, there was a significant interaction between age and stimulus. The two younger groups showed enhanced exploratory activity to the two nipples with the rigid features, suggesting that they differentiated these nipples from those without such features. While the 4-month-olds made these discriminations, too, they made other ones as well. This differential oral behavior, however, may not have been so much exploratory as dictated by the nature of the objects; that is, certain objects may make coordinated sucking impossible. Even so, such oral activity may serve a perceptual function in that it provides a basis for the discriminations shown in various cross-modal oral–visual studies during the early months (Allen, Coronado, Herrera, & Rocha, 1982; Gibson & Walker, 1984; Meltzoff & Borton, 1979).

The findings from the unpublished study by Allen and colleagues (1982) suggest that the sucking response itself may also serve a useful exploratory function. As part of their interest in oral–visual transfer, these investigators assessed a group of 3 1/2-month-olds in oral–oral transfer, using smooth versus nubby spheres (modeled after Meltzoff & Borton, 1979) and smooth versus nubby cylinders. Oral activity was monitored polygraphically. Despite a higher rate of sucking on the smooth pacifier, infants gave evidence of discriminating the objects intramodally; they were significantly slower to initiate sucking in the test phase when the unfamiliar pacifier was substituted for the familiar one.

It is known that the tongue is quite sensitive to pressure changes even in neonates (Thach & Wiffenbach, 1976; Wiffenbach, 1972). Perhaps the pressure changes produced by particular objects lead to a spatial and temporal pattern that could be used for matching or transfer. If this is the case, a decrease with age in threshold to pressure changes could lead to the developmental changes in oral discrimination suggested by Rochat's findings. Rose and colleagues (1981b) found no evidence for oral–visual transfer at 6 months, while they did find evidence for manual–visual transfer. It is possible, however, that, as the hand becomes capable of coordinated exploratory activity, information from the mouth is not picked up as easily, at least during the transition. It is clear that 12-month-olds do indeed pick up some information about objects during oral familiarization (Gottfried et al., 1977).

In both oral and manual tactual perception, we are concerned more with active than with passive touch. Touch is passive when things in the environment impose themselves on a motionless observer. Active touch has been discussed mainly with reference to the hand, and Gibson (1962) writes that it consists of a temporally ordered series of finger and hand movements and positions that involve both the tactual and the kinesthetic systems. Katz (1925; see Krueger, 1970) noted that vibrations are produced when the hand is moved over a surface. He stressed the importance of the observer's self-produced movements in the perception of texture and found that the perceptions of roughness and smoothness were better when the surface was felt actively rather than passively. Gibson (1962) suggested that active touch allows us to perceive corners and edges and is therefore important for the perception of form. Similar patterns of skin deformation, when imposed on a motionless observer, give rise only to rapidly changing sensations, not to a stable perception. Furthermore, there is evidence that passivity impedes storage of tactual information because of the generation of aftersensations (a rarity with active touch) and makes it difficult to perceive the whole object (Heller, 1980; Heller & Leventhal, 1975).

Some of the developmental changes in cross-modal behavior suggested by the current literature may involve changes in the efficiency with which information is obtained through the haptic system. Because infants do not begin to use their hands for controlled manipulation of objects until 5–6 months, it seems fair to say that at that time the tactual system cannot pick up information as readily as the visual system. There is evidence, of course, that it never does (see review by Jones, 1981; Lobb, 1965), but at 6 months there is considerable room for improvement. Increased efficiency is hard to detect just from observation, but we can see that the way the hand is used changes quite dramatically in the second half of the first year (Ruff, 1984). Early on, infants transfer objects from hand to hand, and this activity may lead to general tactual information about the shape of the object. The most noticeable change is that infants begin to finger the surface of objects particurarly when there are small details such as bumps or depressions. This change, in principle, should facilitate the pickup of information about texture and surface detail and could influence visual exploration, especially in cases where the texture is visually subtle. Although it is hard to see how the tactual information could improve on the available visual information, it may provide enough information for success in a cross-modal task where vision would not be simultaneously available. Ruff (1982b) did find that manipulation helped in the recognition of objects when there was some surface structure to be detected and differentiated. Furthermore, the facilitation seemed to come from the haptic component of manipulation rather than that aspect of manipulation directed toward making the object easier to see. Even after new behaviors emerge, there should be changes in the degree to which the behaviors are used in a systematic way. There is evidence that this kind of improvement continues throughout the preschool years (Zaporozhets, 1965).

There is also evidence that the right hemispheric specialization for tactual processing of shape commonly found in older children and adults may emerge during the second year of life (Rose, 1984, 1985). In studies with children aged 1, 2, and 3 years, cross-modal scores were enhanced among 2- and 3-year-olds following palpation with the left as compared with the right hand. This left-hand (right hemisphere) superiority was not evident in the 1-year-olds. Since the right hemisphere is thought to be most activated when holistic rather than analytic processing strategies are engaged, it may be that different information is extracted through tactual exploration with each hand. One-year-olds may be making the cross-modal comparisons on a different, perhaps more primitive basis, or they may not yet have developed hemispheric specialization for this function. If both factors are involved, processing strategies may undergo development with those favoring the pickup of configurational aspects improving as a function of hemispheric development.

THE VISUAL SYSTEM   The visual system matures early, is available for extensive exploration at birth, and reaches almost adult levels of acuity by about 6 months. It is generally considered to be more efficient than the tactual system. The classic distinction between simultaneous apprehension of the object by vision and the successive apprehension of details by the tactual system is not entirely valid. The visual system also samples objects and events discretely in the sense that fixations are separated by eye movements during which there is suppression of input; there are also blinks and head turns in an active observer. On the other hand, given the high acuity of the human system, the speed with which the eyes can move from one fixation point to another is bound to introduce an efficiency into visual exploration that is impossible for tactual exploration; in this sense the visual system may be more adept than the tactual system at picking up information about the whole object. Whether it does or not early in development has been a matter of controversy. Work by Antell and Caron (1985) suggests the possibility that newborns may discriminate and recognize different two-dimensional configurations of the same elements; studies by Milewski (1979) certainly show that 3-month-olds are responsive to simple configurations of elements despite changes in physical parameters, such as size and spacing of elements. Even so, there seems to be a developmental trend toward a greater likelihood that configuration, as opposed to more quantitative variables, will be attended to as the infant matures (Ruff & Turkewitz, 1975, 1979). In addition, more complex configurational properties of objects may not be recognized even by 6-month-olds (Ruff, 1978). This development may be related, in part, to a tendency to scan more widely with age (Haith, Goodman, Goodwyn, & Montgomery, 1982; Salapatek, 1975); before 2 months of age, infants will scan internal features only if those features are moving (Bushnell, 1979), and scanning is generally not as dispersed as later (Haith et al., 1982). Even beyond the infancy period, there is evidence that scanning of objects and scenes becomes more systematic (Vurpillot, 1968). This increase in efficiency is clearly linked to improvements in performance on discrimination tasks, but it may reflect cognitive changes rather than causing better performance directly (Vurpillot & Ball, 1979).

Spatial information about the world can be gathered by both visual and tactual systems. The visual system is unique in its sensitivity to color and brightness differences; this sensitivity means that some edges and boundaries are more easily detected by vision than by touch. On the other hand, the visual system is vulnerable to camouflage where color and brightness differences can hide actual edges. The tactual system cannot be fooled in this way so that touch can be used to clarify ambiguities encountered by the observer.

Because vision is a distal sense it can pick up information from events that are independent of the observer. Although perception is considered to be active in all systems, the ability to observe events without participating directly in them means that the information available to the visual system is potentially much richer and more varied than touch. Disruptions and transformations in the structure of the light reaching the eye reveal much information about the unchanging structure of objects and about the nature of the motions objects make (Gibson, 1979). Even very young infants are exposed, therefore, to all the motion-carried information for the objects and events around them (Ruff, 1980, 1982a). While the extensive transformations available to the visual system may be paralleled in some ways by auditory change and transformations, the same cannot be said for the tactual system. Although there is still a great deal to be learned about the development of the visual system and how visual experience affects the developing infant's ability to perceive the world, it seems safe to conclude that the visual system is inherently more flexible than the tactual system and available in an extensive way earlier in development. In studies of cross-modal transfer, this difference in efficiency could manifest itself in asymmetries of transfer, especially in infancy. That is, the pickup of the necessary information on a paired comparison test trial may be easier visually than tactually leading to visual recognition after tactual familiarization in a shorter time than tactual recognition after visual familiarization.

THE AUDITORY SYSTEM   Since perception necessarily occurs over time, both vision and touch must be sensitive to spatial and temporal changes in stimulation that specify objects and events. In humans, at least those with sight, audition may provide less precise spatial information, but it is clearly designed for the detection of very subtle temporal aspects of signals. The threshold for temporal acuity, that is, the minimum time needed to perceive two signals as successive instead of simultaneous, is markedly lower in the auditory modality than in other modalities. For adults, two identical sounds will be perceived as discrete if separated by only 2 msec, but for neighboring touches at least 10 msec must intervene and for visual signals 100 msec must intervene (Fraisse, 1981). In other words, two visual signals must be separated by an interval 50 times greater than that separating two auditory signals for them to be perceived as discrete! There are also substantial differences between modalities in temporal pattern perception. Morse code signals are learned faster when presented auditorially than when presented visually (Nazzaro & Nazzaro, 1970), and auditory temporal patterns are reproduced more accurately than visual patterns, with the reproduction of patterns presented tactually being intermediate in difficulty (Gault & Goodfellow, 1938).

In the study of infants, there has been little work concerned with infants' perception of temporal patterns, and what there is is exclusively auditory. In terms of auditory perception, the perception of temporal grouping seems finely tuned from early on. The work of Demany, McKenzie, and Vurpillot (1977) shows that infants 1 1/2–3 months of age can discriminate between different patterns of tones, even when the patterns are simple rearrangements of the same temporal intervals separating identical tones. These results are supported by those of Chang and Trehub (1977), who found that 5-month-olds reliably discriminate between tonal patterns with identical components but different temporal groups. Although young infants seem to be able to perceive some sequences as recurring rhythmic groups, there is also a developmental trend for such perception to improve as the infant matures. Using lengthier, more complex sequences of white noise bursts, Morrongiello (1984) found that 12-month-olds surpassed 6-month-olds in discriminating among such perceptual configurations.

Beyond the infancy period, there is evidence that auditory temporal sequences are discriminated better than visual, and that discrimination continues to improve at least between 4 and 11 years (Klapper & Birch, 1971). It is interesting to note that during the same age period there are marked changes in auditory temporal acuity. In a study of auditory fusion, Davis and McCroskey (1980) found that younger children needed longer interpulse intervals to perceive two tones as successive instead of simultaneous. The efficiency with which temporal patterns can be recognized is undoubtedly also a function of their tempo. Auditory patterns are easier to recognize than visual patterns at a fast tempo, with tactual patterns being of intermediate difficulty; such modality differences tend to disappear at slower tempos (Handel & Buffardi, 1969).

The auditory system, therefore, surpasses the visual and tactual systems in the perception of temporal patterns and in many of the processes involved in temporal pattern perception, such as the perception of groupings, tempo, and succession. Although some auditory temporal patterns can be recognized when presented visually, even by infants, this ability increases with development.

How Does Coordination Between Systems Develop?

Since cross-modal abilities are likely to depend in part on experience, we need also to know more about the coordination and mutual influence of the perceptual systems as they act together in normal multimodal situations. We would like to review some of the available evidence and will discuss separately the developing coordination between the haptic and visual systems and between the auditory and visual systems.

There is evidence from a number of sources of a changing response to haptic input from 6 to 12 months. Certainly cross-modal transfer using the familiarization and response to novelty paradigm is much harder to obtain at 6 months than at 12 (Rose et al., 1981b). Bushnell (1982) found reliable evidence that 9 1/2- and 11-

month-olds noticed discrepancies between simultaneous visual and tactual input, but no such evidence for 8-months-olds. Using reaching for and retrieval of an object as the response, Diamond (1981) found that it was not until about 12 months that tactual evidence of an opening in a transparent box, that is, having hands or fingers inside the opening, overrode the visual information for the object as straight ahead and led to indirect reaches. In a study by Harris (1972), there was an increasing tendency from 6 to 12 months to explore manually an object that had been seen before but not touched. Gibson and Riccio (1984) reported that until 12 months ambulatory infants would not cross a walkway if the visual information specified a nonrigid surface despite evidence of its rigidity from tactual exploration. Many of these studies concern conflict between the visual and tactual systems and suggest that vision dominates in the sense that infants trust the visual information more than the tactual.

On the other hand, in some circumstances, infants may be so attentive to tactual information that visual information is ignored. In a recent study by Bushnell, Shaw, and Strauss (1985), the failure of 6-month-olds to respond to temperature–color pairings may have been due to their being tactually "captured" by the temperature and therefore inattentive to the color. This explanation would be consistent with the findings by Casey (1979) and Ruff (1982b), who both found that response to color was diminished in situations where the infant could manipulate the objects and therefore obtain information tactually.

It is possible that young infants have difficulty attending to information from two different sources during their manipulation of objects. Several investigators (Gottfried, Rose, & Bridger, 1978; MacKay-Soroka, Trehub, Bull, & Corter, 1982; Rolfe & Day, 1981; Rose, Gottfried, & Bridger, 1979; Ruff, 1981) have found that infants who could manipulate an object during familiarization failed to respond to the object as familiar during a test in which the familiar and novel objects were presented only visually. On the other hand, they showed recognition of the familiar object if they were able to manipulate on the test as well. These results have been attributed to an effect of the change in context, but it is possible that they are specifically due to a greater salience of information from the tactual modality that would be missing on the visual-only test.

In any case, the fact that tactual information does, with development, come to guide responses suggests an increasing coordination between vision and touch. In the Diamond study, for example, the younger infants apparently fail to use tactual information to make the most adaptive and appropriate response; for adults, the visual information is for an object behind a transparent barrier, but the infant may pick up information only for the object and miss the more subtle information for the barrier. What may happen with development is that the tactual experience focuses the infant's attention on the corresponding visual information and the response accordingly is more appropriate. In the Bushnell studies (1982; Bushnell et al., 1984), the conflict is real and not just apparent; therefore, the evidence for increasing coordination comes from the infant's attempts to explore the mismatched object. In both cases, however, the assumption is that the infant picks up information in two systems and notices the discrepancy. It is of interest that some degree of coordination between manipulation and vision occurs almost as soon as the infant starts to manipulate; that is, both are influenced by the novelty or familiarity of an object (Harris, 1972; Rubenstein, 1976; Ruff, 1976), providing that the dimensions along which the novel and familiar differ are accessible to both vision and touch (Steele & Pederson, 1977). It seems to be only later that the infant clearly notices discrepancies in information from the two sources. Part of this development is surely due to differentiation within the tactual system. We have already discussed ways in which the manipulative behavior of the infant becomes more precise from 6 to 12 months; that is, the infant explores objects in a more differentiated way. This differentiated investigation may itself lead to the pickup of information for finer details of objects.

The coordination of audition and vision appears to exist at some level very early. While there is disagreement about the basis for the responses, it is clear that infants at 3 and 4 months look longer at visual events that match the sound track being played. This is the case for rhythm and related factors and for more qualitative characteristics of sound as well (Bahrick, 1983). Most of these studies capitalize on the amodal properties of events, and it may be that some of these properties require little in the way of experience to perceive. On the other hand, there are instances in which the infant learns to recognize more arbitrary combinations of sounds and visual events; one example is the particular characteristics of the mother's voice and the unique features of her face. It appears that infants can learn to recognize their mothers' voices on some basis shortly after birth or even before birth (DeCasper & Fifer, 1980). At this point we know relatively little about the process by which the relationship between the mother's voice and face is learned; some studies suggest such learning has occurred by 1 month of age (Aronson & Rosenblum, 1971; Carpenter 1974), but these findings have not been replicated.

There are a number of factors that would facilitate such auditory–visual associations. Neonates turn their eyes and heads toward the source of sound (Mendelson & Haith, 1976; Muir, Abraham, Forbes, & Harris, 1979; Turkewitz et al., 1966), an act that leads to simultaneous input from both vision and audition. Infants also visually follow objects more when they make some sound as they move (Lawson & Ruff, 1984); even if this phenomenon is largely due to an increase in arousal in the first 2 months (Lawson & Ruff, 1984), its existence means that the infant is more likely to attend to events in which stimulation to both modalities is present. Auditory localization improves with development (Clifton, Morrongiello, & Dowd, 1984), thus permitting more specific coordination of information about auditorially and visually specified events. In addition, somewhere around 4 months of age, sound localization seems to undergo a change from a reflexive behavior to a voluntary one (Clifton, Morrongiello, Kulig, & Dowd, 1981; Muir et al., 1979). Voluntary head turning could reflect a generally greater flexibility in auditory–visual search. Given the reflexive quality of earlier head turning, one wonders whether infants younger than 4 months are capable of showing the same sorts of auditory–visual matching so characteristic at 4 months of age. Another possible change with development is that the number of constraints on associations increases. While Lawson and Ruff (1984) found 3-month-old infants to be relatively insensitive to the spatial colocation of sound and object, Lawson (1980) found that in 6-month-olds auditory–visual relationships were not established as readily when the sound was not colocated with the object.

Amodal Properties: Their Role in Development

Considering the facility infants seem to have in appreciating amodal properties of objects and events, it is possible that the pickup of amodal properties precedes and facilitates the detection of other intermodal relationships. Objects and events involve some amodal properties (intensity, duration, location, temporal structure) that can be directly detected by two or more systems, and they also have modality-specific properties that can be detected by one but not another system (color, temperature). We would hypothesize that amodal properties of objects and events are perceived earlier and more readily than are relationships between modality-specific properties.

The detection of amodal properties might not only account for initial matches but also facilitate the association or coordination of information about the object that is more specific to the different modalities. Kuhl and Meltzoff (1982) report that 4-month-old infants apparently match the spectral properties of syllables with the structural changes in a moving mouth. Perhaps the infants' detection of these amodal properties helps them learn some arbitrary connections in that event, for example, that a certain pitch and certain characteristics of the face are also associated. If the curvature of an object's surface is picked up by both the tactual and the visual system, then the infant may more readily learn that for that object a particular color and a particular substance are connected.

One way to approach this issue is through a procedure in which true matching is compared to false matching. The technique has been used in the animal literature, but not in the infant literature. Although there has been evidence for some time that apes and monkeys transferred training between vision and touch, it seemed important to show that the long period of training was not leading to an association of two unrelated and nonequivalent stimuli, one in the tactual system and one in the visual system. Weiskrantz and Cowey (1975) trained six monkeys to match either the different or the same shapes in touch and vision. There were six false matching problems in which monkeys were trained to respond, for example, to tactual shape A and visual shape B; in the six true matching problems, tactual shape C, for example, was paired with visual shape C. The monkeys performed above chance in the true matching problems and *below* chance on the false matching problems, suggesting that the monkeys attempted true matches even when such matches were contrary to training.

Even if we assume that the systems are completely independent at birth and require experience to coordinate them, we are still faced with the question of how particular experiences lead to coordination. It is true, for example, that the tonic neck reflex causes the child's head and outstretched arm to be oriented in the same direction, and that a head turn to sound causes the sounding object to enter the visual field as well as centering the sound between the two ears. Both of these reflexive responses might lead to optimal situations for the development of the coordination between vision and touch or vision and audition. On the other hand, there are many situations in which there is, simultaneously, input to one system from one source and input to a second system from another source; for example, the infant may be grasping its blanket and watching its mobile. What is it that keeps the infant from associating those two inputs? One possibility is that it does not connect two inputs unless they come from the same spatial location (Bushnell, 1981). If location were the only constraint, however, the infant's localization skills would have to be very percise. If an infant were looking at an object that was 70 deg from its midline and either listening to a sound or feeling an object that was 90 deg from its midline, would the infant associate them? As already mentioned, another, more powerful source of information is co-occurence of change in time and space. Because objects are part of events that occur over time, their motions or activities are likely to lead to changes in several modalities at the same time and in the same pattern. Location and such conjoint spatial and temporal changes represent information for the amodal properties that we suggest underlies the perception and learning of many cross-modal relationships.

Is Cross-Modal Perception Different from Intramodal Perception?

We have considered developmental changes within the separate modalities, and ways in which coordination among modalities may be achieved. The next issue to be addressed is whether there is any evidence that the development of cross-modal abilities is later or more complicated than the development of intramodal abilities. Although there has been very little effort to compare intramodal with cross-modal abilities in infancy (for exceptions see Allen et al., 1977; Streri et al., 1984), the substantial body of data available from older children suggests that cross-modal transfer is often no more difficult than intramodal transfer. Jones (1981) summarizes much of this evidence and argues strongly that developmental changes in intramodal abilities account for changes in cross-modal transfer. In cross-modal studies the skill under investigation is frequently not carried out with equal facility by the two modalities involved. So, for example, form perception is better visually than tactually; correspondingly, cross-modal transfer tends to be intermediate in difficulty, but to improve in tandem with improvements in the tactual system. Similarly, temporal perception is better auditorially than visually and auditory–visual cross-modal performance improves coincident with improvements in visual temporal perception. In addition, there may be asymmetries in the direction of transfer simply because one system is less efficient than the other in acquiring and using information. Cross-modal transfer, therefore, is constrained by the competence of the inferior of the two modalities involved in a particular task. There are as yet no clear data in the infant literature to suggest another view.

The fact that some investigators find familiarity effects while others find novelty effects may have implications here, in that the occurrence of familiarity or novelty preferences reflects different phases in learning to recognize something. In particular, infants are thought to prefer to look at partially familiar objects early in the process, before all the information is acquired. So, for example, a preference for familiar objects is likely to be observed after brief familiarization times, at younger ages, and with more complex objects since these factors all affect how much information is gathered during familiarization (Hunter, Ames, & Koopman, 1983; Rose, Gottfried, Carminar-Melloy, & Bridger, 1982). Wagner and Sakovitz (in press) have extended these ideas to cross-modal performance, suggesting that cross-modal tasks should require longer familiarization time than intramodal ones. In addition, they argue that, since one can expect an initial period of random responding before enough information is acquired for recognition to occur at any level and a later period of random responding during the transition from familiar to novel preferences, the expected progress of preferences is one of random–familiar–random–novel. They report results that offer some tentative support for the idea that familiarity preferences are more likely to occur cross-modally than intramodally.

There is a methodological problem that is likely to plague anyone trying to compare cross-modal and intramodal conditions, especially when that comparison involves a timed measure such as latency or percentage of time spent looking at novel or familiar objects on a recognition test. The difficulty is that changing the modality of stimulus presentation in and of itself may introduce an element of novelty into the cross-modal condition. With our techniques, infants have to respond to relative degrees of novelty and seem particularly sensitive to changes in the context in which information is gathered (MacKay-Soroka et al., 1982; Rolfe & Day, 1981; Ruff, 1981). Therefore, if a lower percentage of time is spent with the novel object in cross-modal conditions than in intramodal ones, the reason may be that the novel and familiar objects on the cross-modal test of recognition are both novel, albeit to different degrees. It is also possible that the infants are distracted by the switch in modalities and fail to attend to the relevant variables.

Even if the methodological problems could be overcome and it were concluded that cross-modal transfer was more difficult than intramodal transfer, the problem might be not so much a difficulty in translating from one system to another as a difficulty in recognizing objects on the basis of partial information. If one considers the information picked up by the two different systems to be overlapping in some respects and nonoverlapping in others, there would necessarily be more overlap in a test of intramodal transfer than in a test of cross-modal transfer. The study by Streri and colleagues (1984) that was reviewed earlier serves as a good example. In that study, 5-month-old infants demonstrated tactual–tactual transfer and visual–tactual transfer, but not tactual–visual transfer. This pattern of results suggests that the information acquired during tactual familiarization was sufficient only for transfer to a tactual test. Here there would be considerable overlap and any aspect of the object attended to during familiarization would serve as a likely basis for tactual recognition. Tactually salient aspects of the object, or the information to specify them, apparently were not attended to or recognized in the visual test of the tactual–visual condition, perhaps because the overlap was not extensive. The fact that there was visual–tactual transfer may mean that so much information was picked up during visual familiarization that the tactually salient aspect was very likely to be included.

We should also find that any intramodal problem that provides the subject with only partial information on the test should be more difficult than one that provides full information. Rose and colleagues (1983) found just such a result. When 12-month-olds were presented with objects and tested with pictures or line drawings of the objects as well as the objects, there was transfer only to the objects after 15 sec of familiarization, but transfer to all three after 30 sec of familiarization. The longer familiarization may have increased the amount of information obtained and, therefore, the probability that there would be sufficient overlap between familiarization and test experiences to make recognition possible.

A definitive comparison of the relative difficulty of cross-modal and intramodal transfer is not possible until more is known about the nature of the information picked up by different modalities under different conditions. Until we know this, we cannot know how much information is shared by different systems. Until we know how much overlap there is, we cannot begin to specify the mechanisms that underlie the ability to match or transfer information from one modality to another. The critical problem then is to learn more about the nature of the information obtained by the different systems. As we shall indicate next, only an extensive probing of equivalent stimuli can definitively identify the nature of cross-modal equivalences.

Mechanisms Underlying Cross-Modal Abilities

The Issue

A theme throughout this chapter has been that we do not know enough about the bases of the various responses that are made in our cross-modal tasks. Although we refer to the infant's recognition of shape, substance, and temporal pattern, the infant may instead be responding to lower-order variables such as continuities and discontinuities in stimulation. For example, it is possible that the irregular pattern of tactual pressures that originates from sucking a nubby surface is being matched to the discontinuities in luminances produced when the nubby object is viewed. Such a match could be accomplished without any appreciation of that object's overall shape or texture. In many situations, we infer from the overt response that the two experiences provide some common information about the object. Even though the inference may be valid, it is very general; the situation, however, does not allow us to make more specific inferences.

Klüver's (1933) method of equivalent and nonequivalent stimuli provides a good basis for discussion. Klüver suggests that the mechanism underlying a given response cannot be understood if we know only one or two conditions under which the response is evoked; we need to know the range of stimuli to which the subject responds in the same way and the kinds of stimuli to which the subject responds in a different way. Once we have a set of equivalent stimuli and a set of nonequivalent stimuli, we can examine the aspects of stimulation that are common to the equivalent stimuli and absent in the nonequivalent stimuli. Only by doing so can we have a clear understanding of what the basis for the response is; this understanding, in turn, suggests the underlying mechanism. Klüver applied his method to discrimination learning in monkeys; after training the monkeys to respond differentially to a pair of stimuli, he tested them on many other pairs of stimuli. The goal was to see which pairs led to a consistent differential response and which pairs did not; the two groups together then defined the aspect(s) of the original stimuli that were responded to.

The study by Spelke and colleagues (1983) can be used to illustrate the method more specifically. In a matching paradigm, these investigators used the same pairs of sounds with several pairs of visual events. They found that discrete sounds occurring at a particular rate were matched to: (1) a bouncing puppet whose visible impacts with the ground were synchronized to the sounds; (2) a bouncing puppet whose pauses in midair and reversals in direction were synchronized to the sounds; and (3) a circling puppet whose directional reversals, regardless of location, were synchronized to the sounds. In this context, therefore, the three visual displays are equivalent, presumably because of the timing of abrupt breaks in motion and/or changes in direction. If other events have been used, it might have been possible to define a set of displays that were not equivalent to the three displays above. Without such a set, it is logically impossible to define the basis of the response precisely, because it is the nonequivalent stimuli that show what commonalities in the equivalent set are unique to that set. For example, suppose the following three types of display had been tested: (1) a puppet moving continuously in a circle with a sound every time it passed close to the floor; (2) a puppet making abrupt 180-deg turns in synchrony with the sound but not being displaced in space; and (3) a puppet moving in a straight line but pausing every time there was a sound. If, on the basis of synchrony between sound and event, type 2 was equivalent to the three events actually used by these investigators while types 1 and 3 were nonequivalent, the results would be interpreted quite differently than if type 1 and type 3 were equivalent and type 2 was not. What is important to the interpretation, therefore, is that both classes be defined.

The Implication of Using the Method of Equivalent Stimuli

What are the implications of Klüver's argument for the cross-modal studies with infants? There are several that can be illustrated with specific experiments. For example, Meltzoff and Borton found that 1-month-old infants who had sucked on a smooth sphere or a nubby sphere responded more to the familiar object when the two were later paired for visual presentation. The inference they make from their results is that the infants recognized the object they had been sucking on; that is, the oral and visual stimulation specified the same object. The inference is made from very few data, a situation that tends to be accepted because the study involved the same stimuli in the two conditions. What would have happened, however, if the infants had been presented with many different pairs of test objects and differential responses were obtained on several of them? Assuming that spontaneous preferences had been ruled out, how would we account for the differential responses? One possibility, of course, is that the nature of the information picked up was so general that any pair in which one object stimulated the subject along those general lines and the other did not would lead to a differential response. A conjoint comparison of the equivalent and nonequivalent stimuli would help us pinpoint the nature of that information. Turkewitz and colleagues (1984) suggest another possibility; that is, the infants were differentially aroused by sucking the smooth or nubby sphere. The arousal level then differentially affected the visual preferences on the later visual test. Such an alternative could be tested with other pairs of objects that might be expected to lead to differential arousal. The conclusions drawn by Meltzoff and Borton cannot, therefore, be definitive without the kind of probing suggested.

The same comments could be made about most studies of cross-modal transfer where positive results have been obtained. In the study by Rose and colleagues (1983), 12-month-olds, after tactual familiarization with an object, demonstrated recognition of the object, a picture of it, and an outline drawing. The results suggest that infants detected some invariant in all three forms of visual presentation. We could conclude that haptic exploration led to information specifying the contour of the object, but, if other test pairs had been involved, we might have a better idea of the nature of the contour. For example, it could be that the infants were picking up only general information about curvilinearity and rectilinearity rather than the contour specific to the familiarization object.

By the same token, if we get the same results in groups of infants at different ages, we cannot conclude that the same mechanism underlies the responses unless we have sampled widely and see that the equivalent and nonequivalent stimuli at different ages are the same. As an illustration, take the fact that infants 6–12 months old respond differentially to a sphere and a cube presented visually after tactual experience with one of then. Were we to institute Klüver's method systematically we might observe different patterns of response at the different ages even though the responses to the cube and the sphere were the same. The younger infants might transfer the response to any pair of objects in which a curved–straight distinction was maintained, but might fail to transfer to the same shape with a different texture. The older infants, on the other hand, might transfer the response only when the test objects were close to being a sphere and a cube. If this were the case for a number of pairs of objects, we could make a generalization about the increasing specificity of perception with age and increasing generalization of transfer across changes in irrelevant dimensions. If the results went in the opposite direction, then we would draw different conclusions.

Let us take one final example of the usefulness of this approach. Several studies with 12-month-olds have shown that the same discriminations can be made whether there is haptic familiarization and visual test or visual familiarization and haptic test. We can conclude that the information in both modalities was equivalent in some respect, but if we were to cast our net more widely by testing with other pairs of objects, the sets of equivalent and nonequivalent stimuli might differ systematically with the direction of transfer.

As these few examples should make clear, the method of equivalent stimuli represents an approach to the study of cross-modal functioning that requires the investigator to consider a wide variety of possibilities. It is obvious that the choice of stimuli must be based on some prior notion of various alternative interpretations of the phenomena involved, but the method requires that a test of these alternatives involve more than single pairs of objects. Many of the studies that we reviewed serve as demonstrations of the existence of cross-modal matching and transfer and do not probe the processes underlying such behavior. On the other hand, such probing cannot begin until a solid set of findings has been established. We think that the field now has a solid foundation of phenomena to investigate and is ready for the kind of programmatic work that will lead us to a more profound understanding of the mechanisms underlying cross-modal abilities.

REFERENCES

Allen, W. T., Coronado, S., Herrera, J., & Rocha, P. (1982, March). *Object discrimination in oral–oral and oral–visual sensory contexts*. Paper presented at the meeting of the International Conference on Infant Studies, Austin, TX.

Allen, T. W., Walker, K., Symonds, L., & Marcell, M. (1977). Intrasensory and intersensory perception of temporal sequences during infancy. *Developmental Psychology, 13,* 225–229.

Antell, S. E. G., & Caron, A. J. (1985). Neonatal perception of spatial relationships. *Infant Behavior & Development, 8,* 15–24.

Aronson, E., & Rosenblum, S. (1971). Space perception in early infancy: Perception within a common auditory–visual space. *Science, 172,* 1161–1163.

Bahrick, L. E. (1983). Infants' perception of substance and temporal synchrony. *Infant Behavior & Development, 6,* 429–450.

Bahrick, L. E., Walker, A. S., & Neisser, U. (1981). Selective looking by infants. *Cognitive Psychology, 13,* 377–390.

Birch, H. G., & Lefford, A. (1963). Intersensory development in children. *Monographs of the Society for Research in Child Development, 28,* (5, Serial No. 89).

Birch, H. G., & Lefford, A. (1967). Visual differentiation, intersensory integration and voluntary motor control. *Monographs of the Society for Research in Child Development, 32,* (2, Serial No. 110).

Boring, E. G. (1957). *A history of experimental psychology.* New York: Appleton-Century-Crofts.

Bower, T. G. R. (1974). The evolution of sensory systems. In R. B. MacLeod & H. L. Pick, Jr. (Eds.), *Perception: Essays in honor of James J. Gibson* (pp. 141–165). Ithaca, NY: Cornell University Press.

Brown, K. W., Baker, R. A., & Gottfried, A. W. (in press). Development of cross-modal transfer in early infancy. In L. P. Lipsitt & C. K. Rovee-Collier (Eds.), *Advances in infancy research* (Vol. 4). Norwood, NJ: Ablex.

Bryant, P. E., Jones, P., Claxton, V., & Perkins, G. M. (1972). Recognition of shapes across modalities by infants. *Nature, 240,* 303–304.

Bushnell, E. W. (1981). The ontogeny of intermodal relations: Vision and touch in infancy. In R. W. Walk & H. L. Pick (Eds.), *Intersensory perception and sensory integration* (pp. 5–36). New York: Plenum.

Bushnell, E. W. (1982). Visual-tactual knowledge in 8-, 9 1/2-, and 11-month-old infants. *Infant Behavior & Development, 5,* 63–75.

Bushnell, E. W. (in press). The basis of infant visual–tactual functioning—amodal dimensions or multimodal compounds? In L. P. Lipsitt & C. K. Rovee-Collier (Eds.), *Advances in infancy research* (Vol. 4). Norwood, NJ: Ablex.

Bushnell, E. W., Shaw, L., & Strauss, D. (1985). Relationship between visual and tactual exploration in 6-month-olds. *Developmental Psychology, 21,* 591–600.

Bushnell, E. W., Weinberger, N., & Polan, M. B. (1984). What visual–tactual discrepancies do infants detect, and why? Abstract in *Infant Behavior & Development, 7,* 59.

Bushnell, I. W. R. (1979). Modification of the externality effect in young infants. *Journal of Experimental Child Psychology, 28,* 211–229.

Carpenter, C. (1974). Mother's face and the newborn. *New Scientist, 6,* 255–262.

Casey, M. B. (1979). Color versus form discrimination learning in 1-year-old infants. *Developmental Psychology, 15,* 341–343.

Chang, H., & Trehub, S. E. (1977). Infants' perception of temporal grouping in auditory patterns. *Child Development, 48,* 1666–1670.

Clifton, R. K., Morrongiello, B. A., Kulig, J. W., & Dowd, J. M. (1981). Newborns' orientation toward sound: Possible implications for cortical development. *Child Development, 52,* 833–838.

Clifton, R. K., Morrongiello, B. A., & Dowd, J. M. (1984). A developmental look at an auditory illusion: The precedence effect. *Developmental Psychobiology, 17,* 519–536.

Davenport, R. K., Rogers, C. M., & Russell, I. S. (1973). Cross-modal perception in apes. *Neuropsychologia, 11,* 21–28.

Davenport, R. K., Rogers, C. M., & Russell, I. S. (1975). Cross-modal perception in apes: Altered visual cues and delay. *Neuropsychologia, 13,* 229–235.

Davis, S., & McCroskey, R. (1980). Auditory fusion in children. *Child Development, 51,* 75–80.

DeCasper, A. J., & Fifer, W. P. (1980). Of human bonding: Newborns prefer their mothers' voices. *Science, 208,* 1174–1176.

Demany, L., McKenzie, B., & Vurpillot, E. (1977). Rhythm perception in early infancy. *Nature, 266,* 718–719.

Diamond, A. (1981, April). *Retrieval of an object from an open box: The development of visual-tactile control of reaching in the first year of life.* Paper presented at the meetings of the Society for Research in Child Development, Boston.

Dodd, B. (1979). Lip reading in infants: Attention to speech presented in- and out-of-synchrony. *Cognitive Psychology, 11,* 478–484.

Fraisse, P. (1981). Multisensory aspects of rhythm. In R. W. Walk & H. L. Pick (Eds.), *Intersensory perception and sensory integration* (pp. 217–248). New York: Plenum.

Friedes, D. (1974). Human information processing and sensory modality: Cross-modal functions, information complexity, and deficit. *Psychological Bulletin, 81,* 284–310.

Gault, R. H., & Goodfellow, L. D. (1938). An empirical comparison of audition, vision and touch in the discrimination of temporal patterns and ability to reproduce them. *Journal of General Psychology, 18,* 41–47.

Gibson, E. J., Owsley, C. J., & Johnston, J. (1978). Perception of invariants by five-month-old infants: Differentiation of two types of motion. *Developmental Psychology, 14,* 407–415.

Gibson, E. J., Owsley, C. J., Walker, A. S., & Megaw-Nyce, J. (1979). Development of the perception of invariants. *Perception, 8,* 609–619.

Gibson, E. J., & Riccio, G. (1984). Infants' perception of the traversibility of surfaces. Abstract in *Infant Behavior & Development, 7,* 131.

Gibson, E. J., & Walker, A. S. (1984). Development of knowledge of visual–tactual affordances of substance. *Child Development, 55,* 453–460.

Gibson, J. J. (1962). Observations on active touch. *Psychological Review, 69,* 477–491.

Gibson, J. J. (1966). *The senses considered as perceptual systems.* Boston: Houghton-Mifflin.

Gibson, J. J. (1979). *The ecological approach to visual perception.* Boston: Houghton-Mifflin.

Goodnow, J. J. (1969). Eye and hand: Differential sampling of form and orientation properties. *Neuropsychologia, 7,* 365–373.

Gottfried, A. W., Rose, S. A., & Bridger, W. H. (1977). Cross-modal transfer in human infants. *Child Development, 48,* 118–123.

Gottfried, A. W., Rose, S. A., & Bridger, W. H. (1978). Effects of visual, haptic and manipulatory experiences on infants' visual recognition memory of objects. *Developmental Psychology, 14,* 305–312.

Gottfried, A. W., & Rose, S. A. (1980). Tactile recognition memory in infants. *Child Development, 51,* 69–74.

Haith, M. M., Goodman, G. S., Goodwyn, M. A., & Montgomery, L. (1982). A longitudinal study of infant's visual scanning and discrimination of form. Abstract in *Infant Behavior & Development, 5,* 108.

Harris, P. L. (1972). Infants' visual and tactual inspection of objects. *Perception, 1,* 141–146.

Harris, P. L. (1983). Infant cognition. In J. J. Campos & M. M. Haith (Eds.), *Handbook of child psychology* (Vol. 2) (pp. 690–782). New York: Wiley.

Hay, J. C., Pick, H. L., & Ikeda, K. (1965). Visual capture induced by prism spectacles. *Psychonomic Science, 2,* 215–216.

Heller, M. A. (1980). Tactile retention: Reading with the skin. *Perception & Psychophysics, 27,* 125–130.

Heller, M. A. & Leventhal, G. (1975). Delay in retention of forms. *Perceptual & Motor Skills, 41,* 903–906.

Horowitz, F. D. (1975). Visual attention, auditory stimulation, and language discrimination.

Monographs of the Society for Research in Child Development, 39, (5–6, Serial No. 158).

Humphrey, K., Tees, R. C., & Werker, J. (1979) Auditory–visual integration of temporal relations in infants. *Canadian Journal of Psychology, 33,* 347–352.

Hunter, M. A., Ames, E. W., & Koopman, R. (1983). Effects of stimulus complexity and familiarization time on infant preferences for normal and familiar stimuli. *Developmental Psychology, 19,* 338–352.

Jones, B. (1981). The developmental significance of cross-modal matching. In R. W. Walk & H. L. Pick (Eds.), *Intersensory perception and sensory integration* (pp. 109–136). New York: Plenum.

Kinsbourne, M., & Hiscock, M. (1984). The normal and deviant development of functional lateralization of the brain. In M. M. Haith & J. J. Campos (Eds.), *Handbook of child psychology* (Vol. 2) (pp. 158–280). New York: Wiley.

Klapper, Z. S., & Birch, H. G. (1971). Developmental course of temporal patterning in vision and audition. *Perceptual & Motor Skills, 32,* 547–555.

Klüver, H. (1933). *Behavior mechanisms in monkeys.* Chicago: University of Chicago Press.

Knudsen, E. (1983). Early auditory experience aligns the auditory map of space in the optic tectum of the barn owl. *Science, 222,* 939–942.

Krueger, L. (1970). David Katz' "Der aufbau der tastwelt" ("The world of touch"): A synopsis. *Perception & Psychophysics, 7,* 337.

Kuhl, P. K., & Meltzoff, A. N. (1982). The bimodal perception of speech in infancy. *Science, 218,* 1138–1141.

Lawson, K. R. (1980). Spatial and temporal congruity and auditory–visual integration in infants. *Developmental Psychology, 16,* 185–192.

Lawson, K. R., & Ruff, H. A. (1984). Infants' visual following: The effects of size and sound. *Developmental Psychology, 20,* 427–434.

Lewkowicz, D. J. (1985). Bisensory response to temporal frequency in 4-month-old infants. *Developmental Psychology, 21,* 306–317.

Lewkowicz, D. J., & Turkewitz, G. (1980). Cross-modal equivalence in early infancy: Auditory–visual intensity matching. *Developmental Psychology, 16,* 597–607.

Lobb, H. (1965). Vision versus touch in form discrimination. *Canadian Journal of Psychology, 19,* 175–187.

Lyons-Ruth, K. (1977). Bimodal perception in infancy: Response to auditory-visual incongruity. *Child Development, 48,* 820–827.

MacKain, K., Studdert-Kennedy, M., Spieker, S., & Stern, D. (1983). Infant intermodal speech perception is a left-hemisphere function. *Science, 219,* 1347–1349.

MacKay-Soroka, S., Trehub, S. E., Bull, D. H., & Corter, C. M. (1982) Effects of encoding and retrieval conditions on infants' recognition memory. *Child Development, 53,* 815–818.

Marks, L. E. (1978). *The unity of the senses: Interrelations among the modalities.* New York: Academic.

McGurk, H., & MacDonald, J. (1976). Hearing lips and seeing voices. *Nature, 264,* 746–748.

Meck, W. H., & Church, R. M. (1982). Abstraction of temporal attributes. *Journal of Experimental Psychology: Animal Behavior Processes, 8,* 226–243.

Meltzoff, A. N., & Borton, R. W. (1979). Intermodal matching by human neonates. *Nature, 282,* 403–404.

Mendelson, M. J., & Ferland, M. B. (1982). Auditory–visual transfer in four-month-old infants. *Child Development, 53,* 1022–1027.

Mendelson, M., & Haith, M. M. (1976). The relation between audition and vision in the human newborn. *Monographs of the Society for Research in Child Development, 41* (4, Serial No. 167).

Milewski, A. E. (1979). Visual discrimination and detection of configurational invariance in 3-month infants. *Developmental Psychology, 15,* 357–363.

Milner, A. D., & Bryant, P. E. (1980). Cross-modal matching by young children. *Journal of Comparative & Physiological Psychology, 71,* 453–458.

Morrongiello, B. A. (1984). Auditory temporal pattern perception in 6- and 12-month-old infants. *Developmental Psychology, 20,* 441–448.

Morrongiello, B. A., Kulig, J. W., & Clifton, R. K. (1984). Developmental changes in auditory temporal perception. *Child Development, 55,* 461–471.

Muir, D., Abraham, W., Forbes, B., & Harris, L. (1979). The ontogenesis of an auditory localization response from birth to four months of age. *Canadian Journal of Psychology, 33,* 320–332

Nazzaro, J. R., & Nazzaro, J. N. (1970). Auditory versus visual learning of temporal patterns. *Journal of Experimental Psychology, 84,* 477–478.

Piaget, J. (1952). *The origins of intelligence in children.* New York: Norton.

Piaget, J., & Inhelder, B. (1956). *The child's conception of space.* London: Routledge.

Pick, H. L., Jr. (1970). Systems of perceptual and perceptual–motor development. In J. P. Hill (Ed.), *Minnesota Symposia in Child Psychology* (Vol. 4) (pp. 199–219). Minneapolis, MN: University of Minnesota Press.

Pick, H. L., Jr. (1974). Visual coding of nonvisual spatial information. In R. B. MacLeod & H. L. Pick, Jr. (Eds.), *Perception: Essays in honor of James J. Gibson* (pp. 153–165). Ithaca, NY: Cornell University Press.

Pick, H. L., Jr. (in press). Reflections on the data and theory of cross-modal infancy research. In L. P. Lipsitt & C. K. Rovee-Collier (Eds.), *Advances in infancy research,* (Vol. 4). Norwood, NJ: Ablex.

Posner, M. I. (1967). Characteristics of visual and kinesthetic memory. *Journal of Experimental Psychology, 75,* 103–107.

Revesz, G. (1950). *Psychology and art of the blind* (W. A. Wolff, Trans.). New York: Longmens & Green. (Original work published, 1933)

Roberts, S. (1982). Cross-modal use of an internal clock. *Journal of Experimental Psychology: Animal Behavior Processes, 8,* 2–22.

Rochat, P. (1983). Oral touch in young infants: Response to variations of nipple characteristics in the first months of life. *International Journal of Behavioral Development, 6,* 123–134.

Rock, I., & Victor, J. (1964). Vision and touch: An experimentally created conflict between the two senses. *Science, 143,* 594–596.

Rolfe, S. A., & Day, R. H. (1981). Effects of the similarity and dissimilarity between familiarization and test objects on recognition memory in infants following uni- and bimodal familiarization. *Child Development, 52,* 1308–1312.

Rose, S. A. (1983). Differential rates of visual information processing in fullterm and preterm infants. *Child Development, 54,* 1189–1198.

Rose, S. A. (1984). Developmental changes in hemispheric specialization for tactual processing in very young children: Evidence from cross-modal transfer. *Developmental Psychology, 20,* 568–574.

Rose, S. A. (1985). Influence of concurrent auditory input on tactual processing in very young children: Developmental changes. *Developmental Psychology, 21,* 168–175.

Rose, S. A. (in press). Abstraction in infancy: Evidence from cross-modal and cross-dimension transfer. In L. P. Lipsitt & C. Rovee-Collier (Eds.), *Advances in infancy research* (Vol 4). Norwood, NJ: Ablex.

Rose, S. A., Blank, M., & Bridger, W. H. (1972). Intermodal and intramodal retention of visual and tactual information in young children. *Developmental Psychology, 6,* 482–486.

Rose, S. A., Gottfried, A. W., & Bridger, W. H. (1978). Cross-modal transfer in infants: Relationship to prematurity and socio-economic background. *Developmental Psychology, 14,* 643–652.

Rose, S. A., Gottfried, A. W. & Bridger, W. H. (1979). Effects of haptic cues on visual recognition memory in full-term and preterm infants. *Infant Behavior & Development, 2,* 55–67.

Rose, S. A., Gottfried, A. W., & Bridger, W. H. (1981a). Cross-modal transfer and information processing by the sense of touch in infancy. *Developmental Psychology, 17,* 90–98.

Rose, S. A., Gottfried, A. W., & Bridger, W. H. (1981b). Cross-modal transfer in 6-month-old infants. *Developmental Psychology, 17,* 661–669.

Rose, S. A., Gottfried, A. W., & Bridger, W. H. (1983). Infants' cross-modal transfer from solid objects to their graphic representations. *Child Development, 54,* 686–694.

Rose, S. A., Gottfried, A. W., Carminar-Melloy, P. M., & Bridger, W. H. (1982). Familiarity and novelty preferences in infant recognition memory: Implications for information processing. *Developmental Psychology, 5,* 704–713.

Rose, S. A., & Wallace, I. F. (1985). Cross-modal and intramodal transfer as predictors of mental development in fullterm and preterm infants. *Developmental Psychology, 21,* 949–962.

Rubenstein, J. (1974). A concordance of visual and manipulative responsiveness to novel and familiar stimuli in six-month-old infants. *Child Development, 45,* 194–195.

Ruff, H. A. (1976). The coordination of manipulation and visual fixation: A response to Schaffer (1975). *Child Development, 47,* 868–871.

Ruff, H. A. (1978). Infant recognition of the invariant form of objects. *Child Development, 49,* 293–306.

Ruff, H. A. (1980). The development of perception and recognition of objects. *Child Development, 51,* 981–992.

Ruff, H. A. (1981). The effect of context on infants' responses to novel objects. *Developmental Psychology, 17,* 87–89.

Ruff, H. A. (1982a). The development of object perception in infancy. In T. Field, A. Huston, H. C. Quay, L. Troll, & G. E. Finley (Eds.), *Review of Human Development.* New York: Wiley.

Ruff, H. A. (1982b). The role of manipulation in infants' responses to invariant properties of objects. *Developmental Psychology, 18,* 682–691.

Ruff, H. A. (1984). Infants' manipulative exploration of objects: The effects of age and object characteristics. *Developmental Psychology, 20,* 9–20.

Ruff, H. A., & Kohler, C. J. (1978). Tactual–visual transfer in six-month-old infants. *Infant Behavior & Development, 1,* 259–264.

Ruff, H. A., & Turkewitz, G. (1975). Developmental changes in the effectiveness of stimulus intensity on infant visual attention. *Developmental Psychology, 11,* 705–710.

Ruff, H. A., & Turkewitz, G. (1979). The changing role of stimulus intensity in infant visual attention. *Perceptual & Motor Skills, 48,* 815–826.

Salapatek, P. (1975). Pattern perception in early infancy. In L. B. Cohen & P. Salapatek (Eds.), *Infant perception: From sensation to cognition* (Vol. 1) (pp. 133–248). New York: Academic.

Soroka, S. M., Corter, C. M., & Abramovitch, R. (1979). Infants' tactual discrimination of novel and familiar tactual stimuli. *Child Development, 50,* 1251–1253.

Spelke, E. S. (1976). Infants' intermodal perception of events. *Cognitive Psychology, 8,* 533–560.

Spelke, E. S. (1979). Perceiving bimodally specified events in infancy. *Developmental Psychology, 15,* 626–636.

Spelke, E. S. (1981). The infant's acquisition of knowledge of bimodally specified events. *Journal of Experimental Child Psychology, 31,* 279–299.

Spelke, E. S. (1984). The development of intermodal perception. In L. B. Cohen & P. Salapatek (Eds.), *Handbook of infant perception.* New York: Academic.

Spelke, E. S., Born, W. S. & Chu, F. (1983). Perception of moving, sounding objects by four-month-old infants. *Perception, 12,* 719–732.

Spelke, E. S., Owsley, C. J. (1979). Intermodal exploration and knowledge in infancy. *Infant Behavior & Development, 2,* 13–27.

Starkey, P., Spelke, E. S., & Gelman, R. (1983). Detection of intermodal numerical correspondences by human infants. *Science, 222,* 179–181.

Steele, D., & Pederson, D. R. (1977). Stimulus variables which affect the concordance of visual and manipulative exploration in six-month-old infants. *Child Development, 48,* 104–111.

Stern, D. N., Hofer, L., Haft, W., & Dore, J. (1985). Affect attunement: The sharing of feeling states between mother and infant by means of inter-modal fluency. In T. Field & N. Fox (Eds.), *Social perception in infants* (pp. 249–268). Norwood, NJ: Ablex.

Streri, A., Pecheux, M. G., & Vurpillot, E. (1984). Cross-modal transfer of form in 5-month-old infants. Abstract in *Infant Behavior & Development, 5,* 354.

Thach, B. T., & Wiffenbach, J. M. (1976). Quantitative assessment of oral tactile sensitivity in pre-term and term neonates, and comparison with adults. *Developmental Medicine & Child Neurology, 18,* 204–212.

Turkewitz, G., Birch, H. G., Moreau, T., Levy, L., & Cornwell, A. C. (1966). Effects of intensity of auditory stimulation on directional eye movements in the human neonate. *Animal Behaviour, 14,* 93–101.

Turkewitz, G., Gardner, J. M., & Lewkowicz, D. L. (1984). Sensory/perceptual functioning during early infancy: Implications of a quantitative basis of responding. In G. Greenberg & E. Tobach (Eds.), *Conference on levels of integration and evolution of behavior* (pp. 167–195). Hillsdale, NJ: Erlbaum.

Vurpillot, E. (1968). The development of scanning strategies and their relation to visual differentiation. *Journal of Experimental Child Psychology, 6,* 632–650.

Vurpillot, E., & Ball, W. (1979). The concept of identity and children's selective attention. In G. Hale, & M. Lewis (Eds.), *Attention and the development of cognitive skills.* New York: Plenum.

Wagner, S., Winner, E., Cicchetti, D., & Gardner, H. (1981). "Metaphorical" mapping in human infants. *Child Development, 52,* 728–731.

Wagner, S. H., & Sakovits, L. J. (in press). A process analysis of infant visual and cross-modal recognition memory: Implications for an amodal code. In L. P. Lipsitt & C. K. Rovee-Collier (Eds.), *Advances in infancy research,* (Vol. 4). Norwood, NJ: Ablex.

Walker, A. S. (1982). Intermodal perception of expressive behaviors by human infants. *Journal of Experimental Child Psychology, 33,* 514–535.

Walker, A. S., Gibson, E. J., Owsley, C. J., Megaw-Nyce, J., & Bahrick, L. (1980). Detection of elasticity as an invariant property of objects by young infants. *Perception, 9,* 713–718.

Walker-Andrews, A. S., & Gibson, E. J. (in press). What develops in bimodal perception? In L. P. Lipsitt & C. K. Rovee-Collier (Eds.), *Advances in infancy research* (Vol. 4). Norwood, NJ: Ablex.

Walker-Andrews, A. S., & Lennon, E. M. (1985). Auditory–visual perception of changing distance by human infants. *Child Development, 56,* 544–548.

Weiskrantz, L., & Cowey, A. (1975). Cross-modal matching in the rhesus monkey using a single pair of stimuli. *Neuropsychologia, 13,* 257–261.

Welch, R. B., & Warren, D. H. (1980). Immediate perceptual response to intersensory discrepancy. *Psychological Bulletin, 88,* 638–667.

White, B. W., Saunders, F. A., Scadden, L., Bach-y-Rita, P., & Collins, C. C. (1970). Seeing with the skin. *Perception & Psychophysics, 7,* 23–77.

Wiffenbach, J. M. (1972). Discrete elicited motions of the newborn's tongue. In J. F. Bosma (Ed.), *Third symposium on oral sensation and perception* (pp. 347–361). Springfield, IL: Charles C. Thomas.

Worchel, P. (1951). Space perception and orientation in the blind. *Psychological Monographs, 65,* No. 15.

Zaporozhets, A. V. (1965). The development of perception in the preschool child. *Monographs of the Society for Research in Child Development, 30* (2, Serial No. 100).

CHAPTER 7

Developmental Behavioral Genetics and Infancy

ROBERT PLOMIN

The timing is propitious for adding a chapter on behavioral genetics to this hand-book. Although behavioral genetic theory, methods, and research have not previ-ously been reviewed in relation to infancy, some exciting discoveries have recently been made in the application of this approach to the study of development in in-fancy. The purpose of this chapter is to present a brief overview of the field of developmental behavioral genetics as it applies to infant development. The chapter begins with a discussion of the usefulness of quantitative genetics as a general theory of individual differences in development, which also provides background infor-mation needed for the presentation of research results in the second half of the chapter. Although this background material will suffice for most purposes, a recent review of the field of developmental behavioral genetics (Scarr & Kidd, 1984) is strongly recommended because of its review of basic genetic principles, its evolu-tionary flavor, and the overview it provides of the entire field of developmental behavioral genetics, even though infancy is discussed only briefly. For additional discussion of basic issues in quantitative genetic analysis of behavior, several texts on behavioral genetics are available (e.g., Dixon & Johnson, 1980; Fuller & Thomp-son, 1978; Plomin, DeFries, & McClearn, 1980; Vale, 1980).

QUANTITATIVE GENETICS AS A GENERAL THEORY OF INDIVIDUAL DIFFERENCES IN DEVELOPMENT

Theories in developmental psychology tend to be normative theories in the sense that they describe and attempt to explain the average developmental sequence of our species. In contrast, studies of individual differences tend to be atheoretical. The importance of this distinction will be discussed later; however, I would like to begin by proposing that we do have a theory of individual differences in develop-ment, a theory of scope and power rarely seen in the behavioral sciences: quanti-

I am grateful for the helpful comments of Judy Dunn, Robert Emde, Robert McCall, Joy Osofsky, and Sandra Scarr and for the excellent editorial advice of Rebecca Miles. The research described in this chapter on the Colorado Adoption Project was conducted collaboratively with J. C. DeFries and has been supported by the National Institute of Child Health and Human Development (HD-10333) and the National Science Foundation (BNS-8200310).

tative genetic theory. The word *theory* obviously means different things to different psychologists, as illustrated by differences among the best-known theories in psychology, such as personality theories, theories of learning, and Piagetian theory. At a minimum, a theory should be descriptive—it organizes and condenses already existing facts in a reasonable, internally consistent manner. It should make predictions concerning phenomena not yet investigated and permit clear tests of these predictions. A theory must at least be testable, if not falsifiable. Theories should also attempt to explain phenomena as well as to describe and to predict them. Finally, theories should be useful—they should clarify our thinking and be heuristic in suggesting new directions for research.

Is there any theory that meets these minimal criteria? In all the life sciences, no theory is grander than evolutionary theory. It organizes a vast amount of existing facts in a reasonable and internally consistent manner. No theory has spawned more predictions and been more heuristic in so many fields of science. Evolutionary theory is falsifiable: If reproductive differences among individuals in a species do not change the species in the direction of the more fecund individuals, the theory is wrong at its core. Darwin's version of the theory has been shown to be wrong in its less central tenets, primarily in its explanations of processes underlying natural selection. For example, Darwin gave some credence to the prevailing notion of the law of use and disuse as the source of variability upon which natural selection works. Darwin's theory was also wrong in suggesting that the mechanism by which the results of natural selection are passed on from generation to generation is pangenesis, a view that sperm and eggs are miniature replicas of all cells in the parents' bodies. We now know that random mutation of DNA is the source of genetic variability and that the winnowing of natural selection is maintained by the reliable replication of DNA.

All theories take aim at a particular level of explanation. Evolutionary theory paints broad strokes at the level of class, order, and family, and sometimes at the level of genus and species. Even though the foundation for natural selection is genetic variability among individuals in a population, evolutionary theory and predictions emanating from the theory can rarely be brought to bear upon the behavior of individual members of a species.

Quantitative Genetic Theory

Although most theories pale in comparison to the breathtaking scope of evolutionary theory, the theory of quantitative genetics can hold its own because it is the foundation for evolutionary theory: Without genetic differences among individuals in a species, evolution cannot occur. Quantitative genetic theory emerged in the early 1900s from disagreements between Mendelians who rediscovered Mendel's laws of inheritance and so-called biometricians who felt that Mendel's laws derived from experiments with qualitative characteristics in pea plants were not applicable to complex characteristics in higher organisms, which are nearly always distributed quantitatively in a normal bell-shaped curve. When Ronald Fisher (1918) put the finishing touches on the resolution to the dispute, quantitative genetic theory was born. The essence of quantitative genetic theory is that Mendel's mechanism of discrete inheritance also applies to normally distributed complex characteristics if we assume that many genes, each with a small effect, add up to produce observable differences among individuals in a population. If more than three or four genes affect a trait, the observed distribution cannot be distinguished from a normal curve. For example, a trait influenced by two alleles at each of three loci yields 27 different genotypes. Even if the alleles at the different loci equally affect the trait and there is no environmental variation, seven different phenotypes will be observed and will appear to be distributed as a normal curve.

The theory specifies the amount of phenotypic (observed) resemblance expected for different types of family relationships. For example, if genetic differences among individuals completely explain observed differences among individuals for a particular trait, parents and their offspring are expected to be 50 percent similar because they share half of all segregating (varying) gene effects that operate in an additive fashion—that is, gene effects that breed true. If nonadditive genetic variance is important, siblings would be expected to be somewhat more than 50 percent similar genetically because, in addition to 50 percent of the additive genetic variance, siblings share about a quarter of the nonadditive genetic variance. Half-siblings who have only one parent in common share only 25 percent of the additive genetic variance. Assortative mating for a trait increases additive genetic variance for that trait and also increases genetic resemblance among first-degree relatives. Inbreeding lowers the mean value for a trait for inbred individuals when nonadditive genetic variance affects the trait. The classic work on quantitative genetic theory was written by Falconer (1960, revised 1981; for a simpler presentation, see Plomin et al., 1980).

Although quantitative genetic theory makes these rather precise predictions about genetic relatedness, its fundamental point is that genetic differences among individuals can lead to phenotypic differences. The theory also recognizes that environmental influences can contribute to observed variance among individuals and observed covariance between relatives. The essence of quantitative genetic methods is to disentangle genetic and environmental influences.

Methods of Quantitative Genetics

A large part of the power of quantitative genetic theory is that its formulation of the components of variance in a population and of the components of covariance among relatives leads directly to methods to estimate the relative contributions of genetic and environmental influences. As in all experimentation, when two factors potentially influence a dependent variable, the effects of one factor are studied while the other factor is randomized or controlled in some way. The classical twin design comparing phenotypic resemblance in identical and fraternal twins assumes that both types of twins, because members of a pair are reared in the same family, share family environmental influences that potentially make the twin partners similar. However, the two types of twins differ dramatically in terms of genetic components of covariance. Identical twin partners are genetically identical to each other, whereas fraternal twins are about 50 percent similar, on the average, for segregating genes— assortative mating could raise this a bit and nonadditive genetic variance could lower this somewhat. Thus if heredity affects a trait, the twofold greater genetic similarity of identical twins will make them more similar phenotypically than fraternal twins. If identical and fraternal twin correlations do not differ, then heredity is unimportant for the trait.

Adoption designs are particularly powerful. In nonadoptive families, quantitative genetic theory predicts resemblance among relatives to the extent that heredity is important; however, the fact that these family members also share the same family environment makes it possible that observed familial resemblance is due to shared environmental as well as genetic influences. Adoption designs cleanly separate these two types of influence. Genetic background can be randomized while the effects of family environment are evaluated by studying pairs of genetically unrelated individuals in the same family. Similarly, family environment can be randomized while the effects of heredity are assessed by studying pairs of genetically related individuals reared in different families. The resemblance found in the former case (when family environment but not heredity is shared) and the resemblance found in the latter case (when heredity is shared but not family environment) should sum to the resemblance observed in nonadoptive families in which both family environment and heredity are shared.

As in any experiment, potentially confounding effects must be considered. In the twin design, even though twin partners of both types live in the same family, it is possible that identical twins experience more similar family environments than do fraternal twins. If this were the case, some of the greater observed similarity of identical twins might be due to greater similarity of their experiences. This possible confounding effect has been examined and so far does not appear to be a problem for the twin design (Plomin et al., 1980). In the adoption design, the major issue is selective placement, matching of biological parents who relinquish infants for adoption and the adoptive parents of the infants. Selective placement leads to a less clean separation of genetic and environmental influences: Because the phenotypes of the biological parents and adoptive parents are correlated, some of the apparent genetic resemblance between biological parents and their adopted-away offspring could be mediated environmentally, and some of the ostensibly environmental similarity between adoptive parents and their adopted infants could be mediated genetically. Fortunately, the extent of selective placement can be assessed and its effects on genetic and environmental estimates are understood (DeFries & Plomin, 1978).

Beyond Estimates of Genetic and Environmental Influence

The major application of quantitative genetic theory to the study of behavioral development has been to estimate relative contributions of genetic and environmental influences. Although this is a reasonable first step in understanding the variance of a characteristic, quantitative genetic theory can contribute much more toward understanding genetics, environment, and their developmental interface.

Genetic Extensions

It is clear from developmental molecular genetics that genetic regulation is the key to differentiation at a cellular level. One of the most exciting areas for exploration in genetics is the study of the genetic contributions to change for behavioral development as well. Genetic factors are likely to contribute to change, not just to continuity. The concept of age-to-age genetic change, methods to assess it, and findings to date in infancy are discussed at length later in this chapter. (See also Plomin, 1986.)

Another potentially powerful direction for genetic research is to begin to build bridges toward molecular genetics, especially the new techniques emanating from recombinant DNA research. A basic tool in this work is the use of restriction enzymes that cleave DNA at specific nucleotide sequences four to six nucleotide bases in length. If an individual does not have a certain sequence of DNA that is cut by a particular restriction enzyme, his or her DNA will not be cut into fragments of the same length as will that of someone who has this particular DNA sequence. Restriction fragment length polymorphisms (RFLPs, pronounced "riff-lips") have been a boon to linkage studies that map genes to chromosomes. Marker genes have been discovered for all human chromosomes; nearly half of human DNA now has mapped markers nearby, and about two new markers are found each month. RFLPs were responsible for locating the gene for Huntington disease on chromosome 4, the first time that linkage was identified using these techniques for a gene whose protein product was unknown.

Although the complex traits of interest to psychologists are not likely to show single-gene or major-gene effects, it is possible to use a large number of RFLPs to begin to characterize genetic differences among individuals directly rather than indirectly by the traditional methods of quantitative genetics. The problem is that human DNA consists of about 3.5 billion nucleotide base pairs so that an adequate sampling of an individual's DNA would require analysis of hundreds if not thousands of RFLPs. However, most DNA involves introns, stretches of DNA that are spliced out of the messenger RNA copy before it leaves the nucleus of the cell for translation into polypeptides. Thus the amount of functional DNA is much less than is suggested by the presence of 3.5 billion base pairs.

Because the possibilities for applying molecular genetic techniques to the study of behavioral development are still just possibilities, the stunning advances in molecular genetics in general and specifically in the genetic regulation of development will not be discussed further in this chapter. However, it should be mentioned that the new molecular genetic findings such as split genes, transposable genes, and temporal genes do not in the least vitiate the theory of quantitative genetics. Quantitative genetics is the "bottom line" of genetic variability as it affects phenotypic variability. That is, quantitative genetic methods assess the total impact of genetic variability of any kind, regardless of its molecular source.

Environmental Extensions

A major emphasis of this chapter is that quantitative genetics is as useful for studying the environment as it is for studying heredity. In fact, because of the importance of its methods for understanding environmental influence, quantitative *genetic* theory is a misnomer. Two examples are the importance of nonshared environmental influences and genetic mediation of relationships between environmental measures and measures of infant development.

Shared environmental influences, as discussed previously, are those that create phenotypic similarity between family members. For example, the similarity between pairs of adoptees reared in the same adoptive home directly assesses the portion of phenotypic variance that can be accounted for by shared family environment. The rest of the environmental variance—that is, the remainder of the phenotypic variance that cannot be explained by genetic variance or by shared family environment—is due to nonshared environmental influences.

Behavioral genetic research provides the best available evidence for the importance of environmental variance in behavioral development; however, this research strongly suggests that nearly all of this environmental variance is of the nonshared variety, especially for personality and psychopathology (Plomin & Daniels, in press; Rowe & Plomin, 1981). This implies that the unit of environmental transmission is not the family but rather microenvironments within families. This is a momentous conclusion because nearly all previous studies of environmental influences on behavioral development have begun with the assumption that the family is the level at which environments are experienced by children. This assumption has usually been implicit in that one environmental assessment is made and one child's development is studied per family, and then covariance between the environmental measure and children's development is analyzed across families. These studies have yielded few significant and no substantial relationships (Maccoby & Martin, 1983). However, the behavioral genetic data are telling us that the environmental action is within families, not across families. We need to study more than one child per family in order to explore the possible environmental sources of differences between children in the same family.

Rowe and Plomin (1981) suggested categories of nonshared environmental influence. One possible source of such influences is unsystematic, for example, accidents, illnesses, and other idiosyncratic experiences. However, the more interesting possibility is that there are systematic sources of differential sibling experience, such as their differential treatment of each other, differences in treatment by their parents, and differential extrafamilial influences such as interactions with different peer groups. The only category of nonshared environmental influence that has been studied is family structure variables such as birth order, spacing, and gender.

Any traditional measure of family environment can be conceptualized as a possible source of differences within a family. For example, parental affection is a major dimension included in most attempts to measure parental interaction across families by observing parents' affection in interaction with one of their children or by asking parents and children about the parents' affection. Rather than comparing parental affection across families, the same dimension can be assessed within families, asking about *differential* parental affection toward two children. The example of parental affection makes the point that examining environmental relationships within families could yield results quite different from the apparently negligible environmental relationships across families. "Absolute" levels of parental affection (i.e., as compared to parents in other families) might not have important developmental effects. However, slight differences in parental affection toward two children in a family (or siblings' perceptions of such differences regardless of the validity of such perceptions) might have a major impact on children's development.

The interest in nonshared environmental influences is so new that there is not yet much research on the topic; moreover, nearly all of the research that has been done involves adolescents. Results of this research suggest that parental treatment is not a likely source of nonshared family environment because parents usually report that they treat their children similarly and pairs of siblings also perceive similar treatment by their parents (e.g., Daniels, Dunn, Furstenberg, & Plomin, 1985; Daniels & Plomin, 1985). Siblings' interaction with each other and extrafamilial influences such as differential peer experiences are more likely candidates.

This hypothesis is supported by a study of differential parental treatment of infant siblings, a study of 50 families in which mothers were videotaped while interacting with each of two siblings when each child was 12 months old (Dunn, Plomin, & Nettles, 1985). The children were nearly 3 years apart in age, which means that the observations of maternal behavior toward the siblings were separated by nearly 3 years. Maternal behavior was reliably assessed and factor analysis yielded three factors: affection, verbal attention, and control. The results indicate that the mothers were incredibly consistent in their behavior toward their two children at the same age. Corrected for unreliability, the average correlation for maternal behavior toward two siblings was .70. Similar results were obtained at 2 years (Dunn, Plomin, & Daniels, 1986) and at 3 years (Dunn & Plomin, 1986). Other studies on this topic agree that mothers are quite consistent in their behavior toward their children at the same age (Jacobs & Moss, 1976) and somewhat less when siblings are observed at different ages (Abramovitch, Pepler, & Corter, 1982; Dunn & Kendrick, 1982). However, the series of studies by Dunn and her colleagues indicates that even though mothers treat their two children quite similarly when the children are the same age, longitudinal analyses from 12 to 24 months and from 24 to 36 months show little stability for maternal behavior to the same child. Thus, Dunn suggests that rank-ordering of mothers on these dimensions changes during the transition from infancy to early childhood because different mothers respond differently to the developmental advances of their children.

Because so few data are available on nonshared environmental influences in infancy, this important topic will not be discussed further in this chapter. However, data that bear tangentially on the issue will be mentioned as they arise in other contexts.

The second example of the importance of quantitative genetics for studying the environment is genetic mediation of relationships between environmental measures and measures of infant development. Because this topic is discussed at length later in this chapter, it will only be mentioned briefly at this time. All environmental measures in the home are in fact indirect measures of parental behavior—this is obviously true for variables such as parental responsiveness, but it is also applicable to variables such as number of books visible in the home. Because behavioral geneticists are in the business of studying possible genetic links between parental behavior and children's development, they considered the possibility that heredity might mediate relationships between measures intended to assess the home environment and measures of infant development in nonadoptive homes (where the vast majority of environmental studies are conducted). In contrast, in adoptive homes, in which parents share only family environment and not heredity with their children, relationships between environmental measures and measures of development are truly environmental. By comparing environment–development relationships in nonadoptive and adoptive families, the extent of genetic mediation of these relationships can be estimated (Plomin, Loehlin, & DeFries, 1985). Data reviewed later suggest that fully half of the environment–development relationships in infancy are due to genetic mediation.

The Developmental Interface Between Nature and Nurture

As we have seen, quantitative genetic theory can take us well beyond estimates of the relative contributions of genetic and environmental influence. For example, it enables us to examine age-to-age genetic change and continuity and to explore environmental extensions, such as the distinction between shared and nonshared family environmental influence, and the possibility of genetic mediation of environment–development relationships. Moreover, quantitative genetic theory offers a novel perspective on the developmental interplay between genetics and environment. Two examples are genotype–environment interaction and genotype–environment correlation.

Mark Twain once said that everyone talks about the weather but no one does anything about it; interaction is something like the weather in this regard. In quantitative genetics, *genotype–environment interaction* refers to conditional relationships between genotypes and environments—that is, genetic effects that depend upon environmental circumstances or, alternatively, environmental effects that depend upon genotype. Much of what has been written on the topic in the developmental literature is what has been called *interactionism,* "the view that environmental and genetic threads in the fabric of behavior are so tightly interwoven that they are indistinguishable" (Plomin, DeFries, & Loehlin, 1977, p. 309). Frequently cited is the assertion that the "organism is a product of its genes and its past environment" (Anastasi, 1958, p. 197), the point being that there can be no behavior without both environment and genes. This is a truism for the individual, but it is simply irrelevant when one is studying individual differences in a population. If taken seriously at the population level, this view would suggest that environmental influences on development cannot be studied because they interact completely with genetic influences. However, it is notable that the argument is put forward only in the context of genetic studies, not environmental research.

Despite the reasonableness of going beyond genetic and environmental "main effects" to explore the possibility that certain environmental influences are particularly powerful only for certain individuals, interactions of this sort have been difficult to find (Plomin & Daniels, 1984). Even in research with mice in which extreme genotypes and extreme environmental interventions are used, genotype–environment interactions tend to be inconsistent and to account for little overall variance (DeFries, 1979). For example, Cooper and Zubek's (1958) frequently cited study of genotype–environment interaction in maze learning when selected lines of maze-bright and maze-dull rats were reared in either deprived or enriched conditions does not seem to generalize to similar studies in rodents (as reviewed by Fuller & Thompson, 1978).

The adoption design permits analyses of genotype–environment interaction for human data that are analogous to the method used in animal studies in which different strains are reared in different environments (see Plomin et al., 1977). The genotype of adopted children can be estimated from scores of their biological parents, and environmental influences on adopted children can be assessed using any aspect of the children's environment such as characteristics of the adoptive parents or measured features of the home environment. For example, it might be reasonable to expect genetic propensities of children to emerge to a greater extent in permissive environments than in restrictive ones: Adopted children whose biological parents are highly active might not differ from adopted children with less active biological parents in adoptive homes that clamp down on children's activity. However, in permissive adoptive homes, large differences in activity level between the two groups of adopted children might emerge.

Rather than dichotomizing continuous variables such as parental activity or permissiveness, it is preferable to use hierarchical regression to remove main effects of genotype and environment and then to assess their interaction, the joint influence of genotype and environment (Plomin & Daniels, 1984). When this method was used in analyses of the infancy data collected in the Colorado Adoption Project, a longitudinal study of adopted and nonadopted children described in detail later in the chapter, only a chance number of significant genotype-environment interactions was found when genotype was estimated by biological mothers' scores and environment was measured by adoptive parents' scores or by specific measures of the home environment (Plomin & DeFries, 1985). For mental development, 15 genotype-environment interaction analyses were conducted; none was significant. For temperament, 80 genotype-environment analyses yielded only two significant interactions, fewer than would be expected to occur by chance. Finally, for behavioral problems, 30 genotype-environment analyses produced only four significant interactions. Thus taken together the number of significant interactions observed was precisely the number expected on the basis of chance. Nonetheless, the few interactions that emerged warrant further attention because evidence for genotype-environment interaction has not been obtained previously in human studies. The interactions that were found were of the type mentioned in the earlier example—that is, genetic differences among infants emerged more clearly in less constrained environments. For example, genetic differences in infants' emotionality are seen when the rearing parents are low in emotionality, and genetic differences in infants' activity emerge in permissive adoptive families. A similar hypothesis has been offered to explain genotype-environment interactions in mouse research (Henderson, 1970).

Despite the similarity in terms, genotype-environment correlation is very different from genotype-environment interaction. As noted earlier, *genotype-environment interaction* refers to the differential response of genotypes to the same environment, or, alternatively, to environmental effects that depend on genotype. It is quite literally the interaction between genetic deviations and environmental deviations as they predict developmental outcomes. The term *genotype-environment correlation,* on the other hand, refers to the correlation between genetic deviations and environmental deviations. In other words, genotype-environment correlation denotes the extent to which individuals are exposed to environments correlated with their genetic propensities.

Plomin and colleagues (1977) have proposed three types of genotype-environment correlation: passive, reactive, and active. Most quantitative genetic research has been concerned with genotype-environment correlation that arises, for example, when parents provide a family environment correlated with the heredity that they also convey to their children. For instance, to the extent that emotionality is inherited, parents might provide both genes and environment to foster emotionality in their children. This type of genotype-environment correlation is called *passive* because children passively receive family environments correlated with their hereditary propensities. Quantitative genetic research has focused on passive genotype-environment correlation as it relates to IQ using two methods to estimate its importance: comparisons of the variances for adopted and nonadopted children, and modeling approaches using parent–offspring data. Estimates of the importance of passive genotype-environment correlation for IQ vary widely (Plomin, 1986).

Reactive and active types of genotype-environment correlation are likely to be even more important in development. The word *reactive* refers to the fact that individuals who are genetically unrelated to the child can react to the child on the basis of the child's genetic propensities. For example, a child's propensity toward sociability might be rewarded by the response of others to the child's attention and warmth. For the *active* type, a correlation between genotype and environment arises because children actively seek environments compatible with their genotypes. For example, bright children can seek peers, adults, or inanimate aspects of their environment that foster their cognitive development. This has been called niche picking or niche building (Scarr & McCartney, 1983).

The trichotomy of passive, reactive, and active genotype–environment correlation is summarized in Table 7.1. These categories of genotype–environment correlation have been used by Scarr and McCartney (1983) as the cornerstone for a general theory of the processes by which genotype and environments combine during development. They suggest that "the relative importance of the three kinds of genotype–environment effects changes with development. The influence of the passive kind declines from infancy to adolescence, and the importance of the active kind increases over the same period" (p. 427). Rather than calling it *genotype–environment correlation,* Scarr and McCartney refer to it as *genotype→ environment effects* because they propose that "genes drive experience" (p. 425):

> We argue that genetic differences prompt differences in which environments are experienced and what effects they may have. In this view, the genotype, in both its species specificity and its individual variability, largely determines environmental effects on development, because the genotype determines the organism's responsiveness to environmental opportunities. (p. 424)

Also, their goal is to "describe developmental processes over time, not to estimate sources of variance in phenotypes" (p. 426). This provocative theory is likely to serve as a rich heuristic for developmental behavioral genetic research throughout the life span.

It is possible to use adoption data to explore reactive genotype–environment correlation. The strategy for isolating genotype–environment correlation uses biological parents' data to estimate adopted children's genotypes and any measure of adopted children's environment, similar to the test for genotype–environment interaction. Instead of assessing interactions between this genotypic index and environmental measures as they relate to developmental outcomes, the correlation between the genetic and environmental indices is computed. In the absence of selective placement, a significant correlation indicates that the environmental measure in the adoptive home reflects genetic propensities of the adopted children, a reactive genotype–environment correlation. This test will detect reactive genotype–environment

TABLE 7.1.   Three Types of Genotype–Environment Correlation[a]

Type	Description	Pertinent Environment
Passive	Children have genotypes linked to their family environment	Parents and siblings
Reactive	People react to children on the basis of the children's genotypes	Anybody
Active	Children seek an environment conducive to their genotype	Anybody or anything

[a]Adapted from Plomin et al. (1977).

correlation only when there is a heritable relationship between the phenotypes of the biological parent and the adopted child and when there is a relationship between the environmental measure and the adopted infant's phenotype. Although these appear to be quite restrictive limitations, they really define genotype–environment correlation: Genetic differences among children are correlated with differences among their environments.

Analyses of this type using data from the Colorado Adoption Project (Plomin & DeFries, 1983, 1985) find little evidence for reactive genotype–environment correlation in infancy, a finding that is in line with Scarr and McCartney's prediction that passive genotype–environment correlation prevails in infancy, with reactive and active types becoming increasingly important later in childhood. Nonetheless, the hints of reactive genotype–environment correlation that emerged deserve mention because of the novelty of such data. Although no more than a chance number of significant correlations was observed for cognitive development and for behavioral problems, 7 of 28 genotype–environment correlations for temperament reached significance. For example, at both 12 and 24 months, biological mothers' activity level correlated negatively with Caldwell and Bradley's (1978) HOME general factor in adoptive families, suggesting that adoptive parents show less responsivity as assessed by HOME when their children are genetically predisposed toward high activity (Plomin & DeFries, 1985).

Is It a Theory?

Earlier, some minimal criteria for a theory were mentioned: A theory should be descriptive, predictive, explanatory, and useful in a heuristic sense. Quantitative genetic theory more than meets these requirements. To begin with, the theory provides a rationale for expecting genetic differences among children and for expecting these genetic differences to lead to phenotypic differences in the complex behavioral traits that interest psychologists. In this way, quantitative genetic theory organizes a welter of data on individual differences so that they are viewed not as imperfections in the species type or as nuisance error in analysis of variance, but rather as the quintessence of evolution and life. The theory predicts precisely the resemblance to be expected for various family relationships. The armamentarium of quantitative genetic methods for both human and nonhuman research follows closely from the theory and keeps the theory firmly grounded in data, so much so that it sometimes is necessary to emphasize that there is a powerful theory underlying all of the research activity in behavioral genetics.

I cannot think of a psychological theory that begins to match the explanatory precision of quantitative genetic theory. The model starts with single-gene effects, both additive and nonadditive, and then generalizes that model to a polygenic system in which many genes contribute small amounts of variance that mingle with environmental sources of variance. There can be no doubt about the correctness of Mendelian genetics as the mechanism of heredity, and the incredible leaps in knowledge in molecular genetics can be seen as providing a detailed molecular explanation for Mendelian inheritance.

In an interesting discussion of the "hereditarian and environmentalist research programmes," Urbach (1974a, 1974b) suggests that the intractability of the nature–nurture debate is due not to two competing theories, but rather to two competing research programs. Thus rather than comparing the evidence in support of two theories, Urbach chose to ask how the two research programs dealt with anomalies:

> It is relatively easy for any programme to deal with (that is, to make its theories consistent with) any given anomalies. In appraising the programmes, the question is whether they do this in a *progressive* or in a *degenerating* manner. The shift within a research programme from one theory to another is progressive if the new theory not only deals with its predecessor's anomalies but also makes extra predictions, some of which are tested and confirmed. On the other hand, if the new theory does nothing more than accommodate the anomalies, the shift is *ad hoc* and the programme degenerating.
>
> (*Urbach, 1974a, p. 101*)

Urbach reviews quantitative genetic data on IQ and concludes that "the hereditarian programme has anticipated many novel facts. . . . When the environmentalist programme has attempted to account for the novel facts produced by the hereditarian programme, it has been unable to do so except in an *ad hoc* fashion" (p. 133).

For me, the most important benefit of quantitative genetic theory is its heuristic usefulness when it is applied to the phenomena of developmental psychology. The theory has led me to explore the developmental interface of nature and nurture as revealed by genotype–environment interaction and genotype–environment correlation (Plomin et al., 1977); to the understanding that environmental influences on behavioral development primarily operate in such a way as to make two children in the same family no more similar than are children in separate families (Rowe & Plomin, 1981); to the deduction that relationships between environmental measures and children's development can be mediated genetically (Plomin et al., 1985); and to the realization that genes can contribute as much to change as to continuity in development, which has led to the development of methods to analyze genetic change and continuity (Plomin & DeFries, 1981; Plomin, 1986). I have also found quantitative genetic theory useful in thinking about substantive areas, especially mental development (Plomin & DeFries, 1985) and temperament (Buss & Plomin, 1984; Plomin, 1983b). Without hesitation, I predict that quantitative genetic theory and methods will be useful when applied to any topic in infancy research, as long as the research is focused on individual differences rather than normative description.

Individual Differences

Quantitative genetic theory and its behavioral genetic applications are concerned with individual differences in a population, not with normative or average developmental trends. This distinction cannot be overemphasized. Although it is usually difficult to disagree with suggestions for rapprochement between different approaches, and such a truce has been called for by McCall (e.g., 1979) specifically for the individual differences and normative approaches, this is one case in which the differences need to be sharpened rather than smoothed. Mixing these two approaches has led to errors of interpretation in research. For example, problems that arise when language researchers attempt to use individual differences data on the relationship between language-learning environments and language acquisition to address the question of the innateness of language use in the human species have been discussed by Hardy-Brown (1983). Confusion between the two approaches is also responsible for some misguided antipathy toward behavioral genetics; for example, heritability (genetic influence on individual differences in a population) has been mistakenly assumed to be related to innateness (hardwired, species-wide genetic determination that is impervious to environmental influence).

The normative and individual differences perspectives can be thought of in terms of the distinction between means and variances. Descriptions of means and variances are independent. For example, from 12 to 24 months, infants increase in height by 15 percent and in weight by 25 percent on the average. However, these dramatic average changes in height and weight are accompanied by considerable stability of individual differences, with correlations of about .70 from 12 to 24 months. Even more important, explanations of means have no necessary relationship to explanations of individual differences. For example, the rapid average increase in mental development in infancy seems likely to be due to maturational events highly canalized at the species level, yet individual differences in infant mental development appear to be largely environmental in origin, as discussed later in this chapter.

As McCall argues, developmentalists should eventually attempt to explain both species-typical developmental patterns and individual variations on these themes. However, at this time, I suggest that it is important to maintain the distinction between these approaches. I would go further and argue for more theory and research on individual differences. In terms of applying developmental research to the world outside our laboratories, it is individual differences research that is needed because it is to individuals that such research must be applied. For example, it certainly is interesting to try to understand why the human species walks and talks. However, it is critical that we learn why some infants are slow to walk or talk, the extent to which genetic and environmental variation accounts for the observed differences in infants' development, and whether these early differences in developmental rate predict difficulties later in life.

My emphasis on individual differences is not intended to deny the conceptual interest of species-typical approaches to infancy research that focus on average developmental trends in our species. After all, infancy is a mammalian theme that is exaggerated in primates; infant sensorimotor development appears to be highly canalized in the sense that developmental differences among primate species, including *Homo sapiens,* are scant in infancy, and differences among human infants are small compared to differences later in development (Scarr, 1976). However, I view descriptions of normative development as a thematic backdrop against which we can understand variations on the theme. Others (Scarr & Carter, 1983) have been more blunt: "Populations can be described only in statistical terms, because they are *distributions* of individuals. Although one can reify some frequent 'type' as representative of a population, it is quickly apparent that more is lost than gained by typological thinking" (p. 225). The well-known evolutionary biologist Ernst Mayr (1982) considers normative and individual differences approaches as two different worldviews. The former view, which Mayr calls essentialism, sees things in terms of their essence, as physicists view atomic particles. In biology, an essentialist looks at members of a species as representatives of a common type. In contrast, Mayr argues that biology must recognize the uniqueness of individuals within a species; without variation among individual members of the species, evolution cannot occur.

Despite the importance of individual differences, the majority of developmental theory and research is normative. The 28 chapters of the first edition of this handbook, for instance, contain 765 pages of text, excluding references. Of these 765 pages, 519 pages (68 percent) are related to the normative viewpoint and only 246 pages involve individual differences. Some chapters go back and forth between the two perspectives, often invoking the normative perspective for theory and viewing the data in terms of individual differences. Some chapters are difficult to classify. For example, one would expect that the study of perinatal effects on infant development would primarily involve individual differences. However, these studies emphasize the *average* effect of perinatal factors as if there is a specieswide developmental course that is disturbed by perinatal trauma. Although data such as these can be translated into individual differences statistics, the thematic emphasis is normative; thus the chapters on perinatal effects, obstetrical medication, fetal alcohol, and early intervention are primarily tallied as normative. It makes some sense that these chapters emphasize average effects on children because their goal is to describe environmental factors—birth complications, medication, alcohol, and early interventions. However, many of the chapters that focus on infant behavior—for example, chapters on electrophysiology, learning, vision, thought, socioemotional development, and interactions between mothers and infants, fathers and infants, and infants and peers—are also strongly normative in their perspective. Even the two methodology chapters emphasize the normative approach. In fact, the only chapters that focus on individual differences are the chapters on infant assessment, the chapters on physical development, prediction of emotional and social behavior, and prediction of later IQ, and two brief clinical chapters, one on conceptual issues and the other on vulnerability and risk.

The conceptual leap to be made is from a normative to an individual differences perspective; once that leap is accomplished, it is a small step to recognition of the usefulness of quantitative genetic theory. One of the most rewarding professional experiences for me has been seeing experimental psychologists—who have developed ingenious techniques for measuring infant behavior, although always from a normative perspective—become interested in individual differences and then in behavioral genetics. For example, Joseph Fagan III had conducted a decade of research on normative development using Fantz's (1964) novelty preference task. Fagan noticed individual differences among the infants, which persisted despite his best efforts to eradicate them, and began to wonder whether his work might be useful in predicting individual differences in mental development. He obtained school records for some of the children he had tested as infants and found that his measure administered in the first few months of life predicted later IQ (Fagan, 1984). Fagan then set about improving the psychometric properties of his measure because of the increased demands placed upon the measurement of individual differences as compared to group averages. Another step that must be taken is to learn the statistical methods used to analyze individual differences, which focus on variance and covariance rather than means.

Fagan's interest in individual differences led him to behavioral genetics, and we have collaborated by including his measure in the longitudinal Colorado Adoption Project (Plomin & DeFries, 1985). The excitement generated by this collaboration led us to a new research project with David Fulker and Marshall Haith. Various experimental measures of infant development at 6 months of age are being employed to predict adult general cognitive ability using a midparent–midtwin design that, from a genetic viewpoint, provides an "instant" infancy-to-adulthood longitudinal study in addition to yielding estimates of quantitative genetic parameters.

Other experimental paradigms in infancy research will provide equally synergistic interactions when the fresh perspective of quantitative genetics is applied. The first step, however, is to consider individual differences in development, the "very standard deviation" (Levine, Carey, Crocker, & Gross, 1983).

QUANTITATIVE GENETIC RESEARCH IN INFANCY

Because quantitative genetics has only recently been applied to the study of infancy, the contribution of quantitative genetic theory to the study of infant development as described in the first half of this chapter largely remains a promissory note. In the 1870s, the major quantitative genetic designs for the study of human behavior—family, twin, and adoption studies—were proposed by Francis Galton, the father of behavioral genetics. After the turn of the century, these methods were applied increasingly to the study of behavioral development until the 1940s, when nearly 30 years of environmentalism brought a halt to this research. Scarr and Carter (1983) suggest that we have had to rediscover, albeit with elaborated theoretical and methodological bases, facts that were known in the 1930s "because the intervening intellectual history buried them in an avalanche of naive environmentalism" (p. 219).

Only recently have behavioral genetic studies of infancy been reported. Although not impressive in quantity, these few studies have revealed some exciting findings that should stimulate increased interest in the application of quantitative genetic theory to the study of individual differences in infant development. The goal of the second half of this chapter is to provide an overview of these research results. The section begins with mental development and then turns to the study of temperament. The third section describes a new area of research, genetic mediation of relationships between environmental measures and measures of infant development.

Two large-scale longitudinal behavioral genetic studies of infancy are discussed repeatedly in these sections. The first is the Louisville Twin Study (LTS), which was initiated more than 25 years ago. Approximately 25–35 pairs of twins have been recruited each year since 1963, resulting in a sample of about 500 pairs of twins now participating in the longitudinal research program in which the children are studied from 3 months to 15 years of age (Wilson, 1983). The twins are tested at 3, 6, 9, 12, 18, 24, 30, and 36 months and annually thereafter to 9 years of age. A final test session is administered when they are 15 years old. Until recently, the focus of the LTS was IQ and physical growth, although some data relevant to temperament were collected by means of maternal interviews concerning behavioral differences within twin pairs and the Infant Behavior Record, which is rated by the examiner following administration of the Bayley Scales of Infant Development (Bayley, 1969). Beginning in 1976, however, the focus turned to the study of temperament in infant twins using a structured laboratory assessment sequence of "vignettes" that are videotaped and rated later using a modification of the Infant Behavior Record.

The Colorado Adoption Project (CAP) is a longitudinal, prospective adoption study in which adopted children and matched nonadopted children and their home environments are assessed yearly when the children are 1–4 years of age during visits to the adoptive and nonadoptive homes (Plomin & DeFries, 1983). The biological and adoptive parents of the adopted children and the parents of the nonadopted children are tested on a 3-hr battery of diverse measures including assessments of cognitive abilities, personality, and interests and talents. Testing of biological parents began in 1975 and was completed in 1983; the foundation sample consists of 250 adoptive and 250 matched nonadoptive families. Testing of younger siblings of the adopted and nonadopted children in the same manner will eventually yield the important additional comparison of unrelated "siblings" and biological siblings.

The parent–offspring results have been analyzed for the diverse data obtained at 12 and 24 months for 182 adopted infants and 165 nonadopted infants who were tested at both ages. These results have been brought together in a book, *Origins of Individual Differences in Infancy: The Colorado Adoption Project* (Plomin & DeFries, in press), from which the data reported in this chapter are taken. Importantly, the CAP sample is quite representative of metropolitan populations in the United States. For socioeconomic status, the sample is representative of the entire United States population for variance, although its mean is about one standard deviation above the national average. Even more important, selective placement— the matching of adoptive parents to biological parents—is negligible for all traits including cognitive abilities, personality, and demographic characteristics such as socioeconomic status and education.

Mental Development

In this section, twin and adoption data on infant mental development are reviewed. Other topics to be discussed are twin and sibling analyses of age-to-age developmental trends, specific components of mental development, and an amplification model of developmental genetics that suggests some genetic continuity from infancy to adulthood for individual differences in general cognitive ability.

Twin Data on IQ

Although IQ has been the prime target for human behavioral genetic studies, the Louisville Twin Study (LTS) is the only major longitudinal twin study of infant mental development. The Bayley Scales of Infant Development (Bayley, 1969) are administered through 24 months of age, and the Stanford-Binet (Terman & Merrill, 1973) is administered at 30 and 36 months. Figure 7.1 summarizes two decades of research.

After the first 6 months, during which there is no difference between identical and fraternal twin correlations, identical twin correlations are about .10 greater than fraternal twin correlations. The average correlations from 3 to 36 months are .77 for identical twins and .67 for fraternal twins. Compared to twin results for school-age children, adolescents, and adults—for whom identical and fraternal twin correlations are about .85 and .60, respectively (Plomin & DeFries, 1980)—the .10 difference between identical and fraternal twin correlations is not large. However, taken at face value, it suggests that 20 percent of the total variance in Bayley Mental Development Index scores can be explained by genetic variance (see Plomin et al., 1980, for issues related to calculating heritability from twin studies). Explaining 20 percent of the variance of anything in infancy is a remarkable accomplishment.

Even more impressive is the fact that the magnitude of both the identical and

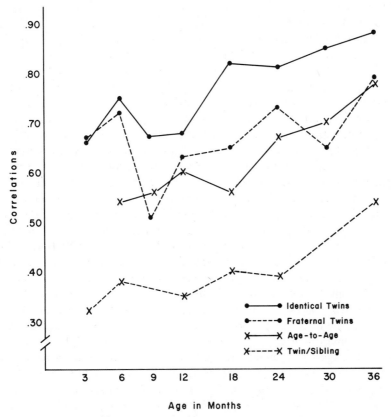

Figure 7.1. Summary of twin and sibling correlations for infant mental development from the longitudinal Louisville Twin Study. (Data from Wilson, 1983: Table 2 for approximately 80 identical and 100 fraternal twin pairs; Figure 4 for twin–sibling correlations for approximately 35 pairs—data not reported at 9 and 30 months; Table 1 for age-to-age correlations, N = 297–424.)

fraternal twin correlations tends to exceed the age-to-age correlations; in other words, twin partners resemble each other at a given age at least as much as they resemble themselves a few months later. This suggests that powerful environmental factors operate to make infant twins similar. The correlation between one twin and a younger sibling tested at the same age, also included in Figure 7.1, indicates that fraternal twins are twice as similar as nontwin siblings during the first year of life. Genetically, of course, fraternal twins are no more similar than nontwin siblings, which implies that the large difference between the correlations must be environmental in origin. One possibility is artifact in that the twins are tested on the same day, whereas the younger siblings are tested a year or so later. However, the fact that the twins are tested by different examiners in different rooms makes it less likely that artifacts of this type could explain such a large difference between the fraternal twin and twin–sibling correlations.

A more likely hypothesis is that twins have substantially more perinatal problems than do singletons and that they share these environmental factors to a much greater extent than do nontwin siblings. Some earlier analyses from the LTS suggest that perinatal factors account for a substantial amount of variance in Bayley scores in the first year of life and then diminish in importance (Wilson, 1977). For over 25,000 infants in the Collaborative Perinatal Project, the correlation between birth weight and 8-month-old Bayley scores was about .20 (Broman, Nichols, & Kenndy, 1975). In twins, however, the correlations are .50, .48, and .30, at 3 months, 6 months, and 12 months, respectively, and they continue to decline—to .14 at 24 months, and .11 at 3 years (Wilson, 1977). The magnitude and pattern of correlations are quite similar when gestational age is correlated with Bayley scores. Twin correlations with birth weight partialed out have not been presented; however, it is safe to hypothesize that the twin correlations during the first year are substantially inflated by shared environmental similarity in the form of prematurity. In fact, if the twin correlations at 3 to 6 months in Figure 7.1 were lowered by about .20, the twin data would be in line with the increasing pattern of correlations shown elsewhere in the figure.

Twin data from the Collaborative Perinatal Project (Nichols & Broman, 1974) at first appear to suggest greater heritability for Bayley scores at 8 months than does the LTS—the correlations are .84 and .55, respectively, for identical and fraternal twins. However, removing data on the 8 percent of the twins who had Bayley scores less than 57 from the analyses reduced the identical twin correlation to .55 and left the fraternal twin correlation unchanged at .55. The latter pattern of correlations of .55 for both identical and fraternal twins suggests no genetic influence and strong shared family environmental influence at 8 months. Although the LTS data reported in Figure 7.1 suggest no genetic influence at 6 months and slight genetic influence at 9 months, those data also indicate substantial shared family environmental variance. Following the Collaborative Perinatal Project report, LTS researchers removed data on retarded pairs from their twin analyses but found the twin correlations essentially unchanged by this procedure (Wilson & Matheny, 1976). Like the LTS, the Collaborative Perinatal Project found a sibling correlation much lower than the fraternal twin correlation. For 8-month Bayley scores for 4347 pairs of nontwin siblings, the sibling correlation is .22 as compared to the fraternal twin correlation of .55. Similarly, McCall (1972) reported a correlation of .24 for 142 pairs of nontwin siblings in the first year of life. As in the LTS, it is likely that the substantially greater correlations for fraternal twins than for nontwin siblings (both of whom share 50 percent of segregating genes) are due to perinatal events that inflate fraternal twin correlations, especially during the first year of life.

One other contribution of the LTS research group will be mentioned. In the 1970s, several tests of infant mental development were constructed within the framework of Piagetian concepts. Matheny (1975) identified 20 Bayley test items administered at 3, 6, 9, and 12 months that are equivalent to items used in Piagetian scales such as the Uzgiris-Hunt Ordinal Scales of Psychological Development (Uzgiris & Hunt, 1975). Scores on these 20 Piagetian-equivalent Bayley items summed across the four ages yielded correlations of .80 for 88 pairs of identical twins and .61 for 44 pairs of fraternal twins. This result is not significantly different from the twin findings for the total Bayley score, for which the identical and fraternal twin correlations are .69 and .63, respectively, averaged across 3, 6, 9, and 12 months. However, these results suggest the possibility that certain components of the Bayley scales might show more genetic influence than others, a topic to which we shall return.

Age-to-Age Patterns of Development

One of the most remarkable findings of the LTS is the high degree of familial patterning of spurts and lags in mental development. Figure 7.2 illustrates longitudinal
profiles of Bayley MDI scores for four pairs of identical twins and four pairs of
fraternal twins. Each pair of identical twins shows a different developmental trend—
up for pair A (from about 75 to about 105), down for pair D (from about 110 to
about 65), and mixed patterns for pairs B and C—but the identical twin partners
are surprisingly similar in their age-to-age changes. The four fraternal twin profiles
show consistent mean differences within pairs but the profiles are also similar, although less so than for the identical twins. *DSI* in the figure refers to a developmental synchronies index, which is a measure of the similarity of the cotwins' profiles. DSI is similar to a twin correlation for each twin pair's deviations across ages.
It is derived from variance components in a repeated-measures analysis developed
by Wilson (1979) to appraise the concordance for both elevation and patterning of
the twin scores during development.

During the first year, the trend correlations based on profiles of tests at 3, 6, 9,
and 12 months are .69 and .63 for identical and fraternal twins, respectively. Profiles
based on scores at 12, 18, 24, and 36 months yield trend correlations of .80 and .72
for the two types of twins, a difference significant at $p < .05$, suggesting that in
the second year of life genetic factors contribute significantly albeit slightly to spurts
and lags. Trend correlations using data at 3, 4, 5, and 6 years are .87 for identical
twins and .65 for fraternal twins, indicating substantial genetic influence on developmental trends after infancy.

Thus despite the remarkable age-to-age profile similarities for identical twins and
the substantial similarities for fraternal twins shown in Figure 7.2, the data for the
entire twin sample suggest at most modest genetic influence on developmental trends
across the second and third years, and no genetic influence during the first year.
However, as indicated earlier, trend correlations include twin similarity both for
overall level and for age-to-age changes—we have already seen that overall level
shows relatively little genetic influence in infancy. It would be interesting to explore
age-to-age genetic correlations, the extent to which genes affecting Bayley MDI
scores at 12 months overlap with genes affecting Bayley MDI scores at 24 months.
Age-to-age correlations are discussed in detail later. Trend correlations are complex
functions of heritabilities at each age and genetic and phenotypic correlations among
the ages.

LTS results for developmental profiles of spurts and lags were questioned because
different results were obtained when nontwin siblings were studied. McCall (McCall,
1970, 1972; McCall, Appelbaum, & Hogarty, 1973) examined developmental profiles of siblings and found a sibling intraclass correlation of .11 for profiles of Gesell
scores at 6, 12, 18, and 24 months from the Fels data. Even this slight similarity
for sibling profiles is probably due to their similarity in overall level of performance.

Reasons for the lower sibling trend correlations as compared to fraternal twin
trend correlations have been debated (McCall, 1976, 1979; Wilson, 1973, 1977).
However, the debate no longer centers around methodological issues concerning
computation of trend correlations because the LTS has now collected a small sample
of about 35 younger siblings of the twins. These trend correlations are substantially

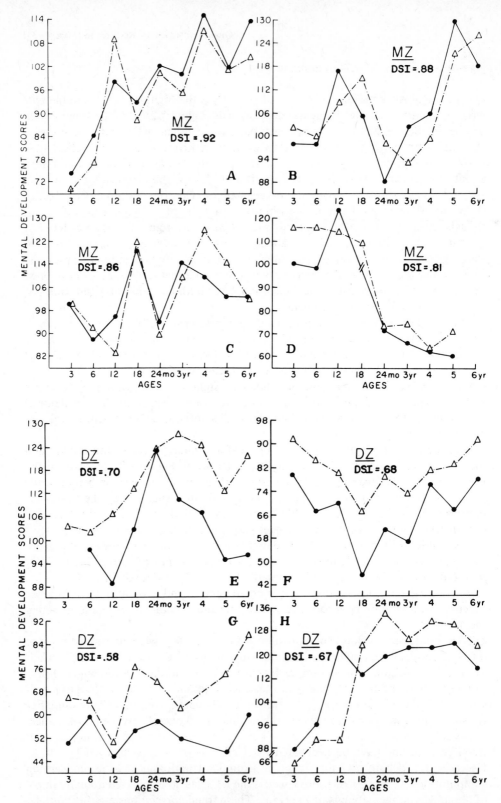

Figure 7.2. Trends in mental development during infancy and early childhood for four identical twin pairs and four fraternal twin pairs. From "Synchronies in Mental Development: An Epigenetic Perspective" by R. S. Wilson, 1978, *Science, 202,* 939–948. Copyright 1978 by the American Association for the Advancement of Science. Reprinted by permission.)

lower than those of fraternal twins, although considerably higher than those obtained by McCall. Across 3, 6, 9, and 12 months, the trend correlation for sibling–twin pairs is .37; across 12, 18, 24, and 36 months, it is .46. In contrast, the
comparable LTS fraternal twin trend correlations are .63 and .72 for the two sets
of ages. After infancy (across 3, 4, 5, and 6 years), the trend correlation for
twin–sibling comparisons (.55) is more similar to the trend correlation for fraternal
twins (.65). A similar pattern of results was seen for single-age assessments: Fraternal twin correlations in infancy are about twice as high as those for nontwin
siblings, and the differences diminish after infancy. The same environmental factors
responsible for the greater similarity of fraternal twins than nontwin siblings for
single-age assessments are likely to be responsible for the greater profile resemblance
for fraternal twins as compared to nontwin siblings. As suggested earlier, perinatal
factors are a likely candidate.

In summary, twin results from the Louisville Twin Study suggest modest genetic
influence on Bayley MDI scores during infancy and increasing genetic influence
during childhood. Developmental trends during the first year of life show no genetic
influence, although slight genetic influence is seen during the second and third years
and, again, it increases during childhood.

Adoption Data on IQ

Data from adoption studies are generally compatible with the twin results in suggesting at most slight genetic influence on general mental development in infancy.
Although over 20 adoption studies involving IQ have been reported, only one large
study has focused on infancy (Plomin & DeFries, 1985).

One of the most frequently cited articles in developmental psychology is Skodak
and Skeels's 1949 report of a longitudinal study of IQ. IQ scores of 100 adopted
children tested four times between early childhood and adolescence were compared
to the educational level and occupational status of their adoptive parents, to education and occupation of their biological parents, and to IQ scores of 63 of the
biological mothers. Although the average age of the children at the first test was 2
years and 3 months, their ages varied from 6 months to 6 years. Thus the frequently
cited correlation of .00 between biological mothers' IQ and the adoptees' scores for
their first testing on the Kuhlman revision of the Binet test could be misleading as
an index of genetic resemblance in infancy. However, from the raw data provided
by Skodak and Skeels, the mother–child correlation for 39 infants tested at 12–24
months has been found to be − .01 (Plomin & DeFries, 1985).

Less well known is an adoption study of IQ reported by Snygg (1938), who studied 227 infants 1–2 years of age. The Kuhlman test was administered to the infants
and the Stanford-Binet to the biological mothers. Unfortunately, there is no doubt
that the biological mothers were a biased sample because "girls who had passed
high school entrance examinations were seldom asked to take psychological tests"
(Snygg, p. 403); their average IQ was only 78.3 and the range was probably restricted, although no information concerning variance was reported. The correlation
between infants and their biological mothers was .08.

In a third adoption study in infancy, infants were tested on the Gesell and biological mothers on the Stanford-Binet (Casler, 1976). For 150 pairs when the infants
were 15 and 21 months, the mean parent–offspring correlation was .09. One small
study of 24 adoptees in the first year of life only included information on the bi-

ological mothers' education and occupation, and these measures did not correlate with infants' mental development scores (Beckwith, 1971).

Until the Colorado Adoption Project, not a single study had compared IQ of adoptive parents and their adopted infants, and, even more surprisingly, there had been only one small IQ study of nonadoptive parents and their infant offspring (Eichorn, 1969). Data from the Colorado Adoption Project (Plomin & DeFries, 1985) add substantially to this literature because the CAP includes a large sample of adopted and nonadopted infants tested at both 12 and 24 months and because general and specific cognitive ability data are available for all parents.

During visits to the homes of the adopted and nonadopted infants, the Ordinal Scales of Psychological Development (OSPD, Uzgiris & Hunt, 1975) are administered at 12 months of age and the Bayley Scales of Infant Development (Bayley, 1969) are administered at both 12 and 24 months. The Bayley Mental Development Index at 12 months is reported to have a split-half reliability of .82 (Bayley, 1969). In the CAP, test–retest reliability for the MDI at 12 months is .80. For the OSPD, four of the seven scales deemed most appropriate for 1-year-olds are administered. Although Uzgiris and Hunt do not advocate combining the scales, the intercorrelations of the scales are positive and data will be presented for a total score. In the CAP, test–retest reliability for the total score is .52; for the four scales, test–retest reliability is .44, .73, .38, and .16, respectively, for Visual Pursuit and the Permanence of Objects, Means of Obtaining Desired Environmental Events, Vocal Imitation, and Gestural Imitation. For the biological, adoptive, and nonadoptive parents, an unrotated first principal component score based on 16 cognitive tests is used as a measure of general cognitive ability or IQ.

The essence of the parent–offspring design of the CAP lies in comparisons of correlations for three types of parents and their offspring: nonadoptive parents and offspring, who share both heredity and family environment; adoptive parent–adoptee pairs, who share only family environment; and biological parent–adopted-away offspring, who share only heredity. This parent–offspring design is restricted in terms of finding genetic variance in infancy because it is limited to revealing genetic variance that is shared by infants and adults; nevertheless, as described later, this limitation adds to the excitement of finding genetic relationships because it implies some genetically mediated continuity between infancy and adulthood. Environmentally, the parent–offspring design is limited to the parental phenotype as a measure of the environment. As discussed later, however, the adoption design provides an opportunity to isolate specific environmental factors unconfounded by genetic bias, regardless of their relationship to the parental phenotype.

The CAP parent–offspring correlations for parental IQ and infant Bayley MDI and Uzgiris-Hunt OSPD scores (Plomin & DeFries, 1985) are listed in Table 7.2 along with familial correlations from other studies. At 24 months, the results are suggestive of both genetic and environmental influences: The "heredity" correlation (weighted biological parent–adoptees correlation) is about .10; the "environmental" correlation (adoptive parents–adoptees) is about .10; and the "heredity plus environment" correlation (control parents–control infants) is about .20. At 12 months, however, the results are less straightforward. The weighted biological parent–adoptee correlation is .17, suggesting genetic influence; the average adoptive parent–adoptee correlation is .06, suggesting slight family environmental influences; but the average control parent–offspring correlation is only .07. Similar results are seen for the OSPD at 12 months. Nonetheless, the hypothesis of genetic influence at 12 months is supported by maximum-likelihood, model-fitting analyses (Fulker & DeFries, 1983), which have considerably more power to detect relationships as weak as these. At 24 months, the pattern of correlations clearly is consistent with the hypothesis of some hereditary influence and some effect of family environment on infant mental development. Taken at face value, these results suggest that about 20 percent of the variance of MDI scores in infancy is due to genetic variance and that about 10 percent is due to family environmental factors shared by parents and their infant offspring. The majority of the variance is left unexplained.

These conclusions are compatible with the results of the other studies of infant mental development that are summarized along with the CAP results in Table 7.2. The table also compares the infancy results with IQ results from adolescence and adulthood. In general, familial correlations in infancy are about half the magnitude of familial correlations later in life: Infant sibling correlations are about .25 rather than about .50, correlations for nonadoptive parents and their infant offspring at 24 months of age are about .20 rather than about .40, correlations for biological parents and their adopted-away infant offspring are about .10 rather than about .20, and correlations for adoptive parents and their adopted infants are about .10 rather than about .20. The exceptions involve twins, for whom correlations in infancy are substantially greater than half the magnitude of correlations later in life, possibly for perinatal reasons mentioned earlier. The data converge on the conclusion that genetic influence on infant mental development, although significant, is substantially less than genetic influence on IQ later in life. Finally, as indicated by the sample sizes for the infancy data and for the adolescent and adult data shown in Table 7.2, much work remains to be done even for global measures of infant mental development. Moreover, as is not the case with research on adolescent and adult IQ, there are no infant studies of twins reared apart, siblings reared apart, half-siblings, cousins, or adoptee–adoptee pairs.

Adoption Data on Specific Components of Mental Development

The twin and adoption data reviewed up until now have focused on *g*, general cognitive ability, or IQ. One important direction for research is to explore the differentiation of specific cognitive abilities in infancy and early childhood. For the adults in the CAP, tests are administered that tap four specific cognitive abilities: verbal, spatial, perceptual speed, and memory. The issue of differentiation of cognitive abilities in infancy has been approached in the CAP at the level of the Bayley total score, Bayley factor scores, and Bayley items as they relate to parental general cognitive ability and specific cognitive abilities (Plomin & DeFries, 1985).

The first level of analysis investigates the relationship of the Bayley total score to parental general and specific cognitive abilities. Even though parental factor scores for specific cognitive abilities are as reliable as IQ, infant Bayley scores correlate only with parental IQ, not with parental specific cognitive abilities. This suggests that infant mental development as measured by the Bayley primarily relates to adult *g* rather than to any specific abilities.

Two types of analyses have been conducted at the factor level, and both point to a similar conclusion: Infant mental development as it predicts adult cognitive abilities is general in nature—that is, not differentiated into specific abilities. The first type involves verbal and nonverbal Bayley items. In a bivariate path analysis

TABLE 7.2. Familial Correlations for Infant General Mental Development

Familial Relationship[a]	Reference	N/Pairs	Age	Infant Test	Correlation
Identical twins reared together (.86 for 4672 pairs)	Nichols and Broman (1974)	110	8 months	Bayley	.55
	Wilson (1983)	80	first year[b]	Bayley	.69
		80	second year[c]	Bayley	.77
Fraternal twins reared together (.60 for 5546 pairs)	Nichols and Broman (1974)	205	8 months	Bayley	.55
	Wilson (1983)	100	first year[b]	Bayley	.63
		100	second year[c]	Bayley	.67
Siblings reared together (.47 for 26,473 pairs)	Nichols and Broman (1974)	4347	8 months	Bayley	.22
	McCall (1972)	142	first year[d]	Gesell	.24
			first and second year[e]	Gesell	.40
	Wilson (1983)	35	first year[b]	Bayley	.35
		35	second year[c]	Bayley	.40
Nonadoptive parents–offspring (.42 for 8433 pairs)	Plomin and DeFries (1985)	157 mothers	12 months	Bayley	.04
		157 fathers	12 months	Bayley	.09
		122 mothers	12 months	Uzgiris-Hunt	.00
		123 fathers	12 months	Uzgiris-Hunt	.09
		157 mothers	24 months	Bayley	.22
		157 fathers	24 months	Bayley	.21
	Eichorn (1969)	not reported	first year[d]	California Preschool[f]	−.14 (−.01)[g]
			second year[h]	California Preschool[f]	.16 (.04)[g]

Biological parents–adoptees (.22 for 814 pairs)	Casler (1976)	141–151 mothers	9 and 15 months[i]	Gesell language and adaptive[j]	.08
			21 and 27 months[k]	Gesell language and adaptive[j]	.11
	Plomin and DeFries (1985)	176 mothers	12 months	Bayley	.12
		41 fathers	12 months	Bayley	.29
		144 mothers	12 months	Uzgiris-Hunt	.16
		36 fathers	12 months	Uzgiris-Hunt	.23
		176 mothers	24 months	Bayley	.06
		41 fathers	24 months	Bayley	.38
	Snygg (1938)	227 mothers	12–24 months	Kuhlman-Binet	.08
	Skodak and Skeels (1949)	39 mothers	12–23 months	Kuhlman-Binet	−.01
Adoptive parents–adoptees (.19 for 1397 pairs)	Plomin and DeFries (1985)	177 mothers	12 months	Bayley	.12
		169 fathers	12 months	Bayley	.00
		143 mothers	12 months	Uzgiris-Hunt	−.04
		138 fathers	12 months	Uzgiris-Hunt	.01
		177 mothers	24 months	Bayley	.10
		169 fathers	24 months	Bayley	.08

[a]In parentheses following each familial relationship is the weighted average correlation primarily for adolescent and adult data from a survey of IQ (Bouchard & McGue, 1981).

[b]Averaged over 3, 6, and 9 months.

[c]Averaged over 12, 18, and 24 months.

[d]Averaged over 6 and 12 months.

[e]Averaged over 6, 12, 18, and 24 months.

[f]Precursor of the Bayley test.

[g]The first correlation is for the parents tested at the same age as the infant in the Berkeley Growth Study; the correlation in parentheses refers to parents' scores at age 17.

[h]Averaged over 18 and 24 months.

[i]Averaged over 9 and 15 months.

[j]Average of correlations for two Gesell subtests.

[k]Averaged over 21 and 27 months.

that compared infant verbal and nonverbal scores to parental verbal and nonverbal scores, parent–offspring correlations for verbal and nonverbal scores suggest a pattern of results similar to those found for the Bayley MDI total score (Baker, 1983). Moreover, cross-correlations (parental verbal vs. infant nonverbal; parental nonverbal vs. infant verbal) are about the same as the isomorphic correlations (parental verbal vs. infant verbal; parental nonverbal vs. infant nonverbal) for all three sets of parents. This suggests that infant verbal and nonverbal abilities are not differentiated genetically or environmentally.

The second type of analysis using Bayley factors involved spatial, verbal, and memory/imitation scales derived from Bayley items according to factor analyses reported by Lewis (1983). The relationship of these factors to parental general and specific cognitive abilities has been investigated (Thompson, Plomin, & DeFries, 1985). Parent–offspring correlations between 12-month Bayley factors and parental cognitive abilities suggest only minimal relationships for both parental g and specific abilities. At 24 months, more parent–offspring resemblance is found; however, Bayley factors that appear to be related to parental cognition are related to parental g, not to specific cognitive abilities.

Finally, item analyses support the emerging conclusion that the nature of infant mental development as it relates to adult cognition is global rather than differentiated. Because of dependencies among the Bayley items, 16 items and 6 scales at 12 months and 4 items and 12 scales at 24 months that avoid item interdependencies were chosen for comparison with parental cognitive abilities in nonadoptive families. Replication of significant nonadoptive family correlations in correlations between biological mothers and their adopted-away offspring suggests genetic links between infancy and adulthood and attenuates the possibility of capitalizing on chance in such analyses. As in the other analyses, insofar as infant items predict adult cognition, they predict IQ, not specific cognitive abilities (Plomin & DeFries, (1985). Interestingly, Bayley items/scales yield three significant correlations with nonadoptive midparent scores at 12 months, and all three of these significant correlations are replicated in correlations between biological mothers and their adopted-away infants. This finding suggests genetic mediation between scores on these Bayley measures and adult IQ. The three Bayley measures are the Tower of Cubes scale, the Pinkboard scale, and an item (115) that involves closing the lid on a round container. These items hint of spatial processes, and it is noteworthy that they do not include language items.

In summary, the same picture emerges no matter how we analyze Bayley scores: Infant mental development as it predicts adult cognitive abilities predicts adult general cognitive ability, not specific cognitive abilities. This suggests that infant mental development is itself general and undifferentiated. It is possible, of course, that the items on the Bayley test lack sufficient diversity to assess adequately the structure of specific cognitive abilities in infancy. We can examine this possibility because, fortunately, the CAP data set includes other measures of two domains of infant mental development: language/communication and attention to novel stimuli.

At 24 months, the Expressive and Receptive scales of the Sequenced Inventory of Communication Development (SICD, Hedrick, Prather, & Tobin, 1975) are administered to provide standardized measures of language production and comprehension. Furthermore, for a subsample of the CAP infants, videotaped communication measures at 12 months of age have been analyzed (Hardy-Brown, 1982; Hardy-Brown, Plomin, & DeFries, 1981). The fact that the SICD correlates .60 with the Lewis verbal scale of Bayley items and .66 with the total Bayley MDI score suggests that the SICD parent–offspring results will be similar to those reported above for the Bayley MDI. That is the case: Parent–offspring correlations are approximately .10, .10, and .20, for the "heredity," "environment," and "heredity-plus-environment" comparisons, respectively (Plomin & DeFries, 1985). However, partialing out the Bayley MDI score indicated that the SICD does not contribute to parent–offspring correlations independently of the Bayley MDI. This fits with the hypothesis that infant mental development as it relates to adult cognitive abilities is general in nature.

Videotaped data on infant communicative responses are in accord with this pattern of results. Numbers of vocalizations, the use of request prosody, syllable structure, and communicative gestures were analyzed for a subsample of 50 adopted and 50 nonadopted CAP 12-month-olds. An unrotated first principal component called "communicative competence" included maternal reports of a word diary and vocal imitation and the scale of Bayley language items, as well as videotaped observations of the use of phonetically consistent forms, vocalization context, vocal signals, true words, use of request prosody, and syllable structure (Hardy-Brown, 1980). When 12-month communicative competence scores were related to parental cognitive abilities, they were correlated only with parental IQ, not with parental specific cognitive abilities (Hardy-Brown, 1982; Hardy-Brown et al., 1981). These parent–offspring results strongly suggest genetic influence in that nonadoptive parent and biological parent IQ scores were found to correlate significantly and substantially with infant communicative competence.

Thus the results of this intensive analysis suggest quite substantial genetic continuity between infant communicative performance and adult IQ. In the sense that infant communicative performance predicts adult IQ, not adult specific cognitive abilities such as verbal ability, these results confirm those described above. However, analyses of the Bayley language items and factors did not suggest that language processes in infancy are the primary precursors of adult IQ. Although genetic influence was suggested for the SICD, the fact that parent–offspring resemblances disappeared when Bayley MDI scores were partialed out suggests that the SICD shows parent–offspring resemblance only by virtue of its correlation with the Bayley MDI. However, when we partialed the Bayley MDI scores from the parent–offspring correlations involving the communicative competence factor, parent–offspring correlations were lowered only slightly—a finding that suggests that communicative competence may involve genetic precursors of adult IQ at 12 months of age that are independent of the processes assessed by the Bayley items (Plomin & DeFries, 1985).

Finally, Fagan's (1982, 1984; Fagan & Singer, 1983) measure of attention to novel stimuli has been administered to CAP infants at 5 and 7 months of age. Twelve follow-up studies assessing attention to novel stimuli had yielded a mean correlation of .44 between scores on this measure at 3–7 months and IQ scores at 2–7 years of age (Fagan, 1984). Because no other measure has been shown to predict school-age IQ from the first year of life, Fagan's measure appeared to be a good candidate for a parent–offspring analysis. Preliminary analyses of data on nonadoptive families indicate some relationship with parental IQ; as we have seen repeatedly, the measure correlates only with parental IQ, not with parental specific cognitive abilities (Thompson & Fagan, 1983).

In summary, the CAP data, which, from a genetic perspective, provide an "instant'' infancy-to-adulthood longitudinal study, lead to the conclusion that the prediction of adult cognitive ability from measures of infant mental development involves g. That is, any measure in infancy that predicts adult cognitive abilities only predicts adult g or IQ, never specific abilities. For example, communicative competence at 12 months relates strongly and genetically to adult IQ, but is not at all related to adult verbal ability. These data suggest that infant mental development is best viewed as undifferentiated. I would expect to find evidence for greater differentiation following the transition from infancy to early childhood. One implication of these findings is that the long-term predictiveness of infant mental tests would be very likely to be improved by focusing on g.

The Amplification Model of Developmental Genetics

One of the major questions for the study of individual differences in infant mental development is why the long-term predictiveness of mental test scores increases steadily during the transition from infancy to childhood. I used to think that the answer would lie in genetic reorganization, so that the genes affecting individual differences in mental test scores in infancy are not related to those that affect individual differences in childhood. That is, I thought that an increase in the genetic correlations between measures at successive ages might be the reason why childhood scores are more predictive of adult IQ than are scores in infancy. However, analyses of the CAP data suggest a dramatically different story.

As mentioned earlier, the use of age-to-age genetic correlations is an exciting advance in our methods for exploring the role of heredity in producing change as well as continuity in development. Change in heritability during development is a form of genetic change—it is essentially a cross-sectional concept, which means that the relative magnitude of genetic and environmental variance changes. For example, data reviewed earlier indicate that the heritability of mental test scores increases dramatically from infancy to childhood. Age-to-age longitudinal genetic correlations are independent of heritability—they indicate the extent to which the genes that affect a trait at one age also affect the trait at another age. This is depicted in Figure 7.3. The genetic correlation, r_G, is the correlation between genetic deviations that affect the trait at Time 1 (G_1) and the genetic deviations that affect the trait at Time 2 (G_2). If there is no genetic change from Time 1 to Time 2, the genetic correlation will be 1.0. A genetic correlation of zero means that genetic effects at Time 1 are unrelated to genetic effects at Time 2.

In Figure 7.3, it can be seen that developmental stability, the phenotypic correlation between Time 1 and Time 2, can be mediated genetically or environmentally. Genetic mediation involves the genetic correlation weighted by the square roots of the heritabilities at the two ages, $h_1 h_2 r_G$. (Paths are standardized partial regressions; thus path h is σ_G/σ_P—the proportion of the phenotypic standard deviation due to the standard deviation of genetic effects on the trait—which is the square root of heritability, V_G/V_P.) Thus the genetic correlation between two ages could be 1.0 even though heritability is low. In other words, even if genetic deviations at Time 1 were perfectly correlated with genetic deviations at Time 2, genetic effects at either age might make only a small contribution to phenotypic variance. Similarly, environmental mediation of phenotypic stability is $e_1 e_2 r_E$. If phenotypic stability is zero between the two ages, both the genetic and the environmental chain of paths must

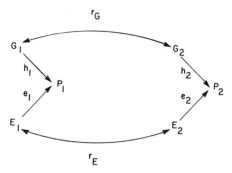

Figure 7.3. Genetic and environmental mediation of phenotypic stability from Time 1 to Time 2.

be zero, except in the unlikely event that a positive genetic correlation is offset by a negative environmental correlation.

Thus the genetic correlation (r_G) answers some questions, and the genetic chain of paths ($h_1 h_2 r_G$) answers others. The genetic chain of paths assesses the genetic contribution to phenotypic stability in development because it standardizes the genetic covariance from age to age in terms of its contribution to phenotypic variance by weighting the genetic correlation by the heritabilities at the two ages. Genetic correlation indicates the extent to which genetic effects overlap at two ages, regardless of their relative contributions to phenotypic variance.

Any quantitative genetic design that can estimate genetic and environmental components of the variance of a single trait can also be used to estimate genetic and environmental components of the covariance of a trait from age to age, assuming that longitudinal data are obtained (see Plomin & DeFries, 1979, for details). For parents and their infant offspring, the *effective* genetic similarity cannot be assumed to be .50 if genetic change occurs from infancy to adulthood. Their effective genetic similarity depends upon the genetic correlation between the ages.

Consider, for example, the similarity between biological parents and their adopted-away infants. As depicted in the path diagram in Figure 7.4, expected similarity between biological parents and their adopted-away infants must take into account the genetic correlation between infancy and adulthood and also recognize the possibility that heritability differs at the two ages. Although this path model looks complicated, it reduces to the usual model of parent–offspring resemblance if the heritabilities for parents and offspring are the same and the genetic correlation is 1.0. This is the case on the left side of the path model, which depicts expected parent–offspring similarity if the parent were an infant of the same age as the adopted-away offspring. Of course, the biological parent is not an infant and, for this reason, the right side of the path diagram indicates that genetic resemblance from infancy to adulthood is a function of the genetic correlation and the heritabilities in infancy and adulthood. From the path model, it can be seen that the expectation for the correlation between biological parents and their adopted-away infants is $\frac{1}{2} h_I h_A r_{GIA}$. If heritabilities are the same in infancy and adulthood and if the genetic correlation between infancy and adulthood is 1.0, this reduces to $\frac{1}{2} h^2$.

Because of these expectations, the parent–offspring design of the CAP is quite limited in terms of detecting genetic influence in infancy. Significant resemblance

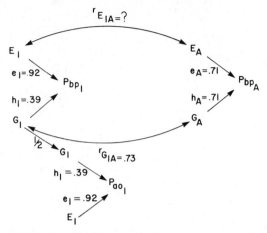

Figure 7.4. Path diagram depicting parent–offspring similarity for mental ability for biological parents (bp) and their adopted-away offspring (ao), taking into account possible genetic change from infancy (I) to adulthood (A) and differing heritabilities in infancy and adulthood. (Adapted from Plomin and DeFries, 1985.)

between biological parents and their adopted-away infants has three prerequisites: The infant measure must be substantially heritable; the adult measure must be substantially heritable; and substantial genetic continuity must exist between infancy and adulthood. That is another way of saying that parent–offspring resemblance depends upon $\frac{1}{2}h_I h_A r_{G_{IA}}$. However, when significant parent–offspring resemblance is observed, these limitations metamorphose into an advantage because they enable us to conclude that both infant and adult measures are substantially heritable and that substantial genetic continuity exists between infancy and adulthood.

In combination with data from twin studies, it is possible to use the CAP data to estimate genetic correlations from infancy to adulthood. Twin data are needed to estimate heritability in infancy (h_I^2) and in adulthood (h_A^2) although the CAP will eventually have enough pairs of adoptive and nonadoptive siblings tested at the same age to provide estimates of h_I^2. At the extreme, if h_I^2 and h_A^2 are significant and the correlation between biological parents and their adopted-away infants is zero, the genetic correlation must equal zero. This would imply that the genes that affect infant variability are completely uncorrelated with those that affect adult variability. At the other extreme, if the parent–offspring correlation for biological parents and their adopted-away infants equals $\frac{1}{2}h_I h_A$ for given heritabilities in infancy and adulthood, the genetic correlation must equal 1.0 because the parent–offspring correlation is $\frac{1}{2}h_I h_A r_{G_{IA}}$. This would mean that the genes that affect individual differences in the trait in infancy correlate perfectly with those that affect individual differences in the trait in adulthood.

Analyses of this type in the CAP have led to some exciting results and to a surprising model of developmental genetics called the amplification model. The CAP infancy results suggest a correlation of about .10 between biological parents' IQ and their adopted-away infants' Bayley MDI scores. At the simplest level, resemblance between biological parents (who are, of course, adults) and their adopted-away infants implies some genetic continuity from infancy to adulthood. Use of the expectation, $\frac{1}{2}h_I h_A r_{GIA}$, permits us to be more precise. We know from the largest data set in the behavioral sciences that the heritability of adult IQ is approximately .50 (Plomin & DeFries, 1980). The LTS suggests a heritability of about .15 for Bayley MDI scores. These estimates suggest that the genetic correlation between Bayley scores in infancy and adult IQ is very high:

$$.10 = \frac{1}{2}h_I h_A r_{GIA}$$

For mental development, it appears that the little genetic variance that exists in infancy covaries substantially with genetic variance in adulthood. The estimate of genetic correlation from infancy to adulthood for IQ is so great that it poses a problem: How can the genetic correlation be so close to 1.0 when genetic variance increases so substantially from infancy to adulthood? This question is what led DeFries (1983) to pose the amplification model of developmental genetics: Genes that affect IQ make only a small contribution to phenotypic variance in infancy, but their effects are amplified through development. Suppose, for example, that genetic differences among infants are responsible for differences among the infants in the formation of dendritic spines during the first few years of life and that complexity of dendritic spines relates to information-processing capabilities. In infancy, these structural differences result in only slight functional differences among infants because so little information has been processed. Gradually, the functional differences are amplified as more and more information is processed by children. The differences snowball as development proceeds, so that a study of these individuals as children will show more genetic variance than was evident in infancy. However, the genetic correlation between the two ages is near unity because the genetic portion of observed variability at both ages originates with the same set of genes whose effects become amplified during development. In other words, even though genetic variance is relatively less important in infancy than in childhood, the little genetic variance that does exist in infancy is substantially related to the genetic variance that affects the trait in adulthood.

It should be noted that the amplification model predicts not high phenotypic correlations from age to age, just high genetic age-to-age correlations. The model does predict that *some* phenotypic stability exists from Bayley scores in infancy to adult IQ scores within individuals. This might seem to contradict the developmental zeitgeist that there is no predictability from infancy to adulthood for IQ. However, closer examination of the extant longitudinal data leaves this question open. A review in the previous edition of this handbook reported a median correlation of .32 for three studies that compared test scores of infants 13–18 months old to their IQ scores at 8–18 years of age (McCall, 1979). The amplification model predicts that phenotypic correlations of Bayley scores in infancy with adult IQ scores should be about .20 for genetic reasons, and environmental mediation of stability could increase the correlation.

It should also be mentioned that the amplification model does not require that the processes underlying the infant and adult measures be isomorphic. For example, genetic continuity from Bayley MDI scores to adult IQ might be due to entirely different processes in infancy and adulthood. "Infancy genes" might affect rate of language acquisition, whereas "adult genes" might affect symbolic reasoning.

Finally, CAP analyses suggest that the amplification model is not limited to mental development; it applies to height, weight, and temperament as well (Plomin & DeFries, 1985). In summary, the amplification model suggests that, as genes come to affect a trait in infancy, they increasingly affect the variance of the trait as their effects are amplified during development. Although genetic continuity is emphasized in the amplification model, the need for the model arises because of observed genetic change in heritabilities. The possibility that genetic effects become amplified as development proceeds seems the only way to explain high age-to-age genetic correlations coupled with developmental increases in heritability.

Temperament

Although everyone knows what personality is, no adequate definition exists. Dictionary definitions refer to the sum total of the characteristics of an individual. In the east, the term is used in this global way (Mangan, 1982). In the west, however, *personality* refers to individual differences in characteristics other than traits such as mental, sensory, and motoric abilities. This still leaves an incredible amount of behavior to study, and dozens of personality traits have been proposed, each of which could turn out to be as complex as intelligence.

While the study of adult personality was suffering from a decade of self-doubt that followed the publication of Mischel's book, *Personality and Assessment,* in 1968, research on personality in children flourished. It has been suggested that the impetus for the rising interest in temperament stems in part from the merging of several contemporary themes in the study of development:

> (1) increasing interest in the description and explanation of individual differences in development, rather than preoccupation with average or normative development; (2) dissatisfaction with the narrow focus of earlier decades on cognitive development; (3) emergence of a view of the child as an active, transacting partner with the environment, reinforcing environmental agents and modifying the impact of the environment; and (4) a shift from exclusive reliance on environmental explanations of behavioral development to a more balanced perspective that recognizes the possibility of biological influences.
>
> *(Plomin, 1983, p. 45)*

The complexity of personality in infancy and early childhood was winnowed by focusing on constitutionally based traits called temperament. Because temperament is the focus of a chapter by Bates in this handbook—see also Plomin and Dunn, 1986—the present discussion will be limited to behavioral genetic data on temperament and especially to one theory of temperament that uses behavioral genetics as its foundation. The temperament theory of Buss and Plomin (1975, 1984) defines temperament as genetically influenced, early-appearing personality traits and suggests that three broad traits meet these criteria: emotionality, activity, and sociability (EAS). Sociability is the key component of extraversion in infancy when the impulsivity facet of adult extraversion is not important; similarly, emotionality is the stripped-down version of adult neuroticism with its anxiety component removed. For adult personality, extraversion and neuroticism are two "superfactors" and appear to be the two most heritable dimensions of personality (Loehlin, 1982). Activity, although obviously an important dimension, is simply not measured in many personality questionnaires for adults, although it is nearly always included in rating instruments for children, perhaps because of the conspicuousness of this dimension in infancy and childhood.

Buss and Plomin (1984) suggest that the EAS temperaments show the best evidence for genetic influence, at least after infancy. In this section, behavioral genetic studies of the EAS traits in infancy will be reviewed.

Emotionality

In Buss and Plomin's theory of temperament, *emotionality* refers to distress, the tendency to become upset easily and intensely, which is assumed to differentiate into fear and anger during the first year of life. Similar dimensions are paramount in nearly every other approach to temperament—for example, Intensity of Reaction, Threshold of Responsiveness, and Quality of Mood in the New York Longitudinal Study approach of Thomas and Chess (1977); the temperament-as-affect approach of Goldsmith and Campos (1982a, 1982b); the reactivity and self-regulation approach of Rothbart and Derryberry (1981); and the work of Kagan and his colleagues on behavioral inhibition (Garcia-Coll et al., 1984; Kagan, 1982).

Four twin studies related to emotionality are summarized in Table 7.3. The studies employed diverse types of measures including parental interviews (Matheny, Wilson, Dolan, & Krantz, 1981), parental questionnaire ratings (Goldsmith & Campos, 1982), tester ratings on Bayley's (1969) Infant Behavior Record (Matheny, Dolan, & Wilson, 1976), and observational ratings in a playroom setting (Matheny & Dolan, 1975). The twin data consistently support the hypothesis that individual differences in emotionality in infancy are strongly affected by genetic factors.

Because parental ratings dominate research in this area, studies using observational ratings of infants in structured settings are particularly noteworthy (Plomin, 1983b). The most widely used instrument is Bayley's Infant Behavior Record (IBR), which is used by testers to rate an infant's behavior during administration of the Bayley mental and motor scales. It offers the important advantages of assessing infants' reactions to a standard, mildly stressful situation and of providing comparable data across studies. The LTS data suggest increasing heritability during infancy for the IBR fearfulness item (Matheny et al., 1976). IBR-like ratings of emotionality in a playroom setting following mother's departure also show significant heritability during infancy (Matheny & Dolan, 1975).

The study by Goldsmith and Campos (1982) includes a laboratory-based assessment of emotionality. Preliminary results suggest genetic influence on the high-arousal emotion of fear in such situations as approach of strangers and the visual cliff at 9 months. Interestingly, less arousing emotional expressiveness of a positive nature such as smiling and laughing show no genetic influence (Goldsmith, 1983b). A similar lack of genetic influence on individual differences in smiling and laughing was found when parental reports were employed in twin analyses (Goldsmith & Campos, 1982). An early report from the LTS also indicated no evidence for genetic influence on smiling during infancy and early childhood (Wilson, Brown, & Matheny, 1971).

A novel application of the repeated-measures analysis of variance to assess age-to-age twin profiles was reported by Matheny and Dolan (1975) for LTS data. The method was used to investigate genetic influence on changes in emotionality from the test situation to the playroom setting. Emotionality scores in the two situations

TABLE 7.3. Behavioral Genetic Studies of Emotionality in Infancy[a]

Reference	Sample (age; number)[b]	Measure	Results[c]			
			6 months	24 months	36 months	
A. Twin studies						
Matheny et al. (1981)	6, 24, and 36 months; 68–78 MZ; 38–48 DZ	Parental interviews concerning twin differences in:	—	37 vs. 13	30 vs. 14	
		hurt feelings	39 vs. 26	41 vs. 15	40 vs. 34	
		temper: frequency	45 vs. 29	46 vs. 28	45 vs. 21	
		irritability	62 vs. 51	59 vs. 39	50 vs. 21	
		crying				
Matheny et al. (1976)	3–12 months; 18–30 months; 47–55 MZ; 27 DZ	Tester ratings on IBR fearfulness item	first year: .74 vs. .54			
			second year: .65 vs. .22			
Matheny and Dolan (1975)	9–30 months; 25–57 MZ; 19–34 DZ	Ratings of emotionality in playroom settings after mother's departure	.66 vs. .30			
Goldsmith and Campos (1982)	9 months; 29 MZ; 61 DZ	Parental ratings of:	.66 vs. .46			
		fear	.77 vs. .35			
		distress to limitations	.71 vs. .69			
		soothability				

B. Parent–offspring adoption study

Colorado Adoption Project (Plomin & DeFries, 1985)	12 and 24 months; 182 adoptive and 164 nonadoptive families	Midparent ratings on CCTI emotionality scale for infants; parents' EAS emotionality-fear and 16 PF second-order factor of neuroticism:	12 months	24 months
		Nonadoptive mothers		
		EAS emotionality	−.02	.01
		16 PF neuroticism	.25[a]	.10
		Nonadoptive fathers		
		EAS emotionality	.17[a]	.21[a]
		16 PF neuroticism	.07	.14
		Biological mothers		
		EAS emotionality	.00	.04
		16 PF neuroticism	.07	.20[a]
		Adoptive mothers		
		EAS emotionality	.16[a]	.15[a]
		16 PF neuroticism	.16[a]	.07
		Adoptive fathers		
		EAS emotionality	.14[a]	.00
		16 PF neuroticism	.09	.03

[a]Adapted from Buss and Plomin (1984).

[b]MZ refers to monozygotic (identical) twins and DZ refers to dizygotic (fraternal) twins; the number denotes pairs.

[c]In Part A, results are presented as twin concordances (Matheny et al., 1981) or as twin correlations (all other studies); parent–offspring correlations are reported in Part B.

[a]$p < .05$.

correlated from .26 to .42 at 9–30 months of age, and the analyses of score profiles across the two situations strongly suggested that genetic influences are important determinants of situational change in emotionality: The average identical twin profile correlation was .67, and the average fraternal twin correlation was .33.

In general, more behavioral genetic data exist for twins than for nontwin family members such as siblings and parents and offspring. Table 7.3 presents some of the results from the parent–offspring design of the CAP. As discussed earlier, the parent–offspring design is limited in terms of finding genetic influence in infancy because it requires genetic continuity from infancy to adulthood. Nonetheless, the data provide a hint of possible genetic influence in that a significant correlation emerges between biological mothers' 16 PF neuroticism and the midparent rating of their adopted-away infants' emotionality.

Activity

Activity is construed in terms of both tempo and vigor (Buss & Plomin, 1984). Measures of activity have been included in six twin studies, one family study, and one adoption study in infancy, as summarized in Table 7.4. The two twin studies that employed parental ratings yielded similar correlations: .75 versus .57 for 9-month-olds (Goldsmith & Campos, 1982) and .78 versus .54 for children 1–5 years of age (Cohen, Dibble, & Grawe, 1977). An LTS analysis based on parental interviews concerning differences within pairs of infant twins showed large differences in concordances for activity for identical and fraternal twins (Matheny et al., 1981).

More twin studies of activity in infancy have used tester ratings than parental ratings. The LTS IBR factors mentioned earlier include activity. During the first 2 years of life, the IBR activity factor yielded average correlations of .40 for identical twins and .17 for fraternal twins (Matheny, 1980). Twin correlations for the IBR items were reported by Matheny et al. (1976), and the results for the Activity and Energy items are included in the table. These items in both the first and second year yield identical twin correlations that are substantially greater than the fraternal twin correlations, although the fraternal twin correlations are too low to fit a simple genetic model. Another twin study using a tester rating instrument similar to the IBR has been reported by Goldsmith and Gottesman (1981), who analyzed twin data on 8-month-old infants in the national Collaborative Perinatal Project. The ratings for activity yielded twin correlations quite similar to those reported for the IBR activity factor in the LTS. Matheny (1983) analyzed trend correlations for twins during infancy for the IBR activity factor. For 66 identical and 40 fraternal twin pairs at 12, 18, and 24 months of age, the trend correlations were significantly higher for identical twins (.52) than for fraternal twins (.18).

One family study of activity (Caldwell & Herscher, 1964) yielded a correlation of .40 between mothers' ratings of their infants' energy level and the mothers' retrospective reports of their energy levels as children. Results from the CAP parent–offspring design suggest at most slight genetic continuity from infancy to adulthood: Parent–offspring correlations in nonadoptive families average .10, and the average biological mother–adopted-away infant correlation is only .06.

In summary, although evidence for genetic continuity from infancy to adulthood is lacking for activity, the twin data without exception point to substantial genetic influence on individual differences among infants in their activity level as assessed by parental report or tester ratings.

TABLE 7.4. Behavioral Genetic Studies of Activity in Infancy[a]

Reference	Sample (age; number)[b]	Measure	Results[c]	
		A. Twin studies		
Matheny (1980)	6, 12, 18, 24, months; 72–91 MZ; 35–50 DZ	Tester ratings on IBR Activity factor	6 months: 12 months: 18 months: 24 months:	.55 vs. .10 .43 vs. .07 .49 vs. .37 .53 vs. .03
Matheny et al. (1976)	3–12 months; 18–30 months; 47–55 MZ; 27 DZ	Tester ratings on IBR Activity item Tester ratings on IBR Energy item	first year: second year: first year: second year:	.34 vs. −.06 .52 vs. .08 .44 vs. .26 .81 vs. .22
Matheny et al. (1981)	6, 24, and 36 months; 68–78 MZ; 38–48 DZ	Parental interview concerning twin differences in activity	6 months: 24 months: 36 months:	32 vs. 13 45 vs. 19 47 vs. 28
Cohen et al. (1977)	1–5 years; 181 MZ; 84 DZ	Childhood Personality Scale (Dibble & Cohen, 1974) maternal ratings of "zestfulness" (energy level)		.78 vs. .54
Goldsmith and Gottesman (1981) Goldsmith and Campos (1982)	8 months; 115 MZ; 209 DZ 9 months; 29 MZ; 61 DZ	Tester ratings of activity Parental ratings of activity		.57 vs. .35 .75 vs. .57
		B. Family study		
Caldwell and Herscher (1964)	1 year; 30 families	Mothers' ratings of energy of infant and self-report of mothers' energy as children		.40
		C. Parent/Offspring Adoption Study		
			12 months	*24 months*
Colorado Adoption Project (Plomin & DeFries, 1985)	12 and 24 months; 182 adoptive and 164 nonadoptive families	Midparent ratings on CCTI activity scale for infants; parents' EAS activity: Nonadoptive mothers Nonadoptive fathers Biological mothers Adoptive mothers Adoptive fathers	 .02 .21[d] .06 −.10 .01	 −.03 .19[d] .05 .02 .01

[a]Adapted from Buss and Plomin (1984).

[b]MZ refers to monozygotic (identical) twins and DZ refers to dizygotic (fraternal) twins; the number denotes pairs.

[c]In Part A, results are presented as twin concordances (Matheny et al., 1981) or as twin correlations (all other studies); parent–offspring correlations are reported in Parts B and C.

[d]p < .05.

Sociability and Shyness

Studies of temperament in infancy have tended to assess shyness (social responding to strangers) rather than sociability (gregariousness), which is more often assessed later in life (Plomin & Daniels, 1986). The results of seven twin studies and one adoption study of sociability and shyness in infancy are presented in Table 7.5.

Two of the twin studies provide evidence for genetic influence based on parental interviews (Matheny et al., 1981, which is an update of an earlier report by Wilson et al., 1971; Torgersen, 1982). Three twin reports involve tester ratings, indicating the trend in temperament research in infancy toward the use of observational ratings of children in structured settings (Plomin, 1983b). LTS analyses of the IBR yielded a Test Affect/Extraversion factor that has been shown to correlate significantly with parental ratings of sociability and shyness (Buss & Plomin, 1984), even though the factor also includes items related to cooperativeness, endurance, and happiness (Matheny, 1980). The LTS results for this factor at 6, 12, 18, and 24 months are shown in Table 7.5. The average twin correlations during the first 2 years of life are .50 for identical twins and .14 for fraternal twins, with no discernible developmental change in the correlations. In an earlier LTS analysis (Matheny et al., 1976), scores on the IBR item, Responsiveness to Persons, were averaged separately for assessments during the first year of life and for second-year assessments. For the first year, the identical twin correlation was significantly greater than the fraternal twin correlation (.63 vs. .34); however, in the second year, no difference was found between the identical and fraternal twin correlations. Moreover, another twin study of 8-month-olds found little evidence of genetic influence on a tester rating of responsiveness to persons (Goldsmith & Gottesman, 1981). A possible reason for this discrepancy is that the IBR item, Responsiveness to Persons, involves rating shyness of infants who have already had time to become familiar with the tester prior to the administration of the Bayley tests.

As described earlier, Matheny (1983) applied the repeated-measures analysis of variance to assess trend correlations during infancy. For 66 identical and 40 fraternal twin pairs at 12, 18, and 24 months of age, the trend correlations for the IBR Test Affect-Extraversion factor are .37 for identical twins and .21 for fraternal twins, suggesting significant genetic involvement in age-to-age stability and instability.

An ethological study of specific behaviors assessed in the homes of infant twins was conducted by Plomin and Rowe (1979). Members of 21 identical twin pairs and 25 same-sex fraternal twin pairs with an average age of 22 months were observed in their homes using time-sampled observations of specific behaviors in seven situations. Each twin partner was rated by a different observer who took an unobtrusive position in the home, kept a neutral facial expression, and did not return overtures for attention from the children. An important feature of the study was that social responding to the stranger and to the mother was recorded in alternating 15-sec intervals. The first situation, warm-up, included measures of the infants' social responding to the mother and to the stranger while they were engaged in discussing the project and attempting to avoid interaction with the children. The measures included infants' approaches, proximity, touches, positive vocalizations, smiles, and looks. In the second episode, stranger approach, the stranger enticed the children to play with him using a standardized protocol. The third situation involved play with the stranger using an interactive toy. The other situations were play with the mother, cuddling with the stranger and mother, and separation from the mother. In the first three situations (when the stranger was strangest), social responding toward the stranger suggested genetic influence. The same social responses directed toward the mother showed no genetic influence. This is one of the few observational studies in behavioral genetics, and it buoys confidence in the assertion that individual differences in shyness, even in infancy, show genetic influence.

Surprisingly, the CAP appears to be the only behavioral genetic study of infant shyness that has used any design other than the twin design. Despite its parent–offspring design, it provides some evidence for genetic influence. Midparent ratings of the infants on the Colorado Childhood Temperament Inventory (Rowe & Plomin, 1977) shyness scale were compared with parents' personality as measured by a "shyness" factor (Factor H) from Cattell's Sixteen Personality Factor questionnaire (Cattell, Eber, & Tatsuoka, 1970) and a sociability scale from the EAS Temperament Survey of Buss and Plomin (1975). Table 7.5 includes these parent–offspring correlations. The correlations for the nonadoptive families suggest that infant shyness is negatively related to parental sociability and positively related to parental shyness. In nonadoptive families, of course, parent–offspring relationships could be mediated either genetically or environmentally. However, the correlations between the biological mothers and their adopted-away offspring at 24 months hint at the influence of heredity. The significant negative correlation between infant shyness and biological mothers' sociability is particularly noteworthy because this correlation involves the biological mothers' self-report of sociability and the adoptive parents' midparent rating of the adoptees' shyness more than 2 years later. Moreover, as discussed earlier in relation to mental development, significant resemblance between biological parents and their adopted-away infants suggests the existence of some genetic continuity from infancy to adulthood.

The correlations between adoptive parents and their adopted infants shown in Table 7.5 suggest a major role for family environmental influences as indexed by parents' personality. Adoptive parents' shyness and sociability are related to shyness of the adopted infants. Thus this first adoption study of shyness suggests parent–offspring similarity even in infancy. This resemblance possibly involves heredity and certainly involves family environmental influence.

Summary

Most of the studies described in this section assessed other traits in addition to emotionality, activity, and sociability; these other traits do not show the consistent pattern of genetic influence shown by the EAS traits. A few studies were not discussed because their sample sizes are so small that their data are likely to be unreliable (Freedman, 1974; Reppucci, 1968; Van den Daele, 1971). One important twin study in infancy included no measures relevant to the EAS traits, but deserves mention because of its novelty. Lytton, Martin, and Eaves (1977) assessed social interaction between mothers and their infants at home and in the laboratory. Measures of attachment (defined behaviorally as a combination of seeking attention, help, and proximity) and compliance revealed no genetic influence and no influence of shared family environment. Observational ratings of specific behaviors in unstructured settings also showed no evidence of genetic influence, though shared fam-

TABLE 7.5. Behavioral Genetic Studies of Shyness and Sociability in Infancy[a]

Reference	Sample (age; number)[b]	Measure	Results[c]		
A. Twin studies					
Torgersen and Kringlen (1978); Torgersen (1982)	2 and 9 months; 34 MZ; 16 DZ	Parental interview data on approach-withdrawal to strangers	Twin correlations not reported; MZ significantly more similar than DZ at 9 months		
Plomin and Rowe (1979)	22 months average; 21 MZ; 25 DZ	Time-sampled observations of social responding during initial interactions with a stranger:			
		Approach	.50 vs. −.05		
		Proximity	.40 vs. −.03		
		Positive vocalizations	.58 vs. .34		
		Smiling	.08 vs. .25		
		Looking	.65 vs. .08		
Cohen et al. (1977)	1–5 years; 181 MZ; 84 DZ	Childhood Personality Scale (Dibble & Cohen, 1974) maternal ratings of shyness	.69 vs. .29		
Matheny (1980)	6, 12, 18, 24 months; 72–91 MZ; 35–50 DZ	Tester ratings on IBR Test Affect-Extraversion factor	6 months: .24 vs. .11 12 months: .33 vs. .28 18 months: .43 vs. .14 24 months: .58 vs. .14		
Matheny et al. (1976)	3–12 months; 18–30 months; 47–55 MZ; 27 DZ	Tester ratings on IBR Persons item	first year: .63 vs. .34 second year: .44 vs. .45		
Goldsmith and Gottesman (1981)	8 months; 115 MZ; 209 DZ	Tester ratings of interest in/responsiveness to persons	.28 vs. .20		
Matheny et al. (1981)	6, 24, and 36 months; 68–78 MZ; 38–48 DZ	Parental interview concerning twin differences in:	*6 months*	*24 months*	*36 months*
		Cuddling	53 vs. 13	41 vs. 11	37 vs. 33
		Accepting people	72 vs. 55	55 vs. 17	40 vs. 9

B. Parent/Offspring Adoption Study

Colorado Adoption Project (Plomin & DeFries, 1985)

12 and 24 months; 182 adoptive and 164 nonadoptive families

Midparent ratings on CCTI shyness scale for infants; parents' 16 PF shyness and EAS sociability:

	12 months	24 months
Nonadoptive mothers		
16 PF shyness	.17[d]	.16[d]
EAS sociability	−.23[d]	−.22[d]
Nonadoptive fathers		
16 PF shyness	−.02	.18[d]
EAS sociability	−.09	−.13
Biological mothers		
16 PF shyness	.08	.10
EAS sociability	−.02	−.15[d]
Adoptive mothers		
16 PF shyness	.11	.04
EAS sociability	−.19[d]	−.24[d]
Adoptive fathers		
16 PF shyness	.07[d]	.19[d]
EAS sociability	−.15[d]	−.25[d]

[a] Adapted from Plomin and Daniels (1986).

[b] MZ refers to monozygotic (identical) twins and DZ refers to dizygotic (fraternal) twins; the number denotes pairs.

[c] In Part A, results are presented as twin concordances (Matheny et al., 1981) or as twin correlations (all other studies); parent–offspring correlations are reported in Part B.

[d] $p < .05$.

ily environment appeared to be more important for these measures. This latter result might be due to procedural artifacts in that a single rater rated both twins. Finally, one ongoing study should be mentioned. The LTS has recently been extended to include structured laboratory episodes designed to elicit emotionality, activity, and sociability (Matheny & Wilson, 1981). These data will be obtained primarily by use of IBR-like ratings, though some specific behavioral observations are also planned. Because of its EAS formulation, the results of this study will be useful for systematically replicating the EAS results of other twin studies. See Wilson (1986) for a preliminary report of this study.

This review indicates that even in infancy the EAS traits appear to show genetic influence. Buss and Plomin (1984) summarize their theory of temperament as follows:

> A major distinction between our theory and other approaches to temperament is that we specify a genetic origin, whereas other theorists tend to be vague about the origins of temperament. We have been impressed during the past decade with the extent to which behavioral genetic data—often obtained by researchers with perspectives quite different from ours—support our major contention that emotionality, activity, and sociability are among the most heritable aspects of personality in early childhood. . . . Another major distinction is that we take a personality perspective, regarding temperaments as a class of personality traits. . . . In describing our theory, we have tried to be specific and to outline ways of testing it. We propose that emotionality, activity, and sociability are the major dimensions of personality in infancy and early childhood; if not, the theory is wrong. We propose that these three traits are heritable; if not, the theory is wrong. If other early-appearing personality traits are shown to be heritable and not derivable from our three temperaments, the theory must be amended. If there are better ways to slice the personality pie early in life, the theory may have to be discarded. (pp. 155–157)

Genetic Mediation of the Environment

Genetic influence on measures of the infant's environment may be one of the most important findings of behavioral genetics. It does not sound so odd to say that genes affect measures of the environment when one realizes that measures of an infant's environment often are measures of parental behavior. Genes can influence parental behaviors and thus indirectly affect measures of the environment; more importantly, genes can affect the relationship between environmental measures and infant development. For example, the two most widely used measures of family environment are Caldwell and Bradley's (1978) Home Observation for Measurement of the Environment (HOME) and the Family Environment Scales (FES) of Moos and Moos (1981). Each of the 45 observation and interview items of the HOME clearly involves parental behavior; for example, the first item is "Mother spontaneously vocalizes to child at least twice during visit." The FES, a 90-item self-report questionnaire, "focuses on the measurement and description of the interpersonal relationships among family members, on the directions of personal growth which are emphasized in the family, and on the basic organizational structure of the family" (Moos, 1974, p. 3).

The adoption design can be used to estimate genetic mediation of ostensibly environmental influences on children's development (Plomin, Loehlin, & DeFries,

1985). In nonadoptive homes, parents share heredity as well as family environment with their children. Thus relationships between environmental measures and measures of children's development could be mediated genetically via parental characteristics. However, in adoptive homes, correlations between measures of the environment and measures of the infants' development cannot be mediated genetically because adoptive parents share only family environment with their adopted children. Thus if genes underlie relationships between environmental measures and children's development, environment–development correlations in nonadoptive homes will be greater than those in adoptive homes.

Figure 7.5 presents a path model illustrating environment–development relationships in nonadoptive and adoptive families. The infant's phenotype, P_i, is assumed to be causally determined by its genotype, G_i, and its environment, E_i, via genetic and environmental paths h and e; the residual arrow impinging on P_i allows for measurement error. Some measured feature of the environment, represented by I, is assumed to act via path f on the immediate environment that affects the trait in question. The environmental measure I is allowed to be correlated, r, with parents' (unmeasured) genotypes.

For nonadoptive families, the correlation between a measured environmental variable and the infant's development can occur in two ways: environmentally via the path fe, or genetically via the parents' and infants' genotype—with a value of $\frac{1}{2}rh$ for the path through each parent, which yields a combined value of rh for the genetic paths. For adoptive families, the measured environmental variable has only an environmental connection to the infant's development, path fe. Thus in nonadoptive homes the correlation between an environmental measure and a measure of infant's development is

$$\text{Nonadoptive } r_{IP_i} = fe + rh$$

In adoptive homes, the environment–development relationship can be represented as

$$\text{Adoptive } r_{IP_i} = fe$$

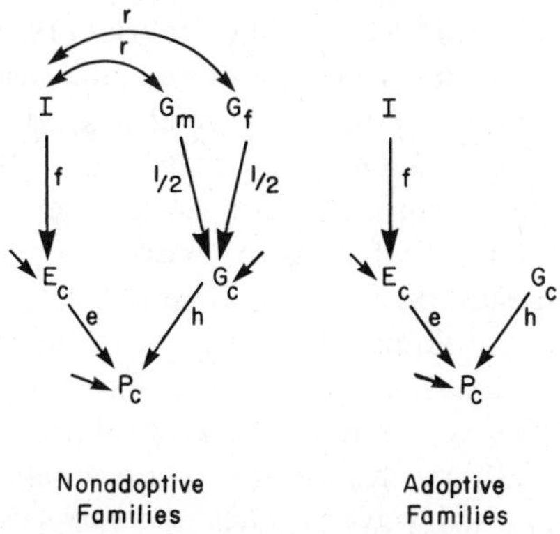

Nonadoptive
Families

Adoptive
Families

Figure 7.5. Path model illustrating environment–development relationships in nonadoptive and adoptive families, I = environmental index; G_m, G_f = genotypes of mother and father; G_c, E_c, P_c = genotype, environment, and phenotype of child; f, e, h, $\frac{1}{2}$, r = values of paths and correlations.

It follows that the difference between the environment–development correlations in nonadoptive and adoptive families yields an estimate of *rh,* the genetic component of the correlation. The correlation in the adoptive families itself provides an estimate of *fe,* the environmental component of the correlation. Thus given suitable data from adoptive families and comparable nonadoptive families one can decompose the correlation between an environmental characteristic and a child's trait into two additive components—one environmental and one genetic.

Plomin and colleagues (1985) discuss assumptions of the model—means and variances of the environmental measures are comparable in adoptive and nonadoptive homes; selective placement is negligible; and genotype-environment correlation is minimal—and show that violations of the latter two assumptions make the model conservative in terms of finding genetic mediation of environmental influences. The authors then examine appropriate data from two previous adoption studies of children 5–14 years old (Burks, 1928; Leahy, 1935) and conclude that "correlations between measures of environment and child's IQ appear to depend at least as much on genetic as on environmental mediation" (p. 391).

Most exciting are infancy data from the CAP (Plomin & DeFries, 1985), which include measures of environment–development relationships for 185 adoptive families and 164 nonadoptive families when the infants are 12 and 24 months old. Two major environmental measures are employed in the CAP: the HOME (Caldwell & Bradley, 1978) at 12 and 24 months, and the FES (Moos & Moos, 1981) at 12 months. Measures of the infants include mental development, language acquisition, temperament, and behavioral problems, as described in detail by Plomin and DeFries (1985). The total score and 6 scales of the HOME and the 10 scales of the FES yielded an unwieldy number of correlations with the various infant measures at 12 and 24 months. In order to reduce the environment–development correlations to a manageable number, composites of the environmental measures were derived using factor analysis. An unrotated first principal component score was used to represent a general HOME factor, and four rotated factors were used to summarize major dimensions of the HOME. Quantitative scoring of the HOME items rather than the traditional dichotomous scoring was also employed in order to increase the variance of the items in middle-class homes. Two second-order factors were derived to summarize the 10 scales of the FES. Details concerning construction of these environmental measures can be found in Plomin and DeFries (1985).

Even after the number of infant and environmental measures had been greatly condensed, 113 environment–development correlations in nonadoptive families and 113 correlations in adoptive families were examined by Plomin and colleagues (1985). Because it makes little sense to assess genetic components of environment–development relationships if no relationship exists between a particular environmental measure and a measure of infant development, the analyses focused on 34 correlations that reached a nominal .05 level of statistical significance in *either* adoptive *or* nonadoptive families. Of the 34 environment–development correlations that were significant in either the adoptive or nonadoptive families, 28 were greater in the nonadoptive families. Furthermore, for 12 correlations that were significantly different in adoptive and nonadoptive families, the correlations in the nonadoptive families were greater. This consistent pattern of greater correlations in the nonadoptive families as compared to the adoptive families suggests genetic involvement in relationships between environmental measures and major domains of infant development. For all 34 correlations, the mean correlation for adoptive families was .09; for nonadoptive families, it was .24. According to the model in Figure 7.5, these data suggest that environment–development correlations for these measures of environment and these measures of infant development are on average approximately 40 percent environmental and 60 percent genetic.

The 34 environment–development correlations that were significant in either adoptive or nonadoptive families were distributed as follows in the four domains of infant development: 10 significant correlations (out of a total of 48) were observed in the domain of behavioral problems; 14 (of 48) were observed for temperament; 6 (of 12) for mental development; and 4 (of 5) for language acquisition. Table 7.6 summarizes the average environment–development correlations in these four domains. All four domains show the pattern of greater environment–development correlations in nonadoptive than in adoptive families.

Although genetic influence appears to be greater for behavioral problems and temperament than for mental and language development, these summary data obscure some important trends. In nonadoptive families, the general factor score for the HOME, the most widely used measure of home environment, correlates .44 with Bayley MDI score at 24 months of age, which is similar to correlations found in other studies of nonadoptive families (reviewed by Gottfried, 1984). The correlation in adoptive families is .29. The HOME is not significantly correlated with Bayley MDI scores at 12 months of age in nonadoptive families (or adoptive families), which also is consistent with the results of other studies. Similar results were obtained for the measure of language development at 24 months of age: The correlation in nonadoptive homes (.50) is significantly greater than that in adoptive homes (.32).

Why do the mean correlations in Table 7.6 for mental and language development suggest only modest genetic influence despite evidence of substantial genetic influence for the HOME general factor? The answer lies in the fact that two of the rotated factors of the HOME, Maternal Involvement and Variety of Experience, show no genetic relationship with the infants' mental or language development. Another HOME factor, Restriction/Punishment, shows no environmental relationships with these measures of development. Only one of the rotated HOME factors, Encouraging Advance (including items such as "Mother consciously encourages developmental advance"), suggests substantial genetic influence. For the adoptive and nonadoptive families, respectively, the correlations are .44 and .22 for the Bayley

TABLE 7.6.   Average Environment–Development Correlations in the Colorado Adoption Project for Adoptive and Nonadoptive Families in which Either Correlation Is Statistically Significant[a,b]

Infant Domain	Number of Correlations	Mean Environment–Development Correlations	
		Adoptive	Nonadoptive
Behavioral problems	10	.07	.23
Temperament	14	.06	.20
Mental development	6	.21	.27
Language development	4	.25	.36

[a]Adapted from Plomin et al. (1985).
[b]Sample size varies from 139 to 180 for adoptive families and from 130 and 163 for nonadoptive families.

MDI and .50 and .27 for the SICD. In both cases, the correlation for the nonadoptive families is significantly greater than that for the adoptive families. In general, these results suggest some specificity of genetic mediation of environment–development relationships.

These results from the Colorado Adoption Project suggest that correlations between widely used environmental measures and major domains of infant development are mediated genetically to a substantial extent, approximately 50 percent on the average. This finding is important at a practical level because implications for intervention in environment–development relationships differ depending on the answer to the question of genetic mediation. Methodologically, it will be important to conduct more environmental studies in adoptive families in order to assess environmental influences free of genetic effects. Conceptually, the possibility of genetic mediation of environment–development relationships highlights the need to explore possible parental mediators of the genetic component of these relationships and to study the developmental processes on which genetic factors exert their effects.

CONCLUSIONS

Quantitative genetics and its subdiscipline of developmental behavioral genetics provide a theory and a set of methodologies of extraordinary power for the description and explanation of individual differences in infancy. The research reviewed in this chapter primarily serves to provide an inkling of the field's heuristic value. Because the amount of developmental behavioral genetic research in infancy is minuscule, at least as compared to other fields of infancy research, most of this potential is as yet unrealized. Nonetheless, some exciting conclusions—or at least hypotheses for future research—are beginning to emerge:

1. Although genetic influence on Bayley Mental Development Index scores in infancy is significant, more impressive is the extent to which the genetic influence in infancy is less than genetic influence on IQ scores later in childhood. About 15 percent of the variance in Bayley scores is due to genetic differences among infants; later in childhood, estimates of genetic influence on IQ scores are closer to 50 percent. One implication of this is that individual differences in infancy might, through genetic mechanisms, predict adult IQ to some slight extent.

2. Individual differences in language acquisition at 12 and 24 months are influenced by heredity.

3. When measures of infant mental development such as Bayley scores or language acquisition scores are related to parental cognitive ability, they are related to general cognitive ability, not to specific cognitive abilities of parents. This suggests that infant mental development is general and undifferentiated.

4. The temperament traits of emotionality, activity, and sociability–shyness evidence significant and possibly substantial genetic influence in infancy.

5. Whenever the relative magnitude of genetic variance changes during development, its impact increases rather than decreases. This is contrary to the

commonly held view that genetic influences are most important early in development.

6. Although genetic influence is generally less in infancy than later in childhood, what little genetic variance exists in infancy covaries highly with genetic variance in adulthood. This suggests an amplification model of developmental genetics: Genes make only a small contribution to phenotypic variance in infancy, but their effects are amplified as development proceeds.

7. Relationships between widely used measures of the home environment and major domains of infant development are mediated genetically to a substantial extent, 50 percent on the average.

In closing, I should perhaps confront a specter that always seems to lurk in the shadows when behavioral genetics enters a new field of research. There is a fear that genetic effects are immutable and that nothing can be done about them. As an antidote to this view, I would suggest that, the more that is known about a trait genetically as well as environmentally, the more likely that rational interventions can be devised. There is also a concern that misguided policy decisions might be made if genetic influence in infancy is found. I suggest that policy decisions involve value judgments and that finding genetic influence in infancy is compatible with a wide range of values and policies. And, in accord with the old-fashioned view of a truth-seeking science, I believe that wiser decisions can be made with knowledge than without it.

The essential anxiety, however, is that genetic influence appears to go against our basic democratic principles. Are not all men created equal? When our founding fathers wrote this, they were not so naive as to think that all men are inherently identical. Even in the seventeenth century, John Locke, whose treatise, *Of Civil Government,* played a key role in the American revolution and in educational thought, had a more balanced view of the nature–nurture question than is usually recognized. By *equality,* Locke clearly meant political equality, not an absence of individual differences (Loehlin, 1983). In a democracy, we do not treat people equally because they are identical—there would be no need for principles of equality if that were true. The essence of democracy is to treat people equally in spite of their differences.

REFERENCES

Abramovitch, R., Pepler, D., & Corter, C. (1982). Patterns of sibling interaction among preschool-age children. In M. Lamb & B. Sutton-Smith (Eds.), *Sibling relationships: Their nature and significance across the lifespan.* Hillsdale, NJ: Erlbaum.

Anastasi, A. (1958). Heredity, environment, and the question "How?" *Psychological Review, 65,* 197–208.

Baker, L. A. (1983). *Bivariate path analysis of verbal and nonverbal abilities in the Colorado Adoption Project.* Unpublished doctoral dissertation, University of Colorado, Boulder.

Bayley, N. (1969). *Manual for the Bayley Scales of Infant Development.* New York: Psychological Corporation.

Beckwith, L. (1971). Relationships between attributes of mothers and their infants' IQ scores. *Child Development, 42,* 1083–1097.

Bouchard, T. J., Jr., & McGue, M. (1981). Familial studies of intelligence: A review. *Science, 212,* 1055–1059.

Broman, S. H., Nichols, P. L., & Kennedy, W. A. (1975). *Preschool IQ: Prenatal and early development correlates.* Hillsdale, NJ: Erlbaum.

Burks, B. (1928). The relative influence of nature and nurture upon mental development: A comparative study of foster parent-foster child resemblance and true parent-true child resemblance. *Twenty-Seventh Yearbook of the National Society for the Study of Education* (Part 1) (pp. 219–316).

Buss, A. H., & Plomin, R. (1975). *A temperament theory of personality development.* New York: Wiley-Interscience.

Buss, A. H., & Plomin, R. (1984). *Temperament: Early developing personality traits.* Hillsdale, NJ: Erlbaum.

Caldwell, B. M., & Bradley, R. H. (1978). *Home Observation for Measurement of the Environment.* Little Rock: University of Arkansas.

Caldwell, B. M., & Herscher, L. (1969). Mother–infant interaction during the first year of life. *Merill-Palmer Quarterly, 10,* 119–128.

Casler, L. (1976). Maternal intelligence and institutionalized children's developmental quotients: A correlational study. *Developmental Psychology, 12,* 64–67.

Cattell, R. B., Eber, H., & Tatsuoka, M. M. (1970). *Handbook for the Sixteen Personality Factor questionnaire.* Champaign, IL: IPAT.

Cohen, D. J., Dibble, E., & Grawe, J. M. (1977). Fathers' and mothers' perceptions of children's personality. *Archives of General Psychiatry, 34,* 480–487.

Cooper, R. M., & Zubek, J. P. (1958). Effects of enriched and restricted early environments on the learning ability of bright and dull rats. *Canadian Journal of Psychology, 12,* 159–164.

Daniels, D., Dunn, J., Furstenberg, F. F., Jr., & Plomin, R. (1985). Environmental differences within the family and adjustment differences within pairs of adolescent siblings. *Child Development, 56,* 764–774.

Daniels, D., & Plomin, R. (1985) Differential experience of siblings in the same family. *Developmental Psychology, 21,* 747–760.

DeFries, J. C. (1979). In J. R. Royce & L. P. Mos (Eds.), *Theoretical advances in behavior genetics.* Alphen aan den Rijn, the Netherlands: Sijthoff & Noordhoff.

DeFries, J. C. (1983). *Amplification model of developmental genetics.* Unpublished manuscript.

DeFries, J. C., & Plomin, R. (1978). Behavioral genetics. *Annual Review of Psychology, 29,* 473–515.

Dixon, L. K., & Johnson, R. C. (1980). *The roots of individuality: A survey of human behavior genetics.* Belmont, CA: Wadsworth.

Dunn, J. F., & Kendrick, C. (1982). *Siblings: Love, envy, and understanding.* London: Grant McIntyre.

Dunn, J., & Plomin, R. (1986). Determinants of maternal behaviour towards 3-year-old siblings. *British Journal of Developmental Psychology, 4,* 127–137.

Dunn, J., Plomin, R., & Daniels, D. (1986). Consistency and change in mothers' behavior towards young siblings. *Child Development, 21,* 1188–1195.

Dunn, J. F., Plomin, R., & Nettles, M. (1985). Consistency of mothers' behavior towards infant siblings. *Developmental Psychology, 21,* 1188–1195.

Eichorn, D. H. (1969). *Developmental parallels in the growth of parents and their children.* Presidential address (Division 7) presented at the meeting of the American Psychological Association, Washington, DC.

Fagan, J. F., III. (1982). A visual recognition test of infant intelligence. *Infant Behavior & Development, 5,* 75.

Fagan, J. F., III. (1984). A new look at infant intelligence. In D. K. Detterman (Ed.), *Current topics in human intelligence.* Norwood, NJ: Ablex.

Fagan, J. F., III, & Singer, L. T. (1983). Infant recognition memory as a measure of intelligence. In L. P. Lipsett (Ed.), *Advances in infancy research.* Norwood, NJ: Ablex.

Falconer, D. S. (1960). *Quantitative genetics.* New York: Ronald Press.

Falconer, D. S. (1981). *Introduction to quantitative genetics.* London: Longman.

Fantz, R. L. (1956). A method for studying early visual development. *Perceptual & Motor Skills, 6,* 13–15.

Fisher, R. A. (1918). The correlation between relatives on the supposition of Mendelian inheritance. *Transactions of the Royal Society of Edinburgh, 52,* 399–433.

Freedman, D. G. (1974). *Human infancy: An evolutionary perspective.* Hillsdale, NJ: Erlbaum.

Fuller, J. L., & Thompson, W. R. (1978). *Foundations of behavior genetics.* St. Louis: Mosby.

Galton, F. (1875). The history of twins as a criterion of the relative powers of nature and nurture. *Journal of the Anthropological Institute, 6,* 391–406.

Garcia-Coll, C., Kagan, J., & Reznick, J. S. (1984). Behavioral inhibition in young children. *Child Development, 55,* 1005–1019.

Goldsmith, H. H. (1983). Emotionality in infant twins: Longitudinal results. *Abstracts of the Fourth International Congress on Twin Studies,* London.

Goldsmith, H. H., & Campos, J. J. (1982). Toward a theory of infant temperament. In R. N. Emde & R. Harmon (Eds.), *The development of attachment and affiliative systems.* New York: Plenum.

Goldsmith, H. H. & Campos, J. J. (1982). Genetic influence on individual differences in emotionality. *Infant Behavior & Development, 5,* 99.

Goldsmith, H. H. & Gottesman, I. I. (1981). Origins of variation in behavioral style: A longitudinal study of temperament in young twins. *Child Development, 52,* 91–103.

Gottfried, A. W. (1984). *Home environment and early cognitive development: Longitudinal research.* New York: Academic.

Hardy-Brown, K. (1980). An analysis of environmental and genetic influence on individual differences in the communicative development of fifty adopted one-year-old children. *Dissertation Abstracts International, 41,* 3025B.

Hardy-Brown, K. (1982). *Communicative development in the first year of life: Genetic and environmental influences.* Paper presented at the meeting of the Behavior Genetics Association, Fort Collins, CO.

Hardy-Brown, K. (1983). Universals and individual differences: Disentangling two approaches to the study of language acquisition. *Developmental Psychology, 19,* 610–624.

Hardy-Brown, K., Plomin, R., & DeFries, J. C. (1981). Genetic and environmental influences on rate of communicative development in the first year of life. *Developmental Psychology, 17,* 704–717.

Hedrick, D. L., Prather, E. M., & Tobin, A. R. (1975). *Sequenced Inventory of Communication Development.* Seattle: University of Washington Press.

Henderson, N. D. (1970). Genetic influences on the behavior of mice can be obscured by laboratory rearing. *Journal of Comparative & Physiological Psychology, 73,* 505–511.

Jacobs, B. S., & Moss, H. A. (1976). Birth order and sex of sibling as determinants of mother–infant interaction. *Child Development, 47,* 315–322.

Kagan, J. (1982). Comments on the construct of difficult temperament. *Merrill-Palmer Quarterly, 28,* 21–24.

Leahy, A. M. (1935). Nature-nurture and intelligence. *Genetic Psychology Monographs, 17,* 236–308.

Levine, M. D., Carey, W. B., Crocker, A. C., & Gross, R. T. (1983). *Developmental-behavioral pediatrics.* Philadelphia: Saunders.

Lewis, M. (1983). On the nature of intelligence: Science or bias? In M. Lewis (Ed.), *Origins of intelligence: Infancy and early childhood.* New York: Plenum.

Loehlin, J. C. (1982). Are personality traits differentially heritable? *Behavior Genetics, 12,* 417–428.

Loehlin, J. C. (1983). John Locke and behavior genetics. *Behavior Genetics, 13,* 117–121.

Lytton, H., Martin, N. G., & Eaves, L. (1977). Environmental and genetical causes of variation in ethological aspects of behavior in two-year-old boys. *Social Biology, 24,* 200–211.

Maccoby, E. E., & Martin, J. A. (1983). Socialization in the context of the family: Parent–child interaction. In P. H. Mussen (Ed.), *Handbook of child psychology: Vol. IV. Socialization, personality, and social development* (4th ed.). New York: Wiley.

Matheny, A. P., Jr. (1975). Twins: Concordance for Piagetian-equivalent items derived from the Bayley Mental Test. *Developmental Psychology, 2,* 224–227.

Matheny, A. P., Jr. (1980). Bayley's Infant Behavior Record: Behavioral components and twin analyses. *Child Development, 51,* 1157–1167.

Matheny, A. P., Jr. (1983). A longitudinal twin study of stability of components from Bayley's Infant Behavior Record. *Child Development, 54,* 356–360.

Matheny, A. P., Jr., & Dolan, A. B. (1975). Persons, situations and time: A genetic view of behavioral change in children. *Journal of Personality & Social Psychology, 14,* 224–234.

Matheny, A. P., Jr., Dolan, A. B., & Wilson, R. S. (1976). Within-pair similarity on Bayley's Infant Behavior Record. *Journal of Genetic Psychology, 128,* 263–270.

Matheny, A. P., Jr., & Wilson, R. S. (1981). Developmental tasks and rating scales for the laboratory assessment of infant temperament. *JSAS Catalog of Selected Documents in Psychology, 11,* 81–82.

Matheny, A. P., Jr., Wilson, R. S., Dolan, A. B., & Krantz, J. Z. (1981). Behavior contrasts in twinships: Stability and patterns of differences in childhood. *Child Development, 52,* 579–588.

Mayr, E. (1982). *The growth of biological thought.* Cambridge, MA: Harvard University Press.

McCall, R. B. (1970). IQ pattern over age: Comparisons among siblings and parent–child pairs. *Science, 170,* 644–648.

McCall, R. B. (1972). Similarity in developmental profile among related pairs of human infants. *Science, 178,* 1004–1005.

McCall, R. B. (1976). Toward an epigenetic conception of mental development in the first three years of life. In M. Lewis (Ed.), *Origins of intelligence.* New York: Plenum.

McCall, R. B. (1979). The development of intellectual functioning in infancy and the prediction of later IQ. In J. D. Osofsky (Ed.), *Handbook of infant development.* New York: Wiley-Interscience.

McCall, R. B., Appelbaum, M. I., & Hogarty, P. S. (1973). Developmental changes in mental performance. *Monographs of the Society for Research in Child Development, 35,* 39–98.

Mischel, W. (1968). *Personality and assessment.* New York: Wiley.

Moos, R. H. (1974). *Preliminary manual for Family Environment Scale, Work Environment Scale, and Group Environment Scale.* Palo Alto, CA: Consulting Psychologists Press.

Moos, R. H., & Moos, B. S. (1981). *Family Environment Scale manual.* Palo Alto, CA: Consulting Psychologists Press.

Nichols, P. L., & Broman, S. H. (1974). Familial resemblance in infant mental development. *Developmental Psychology, 10,* 442–446.

Plomin, R. (1983). Childhood temperament. In B. Lahey & A. Kazdin (Eds.), *Advances in clinical child psychology.* New York: Plenum.

Plomin, R. (1986). *Development, genetics, and psychology.* Hillsdale, NJ: Erlbaum.

Plomin, R., & Daniels, D. (1984). The interaction between temperament and environment: Methodological considerations. *Merrill-Palmer Quarterly, 30,* 149–162.

Plomin, R., & Daniels, D. (1986). Genetics and shyness. In W. H. Jones, J. M. Cheek, & S. R. Briggs (Eds.), *A sourcebook on shyness: Research and treatment.* New York: Plenum.

Plomin, R., & Daniels, D. (in press). Why are two children in the same family so different from each other? *The Behavioral and Brain Sciences.*

Plomin, R., & DeFries, J. C. (1979). Multivariate behavioral genetic analysis of twin data on scholastic abilities. *Behavior Genetics, 9,* 505–517.

Plomin, R., & DeFries, J. C. (1980). Genetics and intelligence: Recent data. *Intelligence, 4,* 15–24.

Plomin, R., & DeFries, J. C. (1981). Multivariate behavioral genetics and development: Twin studies. In L. Gedda, P. Parisi, & W. E. Nance (Eds.), *Twin Research 3, Part B: Intelligence, personality and development.* New York: Liss.

Plomin, R., & DeFries, J. C. (1983). The Colorado Adoption Project. *Child Development, 54,* 276–289.

Plomin, R., & DeFries, J. C. (1985). *Origins of individual differences in infancy: The Colorado Adoption Project.* New York: Academic.

Plomin, R., DeFries, J. C., & Loehlin, J. C. (1977). Genotype–environment interaction and correlation in the analysis of human behavior. *Psychological Bulletin, 84,* 309–322.

Plomin, R., DeFries, J. C., & McClearn, G. E. (1980). *Behavioral genetics: A primer.* San Francisco: Freeman.

Plomin, R., & Dunn, J. (1986). *The study of temperament: Changes, continuities and challenges.* Hillsdale, NJ: Erlbaum.

Plomin, R., Loehlin, J. C., & DeFries, J. C. (1985). Genetic and environmental components of "environmental" influences. *Developmental Psychology, 21,* 391–402.

Plomin, R., & Rowe, D. C. (1979). Genetic and environmental etiology of social behavior in infancy. *Developmental Psychology, 15,* 62–72.

Reppucci, C. M. (1968). *Hereditary influences upon distribution of attention in infancy.* Unpublished doctoral dissertation, Harvard University.

Rothbart, M. K., & Derryberry, D. (1981). Development of individual differences in temperament. In M. E. Lamb & A. L. Brown (Eds.), *Advances in developmental psychology.* Hillsdale, NJ: Erlbaum.

Rowe, D. C., & Plomin, R. (1977). Temperament in early childhood. *Journal of Personality Assessment, 41,* 150–156.

Rowe, D. C., & Plomin, R. (1981). The importance of nonshared environmental influences in behavioral development. *Developmental Psychology, 17,* 517–531.

Scarr, S. (1976). An evolutionary perspective on infant intelligence: Species patterns and individual variations. In M. Lewis (Ed.), *Origins of intelligence.* New York: Plenum.

Scarr, S., & Carter, L. (1983). Genetics and intelligence. In J. L. Fuller & E. C. Simmel (Eds.), *Behavior genetics: Principles and applications.* Hillsdale, NJ: Erlbaum.

Scarr, S., & Kidd, K. K. (1983). Behavior genetics. In M. Haith & J. Campos (Eds.), *Manual of child psychology: Infancy and the biology of development*. New York: Wiley.

Scarr, S., & McCartney, K. (1983). How people make their own environments: A theory of genotype→environment effects. *Child Development, 54,* 424–435.

Skodak, M., & Skeels, H. M. (1949). A final follow-up of one hundred adopted children. *Journal of Genetic Psychology, 75,* 85–125.

Snygg, D. (1938). The relation between the intelligence of mothers and of their children living in foster homes. *Journal of Genetic Psychology, 52,* 401–406.

Terman, L. M., & Merrill, M. A. (1973). *Stanford-Binet intelligence scale: 1972 norms edition.* Boston: Houghton-Mifflin.

Thomas, A., & Chess, S. (1977). *Temperament and development.* New York: Brunner/Mazel.

Thompson, L. A., & Fagan, J. F. (1983). *A family study of infant recognition memory.* Paper presented at the meeting of the Behavior Genetics Association, London.

Thompson, L. A., Plomin, R., & DeFries, J. C. (1985). Parent–infant resemblance for general and specific cognitive abilities in the Colorado Adoption Project. *Intelligence, 9,* 1–13.

Torgersen, A. M. (1982). Influence of genetic factors on temperament development in early childhood. In R. Porter & G. M. Collins (Eds.), *Temperamental differences in infants and young children.* London: Pitman.

Torgersen, A. M., & Kringlen, E. (1978). Genetic aspects of temperamental differences in infants: A study of same-sexed twins. *Journal of the American Academy of Child Psychiatry, 17,* 433–444.

Urbach, P. (1974a). Progress and degeneration in the "IQ debate": I. *British Journal of Philosophy & Science, 25,* 99–135.

Urbach, P. (1974b). Progress and degeneration in the "IQ debate": II. *British Journal of Philosophy & Science, 25,* 235–259.

Uzgiris, I. C., & Hunt, J. McV. (1975). *Assessment in infancy.* Urbana: University of Illinois Press.

Vale, J. R. (1980). *Genes, environment and behavior: An interactionist approach.* New York: Harper & Row.

Van den Daele, L. Infant reactivity to redundant proprioceptive and auditory stimulation: A twin study. (1971). *Journal of Psychology, 78,* 269–276.

Wilson, R. S. (1973). Testing infant intelligence. *Science, 182,* 734–737.

Wilson, R. S. (1977). Mental development in twins. In A. Oliverio (Ed.), *Genetics, environment and intelligence.* Alphen aan den Rijn, the Netherlands: Elsevier.

Wilson, R. S. (1978). Synchronies in mental development: An epigenetic perspective. *Science, 202,* 939–948.

Wilson, R. S. (1979). Analysis of longitudinal twin data. *Acta Geneticae Medicae et Gemellologiae, 28,* 93–105.

Wilson, R. S. (1983). The Louisville Twin Study: Developmental synchronies in behavior. *Child Development, 54,* 298–316.

Wilson, R. S. (1986). Behavior-genetics research in infant temperament: The Louisville Twin Study. In R. Plomin & J. Dunn (Eds.), *The study of temperament: Changes, continuities and challenges.* Hillsdale, NJ: Erlbaum.

Wilson, R. S., Brown, A., & Matheny, A. P., Jr. (1971). Emergence and persistence of behavioral differences in twins. *Child Development, 42,* 1381–1398.

Wilson, R. S., & Matheny, A. P., Jr. (1976). Retardation and twin concordance in infant mental development: A reassessment. *Behavior Genetics, 6,* 353–358.

PART TWO

Social, Emotional, and Interactive Perspectives

Major shifts have occurred in the study of parent–infant relationships since the publication of the first edition of the *Handbook of Infant Development*. A reflection of these shifts is the inclusion in this volume of a single chapter on family interaction, whereas in the first edition separate chapters appeared on mother–infant and father–infant interaction. This chapter, by Ross Parke and Barbara Tinsley, goes further in discussing the influence of social systems. As the authors indicate, there has been increasing focus on the family as a system and on its "transactional" nature. Other important areas that have received increasing interest include the study of the transition to parenthood, the development of the couple's relationship, and the impact of a child on the relationship. Little is known about the continuing impact of infant risk factors on the developing family; however, there is evidence to indicate that a higher level of marital and family disruption occurs in families with high risk infants. We also have much to learn about the effect of the marital relationship on infant and child development. From both theoretical and research perspectives, there has been much growth in knowledge, understanding, and empirical work related to social and emotional development. These advances are reflected in the chapters by Michael Lewis, Carroll Izard and Carol Malatesta, and Karen Barrett and Joseph Campos. Research on parent–infant relationships in western Europe is reviewed in two chapters, one by Peter de Chateau and the other by Hanuš and Mechthild Papoušek.

Lewis points out in his chapter that, although we have many examples to illustrate the social nature of the infant, there are few theories of social development in comparison to the larger number focusing on cognitive and intellectual development. He reviews various models of development and then presents a social network model that goes beyond the dyad or the family system. His chapter provides background material for more specific considerations of parent–infant and family interaction. Another emphasis in his chapter, one that comes up repeatedly throughout the book, concerns the importance of the nature and development of relationships for understanding social development (see also Chapter 21, by Bertrand Cramer, and Chapter 27, by Robert Emde).

Two perspectives on emotional development are presented in the chapters by Izard and Malatesta and Barrett and Campos. Izard and Malatesta view emotional development as the biological, psychological, and sociocultural processes whereby the emotional system interrelates with other systems. Emotional systems according to these authors refer to a set of discrete emotions, such as fear, anger, joy, and surprise, and their interactions. Each fundamental emotion has unique organizational and adaptive functions derived from components characterized by particular developmental processes. Evidence related to these processes is presented in a framework of seven organizing principles, all of which relate to facial expressions. Indeed, a crucial aspect of their theory is the isomorphism that they posit in early development between facial expressions of emotions and internal feeling states. Although they hypothesize concordance between expression and feeling, they discuss the ways in which they become decoupled during socialization. There is a continuity of basic feeling states over the life span. Izard and Malatesta feel that an understanding of the structure, dynamics, and developmental course of facial expressions provides a coherent picture of the relations among components of emotions and the role of emotions in motivation and adaptation.

In their chapter, Barrett and Campos present a functionalist approach to emotions, conceiving of them as bidirectional processes of establishing, maintaining, and/or disrupting significant relationships between an organism and the environment. To counter what they feel is the "reification" of emotion concepts, the authors introduce the interesting concept of emotion families. They conceive of emotions as multifaceted phenomena with no particular criteria (such as facial or autonomic expression) being necessary for the manifestation of a given emotion. Rather, emotions are defined by their functions (such as avoidance in fear, overcoming obstacles to goals in anger), but these functions can be served by many different actions. Because in different contexts, the same action can be in the service of many different emotions, the authors argue that no isomorphism exists between an action and an emotion. The authors also argue that under the right circumstances relatives of each emotion family may be seen very early in development. The notions of individual differences and socialization of emotion are very important for understanding the concept of emotion families; kinship is established based on similarities between emotions in the functions they serve. The socialization of emotion is considered one of the most significant aspects of emotional development, with implications for the elicitation, expression, and functional consequences of emotional states. These two chapters by prominent theoreticians and researchers in the area of emotional development together provide important new perspectives for the field.

Parke and Tinsley consider the marital and family system as a basis for understanding the individual contributions of infants and parents and patterns of interaction. In this framework, it may be important to consider interactions in low- and high-risk families and how the different relationships may develop. The interdependence among roles and functions of all family members is extremely important; for example, parents influence each other as well as their children. Different patterns of relationships may develop in high- and low-risk families that can influence outcomes for both the family as a whole and the individual in the family. A consistent theme running through the Lewis chapter and the Parke and Tinsley chapter is the importance of secular shifts and social changes and the impact that they have on families. The chapters in this section go much beyond their titles in providing perspectives on parenting and the family as a broader system within which many different interactions, combinations, permutations, and trajectories may result. It is important for theoreticians and researchers studying parent–infant and family interactions to recognize this important broader framework.

A cross-cultural perspective is provided in the chapters of de Chateau and the

Papouşĕks. The authors review some of their own work and that of other investigators in western European countries. De Chateau focuses on parent–newborn socialization in western Europe, with particular emphasis on early postnatal contact between newborns and their parents. He raises intriguing questions related to the effects of early contact on the physiology and psychology of the newborn. The Papouşĕks discuss the notion of "intuitive parenting" to explain a type of didactic intervention that may escape the observer's attention because caretakers react this way without being aware of it (this perspective has some similarities to that proposed by Cramer in his chapter on subjective and objective aspects of the parent–infant relationship). Intuitive behaviors are those that hold an intermediate position between innate reflexes and responses requiring rational decision. There is much diversity in this section, providing important theoretical and empirical perspectives on social and interactive issues for parents, infants, and the family system.

CHAPTER 8

Social Development in Infancy and Early Childhood

MICHAEL LEWIS

By nature humans are social animals. From the moment of birth the child is surrounded by other conspecifics, a small portion of which share the child's gene pool, a larger portion of which will influence and in turn be influenced by the child, and finally the largest portion, which forms the background in which these other interactions will take place. The smallest segment we call the family; the larger comprises lovers, friends, acquaintances, and even strangers; and the largest segment is the culture.

Human newborns are surrounded by a large and a diverse social network, and it is within this array that the developmental processes of the organism occur. Given that the major task of the newborn is the adaptation to this environment of people, it seems reasonable to assign to humans the feature of sociability. Not only must the newborn adapt to this world, but there is considerable evidence that many of the sensory and cognitive abilities of infants center around making sense of their social environment. That this adaptation is critical suggests that many skills and biological structures may be in its service.

Much sensory processing seems keyed to this social need. For example, it appears as if infants' discriminatory ability is greater for social than for nonsocial stimuli. By 12 weeks of age English-speaking children can distinguish between social stimuli such as the speech sounds *pa* and *ba* (Eimas, Siqueland, Jusczyk, & Vigorito, 1971). This discriminatory ability appears to be a function of social experience since infants who are not raised in an English-speaking environment are unable to distinguish these subtle differences (Streeter, 1975). Moreover, although young infants are little interested in nonsocial stimuli, they are considerably more attentive—indexed by heart rate changes—to social stimuli. Even brain structures appear more attuned to social than to nonsocial events. For instance, hemispheric differentiation for sound appears to be divided by social or speech sounds and nonsocial or all other sounds (Molfese, Freeman, & Palermo, 1975; Molfese & Molfese, 1979). Of equal importance to the social competence of children is the control of biological functions through social interactions. Important organizational processes, including the regulation of sleep–wake cycles, appear to result from the social interactions between care givers and infants (Papoušek & Papoušek, 1981; Sanders, 1977).

From a more cognitive perspective, Levi-Strauss (1966) has argued that all cognitive activity is essentially social in nature; language and complex symbol systems constitute a social contract. The process of making children social involves to a large

419

extent training them to use the adult forms of communication, thought, and conceptions of reality.

Finally, there appears to be a strong decalage between social and nonsocial schemata in the growth of knowledge. The amount of knowledge that children acquire about their social environment is incredibly vast, and the acquisition occurs rapidly. Lewis and Brooks-Gunn (1979a) have shown that by 9 months infants already have some rudimentary knowledge about themselves. Moreover, children's knowledge about others is also highly developed quite early in life. By 1 month some infants and by 3 months most infants have some understanding of the relationship between people's faces and voices (Brazelton, Koslowski, & Main, 1974; Kuhl & Meltzoff, 1982), and others have shown that infants interact differentially with familiar persons and strangers as early as 5 weeks of age. Sometime between 3 and 6 months children acquire knowledge about human faces, and by 7 months they demonstrate discrimination of emotional expressions (Caron, Caron, & Meyers, 1982). By 3–4 months infants begin to respond differently to children and adults, and by 6–8 months they show differential fear responses to people on the bases of gender and age (Lewis & Brooks, 1974). By 6–8 months infants are surprised at the appearance of a small adult (i.e., a midget) and seem to understand that the height–facial feature integration is unusual in these people (Brooks & Lewis, 1976). Recently, we have found that by 10 months infants are using the facial expression and tonal quality of their mothers in their interactions with strangers. Infants are more friendly to strangers who are treated in a positive manner by their mothers (Feinman & Lewis, 1983).

Thus data suggest that young infants can differentiate between social and nonsocial dimensions and that the social domain appears to be at least as salient for infants as the nonsocial domain. Many more examples of infant social competence exist but are not necessary to demonstrate in order to argue for the social nature of the human child. Given this feature of sociability, it is surprising to find that there are so few theories of social development. Perhaps one difficulty rests in our inability to conceptualize the types of models we need to construct and test in regard to social development. This lack of conceptual activity is in marked contrast to that found in cognitive–intellectual development that has been developed over the last 25 years.

The conceptual schemata for considering cognitive development may be useful for aiding us in our understanding and construction of models of social development. For the most part social development has not been conceptualized by such formal structures; however, it may be instructive to do so. For example, psychoanalytic theory, at least Freud's theory of psychosexual development (1959), can be considered as a stage or discontinuity theory as the areas of excitation are specific and change in a stagelike fashion. Moreover, in that these areas of excitation are biological in origin and nature (libidinal energy is a biological property), we could argue that the theory uses biological explanations of growth. On the other hand, for Freud the social development of the child is a result of biological pressures and *how* the parent or child negotiates them and as such is interactional in nature. Psychoanalytic theory also has an epigenetic flavor, since once the personality is formed, subsequent development is a function of the former structures. We will discuss such epigenetic models further, in particular the Bowlby (1969) and Ainsworth (1969, 1972) theory of attachment, as they relate to developmental models. In general, epigenetic models have as their central thesis the assumption that one set of social experiences is directly connected to the next, while such experiences may have little direct featural similarity. As such they are transformational in nature.

On the other hand, we will consider social network models. Such models lack a transformational feature and rest upon the central premise that social behavior is determined and controlled by social structure (e.g., Luria, 1976). As such, social network models are continuous or incremental in nature. Moreover, models of social development that are linked to a network view allow for the consideration of cultural, individual, and age differences as a function of the differences in social environments. In order to understand social development fully, attention must be given to sociobiological models (DeVore, 1971; Hamilton, 1964; Trivers, 1971; Wilson, 1975). Such models of development have as their central focus our biological nature and seek explanations for our social behavior in our biological dispositions. For the most part these theories are grounded in an evolutionary position, the control of behavior by genetic means and the acquisition of specific characteristics through selective pressures. Little thought has been given to the nature of growth, whether transformational or incremental; however, the source of that growth is to be found in the control of social behavior through genetic–biological factors.

Some of these theories will be taken up in greater detail below; our objective in featuring them now is to point up the need to utilize our existing models, found most often in cognitive development, to think about social development. Moreover, we should be prepared to consider that different aspects of social development may be explained best by different models. Before returning to specific models we will need to undertake several specific tasks. In particular, we need to address the nature and development of relationships, for we hold that central to understanding social development is the careful articulation of the issues surrounding our notion of relationships.

THE NATURE OF RELATIONSHIPS

Although relationships and their establishment, maintenance, and role in human life constitute one of the most important facets of social development, relatively little work has been directed to their study. In the following section we will pay specific attention to relationships, first by defining what we mean by the term, then by positing their general developmental course in the early part of life, and finally by attending to the taxonomy of possible relationships.

Definition of Relationships

The study of early social behavior has focused on interactions between the child and others, usually the mother. The study of interactions, mostly through molecular observational techniques, made available through audiovisual technology, has served as a substitute for the study of relationships. As we shall soon see, interactions, although of considerable interest and having a loose connection to relationships, especially for the developing infant, are not themselves relationships. While many studies have implied that social interactions and relationships are synonymous, due in part to the fact that interactions are relatively easy to measure while relationships are much more difficult to define and to measure, they are not synonomous.

Lewis (Lewis & Brooks-Gunn, 1979; Lewis & Weinraub, 1976; Weinraub, Brooks,

& Lewis, 1977) has tried to make the distinction between interactions and relationships. For us, interactions are specifiable behaviors or sets of behaviors that are observable and therefore measurable. Relationships are inferred from interactions but are difficult to specify and are not easily measurable. For example, the behavior between two people constitutes an interaction, and one might be able to specify the relationship from this interaction. Likewise, knowing a relationship might enable us to predict an interaction. Thus for example a female nursing a baby may indicate a mother–child relationship, or a mother–child relationship may dictate a particular interaction like nursing. However, as we can easily see, the inference of a relationship from an interaction or a set of interactions may be difficult. Likewise, specifying interactions given information about the relationship also is not obvious. Thus females other than the mother can nurse the child (wet nurses), and the mother–child relationship consists of complex and varied interactions including not only nursing and kissing but sometimes even hitting and spanking.

Lewis, Feiring, and Weinraub (1981) have argued that even though mother–child and father–child interactions are different there is no reason to assume that the parent–child relationships are also different. In fact, although one important difference between mother–child and father–child interactions is that they are predicated on different degrees of biological interactions, the relationships may be the same; for example, both may be equally viable attachment relationships.

While the father is undistinguished from other male adults, the mother of the child is biologically obvious—the mother's interactions with the infant clearly distinguish her from all other women. Her biological interaction with the child through pregnancy and childbirth and then nursing makes known to her, to all other individuals, and to the child that she is *mother*. Fathers present a different case. Knowing that a man is the father of a child tells us very little about that man's interactions with the child. This lack of a predictable, biological, predisposed interaction pattern for fathers not only differentiates the father–infant interaction from that of the mother–infant interaction but also makes the nature of the father–infant relationship more difficult to discern. The loose connection between relationships and interactions serves to alert us to the need to study relationships as well as interactions.

Recently, Hinde (1976, 1979) has undertaken such an analysis in an attempt to develop a system for characterizing relationships. For Hinde, there are eight dimensions that can be used to specify relationships:

1. Content or the component interactions include what we have elsewhere called function or goal structures (Lewis & Feiring, 1978, 1979; Lewis & Weinraub, 1976). Here we refer to types of interactions, such as nursing, grooming, play, and education.

2. The diversity of interactions and the structure of the different possible types are a second dimension. As we have indicated, relationships are manifested in various interactions, and it may be the diversity and patterning of these interactions that are critical for understanding relationships.

3. Reciprocity versus complimentarity refers to the status or power aspects of the interactions between people. In other words, interactions involve status dimensions.

4. Interactions also have quality dimensions or components, such as meshing of the dyadic members and turn taking. One in particular, the contingent nature of the interaction, has received much attention (see Coates & Lewis, 1984; Goldberg, 1977; Lewis & Coates, 1980; Lewis & Goldberg, 1969).

5. The relative frequency and patterning of interactions constitute a fifth dimension. Of specific importance for this aspect of relationships is the patterning of *sets* of interactions rather than the patterning of a simple interaction.

6. Multidimensional qualities is a general category used to consider a set of structural qualities of interactions as, for example, the length of a particular interaction and its short- and long-term duration.

7. Cognitive factors, the constructs of the mind, involve those mental processes that allow members of an interaction to think of the other member as well as of themselves. This aspect of interactions and relationships has received very little attention. Moreover, both the extent of the mental processes and the degree of social knowledge necessary to form relationships have been understudied.

8. Penetration, the last variable mentioned by Hinde, is the "extent to which the personality of each is penetrated by the other" (p. 15). It is what we might want to call intimacy.

While we have little quarrel with these aspects of relationships, we would hold that relationships, at least for humans, are based to no small degree on the seventh dimension, the cognitive factors. While specific behaviors influence and play a role in defining relationships, above all are the human abilities to feel, to think, to construct, and to give attribution. These are the qualities that allow us to "go beyond" the behavioral givens or interactions and allow us to form relationships. For example, even though a father may spend little time (low-level interaction) and have poor levels of exchange (poor interactions) with the child, it is possible to attribute the causes of these behaviors to such sources as hard work and/or ignorance and thereby maintain a positive relationship. Or in the extreme of death, one may be able to maintain a relationship *in the absence of behavior*. The cognitive element of relationships is understudied; in fact, it is rarely considered in social development in general and the attachment relationship literature in particular.

A second dimension that needs more thought is the level of penetration or the intimacy of the relationship. Within the developmental literature almost no attention has been given to different types of relationships, and in order to understand social development it is essential to construct a taxonomy of types. This is taken up next.

Types of Relationships

Only one type of relationship has been studied in early childhood in any detail, namely, the attachment relationship. Moreover, the consideration of attachment relationships has resulted in an implicit assumption that there are only two levels of intimacy, that of attached and that of not attached. Given this theoretical inadequacy, we should pause to consider a formulation of relationships possible in our social space. Lewis and Rosenblum (1975, 1979) have attempted to specify the various social objects that occupy the child's social geography. For them the social space of the child is made up of a potentially large number of social objects, including inanimate objects, such as security objects, plants, trees, and so on, and animate objects, including nonhumans, animals, and a wide range of people. Takahashi (1982, 1985, 1986) has studied young children's preferences for different social objects as a function of specific social activities. She finds that among young Japanese children mothers and even fathers are not preferred social objects for all social activities. In like fashion Edwards and Lewis (1979) Lecco and Lewis (1985) found that older children rather than adults are preferred for many social activities. Such findings, including the observation of young children's social networks, (Lewis, Feiring, & Kotsonis, 1984) indicate that a more careful exploration of the types of social relationships, even in young children, is necessary.

Let us consider this problem from a broader perspective in order to explore the range of possible relationships that may exist in human experience. While this analysis relies on an adult perspective, as we shall see, evidence that children may also experience these different types of relationships appears to exist, evidence that will help support the analysis. Figure 8.1 presents these types. We have created a two-dimensional space including sexuality and intimacy. While the space describes eight cells, such a model is meant to imply that (1) these are separate categories—in fact, we view both dimensions (sexual and intimacy) as space with no real boundaries—nor (2) that the space is not permutable, meaning that movement between categories in either direction is possible.

At least four types of relationships can be conceived of. Although we recognize that stranger relationships may be idiosyncratic in that there is relatively no intimacy to be found, there are so many behaviors and interactions related to strangers that it is included as a category. We have also included the dimension of sexuality not

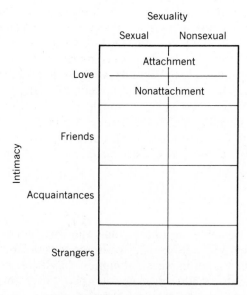

Figure 8.1. Types of relationships.

so much for its relevance for young children as to show that in any general theory such a dimension is necessary.

We all, during our lives, have *love* relationships, *friend* relationships, and *acquaintance* relationships, each with a set of rules governing our actions and goals and each associated with different feeling states. Even within these categories, however, relationships vary and are quite complex.

LOVE RELATIONSHIPS.   First consider love relationships that take place within the family as well as outside of it. Love relationships may be of two kinds: those that are attachment relationships, that is, those that provide a secure base, and those that need not, for it is not clear that a secure base is a necessary part of all love relationships. For example, parents love their children, but children do not necessarily offer a secure base for parents. Love relationships also are divided by sexuality. In some love relationships sexuality will play an important role, such as with a spouse, while in others, such as with mothers, fathers, and children, sexuality is absent. Thus within love relationships the dimensions of secure base (attachment) and sexuality form a complex structure for a variety of different love relationships, all of which exist in our experience. The four cells within love relationships created by an attachment and sexuality matrix might contain: mates as an example of attached and sexual; parents as an example of attached, nonsexual; boy- or girlfriend as nonattached and sexual; and parent *to* child as nonattached and nonsexual. Whether such a complex set of love relationships exists for all children is unknown. Although a role for sexuality during childhood has been suggested (Freud, 1959), it is difficult to study. However, children can and probably do have strong love relationships that both have and do not have an attachment dimension. For example, children love both their parents and their siblings, but they are probably attached to the former and not the latter, especially if the sibling is younger.

FRIENDSHIP RELATIONSHIPS.   Friendship relationships are different from love relationships, and although this may be difficult to describe, it is indicated by the language itself. Friendship relationships also vary along different dimensions and at times may merge with love relationships. Like love, friendship may or may not involve sexual behavior. Friendship relationships tend to vary with the age of the participants; thus they may involve same-age peers or they may exist between older and younger persons, such as between a teacher and student. Like love, friendship relations can be enduring and can exist even without extended interactions.

ACQUAINTANCE RELATIONSHIPS.   Aquaintance relationships are those relationships that tend to be the least enduring and the most specific to the particular interactions that bring them into existence. They usually occur as a consequence of particular and highly structured social exchanges such as with a storekeeper or bank clerk. These relationships vary along a dimension of familiarity, from those in which the members recognize one another, know each other's names, and exchange information (such as between employers and employees or between a shop owner and a customer) to those less familiar interactions with the ticket collector on a train or with people whom we greet casually in passing on the street.

Although people do not have relationships with *strangers,* our analysis requires that this category of nonrelationships be included, especially since so much attention has been paid to children's social interactions with strangers. Strangers are by our definition those people with whom we have no relationship and who are unfamiliar to us. Yet even in this category of nonrelationships there are variations that may be of some importance to our analysis. For example, strangers who possess particular characteristics may elicit different interactions than strangers without those characteristics. Thus strangers of the same sex or racial background as the child are likely to evoke different interactions than strangers of the opposite sex or of another racial background (Lewis, 1980).

In the study of the child's social development, the full array of possible relationships has not been explored or even considered. Attachment relationships, especially to the mother, have been investigated, and some studies of children's friendship patterns have been undertaken (Lewis & Rosenblum, 1975). Unfortunately, very few of these studies have looked at the growth of friendship. Studies of children's reactions to strangers have received attention (Lewis & Rosenblum, 1974a); however, these studies usually have been designed to elicit fear rather than to study children's social behavior with strangers. By removing the mother, leaving the child alone, and requiring strangers to act in an artificial and standardized way such as walking slowly and directly toward the child without talking or altering facial expression, most studies of children's behavior to strangers have been distorted. In fact, one of the most interesting findings in stranger research is the ease with which most young children make friends with a stranger!

For any complete study of social development, it is necessary to recognize that children do have relationships with people other than their parents and to trace the development of these relationships from the child's early social interactions. A complex array of relationships probably exists early in the life of the child, but without delineating the full range of these relationships, it is not possible to explore their development. We will show there is ample evidence that young children are able to establish all three types of major relationships: love (both attachment and nonattachment), friendship, and acquaintance. The developmental sequence and the interconnection between different relationships is an issue that will be addressed when we return to discuss the various models that exist for explaining social development. As we will see, the interconnection between relationships can be considered from an accretional as well as a transformational point of view. In the accretional case the study of the concurrent interconnection centers around the study of different social systems and how one relationship affects another. For example, one might be interested in the number of friends a child has and try to relate the number of friends to such family dimensions as birth order or family size. From a transformational perspective, the study of interconnections is more articulated. This perspective is primarily concerned with the effects of one set of relationships upon another set over time.

THE DEVELOPMENT OF RELATIONSHIPS

Before specifying the types of relationships and how each different type might develop, we need turn our attention to the more primary issue as to the development of relationships in general. That is, it seems reasonable to discuss the development of the child's ability to form relationships prior to specifying the type of relationship. We see this aspect of social development as analogous to cognitive development in that Piaget (1952), for one, has addressed the issue of object permanence development as occurring prior to (or at least concurrent with) the development of specific aspects of object schemata, for example, the development of object permanence as distinct from the development of features of objects such as color or shape. Thus we may discuss the development of *relationship* prior to the development of specific types of relationships.

How are relationships formed? One could attribute their formation to the biological nature of humankind; that is, members of the species possess the ability to form them, or the ability to form relationships may exist to begin with as some have suggested for the development of emotions (Izard, 1977). We would support an alternative view, namely, that relationships grow from a transformation of earlier social acts. This alternative model will be pursued, with the recognition that its formal test is still largely lacking. The transformational model that we will present suggests that interactions generate cognitive structures, which in turn give rise to relationships (see Figure 8.2).

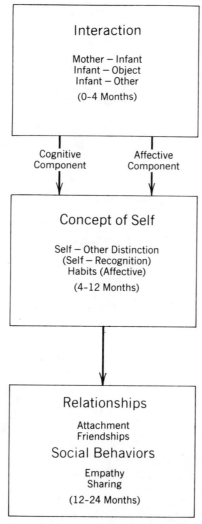

Figure 8.2. Transformational model of the development of relationships.

In the first months of life, the infant's world is occupied primarily by interactions with other people and with objects. In contrast, the adult caregiver experiences both a relationship with the infant and interactions with it. The exploration of this asymmetry between adult and child is necessary in order to understand the growth of the child's social relations from these early interactions.

Of major concern for this transformational model is how these early interactions become relationships for the young child. Elsewhere, Lewis (1982; Lewis & Brooks-Gunn, 1979a; Lewis, Brooks-Gunn, & Jaskir, 1985) has argued that early interactions are the material from which, in part, infants' elaborate cognitive structures derive. If we hold that relationships are predicated, in some measure, on social cognitive structures, then it follows that *interactions lead to relationships through the mediation of these cognitive structures.* Such a view of the child's social development, that relationships derive from interactions through mediating cognitive structures, is missing in research on the antecedents of the specific relationship of attachment (see Ainsworth, 1969; Bowlby, 1969). While early person–child interactions that have particular qualities such as harmony, responsivity, positive reactions to distress, and high stimulation levels, to mention only a few, and are believed to result in various types of attachment relationships (Ainsworth, Belhar, Waters, & Wall, 1978; Belsky, Rovine, & Taylor, 1984; see also Feiring & Lewis, in press), no consideration of the mechanism is given for the connection between interaction and relationship. Since we have argued that interactions and relationships do not and cannot have a one-to-one correspondence, it is necessary to specify the transformational pattern. One particular aspect of the proposed social cognitive structures needed for the development of relationships is the growth of the self (Lewis, 1985).

The formation of self-identity may be the crucial mediating social cognitive variable, since it permits consideration of both self and other. In particular, the development of self fosters more complex social cognitive (even affective) processes such as empathy and sharing. Empathy, the ability to place the self in the role of the other, is critical for the development of relationships (Hoffman, 1979; Youniss, 1980). Sharing is critical in terms of the distribution of actions and objects necessary for the maintenance of relationships. Thus the evolution of the self and therefore the capacity for empathy and sharing are the bases for the development of relationships. The development of self appears to be a consequence of the child's very early interactions and thus may be the mediating variable between interactions and relationships.

Growth of the Self

Before attending to this transformational course, let us attend to the growth of the self. The structure of the self has two components (Lewis & Brooks-Gunn, 1979). The first is the existential self; that is, the distinction of a self separate from other people and objects. To use a perceptual metaphor, it is the emergence of a figure-group relationship, the self being the figure, all else the ground. This self-other distinction occurs before the second component of the self becomes established. This process probably emerges around 8–9 months of age and manifests itself in self-permanence (seen in another form as object permanence). Self-permanence, like object permanence, constitutes one of the first conservation achievements of the child: the ability to maintain an identity independent of setting, persons, or interaction. This self-permanence allows for the development of the second aspect of the self, something we have called the categorical self. The categorical self is that aspect of self-identity that consists of the ways we think about ourselves. Such common and early categories appear to include gender, age, competence, and value (good or bad) but may include others. From the research literature, it is possible to articulate the development of the self schema.

The following is a list of the periods in the development of the self:

Period 1: 0–3 months. This period can be characterized chiefly by a biological determinism. There exist both simple and complex reflexes including responses to others that enhance interactions with the caregivers. Reflexive behavior, at first predominant, declines over this period as early schemata and learning begin to predominate (Lewis 1982; Lipsitt, 1980; Papoušek & Papoušek, 1981). Infants' differentiation among social objects and simple circular reactions can be seen. Through both social and object interactions, the beginnings of a self–other differentiation may make its appearance at the end of this period.

Period 2: 3–8 months. During this period, active learning takes precedence over a waning reflex system. Object interactions and social behavior are facilitated by development of more elaborate schemata. Complex action–outcome pairings occur along with means–ends relationships in both the social and object domains. Primary and secondary circular reactions are almost developed and, as the child learns of its effects on the world, agency and intention can be inferred to be developing. The distinction between self and other is consolidated but cannot be conserved over changes in the nature of the interaction, in terms of either people or objects. Reflected surfaces become of interest due to the contingency between the child's action and the action in the mirror (Dixon, 1957; Rheingold, 1971). While there is little evidence of self-recognition, children are able to adjust their body position in regard to visual changes in spatial cues, indicating elaborate visual–body schemata in spatial knowledge (Butterfield & Hicks, 1977; Lee & Aronson, 1974).

Period 3: 8–12 months. This period can be characterized by two important features. First, at about 8 months infants show general response inhibition when presented with new information or stimuli. Unlike the younger child, the 8-month-old does not respond immediately to the stimulus event; that is, the infant is no longer stimulus bound. This general inhibition allows the child to think about the stimulus before acting on it. It is most often observed in one of its manifestations, that of stranger wariness or fear (Schaeffer, 1974). This milestone of CNS inhibition of action allows for the rapid development of additional schema. One of the most critical schemata of this period is the establishment of self–other schemata differentiation. This differentiation, which was developing through the earlier period, results in the conservation of the self as distinct from the other across a variety of different situations. This conservation of self as subject represents the first important conservation task and is parallel to the child's growing understanding of object existence. Indeed, object permanence and self-permanence are viewed as part of the same process. At this point in time the self as unique and permanent in time and space emerges. Although feature recognition does not exist in any appreciable way, self-recognition can be demonstrated in contingent situations (Lewis & Brooks-Gunn, 1979a). The emergence of self as agent facilitates more complex means–ends relationships and with growing cognitive ability more elaborate plans can be observed.

Period 4: 12–18 months. The period from 12 to 18 months can be characterized as the self-conscious period. During this period the child's emerging sense of self results in a set of emotional states that can be characterized by self-awareness; that is, the child's response in front of mirrors is one of embarrassment if self-recognition is shown. Dixon (1975) calls this the coy stage and Lewis (Lewis & Brooks-Gunn, 1979a; Lewis, Weiss, & Sullivan, 1983) refers to this as the period of self-conscious emotions. Not only does embarrassment in front of the mirror become increasingly apparent, but fear of the loss of the mother also becomes intense. These appear to be additional markers in the self–other differentiation. During this period, self-recognition becomes less dependent on contigency and increasingly more dependent on feature analysis. The self as object becomes more evident in this feature recognition. Pointing behavior emerges, and self-recognition is evidenced through pointing to pictures of the self and through pointing to marks on the nose in reflecting surfaces.

Period 5: 18–30 months. After 18 months, simple language knowledge, the mapping of the lexicon on some features, emerges and allows children to demonstrate knowledge of features of social objects, including themselves. These include gender and age (Edwards & Lewis, 1979; Lewis & Feiring, 1978). Such knowledge supports the belief that the self as object emerges at this time possesses a number of attributes, including goodness or badness and efficacy along with age and gender. Although more empirical exploration is necessary, this mapping of the critical periods of self-development may be useful as an outline for the emergence of this cognitive capacity.

Lewis (1985; Lewis et al., 1985) has shown that the development of the self may have its beginnings in the child's earliest interactions. However, it is not until the infant has a sense of both self- and object permanence that we can speak of a developed self schema. Self-referential behavior demonstrated at 15–18 months, this point marks in self-development. While some self-knowledge may be acquired earlier, it is not until the child has a unique sense of self, independent of the nature of the interaction, that a self-concept can be utilized by the child in forming relationships.

The entire transformational process is schematized in Figure 8.2. In terms of the formation of self, observe that the interactions with objects and people are represented as the cause of the self-development. We have characterized this as taking place at 4–12 months (see listing of the periods in the development of the self, presented earlier). We would suggest that such interactions also lead to the formation of what we call *habits*. Habits are both cognitive and affective structures that derive from the child's associations of people with feeling states. This association is the consequence of interactions in social contexts. Being fed by one's mother is an example of such a habit. These habits are learned associations. Such a notion of habits, affective learned associations, shares a common theme with Cairns (1966). These affective learned associations support early social behavior, and when these associations are disturbed, for example, by the removal of the mother, the young organism becomes affectively unable to act since these associations are broken.

From the data on self-recognition, from the research on mother–infant interactions, and from the attachment literature we suggest that the first phase of the growth of relationships occurs in the first 3–4 months of life. The interactions of the infant with its world are affected by a set of causes still poorly understood. Several investigators, Lipsitt (1980) and Papoušek and Papoušek (1981), for example, have viewed these early interactions in terms of complex unlearned social reflexive behavior. Bower (1975) as well has argued that, rather than thinking of the newborn as possessing only a limited and simple set of initial schemata or structures, as suggested by Piaget (1952), it is necessary to view the child as possessing a set of complex innate reflexes or schemata, some of which seem to be interactive in nature. Early imitation (Meltzoff & Moore, 1977) may be one of these complex reflexes that serve to put the child in interaction with its social environment. Although the imitation phenomenon needs more study (see Hayes & Watson, 1981; Lewis, 1979a; Lewis & Sullivan, 1985), such types of reflexes may be present at birth or soon after and influence other social interactive behaviors.

Another possibility is that, although the child affects the adult's behavior, it is still the adult who controls the interactions (Kaye, 1982; Lewis & Rosenblum, 1974b). Thus the major source of the interactional flow comes not from the infant but from the adult. We know that adults attribute to infants a wide set of abilities, including feeling, thinking, and knowing, long before children are capable of these activities (see Lewis & Sullivan, 1985, and Waite & Lewis, 1979, regarding the influence of parental beliefs on infant imitation; see also Lewis & Michalson, 1983, and Pannabecker, Emde, Johnson, Stenberg, & Davis, 1980, on mothers' perceptions of infants' emotions). In these cases it is the parents' behavior and attribution that sustains the early interactions, and, as with the "clever Hans" phenomenon, the infants' interactions are almost totally controlled by the adults.

The causes of these early interactions are still unclear. The timing may be earlier, the cognitive ability of the newborn greater than previously thought. Even so, interactions occur, habits are formed, and the emergence of the self is observed. The structure of self, then, provides the mediation between interactions and relationships.

Once the infant has formed a rudimentary concept of self and established particular habits, the next stage in the transformation is the utilization of these skills to form relationships. As stated, the mediating cognitive structures necessary for relationships are: (1) a self-schema; and (2) from the self-schema the development of two social affective skills, empathy and sharing. Having discussed the emergence of the self-schema, let us attend next to the emergence of empathy and sharing. Empathy and sharing are receiving considerable attention (Hoffman, 1979; Zahn-Waxler, Radke-Yarrow, & King, 1979). One would agree that empathy (and sharing) is possible only through the recognition of the existence of two selves—oneself and another's self—each having a separate identity and a separate set of needs. Such an analysis requires that we understand both the development of a self-schema and the development of the understanding of the separate nature of selves. The process of growth by which children decenter, that is, begin to consider that all selves are not like oneself, has been dealt with by Piaget (1952), Flavell (1972), and others (cf. Damon, 1977). The timing of this decentering is still unclear. Piaget (1952), for one, did not see these processes as occurring much before 4–6 years, while others see this process as occurring at earlier ages, indeed, as young as 2 years (Borke, 1975; Flavell, 1972; Wellman, 1985). Whatever age we ultimately find as appropriate, it does seem that egocentric thought, that is the use of self to infer actions, thoughts, and feelings of others, and then decentered thought are *both* necessary for the formation and maintenance of empathy and sharing, the basis of relationships (Lewis, 1982).

In this regard our age timing for the movement from self to relationships is used to imply the initial formation of relationships. It is clear that after this initial formation the maturation of these mediating cognitive structures results in changes in the nature of relationships. Nevertheless, the initial appearance of these cognitive mediating variables as marked should be in the second year of life. Certainly by 2 years the child's use of *no* and the onset of the "terrible twos" should alert us to the existence of two selves (child and parent) and the beginning of relationships based on negotiation between them. These mediating cognitive structures must play a criterion role in social development, and no theory of social behavior will be complete without their study. The interested reader should therefore consider their serious study.

To reiterate, from an ontogenetic point of view, the mediating structure between interaction and relationships is the development of self. Even beyond its developmental role, the sense of self may play an important part in interactions and relationships. Relationships are based on both direct and indirect interactions but require a sense of self and an integration of a self with others as in empathy to give them meaning. This is particularly true when we think of the recursive nature of thought. Not only can I think about how I behave to you and how you behave to me, but I can think about how I think you think I behave toward you, and you to me. The complex recursive acts have been captured in Laing's *Knots* and have been discussed as particularly important in social cognition (Lewis, 1983).

EPIGENETIC MODEL OF DEVELOPMENT

The epigenetic model of social development is best characterized by attachment theory. Since this topic is well covered elsewhere, we will focus on some of the broad assumptions which underlie the theory. Although somewhat cultural, it is important to note that many of the features have strong social appeal and account, at least in part, for some of the research findings in social development.

Historical View

It could not have gone unnoticed that the mother, through her unique biological relationship, held a special role vis-à-vis her child. When, exactly, theories having to do with the importance of the child's mother were first developed is difficult to state. Certainly by the turn of the century psychoanalytic theory had described the importance and central role of the mother in the child's life (Freud, 1959). Indeed the most current theory of social development is an extension of that view as first expounded by Freud. Freud's particular epigenetic model was and remains quite specific in holding that: (1) the mother is the first and primary factor in the child's social life; and (2) all subsequent relationships are affected by this early and unique dyadic interaction. Thus if the mother–child relationship is a "good one" the child will have a good social development and conversely if the mother–child relationship is poor the child will subsequently have poor social relationships. As we shall see, this theory relies on three critical features: fixed sequence, determinism, and trait or structural quality.

Fixed Sequence

The epigenetic theory argues for a linear progression in which the infant first adapts to one person within the family network, usually the mother, and from this basic adaptation all subsequent social relationships follow. While some believed in the unique biological relation between mother and infant as the origin of subsequent social adaptation, Bowlby (1969) subscribes to a more general formulation that specifies that attachment is a natural consequence of the infant's early interactions with others and that multiple attachments are possible. Thus the model of adaptation that stressed the child first developed a relationship with the mother, then with father and siblings, and then with others (e.g., peers) is a somewhat modified view of the biological nature of attachment. Although a sequence still exists, it may not be linear. That is, the child's initial attachment relationship can be viewed as plural, with there being a number of others to whom the infant may form an attachment relationship. Even so, a fixed-sequence argument still holds in that all subsequent relationships, such as those with peers, will follow and be a consequence of the earlier attachment relationship(s).

Unfortunately, the number and nature of the other people to whom the infant may be attached have not been studied. Except for the child's mother and father, few other attachment objects have been considered. Moreover, no studies have observed the consequence of the possible attachment combinations to mother and father. This lack of consideration of multiple attachments and attachments only to mother must be the function of a western cultural bias since significant others within an extended family include older siblings, grandparents, uncles, aunts, and cousins. Cross-cultural traditions concerning uncles, aunts, and grandparents should alert us to the fact that, at least for some cultures, these people might also be included in a list of possible attachment objects (Whiting & Whiting, 1975). In some sense, then, the number and nature of attachment figures are dependent on the structure and values of any particular culture. While the infant cannot survive without at least one adult figure caring for it, the nature and number of others involved in the child's life seem to be a function of the values of the larger social network. This issue needs to be examined since it obviously affects the sequential nature of social relationships. It may be a somewhat different model with potentially different consequences to have maternal attachment from which all other relationships follow rather than a multiple-attachment system from which other relationships follow.

Determinism

Not only do the theories of Freud and Bowlby postulate a fixed sequence in the development of relationships but they also assume that later relationships are determined by early ones, particularly the mother–child relationship. This view is still widely held by others who see the mother–infant attachment as determining the child's later peer relationships (Arend, Gove, & Sroufe, 1979; Matas, Arend, & Sroufe, 1978) as well as all others (Main, 1985). While much has been made of the deterministic nature of early relationships on subsequent social relationships, the data are rather limited and the various alternative explanations unexplored. Harlow's (1969) demonstration that motherless monkeys themselves are at risk (1) for dysfunctional peer relationships (they have difficulty mating), and (2) for mothering (they make poor mothers who maltreat and even kill their young), is impressive evidence for the deterministic nature of early relationships. However, such a deterministic view has been challenged by a variety of other data, most of which pertain to the mother–child and child–child relationships.

As has been pointed out repeatedly, the effects of motherless monkeys as reported by Harlow and Harlow (1965) were due not to the lack of mother–child relationships but rather to the complete social isolation in which the monkeys were raised. Baby monkeys raised with other babies showed few of the effects originally reported (Harlow, 1969). This finding not only addresses the deterministic property of relationships but also demonstrates the multiple- as opposed to the fixed-path aspects of social development. Lewis, Young, Brooks, and Michalson (1975) in discussing peer development point out that, rather than being determined in a linear fashion, peer relationships possibly evolve in parallel to other relationships. This view of a multiple-affect system is also offered by Harlow and Harlow (1965) and finds support in a variety of other studies. Thus rather than viewing peer relationships as determined by the mother- or father–child attachment relationship, we can regard them as developing in tandem with the parent–child relationship. For example, a study by Cowen, Pedersen, Balijian, Izzo, and Trost (1973) suggests that there is a greater risk for adult dysfunctional social behavior in individuals with poor peer interaction in childhood. Harlow (1969) also looked at infant monkeys raised by mothers but without peer contact and another group raised with peers but without contact with the mother. Although there are some problems with the design (a mother and infant alone may have disturbed the mother's normal behavior), the general findings indicate that peer attachment in the absence of maternal attachment does not lead to subsequent peer dysfunction while the absence of peer attachment results in serious disturbances. Being reared by a mother alone may have negative consequences for human infants as well; peer experience may be important for peer relationships! These results taken *in toto* indicate that there is no reason to suppose that maternal attachment *per se* will determine successful peer relationships in the absence of peer experience. Moreover, the data seem to indicate that peer experiences (peers and therapists) can overcome poor parental relationships and can influence future peer behavior. For example, Suomi and Harlow (1972) and Novak and Harlow (1975) have shown that the effects of being reared in social isolation (which results in poor peer relationships) can be counteracted through the use of peer therapists, especially if they are younger peers.

Further evidence of the importance of peers can be found in the Furman, Rake, and Hartup study (1979), which located 24 socially withdrawn preschool children. One-third of the children were assigned to a socialization experience with another child who was 15 months younger, another one-third were assigned a child within 3 months of their age, while the remaining one-third received no treatment. Play sessions outside the regular school classroom constituted the intervention. The follow-up to this intervention revealed that social activity of the "younger" therapists' group increased the most, followed by the "same age" therapists' group, the "no treatment" group showing the least social activity. The authors report that the "younger" therapists' group appeared most similar to the general school population. While it is not known for certain, it can be assumed that the maternal attachment in these isolates was inadequate; nevertheless, successful peer experiences produced subsequent adequate peer interactions. This study and ones like it argue against a strict deterministic interconnection between relationships of the kind depicted by the epigenetic model. Hartup (1979) has concluded that peer interactions are central in childhood socialization and the growth of social competence, and the suspicion has grown that such competencies are direct derivations of early experiences in the peer culture.

A more direct approach to the issue of determinism would be to look at groups of children with inadequate attachment relationships to their mothers who at the same time have adequate peer relations. Such a study could offer direct support against or for the deterministic nature of one relationship upon another. Lewis and Schaeffer (1981) studied a group of abused and neglected children—children who have insecure attachment relations with their mothers—to see whether they would have good peer relations if they were placed in a day-care setting for 8 hrs a day and given peer experiences. In this study, two groups of infants aged 6–33 months were observed. Both groups were poor inner-city children and were similar in most respects except that one group had been placed in a day-care center by the state's youth and family services agency because they were maltreated. After 4 months in the day-care setting gross observation could not distinguish the abused children from the nonabused group. Their behavior toward peers, their free-play behavior, and their social interactions with caregivers indicated no obvious and discernible differences between these two groups of children. In order to obtain a more accurate measure of the infants' behavior, twelve 5-min observations of each child were obtained by an observer who did not know what group each child belonged to. These observations were randomly scheduled over 3 weeks, and the only requirement was that the child could not be asleep or feeding. Thus 1 hr of interactive playtime behavior was observed for each child, which indicated almost no difference between these groups. The results of this study, along with those of Furman et al. (1979), confirm the belief that poor infant maternal relationships do not have as a necessary consequence poor peer relationships.

Although evidence of the deterministic nature of one relationship upon another exists (Arend et al., 1979; Matas et al., 1978; Waters, Wippman, & Sroufe, 1979), the majority of the data leave this question open. This is not to imply that one relationship cannot exert an effect on another. Indeed, in our social systems model just such an effect is envisioned. The difference between the positions concerns the deterministic nature of the effect. This will be explored next.

Traits

The issue and controversy surrounding the nature of a trait, or an enduring aspect of personality, have dominated much contemporary thinking (Pervin, 1978). The issue is raised again when considering the effect of one relationship upon another and accounts for the major difference between the epigenetic and social network systems model.

In the epigenetic view the mother–infant or earliest attachment relationship endows the infant with a trait or characteristic that is located within the organism. This trait or its absence then determines subsequent relationships. While the nature of the trait has not been clarified, Sroufe (1979) and Block and Block (1979) have associated it with ego skills; however, it could be a trait such as self-esteem, self-efficacy, or some combination. Whatever its nature, it is the presence or absence of the trait that influences other relationships. An often-used metaphor is that the child is like an empty vessel that needs filling. Once filled, the child can move on to new relationships. If the child is not filled, movement will be inhibited or the new relationships will differ in their nature or degree than if the child is filled. The task of the earliest attachment relationship is to fill the vessel. Thus the explanation for the establishment of relationships rests with a mechanism that resides in the organism.

Also related to this trait issue is the notion of a critical period. Although it is seldom made explicit, it is assumed that the mother–infant relationship in the opening months of life is critical, and if this relationship is inadequate, then the subsequent attachment relationships will be affected, in turn, affecting all other relationships. Thus there is assumed to be a critical period with a beginning and an end after which experience has little effect. This we now know is not so. Attachment relationships do change as a function of the environment of the child (e.g., Thompson & Lamb, 1984).

The notion of a trait provides a mechanism for the deterministic nature of the epigenetic model. One relationship can affect another through the creation of a trait in the child. The child then brings this trait to bear in its next relationship. Moreover, this trait or its absence, based on the outcome of the first relationship, is not easily affected by experience. The question remains, then: How do the data hold up against such trait notions? Certainly from an experiential point of view, early relationships appear to exhibit a strong influence on later ones, and a personality trait appears to be a reasonable mechanism for linking these experiences.

There are now sufficient data that do not fit this model. Interestingly, the motherless monkey literature again provides important information. Recall that the poor mothering behavior of motherless monkeys is used as an example of the consequences of the lack of some trait associated with having good mothering experience. In other words, these monkeys, because of the lack of mothering, become poor mothers. What is not often attended to is the fact that, after their first children, these motherless monkeys appear to be quite normal in their mothering of their second children (Rupenthal, Arling, Harlow, Sackett, & Suomi, 1976; Suomi, 1978). The fact is that the more time a mother spends with the first child, even though she maltreats it, the better mother she appears to be with the second child.

A similar analysis can be applied to the data on peer behavior of maltreated or abused human infants (Lewis & Schaeffer, 1981). If maltreated or abused infants have poor attachment relationships with their mothers and if this leads to a deficiency in a trait, then one would expect this missing trait to result in poor peer relationships. That this effect is eliminated by giving the infants peer experience again suggests that the concept of a trait as the deterministic factor may be in error. Lewis and Schaeffer (1981) have suggested two other ways in which maternal attachment may be related to peer relationships: (1) peer availability; and (2) generalized fear.

PEER AVAILABILITY. Mothers who are inadequate in terms of mothering and who are unable to facilitate a secure attachment relationship may also prevent the infant from having peer experiences. Given that it is the mother who in our culture must facilitate early peer contact, her failure to do so will result in absence of contact and as a consequence the development of inadequate peer interaction skills. In this case, poor attachment and poor peer relationships are related, although the failure of the attachment relationship to the mother is not the cause of poor peer relationships; rather, the cause is a lack of experience with peers.

GENERALIZED FEAR.   Poor mothering resulting in a poor attachment relationship also may produce general fearfulness that has the effect of inhibiting contact with peers. It is this lack of contact, caused by fear, that affects peer relationships. This may explain why younger rather than same-age or older peer therapists are better able to help depressed children; the younger peers may be less frightening to the "patient" since their skills are less developed. Notice in both cases that it is not the absence of a trait caused by a poor interpersonal relationship with the mother that leads to poor subsequent relationships; the effect is more indirect and has to do with the interconnectedness of the social system.

In a study by Lieberman (1977) a secure attachment relationship and previous relationships led to good subsequent peer relationships. The data, however, left open the possibility that either kind of early relationship might have led to similar results. Unless we can separate out the effects of early peer contact from secure maternal attachment relationships, one cannot logically exclude either possibility. This also is true for those studies that show that secure maternal attachments lead to subsequent peer adjustment (Matas et al., 1978; Waters et al., 1979). The role of attachment on peer relationships is just one aspect of the proposition that attachment causes qualitative differences in developmental level or psychopathology that needs to be addressed. Such a review is to be found elsewhere (see Lamb, Thompson, Gardner, & Charnov, 1985). While a trait view might explain the data, there are three developmental models that can be used to explain this connection: (1) trait or child attributes; (2) environmental; and (3) interaction between both sets.

TRAIT.   The child attribute model is similar to a trait notion (Sameroff & Chandler, 1975). Applied to attachment, this model would posit that through early mother–child interaction the child acquires a certain attribute or predisposition to act in a particular way. Later performance is affected by the presence or absence of this attribute in the child. Thus for example a securely attached infant is competent at a later age due to the possession of a competence attribute or is incompetent due to its lack. The use of the term *attribute* does not imply a static or unchanging characteristic; it merely implies that some aspect of the child is affecting its behavior. Such an explanation is less than adequate when applied to attachment given that the attachment classification of an individual child appears stable only as long as the environment in which the child functions remains stable (Thompson & Lamb, 1983; Thompson, Lamb, & Estes, 1982; Vaughn, Egeland, Sroufe & Waters, 1979; Vaughn, Gove, & Egeland, 1980; Waters, 1978). Such findings suggest that environmental attributes must be considered and must play some role in developmental outcomes and psychopathology (Mischel, 1968).

ENVIRONMENTAL.   The second model explains the child's behavior in terms of environmental attributes. Here the early behavior of the child is dependent on the environment, and thus the attachment classification is seen as a manifestation of the environment. Changes in the environment will be reflected in changes in the child's behavior, or attachment classification. The competence of the child at a later point in time reflects a concomitant positive environment. The relationship between the child's early and later behavior is mediated not by the attributes of the child but by the fact that the environments at both points in time are related. Unlike a static trait, the behavior of the child exists only so long as the environment supports or maintains that behavior. The strong environmental (or situational) view is that secure attachment and later competence are no more than measures of a positive environment at two points in time (see Lewis & Feiring, in press).

INTERACTION. The third model proposes that both the attributes of the child and the nature of the environment are necessary to explain the child's behavior. Stability and change are a function of both factors. An infant who is securely attached (as a function of a positive environment in the first year) will show competence at a later age as a function of the early secure attachment as well as the nature of the environment at a later age. Not addressed is whether the attribute exists as an independent factor and interacts with the current environment, thereby producing a new set of behaviors; the former is favored by an interactional view (Lewis, 1972), while the latter is favored by a transactional view (Sameroff & Chandler, 1975). For example, does a securely attached child at t_1 show negative behavior at t_2 because (1) the secure attachment at t_1 has interacted with a negative environment at t_2 to produce negative behavior ($+\text{ATT} \times -\text{E} \rightarrow -\text{BEH}$), or (2) the secure attachment at t_1 has interacted with a negative environment at t_2 to produce an insecure attachment at t_2, and this insecure attachment produces negative behavior ($+\text{ATT} \times -\text{E} \rightarrow -\text{ATT} \rightarrow -\text{BEH}$)?

SOCIAL NETWORK MODEL OF DEVELOPMENT

Social Network Versus the Dyad

In the epigenetic model, it is argued that the earliest relationship with the mother is the single most important aspect for subsequent behavior. Here development is seen as a transformation of the earliest relationship into all other relationships. The mechanism underlying this transformation is the trait characteristic, a feature of the child or the interaction of child and mother, which provides the continuity from one time period to the next. In fact, it is this trait (in interaction with the new experience) that determines the social development outcome. Thus for example child with trait A, obtained from the interaction with the mother, now interacts with peers. Peer interpersonal behavior is a consequence of present peer experiences and past trait A.

The notion of a social network systems model is less transformational and argues instead that the causes of social behavior and development are to be found in the structure of the social system itself. In the social network systems model not only are the changes in growth accretional in nature, but the causes of growth are to be found chiefly in the social structure of the system the infant experiences; not only does such social behavior change in a less transformational fashion, but the sources of the change are to be found in the social structure—when the system is altered, behavior and relations change.

Perhaps an example of the interplay between an individual's or dyad's behavior and a social network will underscore the importance of these issues. Rosenblum and Kaufman (1968) studied both bonnet and pigtail macaque monkeys. Bonnet macaques cluster together in matriarchial groups so that a mother, her sisters, her adult daughters, and their babies might all be found huddled in close proximity. Pigtail macaques, on the other hand, are much more isolate. There are no groups, just the adult female and her baby. Thus in the former case the baby is in close proximity to a large number and varied set of others besides its mother, while in the latter case the baby and mother are alone. The bonnet baby interacts daily and forms relationships with mother, aunts, grandmother, and cousins while the pigtail baby only interacts and forms relationships with its mother, only later forming relationships with others.

When separated from its mother, the pigtail baby first shows marked distress, calling and moving about. This is followed by a state of deep depression. The bonnet baby shows a markedly different pattern. It too is distressed by the withdrawal of the mother; however, it soon recovers as it is "adopted" and cared for by familiar others. This demonstration by Rosenblum and Kaufman (1968) illuminates the effects of the social network. In a system where there is only the mother, her loss constitutes an enormously significant event, one from which the infant is not likely to recover. In Bowlby's (1951) epigenetic terms, the loss of the mother is a life-threatening event. In a system where there are other people, the loss of the mother, while perhaps significant, no longer becomes a life-threatening event, and in fact, given the proper care from others, appears to cause relatively little subsequent disruption. Similar findings have been reported by Robertson and Robertson (1971), Rutter (1979), and Tizard and Tizard (1971), among others, when human infants are studied.

Likewise, in a system where there is only the mother as caregiver, the child's first (and only) relationship will be with her. Other relationships must be sequential (after this first one) and, in part, dependent on this first one. This sequential, deterministic feature (the hallmark of the epigenetic view) does not have to be a biological necessity for the species as some have argued. Rather it is a feature of the social structure. There is little support for the notion that such a structure of mother as sole caregiver is necessary or indeed historically, culturally, or evolutionarily correct. For example, some cultures promote the use of multiple caregiving in the form of both mother and older female sibling or friend (Whiting & Whiting, 1975). Others support day-care settings with multiple adults and children, while others support the mother alone–infant relationships. Work from a variety of sources indicates that mothers are not the only people who interact with these infants; others include fathers (Lamb, 1978), siblings (Dunn & Kendrick, 1979), friends and peers (Lewis & Rosenblum, 1975), and other adults (Landau, 1976). For example, Konner (1975) has shown the evolutionary importance of peers and friends while Landau (1976) has shown in some cultures that only 45 percent of the play activity directed to the infant is by the mother. A social network systems approach appears as an important alternative to the epigenetic view as expressed in the attachment literature.

Socialization theories in the past have stressed the role, at least in early childhood, of the mother. Only recently has there been much work on the role of fathers (Lamb, 1976) and sibling research is understudied during the infancy–early childhood period (Cicirelli, 1975; Dunn & Kendrick, 1979). Although a growing number of studies bear witness to the recognition that other social objects play an important role in the early development of children, there are relatively few theoretical perspectives that can be used to anchor any empirical findings. Bronfenbrenner (1977) and Lewis (Lewis, 1982, 1983; Lewis & Feiring, 1978, 1979; Lewis et al., 1981; Weinraub et al., 1977) have begun to lay out a more theoretical perspective. In each of these views, the child's place in the social network, rather than in a specific dyadic relationship, becomes the primary focus. Lewis (1982), in describing the social network of young children, has suggested that the role of any single relationship cannot be fully appreciated without placing that dyad into the larger framework of the child's life. In particular, when discussing the role of the father, it becomes obvious that part of the father's role is his indirect influence (Lewis & Feiring, 1981).

By refocusing interest on the social system and on the complex nature of this system, two important features of current research interest are addressed. The first is the extension of our concern for the mother–infant relationship as the singularly important dyad to considering other relationships. In particular, research on relationships with fathers, siblings, and peers has now begun in earnest but should be extended to other family members such as grandparents, uncles, and aunts—important people for some children—and teachers and adult friends such as day-care center teachers, baby-sitters, parents' friends, and others. Such an extension will provide information on the entire array of people that inhabit the child's life and that play an important role in socialization. While awareness grows for the study of relationships other than that of mother–child, the emphasis in psychological studies has been for the most part on examining other dyadic relationships, that is, sibling–child (Dunn & Kendrick, 1979) or father–child dyads (Lamb, 1976; Lewis & Weinraub, 1976; Lynn, 1974; Parke, 1979; Pedersen, 1976). Although information on such dyads is important, such a perspective still restricts our conceptualization to dyads and avoids the need to focus on a systems approach.

Biological and Educational Models of the Dyad

Outside of the psychological literature, viewing socialization in terms of multiple caregivers is not new; various sociologists and psychotherapists have applied family or systems models for the last two or three decades (e.g., Aldous, 1978; Bowen, 1972; Hill, 1973; Minuchin, 1974; Parsons & Bales, 1955; Slater, 1974). The failure to utilize this information is due in part to our overemphasis on the role of the dyad, in particular the mother–child dyad. As Lewis (1984) has tried to point out, our emphasis on this unit derives not only from the strong psychoanalytic influence, but from biological models of symbiosis that also stress that the basic social unit is that of the mother–child dyad. Moreover, our educational models reflect this bias: The basic unit is the teacher–student dyad.

In the biological model, the emphasis on the parent–child interaction, in particular the mother–child dyad, is predicated on the belief that this dyad constitutes a biological unit endowed with and possessing unique characteristics that are essential both for survival and for development. The dyad is conceived of as symbiotic (Rosenblum & Moltz, 1983), as a biological imperative having evolutionary significance. It is often perceived as the critical factor in the young organism's development. Animal models, using nonhuman primates or other mammals, demonstrate the importance of the mother–child dyad and of the mother as the single most critical unit in the child's development. Adult males are shown to be either absent or uninterested in the young's development. Data from such studies are impressive in demonstrating the importance of a single adult female's role in her offspring's development and the singularly unimportant role of the biological father. Nevertheless, such models and data often lose sight of the fact that the offspring's development, even though influenced by a mother only, takes place in an environment in which there are large numbers of diverse conspecifics, including younger and older siblings, aunts, adult female and male strangers, and adult males and peers. In the last decade, the importance of other social figures in the child's life has been addressed (Lewis & Feiring, 1978), and although some might still argue for the primary importance of the mother, none would argue that others do not play some role in the child's development.

The teacher–pupil relationship also represents an important dyadic model. This model, focusing on information exchange, holds that the fundamental process through which information is disseminated is a dyadic one, defined as two people: a teacher and a learner. The model of the parent–child dyad, in particular the mother–child, owes much to the teacher–pupil model. The teacher–pupil model of learning focuses on interactions between two members. In the teacher–pupil dyad, it is the adult member for the most part who is believed to educate the pupil. Thus the effects of learning, or, in broader terms, the effects of socialization, occur (1) within the dyadic interaction and (2) as a direct consequence of what the adult member does to the child. The influences of the interaction are the influences of direct information and didactic techniques. These in turn cause the younger member to change, or, in the specific teacher–pupil sense, to learn. Such models of learning, when translated into general dyadic models, clearly emphasize the didactic notion of change. In this view, one member directly influences the other member, and in the most prominent model, the older member influences the younger member. Indeed, the children's learning experience *vis-à-vis* its social environment is often likened to that of teacher and pupil, and in studies of information exchange between parent and child, the teacher model is used. The dimensions thought important in the education of children vis-à-vis school are extended to the home and the family in observing mother–child learning situations (Bee, Van Egeren, Streissguth, Nyman, & Leckie, 1969; Hess & Shipman, 1965). Moreover, both reflect at least in part the unidirectional feature, in which the teacher influences the pupil. Although recognizing that the dyad may be more interactive and multidirectional (Lewis & Rosenblum, 1974b), such models nevertheless suggest that the primary mode of socialization is a dyadic one.

The teacher–pupil dyad model suffers from some of the same problems that are found in the mother–child dyad model. Let us explore some of the common difficulties. To begin with, the dyadic learning model neglects the fact that even in the teaching situation the teacher–pupil interaction occurs in the company of others: other students and at times even other adults. To think of the teacher–pupil dyad as the only significant source of information and therefore of learning is to negate the role of peers (either older or same-age peers) in the learning process. The classroom in which the teacher–pupil dyad is located is also filled with a multitude of dyads, including the teacher–pupil dyads as well as the pupils' interactions with each other.

A second problem occurs when we focus on the processes involved in either change or learning. Both dyadic models (or didactic effects) tend to focus on direct effects as the process inducing change. Although pupils learn directly from what they are given to read or from what their teachers say, there are other important forms of learning that are not didactic in nature. The existence of alternative forms of learning argues against dyadic interactions as the sole or even the predominant model of growth. Observational learning and imitation are examples of such forms of learning, which are not dyadic nor didactic. The process of imitation allows us the opportunity to explore the nondyadic processes that allow children to imitate anyone they choose, be they individuals in positions of power or people who act and/or achieve in a fashion that the imitators wish to emulate. The process of observational learning likewise allows children to learn from anyone, not just the person directly interacting with them. These alternative forms of learning are particularly important in that observing them allows us to consider units larger than two people and therefore allows for the consideration of interactions beyond the dyad.

Language acquisition is a good example of how learning can take place by more than one method. The example of language acquisition can serve as a starting point for this exploration. Most learning theories related to the development of language suggest that the mother–child dyad is chiefly responsible for the child's language acquisition (Lewis & Rosenblum, 1977). Although these theories differ considerably in detail, the major model remains that of the mother's speaking to the child as it affects the child's language ability. However, if we embed the mother–child dyad within a family consisting of a father and an older sibling, the influence of the mother talking to the child becomes only one alternative. In the family unit, there are at least two possible influences on the child's language acquisition: Already discussed is the significance of the mother's speech (or any other person's speech) on the child. In every case, no matter who comprises the dyad, it is the speech of the older member of the dyad to the younger member that is held responsible for development. The second influence, one that is rarely considered, is the impact of other dyads, which do not include the child directly, on the child's language acquisition. In a mother, father, and child interaction, besides two dyads that directly include the child (M$\longleftrightarrow$C; F$\longleftrightarrow$C), there are other dyads that do not include the child: the mother–father dyad, and the parent–older sibling dyad. Research on indirect effects suggests that the language interaction between the mother and the father may influence the child's language acquisition (Lewis & Feiring, 1981). The parental language interaction may affect each parent's direct interaction with the child. For example, if the parents have an argument, they may be less disposed to talk with the child. Thus parental language interaction has two types of indirect effects on the infant. Exactly how the language interaction of the mother–father dyad or the parent–older sibling dyad affects the child is little understood. Nevertheless, these interactions may have significant effects because a young child often witnesses its family members engaging in interactions with each other. Without going into an analysis beyond the dyad it is impossible to study these effects.

Social Proposition of a Social Network Theory

A variety of studies force us to recognize the epigenetic point of view. In fact, they lead to a consideration of a social network systems model. In order to present this model, it is necessary to make explicit the set of propositions which underlie this theory. Some of these propositions have been presented previously but are important enough to the discussion to be presented again.

Proposition 1: Man is by nature a social animal and from birth enters into a social network.

This statement is meant to imply that the human need for social interaction is a biological imperative and is as basic an attribute as the need for air. Moreover, the child is preprogrammed (possesses several reflexes like smiling or imitation) to respond to social stimuli and to elicit responses from others.

Proposition 2: The social network is made up of a variety of social objects, including at least female and male adult caregivers, siblings, other relatives and friends.

This proposition is self-explanatory. It is included merely to emphasize the need to consider social objects other than the mother.

Proposition 3: The social network is made up of social objects, functions, and situations.

The definition of *social object* is difficult. It may be the case that not only persons are responded to as social objects. Certainly many adults (and cultures—e.g., the English) consider animals as possessing those attributes commonly considered human. Children do the same. Even nonanimals such as plants are given human attributes by some adults. What the infant considers "human" is an even more difficult question. Nevertheless, we shall hold to the simple view that the term *social object* refers to a human being, understanding that this is an incomplete definition, since what constitutes a social object may vary both ontogenetically, culturally and historically.

Functions and situations are still harder to define. While some attempts have been made to create a taxonomy of objects—for example, nonliving, animal or vegetable, and so on—there has been little attempt at a taxonomy of functions and situations. Functions include feeding, bathing, changing, and playing. Situations can usually be defined by physical locations—the feeding table, the bathroom, the playground—although feeling states can also be considered, for example, an anxious situation (see Pervin, 1975).

Proposition 4: Social objects, functions, and situations are only partially related.

Social objects refer to people while social functions are those activities that take place within a social network. Situations refer to the context of a social network and as such have a relationship to function. For example, feeding behavior, a social function, takes place under specific situations, although Lewis and Freedle (1973) report that it takes the first year before parents join physical locations (room in the house) with specific functions. While feeding and bathing functions and situations have relatively little variance, we could find functions and situations that are markedly variable. Social objects and social functions are often related. For example, mothering (a function) and mother (an object) are in many cases highly related. We merely wish to point out that the relationships between social object, social function, and social situation may be variable.

Proposition 5: The social network is embedded in and varies as a function of a larger social environment.

Any individual social network must be embedded in both an historical and cultural context and is not invariant with respect to these dimensions.

Proposition 6: The child from birth on is an active participant in the social network.

The child at birth enters into an interactive relationship within the social network. Within this interactive relationship the child's behavior is both initiating and responsive. Moreover, the child's primary mode is active rather than passive in constructing and responding to the network.

Proposition 7: The child's social behavior and the composition of the social network change as a function of developmental status.

Experience and maturation as well as ontogenetic status affect the social network, both to change its composition (objects) and to influence its functions and situations.

Proposition 8: The child has a repertoire of behaviors that are distributed within the social network as befits the objects, function, and situation of the specific interaction. Specific behaviors or subsets of behavior are not restricted to certain social objects but are distributed as a function of the interaction of social objects, functions, and situations.

There are two corollaries to this proposition:

   8a: Within an individual child's social network, certain objects tend to fill certain functions in certain situations.
   8b: When more than one object fulfills the same function, tension is introduced into the system.

Proposition 9: The child acquires knowledge through direct and indirect interaction with the social network.

The child's knowledge is acquired from its social experiences, although the nature and the manner of acquisition of this knowledge are not currently understood. Direct interaction always involves the child as one of the participants in each interaction and occurs when all of the participants are present. It is also possible for the child to be influenced by and to learn from interactions among members of the network when the members themselves are not present. The effects of such interactions might be said to be indirect. The notion of indirect effects has particular importance in any discussion of the role of the father since, in our culture at least, the father is usually not the child's primary caregiver and is often absent during the day.

Proposition 10: Social behavior requires cognition.

In order to understand social behavior we must understand what cognitive processes are necessary for social behavior to occur. This makes no statement regarding the primacy of either social or cognitive behavior.

There is a corollary to this proposition:

10a: *Relationships are a construction of social organisms and as such require cognitive processes; the most important cognitive process, at least in the first two years is the development of the self schema.*

Relationships are not interactions although they may be derived from them. Relationships are cognitive constructions. Thus, they require a self and an understanding of the self in commerce with another self. Thus as a minimum relationships require a referential self.

SYSTEMS THEORY

An alternative view to an epigenetic theory is to consider social systems, and it is toward such a task that we now turn. We will first discuss five characteristics of systems and apply them specifically to social systems. Then we will go on to a discussion of social network theory.

Systems in general and social systems in particular can be characterized by a number of features. In the discussion of the social network system, five features will be considered (1) systems have elements; (2) elements are related; (3) elements are nonadditive; (4) elements operate under a steady-state principle such that they have the ability to change and yet maintain the system; and (5) systems are goal oriented. Social systems at any level—either of the culture or of a family—can be characterized by these features.

Elements

Systems are composed of sets of elements (Monane, 1967; Von Bertalanffy, 1967). Within the family an element represents each individual member—mother, father, child—or it can represent dyads—mother–father, mother–child, father–child—or even triads when there are other children in the family. When one is considering units larger than the family, families themselves can become the elements of the system. There is no constraint on the number of elements or even the stability of the elements themselves. Thus within the family elements can be both individuals and dyads. In a family of four (two children) there are a total of four simple elements, six dyads, and four triads or a total of 14 possible elements. The potential array of different social elements that infants experience, which can influence them and be influenced by them, is large. Unfortunately, there are almost no data on the number of different social contacts and their frequency and intensity as a function of the child's age. In one study of infant friendships, Lewis and colleagues (1975) found that infants had little opportunity to engage in peer contact. Only 20 percent of the mothers (mostly middle- to upper-middle-class northeasterners) surveyed provided their 1-year-old infants with consistent peer exposure. Peer contact, however, can be quite variable; for children in infant day-care programs there is a great deal of peer contact. Peer contact may vary as a function of social class as well as the age of the child. At least for black ghetto children in the inner cities, peer contact is made early and is a chief social contact of even young children (Brown, 1971). Unfortunately, there are no large sets of data concerning the peer contact of infants.

This scarcity of data also applies to other potentially important figures. For example, there are no data as to the number of grandparent or aunt or uncle experiences nor any real count of sibling contacts. Information regarding these relationships is also missing. Clearly, the number of others the child interacts with needs study, especially in light of changing child-rearing practices. Lewis, Feiring, and Kotsonis (1984) collected data on the social networks of over 117 children 3 years old (see Table 8.1). These children live in the area of Princeton and Trenton, New Jersey, and are all from mother- and father-intact homes. Demographically, they represent SES levels I–IV (Hollingshead, 1957) and are equally divided into first, second, third, and fourth birth orders. Each of the terms in Table 8.1 designates frequency of contact (e.g., weekly, monthly, etc.). The children in our sample have approximately 5.8 friends (with a range from 2 to 12). In addition to mother, father, and siblings, the children come in contact with an average of 9.6 relatives (ranging from 4 to 26 relatives) including grandparents, aunts, uncles, and cousins. Mothers report that the children in our sample come in contact with almost all of the people the mother would include as important in her social network, including her friends. The number of adults other than family that the child makes contact with is 7.1. On the average 3.2, 4.4, and 4.4 relatives, friends, and adults other than parents are seen at least once a week.

More work is necessary for us to determine the nature of the social network and the relationships that exist within this network. Moreover, it must be recognized that for some infants the only significant relationship may be between the mother and infant while for others it may include fathers, caregivers (as in day care), siblings, peers, and relatives such as grandparents. Having considered multiple significant relationships, it is now possible to ask which ones exist, how they differ, and what their potential consequences are. While there are relatively few data on infants' relationships with people other than their mothers, some data do exist and will be briefly reviewed.

People in the Child's Network

Mothers are the primary focus in attachment theory, but children form important relationships and attachments with individuals besides their mothers. In this section we introduce other figures such as fathers, siblings, grandparents, and peers. The role of mothers in young children's lives need not be discussed in detail. Mothers are the primary caretakers, even today when many fathers take an active role in child rearing and many mothers hold jobs outside the home. It is the mother who buys clothes for the child, arranges for child care (whether it be hiring a baby-sitter or taking the child to a child-care center), makes medical appointments, and takes the child to the pediatrician's office. Further, even when the child is under someone else's care, the person who normally takes the mother's role is *usually someone else's mother.*

TABLE 8.1. Different Types of People in 3-Year-Olds' Social Networks: Mean Number of People Contacted Daily Through Yearly for the Total Sample (*n* = 117)

	Mean Number of People	Number Seen Daily	Number Seen Weekly	Number Seen Monthly	Number Seen 6-Monthly	Number Seen Yearly
Mother's parents and grandparents	1.77	0.19	0.86	0.53	0.16	0.03
Father's parents and grandparents	1.57	0.08	0.58	0.63	0.21	0.07
Mother's siblings	1.46	0.08	0.50	0.44	0.33	0.11
Other aunts/uncles of child	1.83	0.03	0.41	0.72	0.50	0.17
Cousins of child	1.47	0.0	0.31	0.56	0.51	0.09
Other relatives	1.24	0.03	0.20	0.59	0.27	0.15
Adults known by child	6.04	1.15	2.50	1.61	0.67	0.12
Adult school personnel/teachers	0.68	0.30	0.38	—	—	—
Baby-sitters	0.32	0.03	0.19	0.10	—	—
Male friends (peer)	2.97	0.81	1.57	0.40	0.15	0.03
Female friends (peer)	2.81	0.78	1.33	0.52	0.15	0.03
Nuclear family (parents and siblings)	3.47	3.47	0.0	0.0	0.0	0.0

Fathers

Ten years ago, a visitor from Mars reading the developmental literature would hardly know that American babies usually had fathers living in the same household. The research literature, although still dominated by studies of mother–child, has brought into focus some of the roles fathers play in children's lives. Four questions have been directed toward the father–child relationship. Each of these will be discussed, albeit briefly.

(1) Can fathers do what mothers do? One important question raised about fathers is whether there is any biological difference between mother and father care for the very young. Perhaps mothers take care of infants better than fathers? Parke and O'Leary (1975), in their work with fathers and newborn infants, demonstrate that fathers' care, that is, the interaction patterns between fathers and children, is similar to mothers' care. Thus one would say that fathers can care for their very young infants. While fathers can care, it is apparent that, in general, they do not, especially in the case of the young infant, under 9 months or so. Their daily contact remains low. In spite of the social milieu that makes contact acceptable, the sex-role-appropriate male behavior does not include the care of the very young. Feiring and Lewis (1984) demonstrate that even the increased multiple roles assumed by the mother (mother, worker-out-of-the-home, wife) have not led to an increased involvement of fathers. Without question, the care of infants and very young children remains the domain of women. Thus the shift of child care from mothers to other women demonstrates that there exists strong resistance within the culture for altering traditional male roles. Although they can care for infants as well as mothers can, fathers do not do so readily.

(2) What do fathers do that is different from mothers? While fathers have been shown to be equally capable of caring for young children, there are differences in their interaction patterns that distinguish them from mothers. While maternal interactions are likely to center around child-care activities such as feeding, changing diapers and clothes, bathing, and other caregiving and maternal activities, father's interactions are more likely to include physical playful activities. A number of studies have shown fathers to engage in more rough and tumble, bouncing and tickling activities than their mothers (Lamb, 1976; Lewis & Weinraub, 1976; Parke & Sawin, 1980; Patterson, 1979; Pederson et. al., 1979a,b). While mothers play with their young children, their play is likely to be less active and arousing than that of fathers. Moreover, as the children become older, the father's role is likely to increase, mostly as a function of the declining need for caregiving activities and the increasing needs for exploration, play, and self-initiated action or efficacy vis-à-vis the physical environment (Lewis & Weinraub, 1976). Recently, Mackey (1985) has shown that across many cultures fathers' interactions with young children in public places (zoos, museums, public streets) are quite different than those that can be seen in the home. Although not sufficiently studied, fathers' involvement with their children is probably considerably greater in public than at home while mothers' involvement may be the reverse. This change in roles by situations, with mothers dominating in the home, may be responsible for our rather limited view of fathers' interaction patterns. By studying children in their homes, we may have inadvertently reduced the paternal role.

(3) What are the direct versus the indirect effects of the father? In exploring the role of fathers and mothers, most studies have observed the interactional patterns

of family members. Such patterns, which directly involve the child, we have called fathers' direct effects (Lewis & Feiring, 1982). Of these, we have already mentioned that play and exploration are the major factors. It is also interesting to note that fathers, more than mothers, were influenced by the sex and birth order of their children. In studying families at dinner, Lewis and Feiring (1981) found that the father talked more to first- than later-born and more to male than female children at the table. This is consistent with Aldous (1975), Black (1973), and Margolin and Patterson (1975) data. Fathers also extend their influence on their children in an indirect fashion. That is, they affect their children's lives indirectly by affecting the lives of their wives (Lewis, Feiring, & Weinraub, 1983). These indirect effects include emotional support of the mother. The interdependent nature of the child–parent and parent–parent subsystems has been amply demonstrated. A woman's successful adaptation to pregnancy is associated with the husband's support (Shereshefsky & Yarrow, 1973). Pedersen (1976) has demonstrated how the husband–wife relationship affects the child. Support can include other factors than emotional support. Lynn (1974) reports several studies in which mothers without husbands on a regular or temporary basis describe the difficulties they experience. Hoffman (1971) suggests that women without husbands feel busier, more harassed, and more oriented to immediate goals. This behavior could adversely affect the child.

(4) Are the children attached to their fathers? Surprisingly, the question of whether children are attached to their fathers is rarely asked. Perhaps because theory is oriented toward attachment to the mother, it took many years even to ask the question. The answer is: Of course children are attached to their fathers (Thompson & Lamb, 1984). Ban and Lewis (1974) and Lewis and Weinraub (1974) looked at children's behavior toward their mothers and fathers and found that children directed equal social behavior to each, the only difference being that fathers received somewhat more distal behavior. Lewis and Weinraub also found that over the first 2 years of life proximal behavior toward mothers decreased significantly while no such decrease occurred for fathers. Moreover, fathers received somewhat more distal behavior. These findings, along with those on attachment, should put the question to rest. Still open to consideration is whether there are overall differences in the percentage of security- versus insecurity-attached children vis-à-vis their fathers. Also of interest is the problem of whether secure attachment to one parent disposes the children to a secure attachment with the other. Finally, differences in children and in their developmental outcomes need to be explored for those who are securely attached to one or the other parent, to both, or to neither.

Siblings

Thinking about western myths pertaining to siblings, we come first to the story of Cain and Abel. This story is a prototype of the negative relationship, with competition, rivalry, and even hate between siblings as the prevailing moods. Indeed there are many of these negative attributes associated with siblings. However, there are also many positive features, which tend to be downplayed. At a recent state meeting of school teachers (70 percent female, 30 percent male) the audience was asked how many spoke to one or more of their siblings at least once a week. Fifty-seven percent raised their hands! Such findings force us to conclude that, while both negative and positive aspects are to be found in sibling relationships, siblings play an important, focused, and long-term role in the lives of many.

Very early in a child's life, a sibling can affect the child's behavior (Abramovitch, Corter, & Lando, 1979; Dunn, Kendrick, & MacNamee, 1981) and the child's relationship with and view of the family (Cairns, Clark, Smith, & Lansky, 1979; Dunn & Kendrick, 1980; Kagan, 1956; Koch, 1960). Even the child's view of itself is affected by siblings (Greenbaum, 1965; Tesser, 1980; Yamamoto, 1972). Siblings play a variety of roles vis-à-vis one another, some of which have received some attention in the literature while others have yet to be explored. Siblings protect and help one another. Many mothers note that when they are punishing one of their children the other will protect that child even if the punishment concerns a sibling conflict. Caplow (1968) found that siblings help each other if their mother cannot help. Bryant (1982) found that younger siblings depend on older siblings for help with homework or when they need an ally. Helping with homework is only one way siblings teach one another. Such helping is an example of direct teaching; however, siblings also influence each other through modeling one another's behavior. Dunn and Kendrick (1979, 1982) studied sibling behavior in regard to communication, social interactions, and teachings and found even young siblings (14 months of age and younger) capable of turn taking as well as empathic and teaching behaviors. Siblings provide important social models for each other. Children learn how to share, cooperate, help, and emphathize by watching their siblings. Siblings spend their early lives sharing a variety of objects, experiences, and people. Thus siblings share not only the same parents and grandparents and roughly the same genetic heritage but also possessions (toys, books, clothes, pets), space (sleep in the same room, use the same bathroom, live in the same space), people (mutual playmates, baby-sitters, teachers, doctors, etc.), and even the same life histories (go to the same camps, vacation together, experience disasters together, etc.). They often serve as playmates to one another and when they have friends often involve their siblings with their friends.

Moreover, and most important, siblings seem to form important and long-lasting attachments with each other, although it appears that younger siblings are more often attached to older siblings than the reverse. In a recent survey we asked over 60 adults with siblings which sibling was more likely to call the other. More than 80 percent reported that the younger is more likely to initiate the call to the older, 10 percent said the older, and 10 percent said there was no difference. Infants appear upset by the loss of siblings, or even when the siblings stay away from home overnight or for weekends. Siblings show strong affective bonds, and these relationships show continuity over time (Dunn & Kendrick, 1979; Pepler, Abramovitch, & Corter, 1981; Stillwell & Dunn, 1985). The attachment of siblings to one another has received some attention. Lamb (1978) showed that, while older siblings (20–40 months older) show little attachment to younger siblings, younger siblings showed "inordinate" interest in and were influenced by the older sibling. This earlier attachment, at least by the younger toward the older sibling, persists through time. In a 3-year follow-up study of siblings, the older siblings' verbal descriptions were remarkably related to the kind of behavior they had shown toward their younger siblings (Stillwell, 1984). Such findings of sibling attachment appear in the western child where the sibling role is somewhat different than that in other cultures. Whiting and Whiting (1975) have shown that in some cultures the older sibling may be one of the principal caretakers of the child. One would expect that in such cultures the attachment relationship between siblings would be even stronger. The degree to which siblings become attached to each other should be a function of the values of the family, the cultural expectations, sex, age, and spacing of siblings and more. Even so, many siblings show a strong attachment toward one another that lasts a lifetime. Cicirelli (1982), for example, has found that siblings, especially sisters, are very likely to live together in their old age.

Given these positive features, it is curious to note the negative view assigned to sibling relationships. In part, this may be due to an adult–parent perspective in which sibling rivalry is seen as a predominant factor, neglecting the positive features. Moreover, negative sibling behavior is likely to display itself under (or even be provoked by) the attention and focus of the parents; that is, siblings may be more likely to fight and quarrel in the company of their parents than when alone. In any event, it is clear that sibling aggression, competition, and rivalry do exist. Certainly they must compete for a limited resource, the most important of which is the parent. While it is in the parents' interest that all children survive, it has been suggested by Trivers (1974) that sibling rivalry is unavoidable given that they must share the same parents and given that the attention of a parent *increases* one sibling's likelihood of survival while *decreasing* the likelihood for the other. While physical aggression, including hitting, biting, and pushing, occurs between young siblings, Tooley (1980) has noted that child abuse as we see it today is rarely perpetuated by one child against the other.

Two other negative aspects of the sibling relationship in infancy have received some attention: dethroning and cognitive competence. Dunn and Kendrick (1980) and Feiring and Lewis (1982) have shown the effects of the birth of the second child on the first. In both cases, data revealed that the birth of the second has profound effects on the first and these effects are for the most part negative. Feiring and Lewis (1982) found a significant drop in IQ scores, which improved only 1 year after the birth. Clearly the birth of the second child must have a profound psychological impact on the first given the withdrawal of parental attention, time, and energy, and given the competition engendered by the new child's presence. From a cognitive point of view, Zajonc and Markus (1975) have demonstrated the effect of siblings on IQ. While increases in the size of the family result in lower IQ scores, they also found that children who have younger siblings are smarter than children without. Thus independent of birth order having a younger sibling results in higher IQ scores for the sibling in the next highest position; for example, a third-born with a fourth-born sibling is smarter than a third-born without one. Various possibilities may account for this finding. One suggests that having a younger sibling enables the older child to serve as teacher. In this way the older child learns by teaching. The child without a younger sibling has no opportunity to teach anyone younger.

Parental attitudes and behavior have been found to differ as a function of children's birth order, family size, and sex. For example, Lewis and Kreitzberg (1979), looking at mothers', fathers', and older siblings' behavior toward 3-month-olds, found that parental behavior was inversely related to birth order with firstborns receiving more attention and affection than later-born (see also Moss, 1965). Lewis and Feiring (1982) found that fathers talked more to firstborns than to later-borns. Such findings suggest differential parental behavior toward the children, and these differences along with other family dynamics may account for differential sibling characteristics as well as differential interaction between siblings. Whatever the causes of sibling strife, competition and rivalry as well as affection and influence mark sibling relationships. Moreover, these relationships are long-lived and exist long after the children leave the home. The relationships between siblings are important throughout the life cycle as the siblings themselves constitute the closest family into the next generation.

Grandparents

The failure to consider the possible role of the grandparents in children's development, like that for other social objects, is based on a particular view of social development. The neglect is surprising given the obvious facts that parents of parents exert strong influence on children's development if for no other reason than that they influence the parents. Even the name "grandparent" should make it obvious that such a role carries with it importance for both child and grandparent. Tinsley and Parke (1984) have suggested three important reasons for neglecting the study of grandparents: (1) the focus on only the nuclear family; (2) the focus on only the mother as the important social agent in the child's life; and (3) the limited interest in exploring the full life span development. To these we should add a fourth reason: the focus on only direct effects on the child's development. Clearly, if grandparents do not even live in the same home as the child, how can we focus on only direct effects? As Tinsley and Parke (1984) make clear, however, grandparents exert both direct and indirect effects on their grandchildren. It is clear that the lack of study of influence of grandparents on development reflects a culture that does not value age, that is highly age segregated, and in which intergenerational learning is not encouraged. In cultures such as that of Japan today, cultures where many grandparents, parents, and children live together, the role played by grandparents is more obvious.

Even in our culture the direct effects of grandparents should be considerable given that grandparents generally have contact with their adult children (the parents of the child) at least once a week (Shanas, 1979). Lewis, Feiring, and Kotsonis (1984) reported that grandparents are seen most often when compared to other relatives. Indeed on a weekly basis at least one of the grandparents is seen once for these 3-year-old children. Moreover, Wilson and Tolson (1985) presented data to indicate that hospital visits by grandparents at the time of birth are quite high: More than 90 percent see the child on the first or second day, in spite of the geographic mobility of the child's family.

Two other grandparent characteristics emerge in relationship to direct contact. First, parents of mothers are seen more frequently than the parents of fathers (Lewis, Feiring, & Kotsonis, 1984), reflecting the maternal role of kin keeper (Hill, Foote, Aldous, Carlson, & MacDonald, 1970). Second, grandmothers versus grandfathers are more directly involved in the child's activities, reflecting sex-role differences as an intergenerational phenomena.

Specific direct effects of grandparents included in contact with the child include child care. With large numbers of mothers returning to the work force, the direct care of the child is assumed by grandmothers. The exact figure is unclear, but it appears that lower SES grandmothers may assume this role more than higher SES grandmothers in part because: (1) they live in a multigenerational environment; (2) the poor cannot afford other forms of child care; and (3) grandchild care should also occur more for teenage mothers, again a phenomenon more likely to occur in lower SES groups (Lee, 1980). Grandparents, because of age and intergenerational experiences, can provide unique experiences, introducing their grandchildren to games, events, and words of another time. Grandparents also relate experiences about the children's parents and as such inform the children about the parents' childhood. From the child's point of view, grandparents represent the opportunity to observe how older people behave and what it is like to become old. Sickness and death are often observed firsthand through the interaction of the grandchild and grandparent. Through the observation of older persons (some of whom may be ill or infirm) the child can employ newly acquired prosocial skills in that such conditions of the aged are likely to illicit sympathy and empathy.

Children can observe how their parents interact with *their* parents and thereby learn about how adult children behave. This effect does not involve the child directly. The other indirect effects of grandparents should mirror those of the father except that the grandmother–daughter relationship may supply special support for children through affecting their mothers. Given the mother–daughter relationship and its unique role throughout the life cycle, it should be the case that grandmothers' approval and support have particular importance for mothers, certainly more so than for sons.

The role of the grandparents in the child's social life has been of interest more for sociology than for developmental psychology. Given the interest in social development, it is appropriate to study the influence on children of the parents of their parents.

Aunts, Uncles, and Cousins

Simply stated, there is no research literature on the role of aunts, uncles, or cousins in the development of the child. Within anthropology and animal behavior, the role of these others is well recognized. In many groups, lion prides, for example, the social structure of the group includes the female relatives: mothers, aunts, daughters, and female cousins (if such terms can be used in this context). Moreover, the role of the father's brother and mother's brother has been recognized. In fact, Frazer (1915) points out that at the death of the father the father's brother (uncle) becomes responsible for the family. Jocasta's brother Creon becomes king when Oedipus blinds himself. Hamlet's uncle Claudius becomes king and marries Gertrude when Hamlet's father dies. Thus there is ample evidence for the role of uncles in the lives of families; the role of aunts is more unnoticed. Recently an adult audience was asked whether there are any uncles or aunts who played a support role in their early lives. More than 90 percent of the 300 adults responded that there were such people in their early lives.

Our data on contacts indicate that aunts, uncles, and cousins are present in the child's life (Lewis, Feiring, & Kotsonis, 1984). Given that the previous generation's siblings maintain lifelong contacts, it should come as little surprise that parents' siblings (aunts and uncles) should be a part of the social fabric of the young children. The same reasons for neglecting grandparents apply to these relatives.

Because aunts and uncles are in close contact, their children (cousins) should also be in close contact. In fact, for many children, their first peer contacts and long-lasting ones are with cousins. Thus cousins are likely to play an influential role, and the social network data indicate considerable rate of cousin contact. Cousins are viewed as so close, at least genetically, that in many states there exist laws against marriage between them.

For aunts, uncles, and cousins, differences similar to those already reported for grandparents and siblings are likely to appear. Mothers' siblings, aunts, and uncles and children's cousins are more likely to be in contact than fathers' kin, a finding already reported (Lewis, Feiring, & Kotsonis, 1984). Female cousins and aunts are more likely than uncles and male cousins to maintain contact, a sex-role difference that should appear throughout the social network structure. Moreover, the role of grandparents in the maintenance of sibling contact is probably important. That is, aunt and uncle (and therefore cousin) contact is more likely in some families than in others. The exact nature of the relationship that facilitates this is not well understood.

Clearly, the relationship of aunts, uncles, and cousins is related to sibling contact across the life cycle. As we come to focus on these aspects, the role of these other relatives will become more obvious. Nonetheless, given our limited knowledge of sibling relationships over time, it is reasonable to include these relatives as important for the child's social development.

Peers

Beyond family members there are any number of social objects that play an important role in children's development. Peers are surely the most important, for it is in peer relationships that most of adult social life exists. For this reason, of all social objects beside mothers, early peer relationships have been most studied. For more complete reviews of peers, the reader is referred to Lewis and Rosenblum (1975), Mueller and Brenner (1977), and Hartup (1979).

The failure to examine peer relationships in very early childhood was based on the beliefs that children are: (1) incapable intellectually and (2) emotionally uninterested in peer contact and relationships. Moreover, the role of peers in the child's early life was not explored. These factors are now recognized to be untrue or in need of considerable modification. Piaget's (1952) view on social development argued against early peer interactions; for example, he viewed egocentricity as resulting in parallel play and in the lack of empathy which prevented peer interaction. More recent evidence suggests that egocentric behavior may be overstated for the early life cycle. Young children can engage in interactive play as early as the first year of life, although it is not until the second year that more complex play is observed (Mueller, 1972). Moreover, subjects are capable of taking the perspective of others (Flavell, 1972) and appear capable of empathetic behavior (Borke, 1971; Zahn-Waxler et al., 1979). In terms of perceptual–cognitive ability, infants are capable of discriminating social objects as function of age, learn age-related terms easily, and show that they possess some rudimentary forms of social roles (Brooks-Gunn & Lewis, 1981; Edwards & Lewis, 1979; Lewis, 1984). Thus social skills and perceptual–cognitive abilities are in place quite early to facilitate peer interactions.

The belief that infants had no social or emotional interest in peers due in part to the prevailing view that the social–emotional life of the child primarily involved only the mother also prevented the study of early peer relationships. While the role of the mother is recognized, the role of peers has been shown to be equally important as it is encouraged or inhibited by the social structure. Lewis and Rosenblum (1975), Hartup (1970), and Mueller (1972) have all reviewed the data suggesting that cultural differences in peer contact is the primary factor affecting the degree and amount of social–emotional involvement. In some cultures, peers are given more direct roles in child care (Brown, 1971; Whiting & Whiting, 1975). On the Kibbutz and in Russia, China, and Cuba, for example, we would expect more and earlier peer emotional–social interactions than where group child care is not a part of the culture (e.g., Japan or the United States, although this is changing even now). Peers show interest, enjoyment, and emotional involvement from the earliest opportunities provided in the first year of life. Peer attachment has been shown to exist especially in the absence of adults (Freud & Dann 1951; Gyomrai-Ludowyk, 1963), although it has never been tested sufficiently in the presence of adults.

Children in the first 2 years of life form friendships and are unhappy at their loss (Lewis et al., 1975). Recently, the issue of intersubjectivity, the ability of the subject to realize the separateness but interconnection between self and other, has been suggested to take place within the first 2 years, some suggesting even sooner (Bretherton, 1985). All of these facts argue for the importance of peers even in infancy.

Like siblings, peers perform both positive and negative functions. Peers are good for play (Lewis et al., 1975) and for modeling one's behavior since they share equal or nearly equal abilities and are most like the self. They are also good at teaching, especially somewhat older peers, since their abilities do not differ too markedly (Edwards & Lewis, 1979). Peers protect each other and, most importantly, peers are capable of forming attachments to each other.

The negative features of the peer relationship revolve around the lack of the adult perspective. Thus, for example, while an adult may be able to give up a need for the sake of a child, such behavior may be beyond the ability of young peers. Disputes, therefore, are often settled by power status variables such as strength, age, and gender rather than by true prosocial behavior. Aggressive behavior between peers represents another negative feature, with high physical interaction and direct aggression being two noticeable examples. Clearly, the lack of adult perspective affects levels of knowledge, history, and cultural rules, and this lack should affect the nature of peer interactions. We should not be surprised to see that peer interactions differ from child–adult ones. The issue is not whether they differ but rather their importance in terms of the child's subsequent development. Given these differences, the task is to determine whether outcomes differ in the face of different peer relationships. Given that peer relationships themselves are embedded in the cultural rules, the study of peer behavior needs to be considered in the context of the entire social network. The absence of peer contact in a culture that does not promote contact cannot be taken as evidence for the unimportance of peers in early life.

Teachers, Day-Care Personnel, and Baby-Sitters

Even during the first few months, infants are exposed to nonrelated adults who care for the child while the mother is at work, in school, or at play. Given the increasing number of mothers who work out of the home and the changing family structure (Feiring & Lewis, 1984) there are large numbers of children who are cared for daily by people other than relatives. In some societies, for example, the Soviet Union, China, and Israel, such practices are widely used, while in others, such as the United States, it is a more recent phenomenon.

Whatever the causes, there is increasing frequency of child care by nonrelated adults, usually women. There are few data on children's relationships with these people. Anecdotal evidence suggests that "nannies" play a meaningful role in young children's lives and that strong attachments may exist over many years. Evidence from day-care studies also indicates that young children are capable of forming important relationships with day-care personnel and that these adults are capable in some instances of mitigating some of the difficulties created by the abusing or neglecting mother. In fact, Lewis and Schaeffer (1981) have shown that even for normal (nonabused/neglected) children, the children show similar patterns to both their mothers and their day-care teachers. While the evidence is not strong, there is support for the propositions (1) that children can form multiple attachments, and (2) that they become attached to their day-care teachers. Parenthetically, there should be some concern for the effects of changing teachers often either through day-care personnel turnaround or class change each year.

There has been some research on the transition from home to school—most of it shown to be traumatic for many mothers as well as children (Douglas, 1964; Ferguson & Freeark, 1979; Mitchell & Shepherd, 1966). This should not be surprising given the manner in which children are separated from home, literally torn away without prior training or support. That children have transition difficulties must reflect *both* separation problems and the manner of separation.

The failure to study children's attachment to other adult caregivers may rest on our general bias, which holds to the importance of a single adult attachment figure. Even though Bowlby (1969) does recognize the multiple-attachment capability of the human infant, research to support such a view is rarely performed. Cross-cultural research such as that of Konner (1975) and Greenbaum and Landau (1977) shows that even in the first few weeks infants interact with many adults including nonrelatives to whom they may become attached. Given this possibility and the changing nature of child care it is necessary that we focus on the effects of multiple attachments and the child's relationship to adult caregivers other than parents and relatives.

Other People in Children's Lives

Two classes of people that commonly interact with the child can be considered here: friends of family members and strangers.

FRIENDS OF FAMILY MEMBERS.　Children of all ages are exposed to friends of the family. In fact, one of the important changing characteristics of U.S. society is the movement from family to friends as the major social contact. Lewis, Feiring, and Kotsonis (1984) found that contact with family friends versus family is greater the higher the SES level. Family friends, mother's or father's best friend, for example, should exert some influence on the young child. Not only does the family friend interact directly with the child but the child has the opportunity to observe the parent–friend interaction and in this way learn about adult interactions and parental behavior toward others. Again, when questioned, many people report the significant influence of the family friend in the child's life. In fact, many such friends receive the "honorary" title of uncle or aunt even though they are not relatives.

STRANGERS.　By the time the child is 3 years old it will have been exposed to many people, many of them strangers—medical doctors, occasional baby-sitters, shopkeepers, house visitors, and so on. The response to strangers varies from brief study to fearfulness. Nevertheless, strangers play an important role in our lives—if for no other reason than that most people we come in contact with are strangers and most of our friends were strangers to us at one time. Children differ in their response to these strangers as a function of both child characteristics including, age, sex, and temperament and experience with strangers (Feinman & Lewis, 1983; Kagan, 1974; Lewis & Brooks, 1974). Children also differ in their responses as a function of the characteristics of the stranger—including height, facial configuration, sex, age, and the presence of the mother (Brooks-Gunn & Lewis, 1976; Campos, Emde, Gaensbauer, & Sorce, 1973). These findings should alert us to the fact that response to strangers is not some unitary or single response, elicited by anything unfamiliar.

Strangers are viewed as negative in most theories of social development (Lewis & Rosenblum, 1974a). While the child's response to the initial approach of strangers usually is negative or at least "studied," infants and young children quickly make friends with these strangers (Feiring, Lewis, & Starr, 1984; Rheingold & Eckerman, 1973). Fear of the approach of the stranger has been widely studied and the response of children noted. While a certain amount of attention and concern during approach is appropriate for children once their cognitive capacities mature, which is at around 8 months (Schaffer, 1974), there is little reason to remain fearful once it can be determined that the stranger will do no harm. In fact, without the capacity to transform the initial concern into interest, the young organism would have no opportunity to learn anything new about others who are unfamiliar. Thus strangers should elicit *both* concern and interest. In fact, except for the most fearful children, that is exactly what occurs. Consider children who both hide behind their mothers and look out at the stranger. The competition between the fear and exploratory systems is obvious (Bischof, 1975).

It is necessary to resist the simple notion that strangers play only a negative role in children's early lives. The role of the stranger is complex, and ability to make friends or at least become acquainted with the stranger is an important part of children's social development. The study of this process requires that we consider strangers as not only fear-inducing stimuli but also one way for the child to enlarge its social network. The stranger-to-friend process is a central feature of social development and is in need of study. Although this is not the place to discuss individual differences in sociability of children, it should be recognized that some children will be more open to a variety of social objects while others not (Buss and Plomin, 1984).

This brief review of the various social objects in the child's world should alert us to the complexity of social development. In any discussion of the influence and significance of multiple social objects it must be kept in mind that these cannot be determined apart from the socialization experience itself. For example, to study infants' peer behavior with infants who have no previous peer experience fails to answer the question of the value or need of peer experience and its potential consequences. Only through studying various networks can the relationship between the various social objects be understood. In short, the influences of the social system elements in the young infant's life are not necessarily limited to the mother. The research literature of the past 10 years indicates that the infant is embedded in a complex system of elements including mother, fathers, siblings, other relatives, especially grandparents, uncles and aunts, and peers. Moreover, the infant is capable of interacting with these others and of forming relationships with them. Some of these relationships may be attachments, some love without attachment, and some friendships. The constraints on these relationships probably rest on cultural factors. The first requirement of a social network systems analysis is met: There are a multitude of possible elements.

Interconnection of Elements

Systems are characterized not only by sets of elements, but also by a set of interrelated elements, that is, by elements that are influenced by each other (Monane, 1967). Within the family the interaction of elements can be at several levels. At the simplest level, the infant can affect its parents (Lewis & Rosenblum, 1974b), the parents affect the infant, and the parents affect each other. Such effects come about through the direct interactions between family members. Moreover elements are not only individuals but may be dyads or even larger units. When larger elements are considered, the study of the interrelation of elements becomes more complex. For example, a child can affect not only each parent separately but also the parental interaction. The research on family size (number of children) and age of the child shows that children affect marital satisfaction (Rollins & Galligan, 1978). Likewise, the father can influence the mother and child individually as well as the mother-child interaction. Many different effects of this complex nature have been observed. Pedersen (1975) and Feiring (1975) observed the parental relationship as it affects the mother-child interactions, and several investigators have studied the effect of the father on the mother-child relationship (Clarke-Stewart, 1978; Lamb, 1978b; Lewis & Weinraub, 1976; Parke, 1979; Pedersen, Anderson, & Cain, 1977). Cicirelli (1975) looked at the influence of siblings on the mother-child relationships and Dunn and Kendrick (1979) studied the effect of a newborn child (sibling) on the other child-mother relationship (see Dunn & Kendrick, 1980; Lewis & Rosenblum, 1977; for a review of such studies).

Lewis (Lewis & Feiring, 1982, 1986; Lewis & Weinraub, 1976), Bronfenbrenner (1977), Lamb (1978a, 1978b) and Parke, Power, and Gottman (1979) have discussed some of the various ways that elements within a system may influence each other. Direct and indirect effects have been identified as two major classes (Lewis & Feiring, 1981; Lewis & Weinraub, 1976). We will briefly discuss these classes and return to them later in our discussion. Direct effects are those interactions that represent the influence of one person on the behavior of another when both are engaged in mutual interaction. Direct effects have been studied for each member of the infant's family; mother-infant (Brazelton, Koslowski, & Main, 1974; Lewis, 1972; Stern, 1974), father-infant (Brazelton, Yogman, Als, & Tronick, 1979), and sibling-infant (Greenbaum & Landau, 1977).

Indirect effects refer to two classes of interactions or influence. In the first class are those sets of interactions that affect the target person but that occur in the absence of that person. While these sets of interactions affect the target person, they may be best described as influencing direct effects or interactions. For example, the father, by supporting the mother (both emotionally and physically), affects the mother-infant relationship. Several studies have demonstrated this effect (Barry, 1970; Feiring & Taylor, 1977; Heath, 1976). A second category of indirect effects are those that occur in the presence of the target person even though the interaction is not directed toward or does not involve that person. These effects are based on information that is gathered from sources other than the direct interaction with another person and may be the result of (1) observation of another's interaction with persons or objects or (2) information gathered from another about the attitudes, behavior, traits, or actions of a third person. Such indirect influences have been studied under a wide rubric including identification, modeling, imitation, incidental, vicarious, and observational learning, and more recently, social referencing (see Lewis & Feiring, 1981, in press).

In short, the infant must adapt to a social system containing elements that vary in number and complexity and that influence the infant both directly through their interactions with the child and indirectly through their interactions with each other. The child establishes relationships within a network of already existing relationships.

Nonadditivity

Social systems also possess the quality of nonadditivity; that is, to know everything about the elements that comprise a system will not reveal everything about the operation of the whole. Any set of elements behaves quite differently within the system from the way it does in isolation. This rule holds for simple elements as well as for the more complex ones. Within the family, the way a person behaves alone can be quite different from the way that person behaves in the presence of another. Because observation of a person alone is nearly impossible (and unethical), the study of individual behavior alone is difficult. More common is the observation of a dyad alone or in the presence of a third member. For example, Clarke-Stewart (1978) observed mothers, fathers, and children in dyadic (parent–child) and triadic (mother–father–child) interactions and showed that the quantity and quality of behavior in the mother–child subsystem in isolation are changed when the mother–child subsystem is embedded in the mother–father–child subsystem. The mother initiated less talk, played with the child less, and was also less engaging, reinforcing, directive, and responsive in her child-directed interactions when the father was present than when she was alone with the child. Pedersen and colleagues (1977) report that, while the father/husband frequently divides his behavior between child and spouse in a three-person subsystem, the mother/wife spends much more time in dyadic interaction with the child than with her husband. The child also exerts influence on the parent system. Rosenblatt (1974) found that the presence of one or more children reduced adult–adult touching, talking, and smiling in selected public places such as the zoo, park, or shopping center. Lewis and Feiring (1982) looking at interactions at the dinner table, found that the number of children at the table affects the amount of mother–father verbal interaction as well as the amount of positive affect between the parents. A study by Parke and O'Leary (1975) illustrates the qualities of interdependence and nonadditivity in the family system. When mothers were with their husbands they were more likely to explore the child's body and smile than when they were alone with the child. In addition, when mothers were with their husbands, they tended to touch their sons more than their daughters whereas this difference was not evident when the mother and child were alone.

This rule of nonadditivity presents an obstacle for the study of interactions and relationships. There is some comfort in believing that the interactions one observes between two people remain the same or are invariant across situations or across changing social structures. The rule of nonadditivity suggests that this is not the case. The evidence that the relationships between elements are dependent on the set or subset of elements present suggests the relative nature of interactions. The effect on relationships is not known, although it might well be the case that, while interactions may vary, relationships do not. The relative nature of dyadic interactions makes the study of social behavior more difficult. Indeed, if the rule of nonadditivity is correct, the very act of observation (which introduces another element, the observer) must alter the behavior of those observed.

Steady State

Social systems are characterized by steady states. The term *steady state* describes the process whereby a system maintains itself (e.g., its values or goals) while always changing to some degree. A steady state is characterized by the interplay of flexibility and stability by which a system endeavors to maintain a viable relationship among its elements and its environment. Social systems are defined as goal oriented, and steady-state processes are directed toward goal achievement. However, the same general goal may be served by different patterns of behavior as the system changes to adapt to its environment. Within the family such processes appear essential since one major change that must occur is the development of the child. Since children's skills, knowledge, and behavior continually change, these changes must be accounted for in maintaining stability. For example, Lewis and Weinraub (1974) have shown that the nature of the interactions between child and parent change over the first 2 years of the child's life. The amount of physical proximity, especially touching, decreases while at the same time the amount of distal contact, for example, looking and talking, increases. While the particular behaviors serving the relationship undergo change, the relationship probably remains the same.

The child's functioning in the family is described by adaptation (steady state) and by development of new behavior patterns (flexibility) in the service of prior goals (stability). For example, Dunn and Kendrick (1980) found that firstborn children's independent behavior increased upon the birth of a sibling. Although independent behavior occurred and was encouraged by the mother prior to the birth of the second child and was a developmental goal, the amount, kind, and opportunity for independent behavior changed as the family system changed to include a new member. This consistency in the midst of change has to be an important factor in development that bears on relationships and feelings. This principle of steady states allows for continuity within a changing structure as well as within a changing developmental system where new behaviors and new situations are observed (Lewis & Starr, 1979).

Goals

Social systems are also characterized by their purposeful quality. The family system is generally thought to exist in order to perform certain functions or goal-oriented activities that are necessary both to the survival of its members and to the perpetuation of the specific culture and society. Family functions are often enumerated as procreation and child rearing, which suggests that the family is the principal agent of these societal goals. Beyond this level of generality are numerous other ways of describing and defining family functions (Lewis & Feiring, 1978; Parsons & Bales, 1955).

The epigenetic model not only has restricted the number of the family attachment relationships available to the young child by focusing more or less exclusively on the mother, but also has limited the types of activities or goals engaged in by the other family members. If only caregiving functions or goals are considered, then it makes some sense to study the mother as the most important (and only) element. However, other functions in the child's life include, for example, play and teaching, which may involve family members other than the mother.

The issue of functions, needs, and goals is quite complex. The study of the functions, needs, or goals of the young child is beyond the scope of this chapter. In order to create a list of functions or goals one could utilize Wilson's (1975) adaptive functions or Murrays (1938) need functions. Lewis and Feiring (1979) have also defined some of the functions important for the infant. These include protection, caregiving, nurturance, play, exploration/learning, and social control. *Protection* would include protection from potential sources of danger, including both inanimate (e.g., falling off trees or being burned in fires) and animate sources (e.g., being eaten by a predator, taken by one who is not kin, or attacked by another). *Caregiving* includes feeding and cleaning at the least, and refers to a set of activities that center around biological needs relating to bodily activities. *Nurturance* is the function of love or attachment, as specified by Bowlby (1969). *Play* refers to activities with no immediately obvious goal. These activities are engaged in for their own sake. *Exploration/learning* involves the social activity of finding out about the environment through either watching others, asking for information, or engaging in information acquisition with others. *Social control* represents the restriction of the infant's behavior because it interferes with the behavior of others or because it is useful in teaching specific rules. It differs from exploration/learning in that its major function is to restrict the infant's ongoing behavior. More functions can be considered, but the discussion will be limited to these in order to proceed to the connection between "what people do which things" and the possible outcomes given that certain people do certain things.

Any analysis of the family must consider the range of functions and the nature of the different members who satisfy these functions. Although different family members are generally characterized by particular social functions, it is often the case that persons and functions are only partially related (Lewis & Feiring, 1978, 1979; Lewis, Feiring, & Weinraub, 1981; Lewis & Weinraub, 1976). Consequently, the identity of the family member does not necessarily define the type of range of its social functions. Whereas caregiving (a function) and mother (a person) have been considered to be highly related, recent work indicates that fathers are equally adequate in performing this function. Play, another function, appears to be engaged in more by siblings and fathers than by mothers (Ban & Lewis, 1974; Clarke-Stewart, 1978; Lamb, 1976; Parke & Sawin, 1980).

As indicated previously, a family member may perform several functions within the context of the family system although different family members may be more associated with certain functions than with others. Thus parents may do more caregiving and teaching, but other children do more play. The relative amount of interaction time spent in different activities would certainly be expected to influence the child's development. For example, a child in a family where teaching was the most frequent function (regardless of to whom the teaching was being directed— child, sibling, or parent) would be expected to be different than a child in a family where caregiving was the most frequent activity. In addition, the differential amount of various activities directed by the same individual to the child might influence the child's development. For example, a child whose mother engaged in more caregiving activity than play would be expected to be different from a child whose mother engaged in both equally.

In order to explore this problem, it is necessary to consider the matrix constructed when multiple social objects and needs are related. Lewis (Edwards & Lewis, 1979; Lewis & Feiring, 1978, 1979) has discussed such a matrix, and it has been considered by others as well, for humans as well as animals (Suomi, 1979).

DESCRIPTION AND MEASUREMENT OF THE SOCIAL NETWORK

As an area of research, the study of social networks is about 30 years old (Barnes, 1954). Bott's (1957, 1971) seminal work *The Family and Social Network* is widely known to both sociologists and psychologists. Bott reported that—contrary to popular belief—middle-class couples did not live in isolation but formed coalitions with other middle-class couples in a network of social kinship. Middle-class as compared to working-class families had contact with nonrelative friends on a more daily basis, although they maintained contact with extended family on a less frequent basis. In interviews with couples, Bott discussed with both husbands and wives the type and frequency of contact with people in the categories of relatives, friends, neighbors, and organizations (e.g., school, clubs, unions, religious groups, etc). Couples also kept diaries that helped the researchers determine the nature of the social networks. One interesting result from Bott's work involved the relationship between social network and family roles. Although networks have been examined in regard to adults, relatively little work has been done on networks, roles, and child's development (for exceptions, see Cochran & Brassard, 1979; Feiring & Lewis, 1981; Lewis & Feiring, 1979, Lewis, Feiring, & Kotsonis, 1984).

Since Bott's work, social network theory and research have received the most study and attention from the field of sociology. Attributes of the social network, including size, variety of membership, density, connectedness, reciprocity, and frequency and function of contact, have been studied in regard to the nature of the marital relationship and social and geographic mobility patterns of families (e.g., Lee, 1979). An extensive literature exists that employs quantitative techniques for describing and specifying the characteristics of social networks (e.g., see Holland & Leinhardt, 1979). In general, the examination of the social network, as in Bott's work (1957, 1971), has attempted to delineate through interviews and questionnaires the kind and frequency of contact with kin and nonkin groups. In addition, information about the connectedness of network members (i.e., who knows whom) and the network density (the number of people who know each other relative to those who do not) is often of interest. Once the point of anchorage (e.g., a person, conjugal pair, nuclear family) is determined, information is gathered on kin and nonkin contact (Pattison, 1975). Social networks have also been utilized as the unit of intervention in conducting therapy (e.g., Attneave, 1976; Pattison, 1975). However, there have been few attempts to measure and describe the broad network of people and contacts in a child's social system and to understand the developmental influence they might have, especially in regard to the young child.

In order to describe some basic attributes of the young child's extended social network, data on the composition of children's networks as perceived by their mothers have been collected (Lewis, Feiring, & Kotsonis, 1984). Mothers were asked to complete an adapted version of the Pattison Psychosocial Network Inventory. Each mother was asked to list the persons in the child's social network in the categories of family, relatives, friends of parents, and friends of the child. The mother was asked to specify the relationship of each person listed to the 3-year-old child (e.g., for the relatives' category: cousin, grandparent, etc.) and to indicate the amount of contact the person had with the child. Contact could be on a weekly, monthly, bi-yearly, or yearly basis (contact was defined as including face to face, by phone, or by letter). From the mother's report Lewis, Feiring, and Kotsonis (1984) were able to get an idea of (1) the number of people and the kinds of people who comprised the 3 year-old's network and (2) the frequency of contact with these people. See Table 8.1 for the results of this study.

Self-report data are problematic. When the parent reports on her child's activity there are even more problems. The mother's report will reflect her perception of the child's network and may not yield the most accurate picture of whom the child sees and how often. However, it is not possible to interview young children (or infants) for these data and from a practical research strategy it is not possible to observe the children over a long period to determine whom they saw and how often. Moreover, direct observation itself constitutes an important bias. In order to get an idea of the child's social network, the traditional questionnaire method is a useful technique. Other methods that should be considered are a phone check technique and diary keeping by parents. Although these have been employed, little systematic work using them has been reported.

SOCIAL MATRIX AS A MEASURE OF THE SOCIAL NETWORK: THE RELATION BETWEEN PEOPLE AND NEEDS

Given the varied functions and likelihood of multiple relationships in the life of the child, we need to develop a model that describes how these multiple people and functions operate. Moreover, having such a model enables us to explore how different matrices produce different developmental outcomes. Such a model must focus on the relationship between people and functions.

In the model depicted in Figure 8.3, social objects form the Y axis while social functions form the X axis. Together they form a matrix of objects and functions (Lewis & Feiring, 1979). In this figure P to P_n represents the set of social objects and includes self, mother, father, peer, siblings, grandparent, aunt, plus any other persons to be considered. The array of objects is determined by a variety of factors to be considered in turn. The functions labeled F_1 to F_n consist of protection, caregiving, nurturance, and so forth. The subset of behaviors B_{11}, B_{12}, B_{nn} represents the set of behaviors that can be measured and that are subsumed under the broad heading of a particular function. For example, under **caregiving**, feeding and changing could be included as different behaviors, while under **nurturance**, emotional behaviors such as kissing or responsivity might be considered. The general form of this model provides a framework for considering the complete array of social objects and functions that describe the child's social network. By examining the matrix one can determine which social objects are present, which functions are being sat-

Social Objects

		F_1	F_2	F_3	F_4	F_5	$\ldots F_n$
		Protection $B_{11}\,B_{12}\,B_{13}$	Caregiving $B_{21}\,B_{22}\,B_{23}$	Nurturance $B_{31}\,B_{32}$	Play	Exploration Learning	B_{nn}
			Feeding. Changing	Rock. Kiss			
P_1	Self						
P_2	Mother						
P_3	Father						
P_4	Peer						
P_5	Sibling						
P_6	Grandparent						
P_7	Aunt						
.							
.							
.							
P_n							

(left vertical label: Social Functions)

Figure 8.3. The relationship between social objects and social functions.

isfied, and most important, which functions are achieved by which social object. By examining the horizontal axis of the matrix one can obtain an idea of what functions are characteristic of a particular social object within this particular network. This axis will inform us whether mothers are predominantly concerned with caregiving or fathers with play, a finding that is repeatedly reported. On the other hand, by examining the vertical axis of the matrix, one can study the functions characterizing the network of a particular child. While all of the listed functions are presumed to be important, it might be that for some children caregiving, play, and learning are equally important. Likewise, a child whose network is predominantly concerned with protection will be quite different from one raised in a network concerned with nurturance. However, in order to determine the relationship of object to function, we must turn our attention to the individual cells of the matrix.

The object–function relationship raises the general question of whether some object–function relationships are more important for the child's development than others. For example, what is the consequence of having an older sibling as caregiver as well as the mother instead of just the mother? Or what is the consequence of having a caregiver as provider of care (as in day care) in addition to the mother instead of just the mother?

The answers to questions such as these require that the long-term and higher-order goal structure of the family or society be considered. The value assigned to the consequence of particular outcomes must ultimately play a role in any discussion of social development. For example, if successful peer social adjustment resulting in long-term stable and loving relationships is the goal then one can examine which object–function relationship best produces this outcome. On the other hand, if a socially isolated but artistically successful outcome is desired, then one asks: What produces this? In a word, analysis of a consequence of an object–function matrix must depend on the specification of goals.

Several studies, some of which have already been discussed, have described particular object–function connections. As we have stated, these object–function relationships represent the western cultural values as they now exist and do not necessarily reflect either: (1) the appropriateness across different cultures, or (2) the evaluation concerning which object–function relationship represents the best outcome given a particular goal. The few data that exist suggest that in the general American culture mothers mostly engage in caregiving, protective, and nurturance functions while father, siblings, and peers engage in play. Teaching appears to be performed by parents and older siblings and peers. Similar findings across other cultures have been reported by Whiting and Whiting (1975), although important differences, especially in sibling and peer functions, have been found.

In an attempt to determine whether such an object–function matrix is applicable to young children, Edwards and Lewis (1979) explored how young children perceive the distribution of functions and persons. Persons were represented by dolls of infants, peers, older children, and parent-aged adults. Social functions were created for the child in the form of a story. In the two studies to be discussed, children in the age range of 3–5 years were asked to choose which person they wanted to interact with in a specific social activity. In all the studies, the functions were (1) being helped, (2) teaching about a toy, (3) sharing, and (4) play. For *help,* the adults were selected, while for someone to *play* with, children choose adults and infants last and peers and older children first. For *teaching,* specifically, how to use a toy, older children were selected, while for *sharing,* there were no preference among social objects. In a second study, children were asked to point to photographs of infants, peers, older children, adults (parent-aged), and grandparents in response to the social function questions. The results indicated that older persons were chosen first for *help*. The teaching finding supported the results of the first study in that older children were preferred. Again there was no difference in the social object selected for *sharing*, a replication of the earlier findings. Interestingly, the data on grandparent-aged adults are most similar to that for parent-aged parents.

How early the creation of an object–function connection is made is not known. However, a study by Lewis and colleagues (1975), for example, indicates that by 1 year of age infants play with peers more than with strange adult females or mothers, and mothers are sought after for protection and nurturance more than strange females and peers. Such findings suggest that the discrimination of persons and functions begins very early in life.

The results of the Edwards and Lewis study (1979) also suggest that the persons and functions that describe a child's social system will be influenced by the situation in which the person performs the functions. One important aspect of a social system is the environment in which the system exists. Consequently, the family system, its members, and the functions performed by its members may be different depending on the situation or environment in which the family is interacting. The family system becomes an element in the larger system of the subculture or culture. Thus the quality of the elements can be considered to exist in order to perform certain functions or goal-oriented activities necessary to the survival of its members. Families as elements perform activities for the perpetuation of the specific culture and society.

Some Variables Affecting the Social Matrix

Although individual differences in this matrix exist (e.g., each family may have idiosyncratic features), there are several constraints on the matrix that have to do with both ontogenetic and cultural differences. An examination of these constraints is useful in exploring social development.

Ontogeny

By examining the matrix at different points in a child's life, it should be possible to delineate developmental patterns. One might expect changes both in the composition of the social objects and in the nature of the functions. For example, in our society as children get older, they are likely to come into contact with more people, for example, peers and teachers. Likewise, new functions will emerge as caregiving and nurturance give way to teaching and control. Such changes can be observed in Figure 8.4, which shows a possible matrix for a 3-month-old infant and one for the same child at 6 years. Although the values are fictitious, they demon-

		F_1 Caregiving		F_2 Play	$\ldots F_n$
		B_{11} B_{12} Feeding. Dressing	B_{21}	B_{22} Hide and Seek	B_{nn}
P_1	Self	0		0	
P_2	Mother	30		5	
P_3	Father	10		10	
P_4	Grandmother	5		2	
P_n					
		45		27	

(a)   Social network matrix: target child age 3 months

		F_1 Caregiving		F_2 Play	$\ldots F_n$
		B_{11} B_{12} Feeding. Dressing	B_{21}	B_{22} Hide and Seek	B_{nn}
P_1	Self	10		25	
P_2	Mother	5		5	
P_3	Father	5		15	
P_4	Peer	1		25	
P_5	Teacher	5		15	
P_n					

(b)   Social network matrix: target child age 6 years.

Figure 8.4. Ontogenetic changes in the social network matrix. (The numbers shown do not represent real data, but are for illustrative purposes only.)

strate the point. For the sake of simplicity, the same functions have been maintained, but their values change. When the infant is 3 months, caregiving predominates over play and mother engages in the most caregiving activity. As already reported, fathers may play more with their children than mothers. By the time the child is 6 years old, new objects are added, caregiving gives way to play, and both father and mother play less with the child than do peers or siblings. Such a model is useful in charting the course of social development. Moreover, the use of this model can be used for prediction: Does a particular network at one age predict a later network? For example, what is the outcome for play when early caregiving is shared between several adults rather than one?

Family Structure Factor

Considering the factor of family structure, we can simply point out the possible differences in a matrix for a child of 3 years who is third-born (family size = five). The first effect of interest is the number of objects available for various functions. The only child has no siblings in the vertical ordinate of the matrix, while third-born children will have two older siblings in their matrix. In addition, friends of the child's siblings will probably be present in the social array. Family structure will equally affect the matrix of objects and functions when functions that have to do with missing objects are considered. For example, children may be more likely to play with other children, suggesting that the presence, as compared to the absence, of older siblings may provide more opportunities for play. Thus the function of play may characterize the matrix of a child of a family of five to a greater degree than the matrix of an only child. Another example of how family structure may influence the functions that characterize the child's matrix is suggested by the work of Zajonc and Markus (1975). Small families (e.g., with only one child) may spend more time in the function of information exchange than larger families, thus enhancing the child's early cognitive development. The distribution of function by object will also be affected by family structure. In a family of three, the function of care giving is more than likely performed by the parents while in a family of five caregiving may be taken on by an older sibling as well as the parents. Similarly, a third-born child may spend more time in play with its siblings as compared to its parents, while the only child may have more experience playing with its parents in the absence of sibling companionship. Dunn and Wooding (1977) have reported some interesting data on how family size influences the social functions of play and its distribution among social objects. They have shown that only children received much adult attention that was related to long periods of relatively mature play activity. However, after the birth of a second child a sharp decrease in parental attention to the first child was noted. Lewis and Kreitzberg (1979) reported similar findings in terms of maternal attention as a function of birth order. Older children tend to spend less time playing with their mothers and more time playing with their younger siblings, with the play being characterized by less "mature" activities.

Situational Constraints

Another constraint that operates on the nature of a child's social network matrix is the situation in which interactions take place. For example, a matrix constructed from data taken at a dinnertime situation will most likely limit the social objects to the immediate family members. A dinnertime situation would also constrain the functions that would characterize the matrix. For example, we would expect to see more caregiving than play during a mealtime situation (Lewis and Feiring, 1982).

While functions as they relate to different objects have not been extensively studied, mothers' behavior toward their children as a function of situation has been examined (Lewis & Freedle, 1973, 1977). In one study, the conversational relationships between dyads, 12-week-old infants and their mothers, were examined when the infant was on its mother's lap (presumably when she wished to interact, e.g., play function), and when the infant was in an infant seat (presumably when she wished to do housework and keep her eye on her child, e.g., caregiving function). Under the former, initiation and responsivity were many times greater than under the latter function, even though the total amount of vocalization the mother produced was not different.

Cultural Differences

Cultural differences can also be characterized by differences in the matrix, and the usefulness of this model for this purpose should not be neglected. Figure 8.5 demonstrates differences between 3-month-old Israeli child living in a kibbutz and an American child of the same age. Again there are both object and function differences. Israeli children raised in a kibbutz when compared to American children have many more peers as well as additional adults with whom they interact. This results in a redistribution of the functions with the mother and father in the other. Moreover, there is a radical change in both the distribution and the amount of play when peers are introduced into the matrix. To be noted in such cultural comparisons is the reduction in the caregiving role of the mother (and father) with the appearance of other adults, for example, the *metapelet* in the case of the kibbutz, or other relatives in the case of cultures with extended families. These conclusions are supported by cross-cultural studies of Edwards and Whiting (1976), who found older siblings more involved in caregiving in non-technological cultures. Konner (1975) also found similar results for !Kung San infants as early as 1–13 weeks of age where nonmothers accounted for 20 percent of all physical contact recorded. Although there is little direct evidence, this phenomenon is probably less likely to be observed in the traditional American family where the child is rarely cared for or touched by other adults during this time period.

In a study of functions and objects within the family, Lewis and Feiring (1979) examined the functions of nurturance, caregiving, and information exchange. Although not all functions were observed, it was found that for the 3-year-old target children mothers engaged in more caregiving and nurturance than fathers while both engaged in equal amounts of information exchange. The target children exhibited equal amounts of nurturance to their mothers and fathers although they engaged in more information seeking with their mothers. Interestingly, when family size was considered, that is, when the number of children in the family increased, the object–function nature was altered. In particular, fathers increased their amount of caregiving for the target child as the number of siblings increased; however, the total amount of nurturance for both mother and father decreased. Thus demographic variables such as family size, sex of child, and possibly others should affect this matrix. The fact that these variables can be shown to exert an influence on the matrix provides some support for the validity of our formulation.

	F_1 Caregiving B_{11} Feeding. B_{12} Dressing	$F_2 \ldots F_n$ Play	B_{nn}
P_1 Self	0		
P_2 Metatelet	25	10	
P_3 Mother	5	5	
P_4 Father	2	2	
P_5 Peer	0	15	
P_6 Peer	0	20	
.			
.			
.			
.			
P_n			

(*a*) Social matrix of Israeli child at 3 months of age

	F_1 Caregiving B_{11} Feeding. B_{12} Dressing	$F_2 \ldots F_n$ Play	B_{nn}
P_1 Self	0	0	
P_2 Mother	25	10	
P_3 Father	10	15	
.			
.			
.			
.			
P_n			

(*b*) Social matrix of child from United States at 3 months of age.

Figure 8.5. The effect of culture on the social network matrix. (The numbers shown do not represent real data, but are for illustrative purposes only.)

The construction of the social object–function matrix provides us with a model for understanding the child's social network. The variety of people and functions that comprise this network alters at least as a function of the child's age and culture. Until recently, the focus of most research has been restricted to examining particular cells of the matrix—such as the mother and caregiving functions. At the same time, certain functions and persons have been assumed to be synonymous. Moreover, by using the epigenetic model researchers have assumed that the lack of a particular object–function relationship leads to harmful consequences. If we consider the entire matrix, however, it may be possible to determine whether there are specific object–function relationships, for example, whether mother and mothering are synonymous. In addition, it can be determined whether certain functions can be safely substituted for by others without harmful consequences, as, for example, whether a peer can be substituted for an adult in the functions of nurturance or teaching.

The social network model may best characterize the child's social world as well as reflecting ontogenetic, cultural, and idiographic differences. In the child's life there exist a variety of significant social objects. Which social objects constitute the important relationships for the child depends on the structure and values of the particular culture. We view the social network as a system. The network is established by the culture for the transmission of cultural values. The composition of the network, the nature of the social objects, the functions they fulfill, and the relationship between objects and functions are the parts of the vehicle through which the cultural values are determined. In fact, this structure may be as important as the specific information conveyed; indeed, it may constitute the information itself. Finally, these comments should alert us to the dangers of assuming that the care of children represents some unchanging and absolute process. The care of children is the primary social activity of any society since it represents the single activity wherein the values of the society are preserved. Child care must reflect the values of the culture at large; therefore, one should expect it to change as these values change. The issue of social values must be addressed in order for us to deal with the ideal relationship (if any) between objects and functions and their interaction. The research tasks are to characterize various networks and to determine the outcome of various object–function relationships in regard to a set of goals and values rather than to argue for some ideal biological state.

SOCIAL COGNITIVE SKILLS RELATED TO SYSTEMS

One important problem overlooked in the study of social development has been the growth of cognitive skills that support that development. We have already discussed self-development as one skill that plays a central role in the movement from interactions to relationships. Two important additional cognitive abilities will now be considered. The first deals with the child's conceptualization of social space, that is, the child's growing understanding of persons and their roles. While the relationship between person and role has been discussed previously, we wish to focus more closely on the conceptualization of persons. The second cognitive factor has to do with the effects that influence social growth. We have conceptualized them in terms of direct and indirect effects, which will be presented in more detail.

Social Space

We have shown how it is necessary to consider early social interaction and relationships with a variety of social objects. Given that the infant must learn to make its way through a large and complex social array, how might it go about constructing knowledge? The use of the schematic representation of space presented in Figure 8.6 may offer one possibility. The construction of the child's social world is possible if we allow for the use of only several dimensions. Three dimensions—age, familiarity, and gender—are attributes of the self and of the social world that the child acquires early. These three attributes may be used by the young child as a means to differentiate the social array. Figure 8.6 presents this three-dimensional space along

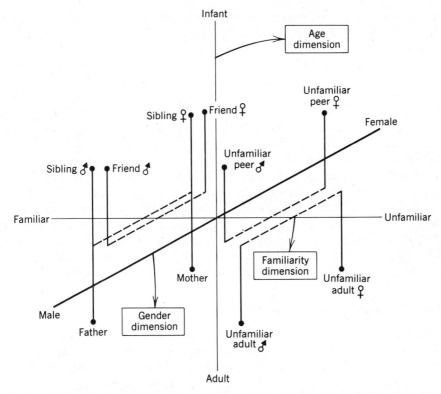

Figure 8.6. Three-dimensional schematic representation of the child's social world. The dimensions of familiarity–unfamiliarity and adult–infant are continuous while the dimension of male–female is dichotomous (although it is possible that, psychologically speaking, from the young child's point of view sex is more or less a continuous variable; e.g., mothers are more female than 5-year-old girls). Siblings and parents have been represented as equally familiar while adult strangers have been represented as less familiar than peer strangers. The points given are merely illustrative of possible locations of persons in a child's social world and may vary depending on the child's perception.

with the placement of some of the more common social objects in the child's life. As these dimensions become more differentiated the social objects within it become differentiated as well. Thus as age becomes differentiated (i.e., larger than a two-category system) one can add grandparents and adolescents, or within the familiarity dimension different degrees of familiar–unfamiliar allow for the placement of strangers, friends, and family.

Whether the infant uses the dimensions referred to above to help create the social array is still to be determined. However, the ability to construct such an array from just three dimensions indicates that it may be possible. From a structural point of view, it appears to be an interesting possibility that should be further explored. There are sources of support for the proposition that very young children have known about such social dimensions of age, familiarity, and gender. For example, Bronson (1972) as well as others (Fogel, 1982) has shown that familiarity in the social world is acquired early and becomes a salient dimension of the child's cognitive structures. Bronson (1972) has demonstrated stranger fear in infants as young as 3 months, while Fogel (1982) and Brazelton (1974) present some data indicating children respond differentially to familiars in terms of their social interactions. The attention literature supports the notion that children are responsive to familiarity soon after birth (e.g., Lewis, Goldberg & Campbell, 1969).

Gender knowledge and gender identity appear quite early and indicate that infants are responsive to gender (Lewis & Weinraub, 1979; Money & Ehrhardt, 1972). Responses to age have been shown repeatedly, both to live subjects (Brooks & Lewis, 1976; Greenberg, Hillman, & Grice, 1973; Lewis & Brooks, 1974) and to pictures (Brooks-Gunn & Lewis, 1981; Lewis, 1985). These and considerably more data could be used to support the argument that the dimensions of gender, age, and familiarity are available for the construction of the social array and that these dimensions are concepts that come into use early in the child's life. Unfortunately, while some evidence exists for the demonstration of knowledge of each of these dimensions of the array, there is no information to allow us to conclude that these dimensions in combination are used. Even so, by allowing for the consideration of the cognitive ability of the young child to organize the considerable and diverse number of social objects, and by using a structural analysis such as the one presented, we have the start of a theory of social cognition based on the complex structure of the social world.

Direct and Indirect Social Effects

Still another cognitive capacity in young children allows them to profit from action around them that does not directly involve them. Such a process as this has been described under such terms as *incidental learning, direct* and *indirect effects,* and more recently, *social referencing.* We will focus on these processes since they allow for the consideration of a systems approach.

Social knowledge and relationships emerge through the child's experiences with people and objects. How children acquire information and how they form relationships are unclear but are usually studied by focusing on the nature of the child's commerce with its environment. In general, models of social interaction, especially in infancy, have tended to be restricted to what has been called direct forms of experience (Bronfenbrenner, 1977; Lewis & Weinraub, 1976) wherein the child acquires knowledge and forms relationships through its interactions with other people and objects. At least two reasons appear to explain why emphasis has been placed almost exclusively on direct effects. In regard to the first, the influence of the experimental paradigm can be seen. Because the paradigm is concerned with the issue of causality, it is necessary to find specific and manipulatable factors that affect specific outcomes. This cause and effect model focuses attention on direct interactions. The second reason for the failure to examine less direct forms of interactions is the overconcern for studying the dyadic relationship of infant and mother. By focusing attention solely on the mother–child relationship as the primary cause of social and cognitive development, an error only now being corrected, we not only eliminated significant others from consideration in the child's development, but, more to the point, we studied only dyadic interactions. The failure to consider more complex interactions restricted our theoretical scope and the consideration of indirect effects.

Certainly, information acquisition and the formation of social relationships require the interaction of the child with the environment. However, relatively little consideration has been given to the types of processes that do not include direct interaction but influence the nature and form of immediate or future interactions. Children acquire information in a variety of indirect ways that are not necessarily characterized by immediate interaction with people or objects. For example, in observational or imitational learning the child learns about the environment by watching an interaction of another or others but not through direct interaction with the object(s) or person(s) being observed. Children also learn about the environment in a less focused manner (e.g., see Hagen & Hale, 1973, for a discussion of incidental learning).

The failure to consider both direct and indirect effects on the child's acquisition of information and formation of social relationships is further exacerbated by the lack of formulations and methods for examining how these two kinds of effects operate separately or in combination to affect socialization. While it has become increasingly clear that both direct and indirect effects need to be considered, relatively little focus on this problem has occurred (see Bronfenbrenner, 1977; Clarke-Stewart, 1978a, 1978b; Lewis & Feiring, 1978; Lewis & Weinraub, 1976; Parke et al., 1979; and more recently Campos & Stenberg, 1981; Feinman & Lewis, 1983; Sorce & Emde, 1981).

Direct Effects

Direct effects have been defined as those interactions that represent the effect or influence of one person on the behaviors of another when both are engaged in mutual interaction (Lewis & Weinraub, 1976). In the study of social behavior, direct effects are usually observed in dyadic interactions but could include more than two people as when a teacher instructs a class of students. Direct effects involve information gathered from participation in an interaction with another person or object and always involve the target person as one of the focused participants in the interaction.

Consider a mother and infant interaction in which an infant vocalizes and then the mother vocalizes back. The responsivity of mother to child directly affects the rate of infant vocalization and before long the infant vocalizes in order to produce the maternal response. Besides the direct reinforcement of the vocalization behavior, the child may have learned a number of different rules, including that people (at least its mother) are responsive, that it can control its environment (a means and ends rule), and that there is turn taking in social exchanges. The learning of these things occurs as a direct relationship between the behavior of mother and that of infant, and the variance to be explained and accounted for can be found in the parameters of each participant's behavior.

It is also possible to study the direct effect of an interaction at one point in time and relate it to the child's developmental status at a subsequent point. Thus for example, Freedle and Lewis (1977) looked at the mother–infant vocalization pattern when the infant was 12 weeks of age and related it to the dyad's linguistic patterns when the child was 2 years old. The finding that prelinguistic turn taking and conversation openings and closings at 12 weeks, as measured in direct interaction, were related to both child's MLU and mother's question asking when the child was 2 years old lends support to the study of direct effects as they influence subsequent development.

Interest and focus on the study of direct effects may be found in the infant learning literature, as well, where the process of information acquisition has received considerable attention. At least four types of learning processes in infants and young children have been studied: classical conditioning (Papoušek, 1967); instrumental conditioning (Lipsitt, 1963); contingency or conjugate learning (Lewis & Goldberg, 1969; Rovee-Collier & Gekoski, 1979); and habituation (Lewis et al., 1969). Although there is some question as to the developmental course of these different forms of learning, all have been shown to be effective ways for infants at an early age to acquire information from their direct interactions with their environment. Further discussion on the importance of examining direct effects is not necessary since it is commonly recognized that the role of direct interaction and learning has a significant effect on the child's (and parent's) concurrent and subsequent developmental status. It is on the role of indirect effects that attention should be focused.

Indirect Effects

The term *indirect effect* refers to two classes of events. In the first class, indirect effects are those sets of interactions that affect the target person but that occur in the absence of that person. These sets of interactions affect the target person but may best be described as influences that play their role in development as they affect direct effects (or interactions).

The second class of indirect effects is comprised of interactions among members of the system that occur in the presence of the target person, even though the interaction is not directed toward or does not involve that person. These kinds of indirect effects are based on information that is gathered from sources other than the direct interaction with another person or object. These effects may be the result of observation of another's interaction with persons or objects or may be the result of information gathered from another about the attitudes, behaviors, traits, or actions of a third person.

In a child's absence, a father can make a mother feel good about herself as wife and as mother. The mother's good feeling about her competence influences her responsiveness to the child in a positive way, making her more likely to praise the child's attempts to master the environment. The mother praises the child's exercise of motor skills, which facilitates the child's ability to contact and explore people and things in the environment. Consequently, the child's development of motor and cognitive skills has been indirectly influenced by the father. The child is not present when the husband praises his wife and compliments her on the development of their child. Neither is the father present and praising the child on the following day. However, the father has an indirect effect on the child's development *vis-à-vis* his support of the mother and the mother's consequent responsiveness to the child. This influence has been discussed in terms of two parameters: marital satisfaction and self-esteem. From a marital satisfaction point of view, the parent (either one) will be capable of better parenting if certain other needs are met, in particular, if adult social relations are satisfactory. The praise of the father for the mother's work in caring for the child has an effect on maternal self-esteem (Barry, 1968, 1970; Feiring, 1976; Heath, 1976; Pedersen, 1975). If care giving constitutes an important activity for the mother, her success in this activity serves to foster feelings of competency and high self-esteem, which in turn should positively affect the mother–infant interaction. While research has only started to explore such influences, there is some suggestion that they do play an important role.

Moreover, fathers influence the direct interactions between child and mother through their sharing of the various tasks that are necessary in the lives of families. Besides the more obvious financial support, adults support one another through the sharing of tasks. The financial burden is currently more equally shared between mother and father, and there has been an increase in the father's sharing of household tasks. While sharing financial and household duties may be important ways in which a couple supports the family and each other's functioning, a most important support function relative to the role of parenting must be in the ability of two adults to discuss the problem of child care. The sharing of tasks, responsibilities, information, and philosophies around child care between parents (or other caregivers) is an important indirect influence that has received too little attention but that nevertheless influences the child's development.

The discussion to follow focuses on those indirect effects that occur in the presence of the child. These are effects that the child experiences but that do not focus on the child and as such have been considered indirect. Indirect forms of information acquisition have been considered under a wide rubric that includes identification, modeling, imitation, and incidental, vicarious, and observational learning. While a distinction between these terms is beyond the scope of this discussion, it should be clear that forms other than direct kinds of information acquisition have received considerable attention (see, e.g., Bandura, 1969, 1973; Freud, 1953; Guillaume, 1971; Hagen & Hale, 1973; Hartup & Coates, 1970; Lewis, 1979a; Parke et al., 1979; Piaget, 1951; Yando, Seitz, & Zigler, 1978).

Recently Lewis (Feinman & Lewis, 1983; Feiring, Lewis, & Starr, 1984; Lewis & Feiring, 1981, in press) and Campos and Emde (1985) have explored indirect effects as they relate to social development. In one study of families at dinner (Lewis & Feiring, 1982), we observed how the behavior of two of the family members affected the behavior of a third member. Specifically, we were interested in the child's vocalization. Vocalization of the father directed to the child was significantly correlated with how much vocalization the child directed to the father. This type of analysis reflects what we have called direct effects; that is, how the father's behavior toward the child affects the child's behavior toward him. An indirect effect in this situation is for example, how the vocalization of the mother directed to the father affects the father–son pattern. An indirect effect would be demonstrated if the amount of vocalization in which the mother and father mutually engage in affects how much the child vocalizes to the father. The findings indicate that mother–father vocalization is significantly correlated with child's vocalization to the father. This finding holds independently of how much the mother vocalizes to the child. At the dinner table how much vocalization mother and father engage in affects how the child will act. This indirect effect influences the child's behavior nearly as much as the direct effect of the father's vocalization.

Other types of indirect effects have been observed. Feinman and Lewis (1983) had mothers talk to approaching strangers in a "stranger approach" paradigm. The mother talked in either a highly positive or a neutral tone. After the mother stopped her conversation her 18-month-old child's response to the stranger's friendly overture was observed. As predicted, children whose mothers responded in a friendly manner to the stranger as opposed to a neutral manner had infants who responded significantly more positively to the strangers. This study indicated that children as young as 10 months of age are able to use their mothers' behavior toward another to inform them and affect their behavior toward that other. Similar findings concerning infants' responses to strangers as a function of others' behavior to those strangers were reported by Feiring et al. (1984).

This indirect effect can also be obtained in regard to young children's response to objects or situations. In a series of studies, children's responses to novel toys, potentially threatening objects, and the deep side of the visual cliff have been shown to be affected by maternal responses. While such studies are best considered related to social referencing, they do indicate that young infants are able to obtain information not only in a direct manner but also indirectly. While most experimental studies have used the mother as the source of the indirect effect, Feiring et al. (1984) used other adults beside mothers. These authors found both mother and others (in this case a stranger) capable, through their interactions, of influencing the child's subsequent behavior. Such findings suggest that indirect effects may operate across a wide number of other social objects. The schema for social objects allows the young child to conceptualize others, and indirect and direct social effects allow for the action of these multiple objects. These two cognitive aspects represent an important vehicle for the child's social commerce in a complex social field. Children by 12 months of age appear capable of utilizing them.

In any theory of social development there is a need to consider these cognitive capacities. It will do social theories little good to ignore the role of cognition in social development (and social development in cognition). The development of self and thus the capacity of the organism to feel empathy, pride, shame, and guilt are important aspects of social development. The child's ability to share and understand the perspective of mother is of central importance to its social behavior. In addition, the development of understanding of others, their nature, and their roles is necessary for appropriate social behavior to emerge. Underlying these developments is the child's ability to learn both directly and indirectly from those around it. Thus these three cognitive capacities have been stressed, although others could be mentioned as well.

SUMMARY AND CONCLUSION

The study of social development in infancy and early childhood is for the most part not theory driven. Given the almost unlimited aspects of social development that could be studied, the literature is vast and difficult to summarize. This chapter has aimed at focusing this literature on the two important guiding theories, those of attachment and social network. A more complete review would have to include the addition of the sociobiological theory, and its omission is recognized. Even in a handbook there is not sufficient space for it. More attention needs to be given to the roles of cognition and affect in social development. While some consideration has been given here to cognition, specifically the development of self and its role in relationships, infants' understanding of people, and people and their roles, more attention needs to be paid to the roles of perception–discrimination, intersensory integration, memory, and categorization. Social development theories, especially attachment theory, suffer by the inadequate attention paid to cognition (a similar complaint could be leveled at the failure of cognitive theories to consider social and affective issues). The role of affect in social behavior and the relationship between them is lacking as well, in part because little attention has been paid to them by others (see Lewis & Michalson, 1984). It is obvious that many social interactions and relationships center around affect as their content and outcome. In the young infant much of the mother–child interaction centers around affect (see Brooks-Gunn & Lewis, 1982; Field, 1981; Lewis & Michalson, 1982; Malatesta & Haviland, 1982).

Also missing from a more complete review is the role of individual differences, in social behavior, particularly temperament. The social interactions and subsequent relationships of a child of "difficult" temperament (see Thomas & Chess, 1981) or of an inhibited child (see Kagan, Reznick, Clarke, Snidman, & Garcia-Coll, 1984) should inform us first, that individual differences are important in helping us understand the range of social behavior and the nature of development, and second, that more work is necessary to expound those other individual difference variables that need consideration. In this regard, sex differences are particularly important as they impact on development. Without question, gender plays a critical role in both the content of social behavior and the developmental process itself (for examples see Lewis et al. 1984; Schaeffer & Bayley, 1963). In many studies, the development of male children and that of female children seems to involve different processes (Lewis, Feiring, McGuffog, & Jaskir, 1984) as well as differences in stability and change (Kagan & Moss, 1963). Finally a consideration of psychopathology would address how social development goes astray. Given the recent interest in developmental psychopathology (Lewis, 1985; Sroufe & Rutter, 1984), consideration of these issues, even with the limited amount of data, is needed. To do justice to all these topics is beyond the capacity of this chapter. Nevertheless, no theory of social development can be considered complete without some attention paid to them.

In this chapter, we have stressed several themes that we feel are necessary for even the most cursory discussion of the topic. First, infants at birth enter into a social world filled with a variety of people performing a variety of behaviors. We suspect that the evolutionary history provides the earliest mechanisms for coping with and adapting to this complex structure. These mechanisms (be they action patterns, reflexes, or instincts) are more complex than originally thought and provide the organism with the behavioral repertoire to enter and engage the social environment. Early social interactions may be in large part made up of these complex interactive patterns. However, it is not until the child's sense of self emerges that we can speak of relationships, and it is on this process that we have focused some attention. For us, in the study of social development in infancy, one of the critical developmental events is the ontogeny of the self-construct. Such development is cognitive in nature and stands as the mediating event between early "primitive" interactional patterns and mature social behavior. In a word or two, *relationships require a self and the negotiation of two selves.*

We have also focused on the wide array of people who inhabit the infant's world. How they behave, what impact they have, and the child's conceptualization of them are topics that any theory of social development must consider. This array is large and varied, and the child's relationship to them is complex. While attachment theory treats this array in a limited fashion, one that is sequential in nature, social network theory treats these relationships simultaneously and suggests that the task of the child is to learn to cope with many at a time. This difference argues for the importance of the social structure as it impacts on roles, people, and relationships, while attachment, grounded in ethology, relies more on universal patterns. While we clearly favor one theory over another, the importance of contrast is in the *test* of their differential prediction. It is our intention not to limit the discussion, but rather to see how differential prediction and test are possible. Not until our social theories are strong enough for this can it be said that we have any real understanding of social development.

REFERENCES

Abramovitch, R., Corter, C., & Lando, B. (1979). Sibling interaction in the home. *Child Development, 50,* 997–1003.

Ainsworth, M. D. S. (1961). *The development of infant–child interaction among the Ganda.* Paper read at Tavistock Study Group on Mother–Infant Interaction, London.

Ainsworth, M. D. S. (1964). Patterns of attachment behavior shown by the infant in inter-action with his mother. *Merrill-Palmer Quarterly, 10,* 51–58.

Ainsworth, M. D. S. (1969). Object relationships, dependency, and attachment: A theoretical review of the infant–mother relationship. *Child Development, 40,* 969–1026.

Ainsworth, M. D. S. (1972). Attachment and dependency: A comparison. In J. L. Gewirtz (Ed.), *Attachment and dependency.* Washington, DC: V. H. Winston.

Ainsworth, M. D. S. (1973). The development of infant–mother attachment. In B. M. Cald-well & H. N. Ricciuti (Eds.), *Review of child development and research* (Vol. 3) Chicago: University of Chicago Press.

Ainsworth, M. D. S., & Bell, S. M. (1969). Some contemporary patterns of mother–infant interaction in the feeding situation. In A. Ambrose (Ed.), *Stimulation in early infancy.* New York: Academic.

Ainsworth, M. D. S., Belhar, M. C., Waters, E., & Wall, S. (1978). *Patterns of attachment: A psychological study of the strange situation.* Hillsdale, NJ: Erlbaum.

Aldous, J. (1975). The search for alternatives: Parental behaviors and children's original problem solutions. *Journal of Marriage & the Family, 37,* 711–722.

Aldous, J. (1978). *Family careers: Developmental change in families.* New York: Wiley.

Anderson, J. W. (1972). Attachment behavior out-of-doors. In Blurton-Jones (Ed.), *Eth-ological studies of human behavior.* London: Cambridge University Press.

Arend, R., Gove, F. L., & Sroufe, L. A. (1979). Continuity of individual adaptation from infant to kindergarten: A predictive study of ego-resilience and curiosity in preschoolers. *Child Development, 50,* 950–959.

Attneave, C. L. (1976). Social networks as the unit of intervention. In P. J. Guerin (Ed.), *Family therapy: Theory and practice.* New York: Gardner.

Baldwin, J. M. (1894). *Handbook of psychology: Feeling and will.* New York: Holt.

Ban, P., & Lewis, M. (1974). Mothers and fathers, girls and boys: Attachment behavior in the one-year-old. *Merrill-Palmer Quarterly, 20* (3), 195–204.

Bandura, A. (1969). *Principles of behavior modification.* New York: Holt, Rinehart, & Win-ston.

Bandura, A. (1973). *Aggression: A social learning analysis.* Englewood Cliffs, NJ: Prentice-Hall.

Barnes, J. A. (1954). Class and committees in a Norwegian island parish. *Human Relations, 7,* 39–58.

Barry, W. A. (1968). *Conflict in marriage: A study of the interactions of newlywed couples in experimentally induced conflicts.* Doctoral dissertation, University of Michigan, Ann Arbor, MI.

Barry, W. A. (1970). Marriage research and conflict: An integrative review. *Psychological Bulletin, 73* (1), 41–54.

Bates, J. E., Maslin, C. A., & Frankel, K. A. (1985). Attachment security, mother–child interaction and temperament as predictors of behavior problem ratings at age three years. In I. Bretherton & E. Waters (Eds.), Growing points of attachment theory and research. *Monographs of the Society for Research in Child Development, 50,* 167–193.

Bee, H. L., Van Egeren, L. F., Streissguth, A. P., Nyman, B. A., & Leckie, M. S. (1969). Social class differences in maternal teaching strategies and speech patterns. *Developmental Psychology, 1* (6), 726–734.

Beilin, H. (1983). The new functionalism and Piaget's program. In E. K. Scholnick (Ed.), *New trends in conceptual representation.* Hillsdale, NJ: Erlbaum.

Belsky, J., Rovine, M., & Taylor, D. G. (1984). The origins of individual differences in infant–mother attachment: Maternal and infant contributions (The Pennsylvania Infant and Family Development Project). *Child Development, 55,* 718–728.

Bischof, N. (1975). A systems approach toward the functional connections of attachment and fear. *Child Development, 46* (4), 801–817.

Blehar, M. C., Lieberman, A., & Ainsworth, M. D. S. (1977). Early face-to-face interaction and its relation to later infant–mother attachment. *Child Development, 48,* 182–194.

Block, J. H. (1973). Conceptions of sex role: Some cross-cultural and longitudinal perspectives. *American Psychologist, 28,* 512–526.

Block, J., & Block, T. H. (1979). The role of ego control and ego resiliency in the organization of behavior. In W. A. Collins (Ed.), *Minnesota Symposium on Child Psychology* (Vol. 13). Hillsdale, NJ: Erlbaum.

Borke, H. (1971). Interpersonal perception of young children: Egocentrism or empathy. *Developmental Psychology, 5,* 263–269.

Borke, H. (1975). Piaget's mountains revisited: Changes in the egocentric landscape. *Developmental Psychology, 11,* 240–243.

Bott, E. (1957). *Family and social network.* London: Tavistock Institute of Human Relations.

Bott, E. (1971). Family and social network (2nd ed.). New York: Free Press.

Bowen, M. (1972). Family therapy and family group therapy. In H. I. Kaplan & B. J. Sadock (Eds.), *Group treatment of mental illness.* New York: Dutton.

Bower, T. G. R. (1974). *Development in infancy.* San Francisco: Freeman.

Bower, T. G. R. (1975). Infant perception of the third dimension and object concept development. In L. B. Cohen & P. Salapatek (Eds.), *Infant perception: From sensation to cognition* (Vol. 2). New York: Academic.

Bowlby, J. (1958). The nature of the child's tie to his mother. *International Journal of Psychoanalysis, 39,* 350–373.

Bowlby, J. (1951). *Maternal care and mental health.* Geneva: World Health Organization. New York: Columbia University Press. (Abridged version published as *Child care and the growth of love* (2nd Ed.). (1965). Harmondsworth: Penguin Books.

Bowlby, J. (1969). *Attachment and loss: Vol. 1. Attachment.* New York: Basic.

Bowlby, J. (1973). *Attachment and loss: Vol. 2. Separation: Anxiety and anger.* London: Hogarth.

Bowlby, J. (1980). *Attachment and loss* (Vol. 3). New York: Basic.

Brazelton, T. B., Koslowski, B., & Main, M. (1974). The origins of reciprocity: The early mother–infant interaction. In M. Lewis & L. Rosenblum (Eds.), *The effect of the infant on its caretaker: The origins of behavior* (Vol. 1). New York: Wiley.

Brazelton, T. B., Yogman, M., Als, H., & Tronick, E. (1979). The infant as a focus for family reciprocity. In M. Lewis & L. Rosenblum (Eds.), *The child and its family: The genesis of behavior* (Vol. 2). New York: Plenum.

Bretherton, I. (1985). Attachment theory: Retrospect and prospect. In I. Bretherton & E. Waters (Eds.), Growing points of attachment, theory and research. *Monographs of the Society for Research in Child Development, 50,* 3–38.

Broman, S. H., Nichols, P. L., & Kennedy, W. A. (1972). Precursors of low IQ in young children. *Proceedings of the Annual Convention of the American Psychological Association, 7,* 77–78.

Bronfenbrenner, U. (1977). Toward an experimental ecology of human development. *American Psychologist, 32,* 513–531.

Bronson, G. W. (1972). Infants' reactions to unfamiliar persons and novel objects. *Monographs of the Society for Research in Child Development, 37.*

Brooks, J., & Lewis, M. (1974). The effect of time on attachment as measured in a free-play situation. *Child Development, 45,* 311–316.

Brooks, J., & Lewis, M. (1976). Infants' responses to strangers: Midget, adult and child. *Child Development, 47,* 323–332.

Brooks-Gunn, J., & Lewis, M. (1981). Infant social perception: Responses to pictures of parents and strangers. *Developmental Psychology, 17,* 647–649.

Brooks-Gunn, J., & Lewis, M. (1982). Affective exchanges between normal and handicapped infants and their mothers. In T. Field & A. Fogel (Eds.), *Emotion and interaction: Normal and high risk infants.* Hillsdale, NJ: Erlbaum.

Brown, C. (1971). *Manchild in the promised land.* New York: Signet.

Bryant, B. K. (1982). Sibling relationships in middle childhood. In M. Lamb & B. Sutton-Smith (Eds.), *Sibling relationships: Their nature and significance across the life-span.* Hillsdale, NJ: Erlbaum.

Burt, C., Jones, E., Miller, E., & Moodie, W. (1934). *How the mind works.* New York: Appleton-Century-Crofts.

Buss, A. H., & Plomin, R. (1984). *Temperament: Early developing personality traits.* Hillsdale, NJ: Erlbaum.

Cairns, R. B. Attachment behavior of mammals. (1966). *Psychological Review, 73,* 409–426.

Cairns, N., Clark, G., Smith, S., & Lansky, S. (1979). Adaptation of siblings to childhood malignancy. *Journal of Pediatrics, 95,* 484–487.

Campos, J., Emde, R. N., Gaensbauer, T., & Sorce, J. (1973). *Cardiac and behavioral responses of human infants to stranger: Effects of mother's absence and of experimental sequence.* Paper presented at the meeting of the Society for Research in Child Development, Philadelphia.

Campos, J. J., & Emde, R. N. (1985). Personal communication.

Campos, J. J., & Stenberg, C. R. (1981). Perception, appraisal, and emotion: The onset of social referencing. In M. Lamb & E. L. Sherrod (Eds.), *Infant social cognition.* Hillsdale, NJ: Erlbaum.

Caplow, T. (1968). *Two against one: Coalition in triads.* Englewood Cliffs, NJ: Prentice-Hall.

Caron, R. F., Caron, A. T., & Myers, R. S. (1982). Abstraction of invariant face expressions in infancy. *Child Development, 53,* 1008–1015.

Caudill, W. & Weinstein, H. (1969). Maternal care and infant behavior in Japan and America. *Psychiatry, 32,* 12–43.

Cicirelli, V. G. (1975). Effects of mother and older sibling on the problem solving behavior of the younger child. *Developmental Psychology, 11,* 749–756.

Cicirelli, V. G. (1982). Sibling influence throughout the lifespan. In M. E. Lamb & B. Sutton-Smith (Eds.), *Sibling relationships: Their nature and significance across the lifespan.* Hillsdale, NJ: Erlbaum.

Clark-Stewart, K. A. (1978a). And daddy makes three: The father's impact on mother and young child. *Child Development, 49*(2), 466–478.

Clarke-Stewart, A. (1978b). Recasting the lone stranger. In J. Glick & A. Clarke-Stewart (Eds.), *Studies in social and cognitive development: The development of social understanding* (Vol. 1). New York: Gardner.

Coates, D., & Lewis, M. (1984). Early mother–infant interaction and infant cognitive status as predictors of school performance and cognitive behavior in six year olds. *Child Development, 55,* 1219–1230.

Cochran, M. M., & Brassard, J. A. (1979). Child development and personal social networks. *Child Development, 50,* 601–616.

Cohen, L. F. (1974). The operational definition of human attachment. *Psychological Bulletin, 81,* 207–217.

Cowen, E., Pedersen, A., Balijian, H., Izzo, L. D., & Trost, M. (1973). A long-term follow-up of early detected vulnerable children. *Journal of Consulting & Clinical Psychology, 41,* 438–446.

Crockenberg, S. (1981). Infant irritability, mother responsiveness, and social support influences on the security of mother–infant attachment. *Child Development, 52,* 857–865.

Cronbach, L. J. (1975). Five decades of public controversy over mental testing. *American Psychologist, 30,* 1.

Damon, W. (1977). *The social world of the child.* San Francisco: Jossey-Bass.

Dennis, W. (1960). Causes of retardation among institutional children: Iran. *Journal of Genetic Psychology, 96,* 47–59.

DeVore, B. I. (1971). The evolution of human society. In J. F. Eisenberg & W. S. Dillon, Eds. (q.v.), *Man and beast: Comparative social behavior.*

Dixon, J. C. (1957). Development of self recognition. *Journal of Genetic Psychology, 91,* 251–256.

Douglas, J. W. B. (1964). *The home and the school.* London: Panther Books.

Dunn, J., & Kendrick, C. (1979). Interaction between young siblings in the context of family relationships. In M. Lewis & L. Rosenblum (Eds.), *The child and its family: The genesis of behavior* (Vol. 2). New York: Plenum.

Dunn, J., & Kendrick, C. (1980) The arrival of a sibling: Changes in interaction between mother and first-born child. *Journal of Child Psychology, 21,* 119–132.

Dunn, J., & Kendrick, C. (1982). *Siblings: Love, envy and understanding.* Cambridge, MA: Harvard University Press.

Dunn, J., Kendrick, C., & MacNamee, R. (1981). The reaction of first-born children to the birth of a sibling: Mother's reports. *Journal of Child Psychology & Psychiatry, 22,* 1–18.

Dunn, J., & Wooding, C. (1977). Play in the home and its implications for learning. In B. Tizard & D. Harvey (Eds.), *The biology of play.* London: Heinemann Medical Books.

Edwards, C. P., & Lewis, M. (1979). Young children's concepts of social relations: Social functions and social objects. In M. Lewis & L. Rosenblum (Eds.), *The child and its family: The genesis of behavior* (Vol. 2). New York: Plenum.

Edwards, C. P., & Whiting, B. B. (1976). Dependency in dyadic context: New meaning for an old construct. Paper presented at the annual meeting of the Eastern Psychological Association, New York.

Egeland, B., & Garber, E. A. (1984). Infant–mother attachment: Factors related to its development and changes over time. *Child Development, 55,* 753–771.

Eimas, P. D., Siqueland, E. R., Jusczyk, P., & Vigorito, H. (1971). Speech perception in infants. *Science, 171,* 303–306.

Emde, R. N. (1983). The prerepresentational self and its affective core. *Psychoanalytic Study of the Child, 38,* 165–192.

Feinman, S., & Lewis, M. (1983). Social inferencing at ten months: A second-order effect on infants' responses to stranger. *Child Development, 54,* 878–887.

Feiring, C. (1975). *The influence of the child and secondary parent on maternal behavior: Toward a social systems view of early infant–mother attachment.* Unpublished doctoral dissertation, University of Pittsburgh.

Feiring, C. (1976). *The preliminary development of a social systems model of early infant–mother attachment.* Paper presented at the meetings of the Eastern Psychological Association, New York.

Feiring, C., & Lewis, M. (1981). Middle class differences in the mother–child interaction and the child's cognitive development. In T. Field (Ed.), *Culture and early interactions.* Hillsdale, NJ: Erlbaum.

Feiring, C., & Lewis, M. (1982). Early mother–child interaction: Families with only and first-born children. In G. L. Fox (Ed.), *The childbearing decision: Fertility attitudes and behavior.* Berkeley, CA: Sage.

Feiring, C., & Lewis, M. (1984). Changing characteristics of the U.S. family: Implications for family relationships and child development. In M. Lewis (Ed.), *Beyond the Dyad.* New York: Plenum.

Feiring, C., & Lewis, M. (1985). *Causal inference and studies of antecedent factors in child development.* Unpublished manuscript.

Feiring, C., Lewis, M., & Starr, M. D. (1984). Indirect effects and infant reactions to strangers. *Developmental Psychology, 20,* 485–491.

Feiring, C., & Taylor, J. (1977). *The influences of the infant and secondary parent on maternal behavior: Toward a social systems view of infant attachment.* Unpublished manuscript, University of Pittsburgh.

Ferguson, L. R., & Freeark, K. (1979). *School entry: Transition for mother and child.* Paper presented at the Society for Research in Child Development, Boston.

Field, T. (1981). Infant arousal, attention, and affect during early interactions. In L. Lipsitt (Ed.), *Advances in infant development* (Vol. 1). Hillsdale, NJ: Erlbaum.

Flavell, J. H. (1972). An analysis of cognitive-developmental sequences. *Genetic Psychology Monographs, 86,* 279–350.

Flavell, J. H. (1974). The genesis of our understanding of persons: Psychological studies. In T. Mischel (Ed.), *Understanding Other Persons.* Totowa, NJ: Rowman & Littlefield.

Fogel, A. (1982). Early adult–infant interaction: Expectable sequences of behavior. *Journal of Pediatric Psychology, 7,* 1–22.

Frazer, J. (1915). *The Golden Bough.* New York: Macmillan.

Freedle, R., & Lewis, M. (1977). Prelinguistic conversations. In M. Lewis & L. Rosenblum (Eds.), *Interaction, conversation and the development of language: The origins of behavior* (Vol. 5). New York: Wiley.

Freud, S. (1953). Three essays on the theory of sexuality. In J. Strachey (Ed. & Trans.) in collaboration with A. Freud, *The standard edition of the complete psychological works of Sigmund Freud* (Vol. 7). London: Hogarth Press and the Institute of Psycho-analysis. (Original work published 1905)

Freud, S. (1959). Instincts and their vicissitudes. *Collected Papers.* New York: Basic Books. (Original work published 1915)

Freud, A., & Dann, S. (1951). An experiment in group upbringing. In R. Eissler, A. Freud, H. Hartmann, & E. Kris (Eds.), *The psychoanalytic study of the child* (Vol. 6). New York: International Universities Press.

Furman, W., Rake, D. F., & Hartup, W. W. (1979). Rehabilitation of socially-withdrawn children through mixed-age and same-age socialization. *Child Development, 50,* 915–922.

Goldberg, S. (1977). *Stimulus properties of the human infant.* Unpublished manuscript.

Goldsmith, H. H., & Campos, J. J. (1982). Toward a theory of infant temperament. In R. N. Emde & R. J. Harmon (Eds.), *The development of attachment and affiliative systems.* New York: Plenum.

Gould, S. J. (1981). *The mismeasurement of man.* New York: Norton.

Greenbaum, M. (1965). Joint sibling interview as a diagnostic procedure. *Journal of Child Psychology & Psychiatry, 6,* 227–232.

Greenbaum, C. W., & Landau, R. (1977). In P. H. Leiderman, S. R. Tulkin, & A. Rosenfeld (Eds.), *Culture and infancy: Variations in the human experience.* New York: Academic.

Greenberg, D. J., Hillman, D., & Grice, D. (1973). Infant and stranger variables related to stranger anxiety in the first year of life. *Developmental Psychology, 9,* 207–212.

Gillaume, D. (1971). *Imitation in children* (E. P. Halperin, Trans.). Chicago: University of Chicago Press. (Original work published 1926)

Gyomroi-Ludowyk, E. (1963). The analysis of a young concentration camp victim. *Psychoanalytic Study of the Child, 18,* 484–510.

Hagen, J., & Hale, G. (1973). The development of attention in children. In A. Pick (Ed.), *Minnesota Symposia on Child Psychology* (Vol. 7). Minneapolis: University of Minnesota Press.

Hamilton, W. D. (1964). The genetical theory of social behavior, I, II. *Journal of Theoretical biology, 7,* 1–52.

Harlow, H. F. (1958). The nature of love. *American Psychologist, 13,* 573–685.

Harlow, H. F. (1969). Age-mate or peer affectional system. In D. S. Lehrman, R. A. Hinde, & E. Shaw (Eds.), *Advances in the study of behavior* (Vol. 2). New York: Academic.

Harlow, H. F., & Harlow, M. D. (1965). The affectional systems. In A. M. Schrier, H. F. Harlow, & F. Stollnitz (Eds.), *Behavior of nonhuman primates* (Vol. 2). New York: Academic.

Hartup, W. W. (1970). Peer interaction and social organization. In P. Mussen (Ed.), *Carmichael's manual of child psychology* (Vol. 2). New York: Wiley.

Hartup, W. W. (1975). The anatomy of attachment. *Contemporary Psychology, 20,* 311–313.

Hartup, W. W. (1979). Two social worlds: Family relations and peer relations. In M. Rutter (Ed.), *Scientific foundations of developmental psychiatry.* London: Heinemann.

Hartup, W. W., & Coates, B. (1970). The role of imitation in childhood socialization. In R. A. Hoppe, G. A. Milton, & E. C. Simmel (Eds.), *Early experiences and the processes of socialization.* New York: Academic.

Hayes, L. A., & Watson, J. S. (1981). Neonatal imitation: Fact or artifact? *Developmental Psychology, 17,* 655–660.

Heath, D. H. (1976). Competent fathers: Their personality and marriage. *Human Development, 19,* 26–39.

Heinicke, C., & Westheimer, I. (1966). *Brief separations.* New York: International University Press.

Hess, E. H. (1959). Imprinting. *Science, 130,* 133–141.

Hess, R. D., & Shipman, V. C. (1965). Early experience and the socialization of cognitive modes in children *Child Development, 36,* 869–886.

Hill, R. (1966). Contemporary developments in family theory. *Journal of Marriage & the Family, 28,* 10–26.

Hill, R. (1973). Modern systems theory and the family: A confrontation. *Social Science Information, 10*(5), 7–26.

Hill, R., Foote, N., Aldous, J., Carlson, R., & MacDonald, R. (1970). *Family development in three generations: A longitudinal study of changing family patterns of planning and achievement.* Cambridge, MA: Schenkman.

Hinde, R. A. (1976). Interactions, relationships, and social structure. *Man, 11,* 1–17.

Hinde, R. A. (1979). *Towards Understanding Relationships.* London: Academic.

Hoffman, M. L. (1971). Father absence and conscience development. *Developmental Psychology, 4,* 400–406.

Hoffman, M. (1979). Empathy, its development and prosocial implications. In B. Keasy (Ed.), *Nebraska Symposium on Motivation* (Vol. 26). Lincoln: University of Nebraska Press.

Holland, P. W., & Leinhardt, S. (Eds.). (1979). *Perspectives on social network research.* New York: Academic.

Hollingshead, A. B. (1957). *Two-factor index of social position.* New Haven, CT: Author.

Hunt, J. McV. (1961). *Intelligence and experience.* New York: Ronald.

Izard, C. E. (1977). *Human emotions.* New York: Plenum.

Jensen, A. R. (1980). *Bias in mental testing.* New York: Free Press.

Kagan, J. (1956). The child's perception of the parent. *Journal of Abnormal & Social Psychology, 53,* 257–258.

Kagan, J. (1974). Discrepancy, temperament and infant distress. In M. Lewis & L. Rosenblum (Eds.), *The origins of fear: The origins of behavior* (Vol. 2). New York: Wiley.

Kagan, J., & Moss, H. A. (1962). *Birth to maturity.* New York: Wiley.

Kagan, J., Reznick, S., Clarke, C., Snidman, N., & Garcia-Coll, C. (1984). Behavioral inhibitions to the unfamiliar. *Child Development, 55,* 2212–2225.

Kaye, K. (1982). *The mental and social life of babies: How parents create persons.* Chicago: University of Chicago Press.

Koch, H. L. (1960). The relation of certain formal attributes of siblings to attitudes held toward each other and toward parents. *Monographs of the Society for Research in Child Development, 25,* 1–124.

Konner, M. (1975). Relations among infants and juveniles in comparative perspective. In M. Lewis & L. Rosenblum (Eds.), *Friendship and peer relations: The origins of behavior* (Vol. 4). New York: Wiley.

Kotelchuck, M. (1972). *The nature of the infant's tie to his father.* Unpublished dissertation, Harvard University.

Kotelchuck, M., Zelazo, P. R., Kagan, J., & Spelke, E. (1975). Infant reactions in parental separations when left with familiar and unfamiliar adults. *Journal of Genetic Psychology, 126,* 255–262.

Kuhl, P. K., & Meltzoff, A. N. (1982). The bimodal perception of speech in infancy. *Science, 218,* 1138–1141.

Laing, R. D. (1970). *Knots,* New York: Pantheon.

Lamb, M. (1974). A defense of the concept of attachment. *Human Development, 17,* 376–385.

Lamb, M. E. (1976). The role of the father: An overview. In M. E. Lamb (Ed.). *The role of the father in child development.* New York: Wiley.

Lamb, M. E. (1978a). Interactions between eighteen-month-olds and their preschool-aged siblings. *Child Development, 49,* 51–59.

Lamb, M. E. (1978b). The father's role in the infant's social world. In J. H. S. Mathews & M. Matthews (Eds.), *Mother/child, father/child relationship.* Washington, DC: National Association for Education of Young Children.

Lamb, M. (Ed.). (1981). *The role of the father in child development* (2nd ed.). New York: Wiley.

Lamb, M., Thompson, R., Gardner, W., & Charnov, E. (1985). *Infant-mother attachment: The origins and developmental significance of individual differences in strange situation behavior.* Hillsdale, NJ: Erlbaum.

Landau, R. (1976). Extent that the mother represents the social stimulation to which the infant is exposed: Findings from a cross-cultural study. *Developmental Psychology, 12,* 399–405.

Lazar, I., & Darlington, R. B. (1982). Lasting effects of early education: A report from the Consortium for Longitudinal Studies. *Monographs of the Society for Research in Child Development, 47,* 1–151.

Lecco, C., & Lewis, M. (1985). *Knowledge of age in children: A study in social cognition.* Unpublished dissertation, Princeton University.

Lee, G. R. (1979). Effects of social networks on the family. In W. R. Burr, R. Hill, F. Nye, & I. Neiss (Eds.), *Contemporary theories about the family: Vol. 1. Research-based theories.*

Lee, G. R. (1980). Kinship in the seventies: A decade review of research and theory. *Journal of Marriage & the Family, 42,* 923–934.

Levi-Strauss, C. (1966). *The savage mind.* Chicago: University of Chicago Press.

Lewis, M. (1972). State as an infant–environment interaction: An analysis of mother–infant interaction as a function of sex. *Merrill-Palmer Quarterly, 18,* 95–121.

Lewis, M. (1979a). *Issues in the study of early imitation.* Paper presented at the meeting of the Society for Research in Child Development, San Francisco.

Lewis, M. (1979b). The self as a developmental concept. *Human Development, 22,* 416–419.

Lewis, M. (1980). Issues in the development of fear. In I. L. Kutash & L. B. Schlesinger (Eds.), *Pressure Point: Perspectives on stress and anxiety.* San Francisco: Jossey-Bass.

Lewis, M. (1982). The social network systems model: Toward a theory of social development. In T. Field (Ed.), *Review of human development* (Vol. 1). New York: Wiley.

Lewis, M. (1983). Newton, Einstein, Piaget and the concept of the self. In L. S. Liben (Ed.), *Piaget and the foundations of knowledge.* Hillsdale, NJ: Erlbaum.

Lewis, M. (1984). Social influences on development: An overview. In M. Lewis (Ed.), *Beyond the dyad.* New York: Plenum.

Lewis, M. (1985). Age as a social dimension. In T. Field & N. Fox (Eds.), *Social perception in infants,* New York: Academic.

Lewis, M. (1986). Origins of self-knowledge and individual differences in early self-recognition. In J. Suls and A. G. Greenwald (Eds.), *Psychological Perspectives on the Self (Vol. 3).* London: Lawrence Erlbaum Associates.

Lewis, M. (in press). Individual differences in early self recognition. In A. Greenwald & J. Suls (Eds.), *Psychological perspective of the self* (Vol. 3). Hillsdale, NJ: Erlbaum.

Lewis, M. (in press). Predicting psychopathology in six year olds from early parental relations. *Integrative Psychiatry.*

Lewis, M. (in press). The role of the self in knowing. In P. Cole (Ed.), *Self and consciousness, Houston Symposium VI.*

Lewis, M., & Ban, P. (1971). *Stability of attachment behavior: A transformational analysis.* Paper presented at the Meeting of the Society for Research in Child Development, Symposium on Attachment: Studies in Stability and Change, Minneapolis.

Lewis, M., & Brooks, J. (1974). Self, other and fear: Infants' reactions to people. In M. Lewis & L. Rosenblum (Eds.), *The origins of fear: The origins of behavior* (Vol. 2). New York: Wiley.

Lewis, M., & Brooks-Gunn, J. (1979). *Social cognition and the acquisition of self.* New York: Plenum.

Lewis, M., Brooks-Gunn, J., & Jaskir, J. (1985). Individual differences in early visual self recognition. *Developmental Psychology, 21.*

Lewis, M., & Coates, D. L. (1980). Mother–infant interactions and cognitive development in twelve-week-old infants. *Infant Behavior & Development, 3,* 95–105.

Lewis, M., & Feiring, C. (1978). The child's social world. In R. M. Lerner & J. D. Spanier (Eds.), *Child influences on marital and family interaction: A life-span perspective.* New York: Academic.

Lewis, M., & Feiring, C. (1979). The child's social network: Social object, social functions and their relationship. In M. Lewis & L. Rosenblum (Eds.), *The child and its family: The genesis of behavior* (Vol. 2). New York: Plenum.

Lewis, M., & Feiring, C. (1981). Direct and indirect interactions in social relationships. In L. Lipsitt (Ed.), *Advances in infancy research* (Vol. 1). New York: Ablex.

Lewis, M., & Feiring, C. (1982). Some American families at dinner. In L. Laosa & I. Sigel (Eds.), *The family as learning environments for children* (Vol. 1). New York: Plenum.

Lewis, M., & Feiring, C. (1986). *Predicting attachment from early social interactions: A prospective study.* Unpublished manuscript.

Lewis, M., & Feiring, C. (in press). Indirect and direct effects and family interaction. In S. Feinman (Ed.), *Social Referencing.* New York: Plenum.

Lewis, M., Feiring, C., & Kotsonis, M. (1984). The social network of the young child: A developmental perspective. In M. Lewis (Ed.), *Beyond the dyad: The genesis of behavior.* New York: Plenum.

Lewis, M., Feiring, C., McGuffog, C., & Jaskir, J. (1984). Predicting psychopathology of six-year-olds from early social relations. *Child Development, 55,* 123–136.

Lewis, M., Feiring, C., & Weinraub, M. (1981). The father as a member of the child's social network. In M. Lamb (Ed.), *The role of the father in child development* (2nd ed). New York: Wiley.

Lewis, M., & Freedle, R. (1973). Mother–infant dyad: The cradle of meaning. In P. Plinet, L. Krames, & T. Alloway (Eds.), *Communication and affect: Language and thought.* New York: Academic.

Lewis, M., & Freedle, R. (1977). The mother and infant communication system: The effects of poverty. In H. McGurk (Ed.), *Ecological factors in human development.* Amsterdam, the Netherlands: North-Holland.

Lewis, M., & Goldberg, S. (1969). Perceptual–cognitive development in infancy: A generalized expectancy model as a function of the mother–infant interaction. *Merrill-Palmer Quarterly, 15*(1), 81–100.

Lewis, M., Goldberg, S., & Campbell, H. (1969). A developmental study of information processing within the first three years of life: Response decrement to a redundant signal. *Monographs of the Society for Research in Child Development, 34.*

Lewis, M., & Kreitzberg, V. (1979). The effects of birth order and spacing on mother–infant interactions. *Developmental Psychology, 15*(6), 617–625.

Lewis, M., & Michalson, L. (1982). Socialization of emotions. In T. Field & A. Fogel (Eds.), *Emotion and early interaction: Normal and high risk infants.* Hillsdale, NJ: Erlbaum.

Lewis, M., & Michalson, L. (1983). *Children's emotions and moods: Developmental theory and measurement.* New York: Plenum.

Lewis, M., & Rosenblum, L. (1974a). Introduction. In M. Lewis & L. Rosenblum (Eds.), *The origins of fear: The origins of behavior* (Vol. 2). New York: Wiley.

Lewis, M., & Rosenblum, L. (1974b). Introduction. In M. Lewis & L. Rosenblum (Eds.), *The effect of the infant on its caretaker: The origins of behavior* (Vol. 1). New York: Wiley.

Lewis, M., & Rosenblum, L. (1975). Introduction. In M. Lewis & L. Rosenblum (Eds.), *Friendship and peer relations: The origins of behavior* (Vol. 4). New York: Wiley.

Lewis, M., & Rosenblum, L. (1977). Introduction. In M. Lewis & L. Rosenblum (Eds.), *Interaction, conversation, and the development of language: The origins of behavior* (Vol. 5). New York: Wiley.

Lewis, M., & Rosenblum, L. (1979). Issues in the study of the social network. In M. Lewis & L. Rosenblum (Eds.), *The child and its family: The genesis of behavior* (Vol. 2). New York: Plenum.

Lewis, M., & Schaeffer, S. (1981). Peer behavior and mother–infant interaction in maltreated children. In M. Lewis & L. Rosenblum (Eds.), *The uncommon child: The genesis of behavior* (Vol. 3). New York: Plenum.

Lewis, M., & Starr, M. (1979). Developmental continuity. In J. Osofsky (Ed.), *Handbook of infant development*. New York: Wiley.

Lewis, M., & Sullivan, M. (1985). Imitation in the first six months of life. *Merrill-Palmer Quarterly, 31,* 315–333.

Lewis, M., & Weinraub, M. (1974). Sex of parent × sex of child. In Friedman, Richart, & Van de Wiele (Eds.), *Sex differences in behavior.* New York: Wiley.

Lewis, M., & Weinraub, M. (1976). The father's role in the infant's social network. In M. Lamb (Ed.), *The role of the father in child development* (Vol. 1). New York: Wiley.

Lewis, M., & Weinraub, M. (1979). Origins of early sex role development. *Sex Roles, 5*(2), 135–153.

Lewis, M., Young, G., Brooks, J., & Michalson, L. (1975). The beginning of friendship. In M. Lewis & L. Rosenblum (Eds.), *Friendship and peer relations: The origins of behavior* (Vol. 4). New York: Wiley.

Lieberman, A. F. (1977). Preschoolers' competence with a peer: Relations with attachment and peer experience. *Child Development, 48,* 1277–1287.

Lipsitt, L. P. (1963). Learning in the first year of life. In L. P. Lipsitt & C. C. Spiker (Eds.), *Advances in child development and behavior* (Vol. 1). New York: Academic.

Lipsitt, L. (1980). *The enduring significance of reflexes in human infancy: Developmental shifts in the first month of life.* Paper presented at the meetings of the Eastern Psychological Association, Hartford, CT.

Littenberg, R., Tulkin, S. R., & Kagan, J. (1971). Cognitive components of separation anxiety. *Developmental Psychology, 4,* 301–305.

Londerville, S., & Main, M. (1981). Security of attachment, compliance, and maternal training methods in the second year of life. *Developmental Psychology, 17,* 289–299.

Luria, A. R. (1976). *Cognitive development: Its cultural and social foundations.* Cambridge, MA: Harvard University Press.

Lynn, D. B. (1974). *The father: His role in child development.* Monterey: Brooks/Cole.

Maccoby, E. E., & Feldman, S. S. (1972). Mother-attachment and stranger-reactions in the third year of life. *Monographs of the Society for Research in Child Development, 37*(1).

Mackey, W. C. (1985). *Fathering behaviors: The dynamics of the man-child bond.* New York: Plenum.

Main, M. (1977). Analysis of a peculiar form of reunion behavior seen in some daycare children: Its history and sequelae in children who are homereared. In R. Webb (Ed.), *Social development in daycare*. Baltimore: John Hopkins University Press.

Main, M. (1985). *An adult attachment classification system*. Paper presented at the biennial meeting of the Society for Research in Child Development, Toronto.

Maletesta, C. Z., & Haviland, J. (1982). Learning display rules: The socialization of emotional expression in infancy. *Child Development, 53,* 991–1003.

Margolin, G., & Patterson, G. R. (1975). Differential consequences provided by mothers and fathers for their sons and daughters. *Developmental Psychology, 11,* 537–538.

Matas, L., Arend, R. A., & Sroufe, L. A. (1978). Continuity of adaptation in the second year: The relationship between quality of attachment and later competence. *Child Development, 49,* 547–556.

McCall, R. B., Applebaum, M. I., & Hogarty, P. S. (1973). Developmental changes in mental performance. *Monographs of the Society for Research in Child Development, 38.*

Meltzoff, A. N., & Moore, M. K. (1977). Imitation of facial and manual gestures by human neonates. *Science, 198,* 75–78.

Minuchin, S. (1974). *Families and family therapy.* Cambridge: Harvard University Press.

Mischel, W. (1968). *Personality and adjustment.* New York: Wiley.

Mitchell, S., & Shepherd, M. (1966). A comparative study of children's behavior at home and at school. *British Journal of Educational Psychology, 36,* 248–254.

Miyake, K., Chen, S. J., & Campos, J. J. (1985). Infant temperament, mother's mode of interaction, and attachment in Japan: An interim report. *Monographs of the Society for Research in Child Development, 50,* 276–297.

Molfese, D. L., Freeman, R. B., & Palermo, D. S. (1975). The ontogeny of brain lateralization for speech and nonspeech stimuli. *Brain & Language, 2,* 356–368.

Molfese, D. L., & Molfese, V. J. (1979). Hemispheric and stimulus differences as reflected in cortical responses of newborn infants' speech stimuli. *Developmental Psychology, 15,* 505–511.

Monane, J. H. (1967). *A sociology of human systems.* New York: Appleton-Century-Crofts.

Money, J., & Ehrhardt, A. (1972). *Man and woman, boy and girl.* Baltimore: Johns Hopkins University Press.

Moss, H. A. (1965). Methodological issues in studying mother–infant interaction. *American Journal of Orthopsychiatry, 35,* 482–486.

Mueller, E. (1972). The maintenance of verbal exchanges between young children. *Child Development, 43,* 930–938.

Mueller, E., & Brenner, J. (1977). The origins of social skills and interaction among playgroup toddlers. *Child Development, 48,* 854–861.

Murray, H. A. (1938). *Explorations in personality.* New York: Oxford University Press.

Novak, M. A., & Harlow, H. F. (1975). Social recovery of monkeys isolated for the first year of life: Rehabilitation and therapy. *Developmental Psychology, 11,* 453–465.

Pannabecker, B. J., Emde, R. N., Johnson, W., Stenberg, C., & Davis, M. (1980). *Maternal perceptions of infant emotions from birth to 18 months: A preliminary report.* Paper presented at the International Conference of Infant Studies Meetings, New Haven, CT.

Papoušek, H. (1967). Experimental studies of appetitional behavior in human newborns and infants. In H. W. Stevenson, E. H. Hess, & H. L. Rheingold (Eds.), *Early behavior: Comparative and developmental approaches.* New York: Wiley.

Papoušek, H., & Papoušek, M. (1981). The common in the uncommon children: Comments on the child's integrative capacities and on initiative parenting. In M. Lewis & L. Rosenblum (Eds.), *The uncommon child: The genesis of behavior* (Vol. 3). New York: Plenum.

Parke, R. (1979). Perspectives in father–infant interaction. In J. Osofsky (Ed.), *Handbook of infant development.* New York: Wiley.

Parke, R. D., & O'Leary, S. (1975). Father–mother–infant interaction in the newborn period: Some findings, some observations, and some unresolved issues. In K. Riegel & J. Meacham (Eds.), *The developing individual in a changing world: Vol. 2. Social and environmental issues.* The Hague: Mouton.

Parke, R. D., Power, T. G., & Gottman, J. M. (1979). Conceptualizing and quantifying influence patterns in the family triad. In M. E. Lamb, S. J. Suomi, & G. R. Stephenson (Eds.), *Social interaction analysis.* Madison: Wisconsin University Press.

Parke, R. D., & Sawin, D. B. (1980). The family in early infancy: Social interactional and attitudinal analyses. In F. A. Pedersen (Ed.), *The father–infant relationship: Observational studies in the family setting.* New York: Praeger.

Parsons, T., & Bales, R. F. (1955). *Family socialization and interaction process.* Glencoe, IL: Free Press.

Pastor, D. L. (1981). The quality of mother–infant attachment and its relationship to toddlers' initial sociability with peers. *Developmental Psychology, 17*(3), 326–335.

Patterson, G. R. (1979). A performance theory for coercive family interaction. In R. B. Cairns (Eds.), *The analysis of social interactions.* Hillsdale, NJ: Erlbaum.

Pattison, M. (1975). A psychosocial kinship model for family therapy. *American Journal of Psychiatry, 132,* 1246–1251.

Pedersen, F. (1975). *Mother, father and infant as an interactive system.* Paper presented at the annual convention of the American Psychological Association, Chicago.

Pedersen, F. A. (1976). Does research on children reared in father-absent families yield information on father influence? *The Family Coordinator, 25,* 459–464.

Pedersen, F. A., Anderson, B. J., & Cain, R. L. (1977). *An approach to understanding linkups between the parent–infant and spouse relationship.* Paper presented at the meeting of the Society for Research in Child Development, New Orleans.

Pedersen, F. A., Rubenstein, O. L., & Yarrow, L. J. (1979). Infant development in father-absent families. *Journal of Genetic Psychology, 135,* 51–61.

Pedersen, F. A., Yarrow, L. J., Anderson, B. J., & Cain, R. L. (1979). Conceptualization of father influences in the infancy period. In M. Lewis & L. Rosenblum (Eds.), *The child and its family.* New York: Plenum.

Pepler, D. J., Abramovitch, R., & Corter, C. (1981). Sibling interaction in the home: A longitudinal study. *Child Development, 52,* 1344–1347.

Pervin, L. A. (1975). *Personality: Theory, assessment and research.* New York: Wiley.

Pervin, L. A. (1978). *Current controversies and issues in personality.* New York: Wiley.

Piaget, J. (1951). Play, dreams, and imitation in childhood (C. Gattegno & F. M. Hodgson, Trans.). New York: Norton. (Original work published, 1945)

Piaget, J. (1952). *The origins of intelligence in children.* New York: Norton.

Plomin, R., & Rowe, D. C. (1978). Genes, environment, and development of temperament in young human twins. In G. M. Gurghardt & M. Bekoff (Eds.), *The development of behavior: Comparative and evolutionary aspects.* New York: Garland STPM Press.

Provence, S., & Lipton, R. C. (1962). *Infants in institutions.* London: Bailey & Swinfer.

Rheingold, H. L. (1971). *Some visual determinants of smiling infants.* Unpublished manuscript.

Rheingold, H. L., & Eckerman, C. O. (1969). The infant's free entry into a new environment. *Journal of Experimental Child Psychology, 8,* 271–283.

Rheingold, H. L., & Eckerman, C. O. (1973). Fear of the stranger: A critical review. In

H. W. Reese (Ed.), *Advances in child development and behavior* (Vol. 8). New York: Academic.

Robertson, J., & Robertson, J. (1971). Young children in brief separation: A fresh look. *Psychoanalytic Study of the Child, 26,* 264–315.

Rollins, B. C., & Galligan, R. (1978). The developing child and marital satisfaction of parents. In R. M. Lerner & G. B. Spanier (Eds.), *Child influences on marital and family interaction.* New York: Academic.

Rosenblatt, P. C. (1974). Behavior in public places: Comparisons of couples accompanied and unaccompanied by children. *Journal of Marriage & the Family, 36,* 750–755.

Rosenblum, L. (1961). *The development of social behavior in the rhesus monkey.* Unpublished dissertation, University of Wisconsin.

Rosenblum, L., & Kaufman, I. C. (1968). Variations in infant development and response to maternal loss in monkeys. *American Journal of Orthopsychiatry, 38,* 418–426.

Rosenblum, L. A., & Moltz, H. (1983). *Symbiosis in parent–offspring interaction.* New York: Plenum.

Rosenthal, M. K. (1973). Attachment and mother–infant interaction: Some research impasses and a suggested change in orientation. *Journal of Child Psychology & Psychiatry, 14,* 201–207.

Rosenzweig, M. R. (1964). Effects of heredity and environment on brain chemistry, brain anatomy, and learning ability in the rat. In A. J. Edwards & J. F. Cawley (Eds.), Symposium on Physiological Determinates of Behavior: Implications for Mental Retardation. *Kansas Studies in Education, 14,* 3–34.

Rovee-Collier, C. K., & Gekoski, M. J. (1979). The economics of infancy: A review of conjugate reinforcement. In H. W. Reese & L. P. Lipsitt (Eds.), *Advances in child development and behavior* (Vol. 13). New York: Academic.

Rupenthal, G. C., Arling, G. L., Harlow, H. F., Sackett, G. P., & Suomi, S. J. (1976). A 10-year perspective of motherless-mother monkey behavior. *Journal of Abnormal Psychology, 85,* 341–349.

Rutter, M. (1971). Parent–child separation: Psychological effects on the children. *Journal of Child Psychology & Psychiatry, 12,* 233–260.

Rutter, M. (1979). Maternal deprivation, 1972–1978: New findings, new concepts, new approaches. *Child Development, 50,* 283–305.

Sameroff, A. J., & Chandler, M. J. (1975). Reproductive risk and the continuum of caretaking casuality. In F. D. Horowitz, M. Hetherington, S. Scarr-Salapatek, & G. Siegel (Eds.), *Review of child development research* (Vol. 4). Chicago: University of Chicago Press.

Sanders, L. W. (1977). Infant and caretaking environment: Investigation and conceptualization of adaptive behavior in a system of increasing complexity. In E. J. Anthony (Ed.), *The child psychiatrist as investigator.* New York: Plenum.

Scarr, S. (1981). Testing for children. *American Psychologist, 36,* 1159–1166.

Schaefer, E. S., & Bayley, N. (1963). Maternal behavior, child behavior and their intercorrelations from infancy through adolescence. *Monographs of Social Research in Child Development, 28.*

Schaffer, H. R. (1974). Cognitive components of the infant's response to strangerness. In M. Lewis & L. Rosenblum (Eds.), *The origins of fear: The origins of behavior* (Vol. 2). New York: Wiley.

Schaffer, H. R., & Emerson, P. E. (1964). The development of social attachments in infancy. *Monographs of the Society for Research in Child Development, 29.*

Scott, J. P. (1962). Genetics and the development of social behavior in mammals. *American Journal of Orthopsychiatry, 32,* 878–893.

Sears, R. (1972). Attachment, dependency, and frustration. In Gewirtz (Ed.), *Attachment and dependency*. Washington, DC: Winston.

Shanas, E. (1979). Social myth as hypothesis: The case of the family relations of old people. *Gerontologist, 19,* 3-9.

Shereshefsky, P. M., & Yarrow, L. J. (1973). Psychological aspects of a first pregnancy and early postnatal adaptation. New York: Raven.

Slater, P. (1974). Parental role differentiation. In R. L. Coser (Ed.), *The family: Its structures and functions* (2nd ed.). New York: St. Martin's.

Sorce, J. F., & Emde, R. N. (1981). Mother's presence is not enough: Effect of emotional availability on infant exploration. *Developmental Psychology, 17,* 737-745.

Spitz, R. A. (1959). *A genetic field theory of ego information: Its implications for pathology.* New York: International University Press.

Sroufe, L. A. (1979). Socioemotional development. In J. D. Osofsky (Ed.), *Handbook of infant development.* New York: Wiley.

Sroufe, L. A., Fox, N. E., & Pancake, V. R. (1983). Attachment and dependency in developmental perspective. *Child Development, 54,* 1615-1627.

Sroufe, L. A., & Rutter, M. (1984). The domain of developmental psychopathology. *Child Development, 55,* 17-29.

Sroufe, L. A., Waters, E., & Matas, L. (1974). Contextual determinants of infant affective response. In M. Lewis & L. Rosenblum (Eds.), *The origins of fear: The origins of behavior* (Vol. 2). New York: Wiley.

Stayton, D. J., Ainsworth, M. D. S., & Main, M. B. (1973). Development of separation behavior in the first year of life: Protest, following, and greeting. *Developmental Psychology, 9,* 213-225.

Stern, D. N. (1974). The goal and structure of mother–infant play. *Journal of the American Academy of Child Psychiatry, 13,* 402-421.

Stillwell, R. (1984). *Social relationships in six-year-olds as viewed by themselves, their mothers and their teachers.* Unpublished dissertation, Cambridge University.

Stillwell, R., & Dunn, J. (1985). Continuities in sibling relationships: Patterns of aggression and friendliness. *Journal of Child Psychology & Psychiatry, 26,* 627-637.

Streeter, L. A. (1975). The effects of linguistic experience on phonetic perception. *Dissertation Abstracts International, 35,* 4696.

Suomi, S. J. (1978). Maternal behavior by socially incompetent monkeys: Neglect and abuse of offspring. *Journal of Pediatric Psychology, 3,* 28-34.

Suomi, S. J. (1979). Differential development of various social relationships by rhesus monkey infants. In M. Lewis & L. Rosenblum (Eds.), *The child and its family: The genesis of behavior* (Vol. 2). New York: Plenum.

Suomi, S. J., & Harlow, H. F. (1972). Social rehabilitation of isolate-reared monkeys. *Developmental Psychology, 6,* 487-496.

Suomi, S. J., & Harlow, H. F. (1975). The role and reason of peer relationships in rhesus monkeys. In M. Lewis & L. A. Rosenblum (Eds.), *Friendship and peer relations.* New York: Wiley.

Takahaski, K. (1982). Attachment behaviors to a female stranger among Japanese two-year-olds. *Journal of Genetic Psychology, 140,* 299-307.

Takahashi, K. (1984-1985). Life-span development of affective relationships. *Annual Report of Research and Clinical Center for Child Development,* Hokkaido University.

Takahashi, K. (in press). Age and gender of adult strangers as determinants of extension of attachment behaviors among Japanese toddlers. *Developmental Psychology.*

Tanner, J. M. (1970). Physical growth. In P. H. Mussen (Ed.), *Carmichael's manual of child psychology.* New York: Wiley.

Tesser, A. (1980). Self-esteem maintenance in family dynamics. *Journal of Personality & Social Psychology, 39,* 77–91.

Thomas, A., & Chess, S. (1981). Temperament in the contributions of individuals to their development. In R. M. Lerner & N. A. Busch-Rossenael (Eds.), *Individuals as producers of their development: A life-span perspective.* New York: Academic.

Thompson, R. A., & Lamb, M. (1983). Security and attachment and stranger sociability in infancy. *Developmental Psychology, 19,* 184–191.

Thompson, R. A., & Lamb, M. E. (1984). Infants, mothers, families, and strangers. In M. Lewis (Ed.), *Beyond the dyad.* New York: Plenum.

Thompson, R. A., Lamb, M. E., & Estes, D. (1982). Stability of infant–mother attachment and its relationship to changing life circumstances in an unselected middle class sample. *Child Development, 53,* 144–148.

Tinsley, B. R., & Parke, R. D. (1984). Grandparents as support and socialization agents. In M. Lewis & L. Rosenblum (Eds.), *Beyond the dyad: The genesis of behavior* (Vol. 4). New York: Plenum.

Tizard, J., & Tizard, B. (1971). The social development of two-year-old children in residential nurseries. In H. R. Schaffer (Ed.), *The origins of human social relations.* New York: Academic.

Tooley, K. M. (1980). The young child as victim of sibling attack. In J. V. Cook & R. Tyler (Eds.), *Child abuse: Commission and omission.* Kent, England: Butterworths Publishing Co.

Trivers, R. L. (1971). The evolution of reciprocal altruism. *Quarterly Review of Biology, 46,* 35–57.

Triver, R. L. (1974). Parent–offspring conflict. *American Zoologist, 14,* 249–264.

Vaughn, B., Egeland, B., Sroufe, L. A., & Waters, E. (1979). Individual differences in infant–mother attachment at twelve and eighteen months: Stability and change in families under stress. *Child Development, 50,* 971–975.

Vaughn, B., Gove, F. L., & Egeland, B. (1980). The relationship between out-of-home care and the quality of infant–mother attachment in an economically disadvantaged population. *Child Development, 51,* 1203–1214.

Von Bertalanffy, L. (1967). *Robots, men and minds.* New York: Brazilles.

Waite, L. H., & Lewis, M. (1979). *Maternal report on the development of social imitation during the first year.* Paper presented at the meeting of the Society for Research in Child Development, San Francisco.

Waters, E. (1978). The reliability and stability of individual differences in infant–mother attachment. *Child Development, 49,* 483–494.

Waters, E., Vaughn, B., & Egeland, B. (1980). Individual differences in infant–mother attachment relationships at age one: Antecedents in neonatal behavior in an urban, economically disadvantaged sample. *Child Development, 51,* 208–216.

Waters, E., Wippman, J., & Sroufe, L. A. (1979). Attachment, positive affect, and competence in the peer group: Two studies in construct validation. *Child Development, 50,* 821–829.

Weinraub, M., Brooks, J., & Lewis, M. (1977). The social network: A reconsideration of the concept of attachment. *Human Development, 20,* 31–47.

Weinraub, M., & Lewis, M. (1974). *Maternal verbalization as a determinant of separation distress in the two-year-old child.* Paper presented at the meeting of the Eastern Psychological Association, Philadelphia.

Weinraub, M., & Lewis, M. (1975). *The determinants of separation distress: A path analysis model.* Paper presented at the meeting of the Eastern Psychological Association, New York.

Wellman, H. M. (1985). A child's theory of mind: The development of conceptions of cognition. In S. Yussen (Ed.), *The growth of reflection in children*. New York: Academic.

Wenar, C. (1972). Executive competence and spontaneous social behavior in one-year-olds. *Child Development, 43,* 256–260.

Whiting, B. B., & Whiting, J. W. M. (1975). *Children of six cultures: A psychocultural analysis*. Cambridge, MA: Harvard University Press.

Wiesel, T. N., & Hubel, D. H. (1965). Comparison of extent of recovery from the effects of visual deprivation in kittens. *Journal of Neurophysiology, 28,* 1060–1072.

Wilson, E. O. (1975). *Sociobiology*. Cambridge: The Belknap Press of Harvard University Press.

Wilson, N., & Tolson, S. H. (1985). *An analysis of adult-child interaction patterns in three generational black families*. Paper presented at the Society for Research in Child Development Symposium on Grandparents and Very Young Children.

Yamamoto, K. (1972). *The child and his image: Self concept in the early years*. Boston: Houghton Mifflin.

Yando, R., Seitz, V., & Zigler, E. (1978). *Imitation: A developmental perspective*. Hillsdale, NJ: Erlbaum.

Yarrow, L. J. (1963). Research in dimensions of early maternal care. *Merrill-Palmer Quarterly, 9,* 101–114.

Yarniss, J. (1980). *Parents and peers in social development: A Sullivan-Piaget perspective*. Chicago: University of Chicago Press.

Zahn-Waxler, C., Radke-Yarrow, M., & King, R. (1979). Child rearing and children's prosocial imitations towards victims of distress. *Child Development, 50,* 319–330.

Zajonc, R. B., & Markus, G. B. (1975). Birth order and intellectual development. *Psychological Review, 82,* 74–88.

CHAPTER 9A

Perspectives on Emotional Development I: Differential Emotions Theory of Early Emotional Development

CARROLL E. IZARD and CAROL Z. MALATESTA

A central premise of differential emotions theory is that emotions—characterized by neurochemical, expressive, and experiential components—are the fundamental motivators of human behavior and that each of the basic emotions has unique adaptive functions including a significant role in the organization of developmental processes. This chapter extends differential emotions theory to provide a framework for the study of emotional development. In early development the expressive component of emotion is seen as pivotal, linked to innate neurochemical substrates and motivational, cue-producing feelings on the one hand and to social communication on the other. The overarching thesis is that an understanding of the structure, dynamics, and developmental course of facial expressions provides a coherent picture of the relations among the components of emotion and the role of the emotions in motivation and adaptation. The approach is framed by seven organizing principles, related to either the biological or the social functions of facial expressions, with special attention to their modifications during development, their role in motivation, socialization, the acquisition of emotion labels, and the development of emotion–cognition relations.

BACKGROUND

Contemporary behavioral scientists have now produced robust evidence that supports Darwin's (1872) once controversial thesis that the expressions of certain basic emotions are innate and universal. This evidence has led to a wider appreciation of the biological bases of emotions and their significance in adaptation and evolution.

The first draft of this paper was based on an invited address by the first author to the Eastern Psychological Association, April 1, 1983. Work on the paper was supported by NSF Grant #BNS 811832 to the first author and by National Research Service Award #1 F32 MH08773–01 to the second author. We are grateful for helpful discussions of neural processes with colleagues Pat Saxton, Tom Scott, Jerry Siegel, and Carl Skeen and of cognitive processes with colleagues Brian Ackerman, James Hoffman, and John McLaughlin, and for very helpful criticisms from Joe Campos and the editor. Special thanks to Sharon Antonio for her care and skill in the processing of the manuscript.

Biologists and philosophers have suggested that the emergence of emotions was essential in the evolution of higher forms of life:

> In the sub-human animal world . . . there has been an evolution of more precise and sensitive sense-organs and . . . [an] ever further-evolving brain, leading to improved capacities of knowledge and *feeling* [italics added][;] . . . the evolution of man is a further step in the same direction. (Waddington, 1957, p. 271)

(Waddington, 1957, p. 271)

"The human being's departure from the normal pattern of animal mentality is a vast and special evolution of *feeling* [italics added] in the hominid stock" (Langer, 1967, pp. xvi–xvii).

We surmise that in phylogenetic development the emotions system began as an affective counterpart or replacement for simple approach and withdrawal reflexes or instincts that had to use fixed efferent programs. That is, mechanisms mediating emotions appropriate to attractive and aversive situations were selected initially to provide the capacity to suppress fixed action patterns and thereby regulate and alter approach and avoidance strategies (cf. Epstein, 1982; Fox & Davidson, 1984). These and other emotions evolved by natural selection, random mutation of genes, and other principles such as genetic assimilation (Waddington, 1962) and inclusive fitness (Trivers, 1971). It is beyond the scope of this chapter to speculate on the precise order of emergence of the discrete emotions and how each contributed to adaptive functioning. The origin of adaptation is still considered by some to be the primary problem of evolutionary biology (Gaylord Simpson, cited in Waddington, 1957). Nevertheless, we assume that in human evolution the emergence of each new emotion added new motivation, cue-producing capacity, and action tendencies, and that the new emotion in interaction with the established affects and with cognition produced new behavioral alternatives and greater flexibility of function.

The great flexibility and spontaneity of emotion-related behavior and of behavior in general obtain as a function of both genetic programs that emerged through phylogeny and experience- or cognition-based structures and abilities acquired in ontogeny. An understanding of these essential features of human behavior calls for a developmental theory of emotion.

Early theories of emotion were patently nondevelopmental (Cannon, 1927; Darwin, 1872; James, 1884, 1890, pp. 442–485). They were concerned primarily with issues relating to the evaluation and significance of the expressions of emotions, emotion activation or causation, and the sequencing of physiological events. Today, although much emotions research is conducted with infants and children (and some work with the aged has begun to appear), there have been only a few attempts to treat emotions systematically within an expressly developmental theoretical framework (Campos & Barrett, 1984; Emde, 1980; Izard, 1977, 1978; Kagan, 1984; Lewis & Michalson, 1983; Malatesta, in press; Malatesta & Izard, 1984b; Sroufe, 1979), and most of these deal only with a limited period of time. The renaissance of research on the emotions over the past decade has resulted in the accumulation of a great deal of new data concerning the role of emotions in development. This has stimulated the present attempt to extend differential emotions theory (Izard, 1971, 1977) and construct a complementary developmental model of emotions with a life span orientation.

We begin with some key definitions and then consider emotional development in the context of overall development, framing the theory in terms of the three (biological, expressive, feeling) components of emotion and seven organizing principles. Two of the principles relate primarily to biological substrates and the biosocial significance of emotion-specific neuromuscular patterns, two to the development of expressive behavior, and three to the subjective or feeling component. All seven principles relate in one way or another to facial expressions of the emotions, which are assumed to be innately linked to neural substrates and feeling states on the one hand and to serve a social–communicative function on the other. The evidence and argument that follow bear on this general organizing theme and on the assumption that the relations among expressions, neural substrates, and feeling states change in the course of development. Most of the data that support these principles come from studies of early development, and much focuses on emotion expression. We recognize that, as work in the field continues to expand, it will be necessary to refine the proposed theoretical framework. Before proceeding, some clarification of terms is in order.

DEFINITIONS AND NOMENCLATURE

Emotions System

The concept of the emotions as a system has been discussed in detail elsewhere (Izard, 1977, pp. 48–55). In brief, *emotions system* refers to the discrete emotions and their relations to one another and to the other systems that operate within the individual. We view the somatic nervous system as primary in emotion activation and emotion regulation. The autonomic nervous system (ANS) is typically activated by emotion and plays a role in sustaining emotion over time. The reticular activating system is involved in the amplification and attenuation of emotions (see Izard, 1977, Chap. 3, for further discussion of these points of general emotion theory).

The emotions system and the neurophysiological life-support, motor, and cognitive systems constitute relatively independent but highly interrelated divisions of functioning (Izard, 1971; cf. Leventhal, 1982; Tomkins, 1962). Normal development proceeds as biological and social processes produce structures or organizations that connect and integrate these systems for adaptive and creative functioning. The definitions that follow make more explicit our conception of the emotions system and its components.

Discrete Emotions

A *discrete emotion* can be defined as a particular set of neural processes that lead to a specific expression and a corresponding specific feeling. Thus an emotion consists of three components—*neural, motor–expressive,* and *mental* processes (feelings)—and the term *emotion* always refers to a three-component system. In the young child the motor component is manifested as facial, vocal, and bodily patterns of emotion expression. In later life other processes influenced by culture and idiosyncratic experience may become substitutable for the instinctlike motor component of innate emotion expressions.

The term *emotion expression* refers primarily to motor–behavioral responses such as facial and vocal expressions and secondarily to postural, gestural, visceral, and glandular activity. *Emotion feeling* refers to the internal, subjectively experienced component that derives directly from the underlying neural and motor processes. Emotion feelings have organizational, motivational, and cue-producing functions. The more general term *affect* refers both to the emotions and to the more cyclic, relatively more stimulus-bound physiological states such as thirst, hunger, and the need for elimination; the affects of sex and pain share characteristics of physiological needs (drives) and emotions (Izard, 1977; Tomkins, 1963).

Fundamental Emotions, Patterns of Emotions, and Affective–Cognitive Structures

We use the term *fundamental emotion* to refer to an emotion that "has (a) a specific innately determined neural substrate, (b) a characteristic neuromuscular–expressive pattern, and (c) a distinct subjective or phenomenological quality" (Izard, 1972, p. 2). There is substantial evidence that criteria (b) and (c) are met by the emotions of interest, joy, surprise, sadness, anger, disgust, contempt, fear, and shame (Eibl-Eibesfeldt, 1972; Ekman, Friesen, & Ellsworth, 1972; Izard, 1971, 1972). The evidence relating to emotion-specific neural substrates is far from complete, yet there is some hard evidence for distinct neural pathways and neurotransmitters (see Izard & Saxton, in press, for a review). Further, emotions that meet criterion (b) must partially meet criterion (a), for distinct efferent neural pathways are required for distinct configurations of movement, and such distinct configurations of movement provide distinct patterns of afferent feedback to the brain.

We hypothesize that shyness and guilt are universal and should also be considered fundamental emotions, but we recognize that the evidence for their meeting the foregoing criteria is meager. According to Tomkins (1963) shame, shyness, and guilt can be considered variants of the same emotion. However, Buss (1979) has presented evidence for the physiological separateness of shame and shyness, and there is some evidence for the distinctness of shame, shyness, and guilt at the level of subjective experience (Blumberg & Izard, 1985; Izard & Hyson, in press; Mosher & White, 1981).

A *pattern of emotions* is two or more discrete emotions that tend to co-occur with some regularity. They may tend to occur in response to particular events and can assume traitlike status. Both innate and learned characteristics of emotions lead to dynamic and relatively stable interrelationships (cf. Darwin, 1872; Tomkins, 1962). For example, depending on the level of stimulation and its rate of onset and change, interest may graduate into surprise and surprise into fear. Theory and experimental evidence suggest that some pairs of emotions tend to be polar opposites or to be counteractive (e.g., interest–disgust, joy–sadness, anger–fear) and that others tend to be activated in blends, combinations, or patterns (e.g., interest and joy, anger and disgust) (Darwin, 1872; Izard, 1972; Plutchik, 1980). Certain psychological disorders are regularly characterized by patterns of emotions that appear to be dynamically related, such as sadness and anger in depression (Blumberg & Izard, 1985; Izard, 1972).

An *affective–cognitive structure* is a feeling-cognition association or bond. Such structures may range from simple (a discrete feeling and the image or symbol of a single object) to highly complex (a pattern of affects and associated images and schemata). The formation of affective–cognitive structures is facilitated by the inherent cue-producing function of emotion feelings.

Anxiety, depression, hostility, love, jealousy, and pride are examples of affective–cognitive structures or emotion–cognition complexes. One could argue that emotion–cognition complexes such as hostility and love should also be considered basic or fundamental. Hostility is common across cultures, but it can include feelings associated with at least three fundamental emotions—anger, disgust, and contempt (Izard, 1977, chap. 13). Love, or at least affective attachment as between mother and infant, is also a characteristic common to our species and many others. Yet students of attachment typically hold that attachment involves more than one emotion (Bowlby, 1969; McGinnes & Izard, 1984). The empathic sadness or anger a parent feels in response to a child's loss or frustration can be considered a part of parental love. For these and other reasons, the foregoing categories are considered not fundamental emotions but emotion–cognition complexes or affective–cognitive structures that typically involve patterns of fundamental emotions, imagery, ideation, and other cognitive processes (Izard, 1972, pp. 1–4, 1977, chap. 3). Although detailed discussion of the development of these complex affective–cognitive structures is beyond the scope of this Chapter, we propose that they emerge after most of the fundamental emotions are functional and after the infant has begun to label emotions and comprehend their causes and consequences (Bretherton & Beeghly-Smith, 1982; Masters & Carlson, 1984).

All emotions and affective–cognitive structures also involve the motor system, in two ways. In early development, emotion is regularly expressed in the striate musculature of the face and body, and it sets up action tendencies in the muscles of instrumental behavior (cf. Arnold, 1960, vol. II, chap. 3; Zajonc & Markus, 1984).

Facial Expression and Emotional Behavior

By *facial expression* we mean the particular facial muscle movements and consequent facial appearance changes that signal emotion. Thus facial expression is a specific part of emotion expression. Izard (1979) has described the anatomical basis for these appearance changes and the formulas for identifying each emotion as combinations or patterns of such appearance changes. The formulas are based on differential emotions theory and empirical evidence. A facial movement that is not part of one of the formulas is hypothesized to have no emotion signal value. Whereas *emotion expression* refers to an integral component of emotion, *emotional behavior* includes both expressive patterns and instrumental acts motivated by emotion feeling.

Innateness

Conceiving of genetic and experiential determinants as a dichotomy is not considered fruitful because virtually all behavior is a joint function of the two. Nevertheless, because we think that the biological bases of emotions and emotion-related behaviors and the role of biological factors in emotional development deserve special attention, we use the term *innate* to underscore the influence of information encoded in the genes. We apply the term *innate* to behavior that is directed or facilitated by genetic programs. We believe that different genetic programs have different degrees of fixity, but we assume that in virtually all cases there are preprogrammed allowances for modification through learning and experience.

Cognition: Our Use of the Concept

Differential emotions theory places some constraints on the concept of *cognition* and makes certain distinctions between *cognitive information processing* and *cognitive representation* on the one hand and *emotion information processing* and *emotion feeling as a quality of consciousness* on the other. Most cognitive theorists would agree that *cognition* is not synonymous with *information processing,* a term we consider quite useful in other contexts. Neurochemical information is processed in DNA molecules, and we believe that affective information is processed in the emotions system. Affective information processing can be independent of cognition, as we shall argue in our discussion of the second principle.

As do many cognitive theorists, we use the term *cognition* to refer to mental operations involving representational processes based on learning or experience. As is not the case with some cognitive theorists (e.g., Lazarus, 1982; Mandler, 1975, 1982; Plutchik, 1980), we assume that cognition is continually influenced by *emotion feelings* that are direct derivatives (unmediated products) of processes in the biological substrates of emotion. There is a neural code for the feeling state associated with each of the fundamental emotions, and an emotion feeling is a direct product of the neural code. Although deciphering these codes will be extremely difficult, we believe it to be a worthy challenge for neuroscience. Given the present state of knowledge relating to this problem, we consider it heuristic to assume that a specific emotion feeling is generated directly from brain activity and that the causal chain from neurophysiological processes to feeling state does *not* require appraisal, matching, or comparison with learned schemata or expectations. Feelings are *mental phenomena* that have important organizing and motivational functions (Izard, 1977, chap. 6).

According to Piaget (1952), the full capacity for cognitive representation as traditionally defined does not emerge until the final (sixth) stage of sensorimotor experience (18 months of age). Recent research, however, tends to support Kagan's (1979) attribution of rudimentary cognitive representation to infants of 3–4 months. Regardless of the age of acquisition of this capacity, not all cognitive theorists believe that all mental representations are a function of learning, experience, or cognitive processes. According to Neisser schemata for physiognomonic perception are probably innate, and "babies are innately prepared to perceive smiles or frowns, soothing tones or harsh inflections, as indications of what others will do next" (Neisser, 1976, p. 191; cf. Werner, 1948).

What we assume to be innate is the capacity for direct mental encoding of discrete emotion feelings, and we assume that these feelings mediate perceptual–cognitive processes and action. Thus the infant is innately prepared, as a function of the innate emotions system and the feelings generated within it, to register and respond to emotion signals without cognitive appraisal. As a function of the *sensory registration* of the stimulus or event, infants respond affectively to facial and vocal signals in the first weeks of life (Field, 1979; Wolff, 1966), when cognitive representation, appraisal, and comparison processes in their conventional sense are not thought to operate. Nonhuman primates are also innately prepared to process and respond affectively to emotion information, independent of learning- or experience-based representation. As Sackett (1966) has demonstrated, infant monkeys reared in isolation still show appropriate fear expression to slides of adult monkeys' threat displays.

Thus we use the term *cognition* to refer to mental operations based on representational processes (e.g., comparisons of events and schemata), processes beyond sensory registration of the stimulus or event. In contrast to cognitive information processing, including Mandler's (1982) evaluative cognitions, the young infant's sensing and responding to emotion signals exemplify what we mean by *emotion information processing*. The infant's smile in response to a high-pitched human voice at 3 weeks of age and to a nodding face at 4–6 weeks (Wolff, 1966) and its *differential responding to different facial expressions* of the care giver at 2–3 months of age (Hembree & Izard, 1985; Lelwica & Haviland, 1983) are all based on emotion information processing and represent an affective rather than a cognitive capacity. The constraints placed on semantic or conceptual and representational processes by the 2-month-old infant's cognitive capacities (Harris, 1983a; Olson & Sherman, 1983) and by its limited skills and knowledge (Bransford, Franks, Morris, & Stein, 1979) point toward a noncognitive process for detecting facial and vocal signals of emotion. In any case, the hypothesized process is not part of cognition as we use the term. Thus our view of the processing of sense data that leads to emotion activation is more akin to Gibson's (1966, 1979) theory of direct perception than to Piaget's (1954) emphasis on constructed concepts.

We surmise that emotion information processing is typically automatic rather than deliberate (cf. Naus & Halasz, 1979) and more like sensory encoding than semantic encoding (cf. Nelson, 1979). Yet it serves an organizing function in that it leads to discrete emotion feelings and causally linked patterned expression, cue-producing motivational experience, and action tendencies.

The constraints we have placed on our use of the term *cognition* should not be misconstrued as restrictions on the importance of cognitive processes for emotion and emotional development. As we shall discuss in later sections, emotions frequently arise in early infancy as a function of a number of noncognitive processes, such as gustation and pain. We also believe that emotion arises in infancy, as well as in later years, as a function of direct perception that does not necessarily involve appraisal or interpretive processes. However, cognitive appraisal, comparison, semantic processing, inference, and imagery are frequent activators of emotion as soon as the requisite cognitive capacities are in place. And emotion–cognition interactions are central in the development of more specific motivations (affective-cognitive structures), temperament, and personality (Izard, 1977, chap. 3).

Overview

The present theoretical approach to emotion development is an extension of differential emotions theory. The central premise is that emotions are the fundamental motivators of human behavior and that each of the basic emotions (interest, joy, surprise, sadness, anger, disgust, contempt, fear, shame, shyness, guilt) has unique adaptive functions, including motivational and cue-producing properties. For ex-

ample, interest motivates approach and exploration, anger the removal of obstruc-
tions, disgust the rejection of distasteful objects, fear avoidance, guilt reparation,
and so on. Similar views on the functions of discrete emotions have been espoused
by a number of other theorists (Campos & Barrett, 1984; Cannon, 1929; Darwin,
1872; McDougall, 1923; Plutchik, 1980; Sroufe, 1979; Tomkins, 1962). It is our
additional explicit assumption that emotions are critical building blocks and prime
movers in human ontogeny, organizing and motivating developmental processes and
all significant human behavior, a position that is elaborated on in the following
pages.

The foregoing definitions and premises and the differential emotions theory of
which they are a part suggest a set of seven principles that organize the present
approach to understanding emotional development. The seven principles are listed
below.

Principle 1.   Innate emotion-specific neuromuscular patterns (facial expressions
of basic emotions) show regularity in form and time of emergence and serve
crucial adaptive functions in development.

Principle 2.   The preadaptedness of emotion-specific expressive behaviors enables the emotions system to function independently of the cognitive system, but
the interaction and interdependence of the two systems become more complex
with development.

Principle 3.   Biological and social forces gradually change full-face instinctlike
expressions to more restricted and controlled emotion signals.

Principle 4.   An innate expression-feeling concordance ensures effective communication with the prelingual infant but learned expression regulation increases
the flexibility of expression-feeling relations.

Principle 5.   The socialization of emotion expressions contributes to the regulation of emotion feelings.

Principle 6.   Emotion feelings are invariant over the life span but their causes
and consequences change with development.

Principle 7.   Facial expressions and expression-feeling concordance facilitate the
development of emotion-cognition relations and affective-cognitive structure.

We shall present first the principles relating to the neurophysiological component, then those relating to the development of the expressive component, and finally the principles relating to developmental processes in relation to emotion feelings or the subjective-experiential component.

The overarching thesis of the present theoretical approach is that an understanding of the structure, dynamics, and developmental course of facial expressions will
provide a coherent picture of the relations among the components of emotion and
the role of emotion in motivation and adaptation. Evidence will show that the facial
expressions of emotions have biological functions of a regulatory nature, social
functions of a communicative nature, and a role in organizing and motivating behavior in the individual via expression-feeling relations and in social interaction via
display of signals.

BIOLOGICAL SUBSTRATES AND THE BIOSOCIAL SIGNIFICANCE OF EMOTION-SPECIFIC NEUROMUSCULAR PATTERNS

Much of our discussion of the biological aspect of emotion relates to the neuromuscular component. We shall argue that a special set of neuromuscular facial patterns is an essential aspect of the biology of emotions and that these patterns are genetically programmed to organize and motivate adaptive infant behavior and care giver–infant interactions. The evidence for biologically determined discrete neuromuscular patterns, each conveying particular affective information, is consistent with a hypothesis of specific neural substrates for each discrete emotion, but firm evidence for such a hypothesis is lacking. However, we shall begin by presenting a brief summary of research on the biological basis of emotions, noting some findings that suggest the fruitfulness of testing the hypothesis of discrete emotion-specific neurochemical substrates. More detailed expositions of the neural pathways and neurotransmitters involved in the emotions system can be found elsewhere (Anisman & Zacharko, 1982; Borod & Koff, 1984; Gray, 1982; Izard & Saxton, in press; Kinsbourne & Bemporad, 1984; Moyer, 1971; Panksepp, 1982; Smith & DeVito, 1984; Tucker & Williamson, 1984; Zuckerman, 1984).

A century of research converges on the conclusion that the neuronatal substrates of the emotions are fundamentally limbic in origin (Isaacson, 1982; MacLean, 1973), but the neural regions included in the limbic brain have expanded since Broca's original designation of the limbic lobe. Today the emotional brain includes not only the limbic cortical areas of the hippocampus and cingulate gyrus but also the amygdala, hypothalamus, ventral midbrain area, and the major pathways connecting these structures with each other and with the frontal lobes. It is possible for the emotional brain to influence all behavior elicited by environmental input, because "all modes of the external sensorium are processed through limbic cortical areas, the amygdala and hippocampus" (Kelly & Stinus, 1984, p. 11).

The structures of the limbic system are clearly related to emotional behavior, as indicated by a wide variety of stimulation and lesion experiments with nonhuman animals (Izard & Saxton, in press). Furthermore, in conscious human patients, stimulation of limbic system structures yields reports of emotion-specific feelings as well as changes in emotional behavior (Heath & Mickle, 1960; King, 1961; Mark & Ervin, 1970). One cannot rule out a hypothesis that the stimulation did not elicit some cognitive process that in turn mediated the emotion. However, research with cats indicates that medial hypothalamic stimulation elicits affective attack by changing the "level setting" in sensory and motor systems (Bandler, 1982). That is, such stimulation leads to the biasing of specific sensorimotor mechanisms that subserve the affective behavior. This leaves open the possibility that a similar scheme operates in humans, with direct brain stimulation mediating emotion via sensorimotor rather than cognitive processes.

Current evidence indicates that limbic structures are best regarded as complex integrative centers mediating outputs, in some cases quite specific outputs. In turn, much of the limbic output is integrated with motor activity in the ventral striatum (Kelly & Stinus, 1984). Here there is a unique confluence of afferents from primary sensory cortex, motor cortex, association cortex, limbic structures, and ascending connections from the midbrain.

Over 15 years of research on the neural substrates of affective attack in the cat led to the conclusion that there were no simple schemes (centers or circuits) in which such behavioral entities are encoded in the brain (Flynn, 1972). Nevertheless, the findings from this and more recent research are consistent with a kind of neural specificity for emotional behavior. In his search for substrates Bandler (1982) used microinjection of glutamic acid to produce a much more specific and localized excitation than can be obtained with electrical stimulation via microelectrodes. He found that glutamate microinjections in the perifornical hypothalamic neurones produced the jaw-opening component of biting, and such injections in the midbrain central gray neurones elicited defensive rage display. Bandler concluded that the microinjections of excitatory amino acids enabled him "to identify the specific location of populations of neurones where excitation has specific behavioral consequences" (p. 394).

Basic homeostatic and autonomic functions are regulated by the hypothalamus and its neural extension through the brain stem. The hypothalamus appears to function as another locus of neural integration for emotional behavior, linking perceptual input from higher centers with behavioral responses involving autonomic nervous system (ANS) activation via the intermediolateral cell columns of the spinal cord. Most interesting of all from the standpoint of differential emotions theory has been the research indicating that there are multiple direct inputs to these spinal cord output cells, allowing for both rapidity of action and specificity. In addition, there is evidence of differential input to the various thoracic cord segments, suggesting discrete patterns of ANS activity as opposed to the older "mass action" model (Smith & DeVito, 1984).

An integral part of the modulation of emotional behavior derives from the activity pattern of chemical neurotransmitters and modulators of synaptic activity present throughout the nervous system, as well as specifically in the limbic structures. New methods of histochemical analysis developed within the last few decades have permitted investigators to map the synaptic pathways involved in certain neurotransmitter systems, and further to localize receptors and minute (picogram) concentrations of peptides occurring, and no doubt modulating activity in, discrete areas of the brain. The monoamine neurotransmitter systems (norepinephrine, dopamine, and serotonin) seem especially concerned with the modulation of the integrative activity of the brain as a whole, and experimental or clinical manipulation of these systems affects emotional behavior in both humans and other animals. Their specific pathways or loci of concentration are described in detail elsewhere (Izard & Saxton, in press; Kelly & Stinus, 1984). For example, dopamine appears to be intimately involved in an animal's motivational arousal and its flexibility in adaptive behavioral responses. In humans, amphetamine, which acts pharmacologically to release dopamine, induces elevation of mood and a sense of well-being, in addition to arousal. Subjective reports of dopamine release include the experience of elation and feelings of friendliness (Johanson & Uhlenhuth, 1980; Martin, Sloan, Sapira, & Jasinski, 1971). Mesolimbic dopamine appears essential for at least some aspects of the exploratory response (Fink & Smith, 1980) and by implication the emotion of interest (cf. Zuckerman, 1984). Evidence of specific neural circuitry and neurotransmitters for affective syndromes or traits such as depression (Anisman & Zacharko, 1982), anxiety (Gray, 1982), and sensation seeking (Zuckerman, 1984) has increased steadily in recent years.

Recent evidence indicates that certain neurotransmitter pathways may be lateralized (Tucker, 1981; Tucker & Williamson, 1984). For example, research with animals and human autopsy studies suggests a left lateralization of the dopamine pathways and a right lateralization of norepinephrine pathways, especially in somatosensory nuclei (Denenberg, 1980; Oke, Keller, Mefford & Adams, 1978; Tucker & Williamson, 1984). These findings are of interest in light of reported lateralization of emotions. Accumulating evidence indicates that the right hemisphere may be more finely tuned to the perception and processing of negative emotions than the left hemisphere and that the left may more readily process stimuli with a positive valence (Davidson, 1984; Fox & Davidson, 1984). Qualitatively different forms of information processing may also be attributable to lateralization of neurotransmitter substances (Tucker & Williamson, 1984). The most stable relevant finding from the lateralization research is that the right hemisphere is more involved than the left in processing emotion information and mediating emotion experience (Sperry, 1982).

As already indicated, the central premises of differential emotions theory give rise to the seven principles that organize the present theoretical approach to emotional development. In particular, the proposition that from the first days of life the emotions serve critical motivational, adaptive functions (Izard, 1979a) leads to Principle 1, the assumption of preadapted emotion mechanisms.

Principle 1: Innate emotion-specific neuromuscular patterns (facial expressions of basic emotions) show regularity in form and time of emergence and serve crucial adaptive functions in development.

The results of the foregoing neurophysiological and neurochemical research provide some leads for examining the assumption of emotion-specific neural mechanisms. The simplistic idea of a unitary or general arousal is being challenged by a view that allows for different types of arousal (Berlyne, 1960; Izard, 1971; Routtenberg, 1968; Zuckerman, 1984). Different types of arousal, each accompanied by its own particular feeling state and action tendency, would seem to require different neurophysiological and biochemical substrates. However, precise specification of the assumed underlying circuitry for each of the fundamental emotions has only begun (e.g., Panksepp, 1982). At present the assumption of distinct neural circuits relies largely on cross-cultural research indicating universality of facial expressions of emotion (Ekman et al., 1972; Izard, 1971), and studies documenting the very early, presumably unlearned emergence of facial expressions of the fundamental emotions in young infants (Eibl-Eibesfeldt, 1972; Hiatt et al., 1979; Izard, Huebner, Risser, McGinnes, & Dougherty, 1980; Steiner, 1973, 1974, 1979). Robust cross-cultural, developmental, and clinical evidence has resolved the issue of the universality of facial expressions. We turn now to more direct evidence of their innateness, ontogeny, and adaptive functions.

Preadapted Genetic Programs for Emotion-Specific Neuromuscular Patterns

The preadaptedness of the emotions system is most evident in the neuromuscular patterns that are reliably identifiable in young infants as facial expressions that convey emotion-specific messages (Huebner & Izard, 1985; Izard, Huebner, Risser, McGinnes, & Dougherty, 1980; Stenberg, 1982; Stenberg, Campos, & Emde, 1983).

The ability of the relatively dependent infant to signal emotion and need states to caregivers who intervene in its behalf is an extremely adaptive one.

The neuromuscular component of the emotions system shows features of both innateness and modifiability. The innate features are directed by genetic programs that have built-in allowances for learning or developmental modifiability. Genetically programmed aspects of development include provisions for (1) capacity for social communication through facial expression, (2) a predictable timetable for the emergence of emotion expressions, and (3) a natural concordance, at least initially, between expression and feeling.

Although certain irregularities in some event–emotion sequences (e.g., inconsistent reactions to stranger approach in infants 8–10 months old) may appear to argue against the preadaptedness of the emotions system, inconsistency in frequency and form of activity in response to apparently invariant stimulus conditions is characteristic of motivated behavior. Such variability in response to external stimuli can be understood as a function of interaction between incentive events and changing internal states (Epstein, 1982). The relative lack of fixed event–emotion sequences is especially adaptive for human beings. Flexibility is necessary for person–environment adaptation.

Genetically Determined Capacity for Social Communication Through Facial Expressions

Virtually all the component muscle movement units of adult facial expressions have been identified in the facial movements of both premature and full-term neonates (Oster, 1978). Two facial expressions present at birth, interest and disgust, and one that emerges in the third or fourth week of life, enjoyment or the social smile, have specifiable links to antecedent and consequent events of adaptive significance. The complete expression of disgust and components of the expression of enjoyment have been shown to be mediated by neural substrates in the very oldest part of the brain, the brain stem, suggesting that these patterned movements are phylogenetic adaptations.

Evidence from several studies suggests that interest sustains attention and visual exploration of social stimuli. If our interpretation of the findings is correct, it can be inferred that interest expression facilitates information processing, social interaction, and learning. Results of one study (Langsdorf, Izard, Rayias, & Hembree, 1983) showed that interest expression is significantly related to gaze behavior or attention focusing, especially in relation to human faces. The investigators showed 2-, 4-, 6-, and 8-month-old infants stimuli that varied in facelikeness—a human face, a manikin, and an inanimate object with scrambled facial features. The more facelike the stimulus, the greater were indices of heart rate deceleration, gaze time or visual fixation, and interest expression. Further, facial indicators of interest predicted visual fixation better than age or heart rate deceleration, suggesting a close relation between interest and attentional behaviors. Kistiakovskaia's (1965) work also suggests a close connection between visual fixation and convergence and the *animation complex,* which includes components of the interest and joy expressions.

Because interest in the infant is preprogrammed for selective attention to the human face (Fantz, 1973) as well as to novelty and movement, we can infer that interest expression facilitates social interaction. The main point here is that the preprogrammed facial movements that signal interest—activated in the newborn by novelty and the human face—serve basic adaptive functions in fostering acquisition of knowledge about the dynamic features of the physical and social environment.

A number of studies of normal and congenitally blind and other atypical infants show that the smiling response is innate and universal (Darwin, 1877; Eibl-Eibesfeldt, 1972; Thompson, 1941). The effectiveness of the caregiver's voice (Wolff, 1963) and face (Spitz & Wolf, 1946) as smile-eliciting stimuli and the power of the infant's smile as a smile elicitor for the caregiver appear to be phylogenetic adaptations. The EMG output from the zygomatic major (the principal muscle in the smile pattern) increases significantly when mothers watch video segments of babies smiling, even when the infants are strangers (Izard, Simons, Gelles, Hembree, & Huebner, 1985).

Although controlled experiments on the long-term effect of smiling on social development and social bonding are lacking for ethical reasons, common sense and studies of institutionalized or deprived infants argue strongly for its adaptive significance (Spitz, 1945, 1946). Provence and Lipton (1962) showed that institutionalized infants who had minimal social interaction suffered severe deficits in social response. Although the preference for human faces and the social smile emerged at the normal time, there was delay in discriminating attendant from stranger and face from mask and in imitation of facial expressions.

Short-term effects of depriving the infant of mother's animated, smiling face have been well documented (Hembree & Izard, 1985; Tronick, Adamson, Wise, Al, & Brazelton, 1975). When mothers maintain silence and a still face, infants as young as 3 months show apparent efforts to reengage the mother in animated social interaction, followed in some cases by perturbation, negative emotion expressions, and withdrawal behaviors. The weight of the evidence from the foregoing studies supports the assumption that the expression of joy is preprogrammed and has adaptive significance in social development.

Steiner's (1973, 1974, 1979) work on facial expression in response to taste and smell stimulation shows that the patterned neuromuscular responses constituting the expression of disgust are preprogrammed. The administration of a bitter substance (0.0003 M of quinine sulfate) to 100 infants between the time of birth and first feeding regularly elicited the disgust expression—frowning, depressed mouth corners, platysma contraction, and retching or spitting. The infants showed different facial reactions to sweet, sour, and bitter substances and judges had little difficulty in discriminating among them. Steiner (1979) concluded that the communicative significance of the disgust expression and other gustofacial responses could be understood in the framework of the caregiver–infant relationship. The adaptive value of these expressive behaviors is universally recognized by caregivers during feeding and related ministrations.

The physical distress expression is also present at birth (Hembree, Ansul, & Izard, 1985). Discomfort or painful stimulation regularly elicits this highly stereotyped pattern (Darwin, 1872; Hembree et al., 1985). It is generally agreed that this expression and the accompanying negative vocalization are an all-out emergency signal that preempts the attention of the caregiver (Emde, Gaensbauer, & Harmon, 1976). As we shall show later, there are significant age-related changes in the relation between aversive stimulation and the physical distress expression, but the adaptive value of this peremptory signal for the health and well-being of the young infant is self-evident.

Four emotion expressions, not present at birth, emerge in the first 7 months of life—surprise, sadness, anger, and fear (Izard, Huebner, Rissen, McGinnes, & Dougherty, 1980). Evidence suggests that the appearance of these expressions is largely a function of biological maturation, but their later appearance makes for relatively greater influence of temperament, learning, and socialization in linking them to specifiable antecedents and consequences. Nevertheless, it has been shown that in young infants painful stimulation induces expressions of anger and sadness (Izard, Hembree, Dougherty, & Spizzirri, 1983), restraint anger (Stenberg, 1982), and highly discrepant or strange stimuli fear (Schwartz & Izard, 1985). That these expressions have adaptive functions is demonstrated by mothers' discriminating their signal value and responding to them differentially (Huebner & Izard, 1985).

Predictable Timetable for the Emergence of Event-Related Emotion Expressions

Current evidence does not provide a precise timetable for the emergence of all the emotion expressions in humans. However, the available data tell us when infants are capable of displaying certain emotion expressions in response to particular events.

At birth, interest expressions are elicited by novelty or movement, physical distress expressions by painful stimulation, and disgust expressions by offensive substances (see Freedman, 1974; Hembree et al., 1985; Izard, Huebner, Risser, McGinnes, & Dougherty, 1980; Steiner, 1973). The social smile emerges sometime between 3 and 6 weeks; it can be elicited by a high-pitched human voice at 3–4 weeks and by a nodding face at 4–6 weeks (Wolff, 1966).

Components of the sadness expression have been observed intermittently during periods of distress induced by a painful medical procedure as early as the first week of life (Hembree et al., 1985). The full expression of sadness has been observed under similar conditions at about 3–4 months (Izard et al., 1980). Over 90 percent of 2-month-old infants displayed the anger expression, intermittently and briefly, in response to the pain of diphtheria–pertussis–tetanus (DPT) inoculation (Izard et al., 1985). A substantial percentage of 4-month-old infants showed anger to arm restraint (Stenberg, 1982). The fear expression has been reliably identified in 7-month-old infants in response to extreme novelty (Schwartz & Izard, 1985; cf. Hebb, 1946), and fear of heights (visual cliff) in self-locomotive infants (7–9 months of age) has been thoroughly documented by Campos and his colleagues (Campos, Hiatt, Ramsay, Henderson, & Svejda, 1978).

At the behavioral level one can argue that early emergence of the powerful emotion of fear would be maladaptive in a young infant with highly limited capacity for locomotion and other instrumental behaviors. Harlow (1971) argued that in infant rhesus monkeys fear always emerges after the capacity for affectional behavior and before the capacity for aggressive behavior. He maintained that this sequence was essential to all later stages of development (p. 68). At the neurophysiological level the relatively later appearance of the fear expression is probably attributable to the immaturity of its substrates.

The emergence of shame, shyness, guilt, and contempt has not been studied systematically, but a number of investigators have presented evidence or theory suggesting that signs of these emotions (not always facial) are observable in the first half of the second year of life (Hoffman, 1984; Izard & Hyson, in press; Scherer, 1984; Zahn-Waxler, Radke-Yarrow, & King, 1979).

In addition to timetables for event-elicited discrete emotions, there may be pre-programmed peaks or growth functions for certain expressions or event–expression relationships. For example, Super and Harkness (1982) reported cross-cultural concurrences in the peak of infant smiling during the first year, and Kagan (1976) reported similar growth functions for separation-induced crying for several cultures.

A Natural Concordance, at Least Initially, Between Expression and Feeling

By *natural concordance* we mean that external signs of affects, such as distressful crying, are accompanied by internal feelings, in this case pain sensations, that are considered congruent with the external signs. We believe that the crucial roles of facial expressions in early development and caregiver–infant interactions could not be sustained without concordant feeling states and their motivational functions. In view of the evidence presented in the foregoing section it seems reasonable, for example, to infer that the *feeling state* of interest motivates visual exploration and that of enjoyment affiliative behaviors. However, because the hypothesis of expression–feeling concordance remains controversial, we discuss it in some detail under Principle 4.

Summary

The evidence reviewed supports the principle that innate emotion-specific neuromuscular patterns (facial expressions of emotions) show regularity in form and time of emergence and serve adaptive functions in development. Three expressions—interest, disgust, physical distress—present at birth have specifiable antecedents and consequences. Novelty and human faces elicit interest and facilitate visual exploration and social interaction. Chemical tastants elicit disgust and the disgust expression aids in the rejection of undesirable substances and alerts caregivers. Discomfort or painful stimulation elicits the physical distress expression, which preempts caregiver attention and brings comforting interventions. The social smile is elicited at 3 weeks by a high-pitched human voice and at 6 weeks by the human face and it very regularly elicits a smile from the caregiver. Both the interest and joy expressions contribute to social bonding and the development of attachment. All four of these facial expressions send affect-specific messages and elicit different caregiver responses.

The emergence of expressions of surprise, sadness, anger, and fear within the first 7 months of life appears to be primarily a function of biological maturation, but learning and socialization may have a relatively greater influence on the early elicitors and consequences of these emotions. With the exception of surprise, which has proved highly elusive in the laboratory (Charlesworth & Kreutzer, 1973), the emergence of all the early infancy expressions follows a fairly predictable timetable, at least in relation to certain incentive events that can be studied in the laboratory. All these basic emotion expressions have discriminable signal value and differential effects on caregivers. Finally, we proposed that the neuromuscular patterns that signal emotion provide sensory feedback to the brain and hence contribute to the activation and regulation of emotion feeling states. This proposition will be discussed further under Principle 4.

We have supported the proposition that the emotion expressions are innate and preadapted to serve significant communicative functions in early development. That emotion expressions emerge largely as a function of biological maturation and that some of them operate from birth with instinctlike precision in response to both positive and stressful stimulation suggest that they can function independent of cognition, the topic of Principle 2.

Principle 2: The preadaptedness of emotion-specific expressive behaviors enables the emotions system to function independently of the cognitive system, but the interaction and interdependence of the two systems become increasingly more complex with development.

We recognize that emotions and cognition, and indeed all systems of the individual, typically function in a highly interactive, interdependent fashion. We maintain, however, that the emotions system can operate independently of cognition and that such functioning plays a significant role in development, especially in early infancy. This assumption is tied to our definitions and nomenclature, particularly with respect to the concepts of emotion, emotions system, and cognition.

Research on facial expressions provides the strongest evidence for the proposition that the emotions system can operate independently of the cognitive system. Several studies show that expressive behavior can be mediated by the brain stem in the absence of limbic and cortical structures (Steiner, 1979) typically considered necessary for the consolidation of memory (Routtenberg, 1980), or for cognition as we have defined it. Some of the earliest data relating to this issue came quite incidentally from studies of ANS and adrenal activity during aggression. Cannon (1928) found that appropriate stimulation of decorticate cats led them to display ferocious attack, defense, and flight behaviors. In a follow-up study, Bard (1928) determined that the emotion-expressive behavior was possible when everything above the brain stem was removed except the posterior hypothalamus. Even without the posterior hypothalamus some components of the emotional behavior could be elicited.

Steiner (1979) studied gustofacial responses, including the disgust expression, in various animal preparations and human infants with brain disorders. Steiner's research showed that the disgust expression is controlled by phylogenetically ancient parts of the central nervous system—brain stem (pontobulbar) mechanisms. Anencephalic and hydroanencephalic newborns encoded expressions to sweet, sour, and bitter substances that were virtually identical to those of normal infants. Autopsies on the malformed infants revealed no cortical structures. The pathway for the disgust expression goes from peripheral receptors via the VIIth (chordatympany) nerve (as well as the taste fibers of the IXth and Xth nerves) to the solitary tract nucleus in the medulla to the motor nucleus of the VIIth nerve, which activates the motoneurons that produce the patterned facial expression. Thus Steiner's work represents strong evidence for brain stem mediation of the expression of at least one of the basic emotions—disgust.

Steiner infers that the brain stem also mediates the feeling state or hedonic aspect of disgust and that the hedonic state associated with the expression is totally unrelated to cognition. In Steiner's view the disgust expression signals "decision" based on a "hedonic monitor system" that is independent of learning and experience. The decision or "discrimination between 'pleasant' and 'aversive' [substances] does not result from cognitive mental processes" (Steiner, 1979, p. 262). Thus Steiner provides strong evidence for the noncognitive, brain stem mediation of the disgust expression and infers that the accompanying hedonic state is mediated similarly.

A quite different line of research lends support to Steiner's position and to Principle 2. Findings from studies of facial feedback can be interpreted as showing that sensory data from expressive behavior generate emotion feeling states independently of cognition. This research will be discussed under Principle 4.

Five other types of empirical findings support the thesis that neural processes alone are sufficient to generate emotion directly without cognitive mediation. First, evidence discussed previously showed that direct manipulation of subcortical brain structures through stimulation and ablation of selected areas can lead to the activation or the elimination of certain emotional behaviors. In the cat, at least, direct brain stimulation apparently produces affective behavior via sensorimotor rather than cognitive processes. It seems reasonable to infer that the sensory data of pain require no cognitive mediation in order to achieve awareness and that, similarly, the neural and motor processes of a particular emotion, say, pain-elicited anger, can automatically generate the feeling of anger in consciousness, independently of cognition.

Second, as Zajonc (1984) has noted, there are receptors and neural pathways that could enable sensory input to affect the limbic system and activate emotion processes prior to cognitive appraisal or evaluation. An example is the retino-hypothalamic tract that enables information from the visual sense to affect an important emotion-related brain structure (hypothalamus) directly. Though this kind of pathway for direct sensory input to the limbic system does not demonstrate the independence of emotion activation from cognitive appraisal, it suggests that there is an anatomical basis that would permit such independence.

Third, emotion responses can be elicited in the human neonate before the infant is thought to have the capacity for cognitive representation or appraisal of incentive events. The evidence we discussed in relation to our restrictions on the use of the term *cognition* is also evidence that the emotions system functions independently of cognition. Also, as discussed earlier, newborns respond emotionally to facial and vocal signals of emotion, long before "mental work" on items represented in memory is thought to be playing a role. Infants in the first weeks of life show preferences in attention (Fantz, 1964). Like Zajonc (1980), we believe such preferences are based on affective rather than cognitive discrimination. Tactile stimulation produces smiling and laughter in infants 4–6 months old, whereas stimuli requiring evaluation are not effective until later ages (Sroufe & Wunsch, 1972). Furthermore, as discussed above, neonates make hedonic "decisions" in relation to tastants and show physical distress to painful medical procedures in the first hours of life before cognition as we have defined it would be expected.

Fourth, evidence from studies of the relation between affect and cognition in children with Down's syndrome suggests that the affective and cognitive systems have some independence. Investigations by Cicchetti and colleagues (Cicchetti & Sroufe, 1978; Motti, Cicchetti, & Sroufe, 1983) have demonstrated that when Down's syndrome babies are matched for mental age with samples of nonhandicapped infants they still show different event–expression sequences that would have been predicted by the view that emotional development is dependent on cognitive development.

Finally, research on brain lateralization suggests the possibility of relatively independent functioning of the emotions system. There is functional differentiation between the cerebral hemispheres, and the bulk of the evidence indicates that the right hemisphere is relatively more involved than the left in the processing of emotion information (Denenberg, 1980; Ray & Cole, 1985; Tucker, 1981; Tucker & Williamson, 1984). Sperry (1982) and his colleagues have shown that in the divided brain (patient with commissurotomy) emotion can be elicited by a stimulus (e.g., photograph of family member) presented to the right hemisphere before the patient can identify and label the stimulus.

All of the foregoing is not to say that cognition and emotion usually operate independently of one another. On the contrary, in adults it is likely that there is almost continuous mutual influence. Because we assume that from birth the human being has a *functioning* emotions system, that some emotion is *always* present in consciousness, and that the ongoing emotion influences all perceptual–cognitive processes in some way, we also assume that emotion is primal. Our view of the primacy of emotion does not conflict with our assumption of the continual reciprocal influences of emotion and cognition. The ongoing emotion in consciousness influences the way we construe objects and events and that construction may in turn alter the ongoing emotion or activate a different one.

The foregoing arguments notwithstanding, the primacy of emotions and other issues relating to emotion–cognition relations are far from settled. Developmental research on cognitive processes (see Fagan & Rovee-Collier, 1983; Harris, 1983a) suggests that we may still tend to underestimate the young infant's cognitive capacities. Research on the emergence of early cognitive and affective responses and other aspects of emotion–cognition relations is much needed.

DEVELOPMENTAL CHANGES IN EMOTION EXPRESSIONS

In humans the observable expressive component of the emotions system consists primarily of actions of the musculature of the face and larynx—facial and vocal expressions and gaze behavior. The muscles that control posture and locomotion are also involved, but their actions in emotions have been the focus of less study. Expressive behaviors act as communicative links with the social environment and contribute to the unique quality of conscious experience that constitutes emotion feeling (Izard, 1971; Laird, 1984; Tomkins, 1962). Expression can also be viewed as the source of specific sociomotivational cues to both the self and others (DePaulo & Rosenthal, 1982; Izard, Huebner, Risser, McGinnes, & Dougherty, 1980). Developmentally, expressive behavior undergoes changes in both *function* and *form*. These developmental shifts occur as a result of both maturational changes in the nervous system, as noted previously, and socialization.

As shown in the discussion of Principles 1 and 2, the mechanisms of emotion expression are innate and preadapted. Much of the preadaptedness relates to the needs of the young infant, served well by instinctlike motivational and social communication systems that derive from the emotions. Increasing complexity of the individual and of individual-environment transactions calls for increasing self-regulation and, particularly, for regulation of the powerful motivational signals of emotion expressions, processes described in Principle 3.

Principle 3: Biological and social forces gradually change full-face instinctlike expression to more restricted and controlled emotion signals.

During the opening weeks of life affective expression shows characteristics of both reflexes and instincts. The early expressions are reflexlike in that they are innate, relatively stereotyped, and some of them (e.g., disgust, physical distress, anger) are elicited rather than being generated spontaneously. They show features typical of instincts in that they are characterized by species-specific efferent programs. However, emotion expressions differ from reflexes and instincts in that they undergo developmental changes through maturation and socialization without ever dropping out of the individual's behavioral repertoire. The developmental changes in facial expressions are discussed below and the role of socialization in expression regulation is taken up under Principle 4.

Although many aspects of early emotional behaviors are apparently tied to genetically dictated species-typical patterns of brain organization and maturational timetables, another species-typical characteristic, *developmental modifiability,* allows for subsequent growth and change in the output side of the emotions system. The term *developmental modifiability* refers to the capacity to transform the more stereotyped and instinctlike aspects of emotional behavior in response to environmental input. Elements of developmental modifiability include (1) the capacity for acquiring learned elicitors of emotion in addition to the natural, unlearned elicitors and (2) modifications of expressive behavior through instrumental learning and the exercise of voluntary control. Learning of this sort is apparently dependent on the maturation of the cortex and pyramidal motor system. For example, in a study of developmental changes in 2-, 4-, 7-, and 19-month-olds' emotion responses to the acute pain of DPT inoculations, Izard and colleagues (1983) found that the inoculation produced a uniquely patterned physical distress expression with great regularity but that the duration of this emergency signal decreased with age, especially markedly after the first half-year of life. The painful stimulation of inoculation also elicited the anger expression, increasingly with age. The decrease in the peremptory distress expression was considered a function of the maturation of inhibitory mechanisms in the central nervous system. The increase in anger expression was interpreted as a joint function of the inhibition of the physical distress expression and a dispositional tendency in animals and humans to respond to aversive stimulation with aggression (cf. Berkowitz, 1983).

The development of expressive behavior involves the modification of innate patterns that are highly adaptive in early infancy (see Zivin, 1985). Genetic programs direct behavior initially, ensuring a certain degree of universality in the expression of emotions (emotion signaling) among individuals from different families and different cultures. At the same time, developmental modifiability, permitting development of the control of certain emotion expressions in accord with social conventions, helps ensure a fit between individuals and their social niche. Although most adult expressive behaviors are regulated, instinctlike facial expressions may occur in intense unanticipated emotion-eliciting situations throughout the life span.

Age-Related Changes in Eliciting Conditions

Emotion expression is dependent on the existence of: (1) intact and functional sensory systems for the sensory registration of emotionally relevant stimuli; (2) a functional neuromuscular system; and (3) central neural programs for the integration of emotion arousal and emotional behavior. By these criteria young infants are expressively competent well within the opening months of life. Human newborns are sensorily precocious, with all sensory systems capable of at least rudimentary function at birth (Werner & Lipsitt, 1981). Thus the early elicitors of affect—tactile, visual, auditory, gustatory, olfactory, and vestibular sensations—can be detected and processed at least on an elementary level.

In the opening years of life the elicitation of emotion is frequently dependent on the physical parameters of stimuli; however, the band of elicitors gradually expands to include stimuli that are more "psychological" or abstract in nature. The disgust expression, initially limited as a response to noxious olfactory or gustatory stimuli, is seen later in development in response to revolting ideas or loathsome persons. Among the early psychological elicitors of emotions are events such as the recognition of familiar persons (for the elicitation of smiling), heights or the sudden approach of a highly discrepant or a strange object (for the elicitation of fear), the perception of change or novelty (for the elicitation of interest), and the resolution of incongruity (for the elicitation of smiling).

In the context of our discussion of Principle 2 we indicated an array of physical stimuli that are capable of eliciting emotion expressions in young infants, including auditory, visual, and tactile stimuli. Many of these same stimuli remain potent elicitors of affective response later in development as well. As children mature, their learning and experience greatly increase the number and variety of elicitors for the various discrete emotions, patterns of emotions, and affective–cognitive structures.

Age-Related Changes in Frequency and Configuration of Expressive Signals

The emotion expressions of young infants appear to be automatic responses to preemptive stimuli, there being little or no ability to postpone or alter the timing or shape of the response (Malatesta & Izard, 1984b). Formal aspects of emotion expression that undergo change with age include the *frequency, range, discreteness,* and *integrity* of the expression.

Changes in the Frequency and Range of Emotion Expressions

Newborn infants have a notoriously low threshold for activation of the distress cry, but by 3–4 months of age they show substantial reduction in the frequency of crying bouts (Emde et al., 1976). By 18 months of age they even show a substantial reduction in the peremptory distress cry in response to the acute pain of inoculation (Izard et al., 1983), about a fourth of them showing a complete absence of the distress expression and others displaying it only briefly.

A study of mother–infant interaction and separation by Malatesta and Haviland (1982) using the Maximally Discriminative Facial Movement Coding System (Max) (Izard, 1979b) suggests that the rate of change of affective displays other than distress also decreases with age. Three-month-old infants changed their facial expressions once every 7 sec whereas 6-month-olds did so once every 9 sec. In terms of hedonic type, there was proportionately less expression of negative affect than of positive affect at 6 versus 3 months.

The only other similar age-related work on expression frequency and range in adults is that of Malatesta and Izard (1984a) in which young, middle-aged, and older women were asked to recount personal experiences under emotion induction conditions. Max coding showed that there is a rich range of expressive behavior in adult women. However, as is not the case with infants, their expressions consist mainly of blends, masking, and partial versions of discrete emotion expressions.

Changes in Discreteness of Expression

When we use the term *discreteness* in the context of emotion expression, we are referring to the extent to which the expression is representative of a discrete category of emotion (e.g., anger). An emotion expression that is completely discrete shows the formal muscle movement pattern or appearance changes of that expression in all regions of the face, unaccompanied by appearance changes associated with any other emotions. Although infants change their facial expressions very rapidly, often creating the impression of "mixed emotions," discrete expressions are more common than blends in infants under the age of 1 year. Demos (1982), who has studied the expressive behaviors of children 7–24 months old under naturalistic conditions, reports that blends were relatively rare at the youngest ages and became increasingly likely with age. Demos's work suggests that children in the second year of life may already be learning to adopt the social smile as a mask. That the smile was at times accompanied by components of negative expression suggested that these infant subjects had not yet fully mastered the strategy of completely concealing negative affect.

By adulthood blended emotion expressions are said to be characteristic (Ekman et al., 1972). The presence of a blended expression may signal actual mixed emotions in the person showing the expression. Alternatively, it may represent a conscious or unconscious attempt to mask a particular feeling, with one type of emotion signal in the blend constituting "leakage" of the underlying feeling state.

Changes in the Integrity of Expressions

The term *integrity of expression* refers to the completeness of the expression, regardless of whether the expression is a discrete or blended one. Adults are said to have the capacity to fragment (Ekman et al., 1972) or miniaturize (Tomkins, 1962) the complete form of the expression. Miniaturization is the process by which a complex patterned expression is compressed almost to the point of invisibility so that the expression is barely perceptible to an observer. It often involves compressing the physical parameters of the signal, as in the compression of a joyful smile into a "thin smile" confined to minimal lip movement and no involvement of the muscles surrounding the eye. In fact, a variety of different smile patterns have been identified in adults; patterns vary in terms of onset, apex, offset, and degree of symmetry (Ekman & Friesen, 1982; Haynes & Stettner, 1983). Preliminary analysis indicates that different smile patterns are associated with different eliciting conditions as well as different feeling states. Another example of fragmenting is the drawing together and lowering of the brows under conditions of anger, unaccompanied by squaring the mouth or compressing the lips. An even more reduced anger expression is the fixed stare. Reduced expressions, by virtue of their loss of information, are more ambiguous, and thus the observer is more dependent on knowledge of the expresser and of the context for accurate decoding of the signal.

There have been only a few studies of the development of the ability to miniaturize expressions and of the course of such changes over the life span. Zivin (1982) has tracked the transformation of two facial signals from preschool into adulthood and finds that they become more abbreviated in form. There are apparently even further changes with advancing age. In the Malatesta and Izard (1984b) study of young, middle-aged, and older women's facial expressions of emotion, it was noted that the older two groups used more partial versions of emotion expressions than did the youngest group, who tended to give more complete expressions.

The foregoing discussion of changes in the functional and formal features of emotion expressions indicates that pronounced changes in expression occur during late infancy and early childhood with continuing refinement through adulthood. The intriguing question is how such remarkable changes are accomplished in such a relatively short period during early development; also of interest are the circumstances that encourage change. We might also ask about the background motivation for such changes; that is, why is affect modulation encouraged by socializing agents and why are the expression changes learned in childhood maintained over time, apparently with only minor modification throughout adulthood and the later years? The processes involved in the socialization of emotions have recently become the focus of considerable interest to developmental psychologists (Lewis & Saarni, in press). Although the process is apparently quite complex, we are beginning to understand something about early socialization of emotion, a topic of discussion under Principle 5.

Unresolved Issues

Although current evidence indicates that there is developmental change from reflex- or instinctlike full-face expressions to more controlled and limited configurations of emotion signals, many important questions need to be investigated before we can understand the underlying processes and effects of these changes in emotion expression. What inhibitory neural mechanisms are involved and what is their developmental course? What are the ANS and experiential correlates of developmental changes in facial expressions? At what stage of cognitive and motor development can the infant begin to exercise some degree of control over emotion expressions? What are the immediate effects of a regulatory process such as suppression of emotion expression on the functioning of the somatic and autonomic nervous system, cognitive processes, and instrumental behavior?

Expression Regulation: Implications for the Communication and Regulation of Emotion Feelings

In the ecological niche of the young infant the higher-order cognitive, social, and motor skills necessary for adaptation reside in the care givers. A principal role of the infant in the social nexus is to communicate its needs and feelings. A second role of the infant is to learn to regulate its emotion expressions, which, in the early months of life, fire with instinctlike rapidity and precision in response to a wide range of incentive events. Such responding on the part of the infant suggests that its internal states or feelings have preprogrammed connections to overt expressive behavior, a central aspect of the next principle, Principle 4. The organizational and motivational functions of affect expressions also suggest that they are linked to concordant feelings, phenomena that have motivational and cue-producing properties (Isen, 1984; Izard, 1971). An initial link between expression and feeling does not mean that the link is continuously functional.

A hypothesis of continuous linkage of expression and feeling throughout the life span is untenable. Therefore, if we assume preprogrammed expression–feeling connections, then it follows that these connections must be modified during development in order to account for the older child and adult's well-known ability to dissimulate expression and feeling, another aspect of Principle 4.

Principle 4: An innate expression–feeling concordance ensures effective communication with the preverbal infant, but learned expression regulation increases the flexibility of expression–feeling relations.

Principle 4 has three distinct but related aspects. The first concerns the assumption of an innate expression–feeling concordance. The second involves the sensory feedback hypothesis of emotion activation, viewed as a mechanism that can explain early expression–feeling concordance and expression-generated emotion feelings in adults. The third aspect focuses on expression regulation and dissimulation, seen as an imperative consequence of innate expression–feeling concordance—learn to control feelings of self and others by controlling emotion expressions.

In the section on terminology, *emotion feeling* was defined as the direct product of the underlying neural and motor processes, as a qualitatively distinct aspect of consciousness that has motivational and organizational functions in relation to cognition and action. Selectivity of perception and organization of behavior exist from birth, and the concept of innate emotion feelings offers a parsimonious explanation of these phenomena. As indicated in the discussion of Principle 1 and the introduction to this section, newborn infants' preferences for novelty, certain types of visual and auditory stimuli, and the human face suggest the underlying motivational state of interest (Fantz, 1973; Wolff, 1965). In response to such stimuli young infants respond in meaningful ways—attending, exploring, tracking, mimicking (Anthony & Graham, 1983; Lelwica & Haviland, 1983; Wolff, 1965).

The Relation Between Expression and Feeling

In contrast to the view that emotion feeling is cognitively or socially constructed (Averill, 1985; Mandler, 1982), we propose that there is an innate concordance of expression and feeling and that the neural processes subserving expression contribute to the activation and regulation of feeling states. Because there are some discrete emotion-specific expressions at birth, we maintain that there are likewise some specific emotion feelings at birth. When other expressions emerge, concordant feelings emerge simultaneously.

It is generally agreed that children do experience concordance of emotion expression and emotion feeling. The question is when and how concordance emerges. It is present from birth or the moment a specific expression emerges, or do expressions and feelings develop in parallel such that their association or concordance has to be learned?

The discussion of the principles relating to the biological substrates, the first component of emotion, emphasized the role of the neuromuscular patterns that are identified as emotion-specific facial expression, the second component of emotion. It was argued that these neuromuscular patterns were innately linked to brain mechanisms and that they served crucial adaptive functions in development. In the discussion that follows, we shall argue that from birth the efferent message that leads to facial expression and the subsequent afferent feedback contribute to a concordant feeling state and that through development the relation between expression and feeling becomes flexible and multidimensional.

Our argument for expression–feeling concordance in young infants assumes that the principal components of the expression are encoded for more than a few milliseconds. We have observed highly fleeting components of emotion expressions in the newborn's response to acute pain and questioned whether such expressions could have concordant feeling states (Hembree et al., 1985). Campos and Barrett (1984) propose that in the newborn period (0–2 months), inappropriate components of emotion expressions may appear very briefly as "overflow" or "noise" in the relevant display, perhaps because of neurological immaturity.

The proposition that emotion feelings are innate by virtue of their initial dependence on innate expressions runs counter to the constructivist view (Averill, 1985; Lewis & Michalson, 1983; Mandler, 1982) that feelings or the subjective component of emotion is a function of experience. The constructivist positions differ in detail, but the common denominator is that emotional experiences or feeling states are products of learning, typically social learning. For most of them the connections between expressions and feelings are also learned. We believe that it is highly improbable that one could ever teach an infant how to *feel* joy or sadness or any emotion. We take the opposite view—that the expression–feeling connection is innate and that it is their uncoupling that has to be learned. Of course the image, symbol, and thought network that gradually becomes associated with a feeling state is largely a function of social and cognitive construction. This is what we refer to as the development of affective–cognitive structures (see Principle 7), and we maintain that it is the innate feeling component of affective–cognitive structures that makes them motivational phenomena.

Innate Expression–Feeling Concordance

There is reason to believe that functional integrity between emotion feeling and emotion expression is preprogrammed because of the role that emotion plays in adaptation. According to Carmichael's (1970) law of anticipatory function in prenatal neurogenesis, many structures (and presumably links between structures and systems) that make for later adaptive responses are functional at a period somewhat prior to the time they must actually be called into use. Preadaptation would seem to be especially useful in the case of the emotions system because emotion-expressive behaviors, acting as signals to caregivers and others, prompt attention to the infant's needs for relief from discomfort, affective contact, and social stimulation. The effectiveness of caregiver ministrations, which differ for different expressions (Huebner & Izard, 1985), suggests concordance of the infant's expression and internal state.

Other empirical considerations also suggest an initial concordance between feelings and expressive behaviors. Infants display facial behaviors that bear a striking resemblance to facial patterns of emotion in adults (Izard, Huebner, Risser, McGinnes, & Dougherty, 1980; Malatesta & Haviland, 1982). In adults, when these specific facial patterns are spontaneous and not dissimulated, they are associated with particular emotion states (Fridlund & Izard, 1983; Fridlund, Schwartz, & Fowler, 1984; Schwartz, Fair, Greenberg, Friedman, & Klerman, 1974).

There is also evidence of covariance between incentive events (which are assumed to produce specific feeling states) and emotional behaviors (which are assumed to be indicators of those states) (Kagan, 1976). For example, Stenberg and colleagues (1983) have demonstrated that facial response components specific to anger, rather than a composite of components belonging to other emotion states, occurred in 4-month-old infants in response to incentive conditions thought to arouse anger (limb restraint). In addition, Hyson and Izard (1984) have observed coherent relations between emotion expressions and instrumental acts in 18-month-olds during brief separation, suggesting an underlying feeling state that motivates and guides instrumental behavior.

In considering the idea that pre–self-conscious, preverbal infants can experience emotions congruent with their expressions, it is helpful to consider the functioning of other sensory systems in infancy. Earlier we noted that the affect of pain does not require cognitive appraisal or comparison (Izard et al., 1983). When young infants encode the physical distress expression in response to DPT inoculation, their heart rates increase an average of 19 beats per minute (Johnston & Strada, 1985). Given the prototypical facial expression and the expected ANS changes, it seems quite reasonable to infer a concomitant feeling state.

The alternative to an innate concordance between a pattern of expressive behavior and a feeling state would be that their association must be a learned one, and the foregoing discussion suggests that this is highly improbable. If the linkages were not genetically programmed or if there were no preparedness in favor of concordance, and linkages were attendant on social learning, there would be too much room for error and pathology in such a crucial adaptive system.

Facial Feedback and Expression–Feeling Concordance

Automatic expression–feeling concordance in infancy is consistent with the hypothesis that the efferent message to the facial muscles and/or the cutaneous and proprioceptive feedback from the patterned facial movements contribute to the *activation* or *generation* of specific emotion feelings (cf. Bandler, 1982; Flynn, 1867). Facial feedback may not be the only mechanism for the activation of discrete emotions in early infancy. It is possible that affective information automatically triggers central processes that generate emotion feelings (Panksepp, personal communication, June 1, 1985; cf. Panksepp, 1982). However, the highly differentiated pattern of efferent and afferent pathways associated with facial expression is the only known neurophysiological mechanism with the required specificity to activate the discrete emotion-specific feelings. Facial skin is particularly well supplied with receptors highly sensitive to the minute stretching or wrinkling resulting from even very subtle expressive movements (Nordin, Hagbarth, Thomander, & Wallin, 1984).

Before briefly reviewing the data supporting the facial feedback hypothesis, three points are in order. First, Cannon's (1927) attack on the James-Lange theory was concerned with visceral feedback and has no bearing on the facial feedback hypothesis (see Izard, 1977, pp. 55–64, for a review). Second, Rinn's (1984) argument that there may be insufficient proprioceptors in the face for discrete patterned feedback does not negate the possibility that cutaneous nociceptive and low-threshold mechanoreceptive (LTM) neurons that project to the face may be adequate to the task (Dubner, Sessle, & Storey, 1978). Additionally, a substantial percentage of the LTM neurons have visceral afferent convergence (Hu, Dostrovsky, & Sessle, 1981), and this is not inconsistent with the notion that somatic feedback from the face may play a role in recruiting visceral activity. The data of Hu and colleagues clearly revealed an anatomical basis for the coordination of facial and visceral afferent input to thalamus and hence to cortex. Third, at the behavioral level, about 16 of 18 experiments that tested the facial feedback hypothesis of emotion activation or emotion regulation have yielded affirmative evidence (Laird, 1984).

More than a dozen experiments have tested a version of the facial feedback hypothesis of feeling state activation (Laird, 1984). In the typical experiment, subjects, unaware of the purpose of the manipulation and its relation to emotion expression, are requested to contract facial muscles such that they assume the expression of a positive or negative emotion while rating positive or negative emotion stimuli. Typically subjects who have been manipulated into a frown pose rate negative emotion stimuli more negatively and positive ones less positively than do subjects manipulated into a smile pattern. Most such experiments indicate that the expression manipulation works, at least in terms of the broad classes of emotion feelings (positive or negative).

In a review of these experiments Laird (1984) claimed that the ratio was 10 to 1 in favor of an emotion-specific expression effect. However, a close examination of the study designs shows this to be an exaggerated claim. As Winton (1985) observed, all the studies except one failed to meet the two criteria necessary to demonstrate emotion-specific effects. Either they did not manipulate two emotions of like valence (e.g., two negative emotions) or they failed to obtain adequately differentiated self-reports of emotion experience. Nevertheless, that the studies yielded substantial evidence that experimenter-manipulated expressions at least activate positive and negative emotion states is supportive of the facial feedback hypothesis.

Although facial feedback is considered an important factor in emotion activation in infancy, differential emotions theory holds that other mechanisms of emotion activation emerge with development. These processes and the role of ANS activity in amplifying and sustaining emotion are discussed elsewhere (Izard, 1877; cf. Fehr & Stern, 1970).

Learned Expression Regulation and Dissimulation Increases the Flexibility of the Expression–Feeling Relation

If there is innate expression–feeling concordance, then learning is definitely necessary to uncouple expression and feelings. The need to manage the expression of one's emotions is a fact of everyday life. In growing up, children have to learn not to cry at minor injuries and upsets, to adopt a brave stance in the face of threats, not to get overexcited in situations where calm should rule, and not to laugh at another's misfortune. They also have to learn to look calm or happy when their security is in doubt or their self-confidence is shaken, to appear happy when receiving a disappointing gift, and to express sadness at another person's loss even though the other person is a rival. The ability to modify emotion expressions is a tremendously adaptive item in anyone's behavioral repertoire both for self-management of feeling and as a means of promoting harmonious social interactions (cf. Campos, Barrett, Lamb, Goldsmith, & Stenberg, 1983).

Several studies have demonstrated that children are aware of the need to conceal their feelings in order to gain advantages in interpersonal situations, to avoid hurting other people's feelings, to defend their self-esteem, and to avoid punishment for revealing negative feelings (Demos, 1974; Saarni, 1979, 1980). They also show a rudimentary ability to dissimulate by the age of 4 (Cole, 1983), a capacity that improves with age (Saarni, 1981).

Expression Regulation in Infancy

Indirect evidence for early expression regulation comes from a study of responses to acute pain. A longitudinal microanalytic study of the facial expressions of infants 2–19 months old to the acute pain of inoculation (the DPT immunization series) showed that the physical distress expression gives ground to the anger expression with increasing age (Izard et al., 1985). By 19 months of age, 28 percent of the infants did not encode the all-out distress expression at all, and all infants displayed far more anger than distress. The investigators reasoned that in the mobile toddler capable of defensive behavior the anger expression is more adaptive than the distress expression. The physical distress expression preempts all available energy, whereas anger mobilizes energy for instrumental action. The findings suggest that maturation of inhibitory neural mechanisms and social learning have enabled the toddler to exercise adaptive expression regulation.

Expression Regulation in Adults

Direct evidence for the role of facial expression in adults' regulation of affective experience and autonomic nervous system (ANS) activity in pain comes from the work of Lanzetta and his colleagues (Colby, Lanzetta, & Kleck, 1977; Kleck, Vaughn, Cartwright-Smith, Vaughn, Colby, & Lanzetta, 1976; Lanzetta, Cartwright-Smith, & Kleck, 1976). The last paper reports three studies that typify this series of experiments. In the first study subjects were instructed to "hide" their overt expressive responses while anticipating painful electric shocks. The results showed that the hide-expression condition significantly reduced a skin conductance index of ANS arousal and decreased self-reported estimates of shock aversiveness. The second experiment of Lanzetta and colleagues replicated the foregoing findings and disconfirmed the alternative hypothesis that the results of experiment one could be a function of attention focusing. The third experiment of Lanzetta and colleagues showed that voluntary regulation of expressive behavior while actually experiencing (rather than anticipating) intense electric shock regulated arousal (skin conductance) and subjective estimates of pain. The investigators interpreted their results as supporting the Darwinian-type sensory feedback models of Gellhorn (1964), Izard (1971), and Tomkins (1962).

Zuckerman, Klorman, Larrance, and Spiegel (1981) extended the studies of Lanzetta and colleagues (1976) using a more elaborate design that included several different types of emotion elicitors, measures of three different ANS functions (skin conductance, heart rate, and digital blood volume), a spontaneous expression as well as expression suppression and expression exaggeration conditions, and a two-phase procedure that permitted both within- and between-subject comparisons. They found that facial expression modulated physiological output (averaged across the three ANS indices) and subjective experience in emotional states (as indexed by a pleasant–unpleasant dimensional scale). The consistency of the results across phases and the similarity to those of Lanzetta and colleagues testify to their robustness and generality. Like Lanzetta and colleagues (1976), Zuckerman and colleagues (1981) interpreted their results as supporting the sensory feedback hypothesis.

Another kind of evidence for expression regulation comes from the work of Ekman and his colleagues. Ekman (1972) and Friesen (1972) found that Japanese and Americans showed the same facial expression when experiencing fear, disgust, and distress if they were alone, but the two cultural samples followed different display rules in responding to the same stimulus situations if they were observed. Ekman and Friesen (1982) have also shown that the smile can be used in regulating or masking other expressions. However, such expression management is difficult even for adults, and "felt, false, and miserable" smiles can be distinguished by careful observation.

Thus it appears that concordance between emotion expression and emotion feeling comes naturally; it is dissimulation that is difficult and depends on the maturation of inhibitory neural systems and on a learned awareness that civilized people do not express their feelings in unrestrained fashion.

Socialization practices in different cultures uniformly include teaching attitudes toward emotions (Izard, 1971) and display rules (Ekman, 1969). Young children receiving a disappointing gift are likely to signal that disliking quite openly; it is only later that they acquire the ability to manage a graceful smile and an expression of gratitude. To assume that feeling state and expressive behavior are disjoined during infancy, become coupled sometime thereafter, resist uncoupling until late childhood, and later become behaviorally variable again presents us with an unparsimonious and unrepresentative example of behavioral development.

The foregoing findings concerning the role of emotion expressions in the regulation and activation of emotion feelings alert us to the possibility that the socialization or cultural shaping of emotion expressions is tantamount to the shaping of emotion experiences and of the emotional life in general. That is, to the extent that the facial feedback hypothesis is valid, modifications in expressive patterns as well as culturally determined inhibition or facilitation of expression or expressive style can be expected to alter the flow of emotion experiences and, by implication, personality development. Although studies of cultural differences in socialization have told us something about these processes, precisely how and to what extent learned modifications in expressions and expressive styles affect social, cognitive, and personality development are important problems for future research.

Summary

Consideration of several developmental processes as well as empirical data from children and adults has led us to posit concordance between expressions and feelings during infancy. Concordance of feelings and expressions seems essential to effective social communication. This is particularly true in the prelinguistic infant for whom expressive behaviors are virtually the sole source of information for guiding the care giver's comforting and nurturant behaviors. Even in the adult, emotion and other nonverbal signals strongly influence the perceived meaning of verbal utterances (Argyle, 1972; Ekman, 1979). We assume that the expression–feeling concordance is highly stable in early infancy where the innate relationship seems to be more adaptive and a more logical possibility than a learned one. We recognize that there is little direct evidence for expression–feeling concordance in infancy and that there is a need for more evidence that converges on this issue. However, there is substantial evidence that one can learn to encode emotion expressions that are not concordant with ongoing feelings. With maturation and socialization, individuals can learn to dissociate completely expression and feeling. There is a need for research on the consequences of discordance and dissociation of feelings and expressions.

Implications of Expression–Feeling Connections for Emotion Socialization

We have presented the evidence for innate concordance of expressions and feelings and for the facial (expression) feedback hypothesis of emotion activation and regulation. The evidence is substantial, though not conclusive, that the manipulation of expressive behavior contributes to the activation and regulation of emotion feelings. Because the socialization of emotions focuses heavily on the control of affect expressions, the evidence for early expression–feeling concordance and for the feedback hypothesis suggests Principle 5, that the socialization of emotion expressions contributes to the regulation of emotion feelings and to the shaping of emotion expression styles and emotion traits.

Principle 5: The socialization of emotion expressions contributes to the regulation of emotion feelings.

The significance of the socialization of emotion expressions becomes clear when we consider the implications of expressions for motivational feelings and the power of expressions in influencing the behavior of others through contagion, modeling, and empathy.

From the moment of birth the facial expressions of the infant influence the behavior of the caregiver and vice versa. Through the life span emotion expressions remain important motivators and regulators of social behavior (Emde, 1980; Izard, 1977). First, they generate emotion responses in others by contagion. *Contagion* has been defined as taking on another's emotion state simply by being exposed to that person's affective behavior (Hoffman, 1978; Izard, 1977). It is an involuntary, reciprocal, and emotion-specific response. Vulnerability to contagion is apparently present as early as the opening days of life, at least as judged by studies of the spreading of crying among nursery infants. Simner (1971) demonstrated that newborns will cry in response to tape-recorded cries of other infants at 70 hr after birth, and Sagi and Hoffman (1976) and Martin and Clark (1982) have extended the finding to even younger infants.

Lelwica and Haviland's (1983) demonstration of different emotion expressions by the infant to different emotion expressions by the mother provided more powerful support for the contagion thesis. They had mothers of 10-week-old infants simulate three types of emotion—happiness, anger, and sadness—both facially and vocally. Infants were found to respond differentially and reciprocally. Instances of infant interest expression increased over modeled trials only to mothers' joy expression; infant anger expressions were increased only to the mothers' modeled anger; almost all infant expressions were inhibited by mothers' modeling of sadness.

Contagion is not limited to infancy, as exemplified by the "group glee" of grade school children and the group excitement and fear that occur under conditions of spectator sports and mob panic, respectively. In addition, under experimental conditions, Vaughn and Lanzetta (1880) have shown that adults who are observing a model's expressions of pain or physical distress in response to electric shock display similar expressions.

Further, emotion signals are informationally important in directing or regulating the observer's subsequent behavior (cf. Campos et al., 1983; Charlesworth, 1982). Children as young as 1 year of age have been shown to use their mothers' facial expressions as a source of information and as a guide to behavior during situations of environmental or interpersonal uncertainty (Campos & Stenberg, 1981; Dickstein, Thompson, Estes, Malkin, & Lamb, 1982). Camras (1977), who studied the role of children's facial expressions in a conflict situation between peers, found that a particular kind of aggressive display could be used, apparently instrumentally, to maintain possession of an object and ward off further aggression.

Whether or not there are further changes in the instrumental use of emotion expressions beyond the childhood years is largely a question for further research. However, there is some preliminary evidence that old people may be less likely to abide by conventional display rules than younger adults. Self-report data from young, middle-aged, and older individuals (Malatesta & Kalnok, 1984) indicated that older people may be more overt and outspoken with their feelings. In this study older subjects rated themselves as significantly more "honest" than younger subjects. They also indicated they were less likely to be bound by conventions concerning emotion concealment. These self-report data appear congruent with assumptions relating to display rules. Conformance with social conventions regarding emotion control may be particularly important during young and middle adulthood when close and frequent interactions with a variety of other adults in important work- and family-related matters call for minimizing the chances of interpersonal friction. Older people retired from the work force would have less to lose by the overt expression of their feelings, including their negative feelings. They might also feel that their age status entitles them to express their opinions and feelings openly.

In summary, emotion expressions induce shared feelings through contagion and empathy and motivate behavior in interpersonal exchange. Salient examples are the effects of mothers' sad faces on infant responses (Tronick, Ricks, & Cohn, 1982) and the effects of mothers' expressions on the infant's behavior on the visual cliff (Klinnert, Campos, Sorce, Emde, & Svejda, 1983). Because overt emotion expressions exert such a powerful influence on feeling and behavior, it is no wonder that all individuals are expected to learn to exercise control over them. The motivational impact of emotion expressions also helps to explain why social conventions for moderating expressive behavior have evolved in all cultures, although their form, enculturation, and effects on the individual vary across cultures. Obviously there will be a need to suppress, attenuate, or transform some types of expressions, most notably the negative emotions such as anger, in order to avoid social contagion, escalation of feelings, and hostile encounters. On the other hand, it is adaptive to be able to encode some emotion expressions at will in order to facilitate interpersonal harmony, as in the use of smiling and attentive gazing to signal liking and deference.

The Socialization of Emotion Expressions

Whereas in early infancy crying always signals aversive stimulation, the toddler may cry to protest separation and recall an absent care giver (Shiller, Izard, & Hembree, 1985), and a 4-year old may use crying to request a favorite treat.

Thus with the maturation of inhibitory neural mechanisms and neuromuscular systems and the development of higher-order cognitive abilities, emotion expressions become increasingly subject to control. They also become increasingly useful as a means of regulating or influencing the behavior of others, with reflex- or instinctlike characteristics typically minimized and subordinated through socialization.

Because facial expressions result from contraction of striate muscles innervated by the somatic (voluntary) nervous system, they are eminently suited for modification by operant conditioning, modeling, and other forms of social learning. They are highly conspicuous to those who function as socializing agents, being conveniently located on a part of the anatomy that is almost always clearly visible and being readily identifiable as expressions of feeling (Izard, Huebner, Risser, McGinnes, & Dougherty, 1980). Rheingold, Gewirtz, and Ross (1959) and Etzel and Gewirtz (1967), in investigating the conditionability of infant behavior, were among the first to produce evidence of the malleability of the infant expressive behavior. They showed that the rate of smiling, crying, and vocalization in young infants could be increased or decreased under conditions of reinforcement and extinction. Studies of the face-to-face interactions of American middle-class mothers and their 3- and 6-month-old infants show contingency patterns and provide evidence of the opportunity for early conditioning of emotion expressions (Malatesta, 1980, 1982; Malatesta & Haviland, 1982). Objective (Max) analysis of the facial movements of young infants and their mothers in face-to-face play showed that infants displayed a wide range of positive and negative expressions. Mothers, however, used a more restricted range than their infants, limiting their expressions almost exclusively to the positive emotions. In addition there was a pronounced tendency for mothers to respond contingently to their infants' changes in expression with expression changes of their own within less than 0.8 sec. Thus mothers' responses to recognizable emotion expressions fell within the optimal temporal range for instrumental conditioning.

More naturalistic studies support these laboratory findings. For example, observations on congenitally blind infants have shown that, although these infants show the same basic range of emotion expressions as sighted infants and a similar developmental timetable for the emergence of the various expressions, those of blind babies eventually become less frequent and more muted (Fraiberg, 1979; Thompson, 1941). Selective extinction of certain emotion expressions can also be seen under natural conditions. For example, among the Utku Eskimos of the Hudson Bay (Briggs, 1970), displays of anger in children after the age of 2 are followed by a "silent treatment." Within a few years there are no tantrums and little interpersonal aggression.

During the course of development children gradually acquire culture-specific attitudes toward emotions (Izard, 1971), what Ekman and Friesen (1975) refer to as display rules, and conventionalized forms of expression (Demos, 1974; Saarni, 1979). These acquired attitudes and knowledge about emotion feelings and emotion expressions are accompanied by a corresponding tendency to regulate (transform, inhibit, mask) expressions when cultural or social norms require it. Children also gradually acquire the ability voluntarily to *enact* or mimic reasonable facsimiles of emotion expressions, and by late childhood their abilities are about as good as those of adults (Blumberg, 1983; Ekman, Roper, & Hager, 1980; Odom & Lemond, 1972). The dual abilities to conceal and enact emotions at will gradually enable the child to conform to the customs and conventions of the larger culture regarding the regulation of emotion expression.

Cultural Differences in Socialization Produce Different Styles of Expression Regulation

There have been two kinds of studies that have specified some of the details of socialization that appear to influence emotion expression in culture-specific ways— field studies of child-rearing practices among culturally diverse peoples and laboratory studies of social interaction. We examine ethnographic studies first.

As Izard (1971) has shown, cultures vary in their attitudes toward and understanding of various emotions. This in turn affects socialization practices relating to emotion and ensures that they will be cross-culturally variable. Geertz (1959) has noted that in order to understand the socialization of emotion we must take into account the *timing, social context,* and *method* by which cultural values concerning emotion are transmitted. In her study of Javanese socialization processes, she observed that the Javanese adults exercise strong control over their emotion expressions. They dislike the intense expression of emotion and rarely quarrel openly or raise their voices in anger. Javanese children under the age of 5 are considered "not yet Javanese," because they are not yet able to control their emotions in an adult manner. Specific practices, apparently linked to developmental stage, gradually transform the "barbarian" child into a civilized Javanese. As infants they are handled in a relaxed, gentle, unemotional manner. Mothers avoid upsetting the child by abrupt weanings, favoring instead a gradual weaning process. In later infancy and early childhood socialization proceeds by giving the child detailed, unemotional instructions unaccompanied by threats of punishment from the parents. At about the age of 5, the father's interaction with the child, which earlier could be characterized as warm and playful, becomes one of distance and reserve and at about the same time the child's behavior seems to undergo a change from spontaneous and playful to a more docile, restrained, and formal demeanor.

Lutz (1982, in press) has shown the effects of social context and parental ethnopsychology in the socialization of emotional behavior among Ifalukians. The growing child learns a set of emotion terms and their culturally constituted emotional meaning, which then directs behavior. For example, on the Micronesian atoll of Ifaluk, emotions (defined by Lutz as we define affective–cognitive structures) are situationally defined and their occasion (or suppression) reflects local cultural ideals of social behavior. Ifalukian values stress nonaggression, cooperation, sharing, and hierarchical obedience. These values are supported by the concept of *metagu. Metagu* may be elicited by an encounter with a malevolent ghost, the "justifiable anger" of another, or unfamiliar surroundings. *Metagu* is viewed as the primary inhibitor of misbehavior in children and adults. Because this affective–cognitive structure is consistent with cultural values and positively regarded, parents encourage its development in their children and do not protect them from experiencing it.

In a detailed analysis of parent–child interaction, Caudill and Weinstein (1969) observed that differences in the emotional behavior of American and Japanese children appeared to be determined by rather specific practices early in life. For example, American mothers were found to stimulate their infants more and to get them aroused; in contrast, Japanese mothers were found to have a more soothing and quieting approach, as indicated by greater lulling, more carrying in the arms, and more rocking. The speech of American mothers to their infants appeared to be directed at reinforcing the happy vocalizations of their infants, whereas in Japanese families, maternal speech to infants usually occurred in the context of trying to soothe them and quell their unhappy vocalizations.

Several other studies provide further insight into the cultural specificity of emotion socialization and the developmental role of very early instruction in emotion expression regulation. Dixon, Tronick, Keeler, and Brazelton (1981) noted that among the Gusii of southwest Kenya attenuation principles rule social interchange between adults; the buildup of both positive and negative affect is avoided by the practice of continual gaze aversion and the use of a bland countenance. Parallels are found in the interactions between Gussi mothers and their infants, where mothers' facial expressions are kept bland rather than animated. Mothers avert their gaze or blink frequently to break visual contact with their infants and restrain their infants' limbs to prevent excessive motor excitement.

Levy's (1973, 1984) work addresses directly the issue of cultural variations in emotion regulation. He did an extensive analysis of emotion expressions and feelings among the Tahitians. He discovered that in their society anger, fear, and shame are hypercognated—overly intellectualized and associated with obsessive-type defenses. On the other hand, sadness and guilt are hypocognated. Levy interpreted these emotion–cognition styles as systems of control and concluded that such emotion control systems varied across cultures. His own psychological ethnographies revealed clearly different control systems for the Tahitians and the Newars of Nepal.

Research with the strange situation procedure (Ainsworth, Blehar, Waters, & Wall, 1878) has provided indirect evidence for the differential effects of socialization on emotion expression and emotion regulation (Grossman, Schwan, & Grossman, in press; Miyake, 1984–1985; Takahashi, 1985). Attachment classification based on the strange situation procedure has been associated with emotion expression style (Ainsworth et al., 1978; Shiller, Izard, & Hembree, 1985), and frequency of secure, avoidant, and ambivalent–resistant attachment types differs significantly among cultures. As compared with the frequencies of attachment types among American infants, the frequency of avoidant babies in Germany is approximately four times as great and that of ambivalent–resistant babies in Japan almost two times as great. Takahashi found no avoidant babies in her Japanese studies, even after she modified the procedure to reduce the level of stress. She explains the cultural differences in frequencies of attachment types in part as a function of cultural differences in emotion expressions.

In Malatesta and Haviland's (1982) study of middle-class American mothers, expression contingency patterns differed according to the infant's age and sex; age and sex differences were interpreted as reflections of implicit goals for culturally defined gender and age norms for emotion expression. The investigators also noted frequent idiosyncratic expressive patterns in mothers superimposed on the more basic patterns. A correlational analysis indicated that individual mother–infant pairs shared expressive commonalities and that the concordance between the expressive behaviors of mothers and their infants was stronger at 6 months than at 3.

The foregoing findings suggest that the patterns or styles of emotion expression in infants are influenced in accordance with cultural norms and experiences provided by caregivers during face-to-face interaction. The hypothesized mechanisms of change include maternal contingent responding (ignoring responses constituting extinction training, contingent changes constituting reinforcement training), as well as observational learning based on the infant's repetitive exposure to a selected class of well-articulated expressions.

Whether young infants can imitate or match expressive patterns and show improved motor output on the basis of observational learning is currently the subject of controversy. A recent review of the literature on infant imitation (Malatesta & Izard, 1984b), however, showed that there is more empirical support in favor of imitation or matching than against it. This review concluded that infants *are* capable of matching (to use the less cognitively laden term) adult facial and vocal gestures, that matching the components of emotion expressions may be easier than matching nonemotional gestures, that infants accommodate their responses over time to match a model, and that they benefit from practice. Given the infant's ability to match its performances to that of another individual and to improve over time, and given that exposure to maternal exemplars of expressive behavior may run as high as 30,000–35,000 episodes during the third to the sixth month (Malatesta, in press), there is ample opportunity for learning and modification of emotional responses. Although we hesitate to impute intentionality to the matching responses of young infants in the opening months of life, the capacity to mimic another seems to be a vital process contributing to the ontogeny of emotions. With the advent of more intentional, goal-directed behavior by about 10 months, another powerful source of behavioral modification is added. Now children can modify their expressive behavior in accordance with feedback from the environment to achieve goals more effectively.

Although most of the available evidence on the socialization of emotion relates to emotion expression, we recognize the great importance of language in all facets of socialization. The contribution of language and other cognitively mediated processes in socialization has been reviewed extensively by Lewis and Michalson (1983). We shall consider the role of cognition and language in emotional development under Principle 7.

Stability of Emotion Expression Style

Are the effects of socialization reflected in stable individual differences in emotion or emotion-related characteristics? This is part of the larger question of continuity in human development. It is a fundamental and complex issue for developmental psychologists and it remains unresolved (cf. Kagan, Kearsley, & Zelazzo, 1978). The research on continuity has produced far more negative than positive results. However, most of the research did not include objective measures of well-defined emotion variables, and so the issue of continuity of emotion expression styles and other functions of the emotions system remains largely unexplored.

A few studies have shown that affective measures in infancy or early childhood predicted later cognitive or psychomotor performance (see Beckwith, 1979, for a review). For example, infant socioemotional variables correlated with intelligence at 3–10 years of age (Birns & Golden, 1972; Haviland, 1976; Yarrow, Goodwin, Manheimer, & Milowe, 1973).

Four studies have shown stability of wariness or fear responses. Scarr and Salapatek (1970) found short-term (2-month interval) stability in fear expression. Infants 6–18 months of age were exposed to a stranger, visual cliff, jack-in-the-box, mechanical dog, masks (horror face, bear), and loud noises. The infants showed similar reactions on both occasions to all stimuli except the noise. Bagley (1956), Bronson (1972), and Kagan and Moss (1962) showed that wariness or fear of strangers in infancy predicted fear or shyness in preschool years.

Washburn's (1929) classic study of smiling and laughing in the first year was also a study of expression styles. Her observations identified three groups. The first group, ambi-expressive, had two subtypes—the parvi-expressive, whose expressive behavior was low in intensity and frequency, and the multi-expressive, whose expressions were high in frequency and varied in form. The second group (misnamed risor-expressive by Washburn because she confused the role of the risorius and the zygomatic muscles in smiling) showed much smiling and laughing and little crying. The third group, depressor-expressive, smiled and laughed infrequently and cried often. Washburn concluded that these expression styles did not vary from observation to observation. Most subjects retained their expressive style (group membership) when they were observed in their second year.

Some investigators (e.g., Thomas, Chess, & Birch, 1968; Matheny, 1985) have reported that temperament dimensions, interpreted by some researchers as emotion-based phenomena (Goldsmith & Campos, 1982), show some stability over time. Thomas and colleagues claimed that temperamentally difficult infants were more likely to have mental health problems in later life, but others (e.g., Block, 1971; MacFarlane, 1963) reported discontinuities in psychological adjustment from infancy to childhood and adulthood.

Kagan (1982) has reported a type of temperamental stability indexed by cardiac response patterns. He has shown that high heart rate and restricted heart rate range in response to events that are relatively difficult to assimilate characterize behaviorally inhibited children. The behavioral inhibition observed in uncertain situations can be interpreted as signs of shyness or anxiety. All of the foregoing studies that dealt explicitly with emotion concepts were completed before the development of objective coding systems for identifying emotion-specific expressive behaviors. These systems have been used in only three longitudinal investigations. These studies lend support to the hypothesis of continuity of emotion expression style. By *emotion expression style* we mean the frequency and duration with which one or more emotions are expressed in particular situations.

In a longitudinal study of emotion responses to the pain of DPT inoculations, using the Max and Affex coding systems (Izard, 1979; Izard et al., 1983), anger expression indices aggregated (averaged) for DPTs 1, 2, and 3 at ages 2, 4, and 6 months predicted anger expression in the DPT inoculation situation at 19 months of age. Separate hierarchical regression analyses with the 2-, 4-, and 6-month expression indices as predictors and the 19-month index as criterion showed that all three early predictors accounted for some unique variance in the criterion. Similar results were obtained for the sadness expression (Izard, Hembree, & Huebner, 1984). In addition, preliminary analyses indicate that mothers' reports of how much their 12-month-old infants "get angry or mad" in daily life compared to the average baby of the same age correlated significantly with the amount of Max/Affex coded anger expression during the 19-month DPT inoculation episode.

Malatesta and Haviland's (1982) study of mother–infant interaction and separation found that infants' expressions at 3–6 months were predictors of infant emotion expression style at 9–12 months. Emotion expression styles have also shown continuity from 13 to 18 months of age during brief mother–infant separation. The Time 1–Time 2 correlations were .61, .90, .53, and .90 for interest, anger, blends, and total negative emotion expression, respectively (Hyson & Izard, 1984).

Some emotion expression indices were found to be significantly related to independent measures of temperament (Infant Behavior Questionnaire [IBQ], Rothbart, 1981). For example, the higher the infants' anger expression scores in brief separation, the higher were their scores on the IBQ Scale of Distress to Limitations, considered by Rothbart as a measure of an anger-related trait of temperament (McGinnes & Izard, 1984).

We have also found significant relationships between indices of mothers' emotion expression style and toddlers' emotion expressions in the strange situation. For example, mothers who reported that they try to suppress or conceal their anger expression were more likely to have children who expressed negative emotion during separation (McGinnes & Izard, 1984).

Unresolved Issues

Several other important questions relating to Principle 5 need to be investigated. Will convergent data from studies of relations among infants' facial expressions, patterns of ANS activity, and overt behavior lend further support to the hypothesis of innate expression–feeling concordance? Is it possible to obtain convincing evidence of the effect of experimenter-manipulated facial expressions on specific emotion feelings independent of contextual stimuli? How generalizable is this effect? Can techniques for obtaining the effect be applied for educational or therapeutic purposes? What are the long-term effects of over- and undercontrol of emotion expressions? Does extensive dissociation of expression and feeling lead to psychopathology?

DEVELOPMENT RELATED TO EMOTION FEELINGS

Differential emotions theory holds that each of the fundamental emotions has unique motivational and adaptive functions. It assumes that the social aspect of emotion motivation is a function of emotion expression and that the intrapsychic aspect of motivation is primarily a function of the subjective experience of emotion—the feeling state. It also postulates innate concordance between facial expressions and feeling states. Some motivational construct seems necessary to explain the organization and directedness of young infant behaviors such as communicative responses (Tronick et al., 1982), tracking novel objects (Wolff, 1966), and memory retrieval (Fagan & Rovee-Collier, 1983).

Anthony and Graham (1983) presented evidence for what can be interpreted as a sensory-selective set mediated by the feeling state of interest in infants as young as 16 weeks. Their study was based on an earlier finding that selective attention can modulate the brain stem blink reflex. They assessed the magnitude of blink reflexes elicited by visual and acoustic probes when probe modality either matched or mismatched the modality of interesting or dull foreground stimulation. Differences in mean heart rate deceleration showed that interesting and dull foregrounds differentially engaged the infants' attention. Blink magnitude was significantly greater and information processing enhanced when modality of interesting foreground stimulation matched modality of probe. The construct of a motivational feeling state of interest offers a parsimonious explanation of such organized, goal-directed behavior.

In discussing the principles of development related to emotion feeling states we shall argue: (1) that emotion expressions and emotion feelings are innately concordant; (2) that sensory feedback from facial expression contributes to the activation and regulation of feelings; (3) that learned expression regulation and dissimulation increase the flexibility of expression–feeling relations; (4) that emotion feelings have stability over time while their causes and consequences change with development; and (5) that facial expressions and expression–feeling concordance facilitate the development of emotion–cognition relations and affective–cognitive structures.

That emotions serve basic motivational functions throughout the life span, have cue-producing functions that reliably guide adaptive behavior, show at least short-term stability in terms of expression styles, and facilitate a sense of individual continuity leads to Principle 6, the proposition of invariance in the essential quality of a given emotion feeling.

Principle 6: Emotion feelings are invariant over the life span but their causes and consequences change with development.

In the discussion of Principles 1 and 2, we were concerned with emotional development at the biological level. Development of neural substrates, particularly inhibitory mechanisms, permits emotion regulation and increases the complexity of connections between discrete emotions and between the emotions and drives and cognitive and motor systems. Development at the biological level also contributes to changes in emotion thresholds. Principles 3, 4, and 5 were concerned with the development of emotion expressions and the relations between expressions and feelings. Development at the expressive level is characterized by a tendency toward minimization and by changes in the frequency, discreteness, and integrity of facial expressions. The evidence suggested that with development the relations between expressions and feelings become flexible.

Principle 6 is concerned with the question of what develops in relation to the third component of emotion, emotion feeling. The first part of Principle 6 maintains that the unique quality of a given emotion feeling is invariant over the life span (cf. Campos & Barrett, 1984). The second part of Principle 6 proposes that what develop are relations between events and feelings, between feelings and cognition percepts, images, and thoughts, and between feelings and actions. Relations among emotion feeling states also develop. Through classical conditioning and other forms of learning one emotion may become closely linked to another. Such linkages among emotions may help account for the well-known sadness–anger pattern commonly found in depressed individuals (Izard, 1972; Izard & Schwartz, 1985). These relations between emotion feelings and other processes or events are typically reciprocal causal relations, with feelings influencing cognition and action and vice versa. It should be remembered that in the present theoretical framework the immediate or proximal cause of a feeling state is a particular pattern of neural activity. Other emotion feelings, drives, imagery, thoughts, and appraisals of events are distal causes or causes of specific neural processes that generate feelings. In fine, emotion–emotion, emotion–drive, and event–feeling–cognition–action relations are what develop.

Invariance of Emotion Feeling

In weighing the invariance claim of Principle 6, one should remember that it is the invariance of emotion *feeling* that is proposed, not the invariance of event–emotion, emotion–cognition, or emotion–behavior relationships. All of these follow a developmental course; they are a large part of the subject matter of emotional development.

Innate Expression–Feeling Concordance Argues for Feeling State Invariance

Although the chief concern in the discussion of this aspect of Principle 6 is the invariance of emotion feelings, it should be noted that arguments for universal facial expressions, innate expression–feeling concordance, and the social signal value of expressions are important complementary ideas. The young infant responds as though the caregiver's smile always has the same meaning. Thus expressions apparently provide the kind of consistency in the socioemotional context that is required for healthy development. The case presented earlier for expression–feeling concordance also supports the hypothesis of invariant feeling states. From these arguments and assumptions it follows that any time in the life span that an expression is spontaneously and veridically encoded the same feeling results. As already noted, the facial expressions of young infants are identical in all essential aspects to adult expressions that have been shown to be universal.

The Adaptiveness of Feeling State Invariance

Emotion feeling as defined here—a direct derivative or unmediated product of certain neural processes—is very basic to animal adaptation, providing cues for interacting with the environment. The survival value of feelings as motivations for goal-directed behaviors calls for invariance of their basic cue-producing function. Perhaps the affect of pain provides the most compelling example of the survival value of invariant feeling states. The necessity of the feeling or experience of pain for health and survival is widely acknowledged (Szasz, 1957). Whether signaled by the uninhibited instinctlike expression of the newborn or by the stoic understatement of the aged terminally ill patient, pain makes the most urgent demand for attention. Pain serves a critical protective function whenever trauma threatens. Throughout life we know the feeling of pain and its basic significance as a demand for change in the quality or intensity of stimulation. Essentially the same can be said of the feeling of disgust, which motivates rejection of distasteful and potentially harmful substances. If the stimulus for disgust is effective, the motivation to reject seems equally compelling at all ages. The feeling of fear also serves a protective function, and it motivates avoidance or escape at any age when threat is perceived. If the feelings and basic cue-producing characteristics of pain, disgust, and fear were variable, one might increase one's injury, consume lethal substances, and run toward danger. A similar case can be made for each of the other fundamental emotions (Izard, 1977).

Emotion feelings may also be viewed as invariant or stable in terms of phylogeny or at the level of the species. That is, certain characteristics of species, including homo sapiens, can be seen as functions of stable emotion–motivational conditions. Empathy, altruism, and social bonding are characteristic of human development, and there is good reason to believe that these phenomena are mediated by invariant emotion experiences. One can infer from Jolly's (1966) work with nonhuman primates that parental interest or empathic enjoyment of juveniles' play behavior contributed to the development of primate social life and intelligence. Averill (1968) has argued persuasively for the role of grief and communal empathy in maintaining group cohesiveness. The ability to share invariant feelings of negative as well as positive emotions by way of distal cues from another person and through symbolic processes is undoubtedly a part of the human evolutionary heritage, a significant contribution to our development as a social species and to our capacity for adaptive prosocial behavior.

Altruism and empathic behavior also seem to be based on a species-stable affective core. Hoffman (1981) made a strong case for biologically based altruism mediated by empathy, particularly the emotion feeling component of empathy. He argued that it was not the altruistic actions themselves but the mediators of such actions that had to emerge through natural selection. He presented evidence supporting his proposition that the feeling state in empathic arousal meets the evolutionary criteria for the basis of an altruistic response system.

Several studies with children and adults have shown that event- or imagery-induced emotions have emotion-specific effects on prosocial and moral behavior (Isen, 1970; Rosenhan, Underwood, & Moore, 1974; Strayer, 1980; Zahn-Waxler et al., 1979; Zahn-Waxler, Friedman, & Cummings, 1983). For example, induced joy increases altruistic behavior (Rosenhan et al., 1974) and resistance to temptation (Fry, 1975). Several investigators (Eisenberg-Berg & Geisheker, 1979; Howard & Barnett, 1981) found that having children focus on the distress of others, especially on facial features, increases altruistic behavior. That the emotion feeling underlying empathy is invariant is suggested by the regularity with which the same kind of behavior (e.g., helping) occurs in empathy at widely different ages.

Social bonding, widely accepted as a characteristic of the human species, also seems to be mediated by emotion feelings that appear invariant (Bowlby, 1969; Hamburg, 1963; Konner, 1982). Drawing on the work of Bowlby (1969), Ainsworth and colleagues (1978), and Kagan (1976), Konner (1982) argued that social bonding or attachment is facilitated and strengthened by the emergence of genetically based social fears that render the primary care giver relatively more attractive and others less so.

Feeling State Invariance, Sense of Continuity, and Self-Concept

We propose that invariant feeling states contribute to the development of the sense of continuity and the development of the self-concept by providing stable referents within the self. Such referents seem necessary for differentiating self from others and for developing relations with the social and physical environment. For example, invariance in the feelings of joy and sadness eventually enables the child to infer the causes and consequences of joy and sadness. The repetition and stability of the feelings of joy or any qualitatively distinct feeling state enable the infant to experience the emotion as its own. Thus feelings may be considered the first element of the concept, or rather the affective–cognitive schema, of self.

Continuity of Expression Styles and Feeling State Invariance

In the discussion of Principle 4, we presented evidence for the continuity of emotion expression styles across situations and over time. In addition, Hyson and Izard (1984) have found the relationships one would expect between facial expressions and instrumental behaviors. Under Principle 5 we made a case for the concordance of expressive behavior and emotion feeling states. Taken together, the evidence for concordance between emotion expression and emotion feeling and between expression and instrumental behavior and the continuity of expressive style argues for invariance in the quality of a given emotion feeling.

Continuity of Emotion Feeling in Consciousness

The significance of invariance in emotion feeling at the level of the individual and of stability at the level of the species argues for the continuity of emotion feeling in consciousness. The latter seems required by the ubiquitous functions of emotions in motivation and adaptation, functions that have been described in various sections of this paper.

Two misconceptions have worked against the acceptance of the idea that feelings are always present in consciousness: (1) the notion that emotions are transient or emergency-type phenomena; and (2) the idea that emotion *must* be represented cognitively. We have presented a case against these notions elsewhere (Izard, 1984). In brief, the argument that feelings are continuous in consciousness depends on the acceptance of two related assumptions: Emotions vary on a dimension of intensity, and the contents of consciousness vary in terms of levels of awareness. Behavioral science has generally ignored emotion that exists at a low intensity or at a low level of awareness.

The proposition that emotion feelings are continuous relates to two previously discussed propositions. The first is that the third component of emotion, the component that achieves awareness, is a *feeling state,* not a cognitively constructed schema or label. Because of the relative independence of emotion and cognition, some level of emotion feeling can exist in consciousness, unlabeled and "uncognized." The absence of emotion labels in the first year of life does not mean the absence of emotion feeling. The second of these propositions is that feeling is a direct derivative of neural processes. Papez's (1937) conception of the limbic lobe as the neural basis of a "*stream* of feeling" (italics added) is consistent with our view that the affective aspect of consciousness is characterized by a continuous flow of feeling that changes qualitatively depending on internal and external events.

One other idea has contributed to misunderstanding regarding the presence of emotion in awareness. *Facial expressions* of emotions are often very brief. The duration of an emotion *feeling,* however, cannot be judged by its external *expression.* The most significant functions of external expression relate to the activation, regulation, and social communication of emotion.

The duration of a given emotion feeling in consciousness is probably a function of several variables, including cognition and the level of particular hormones and neurotransmitters. Beck (1976) and Kovacs and Beck (1979) have shown that cognitive distortions characterize depressive patients whose consciousness is dominated by sadness and other negative emotions for long periods of time. Depression is also characterized by changes in brain neurochemistry (Anisman & Zacharko, 1982; Davis, 1970), as is anxiety (Gray, 1982; Tuma & Maser, in press). These cognitive and biochemical processes play a role establishing moods or sustaining emotions over time. In most normal conditions emotions do not remain at high intensities for very long, but a decrease in intensity does not necessarily mean nonexistence.

The Causes and Consequences of Emotion Feelings Change with Development

Even though the quality of a given emotion feeling is invariant, its distal causes (e.g., appraisals of events) and cognitive or behavioral consequences change with development. These changes occur as a function of neural, cognitive, and motor development and as a function of the characteristics of emotion feelings. Emotion feelings are characterized by a high degree of flexibility with respect to the conditions required to elicit them and the cognitive and motor responses they can motivate (cf. Tomkins, 1962). As the neural substrates of emotions develop they permit an increasing degree of emotion regulation (particularly by means of inhibitory mechanisms) that facilitates the growth in flexibility of event–emotion–cognition–action sequences.

Developmental Changes in Response to Emotion Feelings

In the young child fear motivates only avoidance or escape. In the older child and adult fear or fear anticipation may motivate, at least indirectly or in interaction with interest, an effort to understand and alter the source of threat. Fear drives young children to the protective shelter of the caregiver but may make older children seek ways of managing the threat and increasing their independence. Younger children are likely to escape by using their legs; older children may use language. Eventually, an individual can learn countless ways to respond to feelings of fear, but all of them are designed to reduce, avoid, or escape the perceived threat.

As already noted, affective responses to unanticipated painful stimulation change dramatically with age. In the newborn, the response is uniformly an all-out emergency distress expression. In the toddler the response is more anger expression than physical distress, and by 19 months some children do not show the distress expression at all.

Interest in toys will lead the 10-month-old to explore, manipulate, and bang them. The 14-month-old may relate one toy to another, and the 3-year-old may use them in rich fantasy or imaginative play (Kagan et al., 1978; Singer, 1973). Eventually, interest can engage the individual in virtually anything.

With increasing age and cognitive development, responses to feelings of anger tend to become less gross and physical and more subtle and verbal. Responses to surprise became more subdued, and sadness less frequently leads to tears. These broad types of changes reflect the general effects of emotion regulation. The infinite variety of specific responses to feelings of joy, sadness, anger, fear, and the other emotion feeling states probably reflects individual differences in temperament and personality.

Developmental Changes in Emotion-Eliciting Conditions

At 3 weeks of age the high-pitched human voice elicits a smile. In later life it may elicit fear or anger, depending on the context. In the infant 2–5 months old an unfamiliar human face regularly elicits a smile. In the 9-month-old even a smiling face, under certain conditions, may elicit negative emotions. Mother's departing face may go unnoticed by the 3-month-old, evoke angry protest in many 13-month-olds, and bring joy to the teenager who wants the privacy of the house.

These few examples of variability in emotion-eliciting conditions and in responses to emotion feelings are only suggestive of the myriad ways that the causes and consequences of emotion feelings change with development. With increasing age emotion feelings become linked to a wider range of incentive events, cognitions, and behaviors. Each emotion feeling becomes part of an ever growing, changing array of affective-cognitive structures and emotion-cognition-action patterns. The addition of each such link between the emotion, cognitive, and motor systems increases behavioral alternatives and adaptiveness to changing sociocultural and environmental demands and opportunities.

Invariant Emotion Feelings and Emotion-Cognition Relations

Differential emotions theory holds that during development the association of particular emotion feelings with particular images and symbols leads to affective-cognitive structures and that such structures, which may become stable personality characteristics or traits, become increasingly important motivational phenomena (Izard, 1977). The present theoretical approach to emotional development helps explain these processes. Expression-feeling concordance contributes to the development of affective-cognitive structures because expressions provide a contingent cue for tuition in emotion labeling. Invariant emotion feelings provide a stable framework for organizing emotion-cognition relations. These propositions and the evidence and arguments supporting them lead to Principle 7.

Principle 7: Facial expressions and expression-feeling concordance facilitate the development of emotion-cognition relations and affective-cognitive structure.

The evidence and argument for the motivational functions of emotion expression and emotion feeling and for expression-feeling concordance provide the foundation for the seventh principle of emotional development. Principle 7 reaffirms the assumption that emotions constitute the primary motivational system for human behavior, including cognitive development and language acquisition, and that cognitive development and language, in turn, greatly enhance the complexity and flexibility of the emotions system.

Tomkins (1962) and Izard (1971) have postulated the emotion of interest as crucial in motivating cognitive development. A few empirical studies support this contention. The previously discussed studies of Wolff (1966), Fantz (1973), Anthony and Graham (1983), and Langsdorf and colleagues (1983) suggested that interest enhances information processing. There are several studies with adults that demonstrate the motivational effects of emotion feelings on information processing and cognition. Various emotion induction procedures have been used to influence stereoscopic perception (Izard, Wehmer, Livsey, & Jennings, 1965), precognitive preferences (Zajonc, 1980), and learning and memory (Bower, 1981; Izard, Nagler, Randall, & Fox, 1965). Although some of the findings from this line of research have failed to replicate (see Bower & Mayer, 1984; Mandler & Shebo, 1983), this area seems a highly promising one for future investigations.

Feelings as the First Mental Structures

As discussed elsewhere (Izard, 1978, 1980), the assumption of expression–feeling concordance leads to the conclusion that the first kind of awareness is awareness of feeling and that the first structures of mind are discrete feeling states. If we accept this assumption, then it follows that the ontogeny of emotion expressions indicates that even in the first half-year of life the infant has a varied repertoire of affective mental structures. A first step in transforming these affective structures into affective-cognitive structures is the association of feelings with images, first probably through classical conditioning.

Feelings are by definition phenomena of consciousness or awareness. This does not mean that feeling must be in focal or peak awareness or that feeling must be cognized and labeled. What some theorists call unconscious feeling or motivation is, according to differential emotions theory, feeling that is uncognized or at a low level of awareness. Because awareness of interest and enjoyment is frequently contingent on the perception of the caregiver's face, Principle 7 suggests that the first affective-cognitive structure is an association or bond between positive affect and an image of the caregiver's face. Through similar contingent occurrences of various feeling states with different objects and events the preverbal infant develops a network of related affective-cognitive structures. Because a given feeling state can be associated with a wide range of phenomena, by the end of the prelinguistic period (15–18 months of age) the toddler may have a rather rich repertoire of this type of mental structure.

Awareness of Feelings and Awareness of Self

As discussed previously (Izard, 1978), it seems reasonable that emotion expressions and their concomitant feeling states facilitate the development of the concept or affective-cognitive schema of self. The repeated experiencing of discrete feeling states during the first months of life helps the infant develop a sense of being, separate from the objects and events that occur in relation to its expressions and feeling states. We hypothesize that even in the early months of life these expression–feeling–event sequences begin laying the groundwork for achieving a sense of ownership of feeling states.

We have theorized elsewhere (Izard, 1978) that the frequent association of the infant's emotion expressions and care giver ministrations provides the infant's first opportunity to experience frequent and consistent cause–effect relations (cf. Piaget, 1981). The infant's growing and sharpening awareness of ownership of the feeling states that precede caregiver actions fosters growth of the concept of self as causal agent. This subjective sense of self as capable of eliciting change lays the foundation for the later development of an objective awareness of self with unique characteristics (cf. Harter, 1983; Lewis & Michalson, 1983).

The Development of Affective-Cognitive Structures: The Example of Empathy

Empathy or vicarious emotion also plays a part in the process of associating feelings and feeling–image structures with symbols. Darwin (1872) observed his 5-month-old son match the sad expression of his caregiver, and Lelwica and Haviland (1983) have shown that such matching can occur as early as 10 weeks of age. When vicarious emotion occurs in toddlers (Zahn-Waxler et al., 1979) who are just beginning to use language, they apparently make the seemingly complex connections between caregivers' feelings, their feelings, verbal descriptors of the feelings, and appropriate (reparative) actions.

Hoffman (in press) has presented a theory of emotion–cognition relations that provides a framework for understanding the development of empathy. He begins with a description of basic modes of affect arousal. Four modes are based on properties of the physical stimulus—unconditioned responses, conditioned responses, mimicry, and comparison processes—and two are based on the meaning of the stimulus that is derived by the higher-order cognitive processes of categorization and appraisal. His view that emotion can be generated without comparison, categorization, or appraisal processes (as he defines these terms) is consistent with our distinctions between emotion and cognition and between our categories of noncognitive (sensory registration, drive states, ongoing emotion) and cognitive (appraisal, imagery, thought) processes of emotion activation. Hoffman suggests that the categorical and appraisal modes change with age and with the increasing cognitive complexity of the individual. Following an elaboration of the modes of affect arousal, he discusses the ways that affect may initiate, terminate, or disrupt information processing, organize recall, lead to selective processing, contribute to the formation of emotionally charged schemata, provide input for social cognition, and influence decision making and problem solving.

Hoffman's (1978a, 1984) description of the development of empathy, conceived of as having both affective and cognitive components, provides a good example of the way emotion feelings interact with increasingly higher-order cognitive abilities to produce more sophisticated levels of behavior. According to Hoffman, levels or modes of empathic responding include circular reactions such as distress-induced distress or affect contagion in newborns (Martin & Clark, 1982; Sagi & Hoffman, 1976; Simner, 1971), classical conditioning, direct association, mimicry, language-mediated association, and role taking. The type of eliciting stimulus, the depth of processing, and past experience determine which mode will operate. Hoffman concludes that, whereas the first mode (circular reactions) may drop out after infancy and the sixth mode (role taking) may be used rarely, the four intermediate modes "enter at different points in development and probably continue to operate throughout life" (Hoffman, 1984, p. 106).

A number of studies support Hoffman's concept of empathy as a joint function of affect and cognition that operates in one of several modes, varying to some extent with stage of overall development. Several studies have shown that children, including toddlers of 18 months, respond with appropriate verbalizations to salient affective cues signaling the plight of others (Strayer, 1980; Zahn-Waxler et al., 1979; Zahn-Waxler et al., 1983).

Hoffman's position is generally compatible with differential emotions theory and our approach to emotional development. Consistent with our theory, Hoffman suggested that facial expressions may provide the best stimulus for, and the best index of, empathic arousal or feeling state. In keeping with the overarching thesis of this chapter, the remainder of our discussion focuses mainly on the contribution of emotion expressions and expression feeling concordance to the development of emotion–cognition relations and affective–cognitive structures.

Language, Emotion Labeling, and the Development of Complex Affective–Cognitive Schemata

Another important step in the development of emotion–cognition relations is the association or bonding of verbal symbols to feelings or feeling–image structures. Facial expressions are key agents in this process. Emotion expression is the observable link between the child's feeling state and the caregiver's perception and interpretation of the child's needs and desires. Expressions provide a handle for the caregiver to connect with the child's preverbal mentality and with its efforts to associate verbal symbols with the desired objects and events.

It is now well established that the child begins to label emotion feelings in the second year of life, showing considerable skill in this process by 18 months of age (Bretherton & Beeghly-Smith, 1982). With the emergence of emotion labeling, the development of emotion comprehension and emotion–cognition relations is greatly accelerated. The work of Masters and his colleagues (see Masters & Carlson, 1984) and that of Gomby and Ellsworth (1985), Stein and Jewett (1985), and Schwartz and Trabasso (1984) show that by 3 years of age the child can demonstrate rather sophisticated knowledge of the causes and consequences of emotion and that this knowledge increases with age. DePaulo and Rosenthal (1982) have shown that significant aspects of emotion recognition, or more broadly, sensitivity to nonverbal cues, undergo significant changes with cognitive and social development. Weiner and Graham (1984) have presented a theory of emotional development that emphasizes the importance of attributions about causality as elicitors of emotions. The theory has inspired a number of empirical studies that demonstrate how study of the development of attributional processes contributes to our understanding of the development of emotion–cognition relations. Space does not permit a full discussion of the development of emotion labeling, emotion comprehension, and emotion-related attributional processes, but the integrative papers just cited provide a good background.

If we assume innate expression–feeling concordance and the existence of emotion feeling states from birth, then it follows that in the course of development emotions must be effectively linked with cognitive processes and instrumental behaviors (cf. Cicchetti & Hesse, 1983). In the framework of the present theory, emotional development is in large measure the development of integrative processes and mechanisms that organize emotion, cognition, and action adaptively. We have argued that emotions provide the motivational basis for these organizing and integrative processes.

This conceptualization can be made somewhat more concrete by considering the transition from the prelinguistic infant to the verbally accomplished child. In the early months of life the principal means of social communication is facial and vocal expression (Emde et al., 1976; Malatesta & Izard, 1984b; Sroufe, 1979). Empirical evidence suggests that these expressive signals have some specificity of meaning for the caregiver (Izard, Huebner, Risser, McGinnes, & Dougherty, 1980; Scherer, 1982). Caregiver responses are differentially influenced by these signals (Huebner & Izard, 1983; Malatesta, 1981), and infants are in turn influenced by the caregiver's expressive behavior (Tronick, Als, Adamson, Wise, & Brazelton, 1978).

An analysis of the emotion vocabulary mothers use in interaction with their 3- and 6-month-old infants (Malatesta & Haviland, 1982) revealed that mothers make many direct and indirect comments about their baby's ongoing emotion states. They may encourage an expression ("Smile for mommy"), discourage it ("Don't be mad"), or simply make a neutral comment ("You're feeling sad, aren't you?"). Note that this early emotion commentary exposes young infants to labels for their emotions, and in many instances it also includes a decidedly evaluative component in respect to expression etiquette.

As noted earlier, there is little systematic evidence of explicit instruction in emotion labeling as a part of language acquisition, yet the labeling of internal states shows significant progression during childhood (Izard, 1971; Ridgeway, Waters, & Kuczaj, in press). As children learn language and acquire the labels for emotions and learn attendant proscriptions and prescriptions for the management of these behaviors, further social influence is exerted and self-regulating processes are developed. Linguistic labels for emotions subserve socialization and emotion regulation in a number of ways. First, when others draw attention to the outward signs of emotion through labeling, emotion states that existed in awareness only as feelings eventually enter the domain of reflective self-consciousness. Second, phenomena that have labels are more readily brought within the domain of social scrutiny and can thus become a focus of regulation by the community. Third, language can be used to evoke emotion feelings and expressions.

As the child's capacity for memory, images, and abstract thinking matures developmentally, language becomes an increasingly powerful tool for evoking *remote* emotion processes—emotional events that are anticipated and those that have taken place in the past. The ability to recall emotion experiences and to *anticipate* future emotions makes emotion management easier because one can plan one's responses in advance. The ability to remember *past* emotion experiences also facilitates empathic understanding of the feelings of others, as well as serving as a guide for one's own future expressive behavior. Although there has been no research on the relative contribution of verbal and nonverbal messages in emotion socialization at different developmental periods, we believe that external verbal controls begin to diminish in late childhood, but that nonverbal messages continue to exert potent control over expressive behavior throughout life. Indeed, Zajonc (1980) has suggested that language may always be in second place in significant social interactions. Nevertheless, the process of adding language to the already existing nonverbal communication system is of monumental importance in human development. Eventually the child who was once capable only of experiencing a given emotion directly as a feeling becomes capable of labeling or symbolizing that feeling in consciousness, with or without that particular feeling being present.

It is indeed a landmark in emotional development when feelings and thoughts about feelings can exist in consciousness simultaneously. The child can then have one feeling in consciousness while dealing with others at the symbolic level. This is of great consequence for the development of emotion regulation, empathy, and prosocial behavior (cf. Hoffman, 1978a, 1983; Kagan, 1984).

In the course of development particular feelings and patterns of feelings become associated with particular classes of images, symbols, and actions. The result is the development of complex affective–cognitive schemata and networks. In such affective–cognitive phenomena, emotions constitute the main organizing and motivational forces, influencing perception (Izard, Wehmer, Livsey, & Jennings, 1965; Zajonc, 1980), learning and memory (Bower, 1981; Laird, Wagener, Halal, & Szegda, 1982), and the development of temperament and personality (Goldsmith & Campos, 1982).

CONCLUDING REMARKS

We have taken the position that a focus on the structure, dynamics, and developmental course of facial expressions can provide a useful theoretical approach to the study of emotional development. A case was made for innate expressions, for innate connections among expressions, underlying neural substrates, and concordant feeling states. Support was marshaled for the notion that expressions are both objects and agents of socialization. Evidence and argument were presented for the crucial role of expressions in social communication, cognitive development, the acquisition of language, and the development of affective–cognitive structures, including the affective–cognitive schema of self.

We view the emotions system as one of a set of organismic systems, yet we think that our highlighting of the separate components of emotion is heuristic. We believe that fruitful research can be guided by the recognition that an emotion is a complexly interrelated set of neural, motor, and mental processes. A given emotion will never be fully understood without detailed knowledge of all of its components and their development over time. Only with this knowledge can we fully understand the development of relations among the emotions system, cognition, and the other organismic systems, and the role of emotion in motivation and adaptation.

So the study of emotions invites several specialized approaches, but it also requires collaborative effort in order to build an integrated theory of emotions as discrete systems within the larger emotions system and within the set of systems that operates within the human being and that relates to environment and culture. We believe such a collaborative effort to be a top priority for the behavioral sciences, a belief based on the central premise that the emotions constitute the evolutionary roots of human mentality and the principal motivational system for human behavior.

REFERENCES

Ahrens, R. (1954). Beitrag zur Entwicklung des Physiognomie-und Mimikerkennens I. *Zeitschrift fur Angewandte und Experimentelle Psychologie, 2,* 412–454.

Ainsworth, M. S., Blehar, M. D., Waters, E., & Wall, S. (1978). *Patterns of attachment: A psychological study of the strange situation.* Hillsdale, NJ: Erlbaum.

Anisman, H., & Zacharko, R. M. (1982). Depression: The predisposing influence of stress. *The Behavioral & Brain Sciences, 5,* 89–99.

Anthony, B. J., & Graham, F. K. (1983). Evidence for sensory-selective set in young infants. *Science, 220,* 742–743.

Argyle, N. (1972). Non-verbal communication in human social interaction. In R. A. Hinde (Ed.), *Non-verbal communication.* New York: Cambridge University Press.

Arnold, M. B. (1960). *Emotion and personality: Vol. II. Neurological and physiological aspects.* New York: Columbia University Press.

Averill, J. R. (1968). Grief: Its nature and significance. *Psychological Bulletin, 70,* 721–748.

Bandler, R. (1982). Neural control of aggressive behavior. *Trends in Neuro Sciences, 5*(11), 390–394.

Bard, P. (1934). On emotional expression after decortication with some remarks on certain theoretical views. Part II. *Psychological Review, 41,* 424–449.

Bartlett, E. S., & Izard, C. E. (1972). A dimensional and discrete emotions investigation of the subjective experience of emotion. In C. E. Izard (Ed.), *Patterns of emotions: A new analysis of anxiety and depression.* New York: Academic.

Bayley, N. (1956). Individual patterns of development. *Child Development, 27,* 45–74.

Beck, A. T. (1976). *Cognitive therapy and the emotional disorders.* New York: International Universities Press.

Beckwith, L. (1979). Prediction of emotional and social behavior. In J. Osofsky (Ed.), *Handbook of infant development.* New York: Wiley.

Berkowitz, L. (1983). Aversively stimulated aggression: Some parallels and differences in research with animals and humans. *American Psychologist, 38,* 1135–1144.

Berlyne, D. E. (1960). *Conflict, arousal, and curiosity.* New York: McGraw-Hill.

Birns, B., & Golden, M. (1972). Prediction of intellectual performance at three years from infant tests and personality measures. *Merrill–Palmer Quarterly, 18,* 53–58.

Block, J. (in collaboration with N. Haan). (1971). *Lives through time.* Berkeley: Bancroft.

Blumberg, S. H. (1983). *Affective and cognitive characteristics of depression in ten year old children.* Masters thesis, University of Delaware.

Blumberg, S. H., & Izard, C. E. (in press). Affective and cognitive characteristics of non-depressed and depressed 10-year-old children. *Journal of Personality & Social Psychology.*

Borod, J. C., & Koff, E. (1984). Asymmetries in affective facial expression: Behavior and anatomy. In N. A. Fox & R. J. Davidson (Eds.), *The psychobiology of affective development.* Hillsdale, NJ: Erlbaum.

Bower, G. H. (1981). Emotional mood and memory. *American Psychologist, 36*(2), 129–148.

Bower, G. H., & Mayer, J. D. (1984). *Failure to replicate mood-dependent retrieval.* Unpublished manuscript, Stanford University, Department of Psychology.

Bowlby. J. (1969). *Attachment and loss* (Vol. 1). New York: Basic.

Bowlby, J. (1973). *Attachment and loss: Vol. II. Separation, anxiety, and anger.* New York: Basic Books.

Bransford, J. D., Franks, J. J., Morris, C. D., & Stein, B. S. (1979). Some general constraints on learning and memory research. In L. Cermak & F. Craik (Eds.), *Levels of processing in human memory.* Hillsdale, NJ: Erlbaum.

Bretherton, I., & Beeghly-Smith, M. (1982). Talking about internal states: The acquisition of an explicit theory of mind. *Developmental Psychology, 18,* 906–921.

Briggs, J. (1970). *Never in anger.* Cambridge, MA: Harvard University Press.

Bronson, G. (1972). Infants' reactions to unfamiliar persons and novel objects. *Monographs of the Society for Research in Child Development, 37*(3), Ser. 148.

Buck, R. (1980). Nonverbal behavior and the theory of emotion: The facial feedback hypothesis. *Journal of Personality & Social Psychology, 38*(5), 811–824.

Buss, A. H. (1979). *Self consciousness and social anxiety.* San Francisco: Freeman.

Campos, J. J., & Barrett, K. C. (1984). A new understanding of emotions and their development. In C. E. Izard, J. Kagan, & R. Zajonc (Eds.), *Emotions, cognition, and behavior.* New York: Cambridge University Press.

Campos, J. J., Barrett, K. C., Lamb, M. E., Goldsmith, H. H., & Stenberg, C. (1983). Socioemotional development. In M. M. Haith & J. J. Campos (Eds.), Infancy and developmental psychobiology, Vol. II of P. H. Mussen (Ed.), *Handbook of child psychology* (4th ed.). New York: Wiley.

Campos, J. J., Hiatt, S., Ramsay, D., Henderson, C., & Svejda, M. (1978). The emergence of fear on the visual cliff. In M. Lewis & L. A. Rosenblum (Eds.), *The development of affect: Vol. 1. Genesis of Behavior.* New York: Plenum.

Campos, J. J., & Stenberg, C. (1981). Perception, appraisal and emotion: The onset of social referencing. In M. Lamb & L. Sherrod (Eds.), *Infant social cognition.* Hillsdale, NJ: Erlbaum.

Camras, L. A. (1977). Facial expressions used by children in a conflict situation. *Child Development, 48,* 1431–1435.

Cannon, W. B. (1927). The James-Lange theory of emotions: A critical examination and an alternative theory. *American Journal of Psychology, 39,* 106–124.

Cannon, W. B. (1929). *Bodily changes in pain, hunger, fear and rage: An account of recent researches into the function of emotional excitement* (2nd ed.). New York: Appleton-Century-Crofts.

Carmichael, L. (1970). The onset and early development of behavior. In P. H. Mussen (Ed.), *Carmichael's manual of child psychology.* New York: Wiley.

Caudill, W., & Weinstein, H. (1969). Maternal care and infant behavior in Japan and America. *Psychiatry, 32,* 12–43.

Charlesworth, W. R. (1982). An ethological approach to research on facial expressions. In C. E. Izard (Ed.), *Measuring emotions in infants and children.* New York: Cambridge University Press.

Cicchetti, D., & Hesse, P. (1983). Affect and intellect: Piaget's contributions to the study of infant emotional development. In R. Plutchik & H. Kellerman (Eds.), *Emotion: Theory, research and experience* (Vol. 2). New York: Academic.

Cicchetti, D., & Schneider-Rosen, K. (1984). Theoretical and empirical considerations in the investigation of the relationship between affect and cognition in atypical populations of infants. In C. E. Izard, J. Kagan, & R. Zajonc (Eds.), *Emotions, cognition, and behavior.* New York: Cambridge University Press.

Cicchetti, D., & Schneider-Rosen, K. (in press). An organizational approach to childhood depression. In M. Rutter, C. E. Izard, & P. Read (Eds.), *Depression in young people: Developmental and clinical perspectives.* New York: Guilford.

Cicchetti, D., & Sroufe, L. A. (1976). The relationship between affective and cognitive development in Down's syndrome infants. *Child Development, 47,* 920–929.

Cicchetti, D., & Sroufe, L. A. (1978). An organizational view of affect: Illustration from the study of Down's syndrome infants. In M. Lewis & L. A. Rosenblum (Eds.), *The development of affect.* New York: Plenum.

Colby, C. Z., Lanzetta, J. T., & Kleck, R. E. (1977). Effects of expression of pain on autonomic and pain tolerance responses to subject–controlled pain. *Psychophysiology, 14,* 537–540.

Cole, M. (1983, April). *Preschoolers' emotional display rules.* Paper presented at the biennial meeting of the Society of Research and Child Development, Detroit.

Darwin, C. R. (1872/1965). *The expression of emotions in man and animals.* London: John Murray (Chicago: University of Chicago Press).

Davidson, R. J. (1984). Affect, cognition and hemispheric specialization. In C. E. Izard, J. Kagan, & R. Zajonc (Eds.), *Emotion, cognition and behavior.* New York: Cambridge University Press.

Davis, J. (1970). Theories of biological etiology of affective disorders. *International Review of Neurobiology, 12,* 145–175.

Demos, V. (1974). *Children's understanding and use of affect terms.* Doctoral dissertation, Graduate School of Education, Harvard University.

Demos, V. (1982). Facial expressions of infants and toddlers. In T. Field & A. Fogel (Eds.), *Emotion and early interaction.* Hillsdale, NJ: Erlbaum.

Denenberg, V. (1980). General systems theory, brain organization, and early experience. *American Journal of Physiology, 238,* 3–13.

DePaulo, B. M., & Rosenthal, R. (1982). Measuring the development of sensitivity to non-verbal communication. In C. E. Izard (Ed.), *Measuring emotions in infants and children.* New York: Cambridge University Press.

Dickstein, S., Thompson, R., Estes, D., Malkin, C., & Lamb, M. (1982). *Social referencing and maternal contributions.* Paper presented at the International Conference on Infant Studies, Austin, TX.

Dixon, S., Tronick, E., Keeler, C., & Brazelton, T. B. (1981). Mother–infant interaction among the Gusii of Kenya. In T. M. Field, A. M. Sostek, P. Vietze, & P. H. Leiderman (Eds.), *Culture and early interaction.* Hillsdale, NJ: Erlbaum.

Dubner, R., Sessle, B. J., & Storey, A. T. (1978). *The neural basis of oral and facial function.* New York: Plenum.

Dunn, J. (1985). *Family interaction and the development of emotional understanding.* Paper presented at the meeting of the Society for Research in Child Development, Toronto.

Eibl-Eibesfeldt, I. (1972). Similarities and differences between cultures in expressive movements. In R. A. Hinde (Ed.), *Nonverbal communication.* Cambridge, MA: Cambridge University Press.

Eisenberg, N., & Lennon, R. (1983). Sex differences in empathy and related capacities. *Psychological Bulletin, 94,* 100–131.

Eisenberg-Berg, N., & Geisheker, E. (1979). Content of preachings and power of the model/preacher: The effect on children's generosity. *Developmental Psychology, 10,* 21–28.

Ekman, P. (1965). Communication through nonverbal behavior: A source of information about an interpersonal relationship. In S. S. Tomkins & C. E. Izard (Eds.), *Affect, cognition, and personality.* New York: Springer.

Ekman, P. (1979). About brows: Emotional and conversational signals. In M. von Cranach, K. Foppa, W. Lepenies, & D. Ploog (Eds.), *Human ethology.* London: Cambridge.

Ekman, P., & Friesen, W. V. (1975). *Unmasking the face: A guide to recognizing emotions from facial clues.* Englewood Cliffs, NJ: Prentice-Hall.

Ekman, P., & Friesen, W. V. (1982). Felt, false, and miserable smiles. *Journal of Nonverbal Behavior, 6,* 238–252.

Ekman, P., Friesen, W. V., & Ellsworth, P. (1972). *Emotion in the human face: Guidelines for research and an integration of findings.* New York: Pergamon.

Ekman, P., Roper, G., & Hager, J. C. (1980). Deliberate facial movement. *Child Development, 51,* 886–891.

Emde, R. N. (1980). Levels of meaning for infant emotions: A biosocial view. In W. A. Collins (Ed.), *Development of cognition, affect and social relations. Minnesota Symposia on Child Psychology* (Vol. 13, pp. 1–38). Hillsdale, NJ: Erlbaum.

Emde, R. N., Gaensbauer, T. J., & Harmon, R. J. (1976). *Emotional expression in infancy.* New York: International Universities Press.

Epstein, A. N. (1982). Instinct and motivation as explanations for complex behavior. In D. W. Pfaff (Ed.), *Physiological mechanisms of motivation.* New York: Springer-Verlag.

Etzel, B., & Gerwitz, J. (1967). Experimental modification of caretaker-maintained high rate operant crying in a 6- and a 20-week-old infant (Infans tyrannotearus): Extinction of crying with reinforcement of eye contact and smiling. *Journal of Experimental Child Psychology, 5,* 303–317.

Fagan, J. W., & Rovee-Collier, C. (1983). Memory retrieval: A time-locked process in infancy. *Science, 222,* 1349–1351.

Fantz, R. L. (1964). Visual experience in infants: Decreased attention to familiar patterns relative to novel ones. *Science, 146,* 668–670.

Fehr, F. S., & Stern, J. A. (1970). Peripheral physiological variables and emotion: The James-Lange theory revisited. *Psychological Bulletin, 74,* 411–424.

Field, T. (1979). Visual and cardiac responses to animate and inanimate faces by young term and preterm infants. *Child Development, 50,* 188–194.

Fink, J. S., & Smith, G. P. (1980). Mesolimbicocortical dopamine terminal fields are necessary for normal locomotor and investigatory exploration in rats. *Brain Research, 199,* 359–384.

Flynn, J. P. (1967). The neural basis of aggression in cats. In D. C. Glass (Ed.), *Neurophysiology and emotion.* New York: Rockefeller University Press.

Flynn, J. P. (1972). In J. K. Coles & D. D. Jensen (Eds.), Patterning mechanisms, patterned reflexes and attack behavior in cats. *Nebraska Symposium on Motivation.* Lincoln: University of Nebraska Press.

Fox, N. A., & Davidson, R. J. (1984). *Hemispheric substrates of affect: A developmental model.* In N. A. Fox & R. J. Davidson (Eds.), *The psychobiology of affective development.* Hillsdale, NJ: Erlbaum.

Fraiberg, S. (1979). Blind infants and their mothers: An examination of the sign system. In M. Bullowa (Ed.), *Before speech.* New York: Cambridge University Press.

Freedman, D. G. (1974). *Human infancy: An evolutionary perspective.* Hillsdale, NJ: Erlbaum.

Fridlund, A. J., & Izard, C. E. (1983). Electromyographic studies of facial expressions of emotions and patterns of emotion. In J. T. Cacioppo & R. E. Petty (Eds.), *Social psychophysiology: A sourcebook.* New York: Guilford.

Fridlund, A., Schwartz, G., & Fowler, S. (1984). Pattern recognition of self-reported emotional state from multiple-site facial EMG activity during affective imagery. *Psychophysiology, 21,* 622–637.

Fry, P. S. (1975). Affect and resistance to temptation. *Developmental Psychology, 11,* 466–472.

Gaensbauer, T. J., Connell, J. P., & Schultz, L. A. (1983). Emotion and attachment: Interrelationships in a structured laboratory paradigm. *Developmental Psychology, 19,* 815–831.

Geertz, H. (1959). The vocabulary of emotion. *Psychiatry. 22,* 225–237.

Gellhorn, E. (1964). Motion and emotion: The role of proprioception in the physiology of the emotions. *Psychological Review, 71*(6), 457–472.

Gibson, J. J. (1966). *The senses considered as perceptual systems.* Boston: Houghton-Mifflin.

Gibson, J. J. (1979). *The ecological approach to visual perception.* Boston: Houghton-Mifflin.

Goldsmith, H. H., & Campos, J. J. (1982). Toward a theory of infant temperament. In R. N. Emde & R. J. Harmon (Eds.), *The development of attachment and affiliative systems.* New York: Plenum.

Gomby, D. S., & Ellsworth, P. C. (1985). *Situational determinants of emotional inferences.* Unpublished manuscript, Stanford University.

Gray, J. A. (1982). Precis of the neuropsychology of anxiety: An inquiry into the functions of the septo-hippocampal system. *Behavioral & Brain Sciences, 5,* 469–534.

Grill, J. H., & Norgren, R. (1978). The taste reactivity test. II. Mimetic responses to gustatory stimuli in chronic thalamic and chronic decerebrate rats. *Brain Research, 143,* 281–297.

Grossmann, K. E., Schwan, A., & Grossmann, K. (in press). Infants' communications after brief separation: An analysis of Ainsworth's strange situation. In C. E. Izard & P. B. Read (Eds.), *Measuring emotions in infants and children.* New York: Cambridge University Press.

Guillory, A. W., Self, P. A., Biscoe, B. M., & Cole, C. A. (1982). *The first four months: Development of affect, cognition, and synchrony.* Paper presented at the annual meeting of the American Psychological Association, Washington, DC.

Hagar, J. C., & Ekman, P. (1981). Methodological problems in Tourangeau and Ellsworth's study of facial expression and experience of emotion. *Journal of Personality & Social Psychology, 40,* 358–362.

Haldane, J. B. S. (1932). *The causes of evolution.* London: Longmans Green.

Hamburg, D. A. (1963). Emotions in the perspective of human evolution. In P.H. Knapp (Ed.), *Expression of emotions in man.* New York: International Universities Press.

Harlow, H. F. (1971). *Learning to love.* San Francisco: Albion.

Harris, P. L. (1983a). Infant cognition. In M. M. Haith & J. Campos (Eds.), *Handbook of child psychology: Infancy and developmental psychobiology.* New York: Wiley.

Harris, P. L. (1983b). Children's understanding of the link between situation and emotion. *Journal of Experimental Child Psychology, 36,* 490–509.

Harter, S. (1983). Developmental perspectives on the self-system. In P. H. Mussen (Ed.), *Handbook of child psychology* (Vol. 4). New York: Wiley.

Hass, H. (1970). *The human animal.* New York: Putnam's Sons.

Haviland, J. (1976). Looking smart: The relationship between affect and intelligence in infancy. In M. Lewis (Ed.), *Origins of intelligence.* New York: Plenum.

Haynes, O. M., & Stettner, L. J. (1983, April). *Forms and function in smiling.* Paper presented at the Society for Research in Child Development, Detroit.

Heath, R. G., & Mickle, W. A. (1960). Evaluation of seven years experience with depth electrode studies in human patients. In E. R. Ramey & D. S. O'Doherty (Eds.), *Electrical studies on the unanesthetized brain.* New York: Hoeber.

Hebb, D. (1946). On the nature of fear. *Psychological Review, 53,* 259–276.

Hembree, E. A., Ansul, S., & Izard, C. E. (1985). *Emotion signals in newborns' facial responses to pain.* Unpublished manuscript, Department of Psychology, University of Delaware.

Hembree, E. A., & Izard, C. E. (1984). *Individual differences and developmental changes in emotion expressions in early mother–infant interaction.* Unpublished manuscript, Department of Psychology, University of Delaware.

Hiatt, S., Campos, J. J., & Emde, R. N. (1979). Facial patterning and infant emotional expression: Happiness, surprise, and fear. *Child Development, 50*(4), 1020–1035.

Hoffman, M. L. (1978a). Empathy, its development and prosocial implications. *Nebraska Symposium on Motivation* (Vol. 25, pp. 169–218). Lincoln: University of Nebraska Press.

Hoffman, M. L. (1978b). Toward a theory of empathic arousal and development. In M. Lewis & L. A. Rosenblum (Eds.), *The development of affect.* New York: Plenum.

Hoffman, M. L. (1981). Is altruism part of human nature? *Journal of Personality & Social Psychology, 40,* 121–137.

Hoffman, M. L. (1984). Interaction of affect and cognition in empathy. In C. E. Izard, J. Kagan, & R. Zajonc (Eds.), *Emotions, cognition, and behavior.* New York: Cambridge University Press.

Hoffman, M. L. (in press). Affect, cognition, and motivation. In R. Sorrentino & E. T. Higgins (Eds.), *Handbook of motivation and cognition.* New York: Guilford.

Howard, J. A., & Barnett, M. A. (1981). Arousal of empathy and subsequent generosity in young children. *Journal of Genetic Psychology, 138,* 307–308.

Hu, J. W., Dostrovsky, J. O., & Sessle, B. J. (1981). Functional properties of neurons in cat trigeminal subnucleus caudalis (medullary dorsal horn). I. Responses to oral-facial noxious and nonnoxious stimuli and projections to thalamus and subnucleus oralis. *Journal of Neurophysiology, 45*(2), 173–192.

Huebner, R. R., & Izard, C. E. (1983). *Mothers' responses to infants' facial expressions of sadness, anger, and physical distress.* Unpublished manuscript, Department of Psychology, University of Delaware.

Hyson, M. C., & Izard, C. E. (in press). Continuities and changes in emotion expressions during brief separation at thirteen and eighteen months. *Developmental Psychology.*

Hyson, M. C., & Izard, C. E. (1984). *Relationships between emotion expressions and other behavior during a brief separation.* Unpublished manuscript, Department of Psychology, University of Delaware.

Isaacson, R. L. (1982). *The limbic system.* New York: Plenum.

Isen, A. (1970). Success, failure, attention, and reaction to others: The warm glow of success. *Journal of Personality & Social Psychology, 15*(4), 294–301.

Izard, C. E. (1971). *The face of emotion.* New York: Appleton-Century-Crofts.

Izard, C. E. (1972). *Patterns of emotions: A new analysis of anxiety and depression.* New York: Academic.

Izard, C. E. (1977). *Human Emotions.* New York: Plenum.

Izard, C. E. (1978). On the ontogenesis of emotions and emotion–cognition relationships in infancy. In M. Lewis & L. A. Rosenblum (Eds.), *The development of affect.* New York: Plenum.

Izard, C. E. (1979). *The maximally discriminative facial movement coding system (Max).* Newark, DE: University of Delaware, Instructional Resources Center.

Izard, C. E. (1981). Differential emotions theory and the facial feedback hypothesis of emotion activation: Comments on Tourangeau and Ellsworth's "The role of facial response in the experience of emotion." *Journal of Personality & Social Psychology, 40,* 350–354.

Izard, C. E. (1984). Emotion–cognition relationships and human development. In C. E. Izard, J. Kagan, & R. Zajonc (Eds.), *Emotions, cognition and behavior.* New York: Cambridge University Press.

Izard, C. E., Dougherty, L. M. & Hembree, E. A. (1980). *A system for identifying affect expressions by holistic judgements (Affex).* Newark, DE: University of Delaware, Instructional Resources Center.

Izard, C. E., Gelles, M., Simons, R. F., Hembree, E. A., & Huebner, R. R. (1985). *Mothers' psychophysiological responses to unfamiliar infants' affect expressions.* Unpublished manuscript, University of Delaware.

Izard, C. E., Hembree, E. A., Dougherty, L. M., & Spizzirri, C. L. (1983). Changes in facial expressions of 2- to 19-month-old infants following acute pain. *Developmental Psychology, 19,* 418–426.

Izard, C. E., Hembree, E. A., & Huebner, R. R. (1984). *Infants' emotion expressions to acute pain: Stability and change.* Unpublished manuscript, Department of Psychology, University of Delaware.

Izard, C. E., Huebner, R. R., Risser, D., McGinnes, G., & Dougherty, L. (1980). The young infant's ability to produce discrete emotion expressions. *Developmental Psychology, 16*(2), 132–140.

Izard, C. E., & Hyson, M. C. (in press). Shyness as a discrete emotion. In W. H. Jones (Ed.), *Shyness.* New York: Plenum.

Izard, C. E., Nagler, S., Randall, D. & Fox, J. (1965). The effects of affective picture stimuli on learning, perception and the affective values of previously neutral symbols. In S. S. Tomkins & C. E. Izard (Eds.) *Affect, cognition, and personality.* New York, Springer.

Izard, C. E., & Saxton, P. M. (in press). Emotions. In R. C. Atkinson, R. J. Hernstein, G. Lindzey, D. Luce, & R. Thompson (Eds.), *Steven's handbook of experimental psychology.* New York: Wiley.

Izard, C. E., & Schwartz, G. M. (in press). Patterns of emotion in depression. In M. Rutter, C. E. Izard, & P. Read (Eds.), *Depression in young people: Developmental and clinical perspectives.* New York: Guilford.

Izard, C. E., Wehmer, G. M., Livsey, W., & Jennings, J. R. (1965). Affect, awareness, and performance. In S. S. Tomkins & C. E. Izard (Eds.), *Affect, cognition, and personality* (pp. 2–41). New York: Springer.

James, W. (1884). What is emotion? *Mind 4,* 188–204.

James, W. (1890). *The principles of psychology* (vol. 2). New York: Dover.

Johanson, C. E., & Uhlenhuth, E. H. (1980). Drug preference and mood in humans: d-amphetamine. *Psychopharmacology, 71,* 274–279.

Johnston, C. C., & Strada, M. E. (1985). *Acute pain response in infants: A multidimensional description.* Manuscript submitted for publication.

Jolly, A. (1966). Lemur social behavior and primate intelligence. *Science, 153,* 501–506.

Kagan, J. (1976). Emergent themes in human development. *American Scientist, 64*(2), 186–196.

Kagan, J. (1979). Structure and process in the human infant. The ontogeny of mental representation. In M. H. Bornstein & W. Kessen (Eds.), *Psychological development from infancy: Image to intention.* Hillsdale, NJ: Erlbaum.

Kagan, J. (1984). The idea of emotion in human development. In C. E. Izard, J. Kagan, & R. Zajonc (Eds.), *Emotions, cognition, and behavior.* New York: Cambridge University Press.

Kagan, J., Kearsley, R. B., & Zelazzo, P. R. (1978). *Infancy: Its place in human development.* Cambridge, MA: Harvard University Press.

Kaufman, I. C. (1977). Developmental considerations of anxiety and depression: Psychobiological studies in monkeys. In T. Shapiro (Ed.), *Psychoanalysis and contemporary science: An annual of integrative and interdisciplinary studies* (Vol. 5). New York: International Universities Press.

Kelley, A. E., & Stinus, L. (1984). Neuroanatomical and neurochemical substrates of affective behavior. In N. A. Fox & R. J. Davidson (Eds.), *The psychobiology of affective development* (pp. 1–75). Hillsdale, NJ: Erlbaum.

King, H. E. (1961). Psychological effects of excitation in the limbic system. In D. E. Sheer (Ed.), *Electrical stimulation of the brain.* Austin: University of Texas Press.

Kinsbourne, M., & Bemporad, B. (1984). *Lateralization of emotion: A model and the evidence.* In N. A. Fox & R. J. Davidson (Eds.), *The psychobiology of affective development.* Hillsdale, NJ: Erlbaum.

Kistiakovskaia, M. I. (1965). Stimulus evoking positive emotions in infants in the first months of life. *Soviet Journal of Psychiatry, 3,* 39–48.

Kleck, R. E., Vaughn, R. C., Cartwright-Smith, J., Vaughn, K. B., Colby, C. Z., & Lanzetta, J. T. (1976). Effects of being observed on expressive, subjective, and physiological responses to painful stimuli. *Journal of Personality & Social Psychology, 34*(6), 1211–1218.

Kleinke, C. L., & Walton, J. H. (1982). Influence of reinforced smiling on affective responses in an interview. *Journal of Personality & Social Psychology, 4*(3), 557–565.

Klinnert, M., Campos, J., Sorce, J., Emde, R., & Svejda, M. (1983). Emotions as behavior regulators: The development of social referencing. In R. Plutchik & H. Kellerman (Eds.), *Emotions in early development,* Vol. 2 of *Emotion: Theory, research and experience.* New York: Academic.

Klinnert, M. D., Emde, R. N., Butterfield, P., & Campos, J. J. (in press). Social referencing: The infant's use of emotion signals from a friendly adult with mother present. *Developmental Psychology.*

Konner, M. (1982). Biological aspects of the mother–infant bond. In R. N. Emde & R. J. Harmon (Eds.), *The development of attachment and affiliative systems.* New York: Plenum.

Kovacs, M., & Beck, A. T. (1979). Cognitive–affective processes in depression. In C. E. Izard (Ed.), *Emotions in personality and psychopathology.* New York: Plenum.

Laird, J. D. (1984). The real role of facial response in the experience of emotion: A reply to Tourangeau and Ellsworth, and others. *Journal of Personality & Social Psychology 47,* 909–917.

Laird, J. D., Wagener, J. J. Halal, M., & Szegda, M. (1982). Remembering what you feel: Effects of emotion on memory. *Journal of Personality & Social Psychology, 42*(4), 646–652.

Langer, S. K. (1967). *Mind: An essay on human feeling.* Baltimore: Johns Hopkins Press.

Langsdorf, P., Izard, C., Rayias, M., & Hembree, E. (1983). Interest expression, visual fixation, and heart rate changes in 2- to 8-month-old infants. *Developmental Psychology, 19*(3), 375–386.

Lanzetta, J. T., Cartwright-Smith, J. E., & Kleck, R. E. (1976). Effects of nonverbal dissimulation on emotional experience and autonomic arousal. *Journal of Personality & Social Psychology, 33,* 354–370.

Lazarus, R. S. (1982). Thoughts on the relations between emotion and cognition. *American Psychologist, 37,* 1019–1024.

Lazarus, R. S., Kanner, A. D., & Folkman, S. (1980). Emotions: A cognitive-phenomenological analysis. In R. Plutchik & H. Kellerman (Eds.), *Emotion: Theory, research, and experience* (Vol. 1). New York: Academic.

Lelwica, M., & Haviland, J. M. (1983, April). *Response or imitation: Ten-week-old infants' reactions to three emotion expressions.* Paper presented at the biennial meeting of the Society for Research in Child Development, Detroit.

Leventhal, H. (1982). The integration of emotion and cognition: A view from the perceptual-motor theory of emotion. In M. Clark & S. Fiske (Eds.), *Affect and cognition.* Hillsdale, NJ: Erlbaum.

Levy, R. I. (1984). *On the nature and functions of the emotions: An anthropological perspective.* Unpublished manuscript, University of California, San Diego.

Lewis, M., & Michalson, L. (1983). *Children's emotions and moods: Developmental theory and measurement.* New York: Plenum.

Lewis, M., & Saarni, C. (1985). *Socialization of emotion.* New York: Plenum.

Lipps, T. (1906). Das Wissen von Fremden Ichen. *Psychologische Untersuchnung, 1,* 694–722.

Lorenz, K. (1966). *On aggression.* Harcourt, Brace & World.

Lutz C. (1982). The domain of emotion words on Ifaluk. *American Ethologist, 9,* 113–116.

Lutz, C. (in press). Parental goals, ethnopsychology and the development of emotional meaning. *Ethos.*

Macfarlane, J. W. (1963). From infancy to adulthood. *Childhood Education, 39,* 336–342.

MacLean, P. D. (1958). The limbic system with respect to self-preservation and the preservation of the species. *Journal of Nervous & Mental Disease, 127,* 1–11.

MacLean, P. D. (1967). The brain in relation to empathy and medical education. *Journal of Nervous & Mental Disease, 144,* 374–382.

MacLean, P. D. (1973). *A triune concept of the brain and behavior.* Toronto: University of Toronto Press.

Malatesta. C. Z. (1981). Infant emotion and the vocal affect lexicon. *Motivation & Emotion, 5,* 1–23.

Malatesta, C. Z. (1982). The expression and regulation of emotion: A lifespan perspective. In T. Field & A. Fogel (Eds.), *Emotion and early interaction.* Hillsdale NJ: Erlbaum.

Malatesta, C. Z. (in press). Developmental course of emotion expression in the human infant. In G. Zivin (Ed.), *The development of expressive behavior.* New York: Academic.

Malatesta, C. Z., & Haviland, J. M. (1982). Learning display rules: The socialization of emotion expression in infancy. *Child Development, 53,* 991–1003.

Malatesta C. Z., & Izard, C. E. (1984a). The facial expression of emotion: Young middle-aged, and older adult expressions. In C. Z. Malatesta & C. E. Izard (Eds.), *Emotion in adult development.* Beverly Hills: Sage.

Malatesta, C. Z., & Izard, C. E. (1984b). The ontogenesis of human social signals: From biological imperative to symbol utilization. In N. A. Fox & R. J. Davidson (Eds.), *The psychobiology of affective development.* Hillsdale, NJ: Erlbaum.

Malatesta, C. Z., & Kalnok, M. (1984). Emotional experience in younger and older adults. *Journal of Gerontology, 39,* 301–308.

Mandler, G. (1975). *Mind and emotions.* New York: Wiley.

Mandler, G. (1982). The structure of value: Accounting for taste. In M. S. Clark & S. T. Fiske (Eds.), *Affect and cognition.* New York: Erlbaum.

Mandler, G., & Shebo, B. J. (1983). Knowing and liking. *Motivation & Emotion, 7*(2), 125–144.

Mark, V. H., & Ervin, F. R. (1970). *Violence and the brain.* New York: Harper & Row.

Martin, G., & Clark, R. (1982). Distress crying in neonates: Species and peer specificity. *Developmental Psychology, 18,* 3–9.

Martin, W. R., Sloan, J. W., Sapira, J. D., & Jasinski, D. R. (1971). Physiologic, subjective, and behavioral effects of amphetamine, methamphetamine, ephedrine, phenetrazine and methylphenidate in man. *Clinical Pharmacology & Therapeutics, 12,* 245–258.

Masters, J. C., & Carlson, C. R. (1984). Children's and adult's understanding of the causes and consequences of emotional states. In C. E. Izard, J. Kagan, & R. Zajonc (Eds.), *Emotions, cognition, and behavior.* New York: Cambridge University Press.

Matheny, A. P., Jr., Riese, M. L., & Wilson, R. S. (1985). Rudiments of infant temperament: Newborn to 9 months. *Developmental Psychology, 21,* 486–494.

Maynard-Smith, J. (1964). Group selection and kin selection. *Nature, 201,* 1145–1147.

McDougall, W. (1923). *An introduction to social psychology.* London: Methuen.

McGinnes G., & Izard, C. E. (1984). *Individual differences in infants' responses to separation.* Unpublished manuscript, Department of Psychology, University of Delaware.

Miyake, K. (1984–1985). Relation of temperamental disposition to classification of attachment: Comparison of results obtained in two independent samples. *Research and Clinical Development.* Hokkaido University, Sapporo, Japan.

Moore, B. S., Underwood, B., & Rosenhan, D. L. (1973). Affect and altruism. *Developmental Psychology, 8,* 99–104.

Mosher, D. L., & White, B. B. (1981). On differentiating shame and shyness. *Motivation & Emotion, 5*(1), 61–74.

Motti, F., Cicchetti, D., & Sroufe, A. (1983). From infant affect expression to symbolic play: The coherence of development in Down syndrome children. *Child Development, 54,* 1168–1175.

Moyer, K. E. (1971). *The physiology of hostility.* Chicago: Markham.

Murphy, L. B. (1937). *Social behavior and child personality.* New York: Columbia University Press.

Naus, M. J., & Halasz, F. G. (1979). Developmental perspectives on cognitive processing and semantic memory structure. In L. Cermak & F. Craik (Eds.), *Levels of processing in human memory.* Hillsdale, NJ: Erlbaum.

Neisser, U. (1976). *Cognition and reality*. San Francisco: W. H. Freeman.

Neisser, U. (1982). *Memory observed*. San Francisco: W. H. Freeman.

Nelson, D. L. (1979). Remembering pictures and words: Appearance, significance, and name. In L. Cermak & F. Craik (Eds.), *Levels of processing in human memory*. Hillsdale, NJ: Erlbaum.

Nordin, M., Hagbarth, K. E., Thomander, L., & Wallin, U. (1984). Microneurographic recordings from the trigeminal and facial nerves. *Electroencephalography & Clinical Neurophysiology, 57,* 59.

Norman, D. A. (1980). Twelve issues for cognitive science. In D. A. Norman (Ed.), *Perspectives on cognitive science: Talks from the LaJolla Conference*. Hillsdale, NJ: Erlbaum.

Odom, R. D., & Lemond, L. C. (1972). Developmental differences in the perception and production of facial expressions. *Child Development, 43,* 359-369.

Oke, A., Keller, R., Mefford, I., & Adams, R. (1978). Lateralization of norepinephrine in human thalamus. *Science, 200,* 1411-1413.

Olson, G. M., & Sherman, T. (1983). Attention learning and memory in infants. In M. M. Haith & J. J. Campos (Eds.), *Handbook of child psychology: Infancy and developmental psychobiology*. New York: Wiley.

Oster, H. (1978). Facial expression and affect development. In M. Lewis & L. Rosenblum (Eds.), *The development of affect*. New York: Plenum.

Oster, H. (1981). "Recognition" of emotional expression in infancy? In M. E. Lamb & L. Sherrod (Eds.), *Infant social cognition*. Hillsdale, NJ: Erlbaum.

Panksepp. J. (1982). Toward a general psychobiological theory of emotions. *Behavioral & Brain Sciences, 5,* 407-467.

Papez, J. W. (1937). A proposed mechanism of emotion. *Archives of Neurology and Psychiatry. 38,* 725-743.

Piaget, J. (1952). *The origins of intelligence in children*. New York: International Universities Press.

Piaget, J. (1954). *The construction of reality in the child*. New York: Basic Books.

Plutchik, R. (1980). *Emotion: A psychoevolutionary synthesis*. New York: Harper & Row.

Provence, S., & Lipton, R. C. (1962). *Infants in institutions: A comparison of their development with family-reared infants during the first year of life*. New York: International Universities Press.

Ray, W. J., & Cole, H. W. (1985). EEG alpha activity reflects attentional demands, and beta activity reflects emotional and cognitive processes. *Science, 228,* 750-752.

Rheingold, H., Gerwirtz, J., & Ross, H. (1959). Social conditioning of vocalizations in the infant. *Journal of comparative & physiological psychology, 52,* 68-73.

Ridgeway, D., Waters, E., & Kuczaj, S. (in press). The acquisition of emotion descriptive language: Receptive and productive vocabulary norms for ages 18 months to six years. *Developmental Psychology*.

Rinn, W. E. (1984). The neuropsychology of facial expression: A review of the neurological and psychological mechanisms for producing facial expressions. *Psychological Bulletin, 95,* 52-77.

Rosenhan, D. L., Underwood, B., & Moore, B. (1974). Affect moderates self-gratification and altruism. *Journal of Personality & Social Psychology 30*(4), 546-552.

Rothbart, M. K., & Derryberry, D. (1981). Development of individual differences in temperament. In M. E. Lamb & A. L. Brown (Eds.), *Advances in developmental psychology* (Vol. 1). Hillsdale, NJ: Erlbaum.

Routtenberg, A. (1968). The two-arousal hypothesis: Reticular formation and limbic system. *Psychological Review, 75,* 51–81.

Rutter, M., Izard, C. E., & Read, P. (Eds.). (in press). *Depression in young people: Developmental and clinical perspectives.* New York: Guilford.

Saarni, C. (1979). Children's understanding of display rules for expressive behavior. *Developmental Psychology, 15,* 424–429.

Saarni, C. (1980). Cognitive and communicative features of emotional experience or do you show what you think and feel. In M. Lewis & L. Rosenblum (Eds.), *Development of affect.* New York: Plenum.

Saarni, C. (1981, April). *Emotional experience and regulation of expressive behavior.* Paper presented at the biennial meeting of the Society for Research in Child Development, Boston.

Sackett, G. (1966). Monkeys reared in isolation with pictures as visual input: Evidence for an innate releasing mechanism. *Science, 154,* 1468–1473.

Sackett, G. P. (1982). Can single processes explain effects of postnatal influences on primate development? In R. N. Emde & R. J. Harmon (Ed.), *The development of attachment and affiliative systems.* New York: Plenum.

Sagi, A., & Hoffman, M. (1976). Empathic distress in the newborn. *Developmental Psychology. 12,* 175–176.

Scarr-Salapatek, S. (1976). An evolutionary perspective on infant intelligence: Species patterns and individual variations. In M. Lewis (Ed.), *Origins of intelligence: Infancy and early childhood.* New York: Plenum.

Scherer, K. R. (1982). The assessment of vocal expression in infants and children. In C. E. Izard (Ed.), *Measuring emotions in infants and children.* New York: Cambridge University Press.

Scherer, K. R. (in press). On the nature and function of emotion: A component process approach. In K. R. Scherer & P. Ekman (Eds.), *Approaches to emotion.* Hillsdale, NJ: Erlbaum.

Schwartz, G. E., Fair, P. L., Greenberg, P. S., Friedman, M. J., & Klerman, J. L. (1974). Facial electromyography in the assessment of emotion. *Psychophysiology, 11,* 237.

Schwartz, G., & Izard, C. E. (1985). *Emotion expressions of seven- and fourteen-month-old infants to three-dimensional masks.* Unpublished manuscript, Department of Psychiatry, Medical College of Pennsylvania, Philadelphia.

Schwartz, R. M., & Trabasso, R. (1984). Children's understanding of emotions. In C. E. Izard, J. Kagan, & R. Zajonc (Eds.), *Emotions, Cognition and Behavior.* New York: Cambridge University Press.

Scott, T. R. (1981). Brain involvement in the gustatory neural code. In Y. Katsuki, R. Norgren, & M. Sato (Eds.), *Brain mechanisms of sensation.* New York: Wiley.

Shatz, M., William, H. M., & Silber, S. (1983). The acquisition of mental verbs: A systematic investigation of the first reference to mental states. *Cognition, 14,* 301–321.

Shiller, V. M., Izard, C. E., & Hembree E. A. (1984). *Patterns of emotion expression during separation.* Unpublished paper, Department of Psychology, University of Delaware.

Simner, M. L. (1971). Newborn's response to the cry of another infant. *Developmental Psychology, 5,* 136–150.

Singer, J. L. (1973). *The child's world of make-believe.* New York: Academic.

Smith, O., & DeVito, J. (1984). Central neural integration for the control of autonomic responses associated with emotion. *Annual Review of Neuroscience, 7,* 43–65.

Sperry, R. (1982). Some effects of disconnecting the cerebral hemispheres. *Science, 217,* 1223–1226.

Spitz, R. A. (1945). Hospitalism: An inquiry into the genesis of psychiatric conditions in early childhood. *Psychoanalytic Study of the Child, 1,* 53–74.

Spitz, R. A. (1946). Hospitalism: A follow-up report. *Psychoanalytic Study of the Child, 2,* 113–117.

Sroufe, L. A. (1979). Socioemotional development. In J. D. Osofsky (Ed.), *Handbook of infant development.* New York: Wiley.

Sroufe, L. A., & Wunsch, J. P. (1972). The development of laughter in the first year of life. *Child Development, 42,* 1326–1344.

Stein, N. L., & Jewett, J. L., (1984). A conceptual analysis of the meaning of negative emotions: Implications for a theory of development. In C. E. Izard & P. B. Read (Eds.), *Measuring emotions in infants and children* (Vol. 2). New York: Cambridge University Press.

Steiner, J. E. (1973). The human gustofacial response. In J. F. Bosma (Ed.), *Fourth symposium on oral sensation and perception.* Rockville, MD: U.S. Department of Health, Education, and Welfare.

Stenberg, C. R. (1982). *The development of anger facial expressions in infancy.* Doctoral dissertation, University of Denver.

Stenberg, C., Campos, J., & Emde, R. (1983). The facial expression of anger in seven-month-old infants. *Child Development, 54,* 178–184.

Strayer, J. (1980). A naturalistic study of empathic behaviors and their relation to affective states and perspective-taking skills in preschool children. *Child Development, 15,* 815–822.

Super, C., & Harkness, S. (1982). The development of affect in infancy and early childhood. In D. A. Wagner & H. W. Stevenson (Eds.), *Cultural perspectives on child development.* San Francisco: W. H. Freeman.

Szasz, T. S. (1957). *Pain and pleasure: A study of bodily feelings.* New York: Basic Books.

Takahashi, K. (1985, April). *How do Japanese infants and mothers behave in the strange situation episodes?* Paper presented at the meeting of Society for Research in Child Development, Toronto.

Takahashi, K. (1985, April). *Behavior changes in the strange situation procedure among young Japanese children between the 12th and 23rd months.* Paper presented at the meeting of Society for Research in Child Development, Toronto.

Thelen, E. (1981). Rhythmical behavior in infancy: An ethological perspective. *Developmental Psychology, 17,* 237–257.

Thelen, E., & Fisher, D. (1983). From spontaneous to instrumental behavior: Kinematic analysis of movement changes during very early learning. *Child Development, 54,* 129–140.

Thomas, A., Chess, S., & Birch, H. G. (1968). *Temperament and behavior disorders in children.* New York: New York University Press.

Thompson, J. (1941). Development of facial expression of emotion in blind and seeing children. *Archives of Psychology, 37,* 5–47.

Tomkins, S. S. (1962). *Affect, imagery, and consciousness: Vol. 1. The positive affects.* New York: Springer.

Tomkins, S. S. (1963). *Affect, imagery, and consciousness: Vol. 2. The negative affects.* New York: Springer.

Tomkins, S. S. (1981). The role of facial response in the experience of emotion: A reply to Tourangeau and Ellsworth. *Journal of Personality & Social Psychology, 40,* 355–357.

Trivers, R. L. (1971). The evolution of reciprocal altruism. *Quarterly Review of Biology, 46,* 35–57.

Tronick, E., Adamson, L., Wise, S., Als, H., & Brazelton, T. (1975). *The infant's entrap-

ment between contradictory messages in face to face interaction. Paper presented at the biennial meeting of the Society for Research in Child Development, Denver.

Tronick, E., Als, H., Adamson, L., Wise, S., & Brazelton, B. (1978). The infant's response to entrapment between contradictory messages in face-to-face interaction. *Journal of the American Academy of Child Psychiatry, 17,* 1–13.

Tronick, E., Ricks, M., & Cohn, J. (1982). Maternal and infant affective exchange: Patterns of adaptation. In T. Field & A. Fogel (Eds.), *Emotion and early interaction.* Hillsdale, NJ: Erlbaum.

Tucker, D. M. (1981). Lateral brain function, emotion and conceptualization. *Psychological Bulletin, 89,* 19–46.

Tucker, D. & Williamson, P. (1984). Asymmetric neural control systems in human self-regulation. *Psychological Review, 91,* 185–215.

Tuma, A. H., & Maser, J. D. (Eds.). (in press). *Anxiety and the anxiety disorders.* Hillsdale, NJ: Erlbaum.

Underwood, B., Moore, B. S., & Rosenhan, D. L. (1973). Affect and self-gratification. *Developmental Psychology, 8,* 209–214.

Vaughan, K. B., & Lanzetta, J. T. (1980). Vicarious instigation and conditioning of facial expressive and autonomic responses to a model's expressive display of pain. *Journal of Personality & Social Psychology. 36*(6), 909–923.

Waddington, C. H. (1957). *The strategy of the genes.* London: Allen & Unwin.

Waddington, C. H. (1962). *New patterns in genetics and development.* New York: Columbia University Press.

Washburn, R. W. (1929). A study of the smiling and laughing of infants in the first year of life. *Genetic Psychology Monographs, 6*(5), 397–535.

Weiner, B., & Graham, S. (1984). An attributional approach to emotional development. In C. E. Izard, J. Kagan, & R. Zajonc (Eds.), *Emotions, cognition, and behavior.* New York: Cambridge University Press.

Werner, H. (1948). *The comparative psychology of mental development.* New York: International Universities Press.

Werner, J. S., & Lipsitt, L. P. (1981). The infancy of human sensory systems. In E. S. Gollin (Ed.), *Developmental Plasticity: Behavioral and biological aspects of variations in development.* New York: Academic.

Winton, W. M. (1986). The role of facial response in self-reports of emotion: A critique of Laird. *Journal of Personality & Social Psychology, 50,* 808–812.

Wolff, P. H. (1966). The causes, controls, and organization of behavior in the neonate. *Psychological Issues, 5*(1), Whole No. New York: International Universities Press.

Yarrow, L. J., Goodwin, M. S., Manheimer, H., & Milowe, I. D. (1973). Infancy experiences and cognitive and personality development at ten years. In L. J. Stone, H. T. Smith, & L. B. Murphy (Eds.), *The competent infant.* New York: Basic.

Zahn-Waxler C., Friedman, S. L., & Cummings E. M. (1983). Children's emotions and behaviors in response to infants' cries. *Child development, 1983, 54,* 1522–1528.

Zahn-Waxler C., Radke-Yarrow M., & King R. A. (1979). Child rearing and children's prosocial initiations towards victims of distress. *Child Development, 50,* 319–330.

Zajonc, R. B. (1980). Feeling and thinking: Preferences need no inferences. *American Psychologist, 35*(2), 151–175.

Zajonc, R. B. (1984). On the primacy of affect. *American Psychologist, 39,* 117–123.

Zajonc, R. B., & Markus, H. (1984). Affect and cognition: The hard interface. In C. E. Izard, J. Kagan, & R. Zajonc (Eds.), *Emotions, cognition, and behavior.* New York: Cambridge University Press.

Zivin, G. (1982). Watching the sands shift: Conceptualizing development of nonverbal mastery. In R.S. Feldman (Ed.), *The development of nonverbal behavior in children*. New York: Springer.

Zuckerman, M. (1984). Sensation seeking: A comparative approach to a human trait. *The Behavioral & Brain Sciences, 7,* 413–471.

Zuckerman, M., Klorman, R., Larrance, D., & Spiegel, N. (1981). Facial autonomic, and subjective components of emotion: The facial feedback hypothesis versus the externalizer–internalizer distinction. *Journal of Personality & Social Psychology, 41,* 929–944.

CHAPTER 9B

Perspectives on Emotional Development II: A Functionalist Approach to Emotions

KAREN CAPLOVITZ BARRETT and JOSEPH J. CAMPOS

BACKGROUND: A PARADIGM SHIFT IN THEORIES OF EMOTION

Over the past decade, much has been written regarding a new zeitgeist in psychology—a zeitgeist in which emotion has once again been deemed an appropriate topic for scientific inquiry (e.g., Campos, Barrett, Lamb, Goldsmith, & Stenberg, 1983; Scherer, 1986). Psychologists are grappling with basic issues regarding the elicitation and expression of emotion. A paradigm shift (Kuhn, 1962) is occurring—theories are moving away from simple stimulus–response orientations to orientations emphasizing personal meanings, organismic strivings, and the *functional importance* of emotions.

Yet amid all of this excitement, several disheartening facts remain: (1) most of the new theories of emotion are not applicable to and/or testable in infants; (2) a cavernous gap remains between the new and exciting theoretical positions, on the one hand, and empirical evidence to substantiate or negate those positions, on the other; and (3) theories of emotional *development* remain prisoners of the "old" paradigm.

In this chapter, we will present a position regarding emotionality and emotional development—a position that begins to address the first and third problems above and that is directed at stimulating research to address the second. An inevitable consequence of any paradigm shift is that the existing literature has emerged from the old paradigm and applies only obliquely to new paradigm positions. Much of what we will have to say, therefore, is quite speculative, and some specific predictions may need to be changed as research progresses. We believe, however, that it is important for us, as researchers and theorists, to make clear our position now, in a fashion that is amenable to empirical test. In this way, our position can serve as impetus for progress in the field of emotional development, such that research can catch up to theory.

Before we explicate our position, we will highlight some points of contrast between it and traditional theories regarding emotionality and emotional development. Some unifying characteristics of traditional positions are: (1) attempts to specify a central criterion that is necessary and sufficient for diagnosing presence of an emotion; and (2) views of emotions as *reified wholes* that are present or absent. In addition, most traditional views of emotional development consider changes in emotionality to be *secondary to* changes in cognitive development. We will examine each of these characteristics in turn.

First, the traditional theory proposes a central, definitive criterion for the "diagnosis" of an emotion's presence. It is clear why theorists would wish to involve themselves in such an enterprise. Pinpointing of such criteria would greatly facilitate research, in that an isomorphism could be drawn between the criterion and the emotion. Thus if one wished to study the effects of an emotion on some other process, one would need only to look for the "emotionomic" criterion and study it in relationship to that process.

There have been many different versions of this approach. Emotions have been defined as feeling states, and operationalized as self-reports. Emotions have been viewed as physiological reactions, and/or the feedback from such reactions (e.g., James, 1890; Lange, 1922). Emotions have been viewed as facial responses, and/ or the feedback from such responses (e.g., Izard & Malatesta, Chapter 9A, this volume). And, perhaps most commonly, emotions have been defined in terms of ordinary cognitive processes, sometimes in conjunction with undifferentiated arousal (e.g., Lewis & Brooks-Gunn, 1979; Schachter & Singer, 1962; Sroufe, 1979; Weiner & Graham, 1984).

It is beyond the scope of this chapter to critique each of these approaches in detail. Our overall criticism is that, although the desire to devise such a singular criterion is admirable, it is doomed to failure. None of these variables, in itself, is necessary nor sufficient to indicate presence of emotionality. The presence of a particular emotion is determined not by documenting a particular type of response, but rather by documenting a particular *set of functional relationships* between an organism and the environment.

It is quite clear that the covariation among different "emotion-defining" variables is far from perfect. In fact, individuals vary widely in their propensities to "emote" via various physiological channels (cf. Lacey, 1967) or via facial expressions, even during infancy (cf. Field, 1982; Rosenthal, 1979). Moreover, individuals who are more facially expressive and who report more intense feelings actually may be *less* expressive physiologically (e.g., Buck, 1979; Field, 1982; Jones, 1930). Why should one believe that the person who is facially expressive and electrodermically unexpressive is experiencing more or less emotionality than is the person who displays the opposite configuration?

Some theorists would construe all of these expressions as indicators of an underlying feeling state, and say that the deciding indicator should be verbal report. The attitude implicit in this perspective is that if you want to know how a person feels, the best way of finding out is to ask that person (e.g., Leventhal, 1984).

Yet this method has as many problems (if not more) as any other method. Many have criticized the use of self-report instruments on the grounds that such reports are prone to social desirability and other demand characteristics (cf. Crowne & Marlowe, 1964; Meehl & Hathaway, 1946). Self-reports of emotionality certainly are not immune to these problems. Moreover, self-reports of emotionality are fraught with additional difficulties. When asked to indicate the extent to which one is feeling particular emotions, one must, at least: (1) define for oneself how one feels when experiencing those emotions; (2) be sensitive to such feeling states; (3) be sensitive to the distinction between these and other feeling states; and (4) be able to quantify the extent to which these feeling states are present. Each of these variables is likely to differ widely across individuals, producing untold perturbations in the validity of such measures of feeling. Yet how else does one determine how a person *feels*?

Which brings us to a second problem with defining emotion as feeling—how can one study *feeling* in babies? Izard and Malatesta (Chapter 9A, this volume) provide provocative logic for believing that facial expressions of emotions are connected directly to feeling states. Although one might take issue with this logic, the implications of their theory for research on infantile emotionality do not rise or fall on the connection between expression and feeling. For them, *facial expressions* rather than reports of feeling are emotionomic.

We would agree with Izard that facial expressions are a useful tool in the study of emotionality during infancy. It is clear that neonates are capable of making all of the muscle movements associated with emotionality, as Izard and Malatesta (Chapter 9A, this volume) have indicated (cf. Oster & Ekman, 1978). Moreover, neonates show the facial patterning associated with particular emotions as well (e.g., disgust: Steiner, 1979; REM-state smiling: Emde, Gaensbauer, & Harmon, 1976). Such findings, in conjunction with research indicating the emotion-specific social communicative value of facial expressions, suggest the utility of facial expressions as indices of emotionality. However, that is precisely the way we would wish to view facial expression—as *one* window on emotionality.

This brings us to the second characteristic of traditional perspectives on emotional development—the notion that emotions are *reified wholes,* which *emerge* at some point in development. That is, each emotion, as a whole, is absent until the point in development when criterial conditions are met (usually particular *cognitive developments:* Buss, 1980; Lewis & Brooks-Gunn, 1979; Sroufe, 1979, or *facial expressions:* Izard & Malatesta, Chapter 9A, this volume).

In contrast to such positions, we do not believe that emotions are wholes that emerge at particular points in development. Nor do we believe it useful to characterize emotions as "true" versus "pseudo," based upon a specific criterion. Rather, we conceive of emotions as multifaceted, protean phenomena that are well characterized by Wittgenstein's (1953) concept of *family resemblance.* That is, no particular criterion is *necessary* for the presence of "the real emotion." Relatives of each emotion family might be seen very early in development, given the right circumstances. Moreover, no single criterion provides sufficient information for one to infer emotionality.

There are *intrinsic* but *not invariant* links between specific emotion families and particular (1) appreciations ("hot" cognitions regarding the significance of organism–environment relationships), (2) goals that these appreciations usually regard, (3) action tendencies, (4) vocalic patterns, (5) physiological patterns, (6) facial movement patterns, and (7) adaptive functions. That is, emotion families typically are associated with particular patterns of these characteristics; however, particular instances of an emotion (family members) may not be associated with one or more of the characteristics. In fact, a particular family member may include additional, learned responses that are not associated with other family members (responses that even may be associated with other families: e.g., the smile of embarrassment, an emotion we view as a member of the shame family). Moreover, some *families* may not have all characteristics (e.g., no specific facial muscle movements have been documented for shame: cf. Ekman, 1984).

We believe that emotion families have "fuzzy boundaries" (Rosch, 1978)—not merely in terms of our labels or concepts of them, but in terms of the appreciations and responses associated with them. We believe that one reason researchers have failed to find consistency among different emotional responses is that slightly different emotions, with concomitant differences in responses, are being evoked in different individuals. Moreover, to the extent that different appreciations and responses are evoked, feedback and the subjective experience of the emotion over time should differ as well (Laird, 1984). As we will elaborate later, the way to determine kinship between two emotions is to ascertain the *similarity between those emotions in the functions they serve.*

The third aspect of most traditional approaches concerns the effect of cognitive development on emotional development. The most influential paradigm in developmental psychology has been Piagetian theory. All of us, entrenched in that perspective, think of development in a particular way. The baby *is* a sensorimotor being who is developing a sense of self and other; the young child *is* a preoperational symbolizer. Thus it is only natural that most initial attempts to describe emotional development have tied emotional developments to changes in broad cognitive abilities (e.g., Lewis & Brooks-Gunn, 1979; Sroufe, 1979). Some of our own research provides a vivid example of this, we believe, mistaken, approach.

Consider research and theory regarding the development of fear. Traditionally, fear has been the prototypical "emergent" emotion. It seemed that all kinds of fears blossomed during the third quarter of the first year of life. "All of a sudden," babies were wary of strangers, masks, jack-in-the-boxes, heights, and so on (cf. Campos, Hiatt, Ramsay, Henderson, & Svejda, 1978; Scarr & Salapatek, 1970). Moreover, these fears were being manifested at about the time that Piaget's stage 4 was predicted to begin. Naturally, captives of the existing paradigm that we were, we thought that the sensorimotor achievement might provide a mechanism for the emergence of fear, at least of fear on the visual cliff. But we were wrong.

In the study designed to test the role of sensorimotor development in the development of fear on the visual cliff (Campos et al., 1978), babies were assigned a Piagetian stage based upon their performance on the Uzgiris-Hunt object permanence tasks. Then locomotor and prelocomotor babies at various stages of object permanence were tested on the deep and shallow sides of the visual cliff, using the direct placement heart rate paradigm. Figure 9B.1 presents the results of that study. As the figure indicates, although *locomotor experience* significantly influenced heart rate acceleration on the deep side of the visual cliff, object permanence stage exerted no such influence. Why did locomotor experience succeed while sensorimotor stage failed? We believe it was because locomotion provided infants with the kinds of experiences that endowed heights with *significance* for the infants. We will discuss our concept of significance, and of how events assume significance for the individual, in the model that follows. First, however, it is important to provide an overview of our concept of emotion.

A NEW APPROACH TO EMOTIONAL DEVELOPMENT

Overview

We conceive of emotions as *bidirectional processes of establishing, maintaining, and/or disrupting significant relationships between an organism and the (external or internal) environment.* They are *bidirectional* in that they involve the interdigi-

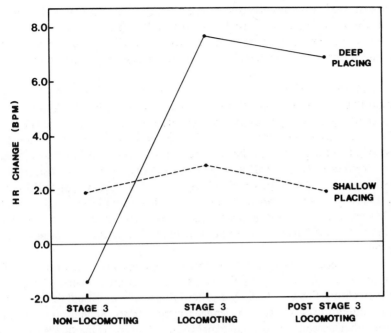

Figure 9B.1. Heart rate responses of 7.3 month old human infants as they are lowered to the deep and shallow sides of the visual cliff.

tating impact of the environment and the organism upon each other. They are *processes* in that both organism and environment are constantly changing in relationship to one another: A change in one evokes a change in the other. They are *relational:* The emotional quality associated with an event is dependent upon how that event affects an organism, and the quality of the organism's emotional response is determined, in part, by the implications of that response for the environmental event. And, finally, the relationships are *significant*—the impact of environment and organism upon each other has implications for that organism's adaptive functioning in that environment.

What Endows Event–Organism Relationships with Significance?

We believe that there are at least three major sources of such significance. First, certain event–organism relationships are significant because they concern biologically given, "prewired" survival goals of the organism. The organism need not *acquire* an appreciation of the significance of these relationships: Biology has endowed the organism with this appreciation because of the implications for the organism's well-being. Examples of this type of significance are the neonate's interactions with gustatory substances—facial disgust to and oral rejection of bitter or sour substances, and ingestive and "savoring" responses to sweet substances (Lipsitt, 1979; Rozin & Fallon, in press; Steiner, 1979). The survival value of such responses is clear—natural substances that are sweet are fit to eat, whereas those that are bitter or sour often may be poisonous or unripe.

Negative emotional responses to abrupt sensory onsets (e.g., sudden loss of support: Irwin, 1932; sudden, loud noises: Gunnar, 1980; explosive visual field expansion: Yonas, 1981) may involve such "prewired" significance as well. Thus the abrupt, vestibular stimulation sensed in a near fall (e.g., a baby plunging its hand down over an edge while crawling) may endow drop-offs with significance, and may be one mechanism for the relationship between crawling experience and fear of heights.

A second source of significance is social communication—another organism's emotional reaction to an event. Babies may be biologically prepared to respond to this source of significance as well; however, the important difference is that another organism's reactions may endow *virtually any ambiguous event* with significance—not just events with properties that nature "anticipates." In other words, although *affective contagion* (e.g., Hoffman, 1977), *affective attunement* (Stern, 1985), or *emotional resonance* (Campos & Stenberg, 1981; Klinnert, Campos, Sorce, Emde, & Svejda, 1983) may be "prewired" processes, they provide a means through which an endless variety of event–organism relationships can *acquire* significance (see Mineka, 1985, for evidence of nonhuman primates' reactions to others' emotional expressions).

There is a plethora of research indicating that infants' reactions to affectively ambiguous events are shaped by the emotional reactions of others (e.g., see Feinman, 1982; Klinnert et al., 1983). We believe that such emotional reactions of others endow ambiguous events with significance for the infants. Such infants do not merely mimic the other person's emotional expressions; their instrumental reactions toward the ambiguous events/objects are shaped by the meaning of the emotional expression. We believe that social communication thus may provide a second mechanism through which babies' locomotor experience helps induce wariness of heights. If an infant almost ventures over a drop-off, its care giver is likely to react emotionally, often by screaming, fearfully, for the baby to stop. In this way, significance of drop-offs may be learned.

However, we do not believe that the influence of social communication is limited to endowing significance to *ambiguous* events. Although there is less evidence of this process, we believe that another's emotional communication can cause an organism to *change* its appreciation of an "unambiguous" (already significant) event. We think that this is an especially important process in the induction of "social emotions," such as shame and guilt (see below). In many situations relevant to these emotions, the organism already *likes* or *desires* to do something, but learns that this action is prohibited. A major vehicle through which the organism learns to avoid engaging in such an act may be a socializer's affective communication regarding it. The socializer's affect-laden reasoning about prohibited acts is associated with increased guilt-relevant behavior (Zahn-Waxler, Radke-Yarrow, & King, 1979). Moreover, in guilt-relevant situations in which the organism has harmed someone, affective communication from the *socializer* may serve to highlight affective communiucation by the *victim* of the wrongdoing (Hoffman, 1970; Zahn-Waxler et al., 1979). We believe that this is an example of how social communication, the second significance-inducing process, might change existing appreciations. We predict that this type of "appreciation change" will be most successful if social communication (1) is provided by an individual whom the organism respects, trusts, and/or views as authoritative and (2) is given repeatedly, over an extended period.

A third source of significance of an event–organism relationship derives from the event's implications for the organism's ongoing goals and strivings. The goals of the organism described in conjunction with the first source of significance were prewired and all-pervasive (survival value always implies significance). In contrast, the goals in this third source may be learned, and regard ends toward which the organism is striving concurrently.

This source of significance results in a highly variable relationship between "stimulus" and emotion. Depending upon a particular individual's strivings, the same stimulus may evoke joy, anger, sadness, or any number of other emotions. For example, if a care giver brings a high chair into the room, a hungry baby may experience joy, whereas a baby who is happily playing may experience anger. Bringing in the high chair implies facilitation of the hungry baby's goals, whereas it implies thwarting of the playing baby's goals.

Moreover, two organisms with *the same goal* should react differently to the same stimulus event if their appreciations differ regarding how that event affects that goal. The requisite studies to test this phenomenon have not been conducted; however, some studies do seem relevant to it. For example, in one study (Caplovitz, Morgan, & Mardashti, 1982), infants all had access to a manipulandum and all observed a jack-in-the-box toy's emergence. No other toys were available, maximizing the likelihood that the manipulandum would be pressed and the jack-in-the-box observed. Infants in a contingent condition *caused* the jack-in-the-box to emerge by pressing the manipulandum, whereas those in a noncontingent condition pressed the manipulandum to no avail. The infants were yoked such that noncontingent and contingent infants received the same number of jack-in-the-box stimuli. The difference between the conditions was that if infants tried to control the jack-in-the-box contingent infants would succeed while noncontingent infants would not.

There was some evidence that noncontingent infants tried to control the jack-in-the-box in that they pressed the manipulandum more frequently if the jack-in-the-box jumped up more frequently. However, whereas contingent infants smiled more as they pressed the manipulandum more, there was no relationship between pressing and smiling in the noncontingent condition. It seemed that contingent infants, who succeeded in controlling the jack-in-the-box, derived joy from the event, whereas noncontingent infants, who did not succeed, did not derive joy from it.

Emotion Families and Characteristics of Those Families

As we stated earlier, we conceive of emotions as members of families, characterized by *intrinsic* but not *invariant* features: (1) particular action tendencies; (2) particular types of appreciations regarding the significance of ongoing event–organism encounters; (3) the goals that these appreciations typically regard; (4) particular vocalic quality/intonation patterns; (5) (at least for certain families, termed *basic emotions* by many theorists) particular patterns of facial movement; (6) particular physiological patterns; and (7) particular adaptive functions.

Before we outline patterns hypothesized for specific families, certain notions should be clarified. First of all, by *intrinsic* we mean that one need not learn to associate the characteristic with the family. The universality of interpretation of certain facial expressions has been best documented (cf. Ekman, 1973; Izard, 1971); moreover, recent research and theory specifying emotion-specific physiological patterns (Ekman, Levenson, & Friesen, 1983) and vocal patterns (Frick, 1985; Scherer, 1986) are quite promising. Much more research is needed to document these physiological and vocalic patterns, and even more is needed to document the virtually unstudied action tendencies we will propose.

By *action tendencies,* we mean *organisms' dispositions to perform behaviors that fulfill a particular function with respect to the environment.* They are *dispositions to act,* which need not actually be realized in overt action. Moreover, the meaning of any resultant overt behavior is defined by a *functional relationship between organism and environment.* Thus an action tendency to approach need not literally lead to approach behavior, especially in older children and adults. A coping behavior that "brings one closer" to something, for example, reading or even thinking about that something, may be utilized instead. Similarly, a baby's action tendency to avoid/protect itself from a fear-inducing event may be realized as a tendency to cling to the caregiver. Action tendencies are particularly intriguing aspects of emotion in that they are *flexible* motor programs, impelling the organism toward a particular functional relationship with the animate and/or inanimate environment. As such, they intervene directly in the emotion process.

Recently, there has been increasing theoretical interest in goal-oriented action (cf. *Human Development, 27* (3–4), 1984); however, remarkably few studies have concerned adaptive behavioral consequences of emotion induction (exceptions include Campos et al., 1978; Frijda, 1986; Gunnar, 1980; Klinnert et al., 1983; Shaver et al., in press).

Moreover, more direct investigation of action *tendencies* is completely lacking. We think it quite likely that subtle movements, more literally congruent with a particular action tendency, could often be detected as initial emotional responses (*preceding* overt behavior). Systems permitting the objective characterization of movement (e.g., Laban, 1974) could be applied to such emotion-relevant movements. However, although objective movement analyses have been used to investigate characteristics of infants' reflexive movements and motor skill acquisition (cf. Thelen, 1984; Thelen & Fisher, 1983), they have not been applied to such emotion-relevant precoping movements. In a recently edited volume regarding *developmental kinesics,* for example, not a single article concerned emotion-relevant functional movements (Hoffer & St. Clair, 1981).

Furthermore, in addition to this type of objective assessment, which only is useful if there is a perceptible movement, it seems possible that EMG could detect even more subtle action tendency movements. Objective characterization of emotion-relevant movement is an important domain for future research.

Still, we emphasize that neither the action tendency nor any of the other characteristics is *invariant:* Only a subset of the attributes may be observable in any particular family member. It may be that, at least in some cases, sensitive measurement might detect low-level, residual emotional responses that have been dampened due to socialization pressures. However, we also think it likely that some, or even most, particular organism—environment relations do not elicit all responses.

Another concept to clarify is that of the *appreciation*—a notion quite similar to many recent characterizations of "hot" cognitions (e.g., Ekman, 1984; Lazarus, 1985; Scherer, 1986). We use the term *appreciation* rather than *appraisal* to underscore the fact that the cognitive process need not be deliberative, conscious, or sophisticated. It may consist, for example, of simple detection that a substance is sweet, with the associated implications to a prewired, organismic goal. The important feature of an appreciation is that *significance* of an organism–event relationship is assessed; the sophistication of processing may range from sensation to abstraction.

Finally, we wish to clarify how our emotion families relate to most theorists' notions of *basic* and *complex* emotions. Unlike many theorists, we do not consider certain emotion families to be basic emotion building blocks, out of which other complex emotions are constructed. We do think it is useful to make distinctions among several "fuzzy categories" of emotions; however, we do not consider any class more fundamental than any other. Furthermore, we acknowledge that there is overlap among the categories. A particular member of an emotion family may fall in one class, even though the majority of family members fall in a different class. Moreover, certain *families* (e.g., affection) "fit" most criteria for one class but are characterized by one or two criteria appropriate for a different class.

We base our classification of emotion families upon the following criteria: (1) the typical processes of attaining significance associated with an emotion family (as these processes were described earlier)—process one (innately determined appreciation of survival value of stimuli), process two (socially communicated significance), or process three (ongoing goal relevance); (2) the extent to which appreciations concern other organisms, as well as the organism itself; (3) the extent to which the *goals* with which the emotion family is concerned have been developed through socialization; and (4) the extent to which the emotion family may be communicated socially via discrete facial expressions versus posture and demeanor.

Class 1 (primordial emotion families) and Class 2 (concurrent-goal emotion families) are two classes that typically have been termed basic emotions by other theorists. Although we think it likely that the appreciations associated with each of these emotion families *may* attain significance via any of the three processes described earlier, each of these classes is most likely to employ particular processes. Class 1, which includes emotions like disgust and fear, usually involves the first and/or second process of attaining significance—innately determined appreciation of survival value of stimuli and/or socially communicated significance. Class 2, on the other hand, which includes families like anger and sadness, usually involves the second or third process of attaining significance—social communication and/or ongoing goal relevance. The implication of this difference is that elicitation of primordia (Class 1) emotions is more closely tied to *particular stimulus parameters* than is elicitation of concurrent-goal (Class 2) emotions. Primordial and concurrent-goal families are similar to one another, however, in that each can be communicated socially by discrete, context-independent facial expressions.

A third group, Class 3 (the social emotions), includes families traditionally characterized as complex, such as shame, guilt, pride, and envy. These families, like Class 2 families, involve the second and third processes of achieving significance. However, the *goals* with which we believe these emotions are concerned are developed through socialization (Campos & Barrett, 1984). In addition, each of these emotions seems associated not only with an appreciation regarding *the organism itself,* but also with an appreciation regarding *others*. Third, these emotions seem to be communicated socially by voice, gesture, posture, and demeanor, but not by discrete, context-free facial expressions.

Table 9B.1 summarizes characteristics of some emotion families, as suggested by

TABLE 9B.1. Characteristics of Some Emotion Families

Emotion Family	Goal	Appreciation re:Self	Appreciation re:Other	Action Tendency
Disgust	Avoiding contamination or illness	This stimulus may contaminate me, or cause illness	[a]	Active rejection
Fear	Maintaining integrity of the self (physical or psychological integrity)	This stimulus threatens my integrity	[a]	Flight; active withdrawal
Anger	Any end state that the organism currently is invested in achieving	There is an obstacle to my obtaining my goal	[a]	Active forward movement, especially to eliminate obstacles
Sadness	Any end state that the organism currently is invested in achieving	My goal is unattainable	[a]	Disengagement; passive withdrawal
Shame	Maintenance of others' respect and affection; preservation of self-esteem	I am bad (self-esteem is perceived to be impaired)	Someone/everyone notices how bad I am	Active or passive withdrawal; avoiding others; hiding of self
Guilt	Meeting one's own internalized standards	I have done something contrary to my standards	Someone has been injured by my act	Outward movement; inclination to make reparation, to inform others, and to punish oneself
Pride	Maintenance of the respect of oneself and others	I am good (I have respect for myself)	Someone/everyone thinks (or will think) I am good	Outward/upward movement; inclination to show/inform others about one's accomplishments

[a] No "appreciation re: other" is *central* to primordial or concurrent-goal emotions; however, certain particular family members might involve such an appreciation.
[b] These facial movements are adapted from Izard (1979).
[c] These facial movements are adapted from Ekman et al. (1983).
[d] Ekman et al. (1983) found increased heart rate with sadness; however, *decreased* heart rate is consistent with our theoretical position on *sadness*. We think it possible that most subjects in Ekman et al.'s study experienced an agitated grief state rather than a sad, "giving-up" state.
[e] These facial movements are adapted from Scherer (1986).

564

Adaptive Functions	Facial Expression[b]	Physiological Reaction[c]	Vocalic Pattern[e]
Avoid contamination and illness; learn about substances/ events/attributes to avoid; alert others re: contamination	Brows lowered, nose wrinkled, with widened nasal root; raised cheeks and upper lip	Low heart rate and skin temperature; increased skin resistance	Nasal, slightly tense, "very narrow," but fairly full and powerful voice
Avoid danger (physical and psychological); learn about events/ attributes that are dangerous; alert others re: danger	Brows raised and often pulled slightly together; eyes very wide and tense, rigidly fixated on stimulus	High, stable heart rate; low skin temperature; "gasping" respiration	"Narrow," extremely tense, very weak, thin, high voice
Attain difficult goals; learn to overcome obstacles and achieve goals; communicate power/dominance	Brows lowered and pulled together; mouth open and square or lips pressed tightly together	High heart rate and skin temperature; facial flushing	"Narrow," medium to very tense, medium to extremely full voice
Conserve energy; learn which goals are realizable; encourage nurturance of others	Inner corners of brows moved upward; corners of mouth pulled downward, often with middle of chin pulled upward	Low heart rate;[d] Low skin temperature and skin resistance	"Narrow," thin, lax, slow, or halting voice
Behave appropriately; learn/maintain social standards; communicate submission to others and to others' standards	—	Low heart rate; blushing	"Narrow," moderately lax, thin voice
Behave prosocially; learn/maintain moral and prosocial behavior; communicate contrition/good intentions	—	High heart rate and skin conductance; irregular respiration	"Narrow," tense, moderately full voice
Behave appropriately; learn/maintain social standards; communicate ability to meet standards	—	High heart rate	"Wide," medium tense, full voice

current research and theory. It lists the type of goals with which each family typically is concerned, despite our realization that emotions induced via social communication may not concern these goals.

Some important features of the model are outlined in this table. First of all, note that not all characteristics are associated with all families—no facial expression is listed for the social emotions (shame, guilt, and pride), and no "appreciation re: other" is listed for either the primordial emotions (disgust and fear) or concurrent-goal emotions (anger and sadness). The omission of an "appreciation re: other" for primordial and concurrent-goal emotions is not meant to imply that these emotion families *never* regard a social situation. Rather it is meant to underscore the fact that, whereas appreciations regarding others are *central* to the social emotions, many instances of the primordial and concurrent-goal emotions involve no social force at all.

Second, note that the goals associated with different classes of emotion differ. Primordial emotions concern specific, pervasive (always significant) goals, with clear survival value; concurrent-goal emotions concern any end state that the organism concurrently is invested in achieving; and social emotions concern goals constructed via socialization.

Third, note that appreciations are expressed in very general terms in Table 9B.1. Thus many different particular organism–environment encounters may be appreciated in each of the ways described in the table, and they may be appreciated at any level of cognitive sophistication.

We also wish to highlight the "action tendencies" and "adaptive functions" columns, because these are attributes that few researchers emphasize (an exception is Frijda, in press).

First, certain attributes of action tendencies should be highlighted. Notice that approach tendencies accompany certain negative as well as certain positive emotions. In fact, inclination to inform others is predicted to accompany both guilt and pride—two emotions that some would consider opposites.

Note also that some emotion families are associated with passive tendencies, and others with active tendencies. The active tendencies are predicted to be accompanied by tensing and activation, with accompanying hypertonic musculature. On the other hand, passive tendencies are predicted to be accompanied by deactivation and hypotonic musculature.

A special comment regarding activation and *sadness* is warranted. As Scherer (1986) points out, some studies regarding arousal and sadness seem to contradict others. We agree with him that the most likely explanation for these contradictions is that *different* emotions are being elicited in different studies—in some cases, a highly arousing, acute anguish/distress is elicited, whereas in others, a deactivating "giving up" (more in keeping with our sadness) is elicited. We wish to reserve the term *sadness* for the *deactivating* form of response. Whether these two forms of sadness serve the same functions (and thus belong to the same family), however, deserves further investigation.

Next, we wish to highlight the "adaptive functions" column. Note that three functions are listed for each family, separated by semicolons. The first function listed concerns behavior-regulatory functions; the second concerns internal-regulatory functions; and the third concerns social-regulatory functions. We consider these three types of functions the hallmark of emotionality—these functions make emotions crucial forces in human development. Unlike language, emotions serve these functions from earliest infancy. Moreover, their functions are never replaced. Even while an individual communicates verbally, his or her vocalics, facial expressions, and body movements provide crucial "metamessages" regarding the *true meaning* of the words and relationship between speaker and listener (Bateson, Jackson, Haley, & Weakland, 1956; Watzlawick, Beavin, & Jackson, 1967).

Emotional Development During Infancy: Overview

Table 9B.1 describes characteristics of emotion families *throughout development.* We believe that these features are associated with particular emotion families throughout the life span. However, we clearly do not believe that emotions remain unchanged during the course of development. On the contrary, we believe that emotional development includes: (1) the addition of new members to emotion families (e.g., addition of "fear of impending financial disaster" to the fear family); (2) an increasing ability to appreciate new organism–environment relationships as significant; (3) increasing responsiveness to multiple aspects of a situation (often resulting in multiple or "mixed" emotions); (4) the development of new strategies for coping or enacting action tendencies; (5) increasing adeptness at using emotional expressions *instrumentally,* to influence others; (6) the development of new goals, and of appreciations regarding those goals; and (7) increasing ability to use language to communicate and/or obfuscate emotions and needs. We believe that two major influences upon these developments are cognitive development and socialization. But, we want to emphasize, cognitive development and socialization result in changes in emotionality *only through their influence upon emotion-relevant attributes—either the attributes in Table 9B.1, or the functions those attributes serve.*

As we indicated earlier, we do not conceive of emotion families as emergent phenomena. That is, we believe that emotion families develop through a process of accretion, in which new family members may become evident later in development, but relatives of those family members were apparent earlier, and remain possible throughout development. Emotions are considered "related" to the extent that they *serve the same or similar functions.*

Table 9B.1 helps in organizing characterization of emotions as "relatives." To the extent that the characteristics in Table 9B.1 are shared between emotions, the associated (1) internal–regulatory functions (for facial expressions, vocalic expressions, physiological expressions, action tendencies, and appreciations), (2) social-regulatory functions (for facial expressions, vocalic expressions, action tendencies, and certain physiological reactions), and/or (3) adaptive behavior–regulatory functions (for action tendencies, appreciations, and physiological responses) are shared as well.

However, as we alluded to earlier, the crucial consideration in judging "kinship" is not whether the *responses* associated with the emotions are identical. Rather, it is the extent to which these three types of functions are the same for the emotions being compared. The similarity of internal-regulatory functions may be examined in studies of the impact of emotion induction upon other processes (e.g., memory). Social-regulatory similarity may be assessed through studies of others' judgments of the expressor's emotion, or through social referencing or social comparison studies, in which the "receiver's" behavior is influenced by the communicator's emotional expression. Adaptive behavior–regulatory functions may be assessed in studies of the impact of emotion induction upon organisms' interactions with the environment. If the emotions being compared serve the same internal-, social-, *and* adaptive behavior–regulatory functions, they belong to the same family. To the extent that one or more of the functions differ, and to the extent that any functional similarity is restricted to a circumscribed set of situations, the emotions are more distantly related. Thus the criteria in Table 9B.1 serve as *guides* in the determination of relatedness of emotions; however, "related" emotions need not share all, or even more, of those characteristics.

Influences of Cognitive Development

Despite our assertions that the emotional development is not *secondary* to cognitive development, we do believe that systematic changes in emotion families occur as a function of cognitive development. In particular, cognitive development: (1) increases the number and variety of organism–environment interactions that can be appreciated as significant; (2) increases the number of aspects of complex organism–environment interaction that can be appreciated as significant (often, with appreciations from several emotion families being provoked in the same situation); (3) increases the variety and number of *coping* responses with which the organism can enact an action tendency; and (4) increases the organism's ability to modulate consciously its emotional reactions, utilizing display rules, coping rules, and/or feeling rules. Thus cognitive development may make important contributions to the *breadth and complexity* of emotionality, *through its influence upon one or more of the aspects of emotion families, or the functions served by those aspects.* Cognitive developments are neither necessary nor sufficient for the developmental onset of particular emotion families; however, they are influential upon emotional development.

Socialization Influences

Perhaps even more influential on emotional development is socialization, and in recent years, increasing attention has been devoted to this topic (cf. Lewis & Saarni, 1985). However, we believe that some of the most important domains of emotion socialization have been neglected, both in theory and in research. We therefore will devote somewhat more space to outlining types of emotion socialization than we did to describing influences of cognitive development, in hopes of highlighting these neglected domains.

Unlike theorists and researchers writing in the 1950s and 1960s, few theorists today speak of the *creation* or *social construction* of discrete emotions through learning principles. In fact, when the typical theorist describes socialization of emotion, he or she focuses upon a very specific domain—the "disconnecting" of feeling from expression, due to display rules (rules regarding socially acceptable expression: see Ekman & Friesen, 1975; Izard & Malatesta, Chapter 9A, this volume; Malatesta & Haviland, 1985).

We agree that display rules exist, and that they may importantly influence emotionality. However, display rules are important not because they disconnect expression from experience, but rather because they serve important social- and internal-regulatory functions.

Furthermore, we emphasize that these rules comprise only one effect of socialization upon emotionality. Socialization does not merely change the way emotions *look and sound;* it changes the very nature of emotionality in later development. Although we would never claim that all emotionality is socially created, we believe that too little emphasis is placed upon how *new members of emotion families may be socially constructed.*

We believe that new members of emotion families are constructed throughout development, via socialization influences upon: (1) the ascription of *significance* to organism–environment relationships; (2) the ability to cope with organism–environment relationships and/or emotional phenomenology—to enact or counteract action tendencies; (3) the "average expectable environment" the person faces (and thus the types of organism–environment relations that occur); and (4) the tendency to display particular facial patterns, vocalic patterns, and/or physiological patterns under particular circumstances.

First, socialization affects ascriptions of significance to organism–environment relationships. Socialization is relevant to all three of the significance-endowing processes we described earlier. Even process 1 (prewired significance) may be affected by socialization, as when one acquires disgust for "sticky sweet" tastes, because one learns from others that sugar is fattening. However, socialization is especially relevant to the second (social communication) and third processes (ongoing goal relevance).

Social communication *is* a process of socialization. We already have described how another's nonverbal emotional expressions may endow novel events with significance, or even known and appreciated events with new significance. We believe this is one of the most important sources of new family members, especially during infancy. However, social communication need not take the form of nonverbal emotional communication, nor need it be conveyed while the "receiving" organism is experiencing an event. It may take the form of verbal emotional communication, as when the parent labels the child's, the parent's own, or another person's emotional reaction (cf. Lewis & Michalson, 1982). Nor only might such labeling provide the child with a lexicon for referring to emotional states, it might enable him or her to make inferences regarding the feelings and organism–environment relations associated with the labeled emotions. Lewis and Michalson (1982) have hypothesized that inappropriate labeling might contribute to the development of psychopathology—children might learn to make the "wrong" inferences, and to experience inappropriate affect.

Social communication also may take the form of verbal information, as when a socializer explicitly highlights particular organism–environment relations contributing to an emotion. Or it may take the form of communication via the media (books, cartoons, television, billboards), as when "He-man" gets angry because "bad guys" do bad things, or when people "have a great time" while drinking beer on a television commercial. It may involve pervasive cultural expectations, communicated in a multiplicity of ways.

Levy (1984) has described how cultures *hypocognize* certain emotions and *hypercognize* others. In given cultures, some emotions do not even warrant a verbal label, whereas others are discussed at length, as part of extensive cultural scripts. Levy notes that even hypocognized feelings seem to be *elicited* by the same organism–environment relations that would elicit those emotions in other cultures.

However, the resulting states are *interpreted* quite differently in the absence of a specific cultural script. For example, in Tahiti, the emotions we call *sadness* or *depression* are given labels like *feeling fatigued* or *feeling heavy*—various terms for general discomfort. Moreover, loss of an end state in which one is invested, such as a relationship with a loved one, is not assigned significance in the generation of sadness. The state is usually ascribed to some physical cause, such as illness or evil spirits.

These cultural beliefs clearly imply a different appreciation of significance than would be expected in middle-class America. The organism–environment relationships that we would hold responsible for the feeling are not noted; the feeling is attributed to physical sources. Moreover, the different appreciations also imply different forms of behavior and internal regulation. In Tahiti, a person who loses a lover might purchase an herbal remedy to assuage the bad feelings, rather than becoming reinvested in more promising relationships. In addition, such an individual would be unlikely to learn from the feeling that he or she truly cared for the lost individual, but rather might "learn" that there are evil spirits in the household. Thus cultural communications regarding feeling states or emotions may shape significance, and with it, the adaptive functions of the emotion family induced.

The third process of endowing significance (ongoing goal relevance) is crucially influenced by socialization as well. This is especially true for goals relevant to the social emotions. The overall goals with which these emotions are concerned (e.g., meeting social standards, for shame and pride) must be endowed with significance through socialization—one must learn that "socially appropriate" behavior is desirable. Moreover, each case of induction of a social emotion involves a particular instantiation of the overall goal. Particular standards, which become the immediate pursuits, are sanctioned explicitly and implicitly both by individual socializers and by the larger culture.

For example, *achievement* is a highly valued goal in certain families and cultures, whereas it is devalued, or even considered undesirable, in others. As a result, in middle-class America, where achievement is valued, an especially high achiever would usually feel pride in his or her accomplishments, and an underachiever would likely feel shame. Even toddlers in our culture may become distressed upon failing to meet an achievement standard (Kagan, 1981). On the other hand, a society stressing cooperation might view the high achiever quite differently—as an individual always in pursuit of his or her own goals, at the expense of striving to help others. A different goal would be valued and focused upon—that of cooperation and helpfulness, rather than achievement. As a result, the exceptionally high achiever would feel *shame* to the extent that the societal standards of cooperation and helpfulness were not fulfilled.

Socialization of goal significance is not limited to social emotions, however. Particular goals for concurrent-goal emotions may acquire significance through socialization as well. For example, an adult may become angry upon hearing that he paid more for a house than he "should have." The goal of getting the best price for a purchase certainly would not be significant to a baby; its significance is learned through socialization.

Not only is *significance* influenced by socialization; *"appropriate" ways of enacting or counteracting action tendencies* are socialized as well—again, both explicitly and implicitly, at the family level and at the societal level. A major function of child rearing is to guide children in coping with emotionally arousing situations in "appropriate" ways. Some families, subcultures, and cultures, for example, encourage overt aggression in response to anger, whereas others advise "turning the other cheek." Popular children's songs reflect such social prescriptions. For example, one song advises counteraction of defeat/depression action tendencies: "Hold out your chest, and lift up your chin. Half the battle is picking up the pieces and starting over again" (Michaelf, 1984). Interestingly, some evidence suggests that it would be more adaptive to "give in" to the inclination to slump—subjects who were positioned in a "slump" following failure (by experimenter instruction) actually persisted longer at working insoluble puzzles than did those who were positioned in a "proud," chest-out demeanor (Riskind, 1984). Such findings highlight the complex internal- and behavior-regulatory impact of socialization of action tendencies.

In addition to these familial and cultural influences on significance and action tendencies, the likelihood of encountering particular organism–environment relationships (and thus of experiencing a particular emotion family) is shaped by these same influences. The "average expectable environment" an organism encounters depends upon familial and cultural norms. For example, most babies in our culture have a primary caregiver but are at times left with a substitute caregiver. On the other hand, most babies in Japan are never left with a substitute caregiver. This factor may contribute to the greater distress Japanese babies seem to exhibit when left with a stranger (Miyake, Chen, & Campos, 1985; Takahashi, 1986).

This average expectable environment may provide one reason for the apparent emergence of some emotion families: The types of experiences that induce these emotions simply are not encountered by most very young infants in our culture. For example, sadness often has been thought to emerge at 6–8 months, when the caregiver becomes a permanent object. However, a case study of an abused child indicates that it is *possible* to show sadness much earlier (Gaensbauer, 1980). The average child is not exposed to the harmful environment that this child experienced, however, and is unlikely to have many occasions for experiencing sadness.

A final effect of socialization upon emotion is to regulate facial, vocalic, and physiological expressions. There is much evidence that adults and children regulate their facial expressions in accordance with social prescriptions, and are aware of such regulation (e.g., Ekman & Friesen, 1975; Feldman, White, & Labato, 1982; Saarni, 1982; Shennum & Bugental, 1982). Moreover, beginning in early infancy, parents respond differentially to their babies' various emotional expressions (Izard & Malatesta, Chapter 9A, this volume; Malatesta & Haviland, 1982). There is less evidence regarding socialization of the other channels (voice and physiology), but such socialization seems to occur as well (cf. Malatesta & Haviland, 1985).

As mentioned earlier, we think that these display rules are important not because they disconnect emotional expression for experience, but because of the internal- and social-regulatory impact of these socialized expressions. In fact, display rules should not disconnect facial expression from physiology or phenomenology. Posed, faked, exaggerated, and neutralized expressions influence physiological arousal and self-reported phenomenology in accordance with their appearance (Ekman et al., 1983; Laird, 1974; Zuckerman, Klorman, Larrance, & Spiegel, 1981). Thus display rules serve not to disconnect expression from experience, but rather to change experience in accordance with expression. We would not expect the experience to be identical for posed and spontaneous expressions; however, neither would we expect the experience to be identical for the "same emotion" when display rules do and do not change the expression.

Moreover, virtually all social discourse relies upon socialized expression. Emotional communications serve as metamessages regarding all else that is said and done (cf. Bateson et al., 1956). "Inappropriate" expressions change the communication and the receiver's evaluation of the communicator. In fact, extreme cases of inappropriateness can lead the receiver to question the communicator's sanity. We believe that these are the most important topics for research on display rule development: how the development of appropriate display rule usage versus *deficits* in display rule usage (in relationship to the norms for that age) affects social communication. We also think it important to study other instrumental uses of expressions, and their effects on social communication at various points in development.

In summary, we believe that every aspect of emotionality is influenced by socialization—including the important functions that emotions serve for the developing organism. Many of the most important topics regarding emotion socialization have been neglected, leaving this as a very important area for future research.

Influence of Emotions upon Other Processes of Development

In the previous sections, we described influences of cognitive development and socialization upon emotional development. In this section, we examine briefly the reciprocal influence of emotion upon cognitive development and socialization/learning.

It is beyond the scope of this chapter to review all of the research regarding the influence of emotion upon cognitive processes and learning (most of which was executed with adults). However, we do wish at least to outline certain points regarding this topic, because this area of research (1) highlights the adaptive significance of emotions to the developing organism and (2), as mentioned earlier, provides a means of determining the "relatedness' of different emotions.

Increasing empirical attention has been devoted to the influence of emotion upon learning and cognitive processing, and the accumulating evidence suggests a multiplicity of such effects. An organism's emotional state (or perhaps, in some cases, its exposure to emotion-relevant meaning) seems to influence: (1) its inclination to continue ongoing learning or rehearsal of learned material (Campos & Barrett, 1984; Piaget, 1962; Sroufe, 1979); (2) its creativity or divergent thinking during problem-solving (Isen, 1984; Matas, Arend, & Sroufe, 1978); (3) the type of material (positive vs. negative) it is most likely to remember (Blaney, 1986; Isen, 1984); (4) its judgments of ambiguous events and/or people (e.g., Bargh & Pietromonaco, 1982); and (5) its formation of hedonic categories (Bell, 1970; Spitz & Wolf, 1946).

Moreover, *another's* emotional communication is likely to influence not only these five aspects of learning, but also: the organism's (6) social–cognitive development (the organism's increasing understanding of others: e.g., Borke, 1971; Gnepp, 1983); (7) likelihood of attending to another's words and behavior (and thus of learning from him or her: Fernald, 1984); and (8) acquisition of language (Bruner, 1977; Fernald, 1984).

In addition, we propose an unstudied hypothesis—that affect induction may serve as an organizer for the encoding of relevant material, in analogy to the function of associative mnemonics. Through its organizing effects, affect might facilitate later recall of that material, even if the mood is not reinstated. Such an effect might be especially important in relationship to guilt, shame, and pride, in that it might lead to rapid, permanent learning of socially and/or morally appropriate behavior when one of these emotions is induced. Kety (1976) has described potential physiological (neurotransmitter) mechanisms for such an effect.

Finally, we predict that these influences are not limited to effects of negative emotionality and positive emotionality: *Specific* effects of *particular* emotion families should be observable as well.

Directions for Future Research

Throughout this chapter, we have suggested important domains for future research. In this final section, we would like to summarize some of those suggestions. First of all, basic research is needed regarding the *functions* of emotions.

What are the *internal-regulatory* effects of different emotions? How does emotion induction influence information processing and learning during infancy? Some research has indicated that active crying may interfere with infants' memorial skills (Fagen, Ohr, Fleckenstein, & Ribner, 1985). However, this research did not indicate clearly that *emotion,* per se, influenced memory. Engaging in any extraneous and/ or competing activity during encoding might have produced the same results. More research is needed on this and other related topics. Do different emotion families differentially affect memory and learning? Might emotions, even "negative" emotions such as shame or guilt, *aid* in the encoding of "relevant" material? How does intensity of each type of emotion affect such processes? Are emotion-laden categories recalled more easily than "neutral" categories? If so, does this depend upon the type of emotion and/or type of material being categorized? These are just some questions for research on internal-regulatory effects of emotion.

Another important research area concerns the adaptive behavior–regulatory effects of different emotions. Research has indicated that brief exposure to another's emotional communication influences infants' behavioral reactions to ongoing ambiguous events (cf. Klinnert et al., 1983). What are the effects of emotional communication that occurs over an extended period, in the baby's natural environment (e.g., as part of socialization at home or in day care)? What are the long-term effects of such emotional communication? Can such communications *change* existing behavioral orientations to events? What are the behavior-regulatory implications of emotions induced by processes other than social communication, such as frustration, prevention, or potentiation of infants' attainment of ongoing goals?

What are the *social*-regulatory implications of babies' emotional expressions? There is evidence that babies' spontaneous facial expressions affect mothers' facial expressions (Malatesta & Haviland, 1982). How do a baby's spontaneous facial expressions impact caregivers' (and other persons') behavior? There is evidence that babies' cries affect their mothers' overt behavior (e.g., Bernal, 1972). How do their noncry vocalics affect others' behavior? What is the developmental course of *instrumental* use of emotional expression? How do children's feigned or instrumental expressions affect others' behavior?

In addition to research regarding *functions* of emotion, research is needed regarding *action tendencies* associated with different emotion families. Are there specific, objectively discriminable action tendencies associated with specific emotion families? How are action tendencies enacted or counteracted in various situations and at various points in development? What socialization factors influence children's ways of enacting/counteracting different action tendencies?

Other topics concern the social emotions, about which little is known for the infancy/toddlerhood period. What is the developmental course of these emotions? What behavioral, facial, vocalic, and physiological responses are associated with them? What socialization factors influence children's susceptibility and style of responding to these emotions? What are the functional implications of the social emotions?

Finally, we want to highlight the need to study the functions of emotion language. It now is clear that toddlers use emotion language almost as soon as they can speak (Bretherton, McNew, & Beeghly-Smith, 1981). Moreover, socializers use emotion terms to label even *preverbal* infants' behavior (Lewis & Michalson, 1982). How does the development of emotion language affect induction, expression, and behavior regulation of the labeled emotions? How does it affect the influence of social communication on emotionality?

These are just some of the many questions that deserve further study. The paradigm shift in theories of emotionality is frustrating in that it uncovers myriad questions that research has not begun to answer. But, much more than frustrating, it is exciting, for we, as researchers, can play a role in answering those questions.

REFERENCES

Bargh, J., & Pietromonaco, P. (1982). Automatic information processing and social perception: The influence of trait information presented outside of conscious awareness on impression formation. *Journal of Personality & Social Psychology, 43,* 437–449.

Bateson, G., Jackson, D., Haley, J., & Weakland, J. (1956). Toward a theory of schizophrenia. *Behavioral Science, 4,* 251–264.

Bell, S. (1970). The development of the concept of the object and its relationship to infant–mother attachment. *Child Development, 41,* 291–312.

Bernal, J. (1972). Crying during the first ten days, and maternal responses. *Developmental Medicine & Child Neurology, 14,* 362–372.

Blaney, P. (1986). Affect and memory: A review. *Psychological Bulletin, 99,* 229–246.

Borke, H. (1971). Interpersonal perceptions of young children: Egocentrism or empathy? *Developmental Psychology, 5,* 263–269.

Bretherton, I., McNew, S., & Beeghly-Smith, M. (1981). Early person knowledge as expressed in gestural and verbal communication. When do infants acquire a "theory of mind"? In M. Lamb & L. Sherrod (Eds.), *Infant social cognition.* Hillsdale, NJ: Erlbaum.

Bruner, J. (1977). Early social interaction and language acquisition. In H. Schaffer (Ed.), *Studies in mother–infant interaction.* New York: Academic.

Buck, R. (1979). Individual differences in nonverbal sending accuracy and electrodermal responding: The externalizing–internalizing dimension. In R. Rosenthal (Ed.), *Skill in nonverbal communication.* Cambridge, MA: Oelgeschlager, Gunn & Hain.

Buss, A. (1980). *Self-consciousness and social anxiety.* San Francisco: W. H. Freeman.

Campos, J., & Barrett, K. (1984). Toward a new understanding of emotions and their development. In C. Izard, J. Kagan, & R. Zajonc (Eds.), *Emotions, cognition, and behavior.* New York: Cambridge University Press.

Campos, J., Barrett, K., Lamb, M., Goldsmith, H., & Stenberg, C. (1983). Socioemotional development. In M. Haith & J. Campos (Eds.), *Infancy and developmental psychobiology, Vol. 2* of P. Mussen, *Handbook of child psychology.* New York: Wiley.

Campos, J., Hiatt, S., Ramsay, D., Henderson, C., & Svejda, M. (1978). The emergence of fear of heights. In M. Lewis & L. Rosenblum (Eds.), *The development of affect.* New York: Plenum.

Campos, J., & Stenberg, C. (1981). Perception, appraisal, and emotion: The onset of social referencing. In M. Lamb & L. Sherrod (Eds.), *Infant social cognition.* Hillsdale, NJ: Erlbaum.

Caplovitz, K., Morgan, G., & Mardashti, S. (1982, June). *Mastery motivation in infancy: What does persistence index?* Paper presented at the meeting of the Developmental Psychobiology Research Group, Estes Park, CO.

Crowne, D., & Marlowe, D. (1964). *The approval motive: Studies in evaluative dependence.* New York: Wiley.

Ekman, P. (1972). Universals and cultural differences in facial expressions of emotion. In J. Cole (Ed.), *Nebraska Symposium on Motivation* (Vol. 19). Lincoln: University of Nebraska Press.

Ekman, P. (1984). Expression and the nature of emotion. In K. Scherer & P. Ekman (Eds.), *Approaches to emotion.* Hillsdale, NJ: Erlbaum.

Ekman, P., & Friesen, W. (1975). *Unmasking the face.* Englewood Cliffs, NJ: Prentice-Hall.

Ekman, P., Levenson, R., & Friesen, W. (1983). Autonomic nervous system activity distinguishes between emotions. *Science, 221,* 1208–1210.

Emde, R., Gaensbauer, T., & Harmon, R. (1976). Emotional expression in infancy: A biobehavioral study. *Psychological Issues* (Vol. 10). New York: International Universities Press.

Fagen, J., Ohr, P., Fleckenstein, L., & Ribner, D. (1985). The effect of crying on long-term memory in infancy. *Child Development, 56,* 1484–1592.

Feinman, S. (1982). Social referencing in infancy. *Merrill-Palmer Quarterly, 28,* 445–470.

Feldman, R., White, J., & Labato, D. (1982). Social skills and nonverbal behavior. In R. Feldman (Ed.), *Development of nonverbal behavior in children.* New York: Springer-Verlag.

Fernald, A. (1984). The perceptual and affective salience of mothers' speech to infants. In L. Feagans, C. Garvey, & R. Galinkoff (Eds.), *The origins of growth of communication.* Norwood, NJ: Ablex.

Field, T. (1982). Individual differences in the expressivity of neonates and young infants. In R. Feldman (Ed.), *Development of nonverbal behavior in children.* New York: Springer-Verlag.

Frick, R. (1985). Communicating emotion: The role of prosodic features. *Psychological Bulletin, 97,* 412–429.

Frijda, N. (in press). *The emotions.* New York: Cambridge University Press.

Gaensbauer, T. (1980). Anaclitic depression in a three-and-a-half-month-old child. *American Journal of Psychiatry, 137,* 841–842.

Gnepp, J. (1983). Children's social sensitivity: Inferring emotions from conflicting cues. *Developmental Psychology, 19,* 805–814.

Gunnar, M. (1980). Control, warning signals, and distress in infancy. *Developmental Psychology, 16,* 281–289.

Hoffer, B., & St. Clair, R. (1981). *Developmental Kinesis.* Baltimore: University Park Press.

Hoffman, M. (1970). Conscience, personality, and socialization techniques. *Human Development, 13,* 90–126.

Hoffman, M. (1977). Empathy, its development and prosocial implications. In C. Keasey (Ed.), *Nebraska Symposium on Motivation*. Lincoln: University of Nebraska Press.

Irwin, O. (1932). Infant responses to vertical movement. *Child Development, 3,* 167–169.

Isen, A. (1984). Toward understanding the role of affect in cognition. In R. Wyer, Jr., & T. Srull (Eds.), *Handbook of social cognition*. Hillsdale, NJ: Erlbaum.

Izard, C. (1979). *The maximally discriminative facial movement scoring system*. Unpublished manuscript, University of Delaware.

James, W. (1890). *The principles of psychology*. New York: Holt.

Jones, H. (1935). The galvanic skin response as related to overt emotional expression. *American Journal of Psychology, 47,* 241–251.

Kagan, J. (1981). *The second year*. Cambridge, MA: Harvard University Press.

Kety, S. (1976). Biological concomitants of affective states and their possible role in memory processes. In M. Rosenzweig & E. Bennett (Eds.), *Neural mechanisms of learning and memory*. Cambridge, MA: M.I.T. Press.

Klinnert, M., Campos, J., Sorce, J., Emde, R., & Svejda, M. (1983). Emotions as behavior regulators: Social referencing in infancy. In R. Plutchik & H. Kellerman (Eds.), *Emotions in early development:* (Vol 2.) The Emotions. New York: Academic.

Kuhn, T. (1962). *The structure of scientific revolutions*. Chicago: University of Chicago Press.

Laban, R. (1974). *The language of movement*. Boston: Plays.

Lacey, J. (1967). Somatic response patterning and stress: Some revisions of activation theory. In M. Appley & R. Trumbull (Eds.), *Psychological stress*. New York: Appleton-Century-Crofts.

Laird, J. (1974). Self-attribution of emotion: The effects of expressive behavior on the quality of emotional experience. *Journal of Personality & Social Psychology, 29,* 475–486.

Lange, C. (1922). The emotions. In C. Lange and W. James (Eds.), *The emotions*. Baltimore: Williams & Wilkins. (Original work published 1885)

Lazarus, R. (1985, August). *Classic issues about emotion from the perspective of a relational and cognitive theory*. Paper presented at the Summer Institute on Cognition-Emotion Relationships, Winter Park, CO.

Leventhal, H. (1984). A perceptual motor theory of emotion. In K. Scherer & P. Ekman (Eds.), *Approaches to emotion*. Hillsdale, NJ: Erlbaum.

Levy, R. (1984). Emotion, knowing, and culture. In R. Shweder & R. Levine (Eds.), *Culture theory*. New York: Cambridge University Press.

Lewis, M., & Brooks-Gunn, J. (1979). *Social cognition and the acquision of self*. New York: Plenum.

Lewis, M., & Michalson, L. (1982). The socialization of emotions. In T. Field & A. Fogel (Eds.), *Emotion and early interaction*. Hillsdale, NJ: Erlbaum.

Lewis, M., & Saarni, C. (1985). *The socialization of emotions*. New York: Plenum.

Lipsitt, L. (1979). The pleasures and annoyances of infants: Approach and avoidant behavior. In E. Thoman (Ed.), *The origins of infants' social responsiveness*. Hillsdale, NJ: Erlbaum.

Malatesta, C., & Haviland, J. (1982). Learning display rules: The socialization of emotion expression in infancy. *Child Development, 53,* 991–1003.

Malatesta, C., & Haviland, J. (1985). Signals, symbols, and socialization: The modification of emotional expression in human development. In M. Lewis & C. Saarni (Eds.), *The socialization of emotions*. New York: Plenum.

Matas, L., Arend, R., & Sroufe, L. A. (1978). Continuity of adaptation in the second year: The relationship between quality of attachment and later competence. *Child Development, 49,* 547–556.

Meehl, P., & Hathaway, S. (1946). The K factor as a suppressor variable in the MMPI. *Journal of Applied Psychology, 30,* 525–564.

Michaelf, S. (1984). Half the battle. In *Ben Franklin in Paris.* New York: Edwin H. Morris.

Mineka, S. (1985). The frightful complexity of the origins of fears. In J. Overmeier & F. Brush (Eds.), *Affect, conditioning, and cognition: Essays on the determinants of behavior.* Hillsdale, NJ: Erlbaum.

Miyake, K., Chen, S., & Campos, J. (1985). Infant temperament, mother's mode of interaction, and attachment in Japan: An interim report. In I. Bretherton & E. Waters (Eds.), *Growing points of attachment theory and research: Vol. 50. Monographs of the Society for Research in Child Development,* pp. 276–297.

Oster, H., & Ekman, P. (1978). Facial behavior in child development. In W. A. Collins (Ed.), *Minnesota Symposia on Child Psychology,* (Vol. 11). Hillsdale, NJ: Erlbaum.

Piaget, J. (1962). *Play, dreams, and imitation in childhood.* New York: Norton.

Riskind, J. (1984). They stoop to conquer: Guiding and self-regulatory functions of physical posture after success and failure. *Journal of Personality & Social Psychology, 47,* 479–493.

Rosch, E. (1978). Principles of categorization. In E. Rosch & B. Lloyd (Eds.), *Cognition and categorization.* Hillsdale, NJ: Erlbaum.

Rosenthal, R. (1979). *Skill in nonverbal communication.* Cambridge, MA: Oelgeschlager, Gunn, & Hain.

Rozin, P., & Fallon, A. (in press). Disgust. *Psychological Review.*

Saarni, C. (1982). Social and affective functions of nonverbal behavior: Developmental concerns. In R. Feldman (Ed.), *Development of nonverbal behavior in children.* New York: Springer-Verlag.

Scarr, S., & Salapatek, P. (1970). Patterns of fear development during infancy. *Merrill-Palmer Quarterly, 16,* 53–90.

Schachter, S., & Singer, J. (1962). Cognitive, social, and physiological determinants of emotional state. *Psychological Review, 69,* 379–399.

Scherer, K. (1986). Vocal affect expression: A review and a model for future research. *Psychological Bulletin, 99,* 143–165.

Shaver, P., Schwartz, J., O'Connor, C., Kirson, D., Marsh, C., & Fischer, S. (in press). Emotions and emotion knowledge: A prototype approach. *Journal of Personality & Social Psychology.*

Shennum, W., & Bugental, D. (1982). The development of control over affective expression in nonverbal behavior. In R. Feldman (Ed.), *Development of nonverbal behavior in children.* New York: Springer-Verlag.

Spitz, R., & Wolf, K. (1946). The smiling response: A contribution to the ontogenesis of social relations. *Genetic Psychology Monographs, 34,* 57–125.

Sroufe, L. A. (1979). Socioemotional development. In J. Osofsky (Ed.), *Handbook of infant development.* New York: Wiley.

Steiner, J. (1979). Human facial expressions in response to taste and smell stimulation. In H. Reese & L. Lipsitt (Eds.), *Advances in child development and behavior* (Vol. 13). New York: Academic.

Stern, D. (1985). *The interpersonal world of the infant.* New York: Basic Books.

Takahashi, K. (1986). Examining the strange situation procedure with Japanese mothers and 12-month-old infants. *Developmental Psychology, 22,* 265–270.

Thelen, E. (1984). Learning to walk: Ecological demands and phylogenetic constraints. In L. Lipsitt & C. Rovee-Collier (Eds.), *Advances in infancy research* (Vol. 3). Norwood, NJ: Ablex.

Thelen, E., & Fisher, D. (1983). From spontaneous to instrumental behavior: Kinematic analysis of movement changes during very early learning. *Child Development, 54,* 129–140.

Watzlawick, P., Beavin, J., & Jackson, D. (1967). *Pragmatics of human communication.* New York: Norton.

Weiner, B., & Graham, S. (1984). An attributional approach to emotional development. In C. Izard, J. Kagan, & R. Zajonc (Eds.), *Emotions, cognition, and behavior.* New York: Cambridge University Press.

Wittgenstein, L. (1953). *Philosophical Investigations.* New York: Macmillan.

Yonas, A. (1981). Infants' responses to optical information for collision. In R. Aslin & M. Peterson (Eds.), *Development of perception: Psychobiological perspectives* (Vol. 2). New York: Academic.

Zahn-Waxler, C., Radke-Yarrow, M., & King, R. (1979). Child rearing and children's prosocial initiations toward victims of distress. *Child Development, 50,* 319–330.

Zuckerman, M., Klorman, R., Larrance, D., & Spiegel, N. (1981). Facial, autonomic, and subjective components of emotion: The facial feedback hypothesis versus the externalizer–internalizer distinction. *Journal of Personality & Social Psychology, 41,* 929–944.

CHAPTER 10

Family Interaction in Infancy

ROSS D. PARKE and BARBARA J. TINSLEY

INTRODUCTION

There has been a significant shift in the domain of parent–infant interaction in the last decade. In part, this change is reflected in the reorganization of the second edition of this handbook. In contrast to the earlier edition, in which there were separate chapters devoted to father–infant and mother–infant interaction, in this present edition a single chapter is devoted to parent–infant interaction. This is a significant shift since it gives explicit recognition to the fact that the relationship of the infant to its caregivers can best be appreciated by the simultaneous consideration of the other members of the family. The aim of the present chapter is to provide an overview of recent research in the area of parent–infant relationships within the context of the family.

Organization of the Chapter

A set of theoretical assumptions that guide research in this area will be outlined. These assumptions both explain the choice of topics and provide an organizational structure for the chapter. Next, some recent methodological advances in this area will be discussed. The substantive portion of the chapter begins with a discussion of the nature of mother–infant and father–infant relationships. Next the chapter moves beyond the dyad to examine the impact of the marital relationship on the parent–infant relationship. Next, the roles of various informal and formal social networks in altering parent–infant relationships are described. Finally, the effect of recent historical changes, namely, shifts in work patterns of family members and changes in the timing of the onset of parenthood, on parent–infant relationships will be reviewed.

Some Underlying Theoretical Assumptions

Certain assumptions guide both our choice of material and our organization of this chapter. First, to understand fully the nature of parent–infant relationships, it is

The preparation of this chapter and the research reported were supported in part by National Institute of Child Health & Human Development Grant No. HD05951 and by National Institute of Child Health & Human Development Training Grant No. HD07205. Finally, thanks to Kathleen Helms and Anita Priester for their assistance in the preparation of the manuscript.

necessary to recognize the interdependence among the roles and functions of all family members. It is being increasingly recognized that families are best viewed as social systems. Consequently, to understand the behavior of one member of a family, the complementary behaviors of other members also need to be recognized and assessed. For example, as men's roles in families shift, changes in women's roles in families must also be monitored.

Second, family members—mothers, fathers, and infants—influence each other both directly and indirectly (Lewis & Feiring, 1981; Parke, Power, & Gottman, 1979). Examples of fathers' indirect impact include various ways in which fathers modify and mediate mother–child relationships. In turn, women affect their children indirectly through their husbands by modifying both the quantity and the quality of father–child interaction. Infants may indirectly influence the husband–wife relationship by altering the behavior of either parent that consequently changes the interaction between spouses.

Third, different units of analysis are necessary in order to understand families in infancy. While the individual level—infant, mother, and father—remains a useful and necessary level of analysis, recognition of relationships among family members as units of analysis is necessary. The marital relationship, the mother–infant, and the father–infant relationship require separate analysis. Finally, the family as a unit that is independent of the individual or dyads within the family requires recognition.

Fourth, recognition is being given to the embeddedness of families within a variety of other social systems, including both formal and informal support systems as well as the cultures in which they exist (Bronfenbrenner, 1979; Cochran & Brassard, 1979; Parke & Tinsley, 1982; Tinsley & Parke, 1984). These include a wide range of extrafamilial influences such as extended families, informal community ties such as friends and neighbors, work sites, and social, educational, and medical institutions (Bronfenbrenner & Crouter, 1982; Hoffman, 1984; Kanter, 1977; Tinsley & Parke, 1984).

A fifth assumption concerns the importance of considering family relationships from a variety of developmental perspectives. Developmental changes in infant perceptual–cognitive and social–emotional capacities represent the most commonly investigated type of development. In addition, a life span perspective (Elder, 1974; Parke & Tinsley, 1984) suggests the importance of examining developmental changes in the adult since parents continue to change and develop during adult years. For example, age at the time of the onset of parenthood can have important implications for how females and males manage their maternal and paternal roles. This involves an exploration of the tasks faced by adults such as self-identity, education, and career and an examination of the relationship between these tasks and the demands of parenting.

Developmental analyses need not be restricted to the level of the individual—either infant or parent. Relationships, such as the marital relationship or the mother–infant or father–infant relationship, may follow separate and partially independent developmental courses over infancy. In turn, the mutual impact of different sets of relationships on each other will vary as a function of the nature of the developmental trajectory of each relationship. Families, as units of analysis, may follow their own developmental trajectory. Families change their structure (e.g., through the addition of a new child or the loss of a member through death, separation, or divorce) over time, as well as their norms, rules, and strategies. Tracking the family unit itself over development is an important and relatively neglected task.

Another assumption involves the recognition of the impact of secular shifts on families. In recent years, there have been a variety of social changes in American society that have had a profound impact on families. These include the decline in fertility and family size, the changes in the timing of the onset of parenthood, the increased participation of women in the work force, the rise in rates of divorce, and the subsequent increase in the number of single-parent families (Feiring & Lewis, 1984; Parke & Tinsley, 1984). The ways in which these societywide changes impact on interaction patterns between parents and infants merit examination.

Another closely related assumption involves the recognition of the importance of the historical time period in which the family interaction is taking place. Historical time periods provide the social conditions for individual and family transitions: Examples include the 1960s (the Vietnam War era), the 1930s (the Great Depression), or the 1980s (Farm Belt Depression). Across these historical time periods, family interaction may, in fact, be quite different due to the peculiar conditions of the particular era.

These distinctions among different developmental trajectories, as well as social change and historical period effects, are important because these different forms of change do not always harmonize (Elder, 1984; Elder & Rockwell, 1979; Hareven, 1977; Parke & Tinsley, 1984). For example, a family event such as the birth of a child—the transition to parenthood—may have very profound effects on a man who has just begun a career in contrast to the effects on one who has advanced to a stable occupational position. Moreover, individual and family developmental trajectories are embedded within both the social conditions and the values of the historical time in which they exist (Hareven, 1977). The role of parents, as is the case with any social role, is responsive to such fluctuations.

A final assumption concerns the role of cognitive factors in understanding parent–infant relationships. Specifically, we assume that the ways in which parents perceive, organize, and understand both their infants and their roles as parents will affect the nature of parent–infant interaction (Goodnow, 1984; Parke, 1978; Sameroff, 1983).

In order to understand the nature of parent–infant relationships within families, a multilevel and dynamic approach is required. Multiple levels of analysis are necessary in order to capture the individual, dyadic, and family unit aspects of operation within the family itself as well as to reflect the embeddedness of families within a variety of extrafamilial social systems. The dynamic quality reflects the multiple developmental trajectories that warrant consideration in understanding the nature of families in infancy.

Recent Methodological Shifts

These shifts in our conceptual orientation have been paralleled by corresponding changes in our methodological strategies. Perhaps the most characteristic feature of current methodological approaches is a strong commitment to a multimethod strategy. Pluralism of methods is increasingly common among researchers as opposed to a doctrinaire commitment to a single methodological strategy.

Observational Strategies

To appreciate better the subtleties of the parent–infant interactive process, there have been major methodological advances in observational research (Bakeman & Gottman, Chapter 15, this volume; Sackett, Chapter 16, this volume). There is less reliance on noninteractive time-sampling techniques and an increasing use of microanalytic strategies that more adequately capture sequences of behavior and the moment-to-moment shifts in patterns of dyadic interaction with both mothers (Stern, 1974, 1985) and fathers (Parke & Sawin, 1980). An understanding of the dynamics of interpersonal synchrony is increasingly the aim of parent–infant interaction research. This reflects the common acceptance of the bidirectional nature of parent–infant interaction. Similarly significant advances have been achieved in techniques for analyzing this type of data such as sequential analysis and time series approaches (Bakeman & Gottman, Chapter 15, this volume; Sackett, 1979, Chapter 16, this volume). While detailed discussion of these approaches is beyond the scope of this chapter, one recent development deserves comment.

At the same time that there has been a heavy reliance on microanalytic techniques, there has been an increased utilization of macroanalytic ratings. In part, this shift has come from the slowly accumulating evidence that ratings may in some cases be a more appropriate level of analysis than more microanalytic approaches. For example, a number of investigators have found that ratings yield higher cross-time stability than frequency-count scores (Clarke-Stewart & Hevey, 1981; Jay & Farran, 1981; Waters, 1978). In one particularly instructive investigation, Bakeman and Brown (1980) examined the relative utility of macroanalytic ratings versus microanalytic scores. In addition to microanalytic coding these researchers rated mother–infant interaction using a variety of global ratings scales (e.g., responsiveness of the infant). The ratings revealed significant relationships between early infancy (first 3 months) and measures of children's social competence at 3 years of age. In contrast the microanalytic scores were not significantly predictive of later social functioning in the preschool period. Bakeman & Brown note:

> We think it may be more fruitful to think of characteristics of early interaction, like responsiveness, not as frequencies or sequences of particular acts, but rather as a disposition which permeates all of the mother's and/or all of the baby's interactive behavior. And in that case global rating scales, and not sequential recording of minute particular behaviors followed by various microanalyses, might be the method of choice.
>
> (*p. 445*)

Few would argue that one approach is superior to another, and, as Bakeman and Brown (1980) suggest, "perhaps most fruitful, would be an approach which combines features of molar (rating-scale) and micro methods" (p. 445). However, it is necessary to develop better guidelines to assist researchers in deciding the appropriate level of analysis for the particular question (Cairns & Green, 1979; Maccoby & Martin, 1983).

Structured Interaction Situations

In spite of the commitment to naturalistic observation, many useful insights have been gained from the use of structured interaction contexts. These situations have distinct advantages since they provide a sample of behavior with low base rate in the natural environment, as well as affording a high degree of control over the interactional assessment situation and standardization of setting across individual pairs or groups of interactants.

A variant on this technique involves systematic introduction of perturbations into the interactional context. For example, Tronick and his colleagues (Cohn & Tronick, 1983; Tronick, Cohn, & Shea, 1986) have successfully utilized a paradigm in which mothers are instructed to feign depression when interacting with their infants. Examination of the infant's response to this reduced display of affective expression provided a useful paradigm within which to examine the importance of mutual contingency in face-to-face interaction as well as the ways in which infants react to novel or unexpected shifts in emotional affect. This approach has been helpful in tracing the emergence of both emotional signaling and emotional understanding in the first years of life (Campos, Chapter 9B, this volume; Tronick, Cohn, & Shea, 1985).

Self-Report Strategies

Another recent methodological shift has been the resurgence of the utilization of parental self-report strategies. These methods assume a variety of forms including parental interviews and questionnaires, parental diaries, and playback techniques (i.e., presenting videotapes of parents' behavior to them to obtain their responses), as well as new approaches to parental attitudes and beliefs.

Parents as Observers and Reporters

Under the weight of considerable criticism concerning the limitations of self-report strategies, especially retrospective accounts, these approaches were relatively unfashionable for the past two decades (see Robins, 1963, Yarrow, Campbell, & Burton, 1968, for critiques). In spite of these criticisms there are clear advantages to these techniques, and many issues of current interest (e.g., nature, extensiveness, and satisfaction with social networks) cannot be investigated without recourse to these techniques.

As Maccoby & Martin (1983) recently wrote:

> Using parents as informants has great potential advantages. For assessment of behavior that varies considerably across situations or behavior that is usually not displayed in public, reliable observational data are difficult to obtain and parent interviews are often the only viable alternative. Parents have an opportunity to observe their children and the patterns of interaction in their families over extended periods of time in a broad range of situations. Thus by virtue of their daily participation in the family system, parents have access to a truly unique body of information about the family, and it is reasonable to tap into this information by questioning them.
>
> (*p. 16*)

A number of significant changes have occurred since the 1960 era that have blunted many of the earlier criticisms. First, parent reports are now used primarily for obtaining concurrent, not retrospective, information about family interaction (Maccoby & Martin, 1983). For example, Patterson (1982) has utilized a Parent Daily

Report instrument that involves soliciting via telephone reports of the occurrence of specific behaviors during the last 24 hours—a procedure that reduces the distortions due to retrospective recall. Second, instead of asking parents to make trait attributions such as "dependent" or "difficult," many researchers ask parents to provide detailed descriptions of specific behaviors, which are presumably less open to subjective interpretation and bias and therefore yield more reliable as well as more valid ratings.

Radke-Yarrow and her colleagues have used another promising strategy that minimizes the problems associated with parental self-reports. These investigators train mothers as observers and teach them to record behaviors in response to certain critical instances. The mothers provide a narrative report of the eliciting events, as well as the child and parental behaviors and affective responses. The correspondence between observers' records and maternal reports of similar types of events is quite high, which attests to the reliability of this approach (Radke-Yarrow & Zahn-Waxler, 1985; Zahn-Waxler & Radke-Yarrow, 1982).

Another approach has involved the use of parental diaries, in which parents record a variety of predesignated parental behaviors such as diapering, bathing, or feeding over a period of days. Recording sheets are organized into time blocks (e.g., 15 or 30 min) to facilitate the task for parents. Parke and Anderson (1986) reported significant relationships between parental diary records and independent reports of parental behavior for these same behavior categories. However, this technique has clear limitations and is not useful for all types of behavior. For example, categories with ambiguous definition and boundaries such as play have not been found to be reliably recorded using this diary technique (Parke & Anderson, 1986). Perhaps with more extensive training parents can be reliable recorders of a wider range of behaviors including play.

In summary, self-report strategies are being much more widely used and recent innovations are making these approaches more effective than in earlier eras.

Parent Beliefs and Parent–Infant Interaction

Another major advance that has occurred in part because of our renewed attention to the value of self-report data is the recognition of the importance of parental belief systems in understanding parent–infant interaction and infant development. Parental beliefs are another characteristic of the infant's caregiving environment, and many researchers have articulated and demonstrated empirical and theoretical relationships among parent beliefs, parent behavior, and child development. Various studies have confirmed that parent beliefs can affect child rearing, socialization, and the quality of the "home as a learning environment" (Johnson & Martin, 1983; Skinner, 1985), and subsequently, child language and cognitive and social development (Brooks-Gunn, 1985; Dix & Grusec, 1985; Marjoribanks, 1979; McGillicuddy-DeLisi, 1982; Miller, 1986; Sigel, 1985).

Parents have complex sets of belief systems concerning child development (McGillicuddy-DeLisi, 1982), and these beliefs appear to guide parents' behavior with respect to their children. Earlier, Parke (1978) suggested that parents' reports of their own behavior did not always match investigators' observations of parent behavior, and that parent report and observational data were two independent sources of data. According to this view, both are necessary to understand the antecedents and consequences of parenting behavior. Recently, researchers have begun to look to parent beliefs and attitudes "as 'the missing link' in their accounts of parent–infant relationships" (Goodnow, 1984, p. 193).

Moreover, it is useful to conceptualize beliefs within a transactional system (Sameroff & Chandler, 1975), with parental beliefs subsequently being modified by child behavior, which leads to subsequent modified parent behavior and child development. Holloway (1985) suggests that two questions are relevant with respect to the influence of parental beliefs: (1) the content of these beliefs and (2) their relationship to child outcome—what do they affect and through what process?

Much of the empirical work in this area has centered around the issue of parental developmental timetables (e.g., Hess, Kashigawi, Azuma, Price, & Dickson, 1980; Sameroff & Feil, 1985), because they provide information about parent goals as well as suggesting the basis upon which parents assess their children relative to others (Goodnow, 1985). Some studies have focused on the accuracy of developmental timetables among different groups, while a group of recent investigations have moved beyond merely documenting differences to show the relationships among beliefs, interaction, and infant development.

Adolescent parents have been an important target of early research efforts on the assumption that the lack of knowledge of norms for infant development may be a contributing factor to less adequate parenting skill (Brooks-Gunn & Furstenberg, 1986). In one study of teenage couples, de Lissovoy (1973) assessed both maternal and paternal knowledge of motor, language, and social developmental norms and found that both parents, but particularly fathers, were not familiar with developmental norms. Teenage parents expected such accomplishments as social smiling, sitting alone, pulling up to standing, first step, and the appearance of the first word to occur much earlier than can realistically be expected. Furthermore, both mothers and fathers expected toilet training to be accomplished by 24 weeks and fathers expected obedience training and recognition of wrongdoing to be achieved by 26 and 40 weeks respectively. In combination with the fathers' unrealistic expectations concerning how frequently infants cry, it is not surprising that de Lissovoy noted a frequent occurrence of physical discipline being used by the fathers in that sample. The lack of knowledge of developmental norms is not limited to teenage parents. De Lissovoy (1973) found similar low levels of knowledge of infant development in a group of unmarried high school students of the same age and socioeconomic status as the teenage parents. However, caution should be taken in interpreting this study in light of the restricted sample (rural working class), the limited range of developmental norms investigated, the absence of statistical treatment of the data, and the lack of a nonadolescent comparison group.

A more methodologically sound investigation by Epstein (1979) confirmed that teenagers' knowledge of infant development is deficient—at least in some areas. In contrast to the earlier work of de Lissovoy (1973), the adolescent females in this sample were accurate in their knowledge of perceptual and motor development but deficient in their knowledge of cognitive, social, and language development. Particularly in the case of younger infants (under 8 months of age), the teenage mothers underestimated the infants' cognitive, social, and language skills. In contrast to the results of the study by de Lissovoy, these mothers expected too little of their infants and viewed them as "creatures of physical needs and growth without corresponding mental activity" (Epstein, p. 4, Note 2). However, this study has limitations. First, no males were included. Second, there was no adult comparison group; therefore, it is not clear whether or not the degree of error is greater for adolescent and non-adolescent parents. Two more recent studies have included adults in their design.

Parks and Smeriglio (1983) compared parenting knowledge of primiparous black adolescent mothers with that of primiparous adult mothers. They found no differences between mothers of different ages. However, since most mothers answered correctly, a ceiling effect may have obscured any potential age-related differences. In the other available study, Field, Widmayer, Stringer, and Ignatoff (1980) compared teenage mothers and older mothers in terms of their knowledge of infant development. Although adult mothers had more realistic expectations regarding developmental milestones than teenage mothers, differences in parity and marital status across the two groups make interpretation difficult.

With the exception of the exploratory study of de Lissovoy (1973), parallel studies of the knowledge of developmental timetables of adolescent fathers are not available. However, in light of the more limited opportunities that males are afforded to learn about child care during their own socialization, it is likely that adolescent males would show even more marked deficiencies. If this lack of knowledge among teenage parents is substantiated by future research, it has important implications since lack of knowledge may affect the nature of their interactions with their infants (Parke, 1978).

Nor are inappropriate parent beliefs and knowledge restricted to adolescent parents. As Field (Chapter 19, this volume) shows, mothers of preterms often have unrealistic expectations concerning developmental timetables for their infants. A recent study by Smith, Leiderman, Selz, MacPherson, and Bingham (1981) will illustrate this point. These investigators found that mothers of preterm infants rated developmental milestones for their own child and a typical child differently. In rating their own children, they predicted substantial lags for their own child until approximately 2 years of age. Beyond 2 years, they expected more rapid development in social, psychomotor, and cognitive development than the rate of progress expected by the mothers of full-term infants. These data suggest that parents of preterm infants may have unrealistic expectations for their young children, which, in turn, may be a contributing factor in later dysfunctional parent–child relationships (Field, Chapter 19, this volume).

Other studies have moved beyond this type of descriptive approach and illustrate the relationship among beliefs, interaction, and infant developmental progress. Specifically, recent studies have examined the impact of modifying parental knowledge of developmental timetables as well as the links between more comprehensive parental belief systems concerning the nature and courses of developmental change.

A study by Field and colleagues (1980) illustrates the first strategy. Field assessed the effect of birth status and parental attitudes, as well as the effect of an intervention program, on the development of a group of infants born to lower-class black teenage and postteenage mothers. The intervention program focused on supplemental infant stimulation and education concerning infant developmental milestones and child-rearing beliefs. Results indicated that the intervention group of teenage mothers demonstrated more realistic developmental expectations and more positive child-rearing beliefs than the teen mothers in the control group. Moreover, preterm infants who received intervention had greater weight and length measurements and higher Denver and Bayley scores than preterm controls at 4 months.

Assessments at 4 months included videotaped mother–infant feeding and face-to-face play interactions. Results indicated that both the teenage mothers and preterm infants in the intervention group received more optimal face-to-face interaction ratings than did the control group dyads. This pattern of results suggests that the more realistic beliefs concerning development, in turn, yielded more adequate parent–infant interaction patterns and more optimal development.

Further support for the importance of the role of knowledge about infant development comes from a study by Dickie and Carnahan (1980). These investigators taught parents of infants 4–12 months old in a series of weekly sessions information about child development, variability in infant temperament, and how to read and respond to infant synads appropriately. The training was guided by Goldberg's (1977) model of parental competence. The effect of this training was assessed by home and laboratory observations of parent–infant interaction. Results indicated that parents who participated in the training showed more anticipation of infants needs, responded more appropriately to infant cues, and were higher than non-trained parents in their level of contingent responsivity. In turn the infants in the experimental group were rated as more responsive than infants of families who did not receive the training. The training had its greatest impact on fathers, who increased their interactions with their infants, while mothers who participated in the training sessions decreased their interactions with their infants. In part, this pattern was mediated through the altered beliefs concerning the fathers' competence; in fact, trained parents, both mothers and fathers, were rated by their spouses as more competent than their untrained counterparts. Possibly as a result of viewing their husbands as more competent, the wives were more willing to relinquish child-rearing tasks to their spouses. Although the training included modification of parental knowledge, further work is necessary to disentangle the role of these cognitive factors from the impact of more explicit behavioral training (e.g., contingent responding; cue reading) on subsequent parent infant interaction.

Finally, Chamberlain (1979) found that mothers who participated in an educational program concerning child development during pediatric well baby visits increased their knowledge of child development. In turn, this gain in knowledge was significantly correlated with the reported occurrence of more positive contact with their infants and children. A related study (Whitt & Casey, 1982) suggests that mothers who were provided with an office-based pediatric intervention program emphasizing physical and preventive child care, developmental norms, and information on infant communication abilities during well baby exams demonstrated more positive relationships with their infants. Again, separation of the role of accurate time-table information per se from other types of training is necessary in future work.

A variety of other studies have explored other aspects of parental belief systems, including attributions, parental child-rearing beliefs, and parental models of development. An example of each approach illustrates the range of activity in this domain.

In a recent longitudinal study from birth through 18 months of age, Affleck, McGrade, Allen, and McQueeny (1985) explored the ways in which parental attributions for infant developmental problems can alter infant developmental progress. These investigators compared the outcomes of 57 infants with severe medical problems or genetic syndromes as influenced by the extent to which their mothers: (1) attributed the infants' conditions to a maternal behavior; (2) blamed others for the condition; or (3) reported no such attributions. Results indicated that mothers' blame of themselves for their infants' conditions was positively associated with more optimal parent perceptions of those infants, parental mood states, and parent–child interaction, and that mothers' blame of others (e.g., the obstetrician) was usually related to poor child outcomes. Such results provide further evidence that maternal beliefs are related to parent behavior and child outcome.

In a study of child-rearing beliefs, Skinner (1985) has tested a well-articulated model of the relationship between parent beliefs and parental sensitive and responsive behavior with very young children. The study included 120 families of 3- and 4-year-old children. Mothers were intensively interviewed concerning their child-rearing beliefs, specifically focusing on the extent to which they showed concern for their children's needs, and the importance of giving children control of their own development and learning. Mothers also participated in a task with their children that was coded for maternal directiveness and responsiveness. Results indicated that mothers who reported that they were attentive to their children and professed to believe that children learn from their own actions were less directive during the performance of the task but highly directive when explaining the task to the child. Maternal responsiveness was curvilinearly related to maternal beliefs, such that mothers who fell in the middle category of beliefs showed the most responsive behavior and mothers who were highest in their beliefs showed the greatest sensitivity in their interactions. However, these complicated results do suggest probable relationships between parental beliefs and behaviors, and they highlight the importance of more work to identify which beliefs should affect which behaviors under which specific conditions.

Finally, Sameroff (1975; Sameroff & Feil, 1985) has developed a hierarchical taxonomy of parents' underlying concepts of development and their relationship to parental behavior and child outcome. Although the results from studies utilizing such models are complex, Sameroff and Feil (1985) found significant correlations between parents' concepts of child development and children's cognitive and social competence. However, with regression analysis, parents' concepts of development explained variance in intelligence scores but not social competence scores when parent mental health was taken into account.

This area is clearly conceptually and empirically young. However, as these pioneering investigations suggest, this area is one that has high potential for intervention attempts to modify parent behavior and child outcome, and is an especially fertile domain for the further development of process-oriented theories of parent–child relationships and their effects.

DYADIC ANALYSES: MOTHER–INFANT AND FATHER–INFANT RELATIONSHIPS

In this section we address the issue of the degree to which mothers and fathers are involved with their infants. As will be evident, there are overall differences in the quantity of involvement for mothers and fathers, but there are important stylistic or qualitative differences as well.

Quantitative Effects

In spite of current shifts in cultural attitudes concerning the appropriateness and desirability of shared roles and equal levels of participation in routine caregiving and interaction for mothers and fathers, the shifts are more apparent than real in the majority of families. Although more mothers are entering the work force, current occupational arrangements still mean that the vast majority of fathers have less opportunity for interaction with their infants than mothers. A number of studies indicate that fathers are less available during babies' awake periods (Pedersen & Robson, 1969) and were present for less time with their infants than mothers (Kotelchuck, 1976). This pattern is present not only in U.S. samples but in other countries such as Great Britain (Richards, Dunn, & Antonis, 1977), Australia (Russell, 1983), and France and Belgium (Szalai, 1972).

Second, mothers and fathers differ in the amount of time that they spend in actual interaction with their infants. A number of naturalistic studies of mother–father–infant interaction support this proposition. In a longitudinal study of middle- and working-class families in which mothers, fathers, and their infants were observed at 1, 3, and 9 months of age, mothers were found to respond to, stimulate, express positive affection toward, and provide more basic care for their infants at all time points. Fathers exceeded mothers in the extent to which they engaged in reading and television viewing (Belsky, Gilstrap, & Rovine, 1984). In a replication study (Belsky & Volling, 1986), a similar pattern of mother–father differences was evident across the observations at 1, 3, and 9 months. Again, mothers exceeded fathers in every behavior except reading and watching TV, where fathers exceeded mothers.

Studies in other cultures confirm these findings. In Israel, Greenbaum and Landau (1982) carried out a cross-sectional study in which they observed 96 middle- and lower-class families under naturalistic conditions at 2, 4, 7, and 11 months. At every age point they found that mothers greatly exceeded fathers in verbal interactions—regardless of social class. However, the focus on verbal stimulation may have overestimated the nature of the mother–father differences in light of fathers' propensity to interact in a physical mode (Parke, 1979, 1981; Parke & Tinsley, 1981; Power & Parke, 1981). Even more impressive evidence of the stability of mother–father differences in involvement comes from the longitudinal study of traditional and nontraditional families in Sweden executed by Lamb and his colleagues (Lamb, Frodi, Hwang, & Frodi, 1982; Lamb, Frodi, Hwang, Frodi, & Steinberg, 1982). In this study, families in which the father elected to stay home as primary caregiver for 1 month or more (nontraditional) were compared with families in which the father elected to be a secondary caregiver (traditional). In an analysis of home observations at 8 months, mothers surpassed fathers in holding and affectional behavior—regardless of family type. Subsequent observations at 16 months confirmed that parental gender exerted an important influence on parental behavior—regardless of the parents' relative involvement in caretaking.

Further support for this pattern of sex-of-parent differences comes from a recent study of kibbutz families (Sagi, Lamb, Shoham, Duir, & Lewkowicz, 1985). Kibbutz-reared infants and their parents were observed in the parents' living quarters when the infants were 8 and 16 months of age. Although child care was the primary responsibility of nonparental caretakers (*metapelet*) rather than either parent, sex differences in parental behavior similar to those observed in the United States and Sweden were found. Kibbutz mothers were more likely to vocalize, laugh, display affection, hold, and engage in care giving than were fathers. Since mothers and fathers on Israeli kibbutzim both work full-time and have their children cared for by other care givers, the findings suggest that "more general sex-role expectations (which certainly exist on the kibbutzim) and/or biological predispositions—rather than immediate competing role demands—appear to account for the widely observed differences between maternal and paternal behavior" (Sagi et al., 1985, p. 282).

In summary, in unstructured naturalistic settings, mothers and fathers clearly differ in terms of their degree of involvement with their infants.

These findings are consistent with the more general proposition that pregnancy and birth of a first child, in particular, are occasions for a shift toward a more traditional division of roles (Arbeit, 1975; Cowan, Cowan, Coie, & Coie, 1978; Shereshefsky & Yarrow, 1973). Other studies confirm these general trends. Hoffman and Manes (1978) found that husbands help less with housework after the arrival of a first child than they did before. Cowan and his co-workers (1983) studied couples before and up to 6 months after the birth of a first child. They reported that the shift was most marked in household tasks, next in family decision-making roles, and least in the baby care items. Of particular interest is the fact that these patterns held regardless of whether their initial role division was traditional or equalitarian. "Despite the current rhetoric and ideology concerning equality of roles for men and women, it seems that couples tend to adopt traditionally defined roles during times of stressful transition such as around the birth of a first child" (Cowan et al., 1978, p. 20).

Competence Versus Performance

However, the lower level of father involvement in feeding does not imply that fathers are less competent than mothers to care for the newborn infant. Competence can be measured in a variety of ways; one approach is to measure the parent's sensitivity to infant cues in the feeding context. Success in caretaking, to a large degree, is dependent on the parent's ability to correctly "read" or interpret the infant's behavior so that his or her own behavior can be regulated to respond appropriately. In this context, one approach to the competence issue involves an examination of the degree to which the caretaker modifies his or her behavior in response to infant cues. Parke and Sawin (1975) found that fathers' sensitivity to an auditory distress signal in the feeding context—sneeze, spit-up, cough—was just as marked as mothers' responsivity to this infant cue. Using a conditional probability analysis, they demonstrated that fathers, like mothers, adjusted their behavior by momentarily ceasing their feeding activity, looking more closely to check on the infant, and vocalizing to their infant. The implication of this analysis is clear: In spite of the fact that they may spend less time overall in caretaking activities, fathers are as sensitive as mothers to infant cues and as responsive to them in the feeding context.

Moreover, the amount of milk consumed by infants with their mothers and fathers in this study was very similar, which suggests that fathers and mothers are not only comparable in their sensitivity but equally successful in feeding the infant based on the amount of milk consumed by the infant. Invoking a competence/performance distinction, fathers may not necessarily be as frequent contributors to infant feeding, but when called upon they have the competence to execute these tasks effectively.

Fathers are just as responsive as mothers to other infant cues such as vocalizations. Both mothers and fathers in this study increased their rate of positive vocalizations following an infant's vocal sound. Both fathers and mothers also touched and looked more closely at the infant after the infant had vocalized. These data indicate that fathers and mothers both react to the newborn infant's cues in a contingent and functional manner. The interaction patterns in the newborn period are reciprocal; although our focus in the Parke and Sawin (1975) study was on the role of infant cues as elicitors of parent behavior, in a later study (Parke & Sawin, 1980) it was shown that parent vocalizations can modify newborn infant behavior such as infant vocalizations. Interaction between fathers and infants—even in the newborn period—is clearly bidirectional in quality; parents and infants mutually regulate each other's behavior in the course of interaction.

Fathers do have the capability to execute caregiving activities competently even though they directly contribute less to this type of activity than mothers. In a later section, some of the conditions that may modify the amount of father participation in routine caregiving are explored.

Qualitative Effects: Stylistic Differences in Mother and Father Interaction

Fathers participate less than mothers in caregiving but spend a greater percentage of the time available for interaction in play activities than mothers do. Kotelchuck (1976) found that fathers spent a greater percentage of their time with their infants in play (37.5 percent) than mothers did (25.8 percent), although in absolute terms mothers spent more time than fathers in play with their children.

Nor are these differences in mother and father participation in play restricted to U.S. families. Similar findings have been reported from a longitudinal investigation of parent–infant interaction in England (Richards et al., 1977). These investigators interviewed mothers concerning fathers' participation in a wide range of activities when the infant was 30 and 60 weeks old. At both ages, playing with their infants was the most common activity of these fathers, and over 90 percent of the fathers played regularly with their infants.

Further evidence comes from Lamb (1977a), who observed interactions among mother, father, and infant in their homes at 7–8 months and again at 12–13 months. Based on 4–8 hr of home observation, Lamb reported marked differences in the reasons that fathers and mothers pick up infants: fathers were more likely to hold the babies simply to play with them, whereas mothers were far more likely to hold them for caretaking purposes.

It is not the quantity of time per se that discriminates between mother and father involvement in infancy; it is the quality of play activity as well. Differences in the style of mother–father play have been examined in a recent series of studies by Yogman and his colleagues (Yogman, 1981; Yogman, Dixon, Tronick, Als, & Brazelton, 1977). They compared mothers, fathers, and strangers in their interactions with infants in a face-to-face play context. Six infants were studied in 2 min of interaction with mother, father, and a stranger when they were from 2 weeks to 6 months of age in a lab arrangement whereby infant and adult face each other with instructions to play without using toys and without removing the infant from an infant seat. Using videotaped records, a variety of microbehavioral analyses of the adult–infant interaction patterns were scored. Adults differed in their play with infants as indicated by differences in vocalization and touching patterns. Mothers vocalized in soft, repetitive, imitative burst–pause talking (47 percent) more often than fathers (20 percent), who did so significantly more often than strangers (12 percent). Fathers, however, touched their infants with rhythmic tapping patterns (44 percent) more often than either mothers (28 percent) or strangers (29 percent). Differences are revealed not only in discrete behaviors but also in the patterns of behavior. As Yogman and colleagues (1977) comment: "These adult behaviors were often part of an interactive 'game' in the sense defined by Stern (1974): 'a series of episodes of mutual attention in which the adult uses a repeating set of behaviors with only minor variations during each episode of mutual attention'" (p. 8). Moreover, Yogman (1980) reported that these games were more likely to occur during sessions with fathers than with mothers. Mothers and infants played games during 75 percent of the face-to-face interaction sessions, while fathers played games during 87 percent of the sessions. The types of games that mothers and fathers played differed as well. Visual games in which the "parent displays distal motor movements that may be observed by the infant and appear to be attempts to maintain the visual attention of the infant" (Yogman, 1980, p. 30) were the most common type of mother's game (31 percent of all games played). For fathers, this type of game represented only 19 percent of the games played. The most common types of father-infant games were tactile and limb movement games. Limb movement games, which were associated with increases in infant arousal, represented 70 percent of all father-infant games and only 4 percent of mother–infant games. In contrast to this type of physically arousing game used by fathers, mothers played physically by utilizing more conventional motor games such as "pat-a-cake," "peek-a-boo," or waving. "The visual games more often played by mothers represent a more distal attention-maintaining form of interactive play than the more proximal, idiosyncratic limb movement games played more often by fathers" (Yogman, 1980, p. 39).

Stylistic differences in mothers' and fathers' play are not restricted to very young infants. In a series of studies by Power and Parke (1981), mothers and fathers were videotaped while playing with their firstborn, 8-month-old infants in a laboratory playroom. Fathers played more bouncing and lifting games than mothers. In contrast, mothers played more watching games in which a toy is presented and made salient by moving or shaking it. The mother–father difference in lifting games was qualified by sex of the infant; the game was played primarily by fathers of boys. In addition to examining the amount of time that mothers and fathers devoted to different types of play, Power and Parke examined the sequencing of various types of play for mothers and fathers. Two further ways in which mothers and fathers differ in interaction style are illustrated by this type of analysis. First, fathers were more likely than mothers to engage in extended physical no-toy play interaction; even if they were engaged in toy-mediated play they were generally less successful than mothers in successfully maintaining play of this type. When fathers failed to elicit their infants' attention in toy play, they often shifted to physical no-toy play. In contrast, mothers were better able to maintain infant attention during toy play, and a loss in infant attention led to continued toy play as opposed to a shift to the physical mode as in the case of fathers. In short, there is a general tendency for parents to rely on familiar and predominant modes of play, particularly when infant interest lessens: For mothers this involves prolonging toy play, while for fathers this involves shifting to physical play.

Recent observations of father- and mother–infant interaction in unstructured home contexts with older infants indicate mother–father differences in style of play. Lamb (1977), in an observational study of infants at 7–8 months and again at 12–13 months in their homes, found that fathers engage in more physical (i.e., rough and tumble) and unusual play activities than mothers. Similar findings emerged from home observations of the infants at 15, 18, 21, and 24 months of age (Lamb, 1977b). Again, fathers played more physical games and engaged in more parallel play with their infants. Mothers, in contrast, engaged in more conventional play activities (e.g., "peek-a-boo," "pat-a-cake"), stimulus toy play (where a toy was jiggled or operated to stimulate the child directly), and reading than fathers. Power and Parke (1981) found that fathers engaged in more physical play than mothers in home observations of 7½- and 10½-month-old infants. Similar differences in the style of play patterns were found by Clarke-Stewart (1980) in a study of infants 15–30-months old and their parents: "Fathers' play was relatively more likely to be physical and arousing rather than intellectual, didactic, or mediated by objects—as in the case of mothers" (Clarke-Stewart, 1977, p. 37).

Nor are these effects evident only in infancy. MacDonald and Parke (1984), in a study of the play interaction patterns between mothers and fathers and their 3- and 4-year-olds, found that fathers engaged in more physical play with their children than mothers. In contrast, mothers engaged in more object-mediated play with their children than fathers. According to a recent survey of 390 families, the fathers' distinctive role in physical play changes with his age; that is, as he becomes older, there is a decreased likelihood that he will engage his children physically (Mac-Donald & Parke, 1986).

In all studies reviewed, a reasonably consistent pattern emerges: Fathers are tactile and physical while mothers tend to be verbal. Clearly, infants and young children experience not more stimulation from their fathers, but a qualitatively different stimulatory pattern.

However, this pattern of mother–father differences in play style may be in part culture bound. Specifically, neither in Sweden (Lamb, Frodi, Hwang, Frodi, & Steinberg, 1982) nor among Israeli kibbutz families were there clear sex-of-parent differences in the tendency to engage in play or in the types of play initiated.

> Perhaps this reflects the more egalitarian arrangements effective (at least during observation periods) in Sweden and Israel than in the United States. This would suggest that at least in regard, sex differences in maternal and paternal behavior, are influenced by the concrete competing demands on the parents' time, as well as by their socialization and biogenetic tendencies.
>
> *(Sagi et al., 1985, p. 283)*

In spite of the possible cultural boundedness of these stylistic differences between mothers' and fathers' play, it remains useful to explore the implications of these differences found in U.S. samples. In a recent study, MacDonald and Parke (1984) examined the relationship between father–toddler play and peer–peer interaction. Specifically, fathers and their 3- and 4-year-old boys and girls were observed in 20 min of structured play in their homes. In addition, teachers ranked these children in terms of their popularity among their preschool classmates. For both boys and girls, fathers who were rated as exhibiting high levels of physical play with their children and elicited high levels of positive affect in their children during the play sessions had children who received the highest peer popularity ratings. For boys, however, this pattern was qualified by the fathers' level of directiveness. Boys whose fathers were both highly physical and low in directiveness received the highest popularity ratings, while the boys whose fathers were highly directive received lower popularity scores. Possibly, children who interact with a physically playful father and at the same time have an opportunity to regulate the pace and tempo of the interaction, a characteristic of low-directive fathers, learn how to recognize and send emotional signals during social interactions.

> Through physically playful interaction with their parents, especially fathers, children may be learning the social communicative value of their own affective displays as well as how to use these signals to regulate the social behavior of others. In turn, they may learn to decode accurately the social and affective signals of other social partners.
>
> *(MacDonald & Parke, 1984, p. 1276)*

This issue clearly merits more attention by researchers (see also Parke, MacDonald, Beitel, & Bhavangri, 1986).

Father's role as playmate shows developmental changes; in the Clarke-Stewart (1978) study, at 15 months the child's primary playmate was the mother, by 20 months the mother and father shared this role, and by 30 months the father played more than the mother. Similarly, the mother's role as caretaker was diminishing over this same period, and by 30 months there was little difference in caretaking between mothers and fathers. Of particular interest is the pattern of relationships between playful behaviors and other behavior patterns. For mothers, positive emotion and physical stimulation were highly correlated with other measures of stimulation and responsiveness. For fathers, on the other hand, expressions of negative emotion, including scolding, criticizing, and speaking sharply, were related to fathers' physical playfulness. Other evidence suggests developmental changes in parent–child play. According to a recent survey (MacDonald & Parke, 1986), the fathers' distinctive role as a physical play partner changes with age. Physical play was highest between fathers and 2-year-olds, and between 2 and 10 years of age there is a decreased likelihood that they will engage their children physically.

Not only do fathers and mothers differ in their play patterns, infants react differently to mother and father play. Lamb (1976b), in his study of infants 8–13-months old, found that the infants' responses to play with their fathers were significantly more positive than responses to play with their mothers.

Consistent with Lamb's observations is Clarke-Stewart's (1978) finding that 20-month-old children were significantly more responsive to playful social interaction initiated by the father than to play initiated by the mother. At 2½ years of age, children were more cooperative, close, involved, excited, and interested in play with their fathers. Over two-thirds of the children chose to play with their fathers first in a choice situation and displayed a stronger preference for him as a playmate.

Just as the structured–unstructured distinction is important in the attachment studies, a similar distinction is useful in the play sphere. Although there were clear mother–father differences in the play-probe sessions, fewer differences in infant initiations occurred in unstructured home observations (Clarke-Stewart, 1978).

Just as fathers and mothers behave differentially toward male and female infants, the infants, in turn, react differently to their mothers and fathers. In the Lamb studies (1977a, 1977b), boys were in proximity of, approached, and fussed to their fathers more than girls; female infants, on the other hand, were in proximity of and fussed to their mothers more than the boys, while they approached their mothers about as often as did boys. Spelke, Zelazo, Kagan, and Kotelchuck (1973) observed that 1-year-old infants vocalized more to the same- than to the opposite-sex parent, while Ban and Lewis (1974) found that 1-year-old boys look more at their fathers than at their mothers. Finally, Lynn and Cross (1974) found that 2-year-old boys prefer to play with their fathers than with their mothers; girls, on the other hand, show a shift between 2 and 4 years of age to preferring mother as a play partner.

In general, this pattern of findings suggests that father involvement in infancy is quantitatively less than mother involvement, but the types of roles that mother and father play clearly differ as well. The fact of less quantity of interaction, however, does not imply that fathers do not have an important impact on infant development. Just as earlier research (e.g., Hoffman & Nye, 1974; Schaeffer & Emerson, 1964; Wachs & Gruen, 1982) has indicated that quality rather than quantity of mother–infant interaction was the important predictor of infant cognitive and social development, it is likely that a similar assumption will hold for fathers.

Beyond the Dyad: The Impact of the Marital Relationship on Parent–Infant Interaction

Models that limit examination of the effects of interaction patterns to only the father–infant and mother–infant dyads and the direct effects of one individual on another are inadequate for understanding the impact of social interaction patterns in families (Belsky, 1981, 1984; Lewis & Feiring, 1981; Parke et. al., 1979; Pedersen, 1980). The full family group must be considered. Second, parents influence their infants indirectly as well. A parent may influence a child through the mediation of another family member's impact (e.g., a father may contribute to the mother's positive affect toward her child by praising her caregiving ability). Another way in which one parent may indirectly influence the child's treatment by other agents is by modifying the infant's behavior. Child behavior patterns that develop as a result of parent–child interaction may in turn affect the child's treatment by other social agents. For example, irritable infant patterns induced by an insensitive and impatient mother may in turn make the infant more difficult for the father to handle and pacify. Thus patterns developed in interaction with one parent may alter interaction patterns with another caregiver. In larger families, siblings can play a similar mediating role.

Parents have been shown to behave differently when alone with their infant than when interacting with the infant in the presence of the other parent. A sizable body of research has indicated that rates of parent–infant interactive behavior decrease in a triadic in comparison to a dyadic context in both the laboratory (Lamb, 1979) and the home (Belsky, 1979; Clarke-Stewart, 1978; Pedersen, Anderson, & Cain, 1980) with infants of varying ages. This difference in quantity of stimulation in a triadic context stems in part from the fact that the infant has two social agents who each provide less input than either would if alone with the infant. Moreover, as Pedersen, Zaslow, Cain, and Anderson (1981) have documented, when the parents are together they have the opportunity to interact with one another, a further condition that generally reduces the levels of focused behavior directed toward the infant.

However, there are significant exceptions (see Schaffer, 1984, for a review). For example, Parke and his colleagues (Parke, Grossman, & Tinsley, 1981; Parke & O'Leary, 1976) have found that certain behaviors increase rather than decrease from dyadic to triadic situations. Specifically, parents expressed more positive affect (smiling) toward their infant and showed a higher level of exploratory behavior in the presence of the spouse. Our hypothesis is that parents verbally stimulate each other by focusing the partner's attention on aspects of the baby's behavior, which in turn stimulates affectionate or exploratory behavior in the partner. It is clear that greater attention should be given to the specification of conditions that are likely to increase as well as decrease parental behavior in the presence of a third person (Parke & Tinsley, 1981; Schaffer, 1984). Overall these studies indicate that parent–infant interaction cannot be understood by a sole focus on the parent–infant dyad.

Other investigations emphasize the importance of studying the family triad in terms of the impact of the husband–wife relationship on the parent–infant interaction process and the influence of the birth of an at risk infant on the cohesiveness of the family. In a pioneering investigation Pedersen (1975) assessed the influence of the husband–wife relationship on the mother–infant interaction in a feeding context. Ratings were made of the quality of the mother–infant relationship in connection with two time-sampling home observations when the infants were 4 weeks old. Of particular interest were the ratings of *feeding competence,* which refers to the appropriateness of the mother in managing feeding. "Mothers rated high are able to pace the feeding well, intersperse feeding and burping without disrupting the baby and seem sensitive to the baby's needs for either stimulation of feeding or brief rest periods during the course of feedings" (Pedersen, 1975, p. 4). In addition, the husband–wife relationship was assessed through an interview; and finally, neonatal assessments (Brazelton, 1973) were available. Pedersen found:

> When the father was more supportive of the mother, that is, evaluated her maternal skills more positively, she was more effective in feeding the baby. Then again, maybe competent mothers elicit more positive evaluations from their husbands. The reverse holds for marital discord. High tension and conflict in the marriage was associated with more inept feeding on the part of the mother.
>
> *(Pedersen, 1975, p. 6)*

The status and well-being of the infant, assessed by Brazelton as scores of alertness and motor maturity, were also related to the marital relationship. With an alert baby, the father evaluated the mother more positively; with a motorically mature baby, there appeared to be less tension and conflict in the marriage. In Pedersen's (1975) view "a good baby and a good marriage go together." In a later study by Pedersen, Anderson, and Cain (1977), 5-month-old infants were observed individually with their fathers and mothers as well as in a triadic situation in their homes. Although there were no significant relationships found between positive affect between the parents and positive affect directed toward the infant, there was a significant positive correlation between the amounts of negative affect between the parents and that directed toward the infant. Similarly, Vincent (1981) found that observational and self-report measures of the parents' marital relationship were predictive of the quality of parent–infant attachment by the end of the infant's first year.

Further support for the importance of the impact of the marital relationship on parent–infant interaction comes from a recent series of longitudinal studies. In one longitudinal study (Belsky et al., 1984), parents and their infants were observed in a family triadic setting at 1, 3, and 9 months after the birth of a first infant. These investigators found that fathers' overall engagement of the infant was reliably and positively related to overall marital engagement at three different times of measurement, whereas maternal engagement was related to the marital relationship only at 1 month of age.

In a second study, mother–infant, father–infant, and husband–wife interaction was observed during three separate naturalistic 1-hour home observations when infants were 1, 3, and 9 months old (Belsky & Volling, 1986). As in the previous study by Belsky and his colleagues, there was a greater degree of relationship between fathering and marital interaction than between mothering and marital interaction. However, this difference is qualified, in part, by the age of the infant, since the patterns are approximately similar at 1 and 3 months, but clearly favoring fathers by 9 months. Further evidence of the differential impact of the quality of the marital relationship on fathers and mothers derives from a further cross-lag analysis. This analysis indicated that marital interaction at 1 month was positively related to father–infant involvement at 3 months in the absence of any significant relationship between fathering at 1 month and marital interaction at 3 months. This finding suggests that positive communication between husband and wife about the baby at 1 month promotes stimulating, responsive, and positively affectionate father involvement at 3 months. However, in light of the absence of further evidence that marital communication fosters father involvement at 9 months or maternal involvement at any time, caution needs to be exercised in drawing prematurely firm conclusions about the links between marital and parent–infant relationships.

Other evidence is consistent with these findings. In a recent study of infants 4–8 months old and their parents, Dickie and Matheson (1984) examined the relationship between parental competence and spousal support. Parental competence was based on home observations and involved a variety of components such as emotional consistency, contingent responding, and warmth and pleasure in parenting. Emotional support, a measure of affection, respect, and satisfaction in the husband–wife relationship, and cognitive support, an index of husband–wife agreement in child care, were positively related to maternal competence. Ragozin, Robinson, and Basham (1983), in a study of 105 preterm and full-term infants 4 months old, found that support from an intimate (spouse, partner) was strongly and consistently related to a variety of measures of maternal parenting attitudes and behavior. Intimate support was related to satisfaction with parenting, as well as maternal behavior (a composite index of responsiveness, affection, and gratification from interaction with infant). Moreover, intimate support was related to infants' responsiveness to the parent as well as a cluster of positive infant behaviors during maternal face-to-face interaction. The impact of support on infants was indirect since intimate support modified maternal behavior, which in turn related to infant behavior.

Moreover, in a recent cross-cultural study in Japan, Durrett, Otaki, and Richards (1984) found that mothers' perception of emotional support from the father was related to the quality of infant–mother attachment. Specifically, mothers of securely attached infants perceived greater emotional support from the father than mothers of anxiously avoidant infants and anxiously resistant infants. "Even though the husband–wife relationship in Japan likely differs from spousal relationships in America, it is interesting to note that if the mother perceives support from the father, the mother/infant relationships are enhanced" (Durrett et al., 1984, p. 174).

Just as paternal support relates positively to maternal competence, there is evidence that maternal support is similarly linked to the father's parenting competence. Dickie and Matheson (1984) found that maternal emotional support and cognitive support were related to paternal competence. In fact, these investigators found that spousal support is a stronger correlate of competence in fathers than in mothers. The level of emotional and cognitive support successfully discriminated high and low competent fathers but failed to do so in the case of mothers. This suggests that spousal support is more critical for adequate parenting on the part of fathers than mothers.

In a short-term longitudinal study of the antecedents of father involvement, Feldman, Nash, and Aschenbrenner (1983) measured a variety of factors, including the marital relationship during the third trimester of the wives' pregnancies and again at 6 months postpartum. In support of the importance of marital factors for understanding parent–infant relationships, they found that quality of marital relations predicted father involvement in caregiving, playfulness, and satisfaction with fatherhood. As Feldman and colleagues note: "In our upper to middle class, highly educated sample, the quality of the marital dyad, whether reported by the husband or wife, is the most consistently powerful predictor of paternal involvement and satisfaction" (1983, p. 1634).

Finally, Lamb and Elster (1985) recently addressed a similar question in a sample of adolescent mothers and their male partners. Using an observational scheme similar to that of Belsky and colleagues (1984), they observed mother, father, and infant at home in an unstructured context for approximately 1 hour. As in earlier studies, father–infant interaction was significantly and positively related to the level of mother–father engagement. By contrast, mother–infant interaction was unrelated to measures of mother–father engagement.

Together these findings suggest that successful paternal parenting is more dependent on a supportive marital relationship than maternal parenting. A number of factors may aid in explaining this relationship. First, there is prior evidence that the father's level of participation is, in part, determined by the extent to which the mother permits participation (Dickie & Carnahan, 1980; Redican, 1976). Second, since the paternal role is less well articulated and defined than the maternal role, spousal support may serve to help crystallize the boundaries of appropriate role behavior. Third, men have fewer opportunities to acquire and practice skills that are central to caregiving activities during socialization and therefore may benefit more than mothers from informational (i.e., cognitive) support. Further research on this issue should be a fruitful vehicle for exploring the antecedents and constraints on performance of both fathering and mothering roles.

THE ROLE OF SOCIAL SUPPORT IN MODIFYING PARENT–INFANT INTERACTION PATTERNS

Families exist as units with other social organizations within society and thus need to be viewed within their social context. Recognition of the role of the community and community agents as modifiers of family modes of interaction is necessary for an adequate theory of early family and infant development.

Recognition of the embeddedness of families in a set of broader social systems such as community and culture or in Brim's (1975) terms in the meso and macro systems is only a first step. The next important tasks are: (1) to articulate the ways in which these other levels of social organization affect family functioning; and (2) to explore the ways in which these influence processes take place. It should be noted that community influence, regardless of its form, can be either positive or negative; this view stands in contrast to the view that a high degree of connectedness with community resources is, ipso facto, necessarily positive. In addition, it is assumed that the relationship between communities and families is bidirectional with the influence moving in both directions. It is assumed that the ways in which communities and families are related will vary across the developmental span. Moreover, the influence of support systems on families may be either direct or indirect in its effects. Finally, both availability and utilization need to be separately considered. Families may have friends, relatives, and neighbors available, but fail to utilize these members of their informal social network in times of stress or crisis or on a day-to-day basis.

Following are some of the mechanisms through which these community and extrafamilial influences operate to modify early parent–infant interaction patterns.

Informal and Formal Support Systems

To explore the mechanisms by which community influence is transmitted to the family, two kinds of support systems need to be distinguished: informal and formal.

Informal Support Systems

Informal support systems are: (1) unstructured social networks, which consist of a person's relatives, friends, neighbors, co-workers, and other acquaintances who interact with the person; and (2) structured social support systems, which include a variety of neighborhood or community-based organizations or groups that are generally not officially generated, controlled, or funded by local or other government officials (Cochran & Brassard, 1979; Parke & Tinsley, 1982). Both of these types of social support systems can help families function in a variety of ways: providing instrumental physical and financial support, providing emotional–social support, and providing informational support (Unger & Powell, 1980).

It is useful to reconceptualize the marital relationship as a social support resource for parents, with the mother functioning as a potential support resource and member of the father's social network and vice versa. In this context, the effect of supportive behavior on the part of the mother or father can be examined for its effect on mother–infant and father–infant interaction. The studies reviewed in the preceding section of this chapter indicate clearly that the husband–wife relationship is an important source of informal support. Parents function as support figures for each other, which in turn facilitates parenting and the quality of parent–infant interaction.

A less often recognized function that spouses may serve is that of mediator to extrafamilial informal social network members. In a recent in-depth study of the maternal social networks in 20 families, Solomon (1982) found that fathers played a multidimensional support role including facilitator of outside support. Specifically, fathers contributed to the receipt of help from neighbors: The average length of time the father was at home was positively associated with the amount of help received from neighbors. Solomon postulates that the fathers' availability to neighbors for such tasks as home repairs, emergencies, or snow shoveling stimulated neighborly reciprocity. Fathers also contributed their salaries for the provision of paid support services.

Extended kin such as grandparents and other relatives often function as an important informal support system for parents. While there has been a general shift in the structure of living arrangements from an extended to a self-contained nuclear family, the support functions of kin remain an important source of assistance to families, including fathers, and an important source of approval (or lack of it) for further father involvement in child care (Tinsley & Parke, 1984; Tinsley & Parke, in press). Estimates indicate that families have relatively frequent contact with grandparents, for example, on the average of one to three times per week (Harris, 1975).

Do fathers utilize grandparents as sources of support? According to a recent study (Tinsley & Parke, in press), fathers and mothers of 7-month-old infants did not differ in the extent to which they utilized grandparents as sources of support. However, fathers did report higher levels of satisfaction with contact with their own parents (paternal grandparents) than with the wives' parents (maternal grandparents). Fathers as well as mothers rely upon extended kin during times of transition, change, and stress as well as on a day-to-day basis. Evidence suggests that fathers increase their contact with their own parents during pregnancy—especially their mothers (Bittman & Zalk, 1978). According to Gladieux (1978), fathers also increase their contact with other members of informal networks during pregnancy, especially friends who are already parents. Moreover, the availability of informal supports—either kin or nonkin—who can serve to provide support was linked with higher satisfaction for expectant fathers in this study.

Families are particularly likely to rely on external social support systems under conditions of high stress or family crisis. The birth of an infant prematurely constitutes one example of this type of situation. Recent evidence (Parke & Tinsley, 1984) indicates that parents are more likely to use social support systems when their infants are born prematurely than when their infants are born at term. While both mothers and fathers use both informal support systems and formal systems when their infant is born prematurely, fathers, overall, utilize informal supports in these circumstances less than mothers. Instead, especially for informational purposes, fathers are more likely to rely on formal rather than informal support agencies, perhaps due to their general lower utilization of informal support (Parke & Anderson, 1986).

In studies of abusive families, it has been found that these families are often socially isolated and lack adequate social support systems (Garbarino & Gilliam, 1980; Parke, 1981c; Parke & Collmer, 1975). Similarly, in their study of divorce, Hetherington, Cox, and Cox (1978) have found that the adequacy of the mother's social support network was positively related to her effectiveness with her children.

Socioeconomic conditions and stresses can also affect the parent–infant relationship, mediated by the availability and utilization of social support. For example, in a study of low-income mothers of infants, Hall, Williams, and Greenberg (1985) found that unemployed women with a poor social network had a substantially greater risk of depression than employed women with low network support. Given the empirical relationship between maternal depression and social, emotional, cognitive, and behavioral risk in children (e.g., Billings & Moos, 1981; Orvaschel, Weissman, & Kidd, 1980), life experiences can interact with social support resources to affect parent–infant interaction. A further example is a study of North African Moslem families who had emigrated to live in Paris, France (Honig & Gardner, 1985). These families were severely stressed along a number of dimensions: living conditions, medical status, and employment status. Intensive interviews and assessment indicated that some families became "overwhelmed" and some coped sufficiently under the same circumstances. A significantly greater number of "overwhelmed" families reported severe father–infant and mother–infant interaction problems and child behavior problems. The availability of support resources was not described in this report. However, the study further demonstrates the role of socioeconomic stressors in parent–child interaction patterns and individual and family differences in coping with stressors.

Of more direct relevance are studies of the relationship between social networks and parent–child interaction. Unger (1979) examined the influence of social networks on mother–infant interaction in a small sample of white low-income mothers and their young infants (under 6 months). Using the HOME Scale (Elardo, Bradley, & Caldwell, 1975) to assess interaction, Unger found that mothers who experienced high levels of stress were found to be more actively involved with their infants when they had weekly contact with friends than when they were infrequently in contact. Parents also appeared more responsive to their infants if they were receiving material resources from their network members. In a related study that also employed the HOME Scale, Pascoe, Loda, Jeffries, and Earp (1981) found a positive relationship between the level of maternal social support and selected subscales from the HOME Scale in a group of families with 3-year-old children. Unfortunately, Pascoe et al. did not examine intrafamilial (i.e., spouse support) and extrafamilial social support separately, which does not permit an evaluation of the relative importance of differing sources of support. However, these two studies of Pascoe and colleagues and Unger and Powell are important in view of the previously established positive relationship between the HOME Scale and mental test performance (Bradley & Caldwell, 1976). These investigations suggest that social support may affect infant and child developmental outcomes indirectly through modifying the nature of parent–child interaction patterns.

In turn these altered interaction patterns may lead to different patterns of infant–parent attachment. Crockenberg (1981) found that the utilization of social support was related to the quality of infant–mother attachment, especially in the case of infants with difficult temperaments (this issue will be discussed further later in the chapter). In a later study Crittenden (1985) provided further support for the impact of social support on mother–infant attachment. Abusive and nonabusive mothers and their infants were assessed by the Strange Situation procedure and various indices of the mothers' social networks. Nonabusive mothers were found to have more supportive and satisfying network interaction than the abusive group of mothers. Maternal patterns of social support were related to infant attachment and accounted for 20 percent of the variance in infant security of attachment quality. Unfortunately, neither Crittenden nor Crockenberg examined the independent contribution of different sources of support (fathers, older siblings, extended family, neighbors, friends, professionals) on infant–mother attachment. Nevertheless, it seems apparent that mothers' social networks are a significant factor influencing child-rearing quality and some infant outcomes.

In view of the importance of the quality of attachment to mother (as well as father) for later social and cognitive functioning, these findings are of special significance. In comparison to securely attached infants, insecurely attached infants are less socially competent in later peer–peer interactions (Pastor, 1981; Waters, Wippman, & Sroufe, 1979), are less able to establish friendly relationships with strange adults (Main & Weston, 1981), and show less involvement, persistence, and enjoyment in problem-solving situations (Easterbrooks & Goldberg, 1984; Matas, Arend, & Sroufe, 1978).

Social support may be of particular importance in cases of increased risk for parenting problems, such as adolescent mothers, single parents, or preterm unhealthy or temperamentally difficult infants.

In a study of adolescent mothers, Colletta (1981) found that mothers who received a high level of support from their family of origin—especially emotional support—were lower in hostility, indifference, and rejection of their infants and toddlers 1–3 years old than mothers who received a low level of family support. Similarly, Mercer, Hackley, and Bostrom (1983), in a study of adolescent mothers at 1 month postpartum, found that emotional support was related to higher feelings of love and affection for their infants and greater gratification in the mothering role. Moreover, instrumental support was associated with stronger feeling of love for their offspring and higher sense of competency in the maternal role. Other studies support the relationship between adolescent maternal attitudes and behavior and the availability of social support (Crockenberg, 1983; Epstein, 1980; Wandersman & Unger, 1983). Although earlier studies have been criticized for failing to control for other potential causal variables that might have accounted for the observed support-behavior relationships (Crockenberg, 1985), more recent work that has controlled for these possible confounding factors has yielded similar results. In this study of adolescent mothers, Crockenberg (1985) found that support continued to be associated with responsiveness to crying, sensitivity, and accessibility—even after partialing out such factors as the mother's separation from her own family early in life, maternal attitudes toward responsive caregiving, ethnicity, and current life stress.

Further support comes from a recent study by Osofsky and Culp (1986) in which they followed the development of adolescent mothers from the prenatal period to 6 months after the birth of the infant. First, there was a high degree of stability in the kind of support—familial, financial, and educational—that the mothers received prenatally and at 6 months. Moreover, higher levels of prenatal support the mother reported receiving from significant others were related to higher levels of maternal self-esteem at 6 months. Although self-esteem and support were unrelated at 6 months, support and depression were negatively related at the later time point. Finally, the amount of support the mother received was positively related to a variety of maternal behaviors, including looking at her infant, eye contact, handling, and cuddling. Together these studies provide impressive support for the relationship between social support and parental competence among adolescent mothers.

Does marital status influence the imput of social support on parent–infant relationships? In a comparative study of the relationship between stress and support in single- and two-parent families, Weinraub and Wolf (1983) found that social support had differential effects on the two groups of parents. Overall single parents tended to be more socially isolated than married parents and received less emotional and parenting support. While there were no differences in the observed quality of parent–child interaction in the two groups, optimal mother–child interaction was predicted by different factors for single- and two-parent families. Predicting optimal mother–child interaction in single-parent families were fewer stressful life events and increased parenting support as well as reduced social contact. In the case of single parents a high level of outside social contact may result in less time with her child, which, in turn, may result in a lower-quality parent–child relationship. However, this relationship merits further examination before any definitive conclusion is drawn (see also Hetherington & Camara, 1984). Predicting optimal interaction in two-parent families were fewer stressful life events, satisfaction with emotional support, and the availability of household help. This study suggests the importance not only of considering marital status in evaluating the effects of support but also of recognizing the multifaceted nature of social support.

Social support may be important in the case of at risk infants such as premature and sick infants. Parke and Anderson (1986) found that parents, especially mothers, are more likely to rely on informal social support systems when an infant is born prematurely when with it is born at term. A number of studies have examined the impact of informal social support on parent–infant interaction in both preterm and full-term infants. Crinic, Greenberg, Ragozin, Robinson, and Basham (1983), using samples of both preterm and full-term 4-month-old infants, reported positive relationships between informal social support and a variety of measures of parenting attitudes and behavior—regardless of the birth status of the infant. In addition to the importance of the spousal relationship discussed earlier, these investigators found that community or neighborhood support was modestly predictive of satisfaction with parenting (borderline effect) while more strongly predictive of mothers' behavior in free play and imitation and vocalization elicitation situations. Mothers with higher levels of community support were more responsive, gratified with the interactions, and affectionate, as were their infants. Although social support did not differentially affect parents of preterm and full-term infants, later research suggests that differential effects can be found if a wider range of infant health status is examined.

In a recent study of the social support networks of mothers with high-risk infants and mother–infant interaction, Feiring, Fox, Jaskir, and Lewis (1985) found a strong relationship among high-risk birth, postnatal illness, mothers' social network, and mother–infant interaction patterns. Ninety mothers and infants, comprising four groups, were studied: healthy and sick preterms and healthy and sick full-term infants. Assessment of mother–infant interaction and description of the mothers' social support utilization were undertaken when the infants were 3 months of age. Results indicated that mothers of sick preterm infants reported fewer friends and fewer total support agents contributing goods than mothers in the other groups, while mothers of both preterm and term sick infants reported receiving less services than mothers of healthy preterm and term infants. Differences in social support and infant birth status varied along three dimensions of mother–infant interaction: proximal, distal, and play behaviors. For all families, mothers who received more goods from support agents were more proximal with their infants. Mothers of sick preterm infants were most distal with their infants, although receipt of goods by these mothers reduced their distal behavior. Mothers who received the most services engaged in the most play with their infants, especially for families with healthy preterm and term infants. The authors of this study suggest an interpretive pattern in the data: cautious network response to sick preterms (associated with less proximal and more distal maternal behavior) and more positive network responses to sick term and healthy preterm and term infants, leading to increasing proximal and decreasing distal mother behavior. A possible model suggests that the support received by the mother was mediated by the birth status of the infant, which in turn modified mother–infant interaction behavior.

Finally, some infant characteristics such as temperament may modify the relationship between social support and parent–infant relationships. Crockenberg (1981) found that the extent to which mothers utilized social support networks was related to the infant's pattern of attachment to its mother. Especially in the case of irritable infants, utilization of social support was associated with secure attachment. Wandersman and Unger (1983), in a longitudinal investigation of 40 adolescent mothers and their infants, found that, for mothers with temperamentally easy infants, social support (provided by family, friends, or the infants' fathers) was positively related to mothers' feelings of satisfaction and happiness. Moreover, for mothers with temperamentally difficult infants, social support (provided by the infants' fathers and relatives) reduced contact with friends, and mothers' knowledge of infants and their maturity were related to scores on the HOME Scale (see also Unger & Wandersman, 1986). These studies provide excellent illustrations of the interplay of individual characteristics (temperament) and the role of the social environment (social support networks) on later patterns of infant–parent interaction.

However, these studies are only suggestive and leave unanswered a variety of questions. First, there are few (e.g., Feiring et al., 1985; Weinraub & Wolf, 1983) direct observational data available that describe in detail the ways in which parent–infant interaction patterns are altered by the availability of social networks. Second, the ways in which the relationships between social networks and parent–infant interaction shift across developmental levels of the infant have not been explored. Third, the relationships between parent–infant interaction and social support have been, for the most part, restricted to mothers; few data concerning these relationships for fathers are yet available. There have been few investigations that have simultaneously assessed the assumed linkages among social support, parent–infant interaction, and infant cognitive and social outcomes. Nevertheless, these studies do underscore the value of expanding our conceptual framework to include the links between the family and external social networks that can function as support systems for families.

Relationship Between Formal Social Support Systems and Family Interaction Patterns

Formal Support Systems

Two types of formal support systems need to be distinguished: (1) general and (2) specific to at risk infants and families. General support systems are the types of formal support systems that are available to all members of the community, including such support systems as health care facilities for both adults and children, counseling services for individuals and families, employment agencies, educational opportunities, social work services to facilitate adoption and placement of infants and children, housing assistance, welfare assistance, and recreational facilities.

AFDC payments vary from state to state, and it is unclear how this money affects family structure. There is some indication that higher payments may allow women to separate from or divorce their husbands. Women in states with higher payment levels are more likely to live alone while those with lower payments tend to remain within their parents' homes. Yet this isolation from family support may be detrimental to children. Although we can reach no conclusions, this reminds us that there may be de facto incentives and disincentives for fathers to be involved with their children.

There are a variety of support systems of special relevance to at risk infants and families. These programs both serve the educational function of providing child care information and alleviate stress associated with premature or ill infants. Support systems that serve an educational function include hospital-based courses in child care and child rearing, nurse visiting programs, well baby clinics, follow-up programs, and parent discussion groups. Some other supportive programs that offer stress relief are family and group day-care facilities, baby-sitting services, mothers' helpers, homemaker and housekeeping services, drop-off centers, crisis nurseries, and hot lines.

In recent years a number of investigators have used the hospital to provide social support for parents, with the postpartum period a convenient time point for initiating supportive services for parents of infants. Parents are accessible at this point, and often motivation for learning about infant development and caregiving skills is high during this time.

Demonstration of Newborn Capacities

One approach has been to demonstrate the sensory, perceptual, and social capacities of the infant to parents. The underlying assumption of this approach is that parental interaction patterns are, in part, a function of the parents' knowledge of the infant's capabilities, and by increasing or correcting the parents' perceptions about their infant's abilities, interaction patterns, in turn, will be modified. This approach is consistent with a cognitive mediational model of parent–infant interaction, which assumes that parental interaction is, in part, determined by the assumptions that parents make about the infant's capabilities (Parke, 1978).

Impact on Mothers

Earlier work with teenage mothers and their preterm infants has shown that a combination of exposure to a demonstration of the Brazelton Neonatal Assessment Scale

(BNAS) and the regular completion of an adaptation of the exam to their infants at birth and at 1-week intervals during the first month by the infants' mothers yielded positive outcomes in a number of domains (Widmayer & Field, 1979, 1981). At 1 and 4 months, parent–infant interaction in both structured feeding and face-to-face situations was rated as more optimal, and the infant scored higher on the Bayley Mental Development Index at 12 months. However, there were few differences between the Brazelton exposure group and an intervention group in which the mothers administered the modified form of the Brazelton exam to their infants for the first month, which suggests that the opportunity actively to administer the exam may be more important than mere passive exposure to the administration of the Brazelton exam.

In a subsequent study, Worobey and Belsky (1982) compared passive exposure to the Brazelton (in which mothers just observed administration of the exam), active exposure to the exam (in which mothers elicited responses themselves), and verbal exposure only (in which mothers simply heard a summary of their infants' performance). Observations at 1 month indicated that only *active exposure* enhanced the responsive, stimulating nature of maternal care. Other evidence suggests that passive visual or verbal exposure was ineffective (McLaughlin, Drake, Deni, & Constantini, 1983) while active exposure was successful in influencing confidence and knowledge of infants.

Impact on Fathers

This intervention strategy has been extended to include fathers in a number of recent investigations. Myers (1982) taught mothers or fathers to perform the Brazelton exam on their own infants with attention being drawn to the infants' most positive interactive and physical abilities. In comparison to control parents, both mothers and fathers in the treatment condition had more knowledge of infant development at both the newborn period and a 4-week follow-up. Moreover, the treatment fathers reported to be more involved in caretaking with their infants at 4 weeks than were control fathers. However, there were no differences in parent–infant interaction during a structured 10-min observation session. Similarly, Pannabecker, Emde, and Austin (1982) found no impact of active exposure to a Brazelton demonstration during the early postnatal period in the hospital. Beal (1984) exposed first-time fathers to a Brazelton demonstration on their infants at 2–3 days old. A control group of fathers received no intervention. To assess the impact of this brief intervention, father–infant interaction was observed at 8 weeks postpartum. During a 2-min father–infant interaction session, the interaction patterns among the intervention group were characterized by a higher degree of father–infant mutuality. In addition, the fathers who received the BNAS demonstration perceived their infants as less difficult than fathers in the control group. These findings suggest that both father–infant interaction patterns and paternal perceptions can be modified by this type of intervention. Since all of the fathers also attended prenatal classes and both labor and delivery, it would be interesting to assess whether this type of demonstration would be effective for less interested and involved fathers.

Impact on Mothers and Fathers as a Unit

In response to conceptual calls to treat the family system rather than merely mother–infant or father–infant alone (Belsky, 1981; Parke, 1979, 1981; Pedersen et al., 1980), two recent studies have examined the impact of exposure to a Brazelton demonstration on mother and father together. This assumes that mothers and fathers may indirectly as well as directly influence their infants and that the influence is often mediated through the mother–father unit. In an Australian intervention study, Dolby, English, and Warren (1982) found that active exposure of mother and father together to the Brazelton exam positively affected both maternal and paternal involvement as indexed by home observations and interviews when infants were 6 months old.

In a further American-based exploration of this issue, Belsky (1985) improved upon the design of Dolby and colleagues. In his study, Belsky targeted either mothers or mothers and fathers together. Families were assigned to either an active exposure (i.e., parent(s) actively elicited responses from the newborn) or a passive exposure (i.e., verbal description of the infant's performance of the exam) to the Brazelton exam. Assessments of mother–infant interaction in the dyad and mother–infant, father–infant, and husband–wife interaction in the triad revealed no effects of experimental intervention across the groups at 1, 3, and 9 months. However, there were modest positive effects on both the paternal and marital measures for a subsample of fathers and mothers who rated the demonstration as interesting and enjoyable and who established rapport with the facilitator. These analyses can only be viewed as suggestive but do indicate that more attention needs to be paid to motivational factors as a possible qualifier of the utility of this type of intervention.

Possibly even more important are the methodological implications of the Belsky study for interpreting previous work. The results of the Belsky study that compared both active and passive exposure groups rather than using a no-treatment control raise questions about earlier studies using only no-treatment controls (e.g., Beal, 1984; Dolby et al., 1982; Myers, 1982). The success of these earlier studies may have been due to a Hawthorne effect rather than exposure to the Brazelton demonstration per se. However, the use of different types of assessment situations (e.g., structured vs. naturalistic) makes direct comparisons difficult. In any case, the inconsistent pattern of results suggests that no definite conclusions can be drawn concerning the effectiveness of this type of hospital-centered intervention. Researchers need to determine whether it is the knowledge imparted, the attention drawn to the parent(s), or the altering of self- or spouse perceptions that serves as the active ingredient. Perhaps then we can understand why results have been equivocal. It may be that for certain subsamples of fathers this intervention is useful.

Direct Teaching of Parenting Skills

A more direct approach involves the actual teaching of parenting skills. The media that are used can vary and include face-to-face demonstrations, the provision of written information, or the use of film or videotape presentation. Often these programs are presented in a hospital setting, and in particular during the postpartum period—a convenient time for initiating supportive services for parents of infants. Parents are accessible at this point, and often motivation for learning about infant development and caregiving skills is high during this time.

The value of hospital-based programs for parents is illustrated in the work of Badger, Burns, and Vietze (1981). Teenage mothers who were assumed to be at risk for later parenting problems were recruited in the hospital during the postpartum period and given a series of weekly classes that were the vehicle for a variety of supportive services. In addition to information and instruction in how to stimulate their infants' social and cognitive skills, provided in group classes, the young mothers received information about infant nutrition, family planning, and health care. Further institutional support was available from a clinic doctor of a health service team during the class sessions. Results indicated that young teenage mothers (16 years or younger) and their infants profited from this intervention effort. Specifically, the infants of high-risk mothers who attended classes had normal Bayley scores at 1 year in contrast to a comparison group who had significantly lower Bayley mental scores, emphasizing that social support can indirectly as well as directly affect family members. Furthermore, the mothers who attended the classes were more physically and emotionally responsive to their infants than mothers in the comparison samples. Unfortunately, the relative contributions of the components that may account for the observed differences in infant functioning are unclear.

The early postpartum period can be effectively utilized to provide support for fathers as well. A recent hospital-based study (Parke, Hymel, Power, & Tinsley, 1980) demonstrates the efficacy of this approach. The project involves an assessment of the effect of exposure to a specially designed intervention during the postpartum hospital period on the attitudes and behavior of fathers. Briefly, one group of fathers saw a 15 min videotape, "Fathers and Infants," while a control group of fathers followed the usual hospital routine and saw no videotape presentation. To assess the impact of the intervention, a variety of attitudinal measures and observational measures of father–infant interaction were secured in the hospital in the early postpartum period and in the home at 3 weeks and 3 months for both intervention and control groups. At 3 months, the typical level of father participation in routine caretaking activities in the home was assessed. The purpose of the project was to assess the effectiveness of this limited intervention on paternal attitudes, interaction patterns, and levels of participation in infant care.

During the mothers' postpartum hospitalization, one group of 16 fathers was shown the videotape designed to increase father–infant interaction and caretaking involvement. A control group of 16 fathers saw no videotape. In the videotape, three different fathers were shown successfully playing with, feeding, and diapering their babies. In addition, a narrator emphasized the wide range of newborn cognitive and social capacities as well as the active role that fathers can assume in early care and stimulation of infants. The videotape was designed to serve four purposes: (1) to modify fathers' sex-role attitudes concerning the appropriateness of infant caretaking for adult males; (2) to provide specific demonstrations of feeding and diapering; (3) to provide information concerning newborn infants' perceptual and cognitive capabilities; and (4) to demonstrate a number of ways in which fathers can play with babies, emphasizing contingent responses to infant cues.

Fathers in the film condition were shown the videotape 1 or 2 days after the birth of their infants. Fathers in both film and control conditions followed a similar schedule of assessments. Briefly, the fathers filled out an attitude questionnaire and were observed during a 20-min period with their infants in the hospital and again at 3 weeks and 3 months in the home. At 3 months, a parental diary of caretaking activity was completed. All assessments for the film group were completed after viewing the film. In comparison to a control group of fathers who saw no videotape, fathers who viewed the film in the hospital increased their knowledge about infant perceptual abilities, believed more strongly that infants need stimulation, and were more responsive to their infants during feeding and play in comparison to fathers who were not exposed to the film. Based on diary reports on caretaking activities in the home at 3 months, fathers of boys who saw the film were more likely to diaper and feed their infants than fathers in the no-film control group. For fathers of girls, exposure to the film did not produce any changes in the amount of either diapering or feeding in the home at 3 months. Since fathers are differentially predisposed to interact more with male infants than female infants, the film may have served to strengthen these already existing tendencies. As discussed elsewhere, there is a substantial body of literature in support of the claim that fathers both expect to and do show higher involvement with male than female infants (cf. Parke, 1979; Pedersen, 1980). Similarly, previous social influence literature suggests that it is easier to produce further change in a direction that is already favored than in a nonfavored direction (McGuire, 1968).

Further evidence of the effectiveness of a film intervention during the postpartum period comes from a recent study by Arbuckle (1983). In this project, Arbuckle used a film intervention developed by Parke, et al. (1980). Entitled ''Becoming a Family,'' the film demonstrated the same behavior, such as feeding and diapering, playing, and recognizing infant capabilities, as was included in the Parke, et al. (1980) film intervention. In contrast to the earlier film, this film depicted *both* mothers and fathers actively engaged in caregiving and game playing. Assessment of the impact of the film 4–6 weeks later indicated that first-time fathers who saw the film in comparison to a no-film control group of fathers had greater knowledge of infant sensory and cognitive capabilities and were higher in their perception of the importance of providing infant affection and stimulation. Moreover, the experimental fathers reported higher levels of involvement in the daily caregiving of their babies 4–6 weeks after the intervention. No sex of infant differences were reported. In spite of the limitation of this study by the reliance on self-report measures, the similarity of the findings across these two film intervention studies underscores the potential value of this approach for modifying paternal behavior. Further work is clearly justified; particularly important would be studies that isolate the effective components of these film intervention programs. Finally, comparison of film interventions with other types of interventions such as medical staff instruction, discussion groups, or informational booklets would be helpful. By addressing the relative effectiveness of different approaches, the most optimal and most cost-effective procedures for different groups will become evident.

Another set of studies illustrates the potential for health care providers to play a supportive role for parents of infants and young children. Although these studies have focused on mothers, these types of interventions could provide a useful strategy for promoting father parenting competence as well. In a study by Chamberlin (1979), mothers who participated in an educational program concerning child development during pediatric well baby visits increased their knowledge of child development and their perceptions of being supported in the caregiving role. A related study (Whitt & Casey, 1982) suggests that mothers who were provided with an office-based pediatric intervention program emphasizing physical and preventive child care, developmental norms, and information on infant communication abilities during well baby exams demonstrated a more positive relationship with their infants. The potential of this type of intervention for fathers will depend, in part, on changes in the flexibility of work schedules, which would permit fathers to participate more regularly in pediatric follow-up visits to the pediatrician. Alternatively, intervention programs should be offered on a more flexible basis, such as evenings and weekends, to accommodate fathers.

Although the full potential of hospital and other health care facilities as settings for providing support for fathers is not yet realized, the studies reviewed in these sections illustrate the value of these settings for modifying the parenting behavior of fathers as well as mothers.

Posthospital Experimental Interventions

Successful intervention is restricted to neither the hospital nor the postpartum period, as recent studies illustrate. Crockenberg (1985) recently investigated the relationship between professional support and the quality of maternal care by adolescent mothers in England and the United States. Professional care was defined as the number of health professionals other than doctors (public health nurses, midwives, health visitors, social workers) who had helped the mother since the baby's birth. Mothers and infants were observed in their homes when the babies were 3–3½ months old. English mothers received more professional support, engaged in more smiling and eye contact and less frequent routine contact, and responded more quickly to their babies' crying than did American mothers. Evidence that professional support—regardless of culture—mediates these linkages with maternal behavior derives from the finding that English–American differences are nonsignificant when professional support is partialed out. This study provides further support for the linkage between formal support systems and parenting competence.

In another study, Dickie and Carnahan (1980) provided training to mothers and fathers of infants 4–12 months old in order to increase their competence. Utilizing Goldberg's notion of competence as parental ability to assess, predict, elicit, and provide contingent response experiences for the infant, these investigators provided eight weekly 2-hr sessions. Training emphasized individual infant variation, knowledge of the infant's temperament and cues, provision of contingent experiences, and awareness of the infant's effect on the parents. Fathers who had participated in the training sessions, in contrast to fathers who had not participated, increased their interactions with their infants; specifically, they talked, touched, held, attended more, and gave more contingent responses to infant smiles and vocalizations. The infants of the trained fathers sought interaction more than infants of fathers in the control group. However, mothers in the trained group decreased their interactions; in view of this fact that training did increase the judgments of the spouses' competence, it is possible that the wives of the trained fathers encouraged their competent husbands to assume a greater share of the infant care and interactional responsibilities. Interestingly, this finding underlines the reciprocal nature of the mother–father relationship and provides further support for viewing the family as a social system in which the activities of one member have an impact on the behavior of other family members. Finally, these data are consistent with nonhuman primate findings that father–infant involvement varies inversely with the degree of maternal restrictiveness (for reviews see Parke & Suomi, 1981; Redican & Taub, 1981).

As a number of recent studies suggest, efforts to modify father–infant interaction need not be restricted to young infants. Zelazo, Kotelchuck, Barber, and David

(1977) selected 20 very-low-interacting fathers and their 12-month-old firstborn sons for an intervention study. These fathers did little caretaking or playing and were present only occasionally when their children were awake. Twelve fathers received an intervention involving playing with their infants for ½ hr a day for 4 weeks in their homes. To facilitate the play interaction, a schedule of games and toys was provided for the father. Using a social learning strategy (cf. Bandura, 1977), the experimenters both demonstrated the games, toys, and styles of interaction and coached the fathers in these activities prior to the intervention period. A control group of eight low-interacting fathers received no intervention. To assess the impact of the intervention on the infants' behavior, a lab-based parent–infant interaction session was held before and after the training period. This consisted of a 20-min free-play period, with both parents in the room reading, followed by a series of maternal and paternal departures. In comparison to the control group, infants in the experimental group increased their interaction with their fathers in the free-play session; these infant boys looked more at their fathers and initiated more interaction with them. Separation protest was not affected by the experimental intervention. This was surprising in view of earlier reports that as father involvement increased separation upset in the presence of a stranger lessened (Kotelchuck, 1972; Spelke et al., 1973). Although it was a pioneering study, there were a number of limitations. First, the fathers were instructed to initiate interactions in the lab sessions, and so it is unclear whether there were increases in father behaviors directed to their infants. Second, it is unfortunate that these investigators did not monitor the amount of interaction between fathers and infants in their homes as a follow-up to their intervention program. In spite of these limitations, the investigation further underlines the modifiability of the father–infant relationship. It also serves as a corrective reminder of the fact that modification of early social interaction patterns is not necessarily limited to a particular "critical" period. As both Zelazo and his colleagues and many earlier intervention studies (Rheingold, 1956; Skeels, 1966) have demonstrated, infant responsiveness can be modified at a variety of age levels. A similar caution applies to the development of parental responsiveness to infants. Moreover, the early contact studies (cf. Klaus & Kennell, 1976, 1981), which suggested the importance of the immediate postpartum period for the facilitation of parental responsiveness, have been seriously challenged (Goldberg, 1983; Lamb & Hwang, 1982). Instead, theorists are now recognizing the capacity of both parents and infants for continual adaptation to shifting social circumstances; in turn, this suggests that there is probably no critical time period for the formation of social relationships (Cairns, 1977).

Preventive Intervention Groups

One strategy for providing support not just for fathers but for couples as well is illustrated in the Cowan and Cowan (1983) Transition to Parenthood project. In this study, couples participated from late pregnancy to 3 months postpartum. Assessments continued until infants were 18 months old. Couples in the intervention group met in a semistructured situation weekly for a 6-month period.

> The group leaders worked to help partners consider how their sense of themselves, their mutual role arrangements in the family, their usual ways of showing and telling

each other about their experiences and expectations of building a new family might all contribute to the quality of their relationship as a couple.

(Cowan & Cowan, 1983, p. 4)

In comparison to couples in a control group who did not receive any intervention, the group participants tended to show increased satisfaction with themselves and continued to maintain their level of marital satisfaction while the nongroup couples' satisfaction with marriage continued to decline. In view of the relationship between marital satisfaction and quality of parenting on the part of both mothers and fathers, these findings are significant (Belsky, 1984; Pedersen et al., 1980). Specification of the components of this complex intervention must await further research. Moreover, since the intervention encompassed before, during, and after the transition to parenthood, the investigation cannot provide guidance concerning the optimal timing of such interventions.

Maximizing Intervention Effectiveness: Matching Parents and Strategies

Parents are not homogeneous, in spite of the fact that families as intervention targets are often assumed to possess similar skills, needs, beliefs, and values (Parke & Beitel, 1986). Parents vary in terms of their role concept, in their actual ability or skills to perform parenting tasks, in their own perception of their skills, and in their degree of self-confidence. The family context in which mothers and fathers are embedded varies in terms of degree of spousal support, level of family stress, and distribution of mother and father responsibility. Each of these variants, in turn, affects mother and father performance and involvement as a parent. Fathers, in particular, also vary in terms of their accessibility for intervention. This articulation of possible variations in parents suggests that assessments should be made prior to the selection of an intervention strategy.

Parents with clearly determined deficits in skill or information are good candidates for short-term interventions, such as Brazelton demonstrations or instructional programs involving infant care techniques. In contrast, it may be unnecessary to provide such programs for parents who are already well informed and/or experienced with infants.

Motivation and role dimensions merit consideration as well. Parents who are highly motivated and express a desire to acquire skills and information are obviously better candidates. Parental role definition has been shown to be a more potent predictor of involvement than attendance at delivery, early infant contact, or childbirth preparation classes. Therefore, fathers, for example, who define their major role as breadwinner and view infant and child care as a woman's responsibility would be poor candidates for skill-oriented interventions. Instead, in these types of traditional families, efforts may be better directed at educating the father about maternal needs for support. Time may be better spent problem solving about arranging for informal and formal social support for the wife since belief systems are unlikely to be changed with short-term interventions. Interventions should be designed to enhance capacities in directions determined by the couple's beliefs.

In assessing the form of intervention required, the full family unit including both the mother and father should be taken into account. Mothers often play a gate-keeper function in relation to caregiving activities by which they control the fathers' access to caregiving opportunities. Therefore, in order to maximize the impact of an intervention to enhance father skill and confidence, a complementary intervention must be aimed at modifying maternal perceptions of fathers' capabilities to contribute to infant care. Over the long term, efforts would need to be made to modify maternal definitions and beliefs concerning the legitimacy of fathers' contributions. In addition, this type of program could involve educating mothers about not only the fathers' need for spousal support but also the benefits of paternal involvement for both their children and themselves.

Accessibility of parents is another dimension that merits consideration. Some fathers, due to either low interest or scheduling conflicts, are not available during the prenatal period but are available during the postpartum hospital period. Although the first 48 hours do not appear to be critical for bonding (Goldberg, 1983), it may be a period of high motivation on the part of the parents. For the father, it may be the first time he recognizes the reality of the situation now that there is a baby he can see and hold. In turn, he may be highly motivated to acquire information and skills to aid him in his new role.

Relationship Between Informal and Formal Support Systems

Although informal and formal support systems can make independent contributions to family functioning, a number of recent studies have shown that these two types of support systems can work in concert in supporting families. Links between formal and informal systems can assume a variety of forms, such as: (1) strengthening the informal network through formal intervention (Powell, 1979); (2) mobilizing existing social networks in times of stress (Ruevni, 1979); and (3) using informal network members to help individuals utilize formal support services (Olds, 1981).

Minde and his colleagues (Minde et al., 1980; Minde, Shosenberg, & Marton, 1981) have recently developed a program of self-help groups for mothers of premature infants, which illustrates the interplay between formal and informal systems and the direct and indirect effects of these supportive systems. Each group met once weekly with an experienced neonatal nurse and a mother for 7–12 weeks following the birth. The groups provided a variety of services including opportunities to share feelings, information about the developmental and medical needs of premature infants, assistance with a variety of daily tasks such as baby-sitters' accommodations and unemployment benefits, and familiarization with local community resources for family support.

In contrast to a control group, these mothers visited their infants significantly more in the hospital and touched, talked to, and looked at their infants more and expressed more confidence in their caretaking abilities. At 3 months after discharge, group mothers continued to show involvement with their babies during feedings and were more concerned about their general development. At 1 year they gave their infants more general freedom and stimulation and judged their competence more appropriately to their biological abilities in contrast to mothers in the control group. In turn, the infants whose mothers participated in the intervention group showed more social and independent behaviors such as general playing, food sharing, and self-feeding.

Although the mechanisms through which these positive outcomes were achieved were not determined by this study, some of the possible factors were isolated by subsequent analyses. Of special interest was the finding that more mothers in the support groups reported that their relationships with one or more significant persons in their life improved. In turn, one would expect that these mothers more effectively were able to use these significant others for support. These mothers were viewed as more autonomous—a construct reflecting the degree of perceived control and alternatives that the mothers felt they had over their lives. Again, the specifics of how this program "worked" remain to be determined; however, the project demonstrates the value of intervening at multiple levels and provides further support for the necessity of expanding our views of the critical social contexts for the development of the preterm infant. Finally, as an illustration of the ways in which formal and informal support systems interact, it should be noted that the "self-support" groups in this study are now being run as an independent organization, by the parents themselves.

The Prenatal/Early Infancy Project developed by Olds (1981) provides a final illustration of how formal and informal support can perform together for adolescent mothers. This investigation has developed a model in which the hospital staff (formal system) identifies and trains members of the parents' informal social network (informal system) to assist at risk families.

Specifically, a nurse/home visitor provides home-based education for improving pregnancy management and early infant development, involves "significant others" who participate in the home visits with the mothers in order to create a supportive informal environment for behavioral change on the part of the parents, and, finally, links families with other health and support services in the community. A serious attempt is made to understand better the process through which the program's effects are mediated, by assessing maternal health habits and child-rearing practices as well as the availability and utilization of informal supports and formal community services. Preliminary results from the pregnancy phase indicate that mothers who had the nurse/visitor were aware of more formal community services, and a larger number (65 percent) were enrolled in childbirth education classes than mothers who were not followed by a nurse (50 percent). In the area of informal support, mothers in the nurse/visitor group were accompanied by a support person to childbirth education classes more often than non–nurse–visited mothers. Similarly, nurse-visited mothers experienced support more frequently during labor from a friend or relative. This is of particular significance in light of the recent findings of Sosa, Kennell, Klaus, Robertson, and Urrutia (1980) that the presence of a supportive other is associated with a shorter labor and less complications in childbirth. The results to date are promising and indicate further the value of a multilevel intervention. Although our emphasis has been on supportive intervention, the Olds project underlines the fact that the same model has implications for prevention (Parke, 1981c) by improving pregnancy outcomes and thereby preventing some preterm births.

These studies illustrate the role that informal and formal social networks together can play in helping families adapt to stressful change. However, we do not yet have all the pieces of the puzzle, and the specific direct and indirect ways in which different types of informal and formal supportive intervention alter different aspects of family interaction and, in turn, infant development are not yet well understood. Descriptive studies of how families spontaneously use and profit from available formal and informal network resources as well as experimental interventions in which the contributions of specific parts of the network are manipulated are both useful strategies for future research.

THE IMPACT OF SOCIAL CHANGE ON EARLY FAMILY RELATIONSHIPS

A number of societywide changes have produced a variety of shifts in the nature of early family relationships. Fertility rates and family size have decreased, the percentage of women in the work force has increased, the timing of onset of parenthood has shifted, divorce rates have risen, and the number of single-parent families has increased (for reviews see Feiring & Lewis, 1984; Parke & Tinsley, 1984). In this section, the effects of two of these changes—timing of parenthood and recent shifts in family employment patterns—are explored in order to illustrate the impact of social change on parent–infant and family relationships. Exploration of these shifts will serve to underscore a second theme, namely, the importance of considering the historical period or era in which social change occurs.

The Impact of Timing of Parenthood on Parent–Infant Relationships

Patterns of the timing of the onset of parenting are changing, although those changes are not evident from an examination of the median age of parents at the time of the birth of their first child. In the first half of the 1950s, the median age of a woman at the birth of her first child was 22.2 years, whereas in the 1975–1979 period it was approximately the same—22.3 years. This apparent pattern of stability, however, masks the impressive expansion of the range of the timing of first births during the 1970s. During this period, women were having babies earlier *and* later than in previous decades. Two particular patterns can be identified. First, there was a dramatic increase in the number of adolescent pregnancies, and, second, there was an increase in the number of women who were postponing childbearing until their thirties. Between 1970 and 1980, there was an increase in the rate of childbirths to adolescent mothers. Similarly, between 1970 and 1979, the number of first babies born to women 30–34 years old doubled. What are the consequences of this divergent pattern of childbearing?

A number of factors need to be considered in order to understand the impact on parenting of childbearing at different ages. First, the *life course context,* which is broadly defined as the point at which the individual has arrived in his or her social, educational, and occupational timetable, is an important determinant. Second, the *historical context,* namely, the societal and economic conditions that prevail at the time of the onset of parenting, interacts with the first factor in determining the effects of variations in timing. Let us consider early and delayed childbirth in light of these issues.

Early-Timed Childbearing

The most significant aspect of early entry into parenthood is that it is a nonnormative event. Achieving parenthood during adolescence can be viewed as an accelerated role transition (Russell, 1980). As McCluskey, Killarney, and Papini (1983) note:

School age parenting may produce heightened stress when it is out of synchrony with a normative life course. Adolescents may be entering parenting at an age when they are not financially, educationally, and emotionally ready to deal with it effectively.

(*McCluskey et al., 1983, p. 49*)

In addition, adolescent childbearers are at higher medical risk due to poorer diets, malnutrition, and less intensive and consistent prenatal care (Brooks-Gunn & Furstenberg, 1986; Hoffreth, 1986). Teenage childbearing is also strongly associated with higher levels of completed fertility, and closer spacing of births (Card & Wise, 1978; Moore & Hoffreth, 1978). In the educational sphere, early childbearing is negatively associated with educational attainment—especially for females (Card & Wise, 1978). Similarly, early onset of parenthood is linked with diminished income and assets as well as poverty, relative to individuals who delay childbearing (Card & Wise, 1978; Presser, 1980); again, the effect is particularly severe for women. In turn, this has long-term occupational consequences, with early childbearers overrepresented in blue-collar jobs and underrepresented in the professions. Another issue is that early childbearing is more likely to be unplanned; according to one estimate (Presser, 1974), for women 15–19 years old, 80 percent of the births were unplanned, whereas for a group of women 24–29 years old only 30 percent were unplanned. Similarly, although only 9 percent of the second group gave birth out of wedlock, 60 percent of the teenagers were unmarried. Other estimates differ but still suggest a higher-than-average probability that adolescents are unmarried at the time of conception and/or at the time of delivery. One estimate (Alan Guttmacher Institute, 1976) suggests that, of U.S. teenagers who give birth, one-third conceive within wedlock, one-third marry during pregnancy, and one-third give birth out of wedlock. However, marriage often occurs in the first 2 years after the delivery; again, estimates vary but approximately one-quarter of the unmarried women tend to marry within 2 years (Furstenberg, 1976; Presser, 1980). However, there is a trend over the past two decades that suggests that more recent cohorts are less likely to marry to legitimate a premarital pregnancy than older cohorts were (O'Connell & Rogers, 1984). Teenage marriages tend to be highly unstable; separation and/or divorce is two to three times as likely among adolescents as among women who are 20 years or older (Baldwin & Cain, 1980).

In part, this pattern is due to the fact that the fathers also are often adolescents, and, as in the case of teenage mothers, are often unprepared financially and emotionally to undertake the responsibilities of parenthood (Parke, Power, & Fisher, 1980). In view of the low rates of marriage and high rates of separation and divorce for adolescents, adolescent fathers, in contrast to "on-schedule" fathers, have less contact with their offspring. However, contact is not absent; in fact, several studies of unmarried adolescent fathers indicate a surprising amount of paternal involvement for extended periods following the birth. For example, in a study of 138 unmarried adolescent mothers in Minnesota, Nettleton and Cline (1975) found that 50 percent of the 45 mothers who did not relinquish custody of their infants dated the father during the infant's first year of life. Moreover, 20 percent of these 45 eventually married the fathers of their children. Similarly, 46 percent of the 180 unwed mothers Lorenzi and his colleagues (Lorenzi, Klerman, & Jekel, 1977) interviewed in New Haven either married the babies' fathers or were seeing them on a regular basis 26 months after the birth. Although the number of women who have regular contact with the men who fathered their children declined over the first 2 years (56 percent at 3 months, 40 percent at 15 months, and 23 percent at 26 months), a small but constant proportion of the mothers at each time point (18 percent) reported that they saw the fathers only occasionally. In addition, most of the fathers who visited the mothers also visited the children. Finally, Furstenberg (1976) noted similar rates of visitation as late as 5 years after the birth. Twenty-one percent of the fathers were living with their children, another 20 percent visited their offspring on a regular basis, whereas 21 percent visited occasionally. An interesting and consistent pattern in these studies is that a significant number of fathers establish a stable live-in relationship with their children after 1 or 2 years (Furstenberg, 1976; Lorenzi et al., 1977)—a period that is often necessary to complete formal education and/or secure regular employment. A delay in regular father–child contact does not necessarily preclude the development of a satisfactory father–child relationship or diminish the father's impact on his child's development. Evidence indicates that adolescent father involvement has a positive impact on the child's social and cognitive development (Furstenberg, 1976).

How have increases in the rate of adolescent childbirth altered the father's role? Or, to pose the question differently, how was being an adolescent father different in a historical period when adolescent childbearing was relatively rare than in a period when the rate is significantly higher? First, as rates of adolescent childbearing rise and the event becomes less nonnormative or deviant, the social stigma associated with the event may decrease. In combination with increased recognition that adolescent fathers have a legitimate and potentially beneficial role to play, adolescent fathers' opportunities for participation have probably expanded. Second, the increased availability of social support systems such as day care may make it easier for adolescent fathers (and mothers) simultaneously to balance educational and occupational demands with parenting demands. Clearly, longitudinal studies of the long-term impact of achieving parenthood during adolescence are necessary, as well as more investigation of the impact of adolescent parenthood during different historical periods (see Parke & Nevelle, 1986).

Finally, there are a variety of deleterious effects of early childbearing for the offspring. First, there is a greater risk of lower IQ (Broman, 1981; Brooks-Gunn & Furstenberg, 1986). It also affects academic achievement and retention in grade (Furstenberg & Brooks-Gunn, 1986; Kinard & Klerman, 1983). Nor are the effects short-lived; they tend to persist throughout the school years (Hoffreth, 1986). Social behavior is affected as well, with several studies showing that children of teenage parents are at greater risk of social impairment (e.g., undercontrol of anger, feelings of inferiority, fearfulness) and mild behavior disorders (e.g., aggressiveness, rebelliousness, impulsivity, etc.) (Furstenberg & Brooks-Gunn, 1986). However, the role of parent–infant interaction as a mediator of these outcomes is not clearly established. Few differences have been found between adolescent and older mothers with the exception of vocalization, which may be linked to lower cognitive scores in preschool (Field, 1981). Instead of a model that implicates parenting skill in mediating offspring outcomes, recent work (McAnarney, 1985) suggests that the effects of maternal age are largely indirect and operate through a young woman's education, family structure, support system, knowledge of child rearing, and child rearing experience (Hayes, 1986).

Postponed Childbearing

A variety of contrasts exist between becoming a parent in adolescence and initiating parenthood 15–20 years later. In contrast to adolescent childbearing, when childbearing is delayed, considerable progress in occupational and educational spheres has potentially already taken place. Education is generally completed and career development is well under way for both males and females.

The aim of a recent study by Daniels and Weingarten (1982) was to determine whether the patterns of parental involvement vary as a function of early- versus later-timed parenthood. These investigators interviewed 72 couples. Half of the couples, who formed the early-timed group, had their first child when the wife was on the average 21.5 years old, whereas the remaining couples who formed the late-timed group began their parenthood when the wife was on the average 30.5 years old. In addition, three generations were represented a decade apart. One-third of the sample (12 early- and 12 late-timed parents) were in their early twenties in 1980, one-third were in their early forties, and one-third were in their early fifties.

The oldest cohort was born in the late 1920s and early 1930s. They had their children in 1945–1955, and early-timed parenthood was the usual pattern. Childbearing began at 21 years of age, approximately 14 months after marriage. Late-timed parenthood was nonnormative. The middle-age cohort was born in the late 1930s; they began their parental careers in the 1955–1970 period. This was a transition sample, which contained parents who were following the older pattern of early parenting as well as parents who were delaying the onset of parenting. The youngest cohort was born in the 1950s, and the children of these parents were born in the 1970s. Late timing was more common, and a longer spread between marriage and childbirth was evident. In this cohort, the average age of marriage was 27 years, but the onset of parenthood was delayed approximately 4 years. Semistructured, open-ended clinical interviews were conducted with both spouses. Although some quantitative results were generated by this method, the main results were qualitative and are of value mainly as hypotheses for future systematic evaluation.

The impact of the timing of the onset of parenthood can best be appreciated by examining the effects on both parents—mothers and fathers—within the context of the family system.

The timing of parenthood has a major impact on career patterns of women. Daniels and Weingarten (1982) distinguish two patterns of work outside the home and parenting: a simultaneous pattern, in which work outside the home and parenting coexist in the parents' lives; and a sequential pattern, in which work outside the home and parenthood follow one another. One of their main findings was that the early-timed mothers were eight times more likely to follow a sequential than a simultaneous pattern, whereas the late-timed mothers were more evenly divided into simultaneous (16 mothers) and sequential (20 mothers) patterns. Suggestive cohort effects are evident among the late-timed mothers. There is a clear trend across the three cohorts, who had children in either the 1950s, 1960s, or 1970s, for mothers to move from a sequential pattern in the 1950s to a simultaneous pattern by the 1970s. In the oldest cohort, twice as many late-timed mothers followed a sequential pattern (8 mothers) rather than a simultaneous pattern (4 mothers); in the middle cohort, 7 mothers followed the sequential pattern and 5 mothers adopted the simultaneous pattern; and in the youngest cohort the reverse was true, where 7 followed the simultaneous pattern and 5 followed a sequential pattern. Although these data require replication with larger samples before confidence can be placed in this trend, the findings underscore the importance of considering how various cohorts manage early- and late-timing decisions. For women in the oldest group, in which delayed childbearing was nonnormative, the compromise involved acceptance of a sequential strategy in which career was temporarily interrupted. In contrast, for women in the youngest cohort, the climate of the 1970s with the more liberal attitudes toward maternal employment led to the pursuit of parenthood and careers simultaneously by more of these women.

Each of these patterns has distinct advantages and disadvantages. When childbearing begins early, career development is typically delayed and less time is available for negotiating both marital and personal identity issues. When parenthood and career begin simultaneously, both may be potentially compromised by the necessity of dividing time and energy across two domains. On the other hand, both career and parenthood are under way by a relatively young age. Delaying the onset of parenting, means that a career is already established, that marital stability may be achieved, and that the issue of personal identity may be more settled. If a sequential pattern is followed, the opportunity to devote oneself to parenting more fully is available, but this approach disrupts career advancement and leads to loss of income. If a simultaneous pattern is followed, there is not the obvious career interruption. There may be work–family conflicts, but these are probably fewer than in the case of the early simultaneous pattern due to greater career security.

Mothers who delay childbearing may also qualitatively interact differently with their infants. Ragozin and her colleagues (Ragozin et al., 1982) found that both maternal attitudes and behavior were affected by maternal age. In a comparison of mothers 18–38 years of age, they found with maternal age there were positive linear increases in the amount of caretaking responsibility and satisfaction with parenting and a negative linear relationship for social time away from their infant. Moreover, observed interaction between mothers and their 4-month-old infants indicated that maternal affect increased with maternal age. Similarly, older mothers were more successful in eliciting vocal and imitative responses from their infants—an index of their social and cognitive teaching skills. However, these mother–infant interaction effects were evident only for primiparous mothers, and as parity increased, the relationships between maternal age and parity became negative. As Ragozin and colleagues note:

> It appears that having previously experienced parenthood, a mother becomes more interested in extra-familial roles as she grows older—more ready to "get on with her life." Thus, older multiparous women exhibit less positive affect and less optimal behavior toward infants. In contrast, the older primiparous woman, having more experience in nonparenting roles, is more committed to the parenting experience.
>
> (*1982, p. 633*)

In summary, not only are career patterns affected by timing of parenthood, but as this study clearly illustrates, maternal roles and behavior are affected as well. Unfortunately, Ragozin and colleagues provide no information concerning the extrafamilial work patterns of these women.

What are the consequences of these patterns for father involvement? Again, as for mothers, both early and late timing have advantages and drawbacks for fathers. Men who have their children early have more energy for certain types of activities that are central to the father role, such as physical play (Parke & Tinsley, 1981). In support of this prediction, MacDonald & Parke (1986) found a negative relationship between amount of physical play and paternal age. Similarly, the economic strain that occurs early is offset by avoiding financial problems in retirement due to the fact that children are grown up and independent earlier. In turn, early fathering generally means beginning grandfathering at a younger age, which in turn permits the early-timed father to be a more active grandparent (for a discussion of these issues, see Tinsley & Parke, 1984). In spite of these advantages, when men become fathers early, there are two main disadvantages: financial strain and time strain, due to the competing demands imposed by trying simultaneously to establish a career and a family. In contrast, the late-timed father avoids these problems. The late-timed father's career is more settled, permitting more flexibility and freedom in balancing the demands of work and family. Second, patterns of preparental collaboration between the parents may already be established and persist into the parenthood period. In their study, Daniels and Weingarten found early-timed fathers are less involved in the daily care of a preschool child. According to Daniels and Weingarten (1982), three times as many late-timed fathers, in contrast to their early-timed counterparts, had regular responsibility for some part of the daily care of a preschool child. Possibly, the increase in paternal responsibility assumed by fathers in late-timed families may account for the more optimal mother–infant interaction patterns observed by Ragozin and colleagues (1982). Observational analyses of father–offspring interaction patterns in early- and late-timed families would be helpful.

Other evidence is consistent with the finding of greater father involvement when childbearing is delayed. Bloom-Feshbach (1979) reported that the older a father is at the time of his first child's birth the more he is practically involved with the caretaking of his infant. However, age of father was not associated with expressive-nurturant aspects of the father–child relationship; possibly infant–father attachment, for example, may not be altered by age of the father. Other research suggests one possible mediator of greater father involvement among older fathers. In a recent short-term longitudinal study, Feldman and colleagues (1983) found that one of the predictors of paternal involvement in infant caregiving was low job salience. Although it is possible that older fathers can afford to invest less in their career and therefore low job salience may be tapping a similar dimension, it is possible that time in career and job salience are independent. Assessment of job salience and its relationship to paternal caregiving in early- and late-timed fathers would help clarify this issue.

As the findings in this section demonstrate, the timing of the onset of parenthood is a powerful organizer of both maternal and paternal roles. In the future, investigators need to examine maternal and paternal interaction patterns not only with each other and their children, but also within the context of careers. More detailed attention to cohort issues is warranted, as indicated by the suggestive findings of Daniels and Weingarten (1982). Presumably the decision to delay the onset of parenthood was easier in the 1970s than in earlier decades because of increased acceptance of maternal employment, less rigid role definitions for men and women, and the greater availability of support services such as day care that would permit a simultaneous family–career option.

THE IMPACT OF WOMEN'S AND MEN'S EMPLOYMENT PATTERNS ON THE PARENTAL ROLES IN THE FAMILY

The relationships between employment patterns of both women and men and their family roles are increasingly being recognized (Bronfenbrenner & Crouter, 1982; Hoffman, 1984). In this section, a variety of issues concerning the links between the worlds of work and family are considered in order to illustrate the impact of recent shifts in work patterns on both men's and women's family roles. The impact of changes in the rate of maternal employment on both quantitative and qualitative aspects of father participation is examined, as well as the influence of variations in family work schedules. Finally, historical changes in the nature of men's work are briefly examined.

Women's Employment

Since the mid–1950s, there has been a dramatic shift in the participation rate of women in the labor force. The rise has been particularly dramatic for married women with children. Between 1950 and 1978, the employment rate more than tripled for married mothers of preschoolers, doubled for those with school-age children only, and increased by one-half for those with no young children (U.S. Bureau of the Census, 1979). How have these shifts affected the quantity and quality of the father's contribution to family tasks such as housework and child care?

Quantitative Effects

Problems arise in interpreting the main data source—time use studies—because these studies often fail to control for the family size and the age of children. As Hoffman (1984) notes, "Since employed-mother families include fewer children, in general, and fewer preschoolers and infants, in particular, there are fewer childcare tasks to perform" (p. 439). Therefore, the differences between families with employed and nonemployed mothers may, in fact, be underestimated. A second problem is that, as noted earlier, the differentiation of tasks performed by fathers is often very crude, and in some studies it is impossible to determine what specific aspects of the father's family work—such as primary child care, non–care-related child contact, or housework—are affected. In spite of these limitations, some trends are clear.

In general, fathers increase the proportion of time that they devote to the total family workload when mothers are employed outside the home. However, this increase often emerges as a result of wives reducing the amount of time they devote to housework and child care rather than as a result of increases in the absolute amount of time men devote to these tasks. Consistent with the classic analysis of Blood and Wolfe (1960), in a more recent time-diary study of housework and child care in Syracuse, New York, Walker and Woods (1976) found that husbands' proportion of all family work (i.e., combining that performed by both husband and wife) rose from 16 percent (1.6 of 9.7 hr) to 25 percent (1.6 of 6.4 hr) when wives were employed. Other studies (see Pleck, 1983) confirm the general finding that fathers' proportional share increases not because they are contributing more absolute time but because mothers are spending less time on home tasks. However, these findings are not without significance because the impact of the mother and the father on children is likely to be different in families in which the father and the mother are more equal in their household participation.

Moreover, there is some recent evidence for absolute increases in fathers' contributions to family work when wives are employed, especially in father–child contact. Robinson (1977), in a diary study of a national sample, found a modest increase of 19 min a day in men's total child contact time, an increase of 16.5 percent, when women were employed outside the home. Similarly, Pleck (1981), in an analysis of a survey using respondents' summary estimates, found that fathers with employed wives performed about ½ hr per day more family work that includes housework, child care, and parent–child contact. Although the proportion of time fathers in the Pleck study spent in child-centered activity and housework was not determined, other evidence indicates that child contact is more likely to increase than housework (Hoffman, 1984). If this hypothesis is supported, these modest absolute increases assume greater importance because they directly affect the nature of the father–child relationship.

Other evidence is consistent with this hypothesis that fathers' involvement with children will be especially likely to increase when mothers are employed. Child variables, such as age, appear to determine whether or not fathers' family work shifts with maternal employment. Walker and Woods (1976) found an increase in fathers' family work with maternal employment when the youngest child was 1 year of age or younger or the couple had five or more children. Similarly, Russell (1982) in a recent study of the impact of maternal employment on Australian fathers found that maternal employment altered fathers' involvement in family work only when there were children under 3 years of age. Fathers in this case were slightly more involved when mothers were employed (4.4 hr vs. 3.15 hr for employed vs. nonemployed, respectively). Moreover, Russell found that when mothers are employed, the quality of responsibility that fathers assume shifts: Fathers with employed wives spent time taking sole responsibility for their children, compared to fathers with nonemployed wives (4.7 hr vs. 1.0 hr).

It is clear that there is an increase in father participation when mothers work outside the home, but the data fit well Rappaport's concept of a *psychosocial lag* (Rappaport, Rappaport, & Strelitz, 1977). According to this concept, men's roles in the family are changing at a slower rate than shifts in women's roles in paid employment. Part of the explanation for the relatively modest size of the shift in men's family work when women enter the job market may be that there has been a "value shift in our culture toward greater family involvement by husbands . . . which has effects even on those husbands whose wives are not employed" (Pleck, 1983, p. 47). A similar trend is found in the reduction in time devoted to household tasks by nonemployed women as well as employed women (Hoffman, 1984; Robinson, 1977).

These shifts in father participation can potentially have a positive effect on the father–child relationship as a result of increased direct interaction between the father and child, but paternal participation can have an indirect effect on the child by modifying the mother–child relationship (Lamb, 1982).

Unfortunately, a number of problems limit the value of these findings to our understanding of historical trends in fathering. First, most of the available data come from cross-sectional comparisons of families in which wives are either employed outside the home or not. Although it is assumed that these concurrent data can be extrapolated backward to provide a picture of how men's participation in family activities has shifted across time as a result of the historically documented increases in women's presence in the work force, longitudinal studies of the same families as well as repeated cross-sectional comparisons across time are necessary to place this issue on a firmer empirical basis.

In current literature, cohort, time of testing, and age of children are often confounded. For example, in the studies that show that the fathers' participation is higher when infants and young children are involved, it is not clear whether this is due only to the age of the children or to the difference in the cohorts whose children are younger at the time of evaluation. Value shifts may elicit greater involvement in the current cohort of new parents that may not have affected more seasoned parents. Moreover, once a pattern of father participation has been established, possibly these families will continue to participate more equally in child rearing. If this analysis is correct, future surveys may indicate that father participation extends into later childhood age periods. Alternatively, fathers who are involved early may feel that they have contributed and do less at later ages. The importance of considering the timing of the mother's employment as a determinant of the degree of father involvement is clear. Age of the child is not the only variable, however; other factors such as employment onset in relationship to the family's developmental cycle as well as the reason for employment need to be considered. Both the age of the parents and their point in the occupation cycle will affect paternal involvement and may interact with maternal employment.

Qualitative Changes in the Father–Child Relationship Accompanying Maternal Employment

Examination of the quantitative shifts in father behavior as a consequence of maternal employment is only one aspect of the problem; it is also necessary to examine the impact of this shift on the quality of the parent–child relationship. Some evidence from interviews of a sample of fathers of infants 7–14 months old suggests that maternal employment is related mainly to the level of fathers' instrumental involvement in child care and not to fathers' nurturant expressive behavior (Bloom-Feshbach, 1979). According to these data, further involvement in practical aspects of child care may be more influenced by shifts in maternal employment than more nurturant expressive aspects of the father–child relationship.

However, this conclusion may be premature, as evidenced by two recent observational studies of shifts in style of parent–infant interaction as a function of maternal employment. In one recent study, Pederson and colleagues (1980) assessed the impact of dual-wage-earner families on mother–infant interaction patterns. These investigators observed single- and dual-wage-earner families for a 1-hr period in the evening with their 5-month-old infants. Fathers in single-wage-earner families tended to play with their infants more than mothers did. However, in the two-wage-earner families, the mothers' rate of social play was higher than the fathers' rate of play. In fact, the fathers in these dual-wage-earner families played at a lower rate than even the mothers in the single-wage-earner families. Because the observations took place in the evenings after both parents returned from their jobs, Pedersen and colleagues suggested that the mother used increased play as a way of reestablishing contact with her infant after being away from home for the day. "It is possible that the working mother's special need to interact with the infant inhibited or crowded out the father in his specialty" (Pedersen et al., 1980, p. 10). This behavior of the mother is consistent with the studies of maternal employment and infant attachment that found no relationship between employment status and the quality of infant–mother attachment (Chase-Lansdale, 1981; Hock, 1980) but found evidence of insecure infant–father attachment in dual-career families, though only for sons and not daughters (Chase-Lansdale, 1981; cited by Hoffman, 1984).

A number of questions about Pedersen and colleagues' (1980) findings remain. It is still unclear whether these patterns of increased mother play continue after the mother–infant relationship is more firmly established than it is at 5 months. Is this pattern of increased play evident in dual-wage-earner families in which the mother begins work when the infant is older? Comparison of families in which the age of the infant differs when the mother returns to work would help to clarify these issues.

The style of interaction that the mothers in these working mother families exhibited was similar to the predominant style of mother play characterized by verbal behavior. Mothers in these families increased the amount of their play with their infants but remained within their stylistic mode. There was no evidence of a shift to a more typically "masculine" style of physical play.

In an even more stringent test of the modifiability of play styles as a function of family organization, Field (1978) compared fathers who act as primary caregivers with fathers who are secondary caregivers, in contrast to families in Pedersen and colleagues' study in which both parents were employed outside the home. Mothers and fathers reversed roles in Field's families. Field found that primary caregiver fathers retained the physical component in their interaction styles just as secondary fathers did. However, in other subtle ways the play styles of primary caregiving fathers were similar to the play styles of mothers. Primary caretakers—both mothers and fathers—exhibited less laughing and more smiling, imitative grimaces and high-pitched vocalizations than secondary caretaker fathers did. However, both primary caregiving and secondary caregiving fathers engaged in less holding of the infants' limbs and in more game playing and poking than mothers. Together with Pedersen and colleagues' (1980) study, these data suggest that both mothers and fathers may exhibit distinctive play styles, even when family role arrangements modify the quantity of their interaction. Further research is necessary to assess more completely the modifiability of these interactive styles as a result of differing family arrangements. A complete comparative study of families in which there is a full reversal of primary and secondary caregiving roles with traditional families in which the father is the secondary caregiver would clarify the extent to which interactional behavior is dependent on the differential distribution of caregiving tasks. Just as investigators are examining the impact of self-defined concepts of masculinity, femininity, and androgyny on caregiving patterns, it would clearly be worthwhile to evaluate the relationship between gender-role attitudes and parental play styles. Perhaps androgynous individuals would exhibit less stereotypically masculine or feminine play styles.

Variations in Work Schedules

A variety of shifts have taken place in recent years that have resulted in either reduced work time or more flexible arrangement of work schedules. One change is the shift from a 6- to a 5-day work week, but some have argued that the shorter work week in the United States may have diminished the working hours only for white-collar occupations such as clerical or low-level administration (Kanter, 1977; Willmott, 1971). Other groups such as higher-level professionals work long hours on the job, whereas blue-collar workers are more likely to have more than one job (Hoffman, 1984; Riesman, 1958; Wilensky, 1961).

Work schedules can vary considerably across households over time, and examination of these schedules may reveal a clearer picture than an undifferentiated focus on employment per se. Men who worked four 10-hr days a week compared with men who worked the five 8-hr days spent a significantly greater amount of time in child care (Maklan, 1976). The men who worked 4 days a week devoted nearly 4 more hrs a week to child care, but there was no difference in the amount of time devoted to housework. These changes toward father assumption of a larger share of child care tasks may not only improve his relationship with his children but may also alter the mother–child relationship by relieving mother of some of the routine child care.

Flexible hours may also give men more time for fathering. Flexible hours, for example, may permit fathers to stay home later in the morning and get their children ready for school or, alternatively, to be at home to greet the children after school. Relationships between children and fathers might vary if fathers shared in these daily child care routines. Recent evidence of the effects of flextime is inconclusive. In one recent study of 700 people in two U.S. government agencies, of which one agency was on flextime and the other on a regular schedule, Bohen and Viveros-Long (1981) found that neither mothers nor fathers who were on flextime reported spending more time with their children than did workers on regular schedules. However, people on flextime generally reported less conflict between their home and work responsibilities than those on regular schedules. Perhaps the quality of the relationship between parent and child may improve—even if the amount of time does not shift. However, more research is necessary to explore the value of flextime for families, avoiding such problems as self-selection, before any firm conclusions about the effects of flexible scheduling can be drawn.

REMAINING ISSUES AND FUTURE TRENDS

A number of issues remain to be examined in future research if we are to describe fully the complexities, specify the determinants and processes, and outline the consequences of parent–infant interaction.

Parent as Manager Versus Direct Interactive Partner

The focus of this chapter has been primarily on face-to-face parent–infant interaction. To a large degree this emphasis reflects the common assumption that parental influence takes place directly through face-to-face contact or indirectly through the impact of the interaction on another family member. Only recently have researchers and theorists begun to recognize the "managerial" function of parents and to appreciate the impact of variations in how this managerial function influences the infant's development (Hartup, 1979; Parke, 1978; Parke et al., 1986). By *managerial,* we refer to the ways in which parents organize and arrange the infant's home environment and set limits on the range of the home setting to which the infant has access and the opportunities for social contact with playmates and socializing agents outside the family. The managerial role may be just as important as the parent's role as stimulator, since the amount of time that infants spend interacting with the inanimate environment far exceeds their social interaction time. Here are some estimates based on extensive home observations by White and his colleagues (White, Kaban, Shapiro, & Attonucci, 1976):

> For 12-month-old to 15-month-old children, the figures were 89.7 percent for nonsocial tasks versus 10.3 percent for social tasks. By 18–21 months the figures are 83.8 percent nonsocial and 16.2 percent social; at 24–27 months 80.0 percent nonsocial and 20.0 percent social and at 30–33 months they were 79.1 percent nonsocial and 20.9 percent social.
>
> *(White et al., 1976, p. 125)*

Others report similar findings (Clarke-Stewart, 1973; Wachs & Gruen, 1981; Wenar, 1972). Secondly, White and colleagues (1976) noted that more than 85 percent of the time infants 12–33 months old initiated their own activities. In short, the way that the mother or other caretaker organizes the child's physical environment may be just as important as the direct social interactions between the child and caretaker.

Moreover, this is an important discriminator between mother and father. Power and Parke (1982) have found in an observational study of 7½ and 10½-month-old infants in the home that mothers were more likely than fathers to play a managerial role. Specifically, mothers restricted their infants' behavior, verbally or physically, three times more often than fathers. (See also Power & Parke, 1986.)

A number of aspects of this managerial role appear to be important for the infant's development. Studies by several investigators (Bradley & Caldwell, 1976; Wachs & Gruen, 1981) show that the level of predictability or regularity in the child's home environment is positively correlated with early cognitive development. Furthermore, the boundaries of the home environment to which the child has access for exploration and play influence the child's cognitive development. White and colleagues (1976) argue that:

> the effective child-rearer makes the living area as safe as possible for the naive newly crawling or walking child and then provides maximum access to the living area for the child. This immediately sets the process of development off in a manner that will lead naturally to the satisfaction of and the further development of the child's curiosity; the opportunity to learn about the world at large; and the opportunity to enter into natural useful relationships with people. The child-rearer not only provides maximum access to the living area, but in addition he or she makes kitchen cabinets attractive and available and then keeps a few materials in reserve for those times when the child may become a bit bored.
>
> *(White et al., 1976, pp. 150–151)*

This hypothesis has been supported in a number of empirical investigations: Positive correlations are often reported between infant cognitive development and floor freedom—the degree to which mothers allow their infants freely to explore the physical environment—(Beckwith, Cohen, Kopp, Parmalee, & Marcy, 1976; Wachs & Gruen, 1981), while negative correlations are generally reported between infant cognitive development and various measures of verbal and physical maternal restrictiveness (Elardo et al., 1975; Wenar, 1976; Wachs & Gruen, 1981).

Another form of management that has clear implications for infants' acquisition of social skills is parental supervision (Parke, MacDonald, Beitel, & Bhavnagri, 1986). As infants are in the process of learning new social skills that may be useful in peer relations, parents can play an active managerial role in facilitating the interactions of their children with young age-mates. In this case the parental managerial role is as a supervisor who directly assists the children to initiate their play together, helps maintain the ongoing interaction, and assists the children in resolving their difficulties and disagreements. Recently, Bhavnagri and Parke (1985) have found that the play of 2-year-olds can be facilitated by the provision of this type of maternal supervision. Briefly, the toddlers played together for longer periods and more cooperatively when supervised than when left on their own without this type of parental managerial assistance. Together these studies provide a strong case for broadening our concept of parental roles in infancy beyond parent–infant interaction to include parental managerial functions as well.

Unit of Analysis

Our conceptual analysis of dyadic and triadic units of analysis is still impoverished (Schaffer, 1984). Considerable progress has been made in describing the behavior of individual interactants (e.g., mother, father, infant) within dyadic and to a lesser extent triadic settings, but less progress has been achieved in developing a language for describing interaction in dyadic and triadic terms. While such terms as *reciprocal* or *synchronous* hold promise, there remains little real advance in this regard. In addition to the dyads and triads as units of analysis, greater attention needs to be given to the family as a unit of analysis.

A number of researchers (Boss, 1980; Reiss, 1981) have offered differing taxonomies of family types or typologies that move us to this level of analysis, but to date little effort has been made to apply these notions systematically to family relationships in infancy.

The Issue of Family Variation

One of the clear advances of the last decade is our recognition of the importance of individual differences in infants; one of the next advances will be the recognition of individual differences among families.

Recognition of individual variability across families implies the necessity of expanding our sampling procedures. In spite of demands for a greater awareness of family diversity, the range of family types that are studied is still relatively narrow. While some progress has been made in describing interaction patterns of parents and infants in different cultures (Field, Sostek, Vietze & Leiderman, 1981) and in different ethnic groups in the United States (Harrison, Serafica, & McAdoo, 1984), this work represents only a beginning.

Another form of diversity that warrants more attention is structural variation. In view of the high rates of single mothers and divorced families, caution is still necessary in generalizing from intact families to single-parent households. Again, the amount of observationally based interactional work in infancy among families of different structure remains meager.

Types of Developmental Change

Developmental issues remain a central but far from solved issue—both conceptually and empirically. While it is common to underscore the importance of describing and explaining developmental changes in parent–infant interaction, the development trajectory for infants in the social context of the family is still far from complete. More detailed assessment of the developmental changes that occur over the first 2 years of life for infants in mother–infant, father–infant, and family contexts is required. Moreover, these developmental shifts need to be more closely articulated with changes in the perceptual, cognitive, and social capacities of the infant. This requires more frequent assessment of infant competencies outside the interaction context as well as measures of social interaction with various social partners.

Continuing to treat development as a single trajectory that applies only to the infant is a serious shortcoming of our current approaches. It is necessary to recognize a second developmental trajectory, namely, adult developmental changes. Adult development in this context can assume two forms. First, as discussed in this chapter, the adults' position in terms of their management of a variety of life course tasks, such as marriage, work, and personal identity, will clearly determine how they will execute parental tasks; in turn, these differences may find expression in measures of parent–infant interaction. Second, the developmental shifts in infant perceptual–cognitive and social development in turn may alter parental attitudes and behaviors and/or the nature of the adults' own developmentally relevant choices, such as work or career commitment. This clearly argues for the recognition of two developmental trajectories—an infant developmental course and an adult developmental sequence. The description of the interplay between these two types of developmental curves is necessary to capture adequately the nature of developmental changes in a familial context in infancy (Parke, 1986).

Monitoring Secular Trends

There is a continuing need to monitor secular trends and to describe their impact on parent–infant interaction patterns. Secular change is complex and clearly does not affect all individuals equally or on all behavior patterns to the same extent. In fact, it is a serious oversimplification to assume that general societal trends can isomorphically be applied across all individual families. Moreover, better guidelines are necessary to illuminate which aspects of processes within families are most likely to be altered by historical events and which processes are less amenable to change. For example, the structural dynamics of early interaction (Stern, 1977) as well as some qualitative aspects of early parent–infant interactive style may be insulated from the influence of secular shifts. Are fathers biologically prepared to interact with their children while mothers are biologically programmed to interact in a less physical and more verbal mode? If this assumption about differences in parental play style is, in fact, true, rates of interactions would be more likely to change than style. Alternatively, the restraints may be more solely environmental, and as opportunities for adult male and female participation in child care and child rearing become more equal, some of the stylistic differences may diminish.

To date, historical events, such as shifts in the timing of parenting or work participation, have been treated relatively independently, but, in fact, these events co-occur rather than operating in any singular fashion. Moreover, the impact of any historical change may be different as a result of its occurrence in the same period as another change or changes. For example, women's increased presence in the workplace and the delay in the onset of parenthood vary and probably each event has different meaning without the other change. This implies the need for multivariate designs that would capture the simultaneous impact of multiple events on parenting activities.

Methodological Issues

It is likely that no single methodological strategy will suffice in order to understand the development of family interaction in infancy. Instead, a wide range of designs and data collection and data analysis strategies are necessary (Parke, 1979; Parke & Tinsley, 1984). To date there is still a paucity of information concerning the interrelationships across different levels of analysis. However, it is becoming increasingly clear that a microanalytic strategy is not always more profitable in terms of describing relationships among interactive partners in infancy; in fact, in some cases, ratings may be a more useful approach. What is required is a set of guidelines concerning the appropriate level of analysis for different questions.

Similarly, greater attention needs to be paid to the role of context in determining parent–infant interaction. How do parent–infant interaction patterns shift across lab and home settings and across different types of interaction contexts such as play, teaching, and caregiving? Moreover, it is important to consider the social as well as the physical context. As emphasized throughout this chapter, recognition of the embeddedness of mothers and fathers in family contexts is critical and, in turn, conceptualizing families as embedded in a variety of extrafamilial social settings is important for understanding variation in family functioning. In this regard, it is necessary to recognize that variations in family structure and in ethnicity and social class will modify significantly the ways in which social networks are organized and utilized. For example, the role of the extended family is much more prominent in some groups, such as blacks or Italians, than in other groups (Tinsley & Parke, 1984). Similarly, single-parent families may be more directly embedded in a community-based social network than two-parent families. Descriptions of these variations are necessary for an adequate understanding of the role of extrafamilial networks on family functioning in infancy.

In conclusion, it is clear that parent–infant interaction has matured in the last decade and is now a more fully contextualized issue. Families in the context of their social networks are increasingly the appropriate point of entry for understanding the issue of parental contributions to early infant development. Our conceptual paradigms clearly continue to outstrip our empirical understanding. To reduce this gap is the challenge of the next decade of research. Both infants and parents will benefit from this increased understanding.

REFERENCES

Affleck, G., McGrade, B. J., Allen, D., & McQueeney, M. (1985). Mothers' beliefs about behavioral causes for their developmentally disabled infant's condition: What do they signify? *Journal of Pediatric Psychology, 10,* 293–298.

Alan Guttmacher Institute (1976). 11 million teenagers: What can be done about the epidemic of adolescent pregnancies in the U.S. New York: Planned Parenthood Federation of America.

Arbeit, S. A. (1975). *A study of women during their first pregnancy.* Unpublished doctoral dissertation, Yale University.

Arbuckle, M. B. (1983). *The effects of educational intervention on fathers' relationships with their infants.* Unpublished doctoral dissertation, University of North Carolina at Greensboro.

Badger, E., Burns, D., & Vietze, P. (1981). Maternal risk factors as predictors of developmental outcome in early childhood. *Infant Mental Health Journal, 2,* 33–43.

Bakeman, R., Brown, J. V. (1980). Early interaction: Consequences for social and mental development at three years. *Child Development, 51,* 437–447.

Baldwin, W., & Cain, V. (1980). The children of teenage parents. *Family Planning Perspectives, 12,* 34–43.

Bandura, A. (1977). *Social learning theory.* Englewood Cliffs, NJ: Prentice-Hall.

Ban, P., & Lewis, M. (1974). Mothers and fathers, girls and boys: Attachment behavior in the one-year-old. *Merrill-Palmer Quarterly, 20,* 195–204.

Beal, J. A. (1984, April). *The effect of demonstration of the Brazelton Neonatal Assessment Scale on the father-infant relationship.* Paper presented at the International Conference of Infant Studies, New York.

Belsky, J. (1981). Early human experience: A family perspective. *Developmental Psychology, 17,* 3–23.

Belsky, J. (1984). Determinants of parenting: A process model. *Child Development, 55,* 83–96.

Belsky, J., Gilstrap, B., & Rovine, M. (1984). The Pennsylvania Infant & Family Development Project, I: Stability & change in mother-infant and father-infant interaction in a family setting at one, three & nine months. *Child Development, 55,* 692–705.

Belsky, J. (1979). Mother-father-infant interaction: A naturalistic observational study. *Developmental Psychology, 15,* 601–607.

Belsky, J. & Volling, B. L. (1986). Mothering, fathering & marital interaction in the family triad: Exploring family systems processes. In P. Berman & F. Pedersen (Eds.), *Men's transition to parenthood: Longitudinal studies of early family experience.* Hillsdale, NJ: Erlbaum.

Bhavnagri, N. & Parke, R. D. (1985, April). Parents as facilitators of peer-peer interaction. Paper presented at the biennial meeting of the Society for research in Child Development, Toronto.

Billings, A. G. & Moos, R. H. (1981). The role of coping response and social resources in attenuating the stress of life events. *Journal of Behavioral Medicine, 4,* 139–157.

Bittman, S., & Zalk, S. R. (1978). *Expectant fathers.* New York: Hawthorn.

Blood, R., & Wolfe, D. (1960). *Husbands and wives.* New York: Free Press.

Bloom-Feshbach, J. (1979). *The beginnings of fatherhood.* Unpublished doctoral dissertation, Yale University.

Bohen, H., & Viveros-Long, A. (1981). *Balancing jobs and family life: Do flexible work schedules help?* Philadelphia: Temple University Press.

Boss, P. (1980). Normative family stress: Family boundary changes across the life span. *Family Relations, 29,* 445–450.

Brazelton, T. B. (1973). *Neonatal Behavioral Assessment Scale.* Philadelphia: Lippincott.

Bradley, R. H., & Caldwell, B.M. (1976). Early home environment and changes in mental test performance in children from 6 to 36 months. *Developmental Psychology, 12,* 93–97.

Brim, O. G. (1975). Macro-structural influences on child development and the need for social indicators. *American Journal of Orthopsychiatry, 45,* 516–624.

Broman, S. H. (1981). Longterm development of children born to teenagers. In K. Scott, T. Field, & E. Robertson (Eds), *Teenage parents and their offspring.* New York: Grune & Stratton.

Bronfenbrenner, U. (1979). *The ecology of human development.* Cambridge, MA: Harvard University Press.

Bronfenbrenner, U., & Crouter, A. (1982). Work and family through time and space. In S. B. Kamerman & C. D. Hayes (Eds.), *Families that work: Children in a changing world.* Washington, DC: National Academy Press.

Brooks-Gunn, J., & Furstenberg, F. F. (in press). The children of adolescent mothers: Physical, academic and psychological outcomes. *Developmental Review.*

Cairns, R. B. (1977). Beyond social attachment: The dynamics of interactional development. In T. A. Alloway, P. Pliner, & L. Krames (Eds.), *Attachment Behavior.* New York: Plenum.

Cairns, R. B., & Green, J. A. (1979). How to assess personality and social patterns: Observations or ratings? In R. B. Cairns (Ed.), *The analysis of social interactions: Methods, issues, and illustrations.* Hillsdale, NJ: Erlbaum.

Card, J., & Wise, L. (1978). Teenage mothers and teenage fathers: The impact of early childbearing on the parents' personal and professional lives. *Family Planning Perspectives, 10,* 199–205.

Chamberlin, R. W. (1979). *Effects of educating mothers about child development in physicians' offices on mother and child functioning over time.* Paper presented at the meeting of the American Psychological Association, New York.

Chase-Lansdale, P. L. (1981). *Effects of maternal employment on mother–infant and father–infant attachment.* Unpublished doctoral dissertation, University of Michigan.

Clarke-Stewart, A. K. (1977, March). The father's impact on mother and child. Paper presented at the biennial meeting of the Society for Research in Child Development, New Orleans.

Clarke-Stewart, K. A. (1978). And daddy makes three: The father's impact on mother and young child. *Child Development, 49,* 466–478.

Clarke-Stewart, K. A. (1980). The father's contribution to children's cognitive and social development in early childhood. In F. Pedersen (Ed.), *The father–infant relationship.* New York: Praeger.

Clarke-Stewart, K. A., & Hevey, C. M. (1981). Longitudinal relations in repeated observations from one to two-and-a-half years. *Developmental Psychology, 17,* 127–145.

Cochran, M. M., & Brassard, J. A. (1979). Child development and personal social networks. *Child Development, 50,* 601–616.

Cohn, J. F., & Tronick, E. (1983). Three-month-old infants' reaction to simulated maternal depression. *Child Development, 54,* 185–193.

Colletta, N. D. (1981). Social support and the risk of maternal rejection. *Journal of Psychology, 109,* 191–197.

Cowan, C. P. & Cowan, P. A. (1983, August). *Individual and couple satisfaction during family formation: A longitudinal study.* Paper presented at the meeting of the American Psychological Association, Anaheim, CA.

Cowan, C. P., Cowan, P. A., Coie, L., & Coie, J. D. (1978). Becoming a family: The impact of a first child's birth on the couple's relationship. In W. B. Miller & L. F. Newman (Eds.), *The First Child and Family Formation.* Chapel Hill: Carolina Population Center.

Crnic, K. A., Greenberg, M. T., Ragozin, A. S., Robinson, N. M., & Basham, R. B. (1983). Effects of stress and social support on mothers and premature and full-term infants. *Child Development, 54,* 209-217.

Crittenden, P. M. (1985). Social networks, quality of child rearing, and child development. *Child Development, 56,* 1299-1313.

Crockenberg, S. (1981). Infant irritability, mother responsiveness, and social influences on the security of infant-mother attachment. *Child Development, 52,* 857-865.

Crockenberg, S. B. (1983, April). *Social support and the maternal behavior of adolescent mothers.* Paper presented at the biennial meeting of the Society for Research in Child Development, Detroit.

Crockenberg, S. B. (1985, April). *Professional support for adolescent mothers: Who gives it, how adolescent mothers evaluate it, what they would prefer.* Paper presented at biennial meeting of the Society for Research in Child Development, Toronto.

Daniels, P., & Weingarten, K. (1982). *Sooner or Later: The timing of parenthood in adult lives.* New York: Norton.

de Lissovoy, U. (1973). Child care by adolescent parents. *Children Today, 4,* 22-25.

Dickie, J., & Carnahan, S. (1980). Training in social competence: The effect on mothers, fathers and infants. *Child Development, 51,* 1248-1251.

Dickie, J. R., & Matheson, P. (1984, August). *Mother-father-infant: Who needs support?* Paper presented at the meeting of the American Psychological Association, Toronto.

Dix, T. H., & Grusec, J. E. (1985). Parent attribution processes in the socialization of children. In I. Sigel (Ed.), *Parent belief systems: The psychological consequences for children.* Hillsdale, NJ: Erlbaum.

Dolby, R., English, B., & Warren, B. (1982, March). *Brazelton demonstrations for mothers and fathers: Impact on the developing parent-infant relationship.* Paper presented at the International Conference on Infant Studies, Austin, TX.

Durrett, M. E., Otaki, M., & Richards, P. (1984). Attachment and the mother's perception of support from the father. *International Journal of Behavioral Development, 7,* 167-176.

Easterbrooks, M. A., & Goldberg, W. A. (1984). Toddler development in the family: Impact of father involvement and parenting characteristics. *Child Development, 55,* 740-752.

Elardo, R., Bradley, R., & Caldwell, B. (1975). The relation of infants' home environments to mental test performance from six to thirty-six months: A longitudinal analysis. *Child Development, 46,* 71-76.

Elder, G. H. (1974). *Children of the great depression.* Chicago: University of Chicago Press.

Elder, G. H., & Rockwell, R. (1979). The life course and human development: An ecological perspective. *International Journal of Behavioral Development, 2,* 1-21.

Elder, G. H. (1984). Families, kin and the life course: A sociological perspective. In R. D. Parke, R. N. Emde, H. P. McAdoo, & G. P. Sackett (Eds.), *Review of child development research: The family* (Vol. 7). Chicago: University of Chicago Press.

Epstein, A. S. (1980). *Assessing the child development information needed by adolescent children.* Final report HEW Grant No. 90-C-1341. Ypsilanti, MI: High/Scope Educational Foundation.

Feiring, C., & Lewis, M. (1984). Changing characteristics of the U.S. family: Implications for family networks, relationships and child development. In M. Lewis (Ed.), *Beyond the dyad*. New York: Plenum.

Feiring, C., Fox, N., Jaskir, J., & Lewis, M. (1985, April). *The relationships between social support, infant risk status and mother–infant interaction*. Paper presented at the biennial meeting of the Society for Research in Child Development, Toronto.

Feldman, S. S., Nash, S. C., & Aschenbrenner, B. G. (1983). Antecedents of fathering. *Child Development, 54,* 1628–1636.

Field, T. M. (1978). Interaction behaviors of primary versus secondary caretaker fathers. *Developmental Psychology, 14,* 183–185.

Field, T. M., (1981). A socio-economic analysis of out-of-wedlock birth among teenagers. In K. Scott, T. Field, & E. Robinson (Eds.), *Teenage parents and their offspring*. New York: Grune and Stratton.

Field, T., Sosteck, A., Vietze, P., & Leiderman, H. (1981). *Culture and early interactions*. Hillsdale, NJ: Erlbaum.

Field, T. M., Widmayer, S. M., Stringer, S., & Ignatoff, E. (1980). Teenage, lower-class, black mothers and their preterm infants: An intervention and developmental follow-up. *Child Development, 51,* 426–436.

Furstenburg, F. F., Jr. (1976). *Unplanned parenthood: The social consequences of teenage childbearing*. New York: Free Press.

Furstenburg, F. F., Jr. (1981). Implicating the family: Teenage parenthood and kinship involvement. In T. Ooms (Ed.), *Teenage pregnancy in a family context*. Philadelphia: Temple University Press.

Furstenburg, F. F., Jr., & Crawford, A. G. (1978). Family support: Helping teenage mothers to cope. *Family Planning Perspectives, 10,* 322–333.

Garbarino, J., & Gilliam, G. (1980). *Understanding abusive families*. Lexington, MA: Lexington Press.

Gladieux, J. D. (1978). Pregnancy—The transition to parenthood: Satisfaction with the pregnancy experience as a function of sex role conceptions, marital relationship and social network. In W. B. Miller & L. F. Newman (Eds.), *The first child and family formation*. Chapel Hill: Carolina Population Center.

Goldberg, S. (1977). Social competence in infancy: A model of parent–infant interaction. *Merrill-Palmer Quarterly, 23,* 163–177.

Goldberg, S. (1983). Parent–infant bonding: Another look. *Child Development, 54,* 1355–1382.

Goodnow, J. J. (1984). Parents' ideas about parenting and development: A review of issues and recent work. In M. Lamb, A Brown, & B. Rogoff (Eds.), *Advances in developmental psychology*. Hillsdale, NJ: Erlbaum.

Goodnow, J. J. (1985). Change and variation in ideas about childhood and parenting. In I. Sigel (Ed.), *Parent belief systems: The psychological consequences for children*. Hillsdale, NJ: Erlbaum.

Greenbaum, C. W., & Landau, R. (1979). The infant's exposure to talk by familiar people: Mothers, fathers and siblings in different environments. In M. Lewis & L. Rosenblum (Eds.), *The child and its family*. New York: Plenum.

Hall, L. A., Williams, C. A., & Greenberg, R. S. (1985). Supports, stressors and depressive symptoms in low-income mothers of young children, *American Journal of Public Health, 75,* 518–522.

Hareven, T. K. (1977). Family time and historical time. *Daedalus, 106,* 57–70.

Harris, L. (1975). *The myth and reality of aging in America,* Washington, DC: National Council on Aging.

Harris, L. (1975). *The myth and reality of aging in America*. Washington, DC: National Council on Aging.

Harrison, A., Serafica, F., & McAdoo, H. (1984). Ethnic families of color. In R. D. Parke, R. N. Emde, H. P. McAdoo & G. P. Sackett (Eds.) *Review of Child Development Research, Vol 7: The Family*, Chicago: University of Chicago Press.

Hartup, W. W. (1979). The social worlds of childhood. *American Psychologist, 34,* 944–950.

Hayes, C. D. (Ed.). (1986). *Adolescent pregnancy and child bearing* (Vol. 1). Washington, DC: National Academy Press.

Hess, R., Kashigawi, K., Azuma, H., Price, G. G., & Dickson, W. (1980). Maternal expectations for early mastery of developmental tasks and cognitive and social competence of preschool children in Japan and the United States. *International Journal of Psychology, 15,* 259–271.

Hetherington, E. M., Cox, M., & Cox, R. (1982). Effects of development on parents and children. In M. E. Lamb (Ed.), *Nontraditional families*. Hillsdale, NJ: Erlbaum.

Hetherington, E. M. & Camara, K. (1984). Families in transition. The processes of dissolution and reconstitution. In R. D. Parke, R. N. Emde, H. P. McAdoo, & G. P. Sackett (Eds.) *Review of Child Development Research: The Family.* Chicago: University of Chicago Press.

Hock, E. (1980). Working and nonworking mothers and their infants: A comparative study of maternal caregiving characteristics and infant social behavior. *Merrill Palmer Quarterly, 26,* 79–101.

Hoffman, L. W. (1984). Work, family and the socialization of the child. In R. D. Parke, R. Emde, H. McAdoo, & G. P. Sackett (Eds.), *Review of child development research: The family* (Vol. 7). Chicago: University of Chicago Press.

Hoffman, L. W., & Manis, J. D. (1978). Influences of children on marital interaction and parental satisfactions and dissatisfactions. In R. Leiner & G. Spanier (Eds.), *Child influence on marital and family interaction: A life-span perspective.* New York: Academic.

Hoffman, L. W. & Nye, F. I. (1974). *Working Mothers.* San Francisco: Jossey-Bass.

Hoffreth, S. (1986). The children of teen childbearers. In S. D. Hoffreth & C. D. Hayes (Eds.), *Adolescent pregnancy and childbearing* (Vol. 2). Washington, DC: National Academy Press.

Holloway, S. D. (1985). *The relationship of mothers' beliefs to children's mathematics achievement: Some effects of child gender.* Paper presented at the biennial meeting of the Society for Research in Child Development, Toronto.

Honig, A. S., & Gardner, C. G. (1985, April). *Overwhelmed mothers of toddlers in immigrant families: Stress factors.* Paper presented at the biennial meeting of the Society for Research in Child Development, Toronto.

Jay, S., & Farran, D. C. (1981). The relative efficacy of predicting IQ from mother–child interactions using ratings versus behavioral count measures. *Journal of Applied Developmental Psychology, 2,* 165–177.

Johnson, J. E., & Martin, C. (1985). Parents' beliefs and home learning environments: Effects on cognitive development. In I. Sigel (Ed.), *Parent belief systems: The psychological consequences for children.* Hillsdale, NJ: Erlbaum.

Kanter, R. M. (1977). *Work and family in the United States: A critical review of research and policy.* New York: Sage.

Kinard, E. M., & Klerman, L. (1983). Effects of early parenthood in the cognitive development of children. In E. McAnarney (Ed.), *Premature adolescent pregnancy and parenthood.* New York: Grune & Stratton.

Klaus, M. H., & Kennell, J. H. (1976). *Parent–infant bonding.* St. Louis: Mosby.

Klaus, M. H., & Kennell, J. H. (1981). *Parent–infant bonding.* (2nd ed.). St. Louis: Mosby.

Kotelchuck, M. (1972). *The nature of the child's tie to his father.* Unpublished doctoral dissertation, Harvard University.

Kotelchuck, M. (1976). The infant's relationship to the father: Experimental evidence. In M. E. Lamb (Ed.), *The role of the father in child development.* New York: Wiley.

Lamb, M. E. (1977a). Father–infant and mother–infant interaction in the first year of life. *Child Development, 48,* 167–181.

Lamb, M. E. (1977b). The development of mother–infant and father–infant attachments in the second year of life. *Developmental Psychology, 13,* 639–649.

Lamb, M. E. (1982). Maternal employment and child development: A review. In M. E. Lamb (Ed.), *Non-traditional families.* Hillsdale, NJ: Erlbaum.

Lamb, M. E. (1979). The effects of social context on dyadic social interaction. In M. E. Lamb, S. T. Suomi, & G. R. Stephenson (Eds.), *Social interaction analysis: Methodological issues.* Madison: University of Wisconsin Press.

Lamb, M. E., & Elster, A. B. (1985). Adolescent mother–infant–father relationships. *Developmental Psychology, 21,* 768–773.

Lamb, M. E., Frodi, A. M., Hwang, C. P., & Frodi, M. (1982). Varying degrees of paternal involvement in infant care: Attitudinal and behavioral correlates. In M. E. Lamb (Ed.), *Nontraditional families.* Hillsdale, NJ: Erlbaum.

Lamb, M. E., Frodi, A. M., Hwang, C. P., Frodi, M., & Steinberg, J. (1982). Effects of gender and caretaking role on parent–infant interaction. In R. M. Emde & R. J. Harmon (Eds.), *Attachment and affiliative systems.* New York: Plenum.

Lamb, M. E., & Hwang, C. (1982). Maternal attachment and mother–infant bonding: A critical review. In M. E. Lamb & A. L. Brown (Eds.), *Advances in developmental psychology* (Vol. 2). Hillsdale, NJ: Erlbaum.

Lee, D. M., & Colletta, N. D. (1983, April). *Family support for adolescent mothers: The positive and negative impact.* Paper presented at the biennial meeting of the Society for Research in Child Development, Detroit.

Lewis, M., & Feiring, C. (1981). Direct and indirect interactions in social relationships. In L. P. Lipsitt (Ed.), *Advances in infancy research* (Vol. 1). New York: Ablex.

Lewis, J. D., & Jones, A. C. (1980). *Psychological stress, social support systems, and pregnancy complications in adolescents.* Paper presented at the meeting of the American Psychological Association, Montreal.

Lorenzi, M. E., Klerman, L. V., & Jekel, J. F. (1977). School-age parents: How permanent a relationship. *Adolescent, 45,* 13–22.

Lynn, D. B., & Cross, A. R. (1974). Parent preference of preschool children. *Journal of Marriage & the Family, 36,* 555–559.

McCluskey, K. A., Killarney, J., & Papini, D. R. (1983). Adolescent pregnancy and parenthood: Implications for development. In E. C. Callahan & K. A. McCluskey (Eds.), *Lifespan developmental psychology: Non-normative life events.* New York: Academic.

Maccoby, E. E., & Martin, J. A. (1983). Socialization in the context of the family: Parent–child interaction. In E. M. Hetherington (Ed.), *Handbook of child psychology* (Vol. 4). New York: Wiley.

MacDonald, K., & Parke, R. D. (1984). Bridging the gap: Parent–child play interaction and peer interactive competence. *Child Development, 55,* 1265–1277.

MacDonald, K. & Parke, R. D. (1986). Parent–child physical play: The effects of sex and age of children and parents, *Sex Roles, 7–8,* 367–379.

Main, M., Weston, D. R. (1981). The quality of the toddler's relationship to mother and to father: Related to conflict behavior and the readiness to establish new relationships. *Child Development, 52,* 932–940.

Maklan, D. (1976). *The four day workweek: Blue collar adjustment to a nonconventional arrangement of work and leisure time.* Unpublished dissertation, University of Michigan.

Majoribanks, K. (1979). *Families and their learning environments: An empirical analysis.* London: Routledge & Kegan Paul.

Matas, L., Arend, R. A., & Sroufe, L. A. (1978). Continuity of adaption in the second year: The relationship between quality of attachment and later competence. *Child Development, 49,* 547–556.

McGillicuddy-DeLisi, A. V. (1982). The relation between family configuration and parental beliefs about child development. In L. M. Laosa & I. E. Sigel (Eds.), *Families as learning environments for children.* New York: Plenum.

McGuire, W. J. (1968). The nature of attitudes and attitude change. In G. Lindzey & E. Aronson (Eds.), *Handbook of social psychology* (Vol. 3). Reading: Addison-Wesley.

McLaughlin, F., Drake, D., Deni, R., & Constantini, F. (1983, April). *Sequential analysis of maternal behavior recorded after possible exposure to Brazelton Neonatal Assessment procedures.* Paper presented at the biennial meeting of the Society for Research in Child Development, Detroit.

Mercer, R. T., Hackley, K. C., & Bostrom, A. (1983). Social support of teenage mothers, *Birth Defects: Original Article Series.*

Miller, S. A. (1986). Parents beliefs about their children's cognitive abilities. *Developmental Psychology, 22,* 276–284.

Minde, K., Shosenberg, N. E., Marton, P., Thompson, J., Ripley, J., & Burns, S. (1980). Self-help groups in a premature nursery—A controlled evaluation. *Journal of Pediatrics, 96,* 933–940.

Minde, K., Shosenberg, N. E., & Marton, P. L. (1981). *The effects of self-help groups in a premature nursery on maternal autonomy and caretaking style one year later.* Unpublished manuscript, University of Toronto.

Moore, K. A., & Hoffreth, S. (1978). *The consequences of age at first birth: Family size. Working paper 1146–1102.* Washington, D.C.: The Urban Institute.

Myers, B. J. (1982). Early intervention using Brazelton training with middle class mothers and fathers of newborns. *Child Development, 53,* 462–171.

Nettleton, C. A., & Cline, D. W. (1975). Dating patterns, sexual relationships and use of contraceptives of 700 unwed mothers during a two-year follow period following delivery. *Adolescence, 37,* 45–57.

O'Connell, M., & Roger, C. C. (1984). Out-of-wedlock births, premarital pregnancies and their effects on family formation and dissolution. *Family Planning Perspectives, 16,* 157–162.

Olds, D. (1981). Improving formal services for mothers and children. In J. Garbarino & S. Holly Stocking (Eds.), *Protecting children from abuse and neglect: Developing and maintaining effective support systems for families.* San Francisco: Jossey-Bass.

Orvaschel, H., Weissman, M., & McKidd, K. K. (1980). The children of depressed parents; the childhood of depressed patients. *Journal of Affective Disorders, 2,* 1–16.

Osofsky, J. D., & Culp, A. M. (1986). *Adolescent mothers and infants: Relationships between prenatal factors and patterns of interaction.* Unpublished manuscript, Menninger Foundation.

Pannabecker, M. J., Emde, R. N., & Austin, B. C. (1982). The effect of early extended contact on father–newborn interaction. *Journal of Genetic Psychology, 141,* 7–17.

Parke, R. D. (1978). Parent–infant interaction: Progress, paradigms and problems. In G. P. Sackett (Ed.), *Observing behavior: Vol. 1. Theory and applications in mental retardation*. Baltimore: University Park Press.

Parke, R. D. (1979). Perspectives of father–infant interaction. In J. Osofsky (Ed.), *A handbook of infant development*. New York: Wiley.

Parke, R. D. (1981). *Fathers*. Cambridge, MA: Harvard University Press.

Parke, R. D. (1986, June). Families and stressful change: A multilevel developmental analysis. Paper presented at Social Science Research Council Conference on Child Development in Life Span Perspective, Woods Hole, Mass.

Parke, R. D., & Anderson, E. (1986). Fathers and their at-risk infants: Conceptual and empirical analyses. In P. Berman & F. Pedersen (Eds.), *Men's transition to parenthood: Longitudinal studies of early family experience*. Hillsdale, NJ: Erlbaum.

Parke, R. D., & Beitel, A. (1986). Hospital based interventions for fathers. In M. E. Lamb (Ed.), *Fatherhood: Applied perspectives*. New York: Wiley.

Parke, R. D., & Collmer, C. W. (1975). Child abuse: An interdisciplinary analysis. In E. M. Hetherington (Ed.), *Review of child development* (Vol. 5). Chicago: University of Chicago Press.

Parke, R. D., Hymel, S., Power, T. G., & Tinsley, B. R. (1980). Fathers and risk: A hospital based model intervention. In D. B. Sawin, R. C. Hawkins, L. O. Walker, & J. H. Penticuff (Eds.), *Psychosocial risks in infant–environment transactions*. New York: Bruner/Mazel.

Parke, R. D., Grossman, K., & Tinsley, B. R. (1981). Father–mother–infant interaction in the newborn period: A German–American comparison. In T. M. Field, A. M. Sostek, P. Vietze, & P. H. Leiderman (Eds.), *Culture and early interactions*. Hillsdale, NJ: Erlbaum.

Parke, R. D., MacDonald, K., Beitel, A., & Bhavangri, N. (in press). The interrelationships among families, fathers and peers. In R. Dev Peters (Ed.), *New approaches to family research*. New York: Bruner/Mazel.

Parke, R. D., & Nevelle, B. (1986). The role of the adolescent male in adolescent pregnancy and childbearing. In S. L. Hoffreth & C. D. Hayes (Eds.), *Adolescent pregnancy and childbearing* (Vol. 2). Washington, DC: National Academy Press.

Parke, R. D., Power, T. G., & Fisher, T. (1980). The adolescent father's impact on the mother and child. *Journal of Social Issues, 36,* 88–106.

Parke, R. D., Power, T. G., & Gottman, J. M. (1979). Conceptualization and quantifying influence patterns in the family triad. In M. E. Lamb, S. J. Suomi, & G. R. Stephenson (Eds.), *Social interaction analysis: Methodological issues*. Madison: University of Wisconsin Press.

Parke, R. D., & Sawin, D. B. (1975, April). *Infant characteristics and behavior as elicitors of maternal and paternal responsibility in the newborn period*. Paper presented at the biennial meeting of the Society for Research in Child Development, Denver.

Parke, R. D., & Sawin, D. B. (1980). The family in early infancy: Social interactional and attitudinal analyses. In F. A. Pedersen (Ed.), *The father–infant relationship: Observational studies in the family setting*. New York: Praeger.

Parke, R. D., & Suomi, S. J. (1981). Adult male–infant relationships: Human and nonhuman primate evidence. In K. Immelmann, G. W. Barlow, L. Petrinovitch, & M. Main (Eds.), *Behavioral development: The Bielefeld Interdisciplinary Project*. New York: Cambridge University Press.

Parke, R. D., & Tinsley, B. R. (1981). The father's role in infancy: Determinants of involvement in caregiving and play. In M. E. Lamb (Ed.), *The role of the father in child development* (2nd ed.). New York: Wiley.

Parke, R. D., & Tinsley, B. R. (1982). The early environment of the at-risk infant: Expanding the social context. In D. Bricker (Ed.), *Intervention with at-risk and handicapped infants: From research to application*. Baltimore: University Park Press.

Parke, R. D., & Tinsley, B. R. (1984). Fatherhood: Historical and contemporary perspectives. In K. McCluskey & H. Reese (Eds.), *Life span development: Historical and generational effects*. New York: Academic.

Parks, P. L., & Smeriglio, V. L. (1983). Parenting knowledge among adolescent mothers. *Journal of Adolescent Health Care, 4,* 163–167.

Pascoe, J. M., Loda, F. A., Jeffries, V., & Earp, J. A. (1981). The association between mothers' social support and provision of stimulation to their children. *Developmental & Behavioral Pediatrics, 2,* 15–19.

Pastor, D. L. (1981). The quality of mother–infant attachment and its relationship to toddlers' initial sociability with peers. *Developmental Psychology, 17,* 326–335.

Patterson, G. R. (1982). *Coercive family process*. Eugene, OR: Castalia.

Pedersen, F. A. (1975, September). *Mother, father and infant as an interactive system*. Paper presented at the Annual Convention of the American Psychological Association, Chicago.

Pedersen, F. A. (Ed.) (1980). *The father–infant relationship: Observational studies in the family setting*. New York: Praeger.

Pedersen, F. A., Anderson, B. J., & Cain, R. L. (1977). *An approach to understanding linkages between the parent–infant and spouse relationships*. Paper presented at the meeting of the Society for Research in Child Development, New Orleans.

Pederson, F. A., Anderson, B. J., Cain, R. L., Jr. (1980). Parent–infant and husband–wife interactions observed at age five months. In F. A. Pedersen (Ed.), *The father–infant relationship*. New York: Praeger.

Pedersen, F. A., Zaslow, M. J., Cain, R. L., & Anderson, B. J. (1981). Caesarean childbirth: Psychological implications for mothers *and* fathers. *Infant Mental Health Journal, 2,* 257–263.

Pedersen, F. A., & Robson, K. S. (1969) Father participation in infancy. *American Journal of Orthopsychiatry, 39,* 466–472.

Pleck, J. H. (1981). *Wives' employment, role demands and adjustment (final report)*. Unpublished manuscript, Wellesley College Center for Research on Women.

Pleck, J. H. (1983). Husbands' paid work and family roles: Current research issues. In H. Z. Lopata & J. H. Pleck (Eds.), *Research on the interview of social roles: Vol 3. Families and jobs*. Greenwich, CT: JAI.

Powell, D. R. (1979). Family–environment relations and early childrearing, the role of social networks and neighborhoods. *Journal of Research & Education, 13,* 1–11.

Power, T. G., & Parke, R. D. (1982). Play as a context for early learning: Lab and home analyses. In I. E. Sigel & L. M. Laosa (Eds.), *The Family as a Learning Environment*. New York: Plenum.

Power, T. G., & Parke, R. D. (1983). Patterns of mother and father play with their 8 month old infant: A multiple analyses approach. *Infant Behavior & Development, 6,* 453–459.

Power, T. G., & Parke, R. D. (1984). Social network factors and the transition to parenthood. *Sex Roles, 10,* 949–972.

Power, T. G. & Parke, R. D. (1986). Patterns of early socialization: Mother and father–infant interaction in the home. *International Journal of Behavioral Development, 9,* 331–341.

Presser, H. (1974). Early motherhood: Ignorance or bliss? *Family Planning Perspectives, 6,* 756–764.

Presser, H. (1980). Sally's Corner: Coping with unmarried motherhood. *Journal of Social Issues, 36,* 107–129.

Radke-Yarrow, M., & Zahn-Waxler, C. (1985). Roots, motives and patterns in children's presocial behavior. In J. Reykowki, J. Karylowski, D. Bar-Tol & E. Staub (Eds.), *Origins and maintainence of prosocial behaviors*. New York: Plenum.

Ragozin, A. S., Bashan, R. B., Crnic, K. A., Greenberg, M. T., & Robinson, N. M. (1982). Effects of maternal age on parenting role. *Developmental Psychology, 18,* 627–634.

Rappaport, R., Rappaport, R. N., & Strelitz, Z. (1977). *Fathers, mothers and society.* New York: Basic.

Redican, W. K. (1976). Adult male–infant interactions in non-human primates. In M. E. Lamb (Ed.), *The role of the father in child development.* New York: Wiley.

Redican, W. K., & Taub, D. M. (1981). Male paternal care in monkeys and apes. In M. E. Lamb (Ed.), *The role of the father in child development* (2nd ed.). New York: Wiley.

Reiss, D. (1981). *The family's construction of reality.* Cambridge, MA: Harvard University Press.

Rheingold, H. L. (1956). The modification of social responsiveness in institutional babies. *Monographs of the Society for Research in Child Development, 21* (63).

Richards, M. P. M., Dunn, J. F., & Antonis, B. (1977). Caretaking in the first year of life: The role of fathers' and mothers' social isolation. *Child: Care, Health & Development, 3,* 23–26.

Riesman, D. (1958). Work and leisure in post-industrial society. In E. Larrabee & R. Meyersohn (Eds.), *Mass leisure.* Glencoe, IL: Free Press.

Robbins, L. C. (1963). The accuracy of parental record of aspects of child development and of child rearing practices. *Journal of Abnormal & Social Psychology, 66,* 261–270.

Robinson, J. P. (1977). *How Americans use time.* New York: Praeger.

Rueveni, U. (1979). *Networking families in crisis.* New York: Human Services Press.

Russell, C. (1980). Unscheduled parenthood: Transition to "parent" for the teenager. *Journal of Social Issues, 36,* 45–63.

Russell, G. (1982). Shared-caregiving families: An Australian study. In M. E. Lamb (Ed.), *Nontraditional families.* Hillsdale, NJ: Erlbaum.

Sackett, G. P. (1979). The lag sequential analysis of contingency and cyclicity in behavioral interaction research. In J. D. Osofsky (Ed.), *Handbook of infant development.* New York: Wiley.

Sagi, A., Lamb, M. E., Shoham, R., Dvir, R., & Lewkowicz, K. S. (1985). Parent–infant interaction in families on Israeli kibbutzim. *International Journal of Behavioral Development, 8,* 273–284.

Sameroff, A. J. (1975). Transactional models in early social relations. *Human Development, 18,* 65–79.

Sameroff, A. J. (1983). Developmental systems: Contexts and evolution. In W. Kessen (Ed.), *Handbook of child psychology* (Vol. 1). New York: Wiley.

Sameroff, A. J., & Chandler, M. J. (1975). Reproductive risk and the continuum of caretaking casualty. In F. D. Horowitz, M. Hetherington, S. Scarr-Salapatek, & G. Siegel (Eds.), *Review of child development research* (Vol. 4). Chicago: University of Chicago Press.

Sameroff, A. J., & Feil, L. A. (1985). Parental concepts of development. In I. Sigel (Ed.), *Parent belief systems: The psychological consequences for children.* Hillsdale, NJ: Erlbaum.

Schaffer, H. R. (1984). *The child's entry into a social world.* New York: Academic.

Schaffer, H. R., & Emerson, P. E. (1964). The development of social attachments in infancy. *Monographs of the Society for Research in Child Development, 29* (3) (No. 94).

Shereshefsky, P. M., & Yarrow, L. J. (1973). *Psychological aspects of a first pregnancy and early postnatal adaption.* New York: Raven.

Sigel, I. E. (Ed.). (1985). *Parent belief systems: The psychological consequences for children.* Hillsdale, NJ: Erlbaum.

Skeels, H. (1966). Adult status of children with contrasting early life experiences. *Monographs of the Society for Research in Child Development, 31* (3).

Skinner, E. A. (1985). Determinants of mother sensitive and contingent-responsive behavior: The role of childrearing beliefs and socioeconomic status. In I. Sigel (Ed.), *Parent belief systems: The psychological consequences for children.* Hillsdale, NJ: Erlbaum.

Smith, C., Leiderman, P. H., Selz, L., MacPherson, L., & Bingham, E. (1981, April). *Maternal expectations and developmental milestones in physically handicapped infants.* Paper presented at the biennial meeting of the Society for Research in Child Development, Boston.

Sosa, R., Kennell, J. H., Klaus, M. H., Robertson, S., & Urrutia, J. (1980). The effect of a supportive companion on perinatal problems, length of labor and mother–infant interaction. *New England Journal of Medicine, 303,* 597–600.

Spelke, E., Zelazo, P., Kagan, J., & Kotelchuck, M. (1973). Father interaction and separation protest. *Developmental Psychology, 9,* 83–90.

Stern, D. N. (1974). Mother and infant at play: The dyadic interaction involving facial, vocal, and gaze behaviors. In M. Lewis & L. A. Rosenblum (Eds.), *The effect of the infant on its caregiver.* New York: Wiley.

Szalai, A. (Ed.). (1972). *The use of time: Daily activities of urban and suburban populations in twelve countries.* The Hague: Mouton.

Tinsley, B. J., & Parke, R. D. (in press). Grandparents as interactive and social support agents for families with young infants. *International Journal of Aging & Human Development.*

Tinsley, B. J., & Parke, R. D. (1984). The contemporary impact of the extended family on the nuclear family: Grandparents as support and socialization agents. In M. Lewis (Ed.), *Beyond the dyad.* New York: Plenum.

Tronick, E. Z., Cohn, J. F., & Shea, E. (1986). The transfer of affect between mothers and infants. In T. B. Brazelton & M. Yogman (Eds.), *Affective development in infancy.* Norwood, NJ: Ablex.

Unger, D. G. (1979). *An ecological approach to the family: The role of social networks, social stress and mother–child interaction.* Unpublished master's thesis, Merrill-Palmer Institute.

Unger, D. G., & Powell, D. R. (1980). Supporting families under stress: The role of social networks. *Family Relations, 29,* 566–574.

Unger, D. G., & Wandersman, L. P. (in press). Social support and adolescent mothers: Action research contributions to theory and application. *Journal of Social Issues.*

Wachs, T. D., & Gruen, G. E. (1981). *Early experience and human development.* New York: Plenum.

Walker, K., & Woods, M. (1976). *Time use: A measure of household production of family goods and services.* Washington, DC: American Home Economics Association.

Wandersman, L. P., & Unger, D. G. (1983, April). *Interaction of infant difficulty and social support in adolescent mothers.* Paper presented at the biennial meeting of the Society for Research in Child Development, Detroit.

Waters, E. (1978). The reliability and stability of individual differences in infant–mother attachment. *Child Development, 49,* 483–494.

Waters, E., Wippman, J., Stroufe, L. A. (1979). Attachment, positive affect, and competence in the peer group: Two studies in construct validation. *Child Development, 3,* 821–829.

Weinraub, M., & Wolf, B. M. (1983). Effects of stress and social supports on mother–child interactions in single- and two-parent families. *Child Development, 54,* 1297–1311.

Whitt, J. K., & Casey, P. H. (1982). The mother–infant relationship and infant development: The effect of pediatric intervention. *Child Development, 53,* 948–956.

Widmayer, S. M., & Field, T. M. (1980). Effects of Brazelton demonstrations on early interactions of preterm infants and their teenage mothers. *Infant Behavior & Development, 3,* 79–89.

Weissman, M. M., & Paykel, E. S. (1972). Moving and depression in women. *Society, 9,* 24–28.

Wilensky, H. L. (1961). The uneven distribution of leisure: The impact of economic growth on "freetime." *Social Problems, 9,* 107–145.

Willmott, P. (1971). Family, work, and leisure conflicts among male employees: Some preliminary findings. *Human Relations, 24,* 575–584.

Worobey, J., & Belsky, J. (1982). Employing the Brazelton Scale to influence mothering: An experimental comparison of three strategies. *Developmental Psychology, 18,* 736–743.

Yarrow, M. R., Campbell, J. D., & Burton, R. V. (1968). *Child Rearing.* San Francisco: Jossey-Bass.

Yogman, M. W. (1983). Development of the father–infant relationship. In H. Fitsgerald, B. Lester, & M. W. Yogman (Eds.), *Theory and research in behavioral pediatrics* (Vol. 1). New York: Plenum.

Yogman, M. J., Dixon, S., Tronick, E., Als, H., & Brazelton, T. B. (1977, March). *The goals and structure of face-to-face interaction between infants and fathers.* Paper presented at the biennial meeting of the Society for Research in Child Development, New Orleans.

Young, A., Bechman, B., & Rehr, H. (1975). Parental influence on the pregnant adolescent. *Social Work, 20,* 387–391.

Zahn-Waxler, C., & Radke-Yarrow, M. (1982). The development of altruism: Alternative research strategies. In N. Eisenberg-Berg (Ed.), *The development of prosocial behavior.* New York: Academic.

Zelazo, P. R., Kotelchuck, M., Barber, L., & David, J. (1977, March). *Fathers and sons: An experimental facilitation of attachment behaviors.* Paper presented at the biennial meeting of the Society for Research in Child Development, New Orleans.

CHAPTER 11

Parent–Infant Socialization in Several Western European Countries

PETER DE CHATEAU

In the last decade, the hypothesis has emerged that early separation between parents and their newborns affects their mutual relationship and the future development of this relationship. The infant's ability and capacity for interaction with its surroundings are significantly greater than have been anticipated before, and the parental receptivity for signals from the newborn is probably also greater than has been appreciated, but needs training and stimulation, as well as exposure. The concept of infant fitness and maternal readiness and ability to interact immediately after an uncomplicated delivery is getting growing support from the literature, as the mother and the infant seem to be in a state of hightened alertness and expectation, fully capable of exploring and mutuality.

Systematic videotape recording of 12 deliveries of normal, healthy mothers giving natural birth to normal, healthy full-term infants in the presence of the fathers revealed a number of interesting observations (Wiberg & Humble, in preparation). The length of the recordings varies from 20 to 90 min, starting a few minutes before the baby is born. All 12 babies cry at birth: 2 stop before being placed on the mothers' abdomens, 6 stop crying instantly thereafter, 3 stop 3–4 min after, and 1 continues to cry at intervals. After this a short period of rest and inactivity follows. The infant then opens its eyes and tries to establish eye-to-eye contact with the mother. Hand-to-mouth contact is seen frequently during the following period, as well as crawling movements and movements toward the breast. Often the mother will understand these signals from the infant and help it to start suckling. The infant's hand-to-mouth movements can be seen as exercises for the rooting and suckling reflexes that are vital for the infant in order to survive. In almost all recordings infant activity seems to trigger parental behavior; thus more parental talking, caressing, touching, and so on is seen after increased activity of the infant. Maternal behavior during these recordings follows otherwise a pattern similar to that described by others (Klaus et al., 1970).

At the time of birth the infant not only tries to achieve state control with the help of its caregivers, but also tries to manage its social situation. What happens in the baby's first experiences when communicating to caregivers is not fully understood. We know now to meet most of the baby's physical needs. But our knowledge of the infant's basic sensory, emotional, and social needs is incomplete (Winberg &

de Chateau, 1982). However, over the last decade our knowledge has increased in regard to assessing especially the abilities and capacities of the neonate, and new methods with which to measure these properties have developed rapidly.

INFANT CAPACITY FOR INTERACTION

The early post partum period has been regarded to have great potential and is one of the opportunities for interaction between parents and infants that can influence the future development of family relations. The mother in particular has been regarded to play a very powerful role, whereas the infant's contribution has been accorded less attention. At birth the human brain is not completely developed. Shapiro and Vukovisch (1970) have shown that in rats the number of synapses in dentrites of pyramid cells is correlated to the amount of sensory stimulation during the first weeks of life. Conel (1970) states that the main period of growth of brain cells and dentrites between cells in the human infant is during fetal life and up to 3 months of age. The myelinization and isolation of axons start in the second trimester of pregnancy and are complete by 2 years (Dobbing, 1970). Malnutrition and/ or understimulation during this period may result in impaired neuron growth and subsequently in relative brain damage.

The individual reactive capacity of the newborn baby and its influence on the environment can be illustrated in a number of ways. Immediately after delivery most infants are able, in the alert state (Prechtl, 1974), to see and follow primitively and rather uncoordinatedly slow movements of bright objects, provided that the mother has given birth with very limited analgesia and without anesthesia. The open eyes of the newborn may also be of major importance for establishing the newborn's contact with its caregiver. Robson (1967) suggested that eye contact may be an inborn releasing mechanism for caretaking, and Klaus and Kennell (1970) pointed out that the mother's evaluation of her newborn is usually based on whether the baby looks or not. Eye contact is also described by parents as a confirmation of mutual attachment and, if this communication is missing, early bonding may be disturbed. Fraiberg (1974) showed, for example, that parents have difficulties in attaching to blind infants; thus it appears that mothers seem to hold a certain expectation in regard to eye contact with the newborn.

Routine instillation of silver nitrate into the eyes of the newborn (so-called Credé prophylaxis, one of the great advances in preventive medicine at its time) and its consequences are worth considering. Elicited by the procedure, for example, are severe conjunctival inflammations with vascular injection, edema, purulent secretion, and temporarily impaired vision. In one study (Wahlberg, 1982) infants were photographed 15 min before and 15 min after the prophylaxis, with automatic exposure every thirtieth second, that is, 60 exposures per infant. This was done in daylight or under ordinary room illumination. Before prophylaxis, the eyes were usually open, sometimes widely so, and the facial expression varied. Mostly an impression is gained of satisfaction, joy, or interest. After instillation, there was a marked change. Not only did the infants pinch up their eyes, but the variability and positiveness of the facial expression changed; the mouth broadened and the corners dropped, the eyebrows became wrinkled, and the whole facial appearance seemed to express dissatisfaction. Open, rounded eyes and an alert, satisfied facial expression can communicate important signals to the parents, eliciting caretaking and assurance, whereas the dissatisfied face does not. Whether or not the Credé procedure contributes to bonding failures, especially in vulnerable child–parent situations, needs more exploration.

The capacity of a neonate to fix, follow, and alert to a visual stimulus has appeared to be good evidence of an intact central nervous system. Fantz (1963) and Fantz and Miranda (1975) demonstrated the presence of discriminatory ability in neonates in selecting different patterns when vision was tested. Miranda (1970) showed that when newborn infants were presented with two identical pictures the infants looked more often at the one on the right than at the one on the left. In about 80 percent of cases, mothers have been reported to hold their infants to the left of the body (de Chateau, Holmberg, & Winberg, 1978; Salk, 1970). The infant's preference for turning to the right and looking to the right may be a species-specific adaption to maternal holding to the left; that is, when looking and turning to the right the baby can see its mother. The infant's preference for right side looking and turning could also be a signal to the mother to favor holding to the left.

Korner and Thoman (1972) found that some infants could be soothed more easily than others. Vestibular-proprioceptive stimulation, as a part of mother–infant body contact, had a highly potent soothing effect. When a crying infant during the first weeks of life is picked up and put to the shoulder, it usually stops crying and becomes bright eyed, thus being able to scan its visual surroundings and provide itself with a great deal of visual stimulation. Crying infants may therefore need to be picked up more than infants capable of providing visual experiences for themselves. Maternal neglect of a crying infant may thus deprive the infant of visual stimulation and influence psychomotor and even affective development. The infant's cry can bring the caregiver into the vicinity and thus start an interaction, although large individual differences have been found and the tolerance of caregivers probably shows a great range (Bell, 1974). During the first year of life a number of types of behavior by mothers in resposne to crying, such as picking up, talking, feeding, touching, have been reported by Bell and Ainsworth (1972), illustrating that individual ways of responding found during the neonatal period also continue later. The early maternal responses to infant signals may therefore also influence social interaction.

Fetal heart rate and gross movement accelerations as reactions to auditory stimulation can be registered during the last trimester of pregnancy by means of objective measurements and are also documented in anecdotal reports from pregnant women. Individual fetal reactions depending on the quality and timing of the arousal stimulus are also well documented. At birth the anatomical structures of the inner ear, the myelinization of the auditory nerve and lower pathways in the auditory parts of the brain stem, are rather well developed, in contrast to the rather apparent immaturity of the auditory cortex (Hecox, 1975). The maturation of the central transmission of auditory impulses seems to take almost the entire first year of life, whereas the peripheral pathways reach an adult level at approximately 6 weeks postpartum (Salamy & McNean, 1976). Cortical evoked responses seem, however, to be present for auditory modalities as well (W. Berg & K. Berg, 1979). Orientation responses in connection with auditory stimuli were tested by Wertheimer (1961). Series of clicks were randomly presented to either side of the newborn's head and, when eye movements were elicited, they were in 80 percent of the cases directed toward the sound source. Turkewitz, Birch, and Cooper (1972) and Butterworth and Castillo (1976), using slightly different methods, documented the threshold of the right ear to be lower than that of the left ear resulting in lateral differentiations and preferences. These results might illustrate a spatial value of sound as well as the complexity of audiovisual coordination in neonates. The human voice seems to be a most powerful stimulus to induce infant head turning, eye movements, and mouth movements (Bullowa, 1976; Condon & Sander, 1974; Turner & MacFarlane, 1978). The infant's isolated hearing is however probably of little use and first of relevant importance in the larger context of other perceptional modalities.

Infant taste and smell have been explored only fragmentarily, because of rather poor methodology and of the misconception of their relative unimportance. For the infant in interacting with its caregiver, odors and the taste of different nutriments might very well be of great importance. The perioral region seems to have an asymmetrical sensitivity toward tactile stimuli (Turkewitz, 1977). Different side orientations in breast-fed and bottle-fed infants may well have their explanation in taste and/or smell appreciation. This can also be illustrated by the fact that the termination in the sucking time is rather law bound in neonates fed on breast milk. This termination seems to be related to the different contents of breast milk throughout the feeding session. In contrast the relative proportions of the different components in bottle milk do not vary much in the course of the feeding. The changes over time in the composition of breast milk seem to signal the infant to stop sucking and terminate the meal. Whether the infant uses his smell, taste, or perception of feeling of satisfaction is still unclear. The chemical formula, for example, the number of carbon atoms in the chain, in certain alcohols seems to be correlated to the discriminative ability in distinct reactions to different odors, already present in the newborn at an early stage (Self, Morowitz, & Paden, 1972). At 5 days of age, clinically normal babies spent significantly more time turning toward their own mothers' breast pad than toward a clean breast pad (MacFarlane, 1978). This difference was not found at 2 days. It may be that after birth the infant gradually develops an awareness of its mother's odors, which becomes more specific the more the infant is exposed to them. Experiences during feeding in the neonatal period may be of special importance; events in the very first feeding of an infant can affect many subsequent feedings (Gunther, 1959). Thoman and her colleagues (Thoman, 1975; Thoman et al., 1971, 1972) in a series of observations concerning parity of mothers, mode of nutrition, breast-feeding versus bottle-feeding, and sex of the infant found evidence that the relationships observed during the first days of contact between mother and infant may be indicative of the subsequent parent–child relationship and significant for development of personality characteristics in the child. Breast-fed and bottle-fed infants already differ shortly after birth. Breast-fed infants are fed for longer periods and cry more than bottle-fed infants right from the start and have a different pattern of interaction with their mothers during the first days of their lives (Bernal, 1972; Bernal & Richards, 1970). Differences in infant behavior found on the eighth day can be seen as the result of both or either of these influences, in combination with the nature and quantity of the nutriment received. Infant behavior and development may thus be influenced by early feeding experiences.

The importance of the infant's state in the study of infant capacities and especially the ability to control state have begun to be more extensively investigated (Brazelton, 1973; Prechtl, 1974; Wolff, 1973). Unfortunately, infant state has very seldom been reported on in different studies of infant competence and has hardly ever been taken into account in interactional observational studies (Winberg & de Chateau, 1982). According to Wolff (1973) strong correlations can be seen between clinical, observational, and laboatory polygraphic registrations, but they vary depending upon criteria and definitions used (Dittrichova, 1969). State organization of infants seems to be a fundamental neurophysiological characteristic through which the newborn regulates its reactions to environmental and internal events (Prechtl, 1973; Wolff, 1965). Little is known about the influence of caregiving, common minor disturbances, or therapeutic procedures on state organization (Winberg & de Chateau, 1982). For example, about half of all newborn babies become moderately jaundiced. In most instances, this is a physiological event. Moderately jaundiced infants show substantial reduction in time spent awake (Prechtl, Theorell, & Blair, 1973), and the duration of time spent in state II (REM sleep) is concordantly increased. These conditions decrease the possibilities for interacting with the caregiver. Phototherapy of jaundiced infants, used to diminish the need for exchange transfusions, has become increasingly popular during the last decade. Several authors have found such infants to behave peculiarly when under the lights, but traditional neurological examination has so far failed to reveal any certain negative neurological effects exerted by this therapy. Lester, Telzrow, and Snyder (1977) found that moderately jaundiced infants treated with phototherapy showed disturbances in their interactive and organizational processes as long as 10 days after cessation of the therapy. Thus far it is not clear whether the cause was jaundice, separation from the mother during the phototherapy, the phototherapy itself, or a combination of those factors. Nor is the long-term significance of these findings clear. Odds seem to favor the phototherapy as a causal factor. Another aspect of the potentially dangerous side effects of light therapy may be a disturbance of the infant's circadian rhythm, which very probably is, in its turn, related to future infant behavior and perhaps even development (Emde, Svedberg, & Suzuki, 1975). In adults the intensity, duration, and time intervals of light exposure have been demonstrated to be able to disrupt the normal cyclic excretion of melatonin (Lewy, Wher, & Goodwin, 1980). Many factors do influence the interactive competence, capacity, and ability of the newborn during its first weeks of life. Some of these factors will alter the infant's development in a less favorable way, while others may have a more positive influence. Our knowledge of the infant's basic sensory, emotional, and social needs is still incomplete (Winberg & de Chateau, 1982). There seems, however, to exist a growing acknowledgment that these needs can partly be met by early interaction between infants and their parents and that separation of healthy babies and their parents hardly can be necessary when anxiety and uncertainty seem to grow under such conditions.

MATERNAL READINESS

Like the infant, the mother has a great potential to start interacting immediately after birth. The transition to motherhood starts, however, much earlier. Many factors influencing this process have been identified, but certainly many other unknown influences also contribute to the final pattern of maternal behavior and subsequently to the developing mother–infant relationship (Bowlby, 1969).

For instance, the mother's genetic and cultural background, her relation to her own parents, and her relation to the infant's father are variables of great importance. Maternal education, occupation, health, and obstetrical history will all be involved in the transitional process. Whether the pregnancy is planned and the infant welcome or not is known to have an impact on the course of the pregnancy and will in its turn influence maternal adaptation to the new situation. During pregnancy a number of crises can occur, some going back to the pregnant woman's own infancy or childhood. Studies on the paranatal emotional adjustment of healthy women have shown that psychiatric symptoms during the postpartum period (and to a lesser extent those already existing during pregnancy) are connected with conflicts in the reproductive function, that is, conflicts between demands of reproduction and ambivalent attitudes toward childbirth (Nilsson, 1970). Mothers who during pregnancy experience a large number of crises and who are unable to solve their problems before delivery experience great difficulties in their adaptation toward the initial needs, both biological and psychological, of their newborn infants.

In France in a large survey of 11,000 deliveries maternal attitudes toward pregnancy were examined (Blondel, 1979). The importance that women gave to their pregnancies was expressed by the quality and quantity of prenatal care as well as by degree of family planning and training for childbirth. Women for whom it was the first or second pregnancy were the most mindful of a good course for their pregnancies, possibly owing to their strong desire to be pregnant and also, among primiparas, to curiosity and anxiety regarding this marked change in their lives. Multiparous mothers less often desired their pregnancies and did not acknowledge the importance of good prenatal care. Women with earlier abortions, whether spontaneous or obtained as a means of birth control, chose more intensive prenatal care than women with previous stillbirths or preterm deliveries.

During the years 1980–1982 a short-term longitudinal cross-cultural study on the timing of first birth was made at the Karolinska Hospital in Stockholm (Welles, 1982). The general research question addressed was: How does timing affect the transition to motherhood of Swedish primiparas entering their reproductive careers at different stages (ages) in the life course. Two cohorts of primigravidas were elicited: a younger sample of 27 first-time-pregnant women aged 20–29 years (cohort I) and an older sample of 24 first-time-pregnant women aged 30–39 years (cohort II). The study period began at about 8 months of pregnancy, continued during the lying-in period, and ended at 4 months postpartum. A multidisciplinary research approach including several methodologies was used. All sample mothers were interviewed three times during the transition to motherhood and all filled out questionnaires after each interview. Maternal biomedical variables were collected during pre- and postpartum periods from the medical records. Infant assessments included the Brazelton Neonatal Behavioral Assessment Scale (BNBAS) (Brazelton, 1973) and were administered blind on days 1 and 3 to 55 percent of the sample infants. Infant biomedical variables were collected during the postpartum period from the infants' medical records. Broussard's Neonatal Perception Inventory (NPI) (Broussard & Hartner, 1971) was administered to all mothers on day 5 after delivery to collect information about the infants' early behaviors and maternal expectations regarding both the average baby and their own infants. Hagekull's Baby Behaviour Questionnaire (BBQ) (Hagekull & Bolin, 1981) was completed by mothers at 4 months postpartum to collect dimensions of infant temperament.

There was no significant variation between cohorts in either pregnancy factors or labor and delivery. However, the infants of the two cohorts varied significantly in regard to birth weight (Table 11.1). This finding was considered in two ways: first, that the cohort II mothers' physiological status was different from that of the younger mothers, resulting in a lighter infant at birth. A social factor might also be considered—namely, that the older mother is more watchful of her weight gain during pregnancy than is the young mother, hence the lighter infant birth weight. The weight gain among cohort II mothers was less than that among cohort I mothers although not significantly so. Infants in cohort II were also less healthy: one was stillborn, and another had minor malformations. All infants in cohort I were healthy. There were no group differences between cohorts on any of the seven BNBAS cluster items. Significant day differences or "recovery" scores for both cohorts were found in the motor cluster ($p < .001$) and the reflex cluster ($p < .001$), that is, better motor control and fewer worrisome reflexes on day 3 than on day 1.

Cohort I mothers had significantly more unplanned pregnancies and less anxiety than did cohort II mothers. The older mothers also tended to remain longer in the hospital after birth than did the younger mothers and reported having more difficulty in establishing breast-feeding. Maternal attitudes regarding breastfeeding showed the same trend as the NPI; that is, cohort II mothers had significantly lower expectations of the "average baby's" nursing ability ($p < .02$) and perceived their own infants as having more trouble establishing breast-feeding than did cohort I mothers ($p < .05$). These mothers were more satisfied with their husbands' involvement during pregnancy than were cohort II mothers ($p < .05$), and they also perceived the father as being more confident in caring for the baby in the postpartum period ($p < .001$). There were no differences between the two cohorts in the length of paternity leave. There were no cohort differences on the infant temperament dimension (BBQ) at 4 months of age or in the mothers diagnostic rating of the difficult baby. Significant relationships were found between baby temperament scores and two of the neonatal behavioral cluster scores. The approach dimension of the BBQ correlated with the orientation cluster of the BNBAS ($p < .05$), meaning that neonates who were high on the orientation scores were infants who later exhibited more initial approach behaviors. The relationship between manageability (BBQ) and the regulation of state (BNBAS) cluster indicated that newborn infants with better state regulation were more manageable at 4 months ($p < .05$).

Psychoprophylaxis and antenatal family education may help to relieve anxiety

TABLE 11.1. Some Differences Between Outcome of First-time Pregnancies in Age-Group 20–29 years (Cohort I) and 30–39 years (Cohort II)

	Cohort I (n = 27)	Cohort II* (n = 26)	p-value t-test
Unplanned pregnancy	13/27	5/26	< .05
Anxious during pregnancy	6/27	11/26	n.s.
Infant weight (gm)	3.769	3.487	< .05
Hospital stay < 7 days	21/27	12/24	< .05
Easy breastfeeding	20/27	12/24	< .05
Stressful routines	6/27	12/24	< .05

*n = 26 during pregnancy, n = 24 after delivery, one infant died and one malformed.

and improve the ability of mothers and fathers to cooperate during delivery, making it a less frightening and painful event. There is little evidence, however, that these practices improve parental competence. Doering and Entwisle (1975) found that among 269 mothers (39 percent primiparas and 61 percent multiparas) those who had been trained in the Lamaze method during pregnancy were significantly more "aware" (roughly, less medicated) at delivery. "Aware" mothers showed more positive reactions to delivery and to the baby, more often chose rooming-in with their infants, and breast-fed for longer periods. Probably the main effect of antenatal preparation was to reduce the frequency of general anesthesia during delivery and thus, through a chain of processes, enhance the mother's tie to her infant. The effect of antenatal preparation seems, however, to be minimal in delivery units where general anesthesia is not used (Lund, 1976).

In a study conducted in Stockholm, the extent to which newly delivered mothers participated in childbirth classes was examined in relation to the ability to cope with labor and delivery (Lund, 1976). A total of 596 randomly selected healthy mothers answered a questionnaire 3–4 days postpartum. Women delivered by cesarean section and with severely ill infants were excluded. Among 306 primiparas, 66 percent participated in the motherhood education program. These women were significantly older, better educated, had higher incomes, were more often married, and more often had planned their pregnancies than nonparticipants. There were no differences among these two groups as to frequency of unemployment or illness. Among the multiparas, only 83 out of 290 (29 percent) attended childbirth classes. No differences were found between participants and nonparticipants in perception of pain during delivery regardless of whether the mothers were primiparous or multiparous.

These results suggest that through the existing system those mothers who are in greatest need—that is, those with low education and low income, those experiencing unplanned pregnancies, and those who are unmarried—are not reached. A new approach, therefore, must be developed to ensure that those families can benefit from social and health services that need them most. For example, many women seem to experience positive emotional support and to secure information from friends and the lay literature. Perhaps the medical and paramedical professions have something to learn about how to disseminate information, support, and security to those who are in need of it. In recent years increased attention has been given to the effects of early mother–infant interaction immediately following delivery (de Chateau, 1979). Very little interest has, however, been shown in how maternal attitudes during pregnancy can influence these possible effects. In a study in Vienna the mother's desire to breast-feed was investigated 1 month prior to delivery (Wimmer-Puchinger, 1982). Ninety-five nulliparas were interviewed on a number of attitude dimensions and randomly assigned to three different experimental groups. The first group was given a breast-feeding contact for 15 min postpartum, the second group only skin-to-skin contact, and the third conventional contact, no breast-feeding nor skin-to-skin contact. Four months after delivery the mothers were questioned about the duration of breast-feeding. The skin contact group mothers breast-fed their infants for 3 months, whereas the other two groups did so for a significantly shorter period of time. These results are in concordance with other similar studies, but differentiate between skin and suckling contact. The most interesting result from this study is, however, the relationship between prenatal attitudes on breast-feeding, type of postnatal contact, and duration of breast-feeding. A careful analysis showed that the condition of mother–infant contact postpartum had a more significant influence on the length of breast-feeding than the attitudes investigated a month prior to delivery. This means that immediate skin or suckling contact after delivery was better correlated to longer breast-feeding than was the prepartum maternal wish for breast-feeding.

Gyra (1982) examined the relationship between maternal personality factors and early maternal attachment. A high quality of object relationship, especially with significant others such as the woman's own mother, was significantly positively correlated with the strength of maternal attachment to the infant as measured by the frequency of two individual attachment behaviors. A similar correlation was found between the quality of dependency relationships and maternal attachment behavior. In contrast, the maternal degree of anxiety about babies, measured prenatally, was negatively correlated to the quality of maternal attachment behavior. The results of this study illustrate that mothers with different personalities (and attitudes) may show different attachment behaviors. Their reactions to the type of postnatal care given to them and their newborns may therefore also be influenced and altered in correlation with earlier experiences.

PATERNAL INVOLVEMENT

The expectant father, like the mother-to-be, shows a wide variety of reactions during pregnancy (Bogren, 1983). Psychosomatic symptoms are common, and the rapid changes in maternal feelings arouse similar reactions in the father. In a Stockholm study first-time fathers were interviewed during their wives' pregnancies and 3–5 days postpartum. (Lund, Norling, & Rosenberg, 1977). During the first and second trimesters, the fathers' participation in preparations for delivery as well as their ideas about the task of fathers was very limited. Later in the pregnancy, childbirth education classes were attended by 85 percent of the fathers, and the majority were positive in their judgments about the quality and content of the courses. The fathers' reactions during delivery seemed to be composed of many feelings. Almost all fathers experienced the delivery positively and felt emotionally involved and affected. Knowledge gained during the lectures was considered to be useful during the delivery itself, although some of the men reacted to the physical pain of their consorts during parturition with distress. Fathers also reported feelings of competition with the obstetrical personnel and uncertainty about their task and role during delivery. Some felt they lacked information about established routines. The actual physical presence and participation in the delivery, however, were felt by all men as the most important part of their transition to parenthood.

The so-called couvade syndrome is relatively common among expectant fathers. In Sweden the frequency is, according to a recent investigation, approximately 20 percent (Bogren, 1985). The syndrome may illustrate future difficulties in coping with fatherhood and could therefore be an early sign identifying fathers in need of support during their transition to parenthood. Fathers with symptoms of weight gain, toothache, loss of appetite, gastrointestinal symptoms, and the like during their consorts' pregnancies are not more commonly cohabiting with women showing the same types of symptoms. They therefore rather increase the number of families in need of support than decrease it.

Greenberg and Morris (1974) used the term *engrossment* to describe the father's engagement with the infant, meaning the father's absorption and preoccupation with the newborn. Fathers who were present at the infant's birth thought that they could distinguish their babies from others better than those fathers who were not present at the birth. Fathers and mothers of sick newborns following complicated pregnancies and deliveries were asked 5 days postpartum about their feeling of importance to their infant (de Chateau, 1976). Fathers judged themselves to be less important for their infants than the mothers did.

The training of fathers to handle their healthy newborns during the neonatal period and the fathers' later involvement in child care were investigated by Westthorp-Johansson (1969). The study was conducted in a general maternity hospital in which rooming-in was practiced and the lying-in period usually consumed 5–7 days. Fathers in an experimental group participated in two evening sessions (with nurses as instructors) in which they handled their infants, bathed them, changed diapers, and gave bottle feedings. Fathers in a control group were not given such opportunities. According to the mothers' judgments 6 weeks postpartum, the fathers in the experimental group participated much more in day-to-day activities than fathers in the control group.

In another study a small group of fathers with healthy babies were given brief information about the physiology and benefits of breast-feeding (de Chateau, Holmberg, Jakobson, & Winberg, 1977). The information, given in the first days after delivery, resulted in a prolongation of breast-feeding time as compared to that of a control group. More important, perhaps, were the mothers' commentaries 6–12 months later, which indicated that the early involvement of the fathers in infant feeding increased later understanding of the needs of the child and mother. These studies suggest that the father's involvement with the family can be influenced through early contact and information. Rödholm and Larsson (1979) have made observations of fathers' first contacts with babies born after cesarean section; these fathers displayed highly stereotyped behaviors at the first meeting, very similar to those observed among mothers (Klaus, Kennell, Plumb, & Zuelke, 1970).

About 80 percent of all newly delivered mothers, irrespective of parity, sex of infant, and handedness, hold their newborn babies against a point to the left of the body midline (de Chateau et al., 1978). Fathers were also observed to hold their newborn infants to the left in the same proportion as the mothers (de Chateau, 1983). Fathers with older infants, approximately 1 year old, display the same preference. Males without children of their own and with or without experience of other children showed significantly less preference for left holding. This example might illustrate that the neonatal period may be of special importance to males in their adjustment to newborn infants and thus can influence further involvement. Studies of early paternal behavior are just beginning. Results suggest thus far that fathers, like mothers, show stereotypic behavior in their contacts with their newborns, but the biological importance of these patterns is not yet understood, nor do we know whether father–infant contact during the first days of life influences attitudes and involvement in child care and family functions on a long-term basis.

EARLY POSTPARTUM INTERACTION

A growing number of studies have been published on possible short- and/or long-term effects of early interaction between the mother and her infant and later outcome. In the original study by Klaus and colleagues (1970) 1 hour of close physical contact with their nude infant within the first 3 hr after delivery and another 15 extra hr of contact in the first 3 days postpartum were given to a group of mothers (extended contact). A control group of mothers were given routine care with their infants, not including the above-described total of 16 extra hr of contact. In follow-up studies 1 month, 1 year, and 2 years after delivery differences between the extended contact and control group were found with regard to maternal attachment behavior and linguistic behavior.

Following this original study some investigators have reported similar effects, while others failed to do so. The problems and inconsistencies in the methods used in studies of this kind are still incompletely explored, but they most probably account for the great diversity in outcome. In a review of studies on maternal attachment and mother–neonate bonding Lamb (1983) concluded that there should be strong doubt as to the proven effects of early parent–infant interaction, but does admit that some short-term effects exist for certain types of mothers. Some highly relevant studies on the effect on the duration of breast-feeding, however, were not included. In my opinion short-term effects, despite the diversity of approaches and methodologies used in the different studies of early contact, are highly likely to exist, whereas long-term effects have not been adequately proven.

The data, on our own longitudinal study (de Chateau & Wiberg, 1977a, 1977b, 1984) of early interaction between mother and newborn and the impact of this on the development of their mutual relationship, were derived from a healthy, normal, homogeneous population of middle-class Swedish families. The study was conducted in a general hospital and included 42 mother–infant pairs randomly divided into two groups: (1) 22 primiparous women given extra contact with their newborn infants followed by routine care (P+) and (2) 20 primiparous women given routine care with their newborn infants (P). Basic conditions for participation in the study were that the mothers were healthy and living in our hospital catchment area and that the pregnancy and delivery were normal. Details on the selection procedure allocation to the two groups and methods used are given elsewhere (de Chateau, 1976). The two primiparous mother–infant groups (P+ and P), those with and those without extra contact, were followed using different modes of investigation at 36 hr, 3 months, 1 year, and 3 years after delivery. A summary of the methods used in these follow-up studies is given in Table 11.2. The aim of these studies has

TABLE 11.2.   Methods Used in Follow-up Studies of Early Postnatal Contact

36 hours	Behavioral observation
3 months	Behavioral observation
	Interview with mother
1 year	Behavioral observation
	Interview with mother
	Child Development
	Child Social Development
	Maternal Personality Scale
3 years	Behavioral observation
	Interview with mother and father
	Child Development
	Child observation
	Hormonal studies

been to investigate whether immediate postpartum contact has short- and/or long-term effects on the infant–mother relationship.

In a comparison of maternal behavior at 36 hours postpartum primiparous mothers with extra contact showed significantly more holding, encompassing, and looking *en face*. The mother's position during observation differed greatly between the two groups. P+ mothers more frequently sat up while P mothers more often lay down or leaned on one elbow. An upright position covaried with eye-to-eye contact in the extra contact group. Strong desire for eye-to-eye contact in the P+ mothers thus may have influenced their position during breast-feeding. Infants of P mothers cried significantly more frequently than P+ infants. Within each sex, mother–infant behavior also differed according to care conditions. In short the effects of early contact seemed to be more pronounced in boys and their mothers. Or, put in another way, the attachment processes may be more vulnerable to early postpartum separation when the offspring are males rather than females.

In group comparisons at 3 months mothers in the extra contact group spent more time looking *en face* and kissing their infants. Holding the infant was equally frequent in both groups, but mothers with extra contact more frequently encompassed their infants. Infant smiling and/or laughing appeared significantly more often in the extra contact infants, whereas crying was significantly more common among routine care babies. Again the differences were more pronounced for boy–mother than girl–mother pairs. Based on the interview at 3 months, the routine care mothers felt that adaptation to their infants was somewhat more difficult. Mothers in this group had help in the household for a longer period after discharge from the maternity ward than those in the P+ group. P+ mothers breast-fed their infants at 3 months twice as often as P mothers. P mothers reported more problems with night feeding, although their infants were given night feeds for a much shorter period.

One year after delivery mothers in the P+ group, in contrast to P mothers, held their infants using close body contact for a larger proportion of the total observation time. Touching and caressing, not related to caregiving, were more frequently seen among the extra contact mothers than among the controls. While control mothers used more direct commands and more often told the children to behave properly during a physical examination, for example, not to cry, scream, or fuss, extra contact mothers were more inclined to comfort their children by saying, "This does not hurt," "It will soon be over," "Mother is staying with you," and so on. The main differences in the Gesell Development Test were found in gross motor and linguistic development. The significances and causes of these differences, however, are difficult to estimate. One may speculate that, if the interaction between the extra contact parents and infants is smooth and synchronous (suggested by the observations at 36 hr and 3 months), children may be more likely to develop satisfactorily. That is, the very early experiences may have an indirect influence on later development.

A short semistructured interview covering socioeconomic and occupational circumstances, health, child-rearing practices, and the fathers' participation in child care was administered at the 1-year follow-up. P+ mothers returned to employment outside the home less frequently than control mothers, even though there were no actual differences between the two groups in terms of occupation, socioeconomic circumstances, or opportunities to resume work. The results therefore suggest that P+ mothers preferred to stay at home with their children for a longer period of time than P mothers. The role of the father in the early development of the mother–infant relationship is rather poorly investigated. According to the mothers, fathers in the P+ group participated to a lesser extent in child care (e.g., feeding, changing diapers, playing, and putting to bed) than did fathers in the control group. Mothers with early suckling contact breast-fed their infants on an average for 2½ months longer than routine care mothers did (P+ group: 175 days vs. P group: 108 days). The mean duration of breast-feeding among routine care mothers is in full concordance with data collected from a larger sample during the same period and in the same area. The mean duration of breast-feeding in both the routine care and the extra contact group is also in full concordance with data from Dundee (Salariya, Easton, & Carter, 1978). Three out of 21 mothers with extra contact were still partly breast-feeding their infants at 1 year as opposed to none of the 19 routine care mothers. Breast-feeding was more common in extra contact mothers; these mothers also gave night feeds for a considerably longer time and experienced less problems with night feeds than did routine care mothers. This might indicate that the early contact had influenced mother–infant cooperation in feeding. Breast-feeding is an act of cooperation between mother and infant, and if extra contact during the early postnatal period does promote mother–infant relations, it should also be associated with more successful breast-feeding. However, the influence of early contact can not rule out all other factors. While the available data indicate that the 2½-month prolongation of breast-feeding is a consequence of the early skin-to-skin and suckling contact, it is obvious that this early contact does not always promote breast-feeding; hence the wide range in the observed nursing periods.

The Denver Developmental Screening Test given at 3 years showed that total scores did not differ between the two groups. In linguistic development and gross motor development no differences at all were found, although fine motor adaptation seemed to be somewhat better developed in the P+ group and personal–social development was better in the P group. None of the children showed delay in psychomotor development. The 3-year questionnaire revealed several interesting differences including earlier use of two-word sentences by P+ children, a larger number of sibling births in P+ families, and a statement by P mothers that the time they had been allowed with their infants after delivery had been insufficient.

During recent years great progress has been made in the area of prespeech and in the study of nonverbal means of communication. A prevalent view is that language acquisition essentially takes place in a dialogue. Protoconversation, probably first found around the age of 3 months, includes the infant's ability to take its turn using nonverbal vocalizations. The basics of this turn taking and its predecessors may appear during interaction in gazes between infant and caretaker, already traceable during the first days following delivery. If early interactional contact immediately after delivery between mother and infant is promoted and the infant is in the alert state, this protoconversation may be founded more easily.

Recently Söderberg (1981) reported on the possible connection between early extra contact during the first hour postpartum and linguistic development 3 years later, using videotapes of our longitudinal study. Analysis of linguistic interaction between mother and child 3 years after delivery has so far been made in 10 out of 38 families.

The linguistic effects of early contact, if present, are supposed to be reciprocal, although the evaluation of the dyads' interaction has been treated as an entity with the mother as the most responsible partner being the linguistically most mature of the two.

Of the three dyads showing the best dialogues, all were early contact pairs. The poorest linguistic interactions were found in three control pairs. Of the remaining four dyads in the middle of the scale, one of the early contact dyads may possibly be assigned within the better half and one of the control dyads in the less prominent one. These preliminary results do not allow us to draw any definite conclusions. The results, however, are interesting enough to motivate further analysis of the remaining 28 dyads in the study, where a greater number of turnpassers will be included.

In a recently published study from Portugal (Gomes-Pedro, Bento de Almeida, Silviera da Costa, & Barbosa, 1984), infant behavior was evaluated using the Brazelton Neonatal Behavior Assessment Scale (BNBAS) (Brazelton, 1973) on two groups of healthy normal infants. Background data were comparable in the two groups. In the experimental group, 30 infants with clothes on were soon after delivery and after routine checkups placed on the chest and abdomen of the mothers for 30 min. Control infants, also 30 in number, were only briefly shown to the mothers after delivery and then taken away to an adjacent room. Until 6 hr after birth all infants were treated equally and kept in the nursery. At 6 hr postpartum rooming-in started. The infants were assessed with the BNBAS 1 day, 3 days, and 28 days after birth and direct observation during feeding on the third day and twenty-eighth day of infant and maternal behavior by means of a standardized procedure was made. On the first day no differences between the two groups of infants on the BNBAS were seen. On the third and twenty-eighth day experimental group babies performed better on several of the individual items of the scale, had significantly higher scores on "interactive processes," and were considered to be more attractive. Mothers in the experimental group obtained higher scores for affectionate behavior on the twenty-eighth day. The better performance of infants with early interaction with their mothers on the BNBAS seemed to be more pronounced sometime after delivery than on the first day postpartum. Also maternal behavior during feeding was more influenced by contact on the twenty-eighth day than earlier on. This latter finding is in contrast with those reported earlier by Carlsson (1979); however, some differences in design and timing between the two studies are obvious and therefore direct comparison is difficult to make. The increase in differences in behavior between early contact and control groups over time, as described in the Portuguese study, is not found in any of the other studies in this field (de Chateau, 1979, 1980) and seems difficult to explain utilizing an existing theoretical framework.

Recently a study on routine care in the delivery room and in the maternity ward was made in Budapest and two other major Hungarian cities (Keri & de Chateau, 1985). In all, 140 mothers were interviewed as well as 55 midwives and nursery nurses. The main topics penetrated in these interviews were: (1) routine procedures in the delivery and perinatal period; (2) early mother–infant interaction; (3) breast-feeding; and (4) what changes and/or improvements were wished for in the existing system. Preliminary results from this study show a substantial lack of possibilities for early mother–infant interaction and therefore a high frequency of mothers being separated from their babies immediately after delivery for prolonged and varying periods of time (Table 11.3). Somewhat more than 70 percent of all deliveries were considered to be normal. Abnormal deliveries involved cesarean section, forceps

TABLE 11.3. Summary of Some Important Background Data and Maternal Opinions on Perinatal Care in Hungary

	Number (140)	Percentage
Normal delivery	102	72.5
Abnormal delivery	38	27.5
First delivery	83	59.3
Second/third delivery	57	40.7

	Number (102)[a]	Percentage
Separation	81	79.5
Breast-feeding	93	91.1
Breast-feeding problems	30	29.5
Wish for improvement	40	59.2

[a]Only 102 mothers with normal deliveries.

delivery, infant birth weight under 2.500 grams, and maternal or infant illness. The majority of the mothers were primiparas, which correlates well with national statistics. Information about the first hours after delivery was obtained in great detail and will be summarized here. The normal routine care after delivery is very similar to that seen in many other countries until the introduction of early postnatal contact. Thus are 79 percent of the mothers and infants separated immediately following delivery and if not separated only a few minutes of interaction, for instance, touching, are allowed for. No skin-to-skin or suckling contact was reported, although midwives mentioned that they were aware of the possible advantages of introducing such routines. Breast-feeding was very common during the first week following delivery, although the rationale for doing so was based mainly on medical grounds, whereas psychological and emotional advantages were hardly mentioned. About 40 percent of the mothers wished for improvements in the general perinatal care, mainly changes in separation, information, education, visiting hours, and breast-feeding routines. None of the fathers had been allowed to be present during their consorts' delivery. Also the hospital staff asked for more possibilities for interaction between parents and infants, but medical safety was put forward as an obstacle in order to achieve this goal.

HOLDING NEWBORN INFANTS

Three independent studies (de Chateau et al., 1978; Salk, 1973; Weiland & Sperber, 1970) have shown that 80 percent of mothers, during the first months after delivery hold their infants at a point to the left of the body midline. Several hypotheses have been proposed about the nature of this preference. The most interesting is Weiland and Sperber's hypothesis that holding to the left reduces anxiety in the holder. Among 264 mothers observed in the maternity ward on their holding preference (de Chateau, 1976), 37 were right-handed and right holding. These 37 mothers were contacted for a follow-up study 3 years after delivery and 35 mothers replied. These 35 mothers were matched with a group of 35 right-handed mothers, who held their infants to the left, on the following criteria: parity of mother, age of mother, sex of infant, and postpartum day of observation. The two groups were further divided, each into two subgroups, depending on the parity of the mothers, resulting in a total of four groups. No mother had been separated from her infant; all pregnancies, deliveries, and neonatal periods had been normal. The infants were born at full term, and no signs of asphyxia or disease had been present at birth. The infants had been healthy during the neonatal period and all had been subject to the same type of care in the same maternity ward.

Three years after delivery half of the families had moved to other parts of the country; therefore all mothers were contacted by means of a questionnaire, consisting of 37 items. These items covered socioeconomic conditions (10), stability of being a mother (17), the relationship between mother and father (2), and child development (8). The answers in the questionnaire were given on a scale from 1 to 7, both yes/no answers and open-ended answers. For analysis of the results the chi-square test was used. Data for the perinatal period and the 3-year-period following were collected from hospital and child health center records.

The results given in Table 11.4 show clearly that multiparous left-holding mothers (ML), although they had more complications during earlier pregnancies and the father was less present at delivery and very little at home the first week mother and

TABLE 11.4. Comparison of All Four Groups—PR, MR, PL, and ML

	PR	MR	PL	ML	Chi-Square Test
1. Mean number of home visits	4.23	3.80	2.24	2.13	PR/ML: $p < 0.05$ PR/PL: $p < 0.05$
2. Mean number of telephone contacts	3.55	1.33	2.52	0.80	PR/MR: $p < 0.05$ PR/ML: $p < 0.001$ PL/ML: $p < 0.05$
3. Mean number of all contacts with child health center	17.45	14.87	15.43	12.73	PR/ML: $p < 0.001$
4. Mean time for mother to feel that the infant is "hers" (1 first—4 latest)	4	2	3	1	ML/PR: $p < 0.001$ MR/PR: $p < 0.05$
5. Complications during earlier pregnancies (0 = low; 1 = high)	0.09	0.27	0.09	0.60	ML/PR: $p < 0.001$ ML/PL: $p < 0.001$
6. Father present at delivery (0 = no; 1 = yes)	0.95	0.79	0.95	0.57	PR/ML: $p < 0.005$ PL/ML: $p < 0.005$
7. Father at home after neonatal week (0 = no; 1 = yes)	0.38	0.57	0.52	0.14	PL/ML: $p < 0.02$
8. Nursing time in intervals	2.57	2.71	2.57	2.07	N.S.
9. Child's reaction to mother's leaving (1 = stays and plays; 0 = follows mother)	0.81	0.86	0.95	1.00	N.S.
10. Child plays alone (0 = seldom; 7 = always)	5.33	6.07	5.95	6.43	PR/ML: $p < 0.05$
11. Child comes to mother during night (0 = always; 7 = never)	3.71	3.93	4.05	3.93	N.S.
12. Mother's identification with her own mother (0 = none; 7 = strong)	3.24	3.43	4.19	3.46	N.S.

Note: Group PR (PL) - Primiparous, nonseparated mothers who held their infants to the right (left) of the body midline during the neonatal week. Group MR (ML) - Multiparous, nonseparated mothers who held their infants to the right (left) of the body midline during the neonatal week.

infant were home after discharge from the maternity ward, had confidence in their role as mothers and did ask and needed less help from public health services. These mothers had no problems separating from their children in a playing situation and their children did play best on their own.

Some of the results seem to support the hypothesis that right-holding mothers are less sure in their relationship with their children than left-holding mothers. Even if not, all results are pointing in the same direction, and many of them are not statistically significant. Right-holding mothers do have twice as many home visits by the district nurse on account of their children, and also the total number of all contacts with the child health center is greater for them. In contrast to this no differences were found between the children's health states in the two groups. Right-holding mothers seem to be more worried about their children and less stable in their relationship to them as they need more contacts with the staff of the child health centers. Furthermore, right-holding mothers had a more negative attitude toward their pregnancies and felt at a later date that the infant was theirs; both are signs of uncertainty in the mother role. A tendency can be found in a growing stability in the relationship to their children from primiparous right-holding mothers (PR) (extreme instability) to multiparous left-holding mothers (ML) (extreme stability). Systematic observations of mothers carrying their newborn infants at the second day after delivery revealed three types of carrying: on the left arm, on he right arm, and "in hands." Neonatal care influenced maternal carrying in primiparas; thus 15–20 min of immediate postpartum contact eliminated carrying in hands and increased the proportion of mothers carrying to the left (Fig. 11.1).

Separation on the other hand was associated with an increase in carrying in hands a decrease in carrying to the left. These observations support the anxiety reduction theory of Weiland and Sperber (1970), although other possible explanations may prove to be of equal interest.

SEPARATION OF SICK NEWBORNS

Separation of the sick newborn infant from the mother and father during observation and treatment in neonatal wards has become routine procedure in many situations. The safety of the infant guides the decision to observe the infant in a neo-

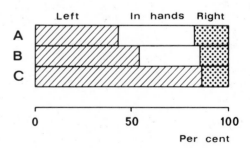

Figure 11.1. Carrying an infant during the first week after delivery in three groups of primiparas. A = separated mothers (*n* = 22); B = nonseparated mothers (*n* = 125); C = "extra contact" mothers (*n* = 21). Carrying to the left (shaded areas), carrying "in the hands" (blank areas), and carrying to the right (dotted areas).

natal ward, but relatively little attention has been paid to the possible harmful consequences for the parent–infant relationship. Several negative effects have been reported, but more specific knowledge is needed about factors influencing the parents' feelings toward their newborn infants. If separation is associated with long-lasting effects on the parent–infant relationship, studies should be made of how negative effects can be neutralized. This should start with an analysis of such factors as the impact of severity of the infant's condition, duration of separation, time of first physical contact between parent and infant, mode of delivery, and so on. In a small-scale study all parents who during a single month gave birth to an infant that was admitted to the neonatal ward immediately after delivery were included. Out of 26 such infants, 1 died the day after birth, another was left for adoption, and there was a set of twins. The number of parent pairs studied was therefore 23. The infants were classified as suffering minor illness, moderately severe illness, severe illness on the basis of eight criteria (de Chateau, 1976).

Parents were allowed to visit their newborn infants at any time during the day and the night. No other visitors were permitted entrance to the ward. Parents were permitted to touch their infants at one of the first visits. They were allowed to take part in feeding, bathing, changing diapers, as soon as the medical state of the infants permitted. This judgment was made by the head nurse and attending pediatrician. A separate room for breast-feeding was available in the ward. Most mothers stayed in the maternity ward during the first 6 days; afterwards they could either live in a "mother's room," located near the neonatal ward, or be discharged to their homes. In the latter case their opportunities to visit the infant were reduced.

A questionnaire consisting of 16 items was given to all mothers on the fifth day after delivery. The questions were in form of statements about parents' perception of the parent–infant relationship and of the hospital stay. Parents were asked to agree or disagree with the statements, using a seven-point scale. To minimize response bias half of the statements were positive and half of them were negative. Most of the statements included a follow-up question with three to five alternative answers. The results of the medical classification on the infants were not known at the time the questionnaire was given to the mothers. Fathers received the questionnaire from the mothers and were asked to return it after they had completed it.

Mothers of infants in the "severe illness" group felt that the infant was theirs later, and they also felt less important to their infants than did mothers with healthier infants. The time lapse after delivery to first touching the infants is shown in Figure 11.2; the time increased from mothers with infants with minor illness to those with infants with severe illness. No correlation was found between the period of time before the mother was first able to touch the infant and her feelings for the baby (Fig. 11.3). Possibly a correlation can be suggested between the severity of the infant's illness and maternal feelings.

Six mothers were delivered by cesarean section (C.S.) under general anesthesia. The infants of these mothers were equally distributed between the three groups in terms of their medical condition. C.S. mothers had to wait at least a day to touch their infants for the first time. They also experienced that they had to wait "too long" before they could touch their infants and reported that it took at least a day for them to get the feeling that the infant really belonged to them. As a group C.S. mothers had to wait significantly longer and felt significantly later that the infant belonged to them than mothers delivered vaginally.

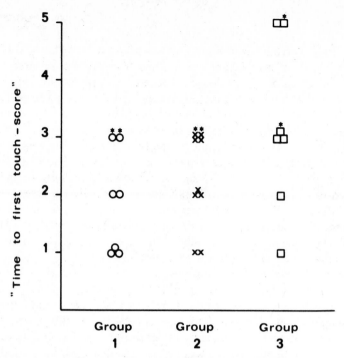

Figure 11.2. Time to first touch: 1 = immediately after delivery; 2 = some hours after delivery; 3 = 2 days after delivery; 4 = a few days after delivery; 5 = later. * = cesarean section; ○ = minor illness; × = moderately severe illness; □ = severe illness.

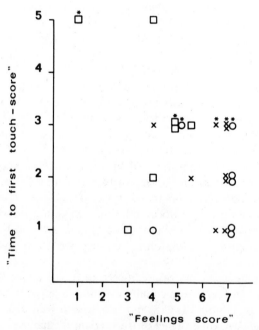

Figure 11.3. Correlations between time of first touch of infant and feeling of importance for the infant on the fifth day after delivery. Explanation of score: Time to first touch—1 = immediately after delivery; 2 = some hours after delivery; 3 = 1 day after delivery; 4 = a few days after delivery; 5 = later. Feeling of importance—1 = not important for the infant; 7 = very important for the infant. * = cesarean section; ○ = minor illness; × = moderately severe illness; □ = severe illness.

660

TABLE 11.5.   Comparison Between Mothers' and Fathers' Answers to the Question: "I Feel Important to my Infant at the Hospital on the Fifth Day After Delivery"

	N	Mean Score*	p (t-test)
Mothers	23	5.1	< 0.001
Fathers	16	2.1	

*score: 1 = disagree very much; 7 = full agreement

Only 65 percent of the fathers completed the questionnaire. Many fathers, moreover, did not fill out the questionnaire completely. An analysis of the drop-out among fathers showed that the lowest socioeconomic class was overrepresented, as were fathers of the infants who were most severely ill. The fathers who answered felt less important to their infants during the hospital stay than mothers did (Table 11.5). This difference might have been even more pronounced if all the fathers of the infants who were most severely ill had answered the questionnaire. Further analysis of the paternal role is desirable as the need for contact between father and infant and for support from the father may be especially great when the infant is ill. From our clinical experience we also get the impression that fathers should be more involved in hospital care. The most important observation in this small study was that mothers of the infants who were most severely ill felt less important and had more difficulty relating to their infants than mothers with healthier infants. This can be seen as an expression of anticipatory grief. The mother's fear that the infant will die may also prevent her from accepting her positive feelings toward the infant in order to avoid some of the pain caused by losing a newborn.

CONCLUDING REMARKS

The socialization of newborns and their parents starts long before delivery. Many influences are at work during pregnancy, dating back to parental experiences in childhood and during development. Genetic and cultural backgrounds as well as parental education, occupation, health, and socioeconomic status all affect the preparation for parenthood and thus the growing parent–infant relationship. More specific maternal attachment and maternal interactional behavior are correlated to maternal parity, obstetrical history, pregnancy, delivery, and perinatal adaptation and care. Also, studies of variations in neonatal care have shown an impact of these variations upon the development of family relationships.

Exciting new data have recently been published on embryonal and fetal movements (Prechtl, 1984). From 7–8 weeks on, increased complexity of movements were observed, from gross movements, upper and lower limb movements, startles, and hiccups to breathing, yawning, sucking, swallowing, and eye movements. According to these studies normal fetal movements are well organized, endogenously generated, and fluent in character, with fluctuations in intensity and complexity. These fetal abilities do resemble later neonatal behaviors, which are needed for survival and probably important signals and messages to caregivers. The question of whether there is a discontinuity of continuity from these movements to neonatal behaviors is however still not settled.

The neonatal sensory ability can be assessed more accurately today, and new methods for measuring these properties as well as neonatal behavior and state have developed rapidly. Their importance for normal parent–infant socialization seems to be increasingly recognized. For instance, our knowledge on infant visual, auditory, tactile, and olfactory perception and early learning processes has rapidly increased. Also, infants' ability to discriminate stimuli in space and to recognize other humans (the mother's voice, odor, etc.) is far better documented and accepted than before. The infant's capacity for early interaction is well developed and necessary for normal development of the infant and its relation to the parents.

The maternal readiness to receive the infant and the parental receptivity do complement this infant ability extraordinarily well. Maternal postpartum behavior follows a given pattern and is a keystone in the process of maternal acknowledgment. Mothers and fathers show throughout the infant's development stage (age) appropriate behavior to secure optimal and continuous emotional and physical growth. Parents learn very quickly to recognize their infants' signals, and these infant activities seem in turn to trigger parental behavior. Maternal attitudes and personality traits influence the complex process of learning and understanding the individual and also the shared needs within the mother–infant dyad.

Fathers show a variety of reactions to pregnancy and display specific behaviors at the first contact with their newborn, much like the behaviors of mothers in the same situation. The couvade syndrome and "engrossment" are examples of the former reaction, and paternal exploring behavior is seen soon after birth if the father is alone with the infant (Rödholm & Larsson, 1979). Early education and training as well as preparation of fathers are of importance for the emotional climate in the family and thus can influence early infant socialization. On a long-term basis, however, our knowledge of these matters is still fragmentary. It is therefore a priority that the important studies of paternal involvement in young infants continue. This field is still rather young but is developing rapidly and needs our profound attention.

In the study of the human adult's behavior with infants, special attention has been given to the preference for holding newborns to the left. In itself the observation of lateralization in behavior is of limited importance. In a larger context, however, mainly psychological and psychodynamic, this phenomenon gains in relevance. The observations of mothers separated from their newborns because of minor medical problems show that preexisting and stabile behavior can be altered under unfavorable conditions. The impact of these conditions not only altered immediate behavior, but also changed attitudes of mothers toward their infants for a prolonged period of time. From these studies it can be postulated that compensation for unfavorable influences can be activated and that perhaps the infant plays an important role in this activating mechanism.

Interpretations of studies concerning the effects of early postnatal contact between mother and newborn merit caution. Much of the current methodology is not well defined; individual differences and cultural variations are not well explored. Nevertheless, concordance in the results from a number of studies suggests that the perinatal period may be a unique and important period for establishing parent–infant relationships.

During this century, a child's birth has changed from being mainly a social event to being a medical and technical one. Concomitantly, there have been revolutionary changes in our way of taking care of newborns and their families. While the outlook for mothers and their babies with regard to physical fitness has improved enormously, there remains the possibility that these changes may have negative effects.

Considering the vulnerability and dependence of the newborn, its safety must have been well guarded during evolution. We can speculate that the infant's needs for protection, warmth, and food would be served if, for example, parental love and affection were complemented with behaviors, partly preprogrammed, that are adapted to the circumstances under which the infant is born. When such behavioral sequences are unfolded under the artificial auspices of modern obstetric and neonatal care, they may become disarranged and disturbed. In some animals, for example, interference with maternal behaviors immediately after birth hampers the mother's ability to take care of her offspring. Similar rules may apply to humans, although the human being's adaptive abilities are considerable. As yet, this is a working hypothesis, and it is against this background that our interest in caregiving during the perinatal period should be seen.

Systematic studies of the effects of early, enriched contact between mother and infant have practical as well as theoretical importance. Such studies could influence practices in delivery, maternity, and neonatal wards. The overarching goal of these studies, however, is to find management recommendations that ensure a balance between providing physical security to mother and infant and meeting social and emotional needs of the baby and its family.

The conditions under which treatment is given have to guarantee maximal medical safety for the newborn. Many of the arguments used to defend separation have during the last decade been shown not to hold very strongly. As our knowledge about the unwanted side effects of separation has grown, also counteractions have been taken. Parents today are allowed free visiting, touching, and participation in the daily care of sick newborn infants in many hospitals. In spite of this, still much anxiety is seen among parents and we have therefore to be constantly active to promote such measurements that can smooth the path for a healthy infant–parent relationship. This part of preventive child psychiatry has to be given high priority.

Parents seem to suffer more from early separation than the babies. Consequently, a reasonable working hypothesis to explain the experimental effects is that short, early contact immediately after delivery influences mainly the mother, and probably also the father. The effects observed in the baby's development thus may be secondary, mediated by changes in the parents' behavior. Our daily experiences suggest that, if a newborn baby lives in an incubator for a long time, the self-confidence and future ability of the parents to adjust to the baby's needs will be much better if they have visited the incubator, touched the baby, and been part of the caregiving team. The infant's situation and stimulation may not be much influenced in this process but, more important, the baby may elicit and enhance appropriate caregiving behaviors in the parents.

In this context important effects have been noted to follow early contact experiences such as the prolongation of breast-feeding (de Chateau, 1976; Salaryia et al., 1978; Wimmer-Puchinger, 1982). Not only was the total duration of breast-feeding prolonged by 2–3 months and night feeding by 2–3 weeks, but the mothers' attitudes toward night feeding were more positive among those who gave the breast early than among control mothers. A reasonable hypothesis to explain these effects would be that the early suckling and skin contact increased the mother's intuitive compliance with the baby's needs.

Incorporating the observed effects of early contact into existing frames of reference in developmental psychology has been a problem. The results of our studies, as well as those of others, have been questioned. Neonatologists have many bitter experiences demonstrating how little our knowledge of infant, child, and adult *physiology* can be applied to newborns. Is there reason to believe that the situation is different with regard to the psychology of the newborn?

In her recently published paper on the process of attachment and bonding, Sylvia Brody (1981) claims that maternal personality traits, the socioeconomic status of the parents, and parental knowledge of infants in general have important effects on the attachment process. As for the infant, Brody says:

> If we assume that after the ordeal of birth a restful and warm skin-to-skin contact relieves an innate thriving to reduce physiological tension that has mounted during delivery then we may suppose that in the skin contact the infant feels a first kind of relief that is pleasurable. (p. 822)

A repetition of this situation may strengthen the pleasure feeling, thus providing for and facilitating the early interactions of the parents and their infants.

REFERENCES

Bell, R. Q. (1974). Contributions of human infants to caregiving and social interaction. In M. Lewis & L. A. Rosenbaum (Eds.), *The effect of the infant on its caregiver.* New York: Wiley.

Bell, S. M., & Ainsworth, M. D. S. (1972). Infants crying and maternal responsiveness. *Child Development, 43,* 1171–1190.

Berg, W. K., & Berg, K. M. (1979). Psychophysiological development in infancy: State, sensory attention, and attention. In J. D. Osofsky (Ed.), *Handbook of infant development.* New York: Wiley.

Bernal, J. (1972). Crying during the first 10 days of life, and maternal responses. *Developmental Medicine and Child Neurology, 14,* 362–372.

Bernal, J., & Richards, M. P. H. (1970). The effects of bottle and breastfeeding on infant development. *Journal of Psychosomatic Research, 14,* 247–252.

Blondel, B. (1979). Attitude of women towards pregnancy according to number and outcome of previous pregnancies. In L. Carenza & L. Zichella (Eds.), *Emotion & Reproduction* (Vol. 20B). London: Academic.

Bogren, L. (1985). The couvade syndrome and side preference in child holding. *Acta Psychiatrica Scandinavica, 68,* 55–65.

Bowlby, J. (1969). *Attachment and loss* (Vol. I). London: Hogarth.

Brazelton, T. B. (1973). Neonatal behavioural assessment scale. In *Clinics in developmental medicine* (No. 50). London: Heinemann.

Brody, S. (1981). The concepts of attachment and bonding. *Journal of the American Psychoanalytical Association, 29,* 815–829.

Broussard, E., & Hartner, M. (1971). Further considerations regarding maternal perception of the first born. In J. Helmuth (Ed.), *The exceptional infant* (Vol. II). New York: Brunner/Mazel.

Bullowa, M. (1976). Infant vocalization: Communication before speech. In W. C. Mc-

Cormack & S. A. Wurm (Eds.), *Language and man. Anthropological issues.* The Hague: Mouton.

Butterworth, G., & Castillo, M. (1976). Coordination of auditory and visual space in newborn infants. *Perception, 5,* 155–60.

Carlsson, S., Fagerberg, H., Horneman, G. Hwang, C. P., Larsson, K., Rödholm, M., & Schaller, J. (1979). Effects of various amounts of contact between mother and child on the mother's nursing behavior: a follow-up study. *Infant Behavior and Development, 2,* 209–214.

Condon, W. S., & Sander, L. B. (1974). Neonate movement is synchronized with adult speech. International participation and language acquisition. *Science, 183,* 99–101.

Conel, J. L. (1970). Life as revealed by the microscope. In F. Vester (Ed.), *Denken, Lernen, Vergessen.* Stuttgart: Deutsche Verlag Anstalt.

De Casper, A. J., & Fifer, W. P. (1980). Of human bonding: Newborns prefer their mothers' voices. *Science, 208,* 1174–1176.

de Chateau, P. (1976). Neonatal care routines. *Medical Dissertation,* New Series No 2. Umeå: University of Umeå, Sweden.

de Chateau, P. (1979). Effects of hospital practices on synchrony in the development of the infant–parent relationship. *Seminars in Perinatology, 3,* 45–60.

de Chateau, P. (1980). Perinatal interaction—Its long-term effects. In E. Simmel (Ed.), *Early experience in early behavior: Application of social development.* New York: Academic.

de Chateau, P. (1983). Left-side preference for holding and carrying newborn infants. IV. Parental holding and carrying during the first week of life. *Journal of Nervous & Mental Disease, 171,* 241–245.

de Chateau, P., Holmberg, H., Jakobson, K., & Winberg, J. (1977). A study of factors promoting and inhibiting lactation. *Developmental Medicine & Child Neurology, 19,* 575–584.

de Chateau, P., Holmberg, H., & Winberg, J. (1978). Left side preference in holding and carrying newborn infants. I. Mothers holding during the first week of life. *Acta Paediatrica Scandinavica, 67,* 169–175.

de Chateau, P., & Wiberg, B. (1977a). Long-term effect on mother–infant behavior of extra contact during the first hour post-partum. I. First observations at 36 hours. *Acta Paediatrica Scandinavica, 66,* 137–144.

de Chateau, P., & Wiberg, B. (1977b). Long-term effect on mother–infant behavior of extra contact during the first hour post-partum. II. A follow-up at three months. *Acta Paediatrica Scandinavica, 66,* 145–151.

de Chateau, P., & Wiberg, B. (1984). Long-term effect on mother–infant behavior of extra contact during the first hour post-partum. III. One year follow-up. *Scandinavian Journal of Social Medicine, 12,* 91–103.

Dittrichova, J. (1969). Development of sleep in infancy. In R. J. Robinson (Ed.), *Brain and Early Behavior.* New York: Academic.

Dobbing, J. (1970). Undernutrition and the developing brain. *American Journal of Diseases of Children, 120,* 411–416.

Doering, S. G., & Entwisle, D. R. (1975). Preparation during pregnancy and ability to cope with labor and delivery. *American Journal of Orthopsychiatry, 45,* 825–837.

Emde, R., Svedberg, J., & Suzuki, B. (1975). Human wakefulness and biological rhythms after birth. *Archives of General Psychiatry, 32,* 780–789.

Fantz, R. L. (1963). Pattern vision in newborn infants. *Science, 140,* 296–297.

Fantz, R. L., & Miranda, S. B. (1975). Newborn infant attention to form and contour. *Child Development, 46,* 224–228.

Field, T. M., Cohen, D., Garcia, R., & Greenberg, R. (1984). Mother–stranger discrimination by the newborn. *Infant Behavior & Development, 7,* 19–25.

Fraiburg, S. (1974). Interaction between blind mothers and infants. In M. Lewis & L. A. Rosenblum (Eds.), *The effect of the infant on its caregiver.* New York: Wiley.

Greenberg, M., & Morris, N. (1974). Engrossment: The newborn's impact upon the father. *American Journal of Orthopsychiatry, 44,* (*4*), 520–530.

Gomes-Pedro, J., Bento de Almeida, J., Silveira da Costa, C., & Barbosa, B. (1984). Influence of early mother–infant contact on dyadic behavior during the first month of life. *Developmental Medicine & Child Neurology, 263,* 657–664.

Gunther, M. (1959). Infant behavior at the breast. In B. M. Foss (Ed.), *Determinants of infant behavior.* New York: Wiley.

Gyra, J. C. (1982). *The relationship of maternal personality factors to early maternal attachment behaviour to the infant.* Unpublished thesis, University of Toronto.

Hagekull, B., & Bolin, G. (1981). Individual stability in dimensions of infant behaviour. *Infant Behavior & Development, 4,* 97–108.

Hecox, K. (1975). Electrophysiological correlates of human auditory development. In L. B. Cohen & P. Salapatel (Eds.), *Infant perception: From sensation to cognition: II. Perception of space, speech and sound.* New York: Academic.

Keri, I., & de Chateau, P. (1985). Unpublished manuscript.

Klaus, M. H., Jerauld, R., Kreger, N., McAlpine, W., Steffa, M., & Kennell, J. (1972). Maternal attachment—Importance of the first postpartum days. *New England Journal of Medicine, 286,* 460–463.

Klaus, M. H., & Kennell, J. H. (1970). Mothers separated from their newborn infants. *Pediatric Clinic of North America, 17,* 1015–1035.

Klaus, M. H., Kennell, J. H., Plumb, N., & Zuelke, S. (1970). Human maternal behavior at the first contact with her young. *Pediatrics, 46,* 187–192.

Korner, A. F., & Thoman, E. B. (1972). The relative efficacy of contact and vestibularproprioceptive stimulation in soothing neonates. *Child Development, 43,* 443–453.

Lamb, M. (1983). Early mother–neonate contact and the mother–child relationship. *Journal of Child Psychology & Psychiatry, 24,* 487–494.

Lester, B., Telzrow, R., & Snyder, D. (1977). *The effects of phototherapy on neonatal behaviour.* Abstract, Meeting of the Society for Research in Child Development, New Orleans.

Lewy, A. J., Wehr, T. A., & Goodwin, F. K. (1980). Light suppressed melatonin secretion in humans. *Science, 210,* 1267–1269.

Lipsitt, L. P. (1977). Taste in human neonates. Its effect on sucking and heartrate. In J. M. Weiffenbach (Ed.), *Taste and development: The genesis of sweet preference* (Publication no. NIH 77-1068). Bethesda: National Institute of Dental Research.

Lock, A. (1978). *Action, gesture and symbol: The emergence of language.* London: Academic.

Lund, W. (1976). *Mödraundervisning.* Stockholm: Natur och Kultur.

Lund, W., Norling, E., & Rosenberg, E. (1977). Mannens roll under graviditet och förlossning. Stockholm: University of Stockholm.

MacFarlane, A. (1975). Olfaction in the development of social preferences in the human neonate. In *Parent–Infant Interaction.* Ciba Foundation Symposium 33, pp. 103–117. Amsterdam: Elsevier.

Miranda, S. B. (1970). Visual abilities and pattern preferences of premature infants and full-term neonates. *Journal of Experimental Child Psychology, 10,* 189–205.

Muir, D., & Field, J. (1979). Newborn infants orient to sounds. *Child Development, 50,* 431–436.

Nilsson, A. (1970). Paranatal emotional adjustment. *Acta Psychiatrica Scandinavica,* Supplementum 220.

Ourth, L., & Brown, B. (1961). Inadequate mothering and disturbance in the neonatal period. *Child Development, 32,* 287–294.

Prechtl, H. F. R. (1974). The behavioral states of the newborn infant. *Brain Research, 76,* 185–189.

Prechtl, H. F. R. (1984). Continuity of neurol functions. In *Clinics in developmental medicine* (No. 94). London: Heinemann.

Prechtl, H. F. R., Theorell, K., & Blair, A. W. (1973). Behavioral state cycles in abnormal infants. *Developmental Medicine & Child Neurology, 15,* 606–615.

Robson, K. S. (1967). The role of eye-to-eye contact in maternal attachment behavior. *Journal of Child Psychology & Psychiatry, 8,* 13–25.

Rovee, C. K. (1972). Olfactory cross-adaptation and facilitation in human neonates. *Journal of Experimental Child Psychology, 13,* 368–381.

Rödholm, M., & Larsson, K. (1979). Father–infant interaction at the first contact after delivery. *Early Human Development, 3,* 21–29.

Salamy, A., & McNean, C. M. (1976). Postnatal development of human brain potentials during the first year of life. *Electroencephalography & Clinical Neurophysiology, 40,* 418–426.

Salariya, F. M., Easton, P. M., & Carter, J. I. (1978). Duration of breast-feeding after early initiation and frequent feeding. *Lancet, 2,* 1141–1143.

Salk, L. (1970). The critical nature of the post partum period in the human for the establishment of the mother–infant bond: A controlled study. *Diseases of Nervous System,* Supplementum 1, pp. 110–116.

Self, P. A., Morowitz, F. D., & Paden, L. Y. (1972). Olfaction in newborn infants. *Developmental Psychology, 7,* 349–363.

Shapiro, S., & Vukovisch, K. R. (1970). Early experience effects upon dendrites. *Science, 167,* 292–294.

Spence, M. J., & De Casper, A. J. (1982). *Human fetuses perceive maternal speech.* Paper presented at the meeting of the International Conference of Infant Studies, Austin, TX.

Söderbergh, R. (1981). *Linguistic effects by three years of age of extra contact during the first hour post partum.* Paper presented at the Second International Congress for the Study of Child Language, Vancouver.

Steiner, J. E. (1977). Facial expressions of the neonate infant indicating the hedonic of food-related chemical stimuli. In J. M. Weiffenbach (Ed.), *Taste and development. The genesis of sweet preference* (Publication No. NIH 77-1068). Bethesda: National Institute of Dental Research.

Thoman, E. B. (1975). Development of synchrony in mother–infant interaction in feeding and other situations. *Federation Proceedings, 34,* 1587–1594.

Thoman, E. B., Barnett, C. R., & Leiderman, P. H. (1971). Feeding behaviour of newborn infants as a function of parity of the mother. *Child Development, 42,* 1471–1483.

Thoman, E. B., Leiderman, P. H. & Olson, J. P. (1972). Neonate mother interaction during breast-feeding. *Developmental Psychology, 6,* 110–129.

Turkewitz, G., Birch, H. G., & Cooper, K. K. (1972). Patterns of responses to different auditory stimuli in the human newborn. *Developmental Medicine & Child Neurology, 14,* 487–491.

Turner, S., & MacFarlane, A. (1978). Localization of human speech by the newborn baby and the effects of Pethidine ("Meperidine"). *Developmental Medicine & Child Neurology, 20,* 727–734.

Wahlberg, V. (1982). Reconsideration of Credé prophylaxis. *Acta Paediatrica Scandinavica,* Supplementum 295.

Welles, B. (1982). *Maternal age and first birth in Sweden: A life course study.* Unpublished thesis, Harvard University.

Weiland, I. K., & Sperber, Z. (1970). Patterns of mother–infant contact: The significance of lateral preference. *The Journal of Genetic Psychology, 117,* 157–165.

Wertheimer, M. (1961). Psychomotor coordination of auditory and visual space at birth. *Science, 137,* 1962–1966.

Westthorp-Johansson, P. (1969). *Instruction for child care in fathers.* Stockholm: University of Stockholm.

Wiberg, B., & Humble, K. (In preparation). *The first hour of life.*

Wimmer-Puchinger, B. (1982). The importance of attitudes during pregnancy and early mother–child contact for breastfeeding behaviour: An empirical study. In H. J. Prill & H. Stauber (Eds.), *Advances in psychosomatic obstetrics and gynecology.* Berlin: Springer Verlag.

Winberg, J., & de Chateau, P. (1982). Early social development: Studies on infant–mother interaction and relationships. In W. W. Hartup (Ed.), *Review of child development research* (Vol. 6). Chicago: University of Chicago Press.

Wolff, P. H. (1965). Organization of behavior in the first three months of life. *Early Development, 51,* 132–153.

Wolff, P. H. (1973). Organization of behavior in the first three months of life. *Early Development, 51,* 132–153.

CHAPTER 12

Intuitive Parenting: A Dialectic Counterpart to the Infant's Integrative Competence

HANUŠ PAPOUŠEK and MECHTHILD PAPOUŠEK

INTRODUCTION: PSYCHOBIOLOGICAL BACKGROUND

The authors' interest in parental behaviors was preceded and motivated by a series of studies on the infant's earliest abilities to learn, cognitively process informational input, and integrate experience from interactions with environment into behavioral adaptations (H. Papoušek, 1961, 1967a, 1977; H. Papoušek & Bernstein, 1969; H. Papoušek & M. Papoušek, 1984a). From those studies as well as from the rich evidence accumulated by other authors (for survey see Sameroff & Cavanaugh, 1979), we can conclude that the human infant, motorically altricial among mammals, is uniquely precocious in the early presence of the rapid postpartum development of integrative capabilities. No other primate, for instance, has the capability of conceptualizing, abstracting across modalities, and symbolizing experience to the degree necessary for the use of meaningful words as human infants do toward the end of the first year of life.

Answers to the initial questions such as: Does the infant learn? How early can the infant learn? or How do complex forms of learning function in the infant? have nourished further interest in the role of integrative capacities in the development of self-regulation or in interactions with environment. The question of the evolution of integrative capacities has drawn attention, too, as it is typical for psychobiological approaches. No matter how difficult this question is and how speculative its treatment necessarily must be at the beginning, a better understanding of both the ontogeny and the phylogeny of integrative capacities is of fundamental importance for infancy research in general.

In the present chapter we will discuss the interrelations between integrative development and social interactions in the infant, in particular the parental contri-

The authors' research was kindly supported by Grant Pa-208/4 from Die Deutsche Forschungsgemeinschaft. Thanks are extended to Dr. Lynne S. Koester for reviewing and correcting the manuscript, to Dr. Gerhard Dirlich and Alexander Yassouridis from the Department of Biostatistics, MPI-P, for statistical consultations, and to Maria-Ernéstine Beck, Monika Haekel, Bettina Moll, Steffen Pöhlmann, Heinz-Dieter Rohde, Doris Winter for their assistance in the collection and analysis of data or in the preparation of the manuscript.

bution to integrative development. Nonetheless, the conception of this aspect will inevitably involve the other difficult questions as well.

Interactional Systems

Let us first consider parent–infant interactions from the "bird's-eye view" of general systems theory. Von Bertalanffy (1968) describes living organisms as systems bearing the features of both open and closed systems in a dialectic unity, and the relations among individual organisms as interactions determined by genetically transmitted programs, by the plasticity of neural regulations, and by time-dependent changes in each of the interacting organisms. This theory would indicate that all interactions among conspecifics are social interactions, and that any behavioral change observable within such interactions bears the character of a social behavior (H. Papoušek & M. Papoušek, 1982a). This is particularly true about social interactions among humans.

Due to interindividual disparity in integrative capacities and amounts of integrated experience, social interactions may become didactic interactions provided the more competent or experienced individual is motivated to share his or her knowledge, and the less competent or inexperienced one is motivated to acquire new knowledge. It would be very difficult to explain the emergence of human culture if similar assumptions were not taken for granted and favored in evolutionary selection. Focusing on parent–infant interactions, we must acknowledge two consequent properties in them: (1) Parent–infant interactions are potential didactic interactions par excellence due to the polar difference in the amount of integrated experience between the interacting individuals; and (2) parent–infant interactions are very special didactic interactions since there is a polar difference in communicative capacities between the adult having advanced speech and the infant lacking any speech.

Within such a broadly defined theory, nonhuman social interactions are potentially didactic; however, they have rarely been looked at as analogous to the human interactions between parents and preverbal infants. There are several reasons for the neglect of early didactic interventions in both human and nonhuman research.

First, didactics have typically been seen as a product of human culture involving verbal communication. Therefore, they have probably not been considered in interactions where speech is absent in at least one partner. In some precursory form, however, didactic tendencies may have been a factor contributing to the emergence of culture. Surprisingly, even Bruner (1971), who is known for admitting various precursors of human competences in the animal world, considers *instruction,* as such, to be strictly a species-typical character of human culture (p. 118) when he discusses the psychobiology of pedagogy. Conversely, Liedtke (1976), after surveying a wealth of comparative material on the presence of both the educational tendencies in animal parents and the need to learn in the young, concluded that the idea of a biological evolution of didactics cannot be rejected.

Second, the neglect of didactic aspects in human parent–infant interactions may have been caused by the lack of knowledge about the infant's integrative competence before this competence became the focus of recent systematic research.

Third, the discussions on infant learning and thought had long been dominated by controversial theories based on artificial dichotomizing of concepts. For example, the human organism has been dichotomized as body versus mind, the regulation of developmental processes as genetic versus environmental, and the course of development as continuous versus discontinuous. Similar theoretical controversies have caused terminological and methodological confusions. Fortunately, the rich interchanges between biological and social sciences in infancy research have helped overcome most difficulties. The major issues of theoretical reorientation have recently been reviewed by Gottlieb (1983) from a psychobiological perspective and by Hinde (1983) from an ethological perspective. A few remaining issues deserve attention in relation to the present chapter.

The classification of behaviors, interactive ones in particular, still represents a problem. On the one hand, there is still an abundance of heterogenic classifications, some based on observable phenomena and others on assumed regulatory functions or biological meanings. In animal studies, for instance, it becomes increasingly difficult to differentiate social behaviors from feeding, grooming, sexual reproduction, or parenting behaviors. As Hinde (1974) points out, introduction of detailed but artificial categories for coding observed behavior does not always improve systems of classification. Additionally, many useful classificatory terms have been polluted with ideological prejudices connoting extreme positions. Often these terms cannot be easily replaced with unpolluted terms.

For instance the terms *learning* and *cognitive capacities* may remind one of former dichotomization between behaviorist and cognitive theoreticians. Yet we see both learning and cognition functioning in a unity. For this reason, we have preferred using the term *integrative capacities* as common to both categories.

Emotions represent another example of problematic categories, too difficult to solve before our knowledge increases. Emotions have frequently been neglected or seen as disturbing noise in theoretical systems by some researchers and theorists, or overestimated as primary factors in the regulation of behavior by others. The restriction to observational methods in infancy research does not allow us to decide what emotions really are. However, neither does it allow us to disregard the participation of emotionality in the infant's interactions with the environment, both social and unsocial. Seeing the close ties between emotionality and integrative development, we have tried to conceptualize them at least in provisional hypotheses.

Although many former attempts to outline hierarchies in behavioral regulations have appeared problematic, there seems to be no doubt that the uniqueness of humans within the world of living organisms can be attributed to the complexity of integrative capacities. In the human it allows spontaneity, symbolism, use of language, and technology of information storing so that the human experience can be integrated across ages, continents, or even planets. In systems theory, von Bertalanffy (1968) derived this conclusion from achievements in comparative biology, ethology, anthropology, neurosciences, and other sciences stressing two related circumstances: (1) the dominant role of such highly adaptive specific capacities in relation to other abilities; and (2) a potential dependence of the specific capacities on adequate supportive factors during both ontogeny and phylogeny. We shall discuss these two points in the following sections about the competences of infants and the competences of parents during parent-child interactions.

The Infant's Competence in Social Interactions

After a long period of scientific ignorance during which preverbal infants were compared with nonhuman animals, we now know that human infants, although different from human adults, are still human in the sense that they are capable of complex integrative processes, self-awareness, autonomy in emotional behaviors, and symbolic communication. The interrelationships among these processes are unknown, but too important to be simply disregarded.

Piaget (1981) discussed interrelationships between affectivity and intelligence in the Sorbonne lectures (1953–1954). When speaking of the first feelings acquired before sensorimotor intelligence, Piaget differentiated feelings linked to perception (in joys, sorrows, pleasantness, and unpleasantness) from those linked to action (in contentment and disappointment). He expressed his belief that there is a constant and dialectic interaction between affectivity and intelligence, that is, that both develop in interconnected ways, but one is not caused by the other (p. 25).

Similarly, Crook (1980) found indicators of interconnected functioning between cognitive abilities and complex social organization in the development of human societies but stressed failures in attempts to assign priority to one or other factor. Reviewing the trends in developmental studies on social and emotional behaviors, Parke (1979) also found it difficult to treat those aspects separately, given the present state of knowledge.

The treatment of interrelationships in cognitive–social–emotional dimensions becomes particularly confusing in relation to their motivational significance. This confusion is exacerbated by the emphasis on specific individual dimensions that seems inherent in each of the various theories of social, emotional, or cognitive development, and by the omission of cognition in most traditional lists of biological needs. Piaget (1952, 1981) considered cognitive constructs (particularly curiosity and play) to have potentially universal relevance for behavioral motivation. From the present neuroscientific positions, Estes (1981) sees motives as organized structures of the cognitive system activating cognitive engagement in problem situations. To us, some degree of cognitive engagement is a fundamental part of all naturalistic interactions between human organism and environment. It is difficult to think of a "biological situation" as being so unproblematic that it never requires cognitive engagement either in processing informational input or in organizing adaptive behavioral responses. Only future research, of course, can replace speculations with factual knowledge. However, if in the future an interconnection is found between successful problem solving and some intrinsic rewarding mechanisms (perhaps secretion of neuropeptides), we may realize that such intrinsic function is a very universal biological phenomenon.

Hitherto, we have used a hypothesis regarding the infant's integrative capacities (H. Papoušek & M. Papoušek, 1979a, 1982a) that we derived from earlier studies on infant learning (H. Papoušek, 1961, 1967a, 1977), problem solving, and concept formation (Papoušek & Bernstein, 1969). Unlike most learning studies, ours included polygraphic records of head movements, general motility, heart rate, and pneumograms in addition to records of stimuli and protocols on globally assessed facial and vocal responses. Such complex evidence allowed us to consider interrelations between motivational systems, integrative processes, and socioemotional behaviors. The core of our hypothesis is a fundamental system of adaptive responses including both observable behaviors serving the function of increasing informational input (scanning, orienting head movements, locomotor approach, exploratory activities) and intrinsic operations necessary for processing perceptual input (constructing concepts and comparing them with preceding concepts already stored in memory) and organizing adaptive responses.

Two substantial aspects relevant to the topic of this presentation have become obvious in our experiments.

First, the infant's fundamental system of adaptive responses appeared to be activated by structural rather than physical properties of environmental stimuli. For example, an infant will orient in response to the perception of a stimulus per se and then habituate to it when no change in the stimulus is evident. Quite a different sequence of events occurs, however, when the infant becomes aware that a given stimulus is followed by another relevant event. In this case, there is increased attention to the stimulus, reflecting the infant's effort to deduce the probability of this combination recurring. Here, the integrative system is evident in the organization of a learned response by the infant, similar to that in associative conditioning. In yet a third situation, the infant may correctly perceive a particular event as following an act organized and executed by the infant. The integrative system is thus activated not only with increased attention, but also with repetitions of the self-initiated behaviors and rather systematic testing of the conditions that lead once more to the desired event. The analogy to instrumental learning is obvious.

Thus simple auditory stimuli selected for experimental stimulation in our studies acquired properties affecting the infant's general behavior in relation to the preceding history of stimuli as manipulated by the researcher. Relatively simple interventions offered opportunities to activate or inhibit infant responsivity and thus also influence the infant's behavioral–emotional state. For instance, stimuli originally used as elicitors of instrumental acts did not remain irrelevant when the learned responses had been extinguished, but showed inhibitory effects upon infant behavior, and if continued, induced sleep (H. Papoušek, 1967a).

Second, emotional and communicative behaviors appeared to be regularly included in the infant's repertoire of responses to experimental stimuli in spite of laboratory circumstances that eliminated social interchanges. We have observed numerous situations in which an infant, faced with a difficult problem-solving task or an overabundance of novelty, shows clear signs of displeasure with both vocal and facial expressions. Similarly, communicative signs of pleasure are displayed by infants upon successful completion or accomplishment of an integrative task. Recognition of a familiar stimulus, control of a contingent occurrence, or fulfillment of an expectation may all be followed by evidence of relaxation and positive affect on the part of the infant. If one admits that expressions of pleasure are indicative of intrinsic motivation then our observations supported the assumption that human infants are motivated for the acquisition of knowledge.

The importance of early learning may be called into question when considered in light of the quite normal phenomenon of infantile amnesia, documented primarily in animal studies. The degree to which humans actually maintain the benefits of early experience has not yet been established. Yet it is important to keep in mind the potential long-term gains in terms of the process of intellectual development, rather than focusing only on the more factual components, before dismissing the impact of infant learning. Studies of amnesia in human adults (such as in Korsakoff syndrome) have shown that it is declarative, data-based information ("know that") that is lost, while more procedural, rule-based information ("know how") is often not lost (Cohen & Squire, 1980). We do not exclude the possibility that human infants also retain the more process-oriented benefits of early experience even though they may appear to lose specific factual knowledge due to diminished exposure to the learning situation or to lack of reminders, as shown in rat infants (Coulter, 1979). Earlier studies of human infants (H. Papoušek, 1967a, 1977) offered perhaps the only experimental evidence suggesting that repeatedly exposing the human infant to stimulation that activates the integrative processes may result in more efficiently organized learning and cognition. Thus the primary long-range benefit from early didactic support might be precisely such procedural improvements, that is, the more action-based "learning how to learn."

The Parents' Competence in Social Interactions

For a psychobiologically oriented infancy researcher it is difficult to take species capabilities into account without asking whether or not some supportive counterpart to them has been selected during evolution. A closer look at the infant's naturalistic niche reveals only a limited set of learning situations resulting from the infant's interaction with the physical, nonliving environment (Newson, 1979; H. Papoušek & M. Papoušek, 1984a). Unparalleled in the physical environment, a wealth of interesting stimulation is provided by the infant's social environment. As we will show in more detail in the next sections of this chapter, social stimulation provided to the infant by caregivers is rich, multimodal, and reciprocal. A microanalytic analysis reveals several episodes interpretable as supportive to infant integrative development during every minute of dyadic interactions between the caregiver and the infant in an alert state. The stimulation provided is so adequate to the infant's integrative competence that it elicits an impression of didactic interventions.

The history of conscious cultural interventions that might be considered didactic is strikingly short. General aspects of child care in historical perspective have been recently surveyed by several authors, such as Aries (1962), Bell and Harper (1977), Borstelmann (1983), Peiper (1958), Rabb and Rotberg (1971), Senn (1975), and Sommerville (1971). As is not the case with the development of somatic factors and quiet sleep, which can be traced to the origins of cultural heritage, almost no evidence can be found on the concern for mental health and development of infants. Peiper's rich documentation (1958) includes translations of Plutarch's (Athens, 50–125 A.D.) recommendations that mothers, and not wet nurses, should nurse infants because infants need a deep love from the very beginning (p. 24–25). Peiper (p. 38) also quotes Galen's (Pergamon, 129–199 A.D.) instruction that fussy newborns can be soothed with three things—nursing, rocking, and singing lullabies. In comparison with detailed medical observations on neonatal and infantile diseases, ancient literature hardly contributed to the psychological knowledge of infancy.

Didactics as a scholarly discipline dealing with methods of conveying knowledge was professionally and scientifically developed during the Enlightenment. Interestingly, Comenius, the author of the seminal work *Opera didactica omnia* (1657), wrote the first manual for the "maternal school," the predecessor of today's nursery schools. In *Schola materni gremii* (1628), Comenius expressed unusually progressive beliefs: (1) that educational care for children should be started during infancy and be based upon parental care; and (2) that education for children in both preschool and school should be carried out playfully. Obviously, Comenius's advice was based on rich empirical experience in educational activities and on the intuitive insight of a loving parent. Comenius was a religious dualistic philosopher, believing in the existence of an immortal soul and stressing mutual interrelations between the mind's needs and bodily health and growth. Comenius acknowledged both the inherited similarity between parents and progeny and the environmental influence upon the minds of children.

However, even if we admit that a call for conscious didactic care for infants can be dated from the early Enlightenment, 350 years of its existence are negligible as a factor influencing the evolution of human precociousness in integrative capacities. Is it then true that the early growth of integrative capacities is merely a question of maturation?

This question has led us to focus on those potential forms of didactic interventions that might escape the observer's attention because caregivers might carry them out without being knowingly aware of them. The didactic interventions might be based upon psychobiological preadaptedness rather than rational sociocultural traditions. We pursued this hypothesis in microanalytic studies of the behaviors in early parent–infant interactions, looking at previously unknown parental behaviors facilitating the conveyance of preverbal information to infants and corresponding to biological precursors of didactic interventions (H. Papoušek & M. Papoušek, 1978). Analyses of these behaviors have shown qualities that assign these behaviors an intermediate position between categories of innate reflexes and responses requiring rational decisions, that is, the position of *intuitive behaviors*. The latency of such behaviors usually occurs at 200-600 msec, which is above the latency of innate simple reflexes and below that of conscious, rational decisions. Individuals are unaware of carrying out these behaviors. They sometimes deny or misinterpret their occurrence and, if they become aware of them, typically find them difficult to control (see the section on methodology).

These intuitive behaviors have been detected in parental interactions with infants and have been found somewhat universally across age, sex, and cultures. Some are present in the infancy period and persist for the entire life span of the individual. The universality of such behaviors indicates the deep phylogenetic roots of observed behavioral patterns. Also indicated is a didactic counterpart to the infant's integrative competence that has been selected during evolution with a certain surplus, crucially important for adaptation. This surplus increases the probability that progeny will find sufficient support for the development of integrative capacities, even during the initial and relatively lengthy period of dependency in the human infant. If parents are not available, almost any experienced member in the social environment is likely to possess similar didactic capabilities with which to complement and enhance the infant's integrative needs. The surplus thus may have played an important role in the past when puerperal maternal mortality was high and in cultures with low frequency of dyadic interchanges between parents and young infants where infants interact mainly with siblings and peers.

Another aspect of parent–infant interactions linked to the history of evolution is the potential parallel between the ontogeny and phylogeny of social interactions, with particular reference to social communication. This consideration is not related to Haeckel's (1891) theory of a recapitulation or Hall's (1916) application of Haeckel's theory in the explanation of psychological development. Rather it is an attempt to investigate at least one way of development from simple origins of social interactions to a complex system of social communication including speech where the evolutionary ways remain obscure due to the paucity of paleontological evidence. Paleontological findings allow only a vague conception of the evolution of human social coexistence and verbal communication.

Since theories on human evolution have paid more attention to aggressive than to prosocial behaviors, the evidence of parental support for speech acquisition during ontogeny calls for a reconsideration of the role of prosocial behaviors in the human evolution. Care for dependent progeny and prosocial behavior in general have recently aroused increased interest among theoreticians of human evolution who doubt the further tenability of the hypothesis that tool use determined human bipedalism. Lovejoy (1981), influenced by new paleontological findings, suggests that bipedalism was an unusual and disadvantageous form of walking that originally resulted from a mere variation in the genetic reproduction but was adopted because of advantages for demographic propagation. Lovejoy's arguments are based on human reproductive rate, short birth spacing (relative to other primates), and longevity on one hand, and monogamic tendencies, strong social bonds, longer period of infant dependency, and intense parenting on the other. According to this theory, the interrelation between reproductive competence and social structures contributed to further divergences of hominids from pongids, and also led to strengthening of monogamic pair bonding and direct involvement of males in bifocal—maternal and paternal—groups allowing higher survivorship of offspring during the Miocene period.

Theories on the evolution of speech have not yet seriously examined the script by which parents help infants acquire their first language. Nevertheless, parents seem universally—albeit unknowingly—to follow similar patterns in guiding the infant from an initial stage of insufficient respiratory control to the stage of using meaningful words in complex ways (M. Papoušek & H. Papoušek, 1981a).

When considering the didactic tendencies in the care for progeny in a broader evolutionary context, one should not overlook the role of playfulness in the acquisition of knowledge. Playfulness was manifestly introduced into didactics by Comenius, as mentioned earlier in the present section, and was viewed by some as a major determinant of human culture. For instance, Huizinga (1955) preferred calling man *Homo ludens* rather than *Homo sapiens*. Comparative research (for reviews, see Bekoff, 1972; Hinde, 1971; Lorenz, 1970, 1971) has called attention to some releasers like "babyishness" of the young and cue signals like the "playsmile" (Van Hooff, 1962) signaling the intention to play and allowing, for instance, the young to attempt threatening behaviors without serious consequences (Blurton Jones, 1972). In congruence with comparative and cross-cultural literature, Bruner (1974, 1983) assumes that children's play was favored during evolution as a pressure-free time during which the subroutines of adult skills could be acquired through observational learning and imitation or problems could be solved with successful solutions serving as a source of pleasure.

Focusing attention on the emergence of play during ontogeny, particularly in vocal play, the present authors (H. Papoušek & M. Papoušek, 1977b, 1978, 1984a; M. Papoušek & H. Papoušek, 1981a; M. Papoušek, H. Papoušek, & Harris, 1986) suggested a hypothesis regarding interrelationships between playfulness and a higher level of the acquisition of knowledge. It was proposed that parallel pathways may lead to play, creativity, humor, arts, and scientific discoveries.

In this conception, the initial confrontation with a novel event compels the integrative system to accumulate information sufficient for the construction of at least a crude concept of the unknown event, thereby avoiding excessive distress or fear of the unknown. These Level One operations may produce rather simple, "black and white," sometimes false or superstitious concepts, and yet the system may adhere to them until an accumulation of similar concepts increases the risk of boredom. To avoid the distress of boredom, the integrative system may activate higher-order Level Two operations, which, if developed properly, reopen the temporary concepts for further exploration and integration under pressure-free conditions. This step may be repeated many times and lead to conceptual improvements that move away from triviality and toward cultural achievements in the forms of various alternatives in play, artistic or scientific creativity, and humor.

As will be shown in connection with vocal communication in the present chapter, caregivers unknowingly give the infant rich opportunities for practicing such Level Two operations. Conversely, of course, such progress may also be arrested by cultural taboos or dogmatic interventions after the infancy period.

It is hardly possible to prove that the acquisition of knowledge during ontogeny or the development of culture during phylogeny has taken the way from Level One operations to Level Two operations. Interestingly, though, there is an analogy between the processes described here and the new models for information processing, recently introduced in the research on artificial intelligence (Hinton & Anderson, 1981; Hinton & Sejnowski, 1983; Smolensky, 1983). In contrast to former theories of information processing, in the new systems, called Boltzmann machines, many processors operate simultaneously and independently. There is no supervising control system that schedules the temporal coordination of operations. Although the overall behavior of such systems appears to be random at the first glance, continued observations reveal that certain new informational structures emerge from initially chaotic states. It is as if such systems "playfully discover" and test new hypotheses on meaningful relations.

In our introduction to this chapter, we have pointed out several open questions regarding the ontogeny and the evolution of human integrative and communicative capacities, such as the precursors of these capacities in preverbal infants or non-human animals, the environmental support of the development of these capacities, and the role of these capacities in behavioral regulation. We have suggested that a psychobiological approach to the problems raised can help overcome the theoretical and methodological confusions caused by former tendencies to dichotomize observed phenomena rather than seeing them in dialectic unities. Our approach has focused attention on the parental contribution to the infant's integrative and communicative capacities. We have indicated that parents provide such support unknowingly in the form of intuitive, relatively universal behaviors. In the following sections we will explain our approach in more detail, beginning with comments on some methodological problems. We will then describe the behavioral repertoire of parental didactics based on the present level of knowledge and discuss its significance for the main integrative processes in the infant.

SOME METHODOLOGICAL PROBLEMS

The introduction of modern technology, making possible the unobtrusive audiovisual documentation of observed events, has brought about significant consequences.

It has substantially improved behavioral analyses in various scientific disciplines. It has also contributed to better cooperation among disciplines since it has made it possible to look at the observed events again and again for additional analyses and to exchange documentation with related disciplines. The Center for Cognitive Studies at Harvard University, directed by Jerome Bruner until 1972, was an outstanding example of a breeding site for infancy research where such an interchange among disciplines flourished. Not only did Bruner point out that infancy studies might lead to solutions of some general problems in psychology, he also brought together developmentalists from zoology, anthropology, psychology, linguistics, pediatrics, and other disciplines, and provided all the modern tools for effective sharing of experience and theories.

The recent and rapid development of technology, especially the widespread use of microprocessors and miniaturization, has provided less expensive and portable equipment. The researcher is capable of taking much of this sophisticated equipment out of the laboratory for studying infants directly in their natural environments. Former paper and pencil documentation has been quickly outdated, and, more important, the narrow limits of behavioral classification that it necessitated have been outdated as well. Students of behavior are no longer compelled to define only a limited list of items a priori; the list can be completed, corrected, or even invented and verified post hoc in successive processing of documentation. This progress has played a particularly significant role in studies of infant social interactions.

In the next sections we shall selectively describe those techniques and outline those general principles that have been found especially useful in our own studies. The reader should keep in mind that the technology of research instruments becomes outdated almost annually with each generation of new apparatus.

Technical Aspects

Filming Versus Videotaping

Although videotaping provides electronic records with perfect synchronization of both picture and sound, it has not completely replaced the use of filming and audiotaping. For the sake of reliable documentation, we have usually combined all three forms of documentation in order to profit from all their specific advantages. Cinematographic pictures allow a better resolution of details and thus also a better reproduction in print. Separate audiotapes are more comfortable to use for subsequent sonography or computer-aided analyses, and necessary of course for a true sound documentation if we decide to use more economic time lapse recording of pictures. An electronically recorded picture permits immediate and innovative manipulations such as split-screen combinations of pictures from several cameras, insertion of a time base or other digital or analog information, instantaneous control of the quality of recording, remote control, simultaneous televised transmission to multiple and remote monitors, and so on (M. Papoušek & H. Papoušek, 1981b; Tronick, Als, & Adamson, 1979). A typical example of a complex combination of filming and videotaping for the study of self-awareness in 5-month-old infants was described by us earlier (H. Papoušek & M. Papoušek, 1974). We reported for the first time on interactions between infants and partners who are available to the infants only on television screens (two screens were used for a preferential design).

The Number of Cameras

One camera seldom guarantees sufficient documentation of dyadic interactions. Valuable information gets lost if subjects turn away from the camera or if the picture of the entire interactional situation brings about a poorer resolution of details, for instance, on visual behaviors. We have preferred using three cameras whenever possible, and have positioned them so as to obtain a good global picture of the entire situation as well as close-up pictures of both interacting faces. The better the audiovisual documentation, the easier it is to carry out additional analyses. Frequently, unexpected episodes occur and reveal unexpected interactional processes or processes for which it is difficult to design laboratory models. We have detected several previously unknown behavioral patterns in the domain of intuitive parenting (H. Papoušek & M. Papoušek, 1983) and found occasional anecdotal and yet convincing evidence of infant integrative capacities otherwise difficult to demonstrate, such as self-recognition or abstraction across sensory modalities (H. Papoušek & M. Papoušek, 1984a).

Time Lapse Recording

It is easier to increase the number of cameras if we can reduce most of the films or tapes with the help of time lapse recording. Moreover, slow, inconspicuous movements can be easily detected in time lapse records in which these movements are displayed as discontinuous jerks. For a reliable synchronization of the entire recording system, we have successfully used an electronic synchronizer (M. Papoušek & H. Papoušek, 1981b). It triggers up to four cameras via remote single-frame control at speeds of 1, 2, 5, 10, 20, 50, or 100 frames/min, and with every tenth frame it sends sound signals to audiotaping systems and switches on spotlight flashes in the visual field of cameras for close-up filming. Simultaneously with every single frame, the synchronizer triggers a silent, luminous display of numbers 0–99 on a small screen in the visual field of the camera photographing the global interactional situation. In this way, all cinematic time lapse records and sound records can be brought onto one common time base given with the sequence of frames in films and evaluated as synchronous in frame-to-frame analyses. The use of time lapse video records or films for the assessment of behavioral states in infancy research has been successfully applied by Anders and Sostek (1976) and Wallin (1984).

For the frame-to-frame evaluation of 16mm movies, there are several types of special projectors on the market. For S-8mm movies, however, we had to have a prototypical piece of equipment constructed (Schmid Co., Straubing), which allows us to operate up to four projectors with one button at various speeds in both directions and thus to display synchronously corresponding frames from all films in question. Each projector has an independent frame counter (H. Papoušek & M. Papoušek, 1979b, 1981). With the help of the Schmid-viewers, the evaluator sees the global pictures and the details of two interacting faces next to each other at one time, and operates all pictures with a single button. Moreover, we have usually videotaped the global situation and had this record available for a control display of picture and sound at natural speed.

Time lapse recording is not easy with video techniques unless expensive equipment is available. At our laboratory, we have used 1-in VIC-471 Videorecorders with a built-in device allowing both recording and playback at seven exactly defined speeds, and a frame-to-frame display of individual half-pictures in both directions (H. Papoušek & M. Papoušek, 1979b; M. Papoušek & H. Papoušek, 1981c). The still-frame display of individual half-pictures (only even or uneven lines are read) reduces the resolution of details, but the display is quiet allowing evaluations of up to 50 pictures per second (the European norm), that is, with a temporal resolution of 20 msec. For a detailed observation of still-frames including both half-pictures, we have been able to store, scan, and enlarge a given frame in an additional Hughes Memory System.

A Reliable Common Time Base

For both a fine-grained analysis of short-lasting behaviors and a united evaluation of information from all recording systems, it is essential to use a reliable, exact time base. For the analysis of films, the simplest way is based on the sequence of frames that may be directly numbered as described in the previous subsection or indirectly on the frame counter of special film viewers. Modern 16mm cameras use light signals for time codes matching analogous ultrasound signals in separate high-quality tape recorders. Sound and picture are then synchronized automatically on the coded time base in film laboratories while producing the final copy of the sound movie. For special laboratory purposes, we have combined an ARI-16 RS camera with a Nagra tape recorder. Otherwise, the above mentioned electronic synchronizer proved sufficient for synchronizing S-8mm films with audiotaping and videotaping.

Video technology has provided an elegant aid to students of interactions by allowing the insertion of a time base onto the picture with an accuracy of 10 msec, using quartz clocks. Every half-picture may thus be labeled for later exact identification, and for measuring the duration of recorded events with the accuracy of 20 msec (again assuming the European norm of 50 half-pictures per second). The insertion of such a time base is included in the new generation of portable, small-format videocameras.

One very important advantage of the common time base is the possibility of arranging data from all used recording systems and their subsequent processing along the time axis for storing in computer memory. Such arrangement permits complex, computer-aided analyses of temporal structures, periodicity, sequential interrelationships, multifactoral analysis of variance, and other statistical procedures.

Insertion of Additional Information into Videorecords

Similar to the insertion of a time base, other digital or analog information can be inserted into or superimposed upon videorecords as well. For instance, we have used Videograph Lemke (M. Papoušek & H. Papoušek, 1981c) for adding one oscillographic display of vocal sounds, and two-digit data on physiological parameters (heart and respiration rates as measured from beat to beat). Using such videopolygraphy we have been able immediately after observations to calculate temporal parameters on vocal sounds in real-time records or to reconstruct melodic contours of the fundamental frequency in the entire range of audible frequencies already at the time when computer-aided analysis could do it only in the range below 700 Hz.

Additional Analysis of Vocal Sounds

Having learned that the analysis of vocal communication provides perhaps the most relevant information for the study of parents' didactic interventions, we extended our methodological repertoire to auditory, sonagraphic, spectrographic, and computer-aided analyses of vocal sounds (M. Papoušek & Sandner, 1981; M. Papoušek & H. Papoušek, 1981a). Most attention has been focused upon the prosodic elements, musical elements, and melodic contours in particular. The use of video-polygraphy mentioned above has proved advantageous for measuring temporal parameters but has been replaced by other methods in regard to frequency measures. For instance, the Digital Sona-Graph TM 7800 (Kay Elemetrics), which we now use, allows analysis of: (1) fundamental frequency even in a high-pitched voice; (2) spectrograms at variable bandwidths; and (3) power spectrum analysis at selectable points, for instance, at the point of maximum fundamental frequency as in our evaluations (H. Papoušek, M. Papoušek, & Koester, 1986). In addition, the contours of fundamental frequency and intensity and the temporal parameters have been analyzed by computers, although only in selected samples for economic reasons. The auditory evaluation by trained co-workers has not been outdated by the use of electronic devices. It still represents an economical and reliable procedure in evaluations of pitch, pitch contours, patterns of stress, quality of voice, and vocal matching, particularly in records including overlapping voices or background noise.

The analysis of lexical content may seem problematic as the majority of utterances in parental speech (baby talk) consist of repetitive interjections, namings, exclamations, sounds matched to infant repertoire, or onomatopoeic sounds with little linguistic information. To us, however, even these types of utterances appeared to be interesting when we related them to a hypothetical script of didactic care for the initial integrative and communicative capacities in infants (H. Papoušek & M. Papoušek, 1983). Quite regularly, we have been able to distinguish two alternating types of utterances in phonetic transcripts of parental speech:

1. References to the interactional context and subprograms for adequate parental interventions. These references have the distinct form of questions or answering statements, and seem to be addressed to the speaker rather than to the infant. Their content indicates a certain assessment of the interactional situation and outlines an adequate intervention.
2. Executions of subprograms indicated in references. In these utterances, which are perhaps only nonsense particles of speech, the parent delivers the proper messages to the infant. The messages are to be looked for not in the lexical content, but in the prosody, particularly in the melodic contours, in rhythmicity, tempo, pausing, and other temporal parameters, in the dynamics of pitch or in the quality of voice.

The following example illustrates such alternations. Mother, approaching the infant who has just awakened and fussed: "You're not alone. Mommy's here." (Reference with soothing melodic contours.) "Yuh, yuh, hoe, hoe, hoe, hoe." (Execution by displaying enhanced soothing contours in prolongated vowels; simultaneous stroking.) To us, the mother evaluated the situation, assessed the reason for the infant's discomfort, and decided to soothe and thus facilitate the transition to quiet waking in her reference. Then she spent some time soothing in various modalities, thus executing the intention indicated in the reference.

If we consider the role of methodological advances in developmental research in general we must admit that, in spite of such radical facilitation of data processing and computation, research still remains tedious and time-consuming. According to our experience, the time that is necessary for recording observations is usually exceeded several hundred times by that required for the evaluation of records. Advances in methodology have opened new areas to scientific investigations and made possible what used to be unthinkable one or two decades ago. Our productivity has increased, but our motivation for attacking the more difficult problems has increased as well. This fact should be kept in mind for calculations of new projects. With the entire available investment, we still evaluate only narrow aspects in the collected material. This circumstance strengthens the need for closer interdisciplinary cooperation and more systematic exchange of documentation for additional evaluations by teams of other specialists.

Comments About Procedural Arrangements and Data Evaluation

The recent rapprochement among developmental sciences and the technical innovations just described have necessarily led to changes in traditional strategies for the arrangement of research designs and choice of methods for the evaluation of data. Again, it would require a monograph to survey these changes. We will mention only those aspects that may be helpful for better understanding of our approaches.

Naturalistic Observations and Laboratory Models

Typically, students of behavior follow the traditions of their disciplines when choosing between observations in naturalistic settings and observations of models under laboratory conditions. Because of technological progress as well as other reasons this dichotomy has become almost superfluous, if not harmful, considering advantages that may be exploited by proper combinations of both alternatives. Naturalistic observations help reveal the entire repertoire of behaviors that may be relevant to our interests, and stimulate the production of adequate hypotheses. Such hypotheses may be best verified in experimental models under strictly controllable laboratory conditions. Nevertheless, a subsequent confrontation of resulting conclusions with naturalistic situations may serve as the crucial test for the adequateness of selected models or point out neglected aspects (H. Papoušek, 1981; Sorenson, 1979).

Our own interests have repeatedly required a similar strategy. For instance, when observing families in a natural setting, we discovered that parents were holding infants in two distinctly different eye-to-eye distances, depending upon the infant's visual attention and interest in the parents' vocal expressions. We analyzed the control of this distance in mothers during the first postpartum days in three standardized modes of interaction (Schoetzau, 1979; Schoetzau & H. Papoušek, 1977). In another naturalistic situation, we discovered that parents were probably using the infant's gestures as visual cues for assessments of the infant's general state (H. Papoušek & M. Papoušek, 1977a). To assess this phenomenon in the laboratory, we prepared drawings of infants in which only these cues were modified. Kestermann (1982) verified the hypothesis under experimental conditions using our drawings, confirmed the effectiveness of hand gestures, and simultaneously proved that intuitive parental behaviors can be studied in nonparents with the help of symbolic representations of infants.

Global Versus Elementary Components of Interpretative Categories

One danger common to analyses of infant social interactions is the use of inadequately defined, overlapping categories for classificatory purposes. The categories may refer to diverse speculative interpretations or correspond to commonsense classifications for the sake of easy comprehension; however, such reference does not justify their use for scientific purposes. Therefore, we have tried to avoid interpretative categories for behavioral evaluations. We use more elementary, descriptive units, making it easier to define, to detect, and to assess behaviors in binary modes (H. Papoušek & M. Papoušek, 1974). In addition to the list of elementary units, more complex, perhaps interpretative categories may be tentatively defined by combining certain elementary units. Then the validity of these categories can be tested in subsequent steps. Quantitative and qualitative scaling may be based upon the number or type of elementary units. Although computer-aided analyses facilitate both exploratory and verifying steps in the search for best-fitting classifications, the search is still very difficult, as we are going to illustrate in connection with vocal communication.

Conscious Awareness of Observed Behaviors

In relation to parent–infant interactions there is more knowledge about the psychobiological preadaptedness of infants than about that of parents. For a long time, parental participation seemed to be tacitly viewed as consisting of consciously performed and culturally determined behaviors. Our earliest observations indicated that parental behaviors also had elements of psychobiological preadaptedness. We saw these elements in universality (across age, sex, and cultures), early functioning during ontogeny, and parents' lack of conscious awareness of these behaviors. For instance, we have interviewed parents after the end of observations to find out to what degree they were aware of their performance and the meaning of their displayed behaviors during the interactions. At other suitable opportunities, we tested the degree to which parents are able to control their behaviors. Obviously parents carry out a set of interactional behaviors with minimal conscious awareness and control. Moreover, the meaning of their behaviors is sometimes discrepant from conscious attitudes. For example, parents try to stay in the middle of the newborn's visual field and to reach direct eye-to-eye visual contact. When they have achieved the contact they display exaggerated "greeting responses." Nevertheless, in interviews they express serious doubts about the possibility that newborns can see at all (Schoetzau & H. Papoušek, 1977). Similarly, parents responded to visual cues in the hand gestures in Kestermann's experiments (1982), but explained in interviews that they were influenced by changes of facial expressions in drawings even though no such changes were present. Parents seem to attribute nonfacial cues unknowingly to the face. They generally observe the face with maximum attention and expect the face to include the crucial information on the infant's state.

Interdyadic Alternation of Partners

For reasons discussed in the introduction to this chapter, the study of dyadic inter-actions between parents and infants accentuates the need for analyses of individual variability in observed behaviors. However, it is much more difficult to analyze individual variability in interactional data than in data obtained from simple stimulus–response designs. In human social interactions in general, individual part-ners not only respond but also act spontaneously from intrinsic motives. Individual partners respond and stimulate simultaneously and with an unusually rich set of behaviors. In parent–infant interactions in particular, both partners differ substan-tially in integrative and communicative competences. The statistical treatment of observational data from parent–infant interactions is particularly difficult when in-dividual variability is to be considered. The situation from which the data originate is a complex process that cannot be described satisfactorily in terms of classical statistical models. The following are a few of the features of parent–infant inter-action that contribute to its formal complexity (H. Papoušek & M. Papoušek, 1985):

1. Interpersonal interaction represents a process determined by global, overall, and relatively stable features of partners (trait factors, e.g., the parent's tem-perament), transitory, instantaneous features of partners (state factors, e.g., the infant's emotional state or the parent's response to a cue signal from the infant), and environmental features (context factors, e.g., effects of labo-ratory settings).

2. The interaction is basically a spontaneous process, influenced by intrinsic motivations, and it is therefore difficult to distinguish a priori dependent and independent variables or to introduce an experimental control of variables.

3. The observed variables are not only dependent on the above factors but also statistically interdependent and thus form multivariate time series.

4. Different types of scales, namely, nominal, ordinal, and interval, have to be used for assessment of the observed behaviors.

5. In parent–infant interactions, the two partners are categorically different in their competences and use unequal sets of behaviors.

So far, no formal model of interaction is available from which statistical models for the variables required in a meaningful description of the process of parent–child interaction could be derived. Primarily we have to restrict our approaches to: (1) invention of special designs, including simple stimulus–response designs, and em-pirical strategies for the introduction of independent variables by systematic vari-ations of experimental conditions, perhaps outside of dyadic interactions; and (2) the use of exploratory and descriptive techniques of data analysis.

In order to overcome some of these difficulties we have asked mothers to alter-nate in interactions with infants so that each mother could be observed in dyadic interactions not only with her own infant but also with two strange infants (H. Papoušek & M. Papoušek, 1985).

Due to predictable organizational difficulties, four mothers were asked to alter-nate so that each mother could dyadically interchange with at least two strange infants. This approach is a compromise between the common paradigm of an in-teraction of a parent with his or her own child and a paradigm in which each parent would interact with each infant. The latter would enable us to apply classical statistical procedures for data analysis such as analyses of variance. The system of alternation applied in our design is illustrated in Figure 12.1.

With this design we obtained observational data for parental and infantile behaviors from 20 mother–infant dyads in five blocks. In order to describe the effects of varying partners, we estimated the intraindividual variation of the data across partners (the interpartner variability) by computing standard deviations s_{Pi} ($i = 1$, n) and s_{Ij} ($j = 1$, n) for the (in general) three interactions observed with parent i, and infant j. The group means of standard deviations $\bar{s}_{Pi}$ and $\bar{s}_{Ij}$ characterize the average interpartner variability for parents and infants respectively. We use the ratio $\bar{s}_{Pi}$ by $\bar{s}_{Ij}$ as a descriptor for the relative determination of observed behaviors by parental and infantile factors. For instance, descriptor values lower than 1 indicate a relatively small interpartner variability for the parent and a relatively large interpartner variability for the infant. This case indicates that the behavior is more strongly determined by the parent.

In addition, we assessed the portion of the variance contributed by parental factors by computing the ratio of the standard deviation of the individual mean values $s_{\bar{x}_{Pi}}$ ($i = 1$, n) by the total standard deviation over all dyads (s_T). Analogously, the ratio of the standard deviation of the individual mean values $s_{x_{Ij}}$ ($j = 1$, n) by the total standard deviation indicated the portion of the variance contributed by infantile factors.

The objectives of this approach are: (1) to classify parents and infants with respect to the degree of variation in individual behaviors while partners are varied; and (2) to analyze interdependencies between observed variability–stability of behaviors and other situational factors. This approach allows us ultimately to explore the reliability and validity of the variables.

For each block consisting of data from four parents and four infants we also carried out an analysis of variance according to the following model for parental behavior (Y) and infantile behavior (Y'):

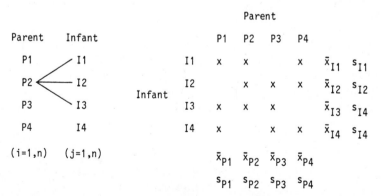

Figure 12.1. Model of Interdyadic Alternations of Parents and Infants: Construction of four-dyad blocks. Left: Symbols for four parents and four infants. Example of one parent (P2) interacting with own infants (I2) and two strange infants (I1, I3). Right: Complete set of interactions within one block of four alternating dyads, which fulfills the requirement that each parent interchanges with own infant and at least two strange infants. $\bar{x}_\pi$ respectively $\bar{x}_{Ij}$ represent intraindividual means; s_π respectively s_{Ij} represent intraindividual standard deviations.

$$Y_{ij} = \mu + \alpha_i + \beta_j + \gamma_{ij}$$
$$Y'_{ij} = \mu' + \alpha'_i + \beta'_j + \gamma'_{ij}$$

This model represents the base of a two-way fixed effect analysis of variance. The symbols μ respectively μ' represent global mean values, α respectively α' represent components characterizing the parental effect, β respectively β' represent the infantile effects, and γ respectively γ' represent the interactional components.

The model presented here aims at an additive decomposition of the values of observed variables. The central assumption underlying the analysis and interpretation of the data is the following: We assume that those behaviors that are minimally affected by the change of partners are more probably determined by the genotype or temperament of the individual, while behaviors that are maximally affected by the change of partners would be more probably determined by the genotype or temperament of the partner. Maximum behavioral fluctuations, co-occurring in both partners, might indicate a strong effect of a common environmental factor, independent of both individuals. On the contrary, fluctuations unrelated to the course of interactional sessions and alternation of partners might indicate the presence of an intrinsic factor, indifferent to both interactive and environmental circumstances. The arguments mentioned above indicate that the model is not fully appropriate for analyses of data related to interactional processes. The model can cautiously be used as a descriptive and exploratory procedure but not as a confirmative one.

Examples of the analyses are given in the following sections. Among others, we have tried to differentiate interactive behaviors according to the degree to which they may be adaptively controlled by each interacting partner during the developmental processes of interactions. We have assumed that, in general, some categories of integrative behaviors as such may show either more plasticity or more rigidity during interactions, perhaps because of their role in evolutionary selection. Consequently, such characteristics might throw more light on the evolution of interactive behaviors.

BEHAVIORAL REPERTOIRE

As we stated previously, we started paying more attention to behaviors that parents carry out unknowingly when we realized how little parents are consciously aware of the infant's integrative competence and of the possibilities of fostering its proper development. The repertoire of human behaviors occurring mostly without conscious awareness is rich and interesting but has been neglected in research. One reason for this neglect may be the view of intuitive behaviors as being undesired relics of animal instincts, although our health and survival would hardly be thinkable without certain sets of autonomic, reflexive, and intuitive responses. The difficulties in studying them may be another reason, since intuitive behaviors cannot be easily separated from rational, culturally determined ones, nor can they be readily classified according to the didactic potential that they may hold in interactions with infants.

For practical reasons, we have listed those behaviors that are potentially significant for intuitive didactic interventions in Table 12.1. The list is not based upon mere speculations. In studies on infant learning, we have learned much ourselves about the assumptions for the successful teaching of infants. Learning in infants requires an alert waking state, a simple structure of stimuli and learning trials, a large number of repetitions of trials, gradual ordering of tasks in terms of complexity, the use of adequate rewards, and sensitivity to feedback signals indicating the limits of tolerance. Somewhat analogous assumptions have been demonstrated for the development of early human communication, namely, consistency in the performance of simple and repetitive communicative elements (Messer, 1980), simultaneous engagement of several modalities (Turkewitz & McGuire, 1978), and fostering of eye-to-eye contact (Fogel, 1977; H. Papoušek & M. Papoušek, 1977a). From similar pieces of evidence, didactic principles could easily be derived for teaching the preverbal infant, much like those used to guide educators of school children. In contrast such principles have only recently been consciously transformed into programs that might become a part of culturally institutionalized interventions.

As stressed earlier, parental behaviors involved in interactions with younger infants will receive the most attention. In this regard, tendencies related to the infant's behavioral and affectional state, to visual contact, and to elementary communicative skills are of particular interest.

Parental Repertoire Related to the Infant's General State

To infancy researchers, the development of behavioral and emotional states, their regulation, circadian cycling, and assessment are all interesting but difficult problems for which they still have divergent methods, concepts, and terminology (W. Berg & K. Berg, 1979; Sostek & Anders, 1981; Thoman & Tynan, 1979; Wolff, 1981). According to Prechtl (1974), only four observable criteria—openness or closedness of eyes, respiration patterns, gross movements, and vocalization—can serve as distinguishing vectors. Prechtl and O'Brien (1982) recommend using the concept of state only in relation to phenomena stable over time (at least in the order of minutes) and occurring in cycles. Unlike students of circadian cycles, students of behavioral development are more interested in the course of waking than that of sleeping in infants (Becker & Thoman, 1982; Koch, 1968; Korner & Thoman, 1970, 1972; H. Papoušek, 1969; Wolff, 1965, 1973). They are also interested in the shorter fluctuations of attention and responsivity that are determined by the interaction with the environment rather than by internally regulated cycles. Many of these environmentally induced state changes (such as those prompted by fluctuations in light, noise, or position) are not only accessible to the researcher for systematic study, but are also a very relevant part of any caregiver's normal interactions with an infant. During social interactions, the use of interesting stimulation (Wolff, 1965) or vestibuloproprioceptive stimulation, produced by lifting the infant upright (Korner & Thoman, 1970, 1972), influences the infant's state. Similarly, infant learning also depends on behavioral states (H. Papoušek, 1969) and on the composition of sleep and feeding cycles (Koch, 1968); however, the course of learning itself influences the subsequent behavioral state (H. Papoušek, 1969). Consequently, it is advisable in terms of didactic success not only to pay attention to the infant's state but also to know that state can be influenced by adequate interventions.

Until recently, caregivers have not been able to utilize the researcher's knowl-

TABLE 12.1. Intuitive Parental Didactics

Expected Didactic Meaning	Observable Behavior	Vocal Behavior
Providing adequate conditions for integrative engagement:		
In general state of infant	Testing muscle tone	References to infant state
	Eliciting and maintaining attention	Alerting messages
	Reducing arousal, soothing, body contact, rhythmic tactile and vestibular stimulation	Soothing messages, singing
In visual contact	Face-to-face position	Calls
	Regulation of eye-to-eye distance	Rhythmic noises
	Greeting as contingent to visual contact	
In fundamental communicative skills:		
Use of nonverbal communication	Enhanced facial expressions and gestures:	References to infant as partner in conversation
	Responses to taste and smell	
	Feeding instructions	
	Articulatory instructions	
	Emotional expressions	
Use of dialogue, reciprocity	Differential responses to infant facial and gestural signals	Turn taking
		Vocal matching and duetting
Identification of caregiver	Individually stable features in behavioral patterns	Individually stable, idiosyncratic voice parameters
Metacommunication	Signals of caregiving approach	Increase of average pitch
	Signals of playfulness	Invitational messages in high-pitch register
		Laughter

Providing adequate stimulation:		
In amount and intensity	Propensity to face-to-face interactions	Propensity to talk to infants Adjusting intensity of prosody to infant level of integrative engagement
In structure	Simplified and enhanced facial expressions	Reduced linguistic complexity Slow rate of articulation Segmentation and repetition Simple prosodic patterns
In meaningfulness	Categorical facial and gestural messages Mediation of environment	Context-dependent references Categorical prosodic messages Differential responses to infant signals
Potential support to integrative processes:		
Cross-modal integration	Multimodality of stimulation	Involvement in multimodal stimulation
Mastery of contingency	Contingent display of behaviors	Contingent vocalization, appraisal
Categorical and conceptual integration	Symbolic and prototypical patterns	Symbolic and prototypical patterns
Imitation	Imitative behaviors and encouraging imitation in games	Vocal matching and imitation
Awareness and control of emotionality	Matching expressions of emotions, attunement, use of emotional expressions in games	Matching vocal expressions of emotions, enhancing or attenuating them Use of emotional expressions in games
Playfulness and creativity	Variations of repetitive behaviors Use of variations as points in games Encouraging infant play	Repetition and variation of prosodic patterns Use of variations as points in games Encouraging infant vocal play
Ritualized, culturally determined games	Universal and stereotypic patterns of games	Stereotypic utterances in games, nursery rhymes, and songs
Acquisition of speech	Pointing and naming Mediation of environment Use of symbolic representation as in toys, pictures, etc.	Modeling protowords and words out of syllables or protowords Naming

edge, and yet it has been the caregiver's task for many generations to make frequent decisions concerning the infant's state and to schedule interventions properly with respect to state cycles. This decision-making process must have been particularly difficult in dealing with very young infants whose state fluctuates frequently and irregularly (Dittrichová, 1969; Sostek & Anders, 1981; Sterman, 1972; Stern, Parmelee, & Harris, 1973). That is, during the first 6–8 weeks of life the innate circadian periodicity is becoming adjusted to environmental reality (H. Papoušek & M. Papoušek, 1982b, 1984b; Stratton, 1982). Sizing up the unknown individuality of the newborn, parents often express through their words uncertainty about the infant's behavioral state. They do not intervene as long as the infant quietly sleeps or is fully awake, but they do tend to help the infant restore one of these two states if the infant becomes passive and drowsy or upset and fussy. In so doing, parents respond immediately to cues signaling a possible deviation from alert waking rather than using some long-term assessment of state. Changes in infant vocalization and ability to maintain dialogic interchange seem to be particularly relevant cues.

At the time when parents verbally express being at a loss whether to play with the infant, to feed, or to prepare the infant for sleep, they regularly carry out one of two exploratory patterns: They either touch with their fingers the infant's oral area, eventually trying to open the infant's mouth by gently pushing the chin downward, or they explore the infant's hands and try to open the palm and stretch the fingers. As described earlier (H. Papoušek & M. Papoušek, 1984a; M. Papoušek & H. Papoušek, 1981d), the common cues in both cases depend on the muscle tone. Muscle tone generally increases during the transition from alert waking to fussiness and cry and makes it more difficult for the caregiver to open the infant's mouth or palm. Tactile palm stimulation at this time elicits a firm, almost spastic grasp in contrast to the soft grasp and gentle finger movements typical for a quiet awake or alert infant. During drowsiness, the responsivity to palmar stimulation strikingly decreases. Similarly, tactile stimulation of the oral area elicits increased oral responses, rooting, sucking, or mouth opening with increasing hunger or fussiness and decreased oral responses and decreased resistance against attempts to open the infant's mouth with the transition to drowsiness and sleep.

However, parents may have other reasons for touching, holding, or exploring infant hands. They may use patterns similar to those described above for a playful stimulation or for responding to the infant's initiative in stretching arms to the caregiver. They may first use the exploration of hands in order to assess infant state and then modify this pattern for arousing. Probably for this reason, we have found a significantly higher occurrence of hand exploration (35.41 percent of interaction time) than mouth exploration (8.09 percent of interaction time) but no significant correlation between both types of exploration in 20 German middle-class mothers interacting with 3-month-olds during laboratory observations (H. Papoušek, M. Papoušek, & Harris, unpublished data). Obviously only a more detailed analysis of the interactional structure can provide further differentiation of observed behaviors.

In this connection, a closer look at the parental baby talk may be particularly helpful. The lexical content in referencing utterances (see the methodological section) frequently indicates to which parental strategy the exploration of infant hands may belong. Executing utterances may then include elements influencing the infant's behavioral–emotional state, such as soothing or arousing melodic contours in the prosody of baby talk, thus confirming the meaning of hand exploration. The melodic contours, so typically enhanced in parental baby talk in general (M. Papoušek

& H. Papoušek, 1981a), have been found to depend significantly on the infant's state and on the interactional context rather than on the syntactic structures as in adult–adult dialogues (H. Papoušek, M. Papoušek, & Koester, 1986). The interrelations between infant state and parental melodic contours are universal across sex as they are equal in both mothers and fathers. They are also dialectical in the sense that parents try to monitor the infant state while responding to it. As we are going to explain later, interventions corresponding to intuitive didactic intentions cannot be overlooked in the classification of the interactional context. In our interpretation, parents, while responding to changes in the infant's state, also try to influence the state particularly by modifying melodic contours for this purpose (see section on relation to integrative processes).

Yet another way to elucidate the meaning of parental behaviors is through experimental analysis. Caregivers certainly collect information on the infant's state through various channels, not only tactile, proprioceptive, and auditory, but also visual. While looking at the infant's face, they can read expressions of emotions as well as transitions between sleep and waking. The position and gestures of infant hands also provide distinct information. Whereas raised, half-open palms, quietly moving fingers, and upper extremities partly stretched toward the parent characterize social interaction in alert infants, prolonged periods of closed fists on both sides are indicative of transitions to fussiness or crying. Conversely, a decrease in muscle tone during transitions to sleep leads to a decrease in finger movements and gradual dropping down of hands and arms until the extremities rest motionless at the sides of the infant (H. Papoušek & M. Papoušek, 1977a). A symbolic representation of these visual cues in our drawings mentioned in the methodological section has offered a convenient possibility for testing the effectiveness of such cues under experimental conditions and in childless populations, and thus for studying the universality of intuitive parental behaviors. In the drawings we modified, for instance, only two cues—eyes either closed or open and hands in positions indicating hunger, social interchange, passivity, and sleep—and combined them concordantly or discordantly. Kestermann (1982) used the drawings as slides for testing girls 7–8 years old, childless women, pregnant women, and mothers and fathers of 6-week-old infants. Subjects were asked to respond by offering one of three available utensils— a milk bottle, a pacifier, a toy—or by turning off a light as if preparing the "infant" for sleep. Inability to decide was to be signaled with the press of a button. The use of nonverbal responses was intended to reduce the role of rational decisions and increase the probability of intuitive behaviors. Kestermann's data confirmed the effectiveness of the selected cues on responses in all examined populations and demonstrated a dependence of appropriate responses and their latency upon the amount of previous experience. For instance, those fathers who had regularly been involved in care of infants did not significantly differ from experienced mothers. Kestermann's data also indicated a universality of the investigated competence across sex and age. Additional interviews revealed that the evidenced caregiving mostly escaped conscious awareness of the subjects.

Parental Repertoire Related to Visual Contact with Infants

No matter how firmly parents may believe that newborns cannot see, they endeavor to achieve a direct, eye-to-eye visual contact with the newborn from the first interchanges. They seek a vertically parallel, face-to-face position toward the infant and use various forms of stimulation in order to increase the probability of visual contact. This parental tendency is rather unique in the animal world. Not even primate parents, other than humans, have been reported to try to capture the infant's sight, although nonhuman primates may carefully observe newborns and infants and sporadically be in eye-to-eye contact with them (Ehardt & Blount, 1984). Looking behavior in primate social groups has not yet received sufficient attention, and has been mainly considered as a function of the dominance network (Chance & Jolly, 1970). Humans, of course, have good reasons for drawing infant attention to the parental face since facial behaviors mediate relevant messages including instructions for a proper production of speech sounds and for oral feeding competence. Moreover, while matching infants' facial expressions parents also provide a "biological mirror," thus contributing to the development of self-awareness in their infants (H. Papoušek & M. Papoušek, 1977a). In an earlier study (H. Papoušek & M. Papoušek, 1974), we developed a method for isolating individual components, characteristic for a mirror picture of self, and demonstrated in a two-choice design that 5-month-old infants detect and prefer eye-to-eye contact with their own mirror image. The reinforcing role of eye-to-eye contact in mother–infant attachment has been discussed by Robson (1967) and Rheingold (1961), among others.

Two nonvocal patterns of parental behaviors during interactions with infants deserve special attention: the regulation of the eye-to-eye distance between parents and infants and the use of a greeting behavior for reinforcing eye-to-eye contact.

Parents regularly use two different eye-to-eye distances. When watching and treating an infant who is not attending to them, parents prefer an "observational distance" of 40–50 cm, which generally corresponds to adult reading distance. However, as soon as the infant shows interest in communicative interchange, parents shorten that distance by half (22.5 cm on the average) using it as a "dialogic distance." As reported earlier (Schoetzau & H. Papoušek, 1977), mothers, both primiparas and multiparas, use such distance regulation on the first postpartum days independently of their knowledge of the visual capacity of newborns. This distance regulation does not depend on the mutual position of mothers and infants. Mothers demonstrate distance regulation when holding newborns in arms, having them on the lap, or standing at a diapering table on which newborns lie. It has remained unclear whether some feedback cues guide the distance regulation (Schoetzau, 1979) or whether the shorter distance may compensate for the newborn's poor visual abilities. Although this hypothesis can be supported by some data on the newborn's insufficient visual acuity and accommodation (Haynes, White, & Held, 1965; Lewis, Maurer, & Kay, 1977; Miranda, 1970), it has been questioned by Salapatek, Bechtold, and Bushnell (1976). Haynes and colleagues (1965) suggested a short distance of 19 cm for optimal visual stimulation of newborns. Salapatek and colleagues showed in a retinoscopic study that the refractive power of the eye lens is not stable, but depends, among other things, on the infant's behavioral state. Another reason for the selection of distance regulation might be a supportive role of size constancy in the infant's conceptualization of parental face. The parental use of the short dialogic distance combined with various arousing stimulations might, therefore, represent a global, manifold compensation for the initial constraints in visual, attentional, and cognitive competences in young infants (see also Aslin, Chapter 1 of this volume).

Once eye-to-eye contact is reached, parents of young infants regularly carry out a greeting behavior beginning with a slight retroflexion of the head, raised eyebrows, widely open eyes (often to the degree of a positive Möbius sign), and slightly opened mouth. This is followed by a smile or a vocal greeting (H. Papoušek & M. Papoušek, 1979b). The latency of the greeting lies between 400 and 800 msec, within the range of intuitive responses, in both mothers and fathers (H. Papoušek, M. Papoušek, & Haekel, unpublished material). Lack of awareness on the part of parents, as shown by interview data, and the inability to control the greeting behavior following experimental instructions confirm the intuitive character of these behaviors. In the social communication of adults and juveniles, a similar greeting (smiling, head tossing, eyebrow flashing, and nodding following visual contact, the so-called distance greeting) has been reported and cross-culturally studied by Eibl-Eibesfeldt (1968, 1972). The greeting response may be functional in prosocial greeting in general or functional in supporting the progeny's integrative development in particular. It is impossible to say which function evolved first. Regardless, the ontogeny of greeting behavior calls for more attention. Lifting eyebrows, for instance, has been reported in infants in the context of imitative capacities and interpreted as a cognitive achievement occurring only above 6 months of age (Meltzoff, 1981). However, lifting eyebrows might also be interpreted as a preadapted, species-specific response to achievement of visual contact, a universal response, gradually emerging during ontogeny. From this view, it is particularly interesting that a rather complete greeting as a response to visual contact has recently been reported by Haekel (1985) in 3-month-old infants.

Parents also try to encourage visual contact with infants by frequent use of two-level melodic contours (an example for which would be a cuckoo call in play) in the prosody of baby talk. In a detailed analysis of maternal baby talk to 21 infants 2 months old, of German, middle-class, urban mothers (M. Papoušek & H. Papoušek, 1984), an intention to reach visual contact was clearly indicated in the lexical content of 35.3 percent of all referencing utterances ($n = 742$). Together referencing and executing utterances in the corresponding subprograms ($n = 2084$) showed a specific profile in the frequency of individual melodic contours that was significantly different from the profile of other subprograms (see section on relation to integrative processes). The two-level contours reached the maximum frequency (45.9 percent). For referencing utterances alone, the peak of two-level contours was even higher (56.9 percent) (H. Papoušek et al., 1986).

Parental Repertoire Related to Elementary Communicative Skills

As is not the case with the communication of other animals, the proportion of genetically transmitted, rather universal, but rigid means of communication among humans is relatively low in comparison to specific, plastic means characterizing individual cultures, communities, and also individual caregivers. Maximum plasticity is found in symbolic communication in humans, especially speech. The most fundamental and universal communicative skills may be the first to be learned during ontogeny and may have a didactic counterpart in intuitive parenting during evolution. At least three aspects of these communicative skills are of particular interest: the participation of nonverbal messages, the use of a dialogic communication, and the cues identifying individual caregivers.

The Use of Nonverbal Communication

Although in comparison with speech, nonverbal communication provides only a limited number of patterns, the human can utilize it for far more variable and adaptive forms of communication than can other mammals or birds. The human attends selectively to invariant features, detecting them in complex configurations, conceptualizing them, and extrapolating them beyond the momentary situational context up to the level of symbolic signs. In our opinion, early during human evolution, it was probably highly relevant to monitor constantly the neighbors' behaviors, and to read in them potential cues not only about the presence of food or predators but also about the neighbors' hostile approach and threatening situations in general. Consequently, a complex capacity to read and interpret various nonverbal behaviors rather than an emission of uniform signals has been favored by selection in human evolution. Most of the nonverbal messages used by humans are composite messages, including combinations of gestures, facial expressions, and vocal prosody. In addition, they include syntactic and metacommunicative elements since their sequential ordering is relevant, and, in some cases, signals communicate on communication. One signal can assign a special meaning to other following signals, such as in play situations where a play-face can signal that none of the following signals, even though aggressive, is meant to be taken seriously.

The fact that nonverbal cues can be read as global expressions of complex interrelations between individual and environment has crucially economized human communication. It has enabled humans to cope with the constraints on the rational processes of thought that allow one to process only a limited amount of information at a time. However, the meaning assigned to nonverbal cues in human cultures seldom corresponds to scientific principles and, therefore, should not mislead, for instance, infancy researchers attempting to classify nonverbal cues. This danger concerns expressions of emotions in particular.

For instance, oral and facial behaviors function not only as expressions of emotions but primarily as physiological mechanisms ensuring either adequate intake of nutrition or elimination of dangerous agents, eaten by accident. These primary functions depend on the chemical properties of such agents. Acids can be detected rather quickly on the tip of the tongue and responded to by firm mouth closing, heavy salivation, and spitting. Other agents can be detected only later on the base of tongue and responded to with vomiting. Resulting observable cues probably served as important monitoring cues to the human as an omnivore earlier during evolution, and elements of them may have been secondarily incorporated as symbolic patterns into other complex configurations of nonverbal messages.

Such reflexive oral and facial responses function in newly born human infants (Steiner, 1977) and rabbit pups (Ganchrow, Oppenheimer, & Steiner, 1979) and have been interpreted as signs of hedonic dimensions. Human infants may respond with similar responses to deviations in the smell or in the taste of breast milk caused by maternal menstruation or by unusual ingredients in the mother's diet. It would be false to interpret such signs of "disgust" as expressions of emotional attitude to the mother.

Similar and perhaps even more relevant may be the history of oral and facial behaviors involved in the production of vocal sounds, and serving not only as models to be imitated by the learners of the first speech but also as components in the

structure of symbolic nonverbal messages. The participation of movements necessary for the production of the "sh" sound in nonverbal messages used for silencing
the social environment can be mentioned as one example.

Theories on emotions, unfortunately, have confused rather than elucidated the
classification of nonverbal behaviors. Here we can only refer the reader to much
more detailed discussions of this problem elsewhere (e.g., Campos, Caplowitz Barrett, Lamb, Goldsmith, & Sternberg, 1983). Our present interest concerns those
categories of nonverbal communication that may be fundamental to didactic interactions, preverbal in particular, and that, therefore, only partly relate to emotional
expressions.

The infant's interest in parental face and voice is extrinsically nourished by parental behaviors mentioned earlier in relation to visual contact. The parent's amount
of vocal stimulation is individually very variable, but on the average quite abundant.
In dialogues between 14 German couples and their 3-month-olds, mothers produced
35.15 (S.D. = 5.89) and fathers 35.06 (S.D. = 8.87) utterances per minute during
2-min spontaneous face-to-face interactions in a homelike laboratory setting (M.
Papoušek, H. Papoušek, & Bornstein, 1985). In a study with alternating interactional partners, 20 German mothers produced 36.80 (S.D. = 9.10) utterances when
interacting with their own 3-month-olds, and 37.69 (S.D. = 8.85) utterances during
interactions with strange 3-month-olds (H. Papoušek & M. Papoušek, unpublished
data). The interindividual variability was similarly high in both mothers and fathers.
However, the intraindividual variability appeared to be low and influenced little by
alternating infants. Parental vocalization, being accompanied with a distinct display
of articulatory movements, provides numerous models to be imitated by the infant
during speech acquisition.

A teaching intention, though unknowing, is even more obvious in feeding situations when parents, both mothers and fathers, instruct infants by demonstrating
oral activities (mouth opening, lip movements, licking) concordant with the situational context (M. Papoušek & H. Papoušek, 1981d). This tendency develops early
and has been demonstrated in infants at the age of 9–12 months when they become
capable of offering food to others. The universality of the behavioral pattern across
sex and age indicates preadaptedness and should be studied across cultures, too.

Other facial expressions may carry less instructional value as such, but especially
when accompanied by corresponding vocalizations may nevertheless communicate
encouragement or discouragement to the infant. One can see a clear gradation in
such parental messages, ranging from pleasure and excited encouragement to rejection, warning, and threat or fear. In previous forms of family life, exposure to
dangers and the display of signs of fear alerting conspecifics were probably more
frequent and more necessary. Due to the domestication of family life in most contemporary cultures, however, it is now less common to observe extreme escalation
of alarming or discouraging signals, particularly in interactions with young infants.
Perhaps one relic of the earlier joint alarm signaling system can be seen in the phenomenon of infants' responding empathetically to the cry of another newborn. Sim-
mer (1971) used a serial analysis to show that vocal properties associated with the
newborn's cry are effective in promoting crying in peers. These findings have since
been confirmed by Sagi and Hoffman (1976) and Martin and Clarke (1982).

With the reduction of visible dangers in modern families, the parent–infant dyad
can afford to pay much more attention to fine-grained qualities of mutual com-

munication in accordance with the infant's integrative development and with the fulfillment of educational expectancies in the parent. Signs indicative of what parents like or dislike, which infant behaviors they tend to support or reject on the one hand and parental interest in feedback signs on the infant's ability to cope with the stimulational offer on the other, represent the prevailing type of nonverbal messages as recorded in our naturalistic observations. In the same vein, we can say that the described circumstances have also significantly increased the potential of didactic support to the infant's integrative competence. The fact that infants actually seek and are differentially influenced by parental nonverbal signals has been elegantly demonstrated by Campos, Hiatt, Ramsay, Henderson, and Svejda (1978) in studies of infants exposed to a visual cliff. These studies have led to the conclusion that infants develop a fear of heights by associating the phenomenon of depth perception with the mother's nonverbal reactions to a "near fall" by her infant.

Various examples illustrate the fine-grained guidance in the prosody of parental talk to infants. In our analyses of 2084 utterances of 21 German, middle-class mothers speaking to 2-month-old infants, encouraging and discouraging maternal tendencies appeared to be related to two distinctly different distributional profiles of melodic contours.

The distribution of encouraging utterances showed maximum rising contours (68.5 percent). Such contours were typically used to encourage goal-directed activities or the achievement of visual contact. Any detectable success was reinforced by mothers with utterances with "praising contours" including maximum (71.0 percent) falling contours or contours with short rise and long fall (bell-right contours of Stern, Spieker, Barnett, & MacKain, 1983; Stern, Spieker, & MacKain, 1982) with strikingly elongated vowels (M. Papoušek & H. Papoušek, 1984). Praising contours were often accompanied by smiles in mothers.

Rejections occurred rarely and were quickly followed by soothing utterances. Fast rhythmical sounds of a staccato type or one-level contours in less elongated vowels characterized discouraging utterances and were often accompanied by facial frowning. Soothing utterances included maximum slowly falling contours and a soft voice at a slow tempo and lower pitch.

A certain metacommunicative significance may be seen in expressions and gestures associated with attempts of prosocial approach, special attention, and care. Both parents and strangers characteristically stretch their hands with open palms toward an infant, hold their heads in an oblique position (lateral flexion), and smile at the infant when approaching. These behaviors serve to signal friendly and helpful intentions in the communication that may follow. Montagner (1978), studying the oblique position of the head in preschool children, assigned a relevant role to this head positioning in the establishment of social relations among children and between children and caregivers. The play-face, comparatively studied by van Hoof (1972), is yet another example of signs signaling that the following interactional communication is going to have a special meaning. In this case, the play-face signals playfulness, that is, that the behaviors to follow are not to be taken seriously. Again, the low degree of conscious awareness of these messages and the high degree of universality across sex, age, cultures, and species indicate an adaptive relevance in evolution.

Not only do parents display their own nonverbal messages to the infant, for example, anticipating or interpreting the potential relevance or impact of a certain environmental event, but they also carefully detect and read the corresponding messages in the behaviors displayed by the infant. Since the infant's behavioral repertoire is richer in facial than in vocal expressiveness during the first months, facial behaviors attract parental attention in particular. Almost all facial expressions of emotions seen in adults are also present in newborns (Oster & Ekman, 1978). The form of these expressions may be less stereotypical and not yet distinctly connected to environmental circumstances, but nevertheless it is clearly identifiable. As mentioned earlier, several specific facial configurations relate to smell and taste (Steiner, 1977) and do not escape parental attention in feeding situations. Emde, Kligman, Reich, and Wade (1978), using data based on ratings of still photographs of 3.5-month-old infants, described three dimensions of emotional expression that can be detected: hedonic (happy vs. unhappy, upset, frustrated); activation (startled, excited, concentrated vs. relaxed, asleep); and external–internal (curious, interested vs. bored, sleepy). Mothers have also reported the gradual emergence of expressions of surprise, fear, and anger in their own infants, although their observations were based on the complex behavior patterns occurring in everyday life (Klinnert, Sorce, Emde, Stenberg, & Gaensbauer, 1984).

Any impression that the nonverbal communication among humans consists of a given set of cues and matching responses would be false. Not only is the human being capable of detecting invariant features in any type of behavior irrespective of its communicative preadaptedness, but many interactive behaviors may gain manifold communicative meanings according to their interactional context. For this reason, it is particularly difficult to interpret matching behaviors that are seen as imitative by some researchers but may mean emotional sharing, duetting, or attunement to others. We shall return to this problem in the next section.

Now that nonverbal messages can be recorded and studied microanalytically, we can begin to understand their role in the early development of communication. Nonverbal communication is seldom a mere background noise during verbal interchanges; more often it represents a separate avenue for fast communication in areas where verbal communication leaves us helpless, for instance, in communication with preverbal infants. Moreover, nonverbal skills of vocal communication may be the sine qua non for the acquisition of human speech, providing the first and abundant opportunities for learning how to code, categorically classify, abstract across sensory modalities, and symbolize so that the first word may then appear and function as an abstract symbol.

Dialogic Structure of Interaction

The introduction of interactional concepts in infancy research has drawn attention to the structure of bidirectional interchanges in the dyadic communication. Both dyadic partners can communicate either in organized alternating or parallel sequences or in independent sequences. Some degree of order facilitates communication for various reasons, such as the mental inability to process larger amounts of simultaneous information or the necessity to use sequential rather than parallel ordering of information in verbal communication. The dialogic structure has obviously been favored in evolution. Disorder is mostly perceived as a disturbance. In studies of preverbal infants, the interest in dialogues has focused on nonvocal behaviors, for example, neonatal sucking (Kaye, 1977, 1984) or visual contact in later preverbal infancy (Kaye & Fogel, 1980; Tronick et al., 1979).

Sucking in human newborns follows a burst–pause pattern, uncommon among other mammals. As Kaye has observed, sucking together with maternal jiggling during pauses may be the first postpartum interchange with a dialogic structure. This interchange is initiated by maternal activity. Around 26 weeks, another form of turn taking was identified by Kaye and Fogel (1980) in facial expressions and visual contacts. Prior to this age the infant's facial expressions are random. Mutual influence and bilateral learning of rules for turn taking become increasingly evident around 6 months and lead to dialoguelike nonvocal interchanges. For instance, during skill teaching, the infant's turning away from the task acts as a signal for the mother to intervene (Kaye, 1984).

We can only speculate on how much such early use of dialogic structures in non-verbal interchanges may contribute to the acquisition of the dialogue skill typical for verbal communications in adults. Nevertheless, this skill is well established already at the age of 1 and 2 years when speech begins (Schaffer, Collis, & Parsons, 1977). Schaffer and colleagues point out that the absence of turn taking may be adaptive in certain cases, for instance, as a warning. Studies of dialogic structures in vocal interchanges between mothers and their 3-month-old infants (Anderson, Vietze, & Dodecki, 1977; Stern, Jaffe, Beebe, & Bennett, 1975) have revealed both coactional vocalizations, sometimes called duetting or chorusing, and alternations. Interestingly, as indicated by Stern and colleagues (1975), alternations were more frequent when mothers were serious or tutorial, whereas coactional vocalizations characterized dyads in positive arousal states. Stern and colleagues concluded that coactional vocalization contributes to the mother–infant attachment.

In dialogues between 21 German mothers and their 2-month-old infants, we (M. Papoušek and H. Papoušek, unpublished data) analyzed 1112 infant utterances and found: (1) that on average 42 percent of the duration of one infant utterance overlapped with the maternal utterance; and (2) that the overlaps increased during times of strongly expressed signs of either pleasure and joy (67 percent) or fussiness and crying (58 percent). In this study, speaker switches occurred on the average 17 times per 3 min. Mothers held the floor for 88.9 percent of the time, while infants did so for 11.1 percent of the time. Maternal turns averaged 8.5 sec while infant turns averaged 0.8 sec.

In another study, comparing 14 fathers and mothers during dialogues with 3-month-old infants (M. Papoušek, H. Papoušek, & Bornstein, 1985), the dialogic structure was more evident than in maternal interchanges with 2-month-old infants. However, parental sex showed no significant influence upon the parameters of dialogic structure. Interindividual variability in effects upon vocal turn taking could be analyzed in the study of interdyadically alternating partners among 20 mothers with their own and two strange infants (M. Papoušek & H. Papoušek, unpublished data). This study revealed that infant individuality had relatively little influence on vocal turn taking. Mothers in all cases represented the main factor giving vocal interchanges the character of a dialogue.

Coactional duetting, mostly associated with vocal matching in pitch and prosodic contours, was typical of vivid, joyful interactions in dyads displaying signs of increased, pleasurable emotionality. Occasionally, mothers were found so talkative and inattentive to their infants' signals that the resulting communication represented a maternal monologue allowing no turn taking. The occurrence of overlaps increased during infantile fussing or crying and, unlike in duetting, was connected with either signs of rejection or more frequently signs of soothing in the prosody of parental speech.

Obviously, a certain degree of organizational order of both vocal and nonverbal interchanges is so advantageous that supportive tendencies have been selected as universal across sex and age and function during the earliest stages of ontogeny. However, the dialogic structure of interchanges is not the only adaptive form. While turn taking may be important for the development of verbal communication in particular, coactional duetting, for instance, may serve to strengthen emotional bonds between interacting individuals under other interactional circumstances. No computer-aided analysis of the temporal structures in vocal interchanges will, therefore, lead to their better understanding unless interactional contexts are taken into consideration and classified as well. A seemingly perfect turn taking can, for instance, be found in situations where, due to various upsetting circumstances, infants reduce vocalizations to short and infrequent utterances while mothers prolong pauses in speech trying to detect the cause of upset.

Identification of Individual Caregivers

Among the higher vertebrates, it is common to many species that individuals are able to distinguish one another by particular signals (Wilson, 1975). For example, the ability to recognize identification calls between parents and the young in birds living in dense, clamorous breeding colonies is astonishing. Equally remarkable is the use of scent marking in many mammal species. Consequently, it should not be surprising to find analogous parent–infant identification functioning in humans in spite of the present lack of evidence. The general necessity to prevent exchange of newborns by sophisticated marking in maternity hospitals refutes the existence of some safe, biologically determined mechanism of mother–infant identification. Conversely, infancy research has provided increasing evidence that the newborn's mind, much as it may be a "tabula rasa" relative to data-based information on the new postpartum environment, is still far from being unprepared in procedural terms to process information, including intrauterine, in complex ways. The set of identifying cues in humans may, therefore, involve more complex and flexible structures of variable cues, like the dynamics of vocal or nonvocal interactional behaviors. Their processing may involve more adaptive operations than mere imprinting or simple conditioning. The identification of the most relevant caregivers is, however, only one aspect of the more complex question of familiarity, which also includes closely connected possibilities of anticipating and controlling parental behaviors according to the infant's own needs.

We now know that vocal sounds alone allow identification of individual human beings with a reliability comparable to fingerprints. Newborns have been reported to differentiate mothers at least roughly from strangers on the base of prenatal experience with maternal voice (De Casper & Fifer, 1980). Within the first 4 months the infant's ability to identify voices increases (Brown, 1979; Mehler, Bertonuci, Barriere, & Jassik-Gerschenfeld, 1978; Mills & Melhuish, 1974). In order to find out which parameters of maternal speech might facilitate the infant's identification of maternal voice we have analyzed vocal interchanges between 20 German mothers and 3-month-old infants in a study using interdyadic alternation of partners (M. Papoušek & H. Papoušek, unpublished data). The design of this study allows assessment of individual variability in dyadic interactions as explained in the section on methodological problems. We have assumed that the more parental behaviors are determined by the genotype or temperament of the parent the less they are affected by the alternation of infant partners. In statistical terms, the identification features in maternal speech correspond to trait factors. In the present chapter, we only want to point out individually stable characteristics in the temporal structure of maternal speech. We have found such characteristics in the onset-to-onset intervals of maternal vocalizations, duration of pauses, number of syllables per utterance, vocalization rate, speech tempo, and the frequency of rhythmic stimulation.

The role of rhythmicity in maternal speech has been neglected in interactional research, for instance, in regard to the intrauterine audible environment of fetuses. Salk (1973) drew attention to another part of this environment—maternal heartbeat—and speculated on the role of heartbeats in fetal imprinting relative to postpartum emotional ties. Among the 20 mothers in our study, a total of 238 rhythmic vocal utterances were found in 15 mothers. There was no difference in the mean periodicity in interactions with own versus strange infants, 3.98 versus 3.99 beats per second, respectively. The distribution of periodicities was in both cases large (S.D. = 1.09 and 1.33, respectively) and asymmetric, showing accumulation in three major areas: (1) musical rhythms as expressed in singing (1.86 beats per second, concerning 5.5 percent of rhythmic utterances); (2) rhythmic repetitive syllables (3.39 beats per second, concerning 56.7 percent of rhythmic utterances); and (3) rhythmic vocal noises (5.33 beats per second, concerning 37.8 percent of rhythmic utterances). Individual subclasses of rhythmicity differed significantly in tempo ($p < .01$) and appeared related to the interactional context. Musical rhythmicity (hummed, whistled, or sung melodies) was used for soothing; rhythmic repetitive syllables were used mainly in playful interactions and less frequently for encouraging visual contact or for soothing; rhythmic vocal noises (e.g., tongue clicking) were used almost exclusively for encouraging visual contact and on rare occasions for soothing. Similarly, the significance of interactional context has recently been evidenced in the rhythmicity of nonvocal, physical patterns of maternal stimulation (Koester, H. Papoušek, & M. Papoušek, 1985).

The presence of multiple types of rhythmicity contradicts any dominant role of either a rhythm derived from maternal heartbeats (approximately 1.0–1.2 beats per second) or a rhythm determined by any other single, common pacemaker. Instead we suggest that the individual rhythmicity depends to some degree on the type of repetitive behaviors, and that only a context-related intraindividual stability can represent one of the cues contributing to identification of caregivers by human infants.

Comments on Individual Variability

The idea that human parental behaviors may be determined at least partly by endogenous trait factors selected during evolution and show not only short-term adjustments to fluctuations in infantile state factors but also long-term strategies of didactic significance accentuates the interest in individual variability of interactional behaviors. Parent–infant relations used to be treated as stimulus–response situations, with parents being viewed as mere stimulators and infants as mere receivers of stimulation with no autonomy. Such conceptions have long been rejected. However, a better understanding, for instance, of the infant's autonomy or of the interactional reciprocity requires a better assessment of the degrees to which parental and infantile behaviors contribute to the variability of interactional processes.

In the section on methodological problems, we explained the difficulties connected with analyses of individual variability in interactional designs, and our attempts to overcome these difficulties. We have found it helpful to utilize both naturalistic observations of dyadic interactions and experimental analyses of selected interactional behaviors under laboratory conditions including narrow stimulus–response designs outside of dyadic interactions. In the same vein, we have applied descriptive statistical models where confirmative ones are not legitimate, using them for guidance in the invention of new empirical ways of verification. One such empirical way has been the design of interdyadic alternation of interacting partners.

Although our approach represents only a beginning of a difficult avenue we want to share with the reader the present state of our conceptions on the determination of interactional behaviors, since any further progress necessitates broad scientific attention. We want to focus upon the question of how far trait factors can be assessed and distinguished from state factors and context factors in dyadic parent–infant interactions. In this type of interaction, the results of statistical analyses can be tested relatively easily with critical logic due to polar differences between partners, for instance, in integrative and communicative competences or in the regulation of behavioral–emotional state that make some outcomes of analyses predictable.

The relative determination of variables in vocal interchanges is characterized by the ratio between the average maternal and infantile interpartner variabilities (see the section on methodological problems). Values lower than 1 indicate that the variable is more strongly determined by the mother. Among maternal variables, values equal to or lower than .6 were found in speech density, speech segmentation, reduction of speech complexity, proportion of whispered utterances, and frequency of rhythmic stimulation. Maternal contribution to the total variance of these variables was high. Such determination of vocal variables corresponds to the assumption that parental didactics tend to provide a qualitatively homogeneous vocal input to young infants (M. Papoušek, H. Papoušek, & Bornstein, 1985); however, the alternation of interacting partners helps differentiate that tendency in detail.

Other variables of maternal vocalizations are more likely to change in response to infant state or to interactional context, and are characterized by values between .6 and .9 in the descriptor of relative determination mentioned above. This category of variables includes the repertoire and forms of melodic contours, verbal and melodic repetitiveness, playfulness in repetitive utterances, turn taking, types of sentences, and elicitation of infant matches in pitch and in pitch contour. Maternal contribution to the total variance was lower than in the preceding category of variables, but still higher than the infant contribution. The effects of two infant states—pleasant excitement and fussiness—were selectively analyzed in samples with no alternation of partners and found significant in the repertoire of melodic contours in parental baby talk (H. Papoušek et al., 1986).

Availability of process variables allowed the use of analysis of variance in relation to speech segmentation and to tempo of articulation. Generally, the main effects for both mothers and infants were significant but relatively small in comparison to strong interaction effects.

On the whole, a series of vocal variables is more or less determined by maternal contributions, part of them as strongly and as independently of alternating partners as to indicate effects of trait factors, probably of an endogenous origin. Similarly strong effects of infantile trait factors have not been revealed with the applied measures. Some vocal variables, namely, the infantile rate of utterances, expression of discomfort, articulatory competence, matching of speech sounds, and elicitation of maternal matching of speech sounds, were affected by infant factors more than by maternal factors; however, the value of the descriptor of relative determination only slightly exceeded 1.1 and the infant's contribution to the total variance remained on the middle level. Trait factors indicated in these findings seem to represent the developmental level of articulatory competence in infants.

The remaining vocal variables appeared to be determined by both partners to the same degree; the value of relative determination moved between .9 and 1.1. Both mothers and infants contributed to the total variance more effectively in relation to maternal prolongation of syllables, tempo of articulation, and tempo of rhythmic stimulation, however, less effectively in relation to the distribution of infant vocal categories, to the frequency of infant matching, and to both frequency and quality of maternal matching. A considerable part of the total variance is thus influenced by context factors.

Thus the analysis of variability in vocal interchanges indicates both the presence of trait factors, evident much more in mothers than in infants, and the contributions of state factors and context factors. Although the effectiveness of trait factors is relatively weak in infants, it is not at all negligible and contradicts the conception of infants as mere receivers of stimulation or as individuals with no autonomy. On the contrary, there is sufficient evidence for reciprocity in the determination of vocal interchange.

In its first application, the design of interdyadic alternation of interactional partners helped maximize trait factors while minimizing state factors and context factors. All interactions were observed under equal laboratory conditions and scheduled so as to eliminate the influence of hunger and circadian changes of waking state. In spite of that, minor fluctuations of behavioral–emotional state could not be prevented in infants; some effects of state fluctuations are known from previous studies (M. Papoušek, H. Papoušek, & Bornstein, 1985). A considerable portion of vocal interchanges are obviously determined by context factors. Since environmental interventions during observations were almost eliminated, the main contextual effect obviously resulted from the interactional process itself. Incidental combinations or sequences of variables might have represented problematic situations to the infant, causing changes in vocalization, or might have elicited various didactic interventions in the mother, for instance, attempts to encourage matching, to offer a playful interchange, or to reinforce the infant's attention with a surprising change in utterances. Rich observational evidence of such episodes helps conceptualize similar context factors; however, their experimental control and analysis are extremely difficult and require further empirical studies.

RELATION TO INTEGRATIVE PROCESSES

The concepts that fundamental participation of integrative processes is involved in the regulation of all behavioral categories and that integrative processes may have evolved in an interaction with supportive interventions from the social environment also lead to the question of what particular integrative processes are involved. Attempts to answer this question may be premature because of the short history of research on intuitive parental didactics and in any event must be speculative since there is a dearth of knowledge about the neurobiological bases of the integrative processes. It may, however, be helpful if we draw more interdisciplinary attention to this topic.

From the recent surveys on early learning and cognitive development (Gratch & Schatz, Chapter 4, Rovee-Collier, Chapter 2, this volume; Harris, 1983; Olson & Sherman, 1983), it is evident that many aspects of cognitive development are still open to question in spite of extensive scientific investigation and seemingly solid theories such as that of Piaget (1983). Theoretical views often tend to narrow and separate phenomena, for instance, for classification, although those phenomena may function in a unity, or to see qualitative changes at the cost of neglecting the continuity of precursors.

For instance, the previous studies by the first author of this chapter on infant learning (H. Papoušek, 1961) revealed complex integrative processes where only the fundamental forms of conditioning were expected according to contemporary theories. The author's first attempt to employ the sucking response in a developmental analysis of conditioning capacities failed because of complex adaptive changes in oral behaviors during the first several months of age. Next, the author employed head turns with much greater success. However, it quickly became evident how complex integration might be involved in simple learning. Once newborns successfully learned an instrumental act for achieving a milk reinforcement under circumstances limited by the presence of an auditory signal, they made it evident within the first postpartum week that they integrated information from proprioceptive (head movement), gustatory (milk reinforcement), and auditory (limiting sound of bell) modalities (H. Papoušek, 1961, 1977). The integrated experience was stored for several days allowing a span of 5 days to be used as a maximum for occasional breaks in the series of consecutive sessions without affecting the whole learning process under investigation (H. Papoušek, 1961, 1967a, p. 253). In discriminative designs where two auditory signals (bell and buzzer) were used for differential responses in a random order, infants detected occasional regularities and used them as superstitious concepts in subsequent responding (H. Papoušek, 1979). The capability of detecting even more complex rules and developing adequate concepts was later confirmed in infants 4–5 months old (H. Papoušek & Bernstein, 1969).

Similarly, observable behaviors displayed by the infants were more complex than the simple head movements expected by the investigators. Head turning, probably as a behavior of high adaptive relevance and potentially representative of purposeful, intentional actions, was regularly accompanied by facial and vocal expressions depending on the course of learning. Earlier we discussed the contribution of such expressions to social interchanges between parents and infants. We remind the reader of this contribution in order to stress two points. First, parents distinctly try to find out what may be taking place in the infant's mind during interactions and depend on specific cues. Second, the infant's integrative engagement can be influenced by simple modifications of applied stimuli. Both points are relevant in relation to didactic interventions.

The rich repertoire of vocal and facial expressions, observable during learning sessions at the earliest age (for photographs of newborns, see H. Papoušek, 1967a, 1967b), was displayed not randomly but regularly in relation to the course of integrative processes under investigation. Difficulties in the integration of adaptive responses resulted in signs of unpleasant feelings, whereas successful adaptation elicited joy. Together with changes in general motility, heart rate, and respiration rate, facial and vocal expressions also indicated that infants often invest enough energy during integrative engagement so as to approach the relatively narrow limits of tolerance available to such young organisms for coping with problematic tasks. Paralleling integrative escalation, we saw overt escalation during problematic tasks starting with knitted eyebrows and proceeding to frowning, closed fists, and bodily stiffness, and finally signs of distress and crying. During the first 2 months, sudden transitions into a sleeplike state reminiscent of "playing possum" or "biological fuse" were also noted (Hopkins & van Wulfften Palthe, 1985; H. Papoušek, 1969; H. Papoušek & M. Papoušek, 1979a). When the infant solved a problematic task, the above facial and vocal expressions decreased in reverse order until smiles and vocal signs of pleasure appeared. The presence of such expressions allowed predictions of the outcome of learned responses and served as feedback information about different degrees of difficulty.

Considering the complexity of the above experiments, originally designed as simple stimulus–response models of learning, we can imagine how difficult it may be to analyze integrative operations involved in an interactional situation. For instance matching of facial expressions between parents and infants can be involved in imitation, empathy, communication of emotions, signs of integrative engagement, referencing, and attunement. Thus matching may serve as a discouraging example to interpreters of interactional situations. In order to make our task easier, we are going to concentrate upon vocal interchanges.

Adequacy of Stimulation in Vocal Interchanges

Vocal interchanges between parents and infants offer perhaps the best opportunities for illustrating didactic tendencies in intuitive caregiving. In order to understand their organization better, let us consider the first didactic goals and means in relation to the infant's integrative development. The first thinkable goal is to establish an initial system of preverbal communication as a prerequisite for the acquisition of speech. The next dominant goal, to support integrative development, is only the less visible side of the same coin. The script for pursuing the given goals must correspond to the special needs and constraints on the side of the less mature interactional partner.

Birth exposes newborns to a radical change in the environment that necessitates many physiological adaptations. For instance, control of breathing is not yet sufficiently regulated and with the exception of crying, infants are unable to modify expiration for communicative purposes. In these first weeks, spontaneous quiet vocalization is minimal in infants. Efforts to promote verbal communication would be dubious. Conversely, drawing infants' attention to oral and facial behaviors, prolonging vowel sounds, and exaggerating facial expressions (often only weakly displayed in adult–adult dialogue) would be meaningful didactically. A clear demonstration of the communicative potential in the prosody of speech, melodic contours of prolonged vowels in particular, offers communicative means that infants can modulate and utilize as early as during presyllabic stage. If there is an endogenous readiness for infants to match, echoing their quiet vocalizations might give a chance to elaborate on these vocalizations and simultaneously to offer infants contingent feedback. Thus infants may not only improve vocal sounds but also learn that their sounds are differentially appreciated by the social world. Typically, for instance, their joyful vocalizations are responded to by approval and fussy vocalizations by rejection. Through the rules and prerequisites of nonverbal communication, infants may become familiar with the caregiver's personality, allowing the infant to identify the caregiver and to manipulate adaptively the most relevant environment represented by the caregiver.

Obviously while describing individual points of this didactic script, we also distinctly relate to the characteristics of baby talk (motherese) and, it is hoped, make it understandable how many teaching lessons may be seen in it. Due to slow and unstable learning in young infants, the first didactic support must be delivered in small portions and simple forms for the infant to benefit. The support must be repeated many times during the infant's short periods of attention. The use of baby talk corresponds to this didactic principle. The general tendency per se to talk to infants is high and has been observed among English, American, Spanish, and Dutch families (Blount & Padgug, 1977; Snow, De Blauw, & von Roosmalen, 1979). Not only do parents talk to newborns immediately after birth (Parke & O'Leary, 1976; Parke, O'Leary, & West, 1972), but female and male strangers tend equally to talk to newborns (Rheingold & Adams, 1980). Parke, Grossmann, and Tinsley (1981) reported equivalent tendencies in American and German parents to talk and display affection to their babies. These tendencies increased when parents were holding infants. The propensity in the adult when talking to babies to modify speech for this purpose in specific, rather universal ways gains a particular significance in this regard.

With this in mind, it is clear why even the earliest qualitative transitions, observed in integrative, social, and emotional development around the age of 8 weeks (for survey see Emde, 1984; H. Papoušek & M. Papoušek, 1984b), cannot be determined merely by maturation or be independent of supportive intervention.

As infants pass into their second month of life, their behaviors become more predictable. Periods of active waking are more regularly distributed and increase. Better motor coordination makes their movements easier to interpret. There is growing attention to human faces and greater variation in fundamental voicing and more distinctly developed features of babyishness. In combination, these characteristics make infants more appreciable interactive partners. The reciprocity of interchanges grows and acquires typical human features. The involvement of integrative processes may become more visible; their visibility, however, soon reveals an astonishing complexity.

Significance for the Main Integrative Processes

In the many studies on infant attention (see Olson & Sherman, 1983, for a survey), it was found that from the very beginning of postnatal learning adaptive behavior is influenced by the degree of prior familiarity with an environmental event and by the degree to which the event is contingent upon the infant's behavior. The adaptive relevance of these interrelations can be seen in their universalities, and also in their close ties to motivation, cognition, and emotion. Piaget (1952) pointed out the motivational function of discrepancy and its facilitative role in cognitive advancement. He also stressed that too much discrepancy between perceptual events and internal schemata may elicit fear or avoidance. Hebb (1949) and Hunt (1965) have similarly incorporated the notion of discrepancy into models of behavioral regulations. Many of our observations have led us to a belief that the infant is as strongly pulled by the expectation of pleasure connected with successful cognitive operations as the infant is pushed by unpleasant feelings resulting from incongruity, dissonance, or failure in adjustment (H. Papoušek & M. Papoušek, 1979a). A similar point of view has recently been expressed by Rheingold (1985). Analogous motivational ties become particularly evident in observable behaviors if the infant detects an event in the environment that can be controlled by the infant's action. These ties are characteristic of instrumental learning in the laboratory and of many episodes occurring during parent–infant interactions under naturalistic circumstances (Goldberg, 1977; H. Papoušek, 1961, 1967a, 1967b, 1977; Watson, 1972). The parental tendency to make oneself familiar, predictable, and controllable in interactions with infants corresponds to the infant's motivation (H. Papoušek, & M. Papoušek, 1984a). As stressed earlier in this chapter, parents offer many opportunities to confront infants with contingencies, for example, in greeting behaviors in response to the achievement of visual contact or in modifications of speech addressed to infants.

In our own analyses of baby talk, various data have indicated the role of an effective didactic tool. Comparing maternal and paternal patterns of baby talk to 3-month-old infants (M. Papoušek, H. Papoušek, & Bornstein, 1985), we have found that both German parents equivalently reduce the average duration of utterances to 1.1 sec and 1.0 sec, respectively, lengthen pauses between utterances, and speak at a slow rate of 3.5 and 3.8 syllables per second of vocalization, respectively. Similar but less pronounced changes were found by Fernald and Simon (1977) in German mothers talking to newborns and by Garnica (1977), Phillips (1973), and Snow (1977) in parents talking to older infants. We have also found in observing 20 German mothers talking to 3-month-old infants that parents reduce the linguistic complexity of utterances. Complete sentences appear in only 33.8 percent of maternal utterances. One-syllable utterances are common, occurring 38.9 percent of the time. Utterances with a maximum of 3 syllables occur 61.2 percent of the time. Since in this sample the design of alternating partners was used, we have been able to assess the relative contribution of infants and mothers to the variability in individual parameters. We found that there were no differences depending on the presence of own versus strange infants. Neither of these parameters was influenced by alternating infants. Mothers in this sample also prolonged syllables (mean duration = 0.32 sec) and decreased the rate of articulation (3.8 syllables per second of vocalization). These parameters were influenced by infant factors and maternal factors to a similar extent.

Parent-to-infant speech is characterized by a higher average pitch in various cultures and in both sexes (Ferguson, 1978; Garnica, 1977; Remick, 1976). Fernald and Simon (1977) reported a significant increase from 203 Hz to 247 Hz among 24 mothers talking to adults versus newborns. But no increase resulted when the mothers attempted to simulate baby talk in absence of newborns. Certain cues in the infant seem to elicit a nearly universal shift in the average pitch of adult speech and thus to distinguish speech addressed to infants. Jacobson, Boersma, Fields, and Olson (1983) asked eight mothers and eight fathers with children and eight female and eight male single adults without children to read two kinds of text under four conditions: baseline, to a pretended but absent child, to a present child, and to a present infant. The fundamental frequency gradually and significantly shifted from 209.1 Hz to 254.5 Hz in females and from 123.0 Hz to 145.8 Hz in males independently of parenthood. The observed shift indicates an unequal proportion of eliciting cues among the four conditions with a maximum in the present infant. The shift as such (3.2 and 2.9 semitones, respectively) seems to us less distinct to perceive than the changes in structure or in prosody of parent-to-infant speech.

When caregivers prolong syllables in baby talk they elongate vowels and modulate the fundamental frequency, thus giving baby talk the character of singsong messages. The increased participation of melody is accompanied by increasing rhythmicity (Blount & Padgug, 1977; Ferguson, 1964; Moerk, 1972; Snow, 1977; Stern & Gibbon, 1979). Seen microanalytically the melodic contours in baby talk are characterized by smoothly gliding pitch transitions and expanded pitch excursions (Fernald & Simon, 1984; M. Papoušek & H. Papoušek, 1981a; M. Papoušek, H. Papoušek, & Bornstein, 1985). Similar patterns appear in adult–adult dialogues only under conditions of increased emotional involvement (Scherer, 1982; Williams & Stevens, 1981).

In contrast to the large variety of inconspicuous prosodic contours in adult–adult dialogues, the prosodic contours in baby talk are less variable and more distinctly categorizable. We have been able to distinguish seven categories in German parents and to show that there are no significant differences in their distribution between mothers and fathers, with the only exception in the frequency of whispered utterances with no melodic contours (M. Papoušek, H. Papoušek, & Bornstein, 1985). Striking was the frequency of one-level and two-level contours that sound like musical tones rather than speech and that rarely appear in adult–adult speech. Complex contours with two or more shifts in direction, which are frequent but inconspicuous in adult dialogue, seldom occurred in baby talk. The expansion of pitch contours in maternal baby talk to 2-month-olds was found to reach 5.9 semitones on the average. Most contours (59.2 percent) belonged to the simplest, unidirectional types, such as one-level, two-level, rising, and falling contours. Bidirectional contours, both U shaped and bell shaped, represented 20.4 percent, tridirectional contours in simple sinusoidal forms represented 7.8 percent, and four-or-more-directional contours represented only 1.3 percent. As evident in baby talk to alternating infants, no differences have been found dependent on the presence of own versus strange infants (M. Papoušek & H. Papoušek, unpublished data). Even more strikingly, the incidence of melodic contours appeared to be unrelated to semantic and linguistic categories. Earlier (H. Papoušek & M. Papoušek, 1984a), we showed examples in which one contour was repeated 37 times within 3 min in utterances with the length varying at 1–7 syllables with 11 different semantic contents. It became obvious that melodic contours might function as specific information carriers per se, detached from the information included in words and syntactic structure.

In order to find out more about the significance of melodic contours we have focused our research on their relation to interactional contexts. One significant relationship involves changes in the infant's behavioral–emotional state, as assessed on the basis of both videotaped observable behaviors and qualitative changes in infant vocal sounds. Two types of state—pleasant excitement and fussiness—were related to two different profiles in contours of parental baby talk: Utterances displayed to fussy infants included maximum falling contours (34.5 percent), utterances displayed to pleasantly excited infants included a higher proportion of rising contours (27.5 percent as opposed to 18.8 percent in utterances to fussy infants) and bi- or tridirectional contours, such as rise–fall (21.3 percent as opposed to 8.9 percent) and sinusoidal patterns (13.5 percent as opposed to 6.5 percent) (M. Papoušek, H. Papoušek, & Bornstein, 1985).

Some contours seem to be typical for certain parental interventions, as is evident in situations where both the interactional context and semantic content in the referencing utterances convincingly elucidate parental intentions. We have been able to categorize 742 utterances on such bases in maternal baby talk of 21 German middle-class mothers to 2-month-old infants. The analysis showed that the distribution of melodic contours was related to four semantically evident intentions: praising; soothing; encouraging vocalization or other behaviors; and appeal for eye-to-eye visual contact. The relationships were highly significant. The maximum of frequencies concerned rise–fall and sinusoidal contours in praising (36.3 percent and 26.3 percent, respectively), falling contours in soothing (80.0 percent), rising contours in encouraging vocalization (29.5 percent), and two-level contours in appeal for visual contact (56.9 percent) (H. Papoušek et al., 1986). Two aspects appeared to be closely interconnected. Melodic contours depended on the infant's behavioral–emotional state and indicated adequate parental interventions. Obviously, any simplified categorization of parental behaviors might hide the manifold interrelations between them and the integrative processes that may be activated in infants. The regularities in the application of melodic contours may serve as contingent stimulations; if varied partially they may maintain increased attention in the infant. Moreover, melodic contours may symbolically represent certain situational contexts or belong to means of parental interventions, such as falling contours participating in soothing and cross-culturally universal lullabies (M. Papoušek & H. Papoušek, 1981a).

In order to verify the validity of the concept of didactic interventions, we have tried to evaluate their relationship to the distribution of melodic contours in maternal speech to 2-month-old infants (M. Papoušek & H. Papoušek, 1984). The total of 2084 utterances collected from 21 German mother–infant dyads was used for an analysis of correlations between melodic contours and five potential determinants: type of sentences, infant state, infant vocal expression, focus of maternal attention, and maternal didactic care. The last determinant is crucial to our hypothesis and was derived from the semantic content of referencing maternal utterances and their observable context. We assumed that mothers use the vocal sounds of infants as feedback on the course of integrative engagement, that is, that transitions from quiet to fussy sounds indicate increasing integrative difficulties, and that transitions to joyful sounds indicate successful engagements. Interestingly, the contingency coefficient was lowest for associations with the type of sentences (.385) and the infant's state (.391), but increased from infant vocal expressions (.461) in the direction of the focus of maternal attention (.630) and reached a maximum in associations with maternal didactic care (.711). This encouraging result should be taken not as a test of the concept, but rather as an example of how our speculations have led to further necessary verifications.

If we add vocal matching to the above consideration, the picture becomes more complex. Nevertheless, matching of individual sound features occurs in parental baby talk at a relatively high frequency. In interdyadic alternation of partners, 6.9 imitative sequences were recorded per 3-min sessions. Mothers followed infants in

62.2 percent of these imitative sequences, mothers vocalized first and were followed by infants in 35.6 percent of the sequences, and both partners vocalized simultaneously, duetting in 2.2 percent of the sequences. From another view, mothers matched 26.4 percent of infants' total utterances and mothers were matched in 13.9 percent of infants' total utterances. Thus mothers roughly match twice as often as infants do. The most frequently imitated sound features were pitch (51.1 percent of maternal matches, 59.4 percent of infant matches), followed by melodic contours, phonetic features, temporal structure, and nonspeech noises in maternal matches, and by melodic contours, temporal structure, and phonetic features in infant matches (M. Papoušek & H. Papoušek, unpublished data).

Since vocal matching produces auditively comparable sounds that do not require transmodal internal processing, it is not surprising that we found it functional in 2-month-old infants. This early occurrence in ontogeny and the fact that infants duplicated, either exactly or one octave higher, their mothers' pitch in a single attempt indicated to us an innate mechanism to account for this phenomenon (H. Papoušek & M. Papoušek, 1982c). Kessen, Levine, and Wendrich (1979) experimentally proved pitch imitation in infants 3–6 months old.

Interpretation of matching in infants as imitation must be done cautiously, because mothers at first increase the average level of pitch after the infant's birth while talking to the newborn. This tendency is common to all caregivers. Moreover, we do not know the history of vocal interchanges preceding our observations.

Imitation has generally been acknowledged as one crucial prerequisite for both social integration and acquisition of speech (Piaget, 1952). Hence matching as an invitation to mutual imitation may be a didactically relevant intervention and function in this sense in playful interactions later during infancy. However, the same invitation may lead to coactional duetting in interactions with pleasantly excited infants and could be interpreted as emotional sharing and contributing to mother–infant bonding. At other times, vocal matching by the mother may be considered a repetition of infant sounds for the purpose of instructive display of models. Matching may also be an important means serving to communicate internal feelings. Stern's concept of attunement (Stern, 1985) adds to the complexity of this problem. Stern points out the possibility of transmodal matching. Matching the dynamic features of a sound in analogous features of a movement can serve as an example, very much like internal feelings expressed by musicians through modulations of tones.

The complexity of interpretations may indicate that researchers have paid too much attention to some invariants while neglecting others. We should not forget that, in spite of so many references to the close ties between actions and thoughts, or actions and language, our knowledge on the perceptual processing of proprioceptive input from the motor system is far from satisfactory. Attention to dynamic parameters in behaviors, for instance, to changes in physical measures related to time, may lead to a better understanding of this difficult area. Dynamic parameters may play the role of common denominators in input from various modalities, thus allowing the nonconscious utilization of nonverbal messages. We cannot rule out a priori the possibility that the discrepancy between the biological relevance of communication based on dynamic and kinesic invariants on the one hand, and our limited awareness of their relevance on the other hand, is still too large to allow a comprehensive conceptualization. Even if it is, a conceptual attempt may serve as a guide to future efforts in infancy research.

The history of studies on intuitive parental didactics is too short to provide direct evidence about the effects of individual didactic interventions on the infant's integrative capacities. Not only ethical reasons but also the universal availability of didactic support make it impossible to isolate and analyze each phenomenon experimentally. Species-specific aspects of human didactics cannot be studied in animal models. However, didactic interventions may be subsumed in general measures of parent–infant interactions used in former studies, for instance, in the duration of dyadic interactions. Effects on infant development related to those general measures may provide indirect evidence as to the role of intuitive didactics.

The universality of didactic interventions seems to cause their qualitative homogeneity, whereas their quantity seems to be variable across social classes and cultures (M. Papoušek, H. Papoušek, & Bornstein, 1985). For instance, traditionally fathers have been reported to talk less to babies than do mothers (Field, 1978; Pedersen, Anderson, & Cain, 1980), and lower-class mothers to talk less than do middle-class mothers in the United States, in England, and in Israel (Field & Pawlby, 1980; Ninio, 1980; Tulkin & Kagan, 1972). Mothers also speak less to babies due to cultural beliefs, for instance, among Guatemalan Indians (Kagan & Klein, 1973) or among African Zambians (Goldberg, 1977).

Bornstein and Ruddy (1984) utilized a natural manipulation of the quantity of maternal stimulation in 22 mothers of twins. As compared to mothers of singletons from a sociologically similar sample, mothers of twins divided their energies between both babies so that only half of maternal activities (talking, encouraging infants' attention verbally or physically) was directed at each twin at 4 months. These deficits caused smaller speaking vocabularies and moderately lower Bayley Scale scores in twins at 1 year than in singletons. The quantity of maternal stimulation at 4 months was reliably related to infant vocabulary size at 12 months ($r = .55$).

In summary, the involvement of integrative processes may be affected by intuitive didactic interventions to a greater extent than we would have predicted a decade ago. Much of didactic intervention may be mediated by nonverbal communication between interacting partners to an extent of which we have only recently become aware. Finer differentiation, employing microanalytic approaches to parent–infant interactions, may clarify the extent and type of mediation. Recent research provides evidence that humans do intervene didactically, although their conscious awareness of such interventions is minimal.

CONCLUSIONS, IMPLICATIONS, AND PERSPECTIVES

In the present chapter, we have tried to outline the development of our engagement in interactional research, focusing primarily on the infant's integrative competence, but leading necessarily to a closer look at the infant's natural counterpart, the parent. This direction was predictable since the time during which the first author had the chance to observe mothers and infants at a lying-in unit designed for research on early mental development. However, a rich experience can accomplish little unless it can be integrated into a solid theoretical concept.

The search for an adequate concept to explain the parental role in infants' development has not been easy. It has moved from one weak theoretical point to another, often across a dangerously soft terrain that could only be bridged by speculative arguments. Such a conceptual path is not unusual and has repeatedly been facilitated by an interdisciplinary orientation. As evident in the introductory section, systems theory, biological sciences, and anthropology, among others, have offered important support in our case. The way across disciplinary borders has often required ideological tolerance, with the resulting benefit that it has also enabled us to combine selectively the strong points of individual approaches, both theoretical and methodological. The view of integrative competence in infants as representing the unity of learning, cognitive, and communicative processes is just one example. Similarly, we could stress the combination of naturalistic observations with stimulus–response designs, thus providing experimental verifications of hypotheses in relation to those difficult tasks inherent to the analyses of interactional processes.

The concept that assigns those parental behaviors displayed toward young infants the meaning of primary didactic interventions gained firmer contours approximately a decade ago. It may upset the reader, as it did us, that to accept this concept necessitates the revision of an enormous number of former assumptions about the infant's early experience—assumptions based on studies in which no attention had been paid to parental behaviors representing fundamental didactic interventions. The discovery of these behaviors in microanalytic studies has certainly enriched our information; however, it has not totally outdated previous knowledge. In many cases the new level of knowledge merely improves the interpretation of data obtained with the help of crude general measures. For instance, the duration of dyadic interactions between parents and infants may still be a sufficient index of crucial parental contributions—and certainly easier than microanalytic measures; without microanalyses, however, duration measures alone will not allow us to interpret the functions of such contributions.

One decade does not give a very small research team enough time to develop a new approach including practical methodological tools and solid verifications of fundamental theoretical assumptions. In some respects we have made intuitive decisions very much as parents seem to do in caring for the infant's integrative progress. In the interest of further progress in the research on parent–infant interactions it is a substantial contribution itself to elicit broader interest and cooperation. In the present chapter we have stressed the importance of comparative and cross-cultural approaches in relation to the question of universality of intuitive didactics. Similarly, we have pointed out the problems of individual variability, and we have intentionally left open the crucial question of abnormal deviations in parental competences.

The puzzling changes in contemporary patterns of marital and family life may throw doubts on any deeper interest in parental capacities. In fact, however, much of the empirical experience motivating our own interest indicates that a neglect of the parental role might imply the neglect of a fundamental source of human happiness. Preliminarily we can say that in more than a tenth of the families selected as normal for our observations we have seen considerable deviations in parental competences co-occuring with a confusion about rationales of infant rearing and with a lack of satisfaction resulting from parenthood. We have not yet been able to analyze potential interrelationships among these phenomena. However, it is difficult not to respond to the urgency of the need for a better understanding of parenthood at a time of such changing attitudes about the role of families in general.

The gaps in our approach for which we may seem to apologize should, therefore, be taken as a challenge.

REFERENCES

Anders, T. F., & Sostek, A. M. (1976). The use of time-lapse video recording of sleep-wake behavior in human infants. *Psychophysics, 13,* 155–158.

Anderson, B. J., Vietze, P., & Dodecki, P. R. (1977). Reciprocity in vocal interactions of mothers and infants. *Child Development, 48,* 1676–1681.

Aries, P. (1962). *Centuries of childhood.* London: Cape.

Becker, P. T., & Thoman, E. B. (1982). "Waking activity": The neglected state of infancy. *Developmental Brain Research, 4,* 395–400.

Bekoff, M. (1972). The development of social interaction, play, and metacommunication in mammals: An anthropological perspective. *Quarterly Review of Biology, 47,* 412–434.

Bell, R. A., & Harper, L. W. (1977). *Child effects on adults.* Hillsdale, NJ: Erlbaum.

Berg, W. K., & Berg, K. M. (1979). Psychophysiological development in infancy: State, sensory function, and attention. In J. D. Osofsky (Ed), *Handbook of infant development.* New York: Wiley.

Bertalanffy, L. von (1968). *Organismic psychology theory.* Barre, MA: Clark University Press with Barre Publishers.

Blount, B. G., & Padgug, E. J. (1977). Prosodic, paralinguistic, and interactional features of parent–child speech: English and Spanish. *Journal of Child Language, 4,* 67–86.

Blurton Jones, N. (1972). Categories in child–child interaction. In N. Blurton Jones (Ed.), *Ethological studies of child behavior.* New York: Cambridge University Press.

Bornstein, M. H., & Ruddy, M. G. (1984). Infant attention and maternal stimulation: Prediction of cognitive and linguistic development in singletons and twins. In H. Bouma & D. G. Bouwhuis (Eds.), *Attention and performance X: Control of language processes.* London: Erlbaum.

Borstelmann, L. J. (1983). Children before psychology: Ideas about children from antiquity to the late 1800s. In W. Kessen (Ed.), History, theory, and methods, Vol. 1 of P. H. Mussen (Ed.), *Handbook of child psychology* (4th ed.). New York: Wiley.

Brown, C. J. (1979). Reactions of infants to their parents' voices. *Infant Behavior & Development, 2,* 295–300.

Bruner, J. (1971). *The relevance of education.* New York: Norton.

Bruner, J. (1983). Play, thought, and language. In P. R. Dodecki & J. R. Newbrough (Eds.), *The legacy of Nicholas Hobbs: Research on education and human development in the public interest* (Part. I). *Peabody Journal of Education, 60,* 60–69.

Bruner, J. S. (1974). Nature and uses of immaturity. In K. Connolly & J. Bruner (Eds.), *The growth of competence.* New York: Academic.

Campos, J. J., Caplowitz Barrett, K., Lamb, M. E., Goldsmith, H. H., & Sternberg, C. (1983). Socioemotional development. In M. M. Haith & J. J. Campos (Eds.), Infancy and developmental psychobiology, Vol. 2 of P. H. Mussen (Ed.), *Handbook of child psychology* (4th ed.). New York: Wiley.

Campos, J. J., Hiatt, S., Ramsay, D., Henderson, C., & Svejda, M. (1978). The emergence of fear on the visual cliff. In M. Lewis & L. A. Rosenblum (Eds.), *The development of affect.* New York: Plenum.

Chance, M. R. A., & Jolly, C. J. (1970). *Social groups of monkeys, apes and men.* New York: Dutton.

Cohen, N. J., & Squire, L. R. (1980). Preserved learning and retention of pattern-analyzing skill in amnesia: Dissociation of knowing how and knowing that. *Science, 210,* 207–210.

Comenius, J. A. (1628). *Schola materni gremii.* German edition in J. Heubach (Ed., 1962), *Informatorium der Mutterschule.* Heidelberg: Quelle & Unger.

Comenius, J. A. (1657). *Opera didactica omnia.* Amsterdam. German edition in A. Flitner (Ed., 1954), *Große Didaktik.* Pädagogische Texte, I. Düsseldorf: Küpper.

Coulter, X. (1979). The determinants of infantile amnesia. In N. E. Spear & B. A. Campbell (Eds.), *Ontogeny of learning and memory.* Hillsdale, NJ: Erlbaum.

Crook, J. H. (1980). *The evolution of human consciousness.* Oxford: Claredon.

DeCasper, A. J., & Fifer, W. P. (1980). Of human bonding: Newborns prefer their mothers' voices. *Science, 208,* 1174–1176.

Dittrichová, J. (1969). Development of sleep in infancy. In R. J. Robinson (Ed.), *Brain and early behaviour. Development in the fetus and infant.* London: Academic.

Ehardt, C. L., & Blount, B. G. (1984). Mother–infant visual interaction in Japanese macaques. *Developmental Psychobiology, 17,* 391–405.

Eibl-Eibesfeldt, I. (1968). Zur Ethologie menschlichen Grussverhaltens. I. Beobachtungen an Balinesen, Papuas und Samoanern nebst vergleichenden Bemerkungen. *Zeitschrift für Tierpsychologie, 25,* 727–744.

Eibl-Eibesfeldt, I. (1972). Similarities and differences between cultures in expressive movements. In R. A. Hinde (Ed.), *Non-verbal communication.* New York: Cambridge University Press.

Emde, R. N. (1984). The affective self: Continuities and transformations from infancy. In J. D. Call, E. Galenson, & R. L. Tyson (Eds.), *Frontiers of infant psychiatry.* New York: Basic.

Emde, R. N., Kligman, D. H., Reich, J. H., & Wade, T. D. (1978). Emotional expression in infancy: I. Initial studies of social signalling and emergent model. In M. Lewis & L. A. Rosenblum (Eds.), *The development of affect.* New York: Plenum.

Estes, W. K. (1981). Intelligence and learning. In M. P. Friedman, J. P. Das, & N. O'Connor (Eds.), *Intelligence and learning.* New York: Plenum.

Ferguson, C. A. (1964). Babytalk in six languages. *American Anthropologist, 66,* 103–114.

Ferguson, C. A. (1978). Talking to children: A search for universals. In J. Greenberg (Ed.), *Universals of human language* (Vol. 1). Stanford: Stanford University Press.

Fernald, A., & Simon, T. (1977). Analyse von Grundfrequenz und Sprach-segmentlänge bei der Kommunikation von Müttern mit Neugeborenen. *Forschungsberichte: Institut für Phonetik und sprachliche Kommunikation der Universität München, 7,* 19–37.

Fernald, A., & Simon, T. (1984). Expanded intonation contours in mothers' speech to newborns. *Developmental Psychology, 20,* 104–113.

Field, T. (1978). Interaction behaviors of primary versus secondary caretaker fathers. *Developmental Psychology, 14,* 183–184.

Field, T., & Pawlby, S. (1980). Early face-to-face interactions of British and American working-and middle-class mother–infant dyads. *Child Development, 51,* 250–253.

Fogel, A. (1977). Temporal organization in mother–infant face-to-face interaction. In H. R. Schaffer (Ed.), *Studies in mother–infant interaction.* London: Academic.

Ganchrow, J. R., Oppenheimer, M., & Steiner, J. E. (1979). Behavioral displays to gustatory stimuli in newborn rabbit pups. *Chemical Senses & Flavour, 4,* 49–61.

Garnica, O. K. (1977). Some prosodic and paralinguistic features of speech to young children. In C. E. Snow & C. A. Ferguson (Eds.), *Talking to children: Language input and acquisition.* New York: Cambridge University Press.

Goldberg, S. (1977). Infant development and mother–infant interaction in urban Zambia. In P. H. Leiderman, S. R. Tulkin, & A. Rosenfeld (Eds.), *Culture and infancy: Variations in the human experience*. New York: Academic.

Gottlieb, G. (1983). The psychobiological approach to developmental issues. In M. M. Haith & J. J. Campos (Eds.), Infancy and developmental psychobiology, Vol. 2 of P. H. Mussen (Ed.), *Handbook of child psychology* (4th ed.). New York: Wiley.

Haeckel, E. (1891). *Anthropogenie oder Entwicklungsgeschichte des Menschen*. (4th rev. and enl. ed.) Leipzig: W. Engelmann.

Haekel, M. (1985, July). Greeting behavior in 3-month-old infants during mother–infant interaction. Presentation at the Eighth Biennial Meetings of the International Society for the Study of Behavioral Development, Tours, France. Abstracted in *Cahiers de psychologie cognitive, 5,* 275–276.

Hall, G. S. (1916). *Adolescence* (Vols. 1, 2). New York: Appleton.

Harris, P. L. (1983). Infant cognition. In M. M. Haith & J. J. Campos (Eds.), Infancy and developmental psychobiology, Vol. 2 of P. H. Mussen (Ed.), *Handbook of child psychology* (4th ed.). New York: Wiley.

Haynes, H., White, B. L., & Held, R. (1965). Visual accommodation in human infants. *Science, 148,* 528–530.

Hebb, D. O. (1949). *The organization of behavior*. New York: Wiley.

Hinde, R. A. (1971). Development of social behavior. In A. M. Schrier & F. Stollnitz (Eds.), *Behavior of nonhuman primates*. New York: Academic.

Hinde, R. A. (1974). *Biological bases of human social behavior*. New York: McGraw-Hill.

Hinde, R. A. (1983). Ethology and child development. In M. M. Haith & J. J. Campos (Eds.), Infancy and developmental psychobiology, Vol. 2 of P. H. Mussen (Ed.), *Handbook of child psychology* (4th ed.). New York: Wiley.

Hinton, G. E., & Anderson, J. A. (Eds.). (1981). *Parallel models of associative memory*. Hillsdale, NJ: Erlbaum.

Hinton, G. E., & Sejnowski, T. J. (1983). *Analyzing cooperative computation*. Proceedings of the Fifth Annual Conference of the Cognitive Science Society, Rochester, NY.

Hopkins, B., & van Wulfften Palthe, T. (1985). Staring in infancy. *Early Human Development, 12,* 261–267.

Huizinga, J. (1955). *Homo ludens*. Boston: Beacon.

Hunt, J. McV. (1965). Intrinsic motivation and its role in development. In D. Levine (Ed.), *Nebraska Symposium on Motivation* (Vol. 13). Lincoln: University of Nebraska Press.

Jacobson, J. L. Boersma, D. C., Fields, R. B., & Olson, K. L. (1983). Paralinguistic features of adult speech to infants and small children. *Child Development, 54,* 436–442.

Kagan, J., & Klein, R. (1973). Cross-cultural perspectives on early development. *American Psychologist, 28,* 947–961.

Kaye, K. (1977). Toward the origin of dialogue. In H. R. Schaffer (Ed.), *Studies in mother–infant interaction*. London: Academic.

Kaye, K. (1984). *The mental and social life of babies. How parents create persons*. London: Methuen.

Kaye, K., & Fogel, A. (1980). The temporal structure of face-to-face communication between mothers and infants. *Developmental Psychology, 16,* 454–464.

Kessen, W., Levine, J., & Wendrich, K. (1979). The imitation of pitch in infants. *Infant Behavior & Development, 2,* 93–99.

Kestermann, G. (1982). *Gestik von Säuglingen: Ihre kommunikative Bedeutung für erfahrene und unerfahrene Bezugspersonen*. Doctoral dissertation, University of Bielefeld, F. R. Germany.

Klinnert, M. D., Sorce, J. F., Emde, R. N., Stenberg, C., & Gaensbauer, T. (1984). Continuities and change in early emotional life. Maternal perceptions of surprise, fear, and anger. In R. N. Emde & R. J. Harmon (Eds.), *Continuities and discontinuities in development*. New York: Plenum.

Koch, J. (1968). The change of conditioned orienting reactions in 5-month-old infants through phase shifts of partial biorhythms. *Human Development, 11,* 124–137.

Koester, L. S., Papoušek, H., & Papoušek, M. (1985, July). Patterns of rhythmic stimulation by mothers with young infants: A comparison of multiple modalities. Presentation at the Eighth Biennial Meetings of the International Society for the Study of Behavioral Development, Tours, France. Abstracted in *Cahiers de psychologie cognitive, 5,* 270–271.

Korner, A. F., & Thoman, E. B. (1970). Visual alertness in neonates as evoked by maternal care. *Journal of Experimental Child Psychology, 10,* 67–78.

Korner, A. F., & Thoman, E. B. (1972). The relative efficacy of contact and vestibular stimulation in soothing neonates. *Child Development, 43,* 443–453.

Lewis, T. L., Maurer, D., & Kay, D. (1978). Newborns' central vision: Whole or hole? *Journal of Experimental Child Psychology, 26,* 193–203.

Liedtke, M. (1976). *Evolution und Erziehung. Ein Beitrag zu integrativen Pädagogischen Anthropologie* (2nd ed.). Göttingen: Vandenhoek & Ruprecht.

Lorenz, K. (1970). *Studies in animal and human behavior* (Vol. 1). Cambridge, MA: Harvard University Press.

Lorenz, K. (1971). *Studies in animal and human behavior* (Vol. 2). Cambridge, MA: Harvard University Press.

Lovejoy, C. O. (1981). The origin of man. *Science, 211,* 341–350.

Martin, G., & Clarke, R. (1982). Distress crying in neonates: Species and peer specificity. *Developmental Psychology, 18,* 3–10.

Mehler, J., Bertonuci, J., Barriere, M., & Jassik-Gerschenfeld, D. (1978). Infant recognition of mother's voice. *Perception, 7,* 491–493.

Meltzoff, A. N. (1981). Imitation, intermodal co-ordination, and representation in early infancy. In G. Butterworth (Ed.), *Infancy and epistemology*. Brighton, England: Harvester.

Messer, D. J. (1980). The episodic structure of maternal speech to young children. *Journal of Child Language, 7,* 29–40.

Mills, M., & Melhuish, E. (1974). Recognition of mother's voice in early infancy. *Science, 252,* 123–124.

Miranda, S. B. (1970). Visual abilities and pattern preferences of premature infants and full-term neonates. *Journal of Experimental Child Psychology, 10,* 189–205.

Moerk, E. (1972). Principles of interaction in language learning. *Merrill-Palmer Quarterly, 18,* 229–257.

Montagner, H. (1978). *L'enfant et la communication. Comment des gestes, des attitudes, des vocalisations deviennent des messages*. Paris: Stock.

Newson, J. (1979). Intentional behaviour in the young infant. In D. Schaffer & J. Dunn (Eds.), *The first year of life. Psychological and medical implications of early experience*. Chichester: Wiley.

Ninio, A. (1980). Picture-book reading in mother–infant dyads belonging to two subgroups in Israel. *Child Development, 51,* 587–590.

Olson, G. M., & Sherman, T. (1983). Attention, learning, and memory in infants. In M. M. Haith & J. J. Campos (Eds.), Infancy and developmental psychobiology, Vol. 2 of P. H. Mussen (Ed.), *Handbook of child psychology* (4th ed.). New York: Wiley.

Oster, H., & Ekman, P. (1978). Facial behavior in child development. In W. A. Collins (Ed.), *Minnesota Symposia on Child Psychology* (Vol. 11). Hillsdale, NJ: Erlbaum.

Papoušek, H. (1961). *Conditioned alimentary motor responses in infants* (Thomayerova Sbírka Přednášek, No. 409). Prague: Státní zdravotnické nakladatelství.

Papoušek, H. (1967a). Experimental studies of appetitional behavior in human newborns and infants. In H. W. Stevenson, E. H. Hess, & H. L. Rheingold (Eds.), *Early behavior: Comparative and developmental approaches.* New York: Wiley.

Papoušek, H. (1967b). Conditioning during early post-natal development. In Y. Brackbill & G. G. Thompson (Eds.), *Behavior in infancy and early childhood.* New York: Free Press.

Papoušek, H. (1969). Individual variability in learned responses in human infants. In R. J. Robinson (Ed.), *Brain and early behaviour. Development in the fetus and infant.* London: Academic.

Papoušek, H. (1977). Entwicklung der Lernfähigkeit im Säuglingsalter. In G. Nissen (Ed.), *Intelligenz, Lernen und Lernstörungen.* Berlin: Springer-Verlag.

Papoušek, H. (1979). From adaptive responses to social cognition: The learning view of development. In M. H. Bornstein & W. Kessen (Eds.), *Psychological development from infancy: Image to intention.* Hillsdale, NJ: Erlbaum.

Papoušek, H. (1981). Audiovisuelle Verhaltensregistrierung mit Hilfe von Film- und Fernsehtechnik. In H. Remschmidt & M. Schmidt (Eds.), *Neuropsychologie des Kindesalters.* Stuttgart: Enke Verlag.

Papoušek, H., & Bernstein, P. (1969). The functions of conditioning stimulation in human neonates and infants. In A. Ambrose (Ed.), *Stimulation in early infancy.* New York: Academic.

Papoušek, H., & Papoušek, M. (1974). Mirror image and self-recognition in young human infants: A new method of experimental analysis. *Developmental Psychobiology, 7,* 149–157.

Papoušek, H., & Papoušek, M. (1977a). Mothering and the cognitive headstart: Psychobiological consideration. In H. R. Schaffer (Ed.), *Studies in mother–infant interactions.* London: Academic.

Papoušek, H., & Papoušek, M. (1977b). Das Spiel in der Frühentwicklung des Kindes. *Suppl. Pädiatrische Praxis, 18,* 17–32.

Papoušek, H., & Papoušek, M. (1978). Interdisciplinary parallels in studies of early human behavior: From physical to cognitive needs, from attachment to dyadic education. *International Journal of Behavioral Development, 1,* 37–49.

Papoušek, H., & Papoušek, M. (1979a). The infant's fundamental adaptive response system in social interaction. In E. B. Thoman (Ed.), *Origins of the infant's social responsiveness.* Hillsdale, NJ: Erlbaum.

Papoušek, H., & Papoušek, M. (1979b). Early ontogeny of human social interaction: Its biological roots and social dimensions. In M. von Cranach, K. Foppa, W. Lepenies, & D. Ploog (Eds.), *Human ethology. Claims and limits of a new discipline.* New York: Cambridge University Press.

Papoušek, H., & Papoušek, M. (1981). Frühentwicklung des Sozialverhaltens und der Kommunikation. In H. Remschmidt & M. Schmidt (Eds.), *Neuropsychologie des Kindesalters.* Stuttgart: Enke Verlag.

Papoušek, H., & Papoušek, M. (1982a). Infant–adult social interactions: Their origins, dimensions, and failures. In T. M. Field, A. Huston, H. C. Quay, L. Troll, & G. E. Finley (Eds.), *Review in developmental psychology.* New York: Wiley.

Papoušek, H., & Papoušek, M. (1982b). Integration into the social world: Survey of research. In P. Stratton (Ed.), *Psychobiology of the human newborn.* New York: Wiley.

Papoušek, H., & Papoušek, M. (1982c, March). Vocal imitations in mother–infant dialogues. Presentation at the Third International Conference on Infant Studies, Austin, TX. Abstracted in *Infant Behavior and Development, 5,* Special ICIS Issue, p. 176.

Papoušek, H., & Papoušek, M. (1983). The psychobiology of the first didactic programs and toys in human infants. In A. Oliverio & M. Zappella (Eds.), *The behavior of human infants.* New York: Plenum.

Papoušek, H., & Papoušek, M. (1984a). Learning and cognition in the everyday life of human infants. In J. S. Rosenblatt, C. Beer, M.-C. Busnel, & P. J. B. Slater (Eds.), *Advances in the study of behavior* (Vol. 14). New York: Academic.

Papoušek, H., & Papoušek, M. (1984b). Qualitative transitions in integrative processes during the first trimester of human postpartum life. In H. F. R. Prechtl (Ed.), *Continuity of neural functions from prenatal to postnatal life.* London: Spastics International Medical Publications.

Papoušek, H., & Papoušek, M. (1985, July). *How does the infant learn in interactions with parents? Individuality in dyadic interactions.* Paper presented at the Eighth Biennial Meetings of the International Society for the Study of Behavioral Development, Tours, France.

Papoušek, H., Papoušek, M., & Koester, L. S. (1986). Sharing emotionality and sharing knowledge: A microanalytic approach to parent–infant communication. In C. E. Izard & P. B. Read (Eds.), *Measuring emotions in infants and children* (Vol. 2). New York: Cambridge University Press.

Papoušek, M., & Papoušek, H. (1981a). Musical elements in the infant's vocalization: Their significance for communication, cognition, and creativity. In L. P. Lipsitt & C. K. Rovee-Collier (Eds.), *Advances in infancy research* (Vol. 1). Norwood, NJ: Ablex.

Papoušek, M., & Papoušek, H. (1981b). Verhaltensmikroanalyse mit Hilfe der Filmtechnik. *Sozialpädiatrie in Praxis und Klinik, 3,* 60–64.

Papoušek, M., & Papoušek, H. (1981c). Verhaltensmikroanalyse mit Hilfe der Fernsehtechnik. *Sozialpädiatrie in Praxis und Klinik, 3,* 137–141.

Papoušek, M., & Papoušek, H. (1981d). Intuitives elterliches Verhalten in Zwiegespräch mit dem Neugeborenen. *Sozialpädiatrie in Praxis und Klinik, 3,* 229–238.

Papoušek, M., & Papoušek, H. (1984, April). Categorical vocal cues in parental communication with presyllabic infants. Paper presented at the Fourth International Conference on Infant Studies, New York. Abstracted in *Infant Behavior & Development, 7,* Special ICIS Issue, p. 283.

Papoušek, M., & Sandner, G. W. (1981). Mikroanalyse musikalischer Ausdruckselemente in Sprache und präverbaler Lautentwicklung. *Sozialpädiatrie in Praxis und Klinik, 3,* 326–331.

Papoušek, M., Papoušek, H., & Bornstein, M. H. (1985). The naturalistic vocal environment of young infants: On the significance of homogeneity and variability in parental speech. In T. M. Field & N. A. Fox (Eds.), *Social perception in infants.* Norwood, NJ: Ablex.

Papoušek, M., Papoušek, H., & Harris, B. J. (1986). The emergence of play in parent–infant interactions. In D. Görlitz & J. F. Wohlwill (Eds.), *Curiosity, imagination, and play. On the development of spontaneous cognitive and motivational processes.* Hillsdale, NJ: Erlbaum.

Parke, R. D. (1979). Emerging themes for social-emotional development. *American Psychologist, 34,* 930–931.

Parke, R. D., O'Leary, S. E., & West, S. (1972). Mother–father–newborn interaction: Effects of maternal medication, labor and sex of infant. *Proceedings of the Eightieth Annual Convention of the American Psychological Association, 7,* 85–86.

Parke, R. D., & O'Leary, S. E. (1976). Family interaction in the newborn period: Some findings, some observations and some unresolved issues. In K. Riegel & J. Meacham (Eds.), *The developing individual in a changing world: Vol. 2. Social and environmental issues.* The Hague: Mouton.

Parke, R. D., Grossman, K., & Tinsley, B. R. (1981). Father–mother–infant interaction in the newborn period: A German-American comparison. In T. Field (Ed.), *Culture and early interactions.* Hillsdale, NJ: Erlbaum.

Pedersen, F. A., Anderson, B., & Cain, R. (1980). Parent–infant and husband–wife interactions observed at the age of 5 months. In F. A. Pedersen (Ed.), *The father–infant relationship: Observational studies in the family setting.* New York: Praeger.

Peiper, A. (1958). *Chronik der Kinderheilkunde* (3rd ed.). Leipzig: Thieme.

Phillips, J. (1973). Syntax and vocabulary of mothers' speech to young children: Age and sex comparisons. *Child Development, 44,* 182–185.

Piaget, J. (1952). *The origins of intelligence in children.* New York: International Universities Press.

Piaget, J. (1981). *Intelligence and affectivity: Their relationship during child development* T. A. Brown & C. E. Kaegi, Palo Alto: Annual Reviews Incorporation.

Piaget, J. (1983). Piaget's theory. In W. Kessen (Ed.), History, theory, and methods, Vol. 1 of P. H. Mussen (Ed.), *Handbook of child psychology* (4th ed.). New York: Wiley.

Prechtl, H. F. R. (1974). The behavioral states of the newborn infant (a review). *Brain Research, 96,* 185–212.

Prechtl, H. F. R., & O'Brien, M. J. (1982). Behavioral states of the full-term newborn. The emergence of a concept. In P. Stratton (Ed.), *Psychobiology of the human newborn.* New York: Wiley.

Rabb, T. K., & Rotberg, R. I. (Eds.). (1971). *The family in history: Interdisciplinary essays.* New York: Harper & Row.

Remick, H. L. N. (1976). Maternal speech to children during language acquisition. In W. von Raffler-Engel & Y. Lebrun (Eds.), *Baby talk and infant speech.* Lisse, Holland: Swets & Zeitlinger.

Rheingold, H. L. (1961). The effect of environmental stimulation upon social and exploratory behaviour in the human infant. In B. M. Foss (Ed.), *Determinants of infant behaviour.* London: Methuen & Co.

Rheingold, H. L. (1985). Development as the acquisition of familiarity. In M. R. Rosenzweig & L. W. Porter (Eds.), *Annual Review of Psychology* (Vol. 36). Palo Alto: Annual Reviews, Inc.

Rheingold, H. L., & Adams, J. L. (1980). The significance of speech to newborns. *Developmental Psychology, 16,* 397–403.

Robson, K. (1967). The role of eye-to-eye contact in maternal–infant attachment. *Journal of Child Psychology & Psychiatry & Allied Disciplines, 8,* 13–25.

Sagi, A., & Hoffman, M. L. (1976). Empathic distress in the newborn. *Developmental Psychology, 12,* 175–176.

Salapatek, P., Bechtold, A. G., & Bushnell, E. W. (1976). Infant visual activity as a function of viewing distance. *Child Development, 47,* 860–863.

Salk, L. (1973). The role of the heartbeat in relations between mother and infant. *Scientific American, 228,* 24–29.

Sameroff, A. J., & Cavanaugh, P. J. (1979). Learning in infancy: A developmental perspective. In J. D. Osofsky (Ed.), *Handbook of infant development.* New York: Wiley.

Schaffer, H. R., Collis, G. M., & Parsons, G. (1977). Vocal interchange and visual regard in verbal and pre-verbal children. In H. R. Schaffer (Ed.), *Studies in mother–infant interaction.* London: Academic.

Scherer, K. R. (1982). The assessment of vocal expression in infants and children. In C. E. Izard (Ed.), *Measuring emotions in infants and children*. New York: Cambridge University Press.

Schoetzau, A. (1979). Effects of viewing distance on looking behavior in neonates. *International Journal of Behavioral Development, 2,* 121–131.

Schoetzau, A., & Papoušek, H. (1977). Mütterliches Verhalten bei der Aufnahme von Blickkontakt mit dem Neugeborenen. *Zeitschrift für Entwicklungspsychologie und pädagogische Psychologie, 9,* 1088–1089.

Senn, M. J. E. (1975). Insights on the child development movement in the United States. *Monographs of the Society for Research in Child Development, 40* (Serial No. 161).

Simner, M. (1971). Newborn's response to the cry of another infant. *Developmental Psychology, 5,* 136–150.

Smolensky, P. (1983). *Harmony Theory: A Mathematical Framework for Stochastic Parallel Processing,* Report No. 8306. Institute for Cognitive Science, University of California, San Diego.

Snow, C. E. (1977). The development of conversation between mothers and babies. *Journal of Child Language, 4,* 1–22.

Snow, C. E., De Blauw, A., & van Roosmalen, G. (1979). Talking and playing with babies: The role of ideologies of child-rearing. In M. Bullowa (Ed.), *Before speech: The beginning of interpersonal communication*. New York: Cambridge University Press.

Sommerville, C. J. (1971). Toward a history of childhood and youth. *The Journal of Interdisciplinary History, 2,* 439–477.

Sorenson, E. R. (1979). Early tactile communication and the patterning of human organization: A New Guinea case study. In M. Bullowa (Ed.), *Before speech: The beginning of interpersonal communication*. New York: Cambridge University Press.

Sostek, A. M., & Anders, T. F. (1981). The biosocial importance and environmental sensitivity of infant sleep-wake behaviors. In K. Bloom (Ed.), *Prospective issues in infancy research*. Hillsdale, NJ: Erlbaum.

Steiner, J. E. (1977). Facial expressions in the neonate infant indicating the hedonics. In J. M. Weiffenbach (Ed.), *Taste and development: The genesis of sweet preference*. Bethesda: U.S. Department of Health, Education & Welfare.

Sterman, M. B. (1972). The basic rest–activity cycle and sleep: Developmental considerations in man and cats. In C. B. Clemente, D. P. Purpura, & F. E. Mayer (Eds.), *Sleep and the maturing nervous system*. New York: Academic.

Stern, D. N. (1985). The interpersonal world of the infant: A view from psychoanalysis and developmental psychology. New York: Basic.

Stern, D. N., & Gibbon, J. (1979). Temporal expectancies of social behaviors in mother–infant play. In E. B. Thoman (Ed.), *Origins of the infant's social responsiveness*. Hillsdale, NJ: Erlbaum.

Stern, D. N., Jaffe, J., Beebe, B., & Bennett, S. L. (1975). Vocalizing in unison and in alternation: Two modes of communication within the mother–infant dyad. *Annals of the New York Academy of Sciences, 263,* 89–100.

Stern, D. N., Spieker, S., & MacKain, K. (1982). Intonation contours as signals in maternal speech to prelinguistic infants. *Developmental Psychology, 18,* 727–735.

Stern, D. N., Spieker, S., Barnett, R. K., & MacKain, K. (1983). The prosody of maternal speech: Infant age and context related changes. *Journal of Child Language, 10,* 1–15.

Stern, E., Parmelee, A., & Harris, M. (1973). Sleep state periodicity in prematures and young infants. *Developmental Psychobiology, 6,* 357–365.

Stratton, P. (1982). Rhythmic functions in the newborn. In P. Stratton (Ed.), *Psychobiology of the human newborn*. Chichester: Wiley.

Thoman, E. B., & Tynan, W. D. (1979). Sleep states and wakefulness in human infants: Profiles from motility monitoring. *Physiology & Behavior, 23,* 519–526.

Tronick, E., Als, H., & Adamson, L. (1979). Structure of early face-to-face communicative interactions. In M. Bullowa (Ed.), *Before speech. The beginning of interpersonal communication.* New York: Cambridge University Press.

Tulkin, S. R., & Kagan, J. (1972). Mother–child interaction in the first year of life. *Child Development, 43,* 31–41.

Turkewitz, G., & McGuire, I. (1978). Intersensory functioning during early development. *Journal of Mental Health, 7,* 165–182.

van Hooff, J. A. R. A. M. (1962). Facial expressions in higher primates. In Evolutionary Aspects of Animal Communication. *Symposium of the Royal Zoological Society,* London, *8,* 97–125.

van Hooff, J. A. R. A. M. (1972). A comparative approach to the phylogeny of laughter and smiling. In R. A. Hinde (Ed.), *Nonverbal communication.* New York: Cambridge University Press.

Wallin, A. (1984). Time-lapse filming of newborn infants. *Acta Paediatrica Scandinavica, 73,* 307–314.

Watson, J. S. (1972). Smiling, cooing, and the "game." *Merrill-Palmer Quarterly, 15,* 323–340.

Williams, C. E., & Stevens, K. N. (1981). Vocal correlates of emotional states. In J. Darby (Ed.), *Speech evaluation in psychiatry.* New York: Grune & Stratton.

Wilson, E. O. (1975). *Sociobiology. The new synthesis.* Cambridge, MA: The Belknap Press of Harvard University Press.

Wolff, P. H. (1965). The development of attention in young children. *Annals of the New York Academy of Sciences, 118,* 815–830.

Wolff, P. H. (1973). Organization of behavior in the first three months of life. In J. L. Nurnberger (Ed.), *Biological and environmental determinants of early development.* Baltimore: Wilkins & Wilkins.

Wolff, P. H. (1981). Normal variation in human maturation. In K. J. Connolly & H. F. R. Prechtl (Eds.), *Maturation and development. Biological and psychological perspectives.* London: Spastics International Medical Publications.

PART THREE

Assessment, Methodology, and Analysis

In the first edition of the *Handbook of Infant Development,* the chapters on methodological issues proved to be so useful for the readers that I decided to include a section in the second edition focusing on different methods of assessment and ways of understanding observational and interaction data. This section includes an overall survey of the behavioral assessment of the newborn, an extensive review of the Brazelton Neonatal Assessment Scale, which is the most widely used scale for assessing the newborn, and two chapters that focus on methodologies and statistical techniques for understanding and analyzing observational and interaction research.

Patricia Francis, Patricia Self, and Frances Degen Horowitz in their chapter on behavioral assessment of the newborn review screening tests, neurological examinations, and behavioral assessment techniques. They cover relationships among assessment procedures and the association with infant–caregiver interaction. Some of the techniques reviewed may also be used with older infants. A chapter is not included in this edition on assessment of older infants as that area was covered extensively in the first edition.

A chapter reviewing research on the Brazelton Neonatal Assessment Scale is included because it is the most widely used newborn assessment measure and has generated a great deal of research related to other measures of the infant and the parent–infant relationship. Brazelton and his colleagues are interested in its value as a communicative system between parents and professionals to enhance understanding of infant interactions as well as its research and clinical use.

The chapters by Gene Sackett and Roger Bakeman and John Gottman discuss methodological and statistical techniques for evaluating observational and interaction research. Bakeman and Gottman present a systematic view of observational methods, with examples of research indicating some of the positives and negatives of various approaches. They focus on developing coding schemes, selecting data recording strategies, and assessing observer agreement. Sackett orients the reader to ways of understanding sequential social interaction data. His widely cited chapter in the first edition provided us with an understanding of lag sequential analysis in behavioral interaction research; this chapter extends our understanding of such methods and adds a discussion of a causal inference model.

CHAPTER 13

The Behavioral Assessment
of the Neonate:
An Overview

PATRICIA L. FRANCIS, PATRICIA A. SELF, and FRANCES DEGEN HOROWITZ

The neonatal period encompasses the infant's first 28 days of extrauterine life. It is during this time that it first becomes possible to examine infant behavior fully, particularly as it may be influenced by environmental input. The significance of the neonatal period in this regard was recognized as early as the 1920s and 1930s by researchers who viewed this period as a proving ground for the nature–nurture controversy. Closer to our time, Stone, Smith, and Murphy (1973) suggested that acknowledgment of the human infant as competent became most evident in our study and understanding of the neonate.

One area of investigation that has reflected, as well as contributed greatly to, our changing conceptualization of the young infant is that of neonatal assessment. We have progressed over the past several hundred years from the largely visual inspection of the neonate to many well-developed tools that permit the structural, functional, and behavioral evaluation of the newborn infant. Other changes in neonatal testing have occurred as well. While many early tests focused on identifying and categorizing exceptional and at risk infants, several procedures currently exist for the express purpose of documenting individual differences in normal babies. Also, as Brooks and Weinraub (1976) note, there is more emphasis today on assessing infants' social competencies, as opposed to assessing only their perceptual capacities or behaviors that may be related to cognitive funtioning.

The purpose of this chapter is to review those tests that are available for the measurement of neonatal behavior. Some of these tests were designed to evaluate not only the neonate but also the infant over the full span of infancy (e.g., the Gesell Developmental Schedules; the Bayley Scales of Infant Development). Procedures are also included that were developed for use solely within the newborn period (e.g., the Brazelton Neonatal Behavioral Assessment Scale, the Postnatal Complications Scale). The tests are categorized as either screening tests, neurological examinations, or behavioral assessment techniques and presented in their respective categories. This classification system is somewhat arbitrary in the sense that all of the procedures that are described rely primarily on behaviors in evaluating the infant. Also, the assessment procedures within categories (particularly the behavioral assessment grouping) are fairly diverse. Still, the three categories have distinct and separate purposes. Screening tests are intended to enable physicians, clinicians, or paraprofessionals to determine quickly whether a neonate needs special attention or care. Neurological examinations primarily assess the infant's sensory capabilities, reflexes, or gestational maturity. Behavioral assessment procedures evaluate an extremely wide range of infant behaviors related to both social and cognitive functioning.

Each test in this chapter will be discussed with respect to the areas of functioning it measures; only items appropriate for evaluating the neonate will be included. Information regarding standardization procedures and reliability and validity estimates will also be provided. Further, a review of the research utilizing each test is included, particularly emphasizing studies conducted subsequent to the review by Self and Horowitz (1979). This chapter is designed to provide the student of neonatal behavior with a convenient overview of the content of available neonatal assessment techniques, as well as information regarding their utility and possible limitations. This review will facilitate the comparison of neonatal assessment techniques and therefore permit the choice of the procedure that is most appropriate to the researcher or clinician's specific needs and purposes.

SCREENING TESTS

Screening tests are relatively simple, inexpensive examinations that indicate whether an infant is in need of further examination or special care. Screening techniques provide for the early identification of children who have various disorders or who are at considerable risk of later experiencing disorders (Meier, 1975). According to Friedlander (1975), early identification provides "the single most powerful means for reducing the impact of exceptionality" (p. 603). In the following review, those screening tests that have received the most widespread utilization by both clinicians and researchers will be described. Other tests, including the developmental screening procedures proposed by Egan, Illingworth, and MacKeith (1969), the Developmental Screening Inventory devised by Knobloch and Pasamanick (1974b), the Kent Infant Development Scale described by Katoff and Reuter (1980), and Noller and Ingrisano's (1984) motor scale, will not be reviewed because of a lack of research conducted on them. Also, medical tests used for screening for specific physical disorders of the mother or child will not be included. For further information about such tests, interested readers might consult Wald (1984) or Meier (1975).

Obstetric Scales

While earlier attempts to identify the at risk neonate focused on the postnatal period, several scales that summarize prenatal and perinatal risk factors have recently been reported. The most commonly used scale appears to be that first offered by Prechtl (1968) in his attempt to describe optimal prenatal and perinatal conditions. Another scale that has received considerable research attention is the Obstetric Complications Scale described by Parmelee and his colleagues (Littman & Parmelee, 1978; Parmelee, 1974b). Although a number of other scales have been reported in the literature, they have not been widely accepted as yet and will therefore not be reviewed. They include the risk index of Siegel (1982), the medical composite score of Mednick, Hocevar, Baker, and Teasdale (1983), the maternal risk score reported by Badger, Burns, and Vietze (1981), and the description of significant perinatal events described by Perkins (1981).

Obstetric Optimality Measures

Prechtl (1968) originally described his concept of optimality with a listing of 42 items. Optimality criteria included items assessing maternal age, parity, maternal blood pressure, condition of the placenta, fetal position, fetal heart rate, spontaneous delivery, birth weight, onset of breathing after birth, gestational age, and the course of postnatal adaptation. Each of the items measuring these conditions was given 1 point if the item possessed the quality; no point was given if the item was not present. The maximum score for the infant was therefore 42 points, although Prechtl (1982) has more recently offered a 62-item scale. Further, Touwen and colleagues (1980) have elaborated the optimality scale to include 74 items. These items are listed in Table 13.1. Several items on the original scale do not appear on the revision; these include proportion of the pelvis, leutic infection, blood group incompatibility, nutritional state of the mother, X-ray of the abdomen, hypermesis, psychological stress of the mother, multiple birth, moderate contractions, vertex intrauterine position of the baby, cardiac regularity and fetal heart rate, cord around the neck, immediate onset of respiration, no resuscitation, no drugs given to the infant, and normal body temperature.

STANDARDIZATION.   Prechtl (1977) provided a distribution of scores for a sample of 1378 newborns. These scores represented a roughly normal distribution, with 50 percent of the infants having scores that were above 40; the lowest score was 27. Prechtl (1982) presented an example of a normalized distribution with the 62-item scale, and cited Michaelis, Dopfer, Gerbig, Dopfer-Feller, and Rogh (1979) for coining the term *reduced optimality* to refer to the difference between optimal and nonoptimal scores. Touwen and colleagues (1980) reported their distribution of optimality scores for a group of 3162 single-born infants. This distribution also mirrored a normal distribution; the median of the distribution was 61, with the tenth, twenty-fifth, seventy-fifth, and ninetieth percentiles at the scores of 66, 63, 57, and 54, respectively. These researchers noted that all infants showed a reduced optimality of at least 3 points.

RELIABILITY.   Touwen and colleagues (1980) noted that their items fell into seven different categories. These categories included social background of the parents (13 items), nonobstetric conditions during pregnancy (9 items), obstetric past history (14 items), obstetric aspects of the present pregnancy (11 items), diagnostic and therapeutic measures (9 items), parturition (11 items), and neonatal conditions immediately after birth (8 items). These investigators reported reliability coefficients of the various items and categories. In four of the seven categories, reliability coefficients measuring the internal consistency of the categories exceeded .40. In the other three categories, the internal consistency of the scales was low due to the small or even negative interitem relationships within these categories. These categories included nonobstetric conditions during pregnancy, obstetric past history, and obstetric aspects of the present pregnancy. The authors also presented the range of interitem correlations for each of the seven categories, and noted that the heterogeneity of the variables probably indicated that they are measuring quite different aspects of the obstetrical history. Finally, each of the seven category subscores cor-

TABLE 13.1. Obstetric Optimality Measures

Variables	Criteria for Optimality

Category 1: Social Background

1. Husband's profession	Managerial functions in industry, commerce and administration, teachers, middle management, both in private and governmental service, secretarial and technical functions, self-employed
2. Profession of gravida's father	Same
3. Marital state at time of delivery[a]	Married
4. Parenthood course	Took part
5. Race and nationality	Dutch, Caucasian
6. Education of gravida	More than elementary
7. Smoking of husband	No smoking
8. Family history of congenital anomalies	No
9. Previous baby with congenital anomalies	No
10. Previous legal abortion[a]	No
11. Height	>161 cm
12. Age[a]	20–31 years
13. Quetelet index (weight/height)	188–242

Category 2: Nonobstetrical Conditions during Pregnancy

14. Smoking	No smoking during whole of pregnancy
15. Illness first trimester[a]	No
16. Surgical therapy during gestation	No
17. Family history of diabetes	No
18. Diabetes (including gestational)	No
19. Heart disease	No
20. Epilepsy	No
21. Hypertension (at or above diast. 90)[a]	No
22. Other diseases	No

Category 3: Obstetrical Past History

23. Preterm delivery	None
24. Late abortion (16–28 weeks)	None
25. Early abortion (< 16 weeks)	Not more than one
26. Late fetal and neonatal loss	None
27. Cesarean section	None
28. Instrumental delivery	None
29. Hypertension in pregnancy	No
30. Placental abruption	None
31. Other complications	None
32. Placenta previa	None
33. Intrauterine growth retardation	No
34. Parity[a]	1
35. Previous infertility[a]	No
36. Induction of ovulation	No

Category 4: Obstetrical Aspects of Pregnancy

37. Vaginal bleeding[a]	No
38. Proteinuria[a]	No
39. Preeclampsis[a]	No

726

TABLE 13.1. (*continued*)

Variables	Criteria for Optimality

Category 4: Obstetrical Aspects of Pregnancy

40. Acetonuria anemia (Hb<110 g/1)[a]	No
41. Mid-trimester	No
42. Third trimester	No
43. Early hypertension (>80 diast.)	No
44. Uncertain or unreliable date of LMP	No
45. Weight gain	8–15 kg
46. Other complications *e graviditate*	No
47. Rhesus sensitization[a]	No

Category 5: Diagnostic and Therapeutic Measures

48. Frequency of prenatal care	9–15 visits
49. Number of admissions including for delivery	1
50. GTT carried out	No
51. Amniocentesis	No
52. Placental function tests, CTG, etc.	No
53. Drugs prescribed or taken prior to sixteenth week	No
54. After sixteenth week	No
55. Cerclage	No

Category 6: Parturition

56. Complications during labor (e.g., prolapse of cord, nuchal cord, rotation disturbances, pelvic anomalies, progress of labor, fever)[a]	None
57. Instrumental delivery including CS	No
58. Presentation at birth[a]	Cephalic
59. Perineal lacerations	Episiotomy
60. Duration first period[a]	10 hr or less
61. Duration second period[a]	50 min or less
62. Amniotic fluid[a]	Clear
63. Start of labor[a]	Spontaneous
64. Augmentation	No
65. Time between rupture of membranes and birth[a]	6 hr or less
66. Sedation or analgesia[a]	None

Category 7: Neonatal Condition Immediately After Birth

67. Duration of gestation[a]	38–42 weeks
68. Birth weight[a]	> 10 p, < 95 p
69. pH (umb v.)	> 7.20
70. First cry	Immediately
71. Apgar score 1 min	8–10
72. Apgar score 3 min	9–10
73. Congenital anomalies	None
74. Transferred to neonatal ward	No

[a]These items appeared on Prechtl's original scale of optimal obstetric conditions.

related significantly with the full optimality score based on the complete list of 74 items.

OTHER INFORMATION.   In addition to information about the utility of the optimality score, the theoretical implications of optimality have been discussed; interested readers are referred especially to Prechtl (1980, 1982). Research that has utilized the optimality score has examined its predictive utility (Prechtl, 1968; Kalverboer, 1979), its relation to neurological scores (Touwen et al., 1980), its relationship to Brazelton and Bayley scores (Coll, Sepkoski, & Lester, 1982), and its relationship to visual behaviors (Caron, Caron, & Glass, 1983).

Prechtl (1968) reported on the relationship of the optimality score to the neurological examination of 1378 infants. The infants were divided into three groups based on their optimality scores: Low-risk, middle-risk, and high-risk. When their scores were compared with scores from selected items from the neurological examination, the low-risk group predominantly showed those responses described as optimal, whereas the high-risk group showed relatively few optimal responses. The middle-risk group fell in between the two groups in the number of optimal responses. Prechtl concluded that there was a high association between obstetric complications as measured by the obstetric scores and the occurrence of neonatal neurological abnormalities. He also noted that there are several problems in pregnancy that may occur in combination with other factors that are likely to predispose an infant to nonoptimality; these include toxemia, instrumental delivery, and fetal distress.

Similarly, Kalverboer (1979) reported on the relationship of the optimality score to neonatal neurological optimality, neonatal neurological syndromes, and preschool neurological optimality scores. Kalverboer found little relationship between the obstetric scales and the neonatal or preschool measures. When the obstetric measures were combined with the neonatal neurological optimality scores (discussed more fully below), weak relationships were found with the neurological syndromes of apathy and hyperexcitability at 5 and 8 years of age.

Touwen and colleagues (1980) explored the relationship of the obstetrical optimality score and the neonatal neurological optimality score. Significant relationships were found in the two types of ratings. It was noted that certain obstetrical conditions had a stronger relationship to neurological morbidity when the obstetrical optimality score was lower. These investigators reported few differences in the obstetric optimality scores related to infant gender.

The relationship of optimality to scores on the Brazelton Neonatal Behavioral Assessment Scale (Brazelton, 1973) and the Bayley Mental and Motor Scales (Bayley, 1969) was explored by Coll and colleagues (1982). These investigators found that infants with higher optimality scores had higher scores on regulation of state items from the Brazelton scale, with infants born to teenage mothers having a wider range of scores. Although these authors also had Bayley measures at 1 year of age, the relationship of optimality scores to these measures was not reported.

Caron and colleagues (1983) examined infants' cognitive functioning with regard to the processing of relational information as a function of the infants' optimality. These investigators did not use the scale as specifically described by Prechtl, but instead measured optimality as a function of eight measures: singleton birth, 40-week gestation, appropriate birth weight, Apgar scores of 8 or better, uneventful pregnancy, normal labor duration, normal delivery, and healthy postnatal period. Any infant who failed to meet any one of these criteria was classed as nonoptimal. The infants were then given a visual fixation task involving habituation. Significant differences were found between the optimal and nonoptimal infants at each of four different ages, with optimal infants exhibiting quicker recovery of visual fixation following habituation.

The Prechtl scales, in summary, seem to capture the flexibility of the young at risk infant. Instead of emphasizing one or two problems in development, investigators have focused on clusters of difficulties, and the possibility that these difficulties will result in less than optimal development. Optimality scores have been related to various neurological indicators, Brazelton scores, and visual fixation. Further research will be required to demonstrate the relationship of reduced optimality to other indices of development.

Complications Scales

The Obstetric Complications Scale (OCS) and the Postnatal Complications Scale (PCS) were both proposed by Parmelee (1974b), and were derived generally from Prechtl's work on optimality. Included in the OCS are maternal characteristics, prior obstetrical history of the mother, pregnancy events, and perinatal measures of the infant. The PCS scores hazardous events that occur after the first few minutes of life, but within the first month of life. In both scales, each nonoptimal event is scored, and only if a chain of events occurs does a deviant nonoptimal score result. The test items for the OCS are presented in Table 13.2, while Table 13.3 contains the items from the PCS; the items in both tables were taken from Littman and Parmelee (1978). These same authors have described a third assessment—the Pediatric Complications Scales (PdCS)—which is used at 4–9 months of age; these scales will not be detailed here.

STANDARDIZATION.   According to Parmelee, Kopp, and Sigman (1976), the OCS and PCS are designed to be applicable to any population; however, the early work of this group focused on premature infants, since they were felt to be more likely to suffer postnatal risk factors. Littman (1977), utilizing a sample of 126 preterm infants, reported frequency distributions for both scales.

RELIABILITY.   While interitem reliability has not been reported for either assessment, it can be assumed that these estimates would be similar to those of the Prechtl scale. Littman (1977) correlated infant scores from the OCS and PCS and reported significant positive relationships between the two assessments. This author also found significant relationships between the PCS and 4- and 9-month PdCS scores.

OTHER INFORMATION.   In addition to the research by Parmelee and his collaborators in examining the utility of the OCS and PCS, Field and her colleagues have used the scales to explore perinatal adaptation (Field & Widmayer, 1980), refine risk measures (Field et al., 1978), and predict later problems (Field, Dempsey, & Shuman, 1983). Also, Prechtl (1982) has noted several conceptual problems with the use of the OCS and the PCS.

Littman and Parmelee (1978) used these procedures to relate neonatal development to Gesell and Bayley scores at 4, 9, and 18 months and at 2 years of age. No

TABLE 13.2.   Obstetric Complications Scale

Items
1. Gestational age (< 37 weeks)
2. Birth weight (< 2.5 kg)
3. Marital status (married)
4. Maternal age (18–30)
5. Previous abortions (none)
6. Previous stillbirths (none)
7. Prolonged unwanted sterility (no)
8. Time since last pregnancy (> 12 months)
9. Parity (1–6)
10. Pelvis (no disproportion)
11. Blood group incompatibility (no)
12. Bleeding during pregnancy (no)
13. Infections or acute medical problems during pregnancy (no)
14. Drugs given during pregnancy (no)
15. Maternal chronic disease (no)
16. Drug abuse (no)
17. Blood pressure during pregnancy (< 140/90 mm Hg)
18. Albuminuria (no)
19. Hyperemesis (no)
20. Hemoglobin at delivery (> 12 gm)
21. Multiple birth (no)
22. Prenatal care during first half of pregnancy (yes)
23. Membranes ruptured prior to delivery (no)
24. Delivery (spontaneous)
25. Forceps (not used)
26. Duration, first stage (3–20 hr)
27. Duration, second stage (10–120 min)
28. Onset of labor (spontaneous)
29. Intrapartum drugs (no)
30. Amniotic fluid (clear)
31. Fetal presentation (vertex)
32. Intrapartum fetal heart rate (100–160 per min)
33. Nuchal or knotted cord (no)
34. Cord prolapse (no)
35. Placental infarction (no)
36. Placenta previa or abruptio (no)
37. Onset of newborn respiration within 6 min (yes)
38. Resuscitation (none needed)
39. Apgar score, 1 min (7–10)
40. Apgar score, 5 min (7–10)

TABLE 13.3.   Postnatal Complications Scale

Items
1. Respiratory distress
2. Ventilatory assistance
3. Infection
4. Noninfectious illness (anomaly, hemorrhage)
5. Metabolic abnormality
6. Convulsion
7. Hyperbilirubinemia or exchange transfusion
8. Temperature disturbance
9. First feeding within 48 hours of birth
10. Surgery

relationships were found between the obstetrical and neonatal events and subsequent development. Field and Widmayer (1980) compared infants who were delivered by cesarean section and under general anesthesia to infants who were born by vaginal delivery with no anesthetic or local–regional anesthetic. Significantly poorer scores were earned by the cesarean-delivered infants on both the OCS and the PCS.

Field and colleagues (1978) compared preterm respiratory distress syndrome infants, postmature infants, and normal infants. In addition to the OCS and PCS, these investigators utilized the Brazelton assessment, the Denver, Carey temperament ratings, Bayley scores at 8 months, and mother–infant interaction measures. The three groups of infants differed significantly with respect to their OCS scores, although only the preterm and normal infants differed on the PCS. The authors suggest that the multiple assessments could be combined to comprise a cumulative risk index that might have utility in predicting later developmental outcome.

Field and colleagues (1983) reported on a 5-year follow-up of these three groups of infants. Correlations of the neonatal measures and later developmental measures revealed a correlation between the OCS and the 4-month mother–infant interaction measures, and between the PCS and the McCarthy Motor Scale at 5 years of age. The authors postulated that the neonatal and postnatal measures may provide "sleeper effects" upon the later measures, and noted the importance of studying these measures further.

Prechtl (1982) has commented in some detail regarding the scales as utilized by Parmelee and his colleagues. For example, he argued that Littman (1977) combined optimality items and obstetric complication items on his scale. Further, Prechtl noted that the optimality concept is not merely a reversal of the complications concept but is actually quite different; that is, while nonoptimality may denote severe pathology, it may also fall within the limits of generally accepted normality.

To conclude, the various complications scales originally described by Parmelee have been used extensively by other investigators. The Obstetric Complications Scale has been related to later developmental scores in at least one study, as has the Postnatal Complications Scale (Field et al., 1983). Still, the objections raised by Prechtl about the conceptual basis of optimality as opposed to complications seem valid; as such, the optimality scales may be the scales of choice in the measurement of pregnancy or neonatal difficulties.

Other Screening Devices

Apgar Scoring System

The Apgar scoring system (Apgar, 1953) has greatly increased in usage since its origination. It involves rating the newborn at 1 and 5 min after birth; five different items are scored on a scale from 0 to 2. Two points are given if the infant is in the best possible condition for a particular sign, no points are assigned if the sign is not present, and 1 point is given for all conditions between 0 and 2. Thus the highest total score an infant can obtain is 10.

TEST ITEMS.   The five signs from which the Apgar score is derived are heart rate, respiratory effort, reflex irritability, muscle tone, and color. If the infant has a heart rate of 100–140 beats per minute, it receives a score of 2. If the heart rate is 100 or below, the infant receives a 1; a 0 is recorded when there is no detectable heart beat. In assessing respiratory effort, regular breathing and lusty crying result in a score of 2; a 0 is given if the infant is apneic, and for all other breathing types (e.g., shallow breathing) the infant receives a score of 1. Reflex irritability is the third sign and refers to a response to some form of stimulation. Since 1958, this stimulation has usually been presented to the soles of the feet. If the infant cries after this stimulation, a score of 2 is given; a grimace or movement receives a value of 1, and no reaction receives a 0. For the fourth sign—muscle tone—an infant whose spontaneously flexed arms and legs resist extension is given 2 points, while a completely flaccid infant receives a 0 score. The fifth and most controversial sign is skin color. Infants receive a score of 2 only when they are entirely pink at 1 min of age. Few children receive such a rating at 1 min, although they often do receive it at 3–5 min of age (Apgar, 1953).

STANDARDIZATION.   According to Apgar, Holaday, James, Weisbrot, and Berrien (1958), 70 percent of a sample of more than 15,000 infants received total scores of 8–10 at 60 sec after birth; 6 percent had scores of 0–2, and 24 percent received scores of 3–7. Further standardization studies have not been reported.

RELIABILITY.   Further tests of reliability of the Apgar scoring system have not been reported since the work of Apgar and colleagues (1958). In that study, the investigators reported that the widest variation in the total score was a disagreement of 1 point. These variations in reported scores occurred most frequently in the mid-range of the scale (i.e., with infants who received scores of 5, 6, or 7). In contrast, variations in scores of infants with high or low scores were rare.

OTHER INFORMATION.   Research utilizing the Apgar scoring system has attempted to relate Apgar scores to maternal health variables, infant birth condition, later anomalies and/or morbidity, and later neurological conditions. With regard to maternal health variables, Zax, Sameroff, and Babigian (1977) noted that infants born to neurotic depressive women had lower Apgar scores and more fetal deaths. Similarly, Lederman, Lederman, Work, and McCann (1981) found that conflict in the acceptance of pregnancy by first-time mothers and their fear of loss of self-esteem associated with pregnancy were correlated with lower Apgar scores in their infants. These researchers also noted the relationship of these measures to a generally higher maternal anxiety score. Finally, Hingson and colleagues (1982) examined whether maternal smoking, drinking, or use of other psychoactive substances was associated with low infant Apgar scores. While none of these factors was significantly correlated with lower scores, other factors such as short gestation, delivery or placental abnormalities, and exposure to general anesthesia were related to lower Apgar ratings.

Other perinatal events have been related to Apgar scores. For instance, Rindfuss, Gortmaker, and Ladinsky (1978) noted the significantly poorer Apgar scores of infants whose mothers underwent elective induction of labor, although the overall difference in scores was less than 1 point. Fetal monitoring and changes in fetal heart rate have also garnered research attention. Neutra, Greenland, and Friedman (1981) found no differences in monitored versus nonmonitored infants until the infants were categorized into risk groups. In high-risk pregnancies, monitored infants had a more favorable distribution of Apgar scores, as did infants who were born prematurely. Acien (1979) correlated fetal heart rate deceleration with the Apgar score and found that an index of fetal heart rate deceleration was associated with decreased 5-min Apgar scores.

The pH value of the infant's blood, both prior to birth and immediately thereafter, has also been correlated with Apgar scores. Weber (1980) reported that by continuous pH monitoring of infants during birth infants with Apgar scores of less than 8 could be determined. Similarly, Fields, Entman, and Boehm (1983) have suggested that all infants with Apgar scores of less than 7 be further evaluated for blood pH to determine acidosis; through the use of the Apgar scores and pH monitoring, these authors argue that a more precise diagnosis may be made of the at risk infant. Sykes, Molloy, Johnson, Stirratt, and Turnbull (1983) examined 850 infants who were continuously or intermittently monitored for fetal heart rate, and who also had pH levels recorded. Apgar scores of less than 7 were found in 87 infants, and low Apgar scores and acidosis were found in 19 infants.

Several other studies have looked at Apgar scores in relation to the progress of delivery, infant EEGs, maternal estriol level prior to delivery, and maternal administration of salbutamol. Rossavik (1978) examined the intrauterine pressure during the first stage of labor and found a significant correlation between this measure and the duration of the second stage of labor, as well as the 1-min Apgar ratings. Borgstedt, Heriot, Rosen, Lawrence, and Sokol (1978) reported on the relationship of fetal EEGs to Apgar scores. These investigators found a prolonged voltage suppression in infants with lower 1- and 5-min Apgar scores. Giussi and colleagues (1979) reported that lower maternal serum estriol levels were associated with infants with depressed Apgar scores (1–6), while oxytocinase and hCS were not associated with lower scores. Hastwell (1980) reported on women in premature labor who were given salbutamol; he found that administrations of salbutamol in the 4 hours prior to birth were associated with a reduced incidence of low Apgar scores.

As reported by Self and Horowitz (1979), data regarding correlations between Apgar scores and later measures of cognitive functioning are conflicting. Serunian and Broman (1975) reported lower 8-month Bayley scores in infants with very low Apgar scores, while Edwards (1968) found significant relationships between Apgar ratings and 4-year IQ scores. However, other investigators have failed to find such relationships (e.g., Broman, Nichols, & Kennedy, 1975; Fysh, Turner, & Dunn, 1982; Richards, Richards, & Roberts, 1968; Shipe, Vandenberg, & Williams, 1968). Similarly, the data continue to be inconclusive with regard to the associations between Apgar scores and later neurological/motor abnormalities. As one example, Nelson and Ellenberg (1981) found in a sample of children with cerebral palsy that the majority had had Apgar scores from 7 to 10; also, of those children who had had low 10-min Apgar ratings (i.e., 0–3) and survived, 80 percent were free of major handicaps at early school age. However, these same authors reported in 1979 that lower 5- and 10-min Apgar scores were associated with an increased incidence of cerebral palsy.

The clearest findings regarding the Apgar test involve its relationship to infant mortality. Early studies documented strong correlations between low Apgar ratings and infant mortality, particularly during the neonatal period (e.g., Drage, Kennedy, & Schwarz, 1964; Richards et al., 1968; Serunian & Broman, 1975). More currently, Atkinson (1983) has summarized North Carolina data collected from 1978 to 1980. Apgar scores alone were found to be just as useful in predicting mortality as was birth weight, although the two measures used in conjunction were much better in predicting neonatal death; these two measures were also better predictors than maternal high-risk factors. In another study, Naeye (1979) found that abnormal 5-min Apgar scores were best correlated with mortality rates and were most often associated with amniotic fluid infections. Nelson and Ellenberg (1979) found decreased 10-min scores to be associated with the greatest risk of early death. However, Atkinson (1983) has noted that Apgar scores are not especially useful in predicting postneonatal mortality.

In a retrospective study of special populations, Lipsitt, Sturner, and Burke (1979) compared 15 infants who succumbed to sudden infant death syndrome (SIDS) with a control group. SIDS infants were found to have received significantly lower Apgar scores than the control infants at 1, 2, and 5 min after birth. Goldson, Fitch, Wendall, and Knapp (1978) examined the Apgar scores of two groups of children, one of which was composed of abused children. The abused children were found to have had lower Apgar scores at 5 min compared to the nonabused group.

The almost universal usage of the Apgar scoring system in western countries attests to its utility to medical personnel. Both observer and test–retest reliability have been well studied. Research on this assessment generally suggests some relationship between Apgar ratings and pre-, peri-, and early neonatal factors. However, relationships to later developmental measures have not been substantiated, especially in studies that have controlled for factors such as race and socioeconomic status (e.g., Broman et al., 1975; Shipe et al., 1968).

Denver Developmental Screening Test

The Denver Developmental Screening Test (DDST) was originally proposed by Frankenburg and Dodds (1967). In 1981, Frankenburg, Fandal, Sciarillo, and Burgess reported on the newly abbreviated and revised Denver Developmental Screening Test (DDST-R). These authors claim that it is the most extensively taught and validated developmental screening test used throughout the United States. It is primarily used by physicians and clinicians to detect children with mild developmental delays and developmental problems. The recent revision of the DDST provides a more graphic portrayal of a child's rate of development and an abbreviation of the original DDST that makes it easier to administer as a routine part of the medical evaluation.

TEST ITEMS.   The items that may be assessed during the first month of life on the Denver include the following: In the gross motor category, the infant should lift its head 45 and 90 deg while prone. In the language category, the infant should respond to a bell and vocalize other than crying. In the fine motor–adaptive category, the infant should follow first to midline, then past midline, and exhibit symmetrical movements. In the personal–social realm, the infant should regard a face and smile spontaneously by 1 month of age.

STANDARDIZATION AND RELIABILITY.   Frankenburg and colleagues (1981) noted that the original DDST was standardized on more than 20,000 children. As such, they have attempted recently only to determine the reliability between the DDST and the DDST-R. In the clinical judgments that are made about children, the DDST and DDST-R have been found to agree 98–100 percent of the time. Individual tester–observer item agreement was reported at 97 percent across all items. Separate estimates have not been provided for the 1-month items.

Standardization data have also been reported from samples from other countries or special populations. Bryant, Davies, and Newcombe (1979) have described norms for a South Glamorgan, Wales, sample, while Ueda (1978a, 1978b) reported on the

Denver's standardization with Tokyo and Okinawa children. Similarly, Jaffe, Harel, Goldberg, Rudolph-Schnitzer, and Winter (1980) reported norms from an Israel population and Solomons (1982) has standardized this test on children from Yucatan, Mexico.

OTHER INFORMATION.   Since the primary utilization of the DDST has been to refer infants for further testing in the event of developmental delay, most of the research attention has focused upon the accuracy of the judgments that are based upon the outcome of the test. In an early study, Frankenburg, Goldstein, and Camp (1971) reported an underreferral rate of 3 percent and an overreferral rate of 11 percent; German, Williams, Herzfeld, and Marshall (1982) reported underreferrals at 0–8 percent and overreferrals at 21–44 percent. In contrast, Applebaum (1978) reported an underreferral rate of 68 percent and no overreferrals. Other studies have examined relationships between DDST scores and later abnormalities (e.g., Ounsted, Moar, & Scott, 1983); however, the majority of this research has utilized infants and children much older than the subject of his review.

In summary, although the DDST is a widely used screening tool for young children, its utility in the early infancy period is limited by the small number of items observable in the first month. In addition, the recent work on the accuracy of referrals based on this test has provided distressing data with regard to both under- and overreferrals. These data suggest that even the screening function of the DDST for young infants is suspect. As such, it is not clear that this test should be used for such a purpose. At the very least, the DDST should be supplemented by other measures when making clinical judgments about a young child.

NEUROLOGICAL EXAMINATIONS

Several neurological evaluations have gained considerable usage with neonatal populations; in addition, measures of gestational age have been derived in part from these examinations. The most popular neurological tests have included those of Prechtl and Beintema (1964), Saint-Anne Dargassies (1977), Touwen (1976), Dubowitz and Dubowitz (1981), Amiel-Tison (1982), and Parmelee (1974a). Since little published information in American journals has been provided regarding the Touwen, Amiel-Tison, and Saint-Anne Dargassies methods, they will not be detailed here; similarly, the Parmelee scale has not received additional attention and will not be reviewed. Following the review of the Prechtl scale, Dubowitz, Dubowitz, and Goldberg's (1970) method for assessing gestational age will be described.

The Neurological Examination of Prechtl

Prechtl and Beintema (1964) described a procedure to diagnose neurological abnormalities of the newborn. Prechtl (1977) has revised this procedure, drawing from increased knowledge of the course of neurological development described by Beintema (1968) and others. He has also benefited from our increased understanding of infant behavior, particularly with respect to state cycles, and from the use of his own concept of optimality (described earlier in the discussion of prenatal and perinatal scales). In addition to the complete neurological examination, Prechtl (1977) has described a short version for screening purposes. It is estimated to take approximately 10 min.

TEST ITEMS.   As in his earlier version, Prechtl (1977) stressed the importance of noting the infant's state during the examination. The most optimal state for eliciting various reflexes is specified, as are states during which a reflex should not be elicited. In addition, Prechtl lists the optimal response for each of the reflexes.

Observational and informational items include: medical history, state, resting posture, spontaneous motor activity, athetoid postures and movements, tremor, other movements, skin condition, respiration, head shape and size, facial features, pupil condition, vertebral column condition, spontaneous movement of the head, and spontaneous crawling movements. Elicited reflexes and behaviors include: Chvostek's reflex, lip, jaw, glabella, abdominal, Cremaster, anal, nystagmus, reaction of the pupils to light, optical blink reflex, acoustic blink reflex, corneal reflex, supine suspension, doll's eye test, asymmetrical tonic neck reflex, resistance against passive movement, power of active movements, range of movements, recoil of forearm, muscular consistency, biceps reflex, knee jerk, ankle clonus, palmar grasp, plantar grasp, Babinski reflex, magnet response, withdrawal reflex, rooting response, sucking response, traction test, control of head movements during sitting posture, Moro response (head drop), Moro response (body drop), ankle jerk, Galant's response, posture of head and limbs in prone suspension, placing response, stepping movements, rotation test, and crying behavior.

STANDARDIZATION.   Prechtl (1977) does not provide standardization information regarding the second revision of the neurological examination. The original Prechtl and Beintema (1964) test was used with 1500 children, and each response and/or reflex was documented with respect to the significance it might have later in development.

RELIABILITY.   Observer and test–retest reliabilities of the Prechtl (1977) neurological examination have not been reported. These figures, however, should be comparable to those provided by Prechtl (1963) and Beintema (1968). Prechtl (1963) reported the observer reliability among three observers to be in the range of .80–.96. In Beintema's (1968) report of 49 infants 1–9 days of age, he noted that neurological examinations in the first 3 days of life are less valid due to the difficulty in altering the state of the infant.

OTHER INFORMATION.   Prechtl's examination, usually the earlier version described by Prechtl and Beintema (1964), has been used in a variety of research endeavors by persons other than Prechtl. The effects of delivery factors and preterm birth have been examined. In addition, comparisons between performance on the neurological examination and the Brazelton test have been noted; long-term follow-up data have also been provided.

Belsey and colleagues (1981) utilized the Prechtl examination across the first 6 weeks of life in a comparison of mothers who received intramuscular pethidine, epidural bupivacaine, or no drugs. In the infants of pethidine mothers, the Prechtl revealed that the spontaneous motor activity when the infant was awake was adversely affected. Bratteby (1981) also examined the effects of obstetric regional anesthesia upon infants with the Prechtl and Beintema test. At the first and fourth day of life, differences between infants born to mothers who received (1) paracervical and pudendal nerve blockage or (2) epidural analgesia with nitrous oxide during contractions were not evident, although some deviations in blood chemistry and other physiologic variables were found.

Leijon (1980) also looked at delivery factors in the examination of vacuum extraction and its effects on 1- and 5-day-old infants. Infants delivered by vacuum extraction had fewer optimal responses on the Prechtl and Beintema examination on day 1 than did the normally delivered infants, although their scores improved by day 5. Infants born with prolonged vacuum extraction (longer than 15 min) or in an occipito-posterior presentation seemed to account for most of the differences between the two groups.

Two studies have examined factors after birth utilizing the Prechtl and Beintema test. Leijon and Finnstrom (1982) correlated a modified Prechtl scale with Brazelton exam scores on days 1 and 5 in 78 healthy newborns. They found that a total neurological score and an optimality score from the Prechtl scale were correlated with motor performance and orientation on the Brazelton. Habituation and state change items on the Brazelton were not generally related to neurological scores. The authors suggests that the low correlations between neurological variables and physiological stability may be explained by inadequate definitions of tremulousness and number of startles on the Brazelton scale.

Forslund and Bjerre (1983) assessed full-term infants and preterm infants at term with a slightly modified version of the Prechtl test; prenatal and perinatal optimality scores were also noted. Compared to the term infants, the preterm infants received lower ratings with respect to muscle tone, resistance to passive movements, arm recoil, degree of head lag, withdrawal, and the Moro reflex but evidenced better head control in the sitting position; also, it was easier to elicit the tonic neck reflex in the preterm group. Low-risk preterms, as determined by prenatal and perinatal optimality scores, were more like full-terms except in their posture in the supine position.

Njiokiktjien and Kurver (1980) classified 144 newborns by optimality in accordance with Prechtl's neurological examination. At 12, 22, and 36 months of age, the parents were queried about the child, and at 22 months the child was assessed using the Gesell and Amatruda (1947) method and other neurological items. Infants judged to be suboptimal on Prechtl's neurological optimality measure were found to be more emotionally labile and to have shorter attention spans. Although a few abnormal responses were found later in the suboptimal group, no clinical syndromes were apparent. Suboptimal male infants were more different from their optimal counterparts than were females.

Kalverboer, Touwen, and Prechtl (1973) also reported a follow-up of infants with obstetric optimality scores and newborn neurological examinations. The children were observed again at 5 years of age with a neurological examination and other measures; school achievement records were also examined. Few correlations were found between the neonatal neurological optimality score and the 5-year neurological optimality measure. Only when newborn and preschool scores were combined were there relationships with observed behaviors, such as motor activity; these relationships were more apparent for boys than for girls.

The neurological examination described by Prechtl (1977) remains the most comprehensive and useful neurological examination available in early infancy. This examination documents adaptations of the infant in the first postnatal days. Surprisingly, recent research has shown little relationship between these scores and later neurological difficulties. However, this may be a function of the generally healthy newborns who are typically sampled.

Dubowitz Assessment of Gestational Age

The procedure described by Dubowitz and colleagues (1970) has become an increasingly popular tool in assessing the infant's gestational age. Recently, Dubowitz and Dubowitz (1981) described a neurological assessment to accompany their gestational age assessment. Since it is the former that has garnered the most research attention, this is the instrument that will be reviewed. Other indices of gestational age have not gained widespread popularity; these include the measurement of nerve conduction velocity by Schulte, Michaelis, Linke, and Nolte (1968), the procedure provided by Lubchenco, Hansman, and Boyd (1966), and the ponderal index (Rohrer, 1921), which is based on the proportion of an infant's weight to length.

Ballard, Novak, and Driver (1979) have described an abbreviated form of the technique of Dubowitz and colleagues. This abbreviated version, they claim, takes approximately half the time required by the full exam yet has adequate reliability. Further published work on the Ballard revision is not yet available, although Park, Shafaie, and Self (1983) reported differences of approximately 1 week in the assessment of gestational age using the two procedures.

TEST ITEMS.   Dubowitz and Dubowitz (1981) provided a one-page scoring sheet for their measurement of gestational age. It includes both reflex items and external criteria. Historical information is requested, including the infant's name, sex, race, hospital number, date and time of birth and of the examination, age, weight, length, and head circumference. Also, a place is provided for totaling the scores of the neurological and external criteria items and estimating the gestational age of the infant.

The neurological and reflex items include: posture, square window (hand flexion), ankle dorsiflexion, arm recoil, leg recoil, popliteal angle, heel-to-ear, scarf sign, head lag, and ventral suspension. External or superficial criteria include the amount of edema, skin texture, skin color, skin opacity, lanugo, plantar creases, nipple formation, breast size, ear form, ear firmness, and genital development.

STANDARDIZATION.   In the report by Dubowitz and colleagues (1970), 167 infants served as the standardization sample. These were infants whose mothers were sure of their last menstrual period. From these infants, Dubowitz and colleagues calculated a regression line for their data, with gestation equaling the total score times 0.2642 + 24.595. Other investigators have noted that the regression line should be altered with differing populations. For instance, Jaroszewicz and Boyd (1973) found with 100 nonwhite infants the regression line should be altered to obtain the best fit, although the two regression lines differed by less than 0.2 weeks in the age range of 30–42 weeks. In another report, Hancock (1973) concluded that the usefulness of the Dubowitz technique was limited with atypical infants, including those who were grossly abnormal, had been resuscitated, or had experienced a breech delivery.

RELIABILITY.   Dubowitz and colleagues (1970) noted that reliability among observers for the scale is excellent. Among four pediatricians scoring independently, no significant differences were obtained. Among naive nursing personnel, however, one of three nurses was noted to score consistently higher than the other two nurses and the trained investigators. Dubowitz and colleagues also reported that the scale can be used as easily on the first day of life as on the next few days, as no significant differences in scoring were found across this time period.

OTHER INFORMATION. The Dubowitz method has been used in the assessment of growth in early infancy and in conjunction with the neurological examination to assess differences in development. Riese (1980) has also studied its utility in assessing gestational age in twins.

In one study, Oakley and Tavare (1979) used the Dubowitz method as they developed a new method for assessing growth in early infancy. Infants judged to be full term by the Dubowitz technique were measured for skin fold thickness at birth and at 6 weeks of age. Those with low skin fold thickness tended to gain more during this time; the authors coined the term *thin for dates* to describe these infants.

Palmer, Dubowitz, Levene, and Dubowitz (1982) compared preterm infants with intraventricular hemorrhage with or without ventricular dilatation to preterm infants who had experienced no hemorrhaging. Infants were measured for gestational age via the Dubowitz technique, given the Dubowitz and Dubowitz (1981) neurological examination, and assessed with the Griffith test at 6, 9, and 12 months of age. When the infants' ages were corrected for prematurity, all of the infants were normal, except for one infant. A higher incidence of neurological abnormality was found in infants with ventricular dilatation following intraventricular hemorrhage.

Riese (1980) utilized the Dubowitz technique in comparing methods for assessing gestational age in twins. In addition to the Dubowitz technique, this author included these methods: date of last menstrual cycle, a physical examination, a neurological examination, an unspecified clinical assessment, and ultrasound cephalometry. Surprisingly, Riese reported that 34 percent of the sample had within-pair discrepancies of gestational age measurements in the range of 2–6½ weeks. The author favored the systematic use of only one method and proposed that modifications might be necessary for the assessment of twins.

One other study, by Sibai, Anderson, Abdella, McCubbin, and Dilts (1983), also used more than a single technique in its examination of the effects of eclampsia. In addition to the technique of Dubowitz and colleagues, these authors used the table and methods described by Lubchenco and colleagues (1966). Generally, these methods utilize the Ponderal Index to tabularize data for infants 26–42 weeks of age; these data can thus be used to estimate gestational age. Sibai and colleagues (1983) used both of these methods to categorize their infants as less or greater than 36 weeks of age. Infants were examined frequently during the first 6 months of life, then every 6 months until they reached 50 months of age. Infants with uncomplicated eclampsia had normal growth and development as measured by the DDST and other measures. Neurological abnormalities were associated with placental abruption or intrauterine growth retardation.

In summary, the procedure of Dubowitz and colleagues for the measurement of gestational age has increased in popularity because of its ease of administration and training for use. Problems with use for estimating gestational age may occur with special samples such as twins, however. In addition, care should be taken to standardize the instrument with the sample on which it is to be used.

BEHAVIORAL ASSESSMENT TECHNIQUES

Compared to the screening tests and the neurological examinations, behavioral assessment techniques are vastly more diverse in intent and design. A particular behavioral assessment may attempt to obtain an estimate of neonatal status, to differentiate between normal and abnormal infants, or to predict behaviors at some later point in time. Other goals of various behavioral assessments include the identification of infant individual differences, with respect to both cognitive capacities and temperament. So diverse is this area of assessment that subcategories will be utilized in the current review. The first subcategory focuses on infant social functioning and includes measures of infant temperament. The last four subcategories relate more to infant abilities; these include measures of neonatal status, psychometric devices, sensorimotor scales, and sensory processing techniques. Of these subcategories, only the measures of temperament and neonatal status were specifically designed to be utilized with the neonate. Subsequently, the psychometric tests, sensorimotor scales, and sensory processing techniques to be reviewed have not been used extensively in research within the first month of life. In the literature review of these tests, then, those studies on the neonate that do exist will be empahsized; however, studies on older infants will also be described briefly in order to provide some perspective on these tests' general research utility.

Measures of Infant Temperament

Considerable research attention has been given in the past 10 or 15 years to the early assessment of infant temperament. As Rutter (1982) noted:

> The temperamental qualities brought by a child to the interactions and situation that he or she encounters therefore play an important part in determining how that encounter proceeds and whether it is likely to result in the development of some form of maladaptive response or emotional–behavioral disturbance. (p. 5)

Most of the techniques that have measured infant temperament have been derived from the work of Thomas and Chess and their co-workers in the New York Longitudinal Studies (e.g., Thomas & Chess, 1977; Thomas, Chess, Birch, Hertzig, & Korn, 1963). However, for the most part these techniques have focused on the older infant (e.g., Bates, Freeland, & Lounsbury, 1979; Carey & McDevitt, 1978; Rothbart, 1981), with few neonatal procedures existing for this purpose. Crockenberg and Smith (1982) used the Brazelton Neonatal Behavioral Assessment Scale (Brazelton, 1973) to measure temperament, by combining various items from that scale into an irritability cluster. However, the most frequently utilized temperament scale for neonates is the Neonatal Perception Inventory, offered by Broussard and Hartner (1971).

Neonatal Perception Inventory

Broussard and Hartner (1971) described several inventories in which mothers rate the "average" infant and then each mother rates her own baby. On the first or second postpartum day, the mother completes the Neonatal Perception Inventory (NPI I); at 1 month, the Neonatal Perception Inventory II (NPI II) is completed, as is the Degree of Bother Inventory. These measures attempt to assess the concerns mothers may have about their young infants, and the comparisons mothers may make to the average infant.

TEST ITEMS.   Table 13.4 describes the NPI I; Tables 13.5 and 13.6 describe the NPI II and the Degree of Bother Inventory. Mothers are asked to provide information about the average baby first, and then they describe their own infant. In the Degree of Bother Inventory, mothers are asked how much they are bothered by their own infants' behavior in a variety of categories, including crying, sleeping, and feeding.

For both NPI scales, each item is assigned a value from 1 to 5 with "none" being assigned a 1 and "a great deal" a 5. The lower value represents the more desirable

TABLE 13.4.   Neonatal Perception Inventory I

Items
How much crying do you think (the average baby does; your baby will do)?
How much trouble do you think (the average baby has; your baby will have) feeding?
How much spitting up or vomiting do you think (the average baby does; your baby will do)?
How much difficulty do you think (the average baby has; your baby will have) sleeping?
How much difficulty (does the average baby have; do you expect your baby to have) with bowel movements?
How much trouble do you think (the average baby has; your baby will have) settling down to a predictable pattern of eating and sleeping?

Note: Each item is rated according to the following scale: 1 = none; 2 = very little; 3 = moderate amount; 4 = a good bit; 5 = a great deal.

TABLE 13.5.   Neonatal Perception Inventory II

Items
How much crying (do you think the average baby does; has your baby done)?
How much trouble (do you think the average baby has; has your baby had) feeding?
How much spitting up or vomiting (do you think the average baby does; has your baby done)?
How much difficulty (do you think the average baby has; has your baby had) in sleeping?
How much difficulty (does the average baby have; has your baby had) with bowel movements?
How much trouble (do you think the average baby has; has your baby had) in settling down to a predictable pattern of eating and sleeping?

Note: Each item is rated according to the following scale: 1 = none; 2 = very little; 3 = moderate amount; 4 = a good bit; 5 = a great deal.

TABLE 13.6.   Degree of Bother Inventory

Items
Crying
Spitting up or vomiting
Sleeping
Feeding
Elimination
Lack of a predictable schedule
Other: (specify)

Note: Each item is rated according to the following scale: 1 = none; 2 = very little; 3 = somewhat; 4 = a great deal.

behavior. The six items are then totaled for the Average Baby section and the Your Baby section. The Neonatal Perception Inventory Score is the score found when the Your Baby score is subtracted from the Average Baby score. Infants rated by their mothers as better than average are considered low risk, whereas infants who are rated by their mothers as not better than average are classified as being at "high risk for subsequent development of emotional difficulty" (Broussard & Hartner, 1971, p. 447). For the Degree of Bother Inventory, each item is scored from 1 to 4 and the score for each item is summed to provide a total problem score.

STANDARDIZATION AND RELIABILITY.   Broussard and Hartner (1971) administered the scales to 318 primiparas on the first or second postpartum day and again at 1 month. For the NPI scales, the investigators reported that the mothers gave total scores in the range of 7–23 (out of a possible range of 6–30). Differences between the Average Baby and Your Baby scores ranged from +9 to −9. At 2 days, 46.5 percent of the mothers rated their infants as better than average; at 1 month 61.2 percent viewed their infants favorably. Those mothers who viewed their infants favorably were less bothered by their infants' behavior (as measured by the Degree of Bother Inventory). Perry (1983) found in her sample of 57 couples that 70 percent of her mothers rated their infants as above average at 2 days of age. Similarly, Palisin (1980) found that 77 percent of her mothers rated their infants favorably at 2 days, and 66 percent did so at 1 month.

Broussard and Hartner (1971) stated that both the NPI I and the NPI II have construct and criterion validity, and that the Degree of Bother Inventory has high face validity; however, they did not provide specific information to support these conclusions.

Freese and Thoman (1978) asked 20 primiparas and 20 multiparas to complete the NPI I and the NPI II and the Degree of Bother Inventory on 2 successive days. Test–retest reliability for the NPI I was .22 for primiparas and .70 for the multiparas; for the NPI II, these reliability estimates were .82 and .70 for primiparous and multiparous mothers, respectively. For the Degree of Bother Inventory, the test–retest reliability was .89 for primiparas and .81 for multiparas. Blumberg (1980) also reported upon the reliability of the NPI scales. In a sample of 100 mothers (40 percent of whom were primiparious) who rated their infants on the first to fifth postpartum days using the NPI I, Blumberg reported alpha reliability coefficients of .63 for the Average Baby scale and .74 for the Your Baby scale.

OTHER INFORMATION.   In one of the first investigations using the NPI, Broussard and Hartner (1971) reported on a follow-up study across 4½ years. In addition, Broussard (1976) followed this same sample through 10–11 years. Palisin (1980) has also provided longitudinal data using the NPI. In other studies, Perry (1983) used the NPI to compare maternal and paternal perceptions of newborns, while Bates and colleagues (1979) have correlated the NPI with other measures of infant temperament.

Broussard and Hartner (1971) in their original report of a 4½ year follow-up on 85 newborns found that the NPI I was not related to the subsequent development of the child at the age of 4½ years. If the NPI I was used in conjunction with the NPI II, however, the predictive capacity of the scales was greater. In general, if the mother had a positive perception of her infant at either 2 days or 1 month, the child was less likely to need intervention at 4½ years.

Broussard (1976) reported on a follow-up of 104 of her original sample when they were between 10 years, 3 months, and 11 years, 9 months of age. Fifty-nine boys and 45 girls were rated according to the probability of a mental disorder. She found that male infants who were viewed negatively at either 2 days or at 1 month by their mothers were much more likely to have an emotional disorder at the follow-up testing. For females, a single negative perception was less likely to be associated with later emotional disorder than it was for males. Among infants viewed negatively at both 2 days and 1 month, only 7.7 percent were judged to be without a mental disorder at 10–11 years; sex differences were not found in these comparisons. When extremes of mental disorder diagnosis were used, the 2-day ratings were not significantly associated with the presence of mental disorders, although the 1-month ratings were. Broussard noted that all of the children who were rated as pathological at 4½ years were categorized as having a mental disorder at 10–11 years.

In contrast, Palisin (1980) tried to replicate the findings reported by Broussard and Hartner (1971) with a sample of 50 children. She was unable to substantiate the utility of either the NPI I or the NPI II in predicting later pathology in her sample. This author suggested, therefore, that the scales may have clinical utility during the neonatal period, but that their predictive validity for later emotional disturbance was not demonstrated.

Perry (1983) used the Neonatal Perception Inventories in conjunction with the Brazelton scale and a modified version of the Brazelton referred to as the Mother's Assessment of the Behavior of Her Infant (MABI) (Field et al., 1978); on the latter, parents are taught to administer the Brazelton test. The NPI was given when the infant was 2 days, 1 week, and 1 month of age. Perry found that Brazelton scores did not significantly predict scores on the NPI for either mothers or fathers. The use of the structured interaction through the MABI, however, did improve mothers' perceptions of their infants. In addition, maternal and paternal perceptions gained in concordance over the 1-month time period.

Bates and colleagues (1979) also used the NPI in conjunction with their measurement of difficultness as determined by the Infant Characteristics Questionnaire. The NPI was administered to 98 mothers when their infants were 1 month and 4–6 months of age. They found that less favorable 1-month descriptions were associated with infants' being described as fussy–difficult at the second testing on the Infant Characteristics Questionnaire. Finally, Blumberg (1980) examined the effects of neonatal risk, maternal attitude, and cognitive style on maternal perceptions. Her sample included infants who were assigned to the intensive care nursery, the premature unit, the isolation unit, or the regular newborn nursery; 35 percent were considered to be at high to moderate risk. On the first to the fifth postpartum days, the mothers were asked to complete the NPI I. Results indicated that higher-risk infants were perceived more negatively by their mothers. Also, mothers who were delivered by cesarean section had more positive perceptions of their infants, and black mothers viewed their infants more negatively. Other factors, such as maternal anxiety, were not systematically related to mothers' perceptions of their neonates.

As noted above, the Neonatal Perception Inventory is one of the few attempts to describe neonatal temperament. Reports on test–retest reliability have not been favorable, except for the Degree of Bother Inventory completed at 1 month or later. Similarly, predictions from these scores to later perceptions or pathology have not generally been impressive. Intervention strategies aimed at altering maternal perceptions have been successful; differences in maternal perceptions in accordance with the at risk status of the infants have also been documented. The scales seem to have their greatest utility, then, in the documentation of maternal perceptions during the neonatal period.

Tests of Neonatal Status

The assessments to be presented in this section were specifically designed for utilization beginning within the first few days of life. Some scales of this type rely on fairly global ratings of the neonate. For example, on the First-Week Evaluation Scale, devised by Cohen, Allen, Pollin, Inoff, Werner, and Dibble (1972), newborn constitution is determined by having two raters review an infant's medical records. These raters then score each infant on a scale of 1 to 5 on these measures: health, physiological adaptation, calmness, vigor, attention, and neurological status. However, the more frequently utilized neonatal assessment devices rely on direct observation of specific newborn behaviors; in addition, examiners on these tests attempt to elicit many of the behaviors to be assessed. Currently, there are two such assessments receiving widespread use—the Graham/Rosenblith Scales and the Brazelton Neonatal Behavioral Assessment Scale.

Graham Behavior Test for Neonates and the Graham/Rosenblith Scales

The Graham Behavior Test for Neonates (Graham, Matarazzo, & Caldwell, 1956) was originally designed to differentiate normal newborns from those that might be brain injured. The original test consisted of five scales: Pain Threshold, Maturational Level, Visual Response, and ratings of Irritability and Muscle Tension. However, Rosenblith (1974a, 1975) has substantially revised the Graham tests, with the resulting examination becoming known as the Graham/Rosenblith Scales. Since Rosenblith's revision is the test that is more commonly used currently, it will be reviewed here.

TEST ITEMS.   In her revision of the Graham test, Rosenblith eliminated the Pain Threshold scale. Table 13.7 provides a listing of the scales that are included on the Graham/Rosenblith examination, as well as behaviors that make up these scales. In addition, the examiner assigns an irritability rating to the infant; criteria for this rating are described below.

With regard to scoring, the Motor and Tactile–Adaptive scales have a 9-point maximum; further, these two scores are summed, yielding a total maturation score. Visual responsiveness is based on a 10-point scale, while auditory responsiveness can receive a score up to 5 points. For the muscle tonus rating, each measure is assigned a value of 1 to 9, with double ratings given in order to take into account the diverse degrees of tonicity in different parts of the body (e.g., the normal differences in neonates' upper and lower limbs). Finally, the irritability score is based upon ratings made by the examiner over the course of the entire examination. These ratings reflect the frequency with which irritable behavior is observed, the ease with which the infant can be soothed, and whether or not the irritable behavior is judged to be appropriate. These are then combined to place the infant into one of five categories: normal, three degrees of irritability, and no crying.

STANDARDIZATION.   The original Graham scales were standardized by Graham and colleagues (1956), who gave the scales to 176 infants without prenatal, perinatal,

TABLE 13.7. Graham/Rosenblith Scales

Scales and Items

Motor Scale

1. Head reaction in prone position
2. Coordinated crawling motions in prone position
3. Vigor of response to cotton and cellophane
4. Strength of pull as measured on a 4- or 5-pound spring balance

Tactile–Adaptive Scale

1. Responses to cotton over the nose
2. Responses to cellophane over the nose and mouth
3. Persistence of responses over the 20-sec period that cotton and cellophane are applied

Visual Responsiveness

1. Fixation/degree of visual pursuit (both horizontal and vertical) of object

Auditory Responsiveness

1. Responses to rattle and bell

Muscle Tonus

1. Nature (flexed or extended) of spontaneous lower limb position
2. Response of all four extremities to limb displacement
3. Response of the lower limbs to having pressure applied to the feet
4. Change in muscle tone in response to being pulled to a sitting position
5. Amount of spontaneous activity
6. Frequency/severity of trembling, where it occurs, and what stimuli evoke it

or postnatal complications, and to 81 infants suffering from anoxia, mechanical birth injury, or disease or infections associated with brain damage. Socioeconomic factors and sex did not influence the scores, although age did in three scales and in two scales race influenced the scores. The test was concluded to have differentiated significantly between normal and traumatized newborns. Further standardization samples have not been reported except the extensive sampling reported by Rosenblith (1974a, 1975) in regard to performance on other standardized infant tests; these data are discussed in the next section.

RELIABILITY.   Interscorer reliability is reported by Rosenblith (1975) from previously unpublished data of Rosenblith and Anderson-Huntington (1972). For 32 infants, the reliability of the Maturation scale was .91; for the Irritability rating it was .875; for Muscle Tonus, .625; and for the Vision score it was .52. Bench and Parker (1970) reported reliabilities to be .77 for Maturation; .71 for Muscle Tonus; and .73 for the Vision score. In the study by Brown and colleagues (1975), inter-observer reliability was established prior to the start of the study, with the range of observer agreement found to be .83 to 1.00, with a mean of .91 across the scales of Motor Strength, Tactile–Adaptive, Visual Responsiveness, and Auditory Responsiveness.

Test–retest reliability data were reported by Rosenblith (1961) on an earlier version of the scale. She found test–retest reliability across 24 hr to be .73 for the Maturation scale, .63 for Vision, .62 for Muscle Tonus, and .62 for Irritability.

OTHER INFORMATION.   While considerable information has been provided regarding the Graham/Rosenblith Scales, most relevant research has been conducted by Rosenblith and her colleagues. In one study, Rosenblith (1974a) reported an extensive comparison of data from over 1500 infants who were part of the Collaborative Perinatal Project. The infants were examined as neonates with the Graham/Rosenblith Scales, and at 9 months of age with the Bayley Scales. She found that by dividing her sample into four separate samples, the relations between neonatal measures and 9 months largely replicated. There were similarities in the patterns of relations between neonatal measures and later measures. Neonatal Motor scale scores correlated with all 8-month criteria, although male and female criteria differed slightly. Neonatal measures were less related to 8-month outcomes for blacks than for whites. When the samples were examined by gestational age, those infants whose gestational age was less than 37 weeks had the greatest number of significant relationships, but those with gestational ages of 37–41 weeks also had a great number of significant relationships.

Follow-up data have been provided on these same infants. Rosenblith (1970, 1975) reported that, at 4 months of age, infants who had low neonatal scores tended to be identified as having more problems. She also noted that infants who did not show visual following during the neonatal period had a greater tendency to fail Visual–Motor items at 8 months of age; also, they were more frequently suspect or abnormal on gross motor development and other measures, despite higher than average IQs and absence of neurological problems. Findings from a 3-year speech and hearing examination indicated that there was little evidence that children who failed to respond to auditory stimuli as neonates showed hearing deficits in later assessments, although a few hard-of-hearing infants were detected during the neonatal period.

In a 4-year follow-up on 400 infants from the original sample, Rosenblith and Anderson-Huntington (1972) utilized 4-year Binet IQ scores and concept formation measures. Relatively few relationships were found, although Motor scale scores did predict later IQ, and newborn irritability was related to irritability and attention at 4 years. Somewhat surprising, then, were the results of analyses examining associations between the neonatal scores and measures taken at 7 years on more than 1000 of the children (Rosenblith, 1979a, 1979b). These analyses revealed quite a few significant correlations; for example, Motor scale scores predicted 7-year IQs, performance on the Draw-A-Person test, and the Arithmetic portion of the Wide Range Achievement Test. Also, neonatal tactile–adaptive measures were related to the Draw-A-Person scores, Bender-Gestalt performance, and whether or not the child had had to repeat a grade in school. Overall, stability of scores across the 7 years was much greater for females and white children. In explaining the larger number of correlations between neonatal and 7-year scores, Rosenblith suggests that children are under greater stress at 7 years, primarily due to school enrollment. As such, deficits indexed by the newborn measures may be more likely to emerge at this time.

In other research, Rosenblith (1974b) found that neonatal scores on the Tactile–Adaptive scale across ethnic subgroups in Hawaii correctly predicted differences in the incidence of sudden infant death syndrome (SIDS). Also, Brown and colleagues (1975) used the Graham/Rosenblith test in conjunction with observations of mother–infant behavior during feeding. Examination behaviors did not predict behavior during feeding, with the exception that infants who were more visually responsive had their eyes open longer during feeding.

In conclusion, the Graham/Rosenblith Scales have been extensively studied by Rosenblith and her colleagues. Further, the evolution of this test is significant in that it represents one of the earliest attempts to assess neonatal status. It has been satisfactorily standardized, and both interobserver and test–retest reliability are, for the most part, more than adequate. However, it should be noted that, particularly compared to the Neonatal Behavioral Assessment Scale offered by Brazelton (1973), the Graham/Rosenblith Scales measure a limited number of neonatal behaviors. Perhaps this partially explains the fact that other researchers have not typically employed these scales.

Brazelton Neonatal Behavioral Assessment Scale

The Brazelton Neonatal Behavioral Assessment Scale (Brazelton, 1973) was designed in "an attempt to score the infant's available responses to his environment, and so, indirectly, his effect on the environment" (p. 4). It was devised for use with the normal newborn, and it samples a broad range of neonatal behaviors, both reflexive/elicited and behavioral. A second edition (Brazelton, 1984) has recently been published; the manual for this edition corrects previous errors and adds items and information.

TEST ITEMS. The reflexive/elicited behaviors that are measured on the Brazelton test include the following: plantar grasp, hand grasp, ankle clonus, Babinski, standing, automatic walking, placing, incurvation, crawling, glabella, tonic deviation of the head/eyes, nystagmus, tonic neck reflex, Moro, rooting, sucking, and passive movements of the limbs. Each of these items is rated on a 3-point scale, depending on whether it is of low, medium, or high intensity; asymmetry and absence of a reflex are noted as well.

Table 13.8 contains a listing of the behavioral items that were included on the original Brazelton test. Recently, however, Horowitz and her colleagues (e.g., Horowitz, Sullivan, & Linn, 1978; Sullivan & Horowitz, 1978) have offered a supplemented version of the Brazelton scale that includes five new behavioral items. This version—referred to as the Neonatal Behavioral Assessment Scale with Kansas Supplements (NBAS-K)—adds these items: orientation—inanimate visual and auditory (now included as a regular item in the second edition), quality of infant alert responsivity, examiner persistence, general irritability, and reinforcement value of the infant's behavior.

In scoring the behavioral items, each is rated on a 9-point scale, with the midpoint of the scale denoting the expected behavior of a normal 3-day-old infant. Two state measures are also noted: initial state of the infant and the infant's predominant state throughout the examination. State is defined in six stages, from deep sleep to crying. The examiner also notes items that describe the conditions under which the test was done and the overall impression of the infant, as well as writing an optional descriptive paragraph. The cover sheet of the scoring sheet provides for recording background data of the parents, birth weight, type of feeding, exact age, and other identifying facts about the infant.

While there is a recommended order for administering the items after the first few, the order is partially determined by the behavior of the infant. There is no limit on the number of times an item might be tried, though the state of the infant during which a particular item is to be administered is specified. Those investigators utilizing the original scale attempt to elicit the infant's best performance on the ori-

TABLE 13.8. Neonatal Behavioral Assessment Scale

Behavioral Items
1. Response decrement to light
2. Response decrement to rattle
3. Response decrement to bell
4. Response decrement to pinprick
5. Inanimate visual orientation response—focusing and following an object
6. Inanimate auditory orientation response—reaction to an auditory stimulus
7. Animate visual orientation—focusing and following a person's face
8. Animate auditory orientation—reaction to a voice
9. Animate visual and auditory orientation—reaction to a person's face and voice
10. Pull-to-sit
11. Defensive movements
12. Degree of alertness
13. General tonus
14. Motor maturity
15. Cuddliness
16. Consolability with intervention
17. Peak of excitement
18. Rapidity of buildup
19. Irritability
20. Activity
21. Tremulousness
22. Amount of startle
23. Lability of skin color
24. Lability of states
25. Self-quieting activity
26. Hand-to-mouth facility
27. Number of smiles

entation and consolability items. However, on the NBAS-K, examiners note a "modal" score (i.e., the infant's characteristic behavior) in addition to a best score.

STANDARDIZATION. To this point the Brazelton scale has not been formally standardized, although Horowitz and her colleagues (in preparation) are currently preparing a normative report based on a sample of 1385 normal infants born in Kansas.

Leijon and Finnstrom (1981) have provided information regarding the distribution of scores for each item on the 9-point scale. Using a sample of 80 infants, these researchers reported that, overall, 16 percent of these babies scored between 1 and 3, 54 percent were rated between 4 and 6, and 26 percent attained scores between 7 and 9 (the percentages do not add to 100 percent because not all infants could be scored on all items). Further, their item analysis revealed most items to be unimodal, with some (e.g., habituation to the rattle) skewing toward the upper end of the scale and others (e.g., startles) skewing toward the lower end of the scale. One exception was self-quieting activity, which demonstrated a "flat" distribution. Finally, for some items the entire 9-point scale was used (e.g., hand-to-mouth facility), while for other items (e.g., activity level) only a narrow range of scores was observed. In this regard, Kestermann (1981) analyzed the extent to which the 1–9 range was utilized for each item. Items found to utilize a wide range of scores included irritability, cuddliness, consolability, hand-to-mouth facility, and lability of skin color; orientation items, in contrast, used a very narrow range. Kestermann concluded, therefore, that some Brazelton items are more valuable in discriminating among normal newborns than others.

RELIABILITY. High interobserver reliability appears to be consistently attainable on the Brazelton examination. For instance, Horowitz and Brazelton (1973) reported in a survey of published research that reliabilities of independent testers trained at the same time ranged from .85 to 1.00. Brazelton and Tryphonopoulou (1972) found that testers can be trained to a .90 criterion of reliability and that these high levels tend to be maintained over time.

By comparison, test–retest reliability on the Brazelton scale has not generally been impressive, particularly when computed using traditional correlational techniques (e.g., Horowitz et al., 1978; Kestermann, 1981; Leijon & Finnstrom, 1981). However, Horowitz and colleagues (1978) have criticized such techniques, advocating instead the use of interval analysis. In this procedure, each infant's score on a particular item is compared to the infant's own performance on that item on another exam, with stability of behavior defined as the same score plus or minus 1 point; percentages are then computed of infants exhibiting such stability. Using this procedure Lancioni, Horowitz, and Sullivan (1980a) reported that 39 percent of their infants exhibited stable Brazelton scores across the first month of life. As these authors note, however, the interval analysis technique does not lend itself to statistical analysis.

In addition to specific methods of computing reliability, other factors appear to influence test–retest stability on the Brazelton examination. For example, Horowitz and colleagues (1977) reported greater stability in an Israeli as compared to an American newborn sample. Also, in comparisons among Brazelton items (e.g., Kestermann, 1981; Sameroff, Krafchuk, & Bakow, 1978) certain areas of the test have been reported more stable than others (e.g., orientation vs. nonorientation, visual vs. auditory orientation). Finally, Linn and Horowitz (1984) have related stability of Brazelton performance to maternal responsivity, with higher stability being found in infants of less responsive mothers.

To summarize, research utilizing the Brazelton assessment consistently reports high interobserver reliability. In contrast, as concluded by Sameroff (1978), the answer to the question of whether Brazelton scores remain stable from day to day still appears to be a qualified no. It should be noted, however, that not all researchers using the Brazelton assessment agree regarding the value of demonstrating behavioral stability during the neonatal period (cf. Horowitz et al., 1978; Kaye, 1978).

OTHER INFORMATION. Since its inception, the Brazelton scale has been used extensively in neonatal research. As noted by Horowitz and Brazelton (1973), investigators utilized early versions of the scale in demonstrating reliable differences between American Caucasian infants and American Orientals (Freedman & Freedman, 1969) and Mexican infants (Brazelton, Robey, & Collier, 1969). The final version has also been used in cross-cultural comparisons (e.g., Coll, Sepkoski, & Lester, 1981; Horowitz et al., 1977; Keefer, Tronick, Dixon, & Brazelton, 1982), as well as in documenting the influence of socioeconomic status on neonatal behavior (Justice, Self, & Gutrecht, 1976) (for a more complete review of the research on the Brazelton exam see Horowitz & Linn, 1982, 1984).

Some early uses of the Brazelton exam included the assessment of differences in neonatal behavior due to maternal medication. In one report, Aleksandrowicz and Aleksandrowicz (1974) concluded that infants' Brazelton performance was affected by medication as late as 28 days after birth. Also, Standley, Soule, Copans, and Duchowny (1974) reported increased irritability in infants whose mothers received anesthesia. In a complex design, Horowitz and colleagues (1973) examined drug effects and ethnicity differences in infants using the Brazelton in the first month of life and the Bayley scales at 3 months of age. Finding few significant medication differences, these investigators concluded that light to moderate levels of obstetrical medication do not appear to affect newborn behavior. Recently, however, such conclusions have been challenged by Lester, Als, and Brazelton (1982), who point out the necessity for considering other factors (e.g., time since first/last drug administration, number of different drugs, length of labor), in addition to level of maternal anesthesia, when assessing medication effects. In this regard, several recent studies have examined Brazelton performance as it relates to actual drug levels present in the umbilical cord (e.g., Belsey et al., 1981; Kuhnert, Harrison, Linn, & Kuhnert, 1984; Rosenblatt et al., 1981); these studies have reported associations between high blood cord levels and depressed Brazelton scores as late as the sixth week of life.

Type of delivery has also been related to Brazelton scores, with Leijon (1980) reporting lower scores in infants born through vacuum extraction compared to babies born without instrumental assistance. However, Field and Widmayer (1980) reported no differences between babies delivered via cesarean section and those experiencing a normal vaginal delivery.

A number of investigators have examined variations in Brazelton scores due to different maternal and infant characteristics. For example, newborn behavior has been reported to be adversely affected by maternal narcotic addiction (Strauss, Lessen-Firestone, Starr, & Ostrea, 1975), methadone treatment (e.g., Marcus, Haus, & Jeremy, 1982; Soule, Standley, Copans, & Davis, 1974), and alcohol use (Streissguth, Barr, & Martin, 1983). Also, poorer infant Brazelton scores have been associated with maternal diabetes (Yogman, Cole, Als, & Lester, 1982) and adolescent childbearing (e.g., Coll et al., 1982; Thompson, Cappleman, & Zeitschel, 1979). In considering infant characteristics, birth weight has been most researched, with average-weight infants performing more optimally on the Brazelton examination compared to both under- and overweight neonates (e.g., Als, Tronick, Adamson, & Brazelton, 1976; Zeskind, 1981). Jaundiced newborns have also been found to score lower on the Brazelton test compared to nonjaundiced babies (Telzrow, Snyder, Tronick, Als, & Brazelton, 1980).

Although the Brazelton scale was originally intended to assess normal newborn behavior, there has been an increasing tendency for researchers to utilize the scale in at risk or atypical infant samples. Comparisons between full-term and premature infants have frequently been made. For instance, Dubowitz, Dubowitz, Morante, and Verghote (1980) used the orientation items to assess visual functioning in preterm neonates. These authors reported that focusing was not generally observed on these items until approximately 33 postconceptual weeks. Field and colleagues (1978), utilizing a preterm sample also characterized by respiratory distress syndrome, described these infants as hypotonic, hard to arouse, and weak in their reflexes. However, it should be noted that studies utilizing "low-risk" preterm babies (i.e., those without serious concomitant problems) have reported minimal differences compared to full-term infants' responsiveness on the Brazelton scale (e.g., Leijon, 1982; Paludetto et al., 1982). Other at risk groups to be studied include postmature samples, who have been found to score lower than term infants on interactive and motoric measures (e.g., Field, Dabiri, Hallock, & Shuman, 1977). Also, some investigators have used the scale with infants suffering from grossly abnormal conditions such as hydranencephaly (Aylward, Lazzara, & Meyer, 1978; Francis, Self, & McCaffree, 1984).

Given the emphasis placed by Brazelton upon the neonate's social nature, it is not surprising that several attempts have been made to relate Brazelton scores to different aspects of mother–infant interaction. To illustrate, Osofsky and Danzger (1974) and Arco, DeMeis, Self, and Gutrecht (1984) found that certain neonatal behaviors, notably social responsiveness, are consistent across the Brazelton testing and interactional contexts. Also, as noted above, stability and variability in Brazelton performance have been related to mother–infant interaction (Linn & Horowitz, 1984).

Higher Brazelton scores have also been found to relate to positive maternal perceptions of the newborn (Meares, Penman, Milgrom-Friedman, & Baker, 1982). Further, there is a growing body of information suggesting that newborn Brazelton scores relate to subsequent interaction measures. For example, Field (1977) reported that lower neonatal interactive scores on the Brazelton exam predicted less infant gazing and less maternal activity during interactions at 3½ months. Similarly, high neonatal irritability has been associated with maternal difficulty in soothing the infant and slower maternal responding to the infant at 3 months (e.g., Crockenberg, 1981; Crockenberg & Smith, 1982). Finally, Waters, Vaughn, and Egeland (1980) reported that low infant scores on the orientation, motor maturity, and regulation items at 7 days of age predicted anxious and resistant attachment patterns toward the mother at 1 year of age.

Perhaps because of these apparent relationships between Brazelton scores and mother–infant interaction measures, a major recent focus in studies utilizing this scale has involved training parents to administer the Brazelton exam. Field and her colleagues (e.g., Field et al., 1978; Widmayer & Field, 1981) have adapted the Brazelton examination to be given by parents, referring to this adaptation as the Mothers' Assessment of the Behavior of her Infant (MABI). According to Field and colleagues (1978), comparisons of maternal and tester ratings are relatively similar in all areas except social interaction, which testers tend to rate higher than the mothers. Further, the MABI has been used to enhance mother–infant interaction in preterm infant samples (e.g., Widmayer & Field, 1980, 1981). Other studies have reported similar results simply through the demonstration of the Brazelton exam to parents (e.g., Liptak, Keller, Feldman, & Chamberlain, 1983; Myers, 1982; Worobey & Belsky, 1982).

Since the original version of the Brazelton scales was published, several investigators have made significant modifications, with respect to both scoring and administration. Major changes in scoring involve the derivation of clusters of items that appear to correlate as opposed to simply utilizing single item scores. Such derivations have typically been attempted through factor analysis (e.g., Osofsky & O'Connell, 1977) and, though the solutions vary across studies, the following areas are usually represented: reactivity/arousal, orientation/responsivity, habituation, motor maturity, and state regulation. Recently, Als and her colleagues (e.g., Adamson, Als, Tronick, & Brazelton, 1975; Als, 1978; Als, Tronick, Lester, & Brazelton, 1977) have criticized statistical means of grouping Brazelton items. Instead, these researchers argue that these groupings should be based upon logical inferences regarding neonatal behavior, and they have offered four such a priori clusters consisting of interactive, physiological, motoric, and state processes. The most recent cluster system, and the one most likely to be widely adopted, is that proposed by Lester (1983); this system includes habituation, orientation, motor performance, range of state, regulation of state, and autonomic regulation clusters. While Sameroff and colleagues (1978) have pointed out problems with both the factor analysis and a priori cluster approaches, most current research utilizing the Brazelton examination does tend to group items in some fashion.

With respect to changes in the actual administration of the Brazelton scale, the most utilized modification is the NBAS-K (Horowitz et al., 1978), previously described. Already the NBAS-K has been examined, and its utility substantiated, in several reports (e.g., Lancioni et al., 1980; Lancioni, Horowitz, & Sullivan, 1980b); further, according to Sullivan and Horowitz (1978), the addition of the new items and the use of the modal scoring system appear to cause no scoring distortion in the rest of the items. Another revision of the Brazelton scale is an abbreviated version that may be adopted for clinical use (Berger, 1981). Finally, Als (1982) has substantially revised this assessment for use with preterm infants, referring to this revision as the Assessment of Preterm Infants' Behavior (APIB).

Some final comments regarding the Brazelton scale involve its relationship to other infant tests and behaviors. As described above, Leijon and Finnstrom (1981) reported that ratings derived from the Prechtl-Beintema test positively related to Brazelton orientation and motor items on 1 day of age; few associations were found on day 5. Brazelton scores have also been reported to predict later infant behaviors and test scores. For example, Horowitz, Self, Paden, Culp, Boyd, and Mann (1971) and McCluskey and Horowitz (1975) reported positive associations between Brazelton performance and later visual responsiveness. Several studies have attempted to examine relationships between Brazelton and Bayley scores. For instance, Sostek and Anders (1977) found that higher Brazelton state control and total scores at 8 days predicted higher MDIs at 10 weeks of age. Similarly, Vaughn, Taraldson, Crichton, and Egeland (1980) reported modest but significant positive correlations between Brazelton scores during the first 2 weeks of life and 9-month performance on the Bayley Mental scale. Field and colleagues (1978), using a sample of preterm infants, reported the neonatal a priori motor scores predicted the Bayley MDI at 8 months, and that a priori motor and interactive scores predicted 12-month MDI levels. Finally, Lester (1983) has investigated a "recovery curve" strategy using Lester cluster score changes over time and relating these changes to later Bayley score performance with some moderate success.

In summary, the Brazelton Neonatal Behavioral Assessment Scale, despite its recent development, has been extensively used for a diverse number of purposes in infant research. It has certainly proved to be extremely effective with respect to distinguishing among normal newborn infants, and has been increasingly employed in at risk and atypical infant samples. Finally, a growing body of literature suggests that Brazelton performance might well be useful in predicting other infant behaviors, both in interaction with the caregiver and on standard infant assessments.

Psychometric Devices

The assessment devices to be discussed in the present section are based on the same assumptions that guided the intelligence testing movement during the late nineteenth and early twentieth centuries. Although infants were not targets of study by early test developers, by the 1920s investigators had become greatly interested in tapping infant intelligence. As noted by Horowitz and Dunn (1978), this interest was stimulated in large part by the potential of the infancy period for testing the relative effects of heredity and environment. The rise in infant intelligence testing is described by Brooks and Weinraub (1976):

> As the testing movement gained momentum and branched out into more areas in the 1920s, a series of investigators in America began intensive studies of infants and preschoolers. This ultimately led to the development of normative scales and intelligence tests such as those developed at Yale, Minnesota, Berkeley, and Iowa. These tests, appearing in the late 1920s and early 1930s, gained widespread acceptance and they led to a series of studies on the stability of scores from month to month, the test-retest reliability from testing to testing, and the predictive validity from infancy to childhood. (p. 19)

Since that time, numerous scales based on the psychometric approach have been developed for infants. The devices to be detailed in this section are the two that have been most commonly utilized in the United States—the Gesell Developmental Schedules and the Bayley Scales of Infant Development.

Gesell Developmental Schedules

The Gesell Developmental Schedules have been widely used by both psychologists and pediatricians since the late 1920s when Arnold Gesell published his first studies. The information included here is taken from Gesell and Amatruda's (1947) *Developmental Diagnosis, Second Edition,* and the third edition of *Developmental Diagnosis,* edited by Knobloch and Pasamanick (1974a). Behavior and development are examined at the key ages of 4, 16, 28, and 40 weeks and 12, 18, 24, and 36 months, with some comments about 48 and 60 months added by Knobloch and Pasamanick.

TEST ITEMS.   In the latest version of the scales (Knobloch & Pasamanick, 1974a), behavior is divided into five areas: Gross Motor, Fine Motor, Adaptive, Language, and Personal–Social. Table 13.9 summarizes the behaviors from each of these areas that are considered typical in the infant at 4 weeks of age. During the course of the test, a minus is assigned if the behavior does not occur (or in older ages, if a less mature behavior occurs), a plus if the behavior occurs, and a double plus if a more mature pattern occurs. At the end of the examination the examiner assesses the infant's behavior in each of the four areas, as well as the overall behavior. This is done not merely by adding the pluses and minuses but by estimating the infant's degree of acceleration or delay in relation to the age norms.

The examiner assigns a representative age to each of the four areas as well as an overall age. These ages can then be used to figure a developmental quotient (DQ), which is maturity age divided by chronological age. Gesell continually stressed that

TABLE 13.9.   Gesell Developmental Schedules

Scales and Items

Gross Motor Scale

1. In supine position, side position head predominates
2. In supine position, the asymmetrical tonic neck reflex postures predominate
3. In supine position, infant can roll partially to side
4. In prone position, when pulled to sit, there is complete or marked head lag
5. In sitting position, the head predominantly sags forward on infant's chest
6. When held prone above a surface, the head droops
7. If placed in prone position, the infant rotates head so it rests on cheek
8. In prone position, the infant will raise head slightly to turn it, so infant can rest on cheek
9. Crawling movements occur in the prone position

Fine Motor Scale

1. Hands are fisted in supine position
2. Hands will clench a rattle on contact

Adaptive Scale

1. A ring or rattle is regarded only momentarily in the line of vision
2. A dangled ring will be followed to midline
3. Infant drops the clenched rattle immediately
4. Infant attends to a bell by diminished activity

Language Scale

1. Infant shows vague and indirect regard to the examiner during the assessment
2. Infant exhibits an impassive face throughout most of the examination period
3. Infant emits small, throaty vocalizations

Personal–Social Scale

1. Infant diminishes activity as it regards an adult face
2. Infant stares indefinitely at surroundings
3. Infant requires two night feedings.

this was not equivalent to an intelligence quotient or any estimate of intelligence in the general sense of the term.

STANDARDIZATION.   The Gesell Developmental Schedules have apparently been standardized extensively, although exact figures are hard to ascertain. One standardization group consisted of 107 healthy children of middle socioeconomic status tested at 15 months and followed up at 18 months, 2, 3, 4, 5, and 6 years of age (Gesell et al., 1940). Another group (possibly comprising part of the aforementioned group) included 107 children (middle socioeconomic status) of whom 2 to 48 were tested at each of 15 age levels, with a total of 524 examinations (Gesell, Thompson, & Amatruda, 1934). Still another group, this one of 90 infants, both normal and abnormal, were seen a total of 429 times, from the time the infants were under 3 months until they were more than 48 months (Gesell, 1928). Standardization data from the latest edition of the schedules have not been reported.

RELIABILITY.   Gesell recognized the problem of examiner reliability as noted by his discussions of having an observer take notes throughout the examination, as well as having the examiner score the exam. Also, he only used trained experimenters for his examinations. The problem of examiner–observer reliability, however, was never investigated statistically.

Knobloch and Pasamanick (1974a) reported reliability of DQ assignment to be .98 among 18 pediatric residents across 100 clinical examinations. They also commented on the impossibility of calculating split-half reliability from the schedules, since equal numbers of items are not available.

Test–retest reliability of the Gesell schedules is apparently high. Gesell (1928) reported that in 90 infants seen 492 times, the first test indicated the overall scores 80 percent of the time; in delayed infants it was 96 percent. Knobloch and Pasamanick (1974a) reported test–retest reliability for 65 infants seen by different pediatricians within 2 to 3 days to be .82. No separate reliability estimates have been reported for the 4-week items.

OTHER INFORMATION.   In a classic series of articles, Fish and her co-workers (e.g., Fish, 1957, 1959, 1960; Fish, Shapiro, Halpern, & Wile, 1965; Fish, Wile, Shapiro, & Halpern, 1966) reported on their attempts to detect and longitudinally follow schizophrenia during infancy. As described in the first report, Fish (1957) administered the Gesell scales to 16 infants beginning at 4–6 weeks of age. On their first evaluation, three infants were judged as being vulnerable to schizophrenia. These judgments were based in large part on the infants' uneven performance on the various Gesell scales. According to this report, these infants were characterized by abnormal patterns of development across the first 18 months of life. In a 10-year follow-up study, Fish and colleagues (1966) had this same sample evaluated by a psychiatrist who was naive as to these children's original diagnoses. The three children who had been classified as vulnerable to schizophrenia as infants were distinguished by the psychiatrist from the other children. According to him, these three children exhibited pathological disorders of thinking, identification, and personality organization. In contrast, none of the other children were identified as pathological, although two were diagnosed as having moderate neurotic problems.

Other than the work of Fish and her colleagues, very little data are available regarding the Gesell test in the first months of life. It should be noted, however, that this assessment has been useful in research on older infants, particularly with regard to the predictive validity of the scale. As just one example, Roe, McClure, and Roe (1983) reported significant correlations between WISC-R scores at 12 years of age and DQ scores at 5, 7, 9, and 15 months; correlations were .64, .66, .62, and .43 respectively. The Gesell test has also been used to examine the development of Down's syndrome infants (e.g., Dicks-Mireaux, 1972) and to document the relationship between infant cognitive level and factors such as maternal intelligence (e.g., Casler, 1976) and birth order (e.g., Cohen & Beckwith, 1977). Finally, there has been much recent interest in relating Gesell scores to measures of infant–caregiver interaction (e.g., Beckwith, Cohen, Kopp, Parmelee, & Marcy, 1976; Cohen & Beckwith, 1979).

In summary, the Gesell Developmental Schedules have been used for clinical and research purposes. Standardization has been extensive and reliability is excellent. Some research suggests their utility for predicting later developmental levels. Also, with older infants they have been successfully employed in demonstrating associations between infant cognition and a number of variables. Overall, however, they do not seem to be used as frequently as the Bayley Scales of Infant Development (Bayley, 1969), in either clinic or research settings.

Bayley Scales of Infant Development

The Bayley Scales of Infant Development (Bayley, 1969) are essentially a revision of the California First Year Mental Scale (Bayley, 1933), the California Preschool Mental Scale (Jaffa, 1934), and the California Infant Scale of Motor Development (Bayley, 1936). The age range for the current Bayley test is 1 month–2½ years. Although this test was originally designed to measure the intellectual capacities of the child, this intention had to be deemphasized when studies failed consistently to demonstrate relationships between infant test scores and later cognitive measures. However, it is widely agreed that the Bayley examination is extremely effective at assessing a child's developmental status at a given age.

TEST ITEMS.   The current revision is composed of three separate scales, each of which is designed to assess a separate component of the child's total developmental status at a certain age. Table 13.10 contains a listing of items from the Mental and Motor scales that can be assessed in the 1-month-old infant. At this age level, the Mental scale primarily measures sensory–perceptual abilities, while items on the Motor scale tend to involve gross body movements and head control. A third part of the Bayley scales—the Infant Behavior Record (IBR)—is completed after the

TABLE 13.10.   Bayley Scales of Infant Development

Scales and Items

Mental Scale

1. Responds to the sound of a bell
2. Quiets when picked up
3. Responds to the sound of a rattle
4. Responds to a sharp sound like a light switch
5. Momentarily regards a red ring
6. Regards a person momentarily
7. Regards the red ring for a prolonged period
8. Exhibits horizontal eye coordination to the red ring
9. Exhibits horizontal eye coordination to a light
10. Visually follows a moving person
11. Responds to a voice
12. Exhibits vertical eye coordination to the light
13. Vocalizes once or twice
14. Exhibits vertical eye coordination to the red ring

Motor Scale

1. Lifts head when held at shoulder
2. Shows postural adjustment when held at shoulder
3. Exhibits lateral head movements in prone position
4. Exhibits crawling movements in prone position
5. Grasps red ring
6. Thrusts arms in play
7. Thrusts legs in play
8. Holds the head erect briefly while in a sitting position

Mental and Motor scales have been administered. The primary purpose of the IBR is to help the clinician assess the infant or child's orientation toward its environment. However, since few of the behaviors measured by the IBR can be observed during the neonatal period, it will not be further described here.

After the infant has been tested on the Bayley Mental scale, its basal level (the last item passed) is noted. The raw score for the scaling is the total number of items the child passed, including all items below the basal level. The raw score is converted to the mental development index (MDI) by consulting the norms for the child's given age as derived by Bayley (1969). The Motor scale is converted similarly except that a different table of normative scores is given; this conversion yields the psychomotor development index (PDI). Bayley does not interpret these scores as intelligence scores. When delayed infants or children are being assessed, Bayley suggests finding the child's raw score in the table of norms in the rows corresponding to an MDI or PDI of 100, then noting the age group column in which the given raw score is nearest that obtained by the child. This she calls an age equivalent or mental age equivalent.

STANDARDIZATION.   The current Bayley Scales of Infant Development were standardized on 1262 children 2–30 months of age. In this sample there were no significant differences related to sex, birth order, geographic location, or parental education. One racial–ethnic group difference was found, with black children obtaining slightly superior (though significant) scores on the Motor scale from 3 through 14 months. In an earlier standardization, Bayley (1965) utilized 87 infants, including a sample of 1-month-olds; for these 1-month-old infants, no differences were observed due to sex, birth order, parental education, or geographic location.

RELIABILITY.   Bayley (1969) did not report interobserver reliability for the latest standardization sample. Werner and Bayley (1966) did report reliability estimates for the immediate precursors of the Mental and Motor scales with 90 infants 8 months old; mean estimates for these scales were 89.4 and 93.4 percent respectively. Agreement was high on the Mental scale items that dealt with object-oriented behaviors and lower on items requiring social interaction. On the Motor scale, high agreement was found on items dealing with independent control of head, trunk, and extremities, compared to items requiring adult assistance.

Test–retest reliability was also investigated by Werner and Bayley (1966) with 28 children returning in 1 week for a retest by the same examiners. Test–retest agreement for the Mental scale was 76.4 percent and for the Motor scale was 75.3 percent. More recently, Horner (1980) examined test–retest stability in Bayley scores across 1 week in 9- and 15-month-old male and female infants. Horner reported that this stability was significant in all but the 9-month-old female group; overall agreement was 84.6 percent in the 9-month group and 84.5 percent in the 15-month group. Items exhibiting the least stability across the 1-week period were vocal/verbal and social–interactional in nature. No separate reliability estimates have been provided for the neonatal period.

OTHER INFORMATION.   Much of the available data on the Bayley test within the first month of life have come from cross-cultural research. For instance, several studies have been reported on the performance of babies from Yucatan, Mexico, on the Motor scale (e.g., Solomons, 1978, 1980; Solomons & Solomons, 1975). In the initial study, Solomons and Solomons (1975) tested these babies every month beginning at 2 weeks of age and continuing for a year. Overall, these reports indicated that the Mexican babies exhibited advanced motor skills until around 6 months of age, at which time they began to lag behind American infants; by 12 months of age, the average PDI for the Mexican infants was 86.

In another study, Metzl (1980) examined the impact of exposing parents to an infant stimulation program on the infant's development; the Bayley scales were administered at 6 weeks and 6 months of age. Results indicated that the greatest increase in infant MDI levels occurred in the group in which both parents were being trained in the stimulation program.

In considering infants after the first month of life, the Bayley scales have been extensively employed as a research tool. To illustrate, they have often been used in studies of prematurity (e.g., Hunt & Rhodes, 1977; Siegel, 1983) and other exceptional conditions (e.g., Pollitt, 1983; Thompson, Eisenberg, & Levin, 1982). Recently these scales have been increasingly employed as an outcome measure in evaluating treatments for conditions such as malnutrition (e.g., Joos, Pollitt, Mueller, & Albright, 1983) and anemia (e.g., Honig & Oski, 1978). In addition, several researchers have demonstrated relationships between Bayley scores and infant–caregiver interaction (e.g., Cohen & Beckwith, 1979; Lee-Painter & Lewis, 1974; Lewis & Coates, 1980; Poresky & Henderson, 1982).

Information also exists regarding relationships among the various Bayley scales, as well as between the Bayley test and other assessments. For instance, Bayley (1969) reported low correlations between MDI and PDI scores. However, significant positive relationships have been found between MDI estimates and factors derived from the IBR (e.g., McGowan, Johnson, & Maxwell, 1981; Matheny, Dolan, & Wilson, 1974). With respect to the Bayley's relationship to other tests, several studies have reported positive associations to Piagetian-based measures (e.g., Gottfried & Brody, 1975; King & Seegmiller, 1973). Further, Siegel (1979) found that both MDI and PDI measures collected through 24 months of age predicted 30- and 36-month Stanford-Binet scores. However, it should be noted that for the most part Bayley performance does not consistently predict later cognitive measures. This is particularly true when socioeconomic status and level of functioning are controlled (e.g., Dubose, 1976; Rubin & Balow, 1979; Willerman, Broman, & Field, 1970).

In summary, the Bayley Scales of Infant Development have been extremely well standardized and have been demonstrated to be very reliable. At this point in time, this test appears to be the most frequently utilized measure of infant cognition. Also, with the possible exception of the Brazelton test, the Bayley scales have had the most extensive use in research of all the behavioral assessment techniques; they have certainly been used more than the Gesell Developmental Schedules in this regard. While they may not necessarily predict later IQ scores, they are probably unrivaled at determining a child's developmental status relative to its age-mates.

Sensorimotor Scales

As noted by several authors (e.g., Dunst, 1982; Uzgiris & Hunt, 1975), Piagetian-based sensorimotor scales differ from tests such as the Gesell and Bayley scales in a number of ways. Generally, psychometric approaches assume that intelligence is a unitary trait, emphasize the infant's chronological age, and fail to consider the importance of interrelationships among demonstrated skills. In contrast, sensorimotor scales assume that infant cognition consists of a number of discrete abilities, emphasize sequential progression rather than age, and place great significance on the interrelationships that exist among achievements in different areas.

To this point, three major sensorimotor scales have been developed. These are the Casati-Lezine Scale (Casati & Lezine, 1968), the Albert Einstein Scales of Sensorimotor Development (Corman & Escalona, 1969), and the Infant Psychological Development Scales (Uzgiris & Hunt, 1975). The Casati-Lezine test measures four areas of sensorimotor development: object search, the use of intermediaries, object exploration, and the combination of objects. The Albert Einstein scales assess sensorimotor functioning in the areas of prehension, object permanence, and space. While both of these scales have been utilized to some degree by infant researchers, they focus almost exclusively on achievements beginning in the third or fourth sensorimotor substage; therefore, they surpass the age range to be covered in the present chapter. This discussion, then, will center upon the Uzgiris-Hunt test, which includes information on 1-month-old infants.

Infant Psychological Development Scales (IPDS)

The IPDS, which Dunst (1982) has referred to as "the most comprehensive and best-constructed Piagetian-based scales" (p. 264) currently in use, is based on the assumption that development proceeds in an ordinal fashion. In explaining the implications of such an assumption for testing, Uzgiris and Hunt (1975) state that:

> ordinal scales imply a hierarchical relationship between achievements at different levels, so that in principle the achievements of the higher level do not incidentally follow, but are intrinsically derived from those at the preceding level and encompass them within the higher level. (p. 11)

Although infant chronological age is not emphasized in the IPDS, the report by Uzgiris and Hunt (1975) was based on 84 infants in the range of 1–23 months of age; in general, the IPDS is appropriate for administration within the first 2 years of life.

TEST ITEMS. The IPDS measures infant development in seven areas: (1) visual pursuit and the permanence of objects, (2) means for obtaining desired environmental events, (3a) vocal imitation, (3b) gestural imitation, (4) operational causality, (5) construction of object relations in space, and (6) schemes for relating to objects. Each subscale consists of a hierarchical ordering of items that is designed to examine the emergence of each concept.

During administration infants are presented with a number of eliciting situations intended to test their level of performance in each area. Uzgiris and Hunt reported that only two subscales—visual pursuit and the performance of objects and vocal imitation—contained items that were exhibited by a majority of infants at the 1-month level. For the visual pursuit/permanence of objects scale, the one item passed at this age involved the momentary perceptual construction of an object; for this item, the infant has to follow a slowly moving object through a complete arc of 180 deg with smooth accommodation. Two items were passed on the vocal imitation scale. The first—the differentiation of the vocalizing scheme—is credited if the infant exhibits nondistress vocalizations (e.g., cooing). The second—recognition of the infant's own sounds—is scored if an infant increases mouthing movements or smiles on hearing sounds it has already made.

Consistent with the theoretical framework underlying the IPDS, Uzgiris and Hunt do not advocate nor present procedures for deriving a score based upon IPDS performance. Rather, infants are simply characterized with respect to their most advanced achievements on each subscale in order to indicate their level of cognitive organization.

STANDARDIZATION.   To this point, no real attempt has been made to standardize the IPDS, which is essentially a reflection of the philosophy on which the scales are based. According to Uzgiris and Hunt, the various levels of cognitive organization are of psychological significance in their own right, and "need not be based on the individual's comparative status in a statistical distribution" (p. x).

RELIABILITY.   For their sample of 84 infants, Uzgiris and Hunt reported the following interobserver reliabilities for the indicated subscales: visual pursuit and permanence of objects, 96.4 percent; means for obtaining desired environmental events, 96.2 percent; vocal imitation, 91.8 percent; gestural imitation, 95.7 percent; operational causality, 93.7 percent; construction of object relations in space, 96.9 percent; and schemes for relating to objects, 93.0 percent. Good interobserver reliability also appears possible in atypical samples, as Kahn (1976) reported reliabilities ranging from 78 to 95 percent among the seven subscales in a group of individuals who were severely to profoundly retarded.

With respect to test–retest reliability, Uzgiris and Hunt provided figures regarding the stability of infant performance over a 48-hr span. Test–retest reliabilities for the subscales were: visual pursuit and permanence of objects, 83.8 percent; means for obtaining desired environmental events, 75.5 percent; vocal imitation, 72.6 percent; gestural imitation, 70.0 percent; operational causality, 71.2 percent; construction of object relations in space, 84.6 percent; and schemes for relating to objects, 79 percent. Higher test–retest reliabilities were demonstrated in the retarded sample utilized by Kahn (1976), who reported figures ranging from 88 to 96 percent from test administrations 1 week apart.

OTHER INFORMATION.   There is almost no information specific to the 1-month-old infant available on the IPDS, although infants this age have been used in attempts to substantiate the ordinality of the scales. Using scalogram analysis, Uzgiris and Hunt (1975) demonstrated that their infants 1–23 months old followed a sequential order of progression on the scales. Ordinality was particularly consistent for operational causality, while both means for obtaining events and schemes for relating to objects exhibited less ordinality. In a longitudinal study, Uzgiris (1973) administered the scales to 12 infants 1–25 months of age. While she reported that the order of the scales was generally verified, some "backsliding" (i.e., slight regressions in performance) was observed for some tasks in certain testing situations. However, as Uzgiris (1976) notes, invariant sequencing is claimed for the sensorimotor stages themselves, not for specific tasks intended to index those stages.

Despite its relatively recent development, considerable information exists regarding the use of the IPDS in research with older babies. Such research has documented socioeconomic differences in IPDS performance (e.g., Wachs, Uzgiris, & Hunt, 1971) and the utility of this test in assessing atypical infant/child populations (e.g.,

Kahn, 1975; Wachs, 1970; Wachs & DeRemer, 1978) and as a clinical/educational tool (e.g., Dunst, 1980, 1982). In addition, as with other tests discussed in this chapter, several authors have analyzed the IPDS using factor analysis (e.g., Silverstein, McLain, Brownlee, & Hubbell, 1976; Wachs & Hubert, 1981).

Final comments involve the relationship between the IPDS and other tests. In one study, King and Seegmiller (1973) reported positive associations between several IPDS subscales and 14-, 18-, and 22-month Bayley scores. The predictive validity of these scales has also been demonstrated with respect to Stanford-Binet scores (e.g., Siegel, 1979; Wachs, 1976). In fact, in her study Siegel (1979) compared the predictive power of the IPDS and the Bayley test and concluded that the IPDS was a "slightly better" predictor.

To conclude, the IPDS has not been as widely utilized in research as other infant tests, undoubtedly due to its relatively recent development; also, extensive standardization of these scales has not been attempted. Still, the existing data suggest that this test is at least as reliable and valid as other infant tests. Further, it provides an alternative to those researchers who would prefer not to utilize a psychometric approach in their study of infant development.

Sensory Processing Techniques

The procedures to be discussed in the present section represent one of the most recent attempts to tap infant abilities. Because to this point no single assessment has been adopted within this framework, it is not possible to present this approach as the other tests in this chapter were presented. Instead, the rationale underlying the development of these procedures will be described, followed by a discussion of the research that has been conducted in this area.

Although the sensory processing approach has been addressed by a variety of researchers utilizing a number of diverse measures, some common themes do appear in the literature. Frequently these themes include a dissatisfaction with the traditional approaches to infant assessment, as well as the belief that, ultimately, continuity can be demonstrated between infant test scores and later cognitive abilities. As Fagan and McGrath (1981) wrote:

> Variations in sensorimotor development during the first year of life bear no significant relationship to levels of childhood intelligence, at least within the normal range of intelligence. The failure to find a correlation between scores on infant tests and later intelligence has been interpreted by many to mean that the growth of intelligence is not constant or that the notion of general intelligence is not applicable to infancy. An alternative explanation for the zero correlation between early and later performance is that standard tests of infant development are composed principally of items that tap the development of simple sensory and motor skills. These are functions which, later in life, are not related to differences in intelligence and, thus, would not be expected to be early indicators of intelligence. Presumably, to predict later intelligence, the task is to sample early behaviors which are similar to behaviors known to be related to later intelligence. (pp. 121–122)

Most often, the early behaviors that have been selected by researchers utilizing the sensory processing approach include measures of attention, discrimination, and memory.

As noted by Fagan and McGrath (1981), a major impetus for the sensory processing approach to infant intelligence was early research that demonstrated differences in visual processing between normal infants and at risk and atypical infants. In one early report, Fantz and Nevis (1967) found that home-reared infants were superior to institutionalized babies on measures of visual discrimination, and that some positive correlations existed between these measures and scores on a standard infant test. Much research has also been conducted comparing normal and Down's syndrome infants (see review by Miranda, 1976) on various measures of visual processing. For instance, Miranda and Fantz (1974) found that normal babies demonstrated a preference for novel visual stimuli several weeks earlier than the Down's syndrome infants. Differences have also been reported between full-term and preterm infants, with full-term babies generally being reported as more attentive and superior at discriminating among stimuli (e.g., Rose, 1980; Rose, Gottfried, & Bridger, 1979; Sigman, 1976; Sigman & Parmelee, 1974).

Following these studies that focused on comparing normal infants with those babies who might be expected to have lower intelligence later on in life, there has been more emphasis on actually testing the predictive validity of these sensory processing measures. Two studies conducted within the newborn period will be discussed in detail. In one of the earliest tests of predictive validity within this approach, Miranda, Hack, Fantz, Fanaroff, and Klaus (1977) compared the efficacy of neurological exams and visual processing measures in detecting infant abnormalities; 33 premature infants were examined at an average of 39 weeks of postconceptional age. From a visual fixation test, infants were classified as normal, suspect, or abnormal. According to this classification scheme, infants who exhibited sustained attention to stimuli and discriminated between patterns were categorized as normal, while abnormal infants failed to do so; infants classified as suspect exhibited behaviors in between what was considered normal and abnormal performances. All infants were then rated as normal, abnormal, or suspect by a pediatrician (who was naive to the infants' other ratings) on the basis of their performance on a standard neurological exam. For follow-up, 7 infants were tested with the Bayley scales by 2 years of age, 19 subjects were given the Stanford-Binet test between 36 and 60 months, and the Cattell Infant Scale was administered to 1 infant at 37 months; 3 infants had died by 14 months of age and 3 were untestable due to severe retardation. Results indicated that the visual fixation test correctly predicted the status of 27 infants, while the neurological examination only predicted the status of 21 infants accurately.

In another study, Harmant, Roucoux, Culee, and Lyon (1983) were particularly interested in the value of visual discrimination in predicting permanent brain damage in a group of 129 preterm infants; a control group of 150 normal infants was also examined. All babies were observed at (corrected) term and at 1, 3, 6, 12, and 18 (corrected) months of age. Measures included a standard neurological assessment and the following visual behaviors: eye opening, attention (fixation and pursuit) to a face and a red ball, and discrimination of abstract patterns. Dramatic differences were found between the preterm infants who developed normally (Group N) and those who presented neurological sequelae (Group S). For example, in Group N 50 percent attended to the face/target at the term testing while 95 percent did so at 1 month of age; comparable figures for Group S were 20 percent and 50 percent, respectively. In considering visual discrimination, Group N was very similar to the normal control group throughout the study. In contrast, no pattern discrimination was observed in infants with severe sequelae before 8 months of age; further, these infants remained delayed in discrimination after the first year. Overall, Harmant and colleagues concluded that the visual discrimination measure was superior to the attention measure in detecting and predicting abnormalities.

In considering research after the newborn period, the existing information on the predictive validity of both attention and discrimination measures is inconclusive. For instance, several authors have reported relationships between infant attention and subsequent tests of cognition (e.g., Kagan, Lapidus, & Moore, 1978; Kopp & Vaughn, 1982); however, these findings were qualified by infant gender or social class confounds. Similar problems exist in studies reporting associations between infants' performance on discrimination tasks and later cognitive development (e.g., O'Connor, 1980; Roe, 1978).

Somewhat stronger support for the sensory processing approach to infant intelligence has come from studies of infant memory. Several authors have demonstrated the predictive validity of habituation measures taken early in infancy. For example, Miller and colleagues (1977) found that faster habituators at 2–4 months attained significantly higher levels on subscales from the IPDS at 15 months of age. In another study, Lewis and Brooks-Gunn (1981) measured habituation and response recovery to novel stimuli in 3-month-old infants. At 24 months of age, both of these measures were significantly related to Bayley MDI scores. In contrast, neither 3-month Bayley nor 3-month Albert Einstein scores were related to the 24-month Bayley scores.

Undoubtedly the most systematic attempt to relate infant visual memory to infant intelligence has been made by Fagan and his colleagues (e.g., Fagan, 1981, 1982a, 1982b; Fagan & McGrath, 1981) utilizing a paired associates paradigm. In a summary of studies, Fagan and McGrath (1981) reported on four samples of children 3.8–7.5 years of age whose visual recognition memory (VRM) had been measured at 4–7 months; childhood assessments included the PPVT, Stanford-Binet, WPPSI, and WISC-R. Dividing the children into a low-CA ($X = 4$ years) and a high-CA ($X = 7$ years) group, Fagan and McGrath reported correlation coefficients between infant visual recognition memory and later intelligence scores of .37 and .57, respectively, in the two age groups; no gender or social class differences were observed. These authors also argue that these correlations are probably artificially low due to the relatively low reliability of the VRM scores (as a function of the small number of problems used in testing) and the limited range of intelligence scores in the sample of children. In this regard, Fagan (1982b) has recently described his attempts to devise a VRM test composed of more problems, as well as to provide norms on this test for infants at various ages. At the time of this report, the test had been administered to 92 infants at 52, 56, 62, and 69 weeks of age; Fagan reported that these infants' visual fixation scores were normally distributed and that test reliability was .60. The test was also administered to 123 infants suspected to be at risk for slower cognitive development; compared to the standardization group, these at risk infants showed lower absolute novelty preferences of 10 of the 12 problems. This difference was statistically significant, therefore supporting the concurrent validity of the VRM test.

Clearly, the sensory processing approach has emerged too recently to allow definitive conclusions regarding its utility. Information is particularly lacking on relationships between normal, full-term neonates' processing abilities and other measures. In addition, the available data on attention and discrimination in older babies must be interpreted cautiously at this point, given the various confounds that have been reported. Still, the assumption that infant tests should emphasize abilities that are known to relate to intelligence later in childhood seems conceptually sound. Also, as noted by McCall (1981), the predictive validity of infant memory measures for later intelligence matches and may even exceed that of standardized infant tests. As such, the use of sensory processing measures appears promising at this time, although extensive study is necessary before we may conclude that this utilization is a viable approach to measuring infant cognitive capacities.

SUMMARY AND CONCLUSIONS

In this chapter we have reviewed many of the assessment procedures that can be used with neonates. Although not all of these procedures were specifically designed to test neonatal functioning, each can yield some information regarding the infant during the first month of life. Perhaps the most important outcome of the present review involves the demonstration of the great number of diverse behaviors that can be measured in infants this young. After such a demonstration, the former widespread acceptance of the "tabula rasa" view of the human infant seems incomprehensible. Clearly, as St. Clair (1978) has noted in her historical review of neonatal assessment, no one procedure fits everyone's needs. Still, the present descriptions of techniques should allow readers to choose that procedure, or combination of procedures, that best matches their needs.

Neonatal assessment is done for a variety of reasons, a fact that is reflected in the classification system utilized in this chapter. For instance, screening tests and neurological examinations are more likely to be used in clinical situations, where decisions must be made regarding the infant's immediate status and, subsequently, special treatment or placement needs. In contrast, behavioral assessment techniques appear to have been utilized more in measuring specific areas of development in normal babies. For that reason, these procedures have been more likely to be employed for basic research purposes. In that regard, the volume of research on behavioral assessment is almost overwhelming. Earlier studies focused on the relationship between assessment scores and different demographic variables and infant birth conditions. More recently, investigators have paid more attention to associations between assessment measures and maternal/infant characteristics, other assessment devices, and measures of infant–caregiver interaction.

Certainly one research question that has been pursued regarding all of the assessment procedures discussed in this review involves their relationship to later measures of infant and child development. In their historical review of infant intelligence testing, Brooks and Weinraub (1976) identified three waves of events in infant testing. During the first two waves, researchers attempted to demonstrate continuity between infant abilities and later child/adult intelligence. By the 1960s, following the repeated failure of such attempts, a third wave was observed, with investigators questioning the value of this search for continuity. At this point, it would appear that a fourth wave has emerged in infant testing, a wave that is best represented by researchers within the sensory processing framework. Perhaps, as McCall (1981) has stated, the attempt to predict subsequent behaviors from earlier ones is simply "sacred" to the developmental psychologist. Regardless of the reason, the predictive validity of measures obtained during the infancy period is still an important and legitimate issue to some researchers. Also, such researchers will always be interested in assessment during the neonatal period, as this period represents the ultimate test of continuity in human behavior and development.

Horowitz and her colleagues (Horowitz, 1984; Horowitz, Linn, & Buddin, 1983; Horowitz, Sullivan, & Linn, 1978) have repeatedly questioned the theoretical basis of expecting neonatal behavioral assessments or measures to be predictive of later developmental status. If infant–environment transactions are considered relevant to subsequent developmental status then the infant's experiences in the environment subsequent to the neonatal period should play a significant role in determining developmental outcome. In such an instance neonatal assessments by themselves should not be expected to predict later developmental status. If environmental experiences during infancy are not relevant to developmental outcome then it is reasonable to expect that neonatal assessments might be predictive of later development. Thus the reasons for using neonatal assessments and the expectations concerning their predictive powers are necessarily affected by the theoretical predilections of developmental investigators.

As the present review has demonstrated, the newborn infant is "available" for evaluation in more areas of development than many people would ever have thought possible. The techniques devised for this evaluation have already proven themselves invaluable, with respect to both helping the atypical infant and documenting the wide range of individual differences among normal newborns. Further, neonatal assessment has made great progress as a discipline in recent years; examples of this progress include the focus on infant social competencies and the combination of assessment procedures.

Still, the field of neonatal assessment may yet reflect what Horowitz and Dunn (1978) refer to as "too simple" a view of development. While it is important to examine relationships between assessment scores and specific target variables (e.g., infant birth condition, maternal characteristics), we must not be content to limit ourselves to such singular examinations. Particularly lacking in the assessment literature at this time are multivariate investigations of the interrelationships that exist between infants' abilities, their social nature, and transactions with their environment. Such investigations are essential if neonatal assessment is to continue to keep pace with our ever-increasing awareness of the human infant's vast complexity.

REFERENCES

Acien, P. (1979). Fetal heart rate deceleration index—Its relation with fetal pH, Apgar score and dips or decelerations. *Journal of Perinatal Medicine, 17,* 7–18.

Adamson, L., Als, H., Tronick, E., & Brazelton, T. B. (1975). *A priori profiles for the Brazelton neonatal assessment.* Unpublished manuscript.

Aleksandrowicz, M. K., & Aleksandrowicz, D. R. (1974). Obstetrical pain-relieving drugs as predictors of infant behavior variability. *Child Development, 45,* 935–945.

Als, H. (1978). Assessing an assessment: Conceptual considerations, methodological issues, and a perspective on the future of the Neonatal Behavioral Assessment Scale. In A. J.

Sameroff (Ed.), Organization and stability of newborn behavior: A commentary on the Brazelton Neonatal Behavioral Assessment Scale. *Monographs of the Society for Research in Child Development, 43* (5–6, Serial No. 177).

Als, H. (1982). Toward a syntactive theory of development: Promise for the assessment and support of infant individuality. *Infant Mental Health Journal, 3,* 229–243.

Als, H., Tronick, E., Adamson, L., & Brazelton, T. B. (1976). The behavior of the fullterm but underweight newborn infant. *Developmental Medicine & Child Neurology, 18,* 590–602.

Als, H., Tronick, E., Lester, B. M., & Brazelton, T. B. (1977). The Brazelton Neonatal Behavioral Assessment Scale (BNBAS). *Journal of Abnormal Child Psychology, 5,* 215–231.

Amiel-Tison, C. (1982). Neurologic signs, aetiology and implications. In P. Stratton (Ed.), *Psychobiology of the human newborn.* New York: Wiley.

Apgar, V. (1953). A proposal for a new method of evaluation of the newborn infant. *Current Researches in Anesthesia & Analgesia, 32,* 260–267.

Apgar, V., Holaday, D. A., James, L. S., Weisbrot, I. M., & Berrien, C. (1958). Evaluation of the newborn infant—Second report. *Journal of the American Medical Association, 168,* 1985–1988.

Applebaum, A. S. (1978). Validity of the Revised Denver Developmental Screening Test for referred and non-referred samples. *Psychological Reports, 43,* 227–233.

Arco, C. M. B., DeMeis, D. K., Self, P. A., & Gutrecht, N. M. (1984). Interrelationships among maternal and infant characteristics during the neonatal period. *Journal of Pediatric Psychology, 9,* 131–147.

Atkinson, D. (1983). An evaluation of Apgar scores as predictors of infant mortality. *North Carolina Medical Journal, 44,* 45–54.

Aylward, B. P., Lazzara, A., & Meyer, J. (1978). Behavioral and neurological characteristics of a hydranencephalic infant. *Developmental Medicine & Child Neurology, 20,* 211–221.

Badger, E., Burns, D., & Vietze, P. (1981). Maternal risk factors as predictors of developmental outcome in early childhood. *Infant Mental Health Journal, 2,* 33–43.

Ballard, J. L., Novak, K. K., & Driver, M. (1979). A simplified score for assessment of fetal maturation of newly born infants. *Journal of Pediatrics, 95,* 769–774.

Bates, J. E., Freeland, C. A., & Lounsbury, M. L. (1979). Measurement of infant difficultness. *Child Development, 50,* 794–803.

Bayley, N. (1933). *The California First-Year Mental Scale.* Berkeley: University of California Press.

Bayley, N. (1936). *The California Infant Scale of Motor Development.* Berkeley: University of California Press.

Bayley, N. (1965). Comparisons of mental and motor tests scores for ages 1–15 months by sex, birth order, race, geographical location, and education of parents. *Child Development, 36,* 369–411.

Bayley, N. (1969). *Manual for the Bayley Scales of Infant Development.* New York: Psychological Corporation.

Beckwith, L., Cohen, S. E., Kopp, C. B., Parmelee, A. H., & Marcy, T. G. (1976). Caregiver–infant interaction and early cognitive development in preterm infants. *Child Development, 47,* 579–587.

Beintema, D. J. (1968). A neurological study of newborn infants (No. 28). *Clinics in Developmental Medicine.* London: Heinemann.

Belsey, E. M., Rosenblatt, D. B., Lieberman, B. A., Redshaw, M., Caldwell, J., Notarianni,

L., Smith, R. L., & Beard, R. W. (1981). The influence of maternal analgesia on neonatal behavior: I. Pethidine. *British Journal of Obstetrics & Gynecology, 887,* 398-406.

Bench, J., & Parker, A. (1970). On the reliability of the Graham/Rosenblith behavior test for neonates. *Journal of Child Psychology & Psychiatry, 11,* 121-131.

Berger, L. R. (1981). Newborns are people too: An abbreviated Brazelton assessment for clinical use. *Journal of Developmental & Behavioral Pediatrics, 2,* 109-111.

Blumberg, N. L. (1980). Effects of neonatal risk, maternal attitude, and cognitive style on early postpartum adjustment. *Journal of Abnormal Psychology, 89,* 139-150.

Borgstedt, A. D., Heriot, J. T., Rosen, M. G., Lawrence, R. A., & Sokol, R. J. (1978). Fetal electroencephalography and one-minute and five-minute Apgar scores. *Journal of the American Medical Women's Association, 33,* 220-222.

Bratteby, L. E. (1981). Effects on the infant of obstetric regional analgesia. *Journal of Perinatal Medicine, 9,* (Supp. 1), 54-56.

Brazelton, T. B. (1973). Neonatal Behavioral Assessment Scale. *National Spastics Society Monograph.* Philadelphia: Lippincott.

Brazelton, T. B. (1984). *Neonatal Behavioral Assessment Scale.* Philadelphia: Lippincott.

Brazelton, T. B., Robey, J. S., & Collier, G. A. (1969). Infant development in the Zinacanteco Indians of Southern Mexico. *Pediatrics, 44,* 274-293.

Brazelton, T. B., & Tryphonopoulou, Y. A. (1972). *A comparative study of the Greek and U. S. neonates.* Unpublished manuscript.

Brooks, J., & Weinraub, M. (1976). A history of infant intelligence testing. In M. Lewis (Ed.), *Origins of intelligence.* New York: Plenum.

Broman, S., Nichols, P., & Kennedy, W. A. (1975). *Preschool I.Q.: Prenatal and early developmental correlates.* Hillsdale, NJ: Erlbaum.

Broussard, E. R. (1976). Neonatal prediction and outcome at 10/11 years. *Child Psychiatry & Human Development, 7,* 85-93.

Broussard, E. R., & Hartner, M. (1971). Further considerations regarding maternal perceptions of the firstborn. In J. Hellmuth (Ed.), *The exceptional infant: Studies in abnormalities.* New York: Brunner/Mazel.

Brown, J. V., Bakeman, R., Snyder, P. A., Fredrickson, W. T., Morgan, S. T., & Hepler, R. (1975). Interactions of black inner-city mothers with their newborn infants. *Child Development, 46,* 677-686.

Bryant, G. M., Davies, K. J., & Newcombe, R. G. (1979). Standardization of the Denver Developmental Screening Test for Cardiff children. *Developmental Medicine & Child Neurology, 21,* 353-364.

Carey, W. B., & McDevitt, S. C. (1978). Revision of the Infant Temperament Questionnaire. *Pediatrics, 61,* 735-739.

Caron, A. J., Caron, R. F., & Glass, P. (1983). Responsiveness to relational information as a measure of cognitive functioning in nonsuspect infants. In T. Field & A. Sostek (Eds.), *Infants born at risk: Physiological, perceptual and cognitive processes.* New York: Grune & Stratton.

Casati, I., & Lezine, I. (1968). *Les etapes de l'intelligence sensorimotorice.* Paris: Editions du Centre de Psychologie Appliquee.

Casler, L. (1976). Maternal intelligence and institutionalized children's developmental quotients: A correlational study. *Developmental Psychology, 12,* 64-67.

Cohen, D. J., Allen, M. G., Pollin, N. W., Inoff, G., Werner, M., & Dibble, E. (1972). Personality development in twins. *Journal of the American Academy of Child Psychiatry, 11,* 625-644.

Cohen, S. E., & Beckwith, L. (1977). Caregiving behaviors and early cognitive development as related to ordinal position in preterm infants. *Child Development, 48,* 152–157.

Cohen, S. E., & Beckwith, L. (1979). Preterm infant interaction with the caregiver in the first year of life and competence at age two. *Child Development, 50,* 767–776.

Coll, C. G., Sepkoski, C., & Lester, B. M. (1981). Cultural and biomedical correlates of neonatal behavior. *Developmental Psychobiology, 14,* 147–154.

Coll, C. G., Sepkoski, C., & Lester, B. M. (1982). Effects of teenage childbearing on neonatal and infant behavior in Puerto Rico. *Infant Behavior & Development, 5,* 227–236.

Corman, H. H., & Escalona, S. K. (1969). Stages of sensorimotor development: A replication study. *Merrill Palmer Quarterly, 15,* 351–361.

Crockenberg, S. B. (1981). Infant irritability, mother responsiveness, and social support influences on the security of infant–mother attachment. *Child Development, 52,* 857–865.

Crockenberg, S. B., & Smith, P. (1982). Antecedents of mother–infant interaction and infant irritability in the first three months of life. *Infant Behavior & Development, 5,* 105–119.

Dicks-Mireaux, M. J. (1972). Mental development of infants with Down's syndrome. *American Journal of Mental Deficiency, 77,* 26–32.

Drage, J. S., Kennedy, C., Berendes, H., Schwarz, B. K., & Weiss, W. (1966). The Apgar score as an index of infant morbidity. *Developmental Medicine & Child Neurology, 8,* 141–148.

Drage, J. S., Kennedy, C., & Schwarz, B. K. (1964). The Apgar score as an index of neonatal mortality. *Obstetrics & Gynecology, 24,* 222–230.

Dubose, R. F. (1976). Predictive value of infant intelligence scales with multiply handicapped children. *American Journal of Mental Deficiency, 81,* 388–390.

Dubowitz, L. M. S., & Dubowitz, V. (1981). *The neurological assessment of the preterm and full-term newborn infant.* London: Heinemann.

Dubowitz, L. M. S., Dubowitz, V., & Goldberg, C. (1970). Clinical assessment of gestational age in the newborn infant. *Journal of Pediatrics, 77,* 1–10.

Dubowitz, L. M. S., Dubowitz, V., Morante, A., & Verghote, M. (1980). Visual function in the preterm and full-term newborn infant. *Developmental Medicine & Child Neurology, 22,* 465–475.

Dunst, C. J. (1980). *A clinical and educational manual for use with the Uzgiris and Hunt Scales of Infant Psychological Development.* Baltimore: University Park Press.

Dunst, C. J. (1982). The clinical utility of Piagetian-based scales of infant development. *Infant Mental Health Journal, 3,* 259–275.

Edwards, N. (1968). The relationship between physical condition immediately after birth and mental and motor performance at age four. *Genetic Psychology Monographs, 78,* 27–289.

Egan, D., Illingworth, R. S., & MacKeith, R. C. (1969). *Developmental screening 0–5 years.* London: Heinemann.

Fagan, J. F., III. (1981). *Infant memory and the prediction of intelligence.* Paper presented at the biennial meetings of the Society for Research in Child Development, Boston.

Fagan, J. F., III. (1982a). New evidence for the prediction of intelligence from infancy. *Infant Mental Health Journal, 3,* 219–228.

Fagan, J. F., III. (1982b). *A visual recognition test of infant intelligence.* Paper presented at the meetings of the International Conference on Infant Studies, Austin, TX.

Fagan, J. F., III, & McGrath, S. K. (1981). Infant recognition memory and later intelligence. *Intelligence, 5,* 121–130.

Fantz, R. L., & Nevis, S. (1967). Pattern preferences and perceptual–cognitive development in early infancy. *Merrill-Palmer Quarterly, 13,* 77–108.

Field, T. M. (1977). Effects of early separation, interactive deficits and experimental manipulations on infant–mother face-to-face interaction. *Child Development, 48,* 763–771.

Field, T. M., Dabiri, C., Hallock, N., & Shuman, H. H. (1977). Developmental effects of prolonged pregnancy and the postmaturity syndrome. *Journal of Pediatrics, 90,* 836–839.

Field, T. M., Dempsey, J., & Shuman, H. H. (1983). Five-year follow-up of preterm respiratory distress syndrome and post-term postmaturity syndrome infants. In T. Field & A. Sostek (Eds.), *Infants born at risk: Physiological, perceptual and cognitive processes.* New York: Grune & Stratton.

Field, T. M., Hallock, N., Ting, G., Dempsey, J., Dabiri, C., & Shuman, H. H. (1978). A first-year follow-up of high-risk infants: Formulating a cumulative risk index. *Child Development, 49,* 119–131.

Field, T. M., & Widmayer, S. M. (1980). Developmental follow-up of infants delivered by Caesarean section and general anesthesia. *Infant Behavior & Development, 3,* 253–264.

Fields, L. M., Entman, S. S., & Boehm, F. H. (1983). Correlation of the one-minute Apgar score and the pH value of umbilical arterial blood. *Southern Medical Journal, 76,* 1477–1479.

Fish, B. (1957). The detection of schizophrenia in infancy. *Journal of Nervous & Mental Disease, 125,* 1–24.

Fish, B. (1959). Longitudinal observations of biological deviations in a schizophrenic infant. *American Journal of Psychiatry, 116,* 25–31.

Fish, B. (1960). Involvement of the central nervous sytem in infants with schizophrenia. *Archives of Neurology, 2,* 115–119.

Fish, B., Shapiro, T., Halpern, F., & Wile, R. (1965). The prediction of schizophrenia in infancy: III. Ten-year follow-up report of neurological and psychological development. *American Journal of Psychiatry, 121,* 768–775.

Fish, B., Wile, R., Shapiro, T., & Halpern, F. (1966). The prediction of schizophrenia in infancy: II. Ten-year follow-up report of predictions made at one month of age. In P. Hoch & J. Zubin (Eds.), *Psychopathology of schizophrenia.* New York: Grune & Stratton.

Forslund, M., & Bjerre, I. (1983). Neurological assessment of preterm infants at term conceptional age in comparison with normal full-term infants. *Early Human Development, 8,* 195–208.

Francis, P. L., Self, P. A., & McCaffree, M. A. (1984). Behavioral assessment of a hydranencephalic neonate. *Child Development, 55,* 262–266.

Frankenburg, W. K., & Dodds, J. B. (1967). The Denver Developmental Screening Test. *Journal of Pediatrics, 71,* 181–191.

Frankenburg, W. K., Fandal, A. W., Sciarillo, W., & Burgess, D. (1981). The newly abbreviated and revised Denver Developmental Screening Test. *Journal of Pediatrics, 99,* 995–999.

Frankenburg, W. K., Goldstein, A. D., & Camp, B. W. (1971). The revised Denver Developmental Screening: Its accuracy as a screening instrument. *Journal of Pediatrics, 79,* 988–995.

Freedman, D. G., & Freedman, N. (1969). Behavioral differences between Chinese-American and European-American newborns. *Nature, 24,* 1227.

Freese, M. P., & Thoman, E. B. (1978). The assessment of maternal characteristics for the study of mother–infant interactions. *Infant Behavior & Development, 1,* 95–105.

Friedlander, B. Z. (1975). Screening: A state of the art survey. In B. Z. Friedlander, G. M. Sterritt, & G. E. Kirk (Eds.). *Exceptional infant: Assessment and intervention* (Vol. 3). New York: Brunner/Mazel.

Fysh, W. J., Turner, G. M., & Dunn, P. M. (1982). Neurological normality after extreme birth asphyxia—Case report. *British Journal of Obstetrics & Gynecology, 89,* 24–26.

German, M. L., Williams, E., Herzfeld, J., & Marshall, R. M. (1982). Utility of the Revised Denver Developmental Screening Test and the Developmental Profile II in identifying preschool children with cognitive, language, and motor problems. *Education & Training of the Mentally Retarded, 17,* 319–324.

Gesell, A. (1928). *Infancy and Human Growth.* New York: Macmillan.

Gesell, A., & Amatruda, C. S. (1947). *Developmental diagnosis* (2nd ed.). New York: Hoeber.

Gesell, A., Halverson, H. M., Ilg, F. L., Thompson, H., Castner, B. M., Ames, L. B., & Amatruda, C. S. (1940). *The first five years of life.* New York: Harper.

Gesell, A., Thompson, H., & Amatruda, C. S. (1934). *Infant behavior: Its genesis and growth.* New York: McGraw-Hill.

Giussi, G., Ballejo, G., Marinho, E., Xercavins, J., Vinacur, J., Nieto, F., Roca, R., & Rieppi, G. (1979). hCS, estriol and oxytocinase in maternal serum and neonatal condition in high risk pregnancies. *Journal of Perinatal Medicine, 7,* 243–249.

Goldson, E., Fitch, M. J., Wendall, T. A., & Knapp, G. (1978). Child abuse: its relationship to birthweight, Apgar score and developmental testing. *American Journal of the Diseases of Children, 132,* 790–793.

Gottfried, A. W., & Brody, D. (1975). Interrelationships between and correlates of psychometric and Piagetian scales of sensorimotor intelligence. *Developmental Psychology, 11,* 379–387.

Graham, F. K., Matarazzo, R. G., & Caldwell, B. M. (1956). Behavioral differences between normal and traumatized newborns: II. Standardization, reliability, and validity. *Psychological Monographs, 70* (21, Whole No. 428).

Hancock, B. W. (1973). Clinical assessment of gestational age in the neonate. *Archives of Diseases in Childhood, 48,* 152–154.

Harmant, K., Roucoux, M., Culee, C., & Lyon, G. (1983). Vision attention and discrimination in infants at risk and neurological outcome. *Behavioral Brain Research, 10,* 203–207.

Hastwell, G. B. (1980). Apgar scores, respiratory distress syndrome and salbutamol. *Medical Journal of Australia, 1,* 174–175.

Hingson, R., Gould, J. B., Morelock, S., Kayne, H., Herren, T., Alpert, J. J., Zuckerman, B., & Day, N. (1982). Maternal cigarette smoking, psychoactive substance use and infant Apgar scores. *American Journal of Obstetrics & Gynecology, 144,* 959–966.

Honig, A. S., & Oski, F. A. (1978). Developmental scores of iron deficient infants and the effects of therapy. *Infant Behavior & Development, 1,* 168–176.

Horner, T. M. (1980). Test-retest and home-clinic characteristics of the Bayley Scales of Infant Development in nine- and fifteen-month-old infants. *Child Development, 51,* 751–758.

Horowitz, F. D., Aleksandrowicz, M., Ashton, L. J., Tims, S., McCluskey, K., Culp, R., & Gallas, H. (1973). *American and Uruguayan infants: Reliabilities, maternal drug histories and population difference using the Brazelton scale.* Paper presented at the biennial meeting of the Society for Research in Child Development, Philadelphia.

Horowitz, F. D., Ashton, J., Culp, R., Gaddis, E., Levin, S., & Reichmann, B. (1977). The effects of obstetrical medication on the behavior of Israeli newborn infants and some comparisons with Uruguayan and American infants. *Child Development, 48,* 1607–1623.

Horowitz, F. D., & Brazelton, T. B. (1973). Research with the Brazelton neonatal scale. In

T. B. Brazelton (Ed.), *Neonatal Behavioral Assessment Scale*. National Spastics Society Monograph. Philadelphia: Lippincott.

Horowitz, F. D., & Dunn, M. (1978). Infant intelligence testing. In F. D. Minifie & L. L. Lloyd (Eds.), *Communicative and cognitive abilities—Early behavioral assessment*. Baltimore: University Park Press.

Horowitz, F. D., & Linn, P. L. (1982). The Neonatal Behavioral Assessment Scale: Assessing the behavioral repertoire of the newborn infant. In M. Wolraich & D. K. Routh (Eds.), *Advances in developmental and behavioral pediatrics*. Greenwich, CT: JAI.

Horowitz, F. D., & Linn, P. L. (1984). Use of the NBAS in research. In T. B. Brazelton (Ed.), *Neonatal Behavioral Assessment Scale*. Philadelphia: Lippincott.

Horowitz, F. D., Linn, P. L., & Buddin, B. J. (1983). Neonatal assessment: Evaluating the potential for plasticity. In T. B. Brazelton & B. M. Lester (Eds.), *New approaches to developmental screening*. New York: Elsevier.

Horowitz, F. D., & Mitchell, D. W. (in preparation). *An atlas of neonatal behavior*. University of Kansas.

Horowitz, F. D., Self, P. A., Paden, L. Y., Culp, R., Boyd, E., & Mann, M. E. (1971). *Newborn and four-week retests on normative population using the Brazelton newborn assessment procedure*. Paper presented at the biennial meeting of the Society for Research in Child Development, Minneapolis.

Horowitz, F. D., Sullivan, J. W., & Linn, P. (1978). Stability and instability in the newborn infant: The quest for elusive threads. In A. J. Sameroff (Ed.), Organization and stability of newborn behavior: A commentary on the Brazelton Neonatal Behavioral Assessment Scale. *Monographs of the Society for Research in Child Development, 43* (5–6, Serial No. 177).

Hunt, J. V., & Rhodes, L. (1977). Mental development of infants during the first year. *Child Development, 49,* 204–210.

Jaffa, A. S. (1934). *The California Preschool Mental Scale*. Berkeley: University of California Press.

Jaffe, M., Harel, J., Goldberg, A., Rudolph-Schnitzer, M., & Winter, S. T. (1980). The use of the Denver Developmental Screening Test in infant welfare clinics. *Developmental Medicine & Child Neurology, 22,* 55–60.

Jaroszewicz, A. M., & Boyd, I. H. (1973). Clinical assessment of gestational age in the newborn. *South African Medical Journal, 47,* 2123–2124.

Joos, S. K., Pollitt, E., Mueller, W. H., & Albright, D. L. (1983). The Bacon Chow study: Maternal nutritional supplementation and infant behavior development. *Child Development, 54,* 669–676.

Justice, L. K., Self, P. A., & Gutrecht, N. M. (1976). *Socioeconomic status and scores on the Brazelton Neonatal Behavioral Assessment Scale*. Paper presented at the Southeastern Conference on Human Development, Nashville.

Kagan, J., Lapidus, D. R., & Moore, M. (1978). Infant antecedents of cognitive functioning: A longitudinal study. *Child Development, 49,* 1005–1023.

Kahn, J. (1975). Relationship of Piaget's sensorimotor period to language acquisition of profoundly retarded children. *American Journal of Mental Deficiency, 79,* 640–643.

Kahn, J. (1976). Utility of the Uzgiris-Hunt scales of sensorimotor development with severely and profoundly retarded children. *American Journal of Mental Deficiency, 80,* 663–665.

Kalverboer, A. F. (1979). Neurobehavioural findings in preschool and school-aged children in relation to pre- and perinatal complications. In D. Shaffer & J. Dunn (Eds.), *The first year of life*. New York: Wiley.

Kalverboer, A. F., Touwen, B. C. L., & Prechtl, H. F. R. (1973). Follow-up of infants at risk of minor brain dysfunction. *Annals of the New York Academy of Sciences, 205,* 173–187.

Katoff, L., & Reuter, J. (1980). Review of developmental screening tests for infants. *Journal of Clinical Child Psychology, 9,* 30–34.

Kaye, K. (1978). Discriminating among normal infants by multivariate analysis of Brazelton scores: Lumping and smoothing. In A. J. Sameroff (Ed.), Organization and stability of newborn behavior: A commentary on the Brazelton Neonatal Behavioral Assessment Scale. *Monographs of the Society for Research in Child Development, 43* (5–6, Serial No. 177).

Keefer, C. H., Tronick, E., Dixon, S., & Brazelton, T. B. (1982). Specific differences in motor performance between Gusii and American newborns and a modification of the Neonatal Behavioral Assessment Scale. *Child Development, 53,* 754–759.

Kestermann, G. (1981). Assessment of individual differences among healthy newborns on the Brazelton scale. *Early Human Development, 5,* 15–27.

King, W. L., & Seegmiller, B. (1973). Performance of 14-to-22 month-old black male infants on two tests of cognitive development: The Bayley scales and the psychological development scale. *Developmental Psychology, 8,* 317–326.

Knobloch, H., & Pasamanick, B. (1974a). *Gesell and Amatruda's Developmental Diagnosis: The evaluation and management of normal and abnormal neuropsychologic development in infancy and early childhood* (3rd ed.). New York: Harper & Row.

Knobloch, H., & Pasamanick, B. (1974b). The Developmental Screening Inventory. In H. Knobloch & B. Pasaminick (Eds.), *Gesell and Amatruda's Developmental Diagnosis, 3rd Edition.* New York: Harper & Row.

Kopp, C. E., & Vaughn, B. E. (1982). Sustained attention during exploratory manipulation as a predictor of cognitive competence in preterm infants. *Child Development, 53,* 174–182.

Kuhnert, B. R., Harrison, M. J., Linn, P. L., & Kuhnert, P. M. (1984). Effects of maternal epidural anesthesia on neonatal behavior. *Anesthesia & Analgesia, 63,* 301–308.

Lancioni, G. E., Horowitz, F. D., & Sullivan, J. W. (1980a). The NBAS-K: I. A study of its stability and structure over the first month of life. *Infant Behavior & Development, 3,* 341–359.

Lancioni, G. E., Horowitz, F. D., & Sullivan, J. W. (1980b). The NBAS-K: II. Reinforcement value of the infant's behavior. *Infant Behavior & Development, 3,* 361–366.

Lederman, E., Lederman, R. P., Work, B. A., & McCann, D. S. (1981). Maternal psychological and physiologic correlates of fetal-newborn health status. *American Journal of Obstetrics & Gynecology, 139,* 956–958.

Lee-Painter, S., & Lewis, M. (1974). *Mother–infant interaction and cognitive development.* Paper presented at the meetings of the Eastern Psychological Association, New York City.

Leijon, I. (1980). Neurology and behaviour of newborn infants delivered by vacuum extraction of maternal indication. *Acta Paediatrica Scandinavica, 69,* 626–631.

Leijon, I. (1982). Assessment of behaviour on the Brazelton scale in healthy preterm infants from 32 conceptional weeks until full-term age. *Early Human Development, 7,* 109–118.

Leijon, I., & Finnstrom, D. (1981). Studies on the Brazelton Neonatal Behavioral Assessment Scale. *Neuropediatrics, 12,* 242–253.

Leijon, I., & Finnstrom, D. (1982). Correlation between neurological examination and behavioural assessment of the newborn infant. *Early Human Development, 7,* 119–130.

Lester, B. M. (1984). Data analysis and prediction. In T. B. Brazelton (Ed.), *Neonatal Behavioral Assessment Scale.* Philadelphia: Lippincott.

Lester, B. M., Als, H., & Brazelton, T. B. (1982). Regional obstetric anesthesia and newborn behavior: A reanalysis toward synergistic effects. *Child Development, 53,* 687–692.

Lewis, M. (1976). What do we mean when we say "infant intelligence scores"? A sociopolitical question. In M. Lewis (Ed.), *Origins of intelligence.* New York: Plenum.

Lewis, M., & Brooks-Gunn, J. (1981). Visual attention at three months as a predictor of cognitive functioning at two years of age. *Intelligence, 5,* 131–140.

Lewis, M., & Coates, D. L. (1980). Mother–infant interaction and cognitive development in twelve-week-old infants. *Infant Behavior & Development, 3,* 95–105.

Linn, P. L., & Horowitz, F. D. (1984). The relationship between infant individual differences and mother–infant interaction during the neonatal period. *Infant Behavior & Development, 6,* 415–427.

Lipsitt, L. P., Sturner, W. Q., & Burke, P. (1979). Perinatal indicators and subsequent crib death. *Infant Behavior & Development, 2,* 325–328.

Liptak, G. S., Keller, B. B., Feldman, A. W., & Chamberlin, R. W. (1983). Enhancing infant development and parent-practitioner interaction with the Brazelton Neonatal Assessment Scale. *Pediatrics, 72,* 71–78.

Littman, B. (1977). *Precursors and correlates of two-year-old competence in preterm children.* Paper presented at the biennial meetings of the Society for Research in Child Development, New Orleans.

Littman, G., & Parmelee, A. H. (1978). Medical correlates of infant development. *Pediatrics, 61,* 470–474.

Lubchenco, L. O., Hansman, C., & Boyd, E. (1966). Intrauterine growth in length and head circumference as estimated from live births at gestational ages from 26 to 42 weeks. *Pediatrics, 37,* 403–408.

Marcus, J., Haus, S. L., & Jeremy, R. J. (1982). Differentiated motor and state functioning in newborns of women on methadone. *Neurobehavioral Toxicology & Teratology, 4,* 459–462.

Matheny, A. P., Dolan, A. B., & Wilson, R. S. (1974). Bayley's Infant Behavior Records: Relations between behaviors and mental test scores. *Developmental Psychology, 10,* 696–702.

McCall, R. B. (1981). Early predictors of later IQ: The search continues. *Intelligence, 5,* 141–147.

McCluskey, K. A., & Horowitz, F. D. (1975). *A comparison of neonatal assessment score with laboratory performance in auditory and visual discrimination tasks between the ages of one and four months.* Paper presented at the biennial meeting of the Society for Research in Child Development, Denver.

McGowan, R. J., Johnson, D. L., & Maxwell, S. E. (1981). Relations between infant behavior ratings and concurrent and subsequent mental test scores. *Developmental Psychology, 17,* 542–553.

Meares, R., Penman, R., Milgrom-Friedman, J., & Baker, K. (1982). Some origins of the 'difficult' child: The Brazelton scale and the mother's view of her newborn's character. *British Journal of Medical Psychology, 55* (Pt. 1), 77–86.

Mednick, B. R., Hocevar, D., Baker, R. L., & Teasdale, T. (1983). Effects of social, familial, and maternal state variables on neonatal and infant health. *Developmental Psychology, 19,* 752–765.

Meier, J. H. (1975). Screening, assessment and intervention for young children at developmental risk. In B. Z. Friedlander, G. M. Sterritt, & G. E. Kirk (Eds.), *Exceptional infant: Assessment and intervention* (Vol. 3). New York: Brunner/Mazel.

Metzl, M. N. (1980). Teaching parents a strategy for enhancing infant development. *Child Development, 51,* 583–586.

Miller, D. J., Ryan, E. B., Short, E. J., Reis, P. G., McGuire, M. D., & Culler, P. M. (1977). Relationships between early habituation and later cognitive performance in infancy. *Child Development, 48,* 658–661.

Miranda, S. B. (1976). Visual attention in defective and high-risk infants. *Merrill-Palmer Quarterly, 22,* 201–228.

Miranda, S. B., & Fantz, R. L. (1974). Recognition memory in Down's syndrome and normal infants. *Child Development, 45,* 651–660.

Miranda, S. B., Hack, M., Fantz, R. L., Fanaroff, A. A., & Klaus, M. H. (1977). Neonatal pattern vision: A predictor of future mental performance. *Journal of Pediatrics, 91,* 642–647.

Myers, B. J. (1982). Early intervention using Brazelton training with middle-class mothers and fathers of newborns. *Child Development, 53,* 462–471.

Naeye, R. L. (1979). Underlying disorders responsible for the neonatal deaths associated with low Apgar scores. *Biology of the Neonate, 35,* 150–155.

Nelson, K. B., & Ellenberg, J. H. (1979). Neonatal signs as predictors of cerebral palsy. *Pediatrics, 64,* 225–232.

Nelson, K. B., & Ellenberg, J. H. (1981). Apgar scores as predictors of chronic neurologic disability. *Pediatrics, 68,* 36–44.

Neutra, R. R., Greenland, S., & Friedman, E. A. (1981). The relationship between electronic fetal monitoring and Apgar score. *American Journal of Obstetrics & Gynecology, 140,* 440–445.

Njiokiktjien, C., & Kurver, P. (1980). Predictive value of neonatal neurological examination for cerebral function in infancy. *Developmental Medicine & Child Neurology, 22,* 736–747.

Noller, K., & Ingrisano, D. (1984). Cross-sectional study of gross and fine motor development. *Physical Therapy, 64,* 308–316.

Oakley, J. R., & Tavare, S. (1979). Another approach to the assessment of growth in early infancy. *Developmental Medicine & Child Neurology, 21,* 186–193.

O'Connor, M. J. (1980). A comparison of preterm and full-term infants on auditory discrimination at 4 months and on Bayley Scales of Infant Development at eighteen months. *Child Development, 51,* 81–88.

Osofsky, J. D., & Danzger, B. (1974). Relationships between neonatal characteristics and mother–infant interaction. *Developmental Psychology, 10,* 124–130.

Osofsky, J. D., & O'Connell, E. J. (1977). Patterning of newborn behavior in an urban population. *Child Development, 48,* 532–536.

Ounsted, M. K., Moar, V. A., & Scott, A. (1983). Small for dates babies at the age of 4 years: Health, handicap, and developmental status. *Early Human Development, 8,* 243–258.

Palisin, H. (1980). The Neonatal Perception Inventory: Failure to replicate. *Child Development, 51,* 737–742.

Palmer, P., Dubowitz, L. M. S., Levene, M. I., & Dubowitz, V. (1982). Developmental and neurological progress of preterm infants with intraventricular hemorrhage and ventricular dilatation. *Archives of Disease in Childhood, 57,* 748–753.

Paludetto, R., Mansi, G., Rinaldi, P., DeLuca, T., Corchia, C., DeCurtis, M., & Andolfi,

M. (1982). Behavior of preterm newborns reaching term without any serious disorders. *Early Human Development, 6,* 357–363.

Park, K. A., Shafaie, Mh. S., & Self, P. A. (1983). *The influence of gestational age upon maternal perceptions: A failure to replicate.* Paper presented at the Eleventh Annual Graduate Conference on Personality and Social Psychology, Norman, OK.

Parmelee, A. H. (1974a). *Newborn neurological examination.* Unpublished manuscript.

Parmelee, A. H. (1974b). *The Obstetric Complications Scales and the Postnatal Complications Scale.* Unpublished manuscript.

Parmelee, A. H., Kopp, C. B., & Sigman, M. (1976). Selection of developmental assessment techniques for infants at risk. *Merrill Palmer Quarterly, 22,* 177–201.

Perkins, R. P. (1981). The neonatal significance of selected perinatal events among infants of low birth weight. *American Journal of Obstetrics & Gynecology, 139,* 546–561.

Perry, S. E. (1983). Parents' perceptions of their newborn following structured interactions. *Nursing Research, 32,* 208–212.

Pollitt, E. (1983). Morbidity and infant development: A hypothesis. *International Journal of Behavioral Development, 6,* 461–475.

Poresky, R. H., & Henderson, M. L. (1982). Infants' mental and motor development: Effects of home environment, maternal attitudes, marital adjustment, and socioeconomic status. *Perceptual & Motor Skills, 54,* 695–702.

Prechtl, H. F. R. (1963). The mother–child interaction in babies with minimal brain damage (a follow-up study). In B. M. Foss (Ed.), *Determinants of infant behavior II.* New York: Wiley.

Prechtl, H. F. R. (1968). Neurological findings in newborn infants after pre- and paranatal complications. In J. H. P. Jonxis, H. K. A. Visser, & J. A. Troelstra (Eds.), *Aspects of prematurity and dysmaturity.* Springfield: C. C. Thomas.

Prechtl, H. F. R. (1977). *The neurological examination of the full term newborn infant* (2nd ed). London: Heinemann.

Prechtl, H. F. R. (1980). The optimality concept. *Early Human Development, 4,* 201–205.

Prechtl, H. F. R. (1982). Assessment methods for the newborn infant, a critical evaluation. In P. Stratton (Ed.), *Psychobiology of the human newborn.* New York: Wiley.

Prechtl, H. F. R., & Beintema, D. (1964). *The neurological examination of the full-term newborn infant.* London: Heinemann.

Richards, F. M., Richards, I. D. G., & Roberts, C. J. (1968). The influence of low Apgar rating on infant mortality and development. In R. MacKeith & M. Bax (Eds.), *Studies in Infancy.* Clinics in Developmental Medicine (No. 27). London: Spastics Society (Heinemann).

Riese, M. L. (1980). Assessment of gestational age in twins: Lack of agreement among procedures. *Journal of Pediatric Psychology, 5,* 9–16.

Rindfuss, R. R., Gortmaker, S. L., & Ladinsky, J. L. (1978). Elective induction and stimulation of labor and the health of the infant. *American Journal of Public Health, 9,* 872–877.

Roe, K. V. (1978). Infants' mother–stranger discrimination at 3 months as a predictor of cognitive development at 3 and 5 years. *Developmental Psychology, 14,* 191–192.

Roe, K. V., McClure, A., & Roe, A. (1983). Infant Gesell scores vs. cognitive skills at age 12. *Journal of Genetic Psychology, 142,* 143–147.

Rorher, F. (1921). Der index der korperfulle als mass des ernahrungszustandes. *Munchner Medizinische Wochenschriff, 68,* 580.

Rose, S. A. (1980). Enhancing visual recognition memory in preterm infants. *Developmental Psychology, 16,* 85–92.

Rose, S. A., Gottfried, A. W., & Bridger, W. H. (1979). Effects of haptic cues on visual recognition memory in full-term and preterm infants. *Infant Behavior & Development, 2*, 55–67.

Rosenblatt, D. B., Belsey, E. M., Lieberman, B. A., Redshaw, M., Caldwell, J., Notarianni, L., Smith, R. L., & Beard, R. W. (1981). The influence of maternal analgesia on neonatal behavior: II. Epidural bupivacaine. *British Journal of Obstretric Gynaecology, 88*, 407–413.

Rosenblith, J. F. (1961). The modified Graham behavior test for neonates: Test–retest reliability, normative data and hypotheses for future work. *Biologia Neonatorium, 3*, 174–192.

Rosenblith, J. F. (1964). Prognostic value of behavioral assessment of neonates. *Biologia Neonatorium, 6*, 76–103.

Rosenblith, J. F. (1970). Are newborn auditory responses prognostic of deafness? *Transactions of American Academy of Ophthalmology & Otolaryngology, 74*, 1215–1228.

Rosenblith, J. F. (1974a). Relations between neonatal behaviors and those at eight months. *Developmental Psychology, 10*, 779–792.

Rosenblith, J. F. (1974b). *Relations between newborn and four-year behaviors.* Paper presented at the meetings of the Eastern Psychological Association, New York City.

Rosenblith, J. F. (1975). Prognostic value of neonatal behavioral tests. In B. Z. Friedlander, G. M. Sterritt, & G. E. Kirk (Eds.), *Exceptional infant: Vol. 3. Assessment and intervention.* New York: Brunner/Mazel.

Rosenblith, J. F. (1979a). *Relations between behaviors in the newborn period and intellectual achievement and IQ at 7 years of age.* Paper presented at the meetings of the International Society for the Study of Behaviour and Development, Lund, Sweden.

Rosenblith, J. F. (1979b). *Relations between Graham/Rosenblith neonatal measures and seven year assessments.* Paper presented at the meetings of the Eastern Psychological Association, Philadelphia.

Rosenblith, J. F., & Anderson-Huntington, R. B. (1972). *Relations between newborn and 4 year behavior.* Abstract Guide of the Twentieth International Congress of Psychology, Tokyo.

Rossavik, I. K. (1978). Relation between total uterine impulse, method of delivery, and one-minute Apgar score. *British Journal of Obstetrics & Gynecology, 85*, 847–851.

Rothbart, M. K. (1981). Measurement of temperament in infancy. *Child Development, 52*, 569–578.

Rubin, R. A., & Balow, B. (1979). Measures of infant development and socio-economic status as predictors of later intelligence and school achievement. *Developmental Psychology, 15*, 225–227.

Rutter, M. (1982). Temperament: Concepts, issues and problems. In *Temperamental differences in infants and young children, Ciba Foundation Symposium 89.* London: Pittman.

Saint-Anne Dargassies, S. (1977). *Neurological development in the full-term and premature neonate.* New York: Elsevier/North Holland.

St. Clair, K. L. (1978). Neonatal assessment procedures: A historical review. *Child Development, 49*, 280–292.

Sameroff, A. J. (1978). Summary and conclusions: The future of neonatal assessment. In A. J. Sameroff (Ed.), Organization and stability of newborn behavior: A commentary on the Brazelton Neonatal Behavioral Assessment Scale. *Monographs of the Society for Research in Child Development, 43* (5–6, Serial No. 177).

Sameroff, A. J., Krafchuk, E. E., & Bakow, H. A. (1978). Issues in grouping items from the Neonatal Behavioral Assessment Scale. In A. J. Sameroff (Ed.), Organization and stability of newborn behavior: A commentary on the Neonatal Behavioral Assessment Scale. *Monographs of the Society for Research in Child Development, 43* (5–6, Serial No. 177).

Schulte, F. J., Michaelis, R., Linke, I., & Nolte, R. (1968). Motor nerve conduction velocity in term, preterm and small-for-dates newborn infants. *Pediatrics, 42,* 17–26.

Self, P. A., & Horowitz, F. D. (1979). The behavioral assessment of the neonate: An overview. In J. D. Osofsky (Ed.), *Handbook of infant development.* New York: Wiley.

Serunian, S. A., & Broman, S. H. (1975). Relationship of Apgar scores and Bayley Mental and Motor scores. *Child Development, 46,* 696–700.

Shipe, D., Vandenberg, S., & Williams, R. D. B. (1968). Neonatal Apgar ratings as related to intelligence and behavior in preschool children. *Child Development, 39,* 861–866.

Sibai, B. M., Anderson, G. D., Abdella, T. N., McCubbin, J. H., & Dilts, P. V. (1983). Eclampsia III: Neonatal outcome, growth and development. *American Journal of Obstetrics & Gynecology, 146,* 307–316.

Siegel, L. S. (1979). Infant perceptual, cognitive, and motor behaviors as predictors of subsequent cognitive and language development. *Canadian Journal of Psychology, 33,* 382–394.

Siegel, L. S. (1982). Reproductive, perinatal, and environmental factors as predictors of the cognitive and language development of preterm and full-term infants. *Child Development, 53,* 963–973.

Siegel, L. S. (1983). Correction for prematurity and its consequences for the assessment of the very low birthweight infant. *Child Development, 54,* 1176–1188.

Sigman, M. (1976). Early development of preterm and full-term infants: Exploratory behavior in eight-month-olds. *Child Development, 47,* 606–612.

Sigman, M., & Parmelee, A. H. (1974). Visual preferences of four-month-old premature and full-term infants. *Child Development, 45,* 959–965.

Silverstein, A. B., McLain, R. E., Brownlee, L., & Hubbell, M. (1976). Structure of ordinal scales of psychological development in infancy. *Educational & Psychological Measurement, 36,* 355–359.

Solomons, G., & Solomons, H. C. (1975). Motor development in Yucatan infants. *Developmental Medicine & Child Neurology, 17,* 41–46.

Solomons, H. C. (1978). The malleability of infant motor development: Cautions based on studies of child-rearing practices in Yucatan. *Clinical Pediatrics, 17,* 836–840.

Solomons, H. C. (1980). Standardization of the Bayley Motor Scale of Infant Development in Yucatan, Mexico. *Developmental Medicine and Child Neurology, 22,* 580–587.

Solomons, H. C. (1982). Standardization of the Denver Developmental Screening Test on infants from Yucatan, Mexico. *International Journal of Rehabilitation Research, 5,* 179–189.

Sostek, A. M., & Anders, T. F. (1977). Relationships among the Brazelton Neonatal Scale, Bayley Infant Scales, and early temperament. *Child Development, 48,* 320–323.

Soule, B., Standley, K., Copans, S., & Davis, M. (1974). Clinical uses of the Brazelton Neonatal Scale. *Pediatrics, 54,* 583–586.

Standley, K., Soule, A. B., Copans, S. A., & Duchowny, M. S. (1974). Local–regional anesthesia during childbirth: Effect on newborn behaviors. *Science, 186,* 634–635.

Stone, L. J., Smith, H., & Murphy, L. (1973). *The competent infant.* New York: Basic.

Strauss, M. E., Lessen-Firestone, J. K., Starr, R. H., & Ostrea, E. M. (1975). Behavior of narcotics-addicted newborns. *Child Development, 46,* 887–893.

Streissguth, A. P., Barr, H. M., & Martin, D. C. (1983). Maternal alcohol use and neonatal habituation assessed with the Brazelton scale. *Child Development, 54,* 1109–1118.

Sullivan, J. W., & Horowitz, F. D. (1978). *Kansas supplements to the Neonatal Behavioral Assessment Scale: A first look*. Paper presented at the International Conference on Infant Studies, Providence.

Sykes, G. S., Molloy, P. M., Johnson, P., Stirratt, G. M., & Turnbull, A. C. (1983). Fetal distress and the condition of newborn infants. *British Medical Journal, 287*, 943–945.

Telzrow, R. W., Snyder, D. M., Tronick, E., Als, H., & Brazelton, T. B. (1980). The behavior of jaundiced infants undergoing phototherapy. *Developmental Medicine & Child Neurology, 22*, 317–326.

Thomas, A., & Chess, S. (1977). *Temperament and development*. New York: Brunner/Mazel.

Thomas, A., Chess, S., Birch, H. G., Hertzig, M. E., & Korn, S. (1963). *Behavioral individuality in early childhood*. New York: New York University Press.

Thompson, M. G., Eisenberg, H. M., & Levin, H. S. (1982). Hydrocephalic infants: Developmental assessment and computed tomography. *Child's Brain, 9*, 400–410.

Thompson, R. J., Jr., Cappleman, M. W., & Zeitschel, K. A. (1979). Neonatal behavior of infants of adolescent mothers. *Developmental Medicine & Child Neurology, 21*, 474–482.

Touwen, B. (1976). *Neurological development in infancy*. London: Heinemann.

Touwen, B., Huisjes, H. J., Jurgens-v.d.Zee, A. D., Bierman-van Eendenburg, M. E. C., Smrkovsky, M., & Olinga, A. A. (1980). Obstetrical condition and neonatal neurological morbidity. An analysis with the help of the optimality concept. *Early Human Development, 4*, 207–228.

Ueda, R. (1978a). Child development in Okinawa compared with Tokyo and Denver, and the implications for developmental screening. *Developmental Medicine & Child Neurology, 20*, 657–663.

Ueda, R. (1978b). Standardization of the Denver Developmental Screening Test on Tokyo children. *Developmental Medicine & Child Neurology, 20*, 647–656.

Uzgiris, I. C. (1973). Patterns of cognitive development in infancy. *Merrill Palmer Quarterly, 19*, 181–204.

Uzgiris, I. C. (1976). Organization of sensorimotor intelligence. In M. Lewis (Ed.), *Origins of intelligence*. New York: Plenum.

Uzgiris, I. C., & Hunt, J. McV. (1975). *Assessment in infancy: Ordinal scales of psychological development*. Urbana: University of Illinois Press.

Vaughn, B., Taraldson, B., Crichton, L., & Egeland, B. (1980). Relationships between neonatal behavioral organization and infant behavior during the first year of life. *Infant Behavior & Development, 3*, 47–66.

Wachs, T. D. (1970). Report on the utility of a Piagetian-based infant scale with older retarded children. *Developmental Psychology, 2*, 449.

Wachs, T. D. (1976). Relation of infants' performance on Piaget scales between twelve and twenty-four months and their Stanford-Binet performance at thirty-one months. *Child Development, 46*, 929–935.

Wachs, T. D., & deRemer, P. A. (1978). Adaptive behavior and Uzgiris-Hunt scale performance of young, developmentally-disabled children. *American Journal of Mental Deficiency, 83*, 171–176.

Wachs, T. D., & Hubert, N. C. (1981). Changes in the structure of cognitive–intellectual performance during the second year of life. *Infant Behavior & Development, 4*, 151–161.

Wachs, T. D., Uzgiris, I., & Hunt, J. McV. (1971). Cognitive development in infants of different age levels and from different environmental backgrounds: An exploratory investigation. *Merrill Palmer Quarterly, 17*, 283–317.

Wald, N. J. (Ed.). (1984). *Antenatal and neonatal screening*. New York: Oxford University Press.

Waters, E., Vaughn, B. E., & Egeland, B. R. (1980). Individual differences in infant–mother attachment relationships at age one: Antecedents in neonatal behavior in an urban, economically disadvantaged sample. *Child Development, 51,* 209–216.

Weber, T. (1980). Continuous fetal pH monitoring and neonatal Apgar score. *Journal of Perinatal Medicine, 8,* 158–163.

Werner, E. E., & Bayley, N. (1966). The reliability of Bayley's revised scale of mental and motor development during the first year of life. *Child Development, 37,* 39–50.

Widmayer, S. M., & Field, T. M. (1980). Effects of Brazelton demonstrations on early interactions of preterm infants and their teenage mothers. *Infant Behavior & Development, 3,* 78–89.

Widmayer, S. M., & Field, T. M. (1981). Effects of Brazelton demonstrations for mothers on the development of preterm infants. *Pediatrics, 67,* 711–714.

Willerman, L., Broman, S. H., & Fielder, M. (1970). Infant development, preschool I. Q., and social class. *Child Development, 41,* 69–77.

Worobey, J., & Belsky, J. (1982). Employing the Brazelton scale to influence mothering: An experimental comparison of three strategies. *Developmental Psychology, 18,* 736–743.

Yogman, M. W., Cole, P., Als, H., & Lester, B. M. (1982). Behavior of newborns of diabetic mothers. *Infant Behavior & Development, 5,* 331–340.

Zax, M., Sameroff, A. J., & Babigian, H. M. (1977). Birth outcomes in the offspring of mentally disordered women. *American Journal of Orthopsychiatry, 47,* 218–230.

Zeskind, P. S. (1981). Behavioral dimensions and cry sounds of infants of differential fetal growth. *Infant Behavior & Development, 4,* 297–306.

CHAPTER 14

Neonatal Behavioral Assessment Scale

T. BERRY BRAZELTON, J. KEVIN NUGENT, and BARRY M. LESTER

INTRODUCTION

The Neonatal Behavioral Assessment Scale (NBAS) was published 14 years ago (Brazelton, 1973). Recently, revisions were made, and the experiences of 10 years were summarized in the revision (NBAS, 2nd ed., Brazelton, 1984). Four centers and eight authors contributed to the revised edition. The scale is in use in over 400 locations; six training centers have been established in the United States, six in Europe, and one in Israel; over 125 published studies have appeared within the United States and in cross-cultural contexts.

In these studies, the characteristics of the NBAS have been explored, evaluated, and criticized. This chapter will summarize the current status of the NBAS and attempt to outline its appropriateness as a research instrument. We have just begun to explore its use as a clinical assessment to assist health professionals in their efforts to join parents in structuring an appropriate caregiving environment for premature, small for dates, or impaired infants. This chapter will also explore some of the conceptual and methodological issues involved in utilizing the NBAS to facilitate communication between parents, professionals, and the new baby. Psychometric issues of reliability and validity, including its use in predicting the baby's later developmental outcome, will also be addressed.

CONCEPTUAL BASE

The original goal for the NBAS was to attempt to describe autonomic, motor, state and social attention systems—which were seen as integrative and interacting with each other in the normal, healthy, full-term infant. The NBAS was seen not as a set of discrete stimulus–response presentations but as an interactive assessment, in which the adult participant played a major role, facilitating the performance and organizational skills of the infant. We hoped to establish the infant's capacities and his limits in contributing to the caregiving environment. We expected to gain a deeper understanding of the meaning of infant behavior as it reflected the relative contribution of these developmental lines. We conceived of a single assessment in the neonatal period as only one brief glimpse into the continuum of the infant's adjustment to labor, delivery, and his new environment. As such, it was expected to reflect his inborn characteristics and the behavioral respones that had already been shaped by the intrauterine environment. We hoped repeated exams would demonstrate his coping capacities and his capacities for utilizing his own inner organization as he began to experience, integrate, and profit developmentally from the environment's stimulation. Thus it was felt that serial exams would reflect the interaction between the infant's inborn characteristics and the shaping of them in the first few weeks.

As we have worked with the NBAS, several issues have become clear. An assessment of the newborn presents an opportunity for looking both forward into the baby's future and backward into his intrauterine experience. The intrauterine influences that shape newborn behavior are becoming more and more commonly recognized. The newborn's behavior at birth is phenotypic and genotypic in that complex behaviors are already shaped by influences in utero that probably act in a synergistic fashion.

Using the scale, we have been impressed by the baby's capacity to seek stimuli in an appropriate range for the level of stimulation the infant can tolerate. This ability in the normal baby fits with Osofsky's thesis (1976) that such a baby is both readable and predictable for his caregiver. Expectable behavior makes it more likely that the parent will nurture him appropriately. The infant's responses of recognition when his receptive range is met is distinctly different from the kind of automatic responses elicited by an observer who is insensitive to his individual range of responses.

The base for the infant's responses to internal and external stimuli can be seen in his use of states of consciousness as an expression of his internal organization and of his ability to master and control his reactions to external stimuli. With an awareness of the infant's use of states of consciousness (we identify six states: deep sleep, light sleep, indeterminate drowsy, wide awake alert, fussy alert, and crying), an examiner can rapidly develop an expectancy for an infant's reactions to stimuli so that, in a sense, state becomes the base for understanding each baby. Behavioral states, then, are seen as reflections of internal organization (e.g., autonomic, motor), as well as of reactions to incoming stimuli and the subsequent responses. We have begun to see alert states as actively prolonged in order to assimilate environmental information, and habituated states or crying utilized actively in order to control overwhelming information from the environment.

The concept of states of arousal as a continuum has been criticized (Prechtl, and O'Brien, 1982), yet this concept helps us as we work to help the infant produce and utilize states that are appropriate to the conditions of the exam. As one works with a newborn, one can help him in prolonging his state of alertness as he attends to stimuli. He can be seen to utilize a habituated sleep state to shut out disturbing stimuli. It soon becomes apparent that these states are not just passively induced by the observer's handling. The neonate's ability to organize his autonomic system in order to suppress interfering motor activity as he prolongs an attentional state becomes observable and repeatable. Each baby must be handled differently, but as one assists him to produce each state, predictable response patterns to negative and positive stimuli can be observed within each state. This predictability is, of course, the base for interscorer reliability in administration of the NBAS. The relatively predictable sequence of states found in an exam suggests that there is a continuum of states in the infant. Whether this induced continuum represents a window into the more spontaneous and natural cycling of states in a day–night continuum remains to be demonstrated. State can be a response to the baby's internal environment as readily as it can be to events outside the baby, to which he adjusts. In the NBAS, state may well be the result of both. External stimuli create autonomic and central nervous system responses to which the baby must adjust. State becomes a measure of the infant's capacity to "control" his environment. He can be seen to move along a continuum of states as he reacts to and adjusts to the stimuli presented by the examiner.

The demands of recovery from labor and delivery and from adjustments to the new environment dominate the infant's ability to respond from day to day. These demands are contingent in part upon the perinatal experience to which he has been exposed. The infant's ability to organize himself to respond to these demands through the postnatal period may reflect his present organization and his future pattern for adapting to his new environment. This, then, has been the concept behind our exploration of recovery curves in the postnatal period. The curve of behavioral recovery may represent not only the capacity of the infant to cope, but his ability to incorporate environmental cues and to begin to learn as he adapts to his internal and external environment (Brazelton, 1979). The recovery curves may give us a window into his future coping capacities.

PREDICTION

The systems within the infant are interactive and interdependent, but the items representing them are not measured in the same ways. Hence the scores are not of equivalent value. Many of the items go from clinically worst to best, but others reach an optimal score in the middle range. We did not want to provide a total "score." Rather, the NBAS represents a profile in which one sees the relative contribution of each developmental line to his ability to respond. This profile will change over time in response to the maturation of his internal capacities and to the external opportunities for learning. Thus the concept of change over time becomes a way of looking dynamically at the different systems that contribute to the baby's development.

Our use of behavioral responses for making predictions about a baby's future—cognitive, motor, and temperament—is based on a concept of change over time—changes within the baby as well as changing demands from the environment (cf. Sameroff & Chandler, 1975). Change in systems is the appropriate mode for prediction, and so far we do not know what change is developmentally appropriate. A conventional prediction might represent no change over time and a kind of inflexibility in the face of changing demands on the infant. Flexibility in responsiveness to changing capacities from within and to increasing demands from without should become the hallmark predicting optimal future function. How to quantify these patterns without losing the individuality of the baby has been one goal in our research. Then and only then can we hope to be able to use the neonate's behavior in a predictive system. Our goal in making predictions about an infant's future is that of being able to identify which at risk babies are most in need of early intervention. This is a major goal for research and clinical applications of the NBAS.

EARLY INTERVENTION

The importance of assessing the behavioral repertoire of the infant as early as possible has now been widely accepted (see Brazelton, 1984 appendix). We could facilitate an optimal outcome for babies if we could recognize neurological difficulties in organizing response systems that make it difficult for an infant to adjust to his environment. We have long recognized the environment's influence in improving or reinforcing potential deficits toward optimal development in high-risk infants.

Recent work in neurophysiology demonstrates the redundancy of neurological pathways in the immature central nervous system (St. James-Roberts, 1979). Unassigned pathways can be captured for substitution of function for damaged or impaired pathways, if such pathways are offered experiences from which they are able to learn. We have been aware in the past that behavioral substitution for impaired sensory or motor areas was possible. For instance, a blind infant uses highly sensitized auditory and tactile cues to replace the usual visual cues. Now, the concept of substitution of these unassigned pathways reinforces the concept of plasticity in the immature nervous system. But we must provide these pathways with information that is appropriate to them for organizing and learning responses rather than disorganizing ones. For example, an impaired brain is likely to be a hypersensitive one, and ordinary stimuli may be inappropriate or disorganizing. Hence a behavioral assessment that can explore for stimuli that are individuated and graded to produce positive responses in a hypersensitive individual might point to the kind of environmental stimuli that would lead toward organization and learning for that baby's future. The best use of the NBAS might be to identify as early a possible the individual differences in receptivity of such babies and to identify each baby's capacity for receiving and utilizing environmental stimuli.

CONTENT OF THE NBAS

The revised NBAS assesses the newborn's behavioral repertoire on 28 behavioral items, each scored on a 9-point scale. Table 14.1 shows the 28 items and the appropriate states in which they should be assessed. The scale measures the coping capacities and the adaptive strategies of the infant that emerge as he recovers from the stresses of labor and delivery and adjusts to the demands of the extrauterine environment. As discussed later, this process of adaptation can be measured by studying patterns of change, called profile or recovery curves (Lester, 1984) over repeated Brazelton examinations.

In order to be able to assess these patterns of change, at least two but preferably three or more examinations are needed for each infant. The first should be done on day 2 or 3, when the immediate stresses of labor and delivery have begun to wear off. The next examination can be done best at 7–10 days, while the third may be done at 14 days or at 1 month. Scores from these successive exams establish a behavioral pattern of change over the first weeks of life. This pattern, in turn, might well become the most important measure of prediction to later developmental outcome (Lester, 1984; Sepkoski, Hoffman, & Brazelton, 1986).

The NBAS also includes an assessment of the newborn's neurological responses.

TABLE 14.1.   Behavioral Items on the Revised Neonatal Behavioral Assessment Scale[a]

1. Response decrement to light (1,2,3)	15. Cuddliness (4,5)
2. Response decrement to rattle (1,2,3)	16. Defensive movements (3,4,5)
3. Response decrement to bell (1,2,3)	17. Consolability (6 to 4,3,2)
4. Response decrement to tactile stimulation of the foot (1,2,3)	18. Peak of excitement (all states)
	19. Rapidity of buildup (all states)
5. Orientation inanimate visual (4,5)	20. Irritability (all awake states)
6. Orientation inanimate auditory (4,5)	21. Activity (alert states)
7. Orientation inanimate visual and auditory (4,5)	22. Tremulousness (all states)
8. Orientation animate visual (4,5)	23. Startle (3,4,5,6)
9. Orientation animate auditory (4,5)	24. Lability of skin color (from 1 to 6)
10. Orientation animate visual and auditory (4,5)	25. Lability of states (all states)
11. Alertness (4,5)	26. Self-quieting activity (6 to 4,3,2,1)
12. General tonus (4,5)	27. Hand–mouth facility (all states)
13. Motor maturity (4,5)	28. Smiles (all states)
14. Pull-to-sit (4,5)	

[a]Numbers in parentheses refer to optimal state for assessment.

Table 14.2 lists the reflex items. Each reflex is scored on a 4-point scale, from 0 to 3. The reflex items will identify gross neurological abnormalities by deviant scores; they are not designed to provide a neurological evaluation. When three abnormal scores are found, the authors suggest a detailed neurological evaluation (e.g., Prechtl, 1968). Elicitation of the reflexes serves as a technique for eliciting other behavioral responses, such as the newborn's state control and his capacity to shut out the disturbing stimuli necessary to produce reflex responses.

In the second edition of the NBAS (Brazelton, 1984), nine supplementary items

TABLE 14.2.   Reflex Behaviors on the Revised Neonatal Behavior Assessment Scale

Reflex Items	X	O	L	M	H	A
Plantar grasp		0	1	2	3	
Hand grasp		0	1	2	3	
Ankle clonus		0	1	2	3	
Babinski		0	1	2	3	
Standing		0	1	2	3	
Automatic walking		0	1	2	3	
Placing		0	1	2	3	
Incurvation		0	1	2	3	
Crawling		0	1	2	3	
Glabella		0	1	2	3	
Tonic deviation of head and eyes		0	1	2	3	
Nystagmus		0	1	2	3	
Tonic neck reflex		0	1	2	3	
Moro		0	1	2	3	
Rooting (intensity)		0	1	2	3	
Sucking (intensity)		0	1	2	3	
Passive movement						
arms R		0	1	2	3	
L		0	1	2	3	
legs R		0	1	2	3	
L		0	1	2	3	

Note: X = response omitted; O = response not elicited; A = asymmetry of response; L = low; M = medium; H = high.

have been added, to be used with the NBAS in the assessment of high-risk infants. It became clear that the NBAS as originally designed was not an appropriate assessment for premature infants before they reached 36 weeks of gestational age (Brazelton, 1984). Furthermore, its use with premature infants after 36 weeks necessitated items that could capture the range and quality of the behavior exhibited by such sensitive, fragile infants. This led to the attempt to develop a number of supplementary items for high-risk fragile infants, based on items utilized in the APIB (Assessment of Preterm Infants' Behavior), (Als, Lester, Tronick, & Brazelton, 1982), and the NBAS-K (Neonatal Behavioral Assessment Scale, Kansas version, Horowitz & Linn, 1978). These items attempt to summarize the quality of the baby's responsiveness, the cost to him of such responses, as well as the amount of input from the examiner necessary to organize his responses. We have utilized these items to reflect the lowered thresholds and the high cost of responsiveness in fragile and at risk infants. We do not feel that the scale in its present form can be utilized before an infant is 36 weeks of gestational age and/or until a fragile infant is off supports and in room air. Only examiners trained specifically to work with high-risk infants should use the NBAS with these populations. These items have been successful in delineating the recovery of these infants and provide us with a window into their current functioning. Following is a description of the nine supplementary items; they will be subject to further investigation and change.

1. *Quality of alert responsiveness.* Assesses the quality of the infant's reponses to animate and inanimate visual and auditory stimuli.

2. *Cost of attention.* Assesses the degree to which the infant's state, motor, and physiological systems are stressed by environmental stimulation.

3. *Examiner persistence.* Measures the degree of facilitation necessary from the examiner in order to elicit the infant's optimal performance.

4. *General irritability.* Measures the amount of irritable crying in response to the various levels of stimulation throughout the exam.

5. *Robustness and endurance.* Describes the level of energy resources the infant has available, and any evidence of exhaustion or overloading.

6. *Regulatory capacities.* Assesses the degree to which the infant is able to maintain himself, as well as the level at which maintenance is achieved.

7. *State regulation.* Measures the range, quality, and stability of the infant's states.

8. *Balance of motor tone.* Examines the balance between flexor and extensor motor tone.

9. *Reinforcement value of the infant's behavior.* This is a rating of the newborn's social attractiveness to the examiner.

Each of these items is scored on a 9-point scale, with higher scores often reflecting better performance. While the supplementary items are regarded as preliminary and optional, we believe that these items have the potential to help us understand the unique behavioral patterns of the premature or fragile infant (Brazelton, 1984).

An additional set of scores has been added to the NBAS by the Kansas group in the NBAS-Kansas version (Horowitz & Linn, 1978). These are referred to as *modal* scores and are designed to capture the infant's typical level of response, rather than his *best performance* score. Modal scores have been added on the orientation, consolability, and defensive movement items. In order to assign a modal score, the item is administered four times so that differences between best and modal performance can be examined (Lancioni, Horowitz, & Sullivan, 1980). The original concept of best performance was suggested in order to (1) overcome subtle, uncontrolled environmental influences that would be apt to influence an infant's responses, and (2) reproduce parents' responses to him. Horowitz argues that modal performance is probably more typical of what a baby is like at home, while we believe that best performance represents a form of "pushing limits," which may be a better estimate of future performance than modal performance. Best performance tells us how the baby performs under the stress of pressures to perform.

TESTING CONDITIONS AND PROCEDURES

Environmental Conditions

Ideally, the NBAS should be administered in a quiet, moderately lighted room, with a temperature of 72–82 deg F. Less than ideal ambient conditions, such as harsh light and unpredictable noise, should be noted on the score sheet, as they will influence the infant's behavior. They will not contribute to his best performance.

The examination should begin when the infant is asleep, preferably in light sleep (state 2). The authors recommend a point midway between feedings as the best time for the exam. It is pointed out that the effects of maternal obstetric medication, jaundice, dehydration, or stressful medical procedures such as circumcision will influence the newborn's responses to the behavioral examination. If it is necessary to use the NBAS under such circumstances, the exam should be scored but the impinging circumstances should be noted.

The NBAS is appropriate for use without adaptation with normal infants 36–44 weeks of gestational age, who are in room air and off supports. While the scale with the supplementary items may be used with fragile infants, it should be done, as already mentioned, by experienced examiners.

Training of Examiners

The NBAS was developed to assess the behavior of the newborn within the dynamic context of the infant–caregiver relationship. It is precisely the interactive character of the scale that distinguishes it from other assessments. Nowhere is this shift of emphasis more apparent than in the training of examiners for the administration of the scale. The training to reliability of examiners on the NBAS has become an issue of importance for many reasons. First, since the field of newborn assessment is a relatively new area of investigation, few health professionals—doctors, nurses, psychologists, social workers, physical or occupational therapists—have been trained to record behaviors in the newborn. Second, medical professionals are trained to search for abnormalities. The aim of the NBAS is to provide a profile of the infant's overall level of organization, documenting and integrating both positive and negative characteristics of behavior. Hence it reflects a radical departure from conventional pathological medical assessment. Third, researchers and clinicians are trained to maintain objectivity as they react to the baby, so that the interactive thrust of the scale constitutes a more systems approach to newborn assessment than the stimulus–response approach to which clinicians and researchers may be accustomed.

Two initial concepts are important: *best performance* and *examiner flexibility*. The ability of the infant to produce best performance is, in turn, linked with the examiner's ability to elicit it by providing optimal conditions. This is dependent on the examiner's flexibility, that is, the ability to vary or change procedures and to modulate input in response to the baby's cues as the examination proceeds. The scale does not have a specified order of administration and so places greater demands on the examiners to adapt their procedures to the responses and cues of the infants. Such flexibility reflects both the examiner's understanding of the newborn's behavior repertoire and the development of sharp observational skills.

It is critical that examiners using and scoring the scale be reliable with each other. Data gathered otherwise cannot be compared.

Training on the scale focuses on achieving examiner reliability, that is, reliability in scoring and competence in administration. *Scoring reliability* means that two observers can achieve an interobserver agreement level of 92 percent by being able accurately to observe the same behavior and score it within 1 point on the 9-point items, 28 in number. The scoring criteria in the manual are well defined so that when inexperienced trainees have administered and scored the examination with 20 or 25 babies, they should have little difficulty reaching the 92 percent interscorer reliability criterion.

Competence in administration refers not merely to examiners' knowledge of administrative procedures but also to their competence in handling the infant and ability to understand and respond to behavioral cues throughout an assessment. Experience in handling babies and in the variations in expectable responses is critical to adequate administration. For this reason it is thought that examiners in training need the experience of testing at least 20 babies.

Nugent and Sepkoski (1984) describe two phases in the training of examiners on the NBAS: (1) self-training phase; and (2) reliability training phase. The initial phase involves familiarization with test items and the administrative and scoring procedures. Prospective examiners should also have an adequate background in infant development in order to interpret the infant's behavior. It is suggested that the trainee then view the training film* that describes the scale. The trainee should also try to observe a demonstration examination performed by a certified examiner, preferably at a training center.**

---

*Available from March of Dimes Birth Defects Foundation, Professional Education Department, 1275 Mamaroneck Ave., White Plains, NY 10605.
**NBAS training centers in North America and overseas:

J. Kevin Nugent, Ph.D., Director
The Children's Hospital
Child Development Unit
300 Longwood Ave.
Boston, MA 02115

Frances D. Horowitz, Ph.D.
Vice Chancellor for Research
Graduate Studies and Public Service, and
Professor, Department of Human Development and Family Life
University of Kansas
Lawrence, Kansas 66045

Kathryn E. Barnard, RN, Ph.D., FAAN
Professor of Nursing
Dept. of Parent-Child Nursing
Res. 212, CDMRC, WJ-10
University of Washington
Seattle, WA 98195

Suzanne Campbell, Ph.D.
Dept. of Medical and Allied Health Professions
University of North Carolina at Chapel Hill
Chapel Hill, NC 27514

Joan Castellan, RN
Regional Center for Infants and Young Children for Washington, Maryland, & Virginia
1432 Fenwick Lane
Silver Spring, MD 20912

Peter Gorski, M.D.
Northwestern University
Chicago, IL

Sherry Boyd, Ph.D.
Oregon Health Sciences University
Portland, OR 97201

USES OF THE NBAS

Since it was first published in 1973, the NBAS has become widely used in the assessment of newborn behavior. Currently, it is also being used as a form of intervention with parents in the newborn period. Among the classifications of studies with the NBAS are the following:

1. Studies of high-risk infants
2. Studies on the effects of obstetric medication
3. Studies on the effects of maternal substance abuse
4. Cross-cultural comparisons of newborn behavior
5. Prediction studies
6. Uses of the NBAS as a form of intervention

A few examples of each of these types of studies will be given.

Studies of High-Risk Infants

Although the NBAS was designed for the assessment of healthy full-term infants, it has been used to examine the effects of a wide range of prenatal and perinatal risk factors such as low birth weight and prematurity on behavior.

In one of the first studies of low birth weight infants, Scarr and Williams (1973), using an early version of the scale, tested 30 neonates ranging in birth weight from 1300 to 1800 g with a mean gestational age of 32.6 weeks; they were tested at 7 days and 4–6 weeks of life. Correlations between birth weight and behavior showed nine significant correlations, while at 1 month the number of correlations at this level did not exceed chance. Finally, both 1-week and 4-week scale scores correlated with Cattell IQ at 1 year, both with simple correlations and with birth weight partialed out. Neonatal observations were more predictive than 4-week observations and centered around behaviors that had to do with responsivity and the organization of responses.

Barry M. Lester, Ph.D.
Bradley Hospital
1011 Veterans Memorial
  Parkway
East Providence, Rhode Island
  02915

Prof. Dr. Hellgard Rauh
Fachbereich Erziehungs - und
  Unterrichtsweissenschaften
Institüt für Psychologie, Freie
  Universität Berlin,
  Habelschwerdler
Allee 45, Berlin 33, West
  Germany

Joao Gomes Pedro, M.D.,
  Ph.D.
Estrada la Luz
128 - 10 E
Lisboa, 1600, Portugal

Hanne Munck, Cand. Psychol.
University of Copenhagen
Institute of Clinical
  Psychology, Njalsgade 90
DK 2300 Copenhagen,
  Denmark

Drs. Dymph van den Boom
Dept. of Developmental
  Psychology
Univ. of Leiden
Hooigracht 15
2312 KM Leiden
Netherlands

Marie Anne Waugh, M.A.
Robin Dolby Ph.D.
Beulah Warren, M.A.
Sydney, New South Wales,
  Australia

Judith Auerbach, Ph.D.
Dept. of Psychology
Hebrew University
Jerusalem, Israel

Dieter Wolke, Dipl. Psych.
Dept. of Psychological
  Medicine
The Hospitals for Sick
  Children
Great Ormonde St.
London WC1N 3JH.
Great Britain

The ponderal index (a ratio of weight to length) used to indicate fetal malnutrition was used by Als, Tronick, Adamson, and Brazelton (1976) to compare full-term underweight for length (below tenth percentile) and average weight for length infants at 1, 3, 5, and 10 days of life on the NBAS. These normal, healthy, but slightly underweight infants differed from controls along behavioral dimensions that are particularly important for caregiving, such as attractiveness, need for stimulation, interactive processes, and motor processes. The groups also differed on reflexive behavior. Moreover, in follow-up by telephone of the underweight infants, mothers reported difficulties in temperamental organization and indications of psychosomatic reaction to stress. Their neonatal behavior predicted difficulties in state behavior in later infancy, with hypersensitivity to stimuli, rapid state changes, and increased crying spells of long duration.

Lester and Zeskind (1978) and Lester (1979) examined infants who were below the third percentile on the ponderal index and showed that these infants exhibited poorer performance across NBAS behavioral dimensions. Correlations between the Brazelton scale dimensions and the acoustic features of babies' cries indicated that poor Brazelton scores were related to differences in cry features. The cry of the underweight for length babies showed a higher and more variable fundamental frequency and more harmonic distortion, in contrast to the generally flat melody form of the cry of the full weight infant. These findings were replicated in a subsequent study by Zeskind (1981) showing that underweight infants differed from average weight babies on the four summary dimensions of the NBAS. Cry features and Brazelton scale scores were highly related, supporting the previous findings. Thus babies' behavior and cry features can reflect intrauterine stress. In a recent study, the NBAS clusters and supplementary items were found to discriminate infants with atypical patterns of fetal growth from infants with appropriate patterns of fetal growth (Lester, Garcia-Coll, Valcarcel, Hoffman, & Brazelton, 1986).

Multiple regression was used to determine the relative contribution of six high-risk variables on factor scores of the Brazelton scale in another study by Lester (Lester, Emory, Hoffman and Eitzman, 1976). Low attention scores were associated with low birth weight babies who were likely to be the infants of younger mothers. Low Apgar scores were associated with babies who scored lower on a temperament arousal dimension. Factor scores representing three dimensions—attention, arousal, and temperament—were compared among the three birth weight groups, with gestational age as a covariate. Both extremes—low and very high birth weight babies—scored lower on attentional behavior than infants of average birth weight. Low birth weight males and high birth weight females scored lower on arousal and temperament than other sex by birth weight groups. Postmature as well as immature babies may be at risk for attentional deficits and poor state control.

In another study using multivariate analyses Sepkoski, Garcia-Coll, and Lester (1982) examined the cumulative effects of risk variables on the Brazelton scores of 150 Puerto Rican neonates. Six risk variables were regressed on the seven a priori behavioral clusters. The regression model for each cluster, with the exception of range of state, was significant, indicating that the variables associated with obstetric risk act in concert to influence most behaviors measured by the Brazelton scale. Three variables reflecting growth, maturity, and fetal nonoptimal conditions were found to have major effects on neonatal behavior. Additionally, the motor cluster was found to be more sensitive to risk than any of the other clusters.

Brazelton, Tryphonopoulou, and Lester (1979) examined three groups of Greek neonates on the NBAS on days 1, 5, and 10. They compared the behavior of infants born to mothers who were cared for in late pregnancy at the Athens orphanage, the Metera, with infants from middle-class and lower-class homes. The Metera infants exhibited the poorest overall performance. It was postulated that their performance was affected by fetal undernutrition in the first few months of their illegitimate pregnancies.

Sell, Luick, Poisson, and Hill (1980) used a modification of the NBAS to study the behavioral characteristics of very low birth weight infants (< 1500 g) born at 28–32 weeks, when they reached a mean age of 38.2 weeks of gestational age. They found less visual responsivity, depressed reflexes, and reduced state lability in these infants when compared with healthy, full-term infants. The recovery of prematures is not complete by 40, or by 44 weeks.

Scanlon, Scanlon, and Tronick (1984) studied 45 very low birth weight infants (VLBW) between 750 and 1500 g with a mean gestational age of 31.1 weeks. They assessed the infants at 7 and 21 days of life, using a version of the NBAS specially modified for extremely premature infants. Using multiple regression to determine the influence of intrapartum and neonatal factors on newborn behavior, they found that evidence of perinatal asphyxia determined by cord pH and low Apgar scores accounted for significant amounts of the variance in the first behavioral examination. Gestational age and birth weight exhibited high correlations with NBAS scores at day 14. At this time Apgar scores and cord pH correlations with behavior were already less significant than on the first examination, signifying these babies' recovery from the insult. The babies who were not improving were predicting to poor CNS function later.

Ferrari, Grosoli, Fontane, and Cavazutti (1983) showed that low-risk preterm infants born at 33 weeks of gestation or less had poorer orientation, motor performance, regulation of state, and autonomic regulation scores than healthy term infants when examined on the NBAS at 40 weeks of gestational age and on the fifth day postterm. Paludetto and colleagues (1984) in another Italian study examined 30 preterm infants born at 27–34 weeks of gestational age, at 35, 38, 40, and 44 weeks on the NBAS. Performance on the orientation and motor clusters of the neonatal scale was poor at first but improved with advanced postconceptual age. Behavioral development did not proceed evenly in all areas, and their data plot uneven recovery.

Studies of the effects of jaundice and of phototherapy on newborn behavior have outlined the effects of these perinatal influences. Telzrow, Snyder, Tronick, Als, and Brazelton (1980) looked at the effects of phototherapy in infants suffering from hyperbilirubinemia by comparing a jaundiced group receiving phototherapy with a jaundiced group without therapy, as well as a nonjaundiced group. They found that the effects of phototherapy may interact with the effects of jaundice to cause disorganization in state modulation that persists beyond the normal week of recovery from jaundice. After 10 days of discontinuation of phototherapy, these infants still showed diminished alertness, social responsivity, and consolability. They remained difficult for their mothers to understand.

Nelson and Horowitz (1982) using the NBAS-K found behavioral differences in infants who were treated with phototherapy at 2 weeks of age. At that time the comparison infants scored higher than the treated infants on items dealing with state control and orientation.

Yogman, Cole, Als, and Lester (1982) studied infants of diabetic mothers and found that newborns of diabetic mothers, who were delivered by elective cesarean section, showed poorer scores on the orientation, motor, and autonomic dimensions of the NBAS than did a comparison group of healthy newborns delivered by cesarean. This seemed to be due to the influence of maternal diabetes.

Field and Widmayer (1980) used the NBAS to examine the effects of cesarean section deliveries on newborn behavior but found no differences in performance between elective cesarean deliveries and spontaneous vaginal deliveries over the first week after delivery.

The NBAS has also been used to study the behavior of infants of teenage mothers. Thompson, Cappelman, and Zeitschel (1979) compared the infants of 30 low socioeconomic teenage (under 18) mothers with 30 older mothers. The infants were examined on the NBAS at 2–5 days of age. Results showed that the infants of adolescent mothers performed less well on the orientation, motor, and state dimensions of the NBAS.

Lester, Emory, Hoffman, and Eitzman (1982), comparing the organization of neonatal behavior of teenage and older mothers in Puerto Rico and Florida, found evidence for the additive effects of maternal age with other biological outcome variables in predicting Brazelton scale factors. And in a study of 303 infants Lester, Garcia-Coll, and Sepkoski (1983) studied maternal age as an independent factor, while controlling for obstetric history and other prenatal and perinatal factors. Results of regression analyses showed that for both Mainland U.S. and Puerto Rican infants none of the bivariate correlations between maternal age and Brazelton scale cluster scores was significant. However, in the Puerto Rican group, a significant Age × Complications interaction effect was found that showed that with fewer obstetric complications infants of teenage mothers spent more time in higher states of arousal, reached a crying state earlier in the exam, and changed state more often than infants of older mothers. They were already more difficult infants.

The NBAS has been useful in documenting the behavioral differences of birth weight—both from prematurity and from intrauterine deprivation (as evidenced by a low ponderal index). The effects on state regulation, on orientation or attention, on autonomic regulation, and on motor and reflex behavior recur in the many studies that have utilized the scale as an outcome measure. So far, too few studies have utilized the scale with repeated measures to document the severity and duration of effects.

The effects of obstetric risk, of maternal variables such as age extremes (e.g., teenage mothers), of undernutrition, or of diabetes do seem to be demonstrated as significant in that they influence the behaviors of the neonate. So far, too few studies have utilized a multivariate approach of the many pre- and perinatal variables that are likely to influence the high-risk neonate's behavioral recovery. We need to assimilate all such variables as we study these different kinds of low birth weight babies. It is not likely that specific behavioral effects from each variable will be found. They need to be used in multivariate analyses.

The disorganization of the central nervous system that results from significant pre- and perinatal variables seems to be generalizable, affecting the many systems of the neonate. Prematurity is likely also to have a general effect on all systems. It is critical that we continue to clarify the physical as well as behavioral measures of both prematurity and intrauterine stress. So far, our measures of gestational age and of intrauterine deprivation are relatively crude, but it is necessary that they be documented carefully in any study of the behavior of high-risk babies. We utilize the Dubowitz exam for gestational age and compare it to the best maternal dates for expected delivery. The ponderal index is utilized for evidence of intrauterine depletion of tissue storage. These measures do not reflect the duration or severity of intrauterine stress or of the effects of an early delivery on the baby's ability to organize himself.

The behavioral assessment can document the degree of the effects of intrauterine stress. By following the change of behaviors over time, the effect is seen on the cluster scores rather than on single items, and following these effects over time, we may "postdict" to the neurological insults in utero and at the time of delivery. The new additions, the supplementary items, may well lead us to a new understanding of the *cost* to the nervous system as it organizes after a CNS insult, or as it recovers from a premature or stressful delivery. We hope that the use of the nine supplementary items will offer further documentation to the effects of such stresses on the organizing central nervous system as it adapts to the extrauterine environment. Localized insults to the developing nervous system may be demonstrated by effect on single items from the scale, but their general effect on all behaviors as they reflect the integrative function of the baby may be more predictive of future recovery of function.

The Effects of Obstetric Medication

There have been many studies examining the effects of obstetric medication on newborn behavior (cf. Sepkoski, 1985). Using a modified version of the scale, Brackbill (1979) compared the analgesic effects of meperedine in full-term healthy infants whose mothers also received epidural anesthesia. Differences between meperedine and nonmeperedine groups were found on the Brazelton scale in terms of a total score and a summary neurologic score and for four of five elicited responses. Group differences were also found for the rate of habituation of the orienting reflex. By contrast, when Standley, Soule, Copans, and Duchowny (1974) compared the effects of analgesia with that of anesthesia using the scale, they found mean differences in the a priori subscales of irritability and motor maturity due to anesthesia with analgesia controlled, but no effects when analgesia was studied with the effects of anesthesia controlled. In another report, Aleksandrowiscz and Aleksandrowiscz (1974) administered the Brazelton scale eight times during the first month of life and found medication effects.

Thus medication routinely administered to mothers certainly seems to affect their newborns' behavior.

Studies have called attention to the possible synergistic effects of medication and other stress factors. In one study (Tronick et al., 1976), strict selection criteria were used to compare the effects of eight drug groups on behavior of full-term, healthy infants whose mothers had problem-free pregnancies, labors, and deliveries. The Brazelton exam was administered on days 1, 2, 3, 4, 5, 7, and 10. Mean differences among the drug groups were sporadic and did not persist. Local anesthesia and analgesic premedication produced few changes in behavior, and while epidural anesthesia did result in an initial diminution in the motor organization of the infant, this effect was transient. Lester and colleagues (1982) reanalyzed these data and found that obstetric medication in combination with length of labor, parity, and the infant's ponderal index score did affect NBAS performance. They suggested that medication may act synergistically with other stress factors in pregnancy or at the time of delivery. In a further prospective investigation of this hypothesis, Sepkoski, Lester, Ostheimer, Hoffman, and Brazelton (1984) examined the effects of bupivacaine epidural anesthesia on the behavior of a sample of 60 babies varying in birth histories. They administered the Brazelton scale at 3 hr, 3 days, 1 week, and 1 month of age. Findings indicated that few effects were found when the drug was administered as a single variable in bivariate correlations, but when bupivacaine was examined with other variables that may increase its rate of placental transfer (e.g., pH of umbilical blood weight of baby and mother), many correlations with behavior were found. The drug was related to decreased performance on six of the seven priori clusters over the first month of life. Behaviors on the motor and autonomic regulation clusters were affected most significantly with effects being greater at 3 hr of age than later in the month. Woodson and DaCosta (1980) in a sample of 113 healthy full-term infants born in Kuala Lumpur found that there was a relationship between length of labor and maternal blood pressure during labor, in combination with medication variables and higher scores on irritability on the NBAS.

Horowitz and colleagues (1977) reported the results of a series of studies comparing Israeli, Uruguayan, and American samples. Infants in the Israeli samples were tested on days 1, 4, and 30 with the Brazelton scale and at 3 months with the Bayley scales. No medication was used at the time of delivery for the Israeli babies as compared with the U.S. sample. The results were dramatic in the few significant effects obtained, especially in view of the large number of statistical tests performed and for the low magnitude of the effects found. The *largest* difference was 1.7 scale points; however, they were in the direction of medication effects. These studies suggested that low levels of obstetric medication in very healthy infant–mother pairs have little or no effect on neonatal behavior. Perhaps medication effects are created when there are two or more interactive variables, such as prenatal stress or undernutrition, coupled with small amounts of medication.

Kuhnert, Harrison, Linn, and Kuhnert (1984) used the NBAS to examine the effects of maternal epidural anesthesia on neonatal behavior, specifically between lidocaine and chloroprocaine. Ninety-nine healthy infants were examined at less than 5 hr and at 3 days of age. Clinical characteristics, pharmacological data, and NBAS scores were analyzed using stepwise multiple regression and repeated analysis of variance. At less than 5 hr of age, the chloroprocaine group performed significantly better on the autonomic cluster. All the cluster scores showed significant improvement with age except for regulation of state. Furthermore, the route of delivery was related to regulation of state, with cesarean section babies performing better. The data suggested that differences in performance on the NBAS associated with lidocaine are subtle and that other perinatal factors can influence performance on the NBAS more than the type of local anesthetic used. This is an example of using the NBAS to compare the effects of two different drugs.

The NBAS is useful in demonstrating subtle as well as more powerful effects of maternal medication on the newborn baby. The depressing effects of medication are seen in all clusters of behavior on the NBAS. The scale can be used to demonstrate short-term effects as well as longer-lasting depression of the CNS. The short-term effects vary with dose, timing of administration before delivery, and other variables that are synergistic with medication. Such variables as (1) fat stores in the mother that absorb medication to protect the fetus, (2) fat stores in the baby that are not present in SGA babies, leaving them vulnerable to lower doses of medication, (3) duration of labor, (4) mild CNS stress that added to medication effects, (5) type of labor (cesarean section), and (6) analgesia plus anesthesia must all be accounted for in any study of medication effects. The short duration and the minimal disorganization from low levels of medication do not seem to affect the performance of a healthy baby. But the additive effects of several variables do. The depressant effects of medication seem to be demonstrated in all behavioral clusters.

It is even more critical to document medication effects over time with multiple exams. The recovery from short-term effects can be seen in healthy infants, whereas poor recovery may point to the effects of other stresses on the baby, and may predict to future dysfunction.

The studies that demonstrate longer-lasting (1 year) or sleeper (3–4 years) effects of maternal medication on the infants' performance have not yet been able to sort out the direct effect of medication on the infants' central and autonomic nervous sytems versus a short-term effect on the infants' behavior that then affects maternal handling. A mother may perceive her baby as depressed and may handle him differently to prolong the apparent effect of medication. This still needs to be studied to identify direct versus indirect effects of medication.

The Effects of Maternal Substance Abuse

Soule, Standley, Copans, and Davis (1974) compared infants of 19 heroin-addicted mothers taking methadone with 41 controls who differed on economic, racial, and medical factors. Mean differences were found for 14 of the 26 items of the scale and reflected the methadone baby's state of narcotic withdrawal. The methadone babies were neurologically irritable as shown by more crying, rapid state changes, tremors, hypertonicity, and poorer motor maturity at birth. An interesting sidelight to this study was that information from the exam was useful in the management of these infants by using consolability maneuvers to avoid the administration of drugs and to alleviate the withdrawal. In a similar report, Kaplan and Kron (1975) found mean differences between narcotic-addicted and control infants on 12 of the items that Soule and colleagues (1974) found to discriminate between the two groups. Kron, Finnegan, Kaplan, Litt, and Phoenix (1975); Strauss, Lessen-Firestone, Starr, and Ostrea (1976); and Strauss, Starr, Ostrea, Chavez, and Struker (1976) also showed that such affected infants had significantly poorer behavioral organization in all dimensions than did control infants. Kaplan and Kron (1975) generated summary scores from the scale and found these scores to be related to measures of sucking and to the birth weight of the baby. The latter finding led to the conclusion that lower birth weight babies were much more affected by the narcotic and demonstrated more serious withdrawal effects than did full birth weight babies. The authors controlled for risk-producing factors other than maternal addiction, since other variables may have affected neonatal behavior. The Brazelton scale was administered to 22 infants of heroin-addicted mothers and 22 controls on days 1 and 2 of life. All infants were full term, full birth weight, and their mothers were similar in terms of age, socioeconomic status, prenatal history, and length of labor; Apgars were also similar. In addition to demonstrating classic behavioral signs of withdrawal such as irritability, tremulousness, state lability, motor immaturity, and resistance to cuddling, these infants differed along dimensions of orientation responsiveness such as habituation, alertness, and auditory and visual orientation. It was felt that the behavior patterns of addicted neonates are likely to tax the ability of the caregiver to adapt to the infant.

Chasnoff, Hatcher, and Burns (1982) studied the effects of different types of maternal addiction on a sample of 95 newborn infants. The subjects were divided into four groups according to the type of primary maternal addiction: (1) heroin/methadone group ($n = 51$); (2) mixed sedative/stimulant group ($n = 22$); (3) pentazocine/tripelenamine group ($n = 3$), and (4) phencyclidine group ($n = 9$). The fifth group was a control group ($n = 27$). The infants were examined once on the NBAS at 2 days of age. The heroin/methadone group had poorer visual and auditory orientation and motor maturity scores than all the other groups. Infants in groups 1 and 3 had significantly lower birth weights and lengths and had smaller head circumferences than did the controls. All four groups had poorer state control, with increased lability of state and poor consolability, as compared to the control group. Chasnoff and colleagues (1982) also found that infants whose mothers abused phencyclidine (PCP) prior to and during pregnancy were more behaviorally labile and more difficult to console than the infants of drug-free mothers. No statistical differences were found on the Bayley Scales of Infant Development at 3 months, and the effects on neonatal behavior seemed to have been compensated for at this time. This is encouraging because it seems to indicate that effective interventions with addicted mothers will help babies recover. If, on the other hand, a mother is allowed to take an addicted baby home without any understanding of his difficult behavior, her own reaction might couple with the baby's difficultness to produce an unnecessarily impaired infant.

Infants born to alcohol-addicted mothers were studied by Streissguth, Ban, and Martin (1983). They examined the effects of intrauterine alcohol exposure in a sample of 417 infants, who were examined once on the NBAS 9–35 hr after delivery. Maternal alcohol usage was obtained by a method of self-report during the fifth month of pregnancy. Factor analysis yielded six factors that were entered into a multiple regression analysis as dependent variables. Maternal alcohol use in mid-pregnancy was related to poorer habituation and to significantly lower arousal in newborns, even after adjusting for smoking and caffeine use, maternal age, and nutrition during pregnancy, for sex and age of the infant, and for obstetric medication. Alcohol levels in the mother seem to affect the baby's central nervous system as reflected by his behavior at birth.

Picone, Allen, Olsen, and Ferris (1982) evaluated the effects of maternal caloric intake, weight gain, smoking, and stress on the pregnancy outcome of 60 women. Serial NBAS examinations were performed at 2, 3, and 14 days postpartum. Multiple and stepwise regression analyses were used to examine the predictive relationship between maternal variables and Brazelton scores. Low weight gain (LWG) in the second trimester was associated with poor habituation, orientation, regulation of state, motor performance, and reflexes over all three test dates. Repeated measures analysis of variance showed that smoking during pregnancy adversely affected auditory and visual habituation scores, orientation, and autonomic regulation over all three test dates. Low weight gain and smoking were found to have significant but separate detrimental effects on newborn behavioral functioning over the first 2 weeks.

Fricker, Hindermann, and Bruppacher (in press) in an epidemiologic investigation of 996 Swiss healthy full-term newborns used the NBAS to examine the effects of tobacco, alcohol, and coffee consumption on neonatal outcome. They found a significant negative effect on the orientation cluster when the mother smoked before pregnancy, and on the habituation cluster when the mother smoked in the third trimester. No effects for alcohol were found. There was a significant relationship between coffee consumption and lower scores on the orientation and motor clusters of the NBAS.

Jacobson, Fein, Jacobson, and Schwartz (1984) studied the effects of maternal exposure to environmental toxins on newborn behavior. They used the NBAS to examine 242 infants born to women who were exposed prenatally to polychlorinated biphenyls (PCBs). PCB exposure was measured directly from cord serum samples, and indirectly from reported maternal consumption of contaminated Lake Michigan fish. Adjusted contaminated fish consumption was regressed on six of the NBAS clusters. Contaminated fish consumption (based on levels both before and during pregnancy) predicted a linear combination of five NBAS clusters. The strongest relationships were with autonomic maturity, number of abnormal reflexes, and range of state. The most highly exposed infants were more likely than controls to be classified as worrisome on the autonomic, range of state, and reflex clusters.

The use of the NBAS to demonstrate effects of maternal ingestion of toxins is expected to be one of the most productive areas for future investigation. Environmental toxins such as PCB and PCP have been shown to affect neonatal behavior, particularly in depressing the ability of the newborn to adjust to and orient to environmental stimuli. Addicted mothers produce addicted babies, and the withdrawal effects of substance abuse generate extreme irritability with intractable crying, poor state control and consolability, motor immaturity with a mixture of tremors, hypertonicity, and hypotonicity. The inability of the baby to be consoled and the hypersensitivity to all environmental stimuli indicate high risk in adjusting to the neonate's future environment. An addicted, high-risk mother will be presented with an irritable, unreachable baby. The forces for failure in the parent–infant interaction are predictable at birth. If they are predictable because of the severity of dysfunction in the infant's behavior, they can be utilized to set up appropriate intervention strategies.

Maternal heroin, methadone, PCP, alcohol, caffeine, and tobacco have effects on the neonate's performance. The last two mainly affect orientation items of the scale. The more powerful addictive drugs affect all segments of the babies' performance; orientation and state control are depressed, consolability is difficult, irritability to stimuli and tremors, startles, and poor motor organization (hypo- and hypertonicity) are the hallmarks of the effects on the baby of prolonged consumption and/or addiction in the mother. Again, the duration of these effects on the baby's behavior may be the best evidence of duration of intrauterine insults, and may best predict future effects on his performance. We need repeated NBAS measures to document this.

Other pre- and perinatal variables need to be carefully controlled that are likely to be synergistic with the effects of such toxins—maternal undernutrition, hypertension, time and duration of ingestion, number of toxins ingested, and so forth. The gestational age and nutritional status of the baby must be carefully measured. Cord blood levels of toxins would be an ideal addition to any study, although they reflect only the recent ingestion. Effects of levels in early pregnancy are more likely to affect the baby's outcome. Again, change of his behavioral orgnization over time is undoubtedly a better reflection of the effects on his central and autonomic nervous systems.

Cross-Cultural Uses of the NBAS

The NBAS has been used to assess neonatal behavioral differences and their natural variations in a wide range of cultural settings. In each case, the scale has been used to identify the prenatal and perinatal influences that affect neonatal behavior. In one of the first studies of Asian and Asian-American infants, using an earlier version of the scale, Freedman and Freedman (1969) compared 24 Chinese-American with 24 European-American neonates and controlled for initial state, 5-min Apgar score, length of labor, obstetrical medication, an the age and parity of the mother. While total Brazelton scores were different between the two groups, item-by-item comparisons showed that these differences were due to behaviors reflecting temperamental dimensions. Specifically, Chinese-American neonates were less "perturbable" to examiner ministrations, habituated more quickly, were better at self-quieting, and soothed more easily when consoled. These differences were interpreted to represent genetic differences.

Freedman (1971) replicated these findings with Japanese-American and Navajo Indian infants. The same pattern of differences described above were again observed in these two samples. He showed that Navajo newborns were consistently quieter and less irritable than Anglo-American newborns. Chisholm (1983) in turn replicated Freedman's results and found Navajo infants to be less irritable, with better self-quieting behaviors, with lower peak of excitement, less rapid build-up, and lower lability of state scores than Anglo-American infants on the NBAS.

Muret-Wagstaff and Moore (in press) examined the behavior of a sample of infants born to Hmong mothers, who had come to the United States from Laos. They compared the behavior of the Hmong infants with a sample of American Caucasian infants on the NBAS on days 1, 3, 7, 14, and 28. The Hmong infants had higher scores on the orientation cluster on days 1, 7, 14, and 28, while Caucasian infants had higher scores on the motor cluster on days 1, 3, and 28. Hmong infants were less irritable than Caucasian infants on all days except day 3.

Recently, two studies of newborn behavior in Asia have been reported. Walsh (in press) studied the effects of low ponderal index on the behavior of a sample of Nepalese infants. Comparing their performance with a U.S. sample of infants with equal nutritional status, she found the Nepalese infants performed better on the motor and autonomic regulation clusters of the NBAS. The author speculated that, since the measure of ponderal index was standardized in the United States, it was probably not an accurate measure of nutritional status in Nepalese infants, so that Nepalese neonates may not in fact have been undernourished.

Landers (in press) examined a sample of healthy full-term South Indian infants on the NBAS on days 1, 3, 5, 7, 10, and 30. She found an increase in performance on the habituation, motor, autonomic stability, and reflex clusters over the first month of life. She concluded that differential performances on the NBAS were influenced by maternal swaddling techniques, the type and quality of motor stimulation, and the mother–infant interaction and its effect on the infant's social responsivity.

Studies using the NBAS with infants from Latin America come from four populations: the Zinacanteco, Mayan Indians of highland Chiapas in southern Mexico; Ladinos of mixed Latin and Mayan ancestry from Guatemala; Latin infants from Puerto Rico; and Queshuq and Aymara Indians from the Andes and a low-altitude sample from Lima.

In an investigation of the Zinacanteco Indians of southern Mexico, five neonates were examined during the first week of life and compared with three Caucasian infants (Brazelton et al., 1969). The Zinacanteco babies seemed to demonstrate a higher-order control of state and motor behavior than the Caucasian infants, which fostered prolonged and repeated responses to auditory, visual, and kinesthetic stimuli during the first week. Observations of mother–infant interaction suggested that the mothers reinforced the quiet alertness of the baby by providing dyadic interaction well suited to the society and a demonstration of the infant's role in shaping the environment's response to him.

The Guatemalan study, by Brazelton, Tronick, Lechtig, Lasky, and Klein (1977) was part of a longitudinal project conducted by the Institute of Nutrition of Central America and Panama to investigate the effects of protein and calorie supplementation on mental, motor, and physical development in four subsistence-level farming villages in eastern Guatemala. Performance on the NBAS was found to improve significantly with increasing gestational age, age of testing, and birth weight. Birth weight in turn was correlated with maternal nutritional history as well as life-style. Infants in the higher socioeconomic groups scored significantly higher on all items than did infants of lower socioeconomic status.

In two studies in Puerto Rico, Puerto Rican infants were compared with black and white American babies, by grouping items according to the typologies of the Brazelton scale (Garcia-Coll, Sepkoski, & Lester, 1981). In the first study, differences were found along all four behavioral dimensions. Puerto Rican infants performed better on social responsiveness and were better able to control their physiologic repsonse to stress. They came rapidly into alert states, were highly responsive to stimulation, and showed much physical activity. They also showed more jerky movements but were successful at self-quieting. The second study also showed striking differences between the Puerto Rican infants and the other two groups.

Saco-Pollitt (1981) compared female infants born at high altitudes (4300 meters) with a low-altitude sample born in Lima (150 meters). She found that the infants born at high altitudes performed less well on the interactive and motor dimensions of the NBAS.

A number of studies using the NBAS have been conducted in Africa. In a study of urban Zambian and American infants, the Brazelton scale was administered to 10 babies from each culture on days 1, 5, and 10 (Brazelton, Koslowski, & Tronick, 1977). Although all infants were full term and normal, the Zambian babies showed pediatric evidence of intrauterine depletion and placental insufficiency. The samples were compared on each item of the scale for each day of the examination. On day 1 the Zambians scored lower than the Americans on items that reflected reactivity, whereas by day 10, although the Zambians still scored low on reactivity measures, they scored higher than Americans on items indicating social attentiveness. The recovery of the Zambian infants was attributed to a combination of inherited (genetic and nongenetic) factors and cultural expectations for responsiveness of the caregiver.

In another study, Dixon, Keefer, Tronick, and Brazelton (1982) studied the behavior of 24 Gusii newborn infants in Kenya. The infants, though born under nonoptimal prenatal and perinatal conditions by standards in technologically advanced cultures, performed within the normal range observed for American infants born under more optimal obstetric conditions. The Gusii infants were motorically more mature, and this was interpreted as a function of the early and constant stimulation by the environment, which reinforced motor behavior.

Winn, Morelli, and Tronick (in press) examined the behavior of a sample of Efe Pygmy newborns, inhabitants of the Ituri forest in northeastern Zaire. The NBAS was administered to 16 Efe newborns within 60 hr postpartum. Two summary measures, arousal and degree of reactivity ranking, were generated to analyze the relationship between newborn behavior and caretaking practices observed at 3, 7, and 18 weeks. While there was a correlation between the degree of reactivity ranking and infant fussing at 3 and 7 weeks, there was no relationship between the two clusters and measures of caretaking at 3, 7, or 18 weeks.

On the strength of these studies, we recommend that several assessments be added in cross-cultural studies. An estimate of gestational age (Brett, 1965; Dubowitz, 1970; Robinson, 1966), of neurological adequacy (Prechtl, 1968), of intrauterine conditions of nutrition (dysmaturity scales of Dubowitz, 1970; Lubchenco, 1970), as well as correct length and weight measurements and Apgar scores, should be added to any behavioral assessment that attempts to evaluate cross-cultural differences in behavior at birth.

Prediction Studies

Several studies have examined the contribution of newborn behavior to mother–infant interactions and developmental outcome in later infancy. In one of the first of these studies, Sameroff, Krafchuk, and Bakow (1978), with a factor analysis of the scale, used the factors to predict infant response clusters and maternal response clusters during a home observation at 4 months. They found that items of one of the two main factors, Alertness, was related to activity in the mother and responsivity in the infant during the home observation session. Similar findings were reported by Osofsky and Danzger (1974) with respect to neonatal style and mother–infant interaction during a feeding situation with infants 2–4 days old. Scale performance was related to infant feeding behavior, which was in turn correlated with the behavior of the mother. This study showed that infant style and responsivity were consistent during the Brazelton assessment and the feeding session—for example, newborns who were alert and responsive according to the scale behaved similarly when fed. Also, patterns of maternal stimulation and style of responding were conistent with the demand and responsivity characteristics of the baby.

Als and Lewis (1975) used the scale six times during the first 3 months of life. They also observed infant–mother interaction during feeding at these same age points. They used eight subscales to derive five temperament types and were interested in the developing organization of the baby during the first few months. They found that by 2–3 months, mother and infant had combined efforts to achieve a well-modulated state in the baby and that the infant's temperament affected the way the mother handled the baby. For example, the mothers learned to stimulate lethargic babies and contain overreactive infants.

Sostek and Anders (1977) found significant relationships between NBAS performance in the first few days of life and Bayley scores at 10 weeks of age. Vaughn, Taraldson, Crichton, and Egeland (1980) reported a significant relationship between NBAS and Bayley Mental scale scores at 9 months. Waters, Vaughn, and Egeland (1980) reported that infants classified as "anxious resistant" on the Strange Situation Paradigm at 1 year had less optimal scores on the orientation, motor maturity, and autonomic regulation dimensions of the NBAS. Bakeman and Brown (1980) found that the NBAS orientation items were correlated with social participation and social competence measures at 3 years of age.

Crockenberg (1981) examined the relationship between newborn behavior as assessed on the NBAS and mothers' ratings of temperament, as assessed by the Infant Behavior Questionnaire (Bates, Freeland, and Lounsbury, 1979) at 3 months. The infants were examined on the NBAS in the infants' homes at 5 and 10 days after birth. The item scores were combined into clusters (Kaye, 1978) and averaged across the two examinations. There was a significant correlation between newborn motor maturity and IBQ smiling and laughter at 3 months. Neither newborn alertness nor irritability predicted IBQ distress scores or newborn consolability, nor did they predict IBQ soothability at 3 months.

Pedro, (1984) in a Portuguese study used the NBAS to evaluate the effects of infants having extended contact with their mothers for a half-hour after delivery and found that these infants as compared to a control group who had no such extra contact had higher scores on the interactive cluster at 3 and 28 days.

In a study of 243 firstborn infants from an economically disadvantaged population, Waters and colleagues (1980) showed that ratings of maternal variables along with assessments of newborn behavior added significantly to the prediction of the quality of maternal caregiving over the first 6 months of life. Linn and Horowitz (1984) also showed that when NBAS measures were combined with some measures of the infant's environment prediction to later measures of mother–infant interaction would be enhanced significantly.

Lester (1984), using patterns of change over repeated NBAS examinations, called profile or recovery curves, has been able to predict 18-month Bayley Mental and Motor Scale scores in term and preterm infants. These profile curve parameters were computed from NBAS cluster scores at 40, 42, and 44 weeks of gestation. SES combined with the medical risk rating scale, the Parmelee neurological, and the NBAS curve factors explained 86 percent of the variance in 18-month MDI scores at 18 months for premature infants. The data supported the hypothesis that repeated assessments of the NBAS are necessary if the NBAS is to be used to correlate with later developmental outcome.

Nugent, Lester, Hoffman, and Brazelton (1984) in a sample of healthy Irish infants also found a significant relationship between patterns of change in neonatal behavior and Stanford-Binet scores at 3 years. Sepkoski, Hoffman, and Brazelton (1986) also found a relationship between NBAS recovery curve profiles and Bayley MDI scores at 1 year and McCarthy scores at 5 years. We are convinced that repeated exams significantly improve the scale's potential for making predictions about future outcome.

From these studies, we have learned that a single assessment is of value only as a screening instrument for gross neurological and behavioral dysfunction. Several consecutive exams are much more sensitive to intrauterine stress, to perinatal factors, as well as to evidence for future organization. Patterns of change over time in the neonatal period, called profile or recovery curves, are likely to be better predictors of future function than are single exams. The pattern of change in behaviors reflects the ability of the neonate both to reorganize after the stress of labor and delivery and to assimilate early environmental stimulation and efforts on the part of the environmental caregiver to assist the baby in this reorganization. To predict that is the goal of the exam.

Certain groups of data (such as orientation, state regulation, consolability, irritability) are likely to change in a positive direction. Motor and reflex items that reflect midbrain function may change less as a response to environmental input. Autonomic regulation is more indicative of internal regulators and may not reflect the appropriateness of environmental input but may be evidence of internal organization or disorganization. Thus if one is concerned with future cognitive or social development, patterns of change in certain groups of data may be more predictive than others. The motor, reflex, and autonomic clusters may predict future motor function better. In studies of prediction we must continue to strive for better indicators of the effects of the cost to the baby to achieve internal regulation as they interplay with environmental input. This then may well correlate with the external displays of cognitive and social performance in the future. We hope that appropriate clusters of the NBAS behaviors with the addition of the nine new descriptors as they change over time will be of more value in predicting future functioning as well as identifying at risk factors in the neonatal period that can be addressed early.

Uses of the NBAS as an Intervention

The NBAS is being used increasingly by health care professionals to help parents understand their newborn infants' competencies, temperament, and individual behavioral patterns. A growing number of studies suggest that observing the administration of the NBAS can enhance parent–infant interaction.

Anderson and Sawin (1983), using a pretest–posttest design, showed that demonstrating the capabilities and individual behavioral characteristics of their newborns to primiparous mothers increased mothers' responsivity scores on the AMIS (Assessment of Mother–Infant Sensitivity Scale, Price, 1983). Liptak, Keller, Feldman, and Chamberlain (1983) found that mothers to whom the NBAS was demonstrated spent more time playing and talking with their infants at 1 and 3 months. Myers (1982) also examined the effectiveness of the NBAS as a parent education tool for a sample of first-time middle-class mothers and fathers. The target parents in the treatment group were taught to administer the Brazelton scale to their own infants. Measures of knowledge of infant behavior, confidence in parenting ability, satisfaction with the infant, father–infant and mother–infant interaction, and father's caretaking were collected in the first month postpartum. Results showed that there were no treatment effects in the observations of mother–infant or father–infant interaction. However, both mothers' and fathers' knowledge of infant behavior showed strong treatment effects in the hospital and at 1 month. Also, treatment fathers were more involved in caretaking with their infants at 4 weeks than were control fathers. Worobey and Belsky (1982) also actively involved mothers in the administration of the NBAS and found that at 4–6 weeks these mothers were more responsive with their infants than mothers who only observed the NBAS being administered to their infants or mothers who did not observe the NBAS.

More recently, Beal (1983) demonstrated 3-day-old behavior to fathers. At 1 and 4 months, fathers were significantly more sensitive to their babies' cues and were more involved with caregiving practices with their babies.

In a study by Widmayer and Field (1981) of 30 healthy preterm neonates born to mothers of lower socioeconomic status, the NBAS was administered in the mother's presence in the hospital, and she was asked to fill out the Mother's Assessment of the Behavior of Her Infant Scale (MABI) at 1-week intervals during the first month. The mothers in the two control groups did not observe the NBAS. At 1 month the experimental groups performed more positively on the NBAS and on feeding and face-to-face play sequences. At 4 months, the experimental group infants performed better on the Denver Developmental Screening Test than the control group. At 1 year, the experimental group infants received significantly higher scores than the control group infants on the mental developmental index of the Bayley Scales of Infant Development.

While the sample sizes for these studies are relatively small and the ways in which the NBAS are used are often not comparable, the studies suggest that the NBAS can be effective in helping sensitize parents to the competencies of their newborns and can facilitate early parent–infant interactions. We are convinced that the demonstration of the scale is not in itself an intervention. However, if the newborn's behavior is used as a way of enlisting the mother and father's responsiveness to the baby, either by active participation or by sharing their concerns and questions with the examiner, we think that the kind of relationship with a supportive caregiver may be enhanced, and its effect will affect the parent–infant interaction as well as the parents' capacity to turn to the caregiver for help in the future (Nugent, 1985). We are documenting maternal responsivity while we demonstrate their normal and difficult infants' behavior and will analyze the maternal behaviors reflecting their involvement.

The different ways to use the scale as an intervention need to be studied more carefully than they have been so far. Simple demonstrations of newborn behavior seem to influence parents' future reactions to their babies in certain instances. Certainly, in our experiences, a demonstration of the behavior of a difficult or disordered baby allows the parent to see that it is the baby that is disorganized even in the hands of an "expert." This, then, can act to relieve the parent of natural feelings of inadequacy. But the next step is even more critical to an effective intervention. If the NBAS demonstrator can utilize the baby's behaviors to elicit the parent's feelings of inadequacy, of helplessness, of guilt, and of anger (at "why me or my baby?"), the stage can be set for future communication and intervention. If, then, repeated demonstrations of the NBAS can be shared with parents as they attempt to organize such a baby, the mechanisms in the baby that lend themselves to disorganizing his behavior can be identified. With this identification, interventions can be adjusted by the demonstrator and the parents to the individual needs of that particular baby. In this way, with a shared demonstration and understanding of the mechanisms that underlie the disorganized behaviors, the examiner can shape the intervention to the needs of each baby and to each set of parents. This, then, is the essence of a meaningful intervention.

METHODOLOGICAL ISSUES

Methodological and psychometric issues with the NBAS have been discussed in the 1979 chapter of this handbook, as well as in the revised NBAS manual (Horowitz & Linn, 1984; Lester, 1984). Our interest here is not to repeat what is available elsewhere but to underscore the main issues and consider new developments.

As mentioned earlier, complete standardization data for the NBAS are not yet available. Studies of normal term infants have been reported but not for the purpose of establishing a normative data base. These studies include attempts to examine psychometric properties of the NBAS (Kaye, 1978; Lester, 1980; Strauss, Starr, Ostrea, Chavez, & Struker, 1976). Part of the difficulty in establishing a normative data base is the selection criteria that would define a normal newborn population. For example, Tronick and colleagues (1976) conducted an intensive study in which 54 infants were tested on days 1, 2, 3, 4, 5, 7, and 10. The purpose of the study was to determine effects of regional obstetric anesthesia and to establish norms for each of those days with a minimally medicated population. The initial report showed virtually no drug effects, which led to the use of this sample as a normative data base (Als et al., 1979; Lester, 1980). More recently, a reanalysis of these data did reveal drug effects when they were combined with other pre- and perinatal variables in a multivariate analysis (Lester et al., 1982). Would a normative data base include only mothers who received no obstetrical medication? Immediately after publication of the study of Tronick and colleagues (1976), a letter appeared in *Pediatrics* suggesting that the absence of drug effects may have been due to the highly restrictive selection criteria for optimality and these babies were not representative of the normal population.

Newborn behavior is influenced by many factors, and while the development of a normative data base is necessary, sufficient attention has not been paid to the population characteristics that would describe such a data base. Horowitz, Sullivan, Byrne, and Mitchell (1984) have approached this by collecting a large sample of over 1300 normal infants, including 200 infants from a previous study of the stability of the NBAS (Lancioni et al., 1980), in which it may be possible to estimate the effects of background variables on behavior. With this information as a base, NBAS scores in other samples could be adjusted for the effects of known influences such as obstetrical medication. We plan to collect the samples from the United States and abroad that are controlled for important, identified pre- and perinatal variables to form such a base.

Data Reduction

The NBAS yields scores on 9-point behavioral scales, 28 in number, and 20 reflexes. Now there are nine additional supplementary items, each scored on a 9-point scale. Data are typically reduced to summary scores that have been conceptually and/or empirically derived. One purpose of data reduction is to reduce the number of statistical tests necessary, thereby reducing the likelihood of spurious results. Many of the items measure common behavioral constructs such as the six orientation items and are highly intercorrelated. A second advantage of data reduction is to increase the reliability of measurement by reducing the error variance introduced by individual items and increasing the variance due to more global individual differences in infant behavior.

There is also an epistemological rationale for constructing summary variables. The assumption has been made that the 9-point rating scale is the best approximation to the behavior in question, given our current knowledge and the constraints of the NBAS. It is not assumed that the phenomena we attempt to measure are intrinsically ordinal in nature. The "true" behavioral processes may have interval or ratio properties. The 9-point rating scale is a limitation of measurement, not a limitation of "reality." Summary scores combine items that approximate common behavioral processes and therefore provide a better estimate of that underlying "reality." For example, six maneuvers measure how the infant tracks visual and auditory animate and inanimate stimuli. When combined they provide a more powerful index of the behavioral process or orientation than each single estimate would provide. The assumption is that multiple estimates of an underlying process that we cannot measure directly are necessary for a reasonable approximation of that process.

The above arguments are meant to imply not that there is no justification for item-by-item analysis, but that for the reasons stated there are advantages to summary scores. It may be of interest to examine single items for population distributions or to test specific hypotheses. For example, within the orientation cluster one may have a hypothesis that involves a comparison of visual with auditory processing items. Also, as discussed below, it is sometimes necessary to examine individual items to understand the direction of certain effects.

One problem in developing summary scores is that for some items the optimal score is toward the middle of the 9-point scale. All of the items are ordinal and linear but not necessarily with respect to optimality. For general tone, the dimension that is scored is the degree of tonicity; a score of 1 is extremely hypotonic while a score of 9 is extremely hypertonic. The clinically optimal score is in the middle. For 18 of the 28 behavioral scales, the higher scores do indicate optimal performance. Curvilinear relationships have been investigated by recoding these items to match the more linear ones. When these items are not recoded, as would be the case in most factor-analytic studies, relationships that are curvilinear with respect to optimal performance cannot be measured.

Factor analysis was used in a number of early empirical attempts to group items based on their statistical interrelationships (cf. Aleksandrowicz & Aleksandrowicz, 1976; Horowitz et al., 1984; Kaye, 1978; Lester et al., 1976; Osofsky & O'Connell, 1977; Sameroff et al., 1978; Strauss & Rourke, 1978). One problem with this approach was that items that were curvilinear with respect to optimal performance could not really be compared with items that were linear with respect to optimal performance. For example, a motor factor that included positive loadings for motor maturity, which is linear, and motor tone, which is curvilinear, would suggest that high factor scores were indicative of infants with smooth, unrestricted movements who were also hypertonic. Of course, this makes no clinical sense. Hence the items had to be reevaluated in order to make them comparable. Such a maneuver can be made before summary scores are constructed.

With factor analysis, large samples are necessary for factor structures to be stable and replicable across studies. Most investigators have followed a principal components analysis with iterative procedures to "rotate" the factors that further contribute to the likelihood of solutions unique to a specific sample. Hence summary scores of small samples would make them easier to use with each other.

Yet there is some consistency of findings of factor-analytic studies across different populations. Most reports agree on two major dimensions of neonatal behavior: an orientation–alertness dimension that has consistently been the strongest, and an irritability–arousal dimension. A third, motor dimension, has been reported in several studies. The fact that these dimensions have been observed across studies that vary in sample characteristics and size probably indicates a fairly robust underlying structure to the NBAS consisting of these two or three dimensions.

A nonparametric grouping of the NBAS items was developed by Adamson, Als, Tronick, and Brazelton (1975) and published in the work of Als et al. (1979). Als et al., note that this method does not depend on linear relationships, normality of distribution, or interval scale coding; they also note that this method uses all of the information in the NBAS and is useful for individual infants. The items are grouped into four dimensions: interactive processes, motoric processes, state control, and response to stress. Qualitative information is used from each item to produce a single score (1, 2, or 3) for each dimension that reflects "optimal," "normal," or "worrisome" performance. The four dimensional scores can then be combined to provide a profile of an individual infant and summarized into a single score (Als et al., 1979). Sostek and Anders (1977) expanded this 3-point to a 5-point scale by creating intermediate categories between normal and worrisome.

We found that there were a number of problems with these four dimensions. The conceptual basis of the groupings was not clinically understandable. For example, the inclusion of cuddliness and consolability with the orientation items and alertness did not seem justified. The 3-point scoring reduced the sensitivity of measurement for most studies. Since the score of 2 was supposed to reflect average performance, the vast majority of infants received the same score. If it can be shown that infants labeled as worrisome did go on to develop abnormally, this approach could still develop into a useful screening tool for the early detection of infants at risk.

A seven-cluster scoring method was developed to improve previous data-reduction procedures and has proven to be more sensitive to the influence of minor prenatal variables such as maternal medication (Lester et al., 1982). The scoring criteria for the seven clusters are shown in Table 14.3. These criteria were revised (Lester, 1984) in the 1984 edition of the NBAS. The seven clusters were developed from a conceptual and an empirical base, by examining the results of published factor-analytic studies and conducting additional analyses of our own using factor analysis (before and after recoding items), as well as correlation and cluster analyses. The items were grouped into conceptual categories that represent constructs of neonatal behavior that had empirical support. Items are rescored so that higher scores indicate more optimal performance. Within cluster, behavior items are averaged together. The distributional properties of the clusters are not truncated, and parametric (or nonparametric) techniques can be readily applied.

The seven clusters include six behavioral clusters and one reflex cluster. *Habituation* is the process of reactivity followed by response inhibition during sleep. *Orientation* includes the ability to attend to visual and auditory stimuli and the quality of the states of alertness. The *motor* cluster measures motor performance and the quality of movement and tone. There are two state clusters. *Range of state* is a measure of arousal level, or arousability. *Regulation of state* is how the infant re-

TABLE 14.3. **Brazelton Neonatal Behavioral Assessment Scale–Seven-Cluster Scoring Criteria**

Items[a]	Clusters
	Habituation
(1) Light	Raw score of each
(2) Rattle	
(3) Bell	
(4) Pinprick	
	Orientation
(5) Inanimate visual	Raw score of each
(6) Inanimate auditory	
(7) Inanimate visual and auditory	
(8) Animate visual	
(9) Animate auditory	
(10) Visual auditory	
(11) Alertness	
	Motor
(12) Tonus	Recode: $9/1=1$; $8/2=2$; $7/3=3$; $4=4$; $5=5$; $6=6$
(13) Maturity	Raw score
(14) Pull to sit	Raw score
(16) Defense	Raw score
(21) Activity	Recode: $9/1=1$; $8/2=2$; $7/3=3$; $4/6=4$; $5=5$
	Range of State
(18) Peak of excitement	Recode: $9/1=1$; $8/2=2$; $4/3=3$; $7/5=4$; $6=5$
(19) Rapidity of buildup	Recode: $9/1=1$; $8/2=2$; $7/3=3$; $4=4$; $5=5$; $6=6$
(20) Irritability	Recode: $9/1=1$; $8=2$; $7=3$; $6=4$; $5=5$; $2,3,4=6$
(25) Lability of state	Recode: $1,7,8,9=1$; $5,6=2$; $4=3$; $3=4$; $2=5$
	Regulation of State
(15) Cuddliness	Raw score of each
(17) Consolability	
(26) Self-quieting	
(27) Hand to mouth	
	Autonomic Stability
(22) Tremors	Recode: Invert: $9=1$ ($1=9$); $8=2$; ($2=8$); etc.
(23) Startles	Recode: If 1, drop; otherwise invert 2–9 on 8-point scale
(24) Skin	Recode: $9,1=1$; $8=2$; $7=3$; $6=4$; $5=5$; $3,4=6$; $2=7$
	Reflexes
	An abnormal score is defined as 0, 1, or 3 for all reflexes except clonus, nystagmus, or TNR where 0, 1, and 2 are normal and 3 is abnormal. Reflex score = total number of abnormal reflex scores

[a]Numbers in parentheses represent Brazelton scale item number.
Source: "Regional Obstetric Anesthesia and Newborn Behavior: A Reanalysis Toward Synergistic Effects" by B. M. Lester, H. Als, and T. B. Brazelton, (1982) *Child Development, 53*, 687–692.

sponds when aroused, which may consist of endogenous mechanisms for lowering arousal or the ability to respond to environmental (examiner-induced) input. The *autonomic* cluster records signs of stress related to homeostatic adjustments of the nervous system. The *reflex* cluster is a simple count of the number of abnormal elicited reflex clusters. On this cluster a higher score indicates a greater number of abnormal reflexes, hence "worse" performance.

The seven clusters have been used in a number of studies; however, little is known about their distributional and psychometric properties. Data on the reliability and validity of the clusters have been reported in two studies (Jacobson et al., 1984; Mitchell, 1980). In our own data, the maximum correlation between clusters was in the range of .50, suggesting that the behavioral constructs that they measure are relatively distinct.

Only one published study has examined the relationship between cluster scores and long-term developmental outcome (Leijon, 1982). The orientation and motor clusters were significantly correlated with developmental scores at 18 months of age in growth-retarded and normal control infants. Data from our unit show significant relationships between the cluster scores and developmental outcome at 3 years of age in a normal sample from Ireland (Nugent, Greene, and Brazelton, 1984), at 1 year and at 5 years of age in a normal Boston sample (Sepkoski, 1986), and at 18 months in term and preterm infants (Lester, 1984).

The practice of recoding curvilinear items was criticized by Jacobson and colleagues (1984) on the grounds that information regarding the direction of the effects is lost (e.g., hyper- vs hypotonic). These authors proposed a revised set of clusters based on a factor analysis of a reasonably sized sample of 162 infants. The use of the recoding procedure is nicely illustrated by their data. For example, in the motor cluster, motor maturity is significantly correlated with the recoded general tonus items and the recoded activity item as we would expect, suggesting that optimal tone is related to smoother, more unrestricted motor movements and moderate activity. When the unrecoded general tonus and activity items are correlated with motor maturity, the correlations are virtually zero, which makes clinical sense. In short, while using unrecoded items does preserve the original information of each item, it makes the combining of items difficult at best; at worst, it results in factors that have little conceptual or clinical validity.

The information lost to the recoding procedure can be recovered by examining original scores for items that were recoded following main effects for clusters in which the items are included. In some cases, a simple plot of the distribution of the item would suffice; in other cases, the investigator may choose to conduct further statistical tests. For example, if main effects were found on the motor cluster, inspection of the unrecoded tonus and activity items would reveal the direction of the effects for these two items. This approach was used in a study of teenage pregnancy and the NBAS (Garcia-Coll et al., 1981; Lester et al., 1982). Following the main effects on the range of state cluster, it was found that infants of teenage mothers changed state more often than infants of older mothers. Horowitz has argued that in any study using the NBAS the mean and standard deviation should be reported for each individual item.

Test–Retest Reliability

The reliability of a test is often defined as the consistency between measurements in a series. The Pearson correlation between two successive measurements has been used to measure test–retest reliability of the NBAS. Most studies have reported low to moderate day-to-day stability for single items, as well as for summary scores. Sameroff and colleagues (1978) reported significant correlations on individual items from day 2 to day 3 of life in the range of .51–.78, with almost half of the items below .33 (.33 was the minimum correlation necessary for statistical significance in this sample). In a report comparing test–retest reliabilities for a sample of 44 Kansas infants and 60 Israeli infants, Horowitz, Ashton, Culp, Gaddis, Levin, and Reichmann (1977) found that repeated examinations produced significant correlations for different items in the range of .20–.50. Kaye (1978), correlating factor scores from day 2 to day 15, did not find significant test–retest correlations. In a sample of 200 Kansas infants tested with the NBAS-K on days 1, 2, and 3, and a subsample of 100 of the infants tested again at 2 weeks and 1 month, Lancioni and colleagues (1980) reported a number of significant test–retest item correlations but at magnitudes considered to be low to moderate.

There is some question as to the appropriateness of evaluating test–retest reliability of the NBAS using the Pearson r strategy, since the Pearson r reflects the relative position of the individual's score within a group on two successive occasions. If one is interested in the degree to which an individual infant performs similarly or differently on two examinations, a more direct measure may be the number of items on which performance is stable or variable across tests (Horowitz et al., 1984). In the original sample of 60 infants on which test–retest stability was computed (Horowitz & Brazelton, 1973), the criterion for reliability was based on the number of items in which the scores were in agreement on two tests, divided by the number of scores in which there was a disagreement. A score that was the same or differed by 1 point on the 9-point scale was considered an agreement. It was found that for individual infants single-item reliabilities were in the range of .23–.85 from 3 days to 1 month of age.

Subsequently, the Kansas group has found that repeated NBAS-K tests on a normative sample of 200 infants over the first 3 days results in approximately half of the infants showing 50 percent or more agreement on item scores over two tests. In a 2-week to 1-month test–retest comparison on the subsample of 100 of these infants, half of the infants showed item score agreement on 60 percent of the items. Infants with high agreement (75 percent during the first 3 days and 60 percent at 2 weeks and 1 month) were designated stable, the remainder variable.

The question of test–retest reliability must therefore be cast in terms of those kinds of questions being posed when the NBAS is used. It is clear that the psychometric measure, the Pearson r, will yield low moderate day-to-day correlations. However, even this information might be useful better to understand the relative stability of different processes of behavioral development. In a multiple regression analysis, six tests collected during the first week of life were used to predict score on day 10 in 54 healthy term infants (Lester, 1980). Correlations were in the range of .25–.91 across the 26 behavior items. The mean test–retest correlation for the items that define the six behavioral clusters reveals a more interesting pattern. The lowest correlations were found for the two clusters that represent behavioral processes that are newly emerging and are expected to be more variable and subject to environmental influence, range of state (.29) and orientation (.42). The highest correlations were found in the habituation (.75) and autonomic (.52) clusters, behavioral processes that should be more stable. The motor and regulation of state clusters showed midrange correlations of .49 and .48, respectively. The point here is that, regardless of how one addresses the issue of stability, it may be necessary to consider the items or clusters in the light of clinically understandable hypotheses regarding the behavioral process that is being measured.

The individually derived measure of day-to-day stability suggested by Horowitz also reveals a different understanding of variability in newborn behavior. Linn and Horowitz (1983) studied mother–infant interaction in infants independently classified as stable or variable on the NBAS as previously described. More responsive mothers related to variable infants, less responsive mothers to the stable infants. It was suggested that variability in infant behavior may be more useful for eliciting maternal responsivity than stability. It may be more appropriate to think of the test–retest properties of the NBAS as a characteristic of the infant than as a criterion measure of the reliability of the test. As Horowitz and Linn (1984) point out, this could pose a challenge to standard psychometric criteria for acceptance of an assessment tool. It is true that from a psychometric point of view we are not used to predicting change in test–retest performance; change or instability is usually thought of as error variance. However, this assumption is only valid if we expect the phenomena under study to be stable.

Another assumption is that the behavioral processing we are studying can be described by linear functions. Polynomial regression analysis has shown that, while there are linear trends in the NBAS over the first 10 days of life for some items, many items show significant quadradic and cubic trends (Lester & Brazelton, 1985). The original concept behind the NBAS was that it measured dynamic aspects of behavior that required repeated examinations (Brazelton, 1973, 1976). It was hypothesized that by describing the individual infant's pattern over repeated examinations one could measure the infant's recovery from the birth process and ability to adapt to the extrauterine environment. How the infant changes, the infant's pattern of change, becomes a measure of the infant's behavioral organization. Figures 14.1 and 14.2 contrast two preterm infants in their patterns of performance on the

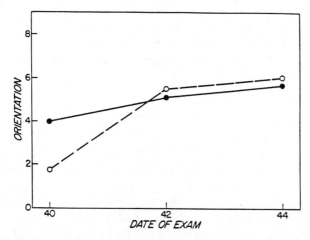

Figure 14.1. Infant A's Bayley MDI score at 18 months was 100. Infant A's predicted score from the curve parameters was 96. Solid line = mean of preterm group; broken line = preterm infant. (*Note:* From "A Longitudinal Study of Term and Preterm Infants: Evidence for the Predictive Validity of the Neonatal Behavioral Assessment Scale" by B. M. Lester, J. Hoffman, and T. B. Brazelton, 1986. Unpublished manuscript.)

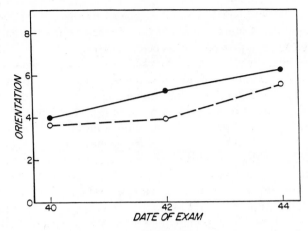

Figure 14.2. Infant B's Bayley MDI score at 18 months was 90. Infant B's predicted score from the curve parameters was 90.2. (*Note:* From "A Longitudinal Study of Term and Preterm Infants: Evidence for the Predictive Validity of the Neonatal Behavioral Assessment Scale" by B. M. Lester, J. Hoffman, and T. B. Brazelton. Manuscript submitted for publication.)

orientation cluster from three exams, at 40, 42, and 44 weeks of gestation. The figures also show how the two infants depart from the mean of the sample from which they were drawn. Mathematically, these curves can be quantified along time-ordered dimensions such as velocity or acceleration and along rank-ordered dimensions such as range and skewness. Rank-ordered variables are important because they preserve nonlinear information in these curves. Preliminary analysis has shown that the dimensions significantly predict 18-month Bayley Mental scale scores in term and preterm infants (Lester, Hoffman, & Brazelton, submitted).

Both linear and nonlinear variables were found to be significant predictors of developmental outcome. It is likely that these curves, computed over the first postnatal month, measure not only the capacity of the infant to cope with the extrauterine environment but also the response of the caretaking environment to the infant. If future research confirms that these curves can be used to predict later developmental outcome at levels that reach clinical as well as statistical significance, it will probably be because they provide an early index to functional organism–environment interaction.

FUTURE DIRECTIONS

Since it was first published 12 years ago, the NBAS has become the most widely used neonatal behavioral assessment instrument. Its use as a research instrument has been validated by many studies. It is a dynamic assessment, and it has taken time to evaluate its psychometric properties. The scale has been shown to have face validity and concurrent validity. Predictive validity seems to depend on the changes seen in repeated tests, and the data so far suggest that when repeated tests are used predictive validity is achieved (Lester, 1984; Lester, Hoffman, & Brazelton, 1986; Nugent, Greene, & Brazelton, 1984; Sepkoski, Hoffman & Brazelton, 1986). Not enough data on its usefulness as a predictor to future outcome have been collected, but it offers us a chance to look at change in the neonatal period as a normative aspect of early infancy. Test–retest stability is not an appropriate measure, as the baby is changing from day to day. This is the only psychometric technique that is inapproprite. The questions are: (1) what aspects of the neonate's behavior might reflect optimality in the baby's increasing organization; and (2) which behaviors reflect early environmental influences. Thus the changes in behavior become the most likely sources for prediction of the baby's future. We have felt limited by the kind of assessments available in later infancy and childhood, since the concept behind the NBAS is that of interacting developmental systems rather than static ones.

The assessment is a global one rather than a test of any one or two systems in the newborn. Since it is so widely used, the next future effort will be to collect and collate the data from the many studies in an attempt to establish a normative data base against which can be tested the many variables that influence neonatal behavior. A multivariate analysis of prenatal factors is one obvious technique.

Establishing the value of it as a clinical assessment for all newborns and in particular for infants at risk between 36 and 44 weeks is another goal for the future. For wide use it may need to be shortened, but we need to do that with full knowledge of the value of each variable. Further, to find a more systems-oriented approach to evaluate the constantly changing but interactive aspects of the systems within the baby as they represent genetic endowment and intrauterine experience and to establish their interactions with perinatal variables and experiential influences become the real challenges. Further, to understand its use as a communicative system between parents and a concerned professional in order to provide intervention and/or an understanding of the baby to enhance the parent–infant interaction may be the most important future goal for the NBAS. How does one utilize it best as a communication system?

REFERENCES

Adamson, L., Als, H., Tronick, E., & Brazelton, T. B. (1977). The development of social reciprocity between a sighted infant and her blind parents. *Journal of the American Academy of Child Psychiatry, 16,* 194–207.

Aleksandrowicz, M. K., & Aleksandrowicz, D. R. (1976). Precursors of ego in neonates: Factor analysis of Brazelton scale data. *Journal of the American Academy of Child Psychiatry, 15,* 257–268.

Als, H., & Lewis, M. (1975). *The contribution of the infant to the interaction with his mother.* Paper presented at Society for Research in Child Development meetings, Denver.

Als, H., Lester, B. M., Tronick, E., & Brazelton, T. B. (1982). Manual for the assessment of preterm infants' behavior (APIB). In H. E. Fitzgerald, B. M. Lester, & M. W. Yogman (Eds.), *Theory and research in behavioral pediatrics,* (Vol. I). New York: Plenum.

Als, H., Tronick, E., Adamson, L., & Brazelton, T. B. (1976). The behavior of the full-term yet underweight newborn. *Developmental Medicine & Child Neurology, 18,* 590.

Als, H., Tronick, E., Lester, B. M., & Brazelton, T. B. (1979). The Brazelton Neonatal Scale (BNBAS). In J. Osofsky (Ed.), *Handbook of infant development.* New York: Wiley.

Anderson, C. J. (1981). Enhancing reciprocity between mother and neonate. *Nursing Research, 30,* 89–93.

Anderson, C., Sawin, D. B. (1983). Enhancing responsiveness in mother–infant interaction. *Infant Behavior and Development, 6*(3): 361–368.

Bakeman, R., & Brown, J. V. (1980). Early intervention: Consequences for social and mental development at three years. *Child Development, 51,* 437–447.

Bates, J. E., Freeland, A. B., & Lounsbury, M. L. (1979). Measurement of infant difficulties. *Child Development, 50,* 744–803.

Beal, J. (1983). *The effect of demonstration of the BNBAS on the father–infant relationship.* Doctoral Dissertation, Boston University School of Nursing.

Brackbill, Y. (1979). Obstetric medication and infant behavior (1979). In J. Osofsky (Ed.), *Handbook of infant development.* New York: Wiley.

Brazelton, T. B. (1973). Neonatal Behavioral Assessment Scale. *Clinics in Developmental Medicine* (No. 50). London: Heinemann; Philadelphia: Lippincott.

Brazelton, T. B., Robey J. S., Collier, G. A. (1969). Infant Development in the Zimancanteco Indians of Southern Mexico. *Pediatrics, 44,* 274–281.

Brazelton, T. B. (1979). Behavioral competence of the newborn infant. *Seminars in Perionatology, 3,* 35–44.

Brazelton, T. B. (1984). *Neonatal Behavioral Assessment Scale* (2nd ed.). Spastics International Medical Publications. London: Blackwell; Philadelphia; Lippincott.

Brazelton, T. B., Koslowski, B., & Tronick, E. (1977). Neonatal behavior among urban Zambians and Americans. *Annual Progress in Child Psychiatry, 15,* 97–107.

Brazelton, T. B., Parker, W. B., & Zuckerman, B. (1976). Importance of behavioral assessment of the neonate. *Current Problems in Pediatrics Monographs* (Vol. 7). Chicago: Yearbook Medical Publications.

Brazelton, T. B., Tronick, N., Lechtig, A., Lasky, R. E., & Klein, R. E. (1977). The behavior of nutritionally deprived Guatemalan infants. *Developmental Medicine & Child Neurology, 19,* 364–372.

Brazelton, T. B., Tryphonopoulou, Y., & Lester, B. M. (1979). A comparative study of the behavior of Greek neonates. *Pediatrics, 63,* 279–285.

Brett, E. (1965). The estimation of fetal maturity by the neurological examination of the neonate. In M. Dawkins & W. G. Macgregor (Eds.), *Gestational age, size, and maturity. Clinics in Developmental Medicine* (No. 19). London: Spastics Society with Heinemann.

Chasnoff, I. J., Hatcher, R., & Burns, W. J. (1982). Polydrug- and methadone-addicted newborns: A continuum of impairment? *Pediatrics, 70,* 210–213.

Chisholm, J. (in press). Biology, culture and the development of temperament: A Navajo example. In J. K. Nugent, B. M. Lester, & T. B. Brazelton (Eds.), *The cultural context of infancy* (Vol. II). New York: Ablex.

Crockenberg, S. B. (1981). Infant irritability, mother responsiveness, and social support influences on the security of infant–mother attachment. *Child Development, 52,* 857–865.

Dixon, S., Keefer, C., Tronick, E., & Brazelton, T. B. (1982). Perinatal circumstances and newborn outcome among the Gusii of Kenya: Assessment of risk. *Infant Behavior & Development, 5,* 11–32.

Dubowitz, L. M. S., Dubowitz, V., & Goldberg, C. (1970). Clinical assessment of gestational age in the newborn infant. *Journal of Pediatrics, 77,* 1–10.

Ferrari, F., Grosoli, M. V., Fontane, G., & Cavazutti, G. B. (1983). Neuro behavioral comparison of low risk preterm and fullterm infants at term conceptual age. *Developmental Medicine & Child Neurology, 25,* 450–458.

Field, T. M., & Widmayer, S. (1980). Developmental follow-up of infants delivered by Cesearean-section and general anesthesia. *Infant Behavior & Development, 43* (5–6), 135–1358.

Field, T. M., Widmayer, S., Stringer, S., & Ignatoff, E. (1980). Teenage, lower-class black mothers and their preterm infants: An intervention and developmental follow-up. *Child Development, 51,* 426–436.

Freedman, D. G. (1971). Genetic differences in behavior. In G. B. A. Stoelinga & Ten Bosch Vanderwolff (Eds.), *Normal and abnormal development of behavior.* Netherlands: Leiden University Press.

Freedman, D. G., & Freedman, N. (1969). Behavioral differences between Chinese-American and European-American newborns. *Nature, 224,* 1127.

Fricker, H. S., Hindermann, R., & Bruppacher, R. (in press). An epidemiological investigation on the course of pregnancy in 996 Swiss women, and its influence on newborn behavior using the Brazelton scale. In J. K. Nugent, B. M. Lester, T. B. Brazelton (Eds.), *The cultural context of infancy.* Norwood, NJ: Ablex.

Garcia-Coll, C. T., Sepkoski, C., & Lester, B. M. (1981). Cultural and biomedical correlates of neonatal behavior. *Developmental Psychobiology, 14,* 147–154.

Horowitz, F. D., & Brazelton, T. B. (1973). Research with the Brazelton neonatal scale. In T. B. Brazelton, Neonatal Behavioral Assessment Scale. *Clinics in Developmental Medicine* (No. 50). Spastics International Medical Publications. London: Heinemann; Philadelphia: Lippincott.

Horowitz, F. D., & Linn, P. L. (1982). The Neonatal Behavioral Assessment Scale. In M. Wolraich & D. K. Routh (Eds.), *Advances in developmental pediatrics* (Vol. 3). Greenwich, CT.

Horowitz, F. D., & Linn, P. L. (1984). Use of the NBAS in research. In T. B. Brazelton (Ed.), *Neonatal Behavioral Assessment Scale* (2nd ed.). Spastics International Medical Publications. London: Blackwell; Philadelphia: Lippincott.

Horowitz, F. D., Ashton, J., Culp, R. E., Gaddis, E., Levin, S., & Reichmann, B. (1977). The effect of obstetric medication on the behavior of Israeli newborns and some comparisons with American and Uruguayan infants. *Child Development, 48,* 1607–1623.

Horowitz, F. D., Sullivan, J. E., Byrne, J. M., & Mitchell, W. (in preparation). An atlas of the newborn infant.

Jacobson, J. L., Fein, G. G., Jacobson, S., & Schwartz, P. M. (1985). Factors and clusters for the Brazelton scale: An investigation of the dimensions of neonatal behavior. *Developmental Psychology, 20,* 339–353.

Kaplan, S. L., Kron, R. E., Litt, M., Finnegan, L. P., & Phoenix, M. D. (1975). Correlations between scores on the Brazelton Neonatal Assessment Scale, measures of newborn sucking behavior, and birthweight in infants born to narcotic addicted mothers. In N. R. Ellis (Ed.), *Aberrant development in infancy: Human and animal studies* (Vol. 8). Hillsdale, NJ: Erlbaum.

Kaye, K. (1978). Discriminating among normal infants by multivariate analysis of Brazelton scores: Lumping and smoothing. *Monographs of the Society for Research in Child Development, 43* (5–6).

Keefer, C. H., Tronick, E., Dixon, S., & Brazelton, T. B. (1982). Specific differences in motor performance between Gusii and American newborns and a modification of the neonatal behavioral assessment scale. *Child Development, 53,* 754–759.

Kron, R. E., Finnegan, L. P., Kaplan, B. L., Litt, M., & Phoenix, M. D. (1975). The assessment of behavioral change in infants undergoing narcotic withdrawal: Comparative data from clinical and objective methods. *Addictive Diseases, 2,* 257–275.

Kuhnert, B. R., Harrison, M. J., Linn, P. L., & Kuhnert, P. M. (1984). Effects of maternal epidural anesthesia on neonatal behavior. *Anesthesia & Analgesia, 63,* 301–308.

Lancioni, G., Horowitz, F. D., & Sullivan, J. (1980). The NBAS-K. I: A study of its stability and structure over the first month of life. II: Reinforcement value of the infant's behavior. *Infant Behavior & Development, 3,* 341–359, 361–366.

Landers, C. (in press). A psychological study of infant development in South India. In J. K. Nugent, B. M. Lester, & T. B. Brazelton (Eds.), *The cultural context of infancy.* Norwood, NJ: Ablex.

Leijon, I., Finnstrom, O., Nilsoon, B., & Ryden, G. (1980). Neurology and behavior of growth-retarded neonates. Relation to biochemical placental function tests in late pregnancy. *Early Human Development, 4,* 257–270.

Lester, B. M. (1979). A synergistic process approach to the study of prenatal malnutrition. *International Journal of Behavioral Development, 2,* 377–393.

Lester, B. M. (1980). Behavioral assessment of the neonate. In E. Sell (Ed.), *Follow-up of the high risk newborn—A practical approach.* Springfield, IL: C. C. Thomas.

Lester, B. M. (1984). Data analysis and prediction. In T. B. Brazelton (Ed.), *Neonatal Behavioral Assessment Scale* (2nd ed.). Spastics International Medical Publications. London: Blackwell; Philadelphia: Lippincott.

Lester, B. M., & Zeskind, P. S. (1979). Brazelton scale and physical size correlates of neonatal cry features. *Infant Behavior & Development, 4,* 393–402.

Lester, B. M., Als, H., & Brazelton, T. B. (1982). Regional obstetric anesthesia and newborn behavior: A reanalysis towards synergistic effects. *Child Development, 53,* 687–692.

Lester, B. M., Garcia-Coll, C. T., & Sepkoski, C. (1982). Teenage pregnancy and neonatal behavior: Effects in Puerto Rico and Florida. *Journal of Youth & Adolescence, 5,* 385–402.

Lester, B. M., Garcia-Coll, C., Valcarcel, M., Hoffman, J., & Brazelton, T. B. (1986). Effects of atypical patterns of fetal growth on newborn (NBS) behavior. *Child Development.*

Lester, B. M., Hoffman, J., & Brazelton, T. B. (1986). A longitudinal study of term and preterm infants: Evidence for the predictive validity of the Neonatal Behavioral Assessment Scale. Unpublished manuscript.

Lester, B. M., Emory, E. K., Hoffman, S. L., & Eitzman, D. V. (1976). A multivariate study of the effects of high-risk factors on performance on the Brazelton Neonatal Assessment Scale. *Child Development, 47,* 515–517.

Lester, B. M., Garcia-Coll, C., & Sepkoski, C. (1983). A cross-cultural study of teenage pregnancy and neonatal behavior. In T. M. Field & A. Sostek (Eds.), *Infants born at risk: Psychological, perceptual, and cognitive processes.* New York: Grune & Stratton.

Linn, P. L., & Horowitz, F. D. (1984). The relationship between infant individual differences and mother–infant interaction during the neonatal period. *Infant Behavior & Development, 6,* 415–427.

Liptak, G. S., Keller, B. B., Feldman, A. W., & Chamberlain, R. W. (1983). Enhancing infant development and parent practitioner interaction with the Brazelton Neonatal Behavioral Assessment Scale. *Pediatrics, 72,* 71–78.

Lubchenco, L. O. (1970). Assessment of gestational age and development at birth. *Pediatric Clinics of North America, 17,* 125–145.

Mitchell, S. (1981). Paper presented at biennial meetings of the Society for Research in Child Development, Boston.

Muret-Wagstaff, S., & Moore, S. G. (in press). The Hmong in America: Infant behavior and rearing practices. In J. K. Nugent, B. M. Lester, & T. B. Brazelton (Eds.), *The cultural context of infancy* (Vol. I). Norwood, NJ: Ablex.

Myers, B. J. (1982). Early intervention using Brazelton training with middle-class mothers and fathers of newborns. *Child Development, 53,* 462–471.

Nelson, C. A., & Horowitz, F. D. (1982). The short-term behavioral sequelae of neonatal jaundice treated with phototherapy. *Infant Behavior & Development, 5,* 289–299.

Nugent, J. K., Greene, S., & Brazelton, T. B. (1984). Predicting 3 year IQ scores from patterns of change in newborn behavior. Presented at the Third International Conference in Infant Studies, New York.

Nugent, J. K., & Sepkoski, C. (1984). The training of NBAS examiners. In T. B. Brazelton

(Ed.), *Neonatal Behavioral Assessment Scale* (2nd ed.). Spastics International Medical Publications. London: Blackwell; Philadelphia: Lippincott.

Osofsky, J. (1976). Neonatal characteristics and mother–infant interaction in two observational situations. *Child Development, 47,* 1138–1147.

Osofsky, J., & Danzger, B. (1974). Relationships between neonatal characteristics and mother–infant interaction. *Developmental Psychology, 10,* 124–130.

Osofsky, J. D., & O'Connell, E. J. (1977). Patterning of newborn behavior in an urban population. *Child Development, 48,* 532–536.

Paludetto, R., Mansi, G., Rinaldi, P., DeLuca, T., Corchia, C., De Curtis, M., & Andolfi, M. (1982). Behaviour of preterm newborns reaching term without any serious disorder. *Early Human Development, 6,* 357–363.

Pedro, J. C. Gomes (in press). The effects of extended contact in the neonatal period on the behavior of a sample of Portuguese mothers and infants. In J. K. Nugent, B. M. Lester, & T. B. Brazelton (Eds.), *The cultural context of infancy* (Vol. I). Norwood, NJ: Ablex.

Pedro, J. Gomes, de Almeida, J. B., & Costa Barbosa, A. (1984). Influence of Early Mother–Infant Contact on Synoptic Behavior during the first month of life. *Developmental Medicine and Child Neurology, 26,* 657–664.

Picone, T. A., Allen, L. H., Olsen, P. N., & Ferris, M. E. (1982). Pregnancy outcome in North American women: II. Effects of diet, cigarette smoking, stress, and weight gain on placentas, and on neonatal physical and behavioral characteristics. *American Journal of Clinical Nutrition, 36,* 1214–1224.

Prechtl, H. F. R., & Beintema, J. (1968). The neurological examination of the full-term newborn infant. *Clinics in Developmental Medicine* (No. 28). London: Spastics International Medical Publications with Heinemann Medical.

Prechtl, H. F. R., & O'Brien, M. J. (1982). Behavioral states of the full-term newborn: the emergence of a concept. In P. Stratton (Ed.). *Psychology of the Human Newborn.* New York: John Wiley & Sons, 1982.

Price, G. M. (1983). Sensitivity in mother–infant interaction: The AMIS scale. *Infant Behavior & Development, 6,* 353–360.

Robinson, R. J. (1966). Assessment of gestational age by neurological examination. *Archives of Disease in Childhood, 41,* 437–447.

Saco-Pollitt, C. (1981). Birth in the Peruvian Andes: Physical and behavioral consequences in the neonate. *Child Development, 52,* 839–846.

St. James-Roberts, I. (1979). Neurological plasticity. In H. Reese & L. Lipsitt (Eds.), *Advances in child development.* New York: Academic.

Sameroff, A. J. (Ed.) (1978). Organization and stability of newborn behavior: A commentary on the Brazelton Neonatal Behavioral Assessment Scale. *Monographs of the Society for Research in Child Development, 43,* (5–6, Serial No. 177).

Sameroff, A. J., & Chandler, M. (1975). Reproductive risk and the continuum of caretaking casualty. In F. D. Horowitz (Ed.), *Review of child development research* (Vol. 4). Chicago: University of Chicago Press.

Sameroff, A. J., Krafchuk, E. E., & Bakow, H. A. (1978). Issues in grouping items from the neonatal behavioral assessment scale. *Monographs of the Society for Research in Child Development, 43* (5–6).

Scanlon, K. B., Scanlon, J. W., & Tronick, E. (1984). The impact of perinatal and neonatal events on the early behavior of the extremely premature human. *Developmental & Behavioral Pediatrics, 5,* 65–73.

Scarr-Salapatek, S., & Williams, M. L. (1973). The effects of early stimulation on low-birth-weight infants. *Child Development, 44,* 94–101.

Sell, E. J., Luick, A., Poisson, S. S., & Hill, S. (1980). Outcome of very low birthweight (VLBW) infants: I. Neonatal behavior of 188 infants. *Journal of Developmental & Behavioral Pediatrics, I,* 78–85.

Sepkoski, C. (1984, April). Neonatal and one-year followup of maternal medication effects. In B. M. Lester (Chair), *Meaning and measurement of change in neonatal behavior.* Symposium conducted at the meeting of the International Congress of Infant Studies, New York.

Sepkoski, C. (1984). *The cumulative effects of bupivacaine epidural anesthesia and obstetric variables on neonatal behavior.* Doctoral dissertation, University of Florida.

Sepkoski, C. (1985). Maternal obstetric medication and newborn behavior. In J. W. Scanlon (Ed.), *Perinatal anesthesia.* London: Blackwell.

Sepkoski, C., Garcia-Coll, C., & Lester, B. M. (1982). The cumulative effects of obstetric risk variables on newborn behavior. In L. P. Lipsitt & T. M. Field (Eds.), *Infant behavior and development: Perinatal risk and newborn behavior.* Norwood, NJ: Ablex.

Sepkoski, C., Hoffman, J., and Brazelton, T. B. (1986). The relationship between NBAS profiles, 1-year Bayley and 5-year McCarthy scores. Presented at the International Congress of Infant Studies, Los Angeles.

Sostek, A. M., & Ander, T. (1977). Relationships among the Brazelton Neonatal Scale, Bayley Infant Scales, and early temperament. *Child Development, 48,* 320–323.

Soule, A. B., Standley, K., Copans, S. A., & Davis, M. (1974). Clinical uses of the Brazelton neonatal scale. *Pediatrics, 54,* 583–586.

Standley, K. Soule, A. B., Copans, S. A. & Duchowny, M. S. (1974). Local-regional anesthesia during childbirth: Effect on newborn behaviors. *Science, 186,* 634–635.

Strauss, M. E., Rourke, D. L. (1978). A multivariate analysis of the Neonatal Behavioral Assessment Scale in several samples. In A. J. Sameroff (Ed.), Organization and stability of newborn behavior: A commentary on the Brazelton Neonatal Behavioral Assessment Scale. *Monographs of the Society for Research in Child Development* (No. 177), *43* (5–6).

Strauss, M. E., Lessen-Firestone, J. K., Starr, R. H., & Ostrea, E. M. (1976). Behavior of narcotics-addicted newborns. *Child Development, 46,* 887–893.

Strauss, M. E., Starr, R. H., Ostrea, E. M., Chavez, C. S., & Struker, J. C. (1976). Behavioral concomitants of prenatal addiction to narcotics. *Journal of Pediatrics, 89,* 842.

Streissguth, A. P., Barr, H. M., & Martin, D. C. (1983). Maternal alcohol use and neonatal habituation assessed with the Brazelton scale. *Child Development, 54,* 1109–1118.

Telzrow, R. W., Snyder, D. M., Tronick, E., Als, H., & Brazelton, T. B. (1980). The behavior of jaundiced infants undergoing phototherapy. *Developmental Medicine & Child Neurology, 22* 317–326.

Thompson, R. J., Cappelman, M. W., & Zeitschel, K. A. (1979). Neonatal behavior of infants of adolescent mothers. *Developmental Medicine & Child Neurology, 21,* 474–482.

Tronick, E., Wise, S., Als, H., Adamson, L., Scanlon, J., & Brazelton, T. B. (1976). Regional obstetric anesthesia and newborn behavior: Effect over the first ten days of life. *Pediatrics, 58,* 94–100.

Vaughn, B. E., Taraldson, B., Crichton, L., & Egeland, B. (1980). Relationships between neonatal behavioral organization and infant behavior during the first year of life. *Infant Behavior & Development, 3,* 47–66.

Walsh Escarce, M. E. (in press). A cross-cultural study of Nepalese neonatal behavior. In J. K. Nugent, B. M. Lester, & T. B. Brazelton (Eds.), *The cultural context of infancy* (Vol. I). Norwood, NJ: Ablex.

Waters, E., Vaughn, B. E., & Egelund, B. (1980). Individual differences in infant–mother attachment relationships at age one: Antecedents in neonatal behavior in an urban, economically disadvantaged sample. *Child Development, 51,* 208–216.

Winn, S., Morelli, G. A., & Tronick, E. The infant and the group: A look at Efe caretaking practices in Zaire. In J. K. Nugent, B. M. Lester, & T. B. Brazelton (Eds.), *The cultural context of infancy* (Vol. I). Norwood, NJ: Ablex.

Widmayer, S. M., & Field, T. M. (1980). Effects of Brazelton demonstrations on early interactions of preterm infants and their teenage mothers. *Infant Behavior & Development, 3,* 79–89.

Worobey, J., & Belsky, J. (1982). Employing the Brazelton scale to influence mothering: An experimental comparison of three strategies. *Developmental Psychology, 18,* 736–743.

Yogman, M. W., Cole, P., Als, H., & Lester, B. M. (1982). Behavior of newborns of diabetic mothers. *Infant Behavior & Development, 5,* 331–340.

Zeskind, P. S. (1981). Behavioral dimensions and cry sounds of infants of differential fetal growth. *Infant Behavior & Development, 4,* 297–306.

CHAPTER 15

Applying Observational Methods: A Systematic View

ROGER BAKEMAN and JOHN M. GOTTMAN

INTRODUCTION

Goals of this Chapter

Because studies using systematic observational techniques are especially popular among infancy researchers, it seems worthwhile to define what distinguishes *observational* from other methods and to delineate particular issues users of observational methods must resolve. Our hope is that researchers practiced in observational methods will recognize the kind of work they do here and perhaps even pick up a new idea or two. Still, this chapter is written primarily for observational neophytes. Our hope is that they will find here the various elements of observational methodology clearly and simply described and will gain a clearer understanding of what work needs to be done and what choices need to be made before observational methods are applied.

Observational Methods Defined

Although a variety of different methods could all be called *observational,* for present purposes we will restrict the term to just one particular approach. We think this reflects current usage fairly accurately. At the same time, it serves to delimit clearly just what this chapter is about. Moreover, the approach we define and describe is a relatively coherent and commonly used one.

As we use the term, *observational methodology* signifies a particular systematic approach to the business of quantifying behavior. The aim is to define beforehand various forms of behavior—forms that are embodied in predefined behavioral codes—and then ask observers to record whenever behavior corresponding to any of the predefined codes occurs. Observer accuracy is a major concern, and typically considerable effort is spent training observers so that they will produce essentially similar records, given that they observed the same stream of behavior. In sum, the

Support from NIHM (MH26131) and NIH (HD11209) to Josephine V. Brown and Roger Bakeman and from NSF (BNS-8012068 and BNS-8300716) to Roger Bakeman and Lauren B. Adamson is gratefully acknowledged; the research it made possible provided many of the examples used here.

two major defining characteristics of observational methods are (1) the use of pre-defined catalogs of behavioral codes, (2) by observers of demonstrated reliability. Thus we would distinguish observational methods from the writing of narrative reports, on the one hand, and from the use of rating scales, on the other.

Observational May Be Experimental

Often, users of observational methods observe behavior in relatively natural, un-manipulated contexts, but this is only an observed correlation, not a logically nec-essary connection. Observational methods provide a way of quantifying behavior, nothing more. The behavior might be observed in experimentally manipulated con-texts (with random assignment of subjects to contexts or with contexts repeated within subjects) or in naturally occurring contexts. The point is that there is nothing inherently nonexperimental (or experimental) about observational methods. If they provide a reasonable way to quantify the behavior under study, they could be used by experimental and nonexperimental studies alike.

Two Examples

Consider, for example, Bornstein, Kessen, and Weiskopf's (1976) elegant demon-stration that infants perceive color categorically. Using a habituation paradigm, in-fants were exposed to light of various wavelengths. The dependent (or criterion, or response) variable was infants' looking time as judged by human observers of known reliability. The "coding scheme" in this case was extremely simple. It consisted of just two codes: (1) infant looking; and (2) infant not looking. Mere simplicity, how-ever, does not change the fact that observational methodology, exactly as we define it, was used here. Still, because the independent (or predictor, or explanatory) var-iable side of this study was considerably more elaborated than the dependent var-iable side, we think most readers would not label this as an observational study, but simply as an example of observational methods embedded within an experimental study.

An example of a study that emphasizes the observational component but is like-wise experimental is provided by Green, Gustafson, and West (1980). One of their questions concerned the effect of infants' locomotion on mother–infant interaction. In order to study this experimentally, they observed infants (who were not yet walk-ing routinely) in walkers and out of walkers. Thus the independent (within-subjects) variable was simply whether infants could locomote freely (aided by walkers) or not (no walkers), while several different dependent measures were derived from Green and colleagues' coding schemes. All "social interactions" were coded for who in-itiated the interaction (and how) and also for their thematic content. Thus Green and Bornstein and their colleagues are alike in that both defined beforehand the behavioral codes of interest and both assessed the reliability of their human ob-servers. But Green and colleagues lavished considerably more time and attention on the process of defining and developing coding schemes that were then used to extract information about several aspects of the behavior they observed. Because of this emphasis, we tend to think of theirs as a paradigmatic observational study.

THE ALTERNATIVES: FROM NARRATIVE REPORTS TO RATING SCALES

We make no claim here for the superiority of observational over other methods. Different methods are "superior," after all, only in relation to how well they further particular research goals. Thus it is instructive to compare observational methods with two of their close cousins, noting the special strengths of each. Such comparisons should help us decide just when observational methods would be an appropriate choice.

Narrative Reports

The writing of narrative reports has a long and venerable history. This subjective approach to understanding has been used far longer than the upstart methods we characterize as scientific. Still, this enterprise lacks what many would consider an essential component of scientific inquiry: replicability of procedures. Narrative reports depend mightily on the individual doing them, and judgments others make about the worth of those reports are inextricably bound up with judgments about the personal qualities of their author. We not only would be surprised but also suspicious if two reports from different authors were identical. When using observational methods, on the other hand, identical reports are the goal; assuming some talent and proper training, the personal qualities of the observers should not matter. It is primarily this drive for replicability that we think earns observational methods the appellation *scientific* and distinguishes them from the writing of narrative reports.

However, the predefined behavioral codes of observational methods act as a filter. While some events are let in, others are necessarily excluded "unseen." Observers are not allowed the full exercise of their sensibility; trivia may be recorded, albeit accurately, while really critical phenomena might go unrecorded. Certainly there is much to learn from the sensitive reports of observers like Selma Freiberg (1974) and T. Berry Brazelton (1974). And certainly narrative reports (whether written by people who call themselves pediatricians, clinical psychologists, participant-observer anthropologists, journalists, ethnomethodologists, or whatever) can contribute greatly to our understanding of infants. Not all authors deserve our attention, of course, but those that do can push our understanding in ways that would prove impossible from the mere numbers produced by observational methods. For example, it seems unlikely that any amount of systematic observation would produce the same kind of understanding of how the world seems to a retarded person as that provided by the first chapter of William Faulkner's *The Sound and the Fury*.

In sum, the relative strengths of narrative reports and observational methods are those usually accorded to humanistic and scientific methods of inquiry, respectively. Nonetheless, preparing narrative reports, or something akin to them, has an important role to play in observational studies. Typically, investigators prepare such reports when developing a new coding scheme. Thus their own (and others') narrative reports often serve users of observational methodology during the pilot phase of a new investigation.

Rating Scales

Users of rating scales and users of observational methods have more in common with each other than either has with authors of narrative reports. Both want to quantify behavior and both want to ensure that different observers or raters would produce replicable results. The use of rating scales, however, has a number of advantages and in many cases might be preferable to the use of observational methods. For example, imagine an intervention study in which an investigator wants to change maternal responsivity to infant cues. What needs to be assessed is clearly stated and is a relatively coherent concept, one that could be defined for raters quite precisely. In such a case, the far less stringent time demands of a rating scale approach would make it the methodology of choice. On the other hand, if an investigator wants to describe exactly how mothers are responsive to their infants on a moment-to-moment basis and how the forms of this responsivity change with infant development, then the more detailed approach of observational methods would be required.

Thus we agree with Cairns and Green (1979; see also Bakeman & Brown, 1978) that ratings are especially useful when investigators want to describe individual differences in behavioral style, but that observational methods are clearly better suited when one wants to understand process or the mechanisms of social patterns. There is no question that observational methods are time-consuming; thus when rating scales can adequately capture the construct of interest, their use is recommended. For example, rating scales are commonly used to characterize the quality of attachment (Ainsworth, Blehar, Waters, & Wall, 1978). Given the task (to assess an individual difference characteristic), this seems exactly the appropriate methodology.

An example of a study that used both rating scales and observational methods to assess early infant–mother interaction is provided by Bakeman and Brown (1980). Interestingly, scores derived from behavioral observations were useful for describing interactive process and how that process differed for preterm and full-term infants. However, only rating scale measures proved predictive (significantly, but weakly) of subsequent cognitive development.

MEASURING BEHAVIOR: THE CODING SCHEME AS INSTRUMENT

The first step in any research, of course, is defining a clear question. When observational methods are used, the next step is developing a coding scheme. Because so much in observational research depends on the coding scheme, this is a step that deserves a good deal of time and attention. After all, the coding scheme is the basic measuring instrument of observational research. But what should be measured? This is where the research question comes in, because without the focus it provides, the essentially infinite variety of potential events muddling along in the passing stream of behavior almost always proves overwhelming.

When one wants to measure temperature, one pulls a thermometer off the shelf and does not worry much about a theory of heat. Measuring behavior is a different matter, and theoretic concerns are difficult to avoid. In fact, we think that designing a coding scheme should be viewed as a theoretic act. By including some events in the coding scheme and not others, the investigator is saying, in effect: These are what I think are important; these are what I want extracted from the passing stream. Thus the coding scheme is a hypothesis of sorts, a lens with which an investigator has chosen to view the world. If that lens is thoughtfully constructed and well formed (and aimed in the right direction), a clearer view of the world should emerge. But if not, no amount of corrective action will bring things into focus later. In such cases, the theoretical underpinnings and assumptions of the coding scheme should be questioned.

The Art of Coding Schemes

Having said this, we are not quite sure what to say next. We are absolutely convinced that the success of observational research stands or falls with the distinctions that early on become enshrined in the coding scheme. At the same time, we know that no mechanical prescriptions guaranteeing successful coding schemes are possible. Just as the art of doing good research is intimately connected with the ability to ask interesting questions, so too the art of observational research involves the ability to construct useful and fruitful coding schemes. But it remains an art that some people master better than others, not a craft that almost anyone can learn mechanically. Nonetheless, there are a number of distinctions that we think almost anyone could find useful while engaged in the often arduous and time-consuming task of coding scheme development (see also Rosenblum, 1978).

Momentary versus Duration Events

In order to avoid the somewhat jargony plural form of *behavior,* let us use the term *event* to signify those aspects of behavior we want coded. Some events are typically quite brief. In such cases, we are usually concerned with how often they occurred, not with how long they lasted. In other cases, the duration of events is very much of concern—either the average length of time an episode or bout lasts or the percentage of total time devoted to that kind of event. Because events of interest to researchers so often fall clearly into one class or the other, many writers have found it convenient to distinguish between momentary events or *frequency behaviors,* on the one hand, and behavioral states or *duration behaviors,* on the other (J. Altman, 1974; Sackett, 1978). The distinction is not absolute, of course, but examples of relatively brief and discrete momentary events could include baby burps, dog yelps, or child points while examples of duration events could include baby in REM sleep, dog hunting, or child engaged in parallel play.

The distinction between momentary and duration events has a number of ramifications. Certain data recording strategies, as well as certain data analyzing techniques, are more appropriate for one than the other. As a result, we find it useful when investigators clearly designate whether duration is an important aspect of the events they code or not. The two examples presented earlier exemplify this distinction nicely. Bornstein and colleagues (1976) were very much concerned with how long infants looked at lights of different wavelengths, while Green and colleagues (1980) were concerned just with how often "social interactions" occurred (and also with who initiated them and what their dominant themes were).

The Case of Behavioral States

One way of conceptualizing duration events is both so useful and so common among infancy researchers that it deserves special comment. Often, researchers view the events they code as *behavioral states.* The assumption is that the "surface" behavior observed reflects some underlying "organization," and that at any given moment, an infant (or an infant–other dyad) will be "in" a particular state. The observers' task then is to segment the stream of behavior into successive episodes of different behavioral states. Perhaps the best-known example is provided by the arousal states usually associated with young infants (quiet, alert, fussy, REM sleep, etc.; Wolff, 1966), but other examples abound.

For example, in order to study the developing communicative abilities of older infants, Bakeman and Adamson (1984) defined six attentional or engagement states. Their states were influenced, in part, by Parten's classic study (1932) of play in young children and characterize an infant's involvement with people and/or objects as follows: (1) unengaged; (2) onlooking; (3) solitary object play; (4) person play; (5) supported (or passive) joint engagement (infant and partner engaged with same object or event, but infant shows no awareness of the other's interest or presence, at least overtly); and (6) coordinated joint engagement (infant and partner engaged with same object or event and infant evidences awareness of the partner, coordinating attention between their shared object and the partner).

The concept of *behavioral state,* as a particular or special kind of duration event, can prove extremely useful in observational research for at least three reasons. First, it is an integrative concept that protects investigators from becoming lost in a morass of detail. Sometimes there is a tendency for observational researchers to code ever more finely detailed acts, which is time-consuming and not necessarily useful. For example, as noted in the previous paragraph, Bakeman and Adamson (1984) were interested in whether infants deployed attention just to objects, just to people, or to the two jointly. Thus it made sense for them to code just that, conceptualized as a behavioral state, instead of coding all the possible attention-directed acts separately.

Second, behavioral state may qualify or modify the meaning of other acts. For example, some time ago Korner (1972) noted that the meaning of many infant acts was affected by the infant's arousal state. Applying this idea, Adamson and Bakeman (1985) were able to show that infants' affective expressions were more likely when infants were engaged jointly with their mothers than when playing with objects alone. The point of this example is to indicate that, once behavioral state is coded, other events can be analyzed relative to the state during which they occur. This, in turn, can be a very useful descriptive and analytic strategy.

Finally, by its very nature a set of behavioral state codes is likely to be mutually exclusive and exhaustive. As discussed in the next paragraph, this often turns out to be a desirable property for coding schemes to have.

Mutually Exclusive and Exhaustive Codes

The coding schemes discussed so far—Kessen and colleagues' infant looking, Green and colleagues' initiation and social interactive theme, and Bakeman and Adamson's engagement state—all have been mutually exclusive and exhaustive. They are mutually exclusive because in each case only one code from the scheme can be associated with a particular event, and they are exhaustive because for each event some code in the scheme applies. Observational research does not require that all coding schemes consist of mutually exclusive and exhaustive codes, but in fact such schemes have several desirable features. Their construction requires a certain amount of conceptual analysis, for example, and their use can simplify data analysis. As a result, such schemes are frequently encountered.

In principle, codes can always be defined in a way that makes them mutually exclusive and exhaustive (S. Altmann, 1965). For example, in one set of studies of mothers and infants engaged in face-to-face play, Stern (1974) was interested in who initiated and who terminated mutual visual regard. His coding scheme could have consisted of just two (non–mutually exclusive) events—mother looking at infant and infant looking at mother. In fact, Stern found it more convenient to define four mutually exclusive and exhaustive "dyadic states"—(1) mutual regard; (2) mother looking at infant but infant looking away; (3) infant looking at mother but mother looking away; and (4) both looking away. Since each successive moment could be described with one, and only one, of these behavioral state codes, Stern was able to describe and quantify the ongoing interaction between mothers and infants in clear and useful ways (see also Bakeman & Brown, 1977).

A set of mutually exclusive and exhaustive codes necessarily categorizes just one aspect of behavior, like looking or attention or interactive theme. Often, however, investigators are concerned with several aspects. In such cases, several schemes can be defined, each consisting of mutually exclusive and exhaustive codes and each dealing with a different aspect of behavior. A good example of this approach is Landesman-Dwyer's Baby Behavior Code (1975; see also Landesman-Dwyer, Keller, & Streissguth, 1978). She defined four aspects of neonatal behavior that might be affected by, for example, mothers' alcohol intake—eyes, face/vocalization, head, and body/limb movements. In addition, a fifth aspect, external stimulation, characterized the current environmental circumstance. For each aspect, 10 mutually exclusive and exhaustive codes were defined. For example, the codes for eyes were: closed, slow rolling, squint, blinking, dazed, bright, tracking, REM, other, and can't see.

In the next section, we will describe how Landesman-Dwyer has observers record data using her coding scheme. For now, we just want to point out an advantage of a scheme structured like this. The overall scheme is a collection of five separate schemes—a hierarchy of five branches, each of which comprises 10 "twigs." There are 50 codes in all, but because of the way they are structured, observers find the scheme relatively easy to learn and easy to use. Thus one advantage of a coding scheme that consists of a set, or sets, of mutually exclusive and exhaustive codes is the way it structures and simplifies the observer's task.

Physically Versus Socially Based Codes

It is sometimes claimed that observational methods are superior to rating scale approaches because the former are "objective" while the latter are "subjective." We do not agree with this statement for at least two reasons. First, in actual cases the distinction is not always all that clear, and, second, codes some might call subjective often turn out to be very useful.

Some behavioral codes are clearly physically based. They classify behavior with clear and well-understood roots in the organism's physiology. Other codes are much more socially based. They deal with behavior whose very classification depends more on ideas in the minds of the researchers than on mechanisms in the body. Instead of following quite clearly from physical features or physical mechanisms in a way that causes almost no disagreement, socially based schemes follow from cultural tradition or current negotiation among people as to a meaningful way to view and categorize the behavior under study.

An excellent and well-known example of a physically based scheme is Ekman and Friesen's (1978) Facial Action Coding System (FACS), which scores facial movement in terms of visible changes in the face brought about by the motion of specific muscle groups. It might code such things as specific brow configuration, while a socially based scheme would code such things as "sadness." In general, socially based schemes require considerably more inference on the part of the observers, but we hesitate to say that such schemes are, for that reason alone, less "real." Socially and physically based schemes simply provide description on different levels. Not all investigators would agree with this. Some, especially those trained in animal behavior and ethology, might argue that, if the problem is analyzed properly, socially based schemes can always be reduced to physically based ones. We disagree with this and would argue instead that often there are very good reasons for using socially based codes.

Physically based schemes like Ekman and Friesen's FACS can be time-consuming to learn and apply, and so just as a practical matter, it may be much easier to use a socially based alternative. Even if it is not, a socially based scheme may more faithfully reflect the level of description appropriate for a given research issue. Often various aspects of the socially created world are exactly what we want to study, and in such cases socially based coding schemes are the appropriate "filter" to capture the behavior of interest.

For example, Adamson and Bakeman (1985) were interested in the communicative functions of expressions of affectivity on the part of infants, especially as they might be related to the emergence of referential communication abilities. Since the communicative effect of infants' affective expressions was central to their thinking, Adamson and Bakeman instructed coders to locate times (on previously recorded videotapes) when an infant's activity would likely signal a relatively sudden heightening of affectivity to most adults (similar to Emde's *episodic salient processes*; see Emde, 1980). Thus Adamson and Bakeman thought of their codes as socially based and self-consciously regarded their observers not as "detectors" of some physical or physiological process but instead as cultural "informants," better able to do their task because of, not in spite of, their human interpretative abilities (see also Shotter, 1978).

The foregoing does not mean that we support inference and interpretation with rich abandon. We can see merit in the advice that investigators should avoid coding schemes that require observers to make judgments about intentionality. Just from the standpoint of observer agreement, there is no reason to ask observers to make more complex judgments (was the baby trying to get its mother's attention?) when simpler ones will do (did the baby approach within 1 m of its mother and look at her?). However, if this advice is followed rigorously, we could end up not studying some very interesting behavior or else defending some possibly quite silly coding schemes.

Other things being equal, we much prefer coding categories that are defined in terms of observable and concrete features, but we are not willing to let this one consideration override all others, especially if the meaningfulness of the data collected or the ability of those data to answer the questions at hand might suffer. It is possible, for example, to record accurately how many times an infant approaches within 1 m of its mother, what proportion of time is spent looking at her, and so forth, and still not be able to gauge validly the quality of the mother–infant relationship (Ainsworth et al., 1978; Sroufe & Waters, 1977).

In sum, we think it more important that codes fit the question at hand than that they be "objective." We know that some investigators will be unhappy unless codes are clearly grounded in the physical world, but we tend to be tolerant of almost any coding scheme as long as it fits the research concerns and as long as—and this is a key proviso—trained observers can demonstrate acceptable levels of agreement using it. This critical matter of observer agreement will be discussed in a subsequent section, but first we want to describe various strategies for recording observational data.

RECORDING DATA: STRATEGIES FOR SELECTION AND COLLECTION

If the first step in designing an observational study is defining the question and the second is developing the coding scheme, then the third is deciding on an appropriate method or strategy for recording data. By *method* we mean considerably more than the mechanics of data recording. In fact, mechanics are discussed only briefly here. Mainly we mean the logic of the way a coding scheme is applied to the passing stream of behavior, extracting from it numbers that can be used for subsequent quantitative analysis.

Based on our reading of the literature, our consulting, and our own work, we have come to identify four major strategies for recording observational data. In actual studies, investigators may use combinations or hybrid forms of these four basic methods; still we find that our coding scheme for recording strategies can usefully classify the methods most researchers use. These four strategies are quite distinct in a number of ways. Each has its particular advantages and disadvantages, and each influences the kinds of analyses that are possible subsequently. As a result, the choice of an appropriate recording method is an important matter. In this section we describe the four methods, including three variants of the first, but first there are two distinctions that need to be made.

What Is Coded? Events versus Intervals

As mentioned earlier, coding schemes are the measuring instruments of observational research. But what is measured? That is, what is the nature of the "unit" to which a code from the scheme is assigned, what is the "thing" categorized? In observational research, the unit categorized is almost always either a particular event or a particular time interval.

The coding of intervals is usually a straightforward affair for observers. A time-keeping device of some sort marks the interval to be coded; observers then need only code that interval. The coding of events can be more complex. Often observers have two tasks. First they need to detect that a codable event has occurred; then they need to code that event. This is an important distinction because, as discussed in the next section, the reliability both for determining event boundaries and for coding the events so bounded may need to be determined separately.

Continuous versus Intermittent Recording

A second distinction concerns not the unit coded but the continuity of coding. If successive events or intervals are coded, we would call the recording continuous. If there are gaps between the events or intervals coded, however, then we would regard recording as intermittent. This distinction matters because, among other things, it determines whether sequential analyses are appropriate for the data recorded.

The two distinctions just described, when arranged as a 2- × -2 table, conveniently generate the four recording strategies outlined below. Although the scheme is not perfect and hazy borderline cases can be found, in general *coding events* and *coding intervals* are continuous recording strategies while *cross-classifying events* and *time-sampling* are intermittent (see Table 15.1).

Method 1a: Coding Events

In the next few paragraphs, we discuss the simplest of all possibilities—coding events without any time information, although we suspect that coding events while preserving time information (recording onset and offset times and timing pattern changes, as discussed in subsequent paragraphs) is far more common. The observer's task in this case is quite simple; he or she simply notes (perhaps using pencil and paper) each time a codable event occurs.

The interpretation of this record depends on the nature of the codes. If codes represent momentary events, then the data consist of tallies for the different codes, and about all investigators can do is report the frequency, or rate (number of tallies divided by length of observation), for those events. If codes represent a set of mutually exclusive and exhaustive behavioral states, however, then the data consist of a sequence or string of codes, and investigators can report percentages or probabilities for each state, indicating how often each code was used, as well as sequential statistics, like event-based transitional probabilities as discussed later on. For example, Adamson and Bakeman (1985) reported that 59 affective expressions occurred per hour, on the average, while Bakeman and Adamson (1984) determined that for 15-month-old infants with their mothers 22 percent of the engagement states were coded supported joint.

In point of fact, because Adamson and Bakeman wanted to relate the occurrence of affective expressions to engagement state, and wanted to know percentages of time spent in each of the engagement states, their recording system preserved time information. Still, if the kind of statistics just given had been sufficient for their purposes, they could have opted for a simpler system, one that just recorded the frequency and sequence of events.

TABLE 15.1. Recording Strategies

Method	Unit Coded	Recording	Advantages	Disadvantages
Coding Events				
Times not recorded	Event	Continuous	Easy and inexpensive	Statistics limited (rates and event-based probabilities)
Onset, offset, or pattern change times recorded			Complete statistics possible	Usually requires electronic recording devices or time-stamped videotapes
Coding Intervals	Interval	Continuous	Easy and inexpensive	Statistics estimated; depending on interval used, may be inaccurate
Cross-classifying events	Event	Intermittent	Easy and inexpensive, highly focused, clear analysis	Statistics limited, highly focused
Time sampling	Interval	Intermittent	Easy and inexpensive, efficient use of observation time	Statistics limited (percentages) and estimated

Method 1b: Recording Onset and Offset Times

Probably the most flexible way to collect observational data is to record times of occurrence along with each event. Certainly this method provides the most options for subsequent data analysis, whether onset and offset times are recorded as described here or whether pattern changes are timed as described next. The major advantages of this approach, then, are the completeness of the record and the options for analysis that completeness allows for. The major disadvantage is that recording occurrence times is almost always best done with electronic instrumentation of some sort, instrumentation that can be complicated to use, requires maintenance, and certainly costs more than the pencils, paper, and stopwatches of a simpler era.

With proper equipment, the observers' task can be quite manageable. Assume, for example, that observers have available a keyboard device of some sort, that codes are entered on the keyboard, and that all timekeeping is accomplished internally by the recording device. Then, whenever a momentary event occurs, observers need only enter the code for that event. The onset time is recorded by the device and, because the event is regarded as momentary, there is no question of offset time. Duration events require that observers enter offset times in addition, but only if they are not organized into mutually exclusive and exhaustive sets. When codes are mutually exclusive and exhaustive, only onset times need be entered, because the onset of another code in the set necessarily means the offset of the last code entered from that set.

For example, Linn and Horowitz (1983) defined 10 sets of mutually exclusive and exhaustive codes, appropriate for coding the behavior of very young infants in interactional situations like feeding. Using an electronic recording device, observers noted whenever a codable event in any of the 10 sets began. From a record like this, a variety of different descriptive statistics can be derived, but one that Linn and Horowitz developed is especially interesting. They computed how likely mothers were to touch or talk to their infants, given that their infants had looked at them or vocalized within the same 5-sec intervals. Mothers were not likely to respond before their babies looked or vocalized, of course, but some mothers were quite likely to respond just after, while others were not. Using these "conditional probability profiles," Linn and Horowitz classified mothers as "responsive" or "unresponsive" and so were able to demonstrate that infants who showed variability on the Kansas version of the Brazelton tended to have mothers who were more responsive to them—a matter of some theoretical importance (see Emde, 1978; Horowitz, Sullivan, & Linn, 1978).

An additional example of this recording strategy is provided by the Bakeman and Adamson (1984) and Adamson and Bakeman (1985) studies cited previously. Working from videotapes, observers recorded onset times for, among other things, the six engagement states defined earlier as well as affective expressions. From this record they were able to determine, for example, that when with their mothers 15-month-old infants spent 23 percent of the observation session engaged in supported joint, on the average. Since 29 percent of the affective expressions tallied occurred during supported joint, that engagement state was the occasion for more than its "share" of affective expressions.

Both of these examples reveal one important strength of creating a record that includes exact onset times (and offset times, as appropriate) for the various events defined in the coding scheme (or schemes). Not only can a variety of standard descriptive statistics for the various events be derived, but also quite different kinds of events, like infants' affective expressions and engagement states, can be related to each other. When working from videotapes, the different kinds of events can be coded at different times on different "runs" through the videotapes. In this way a rich and detailed quantitative record can gradually be built up, allowing for subsequent analyses (and even subsequent coding) to be guided by previous findings.

Method 1c: Timing Pattern Changes

If codes are divided into a small number of mutually exclusive and exhaustive sets (like the Landesman-Dwyer Baby Behavior Code described earlier), then observers can note whenever a codable event begins (as Linn & Horowitz's observers did) or they can note the status of codes in each set whenever there is any change in the overall pattern (as Landesman-Dwyer's observers do). Paradoxically, this approach seems like more work, but many observers prefer it to the simple recording of onset times just discussed.

The method is practical only when there are relatively few sets of codes. For example, the Baby Behavior Code consists of five sets—one each for external stimulation, eyes, face, head, and body. Observers are taught to think of this as a five-digit code: The first digit represents the kind of external stimulation, the second digit represents the eyes, the third the face, and so forth. Thus the code 18440 means that external stimulation was a reflex test (code 1), REM movement was evident in the eyes (code 8), there was a smile on the face (code 4), the head was up (also code 4), and the body was in repose (code 0). If code 18440 were followed by code 18040, it would mean that nothing had changed with respect to external stimulation, eyes, head, and body, but that the face was now in repose (code 0), not smiling as before.

Each time there is a change in codable behavior, even if it involves only one of the five sets, a complete five-digit code is entered. On the surface of it, this seems like more work than necessary. After all, why require observers to enter codes for external stimulation, eyes, head, and body when there has been no change just because there has been a change in facial behavior? In fact, observers who use this approach to recording data report that, once they are trained, it does not seem like extra work at all. Moreover, since the status of all five sets is noted whenever any change occurs, investigators feel confident that changes are seldom missed, which they might not be the case if observers were responsible for monitoring five different domains of behavior separately.

No matter which approach is used—recording onset and offset times or timing pattern changes—the data contain the same information and all the same kinds of descriptive statistics can be extracted. When recording live both methods essentially require an electronic recording device. With such devices, observers do not need to read and record time; that is done automatically for them. Codes are entered as though touch typing, leaving observers free to devote their full attention to the behavior observed. When working from videotapes an electronic recording device is far less essential, but the videotape does need to be "stamped" in some way with a time code.

Method 2: Coding Intervals

Although detecting, coding, and timing events provide a complete and accurate record for the behavior of interest, coding intervals has probably been more frequently used, especially in the older literature. The reason for this, we think, has something to do with historical precedent, a human propensity to impose clock units on passing time, the ready availability and attractive price of lined paper, and the unavailability until relatively recently of electronic recording devices.

The essence of the method is as follows. An infant, a mother–infant dyad, or whatever is observed for a period of time. That period is divided into a number of relatively brief intervals, typically on the order of 10 or 15 sec or so. Observers then categorize each successive interval or else note which codable events, if any, occurred during each successive interval.

The major advantages of this method are its simplicity and the low cost of instrumentation. Usually it requires only pencil, paper, and some sort of simple timing device like a stopwatch or an electronic circuit that delivers a click to the observer's ear at appropriate intervals.

The major disadvantage of interval coding is that neither frequency nor duration information may be rendered very accurately (J. Altmann, 1974: Sackett, 1978). The key consideration is the length chosen for the interval. If that interval is somewhat shorter than the shortest duration typically encountered for a codable event, then little distortion should be introduced into the data (Smith & Connolly, 1972). In fact, we suspect that most investigators who use an interval coding strategy understand perfectly well that the interval used should not be so long as to mask onsets and offsets of events being studied because if it is, then not only will estimates of frequencies, durations, and percentages be inaccurate, but behavioral sequences could be distorted as well.

A second advantage of interval coding is that in some cases observers find it easier to categorize a clearly bounded interval than to determine exactly when in the stream of behavior a particular event began and ended. For example, Brazelton, Tronick, and their co-workers have been interested in whether the waxing and waning of affective and attentional involvement during early mother–infant face-to-face interaction indicates mutual regulation. They defined several sets of mutually exclusive and exhaustive codes, including sets for vocalizations, facial expressions, gaze directions, and body positions for both mother and infant (Tronick, Als, & Adamson, 1977). Observers then viewed videotapes repeatedly, often in slow motion. After each second of real time, they would decide on the one code from each set that best characterized that 1-sec interval. Because a single second is short, relative to the behavior being coded, this particular instance of interval coding probably introduced essentially no distortion into the data. Moreover, it was certainly an excellent, if painstaking, way to capture the highly detailed data concerning affective and attentional involvement that this research team wanted.

In sum, there are two major differences between coding events and coding intervals. First, what it is that stirs observers to record is different. In the case of event coding, it is the occurrence of the events themselves. In the case of interval coding, it is a clock running out, indicating the end of an interval. Second, the end of an interval is determined by a device external to the observer, while when event coding, the observer usually is asked not just to code events, but to detect when they occur as well. The implication is that, when event coding, investigators need to be concerned about the reliability of detection as well as the reliability of coding.

No matter whether events or intervals are coded, as long as continuously alert observers code successive events or intervals, a continuous record results. When coding events without recording time information, event frequencies (or rates), event probabilities (or percentages), and event-based transitional probabilities can be derived. When coding events along with their times of occurrence or when coding intervals using a relatively short interval, then percentages of total time (time budget information), mean episode durations, time-based transitional probabilities, and a variety of other descriptive statistics can be derived as well. For a fuller treatment, detailing some ways such continuously recorded data can be analyzed, see Bakeman and Gottman (1986).

Method 3: Cross-Classifying Events

Of the four methods defined here, the least used in infancy studies is the approach we call cross-classifying events. Nonetheless, it is an approach with a number of powerful advantages. It is like tallying momentary events in that observers are instructed to note whenever a particular kind of event occurs. As is not the case for tallying momentary events, however, usually only one kind of event is defined, and when it occurs, observers classify it on a number of dimensions.

For example, although this takes us somewhat out of the range of infancy, Bakeman and Brownlee (1982) wanted to determine whether social rules apparently govern object conflicts among toddlers and preschoolers. Thus the event of interest to them was an object struggle. Whenever two children disputed possession of an object, observers were asked to record: (1) prior possession—whether the child now attempting to take over the object from its current possessor had played with that object within the previous minute (yes or no); (2) resistance—whether the current possessor resisted the taker's attempt (yes or no); and (3) success—whether the taker was successful in gaining possession of the object (yes or no). Since the dominance ranking of the children had been determined, each object struggle was also categorized as follows: (4) dominance—whether taker was dominant to possessor (yes or no). As the reader can see, these schemes are very simple. There are four sets of mutually exclusive and exhaustive codes, and each set consists of just two codes—yes and no.

This recording strategy has a number of major advantages. First, techniques for analyzing cross-classified data (contingency tables) have received a good deal of attention both historically and currently and are relatively well worked out (e.g., Castellan, 1979; Feinberg, 1980; Upton, 1978). Second, recording such data is extremely simple and straightforward; pencil and paper should suffice. Third, the very structuredness of the coding scheme should require a certain amount of conceptual analysis and forethought. Finally, clear and simple descriptive statistics typically result. For example, Bakeman and Brownlee (1982) reported that, although 75 percent of the take attempt among preschoolers met with resistance overall and 71 percent did when the taker was dominant, only 56 percent encountered resistance when the taker had had prior possession. This suggests that prior possession conferred some advantage, an advantage that was not evident among toddlers, for whom dominance seemed to matter more.

The major disadvantage of cross-classifying events follows from one of its strengths. It is tightly focused and highly structured and requires observers to impose that structure on the passing stream of behavior. As a result, interesting sequences not accounted for in the coding scheme might pass by unseen like ships in the night. Moreover, the amount of descriptive information that can be extracted from cross-classified data is somewhat limited, not at all as varied as that provided by recording event onset and offset times, for example. Still, cross-classifying events is a useful and powerful way for recording data when investigators have fairly specific questions in mind and know exactly on what kinds of events they wish to focus. It is clearly suited for comfirmatory work, but is less useful in an exploratory context.

Method 4: Time Sampling

Perhaps the best-known example of a time sampling strategy, at least from the standpoint of textbooks in developmental psychology, is Parten's (1932) study of social participation among preschool children. She defined six levels or categories of social participation as follows: (1) unoccupied; (2) onlooking; (3) solitary independent play; (4) parallel activity; (5) associative play; and (6) cooperative or organized supplementary play. Then, during the school year of 1926–1927, some 42 children whose ages ranged from not quite 2 to almost 5 years were observed during indoor free play. Each child was observed for 1 min each day and the order of observation was varied systematically so that the 1-min samples would be distributed more or less evenly throughout the hour-long free-play period. Children were observed about 70 different times, on the average, and each time they were observed that 1-min sample was categorized using one of the six codes just listed.

Goodenough (1928) called this the method of repeated short samples. Today it is usually called time sampling, but its purpose remains the same. A number of relatively brief, nonsuccessive time intervals are categorized and the percentage of time intervals assigned a particular code is used to estimate the proportion of time an individual devotes to that kind of activity. For example, one 3-year-old child in Parten's study was observed 100 times. None of the 1-min time samples was coded unoccupied, 18 were coded solitary, 5 onlooking, 51 parallel, 18 associative, and 8 cooperative. It seems reasonable to assume that, had Parten observed this child continuously in a similar situation, hour after hour, day after day, about 51 percent of that child's time would have been spent in parallel play.

As is the case for cross-classifying events, a major advantage of time sampling is the simplicity of the recording instruments required, and as is also the case for cross-classifying events, a major disadvantage is the limited kinds of analysis that are appropriate for the data collected. If all an investigator needs is time budget information (how much time was devoted to different kinds of activities), then time sampling is an efficient way to estimate such scores. However, if any sort of sequential information is required, then this intermittent method of data recording will not do.

One final point: Occasionally investigators claim to have used a time sampling methodology when in fact successive intervals were coded. In such cases, it is difficult to see what was "sampled" and so a phrase like *interval coding* would seem more appropriate.

Recording Devices: Pencil, Paper, and Electronics

Throughout this section we have made occasional comments about recording devices, primarily because some devices seem better suited for certain recording strategies than others. As already noted, an advantage of all the recording strategies defined here, except coding events along with their occurrence times, is the feasibility of pencil and paper recording. More complex means can be used for coding events without time information, for coding intervals, for cross-classifying events, and for time sampling, but almost always pencil and paper will suffice.

This is not an advantage to be dismissed lightly. Pencil and paper are easy to transport and use almost anywhere. Their cost is low and they contain no batteries that may at a critical moment appear mysteriously discharged. The whole record is always on display and parts of it can be modified with nothing more complex than an eraser. Moreover, although paper can be misplaced, it almost never malfunctions. For all these reasons, we would not dismiss the possibility of pencil and paper recording just because it seems unsophisticated.

Electronic devices of various kinds, however, certainly have their uses, especially when events are coded along with their occurrence times. The kinds of devices investigators might find helpful depend as much as anything on whether behavior is viewed live or on videotape. When recording live using a coding scheme like Landesman-Dwyer's or Linn and Horowitz's as described earlier, some sort of electronic recording device is almost indispensable. Such devices typically have a keyboard and an internal clock, are portable, and work as follows: Whenever a codable event occurs, the observer depresses the appropriate keys. A record of the keys "stroked" and the times they were stroked is stored in the device's memory. Once the observation session is completed, the contents of memory are "dumped," either directly to a computer or to audiocassette tape for temporary storage and later processing. Examples of such devices are the OS-3 (Observational Systems, Redmond, WA 98052) and the Datamyte (Electro-General, Minnetonka, MN 55343), although battery-operated portable microcomputers, which have become available only recently, represent another possibility, especially if local programming talent is available. A slightly modified portable microcomputer, already programmed for observational recording and data analysis, is available from S+K Products, Toronto, Canada.

There is essentially no difference between live recording and viewing videotapes if the tapes are played straight through at normal speed without stopping. Usually, however, investigators exploit the unique advantage videotape gives, which is the ability to stop, rewind, and replay important segments, perhaps several times and at varying speeds. In such cases, an electronic recording device is not essential as it is with real-time viewing. What is important for time recording is that the videotapes be "time stamped" in some way. The usual way to do this has been with a date-time generator, an electronic device that incorporates the date and the passing time into the signal when recorded so that it is displayed as part of the picture on playback. Thus the date and time are available to the viewer, but they are not machine readable.

A machine-readable time code would offer videotape-based observers the same advantage the internal clock in an electronic recording device conveys to live observers. It would allow them to concentrate on the events themselves and leave time recording to the machine. Until recently, this advantage has been expensive and complex to achieve, but now with the increasing availability of microcomputers and the option of two audio tracks on ½-in. as well as ¾-in. videotapes, it is becoming more practical. A microcomputer can be programmed to record a time code on an audio track and to read the time code on playback (the OS-3 is already so programmed). An observer then can work as follows: Sitting in front of a video monitor and a microcomputer display, and having available controls for the videocassette recorder as well as the microcomputer keyboard, he or she enters codes when appropriate. The videotape might be stopped at the moment or playing at some speed. In either case, the observer's code along with the last time code read is stored in memory and displayed on the microcomputer's display. The observer thus has visually available and can edit the coding for that session. When done, the entire record is in machine-readable form (no keypunching required) and can be subjected to immediate analysis, depending on how the microcomputer is programmed.

We would like to end this section with a note of caution. Sophisticated recording systems like the one just described appear very attractive because they hold out the promise that, once mastered, savings in time and labor should result. The key phrase here is "once mastered," because almost inevitably such sophisticated equipment requires that users pay an "entry cost." This entry cost includes not just the initial cost of the equipment, but the time it takes to learn how to use the equipment and keep the equipment working properly. Such costs may be justified only if the coding task is quite sizable.

ASSESSING RELIABILITY: CAN AND DO OBSERVERS AGREE?

Any research requires a clear question, of course. And observational research requires a focused coding scheme. Naturally, there can be no data without an appropriate recording strategy. But observer reliability is the sine qua non of observational methods. Without it the author's reports are only as good as our opinion of the author's capabilities.

It is all too easy to see what we want to see, even given the best of intentions and the sincerest of desires. For that reason, elaborate precautions are taken in scientific work to insulate measuring procedures from the investigator's influence. When measurements are recorded automatically or when there is little ambiguity about the measurement, as is often the case in the "hard sciences," the problem of investigator bias is not so severe. But in observational research, especially when what we call socially based coding schemes are employed, it becomes especially important to convince all concerned that what was recorded does not unduly reflect either the investigator's desires or some idiosyncratic worldview of the observer.

The solution to the problem of investigator bias is to keep observers naive as to the hypotheses under investigation—which is just standard scientific practice, but in observational research means that investigators can almost never serve as observers. The solution to the problem of observer idiosyncrasy is to demonstrate that observers who have seen the same events will produce essentially similar records. As noted in the following paragraphs, there are a number of ways to do this.

Why Compute Observer Agreement? Three Reasons

There are at least three reasons that investigators would want to determine how well observers agree, either among themselves or with a standard protocol. First, we need to assure ourselves, as investigators, that observers are coding events in accord with our definitions. Second, we need to provide observers with feedback to aid in their training. And third, we need to assure others (including journal editors and reviewers) that our observers are accurate and our procedures replicable. Depending on which reason is paramount, different procedures and different agreement statistics may be recommended.

To assure ourselves that observers are accurately applying our codes in a way consistent with our understanding, we need to compare their coding of events with one of our own. This could be done live, but is better accomplished with videotapes. Thus even when observers will record live behavior, we recommend using videotapes of similar behavior when training observers. The best strategy is to prepare standard protocols for those training tapes and then use quite stringent statistics to gauge observers agreement with us.

By "stringent statistics" we mean statistics like Cohen's kappa that compare observers' coding on a moment-by-moment or point-by-point basis, not statistics that gauge correlations among summary scores. Not only do stringent statistics give us greater assurance that observers are accurately doing what we want, they also provide better feedback for observers. For example, in a way that will be demonstrated shortly, the procedure for computing Cohen's kappa also pinpoints exactly what kinds of disagreements are occurring and can even indicate whether one observer is more "sensitive" than another.

When convincing others that our procedures are accurate, however, less stringent means can be employed. It depends on what kind of scores we report and analyze. Often investigators collect detailed moment-by-moment data with the intention of deriving a few summary scores from them. For example, an investigator might be interested in a simple percentage like the proportion of time infants spend looking at a particular stimulus or a conditional probability like the probability in a particular 5-sec interval of a mother's vocalization given that her infant vocalized in the previous 5-sec interval. In such cases a reasonable rule would seem to be as follows: It is only necessary to demonstrate reliability for the scores actually analyzed, not necessarily for the data collected. This can be done with nothing more complex than a correlation coefficient, although more sophisticated procedures are available (e.g., Cronbach, Gleser, Nanda, & Rajaratnam, 1972).

There are a number of reasons to stay with a statistic like Cohen's kappa, however. First, it provides helpful feedback to observers. Moreover, if point-by-point agreement is established, then it can generally be assumed that scores derived from the collected data (like conditional probabilities) will also agree. In other words, if agreement at a lower level is demonstrated, agreement at a higher level can be assumed.

As just discussed, the main reasons for assessing observer reliability are to convince first ourselves, then our observers, and finally others that the observers are accurately rendering the passing stream of events. Two other reasons are worth mentioning—calibration between observers and drift within observers. Whenever different observers are used for collecting the same kind of data, we need to ensure that the data collected do not vary as a function of the observer, which means that we need to calibrate observers against each other or, better yet, calibrate all observers against some standard protocol. Similarly, especially when coding continues for some time, we need to ensure that observers' performance does not drift with time, which means that intraobserver reliability needs to be assessed from time to time. The only way to do this, of course, is with videotapes.

Percentage Agreement and Its Problems

A percentage agreement of some sort is probably the most commonly used agreement statistic. At the same time, it is probably the least adequate and should not be used if at all possible. The major problem is this: Given a particular coding scheme and a particular recording strategy, some agreement would occur just by chance alone, even with blindfolded observers, but percentage agreements do not correct for this. Moreover, the amount of chance agreement varies depending on the number of codes in the coding schemes and how often they occur. This means that similar values derived from different studies could represent different levels of agreement. Thus there is no comparability of percentage agreements across studies and it is impossible to establish a common standard for "good" agreement. True, some people think that agreement percentages are "good" if they are in the nineties, but there is no rational basis for this belief.

For example, imagine that two observers coded whether an infant's eyes were open or closed for each of 100 sec. They agreed that the baby's eyes were closed in 90 sec and open in 7 sec. However, they disagreed about 3 sec. As indicated in Table 15.2, observer A thought the infant's eyes were closed for 2 sec when observer B thought they were open, while observer A coded open 1 sec when observer B coded closed. In this case, the proportion of agreement actually observed, P_o, is quite high (N_A refers to the number of agreements while N_D is the number of disagreements):

$$P_o = \frac{N_A}{N_A + N_D} = \frac{97}{97 + 3} = .97$$

(The percentage agreement is $P_o \times 100$, or 97 percent.)

However, the proportion of agreement expected just due to chance, P_c, is also quite high. From basic probability theory, we know that the probability of two events occurring jointly (in this case, both observers coding a second the same), just due to chance, is the product of their simple probabilities. The simple probability for observer A coding closed is .92 and for observer B is .91. Thus the expected joint probability is .8372. Similarly, the expected joint probability for open is .0072 (.08 × .09). Summing the chance probability for each code gives the overall proportion of agreement expected by chance, which in this case is .8444. Since this number is so high, it raises the question: How impressive is a value of .97, the observed proportion of agreement?

Cohen's Kappa and its Advantages

A statistic designed to correct for chance agreement is Cohen's kappa (Cohen, 1960). Since values can thus be compared across studies and since Cohen's kappa does not variously inflate the actual level of agreement, it is almost always preferable to simple agreement percentages. It is defined as follows (P_o is proportion agreement observed and P_c is proportion agreement expected by chance):

$$\kappa = \frac{P_o - P_c}{1 - P_c}$$

TABLE 15.2.   Agreement for Eyes Open or Closed

	Observer B		
Observer A	Closed	Open	Totals
Closed	90	2	92
Open	1	7	8
Totals	91	9	100

For the data given in Table 15.2, the value of kappa would be

$$\kappa = \frac{.9700 - .8444}{1 - .8444} = .8072$$

Now that we know the value of kappa, we are in a position to determine whether the 97 percent agreement observed is really as impressive as it seems.

Fleiss, Cohen, and Everitt (1969) have described the sampling distribution of kappa, and so it is possible to determine whether any given value of kappa differs significantly from zero (see also Hubert, 1977). First the population variance of kappa, assuming that kappa is zero, is estimated from the sample data. Then the value of kappa estimated from the sample data is divided by the standard error (the square root of the estimated variance) and the resulting z score is compared to the normal distribution. If the result were 2.58 or bigger, for example, we could claim that kappa differed significantly from zero at the .01 level. For the data given in Table 15.2, the square root of the variance is .09977 and the z score is 8.09. Thus the observed agreement is significantly better than chance (a FORTRAN subroutine that computes kappa along with its standard error and the associated z score is given in Bakeman & Gottman, 1986).

There seems little doubt that the data presented in Table 15.2 represent respectable agreement. The value of kappa is sizable (.81), it is significantly different from zero, and the percentage agreement is very high. Significance alone, however, may be too weak a criterion for "good" kappas. Just as correlation coefficients that account for little variance in absolute terms are often significant, if the sample is large, so too quite low values of kappa can be significant, which only means that the pattern of agreement observed is greater than would be expected if observers were guessing and not looking. Since we want good agreement, not just better than chance agreement, significance alone is not enough. Our own inclination, based on using kappa with a number of different coding schemes, is to regard kappas less than .7, even when significant, with some concern, but this is only an informal rule of thumb. Fleiss (1981), for example, characterizes kappas of .40–.60 as fair, .60–.75 as good, and over .75 as excellent (see also Cicchetti & Sparrow, 1981).

In sum, major advantages of kappa are that it corrects for chance and that it can be tested for significance. In addition, the table of agreements and disagreements used to compute kappa (sometimes called the agreement matrix or the confusion matrix) provides useful feedback for observers. For example, imagine that two observers were asked to code 100 engagement states using a slightly simplified version of the Bakeman and Adamson engagement state scheme presented earlier and that the agreement data were as presented in Table 15.3. What is clear from

TABLE 15.3. Agreement for Infant's Engagement State

Observer A	Observer B					
	Unengaged	Onlooking	Object	Person	Joint	Totals
Unengaged	5	1	0	0	0	6
Onlooking	0	7	0	3	4	14
Object	0	0	38	0	7	45
Person	0	3	0	4	0	7
Joint	0	0	1	1	26	28
Totals	5	11	39	8	37	100

these data is that observer B, rightly or wrongly, is "sensitive" to joint engagement. Observer B coded joint four times when observer A coded onlooking and seven times when observer A coded object, while observer A never coded joint when observer B coded onlooking and only coded joint once when observer B coded object. On the other hand, the two observers seemed equally prone to confuse onlooking and person. In such a case, we would conclude that more time needs to be spent sharpening the definition of joint engagement.

Cohen's kappa for the data given in Table 15.3 would be computed as follows. First, we would compute the proportion of observed agreement:

$$P_o = \frac{5 + 7 + 38 + 4 + 26}{100} = \frac{80}{100} = .80$$

Then the proportion expected by chance:

$$P_c = \frac{(5 \times 6) + (11 \times 14) + (39 \times 45) + (8 \times 7) + (37 \times 28)}{100 \times 100} =$$

$$\frac{3031}{10000} = .3031$$

And finally kappa itself:

$$\kappa = \frac{.8000 - .3031}{1 - .3031} = \frac{.4969}{.6969} = .7130$$

For the data in Table 15.3, the standard error of kappa is .06006 and the z score comparing kappa to its standard error is 11.9.

Example 1: Time Sampling and Coding Intervals

For the next several paragraphs, we discuss how Cohen's kappa can be applied to data collected with the various recording strategies discussed in the previous section. We begin with time sampling and interval coding because in both cases observers are not responsible for determining the boundaries of the "unit" coded. A clock of some sort marks the intervals instead, either successive intervals in the case of interval coding or intermittent intervals when time sampling. In either case, the application of Cohen's kappa is straightforward. Two observers view the behavior under consideration and independently code intervals. Agreements and disagreements for each interval coded are tallied in an agreement matrix like the ones portrayed in Tables 15.2 and 15.3 and kappa is computed.

If more than one mutually exclusive and exhaustive coding scheme is used to code intervals, then a separate kappa would be computed for each scheme. Some schemes can be quite simple, consisting of just two codes. For example, observers might be asked to check intervals if a particular kind of event occurred during it; this is, in effect, a mutually exclusive and exhaustive scheme with two codes: (1) presence or (2) absence of that event.

Example 2: Cross-Classifying Events

When cross-classifying events, two kinds of agreement need to be considered— agreement as to whether an event occurred and agreement as to how events are classified. Determining to what extent two observers are both detecting the same events is somewhat problematic and may represent one of the few times a percentage agreement is the statistic of choice. For example, during an agreement check Bakeman and Brownlee (1982) asked two observers to detect and cross-classify object conflicts. One observer recorded 50 such conflicts, the other 44, but all 44 of those had also been noted by the first observer. Thus their percentage agreement was 88.0 percent (44 divided by 44 + 6). If only 42 had been recorded by both observers, meaning that the first observer noted 8 conflicts that the second missed while the second noted 2 missed by the first, then the percentage agreement would be 80.8 percent (42 divided by 42 + 8 + 2).

Agreement about coding can only be determined for events both observers cross-classify, of course, but it is easy to do. First, agreement matrices are established for each coding scheme used (i.e., for each dimension classified). Then for each event cross-classified, agreements and disagreements are tallied for each of the dimensions defined and kappas computed. For example, Bakeman and Brownlee reported kappas of .91, .78, and .79 for coding prior possession, resistance, and success respectively.

In sum, because cross-classifying events typically requires recording information about just one kind of relatively infrequent event (like an object conflict), we recommend reporting a percentage agreement for events detected (in addition to kappas for each dimension coded). This at least gives some descriptive sense of how frequently two observers both thought an event of the kind being studied occurred.

Example 3: Timing and Coding Events

When detecting events and timing their onsets and offsets or else their pattern change, however, we have a different recommendation. First, we should point out that in such cases it is not at all obvious how even a percentage agreement would be determined. Consider, for example, the task of coding engagement states referred to earlier. The agreement data given in Table 15.3 assumed that observers had only to code states—that the events presented to coders were already "unitized," the boundaries already drawn. Actually, Bakeman and Adamson asked coders to detect those boundaries, segmenting the stream of behavior into successive engagement states.

If we wanted to compute a percentage agreement in this case, we would first align the two records for easy comparison. But what constitutes an agreement or a disagreement? If both observers code the same state beginning about the same time, that could be an agreement. But what happens if the first observer thinks another state occurs for a time and then reverts back to the initial state, while the second observer codes no interposing state? Is this one disagreement (because the first observer wrongly thought that a state interposed) or two disagreements (because the second observer missed both the switch to the interposing state and the switch back to the initial state)? In practice, a number of questions of this sort arise. Moreover, even if we could develop unambiguous rules for defining agreements and disagreements, the end result would still be an agreement statistic that does not correct for chance.

Our recommendation is as follows. Treat the data as though it all had resulted from interval coding—that is, assume, for example, that observers made coding decisions every second. The choice of an interval is arbitrary, to be sure, but need not be implausible. Bakeman and Adamson's coders, for example, recorded engagement state onset times to the nearest second, and so a 1-sec interval for agreement checking seemed reasonable to them. Given an interval, it is easy to compute kappa. As with interval coding, agreements and disagreements for each interval are tallied in an agreement matrix like the one in Table 15.3. The codes need to be grouped into mutually exclusive and exhaustive sets, of course, but as noted earlier this is easily accomplished. Then kappa is computed for each set.

Based on cautions learned about chi-square, some readers may think changing the interval from 1 sec to a 0.5 sec, for example, might affect the value of kappa, but this is not so. A simple demonstration should convince skeptical readers. Imagine that the data in Table 15.3 were derived from coding 1-sec intervals. If a 0.5-sec interval has been used instead, each tally would be about twice the value given in Table 15.3. Thus the exercise is to double the values in Table 15.3, compute kappa for these doubled data, and see whether it is the same as the kappa computed earlier for the undoubled data.

An advantage of the approach just described, in addition to the advantages that accrue from using kappa, is that it reflects with some fidelity just what observers using a continuous recording strategy are expected to do, and that is to remain continuously alert, making decisions on a moment-by-moment basis. Consider, for example, a very simple coding scheme like the presence or absence of affective expressions. Using a percentage agreement approach, coders would get "credit" just when both noted an affective expression at the same time. They would get no credit for all the times they decided *not* to code an affective expression. With kappa, however, they get credit (corrected for chance) for agreeing on both the presence or the absence of an affective expression.

Example 4: Coding Events without Timing

Paradoxically, what seems like the simplest recording strategy can be the most problematic for determining observer agreement. When the material presented to coders is already "unitized" there is no problem. For example, observers might be given transcripts of a mother's stream of talk and asked to code each sentence. In such cases kappa can be used. However, when observers both detect and code events—and record no time information—it is not so easy. Probably the best approach is to use percentage agreements (although as previously noted defining agreements and disagreements is not always easy) or else to compute correlations between summary scores derived from two observers' records. But neither approach takes chance agreement into account.

In summary, in this section, we have emphasized ways to assess observer agreement that rely on Cohen's kappa. This is not the only way to approach reliability, of course (see, e.g., Hartmann, 1982; Hollenbeck, 1978; Johnson & Bolstad, 1973); as most readers know, a large and specialized literature is devoted to the topic. Still, we think there are good reasons to emphasize kappa. First, unlike many agreement statistics, it corrects for chance and so provides a metric that is comparable across studies. Second, it can be tested for significance. Third, kappa provides a relatively stringent point-by-point or moment-by-moment check on agreement. This is useful not just for convincing ourselves and others concerning the accuracy of our data, but also for giving observers feedback concerning their performance. Finally, as the examples just discussed indicate, kappa can be used with data derived from a number of common recording strategies.

DESCRIBING SEQUENCES: TRANSITIONAL PROBABILITIES AND z SCORES

Two common reasons investigators might have for choosing observational methods in the first place are: (1) a desire to describe how much time is devoted to different activities, in which case either continuous or intermittent recording strategies would work; and (2) a desire to capture something about process, in which case continuous recording strategies are usually required. A concern with process leads naturally to a sequential approach to one's data and to sequential analysis. Much could be said about sequential analysis (see, e.g., Bakeman & Gottman, 1986; Castellan, 1979; Chatfield, 1973; Gottman, 1981; Gottman & Bakeman, 1979). Here we will confine our comments mainly to transitional probabilities and their associated z scores, first because they are such basic descriptive statistics for sequential analysis, and second because so much can be accomplished with them alone.

Transitional Probabilities Defined

A simple or unconditional probability is just the probability with which a particular "target" event occurred. For example, if 100 states were classified and 45 were coded solitary object engagement, then the probability for the solitary state could be .45 (45 divided by 100). If S stands for solitary play with objects, this would be written $p(S)$. Similarly, a conditional probability is the probability with which a particular "target" event occurred, but relative to another "given" event. For example, if 28 of those 100 states were coded joint and if 17 of the states following joint were coded solitary, then we would say that the probability for the solitary state, given a preceding joint, would be .61 (17 divided by 28). If J stands for joint, this would be written $p(S/J)$. Since in this case the conditional probability for solitary was greater than its simple probability, we might suspect that something about the joint state makes solitary engagement a likely consequent.

A transitional probability is one kind of conditional probability. It is distinguished from other conditional probabilities in that the target and given events occur at different times. Often the word *lag* is used to indicate this displacement in time. For example, in the example just given, adjacent or lag 1 events were examined. If S stands for solitary and J for joint, this could be written "$p(S_{+1}/J_0)$," and would be understood as the probability of solitary at lag 1, given joint at lag 0.

Event-Based Versus Time-Based Transitional Probabilities

Data used to compute transitional probabilities could be either a sequence of coded events (event sequence data) or a sequence of coded intervals (time sequence data). For example, in the study cited earlier, Linn and Horowitz (1983) computed lag 3, lag 2, lag 1, lag 0, lag -1, lag -2, and lag -3 time-based transitional probabilities. That is, they computed probabilities for a mother responding to her infant in the third 5-sec interval after her baby had acted, in the second, the first, the same (lag 0), as well as in the 5-sec interval *before* her infant acted (lag -1), and so on. Since Linn and Horowitz were concerned with whether, and how soon, mothers responded to their infants, it made a great deal of sense for them to base their calculations on timed intervals.

Bakeman and Adamson (1984), on the other hand, computed transitional probabilities based just on the sequence of events, ignoring time. Their data-recording strategy preserved time, and so they could have computed time-based transitional probabilities. However, they were interested in the way behavioral states unfolded in time, in whether certain states were more likely to follow some states than others, and this kind of information can be obscured by time-based transitional probabilities. For example, consider the following three time sequences (U = unengaged; S = solitary, J = joint; each code represents an arbitary time interval):

1. U U U S J J
2. U S S S J J
3. U U S S J J

All three of these sequences of coded intervals clearly represents just one kind of event sequence—unoccupied to solitary to joint. However, values for time-based transitional probabilities would be quite different for these three sequences: the $p(J_{+1}/S_0)$ would be 1.00, 0.33, and 0.50 for sequences one to three respectively. No one would actually compute transitional probabilities based just on six intervals, of course, but the point of this example is that when investigators are concerned with just the typical sequencing of events they should ignore any time information that might have collected (even if this seems hard to do). Otherwise what they want to reveal may be obscured instead.

z Scores and How to Compute Them

Transitional probabilities have real merits as a descriptive statistic. Often, for example, it is useful to know that 61 percent of the time after an episode of joint engagement, solitary object play follows. They are somewhat less useful when comparing two infants or when comparing mean values for two groups of infants. This is because the value of a transitional probability is influenced by the simple probability for the target code. Imagine, for example, that the $p(S)$ for one infant was .45 but for another infant was .21. Although it does not follow *necessarily*, it is certainly likely that the value of $p(S_{+1}/J_0)$ will be higher for the first infant simply because more of its behavioral states were coded solitary. In other words, the information provided by a simple probability and an associated transitional probability overlaps somewhat; high values for one imply likely high values for the other.

What is needed is a statistic that indicates just how big (or small) a transitional probability is relative to the simple probability for the target event. The z score is such a statistic. If the given event exerts no influence on the target event, the expected value for the conditional probability is the value observed for the target event. What the z score does is gauge how much the observed value for a conditional probability deviates from this expected value. In effect, z scores "correct" for the target probability baseline value for a particular individual, which is why they are so useful when comparing different individuals.

It is easy enough to compute z scores, especially when one remembers the binomial test. For ease of presentation, here we will consider just the lag 1 case, although the principle is the same for other lags. Also, even though the data could consist of a string of coded events or a string of coded intervals, here we will assume coded events unless otherwise stated. The first task is to tally pairs of events (or intervals) so that we know how often the target event followed the given event (assuming lag 1). Then (f = frequency, p = probability, t = target, g = given)

$$z = \frac{f(g,t) - f(g)p(t)}{\sqrt{f(g)p(t)(1 - p(t))}}$$

The observed frequency is $f(g,t)$, the number of times the given was actually followed by the target event. The expected frequency is $p(t)$, the probability of the target event, times $f(g)$, the number of opportunities the target has for occurring after the given event. Finally, the denominator is the estimated standard deviation for the difference between observed and expected.

With a little bit of algebraic manipulation, the z score formula just given can be rewritten using a transitional probability instead of a joint frequency (N = number of pairs tallied, which is somewhat different than the number of events coded):

$$z = \frac{p(t/g) - p(t)}{\sqrt{\dfrac{p(t)(1 - p(t))}{Np(g)}}}$$

Both formulas give identical results, of course, but before either is used at least four important qualifications should be understood. Two are more conceptual and are discussed in later paragraphs (number of data points required, independence of data points) but the other two are more computational.

The first computational point concerns $p(t)$, the probability for the target event. This is computed as $f(t)$, the frequency for the target event, divided by N *only when adjacent events can be coded the same*. Otherwise, when adjacent events must be different, this is computed as the frequency for the target event divided by $N - f(g)$, the difference between N and the frequency for the given event. (Technical note: To be precise, N is the number of pairs tallied, $f(t)$ is the number of pairs whose second event is coded the target, and $f(g)$ is the number of pairs whose first event is coded the target.)

This may seem like a minor matter but it is not. First, it often occurs that adjacent codes cannot be the same, and second, computing the probability for the target event incorrectly in such cases can seriously distort subsequent calculations and inferences. There is usually no requirement that adjacent codes be different when intervals are coded or when the successive events coded are something like maternal utterances. However, when behavioral states are coded, it is almost always the case that adjacent codes must be different by definition. After all, if two adjacent states were coded the same, they would be not two states, but just one.

The second computational point concerns a criticism Allison and Liker (1982) have made. The *z* score formulas just presented follow Sackett (1974, 1979; see also Bakeman, 1978; Bakeman & Dabbs, 1976; Gottman, 1979). More recently, Gottman (1980) and Allison and Liker (1982) have objected to Sackett's computation, noting that it is too conservative. The standard error for the differences between expected and observed would be correct, they write, only if the probability for the target code were the "true" value instead of an estimate based on sample observations. According to them the correct statistic is

$$z = \frac{f(g,t) - f(g)p(t)}{\sqrt{f(g)p(t)(1 - p(t))(1 - p(g))}} \quad \text{or}$$

$$z = \sqrt{\frac{p(t/g) - p(t)}{\dfrac{p(t)(1 - p(t))(1 - p(g))}{Np(g)}}}$$

Note that these formulas will always yield somewhat higher values than the formulas given earlier (as before, N is number of pairs tallied).

A computer program that computes *z* scores as described here is available (Bakeman, 1983). The program lets the user specify whether adjacent codes must be different or not and whether *z* scores are to be computed as suggested by Sackett or by Allison and Liker.

How Much Data Justify Significance?

Especially when comparing individuals or groups of individuals, the *z* score is often a more useful statistic than a transitional probability. In addition, it can be tested for significance. This is very helpful because it allows us to report, for example, not just that solitary object play followed joint engagement more often than we would expect, given the "base rate" for solitary play, but that the difference was significant.

It is possible to argue that significance testing may not always be appropriate. Perhaps the most important issue concerns the number of events. A computed *z* score is declared significant on the basis of the normal approximation of the binomial distribution, but this is justified only if a relatively large number of events has been coded and used in the computation. How many are enough? According to a widely used rule of thumb suggested by Siegel (1956), $NP(1-P)$ must be at least 9.

Applied to transitional probabilities, Siegel's rule works as follows. N refers to the number of two-event sequences tallied (which will be somewhat less than the number of events coded), while P refers to the absolute probability for the particular two-event sequence under consideration. If adjacent events can be coded the same, then P will be the simple probability for the first event multiplied by the simple probability for the second. However, if adjacent events must be different, then (g = first or given event, t = second or target event):

$$P = p(g)\ \frac{p(t)}{1 - p(g)}$$

instead of $p(g)$ times $p(t)$.

As an example, imagine that $p(g) = .4$, $p(t) = .2$, $N = 70$, and adjacent codes cannot be the same. Then:

$$P = \frac{.2}{1 - .4} = .1333$$

and

$$NP(1 - P) = 70 \times .1333 \times (1 - .1333) = 8.09$$

Seventy coded events may seem like a lot to some investigators, but in this case 8.09 falls short of the required 9, and so according to Siegel's rule of thumb, assigning significance would be dubious in this case (the reader may want to verify that the situation is even worse if adjacent codes can be the same; then the value would be 5.15).

With a little algebraic manipulation, Siegel's rule of thumb can be made pro-scriptive as follows:

$$N = \frac{9}{P(1-P)}$$

Using the same values given in the last paragraph and again assuming that adjacent codes must be different:

$$N = \frac{9}{.1333\ (1 - 1.333)} = 77.9$$

In other words, if significance were to be assigned to the z score associated with the transitional probability for which given and target event probabilities were as stated, then sufficient data would need to be collected so that at least 78 two-event sequences could be tallied. This is a useful way to recast Siegel's rule of thumb

because, assuming a reasonable basis for estimating given and target event probabilities, it gives guidance as to the minimum amount of data that need be collected
if significance testing is even to be a consideration later.

Is Independence a Problem?

Even when sufficient data are available, it is occasionally claimed that assigning
significance to a z score associated with a transitional probability is not justified
because the data (successive coded events or successive coded intervals) are not "independent." In general, we do not find this argument compelling; it arises, we think,
mainly through an overapplication of some basic statistical notions, correct in themselves, but not necessarily correct in this context.

As students in introductory statistics learn, when using chi-square or binomial
tests, some entity (the unit of analysis, which for the examples presented earlier was
a two-event sequence) is categorized. The results of successive categorizations are
then tallied in an appropriate way. In order for the binomial (or chi-square) to be
the appropriate theoretical distribution against which to compare the observed results, the successive categorizations must be independent of each other. What this
means is that the results of any one judgment should not be influenced by whatever
the previous judgment was.

Independence, then, is a procedural, not an empirical, matter. Adjacent events
may or may not be independent in fact—but this is exactly what we want to find
out. The point is, when making successive judgments, there is no reason to think
that a coder's present judgment is unduly affected by the judgment just made. We
conclude that successive events (when coding events) and successive intervals (when
coding intervals) can be regarded as independent, in the sense required to justify
assigning significance to these z scores on the basis of the binomial sampling distribution.

There is at least one exception to the argument just made. Consider, for example,
the Adamson and Bakeman (1985) study of infants' engagement states and affective
expressions cited earlier. Their observers recorded onset times for engagement states
and onset and offset times for affective expressions to the nearest second. For one
set of analyses, they wanted to determine whether affective expressions were used
as "greetings," occurring more often during the first few seconds of coordinated
joint engagement than later on during that state. Arbitrarily, a 1-sec interval was
selected for analysis, and each second of coordinated joint engagement was tallied
in a 2-×-2 table (interval among first 5 sec of state or not, interval coded for affect
or not).

In this case, the interval used for analysis was arbitrarily chosen. It could have
been halved or doubled and this would have affected the value of the z score. We
conclude as follows: When events or time intervals are each coded separately, the
assumption of independence seems reasonable and we would freely assign significance. However, when there is no one-to-one correspondence between time units
used and coding decisions made (as in the example just given) then assigning significance to the z scores seems a dubious matter at best. In such cases, the z score
can still serve as a useful index, especially when comparing different conditions
within a study. For example, Adamson and Bakeman reported that affective expressions characterized the beginning of coordinated joint engagement only when the

infant's partner was a peer. With mothers affective expressions occurred throughout coordinated joint engagement and were not confined to the first several seconds.

How Many Tests Are too Many?

Even when sufficient data are available, and coding decisions have been discretely made, significance testing of transitional probability z scores can still be problematic if too many tests are made. The pitfall of too many significance tests and its attendant courting of type I error is not just a worry for investigators attempting to detect significant sequences, of course. However, observational studies typically use coding schemes with several codes. These many codes generate many more possible sequences. If in the context of an exploratory study the significance of all possible two-event sequences is tested, so many tests can be made that the probability of type I error (of claiming that some sequences are significant when in fact they are not) approaches certainty. For example, when tests are independent and the alpha level for each is .05, the "studywise" alpha level, when k tests are performed, is $1 - .95^k$ (Cohen & Cohen, 1983). Thus if 20 tests were performed, the probability of type I error would be .64, not .05.

To counter this problem, some thought needs to be given to ways for controlling type I error. The best way, of course, is to limit drastically the number of tests made. This is easy enough if a study's intent is largely confirmatory, more difficult when a study is mainly exploratory. In any case, Bonferroni's correction could be used. If k tests are performed and a studywise alpha level of .05 is desired, then the alpha level applied to each test should be not the desired studywise alpha, but that value divided by k instead (see Miller, 1966). For example, if 20 tests are performed, the alpha level for each should be .0025 (.05 divided by 20).

ANALYZING SCORES: THE ADVANTAGES OF FAMILIAR DESIGNS

For a great many purposes, observational data require not exotic statistical techniques, but just the thoughtful use of the rather impressive array of techniques with which psychologists are already familiar. This is not to say that time series analysis (Gottman, 1981), for example, is not useful; it does, however, represent a rather specialized set of techniques. In this section we will focus on more broadly used and understood approaches to data analysis.

Percentages and Other Common Scores

As mentioned at the beginning of the last section, a common reason investigators have for choosing observational methods is a desire to describe how much time is devoted to different activities. Indeed, percentage scores for time spent in different activities or behavioral states, whether derived from time sampling or timing and coding events or coding intervals, are probably the most frequently used kind of summary score in observational studies. But there are other possibilities. Probably the most common are rates (derived from event or interval coding, or cross-classifying events), mean event durations (derived from timing and coding events or coding intervals), event-based transitional probabilities and z scores (derived from coding events or intervals), and time-based transitional probabilities and their z scores (derived from timing and coding events or coding intervals). In addition, any number of special-purpose summary indices limited only by an investigator's needs and imagination could be derived from observational data (e.g., Linn & Horowitz's measure of maternal responsiveness).

Standard Designs and Models

What the kinds of scores just listed have in common is that usually they are interval scaled, which means that all the standard parametric techniques—from simple correlation to multiple regression to the special cases of multiple regression called analysis of variance and covariance (Cohen & Cohen, 1983)—can be brought to bear. This assumes that the investigator's observations are embedded in a specified design, that is, that observations are made for several subjects (infants, mother–infant dyads, etc.) and that subjects belong to different groups (between-subjects factors) and/or are observed under different conditions or at different ages (within-subject factors).

Early in this chapter we commented that observational methods provide a way to quantify behavior, nothing more. That is, they are concerned with the dependent variable side of a study, not the independent variable side. However, when using observational measurement for dependent variables, data analysis is greatly facilitated if the independent variables can be expressed in standard design terms. This may seem so obvious that it hardly needs to be said. Indeed, the advantages of standard designs as a way of investigating the effects of research factors are so obvious and so overwhelming that learning about them is almost always part of a research psychologist's training.

For example, in the study cited earlier, Adamson and Bakeman (1985) computed the rate of infants' affective expressions separately for each infant in each of three conditions (observed with mother, with peer, and alone) at each of four ages. These scores were analyzed with a mixed model analysis of variance design. The between-subjects factor was sex of infant and the within-subject factors were experimental condition and age of infant. The condition effect was partitioned into mother versus peer and others (mother or peer) versus alone contrasts, while the age effect was partitioned into linear, quadratic, and cubic trends. Scores for two cohorts, one observed at 6, 9, 12, 15 and one at 9, 12, 15, and 18 months of age, were analyzed separately. For both cohorts, affective rates were higher when with mothers than when with peers (significant mother vs. peer contrasts), and again for both cohorts, rates increased with age (significant linear trends).

There are a number of reasons that data might fail to fit neatly into the ANOVA mold or that an ANOVA-like analysis might not be appropriate. A study might include just one subject, for example, or too few subjects to justify an analysis of variance. Sometimes no independent variables are specified, an approach that makes sense for some descriptive concerns. Or so few events may be observed that the reliability of summary scores computed for individual cases is questionable.

Under these circumstances descriptive approaches, as well as the use of z scores as described in the previous section, are still available. For example, earlier we described how Adamson and Bakeman (1985) used z scores to determine whether affective expressions characterized the beginning of coordinated joint engagement.

These z scores were based on data pooled across subjects. Because coordinated joint engagement was relatively infrequent with peers, computing individual z scores in this case seemed unwarranted.

Limitations of Transitional Probabilities

One score that should not normally be subjected to analysis of variance is the transitional probability. The reason was alluded to earlier: The value of a transitional probability is too intimately involved with the value of the target code's simple probability. Indeed, the expected value for $p(t/g)$, the transitional probability, is directly related to $p(t)$, the target's simple probability. It is not *necessary*, of course, that observed values agree with their expected values. Still, when analyses of both $p(t/g)$ and $p(t)$ reveal significant group differences, for example, it seems unjustified to claim that the differences with respect to $p(t/g)$ are explained by anything more complex than the differences detected for $p(t)$. Almost always when individual or group differences are at issue, the appropriate score to analyze is not the transitional probability, but its associated z score instead.

An example will illustrate both the usefulness of analyzing z scores within an ANOVA design and the difference between that and just describing the z score. As noted earlier, Bakeman and Adamson (1984) reported that z scores associated with the supported joint to solitary object transition were large and significant, both when infants were observed with mothers and when with peers. In other words, this transition occurred significantly more often than expected, no matter the partner. However, an analysis of variance of individual z scores indicated a significant partner effect favoring the mother. Thus not only was this sequence significantly more likely than expected with both mothers and peers, but the extent to which it exceeded the expected was significantly higher with mothers, compared to peers. As the reader can see, these two analyses provide different information about the sequence in question.

Hewing the Log-Linear Line

When rare events call the reliability of interval scaled individually based summary scores into question, the data might still be suitable for a log-linear analysis. For example, Adamson and Bakeman (1985) asked observers to record whenever infants used a word, pointed, or offered. Coded were videotapes made when infants were 9, 12, and 15 months of age. However, rates for these "conventionalized" acts were often either zero or quite low. Especially at the younger ages and when not with mothers, many infants never engaged in these acts at all. Thus the appropriate dependent variable is categorical (e.g., was a point coded (1) at least once or (2) not at all) and log-linear analyses instead of analyses of variance are appropriate.

In spite of a number of technical differences between analyses of variance and log-linear analyses, their results can be expressed in quite similar ways. For example, terms Adamson and Bakeman considered for their model included a linear term for age, a mother versus peer contrast, and an others (mother or peer) versus alone contrast. For the response variable "offers" a model containing just a linear term for age and the others versus alone contrast fit the data, while for "words" and "points" the mother versus peer contrast was required as well. Adamson and Bakeman concluded that the occurrence, or not, of these conventionalized acts was affected by increasing age, by whether the infant was with others or alone, and—except for offers—by whether the partner was the mother or a peer.

In observational research often dependent variables are categorical, either inherently so or because infrequent events make anything else inappropriate, as in the example just presented. Given enough observations and an appropriate design, log-linear analysis is often a useful technique in such cases, although at present it seems underused by most infancy researchers.

CONCLUSION

The title of this chapter is "Applying Observational Methods: A Systematic View." This title has two possible meanings. First, we remain as convinced as ever that observational methods can and do provide investigators with a systematic view of whatever behavior they study, that such methods are an important instrument in the scientific arsenal. At the same time, we would not want this one truth to stamp out all the rest, and we certainly recognize that other methods also have their uses.

Second, we hope that this chapter has provided both old and new researchers with a systematic view of observational methods themselves, of the choices that need to be made, and of the possibilities and problems those choices imply. We have tended to emphasize "front-end" concerns such as developing coding schemes, selecting data recording strategies, and assessing observer agreement. Partly this is because data-analytic concerns are discussed thoroughly elsewhere (e.g., Bakeman & Gottman, 1986; Gottman, 1981; Gottman & Bakeman, 1979; Sackett, Chapter 16, this volume). But the main reason for our emphasis is the conviction, gained from our own work and consulting with others, that once these front-end concerns are adequately addressed, data almost analyze themselves. When this happy state of affairs obtains, it is easier to get on with the task that occasioned our interest in observational methods in the first place—the study and understanding of infants' development.

REFERENCES

Adamson, L. B., & Bakeman, R. (1985). Affect and attention: Infants observed with mothers and peers. *Child Development, 56,* 587–593.

Adamson, L. B., & Bakeman, R. (1985, April). *Infants' conventionalized acts with mothers and peers.* Paper presented at the biennial meeting of the Society for Research in Child Development, Toronto.

Ainsworth, M. D. S., Blehar, M. C., Waters, E., & Wall, S. (1978). *Patterns of attachment.* Hillsdale, NJ.: Erlbaum.

Allison, P. D., & Liker, J. K. (1982). Analyzing sequential categorical data on dyadic interaction: A comment on Gottman. *Psychological Bulletin, 91,* 393–403.

Altmann, J. (1974). Observational study of behaviour: Sampling methods. *Behaviour, 49,* 227–267.

Altmann, S. A. (1965). Sociobiology of rhesus monkeys. II. Stochastics of social communication. *Journal of Theoretical Biology, 8,* 490–522.

Bakeman, R. (1978). Untangling streams of behavior: Sequential analysis of observation data. In G. P. Sackett (Ed.), *Observing behavior: Vol 2. Data collection and analysis methods.* Baltimore: University Park Press.

Bakeman, R. (1983). Computing lag sequential statistics: The ELAG program. *Behavior Research Methods & Instrumentation, 15,* 530–535.

Bakeman, R., & Adamson, L. B. (1984). Coordinating attention to people and objects in mother–infant and peer–infant interaction. *Child Development, 55,* 1278–1289.

Bakeman, R., & Brown, J. V. (1977). Behavioral dialogues: An approach to the assessment of mother–infant interaction. *Child Development, 49,* 195–203.

Bakeman, R., & Brown, J. V. (1978, April). Assessing early interaction: Methodologies and limitations. In K. G. Scott (Chair), *Social responsiveness of term and preterm infants.* Symposium presented at the biennial meeting of the Southeastern Conference on Human Development, Atlanta, GA.

Bakeman, R., & Brown, J. V. (1980). Early interaction: Consequences for social and mental development at three years. *Child Development, 51,* 437–447.

Bakeman, R., & Brownlee, J. R. (1982). Social rules governing object conflicts in toddlers and preschoolers. In K. H. Rubin & H. S. Ross (Eds.), *Peer relationships and social skills in childhood.* New York: Springer-Verlag.

Bakeman, R., & Dabbs, J. M., Jr. (1976). Social interaction observed: Some approaches to the analysis of behavior streams. *Personality & Social Psychology Bulletin, 2,* 335–345.

Bakeman, R., & Gottman, J. M. (1986). *Observing interaction: An introduction to sequential analysis.* Cambridge, England: Cambridge University Press.

Bornstein, M. H., Kessen, W., & Wieskopf, S. (1976). The categories of hue in infancy. *Science, 191,* 201–202.

Brazelton, T. B., Koslowski, B., & Main, M. (1974). The origins of reciprocity: The early mother–infant interaction. In M. Lewis & L. A. Rosenblum (Eds.), *The effect of the infant on its caregiver.* New York: Wiley.

Cairns, R. B., & Green, J. A. (1979). How to assess personality and social patterns: Observations or ratings? In R. B. Cairns (Ed.), *The analysis of social interactions: Methods, issues, and illustrations.* Hillsdale, NJ: Erlbaum.

Castellan, N. J. (1979). The analysis of behavior sequences. In R. B. Cairns (Ed.), *The analysis of social interactions.* Hillsdale, NJ: Erlbaum.

Chatfield, C. (1973). Statistical inference regarding Markov chain models. *Applied Statistics, 22,* 7–20.

Cicchetti, D. V., & Sparrow, S. S. (1981). Developing criteria for establishing interrater reliability of specific items. Applications to assessment of adaptive behavior. *American Journal of Mental Deficiency, 86,* 127–137.

Cohen, J. (1960). A coefficient of agreement for nominal scales. *Educational & Psychological Measurement, 20,* 37–46.

Cohen, J., & Cohen, P. (1983). *Applied multiple regression/correlation analysis for the behavioral sciences.* Hillsdale, NJ: Erlbaum.

Cronbach, L. J., Gleser, G. C., Nanda, H., & Rajaratnam, N. (1972). *The dependability of behavioral measurements: Theory of generalizability for scores and profiles.* New York: Wiley.

Ekman, P. W., & Friesen, W. (1978). *Manual for the facial affect coding system.* Palo Alto: Consulting Psychologist Press.

Emde, R. N. (1978). Commentary. In A. J. Sameroff (Ed.), Organization and stability of newborn behavior: A commentary on the Brazelton Neonatal Behavioral Assessment Scale. *Monographs of the Society for Research in Child Development, 43,* (5–6, Serial No. 177).

Emde, R. N. (1980). Levels of meaning for infant emotions: A biosocial view. In W. A. Collins (Ed.), *Development of cognition, affect, and social relations.* Hillsdale, NJ: Erlbaum.

Fienberg, S. E. (1980). *The analysis of cross-classified categorical data.* Cambridge, MA: MIT Press.

Fleiss, J. L. (1981). *Statistical methods for rates and proportions.* New York: Wiley.

Fleiss, J. L., Cohen, J., & Everitt, B. S. (1969). Large sample standard errors of kappa and weighted kappa. *Psychological Bulletin, 72,* 323–327.

Fraiberg, S. (1974). Blind infants and their mothers: An examination of the sign system. In M. Lewis & L. A. Rosenblum (Eds.), *The effect of the infant on its caregiver.* New York: Wiley.

Goodenough, F. L. (1928). Measuring behavior traits by means of repeated short samples. *Journal of Juvenile Research, 12,* 230–235.

Gottman, J. M. (1979). *Marital interaction: Experimental investigations.* New York: Academic.

Gottman, J. M. (1980). Analyzing for sequential connection and assessing interobserver reliability for the sequential analysis of observational data. *Behavioral Assessment, 2,* 361–368.

Gottman, J. M. (1981). *Time-series analysis: Introduction for social scientists.* New York: Cambridge University Press.

Gottman, J. M., & Bakeman, R. (1979). The sequential analysis of observational data. In M. E. Lamb, S. J. Suomi, & G. R. Stephenson (Eds.), *Social interaction analysis: Methodological issues.* Madison: University of Wisconsin Press.

Green, J. A., Gustafson, G. E., & West, M. J. (1980). Effects of infant development on mother–infant interaction. *Child Development, 51,* 199–207.

Hartmann, D. P. (1982). Assessing the dependability of observational data. In D. P. Hartmann (Ed.), *Using observers to study behavior: New directions for methodology of social and behavioral science* (No. 14). San Francisco: Jossey-Bass.

Hollenbeck, A. R. (1978). Problems of reliability in observational research. In G. P. Sackett (Ed.), *Observing behavior: Vol. 2. Data collection and analysis methods.* Baltimore: University Park Press.

Horowitz, F. D., Sullivan, J. S., & Linn, P. (1978). Stability and instability in the newborn infant: The quest for elusive threads. In A. J. Sameroff (Ed.), Organization and stability of newborn behavior: A commentary on the Brazelton Neonatal Behavioral Assessment Scale. *Monographs of the Society for Research in Child Development, 43,* (5–6, Serial No. 177).

Hubert, L. (1977). Kappa revisited. *Psychological Bulletin, 84,* 289–297.

Johnson, S. M., & Bolstad, O. D. (1973). Methodological issues in naturalistic observation: Some problems and solutions for field research. In L. A. Hamerlynch, L. C. Handy, & E. J. Mash (Eds.), *Behavior change: Methodology, concepts, and practice.* Champaign, IL: Research Press.

Korner, A. (1972). State as variable, as obstacle, and as mediator of stimulation in infant research. *Merrill-Palmer Quarterly, 18,* 77–92.

Landesman-Dwyer, S. (1975). *The baby behavior code (BBC): Scoring procedures and definitions.* Unpublished manuscript.

Landesman-Dwyer, S., Keller, L. S., & Streissguth, A. P. (1978). Naturalistic observations of newborns: Effects of maternal alcohol intake. *Alcoholism: Clinical & Experimental Research, 2,* 171–177.

Linn, P., & Horowitz, F. D. (1983). The relationship between infant individual differences and mother–infant interaction during the neonatal period. *Infant Behavior and Development, 6,* 415–427.

Miller, R. G. (1966). *Simultaneous statistical inference.* New York: McGraw-Hill.

Osofsky, J. D. (1976). Neonatal characteristics and mother–infant interaction in two observational situations. *Child Development, 47,* 1138–1147.

Parten, M. B. (1932). Social participation among preschool children. *Journal of Abnormal & Social Psychology, 27,* 243–269.

Rosenblum, L. (1978). The creation of a behavioral taxonomy. In G. P. Sackett (Ed.), *Observing behavior: Vol. 2. Data collection and analysis methods.* Baltimore: University Park Press.

Sackett, G. P. (1974). *A nonparametric lag sequential analysis for studying dependency among responses in observational scoring systems.* Unpublished manuscript.

Sackett, G. P. (1978). Measurement in observational research. In G. P. Sackett (Ed.), *Observing behavior: Vol. 2. Data collection and analysis methods.* Baltimore: University Park Press.

Sackett, G. P. (1979). The lag sequential analysis of contingency and cyclicity in behavioral interaction research. In J. D. Osofsky (Ed.), *Handbook of infant development.* New York: Wiley.

Shotter, J. (1978). The cultural context of communication studies: Theoretical and methodological issues. In A. Lock (Ed.), *Action, gesture, and symbol: The emergence of language.* London: Academic Press.

Siegel, S. (1956). *Nonparametric statistics for the behavioral sciences.* New York: McGraw-Hill.

Smith, P. K., & Connolly, K. J. (1972). Patterns of play and social interaction in preschool children. In N. Blurton Jones (Ed.), *Ethological studies of child behavior.* Cambridge, England: Cambridge University Press.

Sroufe, L. A., & Waters, E. (1977). Attachment as an organizational construct. *Child Development, 48,* 1184–1199.

Stern, D. N. (1974). Mother and infant at play: The dyadic interaction involving facial, vocal, and gaze behaviors. In M. Lewis & L. A. Rosenblum (Eds.), *The effect of the infant on its caregiver.* New York: Wiley.

Tronick, E., Als, H., & Adamson, L. (1979). Structure of early face-to-face communicative interactions. In M. Bullowa (Ed.), *Before speech: The beginning of interpersonal communication.* Cambridge, England: Cambridge University Press.

Upton, G. J. G. (1978). *The analysis of cross-tabulated data.* New York: Wiley.

Wolff, P. (1966). The causes, controls, and organization of the neonate. *Psychological Issues, 5* (Whole No. 17).

CHAPTER 16

Analysis of Sequential
Social Interaction Data:
Some Issues,
Recent Developments,
and a Causal
Inference Model

GENE P. SACKETT

A modest amount of work on analyzing sequential social interaction has appeared since the last edition of this volume. Among the topics addressed are analysis of categorical and continuous variables, observer reliability, dominance and bidirectionality in social relations, inferential statistics, and statistical modeling. Some of this effort deals directly or indirectly with two issues: (1) appropriate techniques for assessing the statistical significance of conditional probabilities measuring response contingency, and (2) the effects of serial dependence (autocorrelation) on significance tests and their interpretation. The major purpose of this chapter is to describe these issues, show in commonsense terms why they are important, and offer some suggestions for their resolution. Before undertaking this primary task, let us review a selected set of recent literature.

SOME RECENT LITERATURE

Time Series Analysis

Books by Gottman (1981) and Gregson (1983), written specifically for behavioral scientists, illustrate the theory and application of time series analysis (TSA) to behavioral research. Williams and Gottman (1982) also offered computer programs for implementing the methods in Gottman's book. TSA is used with continuous quantitative temporal measures, such as behavior intensity scales or heart rate, as opposed to the discrete categorical data typical of social interaction studies. Based

Work on this chapter was supported by grant RR00166 from the National Institutes of Health, Animal Resources Branch, to the Regional Primate Research Center at the University of Washington, and by a grant from the John D. and Catherine T. MacArthur Foundation.

on special analysis as employed in engineering, economics, and electrophysiology, TSA generates parameters measuring temporal characteristics of individual dependent variables (autocovariation) and temporal interdependence between two or more dependent variables (crosscovariation). Time series data intervals can vary over seconds, hours, months, or even years.

Possibly the most important TSA statistic for interaction studies is *coherence*. This measure quantifies the degree of covariation between two time series within the behaviors of a single individual or between behaviors of several individuals. Subsequent analysis of phase relations indicates whether one of the coherent time series leads or lags the other. This provides a basis for inferring *temporal causality*— the degree to which one temporal pattern depends on the prior occurrence of a triggering temporal pattern. An application by Lester, Hoffman, and Brazelton (1985) illustrates how TSA can measure the degree of "rhythm" within the behaviors of an infant and its mother and how their rhythms are coupled. TSA methods should be useful for interaction researchers that measure continuous quantities or can generate meaningful quantitative scales from categorical data (e.g., Maxim, 1985).

Observer Reliability

The *kappa* statistic (Fleiss, 1981, chap. 13) is established as the preferred way to measure within- and between-observer reliability with categorical data. This method also identifies the degree to which each category exhibits disagreement errors. Kappa is preferred over simple agreement percentages or product–moment correlations because it includes a correction for agreement by chance. Early work on kappa dealt with only two observers. Conger (1980) and Fleiss, Nee, and Landis (1979) extended the method for more than two observers or for retesting one observer on more than two occasions.

Another approach to observer reliability was detailed by Mitchell (1979), who assessed reliability in the context of repeated-measure analysis of variance (ANOVA). The generalizability of main effects and interactions over two or more observers is studied by including *observers* as an independent group factor in the ANOVA. Thus primary inferential analyses and observer reliability are studied at the same time. This technique seems useful only when each observer collects data under all conditions of a study. Given this situation, it should be an excellent method to combine with time series analyses, as agreement percentage statistics are not easily calculated with continuous temporal variables (e.g., Hollenbeck, 1978).

An important problem, investigated by Kaye (1980), concerns statistical models for estimating observer omission and commission error rates, rather than simply measuring overall agreement. This is especially important with sequential data. Accurately coding events that occur in a given instant, and not coding events that do not occur, are both essential for high-quality data sequences. Kaye suggested that estimates of these error sources might also be used to weight conditional probabilities, increasing the power of statistical tests. A need for such adjustment was made clear by Sutcliff (1980), and an alternative reliability modeling method was presented by Tanner and Young (1985). Although the validity of Kaye's statistical model was called into question by Kraemer (1982), good methods for isolating specific sources of unreliability in sequential analysis studies are clearly required. Development of a valid method for weighting proportions data by measurement and observer error could result in more efficient use of often expensive interaction research data.

Modeling Social Interaction

Interaction modeling has two interrelated purposes. The first is to characterize statistically types of linkage between responses of interactors. This is done by hypothesizing possible linkages, generating statistical parameters measuring these linkages, and testing to see which parameters, if any, best fit the actual interaction data. Statistically, the linkages represent different ways in which interaction processes can operate to restrict random covariation between behaviors. The typical model in almost all past research is that of no linkage, a null hypothesis that contingency probabilities will not differ from unconditional probabilities of the contingent behaviors. The second purpose is to interpret model parameters in terms of possible psychological processes that produce nonrandom statistical linkage. Some modeling methods are directed at both of these purposes, while others study only statistical linkages.

An example of discrete category modeling was provided by Thomas and Malone (1979), who presented models for studying the degree to which the behavior streams of two interactors are self-regulated, depend on prior contingencies, depend on enduring individual predispositions, or are temporarily conditioned by reinforcementlike processes. Psychologically, these models assess the extent to which interactors are sensitive to their own behavior, another person's behavior, and particular combinations of own–other behavior. Their Markovian approach analyzes data at the level of measurement and description of basic behavior categories. Most other models either require a transformation to continuous variables or use factors or latent variables extracted from the basic data to generate model parameters. However, like most other proposed discrete models, the Thomas and Malone approach is limited to two-person interaction. More restrictively, their models were developed for only two possible behavior states. Budescu (1985) developed a similar Markovian model and generalized it to data with many behavior states.

Several other approaches illustrate a broad range of alternatives available for modeling statistical and psychological properties of interaction systems. Gottman and Ringland (1981) detailed the use of spectral analysis to identify unidirectional and reciprocal relations among dyads of children and of mother–infant pairs. Their methods describe cyclicity within each individual's behavior and lagged synchrony in between-individual behavior. Accurate predictions of the degree and direction of synchrony, adjusted for cyclicity, are used to index the psychological qualities of dominance by one individual versus bidirectional influences.

Budescu (1984) presented an important descriptive and inferential approach to modeling the same psychological processes as Gottman and Ringland that does not require data transformations. This method uses a log-linear partition of time or event-lagged conditional probabilities to measure the degree of unidirectional or bidirectional, strong or weak, associations between the behaviors of a dyad. Although developed only for two-person, two-behavior situations, this technique and a related method called logistic regression (e.g., Breslow & Day, 1980; Fleiss, 1981) could be employed in many-person, many-category situations. Wampold and Margolin (1982) illustrated how *chi-square* and *runs test* statistics can also be used to study directionality in lagged categorical data with more than two persons and many categories. Their methods are based on straightforward probability assumptions and well-known nonparametric tests, and most interaction workers should be able to use them without requiring a new statistical education.

Several authors have presented parametric multivariate interaction models. Martin (1981) developed a structural equation, multiple regression model for application to longitudinal mother–offspring data. Category data measuring social signaling are transformed into behavior intensity scales for each dyad member. Equations are generated with parameters measuring various aspects of within- and between-scale temporal relations. These parameters are interpreted as measures of psychological processes such as noninvolvement, responsiveness, tolerance for mismatching behavior by the partner, perseveration, demandingness, and insistence. Martin used a correlation analysis to study consistency of these attributes over time, and multiple regression to determine whether earlier measures predict late behavior styles and traits of the dyad members. Importantly, he showed a way to compare different groups of subjects (e.g., by gender) for stability and predictability over long periods of development. A similar method, using latent structure and path analysis, was developed by Dillon, Madden, and Kumar (1983). Altough complex, their method does not require a data transformation from discrete to continuous variables and can be applied with multiple categories and subjects.

Statistical Analysis

The work previously described is concerned with statistical inference as well as modeling interaction processes. Other articles address statistical inference problems directly. The main issues concern appropriateness of various inferential statistics for different types of data, sampling, and hypotheses, and the analysis of nonindependent proportions due to correlated unconditional probabilities or serial (auto) correlation within categories.

A very accessible book by Fleiss (1981) presents the statistical theory underlying potential interaction data inference methods involving modern techniques for analyzing rates and proportions. Fleiss developed the important concept of *odds ratios* and their logarithm, the *logit* statistic. These provide a way of comparing proportions analogous to the effect size estimates of statistical power analysis (e.g., Cohen, 1969). When used with linear regression methods (e.g., Baker & Nelder, 1978), the logit statistic provides a powerful method for studying main effects and interactions among temporal, continuous, and "dummy coded" categorical independent variables when binomial probabilities are dependent variables. Budescu's (1984) modeling method illustrates a fairly simple application of logistic analysis, and Allison and Liker (1982) applied the technique for studying group differences in lagged probabilities and autocorrelation. Further theoretical work on logistic regression may yield a general data-analytic strategy solving many social interaction inferential and modeling problems.

Proper analysis of correlated proportions, a continuing issue in psychological statistics, is also a major problem in interaction data. Gardner, Hartmann, and Mitchell (1982) illustrated the basic problem using computer simulation data to show how serial dependence can bias contingency table analyses of dyadic interaction. Zwick, Neuhoff, Marascuilo, and Levin (1982) and Serlin, Carr, and Marascuilo (1982) described some general issues and presented methods for studying categorical and rank order correlated data. Of special pertinence to interaction research, Strube

(1985) showed a way to compare and combine significance tests across studies, taking account of the correlation between one or more variables. This technique can be used to compare correlated proportions within a study, exactly the problem in many interaction analyses. A different approach to handling correlations among behavior category summary measures was presented by Mendoza and Graziano (1982), who used multivariate analysis of variance (MANOVA), testing for overall group differences in total variance of all categories before applying univariate ANOVA to individual categories. This approach addresses important alpha error issues, multiple significance tests, and individual significance tests on many highly correlated dependent variables—problems found in most interaction studies.

SOME BASIC SEQUENTIAL ANALYSIS CONCEPTS

The ideas in the rest of this chapter are developed in the context of lag sequential analysis (Sackett, 1979), a method for describing how well past events predict future events using discrete category data. This nonparametric technique, analogous to time series analysis, studies both short and long repetition and cyclicity in temporal connections within and between events. Statistically, lag analysis shares its counting method and many data analysis problems with other contingency analysis procedures, so the content here should have wider implications.

The issues addressed will be illustrated using a mother–infant communication code employed by Vietze, Abernathy, Ashe, and Faulstich (1978) to study normal and developmentally delayed infants. Table 16.1 shows their original infant and mother behaviors and unconditional probabilities estimated from normal dyads. For analysis they collapsed the original codes into the smaller set also shown in the table. Analysis focused on vocal interaction, so all behaviors containing vocalization were pooled into a VOC category. Gazing at the partner was prioritized by pooling behaviors that included looking, but not vocalizing or crying, in the LOOK category. With inclusion of a no-signal category (NONE), this system generates the mutually exclusive and exhaustive partition of possible events necessary for a valid sequential analysis. However, the collapsed code unconditional probabilities are "true" measures of total occurrence only for the VOC and NONE categories. Neither the original nor the collapsed category is exactly the same for the dyad partners, and there are more infant than mother behaviors in the collapsed data. Both conditions are acceptable for a valid sequential analysis.

Real-Time Sequences

Table 16.2 presents hypothetical 20-sec sequences for these behaviors. The left side shows second-by-second data in which a behavior can follow itself in the sequence. This will be used to illustrate some basic concepts.

An *unconditional probability (UCP)* is the frequency of a code divided by the total number of codes in the series. For example, infant NONE occurs eight times in the 20 intervals, so its UCP is $8/20 = .4$. The mother NONE UCP is $4/20 = .2$. The UCP measures the chances of observing a behavior at any randomly selected second.

A *lag probability* measures temporal co-occurrence of behavior pairs within or between interactor sequences. A *criterion* behavior is selected, and counts are made for the number of times the criterion is *matched* by itself (autolag) or by other

TABLE 16.1. Infant and Mother Signaling Behaviors: Original and Collapsed Categories and Their Unconditional Probabilities

	Infant				Mother		
Original Category	Probability	Collapsed Category	Probability	Original Category	Probability	Collapsed Category	Probability
Vocal (V)	.05	I1 = VOC	.19	Vocal (V)	.05	M1 = VOC	.45
Look (L)	.10	I2 = LOOK	.15	Look (L)	.15	M2 = LOOK	.20
Smile (S)	.05	I3 = SMILE	.05	Touch-Play (TP)	.05	M3 = TOUCH-PLAY	.15
Cry (C)	.10	I4 = CRY	.15	L+S (L)	.05	M4 = NONE	.20
L+S (L)	.05	I5 = NONE	.46	V+L (V)	.10		
V+L (V)	.05			V+L+S (V)	.10		
V+L+S (V)	.03			V+TP (V)	.15		
V+S (V)	.06			L+S+TP (TP)	.10		
C+L (C)	.05			V+L+S+TP (V)	.05		
NoSig (N)	.46			NoInfBeh (N)	.20		

Note: Collapsed categories were formed by pooling original categories with those having the same letter code.

TABLE 16.2.   20-Sec Sequential Sample of Infant and Mother Behaviors When a Behavior Can (time) and Cannot (event) Follow Itself

Time or Event	Time Sequence		Event Sequences			
			Infant Triggered		Mother Triggered	
	Infant	Mother	Infant	Mother	Infant	Mother
1	V	N	V	N	V	N
2	N	L	N	L-V	N	L
3	N	V	L	N	N	V
4	N	V	C	TP	L	N
5	L	N	L	V	C	TP
6	C	TP	V	TP	L	V
7	L	V	S	L	V	TP
8	V	TP	N	V	S	L
9	S	L	C	V	N-C	V
10	N	V	V	L	V-N	L
11	N	V	N	L-V-N	N	V
12	C	V	V	V	N	N
13	V	L	C	N	V	V
14	N	L	L	V	C	N
15	N	V	V	TP	L	V
16	N	N			V	TP
17	V	V				
18	C	N				
19	L	V				
20	V	TP				

behaviors (crosslag) at various steps from each criterion occurrence. Infant NONE (N) will be used to illustrate the process. N occurs eight times (intervals 2-4, 10-11, 14-16). N matches itself in the next interval (lag 1) five times ($2\rightarrow3$, $3\rightarrow4$, $10\rightarrow11$, $14\rightarrow15$, $15\rightarrow16$), yielding an autolag 1 probability of $5/8 = .625$. Two steps from each occurrence (lag 2) N matches itself twice ($2\rightarrow4$, $14\rightarrow16$; autolag 2 probability $= 2/8 = .25$). Further lags are counted in the same way up to a maximum lag of interest.

Crosslags can be counted either within the infant series or between the infant and mother series. For example, infant LOOK matches infant NONE once at lag 1 (interval $4\rightarrow5$) and once at lag 2 ($3\rightarrow5$), so both probabilities are $1/8 = .125$. Within the infant series, simultaneous matching cannot occur owing to the mutual exclusion code requirement of sequential data. However, simultaneity (lag 0) can occur between independently generated sequences. Thus infant N is matched by mother N once at lag 0 (interval 16; $p = 1/8 = .125$), twice at lag 1 ($4\rightarrow5$, $15\rightarrow16$; $p = 2/8 = .25$), and three times ($3\rightarrow5$, $14\rightarrow16$, $16\rightarrow18$; $p = 3/8 = .375$) at lag 2. As with autolags, crosslag matching can be carried out to any maximum lag desired, given a sufficiently long data sequence. Criteria for selecting a maximum lag and alternative techniques for initiating (triggering) lag counts from behavior onsets or offsets are detailed elsewhere (Sackett, 1979, 1980).

Generating lag 0 and lag 1 conditional probabilities is identical in all contingency analysis methods. Until recently, such lag 0 and 1 data have been the basis for most interaction studies. Lag analysis differs from its Markovian alternative (e.g., Gottman & Notarius, 1977) in that the former studies contingencies at each lag independent of prior lags, while the latter studies exact patterns over a chain of 2-N sequential events. Thus a lag analysis deals with many fewer probabilities than a Markov analysis, but can describe most of the same relations and more easily detects repetition and cyclicity over many lags.

The fundamental basis for statistical inferences concerning individual conditional probabilities is the same for all contingency analysis methods. A random model, based on UCPs, is assumed to describe the conditional relations. In lag analysis, this null model predicts that a given behavior will match the criterion at any lag in proportion to the matching behavior UCP. A simple one-step Markov analysis assumes that all behavior pairs will match at lag 1 in proportion to the product of their UCPs (the multiplicative probability rule). These random conditional probabilities should then predict higher-order sequences involving chains of three, four, or more behaviors if only random linkages chain the events. Each of these null models assumes that the method of sampling behavior (e.g., real time, discrete event, modified frequency intervals) does not itself restrict the operation of chance.

Event Sequences

A source of confusion for some interaction researchers concerns generation and analysis of sequences of events irrespective of event durations. Some workers believe that lag analysis is not applicable to this data type nor to data with meaningful lag 0 contingency. However, event sequences can be studied by lag methods, and their analysis poses the same problems for all contingency analysis techniques.

The right side of Table 16.2 shows several event series derived from behavior change points in the real-time data on the left. For example, the first infant-triggered event, V, is followed by a single event N derived from the three N's at intervals 2, 3, 4 in real time. The three N's represent a single behavior change. The infant event series contains only 15 data points, which represents its behavior changes during the 20-sec sample.

Two event series are required, one for the infant and one for the mother. This occurs because infant and mother behavior changes do not always happen in the same time interval, and the two series do not contain the same number of total behavior changes. Note that in the "trigger" event series a behavior cannot follow itself, as occurrence of a new behavior is exactly what defines a behavior change.

Confusion arises in aligning the behaviors of the nontrigger individual, as more than one behavior can co-occur with a single event in the triggering sequence. Examples are mother LOOK then VOC co-occurring with the second NONE infant-triggered event, and infant NONE then CRY co-occurring with VOC at the ninth mother-triggered event. This situation presents several problems. First, there usually are more events in nontrigger than in trigger sequences. This is not a problem concerning unconditional probabilities, which can be calculated from overall frequencies in the usual way, with the usual meaning regarding random occurrence. However, generating lag probabilities between the two series is a problem.

In the infant-triggered series, mother LOOK→VOC at event 2 is simultaneous with infant NONE, yet represents a real sequence of two events in the mother series. Actually, mother LOOK is simultaneous with infant NONE onset, while mother VOC occurs at mother lag 1 from infant NONE onset. For event analysis purposes, the mother event series is preserved by considering LOOK the second, VOC the third, and NONE (occurring with event 3 in the infant series) the fourth maternal event. Similarly, the maternal L→V→N sequence at infant event 11 should be considered events 12, 13, and 14 in the mother series. When lagged against infant NONE, mother LOOK at event 2 is at lag 0 (simultaneous), VOC is at lag 1, and maternal NONE is at lag 2. Likewise, lagging from infant NONE at event 11, mother LOOK gets a lag 0 count, VOC is at lag 1, NONE at lag 2, and VOC at lag 3. With this counting method, the maternal event series UCP null method for random matching of infant events is valid.

Alternatively, each of the co-occurring nontrigger series behaviors could be given a lag 0 count for matching criterion events. However, this inflates the number of behaviors occurring at lag 0, relative to the number that can possibly occur at lags greater than 0. It also distorts the real event sequential flow of behavior. Further, the unconditional probabilities of each nontrigger series behavior will not provide a random distribution model when co-occurrences are unequally distributed among the trigger series categories. Co-occurrence probabilities would have to be considered along with UCPs to define a chance model. Although a more complex null model could be defined, the previously described counting method, which preserves the true event sequence, seems preferable.

BIASES IN THE OPERATION OF CHANCE

A number of factors can restrict the operation of chance so that a simple UCP null model may not be valid for testing some contingencies. Autocorrelation and sampling method bias are prominent sources of such restriction. Example data in Table 16.3, using the infant behaviors and UCPs from Table 16.1, illustrate these problems. The second section presents an eight-lag analysis with infant NONE as criterion and each infant category as match. The analysis will be detailed for lag 1, under the assumption that each behavior can follow itself (time sequence).

Data were collected for a total of 600 sec. The criterion, infant NONE (I5), occurs for 276 sec. (UCP = .46). At lag 1, I5 follows itself (autocorrelation) 221 times, yielding an observed matching probability of 221/276 = .801. The other four behaviors have matching frequencies of 19, 15, 5, and 16. When divided by 276, the total N of the criterion available to be matched, the observed crosslag probabilities for following I5 at lag 1 are .069, .054, .018, and .058. An index of discrepancy between the observed matching probability (OP) and the UCP chance probability (EP, top section of the table) is calculated from the normal distribution approximation to the exact binomial probability (e.g., Siegel, 1956, pp. 40–41). These values are given in the third line for each lag. The fourth line will be discussed later. With the autolag 1 contingency as an example,

$$Z_{BI} = OP - EP / \sqrt{(EP * (1 - EP)) / N} \text{ CRIT}$$

$$= .801 - .46 / \sqrt{(.46 * .54)/276} = 11.33$$

Using a rounded value for two-tailed .05 level significance of $Z = 2.00$, the lag 1 results show that I5 follows itself (is excited above its expected value), while the other four behaviors are inhibited (below their expected values).

TABLE 16.3.   Lag Sequential Analysis for Infant Behaviors with I5 = No Signal as the Criterion

	I1 = VOC	I2 = LOOK	I3 = SMILE	I4 = CRY	I5 = NONE	TOT N
Freq	114	90	30	90	276	600
Unc Pr	.19	.15	.05	.15	.46	

2. No Autocorrelation Adjustment

Lag						N CRIT
1 Freq	19	15	5	16	221	276
Obs Pr	.069	.054	.018	.058	.801	
Z_{BI}	−5.12	−4.47	−2.44	−4.28	11.33	
Z_{HG}	−5.69	−4.84	−2.50	−4.64	15.42	
2 Freq	39	31	10	30	166	276
Obs Pr	.141	.112	.036	.109	.601	
Z_{BI}	−2.08	−1.77	−1.07	−1.91	4.70	
Z_{HG}	−2.31	−1.92	−1.10	−2.07	6.40	
3 Freq	78	61	20	62	55	276
Obs Pr	.283	.221	.072	.225	.199	
Z_{BI}	3.94	3.30	1.68	3.49	−8.70	
Z_{HG}	4.38	3.58	1.72	3.78	−11.84	
4 Freq	58	46	15	46	110	275
Obs Pr	.211	.167	.055	.167	.400	
Z_{BI}	0.89	0.79	0.38	0.79	−2.00	
Z_{HG}	0.99	0.86	0.39	0.86	−2.72	
5 Freq	39	31	10	30	164	274
Obs Pr	.142	.113	.036	.109	.599	
Z_{BI}	−2.02	−1.72	−1.06	−1.90	4.62	
Z_{HG}	−2.25	−1.86	−1.09	−2.06	6.28	
6 Freq	24	19	7	22	201	273
Obs Pr	.088	.070	.026	.081	.736	
Z_{BI}	−4.30	−3.70	−1.82	−3.19	9.15	
Z_{HG}	−4.78	−4.02	−1.87	−3.46	12.45	
7 Freq	44	36	12	31	150	273
Obs Pr	.161	.132	.044	.114	.549	
Z_{BI}	−1.22	−0.83	−0.46	−1.67	2.95	
Z_{HG}	−1.36	−0.90	−0.47	−1.81	4.02	
8 Freq	68	53	18	53	80	272
Obs Pr	.250	.195	.066	.195	.294	
Z_{BI}	2.25	2.08	1.21	2.08	−5.49	
Z_{HG}	2.80	2.25	1.24	2.25	−7.48	

3. Adjustment for Autocorrelation

Lag						TOT N_A
N_A	114	90	30	90	—	324
Unc Pr_A	.352	.278	.093	.278	—	
						N CRIT$_A$
1 Obs Pr	.345	.273	.091	.291	—	55
2 Obs Pr	.355	.282	.091	.273	—	110
3 Obs Pr	.353	.276	.090	.281	—	221

4. Lag 1 Data for Criterion Cannot Follow Itself

						N CRIT
Freq	97	77	26	76	—	276
Obs Pr	.357	.279	.094	.275	—	

Note: Section 2—criterion can follow itself, no adjustment for autocorrelation; section 3—adjustments for autocorrelation; section 4—criterion cannot follow itself, lag 1 adjusted. N CRIT = frequency of criterion for lagged statistics; Z_{BI} = estimated binomial probability; Z_{HG} = hypergeometric probability.

Autocorrelation Bias

Figure 16.1 plots infant NONE autocorrelation over the eight lags. Also shown is the expected UCP and its 95 percent confidence band, where

$$CI_{95} = \pm 1.96 * SD \text{ and}$$

$$SD = \sqrt{(EP * (1 - EP)) / N \text{ CRIT}}$$

This autolag function shows pronounced cyclicity. NONE follows itself well above chance at lags 1 and 6, and well below chance at lags 3 and 8. This pattern indicates that a repetitive, probably self-generated, process underlies infant NONE occurrence. The pattern can also be used to illustrate why criterion behavior autocorrelation biases the UCP null model by constraining or expanding the range of opportunity for crosslag occurrence.

NONE occurs with a probability of .801 at lag 1. This is an *excess* of .341 probability units relative to the NONE chance UCP of .46. Therefore, at lag 1, probabilities of the other four infant behaviors cannot reach their composite UCP by .341—the amount of autolag excess. NONE occurs at lag 3 with a probability of .199, a .261 probability unit *deficit* with respect to the .46 UCP. Therefore, at lag 3 there is .261 more opportunity for the other four behaviors to occur than specified by their composite UCP of .54. If crosslag probabilities *within* an individual's repertoire are a major focus of interest, then the following principle holds:

> With criterion autocorrelation above its expected value, one or more other behaviors *cannot* reach their expected values. With criterion autocorrelation below expectation, one or more other behaviors *must* exceed their expected values.

Potential consequences of criterion behavior autocorrelation for interpreting crosslags *between* two sequences will be discussed later.

Adjusting Crosslags for Autolag Bias

The third section of Table 16.3 illustrates a method of correcting autocorrelation bias by modifying the crosslag null model. This method should be applicable with any categorical analysis technique.

1. The overall frequency (N_A) of each crosslag behavior is divided by a new TOT N, the original total frequency minus the overall criterion frequency. Here, the new TOT N is $600 - 276 = 324$. This yields an adjusted set of UCPs (Unc Pr$_A$) based on the total frequency of matching behaviors *independent of* criterion frequency. For example, the infant VOC (I1) UCP changes from unadjusted $114/600 = .19$ to adjusted $114/324 = .352$.

2. The number of criterion occurrences at each lag (N CRIT) is adjusted to reflect only those actually available for matching with the nonautocorrelated behaviors. This is done by subtracting the criterion frequency at a given lag from the original N CRIT. For example, I5 itself occurs 221 times at lag 1. The adjusted N CRIT is then $276 - 221 = 55$.

3. New crosslag probabilities are calculated by dividing the matching frequencies at a given lag by the adjusted N CRIT. For example, the 19 infant VOC lag 1

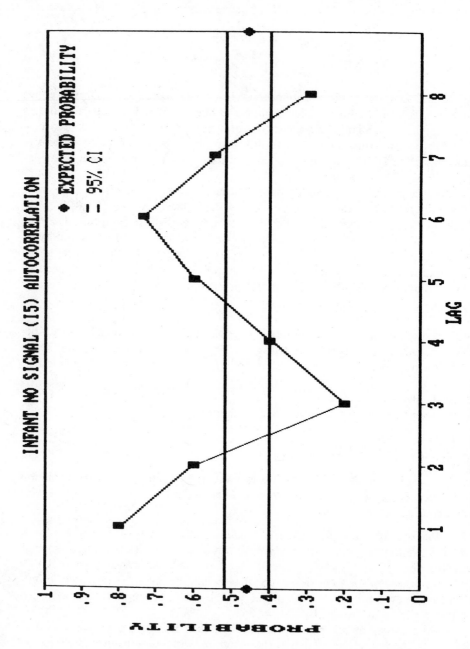

Figure 16.1. Eight-lag autocorrelation function for Infant NONE behavior.

occurrences are divided by 55. This yields an observed probability of .345 rather than the .069 value without adjustment.

The consequences of adjustment are seen by comparing the nonadjusted (section 2) with the adjusted (section 3) lag 1 probabilities and their discrepancies from what is expected. In the unadjusted data, all four matches are well below their UCP expected values. In the adjusted data, all four matches are practically identical to their Unc Pr_A expected values. Thus when corrected for autocorrelation, all of the matching behaviors fit the null chance model. In fact, this is true at each of the eight lags because these data were constructed to reflect no contingency except I5 autocorrelation.

If there were real contingencies in infant behaviors following I5, over and above I5 autocorrelation bias, they would be detected in the adjusted data. However, adjusted tests are always less statistically powerful owing to the reduced N CRIT and consequent increase in Z score standard deviations. But this seems reasonable and intuitively proper, as strong autocorrelation patterns do in fact nonrandomly determine the degree to which other behaviors can occur.

The lesson in this analysis is that autocorrelation must be assessed as a preliminary step in any categorical data sequential analysis. The autolag functions can themselves yield interesting and important substantive information (e.g., Sackett, 1980). This information is lost in studies that analyze only lag 1 relationships. More important, the results and interpretations of such studies are suspect, as what seem to be real contingencies (e.g., lag 1 in the second section of Table 16.3) may be artifacts of autocorrelation.

Sampling Method Bias

The most common sampling method bias involves constraint on the probability of the criterion behavior following itself. All event sequence data have this characteristic. Time sequence data also have this property. The last instance of a consecutive run of a behavior cannot be followed by that behavior. However, the usually large TOT N in a time sequence typically makes bias small. The data in Table 16.3 illustrate the basic problem and its solution.

Suppose that an event sequence had been used to generate the data in Table 16.3. At lag 1, the 221 instances of I5 could not occur, and so must be distributed among the other four behaviors. The bottom section of the table presents one possible distribution of the 276 I5 lag 1 matches and corresponding observed probabilities. If we tested these lag probabilities against the UCPs in the top section, each would generate a Z score *above* 2.00. But this is a logical impossibility. If one behavior in a mutually exclusive, exhaustive set is above its expected value, at least one other must be below its expectation. This shows that the simple UCP null model must be wrong.

The solution is essentially the same as autolag adjustment. Since the criterion cannot occur at lag 1, its UCP must be removed from the null model. This is done by the step 1 procedure listed for autolags; calculate a new TOT N by subtracting the criterion frequency from the original TOT N. This yields nothing more than the sum of the frequencies of the matching behaviors that can occur at lag 1. New UCPs are calculated by dividing each overall matching behavior frequency by the new TOT N. Here, these are exactly the ones shown in the third section of the table. When one compares these Unc Pr_A values with the observed probabilities in the bottom section, one sees that there is almost no difference from the adjusted expected values rather than four above-chance probabilities.

Failure to adjust the null model for sampling method bias results in incorrect conclusions in all contingency analysis methods. Thus interaction data analysts must examine their sampling techniques for biases that can invalidate their null models. This topic needs more study to identify biases in particular sampling methods other than the obvious bias discussed here.

STATISTICAL INFERENCE

Allison and Liker (1982) raised an important issue concerning the use of Z scores for indexing significant contingency in categorical data. They rightly argued that the binomial Z statistic, as defined above and used in many published studies, requires the assumption that criterion behavior probabilities are asymptotic population values not subject to sampling variation. Clearly, with respect to a given subject or dyad, this assumption is untenable unless a very large behavior sample is taken. Their solution is to use the 2-$\times$-2 chi-square hypergeometric distribution for making inferences, as this takes account of sampling variability in both the criterion and matching behavior. Table 16.4 illustrates the procedure using the autolag 1, 2, and 3 data from Table 16.3.

TABLE 16.4.   Chi-Square (Hypergeometric) Tests for Autocorrelation of the Infant NONE data in Table 16.3

		Contingency Table of Lagged Frequencies			$\chi^2_{(1)}$	$\sqrt{\chi^2_{(1)}} = Z_{HG}$
		Lag 0				
		NONE	notNONE	Total		
Lag 1	NONE	221	55	276	238.08	15.43
	notNONE	55	268	323		
	Total	276	323	599		
Lag 2	NONE	166	110	276	40.37	6.35
	notNONE	110	212	322		
	Total	276	322	598		
Lag 3	NONE	55	221	276	142.87	-11.95^a
	notNONE	221	100	321		
	Total	276	321	597		

[a] A negative sign is used when the upper left cell column proportion is smaller than that for the upper right.

Matching frequency data are cast in a 2- × -2 table, with lag 0 (triggering criterion event) as one dimension and any other lag as the second dimension. Here the cells contain the number of times that the criterion behavior NONE is matched or not matched (column 1), and that all other noncriterion behaviors notNONE are matched or not matched at a given lag (column 2). For example, at lag 1 in the upper table, NONE is matched by NONE 221 times and by notNONE 55 times. The notNONE trigger is matched by NONE 55 times and by notNONE 268 times. This all yields a highly significant chi-square with 1 degree of freedom. Note that the total N for this table is 599, not 600. This occurs because the six hundredth event is the end of the data, and cannot be followed at lag 1 (see Sackett, 1979, for more about this). Similarly, lags 2 and 3 can have total frequencies of only 598 and 597 because of "falling off at the end."

With 1 degree of freedom, the square root of the hypergeometric chi-square is exactly equal to Z, the normal distribution statistic. This value is labeled Z_{HG}. At lag 1, Z_{HG} is 15.43. Comparing this value with that of Z_{BI} for NONE at lag 1 in Table 16.3, one can see that the binomial Z is smaller and its square is not equal to the chi-square value for lag 1. A simple transformation of Z_{BI} to account for criterion sampling variability equates the two Z scores (see Allison & Liker, 1982, for more details). The procedure is to divide Z_{BI} by the square root of 1 minus the criterion UCP. In this case,

$$Z_{HG} = Z_{BI} / \sqrt{1 - \text{UCP}_{NONE}}$$
$$= 11.33 / \sqrt{1 - .46} = 15.415$$

This is the same value as that found in the chi-square analysis except for a slight difference owing to different total N's.

One can see the consequences of using Z_{HG} by comparing it with Z_{BI} in Table 16.3. Z_{HG} is always larger, it is proportionately larger for behaviors with higher UCPs, and it suggests significance more often. In effect, Z_{HG} is not a conservative inferential index. Given the biases on randomness, alpha error problems involving many tests on the same data set, and nonindependence of unconditional probabilities found in most sets of observational data, it would seem that the more conservative Z_{BI} index is preferable over Z_{HG}. This is especially true for studies that do not have specific a priori hypotheses about the sequential structure of their data. However, if Z values will be used for subsequent tests of within-group homogeneity or between-group differences (e.g., Sackett, 1980), and the individuals in the study differ markedly in criterion probability or total N, the Z_{HG} values might yield more valid tests because of their criterion variance sensitivity.

DIRECTIONALITY OF CONTINGENT RELATIONSHIPS

In the example data the temporal distribution of infant behavior was constrained only by infant nonsignaling autocorrelation. However, the major purpose of a study such as this is usually to see how mother and infant behaviors covary. Table 16.5 presents possible data for maternal contingency on the most frequent infant behavior, no signaling. Lag 0 simultaneous matching and crosslags 1, 2, and 3 are analyzed using the Z_{BI} statistic calculated with maternal behavior UCPs as the null

TABLE 16.5.   Lag Relationships of Mother Behaviors with Infant NONE (I5) as Criterion

Lag	M1 = VOC	M2 = LOOK	M3 = TP	M4 = NONE	N CRIT
Unc Pr	.45	.20	.15	.20	
0 Freq	57	110	83	26	276
Obs Pr	.207	.399	.301	.094	
Z_{BI}	−8.12	8.26	7.02	−4.40	
1 Freq	179	59	28	10	276
Obs Pr	.649	.214	.101	.036	
Z_{BI}	6.64	0.58	−2.28	−6.81	
2 Freq	152	40	69	15	276
Obs Pr	.551	.145	.250	.054	
Z_{BI}	3.37	−2.28	4.65	−6.06	
3 Freq	120	83	70	3	276
Obs Pr	.435	.301	.254	.011	
Z_{BI}	−0.50	4.20	4.84	−7.85	

model. A different visual display of the results is shown in Figure 16.2, which also plots the $Z = \pm 2.00$ critical range for comparison.

The most probable maternal behaviors occurring simultaneously (lag 0) with infant NONE are LOOK and TOUCH-PLAY, with mother VOC markedly inhibited. No signal (NONE) by the mother is inhibited over the total lag range. At lag 1, only mother VOC occurs at an excited level. At lag 3, both mother VOC and TOUCH-PLAY are excited, while at lag 4, LOOK and TOUCH-PLAY are excited. This pattern suggests that (1) maternal signaling is elicited by infant failure to signal, as such failure *inhibits* mother nonsignaling; (2) infant nonsignaling elicits subsequent maternal vocalization and inhibits looking; and (3) the mother rarely vocalizes while the infant is not signaling. Strong temporal patterning of all maternal behaviors contingent on infant failure to signal is evidenced by the fact that 14 of the 16 Z values are outside the ± 2.00 range. Thus an infant's failure to signal has a strong *unidirectional* effect on the temporal structure of the mother's whole repertoire.

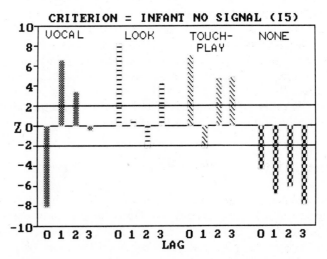

Figure 16.2. Lag contingencies for all maternal behaviors matched against Infant NONE behavior as criterion.

TABLE 16.6. Lag Relationships of Infant Behaviors with Mother VOC (M1) as Criterion

Lag	I1 = VOC	I2 = LOOK	I3 = SMILE	I4 = CRY	I5 = NONE	TOT CRIT
Unc Pr	.19	.15	.05	.15	.46	
0 Freq	75	59	20	59	57	270
Obs Pr	.278	.219	.074	.219	.211	
Z_{BI}	3.69	3.18	1.81	3.18	−8.21	
1 Freq	56	44	14	47	108	269
Obs Pr	.208	.164	.052	.175	.401	
Z_{BI}	0.75	0.69	0.15	1.15	−1.94	
2 Freq	38	30	10	30	160	268
Obs Pr	.142	.112	.037	.112	.597	
Z_{BI}	−2.01	−1.74	−0.98	−1.74	4.50	
3 Freq	23	19	6	19	201	268
Obs Pr	.086	.071	.022	.071	.750	
Z_{BI}	−4.34	−3.62	−2.10	−3.62	9.53	

To assess bidirectional effects, one must measure infant contingencies on maternal behavior. Table 16.6 presents vocalization, the most frequent maternal behavior, as criterion lagged with each infant behavior. Z values for lags 0–3 are plotted in Figure 16.3, where a striking pattern of infant behaviors contingent on maternal VOC is seen. Infant NONE (left curve) is markedly inhibited at lag 0 and rises well above expectation by lag 3. The other four infant behaviors exhibit the opposite pattern, initially above chance and dropping linearly below chance by lag 3. Were this our sole information, we would conclude that infant signaling is inhibited by maternal vocalization. However, from the analysis of infant behaviors in Table 16.3 and Figure 16.1, we know that infant NONE autocorrelation produces just the pattern shown in Figure 16.3. When infant NONE is low, the other infant behaviors must *exceed* their expected values, and when NONE is high, the other behaviors must be *depressed*.

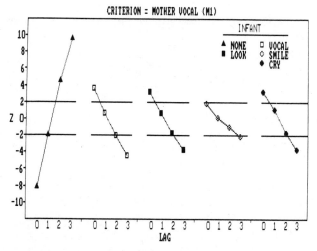

Figure 16.3. Lag contingencies for all infant behaviors lagged against Mother VOC behavior as the criterion.

A hypothesis concerning the process generating these dyadic behaviors is suggested when comparing Figures 16.2 and 16.3. Maternal vocalization is inhibited by infant NONE. Infant NONE is cyclically autocorrelated. Maternal behavior is locked onto this autocorrelation but infant behavior is unaffected by that of the mother.

An Overall Inferential Lag Test

The hypothesis of infant indifference to maternal vocalization can be tested more directly with a chi-square test procedure than with the Z tests. A chi-square procedure can provide an overall test for contingency analogous to using ANOVA before performing individual comparison tests. Such an overall test should be done before performing individual Z tests. A chi-square procedure also solves the variance issue raised by Allison and Liker (1982), providing a better inferential solution than the one they proposed.

Table 16.7 recasts the data of Table 16.6 into 2-×-5 chi-square tables. Occurrence of the mother VOC (M1) criterion versus any other maternal behavior (notM1) is the column variable. The five infant behaviors form the row variables. Table cells contain frequency of infant behavior matches under these two maternal trigger conditions. A separate table is formed for each lag. Each table measures differences in the infant's behavior profile depending on whether the criterion did or did not occur at a prior lag. The results show large significant chi-square values at all lags except lag 1.

These four chi-squares assess the significance of differences between infant behaviors *at each lag* shown in Figure 16.3. At lag 1, four of these five Z values are inside the critical range while one (NONE) is at -2.00. Thus it is not surprising that the overall chi-square test for lag 1 is not significant, even though one of the five behaviors seems to differ from chance at the .05 level.

Like the analysis based on individual Z values (Table 16.6), these chi-square tests suggest that infant behavior is contingent on maternal vocalization. In fact, the profile probabilities in Table 16.7 are exactly those plotted in Figure 16.3, which

TABLE 16.7.   Overall Chi-Square Tests for Significance of Infant Behaviors Lagged Against Mother VOC (M1) as Criterion

		Lag 0		Lag 1		Lag 2		Lag 3	
		M1	notM1	M1	notM1	M1	notM1	M1	notM1
I1 = VOC	Freq	75	39	56	58	37	76	23	91
	Obs Pr	.287	.118	.208	.176	.138	.230	.086	.277
I2 = LOOK	Freq	59	31	44	46	29	60	19	71
	Obs Pr	.219	.094	.164	.139	.108	.261	.071	.216
I3 = SMILE	Freq	20	10	14	16	16	20	6	24
	Obs Pr	.074	.030	.052	.048	.037	.061	.022	.073
I4 = CRY	Freq	59	31	47	43	30	60	19	71
	Obs Pr	.219	.094	.175	.130	.112	.261	.071	.216
I5 = NONE	Freq	57	219	108	167	156	114	201	72
	Obs PR	.211	.664	.401	.506	.582	.345	.750	.219
	Total	270	330	269	330	268	330	268	329
$\chi^2_{(4)}$		122.44		6.91		37.70		167.93	
p		$< .001$		0.15		$< .001$		$< .001$	

suggests an explanation based on infant NONE autocorrelation. To test the hypothesis of no contingencies between infant behavior and maternal vocalization other than that produced by NONE autocorrelation, one can recalculate chi-square values dropping infant NONE from the analysis. The logic of doing this is identical to that for the autocorrelation adjustments applied to within-infant behavior in Table 16.3.

The frequencies in Table 16.8 are identical to those in Table 16.7 except that the column totals are reduced by the frequency of the deleted autocorrelated infant NONE. Consequently, the profile probabilities are changed. Note that now none of the chi-squares even approach significance, and the probabilities across rows are almost identical at each lag. Clearly, after eliminating variation due to NONE autocorrelation—and therefore bias in the chi-square null model due to spurious excesses and deficits in the other infant behaviors—only random infant contingencies remain.

Detailing possible applications of this chi-square approach is beyond the scope of this chapter. Some of the possibilities are described by Budescu (1984) and by Wampold (1984). However, several strengths of the method should be mentioned:

1.   The overall chi-square test guards against type I statistical error.
2.   The method allows testing for contingencies produced by any or all of the behaviors. In developmental research, different dyads may accomplish the same interactive ends using entirely different behaviors. Focusing on a particular pair of behaviors, as is often done in interaction studies, may thus completely miss real linkages.
3.   The chi-square values measure the degree to which one individual's total behavior profile is nonrandomly linked to partner behavior. Under appropriate sample size and distribution conditions, these values can be used to compare different dyads and test groups, and to assess developmental changes. This can be done even if individual dyads are contingent on different behaviors or the behavior categories are not the same at different times of measurement.
4.   The contingency table null models are easily modified to test for effects such as autocorrelation or more complex linkages. This is done by dropping a known contingency source from the data and determining whether there are still any con-

TABLE 16.8.   Chi-Square Tests of Infant Behaviors Lagged Against Mother VOC (M1) as Criterion with the Autocorrelated Effects of Infant NONE removed

		Lag 0		Lag 1		Lag 2		Lag 3	
		M1	notM1	M1	notM1	M1	notM1	M1	notM1
I1 = VOC	Freq	75	39	56	58	37	76	23	91
	Obs Pr	.352	.351	.348	.356	.330	.352	.343	.354
I2 = LOOK	Freq	59	31	44	46	29	60	19	71
	Obs Pr	.277	.279	.273	.282	.256	.278	.284	.276
I3 = SMILE	Freq	20	10	14	16	16	20	6	24
	Obs Pr	.094	.090	.087	.098	.143	.093	.090	.093
I4 = CRY	Freq	59	31	47	43	30	60	19	71
	Obs Pr	.277	.279	.292	.264	.268	.278	.284	.276
	Total	213	111	161	163	112	216	67	257
$\chi^2_{(3)}$		0.01		0.38		1.92		0.05	

tingencies left among the remaining behaviors. In a more complex fashion this is exactly the procedure in log linear and logistic regression models.

5.   Log linear or logistic regression models can be directly applied to these contingency tables (see first section of Chapter). This allows for study of a trend in the lag data, effect size and direction of individual contingencies, main effects and interactions of experimental or naturally occurring independent variables, and covariance adjustments involving quantitative variables. Further, even these more complex analyses proceed at the measurement and interpretation levels of the original categories rather than complex data transformations and higher-order, perhaps imaginary, factors and latent variables.

CAUSAL INFERENCES FROM CONTINGENCY ANALYSES

Contingency analyses are regarded as tests of association, not causality. Although weak causality might be inferred when event X is regularly preceded by event Y, it is clear that this relation could be caused by some other unmeasured event Z. For this reason, manipulative experiments are employed to control irrelevant factors while systematically varying linkages between independent variables and consequent responses. Causality, in the sense of identifying conditions that are at least *sufficient* to produce reliable behavioral variation, is often imputed when the experiment is successful and has achieved positive replications. In the context of interaction research, the following might constitute a manipulative experiment to identify such a causal relationship.

A common development research problem is determining the extent of bidirectional active engagement in social interaction by a mother and her infant. To study the influence of maternal behaviors on infant engagement *experimentally,* an investigator might "program" the mother to behave in different ways following a given infant behavior. For example, when an infant shows no social signaling, its mother could be scheduled to vocalize on half of the occasions and withhold vocalization on the other half. If the infant's subsequent behavior differs under the two conditions, it could be concluded that (1) the infant *pays attention* to what the mother does, and (2) different maternal behaviors cause (are a sufficient condition for) changes in infant behavior.

This exact experiment is embedded in natural sequences of mother–infant interaction. The sole difference is that the proportions of Mother VOC or Mother notVOC following Infant NONE are not controlled. However, given a sufficient sample of each, the same basic statistical tests and interpretive logic as in the controlled experiment would hold. The data in Table 16.8 present such an analysis. The right section is partitioned into two maternal sequences as trigger conditions: Mother VOC at lag 0 followed at lag 1 by either (1) infant NONE ($M1_0 \rightarrow I5_1$) or (2) Infant notNONE ($M1_0 \rightarrow notI5_1$). The rows correspond to all *maternal* behaviors at lag 2 that can follow these two trigger sequences. This table tests the hypothesis that the mother actually pays attention to the infant's behavior and modifies her behavior accordingly. The left section of Table 16.9 tests whether the infant pays attention to what the mother does. The two trigger conditions are Infant NONE at lag 0 followed at lag 1 by (1) Mother VOC ($I5_0 \rightarrow M1_1$) or (2) Mother notVOC ($I5_0 \rightarrow notM1_1$). The rows are all possible *infant* behaviors following the two maternal trigger conditions.

TABLE 16.9.   Mother Attention to Infant NONE (left) and Infant Attention to Mother VOC (right)[a]

	Mother Behavior at Lag 2			Infant Behavior at Lag 2	
	$M1_0 \rightarrow I5_1$	$M1_0 \rightarrow notI5_1$		$I5_0 \rightarrow M1_1$	$I5_0 \rightarrow notM1_1$
M1 = VOC	65 (.607)	46 (.286)	I1 = VOC	35 (.196)	18 (.186)
M2 = LOOK	27 (.252)	30 (.186)	I2 = LOOK	28 (.156)	14 (.144)
M3 = TP	8 (.075)	48 (.298)	I3 = SMILE	9 (.050)	5 (.052)
M4 = NONE	7 (.065)	37 (.230)	I4 = CRY	27 (.151)	14 (.144)
			I5 = NONE	80 (.447)	46 (.474)
$\chi^2_{(3)}$		43.31	$\chi^2_{(4)}$		0.22
p		$< .001$	p		$> .90$

[a]Probabilities in parentheses.

The data reveal two straightforward results. The mother profile at lag 2 is significantly different under the two conditions, indicating that infant behavior causes (is sufficient for) maternal response changes. The infant profile at lag 2 is identical under the two conditions, indicating that infant behavior is unaffected by that of the mother. Thus the infant does not care what the mother does, even though the mother's lag 1 behavior may actually be contingent on the infant lag 0 trigger activity.

This "causal" analysis directly tests the hypothesis offered to explain the example data presented above. The infant's behavior is self-generated in that it is unresponsive to different infant–mother sequences. The mother's behavior is affected by what the infant does. Thus the total relationship, as measurable by this data set, is determined by the infant's unidirectional effect (dominance). According to the analyses earlier in the paper, this effect is generated by the infant NONE autocorrelation. In sum, the mother links with the infant's autocorrelation pattern and modifies her behavior according to its cyclicity.

Combining the analyses in Tables 16.3, 16.7, 16.8 and 16.9 yields results pertinent to several important interaction concepts. The within-infant analysis (Table 16.3) determines the presence or absence of autocorrelation and crosslag patterns in the infant's temporal repertoire. The chi-square lag model (Tables 16.7 and 16.8) determines whether there are *any* nonrandom contingencies between interactor behaviors. Subsequent Z tests identify which specific behaviors are linked, and the excited or inhibited form of the linkage. At this point the analysis yields only association information. Applying the causal model (Table 16.9) determines directionality of influence. A finding of significant profile differences identifies directional influence on the profiled individual. Bidirectionality of influence is present when the causal model shows significant profile differences of *both* dyad members. Reciprocity of influence is revealed by profile differences of similar or dissimilar magnitude when each directional test is compared between individuals. Reciprocity involving the same behaviors is assessed by making the directional tests with the same triggers for each interactor.

Some Strengths of the Causal Analysis

This quasi-experimental causal model provides a solution to the problem of autocorrelation bias in contingency analysis. Each column in Table 16.9 represents a comparison made at the same time, time window, or event away from the criterion trigger event. In the example, all tests are made at lag 2. Therefore, autocorrelation influences are equal for each triggering condition, since all tests are made at the same lag. Of course, if autocorrelation at the test lag is very high, it is correspondingly difficult to achieve significance. In the limiting case, if the lag 0 trigger has a 1.00 probability of recurring at lag 2, there can never be a difference in lag 2 profiles. This again shows why autocorrelation should be studied both for its own sake as a linkage type and to make valid interpretations of contingency test results.

The causal model can be extended to study profile differences of more than two trigger sequences without any change in the basic method. For example, maternal vocalization followed by any infant signaling ($M1_0 \rightarrow notI5_1$) could be split into VOC (I1) versus the other three signals. This would produce a table with three columns, mother VOC at lag 0 followed by (1) infant NONE, (2) infant VOC, and (3) infant OTHER SIGNALS at lag 1, yielding a 3- $\times$ -4 chi-square. With sufficient frequencies of occurrence, all five infant states at lag 1 could be tested, yielding a 5- $\times$ -4 table. Such a model would be powerful for detecting exactly which infant behaviors controlled maternal actions.

An apparent problem in applying the causal model concerns defining "lag 2"— where to make the profile test in the behavior stream. In fact, profile frequencies could be counted at any lag after 1 that seems reasonable. This would usually be the actual lag 2 for event lags, unless a delayed effect of the triggering sequence is suspected. Such might be the case with very young infants or with psychotic mothers.

With time series data the issue is not so clear. A delay in reacting to the trigger sequence is likely, and the "psychological" time base of the partners could be quite different. Rather than examine second-by-second lags, one can define a *time window*. For example, frequencies might be summed for the 5-sec interval after the trigger sequence onset (or offset). According to the chi-square null model, behaviors should occur in this interval according to their marginal probabilities, so the statistical validity of a time window is no different from using a single second as the lag. Using a time window also has the advantage of increasing the total frequency of counts in the table, thereby increasing the power of the profile test. The main caution is not to make the window so large that early contingencies become masked by randomness later in the window. A criterion to define the window, such as mean behavior duration, would guard against masking.

Lastly, the profile data time window need not be the same for each interactor. The infant's reaction time, information processing, and attentional shifts may be quite different from the mother's, so it may be both methodologically and substantively important to use a different window size for each partner.

A CONCLUDING REMARK

Generating sequential observational data has become a popular activity in education and behavior sciences. Advances have been made in conceptualizing and analyzing such data, and a number of new issues and problems have been raised. This chapter has attempted to steer the interested worker toward some of this recent information, to raise an alarm concerning several specific issues, and to offer some potential solutions. As in my previous contribution to this volume, I welcome interest, criticism, and active participation in this research area by those who are more sophisticated than I in statistics and mathematics. With their help, I expect to see a general and powerful analytic system for categorical sequential data developed by the next revision of this volume.

REFERENCES

Allison, P. D., & Liker, J. K. (1982). Analyzing sequential categorical data on dyadic interaction: A comment on Gottmann. *Psychological Bulletin, 91,* 393–403.

Baker, R. J., & Belder, J. A. (1978). *The Grim system.* Oxford: Numerical Algorithms Group.

Breslow, N. E., & Day, N. E. (1980). *Statistical methods in cancer research: Vol. I. The analysis of case-control studies.* Lyon, France: International Agency for Research on Cancer.

Budescu, D. V. (1984). Tests of lagged dominance in sequential dyadic interaction. *Psychological Bulletin, 96,* 402–414.

Budescu, D. V. (1985). Analysis of dichotomous variables in the presence of serial dependence. *Psychological Bulletin, 97,* 547–561.

Cohen, J. (1969). *Statistical power analysis for the behavioral sciences.* New York: Academic.

Conger, A. J. (1980). Integration and generalization of kappas for multiple raters. *Psychological Bulletin, 88,* 322–328.

Dillon, W. R., Madden, T. J., & Kumar, A. (1983). Analyzing sequential categorical data on dyadic interaction: A latent structure approach. *Psychological Bulletin, 94,* 564–583.

Fleiss, J. L. (1981). *Statistical methods for rates and proportions* (2nd ed.). New York: Wiley.

Fleiss, J. L., Nee, J. C. M., & Landis, J. R. (1979). Large sample variance of kappa in the case of different sets of raters. *Psychological Bulletin, 86,* 974–977.

Gardner, W., Hartmann, D. P., & Mitchell, C. (1982). The effects of serial dependency on the use of χ^2 for analyzing sequential data in dyadic interactions. *Behavioral Assessment, 4,* 75–82.

Gottman, J. M. (1981). *Time-series analysis.* Cambridge, England: Cambridge University Press.

Gottman, J. M., & Notarius, C. (1977). Sequential analysis of observational data using Markov chains. In T. Kratochwill (Ed.), *Strategies to evaluate change in single subject research.* New York: Academic.

Gottman, J. M., & Ringland, J. T. (1981). The analysis of dominance and bidirectionality in social development. *Child Development, 52,* 393–412.

Gregson, R. A. (1983). *Time series in psychology.* Hillsdale, NJ: Erlbaum.

Hollenbeck, A. R. (1978). Problems of reliability in observational research. In G. P. Sackett (Ed.), *Observing behavior: Vol. 2. Data collection and analysis methods.* Baltimore: University Park Press.

Kaye, K. (1980). Estimating false alarms and missed events from interobserver agreement: A rationale. *Psychological Bulletin, 88,* 458–469.

Kraemer, H. C. (1982). Estimating false alarms and missed events from interobserver agreement: Comment on Kaye. *Psychological Bulletin, 92,* 749–754.

Lester, B. M., Hoffman, J., & Brazelton, T. B. (1985). The rhythmic structure of mother-infant interaction in term and preterm infants. *Child Development, 56,* 15–27.

Martin, J. A. (1981). A longitudinal study of the consequences of early mother–infant interaction: A microanalytic approach. *Child Development Monographs 46* (Serial No. 190).

Maxim, P. E. (1985). Multidimensional scaling of macaque social interaction. *American Journal of Primatology, 8,* 279–288.

Mendoza, J. L., & Graziano, W. G. (1982). The statistical analysis of dyadic social behavior: A multivariate approach. *Psychological Bulletin, 92,* 532–540.

Mitchell, S. (1979). Interobserver agreement, reliability, and generalizability of data collected in observational studies. *Psychological Bulletin, 86,* 376–390.

Sackett, G. P. (1979). The lag sequential analysis of contingency and cyclicity in behavioral interaction research. In J. Osofsky (Ed.), *Handbook of infant development.* New York: Wiley.

Sackett, G. P. (1980). Lag sequential analysis as a data reduction technique in social inter-action research. In D. Sawin, R. Kawkins, L. Walker, & J. Penticuff (Eds.), *Exceptional infant: Vol. 4. Psychosocial risks during pregnancy and early infancy.* New York: Brun-ner/Mazel.

Serlin, R. C., Carr, J., & Marascuilo, L. A. (1982). A measure of association for selected nonparametric procedures. *Psychological Bulletin, 92,* 786–790.

Siegel, S. (1956). *Nonparametric statistics.* New York: McGraw Hill.

Strube, M. J. (1985). Combining and comparing significance levels from nonindependent hypothesis tests. *Psychological Bulletin, 97,* 334–341.

Sutcliffe, J. P. (1980). On the relationship of reliability to statistical power. *Psychological Bulletin, 88,* 509–515.

Tanner, M. A., & Young, M. A. (1985). Modeling ordinal scale disagreement. *Psychological Bulletin, 98,* 408–415.

Thomas, E. A. C., & Malone, T. W. (1979). On the dynamics of two-person interaction. *Psychological Review, 86,* 331–360.

Vietze, P. M., Abernathy, S. R., Ashe, M. L., & Faulstich, G. (1978). Contingent interaction between mothers and their developmentally delayed infants. In G. P. Sackett (Ed.), *Observing behavior: Vol. 1. Theory and applications in mental retardation.* Baltimore: University Park Press.

Wampold, B. E. (1984). Tests of dominance in sequential categorical data. *Psychological Bulletin, 96,* 424–429.

Wampold, B. E., & Margolin, G. (1982). Nonparametric strategies to test the independence of behavioral states in sequential data. *Psychological Bulletin, 92,* 755–765.

Williams, E. A., & Gottman, J. M. (1982). *A user's guide to the Gottman-Williams time-series analysis computer programs for social scientists.* Cambridge: Cambridge University Press.

Zwick, R., Neuhoff, V., Marascuilo, L. A., & Levin, J. R. (1982). Statistical tests for cor-related proportions: Some extensions. *Psychological Bulletin 92,* 258–271.

PART FOUR

Risk Factors, Clinical Approaches, and Interventions

Intervention approaches with infants have flourished over the last few years. They include proposals to teach infants to read in the first year, studies of the long-term effects of the newborn nursery environment, studies focusing on the effects of biological and environmental stress on outcomes, and the more traditional introduction of some type of stimulation or extra factor in the first few years of life with subsequent study of the outcomes for the infants. This last type of intervention characterizes studies with risk groups of infants.

The chapters in this section provide the opportunity to consider different types of risk factors and intervention approaches with infants, parents, and families. Claire Kopp provides a thorough review of prenatal and perinatal factors that influence early cognitive development. In her chapter, she provides a brief description of how the study of developmental risk has evolved and speculates about implications of this research. The first part of the chapter provides a historical view of the past 40 years of risk research and the second part focuses on research interests prevalent in the 1970s. This latter section is concerned with cognitive functioning of infants who were exposed to risk factors, thus providing some understanding of the effects of risk on early cognition and the questions that remain to be answered in this area.

Charles Vorhees and Elizabeth Mollnow in their chapter on behavioral teratogenesis focus on developmental injuries, particularly those to the central nervous system, which occur during very early development. Developmental injuries have been approached from two perspectives, one examining problems by putative causes and the other studying the target organ of injury. Developmental risk and injury have been studied from a psychological perspective by considering problems of early behavioral, sensory, emotional, and cognitive processes and how these can be measured. While they mention that it is difficult to do justice in a chapter to an area as extensive as behavioral teratogenesis, they have reviewed compounds for which there is a bridge between the human and animal research that permits conclusions to be reached about the hazard potential of each agent for causing prenatal or neonatal CNS injury. They hold much hope that research will continue to provide knowledge to decrease the incidence of damage for infants and children.

Anneliese Korner's chapter is more specific, focusing on the special risks and intervention needs of highrisk newborns and their family systems. She focuses her discussion of preventive intervention on preterm infants, who are the largest group of highrisk newborns that can benefit from such intervention efforts. The long- and short-term benefits of early intervention are reviewed and controlled clinical studies are evaluated.

Tiffany Field's chapter, covering affective disturbances that disrupt the parent–infant interactional system, presents another group for which intervention could be beneficial. Disturbances discussed by Field may occur as a result of a member of the dyad becoming affectively unresponsive or as a result of the relationship being disrupted by separation.

Bertrand Cramer takes intervention a step further, discussing the connections between clinical concerns and research issues. He presents a fascinating perspective on clinical intervention with infants and families—a therapeutic approach only very recently being attempted (see also Emde, Chapter 27 of this volume). The importance of the clinical intervention perspective for the readers of this volume is that it has emerged from an integration of clinical and research approaches.

It is interesting to consider the different ways studies of high-risk parents and infants have enriched our understanding of the parent–infant relationship system. For example, patterns of interaction that are taken for granted in low-risk groups may or may not occur within higher-risk pairs or may develop according to a different developmental timetable. Language or symbolic play interactions that are so much a part of middle-class interaction patterns are often delayed or do not occur in the same way. Affective exchanges between disadvantaged and at risk mothers and infants differ markedly from those between low-risk dyads, with many more distress-laden, angry, and inconsistent interactions occurring in the high-risk groups. How do such differences affect our understanding of the relationship? Do other patterns replace those that do not occur? Are some of them more or less adaptive? What do the differing patterns mean for later development? How are patterns carried on from one generation to another and how can they be changed? Many of these questions are being studied but are as yet unanswered; many are targeted toward the development of appropriate interventions.

CHAPTER 17

Developmental Risk: Historical Reflections

CLAIRE B. KOPP

INTRODUCTION

The phrase *developmental risk* indicates the well-being of children is in jeopardy. Risks, stemming from adverse biological and/or environmental conditions, can begin to influence development before birth, during infancy, or in the childhood years. Their effects on child functioning can be circumscribed or global, their impact minimal to severe, their duration from the short to the long term.

Developmental risks have been studied for years and years, in fact, long before the existence of a formal terminology. The 1884 observation of an acephalic infant (Preyer, reprinted in Dennis, 1972) is a study of risk, and the reports of the handicaps of preterm infants described in the 1920s are studies of risk (see Kopp & Krakow, 1983). In this country, systematic efforts to assess the effects of biologically derived risk factors began to emerge in the 1920s and were often directed to preterm infants (Kopp & Krakow, 1983).

During the ensuing years literally hundreds of studies were initiated, with many having a goal of evaluating some of the developmental consequences of one or another risk factor (e.g., preterm birth, anoxia, rubella, thalidomide, spinabifida, single gene disorders, chromosomal anomalies, dystonias, lead, postnatal infections, etc.). Many investigators adopted the longitudinal paradigm in order to analyze enduring effects, and many focused on intellectual competency as one of the primary measures of outcome. Despite the methodological problems often associated with longitudinal research, the longitudinal studies centered around risk factors have yielded substantive knowledge.

With respect to biologically based risk factors, it is now well documented that:

The earlier the advent of a prenatal risk factor (e.g., ingestion of a toxic drug or serious maternal infection during early pregnancy) the greater the likelihood of adverse long-term developmental effects (see Kopp, 1983).

In recent years, risks arising in the prenatal period account for the largest percentage of individuals with intelligence quotients below 50 and with severe neurological and sensory problems (see Hagberg & Hagberg, 1984).

The long-term outcome of perinatal risk is strongly influenced by environmental factors, with biological risks often ameliorated by supportive and sensitive care giving (e.g., see Sameroff & Chandler, 1975; Werner & Smith, 1982).

The relationship between biological and social risks is complex; nonetheless, the combination of high medical risk and high social risk often portends poor outcomes (Baker & Mednick, 1984; Birch & Gussow, 1970; Broman, Nichols, & Kennedy, 1975; Werner & Smith, 1982).

Risks that arise in the late prenatal, perinatal, or early postnatal periods often appear to show their most serious developmental consequences during infancy and early childhood with amelioration frequently observed during the preschool and school years (e.g., see Graham, Ernhart, Thurston, & Craft, 1962).

With the exception of the most severe risk factors, the *fundamental* forms and sequences of early infancy behaviors are not modified by adverse influences, although the rate of development may be sharply curtailed (e.g., Cicchetti & Sroufe, 1976; Decarie, 1969; Kopp, 1983).

The effects of risks vary depending upon the age of the child and the cognitive and social demands that emanate from the environment (see Chess, 1974).

Risk factors may have deleterious consequences for virtually every domain of functioning (e.g., cognitive, social, emotional, etc.), although most outcomes have been documented with respect to the intellect (e.g., Baker & Mednick, 1984; Werner & Smith, 1982).

It is difficult to predict with any certainty the precise level of intellectual *outcome* for any given child from early infancy to later childhood even in instances where risk is established and there is virtually no chance for normal development (e.g., chromosomal anomaly) (see Kopp & McCall, 1982).

These findings have had important implications for social, research, and intervention policies. They have been used, for example, to marshal additional services and resources for economically disadvantaged at risk infants and young children, to argue for more funding support for the study of reproductive risks, to propose the development of sophisticated analytic models in order to tease out causal biological and social influences, and to press for additional research with groups that are at both biological and social risk (e.g., preterm infants of poor, minority adolescents).

The findings have also served as a catalyst for developmentally oriented investigators. Some have explored the cognitive processing skills of early life in an attempt to understand influences of risk, others have turned to examining mediators in the environment that influence outcome, a few have attempted to find predictors of outcome. Much of this research came about during the 1970s and thereafter.

Despite numerous new studies, the overall gain in recent knowledge has been modest. It is absolutely clear, for example, that virtually any group of infants who are at risk and who are studied with virtually any paradigm will show some variation in behavior (sometimes a lot, sometimes just a bit) when compared with normally developing nonrisk infants. *But it is not at all clear when and how these differences are developmentally meaningful for the short and for the long term.*

The reasons for this very fundamental gap in our knowledge base are complex and manyfold; however, one of the major problems is that the study of mediators and processes influenced by risk factors is itself in its infancy, and its development is very uneven. Some aspects of functioning among risk groups are routinely studied, others not at all; some age groups are studied, others not at all; some diagnostic groups are routinely studied, others not at all; some studies have included a longitudinal component, many have not. Compounding these difficulties is the fact that investigators have not used equivalent samples, paradigms, or specific content domains even when they are ostensibly studying the same domain or process (see Kopp, 1983, for examples). Unfortunately the gaps and diversity of approaches often mean that only the most obvious or general conclusions can be reached.

Perhaps now is an appropriate time to take stock. The exponential growth of the study of infancy and the study of infants at developmental risk has slowed appreciably. Research funding has slackened. The fervor that once suggested infancy research might begin to unravel all aspects of growth and development has given way to more sober-minded expectations. Despite these trends, there is motivation to continue—the analysis of the behaviors of early life has not lost its fascination. And the study of risk with all of its challenges and enigmas has not lost its engrossing qualities.

Thus this chapter is written in the spirit of the times. Primarily reflective in content, it is an attempt to summarize briefly how the study of developmental risk evolved and grew. However, no attempt is made to generate a list of prescriptives; that too will have to evolve and grow.

The first part of the chapter provides a historical overview of the past 60 years of risk research with emphasis on the 1920s to 1960s. Two trends will become apparent. First, some of the most innovative and far-reaching studies of risk did not have their origins either in mainstream psychology or in child development. In fact, only a few "developmentalists" were involved in risk-related research until the late 1960s and 1970s. By far, most of the innovators came from psychiatry, pediatrics, and public health. Their often provocative ideas and findings stimulated arguments and counterarguments and in some cases prompted the growth of theory. In some instances, the research and the ideas were so important that the influence extended far beyond the topic of risk per se. A second point is that even the best ideas need financial support to keep them going. Innovative studies in risk often attracted some level of support. For some this came in the form of research grants, for others in the form of modest stipends. Whatever the source and the level, funds permitted an interest to be translated into reality.

The second part of the chapter picks up the theme of reflection but in this case highlights a focus of research interest that was prevalent in the 1970s. That interest can be broadly classified as a concern with cognitive functioning of infants who had been exposed to risk factors. An analysis of this kind has not been made previously. This brief examination will show advances that have been made in understanding the effects of risk on early cognition and also point to the puzzles that still need solving.

DEVELOPMENTAL RISK WITH A FOCUS ON INFANCY

From the 1920s through the 1960s

To set the stage, the phrase *developmental risk research* (or *risk research*) is used throughout this chapter to refer to studies where the effects of adverse factors were documented with respect to infant development. The nomenclature serves as an organizational tool that integrates many different types of studies. However, it will be helpful to recall that *developmental risk* is a phrase of recent origin, having been introduced and used routinely during the last 15–20 years.

The format of this historical excursion in this first section is primarily a chronological and topical table (see Table 17.1). The first column of the table lists investigators or landmark studies of developmental risk (the emphasis is often but not exclusively on studies done in the United States). In addition to showing major trends, this first column also reveals that some researchers focused on developmental risk from a biological framework and others from an environmental one. The biological emphasis often centered on risk from the prenatal and/or perinatal periods whereas the environmental emphasis focused extensively on adversities in postnatal life. Whatever the orientation, concern was directed to the vulnerability of the infant and very young child.

In addition to a listing of risk researchers or specific kinds of studies, Table 17.1 includes four other columns. These call attention to the evolution of infancy research with normally developing samples and the theoretical or paradigmatic orientations that drove them. These are entered into the table by decade of emergence. The goal here is to show that, by and large, the study of infants at developmental risk and the study of infancy per se were not integrated during these years. The integration did not occur until the 1970s when developmentalists interested in infancy started to extend the use of some of their paradigms and strategies to samples at developmental risk. Often this extension had two goals, which were not mutually exclusive. One was to help clarify a developmental phenomenon or issue, and the other was to determine the capabilities of samples of infants at risk. Examples of researchers who sparked this later trend included Sroufe and his colleagues and Fantz and his collaborators.

The discussion that follows is directed to a brief elaboration of the first column—historical trends in the study of developmental risk. This is done primarily by decade; in certain instances the uniqueness of a particular contribution is highlighted.

The 1920s

We begin with the decade of the 1920s. Several pediatricians were involved in studies of preterm infants (see Kopp & Krakow, 1983, for details), but the giant of the time in terms of the study of developmental risk was pediatrician–psychologist Arnold Gesell.

ARNOLD GESELL.   To this day, Gesell's views are controversial because of his maturational stance, his tie between infant mental life and motor acts, and the small sample used to derive the norms for his developmental test. Yet a reading of the man's output clearly reveals a gifted intellect and a flowing pen. A prodigious reader, influenced by biology, embryology, anthropology, and comparative studies, Gesell had extensive interests but seemed particularly intrigued by all aspects of normal and abnormal growth of human infancy and early childhood. By 1921, he had written about the effects of twin birth on growth of the mind (Gesell, 1921), and by 1929 he had authored *Infancy and Human Growth*. In this book, Gesell documented growth trends of normally developing infants as well as those who had experienced birth injury, preterm birth, and postterm birth and infants who had Down's syndrome (labeled at that time *mongolism*).

Although Gesell had started many of his infancy studies in the early 1920s, the 1926 funding of the Yale Psycho-Clinic by the Laura Spelman Rockefeller memorial surely provided the boost for more extensive, far-reaching studies of both normally developing and at risk infants (his use of cinematography was unmatched at the time). In the 1930s, Gesell wrote extensively about infants and children at risk. His studies of these groups continued for many, many years.

The funding of the Child Study Centers (e.g., at Yale, Minnesota, Iowa, etc.) with Rockefeller monies meant that studies of child development could begin and move forward, which they did. A few researchers involved in the study of normally developing children also turned an occasional look at children who had problems. Thus Mary Shirley (1939) studied the development of preterms, and Florence Goodenough (1932) looked at the emotional development of a deaf and blind child.

By and large, however, with the exception of Gesell, the era of the child study movement was a time to focus upon and to describe the development of the normal infant and child. In a sense Gesell had his own agenda and priorities, and he had the means and skill to go about meeting them.

By the late 1940s until well into the 1970s, Gesell's theories, maturational bent, and descriptive methodologies were an anathema to experimentally, psychodynamically, or environmentally oriented psychologists. Even now, many shun his theoretical views or his quasi-experimental methodologies.

While there is ample justification for discounting some of Gesell's writings, his influence in the study of risk must be acknowledged. His emphasis on prediction of mental growth from infancy particularly for children at risk continues to hold sway in some quarters. His concern about gestational and conceptual age matches among preterms spawned considerable research and controversy on this topic here and abroad. Arthur H. Parmelee, who studied with Gesell, carried forward a concern for this topic as well as research in developmental risk. Gesell's influence can be found in other areas. Early on he documented a short-term attentive precocity among young preterms; in recent times this finding indirectly sparked studies of the sensory abilities of these infants and what this might mean for subsequent development. This list could be extended, but the point seems clear. Gesell's influence may have waxed and waned, but in the long term he has had a lasting impact on risk groups that have been studied and the types of questions posed.

The 1930s and the 1940s

The depression and World War II had profound consequences for the study of children in the United States (see Sears, 1975). Yet in the United States several reports surfaced about infants and children who were at risk because of biological factors (see Kopp & Krakow, 1983) or environmental deprivations of one or another kind (e.g., see Goldfarb, 1944, 1945; Levy, 1937; Powdermaker, Levis, & Touraine, 1937). Early deprivations were believed to cause social, emotional, and cognitive impairments that were long lasting. The decades of the 1930s and 1940s saw a focus on risk due to environmental deprivations, primarily with respect to the infant's mother.

A major impetus for this work came from Europe. The psychoanalytic movement was strong there and several clinician–researchers bred in the tradition of primary process thinking, ego development, fixations, and so forth became involved in the study of effects of institutional life on infants and young children. Katherine Wolf, for example, along with Durfee, in 1933 (cited in Bowlby, 1950) described major developmental effects that institutionalization had on infants. Institutionalization of infants often occurred due to abandonment, death of parents, or in some cases

TABLE 17.1. Trends in Infancy Research: Theoretical and Conceptual Orientations

Decade	Investigators or Landmark Studies	Child Study Movement	
		Focus	Orientation
1920s	Pediatricians, obstetricians: study preterms Gesell: studies of preterms, adoptees, mentally and neurologically impaired, assessment	Child development centers established Infancy research: normative trends, neonates, emotions, neuromuscular maturation, conditioning	*Theoretical:* embryology, maturational, behaviorism-conditioning *Issues:* stages, continuities, early experiences *Methodologies:* observations, films
1930s	Shirley: preterms Spitz, Wolf, others: infants in institutions.		
1940s	Spitz: "hospitalism"		
1950s	Bowlby: homeless infants and children—maternal deprivation Graham: anoxia, assessment of newborns Collaborative Project Kauai Project		
1960s	Koch: longitudinal studies PKU, Down syndrome Decarie: thalidomide infants Chess: rubella Prechtl: assessment of risks—pregnancy, birth; assessment of newborns		
1970s	Parmelee et al.: Infant Studies Project Brazelton et al.: assessment of newborns Fantz, Fagan, Miranda: visual processing preterms, Down's syndrome Ramey et al.: Abecedarian project (infants at environmental risk) Piagetian derived studies		
1980s	Continuing interest in biological factors (e.g., very low birth weight, sex chromosome anomalies, high-risk pregnancies) and environmental conditions (e.g., infant neglect and abuse, adolescent pregnancies and motherhood); efforts made to generate across institution collaborations		

Psychoanalytic		Experimental/Psychophysiological		Piagetian–Cognitive	
Focus	Orientation	Focus	Orientation	Focus	Orientation
Early experiences (e.g., deprivations, institutions), mental health, mothering processes, infant attributes, mother–infant interaction, attachment (pioneering researchers: Spitz, Bowlby, Wolf, Benjamin, Escalona, Mahler, etc.)	*Theoretical:* Freudian theory, biology, embryology, ethology *Issues:* Individual variability, continuities, assessment *Methodologies:* observations, film	Processes related to newborn and infant learning, perception, attention, memory, sleep, sensory responsivity, social interactions, play, etc.	*Theoretical:* behaviorism, learning theory, perceptual affordances, atheoretical *Issues:* processing abilities, capacities *Methodologies:* cardiac responses, EEG, skin responsivity, sucking, visual fixations, motility, preferences, initiations, etc. Laboratory based *Technologies:* computer, video	Sensorimotor intelligence (object permanence, space, causality, etc.)	*Theoretical:* Piaget's theory (active organism, interactionism, stages, foundation of later knowledge) *Issues:* species typicality, decalages, interface cognition and language, sensorimotor assessments

destitute or ill parents. Infant institutions were invariably grim places. Public support was often minimal; therefore caregivers were in very short supply and facilities were bare of all but the most essential amenities. In addition, the social ethic suggested that children who ended up in institutions somehow came from morally bereft families—thus it can be inferred that institutional directors believed that the niceties of child care could be ignored. And they were (for various accounts of abandoned children in the United States see Bremner, 1970; Brophy, 1972; Platt, 1969; Riis, 1957).

The early descriptions and research were some of the catalysts that ultimately led to enormous interest in topics related to deprivations in early life, the importance of the mother, the meaning of both the physical and the social environment, caregiver interactions with normally developing infants and those who were at risk or had handicapping conditions, and the construct of attachment. Rene Spitz and his ideas fostered one strand of this research, and John Bowlby and his ideas another.

RENE SPITZ.   Rene Spitz had strong ties to psychoanalysis and a desire to study the "psychoanalytic psychology of infancy." He noted that in 1935 when he began his studies he "was a lonely figure" (Spitz, 1963, p. xv of Foreward). Earlier, Spitz had written several pieces with a psychoanalytic orientation (for a listing see Gaskill, 1963), but then he became interested in the effects of institutionalization in early life. This led to the historic study, *Hospitalism* (Spitz, 1945). The goal of this study was to extend Wolf's earlier research and isolate the factors that led to aberrant behaviors using a large sample of infants. Findings from the study (which actually included several institutions and spanned two continents) tied institutional life to reduced or impaired levels of exploration and to declines in the rate of development. Spitz attributed a major drop in developmental quotient (DQ) found with one of the study groups to lack of human contact, and he implicated lack of mothering as a critical factor. In another classic paper, "Anaclitic Depression: An Inquiry into the Genesis of Psychiatric Conditions in Early Childhood" (Spitz, 1946), he described psychiatric disturbances in early infancy and linked some severe manifestations to a prolonged loss of mother.

Moving to the United States before the beginning of World War II, Spitz settled in New York (he later moved to Denver) and became active in psychoanalytic circles. He wrote extensively about infant affect, early thought processes, the young ego, early communication, defense mechanisms, and infants who were "troubled" because of deprivations (see Rangell, 1963). He also believed, as did Gesell, in the importance of film for documenting infant behavior (see Emde & Harmon, 1983, for a listing).

Spitz's ideas about the critical role of early experiences and mothering might have been ignored for the most part, but they were not. They received endorsement from some members of the mental health community. One reason is that during the war it began to be apparent that soldiers showed enormous variation in their ability to cope with the experiences of battle. It was felt that these variations in psychological well-being were in part tied to the experiences of early life (Escalona, 1985). The psychoanalytic model appeared to provide a reasonable base from which to study the roots of mental health. The ideas of Spitz, John Benjamin, and Sibylle Escalona received increasing attention. Financial support for research of this nature, including studies of infancy and early life, began to materialize. For example, by the late 1940s the National Institute of Mental Health was formed. Escalona (1985) recalls that she received grant #27 from the newly formed agency. Recognize though that this infancy work (late 1940s and early 1950s) stood relatively alone (see Table 17.1).

Not surprisingly, Spitz's ideas about early life or even the origins of neuroses have not gone unchallenged. As one example, the crucial role of the child's biological mother as a cause of poor performance by institutionalized infants was questioned (e.g., see Casler, 1963). Similarly, Spitz's themes about infant ego, perceptual organization, and emotional development were also challenged (see Campos, 1983). After a while many of his ideas were largely ignored. Despite this, his students and colleagues (e.g., Leon Yarrow, Robert Emde, and others) began to move to the forefront in the study of infancy. Yarrow's 1961 article on reevaluating maternal deprivation in infancy is itself a classic.

Today, Spitz's contribution to infancy research is again being viewed in a positive light. Witness the republication of some of his selected papers (Emde, 1983). But it is not solely because of the interest of a former colleague. Rather, the time is ripe. Currently, there is a belief that the individual's emotional life has been neglected in the cause of studying the intellect; in fact, some consider that cognition and emotion are linked. Now numerous studies have been initiated about affect and emotion and its influences with individuals of all ages. Spitz's discussion of affect now seems to have conceptual value for the organization of contemporary studies of infant emotions (Campos, 1983).

From the standpoint of developmental risk during infancy, Spitz has to be considered as an important innovator. His early emphasis on mothering and the environment of early life forced an appreciation of caregiving per se and its implications for development. Surely his ideas fed into the concern about mothering, caregiving, and the role of the early environment of infants at risk that began to appear during the 1970s. Variations in caregiving (the environment) began to be tied in one or another way to the facilitation or distortion of the course of development of infants at risk.

JOHN BOWLBY. Spitz's contributions do not stand alone in the decade of the 1930s and 1940s. During this time, John Bowlby, also a student of psychoanalysis, began to study and report on the role of the environment in the development of neuroses and in the formation of delinquent behavior (see Bowlby, 1940, 1946). Bowlby was working at the Tavistock Clinic in London when in 1948 the Social Commission of the United Nations decided to implement a study of homeless children. The World Health Organization, particularly the Mental Health Section, provided financial support for the endeavor and Bowlby was asked to head the effort. The work was started in 1950.

The WHO monograph, *Maternal Care and Mental Health* (Bowlby, 1951), provided a statement about the origins of mental health, a review of the untoward effects of maternal deprivation, and prevention of same. A key statement suggested that an essential ingredient for mental health "is that the infant and young child should experience a warm, intimate, and continuous relationship with his mother (or permanent mother-substitute) in which both find satisfaction and enjoyment" (p. 77). The child who does not have this relationship is maternally deprived.

As Bowlby (1969) noted in the preface of his landmark volume, *Attachment,* not only was the WHO report timely, but it helped focus attention on the problems of homeless infants and children and suggested ways to improve their care. Bowlby also commented that reviewers of the book lamented the lack of information about the processes involved in early psychopathology as a result of maternal deprivation. His inability to provide information led to systematic observations of infants and children separated from their mothers for a variety of reasons and for varying lengths of time.

Attachment theory stemmed from the observations Bowlby made with many of his colleagues including James Robertson, Mary Ainsworth, Chris Heinicke, and others. The history of this and related research, the controversies the ideas and the studies engendered, and the growth of an extensive literature have been amply documented elsewhere (e.g., Ainsworth, 1962; Bretherton & Waters, 1985) and do not need to be discussed here.

The point that does need emphasis is that Bowlby's original studies of environmental risk set the stage for coming generations of researchers to look at caregiving with new ideas and new paradigms. The early studies of infants at environmental risk soon gave way to studies of normally developing infants. In a matter of time, attachment theory and attachment processes were used to study infants and young children at risk because of adverse biological factors (see Serafica & Cicchetti, 1978). As was not the case for Gesell and Spitz, interest in Bowlby's ideas has not waxed and waned.

The 1950s and the 1960s

These decades witnessed a proliferation of research around biological risk conditions. This growth was due to many factors. On the positive side, new treatments and technologies improved perinatal mortality rates (see Kopp, 1983), new breakthroughs were forthcoming in the field of genetics, and funding agencies were created by the U.S. government (e.g., the National Institute of Neurological Diseases and Blindness) to begin to support major research efforts to explore risk factors. On the negative side, there were unfortunate epidemics such as rubella in the 1960s. So too there was the thalidomide disaster. Their net result was long-term serious sequelae for thousands of children. These conditions and more sparked the resurgence of interest in biological risk.

The research of the times, the paradigms that guided it, and the major findings have been recounted elsewhere in the past decade and do not need repetition here (e.g., Kopp, 1983; Kopp & Krakow, 1983; Sameroff & Chandler, 1975). It is useful, however, to review briefly some of the events of this period and to call attention to a few of the innovators who individually or collectively moved the study of risk to increasing levels of sophistication.

THE AVANT-GARDE.   During the 1950s several key articles appeared that suggested that adverse developmental and neurological outcomes were linked to complications of pregnancy (e.g., Lilienfeld & Parkhurst, 1951; Lilienfeld & Pasamanick, 1954; Pasamanick & Knobloch, 1961). The *continuum of reproductive casualty* was the phrase that came to signify the relationship between maternal pregnancy complications, perinatal stresses, and poor infant outcome. Of interest, the iatrogenic contributions to poor outcome were not known (indeed they would not be understood until decades later). The phrase *continuum of reproductive casualty* became a call to arms, and battles were waged in order to understand why pregnancies could fail. Notably, the "call" was first sounded by workers in the domain of public health and subsequently taken up by pediatricians and psychologists.

During the 1950s, a massive study of women and their pregnancies was planned, and would be implemented. This was the Collaborative Perinatal Project (see Broman et al., 1975). It was conceived primarily by medical researchers and clinicians, and psychologists were integrated into the research because of their expertise in experimental design and data analysis and their skill in measurement, particularly intelligence. More than a few began to study infants and infants at risk; indeed, the Collaborative Project probably made risk research acceptable to psychologists. In addition to the Collaborative Perinatal Project, the Kauai studies were implemented during this period. This too was an interdisciplinary research project designed to evaluate the pregnancies, births, and subsequent development of all of the children born in Kauai during a single year (see Werner & Smith, 1977, 1982).

Highlights of both of these extraordinary studies are mentioned in Kopp and Krakow (1983) and in Sameroff and Chandler (1975). The critical nature of their findings is the fact that the developmental outcome of *perinatal* risk conditions is often dependent upon the facilitative or detrimental aspects of the child's environment. Outcomes for risks that arose in the early prenatal period, which were often quite serious, were not as tightly linked to the subsequent rearing environment.

The 1950s also witnessed the beginnings of Frances K. Graham's longitudinal studies of infants who had experienced neonatal anoxia (e.g., Graham, Pennoyer, Caldwell, Greenman, & Hartmann, 1957; see summary in Kopp & Krakow, 1983). The research has been preeminent on two counts; it demonstrated, first, that the adverse consequences of a neonatal risk event are often attenuated from infancy to the school years, and, second, that it was and is possible to study developmental risk with scientific rigor and precision. Graham's influence has been far-reaching and steady.

In addition to these often highly publicized studies, there were others that perhaps were not as well known but were equally important. Richard Koch began his longitudinal studies of children who had Down syndrome and those who were diagnosed as having PKU. The Down syndrome studies were particularly detailed and extensive, and clearly documented the developmental course of these children and also revealed when predictions about later intellectual development could be made with some degree of accuracy (e.g., Fishler, Graliker, & Koch, 1964–1965; Share, Webb, & Koch, 1961–1962). An interesting footnote to Koch's research is that he was somewhat reluctant to enter this line of study but did so at the urging of Arthur H. Parmelee, Sr., who also obtained financial support for him (Koch, 1985).

With the exception of Bowlby and Spitz, it has been rare for investigators to approach the study of risk with a strong theoretical underpinning as foundation for research. Most typically a primarily goal is to define the course of development subsequent to a risk event, and possibly to examine the influence of one or more mediating variables. T. Gouin-Decarie (e.g., 1969) provided an exception in her landmark studies of the development of babies and children whose mothers had taken thalidomide early in their pregnancies. The theoretically derived questions asked whether infants who had limited physical means could develop (1) attachments, in the classic Bowlby framework, to their primary caregivers, and (2) sensorimotor intelligence from a Piagetian perspective. In each instance, Gouin-Decarie showed that both attachment and sensorimotor competencies could be attained, although the pathways and processes for the accomplishments might differ from those used by children whose limbs were intact.

Stella Chess (1974, 1977), known primarily for her studies on behavioral individuality and temperament, brought the practiced eye of a psychiatrist to the study of children whose mothers had rubella in pregnancy. These children often showed a variety of severe sensory and physical impairments along with varying degrees of developmental delays. Chess (1977) has shown that, even in cases where the developmental "die" seems set, improvements in level of functioning can occur. And in her rarely cited 1974 article, Chess briefly mentioned a philosophical perspective that probably served as the basis for the questions that she later posed. As one example, she noted that one needed to look for the ramifications of a particular dysfunction on other aspects of behavior. In another comment, she said that the limitations observed at one developmental age might or might not have implications for another. Much depended on the nature of the demands on the child. Chess's insights bear some relationship to current attempts to define child competencies and processing skills in relation to task and situational factors. To my knowledge, attempts to apply these principles to the study of infants at risk have not been undertaken.

THE LEGACY.   The innovators immeasurably added to the understanding of risk factors and their outcomes. In addition to their research findings, they left a legacy of commitment to infants and children who are at risk. They were interested in and studied these children long before others cast a glance at problematic forms of development. They posed questions that went beyond the routine: What are *developmental* consequences? How can we better understand them? The innovators deserve much recognition.

In addition to these contributions, the early years of research on developmental risk may have bestowed a misleading sense of security and rightness. So many questions needed to be asked and answered about developmental risk that concerns about research directions and foci probably seemed irrelevant. Researchers at times pursued an independent and sometimes idiosyncratic course of study. In addition, both government and private agencies had the resources and the interest in funding both large- and small-scale studies of risk.

A belief in an endless supply of money must have been taken as encouragement to continue as before. And indeed, studies on risk expanded in scope and number in the 1970s; decreases began in the 1980s when financial resources diminished. But by then we had the fragmented research findings that are part of our current heritage.

RISK AND COGNITIVE FUNCTIONING DURING INFANCY: THE 1970s ON

Introduction

The 1970s heralded a growth decade for developmental research. Financial support, academic and clinical interest, an abundance of graduate students, and interesting unexplored research topics converged and led to an unprecedented span of productivity. Innovative ideas and methodologies, new theories, and videotape and computer technologies revolutionized the field.

Virtually every domain that was studied with samples of normally developing children was also extended to the study of infants and children at biological risk. Included were children with chromosomal anomalies, or those who were exposed to prenatal infections or embryotoxic substances, or who experienced preterm birth, anoxia, neonatal sepsis, and the like (see Kopp, 1983). Many of these risk conditions had never before been studied in depth, nor had the very young been the focus of research. Assessments of newborns, evaluation of sensorimotor functioning using Piagetian theory, research into attachment and bonding, and studies of visual and auditory processing proliferated rapidly. In addition to documenting the varied nature of problem functioning, investigators attempted to study the processes that might be involved.

A useful gauge of the commitment to risk research can be obtained by noting the number of studies devoted solely to perceptual–cognitive characteristics of preterms. As just one example, 11 studies were published between 1974 and 1980, of which half focused on infants in the first part of the first year (see Kopp, 1983, for details). In like manner, other risk groups and other content domains showed marked increases in research.

Coincident with an interest in research, there were renewed attempts to synthesize and evaluate the implications of past studies. Sameroff and Chandler (1975) confronted the issue of the role of the environment in ameliorating or exacerbating the effects of perinatal stress. Werner and Smith (1982) brought together two decades of longitudinal research from the Kauai studies and attempted to show factors that led to resiliency or vulnerability subsequent to perinatal stress. Kopp and Parmelee (1979) and more recently Kopp (1983) reviewed the multiple nature of prenatal and perinatal risks and provided detailed discussions of research on risk conditions such as preterm birth and Down syndrome. And a new type of synthesis appeared with the publication of volumes devoted solely to studies of risk (Field, Sostek, & Goldberg, 1979; Kearsley & Sigel, 1979; Lipsitt & Field, 1982).

To date, however, the reviews and syntheses have primarily focused upon outcome data related to intellectual, neurological, and educational sequelae. To my knowledge, no attempt has been made to discuss the effect of risk events upon a single domain of functioning during infancy. This section is an attempt to redress this omission. The focus is on cognitive functioning.

The rationale for this effort is straightforward. Every act and every event that involve humans involve cognition. Indeed, "mental processes habitually intrude themselves into virtually *all* human psychological processes and activities" (Flavell, 1985, p. 2). And unfortunately, cognitive processes and activities are often subject to distortion by adverse biological conditions. Indeed, testimony to the incontrovertible association between biological risk and cognitive functioning dates back to antiquity. In more recent times, mental retardation, attentional problems, learning disabilities, and more have been systematically documented for at least some of the individuals who have been exposed to stress during the prenatal and perinatal periods. And even more recently, researchers have noted some of the specific cognitive processing abilities that are *different* or seemingly impaired among some infants at risk.

This section is organized into two parts, which mirror the primary approaches used to study cognitive functioning of either at risk infants or those who had handicapping conditions. One derived from Piagetian theory and the other focused on cognitive processes. Both of these approaches, which overlapped in time, have had strengths and weaknesses.

The research settings that I have been involved with have included both of these orientations. This background experience is used as an organization scheme for this section. Piagetian research is described first and includes mention of conceptual foundations, research findings, and issues that came out of the studies. Following, discussion centers on research focused upon cognitive processes. Where appropriate, the research is linked to other investigators' findings. In keeping with the first part of this review, mention is also made of the financial support that allowed studies to be implemented. While the benefits of support are clearly apparent, it is important to recognize that the source of funding may have implications for the topic that is studied and the specific groups targeted for the research.

Piagetian-Derived Research

During the early part of the 1970s a major trend in the study of risk involved examination of the functioning of at risk and handicapped infants using Piagetian theory as a foundation. In part, this reflected the belief that Piaget's theory provided a conceptual framework for infant cognition. No other theory existed that systematically spelled out an ontogenetic sequence for both the growth of cognition and the contents of the mind. Often referred to as schemata, these contents of infant mind related to growth of understanding of objects, space, time, causality, object relationships, and problem solving. Not only were these achievements important in their own right, but they were, Piaget said, the foundation for later intellectual development (Piaget, 1952, 1954).

The promise of Piaget's theory was so substantial that sensorimotor series had been designed as formal measures of infant cognition. These included series by Casati and Lezine (1968), Escalona and Corman (1967), and Uzgiris and Hunt (1966). It was presumed that these batteries permitted detailed evaluations of infant knowledge in contrast to developmental examinations (e.g., Gesell, Bayley) that only provided an overall assessment of the infant's level of development. Further, it was assumed that when one had the opportunity to define cognition in terms of stages and substages it provided a refinement in measurement that heretofore had been unavailable. Clearly this was appealing.

Accordingly, the stage was set for many to turn to the sensorimotor series for the study of infants at risk and handicapped and mentally retarded children. At the very least, it appeared that research with infants at risk could also reveal how the foundations might be distorted.

Funding was required to put these ideas to the test. During the early 1970s, funding agencies (e.g., National Institute of Child Health and Human Development—NICHD) expressed an interest in longitudinal studies particularly with infants who were at biosocial or environmental risk. The aim was not simply documentation of performance, but extended to attempts to predict performance from early life to later, and to offer interventions should development seem problematic. This focus represented just one of the many different ways that research related to mental retardation was being supported.

In this spirit, the Infant Studies Project (Parmelee, Kopp, & Sigman, 1976) was conceived and implemented with generous support from NICHD. The study was a longitudinal analysis of preterm infants in which primary goals were to gain a better understanding of contemporaneous and future functioning of these infants and to offer interventions as appropriate. A major subgoal of the study was to enhance prediction of outcome (see Parmelee et al., 1976, for details). Cumulative measures of neurophysiological, medical, and behavioral aspects of functioning were evaluated from birth to 9 months of age (corrections made for amount of prematurity), and were used to predict outcome, which was to 24 months of age (the children, now in their late childhood years, are still being followed; e.g., see Cohen & Parmelee, 1983). Within the Infant Studies Project, it seemed that if comprehensive measures were used and measurements taken often enough then accurate prediction might be made relatively early in life.

Because cognitive outcome was an important feature of the study, aspects of cognitive functioning were measured during early infancy including measures of attention, exploratory behavior, sensorimotor schemata, and sensorimotor functioning according to Piaget. All of these were part of the assessment battery (Kopp, 1974, 1976; Kopp, Sigman, & Parmelee, 1973; Kopp, Sigman, Parmelee, & Jeffrey, 1975; Parmelee et al., 1976; Sigman, 1974, 1976; Sigman, Kopp, Littman, & Parmelee, 1977).

Specifically in relation to Piaget's theory, sensorimotor functioning was evaluated using the Casati-Lezine (1968) series. The series had strong theoretical underpinnings, along with organization and administrative strengths. Further, the authors had reported data on a large cross-sectional sample of French infants, and these data were available for some comparisons. In addition, Kopp and colleagues (1973) had collected longitudinal data on a small sample of normally developing full-term infants observed from 7 to 24 months of age. These data suggested what might be expected in the way of developmental trends.

Within the Infant Studies Project, 9 months was selected as the age to administer the series because it was hoped that many of the infants would demonstrate the beginning of two important behaviors—object permanence and intentionality as represented by understanding of means–ends relationships. And, in fact, most of them did.

Since this was one of the first attempts to evaluate preterm infants with a sensorimotor series, many questions arose. These included, for example, the following: (1) whether there were differences in sensorimotor development of term and preterm infants; (2) whether the internal structure of the sensorimotor scales was defined by a single factor or by multiple ones; and (3) whether sensorimotor scales provided a dimension to the measurement of infant cognition above that provided by developmental assessments (Kopp, O'Connor, Sigman, Parmelee, & Marcy, 1975). Later on, the predictive strength of the sensorimotor series in relation to 2-year outcome for the risk sample was evaluated in relation to all other measures (Sigman & Parmelee, 1979).

In order to get at some of the fundamental issues, initial studies used samples of preterms that were developmentally normal. This allowed us to determine whether being *preterm* per se affected performance without having the confounding variable of developmental delay clouding the picture. Findings from these analyses revealed very few differences between terms and preterms in rate of development of stages, virtually none in terms of types of schemata displayed, and only occasionally a minor perturbation in a within-stage sequence (Kopp et al., 1975). But these minor perturbations had also occasionally been found with full-term infants (Kopp et al., 1973). These findings, which were reported for 9-month-old infants, were essentially replicated with the sample when they were 24 months of age (Kopp, 1976). Not surprisingly, when the sensorimotor evaluations were made with the entire sample of preterms, that is, when both normally developing and developmentally delayed infants were included in the sample, then delays in rate of change in sensorimotor performance were noted when compared with the performance of full-terms (Parmelee, 1976).

Using principal components analyses for the 9-month tests, the structural aspects of the subportions of the Casati-Lezine series and the Casati-Lezine were analyzed in relation to the Gesell developmental test. Findings revealed that the measures within the sensorimotor series represented statistically relatively independent variables, and that the sensorimotor evaluation and the Gesell tapped relatively different domains of function (Kopp et al., 1975). These findings were important from both a theoretical and a practical vantage point for they indicated that each type of assessment contributed unique kinds of information about infant functioning. And from a purely applied standpoint, the use of both a developmental examination (e.g., Bayley, Gesell) and a sensorimotor series might be warranted for diagnosis and intervention at least during the first year of an infant at risk.

Predictive analyses done at a later date using first-year test performance to developmental outcome at 2 years showed the sensorimotor series contributing a small but significant amount over and above the rather sizable contribution made by 9-month Gesell performance (Sigman & Parmelee, 1979). However, the contributions were so modest that they had little real significance for individual prediction. Thus the hope that sensorimotor performance would show meaningful ties to later intellectual functioning was not realized, at least for this group of children.

At about the same time that the sensorimotor series was included in the Infant Studies Project, other investigators also turned to sensorimotor tasks as a way of defining or assessing the cognitive status of risk or handicapped groups of infants and children, providing interventions, or examining the relationship between sensorimotor functioning and language abilities (Brassell & Dunst, 1976; Greenwald & Leonard, 1979; Kahn, 1975, 1976; Robinson, 1974). In general, when findings were reported for infants or young children who were developmentally delayed and/or handicapped, the data showed that the rate of growth of sensorimotor functioning was slower than for normally developing children. Stated another way, an infant had to reach some general level of developmental proficiency before successful stage performance could be obtained on any given sensorimotor task. Sensorimotor series were also used with infants who had motor limitations such as cerebral palsy or sensory impairments such as blindness. Findings obtained with some of the motorically impaired were somewhat of a surprise because they indicated that physical restrictions in and of themselves need not distort the growth of object permanence, or causality, or other sensorimotor cognitions (see Decarie, 1969; Kearsley, 1979; Kopp & Shaperman, 1973). These findings ran counter to theory in that Piaget (1970) had explicitly linked motor as well as sensory activities to the growth of cognition.

All of the studies on risk and handicapped groups of infants suggested that with some exceptions the rate of sensorimotor progression had some ties to general developmental functioning. Clearly the intactness of the organism influenced the pace at which sensorimotor cognitions developed. In a sense, these findings complemented other reports that indicated that rate was similarly affected by very adverse environments. What else might be influenced? Could, for example, the sequence of sensorimotor development show major distortions, or could the nature of schemata be changed? This does not seem to be the case—no major distortions of sequence or schemata have ever been reported in the literature (e.g., Cicchetti & Sroufe, 1976; Kopp, 1983).

Overall, then, data showed a striking similarity across all infants (normal, at risk, handicapped) in the nature and sequence of sensorimotor performance when developmental age was taken into account. This conclusion is readily interpretable when considered within the framework of contemporary views of infancy (Scarr-Salapatek, 1976). Sensorimotor behaviors are species-typical, highly canalized means by which infants establish a foothold in a complex and strange object and social world. Sensorimotor behaviors do not have to be taught; they only need some appropriate level of general experiences to emerge. Given these experiences, they emerge sooner or later even if the organism has received an insult with the exception of the most severe.

All of this knowledge is important because we know what can be expected during early development, what may affect the rate of development, and some general types of interventions that might be appropriate should a particular infant show delays in sensorimotor achievements.

In balance, what can be said about continued use of sensorimotor series as a tool to advance understanding of the cognitive competencies of infants who are at developmental risk? Realistically, very little can be gained. Knowing that risk factors can delay the growth of a cognitive ability is significant but is not an end point in and of itself. Why does this happen? What processes might be implicated in delays? Do risk factors distort some cognitive features more than others? Are some children more vulnerable to cognitive dysfunctions than others? Why?

These were and are the issues that ought to be explored but cannot be with sensorimotor series. The limitations are essentially tied to the theory itself. Scholnick (1985) describes Piagetian theory as a theory of content acquisition, and the tasks associated with content acquisition allow only one solution. As a result, task performance does not provide understanding of process or even of the reason for individual differences in rate. And identifying rates of change does not reveal the fundamentals of cognitive abilities.

This is one reason why the past few years have seen a shift away from the "classic" form of Piaget's theory. Now we have neo-Piagetian thinking, information-processing perspectives, renewed interest in individual differences, and even research done without theoretical or conceptual perspectives. Although some of the newer emphases cannot be readily extended to the study of infancy, very little has actually been applied to studies of infants at risk.

A Shift to Cognitive Process Research

The sensorimotor studies that we and others were involved with can be construed as studies of cognitive products, that is, *output of the mind*. But many cognitive processes are involved before a cognitive product is *revealed*. Attending, registering, encoding, evaluating, storing, retrieving, planning, and communicating are among some of the processes that are involved. They are of course critically important to the acquisition of knowledge: It was not surprising that researchers early on wanted to understand the cognitive processing abilities of normally developing infants. During the 1970s this research grew almost exponentially. For the most part these studies were directed toward the analysis of selective attention and recognition memory in early life. These are after all the primary means by which young infants begin to accumulate knowledge of their world.

Soon a few investigators began to study attention and memory with risk and handicapped infants using the models that were part of the burgeoning arena of infancy research with normally developing infants. Sometimes the framework was theoretical—for example, Fantz and Fagan (1976) wanted to determine whether post-conceptional age or postnatal age provided the most accurate evaluation of preterms' attention. At other times, the question was highly pragmatic—in the Infant Studies Project, for example, the issue was whether prediction of later functioning could be enhanced with the inclusion of an attention measure (Parmelee et al., 1976) (this view was not unique to us—Fantz & Nevis, 1967, and Lewis, Goldberg, & Campbell, 1969, among others, suggested that process variables assessed during infancy might serve as indices of cognitive status and predict later mental functioning). Still other times the question was a simple but important one, namely, how does a risk or handicapped group do on a particular cognitive processing measure when compared to normally developing infants (Miranda & Fantz, 1974)? The pace of research on risk accelerated as the number of questions seemed endless and the creativity of investigators appeared to be limitless.

This interest in processing abilities was reflected in the Infant Studies Project. There was an assessment of newborn fixation (e.g., Kopp et al., 1975; Sigman et al., 1973, 1977), measures of visual and auditory attention in 4-month-olds (e.g., O'Connor, 1980; Sigman & Parmelee, 1976), examination of exploratory behavior of 8-month-olds (Sigman, 1977), and an analysis of coordination and the action schemes used by 8-month-olds (Kopp, 1976). The findings obtained from use of these measures have been detailed elsewhere, as has their predictive utility (e.g., Parmelee, 1976; Sigman & Parmelee, 1979).

Because the measure of action schemes eventually became a catalyst for additional research in cognitive processing abilities, it is discussed here in some detail. Approximately 20 visual–manipulative–oral object-related behaviors had been identified as potentially in the repertoire of infants 8–9 months of age. These included mouthing objects, examining them slowly (Uzgiris, 1969), banging, shaking, throwing, and so on. In initial analyses, significant findings emerged around group differences in duration and frequency. Described briefly in Kopp (1976), Birth × Sex interactions were noted in examining and looking at objects, with full-term females showing the longest durations and the other groups (full-term males, preterm males and females) showing shorter durations. A full-term–preterm difference was found for mouthing with full-terms showing significantly more of this activity, but the difference was primarily a function of the very low durations of mouthing shown by preterm males. Mouthing was actually the longest action scheme engaged in by the full-term infants. When the action schemes were organized into conceptual categories related to direct object exploration (examining, mouthing, holding object and looking at it) and those involved in large ballistic movements (waving, banging, etc.) the only significant difference that emerged was that males did more of the latter than did females. Overall then preterm males did not evidence a great deal of direct object exploration (examining, mouthing) but they did engage in ballistic activities. In a very real way, their object exploration was unlike that of full-term males and preterm females. This *different pattern* of action scheme activity begged for more detailed analyses.

Could the modes of object exploration influence how or what an infant learned? Might the findings also have special relevance for preterm males who consistently show a greater number of difficulties than preterm females (e.g., in some longitudinal samples as many as 25 percent had learning difficulties; Davies & Stewart, 1975; Rubin, Rosenblatt, & Balow, 1973).

In a quest to get at some of these issues, Kopp and Vaughn (1982) turned to a reanalysis of the action scheme data, specifically where findings indicated the term and preterm differences in duration scores were most apparent. These were behaviors that related to durations of visual attention and explorations. The action scheme observations were examined with a goal of determining whether higher durations of attention and exploration were related to 2-year outcome as measured by developmental and sensorimotor assessments. A mixed gestational age, gender, ethnic, and social class sample of 76 Infant Studies Project preterm infants (51 males) who were without major delays was used. Again a priori conceptual clusters were established with one containing action schemes that we labeled *explore* (examining, mouthing, holding and looking at objects, and looking without contact) and another labeled *look,* which was nonexploratory attention to mother or around the room. A 9-month Gesell score was also included in the measurement battery. Outcome was in relation to 2-year Bayley MDI, Gesell DQ, sensorimotor test score, and a receptive language measure.

Findings from hierarchical stepwise procedures revealed that for the entire sample Gesell scores, social class, and ethnic status were highly significant predictors to outcome. Of importance, the two duration scores of *explore* and *look* also contributed significantly to outcome. Of equal import was the fact that the scores on the outcome measures differed markedly for males and females. In general, girls received higher scores than boys and Caucasian females scored highest of all groups. Because of this and because of our interest in males, the data were rerun separately by gender.

These analyses showed that for males findings were similar to those obtained with the sample as a whole. That is, the duration measures contributed significantly to outcome scores, and specifically *explore* predicted to Bayley MDI outcome and *look* to Gesell outcome. In contrast, the multiple r's for the female sample were greater than for the sample as a whole, and the duration measures of attention did not provide significant increments for them to outcome prediction.

Thus the results indicated that a duration measure of attention and exploration obtained during infancy with a male sample at risk made a supplemental contribution (above that offered by developmental assessments) to later cognitive functioning. The reason that exploration was more highly related to Bayley performance and social attentiveness to Gesell score may have been partly a function of item content and emphasis within these tests.

The data for the males were consistent with those from other investigators who reported recent studies of the relationship between information-processing abilities (e.g., response to novelty, dishabituation) of infants and later development (e.g., Fagan & McGrath, 1981; Fagan & Singer, 1982; Lewis & Brooks-Gunn, 1981), although gender differences were not reported (even more recent studies, e.g., Caron,

Caron, & Glass, 1983; Rose & Wallace, 1985, affirm the general predictive trend). The data were also consistent with McCall's (1976, 1979) model of mental development in which exploratory manipulation was the first principal component derived from analysis of developmental test data from infants 8–12 months old. Of equal importance, the role of status variables in predicting outcome for the females in the sample is consistent with other studies that found that individual differences in IQ were better predicted by early test data for girls than for boys.

Overall then these preliminary findings on a measure of the way infants use their visual and manipulative abilities to explore were thought-provoking. It seemed possible that what was actually being measured was an analog of the infant's ability to sustain attention to objects. This ability involves both intentional and voluntary input on the part of the infant to stay with a task or situation for informational and/or motivational purposes. In sustained attention, the child is truly *acting* on his or her own behalf. A more systematic study of sustained attention with infants at risk was warranted.

The Study of Sustained Attention as a Cognitive Process: The Early Years

The catalyst that spurred the systematic study of sustained attention came about in the late 1970s when *Project Reach* was funded by the then Bureau for the Education of the Handicapped. *Reach* was part of a large-scale effort designed to obtain fundamental information about the capabilites of handicapped and at risk infants and preschoolers. It was hoped that this information would eventually be used in the implementation of intervention programs.

Sustained attention and self-control became the focus of research for the infancy and toddler studies. In actuality, the Infant Studies Project data and observations served as the basis of interest for studies in both domains. The sustained attention studies were a direct outgrowth of the data, and were reinforced by literature on older handicapped children that indicated sustained attention was a frequent and ongoing source of difficulty for these children. The link to the self-control studies was more indirect. While testing 2-year-olds, I had been impressed by the fact that some of the children were totally out of control (even for children of this age). Repeatedly, the question "why" surfaced. A review of the research literature on older children clearly indicated that self-control was a problematic area of functioning for risk and handicapped groups; this was a second impetus to study this topic.

With my own and others' observations in hand, it seemed reasonable to assume that problems in attention and control could occur as early as the second year of life. The source could be child or caregiver since both enter into major transitions during this time. There are of course the well-documented developmental shifts in cognitive, linguistic, motoric, and social functioning that occur by the end of the second year. It is possible that, if distortions occur in these domains, they may have ramifications for other aspects of behavior both in the short and the long term. Further, the role and influence of caregivers in socializing the child and organizing and directing the child's milieu become increasingly salient, more explicit, and vital with respect to monitoring and teaching the walking, talking, autonomous, and striving 2-year-old.

Accordingly, attention and self-control were studied extensively. Only the sustained attention research is discussed here. The interested reader can find discussions and research on self-control in Kopp (1982), Kopp, Krakow, and Vaughn (1983), Vaughn, Kopp, and Krakow (1984), and other reports.

The first challenge in the sustained attention research was to define the nature of what was being studied. After a lengthy period of observations and pilot studies, sustained attention was operationalized as a *focus upon and continued engagement with objects*. This could include both visual and visual–manipulative actions with objects, and involved exploration as well as play with objects, and the inclusion of others into the activity at hand. The critical properties of this aspect of attention are, first, that the infant is fully focused upon the activity, and, second, that the child is able to disregard extraneous, nonfocal features of the environment (Krakow, Kopp, Vaughn, 1981). The content of activity is unimportant—the child who sits and examines different objects in succession can be as engaged as the one who focuses solely on a single toy.

The definition and the research strategy that was adopted in studying sustained attention differed, by choice, from the theme of selective attention and habituation that has characterized much of the research on early visual attention (Banks, 1980; Cohen & Salapatek, 1975; Haith, 1980). These studies often have relied on two-dimensional stimuli that are selected by the researcher who uses a duration measure to document the amount of time spent looking at particular stimuli.

However, the nature of selective attention and the way it is measured during the early months of life do not appear to be as applicable to the older infant or toddler as they are to the younger one. The fact is that exploration expands dramatically in the first year (Gibson & Rader, 1979) and infants begin to show individualized preferences, and it is often difficult to maintain infant interest in two-dimensional visual targets once they discover their hands and three-dimensional objects.

From a developmental standpoint, it seems reasonable to presume that there is a progression from selective attention to certain visual stimuli to the later-developing voluntary sustained attention that is manifested to objects that are both seen and manipulated. Along the way, however, attention will be pressed into varied service. Early on the infant's discovery of its hands at around 3–4 months heralds a preoccupation that will command the focus of attention for several months (Bruner, 1970). Gradually, with experience, attention can shift from the hands per se to what the hands can do with objects, and finally to the objects themselves (Uzgiris, 1969). Infants will then engage in a variety of exploratory activities with their hands, attending and studying objects for their particular characteristics. This capability seemingly signals the beginning of voluntary sustained attention to objects, or, stated another way, the ability to become engaged in and remain engaged in play and task situations. Sustained attention, Kagan and Kogan (1970) surmised, becomes increasingly important during the first year of life. The Kopp and Vaughn (1982) analysis supported this statement at least in a preliminary fashion.

The plan in studying sustained attention was first to sample a normally developing group of 2- and 3-year-olds in order to determine patterns of functioning and look for developmental trends. With this information in hand, groups of risk and handicapped children would then be examined. That is what occurred. Because findings have been reported in a variety of forums and some have not been published at all, some detail is provided about the children, procedures, and results.

Normally Developing Children

In order to explore developmental trends, normally developing children were observed at 12, 18, 24, and 30 months of age (Krakow et al., 1981). All were healthy children of middle-class parents. Each child was seen in a small carpeted area of a laboratory room that simulated a sparsely furnished living space. The child was told to play and was given a bucket of age-appropriate toys (e.g., doll, necklace, hammer, wheel toy, cars, comb, etc.) placed on the floor. Mother sat nearby and was requested not to initiate interaction with the child, but to respond if the child turned to her, and if the child left the scene to redirect him or her back to the toys. Six minutes were videotaped.

A major dependent measure was seconds on task (or its converse, off time), defined as the cumulative duration of child engagement with the toys. Other dependent measures included the nature of on-task activities (e.g., bringing a toy to mother), off-task activities that were defined as glancing away from the toys for longer than 3 sec, wandering away, initiating social contact unmediated by toys, or manipulating any of the nontoys in the vicinity (e.g., camera, chair). In addition, momentary gazes away (less than 3 sec and intensity of object exploration (ranging from unoccupied to intensely engaged) were also coded.

Findings (Kopp, Krakow, & Vaughn, 1982; Krakow et al., 1981) indicated significant changes (from 12 to 30 months) in time on activity with linear increases from almost 5 min at the youngest ages to almost 6 min at the oldest. Using a small subset sample of children seen longitudinally, cross-time intercorrelations were computed for time on task. The resulting correlation matrix indicated that time on task at 12 months was significantly related to time on task at each subsequent age period.

Although the data from the 12- and 18-month-olds revealed that most of the sample showed a great deal of interest in the assorted play objects and either played with them alone or brought the objects to mother to see, a few children were very social (toward their mothers) and thereby showed somewhat higher levels of off time than the rest of their peers. Although the implications of object versus the somewhat more social patterns of interaction (e.g., differences in developmental performance) were examined, nothing substantive emerged. It may be that the differences were just not very meaningful or that a more fine-grained analysis was needed in order to uncover implications.

In other analyses, additional age-related changes emerged. One involved the intensity of object orientation, which increased markedly from 12 to 18 months. The other related to the very short gazes away from the toys to mother or experimenter around the room (as if monitoring the environs). These decreased significantly.

Overall, the results were interpreted as indicating that with age not only are children able to spend longer periods engaged with objects, but they appear to be more committed to objects of interest, disregarding extraneous nonfocal features of the environment. And although young children still monitor their environs with momentary gazes away, these diminish as they get older. Apparently, these developmental progressions reflect increasing efficiency in information-processing abilities that in part must be tied to a general advance in cognitive development. Finally, the results indicate that there is some stability in individual differences among young children in sustained attention.

It is likely that minor variations in sustained attention hold essentially little in the way of long-term developmental ramifications, but that very high or very low off time might be developmentally meaningful. Vulnerable children may be those who cannot maintain appropriate levels of commitment to tasks or to play (low levels of sustained attention) or children who are consistently and almost exclusively engrossed in their activities (highest levels of sustained attention). In either instance the extremes may limit information intake either around characteristics of the object world or around the monitoring of object or social signals from the environment. Clearly, these speculations require empirical support.

Developmentally Delayed Samples

Sustained attention data were collected using similar procedures with two groups of developmentally delayed children (Down syndrome and delayed due to unknown etiology) and a small group of nondelayed but at risk toddlers. The goal was to determine developmental trends with these children and also the quality of their performance on the sustained attention task.

It seemed essential to generate a sample selection strategy and some preliminary hypotheses for handling data analyses, otherwise the data might be uninterpretable. One reason is that samples constituted with non–normally developing children are often heterogeneous, and confounding and uncontrolled variables abound. In order to make the sample somewhat homogeneous, developmental age was selected as a matching variable. The rationale was that the data with normally developing children had revealed clear evidence of developmental trends. Theoretically, the choice also stemmed from a desire to explore further the controversy around developmental versus different perspectives that often permeates discussions in the mental retardation literature. On the one hand, the developmental view infers that a sample matched on developmental age results in performance that is grossly equivalent (this is akin to the mental age argument of Zigler, 1969). A version of the difference view found in Kopp (1983) suggests that the structure and form of behaviors of children equated on developmental age but who differ in chronological age (e.g., developmentally delayed, mentally retarded) will be grossly similar, but that subtle, albeit meaningful, differences will emerge. In one study, for example, Jones (1980), using developmental age matches, noted that Down syndrome children used low levels of referential eye contact. This involves pausing in an activity, directing eye contact to mother to elicit a response, and on receiving same, returning to the original activity. This chain of events requires the infant to attach some meaning to the act of engaging another person in an activity and then interpreting the meaning and significance of the exchange. Children who do not do this are at a disadvantage for expanding their knowledge base.

Thus the decision was made to equate developmental age and probe for differences in performance. It seemed that differences might emerge in situations where the primary task involved acquisition, encoding, retention, or transformation of information that was not immediately and directly brought to the individual, or in tasks where information was not obvious or had to compete with other stimuli. If these guesses could be experimentally tested, we might further our understanding of the meaning of developmental delays.

For the sustained attention study, each child was tested with a developmental examination (the Gesell, for its ease of administration). In addition, other criteria were established for the sample. The children had to have a developmental quotient (Gesell & Amatruda, 1950) of 50–85, be no more than 5 years of chronological age, and fall within 12–30 months of developmental age. Operating under these constraints, two separate samples were assembled of the developmentally delayed children, one with a mean age of 17 months, the other with a mean age of 26–27 months (eight of the Down syndrome and three of the unknown etiology sample were seen at both ages). Using matching procedures, a group of normally developing children was drawn from the subject pool (previously tested children) to provide a comparison group. Ideally, samples would have been generated that exactly coincided with the ages of the normally developing children that had been studied earlier. Unfortunately, the handicapped subject pool was limited.

The data from two studies of the delayed children, the first documenting findings with the younger group and the second with the older ones, have been reported elsewhere (Krakow & Kopp, 1983). In brief, analyses comparing the normally developing and both groups of delayed revealed one significant difference in the duration of sustained attention at the younger age and none at the older age. It is not apparent why the difference emerged, but the fact that it did not reappear at older ages suggests it may not have been developmentally meaningful. However, this premise is considered tentative because the samples were not followed longitudinally.

Interesting results were obtained with the younger children, who consistently evidenced a mixture of mature and immature behaviors (e.g., three times as much throwing for both of the delayed groups than for the normally developing one) and less monitoring of the environment in terms of short glances away from the play activity. Furthermore, the Down syndrome children turned less frequently to their mothers at both ages than the other groups. In contrast the children delayed of unknown etiology spent a considerable amount of off-task behavior in an unoccupied way (e.g., they did not explore other facets of the room and surroundings) although this was considerably greater at the younger age than the older one. Table 17.2 summarizes these data by showing the percentage of time the children engaged in sustained attention and other activities at each of the ages. Among the older children, differences were also found in off-task behavior as described, and in the quality of play behavior. Specifically, the delayed groups again showed facets of immature behavior in their play (e.g., stereotypic, regressive, repetitive actions) that were exceedingly rare in the play of normally developing children of equivalent developmental age. This mixture of mature and immature behavior is very reminiscent

TABLE 17.2. Sustained Attention: Amount and Content of On- and Off-Task Time

| Behavior Category | Developmental Ages | | | | | |
| | 17 Months | | | 26–27 Months | | |
	ND[a]	DS	UE	ND	DS	UE
Sustained attention (on task)	81[b]	85	69	88	86	90
Off-time activity:						
with other objects	<7	6	1	7	10	11
with social interactions	>7	2	5	4	<1	5
Unoccupied	2	5	23	<1	4	4

[a]ND = normally developing; DS = Down syndrome; UE = developmentally delayed with unknown etiology.
[b]Percentage scores.

of the behavioral shifts from more advanced to more immature and vice versa described by Inhelder (1963) in her studies of mentally retarded individuals.

In sum, it is clear that the delayed young children matched on developmental age had a similar repertoire to children who were not delayed. The delayed groups were able to direct their attention voluntarily and intentionally to objects and people of interest. Further, the developmental age increases documented with the normally developing sample had some counterpart among delayed groups, particularly those with unknown etiology. What the delayed children could not do was consistently show mature behaviors, nor were they able to capitalize and use all of the social and object resources that were available. In this sense they unfortunately limited their information intake around the myriad subdued or subtle cues that abounded in the task situation. To the extent that this pattern continues, the acquisition of knowledge has to be compromised.

The Balance Sheet

The research reported above was an attempt to obtain developmental information and some understanding of individual variability in the young child's ability to sustain attention to objects. The construct was operationalized as a focus upon and continued engagement with objects. A duration score related to on-task time (or the converse) was a primary dependent measure, although numerous other observations were coded, including the nature of the children's activities when they were engaged with toys and when they were not.

The sustained attention procedure appears to be an effective paradigm because it allows the child freedom to focus upon and to choose objects of interest. Given this option, even the 1-year-old child can devote many minutes to continued and rich interactions with objects. The freedom of selection probably accounted for the richness of the data that showed that sustained attention becomes longer over time (12–30 months), but, more important, it becomes more controlled, focused, and intense even during the short period from 12 to 18 months of age. The findings also contributed to our understanding of play as a mediator of social interactions in that most children attempt to involve their mothers at least to some degree in their activities. And the data revealed interesting information about attention deployment. Despite very absorbing play situations, young children take short time-out bouts to monitor their surroundings.

These data highlight the fact that if performance had been examined only in terms of on or off times a great deal of meaningful information would have been missed. And although the measurement of on-task time yielded developmental trends, its value as a gauge of individual differences requires additional study. Clearly, it did not provide the most interesting information about the nature of sustained attention among developmentally delayed young children. The truly provocative findings emerged from the analysis of the content of activities during on and off times. The results further support the view that process-oriented studies of cognition will yield greater understanding of the at risk and handicapped child than will research focused exclusively on product.

A Broader Perspective

Challenges still confront the researcher interested in processing-oriented studies with infants who have problems. Thus far the focus has been primarily on attention and memory to the virtual exclusion of other cognitive mechanisms. Scholnick (1985) has made some cogent appraisals of risk research. She states that, if a goal is to determine where and when distortions in functioning arise, then it is essential to ask which processes show distortions and which do not, and which do or do not show interactions with task demands. She further notes that the speed of processing, attention, and memory depends on the way a task is organized. But to date there does not appear to be a single study of infants at risk for cognitive impairments where variations in task organization have been systematically studied.

Scholnick (1985) also questions the generality inherent in the term *distortions*. Implicitly, if not explicitly, the search for distortions in early functioning has been the impetus for many studies. Scholnick asks: What does a distortion mean? With reference to attention, is it attending less in general, or in certain situations or to certain stimuli, or the use of different attentional mechanisms? Is a distortion the presence of a different pattern of interrelations among abilities ? And she adds:

> Perhaps if there were a way to characterize these distortions we would be closer to understanding how a given etiology has an impact. As we look at component processes such as memory or attention we could see how a task is put together and we could understand performance.

Scholnick's call for specificity is a challenge that ultimately will have to be met—if answers are to be obtained about the how and why of cognitive impairments among infants at risk or with handicapping conditions.

At the very least, documenting distortions may be very difficult, and may require moving beyond quantitative tools to qualitative types of analyses. Consider that normally developing infants and young children show richness and diversity in their behaviors; they attend to their surroundings and show intensity and zest in many of their object and social interactions. These characteristics surface particularly during the last quarter of the first year and are very evident during the second. Although children of this age are not easily thwarted in reaching their goals, and do not have the resources to generate many alternatives when frustrated, they have persistence, goals, and a desire to do.

In contrast, although similar behaviors behavioral qualities can be identified among young children who are mildly to moderately developmentally delayed (e.g., a developmental quotient in the 50–80 range) matched on developmental age, their repertoire of behavior does not appear to function in the same way as that of the normally developing child. In all probability these children have the requisite cognitive processing skills in their repertoire, many show goals and desires, and many demonstrate quite mature behaviors on occasion, but the cognitive processing (e.g., use of cues, attention, comprehension) does not always operate efficiently. The motivation to do may be misplaced for time or situation, and the mature behavior is often not sustained. The net result is insertion of inappropriate behaviors or deletion of appropriate ones for certain object and interpersonal behaviors or deletion of appropriate ones for certain object and interpersonal situations—and a child who is qualitatively different from developmental age–matched peers.

REFERENCES

Ainsworth, M. D. S. (1962). The effects of maternal deprivation: A review of findings and controversy in the context of research strategy. In *Deprivation of maternal care*, Public Health Paper # 14. Geneva: World Health Organization.

Baker, R. L., & Mednick, B. R. (1984). *Influence on human development: A longitudinal perspective*. The Hague: Kluwer-Nijhoff.

Banks, M. (1980). The development of visual accommodation during early infancy. *Child Development, 51,* 646–666.

Bayley, N. (1969). *Manual for the Bayley Scales of Infant Development*. New York: Psychological Corporation.

Birch, H. G., & Gussow, J. D. (1970). *Disadvantaged children: Health, nutrition and social failure*. New York: Harcourt, Brace & World.

Bowlby, J. (1940). The influence of early environment in the development of neurosis and neurotic character. *International Journal of Psychoanalysis, 21,* 154–178.

Bowlby, J. (1946). *Forty-four juvenile thieves, their characters and home life*. London: Bailliere, Tyndall & Cox.

Bowlby, J. (1951). *Maternal care and mental health*. Geneva: World Health Organization.

Bowlby, J. (1969). *Attachment and loss: Vol. 1. Attachment*. London: Hogarth.

Brassell, W. R., & Dunst, C. J. (1976). Comparison of two procedures for fostering the development of the object construct. *American Journal of Mental Deficiency, 80,* 523–528.

Brenner, R. H. (1978). *Children and youth in America: A documentary history: Vol. 1. 1600–1865*. Cambridge, MA: Harvard University Press.

Bretherton, I., & Waters, E. (1985). Growing points of attachment: Theory and research. *Monographs of the Society for Research in Child Development (50,* No. 1–2).

Broman, S. H., Nichols, P. L., & Kennedy, W. A. (1975). *Preschool IQ: Prenatal and early developmental correlates*. Hillsdale, NJ: Erlbaum.

Brophy, A. B. (1972). *Foundlings on the frontier. Racial and religious conflict in Arizona territory, 1904–1905*. Tucson: University of Arizona Press.

Bruner, J. S. (1970). The growth and structure of skill. In K. J. Connolly (Ed.), *Mechanisms of motor skill development*. New York: Academic.

Campos, J. (1983). Psychology. In R. N. Emde (Ed.), *Rene Spitz: Dialogues from infancy. Selected papers*. New York: International Universities Press.

Caron, R. F., Caron, A. J., & Glass, P. (1983). Responsiveness to relational information as a measure of cognitive functioning in non-suspect infants. In T. Field & A. Sostek (Eds.), *Infants born at risk: Physiological, perceptual and cognitive processes*. New York: Grune & Stratton.

Casati, I., & Lezine, I. (1968). *Les etapes de l'intelligence sensori-motrice*. Paris: Editions du Centre de Psychologie Appliquee.

Casler, L. (1963). Maternal deprivation: A critical review of the literature. *Monographs of the Society for Research in Child Development, 26*(2, Serial No. 80).

Chess, S. (1974). The influence of defect on development in children with congenital rubella. *Merrill-Palmer Quarterly, 20,* 255–274.

Chess, S. (1977). Follow-up report on autism in congenital rubella. *Merrill-Palmer Quarterly, 20,* 255–274.

Cicchetti, D., & Sroufe, L. A. (1978). The relationship between affective and cognitive development in Down's syndrome infants. *Child Development, 47,* 920–929.

Cohen, L. B., & Parmelee, A. H. (1983) Prediction of five-year Stanford-Binet scores in preterm infants. *Child Development, 54,* 1242–1253.

Davies, P., & Stewart, A. L. (1975). Low birth-weight infants and neurological sequelae and later intelligence. *British Medical Bulletin, 31,* 85–91.

Decarie, T. G. (1969). A study of the mental and emotional development of the thalidomide child. In B. M. Foss (Ed.), *Determinants of infant behaviour* (Vol. 4). London: Methuen.

Dennis, W. (1972). *Historical readings in development psychology*. New York: Appleton-Century-Crofts.

Emde, R. N. (1983). The prerepresentational self and its affective core. *The Psychoanalytic Study of the Child, 38,* 165–192.

Emde, R. N., & Harmon, R. J. (1983). Endogenous and exogenous smiling systems in early infancy. *Journal of the American Academy of Child Psychiatry, 11,* 77–100.

Escalona, S. K. (1985). Personal communication.

Escalona, S. K., & Corman, H. (1967, March). *The validation of Piaget's hypothesis concerning the development of sensorimotor intelligence: Methodological issues.* Paper presented at the biennial meeting of the Society for Research in Child Development, New York.

Fagan, J. F., & McGrath, S. K. (1981). Infant recognition memory and later intelligence. In K. F. Riegel (Ed.), *Intelligence: Alternative views of a paradigm.* New York: S. Karger.

Fagan, J. F., & Singer, L. (1982). Infant recognition memory as a measure of intelligence. In L. P. Lipsitt (Ed.), *Advances in infancy research* (Vol. 2). Norwood, NJ: Ablex.

Fantz, R. L., & Fagan, J. F. (1975). Visual attention to size and number of pattern details by term and preterm infants during the first six months. *Child Development, 16,* 3–18.

Fantz, R. L., & Nevis, S. (1967). The predictive value of changes in visual preferences in early infancy. In J. Hellmuth (Ed.), *The exceptional infant* (Vol. 1). Seattle: Straub & Hellmuth.

Field, T. M., Sostek, A. M., Goldberg, S., & Shuman, H. H. (Eds.). (1979). *Infants born at risk: Behavior and development.* Jamaica, NY: Spectrum.

Fishler, K., Graliker, B. V., & Koch, R. (1964–1965). The predictability of intelligence with Gesell developmental scales in mentally retarded infants and young children. *American Journal of Mental Deficiency, 69,* 515–525.

Flavell, J. (1985). *Cognitive Development* (2nd ed.). Englewood Cliffs, NJ: Prentice-Hall.

Gaskill, H. S. (1963). *Counterpoint: Libidinal object and subject.* New York: International Universities Press.

Gesell, A. (1921). Hemihypertrophy and mental defect. *Archives of Neurology & Psychiatry, 6,* 400–423.

Gesell, A. (1929). *Infancy and human growth.* New York: Macmillan.

Gesell, A., & Amatruda, C. S. (1950). *Gesell and Amatruda's developmental diagnosis: The evaluation and management of normal and abnormal neuropsychologic development in infancy and early childhood.* Hagerstown, MD: Harper & Row.

Goldfarb, W. (1944). The effects of early institutional care on adolescent personality: Rorschach data. *American Journal of Orthopsychiatry, 14,* 441–447.

Goldfarb, W. (1945). Psychological privation in infancy and subsequent adjustment. *American Journal of Orthopsychiatry, 15,* 247–255.

Goodenough, F. L. (1932). Expression of the emotions in a blind–deaf child. *Journal of Abnormal & Social Psychology, 27,* 328–333.

Gibson, E., & Rader, N. (1979). Attention: The perceiver as performer. In G. A. Hale & M. Lewis (Eds.), *Attention and cognitive development.* New York: Plenum.

Graham, F. K., Ernhart, C. B., Thurston, D. L., & Craft, M. (1962). Development three years after perinatal anoxia and other potentially damaging new born experiences. *Psychological Monographs, 76* (3, Whole No. 522).

Graham, F. K., Pennoyer, M. M., Caldwell, B. M., Greenman, M., & Hartmann, A. T. (1957). Relationships between clinical status and behavior test performance in a newborn group with histories suggesting anoxia. *Journal of Pediatrics, 50,* 177–189.

Greenwald, C. A., & Leonard, L. B. (1979). Communicative and sensorimotor development of Down's syndrome children. *American Journal of Mental Deficiency, 84,* 296–303.

Hagberg, B., & Hagberg, G. (1984). Aspects of prevention of pre-, peri-, and postnatal brain pathology in severe and mild mental retardation. In J. Dobbing, A. D. B. Clarke, J. A. Corbett, J. Hogg, & R. D. Robinson (Eds.), *Scientific studies in mental retardation.* London: Royal Society of Medicine & Macmillan Press Ltd.

Haith, M. (1980). *Rules that babies look by: The organization of newborn visual activity.* Hillsdale, NJ: Erlbaum.

Jones, D. H. M. (1980). Prelinguistic communication skill in Down's syndrome and normal infants. In T. M. Field (Ed.), *High-risk infants and children.* New York: Academic.

Kearsley, R. B. (1979) Iatrogenic retardation: A syndrome of learned incompetence. In R. B. Kearsley & I. Sigel (Eds.), *Infants at risk: Assessment of cognitive functioning.* Hillsdale, NJ: Erlbaum.

Kearsley, R. B., & Sigel, I. E. (Eds.). (1979). *Infants at risk: Assessment of cognitive functioning.* Hillsdale, NJ: Erlbaum.

Kopp, C. B. (in preparation). *On attention in early life.*

Kopp, C. B. (1974). Fine motor behaviors of infants. *Developmental Medicine & Child Neurology, 16,* 629–636.

Kopp, C. B. (1976). Action-schemes of 8-month-old infants. *Developmental Psychology, 12,* 361–362.

Kopp, C. B. (1982). The role of theoretical frameworks in the study of at-risk and handicapped young children. In D. Bricker (Ed.), *Application of research findings to intervention with at-risk and handicapped infants.* Baltimore: University Park Press.

Kopp, C. B. (1983). Risk factors in development. In J. J. Campos & M. Haith (Eds.), *Handbook of child psychology* (Vol. 2). New York: Wiley.

Kopp, C. B., O'Connor, M. J., Sigman, M., Parmelee, A. H., & Marcy, T. G. (1975). *Early cognitive development of pre-term and fullterm infants: Component structure of sensorimotor and developmental examinations.* Denver: Society for Research in Child Development.

Kopp, C. B., & Krakow, J. B. (1983). The developmentalist and the study of biological risk: A view of the past with an eye toward the future. *Child Development, 54,* 1086–1108.

Kopp, C. B., Krakow, J. B., & Vaughn, B. E. (1983). Patterns of self-control in young handicapped children. In M. Perlmutter (Ed.), Development and policy concerning children with special needs. *The Minnesota Symposia on Child Psychology* (Vol. 16). Hillsdale, NJ: Erlbaum.

Kopp, C. B., Krakow, J. B., & Vaughn, B. E. (1982). Unpublished manuscript.

Kopp, C. B., & McCall, R. B. (1982). Predicting later mental performance for normal, at-risk, and handicapped infants. In P. B. Baltes & O. G. Brim (Eds.), *Life-span development and behavior* (Vol. 4). New York: Academic.

Kopp, C. B., O'Connor, M. J., Sigman, M., Parmelee, A. H., & Marcy, T. G. (1975, March). *Early cognitive development of pre-term and fullterm infants: Component structure of sensorimotor and developmental examination.* Paper presented at the Society for Research in Child Development, Denver.

Kopp, C. B., & Parmelee, A. H. (1979). Prenatal and perinatal influences on behavior. In J. D. Osofsky (Ed.), *Handbook of infant development.* New York: Wiley.

Kopp, C. B., & Shaperman, J. (1973). Cognitive development in the absence of object manipulation during infancy. *Developmental Psychology, 9,* 430.

Kopp, C. B., Sigman, M. D., & Parmelee, A. H. (1973). A longitudinal study of sensorimotor development. *Developmental Psychology, 10,* 687–695.

Kopp, C. B., Sigman, M., Parmelee, A. H., & Jeffrey, W. E. (1975). Neurological organization and visual fixation in infants at 40 weeks conceptional age. *Developmental Psychobiology, 8,* 165–171.

Kopp, C. B., & Vaughn, B. E. (1982). Sustained attention during exploratory manipulation as a predictor of cognitive competence in preterm infants. *Child Development, 53,* 174–182.

Krakow, J. B., & Kopp, C. B. (1983). The effects of developmental delay on sustained attention in young infants. *Child Development, 54,* 1143–1155.

Krakow, J. B., Kopp, C. B., & Vaughn, B. E. (1981). *Sustained attention in young children.* Paper presented at biennial meeting of the Society for Research in Child Development, Boston.

Levy, D. M. (1937). Primary affect hunger. *American Journal of Psychiatry, 94,* 643–652.

Lewis, M., & Brooks-Gunn, J. (1981). Visual attention at three months as a predictor of cognitive functioning at two years of age. In K. F. Riegel (Ed.), *Intelligence: Alternative views of a paradigm.* New York: S. Karger.

Lewis, M., Goldberg, S., & Campbell, H. (1969). A developmental study of information processing within the first three years of life; response decrement to a redundant signal. *Monographs of the Society for Research in Child Development, 34* (9, Serial No. 133).

Lilienfeld, A. M., & Parkhurst, E. (1951). A study of the association of factors of pregnancy and parturition with the development of cerebral palsy: A preliminary report. *American Journal of Hygiene, 53,* 262–282.

Lilienfeld, A. M., & Pasamanick, B. (1954). Association of maternal and fetal factors with the development of epilepsy, I: Abnormalities in the prenatal and paranatal periods. *Journal of the American Medical Association, 155,* 719–724.

Lipsitt, L. P., & Field, T. M. (1982). *Infant behavior and development: Perinatal risk and newborn behavior.* Norwood, NJ: Ablex.

McCall, R. B. (1976). Toward an epigenetic conception of mental development in the first three years of life. In M. Lewis (Ed.), *Origins of intelligence: Infancy and early childhood.* New York: Plenum.

McCall, R. B. (1979). Qualitative transitions in behavioral development in the first two years of life. In M. Bornstein & W. Kessen (Eds.), *Psychological development from infancy.* Hillsdale, NJ: Erlbaum.

Miranda, S. B., & Fantz, R. L. (1974). Recognition memory in Down's syndrome and normal infants. *Child Development, 45,* 651–660.

O'Connor, M. J. (1980). A comparison of preterm and fullterm infants on auditory discriminations at four months and on Bayley scales of infant development at eighteen months. *Child Development, 51,* 81–88.

Parmelee, A. H. (1976). *Diagnostic and intervention studies of high-risk infants* (USPHS Contract No. 1-HD-32776). (Report)

Parmelee, A. H., Kopp, C. B., & Sigman, M. (1976). Selection of developmental assessment techniques for infants at risk. *Merrill-Palmer Quarterly, 22,* 177–199.

Pasamanick, B., & Knobloch, H. (1961). Epidemiologic studies on the complications of pregnancy and the birth process. In G. Caplan (Ed.), *Prevention of mental disorders in children.* New York: Plenum.

Piaget, J. (1952). *The origins of intelligence in children.* New York: International Universities Press.

Piaget, J. (1954). *The construction of reality in the child.* New York: Basic.

Piaget, J. (1970). Piaget's theory. In P. H. Mussen (Ed.), *Carmichael's manual of child psychiatry* (3rd ed.) (Vol. 1). New York: Wiley.

Platt, A. M. (1969). *The child savers. The invention of delinquency.* Chicago: University of Chicago Press.

Powdermaker, F., Levis, H. T., & Touraine, G. (1937). Psychopathology and treatment of delinquent girls. *American Journal of Orthopsychiatry, 7,* 58–71.

Rangell, L. (1963). Beyond and between the no and the yes: A tribute to Dr. Rene A. Spitz. In H. S. Gaskill (Ed.), *Counterpoint: Libidinal object and subject.* New York: International Universities Press.

Riis, J. (1957). *How the other half lives. Studies among the tenements of New York.* New York: Hill & Wang.

Robinson, C. (1974). Error patterns in level 4 and level 5 object permanence training. *American Journal of Mental Deficiency, 78,* 389–396.

Rose, S., & Wallace, I. (1985). Cross-modal and intramodel transfer as predictors of mental development in full-term and preterm infants. *Development Psychology, 21,* 949–962.

Rubin, A., Rosenblatt, C., & Balow, B. (1973). Psychological and educational sequelae of prematurity. *Pediatrics, 52,* 352–363.

Sameroff, A. J., & Chandler, M. J. (1975). Reproductive risk and the continuum of caretaking casualty. In F. D. Horowitz, M. Hetherington, S. Scarr-Salapatek, & G. Siegel (Eds.), *Review of child development research* (Vol. 4). Chicago: University of Chicago Press.

Scarr-Salapatek, S. (1976). An evolutionary perspective on infant intelligence: Species patterns and individual variations. In M. Lewis (Ed.), *Origins of intelligence: Infancy and early childhood.* New York: Plenum.

Scholnick, E. (1985). Personal communication.

Sears, R. R. (1975). Your ancients revisited: A history of child development. In E. M. Hetherington (Ed.), *Review of child development research* (Vol. 5). Chicago: University of Chicago Press.

Serafica, F. C., & Cicchetti, D. (1976). Down's syndrome children in a strange situation: Attachment and exploration behaviors. *Merrill-Palmer Quarterly, 22,* 137–150.

Share, J., Webb, A., & Koch, R. (1961–1962). A preliminary investigation of the early developmental status of mongoloid infants. *American Journal of Mental Deficiency, 66,* 238–241.

Shirley, M. (1939). A behavior syndrome characterizing prematurely born children. *Child Development, 9,* 347–360.

Sigman, M. (1976). Early cognitive development of pre-term and full-term infants: Exploratory behavior in eight-month-old infants. *Child Development, 47,* 606–612.

Sigman, M., Kopp, C. B., Littman, B., & Parmelee, A. H. (1977). Social and familial influences on the development of pre-term infants. *Journal of Pediatric Psychology, 6,* 1–12.

Sigman, M., & Parmelee, A. H. (1974). Visual preferences of four-month-old premature and full-term infants. *Child Development, 45,* 959–965.

Sigman, M., & Parmelee, A. H. (1979). Longitudinal evaluation of the preterm infant. In T. M. Field, A. M. Sostek, S. Goldberg, & H. H. Shuman (Eds.), *Infants born at risk: Behavior and development.* Jamaica, NY: Spectrum.

Spitz, R. A. (1945). An inquiry into the genesis of psychiatric conditions in early childhood. *The Psychoanalytic Study of the Child, 1,* 53–74.

Spitz, R. A., & Wolf, M. (1946). Anaclictic depression: An inquiry into the genesis of psychiatric conditions in early childhood, II. *The Psychoanalytic Study of the Child, 2,* 342–363.

Spitz, H. H. (1963). Field theory in mental deficiency. In N. R. Ellis (Ed.), *Handbook of mental deficiency: Psychological theory and research.* New York: McGraw-Hill.

Sroufe, A. L. (1979). Socioemotional development. In J. Osofsky (Ed.), *Handbook of infant development.* New York: Wiley.

Uzgiris, I. C. (1969). Ordinality in the development of schemas for relating to objects. In J. Hellmuth (Ed.), *Exceptional infant* (Vol. 1). Seattle: Special Child Publications.

Uzgiris, I. C., & Hunt, J. (1975). Assessment in infancy: Ordinal scale of psychological development. Urbana: University of Illinois Press.

Vaughn, B. E., Kopp, C. B., & Krakow, J. B. (1984). The emergence and consolidation of self-control from 18 to 30 months of age: Normative trends and individual differences. *Child Development, 55,* 990–1004.

Werner, E. E., Bierman, J. M., & French, F. E. (1971). *The children of Kauai: A longitudinal study from the prenatal period to age ten.* Honolulu: University of Hawaii Press.

Werner, E. E., & Smith, R. S. (1977). *Kauai's children come of age.* Honolulu: University of Hawaii Press.

Werner, E. E., & Smith, R. S. (1982). *Vulnerable but invincible: A longitudinal study of resilient children and youth.* New York: McGraw-Hill.

Yarrow, L. J. (1961). Maternal deprivation: Toward an empirical and conceptual reevaluation. *Psychological Bulletin, 58,* 459–490.

Zigler, E. (1968). Developmental versus differences theories of mental retardation and the problem of motivation. *American Journal of Mental Deficiency, 73,* 536–556.

CHAPTER 18

Behavioral Teratogenesis: Long-Term Influences on Behavior from Early Exposure to Environmental Agents

CHARLES V. VORHEES and ELIZABETH MOLLNOW

INTRODUCTION

This chapter is concerned with developental injury and factors that increase the risk of developmental injury. More specifically, this chapter is about injuries to the central nervous system (CNS) that occur during very early development. Even this is an enormous topic that cannot reasonably be reviewed in a single chapter. To narrow the topic further, the goal here is to review those topics in early CNS injury that have been rarely presented to developmental psychologists. Before beginning, it is worthwhile briefly to outline the scope of the entire area and then provide the rationale for the particular focus of the current discussion.

The topic of developmental injury is vast, encompassing parts of developmental psychology, pediatrics, genetics, developmental biology, developmental neuroscience, obstetrics, and essentially all of developmental toxicology, cytogenetics, teratology, mutagenesis, and behavioral teratology. To understand the basis of this broad topic, one need only consider the generic sources of developmental injury. These include the many genetic and environmental sources of maldevelopment. Genetic types include the single-gene dominant and recessively inherited defects, as well as cytogenetic, multifactorial genetic, and mutagenic abnormalities. Environmental types include nutritional, xenobiotic (drugs, environmental chemicals, and physical agents such as radiation), mechanical (such as trauma), and psychosocial sources of defective development. It is not surprising that such diverse causes of injury require the efforts of the many specialties mentioned above. But not all specialties place equal emphasis on all types of developmental problems. Fundamentally, developmental injuries have been approached from two broad perspectives.

One outlook examines problems by putative causes. Thus genetic approaches have focused extensively on the dominant and recessively inherited single-gene defects, and to a lesser extent on multfactorially caused disorders. Cytogenetic approaches

The writing of this chapter was made possible through the support provided by the Children's Hospital Research Foundation of Cincinnati.

have focused on chromosomal defects, such as Down's syndrome. Mutagenic approaches have focused on environmental agents that may induce DNA or chromosomal damage in otherwise normal organisms. Similarly, toxicological and teratological approaches have focused primarily on exogenous causes of somatic, as opposed to germinal, cell injury caused by drugs, toxins, and radiations. Finally, psychological approaches have focused on psychosocial sources of abnormal development.

A second outlook examines problems by the target organ of injury. Thus teratological approaches have frequently emphasized the study of birth defects (congenital malformations); perinatal approaches emphasize injuries of the newborn; and psychological and neuroscience approaches emphasize neurobehavioral injuries. Whether these disorders are conceptually sliced in different directions in order to facilitate their investigation is not crucial for our purposes, except to the extent that we appreciate that such divergent orientations lead to different research questions and hence to different findings and interpretations. It is clear, however, that no one way of looking at developmental risk and injury has proved superior to the others, while plurality of approach has often been invaluable in understanding these difficult disorders.

Interest in developmental risk and injury from a psychological perspective has led to examination of the problems of early behavioral, sensory, emotional, and cognitive processes and how these can be measured. In this endeavor the populations most often examined have been those with Down's syndrome and familial mental retardation of unknown origin and infants born preterm and/or small for gestational age. An excellent review of these areas has been recently provided by Kopp (1983). As Kopp has noted, the emphasis in these areas has been primarily upon psychological processes of normal and abnormal development, evaluation of status, prediction of outcome, and intervention to alter outcome. By focusing on chromosomal defect syndromes, or physically defined perinatal risks such as preterm birth (Kopp, 1983), these investigations have directed less effort toward trying to uncover as yet unknown causes of CNS damage. There is no shortage of ideas about causes, but obtaining an adequate study sample has proven to be quite difficult. Kopp (1983) has noted some of the substantial design problems attendant upon studying lower-frequency risk factors in human investigations.

Before further delineating the limits of this review, two relevant terms must be more thoroughly defined, that is, *teratology* and *behavioral teratology*. Teratology is the study of birth defects, their cause, pathophysiology, and epidemiology (Wilson, 1973). Narrowly defined, it is the study of congenital malformations alone. More broadly defined, it is considered the study of all types of abnormal development (Wilson, 1973, 1977a). In this broader conceptualization the manifestations of abnormal development range from death at the most severe end of the spectrum, through physical malformation, growth abnormality, and ultimately to aberrations of function, of which CNS damage represents perhaps the major group of serious long-term effects.

Behavioral teratology is the study of damage to the developing brain and its effects on behavior. As a field, behavioral teratology (psychoteratology) traces its origins to animal research on how early differences in experience (e.g., handling) influence behavior and to the causes of birth defects (Vorhees, 1986c, 1986d). Hence the field is rooted in both experimental psychology and teratology. One way of conceptualizing the relationship among the four types of developmental injury encompassed by teratology is to view each as having its own unique relationship to the dose of the agent inducing harm. In this view the four types of injury may be seen, in idealized form, as a set of dose–response curves (Fig. 18.1, Vorhees, 1986b). The slope of each curve, the spacing between curves (their degree of overlap), and even the presence of each effect curve for a given agent depend entirely on the agent. Thus Figure 18.1 represents an idealized case of a family of curve sets. This example represents a case where a drug produces all four types of response, where the dose–response curve for each effect is equally spaced from the others, and where each curve has the same shape (slope). Few agents produce such a symmetrical pattern, but this illustrates the essential features of all of teratology (developmental toxicology).

Thus behavioral teratology is related to the other types of developmental injury (teratogenesis) in a systematic, if not precise, way. Behavioral teratology is interested in the causes of developmental injury whether they be genetic, cytogenetic, or environmental in nature, and it is interested in causes arising both pre- and postnatally. Despite this broad scope, the emphasis in the field continues to be upon pre- and perinatal xenobiotic (chemical and radiation) causes of CNS injury and behavioral dysfunction. This emphasis, although not as comprehensive as the definition just given, will nevertheless be the emphasis of this chapter.

This means that some topics will not be reviewed here. No attempt will be made in this chapter to review the causes of structural teratogenesis, growth retardation, or developmental mortality. Excellent reviews of the influences of drugs and environmental agents on these parameters may be found in Wilson (1977b, 1977c). Another excellent review of the sources of all well-established causes of major malformations in humans has been presented by Kalter and Warkany (1983). Nor will

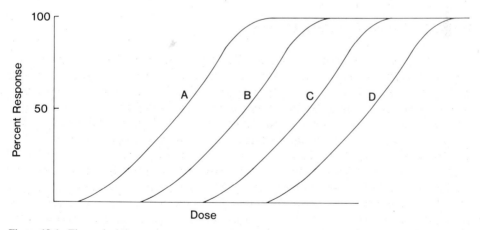

Figure 18.1. Theoretical dose-response curves for the four major outcomes of abnormal prenatal development (teratogenesis). These idealized curves are intended to represent the usual relationship between each type of outcome for those teratogens capable of producing all four types of effects. A is the curve of functional teratogenesis; B is the curve of ponderal teratogenesis (abnormal growth and weight); C is the curve of structural teratogenesis (congenital malformations); and D is the curve for embryolethality. Curve A of functional effects represents, in this instance, the curve for behavioral teratogenesis, but in a more general way it may be taken to represent functional damage to any physiological system. (From: Riley, E. P., & Vorhees, C. V. (Eds.). *Handbook of Behavioral Teratology,* New York: Plenum, in press. Used with permission.)

any attempt be made to review other forms of functional teratogenesis, such as immune competence, cardiovascular capacity, renal function, and so forth. The reader is referred to sources such as Snell (1982), Kimmel and Buelke-Sam (1981), and Johnson and Kochhar (1983) for these topics. As indicated, the present review will focus on the effects defined by the leftmost curve in Figure 18.1, that is, CNS dysfunction, hereafter called behavioral teratogenesis. But even within this realm none of the genetic (single-gene, cytogenetic, mutagenic) causes of behavioral disorders will be reviewed. Some of these topics are briefly presented by Kopp (1983) in the introductory sections of her review. In addition, psychosocial types of environmental causes will not be reviewed.

Finally, because the drugs used during the intrapartum period at the very end of pregnancy have been so well reviewed by Brackbill (1979), this topic has been omitted. Instead, the emphasis here is upon those environmental sources of injury (drugs, other chemicals, radiation) to which women may be exposed throughout pregnancy, particularly during early pregnancy, that may produce postnatal behavioral dysfunction long after the exposure has occurred. Evidence derived from research on both humans and experimental animals will be reviewed in an attempt to reveal convergence and establish causation.

CNS effects are the best investigated of all the dysfunctions represented by the left curve of Figure 18.1, and there are good reasons for this. Of all the organ systems, none is more crucial to the quality of life, more complex in its structure and function, more protracted in its development, or more difficult to measure noninvasively for integrity than the central nervous system. These facts lend a special significance to the investigation of CNS developmental injury and to efforts to understand and prevent it, and explain the rapid emergence of the field of behavioral teratology (Riley & Vorhees, 1986; Yanai, 1984).

THEORETICAL CONSIDERATIONS

The general scheme presented in Figure 18.1 forms the theoretical basis for behavioral teratology. Because of this, a closer examination of the implications of this scheme is important to an understanding of the entire field and the review that follows. Note in Figure 18.1 that at any given point (dose) along the abscissa one should expect the effects observed (as represented by a vertical line drawn from the abscissa) to cross more than one response curve. This expectation has been widely confirmed (Wilson, 1973). In rodents, there are many agents that produce fetal death (resorption) in some members of the litter, malformations in others, and no malformations but growth impairment and/or postnatal dysfunctions in the remainder of the litter. Of course, doses may be found that produce no effects other than functional ones, but if these doses are low enough to have no overlap with any of the other curves, they will most likely produce altered function in only a minority of the offspring. The remainder will be unaffected. This means that most agents given at doses producing only functional effects will inevitably have those effects diluted by the presence of unaffected siblings. This dilution effect is extremely important because it suggests that most behavioral teratology studies tend to underestimate the true magnitude of the effect discovered. This occurs because we have no absolute way of sorting the affected from the unaffected. This is quite unlike the case where malformations are studied, since in this case there is no problem sorting the malformed from the nonmalformed without ambiguity.

The dilution effect for behavior is easily understood in experimental animals since most have multiple offspring per litter, so that within each litter some animals can be affected and others not. In human beings the translation of this effect is that a functional teratogen would affect some children and not others within a given population. The physiological basis for variation in susceptibility to injury is presumed to reside in both genetically and environmentally determined individual differences.

The dilution effect is further complicated because the effects on behavior are graded even within a given litter. For example, if a litter has 60 percent of the offspring affected, 20 percent may be severely affected, 20 percent moderately affected, and 20 percent mildly affected. We cannot do an absolute sort into affected and unaffected individuals in behavioral analyses, in part because we have a broad range in intensity of effects among the exposed individuals. This is why behavioral teratogenesis detection is assumed to be continuously distributed and decisions are generally reached based on the use of parametric statistics. Malformations, by contrast, are usually dichotomously distributed and statistical tests are used somewhat differently, usually to decide whether the rate of malformation exceeds that of controls.

Returning to Figure 18.1, it should be noted that the leftmost curve, although depicted as a single curve, would be more accurately represented as a set of curves. There should be one curve for each organ system that may be functionally compromised by a treatment. This understanding combined with knowledge of the relationship of these curves to the other curves of developmental injury forms the basis of the newer perspective in developmental toxicology. Prenatal injury can no longer be viewed as constituting merely abnormal shape and weight, but must be judged by total organismic integrity. This can only be determined postnatally and longitudinally. From this perspective prenatal injury may represent the most devastating kind of malady, since the outlook for the affected individual is a lifelong impairment of health and well-being. This idea is supported by the evidence. Kopp (1983) has summarized evidence that prenatal injury is generally the most serious, the most intractable to treatment, and hence the type from which the least recovery occurs.

Additional ideas that emerge from the conceptualization represented in Figure 18.1 and the data that support it are worth mentioning (Vorhees & Butcher, 1982). First, not all agents produce all categories of response. Second, even among agents that induce all four types of effects the relative positions of the growth (or ponderal, i.e., as reflected in weight) and functional curves may be separate and distinct for some agents, and virtually indistinguishable for others. Third, among agents that produce functional effects, it has been found that the functional effects are usually the most sensitive index of developmental damage. The only currently known exception might be some rare cases of transplacentally induced cancer, as with diethylstilbestrol (DES). Fourth, because of the dilution effect discussed previously it is difficult to test for effects near the lower end of the functional effects curve, that is, close to the no detectable effect level (NOEL).

The first point, that not all agents produce all categories of effects, requires further explanation. While some dose of any given agent may be found that will produce embryolethality or maternal toxicity, many agents exist that do not produce malformations at any dose. There are also agents known that produce dysfunction and impaired growth, but no malformations even at high doses (Vorhees & Butcher, 1982). And there are agents that produce malformations and/or impaired growth, but no dysfunctions apart from the direct effects of the physical deformity on function (Vorhees, 1986b). When an agent is capable of producing dysfunction, however, it is important to appreciate that the dose–response curve for these effects will be to the left of the other curves as noted above (Fig. 18.1). This means that among the four types of injury abnormalities of function are expected to be the most sensitive ones to a toxic influence. This observation has a profound influence on any rational approach to the protection of public health and safety (Vorhees, 1986b), since under these circumstances, the measurement of functional effects should lower the NOEL and with it the maximum safe level of the agent in question. Interestingly, the evidence suggests that more agents produce growth impairments and maternal toxicity than any other types of developmental deviation (Gray & Kavlock, 1984; Johnson, 1984; Khera, 1984). But even if this is true, the unpredictability of which agents cause functional and structural abnormalities means that these effects will remain the most important, not only because they are more serious forms of damage to the infant than weight loss, but also because as long as we cannot predict which agents do or do not produce these effects we will need to test for them to ensure that they are not occurring. At present we cannot predict which agents are capable of producing postnatal dysfunctions or malformations using nonmammalian systems, although some screening tests now appear promising (Johnson, 1984).

Finally, one question that must be posed, even if not presently answerable, is: What is the role of CNS plasticity and recovery of function in the context of behavioral teratogenesis? CNS plasticity has been studied extensively, and there are data showing that the CNS is capable of substantial recovery after injury (see review by Finger & Stein, 1982). In surgically or electrolytically induced lesion studies it has been shown that the developing CNS sometimes has a greater capacity for recovery than the adult brain (Finger & Stein, 1982). This may also be true for a few types of highly selective neurotoxins, such as 6-hydroxydopamine. Much attention is currently being directed toward trying to understand CNS plasticity and manipulate it for beneficial purposes (Freed, de Medinaceli, & Wyatt, 1985). The problem in behavioral teratology at present is that the evidence shows that some kinds of early CNS injury can lead to remarkable recovery (see review by Hicks & D'Amato, 1978, for X-irradiation-induced injury and recovery in rodents), while other types of early injury produce enduring behavioral disorders from which little recovery occurs (see later discussion on anticonvulsants). This is so despite the fact that the agents producing both types of outcome are no different in their acute toxicity at the time of exposure. Unfortunately, not enough is known at this time to make any statements about what kinds of damage are most and least likely to lead to functional recovery or what mediates such differences. We only know that marked differences exist in susceptibility as a function of type of agent and stage of brain development when the exposure occurs. A deeper understanding must await future research.

An important concept in the functional recovery literature that may have relevance to early brain injury is that of lesion momentum (Finger & Stein, 1982). It has long been known that, the greater the momentum of a brain lesion, that is, the faster it develops, the greater the functional impairment and the worse the recovery.

Lesions that are slow growing (less momentum), or so-called staged or serial lesions, when induced experimentally, lead to much better outcomes: less functional loss and greater recovery. Butcher and Vorhees (1984) have recently discussed the possible applicability of this concept to early brain development. The theory suggests that large-dosage, short-term exposure to damaging agents might be more devastating than longer-term, lower-dosage exposures. Only limited data exist that might bear on this hypothesis. There are findings from studies in monkeys using lead administration postnatally that support the theory. These data show that monkeys given a discrete high dose of lead were more behaviorally impaired later in life than those given chronic low levels (see review by Laughlin, 1986). Whether this theory will withstand the test of future research remains to be seen.

Despite current theoretical limitations, a number of generalizations have been uncovered in recent years about behavioral teratogenesis in animal experiments to warrant inclusion here. These basic generalities should serve as aids in understanding early CNS injury in human beings, and may help direct clinically based as well as animal research designs in the future. These generalizations are the topic of the next section.

PRINCIPLES OF BEHAVIORAL TERATOGENESIS DERIVED FROM ANIMAL RESEARCH

Before reviewing the major identified xenobiotic causes or suspected causes of behavioral teratogenesis it is important to consider the principles of behavioral response to developmental injury. The principles to be described here have been derived from experimental research using laboratory animals. It has been and remains a firm tenet of behavioral teratology that the concepts developed in animals will apply to human beings. Moreover, it is believed that such research will presage directions for human investigation; that it will confirm causality to the exclusion of other factors to a degree impossible in human studies; and that it will enable us to probe pathophysiological and behavioral mechanisms to further our understanding of processes generally not amenable to human investigation. This knowledge will, in turn, enhance our efforts at prevention.

In the following section, it will be noticed that in animal studies doses of the administered agent are sometimes higher than those to which humans are routinely exposed. This presents more an apparent than a real problem for interpretation. The reason is that often the relevant basis for comparison is not administered dose but rather plasma or brain drug level or comparability of pharmacological response across species. On these bases many animal experiments can be compared to human conditions with considerable validity. Another basis for comparison is that in toxicology higher exposures are sometimes used to establish clear-cut causality using moderate numbers of carefully controlled, randomized subjects. The assumption is made that if the drug is found to cause a significant effect then extrapolation of such effects to humans in larger populations in less controlled settings at lower doses constitutes "reasonable inference." While such inferences have sometime been challenged, this standard approach will be assumed to be appropriate and valid in the review of animal studies provided below.

The principles of behavioral teratogenic response described here have been presented in detail elsewhere (Vorhees, 1986d). These principles are extensions and refinements of concepts originally put forth by Wilson (1977a) for all forms of teratogenesis. Those interested in the evolution of these ideas are also referred to a discussion of these issues in an earlier review by Vorhees and Butcher (1982). The 12 principles of behavioral teratogenic response are presented in Table 18.1.

The first 7 principles are the most basic and most well established. All of these apply to the other types of teratogenic effects as well as to behavior.

The first principle embodies the concept of genetic determination. This principle simply acknowledges that genetic factors have a substantial influence on the embryo's response to any form of insult to development. There is extensive evidence of this for malformations in which some inbred strains of mice exhibit a high incidence of defects in response to a drug (susceptible strains), while others show only a low incidence or no response at all (resistant strains). Although less extensively documented for behavioral effects, the existing data show that genetic differences can subtantially influence the behavioral response to agents such as alcohol (Ginsburg, Yanai, & Sze, 1975), methylmercury (cf. Hughes & Annau, 1976; Spyker, Sparber, & Goldberg, 1972), and methylazoxymethanol (Haddad, 1985, personal communication).

The second principle embodies the concept of critical periods. The critical periods concept is well known in psychology, being classically represented by studies on

TABLE 18.1. Principles of Behavioral Teratology

1. *Principle of Genetic Determination:* The type and magnitude of behavioral teratogenic effect depends on the genetic milieu of the organism.
2. *Principle of Critical Periods:* The type and magnitude of behavioral teratogenic effect depends on the stage of development of the organism when affected.
3. *Principle of Specific Mechanisms:* Agents that are behaviorally teratogenic act on the developing nervous system by specific mechanisms to alter development.
4. *Principle of Behavioral Teratogenic Responses:* Behavioral teratogenesis is expressed as impaired cognitive, affective, social, arousal, reproductive, and sensorimotor behavior, delayed behavioral maturation of these capacities, or other indices of compromised behavioral competence.
5. *Principle of Target Access:* The type and magnitude of behavioral teratogenic effect depends on the type of agent and its access to the developing nervous system.
6. *Principle of Dose-Response:* The type and magnitude of the behavioral teratogenic effect depends on the dose of the agent reaching the developing nervous system.
7. *Principle of Environmental Determination:* The type and magnitude of a behavioral teratogenic effect depends on the environmental influences on the organism, including both prenatal and postnatal environmental factors.
8. *Principle of Types of Behavioral Teratogens:* Only those agents that are central nervous system teratogens or, if not CNS teratogens, are psychoactive are capable of producing behavioral teratogenic effects.
9. *Principle of Response Relationships:* Behavioral teratogenic effects are demonstrable at doses below those causing malformations if the agent is capable of producing adverse behavioral effects.
10. *Principle of Maximum Susceptibility:* The period of susceptibility to behavioral teratogenic effects is isomorphic with CNS development, and the period of maximum susceptibility corresponds to the period of maximum susceptibility of the CNS to structural injury; for the CNS this is the period of neurogenesis.
11. *Principle of Limits of Behavioral Teratogenic Susceptibility:* Not all agents that are capable of producing malformations or other types of teratogenic effects are necessarily behavioral teratogens.
12. *Principle of Preconceptional or Transgenerational Effects:* Some agents can induce transmissible damage to their offspring prior to conception that is manifest in the behavior of the offspring. Such damage is mediated through the germ cells by affecting developing spermatozoa or unfertilized ova.

imprinting. In the current context the critical period notion focuses on periods of maximum or special vulnerability to insult. In its simplest form this principle stems from the fact that limbs are most susceptible to deviations in development at those times in embryonic development when the basic cell layers of the limb are first appearing and migrating to their target areas. Disruption at such times disorganizes the cell layers and, if sufficiently large, prevents compensatory adjustments. The results are defective limbs in which bones may be reduced or missing at one extreme, or in the case of distal phalanges, extra or fused digits are manifest. This principle also applies to the CNS. There is a relatively narrow period during embryonic development when some agents can sufficiently alter neural plate fusion that brain and spinal cord malformations occur (Kalter, 1968). Such neural tube defects are important and are relatively common if one considers them in relation to all other types of major congenital defects (Warkany, Lemire, & Cohen, 1981). They are not the subject of this review, however. The focus here is upon more subtle types of defects that do not produce visible CNS defects when examined at autopsy. Critical periods of vulnerability to such subtle forms of damage also exist and have been demonstrated in many experiments in rats for a variety of agents such as excess vitamin A (see Vorhees & Butcher, 1982) and anticonvulsants (Vorhees, 1983). The effect has also been demonstrated with prenatally consumed alcohol, although the effect is less pronounced (Driscoll, Chen, & Riley, 1982). Reasons for the differences in response to alcohol are presently unclear, but the search for critical periods in rats for alcohol has not been extensive. To date, studies researching critical periods for behavioral teratogenesis resulting from alcohol have divided gestation into two fairly broad periods. Since the timing of events in neurogenesis in the rodent CNS is quite critical (Rodier, 1980), broad periods may be too large to dissect out period-specific vulnerabilities. This is an experimentally answerable question that future research should be able to resolve.

The third principle embodies the concept of specific mechanisms. This is a straightforward reductionistic concept asserting that there are neurochemical and/or ultrastructural changes in the CNS that mediate abnormalities in postnatal behavior produced by prenatal exposure to harmful agents. One important concept that has evolved from an appreciation of this principle has been expressed by Wilson as the idea that all types of embryopathy are expressed through a set of final common pathways (Wilson, 1973, 1977a). Empirically, it has long been observed that there is a definable set of birth defects. While the list of defects and combinations of defects may not be short, it is nonetheless finite. The reason for this arises directly from the processes of embryogenesis. The disruption of some embryonic effects is incompatible with survival of the organism, and results in spontaneous abortion or terathanasia (Warkany, 1978), while other effects are survivable, at least intrauterinely. Morphogenetic events necessary for normal development include such things as rotation and fusion of palate shelves and closure of the neural plates. There are many different ways in which processes such as these may be disrupted, but the final common pathway involves the morphogenetic movements that produce apposition and closure of these structures. Failure of closure, regardless of how produced, results in cleft palate and neural tube defects, a final common set of defects. Therefore, one might discover 10,000 agents that are capable of altering palate morphogenesis, but the ultimately observed abnormality, cleft palate, appears the same irrespective of the agent and mechanism that caused it. Phrased another way, if we eventually discover 10,000 new chemicals capable of producing birth defects we will not discover 10,000 new types of birth defects. Indeed we may not find any entirely new types of defects.

This point has tended to go unnoticed in the analysis of behavioral teratogenesis. If it applies to behavioral effects, however, it means that there are a finite number of brain defects that can be produced, and hence a finite number of behavioral dysfunctions that can occur in the offspring. Of course these abnormalities may interact with environmental factors to make the number of manifestations quite large and complex, but it will remain finite. On top of this rests the problem of measurement, and scientists are constantly inventing new methods of measuring behavior. But despite environmental interactions and the changing landscape introduced by better methods of ascertainment it is worth remembering that the number of behavioral disorders is finite, and it may not be surprising to find that agents that are chemically very different may produce behavioral profiles that are quite similar. We must avoid the belief that every newly discovered behavioral teratogen should produce a unique profile of dysfunctions or that people identified with similar dysfunctions perforce arise from a single or closely related set of causes. Finally, we should not regard the task of trying to develop a set of screening tests for behavioral teratogenesis in humans and experimental animals as daunting, but rather we should take some solace from our knowledge that developmental CNS abnormalities are reflected in a definable universe of functional processes for which we can develop appropriate and genuinely representative tests.

The fourth principle embodies the types of responses that are within the domain of behavioral teratology. This principle is self-explanatory.

The fifth principle embodies the concept of agent access to the target. This principle recognizes the influences of pharmacokinetic factors in influencing the absorption, distribution, protein binding, tissue uptake, metabolism, and excretion of all chemical agents that may be behavioral teratogens in determining their ultimate efficacy.

The sixth principle embodies the concept of dose–response relationships and is fundamental to an understanding of all behavioral teratogenic effects. While dose–response relationships for behavior have not always been found (Nelson, 1981), they have been found when diligently sought (see Vorhees, 1986d). Cases where they have not been found appear to be the result of two factors. First, the window for behavioral teratogenesis for many agents is narrow and the dose–response curve steep. Under these conditions the spacing of dose groups is critical. As an example consider the drug phenytoin. Oral administration to rats of 250–300 mg/kg with repeated dosing represents the lower end of the malformation dose–response curve. A dose of 200 mg/kg in one experiment produced striking behavioral teratogenesis, while a dose of 50 mg/kg produced no detectable effects (Vorhees, 1983). Doses within this range, done in a second experiment, produced reliable, graded behavioral effects of increasing severity with increasing dose (Vorhees, 1986a). If only the first experiment had been done one might have concluded that this was another example of the purported all-or-none effect for behavioral teratogenesis, but the second experiment clearly proved otherwise, showing that dose–response effects were present but only within a rather narrow dose range. In sum, one cannot use the log or even half-log dosing approaches so often used in other fields and hope to see dose–response effects on behavior for many agents because with such wide ranges one will often produce marked embryotoxicity at the upper extremes and no effects at the lower extremes. This steep dose–response relationship is not universal. Indeed, newer evidence in rats with the anxiolytic diazepam suggests that it may be a behavioral teratogen at doses far below those that are embryotoxic (Kellogg, Tervo, Ison, Parisi, & Miller, 1980).

The second reason that dose–response effects have been missed in the past may be related to measurement artifacts. Behavioral tests are always constructed to detect functional changes within a specified range. This range is limited by the behavioral repertoire of the animal and by the latitude of the response options allowed by the structure of the test environment. Experimenters frequently refer to these limits on performance as representing floor and ceiling effects. This is done in recognition of the fact that behavioral measures are restricted at both ends of the response continuum. Several well-known examples illustrate these problems. If one has a task on which animals show almost no activity under control conditions, it will be impossible to demonstrate a treatment-induced hypoactivity, even if that is an effect induced by the treatment. Inactive animals cannot exhibit a change toward a less active state. Such a floor effect is a well-known problem of some behavioral tests.

Limits also occur at the upper extremes of activation. While there is no apparatus-imposed restraint on the upper limit of locomotor activity, there are organismic limits. As doses of d-amphetamine are increased rats show progressively more ambulation only up to a certain point; then the behavior emitted changes to stereotypy and ambulation declines thereafter with further increases in dose. This kind of limit is not usually termed a ceiling effect, but it is a limit nonetheless. Thus activity tests have very limited ranges for detection of changes in the target behavior. Among behavioral tests, activity actually has a larger range than many. Tests of shock avoidance behavior are notorious for the narrow range of behaviors that are consistent with what the task is intended to measure. Operant tasks have their own set of detection limits, although usually they are not as constricted as shock avoidance tests. Given this it seems apparent that many "failures" to detect dose–response behavioral teratogenic effects may be related to the narrow range of behaviors that can be detected on many tests, and the highly selective range of tests chosen by experimenters to search for these effects. Until these points can be appropriately addressed experimentally it is unreasonable to conclude that a given prenatally administered agent lacks a systematic dose–response relationship to postnatal behavioral dysfunction.

The seventh principle embodies the concept of environmental determination. The idea that environment has a major influence on behavior is so fundamental to psychology that it hardly requires further explanation here. Only two aspects of this idea require mention at this point. One is that fostering and cross-fostering techniques designed to sort out postnatal maternal influences that might interact with the embryonic treatment, although important, are not necessarily overriding considerations in such research and can sometimes be omitted. The second is that controls to sort out the influence of differential early experience on later behavioral performance are frequently unnecessary. This is because many behaviors are either unaffected by early handling or if affected are altered in ways that do not interact with prenatal drug effects. There is no doubt that both of these concerns are well founded, that is, that maternal changes and handling influences can be shown to interact with some prenatal treatments to alter the expression of these effects (Joffe, 1969). But it is also true that there are a number of drugs that produce postnatal behavioral changes that are little influenced or may be free of influence from significant confounding by postnatal changes in maternal behavior or changes introduced by early handling (see Middaugh, 1986; Vorhees, 1986a). Current evidence from animal research suggests that these two factors are usually secondary in importance to the direct influence of the prenatal drug-induced CNS damage. Therefore, controls for handling and maternal rearing should not determine the research designs in behavioral teratology, but should be subordinated to considerations of the effects of the drug itself on embryonic brain development.

The eighth principle is tentative and is based on current evidence. It appears at present that all agents that are CNS teratogens at higher doses are behavioral teratogens at submalforming doses. Thus the first half of the eighth principle seems firm. The second half of the principle, however, presents problems. We know that there are also compounds that are behavioral teratogens that are not CNS teratogens at any reasonable dose. An example might be d-Amphetamine (Buelke-Sam, 1986), although the evidence that d-amphetamine is a behavioral teratogen in rats is not altogether clear-cut. Diazepam (Kellogg et al., 1980) and phenobarbital (Middaugh, 1986) are examples of agents that seem to be behavioral, but not CNS, teratogens. Other agents such as phenytoin and trimethadione may also fit, but in these cases the malformation data are somewhat conflicting. Neuroleptics may also be behavioral but not CNS teratogens (Vorhees, Brunner, & Butcher, 1979). Propoxyphene (Darvon) also appears to fit in this category (Vorhees et al., 1979). Some pesticides may also meet this definition (Mactutus & Tilson, 1986). What all these agents have in common is that in adults their principal target of pharmacologic effect is the CNS. Thus it is tempting to conclude that all psychopharmacologically active agents may be behavioral teratogens. But such a conclusion would be ill-advised. Acetazolamide, although it acts in all tissues as a carbonic anhydrase inhibitor, is also apparently by some other mechanism a potent centrally acting compound that has clinically useful anticonvulsant activity. Yet acetazolamide appears not to be a behavioral teratogen (Butcher, Hawver, Burbacher, & Scott, 1975). The problem is, therefore, that we know that not all psychoactive compounds are behavioral teratogens, yet we cannot make valid categorical exclusions on which ones these are. At present we can only say that all behavioral teratogens either are CNS teratogens or are psychoactive, but we cannot make the more powerful statement as to which of the psychoactive compounds are always behaviorally teratogenic.

The ninth principle is also tentative, but it is becoming firmer with each passing year. This principle states that, for any agent that is behaviorally teratogenic, the behavioral effects induced can be reliably detected at doses lower than those that produce structural teratogenesis. The principle has specifically been framed in relation to malformations for two reasons: (1) because this is the traditional focus of comparison in teratology; and (2) because this rule may not always apply if one were to consider growth changes as a manifestation of teratogenesis. In other words, although the behavioral dose–response curve is reliably to the left of the malformation curve for any behavioral teratogen, it may not always be to the left of the growth curve (e.g., Vorhees et al., 1979), even though shown to the left of it in Figure 18.1. The behavioral curve is shown to the left of the growth curve because that seems to be the most common finding for known behavioral teratogens, but these two curves may be almost superimposed in some instances.

It is important not to confuse these statements with the oft-expressed but incorrect notion that the behavioral dose–response curve is always to the left of all of the other curves of embryotoxicity. There is no evidence to support this more global supposition, and, although it has often been attributed to behavioral teratologists, a review of the literature raises doubt that such attribution is correct. Those in the field have usually been careful to qualify such statements so that they apply only to cases where the agent in question is a behavioral teratogen. The above statement is usually presented by those seeking to set up a straw man that is then easily assailed. In any event, this misunderstanding of the concept should be put to rest.

The tenth principle is also tentative, but it is worth stating for heuristic value until it is disproved, if that day comes. This principle states that neurogenesis is the period during CNS development when it is most vulnerable compared to any other period, that is, as opposed to periods of synaptogenesis, gliogenesis, or myelinogenesis. Even more specifically, this principle speculates that within the period of neurogenesis the most vulnerable time is the period in midneurogenesis when the CNS is also vulnerable, at higher doses, to structural injury. Evidence that neurogenesis is the most sensitive period for producing behavioral teratogenesis is abundant (see Vorhees, 1986d). That this should be the case is also consistent with the known fact in teratology that the farther along in development an organism is the more difficult it is to disrupt ontogenetic processes (Wilson, 1973). Thus in a real sense this principle represents a parallel form of the concept of progressive resistance to malformation that is well established from experimental embryology and teratology (Wilson, 1973). It is reassuring that the current evidence in behavioral teratology supports this very basic pattern. This relationship may be more complicated than described above, however, as evidenced in the recent review of the behavioral effects of antiproliferative agents by Rodier (1986).

The tenth principle should not be taken, however, as a statement that things cannot be otherwise in special cases. For example, some agents, such as antithyroid drugs, might have no damaging effects prior to thyroid development, but disrupt its function later at a point in development when the thyroid normally becomes operational. In fact, just such evidence exists from the work of Davenport and Dorcy (1972). Similar effects may occur with sex hormones and drugs that can affect them (Gandelman, 1986). At present these instances can only be accommodated as exceptions to the rule. We cannot recast the tenth principle into a more comprehensive and accurate account of the evidence until more data become available.

The eleventh principle merely states that not all birth defect–producing agents are necessarily behavioral teratogens. While this ought to be perfectly obvious, it is a point that has occasionally been missed and therefore warrants inclusion.

The twelfth principle is the newest and has been occasioned by two types of data derived from animal research. The first is that there are effects that can occur on offspring behavior as a result of paternal rather than maternal exposure (Adams, Fabricant, & Legator, 1981). Such effects might be termed male-mediated behavioral teratogenesis or perhaps more aptly, male-mediated behavioral mutagenesis. The second line of evidence also has to do with transgenerational effects, but it stems from the more common maternal type of exposure during pregnancy. In this instance, however, the effects on behavior are demonstrable in the grandoffspring of the exposed animal; that is, these effects appear to be transmitted across more than one generation (Friedler & Wheeling, 1979; Resnick, Morgane, Hasson, & Miller, 1982). Both types of transgenerational effects might be mediated by damage to the germ cells, but to date no exact mechanism has been established. Such findings represent a new and tantalizing area of potentially fruitful future research.

REVIEW OF ENVIRONMENTAL AGENTS CAUSING BEHAVIORAL TERATOGENESIS

As stated in the introduction to this chapter, our goal is to emphasize those topics that have received relatively little attention elsewhere. Thus the review of specific xenobiotic causes of behavioral teratogenesis that follows will not necessarily devote attention to various agents in direct proportion to their known or suspected severity for causing injury, nor in proportion to the number of individuals affected or the number of investigations that have been done on each. Instead, attention has been placed on those agents not thoroughly reviewed elsewhere, and on agents for which both human and animal data are available to provide converging evidence. In the case of agents such as lead that have been extensively reviewed elsewhere, the reader will be referred to those reviews, and an abbreviated discussion will be presented here.

In what follows, the chemical and physical agents have been divided into three groupings. The first grouping is of those agents that by the weight of published scientific evidence have been judged by the author to be well established as behavioral teratogens in both humans and animals. The second grouping is of those agents that have been judged probable behavioral teratogens, although there are some missing pieces of information that make a definitive judgment problematic. The third grouping is of those agents that have been judged possible or suspected behavioral teratogens. For the agents in this grouping some fairly persuasive experimental evidence exists, but the data are far from conclusive. It must be emphasized that these groupings are based on the author's assessment of the literature, not on any government review panel or other established set of rigid criteria. The reason for this is that no such committee review or established set of criteria exists at this time for behavioral teratogens. The author has attempted in this review to be very conservative, and some readers will undoubtedly judge many of the probable behavioral teratogens to be already established. Such differences in judgment can best be resolved by future discussion and evaluation.

AGENTS ESTABLISHED AS BEHAVIORAL TERATOGENS

This section reviews those agents that have been definitively established as behavioral teratogens in both animals and human beings based on the weight of scientific evidence published in peer-reviewed sources. For each of these the strength of the evidence in humans is sufficient itself to establish each of the chemicals as a behavioral teratogen. The animal research is also strong, so that the combined effect is persuasive. Some of the agents in this group are also structural teratogens, and some also affect growth. These effects are important but are less frequent or less potent in affecting the quality of the child's life than are the behavioral defects. The agents in this category are mercury, alcohol, and lead.

Methylmercury and Fetal Minamata Disease

In the late 1950s an industrial plant in Japan discharged a mercury-containing effluent into Minamata Bay. People living in the surrounding communities subsequently began to exhibit evidence of neurotoxicity, and some of the children born were profoundly retarded and neurologically impaired (Reuhl & Chang, 1979). It was determined that the mercury had been gradually taken up by plants and bottom-feeding fishes in the bay and had moved up the food chain of this marine ecosystem. As mercury moved up the food chain it was progressively concentrated because of mercury's deposition in body lipids and slow rate of elimination. Gradually mercury, as methylmercury, accumulated in the larger fish that were caught by local fishermen, thereby allowing this heavy metal to move into the human food supply of the region. Fish was the principal food source for many of the people living around Minamata Bay.

Congenital methylmercury poisoning (or fetal Minamata disease) was eventually fully established as the cause of more than 40 cases of mental retardation and neurological impairments (Reuhl & Chang, 1979). Other cases of mercury neurotoxicity have also occurred in Iraq and elsewhere in Japan (see Chang & Annau, 1984; Hattan, et al., 1983). Such incidents, combined with the widespread environmental distribution of industrially discharged and agriculturally used mercury, prompted the U.S. Food and Drug Administration to set allowable limits on mercury content in the U.S. food supply (Hattan et al., 1983).

By the early 1970s methylmercury was the first clearly established human behavioral teratogen. In this instance, and in several other cases reviewed below, we will see that discovery of behavioral teratogenesis in human beings preceded establishment of comparable relationships in experimental animals. If this seems puzzling, it should not be. While the concept of behavioral teratogenesis can be found in the late 1950s and early 1960s (Werboff & Gottlieb, 1963), the field was not on sufficiently firm scientific ground at that time accurately to predict behavioral teratogenesis or cogently to apprise government regulatory authorities of its significance.

One of the hallmarks of methylmercury neurotoxicity is the striking difference in vulnerability of the adult compared to the embryo, fetus, and child. The principal symptoms of severe toxicity in adult Minamata Bay victims included ataxia, dysarthria, and sensory dysfunctions (constriction of visual fields, perioral numbness, and hearing disturbances) (Reuhl & Chang, 1979; Takeuchi, Eto, & Eto, 1979). Most of the mothers who were exposed to mercury during pregnancy, however, and who delivered fetal Minamata disease children, did not themselves have severe mercury intoxication. Indeed their symptoms were generally mild or absent, and often reversible. By contrast, the symptoms in their infants damaged in utero were usually severe, pervasive, and irreversible. Reuhl and Chang (1979) reviewed 22 cases of fetal Minamata disease and found that 100 percent suffered from mental problems. Ataxia, abnormal gait, abnormal speech, and abnormal chewing and swallowing were neurological symptoms also found in 100 percent of these cases. No other symptoms occurred with the frequencies of the most serious mental and neurological defects, indicating that the CNS was the target organ of the vast majority of the effects of methylmercury on the conceptus. Reuhl and Chang (1979) found that in those cases that were followed for years after being identified some symptoms improved but very few disappeared. Those with growth impairments, for example, sometimes showed catch-up growth and some of their neurological symptoms disappeared, but none of the more severe problems such as mental retardation, hyperkinesis, or dysarthria disappeared. Reuhl and Chang (1979) also noted that, although there was overlap in the neuropathological findings between autopsied adult, infant, and fetal cases, one striking difference was the distribution of the lesions. Whereas adult brains showed localization of the lesions, the fetally exposed brains showed diffuse damage. Brains from childhood cases showed a distribution pattern similar to fetal cases (see Takeuchi et al., 1979). This age-dependent pattern is not unique to fetal methylmercury exposure, but appears to be characteristic of many types of congenitally or neonatally caused mental damage. This observation should guide the search for the mechanisms of action of behavioral teratogens, indicating as it does that many types of prenatal CNS injury will be found to produce diffuse rather than focal damage.

Animal research on the effects of prenatal methylmercury on postnatal behavior began with the work of Spyker and colleagues (1972). They found that 8 mg/kg given to pregnant mice on day 7 or 9 of gestation produced offspring showing defective swimming behavior (characterized by incoordination) and increased open-field backward stepping behavior (a normally rare occurrence in this test).

This experiment has been followed by many others on prenatal methylmercury exposure. For example, Musch, Bornhausen, Kriegel, and Greim (1978) administered much lower doses of methylmercury, 0.5 or 2.0 mg/kg, but for a slightly longer period of time, days 6–9 in rats. Musch and colleagues (1978) found dose-dependent decreases in an appetitively motivated operant conditioning test in the offspring as adults. Musch and colleagues also noted that, despite the fact that the mercury offspring lever-pressed more frequently than controls during training, they were less effective at obtaining reinforcements when a schedule using differential reinforcement of high rates of responding was imposed. The more demanding the schedule, in fact, the worse the mercury offspring performed.

More recently, Eccles and Annau (1982a, 1982b) have found that 5 or 8 mg/kg of methylmercury administered to rats on days 7 or 14 of gestation produced offspring that were hyperactive, impaired on an active avoidance task, and exhibited reduced appetitive operant conditioning on a differential reinforcement of low rates of responding test schedule.

As these representative behavioral experiments in animals show, prenatal methylmercury produces long-term effects on a wide variety of postnatal behaviors. These studies also illustrate that the effects on behavior are a function of both the dose given and the period during embryofetal development when exposure occurs. Finally, the behavioral experiments in animals demonstrate that the effects on offspring behavior are independent of maternal toxicity during gestation (e.g., undernutrition caused by loss of appetite and weight) or postnatal rearing conditions. These four characteristics (dose, exposure period, and pre- and postnatal maternal effects) form a bridge of evidence that methylmercury causes behavioral deficits, and exclude other competing hypotheses that might be suggested to account for the effects observed. The many animal experiments on prenatal methylmercury have resolved each of these points by showing that this toxin acts directly on the embryonic and fetal brain.

Types of evidence besides effects on behavior point unequivocally to methylmercury's neurotoxicity. In both human and animal studies evidence has been gathered that shows that fetal tissues display a trapping effect for methylmercury to a degree not observed in adults. Neuropathologically, methylmercury causes cell death and disruption of cytoarchitecture during development, primarily in the cerebellum and cerebral cortex (Chang & Annau, 1984). New evidence shows that prenatal methylmercury in mice alters the pattern of mitosis in several brain regions, causing mitotic arrest coupled with an apparent compensatory increase in proliferative activity (Rodier, Aschner, & Sager, 1984). Damage to extrapyramidal systems and the hippocampus has also been reported.

These changes and the behavioral experiments have recently been reviewed by Chang and Annau (1984), who describe the cumulative evidence that methylmercury is a behavioral teratogen. Species examined have been mice, rats, hamsters, cats, and monkeys, and all species are affected (Chang & Annau, 1984). The literature on methylmercury's developmental neurotoxicity is remarkable for the consistency with which its effects are reported. All find significant CNS damage from prenatal methylmercury exposure regardless of whether the examinations of the offspring are behavioral, neuropathological, or neurochemical. While there are certainly some inconsistencies in terms of the nature of the behavioral defects in the offspring as reported by different investigators, these appear to arise from major differences between studies in the dose and periods of gestation chosen for methylmercury administration, and the large range of behavioral tests used to assess the functional integrity of the progeny. On balance, methylmercury represents the most clear-cut example of behavioral teratogenesis and today serves as a model compound for the field. Methylmercury could fairly be described as the "thalidomide of behavioral teratogenesis," in the sense that its effects are as clear and remarkable as were those of thalidomide in causing limb deformities.

Alcohol and the Fetal Alcohol Syndrome

Behavioral teratology has been profoundly changed by the discovery, or what some prefer to call the rediscovery (Rosett & Sander, 1979; Shaywitz, 1978), of the prenatal toxicity of alcohol. Those who are interested can find a number of reviews of the ancient and more modern histories of our gradual awakening to an appreciation of alcohol's embryotoxicity (Abel 1980a; Abel, Randall, & Riley, 1983; Rosett & Sander, 1979; Shaywitz, 1978; Streissguth, Landesman-Dwyer, Martin, & Smith, 1980). Meyer and Riley (1986) present a thorough review of this topic with particular attention to alcohol's consequences on behavioral development in animal models of the fetal alcohol syndrome (FAS). No matter how the history of alcohol embryotoxicity is traced, however, it is clear that 1973 marks the year when this issue came into focus in the United States (Jones, Smith, Ulleland, & Streissguth, 1973). Later in 1973 these authors also coined the term *fetal alcohol syndrome* (Jones & Smith, 1973), and in so doing captured the attention of the scientific and lay communities. Rather quickly, basic researchers began trying to develop animal analogues of FAS to better document the clinical findings and to resolve issues that could not be addressed adequately in investigations using human beings.

The clinical features of the FAS have been organized into four clusters. These involve effects on psychological functioning, growth, facial morphology, and structural development of major organs. Together they are felt to constitute a syndrome, but there are still those who dispute such a conceptualization. In brief, the psychological effects involve mild to moderate mental retardation, abnormal reflexes, irritability and state lability in infancy, hyperactivity, and in some cases learning disabilities during childhood (Streissguth et al., 1980). The growth effects involve pre- and postnatal growth retardation and microcephaly. The facial effects involve a series of dysmorphologic features, which together are considered to present a distinct appearance, but which individually are seen in many other developmental disorders or even as variants in normal children. Finally, the structural effects are major malformations. These are not unique to the syndrome, but it is reported that FAS children have an increased incidence of birth defects compared to controls. These defects are most commonly reported to involve the heart, joints, and palate.

By 1975 scientists had found that they could model the major malformation-inducing aspect of FAS in mice (Chernoff, 1975; Randall, Taylor, & Walker, 1977), but rats were found to be largely resistant to alcohol-induced malformations (Fernandez, Caul, Boyd, Henderson, & Michaelis, 1983). Later, it would even be reported that facial dysmorphology could be induced in mice by in utero exposure to alcohol (Sulik, Johnston, & Webb, 1981). In two important recent experiments Blake and Scott (1984a, 1984b) have provided strong evidence that alcohol, rather than its metabolite acetaldehyde, is the proximate teratogen for the production of malformations and resorptions in mice. Blake and Scott also demonstrated that mouse embryos exhibit changing susceptibility as a function of time of alcohol administration during gestation, and that the degree of damage was a direct function of the amount of alcohol reaching embryonic tissues. These data and others from embryoculture demonstrate that alcohol is teratogenic in animals when the influence of altered nutrition and alcohol metabolism are strictly controlled (Fifth Special Report to the U.S. Congress on Alcohol and Health, 1984).

By 1976 behavioral scientists had found rats suitable for demonstrating the functional consequences of prenatal alcohol (Bond & DiGiusto, 1976). Very rapidly there followed a spurt of research on the morphological and behavioral consequences of prenatal alcohol in animal model systems (reviewed by Abel, 1980a, 1981; Meyer & Riley, 1986; Riley & Meyer, 1984).

FAS quickly emerged as the largest and most pervasive line of research in behavioral teratology, helped along by a substantial influx of funds from the National Institute on Alcohol Abuse and Alcoholism. Even today, FAS research remains the dominant area of research in behavioral teratology. With an incidence rate in humans estimated at 1–3 per 1000 births in the United States (Fifth Special Report to the U.S. Congress on Alcohol and Health, 1984), this research emphasis is not hard to understand: FAS represents the largest environmental cause of behavioral teratogenesis yet discovered, and perhaps the largest single environmental cause that will ever be discovered. Thus although the discovery of FAS marks the realization of a new and tragically real source of human maldevelopment, it is also the case that FAS has spurred the growth of scientific research in behavioral teratology in much the same way that the discovery of thalidomide embryopathy spurred research in structural teratology.

Alcohol has also been found to double the risk of spontaneous abortion in heavy drinkers, to shorten pregnancy length, and to increase the incidence of joint and cardiac defects at blood levels in the intoxicated range (100 mg/dl and above). The most reliable of all the physical effects of alcohol, however, is a dose-dependent decrease in birth weight (Abel, 1984). This weight reduction may be as large as 1300 g (mean weight of 2000 g in FAS cases vs. 3300 g in controls) based on a review of cases reported in the literature (Fifth Special Report to the U.S. Congress on Alcohol and Health, 1984), although prospective studies find reductions in heavier drinkers averaging a more modest 200 g. The risk of these effects appears to be most clear for those women who are the heaviest 5–10 percent consumers of alcohol. In addition, the amount of newborn weight reduction has been found to be a function of the number of years of drinking prior to the pregnancy that resulted in an FAS child (reviewed by Rosett, 1980). It has also been noted that women who are heavy drinkers who reduce their consumption during the second and third trimesters of pregnancy do not change their risk of having children with birth defects, as would be expected, but substantially reduce their risk of having a growth-retarded child (Rosett et al., 1983), although others have found this is not the case if the woman has a long history of heavy alcohol consumption (Little, Streissguth, Barr, & Herman, 1980). It is estimated that about 60 percent of American women drink. About 5 percent of American women will admit to drinking 2 or more drinks per day or 14 or more drinks per week. From such data it has been estimated that among heavy drinkers (5 or more drinks per day on average) there appears to be a 30 percent or greater risk of having a child with FAS (Landesman-Dwyer, 1982; Ouellette, Rosett, Rosman, & Weiner, 1977; Sokol, Miller, & Reed, 1980).

It is now concluded by most reviewers of the topic that central nervous system dysfunctions are the most serious consequence of FAS (Fifth Special Report to the U.S. Congress on Alcohol and Health, 1984). Moreover, research has found that moderate drinkers place their offspring at increased risk for a less severe spectrum of effects, often termed *fetal alcohol effects* (FAE) (Abel et al., 1983). When FAE occurs, the most common effects are CNS dysfunction and growth retardation, whereas FAS is most frequently associated with the CNS dysfunctions of mental retardation (usually moderate with an IQ of 60–70), hyperactivity (with shortened attention span), sleep disorders, reflex changes, and several other more specific behavioral changes (Abel et al., 1983; Little, Graham, & Samson, 1982).

Children identified as having FAS and FAE have shown a variety of behavioral dysfunctions. The data on such effects come from two types of studies: retrospectively asertained cases in which FAS children were first identified clinically and then followed up for psychological outcome, and prospectively ascertained cases in studies designed to screen a population for FAE and then follow the children longitudinally on measures of psychological development.

Streissguth, Herman, and Smith (1978a) examined 20 previously diagnosed FAS patients on standardized tests of intelligence and related the findings to the other major symptoms of the disorder. Using the Bayley scales for the youngest, the Stanford-Binet for children 2.5–5 years old, the WISC-R for children 6–15 years old, and the WAIS for those over 16, they found a systematic relationship between lowered IQ scores and severity of dysmorphic features. Those children with the most severe facial abnormalities had IQ scores averaging 55, and those with the mildest features IQ scores averaging 82. Those with moderate abnormalities had IQ scores that on average fell between these values. Occipital–frontal head circumference and height were also related to IQ and to degree of facial dysmorphology, but not as strongly. Seventeen of these children were then retested 1–4 years later using the tests mentioned above according to age in order to determine the stability of their original impairments (Streissguth, Herman, & Smith, 1978b). The results showed IQ scores to be stable for 13 of the individuals; they rose more than 1 standard deviation for two individuals, and fell more than 1 standard deviation for two other individuals. Time between testing and original IQ did not predict the IQ changes in the four cases showing the largest changes at the time of retest.

These same investigators have also conducted a large prospective study in Seattle designed to detect FAS and FAE in an unselected population of women who were enrolled in the study during the fifth month of pregnancy (Streissguth, Martin, Martin, & Barr, 1981). The children from this study had been evaluated physically and psychologically at various points in the ongoing project. The first part involved evaluations of psychological functioning at birth, 8 months, and 18 months of age (Landesman-Dwyer, Keller, & Streissguth, 1978). In most of their reports a cohort of 500 children was selected from the 1529 enrolled. The cohort mothers were matched on multiple socioeconomic, medical, and other criteria but varied in self-reported alcohol intake. Of these, 250 were mothers classified as heavy drinkers and 250 were mothers classified as light drinkers or abstainers (all categories were then further subdivided). Using an observational scoring system on newborns, the authors found significant relationships between maternal alcohol consumption ratings and five infant behaviors during a 60-min observation interval. These behaviors were increased time with eyes opened during observation in a darkened room, increased body tremors, increased time with head turned to the left, decreased vigorous body movement, and increased frequency of hand-to-face motions (Landesman-Dwyer et al., 1978). Also, behaviors termed dazed eyes, yawns, and sneezes significantly interacted (increased) with degree of prenatal exposure to alcohol and nicotine.

Another study from this same sample of 1529 offspring examined newborn conditioning using two appetitive tasks, a conditioned head-turning and conditioned nonnutritive sucking test (Martin, Martin, Lund, & Streissguth, 1977). Significant relationships were found between degree of reported prenatal alcohol and nicotine consumption and acquisition of the target behaviors. Further analyses of the data showed that infants of heavier alcohol-consuming mothers had a weaker sucking response and a longer latency to initiate sucking than did infants of light drinkers and abstainers (Martin, Martin, Streissguth, & Lund, 1979).

At 8 months of age the cohorts used for behavioral analyses were evaluated using the Bayley scales (Streissguth, Barr, Martin, & Herman, 1980). After statistical adjustment for maternal report of caffeine and nicotine consumption and adjustment for known variance predictors such as gestational age at delivery, maternal parity, and maternal education, a significant negative relationship was found between maternal alcohol consumption and infant Bayley development scores. The Bayley mental development index was quadratically related to alcohol dose and the Bayley psychomotor development index was linearly related to alcohol dose. For both measures higher alcohol predicted lower performance scores.

A subsample of this cohort was examined for vigilance at 3–4 years of age (Herman, Kirchner, Streissguth, & Little, 1980). Although a trend existed ($p < .09$), vigilance task performance was not significantly related to maternal drinking history. However, evaluation of the complete cohort at age 4 years with some improvements in the vigilance methodology showed that maternal alcohol was significantly related to increased errors and longer reaction times (Streissguth, Martin, et al., 1984). These relationships remained stable even after statistical adjustment for smoking history, birth order, maternal education, nutrition, and caffeine consumption.

Maternal alcohol consumption was also found to be significantly related to diminished neonatal habituation and to an increased frequency of low arousal states as assessed by the Brazelton Neonatal Behavioral Scale (Streissguth et al., 1981; Streissguth, Barr, & Martin, 1983).

A follow-up study has also been reported on these children when they were 4 years of age (Landesman-Dwyer, Ragozin, & Little, 1981). In this study the children of heavy and light drinking mothers were observed in their homes. After statistically partialing out the influence of maternal use of cigarettes and matching subjects on a variety of other characteristics, the authors found that children of the alcohol users were "less attentive, less compliant with parental commands, and more fidgety during mealtimes" (p. 187) than controls (light drinkers and abstainers).

This prospective study sample has been examined for other alcohol-related effects. The Seattle investigators have found that birth and 8-month infant weights were significantly related to maternal alcohol consumption after correction for other possible influences (Barr, Streissguth, Martin, & Herman, 1984). Most important, although both maternal smoking and alcohol contributed to lowered birth weights, only alcohol contributed significantly to reduced infant weights at 8 months of age. Apgar scores, heart rate changes, and respiratory distress were also found to be related to self-reported amount of maternal alcohol consumed (Streissguth, Barr, & Martin, 1982).

No attempt has been made here to provide an exhaustive review of studies examining the psychological effects of prenatal alcohol exposure in human beings. The focus has been on the Seattle prospective study because there are more data available and they are more thoroughly analyzed than any other data set at this point. It is important to appreciate that all of these studies from the Seattle prospective study cohort use a stratified groups approach. They have not simply examined experimentals (a group of very heavy drinkers) and controls (a group of abstainers), but instead have divided their samples into heavy, moderate-to-heavy, moderate, and light-to-abstention groups and related outcome measures using multiple regression techniques. By doing this they have convincingly demonstrated that many psychological measurements on infants and young children are systematically related to maternal self-reported alcohol consumption during and/or prior to pregnancy. Even more important, they have excluded those women who could be classified as chronic alcoholics who would be at high risk of producing FAS children. By so doing they have been able to show that there is a reliable dose–response relationship between self-reported moderate to heavy alcohol use (but short of alcoholism) and compromised psychological development. This relationship, although influenced on some measures by other factors such as maternal smoking, has been found to occur independent of many other potentially confounding variables.

Overall, these data and others demonstrate that prenatal alcohol is teratogenic and behaviorally teratogenic at high doses in humans. At such high doses intellectual damage is among the most prevalent symptom of alcohol exposure, and when present is the most devastating effect on the child. The data further show that alcohol is a behavioral teratogen at lower doses, doses that do not produce malformations or facial dysmorphology. This observation confirms what would be theoretically expected from experimental behavioral teratology (Vorhees, 1986d). The incidence of such fetal alcohol effects has been estimated to be three to five times higher than the incidence of FAS. Thus the human findings provide a strong case for alcohol as a human behavioral teratogen.

Nonetheless, it is important to bear in mind that many variables cannot be controlled in human studies and some issues cannot thereby be resolved. One of these is that all human investigations must rely upon the self-reports of mothers about their alcohol use. Although mutliple measurement instruments have been used to obtain this information, and studies on the validity of the measures have been made, there remains a significant element of uncertainty that cannot be dispelled using such questionnaires. People are notoriously unreliable as reporters of their own habits, and are particularly sensitive about reporting the use of items such as alcohol. No human investigation on alcohol during pregnancy has been able to overcome this problem entirely. This represents one of several reasons why animal experiments play a vital role in the case linking prenatal alcohol to behavioral teratogenesis.

Since the most serious effect of FAS and often the only effect of FAE is behavioral dysfunction, animal models of these conditions take on pivotal significance for resolving many issues that cannot be reconciled in human investigations. The behavioral teratology of alcohol in experimental animals has been reviewed numerous times (Abel, 1980a, 1981; Abel et al., 1983; Meyer & Riley, 1986; Riley & Meyer, 1984; Vorhees & Butcher, 1982). No attempt will be made here to re-review this extensive literature. Instead the reader is referred to the excellent recent review by Meyer and Riley (1986) for more details. By way of summary, it will be noted that the research in animals on the behavioral effects of prenatal alcohol has established the following: (1) that alcohol-induced postnatal behavioral dysfunction is dose dependent and duration dependent; (2) that alcohol-induced behavioral dysfunction is exposure period dependent; (3) that behavioral dysfunction is substantially independent of postnatal maternal rearing condition, environmental enrichment, or differential handling experience; (4) that alcohol-induced postnatal dysfunction occurs independent of confounding by undernutrition; (5) that the severity and type of behavioral dysfunction induced by alcohol can be influenced by the genetic background of the organism; (6) that dose–response effects are directly related to oral intake and blood alcohol levels within species, and to blood levels but not to oral intake across species; and (7) that no period of prenatal development has yet been established to be dramatically more sensitive to alcohol-induced behavioral dysfunction in animals than any other. The second and seventh are not contradictory, since, although different behavioral effects have been demonstrated after different periods of exposure, no period has been found that can account for all or the majority of the behavioral effects induced by prenatal alcohol exposure.

Examination of the results of behavioral studies in terms of the types of behavioral dysfunctions induced in animals by alcohol shows that the following generalizations are warranted: (1) Alcohol offspring are hyperactive on a number of tests of locomotor activity, some of which include measures of other forms of gross motor movement as well; (2) alcohol offspring generally exhibit a reduced rate of habituation of locomotor activity upon repeated testing; (3) alcohol offspring exhibit perseverative behavior and an impairment of response inhibition, even when response inhibition is adaptive and is being reinforced (using either positive or negative reinforcement procedures); (4) alcohol offspring often exhibit hyperreactivity to challenging situations; (5) alcohol offspring may exhibit abnormal early reflex and sensorimotor development; and (6) alcohol offspring exhibit some types of learning impairments (e.g., in shuttle-box shock avoidance tests), although these effects are not global and many other tests of learning show no effects on learning or show effects that can be accounted for by the performance changes noted above.

The leading hypothesis to explain these behavioral changes is that alcohol offspring have impaired response inhibition (Meyer & Riley, 1986), perhaps mediated by damage to cholinergic fibers in the hippocampus. Other behaviors, such as changes in seizure susceptibility, altered alcohol preference, reductions in sexually dimorphic behaviors, and altered response to psychotropic drug challenges, have also been reported, but insufficient data exist to describe these effects adequately or rely on their replicability. Meyer and Riley (1986) review the evidence for these other effects as well as the well-established ones outlined above.

The animal findings combined with those in human studies on alcohol-induced behavioral dysfunction demonstrate that not only is this compound a behavioral teratogen but its CNS effects may be the most sensitive index of alcohol's developmental toxicity.

Lead

Lead-induced neurotoxicity can be traced back hundreds of years in human history. The special susceptibility of developing organisms to the neurotoxic effects of lead, however, has been appreciated only more recently (reviewed by Silbergeld, 1984). The problem of lead-induced developmental neurotoxicity is quite different from the problems with mercury and alcohol because in the case of lead the timing of the insult is primarily postnatal rather than prenatal, although new evidence is altering this view somewhat (CDC, 1985). Because high levels of lead exposure are so clearly neurotoxic, the focus has switched from examinations of lead-induced encephalopathy to examinations of what is often termed *asymptomatic lead-induced neurotoxicity.*

Lead encephalopathy in children has been described since 1839 (see Bornschein, Pearson, & Reiter, 1980a). Children may appear first with gastrointestinal problems or with encephalopathy. If the presenting sysmptoms are gastrointestinal about 30 percent will exhibit permanent neurological damage, whereas if the presenting symptoms are of encephalopathy about 80 percent sustain permanent neurological damage. Lead encephalopathy consists of one or more of the following: confusion, seizures, lethargy, vomiting, coma, and death. The permanent sequelae of lead-induced encephalopathy are usually seizure disorders and severe mental retardation. In most of the early cases of plumbism blood lead was never measured, making it difficult to determine how high the levels were that caused such severe damage. Today blood lead levels above 80 μg/dl are considered to be high and trigger drug chelation therapy to reduce lead body burdens over a period of days to weeks of continuous treatment. Children with lead-induced encephalopathy generally have blood levels of 80 μg/dl or above.

How big a problem is lead exposure in children? The answer to this depends on the cutoff level used to define asymptomatic plumbism. The U.S. Centers for Disease Control had in the past set a blood lead level of 30 μg/dl as the trigger point for recommending that a child be referred for evaluation and treatment. Using the CDC cutoff, the National Center for Health Statistics completed a nationwide survey showing that 2 percent of all white children in the United States and 12.2 percent of all black children 6 months to 5 years of age have blood lead levels at any given time in excess of 30 μg/dl (Mahaffey, Annest, Roberts, & Murphy, 1982). These rates are even higher if one focuses on urban, lower socioeconomic, black children (18.6 percent). Such findings dramatically illustrate the scope of the lead poisoning problem in this country. This survey was done between 1976 and 1980, long after the removal of lead from paints, after lead abatement plans were undertaken in urban areas, and after lead reduction standards were imposed on gasoline producers. The data illustrate how pervasive lead has become in our surroundings and how difficult it is to remove from the environment even after major sources of lead influx are curtailed. Similar situations exist in other countries. Recently, the CDC has lowered its screening trigger value for blood lead from 30 to 25 μg/dl (CDC, 1985). If the prevalence data cited above were recalculated using the newer CDC trigger value the number of at risk children would rise sharply. One encouraging piece of information that came out of the National Center for Health Statistics survey is that average blood lead levels deceased from 14.6 to 9.2 μg/dl between 1976 and 1980 (Annest, Pirkle, Makuc, Neese, Bayse, & Kovar, 1983). This was attributed to the regulations mandating the use of unleaded gasolines.

Many human investigations have been undertaken to try to document the exact risks and precise nature of the neuropsychological impairments induced by lead exposures in the asymptomatic range (25 or 30 to 80 μg/dl). Bornschein and colleagues (1980a) have provided an excellent critical review of these investigations. In that review, they note that two major problems have plagued most of the human lead studies. First, careful serial blood lead values have not been obtained so that the true history of lead exposure in the study population has not been established. This is obviously a crucial point since the evidence suggests that chronic moderate lead exposure is the primary problem rather than transient elevations. Second, the psychological assessment methods have been inadequate. The methods used could not ensure that actual deficits could be detected if present or that the specific nature of any deficits detected could be elucidated.

Perhaps the best known of the lead studies, and one that avoids most of the problems that plague others in the field, is that by Needleman and colleagues (1979). These investigators did not rely on blood lead, but instead used dentine lead. They surveyed a large number of urban children's teeth and then followed up the upper and lower 10 percent based on lead content using a variety of psychological assessment instruments. The high lead group performed significantly worse than the low lead group on the WISC-R intelligence test (full-scale IQ, verbal IQ, verbal subtests for information, vocabulary, and digit span), Seashore Rhythm Test, Token Test, Sentence Repetition Test, and a reaction time test.

This study has been widely cited as establishing that moderate lead exposure impairs cognitive development (e.g., CDC, 1985). On its behalf one may note that this study was well designed, well conducted, and statistically well analyzed. By using dentine rather than single- or 2-point measurement of blood lead the authors argued that they were measuring chronic lead exposure rather than only recent exposure (Needleman et al., 1979). The strongest findings in this study may be the reaction time data, which showed a consistent and clear deficit in the high lead group using a series of different response delay intervals. Another potentially important area of differences found was teacher rating scales of negative classroom behaviors. The teachers' ratings data are important because not just the upper and lower 10 percent dentine level subgroups were used, but the entire study population. For this analysis children from the entire sample were placed in one of five dentine lead categories. Needleman and colleagues found a dose-dependent relationship between elevated dentine lead and increased frequency of negatively rated classroom behaviors. This is strong evidence that children with higher body burdens of lead exhibit more problem behaviors. The negative behaviors that showed the clearest dose-dependent relationships among those reported by Needleman and colleagues were increased distractibility, disorganization, daydreaming, frustration, and difficulty following directions. Each of these behaviors increased in approximate proportion to increasing dentine lead levels.

Probably the two major drawbacks of this study were: (1) that the relationship between dentine lead and blood lead is not well understood, which makes interpretation of the findings difficult; and (2) that the magnitudes of the behavioral differences obtained were often small. For example, the mean IQ score in the low lead group was 106.6 while in the high lead group it was 102.1. While the difference was statistically significant, it is not clear what the functional or practical significance of such a modest difference is. As for use of dentine lead, it is clear that accompanying serial blood lead levels would have been beneficial to the interpretation of the data obtained by Needleman and colleagues.

Other criticisms of the study by Needleman and colleagues (1979) have also been made. They include the fact that the authors used the study children's fathers' socioeconomic status rather than educational level, that scaled IQ scores were used rather than unscaled scores, and that analysis of covariance was used rather than multiple regression techniques. Recently, Needleman, Geiger, and Frank (1985) have reanalyzed their data taking into account each of these criticisms, and have reported that none of them makes any material difference in the outcome. In fact, some differences are actually slightly larger on reanalysis. On balance, it appears that the study by Needleman and colleagues (1979) should be afforded greater weight than other studies done thus far in humans in evaluating the effects of moderate lead exposure.

Problems in other studies have centered on imprecise subject selection, problematic definition of groups (i.e., what constitutes a high lead versus a low lead group), improper statisical analyses, inadequate subject matching, and questionable control over test administration. The combined effects of these problems led Bornschein and colleagues (1980a) to conclude that no clear case for neurobehavioral damage after moderate lead exposure currently exists. Even among the better studies they reviewed, about half show lead-associated deficits and half do not. But the data of Needleman and colleagues (1979) must certainly not be treated as equal to the rest. The superiority of this study in many respects suggests that it should be given greater credence until convincing evidence is developed to refute it, if that day comes.

Although most of the lead research has focused on childhood lead exposure, as noted above, a recent experiment has investigated possible prenatal influences of lead on psychological function (Bellinger et al., 1984). These investigators conducted a prospective study of children born in a large hospital in Boston. In this study cord blood lead values at delivery were obtained on 11,837 newborns during a 2-year period. Using a subsample of 2500 of these newborns, the investigators selected those infants that were in the highest and lowest 10 percent of the population for blood lead levels. The upper 10 percent group had lead values of > 10 μg/dl and the lower 10 percent group had lead values of < 2 μg/dl. A middle dose lead group was also selected. After exclusion of cases confounded by other conditions (disease, malformations, labor and delivery complications, postnatal distress, etc.) they enrolled 249 infants in the study. The mothers of these 249 infants were predominantly middle-class and were fairly well educated. The authors adjusted statistically for many other factors known to affect neonatal behavioral outcome, and using the Bayley scales, found that Bayley mental development index scores were negatively related to cord lead levels. At 6 months of age, the low lead group's mean mental index score was 110.8 compared to the high lead group's mean score of 105.0. Cord blood levels, however, were not significantly related to Bayley psychomotor development scores. The authors point out that the cord blood lead levels are consistent with recent national survey findings, including the fact that between 1976 and 1980 blood lead values in children have declined appreciably (Annest et al., 1983). Although the magnitudes of the Bayley mental development score differences found by Bellinger and colleagues (1984) were small, they add another piece of evidence to the idea that even relatively mild prenatal lead elevations can have a significant negative impact on early mental development. These data may also point to the importance in future studies of examining more closely the influence of prenatal lead exposures, since this is a period of high sensitivity of the CNS to injury.

There is a preliminary report in humans in another prospective study relating prenatal lead to postnatal outcome (Ernhart et al., 1985). These authors assessed cord blood lead levels at birth and related these to a series of physical and behavioral indices of early development. The behavioral assessments were the Brazelton and part of the Graham-Rosenblith. They found small but significant associations between cord blood lead levels and abnormal infant reflexes and soft neurological signs.

Some of the problems in the human studies have been investigated in animals. Bornschein, Pearson, and Reiter (1980b) have also thoroughly reviewed this literature. Lead-induced neuropathy can be induced in postnatally developing animals. These effects are not in dispute. In general, such overt effects may be considered models of human lead-induced encephalopathy, although species differences are also apparent.

Most of the experimental animal research has focused on the same problem as have the investigations in human beings, namely, the behavioral effects of chronic developmental exposure to moderate levels of lead. Based on the review by Bornschein and colleagues (1980b) the following conclusions may be drawn: (1) Lead-exposed animals consistently exhibit impairments of learning, and these effects occur without regard to the specific type of test (within certain limits, see below); (2) changes in locomotor activity have been reliably found, and usually these have been findings of hyperactivity; (3) pattern discrimination learning is more often affected than other aspects of learning (i.e., compared to reversal learning, extinction, and passive avoidance, which are generally unaffected); (4) the effects on behavior appear long after lead exposure has been discontinued, although it is not possible to conclude that these effects are permanent; (5) the behavioral effects occur independent of undernutrition (reduced weight gain), since they are found at exposures that do not produce significant growth reductions and in studies employing pair-fed controls; and (6) the behavioral effects occur independent of possible confounding influences of altered maternal rearing behavior by lead-exposed dams.

While Bornschein and colleagues (1980b) note many flaws in the individual animal experiments, on balance the studies add significantly to the weight of evidence suggesting that moderate lead exposure during development poses significant risk of untoward neurobehavioral effects. The conclusions noted above based on the review by Bornschein and colleagues (1980b) were based primarily on rodent experiments. Those conclusions have been measurably strengthened by studies reported more recently. Among the most important have been those conducted in monkeys (Bushnell & Bowman, 1979a, 1979b; Mele, Bushnell, & Bowman, 1984). These studies are important because they have achieved what has often been missing in earlier rodent studies, that is, chronic, early, moderate (asymptomatic) lead exposure with careful documentation of blood lead levels, with testing conducted at long intervals after discontinuation of lead exposure, and with evaluation of a wide variety of behaviors (including social interactions, play, activity, and multiple types of learning). As an example Mele and colleagues (1984) treated infant rhesus monkeys with lead during the first year and tested them on an operant task at almost 3 years of age (2 years after treatment). They found that lead-exposed monkeys had a lower index of curvature in learning an operant fixed interval schedule (a measure of learning performance) than controls. For a review of these important primate experiments see the recent discussion by Laughlin (1986). Taken together with the findings on other types of behavioral tests in monkeys, the data support the view that blood lead values of 32–65 μg/dl early in life can produce significant long-term behavioral dysfunctions.

In conclusion, the data show that high levels of lead exposure are severely neurotoxic. The data also support the view that moderate lead exposure during early postnatal, and perhaps prenatal, development is capable of producing milder long-term behavioral deficits. While the lead literature on moderate exposures is not as clear-cut as it is for methylmercury or alcohol, the preponderance of evidence indicts lead as a developmental neurobehavioral toxin.

AGENTS THAT ARE PROBABLE BEHAVIORAL TERATOGENS

The next several groups of compounds are those for which the evidence of behavioral teratogenesis is strong but cannot yet be considered conclusive. As the evidence accumulates these compounds can reasonably be expected to move into the preceding category of known behavioral teratogens. In each of the groups reviewed below, however, there are some significant gaps in the evidence still requiring resolution.

Because of the large number of compounds in this group equal attention cannot be given to each. Anticonvulsants will be reviewed in the greatest detail because the emergence of this area is new and less well known, and because they illustrate a theme of this review, which is how the two prongs of research, human and animal studies, can converge to provide a better picture of a drug's effects. The idea of bringing both human and animal studies to bear will be followed in abbreviated form on subsequent compounds.

The Fetal Anticonvulsant Syndromes

During the last 15–20 years epidemiological evidence has mounted indicating that epileptic women have an increased incidence of children with congenital malformations. There is not complete agreement on how large this increase is, but most investigations have found it to be double to triple the rate found in controls (Janz, 1975, 1982a, 1982b; Kalter & Warkany, 1983). The main concern has been not whether epileptic women have increased risk or not, but instead the cause of the increase. Is the increase the result of the disease itself, or is it related to the anticonvulsant medications being taken to control the seizures? Genetic contributions, pathophysiological processes, and adverse effects of maternal seizures on the conceptus during pregnancy have all been suggested as possible ways in which epilepsy might cause embryonic damage. Major studies can be found that conclude that the increased malformations among children of epileptic women are attributable to the epilepsy (Shapiro et al., 1976), and others conclude that it is attributable to the drugs they take for epilepsy (Nakane, 1979).

Most of the newer evidence points to the anticonvulsant medications themselves, and not to the condition of having epilepsy (Kalter & Warkany, 1983). Some of the most persuasive evidence is that epileptics who have been taken off anticonvulsant medications appear to have malformation rates in their offspring that are well below those of women who continue to take anticonvulsants during pregnancy (Nakane, 1979).

Kalter and Warkany (1983) have recently reviewed the known causes of major malformations. They estimate that 3 percent of all newborns are identified as having major malformations. Of these, more than 60 percent are of unknown cause, 13.5 percent are due to a known mutant allele or chromosomal abnormality, another 20 percent are of complex origin reflecting a mixture of genetic and unidentified contributing factors, leaving less than 20 percent having specifically identifiable causes. Based on data that epileptic women have twice the incidence of defects as the population at large, and that about 0.52 percent of delivering women have epilepsy, the authors calculated that pregnancies of epileptic women accounted for about 1.26 percent of all deliveries. Based on 1981 population statistics, this incidence represents almost 1400 affected births annually in the United States.

Unfortunately, it is not possible simply to remove all epileptic women from medications when they become pregnant, because untreated epilepsy is a major mortality and morbidity risk to the epileptic patient and perhaps to the fetus (Montouris, Fenichel, & McLain, 1979). In addition, it is a difficult task to remove epileptics from their medication during pregnancy even if one decides that such a course of action should be taken. One problem is that by the time pregnancy is verified the epileptic patient would very likely be 4–8 weeks into the pregnancy and would have exposed the embryo to the drug throughout much of organogenesis. Steady-state anticonvulsant medication levels in tissue also require days to be cleared. It has also been observed that the risk of seizures sometimes increases during pregnancy and the dose of the medication is increased during late pregnancy when this occurs (Nakane, 1979).

If we accept for the moment that epilepsy must be controlled because the risks of nontreatment exceed those of treatment, then the next logical task is to find the safest anticonvulsant. There has been little research directed toward this issue. There are some data on structural abnormalities in animals dosed with the major anticonvulsant drugs (Fritz, Muller, & Hess, 1976; Sullivan & McElhatton, 1975, 1977). But malformations do not represent the only hazard to the conceptus from prenatal anticonvulsant drug exposure.

Some anticonvulsants have been shown to produce a more subtle pattern of defects in which major malformations are not the most prominent feature. Although German, Kowal, and Ehlers (1970) described some of the features of this broader pattern for trimethadione, it was not until 1975 that the full patterns of the fetal trimethadione (Zackai, Mellman, Neiderer, & Hanson, 1975) and the fetal hydantoin syndromes (Hanson & Smith, 1975) were described. Broadly, the main features of both syndromes bear some resemblance to those of the fetal alcohol syndrome (FAS), but closer examination also reveals differences.

In general, the fetal hydantoin syndrome is said to consist of facial anomalies, digit hypoplasia, intrauterine growth deficiency, and mental subnormality (Hanson & Smith, 1975); digital hypoplasia has not been reliably associated with cases of FAS. In a small prospective study, it was noted that approximately 11 percent of offspring from epileptic women taking hydantoins had the complete syndrome, and another 31 percent exhibited partial or incomplete expressions of the disorder (Hanson, Myrianthopoulos, Sedgwick-Harvey, & Smith, 1976).

The facial pattern consists of midfacial hypoplasia, epicanthal folds, upturned nares, hypertelorism, ptosis or strabismus, mispositioned ears, and large lips and mouth. Growth is reported to be at 75 percent of normal. Mental and motor deficiency has not been described in detail, but only as being mild to moderate based on unspecified assessment instruments (Hanson et al., 1976). The digital hypoplasia consists of reduced phalanges and/or nails of either the hands or feet.

The fetal trimethadione syndrome is more serious than the fetal hydantoin syndrome and consists of growth deficiency, facial anomalies, and behavioral delay, with other defects occurring less frequently, such as microcephaly, cardiac defects, eye defects, hypospadias, and hernia (Zackai et al., 1975). The facial defects consist of epicanthal folds, mispositioned ears, V-shaped eyebrows, and palate and tooth irregularities. The behavioral effects consist of mild mental retardation and speech difficulties (assessed with unspecified psychological instruments). In 1977, Feldman, Weaver, and Lovrien reviewed the findings on the fetal trimethadione syndrome and noted that 87 percent of pregnancies in which this drug was used and reported worldwide in retrospective case studies were either spontaneously aborted or born with major malformations. Fifty-four percent of the worldwide cases surviving postnatally were said to show speech impairment, and 50 percent mental retardation. Among live births, therefore, the psychological defects show the highest incidence. Visual impairment was also reported in 50 percent of the cases on which vision was examined. All other symptoms, including facial anomalies, were reported to occur in less than 50 percent of the cases. The highest craniofacial defect incidence was 42.5 percent (mispositioned ears); the next highest was 27.5 percent (cleft lip and/or palate); and all other facial defects occurred at incidence rates of 10 percent or below (Feldman et al., 1977).

As has been noted, "the most serious consequence [of trimethadione] is mental deficiency" (Smith, 1977, p. 1337). A similar conclusion was reached for the fetal hydantoin syndrome. In a prospective study Hill and her associates noted that anticonvulsants were significantly associated with a cluster of defects, of which one of the most prominent was low Gesell developmental quotients at 21 months of age (Hill, Verniaud, Horning, McCulley, & Morgan, 1974).

These reports point persuasively toward the existence of fetal hydantoin and trimethadione syndromes. In both cases the behavioral dysfunction is the most serious and often the most consistently observed type of defect. The American Academy of Pediatrics Committee on Drugs, however, makes no recommendation regarding which drugs to avoid during pregnancy for epileptic women, presumably because the data are still inadequate. They recommend that drug treatment for epileptics should be continued throughout pregnancy, stating that women have "a 90% chance of having a normal child, but that the risk of congenital malformations and mental retardation is two to three times greater than average because of her disease or its treatment" (Segal et al., 1979, p. 333).

More recently, descriptions of fetal barbital (Seip, 1976; Smith, 1977) and fetal primidone syndromes (Rudd & Freedom, 1979; Shih, Diamond, & Kushnick, 1979) have also been reported. Mental deficiency has been rather uniformly reported in these cases.

For example, the cases reported by Rudd and Freedom (1979) described two children born to the same woman who were exposed in utero to primidone. The most affected of the two showed mental retardation, stunted growth, hirsutism, microcephaly, cardiac defects, and hypoplastic nails. This pattern is very similar to the fetal hydantoin picture. The description by Seip (1976) of the effects of barbiturates was also on two children born to one woman. She received phenobarbital, primidone, and ethosuximide during the first pregnancy, and phenobarbital and primidone during her second. Both infants showed dysmorphic effects. Both had low nasal bridge, hypertelorism, epicanthal folds, mispositioned ears, wide mouths, and growth deficiency. Only one of the two was reported to be moderately mentally retarded (no mention is made of what test or tests were used to assess cognitive development). Overall, the syndromes described as associated with phenobarbital and primidone are very similar, but not identical in all respects.

One of the major problems encountered in trying to sort out the embryotoxicity of anticonvulsants in human beings is that many epileptics are receiving polytherapy, in which they receive two or three drugs simultaneously to control their seizures (Nakane, 1979). Polytherapy with anticonvulsants is believed to offer significant therapeutic gains over higher doses of a single agent in cases where seizure control with one drug is inadequate. This reduces the availability of cases where single drug effects can be evaluated.

The history of valproate as an anticonvulsant is rather different from that of the drugs already discussed. Not only is it newer, particularly in the United States, but it is chemically very different (Rall & Schleifer, 1980). Valproate has been on the market as an anticonvulsant in Europe since 1964, and in the United States since 1978. There are many scattered clinical reports suggesting that valproate is terato-genic, but the most important recent evidence on this drug comes from data generated from European birth defects registries. In 1982 eight countries pooled their data and found a connection between valproate use in pregnant epileptic women and the occurrence of neural tube defects in their infants, particularly spina bifida (Bjerkedal et al., 1982). They found that about 1 percent of the births in which the mothers were on valproate in Europe had some kind of neural tube defect. In contrast, the data from the United States for the same interval, before valproate was on the market, showed the rate of neural tube defects to be much lower than 1 percent.

A newer report from the Netherlands (Lindhout & Meinardi, 1984), examined defects on a subset of all Dutch births between 1972 and 1983. This preliminary report reviewed about one-third of the total data base and found the incidence rate of spina bifida in those using valproate was three to five times the expected rate (10 cases found instead of the expected 2-3). The authors concluded that valproate is significantly associated with an elevated risk of spina bifida, and perhaps also with a second defect, hypospadias.

Valproate has also been said to produce a broader pattern of effects like that of the drugs discussed above. There are several reports in the literature describing a fetal valproate syndrome. A report of seven cases and review of previous reports is noteworthy (DiLiberti, Farndon, Dennis, & Curry, 1984). The salient features of the syndrome included dysmorphic facies and developmental delay (in three of the cases). The facial dysmorphologies were epicanthal folds, low nasal bridge, small upturned nose, shallow philtrum, small downturned mouth, and thin upper ver-million. The valproate syndrome was differentiated from the fetal hydantoin syndrome by DiLiberti and colleagues by the absence of hypertelorism, broad nasal bridge, and broad bifrontal diameter of the head, all of which are said to be seen in hydantoin syndrome cases. It should be noted, however, that these distinctions are tenuous. The similarities among the facial features of most of the fetal anti-convulsant syndromes are far more striking than the differences.

A review of the published cases reveals another difference between the valproate syndrome and the other anticonvulsant syndromes not noted by DiLiberti and colleagues (1984). The valproate syndrome cases have not been reported to show growth retardation. It remains to be seen whether this observation will be confirmed by future investigations. The three out of seven rate of developmental, intellectual, and/or psychomotor delays observed by DiLiberti and colleagues is interesting, but unfortunately was vaguely described, and it is not possible to determine much about the behavioral impairments at this point. In view of valproate's involvement with spina bifida one might expect that its days of use in epileptic women of childbearing age are numbered, but this too remains to be seen.

Few data are available on the fetal effects of other anticonvulsants. With respect to carbamazepine, McMullin (1971) reported a case of gonadal dysgenesis in an infant whose mother took phenobarbital, primidone, phenytoin, phensuccimide, and carbamazepine during pregnancy. Millar and Nevin (1973) reported an infant with myelomeningocele born to a mother taking phenobarbital and carbamazepine.

Fedrick (1973) reported one out of two infants with birth defects born to women taking carbamazepine during the first trimester. Robertson, Donnai, and D'Souza (1983) reported a case of cranial nerve damage in an infant whose mother took carbamazepine for epilepsy during pregnancy, and Hicks (1979) found one out of two epileptic mothers using carbamazepine had a stillbirth with major defects. Lindhout, Hoppener, and Meinardi (1974) reported that carbamazepine taken with phenobarbital and valproate produced an increased occurrence of children born with anomalies. In these authors' most recent large-scale surveillance study, an association was noted also between carbamazepine and spina bifida (Lindhout & Meinardi, 1984). Although the latter association was small, it provides an additional piece of information that carbamazepine might also be teratogenic. In contrast to these reports, Barry and Danks (1974), Starreveld-Zimmerman, van der Kolk, Meinardi, and Elshove (1973), Niebyl, Blake, Freeman, and Luff (1979), and Granstrom and Hiilesmaa (1982) all reported no association between carbamazepine and malformations. No one appears to have looked yet for a broader spectrum of developmental disabilities or behavioral dysfunctions in children of mothers who took carbamazepine.

Similarly scattered collections of reports are available for several other anticonvulsants. The benzodiazepines, primarily diazepam and clonazepam, represent a unique group requiring special mention. Diazepam is infrequently used to prevent seizures in epileptics, but is used in status epilepticus and as adjunctive anticonvulsant therapy on a short-term basis in those at temporary risk for seizures (Schmidt, 1982). For status epilepticus it is usually given intravenously rather than orally. While there may be overlap between doses producing anticonvulsive action and anxiolytic effects, there are also indications that optimally effective anticonvulsant doses are higher than doses necessary to produce anxiolytic effects. For this reason it is not entirely clear that the same doses should be used to model the use of diazepam as an anticonvulsant as opposed to its use as an anxiolytic agent. Chronic use of diazepam produces tolerance to its anticonvulsant action in 40 percent of patients after 3–6 months of use (Schmidt, 1982). This is one of the reasons this drug has found only limited use as an anticonvulsant agent. This problem is not associated, however, with clonazepam (Dreifuss & Sato, 1982). Unfortunately, there are no data on the behavioral teratogenicity of clonazepam. There are some animal experiments on the effects of prenatal diazepam (Valium®) and chlordiazepoxide (Librium®) exposure as they affect postnatal behavior, and these will be reviewed below in the section on anxiolytics.

The review of behavioral teratogenesis of anticonvulsants in animals will be brief because few studies exist. Nevertheless, these studies have contributed significantly to demonstrating the cause–effect relationship between these agents and postnatal behavioral dysfunction, thus filling in an important gap in the evidence that human investigations have been unable to provide. Data on phenobarbital will not be included here, but are reviewed elsewhere (Middaugh, 1986).

The first experiments reported on the behavioral effects of prenatal phenytoin (Dilantin®) were done by Elmazar and Sullivan (1981). They treated rats throughout organogenesis with 100 mg/kg per day of phenytoin. This dose may seem large when compared to human doses, in the range of roughly 3–10 mg/kg (Rall & Schleifer, 1982), but intestinal absorption of the drug in rats is poor compared to that in humans. This illustrates an important point that applies to all the chemical agents discussed in this chapter. The key index of efficacy is blood or target tissue levels of the agent or its active metabolites rather than administered dose. For phenytoin, the human plasma therapeutic range is 10–25 μg/ml (Kutt, 1982). Elmazar and Sullivan measured plasma phenytoin at several intervals after treatment and found plasma phenytoin levels to be in the low end of the human therapeutic range.

Large delays in the maturation of some reflexes and impairments on several measures of motor coordination (rotorod and narrow path walking tests) were observed in the phenytoin offspring. These same animals also did not habituate as rapidly as controls on a test of exploration. Finally, phenytoin offspring showed impaired impulse control by stepping and jumping down inappropriately from elevated platforms.

Elmazar and Sullivan's (1981) experiments indicate that prenatal phenytoin in doses at the low end of the therapeutic range based on plasma concentrations produces a wide variety of adverse behavioral effects in the offspring. The data on cross-fostering included in these experiments also provided evidence that postnatal maternal influences play only a minor role in modifying offspring behavior.

Mullenix, Tassinari, and Keith (1983) used rats given 1000 mg/kg of sodium phenytoin on only a few days of gestation. They measured plasma phenytoin levels and found them to be in the middle of the human therapeutic range. In a test of activity the phenytoin females were less active during an initial exploratory period, but no differences appeared in the males and no differences were found between groups during the remainder of the testing. Observer-based ratings of activity indicated that males showed slightly increased activity, while female activity was decreased. Although less clear-cut, these data are generally in agreeemnt with those of Elmazar and Sullivan (1981).

The next study reporting on the behavioral teratogenicity of phenytoin was by Vorhees (1983). Blood levels at the highest dose tested were at the upper end of the human therapeutic range. The phenytoin dams showed a modest reduction in weight during pregnancy, and their offspring were initially lighter. Newborn mortality was also increased in the phenytoin group.

The high dose of phenytoin produced almost a full day's delay in the onset of the auditory startle response, more than a doubling of early locomotor behavior, and large delays in swimming development. After weaning, the phenytoin offspring showed more than a 50 percent increase in activity, and the most dramatic effect observed was an almost tripling of errors in a complex spatial maze test. Finally, in a test of memory the phenytoin animals showed a significant impairment in the retention of a learned response when tested 2 weeks after initial learning.

In a second experiment the same dose of phenytoin was again used, but the exposure interval was subdivided into one of three shorter intervals. Instead of dosing the dams on days 7–18 of gestation they were exposed on days 7–10, 11–14, or 15–18.

In all but one behavioral test the phenytoin groups showed effects consistent with findings in the longer exposed group. However, not all exposure intervals showed the same effects. For example, the phenytoin groups exposed on days 11–14 and 15–18 showed increased pivoting locomotion on the same days as the phenytoin group exposed on days 7–18, but the increase was about half as large, and the phenytoin group exposed on days 7–10 showed no increase in pivoting. In the spatial learning test, the phenytoin group exposed on days 11–14 was the most affected, showing an increase in both errors and time in the maze. Neither of the other phenytoin exposure intervals showed any significant increase in maze performance.

On balance, these two experiments show that phenytoin is a powerful behavioral teratogen at nonmalforming doses. The results also show that the effects are specific, affecting multiple indices of behavioral development (pivoting, swimming, activity, maze learning, and memory). These effects are replicable and exhibit very clear-cut period–response specificity. This period-specific sensitivity in rats occurs on days 11–14 of gestation when many brain structures are undergoing neurogenesis (Rodier, 1980).

Recently, we have completed a third behavioral experiment with phenytoin, using additional dose levels (Vorhees, 1986a). In brief, we replicated in a clear dose-dependent fashion our previous findings of increased maze errors and times, and increased activity. We also showed a dose-dependent increase in two other tests of activity, and a delay in the air-righting reflex similar to that found by Elmazar and Sullivan (1981).

These results demonstrate the following points: (1) Phenytoin is a specific and powerful behavioral teratogen whose effects exhibit a remarkable consistency from study to study; (2) phenytoin's effects on postnatal behavior are positively related to maternal blood phenytoin levels; (3) maternal blood levels of phenytoin producing in utero damage are within the human therapeutic range for this anticonvulsant, which raises the concern that this drug is able to produce the brain-damaging effects that are an integral part of the fetal hydantoin syndrome at doses necessary for the control of epilepsy; and (4) new data show dose-dependent changes in postnatal behavior from prenatal phenytoin.

Only one experiment exists reporting on the behavioral effects of prenatal trimethadione exposure (Vorhees, 1983). The methods were identical to those described above in the discussion of phenytoin. Unlike phenytoin, trimethadione (250 mg/kg) produced no effects on preweaning measures of behavioral development. Trimethadione produced three significant effects on postnatal measures of behavior. The trimethadione offspring were significantly more active than controls, exhibited a reduction in their frequency of spontaneous alternation behavior, and showed a significant increase in maze errors.

In the second experiment the exposure period of 7–18 days was divided into three shorter periods as described before with phenytoin. All the trimethadione groups showed small delays in swimming development, while only the exposure group of 15–18 days showed an impairment of maze performance.

In summary, trimethadione was also found to be a behavioral teratogen in rats, but it is not as potent as phenytoin. This contrasts with the interpretation of dysmorphologists who suggest that trimethadione is more potent that phenytoin. It must be borne in mind, however, that the clinical appraisal is based upon data such as fetal death, frequency of major malformations, and percentage of infants with minor anomalies and developmental delays. Such an analysis includes behavioral dysfunction as one cluster that is compared with clusters of growth impairments and dysmorphic features in order to come up with a global assessment. Our conclusion, by contrast, is based on animal data and turns exclusively on the degree of behavioral dysfunction. It may turn out that follow-up of the clinical cases will reveal either that the behavioral dysfunctions associated with phenytoin are more severe than with trimethadione, or that our doses of trimethadione in animals were not high enough to be therapeutically comparable with our phenytoin doses. Since we do not yet have blood level data on our trimethadione model it is not possible to state at present where we were in relation to the human therapeutic range.

Only one experiment has been described at present on the possible behavioral teratogenicity of valproate in experimental animals. Chapman and Cutler (1984) administered 600 mg/L of sodium valproate in the drinking water as the sole fluid source to mice at one of three exposure intervals during development. One group was exposed prior to breeding and throughout both gestation and lactation. A second group received the valproate only during lactation. A third group received valproate only after lactation.

On a test of social behavior, the authors found that at intakes calculated to be 103–158 mg/kg the major effect of valproate exposure was to increase social investigatory behavior. They report that this dose is near the minimum anticonvulsant dose for mice, but no data on blood levels of valproate were provided. While the data of Chapman and Cutler (1984) are quite interesting, the meaning of changes in social investigatory behavior as an index of behavioral teratogenesis is too uncertain to draw firm conclusions about valproate.

Cigarette Smoking and Nicotine

The adverse effects of cigarette smoking during pregnancy on birth weight, complications of pregnancy, and spontaneous abortion risk have been documented for many years (Surgeon General's Report, 1979). The birth weight deficits found in children of smokers are dose dependent and average about 200 g. Perhaps most significantly, the risk of having a low birth weight child (< 2500 g) is doubled among women who smoke. The evidence against smoking is further strengthened by newer evidence showing that intervention programs for smokers to help them stop smoking during pregnancy can significantly ameliorate the smoking-induced weight deficit they would be expected to have as compared to those in which no intervention is attempted (Sexton & Hebel, 1984).

A small number of studies have gone beyond the now classic indices of smoking-induced embryotoxicity. Several of these have included measures of behavioral outcome. Picone, Allen, Olsen, and Ferris (1982) examined a matched sample for the effects of maternal diet, smoking, and weight gain on birth weight and length, length of gestation, placental weight, and Brazelton assessments made on infants at birth and at 2 weeks of age. They found that smokers had significantly lighter infants by about 200 g even though they had dietary calorie intakes and gestation lengths no different from those of nonsmokers. Diet predicted maternal weight gain in nonsmokers, even in those having low birth weight infants, but not among smokers. Brazelton scores showed significant effects of maternal smoking on habituation, orientation, and autonomic regulation. Moreover, the habituation and orientation deficits were specific to auditory stimuli. This finding is consistent with findings by Sexton (1978), who also found auditory changes in infants of smokers based on neonatal examinations using the Brazelton. Butler and Goldstein (1973) in an early study had found 7- and 11-year-old children of smokers (more than 10 cigarettes per day) to be delayed in their development of reading and arithmetic skills.

Research on fetal alcohol effects reviewed above included in their designs examinations for the effects of smoking on the behavior of the offspring. As noted above, several behavioral effects in the children were interactively related to both prenatal alcohol and smoking (Landesman-Dwyer et al., 1978; Martin et al., 1977; Martin et al., 1979).

Recently, Naeye and Peters (1984) examined data derived from the prospective Collaborative Perinatal Study of the National Institute of Neurological and Communicative Disorders and Stroke (data on 50,000 pregnancies collected between 1959 and 1966). They selected only cases from one large center, the Boston Lying-in Hospital, with 12,150 cases. After excluding cases lost to follow-up and with identified prenatal or postnatal complications they had a study sample of 9024 women. They also selected a subsample in which women had at least two pregnancies in the study, one in which they had smoked and one in which they had not, and used offspring of the nonsmoking pregnancies as the controls. All children had standardized testing at 7 years of age. In both the large sample of 9024 cases and the subsample, significant differences were found between children of heavy smokers (20 or more cigarettes per day) and nonsmokers on tests of spelling, reading, attention span, and motor activity. Children of heavy smokers had lower achievement scores on spelling and reading, and displayed more motor activity and shorter attention span than control children. However, the magnitude of the differences on all behavioral measures was quite small. The differences were generally 2-3 percent and never greater than 5 percent. The effects were correlated to neonatal hemoglobin values and weight, but not to maternal weight gain during gestation, suggesting that the effects were related to maternal smoking and not other factors. The magnitudes of the behavioral differences at 7 years of age were sufficiently small that it is not entirely clear whether they have any functional significance.

How might effects of maternal smoking be mediated if it causes prenatal brain injury? The most widely discussed hypothesis is that smoking may induce a hypoxic state in the embryo and fetus. There are several mechanisms by which this might occur. One is that nicotine might reduce blood flow to the fetus. Using fetal monitoring, Gennser, Marsal, and Brantmark (1975) demonstrated that, in pregnant volunteers who were heavy smokers, smoking one cigarette or ingesting an oral dose of nicotine increased episodes of fetal apnea and intermittent breathing. Cigarettes had greater effects than nicotine alone, but both produced similar types of changes. Severe fetal hypoxia and its metabolic consequences are well-established causes of brain injury in both humans (Low et al., 1984) and animals (Myers, 1975a, 1975b, 1977, 1979), but it is unlikely that acute hypoxic or anoxic states are relevant to the conditions produced by chronic smoking because the degree of fetal hypoxia produced by smoking is not severe enough to induce the kind of damage shown by Low and colleagues (1984) and Myers (1975a, 1975b, 1977, 1979) under more extreme circumstances.

Perhaps a better understanding of how maternal smoking may be able to cause prenatal CNS damage comes from research on postnatal behavior and neurochemistry in rats exposed to prenatal carbon monoxide (CO), since smoking is known to raise circulating CO levels. Fechter and Annau (1977) have shown that CO exposure in rats at levels equivalent to those measured in human smokers produces reduced postnatal weight gain, reduced neonatal brain dopamine levels after administration of L-dopa, and reduced preweaning locomotor activity. These findings have been followed up by observations that rats prenatally exposed to these levels of CO also exhibit delayed righting and negative geotaxis reflexes, delayed orientation to their home cage scent (Fechter & Annau, 1980), and impaired acquisition and relearning in a two-way shock avoidance test (Mactutus & Fechter, 1984). These differences could not be accounted for by changes in maternal rearing behavior or by reductions in neonatal weight, growth, or other factors (Mactutus & Fechter, 1985).

Although there are some problems with the data from the human investigations on the behavioral teratogenesis of maternal smoking, the relevant animal data provide a clear link between prenatal CO exposure at levels comparable to those induced by smoking and impaired behavioral development of the offspring. Better human investigations and animal experiments using smoking directly may strengthen the case against maternal smoking, but the existing data are sufficient to regard maternal smoking as a probable behavioral teratogen.

Narcotics

Numerous studies have shown that human infants passively addicted to heroin or methadone prenatally exhibit postnatal behavioral disturbances. It is well established that prenatal opiate exposure at doses sufficient to maintain maternal addiction are behaviorally teratogenic to their children (reviewed by Hans, Marcus, Jeremy, & Auerbach, 1984; Householder, Hatcher, Burns, & Chasnoff, 1982; Hutchings, 1983; Hutchings & Fifer, 1986).

The opiates are rather distinct in that their behavioral teratogenic effects can be classified as occurring in at least two phases (Hutchings, 1983). The first phase is one of withdrawal from the opiate. During this period the addicted infant shows the symptoms of opiate abstinence. There is considerable agreement about these symptoms. The withdrawal symptoms have been described as hyperreflexia, tremors, irritability, abnormal crying, disturbed sleep, and impaired motor control (Hans et al., 1984; Hutchings, 1983). These results have been based on both objective and subjective observation methods and systematic testing, usually using the Brazelton test (Hans et al., 1984). Other methods of documenting neonatal behavioral abnormalities in opiate-addicted infants have been spectral analysis of crying patterns, electronically measured tests of sucking, electromyographic analyses of muscle movements, EEG measurements of sleep patterns, and auditorily and visually evoked potential tests. These measures have confirmed that opiate-addicted infants have an unusual high-pitched cry, suck poorly, are hypertonic with increased muscle rigidity, have less quiet and more active sleep, and show evoked potential differences (Hans et al., 1984). In contrast to smoking, which has been found primarily to affect auditorily evoked orientation and related behaviors, opiates are reliably found to impair visually evoked orientation behaviors and EEG recorded potentials (Hans et al., 1984).

The second longer-term phase of opiate-induced postnatal effects is somewhat less clear, but again depends on time since birth. Effects up to 4 months of age are reliably seen. For example, in a prospective study on behavioral outcome Marcus and associates followed a group of infants whose mothers were on methadone maintenance programs throughout their pregnancies (Bernstein, Jeremy, Hans, & Marcus, 1984; Jeremy & Bernstein, 1984; Marcus & Hans, 1982a, 1982b; Marcus, Hans, & Jeremy, 1982a, 1982b, 1984; Marcus, Hans, Patterson, & Morris, 1984). The data show that when assessed at 4 months of age with the Bayley scales opiate-exposed infants performed more poorly on motor items (they were more tense, more active, and less well coordinated) but were no different on social or cognitive items than matched controls. They also report finding poorer attention in opiate-exposed infants even at 12 months of age. Beyond 12 months the findings on children prenatally exposed to opiates are uneven.

Hutchings (1983), Hutchings and Fifer (1986), and Hans and colleagues (1984) have concluded that no clear findings at later ages have been made, although some hints are emerging that these children may continue to exhibit some attention deficits. Hutchings (1983) has also shown that the effects seen in human newborns and infants are confirmed by many animal experiments. Just as with humans, however, the evidence on long-term effects in animals is still equivocal. Some suggestive data on very long-term effects in animals have been reported by Friedler (1974a, 1974b). Thus prenatal opiates are behaviorally teratogenic, but it appears that their effects dissipate with age. The effects are quite clear in neonates and up to 4 months of age. How long the residual effects of opiates may be detected after 4 months is not yet clear, but there is some evidence to suggest that adverse changes last up to 12 months of age. The reader is referred to the review by Hutchings and Fifer (1986) for an excellent discussion of the design and interpretation issues in both human and animal studies on prenatal opiate effects.

Polychorinated Biphenyls (PCBs)

Polychlorinated biphenyls (PCBs) are a class of 210 compounds that have been used for many years in electrical transformers, carbonless paper, and paint for their insular, adhesive, and stability characteristics (Fein, Jacobson, Jacobson, Schwartz, & Dowler, 1984; Fein, Schwartz, Jacobson, & Jacobson, 1983; Taylor, Lawrence, Hwang, & Paulson, 1984). Although PCBs are no longer being used they are widespread and persistent compounds. Taylor and colleagues (1984) examined women exposed occupationally to PCBs and found significant reductions in birth weight and gestation length of their children. When birth weights were adjusted for gestation length the effect on weight was reduced. Taylor and colleagues (1984) conclude that PCB exposure can shorten gestation by 6–7 days.

In 1973, feed from cattle and chickens in Michigan was contaminated with the chemically related compounds, polybrominated biphenyls (PBBs). No differences in fetal mortality were found between the counties containing the contaminated farms and those that were not contaminated (Humble & Speizer, 1984). Unfortunately, these analyses may be too limited to detect the cumulative effects of these PBB compounds.

PCBs have found their way into waterways and are now a significant contaminant in fish. PCBs, like methylmercury, are sequestered in fat tissue and tend to move up the aquatic food chain, becoming increasingly concentrated and eventually being consumed by human beings. In an interesting prospective study in Michigan, Jacobson, Jacobson, and Fein have taken advantage of this natural human experiment and conducted a study of pregnancy outcome in which groups of women who were lake fish consumers were compared to those who were not. The findings indicated that PCBs cross the placenta (Jacobson, Fein, Jacobson, Schwartz, & Dowler, 1984) and that high and low PCB exposure groups matched on many other variables can be identified (Fein et al., 1984). Further, infants born to the higher exposed mothers were smaller, averaging 175 g less at birth, and had 0.6–0.7 cm smaller head circumferences than infants born to lower exposed controls (Fein et al., 1984). The differences in head circumference remained when the data were adjusted for body weight and gestation length. The head and weight differences also persisted after adjustment for a host of other characteristics, most notably smoking and levels of PBBs. The infants were also tested on the Brazelton and were found to show "motoric immaturity, poorer lability of states, a greater amount of startle, and more abnormally weak (hypoactive) reflexes" (Jacobson, Jacobson, Fein, Schwartz, Dowler, 1984, p. 523).

These results are supported by evidence from animal experiments that presaged such observations. Tilson, Davis, McLachlan, and Lucier (1979) showed that mice exposed to one common PCB formulation during days 10–16 of gestation exhibited marked behavioral deficits in the offspring. The PCB offspring showed turning defects, hyperactivity, forelimb grip deficits, and placement and wire crossing motor impairments, and they acquired a one-way shock avoidance response more slowly than controls. Interestingly, with one exception, mice prenatally exposed to PCBs showed no growth deficit. Recent experiments in monkeys neonatally exposed to PCBs also show that at intervals of up to 3 years after exposure animals are hyperactive and exhibit performance impairments on fixed-interval operant schedules of appetitive learning as a function of exposure dose (Mele & Bowman, 1984).

Although the amount of evidence on PCBs is not great, the consistency of the findings and quality of the research point strongly to the fact that these compounds are behaviorally teratogenic. There are no adequate studies on PBBs.

Hormones

Because of the scope of the topic, no substantive review of the effects of prenatal exposure to hormones will be undertaken here. Recent reviews are those of Gandelman (1986) and Meyer-Bahlburg and Ehrhardt (1980). From these data, it may be said that in humans prenatal hormones have long-term behavioral effects and these effects tend to be on the development of sexually dimorphic behaviors more than on cognitive abilities.

For example, male and female children exposed intrauterinely to a synthetic testosterone-type progestin were found to exhibit more masculine-style responses on standardized tests of personality, masculinity–femininity, self-esteem, and attitudes toward work and family (reviewed by Reinisch & Sanders, 1984). Prenatal exposure of females to androgenic hormones increased their masculine-style responses on similar tests, increased their potential for aggression, and increased their scores on measures of self-sufficiency, self-assuredness, independence, and individualistic behavior (Reinisch & Sanders, 1984). In males, the masculine traits are increased by exogenous androgens. In general, prenatal exposure to androgenic hormones increases masculine-style behaviors consistently in males and females in studies in both humans and nonhuman mammals. Although there is somewhat less evidence, it appears that the absence of androgenic hormones intrauterinely increases feminine traits in male children and adolescents.

Radiation

There is abundant evidence that radiation is both a physical and a behavioral teratogen at high doses (Brent, 1981; Hicks & D'Amato, 1978). The case is most clear for ionizing radiation (Jensh, 1986). Some evidence in animals also exists suggesting possible behavioral teratogenicity from nonionizing radiation. This evidence has been well reviewed recently by Jensh (1986).

Evidence from reanalyses of the mental retardation data in those exposed to the atomic bomb explosions on Hiroshima and Nagasaki has recently been reported by Otake and Schull (1984). Confirming previous findings, these authors report that the incidence of mental retardation is five or more times higher in children exposed to atomic radiation in utero as compared to controls. The authors find the highest risk to occur in those exposed during weeks 8–15 of pregnancy. This is a period in human development that constitutes the end of organogenesis and the early phases of histogenesis. In terms of CNS development, this is a period of rapid proliferation and migration of cortical neurons. This period has also been found to be particularly sensitive to behavioral teratogenesis in rodents (Vorhees, 1986d). Thus these rather precise human atomic bomb radiation findings confirm what has been derived from animal experiments concerning periods of high CNS vulnerability.

While the effects of high levels of ionizing radiation on CNS development are well established, the long-term behavioral effects at low and moderate exposure levels remain unclear in human beings. In animal experiments, ionizing radiation at moderate exposure levels has been found to disrupt postnatal behavior (Jensh, 1986). A reliable desription of the types of behaviors affected is not yet possible, but many studies find increased locomotor activity and impaired passive avoidance behavior, effects associated with histological evidence of hippocampa damage in the same animals.

In conclusion, there are extensive human and animal data (reviewed in detail by Hicks & D'Amato, 1978; Jensh, 1986) that ionizing radiation is behaviorally teratogenic at doses below those producing malformations. At higher energy levels, the evidence for nonionizing radiation as a behavioral teratogen is suggestive in animals, but a great deal more data are needed before these relationships will become clear.

AGENTS SUSPECTED OF BEING BEHAVIORAL TERATOGENS

In this section several other categories of chemicals will be reviewed. For each of these groups there is some evidence, usually from animal experiments, suggesting that the compounds may be behaviorally teratogenic. The findings, however, are not yet adequate to conclude that the drugs involved are behavioral teratogens in human beings.

Because of the extraordinary use of antianxiety (anxiolytic) drugs in our society these drugs will be reviewed in more detail than other possible behavioral teratogens. Also, these data have become available from animal studies only in recent years as compared to the other drugs in this section, most of which have been reviewed previously.

Anxiolytics

The benzodiazepines, particularly diazepam and chlordiazepoxide, are anxiolytic and soporific drugs given to millions of people each year. No attempt will be made here to review the structural teratology data on diazepam and chlordiazepoxide. In general, these drugs have been found to produce malformations in animals at higher doses than those used to investigate their behavioral teratogenic potential. There are no data available on benzodiazepines as human behavioral teratogens. Therefore, the evidence reviewed below will be exclusively that derived from animal research.

Fox, Abendschein, and Lahcen (1977) administered six benzodiazepines to mice during one of three periods of development. The offspring were tested in an appetitive position discrimination test. The authors found that all the benzodiazepines tested produced an increase in general activity that facilitated maze performance. This effect was most evident in those exposed only prenatally and diminished with later (and longer) exposure intervals.

Harris and Case (1979) did a study with 40 mg/kg per day of chlordiazepoxide. Chlordiazepoxide exposure did not alter litter size, survival, or weight gain. The chlordiazepoxide rats had shorter combined avoidance–escape latencies than controls on a one-way shock avoidance test. The chlordiazepoxide rats also showed lower rates of responding in an FR-20 operant task than controls. Chlordiazepoxide also shortened pentobarbital- and ethanol-induced sleeping time.

In an experiment by Barlow, Knight, and Sullivan (1979) diazepam modified the effects of maternal restraint stress. Restraint delayed pinna detachment and increased maze errors. The only significant effect in the diazepam group was a facilitation of auditory startle development. The diazepam restraint group showed a similar startle facilitation, and also exhibited a delay in rotorod performance. Since the diazepam restraint group did not show the delay in pinna detachment or decrease in maze learning, diazepam appears to have blocked these restraint-induced impairments. The fact that diazepam and diazepam restraint facilitated startle may be taken to suggest that diazepam had effects independent of restraint. The delay in rotorod performance in the diazepam restraint group could be interpreted as indicating a possible adverse interaction of the two treatments.

Interestingly, higher doses of diazepam do not increase the severity of the effects observed (Butcher & Vorhees, 1979). Survival of diazepam offspring at higher doses was only slightly reduced ($p < .06$); the behavioral effects seen in the diazepam offspring were delayed swimming angle development, facilitated passive avoidance retention, and facilitated rotorod performance, effects no more dramatic than those seen in studies using much lower doses.

Low doses of diazepam also affect temperature regulation (Shore, Vorhees, Bornschein, & Stemmer, 1983). A 5 mg/kg dose of diazepam produced offspring with significantly lower surface body temperature on day 8 of life of about 0.73 deg C as compared to controls (normal surface body temperature was 34.6 deg C). After isolation from the nest for 40 min, however, the drops in surface body temperature in the 5 mg/kg group and controls were identical (about 3.5 deg C). The drop in surface temperature in a 1 mg/kg group, by contrast, was significantly smaller (about 2.9 deg C). Diazepam also produced a significant reduction for both drug groups in locomotor activity on 1 test day out of 8, but it increased exploration in the female 5 mg/kg offspring in a hold-board test measuring nose poking.

By far the most extensive studies on the effects of prenatal diazepam on postnatal behavior and neurochemistry have been those of Kellogg, Miller, Ison, and Simmons. These experiments have been aimed at determining whether moderate prenatal doses of diazepam given later in gestation produce long-term effects on offspring behavior and brain neurotransmitters. Kellogg and colleagues (1980) found that 2.5, 5, and 10 mg/kg of diazepam administered to rats on days 13–20 of gestation produced no effects on reflexes, but suppressed the normal peak in pre-weaning locomotor behavior. The kind of startle response used by these investigators is considered a test of sensory function and of the integrity of centrally mediated information processing. Kellogg and colleagues found the acoustic startle response to be diminished in diazepam offspring.

The temporal resolution of the acoustic startle response has also been assessed in offspring exposed prenatally to diazepam (Kellogg, Ison, & Miller, 1983). The background noise was interrupted at various intervals and then resumed prior to presentation of the test signal. This pattern of prepulse change normally produces an inhibition of the startle response. Significant differences in the startle response were found at two test ages, days 28 and 70, but not earlier or later. At 28 days the difference was between the 10 mg/kg group and the untreated controls and was a reduced degree of startle inhibition. At 70 days of age the effect was unexpectedly the opposite of that at 28 days, enhanced startle inhibition. The meaning of these differences is presently unknown.

The next study examined the effects of prenatal diazepam on postnatal neurotransmitters (Simmons, Kellogg, & Miller, 1984). Doses ranged from 1 to 10 mg/kg of diazepam given on days 13–20, 13–16, or 17–20 of gestation. A dose-dependent reduction in hypothalamic norepinephrine (NE), but not in dopamine (DA), was found in the offspring as adults. No changes were seen in the cortex or hippocampus. Norepinephrine turnover was also reduced in the hypothalamic region, but not in other regions. DA turnover was not altered. The hypothalamic NE levels and turnover were not reduced in a group receving both diazepam and a benzodiazepine antagoinst (R015-1788), nor in a group receiving only antagonist. This suggests that the effect of prenatal diazepam is specific since it can be blocked by coadministration of a receptor blocking agent. Prenatal diazepam also does not alter benzodiazepine binding sites on GABAergic neurons based on measurements of tritiated ligand-receptor binding, or activity levels of glutamic acid decarboxylase, the enzyme that synthesizes GABA (Kellogg, Chisholm, Simmons, Ison, & Miller, 1983).

Simmons, Miller, and Kellogg (1984) have examined the modifying effects of restraint stress on NE following prenatal diazepam exposure. Restraint stress and/or treatment with a drug that blocks NE synthesis reduced hypothalamic NE levels. Such NE reductions were not seen in those rats prenatally exposed to diazepam. Restraint raised plasma corticosterone and prolactin levels in controls. Prenatal diazepam treatment reduced this increase for corticosterone and enhanced it for prolactin. Treatment with the antagonist prevented diazepam from modifying the restraint-induced rise in corticosterone. These data suggest that prenatal diazepam treatment produces long-term changes in the animals' responses to stress.

Finally, these authors have examined the effect of prenatal diazepam on the release of tritiated NE in vitro (Kellogg, Retell, & Harary, 1984). Potassium chloride–induced NE release was reduced by prenatal diazepam in the hypothalamus, but not in the hippocampus or cerebellum. This effect of diazepam could be blocked by addition of the alpha-receptor blocker phentolamine, suggesting that the effect was specific to alpha-adrenergic neurons. These data further suggest that prenatal diazepam exposure changes hypothalamic NE dynamics.

In sum, the experiments by Kellogg, Miller, Ison, and associates suggest that prenatal diazepam produces both early and late changes in offspring behavior and late changes in hypothalamic NE levels, turnover, and release. Unfortunately, the temporal relationship between the NE changes and the effects on activity and the startle response are not in synchrony. Moreover, the later behavioral effects noted in postweaning animals (changes in gap-induced startle inhibition) show a shifting pattern from ages 28 to 70 ranging from attenuated inhibition to no difference to enhanced inhibition. Also, these experiments all use small numbers of litters per group. The authors have, however, successfully replicated their NE findings. Such replication has not yet been reported for the behavioral observations. Moreover, other investigators have reported different effects from those of Kellogg and associates (Ryan & Pappas, 1986). Using the same doses and exposure period similar to that of Kellogg and colleagues (1980) Ryan and Pappas report no reductions in hypothalamic NE or locomotor activity in rat offspring exposed in utero to diazepam.

Marijuana

The research on the prenatal effects of marijuana and its principal psychoactive component, delta-9-tetrahydrocannabinol (THC), is fragmentary. Human retrospective studies have many well-known pitfalls that compromise their interpretation and will therefore not be reviewed. Human prospective studies have found reductions in birth weight of babies born to women who smoke marijuana heavily during pregnancy and are from lower socioeconomic and educational backgrounds (Hingson et al., 1982). Birth weights in another prospective study with predominantly middle-class women did not find an association between marijuana use during pregnancy and reduced birth weight after adjustment for differences in gestation length (Fried, Watkinson, & Willan, 1984). This study did suggest, however, that marijuana shortened gestation. Examination of children for minor physical anomalies born to women from middle-class backgrounds showed no significant relationship between marijuana use and incidence of anomalies or clusters of anomalies (O'Connell & Fried, 1984). Yet these same authors report that the offspring of regular marijuana users showed behavioral changes (Fried, 1980; Fried, Watkinson, Grant, & Knights, 1980). The behavioral changes seen were lack of response to a light stimulus, failure to habituate to a stimulus, tremors, increased startling, and reduced self-quieting.

The area of the effects of prenatal marijuana on behavior is one where research on animals has thus far provided little insight into the risks to brain development from intrauterine exposure to this drug. Some of the earlier literature has been reviewed by Abel (1980b). As he points out, no consistent effects have been reported on offspring behavior, but methodological problems with most of the studies raise doubts about their interpretive value. The most serious problems have to do with dose and absorption (route of delivery), and there are also some problems with the specific form of marijuana used. As with tobacco, marijuana extract is a mixture of compounds, some of which are psychoactive and some of which are not (Abel, 1980b). In addition, doses used have often been too high to be realistic even after making allowance for the problems associated with the use of crude marijuana extracts and for unreliable drug absorption. Plasma levels of THC are almost never provided so dosage is not adequately documented. THC is a compound that is poorly absorbed by usual routes, and it is not at all clear in many studies that adequate quantities have reached the circulation. Last among these primary problems is the form of marijuana used. Marijuana varies greatly in THC content and yet despite this, many studies have been done using resin extracts. The better studies have used THC directly.

Secondary problems in early animal studies were lack of control for nutritional and maternal rearing changes that may have contributed in indeterminant ways to the experimental outcomes, making it difficult to sort out indirect effects from those solely attributable to marijuana. While Abel's critique fails to provide convincing evidence that these secondary problems had any substantive impact on the findings in studies where no effects were observed, such problems may be important in those few studies where behavioral effects have been found. Since most of the animal experiments are negative and drug absorption has usually not been adequately dealt with, the major problem with the literature appears to center on inadequate consideration of the pharmacological aspects of THC, rather than on the design of the behavioral aspects of the studies.

Two recent animal experiments have shown that late gestation or early postnatal maternal dosing of mice with THC or other cannabinoids can produce significant effects on offspring weight, hormones, and brain biogenic amine neurotransmitter levels (Dalterio, Steger, Mayfield, & Blake, 1984a, 1984b). Such data suggest that behavioral effects may be present under properly controlled conditions.

In summary, there appear to be some behavioral and other nervous system effects of prenatal marijuana or THC exposure in human and animal studies, but the data are far from conclusive. A great deal more research and, in the animal studies, improved research approaches are needed.

Anesthetics

Anesthetic agents may be considered for their behavioral teratogenic potential from one of two major perspectives depending on the nature of the exposure. One exposure type might occur during early and middle pregnancy in individuals either occupationally exposed to anesthetics or exposed during a medical procedure. Follow-up studies of occupationally exposed individuals for behavioral sequelae could not be found. One study examined eight cases of pregnant women exposed to anesthetics for dental purposes (Blair, Hollenbeck, Smith, & Scanlon, 1984). Of these, five were exposed to local and three to general anesthetics. Neonates were tested shortly after birth for time spent looking at various patterns. Exposed infants spent more time looking at block patterns than controls. This study is interesting, but it is difficult to understand how local anesthetics administered in dentally effective doses could produce such delayed effects, although the authors have reported preliminary data supporting this observation (Smith, Wharton, Kurtz, Mattran, & Hollenbeck, 1985). These authors also find delayed reflex development and increased maze errors in rats prenatally exposed to the local anesthetics lidocaine and mepivacaine. The effects seen in the human study were small, however, and it may be that the infants exposed to the general anesthetics were the ones most affected. Unfortunately, the data are presented in such a way that this possibility cannot be assessed.

There are now several reports suggesting that prenatal exposure to halothane produces long-term effects in rat or mouse offspring on measures of learning and activity (Bowman & Smith, 1987; Koeter & Rodier, 1981; Quimby, Aschkenase, & Bowman, 1974; Smith, 1977; Smith, Bowman, & Katz, 1978). There are also several preliminary reports that nitrous oxide may be behaviorally teratogenic in mice and rats (Koeter & Rodier, 1981; Mullenix & Moore, 1985; Rice & Millan, 1985). It is too early to draw any firm conclusions about this diverse group of agents, but the probability that some of them are behaviorally teratogenic now seems increased.

A second, short-term type of exposure to anesthetics often occurs during labor and delivery. This literature has been thoroughly reviewed by Brackbill (1979) and the reader is referred there for discussion of the complex issues involved in sorting out the residual effects on behavior of labor and delivery medications.

Neuroleptics and Antidepressants

The data available on neuroleptics and antidepressants as behavioral teratogens come almost exclusively from animal research. Not only are human studies lacking, but most of the studies done in animals are inconsistent and diffciult to interpret. The animal literature has been reviewed by Coyle, Wayner, and Singer (1980). Most of the studies on neuroleptics have been on chlorpromazine, and as these authors note, present an inconsistent picture precluding clear interpretation. Prochlorperazine (Compazine®) is a neuroleptic often used during pregnancy to control hyperemesis gravidarum because of its potent antiemetic properties. This neuroleptic has been shown in rats to be a functional teratogen producing reductions in litter size, offspring weight, and changes in behavioral ontogeny (Vorhees et al., 1979).

The situation with antidepressants is similar. As Coyle and colleagues (1980) point out in reviewing studies on imipramine, the prototype of this drug class, studies comparing imipramine-exposed and control rat offspring fail to reveal general drug-related effects on behavior. Most of these studies have been done by the reviewers themselves, Coyle and Singer. The most noteworthy effect observed in imipramine-exposed offspring was that those reared in a complex (enriched) environment showed deficits in maze learning compared to those reared in standard (deprived) environments. Since these effects have not been investigated by others it is not possible at present to interpret these observations.

While neuroleptics and antidepressants represent two of the most important classes of psychotherapeutic drugs, research into their possible behavioral teratogenic effects has been sparse and inadequate. It seems odd that such important drugs would be so understudied, but this has occurred, in part, because of a lack of support by the relevant funding agencies. For this reason research on the behavioral teratogenesis of psychiatric drugs continues to languish far behind research on other drugs and environmental chemicals.

Aspirin

Aspirin has long been known as a potent CNS teratogen in experimental animals (Warkany & Takacs, 1959). Indeed, salicylates have been models of CNS teratogenesis in animals (Kalter, 1968; Wilson, Ritter, Scott, & Fradkin, 1977). There has been little support from clinical studies, however, implicating aspirin as a structural teratogen in humans (Kalter & Warkany, 1983; Wilson, 1977a), except perhaps in rare extreme cases. There have been reports that regular prenatal aspirin exposure increases the risk of reduced birth weight and perinatal mortality in humans, but not the risk of malformations (Corby, 1978; Turner & Collins, 1975).

Interestingly, animal experiments have unequivocally demonstrated that salicylates are behaviorally teratogenic in rats at submalforming doses (Butcher, Vorhees, & Kimmel, 1972; Kimmel, Butcher, Vorhees, & Schumacher, 1974; Vorhees, Klein, & Scott, 1982). These results are tantalizing because a recent large prospective human study has found that aspirin use during pregnancy is significantly related to lower childhood IQ using the WPPSI test (Streissguth, Treder, et al., 1984). These data are impressive because the authors statistically adjusted for other potential predictors, such as maternal education, parity, diet, age, smoking, caffeine, alcohol, and antibiotics taken to control infections during pregnancy. Moreover, within the study sample women having similar infection histories and other characteristics, but who took acetaminophen instead of aspirin, showed no similar relationship in their children's IQs.

In sum, there is new human evidence about the behavioral teratogenic potential of aspirin, predated by animal research, that may bring this drug under renewed scrutiny as a hazard to prenatal brain development.

Thalidomide

Thalidomide is the classic human structural teratogen, causing many deformities but mainly the limb reduction deformity, phocomelia (reviewed by McBride, 1977). Less well known are the effects of thalidomide on psychological development. In a study in which 56 thalidomide cases were followed into childhood, McFie and Robertson (1973) found an unexpectedly high proportion of thalidomide children with subnormal IQs. The IQ reduction was present in these children even after allowing for their physical disabilities. A second piece of evidence implicating the effect of thalidomide on CNS development is that 44 percent of their study group were left hand (or foot) dominant. As McFie and Robertson note, this shift in lateral dominance has been seen by others examining children born with thalidomide deformities. That thalidomide should cause CNS effects is not all that surprising when one remembers that it is a psychotropic drug, sold originally as a CNS sedative and antianxiety agent, and has structural similarity to other known structural and behavioral teratogens (Shull, 1984). Thus although thalidomide is the classic structural human teratogen, it appears likely that it also has some behavioral teratogenic effects.

Other Agents

There are other agents that may be behavioral teratogens, but the evidence for these is more fragmentary and is beyond the scope of this chapter. For example, there are a number of maternal infections that place the conceptus at increased risk for congenital anomalies. The most notable of these are toxoplasmosis, rubella, cytomegalovirus (CMV), genital herpes, and syphilis. What has been little appreciated by behavioral scientists is that in a percentage of all such cases the maternal infection results in the birth of children who are mentally retarded (reviewed by Sever, 1983). A recent study has shown an association in two clinical cases between maternal CMV and childhood autism (Stubbs, Ash, & Williams, 1984). Thus there is growing evidence that certain maternal infections are behavioral teratogens. Defining the circumstances under which a maternal infection causes cogenital CNS damage distinct from damage to other organ systems will be a major task of future research on infectious agents.

The data on mercury and lead have already been reviewed, but other heavy metals have also been implicated as behavioral teratogens. Most notable among these have been cadmium (Hastings, 1986) and organic tin compounds (Reiter, 1980). There are many other possible agents, including certain industrial solvents (Nelson, 1986), and insecticides (Mactutus & Tilson, 1986). As evidence on the behavioral teratogenicity of other agents mounts it will become necessary to expand greatly the coverage of reviews such as this in the future.

CONCLUSIONS

The field of behavioral teratology has become so extensive that it is now impossible to do justice to the field in a single chapter such as this. There are now entire books devoted to behavioral teratogenesis (Riley & Vorhees, 1986; Yanai, 1984) and even these are not exhaustive. Thus the foregoing review has necessarily been focused. The focus has been on those compounds for which there is a bridge between the human and animal research that converges and enables some conclusions to be reached as to the hazard potential of each agent for causing prenatal or neonatal CNS injury.

From this standpoint it is concluded that methylmercury, alcohol, lead, and high doses of ionizing radiation are well-established behavioral teratogens that cause significant psychological damage to children, and may justifiably be considered major health hazards. Anticonvulsants (especially phenytoin and trimethadione), cigarette smoking, narcotics, PCBs, hormones, and moderate energy ionizing and higher energy nonionizing radiation are probably behavioral teratogens. These agents all appear to be hazardous, but some gaps in the available evidence continue to exist. Finally, there are some important classes of agents about which far too little is known, but for which some evidence exists suggesting that they may be behavioral teratogens. These include anxiolytics, marijuana, anesthetics, neuroleptics, antidepressants, aspirin, thalidomide, cadmium, organic tin, and certain industrial solvents. At present most of these can only be listed in classes, but it seems likely that some agents within these classes will eventually be shown to be more hazardous to the developing brain than others. We can only hope that through research this knowledge will be gained before additional children are harmed.

REFERENCES

Abel, E. L. (1980a). Fetal alcohol syndrome: Behavioral teratology. *Psychological Bulletin, 87,* 29–50.

Abel, E. L. (1980b). Prenatal exposure to cannabis: A critical review of effects on growth, development, and behavior. *Behavioral & Neural Biology, 29,* 137–156.

Abel, E. L. (1981). Behavioral teratology of alcohol. *Psychological Bulletin, 90,* 564–581.

Abel, E. L. (1984). Prenatal effects of alcohol. *Drug & Alcohol Dependence, 14,* 1–10.

Abel, E. L., Randall, C. L., & Riley, E. P. (1983). Alcohol consumption and prenatal development. In B. Tabakoff, P. B. Sutker, & C. L. Randall (Eds.), *Medical and social aspects of alcohol abuse*. New York: Plenum.

Adams, P. M., Fabricant, J. D., & Legator, M. S. (1981). Cyclophosphamide-induced speratogenic effects detected in the F_1 generation by behavioral testing. *Science, 211*, 80–82.

Annest, J., Pirkle, J., Makus, D., Neese, J., Bayse, D., & Kovar, M. (1983). Chronological trend in blood lead levels between 1976 and 1980. *New England Journal of Medicine, 308*, 1373–1377.

Barlow, S. M., Knight, A. F., & Sullivan, F. M. (1979). Prevention by diazepam of adverse effects of maternal restraint stress on postnatal development and learning in the rat. *Teratology, 19*, 105–110.

Barr, H. M., Streissguth, A. P., Martin, D. C., & Herman, C. S. (1984). Infant size at 8 months of age: Relationship to maternal use of alcohol, nicotine, and caffeine during pregnancy. *Pediatrics, 74*, 336–341.

Barry, J. E., & Danks, D. M. (1974). Anticonvulsants and congenital abnormalities. *Lancet, 2*, 48–49.

Bellinger, D. C., Needleman, H. L., Leviton, A., Waternaux, C., Rabinowitz, M. B., & Nichols, M. L. (1984). Early sensory-motor development and prenatal lead exposure. *Neurobehavioral Toxicology & Teratology, 6*, 387–402.

Bernstein, V., Jeremy, R. J., Hans, S. L., & Marcus, J. (1984). A longitudinal study of offspring born to methadone-maintained women: II. Dyadic interaction and infant behavior at four months. *American Journal of Drug & Alcohol Abuse, 10*, 161–193.

Bjerkedal, T., Czeizel, A., Goujard, J., Kallen, B., Mastroiacove, P., Nevin, N., Oakley, G., & Robert, E. (1982). Valproic acid and spina bifida. *Lancet, 2*, 1096.

Blair, V. W., Hollenbeck, A. R., Smith, R. F., & Scanlon, J. W. (1984). Neonatal preference for visual patterns: Modification by prenatal anesthetic exposure. *Developmental Medicine & Child Neurology, 26*, 476–483.

Blake, P. M., & Scott, W. J. (1984a). Determination of the proximate teratogen of the mouse fetal alcohol syndrome: 1. Teratogenicity of ethanol and acetaldehyde. *Toxicology & Applied Pharmacology, 72*, 355–363.

Blake, P. M., & Scott, W. J. (1984b). Determination of the proximate teratogen of the mouse fetal alcohol syndrome: 2. Pharmacokinetics of the placental transfer of ethanol and acetaldehyde. *Toxicology & Applied Pharmacology, 72*, 364–371.

Bond, N. W., & DiGiusto, E. L. (1976). Effects of prenatal alcohol consumption on open-field behavior and alcohol preference in rats. *Psychopharmacology, 46*, 163–168.

Bornschein, R., Pearson, D., & Reiter, L. (1980a). Behavioral effects of moderate lead exposure in children and animal models: Part 1. Clinical studies. *CRC Critical Reviews in Toxicology, 8*, 43–99.

Bornschein, R., Pearson, D., & Reiter, L. (1980b). Behavioral effects of moderate lead exposure in children and animal models: Part 2. Animal studies. *CRC Critical Reviews in Toxicology, 8*, 101–152.

Bowman, R. E., & Smith, R. F. (1977). Behavioral and neurochemical effects of prenatal halothane. *Environmental Health Perspectives, 21*, 189–193.

Brackbill, Y. (1979). Obstetrical medication and infant behavior. In J. D. Osofsky (Ed.), *Handbook of infant development*. New York: Wiley.

Brent, R. L. (1980). Radiation teratogenesis. *Teratology, 21*, 281–298.

Buelke-Sam, J. (1986). Postnatal functional assessment following CNS stimulant exposure: Amphetamine and caffeine. In E. P. Riley & C. V. Vorhees (Eds.), *Handbook of behavioral teratology*. New York: Plenum.

Bushnell, P. J., & Bowman, R. E. (1979a). Effects of chronic lead ingestion on social development in infant rhesus monkeys. *Neurobehavioral Toxicology, 1,* 207–219.

Bushnell, P. J., & Bowman, R. E. (1979b). Reversal learning deficits in young monkeys exposed to lead. *Pharmacology, Biochemistry & Behavior, 10,* 733–742.

Butcher, R. E., Hawver, K., Burbacher, T., & Scott, W. (1975). In N. R. Ellis (Ed.), *Aberrant development in infancy: Human and animal studies.* Hillsdale, NJ: Erlbaum.

Butcher, R. E., & Vorhees, C. V. (1979). A preliminary test battery for the investigation of the behavioral teratology of selected psychotropic drugs. *Neurobehavioral Toxicology, 1* (Suppl. 1), 207–212.

Butcher, R. E., & Vorhees, C. V. (1984). Behavioral testing in rodents given food additives. In L. D. Stegink & L. J. Filer, Jr. (Eds.), *Aspartame: Physiology and biochemistry.* New York: Marcel Dekker.

Butcher, R. E., Vorhees, C. V., & Kimmel, C. A. (1972). Learning impairment from maternal salicylate treatment in rats. *Nature New Biology, 236,* 211–212.

Butler, N. R., & Goldstein, H. (1973). Smoking in pregnancy and subsequent child development. *British Medical Journal, 4,* 573–575.

Centers for Disease Control (1985). *Preventing lead poisoning in young children: A statement by the Centers for Disease Control.* Washington, DC: U.S. Department of Health and Human Services.

Chang, L. W., & Annau, Z. (1984). Developmental neuropathology and behavioral teratology of methylmercury. In J. Yanai (Ed.), *Neurobehavioral teratology.* Amsterdam: Elsevier.

Chapman, J. B., & Cutler, M. G. (1984). Sodium valproate: Effects on social behaviour and physical development in the mouse. *Psychopharmacology, 83,* 390–396.

Chernoff, G. (1975). A mouse model of the fetal alcohol syndrome. *Teratology, 11,* 14A.

Corby, D. G. (1978). Aspirin in pregnancy: Maternal and fetal effects. *Pediatrics, 62* (Suppl.), 930–937.

Coyle, I., Wayner, M. J., & Singer, G. (1980). Behavioural teratogenesis: A critical evaluation. In T. V. N. Persaud (Ed.), *Advances in the study of birth defects: Vol. 4. Neural and behavioural teratology.* Baltimore: University Park Press.

Dalterio, S., Steger, R., Mayfield, D., & Bartke, A. (1984a). Early cannabinoid exposure influences neuroendocrine and reproductive functions in male mice: I. Prenatal exposure. *Pharmacology, Biochemistry & Behavior, 20,* 107–113.

Dalterio, S., Steger, R., Mayfield, D., & Bartke, A. (1984b). Early cannabinoid exposure influences neuroendocrine and reproductive functions in male mice: II. Postnatal effects. *Pharmacology, Biochemistry & Behavior, 20,* 115–123.

Davenport, J. W., & Dorcey, T. P. (1972). Hypothyroidism: Learning deficit induced in rats by early exposure to thiouracil. *Hormones & Behavior, 3,* 97–112.

DiLiberti, J. H., Farndon, P. A., Dennis, N. R., & Curry, C. J. R. (1984). The fetal valproate syndrome. *American Journal of Medical Genetics, 19,* 473–481.

Dreifuss, F. E., & Sato, S. (1982). Benzodiazepines: Clonazepam. In D. M. Woodbury, J. K. Penry, & C. E. Pippenger (Eds.), *Antiepileptic drugs,* (2nd ed.). New York: Raven.

Driscoll, C. D., Chen, J.-S., & Riley, E. P. (1982). Passive avoidance performance in rats prenatally exposed to alcohol during various periods of gestation. *Neurobehavioral Toxicology & Teratology, 4,* 99–103.

Eccles, C. U., & Annau, Z. (1982a). Prenatal methyl mercury exposure: I. Alterations in neonatal activity. *Neurobehavioral Toxicology & Teratology, 4,* 371–376.

Eccles, C. U., & Annau, Z. (1982b). Prenatal methyl mercury exposure: II. Alteration in learning and psychotropic drug sensitivity in adult offspring. *Neurobehavioral Toxicology & Teratology, 4,* 377–382.

Elmazar, M. M. A., & Sullivan, F. M. (1981). Effect of prenatal phenytoin administration on postnatal development of the rat: A behavioral teratology study. *Teratology, 24,* 115–124.

Ernhart, C. B., Wolf, A. W., Filipovich, H. F., Kennard, M. J., Erhard, P., & Sokol, R. J. (1985). Intrauterine lead exposure. *Teratology, 31,* 7B–8B (abstract).

Fechter, L. D., & Annau, Z. (1977). Toxicity of mild prenatal carbon monoxide exposure. *Science, 197,* 680–682.

Fechter, L. D., & Annau, Z. (1980). Prenatal carbon monoxide exposure alters behavioral development. *Neurobehavioral Toxicology, 2,* 7–11

Fedrick, J. (1973). Epilepsy and pregnancy: A report from the Oxford record linkage study. *British Medical Journal, 2,* 442–448.

Fein, G. G., Jacobson, J. L., Jacobson, S. W., Schwartz, P. M., & Dowler, J. K. (1984). Prenatal exposure to polychlorinated biphenyls: Effects on birth size and gestational age. *Journal of Pediatrics, 105,* 315–320.

Fein, G. G., Schwartz, P. M., Jacobson, S. W., & Jacobson, J. L. (1983). Environmental toxins and behavioral development. *American Psychologist, 38,* 1188–1197.

Feldman, G. L., Weaver, D. D., & Lovrien, E. W. (1977). The fetal trimethadione syndrome. *American Journal Diseases of Children, 131,* 1389–1392.

Fernandez, K., Caul, W. F., Boyd, J. E., Henderson, G. I., & Michaelis, R. C. (1983). Malformations and growth of rat fetuses exposed to brief periods of alcohol in utero. *Teratogenesis, Carcinogenesis, & Mutagenesis, 3,* 457–460.

Fifth Special Report to the U.S. Congress on Alcohol and Health (1984). *Alcohol Health & Research World, 9,* 1–72.

Finger, S., & Stein, D. G. (1982). *Brain damage and recovery: Research and clinical perspectives.* New York: Academic.

Fox, K. A., Abendschein, D. R., & Lahcen, R. B. (1977). Effects of benzodiazepines during gestation and infancy on Y-maze performance of mice. *Pharmacological Research Communications, 9,* 325–338.

Freed, W. J., de Medinaceli, L., & Wyatt, R. J. (1985). Promoting functional plasticity in the damaged nervous system. *Science, 227,* 1544–1552.

Fried, P. A. (1980). Marijuana use by pregnant women: Neurobehavioral effects in neonates. *Drug & Alcohol Dependence, 6,* 415–424.

Fried, P. A., Watkinson, B., Grant, A., & Knights, R. M. (1980). Changing patterns of soft drug use prior to and during pregnancy: A prospective study. *Drug & Alcohol Dependence, 6,* 323–343.

Fried, P. A., Watkinson, B., & Willan, A. (1984). Marijuana use during pregnancy and decreased length of gestation. *American Journal of Obstetrics & Gynecology, 150,* 23–27.

Friedler, G. (1974a). Long-term effects of opiates. In J. Dancis & J. C. Hwang (Eds.), *Perinatal pharmacology: Problems and priorites.* New York: Raven.

Friedler, G. (1974b). Influence of morphine administration to male mice on their progeny. *Proceedings of the Thirty-sixth Annual Meeting of the Committee on Problems of Drug Dependence,* pp. 869–874.

Friedler, G., & Wheeling, H. S. (1979). Behavioral effects in offspring of male mice injected with opioids prior to mating. *Pharmacology, Biochemistry & Behavior, 11* (Suppl. 1). 23–28.

Fritz, H., Muller, D., & Hess, R. (1976). Comparative study of the teratogenicity of phenobarbitone, diphenylhydantoin and carbamazepine in mice. *Toxicology, 6,* 323–330.

Gandelman, R. (1986). Behavioral teratogenicity of gonadal and adrenal steroids. In E. P. Riley & C. V. Vorhees (Eds.), *Handbook of behavioral teratology*. New York: Plenum.

Gennser, G., Marsal, K., & Brantmark, B. (1975). Maternal smoking and fetal breathing movements. *American Journal of Obstetrics & Gynecology, 123,* 861–867.

German, J., Kowal, A., & Ehlers, K. L. (1970). Trimethadione and human teratogenesis. *Teratology, 3,* 349–361.

Ginsburg, B. E., Yanai, J., & Sze, P. Y. (1975). A developmental genetic study of the effects of alcohol consumed by parent mice on the behavior and development of their offspring. In *Proceedings of the Fourth Annual Alcoholism Conference of the National Institute on Alcohol Abuse and Alcoholism,* pp. 183–204. Washington, DC: Department of Health, Education, and Welfare.

Granstrom, M.-L., & Hiilesmaa, V. K. (1982). Malformations and minor anomalies in children of epileptic mothers: Preliminary results of the prospective Helsinki study. In D. Janz, M. Dam, A. Richens, L. Bossi, H. Helge, & D. Schmidt (Eds.), *Epilepsy, pregnancy, and the child*. New York: Raven.

Gray, L. E., & Kavlock, R. J. (1984). An extended evaluation of an in vivo teratology screen utilizing postnatal growth and viability in the mouse. *Teratogenesis, Carcinogenesis, & Mutagenesis, 4,* 403–426.

Hans, S. L., Marcus, J., Jeremy, R. J., & Auerbach, J. G. (1984). Neurobehavioral development of children exposed in utero to opioid drugs. In J. Yanai (Ed.), *Neurobehavioral teratology*. Amsterdam: Elsevier.

Hanson, J. W., Myrianthopoulos, N. C., Sedgwick-Harvey, M. A., & Smith, D. W. (1976). Risks to the offspring of women treated with hydantoin anticonvulsants, with emphasis on the fetal hydantoin syndrome. *Journal of Pediatrics, 89,* 662–668.

Hanson, J. W., & Smith, D. W. (1975). The fetal hydantoin syndrome. *Journal of Pediatrics, 87,* 285–290.

Harris, R. A., & Case, J. (1979). Effects of maternal consumption of ethanol, barbital, or chordiazepoxide on the behavior of the offspring. *Behavioral & Neural Biology, 26,* 234–247.

Hastings, L. (1986). Behavioral teratogenesis resulting from early cadmium exposure. In E. P. Riley & C. V. Vorhees (Eds.), *Handbook of behavioral teratology*. New York: Plenum.

Hattan, D. G., Henry, S. H., Montgomery, S. B., Bleiberg, M. J., Rulis, A. M., & Bolger, P. M. (1983). Role of the Food and Drug Administration in regulation of neuroeffective food additives. In R. J. Wurtman & J. J. Wurtman (Eds.), *Nutrition and the brain,* (Vol. 6). New York: Raven.

Herman, C. S., Kirchner, G. L., Streissguth, A. P., & Little, R. E. (1980). Vigilance paradigm for preschool children used to relate vigilance behavior to IQ and prenatal exposure to alcohol. *Perceptual & Motor Skills, 50,* 863–867.

Hicks, E. P. (1979). Carbamazepine in two pregnancies. *Clinical & Experimental Neurology, 16,* 269–275.

Hicks, S. P., & D'Amato, C. J. (1978). Effects of ionizing radiation on developing brain and behavior. In G. Gottlieb (Ed.), *Studies on the development of behavior and the nervous system: Volume 4. Early influences*. New York: Academic.

Hill, R. M., Verniaud, W. M., Horning, M. G., McCulley, L. B., & Morgan, N. F. (1974). Infants exposed in utero to antiepileptic drugs. *American Journal of Diseases of Children, 127,* 645–653.

Hingson, R., Alper, J., Day, N., Dooling, E., Kayne, H., Morelock, S., Oppenheimer, E., & Zuckerman, B. (1982). Effects on maternal drinking and marijuana use on fetal growth and development. *Pediatrics, 70,* 539–546.

Householder, J., Hatcher, R., Burns, W., & Chasnoff, I. (1982). Infants born to narcotic-addicted mothers. *Psychological Bulletin, 92,* 453–468.

Hughes, J. A., & Annau, Z. (1976). Postnatal behavioral effects in mice after prenatal exposure to methylmercury. *Pharmacology, Biochemistry & Behavior, 4,* 385–391.

Humble, C. G., & Speizer, F. E. (1984). Polybrominated biphenyls and fetal mortality in Michigan. *American Journal of Public Health, 74,* 1130–1132.

Hutchings, D. E. (1983). Behavioral teratology: A new frontier in neurobehavioral research. In E. M. Johnson & D. M. Kochhar (Eds.), *Teratogenesis and reproductive toxicology, handbook of experimental pharmacology* (Vol. 65). Berlin: Springer-Verlag.

Hutchings, D. E., & Fifer, W. P. (1986). Neurobehavioral effects in human and animal offspring following prenatal exposure to methadone. In E. P. Riley & C. V. Vorhees (Eds.), *Handbook of behavioral teratology.* New York: Plenum.

Jacobson, J. L., Fein, G. G., Jacobson, S. W., Schwartz, P. M., & Dowler, J. K. (1984). The transfer of polychlorinated biphenyls (PCBs) and polybrominated biphenyls (PBBs) across the human placenta and into maternal milk. *American Journal of Public Health, 74,* 378–379.

Jacobson, J. L., Jacobson, S. W., Fein, G. G., Schwartz, P. M., & Dowler, J. K. (1984). Prenatal exposure to an environmental toxin: A test of the multiple effects model. *Developmental Psychology, 20,* 523–532.

Janz, D. (1975). The teratogenic risk of antiepileptic drugs. *Epilepsia, 16,* 159–169.

Janz, D. (1982a). Antiepileptic drugs and pregnancy: Altered utilization patterns and teratogenesis. *Epilepsia, 23* (Suppl. 1), S53–S63.

Janz, D. (1982b). On major malformations and minor anomalies in the offspring of parents with epilepsy: Review of the literature. In D. Janz, M. Dam, A. Richens, L. Bossi, H. Helge, & D. Schmidt (Eds.), *Epilepsy, pregnancy, and the child.* New York: Raven.

Jensh, R. (1986). Effects of prenatal irradiation on postnatal psychophysiologic development. In E. P. Riley & C. V. Vorhees (Eds.), *Handbook of behavioral teratology.* New York: Plenum.

Jeremy, R. J., & Bernstein, V. J. (1984). Dyads at risk: Methadone-maintained women and their four-month-old infants. *Child Development, 55,* 1141–1154.

Johnson, E. M. (1984). A prioritization and biological decision tree for developmental toxicity safety evaluations. *Journal of the American College of Toxicology, 3,* 141–147.

Johnson, E. M., & Kochhar, D. M. (Eds.). (1983). *Teratogenesis and reproductive toxicology, handbook of experimental pharmacology* (Vol. 65). Berlin: Springer-Verlag.

Joffe, J. M. (1969). *Prenatal determinants of behaviour.* Oxford: Pergamon.

Jones, K. L., & Smith, D. W. (1973). Recognition of the fetal alcohol syndrome in early infancy. *Lancet, 2,* 999–1001.

Jones, K. L., Smith, D. W., Ulleland, C. N., & Streissguth, A. P. (1973). Pattern of malformation in offspring of chronic alcoholic mothers. *Lancet, 1,* 1267–1271.

Kalter, H. (1968). *Teratology of the central nervous system.* Chicago: University of Chicago Press.

Kalter, H., & Warkany, J. (1983). Congenital malformations: Etiologic factors and their role in prevention. *New England Journal of Medicine, 308,* 424–431, 491–497.

Kellogg, C. K., Chisholm, J., Simmons, R. D., Ison, J. R., & Miller, R. K. (1983). Neural and behavioral consequences of prenatal exposure to diazepam. *Monographs in Neural Science, 9,* 119–129.

Kellogg, C., Ison, J. R., & Miller, R. K. (1983). Prenatal diazepam exposure: Effects on auditory temporal resolution in rats. *Psychopharmacology, 79,* 332–337.

Kellogg, C. K., Retell, T. M., & Harary, N. (1984). Benzodiazepine influence on norepinephrine release: Regional specificity. *Neuroscience Abstracts, 10,* 972.

Kellogg, C., Tervo, D., Ison, J., Parisi, T., & Miller, R. K. (1980). Prenatal exposure to diazepam alters behavioral development in rats. *Science, 207,* 205–207.

Khera, K. S. (1984). Maternal toxicity—A possible factor in fetal malformations in mice. *Teratology, 29,* 411–416.

Kimmel, C. A., & Buelke-Sam, J. (Eds.). (1981). *Developmental toxicology.* New York: Raven.

Kimmel, C. A., Butcher, R. E., Vorhees, C. V., & Schumacher, H. J. (1974). Metal-salt potentiation of salicylate-induced teratogenesis and behavioral changes in rats. *Teratology, 10,* 293–300.

Koeter, H. W. B. M., & Rodier, P. M. (1981). Functional development of mice after pre- and postnatal exposure to inhalant anesthetics. *Teratology, 24,* 56A.

Kopp, C. B. Risk factors in development. In P. Mussen & M. Haith (Eds.), *Handbook of child psychology: Infancy and biological bases* (Vol. 2, 4th ed.). New York: Wiley.

Kutt, H. (1982). Phenytoin: Relation of plasma concentration to seizure control. In D. M. Woodbury, J. K. Penry, & C. E. Pippenger (Eds.), *Antiepileptic drugs* (2nd ed.). New York: Raven.

Landesman-Dwyer, S. (1982). Maternal drinking and pregnancy outcome. *Applied Research in Mental Retardation, 3,* 241–263.

Landesman-Dwyer, S., Keller, L. S., & Streissguth, A. P. (1978). Naturalistic observations of newborns: Effects of maternal alcohol intake. *Alcoholism: Clinical & Experimental Research, 2,* 171–177.

Landesman-Dwyer, S., Ragozin, A. S., & Little, R. E. (1981). Behavioral correlates of prenatal alcohol exposure: A four-year follow-up study. *Neurobehavioral Toxicology & Teratology, 3,* 187–193.

Laughlin, N. K. (1986). Neurobehavioral teratology of lead. In E. P. Riley & C. V. Vorhees (Eds.), *Handbook of behavioral teratology.* New York: Plenum.

Lindhout, D., Hoppener, R. J. E. A., & Meinardi, H. (1974). Teratogenicity of antiepileptic drug combinations with special emphasis on epoxidation (of carbamazepine). *Epilepsia, 25,* 77–83.

Lindhout, D., & Meinardi, H. (1984). Spina bifida and in-utero exposure to valproate. *Lancet, 2,* 396.

Little, R. E., Graham, J. M., & Samson, H. H. (1982). Fetal alcohol effects in humans and animals. *Advances in Alcohol & Substance Abuse, 1,* 103–125.

Little, R. E., Streissguth, A. P., Barr, H. M., & Herman, C. S. (1980). Decreased birth weight in infants of alcoholic women who abstained during pregnancy. *Journal of Pediatrics, 96,* 974–977.

Low, J. A., Galbraith, R. S., Muir, D. W., Killen, H. L., Pater, E. A., & Karchmar, E. J. (1984). Factors associated with motor and cognitive deficits in children after intrapartum fetal hypoxia. *American Journal of Obstetrics & Gynecology, 148,* 533–539.

Mactutus, C. F., & Fechter, L. D. (1984). Prenatal exposure to carbon monoxide: Learning and memory deficits. *Science, 223,* 409–411.

Mactutus, C. F., & Fechter, L. D. (1986). Perinatal hypoxia: Implications for mammalian development. In E. P. Riley & C. V. Vorhees (Eds.), *Handbook of behavioral teratology.* New York: Plenum.

Mactutus, C. F., & Tilson, H. A. (1986). Psychogenic and neurogenic abnormalities after perinatal insecticide exposure: A critical review. In E. P. Riley & C. V. Vorhees (Eds.), *Handbook of behavioral teratology.* New York: Plenum.

Mahaffy, K. R., Annest, J. L., Roberts, J., & Murphy, R. S. (1982). National estimates of blood lead levels: United States 1976–1980: Association with selected demographic and socioeconomic factors. *New England Journal of Medicine, 307,* 573–579.

Marcus, J., & Hans, S. L. (1982a). A methodological model to study the effects of toxins on child development. *Neurobehavioral Toxicology & Teratology, 4,* 483–487.

Marcus, J., & Hans, S. L. (1982b). Electromyographic assessment of neonatal muscle tone. *Psychiatry Research, 6,* 31–40.

Marcus, J., Hans, S. L., & Jeremy, R. J. (1982a). Differential motor and state functioning in newborns of women on methadione. *Neurobehavioral Toxicology & Teratology, 4,* 459–462.

Marcus, J., Hans, S. L., & Jeremy, R. J. (1982b). Patterns of 1-day and 4-month motor functioning in infants of women on methadone. *Neurobehavioral Toxicology & Teratology, 4,* 473–476.

Marcus, J., Hans, S. L., & Jeremy, R. J. (1984). A longitudinal study of offspring born to methadone-maintained women: III. Effects of multiple risk factors on development at 4, 8, and 12 months. *American Journal of Drug and Alcohol Abuse, 10,* 195–207.

Marcus, J., Hans, S. L., Patterson, M. A., & Morris, A. J. (1984). A longitudinal study of offspring born to methadione-maintained women: I. Design, methodology and description of women's resources for functioning. *American Journal of Drug and Alcohol Abuse, 10,* 135–160.

Martin, D. C., Martin, J. C., Streissguth, A. P., & Lund, C. A. (1979). Sucking frequency and amplitude in newborns as a function of maternal drinking and smoking. In M. Galanter (Ed.), *Currents in alcoholism* (Vol. 5). New York: Grune & Stratton.

Martin, J., Martin, D. C., Lund, C. A., & Streissguth, A. P. (1977). Maternal alcohol ingestion and cigarette smoking and their effects on newborn conditioning. *Alcoholism: Clinical & Experimental Research, 1,* 243–247.

McBride, W. G. (1977). Thalidomide embryopathy. *Teratology, 16,* 79–82.

McFie, J., & Robertson, J. (1973). Psychological test results of children with thalidomide deformities. *Developmental Medicine & Child Neurology, 15,* 719–727.

McMullin, G. P. (1971). Teratogenic effects of anticonvulsants. *Lancet, 4,* 430.

Mele, P. C., & Bowman, R. E. (1984). Behavioral evaluation of perinatal PCB exposure in rhesus monkeys: Fixed-interval performance and reinforcement omission. *Society for Neuroscience Abstracts, 10.*

Mele, P. C., Bushnell, P. J., & Bowman, R. E. (1984). Prolonged behavioral effects of early postnatal lead exposure in rhesus monkeys: Fixed-interval responding and interations with scopolamine and pentobarbital. *Neurobehavioral Toxicology & Teratology, 6,* 129–135.

Meyer, L. S., & Riley, E. P. (1986). Behavioral teratology of alcohol. In E. P. Riley & C. V. Vorhees (Eds.), *Handbook of behavioral teratology.* New York: Plenum.

Meyer-Bahlburg, H. F. L., & Ehrhardt, A. A. (1980). Neurobehavioral effects of prenatal origin: Sex hormones. In R. H. Schwarz & S. J. Yaffe (Eds.), *Drug and chemical risks to the fetus and newborn.* New York: Alan R. Liss.

Middaugh, L. D. (1986). Prenatal phenobarbital: Effects on pregnancy and offspring. In E. P. Riley & C. V. Vorhees (Eds.), *Handbook of behavioral teratology.* New York: Plenum.

Millar, J. H. D., & Nevin, N. C. (1973). Congenital malformations and anticonvulsant drugs. *Lancet, 1,* 328.

Montouris, G. D., Fenichel, G. M., & McLain, L. W. (1979). The pregnant epileptic: A review and recommendations. *Archives of Neurology, 36,* 601–603.

Mullenix, P. J., & Moore, P. (1985). Behavioral toxicity of nitrous oxide following prenatal exposure of rats. *Teratology, 30,* 5B–6B.

Mullenix, P., Tassinari, M. S., & Keith, D. A. (1983). Behavioral outcome after prenatal exposure to phenytoin in rats. *Teratology, 27,* 149–157.

Musch, H. R., Bornhausen, M., Kriegel, H., & Greim, H. (1978). Methylmercury chloride induces learning deficits in prenatally treated rats. *Archives of Toxicology, 40,* 103–108.

Myers, R. E. (1975a). Four patterns of perinatal brain damage and their conditions of occurrence in primates. In B. S. Meldrum & C. D. Marsden (Eds.), *Advances in neurology* (Vol. 10). New York: Raven.

Myers, R. E. (1975b). Maternal psychological stress and fetal asphyxia: A study in the monkey. *American Journal of Obstetrics & Gynecology, 122,* 47–59.

Myers, R. E. (1977). Experimental models of perinatal brain damage: Relevance to human pathology. In L. Gluck (Ed.), *Intrauterine asphyxia and the developing fetal brain.* Chicago: Year Book Medical Publishers.

Myers, R. E. (1979). Lactic acid accumulation as cause of brain edema and cerebral necrosis resulting from oxygen deprivation. In R. Korobkin & C. Guilleminault (Eds.), *Advances in perinatal neurology* (Vol. 1). New York: Spectrum.

Naeye, R. L., & Peters, E. C. (1984). Mental development of children whose mothers smoked during pregnancy. *Obstetrics & Gynecology, 64,* 601–607.

Nakane, Y. (1979). Congenital malformation among infants of epileptic mothers treated during pregnancy—The report of a collaborative study group in Japan. *Folia Psychiatrica et Neurologica Japonica, 33,* 363–369.

Needleman, H. L., Geiger, S. K., & Frank, R. (1985). Lead and IQ scores: A reanalysis. *Science, 227,* 701–704.

Needleman, H. L., Gunnoe, C., Leviton, A., Reed, R., Peresie, H., Maher, C., & Barrett, P. (1979). Deficits in psychologic and classroom performance of children with elevated dentine lead levels. *New England Journal of Medicine, 300,* 689–695.

Nelson, B. K. (1981). Dose/effect relationships in developmental neurotoxicology. *Neurobehavioral Toxicology & Teratology, 3,* 255.

Nelson, B. K. (1986). Behavioral teratology of industrial solvents. In E. P. Riley & C. V. Vorhees (Eds.), *Handbook of behavioral teratology.* New York: Plenum.

Niebyl, J. R., Blake, D. A., Freeman, J. M., & Luff, R. D. (1979). Carbamazepine levels in pregnancy and lactation. *Obstetrics & Gynecology, 53,* 139–140.

O'Connell, C. M., & Fried, P. A. (1984). An investigation of prenatal cannabis exposure and minor physical anomalies in a low risk population. *Neurobehavioral Toxicology & Teratology, 6,* 345–350.

Otake, M., & Schull, W. J. (1984). In utero exposure to A-bomb radiation and mental retardation; a reassessment. *British Journal of Radiology, 57,* 409–414.

Ouellette, E. M., Rosett, H. L., Rosman, N. P., & Weiner, L. (1977). Adverse effects on offspring of maternal alcohol abuse during pregnancy. *New England Journal of Medicine, 297,* 528–530.

Picone, T. A., Allen, L. H., Olsen, P. N., & Ferris, M. E. (1982). Pregnancy outcome in North American women: II. Effects of diet, cigarette smoking, stress, and weight gain on placentas, and on neonatal physical and behavioral characteristics. *American Journal of Clinical Nutrition, 36,* 1214–1224.

Quimby, K. L., Aschkenase, L. J., Bowman, R. E., Katz, J., & Chang, L. W. (1974). Enduring learning deficits and cerebral synaptic malformation from exposure to 10 parts of halothane per million. *Science, 185,* 625–627.

Rall, T. W., & Schleifer, L. S. (1980). In A. G. Gilman, L. S. Goodman, & A. Gilman (Eds.), *Goodman and Gilman's the pharmacological basis of therapeutics* (6th ed.). New York: MacMillan.

Randall, C. L., Taylor, W. L., & Walker, D. (1977). Ethanol-induced malformations in mice. Alcoholism: Clinical & Experimental Research, 1, 219–224.

Reinisch, J. M., & Sanders, S. A. (1984). Prenatal gonadal steriodal influences on gender-related behavior. In G. D. DeVries, J. P. C. DeBruin, H. B. M. Uylings, & M. A. Corher (Eds.), Sex differences in the brain: The relation between structure and function, *Progress in Brain Research* (Vol. 61). Amsterdam: Elsevier.

Reiter, L. W. (1980). Short-term vs. long-term neurotoxicity: The comparative behavioral toxicity of triethyltin in newborn and adult rats. In R. M. Gryder & V. H. Frankos (Eds.), *Effects of foods and drugs on the development and function of the nervous system: Methods for predicting toxicity.* Washington, DC: Office of Health Affairs, U.S. Food and Drug Administration.

Resnick, O., Morgane, P. J., Hasson, R., & Miller, M. (1982). Overt and hidden forms of chronic malnutrition in the rat and their relevance to man. *Neuroscience & Biobehavioral Reviews, 6,* 55–75.

Reuhl, K. R., & Chang, L. W. (1979). Effects of methylmercury on the development of the nervous system: A review. *Neurotoxicology, 1,* 21–55.

Rice, S. A., & Millan, D. P. (1985). Behavioral effects of in utero nitrous oxide (N_2O) exposure in adult SW mice. *Teratology, 31,* 6B (abstract).

Riley, E. P., & Meyer, L. S. (1984). Considerations for the design, implementation, and interpretation of animal models of fetal alcohol effects. *Neurobehavioral Toxicology & Teratology, 6,* 97–101.

Riley, E. P., & Vorhees, C. V. (Eds.). (1986). *Handbook of behavioral teratology.* New York: Plenum.

Robertson, I. G., Donnai, D., & D'Souza, S. (1983). Cranial nerve agenesis in a fetus exposed to carbamazepine. *Developmental Medicine & Child Neurology, 25,* 540–541.

Rodier, P. M. (1980). Chronology of neuron development: Animal studies and their clinical implications. *Developmental Medicine & Child Neurology, 22,* 525–545.

Rodier, P. M. (1986). Behavioral effects of antimitotic agents administered during neurogenesis. In E. P. Riley & C. V. Vorhees (Eds.), *Handbook of behavioral teratology.* New York: Plenum.

Rodier, P. M., Aschner, M., & Sager, P. R. (1984). Mitotic arrest in the developing CNS after prenatal exposure to methylmercury. *Neurobehavioral Toxicology & Teratology, 6,* 379–385.

Rosett, H. L. (1980). The effects of alcohol on the fetus and offspring. In O. J. Kalant (Ed.), *Alcohol and drug problems in women: Research advances in alcohol and drug problems* (Vol. 5). New York: Plenum.

Rosett, H. L., & Sander, L. W. (1979). Effects of maternal drinking on neonatal morphology and state regulation. In J. D. Osofsky (Ed.), *Handbook of infant development.* New York: Wiley.

Rosett, H. L., Weiner, L., Lee, A., Zuckerman, B., Dooling, E., & Oppenheimer, E. (1983). Patterns of alcohol consumption and fetal development. *Obstetrics & Gynecology, 61,* 539–546.

Rudd, N. L., & Freedom, R. M. (1979). A possible primidone embryopathy. *Journal of Pediatrics, 94,* 835–837.

Ryan, C. L., & Pappas, B. A. (1986). Intrauterine diazepam exposure: Effects on physical and neurobehavioral development in the rat. *Neurobehavioral Toxicology & Teratology, 7,* 279–286.

Schmidt, D. (1982). Benzodiazepines: Diazepam. In D. M. Woodbury, J. K. Penry, & C. E. Pippenger (Eds.), *Antiepileptic drugs* (2nd ed.). New York: Raven.

Segal, S., Anyan, W. R., Cohen, S. N., Freeman, J., Hill, R. M., Kauffman, R. E., Pruitt, A. W., Shinefield, H. R., & Vickers, S. M. (1979). Anticonvulsants and pregnancy, American Academy of Pediatrics Committee on Drugs. *Pediatrics, 63,* 331–333.

Seip, M. (1976). Growth retardation, dysmorphic facies and minor malformations following massive exposure to phenobarbitone in utero. *Acta Paediatrica Scandanavia, 65,* 617–621.

Sever, J. L. (1983). Maternal infections. In C. C. Brown (Ed.), *Childhood learning disabilities and prenatal risk*. New York: Johnson & Johnson.

Sexton, D. W. (1978). The behavior of infants whose mothers smoke in pregnancy. *Early Human Development, 2,* 363–369.

Sexton, M., & Hebel, J. R. (1984). A clinical trial of change in maternal smoking and its effect on birth weight. *Journal of the American Medical Association, 251,* 911–915.

Shapiro, S., Slone, D., Hartz, S. C., Rosenberg, L., Siskind, V., Monson, R., Mitchell, A. A., Heinonen, O. P., Idanpaan-Heikkila, J., Haro, S., & Saxen, L. (1976). Anticonvulsants and parental epilepsy in the development of birth defects. *Lancet, 1,* 272–275.

Shaywitz, B. A. (1978). Fetal alcohol syndrome: An ancient problem rediscovered. *Drug Therapy,* January, pp. 53–60.

Shih, L. Y., Diamond, N., & Kushnick, T. (1979). Primidone induced teratology—Clinical observations. *Teratology, 19,* 47A.

Shore, C. O., Vorhees, C. V., Bornschein, R. L., & Stemmer, K. (1983). Behavioral consequences of prenatal diazepam exposure in rats. *Neurobehavioral Toxicology & Teratology, 5,* 565–570.

Shull, G. E. (1984). Differential inhibition of protein synthesis: A possible biochemical mechanism of thalidomide teratogenesis. *Journal of Theoretical Biology, 110,* 461–486.

Silbergeld, E. K. (1984). Behavioral teratology of lead. In J. Yanai (Ed.), *Neurobehavioral teratology*. Amsterdam: Elsevier.

Simmons, R. D., Kellogg, C. K., & Miller, R. K. (1984). Prenatal diazepam exposure in rats: Long-lasting, receptor-mediated effects on hypothalamic norepinephrine-containing neurons. *Brain Research, 293,* 73–83.

Simmons, R. D., Miller, R. K., & Kellogg, C. K. (1984). Prenatal exposure to diazepam alters central and peripheral responses to stress in adult rat offspring. *Brain Research, 307,* 39–46.

Smith, D. W. (1977). Teratogenicity of anticonvulsive medications. *American Journal of Diseases of Children, 131,* 1337–1339.

Smith, R. F., Bowman, R. E., & Katz, J. (1978). Behavioral effects of exposure to halothane during early development in the rat: Sensitive period during pregnancy. *Anesthesiology, 49,* 319–323.

Smith, R. F., Wharton, G. G., Kurtz, S. L., Mattran, K. M., & Hollenbeck, A. R. (1985). Behavioral effects of midpregnancy administration of lidocaine and mepivacaine in the rat. *Teratology, 31,* 5B (abstract).

Snell, K. (Ed.). (1982). *Developmental Toxicology.* New York: Praeger.

Sokol, R. J., Miller, S. I., & Reed, G. (1980). Alcohol abuse during pregnancy: An epidemiologic study. *Alcoholism: Clinical & Experimental Research, 4,* 135–145.

Spyker, J. M., Sparber, S. B., & Goldberg, A. M. (1972). Subtle consequences of methylmercury exposure: Behavioral deviations in offspring of treated mothers. *Science, 177,* 621–623.

Starreveld-Zimmerman, A. A. E., van der Kolk, W. J., Meinardi, H., & Elshove, J. (1973). Are anticonvulsants teratogenic? *Lancet, 2,* 48–49.

Streissguth, A. P., Barr, H. M., & Martin, D. C. (1982). Offspring effects and pregnancy complications related to self-reported maternal alcohol use. *Developmental Pharmacology & Therapeutics, 5,* 21–32.

Streissguth, A. P., Barr, H. M., & Martin, D. C. (1983). Maternal alcohol use and neonatal habituation assessed with the Brazelton scale. *Child Development, 54,* 1109–1118.

Streissguth, A. P., Barr, H. M., Martin, D. C., & Herman, C. S. (1980). Effects of maternal alcohol, nicotine, and caffeine use during pregnancy on infant mental and motor development at eight months. *Alcoholism: Clinical & Experimental Research, 4,* 152–164.

Streissguth, A. P., Herman, C. S., & Smith, D. W. (1978a). Intelligence, behavior, and dysmorphogenesis in the fetal alcohol syndrome: A report on 20 patients. *Journal of Pediatrics, 92,* 363–367.

Streissguth, A. P., Herman, C. S., & Smith, D. W. (1978b). Stability of intelligence in the fetal alcohol syndrome: A preliminary report. *Alcoholism: Clinical & Experimental Research, 2,* 165–170.

Streissguth, A. P., Landesman-Dwyer, S., Martin, J. C., & Smith, D. W. (1980). Teratogenic effects of alcohol in humans and laboratory animals. *Science, 209,* 353–361.

Streissguth, A. P., Martin, D. C., Barr, H. M., MacGregor-Sandman, B., Kirchner, G. L., & Darby, B. L. (1984). Intrauterine alcohol and nicotine exposure: Attention and reaction time in 4-year-old children. *Developmental Psychology, 20,* 533–541.

Streissguth, A. P., Martin, D. C., Martin, J. C., & Barr, H. M. (1981). The Seattle longitudinal prospective study on alcohol and pregnancy. *Neurobehavioral Toxicology & Teratology, 3,* 223–233.

Streissguth, A. P., Treder, R., Barr, H. M., Shepard, T., Bleyer, A., & Martin, D. (1984). Prenatal aspirin and offspring IQ in a large group. *Teratology, 29,* 59A–60A.

Stubbs, E. G., Ash, E., & Williams, C. P. S. (1984). Autism and congenital cytomegalovirus. *Journal of Autism & Developmental Disorders, 14,* 183–189.

Sulik, K. K., Johnston, M. C., & Webb, M. A. (1981). Fetal alcohol syndrome: Embryogenesis in a mouse model. *Science, 214,* 936–938.

Sullivan, F. M., & McElhatton, P. R. (1975). Teratogenic activity of the antiepileptic drugs phenobarbital, phenytoin, and primidone in mice. *Toxicology & Applied Pharmacology, 34,* 271–282.

Sullivan, F. M., & McElhatton, P. R. (1977). A comparison of the teratogenic activity of the antiepileptic drugs carbamazepine, clonazepam, ethosuximide, phenobarbital, phenytoin, and primidone in mice. *Toxicology & Applied Pharmacology, 40,* 365–378.

Surgeon General's Report (1979). *Smoking and health: A report of the Surgeon General.* Washington, DC: Public Health Service, U.S. Department of Health, Education and Welfare.

Takeuchi, T., Eto, N., & Eto, K. (1979). Neuropathology of childhood cases of methylmercury poisoning (Minamata disease) with prolonged symptoms, with particular reference to the decortication syndrome. *Neurotoxicology, 1,* 1–20.

Taylor, P. R., Lawrence, C. E., Hwang, H.-L., & Paulson, A. S. (1984). Polychlorinated biphenyls: Influence on birthweight and gestation. *American Journal of Public Health, 74,* 1153–1163.

Tilson, H. A., Davis, G. J., McLachlan, J. A., & Lucier, G. W. (1979). The effects of polychlorinated biphenyls given prenatally on the neurobehavioral development of mice. *Environmental Research, 18,* 466–474.

Turner, G., & Collins, E. (1975). Fetal effects of regular salicylate ingestion in pregnancy. *Lancet, 2,* 338–339.

Vorhees, C. V. (1983). Fetal anticonvulsant syndrome in rats: Dose- and period-response relationships of prenatal diphenylhydantion, trimethadione and phenobarbital exposure on the structural and functional development of the offspring. *Journal of Pharmacology & Experimental Therapeutics, 227,* 274–287.

Vorhees, C. V. (1985). Fetal anticonvulsant syndrome in rats: Effects on postnatal behavior and brain amino acid content. *Neurobehavioral Toxicology & Teratology, 7.*

Vorhees, C. V. (1986a). Behavioral teratology of anticonvulsant and antianxiety medications. In E. P. Riley & C. V. Vorhees (Eds.), *Handbook of behavioral teratology.* New York: Plenum.

Vorhees, C. V. (1986b). Comparison and critique of government regulations for behavioral teratology. In E. P. Riley & C. V. Vorhees (Eds.), *Handbook of behavioral teratology.* New York: Plenum.

Vorhees, C. V. (1986c). Origins of behavioral teratology. In E. P. Riley & C. V. Vorhees (Eds.), *Handbook of behavioral teratology.* New York: Plenum.

Vorhees, C. V. (1986d). Principles of behavioral teratology. In E. P. Riley & C. V. Vorhees (Eds.), *Handbook of behavioral teratology.* New York: Plenum.

Vorhees, C. V., Brunner, R. L., & Butcher, R. E. (1979). Psychotropic drugs as behavioral teratogens. *Science, 205,* 1220–1225.

Vorhees, C. V., & Butcher, R. E. (1982). Behavioral teratogenicity. In K. Snell (Ed.), *Developmental toxicology.* New York: Praeger.

Vorhees, C. V., Klein, K. L., & Scott, W. J. (1982). Aspirin-induced psychoteratogenesis in rats as a function of embryonic age. *Teratogenesis, Carcinogenesis & Mutagenesis, 2,* 77–84.

Warkany, J. (1978). Terathanasia. *Teratology, 17,* 187–192.

Warkany, J., Lemire, R. J., & Cohen, M. M. (1981). *Mental retardation and congenital malformations of the central nervous system.* Chicago: Year Book Medical Publishers.

Warkany, J., & Takacs, E. (1959). Experimental production of congenital malformations in rats by salicylate poisoning. *American Journal of Pathology, 35,* 315–331.

Werboff, J., & Gottlieb, J. S. (1963). Drugs in pregnancy: Behavioral teratology. *Obstetric & Gynecologic Survey, 18,* 420–423.

Wilson, J. G. (1973). *Environment and birth defects.* New York: Academic.

Wilson, J. G. (1977a). Current status of teratology—General principles and mechanisms derived from animal studies. In J. G. Wilson & F. C. Fraser (Eds.), *Handbook of teratology* (Vol. 1). New York: Plenum.

Wilson, J. G. (1977b). Embryotoxicity of drugs in man. In J. G. Wilson & F. C. Fraser (Eds.), *Handbook of teratology* (Vol. 1). New York: Plenum.

Wilson, J. G. (1977c). Environmental chemicals. In J. G. Wilson & F. C. Fraser (Eds.), *Handbook of teratology* (Vol. 1). New York: Plenum.

Wilson, J. G., Ritter, E. J., Scott, W. J., & Fradkin, R. (1977). Comparative distribution and embryotoxicity of acetylsalicylic acid in pregnant rats and rhesus monkeys. *Toxicology & Applied Pharmacology, 41,* 67–78.

Yanai, J. (Ed.) (1984). *Neurobehavioral teratology.* Amsterdam: Elsevier.

Zackai, E. H., Mellman, W. J., Neiderer, B., & Hanson, J. W. (1975). The fetal trimethadione syndrome. *Journal of Pediatrics, 87,* 280–284.

CHAPTER 19

Affective and Interactive Disturbances in Infants

TIFFANY FIELD

INTRODUCTION

Over the past several years a number of researchers have been studying the development of infant affect and affective disturbances in the context of early social interactions. Among the models being assessed is that affective responsivity develops in an interactive relationship that features optimal stimulation and arousal modulation (Brazelton, Koslowski, & Main, 1974; Field, 1982c, 1985a; Lester, Hoffman, & Brazelton, 1985; Stern, 1971, 1974; Tronick, Als, & Brazelton, 1977). While infants appear to differ in their responsivity to social stimulation from birth because of different genetic backgrounds and prenatal and perinatal experiences, mothers (caregivers) learn to read their infants' affective displays (facial expressions, gestures, vocalizations, and gaze behavior) and modulate their stimulation to match their infants' individual stimulation and arousal modulation needs. When this occurs, the infant appears to be affectively responsive, the interaction harmonious (both behaviorally and physiologically), and a normal attachment or relationship appears to develop, thereby fostering the infant's affective development.

If either member of the dyad is affectively unresponsive, or if their relationship is disrupted by separation, then affective and interactive disturbances may occur. The infant may be affectively unresponsive, for example, because of higher sensory thresholds or less developed arousal modulation or information-processing skills secondary to prematurity and perinatal complications, and the mother unable to modulate her stimulation accordingly (Field, 1977; Goldberg, Brachfeld, & DiVitto, 1980). Alternatively, the mother may be the source of affective disturbance by being affectively unresponsive, for example, if she is depressed (Cohn & Tronick, 1983; Field, 1984b). Both may be affectively unresponsive, for example, following a separation for the birth of another child (Dunn, Kendrick, & MacNamee, 1981; Field, 1986). Interaction coaching techniques, typically directed at modifying the mother's sensitivity and responsivity to her infant's interaction behaviors, have alleviated disturbed interactions in several types of mother–infant dyads (Clark & Seifer, 1983;

I would like to thank the infants and parents who participated in these studies and the researchers who collaborated with me in conducting these studies. This research was supported in part by a research scientist development award #1K02MH00331–01 from NIMH.

Field, 1983a). However, the interactive disturbances of some dyads may be more difficult to modify.

Affective and interactive disturbances are especially apparent in dyads featuring a depressed infant (failure to thrive) or a depressed mother (postpartum depression) and in dyads experiencing an early separation. Infants and young children appear to experience pronounced affective disturbances when they are chronically exposed to maternal deprivation in the form of neglect (failure-to-thrive infant) or inadequate stimulation (depressed mother) and when their interactions are disrupted by separations and accompanying changes in their relationship. The maternal deprivation experience may predispose the infant to chronic "depression," and the separation situation may provide a model for reactive or acute depression (Field, 1986; Hofer, 1984; Reite & Capitanio, 1985). The infant's responses to these situations appear to be biphasic with an acute period of agitated behavior followed by a more prolonged period of depressed behavior. Agitation is characterized by a constellation of behavioral changes including increased fussiness, activity level, and heart rate, and depression is manifested by flat affect and diminished activity level and heart rate. Vegetative functions such as sleeping, eating, elimination, and illness are also affected.

According to the model being assessed in these situations, optimal levels of stimulation and arousal modulation differ for individuals and are achieved in an attachment or intimate relationship as each individual becomes attuned to the stimulation and arousal modulation needs of the other (Field, 1986a). In mother–infant interactions the mother carefully modulates her behaviors to those of her infant to provide adequate stimulation and arousal modulation. In the optimal interaction the mother's and infant's affective behaviors and physiological rhythms become synchronized (Brazelton et al., 1974; Field, 1985a; Lester et al., 1985). If the mother is emotionally unavailable or affectively unresponsive (as in maternal deprivation syndrome or maternal depression) or if the dyad is separated and the relationship changes, the infant experiences acute or chronic behavioral disorganization, and the mother's and infant's behavioral and physiological rhythms become asynchronous. This is manifested in acute or chronic affective disturbances and changes in activity level and autonomic and biochemical activity. This may occur because the infant has been deprived, either temporarily or chronically, of an important external regulator (zeitgeber) of stimulation and behavioral and physiological rhythms (the mother), and thus fails to develop or sustain arousal modulation and organized behavioral and physiological rhythms. A similar model has been derived from mother–infant interaction and separation data in other species including rats (Hofer, 1984; Schanberg, Evoniuk, & Kuhn, 1984) and macaque monkeys (Reite & Capitanio, 1985) and will be included in this discussion.

BACKGROUND AND SUPPORTING DATA

In this chapter data are reviewed on individual differences in infants' affective responsivity from birth, on affective synchrony and disturbances during early interactions, and the special case of affective disturbances arising from maternal deprivation and early separation experiences.

Individual Differences in Infants' Affective Responsivity from Birth

Individual differences in infants' affective responsivity may derive from differences in genetic background and in prenatal and perinatal experiences. Elsewhere an externalizer–internalizer model has been developed to describe the continuum of individual differences in neonates' affective responsivity, with some infants being expressive (externalizers) and some not (internalizers) (Field, 1982b; Field & Walden, 1982). A number of investigators have noted individual differences in neonates' "hedonic" (positive–negative) responses as manifested in the facial expressions they make to various olfactory and gustatory stimuli (Fox, 1985; Lipsitt, 1981; Steiner, 1979). As noted in studies on spontaneous facial expressions during neonatal assessments (Field, Greenberg, Woodson, Cohen, & Garcia, 1984), on imitative facial expressions by neonates (Field, Woodson, Cohen, Garcia, & Greenberg, 1983; Field, Woodson, Greenberg, & Cohen, 1982; Meltzoff, 1985; Meltzoff & Moore, 1983), and on neonatal responsivity to mothers' faces (Field, Cohen, Garcia, & Greenberg, 1984), significant individual differences have emerged, with some infants at one extreme being "poker-faced" but physiologically reactive to social stimulation (internalizers) and some at the other extreme being facially expressive but physiologically nonreactive (externalizers). Because there appears to be greater concordance in affective responsivity among monozygotic than dyzygotic twins (Field, 1985b), the intensity of affective responses and the predisposition to be more reactive behaviorally or physiologically may have genetic origins. Others (Buck, 1979; Eysenck, 1973; Izard, 1977; Jones, 1950; Tomkins, 1980) have for some time suggested genetic origins for individual differences in expressivity.

Although confounded with genetic influences, individual differences in affective responsivity may also derive from variable prenatal experiences. In a recent ultrasound study different activity–reactivity levels during the fetal stage and affective responsivity during the neonatal stage were reported for those infants whose mothers experienced pregnancy anxiety or depression (Field, Sandberg, Quetel, Garcia, & Rosario, 1985). Sostek and colleagues (Sostek, Sostek, Murphy, Martin, & Born, 1981) have similarly documented depressed activity and responsivity in neonates born to mothers who had elevated levels of plasma monoamine oxidase (a frequently noted correlate of adult depression).

In addition, individual differences in affective responsivity have been noted in infants with congential abnormalities such as Down's syndrome (Jones, 1980; McQuiston, McCarthy, MacTurk, & Vietze, 1980) and craniofacial anomalies (Field & Vega-Lahr, 1984) and infants with perinatal complications such as prematurity or respiratory distress syndrome (Field, 1982; Goldberg et al., 1980; Lester et al., 1985). Infants experiencing these complications appear to be less active and affectively responsive in several neonatal paradigms including their spontaneous facial expressions during neonatal assessments (Field, Greenberg, Woodson, Cohen, & Garcia, 1984), their imitative responses during modeled facial expressions (Field, Woodson, Cohen, Garcia and Greenberg, 1984), and their responsivity to mother's faces (Field, Cohen, Garcia and Greenberg, 1984).

Some manipulations of neonatal activity and affective responsivity have been moderately successful. For example, in one study, giving ultrasound feedback to pregnant women resulted in reduced pregnancy anxiety, diminished fetal activity, and greater neonatal responsivity (Field, Sandberg, Quetel, Garcia & Rosario, 1985).

In other studies the activity levels and affective responsivity of very premature neo-nates have been modified by providing supplemental stimulation in the form of nonnutritive sucking during invasive medical procedures (Field & Goldson, 1984) and during gavage feedings (Anderson, Burroughs, & Measel, 1983; Field, Ignatoff, Stringer, Brennan, Greenberg, Widmayer, & Anderson, 1982) and in the form of rocking waterbeds (Korner, 1985), breathing teddy bears (Thoman, 1985), and body massage (Field et al., 1986). Although most intervention efforts have been directed at modifying the behavior of the caregiver, for example, by providing demonstrations of the Brazelton assessment to mothers (Widmayer & Field, 1980; Worobey & Belsky, 1982), these supplemental stimulation studies suggest that neonatal responsivity can also be enhanced. Enhancing neonatal responsivity may in turn facilitate early mother–infant interactions, thereby lessening the risk for later affective disturbances among infants who have experienced perinatal complications.

Synchrony and Interactive Disturbances

Affective disturbances of infants have typically been studied in the context of early interactions. This research has usually featured high-risk infants such as preterms (Bakeman & Brown, 1980; Crnic, Ragozin, Greenberg, Robinson, & Barham, 1983), RDS infants (Field, 1982a; Goldberg et al., 1980), postterm postmaturity syndrome infants (Field, 1982a), small-for-dates twins (Field, Walden, Widmayer, & Greenberg, 1982), failure-to-thrive infants (Alfasi, 1982; Goldstein & Field, 1985), Down syndrome infants (Jones, 1980; McQuiston et al., 1980), and craniofacial anomaly infants (Field & Vega-Lahr, 1984) and their interactions with mothers, fathers, strangers, and siblings. Alternatively, interaction studies have featured high-risk mothers including teenage mothers (Field, Widmayer, Greenberg, & Stoller, 1982), lower-income black mothers (Field & Widmayer, 1981), Haitian immigrant mothers (Field & Widmayer, 1986), and postpartum depressed mothers (Field, 1984b; Field, Sandberg, Garcia, Vega-Lahr, Goldstein, & Guy, 1985). Thus affective disturbances have been studied in the context of interacting dyads in which either the infant or the mother was affectively unresponsive.

The model we have been assessing on disturbed interactions suggests that high-risk infants have abnormally high or low thresholds to stimulation and narrower activation bands for attentiveness, affective responsivity, and information processing, such that the mother is faced with a more difficult task of modulating her stimulation to match her infant's stimulation and arousal modulation needs (Field, 1982c). If the mother fails by providing either too much or too little stimulation or by insensitive timing of her stimulation, the infant typically becomes overaroused and withdraws from the interaction. In contrast, during interactions with high-risk mothers (typically mothers with depressed affect), very little agitation was noted in the infants; instead the infants' behaviors appeared to mirror their mothers' depressed activity and affective displays (Field, 1984b). The interactions of both high-risk infants and their mothers and high-risk mothers and their infants were characteristically lacking in affective displays and contingent responsivity and in synchronous behavior patterns and physiological rhythms. These patterns are disconcerting inasmuch as relationships have been reported between early interaction disturbances and later, school-age behavioral and emotional problems including hyperactivity, limited attention span, and disturbed peer interactions (Bakeman &

Brown, 1980; Field, 1984b; Sigman, Cohen, & Forsythe, 1981) as well as affective disturbances diagnosed as depression by DSM-III diagnostic criteria (Widmayer, Bauer, & Field, 1986). Disturbances in early interaction patterns among dyads in which one or the other partner is affectively unresponsive are highlighted by their contrast to the affective displays and behavioral and physiological synchrony noted in typical mother–infant interactions.

Typically, mother–infant interactions illustrate attunement or synchrony of behavioral and physiological rhythms as the mother and infant reach mutually optimal stimulation levels and arousal modulation. In one of the earliest studies of this phenomenon, dyadic gaze patterns were studied in twins and their mother (Stern, 1971). Dramatic differences were noted between the interactions of each twin with its mother; one interaction was synchronous, but in the other the mother and infant were not able to arrive at a mutually optimal level of stimulation. Stern (1974) describes the mother as being affectively alive in providing stimulation that closely corresponds to the range of stimulation to which the infant is constitutionally set to respond. During early interactions, the mother tries to maintain the infant's attention and elicit affective behaviors such as smiles and coos, which in turn elicit in her those behaviors that maintain the infant's attention and arousal. In this way they share a dyadic feedback system. One of the ways the mother approximates an optimal range of stimulation is by her "infantized" behaviors or infant-elicited variations of normal social behavior. For example, verbal and facial expressions are exaggerated, with the expressions often formed slowly and sustained. These exaggerated variations in tempo and degree of display appear to match the infant's endogenous rhythms and rate of processing information. Thus the mother varies stimulus modalities, the intensity, complexity, speed, and so forth, of her stimulation to hold or recapture the infant's attention and elicit affective responses. The infant, in turn, provides the mother an array of stimulating behaviors that provide feedback cues for the mother's modification of her own behavior. According to Stern and his colleagues (Stern, Hofer, Haft, & Dore, 1985), the mother's behavior matches her infant's on shape, intensity, or temporal features (duration, beat, or rhythm). This *affect attunement* has been attributed to a matching of internal states by Stern and colleagues (1985).

Similarly, rhythmic cycles of infant attentiveness and maternal activity have been plotted during mother–infant interactions by Brazelton and colleagues (1974). The mother cycles her behaviors in response to her infant's rhythmic changes in attention. Brazelton and colleagues (1974) suggest that the mother appears to meet her infant's stimulation and arousal modulation needs in one of three ways: (1) by adjusting her rhythm to the infant's, following its gazing and gazing-away cues and affective behaviors with increases and decreases in stimulation; (2) by not responding to the infant's rhythm but continuing her stimulation, thus reinforcing the time the infant spends looking away; or (3) by attempting to establish her own rhythm to regulate the infant's (Brazelton et al., 1974). In some cases, a mother may increase and decrease her stimulation but out of phase with her infant, resulting in shorter periods of interaction between them. Thus the infant and mother appear to synchronize their gaze patterns, and the affective tone of their interaction shifts in tandem, with the mother necessarily being sensitive to arousal changes in the infant and the infant responding to her sensitive behaviors. Mothers who show sensitivity to the affective and attentive rhythms of their infants are able to adjust their behaviors and accordingly bring their infants to a more organized state. Because of the immaturity of the infant, much of the onus for synchrony in interaction is on the part of the mother. If the mother does not provide optimal levels of stimulation and modulate stimulation as the infant's arousal level heightens, the infant shows more gaze aversion and fussiness, disrupting the synchrony of their interaction (Field, 1982a).

Tronick, Als, and Brazelton (1980), similarly, assessed the rhythmic cycles of maternal and infant behavior by segmenting the interaction into monadic phases (combinations of behaviors that can then be scored along a continuum from negative to neutral to positive affect). A separate monadic phase score is then assigned to each member of the dyad for each second of the interaction, creating a time series for each member. An example of these rhythmic cycles of monadic phases can be seen in Figure 19.1.

Using still another system of coding mother–infant involvement, Beebe and Kronen (1985) conducted time-series analyses on behaviors ranging from inhibition of responsivity to high positive affect. They reported a mutual "tracking" or a process of the mother and infant moving in the same direction (positive to negative or the reverse) on the nature and intensity of their affective states. In another study on interpersonal rhythm matching Beebe and her colleagues (Beebe, Jaffe, Feldstein,

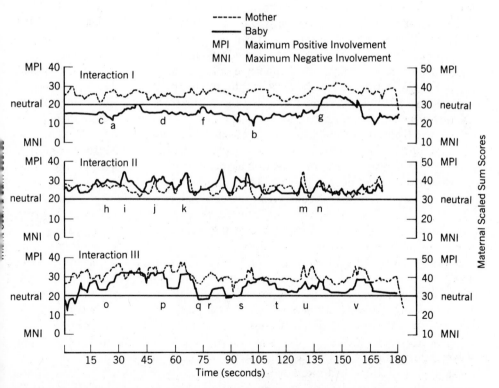

Figure 19.1. Scaled sum scores for each of the infant–mother dyads. The scores range from maximal positive involvement in the interaction through neutral to maximal negative involvement in the interaction for the infant and mother. From Tronick et al. (1980).

Mays, & Alson, 1985) reported that mothers and infants match (in reciprocal or compensatory fashion) the duration of each other's vocal and kinesic behaviors. They propose that "this matching of interpersonal timing provides one way for both partners to enter into each other's temporal world and feeling state" (p. 244). Vocal matching of parents and their young infants including matching of pitch and phonetic and melodic structure has also been demonstrated by M. Papoušek and colleagues (Papoušek, Papoušek, and Bornstein, 1985). And facial expression matching by mothers and their infants has been documented by Malatesta and Izard (1982) and termed *affect matching.*

Finally, in the most definitive demonstrations of the synchrony of mother–infant interactions, the coherence of mother and infant rhythms was studied by spectral and cross-spectral analyses (Gottman, Rose, & Mettetal, 1982; Lester et al., 1985). Coherence is an estimate of the correlation between two time series, providing a measure of the variance in one time series that is attributable to the variance in another time series at each frequency. Higher coherence in this case suggests greater synchrony between infant and maternal cycles of affective behavior. Using the monadic phase system of Tronick and colleagues (1980) Lester and his colleagues created time series for their infants and mothers. By 3 months of age synchrony of behavioral rhythms, as measured by coherence, was demonstrated for normal infant–mother interactions by Lester and colleagues (1985) and by 5 months the coherence had increased. Synchrony, however, was less evident in the interactions of preterm infant–mother dyads at both 3 and 5 months (Lester et al., 1985) Modeled waveforms for these interactions can be seen in Figure 19.2 and spectral densities for the term and preterm infants can be seen in Figure 19.3. Lester and colleagues (1985) suggest that their data provide evidence for behavioral periodicities, which may be biologically based, underlying mother–infant interaction and providing a temporal structure for the organization of cognitive and affective experience.

A series of studies have demonstrated the disturbances that occur during early interactions when the mother is unable to read her infant's signals (Goldberg, 1979) and provide optimal stimulation and arousal modulation (Field, 1982c). Interactions with high-risk infants provide a particularly challenging task for the mother. High-risk infants spend less time looking at their mothers and appear to enjoy their interactions less than normal infants. Their smiles and contingent vocalizations are less frequent and their frowns and cries more frequent than those of normal infants. The greater incidence of negative affective displays among these infants together with their elevated heart rate suggests that interactions may be stressful for high-risk infants and their mothers. In addition, maternal stimulation, infant gaze aversion, negative affect, and heart rate appear to be related. Elevated heart rate, gazing away, and negative affect of the infants may relate to an information overload and elevated arousal level deriving from excessive stimulation. In their natural attempts to elicit positive affect, mothers of high-risk infants appear to provide excessive stimulation and fail to modulate arousal as their infants become distressed. Interestingly, the heart rate curves of these mothers and infants paralleled each other during interactions, with increases in heart rate noted in both mothers and infants during stressful, disturbed interactions, and parallel decreases in heart rate during more harmonious interactions, suggestive of physiological attunement (Field, 1977, 1982a).

Although these studies suggest that infant gaze aversion, negative affect, and

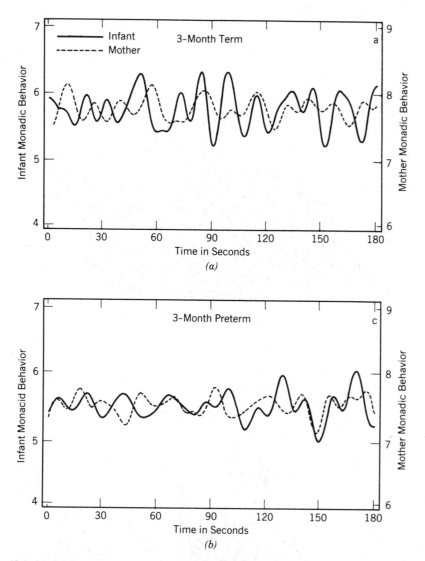

Figure 19.2. Modeled waveforms of social interaction rhythms: (*a*) social interaction rhythms at .022–.10 Hz in 3-month-old term infants and their mothers; (*b*) social interaction rhythms at .122–.10 Hz in 3-month-old preterm infants and their mothers. From Lester et al. (1985).

elevated heart rate may be related to mothers' excessive stimulation and failure to modulate arousal, other studies suggest that these mothers, nonetheless, may be more effective modulators of their infants' behavior than, for example, other family members and strangers (Field, 1983a). It is noteworthy, in this light, that Lester and colleagues (Lester, Hoffman, & Brazelton, 1982), in a study on the coherence of infant and adult behavioral and cardiac rhythms, demonstrated greater synchrony between those rhythms of the infant and mother than those of the infant and a stranger. This finding, they suggest, supports a biological basis for the rhythmic entrainment of both behavior and heart rate during the early dyadic interactions of mothers and infants.

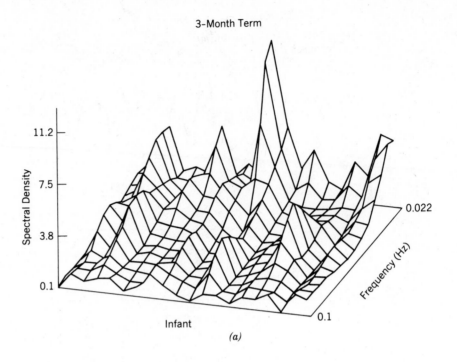

3-Month Term

(a)

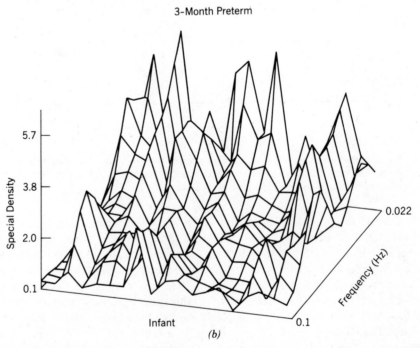

3-Month Preterm

(b)

Figure 19.3. Spectral densities: (*a*) by frequencies at .022–.10 Hz for each term infant at 3 months; (*b*) by frequencies at .022–.10 Hz for each preterm infant at 3 months. From Lester et al. (1985).

Some investigators have suggested that asynchrony in the interactions of high-risk infants and their mothers is related to the limited responsivity of these infants and the overstimulation by their mothers (Crnic et al., 1983; Field, 1977; Goldberg et al., 1980). Relationships between their behavior as neonates and their later interactive behavior suggest some continuity of the limited responsivity of high-risk infants (Field, 1979; Greene, Fox, & Lewis, 1983). Goldberg (1979) has maintained that the basic problem is the unreadability of the high-risk infants' signals. McGehee and Eckerman (1983) similarly suggest that the preterm infant is responsive but unreadable. In a study on the behavioral responses of preterm and term infants at the neonatal stage they noted that the two groups did not differ in their ability to orient visually and sustain en face gaze, but the preterm infants were unable to control erratic body movements and vocalizations and showed more frequent shifts in state (McGehee & Eckerman, 1983). Friedman and colleagues (Friedman, Jacobs, & Werthmann, 1982) have also reported that preterm infants as neonates fuss and cry more, are more difficult to soothe, and change state more frequently than full-term newborns. They continue to be fussier than full-term infants at 4 months (Field, 1979) and 8 months (Goldberg, 1979), and during later interactions the most frequently reported behaviors for these infants are withdrawal behaviors such as gaze aversion, squirming, and fussing, as if the infants are highly aroused, have difficulty modulating their own arousal, and are trying to terminate the interaction. These behaviors have been noted to persist across the first year of life (Crnic et al., 1983).

Tronick and his colleague Gianino (Gianino & Tronick, 1987) have developed an interesting model describing these averting behaviors as the infants' coping strategy for regulating the amount of stimulation they receive. Indeed, they would appear to be effective coping behaviors as they typically signal the mother to modify her stimulation or terminate the interaction. However, if high-risk infants' signals are more difficult to read (Goldberg, 1979), the mothers of those infants may have more difficulty modulating their stimulation.

The picture that emerges from these analyses of different types of interactions (feeding, face-to-face, and floor play) at different stages during the first 2 years of life among preterm infants and their parents is a vicious cycle of the infant being relatively inactive and unresponsive, the parent trying to engage the infant by being more and more active or stimulating, which in turn leads to more inactivity and unresponsivity on the part of the infant. Although the parent's activity appears to be directed at encouraging more activity or responsivity of the infant, this strategy is counterproductive inasmuch as it leads to less instead of more infant responsivity.

Other groups for which similar phenomena have been observed include the Down's syndrome infant and the child with cerebral palsy. Analyses of interactions between Down's syndrome infants and their mothers suggest that the infants engaged in less eye contact and initiated fewer interactions (Jones, 1980; McQuiston et al., 1980). Their mothers were simultaneously noted to be more active and directive during these play interactions. Similarly, cerebral palsied children have been noted to exhibit fewer interactive behaviors, and their mothers are more active and controlling during interactions (Kogan, 1980).

Several speculations have been offered for the frequently observed hyperactivity of the mothers of unresponsive infants labeled at risk due to perinatal complications and/or handicapping conditions (Field, 1980). The most vague interpretation suggests that the frustration of receiving minimal responses from the infant leads to a kind of aggressivity on the part of the mother. Another notion is that the mothers are more active to compensate for the relative inactivity of their infants, perhaps to keep some semblance of an interaction going. A third relates to the mother's wanting her child to perform like the child's agemates and attempting to encourage performance by more frequent modeling of behaviors. Still another interpretation is that the mothers view their infants as fragile and delayed and as a result tend to be overprotective. Overprotectiveness in the extreme is construed as overcontrolling behavior.

The last interpretation, that is, that the mothers may view their infants as fragile and delayed such that their preconceived notions about prematures may affect their behavior, receives some support from the rapidly growing literature on prematurity stereotyping. Frodi and colleagues (Frodi, Lamb, Leavitt, & Donovan, 1978), for example, found that parents reacted with a larger electrodermal response (implying greater arousal) and less sympathy to a videotape of a crying infant who was labeled premature than to a videotape of a crying infant labeled normal. Similarly, Stern and Hildebrandt (1984) found that infants labeled premature were rated more negatively by mothers than infants labeled full term after viewing a videotape of an infant. In still another study in which composite drawings were made of full-term and preterm faces (with the full-terms possessing proportionally wider eyes and rounder heads) the composite drawing of the full-terms evoked more favorable responses from adult judges (Maier, Holmes, Slaymaker, & Reich, 1984). Unfortunately, very few studies have been directed to the other hypotheses. Nonetheless, interventions have been mounted without understanding the dynamics and underlying mechanisms for these interactive disturbances.

That the infant's attentiveness and positive affect can be readily modulated by the behaviors of the mother is demonstrated by interaction coaching studies in which mothers have been requested to modify their behaviors (Clark & Seifer, 1983; Field, 1977; 1983a). The effect of a manipulation in which mothers were requested to imitate their infants' behaviors was that the mothers became less active and more attentive to their infants' cues of being under- or overaroused, and their infants became more attentive and responsive than they had been during spontaneous interactions. Corresponding decreases were noted in tonic heart rate (Field, 1977). Clark and Seifer (1983) also reported that maternal imitation of infant behavior was their most effective interaction coaching technique. Conversely, during an attention-getting manipulation in which mothers were asked to keep their infants' attention, mothers became less sensitive to their infants' behavioral cues, and their activity increased, as did infant gaze aversion and heart rate (Field, 1977). This manipulation was apparently aversive for both members of the dyad as manifested in roughly equivalent, parallel increases in tonic heart rate for both the infants and their mothers. The interpretation made of these data was that high-risk infants may have limited information-processing and/or arousal modulation abilities, thus requiring more frequent breaks in the conversation to process information and modulate arousal. The mother is walking a fine line with these infants in determining the optimal level of stimulation and the points at which arousal modulation is needed. Optimal levels of stimulation may differ for these infants, and they may respond to a narrower range of stimulation, creating the more difficult task for parents of fine-tuning the intensity as well as the amount of stimulation and arousal modulation required by their infants.

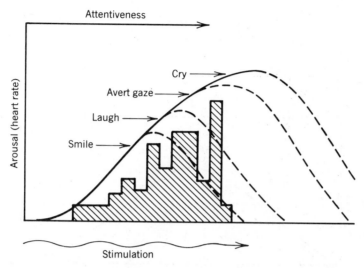

Figure 19.4. A schematic illustration of the progression of infant and mother behavior during game playing. The X axes depict sustained attention of the infant and variation or modulation of stimulation by the mother. The Y axis depicts heart rate. Within the figure the solid ascending curve represents increasing heart rate and the dotted descending curves represent decreasing heart rate. The hatched bars represent variation in the mother's use of stimulus modalities or varying intensity of stimulation.

A schematic illustration of the progression of behaviors during mother–infant interactions can be seen in Figure 19.4. Heart rate is depicted as progressively increasing prior to smiling, laughing, gaze-aversion and crying behaviors. As these behaviors occur, the level of maternal stimulation decreases and heart rate peaks and then gradually returns to baseline. Thus a combination of the infant's affective displays signaling the mother and the mother's diminution of stimulation appears to modulate the arousal level of the infant. If the infant is less able to modulate arousal or the mother is not responsive to the affective cues by modulating her stimulation, the infant's aversive threshold may be exceeded and the infant may avert its gaze and essentially terminate the interaction. Differences between the behavioral curves of normal and high-risk infant–mother dyads are depicted in Figure 19.5.

Determining the nature of optimal stimulation and arousal modulation in complex streams of behavior such as interactions is difficult at best. However, manipulations of interactions such as asking mothers to imitate their infants' behaviors, to silence during infant gaze aversion, and to simplify their behaviors by repetition appear to sensitize mothers to their infants' gaze and affective signals and thereby seem to diminish infant gaze aversion, heart rate, and crying as well as effect increases in attentiveness and positive affective displays such as smiling and laughing (Clark & Seifer, 1983; Field, 1983). Thus as the mother and infant become attuned to each other their interactions become more harmonious. It appears, then, that, even with difficult, high-risk infants whose attentiveness occurs less often and whose affective displays are less frequent and more difficult to read, mothers can be taught ways of providing optimal stimulation and arousal modulation.

Other demonstrations of the critical nature of the mother's provision of optimal stimulation and arousal modulation are provided by studies on interaction pertur-

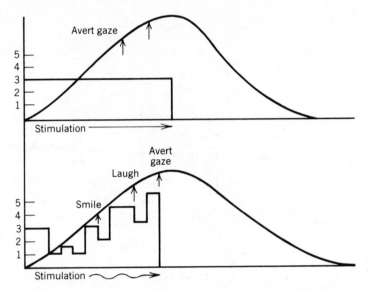

Figure 19.5. The hypothesized differences between the behavioral curves of normal and high-risk infant–mother dyads. The upper curve represents the hypothetical high-risk dyad with the mother stimulating her infant at a level sufficient to attain her infant's attention but then sustaining that level rather than modulating stimulation during infant gaze aversion and crying. The lower curve depicts the normal infant–mother dyad, showing varied or modulated stimulation by the mother as a function of the infant's affective signals and a cessation of behavior at infant gaze aversion with the infant never reaching a crying state.

bations. A frequently studied interaction perturbation is that of the mother's still face (Fogel, Diamond, Langhorst, & Demos, 1982; Stoller & Field, 1982; Tronick, Als, Adamson, Wise, & Brazelton, 1978). In this paradigm, the mother is asked to remain still faced and the infant's responses are recorded. As the mother goes still faced the infant makes several overtures to get the mother to reinstate her natural behavior. When these overtures are not responded to by the mother (she remains still faced), the infant ultimately ceases attempts to reengage her and becomes "depressed" looking. The same kinds of infant behaviors occur when the mother is face to face with her infant but apparently talking to another adult via a mirror reflection arrangement (Murray & Trevarthen, 1985; Trevarthen, 1979). Similarly, in a procedure in which the mother is asked to "look depressed," the infant first attempts to elicit normal behaviors from the mother, then protests her "depressed" behavior by fussing, and finally looks "depressed" and withdrawn (Cohn and Tronick, 1983). Thus with the mother who is not normally depressed but is invited to look depressed, the infant becomes agitated and makes several attempts to reinstate her normal behavior. If, however, the mother is normally "depressed" and is invited to "look depressed" (Field, 1984b), neither the mother's nor the infant's behavior changes across the two situations. It appears that in this sample of depressed mothers their infants had already adapted to their depressed behavior and, indeed, appeared already to have developed their own "depressed" style of interacting.

In another version of the still-face paradigm a brief period of separation was added (Fogel et al., 1982). In this study by Fogel and his colleagues the mothers and their 3-month-old infants first engaged in normal, spontaneous interactions. The mother then left the interaction area and, following a brief separation, returned and emitted a still face. Infants appeared to be distressed by both of these situations. In the case of the mothers' departure the infants extended their arms in their mothers' direction, showed distress brow expressions, and cried, whereas during the stranger departure infants were more likely to yawn. Thus the infants appeared more aroused by the mother separation. In a similar separation study (Stoller & Field, 1982) analyses of heart rate revealed that the mothers' brief departures and still faces were accompanied by significant heart rate accelerations. This manifestation of arousal during disturbed interactions and brief separations is consistent with the model that mothers provide infants optimal levels of stimulation and arousal modulation. In each of these situations, the still-faced mother interaction, the interaction with depressed mothers, and the brief separation of the infant from its mother, the mother is not available to the infant, either in her role of providing optimal stimulation or in her role of attempting to modulate her infant's arousal level. Thus it is not surprising that the infant becomes affectively disturbed and behaviorally and physiologically disorganized.

The Special Case of Maternal Depression

Less favorable affective development has been reported for children reared by depressed mothers as opposed to mothers with other diagnoses or normal mothers (Cytryn, McKnew, Bartko, Lamour, & Hamovitt, 1982; Sameroff & Seifer, 1983). In addition, relationships have been reported between early interaction disturbances and later childhood problems (Bakeman & Brown, 1980; Field, Dempsey, & Shuman, 1983). Despite these apparent relationships, there are very few studies in the literature on early interactions between depressed mothers and their infants. Several studies have featured mothers (e.g., teenage mothers, low-income black mothers, and Haitian immigrant mothers) who appeared to be "depressed"; that is, their activity level and affect were depressed relative to those of normal mothers. However, they would not be considered depressed using standard depression inventories or DSM-III criteria, and efforts to alter their activity level and affective responsivity using interaction coaching techniques have been relatively successful.

An attempt has been made to simulate maternal depression by asking mothers to "look depressed" during interactions with their infants (Cohn & Tronick, 1983). Although it is not clear that their infants responded to their "looking depressed" in the same way that infants would respond to naturally depressed mothers, the interactions in which mothers were instructed to "look depressed" resulted in disorganized, distressed behavior on the part of the infants. During this manipulation the infants more frequently looked wary, averted their gaze, protested, and attempted to elicit responses from the mothers, much as infants interacting with still-faced mothers attempt to reinstate a normal interaction (see Fig. 19.6). In the Cohn and Tronick (1983) study the infants' distressed behavior continued even after the mothers resumed their normal behavior. Although this study was intended to be a simulation of interactions between depressed mothers and infants, it is possible that infants of naturally depressed mothers may be accustomed to their mothers' behavior and may behave very differently. Thus a follow-up to this study was conducted in which infants of naturally depressed mothers (postpartum depression) were compared to infants of nondepressed mothers who were invited to "look depressed" (Field, 1984b).

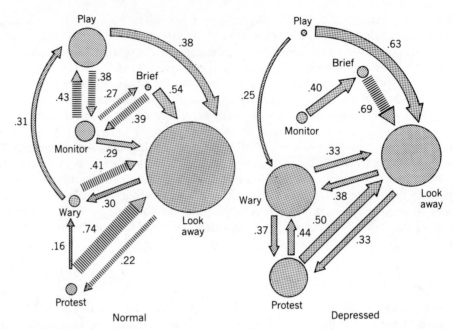

Figure 19.6. State transition diagrams for the depressed and normal conditions. The relative proportion of infant time spent in each state is indicated by size of the circle representing that state. The thickness of the arrows represents the relative size of the conditional probabilities of the event sequence transitions. Striped arrows indicate those transitions for which conditional and unconditional probabilities do not significantly differ, $p < .05$. Only the highest conditional probabilities from each state are shown. The numbers next to the arrows indicate the exact size of conditional probabilities. From Cohn & Tronick (1983).

In this study, the Beck Depression Inventory (Beck, Ward, Mendelson, Mock, & Erbaugh, 1961) was used to identify mothers experiencing postpartum depression (Field, 1984b). The face-to-face interactions of these "depressed" mothers and their infants were then compared to the interactions of nondepressed mothers and their infants. In addition, the infants' and mothers' baseline and interaction heart rates were recorded, and an actometer was attached to the infant for a measure of activity level. Three face-to-face play interactions were recorded, including a spontaneous interaction, an interaction in which the mother was asked to "look depressed," and a "reunion" interaction in which the mother was again asked to behave naturally.

During the "depressed-looking" situation versus the spontaneous interaction the infants of nondepressed mothers versus those of depressed mothers were more disturbed, showing more frequent negative facial expressions, protests, and wary behavior, and higher activity levels and heart rate (see Table 19.1). Thus the request to "look depressed" significantly altered the behavior of nondepressed mothers and their infants, but the behavior of naturally depressed mothers and their infants was not affected by this manipulation.

The data on the nondepressed mothers and their infants support those of Cohn and Tronick (1983), suggesting that these infants noticed the change in their mothers' affect and modified their own affective behavior in response to their mothers "looking depressed." As in the Cohn and Tronick (1983) study much of the infants' behavior appeared to be an attempt to reinstate a normal interaction; failing this,

TABLE 19.1. Infant and Mother Behaviors During Spontaneous, "Depressed," and "Reunion" Interactions (Mean (M), Repeated measures (R), and Interaction (I) effects).* From Field (1984b).

		Nondepressed			Depressed			Effect and p Level
		Spontaneous	Depressed	Reunion	Spontaneous	Depressed	Reunion	
Infant Behaviors								
Positive facial expressions	(frequency)	8.5_a	4.0_b	4.5_b	3.0_c	2.0_c	2.0_c	M^1I^1
Negative facial expressions	(frequency)	1.5_a	8.0_b	6.5_b	5.5_b	5.0_b	4.5_b	I^1
Vocalizations	(frequency)	7.0_a	3.0_b	3.5_b	2.0_c	1.5_c	1.5_c	M^2I^1
Looking away (% time)		21_a	48_b	39_b	38_b	32_b	33_b	I^2
Protesting (% time)		5_a	42_b	37_b	15_c	16_c	17_c	M^2I^4
Looking wary (% time)		7_a	36_b	31_b	11_c	14_c	13_c	M^3I^4
Activity		17_a	26_b	23_b	9_c	11_c	12_c	M^2I^1
Heart rate		148_a	159_b	154_b	140_a	142_a	145_a	M^1I^1
Mother Behaviors								
Positive facial expressions	(frequency)	21.5_a	2.0_b	16.5_a	5.0_b	4.0_b	3.5_b	M^2I^4
Negative facial expressions	(frequency)	2.5_a	8.0_b	3.0_a	9.0_b	11.5_b	10.5_b	M^1I^1
Vocalizations	(frequency)	53_a	21_b	48_a	22_b	26_b	27_b	M^2I^2
Looking at infant (% time)		93_a	89_b	95_a	58_b	65_b	62_b	M^3
Tactile/kinesthetic stimulation (% time)		39_a	11_b	33_a	21_c	11_b	18_c	M^2R^2
Heart rate		79_a	87_b	81_a	71_c	73_c	74_c	M^1I^1

*Means bearing different subscripts (a, b, and c) are different at $p < .05$ or less; SDs can be obtained from the author.

[1] $p < .05$
[2] $p < .01$
[3] $p < .005$
[4] $p < .001$

their distressed behavior (looking away, looking wary, and protesting) carried over into their subsequent "reunion" interaction. These data indicate a carryover of affective behavior or the establishment of a "mood" in the infant. That this may be an anxiety-provoking situation for both the nondepressed mothers and their infants is suggested by their elevated activity level and corresponding increases in heart rate during the "looking depressed" interaction situation.

In contrast, the naturally depressed mothers' behaviors did not appear to change across the three situations. Paralleling the unchanging behavior of the depressed mothers was the unchanging behavior of their infants. The infants of naturally depressed mothers behaved less positively during the spontaneous interaction and showed little change during the "looking depressed" interaction. These data confirm the speculation that infants of naturally depressed mothers may be accustomed to their mothers' depressed behavior and thus may not act distressed when their mothers are invited to "look depressed." The lower heart rate of the depressed mothers and their infants may be mediated by their lower activity levels, as in somatic coupling of activity and heart rate (Obrist, 1981). Lower heart rate has also been associated with situations of helplessness or passive coping (Obrist et al., 1974), and has been attributed to decreased sympathetic adrenergic activity or increased parasympathetic activation and vagal tone (McCabe & Schneiderman, 1985). These data are reminiscent of infant primate studies in which infants do or do not have control in stressful situations (Reite, Short, Seiler, & Pauley, 1981). During brief periods of stress infant monkeys typically show agitated behavior and physiological arousal. During more prolonged stress their activity and physiology were depressed. In the former situation, the primate infant has been said to be actively coping and in the latter, passively coping. The behavior of the infants of depressed mothers versus nondepressed mothers in this study suggests a passive–active coping behavior contrast. The behavior of the infants of depressed mothers appeared to "mirror" the behavior of their mothers, and suggests that by experiencing frequent lack of control during early interactions they may have developed a passive coping, depressed style of interacting. Their "depressed mood" persisted across interactions and may be a well-established defensive posture that may appear in situations regardless of the stimulation provided.

Very little is known about the genetic transmission of depression in families, and genetic susceptibility cannot be ruled out as a possible origin of this behavior, particularly in light of the Sameroff and Seifer (1983) data suggesting that infants of depressed mothers are at unusually high risk for developing depression. An alternative interpretation is that depressed affect may emerge in very young infants as a function of their early interactions with postpartum depressed mothers. Whether the depressed affect of these infants derives from their "mirroring" their mothers' behaviors or simply results from minimal stimulation provided by the mothers is an empirical question. Nonetheless, these data suggest that depression in the mother may be transmitted to her offspring during their very early interactions.

Still another possibility is that these infants were "depressed" prior to experiencing early interactions with their mothers. In another study of this kind mothers who were experiencing postpartum depression but who had also been identified during pregnancy ultrasound examination as being depressed prepartum were filmed interacting with their infants (Field, Sandberg, Garcia, Vega-Lahr, Goldstein, & Guy, 1985). Following delivery their neonates were given a Brazelton neonatal assessment (Brazelton, 1973) and were noted to have "depressed" activity levels and responsivity to social stimulation, not unlike infants of mothers with elevated monoamine oxidase levels (Sostek et al., 1981). At 3 months after delivery, the mothers who had been depressed during pregnancy received scores meeting the criteria for depression on the Beck Depression Inventory and showed flat affect and lower activity levels as well as less contingent responsivity during their interactions with their infants (see Table 19.2). Their infants showed fewer contented expressions and more fussiness as compared to a control group of infants of nondepressed mothers. Thus it is not clear whether the infants' diminished activity level and affective responsivity during their 3-month interactions were merely a behavioral style that persisted from birth or one that largely developed from prolonged exposure to the depressed behavior modeled by their mothers or from minimal stimulation provided by their mothers.

A more intensive longitudinal study across pregnancy and early infancy would be required to assess the origins of this "depressed" behavior in young infants, and a comparison of the infants' behaviors during interactions with their own mothers versus other mothers might indicate whether the depressed affect of these infants

TABLE 19.2.   Mean Rating Scale Scores and *p* Levels Based on Bonferroni *t* Tests (df = 23)

	Depressed	Control	*p* Level
Infant Interaction Behaviors			
State	1.5	2.6	.01
Physical activity	1.6	2.5	.01
Head orientation	2.0	2.2	n.s.
Gaze behavior	2.1	2.3	n.s.
Facial expressions	1.4	2.1	.05
Vocalizations	1.5	1.6	n.s.
Fussiness	1.3	2.2	.01
Summary rating	1.6	2.2	.05
Mother Interaction Behaviors			
State	1.6	2.4	.05
Physical activity	1.8	2.7	.01
Head orientation	2.4	2.5	n.s.
Gaze behavior	2.3	2.5	n.s.
Facial expressions	1.7	2.4	.05
Vocalizations	1.8	1.9	n.s.
Silence during infant gaze aversion	1.5	1.3	n.s.
Imitative behaviors	1.4	2.2	.05
Contingent responsivity	1.5	2.3	.05
Game playing	1.4	2.2	.05
Summay rating	1.7	2.3	.05
Questionnaire Ratings			
CCTI-Emotionality	20	13	.01
EASI-Emotionality	18	12	.01
Childrearing Attitudes	05	01	.05
Locus of Control	28	15	.01
State Anxiety	38	29	.05
Trait Anxiety	51	28	.01
Beck Depression	22	04	.01

is specific to interactions with depressed adults or whether they have already developed a "depressed" style of interacting. Nonetheless, the importance of studying the effects of maternal depression on infant affect is highlighted simply by the incidence of the problem, in the range of 10–12 percent for postpartum depression and 40–70 percent for postpartum blues, with residual effects after 1 year in approximately 4 percent of mothers and a recurrence rate reported at 20–30 percent (Davidson, 1972; Grundy & Roberts, 1975).

The Special Case of Maternal Deprivation Syndrome

A similar constellation of "depressed" behaviors has been reported for the *maternal deprivation syndrome* or the mothers of nonorganic failure-to-thrive infants (Evans, Reinhart, & Succop, 1972; Pollitt, Eichler, & Chan, 1975). Nonorganic failure to thrive has generally been defined as growth retardation with no clear organic etiology and has been attributed to inadequate maternal stimulation (Powell, Brasel, & Blizzard, 1967). Although the maternal deprivation hypothesis has been challenged (Rutter, 1972), investigators continue to describe the syndrome as an interactive process between depressed mothers and affectively unresponsive infants (Drotar, 1975; Ferholt & Provence, 1976; Fischoff, Whitten, & Pettit, 1971; Roberts & Horner, 1979; Shapiro, Fraiberg, & Adelson, 1976). Despite this attribution, there are no published studies on the interactive behaviors of these mothers and infants. Instead, the studies of these dyads have focused on the behaviors of the infants without recording the simultaneous behaviors of the mothers or the behaviors of the mothers without reporting those of the infants.

Descriptive studies of the nonorganic failure-to-thrive infant reveal several behaviors that might readily lead to interactive difficulties including listlessness, minimal smiling, diminished vocalizations, and lack of cuddliness (Leonard, Rhymes, & Solnit, 1966; Powell & Low, 1983). In a study of 12 infants 20 months old the play behaviors of failure-to-thrive infants were described as "emotional blunting" with a decreased range of both positive and negative affective expression (Gaensbauer, 1982). Gaensbauer notes:

> [Their] affective responses appear to be less flexible, less sensitive to environmental events, less prompt in their mobilization, and with a greater tendency for negative emotional states to endure beyond the precipitating stimulus events. The high sadness ratings throughout indicated a skewing of the affective system in the direction of inhibition and withdrawal, possibly representing early vulnerability to depressive moods. (Gaensbauer, 1982 p. 165.)

Similarly, the mothers of failure-to-thrive infants are invariably described as "depressed" or affectively unresponsive. For example, in an observational study by Pollitt and colleagues (1975), mothers were noted to direct less physical and verbal stimulation as well as less affectionate behaviors (kissing, caressing) toward their nonorganic failure-to-thrive infants, and showed significantly fewer instances of positive affect. In another study by Alfasi (1982) the mother of a 3-month-old failure-to-thrive infant was noted to provide extremely high levels of stimulation that were described as intrusive overstimulation resulting in interactional asynchrony; this mother also showed extremely rare positive affect.

One of the reasons nonorganic failure-to-thrive has been labeled the maternal deprivation syndrome is that the infant's growth retardation is often reversed during hospitalization when the infant is reputedly provided more adequate stimulation than is routinely received in the home environment. Pathological disturbances in sleeping, eating, and elimination and autoerotic and self-harming behaviors frequently noted in these infants (Evans et al., 1972; Pollitt & Eichler, 1976; Powell et al., 1967) typically disappear during hospitalization, especially the problems of food intake and weight gain. This association has led some investigators to hypothesize the existence of a physiological pathway whereby emotional deprivation affects the neuroendocrine system regulating growth (Powell et al., 1967). Although the growth hormone data are inconclusive, some researchers have documented relationships between behavioral change and growth gains. In a study comparing normal and organic and nonorganic failure-to-thrive infants, the last group of infants were noted to prefer distal social stimulation and play with inanimate objects as opposed to proximal stimulation such as touching, cuddling, and face-to-face interaction early in their hospitalization (Rosenn, Loeb, & Jura, 1980). Interestingly, in those infants who gained weight during the first week or two of hospitalization, the most substantial weight gain occurred within 1–2 days following a shift to a preference for proximal stimulation. Paradoxically, this effect was not associated with increased caloric consumption.

In a similar study (Goldstein & Field, 1985), the best predictor of weight gain during the final week of hospitalization of nonorganic failure-to-thrive infants was the infants' affective responsivity to stimulation during the preceding week. Because the assessments of the infants' responsivity to social stimulation were conducted at frequent intervals over the course of these investigations, the stimulation associated with the assessments may have served as a form of intervention facilitating weight gain. Touching and handling have been noted to enhance growth in human infants (Field et al., 1986) and growth hormone in rat pups (Schanberg, Evoniuk, & Kuhn, 1984). However, the relationships between stimulation and the constellation of affective, sleeping, and eating behaviors in these infants remain obscure. An unexpected finding in the Goldstein and Field (1985) study poses an interesting paradox. Approximately two-thirds of the nonorganic failure-to-thrive infants gained weight. These infants were from deprived environments and thus, perhaps not surprisingly, gained weight following the more adequate stimulation received in the hospital. The remaining third, however, were from less depriving environments, were affectively responsive during the stimulation assessment conducted upon the infants' admission to the hospital, but became less responsive to stimulation and lost weight during hospitalization. It is conceivable that these infants experienced hospital stimulation as less adequate than maternal stimulation and lost weight, much as occurs with normal infants when separated from their mothers.

The similarities between the affective behavior of depressed mothers and their infants and that of failure-to-thrive infants and their mothers are striking. Both groups of dyads have diminished activity levels and "depressed" affect. Although the failure-to-thrive infants also experience disturbances in vegetative functions including sleeping, eating, and elimination, these problems have not been studied in infants of depressed mothers. In addition, these affective and vegetative disturbances are noted to be persistent or chronic in the failure-to-thrive infants. While chronicity of depressed affect has not been studied in infants of depressed mothers, it is noteworthy that these infants are at high risk for developing childhood depression (Sameroff & Seifer, 1983). While very little is known about either of these groups, the depressed affect of infants of depressed mothers and the depressed affect and vegetative disturbances of the failure-to-thrive infant, nonetheless, suggest a potential model for infant depression. Although sleep studies and biochemical assays have yet to be conducted with these samples, the infants of depressed mothers manifest affective disturbances and the failure-to-thrive infants mimic both the affective and vegetative disturbances noted in childhood depression. The constellation of problems reported for failure-to-thrive infants and infants of depressed mothers are also strikingly similar to those observed in primate and human infants experiencing early separations.

Affective Disturbances Related to Early Separation Experiences

Anaclitic depression has been observed in young infants following separation from their mothers (Spitz, 1946). Bowlby (1969) and others (Robertson & Robertson, 1971) have described the separation experience as a biphasic process of protest followed by despair in infants and young children. Although these descriptions are based on anecdotal case studies, more systematic separation studies have been conducted with young nonhuman primates by several investigators (Harlow & Harlow, 1965; Levine & Coe, 1985; Reite et al., 1981; Suomi, Collins & Harlow, 1976). These primate studies as well as studies on prolonged separations of human infants (Field, 1986) and preschoolers (Field & Reite, 1984) confirm the biphasic response to separation with a period of agitation followed by a period of depression.

Infant pigtail and bonnet monkeys monitored by Reite and his colleagues (Reite, et al., 1981; Reite & Snyder, 1982) via surgically implanted telemetry during mother–infant separations generally reveal behavioral agitation followed by depression during the separation period. Shortly after the separation, infants exhibited an agitation reaction with increased motor activity and frequent distress vocalizations. Depressed behaviors typically emerged shortly thereafter and persisted for the period of separation. The infants moved more slowly than normal, and their play behavior was diminished. Sleep disturbances were characterized by decreases in rapid eye movement (REM) sleep as well as an increase in the number of arousals and time spent awake. The behavioral agitation reaction that occurred immediately after separation was accompanied by increases in both heart rate and body temperature followed by decreases to below baseline (Reite, Short, Kaufman, Stynes, & Pauley, 1978).

In a study of human infants and toddlers (Field, 1986) agitated behavior and physiology were noted during the period of their mothers' hospitalization, and these behaviors were depressed following the mothers' return from the hospital. In this study, the infants' and toddlers' behavioral and physiological responses to separation were monitored before, during, and after their mothers' hospitalization for the birth of a sibling. During these three periods, play sessions were videotaped simultaneously with activity level and heart rate monitoring. In addition, nighttime sleep was time-lapse videotaped, and the parents were administered questionnaires on changes in their infants' and toddlers' behaviors. Increases in fussiness, activity level, heart rate, night wakings, and nighttime crying characterized the hospital period as one of agitation (see Table 19.3). Following the mother's return, decreases

TABLE 19.3. Means for Play and Sleep Behaviors of Infants and Toddlers Prior to, During, and Following Their Mothers' Hospitalization

Behaviors	Baseline	Separation	Reunion	p Level
Play Behaviors (% time sample unit)				
Smiling	9	2	3	.01
Animation	22	15	16	.05
Aggression	2	8	7	.05
Fussiness	15	22	21	.05
Activity level (actometer)	26	35	21	.05
Heart rate (BPM)	117	131	110	.05
Sleep Behaviors				
Total sleep time (minutes)	580	645	575	.05
Latency to sleep (minutes)	28	21	19	.05
Number of night wakings	1	5	4	.05
Crying (minutes)	8	15	14	.05

were noted in positive affect, activity level, heart rate, and active sleep, suggestive of depression. A number of changes noted by the parents were a greater than chance occurrence of clinging and aggressive behaviors, changes in eating and toileting, and sleep disturbances and illnesses that persisted following the mother's return from the hospital.

The infants were clearly agitated by the separation from their mothers, even though they visited them at the hospital during this period and were cared for by their fathers. The depression following the return of their mothers from the hospital may have related to the depressed affect, lesser animation, and exhausted behavior noted in their mothers during this period, which together with the arrival of a new sibling seemed to alter the relationship previously experienced by the mothers and infants. Examples of the infants' disturbance regarding this altered relationship were provided by the parents' comments that the infant, for example, "remained close to the parent," "wanted to be rocked and held," "reverted to baby talk, whining and screaming for attention." "destroyed his playroom," and "threatened to run a truck across the baby's head." In addition, increased fantasy play among the infants and toddlers, interpreted as an act of coping on their part, was characterized by a number of themes that involved aggression against the new sibling, for example, knocking the building blocks onto the new baby.

This biphasic increase followed by a decrease in activity level of the infants and toddlers parallels the sequence of agitation followed by depression reported for young primate separations (Reite et al., 1981). Elevated tonic heart rate during the mother's hospitalization and depressed heart rate following her return may have been mediated by the activity level changes, as in somatic coupling of activity and heart rate (Obrist, 1981). Elevated activity level and heart rate have also been attributed to activation of the sympathetic adrenergic system (Breese et al., 1973). Increased night wakings and crying during the mother's hospitalization are also suggestive of this being an agitated phase for the infants. Longer periods of sleep and more prolonged periods of deep sleep during this phase may be a manifestation of conservation–withdrawal noted to follow physical or emotional stress in young infants (Emde, Harmon, Metcalf, Koenig, & Wagonfeld, 1971; Engel & Schmale, 1972).

The decrease in activity level, depressed heart rate, and shorter periods of active sleep together with depressed or flat affect following the mother's return may be manifestations of depression, a period we have alluded to as one of experienced helplessness on the part of the infant. The decrease in active sleep periods during what appears to be a depressed phase may be a homeostatic coping mechanism, not unlike the infants' and toddlers' more active coping with the stress by increased fantasy play. Depressed activity and heart rate are commonly reported in helpless and passive coping situations, for example, in an avoidance task in which human subjects have no control, a situation in which beta-adrenergic influences are minimal (Obrist et al., 1974). Bradycardia, associated with situations of helplessness, has also been attributed to parasympathetic activitation or vagal tone (McCabe & Schneiderman, 1985). The arrival of a new sibling, a less active, tired mother, and changes in the infants' and toddlers' play interactions may be viewed by them as situations over which they have very little control. Depressed behavior may have been exacerbated in these infants by the arrival of the new sibling and an altered parent–infant relationship.

The primate and human infants may become agitated during separation from the mother due to the loss of an important source of stimulation and arousal modulation. Young monkeys and infants are noted to turn to their mothers for stimulation as well as for comfort in the face of arousing or stressful situations (Ainsworth, 1967; Bowlby, 1969). Although Reite and his colleagues had speculated that bonnet infants would fare better under separation stress than pigtail infants because the bonnet infants are typically adopted by aunts in the social group, the bonnet infants also showed agitation despite being adopted. Similarly, it has been suggested that the human infant may tolerate temporary separation if the father is actively involved and visits to the mother in the hospital are possible (Legg, Sherick, & Wadland, 1974). Yet the infants in the Field (1986) separation study had the advantage of both father involvement and mother visits, but nonetheless were distressed during the hospitalization. Adoptive aunts (in the case of bonnet monkeys) and fathers of human infants may not be as effective as mothers in modulating arousal. Indeed, fathers are consistently noted to engage in more arousing games with their infants (Clarke-Stewart, 1978; Field, 1978, 1981; Lamb, 1975; Parke, 1979; Yogman, 1981).

Heightened levels of arousal may stimulate the sympathetic adrenergic system resulting in agitated behavior, a behavioral complex that is typically associated with active coping, in this case active coping to recall the mother. The emergence of depression as the separation continues may relate to a number of factors. Depression is typically accompanied by increased parasympathetic activation or increases in vagal tone (McCabe & Schneiderman, 1985). This may be a homeostatic mechanism offsetting the sympathetic arousal or agitation in the absence of effective arousal modulation, or it may result from inadequate amounts of stimulation and limited beta-adrenergic activity. Just as the aunts and fathers may be less effective at modulating arousal, they may provide less optimal amounts and types of stimulation by virtue of their lesser familiarity with the infants' stimulation needs. Still another possibility is that the hypothalamic–pituitary adrenocortical system is activated during helpless or passive coping situations (McCabe & Schneiderman, 1985). The monkey infant who fails to recall the mother may experience helplessness just as the human infant who is confronted with an altered relationship due to the arrival of the new sibling may experience helplessness.

Depression may persist following the return of the mother because the mother and/or infant has changed in some way, thus altering the previous relationship. The separations of young primate and human infants are often accompanied by behavior changes that persist even following reunions. These data suggest that separation may be a sufficient condition for behavioral disorganization, but not a necessary condition. In studies by Reite (1983), alterations of the mother–infant relationship (by placing a vest on the mother, with or without holes for sucking, or by the addition of the mother's new baby to the group) induced behavioral and physiological depression, thus highlighting the importance of changes in their relationship independent of separation. The status of the relationship upon reunion may be as important as the separation per se. Changes in the individuals or changes in their relationship may preclude their being in tune with each other upon reunion.

Data on pigtail infants suggest that, although heart rate and arrhythmia values tended to return to baseline following reunion with the mother, the altered cardiac activity persisted for some infants (Seiler, Cullen, Zimmerman, & Reite, 1979). In another study on bonnet monkey infants (Reite & Snyder, 1982), persistent decreases in heart rate and body temperature were noted following reunion with the mother, "possibly reflecting a disturbance in the mother–infant relationship secondary to the mothers having come into estrus during the period of separation" (p. 118). As the authors suggested, "the infant was in a sense reacting physiologically to the persistent disruption of the mother–infant attachment bond, even though the mother was physically present" (p. 118). The mother's being in estrus or returning with a new infant would conceivably alter the previous mother–infant relationship. In still another study by Reite and his colleagues (Reite, 1983), the mother was noted to reject her infant upon reunion, as she very busily groomed other members of the social group in a reputed attempt to reinstate herself in the dominance hierarchy. It was only after a few days of grooming activity that the mother redirected her attention to her infant. The infant's physiology remained depressed during that stressful reunion period even in the presence of the mother.

Similarly, the infants in the Field (1986) separation study remained depressed following the return of their mothers, and this depression was attributed to exhaustion in the mother and an altered relationship between the mother and child during their play together. Thus infants may remain depressed following reunions with their mothers because of temporary disequilibrium in their relationships. Separation may be a sufficient condition for eliciting affective disturbances and disorganized behavior, but not a necessary condition. Affective disturbances may appear even in the presence of an attachment object if the members of the relationship are not in tune with each other.

Thus the effects of separation on primate and human infants appear to be similar even though the context in which the separations of human infants was studied inevitably confounded separation with an altered mother–infant relationship resulting from the arrival of a new sibling. That confound, however, revealed that it is not necessarily separation per se that contributes to the child's depression but a missing source of stimulation and arousal modulation for the infant both during the separation and following their reunion. That separation per se does not necessarily lead to depression is also highlighted by studies in which infants and toddlers were separated from close peers to attend new classes (Field, Vega-Lahr, & Jagadish, 1984) or new schools (Field, 1984a). Aside from highlighting the similarity between the stress associated with parent–child and close peer separations, these studies revealed that the separation from a familiar group of playmates, which is normally stressful, can be ameliorated by transferring close peers together, the close friends serving as a buffer for the separation stress.

As we have hypothesized elsewhere (Field, 1986), a close relationship, whether between parent and offspring or between peers, develops as the behavioral and physiological systems of the two become attuned to each other. Each partner provides meaningful stimulation for the other and has a modulating influence on the other's arousal level leading to a synchrony of their behavioral and physiological rhythms. Separation or a change in the relationship leads to behavioral and physiological disorganization because of the loss of an important source of stimulation and arousal modulation and behavioral and physiological synchrony. Hofer (1984) has advanced a similar model to interpret the effects of separation experiences on a very different species, the rat pup. He, too, maintains that the tranditional Bowlby theory, suggesting that separation stress derives from a disruption of the attachment bond, is circular reasoning and does not explain "what it is about maternal separation that gives it such an impact on the developing infant" (Hofer, 1984, p. 184). While Hofer's independent development of a similar theory from a different data base lends strength to a model of this kind, Hofer's term *maternal regulation* may be too strong for the case of the human infant. Instead the terms *modulation* and *attunement* seem more appropriate inasmuch as these terms imply some adjustment by the mother to the infant's endogenous rhythms, a reciprocal process, rather than a controlling, regulating process or an imposition of the mother's rhythms on those of her infant.

In a study that assessed the attunement hypothesis (Reite & Capitanio, 1985), physiological rhythms were monitored in two peer-reared pigtail infants prior to and during separation as well as during the period following reunion. After subtracting the effects of circadian rhythmicity in both the heart rate and body temperature of each of the animals, the heart rate and body temperature rhythms of one monkey were correlated with those of the other. But the monkey's rhythms were correlated with each other only during baseline and reunion. An asynchrony of their rhythms occurred during separation. Other rhythms such as cortisol cycles have been noted to be synchronized in close child–adult relationships and desynchronized during separations (Lundberg, de Chateau, Winberg, & Frankenhaeuser, 1981; Montagner, Restoin, & Henry, 1982). Separation-induced disorganization of rhythms in infants may be even more pronounced because their behavioral and physiological rhythms are developmentally less mature and more dependent on external modulators.

To return to our original thesis, then, the infant's affective responsivity (both behavioral and physiological) develops in the context of an interactive relationship with the mother (care giver). The mother serves as a modulator (zeitgeber) in providing adequate stimulation, arousal modulation, and the kind of regulation needed for the development of organized behavioral patterns and physiological rhythms. If the mother (caregiver) is affectively unavailable or unresponsive (as in the depressed mother or maternal deprivation syndrome), or if the infant is separated from the mother, behavioral and physiological disorganization will invariably ensue, manifested by disturbances in affective and/or vegetative functions as well as asynchronous rhythms. It is not clear why disturbances occur in these as opposed to other functions. However, several, including affect, activity level, cardiovascular activity, eating, sleeping, cortisol, catecholamine, and growth hormone activity, and the pacemakers for rhythms in all of these functions, appear to share a common center in the CNS (the hypothalamus and extensive connections of the limbic and pituitary adrenocortical systems) that is highly affected by stimulation (McCabe & Schneiderman, 1985).

While some of the effects of inadequate stimulation and arousal modulation on infants' affective behavior have already been demonstrated, further investigations are needed on the asynchrony of behavioral and physiological rhythms and the biochemical changes associated with these affective disturbances. In addition, investigation of differences in affective style, temperament, and coping behaviors may further clarify individual differences in early affective disturbances associated with maternal deprivation and separation.

SUMMARY

Individual differences in affective responsivity from birth suggest that genetic, prenatal, and perinatal events have already influenced infants' affective predispostions. Affective responsivity then further develops in the context of early interactions with caregivers as they learn to adjust their behavior to their infants' individual stimulation and arousal modulation needs. Research on the affective and interactive behavior of normal infants suggests that mothers (caregivers) sensitively provide adequate stimulation and arousal modulation and serve as modulators or pacemakers (zeitgebers) for the developing behavioral patterns and physiological rhythms of their infants. These patterns and rhythms thereby become organized, along with the developing affective displays, gaze patterns, turn taking, and other interaction skills critical to affective development. If mothers, for example, mothers of high-risk infants, do not provide adequate stimulation and arousal modulation, their interactions become disorganized, the mothers' and infants' behavioral patterns and physiological rhythms become asynchronous, and affective disturbances and/or physiological disorganization occurs in the infant.

While intervention studies suggest that disturbed interactions of some dyads can be modified (e.g., the typically overstimulating mothers of preterm infants can be sensitized to their infants' affective signals and thereby modify their behavior), the affective disturbances of other dyads appear to be more chronic, for example, those of the depressed mother and her infant and those of the neglectful mother and her nonorganic failure-to-thrive infant. These two groups of infants may provide a model for chronic depression in infancy inasmuch as the infants show "depressed" affect as early as 3 months of age, and their affective and vegetative disturbances appear to be persistent and to mimic the symptomatology of childhood depression. Although the affective behaviors of these infants have been documented, additional studies are needed to investigate their behavior systematically in an interaction context with their mothers and to assess the correlates of affective disturbance including the behavioral and physiological rhythms of these dyads, vegetative functions such as sleeping and eating behavior, and biochemical activity including catecholamines, cortisol, and growth hormone. In addition, the time course and chronicity of these affective disturbances as well as the generalizability of the behavior across interactions with nondepressed adult caregivers need to be investigated.

The temporary separation of an infant from its mother (the infant's primary source of stimulation and arousal modulation) also results in behavioral and physiological disorganization following a biphasic agitation–depression process. Changes in affect, activity level, heart rate, and vegetative functions (sleeping, eating, elimination, and illness) appear to accompany brief separations such as the mothers' hospitalization for the birth of another child. These changes closely mimic those of separated nonhuman primates traditionally used as an animal model for reactive depression. Because these changes appear to persist following reunion with the mother, an altered relationship in which mothers are less able to meet the infants' stimulation and arousal modulation needs is implicated. An assessment of the synchrony of mothers' and infants' behavioral and physiological rhythms prior to, during, and after the separation would enhance our understanding of what the mother normally provides the infant that is then missing during their separation. Further investigation is needed on separations that are not confounded by altered relationships (e.g., the hospitalization of the infant or separation of the infant from a traveling mother) and on repeated separations (as in commuter parenting or joint custody arrangements) to determine the effects of separation per se and any cumulative effects of early separations. In addition, longer-term follow-ups are needed to chart the adaptation and recuperation process of the infant. Finally, additional measures, for example, assays of catecholamines and cortisol, would enhance our understanding of the underlying CNS mechanisms of separation-related affective disturbances. An additional need for future studies is the delineation of individual difference profiles in affective responsivity, affective disturbance, and coping responses, inasmuch as individual differences have provided some of the most salient data to date on the psychophysiology of affective and interactive disturbances in young infants.

REFERENCES

Ainsworth, M. D. (1967). *Infancy in Uganda.* Baltimore: John Hopkins Press.

Alfasi, G. (1982). A failure-to-thrive infant at play: Applications of microanalysis. *Journal of Pediatric Psychology, 7,* 111–123.

Anderson, G. C., Burroughs, A. K., & Measel, C. P. (1983). Nonnutritive sucking opportunities: A safe and effective treatment for preterm neonates. In T. Field & A. Sostek (Eds.), *Infants born at risk: Physiological, perceptual and cognitive processes.* New York: Grune & Stratton.

Bakeman, R., & Brown, J. (1980). Early interaction: Consequences for social and mental development at three years. *Child Development, 51,* 437–447.

Beck, A. T., Ward, C. H., Mendelson, M., Mock, J. E., & Erbaugh, J. (1961). An inventory for measuring depression. *Archives of General Psychiatry, 4,* 561–571.

Beebe, B., Jaffe, J., Feldstein, S., Mays, K., & Alson, D. (1985). Interpersonal timing: The application of an adult dialogue model to mother–infant vocal and kinesic interaction. In T. Field & N. Fox (Eds.), *Social perception in infants.* Norwood, NJ: Ablex.

Beebe, B., & Kronen, J. (1985). *Mother–infant facial mirroring.* Unpublished manuscript.

Bowlby, J. (1969). *Attachment and Loss: Vol. I. Attachment.* New York: Basic.

Brazelton, T. B. (1973). *Neonatal Behavioral Assessment Scale.* London: Spastic International Medical Publications.

Brazelton, T. B., Koslowski, B., & Main, M. (1974). The origins of reciprocity: The early mother–infant interaction. In M. Lewis & L. Rosenblum (Eds.), *The effect of the infant on its caregiver.* New York: Wiley.

Breese, G. R., Smith, R. D., Mueller, R. A., Howard, J. L., Prange, A. J., Lipton, M. A., Young, L. D., McKinney, W. T., & Lewis, J. K. (1973). Induction of adrenal catecholamine synthesizing enzymes following mother–infant separation. *Nature, New Biology, 246,* 94–96.

Buck, R. (1979). Individual differences in nonverbal sending accuracy and electrodermal responding. The externalizing–internalizing dimension. In R. Rosenthal (Ed.), *Skill in nonverbal communication: Individual differences.* Oelgeschlager: Gunn & Hain.

Clark, G. N., & Seifer, R. (1983). Facilitating mother–infant communication: A treatment model for high-risk and developmentally delayed infants. *Infant Mental Health Journal, 4,* 67–82.

Clarke-Stewart, K. A. (1978). And daddy makes three: The father's impact on mother and child. *Child Development, 49,* 466–478.

Cohn, J. F., & Tronick, E. Z. (1983). Three-month-old infants' reaction to simulated maternal depression. *Child Development, 54,* 185–193.

Crnic, K. A. Ragozin, A. S., Greenberg, M. T., Robinson, N. M., & Barham, R. B. (1983). Social interaction and developmental competence of preterm and full-term infants during the first year of life. *Child Development, 54,* 1199–1210.

Cytryn, L., McKnew, D. H., Bartko, J. J., Lamour, M., & Hamovitt, J. (1982). Offspring of patients with affective disorders. *Journal of the American Academy of Child Psychiatry, 21,* 389–391.

Davidson, J. R. (1972). Post-partum mood changes in Jamaican women. *British Journal of Psychiatry, 121,* 659–663.

Drotar, D. (1975). Mental health intervention in infancy. *Journal of Clinical Child Psychology, 4,* 18–20.

Dunn, J., Kendrick, C., & MacNamee, R. (1981). Reaction of first-born children to the birth of a sibling: Mothers' reports. *Child Psychology & Psychiatry, 22,* 1–18.

Emde, R. N., Harmon, R. J., Metcalf, D., Koenig, K. L., & Wagonfeld, S. (1971). Stress and neonatal sleep. *Psychosomatic Medicine, 33,* 491–497.

Engel, G. L., & Schmale, A. H. (1972). Conservation-withdrawal: A primary regulatory process for organismic homeostasis. In *Ciba Foundation Symposium 8, Physiology, emotion and psychosomatic illness.* Amsterdam: Elsevier.

Evans, S., Reinhart, J., & Succop, R. (1972). Failure-to-thrive: A study of 45 children and their families. *Journal of the American Academy of Child Psychiatry, 11,* 440–448.

Eysenck, H. J. (1973). Eysenck on extraversion. New York: Wiley.

Ferholt, J., & Provence, S. (1976). An infant with psychophysiological vomiting. *Psychoanalytic Study of the Child, 31,* 439–459.

Field, T. (1977). Effects of early separation, interactive deficits, and experimental manipulations on infant–mother face-to-face interaction. *Child Development, 48,* 763–771.

Field, T. (1978). Interaction behaviors of primary vs. secondary caretaker fathers. *Developmental Psychology, 14,* 2, 183–184.

Field, T. (1979). Interaction patterns of high-risk and normal infants. In T. Field, A. Sostek, S. Goldberg, & H. H. Shuman (Eds.), *Infants born at risk.* New York: Spectrum.

Field, T. (1980). Interactions of high-risk infants: Quantitative and qualitative differences. In D. Sawin, R. Hawkins, L. Walker, & J. Penticuff (Eds.), *Current perspectives on psychosocial risks during pregnancy and early infancy.* New York: Brunner/Mazel.

Field, T. (1981). Father's interactions with their high-risk infants. *Infant Mental Health Journal, 2,* 249–256.

Field, T. (1982a). Affective displays of high-risk infants during early interactions. In T. Field & A. Fogel (Eds.), *Emotion and early interaction.* Hillsdale, NJ: Erlbaum.

Field, T. (1982b). Individual differences in the expressivity of neonates and young infants. In R. Feldman (Ed.) *Development of nonverbal behavior in children.* New York: Springer-Verlag.

Field, T. (1982c). Infant arousal, attention and affect during early interactions. In L. Lipsitt (Ed.), *Advances in infant development* (Vol. 1). Norwood, NJ: Ablex.

Field, T. (1983a). Early interactions and interaction coaching of high-risk infants and parents. In M. Perlmutter (Ed.), *Development and policy concerning children with special needs. The Minnesota Symposia on Child Psychology.* Hillsdale, NJ: Erlbaum.

Field, T. (1983b). Social interactions between high-risk infants and their mothers, fathers and grandmothers. In B. Lahey & A. Kazdin (Eds.), *Advances in clinical child psychology.* New York: Plenum.

Field, T. (1984a). Separation stress of young children transferring to new schools. *Developmental Psychology, 20,* 786–792.

Field, T. (1984b). Early interactions between infants and their postpartum depressed mothers. *Infant Behavior & Development, 7,* 527–532.

Field, T. (1985a). Attachment as psychobiological attunement: Being on the same wave length. In M. Reite & T. Field (Eds.), *Psychobiology of attachment.* Orlando, FL: Academic.

Field, T. (1985b). Neonatal perception of people: Maturational and individual differences. In T. Field & N. Fox (Eds.), *Social perception in infants.* Norwood, NJ: Ablex.

Field, T. (1986). Affective responses to separation. In T. B. Brazelton & M. W. Yogman (Eds.), *Affective development in infancy.* Norwood, NJ: Ablex.

Field, T., Cohen, D., Garcia, R., & Greenberg, R. (1984). Mother–stranger face discrimination by the newborn. *Infant Behavior & Development, 7,* 19–26.

Field, T., Dempsey, J., & Shuman, H. H. (1983). Five-year follow-up of preterm respiratory distress syndrome and postterm postmaturity syndrome infants. In T. Field & A. Sostek (Eds.), *Infants born at risk: Physiological, perceptual and cognitive processes.* New York: Grune & Stratton.

Field, T., & Goldson, E. (1984). Pacifying effects of nonnutritive sucking on term and preterm neonates during heelstricks. *Pediatrics, 74,* 1012–1015.

Field, T., Greenberg, R., Woodson, R., Cohen, D., & Garcia, R. (1984). A descriptive study on the facial expressions during Brazelton neonatal assessments. *Infant Mental Health Journal, 5,* 61–71.

Field, T., Ignatoff, E., Stringer, S., Brennan, J., Greenberg, R., Widmayer, S., & Anderson, G. (1982). Nonnutritive sucking during tube feedings: Effects on preterm neonates in an ICU. *Pediatrics, 70,* 381–384.

Field, T., & Reite, M. (1984). Children's responses to separation from mother during the birth of another child. *Child Development, 55,* 1308–1316.

Field, T., Sandberg, D., Garcia, R., Vega-Lahr, N., Goldstein, S., & Guy, L. (1985). Pregnancy problems, postpartum depression and early mother–infant interactions. *Developmental Psychology, 21,* 1152–1156.

Field, T., Sandberg, D., Quetel, T. A., Garcia, R., & Rosario, M. (1985). Effects of ultrasound feedback on pregnancy anxiety, fetal activity and neonatal outcome. *Obstetrics & Gynecology, 66,* 525–528.

Field, T., Schanberg, S., Scafidi, F., Bauer, C., Vega-Lahr, N., Garcia, R., Nystrom, S., & Kuhn, C. M. (1986). Tactile/kinesthetic stimulation effects on preterm neonates. *Pediatrics, 77,* 654–658.

Field, T., & Vega-Lahr, N. (1984). Early interactions between craniofacial anomaly infants and their mothers. *Infant Behavior & Development, 7,* 537–540.

Field, T., Vega-Lahr, N., & Jagadish, S. (1984). Separation stress of nursery school infants and toddlers graduating to new classes. *Infant Behavior & Development, 7,* 277–284.

Field, T., & Walden, T. (1982). Perception and production of facial expressions in infancy and early childhood. In H. Reese & L. Lipsitt (Eds.), *Advances in child development and behavior* (Vol. 16). New York: Academic.

Field, T., Walden, T., Widmayer, S., & Greenberg, R. (1982). The early development of preterm, discordant twin pairs: Brigger is not always better. *Infant Behavior & Development.* Norwood, N.J.: Ablex.

Field, T., & Widmayer, S. (1981). Mother–infant interactions among lower SES black, Cuban, Puerto Rican and South American immigrants. In T. Field, A. Sostek, P. Vietze, & A. H. Leiderman (Eds.), *Culture and early interactions.* Hillsdale, NJ: Erlbaum.

Field, T., & Widmayer, S. (in press). Feeding and face-to-face interactions of Haitian and native black mothers and their 4-month-old twins. *Parenting Studies.*

Field, T., Widmayer, S., Greenberg, R., & Stoller, S. (1982). Effects of parent training on teenage mothers and their infants. *Pediatrics, 69,* 703–707.

Field, T., Woodson, R., Cohen, D., Garcia, R., & Greenberg, R. (1983). Discrimination and imitation of facial expressions by term and preterm neonates. *Infant Behavior & Development, 6,* 485–490.

Field, T., Woodson, R., Greenberg, R., & Cohen, D. (1982). Discrimination and imitation of facial expressions by neonates. *Science, 218,* 179–181.

Fischoff, J., Whitten, C. F., & Pettit, M. A. (1971). A psychiatric study of mothers of infants with growth failure secondary to maternal deprivation. *Journal of Pediatrics, 79,* 209–215.

Fogel, A., Diamond, G. R., Langhorst, B. H., & Demos, V. (1982). Affective and cognitive aspects of the two-month old's participation in face-to-face interaction with its mother. In E. Tronick (Ed.), *Social interchange in infancy: Affect, cognition and communication.* Baltimore, University Park Press.

Fox, N. A. (1985). Sweet/sour–Interest/disgust: The role of approach–withdrawal in the development of emotions. In T. Field & N. Fox (Eds.), *Social perception in infancy.* Norwood, NJ: Ablex.

Friedman, S., Jacobs, B., & Werthmann, M. (1982). Preterms of low medical risk: Spontaneous behaviors and soothability at expected date of birth. *Infant Behavior & Development, 5,* 3–10.

Frodi, A., Lamb, M., Leavitt, L., & Donovan, W. (1978). Fathers' and mothers' responses to infant smiles and cries. *Infant Behavior & Development, 1,* 187–198.

Gaensbauer, T. (1982). Regulation of emotional expression in infants from two contrasting caretaking environments. *Journal of the American Academy of Child Psychiatry, 21,* 163–171.

Gianino, A., & Tronick, E. (1986). The mutual regulation model: Infant self and interactive regulation, coping and defense. In T. Field, P. McCabe & N. Schneiderman (Eds.), *Stress and coping across development.* Hillsdale, NJ: Erlbaum.

Goldberg, S. (1979). Premature birth: Consequences for the parent–infant relationship. *American Scientist, 67,* 214–220.

Goldberg, S., Brachfield, S., & DiVitto, B. (1980). Feeding, fussing and playing parent–infant interaction in the first year as a function of prematurity and perinatal problems. In T. Field, S. Goldberg, D. Stern, & A. Sostek (Eds.), *High-risk infants and children: Adult and peer interactions.* New York: Academic.

Goldstein, S., & Field, T. (1985). Affective behavior and weight changes among hospitalized failure-to-thrive infants. *Infant Mental Health Journal, 6,* 187–194.

Gottman, J., Rose, F. T., & Mettetal, G. (1982). Time-series analysis of social-interaction data. In T. Field & A. Fogel (Eds.), *Emotion and early interaction*. Hillsdale, NJ: Erlbaum.

Greene, J. G., Fox, N. A., & Lewis, M. (1983). The relationship between neonatal characteristics and three-month mother–infant interaction in high-risk infants. *Child Development, 54,* 1286–1296.

Grundy, P. F., & Roberts, C. J. (1975). Observations on the epidemiology of post-partum mental illness. *Psychosomatic Medicine, 53,* 286–290.

Harlow, H. F., & Harlow, M. K. (1965). The affectional systems. In A. M. Schrier, H. F. Harlow, & F. Stollnitz (Eds.), *Behavior of non-human primates* (Vol. 2). New York: Academic.

Hofer, M. A. (1984). Relationships as regulators: A psychobiologic perspective on bereavement. *Psychosomatic Medicine, 46,* 183–197.

Izard, C. E. (1977). *Human emotions.* New York: Plenum.

Jones, H. E. (1950). The study of patterns of emotional expression. In M. Reymert (Ed.), *Feelings and emotions.* New York: McGraw-Hill.

Jones, O. (1980). Mother–child communication in very young Down's syndrome and normal children. In T. Field, S. Goldberg, D. Stern, & A. Sostek (Eds.), *High-risk infants and children: Adult and peer interactions.* New York: Academic.

Kogan, K. L. (1980). Interaction systems between preschool aged handicapped or developmentally delayed children and their parents. In T. Field, S. Goldberg, D. Stern, & A. Sostek (Eds.), *High-risk infants and children: Adult and peer interactions.* New York: Academic.

Korner, A. (1985, April). *Effects of waterbeds on preterm infants.* Paper presented at the biennial meeting of the Society for Research in Child Development, Toronto.

Lamb, M. E. (1975). Fathers: Forgotten contributors to child development. *Human Development, 18,* 245–266.

Legg, C., Sherick, I., & Wadland, W. (1974). Reaction of preschool children to the birth of a sibling. *Child Psychiatry & Human Development, 5,* 3–59.

Leonard, M. F., Rhymes, J. P., & Solnit, A. J. (1966). Fialure to thrive in infants. *American Journal of Diseases in Children, III,* 600–612.

Lester, B. M., Hoffman, J., & Brazelton, T. B. (1982). *Spectral analysis of mother–infant interactions in term and preterm infants.* Paper presented at the meeting of the International Conference on Infant Studies, Austin, TX.

Lester, B. M., Hoffman, J., & Brazelton, T. B. (1985). The rhythmic structure of mother–infant interaction in term and preterm infants. *Child Development, 56,* 15–27.

Levine, S., & Coe, C. L. (1985). The use and abuse of cortisol as a measure of stress. In T. Field, P. McCabe, & N. Schneiderman (Eds.), *Stress and coping* (Vol. I). Hillsdale, NJ: Erlbaum.

Lipsitt, L. (1981). Infant learning. In T. Field, A. Huston, H. Quay, L. Troll, & G. Finley (Eds.), *Review of human development.* New York: Wiley.

Lundberg, U., de Chateau, P., Winberg, J., & Frankenhaeuser, M. (1981). Catecholamine and cortisol excretion patterns in three-year-old children and their parents. *Journal of Human Stress, 10,* 3–11.

Maier, R. A., Holmes, D. L., Slaymaker, F. L., & Reich, J. N. (1984). The perceived attractiveness of preterm infants. *Infant Behavior & Development, 7,* 403–414.

Malatesta, C. Z., & Izard, C. E. (1982). The ontogenesis of human social signals: From biological imperative to symbol utilization. In *Affective development: A psychobiological perspective.* Hillsdale, NJ: Erlbaum.

McCabe, P., & Schneiderman, N. (1985). Psychophysiological reactions to stress. In N.

Schneiderman & J. Tapp (Eds.), *Behavioral medicine: The biopsychosocial approach.* Hillsdale, NJ: Erlbaum.

McGehee, I. J., & Eckerman, C. O. (1983). The preterm infant as a social partner: Responsive but unreadable. *Infant Behavior & Development, 6,* 461–470.

McQuiston, S., McCarthy, M. E., MacTurk, R. H., & Vietze, P. (1980, May). *Mother–infant face-to-face interaction in 3- and 6-month-old Down's syndrome infants.* Paper presented at the annual meeting of the American Association of Mental Deficiency, San Francisco.

Meltzoff, A. N. (1985). The roots of social and cognitive development. Models of man's original nature. In T. Field & N. Fox (Eds.), *Social perception in infants.* Norwood, NJ: Ablex.

Meltzoff, A. N., & Moore, M. K. (1983). Newborns imitate adult facial gestures. *Child Development, 54,* 702–709.

Montagner, H., Restoin, A., & Henry, J. C. (1982). Biological defense rhythms, stress and communication in children. In W. Hartup (Ed.), *Review of child development research* (Vol. 6). Chicago: University of Chicago Press.

Murray, L., & Trevarthem, C. (1985). Emotional regulation of interactions between two-month-olds and their mothers. In T. Field & N. Fox (Eds.), *Social perception in infants.* Norwood, NJ: Ablex.

Obrist, P. A. (1981). *Cardiovascular psychophysiology.* New York: Plenum.

Obrist, P. A., Lawler, J. E., Howard, J. L., Smithson, K. W., Martin, P. L., & Manning, J. (1974). Sympathetic influences on cardiac rate and contractility during acute stress in humans. *Psychophysiology, 11,* 405–427.

Papoušek, M., Papoušek, H., & Bornstein, M. (1985). The naturalisic vocal environment of young infants: On the significance of homogeneity and variability in parental speech. In T. Field & N. Fox (Eds.), *Social perception in infants.* Norwood, NJ: Ablex.

Pollitt, E., & Eichler, A. (1976). Behavioral disturbances among failure to thrive children. *American Journal of Diseases of Children, 130,* 24–29.

Pollitt, E., Eichler, A. W., & Chan, C. K. (1975). Psychosocial development and behavior of mothers of failure to thrive children. *American Journal of Orthopsychiatry, 45,* 525–537.

Powell, G. F., Brasel, J. A., & Blizzard, R. M. (1967). Emotional deprivation and growth retardation simulating idiopathic hypopituitarism. I. Clinical evaluation. *New England Journal of Medicine, 276,* 1271–1278.

Powell, G. F., & Low, J. (1983). Behavior in nonorganic failure to thrive. *Journal of Developmental & Behavioral Pediatrics, 4*(1), 26–33.

Reite, M. (1983, April). *Development of attachment and depression.* Paper presented at the biennial meeting of the Society for Research in Child Development, Detroit.

Reite, M., & Capitanio, J. P. (1985). On the nature of social separation and social attachment. In T. Field & M. Reite (Eds.), *The Psychobiology of attachment and separation.* Orlando, FL: Academic.

Reite, M., Short, R., Kaufman, I. C., Stynes, A. J., & Pauley, J. D. (1978). Heart rate and body temperature in separated monkey infants. *Biological Psychiatry, 13,* 91–105.

Reite, M., Short, R., Seiler, C., & Pauley, J. D. (1981). Attachment, loss and depression. *Journal of Child Psychology and Psychiatry, 22,* 141–169.

Reite, M., & Snyder, D. S. (1982). Physiology of maternal separation in a bonnet macaque infant. *American Journal of Primatology, 2,* 115–120.

Roberts, M. C., & Horner, M. M. (1979). A comprehensive intervention for failure to thrive. *Journal of Clinical Child Psychology, 8,* 10–14.

Robertson, J., & Robertson, J. Young children in brief separation. *Psychoanalytic Study of the Child, 26,* 264–315.

Rosenn, D. W., Loeb, L. S., & Jura, M. B. (1980). Differentiation of organic from non-organic failure to thrive syndrome in infancy. *Pediatrics, 66,* 698–704.

Rutter, M. (1972). *Maternal deprivation reassessed.* Baltimore: Penguin Books.

Sameroff, A. V., & Seifer, R. (1983). Familial risk and child competence. *Child Development, 54,* 1254–1268.

Schanberg, S. M., Evoniuk, G., & Kuhn, C. M. (1984). Tactile and nutritional aspects of maternal care: Specific regulators of neuroendocrine function and cellular development. *Proceedings of the Society for Experimental Biology and Medicine, 175,* 135–146.

Seiler, C., Cullen, J. S., Zimmerman, J., & Reite, M. (1979). Cardiac arrhythmias in infant pigtail monkeys following maternal separation. *Psychophysiology, 16,* 103–135.

Shapiro, V., Fraiberg, S., & Adelson, E. (1976). Infant–parent psychotherapy on behalf of a child in a critical nutritional state. *Psychoanalytic Study of the Child, 31,* 461–491.

Sigman, M., Cohen, S. E., & Forsythe, A. B. (1981). The relations of early infant measures to later development. In S. L. Friedman & M. Sigman (Eds.), *Preterm birth and psychological development.* New York: Academic.

Sostek, A. J., Sostek, A. M., Murphy, D. L., Martin, E. B., & Born, W. S. (1981). Cord blood amine oxidase activities relate to arousal and motor functioning in human newborns. *Life Science, 28(22),* 2561–2568.

Spitz, R. (1946). Anaclitic depression. *Psychoanalytic Study of the Child, 2,* 113–117.

Steiner, J. E. (1979). Human facial expressions in response to taste and smell stimulation. In H. Reese & L. Lipsitt (Eds.), *Advances in child development and behavior* (Vol. 13). New York: Academic.

Stern, D. N. (1971). A micro-analysis of mother–infant interaction: Behavior regulating social contact between a mother and her 3 ½ month-old twins. *Journal of the American Academy of Child Psychiatry, 10,* 501–517.

Stern, D. M. (1974). Mother and infant at play. In M. Lewis & L. Rosenblum (Eds.), *The effect of the infant on its caregiver.* New York: Wiley.

Stern, D. M., Hofer, L., Haft, W., & Dore, J. (1985). Affect attunement: A descriptive account of the intermodal communication of affective states between mothers and infants. In T. Field & N. Fox (Eds.), *Social perception in infants.* Norwood, NJ: Ablex.

Stern, M., & Hildebrandt, K. (1984). A prematurity stereotype: The effects of labeling on adults' perception of infants. *Developmental Psychology, 20,* 360–362.

Stoller, S., & Field, T. (1982). Alteration of mother and infant behavior and heart rate during a still-face interaction. In T. Field & A. Fogel (Eds.), *Emotion and early interactions.* Hillsdale, NJ: Erlbaum.

Suomi, S. J., Collins, H. L., & Harlow, H. F. (1976). Effects of maternal and peer separations on young monekys. *Journal of Child Psychology & Psychiatry, 17,* 101–112.

Thoman, E. (1980). Disruption and asynchrony in early parent–infant interactions. In D. B. Sawin, R. C. Hawkins, L. O. Walker, & J. H. Penticuff (Eds.), *Exceptional infant: Vol. 4. Psychosocial risks in infant–environment transactions.* New York: Brunner/Mazel.

Thoman, E. (1985, April). *Stimulus seeking competence in premature infants.* Paper presented at the biennial meeting of the Society for Research in Child Development, Toronto.

Tomkins, S. (1980). Affect as amplification: Some modification in theory. In R. Plutchik & H. Kellerman (Eds.), *Emotion, Theory, research and experience: Vol. i, Theories of emotion.* New York: Academic.

Trevarthen, C. (1979). Communication and cooperation in infancy. A description of primary intersubjectivity. In M. Bullowa (Eds.), *Before speech: The beginnings of human communication.* Cambridge: Cambridge University Press.

Tronick, E., Als, H., Adamson, L., Wise, S., & Brazelton, T. B. (1978). The infants' response to entrapment between contradictory messages in face-to-face interaction. *Journal of American Academy of Child Psychiatry, 17,* 1–13.

Tronick, E., Als, H., & Brazelton, T. B. (1977). Mutuality in mother–infant interaction. *Journal of Communication, 27,(2),* 74–79.

Tronick, E., Als, H., & Brazelton, T. B. (1980). Monadic phases: A structural descriptive analysis of infant–mother face-to-face interaction. *Merrill-Palmer Quarterly, 26,* 3–13.

Widmayer, S. , Bauer, C. R., & Field, T. (1986). *Affective disorders in children born with perinatal complications.* Manuscript submitted for publication.

Widmayer, S., & Field, T. (1980). Effects of Brazelton demonstrations on early interactions of preterm infants and their teenage mothers. *Infant Behavior & Development, 3,* 78–79.

Worobey, J., & Belsky, J. (1982). Employing the Brazelton scale to influence mothering: An experimental comparison of three strategies. *Developmental Psychology, 18,* 736–743.

Yogman, M. W. (1981). Games fathers and mothers play with their infants. *Infant Mental Health Journal, 2,* 241–248.

CHAPTER 20

Preventive Intervention with High-Risk Newborns: Theoretical, Conceptual, and Methodological Perspectives

ANNELIESE F. KORNER

In recent years, a great deal of intervention research with high-risk newborns has been reported in the literature. There are a number of excellent reviews on this subject that describe the different types of approaches taken by various investigators in implementing intervention. Through the years, such review articles have been written by Cornell and Gottfried (1976), Masi (1979), Field (1980), Schaefer, Hatcher, and Barglow (1980), Campbell (1983), and Burns and Hatcher (1984). Rather than merely updating these reviews, this chapter will focus primarily on the theoretical, conceptual, and methodological issues involved in preventive intervention. Description or citations of particular studies will therefore be selective rather than comprehensive so as to illustrate issues of theory, rationale, and methodology.

THE PROBLEMS OF HIGH-RISK NEONATES TO BE ADDRESSED BY PREVENTIVE INTERVENTION

Methodologists in the field of preventive intervention distinguish between primary, secondary, and tertiary prevention. The distinction is frequently blurred in the minds of those engaged in intervention. Lorion and Lounsbury (1982) describe this distinction very succinctly by stating that "preventive intervention may occur after a disorder has occurred (i.e. tertiary), as it is occurring (i.e. secondary), or before it has occurred (i.e. primary)" p. 28. All three types of preventive intervention are relevant with high-risk newborns.

Preterm infants are by far the largest group of high-risk newborns for whom preventive intervention is relevant. This chapter will therefore concentrate almost exclusively on preventive intervention with this population. There are, of course, full-term high-risk neonates who require preventive intervention. These include infants with congenital anomalies that frequently can be corrected or attenuated by

Preparation of this chapter was assisted by Grant MH-36884 from the National Institute of Mental Health, Prevention Research Branch, Division of Clinical Research. I thank Elaine Reade, Bryna Siegel, and Nancy Lane for their helpful review of this chapter.

tertiary medical intervention. They include full-term infants who are acutely ill because of complications of labor and/or delivery (e.g., asphyxiated infants or infants with acute pulmonary problems) who are the target of secondary medical intervention. They also include full-term infants who are small for dates or who are hyperirritable or lethargic. Primary preventive intervention with the parents designed to help them understand and adaptively deal with their babies' special needs can be particularly rewarding in forestalling the development of secondary problems in the parent–infant interaction or in the infants themselves.

There are very few populations for whom the indications for preventive intervention are as clear-cut as for prematurely born infants. Methodologists like Cowen (1980) and Lorion and Lounsbury (1982) stress the importance of well-documented evidence regarding the incidence of problems and the outcomes to be prevented in any given population *before* preventive intervention is instituted. In the case of preterm infants, there is a very large literature documenting the prevalence of medical, developmental, and social sequelae of prematurity pointing to the need of primary, secondary, and tertiary preventive intervention.

The problems attending prematurity described in the literature are indeed numerous and manifold. Prenatally, for example, the fetus may acquire anomalies that may lead to premature birth. After birth, the preterm infant is forced to cope with vital functions that the maternal organism normally assumes for the fetus. Thus preterm infants are abruptly called upon to regulate their own temperature, to breathe on their own to remain properly oxygenated, to maintain nutritional requirements by food intake through the gastrointestinal tract, and to cope prematurely with the impact of gravity, to name just a few, of the tasks for which these infants are not physiologically prepared. In general, when an organism is called upon to function at a level for which it is too immature, either its attempts collapse or it precociously manages to function, but at the expense of tremendous stress. Both occur in the preterm infant's struggle for survival.

Iatrogenic complications may arise from the very treatments administered to young preterm infants designed to keep them alive. Thus for example blindness may result from too much oxygen therapy, deafness from an excess of certain antibiotics, or bronchopulmonary dysplasia from prolonged ventilator care. Preterm infants are deprived of the sensory stimuli attending intrauterine life that from an evolutionary point of view can be assumed to be conducive to the normal growth and development of the fetus. Instead, preterm infants are placed in the highly artificial, technological environment of intensive care nurseries, which expose them to continuous bright lights and the monotonous white noise generated by the life-support systems. This artificial environment, which fortunately is beginning to be studied systematically (Gottfried & Gaiter, 1984; Lawson, Daum, & Turkewitz, 1977), has been described as one of sensory deprivation (e.g., Hasselmeyer, 1964; Katz, 1971; Neal, 1967) and also as one of sensory bombardment (e.g., Korones, 1976; Lucey, 1977). Although studies with older individuals have shown the disruptive and disorganizing effects of both under- and overstimulation on physiological and psychological functioning (e.g., Frankenhaeuser & Johansson, 1974), we are only beginning to understand the effects of these on preterm infants (e.g., Gorski, 1983; Lucey, 1985). Considering the cumulative effects of all these adversities impinging on the preterm infants' earliest phases of life, it is indeed miraculous that such a large proportion of these infants grow up free of major handicaps.

These achievements notwithstanding, infants born prematurely continue to be overrepresented among the mentally retarded, and among the children who have sensory deficits and/or perceptual–motor problems. Eventually, these problems often lead to learning disorders, hyperactivity, attention deficits, and behavior problems. Even when IQ scores are within normal to low-normal ranges, subtle differences in functioning in prematurely born infants are not uncommon. These deficiencies include signs of minimal brain damage as expressed in deviations of perceptual and visual functioning (Caputo, Goldstein, & Taub, 1979) and subtle deficits in hearing and language production (Field, Dempsey, & Shuman, 1979). For reasons not well understood, prematurely born infants are also overrepresented among victims of sudden infant death.

One of the most common problems is the deleterious effect of the infants' prematurity on the parent–infant interaction. A growing literature describes how most preterm infants do not respond like full-terms even at the expected date of their birth. Papers like those by Field (1979), DiVitto and Goldberg (1979), and Brown and Bakeman (1980) show that preterm infants tend to become overwhelmed, unresponsive, and/or disorganized when treated like full-term infants, with the result that parents often experience them as being very unrewarding. Barnard (1984) observed that, when toward the end of the first year the infants finally become more responsive and rewarding, the parents frequently have become discouraged and less involved. It probably is not a coincidence that a disproportionately high number of children born prematurely are represented among abused and neglected children (e.g., Elmer & Gregg, 1967; Hunter, Kilstrom, Kraybill, & Loda, 1978; Klein & Stern, 1971). Because preterm infants are frequently irritable and difficult to raise and are subject to developmental deviations, they present special challenges and frustrations to their parents. These special difficulties may increase the chance of these children being victimized.

The question, of course, is: How can preventive intervention minimize the deleterious effects of prematurity? Obviously, by far the most effective and most truly preventive intervention is the prevention of premature birth itself. Great strides are being made in this direction, both through improved prenatal care and through labor-suppressant drugs. Once a premature birth has occurred, preventive intervention is primarily concerned with reducing the incidence, prevalence, duration, and severity of the problems that frequently ensue. Once they are born, the ultimate objective of intervention with preterm infants is to normalize their developmental course by whatever means available. Approaches to this task will differ greatly depending on the interveners' discipline, goals, and theoretical persuasion. Implicitly at least, what most intervention approaches have in common are attempts to put prematurely born infants developmentally back on track, be it in the area of physical, neurological, or behavioral development.

DIFFERENCES IN RATIONALE AND METHODS OF APPROACH TO PREVENTIVE INTERVENTION

Interventions Closely Tied to the Care of the Infants

By far the greatest impact of preventive intervention will come about from advances in the field of neonatology. This field is primarily engaged in secondary and tertiary preventive intervention. It is becoming increasingly clear that prematurity in itself is not as damaging as the severe medical complications that attend it. For example, Sostek, Quinn, and Devitt (1979) reported that, in contrast to preterm infants who had major medical complications, preterms with an uncomplicated hospital course tended not to show developmental delays or disabilities on later follow-up. In fact, young, healthy preterm infants did not necessarily fare worse than healthy preterms born at older gestational ages, according to Sostek and colleagues (1979) and others. There seems to be a consensus that preterm infants whose later functioning is most affected are those who suffered massive intracranial hemorrhages or other CNS damage and infants who require prolonged ventilatory care for severe respiratory distress (RDS) (Field et al., 1979; Fritzhardinge et al., 1976; Marriage & Davies, 1977). From this it is clear that preventive intervention resulting from the advances of the rapidly changing field of neonatology will have the greatest impact in eventually preventing or attenuating debilitating medical complications. Great strides have already been made. A good example is the widespread use of betamethasone administered to the mother prior to delivery designed to hasten the formation of surfactant in the infant's lungs. Multicenter collaborative studies have shown that this intervention reduces the incidence of the respiratory distress syndrome (RDS), especially in female, nonwhite infants. In a more recent, still experimental development, surfactant is administered directly to the infants' lungs by endotracheal tubes to achieve the same purpose.

If one views the prematurely born infant as the ultimate case of maternal deprivation, it is not surprising that much of the care provided in intensive care nurseries is designed to support functions that during gestation were automatically regulated by the mother. Thus very young or very ill preterm infants are fed through umbilical catheters and, as they grow older and healthier, they are tube-fed through gavaging. In most nurseries, it is only when the infants are 6–7 weeks prior to term that they are bottle- or breast-fed. As the mother is no longer able to regulate the infant's oxygenation, temperature, and red blood cell production, the infants are given oxygen through different forms of assisted ventilation, are placed in warm incubators, and frequently are given blood transfusions. In some nurseries, young infants are placed on waterbeds to attenuate the premature exposure to the impact of gravity and to provide a soft, warm, fluid support designed to maintain these infants' fragile skin (Korner, Kraemer, Haffner, & Cosper, 1975).

Approaches to intervention in the intensive care nurseries are, of course, not limited to providing support to those functions the mother would have regulated had the infant not been born prematurely. Increasingly, intervention involves attempts to improve both the environment of the intensive care nurseries and the methods used in caring for preterm infants. For example, there is a growing awareness that, with the advent of recent technological advances that save the lives of very young infants who would have died only a few years ago, "intensive care is becoming too intensive" (Lucey, 1977, p. 1064). As a consequence, we are witnessing a return to "minimal handling protocols," usually reserved for very young infants. With the advent of the transcutaneous arterial oxygen tension monitor, which measures noninvasively and continuously $tcpO_2$, it has been found that even older infants sometimes respond with oxygen desaturation when undergoing routine medical treatments or when handled excessively (Gorski, 1983; Lucey, 1985). As a result of his observations, Gorski (1983) advised that multiple medical interventions administered in rapid succession should be avoided. Instead, these ministrations should be staggered to give the infant a chance to recover between procedures.

Recent studies of the physical environment of intensive care nurseries have evoked interest in preventive intervention to offset the potential hazards of this environment for the developing preterm infant (e.g., Gottfried & Gaiter, 1984). Concerns about the noise level inside the incubators date back to the late 1960s and early 1970s (e.g., League, Parker, Valentine, Robinson, & Powell, 1972; Seleny & Streczyn, 1969). Concern is also growing about the continuous, high-intensity illumination to which the infants in the intensive care nursery are exposed for long periods of time. To shield the infants' eyes from the bright lights, some nurseries place blankets over the tops of the incubators. With older, healthier babies who do not have to be watched as closely, other nurseries have dimmed the lights, at least during the night. Obviously, there is much room for biomedical engineering interventions to improve the nursery environment.

Recent research brought about several other types of interventions that involve changes in the care of preterm infants. Simply changing the infants' position at intervals from supine to prone has beneficial effects. According to Martin, Herrell, Rubin, & Fanaroff (1979), quiet sleep significantly increased when infants were placed in the prone and oxygenation improved significantly in this and other states as measured by a transcutaneous oxymeter. Increasingly, preterm infants are placed on sheepskins. This widespread practice started as the result of a study of only six infants (Scott & Richards, 1979), which showed that, when on alternating days the infants were placed on sheepskins, they gained significantly more weight than on the days they were on ordinary bedding. Gene Anderson and her colleagues introduced another interesting approach to changing the care of infants in the intensive care nursery (Anderson, Burroughs, & Measel, 1980). She provided sucking opportunities with a pacifier during gavage feedings to preterm infants. While it had long been known that sucking has an organizing effect on older infants (most studies of visual behavior in newborns use a pacifier to elicit alertness; see also Dowling, 1977), it was not known that sucking had an organizing effect on preterm infants as well. In a later study in which Anderson collaborated with Field and colleagues (1982), it was found that infants provided with pacifiers averaged fewer tube feedings, started bottle feeding earlier, averaged greater weight gains per day, and were discharged 8 days earlier, resulting in considerable savings in hospital costs.

Another intervention that is changing the care of preterm infants in the nursery is the increasing popularity of feeding older infants on demand. Actually this idea is not new but is currently being rediscovered. A study conducted by Horton, Lufchenco, and Gordon back in 1952 showed very clearly that feeding on demand was a safe procedure even with younger infants. Twenty vigorous, healthy preterm infants in the range of 1.55–2.21 kg who participated in this study gained adequate weight on self-demand feedings.

Interventions Involving Compensatory or Environmentally Enriching Forms of Stimulation

Over the last 20 years, a number of intervention studies with preterm infants have used various forms of sensory stimulation that, for the most part, were quite separate from the nursery caregiving routines. Most of the early studies of this type were prompted by the assumption that preterm infants are raised in an environment of sensory deprivation, being confined to "isolettes" and exposed primarily to the monotony of continuous bright lights and the sound of unpatterned white noise. At a later time, it was recognized that it was not a lack of stimulation that preterm infants experienced, but that the forms of stimulation prevailing in the nurseries were noncontingent, unpatterned, asynchronous, tied mostly to the noxious stimuli attending medical procedures, and very unlike the types of stimulation full-term infants receive in their home environments. To remedy this situation, two approaches to intervention based on highly divergent theoretical rationales began to emerge. The aim of one group of studies was to provide types of patterned stimulation that are highly prevalent in utero, aiming to *compensate* for an experiential deficit. The aim of the other group of studies was to provide a more varied, stimulating, naturalistic, and homelike environment to preterm infants, which involved visual, tactile, auditory, and/or social stimulation. Explicitly or implicitly, the goal of the latter group of intervention studies was to *accelerate* the development of preterm infants through sensory enrichment.

Studies Using Compensatory Forms of Stimulation

Most of the investigators who chose to impart compensatory forms of stimulation that are highly prevalent in utero have used vestibular-proprioceptive or movement stimulation, either by itself (Edelman, Kraemer, & Korner, 1982; Freedman, Boverman, & Freedman, 1966; Korner et al., 1975; Korner, Guillemunault, Van den Hoed, & Baldwin, 1978; Korner, Ruppel, & Rho, 1982; Korner, Schneider, & Forrest, 1983) or in conjunction with such auditory stimulation as simulated heartbeats (Barnard, 1972; Barnard & Bee 1983), the human voice (Kramer & Pierpont, 1976), or a recording of intrauterine sounds (Burns, Deddish, Burns, & Hatcher, 1983). The theoretical rationales for choosing movement stimulation varied among investigators as did their methods of providing it. Freedman and colleagues (1966) used a rocker inside the incubator for 30 min twice a day. Neal (1967) used a hammock that rotated inside the incubator three times daily for 30 min each. Barnard in her early study (1972) provided movement stimulation 15 min out of every hour in an incubator equipped with a mattress that moved gently to and fro. In her later study with Bee (1983), Barnard used two additional experimental paradigms in which the infants activated the apparatus through their own quiescence, either as often as this occurred or for a maximum of 15 min per hour. In our studies (Edelman et al., 1982; Korner et al., 1975; Korner et al., 1978; Korner et al., 1982; Korner et al., 1983) and in studies by Kramer and Pierpont (1976) and Burns and colleagues (1983), oscillating waterbeds were used to provide compensatory movement stimulation to the preterm infants.

The rationale for our waterbed studies grew out of developmental research with full-terms and rat pups that we were engaged in for over a decade (Gregg, Haffner, & Korner, 1976; Korner & Grobstein, 1966; Korner & Thoman, 1970, 1972; Thoman & Korner, 1971). In the course of our studies, we found that infants are highly responsive to movement stimulation, very likely because the vestibular system is one of the earliest systems to develop prenatally. It may be precisely the early maturation of the vestibular system that makes it such a good mediator for early stimulation. We also learned from the animal literature that movement stimulation appears to be of fundamental importance for the intactness of early development (Erway, 1975; Gottlieb & Kuo, 1965; Mason, 1968, 1979). The combination of our empirical findings and the evidence in the literature led us to conclude that it might be beneficial to provide compensatory movement stimulation to preterm infants, because they experience a great deal of this type of stimulation prenatally but are largely deprived of it while growing to term in incubators. The most gentle way we could think of to impart such compensatory movement stimulation was through gently oscillating waterbeds. This medium offered, in addition, an opportunity to provide yet another and different type of compensatory stimulation, namely, oscillations that move in the temporal pattern of maternal biological rhythms (Korner, 1979). The possible usefulness of such compensatory stimulation was suggested by Dreyfus-Brisac's (1974) hypothesis that one reason the behavior and sleep of preterm infants are so fragmented is that these babies are deprived of the regulatory influences of maternal biological rhythms. That such influences may exist is suggested by the work of several investigators, such as Sterman (1967), Jeannerod (1969), Hofer (1975, 1976), and Bertini, Antonioli, and Gambi (1978). Hofer's research is particularly relevant to our rationale of providing oscillations in the temporal pattern of maternal biological rhythms in that he repeatedly demonstrated that the disorganized behavior of young rats separated from their mothers disappeared when external stimulation was administered in a time patterning similar to that provided by the mothers' periodic stimulation.

Studies Using an Environmental Enrichment Model

The theoretical rationale of the second group of intervention studies is quite different from that of the compensatory one just outlined. The aim of these studies is largely to make the environment and care of preterm infants more comparable to those of full-terms. To implement this aim, preterm infants were given visual and/or auditory stimulation, extra handling, and social contact, singly or in combination. Probably the earliest study of this type was conducted by Hasselmeyer (1964), who assessed the effects of extra handling on the behavior of preterm infants. She used prescribed ways of stroking the baby's head, neck, cheeks, and chin, sat them up to rub their backs, swaddled them, held them close, and rocked them for extended periods of time. The infants in this study thus not only were touched but experienced containment, vestibular-proprioceptive stimulation, and the upright and undoubtedly also visual stimulation involving the environment and the experimenter. Numerous other "extra handling" studies have been conducted over the years (e.g., Powell, 1974; Rausch, 1981; Rice, 1977; Scarr-Salapatek & Williams, 1973; Solkoff, Yaffe, Weintraub, & Blase, 1969; White & LaBarba, 1975). In all these studies, touch and extra handling involved a great admixture of different forms of stimulation. Scarr-Salapatek and Williams (1973) described that, in addition to the extra handling, the infants were talked to and exposed to mobiles of crib birds and human faces. In fact, this study has had quite an impact on care practices in that visual displays inside the incubator of faces or colorful patterns have become very popular in many intensive care nurseries.

The Continuing Debate

The question as to which types of stimulation are the most relevant for enhancing the development of preterm infants has not been resolved. According to Scarr-Salapatek and Williams, (1973), who, in support of their intervention, which used the environmental enrichment model, argued persuasively against providing compensatory stimulation of the type that is prevalent in utero:

If these infants were still *in utero,* they would not be exposed to visual stimuli but would experience other forms of stimulation. A major consideration, however, in comparing experience in the third trimester fetuses and extra-uterine premature infants is the different functioning of the two organisms. At birth it seems likely that sensory systems change in their organization and functioning just as respiratory and digestive systems alter their modes of operation. Different forms of stimulation may be necessary for extra-uterine development than intrauterine maturation regardless of gestational age. (p. 95)

These points are well taken. Young, prematurely born infants are by no means identical to fetuses of the same postconceptional age. Therefore, even if it were possible, these infants *should not* be exposed to *a simulation* of the intrauterine environment. There is a vast qualitative difference between providing stimulation in a *sensory modality* prevalent in utero and trying to *imitate* what is going on in utero. Unfortunately this distinction is frequently not made, which has led to many careless and fallacious analogies. This has been especially true when the rationale for waterbeds for preterm infants has been discussed in the literature and in the lay press.

It should be stressed that a similar though opposite point could be made to that by Scarr-Salapatek and Williams (1973). While it is true that preterm infants are not like fetuses, neither are they like full-term infants. An increasing number of studies show that preterm infants respond quite differently from full-terms, even at term (Brown & Bakeman, 1980; DiVitto & Goldberg, 1979; Field, 1979). It would be more cogent to argue that, whatever forms of stimulation are given to preterm infants, these should utilize sensory systems that have matured or are in the process of maturing. Gottlieb's work (1971) on the ontogenesis of sensory functions in birds and mammals provides excellent theoretical guidelines in this domain. Much research is, of course, needed to document in human ontogeny what characterizes the sensory processing in different modalities at different postconceptional ages. In the meantime, it seems conceptually reasonable to provide compensatory forms of stimulation similar to those prevailing in utero to young preterm infants and to expose infants closer to term to more complex visual, auditory, tactile, and/or social stimulation.

Primary and Secondary Intervention with the Parents of Preterm Infants

Intervention with the parents of preterm infants is yet another area in which the theoretical rationale and approaches to the task have different greatly. Aims and approaches have included: bringing parents and infants together so that mutual bonding can occur; teaching parents to care for their preterm infants, directly or through modeling; encouraging cognitive mastery through learning about preterm infants in general and the specific needs of their own infants in particular; and giving emotional support through home visits, self-help groups, and/or social service.

Systematic work to help parents of preterm infants began only in 1964 when Barnett, Leiderman, Grobstein, and Klaus (1970) encouraged mothers to touch and care for their preterm infants while they were at the Stanford Premature Research Center. This was quite a departure from previous practices, which prohibited any contact between mothers and infants in intensive care nurseries because of the prevailing fear of introducing infections into the nurseries. The trial to bring mothers and infants together arose from a concern that prolonged separations frequently have deleterious effects on both partners and that poor parenting may ensue. In their theoretical outlook, these investigators were influenced by the imprinting literature, which showed that when goats were separated from their young immediately after birth they frequently refused to accept them back and to nurse them. Thus underlying this research was the hypothesis that the human mother may also have a sensitive period during which attachment to her infant is facilitated. The result of this first trial was that the large majority of the mothers who were introduced to their infants in the intensive care nursery enjoyed this contact. A most important by-product of this study was that the infection rate in the nursery did not rise. This ultimately led to an open-door policy in many nurseries nationwide.

This pilot study was followed by a larger one, which utilized three groups consisting of a separated group receiving routine care, a contact group in which mothers were encouraged to handle and care for their infants in the nursery, and a full-term comparison group. This study was done without Klaus, who by that time had begun collaborating with Kennell at Case Western Reserve. Many publications ensued from both the Leiderman and the Klaus and Kennell groups (e.g., Kennell et al., 1974; Klaus et al., 1972; Leiderman & Seashore, 1975; Leiderman, Leifer, Seashore, Barnett, & Grobstein, 1973). The Leiderman study, which was done with a group of middle-class, predominantly Caucasian families, revealed that the mothers of the contact group had significantly greater self-confidence in caring for their babies on discharge from the hospital and a month later. It was also found that the divorce rate and the giving up of custody of the baby were much greater in the separated group. The Klaus and Kennell studies mostly dealt with mothers whose infants were at high risk not by virtue of prematurity, but as a function of very low socioeconomic backgrounds. In line with the "sensitive period" hypothesis, the randomly assigned mothers in the experimental group were given their naked babies for skin-to-skin contact for 1 hr immediately after birth and for an extra 5 hr on each of the next 3 days. In a series of publications, Klaus and Kennell and their colleagues reported long-term gains for both mothers and children. In particular, mothers in the experimental group showed themselves to be more positive and affectionate than did controls.

Because an unexpected premature birth is almost invariably associated with parental shock, bewilderment, anxiety, and feelings of helplessness, the offer of emotional support to cope with the events can be most helpful. Social workers, interpreters for non–English speaking parents, and a discharge coordinator are therefore essential personnel in intensive care nurseries. For the most part, parents need support not only immediately following the birth of the infants but also during the babies' stay in the nursery and in planning for the eventual homecoming. The time when parents have to take sole charge of the care of their preterm infants can be especially anxiety arousing. To ease parents into this task, some nurseries not only encourage them to help in the care of their preterm infants but also provide a rooming-in facility in which the parents can learn to care for their children just prior to discharge, with help close at hand.

Another approach to helping parents is to facilitate cognitive mastery over the events and the special needs of preterms in general (Harrison & Kositsky, 1983) and their infant in particular (e.g., Blackburn, 1983). Learning to have realistic expectations and to anticipate likely events tends to reduce the feelings of helplessness experienced by most parents of preterm infants.

Self-help groups have become a popular and especially helpful intervention with parents of preterm infants. Such groups provide assistance to parents in many different areas, including mutual emotional support, a reduction of feeling isolated, helpless, and unique, and a degree of cognitive mastery over the events experienced by each member of the group. Additionally, as veterans of the group, members have the opportunity to turn the passive into an active role by becoming group leaders for subsequent parents of preterm infants in the nursery. In a controlled study and follow-up Minde and his colleagues (Minde, Shosenberg, Marton, Thompson, Ripley & Burns, 1980; Minde, Shosenberg, Thompson, & Marton, 1983) beautifully demonstrated these benefits from self-help groups of parents. Even 1 year after the hospital discharge, Minde and colleagues (1983) found the group mothers different from controls: They were more socially stimulating with their infants and provided them with more behavioral autonomy.

METHODOLOGICAL ISSUES

By and large, controlled studies involving intervention with preterm infants share the same general rules governing experimental design and methodological safeguards that are applicable to any other experimental studies. These include: random assignment of subjects to experimental and control groups; appropriate methods of dealing with subject attrition; evaluators of outcome who are "blinded" to the group status of the subjects; and appropriate statistical techniques that deal with the data without loss of power. There are, however, a few methodological problems that are unique to intervention studies with preterm infants. This section will concentrate most heavily on these issues.

The Uncertainty of the Infant's Age

In almost any other studies, the age of the subjects is precisely known. Although there are a number of techniques by which to estimate a preterm infant's gestational age, no matter which technique is used, the result will be an approximate estimate only. Most frequently, gestational age is estimated from the time elapsed since the mother's last menstrual period. Even when this date is reliably known, which is the exception rather than the rule, estimating the infant's gestational age from maternal dates has a minimum error rate of ± 1 week. While it is true that ovulation frequently occurs between the twelfth and sixteenth day of the cycle, there is considerable variation, with ovulation taking place not uncommonly at any time between the eighth and twentieth day (Pritchard, MacDonald, & Gant, 1985). When maternal dates are reliably known, slightly higher error rates (±1.02 weeks) are obtained with the Dubowitz examination (Dubowitz, Dubowitz, & Goldberg, 1970) and with the abbreviated form of that examination (Ballard, Novak, & Driver, 1979). A recent report (Spinnato, Sibai, Shaver, & Anderson, 1984) suggested that the Dubowitz examination may systematically overestimate the gestational age of preterm infants, especially if they are black, born to hypertensive mothers, and if their gestations were less than 33 weeks. Estimates of gestational age by head circumference (Usher & McLean, 1969) and by ultrasound (Campbell, 1969) also have variable error rates that most frequently underestimate the age of infants who are small for dates. Biologically, these variations should not be surprising. After all, the rate of maturation and physical growth varies in older children also.

While the methods of gestational age estimates mentioned above are extremely useful for clinical purposes, the error rates of all of them are of great concern to many investigators who are engaged in developmental studies. If, for example, a study is designed to determine how the sleep or the behavioral functioning of infants 32 weeks of gestational age (or, for that matter, of postconceptional age) differs from that of 34-week-old preterms, erroneous gestational age estimates will greatly affect the clarity of these differences. Or, when in a controlled intervention study assignment to groups is made by using gestational age in a blocked design, errors in gestational age estimates will also blur the results. In our own developmental studies we have tried to cope with this seemingly insurmountable problem by including only those infants whose gestational age estimates are all within a 2-week range. We pay a heavy price for this exclusiveness in that difference in gestational age estimates in excess of 2 weeks is the single most common reason that we have to exclude infants from our studies. We make a further attempt to reduce the error of the gestational age estimation of those infants whose estimates are all within a 2-week range by averaging the two estimates that are most commonly available (gestational age by dates and by Dubowitz). When either one or both of these estimates are missing from the records, estimates by head circumference and/or ultrasound are entered into the averaging process.

Issues of Group Assignment and Randomization

Retrospective control groups, while saving time and getting around the ethical dilemma of not offering intervention to some, are rarely if ever the best methodological approach for comparing experimental and control groups. In the case of intervention studies with preterm infants, retrospective control groups are uniquely contraindicated. There is hardly any field in medicine that changes as quickly as neonatology. Thus differences between an experimental group and a retrospective control group may be purely a function of a cohort effect in the differences in the medical care the infants received.

Randomization to experimental and control groups is by far the safest approach for assigning subjects to groups that may be differently constituted but are a random subset of a single subject pool. Even with randomization, particularly when the samples are small, it may turn out that there will be unequal numbers or unequal representation of certain characteristics in the experimental and control groups. To minimize this chance, we have in the past used a randomization procedure designed by Efron (1971) that randomizes preferentially to the group having the least representation at the time of assignment. This method protects against any great disparity in the number of subjects that will be assigned to the experimental or control groups.

Randomization provides a number of other safeguards also. Studies with preterm infants are frequently protracted so that even within a study, medical care practices may change in the nursery. By randomizing infants to experimental and control groups throughout the study, there will at least be an approximately even number of infants in each group who were treated with the old or with the new medical approach. Another advantage is that the myriad of medical conditions that befall preterm infants will tend to "randomize out" over groups. Some investigators try to cope with the great variability in the medical condition of preterm infants by setting strict selection criteria. Here, too, there are advantages and disadvantages. Doing a study with a homogeneous sample may result in more clear-cut findings. However, these will not generalize to preterm infants at large. Also, the selection criteria may be so stringent that the progress of the study may be even slower than most, as few preterm infants will be eligible for inclusion in the study. This will also increase the chance of cohort effects between early and late entrants into the study.

One very elegant method for eliminating the impact of variability among preterms is to use a design in which each infant serves as its own control in the experimental and control condition. This can either be done in a crossover design in which the order of the experimental and control conditions is randomized or in a pretest and test design in which the test condition will be the experimental one. In this latter design, one of the test conditions will have to be the control condition so that one can be certain that the differences between the pretest and subsequent data are not merely due to age changes. This, of course, means that the crossover design is more parsimonious. However, it is applicable only if investigators can be sure that their intervention will not have a carryover effect that would confound the results obtained (for a more extended review of some of these issues, see Kraemer, 1981).

One very exciting use of the control and the pretest data that is frequently overlooked is that these data are an uncontaminated source of developmental information. For example, we are currently involved in a comparison study of the differential efficacy of different types of waterbeds in which we collect pretest data on a large group of low-risk preterms. These data, by themselves, will yield a great deal of developmental information regarding the sleep and motility characteristics of healthy, growing preterms at different postconceptional ages.

Rather than randomizing over the whole sample, some investigators prefer a blocked design in which experimental and control infants are randomized within each block. There are both advantages and disadvantages to this approach. For example, if blocking is done by gestational age categories, it will be less likely to have very young infants overrepresented in one or the other group. However, there are so many factors that contribute to the variability in the sample (i.e., birth weight, sex, race, and the multitude of different medical conditions that cannot easily be equated and that are common among preterm infants) that one must choose wisely and conservatively among the variables to be blocked, especially when the sample is small. As degrees of freedom and therefore statistical power are lost with each block, care must be taken to block only for those variables that are known to be highly correlated with outcome (Kraemer, Jacob, Jeffery, & Agras, 1979).

Issues of Recruitment and Obtaining Informed Consent

In conducting intervention studies with pereterm infants, parents frequently express disappointment when their infant is assigned to the control group. Many investigators get around this issue by offering two types of interventions, one serving as control for the one under study. While this procedure is apt to attenuate the clarity of the results, it is the only ethical way to proceed if prior studies have established that the intervention under study has some beneficial effects. The situation is quite different when the effects are unknown, for then one can state in all sincerity that it is not known whether the experimental condition confers any advantages. Parents may, of course, insist that their infant be assigned to either the experimental or the control group, in which case one may decide to acquiesce to their wishes, provided that the infant who was not randomly assigned to a group will not be included in the study. We had an interesting experience with one disappointed parent who acquiesced to her infant being in the control group but who put her baby on a waterbed as soon as he was discharged from the hospital. Unfortunately this meant that this infant was lost to us for follow-up. As is true of other studies, one should, of course, have demographic data on those babies whose parents decline consent. Only in this way will it be known whether or not the study sample differs systematically from the subject population available.

One of the best ways for ensuring the randomness of the selection process is to ask for consent on principle to include an infant as either a control or an experimental subject. Consent should be obtained first from the pediatrician in charge of the care of the baby (who should not decide on the basis of how suitable an infant might be for a given treatment) and then from the parents of the child. Until both consents are obtained, the group to which the baby will be randomly assigned should not be known to anyone (including the person obtaining consent), lest knowledge might influence in any way the choices made.

Other Issues of Research Design

Not infrequently, healthy full-term infants are used as a comparison group for preterm infants at term. Compared with full-terms, preterm infants' behavioral responses have been variously described as tending to be disorganized, uneven, obligatory, and/or weak (Dreyfus-Brisac, 1974; Howard, Parmelee, Kopp, & Littman, 1976; Parmelee, 1975; Sigman, Kopp, Littman, & Parmelee, 1977). Certainly a comparison between full-terms and preterms at term is apt to reflect better than anything the extent to which preventive intervention succeeded in putting preterm infants developmentally back on track. However, recent evidence suggests that a comparison group of *just-born* full-terms may highlight differences that will disappear or diminish greatly a few days later. Palmer, Dubowitz, Verghote, & Dubowitz (1982) administered the neurological examination by Dubowitz and Dubowitz (1981) to preterm infants at term and to 1-day-old and 5-day-old full-terms. On day 1, the groups differed significantly on 9 of 11 test items. By day 5, the differences between the groups were no longer significant on 4 items and differences had decreased in magnitude on 4 additional items. Behaviorally, the just-born full-terms had a good deal more flexion and tone than when they were 5 days old. This difference is not surprising considering that 1-day old full-terms had just emerged from a very crowded environment and had gone through the rigors of the birth process, with all its attending physiological adaptations. Clearly, while it is less convenient to study full-terms after they have left the hospital, evidence from this study suggests that this would be the method of choice in any preterm and full-term comparisons.

Most controlled intervention studies are designed to test the *main effects* of a new treatment modality. Using this approach, the question addressed is whether or not a standard treatment produces significant benefits in the experimental group. This design largely ignores the fact that individual infants may respond differently to a given treatment because their particular needs differ. Because of this problem, some investigators strongly advocate that intervention must be based on the individual needs of different infants. With this approach the question becomes: Given interventions tailored to the needs of different babies, do infants respond favorably? While this approach is clinically by far the soundest way to proceed, probably less systematic knowledge will be gained than from the main effects approach. One of the main objectives of the latter is not only to determine what proportion of infants respond positively to a given treatment, but to delineate the characteristics of the nonresponders. When treatment group infants are selected because they are seen clinically as potentially good candidates for a given treatment, it would be much more difficult, maybe impossible, to gain systematic knowledge as to which specific individual characteristics are responsible for some of the treatment group infants' failure to respond. By contrast, when a standard treatment protocol is followed, the factors inherent in the infants that account for their differences in response become much more salient. In our own experience, we learned as much from a single nonresponder as we did from our group results. We found in two studies that infants with a diagnosis of uncomplicated apnea of prematurity responded with significant apnea reduction while they were placed on gently oscillating waterbeds (Korner et al., 1975; Korner et al., 1978). However, one infant's response ran completely counter to that of the group. We found out in a subsequent study that this case was not unique and that highly unstable infants who are being weaned from ventilators or who have major cardiopulmonary or neurological complications or infants who are treated with theophylline are not apt to respond to waterbeds with apnea reduction (Korner, 1981, 1983). Jones (1981), who included in her sample some of these types of infants, made the same observation.

As was already mentioned, some investigators approach intervention by providing multimodal stimulation whereas others attempt to use one modality at a time. The questions posed by the two approaches differ. The multimodal approach is more pragmatic in that it asks: Will the combination of the stimulation package work? This approach cannot determine what exactly brought about the effect. On the other hand, the use of only one form of stimulation at a time can contribute much more basic knowledge. Not only will the effect of a specific form of stimulation become apparent, but it will be possible to learn which forms of stimulation are ontogenetically the most relevant at any given postconceptional age. This, in turn, will eventually lead to a better and more basic understanding of the chronology of maturation in the development of different response systems.

Assessment

Choice of Outcome Variables

The questions posed by a given study should dictate which outcomes should be assessed. It is most important first to define meaningful questions and then to implement the study in the most elegant and parsimonious ways by using flexibly the methodological approaches available in the field. The choice of variables to be assessed should be guided by theoretical considerations and by the findings of other investigators who have conducted studies in the same area. The net of assessments should not be so wide as to result in a fishing expedition with the consequence that some significant differences are found between the groups purely by chance. At the same time, the net should not be so narrow as to preclude serendipitous findings. In our own work, unexpected findings have often led us to pursue new and interesting directions in our subsequent research. To strike a fruitful balance between too broad and too narrow a net of assessments is one of the most difficult methodological challenges.

Choice of Assessment Procedures

All too frequently assessment procedures are used simply because they exist (e.g., the administering of Bayleys whether or not they address the questions asked). In intervention studies, probably the most common and most cogent question asked is whether or not the experimental and control groups differ significantly in their *maturity of functioning* as a result of intervention. There are only a few assessment procedures that were structurally designed to measure longitudinally the maturation of preterm infant functioning (Amiel-Tison, 1968; Brandt, 1979; Korner, Forrest & Schneider, 1981; Korner et al., 1983; Saint-Anne Datgassies, 1966; Korner, Thom, & Forrest, 1984a; Korner, Thom, & Forrest, 1984b and also, in quite a different sense, Als, Lester, Tronick & Brazelton's (1982) APIB examination which is based on its own theoretical model of how behavioral development evolves). Other procedures, even though primarily designed to diagnose neurological impairment, are used also for comparing infants and groups developmentally (Dubowitz & Dubowitz, 1981; Kurtzberg et al., 1979). Still others, like the Brazelton Neonatal Behavioral Assessment Scale (1973) and the Prechtl examination (1977), which were standardized on full-term infants, have been adapted for use in evaluating preterm infants (Als, Tronick, Adamson, & Brazelton, 1976; Aylward, 1981). Since most of these procedures are described in other chapters in this volume and in the literature (e.g., Als, 1984), I will limit myself here to a brief description of a new maturity assessment currently being standardized that was developed specifically to assess the effects of an intervention on the development of preterm infants (Korner, Kraemer, Reade, Forrest, Dimiceli, Thom, in press).

In a longitudinal, randomized study begun in 1977, our aim was to compare in weekly intervals the developmental progress of young preterm infants raised on waterbeds with that of a control group. A review of the existing longitudinal neurobehavioral assessments for preterm infants revealed that none existed that could potentially differentiate performance in less than 2-week age increments. The only longitudinal assessment procedures that were available at the time were the neurological examinations by Saint-Anne Dargassies (1966) and by Amiel-Tison (1968). Neither of these examinations had a numerical scoring system and neither was designed to characterize infant performance in less than 2-week age intervals. Because it was unrealistic to expect that an experimental and control group would differ in the maturity of functioning in excess of 2 weeks, it was necessary to develop a procedure that could reveal more subtle differences in performance. We therefore developed a procedure that used a straightforward, concretely descriptive numerical scoring system that could potentially differentiate performance differences *within* a 2-week age range.

It should be stated that, with the exception of the Brazelton Neonatal Behavioral Assessment Scale (1973), which introduced maneuvers that test examiner–infant interactive processes, most procedures use basically the same test items. This sameness is dictated by the limits of the infants' behavioral and neurological repertoire. The novelty of a procedure is therefore largely a function of the selection and order of presentation of the commonly shared maneuvers, the theoretical rationale underlying the choice of the test items, and the methods of scoring and of analyzing the data.

As the primary purpose of our procedure was to test the *maturity* of the infants' functioning, we selected test items that, according to the literature, promised to show developmental changes over time (Amiel-Tison, 1968; Brandt, 1979; Dubowitz & Dubowitz, 1981; Saint-Anne Dargassies, 1966). In line with the goal of measuring the maturity of functioning, all scaled scores were ordered from the least to the most mature responses as reflected in the literature. Aversive items commonly used in neurobehavioral assessments such as the Moro and pinprick were excluded from the examination. In addition to testing the maturity of the infants' functioning, the examination can point to indications of neurologically abnormal functioning and, if consistent over time, to potential precursors of temperamental differences such as individual proclivities to over- or underreact to stimulation (Korner et al., 1984a; Korner et al., 1984b).

The procedure that is applicable to medically stable infants who are 32 weeks of conceptional age or older and who are on room air has three new features:

1. The psychometric properties of the test items and clusters were thoroughly investigated *before* they were made part of the examination. Starting from what we considered conceptually and clinically important to measure, the test items and clusters retained in the examination had to have a day-to-day test–retest reliability of .6 or above and had to be nonredundant. Clusters that had conceptual face validity had to cohere statistically as well. Also, to be retained in the main part of the examination, single test items and clusters had to demonstrate developmental validity by showing significant changes in functioning with age.

2. A truly invariant sequence is used for administering the test items. This standard sequence is designed to bring about those behavioral states that are likely to elicit the best possible responses from preterm infants. Because a standard sequence of rousing, soothing, and alerting items is built into the procedure, the opportunity to test various functions in appropriate behavioral states is maximized and the need to intervene with some infants more than others is minimized. This prevents the examination from becoming an objectively different experience for each child and at the same time yields an assessment of the states with which infants at different ages respond to a standard sequence of events.

3. Not only have the psychometric properties of this examination been thoroughly investigated, but a new mathematical model (Kraemer, Korner, & Hurwitz, 1985) is being used to analyze the longitudinal test data. This model, in addition to yielding developmental slopes, permits assessment of how birth weight, gestational, conceptional, and chronological age, and other postnatal factors affect the development of different functions, and how "catch-up" time of performance differs according to function.

Correcting for Gestational Age

Some controversy exists at present as to whether to correct the infant's performance for its gestational age. Historically this is interesting because it appears that we are returning to a practice we had given up earlier. Many investigators feel that the biological age of the infant exerts a much greater influence on its performance than its chronological age (e.g., Hunt & Rhodes, 1977; Parmelee, 1975). By contrast, others have felt increasingly that correcting for gestational age tends to exaggerate the maturity of preterm infants (e.g., Caputo, Goldstein, & Taub, 1981; Miller, Dubowitz, & Palmer, 1984; Siegel, 1983). The resolution of this controversy is vitally important not only for intervention research but for guiding parental expectations. Intuitively it makes sense that, the younger the infant evaluated, the more important it is to correct for gestational age. The critical question is to determine empirically when it makes sense to stop correcting for gestational age. We hope that our mathematical model (Kraemer et al., 1985), which is designed to estimate catch-up time, will make a contribution in this domain.

OUTCOME ISSUES

Differences in Outcome

Benefits to preterm infants have been reported from most *published* in-hospital intervention studies. Since some of the benefits accruing from systematic changes in the *care* of preterm infants have already been alluded to in the context of the description of these studies, I will focus here on the benefits reported from studies that used different types of *supplemental stimulation* as a form of preventive intervention of preterm infants. These benefits cut across studies using different theoretical models for providing supplemental stimulation. For example, studies that used vestibular-proprioceptive stimulation to compensate for the movement stimulation so highly prevalent in utero have reported the following benefits in the experimental groups: increased weight gain (e.g., Freedman et al., 1966; Kramer & Pierpont, 1976; Neal, 1967); reductions in apnea and bradycardia (e.g., Korner et al., 1975; Korner et al., 1978); heightened sensory responsiveness (e.g., Barnard & Bee, 1983; Korner et al., 1983; Neal, 1967); reduction in irritability (e.g., Edelman et al., 1982; Korner et al., 1982; Korner et al., 1983); increases in quiet sleep (e.g., Barnard, 1972; Edelman et al., 1982; Korner et al., 1982); quiescence (e.g., Barnard & Bee, 1983; Hasselmeyer, 1964); more modulated spontaneous motility (e.g., Burns et al., 1983; Edelman et al., 1982; Korner et al., 1982; Korner et al., 1983); better neurobehavioral development (e.g., Barnard & Bee, 1983; Burns et al., 1983; Korner et al., 1983; Neal, 1967); and higher Bayley MDIs at 24 months of postnatal age (e.g., Barnard & Bee, 1983).

Similarly, intervention studies with preterm infants based on evironmental enrichment models have reported benefits of various types. Most of these studies have used tactile–kinesthetic stimulation consisting of stroking, caressing, massaging, or other forms of extra handling as their primary intervention. The most common benefit reported in the studies published was that the infants in the experimental group either regained their birth weight earlier or gained more weight than controls. Highly significant differences in weight gain were found in the studies by Scarr-

Salapatek and Williams (1973), White and LaBarba (1975), Rice (1977), and Field and colleagues (1985). Greater, though statistically nonsignificant, weight gain in the experimental groups was reported in the studies by Solkoff and colleagues (1969), Powell (1974), and Rausch (1981). Unfortunately, intervention benefits have at times been described in opposite terms. Thus one of the main benefits reported in the Hasselmeyer (1963) extra handling study was that the infants in the experimental group were more quiescent, while in the Solkoff and Matuszak (1975) study, the infants in the experimental group were more active. Similarly, Hasselmeyer (1963) reported that the infants in the experimental group benefited by defacating less, whereas Rausch (1981) attributed benefits from more frequent stooling in her experimental group. In studies using the environmental enrichment model, infants in the experimental groups also were reported to perform better on the Bayley or the Cattell Infant Intelligence Scale (Powell, 1974; Rice, 1977; Scarr-Salapatek & Williams, 1973). Actually, Scarr-Salapatek and Williams (1973) included in their study a home visiting program in which a social worker provided support, information, and instruction for a special stimulation program. From this study it is thus not clear whether the benefits mostly accrued from the in-hospital intervention or from the after-discharge home visiting program. One of the few environmental enrichment studies that did not use tactile stimulation or any kind of extra handling was the study by Katz (1970). Inside the incubator, Katz presented a 5-min taped monologue of the infant's mother six times a day to preterm infants in the range of 28–32 weeks of gestational age. When the infants were 36 weeks postconceptional age, they were tested with the Rosenblith revision of the Graham test. The results showed that the infants in the experimental group had significantly higher scores in the areas of general maturation, muscle tone, and visual and auditory responses.

Considering the development of central nervous system functioning, it is of theoretical interest that sensory stimulation in one modality can produce gains in functioning in another. For example, Neal (1967) and one of our studies (Korner et al., 1983), which provided vestibular-proprioceptive stimulation to preterm infants, increased performance in the auditory and visual sphere. Similarly, Katz (1970), who provided auditory stimulation to preterms, found gains in muscle tone and other maturational items.

In sum, this very brief review of the effects of intervention studies with preterm infants clearly shows that benefits accrue and that these differ very much in kind. The fact that outcomes of intervention studies vary greatly has been puzzling, if not disturbing, to some reviewers, who view this disagreement as a sign of disarray in this field. Considering the multitudes of different protocols and study populations that have been used in intervention studies, differences in outcome should come as no surprise.

Possible Mechanisms of Action

One can only speculate about what might be the underlying mechanisms accounting for the benefits of intervention and for their differences. Undoubtedly, a large number of factors both singly and in interaction are apt to mediate the different effects of intervention. The following are just a few of these factors: the sensory system stimulated; the quality, intensity, vigor, and duration of the treatment; the regularity, intermittency, and rhythmicity of stimulation, as well as its suddenness of onset;

the length in days or weeks of the treatment; the gestational age at which the infants were born; the conceptional age at which the neural development of different systems can best be activated; and the types of infants studied (sex, race, SGA, AGA, or LGA babies; the acuteness, chronicity, and types of medical complications of the study population, etc.).

We have at least some clues from which we can infer what types of underlying mechanisms may be at work that account for both the common and the diverse benefits reported in the intervention literature. Using animal models, the early experience literature has shown consistently that extra handling of young rodents activates neuroendocrine responses involving the hypothalamic-pituitary-adrenal axis that affect behavioral responses and ultimately behavioral development (e.g., Denenberg, 1975; Levine, 1971). One of the most consistent findings reported in the animal literature is increased weight gain in the handled rats as compared with untreated controls, a finding that Denenberg (1975) attributed to a mild stress response. It is of interest that with two notable exceptions (Hasselmeyer, 1963; Solkoff & Matuszak's 1975 study) all the human studies reviewed above that utilized extra handling reported higher weight gains in the experimental groups. It may not even be the extra handling that was responsible for the increased weight gain in the experimental groups, but that any moderately vigorous, periodic stimulation might bring about the same effect. This is borne out by several studies that reported significant weight gains as a result of moderately vigorous and periodic mechanical rocking (Freedman et al., 1966; Kramer & Pierpont, 1976; Neal, 1967). By contrast, studies that used more gentle and continuous stimulation did not result in increased weight gains in the treatment groups (e.g., Burns et al., 1983; Korner et al., 1983).

With the recent advances in neurochemistry, we are beginning to learn that in rats very specific neuroendocrine responses are activated by different treatment modalities. Even more striking, when the same sensory system is stimulated varying only the intensity of stimulation, differences in neuroendocrine response will result. This is well documented in studies by Evoniuk, Kuhn, and Schanberg (1979) and by Schanberg, Evoniuk, and Kuhn (1984). Evoniuk, for example, maternally deprived rat pups for 2 hr, which resulted in a significant decrease in serum growth hormone (GH) and ornithine decharboxylase (ODC). During maternal separation, the pups were given tactile stimulation differing in quality and intensity. In an attempt to imitate the mothers' grooming behavior, one group was given 10–20 short fairly heavy strokes on the back and head with a moistened brush. Two other groups were given tactile stimulation either by light stroking with the same brush or by tail pinching. In each group, the stimulation was administered every 5 min. It was found that the heavy stroking was the only treatment that prevented a significant decrease in GH and ODC, whereas the other forms of tactile stimulation had no such effect.

Since all reviews of intervention studies agree that preterm infants benefit in various ways from intervention, perhaps the time has come that instead of merely testing whether or not a given intervention package "works," we institute studies that are theory based and that, through systematic variation, test one by one what parameters are responsible for what effects. We are currently engaged in a behavioral study of this type. In two prior studies (Edelman et al., 1982; Korner et al., 1982) we found that our gently oscillating waterbeds increased quiet sleep and decreased irritability and disorganized motility in preterm infants. In a comparison study we are now attempting to determine whether it is the waterbed per se, the oscillations, or the rhythm of the oscillation that is primarily responsible for the effects seen in our two previous studies.

Implications for Replication Studies

Even though replication of findings is deemed absolutely essential by the scientific community, too few investigators are willing to do replication studies and too many journal editors are reluctant to publish them because these studies usually do not break new ground. Those who do undertake replication all too frequently "model" their studies after those already published, using what is usually described as a "modification" of the procedures previously used. When the results of the "replication" study differ, the reliability of the previous findings is frequently challenged because of a so-called "failure to replicate." It should be clear from the above discussion that minor changes in the kind, quality, duration, or interval of stimulation or differences in study population or any other aspects of the research protocol may lead to major differences in outcome. It is clearly indefensible to speak of a "failure to replicate" unless the sample of the replication study is comparable and large enough to test the null hypothesis and unless the identical procedures and research protocols were used in the studies compared. If the results differ between the studies, all that can be said is that there was a failure of the effects to generalize across different protocols or experimental paradigms. This is a much broader issue. Generalization of intervention effects across different protocols, though clinically and practically highly desirable, is even more difficult to achieve than replication.

The Issue of Long-Term Benefits of Intervention

Even though most intervention studies with infants at risk have demonstrated substantial immediate benefits, these effects frequently do not persist. Review articles of the effects of early intervention studies all agree on this point (e.g., Bush & White, 1983; Meisels, 1984; Simeonsson, Cooper, & Scheiner, 1982). Many investigators not only tacitly assume that their intervention will have long-range effects, but view the persistence of effects as the acid test that their intervention was successful. When one considers the odds against finding persistent effects of early intervention in terms of the multitude of other variables impinging on the development of infants, it is indeed surprising that the implicit expectation of long-range effects is so widespread. The following are some of the factors that interfere with the detection of long-range effects:

1. At times, early intervention may really produce only short-range effects either because it was primarily designed to achieve a specific and immediate purpose or because, in comparison to other intervening variables, the intervention was relatively minor in duration, intensity, ontogenetic relevance, breadth, or implementation. For example, it is striking that many studies that in addition to in-hospital intervention provided continued parental support after discharge resulted in distinct long-term benefits (e.g., Barnard & Bee, 1983; Field, Widmayer, Stringer, & Ignatoff, 1980; Scarr-Salapatek & Williams, 1973).

2. Though long-range effects may actually result from early intervention, they

may not come to light, either because the instruments chosen to measure the effects may have little or no relevance to the intervention experienced, or because the assessments used are not sufficiently sensitive to detect subtle differences in infant or family functioning. For example, Bayleys or other developmental tests are commonly used as follow-up measures, even though these assessments may have very little relevance to the earlier intervention and will not assess effects in noncognitive domains.

3. A related point is that it is at times difficult to guess and/or to trace the long-range effects of what is set in motion in the course of early intervention. For example, several studies have shown that early intervention produced infants who were more alert and more capable of responding to visual and auditory interactions with their caregivers than were controls (Barnard & Bee, 1983; Katz, 1971; Korner et al., 1983; Neal, 1967). Because alert and visually responsive infants have an enormous appeal to parents, these qualities in the infants have the potential of facilitating parental attachment, commitment, and delight. What gets set in motion in both the infant and the caregivers as a result of these early interactions is sometimes difficult to trace and to measure. Clearly, many long-range effects of early intervention are transactionally mediated (Sameroff, 1975), entailing sequential and mutual influences in the infant–parent system that continuously change in their overt manifestations.

4. Long-range effects of early intervention are frequently obscured or obliterated by the powerful effects of socioeconomic and/or familial circumstances. This fact is one of the most recurrent themes in the early intervention literature. These effects are well described in Sameroff and Chandler's (1975) review of this topic. Even though it is well known that differing environmental and familial circumstances will either maintain, foster, or diminish the impact of early intervention, it is less clear which specific ingredients in what are globally called socioeconomic and familial circumstances are the most damaging or the most fostering of infant development. Identifying the most important specific ingredients through systematic research would be a great advance not only for intervention research but for understanding developmental issues in general. Considering the powerful impact of socioeconomic and other familial circumstances that impinge on the course of development, it is clear that early intervention, even when beneficial at the time, does not work like an immunization process from which one should automatically expect permanent or even long-lasting effects.

The Pervasive Devaluation of Short-Term Benefits

Reviews of early intervention studies are replete with comments that most interventions lead to only short-term gains that disappear as soon as intervention stops. Implicit in many of these comments from reviewers and investigators alike is a sense of surprise and/or disappointment about the fact that the benefits of intervention are, for the most part, short-lived. A very prevalent view seems to be that unless there are long-term gains, intervention is of relatively little value.

For example, there are several reports in the early intervention literature that preterm infants in the experimental group gained significantly more weight than controls, *but* that these gains were not maintained after intervention stopped. Might not one ask whether this temporary weight gain was an advantage to the preterm infant's well-being and clinical progress at the time that it occurred? In another vein, is it not worthwhile to elicit more positive parental attitudes and greater reciprocity in the mother–infant interaction during the newborn period as a result of parental observation of the Brazelton examination (e.g., Kang, 1974; Ryan, 1973) or to engender more maternal self-confidence in caring for preterm infants as a result of early contact (e.g., Seashore, Leifer, Barnett, & Leiderman, 1973), even if the effects of these interventions cannot be detected at a later time? In our own work, we are frequently asked whether the beneficial effects of waterbeds in reducing apnea or in improving sleep persist after the infants are removed from these beds. Since in the case of our sleep studies the infants are placed on waterbeds for only 4 days, we have no expectations that the beneficial effects will persist. It seems that by placing value primarily on long-range benefits, we are imposing standards upon ourselves that are not shared by any other discipline. For example, who in the field of medicine would argue about the value of reducing apneic spells or about the benefits of a good night's sleep by using a simple intervention that does not produce any side effects? And who in medicine would expect apnea reduction or restful sleep to persist after treatment is withdrawn, if the underlying cause of apnea or disturbed sleep has not been resolved? As behavioral interventionists, we often tend to engage in a bit of magical thinking by expecting that somehow the comfort or the relief of symptoms produced by our intervention should persist beyond the time we are intervening.

Clearly, we must change our mind-set that intervention is trivial unless it has persistent or long-term effects. There is value in *improving the quality of life* at the time intervention occurs. There is value in reducing current stress in infants and/or their parents even if this is short-lived. If one views development as an orderly progression of developmental steps, intervening to rectify or attenuate a disordered sequence in this progression will have a number of salutary effects. Such intervention may prevent current functioning from getting worse, may forestall specific developmental arrests, may facilitate coping better with new developmental tasks, and, in effect, may put the infants developmentally more on track than might have been possible without such intervention. None of these achievements, though important, will guarantee that the developmental course of a given infant will be changed for the better from here on. While this potential exists, it is well known that the vicissitudes of living and the powerful effects of familial circumstances over which we usually have little control will be the prime determiners of whether the effects of intervention will persist.

Selling short the importance of resolving one by one current developmental problems and placing prime emphasis on the importance of long-term gains are self-defeating in that this position raises unrealistic expectations in investigators, the public, and funding agencies alike. It should suffice that early intervention with infants born at risk will produce infants that are more intact, more on track developmentally at the time, and more capable of coping with whatever familial environment they will be entering than would be the case without intervention.

Implications for Follow-up Strategies

In line with the prevailing hope that long-term benefits will accrue from early interventions, prolonged follow-ups have become an ingrained research tradition. In intervention research, prolonged follow-up of research subjects has become quite automatic, its universal usefulness frequently unquestioned. Commonly, the more prolonged the follow-up, the more it is considered valuable. Because of the prevailing hope of finding long-term benefits of intervention no matter what its nature, too few investigators ask themselves whether follow-up is indicated, and if so, what its length should be and what they should reasonably expect to find as a result of the earlier intervention.

To be realistic as well as cost-effective, the length and breadth of follow-up should be proportionate to the duration and intensity of the earlier intervention. In choosing follow-up strategies, it would be cogent to adopt the same guidelines that governed the choice of outcome variables in the earlier assessments of the intervention. Rather than making assessments automatically on the basis of the instruments that are most readily available, follow-up measures should be selected that have some theoretical relevance to the goals of the earlier intervention. Even though one should make some intuitive guesses regarding the areas and direction of infant development and/or family relationships that might have been affected and changed by early intervention, one must guard against the temptation to make too large a number of assessments that inevitably will yield significant findings purely by chance.

Since socioeconomic and familial circumstances have such a powerful effect on maintaining or obliterating the benefits of early intervention, perhaps one fruitful follow-up strategy would be to compare the infants of families who provide the most and the least favorable environments. Such a comparison would be especially meaningful once the potent ingredients that determine favorable and unfavorable environments are better defined. Perhaps this strategy would highlight more clearly the potential long-term effects of early intervention than can the follow-up of a large, heterogeneous group. Extremes always highlight an issue more clearly. This strategy can, of course, only be adopted if the sample contains a sufficiently large number of subjects in the extreme groups to make a reliable comparison.

EARLY INTERVENTION IN CLINICAL CONTEXTS

Paradoxically, clinical intervention with neonates at risk should proceed in quite opposite ways from that used in controlled research studies. Since in clinical intervention one need not adhere to a rigorous research protocol, one can choose flexibly among many different treatment approaches to any given infant. In clinical contexts, one is in the position to assess the characteristics of an infant prior to intervening and one can then use one's intuitive judgment in choosing a form of intervention that clinically appears to be optimal for meeting the individual needs of that particular baby. If the approach selected does not help the infant, one is free to change it and to choose another one. While in the context of a controlled experimental study one could not change the protocol in midstream without losing subjects and thereby biasing the sample, this flexible approach makes ultimate sense in clinical intervention.

As opposed to experimental research designed to test the efficacy of a new treatment modality, clinical intervention confers additional freedoms of action that are inappropriate in the context of controlled research studies. Commonsense changes in the care of infants and in the approach to parents, which aim at improving the quality of life of either or both, can and should be instituted long before research findings definitely prove the efficacy of these changes. Unfortunately, confusion between clinical intervention and intervention research frequently arises when advocacy for changes is legitimized by citing preliminary, inconclusive, or out-of-context research findings as supporting evidence for the need of treatment changes. There should be no need to attempt to legitimize intuitively sensible innovations on scientific grounds. Such innovations are worth trying in their own right.

Unfortunately, in settings where only research findings are valued, suggested changes in the care of infants based on humanistic reasons are frequently devalued and their implementation is impeded. Frequently, in research settings, such changes are allowed to happen *only* in the context of a research study that is to put to the test whether the proposed change can be proven to be effective. Clearly, clinicians and researchers have different agendas that should not be confounded. To be of most help to infants, it would be well to realize that the agenda of each group has its own merits.

REFERENCES

Als, H. (1984). Newborn behavioral assessment. In W. J. Burns & J. V. Lavigne (Eds.), *Progress in pediatric psychology.* New York: Grune & Stratton.

Als, H., Lester, B. M., Tronick, E., & Brazelton, T. B. (1982). Towards a research instrument for the assessment of preterm infants' behavior (APIB). In H. E. Fitzgerald, B. M. Lester, & M. W. Yogman (Eds.), *Theory and research in behavioral pediatrics* (Vol. 1). New York: Plenum.

Als, H., Tronick, E., Adamson, L., & Brazelton, T. B. (1976). The behavior of the full-term yet underweight newborn infant. *Developmental Medicine & Child Neurology, 18,* 590–602.

Amiel-Tison, C. (1968). Neurological evaluation of the maturity of newborn infants. *Archives of Diseases of Childhood, 43,* 89–93.

Anderson, G. E., Burroughs, A. K., & Measel, C. P. (1983). Nonnutritive sucking opportunities: A safe and effective treatment for preterm neonates. In T. Field & A. Sostek (Eds.), *Infants born at risk: Physiological, perceptual, and cognitive processes.* New York: Grune & Stratton.

Aylward, G. P. (1979). Neurologic development in preterm infants. *JSAS Catalog of Selected Documents in Psychology, 11,* 31 (Ms. No. 2245).

Ballard, J. L., Novak, K. K., & Driver, M. (1979). A simplified score for assessment of fetal maturation of newly born infants. *The Journal of Pediatrics, 95*(5), 769–774.

Barnard, K. E. (1972). *The effect of stimulation on the duration and amount of sleep and wakefulness in the premature infants.* University Microfilms No. 72-78, 573, Ann Arbor, Michigan.

Barnard, K. E., & Bee, H. L. (1983). The impact of temporally patterned stimulation on the development of preterm infants. *Child Development, 54,* 1156–1167.

Barnett, C. R., Leiderman, P. H., Grobstein, R., & Klaus, M. (1970). Neonatal separation: The maternal side of interactional deprivation. *Pediatrics, 45*(2), 197–205.

Bertini, M., Antonioli, M., & Gambi, D. (1978). Intrauterine mechanisms of synchronization: In search of the first dialogue. *Totus Homo, X*(8), 73–91.

Blackburn, S. (1983). Fostering behavioral development of high-risk infants. *JOGN Nursing Supplement,* May/June, pp. 76–86.

Brandt, I. (1979). Patterns of early neurological development. In *Human growth—Neurobiology and nutrition* (Vol. 3). New York: Plenum.

Brazelton, T. B. (1973). Neonatal behavioral assessment scale. *Clinics in Developmental Medicine* (No. 50). S.I.M.P. (Spastics International Medical Publications) Philadelphia: Lippincott.

Brown, J. V., & Bakeman, R. (1979). Relationships of human mothers with their infants during the first year of life: Effects of permaturity. In R. W. Bell & W. P. Smotherman (Eds.), *Maternal influences and early behavior.* Holliswood, NY: Spectrum.

Burns, K. A., Deddish, R. B., Burns, W. J., & Hatcher, R. P. (1983). Use of oscillating waterbeds and rhythmic sounds for premature infant stimulation. *Developmental Psychology, 19*(5), 746–751.

Burns, K. A., & Hatcher, R. P. (1984). Developmental intervention with preterm infants. In W. B. Burns & J. V. Lavigne (Eds.), *Progress in pediatric psychology.* New York: Grune & Stratton.

Bush, D. W., & White, K. R. (1983). *The efficacy of early intervention: What can be learned from previous reviews of the literature?* Paper presented at the Annual Meeting of the Rocky Mountain Psychological Association, Snowbird, UT.

Campbell, S. K. (1983). Effects of developmental intervention in the special care nursery. In M. Wolraich & D. K. Routh (Eds.), *Advances in developmental and behavioral pediatrics, 4,* 165–179.

Campbell, S. (1969). The prediction of fetal maturity by ultrasonic measurement of the biparietal diameter. *Journal of Obstetrics & Gynaecology (British Commonwealth), 76,* 603.

Caputo, D. V., Goldstein, K. M., & Taub, H. B. (1979). The development of prematurely born children through middle childhood. In T. M. Field, A. M. Sostek, S. Goldberg, & H. H. Shuman (Eds.), *Infants born at risk.* New York: Spectrum.

Caputo, D. V., Goldstein, K. M., & Taub, H. B. (1981). Neonatal compromise and later psychological development: A 10 year longitudinal study. In S. L. Friedman & M. Sigman (Eds.), *Preterm birth and psychological development.* New York: Academic.

Cornell, E. H., & Gottfried, A. W. (1976). Intervention with permature human infants. *Child Development, 47,* 32–39.

Cowen, E. L. (1980). The wooing of primary prevention. *American Journal of Community Psychology, 8,* 258–284.

Denenberg, V. H. (1975). Effects of exposure to stressors in early life upon later behavioral and biological processes. In L. Levi (Ed.), *Society, stress and disease: Childhood and adolescence.* New York: Oxford University Press.

DiVitto, B., & Goldberg, S. (1979). The effects of newborn medical status on early parent–infant interaction. In T. Field, A. Sostek, S. Goldberg, & H. H. Shuman (Eds.), *Infants born at risk.* New York: Spectrum.

Dowling, S. (1977). Seven infants with esophageal atresia. *The Psychoanalytic Study of the Child, 32,* 215–256.

Dreyfus-Brisac, C. (1974). Organization of sleep in prematures: Implications for caretaking. In M. Lewis & L. A. Rosenblum (Eds.), *The effect of the infant on its caregiver.* New York: Wiley.

Dubowitz, L. M. S., Dubowitz, V., & Goldberg, C. (1970). Clinical assessment of gestational age. *Journal of Pediatrics, 77,* 1–10.

Dubowitz, L. M. S., & Dubowitz, V. (1981). The neurological assessment of the preterm and fullterm newborn infant. *Clinics in Developmental Medicine* (No. 79). S.I.M.P. (Spastics International Medical Publications) London: Heinemann; Philadelphia: Lippincott.

Edelman, A. M., Kraemer, H. C., & Korner, A. F. (1982). Effects of compensatory movement stimulation on the sleep-wake behaviors of preterm infants. *Journal of the American Academy of Child Psychiatry, 21*(6), 555-559.

Efron, B. (1971). Forcing a sequential experiment to be balanced. *Biometrika, 58,* 403-417.

Elmer, E., & Gregg, C. D. (1967). Developmental characteristics of the abused child. *Pediatrics, 40,* 596-602.

Erway, L. C. (1975). Otolith formation and trace elements: A theory of schizophrenic behavior. *The Journal of Orthomolecular Psychiatry, 4,* 16-26.

Evoniuk, G. E., Kuhn, C. M., & Schanberg, S. M. (1979). The effect of tactile stimulation on serum growth hormone and tissue ornithine decarboxylase activity during maternal deprivation in rat pups. *Communication in Psychopharmacology, 3,* 363-370.

Field, T. M. (1979). Interaction patterns of preterm and term infants. In T. Field, A. Sostek, S. Goldberg, & H. H. Shuman (Eds.), *Infants born at risk.* New York: Spectrum.

Field, T. Supplemental stimulation of preterm neonates. *Early Human Development,* 1980, *4/3,* 301-314.

Field, T., Dempsey, J., & Shuman, H. H. (1979) Developmental assessments of infants surviving the respiratory distress syndrome. In T. Field, A. Sostek, S. Goldberg, & H. H. Shuman (Eds.), *Infants born at risk.* New York: Spectrum.

Field, T., Widmayer, S., Stringer, S., & Ignatoff, E. (1980). Teenage, lower class mothers and their preterm infants: An intervention and developmental follow-up. *Child Development, 51,* 426-436.

Field, T., Ignatoff, E., Stringer, S., Brennan, J., Greenberg, S., Widmayer, S., & Anderson, G. C. (1982). Nonnutritive sucking during tube feedings: Effects on preterm neonates in an intensive care unit. *Pediatrics, 70*(3), 381-384.

Field, T. M., Schanberg, S. M., Scafidi, F., Bauer, C. R., Vega-Lahr, N., Garcia, R., Nystrom, J., & Kuhn, C. M. (1985). *Effects of tactile/kinesthetic stimulation on preterm neonates.* Preprint.

Fitzhardinge, P. M., Page, K., Arstrikaitis, M., Boyle, M., Ashby, F., Rowley, A., Netley, C., & Sawyer, P. R. (1976). Mechanical ventilation of infants of less than 1501 grams birthweight: Health, growth and neurological sequelae. *Journal of Pediatrics, 88,* 531-541.

Frankenhaeuser, M., & Johansson, G. (1974). On the psychophysiological consequences of understimulation and overstimulation. *Reports from the Psychological Laboratories of the University of Stockholm* (Suppl. 25).

Freedman, D. G., Boverman, H., & Freedman, N. (1966). *Effects of kinesthetic stimulation on weight gain and on smiling in premature infants.* Paper presented at the Annual Meeting of the American Orthopsychiatric Association, San Francisco.

Gorski, P. A. (1983). Premature infant behavioral and physiological responses to caregiving interventions in the intensive care nursery. In J. D. Call, E. Galenson, & R. L. Tyson (Eds.), *Frontiers of infant psychiatry.* New York: Basic.

Gottfried, A. W., & Gaiter, J. L. (1985). *Infant stress under intensive care.* Baltimore: University Park Press.

Gottlieb, G. (1971). Ontogenesis of sensory function in birds and mammals. In E. Tobach, L. R. Aronson, & E. Shaw (Eds.), *The Biopsychology of Development.* New York & London: Academic.

Gottlieb, G., & Kuo, Z. (1965). Development of behavior in the duck embryo. *Journal of Comparative & Physiological Psychology, 59*(2), 183-188.

Gregg, C. L., Haffner, M. E., & Korner, A. F. (1976). The relative efficacy of vestibular-proprioceptive stimulation and the upright position in enhancing visual pursuit in neonates. *Child Development, 47,* 309–314.

Harrison, H., & Kositsky, A. (1983). *The premature baby book.* New York: St. Martin's Press.

Hasselmeyer, E. G. (1964). The premature neonate's response to handling. *American Nurses Association, 11,* 15–24.

Hofer, M. A. (1975). Infant separation responses and the maternal role. *Biological Psychiatry, 10*(2), 149–153.

Hofer, M. A. (1976). The organization of sleep and wakefulness after maternal separation in young rats. *Developmental Psychobiology, 9*(2), 189–205.

Horton, F. H., Lubchenco, L. O., & Gordon, H. H. (1952). Self-regulatory feeding in a premature nursery. *Yale Journal of Biology and Medicine, 24,* 263–272.

Howard, J., Parmelee, A., Kopp, C., & Littman, B. (1976). A neurologic comparison of preterm and full-term infants at term conceptional age. *Journal of Pediatrics, 88,* 995–1002.

Hunt, J. V., & Rhodes, L. (1977). Mental development of preterm infants during the first year. *Child Development, 48,* 204–210.

Hunter, R. S., Kilstrom, N., Kraybill, E. N., & Loda, F. (1978). Antecedents of child abuse and neglect in premature infants: A prospective study in a newborn intensive care unit. *Pediatrics, 61*(4), 629–635.

Jones, R. A. (1981). A controlled trial of a regularly cycled oscillating waterbed and a non-oscillating waterbed in the prevention of apnea in the preterm infant. *Archives of Disease in Childhood, 56*(11), 889–891.

Jeannerod, M. (1969). Les mouvements du foetus pendant le sommeil de la mère. *Com. Ren. Soc. Biol., 163*(8/9), 1843–1847.

Kang, R. (1974). *The relationship between informing both parents of their infant's behavioral response patterns and the mother's perception of the infant.* Unpublished master's thesis, University of Washington.

Katz, V. (1971). Auditory stimulation and developmental behavior of the premature infant. *Nursing Research, 20,* 196–201.

Kennell, J. H., Jerauld, R., Wolfe, H., Chesler, D., Kreger, N. C., McAlpine, W., Steffa, M., & Klaus, M. H. (1974). Maternal behavior one year after early and extended postpartum contact. *Developmental Medicine & Child Neurology, 16,* 172–179.

Klaus, M. H., Jerauld, R., Kreger, N. C., McAlpine, W., Steffa, M., & Kennell, J. H. (1972). Maternal attachment: Importance of the first post-partum days. *New England Journal of Medicine, 281,* 460–463.

Klein, M., & Stern, L. (1971). Low birthweight and the battered child syndrome. *American Journal of Diseases of Children, 122,* 15–18.

Korner, A. F. (1979). Maternal rhythms and waterbeds: A form of intervention with premature infants. In E. B. Thoman (Ed.), *Origins of the infant's social responsiveness.* Hillsdale, NJ: Erlbaum.

Korner, A. F. (1981). What we don't know about waterbeds and apneic preterm infants. *Pediatrics, 68*(2), 306.

Korner, A. F., & Grobstein, R. (1966). Visual alertness as related to soothing in neonates: Implications for maternal stimulation and early deprivation. *Child Development, 37*(4), 867–876.

Korner, A. F., & Thoman, E. B. (1970). Visual alertness in neonates as evoked by maternal care. *Journal of Experimental Child Psychology, 10,* 67–78.

Korner, A. F., & Thoman, E. B. (1972). Relative efficacy of contact and vestibular stimulation in soothing neonates. *Child Development, 43*(2), 443–453.

Korner, A. F., Kraemer, H. C., Haffner, M. E., & Cosper, L. (1975). Effects of waterbed flotation on premature infants: A pilot study. *Pediatrics, 56*(3), 361–367.

Korner, A. F., Guilleminault, C., Van den Hoed, J., & Baldwin, R. B. (1978). Reduction of sleep apnea and bradycardia in preterm infants on oscillating waterbeds: A controlled polygraphic study. *Pediatrics, 61*(4), 528–533.

Korner, A. F., Forrest, T., & Schneider, P. (1981). *Development of a longitudinal assessment procedure for preterms; Preliminary results from an intervention study.* Paper presented at the Meetings of the Society for Research in Child Development, Boston.

Korner, A. F., Ruppel, E. M., & Rho, J. M. (1982). Effects of waterbeds on the sleep and motility of theophylline-treated preterm infants. *Pediatrics, 70,* 864–869.

Korner, A. F., Schneider, P., & Forrest, T. (1983). Effects of vestibular-proprioceptive stimulation on the neurobehavioral development of preterm infants: A pilot study. *Neuropediatrics, 14*(3), 170–175.

Korner, A. F., Thom, V. A., & Forrest, T. (1984a). Demonstration videotape entitled "Neurobehavioral Maturity Assessment of Preterm Infants (NB-MAP)."

Korner, A. F., Thom, V. A., & Forrest, T. (1984b). Unpublished manual of instructions entitled "Neurobehavioral Maturity Assessment for Preterm Infants (NB-MAP)."

Korner, A. F., Kraemer, H. C., Reade, E. P., Forrest, T., Dimiceli, S., & Thom, V. (in press). A methodological approach to developing an assessment procedure for testing the neurobehavioral maturity of preterm infants. *Child Development.*

Korones, S. B. (1976). Disturbance and infants' rest. In T. D. Moore (Ed.), *Iatrogenic Problems in Neonatal Intensive Care.* Report of the 69th Ross Conference on Pediatric Research, Ross Laboratories, Columbus, Ohio, pp. 94–97.

Kraemer, H. C. (1981). Coping strategies in psychiatric clinical research. *Journal of Consulting & Clinical Psychology, 49*(3), 309–319.

Kraemer, H. C., Jacob, R. G., Jeffery, R. W., & Agras, W. S. (1979). Empirical selection of matching factors in matched-pairs and matched-blocks small-sample research designs. *Behavior Therapy, 10,* 615–628.

Kraemer, H. C., Korner, A. F., & Hurwitz, S. (1985). A model for assessing the development of preterm infants as a function of gestational, conceptional and chronological age. *Developmental Psychology, 21,* 806–812.

Kramer, L. I., & Pierpont, M. E. (1976). Rocking waterbeds and auditory stimuli to enhance growth of preterm infants. *The Journal of Pediatrics, 88*(2), 297–299.

Kurtzberg, D., Vaughan, H. G., Jr., Daum, C., Grellong, B. A., Albin, A., & Rotkin, L. (1970). Neurobehavioral performance of low-birthweight infants at 40 weeks conceptional age: Comparison with normal fullterm infants. *Developmental Medicine & Child Neurology, 21,* 590–607.

Lawson, K., Daum, C., & Turkewitz, G. (1977). Environmental characteristics of a neonatal intensive care unit. *Child Development, 48,* 1633–1639.

League, R., Parker, J., Robertson, M., Valentine, V., & Powell, J. (1972). Acoustical environments in incubators and infant oxygen tents. *Preventive Medicine, 1,* 231–238.

Leiderman, P. H., Leifer, A. D., Seashore, M. J., Barnett, C. R., & Grobstein, R. (1973). Mother–infant interaction: Effects of early deprivation, prior experience and sex of infant. In J. I. Nurnberger (Ed.), *Biological and environmental determinants of early development,* ARNMD (Vol. 51). Baltimore: Williams & Williams.

Leiderman, P. H., & Seashore, M. J. (1975). Mother–infant separation: Some delayed consequences. In Ciba Foundation Symposium 33: *Parent-infant interaction.* Amsterdam: Elsevier.

Levine, S. (1971). Stress and behavior. *Scientific American, 224*(1), 26–31.

Lorion, R. P., & Lounsbury, J. W. (1982). Conceptual and methodological considerations in evaluating prevention interventions. In W. R. Tash & G. Stahler (Eds.), *Innovative approaches to mental health evaluations.* New York: Academic.

Lucey, J. F. (1977). Is intensive care becoming too intensive? *Pediatrics: Neonatology Supplement, 59*(2), 1064–1065.

Lucey, J. F. (1984). The sleeping, dreaming fetus meets the intensive care nursery. In C. C. Brown (Ed.), *The many facets of touch. Johnson & Johnson Pediatric Roundtable, 10,* 75–81.

Marriage, K. J., & Davies, D. A. (1977). Neurological sequelae in children surviving mechanical ventilation in the neonatal period. *Archives of Diseases in Childhood, 52,* 176–182.

Martin, R. J., Herrell, N., Rubin, D., & Faranoff, A. (1979). Effect of supine and prone positions on arterial oxygen tension in the preterm infant. *Pediatrics, 63,* 528–531.

Masi, W. (1979). Supplemental stimulation of the preterm infant. In T. Field, A. Sostek, S. Goldberg, & H. H. Shuman (Eds.), *Infants born at risk.* New York: Spectrum.

Mason, W. A. (1968). Early social deprivation in the non-human primates: Implications for human behavior. In D. C. Glass (Ed.), *Environmental influences.* New York: Rockefeller University Press & Russell Sage Foundation.

Mason, W. A. (1979). Wanting and knowing: A biological perspective on maternal deprivation. In E. B. Thoman (Ed.), *Origins of the infant's social responsiveness.* Hillsdale, NJ: Erlbaum.

Meisels, S. J. (1984). Prediction, prevention, and developmental screening in the EPSDT program. In H. W. Stevenson & A. E. Siegel (Eds.), *Child development research and social policy.* Chicago: University of Chicago Press.

Miller, G., Dubowitz, L. M. S., & Palmer, P. (1984). Follow-up of pre-term infants: Is correction of the developmental quotient for prematurity helpful? *Early Human Development, 9,* 137–144.

Minde, K., Shosenberg, N., Marton, P., Thompson, J., Ripley, J., & Burns, S. (1980). Self-help groups in a premature nursery—A controlled evaluation. *Behavioral Pediatrics, 96*(5), 933–940.

Minde, K., Shosenberg, N., Thompson, J., & Marton, P. (1983). Self-help groups in a premature nursery—Follow-up at one year. In J. D. Call, E. Galenson, & R. L. Tyson (Eds.), *Frontiers of infant psychiatry.* New York: Basic.

Neal, M. V. (1967). *The relationship between a regimen of vestibular stimulation and the developmental behavior of the premature infant.* University Microfilms Inc. No. 70-7342. Ann Arbor, Michigan.

Palmer, P. G., Dubowitz, L. M. S., Verghote, M., & Dubowitz, V. (1982). Neurological and neurobehavioral differences between preterm infants at term and full-term newborn infants. *Neuropediatrics, 13,* 183–189.

Parmelee, A. H. (1975). Neurophysiological and behavioral organization of premature infants in the first months of life. *Biological Psychiatry, 10*(5), 501–512.

Powell, L. F. (1974). The effect of extra stimulation and maternal involvement on the development of low birthweight infants and on maternal behavior. *Child Development, 45,* 106–113.

Prechtl, H. F. (1977). The neurological examination of the full-term newborn infant (2nd ed.). *Clinics in Developmental Medicine* (No. 63). S.I.M.P. (Spastics International Medical Publications) London: Heinemann; Philadelphia: J. B. Lippincott.

Pritchard, J. A., MacDonald, P. C., & Gant, N. F. (Eds.). (1985). *Williams Obstetrics* (17th ed.). Norwalk, CT: Appleton Century-Crofts.

Rausch, P. B. (1981). Effects of tactile and kinesthetic stimulation on premature infants. *JOGN Nursing,* January/February, pp. 34–37.

Rice, R. (1977). Neurophysiological development in premature infants following stimulation. *Developmental Psychology, 13,* 68–76.

Ryan, L. (1973). *Maternal perception of neonatal behavior.* Unpublished master's thesis, University of Washington.

Saint-Anne Dargassies, S. (1966). Neurological maturation of the premature infant of 28 to 41 weeks' gestational age. In F. Falkner (Ed.), *Human development.* Philadelphia and London: Saunders.

Sameroff, A. J. (1975). Early influences on development: Fact or fancy? *Merrill-Palmer Quarterly, 21,* 267–294.

Sameroff, A. J., & Chandler, M. J. (1975). Reproductive risks and the continuum of caretaking casualty. In F. D. Horowitz (Ed.), *Review of child development research, IV.* Chicago: University of Chicago Press.

Scarr-Salapatek, S., & Williams, M. L. (1973). The effects of early stimulation on low birthweight infants. *Child Development, 44,* 94–101.

Schaefer, M., Hatcher, R. P., & Barglow, P. D. (1980). Prematurity and infant stimulation: A review of research. *Child Psychiatry & Human Development, 10,* 199–212.

Schanberg, S. M., Evoniuk, G., & Kuhn, C. (1984). Tactile and nutritional aspects of maternal care: Specific regulators of neuroendocrine function and cellular development. *Proceedings of the Society for Experimental Biology and Medicine, 175,* 135–146.

Scott, S., & Richards, M. (1979). Nursing low-birthweight babies on lambswool. *Lancet, 1*(8124), 1028.

Seashore, M. J., Leifer, A. D., Barnett, C. R., & Leiderman, P. H. (1973). The effects of denial of early mother–infant interaction on maternal self-confidence. *Journal of Personality & Social Psychology, 26,* 369–378.

Seleny, F. L., & Streczyn, M. (1969). Noise characteristics in the baby compartment of incubators. *American Journal of the Disabled Child, 117,* 445–450.

Siegel, L. S. (1983). Correction for prematurity and its consequences for the assessment of the very low birth weight infant. *Child Development, 54,* 1176–1188.

Sigman, M., Kopp, C. B., Littman, B., & Parmelee, A. H. (1977). Infant visual attentiveness in relation to birth condition. *Developmental Psychology, 13*(5), 431–437.

Simeonsson, R. J., Cooper, D. H., & Scheiner, A. P. (1982). A review and analysis of the effectiveness of early intervention programs. *Pediatrics, 69*(5), 635–641.

Solkoff, N., Yaffe, S., Weintraub, D., & Blase, B. (1969). Effects of handling on the subsequent development of premature infants. *Developmental Psychology, 1,* 765–768.

Solkoff, N., & Matuszak, D. Tactile stimulation and behavioral development among low birthweight infants. *Child Psychiatry & Human Development,* 1975, *6,* 33–37.

Sostek, A. M., Quinn, P. O., & Devitt, M. K. Behavior, development and neurological status of premature and full-term infants with varying medical complications. In T. Field, A. Sostek, S. Goldberg, & H. H. Shumann (Eds.), *Infants born at risk.* New York: Spectrum.

Spinnato, J. A., Sibai, B. M., Shaver, D. C., & Anderson, G. D. (1984). Inaccuracy of Dubowitz gestational age in low birth weight infants. *Obstetrics & Gynecology,* 1984, *63*(4), 491–495.

Sterman, M. B. (1967). Relationship of intrauterine fetal activity to maternal sleep stage. *Experimental Neurology* (Suppl. 4), 98–106.

Thoman, E. B., & Korner, A. F. (1971). Effects of vestibular stimulation on the behavior and development of rats. *Developmental Psychology, 5,* 92–98.

Usher, R., & McLean, F. (1969). Intrauterine growth of live-born Caucasian infants at sea level: Standards obtained from measurements in 7 dimensions of infants born between 25 and 44 weeks of gestation. *Journal of Pediatrics, 74*(6), 901–910.

White, J., & Labarba, R. (1976). The effects of tactile and kinesthetic stimulation on neonatal development in the premature infant. *Developmental Psychobiology, 9,* 569–577.

CHAPTER 21

Objective and Subjective Aspects of Parent–Infant Relations: An Attempt at Correlation Between Infant Studies and Clinical Work

BERTRAND G. CRAMER

Recently, increased attention to infancy has reached the domain of clinical work. Clinicians working with at risk infants and with babies presenting various symptoms (especially so-called functional disorders) are eager to test the relevance of infancy studies for their practice.

In this chapter, I will try to assess how cross-fertilization can take place between clinical and research data in this relatively new field of infancy. My point of view—which is that of a clinician—is that certain types of studies, especially those concerning interactions, will be of great benefit for clinical practice and for understanding theoretical issues in psychoanalytically based concepts of development (Stern, 1983). Similarly, I believe that clinical work with parents and infants can contribute to formulating important research questions in the field of infancy.

EPISTEMOLOGICAL PROBLEMS: "BABY MODELS" ARE DIFFERENT IN CLINICAL AND RESEARCH WORK

Before attempting an integration of data stemming from clinical, psychoanalytically derived work and from academic research, one has to acknowledge fundamental differences between these two realms of discourse.

The experimentalist may work on the basis of a model that is so different from that of the clinician that it appears that these two babies have nothing in common. Each field works on the basis of a "metaphor" of the infant that rests on very specific paradigms, corresponding to ideologies that may seem totally at odds.

Kuhn's (1972) work has publicized the notion that what scientists "observe" is predetermined by the model to which they adhere. It is therefore useful to make these epistemological models explicit: We need to assess to what extent the "clinical baby" can be compared to, or even identified with, the "experimental baby." On the other hand, we might see that data from these two fields cannot be integrated, and that, at best, they are complementary.

To date, one is much more impressed by the discrepancies between the two fields; it is very rare in their formulations, and even rarer in their practice, that clinicians use data that they may have gathered in traditional child development journals. Conversely, experimentalists rarely quote work published in clinical or psychoanalytic journals. One must note, however, that infancy offers more potential opportunities for transdisciplinary work (and therefore for "cross-fertilization" of models) than do other age groups because of the fact that in infancy biology and culture seem more intimately intermeshed than later. It is striking that some of the most influential research in the field of interaction has been done by colleagues who have had clinical training but who simultaneously refer frequently to nonclinical work and use experimental methods in their own research (e.g., Brazelton, Emde, Sander, Stern).

SOME BASIC EPISTEMOLOGICAL TRENDS IN INFANCY STUDIES

If we first consider *research*-oriented infancy studies, we can detect the influence of certain models that are generally at odds with those referred to in clinical, psychoanalytically derived studies.

We will review successively:

1. A biological model that stresses the innate rather than outcomes based on learning
2. An adaptive model focusing on healthy development, fostering a positive relationship to the environment, rather than a pathologically based model as is most often found in clinical studies
3. A social model that focuses on motivations explained on an interpersonal basis rather than on a secondary drive model

A Biological Model

The discovery of innate, "wired-in" programs that predispose the infant to have competent interactions with the environment is the single most powerful new model of the infant. This proposition has led to the now widely used phrase *the competent infant,* creating what amounts to a new metaphor—or paradigm—about babies, in marked contrast to the helpless infant of psychoanalytically based, drive-oriented models, or to the "reflex baby" of neurological textbooks.

A kind of biopsychology is thus proposed; such psychological functions as affect reading, role taking, reciprocity, memory, or even "the self" are predicated on the basis of a biologically determined preparedness.

This biology of behavior is linked to several lines of thinking. Among them, a most influential one is evolutionary theory.

Evolutionary Theory

Recently, there has been a revival of Darwinian thinking, and a "wisdom of nature" ideology—strongly supported by the fabulous discoveries of molecular biology—that has been superseding the social and learning theories of former decades.

A foremost example of this point of view is illustrated in the "new" theories of affect. Tomkins's (1962) work on discrete affects derives directly from Darwin's studies on primary affect expression. The infant is now seen as having an innate vocabulary of affect expression (facial features, but also vocalizations) that serves as an amplifier of inner states, as a communication of urgent needs to the caregiver, and also as a facilitator of attachment. Not only affect *expression* but also affect *recognition* is postulated as being inborn. Emde (1984) illustrates this point of view well when he suggests that affect serves as a *central nervous system–based organizer* that will guide the infant's behavior, thus serving adaptation.

There are now a host of data illustrating an innate preadaptedness for exchange with the (human) environment often referred to as resulting, hypothetically, from evolutionary selection in the service of survival. Such preadaptation is inferred in research showing preferences for a human facelike visual gestalt (Fantz, 1963), a feminine voice, and maternal odor (MacFarlane, 1975). It is also inferred when one speaks of early predisposition for synchrony (Condon & Sander, 1974) or for reciprocity (Brazelton, 1974). These data all illustrate the same point, that is, that there is an innate, biologically determined predisposition for human attachment in the service of survival.

Ethology

The field of ethology has also provided important models for infant studies. First, the *primary* nature of attachment has been stressed. Second, models and techniques for observing behaviors have been provided. Surface behaviors were given new credit after being eclipsed by so-called depth theories. The *details* of behavioral sequences, within closely observed time periods, were valued and revealed in microanalytic studies of video recordings. Generally, within this framework, greater attention was paid to what can be called species-specific behaviors, at the expense of personal, individual motivations. Also, the how was now more valued than the why.

Physiological Correlates of Behaviors

The return to biology has also been revealed by the large amount of work carried out on physiological underpinnings of behaviors, such as in studies of sleep, heart rate, and voice spectrography (W. Berg & K. Berg, 1979).

Evolutionary theory, ethology, and the study of physiological correlates of behavior contribute to a massive return of biological models in psychology.

This involves a strong emphasis on innate factors; it also focuses attention on modalities of form rather than content, on the how rather than the why.

There is a definite trend toward eliciting the physical modalities of behaviors at the expense of a search for meaning, such as is typical for psychoanalysis. This is done according to the model of natural sciences, with strong reliance on methods allowing definite objectification of data making statistical methods applicable.

It is important to stress this heavy reliance on natural science–derived models allowing for the study of visible, objective behaviors while precluding the assessment of more experiential subjective factors, which are at the core of clinical studies.

An Adaptive Model

Many infancy studies attempt to answer questions such as: What makes the infant capable of interacting *favorably* with its environment? The accent is thus on successful performances fostering adaptation, and on factors that facilitate attachment and interaction.

This orientation is far from that of classical psychoanalytic studies, which rely most often on pathological cases and in which the problem is that the adaptive mechanisms have failed. The typical approach of psychoanalysis is toward the conflictual basis of behaviors with the accent being placed on genetic, archaic (and unconscious) predeterminants. Behavior is seen as resulting less from efforts toward adaptation than from defensive work against anxiety.

Following Hartmann's (1939) hypotheses concerning the role of conflict-free, autonomous ego functions in fostering adaptation, longitudinal studies of child observation had given the hope that the inner works of adaptation could be documented. Overall they have failed in revealing how reality is recognized by the child, and how the contact to reality is maintained; they have, however, provided many insights into the role of conflict in choices of defenses and modes of object relations.

One must recognize that the psychoanalytic method is not designed to reveal adaptive mechanisms mainly because its technique enhances regressive functioning. A good example of the nonadaptive bias of psychoanalytical models is the persistence—in analytic circles—of notions of the very young infant (Mahler, 1975) as autistic or helpless, or in a nonobject world.

Thus while it is clear that psychoanalysis provides little insight about adaptation, focusing mostly on unconscious conflicts and fantasies, we will try to illustrate later that the psychoanalytic study of infant psychopathology can reveal much on the dynamisms that organize interactions.

A Social Model

One of the main differences in models when one moves from psychoanalytically oriented studies to the "new" infant research is the abandonment of a *secondary drive theory* in favor of a primary attachment one. Bowlby (1959) was most instrumental in this conversion; he rejected the anaclitic model, stating that attachment is not leaning on a drive gratification, but corresponds to a primary need, and is mediated through innate behaviors such as sucking, clinging, following, crying, smiling. Interestingly, Bowlby already used the term *interaction* (rather than the psychoanalytic word *relations*), in this important paper, heralding the development that became so powerful 20 years later.

Freud had described a basically asocial baby; what prompted him into fleeting moments of relations was the search for gratification and tension reduction. This essentially asocial model remained very strong in psychoanalysis; the infant had no relations to speak of, either because it was only invested in drive vicissitudes (i.e., in internal state regulations), or because it was in an undifferentiated phase (Hartmann) allowing for no recognition of the object, or because it was autistic (Mahler). The infant was considered either too narcissistic (i.e., turned inward) or too immature to be able to build relations. The developmental point of view, so widely prevalent in many American and British psychoanalytical groups, did much to fixate this asocial ideology; highly respected American psychoanalysts still state that before age 1 the baby is essentially a neurological organism. From this point of view, the infant is deprived of an inner psychological life, and the timetable of central nervous system maturation is referred to in order to buttress this theory.

Most American psychoanalysts find it very difficult to attribute intrapsychic representations (and conflicts) to the infant; thus object relations proper would start only after symbolic activity develops, which is seen as occurring only after age 1. Even Lichtenberg, who attempted an integration of psychoanalytic theory (of the ego psychology type) with infancy data, did not deviate from this theory: "Only with the maturation of many capacities, beginning after the end of the first year, does the activity develop to create an image of the self" (1983, p. 63); "intrapsychic self and object representations are developments of the second, rather than the first year" (1983, p. 57). No evidence is given for this sudden onset of representational life after the first year; it seems as if Lichtenberg believes that the richness of interactions amply demonstrated in infant studies is a purely behavioral manifestation, with no corresponding inner experience or representation.

Clearly, old theories die hard! And yet a very influential psychoanalytical trend had long advocated that relations exist since birth. Melanie Klein postulated relations to objects in infants, and Balint (1949) talked about primary object love as early as 1937. In France, where ego psychology was never accepted, one would be hard put to find a psychoanalyst today who does not believe in some form of object tie and representational life in infancy. Thus in a paradoxical way, interactional studies postulating sophisticated relations in infancy are much more in harmony with non-American than with ego psychology–derived psychoanalysis.

We will try to illustrate later the opportunities for integration of a primary attachment model with psychoanalytic propositions; clearly, the big problem concerns the nature of *motivation* for attachment and interaction. Can we adhere to a model that postulates a social drive only, or do we have to include pleasures or aversions of another type, such as psychoanalysis proposes?

Problems of the Biological, Adaptive, and Social Models for the Clinician

The biological, adaptive, and social models proposed in most infancy studies present certain challenges for the clinician when trying to integrate them in his usual conceptualizations.

BIOLOGICAL.   With the return to what Ainsworth (1971) has called a behavioral biology comes a natural science ideology and method; the accent is on making objective many aspects of behavior and interactions. The clinician is used to dealing with meaning and subjective experience, especially if he is dynamically oriented. How is he going to reconcile the objective data of infancy studies with the subjective information gathered from his patients?

In what follows, I will argue that when one deals with mother–infant interactions there is a tremendous advantage to taking into account simultaneously objective data defining interactions and their subjective correlates at the level of parental verbalizations. Doing so, one follows the physical properties of interactions such as those characterizing gaze exchange, vocalizations, body contact and the like, and the mental contents of parents that simultaneously define the relationship.

Microanalytic analyses of interactional behaviors are recorded and correlated with the verbal reports that parents make of their inner, subjective experience about the relationship. This bifocal perspective relies on a natural science approach to behavior (as in ethology) as well as on a traditional clinical approach to mental contents. As such it might serve as a bridge between traditional infancy research and clinical work.

ADAPTIVE. Infancy studies use "normal" subjects to illustrate the baby's marvelous adaptive capacities. Can we compare such data with those obtained in clinical work where we are witness—as clinicians—to the failures of adaption and the work of pathology? In what follows I will try to document that symptoms are in fact, a form of communication that the baby establishes in order to remain contingent with the parent's particular, if pathological, set of values, predilections, and inhibitions.

In clinical work we are often confronted with the infant's amazing capacity to respond to the parent's most pressing (and unconscious) demands; they seem to "read" the nature of the parent's psychological needs and in fact *adapt* to them in a way that is equivalent to the capacity for reciprocity described in "normal" babies.

Thus a study of symptomatic interaction and pathology may be highly revealing as to the nature of communication between parents and infants; as such it contributes to overall knowledge of subjects such as contingency, reciprocity, and attunement which were originally described in nonpathological subjects.

SOCIAL. The social model, following Bowlby's definition, describes attachment and interaction as a goal in itself. Some authors go as far as to propose that mothers *and infants* have an *intention* to reciprocate (Cohn and Tronick, 1982), or that they seek "an optimal level of arousal which is affectively positive" (Stern, 1974, p. 210), or that communication is an attractive goal in itself (Emde, 1980), or that the experience of contingency generates pleasure (Papoušek, 1983). It is obvious that mothers and infants like interacting. But unless one proposes a motivational force fueling such pleasurable exchanges, one might end up formulating a tautology: Mothers and babies do interact because they like interacting!

When it comes to motivations, clinical psychoanalysis has some hypotheses to offer that complement the "social" model previously defined: relations are fueled by the need to produce gratifications, to avoid anxiety and loss. While we know very little about the infant's inner experience concerning the motivations for establishing and maintaining relations, we can gather a great deal of information on the parent's need for relationships, and on the influence of this need on shaping interactions. What is more, studying parent–infant interactions clinically can provide information on how the infant learns how to develop intentions on the basis of what he perceives of his parent's motivational preferences.

A main contribution of clinical work with parents and infants concerns the sharing of intentions between partners: parental expectations, values, preferences, and avoidances will determine in a crucial way how infants establish their motivational hierarchies. Thus, when one tries to formulate what fuels interactions, it is not enough to say that both parties like interacting; one needs to study what private values are invloved in determing interactions. In order to carry out such research, one needs to study the parent's mental representations of their relationship to their infant and to the infant's particular way of organizing his contribution to the interactive scenario that is thus created. In order to achieve this goal, we will turn first to the parent's motivational set and its contribution to organizing interactions.

THE PARENTS' SUBJECTIVE CONTRIBUTIONS TO INTERACTION

In classical psychoanalytic studies, the parent–infant relationship was seen as essentially asymmetrical: The infant was seen as helpless and relying for its adaptation on the parent's much greater competence.

Interaction studies attempt to modify this point of view, stressing the infant's competence and its powerful influences on the caregiver (Lewis & Rosenblum, 1974).

Some infant researchers, however, maintain that it is the parents who are the main contributors to the development of mutuality. They subjectively *interpret* the infant's behavior as revealing an intention of mutual exchange.

In his study of the burst-pause pattern of sucking and the mother's reaction to it, Kaye (1982) states: "By making the mother and infant tend to take turns, the pauses and her [the mother's] effect upon them contribute to the mother's *illusion* that she and the baby are communicating" (p. 188). I emphasize the word *illusion* to illustrate the role played by what the mother imagines of the interaction on the development of mutuality. She is the one who injects intentionality into the infant's behavior.

We should be careful to distinguish between the effects of the infant's behavior and the *intended* effects we attribute to it. "The baby is for some time one who is learning first how to intend, and then how to realize intentions" (Dunn, 1982, p. 201).

From the point of view of research strategy, it is thus safer—and certainly much easier—to study how *parents* contribute to the shaping of intentionality in interaction. This point of view is recognized in some infancy research and referred to as the process of *meaning attribution*.

MEANING ATTRIBUTION

The observable interaction is accompanied by a less visible process through which parents attribute meaning to all of the infant's behavior. This attribution is not merely a verbal labeling of the infant's actions and expressions; in fact, it is more like a highly personalized interpretation of the child's behavior.

In clinical settings, as in research settings, when one pays attention to mothers' verbal reports about what they *think* of the interaction, one is always impressed by the great variation in meanings that mothers attribute to identical behaviors in infants. It is important to document these observations because, as we will see later, clinical practice indicates unequivocally that such interpretations play a *crucial role in determining the unfolding of the interaction*. Meaning attribution should be seen as one of the main influencing factors at the level of motivations that explain interactions. As a concept, it provides a potential bridge between research and clinical work. It allows for a potential articulation between what is seen and what is heard, what is in the realm of perception and what is in that of meaning, and what is objective and what is subjective.

Meaning attribution, as an inevitable part of the interaction process, has been referred to by various researchers: Robson (1964) cites the example of a mother who, when she attempts to capture her 3-week-old baby's glance, says: "He looks daggers" (p. 19). Lebovici (1983) presents a case of an infant showing a peculiar forward thrust of his fisted hand when in distress. The mother comments about this gesture saying: "He shows his fist to his father" (p. 300), thus interpreting the child's movement in terms of her own resentment against her husband. Emde (1982) describes a particular form of meaning attribution, referring to the mother's reading of the infant's emotional state; he considers this interpretation to be an essential ingredient of emotional availability. Bruner (1982) describes the crucial importance of meaning attribution in the development of language. The mother acts as if the child has intentions in its mind, thus involving the infant in an adultomorphizing process; this form of attribution is an essential part of the language acquisition device which the mother puts at the service of the child. By attributing meaning to the barest of the infant's utterances, the mother introduces the infant into the symbolic world of the adults; she thus primes the infant for its participation in the world of culture (Bruner, 1982). The notion of entrainment (Brazelton, 1984) might also be used to describe similar phenomena. Parents constantly submit each of the infant's behaviors to influences stemming from their own private set of expectations, ideals, prohibitions, predilections, and so on. Through this process, various aspects of the infant's repertoire are selected and enhanced, while others are censored and extinguished. In this way, cultural and personal sets of values will be transmitted. Shotter and Newson argue that meaning attribution "influences the timing and the manner of the mother's response, and it lays the foundation from which the communication of shared meanings begins to grow" (cited by J. Dunn, 1982, p. 201).

Meaning attribution is at work even during pregnancy, when parents never fail to translate the fetal motility patterns in terms of "strong" or "soft," "active" or "lazy," and so forth, thus laying the foundation for a semantic matrix into which each of the infant's productions will be integrated and invested with meaning. Thus if we take meaning attribution into account, interactions between infants and parents no longer appear symmetrical. The infant displays whatever inner states it experiences with the means at its disposal, that is, affect displays, vocalizations, motor activity, and so on. But only the parents can attribute meaning to these behaviors according to their past history, their cultural heritage, and the social context that predetermines their expectations. The parents' internal representational resources are incomparably richer than those of the infant, and these inner representations will orient all of the parents' behavior and influence the nature, shape, and direction of the interaction. Tremendous pressures are applied on the child's productions and states, embedding them instantaneously into a web of meanings predetermined in the parents' minds. Thus intentions in the infant develop within the constraints and the confines of these parental interpretations; at every moment and at the level of every production, the infant is engulfed in the process that gives a significance to whatever it does. The process of meaning attribution is *always* influential. However, it is much more visible in pathological cases than in normal development, which is why the clinical situation is irreplaceable in revealing the power of such interpretations.

We could not find a better formulation of the importance of meaning attribution than Hinde's: *"What a person thinks about a relationship may be more important than the interaction that actually occurs"* (1976, p. 4).

Hinde stresses that subjective evaluation may be a more influential determinant than the objective factors that we may observe. He adds: "Mothers perpetually overestimate the element of intent in infant behavior: does this mean that the mother–infant relationship depends for its nature on a delusion?" (p. 14). This is indeed an arresting question. An overestimation would be, according to Hinde, a normal, integral part of parenting; in other words, *a false perception, or a distortion of reality, would be basic in the development of parent–infant interactions.* Hinde goes so far as to suggest that this is akin to a delusion, that is, to a pathological process. How could such a "deviant" form of thinking be considered essential for parenting? How could a pathological-like phenomenon (i.e., a delusion) be adaptive?

This paradox is a fundamental question in behavioral science in general and in infant studies in particular. How can we simultaneously take into account the objective aspects of behavior, that is, its formal characteristics, and the subjective meaning that reveals intentions and motivation, and that can appear as deviant or bizarre? If we focus uniquely on signs that can be measured, or counted, or scored, we remain at the level of mechanistic explanations, and lose sight of the fact that identical behaviors might have a totally different relevance according to what sets of private meanings they have for the parents, and for the child. On the other hand, if we remain only at the level of motivations and meanings, we never capture the means through which attachment, communications, and relationships can take place. What is more, while meanings and subjective factors may be easy to detect at the parental level, they cannot be verbalized by infants; in the latter, we might get a glimpse of its experience precisely through the study of behavioral, "objective" correlates.

A PROPOSITION FOR CLINICAL INFANT RESEARCH

My main thesis is that we should be able to study simultaneously these two realms of phenomena: the observable, objective parameters of interactions together with the meanings that underlie them.

In the research literature, one of the best examples of this double-focus approach, touching simultaneously objective and subjective factors, was presented by Stern in his now classical paper on the differential interaction between a mother and her twin boys. (Stern, 1971). In short, Stern demonstrated first that one could make objective marked differences in the gaze exchange between the mother and each boy; that is, with the boy Mark, en face gazing lasted five times longer than with Fred. When Mark and mother were en face, they terminated this position equally frequently, while with Fred, it was *he* who terminated it most often. (In fact, he terminated it nine times more often than did the mother.) These "hard data" were collected by a natural science method, based on a process of objectification of behaviors that were made perceptible with the use of microanalytic study of video recordings. These and other objective data from the interaction process document, in a way that provides a powerful sense of conviction, marked differences in the way the mother and each twin handled and organized their interaction. The differences are striking, with one interactive party doing very well, and the other showing a marked lack of reciprocity or contingency. These differences seem all the more difficult to understand because we are observing twins (although they were fraternal twins).

The researcher has to turn to the clinical approach in order to understand the why of such a difference, which is precisely what Stern did when he shifted from mere looking to listening, and from observing phenomena to questioning the meaning that codetermines them. Stern questioned the mother and she revealed that she felt ambivalent about Fred, *that she saw in him the bad aspects of her husband;* Mark, on the other hand, *represented* her own "good" self.

This work provided an example of the integrated approach that I am advocating as most promising for the field of infant development. Stern's approach objectifies the mechanics of interaction and reveals the process of meaning attribution, showing totally different intentions in the mother's ministration of these two boys. He respects both the formal and the "content" aspects of behaviors, providing a synthetic vista of mechanisms *and* causes.

Clinical research in this field could profit greatly by utilizing such a methodology:

1. Child and parent need to be seen together.
2. Formal aspects of interactions need to be recorded and described.
3. The process of meaning attribution needs to be simultaneously recorded, on the basis of the parents' verbal reports of what they feel or think about the child and about the exchange.
4. In an attempt at synthesizing these two sets of data, particular attention needs to be paid to *coincidences* between the emergence of certain *themes* in the parent's report, and the occurrence of corresponding interactions.

COINCIDENCE BETWEEN THEMES AND INTERACTIONS

Clinical practice teaches us that certain infant behaviors, especially symptomatic behaviors, may coincide with mental contents that the parent, most often the mother, reveals simultaneously. For example, a young mother came into a consultation because she was very anxious about her 2-month-old boy, who presented regurgitations. In spite of reassurance, she was convinced that he would die. Soon after the clinician started to talk with the mother, she revealed that she was still very upset about her brother's death 3 months before the baby's birth. She then reported that on her last visit to him, in the hospital, he looked emaciated, smelled very bad, and kept regurgitating; this impression was so powerful that she fainted. The brother died soon thereafter. She did not cry once, and avoided the burial; clearly, she had not gone through a real mourning process. What was remarkable was the coincidence that occurred: While she was describing this painful scene *the baby suddenly regurgitated.*

It was simple then for the clinician to understand the situation. He simply said: "The baby regurgitates *as* your brother did." This intervention had a powerful effect; the mother started to cry for the first time and spoke at length about her relationship to the lost brother. At the next meeting, she expressed her relief, allowed herself to feel sad about her brother, and no longer felt anxious about her infant.

Two things are worth pointing out:

1. The infant "chose" a symptom—the regurgitation—that had a very precise meaning for its mother. Did this occur by chance? What is more, when she talked about her brother's regurgitations, he "answered" by regurgitating. Again, is this chance only, or is it a form of communication? Couldn't we say that this interaction was dictated by the need—shared by mother and infant—to create a scenario where the child's symptom allowed the mother to avoid the painful realization of her brother's death?

2.   What infant messages was the mother focusing on to orient her interaction with him? Was she reacting to his perceptible messages, to the *reality* of his behavior (as we learn from interaction studies), or was she monitoring her perception of the child through the "delusion" (I am referring here to Hinde's quote) that he represented her dead brother? In other words, was she objectively reading her child's messages, or was she subjectively imagining that the child was her brother, through the identity of symptoms (the regurgitation) that they both shared? Following Fraiberg's (1980) formulations, was the mother reacting to the brother's ghost rather than to the infant itself?

My main point here is that the occurrence of a (symptomatic) behavior, that is, the regurgitation, corresponds to determining factors in the realm of what we may call an imaginary interaction. The regurgitation, which seems maladaptive, or pathological, may be, in fact, highly contingent upon hidden, subjective factors that are as influential as objective forces on the development of the interaction.

It is the systematic study of such coincidences between a visible, objective behavior and a simultaneous process of meaning attribution in the parents that may teach us much about the mutual influences of these two aspects—visible and imaginary—of interactions.

THE RELEVANCE OF CLINICAL WORK FOR INFANT RESEARCH

Clinical situations lend themselves particularly well to the study of coincidences between the visible and imaginary because symptomatic behavior (most often attributed to the infant) leads easily to the unraveling of attendant meaning attribution processes, in the form of anxieties, fantasies, and projections of parental psychic contents. The study of pathological situations can teach us much on processes of communication between parents and infants. Many infant symptoms are closely linked to parental meaning attributions; it often happens in consultation or therapy that the interpretation to the parents of the projection they impose on the child of their own conflicts will transform—or even eradicate—the symptomatic behavior expressed by the infant. In this way, clinical work can reveal major determinants of infant behavior and give us clues as to the causation of interactions at the level of parents' private, subjective meaning attribution.

Such clinical experience allows me to challenge a point of view strongly expressed by many infancy researchers, that is, that the study of pathological conditions biases infant behaviors in a way that obscures issues of adaptation and competence. In fact, many infant symptoms can be understood in terms of an adaptive response to parental communication; they may be seen as contingent upon a particular need expressed by the parent.

Therapy conducted with mothers and infants may be similar, in some ways, to experimental work: In the therapeutic process, we may be able to illustrate coincidences between typical interactive sequences and meaning attributions; if we then show that a clarification of this link is followed by mutations in the interaction, we may consider that meaning attribution and the corresponding interaction are linked in a cause and effect relationship. If meaning attributions are so influential on so-called symptomatic behaviors, we might assume that in normal interactions meaning attributions are—as well—an important codeterminant. The nature of this influence may be understood as not basically different in these two frameworks; pathological conditions may provide a magnifying lens effect on so-called normal types of interactions.

Let us turn now to some clinical examples of the effects of meaning attributions.

CLINICAL EXAMPLES

The most frequent area in which so-called symptoms become the object of much anxiety (and psychiatric referral) for parents is feeding. Most often, parents are concerned that the child does not take in enough food, and, indeed, true anorexias, with or without failure to thrive, are frequently found.

Feeding difficulties are particularly well suited to illustrate failures of contingency; they are frequently characterized by intensive overfeeding, due to anxiety in the parent that does not allow him or her to respect feeding signals coming from the infant. Hunger cues can be ignored with the caregiver reacting more to his or her own inner needs, to the point where the infant's hunger signals are finally totally misread or even distorted.

> Example 1: A mother brought her 22-month-old daughter in for a consultation because of severe feeding difficulties. While we chatted, and the child was quietly playing with a doll, the mother, out of the blue, pulled a bottle from her bag and shoved it into the child's mouth *without any evidence that the child requested it*. I was struck by this lack of contingency and by the intrusive nature of the mother's contribution to this feeding interaction. A few minutes later, as the mother pulled out another bottle, ready to shove it into the child's mouth, I interrupted her action and asked her to refrain from feeding the girl. The mother complied, but reached into her bag again, pulled out a candy, and shoved it *in her own mouth*.

This sequence allowed me to bring to the mother's attention the compulsive, anticontingent nature of her "force-feeding"; moreover, I suggested that feeding the child was a vicarious way of feeding herself. The mother then reported that she harbored severe fears that her child might die of starvation if she did not force-feed her. She went on to report her own unfulfilled wish that her mother had been more of a caring, feeding figure for her and she described intense frustration related to her early relation to her mother.

This vignette demonstrates how an irrational fear (based on a starvation fantasy) for her child determined anticontingent, intrusive feeding behavior. Moreover, one can see that the mother reacted not to hunger signals from the child, but rather to her own frustrated needs for a feeding mother figure, now transferred to the child. This is an example of a mother interposing her own (past) image between herself and her child, creating a marked anticontingency.

> Example 2: In this case, awesome power was attributed to the infant. This 6-month-old girl showed a typical pattern of falling asleep when the mother put her to the breast. The feeding episodes were characterized by much tension on

the mother's part, by their short duration, and by their extreme frequency. This feeding interaction became understandable when the mother revealed her thoughts about Sarah: She thought that her crying was a demonstration of awesome power, and that she could not resist the child's "demandingness."

This attribution of power was linked to two subjective factors:

1. The mother's most enduring childhood tie was to her grandmother, whom she described as exceedingly strong. Sarah was unconsciously expected to be a reproduction of this grandmother, based on the mother's identification of "strength" in child and grandmother.
2. The mother suffered episodes of manic-depressive illness. When she was depressed (as was the case then), she felt weak, and she allocated her "crazy" (manic) strength to Sarah. This made her fear her daughter, as she feared her own "crazy" strength when she felt manic. She could not resist what she felt was strong and demanding in Sarah because at those times she attributed to the child her own unbending will that could not tolerate any frustration when she was manic.

How these attributions are communicated to the child and determine its behavior is a very important point. These "psychic contents" do not pass to the child magically. They follow the rules of interactive communication. It is through acts, facial displays, intonation, "vitality contours," and so on that these attributions determine the infant's response in the interaction.

Let us observe how these communications were mediated in interaction between mother and child: When Sarah was 17 months old, she was seen with her mother. She did not talk to her; she merely emitted willful grunts accompanying a hand gesture to which mother reacted as if they indicated an order to hand her an object. The mother behaved like an obedient (and exhausted) servant. When I tried to play with Sarah, I hid a series of cubes, but she would not look for them. I then offered her a large wooden ring, which she took hold of and pulled. I would not let go, setting the stage for a mini tug-of-war between us; we both pulled on the ring, and neither of us would let go.

I felt there was a normal dose of willfulness and negativism in this child. To my surprise, the mother commented: "She is stronger than you . . . she is really strong!" To the mother, the fact that Sarah refused to play the "hide a cube" game with me was a sign of superior strength, as was the fact that she did not let go of the wooden ring. Each time the mother was confronted with a similar type of interaction, she gave in, letting the child win the contest of wills; this is how she conveyed to Sarah that *she* was the stronger of the two.

This type of interaction was repeated again and again every day, giving the child the conviction that she was the mother's ruler. This pattern had already affected the child's development; her speech development was markedly delayed. In fact, she did not need to learn how to speak, since her wishes were met by the mother even before they were expressed.

The process of meaning attribution that organizes this relationship is based on the idea that the child is all-powerful and should experience no frustration. The mother would persistently favor the development of willfulness and negativism in the child's behavior by attributing to it an awesome power that she really desired for herself. This is how she interpreted Sarah's play as revealing: "She is stronger than you." Again, in this case, we see that the mother did not organize her side of the interaction contingently with the child's messages. Rather, she reacted to an imaginary child; it was the willful, omnipotent part of herself that was revived each time she went through a manic episode.

Clearly, this is a pathological case, with the mother crudely distorting the child's behavior in order to maintain an illusion of an all-powerful girl that she needed. But in "normal" cases, we certainly see how parents transfer onto their babies many signs of power, beauty, and intelligence, with a sense of conviction that more detached onlookers tend to find touching, if somewhat ridiculous. Thus it may be degree and visibility that distinguish normal from pathological interactions.

Example 3: This case is in the realm of feeding difficulty, with obvious pathological consequences for the child. I saw Evelyne when she was 6 weeks old. She had been hospitalized by her pediatrician because of protracted feeding difficulties, leading to a flattening of her growth curve. At 5 weeks, she weighed 200 g less than at birth. Typically, she fell asleep as soon as her mother bottlefed her; what is more, she would do so at the mere *sight* of the bottle!

When we recorded this automatic falling asleep at the bottle on videotape, we noted the following additional aspects of the mother–infant interaction:

1. The mother talked constantly in such a compulsive way that even I felt overwhelmed by this flow.
2. While she talked, the baby was held flat on her lap; she was like a rag doll, motionless, showing no initiative for long stretches of time.
3. When the mother, in response to my suggestion, finally addressed the child, she did so without leaving any room for the infant to take the initiative. She inundated the child with her verbal flow and loomed repeatedly, forcing the child into a too-close face-to-face exchange.
4. Evelyne showed marked and protracted gaze aversion. During a 4-min face-to-face free-play episode, she *never* looked at the mother's face, but did focus on objects such as the mother's earring and my watch.
5. At least on one occasion, we documented the type of coincidence I discussed before: While the mother talked about her own intense yearnings for being held and nurtured, she introduced a pacifier in Evelyne's mouth, despite the fact that the baby showed no sign whatsoever of wanting it.

In summary, the mother–infant interaction was characterized by marked lack of mutuality; it was the mother who always initiated contact or termination, while the baby was forced into passivity. There was lack of contingency; the mother fed the child compulsively, according to her own needs, and not in response to the infant's signals. Evelyne also showed a lack of contingency; when the mother communicated that *she* was ready to feed, the baby fell asleep. When the mother tried to get the child to look at her, Evelyne looked away. These failures in mutuality were so consistent as to suggest to anyone who watched the tapes that these two partners should be separated; this is what led to the child's hospitalization.

Correlation with Meaning Attribution Processes in the Mother

The mother reported a series of thoughts and fantasies that could be correlated with these failures in interaction.

The Death and Reincarnation Theme

The mother conceived her two daughters soon after the main figures in her life died: She wanted children to replace the grandmother and the uncle who had raised her. Certain feelings that she had toward these important persons of her past were transferred directly onto her daughters. For example, she attended her dying uncle during his terminal illness, and saw him progressively wasting away. The mother conceived her first child during that time; with her two daughters, she was obsessed with the idea that they should be fed very generously for fear that they would also waste away. She actually imagined that Evelyne might have a cancer, like her uncle, and that this would explain her diminishing weight.

It became clear that this mother wanted to recreate, through her children, her family or origin; in this way Evelyne and her sister were conceived as props for a "reincarnation" of dead loved ones. This reincarnation theme is very frequently found as the basis for imaginary interaction in pathological but also in normal parent–infant relations. A child is often conceived as such a replacement, and it will be "asked" to maintain a tie to a deceased or lost object. This is how first names are often chosen, with the child carrying the name of a lost one.

This issue has been beautifully described by Fraiberg (1980), who coined the phrase "ghosts in the nursery." In this form of imaginary interaction, the parent reacts contingently to the image of another, lost partner, who is interposed as a "ghost" between the parent and the child. Normally, this reaction does not bring large distortions to the relationship; it may, in fact, enhance the attachment to the new child, who is thus imbued with positive qualities.

But when the relationship to the lost one was bad, or fraught with intense ambivalence, fears of damage to the infant predominate and the interaction is organized around the parental need to *protect* the infant (against the parental ambivalence).

The Feeding Compulsion: Fear of Death

The mother fed the child up to 10 times an hour! She prepared more than 20 bottles at a time, and placed them all over the house in order always to be ready to feed Evelyne. During an interview, she said, while bringing a bottle to Evelyn's mouth, "This is *not* a pleasurable moment." She then explained that each time Evelyne opened her mouth, she shoved a bottle into it and while doing so, talked to the baby, half-jokingly asking her: "Are you afraid of something?"

Force-feeding the child was a must for the mother; she thus protected herself against the danger that the child might waste away and die (like the uncle).

A great deal of anticontingent behavior is motivated in this way by parents. Their ministrations are determined by a defensive need against the emergence of anxieties, often linked to the fear (and the unconscious attendant wish), that the child will die. On the infant's side, the anticontingent behavior (falling asleep during feeds) can be seen as avoidance mechanism; it is as if the infant produced a lowering of state (as in a habituation) to avoid an intrusive overload. We could summarize that *many anticontingent interactions are based on a simultaneous defensive avoidance pattern shared by the two partners.*

Peter Pan Fantasy

This mother explained that she never wanted her children to grow, because their growth must lead to their loss. She wanted to keep them the way they were, like dolls. This corresponds to a Peter Pan fantasy. Thus another meaning was attributed to feeding; proper feeding was unconsciously unwanted because it would lead to growth and loss.

Sexual Meaning Attributions

The mother said that she felt uneasy shoving things forcefully into Evelyne's mouth. She did not like the idea of a totally passive recipient of forced actions. She then explained that she could not stand any form of passivity or tranquility; she had to move and do all the time (and did she ever activate herself!). She did not like sexual relations, hated particularly being penetrated, and *never* showed any sign of pleasure to her 65-year-old husband. Her explanation was, "Then he would totally possess me!" She then explained that she found Evelyne's falling-asleep mechanism quite clever: "That way, she does not have to submit to my force-feeds!"

It is as if this mother transferred onto Evelyne her own fears of being passively penetrated and in this way being possessed. She found relief, paradoxically, in the fact that Evelyne resisted the force-feeding, just as *she* knew how to avoid sexual penetration. In a way, she fostered Evelyne's feeding avoidance, because it protected *her* against anxieties of being intruded upon passively.

In this example, we see again how difficult it is to use the dimension of contingency if one takes into account imaginary aspects of interactions. The mother's intrusive feeding behavior is anticontingent at the level of observable, objective interaction; she imposes, and the child avoids. But at the level of thoughts and fantasies, that is, at the level of imaginary interactions, the mother's and the infant's behavior were contingent upon a particular form of anxiety—the fear of being penetrated and possessed. Thus by avoiding the feeds Evelyne participated in a kind of mutuality with her mother's inner needs. If she showed pleasure in eating, and offered herself willingly to forceful feeds, the mother would become highly anxious, imagining that she would violate and possess her own daughter!

Commentary About Evelyne and Her Mother

I have described four hidden scenarios that powerfully codetermine the interaction between Evelyne and her mother. This is not an exhaustive list of meaning attributions in this case; however, enough material has been presented to provide an understanding of specific interactions and "symptoms."

Two such symptoms were modified during the intervention: Normal feeding resumed after the third session and the weight and height curve recovered slowly thereafter. After four sessions, the amount of time the child gazed at the mother's face increased. These modifications suggest that meaning attribution processes in the mother were causally related to the style of interaction and the formation of symptoms.

Example 4: This was a case in which the "symptoms" of the interaction were lack of physical, proximal contact; this 10-month-old boy and his mother missed the opportunities for body contact.

The mother complained about two things in her son Thomas. First, she felt that he was absolutely not attached to her. Second, he was agitated and when he had tantrums he went red, totally tensed up, and was on the verge of convulsions. He cried a lot and had sleeping difficulties.

During the first interview, a typical "coincidence" episode occurred. At my request, the mother took Thomas on her knees. He stood and soon investigated the mother's face with his fingers, poking, as is quite typical in children of that age, the mother's nose, eyes, and mouth. The mother tensed up (while she was at ease with Thomas on the floor) and said: "Don't hurt me!" and she put him immediately back on the floor. Thomas started yelling. Soon thereafter, she commented: "He doesn't like being held."

This episode occurred as the mother was giving me her physical history, revealing an impressive series of diseases and operations since early childhood. Commenting about her pregnancy, she complained that Thomas "already hurt" her as a fetus. At their first contact after birth, he ripped off the mother's intravenous drip. The coincidence here is twofold: First, while she revealed a subjective feeling of her body being sick, vulnerable, and damaged, she accused her son of further damaging it when he investigated her face. Second, she demonstrated the mechanics of what must have contributed to the marked lack of proximal, body exchange in the observable interaction: When the child initiated body contact (investigating his mother's face), she reacted anticontingently by increasing the distance between them and by pushing the baby down. What is more, we could observe that the child became fidgety and agitated, displaying what the mother felt was *his* symptomatic behavior, when she "rejected" his attempts at body contact. Third, there was a correlation between a fantasy or a subjective gestalt in the mother and a specific form of interaction characterized by mutual avoidance of body contact.

At the next appointment, the mother reported what she called a miraculous change. Thomas now slept well, showed no tantrums, was calmer and, what is more, sought more body contact with her. Telling evidence of a powerful change in the interaction occurred during an interactional episode at the end of the third session. The mother explained that she felt very anxious about a tendency within herself; sometimes she felt the urge to do nothing and to simply sink into total relaxation and let go. This reaction alarmed her, reminding her of similar tendencies to be like a "vegetable" as a child; to fight this tendency she explained that she tried hard to activate herself when she was with Thomas. We came to realize that she had applied a kind of artificial excitement to her interaction with Thomas, for fear of returning to her vegetable-like nature. As we talked about this need, Thomas, who was standing on her knees, progressively leaned against her shoulder, and we ended the interview with the baby totally relaxed, sound asleep against the mother's body. She was flabbergasted, explaining that this form of relaxation had never happened before.

To me, this occurrence was not a matter of chance. By allowing herself to let go of her defensive need to "jazz up" the interaction and to put distance between

Thomas and herself, this mother fostered what was necessary for these two partners to find a relaxed, tension-free body contact, enhancing sleep. Lessening the power of the meaning attribution of "body harm" allowed for such change.

When one witnesses this event on a videotape, with the baby's body nicely relaxed against the mother with her face showing both dismay and relief, one cannot escape the sense of conviction that what is heard and what is seen, the subjective report of the mother and the objective change in the interaction, are tightly knit together in a powerful interconnectedness.

Commentary About the Technique of Observation

These four clinical situations were described in some detail to provide the reader with insights into the clinician's method and means of observation.

The setting for such therapeutic interviews is simple: The baby and the mother (with, at times, the father) are seen for hour-long sessions over periods of weeks or months. Everything is recorded, and on reviewing the tapes attention is paid simultaneously to what is seen and what is heard. During analysis of the tapes, particular attention is paid to coincidence between a specific interaction episode (especially involving the "symptom," e.g., feeding) and attendant verbalization of meaning attributions in the parent. When the therapeutic process is successful, one can observe changes in the modes of parental psychic functioning. It is at this point that one can correlate a modification in meaning attribution and a mutation in the form of interaction. Quite frequently, when the distorting effects of meaning attribution are lessened, one can witness immediate symptom removal. When this occurs, the observer gains a sense of conviction about the close interconnectedness between psychic processes in parents and forms of interactions as well as symptom maintenance. On those occasions, one realizes fully the intimate link between imaginary interactions (in fantasy) and their counterpart at the level of overt visible interaction.

It is with the practice of such "participant observation" that clinicians can make contributions to the field of interaction. What they need to learn is how to practice simultaneously a keen observation of what is seen and a sensitive listening to what is said. In doing so, clinicians might contribute to the building of a bridge between the recent, fascinating discoveries of objective interactions and what they know best, which is the world of meaning and experience.

CONCLUSION

The new research on infant development, and especially on early interactions, provides us with objective criteria allowing for a kind of diagnosis of parent–infant exchange. Concepts such as contingency, emotional availability, attunement, reciprocity, and so forth are highly useful for an assessment of interactions. These criteria were long hoped for in clinical circles, because they held the promise for early screening and intervention in the realm of secondary prevention. These parameters give powerful insights into the mechanics of interactions, revealing their objective correlates, and allowing for the determination of qualitative "interactional profiles."

However, when it comes to explaining the why of interactions, one cannot be satisfied with the somewhat tautological concepts advanced in interactional studies. It is not enough to say that infants and parents are moved to interact because social interaction is a goal in itself. The process of meaning attribution provides us with interesting answers about the parental contribution to the intentions to interact. The study of this process confirms what Hinde (1976) suggested, namely, that "what a person thinks about a relationship may be more important than the interaction that actually occurs."

Both research and clinical reports on infancy indicate that parents always inject an added meaning to whatever goes on in the baby; this meaning is based on their own personal beliefs, ideals, and aversions. It is rooted in their personal history, their past, and their unconscious. It also betrays strong cultural biases, which are recognized in interaction research under the heading of contextual issues. If we look closely at interactions, we see that each of the child's behaviors is embedded in a maze of meanings attributed by parents.

What I suggest in this chapter is that we fully acknowledge the powerful, determining nature of such imaginary factors on the development of interaction. To test this proposition, we need to study, *simultaneously,* the objective and subjective aspects of relations. Indeed, subjective aspects, such as fantasies, anxieties, and ideals, can be made objective, and are worthy of scientific consideration. What is most fascinating for a study of the ontogeny of the human bond is a description of the continuous interplay between these two realms of interactions. This approach can be followed in clinical situations when a child is brought in because of a problem. The symptomatic behavior naturally generates a series of associations in the parent revealing the focus of his or her meaning attribution process. Often, an interaction is produced in coincidence with the revelation of such attributions; this is highly conducive to illustrating the correlation between observable and imaginary interactions. If, in addition, there is therapeutic effect, with a modification of interactive modes, one can establish causal links between the two sides of the interactions that can contribute to a deeper understanding of early bonds.

However, one must acknowledge that if we turn our attention to meaning, as revealed through verbalizations, we will necessarily know much more about the *parental* contributions to imaginary interactions than about the infant's. The dimension of the infant's inner experience remains far from our reach. Yet, as Dunn (1982) put it, "The infant learns how to intend" (p. 201) and we may learn much about the infant's inner world and about its "motivations" if we acknowledge the basic, essential intermeshing that exists between the child's experience and the process of meaning attribution that parents apply to it. The infant discovers its inner states partly through its perceptions according to the parent's face and affect. This is why the work on attunement is so crucial if we want to understand what can be called the fundamental process of shared subjectivity.

The main goal of this chapter has been to provide an impetus and a model for systematic correlation of the "objective" data on interaction with those of shared subjectivity. This correlation should foster new diagnostic and therapeutic tools for clinicians; but it should also widen the scope of research on interactions.

REFERENCES

Ainsworth, M. (1977). Attachment theory, and its utility in crosscultural research. In P. H. Leiderman, S. R. Tulkin, & A. Rosenfeld (Eds.), *Culture and infancy: Variations in the human experience.* New York: Academic.

Balint, M. (1949). Early developmental states of the ego. *International Journal of Psychoanalysis, 30,* 265–273.

Berg, W. K., & Berg, K. (1979). Physiological development in infancy: State, sensory function, and attention. In J. D. Osofsky (Ed.), *Handbook of infant development.* New York: Wiley.

Bowlby, J. (1958). The nature of the child's tie to his mother. *International Journal of Psychoanalysis, 39,* 305–313.

Brazelton, T. B., Koslowski, B., & Main, M. (1974). The origins of reciprocity: The early mother–infant interaction. In M. Lewis & L. A. Rosenblum (Eds.), *The effect of the infant on its caregiver.* New York: Wiley.

Brazelton, T. B. (1984). Why early intervention. In J. Call, E. Galenson, & R. Tyson, *Frontiers of infant psychiatry* (Vol. II). New York: Basic.

Bruner, J. (1982). The organization of action and the nature of the adult–infant transaction. In E. Tronick (Ed.): *Social interchange in infancy.* Baltimore: University Park Press.

Cohn, J. F., & Tronick, E. (1982). Communication rules and the sequential structure of infant during normal and depressed interaction. In E. Tronick (Ed.), *Social interchange in infancy.* Baltimore: University Park Press.

Condon, W. S., & Sander, L. W. (1974). Neonate movement is synchronized with adult speech: Interactional participation and language acquisition. *Science, 182,* 99–101.

Dunn, J. (1982). Comment: Problems and promises in the study of affect and intention. In E. Tronick (Ed.), *Social interchange in infancy.* Baltimore: University Park Press.

Emde, R. (1980). Emotional availability: A reciprocal reward system for infants and parents with implications for prevention of psychosocial disorders. In P. Taylor (Ed.), *Parent-infant relationships.* New York: Grune & Stratton.

Emde, R., & Sorce, J. (1982). The rewards of infancy: Emotional availability and maternal referencing. In J. Call, E. Galenson, & R. Tyson (Eds.), *Frontiers of infant psychiatry* (Vol. 1). New York: Basic.

Emde, R. (1984). The prerepresentational self and its affective core. In S. Kaplan & J. Lichtenberg (Eds.), *Reflections on self psychology.* New York: International Universities Press.

Fantz, R. (1963). Pattern vision in newborn infants. *Science, 140,* 296–297.

Fraiberg, S. (1980). *Clinical studies in infant mental health: The first year of life.* New York: Basic.

Greenspan, S., & Lieberman, A. (1980). Infants, mothers and their interaction. A quantitative clinical approach to developmental assessment. In S. Greenspan & G. Pollock, *The Course of Life.* U.S. Department of Health and Human Services, *80,* 768.

Hartmann, H. (1939). *Ego psychology and the problem of adaptation.* 1958, New York: International Universities Press.

Hinde, R. (1976). On describing relationships. *Journal of Child Psychology and Psychiatry, 17,* 1–19.

Kaye, K. (1982). Organism, apprentice, and person. In E. Tronick, *Social interchange in infancy.* Baltimore: University Park Press.

Kaye, K. (1982). *The mental and social life of babies.* Chicago: University of Chicago Press.

Kuhn, T. (1972). *La structure des révolutions scientifiques.* Paris: Flammarion.

Lebovici, S. (1982). *Le nourrisson, la mère et le psychanalyste.* Paris: Le Centurion.

Lichtenberg, J. (1983). *Psychoanalysis and infant research.* Hillsdale, NJ: Erlbaum.

Lewis, M., & Rosenblum, L. (1974). *The effect of the infant on its caregiver.* New York: Wiley.

Mahler, M. (1975). *The psychological birth of the human infant.* New York: Basic.

Macfarlane, A. (1975). Olfaction in the development of social preferences in the human neonate. In Ciba Foundation Symposium 33, *Parent-infant interaction.* Amsterdam: Elsevier. Excerpta Medica. North Holland. Associated Scientific Publishers.

Papoušek, M. (1983). Interactional failures: Their origins and significance in infant psychiatry. In J. Call, E. Galenson, & R. Tyson (Eds.), *Frontiers of infant psychiatry* (Vol. 1). New York: Basic.

Robson, K. (1964). The role of eye to eye contact in maternal–infant attachment. *Journal of Child Psychology and Psychiatry 8*, 13–15.

Stern, D. (1971). A microanalysis of mother–infant interaction. Behavior regulating social contact between a mother and her three and a half months old twins. *Journal of the American Academy of Child Psychiatry, 10,* 501–517.

Stern, D. (1974). Mothers and infants at play: The dyadic interaction involving facial, vocal and gaze behavior. In M. Lewis & L. Rosenblum (Eds.), *The effect of the infant on its caregiver.* New York: Wiley.

Stern, D. (1983). The early development of schemes of self, of other, and of various experiences of "self with other." In S. Kaplan & J. Lichtenberg (Eds.), *Reflections on self psychology.* New York: International Universities Press.

Stern, D., Hofer, L., Haft, W., & Dore, J. (1984). Affect attunement: The sharing of feeling states between mother and infant by means of inter-modal fluency. In T. Field & N. Fox (Eds.), *Social perception in infants.* Norwood, NJ: Ablex.

Tomkins, S. S. (1962). *Affect, imagery, consciousness.* New York: Springer.

Trevarthen, C. (1977). Descriptive analysis of infant communicative behavior. In H. R. Schaffer (Ed.), *Studies in mother–infant interaction.* London: Academic.

Current Issues and Perspectives

Part Five, "Current Issues and Perspectives," continues major new directions, areas of controversy, and points of integration within the field of infancy. While readers may recognize other areas that could have been included in this section, additional concerns have already been raised in previous chapters in this volume. As the editor, I have requested that the authors of these chapters present the issues in as unbiased a way as possible, while clearly recognizing that each holds a strong and informed opinion about the area that he or she has covered.

Inge Bretherton presents a comprehensive view of theory and research in the area of attachment and places the work in a broader psychoanalytic framework. As is reflected in the monograph published recently in this area (Bretherton & Waters, 1985), there is much breadth and strength in attachment research and literature, and this is likely to be the case for at least the near future. In an integrative way, Bretherton shows how several psychoanalytic theorists (Fairbairn, Sullivan, Mahler, & Stern) who have studied relationships can contribute to our understanding of attachment security, communication, and internal working models. The perspective presented by Bretherton is new, provocative, and important.

Jack Bates emphasizes that temperament is an important element shaping both attachment and continuing interactions with the environment. While he stresses that good longitudinal research is needed, including indices of mother–infant responsiveness, attachment security, and child temperament, an even more important issue relates to the need for better measures of the infant–caregiver relationship both early and late in development. We need to compare the effects of the past history of the relationship, including what has been internalized by the child, with the effects of the current relationship and interactions (see Bretherton's chapter for theoretical perspective).

Jerome Kagan presents perspectives on infancy that are extremely important for our understanding of individual differences and development. He focuses on perceptual, cognitive, and emotional competencies that seem to be biologically prepared. He emphasizes the importance of physiological indices along with behavioral ones and the need to remain receptive to inductively derived constructs. With regard to attachment and temperament issues, Kagan concludes in a moderate way that not only do the classifications reflect the prior history of the infant–parent dyad but they are complex interactive behavioral products of several combined factors as well. He states further that it may not be possible to separate the differential contribution of the various factors.

Robert McCall reviews work related to media, society, and child development research. I felt that it was important to include such a chapter because many of us, particularly in the area of child development, are called on with increasing frequency for a variety of different reasons to speak to and write for the public. McCall reflects his recent work and the knowledge that he has gained in attempting to communicate effectively. The reader who is familiar with the first edition of the Handbook will recall that McCall contributed a methodological chapter on continuities and discontinuities and predictability. In this volume, the area of continuities and discontinuities is covered from a somewhat different perspective by Michael Rutter.

In his chapter, based on both theoretical considerations and empirical data regarding continuities and discontinuities, Rutter points out that evidence runs counter to views that early experiences irrevocably change personality development. However, there are findings indicating that under some conditions indirect effects can be quite long-lasting. He conceptualizes the process as an interactional one, assuming that experiences can change the organism and at the same time recognizing that individuals create their own environment. Thus the result is a complex pattern of continuities and discontinuities.

Infant mental health includes many issues relating developmental science to clinical activity. Emde has been one of the leaders in this area, not only in offering a theoretical understanding of emotional development and its clinical implications, but also in providing empirical studies to test propositions. Dilemmas for infant mental health include the difficult issue of diagnosis in infancy, which in turn leads to consideration of issues of prognosis, the influence of social values, and what we mean by *normality.* Included in his discussion are classical contributions to the field, for instance, those of Bowlby and Spitz, as well as new perspectives from his own work and that of Stern. Finally, he brings into focus the importance of intervention opportunities not only from the point of view of the health care professional who will develop intervention programs, but, perhaps more important, from the perspective of the sensitive infancy researcher who is a developmentalist concerned with individuality and of necessity is involved in a form of intervention.

The chapters in this section were chosen both to highlight important areas of interest and controversy in the field and to point to crucial questions and directions for the future.

CHAPTER 22

New Perspectives on Attachment Relations: Security, Communication, and Internal Working Models

INGE BRETHERTON

The attempt to understand human infant–mother attachment in terms of evolutionary–ethological theory (Bowlby, 1958, 1969) led to a major conceptual breakthrough. Infant behaviors that had previously seemed inexplicable, puzzling, or even irrational made sense within this new framework: the infant's distress upon separation from the mother, the tendency to follow mother about, to use her as a base for exploratory excursions, to keep visual tabs on her while exploring, to retreat to her in the presence of an unfamiliar adult, and to grieve in response to long absences or loss. Human infants' attachment behavior could now be interpreted as homologous with similar behavior shown by nonhuman primate species (see Bowlby, 1969; DeVore, 1965).

The emphasis on the biological function of attachment was important because it drew attention to the fact that the infant's tie to the primary caregiver need not be, indeed, could not be, explained solely in terms of cognitive and socioemotional milestones. On the other hand, specifically human affective, cognitive–representational, and communicative capacities presumably have a major impact on the specifically human development of attachment relations. So far this aspect of attachment has remained underexplored in infant research, but I believe that further progress in understanding the development of attachment in infancy now requires that we pay close attention to what the human ability to construct and share representations means for the development of early attachment relations.

Attachment theory *has* been concerned with the psychological aspect of attachment, but the main focus has been on the experience of young children, adolescents, and adults—not on that of infants (Bowlby, 1973, 1980). The account of attachment in infancy is primarily couched in terms of proximity regulation to a protective figure (Bowlby, 1969). Although Bowlby mentions and explains the concept of internal working models of the self and attachment figures in the 1969 volume (second

During the writing of this paper I received support from the John D. and Catherine T. MacArthur Foundation network for the Transition from Infancy to Early Childhood, which I gratefully acknowledge. I would also like to thank Mary Ainsworth, John Bowlby, Alan Sroufe, and Arietta Slade for helpful comments on prior versions of this manuscript.

edition, 1982), it is only in the second and third volumes of the attachment trilogy (1973, 1980) that he elaborates on the significance of these working models for the functioning and development of attachment relationships. It is in these later writings that the reader is strongly reminded that attachment theory is concerned with some of the same issues that have long been the focus of psychoanalytic theories of (love) object relations.

There were two reasons why Bowlby did not emphasize the subjective–experiential and representational aspect of attachment in his discussions of infancy. First, as I already noted, he wanted to demonstrate the usefulness of the evolutionary–ethological approach in explaining the survival-promoting function of the primate infant's attachment to the mother, and second, research on the early development of self-awareness, emotions, intentional communication via gestures and language, and psychological understanding was practically nonexistent at the time the first detailed account of infant attachment was written. Since the publication of *Attachment* (1969) there has been much empirical work on these topics in infancy (e.g., Bretherton, McNew, & Beeghly-Smith, 1981; Bruner & Scaife, 1975; Emde, 1983; Izard, 1978; Klinnert, Campos, Sorce, Emde, & Svejda, 1983; Lewis & Brooks, 1974, 1978; Trevarthen & Hubley, 1978), and two theoretical statements have appeared that consider the infant's experience of interpersonal relatedness from a psychoanalytic perspective (Mahler, Pine, & Bergman, 1975; Stern, 1985). We are thus in a better position to consider how the infant may experience early relations with caregivers.

In this paper I will first review the evolutionary–ethological basis of attachment theory (Bowlby, 1969, 1973) to provide a basic framework for the discussions that follow. I will then outline Bowlby's views about the construction and function of internal working models of self and attachment figures, of defense mechanisms, and of the intergenerational transmission of attachment patterns. This will be followed by a discussion of Sullivan (1953) and Fairbairn (1952), two psychoanalytic theorists who have proposed ideas that I see as especially closely related to Bowlby's. Although Sullivan and Fairbairn include infant experiences in their account of object relations, neither based his theorizing on actual infant observations. Two recent psychoanalytical formulations of relatedness in infancy, one by Mahler and colleagues (1975) and the other by Stern (1985), do draw on observation of mother–infant interaction. Stern's theory also incorporates insights from academic psychology. After summarizing the highlights of Mahler's and Stern's understanding of the infant's experience of relatedness, I will contrast and compare their views with classical and more recent infant attachment research. In doing so I will attempt to show why secure attachment, open communication, and adequate internal working models go together in development.

THE ETHOLOGICAL–EVOLUTIONARY THEORY OF ATTACHMENT

Human newborns are capable of a variety of signaling behaviors that elicit caregiving and other social responses from adults and that provide feedback regarding the success of caregiving interventions. In the course of the first few weeks and months, these infant social behaviors become more complex and coordinated. At the same time, infants begin to direct them preferentially toward specific caregiving figures. However, it is only during the second half of the first year of life that an infant's proximity-and interaction-seeking behaviors become integrated into a coherent behavioral–motivational system, organized around a particular figure or figures who perform the role of secure base and haven. It is the preferential activation of this proximity- and security-regulating system with respect to a small hierarchy of caregiving figures and its resistance to "refocusing" to which the term *attachment,* as formulated by Bowlby (1982) and Ainsworth (1973), is properly applied.

The claim that around 9 months or so a baby's attachment behaviors come to be organized into a goal-corrected motivational system of proximity and security regulation, focused on specific caregivers, is based on findings of striking changes in infants' separation responses during this period. For example, Yarrow (1967) showed that babies who were moved from a foster home to an adoptive home before the age of 6 months tended to show only mild distress, but when the move to the adoptive home occurred between the ages of 7 and 12 months, the babies tended to be much more deeply upset (with increased crying and clinginess, apathy, eating and sleeping disturbance). The fact that this change more or less coincided with the onset of locomotion (Freedman, 1974; Stayton, Hogan, & Ainsworth, 1971), stranger anxiety (Schaffer & Emerson, 1964; Spitz, 1965), and object permanence (Bell, 1970) made evolutionary sense. A motivational–behavioral system that prevents an infant from straying too far from a protective caregiver during exploratory forays into an unfamiliar physical or social world and that activates search behavior when the protective figure is absent has fairly obvious survival value.

The term *attachment system* refers to a regulatory system hypothesized to exist within a person. Seen from an outside observer's viewpoint the system's set–goal is to regulate behaviors that maintain proximity to and contact with a discriminated protective person, referred to as the *attachment figure(s).* From the psychological vantage point of the attached person, however, the system's set–goal is felt security (Bischof, 1975; Sroufe & Waters, 1977).

In order to clarify the complexity of the system Bowlby (1982) envisaged, I have constructed a diagram (see Fig. 22.1, adapted from Bretherton, 1985). This diagram attempts to spell out the interrelationships among the subsystems comprising and serving the attachment system. It may look unnecessarily intricate, but it is in fact a gross oversimplification. My primary objective was to show interrelations (informational flow between subsystems) rather than to elaborate on the functioning of the separate subsystems.

Several important features of the hypothesized system should be noted. First, although an attachment relationship exists dyadically between two individuals, the system described by Bowlby concerns the organization of a system within the attached person (see also Hinde, 1982; Sroufe & Fleeson, 1986). This system is preferentially organized around specific partners. In some species such a focused system exists in only one of the partners (the parent or the infant). In human and nonhuman primates the attachment relationship is best conceptualized as based on the joint functioning of a filial and a parental attachment system. So far it is largely the human filial system that has been studied, although all studies of the filial system take the complementary functioning of a parental attachment system for granted.

The filial attachment system actively monitors and processes two types of information that are taken in via the sensory systems: clues to danger (physical and psychological) and the accessibility (physical and psychological) of an attachment fig-

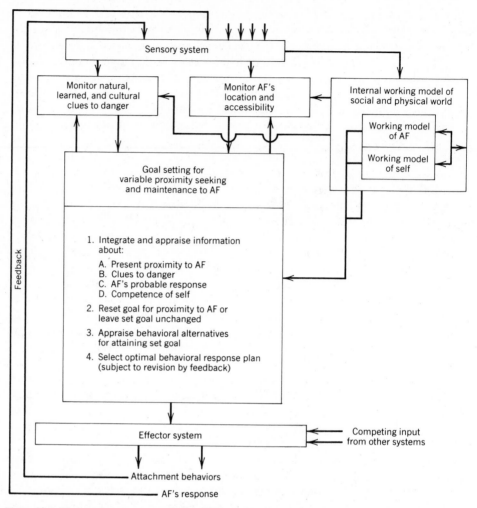

Figure 22.1 The attachment system: A simplified model of a control system for the regulation of proximity to and contact with an attachment figure (AF). (Note: From "Attachment Theory: Retrospect and Prospect: by I. Bretherton, 1982, in I. Bretherton and E. Waters (Eds.), "Growing Points of Attachment Theory and Research," *Monographs of the Society for Research in Child Development, 50* (1–2, Serial No. 209 p. 10.) Reprinted by permission.

ure. Bowlby (1969) originally suggested that the attachment system was activated by perceived danger and deactivated (terminated) by perceived safety. I suggest, however (Bretherton, 1980), that it may be more helpful to think of the system as continuously active, and to postulate that *activation* and *deactivation* refer to the *behaviors* that the system regulates. To do so clarifies and simplifies the relationship between two attachment phenomena that are often regarded as distinct: use of the attachment figure as a secure base for exploration and as a haven of safety when danger threatens. When no clues to danger are perceived and the attachment figure is accessible, the child feels secure and may explore at some distance from the attachment figure. But the attachment system is nevertheless actively monitoring the whereabouts of the attachment figure, and setting limits on how far from the secure base the child will move (Anderson, 1972). When the child perceives the environment as mildly alarming the attachment system's proximity set goal will change, activating proximity-seeking behavior. Persistently nonoptimal supportiveness on the part of the caregiver as well as separation experiences caused by illness or other adverse circumstances tend, however, to affect the set goal of the attachment system more chronically. The resulting clingy behavior is regarded not as a sign of strong attachment but as an indicator that the child is anxious about receiving insufficient security and support. On the other hand, when the exploratory system evaluates a stimulus as highly attractive while the fear system evaluates the same stimulus as somewhat threatening, the child may exhibit oscillating intention movements toward the interest-provoking stimulus and the security-providing attachment figure (Bretherton & Ainsworth, 1974). In situations where the child is uncertain about how to appraise a stimulus, the attachment system may activate information-seeking behavior. This can be seen when infants reference the mother's face during encounters with ambiguous, potentially harmful stimuli as if to discover how mother interprets the event (Campos & Stenberg, 1981; Emde, 1983; Feinman & Lewis, 1983; Klinnert et al., 1983). Finally, if an infant appraises a situation as highly alarming or stressful, mere proximity to an attachment figure is no longer enough. The system now activates contact seeking as well as proximity seeking, with a number of important consequences. If the situation is perceived as threatening by the attachment figure also, both mother and child may leave the situation together. However, if the attachment figure does not perceive the situation as dangerous, he or she can comfort and calm the frightened child. Furthermore, because close bodily contact with attachment figure engenders a greater sense of security, an attachment figure is in an ideal position to teach coping behaviors (Bretherton, 1980).

Bowlby (1980) proposed that attachment behavior rivals mating and feeding behavior in biological importance and that the attachment system has its own distinct internal motivation. Attachment behavior is activated when the attached person is frightened, tired, or sick, and is assuaged when the attachment figure provides protection, help, and soothing. Attachment, in other words, is a crucial component of the infant–mother relationship, but is not meant to comprise all facets of that relationship. Mother in her role as playmate fulfills a different role than mother as attachment figure although the two roles are by no means incompatible (see Bowlby, 1969). In infancy it is important that a primary or secondary attachment figure be physically close and emotionally available. Later the mere knowledge that an attachment figure is potentially accessible and responsive provides a strong and pervasive feeling of security. This holds true throughout the life cycle (Bowlby, 1969). However, in adulthood attachment relationships tend to be mutual, with both partners in a relationship providing security to each other.

Bowlby further proposes that attachments to persons and places as well as fear of the novel and strange can best be understood as governed by a related group of behavioral–motivational control systems whose common function it is to maintain a relatively steady state between an individual and his or her environment (1973). Such homeostatic control systems may be regarded as an "outer ring" of life-maintaining systems complementary to the "inner ring" of systems that maintain physiological homeostasis. As long as the outer ring (the behavioral–motivational systems) is successful at maintaining an individual within a familiar environment, the load placed on the systems maintaining physiological homeostasis is lessened (see Bowlby, 1973, pp. 149–150).

This notion has recently received strong support from studies of nonhuman primates conducted by Reite and his colleagues (Reite, Short, Seiler, & Pauley, 1981). These investigators showed that pigtail macaque infants whose mother was removed from the social group underwent profound physiological changes suggestive of a general impairment of autonomic homeostatic functioning (decreases in heart rate and body temperature, sleep disturbances, and changes in EEG power spectra).

In Bowlby's view the essentially "conservative" homeostatic systems are antithetical to systems mediating exploratory and other forms of information- and stimulation-seeking behaviors such as exploration and playful social interaction. A child's behavior may hence be seen as the outcome of the interplay of several behavioral–motivational systems (Bischof, 1975; Bretherton & Ainsworth, 1974). The propensity for exploration and social interaction with others often takes the child away from the attachment figure, whereas fear and stress experiences take the child toward him or her. The joint operation of these antithetical propensities facilitates exploration under reasonably safe conditions. I would like to caution, however, that it is only from the point of view of an outside observer that one can discuss attachment as a homeostatic system. From the internal perspective of the attached infant and adult, attachment is experienced as a psychological bond to the attachment figure(s) who play(s) the part of secure base and haven.

Attachment theory holds that each infant will become attached to a caregiver, even if the caregiver is not optimally attentive or available. However, individual differences in the quality of caregiver–infant transactions will result in different patterns of relationship. In the early months of the first year the caregiver's availability and responsiveness may be especially influential in patterning the relationship, but by the end of the first year it is probable that both partners are contributing to the stability of individual differences in the relationship. This is due to the fact that the infant has begun to construct *internal working models* of the world, of self and attachment figures. These representations are used by the infant in planning, understanding, and guiding behavior vis-à-vis the caregiver. The concept of internal working model will be discussed in greater detail in the next section.

INTERNALIZATION OF ATTACHMENT RELATIONS: THE CONCEPT OF WORKING MODELS

Bowlby's ideas regarding internal working models are an attempt to rework some of the issues with which psychoanalytic object relations theorists have traditionally been concerned.

Bowlby (1969) suggests that, in the course of interacting with the physical and personal world, an individual constructs internal working models of important aspects of the world. With the aid of working models, the individual perceives and interprets events, forecasts the future, and constructs plans. The notion of internal working models originates from an insightful book by Craik on *The Nature of Explanations* (1943). To quote Craik:

> By a model we thus mean any physical or chemical system which has a similar relation-structure to that of the process it imitates. By "relation-structure" I do not mean some

obscure nonphysical entity which attends the model, but the fact that it is a physical working model which works in the same way as the process it parallels. . . . My hypothesis then is that thought models, or parallels reality. . . . If the organism carries a "small-scale model" of external reality and of its own possible actions within its head, it is able to try out various alternatives, conclude which is the best of them, react to future situations before they arise, utilize the knowledge of past events in dealing with the present and future, and in every way to react in a much fuller, safer and more competent manner to the emergencies which face it. (p.61)

Internal working models need not be fully accurate nor very detailed to be useful, but to fulfill their functional role it is important that the relation–structure of working models be consistent with the reality they represent.

Of special salience within the working model of the world are working models of the self and principal caregiving figures. A key feature of the working model of the self is the notion of how acceptable the self is in the eyes of the attachment figure (Bowlby, 1973). Conversely, a crucial feature in the working model of the attachment figure is the figure's accessibility and emotional supportiveness. Because of their origin in actual interpersonal transactions, the internal working models of self and of attachment figures develop in close complementarity. For example, a child who experiences—and hence represents—attachment figures as primarily rejecting may form a complementary internal working model of the self as unworthy. Similarly a child who experiences a parental figure as emotionally available and supportive will most probably construct a working model of the self as competent and lovable. This construction of complementary internal working models representing the self and attachment figures is a continuous process. As the child develops, attachment relations also undergo change: The child becomes more competent and has more highly differentiated thought processes at his or her disposal leading, in turn, to changes in how the caregiver responds to the child. These changes become reflected in the child's (and the parents') internal working models. In addition, the affective quality of the relationship may change because of external influences on child and caregiver. The attachment figure may gain or lose social support, and experience increases or decreases in life stress.

Although they can change, Bowlby cautions that it would be unwise to think of internal working models of self and caregiving figures as being in a state of continuous flux. Ways of acting and thinking that are at first under deliberate control tend to become less accessible to awareness as they become habitual and automatic (1980). This leads to relative stability in how a person construes the interpersonal world, but increased efficiency is bought at the cost of oversimplification and hence some distortion. Only when the lack of fit between actual interchanges and the corresponding internal working models becomes so great that the model is no longer helpful will the person begin the process of accommodating the models to reality.

However, under some circumstances defensive processes may hinder the adaptive accommodation of internal working models. Bowlby (1980) points out that defense mechanisms can be understood as special cases of the *selective* exclusion of information that we constantly perform when processing input. Until recently it was difficult to envision how a person could (selectively or defensively) exclude aspects of external or internal reality from further appraisal without first becoming aware of them. However, there is now much evidence that information undergoes many stages of selective processing before it reaches awareness, with opportunities for exclusion at each level (see also Erdelyi, 1985).

Because internal working models of the world and the important figures in it guide selective attention and selective processing, some distortion of incoming information in the service of adaptive simplification is normal and unavoidable. However, things become complicated when *defensive* exclusion interferes with the updating of internal working models. Defensive exclusion is believed to occur in response to intolerable mental pain or conflict. Clinical case material suggests that such conflict arises when an attachment figure habitually ridicules a child's security-seeking behaviors, reinterprets rejection of the child as motivated by parental love or otherwise disavows or denies the child's anxious, angry, or loving feelings toward attachment figures (Bowlby, 1973, 1980). Under such circumstances, it is common for a child to exclude defensively from awareness the working model of the "bad" unloving parent, and retain conscious access only to the loving model (the "good" parent). Since the internal working model of an unconditionally loving and supportive parent does not correspond to reality, such an idealized but uncorrectable model is maladaptive. Although defensive processes bring relief because they keep the individual from experiencing unbearable mental pain, confusion, or conflict, they are also bound to make the future accommodation of internal working models to reality problematic. Inadequate working models, in turn, will interfere with effective coping and with optimal development.

In his discussion of defensive exclusion Bowlby draws attention to the distinction between episodic and semantic memory proposed by Tulving (1972; see also Tulving, 1983). Episodic memory stores autobiographical memories of specific events in a person's life history, whereas semantic memory stores generic propositions (general knowledge as opposed to specific memories). Tulving believes that the two memories are based on different storage mechanisms. Be that as it may, Bowlby (1980) emphasizes that autobiographical memory derives from experience, whereas generic knowledge (semantic memory) may be based on information supplied by others. Severe psychic conflict is likely to arise when the two sources of stored information (generalizations built on actual experience and on communications from others) are highly contradictory. Defensive exclusion may be brought to bear on episodically stored memories derived from actual experience as a means of eliminating the conflict.

Finally, Bowlby suggests that internal working models of self and parents developed in childhood play a major part in the intergenerational transmission of attachment patterns (Bowlby, 1973, p. 322). Individuals who grow up to become relatively stable and self-reliant, he postulates, normally have parents who are supportive when called upon, but who also permit and encourage autonomy. Such parents not only tend to engage in fairly frank communication about their own working models of self, of their child, and of others, but also indicate to the child that these working models are open to questioning and revision. To quote Bowlby (1969):

> Because in all these respects children tend unwittingly to identify with parents and therefore to adopt, when they become parents, the same patterns of behaviour towards children that they themselves have experienced during their own childhood, patterns of interaction are transmitted, more or less faithfully, from one generation to another. Thus the inheritance of mental health and of mental ill health through the medium of

family microculture is certainly no less important, and may well be far more important, than is their inheritance through the medium of genes. (p. 323)

Bowlby cites longitudinal studies by Peck and Havighurst (1960), Offer (1969), and Murphey, Silber, Coelho, Hamburg, and Greenberg (1963) in support of these claims. Since then more corroboration has come from Main and Goldwyn (1985), Morris (1980), and Ricks and Noyes (1984); for a summary of these studies see Ricks (1985).

COMPARISON OF ATTACHMENT THEORY WITH TWO OTHER OBJECT RELATIONS THEORIES

Several of Bowlby's notions about the function of internal working models in attachment relations have precursors in the thinking of other psychoanalysts. Many object relations theorists have contributed ideas that are relevant to attachment theory (see Greenberg & Mitchell, 1982, for a review; see also Guntrip, 1971; Kohut, 1977; Winnicott, 1965). In this section I have chosen to discuss Sullivan (1953) and Fairbairn (1952) because their interest in the internalization of love objects, in the effect of defensive processes on interpersonal relationships and on the intergenerational transmission of early relationship patterns seems most congruent with Bowlby's life span theory of attachment. However, because no satisfactory theory about mental representation was available to Sullivan and Fairbairn their ideas were less influential outside clinical circles than they otherwise might have been.

Sullivan and Fairbairn

Sullivan and Fairbairn agree that the infant's most basic need is interpersonal relatedness. The function of the pleasure-giving erogenous zones is to cement or integrate the relationship between infant and mother (Sullivan, 1953) or to serve as "sign-posts to the object" (Fairbairn, 1952, p. 33). Fairbairn objects to classical drive theory because it takes as primary what he regards as secondary, illustrating his argument with the protesting cry of a patient: "You are always talking about my wanting this or that desire satisfied; but what I really want is a father" (Fairbairn, 1952, p. 137).

Sullivan and Fairbairn diverge, however, on how the young baby experiences caregiving events. Sullivan believes that tender care provided by mother and other "mothering ones" is experienced as "good mother," whereas anxious and hence anxiety-provoking care is experienced as "bad mother." Good and bad experiences with caregivers are organized by the infant into two separate personifications. This is how Sullivan (1953) describes the personification of good mother in infancy:

> Thus this personification is not the "real mother"—a particular living being considered as an entity. It is an elaborate organization of the infant's experience. . . . It is important to understand that the infant's personification of the mother is composed of, or made up of, or organized from, or elaborated out of, what has occurred in the infant's relation to what you might call the "real" mother in satisfaction-giving integrations with her. (p. 112)

Only gradually do these separate but generic good and bad personifications (primitive working models) come to be differentiated and integrated into working models of specific caregivers who are both good and bad. The acquisition of language plays an important role in this integration.

Later in the first year the infant also creates personifications of self. "Good me" organizes experience in which tender maternal caregiving was satisfying for the infant, "bad me" organizes experience in which caregiving was associated with anxiety, and "not me" derives from experience that is so intensely anxious that it becomes inaccessible to awareness. Note that the personifications of the mothering one and of "me" are built from the same experiences and, like Bowlby's working models, are complementary. In the course of development, personifications of "mother" and "me" come to be subsumed by the self-system (ego). The self-system protects the person from anxiety through security operations that repress experiences of "bad me" and "not me." Unfortunately, security operations "interfere with observation and analysis, and for this reason prevent the profit one might gain from experience" (Sullivan, 1953, p. 346). Thus in Sullivan's theorizing the desire for security is closely linked to defensive processes, a false security in the framework of attachment theory.

Fairbairn (1952), in contrast to Sullivan, argues that the baby initially experiences mother as whole. However, if relations with the real caregiver are unsatisfactory, the infant has to set up compensatory, internal objects. Once these are internalized, the infant can split off and repress the rejecting and disappointing aspects of the love object, retaining in awareness only the ideal aspect of the object. At the same time complementary parts of the ego are repressed. Hence in an attempt to make the objects in his environment "good" the child ends up by taking upon himself the burden of their apparent "badness."

Sullivan's and Fairbairn's formulations regarding the repression of bad mother or rejecting internal objects resemble some of Bowlby's notions regarding defensive exclusion, but there are important differences too. Bowlby does not agree with Sullivan's postulate that good and bad experiences with caregivers are initially categorized as separate. Like Fairbairn, Bowlby believes that defensive "splitting" of internal working models occurs later as a result of having experienced many painful rejections.

Although both Sullivan and Fairbairn have extended their theories across the life span and across generations, both differ from Bowlby because neither accords a special place to attachment relationships (as opposed to, e.g., sexual relationships). Sullivan delineates a developmental sequence in which needs for different forms of relatedness predominate at different periods during the life span. From 1 to 4 years the child seeks the adult as an audience for play and efforts; from 4 to 8 years the child seeks cooperation, competition, and compromise with other juveniles. From 8 years to puberty the preadolescent needs a "chum" of the same sex while the adolescent seeks an intimate, collaborative, loving, and sexual relationship with someone of the opposite sex. Failure to satisfy each of these interpersonal needs results in loneliness. Even though different forms of relatedness become important at different developmental periods, maladaptive dyadic patterns developed in past interactions tend to be imposed on new relationships (parataxic integrations). Thus "me–you" patterns acquired in early malfunctioning relationships become the basis for distorting later relationships.

Fairbairn's developmental sequence emphasizes increasingly *mature* patterns of relatedness, not differences in partners or content. Infantile compulsive dependence must be followed by a transitional phase that eventually leads to mature dependence. To achieve mature dependence children must give up compulsive attachment to parents and renounce the internalized "good, compensatory" love objects that provided a sort of unreal security. This is possible only if they feel loved as persons in their own right and believe that their own love is welcomed and valued. If not, anxiety over separation is too great, and the transitional phase is never outgrown. The mature dependency of adulthood must be based on reciprocal interdependence, not unilateral dependence. Genitality is one but not the only channel for achieving mature adult relatedness. However, early maladaptive relationship patterns may interfere with the achievement of mature dependence. Some people, Fairbairn says, choose sadistic or unresponsive love objects, and behave toward them so as to elicit these familiar relationships patterns. If one assumes that a person's primary aim is pleasure seeking, this tendency is hard to understand, but it makes sense if the primary aim is interpersonal relatedness (object seeking).

Comparison with Attachment Theory

Bowlby's theory is both more specific and more general than Sullivan's and Fairbairn's. It is more specific because it is concerned with relationships in which one person serves as secure base and secure haven to another, not with relationships in general. It is more general because the construct of internal working model is used to explain the development of healthy as well as pathological relationships. Inspired by Craik's (1943) as well as by Piaget's (1951, 1954) writings, Bowlby emphasizes that the construction of internal working models is a natural consequence of the human ability to represent the world. Internal working models ordinarily fulfill an adaptive function. The development of healthy attachment relationships is based on continued mutual updating and fine-tuning of internal working models. It is in nonoptimal development that defensive exclusion subverts the adaptive function of representation by substituting changes in the internal world for adaptive coping with the external world. Indeed, defensive exclusion is explained as an inappropriate deployment of normal selective attention and normal selective processing. What is still lacking in Bowlby's theorizing is a detailed treatment of precursors to internal working models in early life, before the acquisition of object permanence.

ATTACHMENT THEORY AND TWO PSYCHOANALYTIC THEORIES OF INFANT–MOTHER RELATEDNESS

Unlike Bowlby, Fairbairn and especially Sullivan speculate extensively about how an infant might experience and internalize the early relationship to caregivers, but theirs are reconstructions and intuitions based on retrospective insights obtained from patients, not on systematic infant observations. More recently Mahler (Mahler et al., 1975) and Stern (1985) have put forward psychoanalytic accounts of infants' early experience with their mothers that rely on actual observations. Although both attempt to interpret the development of infant–mother relations from the psychological vantage point of the infant, each emphasizes different issues. Mahler's observations are easily interpretable within attachment theory because issues of attachment and autonomy–exploration were a primary focus. However, Mahler's conceptual framework is very different from Bowlby's (1969) and Ainsworth's (1973). Stern (1985) resembles Bowlby (1969) in his openness to insights from academic developmental psychology, but he focuses much more deeply on infants' intrapsychic processes and intersubjective capabilities. He also places less emphasis on the attachment relationship as distinct from other types of relationship.

Mahler

Many important aspects of Mahler's theory about the psychological birth of the human infant emerged from an attempt to understand the development of schizophrenic or autistic infants in whom, she speculated, the separation–individuation process had not proceeded normally because of unsatisfactory deviations in the mother–infant relationship during the normal symbiotic phase (3–6 months). To validate her hypotheses with normal infants, groups of mother–infant pairs were observed longitudinally in a playroom setting. The findings are presented in summary form, as global conclusions with detailed examples.

Mahler (Mahler et al., 1975) believes that the baby's first experience is that of normal autism. Sensations from within are of primary importance because the baby is somewhat impervious to external stimulation. Additionally, sensations from within and without are not distinguished.

Helped by the caregiving acts of the mother, the baby is able to leave the period of normal autism behind and enter the period of normal symbiosis. During the symbiotic period, the infant becomes interested in the outside world (mainly in the person of the mother), but because a well-demarcated self has not yet developed, the baby experiences the self–mother system as a dual unity. The mother acts as auxiliary ego (Spitz, 1965) for the infant; she tries to be in tune with the baby's communications, "reading the signals," making experiences pleasant, but the baby does not experience her as separate. Satisfactory symbiotic experiences for the baby, according to Mahler, depend "on a certain matching of discharge patterns of the mother and the young infant" (p. 49) and later, on their interactional patterns, behaviorally discernible in mutual cuing, as well as in the infant's early adaptive patterning and in its receptive capacities with the 'good enough' holding behavior of its mother" (a concept derived from Winnicott, 1958). However—in a manner that is not explained—negative feelings are projected by the infant beyond the boundary of the dual unity (replacing the stimulus barrier). During the symbiotic phase, memory begins to play a role in the relationship. Images of the bodily and later of the psychic self emerge from the ever-increasing memory traces of good (pleasurable) and bad (unpleasurable) emotional experiences with mother and from the associated perceptions.

The symbiotic phase leads into the first subphase of the separation–individuation process: *differentiation and the development of the body image.* The baby is now more permanently alert when awake. Attention is increasingly directed outward, and combined with a growing memory store of mother's comings and goings, of good and bad experiences (and mother is confidently expected to relieve the latter). The baby explores mother's face, hair, and body, breaks away physically from lap-hood, checks back to mother, engages in comparative scanning of mother's and stranger's face, shows stranger anxiety. All of this is a sign of somatosensory differentiation of self from mother (7–8 months).

Where the "shielding membrane" of dual unity had been disturbed, the onset of differentiation may be premature or delayed: "optimal situations seem to be those in which awareness of bodily separation in terms of differentiation from mother goes parallel with the toddler's development of independent autonomous functioning—in step with the development of cognition, perception, memory, reality testing" (p. 58).

The differentiation subphase is followed by *practicing,* ushered in by the onset of independent locomotion. During the early practicing subphase mother is the anchor, the center of the world, the stable point, the home base, the beacon of orientation to whom the baby returns from exploratory forays for "emotional refueling" through physical contact. During the later practicing period, marked by the mastery of upright locomotion, the pleasure of exercising skills predominates, and concern about mother's whereabouts is more muted. Quasi-enamored of their own grandeur, elated to escape from fusion with or engulfment by the mother, practicing infants explore the world at some distance from her, though they may become low-keyed if she leaves. Mahler proposes that during these low-keyed episodes children are engaged in "imaging" their absent mothers. However such longing for closeness is absent or diminished where the symbiotic state is unduly prolonged either because symbiosis is parasitic (selfishly motivated on the part of the mother) or because there is no satisfactory symbiosis because mother is impulsive, unpredictable, and somewhat rejecting.

The experience of independent exploration is exhilarating, but ultimately leads toddlers to become more aware of their own separateness and relative helplessness. During the ensuing *rapprochement* subphase, there is waning imperviousness to frustration, a revival of constant concern with mother's whereabouts, and a greater need for her optimal emotional availability (despite toddlers' ambivalence) to support toddlers' positive feelings toward the self. The mother is no longer just home base, but a person with whom toddlers want to share their ever-widening interests in the world. Their preoccupation changes from locomotion–exploration to social interaction with mother. At the same time, toddlers show a certain resistance to having their bodily autonomy violated (being held while dressing), or even to receiving affection when it is not welcome.

All children observed by Mahler and her colleagues showed separation reactions during the rapprochement phase. They wanted to know where mother was. If she was absent for long periods of time the children tended to become low-keyed or restless, or played games that involved losing and finding. Some projected "bad mother" onto the observers who became the object of their impotent rage at having been left (so as to protect the image of "good mother"). However, "good mother" seemed sometimes to exist in fantasy only. When mother returned there were often negative, angry reactions. The impulse to approach mother was frequently accompanied by an impulse to avoid her, as if to ward off further disappointment. Other toddlers responded to separation by seeking out mother's chair. The chair became a kind of bridge to mother. At the same time, many children became better able to leave mother in order to enter the separate toddler playroom on their own, and were able to form relationships with the teacher and with other toddlers.

In the presence of the mother two interesting patterns of behavior were observed: shadowing or following mother's every move (indicating a wish for reunion with the love object) and darting away from mother (indicating fear of engulfment, fear of losing the recently achieved autonomy). At the same time, the representations of self and love object became more differentiated. Fear of losing the love object's love (rather than fear of object loss) became prominent. During this period, some mothers were unable to accept their children's insistent demandingness for social interaction; others found it difficult to accept demands for autonomy.

Mahler hypothesizes that junior toddlers are aware that parents are separate persons, individuals with their own interests and needs. However, if the mother remains quietly available she seems to be able to facilitate the unfolding of the toddler's affective and cognitive capacities. What is important here is not only the emotional growth of the child, but that of the mother, her ability to let go, to give the child encouragement toward independence. Some mothers are unable to do this and, putting their own symbiotic–parasitic needs first, become the shadowers of the child. Other mothers make themselves less than optimally available. If so, such a child will more insistently, even desperately, woo her, even to the extent of interfering with normal affective–cognitive developmental processes. Some of the toddlers in Mahler's project deliberately fell or spilled cookies on the floor with an eye to gaining their mothers' attention. Some used toilet habits to control their mothers.

By 21 months many toddlers had successfully resolved the rapprochement crisis and could function with equanimity at a relative distance from the mother. Mahler characterizes this new subphase as *consolidation of individuality and the beginnings of emotional object constancy.* The child's growing individuation was made possible by language development, but also by internalization processes that could be inferred from the child's identification with "good mother and father," the internalization of parental standards and rules, and the ability to express wishes, fantasies, and mastery in symbolic play.

Emotional object constancy depends for Mahler on the internalization of a positively valued inner image of the mother. This image permits children to function separately from mother despite moderate degrees of longing. Object constancy is much more than Piagetian object permanence: It implies unification of previously separate representations of the good and bad love object into one whole representation. Because of this development mother can now be partially substituted for by a reliable internal image that remains stable despite discomfort. For this reason, the toddler can tolerate longer separations better. Yet if there is a great deal of ambivalence in the relationship, mothers' brief absences even during this phase are wont to stir up considerable anger and longing because the positive image of the mother cannot be sustained.

Mahler provides three examples of separation and reunion behavior during this period of development: A little girl who had been able to utilize play and involvement with other people to ease her concern greeted mother as she returned, made welcoming gestures with toys she brought to mother, and seemed generally pleased to see mother. A little boy, by contrast, showed no pleasure at mother's return. His mother commented that he didn't care. Another little girl responded with visible ambivalence to mother's return. She grimaced, tried to smile, but then looked hurt and angry at her mother. Mahler notes that these reunion responses were intelligible on the basis of the dyads' prior relationship histories. The first child had experienced flexible and responsible mothering; her mother had been consistently available during the prior subphases but had also appropriately encouraged her child's autonomous functioning. This child had developed trust and confidence in mother as well as others and showed good self-esteem. The second mother was unpredictable in her emotional attitudes and her behavior to her child, leading the child to adopt a precocious autonomy, suppressing his emotional need for maternal support. The third mother is not described in detail, but her little girl continued to respond with much anxiety and anger to maternal leave-taking.

Comparison with Attachment Theory

How do Mahler's views align with attachment theory? First, attachment theory has no room for "normal autism." On the other hand, Mahler's description of optimal maternal behavior during the symbiotic period (after 2 months and before locomotion) is strikingly congruent with attachment theory. The major difference is the interpretation of *symbiosis* as an experience of dual unity from which the infant has to separate and differentiate—not to say escape—in order to become an autonomous individual. Because attachment theory is concerned with the balance of attachment and exploratory behaviors, attachment theorists have seen attachment not as an initially symbiotic relationship from which the child must eventually emerge as differentiated and separate, but rather as a relationship that, from the beginning, permits optimal autonomy in the context of emotional support. In the framework of attachment theory, maternal respect for the child's autonomy is an aspect of sensitivity to the infant's signals whereas maternal overconcern (protecting the infant when this seems unnecessary) is interpreted as interference, or insensitivity toward the infant's signals (Ainsworth, Bell, & Stayton, 1974). This will become even clearer when I present findings from Ainsworth's studies of attachment in a later section.

A second major difference is the function of representation. For Bowlby, internal working models of self and attachment figures guide all interactions between child and parents. In fact, the gradual emergence of a *goal-corrected partnership* in attachment during toddlerhood becomes possible only because the child gradually acquires greater ability to take the perspective of the other through internal working models (see Greenberg & Speltz, in press; Marvin, Greenberg, & Mosler, 1976). For Mahler, by contrast, object constancy is most important when the mother is absent. The internalized object becomes in a way a substitute for the external object: "The 'internal mother,' the inner image or intrapsychic representation of the mother, in the course of the third year should become more or less available in order to supply comfort to the child in mother's physical absence" (Mahler et al., 1975, p. 118).

If experiences with mother have been unreliable, or mother has been very intrusive, the internalization of a conflictual inner image is experienced as a foreign body, a "bad" introject. In the attempt to eject this image the child may identify with the bad introject and sweep away the good self-representation along with the good object. These statements make it clear that Mahler's inner image is indeed a static image, not a working model that helps the child forecast mother's behavior whether she is present or absent.

Mahler's conceptualization of emotional object constancy leads to difficulties in describing the child's behavior during separation and reunion. Rejection of substitute care givers (in the example given above) is construed as an attempt to protect the image of "good mother," but subsequent avoidance of mother cannot be explained in the same way. When mother returns and the child rejects her, Mahler claims that "good mother" seems to have existed for the child in fantasy only. Within the framework of attachment theory ambivalent reunion behaviors are, I think, more adequately explained by recourse to internal working models of a less than optimally responsive and hence less trustworthy caregiver.

However, Mahler makes a most valuable contribution in pointing out that the parent—in order to be able to grant the appropriate amount of autonomy and emotional support at different phases of development—must develop in step with the child. Parental development is an area that has been relatively neglected by attachment theorists.

Stern

Stern (1985) makes the case that, in light of what empirical research has taught us about infant development, many central concepts in psychoanalytic theory (including Mahler's explanation of normal autism and normal symbiosis) seem to be less tenable than they once were. However, he also points out that developmental findings are likely to remain sterile if we do not use them to make inferences about the subjective life of the infant, about how the infant comes to experience self and the relationship of self to other. Stern, like Bowlby, views infants as predesigned to engage in interaction with caregivers from birth. He goes beyond Bowlby, however, in postulating several stages in a developing sense of self and of relatedness from birth through the end of toddlerhood.

The Emergent Sense of Self and Relatedness

Stern cites research findings to support his claim that newborns are already capable of experiencing a sense of emergent self-organization. From the many experiments inspired by Gibson's (1979) theory of affordances (see Gibson & Spelke, 1983, for a review) there is now evidence that human perceptual systems are designed to link perception in several modalities into one unified experience (intermodal or amodal perception). It appears that young infants are capable of matching light and sound intensity (Lewkowicz & Turkewitz, 1980), sucked and viewed shapes (Meltzoff & Borton, 1979), visual and auditory rhythms (e.g., Wagner & Sakowitz, 1983), faces with the sound they produce (e.g., MacKain, Studdert-Kennedy, Spieker, & Stern, 1982), and others' facial movements and affect expressions with movements and expressions of their own (Field, Woodson, Greenberg, & Cohen, 1981). These results suggest that the newborn infant can begin to extract self-invariance and other-invariance from the stream of experience.

The Sense of Core Self and Self with Other

Around 2–3 months there is a shift in the way babies relate to others. They make eye contact, smile, coo, learn faster, and engage in effective visual scanning (Emde, Gaensbauer, & Harmon, 1976). Stern suggests that the infant now experiences a sense of core self, based on the experience of self-agency, self-coherence, self-history, and self-affectivity. The sense of *self-agency* derives from the sense of volition that precedes a motor act (Lashley, 1951), the proprioceptive feedback that does or does not occur, the predictability of consequences that follow the act (e.g., during the act of reaching for an object; see Bower, Broughton, & Moore, 1970). These abilities allow the infant to distinguish the self-willed action *of* the self from the other-willed action *on* the self. A sense of *self-coherence* originates in the experience of self as a physically bounded, single entity in distinction to others who are specified by transformations of coherent moving entities seen across a distance, as well as by temporal cohesion of voice and movement (Spelke, 1976, 1979). *Self-affectivity* adds to the sense of core self through the experience of internal patterns of arousal and emotion-specific qualities of feeling. These self-invariants can be experienced with a variety of others, thereby setting the core self apart from the experience of core other. In addition a sense of *self-history* comes into play through the emergence of memory processes. Cued recall of motor acts has been documented in 3-month-olds (e.g., Rovee-Collier & Fagan, 1981; Rovee-Collier & Lipsitt, 1981). Such memories ensure self-continuity over time, although early perceptual recognition may not always be recognized as memory, merely as self-affirming.

The four components of experience—self-agency, self-coherence, self-affectivity, and self-history—taken together constitute the sense of core self. Stern believes that self-invariants are integrated through memory. He proposes that infants store generalized episodes of routine interactions and events and use them in understanding and predicting similar events. A generalized episode is a small coherent chunk of lived experience that stores sensations, goals, affect, and actions in a temporal-physical–causal relationship. Only failed expectations are registered as separate episodes (this is congruent with Schank, 1982, whose work will be discussed in more detail later). Stern calls these generalized memory structures RIGs (*R*epresentations of *I*nteractions that have been *G*eneralized). They are a newer version of *interpersonal process units* proposed in his 1977 book, and constitute the basic units for representing the self and the self with other.

For example, RIGs storing and guiding the processing of attachment experiences would be cuddling or molding to a warm contoured body, and being cuddled; looking into another's eyes, feeling soothed. But there are many other experiences with an other that are not attachment experiences in the technical sense in which the term *attachment* is used in this chapter. Stern believes that all these experiences are registered as changes in self-experience when being with an other, not as Mahlerian dual unity or symbiotic experiences. RIGs are accessed whenever a familiar self-with-other episode recurs, but a RIG may also be activated when the other is not there, but part of a familiar self-with-other episode is reexperienced. Activation of the RIG causes the baby to experience an *evoked companion*. Stern suggests that RIGs could be conceptualized as the building blocks from which a working model of self and other could be constructed.

The Sense of Subjective Self and Intersubjective Relatedness.

Around 9 months there are many changes in the infant's ability to send and understand intentional messages. Infants realize that their subjective experience, their attention, intentions, and affective states can be shared with an other (e.g., Bretherton & Bates, 1979; Klinnert et al., 1983; Trevarthen & Hubley, 1979). Stern suggests that this new ability has phylogenetic roots. Nature has provided ways and means for subjective intermeshings through interintentionality and interaffectivity. Mothers intuitively recognize this change in the baby by engaging in affect sharing with the infant no longer through pure imitation, but instead through *affect at-*

tunement. Affect attunement differs from maternal mirroring or imitation of specific infant behaviors because a different modality is used in attunement. The infant's attention is thereby focused on the shared affect rather than on the match of outward behavior: The mother matches the temporal beat, the intensity contour, the duration of an action, and/or its spatial shape (vertical arm movement with up-and-down head nodding) of her baby's behavior (see Stern, 1985, for details). When asked to give a reason for their attunement the most common explanation given was "to be with" or "join in with" the infant, but most mothers were not fully aware of their attuning behavior. Infants did not generally give an overt response to their mothers' affect attunements, but they did seem to notice misattunements.

Mothers attune not only to categorical affects (joy, sadness) but to dynamic, kinetic qualities of feelings that Stern calls *vitality affects* (the experience of a behavior or event as forceful, gentle, or lethargic). It is clear that attunement plays an important role in the infant's developing ability to recognize that feeling states can be shared with other humans. The converse also holds: Some states will never be attuned to and will therefore be experienced alone, isolated from the interpersonal context. Sometimes mothers "underattune" or "overattune," falling short of or exaggerating the infants' behavior in their attunement. If done consistently, this may undermine the infant's ability to evaluate its own inner states. Indeed, overattunement (exaggerated "overdone" attunement to infant behavior) can become a kind of emotional theft.

The Sense of Verbal Self and Verbal Relatedness

The possible ways of "being with" increase tremendously as the toddler acquires language. Because language makes experience more sharable with others, it allows deeper relations with others (Bretherton, Fritz, Zahn-Waxler, & Rigdeway, 1986; Dunn, Bretherton, & Munn, in press). As Stern argues, old issues of attachment, rejection, and autonomy can now be renegotiated on the verbal level. Language also carries with it the acquisition of an objective sense of self indexed by mirror behavior (Lewis & Brooks, 1978), and the use of names and pronouns (Bretherton, McNew, & Beeghly-Smith, 1981), by empathic behavior (Zahn-Waxler et al., 1979), the establishment of gender identity (Lewis & Brooks, 1978), and symbolic play (Bretherton, 1984; Wolf, Altshuler, & Rygh, 1984). But language, says Stern, is a double-edged sword. It may drive a wedge between experience as lived and as verbally represented, because the domains of core and intersubjective relatedness that continue irrespective of language can be recreated only very partially in the verbal domain. When language does not capture the original experience well the nonverbalized experience may continue to lead an underground existence. Further, although the advent of language brings the ability to narrate (create and recreate) one's own life story with others, the translation into language may alter autobiographical memory in such a way that toddlers may become estranged from their own early experiences.

Comparison with Attachment Theory

Many aspects of Stern's formulation are highly compatible with attachment theory, but there are significant differences as well. The similarities are as follows: Like Bowlby, Stern emphasizes the infant's growing capacity for relatedness that emerges in conjunction with a growing sense of self, although recent research enables Stern to clarify the different communication processes that "carry" the relationship at different periods of development. Stern also specifies more explicitly what may go awry at each new stage in the development of self and relatedness. These formulations about levels of relatedness could fruitfully be applied to the study of attachment. The major difference between Stern and Bowlby lies in Bowlby's focus on the attachment relationship as a special component of the total parent–child relationship (Bowlby, 1982; for more discussion see Bretherton, 1980, 1985). Although Stern's interest in the mother–infant relationship grew out of studies of mother–infant social play, his theorizing applies to the relationship as a whole, not specifically to play or specifically to attachment. For certain purposes separate consideration of the attachment component and the play component of the relationship may not be very useful, and may indeed seem artificial. I regard it as important because more general theories of the mother–infant relationship like Stern's cannot explain why infants show very strong preferences for a few particular caregivers when they are in need of emotional support, comfort, and soothing, whereas they seem to be considerably less choosy about playmates (Bretherton, Stolberg, & Kreye, 1981). Under attachment theory, the function of attachment figures is to provide protection from physical and psychological danger. Indeed, there seem to be cultures where mothers do not engage in much social play with infants (Brazelton, 1977). The function of playmates is to provide social exploration and sociable interaction. The attachment figure can be—but need not be—the infant's favorite playmate, though the relationship is presumably enriched if attachment and playmateship go together. This will become evident in the review of attachment research that follows, although these issues need much more detailed research.

ATTACHMENT RESEARCH IN INFANCY AND TODDLERHOOD

Attachment theory has from the beginning been built on empirical research as well as on clinical insight. It has also, from the beginning, generated much empirical research. Hence the work of Ainsworth and her colleagues (for summaries see Ainsworth, 1982, 1983) is so closely interwoven with Bowlby's theoretical statement of attachment in infancy (1969) that it is difficult to separate the reciprocal contributions of research-inspired theory and theory-inspired empirical work.

Infancy

Because of the scientific climate in which Ainsworth's work was done and because of the ethological basis of attachment theory, results from her studies were primarily couched in behavioral language, emphasizing the protective, survival-promoting function of proximity and interaction regulation. However, the infant's subjective experience with mother can often be inferred from the behavioral descriptions. In this chapter, I will therefore highlight the psychological and affective side of reported findings.

Ainsworth's Baltimore study was based on monthly 4-hr. naturalistic observations of 26 mother–infant dyads in the home. Detailed narrative reports derived from these home observations revealed that mother–infant interactions took on characteristic patterns during the first 3 months, patterns that remained relatively consistent up to the end of the first year of life (see Ainsworth et al., 1978, for an overview; see also Ainsworth, 1982, 1983). The interaction patterns studied in the first quarter concerned feeding, face-to-face interaction, responsiveness to infant crying, and close bodily contact.

Ainsworth and Bell (1969) observed striking differences in how individual mother–infant pairs negotiated the feeding situation during the first 3 months. For some pairs, feeding tended to be an occasion for smooth cooperation. Mother was described as feeding the baby promptly on demand or staving off feedings tactfully, coaxing baby gently, letting it loaf and drowse, feeding solids in such a way as to let baby have the initiative, flexibly interspersing bottle and solid food. For other pairs things did not go so well. Mothers did not adjust their pacing to the baby's cues. They overenlarged the hole in the nipple of the feeding bottle and forced solids. In response their babies tended to struggle, choke, and spit up. Feedings became a battle. Examples of insensitive feeding behavior were teasing a hungry baby by putting a finger in its mouth, or coaxing the baby into taking more food to the point of gagging.

Similar distinctive patterns emerged from the observations of face-to-face interactions between mother and infant during the period from 6 to 15 weeks (Blehar, Lieberman, & Ainsworth, 1977). Some pairs were characterized by primarily happy face-to-face interactions. In such pairs, infants responded with joyful bouncing, smiling, and vocalizing as mother meshed her own playful behavior with that of her baby. The mothers were skilled at pacing and modifying social initiatives in response to the baby's cues, resulting in longer interaction bouts. Babies who experienced many harmonious and happy face-to-face interactions also differentiated significantly in their behavior to mother and observer even at this early age. By contrast, mothers who initiated many face-to-fact interactions without speaking and with an unsmiling expression obtained only muted responses from their babies. Rarely did their babies bounce or vocalize when looking back at them. In these pairs many interactions ended before ever entering a playful phase. The babies of these less responsive mothers also did not differentiate between mother and observer in face-to-face interactions during the first quarter. Furthermore, the data indicate that the mother was the more influential partner in patterning the relationship. Her interactive behavior assessed at 6 and 9 weeks correlated significantly with her later interactive behavior at 12 and 15 weeks. This was not true for the babies.

Findings on close bodily contact were in accord with those on feeding and face-to-face interaction. Some mothers were gentle and tender when picking their babies up. They kissed, hugged, and caressed their babies as they held them, and the babies' experience during holding episodes was rated as pleasurable. Other mothers were frequently inept, tended to provide their babies with unpleasant holding experiences, and verbally expressed their dislike of physical contact (Main & Weston, 1982). An example of inept behavior would be absentmindedly holding the baby upside down while conversing with the observer, or inadvertently banging the baby's head against a hard surface. Mothers who were frequently inept while holding their babies tended to hold them primarily in routine situations such as diapering and feeding.

Similar contrasts were found in maternal responding to infant crying during the first 3 months (Bell & Ainsworth, 1972). There were enormous differences in how many crying episodes a mother ignored (4 percent to 96 percent) and how long she let the baby cry before responding, with average latencies in the range of 2–9 min during the first quarter. Bell and Ainsworth (1972) conclude that "an infant whose mother's responsiveness helps him to achieve his ends develops confidence in his own ability to control what happens to him" (p. 1188). Stern would point out that a baby whose signals are read appropriately also develops a different sense of core self with mother.

The descriptions of harmonious, cooperative, and pleasurable mother–infant interaction provided by Ainsworth and her colleagues are strongly reminiscent of Mahler's accounts of satisfactory symbiotic experiences. In fact, some of Mahler's vignettes (Mahler, Pine & Bergman, 1975) sound like excerpts from the narrative records that formed the basis of Ainsworth's Baltimore study. The major difference lies in the interpretation of the behavior. Mahler saw the close, optimally regulated symbiotic relationship as something from which the baby ultimately had to escape. Ainsworth, by contrast, points out that sensitive maternal behavior lets the infant experience a sense of control. For Ainsworth, unlike Mahler, individuation begins at birth. Hence it makes sense to expect some continuity in the quality of the mother–infant relationship across the first year.

Comparison of the early (first quarter) interactional patterns with patterns observed in the fourth quarter do indeed show considerable consistency. There are two important data sets: Correlations of first-quarter with fourth-quarter interactive patterns and correlations of first-quarter patterns with 1-year-olds' behavior in a laboratory situation known as the Strange Situation.

I will describe the longitudinal correlations of interactive patterns first. Mothers' responsiveness to infant crying was relatively stable from the first to the fourth quarter (r (25) = .49;$p<.01$). During the last quarter, the mean duration of crying had decreased for the sample as a whole, but it was especially noteworthy that babies whose mothers had been most responsive to crying during the early months now tended to cry least (r (25) = -.41;$p<.05$). Instead, these babies tended to rely more on facial expression, gesture, and vocalization to communicate their intentions and wishes to mother (Bell & Ainsworth, 1972). Similarly, infants whose mothers had provided much tender holding early on tended to seek contact with their mothers less often during the fourth quarter, but when bodily contact occurred it was mutually satisfying and affectionate (Ainsworth, Bell, Blehar, & Main, 1971). Ainsworth (Ainsworth et al., 1978) explains these findings by recourse to infants' expectations, based on prior satisfying or rejecting experiences with mother.

First-quarter interactive patterns were also related to infant behavior in the Ainsworth Strange Situation at 12 months. This procedure was originally developed to examine infant exploration in the mother's presence and absence (Ainsworth & Wittig, 1969) but has turned out to be much more interesting as an assessment of attachment patterns. The Strange Situation consists of a standard series of eight episodes, each except the first lasting 3 min. Observations are conducted in a laboratory playroom where, after a brief introductory episode, the baby is first given an opportunity to explore attractive toys in the presence of mother. This is followed by the gradual introduction of a stranger who enters and sits on a chair quietly, then converses with the mother, and finally invites the baby to play. The mother subsequently leaves the baby with the stranger (first separation), returns to be with the baby (first reunion), and then leaves the baby completely alone (second separation). The stranger then rejoins the baby, and finally the mother returns (second reunion).

The infants' behavior during the two reunions with the mother turned out to be even more revealing than the infants' response to separation. Some infants cried on separation, but then approached the mother on her return, asking to be picked up and held. Others, though they did not cry during separation, greeted mother as she returned and sought interaction and/or proximity. These infants were classified as group B. Other infants—who usually did not cry on separation—snubbed or avoided the mother on her return (group A), and yet others responded with intense distress to separation, but showed angry, resistant behavior although they also wanted to be held (group C). I should add that separation episodes are curtailed if the baby becomes very distressed.

Ainsworth was alerted to the avoidant (group A) and resistant (group C) reunion patterns in the Strange Situation because they resembled reunion behaviors typically observed in children after longer, more traumatic separations (e.g., Robertson, 1953; see also Main, Kaplan, & Cassidy, 1985, for a detailed discussion). It is *not* from this direct resemblance that the Strange Situation derives its validity as an assessment of attachment quality, however, but rather from the systematic and extensive correlations of infant behaviors in this situation with maternal and infant behaviors in the home throughout the first year of life. It is noteworthy in this connection that these patterns bear an uncanny resemblance to reunion behaviors noted by Mahler and her colleagues (1975), who also regarded them as resulting from unsatisfactory mother–infant relationships.

Specific patterns of reunion behavior with the mother during the Ainsworth Strange Situation were predictable from early patterns of feeding, face-to-face interaction, close bodily contact, and crying. Group B infants were those who had experienced more harmonious feedings, longer and more pleasurable face-to-face interactions, and tender and affectionate holding, and whose crying was more frequently, promptly, and effectively responded to during the first quarter. Group A and C infants were those who experienced less satisfactory feedings, less contingent pacing, and a more routine manner in face-to-face interaction, less affectionate physical contact, and less responsiveness to crying during the first 3 months of life. The differences between group A and C could be linked to mothers' emotional expressiveness. Mothers of infants classified as group A smiled less in face-to-face interaction and expressed more aversion to physical contact. Mothers of group C infants were more inconsistent.

Reunion behavior in the Strange Situation was also related to the quality of mother–infant interaction in the home during the fourth quarter. Babies classified as group B were more often acknowledged by their mother when she returned after a brief departure (Stayton & Ainsworth, 1973), they experienced more affectionate close bodily contact (Tracy & Ainsworth, 1981), and were only rarely picked up in an interfering manner. Their crying was ignored less frequently (Bell & Ainsworth, 1972). In contrast, group A and C infants experienced positive interactions less frequently and negative interactions more frequently.

In addition to detailed observational codings of discrete behaviors, Ainsworth and her colleagues (Ainsworth et al., 1974) also devised general rating scales to characterize the mother's interactive style toward her infant during the fourth-quarter home visits. These scales assessed four dimensions: (1) *sensitivity-insensitivity;* (2) *acceptance-rejection;* (3) *cooperation-interference; and* (4) *accessibility-*

ignoring. Sensitivity refers to the mother's ability to see things from the baby's point of view, to notice infant cues and interpret them accurately, to respond considerately to infant communications. It also implies that the mother does not distort the baby's communications in light of her own preoccupations, needs, or defenses. *Acceptance* means that the mother temporarily accepts the limitations the maternal role imposes on her other activities, that she does not cast the baby in the role of opponent. *Cooperation* refers to the mother's respect for her baby as a separate person, her skillful intervention when the baby is interrupted in an activity, and her willingness to use gentle persuasion instead of direct control. Finally, *accessibility* denotes the degree to which the mother makes herself psychologically available to the infant when she is present in the room, the degree to which she attends to her infant's signals even when there are distractions or other demands on her attention. Maternal sensitivity and accessibility, taken jointly, closely resemble Emde's conception of *emotional availability* (see Emde, 1980). Like Ainsworth and her colleagues, Emde emphasizes that the mother's emotional availability facilitates the infant's development by fostering security, exploration, and learning, but he also focuses on the reward that both partners experience in a relationship in which each is emotionally available to the other. The baby's appearance and responsive behaviors are rewarding to the caregiver. Achieving harmonious interaction with the baby provides the parent with a sense of fulfillment. Conversely, by reading and appropriately responding to infant signals, parents also reward infants, setting up an expectation that "good things will happen." When mutual rewards are absent, the baby's exploration may be inhibited, and in extreme cases, sadness and depression may ensue.

In Ainsworth's Baltimore study, ratings of maternal sensitivity, acceptance, cooperation, and accessibility during the fourth quarter were significantly higher for infants classified in group B during the Strange Situation than for groups A or C. Mothers whose infants were classified in Group A were especially rejecting. Indeed, rejection of and aversion to close bodily contact and lack of emotional expression were consistently characteristic of mothers whose babies were classified into group A at 1 year of age (Ainsworth et al., 1978). In other words, the patterns of emotional communication in the dyad were relatively stable across the first year of life. One must speculate, however, that by the end of the first year both partners were actively responsible for upholding the stability of mutual interaction patterns because the infants have already begun to construct internal working models of self and mother. A pattern upheld by two partners will be more stable than a pattern due to the behavior of one partner.

Ainsworth and colleagues' (1974) findings concerning the importance of maternal sensitivity and responsiveness have received additional support from a study of attachment in Germany. Grossmann, Grossmann, Spangler, Suess, and Unzner (1985) found that ratings of maternal sensitivity to infant signals at 2 and 6 months were related to later secure attachment classifications in a sample of 50 north German infants, although the differences failed to reach significance at 10 months. They also replicated many of the detailed findings on crying and physical contact. In the United States Egeland and Farber (1984) showed that Ainsworth's sensitivity ratings at 6 months were predictive of later attachment status although the findings were significant only for boys. In addition, Maslin (1983) reported that composite scores of maternal warmth and affectionate behavior during two 3-hr home observations at 6 months predicted secure attachment classifications in the Strange Situation at 12 months. Similarly, Belsky, Rovine, and Taylor (1984; see also Belsky & Isabella, in press) found that a measure which they interpret as an index of maternal sensitivity—obtained during mother–infant interaction in the home—was predictive of secure attachment assessed in the Strange Situation. Finally, Gaensbauer and colleagues (1985) reported that ratings of maternal behavior in the home made by trained lay visitors at 12–14 months were correlated with ratings of security–insecurity in the Strange Situation at 12 months. The security ratings were based on the same dimensions as the traditional Ainsworth classification system, but criteria were more stringent, including only very secure and very insecure infants. Mothers of very securely attached infants were rated as warmer, more responsive, less angry, less fearful, more curious, and happier than mothers of very insecure infants. Taken together, these findings strongly suggest a consistent and therefore measurable influence by the mother on the organization of the emerging attachment relationship, though they do not, of course, rule out infant influences.

Efforts to assess infants' contribution to the quality of later infant–mother attachment have yielded mixed results, with some studies showing effects of infant temperament and many others not (for reviews and discussions see Belsky & Isabella, in press; Bretherton, 1985; Sroufe, 1985). In fact, Ainsworth (1983) speculates that an infant's influence on the mother may be masked by maternal sensitivity. Sensitive maternal interactive behavior is by definition strongly influenced by the individual characteristics of the infant: Maternal sensitive behavior toward an initially irritable baby will be different than sensitive behavior toward an initially well-modulated baby. However, despite the differences in maternal behavior, both babies have a good chance of becoming securely attached. This line of reasoning is corroborated by correlations of maternal responsiveness in the first quarter with less crying in the fourth quarter of the first year, but no correlations between infant crying in the first and fourth quarters (Bell & Ainsworth, 1972). Additional evidence that an initially difficult infant may become an easier infant through dyadic experiences with a sensitive mother comes from Minde (personal communication, May 1984) as well as Belsky and Isabella (in press).

In several reanalyses of their data, the Grossmanns and their collaborators have recently taken the study of communication patterns in attachment relationships a step further. They are now able to pinpoint with more specificity along what dimensions secure and insecure dyads differ. Three studies have been reported so far. In the first study Grossmann and Grossmann (1984) examined tape-recorded maternal and infant vocalizations during 2-hr home observations when the infants were 2, 6, and 10 months old. They were able to identify three maternal conversational styles that they termed sober, tender, and lighthearted. The tender style was characterized by an intermediate tempo of speech, many expressions of quiet pleasure, very few directives, no impatience or tension, a strong tendency to respond to infant vocalizations promptly but without being overly dramatic, a sort of even attentiveness, and prompt and generous soothing in a very calm tone of voice. The lighthearted style was associated with a fast tempo of speech, frequent and sometimes extreme variability in loudness and pitch, much laughing, mock surprise, a frequently demanding voice quality, and intermittent and not always prompt responsiveness to the baby's vocalizations. The sober style was characterized by a relatively slow tempo of speech, fewer and short utterances, an uneven rate of responding to the baby, long reaction time, and somewhat delayed soothing, sometimes accompanied by signs of resignation.

These maternal communication styles were significantly correlated with maternal sensitivity assessed independently but concurrently from narrative reports of mother–infant interactive behavior at home during the same three ages, as well as with the baby's propensity to vocalize. Babies whose mothers had sober or tender conversational styles tended to increase their vocalizations from 6 to 10 months, whereas the babies of lighthearted mothers actually decreased the frequency of their vocalizations. Comparisons of conversational styles to Strange Situation classifications indicated that 50 percent of the B mothers but only 11 percent of A and 10 percent of C mothers used the tender style. The lighthearted style was employed mainly by mothers whose infants were classified A or C. Interestingly, the sober style was common in all three groups (38 percent B, 50 percent A, and 55 percent C). Thus maternal communication styles predict attachment classifications for many but not all infants in the sample, a finding that demands further research.

In a second study, Grossmann, Grossmann, and Schwan (in press) studied communicative behavior in the Ainsworth Strange Situation itself. They focused on infant–mother communication during the three episodes of the Strange Situation when parent and baby were alone together (the low-stress introductory episode and the two high-stress reunion episodes). It turned out that babies' attachment classifications were associated with specific communicative behaviors. Twelve of the 16 secure infants engaged in "direct communication" with mother (by eye contact, facial expression, vocalization, showing and giving of objects) during the introductory episode, but only 12 of 24 infants classified as avoidant did so. During the first reunion episode, 13 of the 16 infants classified as secure communicated directly, while only 7 of 24 infants classified as avoidant did so. In the second reunion episode, 15 out of the 16 secure infants but only 11 of 24 avoidant infants communicated directly. According to the Grossmanns, this demonstrates the emergence of a communication pattern in secure dyads that allows for free affective exchanges. No secure infants stayed away from mother when their mood was negative, and although some infants classified as avoidant did engage in direct communication, they did so only when they were feeling well. Infants classified as avoidant tended not to emit mother-directed signals when distressed, and did not seek bodily contact. With fathers, the results were essentially similar. On reunion with them, a high proportion of infants classified as secure communicated with them directly, but only few of the infants classified as avoidant did so.

In a third study, Escher-Graeub and Grossmann (1983) examined infant–parent communication during a play situation (not in the Strange Situation) at 12 and 18 months. Parents of infants classified as secure in the Strange Situation ignored only 4 percent of their infants' signals during the play session, while parents of avoidant infants ignored 18 percent of the signals addressed to them. Moreover, parents of avoidant infants joined in when the infants were already engrossed in play and withdrew when the infants showed evidence of negative feelings. By contrast, parents of secure infants engaged in mutual play when infants were at a loss but watched quietly when the infants did not need them.

Similar conclusions can be drawn from all three studies. The manner in which parents do or do not respond to their infants' communications modifies the patterning of emotional expressiveness in the developing relationship, and hence its quality. In particular, easy flow of communication between partners or—to use Emde's (1980) term—continued mutual emotional availability seems to require that the parents not selectively discount signals of distress.

Toddlerhood and Early Childhood

Unfortunately we have no home observational studies like Ainsworth's Baltimore project to help us understand the vicissitudes of attachment relations during the second year when autonomy and discipline issues become so prominent. Mahler's notions about increased ambivalence toward mother in the second year and about the shift from practicing to rapprochement to object constancy have not yet been directly studied from the perspective of attachment theory. Instead, researchers have used shortcut methods. By classifying infants in the Strange Situation at 12 and/or 18 months and testing them in a variety of other situations later, investigators have attempted to look for continuity in the relationship. Again communication patterns, especially emotional expressiveness, turned out to be an interesting dimension. Main, Tomasini, and Tolan (1979) found that mothers of toddlers who were classified as securely attached at 12 months were also rated as more sensitive and acceptant when they engaged the toddler in play during a laboratory session at 21 months. Mothers of toddlers earlier classified as avoidant expressed more anger and less pleasure in interaction with them at 21 months. Interestingly, mothers of infants earlier classified as secure also openly communicated their affect when greeting a somewhat familiar woman as she entered the playroom and engaged the toddler in a ballgame. In a second study of toddlers, Matas, Arend, and Sroufe (1978) found that quality of attachment as assessed in the Strange Situation at 12 and 18 months predicted more adaptive communication in a problem-solving task too difficult for 2-year-olds to perform unaided. Toddlers earlier classified as secure tried first to solve the task independently but turned to mother for help when they got stuck. These toddlers also participated in the task with more enthusiasm. Their mothers, conversely, made them feel more comfortable, and helped them to focus on the task. They gave the children space initially (noninterference), but when asked for help (acceptance) they timed and paced their interventions effectively (sensitivity). Effective assistance required that the mothers pay attention to the toddlers' cues and help them to achieve at least part of the solution themselves. Communication between both partners was harmonious in the secure dyads, I believe, because the mothers respected the children's wish for autonomy and the children asked for help only when they could not manage the task on their own. Sensitive responding by the caregiver to infant signals relevant to stress and exploration in the first year of life appears to create the kind of relationship and communication patterns (based on working models) that allow the dyad to negotiate attachment–autonomy issues harmoniously and effectively in the second year of life.

Studies of toddlers who have mothers with bipolar and unipolar depression tend to support these conclusions (Radke-Yarrow, Cummings, Kuczynsky, & Chapman, 1985). Mothers with bipolar depression provided their toddlers with much unpredictable and hence meaningless and confusing affective feedback. In addition, such mothers expressed significantly more negative and significantly less positive affect during several half-days in a homelike laboratory environment. The incidence of insecure attachment was very high in this sample. In addition to the commonly observed avoidant (A) and resistant (C) patterns of insecure reunion behavior in the Strange Situation, an insecure pattern in this sample was characterized by a *combination* of markedly avoidant and markedly resistant reunion behavior (A/C). This pattern was quite uncommon in children of normally functioning mothers, but has been reported for other social risk samples, such as maltreated infants and toddlers (Cicchetti, personal communication, January 1985; Crittenden, 1985).

Findings that link open and effective communication between children and parents to secure attachment are not limited to infancy and toddlerhood. In a recent study of 6-year-olds and their parents Main and colleagues (1985) found that easy and coherent expression of affect was related to security assessed in a variety of ways at 6 years as well as in infancy. Their sample included children who had been classified as secure (B), insecure–avoidant (A), and insecure–disorganized (D) in infancy. The D classification (disorganized–disoriented; for further details see Main & Hesse, in press) has some overlap with the A/C classification reported by Radke-Yarrow and colleagues (1985) and Crittenden (1985). Main and colleagues described the secure 6-year-old as being at ease in exploring feelings and potentialities. The security of parents was rated from transcriptions of an interview about attachment relations in their family of origin. Secure parents, like their children, were characterized by the ease with which positive and negative aspects of attachment experience and feeling were communicated and integrated. Not all of the secure parents studied by Main and colleagues reported favorable childhood experiences, but many did. Thus patterns established in infancy seem to be carried into later relationships, even into relationships that affect parenting of the next generation. In those cases where intergenerational transmission of unfavorable patterns is avoided the parents have reevaluated early relationships with parents and presumably also restructured internal working models of self (see Ricks, 1985, for a review).

SECURITY, COMMUNICATION, AND INTERNAL WORKING MODELS

How does one conceptualize the relationship between open, coherent communication regarding attachment-related issues and infant security? The "easy" answer goes something like this: If an attachment figure adequately and appropriately responds to security- and autonomy-seeking signals, the infant learns a sense of trust that results in an optimal balance of attachment and exploratory behavior. But this begs the question of the criteria by which one judges the adequacy or appropriateness of parental responding. According to my reading of attachment theory, the following argument can be made: The infant is predesigned to expect a caregiver who understands the infant's attachment behaviors. If the attachment figure's internal working model of the caregiving role does not accord with the baby's built-in expectations (e.g., if the caregiver interprets security seeking as overdemandingness, or as not important, or if she or he does not respect the baby's eagerness for independent exploration) the infant's attachment behavior will not be effectively assuaged, eagerness to explore will not be respected, or exploration will be encouraged when the baby signals a desire for comforting and reassurance. As a result, the infant will feel dissatisfied, misunderstood, or disavowed. This has consequences for the working model the infant constructs of self and attachment figure. The clash between the built-in hopes and the actuality leads to a number of less than optimal attachment patterns. This is so because the attachment system is now operating with inadequate working models that distort and partially undermine its functioning and hence also influence the functioning of the exploratory system. The findings reported by Ainsworth and her colleagues (see Ainsworth et al., 1978) suggest that in the early phases of the relationship mother is most influential in "setting the tone," but as memory processes improve it is likely that the child's internal working models serve to uphold already established patterns of attachment. Communication patterns may thus retain qualitative stability, even though the child's communication skills become more complex.

In a recent article, Lieberman and Pawl (in press) describe a number of clinical cases in whom they observed distortions of the attachment–exploration balance because of mother's inability to communicate her availability as secure base and/or haven. One pattern consisted of excessive danger seeking or recklessness, associated with insufficient maternal protection, or maternal discounting of security seeking. Danger-seeking toddlers tended habitually to wander off without checking back to mother, frequently getting lost and/or hurt in the course of exploration (this sounds like a severe form of the darting-away behavior described by Mahler). The toddlers' seemingly intrepid behavior was coupled with high levels of separation anxiety when mother herself left. Danger seeking was also associated with the frequent occurrence of sleep disturbances. A second pattern consisted of excessive danger fleeing (excessive shadowing in Mahler's terms). Danger-fleeing or phobic children showed a restriction of affective range, withdrawal from social interaction with unfamiliar persons, frozen vigilance, and suppressed exploration. It looked as if these children were using self-restraint as self-protection against a mother who, because of her unpredictable punitiveness, was herself perceived as a source of danger. The third pattern was precocious competence (hypercompetence). In hypercompetent children disturbance of the attachment–exploration balance resulted not in direct distortions of exploratory or attachment behavior, but in overconcern for the mother, a phenomenon akin to compulsive caregiving found in pathological mourning (Bowlby, 1980). A hypercompetent child keeps proximity unilaterally, and is overly solicitous of the mother's welfare, especially in situations where one would expect the child to need the mother, not vice versa. The child takes on the role of attachment figure, consoling the mother at separation ("Don't be sad, Mommy."). Hypercompetence may be accompanied by a tendency to refrain from expressing painful and anxious feelings. Lieberman and Pawl report that such children tend to have depressed mothers who are nevertheless invested in them.

In relationships where attachment signals very frequently go unnoticed or uncomprehended or are severely distorted, each partner's internal working models will tend to become and remain inadequate because defensively excluded material now no longer participates in error-correcting feedback. Mutually satisfying communication is impossible without shared working models or a shared understanding of the relationship (albeit at different levels of complexity for the young and for the mature partner). Communication at cross-purposes therefore interferes with the balance between attachment and exploratory behavior in characteristic ways, as described by Lieberman and Pawl (in press). By contrast, in relationships where attachment signals are mutually comprehended and responded to, both partners' internal working models are likely to be more adequate in the first place, and will also remain more open to fine-tuning and updating. Thus in secure dyads we should expect to see continuing efforts at constructing and reconstructing a shared view of the relationship as the child develops greater conceptual, affective, and communication skills.

Peterfreund (1983), a psychoanalyst who has espoused Bowlby's notion of internal working models, describes the patient–analyst relationship in ways that can shed new light on the role of communication in secure infant–parent attachment relationships. Peterfreund emphasizes that it is vital for patients to feel understood by the analyst (attachment figure). What others have called empathy is really to enter into another's working models. But how is this to be achieved? Although many of the processes involved in the activation of working models go on outside awareness, Peterfreund argues that specific processes associated with working models *are* consciously accessible. These processes can be enlisted to assist the analyst in generating images, emotions, fantasies, even nonverbalizable sensorimotor schemata that will be helpful in gaining insight into the patient's working models, always in conjunction with error-correcting feedback from the patient. Many different working models can be brought into play for this purpose: working models of the analysts' relations to others, of his or her own bodily functions, feelings, and thoughts, of average and traumatic infant and child experience, and of the analytic process itself. Working models are useful, Peterfreund emphasizes, because they are experience-near representations that reflect the full richness, strength, depth, vividness, subtlety, and complexity of human thought and feeling. More abstract theories can be thought of as metamodels, developed from the more basic working models. These are less directly useful in conducting therapy.

It seems to me that Peterfreund's ideas can fruitfully be applied to understanding the function of communication in the caregiver–infant relationship. The caregiver also uses a variety of working models—a general model of the world, a normative model about babies in general, models of caregiving patterns derived from experience with parents in childhood—to construct a more or less adequate model of self and infant as attachment partners, in conjunction with error-correcting feedback from the actual infant. Although a parent does not go about the task of building working models with the conscious deliberation of the analyst described by Peterfreund, there is a sense in which parental sensitivity as defined by Ainsworth implies precisely the kind of processes Peterfreund proposes. Sensitivity is grounded in the parent's ability to construct, correct, fine-tune, and update an adequate working model of the infant. Without such a model the parent could not take the baby's perspective, notice what the baby's goals are, and decide what to do about them empathically, or, to phrase it differently, function as an effective secure base.

It is often overlooked that insensitivity as understood by Ainsworth is not necessarily indexed by unpleasant, rejecting, mean, or nasty behavior. *Insensitivity* means that the caregiver is not reading and/or supportively responding to the infant's states or goals, thereby teaching the infant that its signals are irrelevant or counterproductive (see also Stern, 1977, for extensive discussions along similar lines). It is insensitive to deny a distressed or fearful infant the solace of bodily contact (rejection), but it is equally insensitive behavior to insist on affectionate physical contact when the infant is deeply engrossed in some exploratory task (interference). Ainsworth proposed that insensitivity results from mother's inability to take the baby's perspective. One reason for this may be an inadequate working model of self as attachment figure, but insensitivity can also arise due to a caregiver's preoccupation with severe life stresses. We do not know whether these differences matter to the baby, but mismatch based on inadequate working models seems to me to represent a more serious danger.

Stern (1985) illustrates the kind of insensitivity I have in mind with a most poignant example. A paranoid schizophrenic woman who was felt by psychiatric staff to be *overidentified* with her infant was referred to Stern and his team for evaluation. During the affect attunement procedure, this mother showed no attunements at all (they usually occur once a minute). Nevertheless, the mother's behavior with the baby was very gentle at all times. In the course of later therapeutic work it turned out that this mother was making caregiving decisions on the basis of irrelevant signals (such as a car honking outside the window once or twice). The baby had learnt to fall in passively with mother's unpredictable and (in Ainsworth's sense) insensitive behavior.

Refining the Concept of Internal Working Model

The concept of internal working model is proving to be a powerful tool in thinking about attachment and about developing patterns of communication in attachment relationships. Procedures to study internal working models of adults and children have been developed (Cassidy, 1985; Main et al., 1985) and the Grossmanns' studies are pointing the way for how to examine them in infants (Escher-Graeub & Grossmann, 1983; Grossmann et al., in press; Grossmann & Grossmann, 1984). These studies are already changing the way we think about internal working models of self and attachment figures. In addition, it will be useful to follow Bowlby's (1980) example, and continue to incorporate into our research insights from functionalist theories of representation and memory that are currently being developed (see especially Johnson-Laird, 1982; Schank, 1982). Because of their focus on the representation of everyday events these theories are highly compatible with the functionalist perspective on memory required by the concept of working model in attachment theory and, I would add, of object representation in other psychoanalytic theories.

In a recent book entitled *Mental Models* Johnson-Laird (1983) put Craik's (1943) notion of internal working models into an evolutionary perspective. Working models, he pointed out, owe their origin to the survival advantage that they afford an organism by permitting insightful and foresightful behavior. Because the essential feature of a mental model is its functional role in guiding adaptive behavior, structural correspondence between the representation and what is represented (similarity in relation–structure) is vital. The more adequately internal working models can simulate relevant aspects of the world, the better the potential planning and responding capacity of an organism. Humans and the higher apes differ from other animals not only in their ability to construct more complex working models of the physical and social world, but in their ability to construct internal working models of themselves. It is this ability that underlies reflective self-awareness, and the human capacity for intersubjectivity.

Johnson-Laird places great emphasis on the role of internal working models in guiding understanding and in the acquisition of working models by proxy (through communication) but does not discuss how old working models are changed by new input. It is with respect to this issue that I have found some of the theorizing by Mandler (1979), Nelson (Nelson, 1981; Nelson & Gruendel, 1981), and Schank and Abelson (1977) very helpful. These authors describe mental structures called *event schemata* or *scripts* that summarize skeletal information about repeated similar events in a person's life, information about who did what to whom, where, how, and for what reason.

Theories of event representation provide a useful basis for elaborating the notion of working models because event schemata are understood as in some sense isomorphic with the structure of the original experience. They represent its spatial-temporal and causal aspects in connected form, or as Craik (1943) would say, they have the same relation–structure as the represented event. However, there were a number of disadvantages with the initial formulation of script theory (Schank & Abelson, 1977), as Schank himself notes (1982). First, the event structures proposed as basic building blocks of representation consisted of long event sequences (such as what transpires when you visit a restaurant). There was no provision in the theory for making comparisons across similar actions in different scripts (cross-referencing). Secondly, there was little consideration of how scripts change with new contradictory input, and how scripts are related to autobiographical memories. Thirdly, there was scant emphasis on the emotional aspect of represented experience. The revised theory (Schank, 1982), I suggest, provides a more adequate basis for thinking about the acquisition, use, and change of internal working models.

Schank now argues that information derived from episodic or autobiographical memories (including affect) is reprocessed, partitioned, cross-indexed, and summarized in a variety of ways. But all of Schank's hypothesized mental structures preserve a spatiotemporal–causal relation–structure that simulates events in the world. Some of these structures order mini-event representations into coordinated longer event sequences (the former scripts), others generalize across mini-events (feeding situations regardless of context), and yet others generalize across different event sequences (e.g., all caregiving routines). Schank's conceptualization deliberately blurs the distinction between episodic and semantic memory proposed by Tulving (1972, 1983) and substitutes instead a multiply interconnected hierarchy of schemata that are graded from very experience-near to very general. This hierarchy is constructed and continually reconstructed and revised on the basis of new input.

As I already noted, event schemata are generated by processing autobiographical memories. These of schemata in turn guide the processing of new information. Hence the way in which experiences have been encoded in the past (memory) determines how the next similar experience is decoded (processing). When an unexpected turn of events is encountered the new episode is registered as an exception, but if the once unexpected event recurs many times a new schema will be constructed. In addition, the episode will be parsed and information fed into many other structures that represent generalized event information about agents, actions, intentions, goals, and emotions. These parsing and ordering processes can therefore explain how events experienced with attachment figures can influence more general normative working models of the caregiving role, or more generally, how autobiographical memories become incorporated into a variety of more general knowledge structures. They can also provide a new perspective on defensive exclusion (Bowlby, 1980) or biased processing (Erdelyi, 1985). If portions of autobiographical event representations enter into cross-referenced schemata at many hierarchical levels, it is possible to see how material that has been defensively excluded from autobiographical memory can nevertheless influence processing at other levels.

But are these conceptions relevant to infancy? A number of studies (Nelson & Gruendel, 1981; Nelson & Ross, 1982) inspired by the earlier versions of script theory report that even 3-year-olds have a good grasp of the order in which action sequences of routine everyday events take place, especially when event sequences are causally related, and they do not require a large number of exposures to an event in order to construct a schema (Price & Goodman, 1985). With respect to internal working models, it is especially interesting that 3-year-olds who were asked to produce specific memories of a routine event (such as eating dinner last night) tended to produce event schemata or scripts. Only extraordinary events were recalled as episodic memories (Nelson & Gruendel, 1981). At an even younger age toddlers demonstrate in their pretend play that information about everyday events is available to them in schematic form (Bretherton, 1984), and during the preverbal stage, we have evidence that infants anticipate another person's behavior in context (see Izard, 1978; Piaget, 1951; Sroufe, 1979; Stern, 1985).

So far, infant memory has not been examined with a view to studying the development of internal working models of self with other, although Stern's formulation of RIG (representations of interactions that have been generalized) may provide the conceptual tool for studies of working models during the first year of life. In the second year of life, the analysis of communication patterns (e.g., Escher-Graeub & Grossmann, 1983) could serve the same function. From the end of the first year onward, there is reason to suppose that infants can invoke working models to think about and forecast an attachment figure's probable behavior in the future, not only to adjust their behavior to a partner who is present. Anecdotal evidence suggests that by the beginning of the third year toddlers' language may provide a useful window into internal working models of self and attachment figure. Toddlers who reenact separations and reunions with dolls are probably activating their working models of actual experience. A 2-year-old who is upset about mother's repeated trips and reassures herself solemnly "Mommy always coming home" has apparently formed a generic event schema about mother, based on many leave-takings and returns. The same can be said of the child who categorizes long and short maternal absences by whether the hair dryer did or did not remain behind, although the degree to which talk about the hair dryer replaces talk about mother's absence may indicate the onset of defensive exclusion. The opportunity offered by play and language to access a toddler's internal working model of self and attachment figure hence seems promising, but caution is necessary.

As Bowlby (1980), Stern (1985), and Sullivan (1953) point out, language has a rather curious relationship to internal working models. A verbal child can be told by others how to construe specific interpersonal events. Although these imposed construals may diverge from the toddler's own direct acquaintance with the world, it should not be forgotten that they may also fulfill a clarifying and correcting function. The adaptive function of language with respect to attachment is to better align intentions and goals in an attachment partnership (leading to more adequate working models). When defensive exclusion and biased processing become pervasive, however, language may serve to miscommunicate, to create discordances and confusions (though exactly how language enables us to build models of nonexperienced events by proxy is not yet clear). Thus we must look at children's behavior, not merely their language, to infer whether defense mechanisms are already influencing the consciously accessible aspect of working models.

EGO AND INTERNAL WORKING MODELS: CONCLUDING REMARKS

Although I have avoided it so far, I feel that I must now address the classical question of the *I* as knower and the *me* as representation of the self (James, 1890). Some psychoanalytic writers have made a similar distinction between the executive structure called *ego* and self-representations (e.g., Hartmann, 1955), but the I–me relationship is only implicitly or partially addressed by Mahler, Sullivan, Stern, and Bowlby. Yet clarification is crucial. We need to know not only how the executive ego and the working models of self interact with one another, but also how motivational systems communicate with and are influenced by the executive ego. After all, it is the child that engages in proximity and security seeking, not the attachment system.

Perhaps ideas proposed by Johnson-Laird (1982) can prove useful in thinking about these issues. Johnson-Laird suggests that consciousness is the experience we have of our own executive processes. The executive or operating system (the *I*) processes inflow and outflow serially or sequentially by monitoring and controlling information from and to many lower-level processors that operate in parallel. The operating system does not have direct access to the inner workings of these parallel processors. For example, commands for motor movements are couched by the executive system as higher-order instructions for purposeful action, not in terms of individual muscle movements. The lower-level processors automatically convert the high-level commands into specific muscle patterns.

Surely among the most important processors providing input to the operating system are motivational systems. The executive system or *I* can, I suggest, be understood as a metasystem that makes decisions about priorities among the several motivational systems that may be active and that may send conflicting commands to the operating system at a particular point in time. In making these decisions the executive system draws on internal working models of the world, of significant people, and especially of the self. However, as Johnson-Laird points out, the *I* does not seem to have complete control over lower-level processors. They retain some autonomy. The notion of relative willpower, say Johnson-Laird, derives from the degree to which the operating system (the *I*) can enforce its own decisions. Under certain circumstances, executive plans may be interrupted or disrupted by motivational systems that regulate survival-promoting behavior. If this were not so the organism might fail to attend to emergency signals from these systems.

The distinction between the operating or executive control system (ego or *I*) and internal working models of the self (*me*) does not diminish the importance of working models, because working models are instrumental in making sense of events and in guiding purposeful action. In infancy the executive system and working models are still rather primitive. Infants require a caregiver as auxiliary ego (Spitz, 1965) or, in Stern's (1985) terms, a self-regulating other who can help set priorities. Therefore, parents' working models of the baby as needing care, soothing, and protection and of themselves as caregivers play a major role not only in the development of the baby's own working model of self, and in the functioning of the baby's attachment system, but also in the developing organization of the baby's executive control system.

Seen from this perspective, the intergenerational transmission of relationship patterns as well as the continued readiness for transforming old relationship patterns is more easily understood. Changes in a deeply disturbed parent–infant attachment relationship are dependent on parental revisions of internal working models of self in relation to attachment. In a manner not fully understood at present, parents have a tendency to reenact patterns of parenting they themselves experienced; in other words, to identify with the working model of the parent acquired in childhood. As Main and colleagues (1985) have shown, the priority that a parent accords to attachment issues in relating to his or her infant tends to be closely linked to working models of attachment relationships in the family of origin, unless the parent has been able to revise these models during adolescence or early adulthood.

In a seminal paper, Fraiberg, Adelson, and Shapiro (1975) describe severely disturbed young mothers who were unable to provide their infants with the comfort and solace of which they had themselves been deprived as children. For change in the mother–infant relationship to occur, it was not merely a matter of explaining how and why the mother should change her behavior. Because the executive system functions in close collaboration with the internal working model of self, the mother as parent could only change her caregiving behavior after her working model of self as attachment figure had been revised. This was achieved by making it possible for her to relive the emotions appropriate to early experiences of abandonment, severe neglect, and physical abuse. Thus internal working models could not be rebuilt by fiat from the top down; the task had to be achieved from the bottom up, in the context of a therapeutic relationship in which the therapist served as secure base for exploring defensively excluded issues (see also Lieberman & Pawl, in press; Osofsky, 1985). This made it possible for the parent to exorcise the "ghosts in the nursery," or, to put it in attachment terms, to update and reorganize inadequate, distorted internal working models of attachment relations acquired in the past. I assume that in so doing the parent's working model of self became, as it were, unhooked from the complementary model of parents in the family of origin, freeing the parent to become emotionally available to the infant, and to read the infant's signals appropriately. Seen from this perspective, the somewhat abstract concept of internal working model of self and attachment figure demonstrates its enormous practical implications for understanding developmental mental health and pathology.

REFERENCES

Ainsworth, M. D. S. (1973). The development of infant–mother attachment. In B. M. Caldwell & H. N. Ricciuti (Eds.), *Review of child development research* (Vol. 3). Chicago: University of Chicago Press.

Ainsworth, M. D. S. (1982). Attachment: Retrospect and prospect. In C. M. Parkes & J. Stevenson-Hinde (Eds.), *The place of attachment in human behavior.* New York: Basic.

Ainsworth, M. D. S. (1983). Patterns of infant–mother attachment as related to maternal care. In D. Magnusson & V. Allen (Eds.), *Human development: An interactional perspective.* New York: Academic.

Ainsworth, M. D. S., & Bell, S. M. (1969). Some contemporary patterns in the feeding situation. In A. Ambrose (Ed.), *Stimulation in early infancy.* London: Academic.

Ainsworth, M. D. S., Bell, S. M., Blehar, M. C., & Main, M. (1971, April). *Physical contact: A study of infant responsiveness and its relation to maternal handling.* Paper presented at the biennial meeting of the Society for Research in Child Development, Minneapolis.

Ainsworth, M. D. S., Bell, S. M., & Stayton, D. (1974). Infant–mother attachment and social development. In M. P. Richards (Ed.), *The introduction of the child into a social world.* London: Cambridge University Press.

Ainsworth, M. D. S., Blehar, M. C., Waters, E., & Wall, S. (1978). *Patterns of attachment: A psychological study of the strange situation.* Hillsdale, NJ: Erlbaum.

Ainsworth, M. D. S., & Wittig, B. A. (1969). Attachment and the exploratory behaviour of one-year-olds in a strange situation. In B. M. Foss (Ed.), *Determinants of infant behaviour* (Vol. 4). London: Methuen.

Anderson, J. W. (1972). Attachment behaviour out of doors. In N. Blurton Jones (Ed.), *Ethological studies of child behaviour.* Cambridge: Cambridge University Press.

Bell, S. M. (1970). The development of the concept of the object as related to infant–mother attachment. *Child Development, 41,* 291–311.

Bell, S. M., & Ainsworth, M. D. S. (1972). Infant crying and maternal responsiveness. *Child Development, 43,* 1171–1190.

Belsky, J., & Isabella, R. (in press). Maternal, infant, and social–contextual determinants of attachment security. In J. Belsky & T. Nezworkski (Eds.), *Clinical implications of attachment.* Hillsdale, NJ: Erlbaum.

Belsky, J., Rovine, M., & Taylor, D. (1984). The origins of individual differences in infant–mother attachment: Maternal and infant contributions. *Child Development, 55,* 718–728.

Bischof, N. A. (1975). A systems approach toward the functional connections of attachment and fear. *Child Development, 46,* 801–817.

Blehar, M. C., Lieberman, A. F., & Ainsworth, M. D. S. (1977). Early face-to-face interaction and its relation to later infant–mother attachment. *Child Development, 48,* 182–194.

Bower, T. G. R., Broughton, J. M., & Moore, M. K. (1970). Demonstration of intention in the reaching behavior of neonate humans. *Nature, 228,* 679–680.

Bowlby, J. (1958). The nature of the child's tie to his mother. *International Journal of Psycho-Analysis, 39,* 350–373.

Bowlby, J. (1969). *Attachment and loss: Vol. 1: Attachment.* New York: Basic.

Bowlby, J. (1973). *Attachment and loss: Vol. 2: Separation.* New York: Basic.

Bowlby, J. (1980). *Attachment and loss: Vol. 3: Loss, sadness and depression.* New York: Basic.

Brazelton, T. B. (1977). Implications of infant development among the Mayan Indians of Mexico. In P. H. Leiderman, S. R. Tulkin, & A. Rosenfeld (Eds.), *Culture and infancy.* New York: Academic.

Bretherton, I. (1980). Young children in stressful situations: The supporting role of attachment figures and unfamiliar caregivers. In G. V. Coelho & P. Ahmed (Eds.), *Uprooting and development.* New York: Plenum.

Bretherton, I. (1984). Representing the social world in symbolic play: Reality and fantasy. In Bretherton I. (Ed.), *Symbolic play: The development of social understanding.* New York: Academic.

Bretherton, I. (1985). Attachment theory: Retrospect and prospect. In I. Bretherton & E.

Waters (Eds.), Growing points of attachment theory and research. *Monographs of the Society for Research in Child Development, 50* (1-2, Serial No. 209).

Bretherton, I., & Ainsworth, M. D. S. (1974). Responses of one-year-olds to a stranger in a strange situation. In M. Lewis & L. A. Rosenblum (Eds.), *The origins of fear.* New York: Wiley.

Bretherton, I., & Bates, E. (1979). The emergence of intentional communication. In I. Uzgiris (Ed.), *New Directions for Child Development, 4,* 81-100.

Bretherton, I., Fritz, J., Zahn-Waxler, C., & Ridgeway, D. (1986). Learning to talk about emotion: A functionalist perspective. *Child Development, 57,* 530-548.

Bretherton, I., McNew, S., & Beeghly-Smith, M. (1981). Early person knowledge as expressed in verbal and gestural communication: When do infants acquire a "theory of mind"? In M. E. Lamb & L. R. Sherrod (Eds.), *Infant social cognition.* Hillsdale, NJ: Erlbaum.

Bretherton, I., Stolberg, U., & Kreye, M. (1981). Engaging strangers in proximal interaction: Infants' social initiative. *Developmental Psychology, 17,* 746-755.

Campos, J. J., & Stenberg, C. R. (1981). Perception, appraisal and emotion: The onset of social referencing. In M. E. Lamb & L. R. Sherrod (Eds.), *Infant social cognition.* Hillsdale, NJ: Erlbaum.

Cassidy, J. (1985). *Attachment and the self at six.* Unpublished doctoral dissertation, University of Virginia.

Craik, K. (1943). *The nature of explanation.* Cambridge: Cambridge University Press.

Crittenden, P. (1985). Social networks, quality of child-rearing, and child development. *Child Development,* 1299-1313.

DeVore, I. (1965). *Primate behavior: Field studies of monkeys and apes.* New York: Holt, Rinehart & Winston.

Dunn, J., Bretherton, I., & Munn, P. (in press). Coversations about feeling states between mothers and their young children. *Developmental Psychology.*

Egeland, B., & Farber, E. (1984). Infant–mother attachment: Factors related to its development and changes over time. *Child Development, 55,* 753-751.

Emde, R. N. (1983). The prerepresentational self and its affective core. *Psychoanalytic Study of the Child, 38,* 165-192.

Emde, R. N., Gaensbauer, T., & Harmon, R. (1976). Emotional expression in infancy: a biobehavioral study. *Psychological Issues Monograph Series, 10* (1), No. 37.

Erdelyi, H. M. (1985). *Psychoanalysis: Freud's cognitive psychology.* San Fransciso: Freeman.

Escher-Graeub, D., & Grossmann, K. E. (1983). *Bindungssicherheit im zweiten Lebensjahr- die Regensburger Querschnittuntersuchung* (Attachment security in the second year of life: The Regensburg cross-sectional study). Research Report, University of Regensburg.

Feinman, S., & Lewis, M. Social referencing at 10 months: A second order effect on infants' responses to strangers. *Child Development, 54,* 878-887.

Field, T. M., Woodson, R., Greenberg, R., & Cohen, D. (1982). Discrimination and imitation of facial expression. *Science, 218,* 179-181.

Fairbairn, W. R. D. (1952). *Psychoanalytic studies of the personality.* London: Tavistock.

Fraiberg, S., Adelson, E., & Shapiro, V. (1975). Ghosts in the nursery: A psychoanalytic approach to the problems of impaired infant–mother relationships. *Journal of the American Academy of Child Psychiatry, 14,* 387-421.

Freedman, D. G. (1974). *Human infancy: An evolutionary perspective.* Hillsdale, NJ: Erlbaum.

Gaensbauer, T. J., Harmon, R. J., Culp, A. M., Schultz, L. A., van Doornick, W. J., &

Dawson, P. (1985). Relationships between attachment behavior in the laboratory and the caretaking environment. *Infant Behavior& Development, 8,* 355-369.

Gibson, J. J. (1979). *The ecological approach to visual perception.* Boston: Houghton Mifflin.

Gibson, E. J., & Spelke, E. (1983). The development of perception. In J. H. Flavell & E. M. Markman (Eds.), *Handbook of child psychology: Vol. III: Cognitive development.* New York: Wiley.

Greenberg, J. R., & Mitchell, S. A. (1983). *Object relations in psychoanalytic theory.* Cambridge, MA: Harvard University Press.

Greenberg, M. T., & Speltz, M. L. (in press). Contributions of attachment theory to the understanding of conduct problems during the preschool years. In J. Belsky & T. Nezworski (Eds.), *Clinical implications of attachment.* Hillsdale, NJ: Erlbaum.

Grossmann, K. E., Grossmann, K. (1984, September). *The development of conversational styles in the first year of life and its relationship to maternal sensitivity and attachment quality between mother and child.* Paper presented at the congress of the German Society for Psychology, Vienna.

Grossmann, K., Grossmann, K. E., Spangler, G., Suess, G., & Unzner, L. (1985). Maternal sensitivity and newborn orientation responses as related to quality of attachment in Northern Germany. In I. Bretherton & E. Waters (Eds.), Growing points of attachment theory and research. *Monographs of the Society for Research in Child Development, 50* (1-2, Serial No. 209), 233-256.

Grossmann, K. E., Grossmann, K., & Schwan, A. (in press). Capturing the wider view of attachment: A reanalysis of Ainsworth's Strange Situation. In C. E. Izard & P. B. Read (Eds.), *Measuring emotions in infants and children* (Vol. 2). New York: Cambridge University Press.

Guntrip, J. S. (1971). *Psychoanalytic theory, therapy, and the self.* New York: Basic.

Hinde, R. A. (1982). Attachment: Some conceptual and biological issues. In C. M. Parkes & J. Stevenson-Hinde (Eds.), *The place of attachment in human behaviour.* New York: Basic.

Izard, C. E. (1978). Emotions as motivations: An evolutionary–developmental perspective. In R. A. Dienstbier (Eds.), *Nebraska Symposium on motivation* (pp. 163-200). Lincoln, NB: University of Nebraska Press.

James, W. (1890). *The principles of psychology* (Vol. 1). New York: Henry Holt.

Johnson-Laird, P. N. (1983). *Mental models.* Cambridge, MA: Harvard University Press.

Klinnert, M. D., Campos, J. J., Sorce, J. F., Emde, R. N., & Svejda, M. (1983). Emotions as behavior regulators: Social referencing in infancy. In R. Plutchik & Kellerman (Eds.), *The emotions: Vol 2. Emotions in early development.* New York: Academic.

Kohut, H. (1977). *The restoration of the self.* New York: International Universities Press.

Lashley, K. S. (1951). The problem of serial order in behavior. In L. A. Jeffres (Ed.), *Cerebral mechanisms in behavior.* New York: Wiley.

Lewkowicz, D. J., & Turkewitz, G. (1980). Cross-modal equivalence in early infancy: Audio-visual intensity matching. *Developmental Psychology, 16,* 597-607.

Lewis, M., & Brooks-Gunn, J. (1979). *Social cognition and the acquisition of self.* New York: Plenum.

Lieberman, A. F., & Pawl, J. H. (in press). Disorders of attachment in the second year: A clinical developmental perspective. In M. Greenberg, D. Cicchetti, & M. E. Cummings (Eds.), *Attachment in the preschool years: Theory, research and intervention.*

MacKain, K., Studdert-Kennedy, M., Spieker, S., & Stern, D. N. (1982, April). *Infant per-*

ception of audio-visual relations for speech. Paper presented at the International Conference on Infant Studies, Austin, TX.

Mahler, M. S., Pine, F., & Bergman, A. (1975). *The psychological birth of the human infant.* New York: Basic.

Main, M., Kaplan, K., & Cassidy, J. (1985). Security in infancy, childhood and adulthood. A move to the level of representation In I. Bretherton & E. Waters (Eds.), Growing points of attachment theory and research. *Monographs of the Society for Research in Child Development, 50* (1–2, Serial No. 209), 66–104.

Main, M., & Goldwyn, R. (1984). Predicting rejection of her infant from mother's representation of her own experiences: A preliminary report. *International Journal of Child Abuse and Neglect, 8,* 203–217.

Main, M., & Hesse (1985). *Discovery of an insecure disorganized/disoriented attachment pattern: Procedures, findings and implicatons for the classification of behavior.* Unpublished manuscript, University of California, Berkeley.

Main, M., Tomasini, L., & Tolan, W. (1979). Differences among mothers of infants judged to differ in security. *Developmental Psychology, 15,* 472–473.

Main, M., & Weston, D. (1982). Avoidance of the attachment figure in infancy: Descriptions and interpretations. In C. M. Parkes & J. Stevenson-Hinde (Eds.), *The place of attachment in human behaviour.* New York: Basic.

Mandler, J. H. (1979). Categorical and schematic organization in memory. In C. R. Puff (Ed.), *Memory organization and structure.* New York: Academic.

Marvin, R. S., Greenberg, M. T., & Mosler, D. G. (1976). The early development of conceptual perspective-taking: Distinguishing among multiple perspectives. *Child Development, 47,* 511–514.

Maslin, C. A. (1983). *Anxious and secure attachments: Antecedents and consequences in the mother–infant system.* Unpublished doctoral dissertation, Indiana University.

Matas, L., Arend, R. A., & Sroufe, L. A. (1978). Continuity and adaptation in the second year: The relationship between quality of attachment and later competence. *Child Development, 49,* 547–556.

Meltzoff, A. N., & Borton, W. (1979). Intermodal matching by human neonates. *Nature, 282,* 403–404.

Morris, D. (1980). *Infant attachment and problem solving in the toddler: Relations to mother's family history.* Unpublished doctoral dissertation, University of Minnesota.

Murphey, E. B., Silber, E., Coelho, G. V., Hamburg, D. A., & Greenberg, I. (1963). The development of autonomy and parent–child interaction in late adolescence. *American Journal of Orthopsychiatry, 33,* 643–652.

Nelson, K., & Gruendel, J. (1981). Generalized event representations: Basic building blocks of cognitive development. In M. E. Lamb & A. Brown (Eds.), *Advances in developmental psychology* (Vol. 1). Hillsdale, NJ: Erlbaum.

Nelson, K., & Ross, G. (1982). The general and specifics of long-term memory in infants and young children. In M. Perlmutter (Ed.), *Naturalistic approaches to memory.* San Francisco: Jossey-Bass.

Offer, D. (1969). *The psychological world of the teenager: A study of normal adolescent boys.* New York: Basic.

Osofsky, J. D. (1985, August). *The concept of attachment and psychoanalysis.* Paper presented at the meeting of the American Psychological Association, Washington DC.

Peck, R. F., & Havighurst, R. J. (1960). *The psychology of character development.* New York: Wiley.

Peterfreund, E. (1983). *The process of psychoanalytic therapy: Models and strategy.* Hillsdale, NJ: Analytic Press (Erlbaum).

Piaget, J. (1951). *The origin of intelligence in children.* New York: International Universities Press.

Piaget, J. (1954). *The construction of reality in the child.* New York: Basic.

Price, D., & Goodman, G. S. (1985, April). *Preschool children's comprehension of a recurring episode.* Paper presented at the biennial meeting of the Society for Research in Child Development, Toronto.

Radke-Yarrow, M., Cummings, E. M., Kuczynsky, L., & Chapman, M. (1985). Patterns of attachment in two- and three-year-olds in normal families and families with parental depression. *Child Development, 56,* 884–893.

Reite, M., Short, R., Seiler, C., & Pauley, J. D. (1981). Attachment, loss and depression. *Journal of Child Psychology & Psychiatry, 22,* 141–169.

Ricks, M. H. (1985). The social transmission of parenting: Attachment across generations. In I. Bretherton & E. Waters (Eds.), Growing points of attachment theory and research. *Monographs of the Society for Research in Child Development, 50* (1–2, Serial No. 209), 211–227.

Ricks, M. H., & Noyes, D. (1984). *Secure babies have secure mothers.* Unpublished manuscript, University of Massachusetts-Amherst.

Robertson, J. (1953). Some responses of young children to loss of maternal care. *Nursing Care, 49,* 382–386.

Rovee-Collier, C. K., & Fagan, C. W. (1981). The retrieval of memory in early infancy. In L. P. Lipsitt (Ed.), *Advances in infancy research (Vol. 1).* Norwood, NJ: Ablex.

Rovee-Collier, C. K., & Lipsitt, L. P. (1981). Learning, adaptation, and memory. In P. M. Stratton (Ed.), *Psychobiology of the human newborn.* New York: Wiley.

Scaife, M., & Bruner, J. S. (1975). The capacity for joint visual attention in the infant. *Nature, 253,* 265–266.

Schaffer, H. R., & Emerson, P. E. (1964). The development of social attachments in infancy. *Monographs of the Society for Research in Child Development, 29* (Serial No. 94).

Schank, R. C., & Abelson, R. P. (1977). *Scripts, plans, goals and understanding.* Hillsdale, NJ: Erlbaum.

Schank, R. C. (1982). *Dynamic memory: A theory of reminding and learning in computers and people.* Cambridge: Cambridge University Press.

Spelke, E. S. (1976). Infants' intermodal perception of events. *Cognitive Psychology, 8,* 553–560.

Spelke, E. S. (1979). Perceiving bimodally specified events in infancy. *Developmental Psychology, 15,* 626–636.

Spitz, R. (1965). *The first year of life.* New York: International Universities Press.

Sroufe, L. A. (1985). Attachment classification from the perspective of infant–caregiver relationship and infant temperament. *Child Development, 56,* 1–14.

Sroufe, L. A. (1983). Infant–caregiver attachment and patterns of adaptation in preschool: The roots of maladaptation and competence. In M. Perlmutter (Ed.), *Minnesota Symposium in Child Psychology* (Vol. 16, pp. 41–81). Hillsdale, NJ: Erlbaum.

Sroufe, L. A. (1979). Socioemotional development in infancy. In J. Osofsky (Ed.), *Handbook of infant development.* New York: Wiley.

Sroufe, L. A., & Fleeson, J. (1986). Attachment and the construction of relationships. In W. Hartup & Z. Rubin (Eds.), *The nature and development of relationships.* Hillsdale, NJ: Erlbaum.

Sroufe, L. A., & Waters, E. (1977). Attachment as an organizational construct. *Child Development, 48,* 1184–1199.

Stayton, D. J., & Ainsworth, M. D. S. (1973). Individual differences in infant responses to brief everyday separations as related to other infant and maternal behaviors. *Developmental Psychology, 9,* 226–235.

Stayton, D. J., Hogan, R., & Ainsworth, M. D. S. (1971). Infant obedience and maternal behavior: The origins of socialization reconsidered. *Child Development, 42,* 1057–1070.

Stern, D. (1977). *The first relationship: Infant and mother.* Cambridge, MA: Harvard University Press.

Stern, D. N. (1985). *The interpersonal world of the infant.* New York: Basic.

Sullivan, H. S. (1953). *The interpersonal theory of psychiatry.* New York: Norton.

Tracy, R. L., & Ainsworth, M. D. S. (1981). Maternal affectionate behavior and infant mother-attachment patterns. *Child Development, 52,* 1341–1343.

Trevarthen, C., & Hubley, P. (1979). Secondary intersubjectivity: Confidence, confiding, and acts of meaning in the first year. In A. Lock (Ed.), *Action, gesture and symbol.* New York: Academic.

Tulving, E. (1972). Episodic and semantic memory. In E. Tulving & W. Donaldson (Eds.), *Organization of memory.* New York: Academic.

Tulving, E. (1983). *Elements of episodic memory.* New York: Oxford University Press.

Wagner, S., & Sakowitz, L. (1983, April). *Intersensory and intrasensory recognition: A quantitative and developmental evaluation.* Paper presented at the biennial meeting of the Society for Research in Child Development, Detroit.

Winnicott, D. W. (1958). *Collected papers.* London: Tavistock Publications.

Winnicott, D. W. (1965). *The maturational processes and the facilitating environment.* New York: International Universities Press.

Wolf, D. P., Rygh, J., & Altshuler, J. (1984). Agency and experience: Actions and states in play narratives. In I. Bretherton (Ed.), *Symbolic play: The development of social understanding.* New York: Academic.

Yarrow, L. J. (1967). The development of focused relationships during infancy. In J. Hellmuth (Ed.), *Exceptional Infant* (Vol. 1). Seattle: Special Child Publications.

CHAPTER 23

Temperament in Infancy

JOHN E. BATES

Temperament concepts are a way of talking about personal qualities salient from very early in life. Thus temperament is a way of seeing the child as bringing unique social contributions to the world. Minuchin and Fishman (1981) describe two Puerto Rican women talking about the *cuadro* of the younger woman's son. The young boy's *cuadro* (translated as "picture" or "image") is seen (by those who know how) as a spirit floating above the child. (This particular child was seen as a future teacher.) Something like this must occur in many cultures—parents searching for the personality in their infants and young children. Even the youngest child achieves a unique social identity. Bennett (1971) gives an interesting description of the process in three very young babies in a hospital nursery while awaiting placement. Bennett saw the nurses doing two things, first noting characteristics of the infant's functioning, for example, activity level or facial movements, and then using these characteristics to "construct a fantasy about the infant's personality" (p. 334).

In scientific form, this human search for identity is played out in psychological research, especially in the area of temperament. The concept of temperament has recently been a frequent object of psychological definition, measurement, and theory, with special interest from infancy researchers. This chapter will describe the major temperament concepts, existing measures of the concepts, and the ways in which the concepts have proven useful.

The chapter is written from the point of view that temperament concepts are tools, not real entities. The concepts are tools for seeing natural events in more productive ways. What is considered productive varies with the individual researcher or clinician and the aspect of the child she or he most wishes to understand.

Current models of social development attempt to represent many different forces—genetic inheritance, prenatal development, physical environment, psycho-

This chapter owes a debt to colleagues who have read and commented on previous drafts, including D. Kohnstamm, E. Miller, G. Pettit, T. Wachs, S. Crockenberg, and A. Sroufe, and to those who helped with the library research, including the Indiana University Office of Research and Graduate Studies, A. Beltran and P. Riesenman of the Indiana University Library, and E. Miller and P. Sauer. Thanks are also due to the many students and colleagues who have contributed to our research program in the past 10 years. Special thanks go to my friends for their support while I have been preoccupied with this chapter.

logical environment, and cultural and historical forces as well (e.g., see Bronfen-brenner, 1980). It would perhaps be most convenient for model building and testing if temperament concepts and their operationalizations could represent the consti-tutional factor of a systems model of development. However, there is a methodo-logical sticking point that has slowed advance on this convenient path. Most op-erational measures of temperament, if not all, are partially confounded with environmental influences. One's scientific use of presumed temperament measures as representatives of biologically rooted, abstract definitions depends on how the literature allows unconfounding of concepts. The recent literature has indicated some promising steps in validation of temperament concepts. It has at the same time indicated some doubt about whether we could ever adequately measure a pure con-cept of biologically rooted temperament (Bates, 1980; Bates & Bayles, 1984; Sam-eroff, Seifer, & Elias, 1982; Sroufe, 1984).

Different temperament researchers are working on different parts of the general systems model. Some are using temperament most basically as a way of seeing bi-ological processes more clearly, for instance, understanding more about how indi-viduals' emotional systems function and develop. Others are using temperament primarily as a way of understanding socially relevant processes, such as the parent-child relationship, with its theoretically important ramifications for social out-comes. Of course, many researchers would see themselves as testing more than one element of the general model of development. This is required by the systems ap-proach to research. It is also required if one hopes to unconfound the interpretation of temperament measures. However, at the current moment, any given researcher would not likely claim to have measured all elements well. Likewise, this chapter cannot claim to cover all of the implications of temperament.

This chapter is strongly centered in the motive to understand social process, es-pecially process involved in the development of behavior problems. Of course, the chapter will discuss biological concepts of temperament to some extent, even if bi-ological process is not the primary object of study. The chapter, like a Lilliputian trying to subdue and assess a giant, must be able to toss ropes to its partners on the other side of the giant. One notable partner on the biological side is Plomin's Chapter 7 of this volume, on behavior genetics; another is the recent book of Buss and Plomin (1984). Others include Rothbart and Derryberry (1980) and Weissbluth (1982). Each of these works, while emphasizing biological concepts of temperament, also considers environmental factors, just as the more environmentally oriented works also consider biological factors (Bates, 1980; Thomas & Chess, 1977, 1984). From the emerging syntheses of the environmental and biological sides it is possible that we may reach new understandings of the nature and origins of human behavior patterns.

DEFINITIONS OF TEMPERAMENT

Considerable space will be spent on the fundamental concepts of temperament be-fore the chapter turns to research data. There is diversity in what different writers mean by temperament. If we can clarify definitional issues, we may be able to get clearer guidance from research results.

Thomas and Chess

The most widely quoted temperament writers, Thomas and Chess (1977, 1984), define temperament as stylistic qualities of personality, consistent patterns in *how* actions are performed. This is distinct from motivation (the *why*) and the content (*what*) of action. They have operationalized temperament by means of nine dimensions of behavior that could be seen in infants, plus one widely used superordinate construct, difficult temperament, a combination of five of the scales (a second superordinate construct, less widely used, is slow-to-warm-up, which partially resembles difficult temperament). The nine scales are approach versus withdrawal from new experiences, eventual adaptation to changes, positivity versus negativity of moods, intensity of emotional reactions, rhythmicity of biological functioning, persistence in the face of environmental counterforces, distractibility (e.g., soothability when upset), activity level, and threshold of stimulation necessary for a response. The first five of the list are included by Thomas and Chess in their definition of the dimension of difficult temperament.

There has been a great deal of research that uses the Thomas-Chess concepts. One reason for this is the historically timely nature of the Thomas and Chess reintroduction of temperament. Another is their presentation of concepts and data relevant to infancy, an area of increasing interest as a possible substrate for later development. A third reason is the clinical emphasis of Thomas, Chess, and Birch (1968). Thomas and colleagues raised interest in the question of what biological substrates there might be to emerging disorders of social behavior.

Thomas and colleagues' and most other definitions emphasize temperament as early appearing, constitutionally rooted behavioral tendencies. Also in common with most definitions before and since theirs, the Thomas-Chess concept recognizes that temperament is likely to affect personality outcomes only by affecting the social relationships that produce personality. However, beyond these key points of general acceptance, there is much variation from Thomas and Chess in how qualities of temperament are defined. First in contention is whether it is useful to see temperament as style. As several reviewers have noted (e.g., Buss & Plomin, 1984; McNeil, 1976; Rothbart & Derryberry, 1980), the style notion may apply to some of the specific variables used to mark temperament, such as intensity of emotional reactions, but not to others, such as likelihood of withdrawal response to a stranger, where the content of the behavior is more relevant.

Second is the question of which temperament concepts best describe important behavior variations. The field of personality research loves a manageable list, and the Thomas-Chess list of nine traits has been a favorite target for factor analysis. Generally, using various kinds of questionnaire and interview forms of the nine scales, researchers find a difficultness factor that is somewhat like the one Thomas and colleagues (1968) themselves found. On this factor typically load some but not all of the five scales felt a priori to define the difficult infant or child (Bates, 1980; MacPhee, 1982; Maziade, M., Boudreault, M., Thivierge, J., Capéraà, P., & Cote, R., 1984; Persson-Blennow & NcNeil, 1982; Wilson & Matheny, 1983).

Recently, there have been attempts to go even further and evaluate in more molecular fashion the qualities Thomas and colleagues used to define each of the nine temperament dimensions. Hagekull, Lindhagen, and Bohlin (1980) found support for a few of the dimensions, including approach, threshold, and rhythmicity, but generally the support for the nine categories was weak. On the basis of their own research with one questionnaire based on the Thomas-Chess system, Buss and Plomin (1984) concluded that there is very little basis for seeing the nine scales as representing psychometrically meaningful, separate dimensions. Bates, Freeland, and Lounsbury (1979), in a similar vein, but with a focus on the construct of difficultness, found that parent reports of infant temperamental difficultness center primarily on the frequent expression of negative affect through fussing and crying. Items concerning adaptability to new people and situations were slightly correlated with difficultness in parental perceptions of temperament, but they were independent enough to form their own, separate factor. Rhythmicity items were not seen by parents as pertinent to their rating of the infant as difficult, although they did form their own factor.

A third concept of temperament inspired by Thomas and colleagues (1968), more rarely questioned, is that a behavior pattern could show instability across development and still be seen as temperament. Thomas and Chess (1977) feel that there must be environmental influence on temperament traits, and thus high levels of stability must not be demanded of markers of temperament. Many other writers, including Buss and Plomin (1984) and Goldsmith and Campos (1982), support the notion of changeability of temperament. Temperament traits can be changed by life events. This makes some sense. In fact, many measures of temperament, including many of the Thomas-Chess scales, have not shown large cross-age correlations. At adjacent ages in infancy the correlations are modest (i.e., .20's to .40's) to moderate (high .40's to .60's); across ages they are moderate to moderately high (e.g., .75) from middle childhood on; but predicting from infancy to age 6 or beyond, they are usually modest at best (Buss & Plomin, 1984).

However, while the notion of changeability of temperament may allow a better fit to the empirical data now existing, it may also encourage some confusion. If temperament is supposed to be a consistent core of personality, how can something be temperament and be unstable? It will be necessary to show that transformations of temperament can be described in objective, generalizable ways. Otherwise, temperament may become a sort of psychological phlogiston, a concept that is ultimately unable to describe natural events, even if it is a step on the road to our discovery of an important element.

It appears that earnest efforts have begun to specify ways in which changes might occur (Buss & Plomin, 1984); however, these efforts are too new to be proven. In the meantime, perhaps it would be useful to keep in mind the distinction between an imaginary construct, the basic, constitutional disposition toward a temperament trait, and the observable behavior stream from which we infer temperament. We can speak of each of these as temperament, but we should be conscious of the sense in which we speak. The basic trait would be expected to remain essentially constant, while the behavioral expressions would be expected to vary according to environmental presses and developmental processes, including genetic traits that penetrate at particular points in development.

Buss and Plomin

A second major attempt to define temperament is that of Buss and Plomin (1975, 1984). This work will be given special emphasis. Their comparatively strict definition of temperament in the biological sense is congruent with the position of the present chapter. Buss and Plomin emphasize that temperament should not be merely constitutional—this would allow for many kinds of prenatal and other biological influences—but rather, it should derive from genetic inheritance. They emphasize that temperament qualities should show considerable stability, even though they also recognize that the environment will determine the ultimate shape of the personality. Inherited temperamental traits are just factors in the shape of behavior, not necessarily direct determinants. Buss and Plomin (1984) have recently made special effort, however, to speculate on the conditions under which changes in the general trend of temperament would take place, for example, how a parent of one temperament type would react to a young child of another type. This kind of thinking about specific interaction effects involving temperament allows the possibility of research that can accurately track the influence of an early temperament trait. With successes in this kind of research, along with the continuing efforts of behavior genetics to show how much of variance of an observed trait is attributable to genetic inheritance as well as how much to environmental variations, and to discover particular gene locations (Plomin, 1985; Plomin, DeFries, & McClearn, 1980), the next years could show noticeable progress toward resolving definitional questions about temperament.

Buss and Plomin's definition of temperament has the advantage of including a manageable list of specific temperament traits. Rather than the nine of Thomas and colleagues (1968), Buss and Plomin feel that they can cover the concept with three, or possibly four dimensions. Buss and Plomin (1984) suggest that there are three well-supported temperament concepts, emotionality, activity, and sociability. This is supported by the current author's own review of the temperament literature, as well as our data (Bates, in press). The three traits are described below.

Emotionality refers to strong arousal in response to events, with arousal expressed in both behavior and affect. The basis of this tendency is dominance by the sympathetic nervous system, as opposed to the parasympathetic. An emotional infant might be one who has strong general distress, fear, or anger responses as indicated by behavior and psychophysiological changes; this infant might also respond to more minimal aversive stimuli than other infants would respond to, and be less easily mollified than others. General arousal or emotionality tendencies become differentiated with psychological development in the first year. At first, there is a general tendency toward distress; by 2 or 3 months of age, fear can be distinguished from general distress, and after about 7 months of age anger responses can also be seen.* For infants low in emotionality, Buss and Plomin predict a positive correlation between levels of fear and anger, while for infants high in emotionality, they predict an inverse correlation. Among the more emotional, some children's dominant emotionality would be fear, with associated tendencies toward general arousability and distress. Others' would be anger, with less likelihood of both fear and distress. The type of negative affect that predominates is a function of social learning, according to Buss and Plomin. It may also be a function of the other temperament traits of the child. For example, a highly active child would be more likely to respond to threatening stimuli with anger than fear.

---

*The anger onset age estimate is derived from Sroufe (1979); Goldsmith and Campos (1982) imply that anger differences could be detected closer to the third month than the seventh.

The prediction of specialization in anger or fear in high-emotional children is an intriguing one. However, given the general finding in parent reports of behavior problems that the dimensions of anxiety–fearfulness and anger–aggression are independent (Quay, 1979), the hypothesis demands relevant empirical tests. An alternative prediction is that some children will be high on both anger and fearfulness, some low on both, and some of mixed type.

The Buss and Plomin concept of emotionality is closely related to the concept of difficult temperament, at least as we have described it (Bates, 1980, 1983). Our own data offer some support for the Buss and Plomin concept. For one thing, as mentioned above, parents see negative affect as the main correlate of perception of the baby as difficult for caregivers, while the nonemotionality items are relatively independent (Bates & Bayles, 1984). Furthermore, in our recent work we have been searching for distinctions in the general emotionality underlying perception of an infant as difficult (Bates, 1983; Bates, Miller, & Bayles, 1984). This topic will be further discussed in a later section, on the role of temperament in behavior problems.

The emotionality concept of Buss and Plomin is an important one, even if one might disagree with some of its details. It is a core construct in almost all systems of defining and measuring temperament. In fact, there is some thought that a trait like negative emotionality underlies a wide range of adult personality self-report scales, including neuroticism, trait anxiety, ego strength, and social desirability—many of which are not typically seen as reflecting temperament: Watson and Clark's (1984) recent discussion of a concept of negative affectivity, "a dimension of stable and pervasive individual differences in mood and self concept" (p. 483), provides an interesting subjective feelings complement to Buss and Plomin's emphasis on behavioral components of emotionality.

The second major temperament dimension in the Buss and Plomin system is *activity*. This refers to tempo and energy expenditure. The active infant who has attained mobility would be very busy, in an energetic exploration of the environment, with lots of gross motor movement, and a preference for vigorous forms of play. The concept of activity level is common to many systems of temperament variables. One issue concerning activity is the extent to which infancy differences in it are representative of a "true" temperament, a constitutionally based, stable characteristic. Buss and Plomin's (1975) review of the data suggested that activity measures were stable after the first year, but not before that time. Rothbart (1981), however, found moderate levels of stability in parent-reported levels of activity from 3 to 12 months of age. Buss and Plomin (1984) provide some worthwhile criteria for interpreting the nonstability in the first year: Measures of activity should be aggregated over a long enough period to be representative of the activity traits of the child; and the measures should not confound activity temperament with distress, for example, recording a young infant's limb movements while the infant is upset.

The functional value of activity differences is an important issue. Most would doubt that a child's inborn temperamental tendency toward activity directly determines the success of the child's social adaptations. Rather, it would be expected that, to use the automobile engine metaphor (e.g., see Buss & Plomin, 1984), activity level of a child would partially determine the child's distance and speed, but not direction. Some children with high activity levels would tend to do annoying and domineering things, which would lead them into frequent conflict with others, while others would be active in self- and other-edifying ways. Some children low in activity would be dull, perhaps passively resistant, while others would be aware of the world and ready to contribute at the crucial occasions. These adaptational differences within a level of activity temperament could be a product of children's blend of other temperament qualities.

However, it is also quite probable that the child's relations with people help direct the child's energy. Some active children's caregivers are ineffectual in guiding an energetic child, in some instances partly because of their own temperaments. Others help their child to steer a productive course. How such a process occurs and what points a family down a particular path of learning to control activity are not yet clear. In whatever ways the child's activity level is shaped by the environment or itself modifies the environment, it is probable that individual differences in activity have potentially important implications for social development.

On the negative side, an active child may be more likely to have conflicts with control agents than an inactive child. However, an inactive child would also have some potential conflicts with parents. According to Bell (1979), the highly active child appears to trigger upper-limit control behavior, which involves restraint, distraction, and power assertion. The low-active child would be more likely to be pushed toward activity and involvement. In fact, there is some evidence that parents' control patterns with their children are flexibly adjusted according to the activity level of the child, with reduction in parents' restrictive control after the child is given an activity-reducing drug (Barkeley & Cunningham, 1979).

However, high activity trait levels need not be a problem, and indeed may be an advantage. Vaillant's book, *Adaptation to Life,* reports results from a 30-year longitudinal study of Ivy League college men. There is little to suggest that the success of the men in their major life tasks varied meaningfully with their family backgrounds. However, an apparently stable, high level of activity and energy was a consistent way of accounting for success. Thus within the subpopulation of academically and socioeconomically gifted young men, it may have been that a temperament variable was crucial to the attainment of socially valued goals. In another context, however, such as a child in a multistressed, urban family, the same inherent level of activity tendency could mature into acting-out, social conflict patterns of behavior (cf. Thomas et al. 1968; Thomas & Chess, 1977).

The third Buss and Plomin temperament trait is *sociability*, defined as the level of preference for the rewards of being with other people in general. The rewards include such things as presence of and attention from others, and responsive interchange. Not included in the types of rewards sought by a high-sociable person are rewards that depend on the existence of an established relationship, such as sympathy and affection. Thus the concept is more a stranger sociability dimension than a general sociability, although the person high on sociability might be expected to seek attention and social presence and response from family members as well as unrelated people. A sociable infant might be one who frequently initiates contact with a wide range of people, who does not like to be alone, and who responds with warmth in social interchange.

Buss and Plomin (1984) offer some interesting hypotheses about the ecology of sociability. Their predictions about the process that might derive from the match or mismatch between an infant's sociability and the mother's are especially relevant. For example, if the infant is high on sociability while the mother is low, the mother may be prone to irritation by the infant's demands, while the infant is frustrated by the underresponse to his or her needs. Or if the infant is low in need for the social rewards that the mother is high in the need for, the mother will accommodate to the infant's need but be frustrated, and perhaps give special preference to a more sociable sibling of the infant and ultimately appear underresponsive to the infant.

In ongoing work in our laboratory, we have been trying to find ways to assess this kind of process by using longitudinal, observational data and mother descriptions of their infants and their own personalities. We have learned that our concept of difficult temperament may have some relationship to the sociability of the infant. At age 4–6 months, mothers' dominant attribution for their infants' difficultness on the ICQ appears to be the infant's level of demand for social stimulation (Bates, Miller, & Bayles, 1984). Mothers who rated their infants as difficult on the ICQ were more likely to rate their infants as socially demanding than mothers of easier infants.

Thus it remains plausible that the kind of process Buss and Plomin describe, stemming from conflict between the infant's need for social contact and the mother's, might occur. However, it will be a challenge to disentangle the effects of a mismatch in temperament from those of maternal rejection. There could be an infant who makes repeated and strong efforts to achieve social interaction with the caregiver, but who does so because of rejection by the caregiver rather than because of temperament. Perhaps neither the caregiver nor the infant is exceptional in the trait of sociability; the caregiver rejects the infant as part of a neurotic process or lack of skill, and the infant seeks contact because of unmet basic needs (see Sackett & Rupenthal, 1974, for description of an analog of this process in monkeys and their infants).

Lamb (1982) also comments on the ambiguous origins of infant sociability. He argues that the heritability of sociability is small and that there is evidence that qualities of the social environment would be a major source of the infant's sociability. He summarizes findings of a relationship between sociability and secure attachment, for example, interpreting it in environmental terms.

A fourth kind of temperament dimension mentioned by Buss and Plomin is *impulsivity*. Impulsivity is now defined as a combination of inhibitory control and excitement seeking. Buss and Plomin (1984) imply that level of inhibitory control may be a trait that is embedded within or dependent upon the profile of the EAS temperament concepts—emotionality, activity, and sociability. The EAS concepts are thought to represent motive forces in personality, while impulse controls represent brakes on those forces. In contrast to impulse control, excitement seeking does appear to have some coherence and independent status as a trait. Buss and Plomin even suggest that impulse control may be subordinate to the excitement-seeking trait, just as to the EAS traits. However, Buss and Plomin are reluctant to accept excitement seeking as a temperament trait: There is insufficient evidence for its heritability; and there is no evidence that it appears as a trait in infancy.

My own prediction is that a good analog to the impulsivity concept or of the separate traits of impulse control and excitement seeking will be found operating in the first 2 years of life. Just as Buss and Plomin (1984) suggested regarding the activity trait, it is possible that the measurement of it may need to consider developmental factors. In an infant, for example, excitement seeking may be channeled through social interactions more extensively than through nonsocial activities, while in an older child, the reverse may be true. If so, in infants, the trait of excitement seeking might be hidden by the trait of sociability. It will be of great interest to clinical scientists to learn whether it is worthwhile to speak of impulsivity as temperament. There is evidence that the constructs considered here have applicability to the understanding of the concurrent process of behavior disorders, especially the most serious disorders, the acting-out problems. An important question is how impulsive traits come about. Are they something that children bring into the world as a challenge for their caregivers, or are they products of social experience?

This section is concluded with mention of a concept that Buss and Plomin (1984) exclude from their possible temperaments, positive emotionality. Other systems of defining temperament (e.g., Rothbart, 1981; Thomas & Chess, 1984) do include positive emotionality. Buss and Plomin draw some interesting distinctions here. They group positive emotions with the low-arousal emotions, which do not have the same evolutionary significance as the high-arousal emotions, and which do not meet the criteria for being independent temperament dimensions. For example, warmth and affection may have an inherited basis, but are derived via the temperament of sociability, depending on the rewards accrued in social experience.

Summary

In brief, Buss and Plomin (1975, 1984) define temperament as inherited personality traits that appear early in life. They currently propose three dimensions of temperament. The first, emotionality, consists of autonomic nervous system predispositions to respond to stimuli with negative arousal. Negative arousal is a global pattern of distress in the very young infant, and it becomes differentiated into fear and anger tendencies in the older infant. The second, activity, refers to preferred levels of activity and speed of action. The third, sociability, concerns preference for the basic rewards of social interaction, such as attention and responsiveness. Buss and Plomin consider a fourth concept, impulsivity, or at least one of its components, excitement seeking, as a candidate for temperament status. They also exclude a number of other possible temperament traits, such as tendency to express positive emotions, because they are regarded as likely products of the more fundamental EAS dimensions.

Rothbart

The theoretical chapter by Rothbart and Derryberry (1981) is notable for several reasons. First, the chapter provides an interesting, conceptually integrated systems definition of temperament, with an emphasis on temperament in infants. This definition is a hierarchical one. At the first level are constitutional tendencies to show particular patterns of basic psychobiological processes. These tendencies then form the core of affective functioning and motivation, which, in turn, are the core of the child's developing personality. Acting in concert with environmental and maturational variables, they contribute to traits of affect, cognition, and action. The basic processes of temperament are *reactivity* and *self-regulation*. Under the concept of *reactivity,* Rothbart and Derryberry list several response systems, including brain activation processes, autonomic nervous system properties, and endocrine processes. These tendencies interact with the individual's *self-regulation* characteristics in modulating expressions of reactivity. Self-regulation takes the form of attention, motoric approach versus avoidance, self-stimulation or self-soothing, and social communication. The responses to stimuli are characterized by Rothbart and Derryberry along the dimensions of intensity and time. One dimension is the intensity of a stimulus required for a response, the familiar temperament notion of threshold. A second is the intensity of the response itself. How quickly reactions reach their peak and how quickly equilibrium is recovered are two additional dimensions of responses.

The response systems are conceptually nested within "higher-order emotional–motivational patterning" (p. 48). This means that reactivity is expressed via particular profiles of emotional reaction, such as positive affect or distress. The definitional system allows for a great many combinations of features and many individual differences in profile. For example, one infant may have a low threshold to react to a change in the environment, be prone to a negative emotional reaction, and be soothed slowly, whereas another infant could have the same threshold and tendency to negativity, but recover from distress more quickly. This variation not only could affect developmental outcomes through direct effects of the pattern of temperament upon the child's experience, but also could produce indirect effects via the temperament's impact on the social environment. Its complexity and comprehensiveness may ultimately prove appropriate to the topic, but in the meantime, the Rothbart and Derryberry (1981) model has been criticized as being too inclusive, as not drawing a firm enough distinction between temperament and other individual differences in behavior (Buss & Plomin, 1984; Goldsmith & Campos, 1982)(in one degree or another, it seems, the same could be said for any of the temperament models). Rothbart and Derryberry do attempt to distinguish between temperament and the broader construct of personality, saying that personality has a core of temperament, but it also includes more cognitive features, such as self-concept.

A second notable feature of the Rothbart model is the attention paid to development. Rothbart and Derryberry (1981) consider temperament expressions to be modified importantly by development. The main developmental processes are increases in higher-order control of reactivity accompanied by elaboration of the reactivity systems. With advances in cortical functioning, the infant is more and more capable of regulating responses to the environment, for example, through redeployment of attention, through changing the environment itself, or through self-soothing efforts.

A third feature of the Rothbart model is its effort to view temperament as based in specified biological processes, and to make these processes be the ones implicated in studies of adult temperament. Rothbart and Derryberry discuss a variety of neural structure developments and biochemical processes that would have implications for the balance of excitatory and inhibitory processes. This balance is fundamental to temperament. For example, there is some evidence that infants' levels of irritability may be linked to the relative amounts of dopamine and norepinephrine (Rapoport, Pandari, Renfield, Lake, & Ziegler, 1977).

The specific dimensions Rothbart (1981) has focused on in her empirical work were chosen partly on the basis of good psychometric properties. They are (1) activity level, which is defined in terms of gross motor activity; (2) smiling and laughter tendency across situations; (3) fear, or distress and nonapproach responses to new situations; (4) distress to limitations, defined as fussing and crying in response to being made to wait for something or being restrained during caregiving; (5) soothability, or how effectively distress can be reduced; and (6) duration of orienting, or the length of time the child stays involved with a particular object, in the absence of a major change in the stimulus situation. This list of variables has some overlap with both the Thomas and Chess and the Buss and Plomin dimensions. Activity is of course common to the last two systems; fear resembles the Thomas-Chess scales of approach and adaptability; distress to limitations may be conceptually analogous to the Thomas-Chess concept of mood, but it is more closely related to the Buss-Plomin concept of the anger component of emotionality; soothability relates to Thomas and Chess's distractibility, but again, more directly to Buss and Plomin's emotionality concept; and finally, duration of orienting relates well to the Thomas-Chess attention span concept, but does not have an obvious counterpart in the Buss-Plomin system. Concerning the last variable, it is interesting to note that duration of orienting has been found by Rothbart (1981) to be unstable during infancy, thus perhaps supporting its lack of special focus in the Buss-Plomin system.

Summary

Rothbart and Derryberry's (1981) definition of temperament is quite simple at its most basic level, consisting of individual differences in reactivity and self-regulation that are constitutionally based. However, the variations that can result from the interactions between reactive and regulatory processes, from maturation, and from social processes allow for complex distinctions among individual infants. Finally, it should be noted that Rothbart (1981) carefully distinguishes between the behavior of the infant in a particular context, for example, at home, from which temperament traits are inferred, and the temperament itself. The behavior at home is a product of both the temperamental patterns of reactivity and self-regulation and the stimuli present in the particular home.

Goldsmith and Campos

The final definitional system to be presented is that of Goldsmith and Campos (1982). Goldsmith and Campos, although well rooted in psychobiological concepts, suggest the most radically behavioral of the major definitions of temperament. They also offer the definition most radically restricted by developmental era. They see their definition as applicable only to the infancy era, where it is presumed that the effects of social and cognitive development are less likely to mask the underlying temperament.

They describe temperament as structures that organize the expression of emotion. This organization of affect is of special importance to social interaction. The patterning allows easier predictability and hence accommodation to the child by the caregivers. This implies that, for the caregiver, temperament is a working model of the child's response patterns. Such cognitive elements are, in theory, important in the process and outcomes of child rearing, as well argued recently by Parke (1978) and Bell (1979).

Goldsmith and Campos further specify temperament, much as do Rothbart and Derryberry (1981), as consisting of the intensity and time parameters of affect expression. They agree that temperament is important in the infant's sensitivity to stimuli, but also emphasize that temperament is involved in the motivation or initiation of action, too. Unlike Rothbart and Derryberry (1981) they do not assume that the behavioral expressions of temperament must correspond to neurological processes. They also explicitly exclude cognitive processes from the definition of temperament. For example, in assessing the temperamental component in individual differences in frequency, intensity, and other parameters of expressions of fear, it would be necessary to hold constant the infants' individual differences in how they cognitively appraise potential fear stimuli.

Goldsmith and Campos (1982) address the definitional issues of stability and heritability in an interesting way. Basically, they suggest a wait-and-see approach. Like most writers, they say that temperament is found in behavioral patterns, and seeing patterns requires some consistency across situations and time. However, they emphasize that different temperament dimensions might have different breadth. One variable might show much cross-situational consistency, while another shows little. Similarly, cross-age consistency could vary from dimension to dimension and from stage to stage across development. Presumably, temperament stability, if present, should be due to structures or processes within the infant, and not just due to consistent environment.

Goldsmith and Campos's perspective on the heritability criterion (Buss & Plomin, 1975, 1984) is similar. First, is is not necessary to assume that all temperament traits show substantial heritability. Second, even if there is substantial heritability, this would not necessarily mean that heritability could be detected at all ages—a genetic factor could be expressed in some but not other developmental periods. Thus Goldsmith and Campos do not preclude genetic roots and stable characteristics in temperament, but with their radical focus on patterns of affect in social interaction, they do not see these criteria as essential to the definition of temperament. Given these perspectives, it is not surprising that Goldsmith and Campos do not draw a sharp distinction between the general concepts of temperament and personality. They do, however, indicate that social relations with non–caregivers, such as peers, and emerging self-concept are more salient in what is called personality than in what is called temperament.

Goldsmith and Campos (1982) do not propose a particular list of temperament variables, unlike the other workers reviewed in this section. However, they do review the variables proposed by each of the major works (above). They conclude that many of the temperament scales have a component of emotional expression, even though the scales differ according to the degree to which they express discrete affects (e.g., Rothbart's distress to limitations is more specific than Buss and Plomin's emotionality). The scales also differ on the degree to which they measure parameters of temperament versus content dimensions (e.g., Thomas and Chess's intensity measures a parameter of affect across response modalities, while Rothbart's smiling and laughter represents a particular emotional response system).

Summary and Comment

Had this chapter been written a few years ago, it is unlikely that it would have focused so extensively on the definitional issues. However, the exploding research literature using temperament concepts has revealed enough confusion about temperament as a general concept that it appears we must strive to be clear in our use of temperament concepts. The sources emphasized above have made strong efforts in this direction. There are two main senses in which temperament has been defined: First, it is seen as *constitution*—biological characteristics inherent in the child. In talking about temperament in this sense, I would endorse the criteria of Buss and Plomin—temperament should have substantial heritability, appear early, and show considerable stability, at least within development stages. It should account for the core of some personality traits. The heritability criterion will be the one most disputed; I include it primarily because I believe it is included in the popular, traditional concept of temperament. I would also endorse the emphasis Rothbart and Derryberry place on neurological substrates to temperament. This is of clear importance when talking about variability in sensitivity and emotional reactions. Its relevance to other aspects of what is considered temperament, for example, activity and sociability, is less clear. However, ultimately, it would be worthwhile to speculate on specific psychobiological roots for such traits.

Temperament has also been spoken of in the sense of *observable behavior patterns*. All theorists in the above group see emotional behavior as temperament. Some see it as the sine qua non in designating temperament-relevant behavior (Goldsmith & Campos; Rothbart); others indicate that emotional expression is only one of the ways temperament can be seen in behavior (Buss & Plomin; Thomas & Chess). Usually emotional expressions are assumed to be based in corresponding psychobiological traits, but, as seen in Goldsmith and Campos (1982), not always. It is necessary to speak of temperament with referents in observable behavior; otherwise, how could we study it empirically?

However, as all of the above theorists have discussed at length, there is reason to doubt that we will find direct correspondence between the observed behavior patterns of a child, whether observed by the parents or by researchers, and measured biological factors. This could be one factor in the widespread hedging on the issue of stability of temperament. Thomas and Chess's statement has been echoed many, many times: "Temperament is not immutable" (Thomas et al. 1968, p. 4). Virtually all theoretical attempts to define temperament emphasize that temperament is shaped by environmental cues and consequences, even though the children themselves have an impact on the characteristics of their environment. As attempts have been made to develop and validate measures of temperament, it has become apparent that the behavior pattern one calls temperament is not at all likely to be isomorphic with underlying, biological factors (e.g., Bates, 1980, 1983; Rothbart & Derryberry, 1981). The apparently great complexity and subtlety of hypothetical biological factors (e.g., Plomin, Chapter 7, this volume), the likelihood that caregivers alter even young infants' endogenous functioning (Sander, 1975; Sroufe, 1985), and the systems concepts that emphasize the profound linkages between the child's personality and the characteristics of the family (Sroufe & Fleeson, 1984) combine to make it attractive to have a flexible definition of temperament. However, we should be aware of the theoretical pitfalls in this. One is apparent in the empirical literature. Many articles draw misleading interpretations from correlations and noncorrelations involving temperament measures. They uncritically accept the meaning of the temperament measures as equivalent to the name of the scale, under the implicit framework of the abstract, constitutional definition of temperament. This work is far from useless, but it does lack conceptual incisiveness.

How might the dilemma of the two different kinds of meaning of temperament be resolved? Obviously, neither one can be abandoned entirely. One might argue that the biological sense should take definitional priority, that one should be sure that individual differences in a behavior trait are substantially biological before calling the trait *temperament*. That is, temperament should be a clear marker of a biological trait. However, the more social and philosophical use of the term as consisting of a wide range of individual variations in behavior has an ancient and unbroken tradition. Perhaps one should do as some writers do—devise a definition that attempts to include both the biological and the social aspects. However, it is sometimes confusing to have them conflated into one definition. As an attempt to deal with the dilemma, this chapter will try to keep the two kinds of concepts, constitutional and behavioral, separate, for example, as Temperament I and Temperament II. Ultimately, I would hope to see linkups between the two concepts, achieving a good fit between social–behavioral and emotional patterns and more fundamentally biological process, and achieving a good distinction from nontemperamental features of personality. This position implies that my use of *temperament* in the sense of observed behavior is a statement of the hypothesis that conditions like those of Buss and Plomin and Rothbart and Derryberry will ultimately be empirically satisfied; for example, the behavior will be found to have a substantial base in neurological function and genetic inheritance. In referring to behavior patterns not hypothesized to have endogenous origins, one might follow the example of Maccoby, Snow, and Jacklin (1984) and use the term *disposition*.

The empirical work that bridges the current gaps between the constitutional and behavioral concepts will most likely succeed not by linking the *general* concepts of temperament, but rather by establishing links within *specific* operationally measurable dimensions, such as fearfulness or activity level (Bates, 1986). I agree with Goldsmith and Campos (1982) that it is of first importance to study children's behaviors that mark socially important processes in development, behaviors that mark individual differences in the present and future adaptations of the child. This endeavor increases the social value of what might be learned about the biological foundations of the selected behavior dimensions. The point here is that it is more important to choose infant and child behavior dimensions of social relevance than it is to have a comprehensive, watertight definition of temperament. Some of the temperament dimensions we hypothesize will be judged to meet the biological criterion for temperament, and others will not. However, in either case, we can learn things about how children develop, and we can gain further guides as to what general definition for temperament is most useful in our attempts to understand behavior.

The section above has given a detailed summary of the major recent theoretical efforts in the area. It should be pointed out that temperament is a central enough concept that there have been a number of other interesting reviews of the area that have been omitted here. However, two of these are especially worth mention as markers of the range of interest in temperament in the field of child development, and as examples of innovative attempts to resolve major conceptual and methodological issues: See Crockenberg (in press) and Bornstein, Gaughran, and Homel (1984).

Having reviewed temperament as a theoretical concept, the chapter now turns to a review of the empirical work on temperament and infant development. First, measurement issues are considered, and then the empirical data are reviewed.

MEASUREMENT OF TEMPERAMENT

Awareness of issues of measurement is important in selecting and interpreting indexes of individual differences in temperament. The following is not intended as a complete review of the measurement literature. A more comprehensive review can be found in the sources previously reviewed. Another important source is Hubert, Wachs, Peters-Martin, and Gandour's (1982) comprehensive review of child temperament measures. The present section is intended as a summary of the most important issues.

Types of Measure

Parent Report

The dominant type of temperament measure in infancy is parent report. The Thomas-Chess group began with interviews, and this tradition has been carried on in some quarters (e.g., Wolkind & DeSalis, 1982). However, the preferred measure of most investigators now is the questionnaire. One general type of questionnaire is closely based on the nine temperament categories Thomas and Chess used to summarize their interview protocols. There have been numerous questionnaire translations of the concepts of Thomas and colleagues, including ones by the Thomas-Chess group (e.g., Thomas & Chess, 1977), Carey and his colleagues (e.g., Carey & McDevitt, 1978), and a variety of other researchers in many countries (e.g., Hagekull, Bohlin, & Lindhagen, 1982; Hsu, Soong, Stigler, Hong, & Liang, 1981; Huitt & Ashton, 1982; Lerner & Lerner, 1980; Maziade et al., 1984; Pederson, Anderson, & Cain, 1982; Persson-Blennow & McNeil, 1982). Parent questionnaires based on the Thomas-Chess system are the most frequently used operational measures of temperament. A second general category of temperament questionnaire is more loosely based on the Thomas-Chess concepts. This kind of instrument represents Thomas-Chess concepts, but also attempts to measure traits not considered explicitly by Thomas and Chess, including Rothbart (1981), Plomin and his colleagues (see Buss & Plomin, 1984), and Bates and colleagues (1979).

Observation

Another, related way in which temperament has been assessed is through the structured application of the rating scales used in parent questionnaires. Researchers have had observers apply relevant items from temperament questionnaires to the children after observing them at home. Along the lines of observer ratings of naturalistically occurring temperament, another form of temperament measure has been observer coding of relatively specific behavior events, such as an episode of fussing or crying (e.g., Bates, Olson, Pettit, & Bayles, 1982; Maccoby, Snow, & Jacklin, 1984).

Structured observations provide an alternative to parent and observer perceptions of naturally occurring behavior. By standardizing situations, the researcher gains the ability to compare infants' reactions in a known context, which in theory allows a purer measurement of the infant's characteristics. A number of recent studies have used ratings of infants' behavior qualities during tests of mental development (e.g.,

Goldsmith & Gottesman, 1981; Matheny & Wilson, 1980). Others have developed a special situation for assessing a particular trait (e.g., Lamb, 1982). Others have developed a whole battery of situations for measuring several traits (Wilson & Matheny, 1983, 1984).

Goldsmith & Rieser-Danner (1984) have been developing a particulary ambitious battery of tests of temperamental qualities in the vein of Rothbart's categories. This method involves some tests of the infant's reactions to standard situations, as well as tests of the parent's perceptions of the infant, with videotapes of infant behavior in standard situations used to clarify the parent's rating task and give appropriate anchors for the parent's generalizations.

Method and Interpretation Issues

Endogenous Versus Environmental Meanings

The most fundamental issue in interpretation of data was discussed above in the section on definition. This is the issue of how much the behavioral measures of temperament correspond to constitutional as opposed to environmental or experiential factors. For the present, we resolve the issue by using the term *temperament* to summarize behavior patterns that in theory have constitutional origins, while at the same time taking care to view the biological meanings of the term as hypothetical. The possible biological connotations add interest to the task of describing the behavior trait, just as the possible social meanings add interest to the search for the biological processes.

Generalizability

The next important issue, then, is the extent to which a measure really describes generalizable qualities of behavior, wherever these might originate. To this issue can be applied a number of standard, psychometric principles (e.g., as well discussed by Wiggins, 1973). One question is whether the scales that are used are an adequate sampling of the behavior and situations that are relevant to the more theoretical concept of the temperament quality. This question is sometimes referred to as content validity. Another question is whether the scales are being used in a standard way. Here, the concerns are whether different users of the measurement system use it in the same way. Do two trained observers agree on the occurrence of a particular kind of behavior? Do they agree on a more subjective, integrative rating scale? This kind of generalizability is typically considered a type of reliability.

Another type of reliability answers the question of whether the measures will indicate comparable individual differences on different occasions, separated by short intervals of time. Do mothers rate their babies' activity levels in similar ways with a test–retest interval of 2 weeks? Related to this is the question of whether the measure is stable across longer periods. This kind of generalizability often has more theoretical relevance, for example, due to possibly relevant developmental processes, so standards for it are not as clear and universal as they are for short-term stability. It is usually considered not a type of reliability, but rather a type of validity.

Another kind of generalizability is closely related to the concern about whether different users of the measurement system use it in the same way. However, it goes beyond the interest in whether trained observers agree, and is usually considered under the category of validity: Do observers agree with parents in their placement of the child on some behavioral dimension? The typical operationalization of this issue takes the form of correlations between parent and observer indexes of child temperament. The typical correlation is modest (Bates, 1980, 1983). Does this mean that the measure should not be used? Not necessarily. Low convergence between observers and parents could stem from a number of sources; some of the sources are nuisance, others of possible interest for improving measurement and theory. Discrepancies could be due to the vastly different experiential bases of the parent and the observer, the parent interpreting the items differently than the researcher intended them, the parent being unable to perceive the kinds of patterns called for, or the parent seeing the child and the scales in biased ways, for example, tending to describe things in a socially desirable way (Bates & Bayles, 1984; Goldsmith & Campos, 1982; MacPhee, 1983; Plomin, 1983). The discovery of these artifacts has led some to conclude that parent report measures of temperament should not be used.

In principle, the field could discover measures for these artifacts and use them to enhance the predictiveness of the measure or to revise the theoretical root of the concept. For example, there have been a number of independent findings that mother self-reports of anxiety are modestly predictive of a negative perception of the child on temperament and other scales (e.g., Bates & Bayles, 1984; Sameroff et al., 1982; Vaughn, 1983). Mother personality could ultimately be used as a correction factor to give a more realistic picture of the infant. However, what has not been well established is how bias might systematically disagree with an optimally realistic picture of the child. None of the objective measures of child temperament that have been compared to mother personality as a predictor of mother temperament perceptions has yet reached this level of validity. Summarizing over a large number of possible relationships between mother perceptions of the infant, observer perceptions of the infant, and characteristics of the mother, Bates and Bayles (1984) concluded that there is evidence for both objective and subjective factors in the mother perceptions. The subjective factors did not overshadow the objective ones. St. James-Roberts and Wolke (1984) have come to a similar conclusion. Hagekull and colleagues (1982) recently demonstrated in another way that mother perceptions are not necessarily invalid as measures of the child's behavior.

Hagekull and colleagues' results suggest that the degree of overlap between parent and observer may be enhanced by having the mother focus on the same sample of behavior as the observer would, with levels of agreement between mothers and outside observers approaching the level usually attained between two trained observers. This, of course, shows that mothers can in principle see the child in the same way as the observer, not that this is in fact what happens when they fill out a temperament questionnaire under typical conditions. Nor does it mean that either mother or observer is presenting an extremely accurate summary of the child's temperament traits. What each of them sees is influenced by many situational influences on the child's behavior, as well as by the ability to recognize contextual determinants, to notice subtle distinctions in behavior patterns, and to collate patterns occurring at one time with those occurring at another time.

Parent report questionnaires are very important in temperament research. It is not usually practical to record the child's behavior objectively over the range of occasions and situations needed to satisfy the concept of trait; and highly diagnostic, standard contexts for measuring temperament have not been developed yet. Therefore, parents' summaries of their experience with their children are potentially of great value. It is encouraging that research has begun to suggest that there are indeed objective components in parents' perceptions of their young children. However, even if we are never able to disentangle the objective and subjective roots of the ratings, they would still have conceptual value: In theory, the parent's perceptions of the child are or become a major part of reality for the child. For example, if the mother believes her baby to be exceptionally sociable, she may alter the environment in ways that encourage both the perception of sociability and the personality trait, such as by providing the baby many pleasant opportunities for social interaction. As presaged by Bell (1979) and Parke (1978) in their general focus on the role of cognitive activity in parenting, temperament researchers have begun to look for ways of modeling the transactional process between infant behavior, parent behavior, and parent perceptions. One interesting attempt is Wolke and St. James-Roberts's (1984) Recent Event Interview, in which a mother is asked to describe a recent situation where her baby cried, including the relevant general attitudes of the mother, attributions for the crying, action choices the mother saw, how she actually reacted, results, and attributions for the results. Ultimately, perhaps such research will give us knowledge about the perception and the creation of temperament that will allow refinements in definition and measurement.

A final kind of generalizability to be considered is the extent to which a particular measure of a trait converges with other measures of the trait and diverges from measures of theoretically different traits. In some ways the above issues about interobserver reliability and parent–observer correlation could be seen as special cases of this kind of generalizability. However, the way in which this concern is usually addressed is on the level of abstract indexes. In the case of questionnaires, does one item with content relevant to a particular trait correlate with another item with analogous content? Here, factor analysis is a common way of assessing whether parents' perceptions of various items concerning one concept are correlated more with one another than with a cluster of items concerning another concept. Analyses of scale internal consistencies and interscale correlations are alternate methods. On a grander scale, when measures of different sorts are compared, for instance, home and laboratory measures, this kind of generalizability is spoken of as construct validation. In the process of forming a network of abstract concepts, operational measures of those constructs, and relationships and nonrelationships among the measures and constructs, both measures and constructs can be refined and validated.

What has been said above about generalizability of temperament measures has typically been applied most thoughtfully to questionnaire measures. However, the considerations are just as important in appraising naturalistic and structured observation measures, even if they are applied in somewhat different ways.

The evidence concerning the reliability aspects of the measures is considerably more complete at this time than that concerning validity issues. To gain a convenient summary of some of the main psychometric properties of temperament instruments, the reader is referred to the review by Hubert and colleagues (1982). Data relevant to validity issues have been reviewed in the works discussed earlier in the definitional section and will also be considered later in the chapter.

Comment

To conclude the section, it should be noted that, most accurately speaking, reliability and validity are not things that measures attain or have. Rather, they are more like processes we go through in discovering how to interpret existing measures. Sometimes what is discovered is discrepant enough from the main goals that the measure must be refined or dropped. However, other times, even though a measure might be far from perfectly generalizable, it may be sufficiently useful to retain. Even originally unintended meanings might prove useful. The choice of keeping or eliminating a measure is a complex one, ultimately depending on the purposes of the individual researcher and the particular audience he or she hopes to inform.

Many writers emphasize the primacy of reliability in evaluating a measure. It is said that reliability must constrain a measure's validity. Ideally, all measures would meet stringent standards of test–retest reliability, factor purity, and so forth. However, in the current state of temperament research, measures do not generally meet such stringent standards (Hubert et al., 1982). This is not just the result of a lack of proper effort on the part of temperament researchers. Consider an alternate strategy for research—one that places heavier weight on validity than on reliability. Obviously, reliability has to be considered, but if a highly reliable measure fails to point to otherwise interesting features of the child's behavior, the reliability will be useless. In a first stage of research, moderate standards of reliability may be paired with a stronger emphasis on validity. In the second stage, we can refine measures of theoretically important constructs with promising levels of validity. This may indeed be what already happens in the field, despite the emphasis on reliability.

REVIEW OF EMPIRICAL STUDIES

Using a computer-assisted review of the literature from 1967 through most of 1984 and my own files and notes, I noticed six major empirical themes in the temperament research. The themes are (1) direct validation of temperament measures, including correlations between different kinds of temperament measure at the same time, for example, parent versus observer, and correlations between the same or different measures of a trait across development; (2) the role of temperament in socially relevant processes, including parent–child interaction, attachment security, cognitive development, and behavior problems; (3) subjective factors in the perception of temperament; (4) cultural factors; (5) biological processes that might underlie temperament; and (6) the influence of risk conditions, such as premature birth or Down's syndrome. A seventh theme is mentioned in many studies: the question of possible sex differences in temperament. However, remarkably few sex differences in infant temperament have been found, and those that have been found do not form a coherent pattern. The chapter will focus primarily on the first three themes. The other three major themes will be mentioned for the sake of providing entry points for readers who wish more thoroughly to investigate the literature in these areas. The review will also focus on the studies concerning children from birth to age 2 years.

Direct Validation

Mother–Father Agreement

There are a number of ways in which temperament measures have been validated. Mother reports are the major kind of target for validation efforts. The most convenient way to check the meaning of mother perceptions is to correlate them with father perceptions. The father's experience with the baby is comparable to the mother's, even if it is usually less extensive. Studies typically find that mother and father agree to a moderate degree (often correlations of .5–.6), on most scales (see reviews by Bates, 1980; Bates & Bayles, 1984; Hubert et al., 1982; Plomin, 1982). These are the highest validity coefficients obtained in the area. (Small-sample correlations of this size between a mother report scale and a more objective measure are occasionally reported, and occasionally a study will report small interparent agreement, but generally the parental agreements are the highest.) Bates and Bayles (1984), who simultaneously evaluated many different parent report scales and observational measures, asked what the source of the parent–parent overlap is. They concluded that the overlap is not due to the shared perception of the characteristics of the infant that could be seen by the research observer, and suggested that it is due either to the parents seeing objective characteristics that the observer does not or to the mother influencing the father perceptions. Thus while father reports are a convenient means of checking the meaning of mother perception scales, they are not sufficient by themselves.

Parent–Observer Agreement

There are at least 20 studies that have compared mother ratings of infants with observational data. In broad overview, the studies demonstrate that there is a modest to moderate objective basis in the parent perceptions (Bates, 1980). Typical correlations (again, depending on the sample size—studies with small samples sometimes report larger coefficients) are quite modest, usually accounting for 5–15 percent of the variance. Correlations with observer ratings on scales like those filled out by the parent are often found to be a bit larger than those with molecularly coded behavior, such as episodes of fussing and crying.

There are a number of findings of nonrelationship between a parent scale and criterion measure. In some cases, this may be attributable to the poor coherence and relevance of the particular parent report scale; in others, it may be due to the poor psychometric properties or inappropriateness of the criterion measure. At this point, the choice between these two explanations is not obvious, but one can make tentative judgments in particular cases. For example, Vaughn, Taraldson, Crichton, and Egeland (1981) found nonrelationships between their measures of infant behavior and mother reports on the Carey Infant Temperament Questionnaire (ITQ). The original ITQ has major psychometric problems (Hubert et al., 1982—the ITQ-R, or RITQ, is psychometrically better), but we hesitate to assign full responsibility to a lack of validity in the ITQ: Vaughn and colleagues' behavior measures were from a very narrow range of situations, not particularly well suited to the temperament variables of interest. To one degree or another, the same considerations could be applied to many tests of the validity of temperament scales, if not most. Even when significant correlations are found, these correlations are usually too small for one to assume that the main source of the mother's perception has been tapped.

If the observational base of the researcher were closer to that of the mother, would higher validity coefficients be found? This is possible, but the early evidence is mixed. There are hints in the literature that highly salient child characteristics, such as vocabulary in the second year, show more parent–observer convergence (Olson, Bates, & Bayles, 1982; St. James-Roberts & Wolke, 1984). The previously mentioned study of Hagekull and colleagues (1982) suggests that focusing the mother's attention on narrowly bounded domains of infant behavior makes the mother rate more like an observer. However, as said previously, this is not the same as discovering the truest nature of the infant. One should also look at the observer whose experience matches the mother's more natural expertise. Field and Greenberg (1982) found that agreement between parents and infants' all-day nursery school teachers was no higher than has been typically reported for parents and observers.

At the present time, there is more validational evidence for the construct of *difficultness* than for any other single temperament construct. Our own research group has shown that there are small but replicable correlations between mothers' perceptions of the difficultness of their infants on the Infant Characteristics Questionnaire and both observer impressions on the relevant items of the ICQ and molecularly coded amounts of fussing and crying (Bates et al., 1979; Bates et al., 1982; Pettit & Bates, 1984a) (as is the usual case in the validation studies, the more global impressions of the observer tended to correlate a little higher with the mother report than the molecular behavior measures—Bates et al., 1979). Thus amount of crying is central to the ICQ definition of difficult temperament, and the parent perception of difficultness can be partially confirmed in several hours of observation.

Another ICQ item that contributes to the perception of difficultness concerns the intensity of the cry. Lounsbury was able to show that the hunger cries of difficult infants are perceived by unrelated adult listeners as more aversive, demanding, and "spoiled sounding" than those of easy or average infants (Lounsbury & Bates, 1982). This study also found corresponding differences in sound spectrographs of the cries: Those of difficult infants showed higher pitch at peaks of sound intensity, and they showed longer pauses between cry sounds than the other infants' cries. Boukydis, who used the same tape-recorded cries in an independent study, replicated the effects on listeners' ratings of aversiveness, and showed further that the ratings are accompanied by psychophysiological arousal (Boukydis & Burgess, 1982).

The last two studies are part of a growing pattern of evidence suggesting that what parents perceive as difficult about the negative emotionality of infants is that it involves coercive control. A substantial correlate of the difficultness factor, as early as 4–6 months of age, is the mother's perception that her infant demands more attention and stimulation and provides less self-entertainment than other infants (Bates et al., 1982; Bates et al., 1984). This socially demanding, coercive control aspect of difficult temperament could be a factor in the development of behavior problems, as will be discussed below.

Validation for constructs related to the ICQ difficultness concept has also been reported. For example, Sameroff and colleagues (1982) mention convergence between mother ratings on the Carey ITQ mood scale and appropriate home and laboratory observations. Wilson and Matheny (1983) found convergence between a laboratory factor of positive emotional tone and the main factor in the parents' temperament reports, a factor that resembles the Thomas-Chess difficultness definition, including mood, approach, adaptability, and persistence. In related work, Matheny, Wilson, and Nuss (1984) found that laboratory and parent questionnaire measures of tractability correlated.

The above studies have concerned infants 4 months of age or older. Neonatal behavior characteristics may or may not have the same meanings. Crockenberg and Smith (1982) found that neonatal irritability on the Brazelton exam predicted at 3 months how long the infant took to calm when upset, but not how much fussing and crying the infant did overall. This is not a crucial test of whether the construct of difficultness or negative emotionality trait can be measured in earliest infancy, however, the Brazelton exam is widely used, and has been conceptually related to temperament concepts by a number of writers. Yet, most do not regard it as a measure of temperament (Sameroff, 1978; Worobey, 1984). The neonate's performance in the test may reflect relatively transient variables concerning ability to regulate state rather than enduring predispositions.

Crockenberg and Acredolo (1983) found that mother perceptions of overall levels of infant distress on the Rothbart IBQ correlated slightly with the observed frequency of fussing and crying at 3 months. However, on the basis of partial correlations, Crockenberg and Smith (1982) concluded that the total amount of fussing and crying shown by the infant is more the result of mother tendencies, both in attitude and behavior, to respond quickly to infant distress than of infant constitution (Crockenberg & Acredolo, 1983, suggest a potentially better lens on constitutional dispositions than simple counts of the frequency of a particular infant response—instead, assess the infant's tendency to respond to a situation relative to how often the environment provides the relevant stimulus).

Whatever the actual source of the infant's emotionality, whether the pattern of transactions has been set in motion by the mother's attitudes, the infant's constitution, or both, one would predict that alternate measures of emotionality would show the same relation to observed fussing and crying that the IBQ showed. However, Crockenberg (1982), using a very small sample of English teenage mothers, failed to find a relationship between mother-rated emotionality as operationalized by the ICQ and observed fussing and crying or with time to calm after intervention. However, even if amount of negative emotionality seen at 3 months or older could be due to the relationship with the mother over the preceding weeks, most evidence, especially studies of infants past 4 months of age, suggests that mother reports have some objectifiable basis.

The *fear* construct, otherwise referred to as approach/adaptability, or inhibition when meeting unfamiliar people and situations, has received much validation. We found convergence between parent report scales measuring negative adaptation to new situations and observational measures, especially ratings of the fearfulness versus positiveness of the infant's response to an observer at home or Bayley examiner in the laboratory (Bates & Bayles, 1984). Field and Greenberg (1982) found convergence between mother and teacher ratings on adaptability in a group of children

18–60-months old, although not in a group of children 4–12 months old. Perhaps the younger infants have not yet developed stranger anxiety and thus are unable to show consistent individual differences in fear toward strangers. This is suggested by Berberian and Snyder (1982), who reported that difficult children 8–9 months old, defined by mother report on the Carey and McDevitt RITQ, were more fearful in response to the approach of an adult stranger in the laboratory than were easier infants, while easy and difficult children 5–7 months old did not differ. However, the RITQ approach scale itself did correlate even with the younger infants' response to the most extreme intrusion by the stanger. The more withdrawing infants showed a slight but significant tendency to react negatively to the stranger taking the infant's hand. Lamb (1982) summarizes studies showing that a laboratory measure of sociability in response to an approaching stranger correlates with mother reports of approach tendencies. Burg, Quinn, and Rapoport (1978) found that pediatricians' ratings of infant irritability correlated with parent ITQ adaptability. Lemly and Schwarz (1979) found that parent ratings of their 2-year-olds' emotionality (on the Plomin EASI questionnaire) correlated with more negative reactions to a stranger in the laboratory.

By taking the extremes of the fearfulness distribution, Garcia-Coll, Kagan, and Reznick (1984) were able to show a highly interesting pattern. Garcia-Coll and colleagues selected the approximately 50 percent of an unscreened sample of toddlers whose mothers described them as either highly inhibited (withdrawing, in the terms of Thomas & Chess) or highly uninhibited (approaching) in the face of novel situations. They then further selected the most and least inhibited of this sample on the basis of the toddlers' reactions in a series of laboratory situations (about 50 percent of those who were screened via parent report). Parental ratings on the approach scale of the Toddler Temperament Scale (Fullard, McDevitt, & Carey, 1978) correlated, to a moderate degree, with the laboratory behavior measure of inhibition in the group obtained after the first screening for extremes, and to a moderately high degree in the group that passed the second screening.

Furthermore, the extremely inhibited toddlers, compared to the uninhibited ones, showed a tendency to have a high and stable heart rate when facing novel stimuli. Garcia-Coll and colleagues interpret this as due in part to a constitutional tendency toward persistent efforts to assimilate or comprehend an unfamiliar event. The high, stable heart rate that occurs is theoretically due to sympathetic nervous system inhibition of the vagus nerve (recall that Buss & Plomin, 1984, argue that the basis of the emotionality trait is sympathetic dominance). The study of Garcia-Coll and colleagues (1984) is especially stimulating because it integrates behavioral signs of negative response to novelty with specific cognitive and psychophysiological processes. It will be interesting to see how well the findings generalize across the full range of children. It will also be interesting to learn more about the roots of the hypothetical sympathetic dominance. Buss and Plomin (1984) suggest genetic factors here, while Kagan (1983) suggests that uterine environment could affect the balance of cholinergic versus adrenergic ganglia in the child's nervous system, thus affecting the inhibition (fear) versus excitation balance.

Activity constructs have not been as extensively validated in infancy as negative emotionality constructs, but there have been several relevant studies. As indicated in the theory and definition section of the chapter, measurement of a clearly defined trait of activity in infancy has been difficult. Early behaviors thought to tap the trait of activity level may not really be direct measures. In fact, according to Halverson, Moss, and Kearns (1977), in boys the activity shown at 3 months of age may actually be an inverse predictor of activity shown at 3 years (also see Yang & Halverson, 1976, regarding the inversion of intensity hypothesis). However, despite the definitional problems, a few studies do demonstrate that mother reports of infant activity correlate with observations. Hagekull and colleagues (1982) found that mother scores on the intensity/activity factor of their questionnaire correlated with observer scores on the factor. Rothbart (1983) found similar convergence with the IBQ in home observations at 6 and 9 months of age, but not at 3 months. Burg and colleagues (1978) found correlations between mother ITQ ratings of activity and intensity and pediatrician ratings of infants' hyperactivity.

Affleck, Allen, McGrade, and McQueeny (1983) found more indirect validity in a risk sample—mother ratings of activity at 9 months on the Pedersen Perception of Baby Temperament questionnaire were correlated with the observed social responsiveness of the infant and lack of developmental delay. Similarly, Thompson and Lamb (1982) found that IBQ activity was correlated with positive responses to an approaching stranger. However, Stevenson and Leavitt (1980) reported that highly active infants according to the RITQ were less positive to a stranger. The discrepancy between the last two studies could be due to sampling variation (small n in the Stevenson and Leavitt study) or instrument differences (IBQ vs. RITQ). However, age of the infant might be involved, too. In Thompson and Lamb (1982), the positive correlation was found at 19 but not 12 months, and Stevenson and Leavitt (1980) obtained their negative correlation with 12-month-olds. Some other studies have searched for observational correlates of activity and found either null or uninterpretable patterns. Since these studies' null findings are not highly instructive at the present time, because of the questionable relevance of their criterion measures, they will not be reviewed here.

Sociability in the sense used by Buss and Plomin has not often been validated. However, there is a clear support from at least one study: Lemly and Schwarz (1979) reported that parent reports of sociability on the EASI predicted more positive and fewer negative reactions to a stranger in the laboratory.

Stability

Another form of validation of temperament constructs is cross-age stability. As previously discussed, there is some doubt as to how much stability a temperament variable should show. However, in general, there is at least modest to moderate stability for temperament measures. Of course, as Crockenberg (above) and others would argue, it is possible to interpret any stability as due to transactions between the caregiving environment and the infant. It is also possible that consistent perceptual biases might account for stability on parent report instruments. Although the former possibility is indisputable at the moment, the latter possibility is less troubling after some recent findings that show that any perceptual bias is not operating in a global fashion: Bates and Bayles's (1984) analysis of 27 different mother perception variables in a longitudinal sample suggests that the mothers perceive their children in consistently differentiated ways over a period of almost 3 years. For example, rather than seeing the child through a simple filter of general positivity–negativity, the mother's perception of the child in one area was stable and relatively distinct from other variables over the years, for example, difficultness versus negative adaptation to new people and situations. In addition, as mentioned above, the subjective factors one would expect to account for consistency if it were due to bias did not account for larger portions of the variance in mother reports than objective factors. Therefore, consistency in subjective biases might account for some of the cross-age stability in mother reports of temperament, but it cannot account for all of it. In addition, there are findings of stability in observationally based measures of temperament. The parent report and observational findings will be summarized briefly.

First, it is fairly well established that mother reports on emotionality scales are stable across development to at least modest levels. For example, we have found that difficultness on the ICQ is moderately stable from age 6 months to 24 months, despite adjustments in the content of the scale corresponding to developmental changes (Lee & Bates, 1985). However, when the different points on the distribution were examined separately, we found that the easy infants were more stable than the difficult ones. Swets-Gronert (1984) replicated this pattern using a definition of difficultness based on the Thomas-Chess system, finding that the easy constellation was more stable from 6 to 24 months than the difficult category, with slow-to-warm-up not at all stable. Other examples of stability in parent report scales relating to emotionality, including difficultness, negative mood, unsoothability, distress to limitations, and fearfulness, are provided by Hagekull and Bohlin (1981), Maccoby and colleagues (1984), McDevitt and Carey (1981), Peters-Martin and Wachs (1984), Rothbart (1981), and Thomas and Chess (1984). However, there are a few suggestions of the possibility that there may be some discontinuities due to developmental transformations; for example, fearfulness shows stability only in later infancy, according to Rothbart (1981). Kronstadt, Oberklaid, Ferb, and Swartz (1979) emphasize their finding of low stability on a difficultness measure, but this anomaly may be due to poor psychometric properties in their measure.

Second, there are a few studies that suggest that more objective indexes of emotionality show stability. Snow, Jacklin, and Maccoby (1980) showed that a parent diary measure of frequency of crying showed some stability, especially after 9 months of age. Fish and Crockenberg (1981) observed stability in fussing and crying from as early as 1 or 3 months to 9 months of age.

Considering stability in activity indexes, several studies show continuity in mother reports of activity. For example, the IBQ activity scale is moderately stable throughout the first year (Rothbart, 1981). Other studies include Hagekull and Bohlin (1981), Maccoby and colleagues (1984), McDevitt and Carey (1981), and Peters-Martin and Wachs (1984). Evidence for modest levels of stability in more objective indexes of activity comes from Feiring and Lewis (1980) and Matheny (1983). A very early precursor to infancy activity level appears to be neonatal motor maturity, with motorically mature neonates being higher in observed activity as late as 9 months of age (Fish & Crockenberg, 1981; Rosenblith, 1974; Yang & Moss, 1978).

In short, there is evidence that the major temperament concepts are somewhat stable during infancy, whether measured by parent report or direct observation. However, the extent of continuity is typically low enough that one should ask about possible sources of discontinuity as well as continuity. Furthermore, while there may be a constitutional substrate in the continuity that has been found, there may be environmental components too (e.g., as argued by Crockenberg & Acredolo, 1983; Snow et al., 1980, and others). To add a final complication to the interpretation of the stability data, there may even be constitutional roots in the discontinuities that occur, for example, in fear of strangers (see Buss & Plomin, 1984; Goldsmith & Campos, 1982).

To conclude the section on direct validation of temperament measures, there is considerable support for the assertion that temperamentlike variables, especially difficultness, fearful reactions to novelty, and activity, can be measured with some validity: (1) Mothers and fathers agree to a substantial degree; (2) parent reports and observer measures often show some convergence, despite the differences in the experiential base from which parents and observers rate temperament; and (3) in accord with the stability criterion, the major temperament dimensions show some continuity over development. These findings support the assumption that the major parent report and observer measures of early temperament are describing meaningful individual differences. However, there is only a little evidence for the discriminant validity of temperament variables (e.g., Bates & Bayles, 1984), that is, research that shows the extent to which a particular scale relates to conceptually relevant variables and not to irrelevant variables.

Having reviewed the evidence of the most direct forms of generalizability of temperament measures, we now turn to more indirect forms of generalizability. The next major issue is how temperament pertains to social development.

Role of Temperament in Socially Relevant Processes

How might temperament influence the child's social development? This has been the central question in many applications of temperament concepts. Systems models of development recognize that the characteristics of the child play a substantial role in shaping the child's effective environment, including what resources are available, what demands are made, and what conflicts and stresses are present. How to describe the child's role in socialization is a continuing question, but temperament may be one useful description. If we could identify early appearing, relatively stable, biologically rooted personality traits that make a difference in the social environment, we could offer parents better information about what they are dealing with. Clinicians sometimes find that parents are more willing to adjust their practices when their problems with their children are framed as temperament as opposed to parent practices (Thomas & Chess, 1977). Ultimately, refined temperament concepts might allow new approaches to preventing some developmental problems.

Parent–Child Relationship

In studies of the child's earliest social environment, the most important, overarching construct has been *maternal warmth and responsiveness* (Bates et al., 1982; Clarke-Stewart, 1973). There have been many different ways of operationally defining the love and stimulation mothers provide their infants, and there are theory and evidence suggesting that individual differences in such indexes are rooted in an underlying factor and relate to socially relevant outcomes, most clearly to the child's verbal and cognitive competencies (e.g., Bates et al., 1982; Olson, Bates, & Bayles, 1984). Such concepts are theoretically related to other kinds of social competence, including successful supportive interactions with family and peers.

Research gives some grounds for considering mother–infant attachment security as a representative of maternal responsiveness (Ainsworth, Blehar, Waters, & Wall, 1978; Belsky, Rovine, & Taylor, 1984; Egeland & Farber, 1984; Kiser, Bates, Maslin,

& Bayles, 1986; Lamb et al., 1985). However, it certainly does not support equating maternal responsiveness and attachment security. Attachment security predicts later social competencies in some but not all instances (Bates & Bayles, 1985; Bates, Maslin, & Frankel, 1985; Frankel & Bates, 1985; Lamb et al., 1985; Sroufe, 1983). When attachment does predict, *how* it predicts can be debated. It may predict because it indexes stable attitudes toward people, for example, trust versus mistrust, because it indexes stable qualities of the social environment, or some combination of the two. There are convincing formulations of the combination process (Sroufe, 1983), but it has been argued that research has yet to show clearly that both early and later experiences play a role (Lamb et al., 1985). Furthermore, some writers argue that there is a third element in the process—temperament might help shape both the attachment and continuing interactions with the social environment (e.g., Kagan, 1982). Obviously, research is needed that includes good indexes of mother–infant responsiveness qualities as well as attachment security and child temperament and that assesses outcomes longitudinally. This kind of research is just beginning, and it is too soon to give conclusive summaries.

How responsiveness–warmth indexes are interpreted is important in considering the role of temperament. If temperament is to be important in shaping social development, it should do so partly via impact on the child's relationships. Theorists are beginning to specify possible transactions between temperament and environment (see earlier discussion of Buss & Plomin theory). However, in reviewing the literature to this point, it is difficult to say exactly what impact we should have expected to find. On the one hand, temperament qualities must surely have an effect on parents; otherwise they would not be salient enough to assess reliably. On the other hand, however, they may not have any more crucial effect on the qualities of caregiving than other major individual differences in an infant in a typical family setting, such as preferences for foods. Parents would notice and adjust to temperamental traits, keeping the relationship within the limits of effectiveness, and they would also shape the behavioral repertoire of the infant, even in areas that also have psychobiological roots (see Sroufe, 1984).

Considering the research findings, then, the evidence to date does not seriously challenge either of the aforementioned positions. Some studies find temperament scores correlated with parent–infant relationship indexes, while others do not. Our own research with difficult temperament supports the conclusion that there are some direct effects of temperament on the infant's relationships in the first year or so. For example, a difficult infant receives a little more care giver attention in the home than an easy one (Bates et al., 1982; Pettit & Bates, 1984a). However, the effects are far from pervasive, and not likely to be associated with important developmental outcomes. We do not find difficultness to be closely associated with the main factors of maternal warmth–responsiveness–involvement that do relate to developmental outcomes (Bates et al., 1982; Olson et al., 1984).

Thus we have seen some possible ways in which the child's temperament may directly condition interactions with others, but they do not seem to have much social importance in advance of the age of autonomy struggles (the latter qualification will be explained further on, in discussing the data on temperament in relation to parent–child control). We have even checked for some possible statistical interactions, for example, temperament having a different effect on different segments of the socioeconomic continuum, without finding consistent effects (Bates et al., 1982; Bates,

Maslin, & Frankel, 1985). Continued search for context-dependent effects of temperament may prove productive, however, and such research is under way in our laboratory. For example, Sabet-Sharghi and Mathalon are each searching for ways in which mother responsiveness might influence temperament's impact on social development outcomes.

Our own largely null findings to date argue for the position that mother warmth–responsiveness dimensions are not importantly affected by infant temperament. However, although our relationship measures have demonstrated validity in various ways, these findings represent only some of the ways in which the question can be attacked. There are many possible places to look for temperament—different populations, different ways of construing behavior, different situations. Crockenberg's (in press) review of the relevant literature suggests some specific ways researchers might look for temperament–parenting correlations as mediated by factors such as preexisting parent attitudes.

Other studies showing little effect of temperament on parent–child relations include one by Daniels, Plomin, and Greenhalgh (1984). In a large sample of families, Daniels and colleagues found no relationship between a difficultness index based on the RITQ and observer impressions of quality of parenting on the Caldwell HOME scales at 12 and 24 months. Vaughn and colleagues (1981) also used a large sample and failed to find systematic effects of temperament on mother–infant interaction in feeding and play situations. Wachs and Gandour (1981), using a large sample of 6-month olds, found no relationship between difficult versus easy temperament and observed qualities of mother stimulation of the infant (although they did find an interaction between temperament and stimulation in affecting cognitive development).

Other studies have found relationships between parental warmth–responsiveness and infant temperament. The findings are not always easily generalizable, and they sometimes are found only when the interaction between temperament and another variable is examined, but there are enough studies with positive findings in the literature that they should be considered. Campbell (1979) found that mothers in a very small subgroup of difficult infants were less responsive to social bids at both 3 and 8 months than were other mothers. Sample size may be important: In larger samples one is safer in assuming that unmeasured variables will be randomly distributed than in smaller ones. In a study such as Campbell (1979), several of the mothers in the difficult group could be rather broadly disturbed in their functioning, and this could produce a correlation between difficultness and mother responsiveness not found in many other samples. This assumes that psychologically disturbed mothers are more likely than others to see their children as difficult (see evidence presented later) and at the same time to be more unresponsive toward the child. Milliones (1978), like Campbell, found that easier babies had more positive mother behaviors directed toward them than more difficult babies. However, Milliones's sample size (24) and the fact that the mothers were in an urban socioeconomic risk group might limit the generalizability of the findings. It is very possible that the temperament scores could be more a consequence of the mother's attitude and corresponding behavior than a cause. In a similar population, Field, Widmayer, Stringer, and Ignatoff (1980) demonstrated that interventions designed to promote better mother-infant interactions in at risk mothers produced both better interactions and more positive mother perceptions of infant temperament.

In a study of 40 primarily middle-class Israeli mothers "of eastern origin," Klein (1984) found that 6- and 12-month infants who were more difficult on the ITQ received more involved mother behaviors than easier babies, including a variety of positive, stimulating behaviors. However, Klein also found some interactions between temperament and sex; for example, boys high in intensity of emotional reactions got more physical contact than boys with calmer reactions, whereas intense girls received more distal, vocal stimulation than less intense girls. Rendina and Dickersheid (1976), with a sample of 40 6- and 13-month infants, did not reproduce the Klein findings but did find an interaction effect between temperament and sex. There was a gender-mediated relationship between infant temperament and father behavior: Fathers responded to difficult boys by engaging in more social activities than with easy boys, yet were less involved with difficult than with easy girls.

Crockenberg and her colleagues' recent studies show some links between temperamentlike characteristics of infants and mother behavior. However, they also raise the likelihood that the links could be partly a function of preexisting mother characteristics. In Crockenberg and Acredolo (1983), high levels of baby fussing and crying at age 3 months and mother-perceived distress to limits (on the Rothbart IBQ) were correlated with lower levels of mother "involved contact." If fussing and crying and distress to limits are regarded as analogous to difficultness, this finding is parallel to the findings of Campbell (1979) and Milliones (1978), but opposite to the findings of more mother involvement with difficult infants listed above. Based on short-term longitudinal findings in Crockenberg (1982) and Crockenberg and Smith (1982), it appears that mothers' attitudes about responsiveness to infants can be measured as early as the neonatal period, and these attitudes predict both how quickly the mother responds to infant cries and how much the infant cries (as rated by mother and an observer).

In addition, Crockenberg and Acredolo (1983) found that high levels of involved mother contact at 1 month predicted the infant's perceived duration of orienting (IBQ) at 3 months. While Crockenberg and Acredolo do not deny that this link could be due to the effects of the infant's constitution, they favor the interpretation that it is due to the mother's stimulation leading the infant to better organization of attention. Thus in Crockenberg's interpretation observed links between infant temperament and mother behavior could stem from the mother's initial attitudes and behaviors, rather than only from experience with the infant, and a maternal attitude of unresponsiveness is associated with fussing and crying. Indirect support for Crockenberg's interpretation comes from two additional studies: Field and Greenberg (1982) found that handicapped infants were less difficult during a one-to-one play situation with the teacher or mother than they were during ordinary times in the classroom, where they were receiving less involved contact. The other study, by Nover, Shore, Timberlake, and Greenspan (1984), is indirect support of a different sort: Mothers who perceived their 9-month-olds in a more negative way than observers and who were younger and less well educated than other mothers showed less social interaction with the baby in a laboratory play situation. Again, mothers' characteristics predicted the kinds of behavior that could produce the infant behavior that might be viewed as difficult temperament.

A recent study by Easterbrooks and Emde (1984) allows some first steps toward seeing infant temperamentlike behaviors as part of a full family system. This study found in a laboratory assessment that firstborn, 6-month infants were more intrusive during a couple-oriented task when the mothers reported lower marital satisfaction. Furthermore, the mothers were more responsive to the infant intrusions, although fathers were not. Easterbrooks and Emde interpreted this as an effect of the infant on marital adjustment. However, family therapists would often interpret a pattern like this either as a way the parents defuse tension by redirecting attention to the child or as a way the parents communicate with each other via the child. Since social demands are a correlate of perceived difficult temperament, the pattern described by Easterbrooks and Emde could indicate a root of difficultness in marital distress. However, they did not find that infant intrusiveness was related to emotionality-type scales of the IBQ. It was related, in a complex pattern, to perceived smiling and laughter. Mothers rated more intrusive infants as higher in smiling and laughter, but fathers rated both high- and low-intrusive babies as higher on smiling and laughter than intermediate-intrusive babies. Further research along the lines taken by Easterbrooks and Emde could be important in understanding the origins and implications of the behaviors that we now use to define difficult temperament.

Most of the relevant studies on the parent-infant responsiveness correlates of temperament focus on emotionality–difficultness concepts. However, this does not mean that there would not be effects involving other temperament traits. For example, given that infants seen as more active are also more socially responsive, one would be able to predict that activity might be correlated with higher levels of parent involvement. The active baby might be more entertaining to caregivers, and thus receive more attention.

To summarize, there is mixed evidence on the question of whether parents are differentially warm and responsive with difficult versus easy infants. At this point, my own conclusion is that the effects, if they are present, are of low developmental importance, at least within most populations.

A similar conclusion can be drawn from the small group of studies correlating temperament with *attachment security*. None of the many indexes of temperament we used related systematically to attachment security (Bates et al., 1985), a finding that converges with the findings of Egeland and Sroufe and their colleagues (Sroufe, 1982). Similarly, Weber, Levitt, and Clark (1984) reported no infant temperament correlates of attachment security (both Bates et al. and Weber et al., however, did find some correlations between temperament and Strange Situation behavior ratings, e.g., between approach/adaptability indexes and reactions to the stranger). There remains the possibility that temperament links with quality of attachment could be found: Frodi (1983) reports in an abstract (this citation is not based on the full article) that in a group of premature and full-term infants those perceived as easy were more likely to be securely attached.

Sroufe (1984) reviews relevant evidence and argues strongly on the basis of theory that temperament is not directly involved in attachment security. If it does have any effects, they would be found only via the parent–infant relationship; for example, insensitive care with a robust infant might lead to an avoidant pattern of anxious attachment, while similar care with a nonrobust infant might lead to a resistant pattern of anxious attachment. As Sroufe puts it, "the most urgent need is for process studies of how caregivers typically adjust their behavior to accommodate to the particular needs and nature of a given child" (p. 12).

Besides the question of whether temperament might play a role in the levels of parent warmth and responsiveness and ensuing attachment security, one might ask whether temperament influences levels of parental *control and teaching* behaviors. From our research and reviews of the literature, it appears that there are two qualitatively different kinds of maternal control appearing in very early childhood (Lee & Bates, 1985; Pettit & Bates, 1984b). The kind with the most obvious control character is negative or reactive control, a cluster of mother behaviors in response to child trouble behavior, such as scolding, warning, and taking objects away. The other kind is more positive or proactive control, which appears to extend from the mother's early tendency to be warm and responsive, but which also involves the mother directly stimulating cognitive growth in the infant, especially through naming objects and asking the infant to name or bring objects. In positive control the mother is teaching the child concepts and social skills, and is preventing trouble behavior by anticipatory guidance. In fact, low levels of positive control are better predictors of later child behavior problems than levels of negative control (Pettit & Bates, 1984b).

How do temperament scales relate to parental control and teaching behaviors? As mentioned above, in our own research we have not found relationships between difficult temperament and the warmth aspects of the mother–infant relationship. However, by 24 months of age, we did find direct relationships between control and conflict aspects of mother–toddler interaction (Lee & Bates, 1985); for example, difficult toddlers were more likely than others to resist mother efforts to control their explorations, and their mothers were more likely to show reactive kinds of control, such as warning and restraining the child, and the difficult children themselves approached more trouble actions, but did not actually complete more. Interestingly, however, the frequencies of negative emotion behaviors independent of control–conflict context did not correlate with perceived difficultness at age 24 months, unlike at 6 and 13 months. The mothers still reported on the ICQ difficultness factor at 24 months that their difficult toddlers were high in emotionality, but it may be that the emotionality shown by the children in control situations was more salient than emotionality in other contexts. It is also possible that the toddlers' difficultness continued to be based on a general emotionality, but because of the reduced frequency of fussing and crying by 24 months, observers would be more likely to witness sufficient amounts of emotionality in the context of autonomy struggles than in other kinds of situation.

Maccoby and colleagues (1984) studied the relationship of temperamentlike dispositions in infants to mother teaching behavior in laboratory tasks. At 18 months, mothers of difficult boys were making less vigorous teaching efforts, especially of the directive sort, than were mothers of easier boys. Further, compared with dyads where the son was easy at 12 months, where the boy was difficult at 12 months, the mother showed less vigorous teaching effort at 18 months. However, in dyads where the mother showed higher effort at 12 months, boys were lower in difficultness at 18 months. Maccoby and colleagues see these findings as suggesting an escalating cycle in some dyads: If the mother responds to the infant's countercontrol (difficultness) by reducing her teaching pressure, the infant becomes even more likely to be difficult, leading to further withdrawal by the mother. However, for mothers of girls, Maccoby and colleagues saw a tendency to make a stronger teaching effort with difficult as opposed to easy daughters, particularly in the form of encouraging and praising (although the correlation was significant only at 12 months).

Maccoby and colleagues' (1984) Sex × Temperament interaction finding is worth considering, even if it is neither statistically strong nor open to easy interpretation (see Maccoby et al., 1984). This is because of a similar finding by Gordon (1983) in 3-year-olds and their mothers in laboratory tasks. Gordon observed that mothers gave more commands to easy boys than difficult ones, whereas they gave fewer commands to easy girls than to difficult ones. As Maccoby and colleagues suggest regarding their own finding, both of these studies' results could stem from subtle differences in the behavior of difficult girls as opposed to that of difficult boys, for example, more social attentiveness in the girls, or from sex-role stereotypes in the mothers.

Another form of control the parent might have with a child is leading by example. Feinman and Lewis (1983) found that 10-month-olds follow the example of their mothers in being friendly or unfriendly with strangers. They found this social referencing effect to be stronger among easy than among difficult babies. There is not an apparent, direct implication for the parent–child relationship, but it is possible that the difficult infant might learn less about the parent's attitudes than the easy infant, and this eventually contributes to friction between them.

I did not find studies of the effects of infants' activity and sociability characteristics in parent–child relationships, but would expect that effects might be found. With older children, D. Buss (1981) found that activity levels assessed at ages 3 and 4 predicted the quality of parent control at 5 years. More active children's parents showed more physical intervention, impatience, and hostility than less active children's parents, as might be predicted by Bell's notion of upper-limit control. (Buss recognizes that the parents' behavior could be partly due to genetically based activity tendencies shared with the child). If satisfactory operationalizations of activity level in infancy can be developed (see earlier discussion in connection with the A. Buss & Plomin concepts), it seems likely that activity levels may have some interesting correlates in parent–infant relations. It may be that during infancy, however, the activity per se has less important effects than the context in which it occurs. Based on a few clinical observations, I would hypothesize, for example, that a difficult infant who is also high in activity level would be at greater risk for acting-out behavior problems than one who is low in activity.

To summarize, there are some findings of correlation between infant temperament and parent–child relationship indices. However, the findings are not as pervasive as one might have expected. Perhaps this is due to the insensitivity of measures, or perhaps it is an indication that the effects might not be very important in the social development of the child. Alternatively, it may be that whether the child's temperament is related to important characteristics of relations with parents depends on third variables, for example, socioeconomic stresses, or sex and birth order of the child. The literature previously reviewed generally omits the research on older children and their parents. Some interesting work on preschoolers' interactions with parents as related to temperament is emerging now, for example, Stevenson-Hinde and Hinde (1986), and may eventually guide similar efforts with infants.

Behavior Disorders

Considering the hypothetical role of temperament in the development of behavior problems and the wide interest in the origins of behavior problems, there have been relatively few studies on this issue. Thomas and colleagues (1968) have often been cited as showing that difficult infants are at risk for behavior problems. However, in fact, their empirical data did not support this conclusion, since temperament scores generally were associated with behavior problem outcomes only after the age of 3 years (Thomas et al., 1968), by which time the parents' report of temperament could be interpreted as an alternative measure of problem behavior, not necessarily long-standing tendencies in the child.

However, recently a few studies have supported the hypothesis. Cameron (1978) and Korn (personal communication, 1978—see Bates, 1980, for detailed description) reanalyzed the Thomas-Chess data and showed that temperament from as early as age 1 year predicted behavior problems when considered in conjunction with parenting problems and sex of child. For example, Cameron found that the combination of a difficult temperament index from 1 year of age and a parenting problems index from 3 years predicted childhood behavior problems, but only among girls. Carey, Fox, and McDevitt (1977) obtained correlations between infancy temperamental difficultness and school-age reflectivity–impulsivity and adjustment as rated by teachers. The most difficult and the most easy infants were the ones with later problems. Interpretation of this interesting curvilinear effect is difficult (see Bates, 1980).

More direct support comes from our own longitudinal study (Bates et al., 1985; Bates, Pettit, & Bayles, 1985; Pettit & Bates, 1984b). Difficult temperament as indexed by mother ratings on the ICQ as early as 6 months of age predicts later mother perceptions of both acting-out (e.g., aggression) and internalizing (e.g., anxiety) behavior problems at ages 3, 4, and 5 years at modest to moderate levels. Mother perceptions of early activity management problems on the ICQ (e.g., infant will not stop when into something the mother forbids) from as early as 6 months predict later acting-out problems, but not internalizing problems. Early fearfulness (unadaptability to new people and situations) on the ICQ predicts later internalizing but not acting out. The latter two findings represent straightforward continuity of traits; however, the fact that difficultness predicts both anxiety and aggression calls for some new interpretations of difficultness. We set aside for the time being the interpretation that the effect is simply due to a pervasive, stable bias in the way the mother perceives the child. For reasons mentioned above, we feel that such a global bias is not operating—the mother is seeing her infant's personality in a rather highly differentiated way. Furthermore, the relationship between early mother perceptions and later behavior problems has been found not only in the mother reports of behavior problems, but also in observer impressions of the child in the home at age 4 years (Pettit & Bates, 1984b). The interpretation that we have been pursuing involves the further division of difficultness into subtypes, somewhat analogous to the division of emotionality into fear and anger by A. Buss and Plomin (1984).

We note that there could be different reasons for an infant fussing and crying a lot. One is that the infant is demanding attention and stimulation, and this is indeed a major attribution mothers have for difficultness (Bates et al., 1984). We hypothesize that infants of this sort, as well as infants whose difficultness is accompanied by high activity levels or excitement seeking, would be more likely than other infants to fall into a coercive pattern of social control with others, and thus, according to the theory of Patterson (1982), eventually develop aggressive behavior problems. On the other hand, the infant's fussing could be more reflective of an oversensitivity to minor aversive stimuli or due to frequent fear responses to novel events, both of which would hypothetically reflect tendencies toward anxiety. If we can find effective ways of separating the hypothesized components of difficultness, there is the chance that we will be able to make more precise predictions of risk for behavior problems. At this time, the correlations we and others have found between infant temperament and later behavior problems are much too small to be useful for clinical purposes.

Wolkind and DeSalis (1982) also found that difficult temperament, assessed via mother interviews at age 4 months, predicted behavior problems at 42 months. They further suggested a possible mechanism linking the early temperament and the later behavior problems—mother depression. A number of studies have found mother depression concurrently linked with child behavior problems (Lee, 1983). However, Wolkind and DeSalis found that mother depression and behavior problems co-occurred only if the child had been a difficult infant. They suggest that a difficult baby can in some instances contribute to mother depression. A further finding of difficult temperament in the first 2 years predicting behavior problems in the third year is provided by Swets-Gronert (1984), not only with the ICQ but also with the RITQ. Dunn and Kendrick (1982) found that firstborn children's temperament characteristics (average age of assessment 2 years) predicted the appearance of behavior problems in response to the birth of a sibling. For example, high intensity and negative mood predicted greater increases in worries, rituals, and sleep problems than seen in the average child following the birth of the sibling.

Child abuse and neglect are disorders of family functioning that could have roots in child temperamental difficultness. Vietze and his colleagues have provided prospective data to this effect: In follow-ups of large numbers of families, Vietze, Falsey, Sandler, O'Connor, and Altemeier (1980) and Sherrod, Altemeier, O'Connor, and Vietze (1984) found that ITQ perceptions of difficultness in early infancy made very small but significant contributions to the prediction of maltreatment in the next several years, along with other predictors, including the mother's history and personality and stresses on the family.

In summary, the few studies available suggest that infant temperament might mark future disorders of social adjustment. The predictive power has so far been modest, however, and it is clear that other variables, including moderating characteristics of the child, such as infant's activity level or type of difficultness, and environmental characteristics, such as stressful events and parent psychopathology, must be involved in some way. Further research to identify the best predictors and to model their role in development (e.g., through what parent–child interaction process and whether additive or multiplicative effects) could produce important gains in ability to forecast and ultimately prevent disorders.

Cognitive Development

A final type of socially relevant outcome that temperament could have some impact on is cognitive development. In theory temperament has usually been considered orthogonal to cognitive development, but there are enough studies now to suggest that this notion may be inadequate. Lamb (1982) has reviewed a moderately large set of studies that show that the infant's sociability, that is, reaction to strangers, is correlated with performance on tests of cognitive development, such as the Bayley. Lamb notes that some of the overlap between sociability and test score is due to the friendliness and cooperativeness of the infant during the test, but some may be due to more fundamental differences in competence. Lamb ascribes a portion of the sociability to constitutional origins, suggesting that genetic inheritance probably accounts for a portion of the variance, although some of it may be due to experience such as secure attachment, and much of it is unexplained.

An issue in the literature on sociability and cognitive ability that needs further discussion is the extent to which laboratory measures of sociability, in the sense Lamb uses the term, are reflective of fearfulness of novel situations as opposed to sociability in the sense A. Buss and Plomin use the term. Is the infant's sociability in Lamb's (1982) stranger approach procedure composed primarily of fearfulness or behavioral inhibition, as it appears on the surface, or is it also a strong reflection of the child's enjoyment of responsive interactions with people, as A. Buss and Plomin might say? Answering this question will be part of the construct validation process, and will probably require data that can contrast the infant's characteristics in the laboratory stranger approach situation with those at home and in other situations.

Infant difficultness is another temperament construct that could conceivably account for some test performance. If sociability in the Lamb sense really is mostly fearfulness, then the infant's difficultness as defined by Thomas and Chess might also predict cognitive test scores. Or, in the ICQ definition, perhaps the fussiness–difficultness factor would not predict, while the unadaptability factor, closer to the fearfulness construct, would. However, in our own study neither difficult temperament nor unadaptability has been found directly correlated with developmental test scores. Perhaps our testers were able to adjust their test style to the needs of the infants well enough that they did not have a chance to be frustrated. This is certainly the aim of the developmental testing procedures.

Wachs and Gandour (1981) observed an interesting interaction effect involving difficult temperament as defined by the RITQ. They found that, within the group of easy infants, higher amounts of kinesthetic and emotional stimulation were related to advanced sensorimotor development. However, in the difficult group there were no significant correlations between cognitive development and positive environmental features, but there was a correlation between a negative feature, noise and confusion in the home, and slower sensorimotor development. Wachs and Gandour cite this finding as support of the hypothesis that the effective environment depends on the characteristics of the individual organism.

Other dimensions of temperament might also be related to cognitive performance. Matheny and Brown (1971) found that twins higher in activity level also tended to have lower IQs than less active twins at 4 years of age. Matheny and Brown measured temperament in an interesting way: They asked 56 mothers of twins to compare their twins on a wide range of characteristics at 3, 6, and 9 months. The interview data, consisting of many mother anecdotes for each twin, were combed for subtle distinctions between the twins within a pair. Matheny and Brown's finding was opposite to prior findings they reviewed, in which the more active child was more often superior in cognitive development to the inactive child. They noted additional correlates of activity in their subjects that could account for their finding: The more active twin also tended to have the shorter attention span, as well as being more emotional. Thus the Matheny and Brown finding that infancy activity differences predict IQ differences at age 4 could be an artifact of attention span, but it is instructive nevertheless. It indicates that even in a nondeviant sample of moderate size ($n = 56$), there can be third variables operating in ways that are not

universal. Rutter (1982) has concluded that high activity in infants is a positive predictor in at least one population: Active infants are less likely than inactive ones to
show the slow development that is often seen in cases of institutional deprivation.

A final instance of possible temperament effects on the cognitive functioning of
infants concerns infants who do and do not complete laboratory procedures involving habituation. Habituation procedures are a common tool in studying normative features of infant cognitive development. However, according to two recent
studies, there may be some meaningful differences between those infants who complete testing and those who do not; for example, the noncompleters are more difficult (Trieber, 1984; Wachs & Smitherman, 1985).

To summarize, there appear to be some links between temperamentlike characteristics and cognitive development. Infants who are fearful of novelty as assessed
in the laboratory, and perhaps unattracted by the chance to interact with a responsive examiner, tend to score lower on tests of infant development. Difficultness as
perceived by the parents has not been closely connected to development scores, although it is possible that it may mediate the impact of the environment, with easy
infants being sensitive to the positive stimulation in the environment, and difficult
ones being more sensitive to noxious features. Activity in infancy may either facilitate or retard cognitive development, depending perhaps on the presence of another
temperamentlike feature, attention span, and on the particular range of care in the
environment.

Subjective Factors in Perceptions of Temperament

The most general conclusion that can be drawn about subjective factors in parents'
perceptions of their infants' temperament is that tendencies to endorse negative
statements about oneself are correlated with tendencies to see more negative temperamental traits in one's baby. Anxiety, depression, and related indexes of parent
personality have been found to correlate with temperamental difficultness and other
ratings of infants and young children in a number of studies. Studies have used a
variety of parent personality measures and a variety of infant temperament measures, including the Carey ITQ and RITQ (Daniels et al., 1984; Sameroff et al.,
1982; Vaughn, in press), the Rothbart IBQ (Ventura, 1982), and the ICQ (Bates &
Bayles, 1984; Goldsmith, Reiser-Danner, & Pomerantz, 1983; Kohnstamm, 1984),
and the Pedersen Perceptions of Baby Temperament scales (Affleck et al., 1983).
However, while the effect has been replicated, it has not been any stronger, overall,
than the evidence that there are correlates of the perceptions in observed infant
behavior (Bates & Bayles, 1984).

There have been investigations of other possible subjective factors. In a few studies, parents of lower social class have rated their infants more negatively (Affleck
et al., 1983; Bates et al., 1979), but in other studies, SES has been found to have
little direct relationship to temperament (Bates et al., 1982; Bates & Bayles, 1984;
Persson-Blennow & McNeil, 1981). Sameroff and colleagues (1982) found social
class effects for only two of the nine ITQ scales, with lower-class infants being seen
as having lower threshold of responding to stimuli and more intense responses. This
could represent biased perception, but it could also represent consequences of differences in living conditions. Lower-class families may be more likely than upper-
class families to experience conditions that cause developmental problems in early

infancy, such as excessive drug levels and poor nutrition prenatally, and social disorganization or active rejection after birth. However, it seems that many if not most families in the lower economic levels are doing quite well. They have steady social supports and effective skills for making a living and rearing children. Some samples may draw a heavier proportion of lower-class people who are multiply stressed than other samples of lower-class people. Perhaps sample differences, then, account for differences in the studies. It is reasonable to suppose, for example that the presence of considerable psychopathology in the Rochester sample in contrast to the Bloomington sample could account for the contrast between the SES results of Sameroff and colleagues (1982) and those of Bates and colleagues (1982).

Besides the issue of the direct role social class plays in perceiving temperament, there is the issue of its indirect, interactive effects. Kohnstamm (1985) has found that ICQ temperament scores are not correlated with mother education level (we have a similar finding with SES); however, highly educated mothers' scores on one ICQ factor were more independent of those on another factor, as well as more stable across time, compared with less well educated mothers' scores. In a previously unreported analysis (done in conjunction with Bates et al., 1982), we found that upper-middle-class mothers' ratings on the main ICQ fussy–difficult factor were significantly more highly correlated with the observer record of the fussiness of the baby than the lower-middle-class and working-class mothers' ratings. This finding was reserved because it was one of relatively few interactive effects. However, in the context of the Kohnstamm finding, it suggests a general tendency for the higher SES mother to use the temperament rating scales in a more finely differentiated way than the lower SES mothers.

In other tests for subjective effects, extraverted mothers tended to see their babies as less difficult than introverted mothers in the study by Bates and colleagues (1979), but not in the study by Bates and colleagues (1982). Two studies reported no differences between teenage mothers' perceptions of temperament and other mothers' (Garcia-Coll, Sepkoski, & Lester, 1982; Roosa, Fitzgerald, & Carson, 1982). Campbell, Maloni, and Taylor (1979) found that extended contact with the baby in the early postnatal period did not produce any differences in temperament perceptions at age 8 months compared with the regular amount of postnatal contact.

Wolke and St. James-Roberts (1982) contrasted mother perceptions of their newborns with observer ratings. They found that mothers who had had delivery complications rated their babies as less labile than the observers, while mothers who had had optimum deliveries rated their babies as more labile than observers did. Nover and colleagues (1984) found that mothers who rated their 9-month-olds as more difficult than observers tended to see themselves as more anxious than other mothers. They also tended to be less emotionally responsive and more interfering with their infants' explorations.

Halverson and Martin (1981) reported an intriguing pattern in a large-sample longitudinal study: Where mothers had a stable concept of their maternal competence and confidence from the newlywed era onward, their infants were observed to be unstable in their observed activity and irritability from 3 months to 3 years, and the activity–irritability of the child was uncorrelated with the mother's self-concept. However, where mothers were unstable in their self-concept, the child's activity–irritability was highly stable and was well correlated with the mother's confidence at 3 years, even from age 3 months. Halverson and Martin interpret the findings as evidence that mothers with unstable self-concepts are susceptible to control by their infants' activity–irritability characteristics, whereas stable self-concept mothers control the infants' characteristics. In the Halverson and Martin paper, it is not clear whether stable self-concept was always a good sign. Is it possible that the effect differs according to whether a mother has a stable positive or negative self-concept? At the least, however, the study is a start on the kind of research that Sroufe (1985) is calling for, in which we might see the child and the mother shaping each other from the first days.

To conclude, the evidence suggests that characteristics of the parent may affect the perception of the child's temperament, especially in the case of negative emotionality. The parent high in emotionality tends to perceive the child in a similar way. However, the meaning of the correlations between possible subjective factors and temperament is unclear. On the one hand, it makes sense to consider the source of any characterization of a child, and perhaps one could use parental personality and social background as correction factors in producing a "truer" picture of the child (cf. Vaughn, 1983). On the other hand, however, the typical overlap between subjective factors and temperament is small, and in one study where objective and subjective factors were compared, the subjective factors did not outweigh the objective factors (Bates & Bayles, 1984).

Furthermore, the fact that parent characteristics correlate with perceptions of the child does not automatically imply a misleading, useless bias in the temperament report. In fact, there are logical grounds to expect that some of the overlap has an objective basis. For one thing, the parent's personality might affect how one treats the infant, which could shape the child's characteristics. We are interested in the child's characteristics, even if they do not come directly from constitutional sources. For example, Crockenberg (1982) found that mothers with responsive attitudes had infants who were less difficult than mothers with unresponsive attitudes (see above discussion of Crockenberg's position on the maternal contributions to the negative emotionality of infants). The study by Nover and colleagues (1984) may be an example of the same process. Another way in which the overlap between parent characteristics and perceptions of the infant could have an objective basis is through genetic inheritance. It is quite reasonable that parents who see themselves as anxious, for example, have passed on some of the same trait to their children.

Therefore, while subjective factors are quite likely to act as a filter through which the child is perceived, they should not be regarded as merely a source of bias and error variance. They may reflect possible contributions to the personality development of the child through both genetic and parent–child interaction processes. Questions about such processes are fertile grounds for collaboration with areas outside the usual realm of child development research, including social psychology (particularly relevant sources are Darley & Fazio, 1980; Schneider, Hastorff, & Ellsworth, 1979) and behavior genetics (Plomin, Chapter 7, this volume).

Other Issues in Temperament Research

The next three issues will be merely introduced. This priority should not be taken to indicate that they are unimportant issues. I hope to turn to them in more detail in later work, and look for more integrative summaries from greater experts in the areas.

Culture

Very little research relevant to cultural aspects of temperament has appeared in abstracted sources, but the topic has been a common one in other forms of scientific discussion (e.g., Super & Harkness, 1986). Three generalizations seem justified so far. First, parent report infant temperament questionnaires have been translated successfully not only to European but also to Oriental and African languages (e.g., DeVries & Sameroff, 1984; Hsu et al., 1981).

Second, it is also possible that distributions of temperament traits are not identical in all populations. For example, Banks (1981) asserted that Malay parents were similar in many respects to western parents in their temperament ratings, except for one clear difference: Malay children are expected to be sensitive to dirt and uncomfortable clothes and are seen as more sensitive to stimulation that the average U.S. child. DeVries and Sameroff (1984) concluded from a study of infants from three East African groups that the "hypothesis that temperament is influenced by infant experiential factors is strongly supported by our data. The most important factor in producing different infant scores was cultural affiliation" (p. 95). For example, the fact that boys were more difficult in one group of 48 infants is largely attributed to their tribe's patrilineality, whereas the fact that girls were the more difficult in a second group ($n = 53$) is largely credited to this tribe's matrilineal organization. This interpretation should not be fully accepted without replication of the group differences and further description of the societies. There are a great many other important differences among the three tribes that cross-cut the variable of form of descent (M. B. Kendall, personal communication, 1984) and that could provide alternative explanations of the pattern of temperament differences in the event that it does replicate in new samples.

The topic of possible racial differences in temperament variables has not been addressed in this chapter. Well-understood differences between racial groups could contribute to appreciation of the constitutional, psychobiological aspects of temperament. Freedman (1974) argues that there are Oriental versus Caucasian differences in temperament; however, Chisholm (1981) disputes the generality of this on the basis of his recent study in Australia. He replicated Freedman's differences, for example, in oriental newborns being less irritable and more easily soothed, in his study of aboriginal versus white infants. However he found a third variable, not directly related to race, accounted for the effect better than race—aboriginal group mothers had lower blood pressure than white mothers.

The final generalization, implied in the discussion of the second point, is that the cultural differences that have been discussed so far are not well established empirically, nor have the ethnological, ecological, and gene pool bases of the differences been convincingly detailed.

Biological Factors

The work on biological factors in temperament has been much more intensive than the cross-cultural work. There is probably enough research in the area that a reviewer well grounded in biological theory could draw some interesting conclusions. The present chapter will merely mention some of the directions the area is taking. First is of course the behavior genetics area (Plomin, Chapter 7, this volume). As mentioned earlier, behavior geneticists have been moving toward the identification of heritability factors in widely used temperament variables, and perhaps even toward the identification of specific mechanisms of inheritance.

Second, there is a growing body of pediatric studies (Carey, 1984) that suggests physiological bases for some temperament characteristics. Weissbluth's group has been a particularly active contributor to this approach in recent years. Weissbluth and his colleagues have found that, even in normal infants, infants with higher intensity and lower sensory threshold (on the RITQ) tend to score lower on indexes of apneic breathing (Weissbluth et al., 1984). In a related way, Carey (1984) argues that low threshold may be an intrinsic factor in infantile colic.

Temperament may play a role in the health of the infant (Carey, 1984). Weissbluth (1982), for example, includes temperament along with other factors in a model of sudden infant death syndrome. To summarize simply an elegantly complex model, Weissbluth suggests that infants who are at risk for SIDS have congenital deficits in respiratory control that cause elevation in progesterone levels as a means of stimulating breathing. This elevation of progesterone may dull the CNS protective reaction to asphyxiation, making the infant less likely to wake. The disappearance of colic in such infants might be an advance signal of the action of progesterone. Temperament can serve a protective function, in that intense, difficult infants are less likely to die from their congenital problems, even if they do have near-miss episodes of apnea.

Third, there is a psychophysiological tradition, exemplified by Kagan and his colleagues. Garcia-Coll and colleagues (1984), discussed earlier, have suggested a particularly interesting sympathetic versus parasympathetic nervous system process in accounting for some individual differences in children's fearfulness in response to strangers.

Risk and Handicap Conditions

There are at least 20 articles published on temperament in samples of infants with risk or handicap conditions. The pattern of results in the articles I have seen is complex. A few examples include Heffernan, Black, and Poche (1982), who studied a mixed group of young children with neurological problems, including Down's, CP, and epilepsy. This group did not differ significantly from the norms for difficultness on the Toddler Temperament Scale of Fullard and colleagues (1978), but they were lower in activity and persistence. Bridges and Cicchetti (1982) found Down's Syndrome infants to be more difficult than the ITQ norms, and Rothbart and Hanson (1983) got similar findings with the IBQ. Like the biological factors area, the risk area might be ripe for a systematic review of the wide array of data.

SUMMARY AND CONCLUSION

The chapter supports several generalizations about the large and rapidly growing body of literature on temperament in infants. First, there is disagreement about how temperament is to be defined in both abstract and operational ways. However, there is some convergence on temperament as early appearing, somewhat stable traits of the child's behavior that have a constitutional basis. There is also some convergence on a short list of temperament qualities that capture the major dimensions researchers are currently interested in, including the negative emotionality concepts of difficultness and anger and fearfulness of novelty, and the activity and sociability concepts. It is not assumed that this is a definitive list. To some extent our interests as researchers are shaped by the social and philosophical purposes we have for seeking knowledge about temperament. Basic researchers may be interested in different construals of behavior than clinical researchers, and there may be subinterests within the broader groups, for example, the kind of clinical population a researcher is interested in understanding. Such differences in aim make it likely that there will continue to be diverse ways of describing the earliest personality of the child.

Second, operational definitions of temperament, including observational and parent perceptual measures, have demonstrated validity on a wide scale, but validity is a very big question, and much remains to be answered. Temperament measures bear some relation to the observable behavior of the infant. However, they also bear some relation to long-standing characteristics of the parent, as has been fairly well established, and to the observable interaction of the child with the family, which has been less well established. For at least the near future, we must contend, therefore, with ambiguity in the meaning of temperament measures regarding their linkage to the more basic concepts of temperament as hypotheses.

Third, temperament measures in the first and second years have shown some systematic correlations with measures of possible significance for social adaptation. Behavior problems are predicted, with a firm foundation in theory, by temperament indexes. Cognitive development is also predicted, but in a less clear and theoretically well-grounded pattern at the moment.

Fourth, temperament measures show theoretically understandable effects in psychobiological and genetic studies; for instance, extremes of fearfulness of strangers are linked to specific patterns of psychophysiological responses, or, to give another example, fearfulness shows evidence of genetic heritability.

To conclude, despite their conceptual difficulties, temperament concepts are evidently quite useful to early developmental theoreticians, researchers, and clinicians. Clearly, the process of construct validation will continue. Temperament is one of the important threads we are weaving into the theoretical tapestry of early development.

REFERENCES

Affleck, G., Allen, D. A., McGrade, B. J., & McQueeny, M. (1983). Maternal & child characteristics associated with mothers' perceptions of their high risk/developmentally delayed infants. *Journal of Genetic Psychology, 142,* 171–180.

Ainsworth, M. D. S., Blehar, M. C., Waters, E., & Wall, S. (1978). *Patterns of attachment: A psychological study of the Strange Situation.* Hillsdale, NJ: Erlbaum.

Banks, E. (1981, April). *Malay childhood, temperament, and individuality.* Paper presented at Society for Research in Child Development meeting, Boston.

Barkley, R. A., & Cunningham, C. E. (1979). The effects of methylphenidate on the mother–child interactions of hyperactive children. *Archives of General Psychiatry, 36,* 201–208.

Bates, J. E. (1986). The measurement of temperament. In R. Plomin & J. Dunn (Eds.), *The study of temperament: Changes, continuities, and challenges.* Hillsdale, NJ: Erlbaum.

Bates, J. E. (1983). Issues in the assessment of difficult temperament: A reply to Thomas, Chess, and Korn. *Merrill-Palmer Quarterly, 29*(1), 89–97.

Bates, J. E. (1980). The concept of difficult temperament. *Merrill-Palmer Quarterly, 26*(4), 299–319.

Bates, J. E., & Bayles, K. (1984). Objective and subjective components in mothers' perceptions of their children from age 6 months to 3 years. *Merrill-Palmer Quarterly, 30*(2), 111–130.

Bates, J. E., Freeland, C. A. B., & Lounsbury, M. L. (1979). Measurement of infant difficultness. *Child Development, 50,* 794–803.

Bates, J. E., Maslin, C. A., & Frankel, K. A. (1985). Attachment security, mother–child interaction, and temperament as predictors of behavior problem ratings at age three years. In I. Bretherton & E. Waters (Eds.), *SRCD Monographs Special Issue.*

Bates, J. E., Miller E. M., & Bayles, K. (1984, April). *Understanding the link between difficult temperament and behavior problems: Toward identifying subtypes of difficultness.* Paper presented at International Conference on Infant Studies, New York.

Bates, J. E., Olson, S. L., Pettit, G. S., & Bayles, K. (1982). Dimensions of individuality in the mother–infant relationship at 6 months of age. *Child Development, 53,* 446–461.

Bates, J. E., Pettit, G. S., & Bayles, K. (1985, April). *Infancy and preschool antecedents of behavior problems at 5 years.* Paper presented at the biennial meeting of the Society for Research in Child Development, Toronto.

Bell, R. Q. (1979). Parent, child, and reciprocal influences. *American Psychologist, 34,* 821–826.

Belsky, J., Rovine, M., & Taylor, D. G. (1984). The Pennsylvania infant and family development project, III. The origins of individual differences in infant–mother attachment: Maternal and infant contributions. *Child Development, 55,* 718–728.

Bennett, L. (1971). Infant–caretaker interactions. *Journal of the American Academy of Child Psychiatry, 10,* 321–334.

Berberian, K. E., & Snyder, F. F. (1982). The relationship of temperament and stranger reaction for younger and older infants. *Merrill-Palmer Quarterly, 28,* 79–94.

Bornstein, M. H., Gaughran, J., & Homel, P. (1984). Infant temperament: Tradition, critique, new assessments, and prolegomena to future studies. In C. Izard, & P. B. Read (Eds.), *Measurement of emotions in infants and children,* Vol. 2, New York: Cambridge University Press.

Bridges, F. A., Cicchetti, D. (1982). Mothers' ratings of the temperament characteristics of Down syndrome infants. *Developmental Psychology, 18,* 238–244.

Bronfenbrenner, U. (1979). Contexts of child rearing: Problems and Prospects. *American Psychologist, 34*(10), 844–850.

Boukydis, C. Z., & Burgess, R. L. (1982). Adult physiological response to infant cries: Effects of temperament of infant, parental status, and gender. *Child Development, 53,* 1291–1298.

Burg, C., Quinn, P. O., & Rapoport, J. L. (1978). Clinical evaluation of one-year-old infants: Possible predictors of risk for the "hyperactivity syndrome." *Journal of Pediatric Psychology, 3,* 164–167.

Buss, A. H., & Plomin, R. (1984). *Temperament: Early developing personality traits.* Hillsdale, NJ: Erlbaum.

Buss, A. H., & Plomin, R. (1975). *A temperament theory of personality development.* New York: Wiley.

Buss, D. M. (1981). Predicting parent–child interactions from children's activity level. *Developmental Psychology, 17,* 59–65.

Cameron, J. R. (1978). Parental treatment, children's temperament, and the risk of childhood behavioral problems: 2. Initial temperament, parental attitudes, and the incidence and form of behavioral problems. *American Journal of Orthopsychiatry, 48,* 140–147.

Campbell, S. B. (1979). Mother–infant interaction as a function of maternal ratings of temperament. *Child Psychiatry & Human Development, 10,* 67–76.

Campbell, S. B. G., Maloni, J., & Taylor, P. M. (1979, March). *Early contact and maternal perceptions of infant temperament.* Paper presented at the meeting of the Society for Research in Child Development, San Francisco.

Carey, W. B. (1984a, March). *Clinical interactions of temperament.* Presentation to Fifth Occasional Temperament Conference, Keystone, CO.

Carey, W. B. (1984b). "Colic": Primary excessive crying as an infant environment interaction. *Pediatric Clinics of North America, 31,* 993–1005.

Carey, W. B., Fox, M., & McDevitt, S. C. (1977). Temperament as a factor in early school adjustment. *Pediatrics, 60,* 621–624.

Carey, W. B., & McDevitt, S. C. (1978). Revision of the infant temperament questionnaire. *Pediatrics, 61,* 735–739.

Chisholm, J. S. (1981). Prenatal influences on aboriginal-white Australian differences in neonatal irritability. *Ethology & Sociobiology, 2,* 67–73.

Clarke-Stewart, K. A. (1973). Interactions between mothers and their young children: Characteristics and consequences. *Monographs of the Society for Research in Child Development, 38* (Serial No. 153).

Crockenberg, S. (1982). English teenage mothers: Attitudes, behavior, and social support. Unpublished manuscript.

Crockenberg, S. (in press). Are temperamental differences in babies associated with predictable differences in caregiving? In J. V. Lerner & R. M. Lerner (Eds.), "Temperament and psychosocial interaction in childhood," part of the series *New Directions for Child Development.*

Crockenberg, S., & Acredolo, C. (1983). Infant temperament ratings: A function of infants, or mothers, or both? *Infant Behavior & Development, 6,* 61–72.

Crockenberg, S. B., & Smith, P. (1982). Antecedents of mother–infant interaction and infant irritability in the first three months of life. *Infant Behavior & Development, 5,* 105–119.

Daniels, D., Plomin, R., & Greenhalgh, J. (1984). Correlates of difficult temperament in infancy. *Child Development, 55,* 1184–1194.

Darley, J. M., & Fazio, R. H. (1980). Expectancy confirmation processes arising in the social interaction sequence. *American Psychologist, 35,* 867–881.

DeVries, M. W., & Sameroff, A. J. (1984). Culture and temperament: Influences on infant temperament in three East African societies. *American Journal of Orthopsychiatry, 54,* 83–96.

Dunn, J., & Kendrick, C. (1982). Temperamental differences, family relationships, and young children's response to change within the family. In R. Porter & G. M. Collins (Eds.), Ciba Foundation Symposium 89, *Temperamental differences in infants and young children.* London: Pitman.

Easterbrooks, M. A., & Emde, R. N. (1984). Marriage and infant: Different systems linkages for mothers and fathers. Unpulished manuscript.

Egeland, B., & Farber, E. (1984). Infant–mother attachment: Factors related to its development over time. *Child Development, 55,* 753–771.

Feinman, S., & Lewis, M. (1983). Social referencing at ten months: A second-order effect on infants' response to strangers. *Child Development, 54*(4), 878–887.

Feiring, C., & Lewis, M. (1980). Temperament: Sex differences and stability in vigor, activity, and persistence in the first three years of life. *Journal of Genetic Psychology, 136,* 65–75.

Field, T. M., & Greenberg, R. (1982). Temperament ratings by parents and teachers of infants, toddlers, and preschool children. *Child Development, 53,* 160–163.

Field, T. M., Widmayer, S. M., Stringer, S., & Ignatoff, E. (1980). Teenage, lower class, black mothers and their preterm infants: An intervention and developmental follow-up. *Child Development, 51,* 426–436.

Fish, M., & Crockenberg, S. (1981). Correlates and antecedents of nine-month infant behavior and mother–infant interaction. *Infant Behavior & Development, 4,* 69–81.

Frankel, K. A., & Bates, J. E. (1985). Continuity in the mother–child relationship from infant attachment to toddler competence: Further validation of a tool problems test. Unpublished manuscript, Indiana University, Department of Psychology.

Freedman, D. G. (1974). *Human infancy: An evolutionary perspective.* Hillsdale, N.J.: Erlbaum.

Frodi, A. M. (1983). Attachment behavior and sociability with strangers in premature and full-term infants. *Infant Mental Health Journal, 4,* 13–22.

Fullard, W., McDevitt, S., & Carey, W. (1978). *The Toddler Temperament Scale.* Unpublished test form.

Garcia-Coll, C., Kagan, J., & Reznick, J. S. (1984). Behavioral inhibition in young children. *Child Development, 55,* 1005–1019.

Garcia-Coll, C., Sepkoski, C., & Lester, B. M. (1982). Effects of teenage childbearing on neonatal and infant behavior in Puerto Rico. *Infant Behavior & Development, 5,* 227–236.

Goldsmith, H. H. (1983). Genetic influences on personality from infancy to adulthood. *Child Development, 54,* 331–355.

Goldsmith, H. H., & Campos, J. J. (1982). Toward a theory of infant temperament. In R. N. Emde & R. Harmon (Eds.), *The development of attachment and affiliative systems.* New York: Plenum.

Goldsmith, H. H., & Gottesman, I. I. (1981). Origins of variation in behavioral style: A longitudinal study of temperament in young twins. *Child Development, 52,* 91–103.

Goldsmith, H., Reiser-Danner, L., & Pomerantz, S. (1983, April). *Maternal attitude structure as a contributor to the development of temperament.* Paper presented at meeting of Southwestern Psychological Association, San Antonio.

Goldsmith, H. H., & Rieser-Danner, L. (1984, April). The objective assessment of temperament: LAB-TAB and VIDEO-TAB. In M. K. Rothbart, *Developmental perspectives on infant temperament.* Symposium conducted at the International Conference on Infant Studies, New York.

Gordon, B. M. (1983). Maternal perception of child temperament and observed mother-child interaction. *Child Psychiatry & Human Development, 13,* 153–167.

Hagekull, B., & Bohlin, G. (1981). Individual stability in dimensions of infant behavior. *Infant Behavior & Development, 4,* 97–108.

Hagekull, B., Bohlin, G., & Lindhagen, K. (1984). *Validity of parental reports. Infant Behavior & Development, 7,* 77–99.

Hagekull, B., Lindhagen, K., & Bohlin, G. (1980). Behavioral dimensions in one-year-olds and dimensional stability in infancy. *International Journal of Behavioral Development, 3,* 351–364.

Halverson, C. F., & Martin, C. L. (1981, April). *Parent–child stability over time.* Paper presented at the meeting of the Society for Research in Child Development, Boston.

Halverson, C. F., Jr., Moss, H. A., & Kearns, S. J. (1977, March). *Longitudinal antecedents of preschool social behavior.* Paper presented at convention of Society for Research in Child Development, New Orleans.

Heffernan, L., Black, F. W., & Poche, P. (1982). Temperament patterns in young neurologically impaired children. *Journal of Pediatric Psychology, 7,* 415–423.

Hsu, C., Soong, W., Stigler, J. W., Hong, C., & Liang, C. (1981). The temperamental characteristics of Chinese babies. *Child Development, 52,* 1337–1340.

Hubert, N. C., Wachs, T. D., Peters-Martin, P., & Gandour, J. (1982). The study of early temperament: Measurement and conceptual issues. *Child Development, 53,* 571–600.

Huitt, W. G., & Ashton, P. T. (1982). Parents' perception of infant temperament: A psychometric study. *Merrill-Palmer Quarterly, 28,* 95–109.

Kagan, J. (1982). *Psychological research on the human infant: An evaluative summary.* New York: W. T. Grant Foundation.

Kagan, J. (1983). Stress and coping in early development. In N. Garmezy & M. Rutter (Eds.), *Stress, coping, and development in children.* New York: McGraw-Hill.

Kiser, L. J., Bates, J. E., Maslin, C. A., & Bayles, K. (1986). Mother–infant play at six months as a predictor of attachment security at thirteen months. *Journal of the American Academy of Child Psychiatry, 25,* 68–75.

Klein, P. S. (1984). Behavior of Israeli mothers toward infants in relation to infants' perceived temperament. *Child Development, 55,* 1212–1218.

Kohnstamm, G. A. (1984). Bates' Infant Characteristics Questionnaire (ICQ) in the Netherlands. Paper presented at International Conference on Infant Studies, New York, April.

Kohnstamm, G. A. (1985). Some new results obtained with the Dutch translation of the ICQ. Prepared for Workshop on Temperament and Development, Leiden, July.

Kronstadt, D., Oberklaid, F., Ferb, T. E., & Swartz, J. P. (1979). Infant behavior and maternal adaptation in the first six months of life. *American Journal of Orthopsychiatry, 49,* 454–464.

Lamb, M. E. (1982). Individual differences in infant sociability: Their origins and implications for cognitive development. In H. W. Reese & L. P. Lipsett (Eds.), *Advances in child development and behavior* (Vol. 16). New York: Academic.

Lamb, M., Thompson, R. A., Gardner, W., & Charnov, E. L. (1985). *Infant–mother attachment.* Hillsdale, N.J.: Erlbaum.

Lee, C. (1983). *Adult characteristics and their relationship to teaching/disciplinary strategies with compliant and noncompliant children.* Doctoral dissertation, Indiana University.

Lee, C., & Bates, J. (1985). Mother–child interaction at age two years and perceived difficult temperament. *Child Development, 56,* 1314–1325.

Lemly, E. B., & Schwarz, J. C. (1979, March). *Temperament and child rearing antecedents of two-year-olds' reactions to male & female strangers.* Paper presented at Society for Research in Child Development, San Francisco.

Lerner, J. V., & Lerner, R. M. (1983). Temperament and adaptation across life: Theoretical and empirical issues. In P. B. Baltes & O. G. Brim (Eds.), *Life-span development and behavior* (Vol. 5). New York: Academic.

Lounsbury, M. L., & Bates, J. E. (1982). The cries of infants of differing levels of perceived temperamental difficultness: Acoustic properties and effects on listeners. *Child Development, 53,* 677–686.

Maccoby, E. E., Snow, M. E., & Jacklin, C. N. (1984). Children's dispositions and mother–child interaction at 12 and 18 months: A short-term longitudinal study. *Developmental Psychology, 20,* 459–472.

MacPhee, D. (1983, April). *What do ratings of infant temperament really measure?* Paper presented at Society for Research in Child Development, Detroit.

Matheny, A. P. (1983). A longitudinal twin study of stability of components from Bayley's Infant Behavior Record. *Child Development, 54,* 356–360.

Matheny, A. P., & Brown, A. M. (1971). Activity, motor-coordination and attention: Individual differences in twins. *Perceptual & Motor Skills, 32,* 151–158.

Matheny, A. P., Wilson, R. S., & Nuss, S. M. (1984). Toddler temperament: Stability across settings and over ages. *Child Development, 55,* 1200–1211.

Maziade, M., Boudreault, M., Thivierge, J., Capéraà, P., & Coté, R. (1984). Infant temperament: SES and gender differences and reliability of measurement in a large Quebec sample. *Merrill-Palmer Quarterly, 30,* 213–226.

McDevitt, S. C., & Carey, W. B. (1981). Stability of ratings versus perceptions of temperament from early infancy to 1–3 years. *American Journal of Orthopsychiatry, 51*(2), 342–345.

NcNeil, T. F. (1976). *Temperament revisited: A research-oriented critique of the New York longitudinal study of temperament.* Unpublished manuscript, University of Lund, Sweden.

Milliones, J. (1978). Relationship between perceived child temperament and maternal behaviors. *Child Development, 49,*1255–1257.

Minuchin, S., & Fishman, H. C. (1981). *Family Therapy Techniques.* Cambridge: Harvard University Press.

Nover, A., Shore, M. F., Timberlake, E. M., & Greenspan, S. I. (1984). The relationship of maternal perception and maternal behavior: A study of normal mothers and their infants. *American Journal of Orthopsychiatry, 54,* 210–223.

Olson, S. L., Bates, J. E., & Bayles, K. (1984). Mother–infant interaction and the development of individual differences in children's cognitive competence. *Developmental Psychology, 20,* 166–179.

Olson, S. L., Bates, J. E., & Bayles, K. (1982). Maternal perceptions of infant and toddler behavior: A longitudinal construct validation study. *Infant Behavior & Development, 5,* 397–410.

Parke, R. D. (1978). Parent–infant interaction: Progress, paradigms and problems. In G. P. Sackett (Ed.), *Observing behavior (Vol. 1): Theory and applications in mental retardation.* Baltimore: University Park Press.

Patterson, G. (1982). *Coercive family process.* Eugene, OR: Castilia.

Pedersen, F. A., Anderson, B. J., & Cain, R. L., Jr. (1976, April). *A methodology for assessing parental perception of infant temperament.* Paper presented at the Southeastern Conference on Human Development, Nashville.

Persson-Blennow, I., & McNeil, T. F. (1981). Temperament characteristics of children in relation to gender, birth order, and social class. *American Journal of Orthopsychiatry, 51* (4), 710–714.

Persson-Blennow, I., & McNeil, T. F. (1982). Factor analysis of temperament characteristics in children at 6 months, 1 year and 2 years of age. *British Journal of Educational Psychology, 52,* 51–57.

Pettit, G. S., & Bates, J. E. (1984a). Continuity of individual differences in the mother–infant relationship from 6 to 13 months. *Child Development, 55,* 729–739.

Pettit, G. S., & Bates, J. E. (1984b). An age 4 year follow-up of infants and their families. Presented at International Conference on Infant Studies, New York, April.

Plomin, R. (1982). Childhood temperament. In B. Lahey & A. Kazdin (Eds.), *Advances in clinical child psychology* (Vol. 6). New York: Plenum.

Plomin, R. (1985). Developmental behavioral genetics and infancy. In J. D. Osofsky (Ed.), *Handbook of infant development* (2nd ed.). New York: Wiley

Plomin, R., Defries, J. C., & McClearn, G. E. (1980). *Behavioral genetics: a primer.* San Francisco: Freeman.

Quay, H. C. (1979). Classification. In H. C. Quay & J. S. Werry (Eds.), *Psychopathological disorders of childhood*. New York: Wiley.

Rapoport, J. L., Pandari, C., Renfield, M., Lake, C. R., & Ziegler, M. G. (1977). Newborn dopamine-beta-hydroxylase, minor physical anomalies, and infant temperament. *American Journal of Psychiatry, 134,* 676-679.

Rendina, I. & Dickersheid, J. D. (1976). Father involvement with first-born infants. *Family Coordinator, 25,* 373-378.

Roosa, M. W., Fitzgerald, H. E., & Carson, N. A. (1982). Teenage and older mothers and their infants: A descriptive comparison. *Adolescence, 17,* 1-17.

Rosenblith, J. F. (1974). Relations between neonatal behaviors and those at eight months. *Developmental Psychology, 10,* 779-792.

Rothbart, M. K. (1983). Longitudinal observation of infant temperament. Unpublished manuscript, University of Oregon, Department of Psychology.

Rothbart, M. K. (1980, April). *Longitudinal home observation of infant temperament.* Paper presented at International Conference on Infant Studies, New Haven.

Rothbart, M. K. (1981). Measurement of temperament in infancy. *Child Development, 52,* 569-578.

Rothbart, M. K., & Derryberry, D. (1981). Development of individual differences in temperament. In M. E. Lamb (Ed.), *Advances in developmental psychology* (Vol. 1). Hillsdale, NJ: Erlbaum.

Rothbart, M. K., & Hanson, M. J. (1983). A caregiver report comparison of temperamental characteristics of Down syndrome and normal infants. *Developmental Psychology, 19,* 766-769.

Rutter, M. (1983). Stress, coping and development: Some issues and some questions. In N. Garmezy & M. Rutter (Eds.), *Stress, coping and development in children*. New York: McGraw-Hill.

Sackett, G. P., & Ruppenthal, G. C. (1974). Some factors influencing the attraction of adult female macaque monkeys to neonates. In M. Lewis & L. A. Rosenblum (Eds.), *The effect of the infant on its caregiver*. New York: Wiley.

Sameroff, A. J. (1978). Organization and stability of newborn behavior: A commentary on the Brazelton Neonatal Behavior Assessment Scale. *Monographs of the Society for Research in Child Development, 43,* (5-6).

Sameroff, A. J. (1982). Development and the dialectic: The need for a systems approach. In W. A. Collins (Ed.), *Minnesota Symposia on Child Psychology* (Vol. 15). Hillsdale, NJ: Erlbaum.

Sameroff, A. J., Seifer, R., & Elias, P. K. (1982). Sociocultural variability in infant temperament ratings. *Child Development, 53,* 164-173.

Sander, L. W. (1976). Issues in early mother–child interaction. In E. N. Rexford, L. W. Sander, & T. Shapiro (Eds.), *Infant psychiatry: A new synthesis*. New Haven: Yale University Press.

Schneider, D. J., Hastorf, A. H., & Ellsworth, P. C. (1979). *Person perception* (2nd ed.). Reading, MA: Addison-Wesley.

Sherrod, K. B., Altemeier, W. A., O'Connor, L., & Vietze, P. M. (1984). Early prediction of child maltreatment. *Early Child Development & Care, 13,* 335-350.

Snow, M. E., Jacklin, C. N., & Maccoby, E. E. (1980). Crying episodes and sleep-wakefulness transitions in the first 26 months of life. *Infant Behavior & Development, 3,* 387-394.

Sroufe, L. A. (1983). Individual patterns of adaptation from infancy to preschool. In M. Perlmutter (Ed.), *Minnesota Symposia on Child Psychology* (Vol. 16). Hillsdale, NJ: Erlbaum.

Sroufe, L. A. (1979). Socioemotional development. In J. D. Osofsky (Ed.), *Handbook of infant development.* New York: Wiley.

Sroufe, L. A. (1985). Attachment classification from the perspective of infant–caregiver relationships and infant temperament. *Child Development, 56,* 1–14.

Sroufe, L. A., & Fleeson, J. (in press). Attachment and the construction of relationships. In W. W. Hartup & Z. Rubin (Eds.), *Relationships and development.* Hillsdale, NJ: Erlbaum.

Stevenson, M. B., & Leavitt, L. A. (1980, April). *Associations among temperament, sociability, and social experience in one-year-olds.* Paper presented at International Conference on Infant Studies, New Haven.

Stevenson-Hinde, J., & Hinde, R. A. (1986). Changes in associations between characteristics and interactions. In R. Plomin & J. Dunn (Eds.), *The study of temperament: Changes, continuities and challenges.* Hillsdale, NJ: Erlbaum.

St. James-Roberts, I., & Wolke, D. (1984). Toward a systems theory of infant temperament. Paper presented at International Conference on Infant Studies, New York, April.

Super, C. M., & Harkness, S. (1986). Temperament, development and culture. In R. Plomin & J. Dunn (Eds.), *The study of temperament: Changes, continuities and challenges.* Hillsdale, NJ: Erlbaum.

Swets-Gronert, F. (1984, August). *Temperament in young children.* Paper presented at European Conference on Development Psychology, Groningen, the Netherlands.

Thomas, A., Chess, S., Birch, H. G. (1968). *Temperament and behavior disorders in children.* New York: New York University Press.

Thomas, A., & Chess, S. (1984). Genesis and evolution of behavior disorders: From infancy to early adult life. *American Journal of Psychiatry, 141,* 1–9.

Thomas, A., & Chess, S. (1977). *Temperament and development.* New York: Brunner/Mazel.

Thompson, R. A., & Lamb, M. E. (1982). Stranger sociability and its relationships to temperament and social experience in the second year. *Infant Behavior & Development, 5,* 277–287.

Trieber, F. A. (1984). Temperament differences between infants who do and do not complete laboratory testing. *Journal of Psychology, 116,* 95–99.

Vaughn, B. E. (1983, April). *Maternal personality variables measured prenatally predict perceptions of infant temperament.* Paper presented at the biennial meeting of the Society for Research for Child Development, Detroit.

Vaughn, B. E., Taraldson, B. J., Crichton, L., & Egeland, B. (1981). The assessment of infant temperament: A critique of the Carey Infant Temperament Questionnaire. *Infant Behavior & Development, 4,* 1–17.

Ventura, J. N. (1982). Parent coping behaviors, parent functioning, and infant temperament characteristics. *Nursing Research, 31,* 269–273.

Vietze, P., Falsey, S., Sandler, H., O'Connor, S., & Altemeier, W. A. (1980). Transactional approach to prediction of child maltreatment. *Infant Mental Health Journal, 1,* 248–261.

Wachs, T. D., & Gandour, M. J. (1983). Temperament, environment, and six-month cognitive-intellectual development: A test of the organismic specificity hypothesis. *International Journal of Behavioral Development, 6,* 135–152.

Wachs, T. D., & Smitherman, C. (1985). Infant and subject loss in an habituation procedure. *Child Development, 56,* 861–867.

Watson, D., & Clark, L. A. (1984). Negative affectivity: The disposition to experience aversive emotional states. *Psychological Bulletin, 96* (3), 465–490.

Weber, R. A., Levitt, M. J., & Clark M. C. (1984, April). *Maternal and infant temperament as predictors of attachment security and Strange Situation behavior.* Paper presented at the International Conference on Infancy Studies, New York.

Weissbluth, M. (1982). Plasma progesterone levels, infant temperament, arousals from sleep, and the sudden infant death syndrome. *Medical Hypotheses, 9,* 215–222.

Weissbluth, M., Hunt, C. E., Brouillette, R. T., Hanson, D., David, R. J., & Stein, J. M. (1984). *Respiratory patterns during sleep and temperament ratings in normal infant.* Unpublished manuscript, Children's Memorial Hospital, Chicago.

Wiggins, J. S. (1973). *Personality and prediction.* Reading, MA: Addison.

Wilson, R. S., & Matheny, A. P. (1984). Behavior genetics research in infant temperament. In R. Plomin & J. Dunn (Eds.), *The study of temperament: Changes, continuities, and challenges.* Hillsdale, NJ: Erlbaum.

Wilson, R. S., & Matheny, A. P. (1983). Assessment of temperament in infant twins. *Developmental Psychology, 19,* 172–183.

Wolke, D., & St. James-Roberts, I. (1984, April). *Multi-method measurement of the mother-infant system in the first 6 weeks of life.* Paper presented at International Conference on Infant Studies, New York.

Wolke, D., & St. James-Roberts, I. (1983). The influence of pre-, peri- and postnatal variables on newborn behavior: The development of a research instrument. In G. Luer (Ed.), *Bericht uber den 33.* Kongress der DGFPs. Bern: Huber.

Wolkind, S. N., & DeSalis, W. (1982). Infant temperament, maternal mental state and child behavior problems. In R. Porter & G. M. Collins (Eds.), Ciba Foundation Symposium 89, *Temperament differences in young children.* London: Pitman.

Worobey, J. (1984, April). *Temperament ratings in infancy: The saliency of perceived difficulty.* Paper presented at International Conference on Infant Studies, New York.

Yang, R., & Halverson, C. (1976). A study of the "inversion of intensity" between newborn and preschool-age behavior. *Child Development, 47,* 350–359.

Yang, R. K., & Moss, H. A. (1978). Neonatal precursors of infant behavior. *Developmental Psychology, 14,* 607–613.

CHAPTER 24

Perspectives on Infancy

JEROME KAGAN

A comparison of the chapters from the first edition of this handbook with the current set provides a remarkably informative picture of the dramatic changes that history has wrought from the efforts of many investigators over the last 10 years. Although biological processes in development, especially maturing cognitive competences and temperamental dispositions, were minimally represented in the first volume, they are major themes in the current text. Further, the concept of attachment and the controversy surrounding its measurement dominated only 3 of the 28 chapters in the early edition; both are implicit in many more of the current essays. Because these themes are so central to developmental theory this commentary will evaluate the generalizations that are emerging from investigations of these fundamental processes.

A second, more philosophical purpose of this final chapter is to analyze the relation between the meaning of descriptive statements about children and the procedures that form the evidential sources for those propositions. I believe that some behavioral scientists are not sufficiently appreciative of the premise, articulated as part of the philosophy of logical empiricism and generally accepted by most physical and biological scientists, that the meaning of a proposition that describes or explains a relation between phenomena is influenced by its empirical sources. Each of the methods used to gather data is linked to specific, hypothetical mechanisms that mediate the phenomena quantified. If the mechanisms that mediate two different events are not similar, we should not use the same term to summarize the two sources of information, despite our intuition to the contrary.

PERCEPTUAL COMPETENCES: GIVEN AS WELL AS ACQUIRED

Intermodal Schemata

A small but growing group of developmental psychologists is prepared to award to the young infant abilities that older theorists required them to earn through either long, complex chains of stimulus–response associations or effortful, goal-directed actions (see Rose & Ruff, Chapter 6, this volume). This lively return to nativism

Preparation of this chapter was supported, in part, by a grant from the John D. and Catherine T. MacArthur Foundation.

was inevitable, for theories of human nature have oscillated over the past three centuries between an emphasis on endogenous or exogenous influences. After a half-century of excessive commitment to the latter, it was time for the former perspective to recruit enthusiasm.

The contemporary optimism over the influence of endogenous factors takes two forms. One can be found in the reports published after 1975 claiming that newborns possess sophisticated methods for processing information. Most studies before that time were motivated by a desire to understand the conditions that control the infant's attentiveness and mood (Cohen, Gelber, & Lazar, 1971; Fagan, 1973; Kagan, 1971; Fantz, 1965; Haith, 1980; McCall, Kennedy, & Applebaum, 1977). Most investigations were variations on the popular novelty hypothesis, which assumed either a linear or a curvilinear function as the best description of the relation between the infant's attentiveness and the nature of the events being processed. These experiments tacitly assumed a passive organism compelled to stare at one stimulus more than another because of differences in amount of contour, number of elements, curvilinearity, or familiarity. Because these studies explored the stimulus conditions that controlled behavior, they were in a sense loyal to a behavioristic tradition (Kessen, Haith, & Salapatek, 1970; Kessen, Salapatek, & Haith, 1972).

The new frame awards infants structures and competences that permit them to select information and shifts the scepter of control from external stimuli to endogenous processes. This realignment of psychological forces is most apparent in investigations of cross-modal transfer in which infants presumably create a schema for a dimension that is part of an event in one modality—auditory or tactile, for example—and assimilate that same dimension in another modality, often vision. (Some of the most widely cited investigations include Bahrick, 1983; Meltzoff & Borton, 1979; Rose, Gottfried, & Bridger, 1981; Starkey, Spelke, & Gelman, 1983; Wagner, Winner, Cicchetti, & Gardner, 1981. See Brown & Gottfried, 1986; Bushnell, 1986, for counterevidence; Rose & Ruff, Chapter 6, this volume, for a complete review.)

It is tacitly assumed by most investigators that the infant's behavior in the experimental situation not only is based on a learned association between the two modalities, but represents an extraction of the relevant dimensions during the experiment. That is, a 10-month-old infant could have learned at home that the visual appearance of a furry surface produced a distinct tactile sensation when explored with the fingers. Such an infant would show surprise if it saw a furry object while feeling a smooth surface. However, the surprise, which occurs in 11-month-olds but not 8-month-olds, could be explained as a result of acquired expectations and does not necessarily require positing amodal schemata (Bushnell, 1986).

The claim that young infants can detect a dimension present in events from two different modalities (e.g., the dimension of discontinuity or twoness) has significant theoretical implications that require a shift in our traditional view of the infant's mind. Let us explore why this is so by using the study performed by Wagner and his colleagues (1981) as a model. Eleven-month-old infants first heard an intermittent sound and then saw a pair of visual stimuli—a continuous line alongside a discontinuous line. The infants looked longer at the discontinuous line if they had first heard the discontinuous tone, but looked longer at the continuous line if they had been exposed first to the continuous tone, implying that the infants were prepared to extract the quality of *interruptedness* or discontinuity from the two different modalities. This ability appears to be restricted to specific dimensions, for the same infants did not treat an ascending tone as sharing a quality with a line that increased in thickness, nor did they regard a loud tone as sharing qualities with a large rather than a small square. Indeed, most of the cross-modal comparisons attempted in this study did not work, suggesting that the creation of intermodal, or amodal, schemata in infants is probably limited to a small number of dimensions (see Wagner & Sakovits, in press, for a similar result).

In a second persuasive demonstration of intermodal schemata, infants 4–5 months old watched a pair of sound, color films. One depicted two yellow wooden blocks striking each other in an unpredictable pattern. The second film showed two yellow water-soaked sponges being squeezed, alone or against each other, in an equally unpredictable display. The sound tracks for each film were recorded live. Initially, the infants viewed the two films side by side for 90 sec with one sound track playing, and then they viewed the two films for an addition 90 sec with the other sound track. Following a short break, the same two films were shown simultaneously for 3 min, during which there were randomly selected intermittent 5-sec presentations of one of the sound tracks. During the initial phase of the experiment the infants looked significantly longer at the film that matched the sound track. But they showed no preference during the second 90-sec period when the other sound track was played. When one of the sound tracks was played briefly during the subsequent 3 min the infants' first glance was at the film appropriate to the sound track on 57 percent of these occasions—a small but statistically significant deviation from chance (Bahrick, 1983). Bahrick's interpretation of this fact is that the infant extracted the invariant properties of rhythm and temporal synchrony from the visual and auditory events.

Despite the fact that some investigators do not always find robust evidence for cross-modal transfer in infants under 6 months of age (see Bushnell, 1985; Moore, Benenson, Reznick, Peterson, & Kagan, 1986), and the magnitude of the result in confirmatory studies does not have a "between-the-eyes" effect, the positive instances are too numerous to ignore. Hence Rose and Ruff are probably correct in concluding that cross-modal ability exists and urging study of the mechanisms.

Most investigators imply that the dimensions the infant is extracting are those that the scientist is manipulating. For example, in the Meltzoff and Borton experiment, it would seem that nubbiness and smoothness are extracted as invariants by oral manipulation and vision. Rose and Ruff suggest, however, that perhaps the dimension being extracted should be described with a physical metric, such as rate of change or degree of variability in stimulus energy (Turkewitz, Gardner, & Lewkowicz, 1984). Perhaps, in some cases, the dimension being extracted is the intensity of an internal state of arousal—a special application of the James–Lange hypothesis.

This discussion of intermodal schemata invites a consideration of the more fundamental issue of basic processes in psychological function. Consider the extraordinary power and generalizability of the physical concept of energy, which is applicable to phenomena as disparate as sunspots, the dissolving of sugar in water, and the metabolic rate of reptiles. There is no psychological principle with the degree of universality of the second law of thermodynamics, which states that differences in energy between two systems set the occasion for an exchange permitting the systems to approach equality and maximal entropy. Similarly, a major determinant of pattern formation in embryogenesis involves differences in chemical gradients between a cell and its close neighbors less than 1 mm away. In both of these examples of a basic natural law a difference between entities is the occasion for a reaction.

This simple yet powerful idea may have heuristic value for psychological phenomena. Suppose that the infant, like a pair of heat sinks, provides minimally disguised access to basic psychological processes. One characteristic of infants' psychological function is that they are alerted by and attend to those events that contrast with, or are moderately different from, those they have just experienced, or those for which they have established a firm schema. These discrepant events usually provide the occasion for psychological activity. Thus, as with the second law a major condition for mental work is a difference. Indeed, it may be that continuous comparison of present state with the immediate past is a basic characteristic of the brain/mind. When the difference is minimal there is a temporary equilibrium; when the difference falls above a certain threshold mental activity occurs in order to estabish a new equilibrium. Some version of this idea can be found in most psychological theories. In Piagetian theory, *equilibration* refers to the state following successful assimilation of an event the child could not understand initially, while *accommodation* refers to the mental work occasioned by the discrepancy.

Freud's libido, which is an energy metaphor borrowed from nineteenth century physics, flows freely into objects and ideas that bring pleasure. When there is conflict, that is, when the object or act generates anticipations of both pleasure and pain, the mind works to protect the ego and so restructures the energy. If conflict in the Freudian sense is regarded as a discrepancy between the anticipated outcomes of two urges, intentions, or ideas, then again it appears that a discrepancy provokes the mind to do something.

There is an important implication of the twin assumptions that the mind (1) continually evaluates the relation of ongoing experience to its immediately prior states-cum-knowledge, and (2) attempts to remove the difference when there is noticeable discrepancy between the two evaluations. Because maturation of the central nervous system permits the child to detect new sources of discrepancy in the environment, development will be accompanied by more occasions for psychological work. Additionally, because experience provides children with an opportunity to acquire more cognitive structures, they are prepared to detect more discrepancies quickly. Thus both maturation and experience increase the number of occasions when discrepancy will provoke mental work and the construction of new categories. Psychologists have been unable thus far to predict which events will be discrepant, although they have learned that changes in size, color, number of elements, and pattern are usually treated by the infants as discrepancies—but not always (see Bushnell, 1985; Linn, Reznick, Kagan, & Hans, 1982).

This discussion is relevant to the idea of intermodal or amodal schemata. If the infant extracts a salient dimension from an auditory event (say, discontinuity of sound) the subsequent presentation of a visual event will be treated as a discrepancy. As a result, the infant is provoked to attempt an assimilation of the visual event. The fact that the young infant usually (but not always) matches (i.e., looks longer at the event in the new modality that shares a dimension with the one in the first modality) implies that the infant is prepared to search for an event that shares features with the schema established moments ago. But there should be a critical delay between familiarization and test that produces this result. If the delay is too long the infant will not be in the state generated by the familiarization stimulus and behavior should be random. Indeed, if the infant matched following a long delay between the events in the two modalities one would be faced with an even more profound enigma; namely: Why does the infant assume that the two events separated in time are related to each other? In Bahrick's procedure, the infant is fixating two silent films (two blocks or two sponges) and when a sound intrudes into the perceptual space the infant looks initially at the film corresponding to the auditory stimulus. If the intrusion of the sound is treated as a discrepant event, it will provoke mental work. In this case, the mental work is detecting a similarity between what it is hearing and what it is seeing. In most cases, the infant looks at the film that matches the sound track. Bahrick (1983) describes this fact in the following way:

> The detection of the invariance unites the light and the sound for a single event and separates it from other ongoing events that do not share the structure (p. 450).

However, it may not be necessary to assume that the infant extracts a common rhythm or other higher-order structure from the two modalities. Rather, the infant may look at the visual event whose rate of change in sensory energy is similar to that contained in the auditory event. This interpretation of cross-modal functioning acknowledges that the infant detects a common dimension in the two events, but that dimension might be rate of change in stimulus energy. This description has a slightly different sense meaning from the one that claims that infants initially establish a structure for rhythm or discontinuity and recognize that quality in the second event.

In sum, if the perceptual field contains an event that shares features with a schema created from an immediately preceding one, the infant will be attracted to it automatically because it is psychologically easier to work at the assimilation of an event that shares features with a past one than to work at the assimilation of an event that does not. Similarity in rate of change in stimulus energy is a feature that has special priority in guiding the attentiveness of infants under 6 months old. Infant pigtail monkeys 2–4 weeks old showed cross-modal recognition of a visual event after oral manipulation, but older infant monkeys did not (Gunderson, 1983). This interesting fact suggests that the basis for the attentiveness to the matching visual event involves less, rather than more, sophisticated cognitive mechanisms. Hence it is not surprising that evidence for intermodal schemata is much more fragile with infants 4–6 months old than with those 10–12 months old. This fact is also in accord with the finding that infant rhesus monkeys less than 4 months old (comparable to 10–12 months in the human infant) have great difficulty when they have to pick the novel member of a pair of objects and the familiar one was examined 10 sec earlier (Bachevalier & Mishkin, 1984). This difficulty implies that human infants under 10 months do not usually relate the stimulus dimensions of a prior event to one in the present, a process that is assumed in intermodal matching. Further, the most robust demonstrations of intermodal schemata in younger infants always involve events for which differences in rate of change in stimulus energy are salient. A continuous line and a continuous tone contain less change than a discontinuous line and tone; the visual and auditory stimulation accompanying the banging together of two wooden blocks has a faster rate of change than the stimulation accompanying the displacement of two sponges. This explanation does not require us to assume that the young infant creates a higher-order amodal schema from two events. Rather, the baby, alerted by a change in sensory modality, seeks to assimilate the present energy profile to one in the immediate past. The infant is still psychologically active, but a little less creative. Future research will have to determine how abstract the presymbolic, recall-deficient 4-month-old infant is.

If infants can extract a single dimension shared by events in different modalities, psychologists will have to make some alterations in their theories of cognitive function. One of the two most popular views of the infant, due in large part to the work of E. J. Gibson (1969), is that perceptual processes proceed gradually from holistic perception to differentiation. The representation of a single dimension present in visual, auditory, and tactile events should be a slowly acquired skill, not an early gift, even though James Gibson (1966) suggested that the extraction of invariances was autochthonous. The Piagetian view of perception, which holds that cognitive representations are transformations of the products of actions with objects, would also have difficulty explaining intermodal schemata.

Hence the hypothesis of intermodal functioning requires a rewriting of our traditional theories of early cognitive function because it makes infants cognitively analytic, rather than global, in their approach to experience, and describes them as friendly to abstract rather than concrete representations. It will be useful to probe this idea deeply, for should it prove to be correct, seminal aspects of language development that are now mysterious will become understandable. One of the puzzles in early speech forms is the appearance of expressions that were not part of the child's past experience. When a 3-year-old calls a thin slice of lemon a "moon," she is telling us she detected the similarity in form between a piece of lemon lying on a saucer and the picture of a new moon in a coloring book. When she calls a dark cloud "mad," she is informing us that she detected the affective dimension of unpleasantness shared by a storm and an angry face. It has been difficult to explain these intermodal ideas with traditional associationistic mechanisms. If the young child is prepared for such analyses, some of the burden of explanation can be moved to endogenous talents.

Processing of Speech

The ability to process speech syllables as adults do is a second competence recently awarded to the infant (Eimas & Miller, 1980; Kuhl & Meltzoff, 1982; Miller & Eimas, 1983). An additional but related claim is that the processing of a speech unit is context dependent.

The idea of context, which is central to the elegant work on the perception of speech, is a concept with at least three different meanings. *Context* most often refers to the larger, coherent external event in which a particular componential dimension participates. This is the meaning intended by Eimas and Miller, usually named *stimulus context,* and its relevance is affirmed in empirical work. A related meaning, often called *structural context,* treats a set of related cognitive structures, rather than stimulus dimensions, as the coherent unity. A quarter-century ago psychologists would have called these related structures *learned associations.* A frown on the face of a father has an emotional meaning for a 4-year-old that it lacks for a 4-month-old. The child's reactions are to the event cum its associative structures, not just to the event. This meaning of context also involves the expectations and intentions of the individual, which we name *psychological preparedness.* A 2-year-old who expects an adult to ask her a question involving the name of an object will pick up an odd, unfamiliar wooden form if asked, "Give me the *zoob*." A 2-year-old without that expectation will look puzzled, and may cry.

A third meaning of *context* involves physiological states. A child whose heart rate and muscle tone imply high sympathetic arousal will react to the threat of being tested by an adult differently than will a minimally aroused child. Thus children with high sympathetic tone will look frequently at an examiner who is posing questions, while children with low sympathetic tone look less frequently. The differential frequency of glances at the examiner depends, in part, on the physiological state of the child. In a classic study, Valenstein, Cox, and Kakolewski (1968) demonstrated that electrical stimulation of a particular site in the hypothalamus provoked a rat to chew if food were available, to drink when water was present, and to pick up items such as wood chips, if they were on the floor of the cage. However, rats performed none of these acts if the hypothalamic neurons were not electrically stimulated. These three meanings of *context* share a significant feature; namely, the consequences of most events are influenced by the context in which they are but one component.

It is important to note, finally, that at the present time almost all of the basic behavior categories in psychology imply, usually tacitly, that the context of a reaction determines the category to which it is assigned. Consider the basic psychological event of a pigeon in a cage pecking a circular key. No investigator would group all repetitions of this event into one category because each recognizes that the theoretical meaning of the response is inferred from the prior history of the animal (e.g., was the animal shaped to make this response?) and the setting. By contrast, many of the basic categories in chemistry and biology are relatively independent of context. The chemical structure of glucose or cortisol, for example, is the same in blood, saliva, and urine in every place in the world, and a hair cell on the basilar membrane or a muscle cell in the heart has the same structure in all humans. The social sciences, therefore, are unique because their basic categories are conjunctive, combining the features of an agent's reaction (an act, facial expression, or physiological reaction) with features of the context, where *context* refers to the background characteristics of the agent and the setting in which the reaction occurs.

Now let us return to the work of Eimas and Miller, who have reported that perception of the speech syllable *ba* or *wa* depends not only on the duration of the initial formant transition, but also on the transition duration in relation to the duration of the entire syllable (Eimas & Miller, 1980; Miller & Eimas, 1983). There are two ways to interpret the data upon which this inference rests. The interpretation preferred by Eimas and Miller is that, because no percept is fully determined by the information in the signal, the stimulus is referred automatically to a larger frame, a conclusion reminiscent of the early Gestalt writings on perception. The mind evaluates the stimulus with reference to the larger frame in which the signal is embedded. However, a different description of these data is possible if one assumes that events are perceived as perceptual unities, but psychologists, who are interested in determining the components of an event, parse the unity into separate qualities in order to write objectively framed descriptions. Hence the syllable *ba* is described as an event composed of variations in the durations of initial formant transitions and completed syllables. When investigators manipulate each of these dimensions separately they find that the infant's perception of the syllable *ba* or *wa* under one formant transition duration depends on the duration of the syllable and conclude that there is context-dependent perception. This is a proper inference. But, as Garner (1981) implies, the infant's central nervous system may not analyze the stimulus *ba* in the way that the experimenter intended. Hence it is also proper to state that the infant perceives *ba* as a unitary event under one set of conditions, and perceives *wa* as a unitary event under another.

Consider an analogous example in the visual mode. Infants appear to process a pair of bilaterally symmetrical small black circles enclosed in a circular frame as a unity, and not as a pair of black circles plus the larger circular frame. If 5-month-olds are familiarized on a pair of dark circles without a frame and are subsequently presented with a pair of squares, they show clear dishabituation of fixation time and look longer at the pair of squares. But if the same infants are familiarized on a pair of dark circles enclosed in a larger circle and are then presented with a pair of circles and a pair of squares, each in a larger circle, they do not dishabituate to the latter stimulus, even though it is novel (Kagan, 1984). We could conclude that this fact implies either that the perception of a pair of dark circles is context dependent or that a pair of circles without a frame and a pair of circles within a circular frame are two very different perceptual unities that are processed differently.

The physicist Pierre Duhem (1906) regarded the distinction between qualities and quantities as useful. If a new value on a dimension can be formed by addition—like loudness—the dimension can be regarded as a quantity. But if a new phenomenon cannot be formed by adding the separate values on a selected dimension—like the syllable *ba*—it should be regarded as a quality. Although the last section of this chapter will consider the ideas of quality and quantity in more detail, it is useful to present a précis of that argument. Events, like the syllables *ba* and *wa,* contain many different dimensions, some of which can be conceptualized as continuous quantities, others as discrete qualities. There is no quantity that cannot be transformed into a quality by changing the mode of analysis. The preference for conceptualizing an event as composed of continuous quantities or discrete qualities depends on the question being asked and, therefore, the theoretical interest of the scientist. Eimas and Miller are interested in how the central nervous system discriminates among the sounds of human speech. It is particularly useful for that question to view the stimulus events as continua. But for investigators interested in the schematic representation of events, it may be more useful to regard the entire syllable as a unitary, qualitatively distinct event. A pathologist seeking the causes of a new viral disease looks for the unique qualities of that pathogen; but a geneticist interested in putting pathogens into their proper categories will search for sets of continuous characteristics among a group of related viruses.

Psychologists should remain receptive to the new and exciting findings in infant perception and the growth of amodal schemata, even though these ideas originate in investigations that are usually in the confirmatory mode and occasionally ignore failures of prediction. However, this new movement is of such potential significance it would be unwise to be excessively harsh so early.

TEMPERAMENTAL VARIATION

Explanations of differences in mood and social behavior among children during most of this century have emphasized variation in environmental experiences and ignored, sometimes to exclusion, the infant qualities psychologists call *tempera-*

mental. A seminal axiom of the disciplines that study life processes is that the inherent properties of the unit under study make a contribution to the growth of that unit as it reacts to successive encounters with its surroundings. Whenever a generation of theorists overemphasizes the influence of the surroundings and ignores the endogenous characteristics of the unit, or awards too much power to the unit and not enough to the environment, future generations will make the necessary corrections. The disciplines that study behavior are in a transition during which the importance of the child's inherent characteristics, some of which are temperamental predispositions, is being acknowledged. Thomas and Chess (1977), Buss and Plomin (1984), Plomin and Rowe (1979), Rothbart and Derryberry (1981), Carey and McDevitt (1978), Goldsmith and Campos (1982), and many others have helped to effect this change in attitude. This body of work implies that biological sources of variation in the young infant's characteristics invite different treatments by family members and peers and, in addition, exert constraints on the child's psychological choices. There is some resistance to this idea, for it implies that a person's *will* may not always be able to accomplish all he or she desires. Hence acknowledging the relevance of biologically based temperamental qualities is often interpreted (unconsciously and incorrectly) as a restriction on personal freedom and a dilution of the power of individual effort—two beloved ideas in the American ethos.

It is much too early to list the preliminary set of fundamental temperamental dispositions in infants. Bates's excellent summary in this volume reveals that the dimensions that have been posited are influenced in large measure by the particular sources of data gathered by the investigator, a point that will be discussed later. For example, Thomas and Chess posit nine dimensions, with difficult temperament as the most important derived quality. All of these dimensions are derived from parental statements in interviews. Similarly, Rothbart and Derryberry, whose evidence comes from parents' answers to questionnaires about their infants, posit reactivity and self-regulation as primary dimensions, with activity, laughter, fear, distress to constraint, soothability, and duration of attentional involvement as six major temperamental dimensions. In sharp contrast, Buss and Plomin, whose source of evidence is primarily adults' answers to personality scales, posit only three primary dimensions: emotionality, activity, and sociability, with impulsiveness as a derived trait. It is obvious that these three adult dimensions are different from those posited for infants.

Inhibition to the Unfamiliar

Although the research on temperamental dimensions is uneven, in both quantity and quality, a fair inference from existing data is that one important temperamental quality is the child's initial behavioral reaction to unfamiliar people, objects, and situations, especially if that initial reaction is either withdrawal or approach. These complementary styles are moderately stable and are seen clearly during the transition from infancy to early childhood, especially in the child's initial reaction to unfamiliar adults and children. One small group of children 2–3 years old becomes extremely quiet and vigilant and stays close to the caretaker for 5–15 min. But even after the period of inhibition has passed, they rarely approach the unfamiliar peer for the next half-hour. A second, larger group of children begins to play immediately and shows no signs of initial timidity. The former children seem to be young versions of the prototypic introvert; the latter resemble the extravert. These two behavioral profiles with an unfamiliar child are obvious indices of a more general quality, namely, the tendency to display or not to display an initial period of inhibition of speech and play and a retreat to a target of attachment whenever the child encounters the unfamiliar. In searching for concise adjectives to capture the differences between the two kinds of children, recognizing that any word distorts what is observed, the words *restrained, watchful,* and *gentle* capture the essence of the inhibited child, while *free, energetic,* and *spontaneous* reveal the style of the uninhibited youngster. When the inhibited child throws a ball, knocks down a tower of blocks, or hits a large toy clown, the act is monitored, restrained, and almost soft. The same act performed by the uninhibited child seems relaxed and free. Each style represents a preferred reaction to uncertainty that is characteristic of about 10 percent of American children.

The psychological state produced by the unfamiliar or by challenge might be called *uncertainty*, which is a leading candidate among cognitive psychologists as a fundamental metric, even though the units of measurement are not yet consensual. Psychologists typically differentiate among three classes of uncertainty, each of which could produce behavioral inhibition in a child:

1. *Event uncertainty.* The state produced when a person is deciding on the category to which an event belongs.
2. *Response uncertainty.* The state produced when a person is deciding which of several actions to implement.
3. *Consequent uncertainty.* The state produced when a person is attempting to predict a future event or the consequences of an action.

Children differ temperamentally in the ease with which each of these classes of uncertainty is generated. Other investigators have noted the stability of similar qualities in children. Bronson (1970) has found evidence for preservation of individual differences in fearfulness, and Emmerich (1964) has reported that behaviors resembling inhibition and lack of inhibition were preserved among nursery school children observed from 3 to 5 years of age (see also Halverson & Waldrop, 1976; Simpson & Stevenson-Hinde, in press).

Although these behavioral differences are particularly salient in social situations during the second and third years, related or derivative predispositions may be observed throughout the life span, albeit in much different form. Extremely shy preschool children seen in a child guidance clinic were more likely to become adults who chose relatively secure bureaucratic jobs with minimal risk rather than entrepreneurial vocations with their attendant increase in unpredictability (Coolidge, Brodie, & Feeney, 1964; Morris, Soroker, & Burruss, 1954). Further, psychiatrists make a useful distinction between adult patients who are chronic worriers and a much smaller group—less than 10 percent of anxious patients—who are vulnerable to agoraphobia and sudden panic reactions. Many patients in the latter group were extremely fearful and timid during childhood, suggesting that a small proportion of extremely inhibited children may be vulnerable to panic disorder as adults (Gittelman & Klein, 1984).

The 71 members of the Fels Research Institute's longitudinal sample—Caucasian and primarily middle-class—were observed and tested from infancy through adolescence and evaluated again as young adults.Of the many individual qualities quantified during the first 3 years of life, only inhibition and lack of inhibition were preserved across adolescence and young adulthood (Kagan & Moss, 1983). The children who were extremely shy, timid, and fearful during the opening 3 years displayed a coherent cluster of behaviors during the early school years. They avoided dangerous activities, were minimally aggressive, conformed to parental requests, and avoided unfamiliar social encounters. As adolescents, they avoided contact sports and other traditional masculine activities, and the four boys who were most inhibited during the first 6 years chose intellectual careers as adults (music, physics, biology, and psychology). The four boys who were least inhibited during the first 6 years chose more traditional masculine vocations (football coach, salesman, and 2 engineers). Further, the extremely inhibited children became adults who showed more dependency on their love objects and more conscious feelings of anxiety in social situations than did those who were extremely uninhibited as young children.

In a later longitudinal study, Kagan, Kearsley, and Zelazo (1978) compared 53 Chinese-American children with 63 Caucasian children across the 2-year period from 4 to 29 months. Forty-nine of these children were in either full- or part-time day care, while 67 were raised at home without surrogate care. The most significant result was that the Chinese children, whether raised at home or in the day-care center, were consistently more inhibited than the Caucasians during infancy and the transition to childhood. For example, each child was observed in a laboratory setting during which unfamiliar visual and auditory events were presented. On most of the procedures, the Chinese children vocalized and smiled less often than did the Caucasians. The Chinese were more likely than the Caucasians to cry intensely following temporary separation from the mother, and when the 20-month-old children were brought to an unfamiliar room with their mother, a familiar adult, and a stranger, the Chinese children stayed close to their mother for a longer period of time than did the Caucasians. These ethnic differences were most dramatic across the period from 7 to 20 months of age. Additionally, each mother ranked 16 different qualities in her 2-year-old, from most to least characteristic. The Chinese parents regarded fearfulness and timidity as more characteristic of their children than did the Caucasian mothers. For example, the Chinese mothers rated the statement "Stays close to mother" as a salient quality of their children, while the Caucasian mothers regarded talkativeness, a sense of humor, and emotional spontaneity as more characteristic of their children.

One quality that distinguishes the two groups of children provides a clue to the physiological bases for these behaviors. Many of the Chinese children, who were typically inhibited, had stable heart rates while processing unfamiliar visual and auditory information, while more of the Caucasians had variable heart rates. This difference in heart rate variability was the best preserved quality across the 26 months of the investigation. Individual differences in this autonomic variable were much more stable than behavioral qualities like attentiveness, irritability, vocalization, or smiling.

Heart rate variability, as well as absolute heart rate and blood pressure, is regulated by the autonomic nervous system. Heart rate and blood pressure typically increase during inspiration as vagal tone is inhibited, but decrease with expiration as the vagus is disinhibited. As a result, the heart rate of children and adults at rest usually displays a regular cycle of acceleration and deceleration that is yoked to breathing, with the rate moderately variable over epochs of 3–10 sec. However, when the vagal influence is restrained, the cardiac deceleration that normally accompanies expiration is muted, and heart rate rises slightly and becomes much less variable (Bunnell, 1982). It is well established that adults placed under cognitive stress show increases in both epinephrine secretion and heart rate, and a decrease in heart rate variability. A sample of unselected college-age volunteers displayed stable individual differences in the tendency to show large or small sympathetic reactions (changes in blood pressure and heart rate) to laboratory stresses like mental problems or the avoidance of shock (Light, 1984; Light & Obrist, 1983). These changes in physiology are often independent of the adult's introspections about the degree of challenge experienced in the task.

These phenomena are often part of a set of physiological responses to psychological stress initiated in the limbic lobe and hypothalamus, which, in turn, stimulate the pituitary-adrenal axis, the reticular activating system, and the sympathetic arm of the autonomic nervous system—three separate circuits that respond to unfamiliarity and challenge. The action of these circuits leads to release of ACTH from the pituitary and subsequent secretion of glucocorticoids from the adrenal cortex, increased secretion of epinephrine from the adrenal medulla and norepinephrine from the brain stem and sympathetic nerves, leading to a rise in heart rate and dilation of the pupils, and increased discharge of the reticular activating system, leading to subsequent increases in muscle tension (Axelrod & Reisine, 1984; Frankenhaeuser, 1979). A recent review of the factors controlling response to threat and challenge suggests that the paraventricular nucleus of the lateral hypothalamus may be one place where psychological incentives are transduced into important influences on the autonomic nervous system (Smith & DeVito, 1984). When this nucleus is stimulated there is a rise in blood pressure and heart rate and an inhibition of reflex bradycardia. These facts suggest that this area of the lateral hypothalamus is one site of control over emotional responsivity to stressful events, for this region has a monosynaptic connection to the intermediolateral cells of the spinal cord and, thence, to the sympathetic nervous system. Research with animals reveals robust strain differences in the reactivity of these stress circuits to unfamiliarity, challenge, and stress. Reactive strains of rats show frequent defecation in the open-field test while the nonreactive rats do not (Blizard, 1981). Further, Suomi, Kraemer, Baysinger, and DeLizio (1981) and Stevenson-Hinde, Stillwell-Barnes, and Zunz (1980) have found stable individual differences among monkeys in the behavioral signs of fear and inhibition in unfamiliar situations. Finally, a behavioral study of varied dog breeds found that German shepherds were most fearful of novelty while Labrador retrievers were least fearful (Goddard & Beilharz, 1985). These differences among animals and humans bear some resemblance to Pavlov's (1941) distinction between weak and strong nervous systems (the fearful organisms have a weak nervous system while the fearless ones have a strong nervous system), and to Gellhorn's (1967) later distinction between ergotropic and trophotropic factors in the autonomic nervous system.

A Longitudinal Study

Children and adults vary in the ease with which these physiological circuits react to psychological uncertainty. The fact that inhibited children are more likely than uninhibited ones to react with a rise in heart rate and a decrease in heart rate variability, as well as increased pupil dilation, cortisol and norepinephrine levels, and muscle tension, implies a lower threshold of reactivity in one or more of these circuits. The source for these statements is data from ongoing longitudinal studies of two cohorts consisting of equal numbers of inhibited and uninhibited children. One cohort of 46 children has been seen at 21, 48, and 67 months of age; the second cohort of 54 children has been seen at 31, 43, and 67 months of age (Garcia-Coll, Kagan, & Reznick, 1984; Kagan, Reznick, Clarke, Snidman, & Garcia-Coll, 1984; Reznick et al., 1986; Snidman, 1984). The primary index of behavioral inhibition in the preschool years is derived from the child's behavior with an unfamiliar peer of the same age and sex. The inhibited children wait a long time before they talk to or approach the other child and initially spend a long period of time proximal to their mothers while staring at the other child. Even after the inhibited children have become more spontaneous, they are unlikely to initiate an approach or talk to the peer.

Very few uninhibited 20-month-old children became inhibited over the 4 years of the study, and about one-half of the inhibited children remained extremely inhibited. Although the remaining half of the inhibited group changed toward a less inhibited style, they were still far less spontaneous than the typical uninhibited youngster. However, the inhibited children who had displayed high and stable heart rates to cognitive tasks at the early ages were more likely to remain inhibited than were the inhibited children who had low and variable heart rates during the early assessments.

More inhibited than uninhibited children display a rise and stabilization of heart rate and tonically larger pupils over a 1-hr battery of cognitive tests, secrete more cortisol, both under mild stress and at home before the stress of the day has begun, and have higher levels of norepinephrine following the laboratory session. The inhibited children also show less variability in the pitch periods of single-word utterances spoken under mild stress, implying greater tension in the skeletal muscles of the vocal folds and the supporting laryngeal muscles. A mean index of eight physiological variables gathered at age 5½ (derived from the heart, pupil, cortisol, voice, and norepinephrine data) was associated with behavioral inhibition at every age of assessment—the highest correlation was with the original score at 21 months ($r = 0.70$). Further, symptoms suggestive of higher arousal in the stress circuits, especially chronic constipation, allergies, fears, and sleeplessness during the first 2 years of life, were more frequent among inhibited than among uninhibited children, and especially among the inhibited children with high and stable heart rates.

Other evidence suggests that infants who are extremely irritable during the opening days of life are a little more likely to become inhibited during the second and third years than minimally irritable infants. In one study, newborns were observed following withdrawal of a nipple while they were actively sucking. The infants who cried most intensely for a long period and could not be easily soothed showed one of the most distinctive characteristics of inhibited children when they were 31 months old, namely, the tendency to stare frequently at a peer in an ecologically natural social situation. Although a replication failed to reach statistical significance, the direction of the result was the same (Yang & Halverson, 1976). In a second study, Japanese newborns who reacted with extreme distress to repeated removals of a nipple and were not easily placated became fearful and inhibited during early childhood, while newborns who did not show extreme distress were less likely to show the later signs of inhibition (Chen & Miyake, 1983).

Our current view is that a small group of children, no more than 10–15 percent of a normal population of infants, are born with either a high or a low threshold for discharge of some or all of the stress circuits following encounter with the unfamiliar, psychological risk, or challenge. These children are detected by a combination of behavioral and biological qualities, not by any one alone. The group we call temperamentally inhibited showed both consistent withdrawal to unfamiliarity in the second and third years of life, and, during infancy, signs of physiological arousal (including symptoms of extreme irritability, constipation, or allergy), and during the second and third years, a high and stable heart rate and cardiac accelerations to mild cognitive stress. By contrast, the temperamentally uninhibited children show consistent approach behaviors and minimal signs of physiological arousal to cognitive stress. Inhibited behavior alone, without any of the biological signs, is likely to be a reflection of socialization, not temperamental factors. However, whether inhibited and uninhibited children are viewed as qualitatively different groups or as falling on a continuum of uncertainty or arousal will depend on the question of interest and the data awarded priority.

Environmental conditions determine the degree to which the biological tendency favoring inhibition or lack of inhibition will be actualized. It is likely that an unusually benevolent environment that gently promotes an uninhibited coping style might create a socially outgoing demeanor in a child born with a potential for an inhibited temperament. Analogously, an overly stressful environment can create inhibited behavior in a child who is born with a temperamental disposition that favored an uninhibited coping style. Thus only a proportion of shy, timid children—or adults—are born with this temperamental disposition, and even among this group, possession of the biological disposition is not deterministic. The biological mechanisms only make it a little more likely that a child will develop the characteristics of inhibition or lack of inhibition.

As noted earlier, the temperamental differences in children can be viewed as analogous to strain differences among animals in their reactions to challenge. A dramatic example has been provided by Sackett and his colleagues (1981), who found that 6 months of complete isolation of infants who belonged to three different species of macaque monkeys produced different profiles of impairment. Social behavior in rhesus monkeys was severely affected by the isolation, but the social behavior of crab eaters was minimally affected. One possible basis for this result is that crab eaters are normally more social than rhesus; hence this behavioral "system" may be less vulnerable to disturbance. This form of argument seems appropriate for inhibited and uninhibited children. Uninhibited children are harder to frighten; hence chastisement or threat of punishment might not lead to inhibition of asocial behavior as reliably as it does in inhibited children. The implication for those who study family influences is: Look for interactions, not main effects. Unfortunately, this warning is not always heeded, and many scientists continue to expect a uniform effect to emerge from a particular profile of family experiences. Maccoby and Martin's (1983) review of family influences in the *Handbook of Child Psychology* affirms the absence of main effects. Perhaps it is time for developmental scholars to frame their research in terms of expected interactions between a class of experience and a temperamental type, as they do for categories of social class and sex.

The social environment has a continuing influence. A group of extremely inhibited children, most of them boys, became less inhibited over time as their parents imposed gentle pressure on them to adopt a less fearful approach to environmental challenge. A smaller group, most of them girls, changed from uninhibited to mildly inhibited as their parents pressured them to become more cautious. If inhibited children, as they grow to adulthood, find vocational and interpersonal niches that keep uncertainty low but permit adaptation, they will avoid regular rises in uncertainty and arousal and may not be extremely inhibited with friends or family. Further, the modal incentives for uncertainty change with development. An unfamiliar peer is a more potent incentive for 3-year-olds than for 15-year-olds. On the other hand, possible failure at a school task or rejection by a love object is more salient for the adolescent than for the toddler. The changing profile of incentives for uncertainty means that chance or conscious selection of context can lead to increases or decreases in the probability of experiencing uncertainty. Thus the degree of preservation of the behavioral differences between inhibited and uninhibited children will change with development.

Implications for Psychological Theory

Receptivity to the idea that some of the variation among children in timidity, shyness, and fearfulness is due to biological factors present at birth leads investigators to change the relative weights for the characteristics they use to place children into theoretical categories. If one assumes that socialization experiences in the home or with peers are the major determinants of shy, timid, fearful behavior, then classifications like *inhibited* and *uninhibited* will award a greater weight to the child's contemporary behavior and the values and practices of socializing agents. A child who is behaviorally inhibited at 2 but not at 5 years of age will be regarded as belonging to a different category than one who is inhibited at both ages. However, if children born with a lower threshold in the stress circuits are disposed to be inhibited, one is tempted to assign greater weight to biological signs of responsivity in the stress circuits and less weight to overt behavior because many parents try to socialize their inhibited children to be less fearful overtly.

The research on temperament, therefore, will tempt scientists to award a greater weight to early-appearing biological qualities. At present, our major developmental categories are based on age–stage ideas (e.g., the stage of concrete or formal operations), or antecedent social experiences (securely or insecurely attached to the mother). These categories award salience to the child's contemporaneous behavior. A child from an uneducated, economically impoverished family who was classified at age 2 as at risk for school failure will be removed from that category if his reading score at the end of grade 2 is comparable to that of his peers. Similarly, a 1-year-old classified as insecurely attached in the Strange Situation who behaved at age 2 as if she were securely attached would be reclassified because categories based on the influence of environmental events carry the tacit assumption that subsequent experiences can change a child's basic qualities.

However, use of categories based on endogenous characteristics present at birth tends to bias the scientist to regard contemporary behavior as a little less salient and to treat biologically based characteristics as a little more salient because of the unproven assumption that qualities associated with biological processes change more slowly. I do not claim this assumption is valid, but it is the way the minds of Western scientists tend to work. Investigators who believe that intelligence is a heritable quality will classify a 3-year-old with a Stanford Binet IQ score of 120 as intelligent and interpret poor academic performance and an IQ score of 80 in the same child at 10 years of age as due to interfering experiences. They will be reluctant to change that child's classification from high to low intelligence.

Scientists should be continually self-conscious about this issue, for endogenous qualities can change. One of the boys in our longitudinal study was extremely inhibited at 30 months and possessed many of the signs of a low threshold in the stress circuits. But at 4 and 5 years of age he was behaviorally uninhibited and showed few of the biological signs. I suspect that these changes, probably due to socialization, are profound; hence this boy should not be classified as temperamentally inhibited at 5½ years. A child born with known central nervous system damage who displayed an abnormal EEG during the first week of life can, with proper environmental experience, recover and at 10 years of age show no signs of brain damage in either behavior or electrophysiology. It is probably an error to classify this child with other brain-damaged children who did not show psychological repair. Because biological qualities, like exogenously produced ones, are vulnerable to change, it may be useful to apply different descriptive names to the various developmental manifestations of inhibited and uninhibited dispositions, just as we apply the different terms *girl* and *woman* to call attention to the developmental changes in the biology of females, while not rejecting the idea that the genomes of girls and women remain different from those of boys and men from birth to adulthood.

It is likely that future research will reveal that other candidates, perhaps activity level, lability of emotional mood, and even specific affective states, are as stable and as coherent as the qualities of inhibition and lack of inhibition. Each will be expressed in different forms during the successive stages of development and associated with specific biological signs. The empirical strategy used in our research may prove useful in investigations of these other characteristics. Rather than study variation in a volunteer sample, we deliberately selected children who belonged to extreme groups. Psychiatrists and behavioral geneticists interested in the etiology of schizophrenia do not evaluate mood and thought processes in a random sample of children but select subjects who are the offspring of schizophrenic parents because of the reasonable assumption that the qualities that define this category do not fall on a continuum. It may be equally advantageous to supplement studies of volunteer groups with studies of children who fall at the extremes on qualities like activity, regularity of sleep, irritability, frustration, lability of emotional state, and intensity of the expression of anger, sadness, fear, and joy.

Psychological Tone

There is one final dividend that might be realized from continued study of the psychological and physiological attributes of inhibition and lack of inhibition. One of the salient characteristics of scientific disciplines during their most productive phases is a consensus that treats a small number of questions as primary. The bases for the selection are not usually stated, but a combination of readiness for solution, theoretical implications, and a sense of wonder contributes to the choice. The form of motion of the earth, planets, and sun enjoyed such a consensus for over 300 years, until Kepler and Newton removed most of the mystery, permitting successive generations of physicists to ponder the nature of light, heat, magnetism, electricity, and, presently, the structure of matter and the origin of the universe. The function of bodily organs, the mechanisms of reproduction, the evolution of animals, and the chemistry of the gene enjoyed a status that is now awarded to the origin of life.

It is more difficult to find comparable degrees of consensus among contemporary psychologists, although the nature of conscious experience and, later, the mechanisms of learning generated considerable accord among earlier cohorts. I believe that one potentially productive question for contemporary social science deals with the combination of factors that determine a person's continuing *psychological tone*. The phrase *psychological tone* is meant to refer to the coherent sets of psychological and physiological states that accompany different chronic moods, some of which are named *uncertainty, anxiety, depression, serenity, anger,* and *excitement*. Each class of psychological tone is characterized by physiological, behavioral, and subjectively experienced dimensions. For example, the tone of uncertainty involves discharge of the stress circuits, behavioral characteristics like withdrawal, caution, and restraint, and subjective feelings of tension or worry. All three criteria must be met. Discharge of the physiological circuits without the appropriate behaviors or subjective feelings is ambiguous with respect to psychological tone, as is a subjective report of "worry" without the appropriate physiological and behavioral signs. This demand is not too severe. Evolutionary biologists require information on mode of reproduction, anatomy, and biochemistry before they decide on the correct species assignment for a new group of animals.

Both endogenous and exogenous processes influence the psychological tone of uncertainty, and both change over the life span. During infancy, a major determinant of the tone of uncertainty is unpredictability of events related to nurture of states of hunger and cold and the availability of targets of attachment. After age 4, the psychological processes that control tone change more slowly. The existence of an older, competitive or predatory sibling can maintain a tone, and as the child develops beliefs about the self due, in part, to identification with parental figures, anxiety over violating standards becomes influential. In societies with schools, failure in the classroom changes expectations that can influence tone.

There should be a change in tone when youth leave the sphere of the family, the threats associated with siblings and parents are diluted, and adolescents are exposed to new sources of uncertainty. Another time of change in psychological tone occurs after vocational and marital decisions have been made, for each contains new challenges and uncertainties. Thus psychological tone is not a static quality fixed in early childhood, even though early events and temperament can influence its future status to some degree.

Perhaps the most important suggestion is that psychological tone is amenable to initial measurement—a fact that is crucial for consensus among empiricists. It is possible to measure some of the peripheral signs of reactivity of the stress circuits, especially heart rate, heart rate variability, blood pressure, pulse transit time, cortisol, catecholamines, and muscle tension, each of which is a rough index of central processes that mediate emotional tone. Further, the behavioral referents of shyness, withdrawal to the unfamiliar, sleep disturbance, and fears are vulnerable to quantification (even though I do not minimize the measurement complexities), and self-reports of psychological tone are relatively easy to obtain. Finally, the suggestion to study psychological tone is also supported by Sperry (1981), who regards a person's conscious feelings as critical events in a theory of human behavior.

> The new interpretation gives full recognition to the primacy of inner conscious awareness as a causal reality. The phenomena of conscious experience are conceived to play an active, directive role in shaping the flow pattern of cerebral excitation. (p. 7)

And a recent clinical report on a 54-year-old male with resection of parts of the limbic lobe contains the intriguing suggestion that perhaps the amygdala is one place where the moods that are part of self-awareness originate (Hebben, Corkin, Eichenbaum, & Shedlack, 1985).

ATTACHMENT

The idea that variation in the attachment relation between the infant and its caretakers has serious consequences for the child's future has stimulated research and debate over the last quarter-century. The popularity of this theme is attributable in part to historical events local to our society and in part to the availability of an easily implemented methodological innovation. I noted in the first edition of this handbook that since World War I American psychologists have conceptualized the relation of infant to mother in similar ways. Even though one perspective originated in psychoanalytic theory and the other in neobehaviorism, both positions made maternal nurture the primary reason that children learn to treat the caretaker as a source of pleasure, comfort, and safety. In the language of learning theory, the caretaker acquired reward value; in psychoanalytic essays the infant cathected the caretaker. In both frames a passive infant had been transformed by acts of affection, feeding, and protection into a toddler who treated the responses of adults as signals for pleasure, not unlike the state of male albino rats who have learned to run to the right arm of a T-maze in order to find food pellets or a receptive female.

John Bowlby (1969), anticipating contemporary essays on the biological preparedness of the infant, made two important changes in these traditional arguments. First, he shifted the site of agency from caretaker to infant by arguing that the infant's actions toward and with the caretaker contributed to the establishment of an attachment. Second, Bowlby recognized that the pleasure–pain dichotomy referred not only to the sating of hunger, but also to the control of anxiety. He elevated the significance of the second component of the infant–mother bond by suggesting that not only did the caretaker symbolize the pleasure of need satisfaction but she was also effective in muting the infant's anxiety.

This change in the salient affect linking mother and infant implied a new metric for the relation between them, albeit still a qualitative one. The behaviorists' descriptions, which used the phrase *reward value*, implied that the probability of approaching the caretaker was the most sensitive index of the nature of the infant–mother bond. Bowlby, by substituting *degree of security* for *reward value*, suggested that inhibition of distress with the caretaker was a more sensitive index of that bond than probability of approach. This is not a trivial change in emphasis. The objects infants approach are not always the ones that effectively mute distress.

A new rattle, which typically elicits an approach, does not always placate a frightened infant. (As we shall see in the last section of this chapter, the meaning of any construct—attachment is one example—varies with its informational source. Hence the validity of theoretical assertions about attachment varies with the procedures used to measure it.)

There are at least two reasons why Bowlby's writing catapulted the ideas of secure and insecure attachments and their future consequences into prominence. After World War II middle-class American and European society became appreciably more uncertain about the mother–infant bond, in part because of rising divorce rates, adolescent pregnancies, and working mothers who had to leave their babies in daycare centers or in unfamiliar homes with surrogate mothers. The harmonious, reassuring picture of a 25-year-old mother birthing, nursing, and playing with her baby until it skipped off to kindergarten became flawed. Many Americans were threatened by this violation of naturalness and felt that the new profile of care was malevolent. This source of uncertainty, along with the anxiety created by environmental pollution, economic stress, and possible nuclear war, was projected onto the young infant. Thus history had prepared the average citizen in Europe and North America to believe that an infant's emotional security was, after its nutritional state, the most important function to maintain.

Bowley answered those parents who wondered how they might meet this natural need best by suggesting that the infant's sense of security depended upon its attachment bond to a single caretaker. Aware of the requirement for an operational index of the attachment bond, Bowlby had the intuition that separation protest was a sensitive referent of a secured bond. The reason for that guess is found on the first page of the first volume of the trilogy, *Attachment* (1969), where Bowlby suggests that the cry of separation in a 1-year-old resembles the mourning of an adult who has lost spouse or sweetheart because both seem to share the dimension of distress following the loss of a love object. This is not an obviously persuasive rationale. The unrestrained motor tantrums of a 1-year-old following frustration share many qualities with the physical aggression and destructiveness of an 18-year-old delinquent. But very few developmental scholars have suggested that the two phenomena are theoretically similar, and few scientists believe that a 1-year-old who throws trantrums frequently is highly likely to become a violent adolescent.

Thus an important reason for the increased empirical interest in attachment was the ease of implementation of Mary Ainsworth's Strange Situation, which promised to quantify Bowlby's secure and insecure attachments in an objective and therefore scientific manner (Ainsworth, Blehar, Waters, & Wall, 1978; Stayton & Ainsworth, 1973). I suspect that, if Binet and Simon had not constructed an *intelligence test,* McClelland and Atkinson had not invented an objective scoring scheme for *achievement themes* in stories told to pictures, or Piaget had not created the procedure for *conservation of mass,* none of the constructs associated with these procedures would have achieved their deserved importance and fame. The theoretical ideas of intelligence, need for achievement, and conservation became popular because each was linked to a relatively simple, apparently valid procedure that provided referential meaning to the hypothetical construct. And following the productive use of the Strange Situation in many studies, investigators around the world adopted this method because it promised, in less than an hour, to provide them with a window into a profound human characteristic the larger community believed was significant (Arend, Gove, & Sroufe, 1979).

The history of research on attachment and a child's behavior in the Strange Situation during the past decade represent an elegant tribute to the significance of empirical data in clarifying theory. Two creative scientists, John Bowlby and Mary Ainsworth, elaborated a fruitful set of hypotheses tied to a method anyone could use to test the implications of the ideas—a perfect combination for scientific progress. And a decade of investigation by many scholars has permitted some initial judgments about both the ideas and the validity of the method.

Behavior in the Strange Situation

Support for the assumption that the Strange Situation assesses the current emotional relation of the child 1–2 years old to the mother came from early studies revealing that children who were classified as securely attached in the Strange Situation become more resilient, curious, and socially adroit with peers than did infants classified as less securely attached (Arend et al., 1979; Waters, Wippman, & Sroufe, 1979). A monograph edited by Bretherton and Waters (1985) summarizes more recent studies implying that behavior in the Strange Situation does measure qualities in the child that are probably due in part to the history of interaction with the primary caretaker.

However, there is also evidence to suggest that factors other than the child's experiences with the caretaker make a nontrivial contribution to behavior in the Strange Situation. The two most important are, first, the child's temperamental tendency to become uncertain and anxious in unfamiliar situations (Kagan, 1984), and, second, parental socialization practices that teach the infant to control behavioral signs of anxiety (Grossmann, Grossmann, Huber, & Wartner, 1981). If these two factors prove to be as important as they seem at the present time, those who use the Strange Situation would have to evaluate them before generating conclusions about security of attachment based only on the child's behavior in the Strange Situation. Four facts support this skeptical stance.

First, although some investigators find good stability of the attachment classification over the second year of life, others do not. In some studies about one-half of the children change their attachment classification during the second year (Schneider-Rosen, Braunwald, Carlson, & Cicchetti, 1985; Thompson, Lamb, & Estes, 1982). A second, more serious critique is the fact that major differences in the availability and nurture of the caretaker do not always correlate with variations in attachment.

One investigator found no differences in the occurrence of secure attachments when children living with working mothers were compared with those who had nonworking mothers. Moreover, the children whose mothers left home to begin work when the infant was 12–20 months old did not change their attachment classification. The assumptions that lie behind the maintenance of a secure attachment would lead one to expect that at least one child whose mother went to work during the second year would have shifted from secure to less secure status (Owen, Esterbrooks, Chase-Landsdale, & Goldberg, 1984). Additionally, one study did not find that Type A–insecure babies receive less affection, love, or playful interaction than securely attached infants (Belsky, personal communication, 1986). It is also surprising that the proportions of Type A, B, and C infants in a sample of average Swedish families were not significantly different from the proportions found among Swedish infants whose mothers had serious psychiatric disturbance during the first year of life. In fact, the proportion of infants who were securely attached to their mothers tended, if anything, to be slightly higher for mothers who were known to have been psychotic and clearly disturbed. ". . . No evidence was found that serious active maternal mental disturbance during the infant's first year of life relates positively to anxious attachment to the mother at one year of age." (Naslund, Persson-Blennow, McNeil, Kaij, & Malmquist-Larsson, 1984, p. 238)

A third basis for questioning the validity of the Strange Situation derives from the belief that the child's temperamental vulnerability to uncertainty, fear, distress, and behavioral inhibition to the unfamiliar makes some contribution to behavior in the Strange Situation. This suggestion is based on the fact that the child's reunion behavior is correlated with the degree of upset displayed following separation. Children who seriously protest the separation are less likely to be classified as Type A and more likely to be classified as Type C (Connell, 1985). Thompson and Lamb (1984) note:

> Avoidant infants show little or no distress during separation, long latency to onset, and a relatively quick recovery, while resistant infants evince intense separation to stress, brief latency, and slow recovery (p. 440).

There is a great deal of support for the claim that temperamental vulnerability to uncertainty influences behavior in the Strange Situation. A major source for this claim is that infants who are classified as resistant–insecure (Type C infants) at 1 year are psychologically different from securely attached babies from the opening weeks of life. As young infants, Type C children are more irritable, more prone to sleep problems, and generally harder to manage than Type A or B infants. For example, Japanese newborns in the city of Sapporo who would be classified as Type C when they were 1 year old were more likely to cry intensely to the mild frustration of nipple removal than were newborns who would be classified as securely attached. When observed at 1 and 3 months of age in their homes, the former group cried more often and more intensely and, at 7 months, showed more fear to an adult stranger. At 2 years of age, the irritable newborns were more cautious and shy with an unfamiliar child than were securely attached or avoidant children (Chen & Miyake, 1983; Miyake, Chen, Shing-yen, & Campos, 1985).

Although Belsky and Isabella (in press) did not find a predictive relation between early infant irritability and later categories of attachment, Waters, Vaughn, and Egeland (1980) found that extremely irritable newborns were most likely to become Type C infants; almost half (11 of 26) of a group of Type C infants were unusually irritable newborns with a low threshold for arousal. Crockenberg (1981) reported that when highly irritable newborns were raised by mothers with minimal social support, the probability of a Type C classification was even higher. Further, 18-month-olds who were classified as most securely attached (Types B1 and B2) were the least inhibited when playing with an unfamiliar child in a play situation (Easterbrooks & Lamb, 1979), and Israeli children 11–14 months old who were most sociable with a stranger in an unfamiliar context were most likely to be classified as B1 and B2 and least likely to be classified as B4 or C infants (Sagi, Lamb, & Gardner, 1986). Because the peer play and adult stranger situations in the study are similar to the ones our research group uses to assess temperamental inhibition, it is reasonable to suggest that B1 and B2 children are likely to be temperamentally uninhibited (see also Hazen & Durrett, 1982). Even Mary Ainsworth has written that "babies who cry much more frequently than those who cry little tend to protest the mother's departure and to cry when she returns" (Stayton & Ainsworth, 1973, p. 230); "there is no evidence that either in brief separations in an unfamiliar environment or in major separations that last for days or even months, intensity of separation distress is related to persisting anxious relationships with the mother" (Stayton & Ainsworth, 1973, p. 234).

The positive relation between a Type C classification during infancy and later signs of temperamental inhibition is affirmed in a longitudinal study of 113 children who were observed in the Strange Situation at 1 year and assessed at age 6 with the Achenbach-Edelbrock Child Behavior Profile. The 1-year-old boys classified as Type C were judged 5 years later to be less communicative, more withdrawn, and more shy than children who had been A or B infants. Type C females at age 6 were less aggressive and less active than A or B children (Lewis, Feiring, McGuffog, & Jaskir, 1984). This relation is in accord with another study of 96 children observed in the Strange Situation at 12 and 18 months and in a preschool setting at 4–5 years of age. The 10 Type C children were rated as more shy and anxious than the children in groups A or B; the 10 Type A children were rated as more impulsive than the children in groups B or C (Erickson, Sroufe, & Egeland, 1985). This profile is exactly what one would expect if temperamental inhibition and lack of inhibition had some influence on the child's behavior in the Strange Situation.

Perhaps the most persuasive support for this hypothesis is the fact that signs of temperamental inhibition were a better predictor of a Type C classification than a prior history of maltreatment. Comparison of the Strange Situation behavior of maltreated and nonmaltreated children from the same social class at both 19 and 25 months revealed that the children who cried and stayed close to their mothers during the first 3 min of the Strange Situation, as well as during a free-play episode, were most likely to be classified as Type C (Schneider-Rosen, 1984). The child's inhibited or uninhibited behavior with the mother in an unfamiliar room was a better predictor of a Type C classification than almost 2 years of maltreatment at home.

If a low threshold for uncertainty to the unexpected and unfamiliar influences the child's behavior in the Strange Situation to some degree, it will also affect the child's attachment classification. Because the best predictor of seeking contact with the mother when she reenters the room is the degree of upset and distress shown following her departure, infants with a very close relation with the mother who do not become uncertain to the unfamiliar may not cry when the mother leaves and, therefore, will not approach her when she returns. More of these children will be classified Type A. Infants who are moderately vulnerable to uncertainty are more likely to cry when the mother leaves and to approach her when she returns. But because they do not become extremely upset they will be easily placated and classified as securely attached. The children with a very low threshold for uncertainty will become very upset by the unexpected maternal departure and, as a result, are likely to push their mother away as they continue to sob. These infants are likely to be classified as Type C (see Frodi & Thompson, 1985, for empirical support for this claim).

The complete corpus of data is at least suggestive of the hypothesis that the temperamental characteristics associated with the qualities of inhibition and lack of inhibition make some contribution to the classifications of secure and insecure attachment in the Strange Situation, despite Sroufe's claim to the contrary (Sroufe, 1985). Of course, these temperamental qualities probably influence the way parents interact with their children and so behavior in the Strange Situation must reflect, in part, the history of parent–child encounters (see Belsky & Isabella, in press, for a more detailed summary of this position).

A final source of skepticism regarding the validity of the Strange Situation comes from information suggesting that the child's behavior in the Strange Situation is influenced by the degree to which the mother has encouraged her child to control its anxiety over the course of the first year. A child with an attentive and loving mother who has encouraged self-reliance and control of fear is less likely to cry when the mother leaves and, therefore, less likely to approach her when she returns. This child is likely to be classified as avoidant. By contrast, the child whose mother has been protective and less insistent that her child deal with anxiety is more likely to cry and rush to the mother when she reenters the room and so be classified as securely attached (see Hock & Clinger, 1981). This suggestion is affirmed by the behaviors of middle-class West German children (Grossmann et al., 1981). In sharp contrast with the norms for Americans, where three-fourths of 1-year-olds are classified as securely attached, only one-third of these German children behaved in the Strange Situation as if they were securely attached, and almost one-half were avoidant. These data imply not that more German than American children are insecurely attached, but rather that German mothers promote independence and do not like children who cling when they are frightened. Thus both temperamental qualities and prior socialization influence the child's behavior in the Strange Situation.

The total corpus of information poses problems for the traditional interpretation of the primarily experiential origins of Types A, B, and C children. No one, including the author, claims that behavior in the Strange Situation is unrelated to aspects of the prior history of the infant–parent dyad. But the attachment classifications do not reflect only that history. Each is a complex behavioral product that is simultaneously an index of the child's temperamental disposition to be inhibited or uninhibited, prior socialization for the control of fear, and, of course, the emotional relationship to the parent. It may not be possible to separate the differential contribution of these three factors in a single ahistorical assessment at 1 year, as it is not possible to separate the influence of improvement in medical care from that of water purification and health education in explaining the greater longevity of American over Indian citizens during the past year.

Consequences for Future Research

Regardless of the future of the Strange Situation as a method, the research on the construct of attachment has had important benevolent consequences for study of the effect of family experience on the child. Traditional constructs continue to describe, as they have for a century, either the qualities of the child or the qualities in the parents' behavior because of the simplifying assumption that particular parental behaviors produce uniform outcomes in children. The research on attachment, which deals with the relationship between child and adult, has produced a dissatisfaction with this traditional frame, and a small number of investigators are searching for constructs that describe relationships between a profile of parental qualities and a profile in the child. Although similar constructs exist in other disciplines, we do not recognize them as such. For example, when biologists learn the cause of a disease the resulting diagnostic label is, in fact, descriptive of a relation between the pathogen and the symptoms. The construct *poliomyelitis* refers to motor paralysis due to viral infection of the motor neurons—a relation between a specific virus and a specific metabolic process in the spinal cord.

It will be useful to search for analogous constructs in human development. Children vary in their temperamental vulnerability to uncertainty; parents vary in the degree to which they control the child. Suppose that the combination of a controlling parent and a temperamentally uncertain child produces a specific profile different from a controlling mother interacting with an uninhibited child. Another pair of outcomes is generated when a minimally controlling mother interacts with either an inhibited or uninhibited child. The four combinations require four different constructs to capture the relation between the category of child and the category of experience. Currently we do not have such concepts in our vocabulary. The invention of such constructs will advance developmental theory; the motivation to search for these concepts is attributable directly to the work on attachment. Thus in a relatively short time, the work of Bowlby, Ainsworth, and their students has been responsible for major progress in our understanding of early psychological development. Even though slips of the tongue have not proved to be sensitive indices of sexual conflict, Freud's ideas have had a productive influence on our conception of human behavior. A fruitful idea can be more significant than a new method. This conclusion provides a liaison to our final section.

METHODS AND THE MEANING OF PROPOSITIONS

Investigators in young scientific disciplines are tempted to begin their work with a priori concepts they believe refer to phenomena in nature, and to search for ways to measure their actualization in evidence. As a discipline becomes mature, investigators come to recognize that many of their constructs do not reflect essences in nature, but are inexact cognitive inventions that account for robust empirical relations. As a consequence, investigators take the covariation between events more seriously than they do their favorite words. A fifteenth century naturalist's description of flora and fauna usually began with theist ideas; four centuries later botanists used names like *stamen* and *pistil,* which represented newly discovered covariations. It is only in the most mature stage of a discipline that abstract and powerful concepts—like *energy*—become useful. Unfortunately, many parts of psychology are still in the first stage; hence a majority of investigators typically begin their work with abstract words like *intelligence, anxiety,* and *memory,* which they believe have an essence in nature, and look for signs of these essences with procedures they hope will reveal some portion of the event implied by the term.

A comparison of the technical literature in physiology, addressed, let us say, to the effects of drugs, lesions, or imposed stress on animal behavior, with the technical psychological literature on children is instructive. The introductory paragraphs of the former reports rarely contain constructs without a clear referential meaning. The first sentence of the paper is usually a summary of what another investigator has found, and the author implies that the current report is an extension of or an attempt to refute the earlier result. Second, the method sections contain much more detail than psychological papers on children. Angles, speeds, and distances are typically described, while the comparable categories in children's experiments—rate and loudness of speech of the examiner, time of day, and duration of the episode—are usually missing. Finally, the discussion section is typically terse and conservative, while the developmental report is often the occasion for an excursion into possibilities that extend the obtained result far beyond its probable validity.

I am not praising the physiological papers and criticizing the psychological reports. There are scientific advantages and disadvantages to both styles. But it is useful for the psychologist to be aware of the physiologists' acute self-consciousness of the premise that the meanings of the propositions that summarize data derive in part from the specific evidence gathered. Hence each class of empirical procedure potentially imposes a special meaning on the sentences that summarize the evidence.

The Two Meanings of Terms

The meaning of words that describe relations among events is a central problem in all domains of scholarship, but especialy in the behavioral sciences, where many terms originated in folk language. An important insight articulated during the last century is the recognition that words have two different types of meaning. One is contained in the cognitive structures that represent the symbolic dimensions of the word; the other comprises the events to which the word refers. It is understood that a word can have the first type of meaning without the second (Putnam, 1975). Although many scholars have written on this theme, Frege's (1892) distinction between the *sense* and *referential* meanings of words seems to capture the central qualities of the two kinds of meaning. The sense of a word, according to Frege, is the thought it expresses. The referential meaning is contained in the objects and events to which the word points. The morning star and the evening star, which have different senses but the same reference, is a favorite illustration among philosophers. The sense of the word *intelligence* in psychological theory includes the concepts of an alert state, the ability to learn new skills and ideas quickly, efficient and accurate problem solving, and inductive and deductive reasoning talents. Each of these abstract concepts has an ambiguous referent, and there is a disguised presumption that the abstract properties are correlated. By contrast, the referential meanings of *intelligence,* at least in contemporary America, include scores on standardized intelligence and aptitude tests, grades in school and college, receipt of academic prizes, or scores on one or more of the many cognitive tasks psychologists have invented. A correlation among referential meanings is always hoped for but is often unrealized.

There is a general consensus among empirical scientists that the meaning of a theoretical construct should combine both sense and referential meanings; hence any change in the reference has the potential to change the meaning of the construct. Francis Galton regarded sensory acuity as a salient referential feature of *intelligence;* David Wechsler believed size of vocabulary was primary. These two features are typically uncorrelated. When Descartes used the word *body* in sentences devoted to the body–mind problem the primary defining quality he intended was not, as it is for modern neurophysiologists, the columnar organization of neurons in the cerebral cortex. The phrase "sex of a person" can refer in contemporary essays on gender to an individual's chromosomes, gonads, or external genitals; in the eighteenth century the same phrase referred only to the last characteristic.

Contemporary physicists and biologists are much more sensitive to this possibility than are behavioral scientists, in part because psychologists are far less certain than their colleagues in biology or chemistry that the evidence that provides the rationale for a construct captures the desired meaning. Hence behavioral scientists often treat serious changes in reference as having minimal effect on the meaning of the construct. The problem with this attitude, as Frege noted, is that the truth value of a proposition in empirical science applies to the referential, not the sense, meaning. "It is the striving for truth that drives us always to advance from the sense to the reference" (Geach & Black, 1960, p. 63). Even though Putnam (1975) rejects the orthodox form of logical empiricism, he notes that two people can have equivalent sense meanings of a term but different referents; it is the latter that determines whether the term is being used correctly.

The main point of this section is that the source of empirical information—the *referent*—used to award referential meaning to a scientific term is associated with a particular hierarchy of salient, defining features. The features can be regarded as representing selected aspects of the events that are quantified in a particular investigation, usually called the *dependent variables*. Each dependent variable is mediated by specific hypothetical processes, or mechanisms, that are provoked by a procedure. If the processes mediating two phenotypically different sources of empirical information that are presumed to bear on the same construct are different, the propositions summarizing the evidence have different meanings. If, on the other hand, it can be argued, or better yet demonstrated, that the processes mediating the observed events are the same, it is reasonable to treat the two sources of evidence as representative of the same construct. When an outside thermometer reads 90 deg Fahrenheit and many people are perspiring while walking on the sidewalk, we believe both observations are mediated by the kinetic energy of the molecules in the air. Hence each observation reflects the same salient feature that gives meaning to the proposition "The day is hot." But it is less obvious that the same processes mediate precocious standing during the first year of an infant's life, on the one hand, and, on the other, precocious attainment of a large vocabulary in the tenth year. Hence it may be an error to regard both signs as having the same meaning with respect to the construct *intelligence*. When two sets of observations do not share a common process, they should not be regarded as signs of the same construct, no matter what the intuitions of an investigator may be. Because each method used to generate observations is linked to a set of specific, mediating processes, the referential meaning of a scientific term is always influenced by the procedure that produced the relevant data.

One investigator's statements about a child's security of attachment based on a 1-year-old's behavior in the Ainsworth Stange Situation award salience to the child's degree of upset following separation from the mother and ease of being soothed following the mother's return. However, another investigator's statements about security of attachment based on watching a child play with the mother at home award salience to laughter and duration of reciprocal play. These two meanings of attachment may not be equivalent, even though both investigators agree that the basic sense meaning of attachment involves an emotional bond between the infant and the caretaker. For the same reason, the proposition "Anger usually follows an insult" has one meaning if the scientist codes facial expression, a different meaning if plasma catecholamines are quantified, and a third meaning if an interviewer asks the person following the insult, "What emotion are you experiencing?"

Some recent philosophical essays have noted that the meaning of a construct is influenced by the theoretical network of which it is a part (e.g., see Thomas 1979) and have placed less emphasis on referential meaning. However, it is usually the case that the terms that form the logical theoretical network are linked to special procedures and therefore to special sources of evidence. In the psychometric theories of differential intelligence, theoretical terms like *heredity* and *verbal* and *spatial abilities* are linked; in Piaget's theory of the ontogeny of intelligence the linked terms are *equilibrium, assimilation, accommodation,* and the *stages of sensory-motor* and *concrete* and *formal operations.* The theoretical meaning of intelligence is different in the two networks, but it is also obvious that the referents for the terms in the two networks are also very different. The first network refers to IQ scores obtained from monozygotic and dizygotic twins, for example. The second network points to performances on tests for the object concept and assessments of conservation of mass and class inclusion. Indeed, it is not possible to find two different theoretical networks for a given psychological term that refer to identical empirical procedures.

The main claim here is that a conceptual term can exhibit polysemy when it is applied to different sources of evidence, as the meaning of a statement varies with the context of its application. Although this position is similar in spirit to the proposal by Bridgman (1927), and the writings of the scholars who comprised the Vienna circle during the early 1930s, it is more permissive, and avoids its counterintuitive flaws. In Bridgman's view, each concept's central feature was represented by the procedure used to produce the relevant data: "the concept is synonymous to the corresponding set of operations" (1927, p. 5). Because the meaning of a term was synonymous with the procedure, any change in method meant a change in meaning. Thus an orthodox interpretation of Bridgman holds that the meaning of the word *hot* in the proposition "This day is hot" changes if two different types of thermometers are used. But most scholars agree that Bridgman went too far in demanding that every change in procedure implied a new meaning. If different methods produce information referring to the same defining features of a term (because they are linked to the same mediating processes), its meaning remains the same. Thus the meaning of *hot* to describe the temperature of the air is the same with any form of thermometer because the defining feature of *hot* (i.e., kinetic energy of molecules in the air) remains unchanged. But the meaning of *hotter* in the sentence "The piece of iron is hotter than the piece of wood" has one meaning if it refers to the ability of the object to warm a third body, but a different meaning if it refers to a person's sensation of heat upon touching each of the objects, because the defining features of *hotter* are not identical in the two instances (Churchland, 1979).

The opening chapter in Wundt's *An Introduction to Psychology* (1912) provides an example of a tendency among psychologists to be insensitive to the source of information that supports a conclusion. Wundt admits in the first chapter to a difficulty in defining the term *consciousness.* He then proceeds abruptly, and without explanation, to describe a procedure in which a subject reports his perceptions to the beats of a metronome. Because adults hear the beats as varying in intensity, Wundt concludes: "Our consciousness is rhythmically disposed" (p. 5). Although the meaning of that statement is totally dependent upon, and derived from, the procedure with the metronome, Wundt generalized broadly from that specific context to talk of consciousness in general, as Pavlov generalized from the salivation reflex in dogs to the freedom reflex in humans (Boakes, 1984). This habit is still strong among psychologists, who often construct a very narrow procedural context and use a term to describe their data that implies applicability to a broad set of contexts—a leap from the highly particular to the universal.

Weissman cut the tails of more than 20 generations of rats to demonstrate that the principle of inheritance of acquired characteristics was incorrect, apparently convinced that it did not make much difference what particular organ or species was chosen to refute the principle (Sturtevant, 1965). Mendel's early work with the plant *Hieracium* produced data inconsistent with what turned out to be valid hypotheses, but he could not know that *Hieracium* seeds arise without meiosis or fertilization.

> This was the worst possible choice of material for the study of segregation and recombination—for reasons that could not be guessed at the time
>
> > (*Sturtevant, 1965, p. 11*).

The poor vision of white rats makes them inappropriate subjects for experiments that use visual stimuli as conditioned signals, and it now appears that Harlow was lucky to have chosen rhesus macaques and not crab eaters in his research on the effects of isolation (Sackett, Ruppenthal, Fahrenbruch, Holm, & Greenough, 1981). Had Harlow chosen the latter species he would not have seen such severe disturbances in social behavior following isolation, and may not have made the important discovery of the isolation syndrome. Some modern essays on learning theory (Logan, 1979; Prelec, 1982; Staddon, 1984) posit principles containing terms that are completely indifferent to species or class of response.

Psychologists who study habituation would like to believe in the utility of a general term that represents some essential process. Peeke and Petrinovich (1984) urge that psychologists "restrict the use of the term habituation to refer to theoretical processes and never use it as a behavioral description" (1984), p. 5). But habituation of a looking response (duration of fixation to a stimulus) does not always co-occur with habituation of heart rate to the same stimulus (Reznick & Kagan, 1982). Further, there is typically little cross-stimulus generality among infants in rate of habituation of the looking response (Kagan, 1971; Reznick & Kagan, 1982). One 6-month-old who habituates rapidly to checkerboards may habituate slowly to faces, while another infant may show the opposite profile. The descriptor *fast* (or *slow*) *habituator* is usually specific to a class of stimulus events, as well as to a specific response. Hence all sentences of the form "Habituation . . . " followed by a predicate cannot be understood unless the listener knows the source of the information that gives meaning to the term *habituation*.

Propositions about individual differences in personality are especially vulnerable to the problem of meaning ambiguity. Consider the proposition "Introverts become anxious in social situations." There are various meanings of that proposition, depending upon the procedures used to assess *introversion,* on the one hand, and *anxiety in social situations,* on the other. Introversion might have been measured by a questionnaire, observation of behavior in a social setting, or an interviewer's rating based on an interview. Each method might emphasize a different set of features of the concept. Similarly, judgment of anxiety in a social situation could have been based on replies to a questionnaire, behavioral observations, reactions of the autonomic nervous system, or cortisol levels in the blood. Thus a listener might judge as true the proposition "Introverts [based on responses to a self-report questionnaire] become anxious in social situations [based on the frequency of small motor movements in a social situation]" but judge as false the proposition "Introverts [based on a psychiatric interview] are anxious in social situations [based on a rise in heart rate during a group discussion in a laboratory]."

A final example comes from an unpublished study of attitudes among working- and middle-class American mothers. Each of 60 mothers was asked in an interview whether she thought that physical affection was beneficial for infants. Over 90 percent of the mothers said they believed in the benevolent consequences of physical affection; an infant who did not receive affection would be at risk. But when each of the women was asked to recall a taped essay of about 400 words that promoted equally convincing arguments for and against physical affection, the working-class women recalled more of the words supporting the argument against affection, while the middle-class mothers recalled more words supporting the benevolent consequences of affection. This result, which was replicated with three samples of mothers, suggests that working-class American mothers have a weaker commitment to the proposition that physical affection is health giving. The two methods provide different results because the particular essay used for selective recall emphasized some of the dangers of physical affection while the interviewer's questions did not. Hence the validity of the conclusion "American mothers believe physical affection is good for infants" will vary with the procedure. That proposition is more valid for self-report than for selective recall of the essay. These conclusions are not inconsistent. A woman does not have a unified, coherent belief about the importance of physical affection for children. Rather, each mother holds a family of related beliefs about this broad domain. Some investigators who invent the construct *parental attitude about physical affection* presume a unity that may not exist. The anthropologists' practice of relying almost exclusively on reports by informants to reveal beliefs and standards provides only one source of understanding of the mores of a community. Even though the movement called psychological anthropology has not been as successful as many had hoped, its practitioners assumed that application of multiple methods of inquiry would provide a richer picture of a society than informant report alone (Whiting & Whiting, 1959).

Self-Report Procedures

Some investigators write as if the most valid meaning of a term resides with the information produced by self-report, or that information gathered with other procedures must be in accord with the data gathered through self-report. However, there is often little or no relation between a construct like *high self-esteem* based on self-report, on the one hand, and degree of empathic identification with a figure symbolic of someone with high esteem, on the other (Kagan, Hans, Markowitz, Lopez, & Sigal, 1982). Similarly, there is no relation between adults' self-reports of anxiety and changes in finger pulse volume to a stressful situation (Smith, Houston, & Zurawski, 1984). Indeed, there can be no relation between subjects' self-reports of whether or not they were sleeping and their EEGs when awakened at a time the EEG indicated stage 2 sleep (Sewitch, 1984). The author notes: "whatever the underlying internal signals that are detected and used by subjects to report whether they had been awake or asleep, they are not necessarily the same signals that are indexed by polygraphic data" (p. 258).

The term *hurt* provides a particularly persuasive example of the special qualities of self-report information (Wall, 1974). Adults who are administered low levels of electric shock just below or at threshold and asked to say when they feel a sensation display remarkable consensus, both across different laboratories and across time, in the shock level associated with the first report of a sensation. Hence the concept of *sensory threshold for feeling shock* has a stable and clear meaning in this procedural context. However, when the shock level is increased and the subjects are asked to report when they feel that the stimulus hurts, there is far less agreement, both within and across subjects. Why is there consensus, in this context, for the predicate *feel*, but not for the predicate *hurt*? One possibility is that *feel* involves only one judgment made over a short period of time, namely: Is there a difference between one's conscious feelings of a sensation before and after the stimulus? But *hurt* involves more than one judgment. In deciding whether a stimulus hurts, the person implicitly asks other questions, for example, "Is the shock tolerable?" or "Is this feeling similar to other pains I have known?" The answers to these questions are less reliable—or less consistent—because of these additional evaluations.

These additional evaluations are inherent in most, if not all, self-report instruments and answers given in interviews. Every question, whether printed on a scale or asked by an interviewer, forces a subject, unconsciously, to decide on the meaning of the terms, and the investigator cannot assume highly similar understandings of the meanings of questions. The meaning inferred is based on the features of the terms the subject selects as salient, and those features may not be the ones the investigator intended. After discerning meaning, but before answering, the subject relates the comprehended meaning to a larger frame to judge its coherence. For example, suppose a questionnaire asks a mother, "Is your child active—yes or no?" The mother must first decide on the meaning of *active*. The meaning chosen will be influenced by her associations and by the larger frame to which she relates these associations, especially her understanding of her child. If the mother regards her child as intelligent, she may select as a salient feature of *active* the qualities of being curious and exploratory, and so answer "yes." But if she selects the quality of restlessness as a salient dimension of *active*, she may answer "no," if she views restlessness as inconsistent with high intelligence. All parents do not discern the same meaning in a question, in part because of idiosyncratic associations to the words, and in part because of the larger frame to which the question is referred, even after its meaning is comprehended. Perhaps that is why questionnaire studies of activity level in twins reveal heritability while actual observations do not (Plomin & Foch, 1980), and why there is often minimal agreement between a parent's report of the infant's qualities and objective observations of the child (Rothbart & Derryberry, 1981; see Bates, Chapter 23, this volume).

Are There Essences?

The position being promoted here is opposed to the view that theoretically useful psychological terms refer to Platonic essences, each with a best meaning and detectable with an optimally sensitive procedure. The events scientists name, whether ontologically real or invented, consist of sets of correlated qualities.

Investigators who study sleep often write as if there were a more essential form of this state—a unique set of events that is more basically sleep than any other—rather than assuming a family of different states of sleep, each characterized by a set of correlated qualities. The state defined by eyes closed, slow waves in the EEG, no rapid eye movements, and no awareness of being awake when aroused by an experimenter comprises one profile. The state defined by eyes closed, slow waves in the EEG, but rapid eye movements and a consciousness of being awake is another. Each is an equally legitimate example of *sleep*. The state that a particular investigator selects as primary will be a function of his or her theoretical interests. Some features of sleep, dreaming, for example, occur more often in one profile of states than another. The fact that our language contains the word *sleep* tempts us to posit an essence, for words invite, at least in the western mind, the idea of a most fundamental referent in nature for the event named.

Put plainly, although the words behavioral scientists use to describe events are typically abstract universals, the phenomena are coherences of separate, particular events. Hence the words do not map exactly on the events, but are only approximations. I acknowledge, however, that this position probably represents a minority view, for many philosophers, as well as behavioral scientists, prefer to begin their empirical work by first assuming the existence of an abstract process and then searching for the procedure that will reveal its essence in the purest form. The philosopher Paul Churchland (1984), for example, writes as if there is an ontologically real process called *conscious intelligence*: "the activity of a suitably organized matter, and the sophisticated organization responsible for it is . . . the outcome of billions of years of chemical, biological, and neurological evolution" (p. 147). In an earlier work, Churchland (1979) argued that when the terms of modern science replace those of folk psychology the community will come "closer to the ideal of seeing it as it 'really is'" (p. 36); "if we can come to understand much more deeply what it is that the machine between our ears is *doing,* then may we find ourselves able to specify what doing it *best* amounts to" (p. 150).

These statements imply an a priori belief in a set of most essential mental states, not unlike the apriorist mathematician who assumes that his or her mathematical intuition refers to an idealized real state (Kitcher, 1983). I wish to contrast this a priori strategy, characteristic of Wittgenstein in the *Tractatus* (1922), with the more inductive frame adopted in *Philosophical Investigations* (Wittgenstein, 1953) by using the construct of anxiety as the illustration. The position being criticized is one in which a basic state called *anxiety* is assumed to exist in infant and adult humans, as well as animals. Hence scientists apply this term to very different sources of information that may not share the same features, and therefore do not form a coherence. Kandel (1983), for example, uses the word *anxiety* to describe the neuronal physiological processes that accompany reliable changes in the defensive behavior of the sea snail *Aplysia,* and implies that this meaning of *anxiety* shares an essential similarity with the one a psychiatrist intends when describing a father who is worried about his son's grades.

But consider the contrasting situation in which each of four investigators in different laboratories finds a correlation in 4-year-olds among four variables: withdrawal to the mother and reluctance to approach an unfamiliar peer; a rise and stabilization of heart rate to cognitive problems; an increase in pupil size to mild stress; and high cortisol levels in the saliva. Each investigator gives this coherence of four qualities a different name because each focuses on a different dimension of the set of correlated qualities. The first investigator calls the coherence *shyness,* the second, *tension,* the third, *arousal,* and the fourth, *anxiety.* Each of these four terms awards salience to a particular quality in the information generated by the procedures. A fifth investigator who learned about the coherence of the four phenomena might impose a superordinate construct, for example, *vulnerability to uncertainty or fear,* to name the set of covariations. But the meaning of this last phrase is still to be understood in terms of the information produced by the original procedures (Kagan et al., 1984).

The Preservation of Qualities

The theme of essences is relevant to statements about the preservation of individual differences in psychological qualities over long periods of time. Many psychologists assume that when there is statistical evidence for preservation of individual differences in a quality, say, vulnerability to fearfulness, an essence of that quality must be preserved. However, if the procedures that assessed the quality emphasized different features over the period of study, as they often do, I claim that the meanings of the term that describe the quality in question are not identical. That counterintuitive statement creates a problem, for it implies that a particular human quality was not preserved, despite statistical evidence for its continuity. But this may not be as serious a problem as it seems to be on the surface.

Consider an analogy from evolutionary biology. The quality a biologist might call the *cyclicity of female receptivity to mating* has continuously differentiated between mammals and reptiles over the last 30 million years. Differences between the two groups of animals in this quality have been preserved over this long epoch despite major changes in the behavior and physiology of ancient mammals and reptiles, on the one hand, and modern mammals and reptiles, on the other. Thus although the specific cyclic qualities of receptivity to mating have changed, through lawful transformations in both groups, the differences between reptiles and mammals that existed earlier are present today. A better example involves changes in a person's face from infancy to adulthood. The size, shape, and relative distances of the parts of a person's face from the first birthday to age 40 are transformed seriously. Yet is is possible to detect the faces that belong to particular infants and adults because the pattern of differences between the faces has been preserved over the intervening years. Perhaps the same conclusion holds for vulnerability to personality characteristics like fearfulness.

As described earlier in the section on temperamental inhibition, one meaning of a child's *vulnerability to fearfulness* is contained in the behavior of 21-month-olds in a playroom where they encounter an unfamiliar object (a large robot). But a different meaning of the term *vulnerability to fearfulness* is contained in the observations of 4- and 6-year-olds in a testing room with a female examiner (Kagan et al., 1984). The two meanings of *vulnerability to fear* are not identical because the information gathered at the two ages is different. But because the transformations over time are lawful, the psychological differences between fearful and fearless children are preserved. It is not necessary to assume an unchanging essence of some class of *fearfulness* when individual differences in human qualities are preserved. What is preserved is a set of transformations on an original coherence, like the embryological development of the fertilized egg of a frog, or the growth of two faces.

After citing the famous story of Theseus's rebuilt ship, Millikan (1984) writes:

> There is no such thing as identity over or through time. . . . All there is is the identity of the whole collection of temporal stages with that collection, and a principle of unity that collects these stages into a unified whole. For surely we do not want that one temporal stage of an object should be the selfsame as any other temporal stage. (p. 290)

The premise that a current quality is derived from some original event, a thread of connection from past to present, is a central idea in both history and natural science. Both historians who probe the reasons for the battle of Hastings and cosmologists who investigate the origin of our galaxy inquire about an event in the deep past. However, cosmologists have an advantage historians lack for they can use the present as a source of empirical information about the early event. The recent discovery that the current temperature of the cosmos is about 3 deg Kelvin was used to support theorists who favored an original explosion of gases—the "big bang" theory. This inference required a prior faith in a connectedness between an event over 20 billion years ago and the present moment. However, historians interested in conditions that led to the Battle of Hastings can gain no relevant information from the present moment. All they can do is analyze the remnants of eleventh century information.

Psychologists interested in the childhood origins of adult personality assume they can perform empirical operations on the adult that will provide evidence that is informative about the past. A low vulnerability to frustration is regarded as a sign that early childhood was stressful; a confident college-age woman who plans to become a chemist, like her mother, is treated as information permitting conclusions about the quality of parent–child relationship years earlier. Although most psychologists, including the author, regard this assumption of connectedness as reasonable, it is vulnerable. There is the possibility that the adult, like the earth at Hastings this very morning, is a poor source of information about the past. If there were no procedure that could be implemented in the present moment that would alter the truth values of various developmental histories, then explanations of the construction of an adult profile would be like historical essays. But whether or not statements about the past based on present data are more like historical or scientific propositions, the procedures that produce the evidence do affect the meaning of the terms in those statements.

Essences and the Form of the Evidence

The question as to whether essences exist in nature was the source of a deep controversy between Einstein and Bohr regarding the nature of reality. The basis for the controversy, which resembles Helmholtz's disagreement with Mach several decades earlier, rests, in part, on the specific evidence that the scholar uses to describe nature. Einstein believed that reality consists of essential substances whose properties are unaffected by their relation with other substances. Bohr, by contrast, conceptualized reality as a relation between substances; hence each measurement procedure uncovers an intrinsic aspect of that relation, and only in relation to other phenomena (Hubner, 1983). Bohr wrote: "Nothing is necessarily true, but rather . . . every position is dependent upon the particular conditions of its origin" (cited in Hubner, 1983, p. 89).

An observer can describe a fir tree in a forest as an object with an essence or as sets of relations among molecules that are under continuous and dynamic change. These two descriptive frames can also be imposed on mental and physiological processes. But there seems to be a relation between the source of the information about an event and the tendency to treat it either as an entity with an essence or as a set of relations. When the evidence for the tree originates in vision, it appears discrete and unchanging and we are tempted to regard it as an object with an essence. But if the evidence about the tree comes from a summary of a week's measurements of the amounts of oxygen and carbon dioxide exchanged with the air, it will seem more obvious that the tree consists of sets of relations.

There is a different way to state this idea. Reality is composed of objects and events that change at dramatically different rates. Most objects in the perceptible world—rocks, trees, and cups—change very slowly. Others—ripples on the water, clouds, and the invisibile events we name neutrino and synaptic potential—change rapidly. Most events have both rapidly and slowly changing components. The nucleus of a hippocampal neuron changes its shape slowly, but its postsynaptic potentials change quickly. When the rate of change of a quality that is a salient part of an event is very slow, it seem heuristically useful to regard the event as a stable essence, as we do for the neuron's nucleus. It is intuitively less compelling to regard a rapidly changing event, like a synaptic potential, as a stable essence. However, whenever a mathematical argument predicts a quantity in nature with certainty—like the energy of an atomic particle—mathematicians are prone to assume, with Einstein, that there must be an element in reality corresponding to that quantity. A set of mathematical equations and their predicted quantities written on a piece of paper are unchanging—like my percept of a sturdy tree in the forest. However, for Bohr the empiricist, the primary data consist of patterns of physical measurements. Hence, as was the case for the changing values of carbon dioxide and oxygen in the tree, it may have seemed more reasonable to him to treat reality as sets of coherent relations.

I suspect many psychologists, especially those who study humans, prefer Einstein's view because of the procedures used in their experiments. Much of the research on human behavior involves the gathering of verbal responses—whether a patient's answer to an interview, a test probe, or an adult's mark on a printed questionnaire. These signs, like Einstein's equations, do not change. When a mother tells an interviewer, "My baby is afraid," the primary data are static, discrete signs. Hence it is tempting to treat as essences the psychological processes that are presumed to have produced these data. After asking subjects a series of questions about love, Sternberg and Grajek (1984) conclude that "love is primarily a unifactorial entity with possible subfactors" (p. 327). But suppose these same psychologists had measured the subjects' heart rate, galvanic skin response, and EEG while they listened to and answered the same questions. Because the data would now consist of changing relations among the three measurements I suspect the investigators would have sided with Bohr and denied this emotional state essential status.

If the evidence for the construct of anxiety comes from a questionnaire, the investigator writes about anxiety as if it were an essential and relatively stable quality of a person. By contrast, when the data are autonomic reactions or cortisol levels in blood, the investigator is more likely to categorize the quality as a dynamic set of relations. Thus investigators who use data from test anxiety questionnaires write about fearful subjects; those who use physiological data, like Tennes, Downey, and Vernadakis (1977), write about "a difference among individuals in their biochemical state of readiness to respond" (p. 185), a phrase that implies relations among components, rather than a stable essential quality. Those who contend that a sense of self is a stable essence typically rely on a person's verbal replies to questions. But an investigator who measured a person's blood titer for the major hormones and neurotransmitters, together with the power in the EEG at 8–12 Hz, each day for 2 years would find far less stability. Each empirical index has a different rate of change, and, depending on the ones chosen to describe a person, a scientist will conclude that a person has a stable or unstable set of qualities. The source of evidence determines how the event will be conceptualized.

Because modern research on personality relies heavily on words and sentences as primary data, investigators are prone to conceive of the underlying constructs as stable. Indeed, the controversy sparked by Mischel's (1969) suggestion that personality qualities were not stable was due in part to the fact that Mischel based his conclusions in large measure on overt behaviors, while the defenders of stable personality traits more often used verbal responses (projective test protocols and interview data)—a nice example of the main point of this section. Most of the data in psychology fall into three basic classes: words and sentences (or checkmarks to words and sentences), acts, and recordings of physiological reactions. I suggest that the investigator is more likely to regard the underlying construct as a stable essence when the data consist of sentences rather than physiological measurements. Words and sentences have a function in the social sciences similar to that of numbers and equations in physics.

The problem that no philosopher has been able to solve satisfactorily is the invention of a rational defense of a middle position between, on the one hand, a Platonic idealism that assumes an ontologically real essence behind each theoretically useful construct, and, on the other, a skeptical materialism that declares that all any investigator ever has are clusters of correlated events. A century ago Mach wrote, "All that is valuable to us is the discovery of functional relations and that what we want to know is merely the dependence of experiences on one another" (1959, p. 35)—a statement that the fourteenth century Oxford skeptics would have applauded. More recently, Putnam (1983) captured the same idea: "It begins to look as if Kant was right, and science only gives us relations between objects and not the objects themselves" (p. 44). "Not only has modern physics failed to reveal to us any ready-made objects, any objects with a built-in and unique description, but the objects it does postulate are intimately connected with the observer and his ways of observing them" (p. 178). Perhaps all scientists can do is work toward discovering and conceptualizing more robust coherences among dimensions in order to approach, but, of course, never reach, the least adulterated form of the phenomena being pursued.

Qualities and Quantities

This discussion of sources of evidence is relevant to a profound change in frame that is permeating much of contemporary psychology. We have suggested that when the dimensions selected by an investigator are slow to change the related construct is regarded as an essence. When the dimensions are believed to change rapidly the construct is treated as a dynamic family of events. The attraction to essences or families of events is obviously part of the tension over whether dimensions should be viewed as continua or qualities.

As many scholars have noted, any dimension framed as a continuum can be transformed into two qualities. For example, the continuum of caloric energy we call temperature can be transformed into two qualities by selecting a criterion temperature, say, 80 deg, and calling all temperatures above that value hot and all those below it cold. One can treat the biological correlates of inhibited children, especially heart rate, heart rate variability, pupil size, and cortisol level, as reflecting a continuum of arousal. Or one can regard the more unique characteristics of inhibited children—allergies and phobias—as reflecting discrete qualities. Thus inhibited and uninhibited children can be conceived of as differing quantitatively on degree of arousal of the stress circuits, or as qualitatively different groups.

This is not a semantic trick. The idea of coherence among a set of indices is not synonymous with degree of possession of some unitary characteristic. Biologists do not regard a species of bird that sings, has brightly colored wings, and migrates seasonally as possessing more of a continuous biological quality of "avianness" than a barnyard hen. Consider an analogy from medicine. There is a family of events that includes (1) the presence of tubercle bacilli in the body; (2) symptoms of fever, fatigue, and loss of weight; and (3) the presence of blood in the sputum. Individuals can harbor the tubercle bacilli yet not display a fever, fatigue, or blood in the sputum. Physicians give a special diagnostic label to such asymptomatic persons in order to acknowledge their qualitatively unique status, and biologists do not compute an average of the number of tubercle bacilli, body temperature, weight loss, and frequency of discharge of blood and regard that value as representing the abstract physiological state of tuberculosis. Similarly, inhibited children who show signs of reactivity in all the stress circuits might be regarded as qualitatively different from those who show reactivity in only one or two of them.

When two entities—people, animals, events—vary on many relevant dimensions, the investigator can select those that are slow to change, view them as essences, and, as a consequence, create constructs that imply that the entities have distinctive qualities. Or the investigator can select dimensions that change more rapidly and invent constructs that imply continua. Shy behavior following encounter with an unfamiliar child is a response that changes rapidly with time. Indeed, inhibited children usually overcome their shyness with a peer after 20 min of play. And extreme forms of shyness decrease dramatically from 2–5 years of age. Thus if differential shyness were a major dimension used to classify children, the investigator would probably regard it as a dynamic dimension altered by experience and regard the constructs *inhibited* and *uninhibited* as lying on a continuum. However, the association between inhibited behavior on the one hand and on the other a high and stable heart rate and high cortisol level involves qualities that are slower to change over time. Selection of these dimensions invites the conclusion that inhibition and lack of inhibition are qualitatively different psychological characteristics.

The selection of shy behavior or a stable heart rate as the primary dimension is determined by the investigator's prior interests and questions. If he or she is interested in the environmental determinants of behavior, the focus will be on shyness. If, however, the investigator is interested in the genetic determinants of behavior he or she will more likely focus on variables like heart rate variability. Thus the most important influences on the dimensions selected are the investigator's premises about the nature of the phenomenon. This means that if psychologists come to a problem believing that a behavior of interest is under the strong influence of environmental events they will select dimensions that imply a continuum. If, however, the investigor believes the phenomenon is under strong genetic or biological control he or she is more likely to select dimensions that change less and conceive of them as qualities. Nonetheless, the form of the evidence provided by the procedures does play some role, independent of the investigator's premises, because some procedures (e.g., examining the histology of the central nervous system) typically produce evidence that invites the invention of essences, while other sources (the efficiency of a motor performance that changes rapidly) invite a construct of continuous change.

Many psychological constructs can be viewed as either quantitatively continuous or qualitatively discrete, depending upon the source of evidence and mode of analysis, including language ability in humans and symbolic activity in apes, unconscious and conscious processes, recognition and recall memory, and even sexual identity. When student answers to a questionnaire about sex-role interests comprise the evidence, sexual identity is treated as a continuum, because the scores of males and females overlap a great deal. But when the after-school behavior of preadolescents is used as evidence, there is much less overlap, especially for occurrence of aggression, and the investigators are disposed to treat male and female identities as more discrete.

If schizophrenia is the phenomenon of interest the investigator can focus on the dimension of thought disorder, which is slow to change over time, and regard schizophrenia as an essence and schizophrenics as qualitatively different from manic depressives and normals. Or the observer can focus on the ability to maintain social contact in coversation, which changes rapidly, and conceive of a continuum between schizophrenics and other patients.

Psychologists who study human memory can focus on the large differences in digit span between 5-year-old children and 55-year-old adults, which changes little over materials or cultures, and come to regard young children and adults as qualitatively different groups. On the other hand, the investigator can focus on the memory spans of 6-year-olds across different classes of information, note the large variation across contexts, and come to regard the factors that influence recall memory as continuous functions.

We suspect one reason that Mary Ainsworth and her colleagues (Ainsworth et al., 1978) created three qualitatively different attachment groups (groups A, B, and C) rather than describe their findings in terms of the traditional idea of a continuum of security of attachment was that their longitudinal observations on the mother–child pairs led them to expect certain children to become securely attached.

When these particular children cried a moderate amount when the mother left them alone in a strange situation at 1 year, while others cried either much more or much less (the former group was very difficult to soothe when the mother returned), it was difficult to treat this evidence as forming a continuum. Hence the investigators may have been tempted to create three qualitative groups. However, had they selected a different empirical index of attachment they might have invented a continuum.

We chose to emphasize a qualitative difference between inhibited and uninhibited children because we selected behavioral extremes and therefore minimized behavioral overlap in the original selection. Additionally, the forms of the distributions of the behavioral data gathered subsequently (e.g., time proximal to the mother and time staring at an unfamiliar child) did not suggest a continuous trait, for very few uninhibited children spend a long time near their mothers or staring at the unfamiliar child. The pattern of behavioral stabilities and the intercorrelations also favored the hypothesis of qualitatively discrete groups because inhibited children with a high and stable heart rate at 21 months were different at 5½ years from inhibited children with a low and variable heart rate. Further, the fact that some obviously uninhibited children had a high and stable heart rate led us away from the notion of a continuum of arousal. For if there were such a continuum, inhibited behavior and a high and stable heart rate should have covaried better than they did, and there should have been fewer uninhibited children with a high and stable heart rate. Additionally, as our work proceeded, we began to develop the hypothesis that an inhibited temperament might be inherited. As a result, we were tempted to emphasize dimensions that were unique to inhibited children, like their later-born ordinal position, high cortisol levels, and presence of infant symptoms, like colic, allergy, and constipation. These characteristics imply qualitative differences between inhibited and uninhibited children.

However, if we had believed that experience was the primary cause of both inhibited behavior and the correlated physiological signs, we would have selected dimensions belonging to constructs like strength of conditioned anxiety, motivation to control fear, and ability to deal with uncertainty, concepts that seem to apply to all children in differing degrees. As a result, we would have treated the differences between inhibited and uninhibited children as continuous.

Many readers may feel, as I do, that pragmatic factors will decide which description—qualities or quantities—is theoretically more profitable. The description that leads to the more robust predictions and more satisfying explanations is the one to be preferred. This is the central theme in Bohr's famous essay on complementarity, which attempted to resolve the debate as to whether electromagnetic energy should be treated as a continuous wave or as discrete quanta. Bohr suggested that the frame adopted depended upon the question and mode of data analysis. Each perspective was valid in its own domain of inquiry, leading J. J. Thomson to suggest a metaphor of a tiger and a shark to represent the two perspectives; each animal was potent in its own ecological niche, but impotent in the niche of the other.

I believe that contemporary psychology differs from the discipline 30 years ago in ways that are related to these themes. During the 1940s, psychologists were more likely to ask about the relation between environmental events and overt behaviors. They studied the relation between food deprivation and the speed with which an animal ran a maze, between schedule of reinforcement and rate of operant response, between parental punishment and a child's aggressive behavior, between the behavior of a group of confederates and conforming behavior in a subject. Because both the environmental events impinging on the subject and the subject's responses changed over time and conditions the constructs used to explain the discovered relations were seen as continua. The most popular constructs included strength of a habit or a memory trace, intensity of anxiety, or achievement motivation. These constructs were used in propositions that implied a continuum of dynamic forces subject to environmental manipulation and affecting response dispositions regarded as continua.

There is a noticeable shift to a new set of questions in 1987, especially relations between biological events and behavioral or cognitive phenomena, and between classes of cognitive functioning. Thus in the popular chain of boxes that begins with the environment, is followed by events in the brain and cognitive functions, and leads finally, on the right side of the page, to overt behavior, contemporary psychologists ask more often about relations between the middle pair and less often about the relation between the first and last boxes. These questions involve new procedures and therefore produce new data. These new sources of evidence are summarized with constructs that are conceptualized as slower to change and therefore as essences.

Contemporary psychologists study differences in aggressive behavior in mice as a function of their genotype; in the 1940s they studied aggression in mice as a function of rearing conditions. Because genes are treated as essences, contemporary investigators talk about one strain of mice as being qualitatively different from another. Experimental cognitive psychologists using tachistoscopes discovered a phenomenon of sensory memory that had a fixed value of about 0.25 sec. The stability of this value implies an essence, and so sensory memory is treated as qualitatively different from short-term or long-term memory.

More students of the human infant and child now ask about the relation of brain function to perception, cognition, and behavior, while fewer study the effect of parental practices on the child's behavior. This move creates a view of the child as more fixed, and scientists talk about differences among children as more qualitative than quantitative. As more segments of psychology make biological and cognitive processes rather than environmental events the primary causal agents, constructs that imply qualitative differences between entities will replace those that imply continuous variation.

SUMMARY

Contemporary study of the infant is dominated by three issues: (1) specification of those perceptual, cognitive, and emotional competences that seem to be biologically prepared; (2) the etiology and consequences of variations in attachment and the validity of methods purported to measure these variations; and, finally, (3) the role of temperamental variations among infants. I suspect that progress in all three domains will be facilitated if scientists begin to gather relevant physiological indices along with behavioral ones and remain receptive to inductively derived constructs. A few examples of this joint prescription for progress provide a useful way to end this chapter.

The Use of Physiology

A good reason for including relevant physiological variables in some behavioral studies is that the additional evidence can permit discrimination among phenotypically similar behavior profiles that may belong to different etiological constellations. For example, some infant monkeys do not show obvious behavioral changes when they are removed from their mothers if they are placed immediately in a familiar environment (Levine, 1982). Although the seemingly "normal" behavior might be mistaken for absence of emotional distress to the separation, assessment of cortisol levels reveals higher than normal values in the separated monkeys, suggesting that these animals are under high levels of distress.

A recent study of 60 children 3 years old contained a group of 11 children who, over a 1-hr testing session, showed higher and more stable heart rates than the remaining 49 children, despite no obvious differences in overt behavior and relatively similar levels of cognitive performance (Kagan & Reznick, 1984). The presence of the distinctive heart rate pattern implied a level of task involvement that was not obvious in the children's behavior.

One of the most important findings in the work on inhibited and uninhibited children summarized earlier is that the 21-month-old children who were behaviorally inhibited but had consistenly high and stable heart rates were more likely to remain inhibited for the next 4 years than were equally inhibited 21-month-old children who had low and variable heart rates. The cardiac information permitted differentiation of the two classes of inhibited children. However, use of biological data does not imply a reductive philosophy or award priority to such evidence.

Each scientific discipline rests on distinct classes of evidence with special properties. Each property, as described by linguistic or mathematical terms, is salient for its particular source of evidence and is either less salient or absent from other sources. Language provides a persuasive illustration. Spoken or written propositions in English, which are often treated as the primary information to be analyzed, have a unique structure. These propositions consist of noun classes followed by predicates that specify features of the objects or events denoted by the noun class. These features of propositions are so salient that philosophers of language make a major distinction between *extensional* and *intensional* meanings. The former refers to the entities named by the noun class, the latter to the properties of those entities. By contrast, scientists who study the behavior of children first parse and then describe the actions of agents toward objects, animals, and people. Actions do not lend themselves to the descriptive categories *extensional* and *intensional* that are so useful for propositions. Rather the features of actions involve the goals or intentions of the agent, the target of the actions, and the frequency of the responses. And scientists for whom physiological processes (e.g., heart rate, cortisol, and EEG) comprise the primary data choose features like rate, variability, concentration, and latency.

Consider a psychologist interested in an adult's response to a stressful event, like a difficult cognitive task. The investigator who recorded the subject's introspective descriptions during the task would have a set of propositions containing statements like "I feel tense," "I was uneasy," "I was afraid I would fail." These data are usually summarized by adding the number of references to certain internal, intensional properties; in this case, the property of an unpleasant feeling tone. But the investigator who videotaped the subject's behavior during the 1-hr session would be likely to code talking to the examiner, limb movements, attentiveness to the task, and latency to offer an answer. The scientist who coded the subject's heart rate during the testing session would use as evidence changes in heart rate and heart rate variability and, perhaps, the power in the heart rate spectrum at frequencies from 0.05 to 0.5 Hz.

Each of these data sets has a unique structure, and it is not obvious how one relates one source (or one structure) to another. Hence it is reasonable to suggest that complete equivalence of meaning across the different corpora is not possible, although incomplete or partial equivalence is potentially realizable.

Each scholar wants the theoretical entity he or she is studying with the greatest commitment to have equivalences (i.e., to be substitutable with other classes of information). The philosopher of language, for example, wants a class name, like *Einstein*, to be equivalent to *the man who invented relativity theory.* This desire produced a controversy in the philosophy of language. Both Frege and Russell recognized the problem of the identity of two linguistic terms. Their favorite sample was *Scott* and *the author of "Waverley."* Russell insisted that the two terms were not identical because equivalence was not permitted between a proper name (an extensional term) and a property (an intensional feature).

Similarly, a child psychologist interested in aggressive behavior wants to treat *striking a peer, spitting at a peer,* and *throwing a rock at a peer* as equivalent with respect to the category aggression. And a physiologist who studies stress responses would like to treat increases in cortisol, epinephrine, and heart rate as equivalent when a serious stress is imposed. The problem is that because each of these sources of evidence has unique properties identity is not possible; approximate equivalence is the best that can be attained.

Many neuroscientists would like to believe that eventually they will account for the data of human consciousness with evidence based on discharge patterns of neurons in the central nervous system of invertebrates. But because the structure that describes conscious feeling states is different from the structure of the neural discharges, complete equivalence is probably impossible. There is a limit, determined by the structure of the evidence, beyond which formal equivalences are not attainable. Therefore, there is no reason to fear that physiology will gobble up psychology. Psychological constructs will always be vital.

Inductive Constructs

As implied in the earlier discussion on meaning and procedure, disciplines cycle through periods during which the balance between a priori and a posteriori constructs changes. There is always a tension between the drive for evidence and the drive for system (Quine, 1981). Since its formal inception a century ago, psychology has preferred system to evidence—ideas larger than life usually borrowed from philosophy, physics, evolution, and the daily newspaper. The borrowing of metaphors among disciplines is often helpful but on occasion has misleading connotations. That is one reason that modern physicists adopt what seem to others to be playful terms like *charm* and *quark*. This strategy is not in the service of frivolity, but is a self-conscious desire to find completely novel terms that carry no misleading connotations.

Some metaphors originate in everyone's daily experiences; some are historically limited. Aristotle thought that nature consisted of air, water, earth, and fire. Francis

Bacon's seventeenth century theoretical treatise on the essence of nature posited fiery and nonfiery substances as the two basic kinds of matter in the universe (Rees, 1984), because fire was one of the central ideas in the everyday life of most seventeenth century Europeans, who had neither central heating nor electric stoves. Fire brought warmth, prepared food, and melted metals for the manufacture of pragmatic objects. Because few forces were as central to everyday life as fire, it was easy, perhaps inevitable, that a scholar musing about the essential nature of the material world would divide nature into substances that were or were not related to fire (an example of Tversky & Kahneman's principle of availability).

As I noted in the section on attachment, a similar dynamic is probably operating in the modern suggestion that trust and mistrust, or secure and insecure attachments, are the basic experiences of infancy. Humanists and scientists have called this century the era of anxiety. Their evidence, which seems persuasive, includes parents living far from their childhood homes, two world wars, local conflagrations in the Far and Middle East, famine in Africa, the threat of nuclear destruction, pollution of water, air, and food, and a major increase, at least compared with the nineteenth century, in theft, violence, rape, and assassination. There is a great deal to worry about, and, as an added threat, the nineteenth century mother who remained at home creating a haven for her husband and children has been replaced by a working woman who, out of choice or necessity, leaves home as early as her husband, giving her infant to a stranger in an unfamiliar house or group care center. It is as inviting for modern commentators to choose anxiety and its absence as basic categories for human experience as it was for Bacon to choose fire and its absence as fundamental elements in nature three centuries earlier.

Perhaps one of the most frequently exploited ideas in science, also actualized in daily life, is the complementary relation between an active and an inhibitory principle. Salient examples include a person restraining an impulse to insult another, friction slowing a skater, and a squirrel's sudden freezing on a front lawn. It should not be surprising that many theorists have used this complementarity as a serious basis for explanations of behavior. Locke chose pleasure and pain; Pavlov's dichotomy was between excitation and inhibition; Freud selected id and superego; Skinner, reward and punishment; Cannon, fright and flight; Lewin, Schneirla, and Miller, approach and avoidance. Each of these word pairs shares the idea of a force for action and a force for restraint. Even Francis Bacon was friendly to approach–avoidance as a basic dichotomy in nature and projected it onto inanimate objects in his seventeenth century treatise *Natural History*:

> It is certain that all bodies whatsoever, though they have no sense, yet they have perception; for when one body is applied to another there is a kind of election to embrace that which is agreeable, and to exclude or expel that which is ingrate.
>
> (*cited in Whitehead, 1928, p. 61*)

Some metaphors come not from the mundane events of the day, but from sister sciences. Conservation of energy, a salient idea in late nineteenth century physics, had a profound influence on scholars in many domains, each of whom borrowed, consciously or unconsciously, an energy metaphor. Freud named libidinal energy the primary force and explained hysterical paralysis as a derivative of repression of that energy. Pavlov posited differences in the energy contained in the central nervous system and explained hysteria as due to a weak central nervous system that was characterized by inhibition. Pavlov's *inhibition of the energy in the central nervous system* is analogous to Freud's *repression of libidinal energy.*

Some of psychology's favorite ideas include consciousness, intelligence, learning, motivation, morality, self-esteem, memory, language, reasoning, anxiety, and androgyny. These ideas stand for commendably ambitious undertakings, but lack of methodological sophistication has resulted in a rate of progress that is slower than many hoped. I believe that, if the growth of biology is taken as a guide, developmental psychology is circa 1800 when naturalists began to rebel against abstract metaphysical categories and looked at plants and animals in a less prejudiced way (Delaporte, 1982). Darwin and twentieth century biologists used the naturalists' data to invent a set of theoretical entities that turned out to be very different from those that dominated thought several hundred years earlier. The cell, nucleus, DNA, mutation, phosphorylation, calcium pumps, ecological niches, and natural selection are all inductively derived concepts missing from the vocabulary of eighteenth century scientists. However, much research in cognitive science begins, as Linnaeus did, with abstract categories like *consciousness, attention, memory,* and *representation,* rather than beginning in an inductive frame. The contrast between Chomsky's a priori positing of a language acquisition device and Brown's (1973) inductively derived mean length of utterance is illustrative of the two modes. I believe it is time for psychologists to be a bit friendlier to inductively based constructs. That suggestion does not mean abandoning all a priori ideas and slavishly embracing a sterile, dust bowl know-nothing empiricism. Rather, it urges a readiness to relinquish traditional constructs when new functional relations emerge, a resistance to the tendency to assimilate all new discoveries to old ideas, and a willingness to study the child in greater depth with a variety of procedures. Even Einstein, who represents the prototype of the scholar committed to the power of a priori ideas, wrote to his friend Michael Besso in 1918,

"A theory which wishes to deserve trust must be built upon generalizable facts. . . . Never has a truly useful and deep-going theory really been found purely speculatively"

(Holton, 1973, p. 229).

Kessen and colleagues (1970) noted over a decade ago that the defining features of the term *infant* include actions, cognitive processes, and physiological states. Early in this century developmental psychologists awarded salience to the infant's actions. During the past decade study of cognitive functions began its ascent, and it will now move into a phase of rapid acceleration. Perhaps physiological information will be added to research designs in the near future so that psychologists will be able to celebrate their version of a modern synthesis in which all three qualities share power in explanatory essays.

REFERENCES

Ainsworth, M. D. S., Blehar, M. C., Waters, E., & Wall, S. (1978). *Patterns of attachment.* Hillsdale, NJ: Erlbaum.

Arend, R., Gove, F. L., & Sroufe, L. A. (1979). Continuity of individual adaptation from infancy to kindergarten. *Child Development, 50,* 950–959.

Axelrod, J., & Reisine, T. D. (1984). Stress hormones: Their interaction and regulation. *Science, 224,* 452–459.

Bachevalier, J., & Mishkin, M. (1984). An early and a late developing system for learning and retention in infant monkeys. *Behavioral Neuroscience, 98,* 770–778.

Bahrick, L. E. (1983). Infants' perception of substance and temporal synchrony in multimodal events. *Infant Behavior & Development, 6,* 429–451.

Belsky, J., & Isabella R. (in press). Maternal, infant, and social–contextual determinants of attachment security. In J. Belsky & T. Nezworski (Eds.), *Clincial implications of attachment.* Hillsdale, NJ: Erlbaum.

Blizard, D. A. (1981). The Maudsley reactive and non-reactive strains: A North-American perspective. *Behavioral Genetics, 11,* 469–489.

Boakes, R. (1984). *From Darwin to behaviorism.* Cambridge, England: Cambridge University Press.

Bowlby, J. (1969). *Attachment and Loss: Vol. 1. Attachment.* New York: Basic.

Bretherton, I., & Waters, E. (Eds.) (1985). Growing points of attachment theory and research. *Monographs of the Society for Research in Child Development, 50* (1–2).

Bridgman, P. W. (1927). *The logic of modern physics.* New York: Macmillan.

Bronson, G. W. (1970). Fear of visual novelty. *Developmental Psychology, 2,* 33–40.

Brown, K. W., & Gottfried, A. W. (1986). Cross-modal transfer of shape in early infancy. In L. P. Lipsitt & C. K. Rovee-Collier (Eds.), *Advances in infancy research.* Norwood, NJ: Ablex.

Brown, R. W. (1973). *A first language: The early stages.* Cambridge, MA: Harvard University Press.

Bunnell, D. E. (1982). Autonomic myocardial influences as a factor determining intertask consistency of heart rate reactivity. *Psychophysiology, 19,* 442–448.

Bushnell, E. W. (1986). The basis of infant visual–tactual functioning—Amodal dimensions or multimodal compounds? In L. P. Lipsitt & C. K. Rovee-Collier (Eds.), *Advances in infancy research.* Norwood, NJ: Ablex.

Buss, A. & Plomin, R. (1984). *Temperament: Early developing personality traits.* Hillsdale, NJ: Erlbaum.

Carey, W. B., & McDevitt, S. C. (1978). Stability and change in individual temperament diagnoses from infancy to early childhood. *Journal of the American Academy of Child Psychiatry, 17,* 331–337.

Chen, S., & Miyake, K. (1982–1983). Japanese versus United States comparison of mother–infant interaction and infant development. In K. Miyake (Ed.), *Annual Report of the Research and Clinical Center for Child Development.* Hokkaido, Japan: Faculty of Education, Hokkaido University.

Churchland, P. M. (1979). *Scientific realism and the plasticity of mind.* Cambridge: Cambridge University Press.

Churchland, P. M. (1984). *Matter and consciousness.* Cambridge, MA: M.I.T. Press.

Cohen, L. B., Gelber, E. R., & Lazar, M. A. (1971). Infant habituation and generalization to differing degrees of novelty. *Journal of Experimental Child Psychology, 11,* 379–389.

Connell, J. P. (1985). Emotion and social interaction in the Strange Situation. Unpublished manuscript.

Coolidge, J. C., Brodie, R. D., & Feeney, B. (1964). A ten-year follow-up study of sixty-six school phobic children. *American Journal of Orthopsychiatry, 34,* 675–684.

Crockenberg, S. B. (1981). Infant irritability, mother responsiveness, and social support influences on the security of infant mother attachment. *Child Development, 52,* 857–865.

Delaporte, F. (1982). *Nature's second kingdom.* Cambridge, MA: M.I.T. Press.

Duhem, P. (1906). *La theorie physique.* Paris: Chevaliere and Riviere.

Easterbrooks, M. A., & Lamb, M. E. (1979). The relationship between quality of infant–mother attachment and infant competence in initial encounters with a peer. *Child Development, 50,* 380–387.

Eimas, P. D., & Miller, J. L. (1980). Contextual effects in infant speech perception. *Science, 209,* 1140–1141.

Emmerich, W. (1964). Continuity and stability in early social development. *Child Development, 35,* 311–332.

Erickson, M. F., Sroufe, L. A., & Egeland, B. (1985). The relationship between quality of attachment and behavior problems in preschool in a high risk sample. In I. Bretherton & E. Waters (Eds.), Growing points of attachment theory and research. *Monographs of the Society for Research in Child Development, 50,* (1–2).

Fagan, J. F. (1973). Infants' delayed recognition memory and forgetting. *Journal of Experimental Child Psychology, 16,* 424–450.

Fantz, R. L. (1965). Visual perception from birth as shown by pattern activity. *Annals of the New York Academy of Sciences, 118,* 793–814.

Frankenhaeuser, M. (1979). Psychobiological aspects of life stress. In P. H. Venables & M. J. Christie (Eds.), *Research in psychophysiology.* New York: Wiley.

Frodi, A., & Thompson, R. (1985). Infants' affective responses in the Strange Situation. *Child Development, 56,* 1280–1290.

Garcia-Coll, C., Kagan, J., & Reznick, J. S. (1984). Behavioral inhibition in young children. *Child Development, 55,* 1005–1019.

Garner, W. R. (1981). The analysis of unanalyzed perceptions. In M. Kubovy & J. R. Pomerantz (Eds.), *Percpetual organization.* Hillsdale, NJ: Erlbaum.

Geach, P., & Black, M. (Eds.). (1960). *Translations from the philosophical writings of Gottlob Frege.* Oxford: Basic Blackwell.

Gellhorn, E. (1967). *Principles of autonomic-somatic integration.* Minneapolis: University of Minnesota Press.

Gibson, E. J. (1969). *Principles of perceptual learning and development.* New York: Appleton-Century-Crofts.

Gibson, J. J. (1966). *The senses considered as perceptual systems.* Boston: Houghton-Mifflin.

Gittelman, R. & Klein, D. F. (1984). Relationship between separation anxiety and panic and agoraphobic disorders. *Psychopathology* (Suppl. 1), *17,* 56–65.

Goddard, M. E., & Beilharz, R. G. (1985). A multi-variate analysis of the genetics of fearfulness in potential guide dogs. *Behavior Genetics, 15,* 69–89.

Goldsmith, H. H., & Campos, J. J. (1982). Toward a theory of infant temperament. In R. N. Emde & R. Harmon (Eds.), *The development of attachment and affiliative systems.* New York: Plenum.

Grossmann, K., Grossmann, K., Huber, F., & Wartner, U. (1981). German children's behavior toward their mothers at 12 months and their fathers at 18 months in Ainsworth's Strange Situation. *International Journal of Behavioral Development 4,* 157–181.

Gunderson, V. M. (1983). Development of cross-modal recognition in infant pigtail monkeys (*Macaca nemestrina*). *Developmental Psychology, 19,* 398–404.

Haith, M. M. (1980). *Rules that babies look by.* Hillsdale, NJ: Erlbaum.

Halverson, C. F., & Waldrop, M. F. (1976). Relations between preschool activity and aspects of intellectual and social behavior age age seven-and-a-half. *Development Psychology, 12,* 107–112.

Hazen, N. L., & Durrett, M. E. (1982). The relationship of security of attachment to exploration in cognitive mapping abilities in two-year-olds. *Developmental Psychology, 18,* 751–759.

Hebben, N., Corkin, S., Eichenbaum, H., & Shedlack, K. (1985). Diminished ability to interpret and report internal states after bilateral medial temporal resection. *Behavioral Neuroscience, 99,* 1031–1039.

Hock, E., & Clinger, J. B. (1981). Infant coping behaviors. *Journal of Genetic Psychology, 138,* 231–243.

Holton, G. (1973). *Thematic origins of scientific thought.* Cambridge, MA: Harvard University Press.

Hubner, K. (1983). *Critique of scientific reason.* Chicago: University of Chicago Press.

Kagan, J. (1971). *Change and continuity in infancy.* New York: Wiley.

Kagan, J. (1979). Overview: Perspectives on human infancy. In J. D. Osofsky (Ed.), *The handbook of infant development.* New York: Wiley.

Kagan, J. (1984). *The nature of the child.* New York: Basic.

Kagan, J. Hans, S., Markowitz, A., Lopez, D., & Sigal, H. (1982). Validity of children's self-reports of psychological qualities. In B. A. Maher & W. B. Maher (Eds.), *Progress in experimental personality research* (Vol. XI). New York: Academic.

Kagan, J., Kearsley, R. B., & Zelazo, P. R. (1978). *Infancy: Its place in human development.* Cambridge, MA: Harvard University Press.

Kagan, J., & Moss. H. A. (1983). *Birth to maturity.* New Haven, CT: Yale University Press. (Original work published 1962)

Kagan, J., & Reznick, J. S. (1984). Cardiac reaction as an index of task involvement. *Australian Journal of Psychology, 36,* 135–147.

Kagan, J., Reznick, J. S., Clarke, C., Snidman, N., & Garcia-Coll, C. (1984). Behavioral inhibition to the unfamiliar. *Child Development, 55,* 2212–2225.

Kandel, E. R. (1983). From metapsychology to molecular biology: Explorations into the nature of anxiety. *American Journal of Psychiatry, 140,* 1271–1293.

Kessen, W., Haith, M. M., & Salapatek, P. H. (1970). Infancy. In P. H. Mussen (Ed.), *Carmichael's manual of child psychology,* (3rd ed.). New York: Wiley.

Kessen, W., Salapatek, P. H., & Haith, M. M. (1972). The visual response of the human newborn to linear contour. *Journal of Experimental Child Psychology, 13,* 19–20.

Kitcher, P. (1985). *The nature of mathematical knowledge.* New York: Oxford.

Kuhl, P. K., & Meltzoff, A. N. (1982). The biomodal perception of speech in infancy. *Science, 218,* 1138–1141.

Levine, S. (1982). Comparative and psychobiological perspectives on development. In A. Collins (Ed.), The concept of development. *Minnesota Symposium* (Vol. 15). Hillsdale, NJ: Erlbaum.

Lewis, M., Feiring, C., McGuffog, C., & Jaskir, J. (1984). Predicting psychopathology in six-year-olds from early social relations. *Child Development, 55,* 123–136.

Light, K. C. (1984). Cardiovascular and renal responses to competitive mental challenges. In J. F. Orlebeke, G. Mulder, & L. J. P. van Doornen (Eds.), *Cardiovascular psychophysiology: Theory and methods.* New York: Plenum.

Light, K. C., & Obrist, P. A. Task difficulty, heart rate reactivity, and cardiovascular responses to an appetitive reaction time task. *Psychophysiology, 20,* 301–312.

Linn, S., Reznick, J. S., Kagan, J., & Hans, S. (1979). Salience of visual patterns in the human infant. *Developmental Psychology, 18,* 651–657.

Logan, F. A. (1979). Hybrid theory of operant conditioning. *Psychological Review, 86,* 507–541.

Maccoby, E. E., & Martin, J. A. Socialization and the context of the family: Parent–child interaction. In E. M. Hetherington (Ed.), Socialization, personality, and social development (Vol. IV). In P. H. Mussen (Ed.), *Handbook of child psychology* (4th ed.). New York: Wiley.

Mach, E. (1959). *The analysis of sensations.* New York: Dover.

McCall, R. B., Kennedy, C. B., & Applebaum, M. I. (1977). Magnitude of discrepancy and the direction of attention in infants. *Child Development, 48,* 772–785.

Meltzoff, A. N. & Borton, R. W. (1979). Intermodal matching by human neonates. *Nature, 282,* 403–404.

Millikan, R. G. (1984). *Language, thought, and other biological categories: New foundations for realism.* Cambridge, MA: M.I.T. Press.

Mischel, W. (1969). Continuity and change in personality. *American Psychologist, 24,* 1012–1018.

Miyake, K., Chen, S., & Campos, J. J. (1985). Infant temperament, mother's mode of interaction, and attachment in Japan: An interim report. In I. Bretherton & E. Waters (Eds.), Growing points in attachment theory and research. *Monographs of the Society for Research in Child Development, 50,* (1–2).

Miller, J. L., & Eimas, P. D. (1983). Studies on the categorization of speech by infants. *Cognition, 13,* 135–165.

Moore, D., Benenson, J., Reznick, J. S., Peterson, M., & Kagan, J. (1986). *The effect of auditory reception of numerical information on infants' looking behavior: An extension.* Unpub. Manuscript.

Morris, D. P., Soroker, E., & Burruss, G. (1954). Follow-up studies of shy, withdrawn children, I: Evaluation of later adjustment. *American Journal of Orthopsychiatry, 24,* 743–754.

Naslund, B., Persson-Blennow, I., NcNeil, T., Kaij, L., & Malmquist-Larsson, A. (1984). Offspring of women with nonorganic psychosis: Infant attachment to the mother at one year of age. *Acta Psychiatrica Scandinavia, 69,* 231–241.

Owen, M. T., Easterbrooks, M. A., Chase-Lansdale, L., & Goldberg, W. A. (1984). The relation between maternal employment status and the stability of attachments to mother and father. *Child Development, 55,* 1894–1901.

Pavlov, I. (1941). *Lectures on conditioned reflexes: Vol. III. Conditioned Reflexes and psychiatry* (W. H. Gantt, Trans.). New York: International Publishers.

Peeke, H. V. S., & Petrinovich, L. (1984). Approaches, constructs, and terminology for the study of response change in the intact organism. In Peeke, H. V. S., & Petrinovich, L. (Eds.), *Habituation, sensitization, and behavior.* New York: Academic.

Plomin, R., & Foch, T. T. (1980). A twin study of objectively assessed personality in childhood. *Journal of Personality & Social Psychology, 39,* 680–688.

Plomin, R. & Rowe, D. C. (1979). Genetic and environmental etiology of social behavior in infancy. *Developmental Psychology, 15,* 62–72.

Prelec, D. (1982). Matching, maximizing, and the hyperbolic reinforcement feedback function. *Psychological Review, 89,* 189–230.

Putnam, H. (1975). *Mind, language, and reality. Philosophical papers* (Vol. 2). New York: Cambridge University Press.

Putnam, H. (1983). *Realism and reason. Philosophical papers* (Vol 3). New York: Cambridge University Press.

Quine, W. V. (1981). *Theories and things.* Cambridge, MA: Harvard University Press.

Rees, G. (1984). Francis Bacon's biological ideas. In B. Vickers (Ed.), *Occult and scientific mentalities in the Renaissance.* New York: Cambridge University Press.

Reznick, J. S., & Kagan, J. (1982). Category detection in infancy. In L. Lipsitt (Ed.), *Advances in infancy research* (Vol. II). Norwood, NJ: Ablex.

Reznick, J. S., Kagan, J., Snidman, N., Gersten, M., Baak, K., & Rosenberg, A. (1986). Inhibited and uninhibited children: A follow-up study. *Child Development, 57,* 660–680.

Rose, S. A., Gottfried, A. W., & Bridger, W. H. (1981). Cross-modal transfer in six-month-old infants. *Developmental Psychology, 17,* 661–669.

Rothbart, M. K., & Derryberry, D. (1981). Development of individual differences in temperament. In M. E. Lamb & A. L. Brown (Eds.), *Advances in developmental psychology* (Vol. 1). Hillsdale, NJ: Erlbaum.

Sackett, G. A., Ruppenthal, G. G., Fahrenbruch, C. E., Holm, R. A., & Greenough, W. J. (1981). Social isolation rearing effects vary with genotype. *Developmental Psychology, 17,* 313–318.

Sagi, A., Lamb, M. E., & Gardner, W. (in press). Relations between Strange Situation behavior and stranger sociability among infants on Israeli kibbutzim. *Infant Behavior & Development.*

Schneider-Rosen, K. (1984). *Quality of attachment and the development of the self system.* Unpublished doctoral dissertation, Harvard University.

Schneider-Rosen, K., Braunwald, K. G., Carlson, V., & Cicchetti, D. (1985). Current perspectives in attachment theory: Illustration from the study of maltreated infants. In I. Bretherton & E. Waters (Eds.), Growing points of attachment theory and research. *Monographs of the Society for Research in Child Development, 50,* (1–2).

Sewitch, D. E. (1984). The perceptual uncertainty of having slept: The inability to discriminate electroencephalographic sleep from wakefulness. *Psychophysiology, 21,* 243–259.

Simpson, A. E., & Stevenson-Hinde, J. (in press). Temperamental characteristics in three- to four-year-old boys and girls in child–family interactions. *Journal of Comparative & Physiological Psychology.*

Smith, O. A., & DeVito, J. L. (1984). Central neural integration for the control of autonomic responses associated with emotion. In W. M. Cowan (Ed.), *Annual Review of Neuroscience* (Vol. 7). Palo Alto, CA: Annual Reviews.

Smith, T. W., Houston, B. K., & Zurawski, R. M. (1984). Finger pulse volume as a measure of anxiety in response to evaluative threat. *Psychophysiology, 21,* 260–264.

Snidman, N. (1984). *Behavioral restraint and the central nervous system: Predicting performance on cognitive tasks from autonomic nervous system activity.* Unpublished doctoral dissertation, University of California, Los Angeles.

Sperry, R. W. (1981). Changing priorities. *The Annual Review of Neuroscience, 4,* 1–15.

Sroufe, L. A. (1985). Attachment classification from the perspective of infant–caregiver relationships and infant temperament. *Child Development, 56,* 1–14.

Staddon, J. E. R. (1984). Social learning theory and the dynamics of interaction. *Psychological Review, 91,* 502–507.

Starkey, P., Spelke, E. S., & Gelman, R. (1983). Detection of intermodal numerical correspondences by human infants. *Science, 222,* 179–181.

Stayton, D. J., & Ainsworth, M. D. S. (1973). Individual differences in infant responsiveness to brief everyday separations as related to other infant and maternal behavior. *Developmental Psychology, 9,* 226–235.

Sternberg, R. J., & Grajek, S. (1984). The nature of love. *Journal of Personality & Social Psychology, 47,* 312–329.

Stevenson-Hinde, J., Stillwell-Barnes, R., & Zunz, M. (1980). Individual differences in young rhesus monkeys. *Primates, 21,* 498–509.

Sturtevant, A. H. (1965). *A history of genetics.* New York: Harper & Row.

Suomi, S. J., Kraemer, G. W., Baysinger, C. M., & DeLizio, R. D. (1981). Inherited and experiential factors associated with individual differences in anxious behavior displayed by rhesus monkeys. In D. F. Kline & J. Rabkin (Eds.), *Anxiety: New research and changing concepts.* New York: Raven.

Tennes, K., Downey, K., & Vernadakis, A. (1977). Urinary cortisol excretion rates and anxiety in normal one-year-old infants. *Psychosomatic Medicine, 39,* 178–187.

Thomas, D. (1979). *Naturalism and social science.* Cambridge, England: Cambridge University Press.

Thomas, A, & Chess, S. (1977). *Temperament and development.* New York: Brunner/Mazel.

Thompson, R. A., & Lamb, M. E. (1984). Assessing qualitative dimensions of emotional responses in infants: Separation reactions in the Strange Situation. *Infant Behavior and Development, 7,* 423–445.

Thompson, R. A., Lamb, M. E., & Estes, D. (1982). Stability of infant–mother attachment and its relationship to changing life circumstances in an unselected middle-class sample. *Child Development, 53,* 144–148.

Turkewitz, G., Gardner, J. M., & Lewkowicz, D. L. (1984) Sensory/perceptual functioning during early infancy. In G. Greenberg & E. Tobach (Eds.), *Conference on levels of integration and evolution of behavior.* Hillsdale, NJ: Erlbaum.

Valenstein, E. S., Cox, V. C., & Kakolewski, J. W. (1968). Modification of motivated behavior elicited by electrical stimulation of the hypothalamus. *Science, 159,* 1119–1121.

Wagner, S. H., & Sakovits, L. J. (in press). A process analysis of infant visual and cross modal recognition memory. *Advances in infancy research* (Vol. 4). Norwood, NJ: Ablex.

Wagner, S., Winner, E., Cicchetti, D., & Gardner, H. (1981). Metaphorical mapping in human infants. *Child Development, 52,* 728–731.

Wall, P. D. (1974). "My foot hurts me": An analysis of a sentence. In R. Bellairs & E. G. Gray (Eds.), *Essays on the nervous system.* Oxford: Clarendon Press.

Waters, E., Vaughn, N. B., & Egeland, B. R. (1980). Individual differences in infant–mother attachment relationships at age one. *Child Development, 51,* 208–216.

Waters, E., Wippman, J., & Sroufe, L. A. (1979). Attachment, positive affect, and competence in the peer group. *Child Development, 50,* 821–829.

Whitehead, A. N. (1928). *Science and the modern world.* New York: Macmillan.

Whiting, J. W. M., & Whiting, B. B. (1959). Contributions of anthropology to methods of studying child rearing. In P. H. Mussen (Ed.), *Handbook of research methods in child development.* New York: Wiley.

Wittgenstein, L. (1922). *Tractatus logico-philosophicus.* London: Routledge and Kegan Paul.

Wittgenstein, L. (1953). *Philosophical investigations.* New York: Macmillan.

Wundt, W. (1912). *An introduction to psychology.* London: George Allen.

Yang, R. K., & Halverson, C. F. (1976). A study of the inversion of intensity between newborn and preschool age behavior. *Child Development, 47,* 350–359.

CHAPTER 25

The Media, Society, and Child Development Research

ROBERT B. MCCALL

A cartoon (Stevenson, 1977) depicts two dowdy scientists musing over their apparently lackluster careers with the self-consoling caption, "One thing I'll say for us, Meyer—we never stooped to popularizing science."

Despite its humorous intent, the cartoon depicts a truism—"going public" was considered to be one of the lower forms of scientific activity, something upstanding scientists did not do (Goodfield, 1981).

Although no empirical measures are available, the attitudes and behaviors of scientists toward the media seem to be softening recently. Scientists of all disciplines (e.g., Abelson, 1976; Carey, 1977; Goodfield, 1981), including psychologists (Bevan, 1982; Hassett, 1979; Miller, 1969; Rubin, 1980) and child development specialists (Katz, 1984; McCall, 1983a, 1985; McCall & Stocking, 1982), are urging their colleagues to be more cooperative with journalists in communicating the fruits of science to the public. Guidelines for scientists on how to communicate through the media are being written (e.g., Gastel, 1983; McCall, 1983a; McCall, Gregory, & Murray, 1984; N. E. Miller, 1979), and some scientists are arguing that graduate students should be taught how to do it (Mumford, 1984). Universities are encouraging the trend (Watkins, 1984a), believing that the benefits of having their professors in the public eye helps the university gain appropriations and contributions. Communicating with the public, apparently, is not as blasphemous as it once was.

Why the reversal? One can only speculate about the reasons. First, the "golden age" of financial support for science recently ended (Goodfield, 1981), the future of empirical science was threatened, and scientists were forced to justify their existence and to plead for research funds. This threat was particularly severe for social and behavioral scientists, because the administration proposed to eliminate their disciplines altogether from the National Science Foundation budget and drastically cut them back at other agencies. Since legislators and policymakers derive as much or more information about science through the media than through reports of their own agencies (Caplan, Morrison, & Stambaugh, 1975; Weiss, 1974), it is reasonable to tug at legislative purse strings through the media as well as through direct lobbying. As a result, a scientist in the public arena, either in the office of a legislator

I thank Vickie Lattimer, Kathryn Whitmore and Judith Maringo for help in preparing the manuscript and Barbara Lonnborg for her useful suggestions on an earlier draft of the manuscript.

or in the columns of a newspaper, has come to be viewed by some as one making a necessary contribution to the discipline rather than as a pariah.

A second reason may be that the public's attitude toward science has changed in the last three decades, requiring scientists to polish their public image. In the mid-1950s, 88 percent of the public had favorable attitudes toward science (Yankelovich, 1984), perhaps reflecting a rather naive acceptance of and expectation for the scientific enterprise. Then, favorable attitudes toward science dropped dramatically to 52 percent by the mid-1970s, perhaps because of a general skepticism about institutions in America and perhaps because of increased public understanding that science was not perfect, technology could be dehumanizing, and science and technology had the potential to create social ills as well as social goods (Yankelovich, 1984). Today, however, public attitudes toward science have returned to the high levels of the mid-1950s (Yankelovich, 1984). According to Lou Harris (Scientists' Institute for Public Information, 1984), twice as many people say they have "high confidence" in scientists as say they have the same degree of confidence in any other group mentioned, including organized religion, Congress, the White House, state government, and the press itself, whose estate has been declining in public confidence during the last decade (Sanoff, 1982). Since the media are the chief suppliers of science information to nonscientists after their school years (Schramm & Wade, 1967), perhaps science in the media has helped the public understand that, while science is imperfect, it is an intensely human enterprise that has the potential to contribute to the public good (Yankelovich, 1984).

Appropriations for research funds and the public image of science are related, of course (e.g., Brown & Rubinstein, 1985), and both are influenced by the social and political context. For example, in 1957 and 1958, only one in two people believed that human behavior would ever be understood through scientific study (Withey, 1959), and in 1980, 68 percent thought some aspects of human behavior might be understood in scientific terms but only 23 percent thought such understanding would be complete (Miller, Prewitt, & Pearson, 1980). It is not surprising, then, that in 1982 ("Survey Finds Increased Public Support for Social Science," 1984) the public favored federal support for the physical sciences more than for the social sciences (64 vs. 39 percent). But a year later they supported funding for physical and social–behavioral sciences equally (79 vs. 74 percent). Why this improvement occurred is not clear, but the administration's assault on disciplines that studied—however imperfectly—major social problems that touched everyone's lives may have brought out latent public support for the social and behavioral sciences. And it is precisely this relevant character of the social and behavioral sciences that attracts the media to them.

A third possible reason that communicating has become more acceptable, especially for the social and behavioral sciences, is the developing maturity of these disciplines. Keniston (1970) suggested that the adolescent transition to maturity occurs in stages defined by three questions: "Who am I?" "Shall I relate to the wider society with which I often disagree?" And "If I decide to relate to society, how shall I do it?" It can be argued that the social and behavioral sciences have decided "who it is," specifically, that it has knowledge and techniques to understand some behaviors and to contribute to society (Hammel, 1981; Prewitt, 1981; Richter, 1981; Stokoe, 1981; but see Mazur, 1981a). Moreover, at least some behavioral scientists have decided to relate to society more actively through political advocacy, public service, and cooperation with the media. In child development circles, this desire to relate to society is embodied in the Bush Centers on child development and social policy. While the primary focus of these centers is on the legislative process, an increasing emphasis has been on public information and the media (e.g., Brown & Rubinstein, 1985; Gallagher & Sanders, 1981; Muenchow & Lang, 1982).

WHY COMMUNICATE?

While communicating with wider publics may have become a more acceptable topic of discussion, support for such activity is hardly overwhelming, and the goal of a public well educated in the behavioral and developmental sciences has certainly not been achieved. A host of reasons justify why scientists in general and child development specialists in infancy in particular should take an active role in communicating to wider audiences (Stocking, 1978).

Research Support and Image

One reason is that, while the social and behavioral sciences did not die of their financial ills, the convalescence is not complete. Funds for research and social services for infants, children, and families are still tight. While the structures and organizations established to ward off the threat (e.g., special units of APA, APF, COSSA, SRCD, and others) are largely directed at the legislative process, it may be argued that there are no good laws without good public awareness and support (Steinem, 1978). The media are channels for building that constituency, since they are major sources of science information for policymakers (Caplan et al., 1975; Weiss, 1974) and the general public (Schramm & Wade, 1967).

In addition, psychology's public image still needs polishing (Anschuetz, 1979). As indicated above, the public holds only modest hope for scientific psychology, and attitudes may be even less favorable toward service providers. In 1967, for example, only 4–5 percent of the public would contact a psychologist to help them deal with depression or fears that they were becoming mentally ill (Thumin & Zebelman, 1967). More recently, Yankelovich, Skelly, and White (1977) found that families with children under 13 years in a national sample would be most likely to seek help for a child behavior problem from a physician or clergyman and were only slightly less likely to seek assistance from school principals, their friends, their own parents, and juvenile authorities.

Further, it may be more effective in building a positive image and a public constituency to demonstrate the value of science and clinical service to society by giving people information they can use than by directly appealing for public support (McCall, 1985). That is, "a vigorous concern for the public interest is, in the long run, the most enlightened kind of self-interest" (Bevan, 1982, p. 1316). Yet it is estimated that only one cent out of every dollar spent on research goes to dissemination and utilization (Havelock, 1975). No company could survive with that level of commitment, and some wonder if the public, who underwrite science and are taught science by the media (Goodfield, 1981), will continue their support without more feedback.

Public Welfare

Another reason we should communicate is that the primary purpose of research is to contribute to the welfare of society, in our specific case, to the welfare of infants, children, and families. Thus not only do researchers have an obligation to report to their benefactors (McCall & Stocking, 1982; Stocking, 1978; Walum, 1975), but unless the information they acquire escapes the pages of professional journals and finds its way to people who can use that information, science's potential to contribute is strangled. While it is not well established scientifically, the more knowledge about child development parents have, the better skills they have as parents, even after controlling for income and general education (Stevens, 1984), and parents seem to want more information today than they did years ago (Geboy, 1981).

"But it's not my job to communicate," is the rebuttal from scientists content with society's division of labor. True, journalists, television producers, and others are responsible for communicating, but they are dependent on researchers to be sources of information. And if the pillars of the scientific community will not cooperate in providing them accurate, balanced information, other individuals—the very ones who scientists complain have poisoned the science media's well—will continue to provide their own brand of information (Hassett, 1979). As David Leff of *Medical World News* observed, bad communications drive out good communications, so if reliable scientists do not communicate with competent journalists, then charlatans and more sensational media will fill the vacuum. "The choice then is not whether to communicate, but what to communicate and to whom" (Marx, 1976, p. 136). Besides, people do not stop living and behaving without our knowledge; they continue to act, make decisions, and rear their infants and children. As the old saying goes (Stocking, 1978), "While timorous knowledge stands awaiting, audacious ignorance hath done the deed."

The Contribution of Information

But how can communicating the fruits of research on development help people? We do not have 10 easy rules to guide child rearing.

Information on ages and stages, for example, can provide parents with peace of mind and create more realistic expectancies about the development of their infants. Some have suggested that Gessell was popular because he told parents what to expect at which ages, thus relieving anxiety they might feel because their 13-month infant was not yet walking or their 15-month infant had not yet begun to talk. Some have also suggested that unrealistic expectancies about infant and child behavior may contribute to child abuse.

Not only is it helpful to know what to expect when a baby is developing normally, it is also useful to know the signs that something may be wrong (Nunnally, 1961). Although the literature on detecting and predicting from infancy to childhood disability is not definitive (e.g., Kopp & McCall, 1982), well-tempered information can be presented indicating which behaviors may be worth checking and, just as important, which are not very significant (e.g., McCall, 1983b). Sometimes readers of such an article identify a problem and seek treatment that they would not have pursued otherwise (e.g., Landers, 1984). Descriptions of problems also can have a positive effect on parents who do not have the problem. Parents, for example, may be exasperated because their infants are very active and do not sleep through the night, but they may count their blessings after reading an article about colic. And parents who must cope with colic will take some solace in knowing they are not alone.

Even sheer information without obvious implications for parental action can make a contribution. Studies show that most parents seek out reading material on infancy and early childhood not for advice on how to solve a problem, but to become informed about the normal process of human development (Clarke-Stewart, 1978). Simply understanding why a baby cannot walk until a certain age, needs to eat approximately every 4 hr, or seems to be cross-eyed can help a parent avoid worrying about such behaviors. Also, knowing that your parental behavior is on target may be a source of satisfaction, even though it requires you to do nothing differently. Finally, information that makes child development more interesting may contribute to the intellectual and emotional satisfaction of child rearing.

Service Professionals

Professionals who deliver services to infants, children, and their families also have much to gain by communicating (McCall, 1983a). Obviously, services are not terribly useful unless individuals who need them know that they exist. Further, service agencies should be as concerned with prevention as with rehabilitation, and communicating health information through the mass media is sometimes the most cost-effective strategy to amass community resources to treat or prevent the problem. The awareness campaign on infant and child abuse is a case in point. Finally, most social service agencies are continually strapped for funds. Making the community aware of an agency's activities and serving as an information resource can raise the public profile of the agency and create the feeling in potential donors and volunteers that the agency is active and contributing to the public welfare.

Although the primary focus of this chapter is on communications to the general public, specific professional groups, such as service providers, also are exposed to the mass media. For example, adoption agencies could use information on heredity and environment and the consequences of perinatal events; lawyers and judges could use information on divorce, attachment, fathers, and custody; and industrial executives might benefit from information on factors that keep families together, reduce personal stress, and increase happiness, all of which contribute to morale and productivity. The newspaper is *the* multidisciplinary "journal" for most professionals.

Risks

Are there risks and dangers to public communications? Of course. Any activity can be done poorly, and in the case of the mass media, thousands—sometimes millions—of people are exposed to that ineptitude. This can be a special problem for the social and behavioral sciences, because news reports of what people can do to achieve benefit X or avoid detriment Y can often be implemented directly without the intermediate action of a professional, such as a physician, who must diagnose, prescribe, and monitor a new drug (Bressler, 1968). Also, one size of advice does not fit all; the media's very brief presentations do not permit many qualifications about individual differences or matching a course of action or treatment with particular sets of symptoms or circumstances. For example, a description of how to stimulate and play with a normal baby might be disastrous if tried by a mother of a hypersensitive premature infant. And sometimes a well-intended message (e.g., on drug abuse) can have the opposite effect on the audience than the one originally intended (Feingold & Knapp, 1977; Ray & Ward, 1976).

Another risk derives from the fact that researchers do not control the communication process and the message sometimes comes out differently than the professional had wanted. Occasionally it is misleading, inaccurate, unflattering, or trivializing. Even more frustrating is the likelihood (Krieghbaum, 1959) that people will misunderstand, misapply, or transform accurate information to fit their prejudices. So neither communicator nor consumer can be controlled by the scientist, opening the door more widely to undesirable effects.

Any job, scientific research as well as communications, can be done poorly, and people can be misled or harmed, especially if the topic is important. However, the alternative is not to abandon scientific research or communications through the mass media—some information is likely to be better than no information, which would allow "audacious ignorance" or rank prejudice to dominate without restraint. It would be better to improve the quality of communications so that risks are minimized and the benefits outweigh the potential liabilities. Thus while most scientists should conduct research and should not become communicators, just as most journalists should not become scientists, some scientists should help bridge the gap between research and the public by being sources for journalists and otherwise contributing to public education.

To facilitate pursuit of this goal, researchers might benefit from understanding something about communications processes and the requirements, values, and behavior of communicators. Also, those who want to communicate directly might find helpful the experiences of those who have tried their hands. To provide such information is the purpose of this chapter.

COMMUNICATIONS—CONTENTS AND PROCESSES

In oversimplified form, a journalist is trained to report the five *W*'s—the who, what, when, where, and why—and sometimes the how—of an event or phenomenon. Similarly, if scientists are to understand the communications enterprise, they would benefit from knowing something about the five *W*'s of the communications business.

Who—The Audience and the Communicators

Who is the audience, what are they interested in, and who communicates with them?

The Medium

The audience, in part, is determined by the medium. If the message is intended for very large segments of the population, then the mass media are ideal. Recall, for example, the Tylenol scare in which essentially the entire nation was functionally alerted to the potential danger within a few days. Less dramatically, the Developmental Psychology Division of APA sent out six news releases in 1983 to approximately 1200 newspapers and journalists across the country, and something from the set of releases reached an estimated 23 million homes (McCall, 1984). Not only is this audience many times the number of people ever to have read any article in all the professional journals on children in the history of science, but it cost approximately 0.0027 cents to reach each home.

The mass media, however, can also be used to contact a few people who cannot otherwise be identified. For example, a fictional television program on adolescent suicide brought forth a large increase in calls to hotlines ("TV Movie on Suicide Spurs Plenty of Calls to Hot Lines," 1984). While the number of calls was not large, those individuals probably could not have been identified, contacted, and helped in any other way or as inexpensively.

The mass media, however, represent a shotgun approach to communications. They are appropriate when one desires to hit the most people with a single shot or to reach a few hard-to-identify people along with enormous numbers of people who don't really need the message. The alternative, or complementary, approach is "targeted" communications—messages targeted at a specific audience. It is sometimes more effective, for example, to reach "opinion leaders" who influence the ultimate audience than to aim a message directly at the intended group. Service professionals—pediatricians, teachers, school counselors, day-care workers, social service workers, lawyers, clinicians—are opinion leaders who influence parents, infants, and children. Further, a very high percentage can be reached through professional organizations, journals, newsletters, and direct mail. For example, if you have developed a procedure that helps parents deal with the hypersensitivity often characterizing premature infants, it may be best to publish that procedure in a journal or newsletter aimed at pediatricians, since they are likely to be involved directly with parents who have premature infants and since parents are more likely to follow the advice of their doctors than a newspaper report.

The potential advantages of such targeted communications are that they can reach a greater percentage of the individuals actually needing the information and that the professional has greater control over the nature of the message than when the mass media are used. While the cost of producing and distributing a booklet and especially a film or television program can be enormous, an article in a journal or newsletter that reaches the intended audience may cost nothing. Unfortunately, few researchers think of writing for "applied" journals or newsletters outside their fields, and most organizations cannot afford large programs of targeted brochures and booklets like those produced by Boys Town (McCall, Gregory, & Lonnborg, 1985). While specialists in infancy and child development should consider using such "targeted communications" more than they do (Gregory & Stocking, 1981), this chapter will focus on the mass media.

The Audience

Who and how many people are likely to be reached with information about research on infants communicated through the mass media? According to one recent survey (Lichty, 1983), 68 percent of U.S. adults read at least one newspaper every day, 56 percent see network or local news each evening, 24 percent read a major news magazine, and 18 percent listen to an all-news radio station at least once per week. Another survey showed that newspapers and television were seen equally—by 67 percent of the population on any given day (Bogart, 1984). Newspapers, however, are read mainly for news, while TV is watched primarily for entertainment (La-

Follette, 1982; Krieghbaum, 1959), even when people seek information from public affairs and news programs (Hofstetter & Buss, 1981). So despite the potential of television, the newspaper is still the best medium for reaching the masses with information, although magazines may be better suited to communicating science.

Interest in science news is increasing (Goodfield, 1981; Hellemans, 1984; Nunn, 1979; Stipp, 1985), and young adults, who are more likely to be parents of infants, are more interested in science than other age groups (Clark, 1977; Nunn, 1979; Patterson, 1982). Moreover, they would forgo reading many other journalism staples to get more science. In contrast, while several new science magazines have emerged recently (Bennett, 1981; Broad, 1982), they are not always receptive to the social and behavioral sciences. Similarly, newspaper coverage of science (Nunn, 1979) and of the social and behavioral sciences (Singer & Endreny, 1984) has not dramatically increased in the last decade. This is especially ironic for psychology, since surveys indicate that the social and behavioral sciences and human interest topics are more popular among readers than "hard" science and technology (Burgoon, Burgoon, & Wilkinson, 1983; Nunn, 1979). Yet as much (or more) space in the newspaper is devoted to horoscopes and puzzles as to behavioral science and perhaps to all science stories (Nunn, 1979).

The situation is worse with respect to television. Surveys (Weiner, 1980) indicate that the general public, public television viewers, and even PBS managers rate nature and science the most neglected, most missed, and most desired category of programming. But recent science series have not fared well (Angier, 1983), and, for some reason, the behavior of animals seems to be favored over the behavior of people by TV science programmers. So more programs on behavioral science seem unlikely.

The Communicator

Journalists who specialize in science are a small group with a short and unusual history (Dunwoody, 1978, 1980a). Science writing as a specialty was established when major newspapers and wire services sent reporters to cover the manned space shots in the 1960s. Since these reporters had little expertise in science or space technology, they tended to help each other gather and interpret information, despite the fact that many worked for competitive companies. Moreover, the same individuals were assigned to each space event and to scientific conventions and conferences. These periodic "meetings" and the need for cooperation produced a "fraternity" of approximately 25–30 writers who functionally controlled science journalism in the country. Since they cut their teeth on astrophysics and established their specialized reputations by covering the esoteric fields of "hard" science, they do not tend to write about the social and behavioral sciences, which are sometimes considered "garbage science" and to be "fuzzy" at worst or not needing their special expertise at best (Dunwoody, 1980a). Presumably, any journalist can write about social science (Weiss, 1985). Other science writers mix their disdain with acknowledged ignorance: "I'm not very well equipped to evaluate sociology, but it can't hurt anybody so I figure it's not going to do too much damage if I get it a little screwed up" (Dunwoody, 1980a).

Today, the science writing community is larger and broader in orientation than a few years ago, but it is still dominated by approximately 50 people (Mazur, 1981) who retain some bias against behavioral science, although it may be softening (Dunwoody, 1980a, 1983; McCall & Stocking, 1982; Weiss, 1984a). Their editors, however, do not have this prejudice (Dunwoody, 1983), because stories on behavior are more interesting to a larger audience than stories on molecular biology or physics, for instance. Moreover, reporters attending the AAAS convention, for example, know this preference, and file twice as many stories on the behavioral and social sciences as on any other topic (Dunwoody, 1983; Weiss, 1984a). Specifically, for the 1977 AAAS convention, three of the five stores receiving the most play in daily newspapers were on social and behavioral topics, two of which were concerned with children (Dunwoody, 1983). And at the 1982 and 1983 AAAS meetings, the social and behavioral sciences were represented in 23 and 20 percent of the symposia but three or four were among the nine or ten most-covered events, making them approximately twice as likely to receive top media attention as symposia from other disciplines (Weiss, 1984a).

Perhaps as a result of the need to cover the behavioral sciences to please editors, a sample of members of the National Association of Science Writers reported that a course in psychology was in their academic backgrounds and they recommended such a course for science writers now in training more frequently than any other science course (Ryan & Dunwoody, 1975). This survey also revealed that 47 percent of science writers majored in English or journalism, 23 percent achieved an advanced degree, and 62 percent were news reporters or in public relations or advertising before becoming science writers. While only 0.7 percent had doctorates, 42 percent had some experience in a laboratory or with a research project.

More typically, however, behavioral science is not covered by science-writing specialists and not covered as part of a specialized "science beat" (Dunwoody, 1983; Singer & Endreny, 1984; Weiss, 1983). Rather, journalists covering education, women's and life-style topics, crime, economics, health, and children, for example, are assigned stories on these content topics and often rely on social and behavioral researchers as sources (Weiss, 1983). Thus while coverage of the social and behavioral sciences has not increased over the last few years in terms of the number of stories, the number of references to social and behavioral scientists, data, and studies has increased (Singer & Endreny, 1984). In fact, psychologists are 39 percent more likely to be contacted by the press than are "hard scientists" (Dunwoody & Ryan, 1982; Dunwoody & Scott, 1982).

Therefore, although behavioral science is among the most interesting science to readers, trained science writers, who could report it best, favor it least among the sciences. Consequently, behavioral science tends to be written about either by skilled science writers who are biased against the discipline or by writers who have no special training in or understanding of behavioral science.

What—News and Features

The stock in trade of most journalists, whether print or electronic, is news. But the nature of news, while it brings scientists and journalists together, may also keep them worlds apart (Bogart, 1968; Goodfield, 1981).

For one thing, in my experience, scientists typically lack a "nose for news." It is topic selection, more than the "translation" of scientific material into nontechnical language, that separates scientists from journalists. Second, science rarely fits the criteria of news, yet it is typically covered as news. What, then, is news to a journalist?

Recency

Something is news if it is new or recently discovered (Gans, 1980; Weiss, 1984b). The hackneyed phrases "getting a scoop" and "yesterday's news is today's fish wrapper" testify to the journalist's preoccupation with recency.

The journalist's desire for today's news today tends to produce articles that emphasize the results of single studies. This practice hangs the inevitable inconsistency of results directly in front of the public, which spectacle probably diminishes science's credibility because it appears scientists do not know what they are doing (Cobb, 1981). Scientists, however, know that "truth" in science is rarely discovered or even announced in a single day. Instead, scientific principles emerge in fractional increments over scores of studies requiring years to complete, and then only after the inevitable contradictions are sorted out in explicable ways (Weiss, 1984b). More often than not, then, principles emerge in review articles and books, not in single empirical studies. Unfortunately, such reviews are seen by some journalists as a rehash of "old" data and not very newsworthy.

Some single studies, of course, do fit the news model well. Researchers generally chuckle at the notion of a "breakthrough" study, but occasionally one research project deals with a major theoretical or practical issue in a highly comprehensive way and is not likely to be repeated or rivaled in the near future. Examples include the comprehensive evaluation of the milestone early education programs by Lazar, Darlington, and colleagues (1982) and the comprehensive study of divorce by Hetherington, Cox, and Cox (1977).

The journalist's push for recency can also produce ethical problems for scientists. For example, most scientists feel strongly that research must be reviewed, published in a scientific journal, and perhaps even discussed in the scientific community for some months before it is "released" to the press (Culliton, 1972; Ryan, 1979). The press, however, wants to publish the results as soon as they are available (Ryan, 1979)—it is the public's right to know, especially since it is their money that supports the research. This is one of the most profound conflicts between scientists and journalists (Ryan, 1979).

New Information

By definition, news is also *new* information—something that was not known before, contradicts prevailing thought, or is unexpected. You will not see a headline in the *New York Times* stating "World Trade Towers Still Standing" (Burrows, 1980). Everybody expects them to be still standing; it will only be news if one is not. Similarly, you will not see the headline "More Than 900 Dead, 66,000 Injured" to describe the weekly U.S. highway carnage, but you will certainly see "78 Die in Plane Crash" ("Each Week, 900 Die in the Sudden Violence of U.S. Auto Accidents," 1982). The former is not news; it happens every week. The latter is news; it does not. A mother who thoroughly enjoys her infant is not newsworthy; only a mother who abuses her baby makes headlines. This is why more bad than good news gets in the newspapers.

The emphasis on the new also favors information that challenges existing thought, current social institutions, and typical ways of doing things (Gans, 1979; Weiss, 1985). Thus a popular theme for newspaper or magazine stories is to expose common beliefs to be myths, or to feature information that suggests changes should be made in government or the way parents, for example, rear their children. An expression of the latter tendency is the question journalists frequently ask child psychologists, "What is the single biggest mistake parents are making today?"

Conversely, when science validates common wisdom, it is not news (Weiss, 1984b). The "Science for Families" television news feature project (McCall et al., 1984) did a five-part series on divorce featuring Mavis Hetherington and Joan Kelly, but many stations did not use those features because they had already done "something" on divorce. That our features were "science" did not make them newsworthy. Hetherington's research did make news, of course, but mainly because her finding of "no victimless divorces" countered the themes of some popular books and because the public did not expect boys and girls to be influenced differently by divorce.

The Unusual

The emphasis on new information sometimes slips into an emphasis on the unusual, the counterintuitive, and even the bizarre, which also can create antagonism between scientists and journalists (Tichenor, Olien, Harrison, & Donohue, 1970). Scientists feel that journalists sensationalize information to make it unusual, feature rare but extreme cases, or overemphasize minor but unusual results or implications (Tannenbaum, 1963). One study estimated that 10–24 percent of science stories contain statements that are overemphases, value judgments, irrelevancies, or frivolities (Glynn & Tims, 1982).

The desire for the unusual explains why some results receive disproportionate publicity relative to their importance. The birth of quadruplets or quintuplets is always highly publicized, and studies of the purported calming effect of heartbeat sounds on crying infants (Salk, 1962) and the ability of newborn infants to recognize the voices of their mothers (Spence & de Casper, 1982) were also featured because of their unusual results.

Controversy

Journalists, especially in television, also like controversy (Weiss, 1984b). Controversy implies news, because solving the issue is still in progress. Also, issues such as heredity versus environment, the effects of working mothers, infant day care, and creating superbabies often elicit extreme, sometimes bizarre, claims and arguments that make interesting reading and add life to an otherwise dull radio or television talk show.

Presenting several alternatives and their pros and cons is a function researchers should perform, although articles presenting several contrasting views are rare (Tichenor et al., 1971). However, when controversy on a scientific issue is presented in the media (e.g., fluoridation of water, nuclear energy), the public tends to react with conservatism, rejecting the new suggestions or technology in favor of traditional practices (Mazur, 1981b). Apparently, people shun the unknown, and some feel that controversy among "experts" implies that they do not know what they are doing (Cobb, 1981) and that new ventures should be delayed.

The potential of controversy to be disastrous rises, I believe, when academics debate on radio and television. Discussion becomes disagreement, which can quickly become uncivil, rancorous, and ad hominem. In a recent debate on smokers' rights on network television ("Smoking Debate Turns Rough," 1985), one university professor threw a mug of water on another to douse his cigar, the smoker chucked his ashtray at his fire-fighting opponent, and fisticuffs ensued.

Less violently, scholars are trained to "score debating points," not to persuade the lay audience of a particular stance. Such a style becomes only an irrelevant "academic" argument when two professors are involved, but it can be catastrophic when the two protagonists play by different rules. For example, a researcher may respond to claims that a special stimulation program can increase the IQs of infants with the standard "Where's the evidence?" The creator of the program asserts, "We do it every day. It is such a joy to see these babies blossom and their parents have the emotional fulfillment of witnessing their accomplishment. Doctor, are you, as a child psychologist, opposed to helping babies develop their full potential?" From a scientific or debating standpoint, the respondent avoids the question. But he wins the point—he makes the researcher look like a picky, nay-saying, old fuddy-duddy who does not support parents and babies. Persuasion and rules of evidence are different. So some insiders advise that, when controversy calls, namely, a program like "60 Minutes," "hang up." One CBS producer reportedly cautioned a prospective "60 Minutes" guest: "At best you'll be raped, at worse, killed" (Klepper, 1981).

Public Interest

But everything that is recent, new, or controversial is not news. It also must be in the public interest—interesting and relevant to the lives of the public. Unfortunately, a great deal of academic activity is boring to the general public, because it does not relate in any concrete way to their past, present, or future experience, and the greatest sin a communicator can commit is to be boring (Goodfield, 1981). It is this "nose for news," in my opinion, that scientists typically lack; but journalists sometimes commit the complementary error when they exaggerate the relevance or implication of research results for people's lives.

Behavioral scientists often assume that relevancy means telling the public how to do something—for example, how to raise their infants' IQs. Of course, the media do love how-to's, because they relate directly to the audience. But in the author's opinion, researchers overemphasize the media's desire to have practical, how-to information and they underestimate the sheer interest the general public has in descriptive and explanatory research that relates to people's experience. The newly discovered perceptual and mental capabilities of infants, for example, have received substantial coverage without implying prescriptions for parental action.

The Famous

Remarks by a famous scientist (e.g., B. F. Skinner, William Shockley) are more likely to make news than the same remarks by lesser known (but perhaps more competent) people (Goodell, 1977; Goodfield, 1981; Weiss, 1984b). As Walter Sullivan of the *New York Times* reportedly said ("Science, Technology, and the Press; Must the 'Age of Innocence' End?" 1980): "With Linus Pauling, you report it because it's Linus Pauling . . . even if it is *kooky*."

Features

Feature stories, in contrast to news stories, lack the criteria of recency and newness but retain the requirement to be in the public interest. Thus they may be more suited than news stories to communicating behavioral science. Features also are more likely to include different points of view, qualifications, and limitations. Magazines contain more features than news, and thus may be more appropriate for communicating science, but newspapers could carry more features to a wider audience.

Features are often given a "news flavor" by relating the topic to another event that is in the news (Weiss, 1984b). The trial of Larry P. concerning the use of IQ tests by schools was a "news peg" for a variety of features on intelligence, test construction and scoring, and the appropriate interpretation of test results that would never have been published otherwise. Similarly, Father's Day is often a news peg for articles on father behavior.

Conclusion

Despite the differences mentioned, journalists and scientists may actually agree on the newsworthiness of a topic to a greater extent than many scientists believe. Two studies, for example, have found that reporters' rankings of the news value of topics are more similar to scientists' rankings than they are to scientists' estimates of how they think reporters would rank the same topics (R. E. Carter, 1958; Tichenor et al., 1970).

Since I suspect journalism will always cover science as news, scientists must recognize that the press and the public are not interested in "understanding science" or knowing "how scientists study phenomena." Instead, they are interested in *some* of our findings—those that relate to social issues and to their personal experiences and responsibilities. Selecting those findings according to the criteria of newsworthiness is a crucial component of science communications and obviates the need to hype.

Why and How—Newspaper Procedures

Procedures vary depending on the particular medium and even within media, so this section begins with newspaper operations and then describes how other communication channels differ from these procedures.

Time

A major constraint on many journalistic procedures is time (Dunwoody, 1982; Weiss, 1985). A scientist may spend 6 months reviewing literature or 1–5 years conducting a single research study; the local news reporters may perform the journalistic analogue of these projects in an afternoon. Even feature writers at national newspapers and free-lance magazine writers may not have longer than 3–5 days. News reporters covering a major scientific convention may file two stories per day. If scientists would try to write an accurate, balanced, interesting 400-word story on a topic in another discipline in an afternoon, they might have greater understanding of some of the characteristics of newspaper stories that they dislike.

Competition

The time constraint is amplified by competition with other publications to be first with the story and with other reporters for space in their own publication. This explains, in part, the occasional tendency to make a science story somewhat more "newsworthy" than it really is (Weiss, 1985). Scientists sometimes do an analogous thing when they attempt to make their empirical reports appear more scientifically rigorous than they are. After all, "journalists really do perish if they don't publish" (Hassett, 1978). Time and competition undergird many of the procedures described below.

Story Selection

Reporters who specialize in science often have more freedom than many other types of reporters to select their own topics, which they do on the basis of news releases sent by professional organizations (e.g., APA, SRCD, etc.) and private industry, journal articles (e.g., *Science, The New England Journal of Medicine, Nature*), conventions, news pegs, conversations with scientists, and personal interest. Editors, of course, also assign topics.

But story selection for behavioral science is likely to be different, because few reporters specialize in behavioral science. As a result, the social and behavioral sciences tend to be covered by a great variety of reporters who are typically assigned a topic in the news or in the public interest and need research information or expert opinion (Weiss, 1983). Students of infancy, then, are likely to be contacted by general assignment reporters or reporters specializing in education, life-style, or health who are seeking information pertaining to a news peg (e.g., a particularly horrible case of infant abuse, day-care licensing bills in the legislature, proposals to open adoption records) or topics of current social interest (e.g., the development of infants born to teenage mothers, the competence of fathers to care for their infants, the effects of divorce on infants). This means that behavioral scientists often must take more responsibility for conveying accurate and balanced information in a clear and useful way, because the reporter is not trained in science or science reporting. Also, behavioral scientists are more likely to be asked to relate their information to the practical and applied issues of society and child rearing that stimulated the story, and data may or may not be available to help with this task.

Sampling

Which professionals the journalist contacts depends on the nature of the story, whether the publication is oriented toward a local or national audience, and the background of the journalist. News stories—reports of research recently published or presented at a convention—tend to be "single-source" stories. That is, only the author of the research is interviewed. Feature stories in national newspapers and magazines are more likely to involve several sources, because the writers have the time and resources to contact the leading specialists in the country. In contrast, local newspapers often rely on local professionals to provide background information on almost any topic in the field, not just the professional's specialty, and because of time demands, only one or two sources are likely to be contacted.

How these specialists are identified is sometimes controversial. For example, psychologist James Hassett took a year's leave from Boston University to work at *Psy-*

chology Today and discovered the journalistic process of sampling was much different than scientific sampling.

> I didn't understand where all the books were . . . I was quickly informed that journalists don't use books—they use the telephone. What you do is, you find a few key people—usually a friend of a friend—and you call them up and you say, "Who's doing something in this field?" And he tells you a little about what he is doing, and then you talk to all of his friends, and so it goes down the line.
>
> *(Hassett, 1978)*

This "old boy/girl networking" is mixed to varying extents with calls to organizations that specialize in providing sources to journalists (e.g., APA Public Information Office, American Academy of Pediatrics, Scientists' Institute for Public Information, American Association for the Advancement of Science), but even these organizations tend to have their own versions of the "old boy/girl" system.

To some scientists, this strategy produces stories that rely on the same few visible scientists (Goodell, 1977) who seem to be willing to talk about almost any subject, while many more scientifically competent individuals who truly are specialists in the subject matter of the article do not get interviewed. From the journalist's perspective, however, the system works fairly well. A journalist quickly recognizes that a few scientists are unusually cooperative, have a big-picture view, outline the dimensions of the issue succinctly, present a newsworthy and interesting viewpoint clearly, and provide fascinating and crisp quotes (Weiss, 1985). They are "good copy," useful, and efficient. In contrast, a broad selection of scientists often produces a large number who are not cooperative and who are obfuscatory, pedantic, incomprehensible, or irrelevant. Journalists simply do not have the time to help such people communicate.

The actual situation, I believe, falls between these extremes. While a few prominent scientists are frequent media sources, generally speaking, scientific achievement is not related to frequency of media contact (Dunwoody & Scott, 1982; Shepherd, 1979), which may be a sign that journalistic sampling needs improvement and/or that accomplished scientists must take a more active role in public communications.

The implication of this process for scientists is that, when local media call, you may be the most appropriate source in the locality even if the topic is not your specialty. But when a national medium calls, it is your responsibility to represent the discipline as a whole, judge whether you are the most appropriate source in the country for the topic at hand, and refer the journalist to a balanced set of several specialists whether or not you do the interview.

Data Collection

Except for an occasional survey sponsored by a newspaper or television network, the communications media do not collect original scientific data and, with some exceptions, do not read scientific reports. Instead, they communicate what scientists say, usually during an interview, are the conclusions.

The interview process contains two major sources of error: The scientist must communicate the facts correctly, completely, and in a balanced fashion; and the journalist must record those facts and present them correctly, completely, and in a balanced fashion to the public. When errors of fact or emphasis occur in an article, scientists typically blame the journalist. Sometimes they are correct. I have been shattered in my own journalistic activities at the frequency of my errors, including misspellings of the names of colleagues and friends. Further, simply rephrasing results and conclusions can produce unintentional distortions and inaccuracies.

But scientists also make mistakes when presenting the information. The journalistic interview demands that a scientist select the most important and newsworthy information and then present it succinctly, clearly, and interestingly to an alien audience in what amounts to one-draft dictation. Most scientists cannot dictate at all, those who can rarely produce a competent version on the first draft, and few can make the material relevant to a lay audience. For example, in my experience using a tape recorder to interview my colleagues, behavioral scientists often make blatant errors of fact, invariably omit many of the points they later thought should have been included, and even say things that are direct negations of their own data and the conclusion they wish to make. And these errors have been committed by child development's most honored and press-wise citizens. Journalists are not likely to give up the interview, so scientists must learn to do a better job. Guidelines are presented in a later section.

The Story

Scientific articles follow a rigid format that reflects the prototypical chronological sequence of good scientific methodology—theoretical context and predictions, method, results and statistics, and conclusions and implications. News reports, in contrast, are typically written in the opposite sequence—conclusions and implications first, followed by a few details of the method and results, plus quotes from an authority or "sample subject" to flesh out the presentation. In contrast to news, feature stores have a less prescribed format, and may begin with a personal story that provides a context or illustrates the main theme, followed by informational details, pros and cons, and one or more conclusions.

Journalistic sequences are designed to motivate people who otherwise might not read the story, and to provide the main information at the beginning so that readers (and makeup editors) can skip the last portions without serious loss of information. Journalists believe, with some justification (Taylor & Thompson, 1982), that vivid headlines and grabby leads are crucial to recruiting attention of readers (and editors). The "selling" of knowledge to potentially uninterested members of the public may be distasteful to scientists (Ryan, 1979), but it is the only way to reach those most in need of our information who are also likely to be least interested in reading it. Writing a good lead, for example, is very difficult—scientists should try it. They would have more respect for those who do it effectively and responsibly.

The production process typically includes some division of labor that can influence the accuracy of the article. For example, a reporter's story is reviewed by an editor who may make substantial changes in the wording, sequence, and even the theme of the story and who may not check the changes with the reporter. Further, another person writes the headline, a source of considerable dissatisfaction among scientists (Ryan, 1979), and another individual places the story on a page where some material may be eliminated to make the story fit the space. In short, the reporter is only partly responsible for the published version.

Checking

It seems reasonable to scientists that the reporter should call them back to check over the facts before publication. Although some science writers encourage the practice (Perlman, 1974), most journalists—86 percent in one survey of writers of science articles (Tankard & Ryan, 1974)—do not. Indeed, a general assignment reporter may never have encountered such a request until he or she interviews a scientist (Dunwoody, 1982). This point is one of the greatest single differences of opinion between scientists and writers (Ryan, 1979).

Scientists profess that they want to check over the story to make sure that everything is accurate. Journalists, on the other hand, may not have time to have the story checked and do not want to put up with the hassles that checking often entails. Scientists, for example, frequently want to add material, change their quotes, and ignore word limits (Broberg, 1973), and often the revision is not an improvement as far as the journalist is concerned. They also "nitpick" about phraseology, and sometimes they disagree with the themes in the article, even when the basis of their disagreement is not scientific but political, personal preference, or self-interest. In addition, journalists are taught to be independent of their sources, in the same way scientists who write literature reviews or theories are independent of their sources. To refuse sources review privileges safeguards against political censorship and manipulation of the news, a goal most researchers would support, at least when applied to politicians, the military, and big business. Further, the scientific community holds the keys to the facts and the journalist is largely incapable of independently verifying them, which increases the opportunity for science to manage the news and requires even greater vigilance by journalists. Indeed, journalists are even concerned that AAAS manages the news at their convention by deliberately selecting only certain symposia for press conferences (Dunwoody, 1978).

Scientists argue that the facts of social and political events usually are not esoteric; the facts of science, however, are not easily understood by reporters or readers and accuracy checks are more necessary. Indeed, science articles *do* appear less accurate than other news (see section on accuracy), and accuracy does improve when scientists are allowed to review, although they correct only approximately half the errors (Tankard & Ryan, 1974).

Many major magazines, in contrast to most newspapers, face this issue squarely by employing "fact checkers" or "researchers" who document all factual statements and quotes in every article—and there can be up to 300 facts in a 2000-word story (Machalaba, 1981). Authors may be required to supply references, copies of the original technical articles, and telephone numbers of people cited or quoted in the article. Then fact checkers actually check every statement against the sources. *Parents* magazine and *Psychology Today,* for example, follow this procedure. In the author's experience, no technical article is scrutinized as closely as those appearing in these magazines. While such checking is rare at newspapers, there is a trend toward more checking in the popular press as a means of boosting prestige and avoiding lawsuits (Ridder, 1980).

In my view, journalists should recognize that scientific reports are factually more complicated and more easily distorted than are other topics. But scientists also must understand that they "are to journalists what rats are to scientists" (Victor Cohn, cited by Goodfield, 1981). They are the subjects, not the experimenter or the author of the article. Scientists typically do not allow research subjects to check over their data or the researcher's interpretation of their behavior, and they should understand the journalists' tendency to follow the same principles.

Researchers can tactfully volunteer to check stories, (e.g., "I don't mind if you want to call back for more information or to verify facts or quotes"). But, as veteran science writer David Perlman cautioned, if the scientist "asks in a tone that says, 'Hey, buddy, I don't trust you and you are going to screw this story up.' I resent that, because I am as competent in my field as the scientist is in his field. On the other hand, I want to get things right" ("Anatomy of a Science Story," 1984, p. 8). If they are called, scientists need to recognize the distinction between correcting facts and treading on the journalists' turf, independence, and integrity ("Anatomy of a Science Story," 1984). It also helps if scientists keep nitpicking to a minimum, so that the checking procedure is not considered an unreasonable hassle by the journalists.

Public Domain

Most articles written in the popular press are considered to be in the "public domain," which means that other newspapers can reprint the article, in whole or in part, without acquiring permission or citing its origin. In addition, news services provide subscriber newspapers with stories, and a newspaper can, and often does, change the headline, use only part of the original story, or even change the main theme of the article. As with the old game of "pass it on," the story that appears in the *Centerville Weekly* is often substantially different than the original article published in the *New York Times,* perhaps without important qualifiers (Weiss, 1984a).

For some researchers, this "trickled-down" journalism is the ultimate frustration, because neither scientist nor the original journalist has any control or effective recourse over the matter. Both must accept it as part of the process.

Procedures in Other Media

Procedures are different for newspapers of different sizes, magazines, TV and radio news, and TV documentaries and film.

Local Newspapers

Local and small newspapers are less likely to have science and other specialist reporters, and they must use fewer sources, work faster, and check less than reporters of major city or national dailies and magazines. On the other hand, such small newspapers are often pleased to have broadly based material that will be of interest to their readers. Articles in these publications may reach an entirely different audience than an article in the *New York Times,* and local publicity may greatly facilitate acquisition and cooperation of research subjects.

National Publications

Reporters at national newspapers and magazines and free-lance writers tend to have more time (e.g., 4–5 days vs. a few hours to write a feature story) and are more likely to be specialists in a topical area. This means that you can probably spend some time preparing for the interview, they are more likely to use referrals to other specialists, and they are often able to understand and translate some scientific jargon and procedures. Some of these writers are much more broadly versed in child development than most scientists.

Radio and TV News

Radio and television news operate similarly to newspapers, but they seem to have even less time because of the technical requirements of the media. Local TV news-people often arrive having no background information at all on you or the topic, they may or may not discuss the subject matter with you before the cameras start rolling, they seem to have two or three prepared questions that may or may not be relevant to your expertise, the camera may or may not be on you as you speak, and they typically want some "action footage" of your laboratory, (e.g., a baby in the assessment situation, the reporter listening to your answer, etc.). They may be in and out in 30–40 min, you will probably not appear for more than 15 sec in the final version, and that segment may or may not have something to do with the main point you tried to make during the interview. Therefore, I regard radio and TV news appearances as the most risky communications format.

Documentaries

Television documentaries, news magazines, and films operate more like printed magazines than like television news. Typically, one or two researchers background a program or episode by reading articles and interviewing professionals much the way a magazine or newspaper feature writer does. Not only are they collecting information to craft the program, but they are auditioning the professionals as possible on-camera authorities.

A documentary "shoot" is often well planned in contrast to local TV news. The writer and producer already know from the background interview the topics they want you to cover and even some of the things they want you to say. The shoot itself can be very time-consuming—it is not unusual to spend the entire day "on the set" for less than an hour of actual shooting of which nothing to a few minutes may be used in the final product. It is fun and interesting (the first time), but it is also fatiguing. Don't plan anything else that day.

Talk Shows

Radio and television talk shows are booming (B. Carter, Howard, Yang, & Gelman, 1979). They are produced live or without editing, in the studio, usually without much preparation by the interviewer, and with or without audience participation or call-ins. In contrast to the other formats, your personal performance is more crucial in such programs, because you do not have a communicator to translate or to tidy up your language and you do not have the option of being able to use your best "take." Further, because it is live, you must be able to deal on the spot with naive questions and (very rarely) controversy or challenges.

The success of the program will depend in part on your ability to guide the conversation toward useful and interesting topics. In my experience, approximately three of four local interviewers know nothing about what you have to say, although the networks do more preparation. If you have written a book, typical local interviewers will have glanced at the material on the dust jacket and skimmed the table of contents—they almost certainly will not have read it (although they may tell their listeners "it's a great book"). Most simply do not have time, and they welcome a one-page summary of your background and the topics you can cover.

Although many interviewers ask the same banal questions (Fenichell, 1983; Rosen, 1977), some are renaissance people. They have a broad knowledge base, ask interesting questions, and relate your answers to the interests of the audience. The whole affair can be quite stimulating.

SCIENCE AND THE PRESS: LIKE OIL AND WATER?

To hear scientists talk about it, these procedures are so contrary to those of science that they make science and journalism something like oil and water—they don't mix. "In their search for attention-getting headlines and snappy leads," psychologist Zick Rubin complained, "reporters often highlight isolated or unrepresentative results, present them in an oversimplified way, turn minor findings into 'great discoveries,' and generalize from small samples to all of humanity" (1980, p. 7). Sometimes it is worse, as when a paper trivialized Rubin's research on love with the ungrammatical headline "Man Finds Proof Love Between Sexes." Generally, scientists feel that press accounts of their work are oversimplified, sensationalized, and inaccurate (Stipp, 1985; Stocking, 1978). The same complaints about journalists are voiced by business executives (Ricklefs, 1982). In addition, though, scientists feel that going public is demeaning and antiscience (Goodfield, 1981), and that "stooping" (Stevenson, 1977) to do so is not worth the risk (Goodfield, 1981).

Journalists are not willing to accept completely the blame implied by these accusations, and some have sharp words for scientists. June Goodfield (1981), a scientist and a journalist, finds "among journalists a strong feeling that, if there was— or is—a problem, its origin lies squarely with the scientific profession, all too many of whose members have been singularly unconcerned, unhelpful, or just plain arrogant when it comes to explaining science to the nonscientist" (p. 1). Besides lack of interest or contempt, Thistle (1958) observed that scientists who communicate badly "err on two counts: a bumbling, fumbling use of the language itself and a thoroughly mistaken idea of how much detail is required" (p. 955).

Philosophical Dimensions of Difference

These complaints reflect major philosophical differences between the two groups in orientation to knowledge and communication strategies. However, each group thinks the other is more extreme than is actually the case; scientists have less favorable and perhaps less accurate views of journalists than journalists have of scientists, and even those scientists who complain in print (e.g., Rubin, 1980; Walum, 1975; Weigel & Pappas, 1981) ultimately agree with Hassett (1978) that scientists "should spend less time being appalled at the popular press, and more time thinking about how best to deal with it."

Causal Explanation Versus Description

Scientists are mainly concerned with explaining a phenomenon, especially its causes, and they are trained to question, to argue, to debate, and finally to "quibble" (Hassett, 1978). The reporter, in contrast, emphasizes a straightforward description of the main facts (Gans, 1980). "In reporting of a disaster, for example, a scientist looks for causes and a reporter thinks first about effects. . . . There is usually much more 'what' than 'why,' particularly in breaking stories" (Burrows, 1980, p. 15). Most journalists are not trained and have no time or space to integrate causes or factors across studies, understand processes, and compare different solutions to the same problems (Bogart, 1968). The public is "simply interested in knowing when a cure will arrive—how we get to that cure is of no interest" (scientist Robert Weinberg, in "How the Media Cover Cancer," 1983, p. 5).

Abstract Principles Versus Concrete Applications

A major goal of science is to discover general laws or principles that are true under a great variety of specific circumstances. But to a journalist and others who want to apply information—politicians, lawyers, parents, child care workers—an abstraction lacks concrete reality, it is not as interesting or as informative to readers as a concrete example (Funkhouser & Maccoby, 1971; Krieghbaum, 1959), and its successful application usually requires some additional information about the specific situation (Bogart, 1968; Katz, 1984; Revelle, 1975). One kind of concrete presentation, case histories, may influence judgments of readers more than abstractly presented information, because readers underutilize or fail to understand abstract or statistical information (Taylor & Thompson, 1982).

This difference in emphasis is a problem for science communications in at least two ways. First, the scientists' search for general laws sometimes precludes studies of concrete social or technical problems. Scientists often "refer far too much to what is technically possible or technically optimal, rather than what is socially desirable" (scientist John Ziman in Goodfield, 1981, p. 14). And when scientists do get relevant, "it is regrettable, but true, that real-world analyses provide unambiguous answers only for trivial problems" (Goodfield, 1981, p. 12). Second, abstract ideas are difficult to communicate. "Ideas," observes science fiction writer David Gerrold, "in and of themselves, do not photograph well" (Maugh, 1978, p. 37).

Interviewers typically ask scientists for a concrete example or a possible application, and many are at a loss for an answer, often because the scientist usually leaves the task of real-world application to someone else. The "someone else" may be the reporter, and the result may be a bad case of "breakthroughitis" (Judy Randall, *New York Daily News,* in "How the Media Cover Cancer," 1983, p. 1), although scientists also have been known to claim breakthroughs, as in the case of possible explanations of sudden infant death syndrome (Dunwoody, 1980a).

Tentative Versus Certain Conclusions

Scientific data are tentative, vulnerable, changing, and evolving, while the press and presumably the public want finished, unequivocal, permanent truth (Goodfield, 1981; Weiss, 1985). Reporters are trained to get the facts—exactly what happened, confirmed and clear-cut, plus an implication for society. But science rarely can accommodate these criteria (Bogart, 1968).

Sometimes the tentativeness of science is carried to the extreme. Psychologist Hassett (1978) observed that scientists spend pages saying why they don't know anything about a subject, and the journalist wonders why the scientist wrote about it at all. Edward Edelson of the *New York Daily News* discovered the same phenomenon after coauthoring a chemistry text. There is an argument about almost every fact in the book. It is very difficult to get two chemists to agree on the structure of a basic molecule! Coming out of that, I just don't believe 'the facts' anymore ("Science, Technology and the Press," 1980, p. 52).

At one level, the tentativeness of science annoys writers who must cope with the scientist's penchant for perambulating, hedging, and adding innumerable qualifiers. But this tentativeness also distorts the public's image of science. Quibbling scientists look indecisive (Bogart, 1968). If a business executive, lawyer, or politician vacillated between X and Y as do scientists, people would wonder whether they knew what they were doing (Cobb, 1981). What society fails to understand is that, by definition, professionals on the edge of knowledge do *not* know what causes what—scientists are privileged to be able to say so, while most others must make a decision "in audacious ignorance" yet appear certain and confident.

An Audience of Peers Versus the Public

Besides students, scientists ordinarily talk to or write for their scientific peers who presumably understand their specialized vocabulary, methods, theories, and values and may reward the use of esoteric language (Crichton, 1975; Dunwoody, 1980b). As a result, one magazine editor concluded that from the standpoint of the lay public, "most scientists cannot talk or write their way out of a wet paper bag." Even when it is good, "scientific writing stresses accuracy at all costs. . . . The cost . . . is often readability" (Hassett, 1978). In fact, scientists judged a lecture, which was specially composed to contain nonsense, to be clear and stimulating (Naftulin, Ware, & Donnelly, 1973), and the more unintelligible the writing the greater the scientists' ratings of prestige and competence (Armstrong, 1979). However, simpler articles are enjoyed more and can communicate as much information to lay persons as complicated articles (Funkhouser & Maccoby, 1971; Hunsaker, 1979).

Unfortunately, many scientists speak in academic style—"bafflegab" (Stocking & Dunwoody, 1982)—to journalists, who then must select and "translate" the intelligible information into terms appropriate for an audience who shares none of this background (Gans, 1980). And when those scientists see the story, they seem to be primarily concerned not with how the lay public views what they have said, but with how their scientific colleagues will react (Kirsch, 1982; "Science, Technology, and the Press," 1980).

Complete Report Versus a Summary

Scientists know that details make a difference, and, for them, a report is virtually uninterpretable without them. But often the journalist must report the study without those details, perhaps in 300 words—barely more than the length of a journal abstract. The result is that most "errors" scientists detect in science journalism are errors of omission rather than errors of commission, and brief reports of research are seen as simplistic and distorted. In the extreme, one scientist observed, "the public clearly prefers a simple lie to a complicated truth" (Goodfield, 1981, p. 8).

But these criticisms are made from the scientist's, not the layperson's, standpoint. When methodological details are included in stories (e.g., called "precision journalism," Meyer, 1973), the reader, regardless of education, does not judge the story to have greater clarity, accuracy, trustworthiness, or believability (Mosier & Ahlgren, 1981) than matched stories without such details. Moreover, Earl Ubell, a television science reporter, is exasperated with researchers who think that in order to get their message across science stories must cover the topic in minute detail:

> That just isn't true. All the evidence we have suggests that people absorb a good deal from two minutes, and probably don't absorb a hell of a lot more from an hour. . . . A number of experiments have shown that very simplified versions of complicated reports serve the same function in communicating the sense of the report as the entire report itself. So people who scream about oversimplification are just not aware of the way people understand things.
>
> *("The 'Alerting Function' of Television," 1983, p. 8)*

Certainly in terms of memory for specific facts, the data support Ubell.

Truth Versus Profit

Scientists, presumably, objectively seek after truth. In contrast, journalism and the media are businesses—they must provide information that people are willing to buy. Some information, of course, sells better than other information, and the solidity of the empirical basis for an idea does not seem to influence the matter (Hassett, 1978; Weiss, 1984b). But sensational or "vivid" headlines, leads, and stories do attract attention and increase recall of information (Taylor & Thompson, 1982), yet a good many scientists feel that the need to sell newspapers, create interest, and compete for space conflicts with the cautious claims of science, accuracy, and truth. "Given a contrast between truth and profit . . . the truth will always go under" (Goodfield, 1981, p. 8).

Science on television and in books may be even more subject to financial demands than science in newspapers or magazines. Books, for example, are rarely reviewed for scientific accuracy (Hixson, 1981)—factual accuracy is the author's responsibility (Schwarz, 1984), and while newspapers and broadcasters have voluntary codes of ethics, book publishers have none. So "between the hammer of ratings and the anvil of profit, truth, integrity, and literary merit may be squeezed out" (Goodfield, 1981, p. 58), as happened in the case of Rorvik's (1978) book, *In His Image: The Cloning of a Man*. Sadly, good science on commercial television is all but dead for lack of money. The best producers, hosts, communications companies, and advertising agencies have failed to make a commercial success of a television science series, even though they attracted more viewers than NOVA (Angier, 1983). "For, above all, American commercial television is based on the premise of delivering not a program to the audience, but a mass audience to the sponsor, *at once*" (Goodfield, 1981, p. 28). In public television, "NOVA," Cousteau, and the National Geographic were successful because of the good fortune of having consistent sponsorship. Otherwise, much more time may be spent looking for money than producing the program (Goodfield, 1981).

The media's need to sell is especially dangerous, according to scientists, because the media do not check accuracy sufficiently and retractions are not featured as prominently as claims. Some scientists have bemoaned a "double standard" of ethics, in which scientists must answer to their colleagues and to institutional review boards, while the press is allowed to say what it likes under the protection of the First Amendment and the freedom of the press (Garn, 1979). It is akin to the theme of the movie *Absence of Malice*—newspapers don't print the truth, they print what people say is the truth.

But scientists are the ones who presumably are speaking the truth or falsehoods to the press. Although journalists may be influenced by profit motives, scientists are not always paragons of objective selfless virtue either, and many observers have declared that objectivity of both the press and science is a myth (e.g., Burrows, 1980; Goodfield, 1981; Herrnstein, 1982; Kirsch, 1982). According to Edward Edelson of the *New York Daily News:*

> Objective? Are you kidding? . . . You give me a scientist; I'll put 50 cents on the table, and he will tell me 50 cents' worth of what I want to hear. . . . The whole assumption is that scientists are different from us—that they're objective, that they're truth seekers. . . . Some of them are ascetic saints, [but] they're liars, they're cheats . . . some are drunken lechers, some do things just to get their names in the papers . . . some make mistakes at the top of their voices. . . . We meet them all the time and they are just like us.
>
> *("Science, Technology, and the Press," 1980, pp. 55-56)*

David Perlman, veteran science writer for the *San Francisco Chronicle,* agrees that "scientists lie occasionally, like everybody else, and they're going to lie publicly at times" ("Science, Technology, and the Press," 1980, p. 51). But

> I think the tools of science—properly used—can provide a measure of certainty beyond what is provided by pure intuition and hunch. And honest scientists, I believe, spend their professional lives looking for that kind of certainty. But when the scientist becomes a strong partisan and an advocate for a particular position, he begins, like everybody else, to forget about some of the *un*certainty and accept only that which supports his position. (p. 56)

Empirical Dimensions of Difference

The philosophical differences described above are stated in the extreme. When science communication is itself studied scientifically, the perceived differences are more extreme than is actually the case (Goodfield, 1981; McCall & Stocking, 1982; Stocking & Dunwoody, 1982).

Values and Perceptions

The two groups appear to agree on values much more than they disagree. Journalists and scientists from a variety of disciplines, for example, were asked to rank the importance in science communication of accuracy, interest to readers, usefulness to readers, prompt publication, and uniqueness. The scientists, for example, placed accuracy first and felt that reporters would rank it lower. In fact, the two groups ranked all five items identically (Tichenor et al., 1970; Tichenor et al., 1971). Johnson (1963) also found that scientists, science writers, readers, and nonreaders of science news stories all evaluated science news stories primarily on the basis of accuracy and significance. Editors, however, judged stories primarily on the basis of color and excitement.

The two groups, of course, can agree on general values and yet be worlds apart in how they implement them. For example, Ryan (1979) surveyed 122 science writers and editors and 140 scientists from several disciplines whose research had been reported in the press. Of 38 items on the questionnaire, scientists and journalists shared the same general opinion on 32 points, although the degree of agreement differed significantly on half of these. The points of agreement included the following: Science writers should be trained in the fundamentals of research methodology; scientists who deal regularly with the press should have some training in the fundamentals of news communication; newspaper coverage of science news is important for the public and for scientists; news reports of science often omit important information; scientists should not refuse to cooperate with reporters who appear inadequately trained in science; a reporter should not use a word such as *breakthrough* or *cure* unless the scientist believes the term is appropriate when applied to his or her work; scientists have an obligation to work with news reporters to get the results of their research before the public; and scientists should not expect the same level of precision in newspaper science reports that they expect from reports in scientific journals.

With respect to disagreements, researchers tended to think the scientist should review the article before publication, the headlines should be written by the reporter who writes the story, the scientist should release information to the press only after scientific publication, the journalist should rely completely on the scientist to point out the most important contribution of research, and a journalist should not interpret a scientist's technical conclusions. Researchers also felt that journalists often sensationalize scientific news. Journalists tended to disagree with these particular points, which are listed above in order beginning with the point of largest disagreement.

Ryan also had both scientists and journalists rate the items as they felt they would be rated by people in the other profession. Each group perceived the other as being more dissimilar to itself than that group perceived itself to be. Generally, attitudes of journalists and scientists were more similar than different, scientists and journalists believe the gap between the two disciplines is greater than is actually the case, and scientists' stereotypes of journalists and the media are probably too extreme (Stocking & Dunwoody, 1982).

Accuracy

Accuracy is the first concern of scientists and science writers (but perhaps not of editors), and the technical nature of science may make science news reports more prone to error than news reports about other topics. For example, Tankard and Ryan (1974) found that only 8.8 percent of science articles were free of errors, but they reported that other studies of general news stories found error-free rates of 40.1–59.5 percent. Some evidence exists, therefore, that science stories may be less accurate than general news stories. However, it is possible that scientists, who are the judges of accuracy in most of these studies, are more critical than nonscience sources, and that the density of information is greater in science stories, thereby increasing the likelihood of errors. Further, what constitutes an error is debatable—journalists dispute 75 percent of the errors claimed by sources of all kinds (Tillinghast, 1982).

When talking about the media in general, researchers feel accuracy is a major problem. In one study, for example, only 31 percent of scientists from many fields thought science news was generally accurate (Tankard & Ryan, 1974). In another study, 60 percent of the scientists rated science news as generally accurate (Tichenor et al., 1970), approximately the same level as the general public when assessing articles on topics with which they are familiar (Sanoff, 1982). In contrast, 95 percent of the same scientists in this latter study thought an article quoting them was generally accurate, and they said that they would work with that reporter again. Similarly, Pulford (1975, 1976) found that scientists who were featured in articles were 5½ times more likely to regard the article as accurate than as inaccurate. Although these scientists found some error in 71 percent of the articles, they said that 73 percent of the articles were more accurate than inaccurate. The same disparity between perceived and actual accuracy exists for social and behavioral scientists in particular (Weiss, 1984c, 1985). Even if they think the media are generally inaccurate, 75 percent of scientists in one study would "welcome" contact with the press and another 11 percent would "agree" to be interviewed (Dunwoody & Scott, 1982).

What is the nature of the errors that do exist in science reports? In general, they are errors of omission rather than errors of commission or facts (Borman, 1978; Tankard & Ryan, 1971), and the same is true of nonscience stores (Singletary, 1980; Tillinghast, 1982). The scientists in Tankard and Ryan's (1974) survey, for example, were asked which, if any, of 42 kinds of errors occurred in the story about their work. In order of decreasing frequency, the top 9 types of errors were: relevant information about method omitted; relevant information about results omitted; investigator misquoted; names of other investigators on the research team omitted; qualification of statements omitted; headline misleading; investigator quoted out of context; continuity of research with earlier work ignored; and story too brief. Other studies have also shown that omissions and misemphases, rather than errors of fact, are frequent concerns of scientists, and headlines seem to be a particular problem (Pulford, 1975; Tankard & Ryan, 1974; Tichenor et al., 1970). In contrast, 75 percent of social scientists featured in the nation's major media did not feel important information had been omitted (Weiss, 1985).

More specifically, Ryan (1975) subsequently factor-analyzed the scientists' reports of errors (Tankard & Ryan, 1974) and confirmed the distinction between omissions and commissions (also called subjective vs. objective errors by Berry, 1967). Errors of omission dominated the first two factors, while objective mistakes (e.g., misspellings, typographical errors) characterized the third factor. The first factor was a mixture of the omission of relevant information and qualifications with the overstatement of findings, inferences, and the significance of the study or nonscientific aspects of it. Items on the second factor, although mentioned approximately one-fourth as often, implied that the omission of information led to an *under*emphasis of the study's actual significance, generality, applicability, and uniqueness. Underlying both these factors may be the feeling by scientists that the stories written about their work sometimes missed the main point, resulting in exaggerated claims or failure to tout the true implications of the results.

While science reporting may be more errorful than other forms of journalism, it is more accurate than scientists generally believe. Moreover, a good many of the "errors" are errors of omission rather than errors of fact, many of the omissions are simply the result of space limitations (would an abstract from a scholarly journal be judged as errorful?), and the omissions are of greater concern to scientists than they are to the journalist or reading public (Dunwoody, 1982). Finally, as much as scientists dread the apparently simplistic questions by reporters, "What is the main point of your studies and what is the implication for society?," how they are answered and reported is crucial to the scientists' judgment of the accuracy of the story.

It should be noted in these studies of accuracy that, by implication, the errors are attributed to the journalist. But no one tape-records the interview to examine errors of commission—to say nothing of errors of omission—by the scientist source. Certainly, some scientists have irresponsibly claimed to have discovered cures or explanations for particular problems (e.g., SIDS, Dunwoody, 1980), encouraged or allowed journalists to draw unsubstantiated conclusions from their research (e.g., Weigel & Pappas, 1981), and announced results or claims that other scientists find ridiculous (Cowen, 1979). One study of science articles showed that most statements liberally judged to be "sensational" were attributed to sources, not to the reporters (Glynn & Tims, 1982). It is quite possible that the well-honed scientific skill of criticism is really directed at other scientists who express arguable conclusions in the media, and the media get left holding the bag of scientists' dirty laundry (Cowen, 1979).

Another problem with these accuracy reports is that they represent assessments of what scientists call reliability, not validity. Journalists, editors, and fact checkers are predominantly concerned with whether Dr. Jones said what the story quotes him as saying; they spend far less time, often none, checking whether Dr. Jones knows what he is talking about (McCall & Stocking, 1982; Weiss, 1985). Pamela Ridder (1980), a fact checker for the *Columbia Journalism Review,* concluded that a "checker's job is not a quest for truth but a quest for substantiation" (p. 62).

Validity is valued by the press, of course, and it is not totally ignored. But often the criteria, perhaps applied more vigorously to the behavioral sciences, are whether (1) the information is not too counterintuitive and makes "common sense" (although this may conflict with newsworthiness); (2) the source is credible (e.g., professor at a prestigious university); (3) the source seems balanced and fair in treating opposing views; and (4) other scientists vouch for the point (Endreny, 1984; Gans, 1980; Stocking, 1978; Weiss, 1983, 1985). Perhaps the best approach is to have other scientists respond to the claims of a colleague, which, if not supportive, may result in cancelling the entire story, eliminating the point involving the claim, printing the claim and rebuttals or criticisms, or printing the "latest" results (Weiss, 1985).

Factors That Increase Accuracy

While it would seem that experienced reporters would be more accurate than inexperienced writers, journalists specializing in science would be more accurate than those who do not, and reporters from larger newspapers would be more accurate than those from smaller papers, the few studies investigating these differences have failed to show any edge for experience, specialization, or circulation (Tankard & Ryan, 1974; Tichenor et al., 1970). It may be that science writers take more liberties with the material because of their greater experience, novices recognize their need to be careful and accurate, and scientists modify their presentations during the interviews to match the level of the reporter. Scientists who are experienced with the media are more cooperative (Dunwoody & Scott, 1982) but do not have more accurate stories written about them (Tankard & Ryan, 1974).

Accuracy does increase, however, when a story is initiated with a press release, typically prepared and distributed by a university public information office (Berry,

1967; Tichenor et al., 1970). Such releases are often carefully formulated and checked with the sources before they are sent to editors, who assign the topics to reporters, who in turn work hard to please their boss (Tichenor et al., 1971). Some evidence also suggests that the more personal acquaintanceship and contact between scientist and journalist, the more accurate the story (Blankenburg, 1970; Tankard & Ryan, 1974; Tichenor et al., 1971), and a personal interview is associated with fewer errors than a telephone interview (Tankard & Ryan, 1974). But too much contact may lead to *less* accuracy (Tankard & Ryan, 1974; Tichenor et al., 1971).

The Effectiveness of Media Presentations

For most scientists, communicating research information through the mass media is intended to have some positive effect on people beyond entertaining them. Yet the likelihood of an effect and the nature of that effect often have been debated (Atkin, 1979). On the one hand, the advertisers who spend $500,000 for a 30-sec spot during the Super Bowl must know that the ad will influence enough people to make it worth the cost. Further, even single media events, such as the suicide of a fictional character on a soap opera, can be associated with an increase in fatalities across the nation, especially auto accidents (Motto, 1967; Phillips, 1977, 1982; but see Kessler & Stipp, 1984). And single fictional programs on wife abuse or adolescent suicide can produce substantial increases in calls to hotlines ("Battered Wife Film Sparks Calls," 1984; "TV Movie," 1984) or apparent copycat assaults (Karlen & Reese, 1984). On the other hand, it is widely believed that people remember only one or two items from the television news (e.g., Berry, 1983; Woodall, Davis, & Sahin, 1983), and that people rarely change their behavior as a result of media presentations (e.g., Atkin, 1979).

Assessing Media Effects

Several factors help to explain the diversity of views on media effects. One is the way effectiveness is assessed in the media, especially in contrast to the way psychologists usually evaluate effects. Typically, psychologists expect a substantial percentage of subjects or patients to display a clearly observable change in their behavior as a result of a treatment or therapy. In the media, however, the criterion is that a substantial *number* of people, but usually a small percentage, are influenced at a modest *cost per case*. For example, a series of seven television programs on how to stop smoking were shown throughout Finland. Although only 1 percent of the nation's smokers stopped smoking for at least 6 months as a result of the programs, each "cure" was achieved at a cost of approximately $1 (McAlister, Puska, Koskela, Pallonen & Maccoby, 1980), a cost effectiveness that no personal therapist could achieve. Moreover, more intensive campaigns, such as the antismoking media campaign in the United States, can have substantial cumulative effects—a reduction of 36.4 percent in cigarette consumption over estimates of what usage would have been without the campaign (Warner, 1981).

A second reason for the confusing results is that evaluations of media programs or campaigns can be scientifically difficult and very costly—much more expensive than the cost of producing the messages. Ball (1976), reviewing the methodological problems, suggested that "clear and unequivocal evidence of a causal relationship between television in general and social change will probably remain forever a fugitive from our scientific eyes" (p. 8). As a result, few comprehensive, methodologically sound studies of media effects on health promotion are available.

A third difficulty is the dependent variable—media effects on what? Advertisements and health promotion messages usually urge people to take a specific action—buy a particular product, stop smoking, lose weight, send contributions. Such behaviors can be measured precisely. But media messages that are mainly informational, such as reports on infant development, do not tell the audience what to do. Other than having the audience learn some factual information or change their attitudes, it is not clear what effect the message should have or how to measure it. For example, after an informational program on psychotherapy, some people may visit a therapist, some may decide never to seek psychological services, some may conclude they do not need help, many will file the information away possibly to use it at a much later time, others will experience an attitude change that may be expressed much later in different contexts, and most will never use the information. Despite this diversity of actions or inactions, all may have been "helped." Rather than influencing specific overt action (Schramm, 1973), informational programs raise issues in people's minds, suggest how much importance people should attach to such issues (McCombs & Shaw, 1977), reinforce attitudes that people already hold, and create attitudes if none existed before (McQail, 1969). The media, it is said, set agendas—they tell people not so much *what* to think as what to think *about*.

Studies of media effects relevant to this chapter fall into two groups, learning and retention of news information, and the effectiveness of health promotion programming. Almost all the research focuses on television with or without other media; very little is known about the effectiveness of informational print materials (e.g., an article in a newspaper or magazine).

Learning and Memory

A large and confusing literature on recall of news, especially radio and television news, has been reviewed recently by Berry (1983) and Woodall and colleagues (1983). Both reviewers are impressed with the difficulty of such research and lament the lack of coherent findings.

A few conclusions emerge, however. For one thing, while adults can learn and remember substantial amounts from television and radio presentations when exposed and tested under optimal conditions, free or even cued recall minutes or a few hours after an actual broadcast "is strikingly poor" (Berry, 1983, p. 370). For example, viewers can recall only 1 or 2 and rarely more than 3 of the 14–15 items presented on TV news, and 20–50 percent cannot recall *any* item (e.g., Katz, Adoni, & Parness, 1977; Neuman, 1976). Half the viewers of the TV weather segment cannot recall the forecast for tomorrow 15–90 min after the broadcast (Hyatt, Riley, & Sederstrom, 1978).

Why recall is so poor is not known, but substantial percentages of viewers do not pay complete attention to the program (Woodall et al., 1983). Not surprisingly, then, factors that help recruit attention (e.g., importance of the topic to the viewer, newsworthiness, interest value, and vivid pictures, especially of emotionally negative events) aid attention and thus recall (Berry, 1983; Katz et al., 1977; Miller & Barrington, 1981; Wilson, 1974; Woodall et al., 1983). But the information in TV news is primarily presented auditorily (Katz et al., 1977), and more printed information is recalled than material presented on television (Wilson, 1974). Although educated people and those with more background information on the topic recall more, wide variation in recall ability exists (Berry, 1983; Woodall et al., 1983). No one type of news item is clearly remembered better than other types, but viewers tend to recall the who, what, and where of an event (aspects that are frequently reinforced with pictures) more than its causes and consequences (Findall & Hoijer, 1976).

Health Promotion Programs and Campaigns

Despite the apparently dismal evidence for learning and memory for televised information, mass media programs and campaigns to improve health behavior can be successful under certain conditions (Atkin, 1979). For example, in one of the most comprehensive and thoroughly evaluated multimedia health campaigns, researchers found that information provided in the media alone led to reductions in blood pressure and other coronary risk factors in an entire medium-sized town, although the effects were often greater if the media were accompanied by social support and direct reinforcement (Meyer, Nash, McAlister, Maccoby, & Farquhar, 1980).

But results have not always been so impressive or clear, and Atkin (1979) listed several factors that seem to be associated with greater effectiveness. For example, sources of information that are credible, trustworthy, competent, dynamic, attractive, and similar to the members of the audience are relatively more effective. Messages that are perceived to be rewarding and worthy of attention, relevant to the needs of the receiver, entertaining, and attention getting are better. Concentrated bursts of messages are more effective than distributed exposure, and more messages are superior to fewer messages but only up to a point, after which negative effects can be produced. Logical, factual appeals work better for more intelligent audiences, while emotional appeals may be influential in activating those people already convinced or indifferent. Two-sided, balanced messages, especially regarding a highly involving problem, are superior to one-sided appeals when the audience is highly educated, initially opposed to the theme, or likely to be exposed to the opposite point of view. Informative messages may be best presented in print, while television does a better job of arousing emotions and threatening a receiver (which works predominantly in cases in which a simple concrete remedy is advocated, when receivers have low anxiety about the issue, or when a highly credible source delivers the message). Effectiveness is also improved if the audience is interested in or favorably disposed toward the message or needs the information (Ettema, Brown, & Luepker, 1983; Miller & Barrington, 1981). Finally, the media are much better at communicating information and thoughts than at changing attitudes, but attitude change is accomplished more readily than modifying overt behavior.

However, two recent methodologically comprehensive studies have shown substantial changes in attitudes and overt behaviors in areas other than health if programs are deliberately designed to get attention, be entertaining, relate to viewers' needs and interests, model the behaviors to be followed, and show the models rewarded for appropriate actions. In one study (Winett, Leckliter, Chinn, & Stahl, 1984), a single presentation of a 20-min television program dramatizing simple energy conservation techniques resulted in general home energy savings of approximately 10–20 percent over several months, and this was achieved with minimal interpersonal support. In the other study (Ball-Rokeach, Rokeach, & Grube, 1984), a single television program featuring Ed Asner and Sandy Hill (former anchor of *Good Morning America*) that was seen by a very large percentage of people in a few towns changed political values and social attitudes toward the issues of equality, freedom, and the environment. Moreover, it generated substantially more monetary contributions to subsequent appeals (not mentioned in the program) by pro-environment, antiracism, and antisexism groups. Impressively, these effects were just as strong when people who viewed the entire program were compared with those who intended to watch the entire program but were interrupted by extraneous circumstances, thereby controlling for initial attitudes associated with choosing to watch the program.

It appears, then, that it is possible for well-designed television programs to have substantial effects on learning, attitude, and behavioral change, at least under certain conditions. Studies also show, however, that printed materials alone may communicate information more effectively but seem to have far less impact, often none, on attitudes and behavioral change (Atkin, 1979; Winett et al., 1984), although the effectiveness of newspaper and magazine articles has not been investigated as thoroughly as that of television programs.

The Case of Bonding

One of the most dramatic effects of the media in the field of infancy has been the recent conversion of hospital practices to permit early contact and bonding. Recently, I reviewed the research literature, the practitioner literature (e.g., nursing journals), and the popular literature, principally major newspaper and magazine articles. Several points emerged.

One of the first newspaper reports on bonding was published by the *New York Times* (Flaste, 1977), which accurately reflected Klaus and Kennell's (1976) position and also noted that exceptions, such as adoptive parents, exist and that critics have suggested the case for bonding may be overstated. Two years earlier, Kennell (1975) presented the findings in a Johnson and Johnson roundtable that also published the criticisms that subjects might have given the investigators what they wanted and that possibly the increased maternal behavior was not directed at a specific infant and thus did not reflect attachment per se. These early criticisms were dropped in both the scholarly and popular articles thereafter.

Why? Partly, I speculate, because journalism, at least, does not favor qualifiers, but partly because bonding was a message many groups wanted to hear, a factor known to enhance media (and perhaps scientific) influence (Atkin, 1979; Ettema et al., 1983). For example, the nursing community probably believed touching was important before any research was available, having been influenced by their own experiences in the newborn nursery, by Freudian theory, by Ashley Montagu's book on touching (Montagu, 1971), and by Bowlby's emphasis on attachment (Bowlby, 1969), despite the fact that Bowlby states that a critical period in the first few months of life is very unlikely. The result was that the nursing literature generally accepted the research results uncritically and occasionally made rather extreme claims for the benefits of early contact.

The general public was also ready to hear the good news, because the apparent benefits of early contact fit nicely with the movement toward more humane birthing practices. In fact, the popular press typically reported the results and claims of Klaus and Kennell (1976) as only one part of the general theme of humane birth practices. Sometimes, in the press as well as in the joint statement of several medical associations ("Joint Position Statement on the Development of Family-Centered Maternity/Newborn Care in Hospitals," 1978), the bonding results were mentioned almost incidentally in the context of alternative birthing rooms and home deliveries. The social movement was the driving force; early contact was a hanger-on. This single case may illustrate the general principle that science often tends to follow rather than lead society (Rosengren, 1980), and that scientific results, perhaps especially those from social and behavioral science, must fall on sympathetic ears to have a major impact (Atkin, 1979; Ettema et al., 1983; Miller & Barrington, 1981).

More recently, critiques of the early contact literature have appeared (Lamb, 1982; McCall, 1982). The more conservative conclusions reached in these articles have been reported in the media (Brody, 1983; Gordon, 1978; McCall, 1980; McCall & Stocking, 1978), and Klaus and Kennell (1983) have modified their position. But, as usual, retractions get less press than claims.

When a fertile social context exists, research studies need to be especially carefully reviewed and conservatively presented, and popular accounts need to be clear in describing the possible qualifications, limitations, and implications of the findings.

Are Social and Behavioral Sciences Unique?

Except for the work of Weiss, Dunwoody, Singer, and Endreny, the literature cited above is based on research that lumps all sciences together and therefore emphasizes the biological and physical sciences. Is the relationship between the social and behavioral sciences and the press any different than for the biological and physical sciences? Probably it is.

Reporters

As discussed above, journalism covers the social and behavioral sciences differently than the biological and physical sciences. With only a handful of exceptions at major newspapers, specially trained science writers do not tend to write about the social and behavioral sciences (Dunwoody, 1983; Herbert, 1980; Singer & Endreny, 1984; Weiss, 1983), and they rank them low on their list of personal interests (Dunwoody, 1980a). As a result, the social and behavioral sciences are covered by reporters having a great variety of backgrounds, interests, and purposes.

Accuracy

Studies of accuracy typically do not break the data down by topic, but Tankard and Ryan (1974) found that the error rates for the general category of social sciences (6.87 kinds of errors per article) and biology (7.70) were noticeably higher than those for the physical sciences (4.45), but the differences were not significant. Weiss (1984c, 1985) reported the social and behavioral scientists in her study to be as satisfied with media reports of their work as scientists from all disciplines, but she only included stories presented in the major national media, which might be of higher quality than in the other studies. Therefore, it is possible, but not yet convincingly demonstrated, that press reports on social and behavioral science topics are less accurate.

Relevance

In contrast to science reporters, editors tend to favor the social and behavioral sciences (Dunwoody, 1983; Weiss, 1984a), because the topics are relevant to the experiences of the reader (Dunwoody, 1983; Tichenor et al., 1970). In fact, when science writers gather at the meetings of the American Association for the Advancement of Science, more than twice as many articles on social and behavioral science topics are published as on topics from other sciences (Dunwoody, 1983; Weiss, 1984a), because writers know, regardless of their personal preferences, that their editors favor those topics. Besides, writers feel the social and behavioral sciences are easier to read, understand, and write quickly, and thus they can meet their deadlines more readily and with less effort by dashing off a social or behavioral science story (Dunwoody, 1982).

Availability

Social and behavioral scientists are relatively more available to the press and perhaps more favorable (or less unfavorable) toward it (Dunwoody & Ryan, 1983). For example, social and behavioral scientists are 39 percent more likely to be contacted by the press than other scientists in a survey of professors at Ohio State and Ohio universities (Dunwoody & Ryan, 1982; Dunwoody & Scott, 1982). Moreover, social and behavioral scientists regard the "rewards" to them of public communication to be less negative than scientists from other disciplines (Dunwoody & Ryan, 1982). In addition, 10 percent of social and behavioral scientists but 25 percent of scientists from other disciplines were employed in private industry (Dunwoody, 1982). Industry, in contrast to the university, is usually more protective of its knowledge, and reporters often consider industry scientists to be less objective.

Common Sense

Because "everyone fancies him- or herself a psychologist" (but not an astrophysicist), the information provided by a social or behavioral scientist must square with the reporter's and reader's experience (Dunwoody, 1983). This means reporters may feel more confident to judge our information, more skeptical of what we say (Kirsch, 1982), more likely to make their own interpretations of our results, and possibly more prone to trivialize or "editorialize" about us (e.g., "we didn't need a psychologist to tell us that" or "I learned more psychology from the taxi driver on the trip from the airport than at the convention"). Further, there may be a greater favoritism for behavioral results that are somewhat odd or bizarre, because a bizarre theory of sexual behavior, for example, is considerably more interesting to the public than an off-the-wall theory of subatomic particles (who would even know if it was off the wall?).

Terminology

Some of psychology's terminology is deceptively commonplace (Tichenor et al., 1970). For example, journalists may not perceive the need to translate the word *depression*, which a psychologist uses to denote a serious clinical syndrome but which reporters and readers may interpret to mean ordinary *sadness*.

Pseudosciences

While alchemy died years ago, behavioral science must still contend with pseudo-sciences such as astrology and fortune-telling that appear in newspapers and on the airwaves. For example, I once appeared on a call-in talk show on infant behavior and was followed on the program by a fortune-teller. I received only a few calls, but the telephone switchboard lit up like a Christmas tree for the fortune-teller. She told callers the sex of their unborn child, whether they would marry in the next year, and whether they would get the job they wanted. She was a regular feature on the program, but no one called to complain that "you told me my child would be a girl, but he was a boy." It is difficult for a scientist to compete with someone who is unrestrained by rules of evidence.

Implementation

In contrast to other sciences, the social and behavioral sciences are capable of help-ing society more directly, because no intermediary, such as a physician or elaborate equipment, is required to implement the suggestions that some social and behavioral scientists make through the press (Bressler, 1968). Thus psychologists can tell par-ents how to pick a day-care center or how to stimulate the intellectual or emotional growth of their infants, and parents can enact those suggestions directly without professional prescription or monitoring. Some parents could push too much, expect too much, or twist the suggestions to fit their own needs. Because of this ease of application, social and behavioral scientists may be asked to apply their research results to practical issues and to provide "how-to's" more than other scientists.

Therefore, press coverage of the social and behavioral sciences is different from that of other disciplines—it is less likely to be covered as a "beat" by trained science writers; it is reported by writers varying greatly in training, experience, and purpose; it is more popular with editors and readers because it is more relevant to their ex-perience and lives; its relatively commonplace terminology can be more easily mis-interpreted; its findings must meet criteria of "common sense" not applied to other disciplines; it may be more prone to editorializing; and while it has great potential to help, it also has the potential to harm people who may implement behavioral suggestions directly without a professional prescription or monitoring.

HOW TO DO A MEDIA INTERVIEW

Almost every social and behavioral scientist will be contacted by the press at one time or another (Dunwoody & Ryan, 1982; Dunwoody & Scott, 1982), some will appear on broadcast news or on talk shows, and most will be asked to address parent groups, educators, and other practitioners. What follows is a brief set of guidelines on how to do a media interview. Most of the same points are relevant to preparing testimony for legislators, being an expert witness in a court proceeding, or talking to the PTA. The suggestions below are an amalgamation of pointers gained from professional information officers, public relations specialists, and personal expe-rience (Bander, 1983; Gastel, 1983; Hilton & Knoblauch, 1982; Klepper, 1981; McMullen, 1981; Miller, 1979; Read, 1980; Watkins, 1984b).

Preliminaries

Making Contact

Most often, the media come to you. They get your name from the APA, your university public information office, and from other professionals. But under some circumstances you can go to the media. Indeed, in one study of scientists at two Ohio universities, 15 percent said they had initiated contact (Dunwoody & Scott, 1982), and in another study 12 percent had done so (Dunwoody & Ryan, 1983). If you are a professor at a major university, the staff of your university public information office can tell you whether you have a newsworthy topic, write a brief description of your research in the form of a news release, help you formulate quotes that are accurate and interesting, and send the release to local or national media. Some may be willing to get you on talk shows and other broadcasts, even network programs. Although this is unusual, universities are discovering the public relations benefits of keeping professors in the news (Watkins, 1984). If you work at a service agency instead and want to provide information on your agency or on issues in the news (e.g., child abuse, physical punishment in day care), it is best to have a member of your advisory board or some other intermediary call the newspaper and suggest they contact you.

You can, of course, contact a reporter or editor yourself if you have something you believe is in the public interest. However, journalism has an intense paranoia about being used ("Anatomy of a Science Story," 1984). Some science writers even claim to have been contacted by scientists who were up for promotion or had just submitted a grant and who thought publicity would be helpful (Weiss, 1984c). So you may be greeted with skepticism.

Finally, a few scientists seriously want to write their own newspaper article. Even if they can write a model journalistic article, newspapers are unlikely to publish it as news or as a feature article (although it does happen), because it is not written by an "objective reporter." Instead, submit it to the editorial page as a letter to the editor or as an "op-ed" (i.e., "opposite the editorial page") feature.

Basic Information

Assuming the media call you, obtain some basic information before you reflexively say "yes" or "no." If the caller is a print journalist or free-lance writer, politely find out what newspaper or magazine he or she writes for, his or her position (general assignment reporter, science writer), the topic and main point of the story, what information you are to provide, who else the reporter expects to interview, and the reporter's deadline. Usually reporters will volunteer most of this information without being asked.

Generally speaking, the larger the publication and the more experienced and specialized the reporter, the more time he or she will have to work on the story and the more likely he or she will know about the field in general and about science. But there are many fine local reporters, and local publicity may be more important to you than a brief mention in a national publication.

If the caller is from a broadcast medium, determine the nature of the program, the name of the interviewer, the topic and main point of the episode, the program length, the names of other people who will be on the program with you, the information you are to provide or the role you are to play, whether the program will be edited, and whether you will be asked questions by the audience. If it is located in another town, ask if your expenses will be paid (usually *you* pay if you are a news source, but bigger stations may cover expenses).

Generally speaking, documentaries and interview programs that will be edited (except those that thrive on controversy) are the safest but the rarest opportunities; live interview and call-in shows are more common but require special skills; and news programs reach the largest and most diverse audiences but use very little of what you say, have the shortest format, and allow you the least control over what is used.

Decisions

Whatever the medium, your first decision is whether you are the appropriate source or guest. If the newspaper, magazine, or station has a national audience, they want the nation's leading authorities on the topic of interest, and you need to decide whether you are among them. If not, give them the names, locations, and telephone numbers of those authorities. If the program is local, the medium may want the leading *local* authority, and that may be you even if the topic is not your primary specialty. If so, you must decide whether you have sufficient knowledge to do the job without overstepping your expertise, and you should define the limits of that expertise to the caller before going further.

Your next decision is whether you feel comfortable with the role you are to play. Most journalists and interviewers are simply seeking information that is interesting or useful to the public. On the other hand, a very few journalists and interviewers have prejudged the main message, thrive on controversy, or make their reputations at the expense of their guests. You must decide whether you are comfortable with the situation. If you are uncertain, ask to call back in an hour and investigate the reporter or program by calling friends, the television critic of the newspaper in that town, the journalism department of a university, or the state psychological association. Then call back promptly with your decision.

You also need to decide what kind of source or guest you are. If you have an ax to grind, are fond of waxing political, frequently suggest profound changes in society, have something to hide, or advocate an extreme or unusual position, the reporter's job is to challenge you and make you defend those positions. If you ask for controversy, you will probably get it. Otherwise, you will probably not get it.

Also understand that reporters, editors, and interviewers are free to ask you any question they choose. Moreover, they can use only part of what you have to say, embed your comments in a different context, use whatever headline they want, and even interject a different question in front of one of your answers. Further, other newspapers and stations can pick up what you said and use it in ways you had not intended. These are legitimate practices and errors are sometimes made. For these reasons, some universities have policies that they expect professors to follow when dealing with the press (Dunwoody & Ryan, 1983), and you should check this possibility before going further.

Clearly, then, you must accept the fact that in most cases the media are more in control of this enterprise than are you. However, most journalists and interviewers are very responsible, friendly, and cooperative. Further, misuse of material, distortions, and inaccuracies are considered poor, sometimes unethical, journalism. Ultimately, then, it is a relationship of trust, and you need to understand and accept the complementary roles of trust and control.

The vast majority of media contacts are legitimate requests for information and should be accepted. If you decide not to participate, however, decline politely and respectfully and try to refer the caller to an appropriate professional.

Preparation

Written Statements

If you are frequently contacted by the media, if you anticipate that your work or expertise will be of public interest, or if you have time before an interview, prepare a news release or a statement of credentials and expertise.

A news release is a double-spaced statement one to three pages in length that covers the who, what, when, where, why, how, and "so what" of your message. Put the material most important to the public first—the news, findings, conclusion, and implications. Be brief and to the point, avoid technical jargon, and include your name, title, phone number, and one or two credentials in a separate section. Be warned, however, that writing a professional-sounding news release takes skill and practice, and most psychologists could benefit from professional help (e.g., a public information officer at your university, a journalism professor or graduate student).

Alternatively, simply prepare a one-page statement that includes your name, title, phone number, one or two credentials (degree, licensure, number of publications, a book title, or experience relevant to the topic), and a few brief statements indicating the topics of your expertise or the points you want to make. If you have authored a book, the book jacket may suffice; if you have not written a book, look at a few book jackets to get the idea. Give the statement to journalists and talk show interviews before your interview.

Notes

Preparation is also useful even if a newspaper reporter calls you to be a source for a story. For example, during the first call find out the topics the journalist wants covered, ask the journalist to call you back in 30–60 min while you "check some facts," and then jot down points and information you want to cover in the interview. This is especially useful, for example, when several factors contribute to a problem. What often happens in an interview is that you mention one factor, the reporter asks a question or two, and soon the discussion is off on another topic and the remaining factors do not get mentioned. With notes or an outline, you begin answering the question by saying, "There are three important factors. The first is . . . " and make sure, by checking them off on your notes, that all three points are covered.

Whatever you jot down about what you want to say, be sure to prepare answers to likely questions about the who, what, when, where, why, how, and "so what" of the topic. Also try to think of what someone who knows nothing about this topic is likely to ask (What is new that you have found? What is the *single* most important thing parents should do? Why did you write this book and how is it different?). Prepare two-sentence answers plus concrete, commonplace examples to illustrate your points.

The Performance

Display an Attitude of Cooperation and Respect for the Interviewer or Questioner

Treat the interviewer as a professional in his or her occupation. Also avoid continually referring to your book, your research, or yourself. Arrogance is our worst enemy.

Be Brief

Try to answer questions as directly as possible and in one to three sentences. If you are long-winded, you risk being cut off by an interviewer, you invite a journalist to select what he or she thinks is important rather than what you think is important, and you encourage a journalist to paraphrase your words rather than quote you. If your short answer is interesting, you'll be asked to elaborate.

Avoid Jargon

Be conversational, clear, and to the point. Use short, concrete examples that are common to people's experience to illustrate your points.

> *Q:* "Which is more important for IQ, heredity or environment?"
> *A:* "Both are. It's like winning a marathon—you need both natural ability and training."

Always Be "On the Record"

Assume that everything you say to a journalist will be quoted or aired. While most (but not all) reporters will honor a request to speak "off the record" or "on background," that request must be made *before* you speak (Stocking & Dunwoody, 1982). Even then it is not a good habit. You become more casual about what you say, you may forget to label what is on and what is off the record, and the reporter may not be able to judge when you are joking and when you are serious. Protect yourself by assuming that you are always talking to thousands of people through this single person. This is especially true if you like the interviewer and the conversation goes well—you can say things casually that you'll regret seeing in cold black and white. Keep your mind on the task and remember that the real audience is not the reporter or interviewer.

Call a Spade a Spade

Make clear what is known as a result of research, what is mainstream clinical practice, what is your personal judgment, and what is rank speculation. Child development professionals do this less responsibly than laypersons (Robinson, 1982). Be certain about your facts—don't guess or estimate—and use only one or two simple statistics to illustrate a point.

Stay Within Your Competence

It is easy to get carried away and pontificate on something you know little about. Don't be afraid to say you don't know, even during a live broadcast interview, but explain why you don't know (e.g., "No one has really studied that question" or "A physician could answer that more knowledgeably than could I"), or say what you do know about the topic (e.g., "No one knows what causes colic, but it probably is not caused by . . . ").

Watch Your Politics

Some psychologists who are most unhappy with the media are also the most political, frequently recommending extreme or pervasive social changes that reporters feature in their articles or challenge on the air.

Broadcast Interviews Involving Call-ins

Live broadcasts involving call-ins or questions from the audience are similar to journalistic interviews but require additional techniques.

Practice

Definitely rehearse for a broadcast interview with a friend so that you can answer briefly, colloquially, and clearly. Have friends ask you naive questions that laypersons might ask (e.g., "How do I know my child is normal?"). Remember, no one will rephrase your statement, and you get one chance to make your point.

Establish Any Ground Rules Important to You

Before you go on the air, indicate to the producer, host, or hostess, for example, that you cannot diagnose or prescribe treatment for an individual's particular problem, but that you can provide information about the problem in general and describe alternative treatment approaches that are commonly used. Place the emphasis on what you can and cannot *answer,* rather than what you do or do not want *asked,* and, if necessary, appeal to the ethics of your profession, which prohibit personal diagnoses or treatment over the air.

Personal Questions

Answer specific, personal questions with statements about the topic in general.

> *Q:* "My baby is 15 months old and doesn't walk. Is something wrong?"
> *A:* "Approximately 10 to 20 percent of normal infants do not walk by 15 months. . . . "

Alternatively, refer requests for specific advice or therapy to an appropriate professional (e.g., "You should consult a clinical psychologist/physician about that problem. They can be of much greater help to you in person than I could over the air" or "I cannot judge over the air how serious a problem this is, but if you are concerned about it, consult a psychologist/physician . . . ").

Another way to avoid personal diagnoses and prescriptions is to encourage the callers to make these decisions. Carefully ask what alternatives they believe are open to them, what they think might happen if they follow one or another of these courses of action, and which approach appeals to them. In short, teach them to problem-solve.

Complex Questions

A question does not necessarily require a single specific answer. You may respond, for example, "That is an important question, but there's no simple answer to it. It depends on A, B, and C." Alternatively, you can say, "Psychologists take different approaches to that problem. Some recommend A, others suggest B. . . . "

Bridging

Learn how to "bridge." That is, answer the question very briefly and very generally, and then shift the conversation to a topic more to your liking.

> *Q:* *"Isn't it true that it is the quality, not the quantity, of time a parent spends with a baby that is important?"*
>
> *A:* "To a certain extent that is true, but both are really necessary. I feel attachment requires frequent, short, baby-only attention, which can consist of. . . . "

Refocusing

Alternatively, refocus the question, avoiding a direct answer altogether.

> *Q:* "When does a baby first love his or her parents?"
>
> *A:* "The first step in attachment is that babies must be able to see and hear their parents and to recognize them as familiar. Babies can see. . . . "

Fumbling

If the program is live and you hem and haw over an answer, do not go back to correct it unless you have given incorrect information—let inelegancies pass. However, if the program is to be edited (e.g., the local news, a documentary, an edited interview), you can and should request to rephrase a poor answer to an important question, although you will not have the right to pick which answer is actually used in the program.

Attitude

Project a warm, kind, understanding, respectful attitude and try to be sensitive to the feelings and the concerns of the questioner and the audience, which probably contains representatives of nearly all social groups and persuasions. For example, a caller may describe her use of a severe method of disciplining a child. You might respond by saying, "I'm glad this worked for you, but not all parents would like that approach. Some parents might do A, some prefer B, and other have tried C." Also, try to be upbeat. The airwaves are no place for confrontation interviewing, clever put-downs, or hopelessness. Find something positive even in the most dismal circumstances, and provide people with some sympathy and realistic hope that their problem can be solved, even if it requires professional help.

Appearance

Your personal appearance is important, especially for television. You want to convey the impression of confidence, authoritativeness, and professionalism, so dress conservatively (dark suit for men, skirted suit or dress for women). Avoid black and white, bright contrasts in colors or patterns, and flashy jewelry. Navy blue, browns, and solid pastels are good.

Major stations will insist on making up both men and women. Otherwise, women should wear a light application of base and powder. Men may want to wipe their face and forehead with a handkerchief to eliminate shiny spots before going on.

During the show, ignore the camera and the monitor, face and talk directly to the interviewer or questioner, and smile frequently even when you think you are not on camera (sometimes you are, especially when being introduced or when listening to a long question).

Watch tapes of yourself or practice while watching yourself in a mirror to improve your performance.

GOING PUBLIC YOURSELF

Although most researchers will be information sources for professional communicators, the temptation to write for the public yourself is stronger than many scientists care to admit. For example, 30 percent of scientists from all disciplines at two Ohio universities had tried to write something (including press releases) for popular consumption (Dunwoody & Scott, 1982). Since issues of infancy, childhood, and family are popular topics and since professionals are often dissatisfied (if not upset) with the information presented in the media, some will want to try their hand at writing books, magazine articles, and newspaper articles.

To many scientists, it looks easy—all you have to do is translate the technical terminology into common parlance. But good writing for general audiences consists of much more than "translating" vocabulary. It involves selecting material that is inherently interesting to a lay audience, weaving that information around an important and different theme that relates to the experiences of the readers, sprinkling the presentation with real quotes from people who illustrate the main points, writing a lead that attracts attention and is responsible, pulling the reader through the article with transitions (instead of headings), using an active versus a passive style of phrasing, and learning a different style for newspapers, magazines, and even one magazine versus another. While most academics are not trained to write for popular consumption, they can learn, especially if they have the opportunity to be criticized by an expert writer. Further, if child development professionals can write, they have a better than average chance of getting published.

But getting published, especially in popular magazines, is more difficult than getting a technical article accepted. Because the number of people who want to write for magazines is so large relative to the number of articles published, editors must screen proposals and make categorical judgments about who can write and who can produce a piece that is interesting and useful to the particular readers of that magazine. The best sign, for example, that a person can write is a list of publications in popular magazines. So, typically, you cannot get published in magazines until you've published in magazines (*Psychology Today* is a notable exception). The resolution? Write a book for parents or the general public (which is easier to get published) and have the publisher attempt to get portions of it excerpted and published in major magazines, write magazine articles with an established writer who can help compose the piece and get it published, and write letters to the editor or "op-ed" pieces.

Writing Popular Books

Books written for parents, while easier to get published than articles in national magazines, are not easy at that.

Slant

Several hundred books are available for parents. Most focus on infants and young children, and most publishers are experiencing tight economic times and only want to publish a blockbuster. Your first task, then, is carving out a niche for yourself. Merely suggesting that you are going to deliver "the truth" or "baby-science" for parents will not be enough; you need a theme or a slant that is unusual and that will appeal to a substantial number of potential readers. You need to be able to answer the first questions that will be asked by publishers (and talk show hosts): "What is different about this book? Why did you write it?"

Collaboration

Once you have a theme, slant, or (to put it bluntly) "gimmick," you must decide whether you are going to go it alone or work with a writer. Working with a writer has the advantages of obviating the need for you to learn how to write, producing a better written book, benefiting from the writer's experience in how to select and relate material to the needs and interests of the audience, and getting the book published. It has the disadvantages of having the potential to produce conflict over style and control and having to share the royalties.

If you decide to work with a writer, you need to find one. You can call the editors of major magazines and ask for the names of writers they know who might be interested in the topic and project you have in mind, contact the APA Public Information Office, or ask local bookstore owners and newspaper editors if a writer in town (geographical proximity is a substantial asset) might be appropriate. Propose the idea to potential writers, and ask to see a list of published work, some samples of their writing, and, for serious candidates, a list of references. You will want to feel comfortable with the way the writer presents information, confident that the writer can do the job and help get the manuscript published, and certain that the person works cooperatively with sources, especially researchers. To check on the latter point, contact individuals who are quoted in the writer's articles.

A compromise between having someone write the book with you and going it alone is to work with a manuscript editor. Most scientists are not accustomed to being edited at all, since journal articles are modified only for grammar, spelling, and style. But, if you have written a major textbook, you probably have experienced serious copyediting (e.g., sentence structure and paragraph composition), but possibly not intensive manuscript editing, which involves identifying the main theme you want to communicate, structuring the entire chapter to serve that goal, organizing major subsections, and so forth. Ideally you should have someone who is both a good manuscript editor and a good copy editor, but some people are more proficient at one than the other of these skills.

To make either of these strategies work, you must be willing to give up considerable control over the nature of the presentation and to accept many suggestions of how to present your information in a way that is appealing to the potential audience but possibly distasteful to you.

Finances come next. Select a chapter, one you think is the most interesting, and prepare all of the information or a decent draft of that chapter. Then hire the writer for a fixed fee to work on that chapter. If you are happy with the process and the result, arrange to produce two more chapters. If those are satisfactory, discuss arrangements with the writer for the entire manuscript if it were to be published. But will not a publisher provide a manuscript editor at their cost, rather than yours? Maybe, *if* they very much want to publish the manuscript. But your chances of being published are directly proportional to the quality of manuscript you present for review.

After you have produced a detailed table of contents and two or three sample chapters, write a précis. The précis should tell what the book is about, what is unique about it, why it will appeal to a substantial audience, the specific nature and extent of its competition, and why you are the one(s) to write it.

Agents

With these materials in hand, you are ready to consider whether you should work with an agent. Literary agents will evaluate your materials, attempt to locate a publisher, negotiate a contract, arrange for legal services, be your representative in any editorial and financial disputes with the publisher, and help get your royalty checks to you on time (with interest rates high, it is definitely to the publisher's advantage to delay payment, and it happens). Publishing trade books (books intended for the general public) is a cutthroat business with considerably fewer standard practices than publishing textbooks. Royalty rates, advances, subsidiary rights, advertising allowances, promotional tours, and paperback rights are all negotiable within limits, although first-time authors clearly have less bargaining power than do experienced writers (one point for working with an experienced writer). Publishers attempt to get as much control as possible, negotiations and author–publisher relationships can be torturous and strained even when the book is definitely a winner, and thousands of dollars could be at stake.

How do you get an agent? That's not easy, either, and it may be more difficult to get a good agent than to get the manuscript published on your own. Some agents do not accept unsolicited manuscripts from new authors, preferring to take new authors only if they have been recommended to them by someone in the literary or publishing community—another catch-22. Other agents do examine unsolicited manuscripts, and some agents specialize in nonfiction, social and behavioral science, and even child and family. Look through the book *Writer's Market* for a listing of agents or write to college textbook editors for their recommendations, send materials to those suggested to you, and visit those who show some positive response to your overture. Then select one, if you have a choice. Agents may suggest major changes in your approach before they will agree to work with you, and while this may be unsettling to you, they often know what publishers will buy—which is one reason for hiring an agent.

Is it worth it? Financially, if the agent gets one more percentage point of royalty for you, he or she will probably have paid for the 15 percent (of your royalties) commission. Psychologically, most are experienced with the publishing industry and can save you a lot of headaches and uncertainties created by an enterprise you know little about. Although some experienced writers do not work with agents or have had less than positive experiences with them, the majority recommend them in my experience.

Publisher

You are now ready to approach publishers. If you have an agent, the agent will take care of this matter. Otherwise, check *Writer's Market* for publishers who indicate they are interested in publishing your kind of manuscript and are willing to review unsolicited materials (not every publisher does so). Finding a publisher who sells many books in your topical area but does not have one on their list that competes with yours is the ideal. Send your materials with a stamped, self-addressed envelope for return of the manuscript to as many publishers as you feel appropriate, although publishers often frown on simultaneous submissions from unknown authors.

Then wait and realize that the walls of great writers are papered with rejection notices. This is a highly subjective enterprise, and personal opinion and fortuitous circumstances play a large role. Many great books were rejected by other publishers. Your rejection notice may be a duplicated form letter. More likely, though, it will provide a general compliment ("You have presented some useful material and are clearly a leader in your field"), but will state that the manuscript is "not right for our list at this time." Do not expect a substantive critique; most decisions are made after a quick screening of the précis.

Business

If you are offered a contract, you will need to wrestle with business issues. For example, how long can you put off the first offer without risking its withdrawal while you notify other publishers that a bid is out on the manuscript and you are willing to look at any other bids? On the one hand, this is a competitive business, publishers are accustomed to bargaining and making competitive bids, and the interest of one publisher sometimes stimulates another. But on the other hand, you may lack bargaining chips if this is your first book or if the competition is great. If the process gets too thorny or the stakes become too high relative to the potential return, the publisher may withdraw the offer. That's why some writers have agents.

Once you decide on a contract, make sure that you or your agent hires a copyright attorney to check over the contract and negotiate certain points on your behalf. The publisher's attorney represents the publisher, not you. You may want, for example, stipulations and incentives for the publisher to place excerpts in national magazines as part of the promotion of the book. This establishes a list of magazine credits on your behalf, and opens the door to magazine publishing for you.

Be prepared, also, to be asked to help "sell" and promote your book. For example, the contract might stipulate an author tour in which you are expected to appear on talk shows in various cities. How an author comes over on these programs is crucial to the book's success and may even be a factor in whether the book is published in the first place. While it may sound terrifying or glamorous, depending on your perspective, author tours can be both—plus tedious, boring, stressful, and very tiring. The guidelines for interviews given above will help prepare you for the actual interviews but not for the hurry-up-and-wait, the getting across town in 15 minutes to make "Live at Five" and the "Oops, were we supposed to interview you today?"

Magazine Writing

The advice for book authors given above concerning slants and themes, trying your hand at writing, and working with a professional writer also applies to magazine writing. But there are some differences. Elizabeth Crow, editor of *Parents* magazine, gives the following advice to prospective authors, which I have mixed with my experience.

The Magazine

Know the particular audience and character of the magazine you want to approach. Look through the last 12 issues of potential magazines to get an idea of the topics they cover, whether they have published something about your topic recently (which makes them less likely to be interested in another article), and the style of writing and information presented (e.g., heavy on information, mostly fluff, emphasis on personal stories?). Decide two things: which magazines are likely to be interested in your topic and which magazines seem compatible with your style. Then select a theme that is consistent with the audience and the style of the particular magazine. It is likely that you will have a different slant—indeed, a different article—for each of several magazines, even though the basic content you want to communicate is the same. Those themes or slants usually define how the material will be related to the experiences and needs of the magazine's audience. "Infant development," "bonding," "day care," and "the effect of the birth of a child on family members" are topical descriptions of the information, but they are not the slants that appeal to editors. Instead, try "How do infants recognize their parents?" "Will day care benefit or harm my child's development?" "The stressful side of having a baby," or "Sibling rivalry is a myth."

Query

Write a query letter to the editor (*one editor at a time*). *Writer's Market* provides some guidelines. Basically, a query is a one-page letter that describes the slant and general content of your proposed article, why it is an important topic and suitable for this particular magazine, and why you are the one to write it. Writing good query letters is an art in itself, and it will test your mettle as a popular writer. It must be short, fascinating, clear, and compelling. You have essentially two paragraphs—perhaps less—to convince the editor that your topic is worth considering. You will not grab an editor's attention by beginning: "I would like to write an article on the experiences of fathers who stay home full-time with their infants." Instead, you might begin: "'The worst time was about five o'clock,' said one father. 'I would be cooking dinner, the baby would be screaming, some salesman would call on the phone, and I was worried that my wife would have car trouble and I would have to get her. Now I know why mothers look frazzled when their husbands get home—I certainly was.'"

Know that your chances of getting an assignment are slim. *Parents,* for example, receives approximately 1000 proposals each month; 10 percent are worthwhile, but only 5 successful. So your statistical chance at *Parents* is 1 in 200, or about 30 times worse than at *Child Development.* Moreover, most successful proposals are altered in slant or coverage by the editor, and you may be asked to include topics and information that you know little about professionally.

Fees

If you and the editor agree on an article, business matters are next. First, you may bargain for your fee. Recognize, however, that you are not going to get rich as a free-lancer. Although a few very large-selling magazines pay several thousands of dollars for an article, most pay approximately $500 to $1,500 to relatively inexperienced writers, depending on the magazine, the length of the article, the writer's credentials, and the circulation (e.g., under one million). Typically, a magazine will pay a fixed fee if the "piece" is published, possibly pay expenses (e.g., telephone costs) if you can justify and negotiate them, and pay a much smaller "kill fee" instead of the original amount if the final article is not published.

Rights

Negotiating just what "rights" you are selling may be more problematic (Schultz-Brooks, 1984). Once a writer dictates or writes a manuscript, it is copyrighted. When the manuscript is sold, the author signs away some rights to the publisher—as few as possible, preferably. Most desirable from the author's standpoint is to sell *only* "first North American serial rights," which only allows the magazine to be the first to publish the article in North America. After publication, all rights to the article revert to the author. Other assignments may be "all rights North American" (i.e., all publications by the magazine *or other publishers* in North America), "first-time world rights," "world periodical rights," or "all rights" (the magazine may sell the article to anyone forever or during a specified period of time). Another form of the all-rights arrangement is a "work-for-hire" contract in which the writer is treated as an employee of the company and the article then belongs to the company, which may sell it to anyone at any time. Such rights become important when other magazines (e.g., foreign magazines, airline magazines, *Readers Digest*) want to reprint the original article. Usually, articles are reprinted for only $50–$250, but a few magazines (e.g., *Readers Digest*) pay much more. If the author retains all reprint rights, the author may market the article and retain all fees; otherwise, the original publisher may keep all fees or, if stated in a contract, 50 percent of such fees.

Such terms must be negotiated at the time of the assignment. Editors often have several contracts, and may try to gain as many rights as possible (Schultz-Brooks, 1984). Once terms have been reached, ask for a contract or letter of assignment with the details spelled out. Some magazines simply assume they own all rights, or the rights are stated on the back of your check, which becomes a contract when it is signed. While many magazines know that authors, especially professors, are naive and will "take or give up anything," others routinely offer fair and favorable terms (see Schultz-Brooks, 1984).

If your proposal is not successful, accept that gracefully and try again. One professional was rejected 18 times at *Parents* and was then invited to be a columnist. Of course, if you can obtain some feedback from the editor about what topics or slants would be of interest, that helps; but editors are very busy. If the magazine is accustomed to using professionals, volunteer to be a source of background information or referrals in your specialty area. For example, in the September 1984 issue of *Parents,* 37 professionals either authored articles or were cited in them, and *Psychology Today* is almost completely written by psychologists (with much editing) or about psychologists. Such magazines need experts and sources, and if you are good, you'll be loved.

Targeted Communications

Writing books and newspaper and magazine articles is not the only way to communicate.

Writing for Applied Disciplines

For example, you can write articles for the journals and newsletters of applied professions. Pediatricians are very interested in bonding and screening for disabilities, for example, and sometimes it is helpful for research psychologists who specialize in the topic and in relevant methodology to review this literature for those who can and do apply it (e.g., McCall, 1982). In another vein, Michael Wald, a lawyer at Stanford, wrote an article for *Child Development* (Wald, 1976) that outlined the kinds of information that child development researchers could provide lawyers that would be useful with respect to custody, child testimony, abuse, and so forth.

Another strategy is to cooperate with agencies and institutions that routinely produce brochures, booklets, films, and other communication materials for specific audiences (e.g., teachers, legislators, social workers, pediatricians, etc). Such institutions include the university extension services, the Education Commission of the States, Children's Defense Fund, Guttmacher Institute, March of Dimes Birth Defects Foundation, National PTA, Association for Children with Learning Disabilities, drug companies, and others. Typically, these groups employ individuals who specialize in writing, producing, and distributing materials, but they cannot possibly employ people who are experts in all of the topics they cover. As a result, they may be eager to have your voluntary cooperation to supply them with material, and you do not need to be responsible for production and distribution.

The Boys Town Experience

During the last few years, Father Flanagan's Boys' Home has operated a small unit whose purpose is to communicate research information and professional knowledge on children, youth, and families to the general public and to specialized audiences including teachers, parents, social service workers, counselors, pediatricians, lawyers, and others. They have produced films, television programs and series, books, booklets, brochures, and posters, and their staff members have testified before legislatures and appeared as guests on numerous radio and television programs nationwide (McCall, Lonnborg, Gregory, Murray, & Leavitt, 1982; McCall et al., 1984; McCall et al., 1985). Their experience provides guidance to those who want to produce their own targeted communications.

The unit's philosophy specifies that the communication products must be primarily informational as opposed to social or political advocacy; they should attempt to help the consumer better understand an issue and find new ways to solve problems; and the scientific information should be accurate, balanced, and based upon relative consensus in the scientific and professional communities.

Procedurally, the first step is to discern an information need. While it might be desirable to do this with a formal survey, this is not usually practical. Moreover, people typically cannot tell you what they don't know. So in most cases, needs are based on the opinions of researchers who have the knowledge and recognize that it is not being applied by practitioners and on interviews with practitioners who are asked what they do, why they do it, and how they might do it differently if they knew what the researchers or professionals knew.

The next steps are to specify the particular audience, summarize the information they need, and package it in a form that they are likely to read and to use. Literature is summarized by using existing scholarly literature reviews, interviewing a variety of specialists on the topic, and commissioning a specialist to write the review, which staff writers and producers then recast into a communication product appropriate to the audience. This draft is then reviewed by the professionals who supplied the information, other professionals in the field, and members of the intended audience to ensure that the information is accurate, balanced, and responsible; the implications drawn are realistic and practical; the format is appropriate for the audience; and the total product is likely to be useful. Sometimes as many as 100 individuals have reviewed a draft.

Everyone knows, however, that scientists and professionals do not agree among themselves, to say nothing of agreeing with practitioners. Indeed, the principal reason that the American Psychological Association has not passed many resolutions on topics that pertain to scientific literature is the diversity of opinion about the research conclusions. How do you wind up with a product that is accurate, balanced, and useful in the face of such disagreement?

The answer is that someone must make the decisions, and it helps to have a scientist-communicator, even one who does not specialize in the topic at hand, who can put the scientific and practical issues into perspective. Certain techniques also help. If scientists X and Y disagree, the scientist-communicator can attempt to get them to agree on a compromise or they can be told to work out an agreement themselves. Sometimes both have a point and both points should be included in the publication as legitimate differences of opinion or alternative courses of action.

Distribution is the next step. This may be done by direct mail, by advertising in the mass media, or by having a product (e.g., a brochure) distributed by another national organization.

Evaluation is the final stage, but formal procedures are financially impractical. Distribution statistics are as far as most organizations can afford to go. At the end of 1984, for example, Boys Town had produced 34 books, brochures, posters, and films; almost two million copies of these materials had been distributed, 304,693 in 1984 alone, most of them without charge; and these products have won eight national awards from scientific and professional organizations. In addition, the mass media materials reach two to four million households each month. Specific projects are described elsewhere (McCall et al., 1984; McCall et al., 1985).

CONCLUSION

The need to relate to society is likely to persist. "Like it or not," Goodfield (1981) wrote in her personal look at science and the media, "science can no longer take for granted an unquestioning acceptance. . . . That makes the job of communicating science more necessary . . . than at any other time in history" (p. 9). Money for research and social services is likely to remain tight for the foreseeable future, and the media are likely to continue to be interested in the information social and behavioral scientists can contribute about social and personal problems. Although the communication process is imperfect, scientists have long neglected their potential to contribute to its improvement. Science, the media, and society are all likely to benefit from closer cooperation.

REFERENCES

Abelson, P. H. (1976). Communicating with the publics. *Science, 194,* 565.

Anatomy of a science story. (1984). *SIPI Scope, 12,* 1, 3–9.

Angier, J. (1983, September/October). No optimism for TV science series. *SIPI Scope*, pp. 15–16.

Anschvetz, N. (1979). Marketing psychology. *Professional Psychology, 10,* 154–160.

Armstrong, J. S. (1979). *Unintelligible research and academic prestige: Further adventures of Dr. Fox.* Marketing Department Working Paper Series, the Wharton School, University of Pennsylvania, Philadelphia.

Atkin, C. K. (1979). Research evidence on mass mediated health communication campaigns. In D. Nimmo (Ed.), *Communication yearbook 3.* New Brunswick, NJ: Transaction Books.

Ball, S. (1976). Methodological problems in assessing the impact of television programs. *Journal of Social Issues, 32,* 8–17.

Ball-Rokeach, S. J., Rokeach, M., & Grube, J. W. (1984, November). The great American values test. *Psychology Today,* pp. 34–41.

Bander, M. S. (1983). The scientist and the news media. *The New England Journal of Medicine, 308,* 1170–1173.

Battered wife film sparks calls. (1984, October 10). *Omaha World-Herald* (Associated Press).

Bennett, W. (1981, January/February). Science hits the newsstand. *Columbia Journalism Review,* pp. 53–57.

Berry, C. (1983). Learning from television news: A critique of the research. *Journal of Broadcasting, 27,* 359–370.

Berry, F. C., Jr. (1967). A study of accuracy in local news stories of three dailies. *Journalism Quarterly, 44,* 482–490.

Bevan, W. (1982). A sermon of sorts in three plus parts. *American Psychologist, 37,* 1303–1322.

Blankenburg, W. B. (1970). News accuracy: Some findings on the meaning of errors. *Journal of Communication, 20,* 375–386.

Bogart, L. (1968). Social sciences in the mass media. In F.T.C. Yu (Ed.), *Behavioral sciences and the mass media.* New York: Russell Sage.

Bogart, L. (1984). The public's use and perception of newspapers. *Public Opinion Quarterly, 48,* 709–719.

Borman, S. C. (1978). Communication accuracy in magazine science reporting. *Journalism Quarterly, 55,* 345–346.

Bowlby, J. (1969). *Attachment and loss* (Vol. 1). New York: Basic.

Bressler, M. (1968). The potential public uses of the behavioral sciences. In F.T.C. Yu (Ed.), *Behavioral sciences and the mass media.* New York: Russell Sage.

Broad, W. J. (1982). Science magazines: The second wave rolls in. *Science, 215,* 272–273.

Broberg, K. (1973). Scientists' stopping behavior as indicator of writer's skill. *Journalism Quarterly, 50,* 763–767.

Brody, J. E. (1983, March 29). Influential theory on "bonding" at birth is now questioned. *New York Times,* p. C1.

Brown, J. D., & Rubinstein, E. (Eds.). (1985). *The media, social science and social policy for children: Different paths to a common goal.* Norwood, NJ: Ablex.

Burgoon, J. K., Burgoon, M., & Wilkinson, M. (1983). Dimensions of content readership in ten newspaper markets. *Journalism Quarterly, 60,* 74–80.

Burrows, W. E. (1980, April). Science meets the press: Bad chemistry. *The Sciences,* pp. 14–15, 18–19.

Caplan, N., Morrison, A., & Stambaugh, R. J. (1975). *The use of social science knowledge in policy decisions at the national level.* Ann Arbor, MI: University of Michigan, Institute for Social Research, Center for Research on Utilization of Scientific Knowledge.

Carey, W. D. (1977). New directions of AAAS. *Science, 195.*

Carter, B., Howard, L., Yang, J., & Gelman, E. (1979, October 29). Radio's gabfest. *Newsweek,* p. 87.

Carter, R. E. (1958). Newspaper "gatekeepers" and the sources of news. *Public Opinion Quarterly, 22,* 133–144.

Clark, R. (1977). *The world of newspaper readers: Present and potential.* Yankelovich, Skelly and White, Inc.

Clarke-Stewart, K. A. (1978). Popular primers for parents. *American Psychologist, 33,* 359–369.

Cobb, N. (1981, February 2). Medical advice often conflicts: You can't wait for certainty. *Omaha World-Herald.*

Cowen, R. C. (1979). Garbage under glass—What are scientists dishing out? *Technology Review, 82,* 10–11.

Crichton, M. (1975). Medical obfuscation: Structure and function. *New England Journal of Medicine, 293,* 1257–1259.

Culliton, B. J. (1972). Dual publication: "Ingelfinger rule" debated by scientists and press. *Science, 176,* 1403–1405.

Dunwoody, S. (1978, December). *Science writers at work.* Bloomington: Indiana University, Bureau of Media Research, Research Report No. 7.

Dunwoody, S. (1980a). The science writing inner club: A communication link between science and the lay public. *Science, Technology, & Human Values, 5,* 14–22.

Dunwoody, S. (1980b). Why is scientific writing unintelligible? *Cosmic Search,* pp. 8–9.

Dunwoody, S. (1982). A question of accuracy. *IEEE Transactions on Professional Communication, PC–25,* 196–199.

Dunwoody, S. (1983). *Mass media coverage of the social sciences: Some new answers to old questions.* Paper presented at the meetings of the Association for Education in Journalism and Mass Communication, Corvallis, OR.

Dunwoody, S., & Ryan, M. (1982). *Factors influencing scientists as journalistic sources.* Paper presented at the meetings of the Association for Education in Journalism, Athens, OH.

Dunwoody, S., & Ryan, M. (1983). Public information persons as mediators between scientists and journalists. *Journalism Quarterly, 60,* 647–656.

Dunwoody, S., & Scott, B. T. (1982). Scientists as mass media sources. *Journalism Quarterly, 59,* 52–59.

Each week, 900 die in the sudden violence of U.S. auto accidents. (1982, April 14). *Wall Street Journal,* p. 1.

Endreny, P. M. (1984, May). *News values and science values: The editorial role in the presentation of social science news.* Paper presented at the meetings of the American Association for Public Opinion Research and the World Association for Public Opinion Research, Lake Delavan, WI.

Ettema, J. S., Brown, J. W., & Luepker, R. V. (1983). Knowledge gap effects in a health information campaign. *Public Opinion Quarterly, 47,* 516–527.

Feingold, P., & Knapp, M. (1977). Antidrug abuse commercials. *Journal of Communication, 27,* 20–28.

Fenichell, S. (1983, May/June). Talk about talk shows: A view from the sofa. *Channels,* pp. 45–47.

Findall, O., & Hoijer, B. (1976). *Fragments of reality: An experiment with news and TV visuals.* Stockholm, Sweden: Sveriges Radio.

Flaste, R. (1977, August 16). Closeness in the first minutes of life may have lasting effect. *New York Times,* p. 30.

Funkhouser, G. R., & Maccoby, N. (1971). Communicating specialized science information to a lay audience. *Journal of Communication, 21,* 58–71.

Gallagher, J. J., & Sanders, J. (1981). The social scientist, the media, and public policy. *UCLA Educator, 23,* 21–27.

Gans, H. J. (1980). *Deciding what's news.* New York: Vintage.

Garn, S. M. (1979). Social science research ethics. [Letter to the editor]. *Science, 206,* 1022.

Gastel, B. (1983). *Presenting science to the public.* Philadelphia: ISI Press.

Geboy, M. J. (1981). Who is listening to the "experts?" The use of child care materials by parents. *Family Relations, 30,* 205–210.

Glynn, C. J., & Tims, A. R. (1982). Sensationalism in science issues: A case study. *Journalism Quarterly, 59,* 126–131.

Goodell, R. (1977). *The visible scientists.* Boston: Little, Brown & Co.

Goodfield, J. (1981). *Reflections on science and the media.* Washington, DC: American Association for the Advancement of Science.

Gordon, I. J. (1978). Bonding—Is there a critical time? *Parents, 53,* 99.

Gregory, T., & Stocking, S. H. (1981). Communicating science to the public through targeted messages. *Children & Youth Services Review, 3,* 277–289.

Hammel, E. A. (1981). Achievements in social science. [Letter to the editor]. *Science, 213,* 289–290.

Hassett, J. (1978, August). Good science vs. a good story. In D. G. Winter (Chair), *Psychology and the media: Defining and improving our relationship.* Symposium presented at the meeting of the American Psychological Association, Toronto.

Havelock, R. G. (1975). Research on the utilization of knowledge. In M. Kochen (Ed.), *Information for action.* New York: Academic.

Hellemans, A. (1984). Science books for general readers. *Publishers Weekly, 226,* 22–24.

Herbert, W. (1980, October). Humanities and journalism: Akin but worlds apart. *Humanities Report,* pp. 4–8.

Herrnstein, R. J. (1982, August). IQ testing and the media. *The Atlantic Monthly,* pp. 68–74.

Hetherington, E. M., Cox, M., & Cox, R. (1977). The aftermath of divorce. In J. H. Stevens, Jr., & M. Mathews (Eds.), *Mother-child, father-child relations.* Washington, DC: NAEYC.

Hilton, J., & Knoblauch, M. (1982). *On television! A survival guide for media interviews.* New York: AMACOM.

Hixson, V. S. (1981). Caveat lector: Reviewing popular social science. *Journal of Communication, 31,* 168–177.

Hofstetter, C. R., & Buss, T. F. (1981). Motivation for viewing two types of TV programs. *Journalism Quarterly, 58,* 99–103.

How the media cover cancer. (1983). *SIPI Scope, 11,* 3–11.

Hunsaker, A. (1979). Enjoyment and information gain in science articles. *Journalism Quarterly, 56,* 617–619.

Hyatt, D., Riley, K., & Sederstrom, N. (1978). Recall of television weather reports. *Journalism Quarterly, 55,* 306–310.

Johnson, K. G. (1963). Dimensions of judgment of science news studies. *Journalism Quarterly, 40,* 315–322.

Joint position statement on the development of family-centered maternity/newborn care in hospitals. (1978, June). Chicago: American College of Obstetricians and Gynecologists.

Karlen, N., & Reese, M. (1984, October 22). A copycat assault? *Newsweek,* p. 38.

Katz, L. G. (1984, Fall). Some issues in the dissemination of child development knowledge. *Newsletter of the Society for Research in Child Development,* pp. 7–9.

Katz, E., Adoni, H., & Parness, P. (1977). Remembering the news: What the picture adds to recall. *Journalism Quarterly, 54,* 231–239.

Keniston, K. (1970). Youth: A "new" stage of life. *American Scholar, 39,* 631–654.

Kennell, J. (1975). Evidence for a sensitive period in the human mother. In M. H. Klaus, T. Leger, & M. A. Trause (Eds.), *Maternal attachment and mothering disorders: A round table.* New Brunswick, NJ: Johnson and Johnson.

Kessler, R., & Stipp, H. (1984). The impact of fictional television suicide stories on U.S. fatalities: A replication. *American Journal of Sociology, 90,* 151–167.

Kirsch, J. W. (1982). The ethics of going public: Communicating through mass media. *American Behavioral Scientist, 26,* 251–264.

Klaus, M. H., & Kennell, J. H. (1976). Human maternal and paternal behavior. In M. H. Klaus & J. H. Kennell (Eds.), *Maternal–infant bonding: The impact of early separation or loss on family development.* St. Louis: Mosby.

Klaus, M. H., & Kennell, J. H. (1983). *Bonding: The beginning of parent–infant attachment.* New York: New American Library.

Klepper, M. M. (1981, December 28). A TV interview need not be a lynching. *Wall Street Journal,* p. 6.

Kopp, C. B., & McCall, R. B. (1982). Predicting later mental performance for normal, at-risk, and handicapped infants. In P. B. Baltes & O. G. Brim, Jr. (Eds.), *Life-span development and behavior* (Vol. 4). New York: Academic.

Krieghbaum, H. (1959). Public interest in science news. *Science, 129,* 1092–1095.

LaFollette, M. C. (1982, Fall). Science on television: Influences and strategies. *Daedalus,* pp. 183–197.

Lamb, M. E. (1982). Early contact and maternal–infant bonding: One decade later. *Pediatrics, 70,* 763–768.

Landers, A. (1984, November 22). Bizarre behavior is clue to rare Tourette's syndrome. *Omaha World-Herald,* p. 56.

Lazar, I., Darlington, R., et al. (1982). Lasting effects of early education: A report from the consortium for longitudinal studies. *Monographs of the Society for Research in Child Development, 47* (Serial No. 195).

Lichty, L. (1983, February 21). Who gets news from TV—And who does not. *U.S. News & World Report,* p. 52.

Machalaba, D. (1981, December 15). Does Saul Bellow stand on his head? Ask a fact checker. *Wall Street Journal,* p. 1.

Marx, J. L. (1976). Science and the press: Communicating with the public. *Science, 193,* 136.

Maugh, T. H., II. (1978). The media: Image of the scientist is bad. *Science, 200,* 37.

Mazur, A. (1981a). Evaluating the social sciences. [Letter to the editor]. *Science, 212,* 875.

Mazur, A. (1981b). Media coverage and public opinion on scientific controversies. *Journal of Communication, 31,* 106–115.

McAlister, A., Puska, P., Koskela, K., Pallonen, U., & Maccoby, N. (1980). Mass communication and community organization for public health education. *American Psychologist, 35,* 375–379.

McCall, R. B. (1980, September). Parent–infant bonding. *Parents,* p. 92.

McCall, R. B. (1982). A hard look at stimulating and predicting development: The cases of bonding and screening. *Pediatrics in Review, 3,* 205–212.

McCall, R. B. (1983a). Family services and the mass media. *Family Relations, 32,* 315–322.

McCall, R. B. (1983b, June). Is my baby all right? *Parents,* pp. 50–55.

McCall, R. B. (1984, Spring). Report of the public information committee. *Newsletter of the Division on Developmental Psychology of APA,* pp. 17–20.

McCall, R. B. (1985). Child development and society: A primer on disseminating information to the public through the mass media. In I. E. Sigel (Ed.), *Advances in applied developmental psychology* (Vol. II). Norwood, NJ: Ablex.

McCall, R. B., Gregory, T. G., & Lonnborg, B. (1985). Communicating developmental research to the general public: Lessons from the Boys Town Center. In J. D. Brown & E. Rubinstein (Eds.), *The media, social science and social policy for children: Different paths to a common goal.* Norwood, NJ: Ablex.

McCall, R. B., Gregory, T. G., & Murray, J. P. (1984). Communicating developmental research results to the general public through television. *Developmental Psychology, 20,* 45–54.

McCall, R. B., Lonnborg, B., Gregory, T. G., Murray, J. P., & Leavitt, S. (1982, Fall). Communicating developmental research to the public: The Boys Town experience. *Newsletter of the Society for Research in Child Development,* pp. 1–3.

McCall, R. B., & Stocking, H. (1978, June). Parent and child—The bond between them. *Pacific News Service.*

McCall, R. B., & Stocking, S. H. (1982). Between scientists and public: Communicating psychological research through the mass media. *American Psychologist, 37,* 985–995.

McCombs, M. E., & Shaw, D. L. (1972). The agenda-setting function of mass media. *Public Opinion Quarterly, 36,* 176–187.

McMullen, M. (1981). Facing the media: Are your executives ready? *Journal of Communication Management, 11,* 20–21.

McQuail, D. (1969). *Towards a sociology of mass communications.* London: Macmillan.

Meyer, P. (1973). *Precision journalism: A reporter's introduction to social science methods.* Bloomington, IN: Indiana University Press.

Meyer, A. J., Nash, J. D., McAlister, A. L., Maccoby, N., & Farquhar, J. W. (1980). Skills training in a cardiovascular health education campaign. *Journal of Consulting & Clincial Psychology, 48,* 129–142.

Miller, G. A. (1969). Psychology as a means of promoting human welfare. *American Psychologist, 24,* 1063–1075.

Miller, J. D., & Barrington, T. M. (1981). The acquisition and retention of scientific information. *Journal of Communication, 31,* 178–189.

Miller, J. D., Prewitt, K., & Pearson, R. (1980). *The attitude of the U.S. public toward science and technology.* Chicago: National Opinion Research Center, University of Chicago.

Miller, N. E. (1979). *The scientist's responsibility for public communication.* Bethesda, MD: Society for Neuroscience.

Montagu, A. (1971). *Touching: The human significance of the skin.* New York: Columbia University Press.

Mosier, N. R., & Ahlgren, A. (1981). Credibility of precision journalism. *Journalism Quarterly, 58,* 375–380.

Motto, J. A. (1967). Suicide and suggestibility: The role of the press. *American Journal of Psychiatry, 124,* 252–256.

Muenchow, S., & Lang, M. E. (1982). Public education and the media. *The Networker, 11,* 5.

Mumford, G. S. (1984). Basic research and the public. [Letter to the editor]. *Science, 223,* 238.

Naftulin, D. H., Ware, J. E., Jr., & Donnelly, F. A. (1973). The Dr. Fox lecture: A paradigm of educational seduction. *Journal of Medical Education, 48,* 630–635.

Neuman, W. R. (1976). Patterns of recall among television news viewers. *Public Opinion Quarterly, 40,* 115–123.

Nunn, C. Z. (1979). Readership and coverage of science and technology in newspapers. *Journalism Quarterly, 56,* 27–30.

Nunnally, J. C., Jr. (1961). *Popular conceptions of mental health: Their development and change.* New York: Holt, Rinehart, & Winston.

Patterson, J. (1982). A *Q* study of attitudes of young adults about science and science news. *Journalism Quarterly, 59,* 406–413.

Perlman, D. (1974). Science and the mass media. *Daedalus, 103,* 207–222.

Phillips, D. (1977). Motor vehicle fatalities increase just after suicide stories. *Science, 196,* 1464–1465.

Phillips, D. (1982). The impact of fictional TV stories on U.S. adult fatalities: New evidence of the effect of the mass media on violence. *American Journal of Sociology, 87,* 1340–1359.

Prewitt, K. (1981). Usefulness of the social sciences. *Science, 212,* 659.

Pulford, D. L. (1975). *An investigation of accuracy in newspaper science reporting.* Unpublished master's thesis, University of Texas at Austin.

Pulford, D. L. (1976). Follow-up study of science news accuracy. *Journalism Quarterly, 53,* 119–121.

Ray, M., & Ward, S. (1976). Experimentation for pretesting public health programs: The case of the antidrug abuse campaigns. *Advances in Consumer Research, 3,* 278–286.

Read, N. B., Jr. (1980). How to prepare for the TV interview. *IEEE Transactions on Professional Communication, PC-23,* 45–47.

Revelle, R. (1975). The scientist and the politician. *Science, 187,* 1100–1105.

Richter, M. N., Jr. (1981). Achievements in social science. [Letter to the editor]. *Science, 213,* 289.

Ricklefs, R. (1982, September 21). Despite some gripes, bosses say business press is generally good. *Wall Street Journal,* p. 31.

Ridder, P. (1980, November/December). There are TK fact-checkers in the U.S. *Columbia Journalism Review,* pp. 59–62.

Robinson, B. E. (1982). Family experts on television talk shows: Facts, values, and half-truths. *Family Relations, 31,* 369–378.

Rorvik, D. M. (1978). *In his image: The cloning of a man.* Philadelphia: Lippincott.

Rosen, S. (1977). A scientist in television-land. *Television Quarterly, 14,* 81–85.

Rosengren, K. E. (1980). Mass media and social change: Some current approaches. In G. C. Wilhoit & H. DeBock (Eds.), *Mass communication review yearbook* (Vol. 1). New York: Sage.

Rubin, Z. (1980, February). My love-hate relationship with the media. *Psychology Today,* pp. 7, 12, 14.

Ryan, M. (1975). A factor analytic study of scientists' responses to errors. *Journalism Quarterly, 52,* 333–336.

Ryan, M. (1979). Attitudes of scientists and journalists toward media coverage of science news. *Journalism Quarterly, 56,* 18–26, 53.

Ryan, M., & Dunwoody, S. L. (1975). Academic and professional training patterns of science writers. *Journalism Quarterly, 52,* 239–246, 290.

Salk, L. (1962). Mothers' heartbeat as an imprinting stimulus. *Transactions of the New York Academy of Sciences, 24,* 753–763.

Sanoff, A. P. (1982, September 20). The press: In deeper trouble with public. *U.S. News & World Report,* pp. 68–70.

Schramm, W. (1973). *Men, messages, and media: A look at human communication.* New York: Harper & Row.

Schramm, W., & Wade, S. (1967). *Knowledge and the public mind.* Stanford: Stanford University Press.

Schultz-Brooks, T. (1984, January/February). The copyright can. *Columbia Journalism Review,* pp. 33–36.

Schwarz, K. (1984, March 2). Just give us the facts. *Publishers Weekly,* pp. 34–36.

Science, technology and the press: Must the "age of innocence" end? (1980, March/April). *Technology Review,* pp. 46–56.

Scientists' Institute for Public Information. (1984). *Credibility and the media.* New York.

Shepherd, R. G. (1979). Science news of controversy: The case of marijuana. *Journalism Monographs* (No. 62).

Singer, E., & Endreny, P. (1984, May). *Social science in the news: 1970 and 1982.* Paper presented at the meetings of the American Association for Public Opinion Research and the World Association for Public Opinion Research, Lake Delavan, WI.

Singletary, M. (1980, January 25). Accuracy in news reporting: A review of the research. *ANPA News Research Report.*

Smoking debate turns rough. (1985, February 17). *Omaha World-Herald* (United Press International), p. 13-A.

Spence, M. J., & deCasper, A. J. (1982). Human fetuses perceive maternal speech. *Infant Behavior & Development, 5,* 225 (abstract).

Steinem, G. (1978, August 28). Invited address presented at the meetings of the American Psychological Association, Toronto.

Stevens, J. H., Jr. (1984). Child development knowledge and parenting skills. *Family Relations, 33,* 237–244.

Stevenson. (1977, October 24). "One thing I'll say . . . " *New Yorker, 53,* p. 56 (cartoon).

Stipp, D. (1985, March 1). Science gets a big play in the press, but critics question the quality. *Wall Street Journal,* p. 17.

Stocking, S. H. (1978, August). Popular dissemination of research: Perils and promise. In D. G. Winter (Chair), *Psychology and the media: Defining and improving our relationship.* Symposium presented at the meetings of the American Psychological Association, Toronto.

Stocking, S. H., & Dunwoody, S. L. (1982). Social science in the news media: Images and evidence. In J. Sieber (Ed.), *The ethics of social research: Fieldwork, regulation, and publication.* New York: Springer.

Stokoe, W. C. (1981). Achievements in social science. [Letter to the editor]. *Science, 213,* 289.

Survey finds increased public support for social science. (1984, April 6). *COSSA Washington Update,* p. 2.

Tankard, J., & Ryan, M. (1974). News source perceptions of accuracy of science coverage. *Journalism Quarterly, 51,* 219–225, 334.

Tannenbaum, P. H. (1963). Communication of science information. *Science, 140,* 579–583.

Taylor, S. E., & Thompson, S. C. (1982). Stalking the illusive "vividness" effect. *Psychological Review, 89,* 155–181.

Thistle, M. W. (1958). Popularizing science. *Science, 127,* 951–955.

Thumin, F. J., & Zebelman, M. (1967). Psychology vs. psychiatry: A study of public image. *American Psychologist, 22,* 282–286.

Tichenor, P., Olien, C., Harrison, H., & Donohue, G. A. (1970). Mass communication systems and communication accuracy in science news reporting. *Journalism Quarterly, 47,* 673–683.

Tichenor, P. J., et al. (1971, January). *Science, mass media and the public.* Paper presented at U.S. Department of Agriculture Science Writing Seminar, Washington, DC.

Tillinghast, W. A. (1982, August 21). Shop talk at thirty—All about newspaper editors. *Editor & Publisher, 115,* 40, 30.

TV movie on suicide spurs plenty of calls to hot lines. (1984, October 31). *Omaha World-Herald* (Associated Press).

Ubell, E. (1983). The "alerting function" of television. *SIPI Scope, 11,* 8.

Wald, M. S. (1976). Legal policies affecting children: A lawyer's request for aid. *Child Development, 47,* 1–5.

Walum, L. R. (1975). Sociology and the mass media: Some minor problems and modest proposals. *American Sociologist, 10,* 28–32.

Warner, K. E. (1981). Cigarette smoking in the 1970's: The impact of the anti-smoking campaign on consumption. *Science, 211,* 729–731.

Watkins, B. T. (1984a, November 7). Experts from academe: Increasing numbers of professors are appearing in the media. *The Chronicle of Higher Education,* pp. 25–27.

Watkins, B. T. (1984b, November 7). How to get on the 6 o'clock news, and other hints. *The Chronicle of Higher Education,* p. 26.

Weigel, R. H., & Pappas, J. J. (1981). Social science and the press: A case study and its implications. *American Psychologist, 36,* 480–487.

Weiner, J. (1980). Prime time science. *The Sciences, 20,* 6–11.

Weiss, C. H. (1974). What America's leaders read. *The Public Opinion Quarterly, 38,* 1–21.

Weiss, C. H. (1983, March 4). *The national media reports social science.* Paper presented at the meeting of the Eastern Sociological Association, Baltimore, MD.

Weiss, C. H. (1984a, August 27). *Press coverage of social science and science at the American Association for the Advancement of Science Conferences, 1982 and 1983.* Paper presented at the meeting of the American Sociological Association, San Antonio, TX.

Weiss, C. H. (1984b, October 19). *Translation of social science research into public knowledge.* Paper presented at the meeting of the Association for Public Policy Analysis and Management, New Orleans, LA.

Weiss, C. (1984c, September 12). *Social science and the media: The researcher's perspective.* Paper presented at the International Study Group, "On the Relationship between Social Scientists and the 'Real World,'" Haifa, Israel.

Weiss, C. H. (1985, March/April). Media report card for social science. *Society,* pp. 39–47.

Wilson, C. E. (1974). The effect of medium on loss of information. *Journalism Quarterly, 51,* 111–115.

Winett, R. A., Leckliter, I. N., Chinn, D. E., & Stahl, B. (1984). Reducing energy consumption: The long-term effects of a single TV program. *Journal of Communication 34,* 37–51.

Withey, S. B. (1959). Public opinion about science and scientists. *Public Opinion Quarterly, 23,* 382–387.

Woodall, W. G., Davis, D. K., & Sahin, H. (1983). From the boob tube to the black box: Television news comprehension from an information processing perspective. *Journal of Broadcasting, 27,* 1–23.

Yankelovich, D. (1984, Fall). Science and the public process: Why the gap must close. *Issues in Science & Technology,* pp. 6–12.

Yankelovich, Skelly, & White, Inc. (1977). *Raising children in a changing society.* Minneapolis, MN: General Mills.

CHAPTER 26

Continuities and Discontinuities from Infancy

MICHAEL RUTTER

INTRODUCTION

At first glance, it might be thought that the strength of continuities from infancy to later childhood or adult life is a rather dry issue. Empirical data should readily show just how strong the developmental links are. That should be that, leaving rather little room for debate. However, that view represents a most misleading over-simplification; moreover, it is clear that the controversies are far from resolved. The reasons for the continuing dispute are multiple. In the first place, there is not one concept of continuity, but many. Furthermore, there are many ways in which the strength of continuities may be assessed; each has rather different implications. Most of all, however, is the fact that inevitably the varying concepts reflect differences in views regarding the developmental process itself. Equally, the findings on continuities and discontinuities necessarily challenge and test the theoretical constructs postulated as explanations for development. A detailed consideration of these underlying concepts is beyond the scope of this chapter, but some discussion of them is needed in order to understand how and why developmentalists have interpreted the data in such a discrepant fashion. That they have done so is abundantly clear.

Theoretical Considerations

The view that the infancy years are determinative of later development has a long history with adherents in theories as divergent as psychoanalysis, behaviorism, object relations, and cognitive psychology (see reviews by Clarke & Clarke, 1976; Kagan, 1981, 1983, 1984). However, the postulates of these various theories are by no means the same. Thus traditional psychoanalytic theory placed emphasis on the flow of libidinal energies deriving from sexual and aggressive drives, on the laying down of a basic personality structure during the preschool years, and on the shaping of adult personality through partial fixation at particular psychosexual stages (see Baldwin, 1968; Dare, 1985). There was the implication of lasting major sequelae from early psychic traumata and a relative lack of modifiability after the first 5

This work was supported in part by the John D. and Catherine R. MacArthur Foundation Mental Research Network on Risk and Protective Factors in the Major Mental Disorders.

years. These assumptions were reflected in Bowlby's (1951) review of the effects of maternal deprivation in which he argued that the consequences of a lack of mother love in the first 2 years were likely to be permanently damaging. The concept was in keeping with Freud's notion that neurosis could be acquired only during the first 6 years and that the events of the early years were of paramount importance for the whole of the rest of life. As put forward in this strong form, the traditional psychoanalytic view can be rejected, and its consideration need not be taken further here. The notion of libidinal energies is out of keeping with the evidence, the postulates of psychosexual stages are wrong in several key respects, and there are good reasons for rejecting the concept that mother–child relations are built on oral satisfaction and sexual drives (Bowlby, 1969; Kline, 1972; Rutter, 1980). Furthermore there is abundant evidence that the ill effects of early traumata are by no means inevitable and irreversible (see Clarke & Clarke, 1976; Rutter, 1981a), and adult mental disorders differ markedly in their links with childhood (Rutter, 1984a).

Most psychoanalysts no longer adhere to these traditional concepts. However, the postulates of some form of personality "structure" and of a hierarchical development through psychosexual stages continue as theoretical cornerstones, as also they do in Loevinger's (1976) model of ego development, which derives from psychoanalytic thinking. It is not at all easy to see how one would make a critical test of these ideas, but such evidence as there is does not support the hypothesis of stages with a marked horizontal and vertical structure (Flavell, 1982; Hauser, 1976), and the concept of fixation at particular stages seems implausible and out of keeping with the evidence (Rutter, 1984b). Nevertheless it cannot be said that the notion of fixation has been put to the critical test.

Current-day theorists who espouse the concept that events in infancy may have serious lasting sequelae postulate quite disparate mechanisms by which such continuities may arise. Thus Lipsitt (1983) placed emphasis on the ways in which acute stresses may interfere with hedonic adjustment and hence cause a failure in the development of adaptive coping. Emotions rather than cognitions are seen as central, and it is assumed that, although infants have only a minimal capacity for reflection on the past or future, this does not influence the power of experiences to affect later functioning. Accordingly, even events in the neonatal period may have a lasting impact; a recent paper, indeed, argued for a causal connection between perinatal factors and suicide in adolescence (Salk, Lipsitt, Sturner, Riley, & Levatt, 1985).

In contrast, most developmentalists have come to see cognitive processes as the key mediating mechanisms. Thus in discussing the importance of early attachment patterns for the development of later social relationships, Bretherton (1985) suggested that the child establishes internal working models of self and attachment figures—a concept that derives from Bowlby's theorizing. Thus it is a child's translation of maternal rejection into the self-concept of "I am an unlovable person" that is responsible for the persistence of effects. Kagan (1980) has proposed that this cognitive transduction of experiences is crucial and that the lack of a sense of self-awareness before the age of 2 years is the reason that infantile experiences rarely have lasting sequelae. Of course, that strong postulate raises three key issues that will need to be considered in the discussion of continuities and discontinuities: (1) Is it true that experiences during the first 2 years rarely have effects that extend into and beyond middle childhood? (2) Do infants below the age of 2 years lack the cognitive capacities to process experiences in this way? And (3) is this the only (or the main) mechanism by which continuities arise?

A third view suggests that the main process by which early experiences operate is through the shaping of personality traits that become increasingly stabilized. Bloom's (1964) arguments that longitudinal correlations show that the strongest environmental effects are seen in the first 5 years were based on a fundamental misunderstanding of the meaning of correlations (see McCall, 1979), and his concept has fallen into disrepute. On the other hand, there are trait theorists who would see personality growth as largely a matter of the stabilization of biologically determined dimensional features, such as neuroticism or extraversion (Eysenck, 1953, 1967). That adults do indeed tend to have characteristic ways of behaving that to an important extent generalize across situations and persist over time cannot be in serious dispute (Costa, McCrae, & Arenberg, 1980; Eysenck & Eysenck, 1980). Nor can it be doubted that children exhibit temperamental attributes, some of which show a significant degree of consistency over both time and situations. The extent to which they do so from infancy is, however, another matter; this issue will be discussed further later in this chapter.

But, still, there are several reasons for dissatisfaction with the concept of personality as just a collection of traits, whether genetically or environmentally determined (Rutter, 1984b). First, their predictive power is rather weak even in adult life. Second, they provide no explanation for systematic changes in behavior in adult life or childhood, for example, the marked drop in aggressive and delinquent behavior in the early twenties (Rutter & Giller, 1983) and the major rise in affective disturbance during adolescence (Rutter, 1986a). Third, predictive strength does not always lie in behavioral consistency. For example, Dunn and Kendrick (1982) found that girls who had a conflictful relationship with their mothers tended to develop more friendly relationships with their younger siblings; conversely, those with an intense playful relationship with their mothers were more likely to have a poor relationship with their siblings. Similarly Hinde and his colleagues (Hinde, Easton, Meller, & Tamplin, 1983; Hinde & Tamplin, 1983) found a complementarity, and not a similarity, in the characteristics of children's relationships at home and at school. Or, again, Sroufe, Jacobvitz, Mangelsdorf, DeAngelo, and Ward (1985) found that mothers who were seductive to one of their sons tended to be derisive toward their daughters—a psychological coherence but not a generalization of a specific behavior disposition. Fourth, there may be consistencies over time in certain specific situational reactions without any consistency in overall patterns of behavior. For example, Suomi (1983) found stable individual differences in rhesus monkeys' liability to show "depressive" reactions following separation, but such differences were unassociated with the monkeys' behavioral characteristics in stress-free social environments. Finally, adverse childhood experiences may predispose to an increased risk of psychosocial malfunction in adult life without that risk being necessarily mediated through behavioral characteristics evident in childhood (Quinton & Rutter, 1986). Clearly, there is more to personality development than just the stabilization of personality traits, and it is most unlikely that experiences in infancy operate only through effects on such traits.

Psychologists who reject notions of the primacy of experiences in infancy do not necessarily do so for the same reasons. Thus Clarke and Clarke (1976) rejected the idea that infancy constitutes a critical period but put forward a "wedge" hypothesis that suggested a greater potential responsiveness to environmental stimuli in early life (at the thick end), tailing off to a quite limited responsiveness in adulthood (the thin end). Their concept of development is transactional in nature (Sameroff & Chandler, 1975), meaning that spiral effects may arise because children's problematic behavior stemming from early environmental adversity may selectively alter the new environment, making it less satisfactory, which in turn increases the likelihood of further disturbed behavior. Equally, however, such effects may become alleviated in good circumstances. Resilience is inherent, and to an important extent both continuities and discontinuities stem from environmental circumstances (because they remain constant in the former instance and because they change in the latter) and from children's style of engaging or coping with environmental challenges. The concept requires discussion of the evidence both for the possibility of greater environmental effects in early life and for the role of person–environment interactions in continuity.

Kagan's (1984) emphasis has been different in that unlike the Clarkes he has mainly focused on the changes that always occur with development rather than on individual differences. Also, with respect to the latter the focus has been on variations within the normal range rather than the antecedents of psychopathology. In his discussions of the developmental process he has stressed the importance of biologically determined maturational factors (so that, e.g., he argued that the capacity for morality arises from certain intrinsic cognitive developments toward the end of the second year rather than from the experiences of upbringing—Kagan, 1981). Moreover, he has urged that many of these maturational changes involve a reorganization of behavior that is not dependent on earlier experiences and that in essence wipes clean the tape of previous development. Because the cognitive competencies maturing over the first dozen years produce such major changes, it is not reasonable to expect much stability from infancy to adolescence. Further, because, as already noted, the cognitive transduction of experiences is thought to be so important in creating continuities, it is expected that experiences in the first 2 years will rarely have significant sequelae. Finally, Kagan argued that some psychological attributes are better conceptualized in categorical rather than dimensional terms—instancing temperamental inhibition with a high and stable heart rate as an example of this kind. In addition to the issues raised by the Clarkes' views, Kagan's postulates require examination of the extent and importance of behavioral reorganization, of the role of experiential versus maturational factors, and of the possibility that the mechanisms applicable at the extremes may not be the same as those in the middle of the range.

Concepts of Continuity

As various reviewers have discussed (e.g., Emmerich, 1964, 1968; Kagan, 1980; Rutter, 1983; Wohlwill, 1980), there are several quite different concepts of continuity. First, there is the concept of *absolute invariance* or stability—namely, a lack of change during the course of individual development. This would apply, for example, to the acquisition of a skill that, once gained, cannot be lost other than as a consequence of gross disease or extremely abnormal circumstances. This would be the case with the acquisition of object permanence or the quality of self-awareness, for example, and probably too with the ability to form selective social attachments.

Alternatively, it may mean that a skill has reached an asymptote such that there is little subsequent change—so that intelligence remains fairly stable once early adulthood is reached. The phenomenon of absolute invariance is important, but it is not the usual sort of continuity concept applied to development; development is after all concerned with change rather than a lack of change.

Second, there is continuity in the sense of a *regularity in the pattern* of development or in the form of change. Thus it is usual for there to be ups and downs in the course of intellectual development and variations over time in temperamental manifestations. Twin data suggest that to some extent these temporal variations are genetically determined (Matheny, 1984; Wilson, 1977). Thus although there is substantial instability in the sense of both varying levels and varying hierarchical positions in the population, these variations are partially genetically patterned. A rather different example is provided by schizophrenia, in which about half the cases of psychosis with an onset in adult life have been preceded by particular patterns of nonpsychotic abnormalities in childhood (Rutter, 1984a; Rutter & Garmezy, 1983). These childhood precursors are not sufficiently distinctive in form for individual diagnosis to be possible in most cases, but there is no doubt that they represent continuities, or regular patterns, in the disease process.

Third, there is *ipsative stability* or consistency of patterning of behavior within an individual with respect to the pattern of relationships among different personality features (Emmerich, 1968; Thomas, Chess, Birch, Hertzig, & Korn, 1963). In other words an individual may be appropriately described as predominantly anxious (or cheerful or pessimistic), in the sense that although his or her mood may fluctuate a good deal from moment to moment or situation to situation, nevertheless there is a predictable and lasting expectation that more often than not this individual will appear anxious (or cheerful or pessimistic).

Fourth, continuity may be shown by *normative stability*, meaning that the individual maintains the same hierarchical or relative position with regard to some attribute in spite of the fact that the population as a whole changes greatly. Thus both height and IQ show huge changes between the ages of 5 and 15 years, but rank correlations over this time are moderately high, with children who are taller or more intelligent at one age remaining above average in these attributes at a later age.

Fifth, there may be continuity in *structure or process or mechanism*. For example, it is commonly supposed that close personal relationships serve a psychologically protective function throughout life—such that bereavements lead to grief and that the presence of a loved one enhances resilience in the face of stress or adversity (Bowlby, 1969, 1973, 1980). This does not mean that the relationships will be with the same person at all ages, nor even that the *form* of relationships will remain the same. Thus a young girl's relationship with her mother is clearly different from her heterosexual love relationships in adolescence and different yet again from her relationship as a parent with her own child. Yet attachment theory argues that they represent similar functions. It is not necessarily argued that the quality of one relationship predicts the quality of another (indeed, empirical evidence shows that often it does not), nor that the strength of relationships shows any particular consistency. Rather, what is hypothesized is that these relationships throughout the course of development represent the same psychological processes and hence that continuity is to be found in the underlying structure or behavioral organization or biological propensity and not in the surface representations. Of course, such a hypothesis demands evidence that there is some such basic construct. It is not enough to assert its existence, and there have been considerable difficulties deriving from the tendency to use the same term *attachment* to describe both the behavior and the postulated explanatory concept (Hinde, 1982). Also, we require evidence that different forms of relationships do indeed represent similar processes—evidence that is so far rather fragmentary (Hay, 1985).

Finally, continuity may be thought of in terms of a predictable pattern of associations or *causal connections* between events or experiences at an early phase of development and some type of psychological outcome at a later point. For example, attachment theory argues that a lack of stable selective parent–child attachments during the infancy period predisposes to a variety of maladaptive patterns in both later childhood and adult life (Bowlby, 1969, 1973, 1980). It is not suggested that there need be any positive correlations between *behavior* in infancy and that at maturity, nor does attachment theory necessarily assume that there will be other than a weak association between the degree of family instability and the extent of later disturbances. What is does suggest is that a failure to form relationships (or to develop secure attachments) will predictably and substantially increase the risk of disorder during the years that follow.

For obvious reasons these different concepts of continuity predict rather different patterns of statistical associations and, as a result, there is no one direct way of testing for the strength of continuities and discontinuities from the infancy period to alter phases in development. Indeed, there are important pitfalls and hazards to be avoided in the analysis of longitudinal data.

Pitfalls in Longitudinal Analyses

Limitations of Correlations

Most studies of developmental continuities or linkages have relied on correlational analyses. This has been the case both with investigations of the extent to which behavioral or intellectual characteristics at one age predict those at a later age and with those testing associations between early risk factors at later outcomes (see, e.g., the reviews by McCall, 1979; Moss & Susman, 1980; Wohlwill, 1980). Thus critics of the notion that life stress may lead to psychological impairment have frequently noted that simple correlations between the two (i.e., before possible confounding factors are taken into account) are of the order of .3, thus explaining less than 10 percent of the variance (Andrews & Tennant, 1978). In that connection, it is crucial to appreciate that correlations are *not* a measure of the strength of association despite their often being interpreted as such; rather they are an index of the proportion of population variance explained, which is not the same thing at all. The reasons that they are not synonymous derive from several different considerations. First, the size of a correlation is crucially dependent on the base rate of the independent variable. Correlations will be low when there is a very low base rate (meaning that there must be other causes of the outcome being assessed) or one that is very high (meaning that there will be modifiers of effects). The importance of this consideration may readily be appreciated by examination of the findings from the American Perinatal Collaborative Study. Of the 18 variables that differentiated between mental retardation and normal IQ (on a stepwise linear discriminant functions analysis), only 7 appeared in the predictors of IQ based on correlations with IQ in a stepwise multiple regression (Broman, Nichols, & Kennedy, 1975). Thus 1 variable showed a 60-point IQ difference between those with and those without that feature, but a correlation of only .076 with IQ! The variable was Down's syndrome. It is, of course, virtually always causally associated with a substantial intellectual impairment (hence the association with low IQ is very strong indeed), but the correlation is exceedingly low because the base rate is tiny (12 per 25,000 in the population studied) and because mental handicap has many other causes. The same will apply with a very high base rate. For the example, streptococcal sore throats are always caused by the streptococcus, but there will be a rather low correlation between exposure to the bacillus and the clinical infection because only a minority of people exposed to the bacillus develop the disease.

A second rather different consideration is that it is possible for an environmental influence to have a very substantial effect in raising the *mean* level of an outcome variable without it making much, if any, difference to individual variation (and hence without much effect on correlations). Tizard (1975) pointed out the importance of this effect with respect to the role of improved nutrition in bringing about a massive secular trend increase in the height of school children—some 9 cm since the beginning of this century. The same applies to the effects on IQ of the adoption into superior homes of infants from a severely disadvantaged background (Rutter, 1985a; Rutter & Madge, 1976). Ramey, Yeates, and Short (1984) have similarly noted the importance of differentiating between effects on group means and effects on individual differences in their discussion of the benefits associated with preschool intervention programs.

Third, correlations rely on consistency of association across the range (both over time and over the distribution of the variable). Correlations will necessarily drop if that is not the case. For example, Robins, Davis, and Wish (1977) in their study of heroin addiction among Vietnam veterans returning to the United States found that demographic variables correlated very weakly with outcome because although the effects were strong they acted in opposite directions at different points in the time sequence. Inner-city blacks were most likely to use heroin in Vietnam but, among users, whites from rural areas were most likely to remain addicted on return. Correlations will also drop if associations apply differentially at different points in the distribution of either the independent or the dependent variable. This is most obvious with pathological outcomes; thus the genetic factors associated with severe mental handicap (mostly single gene abnormalities) are quite different from those associated with variations in the normal range of IQ (mostly polygenic effects). But the same effect applies within nondisease groups. For example, Lee and Bates (1985) found that temperamental difficultness was associated with increased mother–child conflict only when the difficultness was extreme; Kagan, Reznick, Clarke, Snidman, and Coll (1984) similarly argued that extreme behavioral inhibition in early childhood was better treated on a categorical rather than a dimensional variable (see also Kagan, 1984). Hinde and Dennis (1986) have argued on this basis that for some purposes analyses based on categorization may be preferable to correlational analyses. Similarly, Rutter and Garmezy (1983) noted that pervasive psychopathological disorders tend to differ from situation-specific behavior disturbances in both correlates and course.

The finding that the patterns of associations for boys and girls may be quite different has led to a universal acceptance that associations must be studied separately in the two sexes. The sex differences may be marked in their implications for mechanisms. For example, Simpson and Stevenson-Hinde (1985) found that shyness in boys was associated with *negative* family interactions but in girls it was associated with *positive* ones; Stevenson, Richman, and Graham (1985) found that behavioral problems at 3 years had a strong linear association with disturbance at 8 years in boys, but in girls the association was markedly *U*-shaped (with disorder at 8 most likely when behavior deviance at 3 was either very high or very low); Maccoby, Snow, and Jacklin (1984) found a circular process in boys by which mothers tended to back away from difficult boys, thereby increasing their difficultness, a pattern not present in girls; and Fagot, Hagam, Leinbach, and Kronsberg (1985) found that adults were more likely to respond to boys' whines and demands but to girls' babble, gesture, and talk. It is not only that parents may treat boys and girls somewhat differently, which they do (Block, 1983), but also that the patterns of effects differ between the sexes.

Fourth, correlations are greatly influenced both by unreliability in measures and by changes in their meaning across time periods. It has become common practice to correct correlations over time for attentuation due to unreliability (see, e.g., Olweus, 1979); the consequence of correction is likely to be a marked increase in continuities. The same increase (together with some alteration in the *pattern* of associations) has been found for associations between risk variables and various psychological outcomes (see, e.g., Fergusson & Horwood, in press). However, there is an inevitable lingering doubt on how far the "corrected" statistics represent reality. Even greater problems stem from changes in meaning—a particularly important issue when examining continuities from infancy (Rutter, 1970). Thus crying in the neonate and crying in the adolescent both reflect negative mood, but do they have the same meaning (Rutter, 1982a)? Does activity level as assessed from degree of neonatal kicking in the crib mean the same thing as activity level assessed from adolescent fidgetiness while sitting or from degree of rushing about during leisure time? Korner and colleagues (1985), for example, found that neonatal activity level correlated positively with daytime activity but negatively with nighttime activity levels in middle childhood.

Interactions and Statistical Interaction Effects

A further set of problems in longitudinal analysis stem from the importance of a variety of different kinds of interactions. Such interactions take many forms. For example, individuals with some attribute may respond to a situation in an opposite fashion from those without the attribute. Thus Lutkenhaus, Grossmann, and Grossmann (1985) found that infants with secure attachments at 12 months tended to show *increased* effort following task failure at 3 years whereas those with insecure attachments tended to show *decreased* effort. Similarly, both boys and girls and anxious and nonanxious children tend to respond in opposite ways to negative feedback on their intellectual performance (Dweck & Elliott, 1983). A rather different interaction is evident in the finding that patterns of mother–child interchanges alter if the father is also present (Clarke-Stewart, 1973) or if other children are there (Schaffer & Liddell, 1984). Alternatively, the presence of one stressor may be increased by its association with another or with concurrent or earlier chronic adversity. For example, one hospital admission in early childhood has negligible adverse long-term psychological ill effects, but two admissions constitute a significant risk factor, particularly if associated with long-standing family difficulties (Douglas, 1975; Quinton & Rutter, 1976). The reverse form of interaction is evident in the buffering effect of protective factors on children's reactions to stress events (Rutter, 1985b).

The importance of such interactions is, of course, very well recognized by developmental researchers. What is not so widely appreciated is the extent to which they may be missed by conventional multivariate analyses to detect statistical interaction effects (Rutter, 1983). This is so for many reasons, but six warrant particular mention. First, most statistical packages test only for *multiplicative* interactions and not for additive interactions, which are not the same as simple additive effects in spite of sounding as if they are (Everitt & Smith, 1979). Second, the detection of statistical interaction effects is heavily dependent on the numbers of subjects in key cells. A negative finding may mean that inadequate numbers have prevented any meaningful testing of interactions rather than that in reality there is no interaction. Third, the finding that a variable has a significant main effect after statistically taking into account the effect of other variables is *not* tantamount to a finding that it has an effect in the absence of other variables (see Rutter, 1983). Fourth, sample choice may mean that the findings on interactions are seriously misleading in their general implications. For example, the study of adoptees is a good strategy for separating the effects of genetic and environmental variables just because the biological parentage differs from the social parentage of rearing. But for that very reason estimates of the amount of variance accounted for by gene-environment interactions will constitute underestimates (because the overlap between the two is minimal in adoptees but very great in the general population). A somewhat related issue is the tendency for genetic effects to operate through their influence on people's behavior in shaping their own and others' environments (Scarr & McCartney, 1983). For example, one of the reasons that parental mental disorder constitutes a serious risk factor for the children is that it leads to family discord (Rutter & Quinton, 1984) and disruption (Quinton & Rutter, in press). Fifth, weak continuities may be evident because risk indicators have been mistaken for risk mechanisms. For example, the literature is full of conflicting findings and claims on whether or not parental death in early childhood creates a vulnerability to depression in adult life. Brown, Harris, and Bifulco's (1986) findings indicate that this is likely to be because parental death creates a vulnerability only if it is followed by a lack or distortion of affectionate parental care. Similarly, family breakup creates its main risk for the children not so much through the separations per se that are involved as through the discord before and after the breakup with which it is associated (Rutter, 1971, 1974). Sixth, seriously misleading conclusions may be drawn on the effects of risk factors if apparently confounding variables have in actuality been themselves influenced by the risk variable. Many critiques of the evidence on supposed lasting sequelae from infancy experiences (see, e.g., Clarke & Clarke, 1976; Rutter, 1981a) have drawn attention to the probability that many of the supposed sequelae stem from current adversity rather than past experiences. That is to say, infants exposed to abuse or neglect in the early years may turn out badly not because of what happened in infancy, but rather because in middle childhood and adolescence they are *still* suffering from serious family adversities. There is no question but that this is a real and serious issue to be taken into account when searching for age-specific risk effects. It is for this reason that recent longitudinal studies of environmental effects on cognitive development have usually statistically partialed out the effect of the current environment when seeking to detect a lasting influence from infancy experiences that is independent of current circumstances. There are a host of statistical hazards involved in multivariate procedures designed to examine hypothesized causal effects after controlling for confounding variables (see, e.g., Adams, Brown, & Grant, 1985; Hertzog & Rovine, 1985; Rogosa, 1980). Nevertheless, there are ways of dealing with these statistical problems at least partially. However, the possibility that a confounding variable might have been brought about by the risk factor in question has been investigated rather rarely; the available evidence suggests that this may be more of an issue than usually appreciated.

Brown and colleagues (1986) examined the matter with respect to the associations between parental loss in childhood and adult depression. The usual procedure has been to control for current social class (as low social class tends to be associated with an increased risk of depression in women—at least among those living in inner-city areas). Brown and colleagues showed that this, in effect, served artifactually to reduce the apparent vulnerability effect of parental loss because loss of a parent significantly increased the likelihood that girls would not rise in social class relative to that of their parents. Similarly, Quinton and Rutter (in press) found that the adult outcome of institution-reared women was much more a function of their current marital situation than of whether they had grown up in an institution. The implication would seem to be that current experiences are much more important than past ones. However, that inference was misleading because institution rearing greatly increased the likelihood that the girls would make an unhappy marriage to a deviant man from a similarly disadvantaged background. The main impact on current psychological functioning was indeed that stemming from the women's family circumstances in adult life, but to a major extent such circumstances were a function of their experiences in childhood.

Circular Causal Processes and Chain Effects

A third source of difficulty in the analysis of longitudinal data derives from the effects of possible circular causal processes and chain effects involved in continuities and discontinuities over time. For example, Belsky, Rovine, and Taylor (1984) found that maternal stimulation at 1 month was correlated with infant fussiness at 3 months, which in turn was associated with insecure attachment at 9 months; a cross-lagged analysis suggested that this was indeed the causal chain (infant fussiness at any one age was not correlated with maternal involvement at a later age). The circular process between maternal and infant difficultness in boys (Maccoby, Snow, & Jacklin, 1984) has already been noted.

The data from Dunn and Kendrick's (1982) study of the reaction of young firstborns to the birth of a younger sibling suggest possible ways in which these circular processes may influence continuities and discontinuities over time. Stillwell and Dunn (1985) found a surprisingly high level of consistency in the affective quality of sibling relationships. Thus the level of positive interest shown in the 3-week-old neonate by the firstborn sibling 2–3 years old correlated 0.48 with the positive comments made 3–4 years later by the firstborns about their younger brother or sister. Similarly, the positive and negative approaches to the younger sibling 14 months after birth predicted aggression and extent of sharing between the siblings at the follow-up 3–4 years later (correlations about 0.44–0.55). On the face of it, this degree of continuity in a dyadic relationship is astonishing given that one partner at the beginning was a newborn and at the end was a highly verbal, highly mobile young child. Moreover, the continuity did *not* appear to be a function of the firstborn's temperamental features. Rather it seems that it may have been a function of the pattern of family relationships. A negative relationship between the sibs was more likely to develop after the birth if the previous relationship between the firstborn and mother had been warm and close (a possible jealousy reaction rather than a generalization of behavior); maternal relationships with the firstborn tended to become less involved and more confronting after the arrival of the new baby; this and the mother's warm interactions with the baby tended to increase sibling tensions; mothers tended to scold their sons when they hit their baby siblings; such scoldings in turn were associated with worsening of the sibling relationships. The numbers involved are too small and the complexity of associations too great for analyses to provide any adequate test of this hypothesized causal chain. Nevertheless, there is the strong implication that the continuity in the quality of the sibling relationships stemmed from what was happening in the overall pattern of family interactions rather than from direct effects of the birth of a sibling on the children themselves.

A further key consideration is that lasting effects may stem from the *memory* of past events as well as from effects on current interactions. In other words, people respond on the basis of their expectancies and of the reputations of the other person. Expectancies are evident in the findings from "baby X" studies that adults respond differently to ambiguously dressed infants and toddlers when they think that the child is male than when they think it is female (e.g., Condry & Ross, 1985; Smith & Lloyd, 1978).

Many years ago, Jahoda (1954) noted that Ashanti children tended to behave in accord with cultural expectations of the effects of the day of the week on which they were born (one of the children's given names indicates the day of birth); the effects of public labeling of delinquents may also serve to perpetuate their delinquent behaviour (Rutter & Giller, 1983). To some extent children may come to behave according to what is expected of them.

Reputations are evident in the findings that aggressive children are more likely than other children to *elicit* aggressive behavior from their peers, as well as to show more aggression themselves, and that children's negative reputations may maintain their low social status even after disappearance of the behavioral patterns that gave rise to the initial acquisition of low status (Dodge, 1980). People respond on the basis of a cumulative history of personal interactions and not just the immediate stimulus in the here-and-now situation (Asher, 1983). Nevertheless, it is important to note both how quickly reputations form and how much they affect interactions. For example, Brunk and Henggeler (1984), in an experimental study, showed that children's behavior influenced that of adults with whom they interacted (two 10-year-olds were trained in conduct problem and anxious–withdrawn roles). That adults responded differently according to the children's behavior is not at all surprising, but what was interesting was that during a play session as short as 20 min they were already responding differently to the *same* child behaviors according to the child's overall role. For example, in the anxious–withdrawn condition the child's compliant behavior was rewarded a third of the time, but the same behavior was rewarded only once in 20 times in the conduct disorder condition. It seems that adults are responding as much on the basis of their cognitive sets as on the basis of the child's behavior at that very moment.

Behavioral Reorganization

The fourth issue with respect to longitudinal analyses concerns the examination of discontinuities in development and of apparent major reorganizations of behavior. Kagan (1981, 1984) has argued forcefully for the importance of such discontinuities and reorganization during the process of development. Thus he suggested that "many instances of developmental change can be characterized by replacement of an old structure or process by a new one, with little or no connectedness between the two hypothetical structures. The suggestion implies that some structures or processes vanish" (Kagan, 1981, p. 68). The reality of such massive changes during the course of development cannot be doubted. The hormonal changes at puberty and their huge effects on body stature and proportions (as well as on the emergence of secondary sexual characteristics) provide a dramatic case in point. Kagan (1981) suggested that the emergence of self-awareness in the second year has equally striking psychological effects, and Bowlby (1969) might argue the same for the development of selective attachments in the first year. It may be accepted that the nature of the developmental process carries with it a necessary expectation of an important degree of discontinuity. Nevertheless, as Hinde and Bateson (1985) pointed out, the arguments for discontinuity and reorganization frequently rely on a marked drop in the strength of longitudinal correlations at some age period, and these may arise for a variety of (sometimes trivial) reasons other than a radical reorganization of behavior. Thus correlations may diminish because measures show floor or ceiling effects. This may have been the case, for example, with Kagan's Guatemalan study. The early results appeared to show a major reversal from depressed intellectual performance at 1 year to essentially average performance by mid-childhood (Kagan & Klein, 1973). A later study, however, showed persisting intellectual differences (Kagan, 1979), and it seems likely that the earlier picture of discontinuity was an artifact stemming from ceiling effects in measurement.

Correlations will also drop if individuals in the sample studied vary in timing of their maturational changes. Thus children vary markedly in when they reach puberty so that in any adolescent group of same-aged children some will be prepubertal, some will be just going through puberty, and some will have long since completed puberty. The consequence for longitudinal correlations of height is that (because of the marked growth spurt associated with puberty) correlations with both earlier and late height drop during the age period only to rise again once everyone is through puberty.

A further consequence, however, concerns the psychological correlates of puberty. For example, Magnusson, Stattin, and Allen (1986) found that at age 14 years girls who had reached puberty before 11 years were nine times as likely to have been drunk frequently than those who had only just reached puberty. The question was whether this difference represented initiation into a high-risk behavior associated with later alcohol problems or rather just an early entry into an adult pattern that would be similarly reached by other girls at a later age. The follow-up at age 15 years showed a reduced effect of age of puberty, and by the follow-up 10 years later the effect had entirely disappeared. The same pattern applied to drug usage but it did not for education. Early-maturing girls were less likely to have gone on to tertiary education. In other words, the timing of puberty had a transient effect on alcohol or drug usage but a lasting effect on educational careers; this differentiation could be detected only through longitudinal data that extended well into adult life. The substantive finding is not relevant to continuities from infancy, but the methodological point is. That is, correlations between predictors and outcomes as well as longitudinal correlations for some attribute will be partially influenced by interindividual differences in physical maturity (irrespective of whether physical maturity is included in the analysis).

A final point is that, even when undoubted major reorganizations have indeed taken place, that does not mean that earlier individual differences will necessarily disappear (Hinde & Bateson, 1985). Even metamorphosis does not necessarily erase previous memories. In certain moth species whose larvae can feed on more than one foodstuff, it has been shown that the adult females are prone to lay eggs on the substrate on which they were reared. It seems that experience during the larval phase can affect the behavior of the adult. Comparable effects have also been demonstrated in amphibians.

Conclusions

The net effect of these various considerations in the analysis of longitudinal data is to alert one to the possible complexities involved in continuities and discontinuities in the developmental process. That is not to say that there will not be straightforward direct main effects on outcome from risk variables, nor is it to suggest that continuities will not often derive from intraindividual cognitive or behavioral attributes. But it is to argue that traditional univariate and multivariate correlational analysis may either exaggerate or conceal continuities and discontinuities. Moreover, if the *processes* involved in developmental linkages are to be identified it will be necessary to undertake analyses appropriate for the detection of indirect chain effects and circular causal processes as well as direct main effects. It scarcely needs adding, however, that the greater the complexity of models proposed the greater the opportunity for chance associations. Replication across studies in such instances constitutes a much better test of validity than statistical significance within any one data set. Before considering which mechanisms may actually apply to continuities and discontinuities from infancy it is necessary to consider some of the main findings to be accounted for.

SOME EMPIRICAL FINDINGS ON CONTINUITIES AND DISCONTINUITIES

Cognitive Development

As the research on predictive correlations from early infancy to later childhood for mental performance was well reviewed by McCall (1979) in the first edition of this handbook, the findings may be summarized quite briefly. First, the correlations between infant tests given in the first 30 months of life and IQ assessed at 3–18 years are modest; second, the later the infancy test is given the better the prediction. Thus the median correlation from infant test at 19–30 months to child IQ at 8–18 years was 0.49, but from 13–18 months its was 0.32; from 7–12 months, 0.25, and from the first 6 months of life it was only 0.06. Third, to a slight extent predictions from infancy to earlier childhood tend to be better than to later childhood; and fourth, infant tests are better at predicting mental handicap than they are at differentiating within later levels of performance within the normal range. Subsequent research has supported these conclusions.

The evidence on psychosocial influences on cognitive development has been reviewed by Rutter (1985a), Gottfried (1984), and Wachs and Gruen (1982). This shows that the amount of variance in intellectual performance accounted for by the home environment is quite low (corrected correlations of about 0.15–0.35). The correlations in adoptive families are about half those in biological families, indicating that part of the parental effect on children's intelligence is genetic rather than environmental. Nevertheless, some environmental effect is suggested (a median correlation of about 0.2). Interestingly, longitudinal studies both with intervention (e.g., Ramey et al., 1984) and without it (e.g., Bradley & Caldwell, 1984) have shown that family measures at 2 years or older tend to have a stronger correlation with IQ than do similar measures in infancy. This may be especially the case after correction for parental IQ (Yeates, MacPhee, Campbell, & Ramey, 1983). In other words, the very early family environment seems less influential than that experienced at the toddler age period and later regardless of whether correlations are with contemporaneous or later cognitive measures.

Extreme Conditions

Studies of children exposed to extreme environmental conditions involving gross social isolation and severe physical confinement bring out some other important considerations (Clarke, 1984; Skuse, 1984). At the time of rescue from these grossly abnormal situations, all the children were without spoken language, and most showed gross intellectual retardation. It is clear that serious environmental privation can and does lead to severe cognitive impairment. However, it was usual for the children to show very substantial cognitive improvement after removal from their appalling circumstances (at ages ranging from $2\frac{1}{2}$ to $13\frac{1}{2}$), with 7 out of 10 achieving normal levels of intelligence and language. This improvement was usually evident within months of removal from the extreme environmental conditions, although it took much longer for normal levels to be achieved. It may be inferred that a complete change in environment in early or middle childhood, if it results in good psychosocial conditions, can bring about a marked degree of cognitive recovery. The data are too sparse to draw any conclusions on the degree of completeness of recovery or on the proportion of children who do not recover (let alone why they do not when that is the case—although clearly brain damage is sometimes the explanation).

Adoption

The question of whether environmental effects on intellectual development are greater during the preschool years than they are later in childhood is raised by the evidence that the IQ scores of later-adopted children tend to be slightly lower than those adopted in infancy (see Dennis, 1973). Moreover, longitudinal data suggest that placement in adoptive homes after the age of $4\frac{1}{2}$ does not produce the IQ gains that are usually observed following adoption at earlier ages (Hodges & Tizard, in preparation). The findings raise important issues, but they do not point unequivocally to the greater effect of the early family environment because: (1) It is difficult entirely to rule out selection biases; (2) by definition the late-adopted children have experienced a longer period of disadvantage; and (3) the amount and character of parent–child interaction in middle childhood are very different from those in infancy. It may be added, too, that the findings may reflect enduring effects on social behavior rather than on cognitive competence as such (i.e., that the institutional rearing had had effects on self-esteem or on interaction styles that made the children less able to profit from their experiences).

Preschool Intervention

The related issue of how far the effects of positive early experiences extend into later childhood and adolescence is tackled by the studies of various forms of family and educational intervention during the preschool years. Numerous studies during the 1960s and early 1970s showed that interventions led to immediate IQ gains but that the benefits did not persist for long after the start of regular schooling. The lack of persistence stemmed from a combination of IQ gains in control groups associated with school entry and decrements in the experimental groups. These generally negative findings led to the view that there were no lasting benefits for preschool intervention. Recent evidence, however, has led to a reappraisal resulting in the conclusion that there *are* some effects that persist into middle childhood and adolescence (see Berrueta-Clement, Schweinhart, Barnett, Epstein, & Weikart, 1984; Clarke-Stewart & Fein, 1983; Lazar & Darlington, 1982; Ramey et al., 1984; Rutter, 1985a; Woodhead, 1985). The main findings are as follows: (1) IQ gains do not persist long after school entry unless the intervention also continues; (2) there are some modest lasting increments in scholastic achievement (in some studies only); (3) intervention is followed by some positive changes in the attitudes of children and parents, and of teachers toward the children; and (4) most especially, intervention results in a lower proportion of children requiring special educational treatment. It seems that educational intervention during the preschool years has both a direct impact on cognitive performance and noncognitive effects on children's self-esteem, self-efficacy, and attitudes to learning; on parents' hopes and aspirations; and on teachers' expectations of and responses to the children. The evidence suggests that long-term benefits were dependent on parental support for education, positive role models who demonstrated the value of schooling, a sense of responsibility that extended beyond the self, and an active good-oriented approach to life. The implication is that there are very few persistent *direct* effects but that long-term changes, when they occur, derive from transactional indirect effects stemming from interactions between cognitive and social processes and from a mutually supportive mesh between home and school. It is important that short-lived improvements in competence, when coupled with increased motivation, parental aspirations, and school expectations, may be sufficient to trigger a mutually reinforcing positive cycle of achievement. Nevertheless, it is equally crucial to appreciate that these benefits may be conditional on features of the educational and family context in which the intervention took place and that the benefits mainly apply to well-designed and well-supported interventions for seriously disadvantaged children (Woodhead, 1985). It remains uncertain how far the findings can be generalized to more ordinary circumstances.

Brain Damage

Two developmental issues have been a focus of attention in studies of the possible long-term cognitive deficits associated with brain damage in infancy and early childhood: (1) whether the consequences of acute damage vary according to the age at which it is incurred; and (2) how far the sequelae are dependent on association with psychosocial disadvantage. Little is known on the extent to which there can be cognitive recovery if there are good environmental conditions in later childhood, although a few studies provide some evidence on this matter.

Rutter (1982b, Rutter, Chadwick, & Shaffer, 1983) has reviewed the limited evidence available on age effects. Conclusions are necessarily tentative because of uncertainties on whether lesions at different ages are comparable in nature and in size. Nevertheless, it seems that brain damage may be slightly more likely to give rise to *generalized* intellectual deficits if it occurs in infancy, whereas *specific* effects on language or visuospatial effects resulting from localized lesions may be more differentiated in older children and adults. Early damage to the left hemisphere is less likely than later damage to lead to permanent language impairment (although *some* verbal sequelae are more common than previously suggested); moreover, very early damage tends to result in generally impaired speech development rather than the specifically aphasic-type abnormalities of language associated with later damage.

A variety of mechanisms play a part in these age effects, including the following: (1) The brain is more susceptible to damage in infancy because of its immaturity and rapid growth during this age period; (2) the earlier the brain damage, the greater the reorganization of neuronal connections (however, as well as facilitating recovery in some cases, this may result in greater malfunction through the development of anomalous neuronal connections); (3) there is greater potential for interhemispheric transfer of language functions in infancy; and (4) early brain damage may have different (possibly greater) effects because young children have more *new* learning to undertake than older children and hence less accumulated knowledge and established skills on which to rely. It will be appreciated that these mechanisms may serve to result in either greater or lesser sequelae following brain damage in infancy, depending on the balance between them.

Malnutrition

Cravioto and Arrieta (1983) and Stein and Susser (1985) have summarized the data on cognitive sequelae of malnutrition. It may be concluded that severe malnutrition in infancy rarely results in intellectual impairment unless it is accompanied by social deprivation. Moreover, Winick, Meyer, and Harris's (1975) follow-up study of Korean orphans adopted into American families indicated that, even when social and nutritional privation are combined, a very considerable degree of recovery is possible provided that the later upbringing environment is good. Nevertheless, the results suggested that recovery was not complete for the most severely malnourished subgroup, whose mean IQ of 102 was 10 points below the better nourished, and whose scholastic achievement was nearly 1 standard deviation lower. Inevitably, these conclusions have to be somewhat tentative because of uncertainty over the initial comparability of the subgroups and because a third of the sample were lost to follow-up. The reasons that social disadvantage so greatly increases the ill effects of malnutrition remain obscure. To some extent it clearly represents the summation of two adverse influences, but in addition it seems that there is likely to be some mutual potentiation of damaging effects. In part this may be a consequence of a biologically damaged organism being more susceptible to psychosocial adversities and less able to adapt or cope with life difficulties. However, in addition, there is evidence that handicapped infants are less effective in eliciting appropriate parental behavior.

Perinatal Complications

Comparable issues arise with respect to perinatal complications. Various early studies suggested that, as with malnutrition, persisting cognitive ill effects were largely a consequence of an association with social disadvantage (see Sameroff & Chandler, 1975). However, more recent investigations have indicated that this may not be the case for those with overt brain damage as shown by either abnormal neurological or brain image findings (Stewart, 1983; Vohr & Coll, 1985). The extent to which there are any cognitive sequelae of very low birth weight in the absence of diagnosable brain damage remains quite uncertain, but it is possible that in spite of a lack of effect on IQ there may be more subtle cognitive deficits in some children (Klein, Hack, Gallagher, & Fanaroff, 1985). Nevertheless, it is clear that a major degree of recovery is usual, with lasting deficits minor and largely confined to infants in socially disadvantaged homes (Wilson, 1985). Another type of interaction needs to be considered with respect to other physical hazards arising in the postnatal period. Poor caretaking tends to be associated with an increased exposure of the children to lead toxicity (Dietrich, Krafft, Pearson, Harris, Bornschein, Hammond, & Succop, 1985; Milar, Schroeder, Mushak, Dolcourt, & Grant, 1980) and to head injury (Rutter et al., 1983), both of which create their own biological risks.

Language Development

For the most part the conclusions regarding environmental effects on intelligence apply similarly to language (Puckering & Rutter, in press), but there are some additional issues that require mention. For the most part, language development has such strong self-righting qualities that even after gross deprivation it tends to recover in a more enhancing environment. On the other hand, there is some suggestion that hearing deficits (as from ear infections) during the infancy period when language is ordinarily acquired may sometimes lead to some degree of lasting impairment in verbal skills and in scholastic achievement even though the hearing recovers (Bluestone et al., 1983; Hall & Hill, 1986; Paradise, 1981; Silva, Stewart, Kirkland, & Simpson, 1985). Although the evidence is as yet inconclusive, it may be that this is most likely to occur if the hearing loss is severe and prolonged and if it is combined with other adversities. Nevertheless, there is the possibility of some kind of sensitive period effect.

A further consideration is that, even after children who have been initially delayed in their language development gain normal levels of language, other sequelae may remain (Howlin & Rutter, in press). Impairments in scholastic achievement (especially in reading) are common, and are socioemotional difficulties. Stevenson and colleagues' (1985) longitudinal data show that the latter tend to arise after the infancy period. The mechanisms involved in this continuity from infancy into middle and later childhood remain obscure. To an important extent they may represent continuing biological impairments in language-related skills, but also it seems likely that particularly they reflect secondary consequences stemming from maladaptive patterns of interactions established when young. Thus Siegel, Cunningham, and van der Spuy (1985) found that language-delayed children were less likely than other children to initiate peer interactions.

Temperamental Qualities

It has been a general finding that the correlations from infancy to later childhood or adolescence for temperamental or personality features are very low (Moss & Susman, 1980; Plomin, 1983; Porter & Collins, 1982). For example, the median correlation for individual traits between 3 and 5 years in the New York Longitudinal Study was only 0.19 (Thomas & Chess, 1977). However, it appears that to some extent this very low level of consistency is a function of measuring temperament according to many traits separately considered in dimensional terms. There is some evidence that consistency is greater when extremes of temperamental composites are considered. For example, Coll, Kagan, and Reznick (1984) found a correlation of 0.66 for behavioral inhibition between 21 and 31 months, and Kagan and colleagues (1984) showed a correlation of about 0.5 between 21 months and 4 years (these correlations are based, however, on two extreme groups—a procedure likely to inflate correlations). Similarly, composite extremes tend to provide better predictors of both mother–child conflict (Lee & Bates, 1985) and later behavioral disturbance (Bates, Maslin, & Frankel, 1985; Porter & Collins, 1982). Chess and Thomas (1984) even found a correlation of 0.29 between the overall temperamental set at 3 years and a temperamental measure in adult life, although to a large extent this was a function of the link between temperament and behavioral adjustment in early childhood.

The data on temperamental continuities are too contradictory for firm conclusions to be drawn, particularly as there is little consistency across studies in the measures used or in the ways they are dealt with (see Hubert, Wachs, Peters-Martin, & Gandour, 1982). Clearly, there are major *dis*continuities in temperamental expression between infancy and later childhood, with marked changes being quite common. On the other hand, also there appear to be important threads of continuity—perhaps particularly with those extreme features that impinge on and influence social interactions. It remains uncertain whether this implies that these relatively consistent features have a rather different intrinsic meaning (see earlier discussion with respect to categorical distinctions) or rather that the continuities reside as much in the social interactions provoked as in the qualities themselves.

Psychological Disturbance

Until recently it has generally been assumed that most disturbances in the preschool period are transient and of little long-term significance. However, several recent longitudinal studies has shown this is a mistaken view. Thus Richman, Stevenson, and Graham (1982) showed that 62 percent of the children with problems at 3 years of age had deviant behavior at 8 years compared with 22 percent in the remainder of the population. Continuities were both stronger and more consistent in boys (with persistence mainly applying to conduct disturbance) than in girls, where continuities mainly applied to emotional disturbance (Stevenson et al., 1985). Campbell, Breaus,

Ewing, and Szumowski (1984) showed moderate persistence from 3 to 4 years for inattentive, noncompliant impulsive behavior. Lerner, Inui, Trupin, and Douglas (1985) in a follow-up to adolescence found that children 3–5 years old with a moderate or severe disorder at that age had twice the risk of later disturbance (however, only half the sample were seen at follow-up). Fischer, Rolf, Hasazi, and Cummings (1984) found that continuities from preschool to middle childhood were stronger for "externalizing" than "internalizing" symptoms; Kohn's (1977) findings were similar.

Jenkins, Owen, Bax, and Hart (1984) showed that the patterns of continuity varied somewhat by type of problems; sleep difficulties showed substantial persistence during the first 2 years but much less continuity therafter; for feeding problems and tantrums the main continuity was between 2 and 3 years. The findings reflect, of course, age specificities in the most prevalent forms of disturbance, and the study is less useful in showing which patterns were most predictive of continuity into middle childhood. The findings from other studies suggest that these mainly consist of conduct disturbance or hyperactivity in boys and anxious behavior in girls. Investigations of continuities in middle childhood show that it is unusual for children to move from one extreme to the other on any type of behavior and also that there tends to be substantial consistency in the type of disturbance shown (see Rutter & Garmezy, 1983). It should be added that the evidence on continuities in disturbance mainly applies to persistence from 3 years of age, and very little is known on the links or lack of links with problems in earlier infancy.

The only study with systematic data on family factors that might relate to continuities and discontinuities is the epidemiological/longitudinal study by Richman and colleagues (1982). They found that family adversity was quite strongly related to the *onset* of disorder between 3 and 8 years; of those with adversity at 3 years, 39 percent showed disorder at 8 compared with 16 percent of those in homes without adversity (the link with adversity at 8 was even stronger; 48 vs. 10 percent). Thus family difficulties played a major role in the discontinuity reflected in changes from nondeviance to deviance. Family variables were less powerful in accounting for discontinuity in the opposite direction; however, adverse patterns of interaction between the mother and individual child were associated with persistence of problems (those where the mothers showed low warmth or high criticism were twice as likely to continue to show problem behavior). The implications are that once psychological disturbances become established they tend to show a degree of self-perpetuating qualities and that the factors involved in continuity and discontinuity concern individual patterns of parent–child interaction more than global family difficulties. Of course, it may be that those two features are linked, that is, that continuities stem from adverse patterns of coercive interchange that create a vicious cycle (as suggested by the data of Patterson, 1982, from studies of older children and by the findings on the effects of reputation discussed above).

Qualities of Selective Attachment

Since Ainsworth (1967) and Bowlby (1969) systematically drew attention to the potential developmental significance of infants' first social ties to their parents, there has been a burgeoning of research into the possible continuities between the quality of these early selective attachments are children's later social development. Ainsworth's Strange Situation (or some modification of it) has been most widely used to assess the quality of these ties as conceptualized in terms of "security" of attachment and, although open to various objections (see Lamb, Brown, & Rogoff, 1984), it has proved a most useful tool (see Bretherton & Waters, 1985). Several issues relevant to the theme of continuities and discontinuities in development have been subjected to detailed empirical study. Research has shown that there is little or no concordance between the security of an infant's attachment to its mother and the security of attachment to the father or to other caregivers (Grossmann & Grossmann, 1981; Lamb, 1977; Main & Weston, 1981; Sagi et al., 1985). Thus it is evident that the quality of security applies to a dyadic relationship and not to a behavioral trait of the individual child. On the other hand, although there is little consistency across the infant's dyadic relationships with the two parents, security of mother–infant attachment in infancy has been found to have a substantial degree of prediction to the child's peer relationships and social functioning several years later— and sometimes, but not always, to problem behavior as well (Bates et al., 1985; Erickson, Sroufe, & Egeland, 1985; LaFreniere & Sroufe, 1985; Lewis, Feiring, McGuffoy, & Jaskir, 1984; Main, Kaplan, & Cassidy, 1985; Sroufe, Fox, & Pancake, 1983; Waters, Hay, & Richters, 1985). At first sight this finding of a prediction to the child's functioning with different people in a different situation some considerable time later seems inconsistent with the evidence that "security" measures a dyadic quality that does not predict to other dyads. The reasons for this apparent paradox have yet to be determined, but several possibilities may be considered.

First, there has been the suggestion that, in spite of the relative dyad-specificity of the security measure, perhaps the child's temperamental characteristics are what determine the quality of attachment and, more especially, its links with later functioning. Some studies have shown significant correlations between infant characteristics and security of attachment (e.g., Grossmann, Grossmann, Spangler, Suess, & Unzner, 1985; Miyake, Chen, & Campos, 1985), but others have not (Belsky, Rovine, & Taylor, 1984; Egeland & Farber, 1984) or have found correlations only when neonatal irritability was associated with maternal unresponsiveness and lack of social support (Crockenberg, 1981) or only to some aspects of attachment (Bates et al., 1985). It seems likely that there are some temperamental features that serve to influence the quality of attachments in some circumstances. Nevertheless, it seems equally clear that attachment is far from synonymous with temperament, that the links between temperament and attachment are modest only, and that it is unlikely that the predictive features of attachment security mainly reside in temperamental characteristics (Sroufe, 1985).

A second alternative is that the consistencies over time reside in continuities in the environment rather than in the child. There are marked differences between studies in the extent to which there has been temporal consistency in the measures of security of attachment—some finding changes to be infrequent (Waters, 1983) and others finding changes common (Thompson, Lamb, & Estes, 1982, 1983). However, there appears to be reasonable agreement between investigations in the demonstration that the extent to which alterations in security occur is dependent on the degree of change in the environment (Egeland & Farber, 1984; Thompson et al., 1983). Generally the consistencies over time in parental behavior have been only moderate (Belsky, Gilstrap, & Rovine, 1984; Belsky, Taylor, & Rovine, 1984; Dunn & Plomin, 1986; Pettit & Bates, 1984). Clearly, it is quite possible that to some extent the predictive power of the attachment classification in infancy resides in environmental constancy rather than in any intraindividual psychological processes in the child. However, there are continuities and discontinuities in parental as well as child behavior, and very little is known on the role of environmental continuities as mediators of the link between an infant's attachment to its mother and its social relationships with peers and with adults several years later.

A third possibility is that the cumulative experiences of dyadic relationships serve to shape the child's more general style of social interaction. The evidence on this possibility is meager, but some support is afforded by evidence that the predictions are stronger when the child's relationship with *both* parents shows the same quality of security or insecurity (Main & Weston, 1981) or when the security quality of one dyad shows consistency over time (Erickson et al., 1985; Thompson & Lamb, 1983). On the whole, predictions from mother–infant attachment are stronger than those from father–infant attachment (Main et al., 1985), but it is uncertain whether this reflects the usually greater extent of mother–infant interaction in infancy or rather differences in the nature of father–child and mother–child relationships.

Fourth, increasing attention has been paid in recent years to the possibility that what matters is the way children construe their relationships and the schemes or working models that they develop (Bretherton, 1985). That is, the child is an active participant in the creation of self-perpetuating patterns. Main and colleagues (1985) found that 6-year-olds who had shown insecure attachments at 1 year tended to talk in ways that suggested that they lacked an image of their parents as accessible. Data from adults suggested that those who reported having experienced rejection in childhood adapted better if they accepted the reality of the experience and were able to find reasons outside of themselves to account for it (such as the parents' mental disorder or severe social stresses). Ricks's (1985) adult data indicated the same, but also suggested that later good social experiences might be important in altering individuals' working model of themselves ("That person likes me; maybe I am worthwhile after all") and of their relationships with others (because they have learned that other people can be trusted and will provide emotional support when it is needed).

One puzzling feature of cross-cultural findings is the marked variations in the frequency distribution of secure attachment or of different types of insecurity. For a long while there was the implicit assumption that the secure pattern was the "normal" one, leading to healthy adaptation, an assumption stemming both from the finding that secure attachments constituted the modal pattern in North American studies and the finding that they tended to be associated with sensitive, responsive parenting. However, in North Germany the avoidant pattern predominated in the study of Grossmann and colleagues (1985); in Japan resistant patterns were far more numerous than in the United States (Miyake et al., 1985); and in Israel (Sagi et al., 1985) many kibbutzim infants were unable to complete the separation procedure because of inordinate distress. Hinde (1982) made the important point that, biologically speaking, adaptation is not an absolute quality; rather, behaviors may be adaptive or maladaptive for different situations. It would be wrong to place too much emphasis on cross-cultural variations in that the overall pattern of findings relating to the attachment classification has shown reasonably good agreement across cultures. Nevertheless, the findings have raised important questions on whether infants' responses to the Strange Situation mean the same thing in all circumstances.

Ainsworth's scoring system was devised for essentially normal 1-year-old infants, and increasingly it has become evident that the classification may be misleading when applied to abnormal groups, or to older children. Thus Main and colleagues (1985) have argued for the need for an insecure–disorganized–disoriented category for responses to the Strange Situation in which the infants appear depressed, confused, and apprehensive and show marked avoidance following strong proximity seeking and/or simultaneous display of contradictory behavior patterns (e.g., approaching with averted gaze or gazing strongly away while being held) together with undirected expressions of affect. It is noteworthy that half the infants in this category would have been pronounced "secure" on the Ainsworth classification, yet it predicted difficulties in social functioning at age 6 years. Crittenden (1985) has used an avoidant–ambivalent category that appears to be particularly common in infants subjected to abuse, and Radke-Yarrow, Cummings, Kuczynski, and Chapman (1985) noted that the infants of severely depressed mothers were most likely to show a type of insecurity characterized by both resistance and avoidance together with abnormal affect or stereotyped maladaptive behavior. It seems that with severely disordered families there may be a more pathological variety of insecure attachment that involves disturbances in affect and behavior that extends well beyond the qualities of infants' immediate response to a brief separation. Whether or not this supposedly more abnormal type of insecure attachment shows greater links with later problems in social relationships or functioning remains quite uncertain.

Parent–Infant Bonding

In 1976 Klaus and Kennell proposed that mothers develop "bonds" with their infants during a sensitive period in the first hours after birth; that such bonds are dependent on skin-to-skin contact; and that these supposedly unique developmental changes have a lasting effect on subsequent parent–child relationships and child development. The data to provide a rigorous test of these hypotheses are somewhat meager (Goldberg, 1983), but numerous reviews of the empirical findings suggest that the concept is mistaken in several key respects (Wolkind & Rutter, 1985). The processes in mother and child are not the same; relationships are multifaceted and develop over time rather than being "switched on"; they are not dependent on a simple sensory modality (skin contact); and their establishment is not confined to a short period just after birth. The selective attachments of adopted and nonadopted children are similar in spite of the fact that the former lack early parent–child contact (Singer, Brodzinsky, Ramsay, Steir, & Waters, 1985), and such attachments may develop even as late as 4–7 years of age in late-adopted children (Hodges & Tizard, in press,a; Tizard, 1977). Events in the neonatal period may well influence the development of relationships, and parent–child contact during this time is generally helpful but the effects are not particularly persistent.

The Establishment of First Selective Attachments

The sensitive period hypothesized for the development of children's first selective attachments (Bowlby, 1969) is quite different from that proposed for bonding in two essential respects: It is supposed to occur much later (beginning in the second half of the first year) and to extend over a much longer time span (at least 18 months or so). There is much evidence to show that infants do ordinarily develop their first attachments during that time period and, moreover, that infants of 6–18 months readily switch attachments to new figures if they are separated from their initial caregiver (see, e.g., Dontas, Maratos, Fafoulis, & Karangelis, 1985; Robertson & Robertson, 1971). An institutional upbringing seems to lead to superficial overfriendliness and social disinhibitions if admission is before the age of 2 years but not if admission is at a later age (Wolkind, 1974). Also, it may be that group day care beginning in the first 18 months is more likely to be disruptive than such care beginning at a later age—perhaps particularly if the care is full-time and provides little intensive caregiver interaction, and if there are frequent changes in arrangements (Rutter, 1981a; Vaughan, Dean, & Waters, 1985; Wolkind & Rutter, 1985). Nevertheless, on the whole, it seems that few, if any, effects persist into middle childhood. Even an institutional rearing in the first year seems not to lead to lasting sequelae provided that later conditions are satisfactory (Bohman & Sigvardsson, 1980). However, it does seem that ill effects may be much more likely in genetically high-risk groups, if institutionalization is more prolonged, and if subsequent patterns of upbringing are less good (Crowe, 1974; Parnas, Teasdale, & Schulsinger, 1985). That is to say, not only may risk factors in later childhood add to the effects of those in infancy also but they may *potentiate* the adverse sequelae of infancy experiences.

The extent to which prolonged institutional care in infancy has enduring effects that are independent of later experiences may be examined through the longitudinal study of late-adopted children. The best data (albeit based on a small sample) are provided by Tizard and Hodges' follow-up to age 16 years of infants who spent their first 3–7 years in institutions (Hodges & Tizard, in press,b; Tizard & Hodges, 1978; Tizard & Rees, 1974). The quality of physical care that they received was good, but there was a lack of opportunity to form close continuous relationships with an adult (by 4 years, the children had experienced an average of some 50 caregivers). The 22 children who had been adopted (mostly to above-average homes) were compared with the 13 who returned to their biological parents (mostly to unsatisfactory discordant family circumstances) and with matched general population controls. As already noted, the great majority of adopted children (even those adopted after age of $4\frac{1}{2}$) developed close mutual attachments with their adoptive parents; this happened less often with those restored to their biological parents (where serious family adversity was usual). The key question with respect to continuities and discontinuities from infancy is the degree to which the exinstitutional children's behavior remained different from that of controls at age 16 years. The findings are striking in several respects. First, the level of conduct disturbance (as assessed from parent or teacher ratings or psychiatric referral or delinquency figures) was primarily a function of the children's *current* family situation—being much higher in the restored children than in the adoptees. Second, the adopted children showed somewhat more emotional disturbance at 16 years than their controls (although this had not been the case at the earlier follow-up at 8 years). The suggestion is that being adopted may involve anxieties that are accentuated by adolescent development. Third, the quality of the children's social relationships at 16 years was more a function of their infancy experiences than of their family circumstances at follow-up. As a group, the exinstitutional children stood out as different from their controls in terms of being less discriminating in their friendliness, less likely to have a special friend, and less likely to confide in peers. The differences from controls were substantial, mostly twofold) and the adoptees and restored children were markedly similar in their qualities of relationships in spite of their radically different family circumstances during middle childhood and adolescence. The implication is that *severely* restricted opportunities to develop selective attachments that are present from the first year of life *and* that last at least 2–3 years may have social sequelae that persist right into adolescence even when later conditions or rearing are high quality. Hodges and Tizard's data suggest that these sequelae may be more likely if the children do not develop close attachments with their adoptive parents, but apparently they can occur when they do. The mechanisms involved in this surprisingly strong continuity from infancy remain obscure, but the findings suggest some sort of sensitive period effect (albeit one that is dependent on a lack of social opportunities that persists over several years).

Quinton and Rutter's (in press) follow-up study into adult life of institution-reared girls adds further dimensions to the issue of continuities and discontinuities from infancy. Their sample experienced a variety of adversities that extended through childhood and adolescence. Nevertheless, the subgroup who had experienced severely disrupted parenting during the first 2 years of life had a significantly worse adult outcome (in terms of multiple indices of psychosocial malfunction). The findings suggested some continuity into adult life from adverse infancy experiences (although the continuity was likely to have been strengthened by subsequent maladaptive experiences). Nevertheless, the data indicated that at least part of the continuity stemmed from linkages between environmental circumstances rather than from any changes in the children themselves. Disrupted parenting in infancy was significantly associated with worse family circumstances in late adolescence (because the family breakup when girls were infants meant that in most cases either they had no family to which they could go on leaving the institution or alternatively they returned to a severely discordant family that created stress and did not provide support). Also, adult outcome was much influenced by whether or not the exinstitution woman made a harmonious marriage to a nondeviant man. The great majority of those who had a supportive marital relationship were functioning well in their mid-1920s, suggesting that a substantial degree of improvement in social functioning can still occur in early adult life. The data, however, did not allow any determination of the extent to which this resilience applied to the women who had shown the greatest social deficits in childhood.

RESPONSIVITY TO ENVIRONMENTAL CONDITIONS AND PROCESSING OF EXPERIENCES

As already discussed, there have been arguments that infants are *more* vulnerable to environmental hazards as well as arguments that they are *less* vulnerable. It is clear from the findings outlined above that neither supposition receives unequivocal support. Susceptibilities *do* vary according to age but not in a fashion that adds up to any general statement that infants are more or less affected than older children. The pattern of age variations in responsiveness may be summarized as follows.

Age Variations in Responsivity

First, transient separations seem most likely to result in short-term distress in the case of children from about 6 months to 4 years of age (Rutter, 1981b). The evidence suggests that the distress is in part a function of the threat to the security of the children's selective attachments to their parents. Probably, babies are "protected" because they have yet to develop selective attachments, older children because they have the capacity to maintain relationships over a period of absence. On the whole, a *single* stressful separation (such as a hospital admission) has negligible long-term sequelae, but *multiple* stressful separations are associated with a substantially increased risk of emotional and/or behavioral disturbance in later childhood and adolescence (Douglas, 1975; Quinton & Rutter, 1976). However, for this risk to be present it seems that probably the first admission must have occurred during the preschool years.

Second, the limited available evidence suggests that acute grief reactions of the type seen in adult life following bereavement appear less frequently and tend to be less severe and less prolonged in infancy and early childhood than in adolescence (Rutter, 1966). This age effect may be a consequence of young children's more limited understanding of death (Speece & Brent, 1984) or of their lesser tendency to show depressive reactions (Rutter, 1986a). On the other hand, if *all* types of disturbance are considered these may not be much less frequent following bereavement in early childhood (Black & Urbanowicz, 1985; Van Eerdewegh, Clayton, & Van Eerdewegh, 1985). Also, long-term disorders may be *more* likely following bereavement in early life than in later childhood and adolescence (Rutter, 1966). But this seems to be a function of the impaired child care that follows the parental death rather than a consequence of the death as such (Brown et al., 1986). If so, the greater sequelae are likely to be a function of the greater duration of poor child care rather than the greater vulnerability of very young children.

Third, environmental effects on cognitive development seem less strong in the case of influences in the first 18 months of life than with influences during the age period of 2–5 years. On the other hand, preschool family influences seem to have greater effects than those in middle or later childhood. It has been suggested that the more limited effects in early infancy may be a consequence of a greater canalization of development during that period so that maturational effects dominate (McCall, 1981). Not only are environmental effects greater in the age period 2–5 years, but so are genetic effects. But also, it may be a consequence of the fact that family and school influences tend to have a greater effect on verbal than on visuospatial skills, and verbal skills do not become manifest until the period after early infancy. The explanation for the somewhat reduced environmental impact after the preschool years is likely to be different. To some extent it is likely to be a consequence of the fact that more development has taken place by middle childhood and hence there is less room for influences to make a decisive difference. In addition, however, it may reflect the fact that the type of intensive parent–child interactions likely to affect cognitive development are less characteristic of middle than of early childhood. It should be emphasized, however, that these age differences in environmental responsiveness are relative; major environmental changes (for the better or the worse) have an impact at all ages.

Fourth, a temporary lack of sensory input (of vision and possibly of sound) tends to have a lasting disruptive effect on function only if it occurs in the first few years. Thus an uncorrected strabismus in infancy results in loss of binocular vision whereas one later in childhood does not; possibly, too, a hearing loss is more likely to interfere with verbal development if it occurs early in life than if it occurs after language skills are well established. A lack of input has an effect on developing neural functions that is different from that on established functions.

Fifth, the effects of early brain damage differ somewhat in pattern from those of later brain damage. It cannot be said that infants are generally more or less vulnerable than other children to brain trauma; in some respects they are more and in some respects less so—as a result of a complex mixture of different mechanisms.

Sixth, a lack of opportunity to form selective attachments in the first few years of life may have more enduring effects on the quality of later social relationships than does a similar lack later in childhood when young people have already had attachments that have lasted over a period of some years. Thus institutional rearing in the early years tends to increase the likelihood that peer relationships will lack a certain closeness and emotional intensity whereas a period of institutional care at a later age may not have that effect. Again, this seems to reflect the general rule that the effects of severe traumata (physical or psychological) tend to be greater during developmental phases of rapid growth when skills are just becoming established.

Finally, even though very young infants can detect and respond to differences in caregivers' affective expression (Cohn & Tronick, 1983; Sorce, Emde, Campos, & Klinnert, 1985) and although there do not appear to be any marked age differences in children's susceptibility to the ill effects associated with marked family discord or parental mental disorder, infants react in ways that differ from those seen with older children. Thus Cummings, Zahn-Waxler, and Radke-Yarrow (1981, 1984) showed that, whereas toddlers tend to respond with overt distress or aggression to episodes of anger in the family, school-age children were more likely to exhibit emotional self-control and to employ planful strategies to ameliorate the conflict. Toddlers show disturbances in attachment and dysregulation of effect in response to parental depression (Cytryn, McKnew, Zahn-Waxler, & Gershon, 1986; Radke-Yarrow et al., 1985), whereas older children show a range of emotional and behavioral disturbances including clinical depression (Rutter, 1987). Also, in some circumstances older children and adolescents may be protected from adversity by their ability to take responsibility and cope effectively (Elder, 1974, 1979), features that are less likely to apply with infants.

Age Variations in Processing of Experiences

The long-term consequences of adverse experiences depend not only on children's initial responses but also on their cognitive processing of what has happened to them and on their style of coping with the situation. Age differences may be even more important. To begin with there are developmental changes in children's ability to show anticipatory fear. Up to the age of about 9–12 months, infants may cry when given an inoculation, but they do not cry when the nurse approaches with the syringe, even though they have had previous experience of inoculation (Izard, 1978). Children are less likely to show fear when they have control over the fear object or situation (Gunnar-Vongnechten, 1978), and presumably the extent to which they can control stress circumstances increases as they grow older. Both control and understanding may influence longer-term consequences; thus Ferguson (1979) suggested that the experience of a prior hospital admission might be protective for older children admitted to the hospital but that it increased the likelihood of distress following hospitalization in younger children.

Toward the end of the second year there are important changes in children's self-concepts and self-understanding (Cicchetti & Schneider-Rosen, 1986). Children at that age first become aware of standards, showing upset over broken objects, distress over failure to meet standards set by others, and guilt over their own misdeeds (Kagan, 1981, 1984). Self-control begins to become established then, but self-regulation that involves flexibility in adaptation and some ability to wait for things takes another year or so to appear (Kopp, 1982). Pride and shame do not become established until middle childhood (Harter, 1983), and it may not be until even later that task failure often leads to a generalized sense of helplessness and hopelessness (Dweck & Elliott, 1983). Also, children's understanding of sadness during middle childhood forms an initial tendency to deny the experience, to a linking of sadness with physical hurt, to an attribution to psychological hurt (Glasberg & Abond, 1982).

In recent years there has been a tendency to view attachment patterns in terms of internal working models of relationships (see Bretherton, 1985). The question arises as to when infants first become able to build such models on the basis of their experiences. Adequate data on this issue are lacking, but on the basis of the self-concept findings it seems likely that the ability does not become well developed until toward the end of the second year (or later). However, it may be that the context and circumstances influence the extent to which such models are formed. For example, Hay, Murray, Cecire, and Nash (1985) found that 18-month-old infants were more likely to show generalized modeling if they were actively involved in interactions with the adult model and if verbal explanations were given.

The nature of children's participation in their experiences also alters as they grow older. Dunn and Munn (1985) found that during the second year children became increasingly likely to participate in family interactions that involved conflict; there was a parallel increase in focused teasing and in the appreciation of concepts of approved and disapproved behaviors. At about the same age there was a change from a generalized distress to specific person-focused protest.

Little is known on the extent to which these developmental changes in social cognition and in social interactions influence the persistence or nonpersistence of effects of experiences. However, it may be postulated that persistence of effects is likely to be less in the case of experiences in the first 12–18 months because the more limited cognitive processing that is possible in early infancy means that continuities are less likely to be maintained through lasting alterations in self-concepts, attitudes, or expectations. For the same reason, continuities might become stronger around the age of 2–3 years. They might lessen later in childhood because of children's increasing ability to cope actively to gain control over their environment, and to show active long-term social problem-solving strategies. On the other hand, continuities from adolescence might be stronger because of the increased tendency to develop pervasive helplessness and hopelessness responses. We lack data to test whether or not these inferences are borne out in practice.

MECHANISMS FOR CONTINUITIES AND DISCONTINUITIES

Finally, it is necessary briefly to summarize the various mechanisms that might be involved in the continuities and discontinuities from infancy (Rutter, 1981b, 1983, 1984b, 1986b, in press,b). It is clear that both occur. There are links between behavior and experiences in infancy and functioning in later childhood, but with few exceptions the associations are of no more than moderate strength. The continuities from age 2–3 years are generally stronger than those from the first year of life, but the continuities from all phases of infancy are strongly dependent on later experiences. This does not mean that the infancy experiences are unimportant and that the later environment is the sole determinant of later functioning. The reason that is not so is that to an important extent the later environment is determined by what has gone before.

There are many reasons why major discontinuities between infancy and later childhood are to be expected. First, there is a great deal of development still to occur, and this will be affected by many new influences, both genetic and environmental. Moreover, as new skills accumulate and as new development takes place, the sequelae of infancy constitute a decreasing proportion of the whole. Second, there are crucial biological changes after infancy, and some, such as puberty, do not have strong links with what has gone before. Third, as children develop new capacities (cognitive and noncognitive) and they have new experiences, they will reprocess and reappraise what has happened to them when younger. For example, Bretherton (1985) argued that it is not internal working models of attachment figures per se but rather how people construe those internal models in adulthood that affects their behavior as parents. When their early experiences of rejection are seen as an attribute of their parents and not a reflection of themselves, there is less likelihood that they will repeat the pattern of rejection with their own children.

Continuities from infancy, even extending into adulthood, are to be found in some circumstances, but, as already noted, most of the linkages are indirect rather than direct, and very few are independent of subsequent experiences. A range of rather different processes may be involved.

Structural Changes

Physical traumata can lead to structural changes in the brain, as discussed with respect to head injury, malnutrition, and perinatal complications. These may have lasting effects that derive from the damage to brain development. However, new tissue growth and biological healing processes (as well as psychological adaptations to and strategies for overcoming handicap) usually result in diminishing effects with time. Moreover, even with physical traumata, the consequences may depend on other mechanisms. Thus malnourished children may be less effective in eliciting interactions with their parents and organically damaged infants may behave in ways that are aversive to their parents.

Experiential factors may also have effects on somatic structure and function. For example, it is well established from animal studies that acute stresses of various kinds in early life may lead to lasting changes in the neuroendocrine system that are accompanied by an enhanced resistance to later stress. It is also clear that visual impoverishment in infancy, or severe global environmental privation, may lead to measurable changes in brain structure and chemistry. Human parallels are provided by the effect of a squint in the first 3 years in seriously interfering with the development of binocular vision and, much less certainly, by the effects of conductive hearing losses in early childhood on the development of verbal intelligence. However, it is important to note that these changes are not necessarily irreversible. A degree of brain plasticity persists until late in development (Greenough & Schwark, 1983).

Habits, Attitudes, and Self-Concepts

Kagan (1980) has suggested that the transduction of experiences into the child's belief system constitutes one of the most important mechanisms for behavioral continuities. There is evidence that adverse experiences may impair feelings of self-esteem and self-efficacy and that these are in turn linked with later problems in social adaptation (Harter, 1983). Also, there are grounds for supposing that these changes in self-concept play an important part in the continuities and discontinuities seen in later childhood and adolescence (see, e.g., Brown et al., 1986; Quinton & Rutter, in press). However, even in this age period the evidence is fragmentary and circumstantial, and very little is known on their role in continuities from infancy. As noted above, there are some tentative findings that self-concepts may be crucial in the continuities deriving from early insecurities in parent–child attachments (Bretherton & Waters, 1985). It seems likely that children's feelings about their experiences, the meaning and constructions that they attach to them, and the cognitive sets about themselves and their environment that are derived will greatly influence both the extent and the pattern of continuities from infancy, but empirical data are lacking on how far that is in fact the case.

Vulnerabilities and Sensitivities

A third process concerns the effect of adverse experiences in leading to an increased sensitivity or vulnerability to later stressors. Not much is known on the importance of the mechanism, but there is evidence that it exists. Mention has been made of Suomi's (1983) findings that separation experiences in monkeys resulted in an increased tendency to show "depressive" reactions when they encountered later stressful situations, although there were no behavioral changes evident in stress-free social environments. Similarly, Spencer-Booth and Hinde (1971) found that early separations made monkeys less able to cope with short-term stress later. The finding in humans that multiple hospital admissions increase the risk of later psychological disturbance, although one admission does not, may reflect a similar mechanism. Similarly, Lutkenhaus and colleagues (1985) found that insecure attachment in infancy was associated with an altered response at age 3 years to task failure; Zahn-Waxler, Cummings, McKnew, and Radke-Yarrow (1984) found that young children reared by depressed parents showed an increased rate of distress following conflict; and Quinton and Rutter (in press) found that an institutional rearing was associated with a greater vulnerability to psychosocial adversity in adult life. The mechanism of sensitization (and its counterpart *steeling,* i.e., a reduced susceptibility as a result of early experiences) warrants further investigation in the study of continuities from childhood.

Environmental Linkages

A major factor in the creation of behavioral continuities is provided by the linkages between environments. There are numerous examples of the ways in which one psychosocial hazard leads to a chain of other adversities. For example, parental loss may lead to a lack of affectionate parental care (Brown et al., 1986); parental mental disorder is associated with impaired parenting, family discord, and family disruption (Rutter, 1987); and parenting breakdown may be followed by an institutional upbringing and a disrupted or discordant family setting on leaving the institution in late adolescence (Quinton & Rutter, 1986). The linkages are often multiple, creating chains of effects that are easily overlooked. Thus lack of parental care is associated with an increased risk of adolescent pregnancy, which in turn makes it less likely that the girl will be upwardly socially mobile; then the consequent social disadvantage in adult life may increase the risk of depression (Brown et al., 1986). At any one point, a person's behavior may be most strongly influenced by the current environment, but the very fact that the individual is in that particular environment will have been influenced by the person's earlier behavior and experiences.

Person–Environment Transactions

A child's behavioral response to stress situations is likely to have reciprocal effects on other people's reactions to him or her and hence an effect on the likelihood that the behavior will persist or change. An example was provided in the ways in which the birth of a second child led to changes in the behavior of the firstborn, which went on to influence patterns of family interaction (Dunn & Kendrick, 1982). Toddlers' responses to severely depressed parents may induce further negative experiences in that they tend to act aggressively with both peers and unfamiliar adults (Zahn-Waxler et al., 1984). Similarly, Main and George (1985) reported that physically abused toddlers differed from controls with respect to their tendency to respond to the distress of peers with physical attacks, fear, or anger. Similarly, Crittenden (1985) found that abused toddlers responded to their mothers with patterns of angry difficult behavior that might be expected to maintain their mothers' maltreating style. Yarrow and Klein (1980) suggested that their finding that there was more tension associated with the adoption of older children reflected the effects on the adoptive parents of the children's difficult behavior stemming from experiences in foster care. Dodge (1980; Dodge, Murphy, & Buchsbaum, 1984) found that socially deviant children were less accurate than normal children in identifying prosocial intentions and more liable to make hostile attributions, tendencies likely to increase the deviant children's social difficulties and hence perpetuate their problem behavior.

The above examples refer to negative effects on patterns of interaction. The effects of good-quality preschool education were noted earlier in terms of their positive effects on interaction, effects that served to create chain reactions that predisposed to persistence of benefits. Of course, the same event can serve to produce different responses that have contrasting consequences for later patterns of interaction in different children. For example, Moskowitz (1985) in her follow-up of Freud and Dann's concentration camp children noted how one girl's clinging, whiny behavior alienated her caregivers and led to a negative escalating cycle of frustration, whereas another child's sensitivity elicited sympathy and support.

CONCLUSIONS

The issue of continuities and discontinuities from infancy remains an important one. The evidence runs strongly counter to views that early experiences irrevocably change personality development, but, equally, findings show that in some circumstances indirect effects may be quite long-lasting. Much has still to be learned on what happens to the organism as a result of experiences, and hence much uncertainty remains about the processes involved in continuity and discontinuity. However, it is apparent that acute stressors and chronic adversities can have an important impact on psychological functioning. The experiences impinge on an active, not a passive, organism, and the effects are influenced by how children appraise the situation and respond to the adaptations involved. The very marked individual differences in response have their origins in constitutional variations in susceptibility, in vulnerabilities and resilience created in the social context, and in the particular characteristics of person–environment interactions. Experiences can change the organism, but so do people create their own environments. It is this two-way interaction that results in the complex pattern of continuities and discontinuities that is found. Continuities stem from a multitude of links over time; because each link is incomplete, subject to marked individual variation, and open to modification, there are numerous opportunities for discontinuities to arise. These may serve both to break chains of disadvantage and adversity and to dissipate the benefits of positive experiences.

REFERENCES

Adams, K. M., Brown, G. G., & Grant, I. (1985). Analysis of covariance as a remedy for demographic mismatch of research subject groups: Some sobering simulations. *Journal of Clinical & Experimental Neuropsychology, 7,* 445–462.

Ainsworth, M. D. (1967). *Infancy in Uganda: Infant care and the growth of attachment.* Baltimore: Johns Hopkins Press.

Andrews, G., & Tennant, C. (1978). Life events and psychiatric illness. *Psychological Medicine, 8,* 545–549.

Asher, S. R. (1983). Social competence and peer status: Recent advances and future directions. *Child Development, 54,* 1427–1434.

Baldwin, A. L. (1968). *Theories of child development.* New York: Wiley.

Bates, J. E., Maslin, C. A., & Frankel, K. A. (1985). Attachment security, mother–child interaction and temperament as predictors of behavior-problem ratings at age three years. In I. Bretherton & E. Waters (Eds.), Growing points of attachment theory and research. *Monographs of the Society for Research in Child Development, 50* (1–2, Serial No. 209).

Belsky, J., Gilstrap, B., & Rovine, M. (1984). The Pennsylvania Infant and Family Development Project, I: Stability and change in mother:infant and father:infant interaction in a family setting at one, three and nine months. *Child Development, 55,* 692–705.

Belsky, J., Rovine, M., & Taylor, D. G. (1984). The Pennsylvania Infant and Family Development Project, III: The origins of individual differences in infant:mother attachment:maternal and infant contributions. *Child Development, 55,* 718–728.

Belsky J., Taylor, D. G., & Rovine, M. (1984). The Pennsylvania Infant and Family Development Project, II: The development of reciprocal interactions in the mother:infant dyad. *Child Development, 55,* 706–717.

Berrueta-Clement, J. R., Schweinhart, L. J., Barnett, W. S., Epstein, A. S., & Weikart, D. P. (1984). *Changed lives: The effects of the Perry Preschool Program on youths through age 19.* Ypsilanti, MI: High Scope Press.

Black, D., & Urbanowicz, M. A. (1985). Bereaved children—Family intervention. In J. E.

Stevenson (Ed.), *Recent research in developmental psychopathology.* Oxford: Pergamon.

Block, J. H. (1983). Differential premises arising from differential socialization of the sexes: Some conjectures. *Child Development, 54* (6), 1335–1354.

Bloom, B. S. (1964). *Stability and change in human characteristics.* New York: Wiley.

Bluestone, C. D., Klein, J. O., Paradise, J. L., et al. (1983). Workshop on effects of otitis media on the child. *Pediatrics, 71,* 639–652.

Bohman, M., & Sigvardsson, S. A. (1980). A prospective, longitudinal study of children registered for adoption. A 15 year follow-up. *Acta Psychiatrica Scandinavica, 61,* 339–355.

Bowlby, J. (1951). *Mental care and mental health.* Geneva: W.H.O.

Bowlby, J. (1969). *Attachment and loss: Vol. I. Attachment.* London: Hogarth.

Bowlby, J. (1973). *Attachment and loss: Vol. II. Separation anxiety and anger.* London: Hogarth.

Bowlby, J. (1980). *Attachment and loss: Vol. III. Loss, sadness and depression.* New York: Basic.

Bradley, R. H., & Caldwell, B. M. (1984). The relation of infants' home environment to achievement test performance in first grade: A follow up study. *Child Development, 55,* 803–809.

Bretherton, I. (1985). Attachment theory: Retrospect and prospect. In I. Bretherton & E. Waters (Eds.), Growing points of attachment theory and research. *Monographs of the Society for Research in Child Development, 50* (1–2, Serial No. 209).

Bretherton, I., & Waters, E. (Eds.). (1985). Growing points of attachment theory and research. *Monographs of the Society for Research in Child Development, 50* (1–2, Serial No. 209).

Broman, S. H., Nichols, P. L., & Kennedy, W. A. (1975). *Preschool IQ: Prenatal and early developmental correlates.* Hillsdale, NJ: Erlbaum.

Brown, G. W., Harris, T. O., & Bifulco, A. (1986). The long-term effects of early loss of parent. In M. Rutter, C. E. Izard, & P. B. Read (Eds.), *Depression in young people.* New York: Guilford.

Brunk, M. A., & Henggeler, S. W. (1984). Child influences on adult controls. An experimental investigation. *Developmental Psychology, 20* (6), 1074–1081.

Campbell, S. B., Breaus, A. M., Ewing, L. J., & Szumowski, E. K. (1984). A one-year follow-up study of parent-referred hyperactive preschool children. *Journal of the American Academy of Child Psychiatry, 23* (3), 243–249.

Chess, S., & Thomas, A. (1984). *Origins and evolution of behavior disorders.* New York: Brunner/Mazel.

Cicchetti, D., & Schneider-Rosen, K. (1986). In M. Rutter, C. E. Izard, & P. B. Read (Eds.), *Depression in young people.* New York: Guilford.

Clarke, A. M. (1984). Early experience and cognitive development. *Review of Research in Education, 11,* 125–160.

Clarke, A. M., & Clarke, A. D. B. (1976). *Early experience: Myth and evidence.* London: Open Books.

Clarke-Stewart, K. A. (1973). Interactions between mothers and their young children: Characteristics and consequences. *Monographs of the Society for Research in Child Development, 38* (153).

Clarke-Stewart, K. A., & Fein, G. G. (1983). Early childhood programs. In M. M. Haith & J. J. Campos (Eds.), *Infancy and developmental psychobiology: Vol. 2. Mussen's handbook of child psychology (4th ed).* New York: Wiley.

Cohn, J. F., & Tronick, E. Z. (1983). Three-month old infants' reaction to simulated maternal depression. *Child Development, 54,* 185–193.

Coll, G. C., Kagan, J., & Reznick, J. S. (1984). Behavioral inhibition in young children. *Child Development, 55,* 1005–1019.

Condry, J. C., & Ross, D. F. (1985). Sex and aggression: The influence of gender label on the perception of aggression in children. *Child Development, 56,* 225–233.

Costa, P. T., McCrae, R. R., & Arenberg, D. (1980). Enduring dispositions in adult males. *Journal of Personality & Social Psychology, 38,* 793–800.

Cravioto, J., & Arrieta, R. (1983). Malnutrition in childhood. In M. Rutter (Ed.), *Developmental neuropsychiatry.* New York: Guilford.

Crittenden, P. M. (1985). Maltreated infants: Vulnerability and resilience. *Journal of Child Psychology & Psychiatry, 26* (1), 85–96.

Crockenberg, S. B. (1981). Infant irritability, mother responsiveness, and social support inferences on the security of infant–mother attachment. *Child Development, 52,* 857–865.

Crowe, R. R. (1974). An adoption study of antisocial personality. *Archives of General Psychiatry, 31,* 785–791.

Cummings, E. M., Zahn-Waxler, C., & Radke-Yarrow, M. (1981). Young children's responses to expressions of anger and affection by others in the family. *Child Development, 52,* 1274–1282.

Cummings, E. M., Zahn-Waxler, C., & Radke-Yarrow, M. (1984). Developmental changes in children's reactions to anger in the home. *Journal of Child Psychology & Psychiatry, 25,* 63–74.

Cytryn, L., McKnew, D. H., Zahn-Waxler, C., & Gershon, E. S. (1986). Developmental issues in risk research: The offspring of affectively ill parents. In M. Rutter, C. E., Izard, & P. B. Read (Eds.), *Depression in young people.* New York: Guilford.

Dare. C. (1985). Psychoanalytic theories of development. In M. Rutter & L. Hersov (Eds.), *Child and adolescent psychiatry: Modern approaches* (2nd ed.). Oxford: Blackwell Scientific.

Dennis, W. (1973). *Children of the creche.* New York: Appleton-Century-Crofts.

Dietrich, K. N., Krafft, K. M., Pearson, D. T., Harris, L. C., Bornschein, R. L., Hammond, P. B., & Succop, P. A. (1985). Contributions of social and developmental factors to lead exposure during the first year of life. *Pediatrics, 75* (6), 1114–1119.

Dodge, K. A. (1980). Social cognition and children's aggressive behavior. *Child Development, 51,* 162–172.

Dodge, K. A., Murphy, R. R., & Buchsbaum. K. (1984). The assessment of intention—Cue detection skills in children. Implications for developmental psychopathology. *Child Development, 55,* 163–173.

Dontas, C., Maratos, O., Fafoulis, M., & Karangelis, A. (1985). Early social development in institutionally reared Greek infants: Attachment and peer interaction. In I. Bretherton & E. Waters (Eds.), Growing points of attachment theory and research. *Monographs of the Society for Research in Child Development, 50* (1–2, Serial No. 209).

Douglas, J. W. B. (1975). Early hospital admissions and later disturbances of behaviour and learning. *Developmental Medicine & Child Neurology, 17,* 456–480.

Dunn, J., & Kendrick, C. (1982). *Siblings, love, envy and understanding.* London: Grant McIntyre.

Dunn, J., & Munn, P. (1985). Becoming a family member: Family conflict and the development of social understanding in the second year. *Child Development, 56,* 480–492.

Dunn, J., & Plomin, R. (1986). *Determinants of maternal behaviour towards three-year-old siblings.* Manuscript submitted for publication.

Dweck, C. S., & Elliott, E. S. (1983). Achievement motivation. In E. M. Hetherington (Ed.), *Socialization, personality and social development: Vol. 4. Mussen's handbook of child psychology (4th ed.)*. New York: Wiley.

Egeland, B., & Farber, E. A. (1984). Infant–mother attachment: Factors related to its development and changes over time. *Child Development, 55,* 753–777.

Elder, G. H. (1974). *Children of the Great Depression.* Chicago: University of Chicago Press.

Elder, G. H. (1979). Historical change in life patterns and personality. In P. B. Baltes & O. G. Brim (Eds.), *Life span development and behavior* (Vol. 2). New York: Academic.

Emmerich, W. (1964). Continuity and stability in early social development. *Child Development, 35,* 311–332.

Emmerich, W. (1968). Personality development and concepts of structure. *Child Development, 39,* 671–690.

Erickson, M. F., Sroufe, L. A., & Egeland, B. (1985). The relationship between quality of attachment and behavior problems in preschool in a high-risk sample. In I. Bretherton & E. Waters (Eds.), Growing points of attachment theory and research. *Monographs of the Society for Research in Child Development, 50* (1–2, Serial No. 209).

Everitt, B. S., & Smith, A. M. R. (1979). Interactions in contingency tables: A brief discussion of alternative definitions. *Psychological Medicine, 9,* 581–584.

Eysenck, H. J. (1953). *The structure of human personality.* New York: Wiley.

Eysenck, H. J. (1967). *The biological basis of personality.* Springfield, Il: Chas. C. Thomas.

Eysenck, M. W., & Eysenck, H. J. (1980). Mischel and the concept of personality. *British Journal of Psychology, 71,* 191–204.

Fagot, B. I., Hagam, R., Leinbach, M. D., & Kronsberg, S. (1985). Differential reactions to assertive and communicative acts of toddler boys and girls. *Child Development, 56,* 1499–1505.

Ferguson, B. F. (1979). Preparing young children for hospitalization. *Pediatrics, 64,* 656–664.

Fergusson, D. M., & Horwood, L. J. (in press). Factors related to the trait components of maternal and teacher ratings of childhood conduct disorder. *Journal of Child Psychology & Psychiatry.*

Fischer, M., Rolf, J. E., Hasazi, J. E., & Cummings, L. (1984). Follow-up of a preschool epidemiological sample: Cross age continuities and predictions of later adjustment with internalizing and externalizing dimensions of behavior. *Child Development, 55,* 137–150.

Flavell, J. H. (1982). Structures, stages, and sequences in cognitive development. In W. A. Collins (Ed.), The concept of development. *Minnesota Symposia on Child Psychiatry* (Vol. 15). Hillsdale, NJ: Erlbaum.

Glasberg, R., & Abond, F. (1982). Keeping one's distance from sadness: Children's self reports of emotional experience. *Developmental Psychology, 18,* 287–293.

Goldberg, S. (1983). Parent–infant bonding: Another look. *Child Development, 54,* 1355–1382.

Gottfried, A. W. (Ed.). (1984). *Home environment and early cognitive development: Longitudinal research.* Orlando, FL: Academic.

Greenough, W. T., & Schwark, H. D. (1983). Age related aspects of experience effects upon brain structure. In R. N. Emde & R. J. Harmon (Eds.), *Continuities and discontinuities in development.* New York: Plenum.

Grossmann, K., Grossmann, K. E., Spangler, G., Suess, G., & Unzner, L. (1985). Maternal sensitivity and newborns' orientation responses as related to quality of attachment in Northern Germany. In I. Bretherton & E. Waters (Eds.), Growing points of attachment theory and research. *Monographs of the Society for Research in Child Development, 50* (1–2, Serial No. 209).

Grossmann, K. E., & Grossmann, K. (1981). Parent–infant attachment relationships in Bielefeld. In K. Immelmann, G. Barlow, L. Petrovich, & M. Main (Eds.), *Behavioral development: The Bielefeld Interdisciplinary Project*. New York: Cambridge University Press.

Gunnar-Vongnechten, M. R. (1978). Changing a frightening toy into a pleasant toy by allowing the infant to control its actions. *Developmental Psychology, 14,* 157–162.

Hall, D. M. B., & Hill, P. (1986). When does secretory otitis media affect language development? *Archives of Disease in Childhood, 61,* 42–47.

Harter, S. (1983). Developmental perspectives on self-system. In E. M. Hetherington (Ed.), *Socialization, personality, and social development: Vol. 4. Handbook of child psychology* (4th ed.). New York: Wiley.

Hauser, S. T. (1976). Loevinger's model and measure of ego development: A critical review. *Psychological Bulletin, 83,* 928–955.

Hay, D. F. (1985). Learning to form relationships in infancy: Parallel attainments with parents and peers. *Developmental Review, 5,* 122–161.

Hay, D. F., Murray, P., Cecire, S., & Nash, A. (1985). Social learning of social behavior in early life. *Child Development, 56,* 43–57.

Hertzog, C., & Rovine, M. (1985). Repeated measures analysis of variance in developmental research: Selected issues. *Child Development, 56* (4), 787–809.

Hinde, R. A. (1982). *Ethology.* London: Fontana.

Hinde, R. A., & Bateson, P. (1985). Discontinuities versus continuities in behavioural development and the neglect of process. *International Journal of Behavioural Development, 7,* 129–143.

Hinde, R. A., & Dennis, A. (1986). Categorizing individuals: An alternative to linear analysis. *International Journal of Behavioural Development, 9,* 105–119.

Hinde, R. A., Easton, D. F., Meller, R. E., & Tamplin, A. (1983). Nature and determinants of preschoolers' differential behaviour to adults and peers. *British Journal of Developmental Psychology, 1,* 3–19.

Hinde, R. A., & Tamplin, A. (1983). Relations between mother–child interaction and behaviour in preschool. *British Journal of Developmental Psychology, 1,* 231–257.

Hodges, J., & Tizard, B. (in press,a). IQ and behavioural adjustment of ex-institutional adolescents. *Journal of Child Psychology & Psychiatry.*

Hodges, J., & Tizard, B. (in press,b). The social and family relationships of ex-institutional adolescents. *Journal of Child Psychology & Psychiatry.*

Howlin, P., & Rutter, M. (in press). The consequence of language delay for other aspects of development. In W. Yule, & M. Rutter, (Eds.), *Language development and disorder.* Oxford: MacKeith/Blackwell.

Hubert, N. C., Wachs, T. D., Peters-Martin, P., & Gandour, M. J. (1982). The study of early temperament: Measurement and conceptual issues. *Child Development, 53,* 571–600.

Izard, C. (1978). On the ontogenesis of emotions and emotion-cognitive relationships in infancy. In M. Lewis & L. A. Rosenblum (Eds.), *The Development of Affect.* New York: Plenum.

Jenkins, S., Owen, C., Bax, M., & Hart, H. (1984). Continuities of common behaviour problems in pre-school children. *Journal of Child Psychology & Psychiatry, 25,* 75–89.

Jahoda, G. (1954). A note of Ashanti names and their relationship to personality. *British Journal of Psychology, 45,* 192–195.

Kagan, J. (1979). A cross-cultural study of cognitive development. *Monographs of the Society for Research in Child Development, 44* (5, Series No. 180).

Kagan, J. (1980). Perspectives on continuity. In O. Brim & J. Kagan (Eds.), *Constancy and change in human development.* Cambridge, MA: Harvard University Press.

Kagan, J. (1981). *The second year: The emergence of self-awareness*. Cambridge, MA: Harvard University Press.

Kagan, J. (1983). The emergence of self. *Journal of Child Psychology & Psychiatry, 23,* 363–382.

Kagan, J. (1984). *The nature of the child*. New York: Basic.

Kagan, J., & Klein, R. E. (1973). Cross-cultural perspectives on early development. *American Psychologist, 28,* 947–961.

Kagan, J., Reznick, J. S., Clarke, C., Snidman, N., & Coll, C. G. (1984). Behavioral inhibition to the unfamiliar. *Child Development, 55* (6), 2212–2225.

Klaus, M. H., & Kennell, J. H. (1976). *Maternal–infant bonding: The impact of early separation or loss on family development*. St. Louis, MO: C. V. Mosby.

Klein, N., Hack, M., Gallagher, J., & Fanaroff, A. A. (1985). Preschool performance of children with normal intelligence who were very low-birth-rate infants. *Pediatrics, 75* (3), 531–537.

Kline, P. (1972). *Fact and fantasy in Freudian theory*. London: Methuen.

Kohn, M. (1977). *Social competence, symptoms and underachievement in childhood: A longitudinal perspective*. Washington DC: Winston.

Kopp, C. B. (1982). Antecedents of self organization: A developmental perspective. *Developmental Psychology, 18,* 199–214.

Korner, A. F., Zeanah, C. H., Linden, J., Berkowitz, R. I., Kraemer, H. C., & Agras, W. S. (1985). The relation between neonatal and later activity and temperament. *Child Development, 56,* 38–42.

LaFreniere, P. J., & Sroufe, L. A. (1985). Profiles of peer competence in the preschool: Interrelations between measures, influences of social ecology and relation to attachment history. *Developmental Psychology, 24,* 56–69.

Lamb, M. E. (1977). Father–infant and mother–infant interaction in the first year of life. *Child Development, 48,* 167–181.

Lamb, M. E., Brown, A. L., & Rogoff, B. (Eds.). (1984). *Advances in developmental psychology* (Vol. 3). Hillsdale, NJ: Erlbaum.

Lazar, I., & Darlington, R. B. (1982). Lasting effects of early education. *Monographs of the Society for Research in Child Development, 47* (Serial No. 195).

Lee, C. L., & Bates, J. E. (1985). Mother–child interaction at age two years and perceived difficult temperament. *Child Development, 56,* 1314–1325.

Lerner, J. A., Inui, T. S., Trupin, E. W., & Douglas, E. (1985). Preschool behavior can predict future psychiatric disorders. *Journal of the American Academy of Child Psychiatry, 24,* 42–48.

Lewis, M., Feiring, C., McGuffoy, C., & Jaskir, J. (1984). Predicting psychopathology in six-year-olds from early social relations. *Child Development, 55,* 123–136.

Lipsitt, L. P. (1983). Stress in infancy. In N. Garmezy & M. Rutter (Eds.), *Stress, coping and development in children*. New York: McGraw-Hill.

Loevinger, J. (1976). *Ego development: Conceptions and theories*. San Francisco: Jossey-Bass.

Lütkenhaus, P., Grossmann, K. E., & Grossmann, K. (1985). Infant–mother attachment at twelve months and style of interaction with a stranger at age of three years. *Child Development, 56,* 1535–1542.

Maccoby, E. E., Snow, M. E., & Jacklin, C. N., (1984). Children's dispositions and mother–child interaction at 12 and 18 months: A short term longitudinal study. *Developmental Psychology, 20,* 459–472.

Magnusson, D., Stattin, H., & Allen, V. L. (1986). Differential maturation amongst girls and its relation to social adjustment: A longitudinal perspective. In D. Featherman & R. M. Lerner (Eds.), *Life span development* (Vol. 7). New York: Academic.

Main, M., & George, C. (1985). Responses of abused and disadvantaged toddlers to distress in age mates: A study in the day care setting. *Developmental Psychology, 21* (3), 407–412.

Main, M., Kaplan, N., & Cassidy, J. (1985). Security in infancy, childhood and adulthood. In I. Bretherton & E. Waters (Eds.), Growing points of attachment theory and research. *Monographs of the Society for Research in Child Development, 50* (1–2, Serial No. 209).

Main, M. B., & Weston, D. R. (1981). Security of attachment to mother and father: Related to conflict behavior and the readiness to establish new relationships. *Child Development, 52,* 932–940.

Matheny, A. P., Jr. (1984). Twin similarity in the developmental transformations of infant temperament as measured in a multi-method longitudinal study. *Acta Geneticae Medicae Gemellologiae, 33,* 181–189.

McCall, R. B. (1979). The development of intellectual functioning in infancy and the prediction of late I.Q. In J. D. Osofsky (Ed.), *Handbook of infant development.* New York: Wiley.

McCall, R. B. (1981). Nature–nurture and the two realms of development: A proposed integration with respect to mental development. *Child Development, 52,* 1–12.

Milar, C. B., Schroeder, S. R., Mushak, P., Dolcourt, J. L., & Grant, L. D. (1980). Contributions of the caregiving environment to increase lead burden of children. *American Journal of Mental Deficiency, 84,* 339–344.

Miyake, K., Chen, S., & Campos, J. J. (1985). Infant temperament, mothers' mode of interaction and attachment in Japan: An interim report. In I. Bretherton & E. Waters (Eds.), Growing points of attachment research and development. *Monographs of the Society for Research in Child Development, 50* (1–2, Serial No. 209).

Moskovitz, S. (1985). Longitudinal follow-up of child survivors of the holocaust. *Journal of the American Academy of Child Psychiatry, 24* (4), 401–407.

Moss, H. A., & Susman, E. J. (1980). Longitudinal study of personality development. In O. G. Brim & J. Kagan (Eds.), *Constancy and change in human development.* Cambridge, MA: Havard University Press.

Olweus, D. (1979). Stability of aggressive reaction patterns in males: A review. *Psychological Bulletin, 86,* 852–875.

Paradise, J. L. (1981). Otitis media during early life: How hazardous to development? A critical review of the evidence. *Pediatrics, 65,* 669–673.

Parnas, J., Teasdale, T. W., & Schulsinger, H. (1985). Institutional rearing and diagnostic outcome in children of schizophrenic mothers. *Archives of General Psychiatry, 42,* 762–769.

Patterson, G. R. (1982). *Coercive faculty process.* Eugene, OR: Castalia.

Pettit, G. S. & Bates, J. E. (1984). Continuity of individual differences in the mother–infant relationship from six to thirteen months. *Child Development, 55,* 729–739.

Plomin, R. (1983). Childhood temperament. In B. B. Lahey & A. E. Kazdin (Eds.), *Advances in clinical child psychology* (Vol. 6). New York: Plenum.

Porter, R., & Collins, G. (Eds.) (1982). Temperamental differences in infants and young children. *Ciba Foundation Symposium No. 89.* London: Pitman.

Puckering, C., & Rutter, M. (in press). Environmental influences on language development. In W. Yule, & M. Rutter, (Eds.), *Language development and disorders.* Oxford: Mac-Keith Press/Blackwell.

Quinton, D., & Rutter, M. (1976). Early hospital admissions and later disturbances of Behaviour: An attempted replication of Douglas' findings: *Developmental Medicine and Child Neurology, 18,* 447–459.

Quinton, D., & Rutter, M. (in press). *Parenting breakdown: Making and breaking intergenerational cycles.* Aldershot, Hampshire, England: Gower.

Radke-Yarrow, M., Cummings, E. M., Kuczynski, L., & Chapman, M. (1985). Patterns of attachment in two and three year olds in normal families and families with parental depression. *Child Development, 56,* 884–893.

Ramey, C. T., Yeates, K. O., & Short, E. J. (1984). The plasticity of intellectual development: Insights from preventive intervention. *Child Development, 55* (5), 1913–1925.

Richman, N., Stevenson, J., & Graham, P. J. (1982). *Pre-school to school: A behavioral study.* London: Academic.

Ricks, M. H. (1985). The social transmission of parental behavior: Attachment across generations. In I. Bretherton & E. Waters (Eds.), Growing points of attachment theory and research. *Monographs of the Society for Research in Child Development, 50* (1–2, Serial No. 209).

Robertson, J., & Robertson, J. (1971). Young children in brief separation: A fresh look. *Psychoanalytic Study of the Child, 26,* 264–315.

Robins, L. N., Davis, D. H., & Wish, E. (1977). Detecting predictors of rare events: Demographic family and personal deviance as predictors of stages in the progression towards narcotic addiction. In J. S. Strauss, B. Haroutun, M. Babigian, & Merrill Roff (Eds.), *The origins and course of psychopathology.* New York: Plenum.

Rogosa, D. (1980). A critique of cross-lagged correlation. *Psychological Bulletin, 88,* 245–258.

Rutter, M. (1966). Children of sick parents: An environmental and psychiatric study. *Institute of Psychiatry Maudsley Monographs No. 16.* London: Oxford University Press.

Rutter, M. (1970). Psychological development: Predictions from infancy. *Journal of Child Psychology & Psychiatry, 11,* 49–62.

Rutter, M. (1971). Parent–child separation: Psychological effects on the children. *Journal of Child Psychology & Psychiatry, 12,* 233–260.

Rutter, M. (1974). Epidemiological strategies and psychiatric concepts in research on the vulnerable child. In E. Anthony & C. Koupernik (Eds.), *The child in his family: Children at psychiatric risk* (Vol. 3). New York: Wiley.

Rutter, M. (1980). Psychosexual development. In M. Rutter (Ed.), *Scientific foundations of developmental psychiatry.* London: Heinemann Medical.

Rutter, M. (1981a). *Maternal deprivation reassessed* (2nd Edition). Harmondsworth, Middlesex, England: Penguin.

Rutter, M. (1981b). Stress, coping and development: Some issues and some questions. *Journal of Child Psychology & Psychiatry, 22,* 323–356.

Rutter, M. (1982a). Temperament: Concepts, issues and problems. In R. Porter & G. M. Collins (Eds.), *Temperamental differences in infants and young children. Ciba Foundation Symposium No 89.* London: Pitman.

Rutter, M. (1982b). Developmental neuropsychiatry: Concepts, issues and prospects. *Journal of Clinical Neuropsychology, 4,* 91–115.

Rutter, M. (1983). Statistical and personal interactions: Facets and perspectives. In D. Magnusson & V. Allen (Eds.), *Human development: An interactional perspective.* New York: Academic.

Rutter, M. (1984a). Psychopathology and development: I. Childhood antecedents of adult psychiatric disorder. *Australian & New Zealand Journal of Psychiatry, 18,* 225–234.

Rutter, M. (1984b). Psychopathology and development: II. Childhood experiences and personality development. *Australian & New Zealand Journal of Psychiatry, 18,* 314–327.

Rutter, M. (1985a). Family and school influences on cognitive development. *Journal of Child Psychology & Psychiatry, 26,* 683–704.

Rutter, M. (1985b). Resilience in the face of adversity: Protective factors and resistance to psychiatric disorder. *British Journal of Psychiatry, 147,* 598–611.

Rutter, M. (1985c). Family and school influences on behavioural development. *Journal of Child Psychology & Psychiatry, 26,* 349–368.

Rutter, M. (1986a). The developmental psychopathology of depression: Issues and perspectives. In M. Rutter, C. E. Izard, & P. B. Read (Eds.), *Depression in young people.* New York: Guilford.

Rutter, M. (1986b). Meyerian psychobiology, personality development and the role of life experiences. *American Journal of Psychiatry, 143,* 1077–1087.

Rutter, M. (in press,a). Parental mental disorder as a psychiatric risk factor. In R. E. Hales & A. J. Frances (Eds.), *American Psychiatric Association's Annual Review* (Vol. 6). Washington: APA.

Rutter, M. (in press,b). Intergenerational continuities and discontinuities in serious parenting difficulties. In D. Cicchetti & V. Carlson (Eds.), *Research on the consequences of child maltreatment.* New York: Cambridge University Press.

Rutter, M., Chadwick, O., & Shaffer, D. (1983). Head injury. In M. Rutter (Ed.), *Developmental neuropsychiatry.* New York: Guilford Press.

Rutter, M., & Garmezy, N. (1983). *Stress, coping and development in children.* New York: McGraw-Hill.

Rutter, M., & Giller, H. (1983). *Juvenile delinquency: trends and perspectives.* New York: Guilford.

Rutter, M., & Madge, N. (1976). *Cycles of disadvantage.* London: Heinemann.

Rutter, M., & Quinton, D. (1984). Parental psychiatric disorder: Effects on children. *Psychological Medicine, 14,* 853–880.

Sagi, A., Lamb, M. E., Lewkowicz, K. S., Shoham, R., Dvir, R., & Estes, D. (1985). Security of infant–mother, –father, and metalpelet attachments among kibbutz-reared Israeli children. In I. Bretherton & E. Waters (Eds.), Growing points of attachment theory and research. *Monographs of the Society for Research in Child Development, 50* (1–2, Serial No. 209).

Salk, L., Lipsitt, L. P., Sturner, W. Q., Reilly, B. M., & Levat, R. H. (1985). Relationship of maternal and perinatal conditions to eventual adolescent suicide. *The Lancet,* pp. 624–627.

Sameroff, A. J., & Chandler, M .J. (1975). Reproductive risk and the continuum of caretaking casualty. In F. D. Horowitz (Ed.), *A review of child development research* (Vol. 4). Chicago: University of Chicago Press.

Scarr, S., & McCartney, K. (1983). How people make their own environments: A theory of genotype-environmental effects. *Child Development, 54,* 424–435.

Schaffer, H. R., & Liddell, C. (1984). Adult–child interaction under dyadic and polyadic conditions. *British Journal of Developmental Psychology, 2,* 33–42.

Siegel, L. S., Cunningham, C. E., & van der Spuy, H. I. J. (1985). Interactions of language-delayed and normal preschool boys with their peers. *Journal of Child Psychology & Psychiatry, 26,* 77–84.

Silva, P. A., Stewart, I., Kirkland, C., & Simpson, A. (1985). How impaired are children who experience persistent bilateral otitis media with effusion? In Duane, D. D. and Leong, C. K. (Eds.), *International Study Group on Special Educational Needs Seminar (Mayho),* New York: Plenum.

Simpson, A. E., & Stevenson-Hinde, J. (1985). Temperamental characteristics of three- to four-year-old boys and girls and child–family interactions. *Journal of Child Psychology & Psychiatry, 26,* 43–53.

Singer, L. M., Brodzinsky, D. M., Ramsay, D., Steir, M., & Waters, E. (1985). Mother-infant attachment in adoptive families. *Child Development, 56,* 1543–1551.

Skuse, D. (1984). Extreme deprivation in early childhood: I. Diverse outcomes for three siblings from an extraordinary family. II. Theoretical issues and a comparative review. *Journal of Child Psychology & Psychiatry, 26,* 523–541, 543–572.

Smith, C., & Lloyd, B. (1978). Maternal behavior and perceived sex of infant: Revisited. *Child Development, 40,* 1263–1265.

Sorce, J. F., Emde, R. N., Campos, J., & Klinnert, M. D. (1985). Maternal emotional signaling: Its effects on the visual cliff behavior of 1-year-olds. *Developmental Psychology, 21,* 195–200.

Speece, M. W., & Brent, S. B. (1984). Children's understanding of death: A review of three components of a death concept. *Child Development, 55,* 1671–1686.

Spencer-Booth, Y., & Hinde, R. A. (1971). Effects of brief separations from mothers during infancy on behaviour of rhesus monkeys 6–24 months later. *Journal of Child Psychology & Psychiatry, 12,* 157–172.

Sroufe, L. A. (1985). Attachment classification from the perspective of infant–caregiver relationships and infant temperament. *Child Development, 56,* 1–14.

Sroufe, L. A., Fox, N. E., & Pancake, V. R. (1983). Attachment and dependency in developmental perspective. *Child Development, 54,* 1615–1627.

Sroufe, L. A., Jacobvitz, D., Mangelsdorf. S., DeAngelo, E., & Ward, M. J. (1985). Generational boundary dissolution between mothers and their preschool children: A relationship systems approach. *Child Development, 56,* 317–325.

Stein, Z., & Susser, M. (1985). Effects of early nutrition on neurological and mental competence in human beings. *Psychological Medicine, 15,* 717–726.

Stevenson, J., Richman, N., & Graham, P. (1985). Behaviour problems and language abilities at three years and behavioural deviance at eight years. *Journal of Child Psychology & Psychiatry, 26* (2), 215–230.

Stewart, A. (1983). Severe perinatal hazards. In M. Rutter (Ed.), *Developmental neuropsychiatry.* New York: Churchill Livingstone.

Stillwell, R., & Dunn, J. (1985). Continuities in sibling relationships: Patterns of aggression and friendliness. *Journal of Child Psychology & Psychiatry, 26* (4), 627–638.

Suomi, S. (1983). Models of depression in primates. *Psychological Medicine, 13,* 465–468.

Tennant, C., Bebbington, P., & Hurray, J. (1981). The role of life events in depressive illness: Is there a substantial causal relation? *Psychological Medicine, 11,* 379–389.

Thomas, A., & Chess, S. (1977). *Temperament and development.* New York: Brunner/Mazel.

Thomas, A., & Chess, S. (1980). *The dynamics of psychological development.* New York: Brunner/Mazel.

Thomas, A., Chess, S., Birch, H. G., Hertzig, M., & Korn, S. (1963). *Behavioural individuality in early childhood.* London: University of London Press.

Thompson, R. A., & Lamb, M. E. (1983). Security of attachment and stranger sociability in infancy. *Developmental Psychology, 19,* 184–191.

Thompson, R. A., Lamb, M., & Estes, D. (1982). Stability of infant-mother attachment and its relationship to changing life circumstances in an unselected middle class sample. *Child Development, 53,* 144–148.

Thompson, R. A., Lamb, M. E., & Estes, D. (1983). Harmonizing discordant notes: A reply to Waters. *Child Development, 54,* 521–524.

Tizard, B. (1977). *Adoption: A second chance.* London: Open Books.

Tizard, B., & Hodges, J. (1978). The effect of early institutional rearing on the development of eight-year-old children. *Journal of Child Psychology & Psychiatry, 19,* 99–118.

Tizard, B., & Rees, J. (1974). A comparison of the effects of adoption, restoration to the natural mother, and continued institutionalization on the cognitive development of four-year-old children. *Child Development, 45,* 92–99.

Tizard, J. (1974). Race and IQ: The limits of probability. *New Behaviour, 1,* 6–9.

Van Eerdewegh, M. M., Clayton, P. J., & Van Eerdewegh, P. (1985). The bereaved child: Variables influencing early psychopathology. *British Journal of Psychiatry, 147,* 188–194.

Vaughan, B. E., Deane, K. E., & Waters, E. (1985). The impact of out-of-home care on child–mother attachment quality: Another look at some enduring questions. In I. Bretherton & E. Waters (Eds.), Growing points of attachment theory and research. *Monographs of the Society for Research in Child Development, 50* (1–2, Serial No. 209).

Vohr, B. R., & Coll, C. T. G. (1985). Neurodevelopmental and school performance of very low-birth-weight infants: A seven-year longitudinal study. *Pediatrics, 76* (3), 345–350.

Wachs, T. D., & Gruen, G. E. (1982). *Early experience and human development.* New York: Plenum.

Waters, E. (1983). The stability of individual differences in infant attachment: Comments on the Thompson, Lamb, and Estes contribution. *Child Development, 54,* 516–520.

Waters, E., Hay, D., & Richters, J. (1986). Infant–parent attachment and the origins of prosocial and antisocial behavior. In D. Olweus, J. Block, & M. Radke-Yarrow (Eds.), *Development of antisocial and prosocial Behavior.* New York: Academic.

Wilson, R. S. (1977). Mental development in twins. In A. Oliverio (Ed.), *Genetics, environment and intelligence.* Amsterdam: North Holland.

Wilson, R. S. (1985). Risk and resilience in early mental development. *Developmental Psychology, 21,* 795–805.

Winick, M., Meyer, K. K., & Harris, R. C. (1975). Malnutrition and environmental enrichment by early adoption. *Science, 190,* 1173–1175.

Wohlwill, J. F. (1980). Cognitive development in childhood. In O. G. Brim & J. Kagan (Eds.), *Constancy and change in human development.* Cambridge, MA: Harvard University Press.

Wolkind, S. N. (1974). The components of affectionless psychopathology in institutionalized children. *Journal of Child Psychology & Psychiatry, 15,* 215–220.

Wolkind, S. N., & Rutter, M. (1985). Separation, loss and family relationships. In M. Rutter & L. Hersov (Eds.), *Child and adolescent psychiatry: Modern approaches* (2nd ed.). Oxford: Blackwell Scientific.

Woodhead, M. (1985). Pre-school education has long term effects: But can they be generalized? *Oxford Review of Education, 11* (2), 133–155.

Yarrow, L. J., & Klein, R. P. (1980). Environmental discontinuities associated with transition from foster to adoptive homes. *International Journal of Behavioral Development, 3,* 311–322.

Yeates, K. O., MacPhee, D., Campbell, F. A., & Ramey, C. T. (1983). Maternal IQ and home environment as determinants of early childhood intellectual competence: A developmental analysis. *Developmental Psychology, 19,* 731–739.

Zahn-Waxler, C., Cummings, E. M., McKnew, D. H., & Radke-Yarrow, M. (1984). Altruism, aggression and social interactions in young children with a manic-depressive parent. *Child Development, 55,* 112–122.

CHAPTER 27

Infant Mental Health: Clinical Dilemmas, the Expansion of Meaning, and Opportunities

ROBERT N. EMDE

The last decade has witnessed a burgeoning of clinical activity concerned with emotional problems in infancy. Not only have there been a host of edited volumes and books in this area (e.g., Call, Galenson, & Tyson 1983, 1985; Fraiberg, 1980; Greenspan, 1981; Howell, 1979; Kreisler, 1981; Lebovici, 1983; Provence, 1983), but a journal (*Infant Mental Health Journal*), a bulletin (*Zero to Three*), and three major organizations (National Center for Clinical Infant Programs, International Association for Infant Mental Health, and World Association for Infant Psychiatry and Allied Disciplines) have been established. Still, there is much that at first seems bewildering about this new field, which is usually designated *infant psychiatry*. A variety of mental health disciplines, not just psychiatrists, are working in infancy, and the term *psychiatry* seems problematic when we think of the uncertainties of diagnosis and the lack of predictability from early to later behavior. Our scientific views of the infant are changing, and it is acknowledged that much remains to be learned about emotional and behavioral problems. Compounding the state of uncertainty about infant psychiatry is current health care practice that often recommends the usefulness of a relationship-based developmental approach for clinical work instead of a more traditional approach based on individual diagnosis.

How can we understand recent vigorous clinical activity in the midst of such uncertainty? As the *Handbook of Infant Development* indicates, our knowledge of basic processes is growing, and there is now more of a rationale for turning our attention to clinical problems. But even more compelling is an awareness of the extent of clinical need. We now know what earlier was somehow hidden from us. Infants, who represent our "new beginning" and who are so inherently attractive to us, are also massively vulnerable. They are subject to widespread abuse and neglect, to "turning off," and may suffer a form of reactive depression. They expe-

This work was supported by NIMH project grant #MH22803 and Research Scientist Award #5 K02 MH36808. During the year this was written, the author was a fellow at the Center for Advanced Study in the Behavioral Sciences and received partial support from the John D. and Catherine T. MacArthur Foundation.

rience a variety of adaptive difficulties involving feeding, sleeping, and behavioral regulation. Adaptive difficulties are especially apt to afflict infants born with physical and mental handicaps and those born prematurely. Adaptive difficulties are also more likely to occur in infants born to parents with particular diseases, infants born into particular family constellations, and infants born into disadvantaged environments.

This chapter will develop a perspective in three areas. First, we will consider some dilemmas for infant psychiatry and infant mental health in the light of current developmental thinking. Second, we will consider some frontiers in a new infant psychology that may ultimately provide a better basis for clinical work. Third, we will consider a few developmentally informed guidelines that can serve to illustrate intervention opportunities. The reader may then come to understand why, although there is a shared sense of uncertainty among those diverse professionals who identify themselves with the area of infant psychiatry, there is also a shared optimism.

DILEMMAS FOR AN INFANT PSYCHIATRY

To the extent that *infant psychiatry* implies a separate domain under the heading of psychiatry, such a designation is apt to be misleading. Many disciplines are necessarily involved in understanding and helping with problems of infancy, and recent research and clinical work, by virtue of its being interdisciplinary, has led to a remarkably different view of infancy. The newborn infant is no longer seen as passive, as subject to the tyranny of basic drives, or as an undifferentiated creature waiting to be "shaped." Researchers and clinicians now view the infant as active and participatory in a structured and necessarily supportive social environment. Research has now documented the rich organization of adaptive behavior in early infancy, with more behavior "prepatterned" or programmed by our evolutionary heritage than we had realized. Perhaps even more important, current research seems to be moving toward understanding integrative processes in development. Newer methods are promising the clinician a view of changing relationships over time and a scientific understanding of complex regulatory structures in the face of major developmental transformations. We now appreciate that there are significant maturational events occurring after birth; the field of developmental and behavioral genetics indicates that new modes of understanding are on the horizon, as we contemplate genes turning on and off in the course of development and we think of genes being changed by new cellular substrates (see Plomin, Chapter 7, this volume). We know the infant participates actively in a changing social context. What seems certain is that our scientific views of infancy will continue to change. Hence an interdisciplinary clinical approach will continue to be needed for using new knowledge, treating problems, and promoting health in infancy.

Diagnosis

A poignant dilemma for infant psychiatry concerns diagnosis. The question is a straightforward one: Can we make a psychiatric diagnosis for problems in infancy? Very often it appears we cannot. Not only is our knowledge uncertain, but things are more likely to change with development in this period of life, and much that is problematic is related to environmental context. It is a matter of debate as to whether there can be psychopathology in the infant, and, for those working with clinical problems of infancy, a family assessment approach seems essential. Current diagnostic schemes, based on an individually oriented medical model (DSM-III and ICD-9), are generally not regarded as helpful for diagnosis in infancy. In these schemes, symptom clusters are individually based, and supplemental "axes" or dimensions are not developmental in nature. For infancy, any proposed modifications of such schemes would need to include an assessment of the parent–infant relationship, developmental lines relevant for infancy, and the family environment (Call, 1983; Emde, 1984; Greenspan, 1981; Kreisler & Cramer, 1983). A contrasting approach is represented by a current project that aims to construct a basis for a nosology of relationship disturbances. The latter would be applicable for the first 3 years and might, in some ways, be more useful than a nosology based on assumptions of individual psychopathology within the infant.*

A relationship or family systems approach seems essential for clinical work because of strong mutual influences between infant and family members, important for sustaining development and its disorders. A persistently crying and sleepless baby may reflect a distressed family, a problematic mother–child relationship, or a marriage in trouble. However that sleepless crying got started, it may contribute to a distressed family and then be perpetuated. On the individual level, the baby in question may or may not have physiological upsets such as diarrhea or vomiting, may or may not have learned a maladaptive pattern of behavior, and may or may not be labeled as "the problem" for a health care professional who has been brought on the scene. A systems diagnosis takes account of interrelated systems, both within the individual and beyond the individual. Levels of focus may involve boundaries between psychological and physiological levels and between the infant, dyadic relationship, and family levels. Crying and sleeplessness may therefore reflect a disorder of infancy, but it may be misleading to diagnose the disorder as residing in the infant.

A recent clinical example will have elements familiar to those doing clinical work in infancy. A 7-month-old girl was referred for the problem mentioned above, namely, persistent crying and sleeplessness. The problem had existed since age 2 months but had worsened. Her mother was single, a part-time journalist living with her extended family, which also included two sisters, one soon to get married and the other attending graduate school. Also in the home were her own mother and father (i.e., the infant's grandparents). Grandfather was described as a hard-working professional who worked even harder recently. Mother's plan was to move out of the grandparents' home and get back on her own after the infant was somewhat older and had "settled down." She described grandmother as being extremely attentive, both to her and to her infant. But the crying disrupted everybody.

The infant and her mother were seen in my office. The infant was sociable and engaging, although somewhat cautious toward me initially. There was obvious mutual pleasure between mother and infant; however, at times the infant seemed de-

*Special Project Group of the Center for Advanced Study in the Behavioral Sciences on Developmental Processes in Psychopathology. The group was initiated in 1984–1985 when Drs. Thomas Anders, Robert N. Emde, Herbert Leiderman, Arthur H. Parmelee, Arnold Sameroff, and L. Alan Sroufe were resident fellows at the center and Drs. David Reiss and Daniel Stern were visiting scholars. A monograph is in preparation.

manding of attention from mother who would respond without letting her explore or "settle" on her own. I decided on a home visit and found that the above inter- actional pattern was repeated but now with the addition of grandmother responding to the infant as well as expressing concern about her daughter's sense of frustration. At the home visit, something else became apparent, namely, that the grandparents were aware that they would soon have an "empty nest." Grandmother, especially, was becoming increasingly nervous about what she would do.

There could have been many points of intervention. Suggestions were made about routine sleeping arrangements for the infant, and rather straightforward educational statements were made about the developmental need for the baby to learn to reg- ulate things on her own at times. But most effective, I believe, was an intervention at the family system level. Upon inquiry, it had been discovered that grandmother and grandfather had not been out together "just for fun" in years. A family task was, therefore, given as a prescription. It was framed as essential for the household parenting environment that grandmother and grandfather go out alone at least once a week. This would be difficult, they were told, so at first the entire family should help plan this by discussing it around the dinner table. Results were striking. The grandparents were surprised that this was a difficult task to do, but they did even- tually go out and were able to keep it up during the subsequent weeks. The infant's crying and sleeplessness ceased being a problem. Mother reported by phone that the change at home was like "night and day"—her parents seemed so different. Her baby was doing well, and she was now feeling restless about being more on her own.

Subsequently, this family went through some interesting but quite different strug- gles, but it seems fair to ask what the crying was a symptom of. The infant's be- havioral regulation? Problems between infant and mother, with respect to regula- tion and autonomy? Problems between mother and grandmother? Problems in the grandparents' marriage? Problems involving the family as a whole, with respect to life cycle adaptations? All of these issues seemed relevant.

Prognosis

Prognosis has been central to the art of the clinician since the time of Hippocrates. Correspondingly, predictability has been central to the art of research. Yet prognosis and predictability present a poignant dilemma for infant mental health. Initially, the field was spurred on by the fact that retrospective clinical case histories seemed to highlight special infancy experiences—such as maternal separation or traumatic episodes—for the origin of much later psychopathology. Two decades of research have revealed a far different state of affairs. Such research has come from two directions. First, detailed prospective studies have repeatedly shown that individual variability in infant developmental functions does not predict later variability in the same function; in fact, predictability to later performance is poorest from infancy as compared with later ages (see Kagan, Kearsley, & Zelazo, 1978; McCall, 1979). Second, studies of extreme environmental circumstances in infancy—involving stim- ulus deprivation, parental separation, isolated injuries, and physical handicap— showed the extent to which the effects of early deficit and trauma could be overcome by a subsequent environment that is adequate (see review in Clarke & Clarke, 1977; Emde, 1981; Rutter, 1980; Sameroff & Chandler, 1976; Wolkind & Rutter, 1985). If an adequate environment can be provided in an enduring way, the human infant shows considerable resiliency, with catch-up after earlier environmental or biological deficit. There are now a substantial number of well-documented cases of early deprivation where there has been late adoption with good developmental outcome (Clarke & Clarke, 1977), and the same is true for malnourished war orphan toddlers who were adopted by middle-class American families (Winick, Meyer, & Harris, 1975). Related to resiliency is the fact that infants with severe handicaps are often capable of using alternative pathways to achieve important developmental goals. Two dramatic examples of this are provided by the work of Decarie (1969) with thalidomide infants (tragically born without arms and legs) and the work of Fraiberg (1977) with congenitally blind infants. Both groups of infants were able to achieve object permanence (the capacity to evoke the image of an object in its absence) by using sensory-motor modalities alternative to those than are typical for the non-handicapped.

How do we understand these examples of resiliency? Theoretical biology (Bertalanffy, 1968; Waddington, 1940) has directed our attention to the fact that our evolution has resulted in strong developmental pathways that are crucial for adaptation. Development is, therefore, goal oriented. Corollaries of this view include the following: (1) that biologically important developmental pathways tend to be buffered against stress; (2) that there are multiple pathways for achieving species-important developmental goals; and (3) that there are self-righting tendencies in development after early hurts or deficits (Bell & Harper, 1977; McCall, 1979; Sameroff & Chandler, 1976). A useful model often invoked to describe these relationships is the one constructed by the embryologist Waddington (1940) and contained in his metaphor of *canalization*. The metaphor refers to a strong developmental pathway; the biological predisposition is such that there are strong built-in self-righting tendencies that come into play following any deflection from the pathway due to adverse environmental circumstances. The model is used to array evidence suggesting that mental development is strongly canalized in infancy and less so afterward, meaning that strong self-righting tendencies exist early on. Thus in early infancy severe environmental changes, if temporary, will not necessarily have substantial effects on mental development if the infant is returned to an adequate environment.

What are we to make of this picture? It contains a hopeful image for the clinician in one sense, since its implication is that amelioration through environmental support or change can be substantial. In another sense, however, it presents a major dilemma. How are we to prevent later maladaptive outcomes through early intervention efforts, and how are we to be assured of any continuity from our efforts? Does the clinician face a picture in which there is no continuity at all in early behavior?

As this new edition of the handbook indicates (see Bretherton, Chapter 22; Rutter, Chapter 26) and as has been set forth elsewhere (Emde & Harmon, 1984), the issue of continuities from infancy is by no means settled. Newer research approaches are now yielding evidence of continuities. First and foremost, there are approaches that take the family environment into account as the essential context for early development. Continuity has been found with respect to variables of the parent–infant relationship and with security or insecurity of attachment in infancy predictive of later relationship adjustment (see Bretherton, Chapter 22, this volume; Sroufe, 1979). Parent–infant relationship variables may also account for recent findings of cross-generational continuity in security–insecurity attachment measures (Main, 1985; Ricks, 1985). Another strategy yielding evidence of continuities from infancy concerns subgrouping with respect to variables of interest. Research on a subgroup of infants showing marked behavioral inhibition to the unfamiliar (infants who are typically regarded as very shy) is reviewed by Kagan (Chapter 24, this volume) and suggests strong behavioral continuity extending into the preschool years. Subgrouping is an important strategy because some features of infants may not be distributed normally in the population. Developmental continuities may, therefore, only appear when the investigator looks at a small portion of the distribution (e.g., those infants who are regarded as shy). Continuities may be hidden if one only looks at the entire distribution of a population over time. Other new approaches in the search for infant continuities involve a mapping of antecedent–consequent relations across major times of developmental transformation. Attention is paid to the organization of behavior and to *heterotypic* continuities with predictive relations among behaviors theoretically related but vastly different in form (see Kagan, 1971; Sroufe, 1979). Further, ipsative approaches are now being used in which continuities are being searched for within the behavior of individual infants instead of rank orders within groups of infants; this will be more consonant with the approach of the clinician who must deal with predictability in individual cases.

In sum, the clinician is faced with the dilemma that in infancy the predictability of behavior is less than would be the case for later ages. While disorder and deficit can be recognized and corrected within the context of an appropriate family environment, continuity and any prognosis for enduring change beyond infancy are uncertain. Furthermore, most examples of infant resiliency concern cognitive functions; few have dealt with social and affective functions where adaptation may be more vulnerable to influences from stressful early experience. Newer research approaches may find significant dimensions of continuity from infant experience to later.

Social Values and Action

Another set of dilemmas for the clinician is related to social values. These are likely to influence research, concepts of infant mental health, and what is regarded as problematic or in need of intervention.

We are emotionally aroused by infants. There is a special drawing power or attractiveness about the physical appearance of a young infant, a feature that Lorenz (1943) has referred to in his cross-species comparison as *babiness*. But more than this, we color infancy with our high hopes; infancy embodies our sense of a new beginning; it is a time of promise when there are as yet few disappointments. A family may see the infant as potentially overcoming its social disappointments and as fulfilling its dreams. More broadly, there is a sense that social injustices, those thwarting our egalitarian ideals, can be corrected by intervention in infancy. This sense adds fuel to the infant mental health movement.

Overall, values from the adult world intensify our interpretation of infancy. There is a strong tendency to see the infant's experience as reflecting adult experience. Assumptions tend to be made about complex mental functions, such as fantasy formation, which are then imputed to the infant in the absence of confirmatory evidence. Depending on our beliefs and social setting, this may take several forms.

There may be a tendency to see the normal infant in terms of what we imagine we once had and lost, a tendency to see the infant in terms of a valued scientific theory, or a tendency to see the infant as a diminished or opposite version of what we value as ideal in adults (Kagan et al., 1978). Beyond this, our vision of developmental goals is also colored, to some extent, by our social values at the time (Riegel, 1976; Sameroff & Harris, 1979). Today we value social cooperation and democratic–social ideals more than authoritarian ones. Consequently, our psychology of infant development is more action oriented and participatory, as Sameroff and Harris point out. Today, since egalitarianism is valued as opposed to social Darwinism, our psychology of development acknowledges sexual differences and strengths and encourages exploring a variety of sex roles and options in the parenting environment. Today's clinical practice is likely to welcome biological models that point to multiple pathways in development. We are interested in compensatory factors in the development of physically and mentally handicapped infants who now, as a matter of public policy, are to be "mainstreamed."

Values are likely to influence what the clinician sees as a problem in infancy. This is no minor matter since the diagnosis of a problem and its labeling can be considered a form of social action, bringing with it hazards as well as opportunities for intervention. But there is another aspect to adult values worth bearing in mind. Parents are strongly influenced by such values, not only in terms of what they define as problems in infancy but also in terms of how they encourage normal development. It would seem, in fact, that in parenting, a certain amount of "benign adultomorphism" (Freedman, 1980) is appropriate, in which the parent regards the infant as if he or she were an adult person. In clinical practice, a particularly rewarding question for information gathering is to ask a parent, "Does your baby have a personality yet?" In our experience, parents will typically answer "yes" to this question and elaborate on personality characteristics for even the youngest of infants. Low-risk parents are generally aware that they are "filling in" well beyond the observable and are elaborating according to their own feelings and wishes, which are positive and hopeful. Risk for later problems may be indicated by a "no" answer to this question, by a barrage of negative characteristics attributed to the infant, or by developmentally unrealistic expectations without awareness of "filling in." Kaye (1982) has argued cogently that parents, by virtue of attributing more intentionality and awareness to their infants than they are capable of, teach and lead the way in development. According to Kaye, parents create persons from infants.

Normality

A consideration of what is a problem for infancy now leads us to still another dilemma for an infant psychiatry, namely, that of *normality*. Offer and Sabshin (1974, 1984) have pointed out that there are multiple perspectives of normality. Clinicians are primarily concerned with *normality as health* (a reasonable state of absence of discomfort or disability). But in infancy work, other perspectives are salient and need to be taken into account. What has just been discussed concerning social values relates to what Offer and Sabshin refer to as the *utopian perspective of normality*— that is, normality in terms of what is valued as ideal. Obviously, this perspective changes with context and with the times.

Another perspective has to do with *normality as average* (what is expectable in relation to others). Most developmental tests, such as the Bayley test, use what are called normative age standards. These rely on average, statistical age groupings for mapping how an individual performs in relation to others and for estimating the extent of normality or deviation. Several features about the use of averages in infancy seem important to review.

First, averages are used to typify what is normal about developmental or growth functions in general, that is, for the onset of developmental milestones like smiling, crawling, or grasping, or for the onset of cognitive functions like object permanence. But statistical averages are apt to be misleading when thinking of individuals. Infant development occurs rapidly and is uneven in rate. As a consequence, the group average for some developmental functions will have a lot of variability at certain ages and less for other functions; thus an individual's rate of change will in no way be typified according to a group average (McCall, Eichorn, & Hogarty, 1977).

Second, averages are used to typify differences in the behavior of subgroups of infants. Consider the example of sex differences. Male infants are sometimes characterized as more active, vigorous, and aggressive, while females are more responsive to touch (Maccoby & Jacklin, 1974). But we must be aware of the tendency to convert statements about group differences (differences that are small and based on large numbers of subjects studied) into assumptions about what is average or normal. What is more prominent, in fact, is the range of variability within each sex and the overlap of distributions of functions. Further, such statements tell us nothing about an individual; many normal females are more active than many normal males.

Third, there are important secular trends. As a result of social changes, our subjective (as well as our statistical) standards of average change over time, and these guide our behavior accordingly, as theories of social and cognitive psychology will emphasize. For infancy, the increase in full-time working mothers, the increased participation of fathers in infant caregiving, the diminished birth rate, the decline of the extended family, and the increased divorce rate all have led to a shift in views of what is expectable in the infant's family environment. Changes in the American birthing scene over the last decade have been momentous. Expectations have shifted from that of a necessary surgical ordeal (involving mother, nurse, and doctor) to that of a major opportunity for family development. Expectations are that fathers and mothers (and sometimes siblings) will enthusiastically and actively participate in the labor, childbirth, and postpartum experience. Soon after birth, infants are expected to be socially interactive and awake, whereas a decade ago their social behaviors were not appreciated, and they were expected to be sleepy, a fact we now understand was previously due to effects of sedation given to mothers during labor (Brazelton, 1961; Emde & Robinson, 1979; Klaus & Kennell, 1976).

Fourth, the context of immediate experience also bears on what is expectable. Consider the following common, but different, situations. A mother from a large family with many children sees her persistently fussy 2-month-old as typically irritable; she has seen this kind of behavior before and knows that with patience her infant will grow out of it. Another mother, with a first child and from a small family, sees the same behavior as a major problem; considerably upset, she consults her pediatrician, her infant is pronounced colicky, and intervention takes place with a prescription for medication and a follow-up visit. In another example of contrasts, two Down's syndrome infants are born into different neighborhoods. In one case, the Down's syndrome infant is born into a neighborhood where another Down's infant was born only a month earlier; there are frequent opportunities for comparisons and for group activities with handicapped infants. In the other case, the Down's infant is born into a family that has no neighbors with handicapped children, and they see more behavior as deviant and strange, having few guides for what is "average" under the circumstances. Finally, the importance of context can be dramatized by imagining the attitudes of two families about the normality of a stuffy nose in their infants. In one family, the neighbors recently experienced the tragedy of sudden infant death syndrome. In the other family, there is no such context.

The perspective of *normality as health* in infancy has been strongly influenced by the pediatric concept of risk. For risk, the question is less one of assessing a current state of discomfort or disability and more one of assessing features that make it likely that the infant is in danger of later illness or death. Thus a newborn who is declared small for gestational age is at higher risk for infant morbidity and mortality. Interestingly, although risk is sometimes based on individual factors (such as physiological disturbance), it is usually defined by population variables. That is, compared with a relevant population, the infant is seen from a statistical point of view to be born earlier than normal or to be lighter than normal. For this reason, the concept of risk involves an average perspective as well as a health perspective.

In its psychiatric application, the risk concept has been used primarily in terms of a reference population, for example, infants born to teenage mothers and infants born to parents from an impoverished environment being known to be at increased risk for later psychosocial disorders. But there are individual factors as well. Infants who have physical disabilities, infants who are developmentally retarded, and infants who are regarded as persistently irritable are also at increased risk, depending on environmental context (Rutter, 1980; Thomas & Chess, 1980).

It is worth bearing in mind that from an infant mental health standpoint normality as health is not synonymous with continuity over development. In fact, the low-risk infant may be less predictable than the high-risk counterpart. This makes good biological sense if we think of a range and of variability in behavior as being adaptive, given the variability encountered in human environments.

The last of Offer and Sabshin's normality perspectives deals with *normality as a transactional system,* with what is expectable in the midst of change. In infancy, not only is change rapid but, as has been noted, the wide individual variation in the rates of behavioral change makes for low predictability. It is now recognized that there is a need for new dynamic developmental models to address the question of change, models that can deal with self-regulation in the midst of new integrative transformations. Such models must encompass the changing relations between infant and environment and represent the fact that infant and parent negotiate successive new levels of organization, which cannot be predicted in any linear fashion, from the behavior of one or the other (Sander, 1983).

A transactional perspective makes it impossible to view the infant alone when thinking about normality. We must look at infant and parent, for each is defining the other's normality. In this, there are issues of matching of behaviors, issues of adult developmental changes, and issues of life event changes—all of which must be taken into account. Further, we must be careful not to designate as abnormal what may instead be a transitional process of adaptation to a new and stressful situation.

The normality as transaction perspective seems more difficult to describe and quantify than normality as average or normality as low risk for death or illness. Still, it is the only perspective that directly attempts to view change within complex shifting systems, and therefore researchers and clinicians of infancy have found it increasingly necessary to adopt this perspective.

THE EXPANSION OF MEANING: FRONTIER IN A NEW INFANT PSYCHOLOGY

There is little doubt that the meaning of experience now occupies an active research frontier in the psychology of infancy. Increasingly, investigators seem to be moving toward understanding things that matter to *individual infants,* not just classes of infants. There is an interest in studying what is experienced in the context of a particular life and in the context of a particular caregiving relationship. There is interest in how infant experience is organized into knowledge, how it is carried forward in development, and how it is used in everyday life. Recent advances in our understanding of infant development in its social context have, in turn, made it imperative for us to conceptualize inner knowledge structures; examples in this volume concern the areas of emotional development (Campos, Chapter 9A); attachment (Bretherton, Chapter 22); social development (Lewis, Chapter 8); and early language development (Bates, Chapter 23).

In a sense, we could say a new *psychology of meaning* attempts to address the two core aspects of clinical uncertainties about infancy described in the first section of this chapter: (1) how we can appreciate developmental continuities in the midst of transformations; and (2) how we can appreciate individuality and psychopathology in the midst of a strongly determinative social context. Overall, the psychology of meaning derives from a consideration of the functional aspects of development (what usually happens in the particular adaptive circumstances of the infant) in addition to the formal aspects of development (what can happen according to the developmental timetable and capacities of the infant). There is an interest in meaning structures in addition to competence structures. Further, there is a focus on the embeddedness of the infant's psychological development within the context of the caregiver relationship.

Three examples serve to indicate directions of research of interest to the clinician. These examples concern research on the developing individual's emotions, memory, and sense of reality. They indicate that views are changing in fundamental ways.

Patterned Emotions and Continuity

Chapter 9A of this handbook, by Campos, reviews recent research on emotions and our changing perspective as to their adaptive importance. Whereas before our psychology tended to regard emotions as reactive, intermittent, and disruptive states, they are now more often regarded as active, ongoing, and adaptive processes. Emotions are highly patterned and organized. They not only guide behavior according to what is rewarding or not, but also provide signals that allow us to monitor our behavior. As every clinician knows, our emotions not only allow us to monitor ourselves—our states of well-being and engagement with the world—but also allow us to monitor others, their intentions, their needs, and their states of well-being and engagement. Another adaptive function of our emotions has been suggested by recent research, indicating that emotions are biologically patterned, with a similar organization throughout the life span. Our emotions may provide us with a core of continuity for our self-experience. Because we can get in touch with our own consistent feelings, we know we are the same in spite of the many ways we change. Because of the species-wide consistency of our human affective core, we can also get in touch with the feelings of others and be empathic (Emde, 1983).

Evidence supporting the core of continuity hypothesis comes from several sources. In addition to everyday experience wherein the clinician uses emotions for guides to understanding, considerable research now supports the idea of biological and universal patterning. Discrete, or primary, emotions such as joy, surprise, anger, fear, sadness, and disgust (and, to some extent, interest) show universal patterning of facial expression and recognition across cultures (Ekman, Friesen, & Ellsworth, 1972; Izard, 1971). Not only has this work extended to the vocal channel of expression, but the facial components of emotion have been enumerated in detail (for recent reviews, see Ekman, 1982; Izard, 1982). Further, discrete patterning of emotion has also been found in the facial expressions of infants, at an age before one could easily attribute emotions to particular learning or socialization experiences (see Campos, Chapter 9A). Adding more to the picture of continuity are a number of studies showing a similar organization of emotional expressions in infants, children, and adults. Hedonic tone (pleasure–unpleasure) consistently emerges as the dimension of greatest salience, activation as the second most salient dimension, and a third dimension is variable (see Edme, 1983, for a review of these studies).

Thus our emotions may provide us with a sense of continuity, and, indeed, because we tend to be emotional about those aspects of our experience that are most important to us as individuals, it would seem that our emotion-patterned core allows us to get in touch with the uniqueness of our own (and others') experience. Still, research establishing the continuity of emotional patterning within individuals in longitudinal study is yet to be done. Parental reports of temperament have offered some promising beginnings (see Buss & Plomin, 1984).

What research has documented is that there is a highly patterned emotional signaling system in infancy that guides caregiving and behavior. In early infancy, emotional signals flow predominantly from infant to mother and are used in guiding responses to need states and in finding windows of opportunity for learning and play. Later in infancy, infants seek out emotional expressions from caregivers (and others) in the midst of uncertainty in order to guide their own behavior (see review of infant social referencing research, Campos, Chapter 9A). Throughout infancy, it has been found that the emotional availability of the caregiver is important. This has not only been implicit in investigations of attachment (Bowlby, 1973; Matas, Arend, & Sroufe, 1978) but has also been noted in clinical research and observations (Emde & Easterbrooks, 1985; Emde, Gaensbauer, & Harmon, 1982; Mayler, Pine, & Bergman, 1975; Osofsky, in press). At least one experimental study has documented the effects of mother's emotional availability on infant exploration and play (Sorce & Emde, 1981). In several studies, mother's sensitivity and responsiveness to her infant, rated in early infancy, have been predictive of security of attachment as observed in the infant at 1 year (Bates, Maslin, & Frankel, 1985; Egeland & Farber, 1984; Grossmann, Grossmann, Spangler, Suess, & Unzner, 1985). Some (e.g., Main, 1985; Sroufe, personal communication, 1985) have interpreted this rated characteristic of mother as reflecting her emotional availability, which is apparently needed to promote security and other aspects of development. It seems important to emphasize, however, that emotional availability is a concept having to do with reciprocity within the context of the caregiver–infant relationship. A dampening of emotional availability may be seen as a restricted range of emotions, a shift away from interest and pleasure to a predominance of negative emotions, and a "turning off" of emotional engagement, and, as such, may be a sensitive barometer of current problems or risk of future problems in the infant–caregiver relationship. In the search for meaning, emotional availability represents an area of significance for both researchers and clinicians.

Personal Memory

The study of memory is basic for understanding continuities, and changes in this area of our psychology have been no less dramatic than those in the area of emotions. Again, change has occurred in the search for patterning and for functional–adaptive features. As did Bartlett (1932), Piaget (see Rovee-Collier, Chapter 2, this volume) drew our attention to the holistic and dynamic aspects of memory schemata. Formal phases of competence were enumerated that were based on the experimental testing of children's capacities wherein actions were performed on inanimate objects. More recent research has extended Piaget's work into the social realm (see Bretherton, Chapter 22, this volume) and has begun to consider the more everyday, functional features of memory development. Thus knowledge structures emerging in various contexts have become a topic of research interest in addition to competence structures.

Memory has now been found even more dynamic. Memory can be considered as semantic (prototypic or holistic) as well as episodic (or specific) (Tulving, 1972), and varying degrees of constructive elaboration are found to go into memory scripts or narratives. In early childhood, Nelson and Greundel (1981) describe how memory is laid down according to holistic knowledge structures that they refer to as *generalized event representations* (GERs). These authors demonstrate that children develop knowledge structures according to which they can reconstruct the sequential and general features of an event (e.g., a birthday party) and then fill in the details. Recent attachment theorists, such as Bretherton (1985) and Main (1985), have elaborated on Bowlby's earlier notion of a working model of the attachment relationship (Bowlby, 1969) and have argued for an attachment theory that deals with representational models and knowledge structures in that sense. Stern (1985) has pointed out that, beginning in early infancy, the world of knowledge structures is social—made up not just of generalized event representations, but of generalized interaction representations (GIRs), which are built up as models or holistic expectation sets from recurrent interactions with caregivers (these are structures that Stern refers to as RIGs—*Representations of interactions that are generalized*). How GIRs (or RIGs) develop into specific working models of attachment relationships is a matter for current research and theory building.

While this direction of theory building may seem a bit abstract, it promises to be of considerable importance for the clinician. Theorizing about representations or knowledge structures addresses the conditions of insecure attachments that appear to be at risk for later developmental psychopathology. Further, this kind of theorizing uses a common language that is emerging in the cognitive sciences, artificial intelligence, and psychotherapy research. Because of this, we may eventually find links and transformation rules connecting early knowledge structures and later knowledge structures that emerge in the midst of conflict and developmental psychopathology. It is possible to see the beginnings of a developmental spectrum of knowledge structures in which basic schemata are related to GERs, GIRs, working models of attachment, scripts, narratives, role relationship themes, and core conflictual relationship themes (CCRTs)—the last named as seen in psychotherapy research (Horowitz, Marmar, Krupnick, Wilner, Kaltreider, & Wallerstein, 1984; Luborsky, Crites-Cristoph, & Mellon, 1986).

In infancy, the conceptual framework just presented is generating a research interest in understanding the development of personal memory—that is, the development of knowledge structures about oneself, about others, and about oneself with others. Along this line, evidence seems to be accumulating to support a process-oriented view of personal memory. Although self-awareness, in the sense of self-recognition or self-consciousness, clearly emerges in the middle of the second year (see converging research observations of Amsterdam, 1972; Kagan, 1981; Lewis & Brooks-Gunn, 1979; Schulman & Kaplowitz, 1977; as well as the clinical observations of Mahler et al., 1975; Spitz, 1957), there are, from earliest infancy, accumulated knowledge structures about self that result from experience. In this process-oriented view, a sense of self, a sense of the other, and a sense of the "we" or self with other are seen to have a dynamic developmental course. Stern (1985) has been the most articulate spokesman of this view, which is also contained in a task group report emanating from the Center for Advanced Study in the Behavioral Sciences (Emde & Sameroff, in press).

Shared Reality

The notion of a developing personal memory that contains knowledge structures of a "we," in addition to knowledge structures of a self and of an other, introduces a somewhat different direction for developmental thinking. Views of the infant participating in the development of a shared reality with the caregiver are quite different from our usual form of "I-thou" dialectical thinking (or "I-it" thinking, as one might typify some experimental approaches). In contrast to developmental traditions of Freud and Piaget, this direction of thinking has its historical roots in Cooley (1912), Mead (1934), and Vygotsky (1962). The general idea is that the infant is born preadapted for social interaction and participates actively in a social support system with caregivers. Over time, a preverbal *dialogue* develops between caregiver and infant, as Spitz has called it (Spitz, 1963) and as Bruner has documented more recently (Bruner, 1982). This dialogue has its own set of shared expectancies and rules of operation. By 7–9 months, there is a special quality of this sharing that has been referred to as *intersubjectivity* (Bretherton, McKnew, & Beeghly-Smith, 1981; Stern, 1985; Trevarthen & Hubley, 1979). Intersubjectivity involves the infant's developing sense that its own intentions will correspond to the intentions of the other.

The expectation is that an implicit request in the intentional behavior of the infant, for example, will be met with an appropriate response of the caregiver. That the infant has a shared sense of presuppositions about joint intentionality or about an *interfacing of minds,* as Bretherton and her colleagues have put it (Bretherton et al., 1981), is indicated by failure correction behavior. If the caregiver does not respond according to the infant's expectations, the infant's intentional behavior will persist with varying alterations until the communicative act is met with a successful response. Intersubjectivity, however, involves more than shared intentions with the other. It involves joint referencing of events with the other (Scaife & Bruner, 1975), and it also involves shared feelings (Stern, 1985). Beyond this, intersubjectivity implies "mutual faith in a shared world" as Rommetveit has stated (Rommetveit, 1972, as cited in Bretherton, in press). Without such a faith, communication would be impossible.

Experimental studies of social referencing illustrate a salient aspect of the development of a shared reality. Social referencing is a form of emotional communication that can be demonstrated in the laboratory when the infant is 9 months or older (Feinman, 1983; Gunnar & Stone, in press; Klinnert, in press; Sorce, Emde, Campos, & Klinnert, 1985). When confronted by a situation of uncertainty—such as a modified visual cliff, a robot toy, or a stranger's approach—the infant is observed to seek out emotional information from another, usually by looking to the face. The infant then modifies its patterned behavior as a result of the emotional signal conveyed. Thus as the infant crawls across the visual cliff and notices the uncertain depth, there is a look to mother's face for information. If mother expresses fear or anger, the infant ceases exploration; if mother shows a happy or interested face, the infant continues to explore and moves across the cliff.

The social referencing paradigm has been replicated in many contexts of uncertainty during the last quarter of the first year and the beginning of the second. It is, however, only one aspect of shared meaning. As Bretherton (in press) has argued so cogently, the prolonged one-word stage of infancy, often lasting 10 months or so, is best understood in terms of a building up of progressive understandings of shared presuppositions concerning words used in different social contexts. It is a process in which the "mutual faith in a shared world" is demonstrated over and over again as the child's communicative intent persists with gesture and word; the adult matches words and phrases and often does a considerable amount of guesswork, and the child responds. Words do not have simple definitions from this perspective but, instead, have meaning potentialities as the caregiver helps to teach a more complex language.

The importance of understanding processes in the development of a shared reality has heretofore not been emphasized. We are apt to take shared reality for granted. Yet what could be more profound? Without mutual faith in a shared world, without intersubjectivity, communication and language development would not be possible. Yet we have barely scratched the surface in our investigation of such processes.

The dynamic features in the development of shared reality are important for those interested in infant mental health. In the partnership between parent and infant there is an imbalance. The parent leads the way according to a kind of teaching arrangement that is fine-tuned to the infant's demonstrated level of skill and knowledge. Parental sensitivity and behavior in this area are automatic nonconscious, and, from the investigator's point of view, truly remarkable. The behavior is normative and species typical; it can probably be regarded as another class of intuitive parenting behavior (see Papoušek & Papoušek, Chapter 12, this volume). The metaphor selected to characterize this kind of teaching relationship by those investigators who have described it is that of the apprentice and master (Bruner, 1982; Kaye, 1982). Apprenticeship gives emphasis to the fundamental activity of both partners in the relationship that has a shared goal of expanding the world of opportunity. It operates according to the pull of the greater knowledge of the more experienced one and the push of the eager curiosity of the less experienced one.

The clinician is aware that elements of risk abide in this arrangement. Parental attitudes, when skewed in a negative, mistrustful, and overly conflicted direction, can exert a harsh bias on the shared reality in spite of infant eagerness and a strong developmental push. Indeed, at the individual level, negative parental attitudes in early infancy have been identified as among the most severe of risk factors alerting the clinician to the later possibility of adverse outcomes (Broussard & Hartner, 1970; Gray, Cutler, Dean, & Kempe, 1977). The reader will also note that this line of investigation has other links to our discussion about infant mental health. Findings of cross-generational transmission of infant physical abuse and neglect (see Kempe & Helfer, 1980) and of insecure attachment (Ricks, 1985) point to specific parenting conflicts that are reactivated in infancy. The suggestion is that these conflicts have roots in an aspect of shared reality that has originated in the experience of the parents in being parented. Fraiberg, Adelson, & Shapiro (1975) captured this situation vividly in their classic description of "ghosts in the nursery" wherein intrusions of images from earlier relationship conflicts interfere with the current shared reality of the infancy relationship. Transmission of unconscious parental conflicts in infancy is now the subject of clinical investigation, not only in the United States (Osofsky, in press; Stern, 1985), but in Switzerland (Cramer, 1982) and France (Kreisler, Fair, & Soule, 1974; Lebovici, 1983, 1984). Clinicians can well be excited by the possibility that the perspective provided by a developing shared reality might lead to new advances in our practical understanding. Perhaps we can understand the conditions under which parental *misattunements* (Stern, 1985) can lead to a distorted sense of shared reality. Perhaps we can understand the bases for earlier clinical–intuitive concepts such as the development of a *false self* (Winnicott, 1965) or *not me* experience (Sullivan, 1953) or maladaptive *self-objects* (Kohut, 1971, 1977). All of these concepts have heretofore been given theoretical importance in both infant development and psychopathology in the absence of research evidence.

In entering the realm of an infant psychology that encompasses the meaning of experience, one senses that methods are uncertain and many questions are difficult to frame. But the adventures in trying to understand individual experience are irresistible to those who are interested in infant mental health. The view is vast, and exploration is needed. This brings us to our final section.

INTERVENTION OPPORTUNITIES

Clearly, many intervention opportunities present themselves in infancy, a value-laden time with both hazards and new beginnings. Intervention approaches with high-risk infants and families have been reviewed in the chapters in this volume by Field, Korner, and Cramer (Chapters 19, 20, & 21, respectively). But the search for meaning and intervention are matters that go beyond specific programs designed by health care professionals. A point of view of this chapter is that the sensitive infancy researcher is a developmentalist who is necessarily involved in intervention. Even when engaged in normative studies in nonclinical settings, such a researcher is concerned with individuality and does more to promote infant mental health of subjects than not. The researcher–subject relationship in infancy is a topic that is deserving of more research attention. For now, however, let us review some attitudes that guide intervention. These were originally brought forth as guidelines for health care professionals involved in infancy intervention. Although they are addressed to those dealing with problems and clinical concerns, their application goes beyond consultation settings.

The Importance of an Attitude of Ongoing Assessment

Paradoxically, some of the uncertainty about infancy makes for hopeful intervention. This is so for the following reason: The clinician, in trying to understand the developing system of infant and family, is engaged in a transaction, one in which there is participation in what is being assessed and one in which ongoing attitudes of attempting to understand are apt to be therapeutic. Understanding is not merely the basis for all help; the understanding of another encourages confidence and is, in a very human sense, helpful in itself, particularly if the helping professional is available emotionally as well as physically. Parents struggling with infancy problems will begin to experience help in this way. This is even more true if the clinician's assessment attitude includes an appreciation for the individuality of the infant and its family. Parents cope in unique ways as they match the realities of an illness or crisis with previous, less turbulent expectations and wishes. Families with infancy problems respond favorably to a consultative attitude that appreciates complexity and conveys that there are likely to be multiple meanings of problems and multiple causes of distress and happiness. This is true when considering not only the relations between biology and behavior but also the relations between individuals. In approaching a clinical problem, one must be aware of factors beyond the individual patient; one must appreciate needs and interests, not only of infants, but of their families and their special environments or communities. These diagnostic attitudes will be helpful, especially if the consultant's attitude is nonjudgmental and carries with it an optimism about development.

The Importance of a Developmental Orientation

This brings us to what might be considered most special about therapy in infancy. Under most circumstances, there is a strong developmental thrust on the side of health, not only for the infant, but for the parent who can frequently participate in what might be called a renewing experience. Mothers (and to some extent fathers) can experience new competencies in themselves and rework old conflicts in which there is progress to a new level of development and often a considerably widened world. As Selma Fraiberg has phrased it, even in the most problematic of situations where parents have seemingly not had anything approaching adequate parenting of their own, "it's a little bit like having God on your side" (1980, p. 53). Often it seems as if the therapist assists in removing some impediments to development, and the baby "takes off." That many therapists besides Fraiberg have experienced this optimistic state of affairs is a factor that has spurred recent enthusiasm for infant psychiatry and the infant mental health movement. Interestingly, recent research adds a compelling context for this clinical view. As mentioned before, there are strong self-righting tendencies in infant development, and some developmental functions are canalized or especially resistant to deflection from adaptive pathways; if deflections occur, even through extreme circumstances (such as parental neglect, physical abuse, prolonged hospitalization, or emotional abuse), corrections can occur with an enduring, ameliorative change in the environment (Clarke & Clarke, 1977; Emde, 1981; McCall, 1979; Rutter, 1980; Sameroff & Chandler, 1976; Waddington, 1940). Even with deflection from biological handicap (e.g., congenital blindness, deafness, cerebral palsy), self-righting tendencies are strong, with compensation often occurring through other sensory modalities, providing that the environment is not disadvantaged or problematic. Unfortunately, however, problems in the environment are frequent. Such problems include those related to family isolation and loneliness, financial stress, unresolved grief in parents, misunderstanding and poor communication with professionals, and a lack of knowledge of development under the particular circumstances. In these instances, therapy needs to attend to additional environmental problems as well.

Recent research also indicates that, just as there are strong developmental functions in infants (biologically based pathways with a thrust toward sensory, motor, and social development), there may be strong developmental functions in parents. These functions seem highly specific and activated by the infant in the caregiving situation. Research suggests that they are intuitive, largely nonconscious, compelling, and experienced as rewarding for parents (see Papoušek & Papoušek, 1980, Chapter 12, this volume). Especially prominent in early infancy, they include baby talk, matched contingencies in stimulation, and a variety of visual and postural coordinations that are apparent in both cross-cultural and microanalytic studies of parent–infant interactions.

The Importance of Emotional Availability

Clinicians have long found emotions to be at the center of everyday work. Emotional messages of distress initiate most consultations, and, later, emotional expressions of varying kinds allow for a monitoring of the progress of treatment. In infancy work, the role of emotions in ongoing assessment is probably even greater than at other ages since emotional signals serve as the language of the baby and are essential for caregiving. A few examples may vivify this. Crying communicates distress or pain to the adult and seems to give a universal preemptive message, "Come, change something." Smiling communicates pleasure and conveys, "Stay, keep it up, I like it" (Stechler & Carpenter, 1967). The baby's expression of interest seems to reveal a readiness for exploration and learning, and the expression of surprise may indicate the beginning of assimilation of new information (Charlesworth, 1969). Expressions of fear, anger, and sadness also communicate compelling messages (Emde et al., 1982).

Beyond this, emotions in infancy seem to provide a barometer for the clinician as to whether things are "on track," particularly in social and motivational development. For the infant, emotions initiate and sustain social interchanges and also seem vital for motivating engagement in an expanding world. If development is going well, the clinician will expect to see some sense of sustained pleasure as well as a range of expressed emotions. This would be so in the child, in the parents, and in their interactions. If behavioral development is not going well, the clinician may see evidence of a "turning off," of little pleasure, and of a restriction in the range of emotional expressiveness. In extreme instances, there may be sadness and depression (Emde et al., 1982).

The Importance of Systems Sensitivity

Systems sensitivity is a phrase taken from the teaching literature of psychotherapy and psychoanalysis where it has been used to refer to an empathic registration by the therapist of the quality of functioning of complex personality subsystems and their interactions (Fleming & Benedek, 1966; Lennard & Bernstein, 1960). I find systems sensitivity central for working in infancy. It is that clinical skill that allows us to focus in (or "diagnose") the system(s) appropriate to a workable problem. It requires an appreciation of the simultaneous operation of multiple systems in determining behavior and of the fact that intervention is possible at more than one level. Intervention for an infant with a behavioral or developmental problem is usually intervention with a dyad (caregiver and infant) and sometimes intervention with a family of three or more.

Selma Fraiberg, trained with a psychoanalytic orientation, was also systems sensitive. It was inappropriate, she realized, to work one to one either with infant or with mother. Whenever possible, she worked with both. Furthermore, as she points out in her seminal work (Fraiberg, 1980), however tempting it might be for the therapist to cuddle the baby, play, or demonstrate an aspect of the baby's responsivity, one should usually refrain. Particularly with mothers who are disadvantaged and seeking help, it is important to wait for an opportunity to point out to the mother how the baby is responding to her. There is likely a problem of low self-esteem to begin with, and if the clinician shows how the baby is responsive in ways that mother could not elicit, her self-esteem is apt to suffer more. Butterfield, McCord, Miller, Harmon, and Van Doorninck (1980) used a similar approach in helping mothers of prematures to "read" their babies. Many of these mothers are from disadvantaged environments, and the technique she uses is one of periodically videotaping mothers with their infants. The idea is to point out to the mothers how their babies are responding to them and how they are effective. This educational technique not only increases mother's sensitivity but builds her sense of confidence within the context of her own individuality.

Systems sensitivity in infancy often involves an ability to "stand beside" the dyadic or the family system rather than being in the middle. Rather than relating one to one to a given patient, the clinician observes interactions of others and demonstrates what is working or can work. In this way, adaptive self-righting tendencies inherent in relationships and families can be mobilized. In actuality, systems sensitivity makes use of all the prior intervention attitudes—including ongoing assessment, appreciation of development with its self-righting tendencies, and assessment of emotional availability.

A final case vignette presents a developmental infancy problem that, in the clinical scheme of things would be considered minor. Indeed, this form of intervention opportunity might just as easily have occurred in the midst of a developmental study as in a consultation setting, particularly if the investigator–subject relationship was characterized by trust and availability. The vignette is simple. Still, it illustrates much about the uncertainty, expansion of meaning, and intervention opportunities for infant mental health discussed in this chapter.

A couple came in for consultation with their 22-month-old toddler. Their son had been sleeping in their bed since early infancy, and they felt in a bind. They had adopted him after a long wait for a child. They loved him and wanted to do the very best for him, but somehow they didn't think it was "right" for him to be sleeping with them now. Yet he enjoyed being with them, and he cried and lay awake without them. What to do?

The child was active, engaged, and sociable, obviously developing well and alert. But during the interview, something very interesting happened. Father and mother, who were both health care professionals, told each other for the first time that they wanted to be alone together and that they wanted more sexual intimacy. They were very attracted to each other, but their toddler inhibited them and got in the way. It was easy for me to listen and encourage their talking to each other about this. They told me it was a bit embarrassing for them to talk this way, and they never did so in front of their son.

During the consultation, the toddler ran around my office and bumped his head on two occasions. It was tempting for me to soothe him and interact socially with the youngster, but I refrained. It was clear the child was active, exploring, and got in some difficulty with brief crying, but he soothed himself while his parents were engrossed in discussion with each other. After this had gone on for half an hour, the educational advice seemed natural and simple. Why couldn't they let him cry in his own bed at night and be on his own? They would like to be on their own, and it would seem to make sense. (I think the parents had already decided this on their own; the consultation visit merely provided an opportunity for the change. I was also able to reassure them the child would not be "traumatized.")

A follow-up letter came in 3 weeks. Mother stated that they were relieved to find that it was their problem all along. Johnny cried for 1 hr the first night and went to sleep on his own thereafter.

In conclusion, this chapter has been concerned with issues of infant mental health. Paradoxically, this new field is characterized by a high degree of enthusiasm and optimism even though our scientific views of infancy are changing. The field is interdisciplinary, not limited to psychiatry or to those in the health care professions, and its unifying vitality is found in a developmental orientation. There are many dilemmas, and the field shares a sense of uncertainty. Current strategies in the search for meaning, however, offer hope for more rational assessment and intervention opportunities in the future.

REFERENCES

Amsterdam, B. K. (1972). Mirror self-image reactions before age 2. *Developmental Psychology, 5,* 297–305.

Bartlett, F. C. (1932). *Remembering: A study in experimental and social psychology.* Cambridge, England: Cambridge University Press.

Bates, J. E., Maslin, C. A., & Frankel, K. A. (1985). Attachment security, mother–child interaction, and temperament as predictors of behavior-problem ratings at age three years. In I. Bretherton & E. Waters (Eds.), Growing points in attachment theory and research. *Monographs of the Society for Research in Child Development, 50* (1–2, Serial No. 209).

Bell, R. O., & Harper, L. V. (1977). *Child effects on adults.* Hillsdale, NJ: Erlbaum.

Bertalanffy, L. von. (1968). *General system theory foundations, development, applications.* New York: George Braziller.

Bowlby, J. (1969). *Attachment and loss: Vol. 1. Attachment.* New York: Basic.

Bowlby, J. (1973). *Attachment and loss: Vol. 2. Separation, anxiety, and anger.* New York: Basic.

Brazelton, T. B. (1961). Effect of maternal medication on the neonate and his behavior. *Journal of Pediatrics, 58,* 513–518.

Bretherton, I. (1985). Attachment theory: Retrospect and prospect. In I. Bretherton & E. Waters (Eds.), Growing points in attachment theory and research. *Monographs of the Society for Research in Child Development, 50* (1–2, Serial No. 209).

Bretherton, I. (in press). How to do things with one word: The ontogenesis of message-making in infancy. In J. Locke & M. Smith (Eds.), *The emergent lexicon.* New York: Academic.

Bretherton, I., McKnew, S., & Beeghly-Smith, M. (1981). Early person-knowledge as expressed in gestural and verbal communication: When do infants acquire a "theory of mind"? In M. Lamb & L. Sherrod (Eds.), *Infant social cognition.* Hillsdale, NJ: Erlbaum.

Broussard, E. R., & Hartner, M. S. S. (1970). Maternal perception of the neonate as related to development. *Child Psychiatry & Human Development, 1,* 16–25.

Bruner, J. (1982). *Child's talk: Learning to use language.* New York: Norton.

Buss, A. H., & Plomin, R. (1984). *Temperament: Early developing personality traits.* Hillsdale, NJ: Erlbaum.

Butterfield, P. M., McCord, M. E., Miller, L., Harmon, R., & Van Doorninck, W. (1980). Reciprocity counseling: How to read your baby. In E. Broussard (Ed.), *Prevention of psychosocial disorders in infancy: Emerging perspectives for the 80's.* Pittsburgh, PA: University of Pittsburgh.

Call, J. (1983). Toward a nosology of psychiatric disorders in infancy. In J. Call, E. Galenson, & R. L. Tyson (Eds.), *Frontiers of infant psychiatry.* New York: Basic.

Call, J., Galenson, E., & Tyson, R. L. (Eds.). (1983). *Frontiers of infant psychiatry.* New York: Basic.

Call, J., Galenson, E., & Tyson, R. L. (Eds.). (1985). *Frontiers of infant psychiatry* (Vol. II). New York: Basic.

Charlesworth, W. (1969). The role of surprise in cognitive development. In D. Elkind & J. Flavell (Eds.), *Studies in cognitive development.* London: Oxford University.

Clarke, A. M., & Clarke, A. D. B. (1977). *Early experience: Myth and evidence.* New York: Free Press.

Cooley, C. H. (1912). *Human nature and the social order.* New York: Scribner.

Cramer, B. (1984). La psychiatrie du bebe. In L. Kreisler, R. Schappi, & M. Soule (Eds.), *La Dynamique du Nourrisson.* Paris: Editions ESF.

Decarie, T. G. (1969). A study of the mental and emotional development of the thalidomide child. In B. M. Foss (Ed.), *Determinants of infant behaviour IV.* London: Methuen.

Egeland, B., & Farber, E. (1984). Infant–mother attachment. Factors related to its development and change over time. *Child Development, 55,* 753–771.

Ekman, P. (Ed.). (1982). *Emotion in the human face* (2nd ed.). London: Cambridge University Press.

Ekman, P., Friesen, W., & Ellsworth, P. (1972). *Emotion in the human face: Guidelines for research and an integration of findings.* New York: Pergamon.

Emde, R. N. (1984). Infant psychiatry in a changing world: Optimism and paradox. In J. D. Call, E. Galenson, & R. L. Tyson (Eds.), *Frontiers of infant psychiatry* (Vol. II). New York: Basic.

Emde, R. N. (1981). Changing models of infancy and the nature of early development: Remodeling the foundation. *Journal of the American Psychoanalytic Association, 29*(1), 179–219.

Emde, R. N. (1983). The prerepresentational self and its affective core. *The Psychoanalytic Study of the Child, 38,* 165–192.

Emde, R. N. (1985). Infant psychiatry in a changing world: Optimism and paradox. In J. D. Call, E. Galenson, & R. L. Tyson (Eds.), *Frontiers of infant psychiatry* (Vol. II). New York: Basic.

Emde, R. N., & Easterbrooks, M. A. (1985). Assessing emotional availability in early development. In W. K. Frankenburg, R. N. Emde, & J. Sullivan (Eds.), *Early identification of children at risk: An international perspective.* New York: Plenum.

Emde, R. N., Gaensbauer, T., & Harmon, R. J. (1982). Using our emotions: Principles for appraising emotional development and intervention. In M. Lewis & L. Taft (Eds.), *Developmental disabilities: Theory assessment and intervention.* New York: S. P. Medical and Scientific Books.

Emde, R. N., & Harmon, R. J. (Eds.). (1984). *Continuities and discontinuities in development.* New York: Plenum.

Emde, R. N., & Robinson, J. (1979). The first two months: Recent research in developmental psychobiology and the changing view of the newborn. In J. Noshpitz & J. Call (Eds.), *American handbook of child psychiatry.* New York: Basic.

Emde, R. N., & Sameroff, A. (Eds.). (in press). *A developmental model for understanding relationships and their disturbances.*

Feinman, S. (1983). The effect of maternal touching on infant social referencing. In C. Saarni (Chair), *Processes in the Socialization of Affect.* Symposium conducted at the biennial meeting of the Society for Research in Child Development, Detroit.

Fleming, J., & Benedek, T. (1966). *Psychoanalytic supervision.* New York: Grune & Stratton.

Fraiberg, S. (1977). *Insights from the blind.* New York: Basic.

Fraiberg, S. (1980). *Clinical studies in infant mental health: The first year of life.* New York: Basic.

Fraiberg, S., Adelson, E., & Shapiro, V. (1975). Ghosts in the nursery. *Journal of Child Psychiatry, 14*(3), 387–421.

Freedman, D. (1980). Maturational and Developmental issues in the first year. In S. I. Greenspan and G. H. Pollock (Eds.), *The course of life. Vol I: Infancy and Early Childhood.* Washington, D.C.: DHHS Publication (ADM) 80–786.

Gray, J. D., Cutler, C. A., Dean, J. G., & Kempe, C. H. (1977). Prediction and prevention of child abuse and neglect. *Child Abuse & Neglect, 1,* 45–58.

Greenspan, S. I. (1981). *Psychopathology and adaptation in infancy and early childhood.* New York: International Universities Press.

Grossmann, K., Grossmann, K. E., Spangler, G., Suess, G., & Ungner, L. (1985). Maternal sensitivity and newborns' orientation responses as related to quality of attachment in northern Germany. In I. Bretherton & E. Waters (Eds.), Growing points in attachment theory and research. *Monographs of the Society for Research in Child Development, 50* (1–2, Serial No. 209).

Gunnar, M. R., & Stone, C. (in press). The effects of positive maternal affect on infant responses to pleasant, ambiguous and fear-provoking toys. *Child Development.*

Horowitz, M., Marmar, C., Krupnick, J., Wilner, N., Kaltreider, N., & Wallerstein, R. (1984). *Personality styles and brief psychotherapy.* New York: Basic Books.

Howell, J. G. (1979). *Modern perspectives in the psychiatry of infancy.* New York: Brunner/ Mazel.

Izard, C. (1971). *The face of emotion.* New York: Meredith, Appleton-Century Crofts.

Izard, C. (1982). Measuring emotions in human development. In C. Izard (Ed.), *Measuring emotions in infants and children.* New York: Cambridge University Press.

Kagan, J. (1971). *Change and continuity in infancy.* New York: Wiley.

Kagan, J. (1981). *The second year: The emergence of self-awareness.* Cambridge, MA: Harvard University Press.

Kagan, J., Kearsley, R., & Zelazo, P. (1978). *Infancy, its place in human development.* Cambridge, MA: Harvard University Press.

Kaye, K. (1982). *The mental and social life of babies: How parents create persons.* Chicago: University of Chicago Press.

Kempe, C. H., & Helfer, R. E. (Eds.) (1980). *The battered child,* 3rd edition. Chicago: University of Chicago Press.

Klaus, M. H., & Kennell, J. H. (1976). *Maternal–infant bonding.* St. Louis: C. V. Mosby.

Kohut, H. (1971). *The analysis of the self.* New York: International Universities Press.

Kohut, H. (1977). *The restoration of the self.* New York: International Universities Press.

Kreisler, L. (1981). L'Enfant du Desordre Psychosomatique. Toulouse: Privat.

Kreisler, L., & Cramer, B. (1983). Infant psychopathology: Guidelines for examination, clinical groupings, nosological propositions. In J. D. Call, E. Galenson, & Tyson, R. L. (Eds.), *Frontiers of infant psychiatry.* New York: Basic.

Kreisler, L., Fair, M., & Soule, M. (1974). *L'enfant et son corps.* Paris: Presse Universitaires de France.

Lebovici, S. (1983). *Le nourrisson, la mere et le psychoanalyste: Les interactions precoces.* Paris: Editions du Centurion.

Lebovici, S. (1984). Comments concerning the concept of fantasmic interaction. In J. D. Call, E. Galenson, & R. L. Tyson (Eds.), *Frontiers of infant psychiatry* (Vol. II). New York: Basic.

Lennard, H. L., & Bernstein, A. (1960). *The anatomy of psychotherapy.* New York: Columbia University Press.

Lewis, M., & Brooks-Gunn, J. (1979). *Social cognition and the acquisition of self.* New York: Plenum.

Lorenz, K. Z. (1943). Die Angegorenen Formen Moglicher Erfahrung. *Zeitschrift fur Tierpsychologie, 5,* 235–409.

Luborsky, L., Crites-Cristoph, P., & Mellon, J. (1986). Advent of objective measures of the transference concept. *Journal of Consulting and Clinical Psychology,* 54(1), 39–47.

Maccoby, E. E., & Jacklin, C. N. (1974). *The psychology of sex differences.* Stanford, CA: Stanford University Press.

Mahler, M. S., Pine, E., & Bergman, A. (1975). *The psychological birth of the human infant.* New York: Basic.

Main, M. (1985). Security in infancy, childhood, and adulthood: A move to the level of representation. In I. Bretherton & E. Waters (Eds.), Growing points in attachment theory and research. *Monographs of the Society for Research in Child Development, 50* (1–2, Serial No. 209).

Matas, L., Arend, R., & Sroufe, L. (1978). Continuity of adaptation in the second year: The relationship between quality of attachment and later competence. *Child Development, 49,* 547–556.

McCall, R. B. (1979). The development of intellectual functioning in infancy and the prediction of later I.Q. In J. Osofsky (Ed.), *Handbook of infant development.* New York: Wiley.

McCall, R. B., Eichorn, D. H., & Hogarty, P. S. (1977). Transitions in early mental development. *Monographs of the Society for Research in Child Development, 42* (3, Serial No. 171).

Mead, G. H. (1934). *Mind, self and society: From the standpoint of a social behaviorist.* Chicago: University of Chicago Press.

Nelson, K., & Greundel, J. M. (1981). Generalized event representations: Basic building blocks of cognitive development. In M. E. Lamb & A. L. Brown (Eds.), *Advances in developmental psychology* (Vol. 1). Hillsdale, NJ: Erlbaum.

Offer, D., & Sabshin, M. (1974). *Normality: Theoretical and clinical concepts of mental health.* New York: Basic.

Offer, D., & Sabshin, M. (Eds.). (1984). *Normality and the life cycle.* New York: Basic.

Osofsky, J. D. (in press). Perspectives on infant mental health. In M. Kessler & S. Goldston (Eds.), *A decade of progress in primary prevention.* Hanover: University Press of New England.

Papoušek, H., & Papoušek, M. (1980). *Interactional failures: Their origins and significance in infant psychiatry.* Presented at First World Congress on Infant Psychiatry, Cascais, Portugal.

Provence, S. (1983). Infants and parents: Clinical case reports. *Clinical Infant Reports: Series of the National Center for Clinical Infant Programs* (No. 2). New York: International Universities Press.

Ricks, M. H. (1985). The social transmission of parental behavior: Attachment across generations. In I. Bretherton & E. Waters (Eds.), Growing points in attachment theory and research. *Monographs of the Society for Research in Child Development, 50* (1–2, Serial No. 209).

Riegel, K. (1976). The dialectics of human development. *American Psychologist, 31,* 689–700.

Rutter, M. (Ed.). (1980). *Scientific foundations of developmental psychiatry.* London: William Heineman Medical Books.

Sameroff, A. J., & Chandler, M. (1976). Reproductive risk and the continuum of caretaking casualty. In F. D. Horowitz (Ed.), *Review of child development research* (Vol. 4). Chicago: University of Chicago Press.

Sameroff, A. J., & Harris, A. E. (1979). Dialectical approaches to early thought and language. In M. Bornstein & W. Kessen (Eds.), *Psychological development from infancy: Image to intention.* Hillsdale, NJ: Erlbaum.

Sander, L. H. (1983). Polarity, paradox, and the organizing process in development. In J. D. Call, E. Galenson, & R. L. Tyson (Eds.), *Frontiers of infant psychiatry.* New York: Basic.

Scaife, M., & Bruner, J. S. (1975). The capacity for joint visual attention in the infant. *Nature, 253,* 265–266.

Schulman, A. H., & Kaplowitz, C. (1977). Mirror-image response during the first two years of life. *Developmental Psychobiology, 10,* 133–142.

Sorce, J., & Emde, R. N. (1981). Mother's presence is not enough: Effect of emotional availability on infant exploration. *Developmental Psychology, 17*(6), 737–745.

Sorce, J. F., Emde, R. N., Campos, J., & Klinnert, M. D. (1985). Maternal emotional signaling: Its effect on the visual cliff behavior of 1-year-olds. *Developmental Psychology, 21*(1), 195–200.

Spitz, R. A. (1957). *No and yes.* New York: International Universities Press.

Spitz, R. A. (1963). Life and the dialogue. In H. S. Gaskill (Ed.), *Counterpoint: Libidinal object and subject.* New York: International Universities Press.

Sroufe, L. A. (1979). Socioemotional development. In J. Osofsky (Ed.), *Handbook of infant development.* New York: Wiley.

Stechler, G., & Carpenter, G. (1967). A viewpoint on early affective development. In J. Hellmuth (Ed.), *The exceptional infant: Vol. 1. The normal infant.* Seattle: Special Child Publications.

Stern, D. N. (1985). *The interpersonal world of the infant: A view for psychoanalysts and developmental psychology.* New York: Basic.

Sullivan, H. S. (1953). *The interpersonal theory of psychiatry.* New York: Norton.

Thomas, A., & Chess, S. (1980). *The dynamics of psychological development.* New York: Brunner/Mazel.

Trevarthen, C., & Hubley, P. (1979). Secondary intersubjectivity: Confidence, confiding, and acts of meaning in the first year. In A. Lock (Ed.), Action, gesture and symbol. New York: Academic.

Tulving, E. (1972). Episodic and semantic memory. In E. Tulving & W. Donaldson (Eds.), *Organization of memory.* New York: Academic.

Vygotsky, L. (1962). *Thought and language* (E. Haufmann & G. Vakaer, Eds. & Trans.). Cambridge, MA: M.I.T. Press.

Waddington, C. H. (1940). *Organizers and genes.* London: Cambridge University Press.

Winick, M., Meyer, K. K., & Harris, R. C. (1975). Malnutrition and environmental enrichment by early adoption. *Science, 190,* 1173–1175.

Winnicott, D. W. (1965). Ego distortion in terms of true and false self. In D. W. Winnicott (Ed.), *The maturational processes and the facilitating environment.* New York: International Universities Press.

Wolkind, S., & Rutter, M. (1985). Separation, loss and family relationships. In M. Rutter & L. Hersov (Eds.), *Child and adolescent psychiatry*, 2nd ed. Oxford, England: Blackwell Scientific Publications.

Author Index

Numbers in *italics* indicate pages on which full references appear.

Hudson, R., 114, *140*
Huebner, R. R., 504, 506, 507, 511, 517, 524, 528, 538, *545, 546*
Hufschmidt, H., 260, *307*
Hughes, H. S., 209, *236*
Hughes, J. A., *964*
Huitt, W. G., 1115, *1145*
Huizinga, J., 676, *714*
Hull, C. L., 120, *140*
Hulsebus, R. C., 120, *140*
Humble, C. G., 950, *964*
Humble, K., 642, *668*
Humphrey, B. E., 28, *87*
Humphrey, G. K., 28, *87*
Humphrey, K., 155, *203,* 338, 339, 340, 342, *358*
Hunsaker, A., 1220, *1249*
Hunt, J. McV., 155, 164–165, *202,* 380, 384, *414,* 706, *714,* 758, 759, 760–761, *778,* 894, *912,* 1022, *1032*
Hunt, W. A., 260, *309*
Hunter, M. A., 351, *358*
Hunter, R. S., 1008, *1032*
Hurvich, L. M., 31, *87*
Hurwitz, B., 264, 269, *299*
Hurwitz, S., 1021, *1033*
Hutchings, D. E., 949, 950, *964*
Hutt, S. J., 282, 286, 290, *307, 309*
Hyatt, D., 1227, *1249*
Hwang, C., 589, 593, 611, *635*
Hwang, H. L., 950, *970*
Hymel, S., 608, *637*
Hyson, M. C., 109, 497, 507, 518, 529, 533, *546*

Idanpaan-Heikkila, J., *969*
Ignatoff, E., 586, *633,* 975, *1000,* 1025, *1028, 1031, 1144*
Ihrig, L. H., 124, 125, *144*
Ihsen, E., 124, *142*
Ikeda, K., 322, *357*
Illingworth, R. S., 724, *768*
Ingram, D., 151, 155, *197*
Ingram, E., 114, *140*
Ingrisano, D., 724, 774
Inhelder, B., 320, *359,* 905
Inoff, G., 744, *767*
Inokuma, K., 249, *317*
Inui, T. S., 1274, *1291*
Irwin, O., 559, *576*
Isaacson, R. L., 502, *546*
Isabella, R., 1084, *1095,* 1170, 1172, *1193*
Isen, A., 515, 532, *546,* 572, *576*
Ison, J., 923, 954, *964, 965*
Ison, J. R., 263, 264, *306,* 953, 954, *964, 965*
Ivinskis, A., 13, *85*
Iwase, K., 249, 250, *317*
Izard, C. E., 25, *94,* 427, *484,* 495, 496, 497, 498, 499, 500, 502, 503, 504, 505, 506, 507, 511, 512, 513, 514, 515, 517, 518, 519, 520, 521, 522, 523, 524, 525, 526, 527, 528, 529, 530, 531, 533, 535, 536, 538, 539, *541, 544, 545, 546,* 548, 549, *551,* 556, 557, 561, 564, 568, 571, *576,* 974, 978, *1002,* 1062, 1092, 1097, 1281, *1290,* 1307, *1318*
Izzo, L. D., 434, *481*

Jacklin, C., 271, *310,* 1263, 1265, *1291,* 1304, *1318*
Jacklin, C. N., 1114, 1115, 1125, *1145, 1147*
Jackson, D., 567, *574, 578*
Jackson, J. C., 268, 269, 270, 272, 273, 274, 275, 287, *299, 305, 307*
Jackson, R. W., 15, *79*
Jaco, N. T., 249, *302*
Jacobs, B., 981, *1001*
Jacobs, B. S., 369, *411*
Jacobson, A., 250, *307*
Jacobson, J. L., 706, *714,* 796, 807, *813,* 950, 951, *962, 964*
Jacobson, S., 796, 813
Jacobson, S. W., 950, 951, *962, 964*
Jacobvitz, D., 1258, *1295*
Jaffe, J., 698, *719,* 977–978, *998*
Jaffe, M., 735, *771*
Jagadish, S., 995, *1001*
Jahoda, G., 1266, *1290*
Jakobson, K., 651, *665*
Jakobson, R., 155, 156, *197*
James, L. S., 732, *766*
James, W., 209, 223, 225, *236,* 556, *576,* 1093, 1097
Jampolsky, A., 15, *88*
Janet, P., 209
Janz, D., 940, *964*
Jaroszewicz, A. M., 738, *771*
Jasinski, D. R., 503, *549*
Jaskir, J., 428, 477, *486,* 603, *633,* 1171, *1195,* 1275, *1291*
Jasper, H., 104, *146*
Jassik-Gerschenfeld, D., 67, *91,* 699, *715*
Jay, S., 582, *634*
Jaynes, J., 228, *236*
Jeannerod, M., 245, *307*
Jeffrey, W. E., 100, 102, 104, *140,* 141, 286, *307,* 895, *909*
Jeffries, 601
Jekel, J. F., 616–617, *635*
Jenkins, J. J., 71, *91*
Jenkins, S., 1274, *1290*
Jennerod, 1012
Jennigns, J. R., 535, 539, *547*
Jensh, R., 952, *964*
Jerauld, R., *1032*
Jeremy, R. J., 750, *773,* 949, 960, 963, 964, 966
Jewett, J. L., 538, *552*
Joffe, J. M., 924, *964*
Johanson, C. E., 503, *547*

Subject Index